Upper chart

7.7m (25ft)		8.4m (28ft)		9.1m (30ft)		9.8m (32ft)		10.5m (34ft)		11.2m (37ft)		12.0m (39ft)		12.8m (42ft)		13.6m (45ft)		(48ft)		(50ft)		(53ft)		17.2m (56ft)	
L	U	L	U	L	U	L	U	L	U	L	U	L	U	L	U	L	U	L	U	L	U	L	U	L	U
+6.1	-25.9	+5.9	-26.1	+5.7	-26.3	+5.5	-26.5	+5.3	-26.7	+5.1	-26.9	+4.9	-27.1	+4.7	-27.3	+4.5	-27.5	+4.3	-27.7	+4.1	-27.9	+3.9	-28.1	+3.7	-28.3
6.3	25.7	6.1	25.9	5.9	26.1	5.7	26.3	5.5	26.5	5.3	26.7	5.1	26.9	4.9	27.1	4.7	27.3	4.5	27.5	4.3	27.7	4.1	27.9	3.9	28.1
6.5	25.5	6.3	25.7	6.1	25.9	5.9	26.1	5.7	26.3	5.5	26.5	5.3	26.7	5.1	26.9	4.9	27.1	4.7	27.3	4.5	27.5	4.3	27.7	4.1	27.9
6.7	25.3	6.5	25.5	6.3	25.7	6.1	25.9	5.9	26.1	5.7	26.3	5.5	26.5	5.3	26.7	5.1	26.9	4.9	27.1	4.7	27.3	4.5	27.5	4.3	27.7
6.9	25.1	6.7	25.3	6.5	25.5	6.3	25.7	6.1	25.9	5.9	26.1	5.7	26.3	5.5	26.5	5.3	26.7	5.1	26.9	4.9	27.1	4.7	27.3	4.5	27.5
7.1	24.9	6.9	25.1	6.7	25.3	6.5	25.5	6.3	25.7	6.1	25.9	5.9	26.1	5.7	26.3	5.5	26.5	5.3	26.7	5.1	26.9	4.9	27.1	4.7	27.3
+7.3	-24.7	+7.1	-24.9	+6.9	-25.1	+6.7	-25.3	+6.5	-25.5	+6.3	-25.7	+6.1	-25.9	+5.9	-26.1	+5.7	-26.3	+5.5	-26.5	+5.3	-26.7	+5.1	-26.9	+4.9	-27.1
7.5	24.5	7.3	24.7	7.1	24.9	6.9	25.1	6.7	25.3	6.5	25.5	6.3	25.7	6.1	25.9	5.9	26.1	5.7	26.3	5.5	26.5	5.3	26.7	5.1	26.9
7.7	24.3	7.5	24.5	7.3	24.7	7.1	24.9	6.9	25.1	6.7	25.3	6.5	25.5	6.3	25.7	6.1	25.9	5.9	26.1	5.7	26.3	5.5	26.5	5.3	26.7
7.9	24.1	7.7	24.3	7.5	24.5	7.3	24.7	7.1	24.9	6.9	25.1	6.7	25.3	6.5	25.5	6.3	25.7	6.1	25.9	5.9	26.1	5.7	26.3	5.5	26.5
8.1	23.9	7.9	24.1	7.7	24.3	7.5	24.5	7.3	24.7	7.1	24.9	6.9	25.1	6.7	25.3	6.5	25.5	6.3	25.7	6.1	25.9	5.9	26.1	5.7	26.3
8.3	23.7	8.1	23.9	7.9	24.1	7.7	24.3	7.5	24.5	7.3	24.7	7.1	24.9	6.9	25.1	6.7	25.3	6.5	25.5	6.3	25.7	6.1	25.9	5.9	26.1
8.5	23.5	8.3	23.7	8.1	23.9	7.9	24.1	7.7	24.3	7.5	24.5	7.3	24.7	7.1	24.9	6.9	25.1	6.7	25.3	6.5	25.5	6.3	25.7	6.1	25.9
+8.7	-23.3	+8.5	-23.5	+8.3	-23.7	+8.1	-23.9	+7.9	-24.1	+7.7	-24.3	+7.5	-24.5	+7.3	-24.7	+7.1	-24.9	+6.9	-25.1	+6.7	-25.3	+6.5	-25.5	+6.3	-25.7
8.9	23.1	8.7	23.3	8.5	23.5	8.3	23.7	8.1	23.9	7.9	24.1	7.7	24.3	7.5	24.5	7.3	24.7	7.1	24.9	6.9	25.1	6.7	25.3	6.5	25.5
9.1	22.9	8.9	23.1	8.7	23.3	8.5	23.5	8.3	23.7	8.1	23.9	7.9	24.1	7.7	24.3	7.5	24.5	7.3	24.7	7.1	24.9	6.9	25.1	6.7	25.3
9.3	22.7	9.1	22.9	8.9	23.1	8.7	23.3	8.5	23.5	8.3	23.7	8.1	23.9	7.9	24.1	7.7	24.3	7.5	24.5	7.3	24.7	7.1	24.9	6.9	25.1
9.5	22.5	9.3	22.7	9.1	22.9	8.9	23.1	8.7	23.3	8.5	23.5	8.3	23.7	8.1	23.9	7.9	24.1	7.7	24.3	7.5	24.5	7.3	24.7	7.1	24.9
9.7	22.3	9.5	22.5	9.3	22.7	9.1	22.9	8.9	23.1	8.7	23.3	8.5	23.5	8.3	23.7	8.1	23.9	7.9	24.1	7.7	24.3	7.5	24.5	7.3	24.7
9.9	22.1	9.7	22.3	9.5	22.5	9.3	22.7	9.1	22.9	8.9	23.1	8.7	23.3	8.5	23.5	8.3	23.7	8.1	23.9	7.9	24.1	7.7	24.3	7.5	24.5
+10.1	-21.9	+9.9	-22.1	+9.7	-22.3	+9.5	-22.5	+9.3	-22.7	+9.1	-22.9	+8.9	-23.1	+8.7	-23.3	+8.5	-23.5	+8.3	-23.7	+8.1	-23.9	+7.9	-24.1	+7.7	-24.3
10.3	21.7	10.1	21.9	9.9	22.1	9.7	22.3	9.5	22.5	9.3	22.7	9.1	22.9	8.9	23.1	8.7	23.3	8.5	23.5	8.3	23.7	8.1	23.9	7.9	24.1
10.5	21.5	10.3	21.7	10.1	21.9	9.9	22.1	9.7	22.3	9.5	22.5	9.3	22.7	9.1	22.9	8.9	23.1	8.7	23.3	8.5	23.5	8.3	23.7	8.1	23.9
10.7	21.3	10.5	21.5	10.3	21.7	10.1	21.9	9.9	22.1	9.7	22.3	9.5	22.5	9.3	22.7	9.1	22.9	8.9	23.1	8.7	23.3	8.5	23.5	8.3	23.7
10.9	21.1	10.7	21.3	10.5	21.5	10.3	21.7	10.1	21.9	9.9	22.1	9.7	22.3	9.5	22.5	9.3	22.7	9.1	22.9	8.9	23.1	8.7	23.3	8.5	23.5
11.1	20.9	10.9	21.1	10.7	21.3	10.5	21.5	10.3	21.7	10.1	21.9	9.9	22.1	9.7	22.3	9.5	22.5	9.3	22.7	9.1	22.9	8.9	23.1	8.7	23.3

Lower chart

30.3m (100ft)		31.6m (104ft)		32.9m (108ft)		34.0m (112ft)		35.5m (117ft)		37.0m (121ft)		38.5m (126ft)		40.0m (131ft)		41.5m (135ft)		43.0m (140ft)		44.5m (145ft)		46.0m (150ft)		47.5m (155ft)	
L	U	L	U	L	U	L	U	L	U	L	U	L	U	L	U	L	U	L	U	L	U	L	U	L	U
+1.3	-30.7	+1.1	-30.9	+0.9	-31.1	+0.7	-31.3	+0.5	-31.5	+0.3	-31.7	+0.1	-31.9	-0.1	-32.1	-0.3	-32.3	-0.5	-32.5	-0.7	-32.7	-0.9	-32.9	-1.1	-33.1
1.5	30.5	1.3	30.7	1.1	30.9	0.9	31.1	0.7	31.3	0.5	31.5	0.3	31.7	0.1	31.9	-0.1	32.1	-0.3	32.3	-0.5	32.5	-0.7	32.7	-0.9	32.9
1.7	30.3	1.5	30.5	1.3	30.7	1.1	30.9	0.9	31.1	0.7	31.3	0.5	31.5	0.3	31.7	0.1	31.9	-0.1	32.1	-0.3	32.3	-0.5	32.5	-0.7	32.7
1.9	30.1	1.7	30.3	1.5	30.5	1.3	30.7	1.1	30.9	0.9	31.1	0.7	31.3	0.5	31.5	0.3	31.7	0.1	31.9	-0.1	32.1	-0.3	32.3	-0.5	32.5
2.1	29.9	1.9	30.1	1.7	30.3	1.5	30.5	1.3	30.7	1.1	30.9	0.9	31.1	0.7	31.3	0.5	31.5	0.3	31.7	0.1	31.9	-0.1	32.1	-0.3	32.3
2.3	29.7	2.1	29.9	1.9	30.1	1.7	30.3	1.5	30.5	1.3	30.7	1.1	30.9	0.9	31.1	0.7	31.3	0.5	31.5	0.3	31.7	0.1	31.9	-0.1	32.1
+2.5	-29.5	+2.3	-29.7	+2.1	-29.9	+1.9	-30.1	+1.7	-30.3	+1.5	-30.5	+1.3	-30.7	+1.1	-30.9	+0.9	-31.1	+0.7	-31.3	+0.5	-31.5	+0.3	-31.7	+0.1	-31.9
2.7	29.3	2.5	29.5	2.3	29.7	2.1	29.9	1.9	30.1	1.7	30.3	1.5	30.5	1.3	30.7	1.1	30.9	0.9	31.1	0.7	31.3	0.5	31.5	0.3	31.7
2.9	29.1	2.7	29.3	2.5	29.5	2.3	29.7	2.1	29.9	1.9	30.1	1.7	30.3	1.5	30.5	1.3	30.7	1.1	30.9	0.9	31.1	0.7	31.3	0.5	31.5
3.1	28.9	2.9	29.1	2.7	29.3	2.5	29.5	2.3	29.7	2.1	29.9	1.9	30.1	1.7	30.3	1.5	30.5	1.3	30.7	1.1	30.9	0.9	31.1	0.7	31.3
3.3	28.7	3.1	28.9	2.9	29.1	2.7	29.3	2.5	29.5	2.3	29.7	2.1	29.9	1.9	30.1	1.7	30.3	1.5	30.5	1.3	30.7	1.1	30.9	0.9	31.1
3.5	28.5	3.3	28.7	3.1	28.9	2.9	29.1	2.7	29.3	2.5	29.5	2.3	29.7	2.1	29.9	1.9	30.1	1.7	30.3	1.5	30.5	1.3	30.7	1.1	30.9
3.7	28.3	3.5	28.5	3.3	28.7	3.1	28.9	2.9	29.1	2.7	29.3	2.5	29.5	2.3	29.7	2.1	29.9	1.9	30.1	1.7	30.3	1.5	30.5	1.3	30.7
+3.9	-28.1	+3.7	-28.3	+3.5	-28.5	+3.3	-28.7	+3.1	-28.9	+2.9	-29.1	+2.7	-29.3	+2.5	-29.5	+2.3	-29.7	+2.1	-29.9	+1.9	-30.1	+1.7	-30.3	+1.5	-30.5
4.1	27.9	3.9	28.1	3.7	28.3	3.5	28.5	3.3	28.7	3.1	28.9	2.9	29.1	2.7	29.3	2.5	29.5	2.3	29.7	2.1	29.9	1.9	30.1	1.7	30.3
4.3	27.7	4.1	27.9	3.9	28.1	3.7	28.3	3.5	28.5	3.3	28.7	3.1	28.9	2.9	29.1	2.7	29.3	2.5	29.5	2.3	29.7	2.1	29.9	1.9	30.1
4.5	27.5	4.3	27.7	4.1	27.9	3.9	28.1	3.7	28.3	3.5	28.5	3.3	28.7	3.1	28.9	2.9	29.1	2.7	29.3	2.5	29.5	2.3	29.7	2.1	29.9
4.7	27.3	4.5	27.5	4.3	27.7	4.1	27.9	3.9	28.1	3.7	28.3	3.5	28.5	3.3	28.7	3.1	28.9	2.9	29.1	2.7	29.3	2.5	29.5	2.3	29.7
4.9	27.1	4.7	27.3	4.5	27.5	4.3	27.7	4.1	27.9	3.9	28.1	3.7	28.3	3.5	28.5	3.3	28.7	3.1	28.9	2.9	29.1	2.7	29.3	2.5	29.5
5.1	26.9	4.9	27.1	4.7	27.3	4.5	27.5	4.3	27.7	4.1	27.9	3.9	28.1	3.7	28.3	3.5	28.5	3.3	28.7	3.1	28.9	2.9	29.1	2.7	29.3
+5.3	-26.7	+5.1	-26.9	+4.9	-27.1	+4.7	-27.3	+4.5	-27.5	+4.3	-27.7	+4.1	-27.9	+3.9	-28.1	+3.7	-28.3	+3.5	-28.5	+3.3	-28.7	+3.1	-28.9	+2.9	-29.1
5.5	26.5	5.3	26.7	5.1	26.9	4.9	27.1	4.7	27.3	4.5	27.5	4.3	27.7	4.1	27.9	3.9	28.1	3.7	28.3	3.5	28.5	3.3	28.7	3.1	28.9
5.7	26.3	5.5	26.5	5.3	26.7	5.1	26.9	4.9	27.1	4.7	27.3	4.5	27.5	4.3	27.7	4.1	27.9	3.9	28.1	3.7	28.3	3.5	28.5	3.3	28.7
5.9	26.1	5.7	26.3	5.5	26.5	5.3	26.7	5.1	26.9	4.9	27.1	4.7	27.3	4.5	27.5	4.3	27.7	4.1	27.9	3.9	28.1	3.7	28.3	3.5	28.5
6.1	25.9	5.9	26.1	5.7	26.3	5.5	26.5	5.3	26.7	5.1	26.9	4.9	27.1	4.7	27.3	4.5	27.5	4.3	27.7	4.1	27.9	3.9	28.1	3.7	28.3
6.3	25.7	6.1	25.9	5.9	26.1	5.7	26.3	5.5	26.5	5.3	26.7	5.1	26.9	4.9	27.1	4.7	27.3	4.5	27.5	4.3	27.7	4.1	27.9	3.9	28.1

NORIE'S
NAUTICAL TABLES

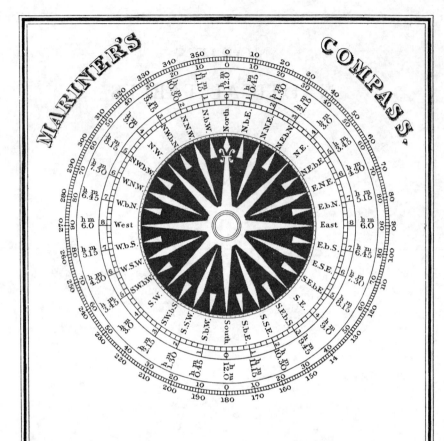

A TABLE OF THE ANGLES

which every Point & Quarter Point of the Compass makes with the Meridian.

NORTH		POINTS	o ' "	POINTS	SOUTH	
		0 – ¼	2 . 48 . 45	0 – ¼		
		0 – ½	5 . 37 . 30	0 – ½		
		0 – ¾	8 . 26 . 15	0 – ¾		
N.b.E.	N.b.W.	1	11 . 15 . 0	1	S.b.E.	S.b.W.
		1 – ¼	14 . 3 . 45	1 – ¼		
		1 – ½	16 . 52 . 30	1 – ½		
		1 – ¾	19 . 41 . 15	1 – ¾		
N.N.E.	N.N.W.	2	22 . 30 . 0	2	S.S.E.	S.S.W.
		2 – ¼	25 . 18 . 45	2 – ¼		
		2 – ½	28 . 7 . 30	2 – ½		
		2 – ¾	30 . 56 . 15	2 – ¾		
N.E.b.N.	N.W.b.N.	3	33 . 45 . 0	3	S.E.b.S.	S.W.b.S.
		3 – ¼	36 . 33 . 45	3 – ¼		
		3 – ½	39 . 22 . 30	3 – ½		
		3 – ¾	42 . 11 . 15	3 – ¾		
N.E.	N.W.	4	45 . 0 . 0	4	S.E.	S.W.
		4 – ¼	47 . 48 . 45	4 – ¼		
		4 – ½	50 . 37 . 30	4 – ½		
		4 – ¾	53 . 26 . 15	4 – ¾		
N.E.b.E.	N.W.b.W.	5	56 . 15 . 0	5	S.E.b.E.	S.W.b.W.
		5 – ¼	59 . 3 . 45	5 – ¼		
		5 – ½	61 . 52 . 30	5 – ½		
		5 – ¾	64 . 41 . 15	5 – ¾		
E.N.E.	W.N.W.	6	67 . 30 . 0	6	E.S.E.	W.S.W.
		6 – ¼	70 . 18 . 45	6 – ¼		
		6 – ½	73 . 7 . 30	6 – ½		
		6 – ¾	75 . 56 . 15	6 – ¾		
E.b.N.	W.b.N.	7	78 . 45 . 0	7	E.b.S.	W.b.S.
		7 – ¼	81 . 33 . 45	7 – ¼		
		7 – ½	84 . 22 . 30	7 – ½		
		7 – ¾	87 . 11 . 15	7 – ¾		
East	West	8	90 . 0 . 0	8	East	West

J.W.Norie deliu͠t

NORIE'S
NAUTICAL TABLES

WITH EXPLANATIONS OF THEIR USE

EDITED BY

CAPTAIN A.G. BLANCE B.Sc.

IMRAY LAURIE NORIE AND WILSON LTD

SAINT IVES CAMBRIDGESHIRE ENGLAND

Published by
Imray Laurie Norie & Wilson Ltd
Wych House, St Ives, Huntingdon, Cambridgeshire PE17 4BT England
☎ 0480 462114 *Fax* 0480 496109

© Imray Laurie Norie & Wilson Ltd 1991

Revised edition 1991

Reprinted 1994

ISBN 0 85288 160 6

British Library Cataloguing in Publication Data
A catalogue record for this book is available from the British Library.

Printed in Great Britain at The Bath Press, Avon.

CONTENTS

PREFACE

One hundred and eighty years of publication involving many new editions and reprints afford a searching test of the usefulness and value of any publication designed to meet the exacting requirements of navigators and the shipping industry. Since J. W. Norie published the first edition of his COMPLETE SET OF NAUTICAL TABLES AND EPITOME OF PRACTICAL NAVIGATION in 1803, the tables have undergone a continuing process of change to maintain their usefulness to the modern practical navigator.

During these years many changes to the tables have been necessary in both content and presentation to conform with changing techniques of navigation, but the aim of the editors has always been to have user friendly navigational tables which could be used quickly and easily under shipboard conditions. This has resulted in many changes to the tables aimed at removing much of the tedium of interpolation, so enabling the navigator to obtain the answers to navigational problems quickly with the minimum of probability of error. Certain tables and data are also included which are not readily available on board ship or are only used in the examination room, but the physical dimensions of the book impose strict limits on what can be included with the result that it is impossible to include all the tables the editor would wish.

In the present edition, the Star's Total Correction Table inside the back cover, the Moon's Total Correction Table and the extended Star's Total Correction Table have been redesigned to reduce interpolation to a minimum.

The editor wishes to thank all those who have suggested improvements to the tables, and will welcome any further helpful criticism which users of the Tables may care to make.

A. G. BLANCE
London 1991

EXPLANATION AND
USE OF THE TABLES

I. COMPUTATION TABLES

TRAVERSE TABLE

(Pages 2 - 93)

These Tables afford an easy and expeditious means of solving all problems that resolve themselves into the solution of right-angled plane triangles. They can thus be applied to all the forms of Sailings except Great Circle Sailing; but they are specially useful in resolving a Traverse. On this account they are called Traverse Tables, and the terms *Course, Distance, Difference of Latitude* and *Departure* are used as names of the different parts involved.

The Traverse Table has now been brought into line with the requirements of the modern compass notation by the inclusion, at the top and foot of each page, of the number of degrees of the new (0–360) circular system of reckoning, corresponding to the value printed at centre of title in conformity with the older quadrantal notation, the latter form being retained for its application to the solution of certain problems in the Sailings and for its utility in the conversion of Departure to Difference of Longitude and vice versa, as explained later in this article.

The figures denoting the number of degrees under the new arrangement are placed in the appropriate quadrants of a small diagrammatic symbol, representing the cardinal points of the compass, and in these positions they introduce the equivalents in the new notation corresponding to the number of degrees of the old system, shown at centre of titles, when pertaining to the respective quadrants. The arrangement will be better understood by reference to an example; thus, on page 58 –'28 DEGREES'

For old	N28°E	S28°E	S28°W	N28°W
Read new	↑ 028°	↑	↑	332° ↑
	|	| 152°	208° |	|

or vice versa, and, as examples of the reverse process, on page 38, but this time from the **foot** with caption '72 DEGREES'—

For new	↑ 072°	↑	↑	288° ↑
	|	| 108°	252° |	|
Read old	N72°E	S72°E	S72°W	N72°W

It will be observed that, in the new notation of the Traverse Table, the three-figure degrees corresponding to Easterly courses are placed in the symbol diagram towards the right-hand side of the page, in contradistinction to those for Westerly equivalents which are printed on the left.

The courses, in both the old and new notation, are displayed at the top and bottom of the pages, while the Distances are arranged in order in the columns marked Dist. The Difference of Latitude and Departure corresponding to any given Run on any given Course will be found in the columns marked D. Lat. and Dep., respectively, of the page for the given Course and opposite the given Distance. But it must most carefully be observed that when the required Course is found at the *top* of the page, the Difference of Latitude and Departure also are to be taken from the columns as named at the *top* of the page; and when the Course appears at the *foot* of the page, the relevant quantities too must be taken from the columns as named at the *foot* of the page.

When any of the given quantities (except the Course which is never to be changed) exceeds the limits of the tables, any aliquot part, as a half or a third, is to be taken, and the quantities found are to be doubled or trebled; that is, they are to be multiplied by the same figure as the given quantity was divided by. And since the Difference of Latitude and Departure corresponding to any given Course and Distance are to be found opposite the Distance on that page which contains the Course, it follows that if any two of the four parts be given, and these two be found in their proper places in the tables, the other two will be found in their respective places on the same page.

The following examples will illustrate the application of the tables to Plane Sailing:—

Example: Find the difference of latitude and departure made good by a ship in sailing 84 miles on a course 112°. (S68°E., Old Style).

Course 112° is found in the Table at foot of page 46. Opposite 84 in the Distance column on that page we get:—D. Lat. 31·5, Dep. 77·9.

The D. Lat. is named S and Departure E, because it is noted that 112° is shown in the South and East quadrant of the compass symbol.

Example: Find the course and distance made good by a ship whose difference of latitude was found to be 431 miles S, and departure 132′ W.

431 and 132 are not to be found alongside each other, but in the Table on page 37 we find 431·3 and 131·9, and these are sufficiently near to the desired value for all practical purposes. These give 197°, or 17° old style, as a course, and 451 as a distance. Hence—

Course S17° W, or 197°, and Distance 451 miles.

These tables may also, as has already been stated, be applied to solving problems in Parallel and Middle Latitude Sailings. In solving these problems the Course (old notation) at the *top* or *bottom* of page becomes the Latitude or Middle Latitude, the Distance column becomes a Diff. Longitude column, and the D. Lat. column becomes a Dep. column. To facilitate the taking out of these quantities the D. Long. and Dep. are bracketed together, and the words *D. Long.*, and *Dep.* are also printed in italics at the top of their respective columns when the Latitude or Middle Latitude, as course, is at the *top;* but at the bottom of their respective columns when Latitude or Middle Latitude, as course is at the *bottom*.

Example: In Latitude or Middle Latitude 47° the departure made good was 260′·5; required the difference of Longitude.

With 47° as course at the *bottom* of the page, look in the column with *Dep.* printed in italics at the *bottom*, just over the end of the bracket; and opposite to 260′·5 will be found 382 in the *D. Long.* column, which is the Difference of Longitude required.

Example: A ship, after sailing East 260′·5, had changed her Longitude 6° 22′. Required the parallel of Latitude on which she sailed.

6° 22′ equals 382′. Opposite 382 in *D. Long.* column is 260′·5 in *Dep.* column entered from the *bottom*, and the parallel on which she sailed is Lat. 47°.

MERIDIONAL PARTS (For the Spheroid)

(Pages 94 - 102)

This table is used in resolving problems by *Mercator's Sailing* and in constructing charts on Mercator's projection. The meridional parts are to be taken out for the degrees answering to the given latitude at the *top* or *bottom*, and for the minutes at either *side* column. Thus, the meridional parts corresponding to the latitude 49° 57′ are 3451·88.

LOGARITHMS

(Pages 103 - 117)

This table gives correct to five significant figures the mantissae (or fractional parts) of the common logarithms of numbers. The operator must decide for himself the integral or whole number part of the logarithm (called the characteristic) according to the position of the decimal point in the natural number.

The rules for determining the characteristic can be demonstrated by the following:

10 000	$= 10^4$	$\therefore$	$\log_{10}$ 10 000	$=$	4
1 000	$= 10^3$	$\therefore$	$\log_{10}$ 1 000	$=$	3
100	$= 10^2$	$\therefore$	$\log_{10}$ 100	$=$	2
10	$= 10^1$	$\therefore$	$\log_{10}$ 10	$=$	1
1	$= 10^0$	$\therefore$	$\log_{10}$ 1	$=$	0
0·1	$= 10^{-1}$	$\therefore$	$\log_{10}$ 0·1	$=$	-1
0·01	$= 10^{-2}$	$\therefore$	$\log_{10}$ 0·01	$=$	-2
0·001	$= 10^{-3}$	$\therefore$	$\log_{10}$ 0·001	$=$	-3
0·0001	$= 10^{-4}$	$\therefore$	$\log_{10}$ 0·0001	$=$	-4

The above, which may be extended infinitely in both directions, shows that the log. of, say, 342 must lie between 2 and 3. Similarly, the log. of 29·64 must be between 1 and 2. From the table it will be found that log. 342 = 2·53403 and log. 29·64 = 1·47188. These statements could be expressed as follows:—

$$10^{2.53403} = 342$$
$$10^{1.47188} = 29·64$$

For numbers greater than 1 the rule for finding the characteristic is—The characteristic is the number which is 1 less than the number of figures before the decimal point. If there are five figures before the decimal point the characteristic is 4; if there is one figure before the decimal point the characteristic is 0, and so on. Thus:—

log. 5378	$=$	3·73062
log. 537·8	$=$	2·73062
log. 53·78	$=$	1·73062
log. 5·378	$=$	0·73062

For numbers less than 1 the rule for finding the characteristic is—The negative characteristic of the log. of a number less than 1 is the number which is 1 more than the number of noughts between the decimal point and the first significant figure. Thus:—

log. 0·5378	$=$	$\bar{1}$·73062
log. 0·05378	$=$	$\bar{2}$·73062
log. 0·005378	$=$	$\bar{3}$·73062
log. 0·0005378	$=$	$\bar{4}$·73062

Tabular logarithms To avoid the negative characteristics, logarithms in tabular form are obtained by adding 10 to the characteristic.

Example: log 0·5378 $= \bar{1}$·73062 or in tabular form 9·73062

log 0·005378 $= \bar{3}$·73062 or in tabular form 7·73062

In the tables of logarithms of trigonometrical functions the characteristic is given in both forms at the top of each column of logarithms.

Example: log. sin. 5° 30′ $= \bar{2}$·98157 or 8·98157

log. cot. 5° 30′ $=$ 1·01642 or 11·01642

Interpolation

When the number whose logarithm is required consists of four significant figures or less the mantissa is taken from the main part of the table. Where there are five significant figures the difference for the fifth figure is obtained from the relevant section of the D column.

Example: log. 140·27 = 2·14675 + 21 = 2·14696

If the number consists of more than six significant figures the approximate logarithm can be found by simple proportion.

Example: log. 140·277 = 2·14675 (from main table) + 21 (from D column)
                                    + 2 (by simple proportion)
                               = 2·14698

To find the number, N, whose log. is known. If the number is required to four significant figures or less all that is necessary is to find the series of digits corresponding to the tabulated mantissa which is *nearest* to the one given. The characteristic of the log. will determine the position of the decimal point. Thus:—

Given log. N = 1·87109.
Nearest tabulated mantissa 87111 gives digits 7432.
The characteristic being 1, there are two figures before the decimal point.
The required number, N, is therefore 74·32.

The following examples will serve to illustrate the procedure when more than four significant figures are required. Suppose the number, N, correct to five significant figures is required when log. N is known to be 2·27104.

Example: log. N = 2·27104
The next less tabulated mantissa ·27091 gives the digits 1866.
But ·27104—·27091 = 13
∴ Entering the 180–189 section of the D column the fifth figure is 6 for a D value of 12 and by simple proportion the sixth figure is therefore 5.
∴ the digits of the number are 186665
The characteristic of the logarithm is 2.
∴ the number N is 186·665

LOGS. of TRIG. FUNCTIONS

(Pages 118 - 241)

Whilst preserving the basic layout which has been a feature of '*Norie's*', and '*Norie's*' alone, since J. W. Norie produced the original edition, changes have been introduced which make the table a much more efficient instrument in conforming with the modern technique of astronomical navigation. For all angles from 0° to 90° the table is now completely *downward* reading and for that reason alone should be practically blunder-proof. In the main part of the table from 4° to 86° the log. functions of angles are tabulated for one minute intervals of the angles and proportional parts for fractions of one minute (from 0'·1 to 0'·9) are given. In the remainder of the table, where that system ceases to be practicable, log. functions are tabulated for intervals of 0'·1 or 0'·2 as necessary and differences between successive tabulations are given. This means that, except in special and rare cases, interpolation is reduced when taking out any log. function of an angle and there is no need to resort to the questionable practice of rounding off angles to the nearest minute in order to 'save trouble'. With this table it is no more of an effort to work accurately than it is to work roughly. How far a navigator is justified in working to tenths of a minute is a matter which can be argued about indefinitely, but since the Nautical Almanac gives hour angles and declinations to tenths of a minute and a modern sextant with a decimal vernier enables readings to be taken to tenths of a minute as well, it would seem only logical to use navigation tables which, with the minimum of effort, provide for the same order of precision.

The characteristic of the logarithm is given at the top of each function's column in indicial form with the tabular form in brackets.

Example: log. sin. 5° 09′ = $\overline{2}$.95310 or 8·95310

Thus the navigator can use whichever form of characteristic is preferred though it must be appreciated that the two forms cannot be interchanged within a calculation.

Occasionally, it may be necessary to find the logs. of trigonometrical functions of angles greater than 90°. No difficulty should be experienced in such cases as the second, third and fourth quadrant equivalents of the first quadrant angles are plainly indicated. It should be noted, however, that the table is *upward* reading for angles between 90° and 180° and also for those between 270° and 360°, but *downward* reading for angles between 180° and 270°. In *all* cases, however, the name of the ratio being used appears at the *top* of the page. When applying proportional parts care should be taken to notice in which direction the log. function is increasing, i.e. upwards or downwards.

Examples:

log. sin.	1° 38′·7	= $\overline{2}$·(45754 + $\frac{88}{2}$)	= $\overline{2}$·45798	or 8·45798
log. tan.	177° 57′·5	= $\overline{2}$·(55240 − $\frac{70}{2}$)	= $\overline{2}$·55205	or 8·55205
log. cosec.	26° 04′·4	= 0·(35712 − 10)	= 0·35702	or 10·35702
log. sec.	333° 25′·3	= 0·(04852 − 2)	= 0·04850	or 10·04850
log. cos.	138° 17′·6	= $\overline{1}$·(87300 + 7)	= $\overline{1}$·87307	or 9·87307
log. sin.	62° 19′·8	= $\overline{1}$·(94720 + 5)	= $\overline{1}$·94725	or 9·94725
log. cot.	117° 53′·0	=	$\overline{1}$·72354	or 9·72354
log. cos.	83° 15′·3	= $\overline{1}$·(07018 − 32)	= $\overline{1}$·06986	or 9·06986

To find the angle whose log. function is given is equally simple. For instance, to find θ when log. sin. θ = $\overline{1}$·66305 or 9·66305, notice that the next *less* tabulated log. sin. is $\overline{1}$·66295 or 9·66295 which gives the angle 27° 24′·0. The excess 10 gives an additional 0′·4. Hence, θ = 27° 24′·4.

In practice, the above processes will, of course, be performed mentally.

HAVERSINES

(Pages 242 - 348)

To make the tables clearer and to make interpolation almost completely unnecessary the tables are presented as follows:—

1. The Log. Haversines are printed in bold type and the Natural Haversines in light type.
2. In the range 0° to 90° and 270° to 360° (the range most frequently used) haversines are tabulated at 0·2′ intervals and the proportional parts for 0·1′ are given at the foot of each page.
3. In the remainder of the table haversines are tabulated at 1·0′ intervals and the proportional parts for 0·2′ are given at the top of each column.
4. The characteristic of the logarithms is given at the top of each column in the negative index form together with the tabular form in brackets.

ANGLE	LOG. HAVERSINE	NAT. HAV.
15° 33'·0	$\overline{2}$·26249 or 8·26249	0·01830
15° 33'·6	$\overline{2}$·26304 or 8·26304	0·01832
15° 33'·7	$\overline{2}$·26313 or 8·26313	0·01832
344° 10'·0	$\overline{2}$·27807 or 8·27807	0·01897
344° 10'·4	$\overline{2}$·27771 or 8·27771	0·01895
344° 10'·5	$\overline{2}$·27762 or 8·27762	0·01895
95° 25'·0	$\overline{1}$·73815 or 9·73815	0·54720
95° 25'·6	$\overline{1}$·73822 or 9·73822	0·54729
263° 37'·0	$\overline{1}$·74475 or 9·74475	0·55559
263° 37'·8	$\overline{1}$·74466 or 9·74466	0·55547

Derivation of Haversine Formulae:

$$\text{Cos. A} = \frac{\text{cos. } a - \text{cos. } b \text{ cos. } c}{\text{sin. } b \text{ sin. } c}, \text{ (fundamental formula)}.$$

$$\therefore 1 - \text{cos. A} = 1 - \frac{\text{cos. } a - \text{cos. } b \text{ cos. } c}{\text{sin.} b \text{ sin. } c}$$

$$\text{i.e. vers A} = \frac{\text{sin. } b. \text{ sin. } c - \text{cos. } a + \text{cos. } b \text{ cos. } c}{\text{sin. } b \text{ sin. } c},$$

$$\therefore \text{cos. } (b \sim c) - \text{cos. } a = \text{sin. } b \text{ sin. } c \text{ vers. A,}$$
$$\text{or } - \text{cos. } a = - \text{cos. } (b \sim c) + \text{sin. } b \text{ sin. } c \text{ vers. A.}$$

By adding unity to each side this becomes—

$$1 - \text{cos. } a = 1 - \text{cos. } (b \sim c) + \text{sin. } b \text{ sin. } c \text{ vers. A,}$$
$$\therefore \text{vers. } a = \text{vers. } (b \sim c) + \text{sin. } b \text{ sin. } c \text{ vers. A,}$$
$$\text{whence hav. } a = \text{hav. } (b \sim c) + \text{sin. } b \text{ sin. } c \text{ hav. A} \ldots\ldots\ldots(1)$$

By transposing we obtain—

$$\text{hav. A} = [\text{hav. } a - \text{hav. } (b \sim c)] \text{ cosec. } b \text{ cosec. } c. \ldots\ldots(2)$$
$$\text{and hav. } (b \sim c) = \text{hav. } a - \text{hav. A sin. } b \text{ sin. } c. \ldots\ldots\ldots\ldots\ldots(3)$$

These three versions of the spherical haversine formula are frequently adapted for navigational purposes as follows.

(1) Hav. z = hav. (l $\pm$ d)* + hav. h cos. l cos. d.
(2) Hav. h = [hav. z — hav. (l $\pm$ d;*] sec. l sec. d.
(3) Hav. mer. zen. dist. = hav. z — hav. h cos. l cos. d.

$$\text{where} \begin{cases} z = \text{zenith distance,} \\ l = \text{latitude,} \\ d = \text{declination,} \\ h = \text{hour angle.} \end{cases}$$

* (l $\sim$ d) when l and d have the same name,
  (l + d) when l and d have different names.

Examples

(1) Find zenith distance when h = 66° 49'·3, 1 = 31° 10'·2 N., d = 19° 24'·7 N.

$$\text{Hav. } z = \text{hav. } h \cos. 1 \cos. d + \text{hav. } (1 \pm d).$$

h ..	66° 49'·3	L. hav. $\overline{1}$·48173 or 9·48173	
1 ..	31° 10'·2	L. cos. $\overline{1}$·93228 or 9·93228	
d ..	19° 24'·7	L. cos. $\overline{1}$·97458 or 9·97458	
		L. hav. $\overline{1}$·38859 or 9·38859	N. hav. 0·24468
(1 ~ d) ..	11° 45'·5	....	N. hav. 0·01049
z ..	60° 40'·9	....	N. hav. 0·25517

Calculated zenith distance = 60° 40'·9 and is used for comparing with the true zenith distance to find the intercept when establishing the position line by the Marc St. Hilaire or Intercept method.

(2) Find the hour angle when 1 = 41° 21'·6 N., d = 9° 34'·1 S., z = 63° 45'·8.

$$\text{Hav. } h = [\text{hav. } z - \text{hav. } (1 \pm d)] \sec. 1 \sec. d.$$

z ..	63° 45'·8	N. hav. 0·27896	
(1 + d) ..	50° 55'·7	N. hav. 0·18485	
		N. hav. 0·09411	L. hav. $\overline{2}$·97364 or 8·97364
1 ..	41° 21'·6	....	L. sec. 0·12461 or 10·12461
d ..	9° 34'·1	....	L. sec. 0·00608 or 10·00608
h ..	41° 46'·9	....	L. hav. $\overline{1}$·10433 or 9·10433

Hour angle = 41° 46'·9 if body is W. of the meridian, or hour angle = 318° 13'·1 if body is E. of the meridian, and is used for finding the computed longitude when establishing the position line by the "chronometer method".

(3) Find the mer. zen. dist. when h = 355° 57'·2, 1 = 48° 12'·5 N., d = 12° 13'·7 S., z = 60° 21'·6.

$$\text{Hav. mer. zen. dist. } = \text{hav. } z - \text{hav. } h \cos. 1 \cos. d.$$

h ..	355° 57'·2	L. hav. $\overline{3}$·09571 or 7·09571	
1 ..	48° 12'·5	L. cos. $\overline{1}$·82375 or 9·82375	
d ..	12° 13'·7	L. cos. $\overline{1}$·99003 or 9·99003	
		L. hav. $\overline{4}$·90949 or 6·90949	N. hav. 0·00081
z ..	60° 21'·6	....	N. hav. 0·25273
mer. zen. dist. ... 60° 15'·2		....	N. hav. 0·25192

The mer. zen. dist., 60° 15'·2, when combined with the declination gives the latitude of the point where the position line (at right angles to the direction of the body) cuts the meridian of D.R. longitude used to compute h. This method of working an ex-meridian sight is, of course, an alternative to using ex-meridian tables.

The haversine formulae and great circle sailing calculations

Formula (1) is used to find the great circle distance from one point to another and formula (2) is used to find the initial and final courses.   The vertex of the track and the latitude of the point where the track cuts any specified meridian can then be found by right angled spherical trigonometry.

Example: Find the great circle distance and the initial course on the track from A (17° 22′ N., 25° 28′ W.) to B (40° 08′ N., 73° 17′ W.).

To find the great circle distance

Hav. AB = hav. (PA ∼ PB) + hav. P sin. PA sin. PB.

P	.. 47° 49′·0	L. hav.	1̄·21550 or 9·21550		
PA	.. 72° 38′·0	L. sin.	1̄·97974 or 9·97974		
PB	.. 49° 52′·0	L. sin.	1̄·88340 or 9·88340		

L. hav. 1̄·07864 or 9·07864   N. hav. 0·11985

(PA ∼ PB) .. 22° 46′·0   ....   N. hav. 0·03896

AB .. 46° 58′·2   ....   N. hav. 0·15881

∴ Great circle distance = 2818·2 miles.

To find the initial course

Hav. A = [hav. PB − hav. (PA ∼ AB)] cosec. PA cosec. AB.

PB   .. 49° 52′·0   N. hav. 0·17772

(PA ∼ AB) .. 25° 39′·8   N. hav. 0·04932

N. hav. 0·12840   L. hav.   1·10856 or 9·10856

PA   .. 72° 38′·0   ....   L. cosec.   0·02026 or 10·02026

AB   .. 46° 58′·2   ....   L. cosec.   0·13609 or 10·13609

A   .. 50° 48′·5   ....   L. hav.   1·26491 or 9·26491

∴ Initial course = N. 50° 48′·5 W. or 309° 11′·5.

NATURAL FUNCTIONS OF ANGLES
(Pages 349-363)

In these tables, which are intended for use with simple pocket calculators, the natural trigonometric functions can be obtained to five decimal places.
Examples:

1. To find tan. 49° 38′:

1·17500   (tan. 49° 36′)
+0·00138   (2′ from difference table against 49°)

tan. 49° 38′ = 1·17638

2. To find cos. 80° 27′:

        0·16677   (cos. 80° 24′)

   −0·00086   (3′ from difference table against 80°, subtracted)

cos. 80° 27′ = 0·16591

3. To find sec. 76° 44′:

       4·34689   (sec. 76° 42′)

   +0·01078   ($\frac{1}{3}$[sec. 76° 42′−sec. 76° 48′]; difference must be

                    obtained by this method because the mean

Sec. 76° 44′ = 4·35767   differences are not sufficiently accurate)

4. To convert 31° 46′ to radians:

$$31° = 0·54105 \text{ radians}$$
$$46′ = 0·01338 \text{ radians}$$

$$31° \ 46′ = 0·55443 \text{ radians}$$

5. To convert 1·648 radians to degrees:

$$1 \text{ radian } = 57° \ 17·7′$$
$$0·648 \text{ radians} = 37° \ 07·7′$$

$$1·648 \text{ radians} = 94° \ 25·4′$$

SQUARES AND CUBES OF NUMBERS

(Pages 364 - 367)

These tables will give squares and cubes of numbers to four significant figures.

To obtain the square or cube of a number:

(a) If the number is between 1 and 10 and consists of three significant figures (or less) the square or cube is taken from the main part of the tables, but if there are four significant figures the Mean Difference section is also used.

Example:

$2·824^2$ = 7·952 (from main table) + 23 (from Mean Difference)

            = 7·975

$7·631^3$ = 58·22 (from main table) + 2 (from Mean Difference)

            = 58·24

(b) All other numbers are converted into scientific notation and the square or cube obtained for the significant figures as before.

Example:

$463·8^2$ = $(4·638 \times 10^2)^2 = 21·51 \times 10^4$

          = $2·151 \times 10^5$ or 215 100

$0·000 \ 07251^3$ = $(7·251 \times 10^{-5})^3 = 381·3 \times 10^{-15}$

          = $3·813 \times 10^{-13}$ or 0·000 000 000 000 3813

SQUARE AND CUBE ROOTS OF NUMBERS

(Pages 368 - 377)

These tables, which give the square and cube roots of numbers to four significant figures, are in the following form:

(a) Square roots of numbers between 1 and 10 and between 10 and 100.

(b) Cube roots of numbers between 1 and 10, between 10 and 100 and between 100 and 1000.

The following examples illustrate the method of obtaining square or cube roots using the tables:

$$\sqrt{839 \cdot 2} \qquad\qquad \sqrt{4523} \qquad\qquad \sqrt[3]{78\ 620\ 000} \qquad\qquad \sqrt[3]{0 \cdot 000\ 7247}$$

1. *Change the number into scientific notation.*

$$= \sqrt{8 \cdot 392 \times 10^2} \qquad = \sqrt{4 \cdot 523 \times 10^3} \qquad = \sqrt[3]{7 \cdot 862 \times 10^7} \qquad = \sqrt[3]{7 \cdot 247 \times 10^{-4}}$$

2. *Adjust the position of the decimal point to make the index of 10 exactly divisible by the root being found.*

$$= \sqrt{8 \cdot 392 \times 10^2} \qquad = \sqrt{45 \cdot 23 \times 10^2} \qquad = \sqrt[3]{78 \cdot 62 \times 10^6} \qquad = \sqrt[3]{724 \cdot 7 \times 10^{-6}}$$

3. *Enter the tables shown below and extract the required root of the significant figures.*

TABLE OF SQUARE ROOTS 1–10	TABLE OF SQUARE ROOTS 10–100	TABLE OF CUBE ROOTS 10–100	TABLE OF CUBE ROOTS 100–1000
$= 2 \cdot 897$	$= 6 \cdot 725$	$= 4 \cdot 284$	$= 8 \cdot 982$

4. *Determine the square or cube root of the power of 10.*

$\sqrt{10^2} = 10$	$\sqrt{10^2} = 10$	$\sqrt[3]{10^6} = 10^2$	$\sqrt[3]{10^{-6}} = 10^{-2}$
$\therefore \sqrt{839 \cdot 2}$	$\therefore \sqrt{45 \cdot 23}$	$\therefore \sqrt[3]{78\ 620\ 000}$	$\therefore \sqrt[3]{0 \cdot 000\ 7247}$
$= 2 \cdot 897 \times 10$	$= 6 \cdot 725 \times 10$	$= 4 \cdot 284 \times 10^2$	$= 8 \cdot 982 \times 10^{-2}$
or $28 \cdot 97$	or $67 \cdot 25$	or $428 \cdot 4$	or $0 \cdot 08982$

Mean Difference columns are not required in the table of square roots of numbers between 5·5 and 9·9 nor in the tables of cube roots of numbers between 1·0 and 10·0 and between 55·0 and 100·0. When any of the above tables are being used to find the roots of numbers with four significant figures interpolation can be carried out mentally.

II. TABLES FOR CELESTIAL NAVIGATION

A, B & C AZIMUTH TABLES

(Pages 380 - 428)

To conform with the method of presenting data in the Nautical Almanac the hour angles in Tables A and B are given in degrees and minutes of arc from 0° 15′ to 359° 45′.

If the H.A. is between 0° and 180° the body is west of the meridian and its hour angle will appear in the upper row of H.A.s at either the top or bottom of the page. If the H.A. is between 180° and 360° the body is east of the meridian and its hour angle will appear in the lower row.

The A, B and C values and the azimuth are derived by employing the well known formula which connects four adjacent parts of a spherical triangle. It can be shown, for instance, that in spherical triangle A B C:—

cot. a sin. b = cot. A sin. C + cos. b cos. C.
∴ cot. a sin. b − cos. C cos. b = sin. C cot. A.

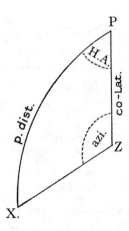

The figure shows the astronomical triangle PZX with the four adjacent parts PX, P, PZ and Z representing, in that order, polar distance, hour angle, co-latitude and azimuth.

Applying the above formula to this particular case, we have:—

cot. PX sin. PZ − cos. P. cos. PZ = P. cot. Z.
Dividing by sin. P. sin. PZ, this becomes—

$$\frac{\text{cot. PX.}}{\text{sin. P}} \cdot \frac{\text{sin. PZ}}{\text{sin. PZ}} - \frac{\text{cos. P}}{\text{sin. P}} \cdot \frac{\text{cos. PZ}}{\text{sin. PZ}} = \frac{\text{sin. P}}{\text{sin. P}} \cdot \frac{\text{cot. Z}}{\text{sin. PZ}}$$

i.e.   cot. PX   cosec. P − cot. P   cot. PZ = cot. Z   cosec. PZ,
or   tan. decl.   cosec. H.A. − cot. H.A. tan. lat.

= cot. azi. sec. lat.

In the tables:—

cot. H.A. tan. lat. is tabulated as A, and tan. decl. cosec. H. A. is tabulated as B.
Hence (A ± B) cos. lat. = cot. azimuth.

(A ± B), referred to for convenience as 'C', forms the primary argument in Table C with lat. as the secondary argument. With these two arguments the azimuth is found.

As an example, consider the case where hour angle = 48°, lat. = 52° N., and decl. = 15° N.

lat.	52° 00′ N	L. tan.	0·10719			
H.A.	48° 00′	L. cot.	9·95444		L. cosec.	0·12893
decl.	15° 00′ N	....			L. tan.	9·42805
		Log. A	0·06163		Log. B	9·55698
		∴A =	1·153 S.		B =	0·361 N.

(A is named opposite to lat.; B has the same name as decl.) (A ± B) = 'C' = 0·792 S. (Same name as A which is numerically greater than B.).

'C'	0·792 S.	Log.	9·89873
lat.	52° 00′ N.	L. cos.	9·78934
Azi.	64° 00′	L. cot.	9·68807

∴ Azimuth = S. 64° W. or 244°.
(The azimuth takes the names of the 'C' factor and hour angle.)

Reference to the tables will show that for the above data A = 1·15 S. and B = 0·36 N. The combination of these is 0·79 S., which in Table C with lat. 52° gives azimuth S. 64°·2 W.

The rules for naming and combining A and B and for naming the azimuth are given on each page of the appropriate table. It is important that they should be applied correctly.

Longitude Correction

The quantity (A ± B) or 'C', besides being one of the arguments for finding the azimuth from table C, is also the 'longitude correction factor' or the error in longitude due to an error of 1′ of latitude. This can often be very useful to those accustomed to working sights by the longitude method.

A simple sketch showing the direction of the position line will at once make it clear which way the longitude correction should be applied. It will easily be apparent that when working a sight by the longitude method:—

(a) when the position line lies N.E./S.W. (body in N.W. or S.E. quadrant), if the assumed latitude is too far north the computed longitude will be too far east, and if the latitude is too far south the longitude will be too far west;

(b) when the position line lies N.W./S.E. (body in N.E. or S.W. quadrant) the reverse holds good.

Example: Suppose a sight worked with lat. 49° 06′ N. gives longitude 179° 46′·0 W. and azimuth S. 70°·5 E., the value of 'C' being 0·54. If the correct latitude turned out to be 49° 46′ N., i.e. 40′ error, the error in longitude would be 40 x 0′·54 or 21′·6. We should therefore have:—

Computed long.	179° 46′·0 W.
Correction	21′·6 E.
Correct long.	179° 24′·4 W.

This is a case where the latitude being too far south, the computed longitude is too far west.

Examples on the use of the tables

In each of the following cases find the longitude correction factor and the true azimuth.

Example 1: H.A. 310°, lat. 48° N., decl. 20° N.
From Table A with H.A. 310°, lat.   48° N.,   A = 0·93 S.
From Table B with H.A. 310°, decl. 20° N.,   B = 0·48 N.

Long. corr'n. factor = A − B =   C = 0·45 S.

From Table C with C 0·45 S., lat. 48° N., T. Azi. = S. 73°·2 E.

A is named S. opposite to lat. because H.A. is *not* between 90° and 270°.
B is named N. because the decl. is N.
C = A − B as A and B have different names, and is named S. as the greater quantity is S.
The azimuth is named S. because C is S., and E. because H.A. is between 180° and 360°.

Example 2: H.A. 244°, lat. 41° S., decl. 5° S.
From Table A with H.A. 244°, lat.   41° S.,   A = 0·42 S.
From Table B with H.A. 244°, decl.   5° S.,   B = 0·10 S.

Long. corr'n. factor = A + B =   C = 0·52 S.

From Table C with C 0·52 S., lat. 41° S., T. Azi. = S. 68°·6 E.

A is named S. same as lat. because H.A. is between 90° and 270°.
B is named S. because the decl. is S.
C = A + B as A and B have the same name (both S.).
The azimuth is named S. because C is S., and E. because H.A. is between 180° and 360°.

Example 3: H.A. 108°, lat. 61° N., decl. 20° N.
From Supplementary Table A with H.A. 108°, lat. 61° N.,   A = 0·59 N.
From Table B with H.A. 108°, decl. 20° N.,   B = 0·38 N.

Long. corr'n. factor = A + B =   C = 0·97 N.

From Table C with C 0·97 N., lat. 61° N., T. Azi. = N. 64°·8 W.

A is named N. same as lat. because H.A. is between 90° and 270°.
B is named N. because the decl. is N.
C = A + B as A and B have the same name (both N.).
The azimuth is named N. because C is N., and W. because H.A. is between 0° and 180°.

Use of ABC Tables for Great Circle Sailing
   These tables provide a ready means of finding the initial great circle course from one point to another.   Suppose, for example, the initial course from P (49° 30′ N., 5° 00′ W.) to Q (46° 00′ N., 53° 00′ W.) is required.   The procedure is simply to treat d. long. as hour angle, lat. of P. as latitude, and lat. of Q as declination.   Thus:—

From Table A with H.A. 48°, lat.   49° 30′ N.,   A = 1·06 S.
From Table B with H.A. 48°, decl. 46° 00′ N.,   B = 1·39 N.

      A − B =   C = 0·33 N.

From Table C with C 0·33 N., lat. 49° 30′ N., T. Azi. = N. 77°·9 W.
    i.e. Initial G.C. Course = N. 77°·9 W. or 282°·1.

   The final course, if required, may be obtained in a similar way by finding the initial course from Q to P and reversing it.

AMPLITUDES and CORRECTIONS

(Explanation with Table)
(Pages 429 - 431)

EX-MERIDIAN TABLE I

(Pages 432 - 443)

'A' is the change in the altitude of a body in seconds of arc during the minute of time immediately preceding or following meridian passage. It is tabulated for latitudes to 83° and declinations to 63°.

This table is in two sections:–

(i) Latitude and Declination SAME NAME. On page 432 - 435 there are bands in which the value of 'A' is omitted. This is because 'A' changes too rapidly for accurate interpolation to be possible, when the body is near the zenith.

(ii) Latitude and Declination DIFFERENT NAME. 'A' for Lower Transit observation is tabulated on the lower parts of pages 440 - 442 of this section and on page 443, although the latitude and declination are of the same name.

'A' is computed using the formula:–

$$A = \frac{1.9635 \times \cos \text{lat} \times \cos \text{dec}}{\sin (\text{lat} \pm \text{dec})}$$

In the denominator the latitude and declination are:–

(a) subtracted at Upper Transit if of the same name;
(b) added at Upper Transit if of different name;
(c) subtracted at Lower Transit.

EX-MERIDIAN TABLE II

(Pages 444 - 447)

The Reduction is the product of 'A' from Table I and the square of the time in minutes that the body is East or West of the meridian. To obtain the True Meridian Altitude, the Reduction is added to the True Altitude of Upper Transit observations and subtracted from the True Altitude of Lower Transit observations of circumpolar bodies.

The table is entered with 'A' and the Local Hour Angle for Upper Transit observations or 'A' and $(180 \sim \text{LHA})$ for Lower Transit observations. If the interpolated value of 'A' from Table I is to one or two decimal places, the Reduction can be obtained to a corresponding accuracy by moving the decimal point the appropriate number of places as shown in the example below:

'A' = 2.45 ; Local Hour Angle = 354° 00'
From the column headed 354° 00':–

Reduction for 2.0 = 19.2
              0.4 = 3.84 (extract the value for 4″ and move the decimal point one place)
             0.05 = 0.48 (extract the value for 5″ and move the decimal point two places)
Reduction for 2.45 = 23.52

Example 1: In D.R. Lat. 48° 13′ N., D.R. Long. 7° 20′ W., the True Altitude of the sun was 19° 52′. Sun's LHA 356° 00′. Declination 21° 39′ S. Determine the Position Line.

Table I	Table II		T. Alt.	19° 52′·0 S.
(Different Name)	LHA 356° 00′		Reduction	5′·6
Lat. 48° 13′ N.		A = 1″·3	T. Mer. Alt.	19° 57′·6 S.
Decl. 21° 39′ S.	Red for. 1″·0 = 4′·3		T. Mer. Z. Dist.	70° 02′·4 N.
A = 1″·3	,, ,, ·3 = 1′·3		Decl.	21° 39′·0 S.
	Reduction = 5′·6		Lat.	48° 23′·4 N.
			True Azimuth	
			from Az. Tables 176°	

Position Line passes 086° and 266° through Lat. 48° 23′·4 N., Long. 7° 20′ W.

Example 2: D.R. Lat. 42° 12′ N., D.R. Long. 24° 32′ W., the True Altitude of Antares was 21° 28′. Star's LHA 357° 00′. Declination 26° 18′ ·0 S. Determine the Position Line.

Table I	Table II		T. Alt.	21° 28′·0 S.
(Different Name)	LHA 357° 00′		Reduction	3′·4
	A = 1″·4			
Lat. 42° 12′ N.	Red. for 1″·0 = 2′·4		T. Mer. Alt.	21° 31′·4 S.
Decl. 26° 18′ S.	,, ,, ·4 = 0′·96		T. Mer. Z. Dist.	68° 28′·6 N.
A = 1″·4			Decl.	26° 18′·0 S.
	Reduction = 3′·36			
			Lat.	42° 10′·6 N.
			True Azimuth	
			from Az. Tables 177°	

Position Line passes 087° and 267° through Lat. 42° 10′·6 N. Long. 24° 32′ W.

Although the latitude and declination of a circumpolar body are always of the same name, 'A' for Lower Transit observations is tabulated in the lower part of the "Latitude and Declination Different Name" section of Table 1.

When near its Lower Transit the Local Hour Angle is less than 180° when west of the meridian and more than 180° when east of it. The Hour Angle to use when entering Table II in this case is (180°∼ LHA).

Example 3: D.R. Lat. 42° 10′ N., Long. 21° 30′ W., the True Altitude of Dubhe was 14° 20′. Star's LHA 176° 30′. Declination 62° 01′ N. Determine the Position Line.

Table I	Table II		T. Alt.	14° 20′·0
(Same Name)	LHA 176° 30′		Reduction	−2′·3
	= 3° 30′			
Lat. 42° 10′ N.	A = 0″·7		T. Mer. Alt.	14° 17′·7
Decl. 62° 01′ N.	Reduction = 2′·29		Polar Dist.	27° 59′·0
A = 0″·7	For Lower Transit—2′·3			
			Lat.	42° 16′·7 N.
			True Azimuth	
			from Az. Tables 358°	

Position Line passes 088° and 268° through Lat. 42° 16′·7 N., Long. 21° 30′ W.

Example 4: D.R. Lat. 50° 02′ S., D.R. Long. 67° 20′ W., the True Altitude of Achernar was 17° 20′. Star's LHA 184° 20′. Declination 57° 29′ S. Determine the Position Line.

Table I	*Table II*	T. Alt.	17° 20′·0
(Same Name)	LHA 184° 20′	Reduction	−3′·5
	= 4° 20′		
Lat. 50° 02′ S.	A = 0″·7	T. Mer. Alt.	17° 16′·5
	Reduction = 3′·5	Polar Dist.	32° 31′·0
Decl. 57° 29′ S.	For Lower Transit—3′·5		
A = 0″·7		Lat.	49° 47′·5 S.
		True Azimuth	
		from Az. Tables	177·5°

Position Line passes 087°·5 and 267°·5 through 49° 47′·5 S., Long. 67° 20′ W.

EX-MERIDIAN TABLE III

(Page 448)

This Table contains a Second Correction, which, when the amount of the Main Correction is considerable, enables the process of Reduction to Meridian to be applied with advantage on much larger hour angles than could otherwise be the case.

Example: D.R. Lat. 31° 00′ N., D.R. Long. 124° 00′ W., the True Altitude of the Sun was 55° 01′. Sun's LHA 347° 30′. Declination 2° 00′ S. Determine the Position Line.

Table I	*Table II*	T. Alt.	55° 01′·0 S.
(Different Name)	LHA 347° 30′	1st Correction	2° 09′·2 +
	A = 3″·1	2nd Correction	3′·6 −
Lat. 31° 00′ N.	Red. for 3″·0 = 125′·0		
Decl. 2° 00′ S.	„ „ ·1 = 4′·2	T. Mer. Alt.	57° 06′·6 S.
A = 3″·1		T. Mer. Z. Dist.	32° 53′·4 N.
	1st Correction = 129′·2	Decl.	2° 00′·0 S.
Entering Table III with 129′ as First Correction		Lat.	30° 53′·4 N.
and 56° as Altitude we have 3·6′ Subtractive		True Azimuth	
for Second Correction.		from Az. Tables	158°

Position Line passes 068° and 248° through Lat. 30° 53′·4 N., Long. 124° 00′ W.

EX-MERIDIAN TABLE IV

(Page 448)

This Table gives the limits of Hour Angle or Time before or after the time of the Meridian Passage when an Ex-Meridian observation can be taken.   When the observation is taken within the time limit prescribed by this Table the Second Correction from Table III is negligible.   The Table is entered with 'A' taken from Table I,

Given Lat. 37° N., Declination 18° N., find the limits of Hour Angle for taking an Ex-Meridian observation.

For Lat. 37° and Declination 18°, 'Same Name', Table I gives 4″·6 for 'A'.   Entering Table IV with 4″·6 as 'A', the time limit abreast is found to be 24 minutes.

CHANGE of HOUR ANGLE with ALTITUDE

(Pages 449 - 450)

The formula used in calculating the values tabulated is:—

Change of H.A. (in mins.) due to 1′ change of Alt. = cosec. Az. sec. Lat.

The table gives in minutes of arc the error in hour angle resulting from an altitude 1′ in error. This is of particular value to those navigators who work their sights by the 'Longitude by Chronometer' method. It will be seen that the error is least in the case of a body on the prime vertical and that it increases as the azimuth decreases—very rapidly as the azimuth becomes very small. From the table the observer can readily find the least azimuth on which the altitude of a body should be observed in order that the resulting longitude may not exceed a chosen limit of error. Another use to which this table can be put is to find the correct longitude when a sight has been worked using an altitude in error by a known amount.

Example 1: In latitude 18° what should be the lowest value of azimuth in order that an error of 1′ in the altitude may not produce more than 2′ of error in the computed longitude?

Under lat. 18° and against azi. 32°, the error for 1′ of alt. is found to be 1′·98. Accordingly, the observation should be taken on a bearing greater than 32°.

(In lat. 36°, it will be seen, an azimuth of about 39° would constitute the limit. In lat. 63° the error would exceed 2′ even when the body was on the P.V.)

Example 2: A sight worked in lat. 54° by the 'Longitude Method' resulted in a deducted longitude of 64° 14′·5 W. and azimuth N. 65° E. Afterwards it was discovered that the sextant index error of 2′ 30″ off the arc had been applied the wrong way. Find the correct longitude.

Since the longitude is found by comparing the L.H.A. of the body with its G.H.A., it is evident that the error in the L.H.A. will be the error in the computed longitude. The index error of 2′·5, which should have been added, was subtracted, so that the altitude used was 5′ too small.

The table shows that in lat. 54°, when the azi. is 65°, the error in H.A. is 1′·88 per 1′ of alt. For 5′, therefore, the error will be 5 × 1′·88 = 9′·40.

As the real altitude was greater than the value used, the observer must be *nearer* to the body than his computed longitude would lead him to suppose. With an *easterly* azimuth this means that the *Westerly* L.H.A. should be greater, and therefore the observer's west longitude should be smaller. Hence:—

Computed long...............	64°	14′·5W.
Error		9′·4 to subtract
Correct long.	64°	05′·1W

It will be appreciated that this is much quicker than re-working the sight.

CHANGE OF ALTITUDE IN ONE MINUTE OF TIME

(Pages 451 - 452)

This Table contains the change in the altitude of a celestial body in minutes and tenths of arc in one minute of time. It is useful for finding the correction to be applied to the computed altitude of a heavenly body when the time of observation differs from that used in the computation of the altitude. When the star is East of the Meridian the correction from the Table is subtractive from the computed altitude if the time of observation is earlier than that used in the computation of the altitude; it is additive if the time of observation is later. When the star is West of the meridian the correction is additive if the time of observation is before that used when computing the altitude, it is subtractive if the time of observation is after.

Formula

Change of altitude in one minute of time = 15′ Sin. Az. Cos. Lat.

The change in 6 seconds of time is found by shifting the decimal point one place to the left.

The change in 1 second of time is found by calling the quantities in the Table seconds instead of minutes.

Example: In Lat. 51° 30′ N. on the Meridian of Greenwich on October 26th, 1925 at 8 h. 0 m. p.m. the computed altitude of the star *Altair* was 37° 09′·2. Find the true altitude at 8 h. 10 m. p.m., the Az. being S.49° 37′ W. Opposite 52° in the Lat. Col. and under 50° in the Az. Col. is 7′·1 of arc which is the change of altitude in 1 min. of time, and 7′·1 × 10 minutes gives 71′ or 1° 11′, which is the correction to apply to the computed altitude.

$$
\begin{array}{lll}
\text{Computed Alt.} \dots\dots\dots\dots & 37° & 09′·2 \\
\text{Corr. to Subt.} \dots\dots\dots\dots & 1° & 11′·0 \\
\hline
\text{True Alt. required} \dots\dots\dots & 35° & 58′·2 \\
\hline\hline
\end{array}
$$

DIP of the SEA HORIZON

(Page 453)

The tabulated values are derived from the formula—Dip (in minutes) = $1·76\sqrt{h}$ where h = height of eye in metres. Thus, for example, when h = 30 m (98 ft), dip. = 9′·6.

Heights of eye are given in metres, ranging from 0·5 m to 50·0 m and also in the equivalent feet (1·5 ft to 164 ft).

MONTHLY MEAN OF THE SUN'S SEMIDIAMETER AND SUN'S PARALLAX IN ALTITUDE

(Page 453)

Correction for parallax is to be taken out opposite the Sun's Altitude and is always *additive*.

Example: The sun's parallax corresponding to 51° of altitude is 0′·1.

AUGMENTATION OF THE MOON'S SEMIDIAMETER

(Page 453)

REDUCTION OF THE MOON'S PARALLAX

(Page 453)

MEAN REFRACTION
(Page 454)

This table contains the Refraction of the heavenly bodies, in minutes and decimals at a mean state of the atmosphere, and corresponding to their apparent altitudes. This correction is always to be *subtracted* from the apparent altitude of the object.

Example: The mean refraction for the apparent altitude 10° 50', is 4·'9.

Caution: For low altitudes all refraction tables are more or less inaccurate.

ADDITIONAL REFRACTION CORRECTIONS
(Page 454)

The mean refraction values given in the Mean Refraction table are for an atmospheric pressure of 1,000 mb (29·5 in) and an air temperature of 10°C (50°F). If the atmospheric pressure or temperature differ from these values additional corrections must be applied to the apparent altitude. These corrections are contained in the tables 'Additional Refraction Corrections for Atmospheric Pressure' and 'Additional Refraction Corrections for Air Temperature'

Example: Find the true altitude of the sun when the observed altitude of the sun's lower limb was 6° 00', height of eye 26 m (85 ft), atmospheric pressure 1020 mb (30·1 in), air temperature 0° C (32° F).

$$
\begin{array}{rcl}
\text{Observed altitude sun's lower limb} & = & 6° \quad 00' \\
\text{Total correction} & = & 0°-01·5' \\
\hline
\text{True altitude} & = & 5° \quad 58·5' \\
\text{Correction for temperature} & = & -0·4' \\
\text{Correction for pressure} & = & -0·2' \\
\hline
\text{Corrected altitude} & = & 5° \quad 57·9' \\
\hline
\end{array}
$$

If the altitude is greater than 5° 00' the error due to applying these corrections to the true altitude can be ignored in practice.

N.B.—To convert barometer readings from mercury inches to millibars, or vice-versa, see page 499. To convert temperatures from Fahrenheit to Celsius, or vice-versa, see page 494 .

The adjustment of mean refraction as shown above is important only when the altitude is small. It should be borne in mind that on account of uncertain refraction position lines obtained from sights taken when the altitude of the body is less than 10° or so should not be relied upon implicitly. Moreover, due to the effect of atmospheric refraction on dip it is unwise to place too much reliance on sights taken, whatever the altitude, when there is cause for abnormal refraction to be suspected.

CORRECTION of MOON'S MERIDIAN PASSAGE

(Page 455)

The correction obtained from this table is to be applied to the time of meridian passage given in the Nautical Almanac (i.e. the time of transit at Greenwich) in order to find the time of the local transit according to the observer's longitude.

$$\text{Correction} = \frac{D \times \text{longitude}}{360}$$ where D is the difference between the times of successive transits.

When the observer is in *East* longitude, D is the difference between the time of transit on the day of observation and the time of transit on the *preceding* day.   When in *West* longitude it is the difference between the times on the day of observation and the *following* day.

Example: From Naut. Alm. L.M.T. of moon's upper transit at Greenwich is:—

	h.	m.
1st July	18	44
	diff. 48m.	
2nd July	19	32
	diff. 53m.	
3rd July	20	25

Find G.M.T. of moon's upper transit on 2nd July (a) in longitude 156° E., (b) in longitude 63° W.

		July	h.	m.
(a)	L.M.T. of transit at Greenwich	2	19	32
	Corr'n. for D 48m., long. 156° E.			−20·8
	L.M.T. of local transit	2	19	11·2
	East longitude in time units		−10	24
	G.M.T. of local transit (156° E.)	2	8	47·2

		July	h.	m.
(b)	L.M.T. of transit at Greenwich	2	19	32
	Corr'n. for D 53m., long. 63° W.			+9·2
	L.M.T. of local transit	2	19	41·2
	West longitude in time units		+4	12
	G.M.T. of local transit (63° W.)	2	23	53·2

SUN'S TOTAL CORRECTION

(Pages 456–461 and Inside Front Cover)

This is a combined table for the correction of both Lower Limb and Upper Limb altitudes of the Sun. To simplify interpolation for intermediate altitudes and heights of eye, the tabulation is based on columnar and linear correction differences of 0.2.

The corrections in the main table give the combined effect of dip, refraction, parallax in altitude and an assumed semi-diameter of 16.0. Subsidiary corrections at the foot of the table give the monthly variations of the semi-diameter from the assumed value of 16.0. The corrections and subsidiary corrections are added to or subtracted from the observed altitude as show in the table.

Example 1				*Example 2*			
Obs. Alt. Sun's L.L.	=	24	57.2	Obs. Alt. Sun's U.L.	=	33	45.6
Corrn. for obs. alt. 25				Corrn. for obs. alt. 34			
and H.E. 12.0m	=	+	8.0	and H.E. 19.7m	=		
		+	0.1	Subsidiary corrn. for June	=	+	0.2
True Alt. of Sun's centre	=	25	05.3	True Alt. of Sun's centre	=	33	20.7

STAR'S TOTAL CORRECTION

(Pages 462–465 and Inside Back Cover)

This table corrects the combined effects of dip and refraction. To simplify interpolation for intermediate altitudes and heights of eye, the table is based on columnar and linear correction differences of 0'.2.

This table can also be used for the correction of observed altitudes of the planets, but in the case of Venus and Mars the small additional correction given in the Nautical Almanac for parallax and phase may be necessary. The size of these corrections vary with the date and the altitude of the planet.

MOON'S TOTAL CORRECTION

(Lower Limb – pages 466–478; Upper Limb – pages 479–491)

This table corrects the combined effects of dip, atmospheric refraction, augmented semi-diameter and parallax in altitude. The dip component used in the main table is a constant 12'.3, therefore the subsidiary correction given at the foot of the pages must be added to the main correction. The argument for this subsidiary correction is the observer's height of eye.

No account has been taken of the reduction with latitude of the moon's horizontal parallax, but in general this is of no practical significance. In cases where a high degree of accuracy is required it will be necessary to apply the corrections separately together with the adjustment of the refraction correction for the prevailing atmospheric pressure and temperature.

The main corrections are ALWAYS added to both the lower limb and upper limb observed altitudes of the moon, the dip correction is then added and for upper limb observations 30' must be subtracted from the result.

Example 1

Moon's Hor. Pax. (from N. Alm.) = 57'.5

Obs. Alt. moon's lower limb	= 38°47'.4
Correction from main table	= + 47'.1
Correction for height of eye 13.5m	= + 5'.8
True altitude of moon	= 39°40'.3

Example 2

Moon's Hor. Pax. (from N. Alm.) = 59'0

Obs. Alt. moon's upper limb	= 69°36'.0
Correction from main table	= + 22'.0
Correction for height of eye 33m	= + 2'.2
	70°00'.2
	− 30'
True altitude of moon	= 69°30'.2

III. TABLES FOR COASTAL NAVIGATION

DAY'S RUN - AVERAGE SPEED TABLE

(Pages 494–500)

This table provides a rapid means of finding the average speed directly from the arguments 'steaming time' and 'distance run'. It will be appreciated that there is no necessity to convert minutes into decimals of a day, and that no logarithms or co-logarithms are required. Simple addition is all that is needed.

The scope of the table has been made wide enough to cover cases of high speed vessels (up to 40 knots or so) on easterly or westerly courses in high latitudes where change of longitude between one local noon and the next may amount to some 30°, or 2 hours of time.

Distances are tabulated as multiples of 100 miles. Increments of speed for multiples of 10 miles and multiples of 1 mile are obtained simply by shifting the decimal point one or two places to the left, respectively.

Example: Given steaming time 23 h. 29 m., distance 582 miles, find the average speed.

Distance in miles	Speed in knots
500	21·291
80*	3·4066
2†	0·08517
582	24·78277

That is, average speed correct to two places of decimals, which are generally considered sufficient, is 24·78 knots.

* Enter with 800 miles and shift decimal point 1 place to the left
† Enter with 200 miles and shift decimal point 2 places to the left

RADAR RANGE TABLE

(Page 501)

RADAR PLOTTER'S SPEED AND DISTANCE TABLE

(Page 502)

MEASURED MILE SPEED TABLE

(Pages 503–509)

This table is arranged in 'critical table' form and gives speeds correct to the nearest hundredth of a knot without interpolation. If the time argument is an exact tabulated value, the speed immediately above it should be taken.

1. If the time recorded for the measured mile is 9 m. 16·2 s., the speed is 6·47 knots.
2. If the time is 4 m. 55·3 s., the speed is 12·19 knots.
3. If the time is 3 m. 52·3 s., the speed is 15·49 knots.
4. Suppose a ship on trials makes six runs over a measured mile, three against the tide and three with the tide, such that the timings by stop-watch are as follows:—

	m.	s.
First run against tide	3	28·8
First run with tide.........................	3	18·4
Second run against tide	3	30·0
Second run with tide	3	17·8
Third run against tide	3	31·1
Third run with tide	3	16·7
Then total time for 6 miles is	20	22·8
∴Average time for 1 mile is	3	23·8

From the table the average speed for the six runs is 17·66 knots.

Strictly speaking, the average speed should be computed by finding the 'mean of means', in which case the work would be arranged as follows.

RUN	m.	s.	SPEED KNOTS	1ST MEAN	2ND MEAN	3RD MEAN	4TH MEAN	MEAN OF MEANS
1st	3	28·8	17·24					
				17·690				
2nd	3	18·4	18·14		17·6650			
				17·640		17·66000		
3rd	3	30·0	17·14		17·6550		17·655625	
				17·670		17·65125		17·6528125
4th	3	17·8	18·20		17·6475		17·650000	
				17·625		17·64875		
5th	3	31·1	17·05		17·6500			
				17·675				
6th	3	16·7	18·30					

6) 106·07	4) 70·6175	
17·68	17·6544	17·68
Ordinary mean speed	*Ordinary mean of second means**	*True mean speed*

At speeds greater than about 19½ knots it will be noticed that in certain cases a change of a tenth of a second in the time will make a difference of more than one hundredth of a knot in the tabulated speed. For example, if the time for one mile is between 2 m. 38·7 s. and 2 m. 38·8 s. the speed, correct to two places of decimals, could be either 22·68 or 22·67 knots.

In very high speed vessels the recorded time for a measured mile may be so small as to be beyond the scope of the table. Even so, a reasonably accurate speed is easily obtained by entering the table with double the recorded time, and then doubling the speed so obtained. For instance, if a mile is run in 1 m. 55·2 s., enter with 3 m. 50·4 s. This gives 15·62 knots which is half the required speed of 31·24 knots (and this will be correct within 0·02 of a knot). By calculation the correct speed is actually 31·250 knots.

* This is usually regarded as being sufficiently accurate

Besides its orthodox use for speed trial purposes, the table will be found useful to navigators for other purposes.

For example, suppose it is decided to alter course after the ship has run 6 miles on a certain heading from a position line obtained at 1432, the speed of the ship being 11·75 knots. The table shows that at this speed the ship will run one mile in a little over 5 m. 6 s., or 6 miles in about 30½ minutes. Therefore, the course should be altered at 1502½.

In certain circumstances it might be considered convenient to plot the radar target of another vessel at regular intervals corresponding to one mile runs of one's own vessel. Suppose the speed to be 9·70 knots, which the table shows to correspond to a mile in about 6 m. 11 s. Then, if the stop-watch is started from zero at the time of the first observation, successive observations should be taken as nearly as practicable when the watch shows 6 m. 11 s., 12 m. 22 s., 18 m. 33s., 24 m. 44 s., and so on.

DISTANCE BY VERTICAL ANGLE

(Pages 510–515)

This table gives the distance of an observer from objects of known height when the angle between base and the summit is known. The tables are for distances up to 7 miles so that the whole object from base to summit will be in view when the height of eye is more than 12 metres (39 feet) Observers whose height of eye is less than this must apply a correction for Dip if their distance from the object exceeds the distance of the sea horizon given for their height of eye in the table Distance of the Sea Horizon (page 486).

The distances given are from the position of the observer to a point at the base vertically below the summit, and it is to this point that the angle should be measured. In places where there is a big rise and fall of tide it would be necessary to make an allowance for the state of the tide, as heights are always given above Mean High Water Springs or Mean Higher High Water. In the case of light-vessels there is no allowance for the state of the tide, as the water plane is always at the same distance with reference to any part of the vessel.

To find the Distance
Measure the angle from summit to base and note the angle; then under the given height find the observed angle, and opposite the angle will be found the distance off in Miles in the *left* hand column.

Example: The vertical angle between the base and summit of a light-house situated 61 m (200 feet) above sea level was 0° 57′. Required the distance.

Under 61 m (200 ft) and opposite the given angle is 2·0 miles, the distance.

To find the Angle to place on the Sextant to pass at a given distance from a Point of Known Height
Opposite the given distance and under the known height will be found the required angle to place on the sextant.

Example: Wishing to pass a point situated 150 m (492 ft) above sea level at a distance of 4 miles, required the angle to place on the sextant.

Opposite 4 miles in the distance column at the *side*, and under 150 m (492 ft) at the *top*, is 1° 10′, the angle required to place on the sextant.

EXTREME RANGE TABLE
(Pages 516–517)

This table has been compiled for the purpose of determining the maximum distance at which an object may be seen at sea according to its elevation and that of the observer's eye. Heights are given in metres with their equivalents in feet.

The arguments with which the table is ordinarily entered are the height of the observer's eye and the height of the distant object which last, however, need not be a terrestrial one but may be the masthead of a vessel, or some other easily defined detail thereof, provided always that the height of the feature or object observed be definitely known. The arguments, too, can be made interchangeable, thus, should the lookout, stationed at the masthead at an elevation exceeding 30 metres observe a low-lying rock having a height of less than that amount, then the terms can be substituted for each other and the 'Height of Eye' can be sought in the 'Height of Object' column, and vice versa.

The tables are computed on the basis of normal atmospheric conditions, refraction and visibility, and, in the case of lights, the quantity taken out as 'Extreme Range' presupposes that the light possesses sufficient power to be discernible at such a distance. It must be remembered also that the heights of lights and shore objects are referred to Mean High Water Springs or Mean Higher Water therefore due allowance should be made when the time of observation does not approximate thereto, particularly if the elevation or distance should be small.

Example 1: At what distance will a tower 60 m (197 ft) high be visible to an observer whose eye is elevated 20 m (66 ft) above the water?

Take 60 m (197 ft) as the 'Height of Object' in the marginal column and in the column under 20 m (66 ft) 'Height of Eye', at the top of the page, will be found the 25·6 miles distance.

Example 2: The officer of the watch, whose eye is elevated 16 m (52 ft) above the water, observes a shore light, with an elevation of 45 m (148 ft), just dipping. At what distance is the ship from the light?

In the column headed 16 m (52 ft) 'Height of Eye' and abreast of 45 m (148 ft) 'Height of Object' will be found the distance 22·4 miles.

DISTANCE of the SEA HORIZON
(Page 518)

The tabulations are derived from the formula—Distance of the sea horizon in nautical miles = $2 \cdot 095 \sqrt{h}$, where h = height of eye in metres. Thus for example, when $h = 50$ m (164 ft) the distance of the sea horizon is 14·8 n. miles.

The following examples show how the table can be used.

Example 1: At what distance in good visibility should an observer whose height of eye is 16 m (52 ft) be able to sight a terrestrial object of height 170 m (558 ft)?

$$\begin{array}{lr} \text{Distance of horizon for height } 16 \text{ m (52 ft)} = & 8 \cdot 4 \text{ miles} \\ \text{\textquotedblright} \qquad \text{\textquotedblright} \qquad 170 \text{ m (558 ft)} = & 27 \cdot 3 \text{ miles} \\ \hline \text{Sum} = & 35 \cdot 7 \text{ miles} \\ \hline \end{array}$$

Hence, the object should be visible at a distance of 35·7 miles.

Example 2: The range of visibility of a light is stated on a chart to be 21 M. At what distance from the light will an observer be at the moment when the light has just dipped below the horizon if his height of eye is 50 feet?

Charted range, i.e. for 15 feet height of eye   21   miles
Subtracting distance of horizon for height 15 feet . . . . . .   4·55   „

Range of light at sea level . . . .   16·45   „
Adding distance of horizon for height 50 feet . . . .   8·30   „

Dipping distance, or maximum range to observer . . . . . .   24·75   „

N.B.—This method is applicable only in the case of a light of adequate power, and the accuracy of the result will probably be affected by the fact that the charted height of a light never includes a fraction of a mile. Abnormal refraction will also affect the accuracy of distances obtained by using this table.

DIP OF THE SHORE HORIZON

(Page 519)

When the part of the horizon immediately under the sun is obstructed by land and the observer is near the shore. the Dip for an observed altitude will be greater than that shown in the Dip of the Sea Horizon table. When correcting the altitude the dip should be taken from this table when obtaining the apparent altitude.

Example: The observed altitude of the sun's lower limb above the shore horizon (distance 1·6 miles) was 22° 30′, Height of Eye 12 m (39 ft).

Observed altitude . . . .   =   22° 30′
Dip of Shore Horizon . . . .   =   −14·7′   (H.E. = 12 m,
                                                      distance = 1·6 miles)
∴Apparent altitude . . . .   =   22° 15·3′

If the refraction is believed to be abnormal the table should be used with caution.

The table can also be used to obtain the approximate range of a ship by measuring the angle between the ship's waterline and the sea horizon.

Example: The sextant angle between a ship's waterline and the sea horizon is 5·0′. Height of Eye = 25 m (82 ft).

From dip of sea horizon table. Dip . . . .   =   8·8′
                                          Observed angle . . . .   =   5·0′

∴Dip of the ship's waterline . . . .   =   14·8
∴From the dip of the shore horizon table, Range . . . .   =   3·5 miles

CORRECTION REQUIRED TO CONVERT A RADIO GREAT CIRCLE BEARING TO MERCATORIAL BEARING

(Page 520)

IV. PHYSICAL AND CONVERSION TABLES

TO CONVERT ARC TO TIME AND TIME TO ARC
(Pages 522–523)

HOURS AND MINUTES TO DECIMAL OF A DAY
(Page 524)

ATMOSPHERIC PRESSURE CONVERSION TABLE
(Page 525)

°FAHRENHEIT - °CELSIUS - °FAHRENHEIT
(Page 526)

SI - BRITISH UNITS
(Pages 527–528)

BRITISH GALLONS - U.S. GALLONS - LITRES
(Pages 529–531)

NAUTICAL MILES, STATUTE MILES, KILOMETRES
(Pages 532–534)

FATHOMS - METRES - FATHOMS
(Page 535)

DECIMAL FRACTIONS OF A DEGREE
(Page 536 and Inside Back Cover)

V. PORTS OF THE WORLD

PORTS OF THE WORLD. LATITUDES AND LONGITUDES

(Pages 538–595)

This section is an alphabetical list of all the ports of the world used by commercial shipping, the positions given to the nearest minute of latitude and longitude being those of the port area, not the centre of the towns or cities. Every effort has been made to ensure that the names and positions given are correct by checking with charts and reliable official sources and publications.

The user should note the following points:-

1 The order of listing is strictly alphabetical   and if two or more ports have the same name they are listed in the sub-order of their countries, alphabetically.

2 A port which has several commonly used names or whose name has been changed recently is entered under each name with the alternative names in brackets.

3 Ports whose names consist of two or more words are entered under each word.

   e.g. Port Chalmers is entered under P as Port Chalmers and under C as Chalmers, Port.

4 To assist in locating a port its country is given in Anglicised form and where it is considered useful the name of the bay, island, river etc. on which it is sited is given in the form used in its country.

5 Accents and diphthongs have been omitted.

I COMPUTATION TABLES

TRAVERSE TABLE
0 Degrees

0°

| 360° / 180° | | | | | 000° / 180° |

D. Lon	Dep.		D. Lon	Dep.		D. Lon	Dep.		D. Lon	Dep.		D. Lon	Dep.	
Dist.	D. Lat.	Dep.	Dist.	D. Lat.	Dep.	Dist.	D. Lat.	Dep.	Dist.	D. Lat.	Dep.	Dist.	D. Lat.	Dep.
1	01·0	00·0	61	61·0	00·0	121	121·0	00·0	181	181·0	00·0	241	241·0	00·0
2	02·0	00·0	62	62·0	00·0	122	122·0	00·0	182	182·0	00·0	242	242·0	00·0
3	03·0	00·0	63	63·0	00·0	123	123·0	00·0	183	183·0	00·0	243	243·0	00·0
4	04·0	00·0	64	64·0	00·0	124	124·0	00·0	184	184·0	00·0	244	244·0	00·0
5	05·0	00·0	65	65·0	00·0	125	125·0	00·0	185	185·0	00·0	245	245·0	00·0
6	06·0	00·0	66	66·0	00·0	126	126·0	00·0	186	186·0	00·0	246	246·0	00·0
7	07·0	00·0	67	67·0	00·0	127	127·0	00·0	187	187·0	00·0	247	247·0	00·0
8	08·0	00·0	68	68·0	00·0	128	128·0	00·0	188	188·0	00·0	248	248·0	00·0
9	09·0	00·0	69	69·0	00·0	129	129·0	00·0	189	189·0	00·0	249	249·0	00·0
10	10·0	00·0	70	70·0	00·0	130	130·0	00·0	190	190·0	00·0	250	250·0	00·0
11	11·0	00·0	71	71·0	00·0	131	131·0	00·0	191	191·0	00·0	251	251·0	00·0
12	12·0	00·0	72	72·0	00·0	132	132·0	00·0	192	192·0	00·0	252	252·0	00·0
13	13·0	00·0	73	73·0	00·0	133	133·0	00·0	193	193·0	00·0	253	253·0	00·0
14	14·0	00·0	74	74·0	00·0	134	134·0	00·0	194	194·0	00·0	254	254·0	00·0
15	15·0	00·0	75	75·0	00·0	135	135·0	00·0	195	195·0	00·0	255	255·0	00·0
16	16·0	00·0	76	76·0	00·0	136	136·0	00·0	196	196·0	00·0	256	256·0	00·0
17	17·0	00·0	77	77·0	00·0	137	137·0	00·0	197	197·0	00·0	257	257·0	00·0
18	18·0	00·0	78	78·0	00·0	138	138·0	00·0	198	198·0	00·0	258	258·0	00·0
19	19·0	00·0	79	79·0	00·0	139	139·0	00·0	199	199·0	00·0	259	259·0	00·0
20	20·0	00·0	80	80·0	00·0	140	140·0	00·0	200	200·0	00·0	260	260·0	00·0
21	21·0	00·0	81	81·0	00·0	141	141·0	00·0	201	201·0	00·0	261	261·0	00·0
22	22·0	00·0	82	82·0	00·0	142	142·0	00·0	202	202·0	00·0	262	262·0	00·0
23	23·0	00·0	83	83·0	00·0	143	143·0	00·0	203	203·0	00·0	263	263·0	00·0
24	24·0	00·0	84	84·0	00·0	144	144·0	00·0	204	204·0	00·0	264	264·0	00·0
25	25·0	00·0	85	85·0	00·0	145	145·0	00·0	205	205·0	00·0	265	265·0	00·0
26	26·0	00·0	86	86·0	00·0	146	146·0	00·0	206	206·0	00·0	266	266·0	00·0
27	27·0	00·0	87	87·0	00·0	147	147·0	00·0	207	207·0	00·0	267	267·0	00·0
28	28·0	00·0	88	88·0	00·0	148	148·0	00·0	208	208·0	00·0	268	268·0	00·0
29	29·0	00·0	89	89·0	00·0	149	149·0	00·0	209	209·0	00·0	269	269·0	00·0
30	30·0	00·0	90	90·0	00·0	150	150·0	00·0	210	210·0	00·0	270	270·0	00·0
31	31·0	00·0	91	91·0	00·0	151	151·0	00·0	211	211·0	00·0	271	271·0	00·0
32	32·0	00·0	92	92·0	00·0	152	152·0	00·0	212	212·0	00·0	272	272·0	00·0
33	33·0	00·0	93	93·0	00·0	153	153·0	00·0	213	213·0	00·0	273	273·0	00·0
34	34·0	00·0	94	94·0	00·0	154	154·0	00·0	214	214·0	00·0	274	274·0	00·0
35	35·0	00·0	95	95·0	00·0	155	155·0	00·0	215	215·0	00·0	275	275·0	00·0
36	36·0	00·0	96	96·0	00·0	156	156·0	00·0	216	216·0	00·0	276	276·0	00·0
37	37·0	00·0	97	97·0	00·0	157	157·0	00·0	217	217·0	00·0	277	277·0	00·0
38	38·0	00·0	98	98·0	00·0	158	158·0	00·0	218	218·0	00·0	278	278·0	00·0
39	39·0	00·0	99	99·0	00·0	159	159·0	00·0	219	219·0	00·0	279	279·0	00·0
40	40·0	00·0	100	100·0	00·0	160	160·0	00·0	220	220·0	00·0	280	280·0	00·0
41	41·0	00·0	101	101·0	00·0	161	161·0	00·0	221	221·0	00·0	281	281·0	00·0
42	42·0	00·0	102	102·0	00·0	162	162·0	00·0	222	222·0	00·0	282	282·0	00·0
43	43·0	00·0	103	103·0	00·0	163	163·0	00·0	223	223·0	00·0	283	283·0	00·0
44	44·0	00·0	104	104·0	00·0	164	164·0	00·0	224	224·0	00·0	284	284·0	00·0
45	45·0	00·0	105	105·0	00·0	165	165·0	00·0	225	225·0	00·0	285	285·0	00·0
46	46·0	00·0	106	106·0	00·0	166	166·0	00·0	226	226·0	00·0	286	286·0	00·0
47	47·0	00·0	107	107·0	00·0	167	167·0	00·0	227	227·0	00·0	287	287·0	00·0
48	48·0	00·0	108	108·0	00·0	168	168·0	00·0	228	228·0	00·0	288	288·0	00·0
49	49·0	00·0	109	109·0	00·0	169	169·0	00·0	229	229·0	00·0	289	289·0	00·0
50	50·0	00·0	110	110·0	00·0	170	170·0	00·0	230	230·0	00·0	290	290·0	00·0
51	51·0	00·0	111	111·0	00·0	171	171·0	00·0	231	231·0	00·0	291	291·0	00·0
52	52·0	00·0	112	112·0	00·0	172	172·0	00·0	232	232·0	00·0	292	292·0	00·0
53	53·0	00·0	113	113·0	00·0	173	173·0	00·0	233	233·0	00·0	293	293·0	00·0
54	54·0	00·0	114	114·0	00·0	174	174·0	00·0	234	234·0	00·0	294	294·0	00·0
55	55·0	00·0	115	115·0	00·0	175	175·0	00·0	235	235·0	00·0	295	295·0	00·0
56	56·0	00·0	116	116·0	00·0	176	176·0	00·0	236	236·0	00·0	296	296·0	00·0
57	57·0	00·0	117	117·0	00·0	177	177·0	00·0	237	237·0	00·0	297	297·0	00·0
58	58·0	00·0	118	118·0	00·0	178	178·0	00·0	238	238·0	00·0	298	298·0	00·0
59	59·0	00·0	119	119·0	00·0	179	179·0	00·0	239	239·0	00·0	299	299·0	00·0
60	60·0	00·0	120	120·0	00·0	180	180·0	00·0	240	240·0	00·0	300	300·0	00·0
Dist.	Dep.	D. Lat.	Dist.	Dep.	D. Lat.	Dist.	Dep.	D. Lat.	Dist.	Dep.	D. Lat.	Dist.	Dep.	D. Lat.
D. Lon		Dep.	D. Lon		Dep.	D. Lon		Dep.	D. Lon		Dep.	D. Lon		Dep.

90°

| W. or / 270° | 90 Degrees | | E. or / 090° | 6h 00m |

TRAVERSE TABLE
0 Degrees

360° 180°						000° 180°			0°

D. Lon	Dep.		D. Lon	Dep.		D. Lon	Dep.		D. Lon	Dep.		D. Lon	Dep.	
Dist.	D. Lat.	Dep.	Dist.	D. Lat.	Dep.	Dist.	D. Lat.	Dep.	Dist.	D. Lat.	Dep.	Dist.	D. Lat.	Dep.
301	301·0	00·0	361	361·0	00·0	421	421·0	00·0	481	481·0	00·0	541	541·0	00·0
302	302·0	00·0	362	362·0	00·0	422	422·0	00·0	482	482·0	00·0	542	542·0	00·0
303	303·0	00·0	363	363·0	00·0	423	423·0	00·0	483	483·0	00·0	543	543·0	00·0
304	304·0	00·0	364	364·0	00·0	424	424·0	00·0	484	484·0	00·0	544	544·0	00·0
305	305·0	00·0	365	365·0	00·0	425	425·0	00·0	485	485·0	00·0	545	545·0	00·0
306	306·0	00·0	366	366·0	00·0	426	426·0	00·0	486	486·0	00·0	546	546·0	00·0
307	307·0	00·0	367	367·0	00·0	427	427·0	00·0	487	487·0	00·0	547	547·0	00·0
308	308·0	00·0	368	368·0	00·0	428	428·0	00·0	488	488·0	00·0	548	548·0	00·0
309	309·0	00·0	369	369·0	00·0	429	429·0	00·0	489	489·0	00·0	549	549·0	00·0
310	310·0	00·0	370	370·0	00·0	430	430·0	00·0	490	490·0	00·0	550	550·0	00·0
311	311·0	00·0	371	371·0	00·0	431	431·0	00·0	491	491·0	00·0	551	551·0	00·0
312	312·0	00·0	372	372·0	00·0	432	432·0	00·0	492	492·0	00·0	552	552·0	00·0
313	313·0	00·0	373	373·0	00·0	433	433·0	00·0	493	493·0	00·0	553	553·0	00·0
314	314·0	00·0	374	374·0	00·0	434	434·0	00·0	494	494·0	00·0	554	554·0	00·0
315	315·0	00·0	375	375·0	00·0	435	435·0	00·0	495	495·0	00·0	555	555·0	00·0
316	316·0	00·0	376	376·0	00·0	436	436·0	00·0	496	496·0	00·0	556	556·0	00·0
317	317·0	00·0	377	377·0	00·0	437	437·0	00·0	497	497·0	00·0	557	557·0	00·0
318	318·0	00·0	378	378·0	00·0	438	438·0	00·0	498	498·0	00·0	558	558·0	00·0
319	319·0	00·0	379	379·0	00·0	439	439·0	00·0	499	499·0	00·0	559	559·0	00·0
320	320·0	00·0	380	380·0	00·0	440	440·0	00·0	500	500·0	00·0	560	560·0	00·0
321	321·0	00·0	381	381·0	00·0	441	441·0	00·0	501	501·0	00·0	561	561·0	00·0
322	322·0	00·0	382	382·0	00·0	442	442·0	00·0	502	502·0	00·0	562	562·0	00·0
323	323·0	00·0	383	383·0	00·0	443	443·0	00·0	503	503·0	00·0	563	563·0	00·0
324	324·0	00·0	384	384·0	00·0	444	444·0	00·0	504	504·0	00·0	564	564·0	00·0
325	325·0	00·0	385	385·0	00·0	445	445·0	00·0	505	505·0	00·0	565	565·0	00·0
326	326·0	00·0	386	386·0	00·0	446	446·0	00·0	506	506·0	00·0	566	566·0	00·0
327	327·0	00·0	387	387·0	00·0	447	447·0	00·0	507	507·0	00·0	567	567·0	00·0
328	328·0	00·0	388	388·0	00·0	448	448·0	00·0	508	508·0	00·0	568	568·0	00·0
329	329·0	00·0	389	389·0	00·0	449	449·0	00·0	509	509·0	00·0	569	569·0	00·0
330	330·0	00·0	390	390·0	00·0	450	450·0	00·0	510	510·0	00·0	570	570·0	00·0
331	331·0	00·0	391	391·0	00·0	451	451·0	00·0	511	511·0	00·0	571	571·0	00·0
332	332·0	00·0	392	392·0	00·0	452	452·0	00·0	512	512·0	00·0	572	572·0	00·0
333	333·0	00·0	393	393·0	00·0	453	453·0	00·0	513	513·0	00·0	573	573·0	00·0
334	334·0	00·0	394	394·0	00·0	454	454·0	00·0	514	514·0	00·0	574	574·0	00·0
335	335·0	00·0	395	395·0	00·0	455	455·0	00·0	515	515·0	00·0	575	575·0	00·0
336	336·0	00·0	396	396·0	00·0	456	456·0	00·0	516	516·0	00·0	576	576·0	00·0
337	337·0	00·0	397	397·0	00·0	457	457·0	00·0	517	517·0	00·0	577	577·0	00·0
338	338·0	00·0	398	398·0	00·0	458	458·0	00·0	518	518·0	00·0	578	578·0	00·0
339	339·0	00·0	399	399·0	00·0	459	459·0	00·0	519	519·0	00·0	579	579·0	00·0
340	340·0	00·0	400	400·0	00·0	460	460·0	00·0	520	520·0	00·0	580	580·0	00·0
341	341·0	00·0	401	401·0	00·0	461	461·0	00·0	521	521·0	00·0	581	581·0	00·0
342	342·0	00·0	402	402·0	00·0	462	462·0	00·0	522	522·0	00·0	582	582·0	00·0
343	343·0	00·0	403	403·0	00·0	463	463·0	00·0	523	523·0	00·0	583	583·0	00·0
344	344·0	00·0	404	404·0	00·0	464	464·0	00·0	524	524·0	00·0	584	584·0	00·0
345	345·0	00·0	405	405·0	00·0	465	465·0	00·0	525	525·0	00·0	585	585·0	00·0
346	346·0	00·0	406	406·0	00·0	466	466·0	00·0	526	526·0	00·0	586	586·0	00·0
347	347·0	00·0	407	407·0	00·0	467	467·0	00·0	527	527·0	00·0	587	587·0	00·0
348	348·0	00·0	408	408·0	00·0	468	468·0	00·0	528	528·0	00·0	588	588·0	00·0
349	349·0	00·0	409	409·0	00·0	469	469·0	00·0	529	529·0	00·0	589	589·0	00·0
350	350·0	00·0	410	410·0	00·0	470	470·0	00·0	530	530·0	00·0	590	590·0	00·0
351	351·0	00·0	411	411·0	00·0	471	471·0	00·0	531	531·0	00·0	591	591·0	00·0
352	352·0	00·0	412	412·0	00·0	472	472·0	00·0	532	532·0	00·0	592	592·0	00·0
353	353·0	00·0	413	413·0	00·0	473	473·0	00·0	533	533·0	00·0	593	593·0	00·0
354	354·0	00·0	414	414·0	00·0	474	474·0	00·0	534	534·0	00·0	594	594·0	00·0
355	355·0	00·0	415	415·0	00·0	475	475·0	00·0	535	535·0	00·0	595	595·0	00·0
356	356·0	00·0	416	416·0	00·0	476	476·0	00·0	536	536·0	00·0	596	596·0	00·0
357	357·0	00·0	417	417·0	00·0	477	477·0	00·0	537	537·0	00·0	597	597·0	00·0
358	358·0	00·0	418	418·0	00·0	478	478·0	00·0	538	538·0	00·0	598	598·0	00·0
359	359·0	00·0	419	419·0	00·0	479	479·0	00·0	539	539·0	00·0	599	599·0	00·0
360	360·0	00·0	420	420·0	00·0	480	480·0	00·0	540	540·0	00·0	600	600·0	00·0
Dist.	Dep.	D. Lat.	Dist.	Dep.	D. Lat.	Dist.	Dep.	D. Lat.	Dist.	Dep.	D. Lat.	Dist.	Dep.	D. Lat.
D. Lon		Dep.	D. Lon		Dep.	D. Lon		Dep.	D. Lon		Dep.	D. Lon		Dep.

W.or 270°	90 Degrees	E.or 090°	6h 00m	90°

TRAVERSE TABLE
1 Degree

1°

359° / 181°												001° / 179°		0h 04m

D. Lon	Dep.		D. Lon	Dep.		D. Lon	Dep.		D. Lon	Dep.		D. Lon	Dep.	
Dist.	D. Lat.	Dep.	Dist.	D. Lat.	Dep.	Dist.	D. Lat.	Dep.	Dist.	D. Lat.	Dep.	Dist.	D. Lat.	Dep.
1	01·0	00·0	61	61·1	01·1	121	121·0	02·1	181	181·0	03·2	241	241·0	04·2
2	02·0	00·0	62	62·0	01·1	122	122·0	02·1	182	182·0	03·2	242	242·0	04·2
3	03·0	00·1	63	63·0	01·1	123	123·0	02·1	183	183·0	03·2	243	243·0	04·2
4	04·0	00·1	64	64·0	01·1	124	124·0	02·2	184	184·0	03·2	244	244·0	04·3
5	05·0	00·1	65	65·0	01·1	125	125·0	02·2	185	185·0	03·2	245	245·0	04·3
6	06·0	00·1	66	66·0	01·2	126	126·0	02·2	186	186·0	03·2	246	246·0	04·3
7	07·0	00·1	67	67·0	01·2	127	127·0	02·2	187	187·0	03·3	247	247·0	04·3
8	08·0	00·1	68	68·0	01·2	128	128·0	02·2	188	188·0	03·3	248	248·0	04·3
9	09·0	00·2	69	69·0	01·2	129	129·0	02·2	189	189·0	03·3	249	249·0	04·3
10	10·0	00·2	70	70·0	01·2	130	130·0	02·3	190	190·0	03·3	250	250·0	04·4
11	11·0	00·2	71	71·0	01·2	131	131·0	02·3	191	191·0	03·3	251	251·0	04·4
12	12·0	00·2	72	72·0	01·3	132	132·0	02·3	192	192·0	03·4	252	252·0	04·4
13	13·0	00·2	73	73·0	01·3	133	133·0	02·3	193	193·0	03·4	253	253·0	04·4
14	14·0	00·2	74	74·0	01·3	134	134·0	02·3	194	194·0	03·4	254	254·0	04·4
15	15·0	00·3	75	75·0	01·3	135	135·0	02·4	195	195·0	03·4	255	255·0	04·4
16	16·0	00·3	76	76·0	01·3	136	136·0	02·4	196	196·0	03·4	256	256·0	04·5
17	17·0	00·3	77	77·0	01·3	137	137·0	02·4	197	197·0	03·4	257	257·0	04·5
18	18·0	00·3	78	78·0	01·4	138	138·0	02·4	198	198·0	03·5	258	258·0	04·5
19	19·0	00·3	79	79·0	01·4	139	139·0	02·4	199	199·0	03·5	259	259·0	04·5
20	20·0	00·3	80	80·0	01·4	140	140·0	02·4	200	200·0	03·5	260	260·0	04·5
21	21·0	00·4	81	81·0	01·4	141	141·0	02·5	201	201·0	03·5	261	261·0	04·5
22	22·0	00·4	82	82·0	01·4	142	142·0	02·5	202	202·0	03·5	262	262·0	04·6
23	23·0	00·4	83	83·0	01·4	143	143·0	02·5	203	203·0	03·5	263	263·0	04·6
24	24·0	00·4	84	84·0	01·5	144	144·0	02·5	204	204·0	03·6	264	264·0	04·6
25	25·0	00·4	85	85·0	01·5	145	145·0	02·5	205	205·0	03·6	265	265·0	04·6
26	26·0	00·5	86	86·0	01·5	146	146·0	02·5	206	206·0	03·6	266	266·0	04·6
27	27·0	00·5	87	87·0	01·5	147	147·0	02·6	207	207·0	03·6	267	267·0	04·7
28	28·0	00·5	88	88·0	01·5	148	148·0	02·6	208	208·0	03·6	268	268·0	04·7
29	29·0	00·5	89	89·0	01·6	149	149·0	02·6	209	209·0	03·7	269	269·0	04·7
30	30·0	00·5	90	90·0	01·6	150	150·0	02·6	210	210·0	03·7	270	270·0	04·7
31	31·0	00·5	91	91·0	01·6	151	151·0	02·6	211	211·0	03·7	271	271·0	04·7
32	32·0	00·6	92	92·0	01·6	152	152·0	02·7	212	212·0	03·7	272	272·0	04·7
33	33·0	00·6	93	93·0	01·6	153	153·0	02·7	213	213·0	03·7	273	273·0	04·8
34	34·0	00·6	94	94·0	01·6	154	154·0	02·7	214	214·0	03·7	274	274·0	04·8
35	35·0	00·6	95	95·0	01·7	155	155·0	02·7	215	215·0	03·8	275	275·0	04·8
36	36·0	00·6	96	96·0	01·7	156	156·0	02·7	216	216·0	03·8	276	276·0	04·8
37	37·0	00·6	97	97·0	01·7	157	157·0	02·7	217	217·0	03·8	277	277·0	04·8
38	38·0	00·7	98	98·0	01·7	158	158·0	02·8	218	218·0	03·8	278	278·0	04·9
39	39·0	00·7	99	99·0	01·7	159	159·0	02·8	219	219·0	03·8	279	279·0	04·9
40	40·0	00·7	100	100·0	01·7	160	160·0	02·8	220	220·0	03·8	280	280·0	04·9
41	41·0	00·7	101	101·0	01·8	161	161·0	02·8	221	221·0	03·9	281	281·0	04·9
42	42·0	00·7	102	102·0	01·8	162	162·0	02·8	222	222·0	03·9	282	282·0	04·9
43	43·0	00·8	103	103·0	01·8	163	163·0	02·8	223	223·0	03·9	283	283·0	04·9
44	44·0	00·8	104	104·0	01·8	164	164·0	02·9	224	224·0	03·9	284	284·0	05·0
45	45·0	00·8	105	105·0	01·8	165	165·0	02·9	225	225·0	03·9	285	285·0	05·0
46	46·0	00·8	106	106·0	01·8	166	166·0	02·9	226	226·0	03·9	286	286·0	05·0
47	47·0	00·8	107	107·0	01·9	167	167·0	02·9	227	227·0	04·0	287	287·0	05·0
48	48·0	00·8	108	108·0	01·9	168	168·0	02·9	228	228·0	04·0	288	288·0	05·0
49	49·0	00·9	109	109·0	01·9	169	169·0	02·9	229	229·0	04·0	289	289·0	05·0
50	50·0	00·9	110	110·0	01·9	170	170·0	03·0	230	230·0	04·0	290	290·0	05·1
51	51·0	00·9	111	111·0	01·9	171	171·0	03·0	231	231·0	04·0	291	291·0	05·1
52	52·0	00·9	112	112·0	02·0	172	172·0	03·0	232	232·0	04·0	292	292·0	05·1
53	53·0	00·9	113	113·0	02·0	173	173·0	03·0	233	233·0	04·1	293	293·0	05·1
54	54·0	00·9	114	114·0	02·0	174	174·0	03·0	234	234·0	04·1	294	294·0	05·1
55	55·0	01·0	115	115·0	02·0	175	175·0	03·1	235	235·0	04·1	295	295·0	05·1
56	56·0	01·0	116	116·0	02·0	176	176·0	03·1	236	236·0	04·1	296	296·0	05·2
57	57·0	01·0	117	117·0	02·0	177	177·0	03·1	237	237·0	04·1	297	297·0	05·2
58	58·0	01·0	118	118·0	02·1	178	178·0	03·1	238	238·0	04·2	298	298·0	05·2
59	59·0	01·0	119	119·0	02·1	179	179·0	03·1	239	239·0	04·2	299	299·0	05·2
60	60·0	01·0	120	120·0	02·1	180	180·0	03·1	240	240·0	04·2	300	300·0	05·2
Dist.	Dep.	D. Lat.	Dist.	Dep.	D. Lat.	Dist.	Dep.	D. Lat.	Dist.	Dep.	D. Lat.	Dist.	Dep.	D. Lat.
D. Lon		Dep.	D. Lon		Dep.	D. Lon		Dep.	D. Lon		Dep.	D. Lon		Dep.

89°

271° / 269°		89 Degrees			089° / 091°	5h 56m

TRAVERSE TABLE
1 Degree

D. Lon / Dist.	Dep. / D. Lat.	Dep.	D. Lon / Dist.	Dep. / D. Lat.	Dep.	D. Lon / Dist.	Dep. / D. Lat.	Dep.	D. Lon / Dist.	Dep. / D. Lat.	Dep.	D. Lon / Dist.	Dep. / D. Lat.	Dep.
301	301·0	05·3	361	360·9	06·3	421	420·9	07·3	481	480·9	08·4	541	540·9	09·4
302	302·0	05·3	362	361·9	06·3	422	421·9	07·4	482	481·9	08·4	542	541·9	09·5
303	303·0	05·3	363	362·9	06·3	423	422·9	07·4	483	482·9	08·4	543	542·9	09·5
304	304·0	05·3	364	363·9	06·4	424	423·9	07·4	484	483·9	08·5	544	543·9	09·5
305	305·0	05·3	365	364·9	06·4	425	424·9	07·4	485	484·9	08·5	545	544·9	09·5
306	306·0	05·3	366	365·9	06·4	426	425·9	07·4	486	485·9	08·5	546	545·9	09·5
307	307·0	05·4	367	366·9	06·4	427	426·9	07·5	487	486·9	08·5	547	546·9	09·5
308	308·0	05·4	368	367·9	06·4	428	427·9	07·5	488	487·9	08·5	548	547·9	09·6
309	309·0	05·4	369	368·9	06·4	429	428·9	07·5	489	488·9	08·5	549	548·9	09·6
310	310·0	05·4	370	369·9	06·5	430	429·9	07·5	490	489·9	08·6	550	549·9	09·6
311	311·0	05·4	371	370·9	06·5	431	430·9	07·5	491	490·9	08·6	551	550·9	09·6
312	312·0	05·4	372	371·9	06·5	432	431·9	07·6	492	491·9	08·6	552	551·9	09·6
313	313·0	05·5	373	372·9	06·5	433	432·9	07·6	493	492·9	08·6	553	552·9	09·7
314	314·0	05·5	374	373·9	06·5	434	433·9	07·6	494	493·9	08·6	554	553·9	09·7
315	315·0	05·5	375	374·9	06·5	435	434·9	07·6	495	494·9	08·7	555	554·9	09·7
316	316·0	05·5	376	375·9	06·6	436	435·9	07·6	496	495·9	08·7	556	555·9	09·7
317	317·0	05·5	377	376·9	06·6	437	436·9	07·6	497	496·9	08·7	557	556·9	09·7
318	318·0	05·5	378	377·9	06·6	438	437·9	07·6	498	497·9	08·7	558	557·9	09·7
319	319·0	05·6	379	378·9	06·6	439	438·9	07·7	499	498·9	08·7	559	558·9	09·8
320	320·0	05·6	380	379·9	06·6	440	439·9	07·7	500	499·9	08·7	560	559·9	09·8
321	321·0	05·6	381	380·9	06·6	441	440·9	07·7	501	500·9	08·7	561	560·9	09·8
322	322·0	05·6	382	381·9	06·7	442	441·9	07·7	502	501·9	08·8	562	561·9	09·8
323	323·0	05·6	383	382·9	06·7	443	442·9	07·7	503	502·9	08·8	563	562·9	09·8
324	324·0	05·7	384	383·9	06·7	444	443·9	07·7	504	503·9	08·8	564	563·9	09·8
325	325·0	05·7	385	384·9	06·7	445	444·9	07·8	505	504·9	08·8	565	564·9	09·9
326	326·0	05·7	386	385·9	06·7	446	445·9	07·8	506	505·9	08·8	566	565·9	09·9
327	327·0	05·7	387	386·9	06·8	447	446·9	07·8	507	506·9	08·8	567	566·9	09·9
328	328·0	05·7	388	387·9	06·8	448	447·9	07·8	508	507·9	08·9	568	567·9	09·9
329	328·9	05·7	389	388·9	06·8	449	448·9	07·8	509	508·9	08·9	569	568·9	09·9
330	329·9	05·8	390	389·9	06·8	450	449·9	07·9	510	509·9	08·9	570	569·9	09·9
331	330·9	05·8	391	390·9	06·8	451	450·9	07·9	511	510·9	08·9	571	570·9	10·0
332	331·9	05·8	392	391·9	06·8	452	451·9	07·9	512	511·9	08·9	572	571·9	10·0
333	332·9	05·8	393	392·9	06·9	453	452·9	07·9	513	512·9	09·0	573	572·9	10·0
334	333·9	05·8	394	393·9	06·9	454	453·9	07·9	514	513·9	09·0	574	573·9	10·0
335	334·9	05·8	395	394·9	06·9	455	454·9	07·9	515	514·9	09·0	575	574·9	10·0
336	335·9	05·9	396	395·9	06·9	456	455·9	08·0	516	515·9	09·0	576	575·9	10·1
337	336·9	05·9	397	396·9	06·9	457	456·9	08·0	517	516·9	09·0	577	576·9	10·1
338	337·9	05·9	398	397·9	06·9	458	457·9	08·0	518	517·9	09·0	578	577·9	10·1
339	338·9	05·9	399	398·9	07·0	459	458·9	08·0	519	518·9	09·1	579	578·9	10·1
340	339·9	05·9	400	399·9	07·0	460	459·9	08·0	520	519·9	09·1	580	579·9	10·1
341	340·9	06·0	401	400·9	07·0	461	460·9	08·0	521	520·9	09·1	581	580·9	10·1
342	341·9	06·0	402	401·9	07·0	462	461·9	08·1	522	521·9	09·1	582	581·9	10·2
343	342·9	06·0	403	402·9	07·0	463	462·9	08·1	523	522·9	09·1	583	582·9	10·2
344	343·9	06·0	404	403·9	07·1	464	463·9	08·1	524	523·9	09·1	584	583·9	10·2
345	344·9	06·0	405	404·9	07·1	465	464·9	08·1	525	524·9	09·2	585	584·9	10·2
346	345·9	06·0	406	405·9	07·1	466	465·9	08·1	526	525·9	09·2	586	585·9	10·2
347	346·9	06·1	407	406·9	07·1	467	466·9	08·2	527	526·9	09·2	587	586·9	10·2
348	347·9	06·1	408	407·9	07·1	468	467·9	08·2	528	527·9	09·2	588	587·9	10·3
349	348·9	06·1	409	408·9	07·1	469	468·9	08·2	529	528·9	09·2	589	588·9	10·3
350	349·9	06·1	410	409·9	07·2	470	469·9	08·2	530	529·9	09·2	590	589·9	10·3
351	350·9	06·1	411	410·9	07·2	471	470·9	08·2	531	530·9	09·3	591	590·9	10·3
352	351·9	06·1	412	411·9	07·2	472	471·9	08·2	532	531·9	09·3	592	591·9	10·3
353	352·9	06·2	413	412·9	07·2	473	472·9	08·3	533	532·9	09·3	593	592·9	10·3
354	353·9	06·2	414	413·9	07·2	474	473·9	08·3	534	533·9	09·3	594	593·9	10·4
355	354·9	06·2	415	414·9	07·2	475	474·9	08·3	535	534·9	09·3	595	594·9	10·4
356	355·9	06·2	416	415·9	07·3	476	475·9	08·3	536	535·9	09·4	596	595·9	10·4
357	356·9	06·2	417	416·9	07·3	477	476·9	08·3	537	536·9	09·4	597	596·9	10·4
358	357·9	06·2	418	417·9	07·3	478	477·9	08·3	538	537·9	09·4	598	597·9	10·4
359	358·9	06·3	419	418·9	07·3	479	478·9	08·4	539	538·9	09·4	599	598·9	10·5
360	359·9	06·3	420	419·9	07·3	480	479·9	08·4	540	539·9	09·4	600	599·9	10·5

| Dist. | Dep. | D. Lat. | Dist. | Dep. | D. Lat. | Dist. | Dep. | D. Lat. | Dist. | Dep. | D. Lat. | Dist. | Dep. | D. Lat. |

TRAVERSE TABLE
2 Degrees

2°   358° / 182°   002° / 178°   0h 08m

D. Lon — Dep.			D. Lon — Dep.			D. Lon — Dep.			D. Lon — Dep.			D. Lon — Dep.		
Dist.	D. Lat	Dep.	Dist.	D. Lat	Dep.	Dist.	D. Lat	Dep.	Dist.	D. Lat	Dep.	Dist.	D. Lat	Dep.
1	01·0	00·0	61	61·0	02·1	121	120·9	04·2	181	180·9	06·3	241	240·9	08·4
2	02·0	00·1	62	62·0	02·2	122	121·9	04·3	182	181·9	06·4	242	241·9	08·4
3	03·0	00·1	63	63·0	02·2	123	122·9	04·3	183	182·9	06·4	243	242·9	08·5
4	04·0	00·1	64	64·0	02·2	124	123·9	04·3	184	183·9	06·4	244	243·9	08·5
5	05·0	00·2	65	65·0	02·3	125	124·9	04·4	185	184·9	06·5	245	244·9	08·6
6	06·0	00·2	66	66·0	02·3	126	125·9	04·4	186	185·9	06·5	246	245·9	08·6
7	07·0	00·2	67	67·0	02·3	127	126·9	04·4	187	186·9	06·5	247	246·8	08·6
8	08·0	00·3	68	68·0	02·4	128	127·9	04·5	188	187·9	06·6	248	247·8	08·7
9	09·0	00·3	69	69·0	02·4	129	128·9	04·5	189	188·9	06·6	249	248·8	08·7
10	10·0	00·3	70	70·0	02·4	130	129·9	04·5	190	189·9	06·6	250	249·8	08·7
11	11·0	00·4	71	71·0	02·5	131	130·9	04·6	191	190·9	06·7	251	250·8	08·8
12	12·0	00·4	72	72·0	02·5	132	131·9	04·6	192	191·9	06·7	252	251·8	08·8
13	13·0	00·5	73	73·0	02·5	133	132·9	04·6	193	192·9	06·7	253	252·8	08·8
14	14·0	00·5	74	74·0	02·6	134	133·9	04·7	194	193·9	06·8	254	253·8	08·9
15	15·0	00·5	75	75·0	02·6	135	134·9	04·7	195	194·9	06·8	255	254·8	08·9
16	16·0	00·6	76	76·0	02·7	136	135·9	04·7	196	195·9	06·9	256	255·8	08·9
17	17·0	00·6	77	77·0	02·7	137	136·9	04·8	197	196·9	06·9	257	256·8	09·0
18	18·0	00·6	78	78·0	02·7	138	137·9	04·8	198	197·9	06·9	258	257·8	09·0
19	19·0	00·7	79	79·0	02·8	139	138·9	04·9	199	198·9	06·9	259	258·8	09·0
20	20·0	00·7	80	80·0	02·8	140	139·9	04·9	200	199·9	07·0	260	259·8	09·1
21	21·0	00·7	81	81·0	02·8	141	140·9	04·9	201	200·9	07·0	261	260·8	09·1
22	22·0	00·8	82	81·9	02·9	142	141·9	05·0	202	201·9	07·0	262	261·8	09·1
23	23·0	00·8	83	82·9	02·9	143	142·9	05·0	203	202·9	07·1	263	262·8	09·2
24	24·0	00·8	84	83·9	02·9	144	143·9	05·0	204	203·9	07·1	264	263·8	09·2
25	25·0	00·9	85	84·9	03·0	145	144·9	05·1	205	204·9	07·2	265	264·8	09·2
26	26·0	00·9	86	85·9	03·0	146	145·9	05·1	206	205·9	07·2	266	265·8	09·3
27	27·0	00·9	87	86·9	03·0	147	146·9	05·1	207	206·9	07·2	267	266·8	09·3
28	28·0	01·0	88	87·9	03·1	148	147·9	05·2	208	207·9	07·3	268	267·8	09·4
29	29·0	01·0	89	88·9	03·1	149	148·9	05·2	209	208·9	07·3	269	268·8	09·4
30	30·0	01·0	90	89·9	03·1	150	149·9	05·2	210	209·9	07·3	270	269·8	09·4
31	31·0	01·1	91	90·9	03·2	151	150·9	05·3	211	210·9	07·4	271	270·8	09·5
32	32·0	01·1	92	91·9	03·2	152	151·9	05·3	212	211·9	07·4	272	271·8	09·5
33	33·0	01·2	93	92·9	03·2	153	152·9	05·3	213	212·9	07·4	273	272·8	09·5
34	34·0	01·2	94	93·9	03·3	154	153·9	05·4	214	213·9	07·5	274	273·8	09·6
35	35·0	01·2	95	94·9	03·3	155	154·9	05·4	215	214·9	07·5	275	274·8	09·6
36	36·0	01·3	96	95·9	03·4	156	155·9	05·4	216	215·9	07·5	276	275·8	09·6
37	37·0	01·3	97	96·9	03·4	157	156·9	05·5	217	216·9	07·6	277	276·8	09·7
38	38·0	01·3	98	97·9	03·4	158	157·9	05·5	218	217·9	07·6	278	277·8	09·7
39	39·0	01·4	99	98·9	03·5	159	158·9	05·5	219	218·9	07·6	279	278·8	09·7
40	40·0	01·4	100	99·9	03·5	160	159·9	05·6	220	219·9	07·7	280	279·8	09·8
41	41·0	01·4	101	100·9	03·5	161	160·9	05·6	221	220·9	07·7	281	280·8	09·8
42	42·0	01·5	102	101·9	03·6	162	161·9	05·7	222	221·9	07·7	282	281·8	09·8
43	43·0	01·5	103	102·9	03·6	163	162·9	05·7	223	222·9	07·8	283	282·8	09·9
44	44·0	01·5	104	103·9	03·6	164	163·9	05·7	224	223·9	07·8	284	283·8	09·9
45	45·0	01·6	105	104·9	03·7	165	164·9	05·8	225	224·9	07·9	285	284·8	09·9
46	46·0	01·6	106	105·9	03·7	166	165·9	05·8	226	225·9	07·9	286	285·8	10·0
47	47·0	01·6	107	106·9	03·7	167	166·9	05·8	227	226·9	07·9	287	286·8	10·0
48	48·0	01·7	108	107·9	03·8	168	167·9	05·9	228	227·9	08·0	288	287·8	10·1
49	49·0	01·7	109	108·9	03·8	169	168·9	05·9	229	228·9	08·0	289	288·8	10·1
50	50·0	01·7	110	109·9	03·8	170	169·9	05·9	230	229·9	08·0	290	289·8	10·1
51	51·0	01·8	111	110·9	03·9	171	170·9	06·0	231	230·9	08·1	291	290·8	10·2
52	52·0	01·8	112	111·9	03·9	172	171·9	06·0	232	231·9	08·1	292	291·8	10·2
53	53·0	01·8	113	112·9	03·9	173	172·9	06·0	233	232·9	08·1	293	292·8	10·2
54	54·0	01·9	114	113·9	04·0	174	173·9	06·1	234	233·9	08·2	294	293·8	10·3
55	55·0	01·9	115	114·9	04·0	175	174·9	06·1	235	234·9	08·2	295	294·8	10·3
56	56·0	02·0	116	115·9	04·0	176	175·9	06·1	236	235·9	08·2	296	295·8	10·3
57	57·0	02·0	117	116·9	04·1	177	176·9	06·2	237	236·9	08·3	297	296·8	10·4
58	58·0	02·0	118	117·9	04·1	178	177·9	06·2	238	237·9	08·3	298	297·8	10·4
59	59·0	02·1	119	118·9	04·2	179	178·9	06·2	239	238·9	08·3	299	298·8	10·4
60	60·0	02·1	120	119·9	04·2	180	179·9	06·3	240	239·9	08·4	300	299·8	10·5
Dist.	Dep.	D. Lat.	Dist.	Dep.	D. Lat.	Dist.	Dep.	D. Lat.	Dist.	Dep.	D. Lat.	Dist.	Dep.	D. Lat.
D. Lon		Dep.	D. Lon		Dep.	D. Lon		Dep.	D. Lon		Dep.	D. Lon		Dep.

88°   272° / 268°   88 Degrees   088° / 092°   5h 52m

TRAVERSE TABLE
2 Degrees

358° / 182°   002° / 178°   0h 08m   **2°**

D. Lon	Dep.		D. Lon	Dep.		D. Lon	Dep.		D. Lon	Dep.		D. Lon	Dep.	
Dist.	D. Lat.	Dep.	Dist.	D. Lat.	Dep.	Dist.	D. Lat.	Dep.	Dist.	D. Lat.	Dep.	Dist.	D. Lat.	Dep.
301	300.8	10.5	361	360.8	12.6	421	420.7	14.7	481	480.7	16.8	541	540.7	18.9
302	301.8	10.5	362	361.8	12.6	422	421.7	14.7	482	481.7	16.8	542	541.7	18.9
303	302.8	10.6	363	362.8	12.7	423	422.7	14.7	483	482.7	16.8	543	542.7	19.0
304	303.8	10.6	364	363.8	12.7	424	423.7	14.8	484	483.7	16.9	544	543.7	19.0
305	304.8	10.6	365	364.8	12.7	425	424.7	14.8	485	484.7	16.9	545	544.7	19.0
306	305.8	10.7	366	365.8	12.8	426	425.7	14.9	486	485.7	16.9	546	545.7	19.1
307	306.8	10.7	367	366.8	12.8	427	426.7	14.9	487	486.7	17.0	547	546.7	19.1
308	307.8	10.7	368	367.8	12.8	428	427.7	14.9	488	487.7	17.0	548	547.7	19.1
309	308.8	10.8	369	368.8	12.9	429	428.7	15.0	489	488.7	17.0	549	548.7	19.2
310	309.8	10.8	370	369.8	12.9	430	429.7	15.0	490	489.7	17.1	550	549.7	19.2
311	310.8	10.8	371	370.8	12.9	431	430.7	15.0	491	490.7	17.1	551	550.7	19.2
312	311.8	10.9	372	371.8	13.0	432	431.7	15.1	492	491.7	17.1	552	551.7	19.3
313	312.8	10.9	373	372.8	13.0	433	432.7	15.1	493	492.7	17.2	553	552.7	19.3
314	313.8	10.9	374	373.8	13.0	434	433.7	15.1	494	493.7	17.2	554	553.7	19.3
315	314.8	11.0	375	374.8	13.1	435	434.7	15.2	495	494.7	17.2	555	554.7	19.4
316	315.8	11.0	376	375.8	13.1	436	435.7	15.2	496	495.7	17.3	556	555.7	19.4
317	316.8	11.0	377	376.8	13.1	437	436.7	15.2	497	496.7	17.3	557	556.7	19.4
318	317.8	11.1	378	377.8	13.2	438	437.7	15.3	498	497.7	17.3	558	557.7	19.5
319	318.8	11.1	379	378.8	13.2	439	438.7	15.3	499	498.7	17.4	559	558.7	19.5
320	319.8	11.2	380	379.8	13.2	440	439.7	15.3	500	499.7	17.4	560	559.7	19.5
321	320.8	11.2	381	380.8	13.3	441	440.7	15.4	501	500.7	17.5	561	560.7	19.6
322	321.8	11.2	382	381.8	13.3	442	441.7	15.4	502	501.7	17.5	562	561.7	19.6
323	322.8	11.3	383	382.8	13.3	443	442.7	15.4	503	502.7	17.5	563	562.7	19.6
324	323.8	11.3	384	383.8	13.4	444	443.7	15.5	504	503.7	17.6	564	563.7	19.7
325	324.8	11.3	385	384.8	13.4	445	444.7	15.5	505	504.7	17.6	565	564.7	19.7
326	325.8	11.4	386	385.8	13.5	446	445.7	15.6	506	505.7	17.6	566	565.7	19.8
327	326.8	11.4	387	386.8	13.5	447	446.7	15.6	507	506.7	17.7	567	566.7	19.8
328	327.8	11.4	388	387.8	13.5	448	447.7	15.6	508	507.7	17.7	568	567.7	19.8
329	328.8	11.5	389	388.8	13.6	449	448.7	15.7	509	508.7	17.7	569	568.7	19.9
330	329.8	11.5	390	389.8	13.6	450	449.7	15.7	510	509.7	17.8	570	569.7	19.9
331	330.8	11.5	391	390.8	13.6	451	450.7	15.7	511	510.7	17.8	571	570.7	19.9
332	331.8	11.6	392	391.8	13.7	452	451.7	15.8	512	511.7	17.9	572	571.7	20.0
333	332.8	11.6	393	392.8	13.7	453	452.7	15.8	513	512.7	17.9	573	572.7	20.0
334	333.8	11.6	394	393.8	13.7	454	453.7	15.8	514	513.7	17.9	574	573.7	20.0
335	334.8	11.7	395	394.8	13.8	455	454.7	15.9	515	514.7	18.0	575	574.6	20.0
336	335.8	11.7	396	395.8	13.8	456	455.7	15.9	516	515.7	18.0	576	575.6	20.1
337	336.8	11.7	397	396.8	13.8	457	456.7	15.9	517	516.7	18.0	577	576.6	20.1
338	337.8	11.8	398	397.8	13.9	458	457.7	16.0	518	517.7	18.1	578	577.6	20.2
339	338.8	11.8	399	398.8	13.9	459	458.7	16.0	519	518.7	18.1	579	578.6	20.2
340	339.8	11.9	400	399.8	13.9	460	459.7	16.0	520	519.7	18.1	580	579.6	20.2
341	340.8	11.9	401	400.8	14.0	461	460.7	16.1	521	520.7	18.2	581	580.6	20.3
342	341.8	11.9	402	401.8	14.0	462	461.7	16.1	522	521.7	18.2	582	581.6	20.3
343	342.8	12.0	403	402.8	14.0	463	462.7	16.1	523	522.7	18.3	583	582.6	20.3
344	343.8	12.0	404	403.8	14.1	464	463.7	16.2	524	523.7	18.3	584	583.6	20.4
345	344.8	12.0	405	404.8	14.1	465	464.7	16.2	525	524.7	18.3	585	584.6	20.4
346	345.8	12.1	406	405.8	14.2	466	465.7	16.2	526	525.7	18.4	586	585.6	20.5
347	346.8	12.1	407	406.8	14.2	467	466.7	16.3	527	526.7	18.4	587	586.6	20.5
348	347.8	12.1	408	407.8	14.2	468	467.7	16.3	528	527.7	18.4	588	587.6	20.5
349	348.8	12.2	409	408.8	14.3	469	468.7	16.4	529	528.7	18.5	589	588.6	20.6
350	349.8	12.2	410	409.8	14.3	470	469.7	16.4	530	529.7	18.5	590	589.6	20.6
351	350.8	12.2	411	410.7	14.3	471	470.7	16.4	531	530.7	18.5	591	590.6	20.6
352	351.8	12.3	412	411.7	14.4	472	471.7	16.5	532	531.7	18.6	592	591.6	20.7
353	352.8	12.3	413	412.7	14.4	473	472.7	16.5	533	532.7	18.6	593	592.6	20.7
354	353.8	12.3	414	413.7	14.4	474	473.7	16.5	534	533.7	18.6	594	593.6	20.8
355	354.8	12.4	415	414.7	14.5	475	474.7	16.6	535	534.7	18.7	595	594.6	20.8
356	355.8	12.4	416	415.7	14.5	476	475.7	16.6	536	535.7	18.7	596	595.6	20.8
357	356.8	12.4	417	416.7	14.5	477	476.7	16.6	537	536.7	18.7	597	596.6	20.8
358	357.8	12.5	418	417.7	14.6	478	477.7	16.7	538	537.7	18.8	598	597.6	20.9
359	358.8	12.5	419	418.7	14.6	479	478.7	16.7	539	538.7	18.8	599	598.6	20.9
360	359.8	12.5	420	419.7	14.6	480	479.7	16.7	540	539.7	18.8	600	599.6	20.9
Dist.	Dep.	D. Lat.	Dist.	Dep.	D. Lat.	Dist.	Dep.	D. Lat.	Dist.	Dep.	D. Lat.	Dist.	Dep.	D. Lat.
D. Lon		Dep.	D. Lon		Dep.	D. Lon		Dep.	D. Lon		Dep.	D. Lon		Dep.

272° / 268°   **88 Degrees**   088° / 092°   5h 52m   **88°**

TRAVERSE TABLE
3 Degrees

D. Lon Dep. Dist.	D. Lat.	Dep.	D. Lon Dep. Dist.	D. Lat.	Dep.	D. Lon Dep. Dist.	D. Lat.	Dep.	D. Lon Dep. Dist.	D. Lat.	Dep.	D. Lon Dep. Dist.	D. Lat.	Dep.
1	01·0	00·1	61	60·9	03·2	121	120·8	06·3	181	180·8	09·5	241	240·7	12·6
2	02·0	00·1	62	61·9	03·2	122	121·8	06·4	182	181·8	09·5	242	241·7	12·7
3	03·0	00·2	63	62·9	03·3	123	122·8	06·4	183	182·7	09·6	243	242·7	12·7
4	04·0	00·2	64	63·9	03·3	124	123·8	06·5	184	183·7	09·6	244	243·7	12·8
5	05·0	00·3	65	64·9	03·4	125	124·8	06·5	185	184·7	09·7	245	244·7	12·8
6	06·0	00·3	66	65·9	03·5	126	125·8	06·6	186	185·7	09·7	246	245·7	12·9
7	07·0	00·4	67	66·9	03·5	127	126·8	06·6	187	186·7	09·8	247	246·7	12·9
8	08·0	00·4	68	67·9	03·6	128	127·8	06·7	188	187·7	09·8	248	247·7	13·0
9	09·0	00·5	69	68·9	03·6	129	128·8	06·8	189	188·7	09·9	249	248·7	13·0
10	10·0	00·5	70	69·9	03·7	130	129·8	06·8	190	189·7	09·9	250	249·7	13·1
11	11·0	00·6	71	70·9	03·7	131	130·8	06·9	191	190·7	10·0	251	250·7	13·1
12	12·0	00·6	72	71·9	03·8	132	131·8	06·9	192	191·7	10·0	252	251·7	13·2
13	13·0	00·7	73	72·9	03·8	133	132·8	07·0	193	192·7	10·1	253	252·7	13·2
14	14·0	00·7	74	73·9	03·9	134	133·8	07·0	194	193·7	10·2	254	253·7	13·3
15	15·0	00·8	75	74·9	03·9	135	134·8	07·1	195	194·7	10·2	255	254·7	13·3
16	16·0	00·8	76	75·9	04·0	136	135·8	07·1	196	195·7	10·3	256	255·6	13·4
17	17·0	00·9	77	76·9	04·0	137	136·8	07·2	197	196·7	10·3	257	256·6	13·5
18	18·0	00·9	78	77·9	04·1	138	137·8	07·2	198	197·7	10·4	258	257·6	13·5
19	19·0	01·0	79	78·9	04·1	139	138·8	07·3	199	198·7	10·4	259	258·6	13·6
20	20·0	01·0	80	79·9	04·2	140	139·8	07·3	200	199·7	10·5	260	259·6	13·6
21	21·0	01·1	81	80·9	04·2	141	140·8	07·4	201	200·7	10·5	261	260·6	13·7
22	22·0	01·2	82	81·9	04·3	142	141·8	07·4	202	201·7	10·6	262	261·6	13·7
23	23·0	01·2	83	82·9	04·3	143	142·8	07·5	203	202·7	10·6	263	262·6	13·8
24	24·0	01·3	84	83·9	04·4	144	143·8	07·5	204	203·7	10·7	264	263·6	13·8
25	25·0	01·3	85	84·9	04·4	145	144·8	07·6	205	204·7	10·7	265	264·6	13·9
26	26·0	01·4	86	85·9	04·5	146	145·8	07·6	206	205·7	10·8	266	265·6	13·9
27	27·0	01·4	87	86·9	04·6	147	146·8	07·7	207	206·7	10·8	267	266·6	14·0
28	28·0	01·5	88	87·9	04·6	148	147·8	07·7	208	207·7	10·9	268	267·6	14·0
29	29·0	01·5	89	88·9	04·7	149	148·8	07·8	209	208·7	10·9	269	268·6	14·1
30	30·0	01·6	90	89·9	04·7	150	149·8	07·9	210	209·7	11·0	270	269·6	14·1
31	31·0	01·6	91	90·9	04·8	151	150·8	07·9	211	210·7	11·0	271	270·6	14·2
32	32·0	01·7	92	91·9	04·8	152	151·8	08·0	212	211·7	11·1	272	271·6	14·2
33	33·0	01·7	93	92·9	04·9	153	152·8	08·0	213	212·7	11·1	273	272·6	14·3
34	34·0	01·8	94	93·9	04·9	154	153·8	08·1	214	213·7	11·2	274	273·6	14·3
35	35·0	01·8	95	94·9	05·0	155	154·8	08·1	215	214·7	11·3	275	274·6	14·4
36	36·0	01·9	96	95·9	05·0	156	155·8	08·2	216	215·7	11·3	276	275·6	14·4
37	36·9	01·9	97	96·9	05·1	157	156·8	08·2	217	216·7	11·4	277	276·6	14·5
38	37·9	02·0	98	97·9	05·1	158	157·8	08·3	218	217·7	11·4	278	277·6	14·5
39	38·9	02·0	99	98·9	05·2	159	158·8	08·3	219	218·7	11·5	279	278·6	14·6
40	39·9	02·1	100	99·9	05·2	160	159·8	08·4	220	219·7	11·5	280	279·6	14·7
41	40·9	02·1	101	100·9	05·3	161	160·8	08·4	221	220·7	11·6	281	280·6	14·7
42	41·9	02·2	102	101·9	05·3	162	161·8	08·5	222	221·7	11·6	282	281·6	14·8
43	42·9	02·3	103	102·9	05·4	163	162·8	08·5	223	222·7	11·7	283	282·6	14·8
44	43·9	02·3	104	103·9	05·4	164	163·8	08·6	224	223·7	11·7	284	283·6	14·9
45	44·9	02·4	105	104·9	05·5	165	164·8	08·6	225	224·7	11·8	285	284·6	14·9
46	45·9	02·4	106	105·9	05·5	166	165·8	08·7	226	225·7	11·8	286	285·6	15·0
47	46·9	02·5	107	106·9	05·6	167	166·8	08·7	227	226·7	11·9	287	286·6	15·0
48	47·9	02·5	108	107·9	05·7	168	167·8	08·8	228	227·7	11·9	288	287·6	15·1
49	48·9	02·6	109	108·9	05·7	169	168·8	08·8	229	228·7	12·0	289	288·6	15·1
50	49·9	02·6	110	109·8	05·8	170	169·8	08·9	230	229·7	12·0	290	289·6	15·2
51	50·9	02·7	111	110·8	05·8	171	170·8	08·9	231	230·7	12·1	291	290·6	15·2
52	51·9	02·7	112	111·8	05·9	172	171·8	09·0	232	231·7	12·1	292	291·6	15·3
53	52·9	02·8	113	112·8	06·0	173	172·8	09·1	233	232·7	12·2	293	292·6	15·3
54	53·9	02·8	114	113·8	06·0	174	173·8	09·1	234	233·7	12·2	294	293·6	15·4
55	54·9	02·9	115	114·8	06·0	175	174·8	09·2	235	234·7	12·3	295	294·6	15·4
56	55·9	02·9	116	115·8	06·1	176	175·8	09·2	236	235·7	12·4	296	295·6	15·5
57	56·9	03·0	117	116·8	06·1	177	176·8	09·3	237	236·7	12·4	297	296·6	15·5
58	57·9	03·0	118	117·8	06·2	178	177·8	09·3	238	237·7	12·5	298	297·6	15·6
59	58·9	03·1	119	118·8	06·2	179	178·8	09·4	239	238·7	12·5	299	298·6	15·6
60	59·9	03·1	120	119·8	06·3	180	179·8	09·4	240	239·7	12·6	300	299·6	15·7
Dist.	Dep.	D. Lat.	Dist.	Dep.	D. Lat.	Dist.	Dep.	D. Lat.	Dist.	Dep.	D. Lat.	Dist.	Dep.	D. Lat.
D. Lon		Dep.	D. Lon		Dep.	D. Lon		Dep.	D. Lon		Dep.	D. Lon		Dep.

TRAVERSE TABLE
3 Degrees

357° / 183°   003° / 177°   0h 12m   **3°**

D. Lon	Dep.		D. Lon	Dep.		D. Lon	Dep.		D. Lon	Dep.		D. Lon	Dep.	
Dist.	D. Lat.	Dep.	Dist.	D. Lat.	Dep.	Dist.	D. Lat.	Dep.	Dist.	D. Lat.	Dep.	Dist.	D. Lat.	Dep.
301	300.6	15.8	361	360.5	18.9	421	420.4	22.0	481	480.3	25.2	541	540.3	28.3
302	301.6	15.8	362	361.5	18.9	422	421.4	22.1	482	481.3	25.2	542	541.3	28.4
303	302.6	15.9	363	362.5	19.0	423	422.4	22.1	483	482.3	25.3	543	542.3	28.4
304	303.6	15.9	364	363.5	19.1	424	423.4	22.2	484	483.3	25.3	544	543.3	28.5
305	304.6	16.0	365	364.5	19.1	425	424.4	22.2	485	484.3	25.4	545	544.3	28.5
306	305.6	16.0	366	365.5	19.2	426	425.4	22.3	486	485.3	25.4	546	545.3	28.6
307	306.6	16.1	367	366.5	19.2	427	426.4	22.3	487	486.3	25.5	547	546.3	28.6
308	307.6	16.1	368	367.5	19.3	428	427.4	22.4	488	487.3	25.5	548	547.2	28.7
309	308.6	16.2	369	368.5	19.3	429	428.4	22.5	489	488.3	25.6	549	548.2	28.7
310	309.6	16.2	370	369.5	19.4	430	429.4	22.5	490	489.3	25.6	550	549.2	28.8
311	310.6	16.3	371	370.5	19.4	431	430.4	22.6	491	490.3	25.7	551	550.2	28.8
312	311.6	16.3	372	371.5	19.5	432	431.4	22.6	492	491.3	25.7	552	551.2	28.9
313	312.6	16.4	373	372.5	19.5	433	432.4	22.7	493	492.3	25.8	553	552.2	28.9
314	313.6	16.4	374	373.5	19.6	434	433.4	22.7	494	493.3	25.9	554	553.2	29.0
315	314.6	16.5	375	374.5	19.6	435	434.4	22.8	495	494.3	25.9	555	554.2	29.0
316	315.6	16.5	376	375.5	19.7	436	435.4	22.8	496	495.3	26.0	556	555.2	29.1
317	316.6	16.6	377	376.5	19.7	437	436.4	22.9	497	496.3	26.0	557	556.2	29.2
318	317.6	16.6	378	377.5	19.8	438	437.4	22.9	498	497.3	26.1	558	557.2	29.2
319	318.6	16.7	379	378.5	19.8	439	438.4	23.0	499	498.3	26.1	559	558.2	29.3
320	319.6	16.7	380	379.5	19.9	440	439.4	23.0	500	499.3	26.2	560	559.2	29.3
321	320.6	16.8	381	380.5	19.9	441	440.4	23.1	501	500.3	26.2	561	560.2	29.4
322	321.6	16.9	382	381.5	20.0	442	441.4	23.1	502	501.3	26.3	562	561.2	29.4
323	322.6	16.9	383	382.5	20.1	443	442.4	23.2	503	502.3	26.3	563	562.2	29.5
324	323.6	17.0	384	383.5	20.1	444	443.4	23.2	504	503.3	26.4	564	563.2	29.5
325	324.6	17.0	385	384.5	20.1	445	444.4	23.3	505	504.3	26.4	565	564.2	29.6
326	325.6	17.1	386	385.5	20.2	446	445.4	23.3	506	505.3	26.5	566	565.2	29.6
327	326.6	17.1	387	386.5	20.3	447	446.4	23.4	507	506.3	26.5	567	566.2	29.7
328	327.6	17.2	388	387.5	20.3	448	447.4	23.4	508	507.3	26.6	568	567.2	29.7
329	328.5	17.2	389	388.5	20.4	449	448.4	23.5	509	508.3	26.6	569	568.2	29.8
330	329.5	17.3	390	389.5	20.4	450	449.4	23.6	510	509.3	26.7	570	569.2	29.8
331	330.5	17.3	391	390.5	20.5	451	450.4	23.6	511	510.3	26.7	571	570.2	29.9
332	331.5	17.4	392	391.5	20.5	452	451.4	23.7	512	511.3	26.8	572	571.2	29.9
333	332.5	17.4	393	392.5	20.6	453	452.4	23.7	513	512.3	26.8	573	572.2	30.0
334	333.5	17.5	394	393.5	20.6	454	453.4	23.8	514	513.3	26.9	574	573.2	30.0
335	334.5	17.5	395	394.5	20.7	455	454.4	23.8	515	514.3	27.0	575	574.2	30.1
336	335.5	17.6	396	395.5	20.7	456	455.4	23.9	516	515.3	27.0	576	575.2	30.1
337	336.5	17.6	397	396.5	20.8	457	456.4	23.9	517	516.3	27.1	577	576.2	30.2
338	337.5	17.7	398	397.5	20.8	458	457.4	24.0	518	517.3	27.1	578	577.2	30.3
339	338.5	17.7	399	398.5	20.9	459	458.4	24.0	519	518.3	27.2	579	578.2	30.3
340	339.5	17.8	400	399.5	20.9	460	459.4	24.1	520	519.3	27.2	580	579.2	30.4
341	340.5	17.8	401	400.5	21.0	461	460.4	24.1	521	520.3	27.3	581	580.2	30.4
342	341.5	17.9	402	401.4	21.0	462	461.4	24.2	522	521.3	27.3	582	581.2	30.5
343	342.5	18.0	403	402.4	21.1	463	462.4	24.2	523	522.3	27.4	583	582.2	30.5
344	343.5	18.0	404	403.4	21.1	464	463.4	24.3	524	523.3	27.4	584	583.2	30.6
345	344.5	18.1	405	404.4	21.2	465	464.4	24.3	525	524.3	27.5	585	584.2	30.6
346	345.5	18.1	406	405.4	21.2	466	465.4	24.4	526	525.3	27.5	586	585.2	30.7
347	346.5	18.2	407	406.4	21.3	467	466.4	24.4	527	526.3	27.6	587	586.2	30.7
348	347.5	18.2	408	407.4	21.4	468	467.4	24.5	528	527.3	27.6	588	587.2	30.8
349	348.5	18.3	409	408.4	21.4	469	468.4	24.5	529	528.3	27.7	589	588.2	30.8
350	349.5	18.3	410	409.4	21.5	470	469.4	24.6	530	529.3	27.7	590	589.2	30.9
351	350.5	18.4	411	410.4	21.5	471	470.4	24.7	531	530.3	27.8	591	590.2	30.9
352	351.5	18.4	412	411.4	21.6	472	471.4	24.7	532	531.3	27.8	592	591.2	31.0
353	352.5	18.5	413	412.4	21.6	473	472.4	24.8	533	532.3	27.9	593	592.2	31.0
354	353.5	18.5	414	413.4	21.7	474	473.4	24.9	534	533.3	27.9	594	593.2	31.1
355	354.5	18.6	415	414.4	21.7	475	474.3	24.9	535	534.3	28.0	595	594.2	31.1
356	355.5	18.6	416	415.4	21.8	476	475.3	24.9	536	535.3	28.1	596	595.2	31.2
357	356.5	18.7	417	416.4	21.8	477	476.3	25.0	537	536.3	28.1	597	596.2	31.2
358	357.5	18.7	418	417.4	21.9	478	477.3	25.0	538	537.3	28.2	598	597.2	31.3
359	358.5	18.8	419	418.4	21.9	479	478.3	25.1	539	538.3	28.2	599	598.2	31.3
360	359.5	18.8	420	419.4	22.0	480	479.3	25.1	540	539.3	28.3	600	599.2	31.4
Dist.	Dep.	D. Lat.	Dist.	Dep.	D. Lat.	Dist.	Dep.	D. Lat.	Dist.	Dep.	D. Lat.	Dist.	Dep.	D. Lat.
D. Lon		Dep.	D. Lon		Dep.	D. Lon		Dep.	D. Lon		Dep.	D. Lon		Dep.

273° / 267°   87 Degrees   087° / 093°   5h 48m   **87°**

TRAVERSE TABLE
4 Degrees

4°   356° / 184°   004° / 176°   0h 16m

Dist.	D. Lat.	Dep.	Dist.	D. Lat.	Dep.	Dist.	D. Lat.	Dep.	Dist.	D. Lat.	Dep.	Dist.	D. Lat.	Dep.
1	01.0	00.1	61	60.9	04.3	121	120.7	08.4	181	180.6	12.6	241	240.4	16.8
2	02.0	00.1	62	61.8	04.3	122	121.7	08.5	182	181.6	12.7	242	241.4	16.9
3	03.0	00.2	63	62.8	04.4	123	122.7	08.6	183	182.6	12.8	243	242.4	17.0
4	04.0	00.3	64	63.8	04.5	124	123.7	08.6	184	183.6	12.8	244	243.4	17.0
5	05.0	00.3	65	64.8	04.5	125	124.7	08.7	185	184.5	12.9	245	244.4	17.1
6	06.0	00.4	66	65.8	04.6	126	125.7	08.8	186	185.5	13.0	246	245.4	17.2
7	07.0	00.5	67	66.8	04.7	127	126.7	08.9	187	186.5	13.0	247	246.4	17.3
8	08.0	00.6	68	67.8	04.7	128	127.7	08.9	188	187.5	13.1	248	247.4	17.3
9	09.0	00.6	69	68.8	04.8	129	128.7	09.0	189	188.5	13.2	249	248.4	17.4
10	10.0	00.7	70	69.8	04.9	130	129.7	09.1	190	189.5	13.3	250	249.4	17.4
11	11.0	00.8	71	70.8	05.0	131	130.7	09.1	191	190.5	13.3	251	250.4	17.5
12	12.0	00.8	72	71.8	05.0	132	131.7	09.2	192	191.5	13.4	252	251.4	17.6
13	13.0	00.9	73	72.8	05.1	133	132.7	09.3	193	192.5	13.5	253	252.4	17.6
14	14.0	01.0	74	73.8	05.2	134	133.7	09.3	194	193.5	13.5	254	253.4	17.7
15	15.0	01.0	75	74.8	05.2	135	134.7	09.4	195	194.5	13.6	255	254.4	17.8
16	16.0	01.1	76	75.8	05.3	136	135.7	09.5	196	195.5	13.7	256	255.4	17.9
17	17.0	01.2	77	76.8	05.4	137	136.7	09.6	197	196.5	13.7	257	256.4	17.9
18	18.0	01.3	78	77.8	05.4	138	137.7	09.6	198	197.5	13.8	258	257.4	18.0
19	19.0	01.3	79	78.8	05.5	139	138.7	09.7	199	198.5	13.9	259	258.4	18.1
20	20.0	01.4	80	79.8	05.6	140	139.7	09.8	200	199.5	14.0	260	259.4	18.1
21	20.9	01.5	81	80.8	05.7	141	140.7	09.8	201	200.5	14.0	261	260.4	18.2
22	21.9	01.5	82	81.8	05.7	142	141.7	09.9	202	201.5	14.1	262	261.4	18.3
23	22.9	01.6	83	82.8	05.8	143	142.7	10.0	203	202.5	14.2	263	262.4	18.3
24	23.9	01.7	84	83.8	05.9	144	143.6	10.0	204	203.5	14.2	264	263.4	18.4
25	24.9	01.7	85	84.8	05.9	145	144.6	10.1	205	204.5	14.3	265	264.4	18.5
26	25.9	01.8	86	85.8	06.0	146	145.6	10.2	206	205.5	14.4	266	265.4	18.6
27	26.9	01.9	87	86.8	06.1	147	146.6	10.3	207	206.5	14.5	267	266.3	18.6
28	27.9	02.0	88	87.8	06.1	148	147.6	10.3	208	207.5	14.5	268	267.3	18.7
29	28.9	02.0	89	88.8	06.2	149	148.6	10.4	209	208.5	14.6	269	268.3	18.8
30	29.9	02.1	90	89.8	06.3	150	149.6	10.5	210	209.5	14.6	270	269.3	18.8
31	30.9	02.2	91	90.8	06.3	151	150.6	10.5	211	210.5	14.7	271	270.3	18.9
32	31.9	02.2	92	91.8	06.4	152	151.6	10.6	212	211.5	14.8	272	271.3	19.0
33	32.9	02.3	93	92.8	06.5	153	152.6	10.7	213	212.5	14.9	273	272.3	19.0
34	33.9	02.4	94	93.8	06.6	154	153.6	10.7	214	213.5	14.9	274	273.3	19.1
35	34.9	02.4	95	94.8	06.6	155	154.6	10.8	215	214.5	15.0	275	274.3	19.2
36	35.9	02.5	96	95.8	06.7	156	155.6	10.9	216	215.5	15.1	276	275.3	19.3
37	36.9	02.6	97	96.8	06.8	157	156.6	11.0	217	216.5	15.1	277	276.3	19.3
38	37.9	02.7	98	97.8	06.8	158	157.6	11.0	218	217.5	15.2	278	277.3	19.4
39	38.9	02.7	99	98.8	06.9	159	158.6	11.1	219	218.5	15.3	279	278.3	19.5
40	39.9	02.8	100	99.8	07.0	160	159.6	11.2	220	219.5	15.3	280	279.3	19.5
41	40.9	02.9	101	100.8	07.0	161	160.6	11.2	221	220.5	15.4	281	280.3	19.6
42	41.9	02.9	102	101.8	07.1	162	161.6	11.3	222	221.5	15.5	282	281.3	19.7
43	42.9	03.0	103	102.7	07.2	163	162.6	11.4	223	222.5	15.6	283	282.3	19.7
44	43.9	03.1	104	103.7	07.3	164	163.6	11.4	224	223.5	15.6	284	283.3	19.8
45	44.9	03.1	105	104.7	07.3	165	164.6	11.5	225	224.5	15.7	285	284.3	19.9
46	45.9	03.2	106	105.7	07.4	166	165.6	11.6	226	225.4	15.8	286	285.3	20.0
47	46.9	03.3	107	106.7	07.5	167	166.6	11.6	227	226.4	15.8	287	286.3	20.0
48	47.9	03.3	108	107.7	07.5	168	167.6	11.7	228	227.4	15.9	288	287.3	20.1
49	48.9	03.4	109	108.7	07.6	169	168.6	11.8	229	228.4	16.0	289	288.3	20.2
50	49.9	03.5	110	109.7	07.7	170	169.6	11.9	230	229.4	16.0	290	289.3	20.2
51	50.9	03.6	111	110.7	07.7	171	170.6	11.9	231	230.4	16.1	291	290.3	20.3
52	51.9	03.6	112	111.7	07.8	172	171.6	12.0	232	231.4	16.2	292	291.3	20.4
53	52.9	03.7	113	112.7	07.9	173	172.6	12.1	233	232.4	16.3	293	292.3	20.4
54	53.9	03.8	114	113.7	08.0	174	173.6	12.1	234	233.4	16.3	294	293.3	20.5
55	54.9	03.8	115	114.7	08.0	175	174.6	12.2	235	234.4	16.4	295	294.3	20.6
56	55.9	03.9	116	115.7	08.1	176	175.6	12.3	236	235.4	16.5	296	295.3	20.6
57	56.9	04.0	117	116.7	08.2	177	176.6	12.3	237	236.4	16.5	297	296.3	20.7
58	57.9	04.0	118	117.7	08.2	178	177.6	12.4	238	237.4	16.6	298	297.3	20.8
59	58.9	04.1	119	118.7	08.3	179	178.6	12.5	239	238.4	16.7	299	298.3	20.9
60	59.9	04.2	120	119.7	08.4	180	179.6	12.6	240	239.4	16.7	300	299.3	20.9

Dist.	Dep.	D. Lat.	Dist.	Dep.	D. Lat.	Dist.	Dep.	D. Lat.	Dist.	Dep.	D. Lat.	Dist.	Dep.	D. Lat.
D. Lon		Dep.	D. Lon		Dep.	D. Lon		Dep.	D. Lon		Dep.	D. Lon		Dep.

86°   274° / 266°   86 Degrees   086° / 094°   5h 44m

TRAVERSE TABLE
4 Degrees

D. Lon	Dep.		D. Lon	Dep.		D. Lon	Dep.		D. Lon	Dep.		D. Lon	Dep.	
Dist.	D. Lat.	Dep.	Dist.	D. Lat.	Dep.	Dist.	D. Lat.	Dep.	Dist.	D. Lat.	Dep.	Dist.	D. Lat.	Dep.
301	300.3	21.0	361	360.1	25.2	421	420.0	29.4	481	479.8	33.6	541	539.7	37.7
302	301.3	21.1	362	361.1	25.3	422	421.0	29.4	482	480.8	33.6	542	540.7	37.8
303	302.3	21.1	363	362.1	25.3	423	422.0	29.5	483	481.8	33.7	543	541.7	37.9
304	303.3	21.2	364	363.1	25.4	424	423.0	29.6	484	482.8	33.8	544	542.7	37.9
305	304.3	21.3	365	364.1	25.5	425	424.0	29.6	485	483.8	33.8	545	543.7	38.0
306	305.3	21.3	366	365.1	25.5	426	425.0	29.7	486	484.8	33.9	546	544.7	38.1
307	306.3	21.4	367	366.1	25.6	427	426.0	29.8	487	485.8	34.0	547	545.7	38.2
308	307.2	21.5	368	367.1	25.7	428	427.0	29.9	488	486.8	34.0	548	546.7	38.2
309	308.2	21.6	369	368.1	25.7	429	428.0	29.9	489	487.8	34.1	549	547.7	38.3
310	309.2	21.6	370	369.1	25.8	430	429.0	30.0	490	488.8	34.2	550	548.7	38.4
311	310.2	21.7	371	370.1	25.9	431	430.0	30.1	491	489.8	34.3	551	549.7	38.4
312	311.2	21.8	372	371.1	25.9	432	430.9	30.1	492	490.8	34.3	552	550.7	38.5
313	312.2	21.8	373	372.1	26.0	433	431.9	30.2	493	491.8	34.4	553	551.7	38.6
314	313.2	21.9	374	373.1	26.1	434	432.9	30.3	494	492.8	34.5	554	552.7	38.6
315	314.2	22.0	375	374.1	26.2	435	433.9	30.3	495	493.8	34.5	555	553.6	38.7
316	315.2	22.0	376	375.1	26.2	436	434.9	30.4	496	494.8	34.6	556	554.6	38.8
317	316.2	22.1	377	376.1	26.3	437	435.9	30.5	497	495.8	34.7	557	555.6	38.9
318	317.2	22.2	378	377.1	26.4	438	436.9	30.6	498	496.8	34.7	558	556.6	38.9
319	318.2	22.3	379	378.1	26.4	439	437.9	30.6	499	497.8	34.8	559	557.6	39.0
320	319.2	22.3	380	379.1	26.5	440	438.9	30.7	500	498.8	34.9	560	558.6	39.0
321	320.2	22.4	381	380.1	26.6	441	439.9	30.8	501	499.8	34.9	561	559.6	39.1
322	321.2	22.5	382	381.1	26.6	442	440.9	30.8	502	500.8	35.0	562	560.6	39.2
323	322.2	22.5	383	382.1	26.7	443	441.9	30.9	503	501.8	35.1	563	561.6	39.3
324	323.2	22.6	384	383.1	26.8	444	442.9	31.0	504	502.8	35.2	564	562.6	39.3
325	324.2	22.7	385	384.1	26.9	445	443.9	31.0	505	503.8	35.2	565	563.6	39.4
326	325.2	22.7	386	385.1	26.9	446	444.9	31.1	506	504.8	35.3	566	564.6	39.5
327	326.2	22.8	387	386.1	27.0	447	445.9	31.2	507	505.8	35.4	567	565.6	39.5
328	327.2	22.9	388	387.1	27.1	448	446.9	31.3	508	506.8	35.4	568	566.6	39.6
329	328.2	22.9	389	388.1	27.1	449	447.9	31.3	509	507.8	35.5	569	567.6	39.7
330	329.2	23.0	390	389.0	27.2	450	448.9	31.4	510	508.8	35.6	570	568.6	39.8
331	330.2	23.1	391	390.0	27.3	451	449.9	31.5	511	509.8	35.6	571	569.6	39.8
332	331.2	23.2	392	391.0	27.3	452	450.9	31.5	512	510.8	35.7	572	570.6	39.9
333	332.2	23.2	393	392.0	27.4	453	451.9	31.6	513	511.8	35.8	573	571.6	40.0
334	333.2	23.3	394	393.0	27.5	454	452.9	31.7	514	512.7	35.9	574	572.6	40.0
335	334.2	23.4	395	394.0	27.6	455	453.9	31.7	515	513.7	35.9	575	573.6	40.1
336	335.2	23.4	396	395.0	27.6	456	454.9	31.8	516	514.7	36.0	576	574.6	40.2
337	336.2	23.5	397	396.0	27.7	457	455.9	31.9	517	515.7	36.1	577	575.6	40.2
338	337.2	23.6	398	397.0	27.8	458	456.9	31.9	518	516.7	36.1	578	576.6	40.3
339	338.2	23.6	399	398.0	27.8	459	457.9	32.0	519	517.7	36.2	579	577.6	40.4
340	339.2	23.7	400	399.0	27.9	460	458.9	32.1	520	518.7	36.3	580	578.6	40.5
341	340.2	23.8	401	400.0	28.0	461	459.9	32.2	521	519.7	36.3	581	579.6	40.5
342	341.2	23.9	402	401.0	28.0	462	460.9	32.2	522	520.7	36.4	582	580.6	40.6
343	342.2	24.0	403	402.0	28.1	463	461.9	32.3	523	521.7	36.5	583	581.6	40.7
344	343.2	24.0	404	403.0	28.2	464	462.9	32.4	524	522.7	36.6	584	582.6	40.7
345	344.2	24.1	405	404.0	28.3	465	463.9	32.4	525	523.7	36.6	585	583.6	40.8
346	345.2	24.1	406	405.0	28.3	466	464.9	32.5	526	524.7	36.7	586	584.6	40.9
347	346.2	24.2	407	406.0	28.4	467	465.9	32.6	527	525.7	36.8	587	585.6	40.9
348	347.2	24.3	408	407.0	28.5	468	466.9	32.6	528	526.7	36.8	588	586.6	41.0
349	348.1	24.3	409	408.0	28.5	469	467.9	32.7	529	527.7	36.9	589	587.6	41.1
350	349.1	24.4	410	409.0	28.6	470	468.9	32.8	530	528.7	37.0	590	588.6	41.2
351	350.1	24.5	411	410.0	28.7	471	469.9	32.9	531	529.7	37.0	591	589.6	41.2
352	351.1	24.6	412	411.0	28.7	472	470.9	32.9	532	530.7	37.1	592	590.6	41.3
353	352.1	24.6	413	412.0	28.8	473	471.8	33.0	533	531.7	37.2	593	591.6	41.4
354	353.1	24.7	414	413.0	28.9	474	472.8	33.1	534	532.7	37.2	594	592.6	41.4
355	354.1	24.8	415	414.0	28.9	475	473.8	33.1	535	533.7	37.3	595	593.6	41.5
356	355.1	24.8	416	415.0	29.0	476	474.8	33.2	536	534.7	37.4	596	594.5	41.6
357	356.1	24.9	417	416.0	29.1	477	475.8	33.3	537	535.7	37.5	597	595.5	41.6
358	357.1	25.0	418	417.0	29.2	478	476.8	33.3	538	536.7	37.5	598	596.5	41.7
359	358.1	25.0	419	418.0	29.2	479	477.8	33.4	539	537.7	37.6	599	597.5	41.8
360	359.1	25.1	420	419.0	29.3	480	478.8	33.5	540	538.7	37.7	600	598.5	41.9
Dist.	Dep.	D. Lat.	Dist.	Dep.	D. Lat.	Dist.	Dep.	D. Lat.	Dist.	Dep.	D. Lat.	Dist.	Dep.	D. Lat.
D. Lon		Dep.	D. Lon		Dep.	D. Lon		Dep.	D. Lon		Dep.	D. Lon		Dep.

TRAVERSE TABLE
5 Degrees

	355° / 185°										005° / 175°	0h 20m

D. Lon	Dep.		D. Lon	Dep.		D. Lon	Dep.		D. Lon	Dep.		D. Lon	Dep.	
Dist.	D. Lat.	Dep.	Dist.	D. Lat.	Dep.	Dist.	D. Lat.	Dep.	Dist.	D. Lat.	Dep.	Dist.	D. Lat.	Dep.
1	01·0	00·1	61	60·8	05·3	121	120·5	10·5	181	180·3	15·8	241	240·1	21·0
2	02·0	00·2	62	61·8	05·4	122	121·5	10·6	182	181·3	15·9	242	241·1	21·1
3	03·0	00·3	63	62·8	05·5	123	122·5	10·7	183	182·3	15·9	243	242·1	21·2
4	04·0	00·3	64	63·8	05·6	124	123·5	10·8	184	183·3	16·0	244	243·1	21·3
5	05·0	00·4	65	64·8	05·7	125	124·5	10·9	185	184·3	16·1	245	244·1	21·4
6	06·0	00·5	66	65·7	05·8	126	125·5	11·0	186	185·3	16·2	246	245·1	21·4
7	07·0	00·6	67	66·7	05·8	127	126·5	11·1	187	186·3	16·3	247	246·1	21·5
8	08·0	00·7	68	67·7	05·9	128	127·5	11·2	188	187·3	16·4	248	247·1	21·6
9	09·0	00·8	69	68·7	06·0	129	128·5	11·2	189	188·3	16·5	249	248·1	21·7
10	10·0	00·9	70	69·7	06·1	130	129·5	11·3	190	189·3	16·6	250	249·0	21·8
11	11·0	01·0	71	70·7	06·2	131	130·5	11·4	191	190·3	16·6	251	250·0	21·9
12	12·0	01·0	72	71·7	06·3	132	131·5	11·5	192	191·3	16·7	252	251·0	22·0
13	13·0	01·1	73	72·7	06·4	133	132·5	11·6	193	192·3	16·8	253	252·0	22·1
14	13·9	01·2	74	73·7	06·4	134	133·5	11·7	194	193·3	16·9	254	253·0	22·1
15	14·9	01·3	75	74·7	06·5	135	134·5	11·8	195	194·3	17·0	255	254·0	22·2
16	15·9	01·4	76	75·7	06·6	136	135·5	11·9	196	195·3	17·1	256	255·0	22·3
17	16·9	01·5	77	76·7	06·7	137	136·5	11·9	197	196·3	17·2	257	256·0	22·4
18	17·9	01·6	78	77·7	06·8	138	137·5	12·0	198	197·2	17·3	258	257·0	22·5
19	18·9	01·7	79	78·7	06·9	139	138·5	12·1	199	198·2	17·3	259	258·0	22·6
20	19·9	01·7	80	79·7	07·0	140	139·5	12·2	200	199·2	17·4	260	259·0	22·7
21	20·9	01·8	81	80·7	07·1	141	140·5	12·3	201	200·2	17·5	261	260·0	22·7
22	21·9	01·9	82	81·7	07·1	142	141·5	12·4	202	201·2	17·6	262	261·0	22·8
23	22·9	02·0	83	82·7	07·2	143	142·5	12·5	203	202·2	17·7	263	262·0	22·9
24	23·9	02·1	84	83·7	07·3	144	143·5	12·6	204	203·2	17·8	264	263·0	23·0
25	24·9	02·2	85	84·7	07·4	145	144·4	12·6	205	204·2	17·9	265	264·0	23·1
26	25·9	02·3	86	85·7	07·5	146	145·4	12·7	206	205·2	18·0	266	265·0	23·2
27	26·9	02·4	87	86·7	07·6	147	146·4	12·8	207	206·2	18·0	267	266·0	23·3
28	27·9	02·4	88	87·7	07·7	148	147·4	12·9	208	207·2	18·1	268	267·0	23·4
29	28·9	02·5	89	88·7	07·8	149	148·4	13·0	209	208·2	18·2	269	268·0	23·4
30	29·9	02·6	90	89·7	07·8	150	149·4	13·1	210	209·2	18·3	270	269·0	23·5
31	30·9	02·7	91	90·7	07·9	151	150·4	13·2	211	210·2	18·4	271	270·0	23·6
32	31·9	02·8	92	91·6	08·0	152	151·4	13·2	212	211·2	18·5	272	271·0	23·7
33	32·9	02·9	93	92·6	08·1	153	152·4	13·3	213	212·2	18·6	273	272·0	23·8
34	33·9	03·0	94	93·6	08·2	154	153·4	13·4	214	213·2	18·7	274	273·0	23·9
35	34·9	03·1	95	94·6	08·3	155	154·4	13·5	215	214·2	18·7	275	274·0	24·0
36	35·9	03·1	96	95·6	08·4	156	155·4	13·6	216	215·2	18·8	276	274·9	24·1
37	36·9	03·2	97	96·6	08·5	157	156·4	13·7	217	216·2	18·9	277	275·9	24·1
38	37·9	03·3	98	97·6	08·5	158	157·4	13·8	218	217·2	19·0	278	276·9	24·2
39	38·9	03·4	99	98·6	08·6	159	158·4	13·9	219	218·2	19·1	279	277·9	24·3
40	39·8	03·5	100	99·6	08·7	160	159·4	13·9	220	219·2	19·2	280	278·9	24·4
41	40·8	03·6	101	100·6	08·8	161	160·4	14·0	221	220·2	19·3	281	279·9	24·5
42	41·8	03·7	102	101·6	08·9	162	161·4	14·1	222	221·2	19·3	282	280·9	24·6
43	42·8	03·7	103	102·6	09·0	163	162·4	14·2	223	222·2	19·4	283	281·9	24·7
44	43·8	03·8	104	103·6	09·1	164	163·4	14·3	224	223·1	19·5	284	282·9	24·8
45	44·8	03·9	105	104·6	09·2	165	164·4	14·4	225	224·1	19·6	285	283·9	24·8
46	45·8	04·0	106	105·6	09·2	166	165·4	14·5	226	225·1	19·7	286	284·9	24·9
47	46·8	04·1	107	106·6	09·3	167	166·4	14·6	227	226·1	19·8	287	285·9	25·0
48	47·8	04·2	108	107·6	09·4	168	167·4	14·6	228	227·1	19·9	288	286·9	25·1
49	48·8	04·3	109	108·6	09·5	169	168·4	14·7	229	228·1	20·0	289	287·9	25·2
50	49·8	04·4	110	109·6	09·6	170	169·4	14·8	230	229·1	20·0	290	288·9	25·3
51	50·8	04·4	111	110·6	09·7	171	170·3	14·9	231	230·1	20·1	291	289·9	25·4
52	51·8	04·5	112	111·6	09·8	172	171·3	15·0	232	231·1	20·2	292	290·9	25·4
53	52·8	04·6	113	112·6	09·8	173	172·3	15·1	233	232·1	20·3	293	291·9	25·5
54	53·8	04·7	114	113·6	09·9	174	173·3	15·2	234	233·1	20·4	294	292·9	25·6
55	54·8	04·8	115	114·6	10·0	175	174·3	15·3	235	234·1	20·5	295	293·9	25·7
56	55·8	04·9	116	115·6	10·1	176	175·3	15·3	236	235·1	20·6	296	294·9	25·8
57	56·8	05·0	117	116·6	10·2	177	176·3	15·4	237	236·1	20·7	297	295·9	25·9
58	57·8	05·1	118	117·6	10·3	178	177·3	15·5	238	237·1	20·7	298	296·9	26·0
59	58·8	05·1	119	118·5	10·4	179	178·3	15·6	239	238·1	20·8	299	297·9	26·1
60	59·8	05·2	120	119·5	10·5	180	179·3	15·7	240	239·1	20·9	300	298·9	26·1
Dist.	Dep.	D. Lat.	Dist.	Dep.	D. Lat.	Dist.	Dep.	D. Lat.	Dist.	Dep.	D. Lat.	Dist.	Dep.	D. Lat.
D. Lon		Dep.	D. Lon		Dep.	D. Lon		Dep.	D. Lon		Dep.	D. Lon		Dep.

275° / 265°	85 Degrees	085° / 095°	5h 40m

TRAVERSE TABLE
5 Degrees

D. Lon	Dep.		D. Lon	Dep.		D. Lon	Dep.		D. Lon	Dep.		D. Lon	Dep.	
Dist.	D. Lat.	Dep.	Dist.	D. Lat.	Dep.	Dist.	D. Lat.	Dep.	Dist.	D. Lat.	Dep.	Dist.	D. Lat.	Dep.
301	299.9	26.2	361	359.6	31.5	421	419.4	36.7	481	479.2	41.9	541	538.9	47.2
302	300.9	26.3	362	360.6	31.6	422	420.4	36.8	482	480.2	42.0	542	539.9	47.2
303	301.8	26.4	363	361.6	31.6	423	421.4	36.9	483	481.2	42.1	543	540.9	47.3
304	302.8	26.5	364	362.6	31.7	424	422.4	37.0	484	482.2	42.2	544	541.9	47.4
305	303.8	26.6	365	363.6	31.8	425	423.4	37.0	485	483.2	42.3	545	542.9	47.5
306	304.8	26.7	366	364.6	31.9	426	424.4	37.1	486	484.2	42.4	546	543.9	47.6
307	305.8	26.8	367	365.6	32.0	427	425.4	37.2	487	485.1	42.4	547	544.9	47.7
308	306.8	26.8	368	366.6	32.1	428	426.4	37.3	488	486.1	42.5	548	545.9	47.8
309	307.8	26.9	369	367.6	32.2	429	427.4	37.4	489	487.1	42.6	549	546.9	47.8
310	308.8	27.0	370	368.6	32.2	430	428.4	37.5	490	488.1	42.7	550	547.9	47.9
311	309.8	27.1	371	369.6	32.3	431	429.4	37.6	491	489.1	42.8	551	548.9	48.0
312	310.8	27.2	372	370.6	32.4	432	430.4	37.7	492	490.1	42.9	552	549.9	48.1
313	311.8	27.3	373	371.6	32.5	433	431.4	37.7	493	491.1	43.0	553	550.9	48.2
314	312.8	27.4	374	372.6	32.6	434	432.3	37.8	494	492.1	43.1	554	551.9	48.3
315	313.8	27.5	375	373.6	32.7	435	433.3	37.9	495	493.1	43.1	555	552.9	48.4
316	314.8	27.5	376	374.6	32.8	436	434.3	38.0	496	494.1	43.2	556	553.9	48.5
317	315.8	27.6	377	375.6	32.9	437	435.3	38.1	497	495.1	43.3	557	554.9	48.5
318	316.8	27.7	378	376.6	33.0	438	436.3	38.2	498	496.1	43.4	558	555.9	48.6
319	317.8	27.8	379	377.6	33.0	439	437.3	38.3	499	497.1	43.5	559	556.9	48.7
320	318.8	27.9	380	378.6	33.1	440	438.3	38.3	500	498.1	43.6	560	557.9	48.8
321	319.8	28.0	381	379.6	33.2	441	439.3	38.4	501	499.1	43.7	561	558.9	48.9
322	320.8	28.1	382	380.5	33.3	442	440.3	38.5	502	500.1	43.8	562	559.9	49.0
323	321.8	28.2	383	381.5	33.4	443	441.3	38.6	503	501.1	43.8	563	560.9	49.1
324	322.8	28.2	384	382.5	33.5	444	442.3	38.7	504	502.1	43.9	564	561.9	49.2
325	323.8	28.3	385	383.5	33.6	445	443.3	38.8	505	503.1	44.0	565	562.9	49.3
326	324.8	28.4	386	384.5	33.6	446	444.3	38.9	506	504.1	44.1	566	563.8	49.3
327	325.8	28.5	387	385.5	33.7	447	445.3	39.0	507	505.1	44.2	567	564.8	49.4
328	326.8	28.6	388	386.5	33.8	448	446.3	39.0	508	506.1	44.3	568	565.8	49.5
329	327.7	28.7	389	387.5	33.9	449	447.3	39.1	509	507.1	44.4	569	566.8	49.6
330	328.7	28.8	390	388.5	34.0	450	448.3	39.2	510	508.1	44.4	570	567.8	49.7
331	329.7	28.8	391	389.5	34.1	451	449.3	39.3	511	509.1	44.5	571	568.8	49.8
332	330.7	28.9	392	390.5	34.2	452	450.3	39.4	512	510.1	44.6	572	569.8	49.9
333	331.7	29.0	393	391.5	34.3	453	451.3	39.5	513	511.0	44.7	573	570.8	49.9
334	332.7	29.1	394	392.5	34.3	454	452.3	39.6	514	512.0	44.8	574	571.8	50.0
335	333.7	29.2	395	393.5	34.4	455	453.3	39.7	515	513.0	44.9	575	572.8	50.1
336	334.7	29.3	396	394.5	34.5	456	454.3	39.7	516	514.0	45.0	576	573.8	50.2
337	335.7	29.4	397	395.5	34.6	457	455.3	39.8	517	515.0	45.1	577	574.8	50.4
338	336.7	29.5	398	396.5	34.7	458	456.3	39.9	518	516.0	45.1	578	575.8	50.4
339	337.7	29.6	399	397.5	34.8	459	457.3	40.0	519	517.0	45.2	579	576.8	50.5
340	338.7	29.6	400	398.5	34.9	460	458.2	40.1	520	518.0	45.3	580	577.8	50.6
341	339.7	29.7	401	399.5	34.9	461	459.2	40.2	521	519.0	45.4	581	578.8	50.6
342	340.7	29.8	402	400.5	35.0	462	460.2	40.3	522	520.0	45.5	582	579.8	50.7
343	341.7	29.9	403	401.5	35.1	463	461.2	40.4	523	521.0	45.6	583	580.8	50.8
344	342.7	30.0	404	402.5	35.2	464	462.2	40.4	524	522.0	45.7	584	581.8	50.9
345	343.7	30.1	405	403.5	35.3	465	463.2	40.5	525	523.0	45.8	585	582.8	51.0
346	344.7	30.2	406	404.5	35.4	466	464.2	40.6	526	524.0	45.8	586	583.8	51.1
347	345.7	30.2	407	405.5	35.5	467	465.2	40.7	527	525.0	45.9	587	584.8	51.2
348	346.7	30.3	408	406.4	35.6	468	466.2	40.8	528	526.0	46.0	588	585.8	51.2
349	347.7	30.4	409	407.4	35.6	469	467.2	40.9	529	527.0	46.1	589	586.8	51.3
350	348.7	30.5	410	408.4	35.7	470	468.2	41.0	530	528.0	46.2	590	587.8	51.4
351	349.7	30.6	411	409.4	35.8	471	469.2	41.1	531	529.0	46.3	591	588.8	51.5
352	350.7	30.7	412	410.4	35.9	472	470.2	41.1	532	530.0	46.4	592	589.7	51.6
353	351.7	30.8	413	411.4	36.0	473	471.2	41.2	533	531.0	46.5	593	590.7	51.7
354	352.7	30.9	414	412.4	36.1	474	472.2	41.3	534	532.0	46.5	594	591.7	51.8
355	353.6	30.9	415	413.4	36.2	475	473.2	41.4	535	533.0	46.6	595	592.7	51.9
356	354.6	31.0	416	414.4	36.3	476	474.2	41.5	536	534.0	46.7	596	593.7	51.9
357	355.6	31.1	417	415.4	36.3	477	475.2	41.6	537	535.0	46.8	597	594.7	52.0
358	356.6	31.2	418	416.4	36.4	478	476.2	41.7	538	536.0	46.9	598	595.7	52.1
359	357.6	31.3	419	417.4	36.5	479	477.2	41.7	539	536.9	47.0	599	596.7	52.2
360	358.6	31.4	420	418.4	36.6	480	478.2	41.8	540	537.9	47.1	600	597.7	52.3
Dist.	Dep.	D. Lat.	Dist.	Dep.	D. Lat.	Dist.	Dep.	D. Lat.	Dist.	Dep.	D. Lat.	Dist.	Dep.	D. Lat.
D. Lon		Dep.	D. Lon		Dep.	D. Lon		Dep.	D. Lon		Dep.	D. Lon		Dep.

TRAVERSE TABLE
6 Degrees

| 354° / 186° | | | | | | | | | 006° / 174° | | 0h 24m |

D. Lon	Dep.		D. Lon	Dep.		D. Lon	Dep.		D. Lon	Dep.		D. Lon	Dep.	
Dist.	D. Lat.	Dep.	Dist.	D. Lat.	Dep.	Dist.	D. Lat.	Dep.	Dist.	D. Lat.	Dep.	Dist.	D. Lat.	Dep.
1	01·0	00·1	61	60·7	06·4	121	120·3	12·6	181	180·0	18·9	241	239·7	25·2
2	02·0	00·2	62	61·7	06·8	122	121·3	12·8	182	181·0	19·0	242	240·7	25·3
3	03·0	00·3	63	62·7	06·6	123	122·3	12·9	183	182·0	19·1	243	241·7	25·4
4	04·0	00·4	64	63·6	06·7	124	123·3	13·0	184	183·0	19·2	244	242·7	25·5
5	05·0	00·5	65	64·6	06·8	125	124·3	13·1	185	184·0	19·3	245	243·7	25·6
6	06·0	00·6	66	65·6	06·9	126	125·3	13·2	186	185·0	19·4	246	244·7	25·7
7	07·0	00·7	67	66·6	07·0	127	126·3	13·3	187	186·0	19·5	247	245·6	25·8
8	08·0	00·8	68	67·6	07·1	128	127·3	13·4	188	187·0	19·7	248	246·6	25·9
9	09·0	00·9	69	68·6	07·2	129	128·3	13·5	189	188·0	19·8	249	247·6	26·0
10	09·9	01·0	70	69·6	07·3	130	129·3	13·6	190	189·0	19·9	250	248·6	26·1
11	10·9	01·1	71	70·6	07·4	131	130·3	13·7	191	190·0	20·0	251	249·6	26·2
12	11·9	01·3	72	71·6	07·5	132	131·3	13·8	192	190·9	20·1	252	250·6	26·3
13	12·9	01·4	73	72·6	07·6	133	132·3	13·9	193	191·9	20·2	253	251·6	26·4
14	13·9	01·5	74	73·6	07·7	134	133·3	14·0	194	192·9	20·3	254	252·6	26·6
15	14·9	01·6	75	74·6	07·8	135	134·3	14·1	195	193·9	20·4	255	253·6	26·7
16	15·9	01·7	76	75·6	07·9	136	135·3	14·2	196	194·9	20·5	256	254·6	26·8
17	16·9	01·8	77	76·6	08·0	137	136·2	14·3	197	195·9	20·6	257	255·6	26·9
18	17·9	01·9	78	77·6	08·2	138	137·2	14·4	198	196·9	20·7	258	256·6	27·0
19	18·9	02·0	79	78·6	08·3	139	138·2	14·5	199	197·9	20·8	259	257·6	27·1
20	19·9	02·1	80	79·6	08·4	140	139·2	14·6	200	198·9	20·9	260	258·6	27·2
21	20·9	02·2	81	80·6	08·5	141	140·2	14·7	201	199·9	21·0	261	259·6	27·3
22	21·9	02·3	82	81·6	08·6	142	141·2	14·8	202	200·9	21·1	262	260·6	27·4
23	22·9	02·4	83	82·5	08·7	143	142·2	14·9	203	201·9	21·2	263	261·6	27·5
24	23·9	02·5	84	83·5	08·8	144	143·2	15·1	204	202·9	21·3	264	262·6	27·6
25	24·9	02·6	85	84·5	08·9	145	144·2	15·2	205	203·9	21·4	265	263·5	27·7
26	25·9	02·7	86	85·5	09·0	146	145·2	15·3	206	204·9	21·5	266	264·5	27·8
27	26·9	02·8	87	86·5	09·1	147	146·2	15·4	207	205·9	21·6	267	265·5	27·9
28	27·8	02·9	88	87·5	09·2	148	147·2	15·5	208	206·9	21·7	268	266·5	28·0
29	28·8	03·0	89	88·5	09·3	149	148·2	15·6	209	207·9	21·8	269	267·5	28·1
30	29·8	03·1	90	89·5	09·4	150	149·2	15·7	210	208·8	22·0	270	268·5	28·2
31	30·8	03·2	91	90·5	09·5	151	150·2	15·8	211	209·8	22·1	271	269·5	28·3
32	31·8	03·3	92	91·5	09·6	152	151·2	15·9	212	210·8	22·2	272	270·5	28·4
33	32·8	03·4	93	92·5	09·7	153	152·2	16·0	213	211·8	22·3	273	271·5	28·5
34	33·8	03·6	94	93·5	09·8	154	153·2	16·1	214	212·8	22·4	274	272·5	28·6
35	34·8	03·7	95	94·5	09·9	155	154·2	16·2	215	213·8	22·5	275	273·5	28·7
36	35·8	03·8	96	95·5	10·0	156	155·1	16·3	216	214·8	22·6	276	274·5	28·8
37	36·8	03·9	97	96·5	10·1	157	156·1	16·4	217	215·8	22·7	277	275·5	29·0
38	37·8	04·0	98	97·5	10·2	158	157·1	16·5	218	216·8	22·8	278	276·5	29·1
39	38·8	04·1	99	98·5	10·3	159	158·1	16·6	219	217·8	22·9	279	277·5	29·2
40	39·8	04·2	100	99·5	10·5	160	159·1	16·7	220	218·8	23·0	280	278·5	29·3
41	40·8	04·3	101	100·4	10·6	161	160·1	16·8	221	219·8	23·1	281	279·5	29·4
42	41·8	04·4	102	101·4	10·7	162	161·1	16·9	222	220·8	23·2	282	280·5	29·5
43	42·8	04·5	103	102·4	10·8	163	162·1	17·0	223	221·8	23·3	283	281·4	29·6
44	43·8	04·6	104	103·4	10·9	164	163·1	17·1	224	222·8	23·4	284	282·4	29·7
45	44·8	04·7	105	104·4	11·0	165	164·1	17·2	225	223·8	23·5	285	283·4	29·8
46	45·7	04·8	106	105·4	11·1	166	165·1	17·4	226	224·8	23·6	286	284·4	29·9
47	46·7	04·9	107	106·4	11·2	167	166·1	17·5	227	225·8	23·7	287	285·4	30·0
48	47·7	05·0	108	107·4	11·3	168	167·1	17·6	228	226·8	23·8	288	286·4	30·1
49	48·7	05·1	109	108·4	11·4	169	168·1	17·7	229	227·7	23·9	289	287·4	30·2
50	49·7	05·2	110	109·4	11·5	170	169·1	17·8	230	228·7	24·0	290	288·4	30·3
51	50·7	05·3	111	110·4	11·6	171	170·1	17·9	231	229·7	24·1	291	289·4	30·4
52	51·7	05·4	112	111·4	11·7	172	171·1	18·0	232	230·7	24·3	292	290·4	30·5
53	52·7	05·5	113	112·4	11·8	173	172·1	18·1	233	231·7	24·4	293	291·4	30·6
54	53·7	05·6	114	113·4	11·9	174	173·0	18·2	234	232·7	24·5	294	292·4	30·7
55	54·7	05·7	115	114·4	12·0	175	174·0	18·3	235	233·7	24·6	295	293·4	30·8
56	55·7	05·9	116	115·4	12·1	176	175·0	18·4	236	234·7	24·7	296	294·4	30·9
57	56·7	06·0	117	116·4	12·2	177	176·0	18·5	237	235·7	24·8	297	295·4	31·0
58	57·7	06·1	118	117·4	12·3	178	177·0	18·6	238	236·7	24·9	298	296·4	31·1
59	58·7	06·2	119	118·3	12·4	179	178·0	18·7	239	237·7	25·0	299	297·4	31·3
60	59·7	06·3	120	119·3	12·5	180	179·0	18·8	240	238·7	25·1	300	298·4	31·4
Dist.	Dep.	D. Lat.	Dist.	Dep.	D. Lat.	Dist.	Dep.	D. Lat.	Dist.	Dep.	D. Lat.	Dist.	Dep.	D. Lat.
D. Lon		Dep.	D. Lon		Dep.	D. Lon		Dep.	D. Lon		Dep.	D. Lon		Dep.

| 276° / 264° | | | | 84 Degrees | | | | 084° / 096° | 5h 36m |

TRAVERSE TABLE

	354° / 186°			6 Degrees						006° / 174°		0h 24m

D. Lon	Dep.		D. Lon	Dep.		D. Lon	Dep.		D. Lon	Dep.		D. Lon	Dep.	
Dist.	D. Lat.	Dep.	Dist.	D. Lat.	Dep.	Dist.	D. Lat.	Dep.	Dist.	D. Lat.	Dep.	Dist.	D. Lat.	Dep.
301	299·4	31·5	361	359·0	37·7	421	418·7	44·0	481	478·4	50·3	541	538·0	56·7
302	300·3	31·6	362	360·0	37·8	422	419·7	44·1	482	479·4	50·4	542	539·0	56·7
303	301·3	31·7	363	361·0	37·9	423	420·7	44·2	483	480·4	50·5	543	540·0	56·8
304	302·3	31·8	364	362·0	38·0	424	421·7	44·3	484	481·3	50·6	544	541·0	56·9
305	303·3	31·9	365	363·0	38·2	425	422·7	44·4	485	482·3	50·7	545	542·0	57·0
306	304·3	32·0	366	364·0	38·3	426	423·7	44·5	486	483·3	50·8	546	543·0	57·1
307	305·3	32·1	367	365·0	38·4	427	424·7	44·6	487	484·3	50·9	547	544·0	57·2
308	306·3	32·2	368	366·0	38·5	428	425·7	44·7	488	485·3	51·0	548	545·0	57·3
309	307·3	32·3	369	367·0	38·6	429	426·6	44·8	489	486·3	51·1	549	546·0	57·4
310	308·3	32·4	370	368·0	38·7	430	427·6	44·9	490	487·3	51·2	550	547·0	57·5
311	309·3	32·5	371	369·0	38·8	431	428·6	45·1	491	488·3	51·3	551	548·0	57·6
312	310·3	32·6	372	370·0	38·9	432	429·6	45·2	492	489·3	51·4	552	549·0	57·7
313	311·3	32·7	373	371·0	39·0	433	430·6	45·3	493	490·3	51·5	553	550·0	57·7
314	312·3	32·8	374	372·0	39·1	434	431·6	45·4	494	491·3	51·6	554	551·0	57·9
315	313·3	32·9	375	372·9	39·2	435	432·6	45·5	495	492·3	51·7	555	552·0	58·0
316	314·3	33·0	376	373·9	39·3	436	433·6	45·6	496	493·3	51·8	556	553·0	58·1
317	315·3	33·1	377	374·9	39·4	437	434·6	45·7	497	494·3	52·0	557	553·9	58·2
318	316·3	33·2	378	375·9	39·5	438	435·6	45·8	498	495·3	52·1	558	554·9	58·3
319	317·3	33·3	379	376·9	39·6	439	436·6	45·9	499	496·3	52·2	559	555·9	58·4
320	318·2	33·4	380	377·9	39·7	440	437·6	46·0	500	497·3	52·3	560	556·9	58·5
321	319·2	33·6	381	378·9	39·8	441	438·6	46·1	501	498·3	52·4	561	557·9	58·6
322	320·2	33·7	382	379·9	39·9	442	439·6	46·2	502	499·2	52·5	562	558·9	58·7
323	321·2	33·8	383	380·9	40·0	443	440·6	46·3	503	500·2	52·6	563	559·9	58·8
324	322·2	33·9	384	381·9	40·1	444	441·6	46·4	504	501·2	52·7	564	560·9	59·0
325	323·2	34·0	385	382·9	40·2	445	442·6	46·5	505	502·2	52·8	565	561·9	59·1
326	324·2	34·1	386	383·9	40·3	446	443·6	46·6	506	503·2	52·9	566	562·9	59·2
327	325·2	34·2	387	384·9	40·5	447	444·6	46·7	507	504·2	53·0	567	563·9	59·3
328	326·2	34·3	388	385·9	40·6	448	445·5	46·8	508	505·2	53·1	568	564·9	59·4
329	327·2	34·4	389	386·9	40·7	449	446·5	46·9	509	506·2	53·2	569	565·9	59·5
330	328·2	34·5	390	387·9	40·8	450	447·5	47·0	510	507·2	53·3	570	566·9	59·6
331	329·2	34·6	391	388·9	40·9	451	448·5	47·1	511	508·2	53·4	571	567·9	59·7
332	330·2	34·7	392	389·9	41·0	452	449·5	47·2	512	509·2	53·5	572	568·9	59·8
333	331·2	34·8	393	390·8	41·1	453	450·5	47·4	513	510·2	53·6	573	569·9	59·9
334	332·2	34·9	394	391·8	41·2	454	451·5	47·5	514	511·2	53·7	574	570·9	60·0
335	333·2	35·0	395	392·8	41·3	455	452·5	47·6	515	512·2	53·8	575	571·9	60·1
336	334·2	35·1	396	393·8	41·4	456	453·5	47·7	516	513·2	53·9	576	572·8	60·2
337	335·2	35·2	397	394·8	41·5	457	454·5	47·8	517	514·2	54·0	577	573·8	60·3
338	336·1	35·3	398	395·8	41·6	458	455·5	47·9	518	515·2	54·1	578	574·8	60·4
339	337·1	35·4	399	396·8	41·7	459	456·5	48·0	519	516·2	54·3	579	575·8	60·5
340	338·1	35·5	400	397·8	41·8	460	457·5	48·1	520	517·2	54·4	580	576·8	60·6
341	339·1	35·6	401	398·8	41·9	461	458·5	48·2	521	518·1	54·5	581	577·8	60·7
342	340·1	35·7	402	399·8	42·0	462	459·5	48·3	522	519·1	54·6	582	578·8	60·8
343	341·1	35·9	403	400·8	42·1	463	460·5	48·4	523	520·1	54·7	583	579·8	60·9
344	342·1	36·0	404	401·8	42·2	464	461·5	48·5	524	521·1	54·8	584	580·8	61·0
345	343·1	36·1	405	402·8	42·3	465	462·5	48·6	525	522·1	54·9	585	581·8	61·1
346	344·1	36·2	406	403·8	42·4	466	463·4	48·7	526	523·1	55·0	586	582·8	61·3
347	345·1	36·3	407	404·8	42·5	467	464·4	48·8	527	524·1	55·1	587	583·8	61·4
348	346·1	36·4	408	405·8	42·6	468	465·4	48·9	528	525·1	55·2	588	584·8	61·5
349	347·1	36·5	409	406·8	42·8	469	466·4	49·0	529	526·1	55·3	589	585·8	61·6
350	348·1	36·6	410	407·8	42·9	470	467·4	49·1	530	527·1	55·4	590	586·8	61·7
351	349·1	36·7	411	408·7	43·0	471	468·4	49·2	531	528·1	55·5	591	587·8	61·8
352	350·1	36·8	412	409·7	43·1	472	469·4	49·3	532	529·1	55·6	592	588·8	61·9
353	351·1	36·9	413	410·7	43·2	473	470·4	49·5	533	530·1	55·7	593	589·8	62·0
354	352·1	37·0	414	411·7	43·3	474	471·4	49·5	534	531·1	55·8	594	590·7	62·1
355	353·1	37·1	415	412·7	43·4	475	472·4	49·7	535	532·1	55·9	595	591·7	62·2
356	354·0	37·2	416	413·7	43·5	476	473·4	49·8	536	533·1	56·0	596	592·7	62·3
357	355·0	37·3	417	414·7	43·6	477	474·4	49·9	537	534·1	56·1	597	593·7	62·4
358	356·0	37·4	418	415·7	43·7	478	475·4	50·0	538	535·1	56·3	598	594·7	62·5
359	357·0	37·5	419	416·7	43·8	479	476·4	50·1	539	536·0	56·3	599	595·7	62·6
360	358·0	37·6	420	417·7	43·9	480	477·4	50·2	540	537·0	56·4	600	596·7	62·7
Dist.	Dep.	D. Lat.	Dist.	Dep.	D. Lat.	Dist.	Dep.	D. Lat.	Dist.	Dep.	D. Lat.	Dist.	Dep.	D. Lat.
D. Lon		Dep.	D. Lon		Dep.	D. Lon		Dep.	D. Lon		Dep.	D. Lon		Dep.

	276° / 264°			84 Degrees						084° / 096°		5h 36m

TRAVERSE TABLE
7 Degrees

7°

353° / 187°   007° / 173°   0h 28m

Dist.	D. Lat.	Dep.	Dist.	D. Lat.	Dep.	Dist.	D. Lat.	Dep.	Dist.	D. Lat.	Dep.	Dist.	D. Lat.	Dep.
1	01.0	00.1	61	60.5	07.4	121	120.1	14.7	181	179.7	22.1	241	239.2	29.4
2	02.0	00.2	62	61.5	07.6	122	121.1	14.9	182	180.6	22.2	242	240.2	29.5
3	03.0	00.4	63	62.5	07.7	123	122.1	15.0	183	181.6	22.3	243	241.2	29.6
4	04.0	00.5	64	63.5	07.8	124	123.1	15.1	184	182.6	22.4	244	242.2	29.7
5	05.0	00.6	65	64.5	07.9	125	124.1	15.2	185	183.6	22.5	245	243.2	29.9
6	06.0	00.7	66	65.5	08.0	126	125.1	15.4	186	184.6	22.7	246	244.2	30.0
7	06.9	00.9	67	66.5	08.2	127	126.1	15.5	187	185.6	22.8	247	245.2	30.1
8	07.9	01.0	68	67.5	08.3	128	127.0	15.6	188	186.6	22.9	248	246.2	30.2
9	08.9	01.1	69	68.5	08.4	129	128.0	15.7	189	187.6	23.0	249	247.1	30.3
10	09.9	01.2	70	69.5	08.5	130	129.0	15.8	190	188.6	23.2	250	248.1	30.5
11	10.9	01.3	71	70.5	08.7	131	130.0	16.0	191	189.6	23.3	251	249.1	30.6
12	11.9	01.5	72	71.5	08.8	132	131.0	16.1	192	190.6	23.4	252	250.1	30.7
13	12.9	01.6	73	72.5	08.9	133	132.0	16.2	193	191.6	23.5	253	251.1	30.8
14	13.9	01.7	74	73.4	09.0	134	133.0	16.3	194	192.6	23.6	254	252.1	31.0
15	14.9	01.8	75	74.4	09.1	135	134.0	16.5	195	193.5	23.8	255	253.1	31.1
16	15.9	01.9	76	75.4	09.3	136	135.0	16.6	196	194.5	23.9	256	254.1	31.2
17	16.9	02.1	77	76.4	09.4	137	136.0	16.7	197	195.5	24.0	257	255.1	31.3
18	17.9	02.2	78	77.4	09.5	138	137.0	16.8	198	196.5	24.1	258	256.1	31.4
19	18.9	02.3	79	78.4	09.6	139	138.0	16.9	199	197.5	24.3	259	257.1	31.6
20	19.9	02.4	80	79.4	09.7	140	139.0	17.1	200	198.5	24.4	260	258.1	31.7
21	20.8	02.6	81	80.4	09.9	141	139.9	17.2	201	199.5	24.5	261	259.1	31.8
22	21.8	02.7	82	81.4	10.0	142	140.9	17.3	202	200.5	24.6	262	260.0	31.9
23	22.8	02.8	83	82.4	10.1	143	141.9	17.4	203	201.5	24.7	263	261.0	32.1
24	23.8	02.9	84	83.4	10.2	144	142.9	17.5	204	202.5	24.9	264	262.0	32.2
25	24.8	03.0	85	84.4	10.4	145	143.9	17.7	205	203.5	25.0	265	263.0	32.3
26	25.8	03.2	86	85.4	10.5	146	144.9	17.8	206	204.5	25.1	266	264.0	32.4
27	26.8	03.3	87	86.4	10.6	147	145.9	17.9	207	205.5	25.2	267	265.0	32.5
28	27.8	03.4	88	87.3	10.7	148	146.9	18.0	208	206.4	25.3	268	266.0	32.7
29	28.8	03.5	89	88.3	10.8	149	147.9	18.2	209	207.4	25.5	269	267.0	32.8
30	29.8	03.7	90	89.3	11.0	150	148.9	18.3	210	208.4	25.6	270	268.0	32.9
31	30.8	03.8	91	90.3	11.1	151	149.9	18.4	211	209.4	25.7	271	269.0	33.0
32	31.8	03.9	92	91.3	11.2	152	150.9	18.5	212	210.4	25.8	272	270.0	33.1
33	32.8	04.0	93	92.3	11.3	153	151.9	18.6	213	211.4	26.0	273	271.0	33.3
34	33.7	04.1	94	93.3	11.5	154	152.9	18.8	214	212.4	26.1	274	272.0	33.4
35	34.7	04.3	95	94.3	11.6	155	153.8	18.9	215	213.4	26.2	275	273.0	33.5
36	35.7	04.4	96	95.3	11.7	156	154.8	19.0	216	214.4	26.3	276	273.9	33.6
37	36.7	04.5	97	96.3	11.8	157	155.8	19.1	217	215.4	26.4	277	274.9	33.8
38	37.7	04.6	98	97.3	11.9	158	156.8	19.3	218	216.4	26.6	278	275.9	33.9
39	38.7	04.8	99	98.3	12.1	159	157.8	19.4	219	217.4	26.7	279	276.9	34.0
40	39.7	04.9	100	99.3	12.2	160	158.8	19.5	220	218.4	26.8	280	277.9	34.1
41	40.7	05.0	101	100.2	12.3	161	159.8	19.6	221	219.4	26.9	281	278.9	34.2
42	41.7	05.1	102	101.2	12.4	162	160.8	19.7	222	220.3	27.1	282	279.9	34.4
43	42.7	05.2	103	102.2	12.6	163	161.8	19.9	223	221.3	27.2	283	280.9	34.5
44	43.7	05.4	104	103.2	12.7	164	162.8	20.0	224	222.3	27.3	284	281.9	34.6
45	44.7	05.5	105	104.2	12.8	165	163.8	20.1	225	223.3	27.4	285	282.9	34.7
46	45.7	05.6	106	105.2	12.9	166	164.8	20.2	226	224.3	27.5	286	283.9	34.9
47	46.6	05.7	107	106.2	13.0	167	165.8	20.4	227	225.3	27.7	287	284.9	35.0
48	47.6	05.8	108	107.2	13.2	168	166.7	20.5	228	226.3	27.8	288	285.9	35.1
49	48.6	06.0	109	108.2	13.3	169	167.7	20.6	229	227.3	27.9	289	286.8	35.2
50	49.6	06.1	110	109.2	13.4	170	168.7	20.7	230	228.3	28.0	290	287.8	35.3
51	50.6	06.2	111	110.2	13.5	171	169.7	20.8	231	229.3	28.2	291	288.8	35.5
52	51.6	06.3	112	111.2	13.6	172	170.7	21.0	232	230.3	28.3	292	289.8	35.6
53	52.6	06.5	113	112.2	13.8	173	171.7	21.1	233	231.3	28.4	293	290.8	35.7
54	53.6	06.6	114	113.2	13.9	174	172.7	21.2	234	232.3	28.5	294	291.8	35.8
55	54.6	06.7	115	114.1	14.0	175	173.7	21.3	235	233.2	28.6	295	292.8	36.0
56	55.6	06.8	116	115.1	14.1	176	174.7	21.4	236	234.2	28.8	296	293.8	36.1
57	56.6	06.9	117	116.1	14.3	177	175.7	21.6	237	235.2	28.9	297	294.8	36.2
58	57.6	07.1	118	117.1	14.4	178	176.7	21.7	238	236.2	29.0	298	295.8	36.3
59	58.6	07.2	119	118.1	14.5	179	177.7	21.8	239	237.2	29.1	299	296.8	36.4
60	59.6	07.3	120	119.1	14.6	180	178.7	21.9	240	238.2	29.2	300	297.8	36.6
Dist.	Dep.	D. Lat.	Dist.	Dep.	D. Lat.	Dist.	Dep.	D. Lat.	Dist.	Dep.	D. Lat.	Dist.	Dep.	D. Lat.

D. Lon — Dep. (top); Dist. / D. Lon — Dep. (bottom)

83°

277° / 263°   83 Degrees   083° / 097°   5h 32m

TRAVERSE TABLE
7 Degrees

D. Lon	Dep.		D. Lon	Dep.		D. Lon	Dep.		D. Lon	Dep.		D. Lon	Dep.	
Dist.	D. Lat.	Dep.	Dist.	D. Lat.	Dep.	Dist.	D. Lat.	Dep.	Dist.	D. Lat.	Dep.	Dist.	D. Lat.	Dep.
301	298.8	36.7	361	358.3	44.0	421	417.9	51.3	481	477.4	58.6	541	537.0	65.9
302	299.7	36.8	362	359.3	44.1	422	418.9	51.4	482	478.4	58.7	542	538.0	66.1
303	300.7	36.9	363	360.3	44.2	423	419.8	51.6	483	479.4	58.9	543	539.0	66.2
304	301.7	37.0	364	361.3	44.4	424	420.8	51.7	484	480.4	59.0	544	539.9	66.3
305	302.7	37.2	365	362.3	44.5	425	421.8	51.8	485	481.4	59.1	545	540.9	66.4
306	303.7	37.3	366	363.3	44.6	426	422.8	51.9	486	482.4	59.2	546	541.9	66.5
307	304.7	37.4	367	364.3	44.7	427	423.8	52.0	487	483.4	59.4	547	542.9	66.7
308	305.7	37.5	368	365.3	44.8	428	424.8	52.2	488	484.4	59.5	548	543.9	66.8
309	306.7	37.6	369	366.2	45.0	429	425.8	52.3	489	485.4	59.6	549	544.9	66.9
310	307.7	37.8	370	367.2	45.1	430	426.8	52.4	490	486.3	59.7	550	545.9	67.0
311	308.7	37.9	371	368.2	45.2	431	427.8	52.5	491	487.3	59.8	551	546.9	67.1
312	309.7	38.0	372	369.2	45.3	432	428.8	52.6	492	488.3	60.0	552	547.9	67.3
313	310.7	38.1	373	370.2	45.5	433	429.8	52.8	493	489.3	60.1	553	548.9	67.4
314	311.7	38.3	374	371.2	45.6	434	430.8	52.9	494	490.3	60.2	554	549.9	67.5
315	312.7	38.4	375	372.2	45.7	435	431.8	53.0	495	491.3	60.3	555	550.9	67.6
316	313.6	38.5	376	373.2	45.8	436	432.8	53.1	496	492.3	60.4	556	551.9	67.8
317	314.6	38.6	377	374.2	45.9	437	433.7	53.3	497	493.3	60.6	557	552.8	67.9
318	315.6	38.8	378	375.2	46.1	438	434.7	53.4	498	494.3	60.7	558	553.8	68.0
319	316.6	38.9	379	376.2	46.2	439	435.7	53.5	499	495.3	60.8	559	554.8	68.1
320	317.6	39.0	380	377.2	46.3	440	436.7	53.6	500	496.3	60.9	560	555.8	68.2
321	318.6	39.1	381	378.2	46.4	441	437.7	53.7	501	497.3	61.1	561	556.8	68.4
322	319.6	39.2	382	379.2	46.6	442	438.7	53.9	502	498.3	61.2	562	557.8	68.5
323	320.6	39.4	383	380.1	46.7	443	439.7	54.0	503	499.3	61.3	563	558.8	68.6
324	321.6	39.5	384	381.1	46.8	444	440.7	54.1	504	500.2	61.4	564	559.8	68.7
325	322.6	39.6	385	382.1	46.9	445	441.7	54.2	505	501.2	61.5	565	560.8	68.9
326	323.6	39.7	386	383.1	47.0	446	442.7	54.4	506	502.2	61.7	566	561.8	69.0
327	324.6	39.8	387	384.1	47.2	447	443.7	54.5	507	503.2	61.8	567	562.8	69.1
328	325.6	40.0	388	385.1	47.3	448	444.7	54.6	508	504.2	61.9	568	563.8	69.2
329	326.5	40.1	389	386.1	47.4	449	445.7	54.7	509	505.2	62.0	569	564.8	69.3
330	327.5	40.2	390	387.1	47.5	450	446.6	54.8	510	506.2	62.2	570	565.8	69.5
331	328.5	40.3	391	388.1	47.7	451	447.6	55.0	511	507.2	62.3	571	566.7	69.6
332	329.5	40.5	392	389.1	47.8	452	448.6	55.1	512	508.2	62.4	572	567.7	69.7
333	330.5	40.6	393	390.1	47.9	453	449.6	55.2	513	509.2	62.5	573	568.7	69.8
334	331.5	40.7	394	391.1	48.0	454	450.6	55.3	514	510.2	62.6	574	569.7	70.0
335	332.5	40.8	395	392.1	48.1	455	451.6	55.5	515	511.2	62.8	575	570.7	70.1
336	333.5	40.9	396	393.0	48.3	456	452.6	55.6	516	512.2	62.9	576	571.7	70.2
337	334.5	41.1	397	394.0	48.4	457	453.6	55.7	517	513.1	63.0	577	572.7	70.3
338	335.5	41.2	398	395.0	48.5	458	454.6	55.8	518	514.1	63.1	578	573.7	70.4
339	336.5	41.3	399	396.0	48.6	459	455.6	55.9	519	515.1	63.3	579	574.7	70.6
340	337.5	41.4	400	397.0	48.7	460	456.6	56.1	520	516.1	63.4	580	575.7	70.7
341	338.5	41.6	401	398.0	48.9	461	457.6	56.2	521	517.1	63.5	581	576.7	70.8
342	339.5	41.7	402	399.0	49.0	462	458.6	56.3	522	518.1	63.6	582	577.7	70.9
343	340.4	41.8	403	400.0	49.1	463	459.5	56.4	523	519.1	63.7	583	578.7	71.0
344	341.4	41.9	404	401.0	49.2	464	460.5	56.5	524	520.1	63.9	584	579.6	71.2
345	342.4	42.0	405	402.0	49.4	465	461.5	56.7	525	521.1	64.0	585	580.6	71.3
346	343.4	42.2	406	403.0	49.5	466	462.5	56.8	526	522.1	64.1	586	581.6	71.4
347	344.4	42.3	407	404.0	49.6	467	463.5	56.9	527	523.1	64.2	587	582.6	71.5
348	345.4	42.3	408	405.0	49.7	468	464.5	57.0	528	524.1	64.3	588	583.6	71.7
349	346.4	42.5	409	406.0	49.8	469	465.5	57.2	529	525.1	64.5	589	584.6	71.8
350	347.4	42.7	410	406.9	50.0	470	466.5	57.3	530	526.0	64.6	590	585.6	71.9
351	348.4	42.8	411	407.9	50.1	471	467.5	57.4	531	527.0	64.7	591	586.6	72.0
352	349.4	42.9	412	408.9	50.2	472	468.5	57.5	532	528.0	64.8	592	587.6	72.1
353	350.4	43.0	413	409.9	50.3	473	469.5	57.6	533	529.0	65.0	593	588.6	72.3
354	351.4	43.1	414	410.9	50.5	474	470.5	57.8	534	530.0	65.1	594	589.6	72.4
355	352.4	43.3	415	411.9	50.6	475	471.5	57.9	535	531.0	65.2	595	590.6	72.5
356	353.3	43.4	416	412.9	50.7	476	472.5	58.0	536	532.0	65.3	596	591.5	72.6
357	354.3	43.5	417	413.9	50.8	477	473.4	58.1	537	533.0	65.4	597	592.5	72.8
358	355.3	43.6	418	414.9	50.9	478	474.4	58.3	538	534.0	65.6	598	593.5	72.9
359	356.3	43.7	419	415.9	51.1	479	475.4	58.4	539	535.0	65.7	599	594.5	73.0
360	357.3	43.8	420	416.9	51.2	480	476.4	58.5	540	536.0	65.8	600	595.5	73.1
Dist.	Dep.	D. Lat.	Dist.	Dep.	D. Lat.	Dist.	Dep.	D. Lat.	Dist.	Dep.	D. Lat.	Dist.	Dep.	D. Lat.
D. Lon		Dep.	D. Lon		Dep.	D. Lon		Dep.	D. Lon		Dep.	D. Lon		Dep.

TRAVERSE TABLE
8 Degrees

8° | 352° / 188° | 008° / 172° 0h 32m

D. Lon	Dep.		D. Lon	Dep.		D. Lon	Dep.		D. Lon	Dep.		D. Lon	Dep.	
Dist.	D. Lat.	Dep.	Dist.	D. Lat.	Dep.	Dist.	D. Lat.	Dep.	Dist.	D. Lat.	Dep.	Dist.	D. Lat.	Dep.
1	01·0	00·1	61	60·4	08·5	121	119·8	16·8	181	179·2	25·2	241	238·7	33·5
2	02·0	00·3	62	61·4	08·6	122	120·8	17·0	182	180·2	25·3	242	239·6	33·7
3	03·0	00·4	63	62·4	08·8	123	121·8	17·1	183	181·2	25·5	243	240·6	33·8
4	04·0	00·6	64	63·4	08·9	124	122·8	17·3	184	182·2	25·6	244	241·6	34·0
5	05·0	00·7	65	64·4	09·0	125	123·8	17·4	185	183·2	25·7	245	242·6	34·1
6	05·9	00·8	66	65·4	09·2	126	124·8	17·5	186	184·2	25·9	246	243·6	34·2
7	06·9	01·0	67	66·3	09·3	127	125·8	17·7	187	185·2	26·0	247	244·6	34·4
8	07·9	01·1	68	67·3	09·5	128	126·8	17·8	188	186·2	26·2	248	245·6	34·5
9	08·9	01·3	69	68·3	09·6	129	127·7	18·0	189	187·2	26·3	249	246·6	34·7
10	09·9	01·4	70	69·3	09·7	130	128·7	18·1	190	188·2	26·4	250	247·6	34·8
11	10·9	01·5	71	70·3	09·9	131	129·7	18·2	191	189·1	26·6	251	248·6	34·9
12	11·9	01·7	72	71·3	10·0	132	130·7	18·4	192	190·1	26·7	252	249·5	35·1
13	12·9	01·8	73	72·3	10·2	133	131·7	18·5	193	191·1	26·9	253	250·5	35·2
14	13·9	01·9	74	73·3	10·3	134	132·7	18·6	194	192·1	27·0	254	251·5	35·3
15	14·9	02·1	75	74·3	10·4	135	133·7	18·8	195	193·1	27·1	255	252·5	35·5
16	15·8	02·2	76	75·3	10·6	136	134·7	18·9	196	194·1	27·3	256	253·5	35·6
17	16·8	02·4	77	76·3	10·7	137	135·7	19·1	197	195·1	27·4	257	254·5	35·8
18	17·8	02·5	78	77·2	10·9	138	136·7	19·2	198	196·1	27·6	258	255·5	35·9
19	18·8	02·6	79	78·2	11·0	139	137·7	19·3	199	197·1	27·7	259	256·5	36·0
20	19·8	02·8	80	79·2	11·1	140	138·6	19·5	200	198·1	27·8	260	257·5	36·2
21	20·8	02·9	81	80·2	11·3	141	139·6	19·6	201	199·0	28·0	261	258·5	36·3
22	21·8	03·1	82	81·2	11·4	142	140·6	19·8	202	200·0	28·1	262	259·5	36·5
23	22·8	03·2	83	82·2	11·6	143	141·6	19·9	203	201·0	28·3	263	260·4	36·6
24	23·8	03·3	84	83·2	11·7	144	142·6	20·0	204	202·0	28·4	264	261·4	36·7
25	24·8	03·5	85	84·2	11·8	145	143·6	20·2	205	203·0	28·5	265	262·4	36·9
26	25·7	03·6	86	85·2	12·0	146	144·6	20·3	206	204·0	28·7	266	263·4	37·0
27	26·7	03·8	87	86·2	12·1	147	145·6	20·5	207	205·0	28·8	267	264·4	37·2
28	27·7	03·9	88	87·1	12·2	148	146·6	20·6	208	206·0	28·9	268	265·4	37·3
29	28·7	04·0	89	88·1	12·4	149	147·5	20·7	209	207·0	29·1	269	266·4	37·4
30	29·7	04·2	90	89·1	12·5	150	148·5	20·9	210	208·0	29·2	270	267·4	37·6
31	30·7	04·3	91	90·1	12·7	151	149·5	21·0	211	208·9	29·4	271	268·4	37·7
32	31·7	04·5	92	91·1	12·8	152	150·5	21·2	212	209·9	29·5	272	269·4	37·9
33	32·7	04·6	93	92·1	12·9	153	151·5	21·3	213	210·9	29·6	273	270·3	38·0
34	33·7	04·7	94	93·1	13·1	154	152·5	21·4	214	211·9	29·8	274	271·3	38·1
35	34·7	04·9	95	94·1	13·2	155	153·5	21·6	215	212·9	29·9	275	272·3	38·3
36	35·6	05·0	96	95·1	13·4	156	154·5	21·7	216	213·9	30·1	276	273·3	38·4
37	36·6	05·1	97	96·1	13·5	157	155·5	21·9	217	214·9	30·2	277	274·3	38·6
38	37·6	05·3	98	97·0	13·6	158	156·5	22·0	218	215·9	30·3	278	275·3	38·7
39	38·6	05·4	99	98·0	13·8	159	157·5	22·1	219	216·9	30·5	279	276·3	38·8
40	39·6	05·6	100	99·0	13·9	160	158·4	22·3	220	217·9	30·6	280	277·3	39·0
41	40·6	05·7	101	100·0	14·1	161	159·4	22·4	221	218·8	30·8	281	278·3	39·1
42	41·6	05·8	102	101·0	14·2	162	160·4	22·5	222	219·8	30·9	282	279·3	39·2
43	42·6	06·0	103	102·0	14·3	163	161·4	22·7	223	220·8	31·0	283	280·2	39·4
44	43·6	06·1	104	103·0	14·5	164	162·4	22·8	224	221·8	31·2	284	281·2	39·5
45	44·6	06·3	105	104·0	14·6	165	163·4	23·0	225	222·8	31·3	285	282·2	39·7
46	45·6	06·4	106	105·0	14·8	166	164·4	23·1	226	223·8	31·5	286	283·2	39·8
47	46·5	06·5	107	106·0	14·9	167	165·4	23·2	227	224·8	31·6	287	284·2	39·9
48	47·5	06·7	108	106·9	15·0	168	166·4	23·4	228	225·8	31·7	288	285·2	40·1
49	48·5	06·8	109	107·9	15·2	169	167·4	23·5	229	226·8	31·9	289	286·2	40·2
50	49·5	07·0	110	108·9	15·3	170	168·3	23·7	230	227·8	32·0	290	287·2	40·4
51	50·5	07·1	111	109·9	15·4	171	169·3	23·8	231	228·8	32·1	291	288·2	40·5
52	51·5	07·2	112	110·9	15·6	172	170·3	23·9	232	229·7	32·3	292	289·2	40·6
53	52·5	07·4	113	111·9	15·7	173	171·3	24·1	233	230·7	32·4	293	290·1	40·8
54	53·5	07·5	114	112·9	15·9	174	172·3	24·2	234	231·7	32·6	294	291·1	40·9
55	54·5	07·7	115	113·9	16·0	175	173·3	24·4	235	232·7	32·7	295	292·1	41·1
56	55·5	07·8	116	114·9	16·1	176	174·3	24·5	236	233·7	32·8	296	293·1	41·2
57	56·4	07·9	117	115·9	16·3	177	175·3	24·6	237	234·7	33·0	297	294·1	41·3
58	57·4	08·1	118	116·9	16·4	178	176·3	24·8	238	235·7	33·1	298	295·1	41·5
59	58·4	08·2	119	117·8	16·6	179	177·3	24·9	239	236·7	33·3	299	296·1	41·6
60	59·4	08·4	120	118·8	16·7	180	178·2	25·1	240	237·7	33·4	300	297·1	41·8
Dist.	Dep.	D. Lat.	Dist.	Dep.	D. Lat.	Dist.	Dep.	D. Lat.	Dist.	Dep.	D. Lat.	Dist.	Dep.	D. Lat.
D. Lon		Dep.	D. Lon		Dep.	D. Lon		Dep.	D. Lon		Dep.	D. Lon		Dep.

82° | 278° / 262° | **82 Degrees** | 082° / 098° 5h 28m

TRAVERSE TABLE
8 Degrees

D. Lon	Dep.		D. Lon	Dep.		D. Lon	Dep.		D. Lon	Dep.		D. Lon	Dep.	
Dist.	D. Lat.	Dep.	Dist.	D. Lat.	Dep.	Dist.	D. Lat.	Dep.	Dist.	D. Lat.	Dep.	Dist.	D. Lat.	Dep.
301	298·1	41·9	361	357·5	50·2	421	416·9	58·6	481	476·3	66·9	541	535·7	75·3
302	299·1	42·0	362	358·5	50·4	422	417·9	58·7	482	477·3	67·1	542	536·7	75·4
303	300·1	42·2	363	359·5	50·5	423	418·9	58·9	483	478·3	67·2	543	537·7	75·6
304	301·0	42·3	364	360·5	50·7	424	419·9	59·0	484	479·3	67·4	544	538·7	75·7
305	302·0	42·4	365	361·4	50·8	425	420·9	59·1	485	480·3	67·5	545	539·7	75·8
306	303·0	42·6	366	362·4	50·9	426	421·9	59·3	486	481·3	67·6	546	540·7	76·0
307	304·0	42·7	367	363·4	51·1	427	422·8	59·4	487	482·3	67·8	547	541·7	76·1
308	305·0	42·9	368	364·4	51·2	428	423·8	59·6	488	483·3	67·9	548	542·7	76·3
309	306·0	43·0	369	365·4	51·4	429	424·8	59·7	489	484·2	68·1	549	543·7	76·4
310	307·0	43·1	370	366·4	51·5	430	425·8	59·8	490	485·2	68·2	550	544·6	76·5
311	308·0	43·3	371	367·4	51·6	431	426·8	60·0	491	486·2	68·3	551	545·6	76·7
312	309·0	43·4	372	368·4	51·8	432	427·8	60·1	492	487·2	68·5	552	546·6	76·8
313	310·0	43·6	373	369·4	51·9	433	428·8	60·3	493	488·2	68·6	553	547·6	77·0
314	310·9	43·7	374	370·4	52·1	434	429·8	60·4	494	489·2	68·8	554	548·6	77·1
315	311·9	43·8	375	371·4	52·2	435	430·8	60·5	495	490·2	68·9	555	549·6	77·2
316	312·9	44·0	376	372·3	52·3	436	431·8	60·7	496	491·2	69·0	556	550·6	77·4
317	313·9	44·1	377	373·3	52·5	437	432·7	60·8	497	492·2	69·2	557	551·6	77·5
318	314·9	44·3	378	374·3	52·6	438	433·7	61·0	498	493·2	69·2	558	552·6	77·7
319	315·9	44·4	379	375·3	52·7	439	434·7	61·1	499	494·1	69·4	559	553·6	77·8
320	316·9	44·5	380	376·3	52·9	440	435·7	61·2	500	495·1	69·6	560	554·6	77·9
321	317·9	44·7	381	377·3	53·0	441	436·7	61·4	501	496·1	69·7	561	555·5	78·1
322	318·9	44·8	382	378·3	53·2	442	437·7	61·5	502	497·1	69·9	562	556·5	78·2
323	319·9	45·0	383	379·3	53·3	443	438·7	61·7	503	498·1	70·0	563	557·5	78·4
324	320·8	45·1	384	380·3	53·4	444	439·7	61·8	504	499·1	70·1	564	558·5	78·5
325	321·8	45·2	385	381·3	53·6	445	440·7	61·9	505	500·1	70·3	565	559·5	78·6
326	322·8	45·4	386	382·2	53·7	446	441·7	62·1	506	501·1	70·4	566	560·5	78·8
327	323·8	45·5	387	383·2	53·9	447	442·6	62·2	507	502·1	70·6	567	561·5	78·9
328	324·8	45·6	388	384·2	54·0	448	443·6	62·3	508	503·1	70·7	568	562·5	79·1
329	325·8	45·8	389	385·2	54·1	449	444·6	62·5	509	504·0	70·8	569	563·5	79·2
330	326·8	45·9	390	386·2	54·3	450	445·6	62·6	510	505·0	71·0	570	564·5	79·3
331	327·8	46·1	391	387·2	54·4	451	446·6	62·8	511	506·0	71·1	571	565·4	79·5
332	328·8	46·2	392	388·2	54·6	452	447·6	62·9	512	507·0	71·3	572	566·4	79·6
333	329·8	46·3	393	389·1	54·7	453	448·6	63·0	513	508·0	71·4	573	567·4	79·7
334	330·7	46·5	394	390·1	54·8	454	449·6	63·2	514	509·0	71·5	574	568·4	79·9
335	331·7	46·6	395	391·1	55·0	455	450·6	63·3	515	510·0	71·7	575	569·4	80·0
336	332·7	46·8	396	392·1	55·1	456	451·6	63·5	516	511·0	71·8	576	570·4	80·2
337	333·7	46·9	397	393·1	55·3	457	452·6	63·6	517	512·0	72·0	577	571·4	80·3
338	334·7	47·0	398	394·1	55·4	458	453·5	63·7	518	513·0	72·1	578	572·4	80·4
339	335·7	47·2	399	395·1	55·5	459	454·5	63·9	519	513·9	72·2	579	573·4	80·6
340	336·7	47·3	400	396·1	55·7	460	455·5	64·0	520	514·9	72·4	580	574·4	80·7
341	337·7	47·5	401	397·1	55·8	461	456·5	64·2	521	515·9	72·5	581	575·3	80·9
342	338·7	47·6	402	398·1	55·9	462	457·5	64·3	522	516·9	72·6	582	576·3	81·0
343	339·7	47·7	403	399·1	56·1	463	458·5	64·4	523	517·9	72·8	583	577·3	81·1
344	340·7	47·9	404	400·1	56·2	464	459·5	64·6	524	518·9	72·9	584	578·3	81·3
345	341·6	48·0	405	401·1	56·4	465	460·5	64·7	525	519·9	73·1	585	579·3	81·4
346	342·6	48·2	406	402·0	56·5	466	461·5	64·9	526	520·9	73·2	586	580·3	81·6
347	343·6	48·3	407	403·0	56·6	467	462·5	65·0	527	521·9	73·3	587	581·3	81·7
348	344·6	48·4	408	404·0	56·8	468	463·4	65·1	528	522·9	73·5	588	582·3	81·8
349	345·6	48·6	409	405·0	56·9	469	464·4	65·3	529	523·9	73·6	589	583·3	82·0
350	346·6	48·7	410	406·0	57·1	470	465·4	65·4	530	524·8	73·8	590	584·3	82·1
351	347·6	48·8	411	407·0	57·2	471	466·4	65·6	531	525·8	73·9	591	585·2	82·3
352	348·6	49·0	412	408·0	57·3	472	467·4	65·7	532	526·8	74·1	592	586·2	82·4
353	349·6	49·1	413	409·0	57·5	473	468·4	65·8	533	527·8	74·2	593	587·2	82·5
354	350·6	49·3	414	410·0	57·6	474	469·4	66·0	534	528·8	74·3	594	588·2	82·7
355	351·5	49·4	415	411·0	57·8	475	470·4	66·1	535	529·8	74·5	595	589·2	82·8
356	352·5	49·5	416	412·0	57·9	476	471·4	66·2	536	530·8	74·6	596	590·2	82·9
357	353·5	49·7	417	412·9	58·0	477	472·4	66·4	537	531·8	74·7	597	591·2	83·1
358	354·5	49·8	418	413·9	58·2	478	473·3	66·5	538	532·8	74·9	598	592·2	83·2
359	355·5	50·0	419	414·9	58·3	479	474·3	66·7	539	533·8	75·0	599	593·2	83·4
360	356·5	50·1	420	415·9	58·5	480	475·3	66·8	540	534·7	75·2	600	594·2	83·5
Dist.	Dep.	D. Lat.	Dist.	Dep.	D. Lat.	Dist.	Dep.	D. Lat.	Dist.	Dep.	D. Lat.	Dist.	Dep.	D. Lat.
D. Lon		Dep.	D. Lon		Dep.	D. Lon		Dep.	D. Lon		Dep.	D. Lon		Dep.

TRAVERSE TABLE
9 Degrees

9°   351° / 189°   009° / 171°   0h 36m

D. Lon	Dep.		D. Lon	Dep.		D. Lon	Dep.		D. Lon	Dep.		D. Lon	Dep.	
Dist.	D. Lat.	Dep.	Dist.	D. Lat.	Dep.	Dist.	D. Lat.	Dep.	Dist.	D. Lat.	Dep.	Dist.	D. Lat.	Dep.
1	01.0	00.2	61	60.2	09.5	121	119.5	18.9	181	178.8	28.3	241	238.0	37.7
2	02.0	00.3	62	61.2	09.7	122	120.5	19.1	182	179.8	28.5	242	239.0	37.9
3	03.0	00.5	63	62.2	09.9	123	121.5	19.2	183	180.7	28.6	243	240.0	38.0
4	04.0	00.6	64	63.2	10.0	124	122.5	19.4	184	181.7	28.8	244	241.0	38.2
5	04.9	00.8	65	64.2	10.2	125	123.5	19.6	185	182.7	28.9	245	242.0	38.3
6	05.9	00.9	66	65.2	10.3	126	124.4	19.7	186	183.7	29.1	246	243.0	38.5
7	06.9	01.1	67	66.2	10.5	127	125.4	19.9	187	184.7	29.3	247	244.0	38.6
8	07.9	01.3	68	67.2	10.6	128	126.4	20.0	188	185.7	29.4	248	244.9	38.8
9	08.9	01.4	69	68.2	10.8	129	127.4	20.2	189	186.7	29.6	249	245.9	39.0
10	09.9	01.6	70	69.1	11.0	130	128.4	20.3	190	187.7	29.7	250	246.9	39.1
11	10.9	01.7	71	70.1	11.1	131	129.4	20.5	191	188.6	29.9	251	247.9	39.3
12	11.9	01.9	72	71.1	11.3	132	130.4	20.6	192	189.6	30.0	252	248.9	39.4
13	12.8	02.0	73	72.1	11.4	133	131.4	20.8	193	190.6	30.2	253	249.9	39.6
14	13.8	02.2	74	73.1	11.6	134	132.4	21.0	194	191.6	30.3	254	250.9	39.7
15	14.8	02.3	75	74.1	11.7	135	133.3	21.1	195	192.6	30.5	255	251.9	39.9
16	15.8	02.5	76	75.1	11.9	136	134.3	21.3	196	193.6	30.7	256	252.8	40.0
17	16.8	02.7	77	76.1	12.0	137	135.3	21.4	197	194.6	30.8	257	253.8	40.2
18	17.8	02.8	78	77.0	12.2	138	136.3	21.6	198	195.6	31.0	258	254.8	40.4
19	18.8	03.0	79	78.0	12.4	139	137.3	21.7	199	196.5	31.1	259	255.8	40.5
20	19.8	03.1	80	79.0	12.5	140	138.3	21.9	200	197.5	31.3	260	256.8	40.7
21	20.7	03.3	81	80.0	12.7	141	139.3	22.1	201	198.5	31.4	261	257.8	40.8
22	21.7	03.4	82	81.0	12.8	142	140.3	22.2	202	199.5	31.6	262	258.8	41.0
23	22.7	03.6	83	82.0	13.0	143	141.2	22.4	203	200.5	31.8	263	259.8	41.1
24	23.7	03.8	84	83.0	13.1	144	142.2	22.5	204	201.5	31.9	264	260.7	41.3
25	24.7	03.9	85	84.0	13.3	145	143.2	22.7	205	202.5	32.1	265	261.7	41.5
26	25.7	04.1	86	84.9	13.5	146	144.2	22.8	206	203.5	32.2	266	262.7	41.6
27	26.7	04.2	87	85.9	13.6	147	145.2	23.0	207	204.5	32.4	267	263.7	41.8
28	27.7	04.4	88	86.9	13.8	148	146.2	23.2	208	205.4	32.5	268	264.7	41.9
29	28.6	04.5	89	87.9	13.9	149	147.2	23.3	209	206.4	32.7	269	265.7	42.1
30	29.6	04.7	90	88.9	14.1	150	148.2	23.5	210	207.4	32.9	270	266.7	42.2
31	30.6	04.8	91	89.9	14.2	151	149.1	23.6	211	208.4	33.0	271	267.7	42.4
32	31.6	05.0	92	90.9	14.4	152	150.1	23.8	212	209.4	33.2	272	268.7	42.6
33	32.6	05.2	93	91.9	14.5	153	151.1	23.9	213	210.4	33.3	273	269.7	42.7
34	33.6	05.3	94	92.8	14.7	154	152.1	24.1	214	211.4	33.5	274	270.6	42.9
35	34.6	05.5	95	93.8	14.9	155	153.1	24.2	215	212.4	33.6	275	271.6	43.0
36	35.6	05.6	96	94.8	15.0	156	154.1	24.4	216	213.3	33.8	276	272.6	43.2
37	36.5	05.8	97	95.8	15.2	157	155.1	24.6	217	214.3	33.9	277	273.6	43.3
38	37.5	05.9	98	96.8	15.3	158	156.1	24.7	218	215.3	34.1	278	274.6	43.5
39	38.5	06.1	99	97.8	15.5	159	157.0	24.9	219	216.3	34.3	279	275.6	43.6
40	39.5	06.3	100	98.8	15.6	160	158.0	25.0	220	217.3	34.4	280	276.6	43.8
41	40.5	06.4	101	99.8	15.8	161	159.0	25.2	221	218.3	34.6	281	277.5	44.0
42	41.5	06.6	102	100.7	16.0	162	160.0	25.3	222	219.3	34.7	282	278.5	44.1
43	42.5	06.7	103	101.7	16.1	163	161.0	25.5	223	220.3	34.9	283	279.5	44.3
44	43.5	06.9	104	102.7	16.3	164	162.0	25.7	224	221.2	35.0	284	280.5	44.4
45	44.4	07.0	105	103.7	16.4	165	163.0	25.8	225	222.2	35.2	285	281.5	44.6
46	45.4	07.2	106	104.7	16.6	166	164.0	26.0	226	223.2	35.4	286	282.5	44.7
47	46.4	07.4	107	105.7	16.7	167	164.9	26.1	227	224.2	35.5	287	283.5	44.9
48	47.4	07.5	108	106.7	16.9	168	165.9	26.3	228	225.2	35.7	288	284.5	45.1
49	48.4	07.7	109	107.7	17.1	169	166.9	26.4	229	226.2	35.8	289	285.4	45.2
50	49.4	07.8	110	108.6	17.2	170	167.9	26.6	230	227.2	36.0	290	286.4	45.4
51	50.4	08.0	111	109.6	17.4	171	168.9	26.8	231	228.2	36.1	291	287.4	45.5
52	51.4	08.1	112	110.6	17.5	172	169.9	26.9	232	229.1	36.3	292	288.4	45.7
53	52.3	08.3	113	111.6	17.7	173	170.9	27.1	233	230.1	36.4	293	289.4	45.8
54	53.3	08.4	114	112.6	17.8	174	171.9	27.2	234	231.1	36.6	294	290.4	46.0
55	54.3	08.6	115	113.6	18.0	175	172.8	27.4	235	232.1	36.8	295	291.4	46.1
56	55.3	08.8	116	114.6	18.1	176	173.8	27.5	236	233.1	36.9	296	292.4	46.3
57	56.3	08.9	117	115.6	18.3	177	174.8	27.7	237	234.1	37.1	297	293.4	46.4
58	57.3	09.1	118	116.5	18.5	178	175.8	27.8	238	235.1	37.2	298	294.3	46.6
59	58.3	09.2	119	117.5	18.6	179	176.8	28.0	239	236.1	37.4	299	295.3	46.8
60	59.3	09.4	120	118.5	18.8	180	177.8	28.2	240	237.0	37.5	300	296.3	46.9
Dist.	Dep.	D. Lat.	Dist.	Dep.	D. Lat.	Dist.	Dep.	D. Lat.	Dist.	Dep.	D. Lat.	Dist.	Dep.	D. Lat.
D. Lon		Dep.	D. Lon		Dep.	D. Lon		Dep.	D. Lon		Dep.	D. Lon		Dep.

81°   279° / 261°   81 Degrees   081° / 099°   5h 24m

TRAVERSE TABLE
9 Degrees

351° / 189°   009° / 171°   0h 36m   **9°**

D. Lon	Dep.		D. Lon	Dep.		D. Lon	Dep.		D. Lon	Dep.		D. Lon	Dep.	
Dist.	D. Lat.	Dep.	Dist.	D. Lat.	Dep.	Dist.	D. Lat.	Dep.	Dist.	D. Lat.	Dep.	Dist.	D. Lat.	Dep.
301	297·3	47·1	361	356·6	56·5	421	415·8	65·9	481	475·1	75·2	541	534·3	84·6
302	298·3	47·2	362	357·5	56·6	422	416·8	66·0	482	476·1	75·4	542	535·3	84·8
303	299·3	47·4	363	358·5	56·8	423	417·8	66·2	483	477·1	75·6	543	536·3	84·9
304	300·3	47·6	364	359·5	56·9	424	418·8	66·3	484	478·0	75·7	544	537·3	85·1
305	301·2	47·7	365	360·5	57·1	425	419·8	66·5	485	479·0	75·9	545	538·3	85·3
306	302·2	47·9	366	361·5	57·3	426	420·8	66·6	486	480·0	76·0	546	539·3	85·4
307	303·2	48·0	367	362·5	57·4	427	421·7	66·8	487	481·0	76·2	547	540·3	85·6
308	304·2	48·2	368	363·5	57·6	428	422·7	67·0	488	482·0	76·3	548	541·3	85·7
309	305·2	48·3	369	364·5	57·7	429	423·7	67·1	489	483·0	76·5	549	542·2	85·9
310	306·2	48·5	370	365·4	57·9	430	424·7	67·3	490	484·0	76·7	550	543·2	86·0
311	307·2	48·7	371	366·4	58·0	431	425·7	67·4	491	485·0	76·8	551	544·2	86·2
312	308·2	48·8	372	367·4	58·2	432	426·7	67·6	492	485·9	77·0	552	545·2	86·4
313	309·1	49·0	373	368·4	58·4	433	427·7	67·7	493	486·9	77·1	553	546·2	86·5
314	310·1	49·1	374	369·4	58·5	434	428·7	67·9	494	487·9	77·3	554	547·2	86·7
315	311·1	49·3	375	370·4	58·7	435	429·6	68·0	495	488·9	77·4	555	548·2	86·8
316	312·1	49·4	376	371·4	58·8	436	430·6	68·2	496	489·9	77·6	556	549·2	87·0
317	313·1	49·6	377	372·4	59·0	437	431·6	68·4	497	490·9	77·7	557	550·1	87·1
318	314·1	49·7	378	373·3	59·1	438	432·6	68·5	498	491·9	77·9	558	551·1	87·3
319	315·1	49·9	379	374·3	59·3	439	433·6	68·7	499	492·9	78·1	559	552·1	87·4
320	316·1	50·1	380	375·3	59·4	440	434·6	68·8	500	493·8	78·2	560	553·1	87·6
321	317·0	50·2	381	376·3	59·6	441	435·6	69·0	501	494·8	78·4	561	554·1	87·8
322	318·0	50·4	382	377·3	59·8	442	436·6	69·1	502	495·8	78·5	562	555·1	87·9
323	319·0	50·5	383	378·3	59·9	443	437·5	69·3	503	496·8	78·7	563	556·1	88·1
324	320·0	50·7	384	379·3	60·1	444	438·5	69·5	504	497·8	78·8	564	557·1	88·2
325	321·0	50·8	385	380·3	60·2	445	439·5	69·6	505	498·8	79·0	565	558·0	88·4
326	322·0	51·0	386	381·2	60·4	446	440·5	69·8	506	499·8	79·2	566	559·0	88·5
327	323·0	51·2	387	382·2	60·5	447	441·5	69·9	507	500·8	79·3	567	560·0	88·7
328	324·0	51·3	388	383·2	60·7	448	442·5	70·1	508	501·7	79·5	568	561·0	88·9
329	324·9	51·5	389	384·2	60·9	449	443·5	70·2	509	502·7	79·6	569	562·0	89·0
330	325·9	51·6	390	385·2	61·0	450	444·5	70·4	510	503·7	79·8	570	563·0	89·2
331	326·9	51·8	391	386·2	61·2	451	445·4	70·6	511	504·7	79·9	571	564·0	89·3
332	327·9	51·9	392	387·2	61·3	452	446·4	70·7	512	505·7	80·1	572	565·0	89·5
333	328·9	52·1	393	388·2	61·5	453	447·4	70·9	513	506·7	80·3	573	565·9	89·6
334	329·9	52·2	394	389·1	61·6	454	448·4	71·0	514	507·7	80·4	574	566·9	89·8
335	330·9	52·4	395	390·1	61·8	455	449·4	71·2	515	508·7	80·6	575	567·9	89·9
336	331·9	52·6	396	391·1	61·9	456	450·4	71·3	516	509·6	80·7	576	568·9	90·1
337	332·9	52·7	397	392·1	62·1	457	451·4	71·5	517	510·6	80·9	577	569·9	90·3
338	333·8	52·9	398	393·1	62·3	458	452·4	71·6	518	511·6	81·0	578	570·9	90·4
339	334·8	53·0	399	394·1	62·4	459	453·3	71·8	519	512·6	81·2	579	571·9	90·6
340	335·8	53·2	400	395·1	62·6	460	454·3	72·0	520	513·6	81·3	580	572·9	90·7
341	336·8	53·3	401	396·1	62·7	461	455·3	72·1	521	514·6	81·5	581	573·8	90·9
342	337·8	53·5	402	397·1	62·9	462	456·3	72·3	522	515·6	81·7	582	574·8	91·0
343	338·8	53·7	403	398·0	63·0	463	457·3	72·4	523	516·6	81·8	583	575·8	91·2
344	339·8	53·8	404	399·0	63·2	464	458·3	72·6	524	517·5	82·0	584	576·8	91·4
345	340·8	54·0	405	400·0	63·4	465	459·3	72·7	525	518·5	82·1	585	577·8	91·5
346	341·7	54·1	406	401·0	63·5	466	460·3	72·9	526	519·5	82·3	586	578·8	91·7
347	342·7	54·3	407	402·0	63·7	467	461·3	73·1	527	520·5	82·4	587	579·8	91·8
348	343·7	54·4	408	403·0	63·8	468	462·2	73·2	528	521·5	82·6	588	580·8	92·0
349	344·7	54·6	409	404·0	64·0	469	463·2	73·4	529	522·5	82·8	589	581·7	92·1
350	345·7	54·8	410	405·0	64·1	470	464·2	73·5	530	523·5	82·9	590	582·7	92·3
351	346·7	54·9	411	405·9	64·3	471	465·2	73·7	531	524·5	83·1	591	583·7	92·5
352	347·7	55·1	412	406·9	64·5	472	466·2	73·8	532	525·5	83·2	592	584·7	92·6
353	348·7	55·2	413	407·9	64·6	473	467·2	74·0	533	526·4	83·4	593	585·7	92·8
354	349·6	55·4	414	408·9	64·8	474	468·2	74·1	534	527·4	83·5	594	586·7	92·9
355	350·6	55·5	415	409·9	64·9	475	469·2	74·3	535	528·4	83·7	595	587·7	93·1
356	351·6	55·7	416	410·9	65·1	476	470·1	74·5	536	529·4	83·8	596	588·7	93·2
357	352·6	55·8	417	411·9	65·2	477	471·1	74·6	537	530·4	84·0	597	589·6	93·4
358	353·6	56·0	418	412·9	65·4	478	472·1	74·8	538	531·4	84·2	598	590·6	93·5
359	354·6	56·2	419	413·8	65·5	479	473·1	74·9	539	532·4	84·3	599	591·6	93·7
360	355·6	56·3	420	414·8	65·7	480	474·1	75·1	540	533·4	84·5	600	592·6	93·9
Dist.	Dep.	D. Lat.	Dist.	Dep.	D. Lat.	Dist.	Dep.	D. Lat.	Dist.	Dep.	D. Lat.	Dist.	Dep.	D. Lat.
D. Lon		Dep.	D. Lon		Dep.	D. Lon		Dep.	D. Lon		Dep.	D. Lon		Dep.

279° / 261°   81 Degrees   081° / 099°   5h 24m   **81°**

TRAVERSE TABLE
10 Degrees

| 10° | 350°/190° | | | | 010°/170° | 0h 40m |

D. Lon	Dep.		D. Lon	Dep.		D. Lon	Dep.		D. Lon	Dep.		D. Lon	Dep.	
Dist.	D. Lat.	Dep.	Dist.	D. Lat.	Dep.	Dist.	D. Lat.	Dep.	Dist.	D. Lat.	Dep.	Dist.	D. Lat.	Dep.
1	01·0	00·2	61	60·1	10·6	121	119·2	21·0	181	178·3	31·4	241	237·3	41·8
2	02·0	00·3	62	61·1	10·8	122	120·1	21·2	182	179·2	31·6	242	238·3	42·0
3	03·0	00·5	63	62·0	10·9	123	121·1	21·4	183	180·2	31·8	243	239·3	42·2
4	03·9	00·7	64	63·0	11·1	124	122·1	21·5	184	181·2	32·0	244	240·3	42·4
5	04·9	00·9	65	64·0	11·3	125	123·1	21·7	185	182·2	32·1	245	241·3	42·5
6	05·9	01·0	66	65·0	11·5	126	124·1	21·9	186	183·2	32·3	246	242·3	42·7
7	06·9	01·2	67	66·0	11·6	127	125·1	22·1	187	184·2	32·5	247	243·2	42·9
8	07·9	01·4	68	67·0	11·8	128	126·1	22·2	188	185·1	32·6	248	244·2	43·1
9	08·9	01·6	69	68·0	12·0	129	127·0	22·4	189	186·1	32·8	249	245·2	43·2
10	09·8	01·7	70	68·9	12·2	130	128·0	22·6	190	187·1	33·0	250	246·2	43·4
11	10·8	01·9	71	69·9	12·3	131	129·0	22·7	191	188·1	33·2	251	247·2	43·6
12	11·8	02·1	72	70·9	12·5	132	130·0	22·9	192	189·1	33·3	252	248·2	43·8
13	12·8	02·3	73	71·9	12·7	133	131·0	23·1	193	190·1	33·5	253	249·2	43·9
14	13·8	02·4	74	72·9	12·8	134	132·0	23·3	194	191·0	33·7	254	250·1	44·1
15	14·8	02·6	75	73·9	13·0	135	132·9	23·4	195	192·0	33·9	255	251·1	44·3
16	15·8	02·8	76	74·8	13·2	136	133·9	23·6	196	193·0	34·0	256	252·1	44·5
17	16·7	03·0	77	75·8	13·4	137	134·9	23·8	197	194·0	34·2	257	253·1	44·6
18	17·7	03·1	78	76·8	13·5	138	135·9	24·0	198	195·0	34·4	258	254·1	44·8
19	18·7	03·3	79	77·8	13·7	139	136·9	24·1	199	196·0	34·6	259	255·1	45·0
20	19·7	03·5	80	78·8	13·9	140	137·9	24·3	200	197·0	34·7	260	256·1	45·1
21	20·7	03·6	81	79·8	14·1	141	138·9	24·5	201	197·9	34·9	261	257·0	45·3
22	21·7	03·8	82	80·8	14·2	142	139·8	24·7	202	198·9	35·1	262	258·0	45·5
23	22·7	04·0	83	81·7	14·4	143	140·8	24·8	203	199·9	35·3	263	259·0	45·7
24	23·6	04·2	84	82·7	14·6	144	141·8	25·0	204	200·9	35·4	264	260·0	45·8
25	24·6	04·3	85	83·7	14·8	145	142·8	25·2	205	201·9	35·6	265	261·0	46·0
26	25·6	04·5	86	84·7	14·9	146	143·8	25·4	206	202·9	35·8	266	262·0	46·2
27	26·6	04·7	87	85·7	15·1	147	144·8	25·5	207	203·9	35·9	267	262·9	46·4
28	27·6	04·9	88	86·7	15·3	148	145·8	25·7	208	204·8	36·1	268	263·9	46·5
29	28·6	05·0	89	87·6	15·5	149	146·7	25·9	209	205·8	36·3	269	264·9	46·7
30	29·5	05·2	90	88·6	15·6	150	147·7	26·0	210	206·8	36·5	270	265·9	46·9
31	30·5	05·4	91	89·6	15·8	151	148·7	26·2	211	207·8	36·6	271	266·9	47·1
32	31·5	05·6	92	90·6	16·0	152	149·7	26·4	212	208·8	36·8	272	267·9	47·2
33	32·5	05·7	93	91·6	16·1	153	150·7	26·6	213	209·8	37·0	273	268·9	47·4
34	33·5	05·9	94	92·6	16·3	154	151·7	26·7	214	210·7	37·2	274	269·8	47·6
35	34·5	06·1	95	93·6	16·5	155	152·6	26·9	215	211·7	37·3	275	270·8	47·8
36	35·5	06·3	96	94·5	16·7	156	153·6	27·1	216	212·7	37·5	276	271·8	47·9
37	36·4	06·4	97	95·5	16·8	157	154·6	27·3	217	213·7	37·7	277	272·8	48·1
38	37·4	06·6	98	96·5	17·0	158	155·6	27·4	218	214·7	37·9	278	273·8	48·3
39	38·4	06·8	99	97·5	17·2	159	156·6	27·6	219	215·7	38·0	279	274·8	48·4
40	39·4	06·9	100	98·5	17·4	160	157·6	27·8	220	216·7	38·2	280	275·7	48·6
41	40·4	07·1	101	99·5	17·5	161	158·6	28·0	221	217·6	38·4	281	276·7	48·8
42	41·4	07·3	102	100·5	17·7	162	159·5	28·1	222	218·6	38·5	282	277·7	49·0
43	42·3	07·5	103	101·4	17·9	163	160·5	28·3	223	219·6	38·7	283	278·7	49·1
44	43·3	07·6	104	102·4	18·1	164	161·5	28·5	224	220·6	38·9	284	279·7	49·3
45	44·3	07·8	105	103·4	18·2	165	162·5	28·7	225	221·6	39·1	285	280·7	49·5
46	45·3	08·0	106	104·4	18·4	166	163·5	28·8	226	222·6	39·2	286	281·7	49·7
47	46·3	08·2	107	105·4	18·6	167	164·5	29·0	227	223·6	39·4	287	282·6	49·8
48	47·3	08·3	108	106·4	18·8	168	165·4	29·2	228	224·5	39·6	288	283·6	50·0
49	48·3	08·5	109	107·3	18·9	169	166·4	29·3	229	225·5	39·8	289	284·6	50·2
50	49·2	08·7	110	108·3	19·1	170	167·4	29·5	230	226·5	39·9	290	285·6	50·4
51	50·2	08·9	111	109·3	19·3	171	168·4	29·7	231	227·5	40·1	291	286·6	50·5
52	51·2	09·0	112	110·3	19·4	172	169·4	29·9	232	228·5	40·3	292	287·6	50·7
53	52·2	09·2	113	111·3	19·6	173	170·4	30·0	233	229·5	40·5	293	288·5	50·9
54	53·2	09·4	114	112·3	19·8	174	171·4	30·2	234	230·4	40·6	294	289·5	51·1
55	54·2	09·6	115	113·3	20·0	175	172·3	30·4	235	231·4	40·8	295	290·5	51·2
56	55·1	09·7	116	114·2	20·1	176	173·3	30·6	236	232·4	41·0	296	291·5	51·4
57	56·1	09·9	117	115·2	20·3	177	174·3	30·7	237	233·4	41·2	297	292·5	51·6
58	57·1	10·1	118	116·2	20·5	178	175·3	30·9	238	234·4	41·3	298	293·5	51·7
59	58·1	10·2	119	117·2	20·7	179	176·3	31·1	239	235·4	41·5	299	294·5	51·9
60	59·1	10·4	120	118·2	20·8	180	177·3	31·3	240	236·4	41·7	300	295·4	52·1
Dist.	Dep.	D. Lat.	Dist.	Dep.	D. Lat.	Dist.	Dep.	D. Lat.	Dist.	Dep.	D. Lat.	Dist.	Dep.	D. Lat.
D. Lon		Dep.	D. Lon		Dep.	D. Lon		Dep.	D. Lon		Dep.	D. Lon		Dep.

| 80° | 280°/260° | | | 80 Degrees | | 080°/100° | 5h 20m |

TRAVERSE TABLE
10 Degrees

D. Lon	Dep.		D. Lon	Dep.		D. Lon	Dep.		D. Lon	Dep.		D. Lon	Dep.	
Dist.	D. Lat.	Dep.	Dist.	D. Lat.	Dep.	Dist.	D. Lat.	Dep.	Dist.	D. Lat.	Dep.	Dist.	D. Lat.	Dep.
301	296·4	52·3	361	355·5	62·7	421	414·6	73·1	481	473·7	83·5	541	532·8	93·9
302	297·4	52·4	362	356·5	62·9	422	415·6	73·3	482	474·7	83·7	542	533·8	94·1
303	298·4	52·6	363	357·5	63·0	423	416·6	73·5	483	475·7	83·9	543	534·8	94·3
304	299·4	52·8	364	358·5	63·2	424	417·6	73·6	484	476·6	84·1	544	535·7	94·5
305	300·4	53·0	365	359·5	63·4	425	418·5	73·8	485	477·6	84·2	545	536·7	94·6
306	301·4	53·1	366	360·4	63·6	426	419·5	74·0	486	478·6	84·4	546	537·7	94·8
307	302·3	53·3	367	361·4	63·7	427	420·5	74·1	487	479·6	84·6	547	538·7	95·0
308	303·3	53·5	368	362·4	63·9	428	421·5	74·3	488	480·6	84·7	548	539·7	95·2
309	304·3	53·7	369	363·4	64·1	429	422·5	74·5	489	481·6	84·9	549	540·7	95·3
310	305·3	53·8	370	364·4	64·2	430	423·5	74·7	490	482·6	85·1	550	541·6	95·5
311	306·3	54·0	371	365·4	64·4	431	424·5	74·8	491	483·5	85·2	551	542·6	95·7
312	307·3	54·2	372	366·4	64·6	432	425·4	75·0	492	484·5	85·4	552	543·6	95·9
313	308·2	54·4	373	367·3	64·8	433	426·4	75·2	493	485·5	85·6	553	544·6	96·0
314	309·2	54·5	374	368·3	64·9	434	427·4	75·4	494	486·5	85·8	554	545·6	96·2
315	310·2	54·7	375	369·3	65·1	435	428·4	75·5	495	487·5	85·9	555	546·6	96·4
316	311·2	54·9	376	370·3	65·3	436	429·4	75·7	496	488·5	86·1	556	547·6	96·5
317	312·2	55·0	377	371·3	65·5	437	430·4	75·9	497	489·4	86·3	557	548·5	96·7
318	313·2	55·2	378	372·3	65·6	438	431·3	76·1	498	490·4	86·5	558	549·5	96·9
319	314·2	55·4	379	373·2	65·8	439	432·3	76·2	499	491·4	86·6	559	550·5	97·1
320	315·1	55·6	380	374·2	66·0	440	433·3	76·4	500	492·4	86·8	560	551·5	97·2
321	316·1	55·7	381	375·2	66·2	441	434·3	76·6	501	493·4	87·0	561	552·5	97·4
322	317·1	55·9	382	376·2	66·3	442	435·3	76·8	502	494·4	87·2	562	553·5	97·6
323	318·1	56·1	383	377·2	66·5	443	436·3	76·9	503	495·4	87·3	563	554·4	97·8
324	319·1	56·3	384	378·2	66·7	444	437·3	77·1	504	496·3	87·5	564	555·4	97·9
325	320·1	56·4	385	379·2	66·9	445	438·2	77·3	505	497·3	87·7	565	556·4	98·1
326	321·0	56·6	386	380·1	67·0	446	439·2	77·5	506	498·3	87·9	566	557·4	98·3
327	322·0	56·8	387	381·1	67·2	447	440·2	77·6	507	499·3	88·0	567	558·4	98·5
328	323·0	57·0	388	382·1	67·4	448	441·2	77·8	508	500·3	88·2	568	559·4	98·6
329	324·0	57·1	389	383·1	67·5	449	442·2	78·0	509	501·3	88·4	569	560·4	98·8
330	325·0	57·3	390	384·1	67·7	450	443·2	78·1	510	502·3	88·6	570	561·3	99·0
331	326·0	57·5	391	385·1	67·9	451	444·1	78·3	511	503·2	88·7	571	562·3	99·2
332	327·0	57·7	392	386·0	68·1	452	445·1	78·5	512	504·2	88·9	572	563·3	99·3
333	327·9	57·8	393	387·0	68·2	453	446·1	78·7	513	505·2	89·1	573	564·3	99·5
334	328·9	58·0	394	388·0	68·4	454	447·1	78·8	514	506·2	89·2	574	565·3	99·7
335	329·9	58·2	395	389·0	68·6	455	448·1	79·0	515	507·2	89·4	575	566·3	99·8
336	330·9	58·3	396	390·0	68·8	456	449·1	79·2	516	508·2	89·6	576	567·2	100·0
337	331·9	58·5	397	391·0	68·9	457	450·1	79·4	517	509·1	89·8	577	568·2	100·2
338	332·9	58·7	398	392·0	69·1	458	451·0	79·5	518	510·1	89·9	578	569·2	100·4
339	333·8	58·9	399	392·9	69·3	459	452·0	79·7	519	511·1	90·1	579	570·2	100·5
340	334·8	59·0	400	393·9	69·5	460	453·0	79·9	520	512·1	90·3	580	571·2	100·7
341	335·8	59·2	401	394·9	69·6	461	454·0	80·1	521	513·1	90·5	581	572·2	100·9
342	336·8	59·4	402	395·9	69·8	462	455·0	80·2	522	514·1	90·6	582	573·2	101·1
343	337·8	59·6	403	396·9	70·0	463	456·0	80·4	523	515·1	90·8	583	574·1	101·2
344	338·8	59·7	404	397·9	70·2	464	457·0	80·6	524	516·0	91·0	584	575·1	101·4
345	339·8	59·9	405	398·9	70·3	465	457·9	80·7	525	517·0	91·2	585	576·1	101·6
346	340·7	60·1	406	399·8	70·5	466	458·9	80·9	526	518·0	91·3	586	577·1	101·8
347	341·7	60·3	407	400·8	70·7	467	459·9	81·1	527	519·0	91·5	587	578·1	101·9
348	342·7	60·4	408	401·8	70·8	468	460·9	81·3	528	520·0	91·7	588	579·1	102·1
349	343·7	60·6	409	402·8	71·0	469	461·9	81·4	529	521·0	91·9	589	580·1	102·3
350	344·7	60·8	410	403·8	71·2	470	462·9	81·6	530	521·9	92·0	590	581·0	102·5
351	345·7	61·0	411	404·8	71·4	471	463·8	81·8	531	522·9	92·2	591	582·0	102·6
352	346·7	61·1	412	405·7	71·5	472	464·8	82·0	532	523·9	92·4	592	583·0	102·8
353	347·6	61·3	413	406·7	71·7	473	465·8	82·1	533	524·9	92·6	593	584·0	103·0
354	348·6	61·5	414	407·7	71·9	474	466·8	82·3	534	525·9	92·7	594	585·0	103·1
355	349·6	61·6	415	408·7	72·1	475	467·8	82·5	535	526·9	92·9	595	586·0	103·3
356	350·6	61·8	416	409·7	72·2	476	468·8	82·7	536	527·9	93·1	596	586·9	103·5
357	351·6	62·0	417	410·7	72·4	477	469·8	82·8	537	528·8	93·2	597	587·9	103·7
358	352·6	62·2	418	411·6	72·6	478	470·7	83·0	538	529·8	93·4	598	588·9	103·8
359	353·5	62·3	419	412·6	72·8	479	471·7	83·2	539	530·8	93·6	599	589·9	104·0
360	354·5	62·5	420	413·6	72·9	480	472·7	83·4	540	531·8	93·8	600	590·9	104·2
Dist.	Dep.	D. Lat.	Dist.	Dep.	D. Lat.	Dist.	Dep.	D. Lat.	Dist.	Dep.	D. Lat.	Dist.	Dep.	D. Lat.
D. Lon		Dep.	D. Lon		Dep.	D. Lon		Dep.	D. Lon		Dep.	D. Lon		Dep.

TRAVERSE TABLE
11 Degrees

| 349° / 191° | | | | 011° / 169° | 0h 44m |

D. Lon	Dep.		D. Lon	Dep.		D. Lon	Dep.		D. Lon	Dep.		D. Lon	Dep.	
Dist.	D. Lat.	Dep.	Dist.	D. Lat.	Dep.	Dist.	D. Lat.	Dep.	Dist.	D. Lat.	Dep.	Dist.	D. Lat.	Dep.
1	01·0	00·2	61	59·9	11·6	121	118·8	23·1	181	177·7	34·5	241	236·6	46·0
2	02·0	00·4	62	60·9	11·8	122	119·8	23·3	182	178·7	34·7	242	237·6	46·2
3	02·9	00·6	63	61·8	12·0	123	120·7	23·5	183	179·6	34·9	243	238·5	46·4
4	03·9	00·8	64	62·8	12·2	124	121·7	23·7	184	180·6	35·1	244	239·5	46·6
5	04·9	01·0	65	63·8	12·4	125	122·7	23·9	185	181·6	35·3	245	240·5	46·7
6	05·9	01·1	66	64·8	12·6	126	123·7	24·0	186	182·6	35·5	246	241·5	46·9
7	06·9	01·3	67	65·8	12·8	127	124·7	24·2	187	183·6	35·7	247	242·5	47·1
8	07·9	01·5	68	66·8	13·0	128	125·6	24·4	188	184·5	35·9	248	243·4	47·3
9	08·8	01·7	69	67·7	13·2	129	126·6	24·6	189	185·5	36·1	249	244·4	47·5
10	09·8	01·9	70	68·7	13·4	130	127·6	24·8	190	186·5	36·3	250	245·4	47·7
11	10·8	02·1	71	69·7	13·5	131	128·6	25·0	191	187·5	36·4	251	246·4	47·9
12	11·8	02·3	72	70·7	13·7	132	129·6	25·2	192	188·5	36·6	252	247·4	48·1
13	12·8	02·5	73	71·7	13·9	133	130·6	25·4	193	189·5	36·8	253	248·4	48·3
14	13·7	02·7	74	72·6	14·1	134	131·5	25·6	194	190·4	37·0	254	249·3	48·5
15	14·7	02·9	75	73·6	14·3	135	132·5	25·8	195	191·4	37·2	255	250·3	48·7
16	15·7	03·1	76	74·6	14·5	136	133·5	26·0	196	192·4	37·4	256	251·3	48·8
17	16·7	03·2	77	75·6	14·7	137	134·5	26·1	197	193·4	37·6	257	252·3	49·0
18	17·7	03·4	78	76·6	14·9	138	135·5	26·3	198	194·4	37·8	258	253·3	49·2
19	18·7	03·6	79	77·5	15·1	139	136·4	26·5	199	195·3	38·0	259	254·2	49·4
20	19·6	03·8	80	78·5	15·3	140	137·4	26·7	200	196·3	38·2	260	255·2	49·6
21	20·6	04·0	81	79·5	15·5	141	138·4	26·9	201	197·3	38·4	261	256·2	49·8
22	21·6	04·2	82	80·5	15·6	142	139·4	27·1	202	198·3	38·5	262	257·2	50·0
23	22·6	04·4	83	81·5	15·8	143	140·4	27·3	203	199·3	38·7	263	258·2	50·2
24	23·6	04·6	84	82·5	16·0	144	141·4	27·5	204	200·3	38·9	264	259·1	50·4
25	24·5	04·8	85	83·4	16·2	145	142·3	27·7	205	201·2	39·1	265	260·1	50·6
26	25·5	05·0	86	84·4	16·4	146	143·3	27·9	206	202·2	39·3	266	261·1	50·8
27	26·5	05·2	87	85·4	16·6	147	144·3	28·0	207	203·2	39·5	267	262·1	50·9
28	27·5	05·3	88	86·4	16·8	148	145·3	28·2	208	204·2	39·7	268	263·1	51·1
29	28·5	05·5	89	87·4	17·0	149	146·3	28·4	209	205·2	39·9	269	264·1	51·3
30	29·4	05·7	90	88·3	17·2	150	147·2	28·6	210	206·1	40·1	270	265·0	51·5
31	30·4	05·9	91	89·3	17·4	151	148·2	28·8	211	207·1	40·3	271	266·0	51·7
32	31·4	06·1	92	90·3	17·6	152	149·2	29·0	212	208·1	40·5	272	267·0	51·9
33	32·4	06·3	93	91·3	17·7	153	150·2	29·2	213	209·1	40·6	273	268·0	52·1
34	33·4	06·5	94	92·3	17·9	154	151·2	29·4	214	210·1	40·8	274	269·0	52·3
35	34·4	06·7	95	93·3	18·1	155	152·2	29·6	215	211·1	41·0	275	269·9	52·5
36	35·3	06·9	96	94·2	18·3	156	153·1	29·8	216	212·0	41·2	276	270·9	52·7
37	36·3	07·1	97	95·2	18·5	157	154·1	30·0	217	213·0	41·4	277	271·9	52·9
38	37·3	07·3	98	96·2	18·7	158	155·1	30·1	218	214·0	41·6	278	272·9	53·0
39	38·3	07·4	99	97·2	18·9	159	156·1	30·3	219	215·0	41·8	279	273·9	53·2
40	39·3	07·6	100	98·2	19·1	160	157·1	30·5	220	216·0	42·0	280	274·9	53·4
41	40·2	07·8	101	99·1	19·3	161	158·0	30·7	221	216·9	42·2	281	275·8	53·6
42	41·2	08·0	102	100·1	19·5	162	159·0	30·9	222	217·9	42·4	282	276·8	53·8
43	42·2	08·2	103	101·1	19·7	163	160·0	31·1	223	218·9	42·6	283	277·8	54·0
44	43·2	08·4	104	102·1	19·8	164	161·0	31·3	224	219·9	42·7	284	278·8	54·2
45	44·2	08·6	105	103·1	20·0	165	162·0	31·5	225	220·9	42·9	285	279·8	54·4
46	45·2	08·8	106	104·1	20·2	166	163·0	31·7	226	221·8	43·1	286	280·7	54·6
47	46·1	09·0	107	105·0	20·4	167	163·9	31·9	227	222·8	43·3	287	281·7	54·8
48	47·1	09·2	108	106·0	20·6	168	164·9	32·1	228	223·8	43·5	288	282·7	55·0
49	48·1	09·3	109	107·0	20·8	169	165·9	32·2	229	224·8	43·7	289	283·7	55·1
50	49·1	09·5	110	108·0	21·0	170	166·9	32·4	230	225·8	43·9	290	284·7	55·3
51	50·1	09·7	111	109·0	21·2	171	167·9	32·6	231	226·8	44·1	291	285·7	55·5
52	51·0	09·9	112	109·9	21·4	172	168·8	32·8	232	227·7	44·3	292	286·6	55·7
53	52·0	10·1	113	110·9	21·6	173	169·8	33·0	233	228·7	44·5	293	287·6	55·9
54	53·0	10·3	114	111·9	21·8	174	170·8	33·2	234	229·7	44·6	294	288·6	56·1
55	54·0	10·5	115	112·9	21·9	175	171·8	33·4	235	230·7	44·8	295	289·6	56·3
56	55·0	10·7	116	113·9	22·1	176	172·8	33·6	236	231·7	45·0	296	290·6	56·5
57	56·0	10·9	117	114·9	22·3	177	173·7	33·8	237	232·6	45·2	297	291·5	56·7
58	56·9	11·1	118	115·8	22·5	178	174·7	34·0	238	233·6	45·4	298	292·5	56·9
59	57·9	11·3	119	116·8	22·7	179	175·7	34·2	239	234·6	45·6	299	293·5	57·1
60	58·9	11·4	120	117·8	22·9	180	176·7	34·3	240	235·6	45·8	300	294·5	57·2
Dist.	Dep.	D. Lat.	Dist.	Dep.	D. Lat.	Dist.	Dep.	D. Lat.	Dist.	Dep.	D. Lat.	Dist.	Dep.	D. Lat.
D. Lon		Dep.	D. Lon		Dep.	D. Lon		Dep.	D. Lon		Dep.	D. Lon		Dep.

| 281° / 259° | | | | 079° / 101° | 5h 16m |

79 Degrees

TRAVERSE TABLE

11 Degrees

11°

D. Lon	Dep.		D. Lon	Dep.		D. Lon	Dep.		D. Lon	Dep.		D. Lon	Dep.	
Dist.	D. Lat.	Dep.	Dist.	D. Lat.	Dep.	Dist.	D. Lat.	Dep.	Dist.	D. Lat.	Dep.	Dist.	D. Lat.	Dep.
301	295·5	57·4	361	354·4	68·9	421	413·3	80·3	481	472·2	91·8	541	531·1	103·2
302	296·5	57·6	362	355·3	69·1	422	414·2	80·5	482	473·1	92·0	542	532·0	103·4
303	297·4	57·8	363	356·3	69·3	423	415·2	80·7	483	474·1	92·2	543	533·0	103·6
304	298·4	58·0	364	357·3	69·5	424	416·2	80·9	484	475·1	92·4	544	534·0	103·8
305	299·4	58·2	365	358·3	69·6	425	417·2	81·1	485	476·1	92·5	545	535·0	104·0
306	300·4	58·4	366	359·3	69·8	426	418·2	81·3	486	477·1	92·7	546	536·0	104·2
307	301·4	58·6	367	360·3	70·0	427	419·2	81·5	487	478·1	92·9	547	537·0	104·4
308	302·3	58·8	368	361·2	70·2	428	420·1	81·7	488	479·0	93·1	548	537·9	104·6
309	303·3	59·0	369	362·2	70·4	429	421·1	81·9	489	480·0	93·3	549	538·9	104·8
310	304·3	59·2	370	363·2	70·6	430	422·1	82·0	490	481·0	93·5	550	539·9	104·9
311	305·3	59·3	371	364·2	70·8	431	423·1	82·2	491	482·0	93·7	551	540·9	105·1
312	306·3	59·5	372	365·2	71·0	432	424·1	82·4	492	483·0	93·9	552	541·9	105·3
313	307·2	59·7	373	366·1	71·2	433	425·0	82·6	493	483·9	94·1	553	542·8	105·5
314	308·2	59·9	374	367·1	71·4	434	426·0	82·8	494	484·9	94·3	554	543·8	105·7
315	309·2	60·1	375	368·1	71·6	435	427·0	83·0	495	485·9	94·5	555	544·8	105·9
316	310·2	60·3	376	369·1	71·7	436	428·0	83·2	496	486·9	94·6	556	545·8	106·1
317	311·2	60·5	377	370·1	71·9	437	429·0	83·4	497	487·9	94·8	557	546·8	106·3
318	312·2	60·7	378	371·1	72·1	438	430·0	83·6	498	488·9	95·0	558	547·7	106·5
319	313·1	60·9	379	372·0	72·3	439	430·9	83·8	499	489·8	95·2	559	548·7	106·7
320	314·1	61·1	380	373·0	72·5	440	431·9	84·0	500	490·8	95·4	560	549·7	106·9
321	315·1	61·2	381	374·0	72·7	441	432·9	84·1	501	491·8	95·6	561	550·7	107·0
322	316·1	61·4	382	375·0	72·9	442	433·9	84·3	502	492·8	95·8	562	551·7	107·2
323	317·1	61·6	383	376·0	73·1	443	434·9	84·5	503	493·8	96·0	563	552·7	107·4
324	318·0	61·8	384	376·9	73·3	444	435·8	84·7	504	494·7	96·2	564	553·6	107·6
325	319·0	62·0	385	377·9	73·5	445	436·8	84·9	505	495·7	96·4	565	554·6	107·8
326	320·0	62·2	386	378·9	73·7	446	437·8	85·1	506	496·7	96·5	566	555·6	108·0
327	321·0	62·4	387	379·9	73·8	447	438·8	85·3	507	497·7	96·7	567	556·6	108·2
328	322·0	62·6	388	380·9	74·0	448	439·8	85·5	508	498·7	96·9	568	557·6	108·4
329	323·0	62·8	389	381·9	74·2	449	440·8	85·7	509	499·6	97·1	569	558·5	108·6
330	323·9	63·0	390	382·8	74·4	450	441·7	85·9	510	500·6	97·3	570	559·5	108·8
331	324·9	63·2	391	383·8	74·6	451	442·7	86·1	511	501·6	97·5	571	560·5	109·0
332	325·9	63·3	392	384·8	74·8	452	443·7	86·2	512	502·6	97·7	572	561·5	109·1
333	326·9	63·5	393	385·8	75·0	453	444·7	86·4	513	503·6	97·9	573	562·5	109·3
334	327·9	63·7	394	386·8	75·2	454	445·7	86·6	514	504·6	98·1	574	563·5	109·5
335	328·8	63·9	395	387·7	75·4	455	446·6	86·8	515	505·5	98·3	575	564·4	109·7
336	329·8	64·1	396	388·7	75·6	456	447·6	87·0	516	506·5	98·5	576	565·4	109·9
337	330·8	64·3	397	389·7	75·8	457	448·6	87·2	517	507·5	98·6	577	566·4	110·1
338	331·8	64·5	398	390·7	75·9	458	449·6	87·4	518	508·5	98·8	578	567·4	110·3
339	332·8	64·7	399	391·7	76·1	459	450·6	87·6	519	509·5	99·0	579	568·4	110·5
340	333·8	64·9	400	392·7	76·3	460	451·5	87·8	520	510·4	99·2	580	569·3	110·7
341	334·7	65·1	401	393·6	76·5	461	452·5	88·0	521	511·4	99·4	581	570·3	110·9
342	335·7	65·3	402	394·6	76·7	462	453·5	88·2	522	512·4	99·6	582	571·3	111·1
343	336·7	65·4	403	395·6	76·9	463	454·5	88·3	523	513·4	99·8	583	572·3	111·2
344	337·7	65·6	404	396·6	77·1	464	455·5	88·5	524	514·4	100·0	584	573·3	111·4
345	338·7	65·8	405	397·6	77·3	465	456·5	88·7	525	515·4	100·2	585	574·3	111·6
346	339·6	66·0	406	398·5	77·5	466	457·4	88·9	526	516·3	100·4	586	575·2	111·8
347	340·6	66·2	407	399·5	77·7	467	458·4	89·1	527	517·3	100·6	587	576·2	112·1
348	341·6	66·4	408	400·5	77·9	468	459·4	89·3	528	518·3	100·7	588	577·2	112·3
349	342·6	66·6	409	401·5	78·0	469	460·4	89·5	529	519·3	100·9	589	578·2	112·4
350	343·6	66·8	410	402·5	78·2	470	461·4	89·7	530	520·3	101·1	590	579·2	112·6
351	344·6	67·0	411	403·4	78·4	471	462·3	89·9	531	521·2	101·3	591	580·1	112·8
352	345·5	67·2	412	404·4	78·6	472	463·3	90·1	532	522·2	101·5	592	581·1	113·0
353	346·5	67·4	413	405·4	78·8	473	464·3	90·3	533	523·2	101·7	593	582·1	113·2
354	347·5	67·5	414	406·4	79·0	474	465·3	90·4	534	524·2	101·9	594	583·1	113·3
355	348·5	67·7	415	407·4	79·2	475	466·3	90·6	535	525·2	102·1	595	584·1	113·5
356	349·5	67·9	416	408·4	79·4	476	467·3	90·8	536	526·2	102·3	596	585·0	113·7
357	350·4	68·1	417	409·3	79·6	477	468·2	91·0	537	527·1	102·5	597	586·0	113·9
358	351·4	68·3	418	410·3	79·8	478	469·2	91·2	538	528·1	102·7	598	587·0	114·1
359	352·4	68·5	419	411·3	79·9	479	470·2	91·4	539	529·1	102·8	599	588·0	114·3
360	353·4	68·7	420	412·3	80·1	480	471·2	91·6	540	530·1	103·0	600	589·0	114·5
Dist.	Dep.	D. Lat.	Dist.	Dep.	D. Lat.	Dist.	Dep.	D. Lat.	Dist.	Dep.	D. Lat.	Dist.	Dep.	D. Lat.
D. Lon		Dep.	D. Lon		Dep.	D. Lon		Dep.	D. Lon		Dep.	D. Lon		Dep.

79 Degrees

79°

TRAVERSE TABLE
12 Degrees

348° / 192°		012° / 168°	0h 48m

D. Lon	Dep.		D. Lon	Dep.		D. Lon	Dep.		D. Lon	Dep.		D. Lon	Dep.	
Dist.	D. Lat.	Dep.	Dist.	D. Lat.	Dep.	Dist.	D. Lat.	Dep.	Dist.	D. Lat.	Dep.	Dist.	D. Lat.	Dep.
1	01.0	00.2	61	59.7	12.7	121	118.4	25.2	181	177.0	37.6	241	235.7	50.1
2	02.0	00.4	62	60.6	12.9	122	119.3	25.4	182	178.0	37.8	242	236.7	50.3
3	02.9	00.6	63	61.6	13.1	123	120.3	25.6	183	179.0	38.0	243	237.7	50.5
4	03.9	00.8	64	62.6	13.3	124	121.3	25.8	184	180.0	38.3	244	238.7	50.7
5	04.9	01.0	65	63.6	13.5	125	122.3	26.0	185	181.0	38.5	245	239.6	50.9
6	05.9	01.2	66	64.6	13.7	126	123.2	26.2	186	181.9	38.7	246	240.6	51.1
7	06.8	01.5	67	65.5	13.9	127	124.2	26.4	187	182.9	38.9	247	241.6	51.4
8	07.8	01.7	68	66.5	14.1	128	125.2	26.6	188	183.9	39.1	248	242.6	51.6
9	08.8	01.9	69	67.5	14.3	129	126.2	26.8	189	184.9	39.3	249	243.6	51.8
10	09.8	02.1	70	68.5	14.6	130	127.2	27.0	190	185.8	39.5	250	244.5	52.0
11	10.8	02.3	71	69.4	14.8	131	128.1	27.2	191	186.8	39.7	251	245.5	52.2
12	11.7	02.5	72	70.4	15.0	132	129.1	27.4	192	187.8	39.9	252	246.5	52.4
13	12.7	02.7	73	71.4	15.2	133	130.1	27.7	193	188.8	40.1	253	247.5	52.6
14	13.7	02.9	74	72.4	15.4	134	131.1	27.9	194	189.8	40.3	254	248.4	52.8
15	14.7	03.1	75	73.4	15.6	135	132.0	28.1	195	190.7	40.5	255	249.4	53.0
16	15.7	03.3	76	74.3	15.8	136	133.0	28.3	196	191.7	40.8	256	250.4	53.2
17	16.6	03.5	77	75.3	16.0	137	134.0	28.5	197	192.7	41.0	257	251.4	53.4
18	17.6	03.7	78	76.3	16.2	138	135.0	28.7	198	193.7	41.2	258	252.4	53.6
19	18.6	04.0	79	77.3	16.4	139	136.0	28.9	199	194.7	41.4	259	253.3	53.8
20	19.6	04.2	80	78.3	16.6	140	136.9	29.1	200	195.6	41.6	260	254.3	54.1
21	20.5	04.4	81	79.2	16.8	141	137.9	29.3	201	196.6	41.8	261	255.3	54.3
22	21.5	04.6	82	80.2	17.0	142	138.9	29.5	202	197.6	42.0	262	256.3	54.5
23	22.5	04.8	83	81.2	17.3	143	139.9	29.7	203	198.6	42.2	263	257.3	54.7
24	23.5	05.0	84	82.2	17.5	144	140.9	29.9	204	199.5	42.4	264	258.2	54.9
25	24.5	05.2	85	83.1	17.7	145	141.8	30.1	205	200.5	42.6	265	259.2	55.1
26	25.4	05.4	86	84.1	17.9	146	142.8	30.4	206	201.5	42.8	266	260.2	55.3
27	26.4	05.6	87	85.1	18.1	147	143.8	30.6	207	202.5	43.0	267	261.2	55.5
28	27.4	05.8	88	86.1	18.3	148	144.8	30.8	208	203.5	43.2	268	262.1	55.7
29	28.4	06.0	89	87.1	18.5	149	145.7	31.0	209	204.4	43.5	269	263.1	55.9
30	29.3	06.2	90	88.0	18.7	150	146.7	31.2	210	205.4	43.7	270	264.1	56.1
31	30.3	06.4	91	89.0	18.9	151	147.7	31.4	211	206.4	43.9	271	265.1	56.3
32	31.3	06.7	92	90.0	19.1	152	148.7	31.6	212	207.4	44.1	272	266.1	56.6
33	32.3	06.9	93	91.0	19.3	153	149.7	31.8	213	208.3	44.3	273	267.0	56.8
34	33.3	07.1	94	91.9	19.5	154	150.6	32.0	214	209.3	44.5	274	268.0	57.0
35	34.2	07.3	95	92.9	19.8	155	151.6	32.2	215	210.3	44.7	275	269.0	57.2
36	35.2	07.5	96	93.9	20.0	156	152.6	32.4	216	211.3	44.9	276	270.0	57.4
37	36.2	07.7	97	94.9	20.2	157	153.6	32.6	217	212.3	45.1	277	270.9	57.6
38	37.2	07.9	98	95.9	20.4	158	154.5	32.9	218	213.2	45.3	278	271.9	57.8
39	38.1	08.1	99	96.8	20.6	159	155.5	33.1	219	214.2	45.5	279	272.9	58.0
40	39.1	08.3	100	97.8	20.8	160	156.5	33.3	220	215.2	45.7	280	273.9	58.2
41	40.1	08.5	101	98.8	21.0	161	157.5	33.5	221	216.2	45.9	281	274.9	58.4
42	41.1	08.7	102	99.8	21.2	162	158.5	33.7	222	217.1	46.2	282	275.8	58.6
43	42.1	08.9	103	100.7	21.4	163	159.4	33.9	223	218.1	46.4	283	276.8	58.8
44	43.0	09.1	104	101.7	21.6	164	160.4	34.1	224	219.1	46.6	284	277.8	59.0
45	44.0	09.4	105	102.7	21.8	165	161.4	34.3	225	220.1	46.8	285	278.8	59.3
46	45.0	09.6	106	103.7	22.0	166	162.4	34.5	226	221.1	47.0	286	279.8	59.5
47	46.0	09.8	107	104.7	22.2	167	163.4	34.7	227	222.0	47.2	287	280.7	59.7
48	47.0	10.0	108	105.6	22.5	168	164.3	34.9	228	223.0	47.4	288	281.7	59.9
49	47.9	10.2	109	106.6	22.7	169	165.3	35.1	229	224.0	47.6	289	282.7	60.1
50	48.9	10.4	110	107.6	22.9	170	166.3	35.3	230	225.0	47.8	290	283.7	60.3
51	49.9	10.6	111	108.6	23.1	171	167.3	35.6	231	226.0	48.0	291	284.6	60.5
52	50.9	10.8	112	109.6	23.3	172	168.2	35.8	232	226.9	48.2	292	285.6	60.7
53	51.8	11.0	113	110.5	23.5	173	169.2	36.0	233	227.9	48.4	293	286.6	60.9
54	52.8	11.2	114	111.5	23.7	174	170.2	36.2	234	228.9	48.7	294	287.6	61.1
55	53.8	11.4	115	112.5	23.9	175	171.2	36.4	235	229.9	48.9	295	288.6	61.3
56	54.8	11.6	116	113.5	24.1	176	172.2	36.6	236	230.8	49.1	296	289.5	61.5
57	55.8	11.9	117	114.4	24.3	177	173.1	36.8	237	231.8	49.3	297	290.5	61.7
58	56.7	12.1	118	115.4	24.5	178	174.1	37.0	238	232.8	49.5	298	291.5	62.0
59	57.7	12.3	119	116.4	24.7	179	175.1	37.2	239	233.8	49.7	299	292.5	62.2
60	58.7	12.5	120	117.4	24.9	180	176.1	37.4	240	234.8	49.9	300	293.4	62.4
Dist.	Dep.	D. Lat.	Dist.	Dep.	D. Lat.	Dist.	Dep.	D. Lat.	Dist.	Dep.	D. Lat.	Dist.	Dep.	D. Lat.
D. Lon		Dep.	D. Lon		Dep.	D. Lon		Dep.	D. Lon		Dep.	D. Lon		Dep.

282° / 258°	78 Degrees	078° / 102°	5h 12m

TRAVERSE TABLE
12 Degrees

348° / 192°   012° / 168°   0h 48m   **12°**

| D. Lon | Dep. | | D. Lon | Dep. | | D. Lon | Dep. | | D. Lon | Dep. | | D. Lon | Dep. | |
Dist.	D. Lat.	Dep.	Dist.	D. Lat.	Dep.	Dist.	D. Lat.	Dep.	Dist.	D. Lat.	Dep.	Dist.	D. Lat.	Dep.
301	294.4	62.6	361	353.1	75.1	421	411.8	87.5	481	470.5	100.0	541	529.2	112.5
302	295.4	62.8	362	354.1	75.3	422	412.8	87.7	482	471.5	100.2	542	530.2	112.7
303	296.4	63.0	363	355.1	75.5	423	413.8	87.9	483	472.4	100.4	543	531.1	112.9
304	297.4	63.2	364	356.0	75.7	424	414.7	88.2	484	473.4	100.6	544	532.1	113.1
305	298.3	63.4	365	357.0	75.9	425	415.7	88.4	485	474.4	100.8	545	533.1	113.3
306	299.3	63.6	366	358.0	76.1	426	416.7	88.6	486	475.4	101.0	546	534.1	113.5
307	300.3	63.8	367	359.0	76.3	427	417.7	88.8	487	476.4	101.3	547	535.0	113.7
308	301.3	64.0	368	360.0	76.5	428	418.6	89.0	488	477.3	101.5	548	536.0	113.9
309	302.2	64.2	369	360.9	76.7	429	419.6	89.2	489	478.3	101.7	549	537.0	114.1
310	303.2	64.5	370	361.9	76.9	430	420.6	89.4	490	479.3	101.9	550	538.0	114.4
311	304.2	64.7	371	362.9	77.1	431	421.6	89.6	491	480.3	102.1	551	539.0	114.6
312	305.2	64.9	372	363.9	77.3	432	422.6	89.8	492	481.2	102.3	552	539.9	114.8
313	306.2	65.1	373	364.8	77.6	433	423.5	90.0	493	482.2	102.5	553	540.9	115.0
314	307.1	65.3	374	365.8	77.8	434	424.5	90.2	494	483.2	102.7	554	541.9	115.2
315	308.1	65.5	375	366.8	78.0	435	425.5	90.4	495	484.2	102.9	555	542.9	115.4
316	309.1	65.7	376	367.8	78.2	436	426.5	90.6	496	485.2	103.1	556	543.9	115.6
317	310.1	65.9	377	368.8	78.4	437	427.5	90.9	497	486.1	103.3	557	544.8	115.8
318	311.1	66.1	378	369.7	78.6	438	428.4	91.1	498	487.1	103.5	558	545.8	116.0
319	312.0	66.3	379	370.7	78.8	439	429.4	91.3	499	488.1	103.7	559	546.8	116.2
320	313.0	66.5	380	371.7	79.0	440	430.4	91.5	500	489.1	104.0	560	547.8	116.4
321	314.0	66.7	381	372.7	79.2	441	431.4	91.7	501	490.1	104.2	561	548.7	116.6
322	315.0	66.9	382	373.7	79.4	442	432.3	91.9	502	491.0	104.4	562	549.7	116.8
323	315.9	67.2	383	374.6	79.6	443	433.3	92.1	503	492.0	104.6	563	550.7	117.1
324	316.9	67.4	384	375.6	79.8	444	434.3	92.3	504	493.0	104.8	564	551.7	117.3
325	317.9	67.6	385	376.6	80.0	445	435.3	92.5	505	494.0	105.0	565	552.7	117.5
326	318.9	67.8	386	377.6	80.3	446	436.3	92.7	506	494.9	105.2	566	553.6	117.7
327	319.9	68.0	387	378.5	80.5	447	437.2	92.9	507	495.9	105.4	567	554.6	117.9
328	320.8	68.2	388	379.5	80.7	448	438.2	93.1	508	496.9	105.6	568	555.6	118.1
329	321.8	68.4	389	380.5	80.9	449	439.2	93.4	509	497.9	105.8	569	556.6	118.3
330	322.8	68.6	390	381.5	81.1	450	440.2	93.6	510	498.9	106.0	570	557.5	118.5
331	323.8	68.8	391	382.5	81.3	451	441.1	93.8	511	499.8	106.2	571	558.5	118.7
332	324.7	69.0	392	383.4	81.5	452	442.1	94.0	512	500.8	106.5	572	559.5	118.9
333	325.7	69.2	393	384.4	81.7	453	443.1	94.2	513	501.8	106.7	573	560.5	119.1
334	326.7	69.4	394	385.4	81.9	454	444.1	94.4	514	502.8	106.9	574	561.5	119.3
335	327.7	69.7	395	386.4	82.1	455	445.1	94.6	515	503.7	107.1	575	562.4	119.5
336	328.7	69.9	396	387.3	82.3	456	446.0	94.8	516	504.7	107.3	576	563.4	119.8
337	329.6	70.1	397	388.3	82.5	457	447.0	95.0	517	505.7	107.5	577	564.4	120.0
338	330.6	70.3	398	389.3	82.7	458	448.0	95.2	518	506.7	107.7	578	565.4	120.2
339	331.6	70.5	399	390.3	83.0	459	449.0	95.4	519	507.7	107.9	579	566.3	120.4
340	332.6	70.7	400	391.3	83.2	460	449.9	95.6	520	508.6	108.1	580	567.3	120.6
341	333.5	70.9	401	392.2	83.4	461	450.9	95.8	521	509.6	108.3	581	568.3	120.8
342	334.5	71.1	402	393.2	83.6	462	451.9	96.1	522	510.6	108.5	582	569.3	121.0
343	335.5	71.3	403	394.2	83.8	463	452.9	96.3	523	511.6	108.7	583	570.3	121.2
344	336.5	71.5	404	395.2	84.0	464	453.9	96.5	524	512.5	108.9	584	571.2	121.4
345	337.5	71.7	405	396.2	84.2	465	454.8	96.7	525	513.5	109.2	585	572.2	121.6
346	338.4	71.9	406	397.1	84.4	466	455.8	96.9	526	514.5	109.4	586	573.2	121.8
347	339.4	72.1	407	398.1	84.6	467	456.8	97.1	527	515.5	109.6	587	574.2	122.0
348	340.4	72.4	408	399.1	84.8	468	457.8	97.3	528	516.5	109.8	588	575.2	122.3
349	341.4	72.6	409	400.1	85.0	469	458.8	97.5	529	517.4	110.0	589	576.1	122.5
350	342.4	72.8	410	401.0	85.2	470	459.7	97.7	530	518.4	110.2	590	577.1	122.7
351	343.3	73.0	411	402.0	85.5	471	460.7	97.9	531	519.4	110.4	591	578.1	122.9
352	344.3	73.2	412	403.0	85.7	472	461.7	98.1	532	520.4	110.6	592	579.1	123.1
353	345.3	73.4	413	404.0	85.9	473	462.7	98.3	533	521.4	110.8	593	580.0	123.3
354	346.3	73.6	414	405.0	86.1	474	463.6	98.6	534	522.3	111.0	594	581.0	123.5
355	347.2	73.8	415	405.9	86.3	475	464.6	98.8	535	523.3	111.2	595	582.0	123.7
356	348.2	74.0	416	406.9	86.5	476	465.6	99.0	536	524.3	111.4	596	583.0	123.9
357	349.2	74.2	417	407.9	86.7	477	466.6	99.2	537	525.3	111.6	597	584.0	124.1
358	350.2	74.4	418	408.9	86.9	478	467.6	99.4	538	526.2	111.9	598	584.9	124.3
359	351.2	74.6	419	409.8	87.1	479	468.5	99.6	539	527.2	112.1	599	585.9	124.5
360	352.1	74.8	420	410.8	87.3	480	469.5	99.8	540	528.2	112.3	600	586.9	124.7

| Dist. | Dep. | D. Lat. | Dist. | Dep. | D. Lat. | Dist. | Dep. | D. Lat. | Dist. | Dep. | D. Lat. | Dist. | Dep. | D. Lat. |
| D. Lon | | Dep. | D. Lon | | Dep. | D. Lon | | Dep. | D. Lon | | Dep. | D. Lon | | Dep. |

282° / 258°   **78 Degrees**   078° / 102°   5h 12m   **78°**

TRAVERSE TABLE
13 Degrees

13° | 347° / 193° | 013° / 167° | 0h 52m

D. Lon Dist.	Dep. D. Lat.	Dep.	D. Lon Dist.	Dep. D. Lat.	Dep.	D. Lon Dist.	Dep. D. Lat.	Dep.	D. Lon Dist.	Dep. D. Lat.	Dep.	D. Lon Dist.	Dep. D. Lat.	Dep.
1	01·0	00·2	61	59·4	13·7	121	117·9	27·2	181	176·4	40·7	241	234·8	54·2
2	01·9	00·4	62	60·4	13·9	122	118·9	27·4	182	177·3	40·9	242	235·8	54·4
3	02·9	00·7	63	61·4	14·2	123	119·8	27·7	183	178·3	41·2	243	236·8	54·7
4	03·9	00·9	64	62·4	14·4	124	120·8	27·9	184	179·3	41·4	244	237·7	54·9
5	04·9	01·1	65	63·3	14·6	125	121·8	28·1	185	180·3	41·6	245	238·7	55·1
6	05·8	01·3	66	64·3	14·8	126	122·8	28·3	186	181·2	41·8	246	239·7	55·3
7	06·8	01·6	67	65·3	15·1	127	123·7	28·6	187	182·2	42·1	247	240·7	55·6
8	07·8	01·8	68	66·3	15·3	128	124·7	28·8	188	183·2	42·3	248	241·6	55·8
9	08·8	02·0	69	67·2	15·5	129	125·7	29·0	189	184·2	42·5	249	242·6	56·0
10	09·7	02·2	70	68·2	15·7	130	126·7	29·2	190	185·1	42·7	250	243·6	56·2
11	10·7	02·5	71	69·2	16·0	131	127·6	29·5	191	186·1	43·0	251	244·6	56·5
12	11·7	02·7	72	70·2	16·2	132	128·6	29·7	192	187·1	43·2	252	245·5	56·7
13	12·7	02·9	73	71·1	16·4	133	129·6	29·9	193	188·1	43·4	253	246·5	56·9
14	13·6	03·1	74	72·1	16·6	134	130·6	30·1	194	189·0	43·6	254	247·5	57·1
15	14·6	03·4	75	73·1	16·9	135	131·5	30·4	195	190·0	43·9	255	248·5	57·4
16	15·6	03·6	76	74·1	17·1	136	132·5	30·6	196	191·0	44·1	256	249·4	57·6
17	16·6	03·8	77	75·0	17·3	137	133·5	30·8	197	192·0	44·3	257	250·4	57·8
18	17·5	04·0	78	76·0	17·5	138	134·5	31·0	198	192·9	44·5	258	251·4	58·0
19	18·5	04·3	79	77·0	17·8	139	135·4	31·3	199	193·9	44·8	259	252·4	58·3
20	19·5	04·5	80	77·9	18·0	140	136·4	31·5	200	194·9	45·0	260	253·3	58·5
21	20·5	04·7	81	78·9	18·2	141	137·4	31·7	201	195·8	45·2	261	254·3	58·7
22	21·4	04·9	82	79·9	18·4	142	138·4	31·9	202	196·8	45·4	262	255·3	58·9
23	22·4	05·2	83	80·9	18·7	143	139·3	32·2	203	197·8	45·7	263	256·3	59·2
24	23·4	05·4	84	81·8	18·9	144	140·3	32·4	204	198·8	45·9	264	257·2	59·4
25	24·4	05·6	85	82·8	19·1	145	141·3	32·6	205	199·7	46·1	265	258·2	59·6
26	25·3	05·8	86	83·8	19·3	146	142·3	32·8	206	200·7	46·3	266	259·2	59·8
27	26·3	06·1	87	84·8	19·6	147	143·2	33·1	207	201·7	46·6	267	260·2	60·1
28	27·3	06·3	88	85·7	19·8	148	144·2	33·3	208	202·7	46·8	268	261·1	60·3
29	28·3	06·5	89	86·7	20·0	149	145·2	33·5	209	203·6	47·0	269	262·1	60·5
30	29·2	06·7	90	87·7	20·2	150	146·2	33·7	210	204·6	47·2	270	263·1	60·7
31	30·2	07·0	91	88·7	20·5	151	147·1	34·0	211	205·6	47·5	271	264·1	61·0
32	31·2	07·2	92	89·6	20·7	152	148·1	34·2	212	206·6	47·7	272	265·0	61·2
33	32·2	07·4	93	90·6	20·9	153	149·1	34·4	213	207·5	47·9	273	266·0	61·4
34	33·1	07·6	94	91·6	21·1	154	150·1	34·6	214	208·5	48·1	274	267·0	61·6
35	34·1	07·9	95	92·6	21·4	155	151·0	34·9	215	209·5	48·4	275	268·0	61·9
36	35·1	08·1	96	93·5	21·6	156	152·0	35·1	216	210·5	48·6	276	268·9	62·1
37	36·1	08·3	97	94·5	21·8	157	153·0	35·3	217	211·4	48·8	277	269·9	62·3
38	37·0	08·5	98	95·5	22·0	158	154·0	35·5	218	212·4	49·0	278	270·9	62·5
39	38·0	08·8	99	96·5	22·3	159	154·9	35·8	219	213·4	49·3	279	271·8	62·8
40	39·0	09·0	100	97·4	22·5	160	155·9	36·0	220	214·4	49·5	280	272·8	63·0
41	39·9	09·2	101	98·4	22·7	161	156·9	36·2	221	215·3	49·7	281	273·8	63·2
42	40·9	09·4	102	99·4	22·9	162	157·8	36·4	222	216·3	49·9	282	274·8	63·4
43	41·9	09·7	103	100·4	23·2	163	158·8	36·7	223	217·3	50·2	283	275·7	63·7
44	42·9	09·9	104	101·3	23·4	164	159·8	36·9	224	218·3	50·4	284	276·7	63·9
45	43·8	10·1	105	102·3	23·6	165	160·8	37·1	225	219·2	50·6	285	277·7	64·1
46	44·8	10·3	106	103·3	23·8	166	161·7	37·3	226	220·2	50·8	286	278·7	64·3
47	45·8	10·6	107	104·3	24·1	167	162·7	37·6	227	221·2	51·1	287	279·6	64·6
48	46·8	10·8	108	105·2	24·3	168	163·7	37·8	228	222·2	51·3	288	280·6	64·8
49	47·7	11·0	109	106·2	24·5	169	164·7	38·0	229	223·1	51·5	289	281·6	65·0
50	48·7	11·2	110	107·2	24·7	170	165·6	38·2	230	224·1	51·7	290	282·6	65·2
51	49·7	11·5	111	108·2	25·0	171	166·6	38·5	231	225·1	52·0	291	283·5	65·5
52	50·7	11·7	112	109·1	25·2	172	167·6	38·7	232	226·1	52·2	292	284·5	65·7
53	51·6	11·9	113	110·1	25·4	173	168·6	38·9	233	227·0	52·4	293	285·5	65·9
54	52·6	12·1	114	111·1	25·6	174	169·5	39·1	234	228·0	52·6	294	286·5	66·1
55	53·6	12·4	115	112·1	25·9	175	170·5	39·4	235	229·0	52·9	295	287·4	66·4
56	54·6	12·6	116	113·0	26·1	176	171·5	39·6	236	230·0	53·1	296	288·4	66·6
57	55·5	12·8	117	114·0	26·3	177	172·5	39·8	237	230·9	53·3	297	289·4	66·8
58	56·5	13·0	118	115·0	26·5	178	173·4	40·0	238	231·9	53·5	298	290·4	67·0
59	57·5	13·3	119	116·0	26·8	179	174·4	40·3	239	232·9	53·8	299	291·3	67·3
60	58·5	13·5	120	116·9	27·0	180	175·4	40·5	240	233·8	54·0	300	292·3	67·5

| Dist. | Dep. | D. Lat. | Dist. | Dep. | D. Lat. | Dist. | Dep. | D. Lat. | Dist. | Dep. | D. Lat. | Dist. | Dep. | D. Lat. |
| D. Lon | | Dep. | D. Lon | | Dep. | D. Lon | | Dep. | D. Lon | | Dep. | D. Lon | | Dep. |

77° | 283° / 257° | 77 Degrees | 077° / 103° | 5h 08m

TRAVERSE TABLE
13 Degrees

347° / 193°   013° / 167°   0h 52m   **13°**

D. Lon	Dep.		D. Lon	Dep.		D. Lon	Dep.		D. Lon	Dep.		D. Lon	Dep.	
Dist.	D. Lat.	Dep.	Dist.	D. Lat.	Dep.	Dist.	D. Lat.	Dep.	Dist.	D. Lat.	Dep.	Dist.	D. Lat.	Dep.
301	293·3	67·7	361	351·7	81·2	421	410·2	94·7	481	468·7	108·2	541	527·1	121·7
302	294·3	67·9	362	352·7	81·4	422	411·2	94·9	482	469·6	108·4	542	528·1	121·9
303	295·2	68·2	363	353·7	81·7	423	412·2	95·2	483	470·6	108·7	543	529·1	122·1
304	296·2	68·4	364	354·7	81·9	424	413·1	95·4	484	471·6	108·9	544	530·1	122·4
305	297·2	68·6	365	355·6	82·1	425	414·1	95·6	485	472·6	109·1	545	531·0	122·6
306	298·2	68·8	366	356·6	82·3	426	415·1	95·8	486	473·5	109·3	546	532·0	122·8
307	299·1	69·1	367	357·6	82·6	427	416·1	96·1	487	474·5	109·6	547	533·0	123·0
308	300·1	69·3	368	358·6	82·8	428	417·0	96·3	488	475·5	109·8	548	534·0	123·3
309	301·1	69·5	369	359·5	83·0	429	418·0	96·5	489	476·5	110·0	549	534·9	123·5
310	302·1	69·7	370	360·5	83·2	430	419·0	96·7	490	477·4	110·2	550	535·9	123·7
311	303·0	70·0	371	361·5	83·5	431	420·0	97·0	491	478·4	110·5	551	536·9	123·9
312	304·0	70·2	372	362·5	83·7	432	420·9	97·2	492	479·4	110·7	552	537·9	124·2
313	305·0	70·4	373	363·4	83·9	433	421·9	97·4	493	480·4	110·9	553	538·8	124·4
314	306·0	70·6	374	364·4	84·1	434	422·9	97·6	494	481·3	111·1	554	539·8	124·6
315	306·9	71·1	375	365·4	84·4	435	423·9	97·9	495	482·3	111·4	555	540·8	124·8
316	307·9	71·1	376	366·4	84·6	436	424·8	98·1	496	483·3	111·6	556	541·7	125·1
317	308·9	71·3	377	367·3	84·8	437	425·8	98·3	497	484·3	111·8	557	542·7	125·3
318	309·8	71·5	378	368·3	85·0	438	426·8	98·5	498	485·2	112·0	558	543·7	125·5
319	310·8	71·8	379	369·3	85·3	439	427·7	98·8	499	486·2	112·3	559	544·7	125·7
320	311·8	72·0	380	370·3	85·5	440	428·7	99·0	500	487·2	112·5	560	545·6	126·0
321	312·8	72·2	381	371·2	85·7	441	429·7	99·2	501	488·2	112·7	561	546·6	126·2
322	313·7	72·4	382	372·2	85·9	442	430·7	99·4	502	489·1	112·9	562	547·6	126·4
323	314·7	72·7	383	373·2	86·2	443	431·6	99·7	503	490·1	113·2	563	548·6	126·6
324	315·7	72·9	384	374·2	86·4	444	432·6	99·9	504	491·1	113·4	564	549·5	126·9
325	316·7	73·1	385	375·1	86·6	445	433·6	100·1	505	492·1	113·6	565	550·5	127·1
326	317·6	73·3	386	376·1	86·8	446	434·6	100·3	506	493·0	113·8	566	551·5	127·3
327	318·6	73·6	387	377·1	87·1	447	435·5	100·6	507	494·0	114·1	567	552·5	127·5
328	319·6	73·8	388	378·1	87·3	448	436·5	100·8	508	495·0	114·3	568	553·4	127·7
329	320·6	74·0	389	379·0	87·5	449	437·5	101·0	509	496·0	114·5	569	554·4	128·0
330	321·5	74·2	390	380·0	87·7	450	438·5	101·2	510	496·9	114·7	570	555·4	128·2
331	322·5	74·5	391	381·0	88·0	451	439·4	101·5	511	497·9	115·0	571	556·4	128·4
332	323·5	74·7	392	382·0	88·2	452	440·4	101·7	512	498·9	115·2	572	557·3	128·7
333	324·5	74·9	393	382·9	88·4	453	441·4	101·9	513	499·9	115·4	573	558·3	128·9
334	325·4	75·1	394	383·9	88·6	454	442·4	102·1	514	500·8	115·6	574	559·3	129·1
335	326·4	75·4	395	384·9	88·9	455	443·3	102·4	515	501·8	115·8	575	560·3	129·3
336	327·4	75·6	396	385·9	89·1	456	444·3	102·6	516	502·8	116·1	576	561·2	129·6
337	328·4	75·8	397	386·8	89·3	457	445·3	102·8	517	503·7	116·3	577	562·2	129·8
338	329·3	76·0	398	387·8	89·5	458	446·3	103·0	518	504·7	116·5	578	563·2	130·0
339	330·3	76·3	399	388·8	89·8	459	447·2	103·3	519	505·7	116·7	579	564·2	130·2
340	331·3	76·5	400	389·7	90·0	460	448·2	103·5	520	506·7	117·0	580	565·1	130·5
341	332·3	76·7	401	390·7	90·2	461	449·2	103·7	521	507·6	117·2	581	566·1	130·7
342	333·2	76·9	402	391·7	90·4	462	450·2	103·9	522	508·6	117·5	582	567·1	130·9
343	334·2	77·2	403	392·7	90·7	463	451·1	104·2	523	509·6	117·6	583	568·1	131·1
344	335·2	77·4	404	393·6	90·9	464	452·1	104·4	524	510·6	117·9	584	569·0	131·4
345	336·2	77·6	405	394·6	91·1	465	453·1	104·6	525	511·5	118·1	585	570·0	131·6
346	337·1	77·8	406	395·6	91·3	466	454·1	104·8	526	512·5	118·3	586	571·0	131·8
347	338·1	78·1	407	396·6	91·6	467	455·0	105·1	527	513·5	118·5	587	572·0	132·0
348	339·1	78·3	408	397·5	91·8	468	456·0	105·3	528	514·5	118·8	588	572·9	132·3
349	340·1	78·5	409	398·5	92·0	469	457·0	105·5	529	515·4	119·0	589	573·9	132·5
350	341·0	78·7	410	399·5	92·2	470	458·0	105·7	530	516·4	119·2	590	574·9	132·7
351	342·0	79·0	411	400·5	92·5	471	458·9	106·0	531	517·4	119·4	591	575·9	132·9
352	343·0	79·2	412	401·4	92·7	472	459·9	106·2	532	518·4	119·7	592	576·8	133·2
353	344·0	79·4	413	402·4	92·9	473	460·9	106·4	533	519·3	119·9	593	577·8	133·4
354	344·9	79·6	414	403·4	93·1	474	461·9	106·6	534	520·3	120·1	594	578·8	133·6
355	345·9	79·9	415	404·4	93·4	475	462·8	106·9	535	521·3	120·3	595	579·8	133·8
356	346·9	80·1	416	405·3	93·6	476	463·8	107·1	536	522·3	120·6	596	580·7	134·1
357	347·9	80·3	417	406·3	93·8	477	464·8	107·3	537	523·2	120·8	597	581·7	134·3
358	348·8	80·5	418	407·3	94·0	478	465·7	107·5	538	524·2	121·0	598	582·7	134·5
359	349·8	80·8	419	408·3	94·3	479	466·7	107·8	539	525·2	121·2	599	583·6	134·7
360	350·8	81·0	420	409·2	94·5	480	467·7	108·0	540	526·2	121·5	600	584·6	135·0
Dist.	Dep.	D. Lat.	Dist.	Dep.	D. Lat.	Dist.	Dep.	D. Lat.	Dist.	Dep.	D. Lat.	Dist.	Dep.	D. Lat.
D. Lon		Dep.	D. Lon		Dep.	D. Lon		Dep.	D. Lon		Dep.	D. Lon		Dep.

283° / 257°   77 Degrees   077° / 103°   5h 08m   **77°**

TRAVERSE TABLE
14 Degrees

14°

346° / 194° • 014° / 166° • 0h 56m

D. Lon	Dep.		D. Lon	Dep.		D. Lon	Dep.		D. Lon	Dep.		D. Lon	Dep.	
Dist.	D. Lat.	Dep.	Dist.	D. Lat.	Dep.	Dist.	D. Lat.	Dep.	Dist.	D. Lat.	Dep.	Dist.	D. Lat.	Dep.
1	01·0	00·2	61	59·2	14·8	121	117·4	29·3	181	175·6	43·8	241	233·8	58·3
2	01·9	00·5	62	60·2	15·0	122	118·4	29·5	182	176·6	44·0	242	234·8	58·5
3	02·9	00·7	63	61·1	15·2	123	119·3	29·8	183	177·6	44·3	243	235·8	58·8
4	03·9	01·0	64	62·1	15·5	124	120·3	30·0	184	178·5	44·5	244	236·8	59·0
5	04·9	01·2	65	63·1	15·7	125	121·3	30·2	185	179·5	44·8	245	237·7	59·3
6	05·8	01·5	66	64·0	16·0	126	122·3	30·5	186	180·5	45·0	246	238·7	59·5
7	06·8	01·7	67	65·0	16·2	127	123·2	30·7	187	181·4	45·2	247	239·7	59·8
8	07·8	01·9	68	66·0	16·5	128	124·2	31·0	188	182·4	45·5	248	240·6	60·0
9	08·7	02·2	69	67·0	16·7	129	125·2	31·2	189	183·4	45·7	249	241·6	60·2
10	09·7	02·4	70	67·9	16·9	130	126·1	31·4	190	184·4	46·0	250	242·6	60·5
11	10·7	02·7	71	68·9	17·2	131	127·1	31·7	191	185·3	46·2	251	243·5	60·7
12	11·6	02·9	72	69·9	17·4	132	128·1	31·9	192	186·3	46·4	252	244·5	61·0
13	12·6	03·1	73	70·8	17·7	133	129·0	32·2	193	187·3	46·7	253	245·5	61·2
14	13·6	03·4	74	71·8	17·9	134	130·0	32·4	194	188·2	46·9	254	246·5	61·4
15	14·6	03·6	75	72·8	18·1	135	131·0	32·7	195	189·2	47·2	255	247·4	61·7
16	15·5	03·9	76	73·7	18·4	136	132·0	32·9	196	190·2	47·4	256	248·4	61·9
17	16·5	04·1	77	74·7	18·6	137	132·9	33·1	197	191·1	47·7	257	249·4	62·2
18	17·5	04·4	78	75·7	18·9	138	133·9	33·4	198	192·1	47·9	258	250·3	62·4
19	18·4	04·6	79	76·7	19·1	139	134·9	33·6	199	193·1	48·1	259	251·3	62·7
20	19·4	04·8	80	77·6	19·4	140	135·8	33·9	200	194·1	48·4	260	252·3	62·9
21	20·4	05·1	81	78·6	19·6	141	136·8	34·1	201	195·0	48·6	261	253·2	63·1
22	21·3	05·3	82	79·6	19·8	142	137·8	34·4	202	196·0	48·9	262	254·2	63·4
23	22·3	05·6	83	80·5	20·1	143	138·8	34·6	203	197·0	49·1	263	255·2	63·6
24	23·3	05·8	84	81·5	20·3	144	139·7	34·8	204	197·9	49·4	264	256·2	63·9
25	24·3	06·0	85	82·5	20·6	145	140·7	35·1	205	198·9	49·6	265	257·1	64·1
26	25·2	06·3	86	83·4	20·8	146	141·7	35·3	206	199·9	49·8	266	258·1	64·4
27	26·2	06·5	87	84·4	21·0	147	142·6	35·6	207	200·9	50·1	267	259·1	64·6
28	27·2	06·8	88	85·4	21·3	148	143·6	35·8	208	201·8	50·3	268	260·0	64·8
29	28·1	07·0	89	86·4	21·5	149	144·6	36·0	209	202·8	50·6	269	261·0	65·1
30	29·1	07·3	90	87·3	21·8	150	145·5	36·3	210	203·8	50·8	270	262·0	65·3
31	30·1	07·5	91	88·3	22·0	151	146·5	36·5	211	204·7	51·0	271	263·0	65·6
32	31·0	07·7	92	89·3	22·3	152	147·5	36·8	212	205·7	51·3	272	263·9	65·8
33	32·0	08·0	93	90·2	22·5	153	148·5	37·0	213	206·7	51·5	273	264·9	66·0
34	33·0	08·2	94	91·2	22·7	154	149·4	37·3	214	207·6	51·8	274	265·9	66·3
35	34·0	08·5	95	92·2	23·0	155	150·4	37·5	215	208·6	52·0	275	266·8	66·5
36	34·9	08·7	96	93·1	23·2	156	151·4	37·7	216	209·6	52·3	276	267·8	66·8
37	35·9	09·0	97	94·1	23·5	157	152·3	38·0	217	210·6	52·5	277	268·8	67·0
38	36·9	09·2	98	95·1	23·7	158	153·3	38·2	218	211·5	52·7	278	269·7	67·3
39	37·8	09·4	99	96·1	24·0	159	154·3	38·5	219	212·5	53·0	279	270·7	67·5
40	38·8	09·7	100	97·0	24·2	160	155·2	38·7	220	213·5	53·2	280	271·7	67·7
41	39·8	09·9	101	98·0	24·4	161	156·2	38·9	221	214·4	53·5	281	272·7	68·0
42	40·8	10·2	102	99·0	24·7	162	157·2	39·2	222	215·4	53·7	282	273·6	68·2
43	41·7	10·4	103	99·9	24·9	163	158·2	39·4	223	216·4	53·9	283	274·6	68·5
44	42·7	10·6	104	100·9	25·2	164	159·1	39·7	224	217·3	54·2	284	275·6	68·7
45	43·7	10·9	105	101·9	25·4	165	160·1	39·9	225	218·3	54·4	285	276·5	68·9
46	44·6	11·1	106	102·9	25·6	166	161·1	40·2	226	219·3	54·7	286	277·5	69·2
47	45·6	11·4	107	103·8	25·9	167	162·0	40·4	227	220·3	54·9	287	278·5	69·4
48	46·6	11·6	108	104·8	26·1	168	163·0	40·6	228	221·2	55·2	288	279·4	69·7
49	47·5	11·9	109	105·8	26·4	169	164·0	40·9	229	222·2	55·4	289	280·4	69·9
50	48·5	12·1	110	106·7	26·6	170	165·0	41·1	230	223·2	55·6	290	281·4	70·2
51	49·5	12·3	111	107·7	26·9	171	165·9	41·4	231	224·1	55·9	291	282·4	70·4
52	50·5	12·6	112	108·7	27·1	172	166·9	41·6	232	225·1	56·1	292	283·3	70·6
53	51·4	12·8	113	109·6	27·3	173	167·9	41·9	233	226·1	56·4	293	284·3	70·9
54	52·4	13·1	114	110·6	27·6	174	168·8	42·1	234	227·0	56·6	294	285·3	71·1
55	53·4	13·3	115	111·6	27·8	175	169·8	42·3	235	228·0	56·9	295	286·2	71·4
56	54·3	13·5	116	112·6	28·1	176	170·8	42·6	236	229·0	57·1	296	287·2	71·6
57	55·3	13·8	117	113·5	28·3	177	171·7	42·8	237	230·0	57·3	297	288·2	71·9
58	56·3	14·0	118	114·5	28·6	178	172·7	43·1	238	230·9	57·6	298	289·1	72·1
59	57·2	14·3	119	115·5	28·8	179	173·7	43·3	239	231·9	57·8	299	290·1	72·3
60	58·2	14·5	120	116·4	29·0	180	174·7	43·5	240	232·9	58·1	300	291·1	72·6
Dist.	Dep.	D. Lat.	Dist.	Dep.	D. Lat.	Dist.	Dep.	D. Lat.	Dist.	Dep.	D. Lat.	Dist.	Dep.	D. Lat.
D. Lon		Dep.	D. Lon		Dep.	D. Lon		Dep.	D. Lon		Dep.	D. Lon		Dep.

76°

284° / 256° • 76 Degrees • 076° / 104° • 5h 04m

TRAVERSE TABLE
14 Degrees

Dist.	D. Lat.	Dep.	Dist.	D. Lat.	Dep.	Dist.	D. Lat.	Dep.	Dist.	D. Lat.	Dep.	Dist.	D. Lat.	Dep.
301	292.1	72.8	361	350.3	87.3	421	408.5	101.8	481	466.7	116.4	541	524.9	130.9
302	293.0	73.1	362	351.2	87.6	422	409.5	102.1	482	467.7	116.6	542	525.9	131.1
303	294.0	73.3	363	352.2	87.8	423	410.4	102.3	483	468.7	116.8	543	526.9	131.4
304	295.0	73.5	364	353.2	88.1	424	411.4	102.6	484	469.6	117.1	544	527.8	131.6
305	295.9	73.8	365	354.2	88.3	425	412.4	102.8	485	470.6	117.3	545	528.8	131.8
306	296.9	74.0	366	355.1	88.5	426	413.3	103.1	486	471.6	117.6	546	529.8	132.1
307	297.9	74.3	367	356.1	88.8	427	414.3	103.3	487	472.5	117.8	547	530.8	132.3
308	298.9	74.5	368	357.1	89.0	428	415.3	103.5	488	473.5	118.1	548	531.7	132.6
309	299.8	74.8	369	358.0	89.3	429	416.3	103.8	489	474.5	118.3	549	532.7	132.8
310	300.8	75.0	370	359.0	89.5	430	417.2	104.0	490	475.4	118.5	550	533.7	133.1
311	301.8	75.2	371	360.0	89.8	431	418.2	104.3	491	476.4	118.8	551	534.6	133.3
312	302.7	75.5	372	361.0	90.0	432	419.1	104.5	492	477.4	119.0	552	535.6	133.5
313	303.7	75.7	373	361.9	90.2	433	420.1	104.8	493	478.4	119.3	553	536.6	133.8
314	304.6	76.0	374	362.9	90.5	434	421.1	105.0	494	479.3	119.5	554	537.5	134.0
315	305.6	76.2	375	363.9	90.7	435	422.0	105.2	495	480.3	119.6	555	538.5	134.3
316	306.6	76.4	376	364.8	91.0	436	423.0	105.5	496	481.3	120.0	556	539.5	134.5
317	307.6	76.7	377	365.8	91.2	437	424.0	105.7	497	482.2	120.2	557	540.5	134.8
318	308.6	76.9	378	366.8	91.4	438	425.0	106.0	498	483.2	120.5	558	541.4	135.0
319	309.5	77.2	379	367.7	91.7	439	426.0	106.2	499	484.2	120.7	559	542.4	135.2
320	310.5	77.4	380	368.7	91.9	440	426.9	106.4	500	485.1	121.0	560	543.4	135.5
321	311.5	77.7	381	369.7	92.2	441	427.9	106.7	501	486.1	121.2	561	544.3	135.7
322	312.4	77.9	382	370.7	92.4	442	428.9	106.9	502	487.1	121.4	562	545.3	136.0
323	313.4	78.1	383	371.6	92.7	443	429.8	107.2	503	488.1	121.7	563	546.3	136.2
324	314.4	78.4	384	372.6	92.9	444	430.8	107.4	504	489.0	121.9	564	547.2	136.4
325	315.3	78.6	385	373.6	93.1	445	431.8	107.7	505	490.0	122.2	565	548.2	136.7
326	316.3	78.9	386	374.5	93.4	446	432.8	107.9	506	491.0	122.4	566	549.2	136.9
327	317.3	79.1	387	375.5	93.6	447	433.7	108.1	507	491.9	122.7	567	550.2	137.2
328	318.3	79.4	388	376.4	93.9	448	434.7	108.4	508	492.9	122.9	568	551.1	137.4
329	319.2	79.6	389	377.4	94.1	449	435.7	108.6	509	493.9	123.1	569	552.1	137.7
330	320.2	79.8	390	378.4	94.3	450	436.6	108.9	510	494.9	123.4	570	553.1	137.9
331	321.2	80.1	391	379.4	94.6	451	437.6	109.1	511	495.8	123.6	571	554.0	138.1
332	322.1	80.3	392	380.4	94.8	452	438.6	109.3	512	496.8	123.9	572	555.0	138.4
333	323.1	80.6	393	381.3	95.1	453	439.5	109.6	513	497.8	124.1	573	556.0	138.6
334	324.1	80.8	394	382.3	95.3	454	440.5	109.8	514	498.7	124.3	574	556.9	138.9
335	325.0	81.0	395	383.3	95.6	455	441.5	110.1	515	499.7	124.6	575	557.9	139.1
336	326.0	81.3	396	384.2	95.8	456	442.5	110.3	516	500.7	124.8	576	558.9	139.3
337	327.0	81.5	397	385.2	96.0	457	443.4	110.6	517	501.6	125.1	577	559.9	139.6
338	328.0	81.8	398	386.2	96.3	458	444.4	110.8	518	502.6	125.3	578	560.8	139.8
339	328.9	82.0	399	387.1	96.5	459	445.4	111.0	519	503.6	125.6	579	561.8	140.1
340	329.9	82.3	400	388.1	96.8	460	446.3	111.3	520	504.6	125.8	580	562.8	140.3
341	330.8	82.5	401	389.1	97.0	461	447.3	111.5	521	505.5	126.0	581	563.7	140.6
342	331.8	82.7	402	390.1	97.3	462	448.3	111.8	522	506.5	126.3	582	564.7	140.8
343	332.8	83.0	403	391.0	97.5	463	449.2	112.0	523	507.5	126.5	583	565.7	141.0
344	333.8	83.2	404	392.0	97.7	464	450.2	112.3	524	508.4	126.8	584	566.7	141.3
345	334.8	83.5	405	393.0	98.0	465	451.2	112.5	525	509.4	127.0	585	567.6	141.5
346	335.7	83.7	406	393.9	98.2	466	452.2	112.7	526	510.4	127.3	586	568.6	141.8
347	336.7	83.9	407	394.9	98.5	467	453.1	113.0	527	511.3	127.5	587	569.6	142.0
348	337.7	84.2	408	395.9	98.7	468	454.1	113.2	528	512.3	127.7	588	570.5	142.3
349	338.6	84.4	409	396.9	98.9	469	455.1	113.5	529	513.3	128.0	589	571.5	142.5
350	339.6	84.7	410	397.8	99.2	470	456.0	113.7	530	514.3	128.2	590	572.5	142.7
351	340.6	84.9	411	398.8	99.4	471	457.0	113.9	531	515.2	128.5	591	573.4	143.0
352	341.5	85.2	412	399.8	99.7	472	458.0	114.2	532	516.2	128.8	592	574.4	143.2
353	342.5	85.4	413	400.7	99.9	473	458.9	114.4	533	517.2	128.9	593	575.4	143.5
354	343.5	85.6	414	401.7	100.2	474	459.9	114.7	534	518.1	129.2	594	576.4	143.7
355	344.5	85.9	415	402.7	100.4	475	460.9	114.9	535	519.1	129.4	595	577.3	143.9
356	345.4	86.1	416	403.6	100.6	476	461.9	115.2	536	520.1	129.7	596	578.3	144.2
357	346.4	86.4	417	404.6	100.9	477	462.8	115.4	537	521.0	129.9	597	579.3	144.4
358	347.4	86.6	418	405.6	101.1	478	463.8	115.6	538	522.0	130.2	598	580.2	144.7
359	348.3	86.8	419	406.6	101.4	479	464.8	115.9	539	523.0	130.4	599	581.2	144.9
360	349.3	87.1	420	407.5	101.6	480	465.7	116.1	540	524.0	130.6	600	582.2	145.2

Dist.	Dep.	D. Lat.	Dist.	Dep.	D. Lat.	Dist.	Dep.	D. Lat.	Dist.	Dep.	D. Lat.	Dist.	Dep.	D. Lat.

TRAVERSE TABLE
15 Degrees

15°

345° / 195°   015° / 165°   1h 00m

| D. Lon Dep. | | | D. Lon Dep. | | | D. Lon Dep. | | | D. Lon Dep. | | | D. Lon Dep. | | |
Dist.	D. Lat.	Dep.	Dist.	D. Lat.	Dep.	Dist.	D. Lat.	Dep.	Dist.	D. Lat.	Dep.	Dist.	D. Lat.	Dep.
1	01.0	00.3	61	58.9	15.8	121	116.9	31.3	181	174.8	46.8	241	232.8	62.4
2	01.9	00.5	62	59.9	16.0	122	117.8	31.6	182	175.8	47.1	242	233.8	62.6
3	02.9	00.8	63	60.9	16.3	123	118.8	31.8	183	176.8	47.4	243	234.7	62.9
4	03.9	01.0	64	61.8	16.6	124	119.8	32.1	184	177.7	47.6	244	235.7	63.2
5	04.8	01.3	65	62.8	16.8	125	120.7	32.4	185	178.7	47.9	245	236.7	63.4
6	05.8	01.6	66	63.8	17.1	126	121.7	32.6	186	179.7	48.1	246	237.6	63.7
7	06.8	01.8	67	64.7	17.3	127	122.7	32.9	187	180.6	48.4	247	238.6	63.9
8	07.7	02.1	68	65.7	17.6	128	123.6	33.1	188	181.6	48.7	248	239.5	64.2
9	08.7	02.3	69	66.6	17.9	129	124.6	33.4	189	182.6	48.9	249	240.5	64.4
10	09.7	02.6	70	67.6	18.1	130	125.6	33.6	190	183.5	49.2	250	241.5	64.7
11	10.6	02.8	71	68.6	18.4	131	126.5	33.9	191	184.5	49.4	251	242.4	65.0
12	11.6	03.1	72	69.5	18.6	132	127.5	34.2	192	185.5	49.7	252	243.4	65.2
13	12.6	03.4	73	70.5	18.9	133	128.5	34.4	193	186.4	50.0	253	244.4	65.5
14	13.5	03.6	74	71.5	19.2	134	129.4	34.7	194	187.4	50.2	254	245.3	65.7
15	14.5	03.9	75	72.4	19.4	135	130.4	34.9	195	188.4	50.5	255	246.3	66.0
16	15.5	04.1	76	73.4	19.7	136	131.4	35.2	196	189.3	50.7	256	247.3	66.3
17	16.4	04.4	77	74.4	19.9	137	132.3	35.5	197	190.3	51.0	257	248.2	66.5
18	17.4	04.7	78	75.3	20.2	138	133.3	35.7	198	191.3	51.2	258	249.2	66.8
19	18.4	04.9	79	76.3	20.4	139	134.3	36.0	199	192.2	51.5	259	250.2	67.0
20	19.3	05.2	80	77.3	20.7	140	135.2	36.2	200	193.2	51.8	260	251.1	67.3
21	20.3	05.4	81	78.2	21.0	141	136.2	36.5	201	194.2	52.0	261	252.1	67.6
22	21.3	05.7	82	79.2	21.2	142	137.2	36.8	202	195.1	52.3	262	253.1	67.8
23	22.2	06.0	83	80.2	21.5	143	138.1	37.0	203	196.1	52.5	263	254.0	68.1
24	23.2	06.2	84	81.1	21.7	144	139.1	37.3	204	197.0	52.8	264	255.0	68.3
25	24.1	06.5	85	82.1	22.0	145	140.1	37.5	205	198.0	53.1	265	256.0	68.6
26	25.1	06.7	86	83.1	22.3	146	141.0	37.8	206	199.0	53.3	266	256.9	68.8
27	26.1	07.0	87	84.0	22.5	147	142.0	38.0	207	199.9	53.6	267	257.9	69.1
28	27.0	07.2	88	85.0	22.8	148	143.0	38.3	208	200.9	53.8	268	258.9	69.4
29	28.0	07.5	89	86.0	23.0	149	143.9	38.6	209	201.9	54.1	269	259.8	69.6
30	29.0	07.8	90	86.9	23.3	150	144.9	38.8	210	202.8	54.4	270	260.8	69.9
31	29.9	08.0	91	87.9	23.6	151	145.9	39.1	211	203.8	54.6	271	261.8	70.1
32	30.9	08.3	92	88.9	23.8	152	146.8	39.3	212	204.8	54.9	272	262.7	70.4
33	31.9	08.5	93	89.8	24.1	153	147.8	39.6	213	205.7	55.1	273	263.7	70.7
34	32.8	08.8	94	90.8	24.3	154	148.8	39.9	214	206.7	55.4	274	264.7	70.9
35	33.8	09.1	95	91.8	24.6	155	149.7	40.1	215	207.7	55.6	275	265.6	71.2
36	34.8	09.3	96	92.7	24.8	156	150.7	40.4	216	208.6	55.9	276	266.6	71.4
37	35.7	09.6	97	93.7	25.1	157	151.7	40.6	217	209.6	56.2	277	267.6	71.7
38	36.7	09.8	98	94.7	25.4	158	152.6	40.9	218	210.6	56.4	278	268.5	72.0
39	37.7	10.1	99	95.6	25.6	159	153.6	41.2	219	211.5	56.7	279	269.5	72.2
40	38.6	10.4	100	96.6	25.9	160	154.5	41.4	220	212.5	56.9	280	270.5	72.5
41	39.6	10.6	101	97.6	26.1	161	155.5	41.7	221	213.5	57.2	281	271.4	72.7
42	40.6	10.9	102	98.5	26.4	162	156.5	41.9	222	214.4	57.5	282	272.4	73.0
43	41.5	11.1	103	99.5	26.7	163	157.4	42.2	223	215.4	57.7	283	273.4	73.2
44	42.5	11.4	104	100.5	26.9	164	158.4	42.4	224	216.4	58.0	284	274.3	73.5
45	43.5	11.6	105	101.4	27.2	165	159.4	42.7	225	217.3	58.2	285	275.3	73.8
46	44.4	11.9	106	102.4	27.4	166	160.3	43.0	226	218.3	58.5	286	276.3	74.0
47	45.4	12.2	107	103.4	27.7	167	161.3	43.2	227	219.3	58.8	287	277.2	74.3
48	46.4	12.4	108	104.3	28.0	168	162.3	43.5	228	220.2	59.0	288	278.2	74.5
49	47.3	12.7	109	105.3	28.2	169	163.2	43.7	229	221.2	59.3	289	279.2	74.8
50	48.3	12.9	110	106.3	28.5	170	164.2	44.0	230	222.2	59.5	290	280.1	75.1
51	49.3	13.2	111	107.2	28.7	171	165.2	44.3	231	223.1	59.8	291	281.1	75.3
52	50.2	13.5	112	108.2	29.0	172	166.1	44.5	232	224.1	60.0	292	282.1	75.6
53	51.2	13.7	113	109.1	29.2	173	167.1	44.8	233	225.1	60.3	293	283.0	75.8
54	52.2	14.0	114	110.1	29.5	174	168.1	45.0	234	226.0	60.6	294	284.0	76.1
55	53.1	14.2	115	111.1	29.8	175	169.0	45.3	235	227.0	60.8	295	284.9	76.4
56	54.1	14.5	116	112.0	30.0	176	170.0	45.6	236	228.0	61.1	296	285.9	76.6
57	55.1	14.8	117	113.0	30.3	177	171.0	45.8	237	228.9	61.3	297	286.9	76.9
58	56.0	15.0	118	114.0	30.5	178	171.9	46.1	238	229.9	61.6	298	287.8	77.1
59	57.0	15.3	119	114.9	30.8	179	172.9	46.3	239	230.9	61.9	299	288.8	77.4
60	58.0	15.5	120	115.9	31.1	180	173.9	46.6	240	231.8	62.1	300	289.8	77.6

| Dist. | Dep. | D. Lat. | Dist. | Dep. | D. Lat. | Dist. | Dep. | D. Lat. | Dist. | Dep. | D. Lat. | Dist. | Dep. | D. Lat. |
| D. Lon | | Dep. | D. Lon | | Dep. | D. Lon | | Dep. | D. Lon | | Dep. | D. Lon | | Dep. |

75°

285° / 255°   075° / 105°   5h 00m

75 Degrees

TRAVERSE TABLE
15 Degrees

Dist.	D. Lat.	Dep.	Dist.	D. Lat.	Dep.	Dist.	D. Lat.	Dep.	Dist.	D. Lat.	Dep.	Dist.	D. Lat.	Dep.
301	290.7	77.9	361	348.7	93.4	421	406.7	109.0	481	464.6	124.5	541	522.6	140.0
302	291.7	78.2	362	349.7	93.7	422	407.6	109.2	482	465.6	124.8	542	523.5	140.3
303	292.7	78.4	363	350.6	94.0	423	408.6	109.5	483	466.5	125.0	543	524.5	140.5
304	293.6	78.7	364	351.6	94.2	424	409.6	109.7	484	467.5	125.3	544	525.5	140.8
305	294.6	78.9	365	352.6	94.5	425	410.5	110.0	485	468.5	125.5	545	526.4	141.1
306	295.6	79.2	366	353.5	94.7	426	411.5	110.3	486	469.4	125.8	546	527.4	141.3
307	296.5	79.5	367	354.5	95.0	427	412.5	110.5	487	470.4	126.0	547	528.4	141.6
308	297.5	79.7	368	355.5	95.2	428	413.4	110.8	488	471.4	126.3	548	529.3	141.8
309	298.5	80.0	369	356.4	95.5	429	414.4	111.0	489	472.3	126.6	549	530.3	142.1
310	299.4	80.2	370	357.4	95.8	430	415.3	111.3	490	473.3	126.8	550	531.3	142.4
311	300.4	80.5	371	358.4	96.0	431	416.3	111.6	491	474.3	127.1	551	532.2	142.6
312	301.4	80.8	372	359.3	96.3	432	417.3	111.8	492	475.2	127.3	552	533.2	142.9
313	302.3	81.0	373	360.3	96.5	433	418.2	112.1	493	476.2	127.6	553	534.2	143.1
314	303.3	81.3	374	361.3	96.8	434	419.2	112.3	494	477.2	127.9	554	535.1	143.4
315	304.3	81.5	375	362.2	97.1	435	420.2	112.6	495	478.1	128.1	555	536.1	143.6
316	305.2	81.8	376	363.2	97.3	436	421.1	112.8	496	479.1	128.4	556	537.1	143.9
317	306.2	82.0	377	364.2	97.6	437	422.1	113.1	497	480.1	128.6	557	538.0	144.2
318	307.2	82.3	378	365.1	97.8	438	423.1	113.4	498	481.0	128.9	558	539.0	144.4
319	308.1	82.6	379	366.1	98.1	439	424.0	113.6	499	482.0	129.2	559	540.0	144.7
320	309.1	82.8	380	367.1	98.4	440	425.0	113.9	500	483.0	129.4	560	540.9	144.9
321	310.1	83.1	381	368.0	98.6	441	426.0	114.1	501	483.9	129.7	561	541.9	145.2
322	311.0	83.3	382	369.0	98.9	442	426.9	114.4	502	484.9	129.9	562	542.9	145.5
323	312.0	83.6	383	369.9	99.1	443	427.9	114.7	503	485.9	130.2	563	543.8	145.7
324	313.0	83.9	384	370.9	99.4	444	428.9	114.9	504	486.8	130.4	564	544.8	146.0
325	313.9	84.1	385	371.9	99.6	445	429.8	115.2	505	487.8	130.7	565	545.7	146.2
326	314.9	84.4	386	372.8	99.9	446	430.8	115.4	506	488.8	131.0	566	546.7	146.5
327	315.9	84.6	387	373.8	100.2	447	431.8	115.7	507	489.7	131.2	567	547.7	146.8
328	316.8	84.9	388	374.8	100.4	448	432.7	116.0	508	490.7	131.5	568	548.6	147.0
329	317.8	85.2	389	375.7	100.7	449	433.7	116.2	509	491.7	131.7	569	549.6	147.3
330	318.8	85.4	390	376.7	100.9	450	434.7	116.5	510	492.6	132.0	570	550.6	147.5
331	319.7	85.7	391	377.7	101.2	451	435.6	116.7	511	493.6	132.3	571	551.5	147.8
332	320.7	85.9	392	378.6	101.5	452	436.6	117.0	512	494.6	132.5	572	552.5	148.0
333	321.7	86.2	393	379.6	101.7	453	437.6	117.2	513	495.5	132.8	573	553.5	148.3
334	322.6	86.4	394	380.6	102.0	454	438.5	117.5	514	496.5	133.0	574	554.4	148.6
335	323.6	86.7	395	381.5	102.2	455	439.5	117.8	515	497.5	133.3	575	555.4	148.8
336	324.6	87.0	396	382.5	102.5	456	440.5	118.0	516	498.4	133.6	576	556.4	149.1
337	325.5	87.2	397	383.5	102.8	457	441.4	118.3	517	499.4	133.8	577	557.3	149.3
338	326.5	87.5	398	384.4	103.0	458	442.4	118.5	518	500.3	134.1	578	558.3	149.6
339	327.4	87.7	399	385.4	103.3	459	443.4	118.8	519	501.3	134.3	579	559.3	149.8
340	328.4	88.0	400	386.4	103.5	460	444.3	119.1	520	502.3	134.6	580	560.2	150.1
341	329.4	88.3	401	387.3	103.8	461	445.3	119.3	521	503.2	134.8	581	561.2	150.4
342	330.3	88.5	402	388.3	104.0	462	446.3	119.6	522	504.2	135.1	582	562.2	150.6
343	331.3	88.8	403	389.3	104.3	463	447.2	119.8	523	505.2	135.4	583	563.1	150.9
344	332.3	89.0	404	390.2	104.6	464	448.2	120.1	524	506.1	135.6	584	564.1	151.2
345	333.2	89.3	405	391.2	104.8	465	449.2	120.4	525	507.1	135.9	585	565.1	151.4
346	334.2	89.6	406	392.2	105.1	466	450.1	120.6	526	508.1	136.1	586	566.0	151.6
347	335.2	89.8	407	393.1	105.3	467	451.1	120.9	527	509.0	136.4	587	567.0	151.9
348	336.1	90.1	408	394.1	105.6	468	452.1	121.1	528	510.0	136.7	588	568.0	152.2
349	337.1	90.3	409	395.1	105.9	469	453.0	121.4	529	511.0	136.9	589	568.9	152.4
350	338.1	90.6	410	396.0	106.1	470	454.0	121.6	530	511.9	137.2	590	569.9	152.7
351	339.0	90.8	411	397.0	106.4	471	455.0	121.9	531	512.9	137.4	591	570.9	153.0
352	340.0	91.1	412	398.0	106.6	472	455.9	122.2	532	513.9	137.7	592	571.8	153.2
353	341.0	91.4	413	398.9	106.9	473	456.9	122.4	533	514.8	138.0	593	572.8	153.5
354	341.9	91.6	414	399.9	107.2	474	457.8	122.7	534	515.8	138.2	594	573.8	153.7
355	342.9	91.9	415	400.9	107.4	475	458.8	122.9	535	516.8	138.5	595	574.7	154.0
356	343.9	92.1	416	401.8	107.7	476	459.8	123.2	536	517.7	138.7	596	575.7	154.3
357	344.8	92.4	417	402.8	107.9	477	460.7	123.5	537	518.7	139.0	597	576.7	154.5
358	345.8	92.7	418	403.8	108.2	478	461.7	123.7	538	519.7	139.2	598	577.6	154.8
359	346.8	92.9	419	404.7	108.4	479	462.7	124.0	539	520.6	139.5	599	578.6	155.0
360	347.7	93.2	420	405.7	108.7	480	463.6	124.2	540	521.6	139.8	600	579.6	155.3

Dist.	Dep.	D. Lat.	Dist.	Dep.	D. Lat.	Dist.	Dep.	D. Lat.	Dist.	Dep.	D. Lat.	Dist.	Dep.	D. Lat.

TRAVERSE TABLE
16 Degrees

16°

344° / 196°   016° / 164°   1h 04m

Dist.	D. Lat.	Dep.	Dist.	D. Lat.	Dep.	Dist.	D. Lat.	Dep.	Dist.	D. Lat.	Dep.	Dist.	D. Lat.	Dep.
1	01·0	00·3	61	58·6	16·8	121	116·3	33·4	181	174·0	49·9	241	231·7	66·4
2	01·9	00·6	62	59·6	17·1	122	117·3	33·6	182	174·9	50·2	242	232·6	66·7
3	02·9	00·8	63	60·6	17·4	123	118·2	33·9	183	175·9	50·4	243	233·6	67·0
4	03·8	01·1	64	61·5	17·6	124	119·2	34·2	184	176·9	50·7	244	234·5	67·3
5	04·8	01·4	65	62·5	17·9	125	120·2	34·5	185	177·8	51·0	245	235·5	67·5
6	05·8	01·7	66	63·4	18·2	126	121·1	34·7	186	178·8	51·3	246	236·5	67·8
7	06·7	01·9	67	64·4	18·5	127	122·1	35·0	187	179·8	51·5	247	237·4	68·1
8	07·7	02·2	68	65·4	18·7	128	123·0	35·3	188	180·7	51·8	248	238·4	68·4
9	08·7	02·5	69	66·3	19·0	129	124·0	35·6	189	181·7	52·1	249	239·4	68·6
10	09·6	02·8	70	67·3	19·3	130	125·0	35·8	190	182·6	52·4	250	240·3	68·9
11	10·6	03·0	71	68·2	19·6	131	125·9	36·1	191	183·6	52·6	251	241·3	69·2
12	11·5	03·3	72	69·2	19·8	132	126·9	36·4	192	184·6	52·9	252	242·2	69·5
13	12·5	03·6	73	70·2	20·1	133	127·8	36·7	193	185·5	53·2	253	243·2	69·7
14	13·5	03·9	74	71·1	20·4	134	128·8	36·9	194	186·5	53·5	254	244·2	70·0
15	14·4	04·1	75	72·1	20·7	135	129·8	37·2	195	187·4	53·7	255	245·1	70·3
16	15·4	04·4	76	73·1	20·9	136	130·7	37·5	196	188·4	54·0	256	246·1	70·6
17	16·3	04·7	77	74·0	21·2	137	131·7	37·8	197	189·4	54·3	257	247·0	70·8
18	17·3	05·0	78	75·0	21·5	138	132·7	38·0	198	190·3	54·6	258	248·0	71·1
19	18·3	05·2	79	75·9	21·8	139	133·6	38·3	199	191·3	54·9	259	249·0	71·4
20	19·2	05·5	80	76·9	22·1	140	134·6	38·6	200	192·3	55·1	260	249·9	71·7
21	20·2	05·8	81	77·9	22·3	141	135·5	38·9	201	193·2	55·4	261	250·9	71·9
22	21·1	06·1	82	78·8	22·6	142	136·5	39·1	202	194·2	55·7	262	251·9	72·2
23	22·1	06·3	83	79·8	22·9	143	137·5	39·4	203	195·1	56·0	263	252·8	72·5
24	23·1	06·6	84	80·7	23·2	144	138·4	39·7	204	196·1	56·2	264	253·8	72·8
25	24·0	06·9	85	81·7	23·4	145	139·4	40·0	205	197·1	56·5	265	254·7	73·0
26	25·0	07·2	86	82·7	23·7	146	140·3	40·2	206	198·0	56·8	266	255·7	73·3
27	26·0	07·4	87	83·6	24·0	147	141·3	40·5	207	199·0	57·1	267	256·7	73·6
28	26·9	07·7	88	84·6	24·3	148	142·3	40·8	208	199·9	57·3	268	257·6	73·9
29	27·9	08·0	89	85·6	24·5	149	143·2	41·1	209	200·9	57·6	269	258·6	74·1
30	28·8	08·3	90	86·5	24·8	150	144·2	41·3	210	201·9	57·9	270	259·5	74·4
31	29·8	08·5	91	87·5	25·1	151	145·2	41·6	211	202·8	58·2	271	260·5	74·7
32	30·8	08·8	92	88·4	25·4	152	146·1	41·9	212	203·8	58·4	272	261·5	75·0
33	31·7	09·1	93	89·4	25·6	153	147·1	42·2	213	204·7	58·7	273	262·4	75·2
34	32·7	09·4	94	90·4	25·9	154	148·0	42·4	214	205·7	59·0	274	263·4	75·5
35	33·6	09·6	95	91·3	26·2	155	149·0	42·7	215	206·7	59·3	275	264·3	75·8
36	34·6	09·9	96	92·3	26·5	156	150·0	43·0	216	207·6	59·5	276	265·3	76·1
37	35·6	10·2	97	93·2	26·7	157	150·9	43·3	217	208·6	59·8	277	266·3	76·4
38	36·5	10·5	98	94·2	27·0	158	151·9	43·5	218	209·6	60·1	278	267·2	76·6
39	37·5	10·7	99	95·2	27·3	159	152·8	43·8	219	210·5	60·4	279	268·2	76·9
40	38·5	11·0	100	96·1	27·6	160	153·8	44·1	220	211·5	60·6	280	269·2	77·2
41	39·4	11·3	101	97·1	27·8	161	154·8	44·4	221	212·4	60·9	281	270·1	77·5
42	40·4	11·6	102	98·0	28·1	162	155·7	44·7	222	213·4	61·2	282	271·1	77·7
43	41·3	11·9	103	99·0	28·4	163	156·7	44·9	223	214·4	61·5	283	272·0	78·0
44	42·3	12·1	104	100·0	28·7	164	157·6	45·2	224	215·3	61·7	284	273·0	78·3
45	43·3	12·4	105	100·9	28·9	165	158·6	45·5	225	216·3	62·0	285	274·0	78·6
46	44·2	12·7	106	101·9	29·2	166	159·6	45·8	226	217·2	62·3	286	274·9	78·8
47	45·2	13·0	107	102·9	29·5	167	160·5	46·0	227	218·2	62·6	287	275·9	79·1
48	46·1	13·2	108	103·8	29·8	168	161·5	46·3	228	219·2	62·8	288	276·8	79·4
49	47·1	13·5	109	104·8	30·0	169	162·5	46·6	229	220·1	63·1	289	277·8	79·7
50	48·1	13·8	110	105·7	30·3	170	163·4	46·9	230	221·1	63·4	290	278·8	79·9
51	49·0	14·1	111	106·7	30·6	171	164·4	47·1	231	222·1	63·7	291	279·7	80·2
52	50·0	14·3	112	107·7	30·9	172	165·3	47·4	232	223·0	63·9	292	280·7	80·5
53	50·9	14·6	113	108·6	31·1	173	166·3	47·7	233	224·0	64·2	293	281·6	80·8
54	51·9	14·9	114	109·6	31·4	174	167·3	48·0	234	224·9	64·5	294	282·6	81·0
55	52·9	15·2	115	110·5	31·7	175	168·2	48·2	235	225·9	64·8	295	283·6	81·3
56	53·8	15·4	116	111·5	32·0	176	169·2	48·5	236	226·9	65·1	296	284·5	81·6
57	54·8	15·7	117	112·5	32·2	177	170·1	48·8	237	227·8	65·3	297	285·5	81·9
58	55·8	16·0	118	113·4	32·5	178	171·1	49·1	238	228·8	65·6	298	286·5	82·1
59	56·7	16·3	119	114·4	32·8	179	172·1	49·3	239	229·7	65·9	299	287·4	82·4
60	57·7	16·5	120	115·4	33·1	180	173·0	49·6	240	230·7	66·2	300	288·4	82·7

| Dist. | Dep. | D. Lat. | Dist. | Dep. | D. Lat. | Dist. | Dep. | D. Lat. | Dist. | Dep. | D. Lat. | Dist. | Dep. | D. Lat. |

74°

286° / 254°   74 Degrees   074° / 106°   4h 56m

TRAVERSE TABLE
16 Degrees

16°

Dist.	D. Lat.	Dep.	Dist.	D. Lat.	Dep.	Dist.	D. Lat.	Dep.	Dist.	D. Lat.	Dep.	Dist.	D. Lat.	Dep.
301	289·3	83·0	361	347·0	99·5	421	404·7	116·0	481	462·4	132·6	541	520·0	149·1
302	290·3	83·2	362	348·0	99·8	422	405·7	116·3	482	463·3	132·9	542	521·0	149·4
303	291·3	83·5	363	348·9	100·1	423	406·6	116·6	483	464·3	133·1	543	522·0	149·7
304	292·2	83·8	364	349·9	100·3	424	407·6	116·9	484	465·3	133·4	544	522·9	149·9
305	293·2	84·1	365	350·9	100·6	425	408·5	117·0	485	466·2	133·7	545	523·9	150·2
306	294·1	84·3	366	351·8	100·9	426	409·5	117·4	486	467·2	134·0	546	524·8	150·5
307	295·1	84·6	367	352·8	101·2	427	410·5	117·7	487	468·1	134·2	547	525·8	150·8
308	296·1	84·9	368	353·7	101·4	428	411·4	118·0	488	469·1	134·5	548	526·8	151·0
309	297·0	85·2	369	354·7	101·7	429	412·4	118·2	489	470·1	134·8	549	527·7	151·3
310	298·0	85·4	370	355·7	102·0	430	413·3	118·5	490	471·0	135·1	550	528·7	151·6
311	299·0	85·7	371	356·6	102·3	431	414·3	118·8	491	472·0	135·3	551	529·7	151·9
312	299·9	86·0	372	357·6	102·5	432	415·3	119·1	492	472·9	135·6	552	530·6	152·2
313	300·9	86·3	373	358·6	102·8	433	416·2	119·4	493	473·9	135·9	553	531·6	152·4
314	301·8	86·6	374	359·5	103·1	434	417·2	119·6	494	474·9	136·2	554	532·5	152·7
315	302·8	86·9	375	360·5	103·4	435	418·1	119·9	495	475·8	136·4	555	533·5	153·0
316	303·8	87·1	376	361·4	103·6	436	419·1	120·2	496	476·8	136·7	556	534·5	153·3
317	304·7	87·4	377	362·4	103·9	437	420·1	120·5	497	477·7	137·0	557	535·4	153·5
318	305·7	87·7	378	363·4	104·2	438	421·0	120·7	498	478·7	137·3	558	536·4	153·8
319	306·6	87·9	379	364·3	104·5	439	422·0	121·0	499	479·7	137·5	559	537·3	154·1
320	307·6	88·2	380	365·3	104·7	440	423·0	121·3	500	480·6	137·8	560	538·3	154·4
321	308·6	88·5	381	366·2	105·0	441	423·9	121·6	501	481·6	138·1	561	539·3	154·6
322	309·5	88·8	382	367·2	105·3	442	424·9	121·8	502	482·6	138·4	562	540·2	154·9
323	310·5	89·0	383	368·2	105·6	443	425·8	122·1	503	483·5	138·6	563	541·2	155·2
324	311·4	89·3	384	369·1	105·8	444	426·8	122·4	504	484·5	138·9	564	542·2	155·5
325	312·4	89·6	385	370·1	106·1	445	427·8	122·7	505	485·4	139·2	565	543·1	155·7
326	313·4	89·9	386	371·0	106·4	446	428·7	122·9	506	486·4	139·5	566	544·1	156·0
327	314·3	90·1	387	372·0	106·7	447	429·7	123·2	507	487·4	139·7	567	545·0	156·3
328	315·3	90·4	388	373·0	106·9	448	430·6	123·5	508	488·3	140·0	568	546·0	156·6
329	316·3	90·7	389	373·9	107·2	449	431·6	123·8	509	489·3	140·3	569	547·0	156·8
330	317·2	91·0	390	374·9	107·5	450	432·6	124·0	510	490·2	140·6	570	547·9	157·1
331	318·2	91·2	391	375·9	107·8	451	433·5	124·3	511	491·2	140·9	571	548·9	157·4
332	319·1	91·5	392	376·8	108·0	452	434·5	124·6	512	492·2	141·1	572	549·8	157·7
333	320·1	91·8	393	377·8	108·3	453	435·5	124·9	513	493·1	141·4	573	550·8	157·9
334	321·1	92·1	394	378·7	108·6	454	436·4	125·1	514	494·1	141·7	574	551·8	158·2
335	322·0	92·3	395	379·7	108·9	455	437·4	125·4	515	495·0	142·0	575	552·7	158·5
336	323·0	92·6	396	380·7	109·2	456	438·3	125·7	516	496·0	142·2	576	553·7	158·8
337	323·9	92·9	397	381·6	109·4	457	439·3	126·0	517	497·0	142·5	577	554·6	159·0
338	324·9	93·2	398	382·6	109·7	458	440·3	126·2	518	497·9	142·8	578	555·6	159·3
339	325·8	93·4	399	383·5	110·0	459	441·2	126·5	519	498·9	143·1	579	556·6	159·6
340	326·8	93·7	400	384·5	110·3	460	442·2	126·8	520	499·9	143·3	580	557·5	159·9
341	327·8	94·0	401	385·5	110·5	461	443·1	127·1	521	500·8	143·6	581	558·5	160·1
342	328·8	94·3	402	386·4	110·8	462	444·1	127·3	522	501·8	143·9	582	559·5	160·4
343	329·7	94·5	403	387·4	111·1	463	445·1	127·6	523	502·7	144·2	583	560·4	160·6
344	330·7	94·8	404	388·3	111·4	464	446·0	127·9	524	503·7	144·4	584	561·4	161·0
345	331·6	95·1	405	389·3	111·6	465	447·0	128·2	525	504·7	144·7	585	562·3	161·2
346	332·6	95·4	406	390·3	111·9	466	447·9	128·4	526	505·6	145·0	586	563·3	161·5
347	333·6	95·6	407	391·2	112·2	467	448·9	128·7	527	506·6	145·3	587	564·3	161·8
348	334·5	95·9	408	392·2	112·5	468	449·9	129·0	528	507·5	145·5	588	565·2	162·1
349	335·5	96·2	409	393·2	112·7	469	450·8	129·3	529	508·5	145·8	589	566·2	162·4
350	336·4	96·5	410	394·1	113·0	470	451·8	129·5	530	509·5	146·1	590	567·1	162·6
351	337·4	96·7	411	395·1	113·3	471	452·8	129·8	531	510·4	146·4	591	568·1	162·9
352	338·4	97·0	412	396·0	113·6	472	453·7	130·1	532	511·4	146·6	592	569·1	163·2
353	339·3	97·3	413	397·0	113·8	473	454·7	130·4	533	512·4	146·9	593	570·0	163·5
354	340·3	97·6	414	398·0	114·1	474	455·6	130·7	534	513·3	147·2	594	571·0	163·7
355	341·2	97·9	415	398·9	114·4	475	456·6	130·9	535	514·3	147·5	595	572·0	164·0
356	342·2	98·1	416	399·9	114·7	476	457·6	131·2	536	515·2	147·7	596	572·9	164·3
357	343·2	98·4	417	400·8	114·9	477	458·5	131·5	537	516·2	148·0	597	573·9	164·6
358	344·1	98·7	418	401·8	115·2	478	459·5	131·8	538	517·2	148·3	598	574·8	164·8
359	345·1	99·0	419	402·8	115·5	479	460·4	132·0	539	518·1	148·6	599	575·8	165·1
360	346·1	99·2	420	403·7	115·8	480	461·4	132·3	540	519·1	148·8	600	576·8	165·4

Dist.	Dep.	D. Lat.	Dist.	Dep.	D. Lat.	Dist.	Dep.	D. Lat.	Dist.	Dep.	D. Lat.	Dist.	Dep.	D. Lat.
D. Lon		Dep.	D. Lon		Dep.	D. Lon		Dep.	D. Lon		Dep.	D. Lon		Dep.

74°

TRAVERSE TABLE

17°

17 Degrees

1h 08m

Dist.	D. Lat.	Dep.	Dist.	D. Lat.	Dep.	Dist.	D. Lat.	Dep.	Dist.	D. Lat.	Dep.	Dist.	D. Lat.	Dep.
1	01·0	00·3	61	58·3	17·8	121	115·7	35·4	181	173·1	52·9	241	230·5	70·5
2	01·9	00·6	62	59·3	18·1	122	116·7	35·7	182	174·0	53·2	242	231·4	70·8
3	02·9	00·9	63	60·2	18·4	123	117·6	36·0	183	175·0	53·5	243	232·4	71·0
4	03·8	01·2	64	61·2	18·7	124	118·6	36·3	184	176·0	53·8	244	233·3	71·3
5	04·8	01·5	65	62·2	19·0	125	119·5	36·5	185	176·9	54·1	245	234·3	71·6
6	05·7	01·8	66	63·1	19·3	126	120·5	36·8	186	177·9	54·4	246	235·3	71·9
7	06·7	02·0	67	64·1	19·6	127	121·5	37·1	187	178·8	54·7	247	236·2	72·2
8	07·7	02·3	68	65·0	19·9	128	122·4	37·4	188	179·8	55·0	248	237·2	72·5
9	08·6	02·6	69	66·0	20·2	129	123·4	37·7	189	180·7	55·3	249	238·1	72·8
10	09·6	02·9	70	66·9	20·5	130	124·3	38·0	190	181·7	55·6	250	239·1	73·1
11	10·5	03·2	71	67·9	20·8	131	125·3	38·3	191	182·7	55·8	251	240·0	73·4
12	11·5	03·5	72	68·9	21·1	132	126·2	38·6	192	183·6	56·1	252	241·0	73·7
13	12·4	03·8	73	69·8	21·3	133	127·2	38·9	193	184·6	56·4	253	241·9	74·0
14	13·4	04·1	74	70·8	21·6	134	128·1	39·2	194	185·5	56·7	254	242·9	74·3
15	14·3	04·4	75	71·7	21·9	135	129·1	39·5	195	186·5	57·0	255	243·9	74·6
16	15·3	04·7	76	72·7	22·2	136	130·1	39·8	196	187·4	57·3	256	244·8	74·8
17	16·3	05·0	77	73·6	22·5	137	131·0	40·1	197	188·4	57·6	257	245·8	75·1
18	17·2	05·3	78	74·6	22·8	138	132·0	40·3	198	189·3	57·9	258	246·7	75·4
19	18·2	05·6	79	75·5	23·1	139	132·9	40·6	199	190·3	58·2	259	247·7	75·7
20	19·1	05·8	80	76·5	23·3	140	133·9	40·9	200	191·3	58·5	260	248·6	76·0
21	20·1	06·1	81	77·5	23·7	141	134·8	41·2	201	192·2	58·8	261	249·6	76·3
22	21·0	06·4	82	78·4	24·0	142	135·8	41·5	202	193·2	59·1	262	250·6	76·6
23	22·0	06·7	83	79·4	24·3	143	136·8	41·8	203	194·1	59·4	263	251·5	76·9
24	23·0	07·0	84	80·3	24·6	144	137·7	42·1	204	195·1	59·6	264	252·5	77·2
25	23·9	07·3	85	81·3	24·9	145	138·7	42·4	205	196·0	59·9	265	253·4	77·5
26	24·9	07·6	86	82·2	25·1	146	139·6	42·7	206	197·0	60·2	266	254·4	77·8
27	25·8	07·9	87	83·2	25·4	147	140·6	43·0	207	198·0	60·5	267	255·3	78·1
28	26·8	08·2	88	84·2	25·7	148	141·5	43·3	208	198·9	60·8	268	256·3	78·4
29	27·7	08·5	89	85·1	26·0	149	142·5	43·6	209	199·9	61·1	269	257·2	78·6
30	28·7	08·8	90	86·1	26·3	150	143·4	43·9	210	200·8	61·4	270	258·2	78·9
31	29·6	09·1	91	87·0	26·6	151	144·4	44·1	211	201·8	61·7	271	259·2	79·2
32	30·6	09·4	92	88·0	26·9	152	145·4	44·4	212	202·7	62·0	272	260·1	79·5
33	31·6	09·6	93	88·9	27·2	153	146·3	44·7	213	203·7	62·3	273	261·1	79·8
34	32·5	09·9	94	89·9	27·5	154	147·3	45·0	214	204·6	62·6	274	262·0	80·1
35	33·5	10·2	95	90·8	27·8	155	148·2	45·3	215	205·6	62·9	275	263·0	80·4
36	34·4	10·5	96	91·8	28·1	156	149·2	45·6	216	206·6	63·2	276	263·9	80·7
37	35·4	10·8	97	92·8	28·4	157	150·1	45·9	217	207·5	63·4	277	264·9	81·0
38	36·3	11·1	98	93·7	28·7	158	151·1	46·2	218	208·5	63·7	278	265·9	81·3
39	37·3	11·4	99	94·7	28·9	159	152·1	46·5	219	209·4	64·0	279	266·8	81·6
40	38·3	11·7	100	95·6	29·2	160	153·0	46·8	220	210·4	64·3	280	267·8	81·9
41	39·2	12·0	101	96·6	29·5	161	154·0	47·1	221	211·3	64·6	281	268·7	82·2
42	40·2	12·3	102	97·5	29·8	162	154·9	47·4	222	212·3	64·9	282	269·7	82·4
43	41·1	12·6	103	98·5	30·1	163	155·9	47·7	223	213·3	65·2	283	270·6	82·7
44	42·1	12·9	104	99·5	30·4	164	156·8	47·9	224	214·2	65·5	284	271·6	83·0
45	43·0	13·2	105	100·4	30·7	165	157·8	48·2	225	215·2	65·8	285	272·5	83·3
46	44·0	13·4	106	101·4	31·0	166	158·7	48·5	226	216·1	66·1	286	273·5	83·6
47	44·9	13·7	107	102·3	31·3	167	159·7	48·8	227	217·1	66·4	287	274·5	83·9
48	45·9	14·0	108	103·3	31·6	168	160·7	49·1	228	218·0	66·7	288	275·4	84·2
49	46·9	14·3	109	104·2	31·9	169	161·6	49·4	229	219·0	67·0	289	276·4	84·5
50	47·8	14·6	110	105·2	32·2	170	162·6	49·7	230	220·0	67·2	290	277·3	84·8
51	48·8	14·9	111	106·1	32·5	171	163·5	50·0	231	220·9	67·5	291	278·3	85·1
52	49·7	15·2	112	107·1	32·7	172	164·5	50·3	232	221·9	67·8	292	279·2	85·4
53	50·7	15·5	113	108·1	33·0	173	165·4	50·6	233	222·8	68·1	293	280·2	85·7
54	51·6	15·8	114	109·0	33·3	174	166·4	50·9	234	223·8	68·4	294	281·2	86·0
55	52·6	16·1	115	110·0	33·6	175	167·4	51·2	235	224·7	68·7	295	282·1	86·2
56	53·6	16·4	116	110·9	33·9	176	168·3	51·5	236	225·7	69·0	296	283·1	86·5
57	54·5	16·7	117	111·9	34·2	177	169·3	51·7	237	226·6	69·3	297	284·0	86·8
58	55·5	17·0	118	112·8	34·5	178	170·2	52·0	238	227·6	69·6	298	285·0	87·1
59	56·4	17·2	119	113·8	34·8	179	171·2	52·3	239	228·6	69·9	299	285·9	87·4
60	57·4	17·5	120	114·8	35·1	180	172·1	52·6	240	229·5	70·2	300	286·9	87·7

| Dist. | Dep. | D. Lat. | Dist. | Dep. | D. Lat. | Dist. | Dep. | D. Lat. | Dist. | Dep. | D. Lat. | Dist. | Dep. | D. Lat. |

73°

73 Degrees

4h 52m

TRAVERSE TABLE
17 Degrees

D. Lon	Dep.		D. Lon	Dep.		D. Lon	Dep.		D. Lon	Dep.		D. Lon	Dep.	
Dist.	D. Lat.	Dep.	Dist.	D. Lat.	Dep.	Dist.	D. Lat.	Dep.	Dist.	D. Lat.	Dep.	Dist.	D. Lat.	Dep.
301	287·8	88·0	361	345·2	105·5	421	402·6	123·1	481	460·0	140·6	541	517·4	158·2
302	288·8	88·3	362	346·2	105·8	422	403·6	123·4	482	460·9	140·9	542	518·3	158·5
303	289·8	88·6	363	347·1	106·1	423	404·5	123·7	483	461·9	141·2	543	519·3	158·8
304	290·7	88·9	364	348·1	106·4	424	405·5	124·0	484	462·9	141·5	544	520·2	159·1
305	291·7	89·2	365	349·1	106·7	425	406·4	124·3	485	463·8	141·8	545	521·2	159·3
306	292·6	89·5	366	350·0	107·0	426	407·4	124·6	486	464·8	142·1	546	522·1	159·6
307	293·6	89·8	367	351·0	107·3	427	408·3	124·8	487	465·7	142·4	547	523·1	159·9
308	294·5	90·1	368	351·9	107·6	428	409·3	125·1	488	466·7	142·7	548	524·1	160·2
309	295·5	90·3	369	352·9	107·9	429	410·3	125·4	489	467·6	143·0	549	525·0	160·5
310	296·5	90·6	370	353·8	108·2	430	411·2	125·7	490	468·6	143·3	550	526·0	160·8
311	297·4	90·9	371	354·8	108·5	431	412·2	126·0	491	469·5	143·6	551	526·9	161·1
312	298·4	91·2	372	355·7	108·8	432	413·1	126·3	492	470·5	143·8	552	527·9	161·4
313	299·3	91·5	373	356·7	109·1	433	414·1	126·6	493	471·5	144·1	553	528·8	161·7
314	300·3	91·8	374	357·7	109·3	434	415·0	126·9	494	472·4	144·4	554	529·8	162·0
315	301·2	92·1	375	358·6	109·6	435	416·0	127·2	495	473·4	144·7	555	530·7	162·3
316	302·2	92·4	376	359·6	109·9	436	416·9	127·5	496	474·3	145·0	556	531·7	162·6
317	303·1	92·7	377	360·5	110·2	437	417·9	127·8	497	475·3	145·3	557	532·7	162·9
318	304·1	93·0	378	361·5	110·5	438	418·9	128·1	498	476·2	145·6	558	533·6	163·1
319	305·1	93·3	379	362·4	110·8	439	419·8	128·4	499	477·2	145·9	559	534·6	163·4
320	306·0	93·6	380	363·4	111·1	440	420·8	128·6	500	478·2	146·2	560	535·5	163·7
321	307·0	93·9	381	364·4	111·4	441	421·7	128·9	501	479·1	146·5	561	536·5	164·0
322	307·9	94·1	382	365·3	111·7	442	422·7	129·2	502	480·1	146·8	562	537·4	164·3
323	308·9	94·4	383	366·3	112·0	443	423·6	129·5	503	481·0	147·1	563	538·4	164·6
324	309·8	94·7	384	367·2	112·3	444	424·6	129·8	504	482·0	147·4	564	539·4	164·9
325	310·8	95·0	385	368·2	112·6	445	425·6	130·1	505	482·9	147·6	565	540·3	165·2
326	311·8	95·3	386	369·1	112·9	446	426·5	130·4	506	483·9	147·9	566	541·3	165·5
327	312·7	95·6	387	370·1	113·1	447	427·5	130·7	507	484·8	148·2	567	542·2	165·8
328	313·6	95·9	388	371·0	113·4	448	428·4	131·0	508	485·8	148·5	568	543·2	166·1
329	314·6	96·2	389	372·0	113·7	449	429·4	131·3	509	486·8	148·8	569	544·1	166·4
330	315·5	96·5	390	373·0	114·0	450	430·3	131·6	510	487·7	149·1	570	545·1	166·7
331	316·5	96·8	391	373·9	114·3	451	431·3	131·9	511	488·7	149·4	571	546·1	166·9
332	317·5	97·1	392	374·9	114·6	452	432·2	132·2	512	489·6	149·7	572	547·0	167·2
333	318·4	97·4	393	375·8	114·9	453	433·2	132·4	513	490·6	150·0	573	548·0	167·5
334	319·4	97·7	394	376·8	115·2	454	434·2	132·7	514	491·5	150·3	574	548·9	167·8
335	320·4	97·9	395	377·7	115·5	455	435·1	133·0	515	492·5	150·6	575	549·9	168·1
336	321·3	98·2	396	378·7	115·8	456	436·1	133·3	516	493·5	150·9	576	550·8	168·4
337	322·3	98·5	397	379·7	116·1	457	437·0	133·6	517	494·4	151·2	577	551·8	168·7
338	323·2	98·8	398	380·6	116·4	458	438·0	133·9	518	495·4	151·4	578	552·7	169·0
339	324·2	99·1	399	381·6	116·7	459	438·9	134·2	519	496·3	151·7	579	553·7	169·3
340	325·1	99·4	400	382·5	116·9	460	439·9	134·5	520	497·3	152·0	580	554·7	169·6
341	326·1	99·7	401	383·5	117·2	461	440·9	134·8	521	498·2	152·3	581	555·6	169·9
342	327·1	100·0	402	384·4	117·5	462	441·8	135·1	522	499·2	152·6	582	556·6	170·2
343	328·0	100·3	403	385·4	117·8	463	442·8	135·4	523	500·1	152·9	583	557·5	170·5
344	329·0	100·6	404	386·3	118·1	464	443·7	135·7	524	501·1	153·2	584	558·5	170·7
345	329·9	100·9	405	387·3	118·4	465	444·7	136·0	525	502·1	153·5	585	559·4	171·0
346	330·8	101·2	406	388·3	118·7	466	445·6	136·2	526	503·0	153·8	586	560·4	171·3
347	331·8	101·5	407	389·2	119·0	467	446·6	136·5	527	504·0	154·1	587	561·4	171·6
348	332·8	101·7	408	390·2	119·3	468	447·6	136·8	528	504·9	154·4	588	562·3	171·9
349	333·8	102·0	409	391·1	119·6	469	448·5	137·1	529	505·9	154·7	589	563·3	172·2
350	334·7	102·3	410	392·1	119·9	470	449·5	137·4	530	506·8	155·0	590	564·2	172·5
351	335·7	102·6	411	393·0	120·2	471	450·4	137·7	531	507·8	155·2	591	565·2	172·8
352	336·6	102·9	412	394·0	120·5	472	451·4	138·0	532	508·8	155·5	592	566·1	173·1
353	337·6	103·2	413	394·9	120·7	473	452·3	138·3	533	509·7	155·8	593	567·1	173·4
354	338·5	103·5	414	395·9	121·0	474	453·3	138·6	534	510·7	156·1	594	568·0	173·7
355	339·5	103·8	415	396·8	121·3	475	454·2	138·9	535	511·6	156·4	595	569·0	174·0
356	340·4	104·1	416	397·8	121·6	476	455·2	139·2	536	512·6	156·7	596	570·0	174·3
357	341·4	104·4	417	398·7	121·9	477	456·2	139·5	537	513·5	157·0	597	570·9	174·5
358	342·4	104·7	418	399·7	122·2	478	457·1	139·8	538	514·5	157·3	598	571·9	174·8
359	343·3	105·0	419	400·7	122·5	479	458·1	140·0	539	515·4	157·6	599	572·8	175·1
360	344·3	105·3	420	401·6	122·8	480	459·0	140·3	540	516·4	157·9	600	573·8	175·4
Dist.	Dep.	D. Lat.	Dist.	Dep.	D. Lat.	Dist.	Dep.	D. Lat.	Dist.	Dep.	D. Lat.	Dist.	Dep.	D. Lat.
D. Lon		Dep.	D. Lon		Dep.	D. Lon		Dep.	D. Lon		Dep.	D. Lon		Dep.

TRAVERSE TABLE
18 Degrees

18°

D. Lon	Dep.		D. Lon	Dep.		D. Lon	Dep.		D. Lon	Dep.		D. Lon	Dep.	
Dist.	D. Lat.	Dep.	Dist.	D. Lat.	Dep.	Dist.	D. Lat.	Dep.	Dist.	D. Lat.	Dep.	Dist.	D. Lat.	Dep.
1	01.0	00.3	61	58.0	18.9	121	115.1	37.4	181	172.1	55.9	241	229.2	74.5
2	01.9	00.6	62	59.0	19.2	122	116.0	37.7	182	173.1	56.2	242	230.2	74.8
3	02.9	00.9	63	59.9	19.5	123	117.0	38.0	183	174.0	56.6	243	231.1	75.1
4	03.8	01.2	64	60.9	19.8	124	117.9	38.3	184	175.0	56.9	244	232.1	75.4
5	04.8	01.5	65	61.8	20.1	125	118.9	38.6	185	175.9	57.2	245	233.0	75.7
6	05.7	01.9	66	62.8	20.4	126	119.8	38.9	186	176.9	57.5	246	234.0	76.0
7	06.7	02.2	67	63.7	20.7	127	120.8	39.2	187	177.8	57.8	247	234.9	76.3
8	07.6	02.5	68	64.7	21.0	128	121.7	39.6	188	178.8	58.1	248	235.9	76.6
9	08.6	02.8	69	65.6	21.3	129	122.7	39.9	189	179.7	58.4	249	236.8	76.9
10	09.5	03.1	70	66.6	21.6	130	123.6	40.2	190	180.7	58.7	250	237.8	77.3
11	10.5	03.4	71	67.5	21.9	131	124.6	40.5	191	181.7	59.0	251	238.7	77.6
12	11.4	03.7	72	68.5	22.2	132	125.5	40.8	192	182.6	59.3	252	239.7	77.9
13	12.4	04.0	73	69.4	22.6	133	126.5	41.1	193	183.6	59.6	253	240.6	78.2
14	13.3	04.3	74	70.4	22.9	134	127.4	41.4	194	184.5	59.9	254	241.6	78.5
15	14.3	04.6	75	71.3	23.2	135	128.4	41.7	195	185.5	60.3	255	242.5	78.8
16	15.2	04.9	76	72.3	23.5	136	129.3	42.0	196	186.4	60.6	256	243.5	79.1
17	16.2	05.3	77	73.2	23.8	137	130.3	42.3	197	187.4	60.9	257	244.4	79.4
18	17.1	05.6	78	74.2	24.1	138	131.2	42.6	198	188.3	61.2	258	245.4	79.7
19	18.1	05.9	79	75.1	24.4	139	132.2	43.0	199	189.3	61.5	259	246.3	80.0
20	19.0	06.2	80	76.1	24.7	140	133.1	43.3	200	190.2	61.8	260	247.3	80.3
21	20.0	06.5	81	77.0	25.0	141	134.1	43.6	201	191.2	62.1	261	248.2	80.7
22	20.9	06.8	82	78.0	25.3	142	135.1	43.9	202	192.1	62.4	262	249.2	81.0
23	21.9	07.1	83	78.9	25.6	143	136.0	44.2	203	193.1	62.7	263	250.1	81.3
24	22.8	07.4	84	79.9	26.0	144	137.0	44.5	204	194.0	63.0	264	251.1	81.6
25	23.8	07.7	85	80.8	26.3	145	137.9	44.8	205	195.0	63.3	265	252.0	81.9
26	24.7	08.0	86	81.8	26.6	146	138.9	45.1	206	195.9	63.7	266	253.0	82.2
27	25.7	08.3	87	82.7	26.9	147	139.8	45.4	207	196.9	64.0	267	253.9	82.5
28	26.6	08.7	88	83.7	27.2	148	140.8	45.7	208	197.8	64.3	268	254.9	82.8
29	27.6	09.0	89	84.6	27.5	149	141.7	46.0	209	198.8	64.6	269	255.8	83.1
30	28.5	09.3	90	85.6	27.8	150	142.7	46.4	210	199.7	64.9	270	256.8	83.4
31	29.5	09.6	91	86.5	28.1	151	143.6	46.7	211	200.7	65.2	271	257.7	83.7
32	30.4	09.9	92	87.5	28.4	152	144.6	47.0	212	201.6	65.5	272	258.7	84.1
33	31.4	10.2	93	88.4	28.7	153	145.5	47.3	213	202.6	65.8	273	259.6	84.4
34	32.3	10.5	94	89.4	29.0	154	146.5	47.6	214	203.5	66.1	274	260.6	84.7
35	33.3	10.8	95	90.4	29.4	155	147.4	47.9	215	204.5	66.4	275	261.5	85.0
36	34.2	11.1	96	91.3	29.7	156	148.4	48.2	216	205.4	66.7	276	262.5	85.3
37	35.2	11.4	97	92.3	30.0	157	149.3	48.5	217	206.4	67.1	277	263.4	85.6
38	36.1	11.7	98	93.2	30.3	158	150.3	48.8	218	207.3	67.4	278	264.4	85.9
39	37.1	12.1	99	94.2	30.6	159	151.2	49.1	219	208.3	67.7	279	265.3	86.2
40	38.0	12.4	100	95.1	30.9	160	152.2	49.4	220	209.2	68.0	280	266.3	86.5
41	39.0	12.7	101	96.1	31.2	161	153.1	49.8	221	210.2	68.3	281	267.2	86.8
42	39.9	13.0	102	97.0	31.5	162	154.1	50.1	222	211.1	68.6	282	268.2	87.1
43	40.9	13.3	103	98.0	31.8	163	155.0	50.4	223	212.1	68.9	283	269.1	87.5
44	41.8	13.6	104	98.9	32.1	164	156.0	50.7	224	213.0	69.2	284	270.1	87.8
45	42.8	13.9	105	99.9	32.4	165	156.9	51.0	225	214.0	69.5	285	271.1	88.1
46	43.7	14.2	106	100.8	32.8	166	157.9	51.3	226	214.9	69.8	286	272.0	88.4
47	44.7	14.5	107	101.8	33.1	167	158.8	51.6	227	215.9	70.1	287	273.0	88.7
48	45.7	14.8	108	102.7	33.4	168	159.8	51.9	228	216.8	70.5	288	273.9	89.0
49	46.6	15.1	109	103.7	33.7	169	160.7	52.2	229	217.8	70.8	289	274.9	89.3
50	47.6	15.5	110	104.6	34.0	170	161.7	52.5	230	218.7	71.1	290	275.8	89.6
51	48.5	15.8	111	105.6	34.3	171	162.6	52.8	231	219.7	71.4	291	276.8	89.9
52	49.5	16.1	112	106.5	34.6	172	163.6	53.2	232	220.6	71.7	292	277.7	90.2
53	50.4	16.4	113	107.5	34.9	173	164.5	53.5	233	221.6	72.0	293	278.7	90.5
54	51.4	16.7	114	108.4	35.2	174	165.5	53.8	234	222.5	72.3	294	279.6	90.9
55	52.3	17.0	115	109.4	35.5	175	166.4	54.1	235	223.5	72.6	295	280.6	91.2
56	53.3	17.3	116	110.3	35.8	176	167.4	54.4	236	224.4	72.9	296	281.5	91.5
57	54.2	17.6	117	111.3	36.2	177	168.3	54.7	237	225.4	73.2	297	282.5	91.8
58	55.2	17.9	118	112.2	36.5	178	169.3	55.0	238	226.4	73.5	298	283.4	92.1
59	56.1	18.2	119	113.2	36.8	179	170.2	55.3	239	227.3	73.9	299	284.4	92.4
60	57.1	18.5	120	114.1	37.1	180	171.2	55.6	240	228.3	74.2	300	285.3	92.7
Dist.	Dep.	D. Lat.	Dist.	Dep.	D. Lat.	Dist.	Dep.	D. Lat.	Dist.	Dep.	D. Lat.	Dist.	Dep.	D. Lat.
D. Lon		Dep.	D. Lon		Dep.	D. Lon		Dep.	D. Lon		Dep.	D. Lon		Dep.

72°

TRAVERSE TABLE
18 Degrees

D. Lon	Dep.		D. Lon	Dep.		D. Lon	Dep.		D. Lon	Dep.		D. Lon	Dep.	
Dist.	D. Lat.	Dep.	Dist.	D. Lat.	Dep.	Dist.	D. Lat.	Dep.	Dist.	D. Lat.	Dep.	Dist.	D. Lat.	Dep.
301	286.3	93.0	361	343.3	111.6	421	400.4	130.1	481	457.5	148.6	541	514.5	167.2
302	287.2	93.3	362	344.3	111.9	422	401.3	130.4	482	458.4	148.9	542	515.5	167.5
303	288.2	93.6	363	345.2	112.2	423	402.3	130.7	483	459.4	149.3	543	516.4	167.8
304	289.1	93.9	364	346.2	112.5	424	403.2	131.0	484	460.3	149.6	544	517.4	168.1
305	290.1	94.3	365	347.1	112.8	425	404.2	131.3	485	461.3	149.9	545	518.3	168.4
306	291.0	94.6	366	348.1	113.1	426	405.2	131.6	486	462.2	150.2	546	519.3	168.7
307	292.0	94.9	367	349.0	113.4	427	406.1	132.0	487	463.2	150.5	547	520.2	169.0
308	292.9	95.2	368	350.0	113.7	428	407.1	132.3	488	464.1	150.8	548	521.2	169.3
309	293.9	95.5	369	350.9	114.0	429	408.0	132.6	489	465.1	151.1	549	522.1	169.7
310	294.8	95.8	370	351.9	114.3	430	409.0	132.9	490	466.0	151.4	550	523.1	170.0
311	295.8	96.1	371	352.8	114.6	431	409.9	133.2	491	467.0	151.7	551	524.0	170.3
312	296.7	96.4	372	353.8	115.0	432	410.9	133.5	492	467.9	152.0	552	525.0	170.6
313	297.7	96.7	373	354.7	115.3	433	411.8	133.8	493	468.9	152.3	553	525.9	170.9
314	298.6	97.0	374	355.7	115.6	434	412.8	134.1	494	469.8	152.7	554	526.9	171.2
315	299.6	97.3	375	356.6	115.9	435	413.7	134.4	495	470.8	153.0	555	527.8	171.5
316	300.5	97.6	376	357.6	116.2	436	414.7	134.7	496	471.7	153.3	556	528.8	171.8
317	301.5	98.0	377	358.5	116.5	437	415.6	135.0	497	472.7	153.6	557	529.7	172.1
318	302.4	98.3	378	359.5	116.8	438	416.6	135.3	498	473.6	153.9	558	530.7	172.4
319	303.4	98.6	379	360.5	117.1	439	417.5	135.7	499	474.6	154.2	559	531.6	172.7
320	304.3	98.9	380	361.4	117.4	440	418.5	136.0	500	475.5	154.5	560	532.6	173.0
321	305.3	99.2	381	362.4	117.7	441	419.4	136.3	501	476.5	154.8	561	533.5	173.4
322	306.2	99.5	382	363.3	118.0	442	420.4	136.6	502	477.4	155.1	562	534.5	173.7
323	307.2	99.8	383	364.3	118.4	443	421.3	136.9	503	478.4	155.4	563	535.4	174.0
324	308.2	100.1	384	365.2	118.7	444	422.3	137.2	504	479.3	155.7	564	536.4	174.3
325	309.1	100.4	385	366.2	119.0	445	423.2	137.5	505	480.3	156.1	565	537.3	174.6
326	310.0	100.7	386	367.1	119.3	446	424.2	137.8	506	481.2	156.4	566	538.3	174.9
327	311.0	101.0	387	368.1	119.6	447	425.1	138.1	507	482.2	156.7	567	539.2	175.2
328	311.9	101.4	388	369.0	119.9	448	426.1	138.4	508	483.1	157.0	568	540.2	175.5
329	312.9	101.7	389	370.0	120.2	449	427.0	138.7	509	484.1	157.3	569	541.2	175.8
330	313.8	102.0	390	370.9	120.5	450	428.0	139.1	510	485.0	157.6	570	542.1	176.1
331	314.8	102.3	391	371.9	120.8	451	428.9	139.4	511	486.0	157.9	571	543.1	176.4
332	315.8	102.6	392	372.8	121.1	452	429.9	139.7	512	486.9	158.2	572	544.0	176.8
333	316.7	102.9	393	373.8	121.4	453	430.8	140.0	513	487.9	158.5	573	545.0	177.1
334	317.7	103.2	394	374.7	121.8	454	431.8	140.3	514	488.8	158.8	574	545.9	177.4
335	318.6	103.5	395	375.7	122.1	455	432.7	140.6	515	489.8	159.1	575	546.9	177.7
336	319.6	103.8	396	376.6	122.4	456	433.7	140.9	516	490.7	159.5	576	547.8	178.0
337	320.5	104.1	397	377.6	122.7	457	434.6	141.2	517	491.7	159.8	577	548.8	178.3
338	321.5	104.4	398	378.5	123.0	458	435.6	141.5	518	492.6	160.1	578	549.7	178.6
339	322.4	104.8	399	379.5	123.3	459	436.5	141.8	519	493.6	160.4	579	550.7	178.9
340	323.4	105.1	400	380.4	123.6	460	437.5	142.1	520	494.5	160.7	580	551.6	179.2
341	324.3	105.4	401	381.4	123.9	461	438.4	142.5	521	495.5	161.0	581	552.6	179.5
342	325.3	105.7	402	382.3	124.2	462	439.4	142.8	522	496.5	161.3	582	553.5	179.8
343	326.2	106.0	403	383.3	124.5	463	440.3	143.1	523	497.4	161.6	583	554.5	180.2
344	327.2	106.3	404	384.2	124.8	464	441.3	143.4	524	498.4	161.9	584	555.4	180.5
345	328.1	106.6	405	385.2	125.2	465	442.2	143.7	525	499.3	162.2	585	556.4	180.8
346	329.1	106.9	406	386.1	125.5	466	443.2	144.0	526	500.3	162.5	586	557.3	181.1
347	330.0	107.2	407	387.1	125.8	467	444.1	144.3	527	501.2	162.9	587	558.3	181.4
348	331.0	107.5	408	388.0	126.1	468	445.1	144.6	528	502.2	163.2	588	559.2	181.7
349	331.9	107.8	409	389.0	126.4	469	446.0	144.9	529	503.1	163.5	589	560.2	182.0
350	332.9	108.2	410	389.9	126.7	470	447.0	145.2	530	504.1	163.8	590	561.1	182.3
351	333.8	108.5	411	390.9	127.0	471	447.9	145.5	531	505.0	164.1	591	562.1	182.6
352	334.8	108.8	412	391.8	127.3	472	448.9	145.9	532	506.0	164.4	592	563.0	182.9
353	335.7	109.1	413	392.8	127.6	473	449.8	146.2	533	506.9	164.7	593	564.0	183.2
354	336.7	109.4	414	393.7	127.9	474	450.8	146.5	534	507.9	165.0	594	564.9	183.6
355	337.6	109.7	415	394.7	128.2	475	451.8	146.8	535	508.8	165.3	595	565.9	183.9
356	338.6	110.0	416	395.6	128.6	476	452.7	147.1	536	509.8	165.6	596	566.8	184.2
357	339.5	110.3	417	396.6	128.9	477	453.7	147.4	537	510.7	165.9	597	567.8	184.5
358	340.5	110.6	418	397.5	129.2	478	454.6	147.7	538	511.7	166.3	598	568.7	184.8
359	341.4	110.9	419	398.5	129.5	479	455.6	148.0	539	512.6	166.6	599	569.7	185.1
360	342.4	111.2	420	399.4	129.8	480	456.5	148.3	540	513.6	166.9	600	570.6	185.4
Dist.	Dep.	D. Lat.	Dist.	Dep.	D. Lat.	Dist.	Dep.	D. Lat.	Dist.	Dep.	D. Lat.	Dist.	Dep.	D. Lat.
D. Lon		Dep.	D. Lon		Dep.	D. Lon		Dep.	D. Lon		Dep.	D. Lon		Dep.

TRAVERSE TABLE
19 Degrees

19°   341°/199°   019°/161°   1h 16m

Dist.	D. Lat.	Dep.	Dist.	D. Lat.	Dep.	Dist.	D. Lat.	Dep.	Dist.	D. Lat.	Dep.	Dist.	D. Lat.	Dep.
1	00.9	00.3	61	57.7	19.9	121	114.4	39.4	181	171.1	58.9	241	227.9	78.5
2	01.9	00.7	62	58.6	20.2	122	115.4	39.7	182	172.1	59.3	242	228.8	78.8
3	02.8	01.0	63	59.6	20.5	123	116.3	40.0	183	173.0	59.6	243	229.8	79.1
4	03.8	01.3	64	60.5	20.8	124	117.2	40.4	184	174.0	59.9	244	230.7	79.4
5	04.7	01.6	65	61.5	21.2	125	118.2	40.7	185	174.9	60.2	245	231.7	79.8
6	05.7	02.0	66	62.4	21.5	126	119.1	41.0	186	175.9	60.6	246	232.6	80.1
7	06.6	02.3	67	63.3	21.8	127	120.1	41.3	187	176.8	60.9	247	233.5	80.4
8	07.6	02.6	68	64.3	22.1	128	121.0	41.7	188	177.8	61.2	248	234.5	80.7
9	08.5	02.9	69	65.2	22.5	129	122.0	42.0	189	178.7	61.5	249	235.4	81.1
10	09.5	03.3	70	66.2	22.8	130	122.9	42.3	190	179.6	61.9	250	236.4	81.4
11	10.4	03.6	71	67.1	23.1	131	123.9	42.6	191	180.6	62.2	251	237.3	81.7
12	11.3	03.9	72	68.1	23.4	132	124.8	43.0	192	181.5	62.5	252	238.3	82.0
13	12.3	04.2	73	69.0	23.8	133	125.8	43.3	193	182.5	62.8	253	239.2	82.4
14	13.2	04.6	74	70.0	24.1	134	126.7	43.6	194	183.4	63.2	254	240.2	82.7
15	14.2	04.9	75	70.9	24.4	135	127.6	44.0	195	184.4	63.5	255	241.1	83.0
16	15.1	05.2	76	71.9	24.7	136	128.6	44.3	196	185.3	63.8	256	242.1	83.3
17	16.1	05.5	77	72.8	25.1	137	129.5	44.6	197	186.3	64.1	257	243.0	83.7
18	17.0	05.9	78	73.8	25.4	138	130.5	44.9	198	187.2	64.5	258	243.9	84.0
19	18.0	06.2	79	74.7	25.7	139	131.4	45.3	199	188.2	64.8	259	244.9	84.3
20	18.9	06.5	80	75.6	26.0	140	132.4	45.6	200	189.1	65.1	260	245.8	84.6
21	19.9	06.8	81	76.6	26.4	141	133.3	45.9	201	190.0	65.4	261	246.8	85.0
22	20.8	07.2	82	77.5	26.7	142	134.3	46.2	202	191.0	65.8	262	247.7	85.3
23	21.7	07.5	83	78.5	27.0	143	135.2	46.6	203	191.9	66.1	263	248.7	85.6
24	22.7	07.8	84	79.4	27.3	144	136.2	46.9	204	192.9	66.4	264	249.6	86.0
25	23.6	08.1	85	80.4	27.7	145	137.1	47.2	205	193.8	66.7	265	250.6	86.3
26	24.6	08.5	86	81.3	28.0	146	138.0	47.5	206	194.8	67.1	266	251.5	86.6
27	25.5	08.8	87	82.3	28.3	147	139.0	47.9	207	195.7	67.4	267	252.5	86.9
28	26.5	09.1	88	83.2	28.7	148	139.9	48.2	208	196.7	67.7	268	253.4	87.3
29	27.4	09.4	89	84.2	29.0	149	140.9	48.5	209	197.6	68.0	269	254.3	87.6
30	28.4	09.8	90	85.1	29.3	150	141.8	48.8	210	198.6	68.4	270	255.3	87.9
31	29.3	10.1	91	86.0	29.6	151	142.8	49.2	211	199.5	68.7	271	256.2	88.2
32	30.3	10.4	92	87.0	30.0	152	143.7	49.5	212	200.4	69.0	272	257.2	88.6
33	31.2	10.7	93	87.9	30.3	153	144.7	49.8	213	201.4	69.3	273	258.1	88.9
34	32.1	11.1	94	88.9	30.6	154	145.6	50.1	214	202.3	69.7	274	259.1	89.2
35	33.1	11.4	95	89.8	30.9	155	146.6	50.5	215	203.3	70.0	275	260.0	89.5
36	34.0	11.7	96	90.8	31.3	156	147.5	50.8	216	204.2	70.3	276	261.0	89.9
37	35.0	12.0	97	91.7	31.6	157	148.4	51.1	217	205.2	70.6	277	261.9	90.2
38	35.9	12.4	98	92.7	31.9	158	149.4	51.4	218	206.1	71.0	278	262.9	90.5
39	36.9	12.7	99	93.6	32.2	159	150.3	51.8	219	207.1	71.3	279	263.8	90.8
40	37.8	13.0	100	94.6	32.6	160	151.3	52.1	220	208.0	71.6	280	264.7	91.2
41	38.8	13.3	101	95.5	32.9	161	152.2	52.4	221	209.0	72.0	281	265.7	91.5
42	39.7	13.7	102	96.4	33.2	162	153.2	52.7	222	209.9	72.3	282	266.6	91.8
43	40.7	14.0	103	97.4	33.5	163	154.1	53.1	223	210.9	72.6	283	267.6	92.1
44	41.6	14.3	104	98.3	33.9	164	155.1	53.4	224	211.8	72.9	284	268.5	92.5
45	42.5	14.7	105	99.3	34.2	165	156.0	53.7	225	212.7	73.3	285	269.5	92.8
46	43.5	15.0	106	100.2	34.5	166	157.0	54.0	226	213.7	73.6	286	270.4	93.1
47	44.4	15.3	107	101.2	34.8	167	157.9	54.4	227	214.6	73.9	287	271.4	93.4
48	45.4	15.6	108	102.1	35.2	168	158.8	54.7	228	215.6	74.2	288	272.3	93.8
49	46.3	16.0	109	103.1	35.5	169	159.8	55.0	229	216.5	74.6	289	273.3	94.1
50	47.3	16.3	110	104.0	35.8	170	160.7	55.3	230	217.5	74.9	290	274.2	94.4
51	48.2	16.6	111	105.0	36.1	171	161.7	55.7	231	218.4	75.2	291	275.1	94.7
52	49.2	16.9	112	105.9	36.5	172	162.6	56.0	232	219.4	75.5	292	276.1	95.1
53	50.1	17.3	113	106.8	36.8	173	163.6	56.3	233	220.3	75.9	293	277.0	95.4
54	51.1	17.6	114	107.8	37.1	174	164.5	56.6	234	221.3	76.2	294	278.0	95.7
55	52.0	17.9	115	108.7	37.4	175	165.5	57.0	235	222.2	76.5	295	278.9	96.0
56	52.9	18.2	116	109.7	37.8	176	166.4	57.3	236	223.1	76.8	296	279.9	96.4
57	53.9	18.6	117	110.6	38.1	177	167.4	57.6	237	224.1	77.2	297	280.8	96.7
58	54.8	18.9	118	111.6	38.4	178	168.3	58.0	238	225.0	77.5	298	281.8	97.0
59	55.8	19.2	119	112.5	38.7	179	169.2	58.3	239	226.0	77.8	299	282.7	97.3
60	56.7	19.5	120	113.5	39.1	180	170.2	58.6	240	226.9	78.1	300	283.7	97.7

Dist.	Dep.	D. Lat.	Dist.	Dep.	D. Lat.	Dist.	Dep.	D. Lat.	Dist.	Dep.	D. Lat.	Dist.	Dep.	D. Lat.

71°   289°/251°   71 Degrees   071°/109°   4h 44m

TRAVERSE TABLE
19 Degrees

19°

D. Lon	Dep.		D. Lon	Dep.		D. Lon	Dep.		D. Lon	Dep.		D. Lon	Dep.	
Dist.	D. Lat.	Dep.	Dist.	D. Lat.	Dep.	Dist.	D. Lat.	Dep.	Dist.	D. Lat.	Dep.	Dist.	D. Lat.	Dep.
301	284·6	98·0	361	341·3	117·5	421	398·1	137·1	481	454·8	156·6	541	511·5	176·1
302	285·5	98·3	362	342·3	117·9	422	399·0	137·4	482	455·7	156·9	542	512·5	176·5
303	286·5	98·6	363	343·2	118·2	423	400·0	137·7	483	456·7	157·2	543	513·4	176·8
304	287·4	99·0	364	344·2	118·5	424	400·9	138·0	484	457·6	157·6	544	514·4	177·1
305	288·4	99·3	365	345·1	118·8	425	401·8	138·4	485	458·6	157·9	545	515·3	177·4
306	289·3	99·6	366	346·1	119·2	426	402·8	138·7	486	459·5	158·2	546	516·3	177·8
307	290·3	99·9	367	347·0	119·5	427	403·7	139·0	487	460·5	158·6	547	517·2	178·1
308	291·2	100·3	368	348·0	119·8	428	404·7	139·3	488	461·4	158·9	548	518·1	178·4
309	292·2	100·6	369	348·9	120·1	429	405·6	139·7	489	462·4	159·2	549	519·1	178·7
310	293·1	100·9	370	349·8	120·5	430	406·6	140·0	490	463·3	159·5	550	520·0	179·1
311	294·1	101·3	371	350·8	120·8	431	407·5	140·3	491	464·2	159·9	551	521·0	179·4
312	295·0	101·6	372	351·7	121·1	432	408·5	140·6	492	465·2	160·2	552	521·9	179·7
313	295·9	101·9	373	352·7	121·4	433	409·4	141·0	493	466·1	160·5	553	522·9	180·0
314	296·9	102·2	374	353·6	121·8	434	410·4	141·3	494	467·1	160·8	554	523·8	180·4
315	297·8	102·6	375	354·6	122·1	435	411·3	141·6	495	468·0	161·2	555	524·8	180·7
316	298·8	102·9	376	355·5	122·4	436	412·2	141·9	496	469·0	161·5	556	525·7	181·0
317	299·7	103·2	377	356·5	122·7	437	413·2	142·3	497	469·9	161·8	557	526·7	181·3
318	300·7	103·5	378	357·4	123·1	438	414·1	142·6	498	470·9	162·1	558	527·6	181·7
319	301·6	103·8	379	358·4	123·4	439	415·1	142·9	499	471·8	162·5	559	528·5	182·0
320	302·6	104·2	380	359·3	123·7	440	416·0	143·3	500	472·8	162·8	560	529·5	182·3
321	303·5	104·5	381	360·2	124·0	441	417·0	143·6	501	473·7	163·1	561	530·4	182·6
322	304·5	104·8	382	361·2	124·4	442	417·9	143·9	502	474·7	163·4	562	531·4	183·0
323	305·4	105·2	383	362·1	124·7	443	418·9	144·2	503	475·6	163·8	563	532·3	183·3
324	306·3	105·5	384	363·1	125·0	444	419·8	144·6	504	476·5	164·1	564	533·3	183·6
325	307·3	105·8	385	364·0	125·3	445	420·8	144·9	505	477·5	164·4	565	534·2	183·9
326	308·2	106·1	386	365·1	125·7	446	421·7	145·2	506	478·4	164·7	566	535·2	184·3
327	309·2	106·5	387	365·9	126·0	447	422·6	145·5	507	479·4	165·1	567	536·1	184·6
328	310·1	106·8	388	366·9	126·3	448	423·6	145·9	508	480·3	165·4	568	537·1	184·9
329	311·1	107·1	389	367·8	126·6	449	424·5	146·2	509	481·3	165·7	569	538·0	185·2
330	312·0	107·4	390	368·8	127·0	450	425·5	146·5	510	482·2	166·0	570	538·9	185·6
331	313·0	107·8	391	369·7	127·3	451	426·4	146·8	511	483·2	166·4	571	539·9	185·9
332	313·9	108·1	392	370·6	127·6	452	427·4	147·2	512	484·1	166·7	572	540·8	186·2
333	314·9	108·4	393	371·6	127·9	453	428·3	147·5	513	485·1	167·0	573	541·8	186·6
334	315·8	108·7	394	372·5	128·3	454	429·3	147·8	514	486·0	167·3	574	542·7	186·9
335	316·7	109·1	395	373·5	128·6	455	430·2	148·1	515	486·9	167·7	575	543·7	187·2
336	317·7	109·4	396	374·4	128·9	456	431·2	148·5	516	487·9	168·0	576	544·6	187·5
337	318·6	109·7	397	375·4	129·3	457	432·1	148·8	517	488·8	168·3	577	545·6	187·9
338	319·6	110·0	398	376·3	129·6	458	433·0	149·1	518	489·7	168·6	578	546·5	188·2
339	320·5	110·4	399	377·3	129·9	459	434·0	149·4	519	490·7	169·0	579	547·5	188·5
340	321·5	110·7	400	378·2	130·2	460	434·9	149·8	520	491·6	169·3	580	548·4	188·8
341	322·4	111·0	401	379·2	130·6	461	435·9	150·1	521	492·6	169·6	581	549·3	189·2
342	323·4	111·3	402	380·1	130·9	462	436·8	150·4	522	493·6	169·9	582	550·3	189·5
343	324·3	111·7	403	381·0	131·2	463	437·8	150·7	523	494·5	170·3	583	551·2	189·8
344	325·3	112·0	404	382·0	131·5	464	438·7	151·1	524	495·5	170·6	584	552·2	190·1
345	326·2	112·3	405	382·9	131·9	465	439·7	151·4	525	496·4	170·9	585	553·1	190·5
346	327·1	112·6	406	383·9	132·2	466	440·6	151·7	526	497·3	171·2	586	554·1	190·8
347	328·1	113·0	407	384·8	132·5	467	441·6	152·0	527	498·3	171·6	587	555·0	191·1
348	329·0	113·3	408	385·8	132·8	468	442·5	152·4	528	499·2	171·9	588	556·0	191·4
349	330·0	113·6	409	386·7	133·2	469	443·4	152·7	529	500·2	172·2	589	556·9	191·8
350	330·9	113·9	410	387·7	133·5	470	444·4	153·0	530	501·1	172·6	590	557·9	192·0
351	331·9	114·3	411	388·6	133·8	471	445·3	153·3	531	502·1	172·9	591	558·8	192·4
352	332·8	114·6	412	389·6	134·1	472	446·3	153·7	532	503·0	173·2	592	559·7	192·7
353	333·8	114·9	413	390·5	134·5	473	447·2	154·0	533	504·0	173·5	593	560·7	193·1
354	334·7	115·3	414	391·4	134·8	474	448·2	154·3	534	504·9	173·9	594	561·6	193·4
355	335·7	115·6	415	392·4	135·1	475	449·1	154·6	535	505·9	174·2	595	562·6	193·7
356	336·6	115·9	416	393·3	135·4	476	450·1	155·0	536	506·8	174·5	596	563·5	194·0
357	337·6	116·2	417	394·3	135·8	477	451·0	155·3	537	507·7	174·8	597	564·5	194·4
358	338·5	116·6	418	395·2	136·1	478	452·0	155·6	538	508·7	175·2	598	565·4	194·7
359	339·4	116·9	419	396·2	136·4	479	452·9	155·9	539	509·6	175·5	599	566·4	195·0
360	340·4	117·2	420	397·1	136·7	480	453·8	156·3	540	510·6	175·8	600	567·3	195·3
Dist.	Dep.	D. Lat.	Dist.	Dep.	D. Lat.	Dist.	Dep.	D. Lat.	Dist.	Dep.	D. Lat.	Dist.	Dep.	D. Lat.
D. Lon		Dep.	D. Lon		Dep.	D. Lon		Dep.	D. Lon		Dep.	D. Lon		Dep.

71°

TRAVERSE TABLE
20 Degrees

20°

D. Lon	Dep.		D. Lon	Dep.		D. Lon	Dep.		D. Lon	Dep.		D. Lon	Dep.	
Dist.	D. Lat.	Dep.	Dist.	D. Lat.	Dep.	Dist.	D. Lat.	Dep.	Dist.	D. Lat.	Dep.	Dist.	D. Lat.	Dep.
1	00.9	00.3	61	57.3	20.9	121	113.7	41.4	181	170.1	61.9	241	226.5	82.4
2	01.9	00.7	62	58.3	21.2	122	114.6	41.7	182	171.0	62.2	242	227.4	82.8
3	02.8	01.0	63	59.2	21.5	123	115.6	42.1	183	172.0	62.6	243	228.3	83.1
4	03.8	01.4	64	60.1	21.9	124	116.5	42.4	184	172.9	62.9	244	229.3	83.5
5	04.7	01.7	65	61.1	22.2	125	117.5	42.8	185	173.8	63.3	245	230.2	83.8
6	05.6	02.1	66	62.0	22.6	126	118.4	43.1	186	174.8	63.6	246	231.2	84.2
7	06.6	02.4	67	63.0	22.9	127	119.3	43.4	187	175.7	64.0	247	232.1	84.5
8	07.5	02.7	68	63.9	23.3	128	120.3	43.8	188	176.7	64.3	248	233.0	84.8
9	08.5	03.1	69	64.8	23.6	129	121.2	44.1	189	177.6	64.6	249	234.0	85.2
10	09.4	03.4	70	65.8	23.9	130	122.2	44.5	190	178.5	65.0	250	234.9	85.5
11	10.3	03.8	71	66.7	24.3	131	123.1	44.8	191	179.5	65.3	251	235.9	85.8
12	11.3	04.1	72	67.7	24.6	132	124.0	45.1	192	180.4	65.7	252	236.8	86.2
13	12.2	04.4	73	68.6	25.0	133	125.0	45.5	193	181.4	66.0	253	237.7	86.5
14	13.2	04.8	74	69.5	25.3	134	125.9	45.8	194	182.3	66.4	254	238.7	86.9
15	14.1	05.1	75	70.5	25.7	135	126.9	46.2	195	183.2	66.7	255	239.6	87.2
16	15.0	05.5	76	71.4	26.0	136	127.8	46.5	196	184.2	67.0	256	240.6	87.6
17	16.0	05.8	77	72.4	26.3	137	128.7	46.9	197	185.1	67.4	257	241.5	87.9
18	16.9	06.2	78	73.3	26.7	138	129.7	47.2	198	186.1	67.7	258	242.4	88.2
19	17.9	06.5	79	74.2	27.0	139	130.6	47.5	199	187.0	68.1	259	243.4	88.6
20	18.8	06.8	80	75.2	27.4	140	131.6	47.9	200	187.9	68.4	260	244.3	88.9
21	19.7	07.2	81	76.1	27.7	141	132.5	48.2	201	188.9	68.7	261	245.3	89.3
22	20.7	07.5	82	77.1	28.0	142	133.4	48.6	202	189.8	69.1	262	246.2	89.6
23	21.6	07.9	83	78.0	28.4	143	134.4	48.9	203	190.8	69.4	263	247.1	90.0
24	22.6	08.2	84	78.9	28.7	144	135.3	49.3	204	191.7	69.8	264	248.1	90.3
25	23.5	08.6	85	79.9	29.1	145	136.3	49.6	205	192.6	70.1	265	249.0	90.6
26	24.4	08.9	86	80.8	29.4	146	137.2	49.9	206	193.6	70.5	266	250.0	91.0
27	25.4	09.2	87	81.8	29.8	147	138.1	50.3	207	194.5	70.8	267	250.9	91.3
28	26.3	09.6	88	82.7	30.1	148	139.1	50.6	208	195.5	71.1	268	251.8	91.7
29	27.3	09.9	89	83.6	30.4	149	140.0	51.0	209	196.4	71.5	269	252.8	92.0
30	28.2	10.3	90	84.6	30.8	150	141.0	51.3	210	197.3	71.8	270	253.7	92.3
31	29.1	10.6	91	85.5	31.1	151	141.9	51.6	211	198.3	72.2	271	254.7	92.7
32	30.1	10.9	92	86.5	31.5	152	142.8	52.0	212	199.2	72.5	272	255.6	93.0
33	31.0	11.3	93	87.4	31.8	153	143.8	52.3	213	200.2	72.9	273	256.5	93.4
34	31.9	11.6	94	88.3	32.1	154	144.7	52.7	214	201.1	73.2	274	257.5	93.7
35	32.9	12.0	95	89.3	32.5	155	145.7	53.0	215	202.0	73.5	275	258.4	94.1
36	33.8	12.3	96	90.2	32.8	156	146.6	53.4	216	203.0	73.9	276	259.4	94.4
37	34.8	12.7	97	91.2	33.2	157	147.5	53.7	217	203.9	74.2	277	260.3	94.7
38	35.7	13.0	98	92.1	33.5	158	148.5	54.0	218	204.9	74.6	278	261.2	95.1
39	36.6	13.3	99	93.0	33.9	159	149.4	54.4	219	205.8	74.9	279	262.2	95.4
40	37.6	13.7	100	94.0	34.2	160	150.4	54.7	220	206.7	75.2	280	263.1	95.8
41	38.5	14.0	101	94.9	34.5	161	151.3	55.1	221	207.7	75.6	281	264.1	96.1
42	39.5	14.4	102	95.8	34.9	162	152.2	55.4	222	208.6	75.9	282	265.0	96.4
43	40.4	14.7	103	96.8	35.2	163	153.2	55.7	223	209.6	76.3	283	265.9	96.8
44	41.3	15.0	104	97.7	35.6	164	154.1	56.1	224	210.5	76.6	284	266.9	97.1
45	42.3	15.4	105	98.7	35.9	165	155.0	56.4	225	211.4	77.0	285	267.8	97.5
46	43.2	15.7	106	99.6	36.3	166	156.0	56.8	226	212.4	77.3	286	268.8	97.8
47	44.2	16.1	107	100.5	36.6	167	156.9	57.1	227	213.3	77.6	287	269.7	98.2
48	45.1	16.4	108	101.5	36.9	168	157.9	57.5	228	214.2	78.0	288	270.6	98.5
49	46.0	16.8	109	102.4	37.3	169	158.8	57.8	229	215.2	78.3	289	271.6	98.8
50	47.0	17.1	110	103.4	37.6	170	159.7	58.1	230	216.1	78.7	290	272.5	99.2
51	47.9	17.4	111	104.3	38.0	171	160.7	58.5	231	217.1	79.0	291	273.5	99.5
52	48.9	17.8	112	105.2	38.3	172	161.6	58.8	232	218.0	79.3	292	274.4	99.9
53	49.8	18.1	113	106.2	38.6	173	162.6	59.2	233	218.9	79.7	293	275.3	100.2
54	50.7	18.5	114	107.1	39.0	174	163.5	59.5	234	219.9	80.0	294	276.3	100.6
55	51.7	18.8	115	108.1	39.3	175	164.4	59.9	235	220.8	80.4	295	277.2	100.9
56	52.6	19.2	116	109.0	39.7	176	165.4	60.2	236	221.8	80.7	296	278.1	101.2
57	53.6	19.5	117	109.9	40.0	177	166.3	60.5	237	222.7	81.1	297	279.1	101.6
58	54.5	19.8	118	110.9	40.4	178	167.3	60.9	238	223.6	81.4	298	280.0	101.9
59	55.4	20.2	119	111.8	40.7	179	168.2	61.2	239	224.6	81.7	299	281.0	102.3
60	56.4	20.5	120	112.8	41.0	180	169.1	61.6	240	225.5	82.1	300	281.9	102.6
Dist.	Dep.	D. Lat.	Dist.	Dep.	D. Lat.	Dist.	Dep.	D. Lat.	Dist.	Dep.	D. Lat.	Dist.	Dep.	D. Lat.
D. Lon		Dep.	D. Lon		Dep.	D. Lon		Dep.	D. Lon		Dep.	D. Lon		Dep.

TRAVERSE TABLE
20 Degrees

Dist.	D. Lat.	Dep.	Dist.	D. Lat.	Dep.	Dist.	D. Lat.	Dep.	Dist.	D. Lat.	Dep.	Dist.	D. Lat.	Dep.
301	282·8	102·9	361	339·2	123·5	421	395·6	144·0	481	452·0	164·5	541	508·4	185·0
302	283·8	103·3	362	340·2	123·8	422	396·6	144·3	482	452·9	164·9	542	509·3	185·4
303	284·7	103·6	363	341·1	124·2	423	397·5	144·7	483	453·9	165·2	543	510·3	185·7
304	285·7	104·0	364	342·0	124·5	424	398·4	145·0	484	454·8	165·5	544	511·2	186·1
305	286·6	104·3	365	343·0	124·8	425	399·4	145·4	485	455·8	165·9	545	512·1	186·4
306	287·5	104·7	366	343·9	125·2	426	400·3	145·7	486	456·7	166·2	546	513·1	186·7
307	288·5	105·0	367	344·9	125·5	427	401·2	146·0	487	457·6	166·6	547	514·0	187·1
308	289·4	105·3	368	345·8	125·9	428	402·2	146·4	488	458·6	166·9	548	515·0	187·4
309	290·4	105·7	369	346·7	126·2	429	403·1	146·7	489	459·5	167·2	549	515·9	187·8
310	291·3	106·0	370	347·7	126·5	430	404·1	147·1	490	460·4	167·6	550	516·8	188·1
311	292·2	106·4	371	348·6	126·9	431	405·0	147·4	491	461·4	167·9	551	517·8	188·5
312	293·2	106·7	372	349·6	127·2	432	405·9	147·8	492	462·3	168·3	552	518·7	188·8
313	294·1	107·1	373	350·5	127·6	433	406·9	148·1	493	463·3	168·6	553	519·7	189·1
314	295·1	107·4	374	351·4	127·9	434	407·8	148·4	494	464·2	169·0	554	520·6	189·5
315	296·0	107·7	375	352·4	128·3	435	408·8	148·8	495	465·1	169·3	555	521·5	189·8
316	296·9	108·1	376	353·3	128·6	436	409·7	149·1	496	466·1	169·6	556	522·5	190·2
317	297·9	108·4	377	354·3	128·9	437	410·6	149·5	497	467·0	170·0	557	523·4	190·5
318	298·8	108·8	378	355·3	129·3	438	411·6	149·8	498	468·0	170·3	558	524·3	190·8
319	299·8	109·1	379	356·1	129·6	439	412·5	150·1	499	468·9	170·7	559	525·3	191·2
320	300·7	109·4	380	357·1	130·0	440	413·5	150·5	500	469·8	171·0	560	526·2	191·5
321	301·6	109·8	381	358·0	130·3	441	414·4	150·8	501	470·8	171·4	561	527·2	191·9
322	302·6	110·1	382	359·0	130·7	442	415·3	151·2	502	471·7	171·7	562	528·1	192·2
323	303·5	110·5	383	359·9	131·0	443	416·3	151·5	503	472·7	172·0	563	529·0	192·6
324	304·5	110·8	384	360·8	131·3	444	417·2	151·9	504	473·6	172·4	564	530·0	192·9
325	305·4	111·2	385	361·8	131·7	445	418·2	152·2	505	474·5	172·7	565	530·9	193·2
326	306·3	111·5	386	362·7	132·0	446	419·1	152·5	506	475·5	173·1	566	531·9	193·6
327	307·3	111·8	387	363·7	132·4	447	420·0	152·9	507	476·4	173·4	567	532·8	193·9
328	308·2	112·2	388	364·6	132·7	448	421·0	153·2	508	477·4	173·7	568	553·7	194·3
329	309·2	112·5	389	365·5	133·0	449	421·9	153·6	509	478·3	174·1	569	534·7	194·6
330	310·1	112·9	390	366·5	133·4	450	422·9	153·9	510	479·2	174·4	570	535·6	195·0
331	311·0	113·2	391	367·4	133·7	451	423·8	154·3	511	480·2	174·8	571	536·6	195·3
332	312·0	113·6	392	368·4	134·1	452	424·7	154·6	512	481·1	175·1	572	537·5	195·6
333	312·9	113·9	393	369·3	134·4	453	425·7	154·9	513	482·1	175·5	573	538·4	196·0
334	313·9	114·2	394	370·2	134·8	454	426·6	155·3	514	483·0	175·8	574	539·4	196·3
335	314·8	114·6	395	371·2	135·1	455	427·6	155·6	515	483·9	176·1	575	540·3	196·7
336	315·7	114·9	396	372·1	135·4	456	428·5	156·0	516	484·9	176·5	576	541·3	197·0
337	316·7	115·3	397	373·1	135·8	457	429·4	156·3	517	485·8	176·8	577	542·2	197·3
338	317·6	115·6	398	374·0	136·1	458	430·4	156·6	518	486·8	177·2	578	543·1	197·7
339	318·6	115·9	399	374·9	136·5	459	431·3	157·0	519	487·7	177·5	579	544·1	198·0
340	319·5	116·3	400	375·9	136·8	460	432·2	157·3	520	488·6	177·9	580	545·0	198·4
341	320·4	116·6	401	376·8	137·2	461	433·2	157·7	521	489·6	178·2	581	546·0	198·7
342	321·4	117·0	402	377·8	137·5	462	434·1	158·0	522	490·5	178·5	582	546·9	199·1
343	322·3	117·3	403	378·7	137·8	463	435·1	158·4	523	491·5	178·9	583	547·8	199·4
344	323·3	117·7	404	379·6	138·2	464	436·0	158·7	524	492·4	179·2	584	548·8	199·7
345	324·2	118·0	405	380·6	138·5	465	437·0	159·0	525	493·3	179·6	585	549·7	200·1
346	325·1	118·3	406	381·5	138·9	466	437·9	159·4	526	494·3	179·9	586	550·7	200·4
347	326·1	118·7	407	382·5	139·2	467	438·8	159·7	527	495·2	180·2	587	551·6	200·8
348	327·0	119·0	408	383·4	139·5	468	439·8	160·1	528	496·2	180·6	588	552·5	201·2
349	328·0	119·4	409	384·3	139·9	469	440·7	160·4	529	497·1	180·9	589	553·5	201·4
350	328·9	119·7	410	385·3	140·2	470	441·7	160·7	530	498·0	181·3	590	554·4	201·8
351	329·8	120·0	411	386·2	140·6	471	442·6	161·1	531	499·0	181·6	591	555·4	202·1
352	330·8	120·4	412	387·2	140·9	472	443·5	161·4	532	499·9	182·0	592	556·3	202·5
353	331·7	120·7	413	388·1	141·3	473	444·5	161·8	533	500·9	182·3	593	557·2	202·8
354	332·7	121·1	414	389·0	141·6	474	445·4	162·1	534	501·8	182·6	594	558·2	203·2
355	333·6	121·4	415	390·0	141·9	475	446·4	162·5	535	502·7	183·0	595	559·1	203·5
356	334·5	121·8	416	390·9	142·3	476	447·3	162·8	536	503·7	183·3	596	560·1	203·8
357	335·5	122·1	417	391·9	142·6	477	448·2	163·1	537	504·6	183·7	597	561·0	204·2
358	336·4	122·4	418	392·8	143·0	478	449·2	163·5	538	505·6	184·0	598	561·9	204·5
359	337·4	122·8	419	393·7	143·3	479	450·1	163·8	539	506·5	184·3	599	562·9	204·9
360	338·3	123·1	420	394·7	143·6	480	451·1	164·2	540	507·4	184·7	600	563·8	205·2

Dist.	Dep.	D. Lat.	Dist.	Dep.	D. Lat.	Dist.	Dep.	D. Lat.	Dist.	Dep.	D. Lat.	Dist.	Dep.	D. Lat.
D. Lon		Dep.	D. Lon		Dep.	D. Lon		Dep.	D. Lon		Dep.	D. Lon		Dep.

TRAVERSE TABLE
21 Degrees

21° 339° / 201° 021° / 159° 1h 24m

Dist.	D. Lat.	Dep.	Dist.	D. Lat.	Dep.	Dist.	D. Lat.	Dep.	Dist.	D. Lat.	Dep.	Dist.	D. Lat.	Dep.
1	00.9	00.4	61	56.9	21.9	121	113.0	43.4	181	169.0	64.9	241	225.0	86.4
2	01.9	00.7	62	57.9	22.2	122	113.9	43.7	182	169.9	65.2	242	225.9	86.7
3	02.8	01.1	63	58.8	22.6	123	114.8	44.1	183	170.8	65.6	243	226.9	87.1
4	03.7	01.4	64	59.7	22.9	124	115.8	44.4	184	171.8	65.9	244	227.8	87.4
5	04.7	01.8	65	60.7	23.3	125	116.7	44.8	185	172.7	66.3	245	228.7	87.8
6	05.6	02.2	66	61.6	23.7	126	117.6	45.2	186	173.6	66.7	246	229.7	88.2
7	06.5	02.5	67	62.5	24.0	127	118.6	45.5	187	174.6	67.0	247	230.6	88.5
8	07.5	02.9	68	63.5	24.4	128	119.5	45.9	188	175.5	67.4	248	231.5	88.9
9	08.4	03.2	69	64.4	24.7	129	120.4	46.2	189	176.4	67.7	249	232.5	89.2
10	09.3	03.6	70	65.4	25.1	130	121.4	46.6	190	177.4	68.1	250	233.4	89.6
11	10.3	03.9	71	66.3	25.4	131	122.3	46.9	191	178.3	68.4	251	234.3	90.0
12	11.2	04.3	72	67.2	25.8	132	123.2	47.3	192	179.2	68.8	252	235.3	90.3
13	12.1	04.7	73	68.2	26.2	133	124.2	47.7	193	180.2	69.2	253	236.2	90.7
14	13.1	05.0	74	69.1	26.5	134	125.1	48.0	194	181.1	69.5	254	237.1	91.0
15	14.0	05.4	75	70.0	26.9	135	126.0	48.4	195	182.0	69.9	255	238.1	91.4
16	14.9	05.7	76	71.0	27.2	136	127.0	48.7	196	183.0	70.2	256	239.0	91.7
17	15.9	06.1	77	71.9	27.6	137	127.9	49.1	197	183.9	70.6	257	239.9	92.1
18	16.8	06.5	78	72.8	28.0	138	128.8	49.5	198	184.8	71.0	258	240.9	92.5
19	17.7	06.8	79	73.8	28.3	139	129.8	49.8	199	185.8	71.3	259	241.8	92.8
20	18.7	07.2	80	74.7	28.7	140	130.7	50.2	200	186.7	71.7	260	242.7	93.2
21	19.6	07.5	81	75.6	29.0	141	131.6	50.5	201	187.6	72.0	261	243.7	93.5
22	20.5	07.9	82	76.6	29.4	142	132.6	50.9	202	188.6	72.4	262	244.6	93.9
23	21.5	08.2	83	77.5	29.7	143	133.5	51.2	203	189.5	72.7	263	245.5	94.3
24	22.4	08.6	84	78.4	30.1	144	134.4	51.6	204	190.4	73.1	264	246.5	94.6
25	23.3	09.0	85	79.4	30.5	145	135.4	52.0	205	191.4	73.5	265	247.4	95.0
26	24.3	09.3	86	80.3	30.8	146	136.3	52.3	206	192.3	73.8	266	248.3	95.3
27	25.2	09.7	87	81.2	31.2	147	137.2	52.7	207	193.3	74.2	267	249.3	95.7
28	26.1	10.0	88	82.2	31.5	148	138.2	53.0	208	194.2	74.5	268	250.2	96.0
29	27.1	10.4	89	83.1	31.9	149	139.1	53.4	209	195.1	74.9	269	251.1	96.4
30	28.0	10.8	90	84.0	32.3	150	140.0	53.8	210	196.1	75.3	270	252.1	96.8
31	28.9	11.1	91	85.0	32.6	151	141.0	54.1	211	197.0	75.6	271	253.0	97.1
32	29.9	11.5	92	85.9	33.0	152	141.9	54.5	212	197.9	76.0	272	253.9	97.5
33	30.8	11.8	93	86.8	33.3	153	142.8	54.8	213	198.9	76.3	273	254.9	97.8
34	31.7	12.2	94	87.8	33.7	154	143.8	55.2	214	199.8	76.7	274	255.8	98.2
35	32.7	12.5	95	88.7	34.0	155	144.7	55.5	215	200.7	77.0	275	256.7	98.6
36	33.6	12.9	96	89.6	34.4	156	145.6	55.9	216	201.7	77.4	276	257.7	98.9
37	34.5	13.3	97	90.6	34.8	157	146.6	56.3	217	202.6	77.8	277	258.6	99.3
38	35.5	13.6	98	91.5	35.1	158	147.5	56.6	218	203.5	78.1	278	259.5	99.6
39	36.4	14.0	99	92.4	35.5	159	148.4	57.0	219	204.5	78.5	279	260.5	100.0
40	37.3	14.3	100	93.4	35.8	160	149.4	57.3	220	205.4	78.8	280	261.4	100.3
41	38.3	14.7	101	94.3	36.2	161	150.3	57.7	221	206.3	79.2	281	262.3	100.7
42	39.2	15.1	102	95.2	36.6	162	151.2	58.1	222	207.3	79.6	282	263.3	101.1
43	40.1	15.4	103	96.2	36.9	163	152.2	58.4	223	208.2	79.9	283	264.2	101.4
44	41.1	15.8	104	97.1	37.3	164	153.1	58.8	224	209.1	80.3	284	265.1	101.8
45	42.0	16.1	105	98.0	37.6	165	154.0	59.1	225	210.1	80.6	285	266.1	102.1
46	42.9	16.5	106	99.0	38.0	166	155.0	59.5	226	211.0	81.0	286	267.0	102.5
47	43.9	16.8	107	99.9	38.3	167	155.9	59.8	227	211.9	81.3	287	267.9	102.9
48	44.8	17.2	108	100.8	38.7	168	156.8	60.2	228	212.9	81.7	288	268.9	103.2
49	45.7	17.6	109	101.8	39.1	169	157.8	60.6	229	213.8	82.1	289	269.8	103.6
50	46.7	17.9	110	102.7	39.4	170	158.7	60.9	230	214.7	82.4	290	270.7	103.9
51	47.6	18.3	111	103.6	39.8	171	159.6	61.3	231	215.7	82.8	291	271.7	104.3
52	48.5	18.6	112	104.6	40.1	172	160.6	61.6	232	216.6	83.1	292	272.6	104.6
53	49.5	19.0	113	105.5	40.5	173	161.5	62.0	233	217.5	83.5	293	273.5	105.0
54	50.4	19.4	114	106.4	40.9	174	162.4	62.4	234	218.5	83.9	294	274.5	105.4
55	51.3	19.7	115	107.4	41.2	175	163.4	62.7	235	219.4	84.2	295	275.4	105.7
56	52.3	20.1	116	108.3	41.6	176	164.3	63.1	236	220.3	84.6	296	276.3	106.1
57	53.2	20.4	117	109.2	41.9	177	165.2	63.4	237	221.3	84.9	297	277.3	106.4
58	54.1	20.8	118	110.2	42.3	178	166.2	63.8	238	222.2	85.3	298	278.2	106.8
59	55.1	21.1	119	111.1	42.6	179	167.1	64.1	239	223.1	85.6	299	279.1	107.2
60	56.0	21.5	120	112.0	43.0	180	168.0	64.5	240	224.1	86.0	300	280.1	107.5

| Dist. | Dep. | D. Lat. | Dist. | Dep. | D. Lat. | Dist. | Dep. | D. Lat. | Dist. | Dep. | D. Lat. | Dist. | Dep. | D. Lat. |

D. Lon — Dep.

69° 291° / 249° 069° / 111° 4h 36m

69 Degrees

TRAVERSE TABLE
21 Degrees

D. Lon	Dep.		D. Lon	Dep.		D. Lon	Dep.		D. Lon	Dep.		D. Lon	Dep.	
Dist.	D. Lat.	Dep.	Dist.	D. Lat.	Dep.	Dist.	D. Lat.	Dep.	Dist.	D. Lat.	Dep.	Dist.	D. Lat.	Dep.
301	281·0	107·9	361	337·0	129·4	421	393·0	150·9	481	449·1	172·4	541	505·1	193·9
302	281·9	108·2	362	338·0	129·7	422	394·0	151·2	482	450·0	172·7	542	506·0	194·2
303	282·9	108·6	363	338·9	130·1	423	394·9	151·6	483	450·9	173·1	543	506·9	194·6
304	283·8	108·9	364	339·8	130·4	424	395·8	151·9	484	451·9	173·5	544	507·9	195·0
305	284·7	109·3	365	340·8	130·8	425	396·8	152·3	485	452·8	173·8	545	508·8	195·3
306	285·7	109·7	366	341·7	131·2	426	397·7	152·7	486	453·7	174·2	546	509·7	195·7
307	286·6	110·0	367	342·6	131·5	427	398·6	153·0	487	454·7	174·5	547	510·7	196·0
308	287·5	110·4	368	343·6	131·9	428	399·6	153·4	488	455·6	174·9	548	511·6	196·4
309	288·5	110·7	369	344·5	132·2	429	400·5	153·7	489	456·5	175·2	549	512·5	196·7
310	289·4	111·1	370	345·4	132·6	430	401·4	154·1	490	457·5	175·6	550	513·5	197·1
311	290·3	111·5	371	346·4	133·0	431	402·4	154·5	491	458·4	176·0	551	514·4	197·5
312	291·3	111·8	372	347·3	133·3	432	403·3	154·8	492	459·3	176·3	552	515·3	197·8
313	292·2	112·2	373	348·2	133·7	433	404·2	155·2	493	460·3	176·7	553	516·3	198·2
314	293·1	112·5	374	349·1	134·0	434	405·2	155·5	494	461·2	177·0	554	517·2	198·5
315	294·1	112·9	375	350·1	134·4	435	406·1	155·9	495	462·1	177·4	555	518·1	198·9
316	295·0	113·2	376	351·0	134·7	436	407·0	156·2	496	463·1	177·8	556	519·1	199·3
317	295·9	113·6	377	352·0	135·1	437	408·0	156·6	497	464·0	178·1	557	520·0	199·6
318	296·9	114·0	378	352·9	135·5	438	408·9	157·0	498	464·9	178·5	558	520·9	200·0
319	297·8	114·3	379	353·8	135·8	439	409·8	157·3	499	465·9	178·8	559	521·9	200·3
320	298·7	114·7	380	354·8	136·2	440	410·8	157·7	500	466·8	179·2	560	522·8	200·7
321	299·7	115·0	381	355·7	136·5	441	411·7	158·0	501	467·7	179·5	561	523·7	201·0
322	300·6	115·4	382	356·6	136·9	442	412·6	158·4	502	468·7	179·9	562	524·7	201·4
323	301·5	115·8	383	357·6	137·3	443	413·6	158·8	503	469·6	180·3	563	525·6	201·8
324	302·5	116·1	384	358·5	137·6	444	414·5	159·1	504	470·5	180·6	564	526·5	202·1
325	303·4	116·5	385	359·4	138·0	445	415·4	159·5	505	471·5	181·0	565	527·5	202·5
326	304·3	116·8	386	360·4	138·3	446	416·4	159·8	506	472·4	181·3	566	528·4	202·8
327	305·3	117·2	387	361·3	138·7	447	417·3	160·2	507	473·3	181·7	567	529·3	203·2
328	306·2	117·5	388	362·2	139·0	448	418·2	160·5	508	474·3	182·1	568	530·3	203·6
329	307·1	117·9	389	363·2	139·4	449	419·2	160·9	509	475·2	182·4	569	531·2	203·9
330	308·1	118·3	390	364·1	139·8	450	420·1	161·3	510	476·1	182·8	570	532·1	204·3
331	309·0	118·6	391	365·0	140·1	451	421·0	161·6	511	477·1	183·1	571	533·1	204·6
332	309·9	119·0	392	365·9	140·5	452	422·0	162·0	512	478·0	183·5	572	534·0	205·0
333	310·9	119·3	393	366·9	140·8	453	422·9	162·3	513	478·9	183·8	573	534·9	205·3
334	311·8	119·7	394	367·8	141·2	454	423·8	162·7	514	479·9	184·2	574	535·9	205·7
335	312·7	120·1	395	368·8	141·6	455	424·8	163·1	515	480·8	184·6	575	536·8	206·1
336	313·7	120·4	396	369·7	141·9	456	425·7	163·4	516	481·7	184·9	576	537·7	206·4
337	314·6	120·8	397	370·6	142·3	457	426·6	163·8	517	482·7	185·3	577	538·7	206·8
338	315·6	121·1	398	371·6	142·6	458	427·4	164·1	518	483·6	185·6	578	539·6	207·1
339	316·5	121·5	399	372·5	143·0	459	428·5	164·5	519	484·5	186·0	579	540·5	207·5
340	317·4	121·8	400	373·4	143·3	460	429·4	164·8	520	485·5	186·4	580	541·5	207·9
341	318·4	122·2	401	374·4	143·7	461	430·4	165·2	521	486·4	186·7	581	542·4	208·2
342	319·3	122·6	402	375·3	144·1	462	431·3	165·6	522	487·3	187·1	582	543·3	208·6
343	320·2	122·9	403	376·2	144·4	463	432·2	165·9	523	488·3	187·4	583	544·3	208·9
344	321·2	123·3	404	377·1	144·8	464	433·2	166·3	524	489·2	187·8	584	545·2	209·3
345	322·1	123·6	405	378·1	145·1	465	434·1	166·6	525	490·1	188·2	585	546·1	209·6
346	323·0	124·0	406	379·0	145·5	466	435·0	167·0	526	491·1	188·5	586	547·1	210·0
347	324·0	124·4	407	379·9	145·9	467	436·0	167·4	527	492·0	188·9	587	548·0	210·4
348	324·9	124·7	408	380·9	146·2	468	436·9	167·7	528	492·9	189·2	588	548·9	210·7
349	325·8	125·1	409	381·8	146·6	469	437·8	168·1	529	493·9	189·6	589	549·9	211·1
350	326·8	125·4	410	382·8	146·9	470	438·8	168·4	530	494·8	189·9	590	550·8	211·4
351	327·7	125·8	411	383·7	147·3	471	439·7	168·8	531	495·7	190·3	591	551·7	211·8
352	328·6	126·1	412	384·6	147·6	472	440·6	169·1	532	496·7	190·7	592	552·7	212·2
353	329·6	126·5	413	385·6	148·0	473	441·6	169·5	533	497·6	191·0	593	553·6	212·5
354	330·5	126·9	414	386·5	148·4	474	442·5	169·9	534	498·5	191·4	594	554·5	212·9
355	331·4	127·2	415	387·4	148·7	475	443·5	170·2	535	499·5	191·7	595	555·5	213·2
356	332·4	127·6	416	388·4	149·1	476	444·4	170·6	536	500·4	192·1	596	556·4	213·6
357	333·3	127·9	417	389·3	149·4	477	445·3	170·9	537	501·3	192·4	597	557·3	213·9
358	334·2	128·3	418	390·2	149·8	478	446·3	171·3	538	502·3	192·8	598	558·2	214·3
359	335·2	128·7	419	391·2	150·2	479	447·2	171·7	539	503·2	193·2	599	559·2	214·7
360	336·1	129·0	420	392·1	150·5	480	448·1	172·0	540	504·1	193·5	600	560·1	215·1
Dist.	Dep.	D. Lat.	Dist.	Dep.	D. Lat.	Dist.	Dep.	D. Lat.	Dist.	Dep.	D. Lat.	Dist.	Dep.	D. Lat.
D. Lon		Dep.	D. Lon		Dep.	D. Lon		Dep.	D. Lon		Dep.	D. Lon		Dep.

291°
249°

69 Degrees

069°   4h 36m
111°

69°

TRAVERSE TABLE
22 Degrees

22°   338° / 202°   022° / 158°   1h 28m

D. Lon	Dep.		D. Lon	Dep.		D. Lon	Dep.		D. Lon	Dep.		D. Lon	Dep.	
Dist.	D. Lat.	Dep.	Dist.	D. Lat.	Dep.	Dist.	D. Lat.	Dep.	Dist.	D. Lat.	Dep.	Dist.	D. Lat.	Dep.
1	00·9	00·4	61	56·6	22·9	121	112·2	45·3	181	167·8	67·8	241	223·5	90·3
2	01·9	00·7	62	57·5	23·2	122	113·1	45·7	182	168·7	68·2	242	224·4	90·7
3	02·8	01·1	63	58·4	23·6	123	114·0	46·1	183	169·7	68·6	243	225·3	91·0
4	03·7	01·5	64	59·3	24·0	124	115·0	46·5	184	170·6	68·9	244	226·2	91·4
5	04·6	01·9	65	60·3	24·3	125	115·9	46·8	185	171·5	69·3	245	227·2	91·8
6	05·6	02·2	66	61·2	24·7	126	116·8	47·2	186	172·5	69·7	246	228·1	92·2
7	06·5	02·6	67	62·1	25·1	127	117·8	47·6	187	173·4	70·1	247	229·0	92·5
8	07·4	03·0	68	63·0	25·5	128	118·7	47·9	188	174·3	70·4	248	229·9	92·9
9	08·3	03·4	69	64·0	25·8	129	119·6	48·3	189	175·2	70·8	249	230·9	93·3
10	09·3	03·7	70	64·9	26·2	130	120·5	48·7	190	176·2	71·2	250	231·8	93·7
11	10·2	04·1	71	65·8	26·6	131	121·5	49·1	191	177·1	71·5	251	232·7	94·0
12	11·1	04·5	72	66·8	27·0	132	122·4	49·4	192	178·0	71·9	252	233·7	94·4
13	12·1	04·9	73	67·7	27·3	133	123·3	49·8	193	178·9	72·3	253	234·6	94·8
14	13·0	05·2	74	68·6	27·7	134	124·2	50·2	194	179·9	72·7	254	235·5	95·2
15	13·9	05·6	75	69·5	28·1	135	125·2	50·6	195	180·8	73·0	255	236·4	95·5
16	14·8	06·0	76	70·5	28·5	136	126·1	50·9	196	181·7	73·4	256	237·4	95·9
17	15·8	06·4	77	71·4	28·8	137	127·0	51·3	197	182·7	73·8	257	238·3	96·3
18	16·7	06·7	78	72·3	29·2	138	128·0	51·7	198	183·6	74·2	258	239·2	96·6
19	17·6	07·1	79	73·2	29·6	139	128·9	52·1	199	184·5	74·5	259	240·1	97·0
20	18·5	07·5	80	74·2	30·0	140	129·8	52·4	200	185·4	74·9	260	241·1	97·4
21	19·5	07·9	81	75·1	30·3	141	130·7	52·8	201	186·4	75·3	261	242·0	97·8
22	20·4	08·2	82	76·0	30·7	142	131·7	53·2	202	187·3	75·7	262	242·9	98·1
23	21·3	08·6	83	77·0	31·1	143	132·6	53·6	203	188·2	76·0	263	243·8	98·5
24	22·3	09·0	84	77·9	31·5	144	133·5	53·9	204	189·1	76·4	264	244·8	98·9
25	23·2	09·4	85	78·8	31·8	145	134·4	54·3	205	190·1	76·8	265	245·7	99·3
26	24·1	09·7	86	79·7	32·2	146	135·4	54·7	206	191·0	77·2	266	246·6	99·6
27	25·0	10·1	87	80·7	32·6	147	136·3	55·1	207	191·9	77·5	267	247·6	100·0
28	26·0	10·5	88	81·6	33·0	148	137·2	55·4	208	192·9	77·9	268	248·5	100·4
29	26·9	10·9	89	82·5	33·3	149	138·2	55·8	209	193·8	78·3	269	249·4	100·8
30	27·8	11·2	90	83·4	33·7	150	139·1	56·2	210	194·7	78·7	270	250·3	101·1
31	28·7	11·6	91	84·4	34·1	151	140·0	56·6	211	195·6	79·0	271	251·3	101·5
32	29·7	12·0	92	85·3	34·5	152	140·9	56·9	212	196·6	79·4	272	252·2	101·9
33	30·6	12·4	93	86·2	34·8	153	141·9	57·3	213	197·5	79·8	273	253·1	102·3
34	31·5	12·7	94	87·2	35·2	154	142·8	57·7	214	198·4	80·2	274	254·0	102·6
35	32·5	13·1	95	88·1	35·6	155	143·7	58·1	215	199·3	80·5	275	255·0	103·0
36	33·4	13·5	96	89·0	36·0	156	144·6	58·4	216	200·3	80·9	276	255·9	103·4
37	34·3	13·9	97	89·9	36·3	157	145·6	58·8	217	201·2	81·3	277	256·8	103·8
38	35·2	14·2	98	90·9	36·7	158	146·5	59·2	218	202·1	81·7	278	257·8	104·1
39	36·2	14·6	99	91·8	37·1	159	147·4	59·6	219	203·1	82·0	279	258·7	104·5
40	37·1	15·0	100	92·7	37·5	160	148·3	59·9	220	204·0	82·4	280	259·6	104·9
41	38·0	15·4	101	93·6	37·8	161	149·3	60·3	221	204·9	82·8	281	260·5	105·3
42	38·9	15·7	102	94·6	38·2	162	150·2	60·7	222	205·8	83·2	282	261·5	105·6
43	39·9	16·1	103	95·5	38·6	163	151·1	61·1	223	206·8	83·5	283	262·4	106·0
44	40·8	16·5	104	96·4	39·0	164	152·1	61·4	224	207·7	83·9	284	263·3	106·4
45	41·7	16·9	105	97·4	39·3	165	153·0	61·8	225	208·6	84·3	285	264·2	106·8
46	42·7	17·2	106	98·3	39·7	166	153·9	62·2	226	209·5	84·7	286	265·2	107·1
47	43·6	17·6	107	99·2	40·1	167	154·8	62·6	227	210·5	85·0	287	266·1	107·5
48	44·5	18·0	108	100·1	40·5	168	155·8	62·9	228	211·4	85·4	288	267·0	107·9
49	45·4	18·4	109	101·1	40·8	169	156·7	63·3	229	212·3	85·8	289	268·0	108·3
50	46·4	18·7	110	102·0	41·2	170	157·6	63·7	230	213·3	86·2	290	268·9	108·6
51	47·3	19·1	111	102·9	41·6	171	158·5	64·1	231	214·2	86·5	291	269·8	109·0
52	48·2	19·5	112	103·8	42·0	172	159·5	64·4	232	215·1	86·9	292	270·7	109·4
53	49·1	19·9	113	104·8	42·3	173	160·4	64·8	233	216·0	87·3	293	271·7	109·8
54	50·1	20·2	114	105·7	42·7	174	161·3	65·2	234	217·0	87·7	294	272·6	110·1
55	51·0	20·6	115	106·6	43·1	175	162·3	65·6	235	217·9	88·0	295	273·5	110·5
56	51·9	21·0	116	107·6	43·5	176	163·2	65·9	236	218·8	88·4	296	274·4	110·9
57	52·8	21·4	117	108·5	43·8	177	164·1	66·3	237	219·7	88·8	297	275·4	111·3
58	53·8	21·7	118	109·4	44·2	178	165·0	66·7	238	220·7	89·2	298	276·3	111·6
59	54·7	22·1	119	110·3	44·6	179	166·0	67·1	239	221·6	89·5	299	277·2	112·0
60	55·6	22·5	120	111·3	45·0	180	166·9	67·4	240	222·5	89·9	300	278·2	112·4
Dist.	Dep.	D. Lat.	Dist.	Dep.	D. Lat.	Dist.	Dep.	D. Lat.	Dist.	Dep.	D. Lat.	Dist.	Dep.	D. Lat.
D. Lon		Dep.	D. Lon		Dep.	D. Lon		Dep.	D. Lon		Dep.	D. Lon		Dep.

68°   292° / 248°   68 Degrees   068° / 112°   4h 32m

TRAVERSE TABLE
22 Degrees

Dist.	D. Lat.	Dep.	Dist.	D. Lat.	Dep.	Dist.	D. Lat.	Dep.	Dist.	D. Lat.	Dep.	Dist.	D. Lat.	Dep.
301	279.1	112.8	361	334.7	135.2	421	390.3	157.7	481	446.0	180.2	541	501.6	202.7
302	280.0	113.1	362	335.6	135.6	422	391.3	158.1	482	446.9	180.6	542	502.5	203.0
303	280.9	113.5	363	336.6	136.0	423	392.2	158.5	483	447.8	180.9	543	503.5	203.4
304	281.9	113.9	364	337.5	136.4	424	393.1	158.8	484	448.8	181.3	544	504.5	203.8
305	282.8	114.3	365	338.4	136.7	425	394.1	159.2	485	449.7	181.7	545	505.3	204.2
306	283.7	114.6	366	339.3	137.1	426	395.0	159.6	486	450.6	182.1	546	506.2	204.5
307	284.6	115.0	367	340.3	137.5	427	395.9	160.0	487	451.5	182.4	547	507.2	204.9
308	285.6	115.4	368	341.2	137.9	428	396.8	160.3	488	452.5	182.8	548	508.1	205.3
309	286.5	115.8	369	342.1	138.2	429	397.8	160.7	489	453.4	183.2	549	509.0	205.7
310	287.4	116.1	370	343.1	138.6	430	398.7	161.1	490	454.3	183.6	550	510.0	206.0
311	288.4	116.5	371	344.0	139.0	431	399.6	161.5	491	455.2	184.0	551	510.9	206.4
312	289.3	116.9	372	344.9	139.4	432	400.5	161.8	492	456.2	184.3	552	511.8	206.8
313	290.2	117.3	373	345.8	139.7	433	401.5	162.2	493	457.1	184.7	553	512.7	207.2
314	291.1	117.6	374	346.8	140.1	434	402.4	162.6	494	458.0	185.1	554	513.7	207.5
315	292.1	118.0	375	347.7	140.5	435	403.3	163.0	495	459.0	185.4	555	514.6	207.9
316	293.0	118.4	376	348.6	140.9	436	404.3	163.3	496	459.9	185.8	556	515.5	208.3
317	293.9	118.8	377	349.5	141.2	437	405.2	163.7	497	460.8	186.2	557	516.4	208.7
318	294.8	119.1	378	350.5	141.6	438	406.1	164.1	498	461.7	186.6	558	517.4	209.0
319	295.8	119.5	379	351.4	142.0	439	407.0	164.5	499	462.7	186.9	559	518.3	209.4
320	296.7	119.9	380	352.3	142.4	440	408.0	164.8	500	463.6	187.3	560	519.2	209.8
321	297.6	120.2	381	353.3	142.7	441	408.9	165.2	501	464.5	187.7	561	520.2	210.2
322	298.6	120.6	382	354.2	143.1	442	409.8	165.6	502	465.4	188.1	562	521.1	210.5
323	299.5	121.0	383	355.1	143.5	443	410.7	166.0	503	466.4	188.4	563	522.0	210.9
324	300.4	121.4	384	356.0	143.8	444	411.7	166.3	504	467.3	188.8	564	522.9	211.3
325	301.3	121.7	385	357.0	144.2	445	412.6	166.7	505	468.2	189.2	565	523.9	211.7
326	302.3	122.1	386	357.9	144.6	446	413.5	167.1	506	469.2	189.6	566	524.8	212.0
327	303.2	122.5	387	358.8	145.0	447	414.5	167.4	507	470.1	189.9	567	525.7	212.4
328	304.1	122.9	388	359.7	145.3	448	415.4	167.8	508	471.0	190.3	568	526.6	212.8
329	305.0	123.2	389	360.7	145.7	449	416.3	168.2	509	471.9	190.7	569	527.6	213.2
330	306.0	123.6	390	361.6	146.1	450	417.2	168.6	510	472.9	191.0	570	528.5	213.5
331	306.9	124.0	391	362.5	146.5	451	418.2	168.9	511	473.8	191.4	571	529.4	213.9
332	307.8	124.4	392	363.5	146.8	452	419.1	169.3	512	474.7	191.8	572	530.3	214.3
333	308.8	124.7	393	364.4	147.2	453	420.0	169.7	513	475.6	192.2	573	531.3	214.6
334	309.7	125.1	394	365.3	147.6	454	420.9	170.1	514	476.6	192.5	574	532.2	215.0
335	310.6	125.5	395	366.2	148.0	455	421.9	170.4	515	477.5	192.9	575	533.1	215.4
336	311.5	125.9	396	367.2	148.3	456	422.8	170.8	516	478.4	193.3	576	534.1	215.8
337	312.5	126.2	397	368.1	148.7	457	423.7	171.2	517	479.4	193.7	577	535.0	216.1
338	313.4	126.6	398	369.0	149.1	458	424.7	171.6	518	480.3	194.0	578	535.9	216.5
339	314.3	127.0	399	369.9	149.5	459	425.6	171.9	519	481.2	194.4	579	536.8	216.9
340	315.2	127.4	400	370.9	149.8	460	426.5	172.3	520	482.1	194.8	580	537.8	217.3
341	316.2	127.7	401	371.8	150.2	461	427.4	172.7	521	483.1	195.2	581	538.7	217.6
342	317.1	128.1	402	372.7	150.6	462	428.4	173.1	522	484.0	195.5	582	539.6	218.0
343	318.0	128.5	403	373.7	151.0	463	429.3	173.4	523	484.9	195.9	583	540.5	218.4
344	319.0	128.9	404	374.6	151.3	464	430.2	173.8	524	485.8	196.3	584	541.5	218.8
345	319.9	129.2	405	375.5	151.7	465	431.1	174.2	525	486.8	196.7	585	542.4	219.1
346	320.8	129.6	406	376.4	152.1	466	432.1	174.6	526	487.7	197.0	586	543.3	219.5
347	321.7	130.0	407	377.4	152.5	467	433.0	174.9	527	488.6	197.4	587	544.3	219.9
348	322.7	130.4	408	378.3	152.8	468	433.9	175.3	528	489.6	197.8	588	545.2	220.3
349	323.6	130.7	409	379.2	153.2	469	434.8	175.7	529	490.5	198.2	589	546.1	220.6
350	324.5	131.1	410	380.1	153.6	470	435.8	176.1	530	491.4	198.5	590	547.0	221.0
351	325.4	131.5	411	381.1	154.0	471	436.7	176.4	531	492.3	198.9	591	548.0	221.4
352	326.4	131.9	412	382.0	154.3	472	437.6	176.8	532	493.3	199.3	592	548.9	221.8
353	327.3	132.2	413	382.9	154.7	473	438.6	177.2	533	494.2	199.7	593	549.8	222.1
354	328.2	132.6	414	383.9	155.1	474	439.5	177.6	534	495.1	200.0	594	550.7	222.5
355	329.2	133.0	415	384.8	155.5	475	440.4	177.9	535	496.0	200.4	595	551.7	222.9
356	330.1	133.4	416	385.7	155.8	476	441.3	178.3	536	497.0	200.8	596	552.6	223.3
357	331.0	133.7	417	386.6	156.2	477	442.3	178.7	537	497.9	201.2	597	553.5	223.6
358	332.0	134.1	418	387.6	156.6	478	443.2	179.1	538	498.8	201.5	598	554.5	224.0
359	332.9	134.5	419	388.5	157.0	479	444.1	179.4	539	499.8	201.9	599	555.4	224.4
360	333.8	134.9	420	389.4	157.3	480	445.0	179.8	540	500.7	202.3	600	556.3	224.8

Dist.	Dep.	D. Lat.	Dist.	Dep.	D. Lat.	Dist.	Dep.	D. Lat.	Dist.	Dep.	D. Lat.	Dist.	Dep.	D. Lat.

TRAVERSE TABLE
23 Degrees

23°

D. Lon	Dep.		D. Lon	Dep.		D. Lon	Dep.		D. Lon	Dep.		D. Lon	Dep.	
Dist.	D. Lat.	Dep.	Dist.	D. Lat.	Dep.	Dist.	D. Lat.	Dep.	Dist.	D. Lat.	Dep.	Dist.	D. Lat.	Dep.
1	00·9	00·4	61	56·2	23·8	121	111·4	47·3	181	166·6	70·7	241	221·8	94·2
2	01·8	00·8	62	57·1	24·2	122	112·3	47·7	182	167·5	71·1	242	222·8	94·5
3	02·8	01·2	63	58·0	24·6	123	113·2	48·1	183	168·5	71·5	243	223·7	94·9
4	03·7	01·6	64	58·9	25·0	124	114·1	48·5	184	169·4	71·9	244	224·6	95·3
5	04·6	02·0	65	59·8	25·4	125	115·1	48·8	185	170·3	72·3	245	225·5	95·7
6	05·5	02·3	66	60·8	25·8	126	116·0	49·2	186	171·2	72·7	246	226·4	96·1
7	06·4	02·7	67	61·7	26·2	127	116·9	49·6	187	172·1	73·1	247	227·4	96·5
8	07·4	03·1	68	62·6	26·6	128	117·8	50·0	188	173·1	73·5	248	228·3	96·9
9	08·3	03·5	69	63·5	27·0	129	118·7	50·4	189	174·0	73·8	249	229·2	97·3
10	09·2	03·9	70	64·4	27·4	130	119·7	50·8	190	174·9	74·2	250	230·1	97·7
11	10·1	04·3	71	65·4	27·7	131	120·6	51·2	191	175·8	74·6	251	231·0	98·1
12	11·0	04·7	72	66·3	28·1	132	121·5	51·6	192	176·7	75·0	252	232·0	98·5
13	12·0	05·1	73	67·2	28·5	133	122·4	52·0	193	177·7	75·4	253	232·9	98·9
14	12·9	05·5	74	68·1	28·9	134	123·3	52·4	194	178·6	75·8	254	233·8	99·2
15	13·8	05·9	75	69·0	29·3	135	124·3	52·7	195	179·5	76·2	255	234·7	99·6
16	14·7	06·3	76	70·0	29·7	136	125·2	53·1	196	180·4	76·6	256	235·6	100·0
17	15·6	06·6	77	70·9	30·1	137	126·1	53·5	197	181·3	77·0	257	236·6	100·4
18	16·6	07·0	78	71·8	30·5	138	127·0	53·9	198	182·3	77·4	258	237·5	100·8
19	17·5	07·4	79	72·7	30·9	139	128·0	54·3	199	183·2	77·8	259	238·4	101·2
20	18·4	07·8	80	73·6	31·3	140	128·9	54·7	200	184·1	78·1	260	239·3	101·6
21	19·3	08·2	81	74·6	31·6	141	129·8	55·1	201	185·0	78·5	261	240·3	102·0
22	20·3	08·6	82	75·5	32·0	142	130·7	55·5	202	185·9	78·9	262	241·2	102·4
23	21·2	09·0	83	76·4	32·4	143	131·6	55·9	203	186·9	79·3	263	242·1	102·8
24	22·1	09·4	84	77·3	32·8	144	132·6	56·3	204	187·8	79·7	264	243·0	103·2
25	23·0	09·8	85	78·2	33·2	145	133·5	56·7	205	188·7	80·1	265	243·9	103·5
26	23·9	10·2	86	79·2	33·6	146	134·4	57·0	206	189·6	80·5	266	244·9	103·9
27	24·9	10·5	87	80·1	34·0	147	135·3	57·4	207	190·5	80·9	267	245·8	104·3
28	25·8	10·9	88	81·0	34·4	148	136·2	57·8	208	191·5	81·3	268	246·7	104·7
29	26·7	11·3	89	81·9	34·8	149	137·2	58·2	209	192·4	81·7	269	247·6	105·1
30	27·6	11·7	90	82·8	35·2	150	138·1	58·6	210	193·3	82·1	270	248·5	105·5
31	28·5	12·1	91	83·8	35·6	151	139·0	59·0	211	194·2	82·4	271	249·5	105·9
32	29·5	12·5	92	84·7	35·9	152	139·9	59·4	212	195·1	82·8	272	250·4	106·3
33	30·4	12·9	93	85·6	36·3	153	140·8	59·8	213	196·1	83·2	273	251·3	106·7
34	31·3	13·3	94	86·5	36·7	154	141·8	60·2	214	197·0	83·6	274	252·2	107·1
35	32·2	13·7	95	87·4	37·1	155	142·7	60·6	215	197·9	84·0	275	253·1	107·5
36	33·1	14·1	96	88·4	37·5	156	143·6	61·0	216	198·8	84·4	276	254·1	107·8
37	34·1	14·5	97	89·3	37·9	157	144·5	61·3	217	199·7	84·8	277	255·0	108·2
38	35·0	14·8	98	90·2	38·3	158	145·4	61·7	218	200·7	85·2	278	255·9	108·6
39	35·9	15·2	99	91·1	38·7	159	146·4	62·1	219	201·6	85·6	279	256·8	109·0
40	36·8	15·6	100	92·1	39·1	160	147·3	62·5	220	202·5	86·0	280	257·7	109·4
41	37·7	16·0	101	93·0	39·5	161	148·2	62·9	221	203·4	86·4	281	258·7	109·8
42	38·7	16·4	102	93·9	39·9	162	149·1	63·3	222	204·4	86·7	282	259·6	110·2
43	39·6	16·8	103	94·8	40·2	163	150·0	63·7	223	205·3	87·1	283	260·5	110·6
44	40·5	17·2	104	95·7	40·6	164	151·0	64·1	224	206·2	87·5	284	261·4	111·0
45	41·4	17·6	105	96·7	41·0	165	151·9	64·5	225	207·1	87·9	285	262·3	111·4
46	42·3	18·0	106	97·6	41·4	166	152·8	64·9	226	208·0	88·3	286	263·3	111·7
47	43·3	18·4	107	98·5	41·8	167	153·7	65·3	227	209·0	88·7	287	264·2	112·1
48	44·2	18·8	108	99·4	42·2	168	154·6	65·6	228	209·9	89·1	288	265·1	112·5
49	45·1	19·1	109	100·3	42·6	169	155·6	66·0	229	210·8	89·5	289	266·0	112·9
50	46·0	19·5	110	101·3	43·0	170	156·5	66·4	230	211·7	89·9	290	266·9	113·3
51	46·9	19·9	111	102·2	43·4	171	157·4	66·8	231	212·6	90·3	291	267·9	113·7
52	47·9	20·3	112	103·1	43·8	172	158·3	67·2	232	213·6	90·6	292	268·8	114·1
53	48·8	20·7	113	104·0	44·2	173	159·2	67·6	233	214·5	91·0	293	269·7	114·5
54	49·7	21·1	114	104·9	44·5	174	160·2	68·0	234	215·4	91·4	294	270·6	114·9
55	50·6	21·5	115	105·9	44·9	175	161·1	68·4	235	216·3	91·8	295	271·5	115·3
56	51·5	21·9	116	106·8	45·3	176	162·0	68·8	236	217·2	92·2	296	272·5	115·7
57	52·5	22·3	117	107·7	45·7	177	162·9	69·2	237	218·2	92·6	297	273·4	116·0
58	53·4	22·7	118	108·6	46·1	178	163·8	69·6	238	219·1	93·0	298	274·3	116·4
59	54·3	23·1	119	109·5	46·5	179	164·8	69·9	239	220·0	93·4	299	275·2	116·8
60	55·2	23·4	120	110·5	46·9	180	165·7	70·3	240	220·9	93·8	300	276·2	117·2
Dist.	Dep.	D. Lat.	Dist.	Dep.	D. Lat.	Dist.	Dep.	D. Lat.	Dist.	Dep.	D. Lat.	Dist.	Dep.	D. Lat.
D. Lon		Dep.	D. Lon		Dep.	D. Lon		Dep.	D. Lon		Dep.	D. Lon		Dep.

67°

67 Degrees

TRAVERSE TABLE
23 Degrees

D. Lon	Dep.		D. Lon	Dep.		D. Lon	Dep.		D. Lon	Dep.		D. Lon	Dep.	
Dist.	D. Lat.	Dep.	Dist.	D. Lat.	Dep.	Dist.	D. Lat.	Dep.	Dist.	D. Lat.	Dep.	Dist.	D. Lat.	Dep.
301	277·1	117·6	361	332·3	141·1	421	387·5	164·5	481	442·8	187·9	541	498·0	211·4
302	278·0	118·0	362	333·2	141·4	422	388·5	164·9	482	443·7	188·3	542	498·9	211·8
303	278·9	118·4	363	334·1	141·8	423	389·4	165·3	483	444·6	188·7	543	499·8	212·2
304	279·8	118·8	364	335·1	142·2	424	390·3	165·7	484	445·5	189·1	544	500·8	212·6
305	280·8	119·2	365	336·0	142·6	425	391·2	166·1	485	446·4	189·5	545	501·7	212·9
306	281·7	119·6	366	336·9	143·0	426	392·1	166·5	486	447·4	189·9	546	502·6	213·3
307	282·6	120·0	367	337·8	143·4	427	393·1	166·8	487	448·3	190·3	547	503·5	213·7
308	283·5	120·3	368	338·7	143·8	428	394·0	167·2	488	449·2	190·7	548	504·4	214·1
309	284·4	120·7	369	339·7	144·2	429	394·9	167·6	489	450·1	191·1	549	505·4	214·5
310	285·4	121·1	370	340·6	144·6	430	395·8	168·0	490	451·0	191·5	550	506·3	214·9
311	286·3	121·5	371	341·5	145·0	431	396·7	168·4	491	452·0	191·8	551	507·2	215·3
312	287·2	121·9	372	342·4	145·4	432	397·7	168·8	492	452·9	192·2	552	508·1	215·7
313	288·1	122·3	373	343·3	145·7	433	398·6	169·2	493	453·8	192·6	553	509·0	216·1
314	289·0	122·7	374	344·3	146·1	434	399·5	169·6	494	454·7	193·0	554	510·0	216·5
315	290·0	123·1	375	345·2	146·5	435	400·4	170·0	495	455·6	193·4	555	510·9	216·9
316	290·9	123·5	376	346·1	146·9	436	401·3	170·4	496	456·6	193·8	556	511·8	217·2
317	291·8	123·9	377	347·0	147·3	437	402·3	170·7	497	457·5	194·2	557	512·7	217·6
318	292·7	124·3	378	348·0	147·7	438	403·2	171·1	498	458·4	194·6	558	513·6	218·0
319	293·6	124·6	379	348·9	148·1	439	404·1	171·5	499	459·3	195·0	559	514·6	218·4
320	294·6	125·0	380	349·8	148·5	440	405·0	171·0	500	460·3	195·4	560	515·5	218·8
321	295·5	125·4	381	350·7	148·9	441	405·9	172·3	501	461·2	195·8	561	516·4	219·2
322	296·4	125·8	382	351·6	149·3	442	406·9	172·7	502	462·1	196·1	562	517·3	219·6
323	297·3	126·2	383	352·6	149·7	443	407·8	173·1	503	463·0	196·5	563	518·2	220·0
324	298·2	126·6	384	353·5	150·0	444	408·7	173·5	504	463·9	196·9	564	519·2	220·4
325	299·2	127·0	385	354·4	150·4	445	409·6	173·9	505	464·9	197·3	565	520·1	220·8
326	300·1	127·4	386	355·3	150·8	446	410·5	174·3	506	465·8	197·7	566	521·0	221·2
327	301·0	127·8	387	356·2	151·2	447	411·5	174·7	507	466·7	198·1	567	521·9	221·5
328	301·9	128·2	388	357·2	151·6	448	412·4	175·0	508	467·6	198·5	568	522·8	221·9
329	302·8	128·6	389	358·1	152·0	449	413·3	175·4	509	468·5	198·9	569	523·8	222·3
330	303·8	128·9	390	359·0	152·4	450	414·2	175·8	510	469·5	199·3	570	524·7	222·7
331	304·7	129·3	391	359·9	152·8	451	415·1	176·2	511	470·4	199·7	571	525·6	223·1
332	305·6	129·7	392	360·8	153·2	452	416·1	176·6	512	471·3	200·1	572	526·5	223·5
333	306·5	130·1	393	361·8	153·6	453	417·0	177·0	513	472·2	200·4	573	527·4	223·9
334	307·4	130·5	394	362·7	153·9	454	417·9	177·4	514	473·1	200·8	574	528·4	224·3
335	308·4	130·9	395	363·6	154·3	455	418·8	177·8	515	474·1	201·2	575	529·3	224·7
336	309·3	131·3	396	364·5	154·7	456	419·8	178·2	516	475·0	201·6	576	530·2	225·1
337	310·2	131·7	397	365·4	155·1	457	420·7	178·6	517	475·9	202·0	577	531·1	225·5
338	311·1	132·1	398	366·4	155·5	458	421·6	179·0	518	476·8	202·4	578	532·1	225·8
339	312·1	132·5	399	367·3	155·9	459	422·5	179·3	519	477·7	202·8	579	533·0	226·2
340	313·0	132·8	400	368·2	156·3	460	423·4	179·7	520	478·7	203·2	580	533·9	226·6
341	313·9	133·2	401	369·1	156·7	461	424·4	180·1	521	479·6	203·6	581	534·8	227·0
342	314·8	133·6	402	370·0	157·1	462	425·3	180·5	522	480·5	204·0	582	535·7	227·4
343	315·7	134·0	403	371·0	157·5	463	426·2	180·9	523	481·4	204·4	583	536·7	227·8
344	316·7	134·4	404	371·9	157·9	464	427·1	181·3	524	482·3	204·7	584	537·6	228·2
345	317·6	134·8	405	372·8	158·2	465	428·0	181·7	525	483·3	205·1	585	538·5	228·6
346	318·5	135·2	406	373·7	158·6	466	429·0	182·1	526	484·2	205·5	586	539·4	229·0
347	319·4	135·6	407	374·6	159·0	467	429·9	182·5	527	485·1	205·9	587	540·3	229·4
348	320·3	136·0	408	375·6	159·4	468	430·8	182·9	528	486·0	206·3	588	541·3	229·7
349	321·3	136·4	409	376·5	159·8	469	431·7	183·3	529	486·9	206·7	589	542·2	230·1
350	322·2	136·8	410	377·4	160·2	470	432·6	183·6	530	487·9	207·1	590	543·1	230·5
351	323·1	137·1	411	378·3	160·6	471	433·6	184·0	531	488·8	207·5	591	544·0	230·9
352	324·0	137·5	412	379·2	161·0	472	434·5	184·4	532	489·7	207·9	592	544·9	231·3
353	324·9	137·9	413	380·2	161·4	473	435·4	184·8	533	490·6	208·3	593	545·9	231·7
354	325·9	138·3	414	381·1	161·8	474	436·3	185·2	534	491·5	208·7	594	546·8	232·1
355	326·8	138·7	415	382·0	162·2	475	437·2	185·6	535	492·5	209·0	595	547·7	232·5
356	327·7	139·1	416	382·9	162·5	476	438·2	186·0	536	493·4	209·4	596	548·6	232·9
357	328·6	139·5	417	383·9	162·9	477	439·1	186·4	537	494·3	209·8	597	549·5	233·3
358	329·5	139·9	418	384·8	163·3	478	440·0	186·8	538	495·2	210·2	598	550·5	233·7
359	330·5	140·3	419	385·7	163·7	479	440·9	187·2	539	496·2	210·6	599	551·4	234·0
360	331·4	140·7	420	386·6	164·1	480	441·8	187·6	540	497·2	211·0	600	552·3	234·4
Dist.	Dep.	D. Lat.	Dist.	Dep.	D. Lat.	Dist.	Dep.	D. Lat.	Dist.	Dep.	D. Lat.	Dist.	Dep.	D. Lat.
D. Lon		Dep.	D. Lon		Dep.	D. Lon		Dep.	D. Lon		Dep.	D. Lon		Dep.

TRAVERSE TABLE
24 Degrees

24° 336° / 204°   024° / 156°   1h 36m

Dist.	D. Lat.	Dep.	Dist.	D. Lat.	Dep.	Dist.	D. Lat.	Dep.	Dist.	D. Lat.	Dep.	Dist.	D. Lat.	Dep.
1	00·9	00·4	61	55·7	24·8	121	110·5	49·2	181	165·4	73·6	241	220·2	98·0
2	01·8	00·8	62	56·6	25·2	122	111·5	49·6	182	166·3	74·0	242	221·1	98·4
3	02·7	01·2	63	57·6	25·6	123	112·4	50·0	183	167·2	74·4	243	222·0	98·8
4	03·7	01·6	64	58·5	26·0	124	113·3	50·4	184	168·1	74·8	244	222·9	99·2
5	04·6	02·0	65	59·4	26·4	125	114·2	50·8	185	169·0	75·2	245	223·8	99·7
6	05·5	02·4	66	60·3	26·8	126	115·1	51·2	186	169·9	75·7	246	224·7	100·1
7	06·4	02·8	67	61·2	27·3	127	116·0	51·7	187	170·8	76·1	247	225·6	100·5
8	07·3	03·3	68	62·1	27·7	128	116·9	52·1	188	171·7	76·5	248	226·6	100·9
9	08·2	03·7	69	63·0	28·1	129	117·8	52·5	189	172·7	76·9	249	227·5	101·3
10	09·1	04·1	70	63·9	28·5	130	118·8	52·9	190	173·6	77·3	250	228·4	101·7
11	10·0	04·5	71	64·9	28·9	131	119·7	53·3	191	174·5	77·7	251	229·3	102·1
12	11·0	04·9	72	65·8	29·3	132	120·6	53·7	192	175·4	78·1	252	230·2	102·5
13	11·9	05·3	73	66·7	29·7	133	121·5	54·1	193	176·3	78·5	253	231·1	102·9
14	12·8	05·7	74	67·6	30·1	134	122·4	54·5	194	177·2	78·9	254	232·0	103·3
15	13·7	06·1	75	68·5	30·5	135	123·3	54·9	195	178·1	79·3	255	233·0	103·7
16	14·6	06·5	76	69·4	30·9	136	124·2	55·3	196	179·1	79·7	256	233·9	104·1
17	15·5	06·9	77	70·3	31·3	137	125·2	55·7	197	180·0	80·1	257	234·8	104·5
18	16·4	07·3	78	71·3	31·7	138	126·1	56·1	198	180·9	80·5	258	235·7	104·9
19	17·4	07·7	79	72·2	32·1	139	127·0	56·5	199	181·8	80·9	259	236·6	105·3
20	18·3	08·1	80	73·1	32·5	140	127·9	56·9	200	182·7	81·3	260	237·5	105·8
21	19·2	08·5	81	74·0	32·9	141	128·8	57·3	201	183·6	81·8	261	238·4	106·2
22	20·1	08·9	82	74·9	33·4	142	129·7	57·8	202	184·5	82·2	262	239·3	106·6
23	21·0	09·4	83	75·8	33·8	143	130·6	58·2	203	185·4	82·6	263	240·3	107·0
24	21·9	09·8	84	76·7	34·2	144	131·6	58·6	204	186·4	83·0	264	241·2	107·4
25	22·8	10·2	85	77·7	34·6	145	132·5	59·0	205	187·3	83·4	265	242·1	107·8
26	23·8	10·6	86	78·6	35·0	146	133·4	59·4	206	188·2	83·8	266	243·0	108·2
27	24·7	11·0	87	79·5	35·4	147	134·3	59·8	207	189·1	84·2	267	243·9	108·6
28	25·6	11·4	88	80·4	35·8	148	135·2	60·2	208	190·0	84·6	268	244·8	109·0
29	26·5	11·8	89	81·3	36·2	149	136·1	60·6	209	190·9	85·0	269	245·7	109·4
30	27·4	12·2	90	82·2	36·6	150	137·0	61·0	210	191·8	85·4	270	246·7	109·8
31	28·3	12·6	91	83·1	37·0	151	137·9	61·4	211	192·8	85·8	271	247·6	110·2
32	29·2	13·0	92	84·0	37·4	152	138·9	61·8	212	193·7	86·2	272	248·5	110·6
33	30·1	13·4	93	85·0	37·8	153	139·8	62·2	213	194·6	86·6	273	249·4	111·0
34	31·1	13·8	94	85·9	38·2	154	140·7	62·6	214	195·5	87·0	274	250·3	111·4
35	32·0	14·2	95	86·8	38·6	155	141·6	63·0	215	196·4	87·4	275	251·2	111·9
36	32·9	14·6	96	87·7	39·0	156	142·5	63·5	216	197·3	87·9	276	252·1	112·3
37	33·8	15·0	97	88·6	39·5	157	143·4	63·9	217	198·2	88·3	277	253·1	112·7
38	34·7	15·5	98	89·5	39·9	158	144·3	64·3	218	199·2	88·7	278	254·0	113·1
39	35·6	15·9	99	90·4	40·3	159	145·3	64·7	219	200·1	89·1	279	254·9	113·5
40	36·5	16·3	100	91·4	40·7	160	146·2	65·1	220	201·0	89·5	280	255·8	113·9
41	37·5	16·7	101	92·3	41·1	161	147·1	65·5	221	201·9	89·9	281	256·7	114·3
42	38·4	17·1	102	93·2	41·5	162	148·0	65·9	222	202·8	90·3	282	257·6	114·7
43	39·3	17·5	103	94·1	41·9	163	148·9	66·3	223	203·7	90·7	283	258·5	115·1
44	40·2	17·9	104	95·0	42·3	164	149·8	66·7	224	204·6	91·1	284	259·4	115·5
45	41·1	18·3	105	95·9	42·7	165	150·7	67·1	225	205·5	91·5	285	260·4	115·9
46	42·0	18·7	106	96·8	43·1	166	151·6	67·5	226	206·5	91·9	286	261·3	116·3
47	42·9	19·1	107	97·7	43·5	167	152·6	67·9	227	207·4	92·3	287	262·2	116·7
48	43·9	19·5	108	98·7	43·9	168	153·5	68·3	228	208·3	92·7	288	263·1	117·1
49	44·8	19·9	109	99·6	44·3	169	154·4	68·7	229	209·2	93·1	289	264·0	117·5
50	45·7	20·3	110	100·5	44·7	170	155·3	69·1	230	210·1	93·5	290	264·9	118·0
51	46·6	20·7	111	101·4	45·1	171	156·2	69·6	231	211·0	94·0	291	265·8	118·4
52	47·5	21·2	112	102·3	45·6	172	157·1	70·0	232	211·9	94·4	292	266·8	118·8
53	48·4	21·6	113	103·2	46·0	173	158·0	70·4	233	212·9	94·8	293	267·7	119·2
54	49·3	22·0	114	104·1	46·4	174	159·0	70·8	234	213·8	95·2	294	268·6	119·6
55	50·2	22·4	115	105·1	46·8	175	159·9	71·2	235	214·7	95·6	295	269·5	120·0
56	51·2	22·8	116	106·0	47·2	176	160·8	71·6	236	215·6	96·0	296	270·4	120·4
57	52·1	23·2	117	106·9	47·6	177	161·7	72·0	237	216·5	96·4	297	271·3	120·8
58	53·0	23·6	118	107·8	48·0	178	162·6	72·4	238	217·4	96·8	298	272·2	121·2
59	53·9	24·0	119	108·7	48·4	179	163·5	72·8	239	218·3	97·2	299	273·2	121·6
60	54·8	24·4	120	109·6	48·8	180	164·4	73·2	240	219·3	97·6	300	274·1	122·0

| Dist. | Dep. | D. Lat. | Dist. | Dep. | D. Lat. | Dist. | Dep. | D. Lat. | Dist. | Dep. | D. Lat. | Dist. | Dep. | D. Lat. |

66° 294° / 246°   **66 Degrees**   066° / 114°   4h 24m

TRAVERSE TABLE
24 Degrees

336° / 204°   024° / 156°   1h 36m   **24°**

D. Lon	Dep.		D. Lon	Dep.		D. Lon	Dep.		D. Lon	Dep.		D. Lon	Dep.	
Dist.	D. Lat.	Dep.	Dist.	D. Lat.	Dep.	Dist.	D. Lat.	Dep.	Dist.	D. Lat.	Dep.	Dist.	D. Lat.	Dep.
301	275·0	122·4	361	329·8	146·8	421	384·6	171·2	481	439·4	195·6	541	494·2	220·0
302	275·9	122·8	362	330·7	147·2	422	385·5	171·6	482	440·3	196·0	542	495·1	220·5
303	276·8	123·2	363	331·6	147·6	423	386·4	172·0	483	441·2	196·5	543	496·1	220·9
304	277·7	123·6	364	332·5	148·1	424	387·3	172·5	484	442·2	196·9	544	497·0	221·3
305	278·6	124·1	365	333·4	148·5	425	388·3	172·9	485	443·1	197·3	545	497·9	221·7
306	279·5	124·5	366	334·4	148·9	426	389·2	173·3	486	444·0	197·7	546	498·8	222·1
307	280·5	124·9	367	335·3	149·3	427	390·1	173·7	487	444·9	198·1	547	499·7	222·5
308	281·4	125·3	368	336·2	149·7	428	391·0	174·1	488	445·8	198·5	548	500·6	222·9
309	282·3	125·7	369	337·1	150·1	429	391·9	174·5	489	446·7	198·9	549	501·5	223·3
310	283·2	126·1	370	338·0	150·5	430	392·8	174·9	490	447·6	199·3	550	502·5	223·7
311	284·1	126·5	371	338·9	150·9	431	393·7	175·3	491	448·6	199·7	551	503·4	224·1
312	285·0	126·9	372	339·8	151·3	432	394·7	175·7	492	449·5	200·1	552	504·3	224·5
313	285·9	127·3	373	340·7	151·7	433	395·6	176·1	493	450·4	200·5	553	505·2	224·9
314	286·9	127·7	374	341·7	152·1	434	396·5	176·5	494	451·3	200·9	554	506·1	225·3
315	287·8	128·1	375	342·6	152·5	435	397·4	176·9	495	452·2	201·3	555	507·0	225·7
316	288·7	128·5	376	343·5	152·9	436	398·3	177·3	496	453·1	201·7	556	507·9	226·0
317	289·6	128·9	377	344·4	153·3	437	399·2	177·7	497	454·0	202·1	557	508·8	226·6
318	290·5	129·3	378	345·3	153·7	438	400·1	178·2	498	454·9	202·6	558	509·8	227·0
319	291·4	129·7	379	346·2	154·2	439	401·0	178·6	499	455·9	203·0	559	510·7	227·4
320	292·3	130·2	380	347·1	154·6	440	402·0	179·0	500	456·8	203·4	560	511·6	227·8
321	293·2	130·6	381	348·1	155·0	441	402·9	179·4	501	457·7	203·8	561	512·5	228·2
322	294·2	131·0	382	349·0	155·4	442	403·8	179·8	502	458·6	204·2	562	513·4	228·6
323	295·1	131·4	383	349·9	155·8	443	404·7	180·2	503	459·5	204·6	563	514·3	229·0
324	296·0	131·8	384	350·8	156·2	444	405·6	180·6	504	460·4	205·0	564	515·2	229·4
325	296·9	132·2	385	351·7	156·6	445	406·5	181·0	505	461·3	205·4	565	516·2	229·8
326	297·8	132·6	386	352·6	157·0	446	407·4	181·4	506	462·3	205·8	566	517·1	230·2
327	298·7	133·0	387	353·5	157·4	447	408·4	181·8	507	463·2	206·2	567	518·0	230·6
328	299·6	133·4	388	354·5	157·8	448	409·3	182·2	508	464·1	206·6	568	518·9	231·0
329	300·6	133·8	389	355·4	158·2	449	410·2	182·6	509	465·0	207·0	569	519·8	231·4
330	301·5	134·2	390	356·3	158·6	450	411·1	183·0	510	465·9	207·4	570	520·7	231·8
331	302·4	134·6	391	357·2	159·0	451	412·0	183·4	511	466·8	207·8	571	521·6	232·2
332	303·3	135·0	392	358·1	159·4	452	412·9	183·8	512	467·7	208·2	572	522·5	232·7
333	304·2	135·4	393	359·0	159·8	453	413·8	184·3	513	468·6	208·7	573	523·5	233·1
334	305·1	135·9	394	359·9	160·3	454	414·7	184·7	514	469·6	209·1	574	524·4	233·5
335	306·0	136·3	395	360·9	160·7	455	415·7	185·1	515	470·5	209·5	575	525·3	233·9
336	307·0	136·7	396	361·8	161·1	456	416·6	185·5	516	471·4	209·9	576	526·2	234·3
337	307·9	137·1	397	362·7	161·5	457	417·5	185·9	517	472·3	210·3	577	527·1	234·7
338	308·8	137·5	398	363·6	161·9	458	418·4	186·3	518	473·2	210·7	578	528·0	235·1
339	309·7	137·9	399	364·5	162·3	459	419·3	186·7	519	474·1	211·1	579	528·9	235·5
340	310·6	138·3	400	365·4	162·7	460	420·0	187·1	520	475·0	211·5	580	529·9	235·9
341	311·5	138·7	401	366·3	163·1	461	421·1	187·5	521	476·0	211·9	581	530·8	236·3
342	312·4	139·1	402	367·2	163·5	462	422·1	187·9	522	476·9	212·3	582	531·7	236·7
343	313·3	139·5	403	368·2	163·9	463	423·0	188·3	523	477·8	212·7	583	532·6	237·1
344	314·3	139·9	404	369·1	164·3	464	423·9	188·7	524	478·7	213·1	584	533·5	237·5
345	315·2	140·3	405	370·0	164·7	465	424·8	189·1	525	479·6	213·5	585	534·4	237·9
346	316·1	140·7	406	370·9	165·1	466	425·7	189·5	526	480·5	213·9	586	535·3	238·3
347	317·0	141·1	407	371·8	165·5	467	426·6	189·9	527	481·4	214·4	587	536·3	238·8
348	317·9	141·5	408	372·7	165·9	468	427·5	190·4	528	482·4	214·8	588	537·2	239·2
349	318·8	142·0	409	373·6	166·4	469	428·5	190·8	529	483·3	215·2	589	538·1	239·6
350	319·7	142·4	410	374·6	166·8	470	429·4	191·2	530	484·2	215·6	590	539·0	240·0
351	320·7	142·8	411	375·5	167·2	471	430·3	191·6	531	485·1	216·0	591	539·9	240·4
352	321·6	143·2	412	376·4	167·6	472	431·2	192·0	532	486·0	216·4	592	540·8	240·8
353	322·5	143·6	413	377·3	168·0	473	432·1	192·4	533	486·9	216·8	593	541·7	241·2
354	323·4	144·0	414	378·2	168·4	474	433·0	192·8	534	487·8	217·2	594	542·6	241·6
355	324·3	144·4	415	379·1	168·8	475	433·9	193·2	535	488·7	217·6	595	543·6	242·0
356	325·2	144·8	416	380·0	169·2	476	434·8	193·6	536	489·7	218·0	596	544·5	242·4
357	326·1	145·2	417	380·9	169·6	477	435·8	194·0	537	490·6	218·4	597	545·4	242·8
358	327·0	145·6	418	381·9	170·0	478	436·7	194·4	538	491·5	218·8	598	546·3	243·2
359	328·0	146·0	419	382·8	170·4	479	437·6	194·8	539	492·4	219·2	599	547·2	243·6
360	328·9	146·4	420	383·7	170·8	480	438·5	195·2	540	493·3	219·6	600	548·1	244·0
Dist.	Dep.	D. Lat.	Dist.	Dep.	D. Lat.	Dist.	Dep.	D. Lat.	Dist.	Dep.	D. Lat.	Dist.	Dep.	D. Lat.
D. Lon		Dep.	D. Lon		Dep.	D. Lon		Dep.	D. Lon		Dep.	D. Lon		Dep.

294° / 246°   66 Degrees   066° / 114°   4h 24m   **66°**

TRAVERSE TABLE
25 Degrees

25° $\frac{335°}{205°}$ $\frac{025°}{155°}$ 1h 40m

D. Lon	Dep.		D. Lon	Dep.		D. Lon	Dep.		D. Lon	Dep.		D. Lon	Dep.	
Dist.	D. Lat.	Dep.	Dist.	D. Lat.	Dep.	Dist.	D. Lat.	Dep.	Dist.	D. Lat.	Dep.	Dist.	D. Lat.	Dep.
1	00·9	00·4	61	55·3	25·8	121	109·7	51·1	181	164·0	76·5	241	218·4	101·9
2	01·8	00·8	62	56·2	26·2	122	110·6	51·6	182	164·9	76·9	242	219·3	102·3
3	02·7	01·3	63	57·1	26·6	123	111·5	52·0	183	165·9	77·3	243	220·2	102·7
4	03·6	01·7	64	58·0	27·0	124	112·4	52·4	184	166·8	77·8	244	221·1	103·1
5	04·5	02·1	65	58·9	27·5	125	113·3	52·8	185	167·7	78·2	245	222·0	103·5
6	05·4	02·5	66	59·8	27·9	126	114·2	53·2	186	168·6	78·6	246	223·0	104·0
7	06·3	03·0	67	60·7	28·3	127	115·1	53·7	187	169·5	79·0	247	223·9	104·4
8	07·3	03·4	68	61·6	28·7	128	116·0	54·1	188	170·4	79·5	248	224·8	104·8
9	08·2	03·8	69	62·5	29·2	129	116·9	54·5	189	171·3	79·9	249	225·7	105·2
10	09·1	04·2	70	63·4	29·6	130	117·8	54·9	190	172·2	80·3	250	226·6	105·7
11	10·0	04·6	71	64·3	30·0	131	118·7	55·4	191	173·1	80·7	251	227·5	106·1
12	10·9	05·1	72	65·3	30·4	132	119·6	55·8	192	174·0	81·1	252	228·4	106·5
13	11·8	05·5	73	66·2	30·9	133	120·5	56·2	193	174·9	81·6	253	229·3	106·9
14	12·7	05·9	74	67·1	31·3	134	121·4	56·6	194	175·8	82·0	254	230·2	107·3
15	13·6	06·3	75	68·0	31·7	135	122·4	57·1	195	176·7	82·4	255	231·1	107·8
16	14·5	06·8	76	68·9	32·1	136	123·3	57·5	196	177·6	82·8	256	232·0	108·2
17	15·4	07·2	77	69·8	32·5	137	124·2	57·9	197	178·5	83·3	257	232·9	108·6
18	16·3	07·6	78	70·7	33·0	138	125·1	58·3	198	179·4	83·7	258	233·8	109·0
19	17·2	08·0	79	71·6	33·4	139	126·0	58·7	199	180·4	84·1	259	234·7	109·5
20	18·1	08·5	80	72·5	33·8	140	126·9	59·2	200	181·3	84·5	260	235·6	109·9
21	19·0	08·9	81	73·4	34·2	141	127·8	59·6	201	182·2	84·9	261	236·5	110·3
22	19·9	09·3	82	74·3	34·7	142	128·7	60·0	202	183·1	85·4	262	237·5	110·7
23	20·8	09·7	83	75·2	35·1	143	129·6	60·4	203	184·0	85·8	263	238·4	111·1
24	21·8	10·1	84	76·1	35·5	144	130·5	60·9	204	184·9	86·2	264	239·3	111·6
25	22·7	10·6	85	77·0	35·9	145	131·4	61·3	205	185·8	86·6	265	240·2	112·0
26	23·6	11·0	86	77·9	36·3	146	132·3	61·7	206	186·7	87·1	266	241·1	112·4
27	24·5	11·4	87	78·8	36·8	147	133·2	62·1	207	187·6	87·5	267	242·0	112·8
28	25·4	11·8	88	79·8	37·2	148	134·1	62·5	208	188·5	87·9	268	242·9	113·3
29	26·3	12·3	89	80·7	37·6	149	135·0	63·0	209	189·4	88·3	269	243·8	113·7
30	27·2	12·7	90	81·6	38·0	150	135·9	63·4	210	190·3	88·7	270	244·7	114·1
31	28·1	13·1	91	82·5	38·5	151	136·9	63·8	211	191·2	89·2	271	245·6	114·5
32	29·0	13·5	92	83·4	38·9	152	137·8	64·2	212	192·1	89·6	272	246·5	115·0
33	29·9	13·9	93	84·3	39·3	153	138·7	64·7	213	193·0	90·0	273	247·4	115·4
34	30·8	14·4	94	85·2	39·7	154	139·6	65·1	214	193·9	90·4	274	248·3	115·8
35	31·7	14·8	95	86·1	40·1	155	140·5	65·5	215	194·9	90·9	275	249·2	116·2
36	32·6	15·2	96	87·0	40·6	156	141·4	65·9	216	195·8	91·3	276	250·1	116·6
37	33·5	15·6	97	87·9	41·0	157	142·3	66·4	217	196·7	91·7	277	251·0	117·1
38	34·4	16·1	98	88·8	41·4	158	143·2	66·8	218	197·6	92·1	278	252·0	117·5
39	35·3	16·5	99	89·7	41·8	159	144·1	67·2	219	198·5	92·6	279	252·9	117·9
40	36·3	16·9	100	90·6	42·3	160	145·0	67·6	220	199·4	93·0	280	253·8	118·3
41	37·2	17·3	101	91·5	42·7	161	145·9	68·0	221	200·3	93·4	281	254·7	118·8
42	38·1	17·7	102	92·4	43·1	162	146·8	68·5	222	201·2	93·8	282	255·6	119·2
43	39·0	18·2	103	93·3	43·5	163	147·7	68·9	223	202·1	94·2	283	256·5	119·6
44	39·9	18·6	104	94·3	44·0	164	148·6	69·3	224	203·0	94·7	284	257·4	120·0
45	40·8	19·0	105	95·2	44·4	165	149·5	69·7	225	203·9	95·1	285	258·3	120·4
46	41·7	19·4	106	96·1	44·8	166	150·4	70·2	226	204·8	95·5	286	259·2	120·9
47	42·6	19·9	107	97·0	45·2	167	151·4	70·6	227	205·7	95·9	287	260·1	121·3
48	43·5	20·3	108	97·9	45·6	168	152·3	71·0	228	206·6	96·4	288	261·0	121·7
49	44·4	20·7	109	98·8	46·1	169	153·2	71·4	229	207·5	96·8	289	261·9	122·1
50	45·3	21·1	110	99·7	46·5	170	154·1	71·8	230	208·5	97·2	290	262·8	122·6
51	46·2	21·6	111	100·6	46·9	171	155·0	72·3	231	209·4	97·6	291	263·7	123·0
52	47·1	22·0	112	101·5	47·3	172	155·9	72·7	232	210·3	98·0	292	264·6	123·4
53	48·0	22·4	113	102·4	47·8	173	156·8	73·1	233	211·2	98·5	293	265·5	123·8
54	48·9	22·8	114	103·3	48·2	174	157·7	73·5	234	212·1	98·9	294	266·5	124·2
55	49·8	23·2	115	104·2	48·6	175	158·6	74·0	235	213·0	99·3	295	267·4	124·7
56	50·8	23·7	116	105·1	49·0	176	159·5	74·4	236	213·9	99·7	296	268·3	125·1
57	51·7	24·1	117	106·0	49·4	177	160·4	74·8	237	214·8	100·2	297	269·2	125·5
58	52·6	24·5	118	106·9	49·9	178	161·3	75·2	238	215·7	100·6	298	270·1	125·9
59	53·5	24·9	119	107·9	50·3	179	162·2	75·6	239	216·6	101·0	299	271·0	126·4
60	54·4	25·4	120	108·8	50·7	180	163·1	76·1	240	217·5	101·4	300	271·9	126·8
Dist.	Dep.	D. Lat.	Dist.	Dep.	D. Lat.	Dist.	Dep.	D. Lat.	Dist.	Dep.	D. Lat.	Dist.	Dep.	D. Lat.
D. Lon		Dep.	D. Lon		Dep.	D. Lon		Dep.	D. Lon		Dep.	D. Lon		Dep.

65° $\frac{295°}{245°}$ 65 Degrees $\frac{065°}{115°}$ 4h 20m

TRAVERSE TABLE
25 Degrees

D. Lon Dep. Dist.	D. Lat.	Dep.	D. Lon Dep. Dist.	D. Lat.	Dep.	D. Lon Dep. Dist.	D. Lat.	Dep.	D. Lon Dep. Dist.	D. Lat.	Dep.	D. Lon Dep. Dist.	D. Lat.	Dep.
301	272·8	127·2	361	327·2	152·6	421	381·6	177·9	481	435·9	203·3	541	490·3	228·6
302	273·7	127·6	362	328·0	153·0	422	382·5	178·3	482	436·8	203·7	542	491·2	229·1
303	274·6	128·1	363	329·0	153·4	423	383·4	178·8	483	437·7	204·1	543	492·1	229·5
304	275·5	128·5	364	329·9	153·8	424	384·3	179·2	484	438·7	204·5	544	493·0	229·9
305	276·4	128·9	365	330·8	154·3	425	385·2	179·6	485	439·6	205·0	545	493·9	230·3
306	277·3	129·3	366	331·7	154·7	426	386·1	180·0	486	440·5	205·4	546	494·8	230·7
307	278·2	129·7	367	332·6	155·1	427	387·0	180·5	487	441·4	205·8	547	495·8	231·2
308	279·1	130·2	368	333·5	155·5	428	387·9	180·9	488	442·3	206·2	548	496·7	231·6
309	280·0	130·6	369	334·4	155·9	429	388·8	181·3	489	443·2	206·7	549	497·6	232·0
310	281·0	131·0	370	335·3	156·4	430	389·7	181·7	490	444·1	207·1	550	498·5	232·4
311	281·9	131·4	371	336·2	156·8	431	390·6	182·1	491	445·0	207·5	551	499·4	232·9
312	282·8	131·9	372	337·1	157·2	432	391·5	182·6	492	445·9	207·9	552	500·3	233·3
313	283·7	132·3	373	338·1	157·6	433	392·4	183·0	493	446·8	208·4	553	501·2	233·7
314	284·6	132·7	374	339·0	158·1	434	393·3	183·4	494	447·7	208·8	554	502·1	234·1
315	285·5	133·1	375	339·9	158·5	435	394·2	183·8	495	448·6	209·2	555	503·0	234·6
316	286·4	133·4	376	340·8	158·8	436	395·2	184·3	496	449·5	209·6	556	503·9	235·0
317	287·3	133·9	377	341·7	159·3	437	396·1	184·7	497	450·4	210·0	557	504·8	235·4
318	288·2	134·4	378	342·5	159·7	438	397·0	185·1	498	451·3	210·5	558	505·7	235·8
319	289·1	134·8	379	343·5	160·2	439	397·9	185·5	499	452·2	210·9	559	506·6	236·2
320	290·0	135·2	380	344·4	160·6	440	398·8	186·0	500	453·2	211·3	560	507·5	236·7
321	290·9	135·7	381	345·3	161·0	441	399·6	186·4	501	454·1	211·7	561	508·4	237·1
322	291·8	136·1	382	346·2	161·4	442	400·6	186·8	502	455·0	212·2	562	509·3	237·5
323	292·7	136·5	383	347·1	161·9	443	401·5	187·2	503	455·9	212·6	563	510·3	237·9
324	293·6	136·9	384	348·0	162·3	444	402·4	187·6	504	456·8	213·0	564	511·2	238·4
325	294·6	137·4	385	348·9	162·7	445	403·3	188·1	505	457·7	213·4	565	512·1	238·8
326	295·5	137·8	386	349·8	163·1	446	404·2	188·5	506	458·6	213·8	566	513·0	239·2
327	296·4	138·2	387	350·7	163·6	447	405·1	188·9	507	459·5	214·3	567	513·9	239·6
328	297·3	138·6	388	351·6	164·0	448	406·0	189·3	508	460·4	214·7	568	514·8	240·0
329	298·2	139·0	389	352·6	164·4	449	406·9	189·8	509	461·3	215·1	569	515·7	240·5
330	299·1	139·5	390	353·5	164·8	450	407·8	190·2	510	462·2	215·5	570	516·6	240·9
331	300·0	139·9	391	354·4	165·2	451	408·7	190·6	511	463·1	216·0	571	517·5	241·3
332	300·9	140·3	392	355·3	165·6	452	409·7	191·0	512	464·0	216·4	572	518·4	241·7
333	301·8	140·7	393	356·2	166·1	453	410·6	191·4	513	464·9	216·8	573	519·3	242·2
334	302·7	141·2	394	357·1	166·5	454	411·5	191·9	514	465·8	217·2	574	520·2	242·6
335	303·6	141·6	395	358·0	166·9	455	412·4	192·3	515	466·7	217·6	575	521·1	243·0
336	304·5	142·0	396	358·9	167·4	456	413·3	192·7	516	467·7	218·1	576	522·0	243·4
337	305·4	142·4	397	359·8	167·8	457	414·2	193·1	517	468·6	218·5	577	522·9	243·9
338	306·3	142·8	398	360·7	168·2	458	415·1	193·6	518	469·5	218·9	578	523·8	244·3
339	307·2	143·3	399	361·6	168·6	459	416·0	194·0	519	470·4	219·3	579	524·8	244·7
340	308·1	143·7	400	362·5	169·0	460	416·9	194·4	520	471·3	219·8	580	525·7	245·1
341	309·1	144·1	401	363·4	169·5	461	417·8	194·8	521	472·2	220·2	581	526·6	245·5
342	310·0	144·5	402	364·3	169·9	462	418·7	195·2	522	473·1	220·6	582	527·5	246·0
343	310·9	145·0	403	365·2	170·3	463	419·6	195·7	523	474·0	221·0	583	528·4	246·4
344	311·8	145·4	404	366·1	170·7	464	420·5	196·1	524	474·9	221·5	584	529·3	246·8
345	312·7	145·8	405	367·1	171·2	465	421·4	196·5	525	475·8	221·9	585	530·2	247·2
346	313·6	146·2	406	368·0	171·6	466	422·3	196·9	526	476·7	222·3	586	531·1	247·7
347	314·5	146·5	407	368·9	172·0	467	423·2	197·4	527	477·6	222·7	587	532·0	248·1
348	315·4	147·1	408	369·8	172·4	468	424·2	197·8	528	478·5	223·1	588	532·9	248·5
349	316·3	147·5	409	370·7	172·9	469	425·1	198·2	529	479·4	223·6	589	533·8	248·9
350	317·2	147·9	410	371·6	173·3	470	426·0	198·6	530	480·3	224·0	590	534·7	249·3
351	318·1	148·3	411	372·5	173·7	471	426·9	199·1	531	481·2	224·4	591	535·6	249·8
352	319·0	148·8	412	373·4	174·1	472	427·8	199·5	532	482·2	224·8	592	536·5	250·2
353	319·9	149·2	413	374·3	174·5	473	428·7	199·9	533	483·1	225·3	593	537·4	250·6
354	320·8	149·6	414	375·2	175·0	474	429·6	200·3	534	484·0	225·7	594	538·3	251·0
355	321·7	150·0	415	376·1	175·4	475	430·5	200·7	535	484·9	226·1	595	539·3	251·5
356	322·6	150·5	416	377·0	175·8	476	431·4	201·2	536	485·8	226·5	596	540·2	251·9
357	323·6	150·9	417	377·9	176·2	477	432·3	201·6	537	486·7	226·9	597	541·1	252·3
358	324·5	151·3	418	378·8	176·7	478	433·2	202·0	538	487·6	227·4	598	542·0	252·7
359	325·4	151·7	419	379·7	177·1	479	434·1	202·4	539	488·5	227·8	599	542·9	253·1
360	326·3	152·1	420	380·6	177·5	480	435·0	202·9	540	489·4	228·2	600	543·8	253·6

Dist.	Dep.	D. Lat.	Dist.	Dep.	D. Lat.	Dist.	Dep.	D. Lat.	Dist.	Dep.	D. Lat.	Dist.	Dep.	D. Lat.
D. Lon		Dep.	D. Lon		Dep.	D. Lon		Dep.	D. Lon		Dep.	D. Lon		Dep.

26°

TRAVERSE TABLE
26 Degrees

334° / 206° 026° / 154° 1h 44m

Dist.	D. Lat.	Dep.	Dist.	D. Lat.	Dep.	Dist.	D. Lat.	Dep.	Dist.	D. Lat.	Dep.	Dist.	D. Lat.	Dep.
1	00.9	00.4	61	54.8	26.7	121	108.8	53.0	181	162.7	79.3	241	216.6	105.6
2	01.8	00.9	62	55.7	27.2	122	109.7	53.5	182	163.6	79.8	242	217.5	106.1
3	02.7	01.3	63	56.6	27.6	123	110.6	53.9	183	164.5	80.2	243	218.4	106.5
4	03.6	01.8	64	57.5	28.1	124	111.5	54.4	184	165.4	80.7	244	219.3	107.0
5	04.5	02.2	65	58.4	28.5	125	112.3	54.8	185	166.3	81.1	245	220.2	107.4
6	05.4	02.6	66	59.3	28.9	126	113.2	55.2	186	167.2	81.5	246	221.1	107.8
7	06.3	03.1	67	60.2	29.4	127	114.1	55.7	187	168.1	82.0	247	222.0	108.3
8	07.2	03.5	68	61.1	29.8	128	115.0	56.1	188	169.0	82.4	248	222.9	108.7
9	08.1	03.9	69	62.0	30.2	129	115.9	56.5	189	169.9	82.9	249	223.8	109.2
10	09.0	04.4	70	62.9	30.7	130	116.8	57.0	190	170.8	83.3	250	224.7	109.6
11	09.9	04.8	71	63.8	31.1	131	117.7	57.4	191	171.7	83.7	251	225.6	110.0
12	10.8	05.3	72	64.7	31.6	132	118.6	57.9	192	172.6	84.2	252	226.5	110.5
13	11.7	05.7	73	65.6	32.0	133	119.5	58.3	193	173.5	84.6	253	227.4	110.9
14	12.6	06.1	74	66.5	32.4	134	120.4	58.7	194	174.4	85.0	254	228.3	111.3
15	13.5	06.6	75	67.4	32.9	135	121.3	59.2	195	175.3	85.5	255	229.2	111.8
16	14.4	07.0	76	68.3	33.3	136	122.2	59.6	196	176.2	85.9	256	230.1	112.2
17	15.3	07.5	77	69.2	33.8	137	123.1	60.1	197	177.1	86.4	257	231.0	112.7
18	16.2	07.9	78	70.1	34.2	138	124.0	60.5	198	178.0	86.8	258	231.9	113.1
19	17.1	08.3	79	71.0	34.6	139	124.9	60.9	199	178.9	87.2	259	232.8	113.5
20	18.0	08.8	80	71.9	35.1	140	125.8	61.4	200	179.8	87.7	260	233.7	114.0
21	18.9	09.2	81	72.8	35.5	141	126.7	61.8	201	180.7	88.1	261	234.6	114.4
22	19.8	09.6	82	73.7	35.9	142	127.6	62.2	202	181.6	88.6	262	235.5	114.9
23	20.7	10.1	83	74.6	36.4	143	128.5	62.7	203	182.5	89.0	263	236.4	115.3
24	21.6	10.5	84	75.5	36.8	144	129.4	63.1	204	183.4	89.4	264	237.3	115.7
25	22.5	11.0	85	76.4	37.3	145	130.3	63.6	205	184.3	89.9	265	238.2	116.2
26	23.4	11.4	86	77.3	37.7	146	131.2	64.0	206	185.2	90.3	266	239.1	116.6
27	24.3	11.8	87	78.2	38.1	147	132.1	64.4	207	186.1	90.7	267	240.0	117.0
28	25.2	12.3	88	79.1	38.6	148	133.0	64.9	208	186.9	91.2	268	240.9	117.5
29	26.1	12.7	89	80.0	39.0	149	133.9	65.3	209	187.8	91.6	269	241.8	117.9
30	27.0	13.2	90	80.9	39.5	150	134.8	65.8	210	188.7	92.1	270	242.7	118.4
31	27.9	13.6	91	81.8	39.9	151	135.7	66.2	211	189.6	92.5	271	243.6	118.8
32	28.8	14.0	92	82.7	40.3	152	136.6	66.6	212	190.5	92.9	272	244.5	119.2
33	29.7	14.5	93	83.6	40.8	153	137.5	67.1	213	191.4	93.4	273	245.4	119.7
34	30.6	14.9	94	84.5	41.2	154	138.4	67.5	214	192.3	93.8	274	246.3	120.1
35	31.5	15.3	95	85.4	41.6	155	139.3	67.9	215	193.2	94.2	275	247.2	120.6
36	32.4	15.8	96	86.3	42.1	156	140.2	68.4	216	194.1	94.7	276	248.1	121.0
37	33.3	16.2	97	87.2	42.5	157	141.1	68.8	217	195.0	95.1	277	249.0	121.4
38	34.2	16.7	98	88.1	43.0	158	142.0	69.3	218	195.9	95.6	278	249.9	121.9
39	35.1	17.1	99	89.0	43.4	159	142.9	69.7	219	196.8	96.0	279	250.8	122.3
40	36.0	17.5	100	89.9	43.8	160	143.8	70.1	220	197.7	96.4	280	251.7	122.7
41	36.9	18.0	101	90.8	44.3	161	144.7	70.6	221	198.6	96.9	281	252.6	123.2
42	37.7	18.4	102	91.7	44.7	162	145.6	71.0	222	199.5	97.3	282	253.5	123.6
43	38.6	18.8	103	92.6	45.2	163	146.5	71.5	223	200.4	97.8	283	254.4	124.1
44	39.5	19.3	104	93.5	45.6	164	147.4	71.9	224	201.3	98.2	284	255.3	124.5
45	40.4	19.7	105	94.4	46.0	165	148.3	72.3	225	202.2	98.6	285	256.2	124.9
46	41.3	20.2	106	95.3	46.5	166	149.2	72.8	226	203.1	99.1	286	257.1	125.4
47	42.2	20.6	107	96.2	46.9	167	150.1	73.2	227	204.0	99.5	287	258.0	125.8
48	43.1	21.0	108	97.1	47.3	168	151.0	73.6	228	204.9	99.9	288	258.9	126.3
49	44.0	21.5	109	98.0	47.8	169	151.9	74.1	229	205.8	100.4	289	259.8	126.7
50	44.9	21.9	110	98.9	48.2	170	152.8	74.5	230	206.7	100.8	290	260.7	127.1
51	45.8	22.4	111	99.8	48.7	171	153.7	75.0	231	207.6	101.3	291	261.5	127.6
52	46.7	22.8	112	100.7	49.1	172	154.6	75.4	232	208.5	101.7	292	262.4	128.0
53	47.6	23.2	113	101.6	49.5	173	155.5	75.8	233	209.4	102.1	293	263.3	128.4
54	48.5	23.7	114	102.5	50.0	174	156.4	76.3	234	210.3	102.6	294	264.2	128.9
55	49.4	24.1	115	103.4	50.4	175	157.3	76.7	235	211.2	103.0	295	265.1	129.3
56	50.3	24.5	116	104.3	50.9	176	158.2	77.2	236	212.1	103.5	296	266.0	129.8
57	51.2	25.0	117	105.2	51.3	177	159.1	77.6	237	213.0	103.9	297	266.9	130.2
58	52.1	25.4	118	106.1	51.7	178	160.0	78.0	238	213.9	104.3	298	267.8	130.6
59	53.0	25.9	119	107.0	52.2	179	160.9	78.5	239	214.8	104.8	299	268.7	131.1
60	53.9	26.3	120	107.9	52.6	180	161.8	78.9	240	215.7	105.2	300	269.6	131.5

Dist.	Dep.	D. Lat.	Dist.	Dep.	D. Lat.	Dist.	Dep.	D. Lat.	Dist.	Dep.	D. Lat.	Dist.	Dep.	D. Lat.

296° / 244° 064° / 116°

64°

64 Degrees

4h 16m

TRAVERSE TABLE
26 Degrees

Dist.	D. Lat.	Dep.	Dist.	D. Lat.	Dep.	Dist.	D. Lat.	Dep.	Dist.	D. Lat.	Dep.	Dist.	D. Lat.	Dep.
301	270.5	131.9	361	324.5	158.3	421	378.4	184.6	481	432.3	210.9	541	486.2	237.2
302	271.4	132.4	362	325.4	158.7	422	379.3	185.0	482	433.2	211.3	542	487.1	237.6
303	272.3	132.8	363	326.3	159.1	423	380.2	185.4	483	434.1	211.7	543	488.0	238.0
304	273.2	133.3	364	327.2	159.6	424	381.1	185.9	484	435.0	212.2	544	488.9	238.5
305	274.1	133.7	365	328.1	160.0	425	382.0	186.3	485	435.9	212.6	545	489.8	238.9
306	275.0	134.1	366	329.0	160.4	426	382.9	186.7	486	436.8	213.0	546	490.7	239.4
307	275.9	134.6	367	329.9	160.9	427	383.8	187.2	487	437.7	213.5	547	491.6	239.8
308	276.8	135.0	368	330.8	161.3	428	384.7	187.6	488	438.6	213.9	548	492.5	240.2
309	277.7	135.5	369	331.7	161.8	429	385.6	188.1	489	439.5	214.4	549	493.4	240.7
310	278.6	135.9	370	332.6	162.2	430	386.5	188.5	490	440.4	214.8	550	494.3	241.1
311	279.5	136.3	371	333.5	162.6	431	387.4	188.9	491	441.3	215.2	551	495.2	241.5
312	280.4	136.8	372	334.4	163.1	432	388.3	189.4	492	442.2	215.7	552	496.1	242.0
313	281.3	137.2	373	335.3	163.5	433	389.2	189.8	493	443.1	216.1	553	497.0	242.4
314	282.2	137.6	374	336.1	164.0	434	390.1	190.3	494	444.0	216.6	554	497.9	242.9
315	283.1	138.1	375	337.0	164.4	435	391.0	190.7	495	444.9	217.0	555	498.8	243.3
316	284.0	138.5	376	337.9	164.8	436	391.9	191.1	496	445.8	217.4	556	499.7	243.7
317	284.9	139.0	377	338.8	165.3	437	392.8	191.6	497	446.7	217.9	557	500.6	244.2
318	285.8	139.4	378	339.7	165.7	438	393.7	192.0	498	447.6	218.3	558	501.5	244.6
319	286.7	139.8	379	340.6	166.1	439	394.6	192.4	499	448.5	218.7	559	502.4	245.0
320	287.6	140.3	380	341.5	166.6	440	395.5	192.9	500	449.4	219.2	560	503.3	245.5
321	288.5	140.7	381	342.4	167.0	441	396.4	193.3	501	450.3	219.6	561	504.2	245.9
322	289.4	141.2	382	343.3	167.5	442	397.3	193.8	502	451.2	220.1	562	505.1	246.4
323	290.3	141.6	383	344.2	167.9	443	398.2	194.2	503	452.1	220.5	563	506.0	246.8
324	291.2	142.0	384	345.1	168.3	444	399.1	194.6	504	453.0	220.9	564	506.9	247.2
325	292.1	142.5	385	346.0	168.8	445	400.0	195.1	505	453.9	221.4	565	507.8	247.7
326	293.0	142.9	386	346.9	169.2	446	400.9	195.5	506	454.8	221.8	566	508.7	248.1
327	293.9	143.3	387	347.8	169.6	447	401.8	196.0	507	455.7	222.3	567	509.6	248.6
328	294.8	143.8	388	348.7	170.1	448	402.7	196.4	508	456.6	222.7	568	510.5	249.0
329	295.7	144.2	389	349.6	170.5	449	403.6	196.8	509	457.5	223.1	569	511.4	249.4
330	296.6	144.7	390	350.5	171.0	450	404.5	197.3	510	458.4	223.6	570	512.3	249.9
331	297.5	145.1	391	351.4	171.4	451	405.4	197.7	511	459.3	224.0	571	513.2	250.3
332	298.4	145.5	392	352.3	171.8	452	406.3	198.1	512	460.2	224.4	572	514.1	250.7
333	299.3	146.0	393	353.2	172.3	453	407.2	198.6	513	461.1	224.9	573	515.0	251.2
334	300.2	146.4	394	354.1	172.7	454	408.1	199.0	514	462.0	225.3	574	515.9	251.6
335	301.1	146.9	395	355.0	173.2	455	409.0	199.5	515	462.9	225.8	575	516.8	252.1
336	302.0	147.3	396	355.9	173.6	456	409.9	199.9	516	463.8	226.2	576	517.7	252.5
337	302.9	147.7	397	356.8	174.0	457	410.7	200.3	517	464.7	226.6	577	518.6	252.9
338	303.8	148.2	398	357.7	174.5	458	411.6	200.8	518	465.6	227.1	578	519.5	253.4
339	304.7	148.6	399	358.6	174.9	459	412.5	201.2	519	466.5	227.5	579	520.4	253.8
340	305.6	149.0	400	359.5	175.3	460	413.3	201.7	520	467.4	228.0	580	521.3	254.3
341	306.5	149.5	401	360.4	175.8	461	414.3	202.1	521	468.3	228.4	581	522.2	254.7
342	307.4	149.9	402	361.3	176.2	462	415.2	202.5	522	469.2	228.8	582	523.1	255.1
343	308.3	150.4	403	362.2	176.7	463	416.1	203.0	523	470.1	229.3	583	524.0	255.6
344	309.2	150.8	404	363.1	177.1	464	417.0	203.4	524	471.0	229.7	584	524.9	256.0
345	310.1	151.2	405	364.0	177.5	465	417.9	203.8	525	471.9	230.1	585	525.8	256.4
346	311.0	151.7	406	364.9	178.0	466	418.8	204.3	526	472.8	230.6	586	526.7	256.9
347	311.9	152.1	407	365.8	178.4	467	419.7	204.7	527	473.7	231.0	587	527.6	257.3
348	312.8	152.6	408	366.7	178.9	468	420.6	205.2	528	474.6	231.5	588	528.5	257.8
349	313.7	153.0	409	367.6	179.3	469	421.5	205.6	529	475.5	231.9	589	529.4	258.2
350	314.6	153.4	410	368.5	179.7	470	422.4	206.0	530	476.4	232.3	590	530.3	258.6
351	315.5	153.9	411	369.4	180.2	471	423.3	206.5	531	477.3	232.8	591	531.2	259.1
352	316.4	154.3	412	370.3	180.6	472	424.2	206.9	532	478.2	233.2	592	532.1	259.5
353	317.3	154.7	413	371.2	181.0	473	425.1	207.3	533	479.1	233.7	593	533.0	260.0
354	318.2	155.2	414	372.1	181.5	474	426.0	207.8	534	480.0	234.1	594	533.9	260.4
355	319.1	155.6	415	373.0	181.9	475	426.9	208.2	535	480.9	234.5	595	534.8	260.8
356	320.0	156.1	416	373.9	182.4	476	427.8	208.7	536	481.8	235.0	596	535.7	261.3
357	320.9	156.5	417	374.8	182.8	477	428.7	209.1	537	482.7	235.4	597	536.6	261.7
358	321.8	156.9	418	375.7	183.2	478	429.6	209.5	538	483.6	235.8	598	537.5	262.1
359	322.7	157.4	419	376.6	183.7	479	430.5	210.0	539	484.4	236.3	599	538.4	262.6
360	323.6	157.8	420	377.5	184.1	480	431.4	210.4	540	485.3	236.7	600	539.3	263.0

Dist.	Dep.	D. Lat.	Dist.	Dep.	D. Lat.	Dist.	Dep.	D. Lat.	Dist.	Dep.	D. Lat.	Dist.	Dep.	D. Lat.

TRAVERSE TABLE
27 Degrees

27°

D. Lon	Dep.		D. Lon	Dep.		D. Lon	Dep.		D. Lon	Dep.		D. Lon	Dep.	
Dist.	D. Lat.	Dep.	Dist.	D. Lat.	Dep.	Dist.	D. Lat.	Dep.	Dist.	D. Lat.	Dep.	Dist.	D. Lat.	Dep.
1	00.9	00.5	61	54.4	27.7	121	107.8	54.9	181	161.3	82.2	241	214.7	109.4
2	01.8	00.9	62	55.2	28.1	122	108.7	55.4	182	162.2	82.6	242	215.6	109.9
3	02.7	01.4	63	56.1	28.6	123	109.6	55.8	183	163.1	83.1	243	216.5	110.3
4	03.6	01.8	64	57.0	29.1	124	110.5	56.3	184	163.9	83.5	244	217.4	110.8
5	04.5	02.3	65	57.9	29.5	125	111.4	56.7	185	164.8	84.0	245	218.3	111.2
6	05.3	02.7	66	58.8	30.0	126	112.3	57.2	186	165.7	84.4	246	219.2	111.7
7	06.2	03.2	67	59.7	30.4	127	113.2	57.7	187	166.6	84.9	247	220.1	112.1
8	07.1	03.6	68	60.6	30.9	128	114.0	58.1	188	167.5	85.3	248	221.0	112.6
9	08.0	04.1	69	61.5	31.3	129	114.9	58.6	189	168.4	85.8	249	221.9	113.0
10	08.9	04.5	70	62.4	31.8	130	115.8	59.0	190	169.3	86.3	250	222.8	113.5
11	09.8	05.0	71	63.3	32.2	131	116.7	59.5	191	170.2	86.7	251	223.6	114.0
12	10.7	05.4	72	64.2	32.7	132	117.6	59.9	192	171.1	87.2	252	224.5	114.4
13	11.6	05.9	73	65.0	33.1	133	118.5	60.4	193	172.0	87.6	253	225.4	114.9
14	12.5	06.4	74	65.9	33.6	134	119.4	60.8	194	172.9	88.1	254	226.3	115.3
15	13.4	06.8	75	66.8	34.0	135	120.3	61.3	195	173.7	88.5	255	227.2	115.8
16	14.3	07.3	76	67.7	34.5	136	121.2	61.7	196	174.6	89.0	256	228.1	116.2
17	15.1	07.7	77	68.6	35.0	137	122.1	62.2	197	175.5	89.4	257	229.0	116.7
18	16.0	08.2	78	69.5	35.4	138	123.0	62.7	198	176.4	89.9	258	229.9	117.1
19	16.9	08.6	79	70.4	35.9	139	123.8	63.1	199	177.3	90.3	259	230.8	117.6
20	17.8	09.1	80	71.3	36.3	140	124.7	63.6	200	178.2	90.8	260	231.7	118.0
21	18.7	09.5	81	72.2	36.8	141	125.6	64.0	201	179.1	91.3	261	232.6	118.5
22	19.6	10.0	82	73.1	37.2	142	126.5	64.5	202	180.0	91.7	262	233.4	118.9
23	20.5	10.4	83	74.0	37.7	143	127.4	64.9	203	180.9	92.2	263	234.3	119.4
24	21.4	10.9	84	74.8	38.1	144	128.3	65.4	204	181.8	92.6	264	235.2	119.9
25	22.3	11.3	85	75.7	38.6	145	129.2	65.8	205	182.7	93.1	265	236.1	120.3
26	23.2	11.8	86	76.6	39.0	146	130.1	66.3	206	183.5	93.5	266	237.0	120.8
27	24.1	12.3	87	77.5	39.5	147	131.0	66.7	207	184.4	94.0	267	237.9	121.2
28	24.9	12.7	88	78.4	40.0	148	131.9	67.2	208	185.3	94.4	268	238.8	121.7
29	25.8	13.2	89	79.3	40.4	149	132.8	67.6	209	186.2	94.9	269	239.7	122.1
30	26.7	13.6	90	80.2	40.9	150	133.7	68.1	210	187.1	95.3	270	240.6	122.6
31	27.6	14.1	91	81.1	41.3	151	134.5	68.6	211	188.0	95.8	271	241.5	123.0
32	28.5	14.5	92	82.0	41.8	152	135.4	69.0	212	188.9	96.2	272	242.4	123.5
33	29.4	15.0	93	82.9	42.2	153	136.3	69.5	213	189.8	96.7	273	243.2	123.9
34	30.3	15.4	94	83.8	42.7	154	137.2	69.9	214	190.7	97.2	274	244.1	124.4
35	31.2	15.9	95	84.6	43.1	155	138.1	70.4	215	191.6	97.6	275	245.0	124.8
36	32.1	16.3	96	85.5	43.6	156	139.0	70.8	216	192.5	98.1	276	245.9	125.3
37	33.0	16.8	97	86.4	44.0	157	139.9	71.3	217	193.3	98.5	277	246.8	125.8
38	33.9	17.3	98	87.3	44.5	158	140.8	71.7	218	194.2	99.0	278	247.7	126.2
39	34.7	17.7	99	88.2	44.9	159	141.7	72.2	219	195.1	99.4	279	248.6	126.7
40	35.6	18.2	100	89.1	45.4	160	142.6	72.6	220	196.0	99.9	280	249.5	127.1
41	36.5	18.6	101	90.0	45.9	161	143.5	73.1	221	196.9	100.3	281	250.4	127.6
42	37.4	19.1	102	90.9	46.3	162	144.3	73.5	222	197.8	100.8	282	251.3	128.0
43	38.3	19.5	103	91.8	46.8	163	145.2	74.0	223	198.7	101.2	283	252.2	128.5
44	39.2	20.0	104	92.7	47.2	164	146.1	74.5	224	199.6	101.7	284	253.0	128.9
45	40.1	20.4	105	93.6	47.7	165	147.0	74.9	225	200.5	102.1	285	253.9	129.4
46	41.0	20.9	106	94.4	48.1	166	147.9	75.4	226	201.4	102.6	286	254.8	129.8
47	41.9	21.3	107	95.3	48.6	167	148.8	75.8	227	202.3	103.1	287	255.7	130.3
48	42.8	21.8	108	96.2	49.0	168	149.7	76.3	228	203.1	103.5	288	256.6	130.7
49	43.7	22.2	109	97.1	49.5	169	150.6	76.7	229	204.0	104.0	289	257.5	131.2
50	44.6	22.7	110	98.0	49.9	170	151.5	77.2	230	204.9	104.4	290	258.4	131.7
51	45.4	23.2	111	98.9	50.4	171	152.4	77.6	231	205.8	104.9	291	259.3	132.1
52	46.3	23.6	112	99.8	50.8	172	153.3	78.1	232	206.7	105.3	292	260.2	132.6
53	47.2	24.1	113	100.7	51.3	173	154.1	78.5	233	207.6	105.8	293	261.1	133.0
54	48.1	24.5	114	101.6	51.8	174	155.0	79.0	234	208.5	106.2	294	262.0	133.5
55	49.0	25.0	115	102.5	52.2	175	155.9	79.4	235	209.4	106.7	295	262.8	133.9
56	49.9	25.4	116	103.4	52.7	176	156.8	79.9	236	210.3	107.1	296	263.7	134.4
57	50.8	25.9	117	104.2	53.1	177	157.7	80.4	237	211.2	107.6	297	264.6	134.8
58	51.7	26.3	118	105.1	53.6	178	158.6	80.8	238	212.1	108.0	298	265.5	135.3
59	52.6	26.8	119	106.0	54.0	179	159.5	81.3	239	213.0	108.5	299	266.4	135.7
60	53.5	27.2	120	106.9	54.5	180	160.4	81.7	240	213.8	109.0	300	267.3	136.2
Dist.	Dep.	D. Lat.	Dist.	Dep.	D. Lat.	Dist.	Dep.	D. Lat.	Dist.	Dep.	D. Lat.	Dist.	Dep.	D. Lat.
D. Lon		Dep.	D. Lon		Dep.	D. Lon		Dep.	D. Lon		Dep.	D. Lon		Dep.

63°

TRAVERSE TABLE
27 Degrees

D. Lon	Dep.		D. Lon	Dep.		D. Lon	Dep.		D. Lon	Dep.		D. Lon	Dep.	
Dist.	D. Lat.	Dep.	Dist.	D. Lat.	Dep.	Dist.	D. Lat.	Dep.	Dist.	D. Lat.	Dep.	Dist.	D. Lat.	Dep.
301	268·2	136·7	361	321·7	163·9	421	375·1	191·1	481	428·6	218·4	541	482·0	245·6
302	269·1	137·1	362	322·5	164·3	422	376·0	191·6	482	429·5	218·8	542	482·9	246·1
303	270·0	137·6	363	323·4	164·8	423	376·9	192·0	483	430·4	219·3	543	483·8	246·5
304	270·9	138·0	364	324·3	165·3	424	377·8	192·5	484	431·2	219·7	544	484·7	247·0
305	271·8	138·5	365	325·2	165·7	425	378·7	192·9	485	432·1	220·2	545	485·6	247·9
306	272·6	138·9	366	326·1	166·2	426	379·6	193·4	486	433·0	220·6	546	486·5	247·9
307	273·5	139·4	367	327·0	166·6	427	380·5	193·9	487	433·9	221·1	547	487·4	248·3
308	274·4	139·8	368	327·9	167·1	428	381·4	194·3	488	434·8	221·5	548	488·3	248·8
309	275·3	140·3	369	328·8	167·5	429	382·2	194·8	489	435·7	222·0	549	489·2	249·2
310	276·2	140·7	370	329·7	168·0	430	383·1	195·2	490	436·6	222·5	550	490·1	249·7
311	277·1	141·2	371	330·6	168·4	431	384·0	195·7	491	437·5	222·9	551	490·9	250·1
312	278·0	141·6	372	331·5	168·9	432	384·9	196·1	492	438·4	223·4	552	491·8	250·6
313	278·9	142·1	373	322·3	169·3	433	385·8	196·6	493	439·3	223·8	553	492·7	251·1
314	279·8	142·6	374	333·2	169·8	434	386·7	197·0	494	440·2	224·3	554	493·6	251·5
315	280·7	143·0	375	334·1	170·2	435	387·6	197·5	495	441·0	224·7	555	494·5	252·0
316	281·6	143·5	376	335·0	170·7	436	388·5	197·9	496	441·9	225·2	556	495·4	252·4
317	282·4	143·9	377	335·9	171·2	437	389·4	198·4	497	442·8	225·6	557	496·3	252·9
318	283·3	144·4	378	336·8	171·6	438	390·3	198·8	498	443·7	226·1	558	497·2	253·3
319	284·2	144·8	379	337·7	172·1	439	391·2	199·3	499	444·6	226·5	559	498·1	253·8
320	285·1	145·3	380	338·6	172·5	440	392·0	199·8	500	445·5	227·0	560	499·0	254·2
321	286·0	145·7	381	339·5	173·0	441	392·9	200·2	501	446·4	227·4	561	499·9	254·7
322	286·9	146·2	382	340·4	173·4	442	393·8	200·7	502	447·3	227·9	562	500·7	255·1
323	287·8	146·6	383	341·3	173·9	443	394·7	201·1	503	448·2	228·4	563	501·6	255·6
324	288·7	147·1	384	342·1	174·3	444	395·6	201·6	504	449·1	228·8	564	502·5	256·1
325	289·6	147·5	385	343·0	174·8	445	396·5	202·0	505	450·0	229·3	565	503·4	256·5
326	290·5	148·0	386	343·9	175·2	446	397·4	202·5	506	450·8	229·7	566	504·3	257·0
327	291·4	148·5	387	344·8	175·7	447	398·3	202·9	507	451·7	230·2	567	505·2	257·4
328	292·3	148·9	388	345·7	176·1	448	399·2	203·4	508	452·6	230·6	568	506·1	257·9
329	293·1	149·4	389	346·6	176·6	449	400·1	203·8	509	453·5	231·1	569	507·0	258·3
330	294·0	149·8	390	347·5	177·1	450	401·0	204·3	510	454·4	231·5	570	507·9	258·8
331	294·9	150·3	391	348·4	177·5	451	401·8	204·7	511	455·3	232·0	571	508·8	259·2
332	295·8	150·7	392	349·3	178·0	452	402·7	205·2	512	456·2	232·4	572	509·6	259·7
333	296·7	151·2	393	350·2	178·4	453	403·6	205·7	513	457·1	232·9	573	510·5	260·1
334	297·6	151·6	394	351·1	178·9	454	404·5	206·1	514	458·0	233·4	574	511·4	260·6
335	298·5	152·1	395	351·9	179·3	455	405·4	206·6	515	458·9	233·8	575	512·3	261·0
336	299·4	152·5	396	352·8	179·8	456	406·3	207·0	516	459·8	234·3	576	513·2	261·5
337	300·3	153·0	397	353·7	180·2	457	407·2	207·5	517	460·7	234·7	577	514·1	262·0
338	301·2	153·4	398	354·6	180·7	458	408·1	207·9	518	461·5	235·2	578	515·0	262·4
339	302·1	153·9	399	355·5	181·1	459	409·0	208·4	519	462·4	235·6	579	515·9	262·9
340	302·9	154·4	400	356·4	181·6	460	409·9	208·8	520	463·3	236·1	580	516·8	263·4
341	303·8	154·8	401	357·3	182·1	461	410·8	209·3	521	464·2	236·5	581	517·7	263·8
342	304·7	155·3	402	358·2	182·5	462	411·6	209·7	522	465·1	237·0	582	518·6	264·2
343	305·6	155·7	403	359·1	183·0	463	412·5	210·2	523	466·0	237·4	583	519·5	264·7
344	306·5	156·2	404	360·0	183·4	464	413·4	210·7	524	466·9	237·9	584	520·3	265·1
345	307·4	156·6	405	360·9	183·9	465	414·3	211·1	525	467·8	238·3	585	521·2	265·6
346	308·3	157·1	406	361·8	184·3	466	415·2	211·6	526	468·7	238·8	586	522·1	266·0
347	309·2	157·5	407	362·6	184·8	467	416·1	212·0	527	469·6	239·3	587	523·0	266·5
348	310·1	158·0	408	363·5	185·2	468	417·0	212·5	528	470·5	239·7	588	523·9	266·9
349	311·0	158·4	409	364·4	185·7	469	417·9	212·9	529	471·3	240·2	589	524·8	267·4
350	311·9	158·9	410	365·3	186·1	470	418·8	213·4	530	472·2	240·6	590	525·7	267·9
351	312·7	159·4	411	366·2	186·6	471	419·7	213·8	531	473·1	241·1	591	526·6	268·3
352	313·6	159·8	412	367·1	187·0	472	420·6	214·3	532	474·0	241·5	592	527·5	268·8
353	314·5	160·3	413	368·0	187·5	473	421·4	214·7	533	474·9	242·0	593	528·4	269·2
354	315·4	160·7	414	368·9	188·0	474	422·3	215·2	534	475·8	242·4	594	529·3	269·7
355	316·3	161·2	415	369·8	188·4	475	423·2	215·6	535	476·7	242·9	595	530·1	270·1
356	317·2	161·6	416	370·7	188·9	476	424·1	216·1	536	477·6	243·3	596	531·0	270·6
357	318·1	162·1	417	371·5	189·3	477	425·0	216·6	537	478·5	243·8	597	531·9	271·0
358	319·0	162·5	418	372·4	189·8	478	425·9	217·0	538	479·4	244·2	598	532·8	271·5
359	319·9	163·0	419	373·3	190·2	479	426·8	217·5	539	480·3	244·7	599	533·7	271·9
360	320·8	163·4	420	374·2	190·7	480	427·7	217·9	540	481·1	245·2	600	534·6	272·4
Dist.	Dep.	D. Lat.	Dist.	Dep.	D. Lat.	Dist.	Dep.	D. Lat.	Dist.	Dep.	D. Lat.	Dist.	Dep.	D. Lat.
D. Lon		Dep.	D. Lon		Dep.	D. Lon		Dep.	D. Lon		Dep.	D. Lon		Dep.

TRAVERSE TABLE
28 Degrees

28°

D. Lon	Dep.		D. Lon	Dep.		D. Lon	Dep.		D. Lon	Dep.		D. Lon	Dep.	
Dist.	D. Lat.	Dep.	Dist.	D. Lat.	Dep.	Dist.	D. Lat.	Dep.	Dist.	D. Lat.	Dep.	Dist.	D. Lat.	Dep.
1	00·9	00·5	61	53·9	28·6	121	106·8	56·8	181	159·8	85·0	241	212·8	113·1
2	01·8	00·9	62	54·7	29·1	122	107·7	57·3	182	160·7	85·4	242	213·7	113·6
3	02·6	01·4	63	55·6	29·6	123	108·6	57·7	183	161·6	85·9	243	214·6	114·1
4	03·5	01·9	64	56·5	30·0	124	109·5	58·2	184	162·5	86·4	244	215·4	114·6
5	04·4	02·3	65	57·4	30·5	125	110·4	58·7	185	163·3	86·9	245	216·3	115·0
6	05·3	02·8	66	58·3	31·0	126	111·3	59·2	186	164·2	87·3	246	217·2	115·5
7	06·2	03·3	67	59·2	31·5	127	112·1	59·6	187	165·1	87·8	247	218·1	116·0
8	07·1	03·8	68	60·0	31·9	128	113·0	60·1	188	166·0	88·3	248	219·0	116·4
9	08·0	04·2	69	60·9	32·4	129	113·9	60·6	189	166·9	88·7	249	219·9	116·9
10	08·8	04·7	70	61·8	32·9	130	114·8	61·0	190	167·8	89·2	250	220·7	117·4
11	09·7	05·2	71	62·7	33·3	131	115·7	61·5	191	168·6	89·7	251	221·6	117·9
12	10·6	05·6	72	63·6	33·8	132	116·5	62·0	192	169·5	90·1	252	222·5	118·3
13	11·5	06·1	73	64·5	34·3	133	117·4	62·4	193	170·4	90·6	253	223·4	118·8
14	12·4	06·6	74	65·3	34·7	134	118·3	62·9	194	171·3	91·1	254	224·3	119·2
15	13·2	07·0	75	66·2	35·2	135	119·2	63·4	195	172·2	91·5	255	225·2	119·7
16	14·1	07·5	76	67·1	35·7	136	120·1	63·8	196	173·1	92·0	256	226·0	120·2
17	15·0	08·0	77	68·0	36·1	137	121·0	64·3	197	173·9	92·5	257	226·9	120·7
18	15·9	08·5	78	68·9	36·6	138	121·8	64·8	198	174·8	93·0	258	227·8	121·1
19	16·8	08·9	79	69·8	37·1	139	122·7	65·3	199	175·7	93·4	259	228·7	121·6
20	17·7	09·4	80	70·6	37·6	140	123·6	65·7	200	176·6	93·9	260	229·6	122·1
21	18·5	09·9	81	71·5	38·0	141	124·5	66·2	201	177·5	94·4	261	230·4	122·5
22	19·4	10·3	82	72·4	38·5	142	125·4	66·7	202	178·4	94·8	262	231·3	123·0
23	20·3	10·8	83	73·3	39·0	143	126·3	67·1	203	179·2	95·3	263	232·2	123·5
24	21·2	11·3	84	74·2	39·4	144	127·1	67·6	204	180·1	95·8	264	233·1	123·9
25	22·1	11·7	85	75·1	39·9	145	128·0	68·1	205	181·0	96·2	265	234·0	124·4
26	23·0	12·2	86	75·9	40·4	146	128·9	68·5	206	181·9	96·7	266	234·9	124·9
27	23·8	12·7	87	76·8	40·8	147	129·8	69·0	207	182·8	97·2	267	235·7	125·3
28	24·7	13·1	88	77·7	41·3	148	130·7	69·5	208	183·7	97·7	268	236·6	125·8
29	25·6	13·6	89	78·6	41·8	149	131·6	70·0	209	184·5	98·1	269	237·5	126·3
30	26·5	14·1	90	79·5	42·3	150	132·4	70·4	210	185·4	98·6	270	238·4	126·8
31	27·4	14·6	91	80·3	42·7	151	133·3	70·9	211	186·3	99·1	271	239·3	127·2
32	28·3	15·0	92	81·2	43·2	152	134·2	71·4	212	187·2	99·5	272	240·2	127·7
33	29·1	15·5	93	82·1	43·7	153	135·1	71·8	213	188·1	100·0	273	241·0	128·2
34	30·0	16·0	94	83·0	44·1	154	136·0	72·3	214	189·0	100·5	274	241·9	128·6
35	30·9	16·4	95	83·9	44·6	155	136·9	72·8	215	189·8	100·9	275	242·8	129·1
36	31·8	16·9	96	84·8	45·1	156	137·7	73·2	216	190·7	101·4	276	243·7	129·6
37	32·7	17·4	97	85·6	45·5	157	138·6	73·7	217	191·6	101·9	277	244·6	130·0
38	33·6	17·8	98	86·5	46·0	158	139·5	74·2	218	192·5	102·3	278	245·5	130·5
39	34·4	18·3	99	87·4	46·5	159	140·4	74·6	219	193·4	102·8	279	246·3	131·0
40	35·3	18·8	100	88·3	46·9	160	141·3	75·1	220	194·2	103·3	280	247·2	131·5
41	36·2	19·2	101	89·2	47·4	161	142·2	75·6	221	195·1	103·8	281	248·1	131·9
42	37·1	19·7	102	90·1	47·9	162	143·0	76·1	222	196·0	104·2	282	249·0	132·4
43	38·0	20·2	103	90·9	48·4	163	143·9	76·5	223	196·9	104·7	283	249·9	132·9
44	38·8	20·7	104	91·8	48·8	164	144·8	77·0	224	197·8	105·2	284	250·8	133·3
45	39·7	21·1	105	92·7	49·3	165	145·7	77·5	225	198·7	105·6	285	251·6	133·8
46	40·6	21·6	106	93·6	49·8	166	146·6	77·9	226	199·5	106·1	286	252·5	134·3
47	41·5	22·1	107	94·5	50·2	167	147·5	78·4	227	200·4	106·6	287	253·4	134·7
48	42·4	22·5	108	95·4	50·7	168	148·3	78·9	228	201·3	107·0	288	254·3	135·2
49	43·3	23·0	109	96·2	51·2	169	149·2	79·3	229	202·2	107·5	289	255·2	135·7
50	44·1	23·5	110	97·1	51·6	170	150·1	79·8	230	203·1	108·0	290	256·1	136·1
51	45·0	23·9	111	98·0	52·1	171	151·0	80·3	231	204·0	108·4	291	256·9	136·6
52	45·9	24·4	112	98·9	52·6	172	151·9	80·7	232	204·8	108·9	292	257·8	137·1
53	46·8	24·9	113	99·8	53·0	173	152·7	81·2	233	205·7	109·4	293	258·7	137·6
54	47·7	25·4	114	100·7	53·5	174	153·6	81·7	234	206·6	109·9	294	259·6	138·0
55	48·6	25·8	115	101·5	54·0	175	154·5	82·2	235	207·5	110·3	295	260·5	138·5
56	49·4	26·3	116	102·4	54·5	176	155·4	82·6	236	208·4	110·8	296	261·3	139·0
57	50·3	26·8	117	103·3	54·9	177	156·3	83·1	237	209·3	111·3	297	262·2	139·4
58	51·2	27·2	118	104·2	55·4	178	157·2	83·6	238	210·1	111·7	298	263·1	139·9
59	52·1	27·7	119	105·1	55·9	179	158·0	84·0	239	211·0	112·2	299	264·0	140·4
60	53·0	28·2	120	106·0	56·3	180	158·9	84·5	240	211·9	112·7	300	264·9	140·8
Dist.	Dep.	D. Lat.	Dist.	Dep.	D. Lat.	Dist.	Dep.	D. Lat.	Dist.	Dep.	D. Lat.	Dist.	Dep.	D. Lat.
D. Lon		Dep.	D. Lon		Dep.	D. Lon		Dep.	D. Lon		Dep.	D. Lon		Dep.

62°

TRAVERSE TABLE
28 Degrees

Dist.	D. Lat.	Dep.	Dist.	D. Lat.	Dep.	Dist.	D. Lat.	Dep.	Dist.	D. Lat.	Dep.	Dist.	D. Lat.	Dep.
301	265·8	141·3	361	318·7	169·5	421	371·7	197·6	481	424·7	225·8	541	477·7	254·0
302	266·7	141·8	362	319·6	169·9	422	372·6	198·1	482	425·6	226·3	542	478·6	254·5
303	267·5	142·2	363	320·5	170·4	423	373·5	198·6	483	426·5	226·8	543	479·4	254·9
304	268·4	142·7	364	321·4	170·9	424	374·4	199·1	484	427·3	227·2	544	480·3	255·4
305	269·3	143·2	365	322·3	171·4	425	375·3	199·5	485	428·2	227·7	545	481·2	255·9
306	270·2	143·7	366	323·2	171·8	426	376·1	200·0	486	429·1	228·2	546	482·1	256·3
307	271·1	144·1	367	324·0	172·3	427	377·0	200·5	487	430·0	228·6	547	483·0	256·8
308	271·9	144·6	368	324·9	172·8	428	377·9	200·9	488	430·9	229·1	548	483·9	257·3
309	272·8	145·1	369	325·8	173·2	429	378·8	201·4	489	431·8	229·6	549	484·7	257·7
310	273·7	145·5	370	326·7	173·7	430	379·7	201·9	490	432·6	230·0	550	485·6	258·2
311	274·6	146·0	371	327·6	174·2	431	380·6	202·3	491	433·5	230·5	551	486·5	258·7
312	275·5	146·5	372	328·5	174·6	432	381·4	202·8	492	434·4	231·0	552	487·4	259·1
313	276·4	146·9	373	329·3	175·1	433	382·3	203·3	493	435·3	231·4	553	488·3	259·6
314	277·2	147·4	374	330·2	175·6	434	383·2	203·8	494	436·2	231·9	554	489·2	260·1
315	278·1	147·9	375	331·1	176·1	435	384·1	204·2	495	437·1	232·4	555	490·0	260·6
316	279·0	148·4	376	332·0	176·5	436	385·0	204·7	496	437·9	232·9	556	490·9	261·0
317	279·9	148·8	377	332·9	177·0	437	385·8	205·2	497	438·8	233·3	557	491·8	261·5
318	280·8	149·3	378	333·8	177·5	438	386·7	205·6	498	439·7	233·8	558	492·7	262·0
319	281·7	149·8	379	334·6	177·9	439	387·6	206·1	499	440·6	234·3	559	493·6	262·4
320	282·5	150·2	380	335·5	178·4	440	388·5	206·6	500	441·5	234·7	560	494·5	262·9
321	283·4	150·7	381	336·4	178·9	441	389·4	207·0	501	442·4	235·2	561	495·3	263·4
322	284·3	151·2	382	337·3	179·3	442	390·3	207·5	502	443·2	235·7	562	496·2	263·8
323	285·2	151·6	383	338·2	179·8	443	391·1	208·0	503	444·1	236·1	563	497·1	264·3
324	286·1	152·1	384	339·1	180·3	444	392·0	208·4	504	445·0	236·6	564	498·0	264·8
325	287·0	152·6	385	339·9	180·7	445	392·9	208·9	505	445·9	237·1	565	498·9	265·3
326	287·8	153·0	386	340·8	181·2	446	393·8	209·4	506	446·8	237·6	566	499·7	265·7
327	288·7	153·5	387	341·7	181·7	447	394·7	209·9	507	447·7	238·0	567	500·6	266·2
328	289·6	154·0	388	342·6	182·2	448	395·6	210·3	508	448·5	238·5	568	501·5	266·7
329	290·5	154·5	389	343·5	182·6	449	396·4	210·8	509	449·4	239·0	569	502·4	267·1
330	291·4	154·9	390	344·3	183·1	450	397·3	211·3	510	450·3	239·4	570	503·3	267·6
331	292·3	155·4	391	345·2	183·6	451	398·2	211·7	511	451·2	239·9	571	504·2	268·1
332	293·1	155·9	392	346·1	184·0	452	399·1	212·2	512	452·1	240·4	572	505·0	268·5
333	294·0	156·3	393	347·0	184·5	453	400·0	212·7	513	453·0	240·8	573	505·9	269·0
334	294·9	156·8	394	347·9	185·0	454	400·9	213·1	514	453·8	241·3	574	506·8	269·5
335	295·8	157·3	395	348·8	185·4	455	401·7	213·6	515	454·7	241·8	575	507·7	269·9
336	296·7	157·7	396	349·6	185·9	456	402·6	214·1	516	455·6	242·2	576	508·6	270·4
337	297·6	158·2	397	350·5	186·4	457	403·5	214·5	517	456·5	242·7	577	509·5	270·9
338	298·4	158·7	398	351·4	186·8	458	404·4	215·0	518	457·4	243·2	578	510·3	271·4
339	299·3	159·2	399	352·3	187·3	459	405·3	215·5	519	458·2	243·7	579	511·2	271·8
340	300·2	159·6	400	353·2	187·8	460	406·2	216·0	520	459·1	244·1	580	512·1	272·3
341	301·1	160·1	401	354·1	188·3	461	407·0	216·4	521	460·0	244·6	581	513·0	272·8
342	302·0	160·6	402	354·9	188·7	462	407·9	216·9	522	460·9	245·1	582	513·9	273·2
343	302·9	161·0	403	355·8	189·2	463	408·8	217·4	523	461·8	245·5	583	514·8	273·7
344	303·7	161·5	404	356·7	189·7	464	409·7	217·8	524	462·7	246·0	584	515·6	274·2
345	304·6	162·0	405	357·6	190·1	465	410·6	218·3	525	463·5	246·5	585	516·5	274·6
346	305·5	162·4	406	358·5	190·6	466	411·5	218·8	526	464·4	246·9	586	517·4	275·1
347	306·4	162·9	407	359·4	191·1	467	412·3	219·2	527	465·3	247·4	587	518·3	275·4
348	307·3	163·4	408	360·2	191·5	468	413·2	219·7	528	466·2	247·9	588	519·2	276·0
349	308·1	163·8	409	361·1	192·0	469	414·1	220·2	529	467·1	248·4	589	520·1	276·5
350	309·0	164·3	410	362·0	192·5	470	415·0	220·7	530	468·0	248·8	590	520·9	277·0
351	309·9	164·8	411	362·9	193·0	471	415·9	221·1	531	468·8	249·3	591	521·8	277·5
352	310·8	165·3	412	363·8	193·4	472	416·8	221·6	532	469·7	249·8	592	522·7	277·9
353	311·7	165·7	413	364·7	193·9	473	417·6	222·1	533	470·7	250·2	593	523·6	278·4
354	312·6	166·2	414	365·5	194·4	474	418·5	222·5	534	471·5	250·7	594	524·5	278·9
355	313·4	166·7	415	366·4	194·8	475	419·4	223·0	535	472·4	251·2	595	525·4	279·3
356	314·3	167·1	416	367·3	195·3	476	420·3	223·5	536	473·3	251·6	596	526·2	279·8
357	315·2	167·6	417	368·2	195·8	477	421·2	223·9	537	474·1	252·1	597	527·1	280·3
358	316·1	168·1	418	369·1	196·2	478	422·0	224·4	538	475·0	252·6	598	528·0	280·7
359	317·0	168·5	419	370·0	196·7	479	422·9	224·9	539	475·9	253·0	599	528·9	281·2
360	317·9	169·0	420	370·8	197·2	480	423·8	225·3	540	476·8	253·5	600	529·8	281·7

Dist.	Dep.	D. Lat.	Dist.	Dep.	D. Lat.	Dist.	Dep.	D. Lat.	Dist.	Dep.	D. Lat.	Dist.	Dep.	D. Lat.
D. Lon		Dep.	D. Lon		Dep.	D. Lon		Dep.	D. Lon		Dep.	D. Lon		Dep.

TRAVERSE TABLE
29 Degrees

29°

Dist.	D. Lat.	Dep.	Dist.	D. Lat.	Dep.	Dist.	D. Lat.	Dep.	Dist.	D. Lat.	Dep.	Dist.	D. Lat.	Dep.
1	00·9	00·5	61	53·4	29·6	121	105·8	58·7	181	158·3	87·8	241	210·8	116·8
2	01·7	01·0	62	54·2	30·1	122	106·7	59·1	182	159·2	88·2	242	211·7	117·3
3	02·6	01·5	63	55·1	30·5	123	107·6	59·6	183	160·1	88·7	243	212·5	117·8
4	03·5	01·9	64	56·0	31·0	124	108·5	60·1	184	160·9	89·2	244	213·4	118·3
5	04·4	02·4	65	56·9	31·5	125	109·3	60·6	185	161·8	89·7	245	214·3	118·8
6	05·2	02·9	66	57·7	32·0	126	110·2	61·1	186	162·7	90·2	246	215·2	119·3
7	06·1	03·4	67	58·6	32·5	127	111·1	61·6	187	163·6	90·7	247	216·0	119·7
8	07·0	03·9	68	59·5	33·0	128	112·0	62·1	188	164·4	91·1	248	216·9	120·2
9	07·9	04·4	69	60·3	33·5	129	112·8	62·5	189	165·3	91·6	249	217·8	120·7
10	08·7	04·8	70	61·2	33·9	130	113·7	63·0	190	166·2	92·1	250	218·7	121·2
11	09·6	05·3	71	62·1	34·4	131	114·6	63·5	191	167·1	92·6	251	219·5	121·7
12	10·5	05·8	72	63·0	34·9	132	115·4	64·0	192	167·9	93·1	252	220·4	122·2
13	11·4	06·3	73	63·8	35·4	133	116·3	64·5	193	168·8	93·6	253	221·3	122·7
14	12·2	06·8	74	64·7	35·9	134	117·2	65·0	194	169·7	94·1	254	222·2	123·1
15	13·1	07·3	75	65·6	36·4	135	118·1	65·4	195	170·6	94·5	255	223·0	123·6
16	14·0	07·8	76	66·5	36·8	136	118·9	65·9	196	171·4	95·0	256	223·9	124·1
17	14·9	08·2	77	67·3	37·3	137	119·8	66·4	197	172·3	95·5	257	224·8	124·6
18	15·7	08·7	78	68·2	37·8	138	120·7	66·9	198	173·2	96·0	258	225·7	125·1
19	16·6	09·2	79	69·1	38·3	139	121·6	67·4	199	174·0	96·5	259	226·5	125·6
20	17·5	09·7	80	70·0	38·8	140	122·4	67·9	200	174·9	97·0	260	227·4	126·1
21	18·4	10·2	81	70·8	39·3	141	123·3	68·4	201	175·8	97·4	261	228·3	126·5
22	19·2	10·7	82	71·7	39·8	142	124·2	68·8	202	176·7	97·9	262	229·2	127·0
23	20·1	11·2	83	72·6	40·2	143	125·1	69·3	203	177·5	98·4	263	230·0	127·5
24	21·0	11·6	84	73·5	40·7	144	125·9	69·8	204	178·4	98·9	264	230·9	128·0
25	21·9	12·1	85	74·3	41·2	145	126·8	70·3	205	179·3	99·4	265	231·8	128·5
26	22·7	12·6	86	75·2	41·7	146	127·7	70·8	206	180·2	99·9	266	232·6	129·0
27	23·6	13·1	87	76·1	42·2	147	128·6	71·3	207	181·0	100·4	267	233·5	129·4
28	24·5	13·6	88	77·0	42·7	148	129·4	71·8	208	181·9	100·8	268	234·4	129·9
29	25·4	14·1	89	77·8	43·1	149	130·3	72·2	209	182·8	101·3	269	235·3	130·4
30	26·2	14·5	90	78·7	43·6	150	131·2	72·7	210	183·7	101·8	270	236·1	130·9
31	27·1	15·0	91	79·6	44·1	151	132·1	73·2	211	184·5	102·3	271	237·0	131·4
32	28·0	15·5	92	80·5	44·6	152	132·9	73·7	212	185·4	102·8	272	237·9	131·9
33	28·9	16·0	93	81·3	45·1	153	133·8	74·2	213	186·3	103·3	273	238·8	132·4
34	29·7	16·5	94	82·2	45·6	154	134·7	74·7	214	187·2	103·7	274	239·6	132·8
35	30·6	17·0	95	83·1	46·1	155	135·6	75·1	215	188·0	104·2	275	240·5	133·3
36	31·5	17·5	96	84·0	46·5	156	136·4	75·6	216	188·9	104·7	276	241·4	133·8
37	32·4	17·9	97	84·8	47·0	157	137·3	76·1	217	189·8	105·2	277	242·3	134·3
38	33·2	18·4	98	85·7	47·5	158	138·2	76·6	218	190·7	105·7	278	243·1	134·8
39	34·1	18·9	99	86·6	48·0	159	139·1	77·1	219	191·5	106·2	279	244·0	135·3
40	35·0	19·4	100	87·5	48·5	160	139·9	77·6	220	192·4	106·7	280	244·9	135·7
41	35·9	19·9	101	88·3	49·0	161	140·8	78·1	221	193·3	107·1	281	245·8	136·2
42	36·7	20·4	102	89·2	49·5	162	141·7	78·5	222	194·2	107·6	282	246·6	136·7
43	37·6	20·8	103	90·1	49·9	163	142·6	79·0	223	195·0	108·1	283	247·5	137·2
44	38·5	21·3	104	91·0	50·4	164	143·4	79·5	224	195·9	108·6	284	248·4	137·7
45	39·4	21·8	105	91·8	50·9	165	144·3	80·0	225	196·8	109·1	285	249·3	138·2
46	40·2	22·3	106	92·7	51·4	166	145·2	80·5	226	197·7	109·6	286	250·1	138·7
47	41·1	22·8	107	93·6	51·9	167	146·1	81·0	227	198·5	110·1	287	251·0	139·1
48	42·0	23·3	108	94·5	52·4	168	146·9	81·4	228	199·4	110·5	288	251·9	139·6
49	42·9	23·8	109	95·3	52·8	169	147·8	81·9	229	200·3	111·0	289	252·8	140·1
50	43·7	24·2	110	96·2	53·3	170	148·7	82·4	230	201·2	111·5	290	253·6	140·6
51	44·6	24·7	111	97·1	53·8	171	149·6	82·9	231	202·0	112·0	291	254·5	141·1
52	45·5	25·2	112	98·0	54·3	172	150·4	83·4	232	202·9	112·5	292	255·4	141·6
53	46·4	25·7	113	98·8	54·8	173	151·3	83·9	233	203·8	113·0	293	256·3	142·0
54	47·2	26·2	114	99·7	55·3	174	152·2	84·4	234	204·7	113·4	294	257·1	142·5
55	48·1	26·7	115	100·6	55·8	175	153·1	84·8	235	205·5	113·9	295	258·0	143·0
56	49·0	27·1	116	101·5	56·2	176	153·9	85·3	236	206·4	114·4	296	258·9	143·5
57	49·9	27·6	117	102·3	56·7	177	154·8	85·8	237	207·3	114·9	297	259·8	144·0
58	50·7	28·1	118	103·2	57·2	178	155·7	86·3	238	208·2	115·4	298	260·6	144·5
59	51·6	28·6	119	104·1	57·7	179	156·6	86·8	239	209·0	115·9	299	261·5	145·0
60	52·5	29·1	120	105·0	58·2	180	157·4	87·3	240	209·9	116·4	300	262·4	145·4

61°

| Dist. | Dep. | D. Lat. | Dist. | Dep. | D. Lat. | Dist. | Dep. | D. Lat. | Dist. | Dep. | D. Lat. | Dist. | Dep. | D. Lat. |

TRAVERSE TABLE
29 Degrees

Dist.	D. Lat.	Dep.	Dist.	D. Lat.	Dep.	Dist.	D. Lat.	Dep.	Dist.	D. Lat.	Dep.	Dist.	D. Lat.	Dep.
301	263·3	145·9	361	315·7	175·0	421	368·2	204·1	481	420·7	233·2	541	473·2	262·3
302	264·1	146·4	362	316·6	175·5	422	369·1	204·6	482	421·6	233·7	542	474·0	262·8
303	265·0	146·9	363	317·5	176·0	423	370·0	205·1	483	422·4	234·2	543	474·9	263·3
304	265·9	147·4	364	318·4	176·5	424	370·8	205·6	484	423·3	234·6	544	475·8	263·7
305	266·8	147·9	365	319·2	177·0	425	371·7	206·0	485	424·2	235·1	545	476·7	264·2
306	267·6	148·4	366	320·1	177·4	426	372·6	206·5	486	425·1	235·6	546	477·5	264·7
307	268·5	148·8	367	321·0	177·9	427	373·5	207·0	487	425·9	236·1	547	478·4	265·2
308	269·4	149·3	368	321·9	178·4	428	374·3	207·5	488	426·8	236·6	548	479·3	265·7
309	270·3	149·8	369	322·7	178·9	429	375·2	208·0	489	427·7	237·1	549	480·2	266·2
310	271·1	150·3	370	323·6	179·4	430	376·1	208·5	490	428·6	237·6	550	481·0	266·6
311	272·0	150·8	371	324·5	179·9	431	377·0	209·0	491	429·4	238·0	551	481·9	267·1
312	272·9	151·3	372	325·4	180·3	432	377·8	209·4	492	430·3	238·5	552	482·8	267·6
313	273·8	151·7	373	326·2	180·8	433	378·7	209·9	493	431·2	239·0	553	483·7	268·1
314	274·6	152·2	374	327·1	181·3	434	379·6	210·4	494	432·1	239·5	554	484·5	268·6
315	275·5	152·7	375	328·0	181·8	435	380·5	210·9	495	432·9	240·0	555	485·4	269·1
316	276·4	153·2	376	328·9	182·3	436	381·3	211·4	496	433·8	240·5	556	486·3	269·6
317	277·3	153·7	377	329·7	182·8	437	382·2	211·9	497	434·7	241·0	557	487·5	270·0
318	278·1	154·2	378	330·6	183·3	438	383·1	212·3	498	435·6	241·4	558	488·0	270·5
319	279·0	154·7	379	331·5	183·7	439	384·0	212·8	499	436·4	241·9	559	488·9	271·0
320	279·9	155·1	380	332·4	184·2	440	384·8	213·3	500	437·3	242·4	560	489·8	271·5
321	280·8	155·6	381	333·2	184·7	441	385·7	213·8	501	438·2	242·9	561	490·7	272·0
322	281·6	156·1	382	334·1	185·2	442	386·6	214·3	502	439·1	243·4	562	491·5	272·5
323	282·5	156·6	383	335·0	185·7	443	387·5	214·8	503	439·9	243·9	563	492·4	272·9
324	283·4	157·1	384	335·9	186·2	444	388·3	215·3	504	440·8	244·3	564	493·3	273·4
325	284·3	157·6	385	336·7	186·7	445	389·2	215·7	505	441·7	244·8	565	494·2	273·9
326	285·1	158·0	386	337·6	187·1	446	390·1	216·2	506	442·6	245·3	566	495·0	274·4
327	286·0	158·5	387	338·5	187·6	447	391·0	216·7	507	443·4	245·8	567	495·9	274·9
328	286·9	159·0	388	339·4	188·1	448	391·8	217·2	508	444·3	246·3	568	496·8	275·4
329	287·7	159·5	389	340·2	188·6	449	392·7	217·7	509	445·2	246·8	569	497·7	275·9
330	288·6	160·0	390	341·1	189·1	450	393·6	218·2	510	446·1	247·3	570	498·5	276·3
331	289·5	160·5	391	342·0	189·6	451	394·5	218·6	511	446·9	247·7	571	499·4	276·8
332	290·4	161·0	392	342·9	190·0	452	395·3	219·1	512	447·8	248·2	572	500·3	277·3
333	291·2	161·4	393	343·7	190·5	453	396·2	219·6	513	448·7	248·7	573	501·2	277·8
334	292·1	161·9	394	344·6	191·0	454	397·1	220·1	514	449·6	249·2	574	502·0	278·3
335	293·0	162·4	395	345·5	191·5	455	398·0	220·6	515	450·4	249·7	575	502·9	278·8
336	293·9	162·9	396	346·3	192·0	456	398·8	221·1	516	451·3	250·2	576	503·8	279·3
337	294·7	163·4	397	347·2	192·5	457	399·7	221·6	517	452·2	250·6	577	504·7	279·7
338	295·6	163·9	398	348·1	193·0	458	400·6	222·0	518	453·1	251·1	578	505·5	280·2
339	296·5	164·4	399	349·0	193·4	459	401·5	222·5	519	453·9	251·6	579	506·4	280·7
340	297·4	164·8	400	349·8	193·9	460	402·3	223·0	520	454·8	252·1	580	507·3	281·2
341	298·2	165·3	401	350·7	194·4	461	403·2	223·5	521	455·7	252·6	581	508·2	281·7
342	299·1	165·8	402	351·6	194·9	462	404·1	224·0	522	456·6	253·1	582	509·0	282·2
343	300·0	166·3	403	352·5	195·4	463	404·9	224·5	523	457·4	253·6	583	509·9	282·6
344	300·9	166·8	404	353·3	195·9	464	405·8	225·0	524	458·3	254·0	584	510·7	283·1
345	301·7	167·3	405	354·2	196·3	465	406·7	225·4	525	459·2	254·5	585	511·7	283·6
346	302·6	167·7	406	355·1	196·8	466	407·6	225·9	526	460·0	255·0	586	512·5	284·1
347	303·5	168·2	407	356·0	197·3	467	408·4	226·4	527	460·9	255·5	587	513·4	284·6
348	304·4	168·7	408	356·8	197·8	468	409·3	226·9	528	461·8	256·0	588	514·3	285·1
349	305·2	169·2	409	357·7	198·3	469	410·2	227·4	529	462·7	256·5	589	515·2	285·6
350	306·1	169·7	410	358·6	198·8	470	411·1	227·9	530	463·5	256·9	590	516·0	286·0
351	307·0	170·2	411	359·5	199·3	471	411·9	228·3	531	464·4	257·4	591	516·9	286·5
352	307·9	170·7	412	360·3	199·7	472	412·8	228·8	532	465·3	257·9	592	517·8	287·0
353	308·7	171·1	413	361·2	200·2	473	413·7	229·3	533	466·2	258·4	593	518·6	287·5
354	309·6	171·6	414	362·1	200·7	474	414·6	229·8	534	467·0	258·9	594	519·5	288·0
355	310·5	172·1	415	363·0	201·2	475	415·4	230·3	535	467·9	259·4	595	520·4	288·5
356	311·4	172·6	416	363·8	201·7	476	416·3	230·8	536	468·8	259·9	596	521·3	288·9
357	312·2	173·1	417	364·7	202·2	477	417·2	231·3	537	469·6	260·3	597	522·1	289·4
358	313·1	173·6	418	365·6	202·7	478	418·1	231·7	538	470·5	260·8	598	523·0	289·9
359	314·0	174·0	419	366·5	203·1	479	418·9	232·2	539	471·4	261·3	599	523·9	290·4
360	314·9	174·5	420	367·3	203·6	480	419·8	232·7	540	472·3	261·8	600	524·8	290·9

| Dist. | Dep. | D. Lat. | Dist. | Dep. | D. Lat. | Dist. | Dep. | D. Lat. | Dist. | Dep. | D. Lat. | Dist. | Dep. | D. Lat. |

TRAVERSE TABLE
30 Degrees

30°   330° / 210°   030° / 150°   2h 00m

D. Lon	Dep.		D. Lon	Dep.		D. Lon	Dep.		D. Lon	Dep.		D. Lon	Dep.	
Dist.	D. Lat.	Dep.	Dist.	D. Lat.	Dep.	Dist.	D. Lat.	Dep.	Dist.	D. Lat.	Dep.	Dist.	D. Lat.	Dep.
1	00.9	00.5	61	52.8	30.5	121	104.8	60.5	181	156.8	90.5	241	208.7	120.5
2	01.7	01.0	62	53.7	31.0	122	105.7	61.0	182	157.6	91.0	242	209.6	121.0
3	02.6	01.5	63	54.6	31.5	123	106.5	61.5	183	158.5	91.5	243	210.4	121.5
4	03.5	02.0	64	55.4	32.0	124	107.4	62.0	184	159.3	92.0	244	211.3	122.0
5	04.3	02.5	65	56.3	32.5	125	108.3	62.5	185	160.2	92.5	245	212.2	122.5
6	05.2	03.0	66	57.2	33.0	126	109.1	63.0	186	161.1	93.0	246	213.0	123.0
7	06.1	03.5	67	58.0	33.5	127	110.0	63.5	187	161.9	93.5	247	213.9	123.5
8	06.9	04.0	68	58.9	34.0	128	110.9	64.0	188	162.8	94.0	248	214.8	124.0
9	07.8	04.5	69	59.8	34.5	129	111.7	64.5	189	163.7	94.5	249	215.6	124.5
10	08.7	05.0	70	60.6	35.0	130	112.6	65.0	190	164.5	95.0	250	216.5	125.0
11	09.5	05.5	71	61.5	35.5	131	113.4	65.5	191	165.4	95.5	251	217.4	125.5
12	10.4	06.0	72	62.4	36.0	132	114.3	66.0	192	166.3	96.0	252	218.2	126.0
13	11.3	06.5	73	63.2	36.5	133	115.2	66.5	193	167.1	96.5	253	219.1	126.5
14	12.1	07.0	74	64.1	37.0	134	116.0	67.0	194	168.0	97.0	254	220.0	127.0
15	13.0	07.5	75	65.0	37.5	135	116.9	67.5	195	168.9	97.5	255	220.8	127.5
16	13.9	08.0	76	65.8	38.0	136	117.8	68.0	196	169.7	98.0	256	221.7	128.0
17	14.7	08.5	77	66.7	38.5	137	118.6	68.5	197	170.6	98.5	257	222.6	128.5
18	15.6	09.0	78	67.5	39.0	138	119.5	69.0	198	171.5	99.0	258	223.4	129.0
19	16.5	09.5	79	68.4	39.5	139	120.4	69.5	199	172.3	99.5	259	224.3	129.5
20	17.3	10.0	80	69.3	40.0	140	121.2	70.0	200	173.2	100.0	260	225.2	130.0
21	18.2	10.5	81	70.1	40.5	141	122.1	70.5	201	174.1	100.5	261	226.0	130.5
22	19.1	11.0	82	71.0	41.0	142	123.0	71.0	202	174.9	101.0	262	226.9	131.0
23	19.9	11.5	83	71.9	41.5	143	123.8	71.5	203	175.8	101.5	263	227.8	131.5
24	20.8	12.0	84	72.7	42.0	144	124.7	72.0	204	176.7	102.0	264	228.6	132.0
25	21.7	12.5	85	73.6	42.5	145	125.6	72.5	205	177.5	102.5	265	229.5	132.5
26	22.5	13.0	86	74.5	43.0	146	126.4	73.0	206	178.4	103.0	266	230.4	133.0
27	23.4	13.5	87	75.3	43.5	147	127.3	73.5	207	179.3	103.5	267	231.2	133.5
28	24.2	14.0	88	76.2	44.0	148	128.2	74.0	208	180.1	104.0	268	232.1	134.0
29	25.1	14.5	89	77.1	44.5	149	129.0	74.5	209	181.0	104.5	269	233.0	134.5
30	26.0	15.0	90	77.9	45.0	150	129.9	75.0	210	181.9	105.0	270	233.8	135.0
31	26.8	15.5	91	78.8	45.5	151	130.8	75.5	211	182.7	105.5	271	234.7	135.5
32	27.7	16.0	92	79.7	46.0	152	131.6	76.0	212	183.6	106.0	272	235.6	136.0
33	28.6	16.5	93	80.5	46.5	153	132.5	76.5	213	184.5	106.5	273	236.4	136.5
34	29.4	17.0	94	81.4	47.0	154	133.4	77.0	214	185.3	107.0	274	237.3	137.0
35	30.3	17.5	95	82.3	47.5	155	134.2	77.5	215	186.2	107.5	275	238.2	137.5
36	31.2	18.0	96	83.1	48.0	156	135.1	78.0	216	187.1	108.0	276	239.0	138.0
37	32.0	18.5	97	84.0	48.5	157	136.0	78.5	217	187.9	108.5	277	239.9	138.5
38	32.9	19.0	98	84.9	49.0	158	136.8	79.0	218	188.8	109.0	278	240.8	139.0
39	33.8	19.5	99	85.7	49.5	159	137.7	79.5	219	189.7	109.5	279	241.6	139.5
40	34.6	20.0	100	86.6	50.0	160	138.6	80.0	220	190.5	110.0	280	242.5	140.0
41	35.5	20.5	101	87.5	50.5	161	139.4	80.5	221	191.4	110.5	281	243.4	140.5
42	36.4	21.0	102	88.3	51.0	162	140.3	81.0	222	192.3	111.0	282	244.2	141.0
43	37.2	21.5	103	89.2	51.5	163	141.2	81.5	223	193.1	111.5	283	245.1	141.5
44	38.1	22.0	104	90.1	52.0	164	142.0	82.0	224	194.0	112.0	284	246.0	142.0
45	39.0	22.5	105	90.9	52.5	165	142.9	82.5	225	194.9	112.5	285	246.8	142.5
46	39.8	23.0	106	91.8	53.0	166	143.8	83.0	226	195.7	113.0	286	247.7	143.0
47	40.7	23.5	107	92.7	53.5	167	144.6	83.5	227	196.6	113.5	287	248.5	143.5
48	41.6	24.0	108	93.5	54.0	168	145.5	84.0	228	197.5	114.0	288	249.4	144.0
49	42.4	24.5	109	94.4	54.5	169	146.4	84.5	229	198.3	114.5	289	250.3	144.5
50	43.3	25.0	110	95.3	55.0	170	147.2	85.0	230	199.2	115.0	290	251.1	145.0
51	44.2	25.5	111	96.1	55.5	171	148.1	85.5	231	200.1	115.5	291	252.0	145.5
52	45.0	26.0	112	97.0	56.0	172	149.0	86.0	232	200.9	116.0	292	252.9	146.0
53	45.9	26.5	113	97.9	56.5	173	149.8	86.5	233	201.8	116.5	293	253.7	146.5
54	46.8	27.0	114	98.7	57.0	174	150.7	87.0	234	202.6	117.0	294	254.6	147.0
55	47.6	27.5	115	99.6	57.5	175	151.6	87.5	235	203.5	117.5	295	255.5	147.5
56	48.5	28.0	116	100.5	58.0	176	152.4	88.0	236	204.4	118.0	296	256.3	148.0
57	49.4	28.5	117	101.3	58.5	177	153.3	88.5	237	205.2	118.5	297	257.2	148.5
58	50.2	29.0	118	102.2	59.0	178	154.2	89.0	238	206.1	119.0	298	258.1	149.0
59	51.1	29.5	119	103.1	59.5	179	155.0	89.5	239	207.0	119.5	299	258.9	149.5
60	52.0	30.0	120	103.9	60.0	180	155.9	90.0	240	207.8	120.0	300	259.8	150.0

Dist.	Dep.	D. Lat.	Dist.	Dep.	D. Lat.	Dist.	Dep.	D. Lat.	Dist.	Dep.	D. Lat.	Dist.	Dep.	D. Lat
D. Lon		Dep.	D. Lon		Dep.	D. Lon		Dep.	D. Lon		Dep.	D. Lon		Dep.

60°   300° / 240°   60 Degrees   060° / 120°   4h 00m

TRAVERSE TABLE
30 Degrees

| 330° / 210° | 030° / 150° 2h 00m |

D. Lon	Dep.		D. Lon	Dep.		D. Lon	Dep.		D. Lon	Dep.		D. Lon	Dep.	
Dist.	D. Lat.	Dep.	Dist.	D. Lat.	Dep.	Dist.	D. Lat.	Dep.	Dist.	D. Lat.	Dep.	Dist.	D. Lat.	Dep.
301	260·7	150·5	361	312·6	180·5	421	364·6	210·5	481	416·6	240·5	541	468·5	270·5
302	261·5	151·0	362	313·5	181·0	422	365·5	211·0	482	417·4	241·0	542	469·4	271·0
303	262·4	151·5	363	314·4	181·5	423	366·3	211·5	483	418·3	241·5	543	470·3	271·5
304	263·3	152·0	364	315·2	182·0	424	367·2	212·0	484	419·2	242·0	544	471·1	272·0
305	264·1	152·5	365	316·1	182·5	425	368·1	212·5	485	420·0	242·5	545	472·0	272·5
306	265·0	153·0	366	317·0	183·0	426	368·9	213·0	486	420·9	243·0	546	472·8	273·0
307	265·9	153·5	367	317·8	183·5	427	369·8	213·5	487	421·8	243·5	547	473·7	273·5
308	266·7	154·0	368	318·7	184·0	428	370·7	214·0	488	422·6	244·0	548	474·6	274·0
309	267·6	154·5	369	319·6	184·5	429	371·5	214·5	489	423·5	244·5	549	475·4	274·5
310	268·5	155·0	370	320·4	185·0	430	372·4	215·0	490	424·4	245·0	550	476·3	275·0
311	269·3	155·5	371	321·3	185·5	431	373·3	215·5	491	425·2	245·5	551	477·2	275·5
312	270·2	156·0	372	322·2	186·0	432	374·1	216·0	492	426·1	246·0	552	478·0	276·0
313	271·1	156·5	373	323·0	186·5	433	375·0	216·5	493	427·0	246·5	553	478·9	276·5
314	271·9	157·0	374	323·9	187·0	434	375·9	217·0	494	427·8	247·0	554	479·8	277·0
315	272·8	157·5	375	324·8	187·5	435	376·7	217·5	495	428·7	247·5	555	480·6	277·5
316	273·7	158·0	376	325·6	188·0	436	377·6	218·0	496	429·5	248·0	556	481·5	278·0
317	274·5	158·5	377	326·5	188·5	437	378·5	218·5	497	430·4	248·5	557	482·4	278·5
318	275·4	159·0	378	327·4	189·0	438	379·3	219·0	498	431·3	249·0	558	483·2	279·0
319	276·3	159·5	379	328·2	189·5	439	380·2	219·5	499	432·1	249·5	559	484·1	279·5
320	277·1	160·0	380	329·1	190·0	440	381·1	220·0	500	433·0	250·0	560	485·0	280·0
321	278·0	160·5	381	330·0	190·5	441	381·9	220·5	501	433·9	250·5	561	485·8	280·5
322	278·9	161·0	382	330·8	191·0	442	382·8	221·0	502	434·7	251·0	562	486·7	281·0
323	279·7	161·5	383	331·7	191·5	443	383·6	221·5	503	435·6	251·5	563	487·6	281·5
324	280·6	162·0	384	332·6	192·0	444	384·5	222·0	504	436·5	252·0	564	488·4	282·0
325	281·5	162·5	385	333·4	192·5	445	385·4	222·5	505	437·3	252·5	565	489·3	282·5
326	282·3	163·0	386	334·3	193·0	446	386·3	223·0	506	438·2	253·0	566	490·2	283·0
327	283·2	163·5	387	335·2	193·5	447	387·1	223·5	507	439·1	253·5	567	491·0	283·5
328	284·1	164·0	388	336·0	194·0	448	388·0	224·0	508	439·9	254·0	568	491·9	284·0
329	284·9	164·5	389	336·9	194·5	449	388·8	224·5	509	440·8	254·5	569	492·8	284·5
330	285·8	165·0	390	337·7	195·0	450	389·7	225·0	510	441·7	255·0	570	493·6	285·0
331	286·7	165·5	391	338·6	195·5	451	390·6	225·5	511	442·5	255·5	571	494·5	285·5
332	287·5	166·0	392	339·5	196·0	452	391·4	226·0	512	443·4	256·0	572	495·4	286·0
333	288·4	166·5	393	340·3	196·5	453	392·3	226·5	513	444·3	256·5	573	496·2	286·5
334	289·3	167·0	394	341·2	197·0	454	393·2	227·0	514	445·1	257·0	574	497·1	287·0
335	290·1	167·5	395	342·1	197·5	455	394·0	227·5	515	446·0	257·5	575	498·0	287·5
336	291·0	168·0	396	342·9	198·0	456	394·9	228·0	516	446·9	258·0	576	498·8	288·0
337	291·9	168·5	397	343·8	198·5	457	395·8	228·5	517	447·7	258·5	577	499·7	288·5
338	292·7	169·0	398	344·7	199·0	458	396·6	229·0	518	448·6	259·0	578	500·6	289·0
339	293·6	169·5	399	345·5	199·5	459	397·5	229·5	519	449·5	259·5	579	501·3	289·5
340	294·5	170·0	400	346·4	200·0	460	398·4	230·0	520	450·3	260·0	580	502·3	290·0
341	295·3	170·5	401	347·3	200·5	461	399·2	230·5	521	451·2	260·5	581	503·2	290·5
342	296·2	171·0	402	348·1	201·0	462	400·1	231·0	522	452·1	261·0	582	504·0	291·0
343	297·0	171·5	403	349·0	201·5	463	401·0	231·5	523	452·9	261·5	583	504·9	291·5
344	297·9	172·0	404	349·9	202·0	464	401·8	232·0	524	453·8	262·0	584	505·8	292·0
345	298·8	172·5	405	350·7	202·5	465	402·7	232·5	525	454·7	262·5	585	506·6	292·5
346	299·6	173·0	406	351·6	203·0	466	403·6	233·0	526	455·5	263·0	586	507·5	293·0
347	300·5	173·5	407	352·5	203·5	467	404·4	233·5	527	456·4	263·5	587	508·4	293·5
348	301·4	174·0	408	353·3	204·0	468	405·3	234·0	528	457·3	264·0	588	509·2	294·0
349	302·2	174·5	409	354·2	204·5	469	406·2	234·5	529	458·1	264·5	589	510·1	294·5
350	303·1	175·0	410	355·1	205·0	470	407·0	235·0	530	459·0	265·0	590	511·0	295·0
351	304·0	175·5	411	355·9	205·5	471	407·9	235·5	531	459·9	265·5	591	511·8	295·5
352	304·8	176·0	412	356·8	206·0	472	408·8	236·0	532	460·7	266·0	592	512·7	296·0
353	305·7	176·5	413	357·7	206·5	473	409·6	236·5	533	461·6	266·5	593	513·6	296·5
354	306·6	177·0	414	358·5	207·0	474	410·5	237·0	534	462·5	267·0	594	514·4	297·0
355	307·4	177·5	415	359·4	207·5	475	411·4	237·5	535	463·3	267·5	595	515·3	297·5
356	308·3	178·0	416	360·3	208·0	476	412·2	238·0	536	464·2	268·0	596	516·2	298·0
357	309·2	178·5	417	361·1	208·5	477	413·1	238·5	537	465·1	268·5	597	517·0	298·5
358	310·0	179·0	418	362·0	209·0	478	414·0	239·0	538	465·9	269·0	598	517·9	299·0
359	310·9	179·5	419	362·9	209·5	479	414·8	239·5	539	466·8	269·5	599	518·7	299·5
360	311·8	180·0	420	363·7	210·0	480	415·7	240·0	540	467·7	270·0	600	519·6	300·0
Dist.	Dep.	D. Lat.	Dist.	Dep.	D. Lat.	Dist.	Dep.	D. Lat.	Dist.	Dep.	D. Lat.	Dist.	Dep.	D. Lat.
D. Lon		Dep.	D. Lon		Dep.	D. Lon		Dep.	D. Lon		Dep.	D. Lon		Dep.

TRAVERSE TABLE
31 Degrees

31° 329° / 211°   031° / 149°   2h 04m

D. Lon / Dist.	D. Lat.	Dep.	D. Lon / Dist.	D. Lat.	Dep.	D. Lon / Dist.	D. Lat.	Dep.	D. Lon / Dist.	D. Lat.	Dep.	D. Lon / Dist.	D. Lat.	Dep.
1	00.9	00.5	61	52.3	31.4	121	103.7	62.3	181	155.1	93.2	241	206.6	124.1
2	01.7	01.0	62	53.1	31.9	122	104.6	62.8	182	156.0	93.7	242	207.4	124.6
3	02.6	01.5	63	54.0	32.4	123	105.4	63.3	183	156.9	94.3	243	208.3	125.2
4	03.4	02.1	64	54.9	33.0	124	106.3	63.9	184	157.7	94.8	244	209.1	125.7
5	04.3	02.6	65	55.7	33.5	125	107.1	64.4	185	158.6	95.3	245	210.0	126.2
6	05.1	03.1	66	56.6	34.0	126	108.0	64.9	186	159.4	95.8	246	210.9	126.7
7	06.0	03.6	67	57.4	34.5	127	108.9	65.4	187	160.3	96.3	247	211.7	127.2
8	06.9	04.1	68	58.3	35.0	128	109.7	65.9	188	161.1	96.8	248	212.6	127.7
9	07.7	04.6	69	59.1	35.5	129	110.6	66.4	189	162.0	97.3	249	213.4	128.2
10	08.6	05.2	70	60.0	36.1	130	111.4	67.0	190	162.9	97.9	250	214.3	128.8
11	09.4	05.7	71	60.9	36.6	131	112.3	67.5	191	163.7	98.4	251	215.1	129.3
12	10.3	06.2	72	61.7	37.1	132	113.1	68.0	192	164.6	98.9	252	216.0	129.8
13	11.1	06.7	73	62.6	37.6	133	114.0	68.5	193	165.4	99.4	253	216.9	130.3
14	12.0	07.2	74	63.4	38.1	134	114.9	69.0	194	166.3	99.9	254	217.7	130.8
15	12.9	07.7	75	64.3	38.6	135	115.7	69.5	195	167.1	100.4	255	218.6	131.3
16	13.7	08.2	76	65.1	39.1	136	116.6	70.0	196	168.0	100.9	256	219.4	131.8
17	14.6	08.8	77	66.0	39.7	137	117.4	70.6	197	168.9	101.5	257	220.3	132.4
18	15.4	09.3	78	66.9	40.2	138	118.3	71.1	198	169.7	102.0	258	221.1	132.9
19	16.3	09.8	79	67.7	40.7	139	119.1	71.6	199	170.6	102.5	259	222.0	133.4
20	17.1	10.3	80	68.6	41.2	140	120.0	72.1	200	171.4	103.0	260	222.9	133.9
21	18.0	10.8	81	69.4	41.7	141	120.9	72.6	201	172.3	103.5	261	223.7	134.4
22	18.9	11.3	82	70.3	42.2	142	121.7	73.1	202	173.1	104.0	262	224.6	134.9
23	19.7	11.8	83	71.1	42.7	143	122.6	73.7	203	174.0	104.6	263	225.4	135.5
24	20.6	12.4	84	72.0	43.3	144	123.4	74.2	204	174.9	105.1	264	226.3	136.0
25	21.4	12.9	85	72.9	43.8	145	124.3	74.7	205	175.7	105.6	265	227.1	136.5
26	22.3	13.4	86	73.7	44.3	146	125.1	75.2	206	176.6	106.1	266	228.0	137.0
27	23.1	13.9	87	74.6	44.8	147	126.0	75.7	207	177.4	106.6	267	228.9	137.5
28	24.0	14.4	88	75.4	45.3	148	126.9	76.2	208	178.3	107.1	268	229.7	138.0
29	24.9	14.9	89	76.3	45.8	149	127.7	76.7	209	179.1	107.6	269	230.6	138.5
30	25.7	15.5	90	77.1	46.4	150	128.6	77.3	210	180.0	108.2	270	231.4	139.1
31	26.6	16.0	91	78.0	46.9	151	129.4	77.8	211	180.9	108.7	271	232.3	139.6
32	27.4	16.5	92	78.9	47.4	152	130.3	78.3	212	181.7	109.2	272	233.1	140.1
33	28.3	17.0	93	79.7	47.9	153	131.1	78.8	213	182.6	109.7	273	234.0	140.6
34	29.1	17.5	94	80.6	48.4	154	132.0	79.3	214	183.4	110.2	274	234.9	141.1
35	30.0	18.0	95	81.4	48.9	155	132.9	79.8	215	184.3	110.7	275	235.7	141.6
36	30.9	18.5	96	82.3	49.4	156	133.7	80.3	216	185.1	111.2	276	236.6	142.2
37	31.7	19.1	97	83.1	50.0	157	134.6	80.9	217	186.0	111.8	277	237.4	142.7
38	32.6	19.6	98	84.0	50.5	158	135.4	81.4	218	186.9	112.3	278	238.3	143.2
39	33.4	20.1	99	84.9	51.0	159	136.3	81.9	219	187.7	112.8	279	239.1	143.7
40	34.3	20.6	100	85.7	51.5	160	137.1	82.4	220	188.6	113.3	280	240.0	144.2
41	35.1	21.1	101	86.6	52.0	161	138.0	82.9	221	189.4	113.8	281	240.9	144.7
42	36.0	21.6	102	87.4	52.5	162	138.9	83.4	222	190.3	114.3	282	241.7	145.2
43	36.9	22.1	103	88.3	53.0	163	139.7	84.0	223	191.1	114.9	283	242.6	145.8
44	37.7	22.7	104	89.1	53.6	164	140.6	84.5	224	192.0	115.4	284	243.4	146.3
45	38.6	23.2	105	90.0	54.1	165	141.4	85.0	225	192.9	115.9	285	244.3	146.8
46	39.4	23.7	106	90.9	54.6	166	142.3	85.5	226	193.7	116.4	286	245.1	147.3
47	40.3	24.2	107	91.7	55.1	167	143.1	86.0	227	194.6	116.9	287	246.0	147.8
48	41.1	24.7	108	92.6	55.6	168	144.0	86.5	228	195.4	117.4	288	246.9	148.3
49	42.0	25.2	109	93.4	56.1	169	144.9	87.0	229	196.3	117.9	289	247.7	148.8
50	42.9	25.8	110	94.3	56.7	170	145.7	87.6	230	197.1	118.5	290	248.6	149.4
51	43.7	26.3	111	95.1	57.2	171	146.6	88.1	231	198.0	119.0	291	249.4	149.9
52	44.6	26.8	112	96.0	57.7	172	147.4	88.6	232	198.9	119.5	292	250.3	150.4
53	45.4	27.3	113	96.9	58.2	173	148.3	89.1	233	199.7	120.0	293	251.2	150.9
54	46.3	27.8	114	97.7	58.7	174	149.1	89.6	234	200.6	120.5	294	252.0	151.4
55	47.1	28.3	115	98.6	59.2	175	150.0	90.1	235	201.4	121.0	295	252.9	151.9
56	48.0	28.8	116	99.4	59.7	176	150.9	90.6	236	202.3	121.5	296	253.7	152.5
57	48.9	29.4	117	100.3	60.3	177	151.7	91.2	237	203.1	122.1	297	254.6	153.0
58	49.7	29.9	118	101.1	60.8	178	152.6	91.7	238	204.0	122.6	298	255.4	153.5
59	50.6	30.4	119	102.0	61.3	179	153.4	92.2	239	204.9	123.1	299	256.3	154.0
60	51.4	30.9	120	102.9	61.8	180	154.3	92.7	240	205.7	123.6	300	257.1	154.5

| Dist. | Dep. | D. Lat. | Dist. | Dep. | D. Lat. | Dist. | Dep. | D. Lat. | Dist. | Dep. | D. Lat. | Dist. | Dep. | D. Lat. |

D. Lon ... Dep.

59° 301° / 239°   59 Degrees   059° / 121°   3h 56m

TRAVERSE TABLE
31 Degrees

329° / 211° 031° / 149° 2h 04m **31°**

Dist.	D. Lat.	Dep.	Dist.	D. Lat.	Dep.	Dist.	D. Lat.	Dep.	Dist.	D. Lat.	Dep.	Dist.	D. Lat.	Dep.
301	258·0	155·0	361	309·4	185·9	421	360·9	216·8	481	412·3	247·7	541	463·7	278·6
302	258·9	155·5	362	310·3	186·4	422	361·7	217·3	482	413·2	248·2	542	464·6	279·2
303	259·7	156·1	363	311·2	187·0	423	362·6	217·9	483	414·0	248·8	543	465·4	279·7
304	260·6	156·6	364	312·0	187·5	424	363·4	218·4	484	414·9	249·3	544	466·3	280·2
305	261·4	157·1	365	312·9	188·0	425	364·3	218·9	485	415·7	249·8	545	467·2	280·7
306	262·3	157·6	366	313·7	188·5	426	365·2	219·4	486	416·6	250·3	546	468·0	281·2
307	263·2	158·1	367	314·6	189·0	427	366·0	219·9	487	417·4	250·8	547	468·9	281·7
308	264·0	158·6	368	315·4	189·5	428	366·9	220·4	488	418·3	251·3	548	469·7	282·2
309	264·9	159·1	369	316·3	190·0	429	367·7	221·0	489	419·2	251·9	549	470·6	282·8
310	265·7	159·7	370	317·2	190·6	430	368·6	221·5	490	420·0	252·4	550	471·4	283·3
311	266·6	160·2	371	318·0	191·1	431	369·4	222·0	491	420·9	252·9	551	472·3	283·8
312	267·4	160·7	372	318·9	191·6	432	370·3	222·5	492	421·7	253·4	552	473·2	284·3
313	268·3	161·2	373	319·7	192·1	433	371·2	223·0	493	422·6	253·9	553	474·0	284·8
314	269·2	161·7	374	320·6	192·6	434	372·0	223·5	494	423·4	254·4	554	474·9	285·3
315	270·0	162·2	375	321·4	193·1	435	372·9	224·0	495	424·3	254·9	555	475·7	285·8
316	270·9	162·8	376	322·3	193·7	436	373·7	224·6	496	425·2	255·5	556	476·6	286·4
317	271·7	163·3	377	323·2	194·2	437	374·6	225·1	497	426·0	256·0	557	477·4	286·9
318	272·6	163·8	378	324·0	194·7	438	375·4	225·6	498	426·9	256·5	558	478·3	287·4
319	273·4	164·3	379	324·9	195·2	439	376·3	226·1	499	427·7	257·0	559	479·2	287·9
320	274·3	164·8	380	325·7	195·7	440	377·2	226·6	500	428·6	257·5	560	480·0	288·4
321	275·2	165·3	381	326·6	196·2	441	378·0	227·1	501	429·4	258·0	561	480·9	288·9
322	276·0	165·8	382	327·4	196·7	442	378·9	227·6	502	430·3	258·5	562	481·7	289·5
323	276·9	166·4	383	328·3	197·3	443	379·7	228·2	503	431·2	259·1	563	482·6	290·0
324	277·7	166·9	384	329·2	197·8	444	380·6	228·7	504	432·0	259·6	564	483·4	290·5
325	278·6	167·4	385	330·0	198·3	445	381·4	229·2	505	432·9	260·1	565	484·3	291·0
326	279·4	167·9	386	330·9	198·8	446	382·3	229·7	506	433·7	260·6	566	485·2	291·5
327	280·3	168·4	387	331·7	199·3	447	383·2	230·2	507	434·6	261·1	567	486·0	292·0
328	281·2	168·9	388	332·6	199·8	448	384·0	230·7	508	435·4	261·6	568	486·9	292·5
329	282·0	169·4	389	333·4	200·3	449	384·9	231·3	509	436·3	262·2	569	487·7	293·1
330	232·9	170·0	390	334·3	200·9	450	385·7	231·8	510	437·2	262·7	570	488·6	293·6
331	283·7	170·5	391	335·2	201·4	451	386·6	232·3	511	438·0	263·2	571	489·4	294·1
332	284·6	171·0	392	336·0	201·9	452	387·4	232·8	512	438·9	263·7	572	490·3	294·6
333	285·4	171·5	393	336·9	202·4	453	388·3	233·3	513	439·7	264·2	573	491·2	295·1
334	286·3	172·0	394	337·7	202·9	454	389·2	233·8	514	440·6	264·7	574	492·0	295·6
335	287·2	172·5	395	338·6	203·4	455	390·0	234·3	515	441·4	265·2	575	492·9	296·1
336	288·0	173·1	396	339·4	204·0	456	390·9	234·9	516	442·3	265·8	576	493·7	296·7
337	288·9	173·6	397	340·3	204·5	457	391·7	235·4	517	443·2	266·3	577	494·6	297·2
338	289·7	174·1	398	341·2	205·0	458	392·6	235·9	518	444·0	266·8	578	495·4	297·7
339	290·6	174·6	399	342·0	205·5	459	393·4	236·4	519	444·9	267·3	579	496·3	298·2
340	291·4	175·1	400	342·9	206·0	460	394·3	236·9	520	445·7	267·8	580	497·2	298·7
341	292·3	175·6	401	343·7	206·5	461	395·2	237·4	521	446·6	268·3	581	498·0	299·2
342	293·2	176·1	402	344·6	207·0	462	396·0	237·9	522	447·4	268·8	582	498·9	299·8
343	294·0	176·7	403	345·4	207·6	463	396·9	238·5	523	448·3	269·4	583	499·7	300·3
344	294·9	177·2	404	346·3	208·1	464	397·7	239·0	524	449·2	269·9	584	500·6	300·8
345	295·7	177·7	405	347·2	208·6	465	398·6	239·5	525	450·0	270·4	585	501·4	301·3
346	296·6	178·2	406	348·0	209·1	466	399·4	240·0	526	450·9	270·9	586	502·3	301·8
347	297·4	178·7	407	348·9	209·6	467	400·3	240·5	527	451·7	271·4	587	503·2	302·3
348	298·3	179·2	408	349·7	210·1	468	401·2	241·0	528	452·6	271·9	588	504·0	302·8
349	299·2	179·7	409	350·6	210·7	469	402·2	241·6	529	453·4	272·5	589	504·9	303·4
350	300·0	180·3	410	351·4	211·2	470	402·9	242·1	530	454·3	273·0	590	505·7	303·9
351	300·9	180·8	411	352·3	211·7	471	403·7	242·6	531	455·2	273·5	591	506·6	304·4
352	301·7	181·3	412	353·2	212·2	472	404·6	243·1	532	456·0	274·0	592	507·4	304·9
353	302·6	181·8	413	354·0	212·7	473	405·4	243·6	533	456·9	274·5	593	508·3	305·4
354	303·4	182·3	414	354·9	213·2	474	406·3	244·1	534	457·7	275·0	594	509·2	305·9
355	304·3	182·8	415	355·7	213·7	475	407·2	244·6	535	458·6	275·5	595	510·0	306·4
356	305·2	183·4	416	356·6	214·3	476	408·0	245·2	536	459·4	276·1	596	510·9	307·0
357	306·0	183·9	417	357·4	214·8	477	408·9	245·7	537	460·3	276·6	597	511·7	307·5
358	306·9	184·4	418	358·3	215·3	478	409·7	246·2	538	461·2	277·1	598	512·6	308·0
359	307·7	184·9	419	359·2	215·8	479	410·6	246·7	539	462·0	277·6	599	513·4	308·5
360	308·6	185·4	420	360·0	216·3	480	411·4	247·2	540	462·9	278·1	600	514·3	309·0

| Dist. | Dep. | D. Lat. | Dist. | Dep. | D. Lat. | Dist. | Dep. | D. Lat. | Dist. | Dep. | D. Lat. | Dist. | Dep. | D. Lat. |

D. Lon Dep.

301° / 239° **59 Degrees** 059° / 121° 3h 56m **59°**

TRAVERSE TABLE
32 Degrees

32°

328° / 212° 032° / 148° 2h 08m

D. Lon	Dep.		D. Lon	Dep.		D. Lon	Dep.		D. Lon	Dep.		D. Lon	Dep.	
Dist.	D. Lat.	Dep.	Dist.	D. Lat.	Dep.	Dist.	D. Lat.	Dep.	Dist.	D. Lat.	Dep.	Dist.	D. Lat.	Dep.
1	00·8	00·5	61	51·7	32·3	121	102·6	64·1	181	153·5	95·9	241	204·4	127·7
2	01·7	01·1	62	52·6	32·9	122	103·5	64·7	182	154·3	96·4	242	205·2	128·2
3	02·5	01·6	63	53·4	33·4	123	104·3	65·2	183	155·2	97·0	243	206·1	128·8
4	03·4	02·1	64	54·3	33·9	124	105·2	65·7	184	156·0	97·5	244	206·9	129·3
5	04·2	02·6	65	55·1	34·4	125	106·0	66·2	185	156·9	98·0	245	207·8	129·8
6	05·1	03·2	66	56·0	35·0	126	106·9	66·8	186	157·7	98·6	246	208·6	130·4
7	05·9	03·7	67	56·8	35·5	127	107·7	67·3	187	158·6	99·1	247	209·5	130·9
8	06·8	04·2	68	57·7	36·0	128	108·6	67·8	188	159·4	99·6	248	210·3	131·4
9	07·6	04·8	69	58·5	36·6	129	109·4	68·4	189	160·3	100·2	249	211·2	131·9
10	08·5	05·3	70	59·4	37·1	130	110·2	68·9	190	161·1	100·7	250	212·0	132·5
11	09·3	05·8	71	60·2	37·6	131	111·1	69·4	191	162·0	101·2	251	212·9	133·0
12	10·2	06·4	72	61·1	38·2	132	111·9	69·9	192	162·8	101·7	252	213·7	133·5
13	11·0	06·9	73	61·9	38·7	133	112·8	70·5	193	163·7	102·3	253	214·6	134·1
14	11·9	07·4	74	62·8	39·2	134	113·6	71·0	194	164·5	102·8	254	215·4	134·6
15	12·7	07·9	75	63·6	39·7	135	114·5	71·5	195	165·4	103·3	255	216·3	135·1
16	13·6	08·5	76	64·5	40·3	136	115·3	72·1	196	166·2	103·9	256	217·1	135·7
17	14·4	09·0	77	65·3	40·8	137	116·2	72·6	197	167·1	104·4	257	217·9	136·2
18	15·3	09·5	78	66·1	41·3	138	117·0	73·1	198	167·9	104·9	258	218·8	136·7
19	16·1	10·1	79	67·0	41·9	139	117·9	73·7	199	168·8	105·5	259	219·6	137·2
20	17·0	10·6	80	67·8	42·4	140	118·7	74·2	200	169·6	106·0	260	220·5	137·8
21	17·8	11·1	81	68·7	42·9	141	119·6	74·7	201	170·5	106·5	261	221·3	138·3
22	18·7	11·7	82	69·5	43·5	142	120·4	75·2	202	171·3	107·0	262	222·2	138·8
23	19·5	12·2	83	70·4	44·0	143	121·3	75·8	203	172·2	107·6	263	223·0	139·4
24	20·4	12·7	84	71·2	44·5	144	122·1	76·3	204	173·0	108·1	264	223·9	139·9
25	21·2	13·2	85	72·1	45·0	145	123·0	76·8	205	173·8	108·6	265	224·7	140·4
26	22·0	13·8	86	72·9	45·6	146	123·8	77·4	206	174·7	109·2	266	225·6	141·0
27	22·9	14·3	87	73·8	46·1	147	124·7	77·9	207	175·5	109·7	267	226·4	141·5
28	23·7	14·8	88	74·6	46·6	148	125·5	78·4	208	176·4	110·2	268	227·3	142·0
29	24·6	15·4	89	75·5	47·2	149	126·4	79·0	209	177·2	110·8	269	228·1	142·5
30	25·4	15·9	90	76·3	47·7	150	127·2	79·5	210	178·1	111·3	270	229·0	143·1
31	26·3	16·4	91	77·2	48·2	151	128·1	80·0	211	178·9	111·8	271	229·8	143·6
32	27·1	17·0	92	78·0	48·8	152	128·9	80·5	212	179·8	112·3	272	230·7	144·1
33	28·0	17·5	93	78·9	49·3	153	129·8	81·1	213	180·6	112·9	273	231·5	144·7
34	28·8	18·0	94	79·7	49·8	154	130·6	81·6	214	181·5	113·4	274	232·4	145·2
35	29·7	18·5	95	80·6	50·3	155	131·4	82·1	215	182·3	113·9	275	233·2	145·7
36	30·5	19·1	96	81·4	50·9	156	132·3	82·7	216	183·2	114·5	276	234·1	146·3
37	31·4	19·6	97	82·3	51·4	157	133·1	83·2	217	184·0	115·0	277	234·9	146·8
38	32·2	20·1	98	83·1	51·9	158	134·0	83·7	218	184·9	115·5	278	235·8	147·3
39	33·1	20·7	99	84·0	52·5	159	134·8	84·3	219	185·7	116·1	279	236·6	147·8
40	33·9	21·2	100	84·8	53·0	160	135·7	84·8	220	186·6	116·6	280	237·5	148·4
41	34·8	21·7	101	85·7	53·5	161	136·5	85·3	221	187·4	117·1	281	238·3	148·9
42	35·6	22·3	102	86·5	54·1	162	137·4	85·8	222	188·3	117·6	282	239·1	149·4
43	36·5	22·8	103	87·3	54·6	163	138·2	86·4	223	189·1	118·2	283	240·0	150·0
44	37·3	23·3	104	88·2	55·1	164	139·1	86·9	224	190·0	118·7	284	240·8	150·5
45	38·2	23·8	105	89·0	55·6	165	139·9	87·4	225	190·8	119·2	285	241·7	151·0
46	39·0	24·4	106	89·9	56·2	166	140·8	88·0	226	191·7	119·8	286	242·5	151·6
47	39·9	24·9	107	90·7	56·7	167	141·6	88·5	227	192·5	120·3	287	243·4	152·1
48	40·7	25·4	108	91·6	57·2	168	142·5	89·0	228	193·4	120·8	288	244·2	152·6
49	41·6	26·0	109	92·4	57·8	169	143·3	89·6	229	194·2	121·4	289	245·1	153·1
50	42·4	26·5	110	93·3	58·3	170	144·2	90·1	230	195·1	121·9	290	245·9	153·7
51	43·3	27·0	111	94·1	58·8	171	145·0	90·6	231	195·9	122·4	291	246·8	154·2
52	44·1	27·6	112	95·0	59·4	172	145·9	91·1	232	196·7	122·9	292	247·6	154·7
53	44·9	28·1	113	95·8	59·9	173	146·7	91·7	233	197·6	123·5	293	248·5	155·3
54	45·8	28·6	114	96·7	60·4	174	147·6	92·2	234	198·4	124·0	294	249·3	155·8
55	46·6	29·1	115	97·5	60·9	175	148·4	92·7	235	199·3	124·5	295	250·2	156·3
56	47·5	29·7	116	98·4	61·5	176	149·3	93·3	236	200·1	125·1	296	251·0	156·9
57	48·3	30·2	117	99·2	62·0	177	150·1	93·8	237	201·0	125·6	297	251·9	157·4
58	49·2	30·7	118	100·1	62·5	178	151·0	94·3	238	201·8	126·1	298	252·7	157·9
59	50·0	31·3	119	100·9	63·1	179	151·8	94·9	239	202·7	126·7	299	253·6	158·4
60	50·9	31·8	120	101·8	63·6	180	152·6	95·4	240	203·5	127·2	300	254·4	159·0
Dist.	Dep.	D. Lat.	Dist.	Dep.	D. Lat.	Dist.	Dep.	D. Lat.	Dist.	Dep.	D. Lat.	Dist.	Dep.	D. Lat.
D. Lon		Dep.	D. Lon		Dep.	D. Lon		Dep.	D. Lon		Dep.	D. Lon		Dep.

58°

302° / 238° 58 Degrees 058° / 122° 3h 52m

TRAVERSE TABLE
32 Degrees

D. Lon	Dep.		D. Lon	Dep.		D. Lon	Dep.		D. Lon	Dep.		D. Lon	Dep.	
Dist.	D. Lat.	Dep.	Dist.	D. Lat.	Dep.	Dist.	D. Lat.	Dep.	Dist.	D. Lat.	Dep.	Dist.	D. Lat.	Dep.
301	255·3	159·5	361	306·1	191·3	421	357·0	223·1	481	407·9	254·9	541	458·8	286·7
302	256·1	160·0	362	307·0	191·8	422	357·9	223·6	482	408·8	255·4	542	459·6	287·2
303	257·0	160·6	363	307·8	192·4	423	358·7	224·2	483	409·6	256·0	543	460·5	287·7
304	257·8	161·1	364	308·7	192·9	424	359·6	224·7	484	410·5	256·5	544	461·3	288·3
305	258·7	161·6	365	309·5	193·4	425	360·4	225·2	485	411·3	257·0	545	462·2	288·8
306	259·5	162·2	366	310·4	194·0	426	361·3	225·7	486	412·2	257·5	546	463·0	289·3
307	260·4	162·7	367	311·2	194·5	427	362·1	226·3	487	413·0	258·1	547	463·9	289·9
308	261·2	163·2	368	312·1	195·0	428	363·0	226·8	488	413·8	258·6	548	464·7	290·4
309	262·0	163·7	369	312·9	195·5	429	363·8	227·3	489	414·7	259·1	549	465·6	290·9
310	262·9	164·3	370	313·8	196·1	430	364·7	227·9	490	415·5	259·7	550	466·4	291·5
311	263·7	164·8	371	314·6	196·6	431	365·5	228·4	491	416·4	260·2	551	467·3	292·0
312	264·6	165·3	372	315·5	197·1	432	366·4	228·9	492	417·2	260·7	552	468·1	292·5
313	265·4	165·9	373	316·3	197·7	433	367·2	229·5	493	418·1	261·3	553	469·0	293·0
314	266·3	166·4	374	317·2	198·2	434	368·1	230·0	494	418·9	261·8	554	469·8	293·6
315	267·1	166·9	375	318·0	198·7	435	368·9	230·5	495	419·8	262·3	555	470·7	294·1
316	268·0	167·5	376	318·9	199·2	436	369·7	231·0	496	420·6	262·8	556	471·5	294·6
317	268·8	168·0	377	319·7	199·8	437	370·6	231·6	497	421·5	263·4	557	472·4	295·2
318	269·7	168·5	378	320·6	200·3	438	371·4	232·1	498	422·3	263·9	558	473·2	295·7
319	270·5	169·0	379	321·4	200·8	439	372·3	232·6	499	423·2	264·4	559	474·1	296·2
320	271·4	169·6	380	322·3	201·4	440	373·1	233·2	500	424·0	265·0	560	474·9	296·8
321	272·2	170·1	381	323·1	201·9	441	374·0	233·7	501	424·9	265·5	561	475·8	297·3
322	273·1	170·6	382	324·0	202·4	442	374·8	234·2	502	425·7	266·0	562	476·6	297·8
323	273·9	171·2	383	324·8	203·0	443	375·7	234·8	503	426·6	266·5	563	477·5	298·3
324	274·8	171·7	384	325·7	203·5	444	376·5	235·3	504	427·4	267·1	564	478·3	298·9
325	275·6	172·2	385	326·5	204·0	445	377·4	235·8	505	428·3	267·6	565	479·1	299·4
326	276·5	172·8	386	327·3	204·5	446	378·2	236·3	506	429·1	268·1	566	480·0	299·9
327	277·3	173·3	387	328·2	205·1	447	379·1	236·9	507	430·0	268·7	567	480·8	300·5
328	278·2	173·8	388	329·0	205·6	448	379·9	237·4	508	430·8	269·2	568	481·7	301·0
329	279·0	174·3	389	329·9	206·1	449	380·8	237·9	509	431·7	269·7	569	482·5	301·5
330	279·9	174·9	390	330·7	206·7	450	381·6	238·5	510	432·5	270·3	570	483·4	302·1
331	280·7	175·4	391	331·6	207·2	451	382·5	239·0	511	433·4	270·8	571	484·2	302·6
332	281·6	175·9	392	332·4	207·7	452	383·3	239·5	512	434·2	271·3	572	485·1	303·1
333	282·4	176·5	393	333·3	208·3	453	384·2	240·1	513	435·0	271·9	573	485·9	303·6
334	283·2	177·0	394	334·1	208·8	454	385·0	240·6	514	435·9	272·4	574	486·8	304·2
335	284·1	177·5	395	335·0	209·3	455	385·9	241·1	515	436·7	272·9	575	487·6	304·7
336	284·9	178·1	396	335·8	209·8	456	386·7	241·6	516	437·6	273·4	576	488·5	305·2
337	285·8	178·6	397	336·7	210·4	457	387·6	242·2	517	438·4	274·0	577	489·3	305·8
338	286·6	179·1	398	337·5	210·9	458	388·4	242·7	518	439·3	274·5	578	490·2	306·3
339	287·5	179·6	399	338·4	211·4	459	389·3	243·2	519	440·1	275·0	579	491·0	306·8
340	288·3	180·2	400	339·2	212·0	460	390·1	243·8	520	441·0	275·6	580	491·9	307·4
341	289·2	180·7	401	340·1	212·5	461	391·0	244·3	521	441·8	276·1	581	492·7	307·9
342	290·0	181·2	402	340·9	213·0	462	391·8	244·8	522	442·7	276·6	582	493·6	308·4
343	290·9	181·8	403	341·8	213·6	463	392·6	245·4	523	443·5	277·1	583	494·4	308·9
344	291·7	182·3	404	342·6	214·1	464	393·5	245·9	524	444·4	277·7	584	495·3	309·5
345	292·6	182·8	405	343·5	214·6	465	394·3	246·4	525	445·2	278·2	585	496·1	310·0
346	293·4	183·4	406	344·3	215·1	466	395·2	246·9	526	446·1	278·7	586	497·0	310·5
347	294·3	183·9	407	345·2	215·7	467	396·0	247·5	527	446·9	279·3	587	497·8	311·1
348	295·1	184·4	408	346·0	216·2	468	396·9	248·0	528	447·8	279·8	588	498·7	311·6
349	296·0	184·9	409	346·9	216·7	469	397·7	248·5	529	448·6	280·3	589	499·5	312·1
350	296·8	185·5	410	347·7	217·3	470	398·6	249·1	530	449·5	280·9	590	500·3	312·7
351	297·7	186·0	411	348·5	217·8	471	399·4	249·6	531	450·3	281·4	591	501·2	313·2
352	298·5	186·5	412	349·4	218·3	472	400·3	250·1	532	451·2	281·9	592	502·0	313·7
353	299·4	187·1	413	350·2	218·9	473	401·1	250·7	533	452·0	282·4	593	502·9	314·2
354	300·2	187·6	414	351·1	219·4	474	402·0	251·2	534	452·9	283·0	594	503·7	314·8
355	301·1	188·1	415	351·9	219·9	475	402·8	251·7	535	453·7	283·5	595	504·6	315·3
356	301·9	188·7	416	352·8	220·4	476	403·7	252·2	536	454·6	284·0	596	505·4	315·8
357	302·8	189·2	417	353·6	221·0	477	404·5	252·8	537	455·4	284·6	597	506·3	316·4
358	303·6	189·7	418	354·5	221·5	478	405·4	253·3	538	456·2	285·1	598	507·1	316·9
359	304·4	190·2	419	355·3	222·0	479	406·2	253·8	539	457·1	285·6	599	508·0	317·4
360	305·3	190·8	420	356·2	222·6	480	407·1	254·4	540	457·9	286·2	600	508·8	318·0
Dist.	Dep.	D. Lat.	Dist.	Dep.	D. Lat.	Dist.	Dep.	D. Lat.	Dist.	Dep.	D. Lat.	Dist.	Dep.	D. Lat.
D. Lon		Dep.	D. Lon		Dep.	D. Lon		Dep.	D. Lon		Dep.	D. Lon		Dep.

TRAVERSE TABLE
33 Degrees

33° 327°/213° 033°/147° 2h 12m

Dist.	D. Lat.	Dep.	Dist.	D. Lat.	Dep.	Dist.	D. Lat.	Dep.	Dist.	D. Lat.	Dep.	Dist.	D. Lat.	Dep.
1	00·8	00·5	61	51·2	33·2	121	101·5	65·9	181	151·8	98·6	241	202·1	131·3
2	01·7	01·1	62	52·0	33·8	122	102·3	66·4	182	152·6	99·1	242	203·0	131·8
3	02·5	01·6	63	52·8	34·3	123	103·2	67·0	183	153·5	99·7	243	203·8	132·3
4	03·4	02·2	64	53·7	34·9	124	104·0	67·5	184	154·3	100·2	244	204·6	132·9
5	04·2	02·7	65	54·5	35·4	125	104·8	68·1	185	155·2	100·8	245	205·5	133·4
6	05·0	03·3	66	55·4	35·9	126	105·7	68·6	186	156·0	101·3	246	206·3	134·0
7	05·9	03·8	67	56·2	36·5	127	106·5	69·2	187	156·8	101·8	247	207·2	134·5
8	06·7	04·4	68	57·0	37·0	128	107·3	69·7	188	157·7	102·4	248	208·0	135·1
9	07·5	04·9	69	57·9	37·6	129	108·2	70·3	189	158·5	102·9	249	208·8	135·6
10	08·4	05·4	70	58·7	38·1	130	109·0	70·8	190	159·3	103·5	250	209·7	136·2
11	09·2	06·0	71	59·5	38·7	131	109·9	71·3	191	160·2	104·0	251	210·5	136·7
12	10·1	06·5	72	60·4	39·2	132	110·7	71·9	192	161·0	104·6	252	211·3	137·2
13	10·9	07·1	73	61·2	39·8	133	111·5	72·4	193	161·9	105·1	253	212·2	137·8
14	11·7	07·6	74	62·1	40·3	134	112·4	73·0	194	162·7	105·7	254	213·0	138·3
15	12·6	08·2	75	62·9	40·8	135	113·2	73·5	195	163·5	106·2	255	213·9	138·9
16	13·4	08·7	76	63·7	41·4	136	114·1	74·1	196	164·4	106·7	256	214·7	139·4
17	14·3	09·3	77	64·6	41·9	137	114·9	74·6	197	165·2	107·3	257	215·5	140·0
18	15·1	09·8	78	65·4	42·5	138	115·7	75·2	198	166·1	107·8	258	216·4	140·5
19	15·9	10·3	79	66·3	43·0	139	116·6	75·7	199	166·9	108·4	259	217·2	141·1
20	16·8	10·9	80	67·1	43·6	140	117·4	76·2	200	167·7	108·9	260	218·1	141·6
21	17·6	11·4	81	67·9	44·1	141	118·3	76·8	201	168·6	109·5	261	218·9	142·2
22	18·5	12·0	82	68·8	44·7	142	119·1	77·3	202	169·4	110·0	262	219·7	142·7
23	19·3	12·5	83	69·6	45·2	143	119·9	77·9	203	170·3	110·6	263	220·6	143·2
24	20·1	13·1	84	70·4	45·7	144	120·8	78·4	204	171·1	111·1	264	221·4	143·8
25	21·0	13·6	85	71·3	46·3	145	121·6	79·0	205	171·9	111·7	265	222·2	144·3
26	21·8	14·2	86	72·1	46·8	146	122·4	79·5	206	172·8	112·2	266	223·1	144·9
27	22·6	14·7	87	73·0	47·4	147	123·3	80·1	207	173·6	112·7	267	223·9	145·4
28	23·5	15·2	88	73·8	47·9	148	124·1	80·6	208	174·4	113·3	268	224·8	146·0
29	24·3	15·8	89	74·6	48·5	149	125·0	81·2	209	175·3	113·8	269	225·6	146·5
30	25·2	16·3	90	75·5	49·0	150	125·8	81·7	210	176·1	114·4	270	226·4	147·1
31	26·0	16·9	91	76·3	49·6	151	126·6	82·2	211	177·0	114·9	271	227·3	147·6
32	26·8	17·4	92	77·2	50·1	152	127·5	82·8	212	177·8	115·5	272	228·1	148·1
33	27·7	18·0	93	78·0	50·7	153	128·3	83·3	213	178·6	116·0	273	229·0	148·7
34	28·5	18·5	94	78·8	51·2	154	129·2	83·9	214	179·5	116·6	274	229·8	149·2
35	29·4	19·1	95	79·7	51·7	155	130·0	84·4	215	180·3	117·1	275	230·6	149·8
36	30·2	19·6	96	80·5	52·3	156	130·8	85·0	216	181·2	117·6	276	231·5	150·3
37	31·0	20·2	97	81·4	52·8	157	131·7	85·5	217	182·0	118·2	277	232·3	150·9
38	31·9	20·7	98	82·2	53·4	158	132·5	86·1	218	182·8	118·7	278	233·2	151·4
39	32·7	21·2	99	83·0	53·9	159	133·3	86·6	219	183·7	119·3	279	234·0	152·0
40	33·5	21·8	100	83·9	54·5	160	134·2	87·1	220	184·5	119·8	280	234·8	152·5
41	34·4	22·3	101	84·7	55·0	161	135·0	87·7	221	185·3	120·4	281	235·7	153·0
42	35·2	22·9	102	85·5	55·6	162	135·9	88·2	222	186·2	120·9	282	236·5	153·6
43	36·1	23·4	103	86·4	56·1	163	136·7	88·8	223	187·0	121·5	283	237·3	154·1
44	36·9	24·0	104	87·2	56·6	164	137·5	89·3	224	187·9	122·0	284	238·2	154·7
45	37·7	24·5	105	88·1	57·2	165	138·4	89·9	225	188·7	122·5	285	239·0	155·2
46	38·6	25·1	106	88·9	57·7	166	139·2	90·4	226	189·5	123·1	286	239·9	155·8
47	39·4	25·6	107	89·7	58·3	167	140·1	91·0	227	190·4	123·6	287	240·7	156·3
48	40·3	26·1	108	90·6	58·8	168	140·9	91·5	228	191·2	124·2	288	241·5	156·9
49	41·1	26·7	109	91·4	59·4	169	141·7	92·0	229	192·1	124·7	289	242·4	157·4
50	41·9	27·2	110	92·3	59·9	170	142·6	92·6	230	192·9	125·3	290	243·2	157·9
51	42·8	27·8	111	93·1	60·5	171	143·4	93·1	231	193·7	125·8	291	244·1	158·5
52	43·6	28·3	112	93·9	61·0	172	144·3	93·7	232	194·6	126·4	292	244·9	159·0
53	44·4	28·9	113	94·8	61·5	173	145·1	94·2	233	195·4	126·9	293	245·7	159·6
54	45·3	29·4	114	95·6	62·1	174	145·9	94·8	234	196·2	127·4	294	246·6	160·1
55	46·1	30·0	115	96·4	62·6	175	146·8	95·3	235	197·1	128·0	295	247·4	160·7
56	47·0	30·5	116	97·3	63·2	176	147·6	95·9	236	197·9	128·5	296	248·2	161·2
57	47·8	31·0	117	98·1	63·7	177	148·4	96·4	237	198·9	129·1	297	249·1	161·8
58	48·6	31·6	118	99·0	64·3	178	149·3	96·9	238	199·6	129·6	298	249·9	162·3
59	49·5	32·1	119	99·8	64·8	179	150·1	97·5	239	200·4	130·2	299	250·8	162·8
60	50·3	32·7	120	100·6	65·4	180	151·0	98·0	240	201·3	130·7	300	251·6	163·4

Dist.	Dep.	D. Lat.	Dist.	Dep.	D. Lat.	Dist.	Dep.	D. Lat.	Dist.	Dep.	D. Lat.	Dist.	Dep.	D. Lat.

57° 303°/237° 57 Degrees 057°/123° 3h 48m

TRAVERSE TABLE
33 Degrees

327° / 213° 033° / 147° 2h 12m **33°**

D. Lon Dep. Dist	D. Lat	Dep.	D. Lon Dep. Dist	D. Lat	Dep.	D. Lon Dep. Dist	D. Lat	Dep.	D. Lon Dep. Dist	D. Lat	Dep.	D. Lon Dep. Dist	D. Lat	Dep.
301	252·4	163·9	361	302·8	196·6	421	353·1	229·3	481	403·4	262·0	541	453·7	294·6
302	253·3	164·5	362	303·6	197·2	422	353·9	229·8	482	404·2	262·5	542	454·6	295·2
303	254·1	165·0	363	304·4	197·7	423	354·8	230·4	483	405·1	263·1	543	455·4	295·7
304	255·0	165·6	364	305·3	198·2	424	355·6	230·9	484	405·9	263·6	544	456·2	296·3
305	255·8	166·1	365	306·1	198·8	425	356·4	231·5	485	406·8	264·1	545	457·1	296·8
306	256·6	166·7	366	307·0	199·3	426	357·3	232·0	486	407·6	264·7	546	457·9	297·4
307	257·5	167·2	367	307·8	199·9	427	358·1	232·6	487	408·4	265·2	547	458·8	297·9
308	258·3	167·7	368	308·6	200·4	428	359·0	233·1	488	409·3	265·8	548	459·6	298·5
309	259·1	168·3	369	309·5	201·0	429	359·8	233·7	489	410·1	266·3	549	460·4	299·0
310	260·0	168·8	370	310·3	201·5	430	360·6	234·2	490	410·9	266·9	550	461·3	299·6
311	260·8	169·4	371	311·1	202·1	431	361·5	234·7	491	411·8	267·4	551	462·1	300·1
312	261·7	169·9	372	312·0	202·6	432	362·3	235·3	492	412·6	268·0	552	462·9	300·6
313	262·5	170·5	373	312·8	203·2	433	363·1	235·8	493	413·5	268·5	553	463·8	301·2
314	263·3	171·0	374	313·7	203·7	434	364·0	236·4	494	414·3	269·0	554	464·6	301·7
315	264·2	171·6	375	314·5	204·2	435	364·8	236·9	495	415·1	269·6	555	465·5	302·3
316	265·0	172·1	376	315·3	204·7	436	365·7	237·5	496	416·0	270·1	556	466·3	302·8
317	265·9	172·7	377	316·2	205·3	437	366·5	238·0	497	416·8	270·7	557	467·1	303·4
318	266·7	173·2	378	317·0	205·9	438	367·3	238·6	498	417·7	271·2	558	468·0	303·9
319	267·5	173·7	379	317·9	206·4	439	368·2	239·1	499	418·5	271·8	559	468·8	304·5
320	268·4	174·3	380	318·7	207·0	440	369·2	239·6	500	419·3	272·3	560	469·7	305·0
321	269·2	174·8	381	319·5	207·5	441	369·9	240·2	501	420·2	272·9	561	470·5	305·5
322	270·1	175·4	382	320·4	208·1	442	370·7	240·7	502	421·0	273·4	562	471·3	306·1
323	270·9	175·9	383	321·2	208·6	443	371·5	241·3	503	421·9	274·0	563	472·2	306·6
324	271·7	176·5	384	322·0	209·1	444	372·4	241·8	504	422·7	274·5	564	473·0	307·2
325	272·6	177·0	385	322·9	209·7	445	373·2	242·4	505	423·5	275·0	565	473·8	307·7
326	273·4	177·6	386	323·7	210·2	446	374·0	242·9	506	424·4	275·6	566	474·7	308·3
327	274·2	178·1	387	324·6	210·8	447	374·9	243·5	507	425·2	276·1	567	475·5	308·8
328	275·1	178·6	388	325·4	211·3	448	375·7	244·0	508	426·0	276·7	568	476·4	309·4
329	275·9	179·2	389	326·2	211·9	449	376·6	244·5	509	426·9	277·2	569	477·2	309·9
330	276·8	179·7	390	327·1	212·4	450	377·4	245·1	510	427·7	277·8	570	478·0	310·4
331	277·6	180·3	391	327·9	213·0	451	378·2	245·6	511	428·6	278·3	571	478·9	311·0
332	278·4	180·8	392	328·8	213·5	452	379·1	246·2	512	429·4	278·9	572	479·7	311·5
333	279·3	181·4	393	329·6	214·0	453	379·9	246·7	513	430·2	279·4	573	480·6	312·1
334	280·1	181·9	394	330·4	214·6	454	380·8	247·3	514	431·1	279·9	574	481·4	312·6
335	281·0	182·5	395	331·3	215·1	455	381·6	247·8	515	431·9	280·5	575	482·2	313·2
336	281·8	183·0	396	332·1	215·7	456	382·4	248·4	516	432·8	281·0	576	483·1	313·7
337	282·6	183·5	397	333·0	216·2	457	383·3	248·9	517	433·6	281·6	577	483·9	314·3
338	283·5	184·1	398	333·8	216·8	458	384·1	249·4	518	434·4	282·1	578	484·8	314·8
339	284·3	184·6	399	334·6	217·3	459	384·9	250·0	519	435·3	282·7	579	485·6	315·3
340	285·1	185·2	400	335·5	217·9	460	385·8	250·5	520	436·1	283·2	580	486·4	315·9
341	286·0	185·7	401	336·3	218·4	461	386·6	251·1	521	436·9	283·8	581	487·3	316·4
342	286·8	186·3	402	337·1	218·9	462	387·5	251·6	522	437·8	284·3	582	488·1	317·0
343	287·7	186·8	403	338·0	219·5	463	388·3	252·2	523	438·6	284·8	583	488·9	317·5
344	288·5	187·4	404	338·8	220·0	464	389·1	252·7	524	439·5	285·4	584	489·8	318·1
345	289·3	187·9	405	339·7	220·6	465	390·0	253·3	525	440·3	285·9	585	490·6	318·6
346	290·2	188·4	406	340·5	221·1	466	390·8	253·8	526	441·1	286·5	586	491·5	319·2
347	291·0	189·0	407	341·3	221·7	467	391·7	254·3	527	442·0	287·0	587	492·3	319·7
348	291·9	189·5	408	342·2	222·2	468	392·5	254·9	528	442·8	287·6	588	493·1	320·2
349	292·7	190·1	409	343·0	222·8	469	393·3	255·4	529	443·7	288·1	589	494·0	320·8
350	293·5	190·6	410	343·9	223·3	470	394·2	256·0	530	444·5	288·7	590	494·8	321·3
351	294·4	191·2	411	344·7	223·8	471	395·0	256·5	531	445·3	289·2	591	495·7	321·9
352	295·2	191·7	412	345·5	224·5	472	395·9	257·1	532	446·2	289·7	592	496·5	322·4
353	296·1	192·3	413	346·4	224·9	473	396·7	257·6	533	447·0	290·3	593	497·3	323·0
354	296·9	192·8	414	347·2	225·5	474	397·5	258·2	534	447·9	290·8	594	498·2	323·5
355	297·7	193·3	415	348·0	226·0	475	398·4	258·7	535	448·7	291·4	595	499·0	324·1
356	298·6	193·9	416	348·9	226·6	476	399·2	259·2	536	449·5	291·9	596	499·8	324·6
357	299·4	194·4	417	349·7	227·1	477	400·0	259·8	537	450·4	292·5	597	500·7	325·1
358	300·2	195·0	418	350·6	227·7	478	400·9	260·3	538	451·2	293·0	598	501·5	325·7
359	301·1	195·5	419	351·4	228·2	479	401·7	260·9	539	452·0	293·6	599	502·4	326·2
360	301·9	196·1	420	352·2	228·7	480	402·6	261·4	540	452·9	294·1	600	503·2	326·8

| Dist. | Dep. | D. Lat. | Dist. | Dep. | D. Lat. | Dist. | Dep. | D. Lat. | Dist. | Dep. | D. Lat. | Dist. | Dep. | D. Lat. |

D. Lon Dep.

303° / 237° 57 Degrees 057° / 123° 3h 48m **57°**

TRAVERSE TABLE

34°

	326° / 214°					34 Degrees								034° / 146° 2h 16m	

D. Lon	Dep.		D. Lon	Dep.		D. Lon	Dep.		D. Lon	Dep.		D. Lon	Dep.	
Dist.	D. Lat.	Dep.	Dist.	D. Lat.	Dep.	Dist.	D. Lat.	Dep.	Dist.	D. Lat.	Dep.	Dist.	D. Lat.	Dep.
1	00·8	00·6	61	50·6	34·1	121	100·3	67·7	181	150·1	101·2	241	199·8	134·8
2	01·7	01·1	62	51·4	34·7	122	101·1	68·2	182	150·9	101·8	242	200·6	135·3
3	02·5	01·7	63	52·2	35·2	123	102·0	68·8	183	151·7	102·3	243	201·5	135·9
4	03·3	02·2	64	53·1	35·8	124	102·8	69·3	184	152·5	102·9	244	202·3	136·4
5	04·1	02·8	65	53·9	36·3	125	103·6	69·9	185	153·4	103·5	245	203·1	137·0
6	05·0	03·4	66	54·7	36·9	126	104·5	70·5	186	154·2	104·0	246	203·9	137·6
7	05·8	03·9	67	55·5	37·5	127	105·3	71·0	187	155·0	104·6	247	204·8	138·1
8	06·6	04·5	68	56·4	38·0	128	106·1	71·6	188	155·9	105·1	248	205·6	138·7
9	07·5	05·0	69	57·2	38·6	129	106·9	72·1	189	156·7	105·7	249	206·4	139·2
10	08·3	05·6	70	58·0	39·1	130	107·8	72·7	190	157·5	106·2	250	207·3	139·8
11	09·1	06·2	71	58·9	39·7	131	108·6	73·3	191	158·3	106·8	251	208·1	140·4
12	09·9	06·7	72	59·7	40·3	132	109·4	73·8	192	159·2	107·4	252	208·9	140·9
13	10·8	07·3	73	60·5	40·8	133	110·3	74·4	193	160·0	107·9	253	209·7	141·5
14	11·6	07·8	74	61·3	41·4	134	111·1	74·9	194	160·8	108·5	254	210·6	142·0
15	12·4	08·4	75	62·2	41·9	135	111·9	75·5	195	161·7	109·0	255	211·4	142·6
16	13·3	08·9	76	63·0	42·5	136	112·7	76·1	196	162·5	109·6	256	212·2	143·2
17	14·1	09·5	77	63·8	43·1	137	113·6	76·6	197	163·3	110·2	257	213·1	143·7
18	14·9	10·1	78	64·7	43·6	138	114·4	77·2	198	164·1	110·7	258	213·9	144·3
19	15·8	10·6	79	65·5	44·2	139	115·2	77·7	199	165·0	111·3	259	214·7	144·8
20	16·6	11·2	80	66·3	44·7	140	116·1	78·3	200	165·8	111·8	260	215·5	145·4
21	17·4	11·7	81	67·2	45·3	141	116·9	78·8	201	166·6	112·4	261	216·4	145·9
22	18·2	12·3	82	68·0	45·9	142	117·7	79·4	202	167·5	113·0	262	217·2	146·5
23	19·1	12·9	83	68·8	46·4	143	118·6	80·0	203	168·3	113·5	263	218·0	147·1
24	19·9	13·4	84	69·6	47·0	144	119·4	80·5	204	169·1	114·1	264	218·9	147·6
25	20·7	14·0	85	70·5	47·5	145	120·2	81·1	205	170·0	114·6	265	219·7	148·2
26	21·6	14·5	86	71·3	48·1	146	121·0	81·6	206	170·8	115·2	266	220·5	148·7
27	22·4	15·1	87	72·1	48·6	147	121·9	82·2	207	171·6	115·8	267	221·4	149·3
28	23·2	15·7	88	73·0	49·2	148	122·7	82·8	208	172·4	116·3	268	222·2	149·9
29	24·0	16·2	89	73·8	49·8	149	123·5	83·3	209	173·3	116·9	269	223·0	150·4
30	24·9	16·8	90	74·6	50·3	150	124·4	83·9	210	174·1	117·4	270	223·8	151·0
31	25·7	17·3	91	75·4	50·9	151	125·2	84·4	211	174·9	118·0	271	224·7	151·5
32	26·5	17·9	92	76·3	51·4	152	126·0	85·0	212	175·8	118·5	272	225·5	152·1
33	27·4	18·5	93	77·1	52·0	153	126·8	85·6	213	176·6	119·1	273	226·3	152·7
34	28·2	19·0	94	77·9	52·6	154	127·7	86·1	214	177·4	119·7	274	227·2	153·2
35	29·0	19·6	95	78·8	53·1	155	128·5	86·7	215	178·2	120·2	275	228·0	153·8
36	29·8	20·1	96	79·6	53·7	156	129·3	87·2	216	179·1	120·8	276	228·8	154·3
37	30·7	20·7	97	80·4	54·2	157	130·2	87·8	217	179·9	121·3	277	229·6	154·9
38	31·5	21·2	98	81·2	54·8	158	131·0	88·4	218	180·7	121·9	278	230·5	155·5
39	32·3	21·8	99	82·1	55·4	159	131·8	88·9	219	181·6	122·5	279	231·3	156·0
40	33·2	22·4	100	82·9	55·9	160	132·6	89·5	220	182·4	123·0	280	232·1	156·6
41	34·0	22·9	101	83·7	56·5	161	133·5	90·0	221	183·2	123·6	281	233·0	157·1
42	34·8	23·5	102	84·6	57·0	162	134·3	90·6	222	184·0	124·1	282	233·8	157·7
43	35·6	24·0	103	85·4	57·6	163	135·1	91·1	223	184·9	124·7	283	234·6	158·3
44	36·5	24·6	104	86·2	58·2	164	136·0	91·7	224	185·7	125·3	284	235·4	158·8
45	37·3	25·2	105	87·0	58·7	165	136·8	92·3	225	186·5	125·8	285	236·3	159·4
46	38·1	25·7	106	87·9	59·3	166	137·6	92·8	226	187·4	126·4	286	237·1	159·9
47	39·0	26·3	107	88·7	59·8	167	138·4	93·4	227	188·2	126·9	287	237·9	160·5
48	39·8	26·8	108	89·5	60·4	168	139·3	93·9	228	189·0	127·5	288	238·8	161·0
49	40·6	27·4	109	90·4	61·0	169	140·1	94·5	229	189·8	128·1	289	239·6	161·6
50	41·5	28·0	110	91·2	61·5	170	140·9	95·1	230	190·7	128·6	290	240·4	162·2
51	42·3	28·5	111	92·0	62·1	171	141·8	95·6	231	191·5	129·2	291	241·2	162·7
52	43·1	29·1	112	92·9	62·6	172	142·6	96·2	232	192·3	129·7	292	242·1	163·3
53	43·9	29·6	113	93·7	63·2	173	143·4	96·7	233	193·2	130·3	293	242·9	163·8
54	44·8	30·2	114	94·5	63·7	174	144·3	97·3	234	194·0	130·9	294	243·7	164·4
55	45·6	30·8	115	95·3	64·3	175	145·1	97·9	235	194·8	131·4	295	244·6	165·0
56	46·4	31·3	116	96·2	64·9	176	145·9	98·4	236	195·7	132·0	296	245·4	165·5
57	47·3	31·9	117	97·0	65·4	177	146·7	99·0	237	196·5	132·5	297	246·2	166·1
58	48·1	32·4	118	97·8	66·0	178	147·6	99·5	238	197·3	133·1	298	247·1	166·6
59	48·9	33·0	119	98·7	66·5	179	148·4	100·1	239	198·1	133·6	299	247·9	167·2
60	49·7	33·6	120	99·5	67·1	180	149·2	100·7	240	199·0	134·2	300	248·7	167·8
Dist.	Dep.	D. Lat.	Dist.	Dep.	D. Lat.	Dist.	Dep.	D. Lat.	Dist.	Dep.	D. Lat.	Dist.	Dep.	D. Lat.
D. Lon		Dep.	D. Lon		Dep.	D. Lon		Dep.	D. Lon		Dep.	D. Lon		Dep.

	304° / 236°					56 Degrees								056° / 124° 3h 44m	

TRAVERSE TABLE
34 Degrees

Dist.	D. Lat.	Dep.	Dist.	D. Lat.	Dep.	Dist.	D. Lat.	Dep.	Dist.	D. Lat.	Dep.	Dist.	D. Lat.	Dep.
301	249·5	168·3	361	299·3	201·9	421	349·0	235·4	481	398·8	269·0	541	448·5	302·5
302	250·4	168·9	362	300·1	202·4	422	349·9	236·0	482	399·6	269·5	542	449·3	303·1
303	251·2	169·4	363	300·9	203·0	423	350·7	236·5	483	400·4	270·1	543	450·2	303·6
304	252·0	170·0	364	301·8	203·5	424	351·5	237·1	484	401·3	270·6	544	451·0	304·2
305	252·9	170·6	365	302·6	204·1	425	352·3	237·7	485	402·1	271·2	545	451·8	304·8
306	253·7	171·1	366	303·4	204·7	426	353·2	238·2	486	402·9	271·8	546	452·7	305·3
307	254·5	171·7	367	304·3	205·2	427	354·0	238·8	487	403·7	272·3	547	453·5	305·9
308	255·3	172·2	368	305·1	205·8	428	354·8	239·3	488	404·6	272·9	548	454·3	306·4
309	256·2	172·8	369	305·9	206·3	429	355·7	239·9	489	405·4	273·4	549	455·1	307·0
310	257·0	173·3	370	306·7	206·9	430	356·5	240·5	490	406·2	274·0	550	456·0	307·6
311	257·8	173·9	371	307·6	207·5	431	357·3	241·0	491	407·1	274·6	551	456·8	308·1
312	258·7	174·5	372	308·4	208·0	432	358·1	241·6	492	407·9	275·1	552	457·6	308·7
313	259·5	175·0	373	309·2	208·6	433	359·0	242·1	493	408·7	275·7	553	458·5	309·2
314	260·3	175·6	374	310·1	209·1	434	359·8	242·7	494	409·5	276·2	554	459·3	309·8
315	261·1	176·1	375	310·9	209·7	435	360·6	243·2	495	410·4	276·8	555	460·1	310·4
316	262·0	176·7	376	311·7	210·3	436	361·5	243·8	496	411·2	277·4	556	460·9	310·9
317	262·8	177·3	377	312·5	210·8	437	362·3	244·4	497	412·0	277·9	557	461·8	311·5
318	263·6	177·8	378	313·4	211·4	438	363·1	244·9	498	412·9	278·5	558	462·6	312·0
319	264·5	178·4	379	314·2	211·9	439	363·9	245·5	499	413·7	279·0	559	463·4	312·6
320	265·3	178·9	380	315·0	212·5	440	364·8	246·0	500	414·5	279·6	560	464·3	313·1
321	266·1	179·5	381	315·9	213·1	441	365·6	246·6	501	415·3	280·2	561	465·1	313·7
322	267·0	180·1	382	316·7	213·6	442	366·4	247·2	502	416·2	280·7	562	465·9	314·3
323	267·8	180·6	383	317·5	214·2	443	367·3	247·7	503	417·0	281·3	563	466·7	314·8
324	268·6	181·2	384	318·4	214·7	444	368·1	248·3	504	417·8	281·8	564	467·6	315·5
325	269·4	181·7	385	319·2	215·3	445	368·9	248·8	505	418·7	282·4	565	468·4	315·9
326	270·3	182·3	386	320·0	215·8	446	369·8	249·4	506	419·5	283·0	566	469·2	316·5
327	271·1	182·9	387	320·8	216·4	447	370·6	250·0	507	420·3	283·5	567	470·1	317·1
328	271·9	183·4	388	321·7	217·0	448	371·4	250·5	508	421·2	284·1	568	470·9	317·6
329	272·8	184·0	389	322·5	217·5	449	372·2	251·1	509	422·0	284·6	569	471·7	318·2
330	273·6	184·5	390	323·3	218·1	450	373·1	251·6	510	422·8	285·2	570	472·6	318·7
331	274·4	185·1	391	324·2	218·6	451	373·9	252·2	511	423·6	285·7	571	473·4	319·3
332	275·2	185·7	392	325·0	219·2	452	374·7	252·8	512	424·5	286·3	572	474·2	319·9
333	276·1	186·2	393	325·8	219·8	453	375·6	253·3	513	425·3	287·0	573	475·0	320·4
334	276·9	186·8	394	326·6	220·3	454	376·4	253·9	514	426·1	287·4	574	475·9	321·0
335	277·7	187·3	395	327·5	220·9	455	377·2	254·4	515	427·0	288·0	575	476·7	321·5
336	278·6	187·9	396	328·3	221·4	456	378·0	255·0	516	427·8	288·5	576	477·5	322·1
337	279·4	188·4	397	329·1	222·0	457	378·9	255·6	517	428·6	289·1	577	478·4	322·7
338	280·2	189·0	398	330·0	222·6	458	379·7	256·1	518	429·4	289·7	578	479·2	323·2
339	281·0	189·6	399	330·8	223·1	459	380·5	256·7	519	430·3	290·2	579	480·0	323·8
340	281·9	190·1	400	331·6	223·7	460	381·4	257·2	520	431·1	290·8	580	480·8	324·3
341	282·7	190·7	401	332·4	224·2	461	382·2	257·8	521	431·9	291·3	581	481·7	324·9
342	283·5	191·2	402	333·2	224·8	462	383·0	258·3	522	432·8	291·9	582	482·5	325·4
343	284·4	191·8	403	334·1	225·4	463	383·8	258·9	523	433·6	292·5	583	483·3	326·0
344	285·2	192·4	404	334·9	225·9	464	384·7	259·5	524	434·4	293·0	584	484·2	326·6
345	286·0	192·9	405	335·8	226·5	465	385·5	260·0	525	435·2	293·6	585	485·0	327·1
346	286·8	193·5	406	336·6	227·0	466	386·3	260·6	526	436·1	294·1	586	485·8	327·7
347	287·7	194·0	407	337·4	227·6	467	387·2	261·1	527	436·9	294·7	587	486·6	328·2
348	288·5	194·6	408	338·2	228·2	468	388·0	261·7	528	437·7	295·3	588	487·5	328·8
349	289·3	195·2	409	339·1	228·7	469	388·8	262·3	529	438·6	295·8	589	488·3	329·4
350	290·2	195·7	410	339·9	229·3	470	389·6	262·8	530	439·4	296·4	590	489·1	329·9
351	291·0	196·3	411	340·7	229·8	471	390·5	263·4	531	440·2	296·9	591	490·0	330·5
352	291·8	196·8	412	341·6	230·4	472	391·3	263·9	532	441·0	297·5	592	490·8	331·0
353	292·7	197·4	413	342·4	230·9	473	392·1	264·5	533	441·9	298·0	593	491·6	331·6
354	293·5	198·0	414	343·2	231·5	474	393·0	265·1	534	442·7	298·6	594	492·4	332·2
355	294·3	198·5	415	344·1	232·1	475	393·8	265·6	535	443·5	299·2	595	493·3	332·7
356	295·1	199·1	416	344·9	232·6	476	394·6	266·2	536	444·4	299·7	596	494·1	333·3
357	296·0	199·6	417	345·7	233·2	477	395·5	266·7	537	445·3	300·3	597	494·9	333·8
358	296·8	200·2	418	346·5	233·7	478	396·3	267·3	538	446·0	300·8	598	495·8	334·4
359	297·6	200·8	419	347·4	234·4	479	397·1	267·9	539	446·9	301·4	599	496·6	335·0
360	298·5	201·3	420	348·2	234·9	480	397·9	268·4	540	447·7	302·0	600	497·4	335·5

Dist.	Dep.	D. Lat.	Dist.	Dep.	D. Lat.	Dist.	Dep.	D. Lat.	Dist.	Dep.	D. Lat.	Dist.	Dep.	D. Lat.

TRAVERSE TABLE
35 Degrees

| | 325° / 215° | | | | | | | | | | 035° / 145° | 2h 20m |

D. Lon	Dep.		D. Lon	Dep.		D. Lon	Dep.		D. Lon	Dep.		D. Lon	Dep.	
Dist.	D. Lat.	Dep.	Dist.	D. Lat.	Dep.	Dist.	D. Lat.	Dep.	Dist.	D. Lat.	Dep.	Dist.	D. Lat.	Dep.
1	00·8	00·6	61	50·0	35·0	121	99·1	69·4	181	148·3	103·8	241	197·4	138·2
2	01·6	01·1	62	50·8	35·6	122	99·9	70·0	182	149·1	104·4	242	198·2	138·8
3	02·5	01·7	63	51·6	36·1	123	100·8	70·5	183	149·9	105·0	243	199·1	139·4
4	03·3	02·3	64	52·4	36·7	124	101·6	71·1	184	150·7	105·5	244	199·9	140·0
5	04·1	02·9	65	53·2	37·3	125	102·4	71·7	185	151·5	106·1	245	200·7	140·5
6	04·9	03·4	66	54·1	37·9	126	103·2	72·3	186	152·4	106·7	246	201·5	141·1
7	05·7	04·0	67	54·9	38·4	127	104·0	72·8	187	153·2	107·3	247	202·3	141·7
8	06·6	04·6	68	55·7	39·0	128	104·9	73·4	188	154·0	107·8	248	203·1	142·2
9	07·4	05·2	69	56·5	39·6	129	105·7	74·0	189	154·8	108·4	249	204·0	142·8
10	08·2	05·7	70	57·3	40·2	130	106·5	74·6	190	155·6	109·0	250	204·8	143·4
11	09·0	06·3	71	58·2	40·7	131	107·3	75·1	191	156·5	109·6	251	205·6	144·0
12	09·8	06·9	72	59·0	41·3	132	108·1	75·7	192	157·3	110·1	252	206·4	144·5
13	10·6	07·5	73	59·8	41·9	133	108·9	76·3	193	158·1	110·7	253	207·2	145·1
14	11·5	08·0	74	60·6	42·4	134	109·8	76·9	194	158·9	111·3	254	208·1	145·7
15	12·3	08·6	75	61·4	43·0	135	110·6	77·4	195	159·7	111·8	255	208·9	146·3
16	13·1	09·2	76	62·3	43·6	136	111·4	78·0	196	160·6	112·4	256	209·7	146·8
17	13·9	09·8	77	63·1	44·2	137	112·2	78·6	197	161·4	113·0	257	210·5	147·4
18	14·7	10·3	78	63·9	44·7	138	113·0	79·2	198	162·2	113·6	258	211·3	148·0
19	15·6	10·9	79	64·7	45·3	139	113·9	79·7	199	163·0	114·1	259	212·2	148·6
20	16·4	11·5	80	65·5	45·9	140	114·7	80·3	200	163·8	114·7	260	213·0	149·1
21	17·2	12·0	81	66·4	46·5	141	115·5	80·9	201	164·6	115·3	261	213·8	149·7
22	18·0	12·6	82	67·2	47·0	142	116·3	81·4	202	165·5	115·9	262	214·6	150·3
23	18·8	13·2	83	68·0	47·6	143	117·1	82·0	203	166·3	116·4	263	215·4	150·9
24	19·7	13·8	84	68·8	48·2	144	118·0	82·6	204	167·1	117·0	264	216·3	151·4
25	20·5	14·3	85	69·6	48·8	145	118·8	83·2	205	167·9	117·6	265	217·1	152·0
26	21·3	14·9	86	70·4	49·3	146	119·6	83·7	206	168·7	118·2	266	217·9	152·6
27	22·1	15·5	87	71·3	49·9	147	120·4	84·3	207	169·6	118·7	267	218·7	153·1
28	22·9	16·1	88	72·1	50·5	148	121·2	84·9	208	170·4	119·3	268	219·5	153·7
29	23·8	16·6	89	72·9	51·0	149	122·1	85·5	209	171·2	119·9	269	220·4	154·3
30	24·6	17·2	90	73·7	51·6	150	122·9	86·0	210	172·0	120·5	270	221·2	154·9
31	25·4	17·8	91	74·5	52·2	151	123·7	86·6	211	172·8	121·0	271	222·0	155·4
32	26·2	18·4	92	75·4	52·8	152	124·5	87·2	212	173·7	121·6	272	222·8	156·0
33	27·0	18·9	93	76·2	53·3	153	125·3	87·8	213	174·5	122·2	273	223·6	156·6
34	27·9	19·5	94	77·0	53·9	154	126·1	88·3	214	175·3	122·7	274	224·4	157·2
35	28·7	20·1	95	77·8	54·5	155	127·0	88·9	215	176·1	123·3	275	225·3	157·7
36	29·5	20·6	96	78·6	55·1	156	127·8	89·5	216	176·9	123·9	276	226·1	158·3
37	30·3	21·2	97	79·5	55·6	157	128·6	90·1	217	177·8	124·5	277	226·9	158·9
38	31·1	21·8	98	80·3	56·2	158	129·4	90·6	218	178·6	125·0	278	227·7	159·5
39	31·9	22·4	99	81·1	56·8	159	130·2	91·2	219	179·4	125·6	279	228·5	160·0
40	32·8	22·9	100	81·9	57·4	160	131·1	91·8	220	180·2	126·2	280	229·4	160·6
41	33·6	23·5	101	82·7	57·9	161	131·9	92·3	221	181·0	126·8	281	230·2	161·2
42	34·4	24·1	102	83·6	58·5	162	132·7	92·9	222	181·9	127·3	282	231·0	161·7
43	35·2	24·7	103	84·4	59·1	163	133·5	93·5	223	182·7	127·9	283	231·8	162·3
44	36·0	25·2	104	85·2	59·7	164	134·3	94·1	224	183·5	128·5	284	232·6	162·9
45	36·9	25·8	105	86·0	60·2	165	135·2	94·6	225	184·3	129·1	285	233·5	163·5
46	37·7	26·4	106	86·8	60·8	166	136·0	95·2	226	185·1	129·6	286	234·3	164·0
47	38·5	27·0	107	87·6	61·4	167	136·8	95·8	227	185·9	130·2	287	235·1	164·6
48	39·3	27·5	108	88·5	61·9	168	137·6	96·4	228	186·8	130·8	288	235·9	165·2
49	40·1	28·1	109	89·3	62·5	169	138·4	96·9	229	187·6	131·3	289	236·7	165·8
50	41·0	28·7	110	90·1	63·1	170	139·3	97·5	230	188·4	131·9	290	237·6	166·3
51	41·8	29·3	111	90·9	63·7	171	140·1	98·1	231	189·2	132·5	291	238·4	166·9
52	42·6	29·8	112	91·7	64·2	172	140·9	98·7	232	190·0	133·1	292	239·2	167·5
53	43·4	30·4	113	92·6	64·8	173	141·7	99·2	233	190·9	133·6	293	240·0	168·0
54	44·2	31·0	114	93·4	65·4	174	142·5	99·8	234	191·7	134·2	294	240·8	168·6
55	45·1	31·5	115	94·2	66·0	175	143·4	100·4	235	192·5	134·8	295	241·6	169·2
56	45·9	32·1	116	95·0	66·5	176	144·2	100·9	236	193·3	135·4	296	242·5	169·8
57	46·7	32·7	117	95·8	67·1	177	145·0	101·5	237	194·1	135·9	297	243·3	170·4
58	47·5	33·3	118	96·7	67·7	178	145·8	102·1	238	195·0	136·5	298	244·1	170·9
59	48·3	33·8	119	97·5	68·3	179	146·6	102·7	239	195·8	137·1	299	244·9	171·5
60	49·1	34·4	120	98·3	68·8	180	147·4	103·2	240	196·6	137·7	300	245·7	172·1
Dist.	Dep.	D. Lat.	Dist.	Dep.	D. Lat.	Dist.	Dep.	D. Lat.	Dist.	Dep.	D. Lat.	Dist.	Dep.	D. Lat.
D. Lon		Dep.	D. Lon		Dep.	D. Lon		Dep.	D. Lon		Dep.	D. Lon		Dep.

| 305° / 235° | | 55 Degrees | | 055° / 125° | 3h 40m |

TRAVERSE TABLE
35 Degrees

D. Lon	Dep.		D. Lon	Dep.		D. Lon	Dep.		D. Lon	Dep.		D. Lon	Dep.	
Dist.	D. Lat.	Dep.	Dist.	D. Lat.	Dep.	Dist.	D. Lat.	Dep.	Dist.	D. Lat.	Dep.	Dist.	D. Lat.	Dep.
301	246.6	172.6	361	295.7	207.1	421	344.9	241.5	481	394.0	275.9	541	443.2	310.3
302	247.4	173.2	362	296.5	207.6	422	345.7	242.0	482	394.8	276.5	542	444.0	310.9
303	248.2	173.8	363	297.4	208.2	423	346.5	242.6	483	395.7	277.0	543	444.8	311.5
304	249.0	174.4	364	298.2	208.8	424	347.3	243.2	484	396.5	277.6	544	445.6	312.0
305	249.8	174.9	365	299.0	209.4	425	348.1	243.8	485	397.3	278.2	545	446.4	312.6
306	250.7	175.5	366	299.8	209.9	426	349.0	244.3	486	398.1	278.8	546	447.3	313.2
307	251.5	176.1	367	300.6	210.5	427	349.8	244.9	487	398.9	279.3	547	448.1	313.7
308	252.3	176.7	368	301.4	211.1	428	350.6	245.5	488	399.7	279.9	548	448.9	314.3
309	253.1	177.2	369	302.3	211.6	429	351.4	246.1	489	400.6	280.5	549	449.7	314.9
310	253.9	177.8	370	303.1	212.2	430	352.2	246.6	490	401.4	281.1	550	450.5	315.5
311	254.8	178.4	371	303.9	212.8	431	353.1	247.2	491	402.2	281.6	551	451.4	316.0
312	255.6	179.0	372	304.7	213.4	432	353.9	247.8	492	403.0	282.2	552	452.2	316.6
313	256.4	179.5	373	305.5	213.9	433	354.7	248.4	493	403.8	282.8	553	453.0	317.2
314	257.2	180.1	374	306.4	214.5	434	355.5	248.9	494	404.7	283.3	554	453.8	317.8
315	258.0	180.7	375	307.2	215.1	435	356.3	249.5	495	405.5	283.9	555	454.6	318.3
316	258.9	181.3	376	308.0	215.7	436	357.2	250.1	496	406.3	284.5	556	455.4	318.9
317	259.7	181.8	377	308.8	216.2	437	358.0	250.7	497	407.1	285.1	557	456.3	319.5
318	260.5	182.4	378	309.6	216.8	438	358.8	251.2	498	407.9	285.6	558	457.1	320.1
319	261.3	183.0	379	310.5	217.4	439	359.6	251.8	499	408.8	286.2	559	457.9	320.6
320	262.1	183.5	380	311.3	218.0	440	360.4	252.4	500	409.6	286.8	560	458.7	321.2
321	262.9	184.1	381	312.1	218.5	441	361.2	252.9	501	410.4	287.4	561	459.5	321.8
322	263.8	184.7	382	312.9	219.1	442	362.1	253.5	502	411.2	287.9	562	460.4	322.3
323	264.6	185.3	383	313.7	219.7	443	362.9	254.1	503	412.0	288.5	563	461.2	322.9
324	265.4	185.8	384	314.6	220.3	444	363.7	254.7	504	412.9	289.1	564	462.0	323.5
325	266.2	186.4	385	315.4	220.8	445	364.5	255.2	505	413.7	289.7	565	462.8	324.1
326	267.0	187.0	386	316.2	221.4	446	365.3	255.8	506	414.5	290.2	566	463.6	324.6
327	267.9	187.6	387	317.0	222.0	447	366.2	256.4	507	415.3	290.8	567	464.5	325.2
328	268.7	188.1	388	317.8	222.5	448	367.0	257.0	508	416.1	291.4	568	465.3	325.8
329	269.5	188.7	389	318.7	223.1	449	367.8	257.5	509	416.9	292.0	569	466.1	326.4
330	270.3	189.3	390	319.5	223.7	450	368.6	258.1	510	417.8	292.5	570	466.9	326.9
331	271.1	189.9	391	320.3	224.3	451	369.4	258.7	511	418.6	293.1	571	467.7	327.5
332	272.0	190.4	392	321.1	224.8	452	370.3	259.3	512	419.4	293.7	572	468.6	328.1
333	272.8	191.0	393	321.9	225.4	453	371.1	259.8	513	420.2	294.2	573	469.4	328.7
334	273.6	191.6	394	322.7	226.0	454	371.9	260.4	514	421.0	294.8	574	470.2	329.2
335	274.4	192.1	395	323.6	226.6	455	372.7	261.0	515	421.9	295.4	575	471.0	329.8
336	275.2	192.7	396	324.4	227.1	456	373.5	261.6	516	422.7	296.0	576	471.8	330.4
337	276.1	193.3	397	325.2	227.7	457	374.4	262.1	517	423.5	296.5	577	472.7	331.0
338	276.9	193.9	398	326.0	228.3	458	375.2	262.7	518	424.3	297.1	578	473.5	331.5
339	277.7	194.4	399	326.8	228.9	459	376.0	263.3	519	425.1	297.7	579	474.3	332.1
340	278.5	195.0	400	327.7	229.4	460	376.8	263.8	520	426.0	298.3	580	475.1	332.7
341	279.3	195.6	401	328.5	230.0	461	377.6	264.4	521	426.8	298.8	581	475.9	333.2
342	280.1	196.2	402	329.3	230.6	462	378.4	265.0	522	427.6	299.4	582	476.7	333.8
343	281.0	196.7	403	330.1	231.2	463	379.3	265.6	523	428.4	300.0	583	477.6	334.4
344	281.8	197.3	404	330.9	231.7	464	380.1	266.1	524	429.2	300.6	584	478.4	335.0
345	282.6	197.9	405	331.8	232.3	465	380.9	266.7	525	430.1	301.1	585	479.2	335.5
346	283.4	198.5	406	332.6	232.9	466	381.7	267.3	526	430.9	301.7	586	480.0	336.1
347	284.2	199.0	407	333.4	233.4	467	382.5	267.9	527	431.7	302.3	587	480.8	336.7
348	285.1	199.6	408	334.2	234.0	468	383.4	268.4	528	432.5	302.8	588	481.7	337.3
349	285.9	200.2	409	335.0	234.6	469	384.2	269.0	529	433.3	303.4	589	482.5	337.8
350	286.7	200.8	410	335.9	235.2	470	385.0	269.6	530	434.2	304.0	590	483.3	338.4
351	287.5	201.3	411	336.7	235.7	471	385.8	270.2	531	435.0	304.6	591	484.1	339.0
352	288.3	201.9	412	337.5	236.3	472	386.6	270.7	532	435.8	305.1	592	484.9	339.6
353	289.2	202.5	413	338.3	236.9	473	387.5	271.3	533	436.6	305.7	593	485.8	340.1
354	290.0	203.0	414	339.1	237.5	474	388.3	271.9	534	437.4	306.3	594	486.6	340.7
355	290.8	203.6	415	339.9	238.0	475	389.1	272.4	535	438.2	306.9	595	487.4	341.3
356	291.6	204.2	416	340.8	238.6	476	389.9	273.0	536	439.1	307.4	596	488.2	341.9
357	292.4	204.8	417	341.6	239.2	477	390.7	273.6	537	439.9	308.0	597	489.0	342.4
358	293.3	205.3	418	342.4	239.8	478	391.6	274.2	538	440.7	308.6	598	489.9	343.0
359	294.1	205.9	419	343.2	240.3	479	392.4	274.7	539	441.5	309.2	599	490.7	343.6
360	294.9	206.5	420	344.0	240.9	480	393.2	275.3	540	442.3	309.7	600	491.5	344.1
Dist.	Dep.	D. Lat.	Dist.	Dep.	D. Lat.	Dist.	Dep.	D. Lat.	Dist.	Dep.	D. Lat.	Dist.	Dep.	D. Lat.
D. Lon		Dep.	D. Lon		Dep.	D. Lon		Dep.	D. Lon		Dep.	D. Lon		Dep.

TRAVERSE TABLE
36 Degrees

36°   324° / 216°   036° / 144°   2h 24m

Dist.	D. Lat.	Dep.	Dist.	D. Lat.	Dep.	Dist.	D. Lat.	Dep.	Dist.	D. Lat.	Dep.	Dist.	D. Lat.	Dep.
1	00.8	00.6	61	49.4	35.9	121	97.9	71.1	181	146.4	106.4	241	195.0	141.7
2	01.6	01.2	62	50.2	36.4	122	98.7	71.7	182	147.2	107.0	242	195.8	142.2
3	02.4	01.8	63	51.0	37.0	123	99.5	72.3	183	148.1	107.6	243	196.6	142.8
4	03.2	02.4	64	51.8	37.6	124	100.3	72.9	184	148.9	108.2	244	197.4	143.4
5	04.0	02.9	65	52.6	38.2	125	101.1	73.5	185	149.7	108.7	245	198.2	144.0
6	04.9	03.5	66	53.4	38.8	126	101.9	74.1	186	150.5	109.3	246	199.0	144.6
7	05.7	04.1	67	54.2	39.4	127	102.7	74.6	187	151.3	109.9	247	199.8	145.2
8	06.5	04.7	68	55.0	40.0	128	103.6	75.2	188	152.1	110.5	248	200.6	145.8
9	07.3	05.3	69	55.8	40.6	129	104.4	75.8	189	152.9	111.1	249	201.4	146.4
10	08.1	05.9	70	56.6	41.1	130	105.2	76.4	190	153.7	111.7	250	202.3	146.9
11	08.9	06.5	71	57.4	41.7	131	106.0	77.0	191	154.5	112.3	251	203.1	147.5
12	09.7	07.1	72	58.2	42.3	132	106.8	77.6	192	155.3	112.9	252	203.9	148.1
13	10.5	07.6	73	59.1	42.9	133	107.6	78.2	193	156.1	113.4	253	204.7	148.7
14	11.3	08.2	74	59.9	43.5	134	108.4	78.8	194	156.9	114.0	254	205.5	149.3
15	12.1	08.8	75	60.7	44.1	135	109.2	79.4	195	157.8	114.6	255	206.3	149.9
16	12.9	09.4	76	61.5	44.7	136	110.0	79.9	196	158.6	115.2	256	207.1	150.5
17	13.8	10.0	77	62.3	45.3	137	110.8	80.5	197	159.4	115.8	257	207.9	151.1
18	14.6	10.6	78	63.1	45.8	138	111.6	81.1	198	160.2	116.4	258	208.7	151.6
19	15.4	11.2	79	63.9	46.4	139	112.5	81.7	199	161.0	117.0	259	209.5	152.2
20	16.2	11.8	80	64.7	47.0	140	113.3	82.3	200	161.8	117.6	260	210.3	152.8
21	17.0	12.3	81	65.5	47.6	141	114.1	82.9	201	162.6	118.1	261	211.2	153.4
22	17.8	12.9	82	66.3	48.2	142	114.9	83.5	202	163.4	118.7	262	212.0	154.0
23	18.6	13.5	83	67.1	48.8	143	115.7	84.1	203	164.2	119.3	263	212.8	154.6
24	19.4	14.1	84	68.0	49.4	144	116.5	84.6	204	165.0	119.9	264	213.6	155.2
25	20.2	14.7	85	68.8	50.0	145	117.3	85.2	205	165.8	120.5	265	214.4	155.8
26	21.0	15.3	86	69.6	50.5	146	118.1	85.8	206	166.7	121.1	266	215.2	156.4
27	21.8	15.9	87	70.4	51.1	147	118.9	86.4	207	167.5	121.7	267	216.0	156.9
28	22.7	16.5	88	71.2	51.7	148	119.7	87.0	208	168.3	122.3	268	216.8	157.5
29	23.5	17.0	89	72.0	52.3	149	120.5	87.6	209	169.1	122.8	269	217.6	158.1
30	24.3	17.6	90	72.8	52.9	150	121.4	88.2	210	169.9	123.4	270	218.4	158.7
31	25.1	18.2	91	73.6	53.5	151	122.2	88.8	211	170.7	124.0	271	219.2	159.3
32	25.9	18.8	92	74.4	54.1	152	123.0	89.3	212	171.5	124.6	272	220.1	159.9
33	26.7	19.4	93	75.2	54.7	153	123.8	89.9	213	172.3	125.2	273	220.9	160.5
34	27.5	20.0	94	76.0	55.3	154	124.6	90.5	214	173.1	125.8	274	221.7	161.1
35	28.3	20.6	95	76.9	55.8	155	125.4	91.1	215	173.9	126.4	275	222.5	161.6
36	29.1	21.2	96	77.7	56.4	156	126.2	91.7	216	174.7	127.0	276	223.3	162.2
37	29.9	21.7	97	78.5	57.0	157	127.0	92.3	217	175.6	127.5	277	224.1	162.8
38	30.7	22.3	98	79.3	57.6	158	127.8	92.9	218	176.4	128.1	278	224.9	163.4
39	31.6	22.9	99	80.1	58.2	159	128.6	93.5	219	177.2	128.7	279	225.7	164.0
40	32.4	23.5	100	80.9	58.8	160	129.4	94.0	220	178.0	129.3	280	226.5	164.6
41	33.2	24.1	101	81.7	59.4	161	130.3	94.6	221	178.8	129.9	281	227.3	165.2
42	34.0	24.7	102	82.5	60.0	162	131.1	95.2	222	179.6	130.5	282	228.1	165.8
43	34.8	25.3	103	83.3	60.5	163	131.9	95.8	223	180.4	131.1	283	229.0	166.3
44	35.6	25.9	104	84.1	61.1	164	132.7	96.4	224	181.2	131.7	284	229.8	166.9
45	36.4	26.5	105	84.9	61.7	165	133.5	97.0	225	182.0	132.3	285	230.6	167.5
46	37.2	27.0	106	85.8	62.3	166	134.3	97.6	226	182.8	132.8	286	231.4	168.1
47	38.0	27.6	107	86.6	62.9	167	135.1	98.2	227	183.6	133.4	287	232.2	168.7
48	38.8	28.2	108	87.4	63.5	168	135.9	98.7	228	184.5	134.0	288	233.0	169.3
49	39.6	28.8	109	88.2	64.1	169	136.7	99.3	229	185.3	134.6	289	233.8	169.9
50	40.5	29.4	110	89.0	64.7	170	137.5	99.9	230	186.1	135.2	290	234.6	170.5
51	41.3	30.0	111	89.8	65.2	171	138.3	100.5	231	186.9	135.8	291	235.4	171.0
52	42.1	30.6	112	90.6	65.8	172	139.2	101.1	232	187.7	136.4	292	236.2	171.6
53	42.9	31.2	113	91.4	66.4	173	140.0	101.7	233	188.5	137.0	293	237.0	172.2
54	43.7	31.7	114	92.2	67.0	174	140.8	102.3	234	189.3	137.5	294	237.9	172.8
55	44.5	32.3	115	93.0	67.6	175	141.6	102.9	235	190.1	138.1	295	238.7	173.4
56	45.3	32.9	116	93.8	68.2	176	142.4	103.5	236	190.9	138.7	296	239.5	174.0
57	46.1	33.5	117	94.7	68.8	177	143.2	104.0	237	191.7	139.3	297	240.3	174.6
58	46.9	34.1	118	95.5	69.4	178	144.0	104.6	238	192.5	139.9	298	241.1	175.2
59	47.7	34.7	119	96.3	69.9	179	144.8	105.2	239	193.4	140.5	299	241.9	175.7
60	48.5	35.3	120	97.1	70.5	180	145.6	105.8	240	194.2	141.1	300	242.7	176.3

| Dist. | Dep. | D. Lat. | Dist. | Dep. | D. Lat. | Dist. | Dep. | D. Lat. | Dist. | Dep. | D. Lat. | Dist. | Dep. | D. Lat. |

54°   306° / 234°   54 Degrees   054° / 126°   3h 36m

TRAVERSE TABLE

36 Degrees

D. Lon	Dep.		D. Lon	Dep.		D. Lon	Dep.		D. Lon	Dep.		D. Lon	Dep.	
Dist.	D. Lat.	Dep.	Dist.	D. Lat.	Dep.	Dist.	D. Lat.	Dep.	Dist.	D. Lat.	Dep.	Dist.	D. Lat.	Dep.
301	243·5	176·9	361	292·1	212·2	421	340·6	247·5	481	389·1	282·7	541	437·7	318·0
302	244·3	177·5	362	292·9	212·8	422	341·4	248·0	482	389·9	283·3	542	438·5	318·6
303	245·1	178·1	363	293·7	213·4	423	342·2	248·6	483	390·8	283·9	543	439·3	319·2
304	245·9	178·7	364	294·5	214·0	424	343·0	249·2	484	391·6	284·5	544	440·2	319·8
305	246·8	179·3	365	295·3	214·5	425	343·8	249·8	485	392·4	285·1	545	440·9	320·3
306	247·6	179·9	366	296·1	215·1	426	344·6	250·4	486	393·2	285·7	546	441·7	320·9
307	248·4	180·5	367	296·9	215·7	427	345·5	251·0	487	394·0	286·3	547	442·5	321·5
308	249·2	181·0	368	297·7	216·3	428	346·3	251·6	488	394·8	286·8	548	443·3	322·1
309	250·0	181·6	369	298·5	216·9	429	347·1	252·2	489	395·6	287·4	549	444·2	322·7
310	250·8	182·2	370	299·3	217·5	430	347·9	252·7	490	396·4	288·0	550	445·0	323·3
311	251·6	182·8	371	300·1	218·1	431	348·7	253·3	491	397·2	288·6	551	445·8	323·9
312	252·4	183·4	372	301·0	218·7	432	349·5	253·9	492	398·0	289·2	552	446·6	324·5
313	253·2	184·0	373	301·8	219·2	433	350·3	254·5	493	398·8	289·8	553	447·4	325·0
314	254·0	184·6	374	302·6	219·8	434	351·1	255·1	494	399·7	290·4	554	448·2	325·6
315	254·8	185·2	375	303·4	220·4	435	351·9	255·7	495	400·5	291·0	555	449·0	326·2
316	255·6	185·7	376	304·2	221·0	436	352·7	256·3	496	401·3	291·5	556	449·8	326·8
317	256·5	186·3	377	305·0	221·6	437	353·5	256·9	497	402·1	292·1	557	450·6	327·4
318	257·3	186·9	378	305·8	222·2	438	354·3	257·4	498	402·9	292·7	558	451·4	328·0
319	258·1	187·5	379	306·6	222·8	439	355·2	258·0	499	403·7	293·3	559	452·2	328·6
320	258·9	188·1	380	307·4	223·4	440	356·0	258·6	500	404·5	293·9	560	453·0	329·2
321	259·7	188·7	381	308·2	223·9	441	356·8	259·2	501	405·3	294·5	561	453·9	329·7
322	260·5	189·3	382	309·0	224·5	442	357·6	259·8	502	406·1	295·1	562	454·7	330·3
323	261·3	189·9	383	309·9	225·1	443	358·4	260·4	503	406·9	295·7	563	455·5	330·9
324	262·1	190·4	384	310·7	225·7	444	359·2	261·0	504	407·7	296·2	564	456·3	331·5
325	262·9	191·0	385	311·5	226·3	445	360·0	261·6	505	408·6	296·8	565	457·1	332·1
326	263·7	191·6	386	312·3	226·9	446	360·8	262·2	506	409·4	297·4	566	457·9	332·7
327	264·5	192·2	387	313·1	227·5	447	361·6	262·7	507	410·2	298·0	567	458·7	333·3
328	265·4	192·8	388	313·9	228·1	448	362·4	263·3	508	411·0	298·6	568	459·5	333·9
329	266·2	193·4	389	314·7	228·6	449	363·2	263·9	509	411·8	299·2	569	460·3	334·4
330	267·0	194·0	390	315·5	299·2	450	364·1	264·5	510	412·6	299·8	570	461·1	335·0
331	267·8	194·6	391	316·3	229·8	451	364·9	265·1	511	413·4	300·4	571	461·9	335·6
332	268·6	195·1	392	317·1	230·4	452	365·7	265·7	512	414·2	300·9	572	462·8	336·2
333	269·4	195·7	393	317·9	231·0	453	366·5	266·3	513	415·0	301·5	573	463·6	336·8
334	270·2	196·3	394	318·8	231·6	454	367·3	266·9	514	415·8	302·1	574	464·4	337·4
335	271·0	196·9	395	319·6	232·2	455	368·1	267·4	515	416·6	302·7	575	465·2	338·0
336	271·8	197·5	396	320·4	232·8	456	368·9	268·0	516	417·5	303·3	576	466·0	338·6
337	272·6	198·1	397	321·2	233·4	457	369·7	268·6	517	418·3	303·9	577	466·8	339·2
338	273·4	198·7	398	322·0	233·9	458	370·5	269·2	518	419·1	304·5	578	467·6	339·7
339	274·3	199·3	399	322·8	234·5	459	371·3	269·8	519	419·9	305·1	579	468·4	340·3
340	275·1	199·8	400	323·6	235·1	460	372·1	270·4	520	420·7	305·6	580	469·2	340·9
341	275·9	200·4	401	324·4	235·7	461	373·0	271·0	521	421·5	306·2	581	470·0	341·5
342	276·7	201·0	402	325·2	236·3	462	373·8	271·6	522	422·3	306·8	582	470·8	342·1
343	277·5	201·6	403	326·0	236·9	463	374·6	272·1	523	423·1	307·4	583	471·7	342·7
344	278·3	202·2	404	326·9	237·5	464	375·4	272·7	524	423·9	308·0	584	472·5	343·3
345	279·1	202·8	405	327·7	238·1	465	376·2	273·3	525	424·7	308·6	585	473·3	343·9
346	279·9	203·4	406	328·5	238·7	466	377·0	273·9	526	425·5	309·2	586	474·1	344·4
347	280·7	204·0	407	329·3	239·2	467	377·8	274·5	527	426·4	309·8	587	474·9	345·0
348	281·5	204·5	408	330·1	239·8	468	378·6	275·1	528	427·2	310·4	588	475·7	345·6
349	282·3	205·1	409	330·9	240·4	469	379·4	275·7	529	428·0	310·9	589	476·5	346·2
350	283·2	205·7	410	331·7	241·0	470	380·2	276·3	530	428·8	311·5	590	477·3	346·8
351	284·0	206·3	411	332·5	241·6	471	381·1	276·8	531	429·6	312·1	591	478·1	347·4
352	284·8	206·9	412	333·3	242·2	472	381·9	277·4	532	430·4	312·7	592	478·9	348·0
353	285·6	207·5	413	334·1	242·8	473	382·7	278·0	533	431·2	313·3	593	479·7	348·6
354	286·4	208·1	414	334·9	243·3	474	383·5	278·6	534	432·0	313·9	594	480·6	349·1
355	287·2	208·7	415	335·7	243·9	475	384·3	279·2	535	432·8	314·5	595	481·4	349·7
356	288·0	209·3	416	336·6	244·5	476	385·1	279·8	536	433·6	315·1	596	482·2	350·3
357	288·8	209·8	417	337·4	245·1	477	385·9	280·4	537	434·4	315·6	597	483·0	350·9
358	289·6	210·4	418	338·2	245·7	478	386·7	281·0	538	435·3	316·2	598	483·8	351·5
359	290·4	211·0	419	339·0	246·3	479	387·5	281·5	539	436·1	316·8	599	484·6	352·1
360	291·2	211·6	420	339·8	246·9	480	388·3	282·1	540	436·9	317·4	600	485·4	352·7

Dist.	Dep.	D. Lat.	Dist.	Dep.	D. Lat.	Dist.	Dep.	D. Lat.	Dist.	Dep.	D. Lat.	Dist.	Dep.	D. Lat.
D. Lon		Dep.	D. Lon		Dep.	D. Lon		Dep.	D. Lon		Dep.	D. Lon		Dep.

TRAVERSE TABLE

37 Degrees

323° / 217°   037° / 143°   2h 28m

Dist.	D. Lat.	Dep.	Dist.	D. Lat.	Dep.	Dist.	D. Lat.	Dep.	Dist.	D. Lat.	Dep.	Dist.	D. Lat.	Dep.
1	00.8	00.6	61	48.7	36.7	121	96.6	72.8	181	144.6	108.9	241	192.5	145.0
2	01.6	01.2	62	49.5	37.3	122	97.4	73.4	182	145.4	109.5	242	193.3	145.6
3	02.4	01.8	63	50.3	37.9	123	98.2	74.0	183	146.2	110.1	243	194.1	146.2
4	03.2	02.4	64	51.1	38.5	124	99.0	74.6	184	146.9	110.7	244	194.9	146.8
5	04.0	03.0	65	51.9	39.1	125	99.8	75.2	185	147.7	111.3	245	195.7	147.4
6	04.8	03.6	66	52.7	39.7	126	100.6	75.8	186	148.5	111.9	246	196.5	148.0
7	05.6	04.2	67	53.5	40.3	127	101.4	76.4	187	149.3	112.5	247	197.3	148.6
8	06.4	04.8	68	54.3	40.9	128	102.2	77.0	188	150.1	113.1	248	198.1	149.3
9	07.2	05.4	69	55.1	41.5	129	103.0	77.6	189	150.9	113.7	249	198.9	149.9
10	08.0	06.0	70	55.9	42.1	130	103.8	78.2	190	151.7	114.3	250	199.7	150.5
11	08.8	06.6	71	56.7	42.7	131	104.6	78.8	191	152.5	114.9	251	200.5	151.1
12	09.6	07.2	72	57.5	43.3	132	105.4	79.4	192	153.3	115.5	252	201.3	151.7
13	10.4	07.8	73	58.3	43.9	133	106.2	80.0	193	154.1	116.2	253	202.1	152.3
14	11.2	08.4	74	59.1	44.5	134	107.0	80.6	194	154.9	116.8	254	202.9	152.9
15	12.0	09.0	75	59.9	45.1	135	107.8	81.2	195	155.7	117.4	255	203.7	153.5
16	12.8	09.6	76	60.7	45.7	136	108.6	81.8	196	156.5	118.0	256	204.5	154.1
17	13.6	10.2	77	61.5	46.3	137	109.4	82.4	197	157.3	118.6	257	205.2	154.7
18	14.4	10.8	78	62.3	46.9	138	110.2	83.1	198	158.1	119.2	258	206.0	155.3
19	15.2	11.4	79	63.1	47.5	139	111.0	83.7	199	158.9	119.8	259	206.8	155.9
20	16.0	12.0	80	63.9	48.1	140	111.8	84.3	200	159.7	120.4	260	207.6	156.5
21	16.8	12.6	81	64.7	48.7	141	112.6	84.9	201	160.5	121.0	261	208.4	157.1
22	17.6	13.2	82	65.5	49.3	142	113.4	85.5	202	161.3	121.6	262	209.2	157.7
23	18.4	13.8	83	66.3	50.0	143	114.2	86.1	203	162.1	122.2	263	210.0	158.3
24	19.2	14.4	84	67.1	50.6	144	115.0	86.7	204	162.9	122.8	264	210.8	158.9
25	20.0	15.0	85	67.9	51.2	145	115.8	87.3	205	163.7	123.4	265	211.6	159.5
26	20.8	15.6	86	68.7	51.8	146	116.6	87.9	206	164.5	124.0	266	212.4	160.1
27	21.6	16.2	87	69.5	52.4	147	117.4	88.5	207	165.3	124.6	267	213.2	160.7
28	22.4	16.9	88	70.3	53.0	148	118.2	89.1	208	166.1	125.2	268	214.0	161.3
29	23.2	17.5	89	71.1	53.6	149	119.0	89.7	209	166.9	125.8	269	214.8	161.9
30	24.0	18.1	90	71.9	54.2	150	119.8	90.3	210	167.7	126.4	270	215.6	162.5
31	24.8	18.7	91	72.7	54.8	151	120.6	90.9	211	168.5	127.0	271	216.4	163.1
32	25.6	19.3	92	73.5	55.4	152	121.4	91.5	212	169.3	127.6	272	217.2	163.7
33	26.4	19.9	93	74.3	56.0	153	122.2	92.1	213	170.1	128.2	273	218.0	164.3
34	27.2	20.5	94	75.1	56.6	154	123.0	92.7	214	170.9	128.8	274	218.8	164.9
35	28.0	21.1	95	75.9	57.2	155	123.8	93.3	215	171.7	129.4	275	219.6	165.5
36	28.8	21.7	96	76.7	57.8	156	124.6	93.9	216	172.5	130.0	276	220.4	166.1
37	29.5	22.3	97	77.5	58.4	157	125.4	94.5	217	173.3	130.6	277	221.2	166.7
38	30.3	22.9	98	78.3	59.0	158	126.2	95.1	218	174.1	131.2	278	222.0	167.3
39	31.1	23.5	99	79.1	59.6	159	127.0	95.7	219	174.9	131.8	279	222.8	167.9
40	31.9	24.1	100	79.9	60.2	160	127.8	96.3	220	175.7	132.4	280	223.6	168.5
41	32.7	24.7	101	80.7	60.8	161	128.6	96.9	221	176.5	133.0	281	224.4	169.1
42	33.5	25.3	102	81.5	61.4	162	129.4	97.5	222	177.3	133.6	282	225.2	169.7
43	34.3	25.9	103	82.3	62.0	163	130.2	98.1	223	178.1	134.2	283	226.0	170.3
44	35.1	26.5	104	83.1	62.6	164	131.0	98.7	224	178.9	134.8	284	226.8	170.9
45	35.9	27.1	105	83.9	63.2	165	131.8	99.3	225	179.7	135.4	285	227.6	171.5
46	36.7	27.7	106	84.7	63.8	166	132.6	99.9	226	180.5	136.0	286	228.4	172.1
47	37.5	28.3	107	85.5	64.4	167	133.4	100.5	227	181.3	136.6	287	229.2	172.7
48	38.3	28.9	108	86.3	65.0	168	134.2	101.1	228	182.1	137.2	288	230.0	173.3
49	39.1	29.5	109	87.1	65.6	169	135.0	101.7	229	182.9	137.8	289	230.8	173.9
50	39.9	30.1	110	87.8	66.2	170	135.8	102.3	230	183.7	138.4	290	231.6	174.5
51	40.7	30.7	111	88.6	66.8	171	136.6	102.9	231	184.5	139.0	291	232.4	175.1
52	41.5	31.3	112	89.4	67.4	172	137.4	103.5	232	185.3	139.6	292	233.2	175.7
53	42.3	31.9	113	90.2	68.0	173	138.2	104.1	233	186.1	140.2	293	234.0	176.3
54	43.1	32.5	114	91.0	68.6	174	139.0	104.7	234	186.9	140.8	294	234.8	176.9
55	43.9	33.1	115	91.8	69.2	175	139.8	105.3	235	187.7	141.4	295	235.6	177.5
56	44.7	33.7	116	92.6	69.8	176	140.6	105.9	236	188.5	142.0	296	236.4	178.1
57	45.5	34.3	117	93.4	70.4	177	141.4	106.5	237	189.3	142.6	297	237.2	178.7
58	46.3	34.9	118	94.2	71.0	178	142.2	107.1	238	190.1	143.2	298	238.0	179.3
59	47.1	35.5	119	95.0	71.6	179	143.0	107.7	239	190.9	143.8	299	238.8	179.9
60	47.9	36.1	120	95.8	72.2	180	143.8	108.3	240	191.7	144.4	300	239.6	180.5
Dist.	Dep.	D. Lat.	Dist.	Dep.	D. Lat.	Dist.	Dep.	D. Lat.	Dist.	Dep.	D. Lat.	Dist.	Dep.	D. Lat.

307° / 233°   **53 Degrees**   053° / 127°   3h 32m

TRAVERSE TABLE

37 Degrees

D. Lon	Dep.		D. Lon	Dep.		D. Lon	Dep.		D. Lon	Dep.		D. Lon	Dep.	
Dist.	D. Lat.	Dep.	Dist.	D. Lat.	Dep.	Dist.	D. Lat.	Dep.	Dist.	D. Lat.	Dep.	Dist.	D. Lat.	Dep.
301	240·4	181·1	361	288·3	217·3	421	336·2	253·4	481	384·1	289·5	541	432·1	325·6
302	241·2	181·7	362	289·1	217·9	422	337·0	254·0	482	384·9	290·1	542	432·9	326·2
303	242·0	182·3	363	289·9	218·5	423	337·8	254·6	483	385·7	290·7	543	433·7	326·8
304	242·7	183·0	364	290·7	219·1	424	338·6	255·2	484	386·5	291·3	544	434·5	327·4
305	243·6	183·6	365	291·5	219·7	425	339·4	255·8	485	387·3	291·9	545	435·3	328·0
306	244·4	184·2	366	292·3	220·3	426	340·2	256·4	486	388·1	292·5	546	436·1	328·6
307	245·2	184·8	367	293·1	220·9	427	341·0	257·0	487	388·9	293·1	547	436·9	329·2
308	246·0	185·4	368	293·9	221·5	428	341·8	257·6	488	389·7	293·7	548	437·7	329·8
309	246·8	186·0	369	294·7	222·1	429	342·6	258·2	489	390·5	294·3	549	438·5	330·4
310	247·6	186·6	370	295·5	222·7	430	343·4	258·8	490	391·3	294·9	550	439·2	331·0
311	248·4	187·2	371	296·3	223·3	431	344·2	259·4	491	392·1	295·5	551	440·0	331·6
312	249·2	187·8	372	297·1	223·9	432	345·0	260·0	492	392·9	296·1	552	440·8	332·2
313	250·0	188·4	373	297·9	224·5	433	345·8	260·6	493	393·7	296·7	553	441·6	332·8
314	250·8	189·0	374	298·7	225·1	434	346·6	261·2	494	394·5	297·3	554	442·4	333·4
315	251·6	189·6	375	299·5	225·7	435	347·4	261·8	495	395·3	297·9	555	443·2	334·0
316	252·4	190·2	376	300·3	226·3	436	348·2	262·4	496	396·1	298·5	556	444·0	334·6
317	253·2	190·8	377	301·1	226·9	437	349·0	263·0	497	396·9	299·1	557	444·8	335·2
318	254·0	191·4	378	301·9	227·5	438	349·8	263·6	498	397·7	299·7	558	445·6	335·8
319	254·8	192·0	379	302·7	228·1	439	350·6	264·2	499	398·5	300·3	559	446·4	336·4
320	255·6	192·6	380	303·5	228·7	440	351·4	264·8	500	399·3	300·9	560	447·2	337·0
321	256·4	193·2	381	304·3	229·3	441	352·2	265·4	501	400·1	301·5	561	448·0	337·6
322	257·2	193·8	382	305·1	229·9	442	353·0	266·0	502	400·9	302·1	562	448·8	338·2
323	258·0	194·4	383	305·9	230·5	443	353·8	266·6	503	401·7	302·7	563	449·6	338·8
324	258·8	195·0	384	306·7	231·1	444	354·6	267·2	504	402·5	303·3	564	450·4	339·4
325	259·6	195·6	385	307·5	231·7	445	355·4	267·8	505	403·3	303·9	565	451·2	340·0
326	260·4	196·2	386	308·3	232·3	446	356·2	268·4	506	404·1	304·5	566	452·0	340·6
327	261·2	196·8	387	309·1	232·9	447	357·0	269·0	507	404·9	305·1	567	452·8	341·2
328	262·0	197·4	388	309·9	233·5	448	357·8	269·6	508	405·7	305·7	568	453·6	341·8
329	262·8	198·0	389	310·7	234·1	449	358·6	270·2	509	406·5	306·3	569	454·4	342·4
330	263·5	198·6	390	311·5	234·7	450	359·4	270·8	510	407·3	306·9	570	455·2	343·0
331	264·3	199·2	391	312·3	235·3	451	360·2	271·4	511	408·1	307·5	571	456·0	343·6
332	265·1	199·8	392	313·1	235·9	452	361·0	272·0	512	408·9	308·1	572	456·8	344·2
333	265·9	200·4	393	313·9	236·5	453	361·8	272·6	513	409·7	308·7	573	457·6	344·8
334	266·7	201·0	394	314·7	237·1	454	362·6	273·2	514	410·5	309·3	574	458·4	345·4
335	267·5	201·6	395	315·5	237·7	455	363·4	273·8	515	411·3	309·9	575	459·2	346·0
336	268·3	202·2	396	316·3	238·3	456	364·2	274·4	516	412·1	310·5	576	460·0	346·6
337	269·1	202·8	397	317·1	238·9	457	365·0	275·0	517	412·9	311·1	577	460·8	347·2
338	269·9	203·4	398	317·9	239·5	458	365·8	275·6	518	413·7	311·7	578	461·6	347·8
339	270·7	204·0	399	318·7	240·1	459	366·6	276·2	519	414·5	312·3	579	462·4	348·5
340	271·5	204·6	400	319·5	240·7	460	367·4	276·8	520	415·3	312·9	580	463·2	349·1
341	272·3	205·2	401	320·3	241·3	461	368·2	277·4	521	416·1	313·5	581	464·0	349·7
342	273·1	205·8	402	321·1	241·9	462	369·0	278·0	522	416·9	314·1	582	464·8	350·3
343	273·9	206·4	403	321·9	242·5	463	369·8	278·6	523	417·7	314·7	583	465·6	350·9
344	274·7	207·0	404	322·6	243·1	464	370·6	279·2	524	418·5	315·4	584	466·4	351·5
345	275·5	207·6	405	323·4	243·7	465	371·4	279·8	525	419·3	316·0	585	467·2	352·1
346	276·3	208·2	406	324·2	244·3	466	372·2	280·4	526	420·1	316·6	586	468·0	352·7
347	277·1	208·8	407	325·0	244·9	467	373·0	281·0	527	420·9	317·2	587	468·8	353·3
348	277·9	209·4	408	325·8	245·5	468	373·8	281·6	528	421·7	317·8	588	469·6	353·9
349	278·7	210·0	409	326·6	246·1	469	374·6	282·3	529	422·5	318·4	589	470·4	354·5
350	279·5	210·6	410	327·4	246·7	470	375·4	282·9	530	423·3	319·0	590	471·2	355·1
351	280·3	211·2	411	328·2	247·3	471	376·2	283·5	531	424·1	319·6	591	472·0	355·7
352	281·1	211·8	412	329·0	247·9	472	377·0	284·1	532	424·9	320·2	592	472·8	356·3
353	281·9	212·4	413	329·8	248·5	473	377·8	284·7	533	425·7	320·8	593	473·6	356·9
354	282·7	213·0	414	330·6	249·2	474	378·6	285·3	534	426·5	321·4	594	474·4	357·5
355	283·5	213·6	415	331·4	249·8	475	379·4	285·9	535	427·3	322·0	595	475·2	358·1
356	284·3	214·3	416	332·2	250·4	476	380·2	286·5	536	428·1	322·6	596	476·0	358·7
357	285·1	214·8	417	333·0	251·0	477	380·9	287·1	537	428·9	323·2	597	476·8	359·3
358	285·9	215·4	418	333·8	251·6	478	381·7	287·7	538	429·7	323·8	598	477·6	359·9
359	286·7	216·1	419	334·6	252·2	479	382·5	288·3	539	430·5	324·4	599	478·4	360·5
360	287·5	216·7	420	335·4	252·8	480	383·3	288·9	540	431·3	325·0	600	479·2	361·1
Dist.	Dep.	D. Lat.	Dist.	Dep.	D. Lat.	Dist.	Dep.	D. Lat.	Dist.	Dep.	D. Lat.	Dist.	Dep.	D. Lat.
D. Lon		Dep.	D. Lon		Dep.	D. Lon		Dep.	D. Lon		Dep.	D. Lon		Dep.

TRAVERSE TABLE
38 Degrees

38°

322° / 218°   038° / 142°   2h 32m

D. Lon		Dep.	D. Lon		Dep.	D. Lon		Dep.	D. Lon		Dep.	D. Lon		Dep.
Dist.	D. Lat.	Dep.	Dist.	D. Lat.	Dep.	Dist.	D. Lat.	Dep.	Dist.	D. Lat.	Dep.	Dist.	D. Lat.	Dep.
1	00·8	00·6	61	48·1	37·6	121	95·3	74·5	181	142·6	111·4	241	189·9	148·4
2	01·6	01·2	62	48·9	38·2	122	96·1	75·1	182	143·4	112·1	242	190·7	149·0
3	02·4	01·8	63	49·6	38·8	123	96·9	75·7	183	144·2	112·7	243	191·5	149·6
4	03·2	02·5	64	50·4	39·4	124	97·7	76·3	184	145·0	113·3	244	192·3	150·2
5	03·9	03·1	65	51·2	40·0	125	98·5	77·0	185	145·8	113·9	245	193·1	150·8
6	04·7	03·7	66	52·0	40·6	126	99·3	77·6	186	146·6	114·5	246	193·9	151·5
7	05·5	04·3	67	52·8	41·2	127	100·1	78·2	187	147·4	115·1	247	194·6	152·1
8	06·3	04·9	68	53·6	41·9	128	100·9	78·8	188	148·1	115·7	248	195·4	152·7
9	07·1	05·5	69	54·4	42·5	129	101·7	79·4	189	148·9	116·4	249	196·2	153·3
10	07·9	06·2	70	55·2	43·1	130	102·4	80·0	190	149·7	117·0	250	197·0	153·9
11	08·7	06·8	71	55·9	43·7	131	103·2	80·7	191	150·5	117·6	251	197·8	154·5
12	09·5	07·4	72	56·7	44·3	132	104·0	81·3	192	151·3	118·2	252	198·6	155·1
13	10·2	08·0	73	57·5	44·9	133	104·8	81·9	193	152·1	118·8	253	199·4	155·8
14	11·0	08·6	74	58·3	45·6	134	105·6	82·5	194	152·9	119·4	254	200·2	156·4
15	11·8	09·2	75	59·1	46·2	135	106·4	83·1	195	153·7	120·1	255	200·9	157·0
16	12·6	09·9	76	59·9	46·8	136	107·2	83·7	196	154·5	120·7	256	201·7	157·6
17	13·4	10·5	77	60·7	47·4	137	108·0	84·3	197	155·2	121·3	257	202·5	158·2
18	14·2	11·1	78	61·5	48·0	138	108·7	85·0	198	156·0	121·9	258	203·3	158·8
19	15·0	11·7	79	62·3	48·6	139	109·5	85·6	199	156·8	122·5	259	204·1	159·5
20	15·8	12·3	80	63·0	49·3	140	110·3	86·2	200	157·6	123·1	260	204·9	160·1
21	16·5	12·9	81	63·8	49·9	141	111·1	86·8	201	158·4	123·7	261	205·7	160·7
22	17·3	13·5	82	64·6	50·5	142	111·9	87·4	202	159·2	124·4	262	206·5	161·3
23	18·1	14·2	83	65·4	51·1	143	112·7	88·0	203	160·0	125·0	263	207·2	161·9
24	18·9	14·8	84	66·2	51·7	144	113·5	88·7	204	160·8	125·6	264	208·0	162·5
25	19·7	15·4	85	67·0	52·3	145	114·3	89·3	205	161·5	126·2	265	208·8	163·2
26	20·5	16·0	86	67·8	52·9	146	115·0	89·9	206	162·3	126·8	266	209·6	163·8
27	21·3	16·6	87	68·6	53·6	147	115·8	90·5	207	163·1	127·4	267	210·4	164·4
28	22·1	17·2	88	69·3	54·2	148	116·6	91·1	208	163·9	128·1	268	211·2	165·0
29	22·9	17·9	89	70·1	54·8	149	117·4	91·7	209	164·7	128·7	269	212·0	165·6
30	23·6	18·5	90	70·9	55·4	150	118·2	92·3	210	165·5	129·3	270	212·8	166·2
31	24·4	19·1	91	71·7	56·0	151	119·0	93·0	211	166·3	129·9	271	213·6	166·8
32	25·2	19·7	92	72·5	56·6	152	119·8	93·6	212	167·1	130·5	272	214·3	167·5
33	26·0	20·3	93	73·3	57·3	153	120·6	94·2	213	167·8	131·1	273	215·1	168·1
34	26·8	20·9	94	74·1	57·9	154	121·4	94·8	214	168·6	131·8	274	215·9	168·7
35	27·6	21·5	95	74·9	58·5	155	122·1	95·4	215	169·4	132·4	275	216·7	169·3
36	28·4	22·2	96	75·6	59·1	156	122·9	96·0	216	170·2	133·0	276	217·5	169·9
37	29·2	22·8	97	76·4	59·7	157	123·7	96·7	217	171·0	133·6	277	218·3	170·5
38	29·9	23·4	98	77·2	60·3	158	124·5	97·3	218	171·8	134·2	278	219·1	171·2
39	30·7	24·0	99	78·0	61·0	159	125·3	97·9	219	172·6	134·8	279	219·9	171·8
40	31·5	24·6	100	78·8	61·6	160	126·1	98·5	220	173·4	135·4	280	220·6	172·4
41	32·3	25·2	101	79·6	62·2	161	126·9	99·1	221	174·2	136·1	281	221·4	173·0
42	33·1	25·9	102	80·4	62·8	162	127·7	99·7	222	174·9	136·7	282	222·2	173·6
43	33·9	26·5	103	81·2	63·4	163	128·4	100·4	223	175·7	137·3	283	223·0	174·2
44	34·7	27·1	104	82·0	64·0	164	129·2	101·0	224	176·5	137·9	284	223·8	174·8
45	35·5	27·7	105	82·7	64·6	165	130·0	101·6	225	177·3	138·5	285	224·6	175·5
46	36·2	28·3	106	83·5	65·3	166	130·8	102·2	226	178·1	139·1	286	225·4	176·1
47	37·0	28·9	107	84·3	65·9	167	131·6	102·8	227	178·9	139·8	287	226·2	176·7
48	37·8	29·6	108	85·1	66·5	168	132·4	103·4	228	179·7	140·4	288	226·9	177·3
49	38·6	30·2	109	85·9	67·1	169	133·2	104·0	229	180·5	141·0	289	227·7	177·9
50	39·4	30·8	110	86·7	67·7	170	134·0	104·7	230	181·2	141·6	290	228·5	178·5
51	40·2	31·4	111	87·5	68·3	171	134·7	105·3	231	182·0	142·2	291	229·3	179·2
52	41·0	32·0	112	88·3	69·0	172	135·5	105·9	232	182·8	142·8	292	230·1	179·8
53	41·8	32·6	113	89·0	69·6	173	136·3	106·5	233	183·6	143·4	293	230·9	180·4
54	42·6	33·2	114	89·8	70·2	174	137·1	107·1	234	184·4	144·1	294	231·7	181·0
55	43·3	33·9	115	90·6	70·8	175	137·9	107·7	235	185·2	144·7	295	232·5	181·6
56	44·1	34·5	116	91·4	71·4	176	138·7	108·4	236	186·0	145·3	296	233·3	182·2
57	44·9	35·1	117	92·2	72·0	177	139·5	109·0	237	186·8	145·9	297	234·0	182·9
58	45·7	35·7	118	93·0	72·6	178	140·3	109·6	238	187·5	146·5	298	234·8	183·5
59	46·5	36·3	119	93·8	73·3	179	141·1	110·2	239	188·3	147·1	299	235·6	184·1
60	47·3	36·9	120	94·6	73·9	180	141·8	110·8	240	189·1	147·8	300	236·4	184·7
Dist.	Dep.	D. Lat.	Dist.	Dep.	D. Lat.	Dist.	Dep.	D. Lat.	Dist.	Dep.	D. Lat.	Dist.	Dep.	D. Lat.
D. Lon		Dep.	D. Lon		Dep.	D. Lon		Dep.	D. Lon		Dep.	D. Lon		Dep.

52°

308° / 232°   52 Degrees   052° / 128°   3h 28m

TRAVERSE TABLE
38 Degrees

D. Lon	Dep.		D. Lon	Dep.		D. Lon	Dep.		D. Lon	Dep.		D. Lon	Dep.	
Dist.	D. Lat.	Dep.	Dist.	D. Lat.	Dep.	Dist.	D. Lat.	Dep.	Dist.	D. Lat.	Dep.	Dist.	D. Lat.	Dep.
301	237·2	185·3	361	284·5	222·3	421	331·8	259·2	481	379·0	296·1	541	426·3	333·1
302	238·0	185·9	362	285·3	222·9	422	332·5	259·8	482	379·8	296·7	542	427·1	333·7
303	238·8	186·5	363	286·0	223·5	423	333·3	260·4	483	380·6	297·4	543	427·9	334·3
304	239·6	187·2	364	286·8	224·1	424	334·1	261·0	484	381·4	298·0	544	428·7	334·9
305	240·3	187·8	365	287·6	224·7	425	334·9	261·7	485	382·2	298·6	545	429·5	335·5
306	241·1	188·4	366	288·4	225·3	426	335·7	262·3	486	383·0	299·2	546	430·3	336·2
307	241·9	189·0	367	289·2	225·9	427	336·5	262·9	487	383·8	299·8	547	431·0	336·8
308	242·7	189·6	368	290·0	226·6	428	337·3	263·5	488	384·5	300·4	548	431·8	337·4
309	243·5	190·2	369	290·8	227·2	429	338·1	264·1	489	385·3	301·1	549	432·6	338·0
310	244·3	190·9	370	291·6	227·8	430	338·8	264·7	490	386·1	301·7	550	433·4	338·6
311	245·1	191·5	371	292·4	228·4	431	339·6	265·4	491	386·9	302·3	551	434·2	339·2
312	245·9	192·1	372	293·1	229·0	432	340·4	266·0	492	387·7	302·9	552	435·0	339·8
313	246·6	192·7	373	293·9	229·6	433	341·2	266·6	493	388·5	303·5	553	435·8	340·5
314	247·4	193·3	374	294·7	230·3	434	342·0	267·2	494	389·3	304·1	554	436·6	341·1
315	248·2	193·9	375	295·5	230·9	435	342·8	267·8	495	390·1	304·8	555	437·3	341·7
316	249·0	194·5	376	296·3	231·5	436	343·6	268·4	496	390·9	305·4	556	438·1	342·3
317	249·8	195·2	377	297·1	232·1	437	344·4	269·0	497	391·6	306·0	557	438·9	342·9
318	250·6	195·8	378	297·9	232·7	438	345·1	269·7	498	392·4	306·6	558	439·7	343·5
319	251·4	196·4	379	298·7	233·3	439	345·9	270·3	499	393·2	307·2	559	440·5	344·2
320	252·2	197·0	380	299·4	234·0	440	346·7	270·9	500	394·0	307·8	560	441·3	344·8
321	253·0	197·6	381	300·2	234·6	441	347·5	271·5	501	394·8	308·4	561	442·1	345·4
322	253·7	198·2	382	301·0	235·2	442	348·3	272·1	502	395·6	309·1	562	442·9	346·0
323	254·5	198·9	383	301·8	235·8	443	349·1	272·7	503	396·4	309·7	563	443·7	346·6
324	255·3	199·5	384	302·6	236·4	444	349·9	273·4	504	397·2	310·3	564	444·4	347·2
325	256·1	200·1	385	303·4	237·0	445	350·7	274·0	505	397·9	310·9	565	445·2	347·8
326	256·9	200·7	386	304·2	237·6	446	351·5	274·6	506	398·7	311·5	566	446·0	348·5
327	257·7	201·3	387	305·0	238·3	447	352·2	275·2	507	399·5	312·1	567	446·8	349·1
328	258·5	201·9	388	305·7	238·9	448	353·0	275·8	508	400·3	312·8	568	447·6	349·7
329	259·3	202·6	389	306·5	239·5	449	353·8	276·4	509	401·1	313·4	569	448·4	350·3
330	260·0	203·2	390	307·3	240·1	450	354·6	277·0	510	401·9	314·0	570	449·2	350·9
331	260·8	203·8	391	308·1	240·7	451	355·4	277·7	511	402·7	314·6	571	450·0	351·5
332	261·6	204·4	392	308·9	241·3	452	356·2	278·3	512	403·5	315·2	572	450·7	352·2
333	262·4	205·0	393	309·7	242·0	453	357·0	278·9	513	404·2	315·8	573	451·5	352·8
334	263·2	205·6	394	310·5	242·6	454	357·8	279·5	514	405·0	316·5	574	452·3	353·4
335	264·0	206·2	395	311·3	243·2	455	358·5	280·1	515	405·8	317·1	575	453·1	354·0
336	264·8	206·9	396	312·1	243·8	456	359·3	280·7	516	406·6	317·7	576	453·9	354·6
337	265·6	207·5	397	312·8	244·4	457	360·1	281·4	517	407·4	318·3	577	454·7	355·2
338	266·3	208·1	398	313·6	245·0	458	360·9	282·0	518	408·2	318·9	578	455·5	355·7
339	267·1	208·7	399	314·4	245·6	459	361·7	282·6	519	409·0	319·5	579	456·3	356·5
340	267·9	209·3	400	315·2	246·3	460	362·5	283·2	520	409·8	320·1	580	457·0	357·1
341	268·7	209·9	401	316·0	246·9	461	363·3	283·8	521	410·6	320·8	581	457·8	357·7
342	269·5	210·6	402	316·8	247·5	462	364·1	284·4	522	411·3	321·4	582	458·6	358·3
343	270·3	211·2	403	317·6	248·1	463	364·8	285·1	523	412·1	322·0	583	459·4	358·9
344	271·1	211·8	404	318·4	248·7	464	365·6	285·7	524	412·9	322·6	584	460·2	359·5
345	271·9	212·4	405	319·1	249·3	465	366·4	286·3	525	413·7	323·2	585	461·0	360·2
346	272·7	213·0	406	319·9	250·0	466	367·2	286·9	526	414·5	323·8	586	461·8	360·8
347	273·4	213·6	407	320·7	250·6	467	368·0	287·5	527	415·3	324·5	587	462·6	361·4
348	274·2	214·3	408	321·5	251·2	468	368·8	288·1	528	416·1	325·1	588	463·4	362·0
349	275·0	214·9	409	322·3	251·8	469	369·6	288·7	529	416·9	325·7	589	464·1	362·6
350	275·8	215·5	410	323·1	252·4	470	370·4	289·4	530	417·6	326·3	590	464·9	363·2
351	276·6	216·1	411	323·9	253·0	471	371·2	290·0	531	418·4	326·9	591	465·7	363·9
352	277·4	216·7	412	324·7	253·7	472	371·9	290·6	532	419·2	327·5	592	466·5	364·5
353	278·2	217·3	413	325·4	254·3	473	372·7	291·2	533	420·0	328·1	593	467·3	365·1
354	279·0	217·9	414	326·2	254·9	474	373·5	291·8	534	420·8	328·8	594	468·1	365·7
355	279·7	218·6	415	327·0	255·5	475	374·3	292·4	535	421·6	329·4	595	468·9	366·3
356	280·5	219·2	416	327·8	256·1	476	375·1	293·1	536	422·4	330·0	596	469·7	366·9
357	281·3	219·8	417	328·6	256·7	477	375·9	293·7	537	423·2	330·6	597	470·4	367·5
358	282·1	220·4	418	329·4	257·3	478	376·7	294·3	538	423·9	331·2	598	471·2	368·2
359	282·9	221·0	419	330·2	258·0	479	377·5	294·9	539	424·7	331·8	599	472·0	368·8
360	283·7	221·6	420	331·0	258·6	480	378·2	295·5	540	425·5	332·5	600	472·8	369·4
Dist.	Dep.	D. Lat.	Dist.	Dep.	D. Lat.	Dist.	Dep.	D. Lat.	Dist.	Dep.	D. Lat.	Dist.	Dep.	D. Lat.
D. Lon		Dep.	D. Lon		Dep.	D. Lon		Dep.	D. Lon		Dep.	D. Lon		Dep.

TRAVERSE TABLE
39 Degrees

	321° / 219°										039° / 141°		2h 36m

Dist.	D. Lat.	Dep.	Dist.	D. Lat.	Dep.	Dist.	D. Lat.	Dep.	Dist.	D. Lat.	Dep.	Dist.	D. Lat.	Dep.
1	00·8	00·6	61	47·4	38·4	121	94·0	76·1	181	140·7	113·9	241	187·3	151·7
2	01·6	01·3	62	48·2	39·0	122	94·8	76·8	182	141·4	114·5	242	188·1	152·3
3	02·3	01·9	63	49·0	39·6	123	95·6	77·4	183	142·2	115·2	243	188·8	152·9
4	03·1	02·5	64	49·7	40·3	124	96·4	78·0	184	143·0	115·8	244	189·6	153·6
5	03·9	03·1	65	50·5	40·9	125	97·1	78·7	185	143·8	116·4	245	190·4	154·2
6	04·7	03·8	66	51·3	41·5	126	97·9	79·3	186	144·5	117·1	246	191·2	154·8
7	05·4	04·4	67	52·1	42·2	127	98·7	79·9	187	145·3	117·7	247	192·0	155·4
8	06·2	05·0	68	52·8	42·8	128	99·5	80·6	188	146·1	118·3	248	192·7	156·1
9	07·0	05·7	69	53·6	43·4	129	100·3	81·2	189	146·9	118·9	249	193·5	156·7
10	07·8	06·3	70	54·4	44·1	130	101·0	81·8	190	147·7	119·6	250	194·3	157·3
11	08·5	06·9	71	55·2	44·7	131	101·8	82·4	191	148·4	120·2	251	195·1	158·0
12	09·3	07·6	72	56·0	45·3	132	102·6	83·1	192	149·2	120·8	252	195·8	158·6
13	10·1	08·2	73	56·7	45·9	133	103·4	83·7	193	150·0	121·5	253	196·6	159·2
14	10·9	08·8	74	57·5	46·6	134	104·1	84·3	194	150·8	122·1	254	197·4	159·8
15	11·7	09·4	75	58·3	47·2	135	104·9	85·0	195	151·5	122·7	255	198·2	160·5
16	12·4	10·1	76	59·1	47·8	136	105·7	85·6	196	152·3	123·3	256	198·9	161·1
17	13·2	10·7	77	59·8	48·5	137	106·5	86·2	197	153·1	124·0	257	199·7	161·7
18	14·0	11·3	78	60·6	49·1	138	107·2	86·8	198	153·9	124·6	258	200·5	162·4
19	14·8	12·0	79	61·4	49·7	139	108·0	87·5	199	154·7	125·2	259	201·3	163·0
20	15·5	12·6	80	62·2	50·3	140	108·8	88·1	200	155·4	125·9	260	202·1	163·6
21	16·3	13·2	81	62·9	51·0	141	109·6	88·7	201	156·2	126·5	261	202·8	164·3
22	17·1	13·8	82	63·7	51·6	142	110·4	89·4	202	157·0	127·1	262	203·6	164·9
23	17·9	14·5	83	64·5	52·2	143	111·1	90·0	203	157·8	127·8	263	204·4	165·5
24	18·7	15·1	84	65·3	52·9	144	111·9	90·6	204	158·5	128·4	264	205·2	166·1
25	19·4	15·7	85	66·1	53·5	145	112·7	91·3	205	159·3	129·0	265	205·9	166·8
26	20·2	16·4	86	66·8	54·1	146	113·5	91·9	206	160·1	129·6	266	206·7	167·4
27	21·0	17·0	87	67·6	54·8	147	114·2	92·5	207	160·9	130·3	267	207·5	168·0
28	21·8	17·6	88	68·4	55·4	148	115·0	93·1	208	161·6	130·9	268	208·3	168·7
29	22·5	18·3	89	69·2	56·0	149	115·8	93·8	209	162·4	131·5	269	209·1	169·3
30	23·3	18·9	90	69·9	56·6	150	116·6	94·4	210	163·2	132·2	270	209·8	169·9
31	24·1	19·5	91	70·7	57·3	151	117·3	95·0	211	164·0	132·8	271	210·6	170·5
32	24·9	20·1	92	71·5	57·9	152	118·1	95·7	212	164·8	133·4	272	211·4	171·1
33	25·6	20·8	93	72·3	58·5	153	118·9	96·3	213	165·5	134·0	273	212·2	171·8
34	26·4	21·4	94	73·1	59·2	154	119·7	96·9	214	166·3	134·7	274	212·9	172·4
35	27·2	22·0	95	73·8	59·8	155	120·5	97·5	215	167·1	135·3	275	213·7	173·1
36	28·0	22·7	96	74·6	60·4	156	121·2	98·2	216	167·9	135·9	276	214·5	173·7
37	28·8	23·3	97	75·4	61·0	157	122·0	98·8	217	168·6	136·6	277	215·3	174·3
38	29·5	23·9	98	76·2	61·7	158	122·8	99·4	218	169·4	137·2	278	216·0	175·0
39	30·3	24·5	99	76·9	62·3	159	123·6	100·1	219	170·2	137·8	279	216·8	175·6
40	31·1	25·2	100	77·7	62·9	160	124·3	100·7	220	171·0	138·5	280	217·6	176·2
41	31·9	25·8	101	78·5	63·6	161	125·1	101·3	221	171·7	139·1	281	218·4	176·8
42	32·6	26·4	102	79·3	64·2	162	125·9	101·9	222	172·5	139·7	282	219·2	177·5
43	33·4	27·1	103	80·0	64·8	163	126·7	102·6	223	173·3	140·3	283	219·9	178·1
44	34·2	27·7	104	80·8	65·4	164	127·5	103·2	224	174·1	141·0	284	220·7	178·7
45	35·0	28·3	105	81·6	66·1	165	128·2	103·8	225	174·9	141·6	285	221·5	179·4
46	35·7	28·9	106	82·4	66·7	166	129·0	104·5	226	175·6	142·2	286	222·3	180·0
47	36·5	29·6	107	83·2	67·3	167	129·8	105·1	227	176·4	142·9	287	223·0	180·6
48	37·3	30·2	108	83·9	68·0	168	130·6	105·7	228	177·2	143·5	288	223·8	181·2
49	38·1	30·8	109	84·7	68·6	169	131·3	106·4	229	178·0	144·1	289	224·6	181·9
50	38·9	31·5	110	85·5	69·2	170	132·1	107·0	230	178·7	144·7	290	225·4	182·5
51	39·6	32·1	111	86·3	69·9	171	132·9	107·6	231	179·5	145·4	291	226·1	183·1
52	40·4	32·7	112	87·0	70·5	172	133·7	108·2	232	180·3	146·0	292	226·9	183·8
53	41·2	33·4	113	87·8	71·1	173	134·4	108·9	233	181·1	146·6	293	227·7	184·4
54	42·0	34·0	114	88·6	71·7	174	135·2	109·5	234	181·9	147·3	294	228·5	185·0
55	42·7	34·6	115	89·4	72·4	175	136·0	110·1	235	182·6	147·9	295	229·3	185·6
56	43·5	35·2	116	90·1	73·0	176	136·8	110·8	236	183·4	148·5	296	230·0	186·3
57	44·3	35·9	117	90·9	73·6	177	137·6	111·4	237	184·2	149·1	297	230·8	186·9
58	45·1	36·5	118	91·7	74·3	178	138·3	112·0	238	185·0	149·8	298	231·6	187·5
59	45·9	37·1	119	92·5	74·9	179	139·1	112·6	239	185·7	150·4	299	232·4	188·2
60	46·6	37·8	120	93·3	75·5	180	139·9	113·3	240	186·5	151·0	300	233·1	188·8

Dist.	Dep.	D. Lat.	Dist.	Dep.	D. Lat.	Dist.	Dep.	D. Lat.	Dist.	Dep.	D. Lat.	Dist.	Dep.	D. Lat.
D. Lon		Dep.	D. Lon		Dep.	D. Lon		Dep.	D. Lon		Dep.	D. Lon		Dep.

309° / 231°		51 Degrees		051° / 129°	3h 24m

TRAVERSE TABLE
39 Degrees

D. Lon	Dep.		D. Lon	Dep.		D. Lon	Dep.		D. Lon	Dep.		D. Lon	Dep.	
Dist.	D. Lat.	Dep.	Dist.	D. Lat.	Dep.	Dist.	D. Lat.	Dep.	Dist.	D. Lat.	Dep.	Dist.	D. Lat.	Dep.
301	233.9	189.4	361	280.5	227.2	421	327.2	264.9	481	373.8	302.7	541	420.4	340.5
302	234.7	190.1	362	281.3	227.8	422	328.0	265.6	482	374.6	303.3	542	421.2	341.1
303	235.5	190.7	363	282.1	228.4	423	328.7	266.2	483	375.4	304.0	543	422.0	341.7
304	236.3	191.3	364	282.9	229.1	424	329.5	266.8	484	376.1	304.6	544	422.8	342.2
305	237.0	191.9	365	283.7	229.7	425	330.3	267.5	485	376.9	305.2	545	423.5	343.0
306	237.8	192.6	366	284.4	230.3	426	331.1	268.1	486	377.7	305.8	546	424.3	343.6
307	238.6	193.2	367	285.2	231.0	427	331.8	268.7	487	378.5	306.5	547	425.1	344.2
308	239.4	193.8	368	286.0	231.5	428	332.6	269.3	488	379.2	307.1	548	425.9	344.9
309	240.1	194.5	369	286.8	232.2	429	333.4	270.0	489	380.0	307.7	549	426.7	345.5
310	240.9	195.1	370	287.5	232.8	430	334.2	270.6	490	380.8	308.4	550	427.4	346.1
311	241.7	195.7	371	288.3	233.5	431	334.9	271.2	491	381.6	309.0	551	428.2	346.8
312	242.5	196.3	372	289.1	234.1	432	335.7	271.9	492	382.4	309.6	552	429.0	347.4
313	243.2	197.0	373	289.9	234.7	433	336.5	272.5	493	383.1	310.3	553	429.8	348.0
314	244.0	197.6	374	290.7	235.4	434	337.3	273.1	494	383.9	310.9	554	430.5	348.6
315	244.8	198.2	375	291.4	236.0	435	338.1	273.8	495	384.7	311.5	555	431.3	349.3
316	245.6	198.9	376	292.2	236.6	436	338.8	274.4	496	385.5	312.1	556	432.1	349.9
317	246.4	199.5	377	293.0	237.3	437	339.6	275.0	497	386.2	312.8	557	432.9	350.5
318	247.1	200.1	378	293.8	237.9	438	340.4	275.6	498	387.0	313.4	558	433.6	351.2
319	247.9	200.8	379	294.5	238.5	439	341.2	276.3	499	387.8	314.0	559	434.4	351.8
320	248.7	201.4	380	295.3	239.1	440	341.9	276.9	500	388.6	314.7	560	435.2	352.4
321	249.5	202.0	381	296.1	239.8	441	342.7	277.5	501	389.4	315.3	561	436.0	353.0
322	250.2	202.6	382	296.9	240.4	442	343.5	278.2	502	390.1	315.9	562	436.8	353.7
323	251.0	203.3	383	297.6	241.0	443	344.3	278.8	503	390.9	316.5	563	437.5	354.3
324	251.8	203.9	384	298.4	241.7	444	345.1	279.4	504	391.7	317.2	564	438.3	354.9
325	252.6	204.5	385	299.2	242.3	445	345.8	280.0	505	392.5	317.8	565	439.1	355.5
326	253.3	205.2	386	300.0	242.9	446	346.6	280.7	506	393.2	318.4	566	439.9	356.2
327	254.1	205.8	387	300.8	243.5	447	347.4	281.3	507	394.0	319.1	567	440.6	356.8
328	254.9	206.4	388	301.5	244.2	448	348.2	281.9	508	394.8	319.7	568	441.4	357.5
329	255.7	207.0	389	302.3	244.8	449	348.9	282.6	509	395.6	320.3	569	442.2	358.1
330	256.5	207.7	390	303.1	245.4	450	349.7	283.2	510	396.3	321.0	570	443.0	358.7
331	257.2	208.3	391	303.9	246.1	451	350.5	283.8	511	397.1	321.6	571	443.8	359.3
332	258.0	208.9	392	304.6	246.7	452	351.3	284.5	512	397.9	322.2	572	444.5	360.0
333	258.8	209.6	393	305.4	247.3	453	352.0	285.1	513	398.7	322.8	573	445.3	360.6
334	259.6	210.2	394	306.2	248.0	454	352.8	285.7	514	399.5	323.5	574	446.1	361.2
335	260.3	210.8	395	307.0	248.6	455	353.6	286.3	515	400.2	324.1	575	446.9	361.9
336	261.1	211.5	396	307.7	249.2	456	354.4	287.0	516	401.0	324.7	576	447.7	362.5
337	261.9	212.1	397	308.5	249.8	457	355.2	287.6	517	401.8	325.4	577	448.4	363.1
338	262.7	212.7	398	309.3	250.5	458	355.9	288.2	518	402.6	326.0	578	449.2	363.7
339	263.5	213.3	399	310.1	251.1	459	356.7	288.9	519	403.3	326.6	579	450.0	364.4
340	264.2	214.0	400	310.9	251.7	460	357.5	289.5	520	404.1	327.2	580	450.7	365.0
341	265.0	214.6	401	311.6	252.4	461	358.3	290.1	521	404.9	327.9	581	451.5	365.6
342	265.8	215.2	402	312.4	253.0	462	359.0	290.7	522	405.7	328.5	582	452.3	366.3
343	266.6	215.9	403	313.2	253.6	463	359.8	291.4	523	406.4	329.1	583	453.1	366.9
344	267.3	216.5	404	314.0	254.2	464	360.6	292.0	524	407.2	329.8	584	453.9	367.5
345	268.1	217.1	405	314.7	254.9	465	361.4	292.6	525	408.0	330.4	585	454.6	368.2
346	268.9	217.7	406	315.5	255.5	466	362.2	293.3	526	408.8	331.0	586	455.4	368.8
347	269.7	218.4	407	316.3	256.1	467	362.9	293.9	527	409.6	331.7	587	456.2	369.4
348	270.4	219.0	408	317.1	256.8	468	363.7	294.5	528	410.3	332.3	588	457.0	370.0
349	271.2	219.6	409	317.9	257.4	469	364.5	295.2	529	411.1	332.9	589	457.8	370.7
350	272.0	220.3	410	318.6	258.0	470	365.3	295.8	530	411.9	333.5	590	458.5	371.3
351	272.8	220.9	411	319.4	258.7	471	366.0	296.4	531	412.7	334.2	591	459.3	371.9
352	273.6	221.5	412	320.2	259.3	472	366.8	297.0	532	413.4	334.8	592	460.1	372.6
353	274.3	222.2	413	321.0	259.9	473	367.6	297.7	533	414.2	335.4	593	460.8	373.2
354	275.1	222.7	414	321.7	260.5	474	368.4	298.3	534	415.0	336.1	594	461.6	373.8
355	275.9	223.4	415	322.5	261.2	475	369.1	298.9	535	415.8	336.7	595	462.4	374.4
356	276.7	224.0	416	323.3	261.8	476	369.9	299.6	536	416.6	337.3	596	463.2	375.1
357	277.4	224.7	417	324.1	262.4	477	370.7	300.2	537	417.3	337.9	597	464.0	375.7
358	278.2	225.3	418	324.8	263.1	478	371.5	300.8	538	418.1	338.6	598	464.7	376.3
359	279.0	225.9	419	325.6	263.7	479	372.3	301.4	539	418.9	339.2	599	465.5	376.9
360	279.8	226.6	420	326.4	264.3	480	373.0	302.1	540	419.7	339.8	600	466.3	377.6
Dist.	Dep.	D. Lat.	Dist.	Dep.	D. Lat.	Dist.	Dep.	D. Lat.	Dist.	Dep.	D. Lat.	Dist.	Dep.	D. Lat.
D. Lon		Dep.	D. Lon		Dep.	D. Lon		Dep.	D. Lon		Dep.	D. Lon		Dep.

TRAVERSE TABLE
40 Degrees

40°   320° / 220°   040° / 140°   2h 40m

Dist.	D. Lat.	Dep.	Dist.	D. Lat.	Dep.	Dist.	D. Lat.	Dep.	Dist.	D. Lat.	Dep.	Dist.	D. Lat.	Dep.
1	00·8	00·6	61	46·7	39·2	121	92·7	77·8	181	138·7	116·3	241	184·6	154·9
2	01·5	01·3	62	47·5	39·9	122	93·5	78·4	182	139·4	117·0	242	185·4	155·6
3	02·3	01·9	63	48·3	40·5	123	94·2	79·1	183	140·2	117·6	243	186·1	156·2
4	03·1	02·6	64	49·0	41·1	124	95·0	79·7	184	141·0	118·3	244	186·9	156·8
5	03·8	03·2	65	49·8	41·8	125	95·8	80·3	185	141·7	118·9	245	187·7	157·5
6	04·6	03·9	66	50·6	42·4	126	96·5	81·0	186	142·5	119·6	246	188·4	158·1
7	05·4	04·5	67	51·3	43·1	127	97·3	81·6	187	143·3	120·2	247	189·2	158·8
8	06·1	05·1	68	52·1	43·7	128	98·1	82·3	188	144·0	120·8	248	190·0	159·4
9	06·9	05·8	69	52·9	44·4	129	98·8	82·9	189	144·8	121·5	249	190·7	160·1
10	07·7	06·4	70	53·6	45·0	130	99·6	83·6	190	145·5	122·1	250	191·5	160·7
11	08·4	07·1	71	54·4	45·6	131	100·4	84·2	191	146·3	122·8	251	192·3	161·3
12	09·2	07·7	72	55·2	46·3	132	101·1	84·8	192	147·1	123·4	252	193·0	162·0
13	10·0	08·4	73	55·9	46·9	133	101·9	85·5	193	147·8	124·1	253	193·8	162·6
14	10·7	09·0	74	56·7	47·6	134	102·6	86·1	194	148·6	124·7	254	194·6	163·3
15	11·5	09·6	75	57·5	48·2	135	103·4	86·8	195	149·4	125·3	255	195·3	163·9
16	12·3	10·3	76	58·2	48·9	136	104·2	87·4	196	150·1	126·0	256	196·1	164·6
17	13·0	10·9	77	59·0	49·5	137	104·9	88·1	197	150·9	126·6	257	196·9	165·2
18	13·8	11·6	78	59·8	50·1	138	105·7	88·7	198	151·7	127·3	258	197·6	165·8
19	14·6	12·2	79	60·5	50·8	139	106·5	89·3	199	152·4	127·9	259	198·4	166·5
20	15·3	12·9	80	61·3	51·4	140	107·2	90·0	200	153·2	128·6	260	199·2	167·1
21	16·1	13·5	81	62·0	52·1	141	108·0	90·6	201	154·0	129·2	261	199·9	167·8
22	16·9	14·1	82	62·8	52·7	142	108·8	91·3	202	154·7	129·8	262	200·7	168·4
23	17·6	14·8	83	63·6	53·4	143	109·5	91·9	203	155·5	130·5	263	201·5	169·1
24	18·4	15·4	84	64·3	54·0	144	110·3	92·6	204	156·3	131·1	264	202·2	169·7
25	19·2	16·1	85	65·1	54·6	145	111·1	93·2	205	157·0	131·8	265	203·0	170·3
26	19·9	16·7	86	65·9	55·3	146	111·8	93·8	206	157·8	132·4	266	203·8	171·0
27	20·7	17·4	87	66·6	55·9	147	112·6	94·5	207	158·6	133·1	267	204·5	171·6
28	21·4	18·0	88	67·4	56·6	148	113·4	95·1	208	159·3	133·7	268	205·3	172·3
29	22·2	18·6	89	68·2	57·2	149	114·1	95·8	209	160·1	134·3	269	206·1	172·9
30	23·0	19·3	90	68·9	57·9	150	114·9	96·4	210	160·9	135·0	270	206·8	173·6
31	23·7	19·9	91	69·7	58·5	151	115·7	97·1	211	161·6	135·6	271	207·6	174·2
32	24·5	20·6	92	70·5	59·1	152	116·4	97·7	212	162·4	136·3	272	208·4	174·8
33	25·3	21·2	93	71·2	59·8	153	117·2	98·3	213	163·2	136·9	273	209·1	175·5
34	26·0	21·9	94	72·0	60·4	154	118·0	99·0	214	163·9	137·6	274	209·9	176·1
35	26·8	22·5	95	72·8	61·1	155	118·7	99·6	215	164·7	138·2	275	210·7	176·8
36	27·6	23·1	96	73·5	61·7	156	119·5	100·3	216	165·5	138·8	276	211·4	177·4
37	28·3	23·8	97	74·3	62·4	157	120·3	100·9	217	166·2	139·5	277	212·2	178·1
38	29·1	24·4	98	75·1	63·0	158	121·0	101·6	218	167·0	140·1	278	213·0	178·7
39	29·9	25·1	99	75·8	63·6	159	121·8	102·2	219	167·8	140·8	279	213·7	179·3
40	30·6	25·7	100	76·6	64·3	160	122·6	102·8	220	168·5	141·4	280	214·5	180·0
41	31·4	26·4	101	77·4	64·9	161	123·3	103·5	221	169·3	142·1	281	215·3	180·6
42	32·2	27·0	102	78·1	65·6	162	124·1	104·1	222	170·1	142·7	282	216·0	181·3
43	32·9	27·6	103	78·9	66·2	163	124·9	104·8	223	170·8	143·3	283	216·8	181·9
44	33·7	28·3	104	79·7	66·8	164	125·6	105·4	224	171·6	144·0	284	217·6	182·6
45	34·5	28·9	105	80·4	67·5	165	126·4	106·1	225	172·4	144·6	285	218·3	183·2
46	35·2	29·6	106	81·2	68·1	166	127·2	106·7	226	173·1	145·3	286	219·1	183·8
47	36·0	30·2	107	82·0	68·8	167	127·9	107·3	227	173·9	145·9	287	219·9	184·5
48	36·8	30·9	108	82·7	69·4	168	128·7	108·0	228	174·7	146·6	288	220·6	185·1
49	37·5	31·5	109	83·5	70·1	169	129·5	108·6	229	175·4	147·2	289	221·4	185·8
50	38·3	32·1	110	84·3	70·7	170	130·2	109·3	230	176·2	147·8	290	222·2	186·4
51	39·1	32·8	111	85·0	71·3	171	131·0	109·9	231	177·0	148·5	291	222·9	187·1
52	39·8	33·4	112	85·8	72·0	172	131·8	110·6	232	177·7	149·1	292	223·7	187·7
53	40·6	34·1	113	86·6	72·6	173	132·5	111·2	233	178·5	149·8	293	224·5	188·3
54	41·4	34·7	114	87·3	73·3	174	133·3	111·8	234	179·3	150·4	294	225·2	189·0
55	42·1	35·4	115	88·1	73·9	175	134·1	112·5	235	180·0	151·1	295	226·0	189·6
56	42·9	36·0	116	88·9	74·6	176	134·8	113·1	236	180·8	151·7	296	226·7	190·3
57	43·7	36·6	117	89·6	75·2	177	135·6	113·8	237	181·6	152·3	297	227·5	190·9
58	44·4	37·3	118	90·4	75·8	178	136·4	114·4	238	182·3	153·0	298	228·3	191·6
59	45·2	37·9	119	91·2	76·5	179	137·1	115·1	239	183·1	153·6	299	229·0	192·2
60	46·0	38·6	120	91·9	77·1	180	137·9	115·7	240	183·9	154·3	300	229·8	192·8
Dist.	**Dep.**	**D. Lat.**	**Dist.**	**Dep.**	**D. Lat.**	**Dist.**	**Dep.**	**D. Lat.**	**Dist.**	**Dep.**	**D. Lat.**	**Dist.**	**Dep.**	**D. Lat.**

50°   310° / 230°   50 Degrees   050° / 130°   3h 20m

TRAVERSE TABLE
40 Degrees

D. Lon	Dep.		D. Lon	Dep.		D. Lon	Dep.		D. Lon	Dep.		D. Lon	Dep.	
Dist.	D. Lat.	Dep.	Dist.	D. Lat.	Dep.	Dist.	D. Lat.	Dep.	Dist.	D. Lat.	Dep.	Dist.	D. Lat.	Dep.
301	230.6	193.5	361	276.5	232.0	421	322.5	270.6	481	368.5	309.2	541	414.4	347.7
302	231.3	194.1	362	277.3	232.7	422	323.3	271.3	482	369.2	309.8	542	415.2	348.4
303	232.1	194.8	363	278.1	233.3	423	324.0	271.9	483	370.0	310.5	543	416.0	349.0
304	232.9	195.4	364	278.8	234.0	424	324.8	272.5	484	370.8	311.1	544	416.7	349.7
305	233.6	196.1	365	279.6	234.6	425	325.6	273.2	485	371.5	311.8	545	417.5	350.3
306	234.4	196.7	366	280.4	235.3	426	326.3	273.8	486	372.3	312.4	546	418.3	351.0
307	235.2	197.3	367	281.1	235.9	427	327.1	274.5	487	373.1	313.0	547	419.0	351.6
308	235.9	198.0	368	281.9	236.5	428	327.9	275.1	488	373.8	313.7	548	419.8	352.2
309	236.7	198.6	369	282.7	237.2	429	328.6	275.8	489	374.6	314.3	549	420.6	352.9
310	237.5	199.3	370	283.4	237.8	430	329.4	276.4	490	375.4	315.0	550	421.3	353.5
311	238.2	199.9	371	284.2	238.5	431	330.2	277.0	491	376.1	315.6	551	422.1	354.2
312	239.0	200.5	372	285.0	239.1	432	330.9	277.7	492	376.9	316.3	552	422.9	354.8
313	239.8	201.2	373	285.7	239.8	433	331.7	278.3	493	377.7	316.9	553	423.6	355.5
314	240.5	201.8	374	286.5	240.4	434	332.5	279.0	494	378.4	317.5	554	424.4	356.1
315	241.3	202.5	375	287.3	241.0	435	333.2	279.6	495	379.2	318.2	555	425.2	356.7
316	242.1	203.1	376	288.0	241.7	436	334.0	280.3	496	380.0	318.8	556	425.9	357.4
317	242.8	203.8	377	288.8	242.3	437	334.8	280.9	497	380.7	319.5	557	426.7	358.0
318	243.6	204.4	378	289.6	243.0	438	335.5	281.5	498	381.5	320.1	558	427.5	358.7
319	244.4	205.0	379	290.3	243.6	439	336.3	282.2	499	382.3	320.8	559	428.2	359.3
320	245.1	205.7	380	291.1	244.3	440	337.1	282.8	500	383.0	321.4	560	429.0	360.0
321	245.9	206.3	381	291.9	244.9	441	337.8	283.5	501	383.8	322.0	561	429.8	360.6
322	246.7	207.0	382	292.6	245.5	442	338.6	284.1	502	384.6	322.7	562	430.5	361.2
323	247.4	207.6	383	293.4	246.2	443	339.4	284.8	503	385.3	323.3	563	431.3	361.9
324	248.2	208.3	384	294.2	246.8	444	340.1	285.4	504	386.1	324.0	564	432.0	362.5
325	249.0	208.9	385	294.9	247.5	445	340.9	286.0	505	386.9	324.6	565	432.8	363.2
326	249.7	209.5	386	295.7	248.1	446	341.7	286.7	506	387.6	325.3	566	433.6	363.8
327	250.5	210.2	387	296.5	248.8	447	342.4	287.3	507	388.4	325.9	567	434.3	364.5
328	251.3	210.8	388	297.2	249.4	448	343.2	288.0	508	389.2	326.5	568	435.1	365.1
329	252.0	211.5	389	298.0	250.0	449	344.0	288.6	509	389.9	327.2	569	435.9	365.7
330	252.8	212.1	390	298.8	250.7	450	344.7	289.3	510	390.7	327.8	570	436.6	366.4
331	253.6	212.8	391	299.5	251.3	451	345.5	289.9	511	391.4	328.5	571	437.4	367.0
332	254.3	213.4	392	300.3	252.0	452	346.3	290.5	512	392.2	329.1	572	438.2	367.7
333	255.1	214.0	393	301.1	252.6	453	347.0	291.2	513	393.0	329.8	573	438.9	368.3
334	255.9	214.7	394	301.8	253.3	454	347.8	291.8	514	393.7	330.4	574	439.7	369.0
335	256.6	215.3	395	302.6	253.9	455	348.6	292.5	515	394.5	331.0	575	440.5	369.6
336	257.4	216.0	396	303.4	254.5	456	349.3	293.1	516	395.3	331.7	576	441.2	370.2
337	258.2	216.6	397	304.1	255.2	457	350.1	293.8	517	396.0	332.3	577	442.0	370.9
338	258.9	217.3	398	304.9	255.8	458	350.8	294.4	518	396.8	333.0	578	442.8	371.5
339	259.7	217.9	399	305.7	256.5	459	351.6	295.0	519	397.6	333.6	579	443.5	372.2
340	260.5	218.5	400	306.4	257.1	460	352.4	295.7	520	398.3	334.2	580	444.2	372.8
341	261.2	219.2	401	307.2	257.8	461	353.1	296.3	521	399.1	334.9	581	445.1	373.5
342	262.0	219.8	402	307.9	258.4	462	353.9	297.0	522	399.9	335.5	582	445.8	374.1
343	262.8	220.5	403	308.7	259.0	463	354.7	297.6	523	400.6	336.2	583	446.6	374.7
344	263.5	221.1	404	309.5	259.7	464	355.4	298.3	524	401.4	336.8	584	447.4	375.4
345	264.3	221.8	405	310.2	260.3	465	356.2	298.9	525	402.2	337.5	585	448.1	376.0
346	265.1	222.4	406	311.0	261.0	466	357.0	299.5	526	402.9	338.1	586	448.9	376.7
347	265.8	223.0	407	311.8	261.6	467	357.7	300.2	527	403.7	338.7	587	449.7	377.3
348	266.6	223.7	408	312.5	262.3	468	358.5	300.8	528	404.5	339.4	588	450.4	378.0
349	267.3	224.3	409	313.3	262.9	469	359.3	301.5	529	405.2	340.0	589	451.2	378.6
350	268.1	225.0	410	314.1	263.5	470	360.0	302.1	530	406.0	340.7	590	452.0	379.2
351	268.9	225.6	411	314.8	264.2	471	360.8	302.8	531	406.8	341.3	591	452.7	379.9
352	269.6	226.3	412	315.6	264.8	472	361.6	303.4	532	407.5	342.0	592	453.5	380.5
353	270.4	226.9	413	316.4	265.5	473	362.3	304.0	533	408.3	342.6	593	454.3	381.2
354	271.2	227.5	414	317.1	266.1	474	363.1	304.7	534	409.1	343.2	594	455.0	381.8
355	271.9	228.2	415	317.9	266.8	475	363.9	305.3	535	409.8	343.9	595	455.8	382.5
356	272.7	228.8	416	318.7	267.4	476	364.6	306.0	536	410.6	344.5	596	456.6	383.1
357	273.5	229.5	417	319.4	268.0	477	365.4	306.6	537	411.4	345.2	597	457.3	383.7
358	274.2	230.1	418	320.2	268.7	478	366.2	307.3	538	412.1	345.8	598	458.1	384.4
359	275.0	230.8	419	321.0	269.3	479	366.9	307.9	539	412.9	346.5	599	458.9	385.0
360	275.8	231.4	420	321.7	270.0	480	367.7	308.5	540	413.7	347.1	600	459.6	385.7
Dist.	Dep.	D. Lat.	Dist.	Dep.	D. Lat.	Dist.	Dep.	D. Lat.	Dist.	Dep.	D. Lat.	Dist.	Dep.	D. Lat.
D. Lon		Dep.	D. Lon		Dep.	D. Lon		Dep.	D. Lon		Dep.	D. Lon		Dep.

41°

TRAVERSE TABLE
41 Degrees

319° / 221°   041° / 139°   2h 44m

| D. Lon | Dep. | | D. Lon | Dep. | | D. Lon | Dep. | | D. Lon | Dep. | | D. Lon | Dep. | |
Dist.	D. Lat.	Dep.	Dist.	D. Lat.	Dep.	Dist.	D. Lat.	Dep.	Dist.	D. Lat.	Dep.	Dist.	D. Lat.	Dep.
1	00.8	00.7	61	46.0	40.0	121	91.3	79.4	181	136.6	118.7	241	181.9	158.1
2	01.5	01.3	62	46.8	40.7	122	92.1	80.0	182	137.4	119.4	242	182.6	158.8
3	02.3	02.0	63	47.5	41.3	123	92.8	80.7	183	138.1	120.1	243	183.4	159.4
4	03.0	02.6	64	48.3	42.0	124	93.6	81.4	184	138.9	120.7	244	184.1	160.1
5	03.8	03.3	65	49.1	42.6	125	94.3	82.0	185	139.6	121.4	245	184.9	160.7
6	04.5	03.9	66	49.8	43.3	126	95.1	82.7	186	140.4	122.0	246	185.7	161.4
7	05.3	04.6	67	50.6	44.0	127	95.8	83.3	187	141.1	122.7	247	186.4	162.0
8	06.0	05.2	68	51.3	44.6	128	96.6	84.0	188	141.9	123.3	248	187.2	162.7
9	06.8	05.9	69	52.1	45.3	129	97.4	84.6	189	142.6	124.0	249	187.9	163.4
10	07.5	06.6	70	52.8	45.9	130	98.1	85.3	190	143.4	124.7	250	188.7	164.0
11	08.3	07.2	71	53.6	46.6	131	98.9	85.9	191	144.1	125.3	251	189.4	164.7
12	09.1	07.9	72	54.3	47.2	132	99.6	86.6	192	144.9	126.0	252	190.2	165.3
13	09.8	08.5	73	55.1	47.9	133	100.4	87.3	193	145.7	126.6	253	190.9	166.0
14	10.6	09.2	74	55.8	48.5	134	101.1	87.9	194	146.4	127.3	254	191.7	166.6
15	11.3	09.8	75	56.6	49.2	135	101.9	88.6	195	147.2	127.9	255	192.5	167.3
16	12.1	10.5	76	57.4	49.9	136	102.6	89.2	196	147.9	128.6	256	193.2	168.0
17	12.8	11.2	77	58.1	50.5	137	103.4	89.9	197	148.7	129.2	257	194.0	168.6
18	13.6	11.8	78	58.9	51.2	138	104.1	90.5	198	149.4	129.9	258	194.7	169.3
19	14.3	12.5	79	59.6	51.8	139	104.9	91.2	199	150.2	130.6	259	195.5	169.9
20	15.1	13.1	80	60.4	52.5	140	105.7	91.8	200	150.9	131.2	260	196.2	170.6
21	15.8	13.8	81	61.1	53.1	141	106.4	92.5	201	151.7	131.9	261	197.0	171.2
22	16.6	14.4	82	61.9	53.8	142	107.2	93.2	202	152.5	132.5	262	197.7	171.9
23	17.4	15.1	83	62.6	54.5	143	107.9	93.8	203	153.2	133.2	263	198.5	172.5
24	18.1	15.7	84	63.4	55.1	144	108.7	94.5	204	154.0	133.8	264	199.2	173.2
25	18.9	16.4	85	64.2	55.8	145	109.4	95.1	205	154.7	134.5	265	200.0	173.9
26	19.6	17.1	86	64.9	56.4	146	110.2	95.8	206	155.5	135.1	266	200.8	174.5
27	20.4	17.7	87	65.7	57.1	147	110.9	96.4	207	156.2	135.8	267	201.5	175.2
28	21.1	18.4	88	66.4	57.7	148	111.7	97.1	208	157.0	136.5	268	202.3	175.8
29	21.9	19.0	89	67.2	58.4	149	112.5	97.8	209	157.7	137.1	269	203.0	176.5
30	22.6	19.7	90	67.9	59.0	150	113.2	98.4	210	158.5	137.8	270	203.8	177.1
31	23.4	20.3	91	68.7	59.7	151	114.0	99.1	211	159.2	138.4	271	204.5	177.8
32	24.2	21.0	92	69.4	60.4	152	114.7	99.7	212	160.0	139.1	272	205.3	178.4
33	24.9	21.6	93	70.2	61.0	153	115.5	100.4	213	160.8	139.7	273	206.0	179.1
34	25.7	22.3	94	70.9	61.7	154	116.2	101.0	214	161.5	140.4	274	206.8	179.8
35	26.4	23.0	95	71.7	62.3	155	117.0	101.7	215	162.3	141.1	275	207.5	180.4
36	27.2	23.6	96	72.5	63.0	156	117.7	102.3	216	163.0	141.7	276	208.3	181.1
37	27.9	24.3	97	73.2	63.6	157	118.5	103.0	217	163.8	142.4	277	209.1	181.7
38	28.7	24.9	98	74.0	64.3	158	119.2	103.7	218	164.5	143.0	278	209.8	182.4
39	29.4	25.6	99	74.7	64.9	159	120.0	104.3	219	165.3	143.7	279	210.6	183.0
40	30.2	26.2	100	75.5	65.6	160	120.8	105.0	220	166.0	144.3	280	211.3	183.7
41	30.9	26.9	101	76.2	66.3	161	121.5	105.6	221	166.8	145.0	281	212.1	184.4
42	31.7	27.6	102	77.0	66.9	162	122.3	106.3	222	167.5	145.6	282	212.8	185.0
43	32.5	28.2	103	77.7	67.6	163	123.0	106.9	223	168.3	146.3	283	213.6	185.7
44	33.2	28.9	104	78.5	68.2	164	123.8	107.6	224	169.1	147.0	284	214.3	186.3
45	34.0	29.5	105	79.2	68.9	165	124.5	108.2	225	169.8	147.6	285	215.1	187.0
46	34.7	30.2	106	80.0	69.5	166	125.3	108.9	226	170.6	148.3	286	215.8	187.6
47	35.5	30.8	107	80.8	70.2	167	126.0	109.6	227	171.3	148.9	287	216.6	188.3
48	36.2	31.5	108	81.5	70.9	168	126.8	110.2	228	172.1	149.6	288	217.4	188.9
49	37.0	32.1	109	82.3	71.5	169	127.5	110.9	229	172.8	150.2	289	218.1	189.6
50	37.7	32.8	110	83.0	72.2	170	128.3	111.5	230	173.6	150.9	290	218.9	190.3
51	38.5	33.5	111	83.8	72.8	171	129.1	112.2	231	174.3	151.5	291	219.6	190.9
52	39.2	34.1	112	84.5	73.5	172	129.8	112.8	232	175.1	152.2	292	220.4	191.6
53	40.0	34.8	113	85.3	74.1	173	130.6	113.5	233	175.8	152.9	293	221.1	192.2
54	40.8	35.4	114	86.0	74.8	174	131.3	114.2	234	176.6	153.5	294	221.9	192.9
55	41.5	36.1	115	86.8	75.4	175	132.1	114.8	235	177.4	154.2	295	222.6	193.5
56	42.3	36.7	116	87.5	76.1	176	132.8	115.5	236	178.1	154.8	296	223.4	194.2
57	43.0	37.4	117	88.3	76.8	177	133.6	116.1	237	178.9	155.5	297	224.1	194.8
58	43.8	38.1	118	89.1	77.4	178	134.3	116.8	238	179.6	156.1	298	224.9	195.5
59	44.5	38.7	119	89.8	78.1	179	135.1	117.4	239	180.4	156.8	299	225.7	196.2
60	45.3	39.4	120	90.6	78.7	180	135.8	118.1	240	181.1	157.5	300	226.4	196.8
Dist.	Dep.	D. Lat.	Dist.	Dep.	D. Lat.	Dist.	Dep.	D. Lat.	Dist.	Dep.	D. Lat.	Dist.	Dep.	D. Lat.
D. Lon		Dep.	D. Lon		Dep.	D. Lon		Dep.	D. Lon		Dep.	D. Lon		Dep.

311° / 229°   49 Degrees   049° / 131°   3h 16m

49°

TRAVERSE TABLE
41 Degrees

319°
221°

041°	2h 44m
139°	

41°

D. Lon	Dep.		D. Lon	Dep.		D. Lon	Dep.		D. Lon	Dep.		D. Lon	Dep.	
Dist.	D. Lat.	Dep.	Dist.	D. Lat.	Dep.	Dist.	D. Lat.	Dep.	Dist.	D. Lat.	Dep.	Dist.	D. Lat.	Dep.
301	227·2	197·5	361	272·5	236·8	421	317·7	276·2	481	363·0	315·6	541	408·3	354·9
302	227·9	198·1	362	273·2	237·5	422	318·5	276·9	482	363·8	316·2	542	409·1	355·5
303	228·7	198·8	363	274·0	238·1	423	319·2	277·5	483	364·5	316·9	543	409·8	356·2
304	229·4	199·4	364	274·7	238·8	424	320·0	278·2	484	365·3	317·5	544	410·6	356·9
305	230·2	200·1	365	275·5	239·5	425	320·8	278·8	485	366·0	318·2	545	411·3	357·6
306	230·9	200·8	366	276·2	240·1	426	321·5	279·5	486	366·8	318·8	546	412·1	358·2
307	231·7	201·4	367	277·0	240·8	427	322·3	280·1	487	367·5	319·5	547	412·8	358·9
308	232·5	202·1	368	277·7	241·4	428	323·0	280·8	488	368·3	320·2	548	413·6	359·5
309	233·2	202·7	369	278·5	242·1	429	323·8	281·4	489	369·1	320·8	549	414·3	360·2
310	234·0	203·4	370	279·2	242·7	430	324·5	282·1	490	369·8	321·5	550	415·1	360·8
311	234·7	204·0	371	280·0	243·4	431	325·3	282·8	491	370·6	322·1	551	415·8	361·5
312	235·5	204·7	372	280·8	244·1	432	326·0	283·4	492	371·3	322·8	552	416·6	362·1
313	236·2	205·3	373	281·5	244·7	433	326·8	284·1	493	372·1	323·4	553	417·4	362·8
314	237·0	206·0	374	282·3	245·4	434	327·5	284·7	494	372·8	324·1	554	418·1	363·5
315	237·7	206·7	375	283·0	246·0	435	328·3	285·4	495	373·6	324·7	555	418·9	364·1
316	238·5	207·3	376	283·8	246·7	436	329·1	286·0	496	374·3	325·4	556	419·6	364·8
317	239·2	208·0	377	284·5	247·3	437	329·8	286·7	497	375·1	326·1	557	420·4	365·4
318	240·0	208·6	378	285·3	248·0	438	330·6	287·4	498	375·8	326·7	558	421·1	366·1
319	240·8	209·3	379	286·0	248·6	439	331·3	288·0	499	376·6	327·4	559	421·9	366·7
320	241·5	209·9	380	286·8	249·3	440	332·1	288·7	500	377·4	328·0	560	422·6	367·4
321	242·3	210·6	381	287·5	250·0	441	332·8	289·3	501	378·1	328·7	561	423·4	368·0
322	243·0	211·3	382	288·3	250·6	442	333·6	290·0	502	378·9	329·3	562	424·1	368·7
323	243·8	211·9	383	289·1	251·3	443	334·3	290·6	503	379·6	330·0	563	424·9	369·4
324	244·5	212·6	384	289·8	251·9	444	335·1	291·3	504	380·4	330·7	564	425·7	370·0
325	245·3	213·2	385	290·6	252·6	445	335·8	291·9	505	381·1	331·3	565	426·4	370·7
326	246·0	213·9	386	291·3	253·2	446	336·6	292·6	506	381·9	332·0	566	427·2	371·3
327	246·8	214·5	387	292·1	253·9	447	337·4	293·3	507	382·6	332·6	567	427·9	372·0
328	247·5	215·2	388	292·8	254·6	448	338·1	293·9	508	383·4	333·3	568	428·7	372·6
329	248·3	215·8	389	293·6	255·2	449	338·9	294·6	509	384·1	333·9	569	429·4	373·3
330	249·1	216·5	390	294·3	255·9	450	339·6	295·2	510	384·9	334·6	570	430·2	374·0
331	249·8	217·2	391	295·1	256·5	451	340·4	295·9	511	385·7	335·2	571	430·9	374·6
332	250·6	217·8	392	295·8	257·2	452	341·1	296·5	512	386·4	335·9	572	431·7	375·3
333	251·3	218·5	393	296·6	257·8	453	341·9	297·2	513	387·2	336·6	573	432·4	375·9
334	252·1	219·1	394	297·4	258·5	454	342·6	297·9	514	387·9	337·2	574	433·2	376·6
335	252·8	219·8	395	298·1	259·1	455	343·4	298·5	515	388·7	337·9	575	434·0	377·2
336	253·6	220·4	396	298·9	259·8	456	344·1	299·2	516	389·4	338·5	576	434·7	377·9
337	254·3	221·1	397	299·6	260·5	457	344·9	299·8	517	390·2	339·2	577	435·5	378·5
338	255·1	221·7	398	300·4	261·1	458	345·7	300·5	518	390·9	339·8	578	436·2	379·2
339	255·8	222·4	399	301·1	261·8	459	346·4	301·1	519	391·7	340·5	579	437·0	379·9
340	256·6	223·1	400	301·9	262·4	460	347·2	301·8	520	392·4	341·2	580	437·7	380·5
341	257·4	223·7	401	302·6	263·1	461	347·9	302·4	521	393·2	341·8	581	438·5	381·2
342	258·1	224·4	402	303·4	263·7	462	348·7	303·1	522	394·0	342·5	582	439·2	381·8
343	258·9	225·0	403	304·1	264·4	463	349·4	303·8	523	394·7	343·1	583	440·0	382·5
344	259·6	225·7	404	304·9	265·0	464	350·2	304·4	524	395·5	343·8	584	440·8	383·1
345	260·4	226·3	405	305·7	265·7	465	350·9	305·1	525	396·2	344·4	585	441·5	383·8
346	261·1	227·0	406	306·4	266·4	466	351·7	305·7	526	397·0	345·1	586	442·3	384·5
347	261·9	227·7	407	307·2	267·0	467	352·4	306·4	527	397·7	345·7	587	443·0	385·1
348	262·6	228·3	408	307·9	267·7	468	353·2	307·0	528	398·5	346·4	588	443·8	385·8
349	263·4	229·0	409	308·7	268·3	469	354·0	307·7	529	399·2	347·1	589	444·5	386·4
350	264·1	229·6	410	309·4	269·0	470	354·7	308·5	530	400·0	347·7	590	445·3	387·1
351	264·9	230·3	411	310·2	269·6	471	355·5	309·0	531	400·8	348·4	591	446·0	387·7
352	265·7	230·9	412	310·9	270·3	472	356·2	309·7	532	401·5	349·0	592	446·8	388·4
353	266·4	231·6	413	311·7	271·0	473	357·0	310·3	533	402·3	349·7	593	447·5	389·0
354	267·2	232·2	414	312·4	271·6	474	357·7	311·0	534	403·0	350·3	594	448·3	389·7
355	267·9	232·9	415	313·2	272·3	475	358·5	311·6	535	403·8	351·0	595	449·1	390·4
356	268·7	233·6	416	314·0	272·9	476	359·2	312·3	536	404·5	351·6	596	449·8	391·0
357	269·4	234·2	417	314·7	273·6	477	360·0	312·9	537	405·3	352·3	597	450·6	391·7
358	270·2	234·9	418	315·5	274·2	478	360·8	313·6	538	406·0	353·0	598	451·3	392·3
359	270·9	235·5	419	316·2	274·9	479	361·5	314·3	539	406·8	353·6	599	452·1	393·0
360	271·7	236·2	420	317·0	275·5	480	362·3	314·9	540	407·5	354·3	600	452·8	393·6
Dist.	Dep.	D. Lat.	Dist.	Dep.	D. Lat.	Dist.	Dep.	D. Lat.	Dist.	Dep.	D. Lat.	Dist.	Dep.	D. Lat.
D. Lon		Dep.	D. Lon		Dep.	D. Lon		Dep.	D. Lon		Dep.	D. Lon		Dep.

TRAVERSE TABLE
42 Degrees

42° 318° / 222°   042° / 138°   2h 48m

D. Lon	Dep.		D. Lon	Dep.		D. Lon	Dep.		D. Lon	Dep.		D. Lon	Dep.	
Dist.	D. Lat.	Dep.	Dist.	D. Lat.	Dep.	Dist.	D. Lat.	Dep.	Dist.	D. Lat.	Dep.	Dist.	D. Lat.	Dep.
1	00.7	00.7	61	45.3	40.8	121	89.9	81.0	181	134.5	121.1	241	179.1	161.3
2	01.5	01.3	62	46.1	41.5	122	90.7	81.6	182	135.3	121.8	242	179.8	161.9
3	02.2	02.0	63	46.8	42.2	123	91.4	82.3	183	136.0	122.5	243	180.6	162.6
4	03.0	02.7	64	47.6	42.8	124	92.1	83.0	184	136.7	123.1	244	181.3	163.3
5	03.7	03.3	65	48.3	43.5	125	92.9	83.6	185	137.5	123.8	245	182.1	163.9
6	04.5	04.0	66	49.0	44.2	126	93.6	84.3	186	138.2	124.5	246	182.8	164.6
7	05.2	04.7	67	49.8	44.8	127	94.4	85.0	187	139.0	125.1	247	183.6	165.3
8	05.9	05.4	68	50.5	45.5	128	95.1	85.6	188	139.7	125.8	248	184.3	165.9
9	06.7	06.0	69	51.3	46.2	129	95.9	86.3	189	140.5	126.5	249	185.0	166.6
10	07.4	06.7	70	52.0	46.8	130	96.6	87.0	190	141.2	127.1	250	185.8	167.3
11	08.2	07.4	71	52.8	47.5	131	97.4	87.7	191	141.9	127.8	251	186.5	168.0
12	08.9	08.0	72	53.5	48.2	132	98.1	88.3	192	142.7	128.5	252	187.3	168.6
13	09.7	08.7	73	54.2	48.8	133	98.8	89.0	193	143.4	129.1	253	188.0	169.3
14	10.4	09.4	74	55.0	49.5	134	99.6	89.7	194	144.2	129.8	254	188.8	170.0
15	11.1	10.0	75	55.7	50.2	135	100.3	90.3	195	144.9	130.5	255	189.5	170.6
16	11.9	10.7	76	56.5	50.8	136	101.1	91.0	196	145.7	131.1	256	190.2	171.3
17	12.6	11.4	77	57.2	51.5	137	101.8	91.7	197	146.4	131.8	257	191.0	172.0
18	13.4	12.0	78	58.0	52.2	138	102.6	92.3	198	147.1	132.5	258	191.7	172.6
19	14.1	12.7	79	58.7	52.9	139	103.3	93.0	199	147.9	133.2	259	192.5	173.3
20	14.9	13.4	80	59.5	53.5	140	104.0	93.7	200	148.6	133.8	260	193.2	174.0
21	15.6	14.1	81	60.2	54.2	141	104.8	94.3	201	149.4	134.5	261	194.0	174.6
22	16.3	14.7	82	60.9	54.9	142	105.5	95.0	202	150.1	135.2	262	194.7	175.3
23	17.1	15.4	83	61.7	55.5	143	106.3	95.7	203	150.9	135.8	263	195.4	176.0
24	17.8	16.1	84	62.4	56.2	144	107.0	96.4	204	151.6	136.5	264	196.2	176.7
25	18.6	16.7	85	63.2	56.9	145	107.8	97.0	205	152.3	137.2	265	196.9	177.3
26	19.3	17.4	86	63.9	57.5	146	108.5	97.7	206	153.1	137.8	266	197.7	178.0
27	20.1	18.1	87	64.7	58.2	147	109.2	98.4	207	153.8	138.5	267	198.4	178.7
28	20.8	18.7	88	65.4	58.9	148	110.0	99.0	208	154.6	139.2	268	199.2	179.3
29	21.6	19.4	89	66.1	59.6	149	110.7	99.7	209	155.3	139.8	269	199.9	180.0
30	22.3	20.1	90	66.9	60.2	150	111.5	100.4	210	156.1	140.5	270	200.6	180.7
31	23.0	20.7	91	67.6	60.9	151	112.2	101.0	211	156.8	141.2	271	201.4	181.3
32	23.8	21.4	92	68.4	61.6	152	113.0	101.7	212	157.5	141.9	272	202.1	182.0
33	24.5	22.1	93	69.1	62.2	153	113.7	102.4	213	158.3	142.5	273	202.9	182.7
34	25.3	22.8	94	69.9	62.9	154	114.4	103.0	214	159.0	143.2	274	203.6	183.3
35	26.0	23.4	95	70.6	63.6	155	115.2	103.7	215	159.8	143.9	275	204.4	184.0
36	26.8	24.1	96	71.3	64.2	156	115.9	104.4	216	160.5	144.5	276	205.1	184.7
37	27.5	24.8	97	72.1	64.9	157	116.7	105.1	217	161.3	145.2	277	205.9	185.3
38	28.2	25.4	98	72.8	65.6	158	117.4	105.7	218	162.0	145.9	278	206.6	186.0
39	29.0	26.1	99	73.6	66.2	159	118.2	106.4	219	162.7	146.5	279	207.3	186.7
40	29.7	26.8	100	74.3	66.9	160	118.9	107.1	220	163.5	147.2	280	208.1	187.4
41	30.5	27.4	101	75.1	67.6	161	119.6	107.7	221	164.2	147.9	281	208.8	188.0
42	31.2	28.1	102	75.8	68.3	162	120.4	108.4	222	165.0	148.5	282	209.6	188.7
43	32.0	28.8	103	76.5	68.9	163	121.1	109.1	223	165.7	149.2	283	210.3	189.4
44	32.7	29.4	104	77.3	69.6	164	121.9	109.7	224	166.5	149.9	284	211.1	190.0
45	33.4	30.1	105	78.0	70.3	165	122.6	110.4	225	167.2	150.6	285	211.8	190.7
46	34.2	30.8	106	78.8	70.9	166	123.4	111.1	226	168.0	151.2	286	212.5	191.4
47	34.9	31.4	107	79.5	71.6	167	124.1	111.7	227	168.7	151.9	287	213.3	192.0
48	35.7	32.1	108	80.3	72.3	168	124.8	112.4	228	169.4	152.6	288	214.0	192.7
49	36.4	32.8	109	81.0	72.9	169	125.6	113.1	229	170.2	153.2	289	214.8	193.4
50	37.2	33.5	110	81.7	73.6	170	126.3	113.8	230	170.9	153.9	290	215.5	194.0
51	37.9	34.1	111	82.5	74.3	171	127.1	114.4	231	171.7	154.6	291	216.3	194.7
52	38.6	34.8	112	83.2	74.9	172	127.8	115.1	232	172.4	155.2	292	217.0	195.4
53	39.4	35.5	113	84.0	75.6	173	128.6	115.8	233	173.2	155.9	293	217.7	196.1
54	40.1	36.1	114	84.7	76.3	174	129.3	116.4	234	173.9	156.6	294	218.5	196.7
55	40.9	36.8	115	85.5	77.0	175	130.1	117.1	235	174.6	157.2	295	219.2	197.4
56	41.6	37.5	116	86.2	77.6	176	130.8	117.8	236	175.4	157.9	296	220.0	198.1
57	42.4	38.1	117	86.9	78.3	177	131.5	118.4	237	176.1	158.6	297	220.7	198.7
58	43.1	38.8	118	87.7	79.0	178	132.3	119.1	238	176.9	159.3	298	221.5	199.4
59	43.8	39.5	119	88.4	79.6	179	133.0	119.8	239	177.6	159.9	299	222.2	200.1
60	44.6	40.1	120	89.2	80.3	180	133.8	120.4	240	178.4	160.6	300	222.9	200.7

| Dist. | Dep. | D. Lat. | Dist. | Dep. | D. Lat. | Dist. | Dep. | D. Lat. | Dist. | Dep. | D. Lat. | Dist. | Dep. | D. Lat |
| D. Lon | | Dep. | D. Lon | | Dep. | D. Lon | | Dep. | D. Lon | | Dep. | D. Lon | | Dep. |

48°   312° / 228°   48 Degrees   048° / 132°   3h 12m

TRAVERSE TABLE
42 Degrees

D. Lon Dep.			D. Lon Dep.			D. Lon Dep.			D. Lon Dep.			D. Lon Dep.		
Dist.	D. Lat.	Dep.	Dist.	D. Lat.	Dep.	Dist.	D. Lat.	Dep.	Dist.	D. Lat.	Dep.	Dist.	D. Lat.	Dep.
301	223.7	201.4	361	268.3	241.6	421	312.9	281.7	481	357.5	321.9	541	402.0	362.0
302	224.4	202.1	362	269.0	242.2	422	313.6	282.4	482	358.2	322.5	542	402.8	362.7
303	225.2	202.7	363	269.8	242.9	423	314.4	283.0	483	358.9	323.2	543	403.5	363.3
304	225.9	203.4	364	270.5	243.6	424	315.1	283.7	484	359.7	323.9	544	404.3	364.0
305	226.7	204.1	365	271.2	244.2	425	315.8	284.4	485	360.4	324.5	545	405.0	364.7
306	227.4	204.8	366	272.0	244.9	426	316.6	285.0	486	361.2	325.2	546	405.8	365.3
307	228.1	205.4	367	272.7	245.6	427	317.3	285.7	487	361.9	325.9	547	406.5	366.0
308	228.9	206.1	368	273.5	246.2	428	318.1	286.4	488	362.7	326.5	548	407.2	366.7
309	229.6	206.8	369	274.2	246.9	429	318.8	287.1	489	363.4	327.2	549	408.0	367.4
310	230.4	207.4	370	275.0	247.6	430	319.6	287.7	490	364.1	327.9	550	408.7	368.0
311	231.1	208.1	371	275.7	248.2	431	320.3	288.4	491	364.9	328.5	551	409.5	368.7
312	231.9	208.8	372	276.4	248.9	432	321.0	289.1	492	365.6	329.2	552	410.2	369.4
313	232.6	209.4	373	277.2	249.6	433	321.8	289.7	493	366.4	329.9	553	411.0	370.0
314	233.3	210.1	374	277.9	250.3	434	322.5	290.4	494	367.1	330.6	554	411.7	370.7
315	234.1	210.8	375	278.7	250.9	435	323.3	291.1	495	367.9	331.2	555	412.4	371.4
316	234.8	211.4	376	279.4	251.6	436	324.0	291.7	496	368.6	331.9	556	413.2	372.0
317	235.6	212.1	377	280.2	252.3	437	324.8	292.4	497	369.3	332.5	557	413.9	372.7
318	236.3	212.8	378	280.9	252.9	438	325.5	293.1	498	370.1	333.2	558	414.7	373.4
319	237.1	213.5	379	281.7	253.6	439	326.2	293.7	499	370.8	333.9	559	415.4	374.0
320	237.8	214.1	380	282.4	254.3	440	327.0	294.4	500	371.6	334.6	560	416.2	374.7
321	238.5	214.8	381	283.1	254.9	441	327.7	295.1	501	372.3	335.2	561	416.9	375.4
322	239.3	215.5	382	283.9	255.6	442	328.5	295.8	502	373.1	335.9	562	417.6	376.1
323	240.0	216.1	383	284.6	256.3	443	329.2	296.4	503	373.8	336.6	563	418.4	376.7
324	240.8	216.8	384	285.4	256.9	444	330.0	297.1	504	374.5	337.2	564	419.1	377.4
325	241.5	217.5	385	286.1	257.6	445	330.7	297.8	505	375.3	337.9	565	419.9	378.1
326	242.3	218.1	386	286.9	258.3	446	331.4	298.4	506	376.0	338.6	566	420.6	378.7
327	243.0	218.8	387	287.6	259.0	447	332.2	299.1	507	376.8	339.2	567	421.4	379.4
328	243.8	219.5	388	288.3	259.6	448	332.9	299.8	508	377.5	339.9	568	422.1	380.1
329	244.5	220.1	389	289.1	260.3	449	333.7	300.4	509	378.3	340.6	569	422.8	380.7
330	245.2	220.8	390	289.8	261.0	450	334.4	301.1	510	379.0	341.3	570	423.6	381.4
331	246.0	221.5	391	290.6	261.6	451	335.2	301.8	511	379.7	341.9	571	424.3	382.1
332	246.7	222.2	392	291.3	262.3	452	335.9	302.4	512	380.5	342.6	572	425.1	382.7
333	247.5	222.8	393	292.1	263.0	453	336.6	303.1	513	381.2	343.3	573	425.8	383.4
334	248.2	223.5	394	292.8	263.6	454	337.4	303.8	514	382.0	343.9	574	426.6	384.1
335	249.0	224.2	395	293.5	264.3	455	338.1	304.5	515	382.7	344.6	575	427.3	384.8
336	249.7	224.8	396	294.3	265.0	456	338.9	305.1	516	383.5	345.3	576	428.1	385.4
337	250.4	225.5	397	295.0	265.6	457	339.6	305.8	517	384.2	345.9	577	428.8	386.1
338	251.2	226.2	398	295.8	266.3	458	340.4	306.5	518	384.9	346.6	578	429.5	386.8
339	251.9	226.8	399	296.5	267.0	459	341.1	307.1	519	385.7	347.3	579	430.3	387.4
340	252.7	227.5	400	297.3	267.7	460	341.8	307.8	520	386.4	347.9	580	431.0	388.1
341	253.4	228.2	401	298.0	268.3	461	342.6	308.5	521	387.2	348.6	581	431.8	388.8
342	254.2	228.8	402	298.7	269.0	462	343.3	309.1	522	387.9	349.3	582	432.5	389.4
343	254.9	229.5	403	299.5	269.7	463	344.1	309.8	523	388.7	350.0	583	433.3	390.1
344	255.6	230.2	404	300.2	270.3	464	344.8	310.5	524	389.4	350.6	584	434.0	390.8
345	256.4	230.9	405	301.0	271.0	465	345.6	311.1	525	390.2	351.3	585	434.7	391.4
346	257.1	231.5	406	301.7	271.7	466	346.3	311.8	526	390.9	352.0	586	435.5	392.1
347	257.9	232.2	407	302.5	272.3	467	347.0	312.5	527	391.6	352.6	587	436.2	392.8
348	258.6	232.9	408	303.2	273.0	468	347.8	313.2	528	392.4	353.3	588	437.0	393.4
349	259.4	233.5	409	303.9	273.7	469	348.5	313.8	529	393.1	354.0	589	437.7	394.1
350	260.1	234.2	410	304.7	274.3	470	349.3	314.5	530	393.9	354.6	590	438.5	394.8
351	260.8	234.9	411	305.4	275.0	471	350.0	315.2	531	394.6	355.3	591	439.2	395.5
352	261.6	235.5	412	306.2	275.7	472	350.8	315.8	532	395.4	356.0	592	439.9	396.1
353	262.3	236.2	413	306.9	276.4	473	351.5	316.5	533	396.1	356.6	593	440.7	396.8
354	263.1	236.9	414	307.7	277.0	474	352.3	317.2	534	396.8	357.3	594	441.4	397.5
355	263.8	237.5	415	308.4	277.7	475	353.0	317.8	535	397.6	358.0	595	442.2	398.1
356	264.6	238.2	416	309.1	278.4	476	353.7	318.5	536	398.3	358.7	596	442.9	398.8
357	265.3	238.9	417	309.9	279.0	477	354.5	319.2	537	399.1	359.3	597	443.7	399.5
358	266.0	239.5	418	310.6	279.7	478	355.2	319.8	538	399.8	360.0	598	444.4	400.1
359	266.8	240.2	419	311.4	280.4	479	356.0	320.5	539	400.6	360.7	599	445.1	400.8
360	267.5	240.9	420	312.1	281.0	480	356.7	321.2	540	401.3	361.3	600	445.9	401.5
Dist.	Dep.	D. Lat.	Dist.	Dep.	D. Lat.	Dist.	Dep.	D. Lat.	Dist.	Dep.	D. Lat.	Dist.	Dep.	D. Lat.
D. Lon		Dep.	D. Lon		Dep.	D. Lon		Dep.	D. Lon		Dep.	D. Lon		Dep.

TRAVERSE TABLE
43 Degrees

43° | 317° / 223° | | 043° / 137° | 2h 52m

Dist.	D. Lat	Dep.	Dist.	D. Lat	Dep.	Dist.	D. Lat	Dep.	Dist.	D. Lat	Dep.	Dist.	D. Lat	Dep.
1	00.7	00.7	61	44.6	41.6	121	88.5	82.5	181	132.4	123.4	241	176.3	164.4
2	01.5	01.4	62	45.3	42.3	122	89.2	83.2	182	133.1	124.1	242	177.0	165.0
3	02.2	02.0	63	46.1	43.0	123	90.0	83.9	183	133.8	124.8	243	177.7	165.7
4	02.9	02.7	64	46.8	43.6	124	90.7	84.6	184	134.6	125.5	244	178.5	166.4
5	03.7	03.4	65	47.5	44.3	125	91.4	85.2	185	135.3	126.2	245	179.2	167.1
6	04.4	04.1	66	48.3	45.0	126	92.2	85.9	186	136.0	126.9	246	179.9	167.8
7	05.1	04.8	67	49.0	45.7	127	92.9	86.6	187	136.8	127.5	247	180.6	168.5
8	05.9	05.5	68	49.7	46.4	128	93.6	87.3	188	137.5	128.2	248	181.4	169.1
9	06.6	06.1	69	50.5	47.1	129	94.3	88.0	189	138.2	128.9	249	182.1	169.8
10	07.3	06.8	70	51.2	47.7	130	95.1	88.7	190	139.0	129.6	250	182.8	170.5
11	08.0	07.5	71	51.9	48.4	131	95.8	89.3	191	139.7	130.3	251	183.6	171.2
12	08.8	08.2	72	52.7	49.1	132	96.5	90.0	192	140.4	130.9	252	184.3	171.9
13	09.5	08.9	73	53.4	49.8	133	97.3	90.7	193	141.2	131.6	253	185.0	172.5
14	10.2	09.5	74	54.1	50.5	134	98.0	91.4	194	141.9	132.3	254	185.8	173.2
15	11.0	10.2	75	54.9	51.1	135	98.7	92.1	195	142.6	133.0	255	186.5	173.9
16	11.7	10.9	76	55.6	51.8	136	99.5	92.8	196	143.3	133.7	256	187.2	174.6
17	12.4	11.6	77	56.3	52.5	137	100.2	93.4	197	144.1	134.4	257	188.0	175.3
18	13.2	12.3	78	57.0	53.2	138	100.9	94.1	198	144.8	135.0	258	188.7	176.0
19	13.9	13.0	79	57.8	53.9	139	101.7	94.8	199	145.5	135.7	259	189.4	176.6
20	14.6	13.6	80	58.5	54.6	140	102.4	95.5	200	146.3	136.4	260	190.2	177.3
21	15.4	14.3	81	59.2	55.2	141	103.1	96.2	201	147.0	137.1	261	190.9	178.0
22	16.1	15.0	82	60.0	55.9	142	103.9	96.8	202	147.7	137.8	262	191.6	178.7
23	16.8	15.7	83	60.7	56.6	143	104.6	97.5	203	148.5	138.4	263	192.3	179.4
24	17.6	16.4	84	61.4	57.3	144	105.3	98.2	204	149.2	139.1	264	193.1	180.0
25	18.3	17.0	85	62.2	58.0	145	106.0	98.9	205	149.9	139.8	265	193.8	180.7
26	19.0	17.7	86	62.9	58.7	146	106.8	99.6	206	150.7	140.5	266	194.5	181.4
27	19.7	18.4	87	63.6	59.3	147	107.5	100.3	207	151.4	141.2	267	195.3	182.1
28	20.5	19.1	88	64.4	60.0	148	108.2	100.9	208	152.1	141.9	268	196.0	182.8
29	21.2	19.8	89	65.1	60.7	149	109.0	101.6	209	152.9	142.5	269	196.7	183.5
30	21.9	20.5	90	65.8	61.4	150	109.7	102.3	210	153.6	143.2	270	197.5	184.1
31	22.7	21.1	91	66.6	62.1	151	110.4	103.0	211	154.3	143.9	271	198.2	184.8
32	23.4	21.8	92	67.3	62.7	152	111.2	103.7	212	155.0	144.6	272	198.9	185.5
33	24.1	22.5	93	68.0	63.4	153	111.9	104.3	213	155.8	145.3	273	199.7	186.2
34	24.9	23.2	94	68.7	64.1	154	112.6	105.0	214	156.5	145.9	274	200.4	186.9
35	25.6	23.9	95	69.5	64.8	155	113.4	105.7	215	157.2	146.6	275	201.1	187.5
36	26.3	24.6	96	70.2	65.5	156	114.1	106.4	216	158.0	147.3	276	201.9	188.2
37	27.1	25.2	97	70.9	66.2	157	114.8	107.1	217	158.7	148.0	277	202.6	188.9
38	27.8	25.9	98	71.7	66.8	158	115.6	107.8	218	159.4	148.7	278	203.3	189.6
39	28.5	26.6	99	72.4	67.5	159	116.3	108.4	219	160.2	149.4	279	204.0	190.3
40	29.3	27.3	100	73.1	68.2	160	117.0	109.1	220	160.9	150.0	280	204.8	191.0
41	30.0	28.0	101	73.9	68.9	161	117.7	109.8	221	161.6	150.7	281	205.5	191.6
42	30.7	28.6	102	74.6	69.6	162	118.5	110.5	222	162.4	151.4	282	206.2	192.3
43	31.4	29.3	103	75.3	70.2	163	119.2	111.2	223	163.1	152.1	283	207.0	193.0
44	32.2	30.0	104	76.1	70.9	164	119.9	111.8	224	163.8	152.8	284	207.7	193.7
45	32.9	30.7	105	76.8	71.6	165	120.7	112.5	225	164.6	153.4	285	208.4	194.4
46	33.6	31.4	106	77.5	72.3	166	121.4	113.2	226	165.3	154.1	286	209.2	195.1
47	34.4	32.1	107	78.3	73.0	167	122.1	113.9	227	166.0	154.8	287	209.9	195.7
48	35.1	32.7	108	79.0	73.7	168	122.9	114.6	228	166.7	155.5	288	210.6	196.4
49	35.8	33.4	109	79.7	74.3	169	123.6	115.3	229	167.5	156.2	289	211.4	197.1
50	36.6	34.1	110	80.4	75.0	170	124.3	115.9	230	168.2	156.9	290	212.1	197.8
51	37.3	34.8	111	81.2	75.7	171	125.1	116.6	231	168.9	157.5	291	212.8	198.5
52	38.0	35.5	112	81.9	76.4	172	125.8	117.3	232	169.7	158.2	292	213.6	199.1
53	38.8	36.1	113	82.6	77.1	173	126.5	118.0	233	170.4	158.9	293	214.3	199.8
54	39.5	36.8	114	83.4	77.7	174	127.3	118.7	234	171.1	159.6	294	215.0	200.5
55	40.2	37.5	115	84.1	78.4	175	128.0	119.3	235	171.9	160.3	295	215.7	201.2
56	41.0	38.2	116	84.8	79.1	176	128.7	120.0	236	172.6	161.0	296	216.5	201.9
57	41.7	38.9	117	85.6	79.8	177	129.4	120.7	237	173.3	161.6	297	217.2	202.6
58	42.4	39.6	118	86.3	80.5	178	130.2	121.4	238	174.1	162.3	298	217.9	203.2
59	43.1	40.2	119	87.0	81.2	179	130.9	122.1	239	174.8	163.0	299	218.7	203.9
60	43.9	40.9	120	87.8	81.8	180	131.6	122.8	240	175.5	163.7	300	219.4	204.6

| Dist. | Dep. | D. Lat. | Dist. | Dep. | D. Lat. | Dist. | Dep. | D. Lat. | Dist. | Dep. | D. Lat. | Dist. | Dep. | D. Lat |

47° | 313° / 227° | | 47 Degrees | | 047° / 133° | 3h 08m

TRAVERSE TABLE
43 Degrees

D. Lon	Dep.		D. Lon	Dep.		D. Lon	Dep.		D. Lon	Dep.		D. Lon	Dep.	
Dist.	D. Lat.	Dep.	Dist.	D. Lat.	Dep.	Dist.	D. Lat.	Dep.	Dist.	D. Lat.	Dep.	Dist.	D. Lat.	Dep.
301	220·1	205·3	361	264·0	246·2	421	307·9	287·1	481	351·8	328·0	541	395·7	369·0
302	220·9	206·0	362	264·8	246·9	422	308·6	287·8	482	352·5	328·7	542	396·4	369·6
303	221·6	206·6	363	265·5	247·6	423	309·4	288·5	483	353·2	329·4	543	397·1	370·3
304	222·3	207·3	364	266·2	248·2	424	310·1	289·2	484	354·0	330·1	544	397·9	371·0
305	223·1	208·0	365	266·9	248·9	425	310·8	289·8	485	354·7	330·8	545	398·6	371·7
306	223·8	208·7	366	267·7	249·6	426	311·6	290·5	486	355·4	331·5	546	399·3	372·4
307	224·5	209·4	367	268·4	250·3	427	312·3	291·2	487	356·2	332·1	547	400·1	373·1
308	225·3	210·1	368	269·1	251·0	428	313·0	291·9	488	356·9	332·8	548	400·8	373·7
309	226·0	210·7	369	269·9	251·7	429	313·8	292·6	489	357·6	333·5	549	401·5	374·4
310	226·7	211·4	370	270·6	252·3	430	314·5	293·3	490	358·4	334·2	550	402·2	375·1
311	227·5	212·1	371	271·3	253·0	431	315·2	293·9	491	359·1	334·9	551	403·0	375·8
312	228·2	212·8	372	272·1	253·7	432	315·9	294·6	492	359·8	335·5	552	403·7	376·5
313	228·9	213·5	373	272·8	254·4	433	316·7	295·3	493	360·6	336·2	553	404·4	377·1
314	229·6	214·1	374	273·5	255·1	434	317·4	296·0	494	361·3	336·9	554	405·2	377·8
315	230·4	214·8	375	274·3	255·7	435	318·1	296·7	495	362·0	337·6	555	405·9	378·5
316	231·1	215·5	376	275·0	256·4	436	318·9	297·4	496	362·8	338·3	556	406·6	379·2
317	231·8	216·2	377	275·7	257·1	437	319·6	298·0	497	363·5	339·0	557	407·4	379·9
318	232·6	216·9	378	276·5	257·8	438	320·3	298·7	498	364·2	339·6	558	408·1	380·6
319	233·3	217·6	379	277·2	258·5	439	321·1	299·4	499	364·9	340·3	559	408·8	381·2
320	234·0	218·2	380	277·9	259·2	440	321·8	300·1	500	365·7	341·0	560	409·6	381·9
321	234·8	218·9	381	278·6	259·8	441	322·5	300·8	501	366·4	341·7	561	410·3	382·6
322	235·5	219·6	382	279·4	260·5	442	323·3	301·4	502	367·1	342·4	562	411·0	383·3
323	236·2	220·3	383	280·1	261·2	443	324·0	302·1	503	367·9	343·0	563	411·8	384·0
324	237·0	221·0	384	280·8	261·9	444	324·7	302·8	504	368·6	343·7	564	412·5	384·6
325	237·7	221·6	385	281·6	262·6	445	325·5	303·5	505	369·3	344·4	565	413·2	385·3
326	238·4	222·3	386	282·3	263·3	446	326·2	304·2	506	370·1	345·1	566	413·9	386·0
327	239·2	223·0	387	283·0	263·9	447	326·9	304·9	507	370·8	345·8	567	414·7	386·7
328	239·9	223·7	388	283·8	264·6	448	327·6	305·5	508	371·5	346·5	568	415·4	387·4
329	240·6	224·4	389	284·5	265·3	449	328·4	306·2	509	372·3	347·1	569	416·1	388·1
330	241·3	225·1	390	285·2	266·0	450	329·1	306·9	510	373·0	347·8	570	416·9	388·7
331	242·1	225·7	391	286·0	266·7	451	329·9	307·6	511	373·7	348·5	571	417·6	389·4
332	242·8	226·4	392	286·7	267·3	452	330·6	308·3	512	374·5	349·2	572	418·3	390·1
333	243·5	227·1	393	287·4	268·0	453	331·3	308·9	513	375·2	349·9	573	419·1	390·8
334	244·3	227·8	394	288·2	268·7	454	332·0	309·6	514	375·9	350·5	574	419·8	391·5
335	245·0	228·5	395	288·9	269·4	455	332·8	310·3	515	376·6	351·2	575	420·5	392·1
336	245·7	229·2	396	289·6	270·1	456	333·5	311·0	516	377·4	351·9	576	421·3	392·8
337	246·5	229·8	397	290·3	270·8	457	334·2	311·7	517	378·1	352·6	577	422·0	393·5
338	247·2	230·5	398	291·1	271·4	458	335·0	312·4	518	378·8	353·3	578	422·7	394·2
339	247·9	231·2	399	291·8	272·1	459	335·7	313·0	519	379·6	354·0	579	423·5	394·9
340	248·7	231·9	400	292·5	272·8	460	336·4	313·7	520	380·3	354·6	580	424·2	395·6
341	249·4	232·6	401	293·3	273·5	461	337·2	314·4	521	381·0	355·3	581	424·9	396·2
342	250·1	233·2	402	294·0	274·2	462	337·9	315·1	522	381·8	356·0	582	425·6	396·9
343	250·9	233·9	403	294·7	274·8	463	338·6	315·8	523	382·5	356·7	583	426·4	397·6
344	251·6	234·6	404	295·5	275·5	464	339·3	316·4	524	383·2	357·4	584	427·1	398·3
345	252·3	235·3	405	296·2	276·2	465	340·1	317·1	525	384·0	358·0	585	427·8	399·0
346	253·0	236·0	406	296·9	276·9	466	340·8	317·8	526	384·7	358·7	586	428·6	399·7
347	253·8	236·7	407	297·7	277·6	467	341·5	318·5	527	385·4	359·4	587	429·3	400·3
348	254·5	237·3	408	298·4	278·3	468	342·3	319·2	528	386·2	360·1	588	430·0	401·0
349	255·2	238·0	409	299·1	278·9	469	343·0	319·9	529	386·9	360·8	589	430·8	401·7
350	256·0	238·7	410	299·9	279·6	470	343·7	320·5	530	387·6	361·5	590	431·5	402·4
351	256·7	239·4	411	300·6	280·3	471	344·5	321·2	531	388·3	362·1	591	432·2	403·1
352	257·4	240·1	412	301·3	281·0	472	345·2	321·9	532	389·1	362·8	592	433·0	403·7
353	258·2	240·7	413	302·0	281·7	473	345·9	322·6	533	389·8	363·5	593	433·7	404·4
354	258·9	241·4	414	302·8	282·3	474	346·7	323·3	534	390·5	364·2	594	434·4	405·1
355	259·6	242·1	415	303·5	283·0	475	347·4	323·9	535	391·3	364·9	595	435·2	405·8
356	260·4	242·8	416	304·3	283·7	476	348·1	324·6	536	392·0	365·6	596	435·9	406·5
357	261·1	243·5	417	305·0	284·4	477	348·9	325·3	537	392·7	366·2	597	436·6	407·2
358	261·8	244·2	418	305·7	285·1	478	349·6	326·0	538	393·5	366·9	598	437·3	407·8
359	262·6	244·8	419	306·4	285·8	479	350·3	326·7	539	394·2	367·6	599	438·1	408·5
360	263·3	245·5	420	307·2	286·4	480	351·0	327·4	540	394·9	368·3	600	438·8	409·2
Dist.	Dep.	D. Lat.	Dist.	Dep.	D. Lat.	Dist.	Dep.	D. Lat.	Dist.	Dep.	D. Lat.	Dist.	Dep.	D. Lat.
D. Lon		Dep.	D. Lon		Dep.	D. Lon		Dep.	D. Lon		Dep.	D. Lon		Dep.

TRAVERSE TABLE
44 Degrees

| | 316° / 224° | | | | | | | | | 044° / 136° | 2h 56m |

D. Lon	Dep.		D. Lon	Dep.		D. Lon	Dep.		D. Lon	Dep.		D. Lon	Dep.	
Dist.	D. Lat.	Dep.	Dist.	D. Lat.	Dep.	Dist.	D. Lat.	Dep.	Dist.	D. Lat.	Dep.	Dist.	D. Lat.	Dep.
1	00·7	00·7	61	43·9	42·4	121	87·0	84·1	181	130·2	125·7	241	173·4	167·4
2	01·4	01·4	62	44·6	43·1	122	87·8	84·7	182	130·9	126·4	242	174·1	168·1
3	02·2	02·1	63	45·3	43·8	123	88·5	85·4	183	131·6	127·1	243	174·8	168·8
4	02·9	02·8	64	46·0	44·5	124	89·2	86·1	184	132·4	127·8	244	175·5	169·5
5	03·6	03·5	65	46·8	45·2	125	89·9	86·8	185	133·1	128·5	245	176·2	170·2
6	04·3	04·2	66	47·5	45·8	126	90·6	87·5	186	133·8	129·2	246	177·0	170·9
7	05·0	04·9	67	48·2	46·5	127	91·4	88·2	187	134·5	129·9	247	177·7	171·6
8	05·8	05·6	68	48·9	47·2	128	92·1	88·9	188	135·2	130·6	248	178·4	172·3
9	06·5	06·3	69	49·6	47·9	129	92·8	89·6	189	136·0	131·3	249	179·1	173·0
10	07·2	06·9	70	50·4	48·6	130	93·5	90·3	190	136·7	132·0	250	179·8	173·7
11	07·9	07·6	71	51·1	49·3	131	94·2	91·0	191	137·4	132·7	251	180·6	174·4
12	08·6	08·3	72	51·8	50·0	132	95·0	91·7	192	138·1	133·4	252	181·3	175·1
13	09·4	09·0	73	52·5	50·7	133	95·7	92·4	193	138·8	134·1	253	182·0	175·7
14	10·1	09·7	74	53·2	51·4	134	96·4	93·1	194	139·6	134·8	254	182·7	176·4
15	10·8	10·4	75	54·0	52·1	135	97·1	93·8	195	140·3	135·5	255	183·4	177·1
16	11·5	11·1	76	54·7	52·8	136	97·8	94·5	196	141·0	136·2	256	184·2	177·8
17	12·2	11·8	77	55·4	53·5	137	98·5	95·2	197	141·7	136·8	257	184·9	178·5
18	12·9	12·5	78	56·1	54·2	138	99·3	95·9	198	142·4	137·5	258	185·6	179·2
19	13·7	13·2	79	56·8	54·9	139	100·0	96·6	199	143·1	138·2	259	186·3	179·9
20	14·4	13·9	80	57·5	55·6	140	100·7	97·3	200	143·9	138·9	260	187·0	180·6
21	15·1	14·6	81	58·3	56·3	141	101·4	97·9	201	144·6	139·6	261	187·7	181·3
22	15·8	15·3	82	59·0	57·0	142	102·1	98·6	202	145·3	140·3	262	188·5	182·0
23	16·5	16·0	83	59·7	57·7	143	102·9	99·3	203	146·0	141·0	263	189·2	182·7
24	17·3	16·7	84	60·4	58·4	144	103·6	100·0	204	146·7	141·7	264	189·9	183·4
25	18·0	17·4	85	61·1	59·0	145	104·3	100·7	205	147·5	142·4	265	190·6	184·1
26	18·7	18·1	86	61·9	59·7	146	105·0	101·4	206	148·2	143·1	266	191·3	184·8
27	19·4	18·8	87	62·6	60·4	147	105·7	102·1	207	148·9	143·8	267	192·1	185·5
28	20·1	19·5	88	63·3	61·1	148	106·5	102·8	208	149·6	144·5	268	192·8	186·2
29	20·9	20·1	89	64·0	61·8	149	107·2	103·5	209	150·3	145·2	269	193·5	186·9
30	21·6	20·8	90	64·7	62·5	150	107·9	104·2	210	151·1	145·9	270	194·2	187·6
31	22·3	21·5	91	65·5	63·2	151	108·6	104·9	211	151·8	146·6	271	194·9	188·3
32	23·0	22·2	92	66·2	63·9	152	109·3	105·6	212	152·5	147·3	272	195·7	188·9
33	23·7	22·9	93	66·9	64·6	153	110·1	106·3	213	153·2	148·0	273	196·4	189·6
34	24·5	23·6	94	67·6	65·3	154	110·8	107·0	214	153·9	148·7	274	197·1	190·3
35	25·2	24·3	95	68·3	66·0	155	111·5	107·7	215	154·7	149·4	275	197·8	191·0
36	25·9	25·0	96	69·1	66·7	156	112·2	108·4	216	155·4	150·0	276	198·5	191·7
37	26·6	25·7	97	69·8	67·4	157	112·9	109·1	217	156·1	150·7	277	199·3	192·4
38	27·3	26·4	98	70·5	68·1	158	113·7	109·8	218	156·8	151·4	278	200·0	193·1
39	28·1	27·1	99	71·2	68·8	159	114·4	110·5	219	157·5	152·1	279	200·7	193·8
40	28·8	27·8	100	71·9	69·5	160	115·1	111·1	220	158·3	152·8	280	201·4	194·5
41	29·5	28·5	101	72·7	70·2	161	115·8	111·8	221	159·0	153·5	281	202·1	195·2
42	30·2	29·2	102	73·4	70·9	162	116·5	112·5	222	159·7	154·2	282	202·9	195·9
43	30·9	29·9	103	74·1	71·5	163	117·3	113·2	223	160·4	154·9	283	203·6	196·6
44	31·7	30·6	104	74·8	72·2	164	118·0	113·9	224	161·1	155·6	284	204·3	197·3
45	32·4	31·3	105	75·5	72·9	165	118·7	114·6	225	161·9	156·3	285	205·0	198·0
46	33·1	32·0	106	76·3	73·6	166	119·4	115·3	226	162·6	157·0	286	205·7	198·7
47	33·8	32·6	107	77·0	74·3	167	120·1	116·0	227	163·3	157·7	287	206·5	199·4
48	34·5	33·3	108	77·7	75·0	168	120·8	116·7	228	164·0	158·4	288	207·2	200·1
49	35·2	34·0	109	78·4	75·7	169	121·6	117·4	229	164·7	159·1	289	207·9	200·8
50	36·0	34·7	110	79·1	76·4	170	122·3	118·1	230	165·4	159·8	290	208·6	201·5
51	36·7	35·4	111	79·8	77·1	171	123·0	118·8	231	166·2	160·5	291	209·3	202·1
52	37·4	36·1	112	80·6	77·8	172	123·7	119·5	232	166·9	161·2	292	210·0	202·8
53	38·1	36·8	113	81·3	78·5	173	124·4	120·2	233	167·6	161·9	293	210·8	203·5
54	38·8	37·5	114	82·0	79·2	174	125·2	120·9	234	168·3	162·6	294	211·5	204·2
55	39·6	38·2	115	82·7	79·9	175	125·9	121·6	235	169·0	163·2	295	212·2	204·9
56	40·3	38·9	116	83·4	80·6	176	126·6	122·3	236	169·8	163·9	296	212·9	205·6
57	41·0	39·6	117	84·2	81·3	177	127·3	123·0	237	170·5	164·6	297	213·6	206·3
58	41·7	40·3	118	84·9	82·0	178	128·0	123·6	238	171·2	165·3	298	214·4	207·0
59	42·4	41·0	119	85·6	82·7	179	128·8	124·3	239	171·9	166·0	299	215·1	207·7
60	43·2	41·7	120	86·3	83·4	180	129·5	125·0	240	172·6	166·7	300	215·8	208·4
Dist.	Dep.	D. Lat.	Dist.	Dep.	D. Lat.	Dist.	Dep.	D. Lat.	Dist.	Dep.	D. Lat.	Dist.	Dep.	D. Lat.
D. Lon		Dep.	D. Lon		Dep.	D. Lon		Dep.	D. Lon		Dep.	D. Lon		Dep.

| | 314° / 226° | | | | | 46 Degrees | | | | | | 046 / 134° | 3h 04m |

TRAVERSE TABLE
44 Degrees

| | 316° / 224° | | | | | | | | | | 044° / 136° | 2h 56m | **44°** |

D. Lon	Dep.		D. Lon	Dep.		D. Lon	Dep.		D. Lon	Dep.		D. Lon	Dep.	
Dist.	D. Lat.	Dep.	Dist.	D. Lat.	Dep.	Dist.	D. Lat.	Dep.	Dist.	D. Lat.	Dep.	Dist.	D. Lat.	Dep.
301	216·5	209·1	361	259·7	250·8	421	302·8	292·5	481	346·0	334·1	541	389·2	375·8
302	217·2	209·8	362	260·4	251·5	422	303·6	293·1	482	346·7	334·8	542	389·9	376·5
303	218·0	210·5	363	261·1	252·2	423	304·3	293·8	483	347·4	335·5	543	390·6	377·2
304	218·7	211·2	364	261·8	252·9	424	305·0	294·5	484	348·2	336·2	544	391·3	377·9
305	219·4	211·9	365	262·6	253·6	425	305·7	295·2	485	348·9	336·9	545	392·0	378·6
306	220·1	212·6	366	263·3	254·2	426	306·4	295·9	486	349·6	337·6	546	392·8	379·3
307	220·8	213·3	367	264·0	254·9	427	307·2	296·6	487	350·3	338·3	547	393·5	380·0
308	221·6	214·0	368	264·7	255·6	428	307·9	297·3	488	351·0	339·0	548	394·2	380·7
309	222·3	214·6	369	265·4	256·3	429	308·6	298·0	489	351·7	339·7	549	394·9	381·4
310	223·0	215·3	370	266·2	257·0	430	309·3	298·7	490	352·5	340·4	550	395·6	382·1
311	223·7	216·0	371	266·9	257·7	431	310·0	299·4	491	353·2	341·1	551	396·4	382·8
312	224·4	216·7	372	267·6	258·4	432	310·8	300·1	492	353·9	341·8	552	397·1	383·5
313	225·2	217·4	373	268·3	259·1	433	311·5	300·8	493	354·6	342·5	553	397·8	384·1
314	225·9	218·1	374	269·0	259·8	434	312·2	301·5	494	355·4	343·2	554	398·5	384·8
315	226·6	218·8	375	269·8	260·5	435	312·9	302·2	495	356·1	343·9	555	399·2	385·5
316	227·3	219·5	376	270·5	261·2	436	313·6	302·9	496	356·8	344·6	556	400·0	386·2
317	228·0	220·2	377	271·2	261·9	437	314·4	303·6	497	357·5	345·2	557	400·7	386·9
318	228·8	220·9	378	271·9	262·6	438	315·1	304·3	498	358·2	345·9	558	401·4	387·6
319	229·5	221·6	379	272·6	263·3	439	315·8	305·0	499	359·0	346·6	559	402·1	388·3
320	230·2	222·3	380	273·3	264·0	440	316·6	305·6	500	359·7	347·3	560	402·8	389·0
321	230·9	223·0	381	274·1	264·7	441	317·2	306·3	501	360·4	348·0	561	403·5	389·7
322	231·6	223·7	382	274·8	265·4	442	317·9	307·0	502	361·1	348·7	562	404·3	390·4
323	232·3	224·4	383	275·5	266·1	443	318·7	307·7	503	361·8	349·4	563	405·0	391·1
324	233·1	225·1	384	276·2	266·7	444	319·4	308·4	504	362·5	350·1	564	405·7	391·8
325	233·8	225·8	385	276·9	267·4	445	320·1	309·1	505	363·3	350·8	565	406·4	392·5
326	234·5	226·5	386	277·7	268·1	446	320·8	309·8	506	364·0	351·5	566	407·1	393·2
327	235·2	227·2	387	278·4	268·8	447	321·5	310·5	507	364·7	352·2	567	407·9	393·9
328	235·9	227·8	388	279·1	269·5	448	322·3	311·2	508	365·4	352·9	568	408·6	394·6
329	236·7	228·5	389	279·8	270·2	449	323·0	311·9	509	366·1	353·6	569	409·3	395·3
330	237·4	229·2	390	280·5	270·9	450	323·7	312·6	510	366·9	354·3	570	410·0	396·0
331	238·1	229·9	391	281·3	271·6	451	324·4	313·3	511	367·6	355·0	571	410·7	396·6
332	238·8	230·6	392	282·0	272·3	452	325·1	314·0	512	368·3	355·7	572	411·5	397·3
333	239·5	231·3	393	282·7	273·0	453	325·9	314·7	513	369·0	356·4	573	412·2	398·0
334	240·3	232·0	394	283·4	273·7	454	326·6	315·4	514	369·7	357·1	574	412·9	398·7
335	241·0	232·7	395	284·1	274·4	455	327·3	316·1	515	370·5	357·7	575	413·6	399·4
336	241·7	233·4	396	284·9	275·1	456	328·0	316·8	516	371·2	358·4	576	414·3	400·1
337	242·4	234·1	397	285·6	275·8	457	328·7	317·5	517	371·9	359·1	577	415·1	400·8
338	243·1	234·8	398	286·3	276·5	458	329·5	318·2	518	372·6	359·8	578	415·8	401·5
339	243·9	235·5	399	287·0	277·2	459	330·2	318·8	519	373·3	360·5	579	416·5	402·2
340	244·6	236·2	400	287·7	277·9	460	330·9	319·5	520	374·1	361·2	580	417·2	402·9
341	245·3	236·9	401	288·5	278·6	461	331·6	320·2	521	374·8	361·9	581	417·9	403·6
342	246·0	237·6	402	289·2	279·3	462	332·3	320·9	522	375·5	362·6	582	418·7	404·3
343	246·7	238·3	403	289·9	279·9	463	333·1	321·6	523	376·2	363·3	583	419·4	405·0
344	247·5	239·0	404	290·6	280·6	464	333·8	322·3	524	376·9	364·0	584	420·1	405·7
345	248·2	239·7	405	291·3	281·3	465	334·5	323·0	525	377·7	364·7	585	420·8	406·4
346	248·9	240·4	406	292·1	282·0	466	335·2	323·7	526	378·4	365·4	586	421·5	407·1
347	249·6	241·0	407	292·8	282·7	467	335·9	324·4	527	379·1	366·1	587	422·3	407·8
348	250·3	241·7	408	293·5	283·4	468	336·7	325·1	528	379·8	366·8	588	423·0	408·5
349	251·0	242·4	409	294·2	284·1	469	337·4	325·8	529	380·5	367·5	589	423·7	409·2
350	251·8	243·1	410	294·9	284·8	470	338·1	326·5	530	381·3	368·2	590	424·4	409·8
351	252·5	243·8	411	295·6	285·5	471	338·8	327·2	531	382·0	368·9	591	425·1	410·5
352	253·2	244·5	412	296·4	286·2	472	339·5	327·9	532	382·7	369·6	592	425·8	411·2
353	253·9	245·2	413	297·1	286·9	473	340·2	328·6	533	383·4	370·3	593	426·6	411·9
354	254·6	245·9	414	297·8	287·6	474	341·0	329·3	534	384·1	370·9	594	427·3	412·6
355	255·4	246·6	415	298·5	288·3	475	341·7	330·0	535	384·8	371·6	595	428·0	413·3
356	256·1	247·3	416	299·2	289·0	476	342·4	330·7	536	385·6	372·3	596	428·7	414·0
357	256·8	248·0	417	300·0	289·7	477	343·1	331·4	537	386·3	373·0	597	429·4	414·7
358	257·5	248·7	418	300·7	290·4	478	343·8	332·0	538	387·0	373·7	598	430·2	415·4
359	258·2	249·4	419	301·4	291·1	479	344·6	332·7	539	387·7	374·4	599	430·9	416·1
360	259·0	250·1	420	302·1	291·8	480	345·3	333·4	540	388·4	375·1	600	431·6	416·8
Dist.	Dep.	D. Lat.	Dist.	Dep.	D. Lat.	Dist.	Dep.	D. Lat.	Dist.	Dep.	D. Lat.	Dist.	Dep.	D. Lat.
D. Lon		Dep.	D. Lon		Dep.	D. Lon		Dep.	D. Lon		Dep.	D. Lon		Dep.

| 314° / 226° | 46 Degrees | 046° / 134° | 3h 04m | **46°** |

TRAVERSE TABLE
45 Degrees

D. Lon	Dep.		D. Lon	Dep.		D. Lon	Dep.		D. Lon	Dep.		D. Lon	Dep.	
Dist.	D. Lat.	Dep.	Dist.	D. Lat.	Dep.	Dist.	D. Lat.	Dep.	Dist.	D. Lat.	Dep.	Dist.	D. Lat.	Dep.
1	00·7	00·7	61	43·1	43·1	121	85·6	85·6	181	128·0	128·0	241	170·4	170·4
2	01·4	01·4	62	43·8	43·8	122	86·3	86·3	182	128·7	128·7	242	171·1	171·1
3	02·1	02·1	63	44·5	44·5	123	87·0	87·0	183	129·4	129·4	243	171·8	171·8
4	02·8	02·8	64	45·3	45·3	124	87·7	87·7	184	130·1	130·1	244	172·5	172·5
5	03·5	03·5	65	46·0	46·0	125	88·4	88·4	185	130·8	130·8	245	173·2	173·2
6	04·2	04·2	66	46·7	46·7	126	89·1	89·1	186	131·5	131·5	246	173·9	173·9
7	04·9	04·9	67	47·4	47·4	127	89·8	89·8	187	132·2	132·2	247	174·7	174·7
8	05·7	05·7	68	48·1	48·1	128	90·5	90·5	188	132·9	132·9	248	175·4	175·4
9	06·4	06·4	69	48·8	48·8	129	91·2	91·2	189	133·6	133·6	249	176·1	176·1
10	07·1	07·1	70	49·5	49·5	130	91·9	91·9	190	134·3	134·3	250	176·8	176·8
11	07·8	07·8	71	50·2	50·2	131	92·6	92·6	191	135·1	135·1	251	177·5	177·5
12	08·5	08·5	72	50·9	50·9	132	93·3	93·3	192	135·8	135·8	252	178·2	178·2
13	09·2	09·2	73	51·6	51·6	133	94·0	94·0	193	136·5	136·5	253	178·9	178·9
14	09·9	09·9	74	52·3	52·3	134	94·8	94·8	194	137·2	137·2	254	179·6	179·6
15	10·6	10·6	75	53·0	53·0	135	95·5	95·5	195	137·9	137·9	255	180·3	180·3
16	11·3	11·3	76	53·7	53·7	136	96·2	96·2	196	138·6	138·6	256	181·0	181·0
17	12·0	12·0	77	54·4	54·4	137	96·9	96·9	197	139·3	139·3	257	181·7	181·7
18	12·7	12·7	78	55·2	55·2	138	97·6	97·6	198	140·0	140·0	258	182·4	182·4
19	13·4	13·4	79	55·9	55·9	139	98·3	98·3	199	140·7	140·7	259	183·1	183·1
20	14·1	14·1	80	56·6	56·6	140	99·0	99·0	200	141·4	141·4	260	183·8	183·8
21	14·8	14·8	81	57·3	57·3	141	99·7	99·7	201	142·1	142·1	261	184·6	184·6
22	15·6	15·6	82	58·0	58·0	142	100·4	100·4	202	142·8	142·8	262	185·3	185·3
23	16·3	16·3	83	58·7	58·7	143	101·1	101·1	203	143·5	143·5	263	186·0	186·0
24	17·0	17·0	84	59·4	59·4	144	101·8	101·8	204	144·2	144·2	264	186·7	186·7
25	17·7	17·7	85	60·1	60·1	145	102·5	102·5	205	145·0	145·0	265	187·4	187·4
26	18·4	18·4	86	60·8	60·8	146	103·2	103·2	206	145·7	145·7	266	188·1	188·1
27	19·1	19·1	87	61·5	61·5	147	103·9	103·9	207	146·4	146·4	267	188·8	188·8
28	19·8	19·8	88	62·2	62·2	148	104·7	104·7	208	147·1	147·1	268	189·5	189·5
29	20·5	20·5	89	62·9	62·9	149	105·4	105·4	209	147·8	147·8	269	190·2	190·2
30	21·2	21·2	90	63·6	63·6	150	106·1	106·1	210	148·5	148·5	270	190·9	190·9
31	21·9	21·9	91	64·3	64·3	151	106·8	106·8	211	149·2	149·2	271	191·6	191·6
32	22·6	22·6	92	65·1	65·1	152	107·5	107·5	212	149·9	149·9	272	192·3	192·3
33	23·3	23·3	93	65·8	65·8	153	108·2	108·2	213	150·6	150·6	273	193·0	193·0
34	24·0	24·0	94	66·5	66·5	154	108·9	108·9	214	151·3	151·3	274	193·7	193·7
35	24·7	24·7	95	67·2	67·2	155	109·6	109·6	215	152·0	152·0	275	194·5	194·5
36	25·5	25·5	96	67·9	67·9	156	110·3	110·3	216	152·7	152·7	276	195·2	195·2
37	26·2	26·2	97	68·6	68·6	157	111·0	111·0	217	153·4	153·4	277	195·9	195·9
38	26·9	26·9	98	69·3	69·3	158	111·7	111·7	218	154·1	154·1	278	196·6	196·6
39	27·6	27·6	99	70·0	70·0	159	112·4	112·4	219	154·9	154·9	279	197·3	197·3
40	28·3	28·3	100	70·7	70·7	160	113·1	113·1	220	155·6	155·6	280	198·0	198·0
41	29·0	29·0	101	71·4	71·4	161	113·8	113·8	221	156·3	156·3	281	198·7	198·7
42	29·7	29·7	102	72·1	72·1	162	114·5	114·5	222	157·0	157·0	282	199·4	199·4
43	30·4	30·4	103	72·8	72·8	163	115·3	115·3	223	157·7	157·7	283	200·1	200·1
44	31·1	31·1	104	73·5	73·5	164	116·0	116·0	224	158·4	158·4	284	200·8	200·8
45	31·8	31·8	1C5	74·2	74·2	165	116·7	116·7	225	159·1	159·1	285	201·5	201·5
46	32·5	32·5	106	75·0	75·0	166	117·4	117·4	226	159·8	159·8	286	202·2	202·2
47	33·2	33·2	107	75·7	75·7	167	118·1	118·1	227	160·5	160·5	287	202·9	202·9
48	33·9	33·9	108	76·4	76·4	168	118·8	118·8	228	161·2	161·2	288	203·6	203·6
49	34·6	34·6	109	77·1	77·1	169	119·5	119·5	229	161·9	161·9	289	204·3	204·3
50	35·4	35·4	110	77·8	77·8	170	120·2	120·2	230	162·6	162·6	290	205·1	205·1
51	36·1	36·1	111	78·5	78·5	171	120·9	120·9	231	163·3	163·3	291	205·8	205·8
52	36·8	36·8	112	79·2	79·2	172	121·6	121·6	232	164·0	164·0	292	206·5	206·5
53	37·5	37·5	113	79·9	79·9	173	122·3	122·3	233	164·8	164·8	293	207·2	207·2
54	38·2	38·2	114	80·6	80·6	174	123·0	123·0	234	165·5	165·5	294	207·9	207·9
55	38·9	38·9	115	81·3	81·3	175	123·7	123·7	235	166·2	166·2	295	208·6	208·6
56	39·6	39·6	116	82·0	82·0	176	124·4	124·4	236	166·9	166·9	296	209·3	209·3
57	40·3	40·3	117	82·7	82·7	177	125·2	125·2	237	167·6	167·6	297	210·0	210·0
58	41·0	41·0	118	83·4	83·4	178	125·9	125·9	238	168·3	168·3	298	210·7	210·7
59	41·7	41·7	119	84·1	84·1	179	126·6	126·6	239	169·0	169·0	299	211·4	211·4
60	42·4	42·4	120	84·9	84·9	180	127·3	127·3	240	169·7	169·7	300	212·1	212·1
Dist.	Dep.	D. Lat.	Dist.	Dep.	D. Lat.	Dist.	Dep.	D. Lat.	Dist.	Dep.	D. Lat.	Dist.	Dep.	D. Lat
D. Lon		Dep.	D. Lon		Dep.	D. Lon		Dep.	D. Lon		Dep.	D. Lon		Dep.

TRAVERSE TABLE
45 Degrees

315° / 225°   045° / 135°   3h 00m   **45°**

D. Lon Dep. Dist.	D. Lat.	Dep.	Dist.	D. Lat.	Dep.	Dist.	D. Lat.	Dep.	Dist.	D. Lat.	Dep.	Dist.	D. Lat.	Dep.
301	212·8	212·8	361	255·3	255·3	421	297·7	297·7	481	340·1	340·1	541	382·5	382·5
302	213·5	213·5	362	256·0	256·0	422	298·4	298·4	482	340·8	340·8	542	383·3	383·3
303	214·3	214·3	363	256·7	256·7	423	299·1	299·1	483	341·5	341·5	543	384·0	384·0
304	215·0	215·0	364	257·4	257·4	424	299·8	299·8	484	342·2	342·2	544	384·7	384·7
305	215·7	215·7	365	258·1	258·1	425	300·5	300·5	485	342·9	342·9	545	385·4	385·4
306	216·4	216·4	366	258·8	258·8	426	301·2	301·2	486	343·7	343·7	546	386·1	386·1
307	217·1	217·1	367	259·5	259·5	427	301·9	301·9	487	344·4	344·4	547	386·8	386·8
308	217·8	217·8	368	260·2	260·2	428	302·6	302·6	488	345·1	345·1	548	387·5	387·5
309	218·5	218·5	369	260·9	260·9	429	303·3	303·3	489	345·8	345·8	549	388·2	388·2
310	219·2	219·2	370	261·6	261·6	430	304·1	304·1	490	346·5	346·5	550	388·9	388·9
311	219·9	219·9	371	262·3	262·3	431	304·8	304·8	491	347·2	347·2	551	389·6	389·6
312	220·6	220·6	372	263·0	263·0	432	305·5	305·5	492	347·9	347·9	552	390·3	390·3
313	221·3	221·3	373	263·8	263·8	433	306·2	306·2	493	348·6	348·6	553	391·0	391·0
314	222·0	222·0	374	264·5	264·5	434	306·9	306·9	494	349·3	349·3	554	391·7	391·7
315	222·7	222·7	375	265·2	265·2	435	307·6	307·6	495	350·0	350·0	555	392·4	392·4
316	223·4	223·4	376	265·9	265·9	436	308·3	308·3	496	350·7	350·7	556	393·2	393·2
317	224·2	224·2	377	266·6	266·6	437	309·0	309·0	497	351·4	351·4	557	393·9	393·9
318	224·9	224·9	378	267·3	267·3	438	309·7	309·7	498	352·1	352·1	558	394·6	394·6
319	225·6	225·6	379	268·0	268·0	439	310·4	310·4	499	352·8	352·8	559	395·3	395·3
320	226·3	226·3	380	268·7	268·7	440	311·1	311·1	500	353·6	353·6	560	396·0	396·0
321	227·0	227·0	381	269·4	269·4	441	311·8	311·8	501	354·3	354·3	561	396·7	396·7
322	227·7	227·7	382	270·1	270·1	442	312·5	312·5	502	355·0	355·0	562	397·4	397·4
323	228·4	228·4	383	270·8	270·8	443	313·2	313·2	503	355·7	355·7	563	398·1	398·1
324	229·1	229·1	384	271·5	271·5	444	314·0	314·0	504	356·4	356·4	564	398·8	398·8
325	229·8	229·8	385	272·2	272·2	445	314·7	314·7	505	357·1	357·1	565	399·5	399·5
326	230·5	230·5	386	272·9	272·9	446	315·4	315·4	506	357·8	357·8	566	400·2	400·2
327	231·2	231·2	387	273·7	273·7	447	316·1	316·1	507	358·5	358·5	567	400·9	400·9
328	231·9	231·9	388	274·4	274·4	448	316·8	316·8	508	359·2	359·2	568	401·6	401·6
329	232·6	232·6	389	275·1	275·1	449	317·5	317·5	509	359·9	359·9	569	402·3	402·3
330	233·3	233·3	390	275·8	275·8	450	318·2	318·2	510	360·6	360·6	570	403·1	403·1
331	234·1	234·1	391	276·5	276·5	451	318·9	318·9	511	361·3	361·3	571	403·8	403·8
332	234·8	234·8	392	277·2	277·2	452	319·6	319·6	512	362·0	362·0	572	404·5	404·5
333	235·5	235·5	393	277·9	277·9	453	320·3	320·3	513	362·7	362·7	573	405·2	405·2
334	236·2	236·2	394	278·6	278·6	454	321·0	321·0	514	363·5	363·5	574	405·9	405·9
335	236·9	236·9	395	279·3	279·3	455	321·7	321·7	515	364·2	364·2	575	406·6	406·6
336	237·6	237·6	396	280·0	280·0	456	322·4	322·4	516	364·9	364·9	576	407·3	407·3
337	238·3	238·3	397	280·7	280·7	457	323·1	323·1	517	365·6	365·6	577	408·0	408·0
338	239·0	239·0	398	281·4	281·4	458	323·9	323·9	518	366·3	366·3	578	408·7	408·7
339	239·7	239·7	399	282·1	282·1	459	324·6	324·6	519	367·0	367·0	579	409·4	409·4
340	240·4	240·4	400	282·8	282·8	460	325·3	325·3	520	367·7	367·7	580	410·1	410·1
341	241·1	241·1	401	283·5	283·5	461	326·0	326·0	521	368·4	368·4	581	410·8	410·8
342	241·8	241·8	402	284·3	284·3	462	326·7	326·7	522	369·1	369·1	582	411·5	411·5
343	242·5	242·5	403	285·0	285·0	463	327·4	327·4	523	369·8	369·8	583	412·2	412·2
344	243·2	243·2	404	285·7	285·7	464	328·1	328·1	524	370·5	370·5	584	413·0	413·0
345	244·0	244·0	405	286·4	286·4	465	328·8	328·8	525	371·2	371·2	585	413·7	413·7
346	244·7	244·7	406	287·1	287·1	466	329·5	329·5	526	371·9	371·9	586	414·4	414·4
347	245·4	245·4	407	287·8	287·8	467	330·2	330·2	527	372·6	372·6	587	415·1	415·1
348	246·1	246·1	408	288·5	288·5	468	330·9	330·9	528	373·4	373·4	588	415·8	415·8
349	246·8	246·8	409	289·2	289·2	469	331·6	331·6	529	374·1	374·1	589	416·5	416·5
350	247·5	247·5	410	289·9	289·9	470	332·3	332·3	530	374·8	374·8	590	417·2	417·2
351	248·2	248·2	411	290·6	290·6	471	333·0	333·0	531	375·5	375·5	591	417·9	417·9
352	248·9	248·9	412	291·3	291·3	472	333·8	333·8	532	376·2	376·2	592	418·6	418·6
353	249·6	249·6	413	292·0	292·0	473	334·5	334·5	533	376·9	376·9	593	419·3	419·3
354	250·3	250·3	414	292·7	292·7	474	335·2	335·2	534	377·6	377·6	594	420·0	420·0
355	251·0	251·0	415	293·4	293·4	475	335·9	335·9	535	378·3	378·3	595	420·7	420·7
356	251·7	251·7	416	294·2	294·2	476	336·6	336·6	536	379·0	379·0	596	421·4	421·4
357	252·4	252·4	417	294·9	294·9	477	337·3	337·3	537	379·7	379·7	597	422·1	422·1
358	253·1	253·1	418	295·6	295·6	478	338·0	338·0	538	380·4	380·4	598	422·8	422·8
359	253·9	253·9	419	296·3	296·3	479	338·7	338·7	539	381·1	381·1	599	423·6	423·6
360	254·6	254·6	420	297·0	297·0	480	339·4	339·4	540	381·8	381·8	600	424·3	424·3

| Dist. | Dep. | D. Lat. | Dist. | Dep. | D. Lat. | Dist. | Dep. | D. Lat. | Dist. | Dep. | D. Lat. | Dist. | Dep. | D. Lat. |

D. Lon Dep.

315° / 225°   **45 Degrees**   045° / 135°   3h 00m   **45°**

| | | | | | Terrestrial Spheroid | | **MERIDIONAL PARTS** | | Compression $\frac{1}{293.465}$ | | | |

M	0°	1°	2°	3°	4°	5°	6°	7°	8°	9°	10°	M
0	0·00	59·60	119·21	178·86	238·56	298·34	358·22	418·20	478·31	538·58	599·01	0
1	0·99	60·59	120·20	179·85	239·56	299·34	359·21	419·20	479·31	539·58	600·02	1
2	1·99	61·58	121·20	180·85	240·55	300·34	360·21	420·20	480·32	540·59	601·03	2
3	2·98	62·58	122·19	181·84	241·55	301·33	361·21	421·20	481·32	541·59	602·04	3
4	3·97	63·57	123·18	182·84	242·55	302·33	362·21	422·20	482·32	542·60	603·04	4
5	4·97	64·56	124·18	183·83	243·54	303·33	363·21	423·20	483·33	543·60	604·05	5
6	5·96	65·56	125·17	184·82	244·54	304·32	364·21	424·20	484·33	544·61	605·06	6
7	6·95	66·55	126·17	185·82	245·53	305·32	365·21	425·20	485·33	545·62	606·07	7
8	7·95	67·54	127·16	186·81	246·53	306·32	366·21	426·20	486·34	546·62	607·08	8
9	8·94	68·54	128·15	187·81	247·53	307·32	367·20	427·21	487·34	547·63	608·09	9
10	9·93	69·53	129·15	188·80	248·52	308·31	368·20	428·21	488·34	548·64	609·10	10
11	10·92	70·52	130·14	189·80	249·52	309·31	369·20	429·21	489·35	549·64	610·11	11
12	11·92	71·52	131·14	190·79	250·51	310·31	370·20	430·21	490·35	550·65	611·12	12
13	12·91	72·51	132·13	191·79	251·51	311·31	371·20	431·21	491·36	551·65	612·13	13
14	13·90	73·50	133·12	192·78	252·50	312·30	372·20	432·21	492·36	552·66	613·14	14
15	14·90	74·50	134·12	193·78	253·50	313·30	373·20	433·21	493·36	553·67	614·15	15
16	15·89	75·49	135·11	194·77	254·50	314·30	374·20	434·21	494·37	554·67	615·15	16
17	16·88	76·48	136·11	195·77	255·49	315·30	375·20	435·22	495·37	555·68	616·16	17
18	17·88	77·48	137·10	196·76	256·49	316·29	376·20	436·22	496·37	556·69	617·17	18
19	18·87	78·47	138·09	197·76	257·48	317·29	377·20	437·22	497·38	557·69	618·18	19
20	19·86	79·46	139·09	198·75	258·48	318·29	378·20	438·22	498·38	558·70	619·19	20
21	20·86	80·46	140·08	199·75	259·48	319·29	379·20	439·22	499·39	559·71	620·20	21
22	21·85	81·45	141·08	200·74	260·47	320·28	380·19	440·22	500·39	560·71	621·21	22
23	22·84	82·44	142·07	201·74	261·47	321·28	381·19	441·23	501·39	561·72	622·22	23
24	23·84	83·44	143·06	202·73	262·46	322·28	382·19	442·23	502·40	562·73	623·23	24
25	24·83	84·43	144·06	203·73	263·46	323·28	383·19	443·23	503·40	563·73	624·24	25
26	25·82	85·42	145·05	204·72	264·46	324·27	384·19	444·23	504·41	564·74	625·25	26
27	26·82	86·42	146·05	205·72	265·45	325·27	385·19	445·23	505·41	565·75	626·26	27
28	27·81	87·41	147·04	206·71	266·45	326·27	386·19	446·23	506·41	566·75	627·27	28
29	28·80	88·40	148·03	207·71	267·45	327·27	387·19	447·24	507·42	567·76	628·28	29
30	29·80	89·40	149·03	208·70	268·44	328·27	388·19	448·24	508·42	568·77	629·29	30
31	30·79	90·39	150·02	209·70	269·44	329·26	389·19	449·24	509·43	569·78	630·30	31
32	31·78	91·39	151·02	210·69	270·43	330·26	390·19	450·24	510·43	570·78	631·31	32
33	32·78	92·38	152·01	211·69	271·43	331·26	391·19	451·24	511·44	571·79	632·33	33
34	33·77	93·37	153·00	212·68	272·43	332·26	392·19	452·25	512·44	572·80	633·34	34
35	34·76	94·37	154·00	213·68	273·42	333·26	393·19	453·25	513·45	573·81	634·35	35
36	35·76	95·36	154·99	214·67	274·42	334·25	394·19	454·25	514·45	574·81	635·36	36
37	36·75	96·35	155·99	215·67	275·42	335·25	395·19	455·25	515·45	575·82	636·37	37
38	37·74	97·35	156·98	216·66	276·41	336·25	396·19	456·25	516·46	576·83	637·38	38
39	38·74	98·34	157·97	217·66	277·41	337·25	397·19	457·25	517·46	577·84	638·39	39
40	39·73	99·33	158·97	218·65	278·41	338·25	398·19	458·26	518·47	578·84	639·40	40
41	40·72	100·33	159·96	219·65	279·40	339·24	399·19	459·26	519·47	579·85	640·41	41
42	41·72	101·32	160·96	220·64	280·40	340·24	400·19	460·26	520·48	580·86	641·42	42
43	42·71	102·31	161·95	221·64	281·40	341·24	401·19	461·26	521·48	581·87	642·43	43
44	43·70	103·31	162·95	222·64	282·39	342·24	402·19	462·27	522·49	582·87	643·44	44
45	44·70	104·30	163·94	223·63	283·39	343·24	403·19	463·27	523·49	583·88	644·46	45
46	45·69	105·30	164·94	224·63	284·39	344·23	404·19	464·27	524·50	584·89	645·47	46
47	46·68	106·29	165·93	225·62	285·38	345·23	405·19	465·27	525·50	585·90	646·48	47
48	47·68	107·28	166·92	226·62	286·38	346·23	406·19	466·28	526·51	586·91	647·49	48
49	48·67	108·28	167·92	227·61	287·38	347·23	407·19	467·28	527·51	587·91	648·50	49
50	49·66	109·27	168·91	228·61	288·37	348·23	408·19	468·28	528·52	588·92	649·51	50
51	50·66	110·26	169·91	229·60	289·37	349·23	409·19	469·29	529·52	589·93	650·52	51
52	51·65	111·26	170·90	230·60	290·37	350·23	410·19	470·29	530·53	590·94	651·53	52
53	52·64	112·25	171·90	231·59	291·36	351·22	411·19	471·29	531·54	591·95	652·55	53
54	53·64	113·24	172·89	232·59	292·36	352·22	412·19	472·29	532·54	592·96	653·56	54
55	54·63	114·24	173·88	233·59	293·36	353·22	413·19	473·30	533·55	593·96	654·57	55
56	55·62	115·23	174·88	234·58	294·35	354·22	414·19	474·30	534·55	594·97	655·58	56
57	56·62	116·23	175·87	235·58	295·35	355·22	415·20	475·30	535·56	595·98	656·59	57
58	57·61	117·22	176·87	236·57	296·35	356·22	416·20	476·30	536·57	596·99	657·60	58
59	58·60	118·21	177·86	237·57	297·35	357·22	417·20	477·31	537·57	598·00	658·62	59
60	59·60	119·21	178·86	238·56	298·34	358·22	418·20	478·31	538·58	599·01	659·63	60
M	0°	1°	2°	3°	4°	5°	6°	7°	8°	9°	10°	M

Terrestrial Spheroid	**MERIDIONAL PARTS**	*Compression* $\frac{1}{293.465}$

M	11°	12°	13°	14°	15°	16°	17°	18°	19°	20°	M
0	659·63	720·46	781·52	842·83	904·41	966·28	1028·46	1090·99	1153·87	1217·14	0
1	660·64	721·47	782·54	843·85	905·43	967·31	1029·50	1092·03	1154·92	1218·19	1
2	661·65	722·49	783·56	844·88	906·46	968·35	1030·54	1093·08	1155·97	1219·25	2
3	662·67	723·51	784·58	845·90	907·49	969·38	1031·58	1094·12	1157·02	1220·31	3
4	663·68	724·52	785·60	846·92	908·52	970·41	1032·62	1095·17	1158·08	1221·37	4
5	664·69	725·54	786·62	847·95	909·55	971·45	1033·66	1096·21	1159·13	1222·43	5
6	665·70	726·55	787·64	848·98	910·58	972·48	1034·70	1097·26	1160·18	1223·49	6
7	666·72	727·57	788·66	850·00	911·61	973·52	1035·74	1098·30	1161·23	1224·54	7
8	667·73	728·59	789·68	851·02	912·64	974·55	1036·78	1099·35	1162·28	1225·60	8
9	668·74	729·60	790·70	852·05	913·67	975·59	1037·82	1100·40	1163·34	1226·66	9
10	669·75	730·62	791·72	853·07	914·70	976·62	1038·86	1101·44	1164·39	1227·72	10
11	670·77	731·64	792·74	854·10	915·73	977·66	1039·90	1102·49	1165·44	1228·78	11
12	671·78	732·65	793·76	855·12	916·76	978·69	1040·94	1103·53	1166·49	1229·84	12
13	672·79	733·67	794·78	856·14	917·79	979·72	1041·98	1104·58	1167·55	1230·90	13
14	673·80	734·69	795·80	857·17	918·82	980·76	1043·02	1105·63	1168·60	1231·96	14
15	674·82	735·70	796·82	858·19	919·85	981·79	1044·06	1106·67	1169·65	1233·02	15
16	675·83	736·72	797·84	859·22	920·88	982·83	1045·10	1107·72	1170·70	1234·08	16
17	676·84	737·74	798·86	860·25	921·91	983·86	1046·14	1108·77	1171·76	1235·14	17
18	677·86	738·75	799·88	861·27	922·94	984·90	1047·18	1109·81	1172·81	1236·20	18
19	678·87	739·77	800·90	862·30	923·97	985·93	1048·23	1110·86	1173·86	1237·26	19
20	679·88	740·79	801·93	863·32	925·00	986·97	1049·27	1111·91	1174·92	1238·32	20
21	680·90	741·80	802·95	864·35	926·03	988·01	1050·31	1112·95	1175·97	1239·38	21
22	681·91	742·82	803·97	865·37	927·06	989·04	1051·35	1114·00	1177·02	1240·44	22
23	682·92	743·84	804·99	866·40	928·09	990·08	1052·39	1115·05	1178·08	1241·50	23
24	683·94	744·85	806·01	867·42	929·12	991·11	1053·43	1116·10	1179·13	1242·56	24
25	684·95	745·87	807·03	868·45	930·15	992·15	1054·47	1117·14	1180·18	1243·62	25
26	685·96	746·89	808·05	869·48	931·18	993·19	1055·51	1118·19	1181·24	1244·68	26
27	686·98	747·91	809·07	870·50	932·21	994·22	1056·56	1119·24	1182·29	1245·74	27
28	687·99	748·92	810·10	871·53	933·24	995·26	1057·60	1120·29	1183·35	1246·80	28
29	689·00	749·94	811·12	872·55	934·27	996·29	1058·64	1121·33	1184·40	1247·86	29
30	690·02	750·96	812·14	873·58	935·30	997·33	1059·68	1122·38	1185·45	1248·92	30
31	691·03	751·98	813·16	874·61	936·33	998·37	1060·72	1123·43	1186·51	1249·98	31
32	692·04	752·99	814·18	875·63	937·37	999·40	1061·77	1124·48	1187·56	1251·04	32
33	693·06	754·01	815·21	876·66	938·40	1000·44	1062·81	1125·53	1188·62	1252·11	33
34	694·07	755·03	816·23	877·69	939·43	1001·48	1063·85	1126·58	1189·67	1253·17	34
35	695·09	756·05	817·25	878·71	940·46	1002·51	1064·89	1127·62	1190·73	1254·23	35
36	696·10	757·07	818·27	879·74	941·49	1003·55	1065·94	1128·67	1191·78	1255·29	36
37	697·12	758·08	819·29	880·77	942·52	1004·59	1066·98	1129·72	1192·84	1256·35	37
38	698·13	759·10	820·32	881·79	943·56	1005·62	1068·02	1130·77	1193·89	1257·41	38
39	699·14	760·12	821·34	882·82	944·59	1006·66	1069·06	1131·82	1194·95	1258·48	39
40	700·16	761·14	822·36	883·85	945·62	1007·70	1070·11	1132·87	1196·00	1259·54	40
41	701·17	762·16	823·38	884·88	946·65	1008·74	1071·15	1133·92	1197·05	1260·60	41
42	702·19	763·18	824·41	885·90	947·68	1009·77	1072·19	1134·97	1198·12	1261·66	42
43	703·20	764·19	825·43	886·93	948·72	1010·81	1073·24	1136·02	1199·17	1262·73	43
44	704·22	765·21	826·45	887·96	949·75	1011·85	1074·28	1137·07	1200·23	1263·79	44
45	705·23	766·23	827·47	888·99	950·78	1012·89	1075·32	1138·11	1201·28	1264·85	45
46	706·25	767·25	828·50	890·01	951·81	1013·92	1076·37	1139·16	1202·34	1265·92	46
47	707·26	768·27	829·52	891·04	952·85	1014·96	1077·41	1140·21	1203·40	1266·98	47
48	708·28	769·29	830·54	892·07	953·88	1016·00	1078·46	1141·26	1204·45	1268·04	48
49	709·29	770·31	831·57	893·10	954·91	1017·04	1079·50	1142·31	1205·51	1269·11	49
50	710·31	771·32	832·59	894·12	955·94	1018·08	1080·54	1143·36	1206·57	1270·17	50
51	711·32	772·34	833·61	895·15	956·98	1019·11	1081·59	1144·41	1207·62	1271·23	51
52	712·34	773·36	834·64	896·18	958·01	1020·15	1082·63	1145·46	1208·68	1272·30	52
53	713·35	774·38	835·66	897·21	959·04	1021·19	1083·68	1146·51	1209·74	1273·36	53
54	714·37	775·40	836·68	898·24	960·08	1022·23	1084·72	1147·56	1210·79	1274·43	54
55	715·38	776·42	837·71	899·26	961·11	1023·27	1085·76	1148·62	1211·85	1275·49	55
56	716·40	777·44	838·73	900·29	962·14	1024·31	1086·81	1149·67	1212·91	1276·55	56
57	717·41	778·46	839·76	901·32	963·18	1025·35	1087·85	1150·72	1213·96	1277·62	57
58	718·43	779·48	840·78	902·35	964·21	1026·39	1088·90	1151·77	1215·02	1278·68	58
59	719·44	780·50	841·80	903·38	965·24	1027·42	1089·94	1152·82	1216·08	1279·75	59
60	720·46	781·52	842·83	904·41	966·28	1028·46	1090·99	1153·87	1217·14	1280·81	60
M	11°	12°	13°	14°	15°	16°	17°	18°	19°	20°	M

| | *Terrestrial Spheroid* | | **MERIDIONAL PARTS** | | | | | | *Compression* $\frac{1}{293.465}$ | | |

M	21°	22°	23°	24°	25°	26°	27°	28°	29°	30°	M
0	1280·81	1344·92	1409·49	1474·54	1540·11	1606·21	1672·89	1740·18	1808·09	1876·67	0
1	1281·88	1345·99	1410·57	1475·63	1541·20	1607·32	1674·01	1741·30	1809·23	1877·82	1
2	1282·94	1347·07	1411·65	1476·72	1542·30	1608·43	1675·13	1742·43	1810·37	1878·97	2
3	1284·01	1348·14	1412·73	1477·81	1543·40	1609·53	1676·24	1743·56	1811·50	1880·12	3
4	1285·07	1349·21	1413·81	1478·89	1544·50	1610·64	1677·36	1744·68	1812·64	1881·27	4
5	1286·14	1350·28	1414·89	1479·98	1545·59	1611·75	1678·48	1745·81	1813·78	1882·42	5
6	1287·20	1351·36	1415·97	1481·07	1546·69	1612·86	1679·59	1746·94	1814·92	1883·57	6
7	1288·27	1352·43	1417·05	1482·16	1547·79	1613·96	1680·71	1748·07	1816·06	1884·72	7
8	1289·33	1353·50	1418·13	1483·25	1548·89	1615·07	1681·83	1749·19	1817·20	1885·87	8
9	1290·40	1354·58	1419·21	1484·34	1549·99	1616·18	1682·95	1750·32	1818·34	1887·02	9
10	1291·47	1355·65	1420·30	1485·43	1551·09	1617·29	1684·06	1751·45	1819·47	1888·17	10
11	1292·53	1356·72	1421·38	1486·52	1552·18	1618·39	1685·18	1752·58	1820·61	1889·32	11
12	1293·60	1357·80	1422·46	1487·61	1553·28	1619·50	1686·30	1753·71	1821·75	1890·47	12
13	1294·66	1358·87	1423·54	1488·70	1554·38	1620·61	1687·42	1754·84	1822·89	1891·62	13
14	1295·73	1359·94	1424·62	1489·79	1555·48	1621·72	1688·54	1755·96	1824·03	1892·78	14
15	1296·80	1361·02	1425·70	1490·88	1556·58	1622·83	1689·66	1757·09	1825·17	1893·93	15
16	1297·86	1362·09	1426·79	1491·97	1557·68	1623·94	1690·78	1758·22	1826·31	1895·08	16
17	1298·93	1363·17	1427·87	1493·06	1558·78	1625·05	1691·90	1759·35	1827·45	1896·23	17
18	1300·00	1364·24	1428·95	1494·16	1559·88	1626·16	1693·01	1760·48	1828·59	1897·38	18
19	1301·06	1365·32	1430·03	1495·25	1560·98	1627·27	1694·13	1761·61	1829·74	1898·54	19
20	1302·13	1366·39	1431·12	1496·34	1562·08	1628·38	1695·25	1762·74	1830·88	1899·69	20
21	1303·20	1367·47	1432·20	1497·43	1563·18	1629·49	1696·37	1763·87	1832·02	1900·84	21
22	1304·27	1368·54	1433·28	1498·52	1564·28	1630·60	1697·49	1765·00	1833·16	1901·99	22
23	1305·33	1369·62	1434·37	1499·61	1565·38	1631·71	1698·61	1766·13	1834·30	1903·15	23
24	1306·40	1370·69	1435·45	1500·70	1566·48	1632·82	1699·73	1767·26	1835·44	1904·30	24
25	1307·47	1371·77	1436·53	1501·80	1567·58	1633·93	1700·85	1768·39	1836·58	1905·46	25
26	1308·54	1372·84	1437·62	1502·89	1568·68	1635·04	1701·97	1769·53	1837·73	1906·61	26
27	1309·61	1373·92	1438·70	1503·98	1569·79	1636·15	1703·09	1770·66	1838·87	1907·76	27
28	1310·67	1374·99	1439·78	1505·07	1570·89	1637·26	1704·22	1771·79	1840·01	1908·92	28
29	1311·74	1376·07	1440·87	1506·16	1571·99	1638·37	1705·34	1772·92	1841·15	1910·07	29
30	1312·81	1377·14	1441·95	1507·26	1573·09	1639·48	1706·46	1774·05	1842·30	1911·23	30
31	1313·88	1378·22	1443·04	1508·35	1574·19	1640·59	1707·58	1775·18	1843·44	1912·38	31
32	1314·95	1379·30	1444·12	1509·44	1575·29	1641·70	1708·70	1776·32	1844·58	1913·54	32
33	1316·02	1380·37	1445·20	1510·54	1576·40	1642·82	1709·82	1777·45	1845·73	1914·69	33
34	1317·09	1381·45	1446·29	1511·63	1577·50	1643·93	1710·94	1778·58	1846·87	1915·85	34
35	1318·15	1382·53	1447·37	1512·72	1578·60	1645·04	1712·07	1779·71	1848·01	1917·00	35
36	1319·22	1383·60	1448·46	1513·82	1579·70	1646·15	1713·19	1780·85	1849·16	1918·16	36
37	1320·29	1384·68	1449·54	1514·91	1580·81	1647·26	1714·31	1781·98	1850·30	1919·31	37
38	1321·36	1385·76	1450·63	1516·00	1581·91	1648·38	1715·43	1783·11	1851·45	1920·47	38
39	1322·43	1386·84	1451·72	1517·10	1583·01	1649·49	1716·56	1784·25	1852·59	1921·63	39
40	1323·50	1387·91	1452·80	1518·19	1584·12	1650·60	1717·68	1785·38	1853·74	1922·78	40
41	1324·57	1388·99	1453·89	1519·29	1585·22	1651·72	1718·80	1786·51	1854·88	1923·94	41
42	1325·64	1390·07	1454·97	1520·38	1586·32	1652·83	1719·93	1787·65	1856·03	1925·10	42
43	1326·71	1391·15	1456·06	1521·48	1587·43	1653·94	1721·05	1788·78	1857·17	1926·25	43
44	1327·78	1392·22	1457·14	1522·57	1588·53	1655·06	1722·17	1789·92	1858·32	1927·41	44
45	1328·85	1393·30	1458·23	1523·67	1589·63	1656·17	1723·30	1791·05	1859·46	1928·57	45
46	1329·92	1394·38	1459·32	1524·76	1590·74	1657·28	1724·42	1792·19	1860·61	1929·73	46
47	1330·99	1395·46	1460·40	1525·86	1591·84	1658·40	1725·54	1793·32	1861·76	1930·89	47
48	1332·06	1396·54	1461·49	1526·95	1592·95	1659·51	1726·67	1794·46	1862·90	1932·04	48
49	1333·13	1397·61	1462·58	1528·05	1594·05	1660·63	1727·79	1795·59	1864·05	1933·20	49
50	1334·20	1398·69	1463·66	1529·14	1595·16	1661·74	1728·92	1796·73	1865·20	1934·36	50
51	1335·28	1399·77	1464·75	1530·24	1596·26	1662·86	1730·04	1797·86	1866·34	1935·52	51
52	1336·35	1400·85	1465·84	1531·33	1597·37	1663·97	1731·17	1799·00	1867·49	1936·68	52
53	1337·42	1401·93	1466·92	1532·43	1598·47	1665·08	1732·29	1800·13	1868·64	1937·84	53
54	1338·49	1403·01	1468·01	1533·53	1599·58	1666·20	1733·42	1801·27	1869·78	1939·00	54
55	1339·56	1404·09	1469·10	1534·62	1600·68	1667·32	1734·54	1802·41	1870·93	1940·16	55
56	1340·63	1405·17	1470·19	1535·72	1601·79	1668·43	1735·67	1803·54	1872·08	1941·32	56
57	1341·70	1406·25	1471·28	1536·82	1602·90	1669·55	1736·80	1804·68	1873·23	1942·48	57
58	1342·78	1407·33	1472·36	1537·91	1604·00	1670·66	1737·92	1805·82	1874·38	1943·64	58
59	1343·85	1408·41	1473·45	1539·01	1605·11	1671·78	1739·05	1806·95	1875·53	1944·80	59
60	1344·92	1409·49	1474·54	1540·11	1606·21	1672·89	1740·18	1808·09	1876·67	1945·96	60

| M | 21° | 22° | 23° | 24° | 25° | 26° | 27° | 28° | 29° | 30° | M |

| | *Terrestrial Spheroid* | | **MERIDIONAL PARTS** | | | | | *Compression* $\frac{1}{293.465}$ | | | |

M	31°	32°	33°	34°	35°	36°	37°	38°	39°	40°	M
0	1945·96	2015·98	2086·78	2158·39	2230·86	2304·23	2378·54	2453·85	2530·20	2607·64	0
1	1947·12	2017·15	2087·97	2159·59	2232·08	2305·46	2379·79	2455·11	2531·48	2608·94	1
2	1948·28	2018·33	2089·15	2160·79	2233·29	2306·69	2381·04	2456·38	2532·76	2610·24	2
3	1949·44	2019·50	2090·34	2161·99	2234·51	2307·92	2382·28	2457·64	2534·04	2611·54	3
4	1950·60	2020·68	2091·53	2163·20	2235·72	2309·15	2383·53	2458·91	2535·33	2612·84	4
5	1951·77	2021·85	2092·72	2164·40	2236·94	2310·39	2384·78	2460·17	2536·61	2614·15	5
6	1952·93	2023·03	2093·90	2165·60	2238·16	2311·62	2386·03	2461·44	2537·89	2615·45	6
7	1954·09	2024·20	2095·09	2166·80	2239·37	2312·85	2387·28	2462·70	2539·13	2616·75	7
8	1955·25	2025·38	2096·28	2168·00	2240·59	2314·08	2388·53	2463·97	2540·46	2618·05	8
9	1956·41	2026·55	2097·47	2169·21	2241·81	2315·32	2389·77	2465·23	2541·74	2619·36	9
10	1957·58	2027·73	2098·66	2170·41	2243·03	2316·55	2391·02	2466·50	2543·03	2620·66	10
11	1958·74	2028·90	2099·85	2171·61	2244·24	2317·78	2392·27	2467·77	2544·31	2621·96	11
12	1959·90	2030·08	2101·04	2172·82	2245·46	2319·02	2393·52	2469·03	2545·60	2623·27	12
13	1961·07	2031·25	2102·23	2174·02	2246·68	2320·25	2394·77	2470·30	2546·88	2624·57	13
14	1962·23	2032·43	2103·42	2175·22	2247·90	2321·48	2396·02	2471·57	2548·17	2625·88	14
15	1963·39	2033·61	2104·61	2176·43	2249·12	2322·72	2397·27	2472·84	2549·45	2627·18	15
16	1964·56	2034·78	2105·80	2177·63	2250·34	2323·95	2398·53	2474·10	2550·74	2628·49	16
17	1965·72	2035·96	2106·99	2178·84	2251·56	2325·19	2399·78	2475·37	2552·03	2629·79	17
18	1966·89	2037·14	2108·18	2180·04	2252·78	2326·42	2401·03	2476·64	2553·31	2631·10	18
19	1968·05	2038·31	2109·37	2181·25	2254·00	2327·66	2402·28	2477·91	2554·60	2632·40	19
20	1969·22	2039·49	2110·56	2182·45	2255·22	2328·89	2403·53	2479·18	2555·89	2633·71	20
21	1970·38	2040·67	2111·75	2183·66	2256·44	2330·13	2404·78	2480·45	2557·18	2635·02	21
22	1971·55	2041·85	2112·94	2184·86	2257·66	2331·37	2406·04	2481·72	2558·46	2636·32	22
23	1972·71	2043·03	2114·13	2186·07	2258·88	2332·60	2407·29	2482·99	2559·75	2637·63	23
24	1973·88	2044·20	2115·32	2187·27	2260·10	2333·84	2408·54	2484·26	2561·04	2638·94	24
25	1975·04	2045·38	2116·52	2188·48	2261·32	2335·08	2409·80	2485·53	2562·33	2640·25	25
26	1976·21	2046·56	2117·71	2189·69	2262·54	2336·31	2411·05	2486·80	2563·62	2641·56	26
27	1977·38	2047·74	2118·90	2190·89	2263·76	2337·55	2412·30	2488·07	2564·91	2642·86	27
28	1978·54	2048·92	2120·10	2192·10	2264·98	2338·79	2413·56	2489·35	2566·20	2644·17	28
29	1979·71	2050·10	2121·29	2193·31	2266·21	2340·03	2414·81	2490·62	2567·49	2645·48	29
30	1980·88	2051·28	2122·48	2194·52	2267·43	2341·27	2416·07	2491·89	2568·78	2646·79	30
31	1982·04	2052·46	2123·68	2195·73	2268·65	2342·50	2417·32	2493·16	2570·07	2648·10	31
32	1983·21	2053·64	2124·87	2196·93	2269·88	2343·74	2418·58	2494·44	2571·36	2649·41	32
33	1984·38	2054·82	2126·06	2198·14	2271·10	2344·98	2419·83	2495·71	2572·65	2650·72	33
34	1985·55	2056·00	2127·26	2199·35	2272·32	2346·22	2421·09	2496·98	2573·94	2652·03	34
35	1986·71	2057·18	2128·45	2200·56	2273·55	2347·46	2422·35	2498·26	2575·24	2653·35	35
36	1987·88	2058·36	2129·65	2201·77	2274·77	2348·70	2423·60	2499·53	2576·53	2654·66	36
37	1989·05	2059·55	2130·84	2202·98	2276·00	2349·94	2424·86	2500·80	2577·82	2655·97	37
38	1990·22	2060·73	2132·04	2204·19	2277·22	2351·18	2426·12	2502·08	2579·12	2657·28	38
39	1991·39	2061·91	2133·23	2205·40	2278·45	2352·42	2427·38	2503·35	2580·41	2658·60	39
40	1992·56	2063·09	2134·43	2206·61	2279·67	2353·66	2428·63	2504·63	2581·70	2659·91	40
41	1993·73	2064·27	2135·62	2207·82	2280·90	2354·91	2429·89	2505·90	2583·00	2661·22	41
42	1994·90	2065·46	2136·82	2209·03	2282·12	2356·15	2431·15	2507·18	2584·29	2662·54	42
43	1996·06	2066·64	2138·02	2210·24	2283·35	2357·39	2432·41	2508·46	2585·58	2663·85	43
44	1997·23	2067·82	2139·21	2211·45	2284·57	2358·63	2433·67	2509·73	2586·88	2665·16	44
45	1998·40	2069·01	2140·41	2212·66	2285·80	2359·87	2434·93	2511·01	2588·17	2666·48	45
46	1999·57	2070·19	2141·61	2213·87	2287·03	2361·12	2436·19	2512·29	2589·47	2667·79	46
47	2000·74	2071·37	2142·81	2215·09	2288·25	2362·36	2437·45	2513·56	2590·77	2669·11	47
48	2001·92	2072·56	2144·00	2216·30	2289·48	2363·60	2438·71	2514·84	2592·06	2670·42	48
49	2003·09	2073·74	2145·20	2217·51	2290·71	2364·85	2439·97	2516·12	2593·36	2671·74	49
50	2004·26	2074·92	2146·40	2218·72	2291·94	2366·09	2441·23	2517·40	2594·66	2673·06	50
51	2005·43	2076·11	2147·60	2219·94	2293·17	2367·33	2442·49	2518·68	2595·95	2674·37	51
52	2006·60	2077·29	2148·80	2221·15	2294·39	2368·58	2443·75	2519·96	2597·25	2675·69	52
53	2007·77	2078·48	2149·99	2222·36	2295·62	2369·82	2445·01	2521·23	2598·55	2677·01	53
54	2008·94	2079·66	2151·19	2223·57	2296·85	2371·07	2446·27	2522·51	2599·85	2678·33	54
55	2010·12	2080·85	2152·39	2224·79	2298·08	2372·31	2447·53	2523·79	2601·14	2679·64	55
56	2011·29	2082·03	2153·59	2226·00	2299·31	2373·56	2448·80	2525·07	2602·44	2680·96	56
57	2012·46	2083·22	2154·79	2227·22	2300·54	2374·80	2450·06	2526·35	2603·74	2682·28	57
58	2013·63	2084·41	2155·99	2228·43	2301·77	2376·05	2451·32	2527·63	2605·04	2683·60	58
59	2014·81	2085·59	2157·19	2229·65	2303·00	2377·30	2452·58	2528·92	2606·34	2684·92	59
60	2015·98	2086·78	2158·39	2230·86	2304·23	2378·54	2453·85	2530·20	2607·64	2686·24	60
M	31°	32°	33°	34°	35°	36°	37°	38°	39°	40°	M

						MERIDIONAL PARTS					

Terrestrial Spheroid — MERIDIONAL PARTS — *Compression* $\dfrac{1}{293.465}$

M	41°	42°	43°	44°	45°	46°	47°	48°	49°	50°	M
0	2686·24	2766·05	2847·13	2929·55	3013·38	3098·70	3185·59	3274·13	3364·41	3456·53	0
1	2687·56	2767·39	2848·49	2930·93	3014·79	3100·14	3187·05	3275·62	3365·93	3458·08	1
2	2688·88	2768·73	2849·85	2932·32	3016·20	3101·57	3188·51	3277·11	3367·45	3459·64	2
3	2690·20	2770·07	2851·22	2933·71	3017·61	3103·01	3189·97	3278·60	3368·97	3461·19	3
4	2691·52	2771·41	2852·58	2935·09	3019·02	3104·44	3191·44	3280·09	3370·49	3462·74	4
5	2692·84	2772·75	2853·94	2936·48	3020·43	3105·88	3192·90	3281·58	3372·01	3464·29	5
6	2694·16	2774·10	2855·31	2937·87	3021·85	3107·32	3194·36	3283·07	3373·54	3465·85	6
7	2695·49	2775·44	2856·67	2939·26	3023·26	3108·76	3195·83	3284·57	3375·06	3467·40	7
8	2696·81	2776·78	2858·04	2940·64	3024·67	3110·19	3197·29	3286·06	3376·58	3468·96	8
9	2698·13	2778·13	2859·40	2942·03	3026·08	3111·63	3198·76	3287·55	3378·11	3470·52	9
10	2699·45	2779·47	2860·77	2943·42	3027·50	3113·07	3200·23	3289·05	3379·63	3472·07	10
11	2700·78	2780·81	2862·14	2944·81	3028·91	3114·51	3201·69	3290·54	3381·16	3473·63	11
12	2702·10	2782·16	2863·50	2946·20	3030·32	3115·95	3203·16	3292·04	3382·68	3475·19	12
13	2703·42	2783·50	2864·87	2947·59	3031·74	3117·39	3204·63	3293·54	3384·21	3476·75	13
14	2704·75	2784·85	2866·24	2948·98	3033·15	3118·83	3206·10	3295·03	3385·73	3478·30	14
15	2706·07	2786·19	2867·60	2950·37	3034·57	3120·27	3207·56	3296·53	3387·26	3479·86	15
16	2707·40	2787·54	2868·97	2951·76	3035·99	3121·71	3209·03	3298·03	3388·79	3481·42	16
17	2708·72	2788·89	2870·34	2953·15	3037·40	3123·16	3210·50	3299·52	3390·32	3482·98	17
18	2710·05	2790·23	2871·71	2954·55	3038·82	3124·60	3211·97	3301·02	3391·85	3484·54	18
19	2711·38	2791·58	2873·08	2955·94	3040·23	3126·04	3213·44	3302·52	3393·38	3486·11	19
20	2712·70	2792·93	2874·45	2957·33	3041·65	3127·49	3214·91	3304·02	3394·91	3487·67	20
21	2714·03	2794·28	2875·82	2958·73	3043·07	3128·93	3216·38	3305·52	3396·44	3489·23	21
22	2715·36	2795·62	2877·19	2960·12	3044·49	3130·37	3217·86	3307·02	3397·97	3490·79	22
23	2716·68	2796·97	2878·56	2961·51	3045·91	3131·82	3219·33	3308·52	3399·50	3492·36	23
24	2718·01	2798·32	2879·93	2962·91	3047·33	3133·26	3220·80	3310·02	3401·03	3493·92	24
25	2719·34	2799·67	2881·30	2964·30	3048·75	3134·71	3222·27	3311·53	3402·56	3495·49	25
26	2720·67	2801·02	2882·67	2965·70	3050·17	3136·15	3223·75	3313·03	3404·10	3497·05	26
27	2722·00	2802·37	2884·05	2967·09	3051·59	3137·60	3225·22	3314·53	3405·63	3498·62	27
28	2723·33	2803·72	2885·42	2968·49	3053·01	3139·05	3226·69	3316·03	3407·16	3500·18	28
29	2724·66	2805·07	2886·79	2969·89	3054·43	3140·49	3228·17	3317·54	3408·70	3501·75	29
30	2725·99	2806·42	2888·17	2971·28	3055·85	3141·94	3229·64	3319·04	3410·23	3503·32	30
31	2727·32	2807·77	2889·54	2972·68	3057·27	3143·39	3231·12	3320·55	3411·77	3504·89	31
32	2728·65	2809·13	2890·91	2974·08	3058·70	3144·84	3232·60	3322·05	3413·30	3506·45	32
33	2729·98	2810·48	2892·29	2975·48	3060·12	3146·29	3234·07	3323·56	3414·84	3508·02	33
34	2731·31	2811·83	2893·66	2976·88	3061·54	3147·74	3235·55	3325·07	3416·38	3509·59	34
35	2732·64	2813·18	2895·04	2978·28	3062·97	3149·19	3237·03	3326·57	3417·92	3511·16	35
36	2733·97	2814·54	2896·42	2979·68	3064·39	3150·64	3238·51	3328·08	3419·45	3512·73	36
37	2735·31	2815·89	2897·79	2981·08	3065·81	3152·09	3239·98	3329·59	3420·99	3514·31	37
38	2736·64	2817·25	2899·17	2982·48	3067·24	3153·54	3241·46	3331·10	3422·53	3515·88	38
39	2737·97	2818·60	2900·54	2983·88	3068·66	3154·99	3242·94	3332·60	3424·07	3517·45	39
40	2739·30	2819·95	2901·92	2985·28	3070·09	3156·45	3244·42	3334·11	3425·61	3519·02	40
41	2740·64	2821·31	2903·30	2986·68	3071·52	3157·90	3245·90	3335·62	3427·15	3520·60	41
42	2741·97	2822·67	2904·68	2988·08	3072·94	3159·35	3247·38	3337·13	3428·70	3522·17	42
43	2743·31	2824·02	2906·06	2989·48	3074·37	3160·81	3248·87	3338·65	3430·24	3523·75	43
44	2744·64	2825·38	2907·43	2990·88	3075·80	3162·26	3250·35	3340·16	3431·78	3525·32	44
45	2745·98	2826·73	2908·81	2992·29	3077·23	3163·71	3251·83	3341·67	3433·32	3526·90	45
46	2747·31	2828·09	2910·19	2993·69	3078·66	3165·17	3253·31	3343·18	3434·87	3528·47	46
47	2748·65	2829·45	2911·57	2995·09	3080·09	3166·62	3254·80	3344·69	3436·41	3530·05	47
48	2749·98	2830·81	2912·95	2996·50	3081·52	3168·08	3256·28	3346·21	3437·95	3531·63	48
49	2751·32	2832·16	2914·33	2997·90	3082·95	3169·54	3257·77	3347·72	3439·50	3533·21	49
50	2752·66	2833·52	2915·72	2999·31	3084·38	3170·99	3259·25	3349·24	3441·05	3534·79	50
51	2754·00	2834·88	2917·10	3000·71	3085·81	3172·45	3260·74	3350·75	3442·59	3536·37	51
52	2755·33	2836·24	2918·48	3002·12	3087·24	3173·91	3262·22	3352·27	3444·14	3537·95	52
53	2756·67	2837·60	2919·86	3003·53	3088·67	3175·37	3263·71	3353·78	3445·69	3539·53	53
54	2758·01	2838·96	2921·24	3004·93	3090·10	3176·83	3265·20	3355·30	3447·23	3541·11	54
55	2759·35	2840·32	2922·63	3006·34	3091·53	3178·28	3266·68	3356·82	3448·78	3542·69	55
56	2760·69	2841·68	2924·01	3007·75	3092·97	3179·74	3268·17	3358·33	3450·33	3544·27	56
57	2762·03	2843·04	2925·39	3009·16	3094·40	3181·20	3269·66	3359·85	3451·88	3545·85	57
58	2763·37	2844·40	2926·78	3010·56	3095·83	3182·66	3271·15	3361·37	3453·43	3547·44	58
59	2764·71	2845·77	2928·16	3011·97	3097·27	3184·13	3272·64	3362·89	3454·98	3549·02	59
60	2766·05	2847·13	2929·55	3013·38	3098·70	3185·59	3274·13	3364·41	3456·53	3550·60	60
M	41°	42°	43°	44°	45°	46°	47°	48°	49°	50°	M

| | *Terrestrial Spheroid* | **MERIDIONAL PARTS** | | | | | *Compression* $\dfrac{1}{293.465}$ | | | | |

M	51°	52°	53°	54°	55°	56°	57°	58°	59°	60°	M
0	3550·60	3646·74	3745·05	3845·69	3948·78	4054·48	4162·97	4274·43	4389·06	4507·08	0
1	3552·19	3648·36	3746·71	3847·38	3950·52	4056·27	4164·81	4276·31	4391·00	4509·07	1
2	3553·77	3649·98	3748·37	3849·08	3952·26	4058·05	4166·64	4278·20	4392·94	4511·07	2
3	3555·36	3651·60	3750·03	3850·78	3954·00	4059·84	4168·47	4280·08	4394·88	4513·07	3
4	3556·95	3653·22	3751·69	3852·48	3955·74	4061·63	4170·31	4281·97	4396·82	4515·07	4
5	3558·53	3654·84	3753·35	3854·18	3957·48	4063·41	4172·14	4283·86	4398·76	4517·07	5
6	3560·12	3656·47	3755·01	3855·88	3959·23	4065·20	4173·98	4285·75	4400·70	4519·08	6
7	3561·71	3658·09	3756·67	3857·58	3960·97	4066·99	4175·82	4287·64	4402·65	4521·08	7
8	3563·30	3659·72	3758·33	3859·29	3962·72	4068·78	4177·66	4289·53	4404·59	4523·08	8
9	3564·89	3661·34	3760·00	3860·99	3964·46	4070·57	4179·50	4291·42	4406·54	4525·09	9
10	3566·48	3662·97	3761·66	3862·69	3966·21	4072·37	4181·34	4293·31	4408·49	4527·09	10
11	3568·07	3664·59	3763·33	3864·40	3967·95	4074·16	4183·18	4295·20	4410·43	4529·10	11
12	3569·66	3666·22	3764·99	3866·10	3969·70	4075·95	4185·02	4297·09	4412·38	4531·11	12
13	3571·25	3667·85	3766·66	3867·81	3971·45	4077·75	4186·86	4298·99	4414·33	4533·12	13
14	3572·85	3669·48	3768·32	3869·52	3973·20	4079·54	4188·71	4300·89	4416·28	4535·13	14
15	3574·44	3671·11	3769·99	3871·22	3974·95	4081·34	4190·55	4302·78	4418·24	4537·14	15
16	3576·03	3672·74	3771·66	3872·93	3976·70	4083·13	4192·40	4304·68	4420·19	4539·15	16
17	3577·63	3674·37	3773·33	3874·64	3978·46	4084·93	4194·24	4306·58	4422·14	4541·17	17
18	3579·22	3676·00	3774·99	3876·35	3980·21	4086·73	4196·09	4308·48	4424·10	4543·18	18
19	3580·82	3677·63	3776·66	3878·06	3981·96	4088·53	4197·94	4310·38	4426·05	4545·20	19
20	3582·41	3679·26	3778·33	3879·77	3983·71	4090·33	4199·79	4312·28	4428·01	4547·21	20
21	3584·01	3680·89	3780·00	3881·48	3985·47	4092·13	4201·64	4314·18	4429·97	4549·23	21
22	3585·61	3682·53	3781·68	3883·19	3987·22	4093·93	4203·49	4316·08	4431·93	4551·25	22
23	3587·20	3684·16	3783·35	3884·91	3988·98	4095·73	4205·34	4317·98	4433·89	4553·27	23
24	3588·80	3685·79	3785·02	3886·62	3990·74	4097·54	4207·19	4319·89	4435·85	4555·29	24
25	3590·40	3687·43	3786·69	3888·33	3992·49	4099·34	4209·04	4321·79	4437·81	4557·31	25
26	3592·00	3689·07	3788·37	3890·05	3994·25	4101·14	4210·90	4323·70	4439·77	4559·33	26
27	3593·60	3690·70	3790·04	3891·76	3996·01	4102·95	4212·75	4325·61	4441·73	4561·36	27
28	3595·20	3692·34	3791·72	3893·48	3997·77	4104·75	4214·61	4327·52	4443·70	4563·38	28
29	3596·80	3693·98	3793·40	3895·20	3999·53	4106·56	4216·46	4329·42	4445·66	4565·41	29
30	3598·40	3695·61	3795·07	3896·91	4001·29	4108·37	4218·32	4331·33	4447·63	4567·44	30
31	3600·01	3697·25	3796·75	3898·63	4003·06	4110·18	4220·18	4333·24	4449·60	4569·46	31
32	3601·61	3698·89	3798·43	3900·35	4004·82	4111·99	4222·04	4335·16	4451·56	4571·49	32
33	3603·21	3700·53	3800·11	3902·07	4006·58	4113·80	4223·90	4337·07	4453·53	4573·52	33
34	3604·82	3702·17	3801·79	3903·79	4008·35	4115·61	4225·76	4338·98	4455·50	4575·55	34
35	3606·42	3703·82	3803·47	3905·51	4010·11	4117·42	4227·62	4340·90	4457·48	4577·59	35
36	3608·03	3705·46	3805·15	3907·24	4011·88	4119·23	4229·48	4342·81	4459·45	4579·62	36
37	3609·63	3707·10	3806·83	3908·96	4013·64	4121·05	4231·34	4344·73	4461·42	4581·65	37
38	3611·24	3708·74	3808·51	3910·68	4015·41	4122·86	4233·21	4346·65	4463·40	4583·69	38
39	3612·85	3710·39	3810·19	3912·41	4017·18	4124·67	4235·07	4348·56	4465·37	4585·72	39
40	3614·46	3712·03	3811·88	3914·13	4018·95	4126·49	4236·94	4350·48	4467·35	4587·76	40
41	3616·06	3713·68	3813·56	3915·86	4020·72	4128·31	4238·80	4352·40	4469·32	4589·80	41
42	3617·67	3715·32	3815·25	3917·58	4022·49	4130·12	4240·67	4354·32	4471·30	4591·84	42
43	3619·28	3716·97	3816·93	3919·31	4024·26	4131·94	4242·54	4356·25	4473·28	4593·88	43
44	3620·89	3718·62	3818·62	3921·04	4026·03	4133·76	4244·41	4358·17	4475·26	4595·92	44
45	3622·50	3720·26	3820·30	3922·77	4027·80	4135·58	4246·28	4360·09	4477·24	4597·96	45
46	3624·12	3721·91	3821·99	3924·50	4029·58	4137·40	4248·15	4362·02	4479·22	4600·01	46
47	3625·73	3723·56	3823·68	3926·23	4031·35	4139·22	4250·02	4363·94	4481·21	4602·05	47
48	3627·34	3725·21	3825·37	3927·96	4033·13	4141·04	4251·89	4365·87	4483·19	4604·10	48
49	3628·95	3726·86	3827·06	3929·69	4034·90	4142·87	4253·77	4367·80	4485·18	4606·15	49
50	3630·57	3728·51	3828·75	3931·42	4036·68	4144·69	4255·64	4369·72	4487·16	4608·19	50
51	3632·18	3730·16	3830·44	3933·15	4038·45	4146·52	4257·52	4371·65	4489·15	4610·24	51
52	3633·80	3731·81	3832·13	3934·88	4040·23	4148·34	4259·39	4373·58	4491·14	4612·29	52
53	3635·41	3733·47	3833·82	3936·62	4042·01	4150·17	4261·27	4375·51	4493·13	4614·34	53
54	3637·03	3735·12	3835·52	3938·35	4043·79	4151·99	4263·15	4377·45	4495·12	4616·40	54
55	3638·64	3736·77	3837·21	3940·09	4045·57	4153·82	4265·02	4379·38	4497·11	4618·45	55
56	3640·26	3738·43	3838·90	3941·83	4047·35	4155·65	4266·90	4381·31	4499·10	4620·50	56
57	3641·88	3740·08	3840·60	3943·56	4049·13	4157·48	4268·78	4383·25	4501·09	4622·56	57
58	3643·50	3741·74	3842·29	3945·30	4050·92	4159·31	4270·67	4385·18	4503·09	4624·62	58
59	3645·12	3743·40	3843·99	3947·04	4052·70	4161·14	4272·55	4387·12	4505·08	4626·67	59
60	3646·74	3745·05	3845·69	3948·78	4054·48	4162·97	4274·43	4389·06	4507·08	4628·73	60
M	51°	52°	53°	54°	55°	56°	57°	58°	59°	60°	M

| | | | Terrestrial Spheroid | | | MERIDIONAL PARTS | | | Compression $\frac{1}{293.465}$ | | |

M	61°	62°	63°	64°	65°	66°	67°	68°	69°	70°	M
0	4628·73	4754·29	4884·06	5018·36	5157·57	5302·11	5452·43	5609·09	5772·68	5943·89	0
1	4630·79	4756·42	4886·26	5020·64	5159·93	5304·56	5454·99	5611·76	5775·47	5946·82	1
2	4632·85	4758·55	4888·46	5022·92	5162·30	5307·02	5457·55	5614·43	5778·26	5949·74	2
3	4634·92	4760·68	4890·66	5025·20	5164·67	5309·48	5460·11	5617·10	5781·05	5952·67	3
4	4636·98	4762·81	4892·87	5027·48	5167·04	5311·94	5462·67	5619·77	5783·85	5955·60	4
5	4639·04	4764·94	4895·07	5029·77	5169·41	5314·40	5465·24	5622·45	5786·65	5958·53	5
6	4641·11	4767·08	4897·28	5032·05	5171·78	5316·87	5467·81	5625·13	5789·45	5961·47	6
7	4643·17	4769·21	4899·49	5034·34	5174·15	5319·34	5470·37	5627·81	5792·25	5964·40	7
8	4645·24	4771·35	4901·70	5036·63	5176·52	5321·80	5472·94	5630·49	5795·05	5967·34	8
9	4647·31	4773·48	4903·91	5038·92	5178·90	5324·27	5475·51	5633·17	5797·86	5970·28	9
10	4649·38	4775·62	4906·12	5041·21	5181·28	5326·74	5478·09	5635·86	5800·66	5973·23	10
11	4651·45	4777·76	4908·33	5043·50	5183·66	5329·22	5480·66	5638·54	5803·47	5976·17	11
12	4653·52	4779·90	4910·55	5045·80	5186·04	5331·69	5483·24	5641·23	5806·29	5979·12	12
13	4655·60	4782·04	4912·76	5048·09	5188·42	5334·17	5485·82	5643·92	5809·10	5982·07	13
14	4657·67	4784·18	4914·98	5050·39	5190·80	5336·65	5488·40	5646·62	5811·92	5985·03	14
15	4659·75	4786·33	4917·20	5052·69	5193·19	5339·13	5490·98	5649·31	5814·74	5987·98	15
16	4661·82	4788·47	4919·42	5054·99	5195·57	5341·61	5493·57	5652·01	5817·56	5990·94	16
17	4663·90	4790·62	4921·64	5057·29	5197·96	5344·09	5496·15	5654·71	5820·38	5993·90	17
18	4665·98	4792·77	4923·86	5059·59	5200·35	5346·57	5498·74	5657·41	5823·21	5996·86	18
19	4668·06	4794·92	4926·08	5061·89	5202·74	5349·06	5501·33	5660·11	5826·04	5999·83	19
20	4670·14	4797·07	4928·30	5064·20	5205·14	5351·55	5503·92	5662·82	5828·87	6002·80	20
21	4672·22	4799·22	4930·53	5066·51	5207·53	5354·04	5506·51	5665·52	5831·70	6005·77	21
22	4674·30	4801·37	4932·76	5068·81	5209·92	5356·53	5509·11	5668·23	5834·53	6008·74	22
23	4676·39	4803·52	4934·99	5071·12	5212·32	5359·02	5511·71	5670·94	5837·37	6011·72	23
24	4678·47	4805·68	4937·22	5073·43	5214·72	5361·51	5514·31	5673·66	5840·21	6014·69	24
25	4680·56	4807·83	4939·45	5075·75	5217·12	5364·01	5516·91	5676·37	5843·05	6017·67	25
26	4682·65	4809·99	4941·68	5078·06	5219·52	5366·51	5519·51	5679·09	5845·89	6020·66	26
27	4684·74	4812·15	4943·91	5080·37	5221·93	5369·01	5522·11	5681·81	5848·74	6023·64	27
28	4686·83	4814·31	4946·15	5082·69	5224·33	5371·51	5524·72	5684·53	5851·58	6026·63	28
29	4688·92	4816·47	4948·38	5085·01	5226·74	5374·01	5527·33	5687·25	5854·43	6029·62	29
30	4691·01	4818·63	4950·62	5087·33	5229·14	5376·51	5529·94	5689·98	5857·29	6032·61	30
31	4693·10	4820·79	4952·86	5089·65	5231·55	5379·02	5532·55	5692·70	5860·14	6035·60	31
32	4695·19	4822·96	4955·10	5091·97	5233·96	5381·53	5535·16	5695·43	5863·00	6038·60	32
33	4697·29	4825·12	4957·34	5094·29	5236·38	5384·04	5537·78	5698·16	5865·86	6041·60	33
34	4699·39	4827·29	4959·58	5096·62	5238·79	5386·55	5540·39	5700·90	5868·72	6044·60	34
35	4701·48	4829·46	4961·83	5098·94	5241·21	5389·06	5543·01	5703·63	5871·58	6047·61	35
36	4703·58	4831·63	4964·07	5101·27	5243·62	5391·57	5545·63	5706·37	5874·44	6050·62	36
37	4705·68	4833·80	4966·32	5103·60	5246·04	5394·09	5548·25	5709·11	5877·31	6053·63	37
38	4707·78	4835·97	4968·57	5105·93	5248·46	5396·61	5550·88	5711·85	5880·18	6056·64	38
39	4709·89	4838·14	4970·82	5108·26	5250·88	5399·13	5553·50	5714·59	5883·05	6059·65	39
40	4711·99	4840·32	4973·07	5110·60	5253·31	5401·65	5556·13	5717·34	5885·93	6062·67	40
41	4714·09	4842·49	4975·32	5112·93	5255·73	5404·17	5558·76	5720·09	5888·80	6065·69	41
42	4716·20	4844·67	4977·57	5115·27	5258·16	5406·70	5561·39	5722·84	5891·68	6068·71	42
43	4718·30	4846·85	4979·83	5117·61	5260·59	5409·22	5564·03	5725·59	5894·56	6071·73	43
44	4720·41	4849·03	4982·08	5119·95	5263·02	5411·75	5566·66	5728·34	5897·45	6074·76	44
45	4722·52	4851·21	4984·34	5122·29	5265·45	5414·28	5569·30	5731·10	5900·33	6077·79	45
46	4724·63	4853·39	4986·60	5124·63	5267·88	5416·81	5571·94	5733·85	5903·22	6080·82	46
47	4726·74	4855·57	4988·86	5126·97	5270·31	5419·34	5574·58	5736·61	5906·11	6083·86	47
48	4728·86	4857·76	4991·12	5129·32	5272·75	5421·88	5577·23	5739·37	5909·00	6086·90	48
49	4730·97	4859·94	4993·38	5131·66	5275·19	5424·42	5579·87	5742·14	5911·90	6089·94	49
50	4733·08	4862·13	4995·65	5134·01	5277·63	5426·96	5582·52	5744·90	5914·80	6092·98	50
51	4735·20	4864·31	4997·91	5136·36	5280·07	5429·50	5585·17	5747·67	5917·70	6096·02	51
52	4737·32	4866·50	5000·18	5138·71	5282·51	5432·04	5587·82	5750·44	5920·60	6099·07	52
53	4739·43	4868·69	5002·45	5141·06	5284·95	5434·58	5590·47	5753·21	5923·50	6102·12	53
54	4741·55	4870·88	5004·72	5143·42	5287·40	5437·13	5593·12	5755·99	5926·41	6105·17	54
55	4743·67	4873·08	5006·99	5145·77	5289·85	5439·67	5595·78	5758·76	5929·32	6108·23	55
56	4745·80	4875·27	5009·26	5148·13	5292·30	5442·22	5598·44	5761·54	5932·23	6111·28	56
57	4747·92	4877·47	5011·53	5150·49	5294·75	5444·77	5601·10	5764·32	5935·14	6114·34	57
58	4750·04	4879·66	5013·81	5152·85	5297·20	5447·32	5603·76	5767·11	5938·06	6117·41	58
59	4752·17	4881·86	5016·08	5155·21	5299·65	5449·88	5606·42	5769·89	5940·97	6120·47	59
60	4754·29	4884·06	5018·36	5157·57	5302·11	5452·43	5609·09	5772·68	5943·89	6123·54	60
M	61°	62°	63°	64°	65°	66°	67°	68°	69°	70°	M

	Terrestrial Spheroid		**MERIDIONAL PARTS**					Compression $\dfrac{1}{293.465}$			
M	**71°**	**72°**	**73°**	**74°**	**75°**	**76°**	**77°**	**78°**	**79°**	**80°**	**M**
0	6123·54	6312·55	6512·01	6723·21	6947·70	7187·33	7444·37	7721·64	8022·70	8352·11	0
1	6126·61	6315·78	6515·43	6726·84	6951·56	7191·46	7448·81	7726·45	8027·94	8357·87	1
2	6129·68	6319·02	6518·85	6730·47	6955·43	7195·60	7453·26	7731·27	8033·19	8363·65	2
3	6132·76	6322·26	6522·28	6734·11	6959·30	7199·74	7457·72	7736·09	8038·45	8369·43	3
4	6135·84	6325·51	6525·71	6737·75	6963·18	7203·89	7462·19	7740·92	8043·72	8375·22	4
5	6138·92	6328·75	6529·14	6741·39	6967·06	7208·05	7466·66	7745·76	8048·99	8381·02	5
6	6142·00	6332·00	6532·58	6745·04	6970·95	7212·21	7471·13	7750·61	8054·27	8386·83	6
7	6145·09	6335·26	6536·02	6748·69	6974·84	7216·37	7475·61	7755·46	8059·56	8392·65	7
8	6148·18	6338·51	6539·46	6752·34	6978·73	7220·54	7480·10	7760·32	8064·86	8398·48	8
9	6151·27	6341·77	6542·91	6756·00	6982·63	7224·71	7484·59	7765·18	8070·17	8404·32	9
10	6154·37	6345·03	6546·36	6759·66	6986·53	7228·89	7489·09	7770·05	8075·49	8410·17	10
11	6157·46	6348·30	6549·81	6763·32	6990·44	7233·07	7493·59	7774·93	8080·81	8416·03	11
12	6160·56	6351·57	6553·27	6766·99	6994·35	7237·26	7498·10	7779·82	8086·14	8421·90	12
13	6163·66	6354·84	6556·73	6770·67	6998·26	7241·45	7502·62	7784·71	8091·48	8427·78	13
14	6166·77	6358·11	6560·19	6774·34	7002·18	7245·65	7507·14	7789·61	8096·83	8433·67	14
15	6169·88	6361·39	6563·65	6778·02	7006·11	7249·85	7511·66	7794·51	8102·18	8439·56	15
16	6172·99	6364·67	6567·12	6781·71	7010·03	7254·06	7516·19	7799·43	8107·55	8445·47	16
17	6176·10	6367·95	6570·60	6785·40	7013·97	7258·27	7520·73	7804·35	8112·92	8451·39	17
18	6179·21	6371·23	6574·07	6789·09	7017·90	7262·49	7525·28	7809·27	8118·30	8457·32	18
19	6182·33	6374·52	6577·55	6792·78	7021·84	7266·72	7529·83	7814·21	8123·69	8463·26	19
20	6185·45	6377·81	6581·04	6796·48	7025·79	7270·95	7534·38	7819·15	8129·09	8469·21	20
21	6188·58	6381·11	6584·52	6800·18	7029·74	7275·18	7538·94	7824·09	8134·49	8475·17	21
22	6191·70	6384·41	6588·01	6803·89	7033·69	7279·42	7543·51	7829·05	8139·91	8481·14	22
23	6194·83	6387·71	6591·50	6807·60	7037·65	7283·66	7548·09	7834·01	8145·33	8487·12	23
24	6197·97	6391·01	6595·00	6811·32	7041·62	7287·91	7552·67	7838·98	8150·76	8493·11	24
25	6201·10	6394·32	6598·50	6815·04	7045·58	7292·16	7557·25	7843·95	8156·20	8499·11	25
26	6204·24	6397·63	6602·01	6818·76	7049·56	7296·42	7561·84	7848·93	8161·65	8505·12	26
27	6207·38	6400·94	6605·51	6822·49	7053·53	7300·69	7566·44	7853·92	8167·10	8511·14	27
28	6210·52	6404·26	6609·02	6826·22	7057·51	7304·95	7571·05	7858·92	8172·57	8517·17	28
29	6213·66	6407·58	6612·54	6829·95	7061·50	7309·23	7575·66	7863·93	8178·04	8523·21	29
30	6216·81	6410·90	6616·05	6833·69	7065·49	7313·51	7580·27	7868·94	8183·52	8529·26	30
31	6219·96	6414·22	6619·57	6837·43	7069·48	7317·79	7584·89	7873·95	8189·01	8535·33	31
32	6223·12	6417·55	6623·10	6841·18	7073·48	7322·08	7589·52	7878·98	8194·51	8541·40	32
33	6226·27	6420·88	6626·63	6844·93	7077·49	7326·38	7594·15	7884·01	8200·02	8547·49	33
34	6229·43	6424·22	6630·16	6848·68	7081·49	7330·68	7598·79	7889·05	8205·54	8553·58	34
35	6232·59	6427·55	6633·69	6852·44	7085·51	7334·98	7603·44	7894·10	8211·06	8559·69	35
36	6235·76	6430·89	6637·23	6856·20	7089·52	7339·29	7608·09	7899·15	8216·60	8565·80	36
37	6238·92	6434·24	6640·77	6859·97	7093·54	7343·61	7612·75	7904·21	8222·14	8571·93	37
38	6242·09	6437·58	6644·32	6863·74	7097·57	7347·93	7617·42	7909·28	8227·69	8578·07	38
39	6245·27	6440·93	6647·87	6867·51	7101·60	7352·26	7622·09	7914·36	8233·25	8584·22	39
40	6248·44	6444·29	6651·42	6871·29	7105·64	7356·59	7626·76	7919·44	8238·82	8590·38	40
41	6251·62	6447·64	6654·97	6875·07	7109·68	7360·93	7631·45	7924·53	8244·40	8596·55	41
42	6254·80	6451·00	6658·53	6878·86	7113·72	7365·27	7636·14	7929·63	8249·98	8602·73	42
43	6257·99	6454·36	6662·10	6882·65	7117·77	7369·62	7640·83	7934·74	8255·58	8608·92	43
44	6261·17	6457·73	6665·66	6886·44	7121·83	7373·97	7645·53	7939·85	8261·19	8615·12	44
45	6264·36	6461·10	6669·23	6890·24	7125·88	7378·33	7650·24	7944·97	8266·80	8621·34	45
46	6267·56	6464·47	6672·81	6894·04	7129·95	7382·69	7654·96	7950·10	8272·42	8627·56	46
47	6270·75	6467·84	6676·38	6897·85	7134·02	7387·06	7659·68	7955·24	8278·05	8633·80	47
48	6273·95	6471·22	6679·96	6901·66	7138·09	7391·44	7664·41	7960·38	8283·70	8640·05	48
49	6277·15	6474·60	6683·55	6905·47	7142·17	7395·82	7669·14	7965·53	8289·35	8646·31	49
50	6280·35	6477·99	6687·14	6909·29	7146·25	7400·21	7673·88	7970·69	8295·01	8652·58	50
51	6283·56	6481·38	6690·73	6913·11	7150·33	7404·60	7678·63	7975·85	8300·68	8658·86	51
52	6286·77	6484·77	6694·32	6916·94	7154·42	7408·99	7683·38	7981·03	8306·35	8665·15	52
53	6289·98	6488·16	6697·92	6920·77	7158·52	7413·40	7688·14	7986·21	8312·04	8671·46	53
54	6293·20	6491·56	6701·52	6924·60	7162·62	7417·80	7692·90	7991·40	8317·74	8677·77	54
55	6296·42	6494·96	6705·13	6928·44	7166·73	7422·22	7697·68	7996·59	8323·44	8684·10	55
56	6299·64	6498·36	6708·74	6932·28	7170·84	7426·64	7702·46	8001·80	8329·16	8690·44	56
57	6302·86	6501·77	6712·35	6936·13	7174·95	7431·06	7707·24	8007·01	8334·88	8696·79	57
58	6306·09	6505·18	6715·97	6939·98	7179·07	7435·49	7712·03	8012·23	8340·62	8703·15	58
59	6309·32	6508·59	6719·59	6943·84	7183·20	7439·93	7716·83	8017·46	8346·36	8709·52	59
60	6312·55	6512·01	6723·21	6947·70	7187·33	7444·37	7721·64	8022·70	8352·11	8715·91	60
M	**71°**	**72°**	**73°**	**74°**	**75°**	**76°**	**77°**	**78°**	**79°**	**80°**	**M**

					MERIDIONAL PARTS					

Terrestrial Spheroid — **MERIDIONAL PARTS** — *Compression* $\frac{1}{293.465}$

M	81°	82°	83°	84°	85°	86°	87°	88°	89°	M
0	8715·91	9122·25	9582·55	10113·57	10741·27	11509·13	12498·70	13893·00	16276·12	0
1	8722·31	9129·44	9590·77	10123·15	10752·76	11523·50	12517·86	13921·78	16333·90	1
2	8728·72	9136·65	9599·00	10132·76	10764·29	11537·92	12537·12	13950·79	16392·67	2
3	8735·14	9143·87	9607·26	10142·39	10775·86	11552·41	12556·50	13980·06	16452·46	3
4	8741·57	9151·10	9615·53	10152·05	10787·47	11566·96	12575·99	14009·57	16513·31	4
5	8748·01	9158·35	9623·82	10161·74	10799·12	11581·56	12595·59	14039·34	16575·25	5
6	8754·47	9165·62	9632·13	10171·45	10810·80	11596·23	12615·29	14069·37	16638·34	6
7	8760·94	9172·90	9640·47	10181·19	10822·53	11610·97	12635·11	14099·66	16702·60	7
8	8767·42	9180·20	9648·82	10190·96	10834·30	11625·77	12655·05	14130·23	16768·08	8
9	8773·91	9187·51	9657·19	10200·76	10846·10	11640·63	12675·10	14161·06	16834·84	9
10	8780·42	9194·84	9665·59	10210·58	10857·95	11655·55	12695·27	14192·18	16902·92	10
11	8786·94	9202·19	9674·00	10220·43	10869·84	11670·54	12715·56	14223·58	16972·37	11
12	8793·47	9209·55	9682·43	10230·31	10881·77	11685·60	12735·97	14255·27	17043·26	12
13	8800·01	9216·92	9690·89	10240·22	10893·74	11700·72	12756·50	14287·25	17115·64	13
14	8806·56	9224·31	9699·37	10250·16	10905·75	11715·91	12777·16	14319·54	17189·57	14
15	8813·13	9231·72	9707·86	10260·13	10917·81	11731·16	12797·94	14352·13	17265·13	15
16	8819·71	9239·14	9716·38	10270·12	10929·91	11746·49	12818·85	14385·03	17342·39	16
17	8826·30	9246·58	9724·92	10280·15	10942·05	11761·88	12839·88	14418·25	17421·42	17
18	8832·90	9254·04	9733·48	10290·20	10954·23	11777·34	12861·04	14451·79	17502·32	18
19	8839·52	9261·51	9742·06	10300·28	10966·45	11792·87	12882·34	14485·67	17585·16	19
20	8846·15	9268·99	9750·66	10310·39	10978·72	11808·47	12903·77	14519·68	17670·05	20
21	8852·79	9276·50	9759·28	10320·54	10991·03	11824·14	12925·32	14554·44	17757·09	21
22	8859·44	9284·02	9767·93	10330·71	11003·39	11839·89	12947·02	14589·34	17846·39	22
23	8866·11	9291·55	9776·60	10340·91	11015·79	11855·70	12968·86	14624·60	17938·07	23
24	8872·79	9299·10	9785·29	10351·14	11028·24	11871·59	12990·83	14660·23	18032·26	24
25	8879·48	9306·67	9794·00	10361·40	11040·73	11887·55	13012·94	14696·24	18129·11	25
26	8886·19	9314·26	9802·73	10371·70	11053·27	11903·59	13035·20	14732·62	18228·76	26
27	8892·91	9321·86	9811·48	10382·02	11065·85	11919·70	13057·61	14769·39	18331·39	27
28	8899·64	9329·48	9820·26	10392·37	11078·48	11935·89	13080·15	14806·56	18437·18	28
29	8906·38	9337·11	9829·06	10402·76	11091·15	11952·15	13102·85	14844·14	18546·32	29
30	8913·14	9344·76	9837·88	10413·18	11103·87	11968·49	13125·70	14882·13	18659·05	30
31	8919·91	9352·43	9846·73	10423·63	11116·64	11984·91	13148·70	14920·54	18775·59	31
32	8926·70	9360·12	9855·59	10434·11	11129·46	12001·41	13171·86	14959·39	18896·23	32
33	8933·50	9367·82	9864·48	10444·62	11142·32	12017·99	13195·18	14998·68	19021·25	33
34	8940·31	9375·54	9873·39	10455·16	11155·23	12034·65	13218·65	15038·43	19150·99	34
35	8947·13	9383·28	9882·33	10465·74	11168·19	12051·38	13242·28	15078·64	19285·83	35
36	8953·97	9391·03	9891·29	10476·35	11181·20	12068·20	13266·08	15119·33	19426·16	36
37	8960·82	9398·80	9900·27	10486·99	11194·26	12085·11	13290·04	15160·51	19572·47	37
38	8967·68	9406·59	9909·28	10497·66	11207·37	12102·09	13314·17	15202·18	19725·29	38
39	8974·56	9414·40	9918·31	10508·37	11220·53	12119·16	13338·48	15244·36	19885·21	39
40	8981·45	9422·23	9927·36	10519·11	11233·73	12136·32	13362·95	15287·07	20052·94	40
41	8988·36	9430·07	9936·44	10529·89	11246·99	12153·56	13387·60	15330·32	20229·28	41
42	8995·28	9437·93	9945·54	10540·70	11260·30	12170·89	13412·43	15374·12	20415·15	42
43	9002·21	9445·81	9954·66	10551·54	11273·67	12188·30	13437·44	15418·48	20611·64	43
44	9009·16	9453·70	9963·81	10562·42	11287·08	12205·81	13462·63	15463·42	20820·06	44
45	9016·12	9461·62	9972·98	10573·33	11300·55	12223·40	13488·01	15508·96	21041·92	45
46	9023·09	9469·55	9982·18	10584·27	11314·07	12241·08	13513·57	15555·11	21279·11	46
47	9030·08	9477·50	9991·40	10595·25	11327·64	12258·86	13539·33	15601·88	21533·87	47
48	9037·09	9485·47	10000·65	10606·27	11341·27	12276·73	13565·28	15649·31	21809·04	48
49	9044·11	9493·46	10009·92	10617·32	11354·95	12294·69	13591·43	15697·39	22108·16	49
50	9051·14	9501·46	10019·21	10628·40	11368·68	12312·74	13617·78	15746·16	22435·81	50
51	9058·18	9509·48	10028·53	10639·52	11382·47	12330·89	13644·33	15795·63	22798·02	51
52	9065·24	9517·53	10037·88	10650·68	11396·32	12349·14	13671·09	15845·81	23202·93	52
53	9072·32	9525·59	10047·25	10661·88	11410·22	12367·48	13698·06	15896·75	23661·97	53
54	9079·41	9533·67	10056·65	10673·11	11424·18	12385·92	13725·24	15948·45	24191·91	54
55	9086·51	9541·77	10066·07	10684·37	11438·19	12404·46	13752·64	16000·94	24818·68	55
56	9093·63	9549·89	10075·52	10695·68	11452·26	12423·10	13780·26	16054·24	25585·79	56
57	9100·76	9558·03	10084·99	10707·02	11466·39	12441·85	13808·10	16108·38	26574·77	57
58	9107·91	9566·18	10094·49	10718·40	11480·57	12460·69	13836·17	16163·39	27968·66	58
59	9115·07	9574·36	10104·02	10729·82	11494·83	12479·64	13864·47	16219·30	30351·52	59
60	9122·25	9582·55	10113·57	10741·27	11509·13	12498·70	13893·00	16276·12		60
M	81°	82°	83°	84°	85°	86°	87°	88°	89°	M

LOGARITHMS

No. 1000———1599   Log. 00000———20385

	0	1	2	3	4	5	6	7	8	9		5th fig.	D
100	00000	00043	00087	00130	00173	00217	00260	00303	00346	00389	100		
101	00432	00475	00518	00561	00604	00647	00689	00732	00775	00817	101	1	4
102	00860	00903	00945	00988	01030	01072	01115	01157	01199	01242	102	2	8
103	01284	01326	01368	01410	01452	01494	01536	01578	01620	01662	103	3	12
104	01703	01745	01787	01828	01870	01912	01953	01995	02036	02078	104	4	16
105	02119	02160	02202	02243	02284	02325	02366	02408	02449	02490	105	5	21
106	02531	02572	02612	02653	02694	02735	02776	02816	02857	02898	106	6	25
107	02938	02979	03020	03060	03100	03141	03181	03222	03262	03302	107	7	28
108	03342	03383	03423	03463	03503	03543	03583	03623	03663	03703	108	8	33
109	03743	03783	03822	03862	03902	03941	03981	04021	04060	04100	109	9	37
110	04139	04179	04218	04258	04297	04336	04376	04415	04454	04493	110		
111	04532	04571	04611	04650	04689	04728	04766	04805	04844	04883	111	1	4
112	04922	04961	04999	05038	05077	05115	05154	05192	05231	05269	112	2	8
113	05308	05346	05385	05423	05461	05500	05538	05576	05614	05652	113	3	11
114	05691	05729	05767	05805	05843	05881	05919	05956	05994	06032	114	4	15
115	06070	06108	06145	06183	06221	06258	06296	06333	06371	06408	115	5	19
116	06446	06483	06521	06558	06595	06633	06670	06707	06744	06781	116	6	23
117	06819	06856	06893	06930	06967	07004	07041	07078	07115	07151	117	7	26
118	07188	07225	07262	07299	07335	07372	07409	07445	07482	07518	118	8	30
119	07555	07591	07628	07664	07700	07737	07773	07809	07846	07882	119	9	34
120	07918	07954	07990	08027	08063	08099	08135	08171	08207	08243	120		
121	08279	08314	08350	08386	08422	08458	08493	08529	08565	08600	121	1	3
122	08636	08672	08707	08743	08778	08814	08849	08885	08920	08955	122	2	7
123	08991	09026	09061	09096	09132	09167	09202	09237	09272	09307	123	3	10
124	09342	09377	09412	09447	09482	09517	09552	09587	09622	09656	124	4	14
125	09691	09726	09760	09795	09830	09864	09899	09934	09968	10003	125	5	17
126	10037	10072	10106	10140	10175	10209	10243	10278	10312	10346	126	6	21
127	10380	10415	10449	10483	10517	10551	10585	10619	10653	10687	127	7	24
128	10721	10755	10789	10823	10857	10890	10924	10958	10992	11025	128	8	28
129	11059	11093	11126	11160	11193	11227	11261	11294	11328	11361	129	9	31
130	11394	11428	11461	11494	11528	11561	11594	11628	11661	11694	130		
131	11727	11760	11793	11827	11860	11893	11926	11959	11992	12025	131	1	3
132	12057	12090	12123	12156	12189	12222	12254	12287	12320	12353	132	2	6
133	12385	12418	12450	12483	12516	12548	12581	12613	12646	12678	133	3	10
134	12711	12743	12775	12808	12840	12872	12905	12937	12969	13001	134	4	13
135	13033	13066	13098	13130	13162	13194	13226	13258	13290	13322	135	5	16
136	13354	13386	13418	13450	13481	13513	13545	13577	13609	13640	136	6	19
137	13672	13704	13735	13767	13799	13830	13862	13893	13925	13956	137	7	22
138	13988	14019	14051	14082	14114	14145	14176	14208	14239	14270	138	8	26
139	14302	14333	14364	14395	14426	14457	14489	14520	14551	14582	139	9	29
140	14613	14644	14675	14706	14737	14768	14799	14829	14860	14891	140		
141	14922	14953	14984	15014	15045	15076	15106	15137	15168	15198	141	1	3
142	15229	15259	15290	15321	15351	15382	15412	15442	15473	15503	142	2	6
143	15534	15564	15594	15625	15655	15685	15715	15746	15776	15806	143	3	9
144	15836	15866	15897	15927	15957	15987	16017	16047	16077	16107	144	4	12
145	16137	16167	16197	16227	16256	16286	16316	16346	16376	16406	145	5	15
146	16435	16465	16495	16524	16554	16584	16613	16643	16673	16702	146	6	18
147	16732	16761	16791	16820	16850	16879	16909	16938	16967	16997	147	7	21
148	17026	17056	17085	17114	17143	17173	17202	17231	17260	17290	148	8	24
149	17319	17348	17377	17406	17435	17464	17493	17522	17551	17580	149	9	27
150	17609	17638	17667	17696	17725	17754	17783	17811	17840	17869	150		
151	17898	17926	17955	17984	18013	18041	18070	18099	18127	18156	151	1	3
152	18184	18213	18242	18270	18299	18327	18355	18384	18412	18441	152	2	6
153	18469	18498	18526	18554	18583	18611	18639	18667	18696	18724	153	3	8
154	18752	18780	18808	18837	18865	18893	18921	18949	18977	19005	154	4	11
155	19033	19061	19089	19117	19145	19173	19201	19229	19257	19285	155	5	14
156	19313	19340	19368	19396	19424	19451	19479	19507	19535	19562	156	6	17
157	19590	19618	19645	19673	19701	19728	19756	19783	19811	19838	157	7	20
158	19866	19893	19921	19948	19976	20003	20030	20058	20085	20112	158	8	22
159	20140	20167	20194	20222	20249	20276	20303	20331	20358	20385	159	9	25

| | 0 | 1 | 2 | 3 | 4 | 5 | 6 | 7 | 8 | 9 | | | |

LOGARITHMS

	0	1	2	3	4	5	6	7	8	9	5th fig.	D
160	20412	20439	20466	20493	20520	20548	20575	20602	20629	20656	160	
161	20683	20710	20737	20763	20790	20817	20844	20871	20898	20925	161	1 3
162	20952	20978	21005	21032	21059	21085	21112	21139	21165	21192	162	2 5
163	21219	21245	21272	21299	21325	21352	21378	21405	21431	21458	163	3 8
164	21484	21511	21537	21564	21590	21617	21643	21669	21696	21722	164	4 11
165	21748	21775	21801	21827	21854	21880	21906	21932	21958	21985	165	5 13
166	22011	22037	22063	22089	22115	22141	22168	22194	22220	22246	166	6 16
167	22272	22298	22324	22350	22376	22402	22427	22453	22479	22505	167	7 18
168	22531	22557	22583	22608	22634	22660	22686	22712	22737	22763	168	8 21
169	22789	22814	22840	22866	22891	22917	22943	22968	22994	23019	169	9 24
170	23045	23070	23096	23122	23147	23172	23198	23223	23249	23274	170	
171	23300	23325	23350	23376	23401	23426	23452	23477	23502	23528	171	1 2
172	23553	23578	23603	23629	23654	23679	23704	23729	23754	23780	172	2 5
173	23805	23830	23855	23880	23905	23930	23955	23980	24005	24030	173	3 7
174	24055	24080	24105	24130	24155	24180	24204	24229	24254	24279	174	4 10
175	24304	24329	24353	24378	24403	24428	24452	24477	24502	24527	175	5 12
176	24551	24576	24601	24625	24650	24675	24699	24724	24748	24773	176	6 15
177	24797	24822	24846	24871	24895	24920	24944	24969	24993	25018	177	7 17
178	25042	25066	25091	25115	25140	25164	25188	25213	25237	25261	178	8 20
179	25285	25310	25334	25358	25382	25406	25431	25455	25479	25503	179	9 22
180	25527	25551	25576	25600	25624	25648	25672	25696	25720	25744	180	
181	25768	25792	25816	25840	25864	25888	25912	25936	25959	25983	181	1 2
182	26007	26031	26055	26079	26103	26126	26150	26174	26198	26221	182	2 5
183	26245	26269	26293	26316	26340	26364	26387	26411	26435	26458	183	3 7
184	26482	26505	26529	26553	26576	26600	26623	26647	26670	26694	184	4 9
185	26717	26741	26764	26788	26811	26834	26858	26881	26905	26928	185	5 12
186	26951	26975	26998	27021	27045	27068	27091	27114	27138	27161	186	6 14
187	27184	27207	27231	27254	27277	27300	27323	27346	27370	27393	187	7 16
188	27416	27439	27462	27485	27508	27531	27554	27577	27600	27623	188	8 19
189	27646	27669	27692	27715	27738	27761	27784	27807	27830	27853	189	9 21
190	27875	27898	27921	27944	27967	27990	28012	28035	28058	28081	190	
191	28103	28126	28149	28172	28194	28217	28240	28262	28285	28308	191	1 2
192	28330	28353	28375	28398	28421	28443	28466	28488	28511	28533	192	2 4
193	28556	28578	28601	28623	28646	28668	28691	28713	28735	28758	193	3 7
194	28780	28803	28825	28847	28870	28892	28914	28937	28959	28981	194	4 9
195	29004	29026	29048	29070	29093	29115	29137	29159	29181	29203	195	5 11
196	29226	29248	29270	29292	29314	29336	29358	29380	29403	29425	196	6 13
197	29447	29469	29491	29513	29535	29557	29579	29601	29623	29645	197	7 16
198	29667	29688	29710	29732	29754	29776	29798	29820	29842	29864	198	8 18
199	29885	29907	29929	29951	29973	29994	30016	30038	30060	30081	199	9 20
200	30103	30125	30146	30168	30190	30211	30233	30255	30276	30298	200	
201	30320	30341	30363	30384	30406	30428	30449	30471	30492	30514	201	1 2
202	30535	30557	30578	30600	30621	30643	30664	30685	30707	30728	202	2 4
203	30750	30771	30792	30814	30835	30856	30878	30899	30920	30942	203	3 6
204	30963	30984	31006	31027	31048	31069	31091	31112	31133	31154	204	4 8
205	31175	31197	31218	31239	31260	31281	31302	31323	31345	31366	205	5 11
206	31387	31408	31429	31450	31471	31492	31513	31534	31555	31576	206	6 13
207	31597	31618	31639	31660	31681	31702	31723	31744	31765	31785	207	7 15
208	31806	31827	31848	31869	31890	31911	31931	31952	31973	31994	208	8 17
209	32015	32035	32056	32077	32098	32118	32139	32160	32181	32201	209	9 19
210	32222	32243	32263	32284	32305	32325	32346	32367	32387	32408	210	
211	32428	32449	32469	32490	32511	32531	32552	32572	32593	32613	211	1 2
212	32634	32654	32675	32695	32716	32736	32756	32777	32797	32818	212	2 4
213	32838	32858	32879	32899	32919	32940	32960	32981	33001	33021	213	3 6
214	33041	33062	33082	33102	33123	33143	33163	33183	33203	33224	214	4 8
215	33244	33264	33284	33304	33325	33345	33365	33385	33405	33425	215	5 10
216	33445	33466	33486	33506	33526	33546	33566	33586	33606	33626	216	6 12
217	33646	33666	33686	33706	33726	33746	33766	33786	33806	33826	217	7 14
218	33846	33866	33886	33905	33925	33945	33965	33985	34005	34025	218	8 16
219	34044	34064	34084	34104	34124	34144	34163	34183	34203	34223	219	9 18

| | 0 | 1 | 2 | 3 | 4 | 5 | 6 | 7 | 8 | 9 | | |

LOGARITHMS

No. 2200———2799   Log. 34242———44700

	0	1	2	3	4	5	6	7	8	9	5th Fig	D	
220	34242	34262	34282	34301	34321	34341	34361	34380	34400	34420	220		
221	34439	34459	34479	34498	34518	34537	34557	34577	34596	34616	221	1	2
222	34635	34655	34674	34694	34714	34733	34753	34772	34792	34811	222	2	4
223	34831	34850	34869	34889	34908	34928	34947	34967	34986	35005	223	3	6
224	35025	35044	35064	35083	35102	35122	35141	35160	35180	35199	224	4	8
225	35218	35238	35257	35276	35295	35315	35334	35353	35372	35392	225	5	10
226	35411	35430	35449	35469	35488	35507	35526	35545	35564	35583	226	6	12
227	35603	35622	35641	35660	35679	35698	35717	35736	35755	35774	227	7	14
228	35794	35813	35832	35851	35870	35889	35908	35927	35946	35965	228	8	15
229	35984	36003	36022	36040	36059	36078	36097	36116	36135	36154	229	9	17
230	36173	36192	36211	36229	36248	36267	36286	36305	36324	36342	230		
231	36361	36380	36399	36418	36436	36455	36474	36493	36511	36530	231	1	2
232	36549	36568	36586	36605	36624	36642	36661	36680	36698	36717	232	2	4
233	36736	36754	36773	36792	36810	36829	36847	36866	36884	36903	233	3	6
234	36922	36940	36959	36977	36996	37014	37033	37051	37070	37088	234	4	7
235	37107	37125	37144	37162	37181	37199	37218	37236	37254	37273	235	5	9
236	37291	37310	37328	37346	37365	37383	37402	37420	37438	37457	236	6	11
237	37475	37493	37512	37530	37548	37566	37585	37603	37621	37639	237	7	13
238	37658	37676	37694	37712	37731	37749	37767	37785	37803	37822	238	8	15
239	37840	37858	37876	37894	37912	37931	37949	37967	37985	38003	239	9	17
240	38021	38039	38057	38075	38093	38112	38130	38148	38166	38184	240		
241	38202	38220	38238	38256	38274	38292	38310	38328	38346	38364	241	1	2
242	38382	38400	38417	38435	38453	38471	38489	38507	38525	38543	242	2	4
243	38561	38579	38596	38614	38632	38650	38668	38686	38703	38721	243	3	5
244	38739	38757	38775	38792	38810	38828	38846	38863	38881	38899	244	4	6
245	38917	38934	38952	38970	38988	39005	39023	39041	39058	39076	245	5	9
246	39094	39111	39129	39146	39164	39182	39199	39217	39235	39252	246	6	11
247	39270	39287	39305	39322	39340	39358	39375	39393	39410	39428	247	7	12
248	39445	39463	39480	39498	39515	39533	39550	39568	39585	39603	248	8	14
249	39620	39637	39655	39672	39690	39707	39725	39742	39759	39777	249	9	16
250	39794	39811	39829	39846	39863	39881	39898	39915	39933	39950	250		
251	39967	39985	40002	40019	40037	40054	40071	40088	40106	40123	251	1	2
252	40140	40157	40175	40192	40209	40226	40243	40261	40278	40295	252	2	3
253	40312	40329	40346	40364	40381	40398	40415	40432	40449	40466	253	3	5
254	40483	40501	40518	40535	40552	40569	40586	40603	40620	40637	254	4	7
255	40654	40671	40688	40705	40722	40739	40756	40773	40790	40807	255	5	9
256	40824	40841	40858	40875	40892	40909	40926	40943	40960	40976	256	6	10
257	40993	41010	41027	41044	41061	41078	41095	41111	41128	41145	257	7	12
258	41162	41179	41196	41212	41229	41246	41263	41280	41296	41313	258	8	14
259	41330	41347	41364	41380	41397	41414	41431	41447	41464	41481	259	9	15
260	41497	41514	41531	41547	41564	41581	41597	41614	41631	41647	260		
261	41664	41681	41697	41714	41731	41747	41764	41780	41797	41814	261	1	2
262	41830	41847	41863	41880	41896	41913	41930	41946	41963	41979	262	2	3
263	41996	42012	42029	42045	42062	42078	42095	42111	42128	42144	263	3	5
264	42160	42177	42193	42210	42226	42243	42259	42275	42292	42308	264	4	7
265	42325	42341	42357	42374	42390	42406	42423	42439	42456	42472	265	5	8
266	42488	42505	42521	42537	42553	42570	42586	42602	42619	42635	266	6	10
267	42651	42667	42684	42700	42716	42732	42749	42765	42781	42797	267	7	11
268	42814	42830	42846	42862	42878	42894	42911	42927	42943	42959	268	8	13
269	42975	42991	43008	43024	43040	43056	43072	43088	43104	43120	269	9	15
270	43136	43153	43169	43185	43201	43217	43233	43249	43265	43281	270		
271	43297	43313	43329	43345	43361	43377	43393	43409	43425	43441	271	1	2
272	43457	43473	43489	43505	43521	43537	43553	43569	43584	43600	272	2	3
273	43616	43632	43648	43664	43680	43696	43712	43728	43743	43759	273	3	5
274	43775	43791	43807	43823	43838	43854	43870	43886	43902	43918	274	4	6
275	43933	43949	43965	43981	43996	44012	44028	44044	44059	44075	275	5	8
276	44091	44107	44122	44138	44154	44170	44185	44201	44217	44232	276	6	10
277	44248	44264	44279	44295	44311	44326	44342	44358	44373	44389	277	7	11
278	14405	44420	44436	44451	44467	44483	44498	44514	44529	44545	278	8	13
279	44560	44576	44592	44607	44623	44638	44654	44669	44685	44700	279	9	14
	0	1	2	3	4	5	6	7	8	9			

LOGARITHMS

No. 2800——3399　　　　　　　　　　Log. 44716——53135

	0	1	2	3	4	5	6	7	8	9	5th fig.	D
280	44716	44731	44747	44762	44778	44793	44809	44824	44840	44855	280		
281	44871	44886	44902	44917	44932	44948	44963	44979	44994	45010	281	1 2
282	45025	45040	45056	45071	45087	45102	45117	45133	45148	45163	282	2 3
283	45179	45194	45209	45225	45240	45255	45271	45286	45301	45317	283	3 5
284	45332	45347	45362	45378	45393	45408	45424	45439	45454	45469	284	4 6
285	45485	45500	45515	45530	45545	45561	45576	45591	45606	45621	285	5 8
286	45637	45652	45667	45682	45697	45713	45728	45743	45758	45773	286	6 9
287	45788	45803	45818	45834	45849	45864	45879	45894	45909	45924	287	7 11
288	45939	45954	45969	45985	46000	46015	46030	46045	46060	46075	288	8 12
289	46090	46105	46120	46135	46150	46165	46180	46195	46210	46225	289	9 14
290	46240	46255	46270	46285	46300	46315	46330	46345	46359	46374	290		
291	46389	46404	46419	46434	46449	46464	46479	46494	46509	46523	291	1 1
292	46538	46553	46568	46583	46598	46613	46627	46642	46657	46672	292	2 3
293	46687	46702	46716	46731	46746	46761	46776	46790	46805	46820	293	3 4
294	46835	46850	46864	46879	46894	46909	46923	46938	46953	46968	294	4 6
295	46982	46997	47012	47026	47041	47056	47070	47085	47100	47115	295	5 7
296	47129	47144	47159	47173	47188	47203	47217	47232	47246	47261	296	6 9
297	47276	47290	47305	47320	47334	47349	47363	47378	47393	47407	297	7 10
298	47422	47436	47451	47465	47480	47494	47509	47524	47538	47553	298	8 12
299	47567	47582	47596	47611	47625	47640	47654	47669	47683	47698	299	9 13
300	47712	47727	47741	47756	47770	47784	47799	47813	47828	47842	300		
301	47857	47871	47886	47900	47914	47929	47943	47958	47972	47986	301	1 1
302	48001	48015	48029	48044	48058	48073	48087	48101	48116	48130	302	2 3
303	48144	48159	48173	48187	48202	48216	48230	48245	48259	48273	303	3 4
304	48287	48302	48316	48330	48345	48359	48373	48387	48402	48416	304	4 6
305	48430	48444	48458	48473	48487	48501	48515	48530	48544	48558	305	5 7
306	48572	48586	48601	48615	48629	48643	48657	48671	48686	48700	306	6 9
307	48714	48728	48742	48756	48770	48785	48799	48813	48827	48841	307	7 10
308	48855	48869	48883	48897	48911	48926	48940	48954	48968	48982	308	8 11
309	48996	49010	49024	49038	49052	49066	49080	49094	49108	49122	309	9 13
310	49136	49150	49164	49178	49192	49206	49220	49234	49248	49262	310		
311	49276	49290	49304	49318	49332	49346	49360	49374	49388	49402	311	1 1
312	49416	49429	49443	49457	49471	49485	49499	49513	49527	49541	312	2 3
313	49554	49568	49582	49596	49610	49624	49638	49651	49665	49679	313	3 4
314	49693	49707	49721	49734	49748	49762	49776	49790	49804	49817	314	4 6
315	49831	49845	49859	49872	49886	49900	49914	49928	49941	49955	315	5 7
316	49969	49982	49996	50010	50024	50037	50051	50065	50079	50092	316	6 8
317	50106	50120	50133	50147	50161	50174	50188	50202	50215	50229	317	7 10
318	50243	50256	50270	50284	50297	50311	50325	50338	50352	50365	318	8 11
319	50379	50393	50406	50420	50434	50447	50461	50474	50488	50501	319	9 12
320	50515	50529	50542	50556	50569	50583	50596	50610	50623	50637	320		
321	50651	50664	50678	50691	50705	50718	50732	50745	50759	50772	321	1 1
322	50786	50799	50813	50826	50840	50853	50866	50880	50893	50907	322	2 3
323	50920	50934	50947	50961	50974	50987	51001	51014	51028	51041	323	3 4
324	51055	51068	51081	51095	51108	51122	51135	51148	51162	51175	324	4 5
325	51188	51202	51215	51228	51242	51255	51268	51282	51295	51308	325	5 7
326	51322	51335	51348	51362	51375	51388	51402	51415	51428	51442	326	6 8
327	51455	51468	51481	51495	51508	51521	51534	51548	51561	51574	327	7 9
328	51587	51601	51614	51627	51640	51654	51667	51680	51693	51706	328	8 11
329	51720	51733	51746	51759	51772	51786	51799	51812	51825	51838	329	9 12
330	51851	51865	51878	51891	51904	51917	51930	51943	51957	51970	330		
331	51983	51996	52009	52022	52035	52048	52061	52075	52088	52101	331	1 1
332	52114	52127	52140	52153	52166	52179	52192	52205	52218	52231	332	2 3
333	52244	52258	52271	52284	52297	52310	52323	52336	52349	52362	333	3 4
334	52375	52388	52401	52414	52427	52440	52453	52466	52479	52492	334	4 5
335	52505	52517	52530	52543	52556	52569	52582	52595	52608	52621	335	5 6
336	52634	52647	52660	52673	52686	52699	52711	52724	52737	52750	336	6 8
337	52763	52776	52789	52802	52815	52827	52840	52853	52866	52879	337	7 9
338	52892	52905	52917	52930	52943	52956	52969	52982	52994	53007	338	8 10
339	53020	53033	53046	53058	53071	53084	53097	53110	53122	53135	339	9 12

| | 0 | 1 | 2 | 3 | 4 | 5 | 6 | 7 | 8 | 9 | | |

LOGARITHMS

	0	1	2	3	4	5	6	7	8	9		5th fig.	D
340	53148	53161	53173	53186	53199	53212	53225	53237	53250	53263	340		
341	53275	53288	53301	53314	53326	53339	53352	53365	53377	53390	341	1	1
342	53403	53415	53428	53441	53453	53466	53479	53491	53504	53517	342	2	3
343	53529	53542	53555	53567	53580	53593	53605	53618	53631	53643	343	3	4
344	53656	53669	53681	53694	53706	53719	53732	53744	53757	53769	344	4	5
345	53782	53795	53807	53820	53832	53845	53857	53870	53883	53895	345	5	6
346	53908	53920	53933	53945	53958	53970	53983	53995	54008	54020	346	6	8
347	54033	54046	54058	54071	54083	54096	54108	54121	54133	54145	347	7	9
348	54158	54170	54183	54195	54208	54220	54233	54245	54258	54270	348	8	10
349	54283	54295	54307	54320	54332	54345	54357	54370	54382	54394	349	9	11
350	54407	54419	54432	54444	54456	54469	54481	54494	54506	54518	350		
351	54531	54543	54555	54568	54580	54593	54605	54617	54630	54642	351	1	1
352	54654	54667	54679	54691	54704	54716	54728	54741	54753	54765	352	2	2
353	54778	54790	54802	54814	54827	54839	54851	54864	54876	54888	353	3	4
354	54900	54913	54925	54937	54949	54962	54974	54986	54998	55011	354	4	5
355	55023	55035	55047	55060	55072	55084	55096	55108	55121	55133	355	5	6
356	55145	55157	55169	55182	55194	55206	55218	55230	55243	55255	356	6	7
357	55267	55279	55291	55303	55315	55328	55340	55352	55364	55376	357	7	9
358	55388	55400	55413	55425	55437	55449	55461	55473	55485	55497	358	8	10
359	55509	55522	55534	55546	55558	55570	55582	55594	55606	55618	359	9	11
360	55630	55642	55654	55666	55679	55691	55703	55715	55727	55739	360		
361	55751	55763	55775	55787	55799	55811	55823	55835	55847	55859	361	1	1
362	55871	55883	55895	55907	55919	55931	55943	55955	55967	55979	362	2	2
363	55991	56003	56015	56027	56039	56050	56062	56074	56086	56098	363	3	4
364	56110	56122	56134	56146	56158	56170	56182	56194	56206	56217	364	4	5
365	56229	56241	56253	56265	56277	56289	56301	56313	56324	56336	365	5	6
366	56348	56360	56372	56384	56396	56407	56419	56431	56443	56455	366	6	7
367	56467	56478	56490	56502	56514	56526	56538	56549	56561	56573	367	7	8
368	56585	56597	56608	56620	56632	56644	56656	56667	56679	56691	368	8	10
369	56703	56714	56726	56738	56750	56761	56773	56785	56797	56808	369	9	11
370	56820	56832	56844	56855	56867	56879	56891	56902	56914	56926	370		
371	56937	56949	56961	56973	56984	56996	57008	57019	57031	57043	371	1	1
372	57054	57066	57078	57089	57101	57113	57124	57136	57148	57159	372	2	2
373	57171	57183	57194	57206	57217	57229	57241	57252	57264	57276	373	3	4
374	57287	57299	57310	57322	57334	57345	57357	57368	57380	57392	374	4	5
375	57403	57415	57426	57438	57449	57461	57473	57484	57496	57507	375	5	6
376	57519	57530	57542	57553	57565	57577	57588	57600	57611	57623	376	6	7
377	57634	57646	57657	57669	57680	57692	57703	57715	57726	57738	377	7	8
378	57749	57761	57772	57784	57795	57807	57818	57830	57841	57853	378	8	9
379	57864	57875	57887	57898	57910	57921	57933	57944	57956	57967	379	9	10
380	57978	57990	58001	58013	58024	58036	58047	58058	58070	58081	380		
381	58093	58104	58115	58127	58138	58150	58161	58172	58184	58195	381	1	1
382	58206	58218	58229	58240	58252	58263	58275	58286	58297	58309	382	2	2
383	58320	58331	58343	58354	58365	58377	58388	58399	58411	58422	383	3	3
384	58433	58444	58456	58467	58478	58490	58501	58512	58524	58535	384	4	5
385	58546	58557	58569	58580	58591	58602	58614	58625	58636	58648	385	5	6
386	58659	58670	58681	58693	58704	58715	58726	58737	58749	58760	386	6	7
387	58771	58782	58794	58805	58816	58827	58838	58850	58861	58872	387	7	8
388	58883	58894	58906	58917	58928	58939	58950	58962	58973	58984	388	8	9
389	58995	59006	59017	59028	59040	59051	59062	59073	59084	59095	389	9	10
390	59107	59118	59129	59140	59151	59162	59173	59184	59196	59207	390		
391	59218	59229	59240	59251	59262	59273	59284	59295	59306	59318	391	1	1
392	59329	59340	59351	59362	59373	59384	59395	59406	59417	59428	392	2	2
393	59439	59450	59461	59472	59483	59495	59506	59517	59528	59539	393	3	3
394	59550	59561	59572	59583	59594	59605	59616	59627	59638	59649	394	4	4
395	59660	59671	59682	59693	59704	59715	59726	59737	59748	59759	395	5	6
396	59770	59781	59791	59802	59813	59824	59835	59846	59857	59868	396	6	7
397	59879	59890	59901	59912	59923	59934	59945	59956	59967	59977	397	7	8
398	59988	59999	60010	60021	60032	60043	60054	60065	60076	60086	398	8	9
399	60097	60108	60119	60130	60141	60152	60163	60173	60184	60195	399	9	10

| | 0 | 1 | 2 | 3 | 4 | 5 | 6 | 7 | 8 | 9 | |

LOGARITHMS

No. 4000————4599   Log. 60206————66266

	0	1	2	3	4	5	6	7	8	9		5th fig.	D
400	60206	60217	60228	60239	60249	60260	60271	60282	60293	60304	400		
401	60314	60325	60336	60347	60358	60369	60379	60390	60401	60412	401	1	1
402	60423	60433	60444	60455	60466	60477	60487	60498	60509	60520	402	2	2
403	60531	60541	60552	60563	60574	60584	60595	60606	60617	60627	403	3	3
404	60638	60649	60660	60670	60681	60692	60703	60713	60724	60735	404	4	4
405	60746	60756	60767	60778	60788	60799	60810	60821	60831	60842	405	5	5
406	60853	60863	60874	60885	60895	60906	60917	60927	60938	60949	406	6	6
407	60959	60970	60981	60991	61002	61013	61023	61034	61045	61055	407	7	8
408	61066	61077	61087	61098	61109	61119	61130	61141	61151	61162	408	8	9
409	61172	61183	61194	61204	61215	61225	61236	61247	61257	61268	409	9	10
410	61278	61289	61300	61310	61321	61331	61342	61353	61363	61374	410		
411	61384	61395	61405	61416	61426	61437	61448	61458	61469	61479	411	1	1
412	61490	61500	61511	61521	61532	61542	61553	61563	61574	61585	412	2	2
413	61595	61606	61616	61627	61637	61648	61658	61669	61679	61690	413	3	3
414	61700	61711	61721	61732	61742	61752	61763	61773	61784	61794	414	4	4
415	61805	61815	61826	61836	61847	61857	61868	61878	61888	61899	415	5	5
416	61909	61920	61930	61941	61951	61962	61972	61982	61993	62003	416	6	6
417	62014	62024	62034	62045	62055	62066	62076	62086	62097	62107	417	7	7
418	62118	62128	62138	62149	62159	62170	62180	62190	62201	62211	418	8	8
419	62221	62232	62242	62253	62263	62273	62284	62294	62304	62315	419	9	9
420	62325	62335	62346	62356	62366	62377	62387	62397	62408	62418	420		
421	62428	62439	62449	62459	62469	62480	62490	62500	62511	62521	421	1	1
422	62531	62542	62552	62562	62572	62583	62593	62603	62614	62624	422	2	2
423	62634	62644	62655	62665	62675	62685	62696	62706	62716	62726	423	3	3
424	62737	62747	62757	62767	62778	62788	62798	62808	62818	62829	424	4	4
425	62839	62849	62859	62870	62880	62890	62900	62910	62921	62931	425	5	5
426	62941	62951	62961	62972	62982	62992	63002	63012	63022	63033	426	6	6
427	63043	63053	63063	63073	63083	63094	63104	63114	63124	63134	427	7	7
428	63144	63155	63165	63175	63185	63195	63205	63215	63226	63236	428	8	8
429	63246	63256	63266	63276	63286	63296	63306	63317	63327	63337	429	9	9
430	63347	63357	63367	63377	63387	63397	63407	63418	63428	63438	430		
431	63448	53458	63468	63478	63488	63498	63508	63518	63528	63538	431	1	1
432	63548	63558	63569	63579	63589	63599	63609	63619	63629	63639	432	2	2
433	63649	63659	63669	63679	63689	63699	63709	63719	63729	63739	433	3	3
434	63749	63759	63769	63779	63789	63799	63809	63819	63829	63839	434	4	4
435	63849	63859	63869	63879	63889	63899	63909	63919	63929	63939	435	5	5
436	63949	63959	63969	63979	63989	63998	64008	64018	64028	64038	436	6	6
437	64048	64058	64068	64078	64088	64098	64108	64118	64128	64138	437	7	7
438	64147	64157	64167	64177	64187	64197	64207	64217	64227	64237	438	8	8
439	64246	64256	64266	64276	64286	64296	64306	64316	64326	64335	439	9	9
440	64345	64355	64365	64375	64385	64395	64404	64414	64424	64434	440		
441	64444	64454	64464	64473	64483	64493	64503	64513	64523	64532	441	1	1
442	64542	64552	64562	64572	64582	64591	64601	64611	64621	64631	442	2	2
443	64640	64650	64660	64670	64680	64689	64699	64709	64719	64729	443	3	3
444	64738	64748	64758	64768	64777	64787	64797	64807	64817	64826	444	4	4
445	64836	64846	64856	64865	64875	64885	64895	64904	64914	64924	445	5	5
446	64934	64943	64953	64963	64972	64982	64992	65002	65011	65021	446	6	6
447	65031	65041	65050	65060	65070	65079	65089	65099	65108	65118	447	7	7
448	65128	65138	65147	65157	65167	65176	65186	65196	65205	65215	448	8	8
449	65225	65234	65244	65254	65263	65273	65283	65292	65302	65312	449	9	9
450	65321	65331	65341	65350	65360	65370	65379	65389	65398	65408	450		
451	65418	65427	65437	65447	65456	65466	65475	65485	65495	65504	451	1	1
452	65514	65523	65533	65543	65552	65562	65571	65581	65591	65600	452	2	2
453	65610	65619	65629	65639	65648	65658	65667	65677	65686	65696	453	3	3
454	65706	65715	65725	65734	65744	65753	65763	65773	65782	65792	454	4	4
455	65801	65811	65820	65830	65839	65849	65858	65868	65877	65887	455	5	5
456	65897	65906	65916	65925	65935	65944	65954	65963	65973	65982	456	6	6
457	65992	66001	66011	66020	66030	66039	66049	66058	66068	66077	457	7	7
458	66087	66096	66106	66115	66125	66134	66143	66153	66162	66172	458	8	8
459	66181	66191	66200	66210	66219	66229	66238	66247	66257	66266	459	9	9

| | 0 | 1 | 2 | 3 | 4 | 5 | 6 | 7 | 8 | 9 | | | |

LOGARITHMS

No. 4600 —— 5199   Log. 66276———71592

	0	1	2	3	4	5	6	7	8	9		5th fig.	D
460	66276	66285	66295	66304	66314	66323	66332	66342	66351	66361	460		
461	66370	66380	66389	66398	66408	66417	66427	66436	66445	66455	461	1	1
462	66464	66474	66483	66492	66502	66511	66521	66530	66539	66549	462	2	2
463	66558	66568	66577	66586	66596	66605	66614	66624	66633	66642	463	3	3
464	66652	66661	66671	66680	66689	66699	66708	66717	66727	66736	464	4	4
465	66745	66755	66764	66773	66783	66792	66801	66811	66820	66829	465	5	5
466	66839	66848	66857	66867	66876	66885	66895	66904	66913	66922	466	6	6
467	66932	66941	66950	66960	66969	66978	66988	66997	67006	67015	467	7	7
468	67025	67034	67043	67052	67062	67071	67080	67090	67099	67108	468	8	7
469	67117	67127	67136	67145	67154	67164	67173	67182	67191	67201	469	9	8
470	67210	67219	67228	67238	67247	67256	67265	67274	67284	67293	470		
471	67302	67311	67321	67330	67339	67348	67357	67367	67376	67385	471	1	1
472	67394	67403	67413	67422	67431	67440	67449	67459	67468	67477	472	2	2
473	67486	67495	67505	67514	67523	67532	67541	67550	67560	67569	473	3	3
474	67578	67587	67596	67605	67614	67624	67633	67642	67651	67660	474	4	4
475	67669	67679	67688	67697	67706	67715	67724	67733	67742	67752	475	5	5
476	67761	67770	67779	67788	67797	67806	67815	67825	67834	67843	476	6	5
477	67852	67861	67870	67879	67888	67897	67906	67916	67925	67934	477	7	6
478	67943	67952	67961	67970	67979	67988	67997	68006	68015	68025	478	8	7
479	68034	68043	68052	68061	68070	68079	68088	68097	68106	68115	479	9	8
480	68124	68133	68142	68151	68160	68169	68178	68187	68196	68206	480		
481	68215	68224	68233	68242	68251	68260	68269	68278	68287	68296	481	1	1
482	68305	68314	68323	68332	68341	68350	68359	68368	68377	68386	482	2	2
483	68395	68404	68413	68422	68431	68440	68449	68458	68467	68476	483	3	3
484	68485	68494	68503	68511	68520	68529	68538	68547	68556	68565	484	4	4
485	68574	68583	68592	68601	68610	68619	68628	68637	68646	68655	485	5	4
486	68664	68673	68682	68690	68699	68708	68717	68726	68735	68744	486	6	5
487	68753	68762	68771	68780	68789	68798	68806	68815	68824	68833	487	7	6
488	68842	68851	68860	68869	68878	68887	68895	68904	68913	68922	488	8	7
489	68931	68940	68949	68958	68966	68975	68984	68993	69002	69011	489	9	8
490	69020	69029	69037	69046	69055	69064	69073	69082	69091	69099	490		
491	69108	69117	69126	69135	69144	69152	69161	69170	69179	69188	491	1	1
492	69197	69205	69214	69223	69232	69241	69249	69258	69267	69276	492	2	2
493	69285	69294	69302	69311	69320	69329	69338	69346	69355	69364	493	3	3
494	69373	69382	69390	69399	69408	69417	69425	69434	69443	69452	494	4	4
495	69461	69469	69478	69487	69496	69504	69513	69522	69531	69539	495	5	4
496	69548	69557	69566	69574	69583	69592	69601	69609	69618	69627	496	6	5
497	69636	69644	69653	69662	69671	69679	69688	69697	69706	69714	497	7	6
498	69723	69732	69740	69749	69758	69767	69775	69784	69793	69801	498	8	7
499	69810	69819	69828	69836	69845	69854	69862	69871	69880	69888	499	9	8
500	69897	69906	69914	69923	69932	69940	69949	69958	69966	69975	500		
501	69984	69992	70001	70010	70018	70027	70036	70044	70053	70062	501	1	1
502	70070	70079	70088	70096	70105	70114	70122	70131	70140	70148	502	2	2
503	70157	70165	70174	70183	70191	70200	70209	70217	70226	70234	503	3	3
504	70243	70252	70260	70269	70278	70286	70295	70303	70312	70321	504	4	4
505	70329	70338	70346	70355	70364	70372	70381	70389	70398	70407	505	5	4
506	70415	70424	70432	70441	70449	70458	70467	70475	70484	70492	506	6	5
507	70501	70509	70518	70527	70535	70544	70552	70561	70569	70578	507	7	6
508	70586	70595	70604	70612	70621	70629	70638	70646	70655	70663	508	8	7
509	70672	70680	70689	70697	70706	70714	70723	70732	70740	70749	509	9	8
510	70757	70766	70774	70783	70791	70800	70808	70817	70825	70834	510		
511	70842	70851	70859	70868	70876	70885	70893	70902	70910	70919	511	1	1
512	70927	70936	70944	70952	70961	70969	70978	70986	70995	71003	512	2	2
513	71012	71020	71029	71037	71046	71054	71063	71071	71079	71088	513	3	3
514	71096	71105	71113	71122	71130	71139	71147	71155	71164	71172	514	4	3
515	71181	71189	71198	71206	71214	71223	71231	71240	71248	71257	515	5	4
516	71265	71273	71282	71290	71299	71307	71315	71324	71332	71341	516	6	5
517	71349	71357	71366	71374	71383	71391	71399	71408	71416	71425	517	7	6
518	71433	71441	71450	71458	71467	71475	71483	71492	71500	71508	518	8	7
519	71517	71525	71534	71542	71550	71559	71567	71575	71584	71592	519	9	8

| | 0 | 1 | 2 | 3 | 4 | 5 | 6 | 7 | 8 | 9 | | |

LOGARITHMS

No. 5200———5799   Log. 71600———76335

	0	1	2	3	4	5	6	7	8	9	5th fig.		D
520	71600	71609	71617	71625	71634	71642	71650	71659	71667	71675	520		
521	71684	71692	71700	71709	71717	71725	71734	71742	71750	71759	521	1	1
522	71767	71775	71784	71792	71800	71809	71817	71825	71834	71842	522	2	2
523	71850	71859	71867	71875	71883	71892	71900	71908	71917	71925	523	3	3
524	71933	71941	71950	71958	71966	71975	71983	71991	71999	72008	524	4	3
525	72016	72024	72033	72041	72049	72057	72066	72074	72082	72090	525	5	4
526	72099	72107	72115	72123	72132	72140	72148	72156	72165	72173	526	6	5
527	72181	72189	72198	72206	72214	72222	72231	72239	72247	72255	527	7	6
528	72263	72272	72280	72288	72296	72305	72313	72321	72329	72337	528	8	7
529	72346	72354	72362	72370	72378	72387	72395	72403	72411	72419	529	9	8
530	72428	72436	72444	72452	72460	72469	72477	72485	72493	72501	530		
531	72510	72518	72526	72534	72542	72550	72559	72567	72575	72583	531	1	1
532	72591	72599	72608	72616	72624	72632	72640	72648	72656	72665	532	2	2
533	72673	72681	72689	72697	72705	72713	72722	72730	72738	72746	533	3	3
534	72754	72762	72770	72779	72787	72795	72803	72811	72819	72827	534	4	3
535	72835	72844	72852	72860	72868	72876	72884	72892	72900	72908	535	5	4
536	72917	72925	72933	72941	72949	72957	72965	72973	72981	72989	536	6	5
537	72997	73006	73014	73022	73030	73038	73046	73054	73062	73070	537	7	6
538	73078	73086	73094	73102	73111	73119	73127	73135	73143	73151	538	8	7
539	73159	73167	73175	73183	73191	73199	73207	73215	73223	73231	539	9	8
540	73239	73247	73256	73264	73272	73280	73288	73296	73304	73312	540		
541	73320	73328	73336	73344	73352	73360	73368	73376	73384	73392	541	1	1
542	73400	73408	73416	73424	73432	73440	73448	73456	73464	73472	542	2	2
543	73480	73488	73496	73504	73512	73520	73528	73536	73544	73552	543	3	2
544	73560	73568	73576	73584	73592	73600	73608	73616	73624	73632	544	4	3
545	73640	73648	73656	73664	73672	73680	73687	73695	73703	73711	545	5	4
546	73719	73727	73735	73743	73751	73759	73767	73775	73783	73791	546	6	5
547	73799	73807	73815	73823	73831	73838	73846	73854	73862	73870	547	7	6
548	73878	73886	73894	73902	73910	73918	73926	73934	73941	73949	548	8	6
549	73957	73965	73973	73981	73989	73997	74005	74013	74021	74028	549	9	7
550	74036	74044	74052	74060	74068	74076	74084	74092	74099	74107	550		
551	74115	74123	74131	74139	74147	74155	74162	74170	74178	74186	551	1	1
552	74194	74202	74210	74218	74225	74233	74241	74249	74257	74265	552	2	2
553	74273	74280	74288	74296	74304	74312	74320	74328	74335	74343	553	3	2
554	74351	74359	74367	74375	74382	74390	74398	74406	74414	74422	554	4	3
555	74429	74437	74445	74453	74461	74468	74476	74484	74492	74500	555	5	4
556	74508	74515	74523	74531	74539	74547	74554	74562	74570	74578	556	6	4
557	74586	74593	74601	74609	74617	74625	74632	74640	74648	74656	557	7	5
558	74663	74671	74679	74687	74695	74702	74710	74718	74726	74733	558	8	6
559	74741	74749	74757	74765	74772	74780	74788	74796	74803	74811	559	9	7
560	74819	74827	74834	74842	74850	74858	74865	74873	74881	74889	560		
561	74896	74904	74912	74920	74927	74935	74943	74950	74958	74966	561	1	1
562	74974	74981	74989	74997	75005	75012	75020	75028	75035	75043	562	2	2
563	75051	75059	75066	75074	75082	75089	75097	75105	75113	75120	563	3	2
564	75128	75136	75143	75151	75159	75166	75174	75182	75190	75197	564	4	3
565	75205	75213	75220	75228	75236	75243	75251	75259	75266	75274	565	5	4
566	75282	75289	75297	75305	75312	75320	75328	75335	75343	75351	566	6	5
567	75358	75366	75374	75381	75389	75397	75404	75412	75420	75427	567	7	5
568	75435	75443	75450	75458	75465	75473	75481	75488	75496	75504	568	8	6
569	75511	75519	75527	75534	75542	75549	75557	75565	75572	75580	569	9	7
570	75588	75595	75603	75610	75618	75626	75633	75641	75648	75656	570		
571	75664	75671	75679	75686	75694	75702	75709	75717	75724	75732	571	1	1
572	75740	75747	75755	75762	75770	75778	75785	75793	75800	75808	572	2	2
573	75816	75823	75831	75838	75846	75853	75861	75869	75876	75884	573	3	2
574	75891	75899	75906	75914	75921	75929	75937	75944	75952	75959	574	4	3
575	75967	75974	75982	75989	75997	76005	76012	76020	76027	76035	575	5	4
576	76042	76050	76057	76065	76072	76080	76088	76095	76103	76110	576	6	5
577	76118	76125	76133	76140	76148	76155	76163	76170	76178	76185	577	7	5
578	76193	76200	76208	76215	76223	76230	76238	76245	76253	76260	578	8	6
579	76268	76275	76283	76290	76298	76305	76313	76320	76328	76335	579	9	7
	0	1	2	3	4	5	6	7	8	9			

LOGARITHMS

No. 5800————6399   Log. 76343————80611

	0	1	2	3	4	5	6	7	8	9		5th fig.	D
580	76343	76350	76358	76365	76373	76380	76388	76395	76403	76410	580		
581	76418	76425	76433	76440	76448	76455	76462	76470	76477	76485	581	1	1
582	76492	76500	76507	76515	76522	76530	76537	76545	76552	76559	582	2	2
583	76567	76574	76582	76589	76597	76604	76612	76619	76626	76634	583	3	2
584	76641	76649	76656	76664	76671	76679	76686	76693	76701	76708	584	4	3
585	76716	76723	76730	76738	76745	76753	76760	76768	76775	76782	585	5	4
586	76790	76797	76805	76812	76819	76827	76834	76842	76849	76856	586	6	5
587	76864	76871	76879	76886	76893	76901	76908	76916	76923	76930	587	7	5
588	76938	76945	76953	76960	76967	76975	76982	76989	76997	77004	588	8	6
589	77012	77019	77026	77034	77041	77048	77056	77063	77071	77078	589	9	7
590	77085	77093	77100	77107	77115	77122	77129	77137	77144	77151	590		
591	77159	77166	77173	77181	77188	77196	77203	77210	77218	77225	591	1	1
592	77232	77240	77247	77254	77262	77269	77276	77284	77291	77298	592	2	1
593	77306	77313	77320	77327	77335	77342	77349	77357	77364	77371	593	3	2
594	77379	77386	77393	77401	77408	77415	77423	77430	77437	77444	594	4	3
595	77452	77459	77466	77474	77481	77488	77496	77503	77510	77517	595	5	3
596	77525	77532	77539	77547	77554	77561	77568	77576	77583	77590	596	6	4
597	77597	77605	77612	77619	77627	77634	77641	77648	77656	77663	597	7	5
598	77670	77677	77685	77692	77699	77706	77714	77721	77728	77735	598	8	6
599	77743	77750	77757	77764	77772	77779	77786	77793	77801	77808	599	9	7
600	77815	77822	77830	77837	77844	77851	77859	77866	77873	77880	600		
601	77887	77895	77902	77909	77916	77924	77931	77938	77945	77952	601	1	1
602	77960	77967	77974	77981	77989	77996	78003	78010	78017	78025	602	2	1
603	78032	78039	78046	78053	78061	78068	78075	78082	78089	78097	603	3	2
604	78104	78111	78118	78125	78132	78140	78147	78154	78161	78168	604	4	3
605	78176	78183	78190	78197	78204	78211	78219	78226	78233	78240	605	5	4
606	78247	78254	78262	78269	78276	78283	78290	78297	78305	78312	606	6	5
607	78319	78326	78333	78340	78348	78355	78362	78369	78376	78383	607	7	5
608	78390	78398	78405	78412	78419	78426	78433	78440	78448	78455	608	8	6
609	78462	78469	78476	78483	78490	78497	78505	78512	78519	78526	609	9	7
610	78533	78540	78547	78554	78562	78569	78576	78583	78590	78597	610		
611	78604	78611	78618	78625	78633	78640	78647	78654	78661	78668	611	1	1
612	78675	78682	78689	78696	78704	78711	78718	78725	78732	78739	612	2	2
613	78746	78753	78760	78767	78774	78782	78789	78796	78803	78810	613	3	2
614	78817	78824	78831	78838	78845	78852	78859	78866	78873	78880	614	4	3
615	78888	78895	78902	78909	78916	78923	78930	78937	78944	78951	615	5	4
616	78958	78965	78972	78979	78986	78993	79000	79007	79014	79022	616	6	4
617	79029	79036	79043	79050	79057	79064	79071	79078	79085	79092	617	7	5
618	79099	79106	79113	79120	79127	79134	79141	79148	79155	79162	618	8	6
619	79169	79176	79183	79190	79197	79204	79211	79218	79225	79232	619	9	6
620	79239	79246	79253	79260	79267	79274	79281	79288	79295	79302	620		
621	79309	79316	79323	79330	79337	79344	79351	79358	79365	79372	621	1	1
622	79379	79386	79393	79400	79407	79414	79421	79428	79435	79442	622	2	1
623	79449	79456	79463	79470	79477	79484	79491	79498	79505	79512	623	3	2
624	79519	79525	79532	79539	79546	79553	79560	79567	79574	79581	624	4	3
625	79588	79595	79602	79609	79616	79623	79630	79637	79644	79651	625	5	3
626	79657	79664	79671	79678	79685	79692	79699	79706	79713	79720	626	6	4
627	79727	79734	79741	79748	79755	79761	79768	79775	79782	79789	627	7	5
628	79796	79803	79810	79817	79824	79831	79837	79844	79851	79858	628	8	6
629	79865	79872	79879	79886	79893	79900	79907	79913	79920	79927	629	9	6
630	79934	79941	79948	79955	79962	79969	79975	79982	79989	79996	630		
631	80003	80010	80017	80024	80031	80037	80044	80051	80058	80065	631	1	1
632	80072	80079	80085	80092	80099	80106	80113	80120	80127	80134	632	2	1
633	80140	80147	80154	80161	80168	80175	80182	80188	80195	80202	633	3	2
634	80209	80216	80223	80230	80236	80243	80250	80257	80264	80271	634	4	3
635	80277	80284	80291	80298	80305	80312	80318	80325	80332	80339	635	5	4
636	80346	80353	80359	80366	80373	80380	80387	80394	80400	80407	636	6	4
637	80414	80421	80428	80434	80441	80448	80455	80462	80469	80475	637	7	5
638	80482	80489	80496	80503	80509	80516	80523	80530	80537	80543	638	8	6
639	80550	80557	80564	80571	80577	80584	80591	80598	80604	80611	639	9	6
	0	1	2	3	4	5	6	7	8	9			

LOGARITHMS

No. 6400 —— 6999   **Log. 80618 —— 84504**

	0	1	2	3	4	5	6	7	8	9		5th fig.	D
640	80618	80625	80632	80638	80645	80652	80659	80666	80672	80679	640		
641	80686	80693	80699	80706	80713	80720	80726	80733	80740	80747	641	1	1
642	80754	80760	80767	80774	80781	80787	80794	80801	80808	80814	642	2	1
643	80821	80828	80835	80841	80848	80855	80862	80868	80875	80882	643	3	2
644	80889	80895	80902	80909	80916	80922	80929	80936	80943	80949	644	4	3
645	80956	80963	80969	80976	80983	80990	80996	81003	81010	81017	645	5	4
646	81023	81030	81037	81043	81050	81057	81064	81070	81077	81084	646	6	4
647	81090	81097	81104	81111	81117	81124	81131	81137	81144	81151	647	7	5
648	81158	81164	81171	81178	81184	81191	81198	81204	81211	81218	648	8	6
649	81225	81231	81238	81245	81251	81258	81265	81271	81278	81285	649	9	6
650	81291	81298	81305	81311	81318	81325	81331	81338	81345	81351	650		
651	81358	81365	81371	81378	81385	81391	81398	81405	81411	81418	651	1	1
652	81425	81431	81438	81445	81451	81458	81465	81471	81478	81485	652	2	1
653	81491	81498	81505	81511	81518	81525	81531	81538	81545	81551	653	3	2
654	81558	81564	81571	81578	81584	81591	81598	81604	81611	81618	654	4	3
655	81624	81631	81637	81644	81651	81657	81664	81671	81677	81684	655	5	3
656	81690	81697	81704	81710	81717	81724	81730	81737	81743	81750	656	6	4
657	81757	81763	81770	81776	81783	81790	81796	81803	81809	81816	657	7	5
658	81823	81829	81836	81842	81849	81856	81862	81869	81875	81882	658	8	6
659	81889	81895	81902	81908	81915	81922	81928	81935	81941	81948	659	9	6
660	81954	81961	81968	81974	81981	81987	81994	82000	82007	82014	660		
661	82020	82027	82033	82040	82046	82053	82060	82066	82073	82079	661	1	1
662	82086	82092	82099	82106	82112	82119	82125	82132	82138	82145	662	2	1
663	82151	82158	82164	82171	82178	82184	82191	82197	82204	82210	663	3	2
664	82217	82223	82230	82236	82243	82250	82256	82263	82269	82276	664	4	3
665	82282	82289	82295	82302	82308	82315	82321	82328	82334	82341	665	5	3
666	82347	82354	82361	82367	82374	82380	82387	82393	82400	82406	666	6	4
667	82413	82419	82426	82432	82439	82445	82452	82458	82465	82471	667	7	5
668	82478	82484	82491	82497	82504	82510	82517	82523	82530	82536	668	8	5
669	82543	82549	82556	82562	82569	82575	82582	82588	82595	82601	669	9	6
670	82608	82614	82620	82627	82633	82640	82646	82653	82659	82666	670		
671	82672	82679	82685	82692	82698	82705	82711	82718	82724	82731	671	1	1
672	82737	82743	82750	82756	82763	82769	82776	82782	82789	82795	672	2	1
673	82802	82808	82814	82821	82827	82834	82840	82847	82853	82860	673	3	2
674	82866	82872	82879	82885	82892	82898	82905	82911	82918	82924	674	4	3
675	82930	82937	82943	82950	82956	82963	82969	82975	82982	82988	675	5	3
676	82995	83001	83008	83014	83020	83027	83033	83040	83046	83053	676	6	4
677	83059	83065	83072	83078	83085	83091	83097	83104	83110	83117	677	7	5
678	83123	83129	83136	83142	83149	83155	83161	83168	83174	83181	678	8	5
679	83187	83193	83200	83206	83213	83219	83225	83232	83238	83245	679	9	6
680	83251	83257	83264	83270	83276	83283	83289	83296	83302	83308	680		
681	83315	83321	83328	83334	83340	83347	83353	83359	83366	83372	681	1	1
682	83378	83385	83391	83398	83404	83410	83417	83423	83429	83436	682	2	1
683	83442	83448	83455	83461	83468	83474	83480	83487	83493	83499	683	3	2
684	83506	83512	83518	83525	83531	83537	83544	83550	83556	83563	684	4	3
685	83569	83575	83582	83588	83594	83601	83607	83613	83620	83626	685	5	3
686	83632	83639	83645	83651	83658	83664	83670	83677	83683	83689	686	6	4
687	83696	83702	83708	83715	83721	83727	83734	83740	83746	83753	687	7	5
688	83759	83765	83772	83778	83784	83790	83797	83803	83809	83816	688	8	5
689	83822	83828	83835	83841	83847	83853	83860	83866	83872	83879	689	9	6
690	83885	83891	83898	83904	83910	83916	83923	83929	83935	83942	690		
691	83948	83954	83960	83967	83973	83979	83986	83992	83998	84004	691	1	1
692	84011	84017	84023	84029	84036	84042	84048	84055	84061	84067	692	2	1
693	84073	84080	84086	84092	84098	84105	84111	84117	84123	84130	693	3	2
694	84136	84142	84149	84155	84161	84167	84174	84180	84186	84192	694	4	3
695	84199	84205	84211	84217	84224	84230	84236	84242	84248	84255	695	5	3
696	84261	84267	84273	84280	84286	84292	84298	84305	84311	84317	696	6	4
697	84323	84330	84336	84342	84348	84354	84361	84367	84373	84379	697	7	5
698	84386	84392	84398	84404	84410	84417	84423	84429	84435	84442	698	8	5
699	84448	84454	84460	84466	84473	84479	84485	84491	84497	84504	699	9	6
	0	1	2	3	4	5	6	7	8	9			

LOGARITHMS

No. 7000———7599 Log. 84510———88076

	0	1	2	3	4	5	6	7	8	9		5th fig.	D
700	84510	84516	84522	84528	84535	84541	84547	84553	84559	84566	700		
701	84572	84578	84584	84590	84597	84603	84609	84615	84621	84628	701	1	1
702	84634	84640	84646	84652	84658	84665	84671	84677	84683	84689	702	2	1
703	84696	84702	84708	84714	84720	84726	84733	84739	84745	84751	703	3	2
704	84757	84763	84770	84776	84782	84788	84794	84800	84807	84813	704	4	2
705	84819	84825	84831	84837	84844	84850	84856	84862	84868	84874	705	5	3
706	84881	84887	84893	84899	84905	84911	84917	84924	84930	84936	706	6	4
707	84942	84948	84954	84960	84967	84973	84979	84985	84991	84997	707	7	4
708	85003	85010	85016	85022	85028	85034	85040	85046	85052	85059	708	8	5
709	85065	85071	85077	85083	85089	85095	85101	85108	85114	85120	709	9	5
710	85126	85132	85138	85144	85150	85156	85163	85169	85175	85181	710		
711	85187	85193	85199	85205	85211	85218	85224	85230	85236	85242	711	1	1
712	85248	85254	85260	85266	85272	85279	85285	85291	85297	85303	712	2	1
713	85309	85315	85321	85327	85333	85339	85346	85352	85358	85364	713	3	2
714	85370	85376	85382	85388	85394	85400	85406	85412	85419	85425	714	4	2
715	85431	85437	85443	85449	85455	85461	85467	85473	85479	85485	715	5	3
716	85491	85497	85503	85510	85516	85522	85528	85534	85540	85546	716	6	4
717	85552	85558	85564	85570	85576	85582	85588	85594	85600	85606	717	7	4
718	85612	85619	85625	85631	85637	85643	85649	85655	85661	85667	718	8	5
719	85673	85679	85685	85691	85697	85703	85709	85715	85721	85727	719	9	5
720	85733	85739	85745	85751	85757	85763	85769	85775	85782	85788	720		
721	85794	85800	85806	85812	85818	85824	85830	85836	85842	85848	721	1	1
722	85854	85860	85866	85872	85878	85884	85890	85896	85902	85908	722	2	1
723	85914	85920	85926	85932	85938	85944	85950	85956	85962	85968	723	3	2
724	85974	85980	85986	85992	85998	86004	86010	86016	86022	86028	724	4	2
725	86034	86040	86046	86052	86058	86064	86070	86076	86082	86088	725	5	3
726	86094	86100	86106	86112	86118	86124	86130	86136	86142	86148	726	6	4
727	86153	86159	86165	86171	86177	86183	86189	86195	86201	86207	727	7	4
728	86213	86219	86225	86231	86237	86243	86249	86255	86261	86267	728	8	5
729	86273	86279	86285	86291	86297	86303	86309	86314	86320	86326	729	9	5
730	86332	86338	86344	86350	86356	86362	86368	86374	86380	86386	730		
731	86392	86398	86404	86410	86416	86421	86427	86433	86439	86445	731	1	1
732	86451	36457	86643	86469	86475	86481	86487	86493	86499	86505	732	2	1
733	86510	86516	86522	86528	86534	86540	86546	86552	86558	86564	733	3	2
734	86570	86576	86581	86587	86593	86599	86605	86611	86617	86623	734	4	2
735	86629	86635	86641	86647	86652	86658	86664	86670	86676	86682	735	5	3
736	86688	86694	86700	86706	86711	86717	86723	86729	86735	86741	736	6	4
737	86747	86753	86759	86764	86770	86776	86782	86788	86794	86800	737	7	4
738	86806	86812	86817	86823	86829	86835	86841	86847	86853	86859	738	8	5
739	86864	86870	86876	86882	86888	86894	86900	86906	86911	86917	739	9	5
740	86923	86929	86935	86941	86947	86953	86958	86964	86970	86976	740		
741	86982	86988	86994	86999	87005	87011	87017	87023	87029	87035	741	1	1
742	87040	87046	87052	87058	87064	87070	87076	87081	87087	87093	742	2	1
743	87099	87105	87111	87116	87122	87128	87134	87140	87146	87152	743	3	2
744	87157	87163	87169	87175	87181	87187	87192	87198	87204	87210	744	4	2
745	87216	87222	87227	87233	87239	87245	87251	87256	87262	87268	745	5	3
746	87274	87280	87286	87291	87297	87303	87309	87315	87320	87326	746	6	4
747	87332	87338	87344	87350	87355	87361	87367	87373	87379	87384	747	7	4
748	87390	87396	87402	87408	87413	87419	87425	87431	87437	87442	748	8	5
749	87448	87454	87460	87466	87471	87477	87483	87489	87495	87500	749	9	5
750	87506	87512	87518	87524	87529	87535	87541	87547	87552	87558	750		
751	87564	87570	87576	87581	87587	87593	87599	87604	87610	87616	751	1	1
752	87622	87628	87633	87639	87645	87651	87656	87662	87668	87674	752	2	1
753	87680	87685	87691	87697	87703	87708	87714	87720	87726	87731	753	3	2
754	87737	87743	87749	87754	87760	87766	87772	87777	87783	87789	754	4	2
755	87795	87800	87806	87812	87818	87823	87829	87835	87841	87846	755	5	3
756	87852	87858	87864	87869	87875	87881	87887	87892	87898	87904	756	6	4
757	87910	87915	87921	87927	87933	87938	87944	87950	87956	87961	757	7	4
758	87967	87973	87978	87984	87990	87996	88001	88007	88013	88019	758	8	5
759	88024	88030	88036	88041	88047	88053	88059	88064	88070	88076	759	9	5
	0	1	2	3	4	5	6	7	8	9			

LOGARITHMS

No. 7600———8199　　　　　　　　Log. 88081———91376

	0	1	2	3	4	5	6	7	8	9		5th fig.	D
760	88081	88087	88093	88099	88104	88110	88116	88121	88127	88133	760		
761	88139	88144	88150	88156	88161	88167	88173	88178	88184	88190	761	1	1
762	88196	88201	88207	88213	88218	88224	88230	88235	88241	88247	762	2	1
763	88252	88258	88264	88270	88275	88281	88287	88292	88298	88304	763	3	2
764	88309	88315	88321	88326	88332	88338	88343	88349	88355	88361	764	4	2
765	88366	88372	88378	88383	88389	88395	88400	88406	88412	88417	765	5	3
766	88423	88429	88434	88440	88446	88451	88457	88463	88468	88474	766	6	4
767	88480	88485	88491	88497	88502	88508	88514	88519	88525	88531	767	7	4
768	88536	88542	88547	88553	88559	88564	88570	88576	88581	88587	768	8	5
769	88593	88598	88604	88610	88615	88621	88627	88632	88638	88643	769	9	5
770	88649	88655	88660	88666	88672	88677	88683	88689	88694	88700	770		
771	88705	88711	88717	88722	88728	88734	88739	88745	88751	88756	771	1	1
772	88762	88767	88773	88779	88784	88790	88796	88801	88807	88812	772	2	1
773	88818	88824	88829	88835	88840	88846	88852	88857	88863	88869	773	3	2
774	88874	88880	88885	88891	88897	88902	88908	88913	88919	88925	774	4	2
775	88930	88936	88941	88947	88953	88958	88964	88969	88975	88981	775	5	3
776	88986	88992	88997	89003	89009	89014	89020	89025	89031	89037	776	6	3
777	89042	89048	89053	89059	89064	89070	89076	89081	89087	89092	777	7	4
778	89098	89104	89109	89115	89120	89126	89131	89137	89143	89148	778	8	4
779	89154	89159	89165	89171	89176	89182	89187	89193	89198	89204	779	9	5
780	89210	89215	89221	89226	89232	89237	89243	89248	89254	89260	780		
781	89265	89271	89276	89282	89287	89293	89299	89304	89310	89315	781	1	1
782	89321	89326	89332	89337	89343	89348	89354	89360	89365	89371	782	2	1
783	89376	89382	89387	89393	89398	89404	89409	89415	89421	89426	783	3	2
784	89432	89437	89443	89448	89454	89459	89465	89470	89476	89481	784	4	3
785	89487	89493	89498	89504	89509	89515	89520	89526	89531	89537	785	5	3
786	89542	89548	89553	89559	89564	89570	89575	89581	89586	89592	786	6	4
787	89598	89603	89609	89614	89620	89625	89631	89636	89642	89647	787	7	4
788	89653	89658	89664	89669	89675	89680	89686	89691	89697	89702	788	8	5
789	89708	89713	89719	89724	89730	89735	89741	89746	89752	89757	789	9	5
790	89763	89768	89774	89779	89785	89790	89796	89801	89807	89812	790		
791	89818	89823	89829	89834	89840	89845	89851	89856	89862	89867	791	1	1
792	89873	89878	89884	89889	89894	89900	89905	89911	89916	89922	792	2	1
793	89927	89933	89938	89944	89949	89955	89960	89966	89971	89977	793	3	2
794	89982	89988	89993	89999	90004	90009	90015	90020	90026	90031	794	4	2
795	90037	90042	90048	90053	90059	90064	90070	90075	90080	90086	795	5	3
796	90091	90097	90102	90108	90113	90119	90124	90130	90135	90140	796	6	4
797	90146	90151	90157	90162	90168	90173	90179	90184	90189	90195	797	7	4
798	90200	90206	90211	90217	90222	90228	90233	90238	90244	90249	798	8	5
799	90255	90260	90266	90271	90276	90282	90287	90293	90298	90304	799	9	5
800	90309	90314	90320	90325	90331	90336	90342	90347	90352	90358	800		
801	90363	90369	90374	90380	90385	90390	90396	90401	90407	90412	801	1	1
802	90417	90423	90428	90434	90439	90445	90450	90455	90461	90466	802	2	1
803	90472	90477	90482	90488	90493	90499	90504	90509	90515	90520	803	3	2
804	90526	90531	90536	90542	90547	90553	90558	90563	90569	90574	804	4	2
805	90580	90585	90590	90596	90601	90607	90612	90617	90623	90628	805	5	3
806	90634	90639	90644	90650	90655	90660	90666	90671	90677	90682	806	6	3
807	90687	90693	90698	90704	90709	90714	90720	90725	90730	90736	807	7	4
808	90741	90747	90752	90757	90763	90768	90773	90779	90784	90790	808	8	4
809	90795	90800	90806	90811	90816	90822	90827	90832	90838	90843	809	9	5
810	90849	90854	90859	90865	90870	90875	90881	90886	90891	90897	810		
811	90902	90907	90913	90918	90924	90929	90934	90940	90945	90950	811	1	1
812	90956	90961	90966	90972	90977	90982	90988	90993	90998	91004	812	2	1
813	91009	91014	91020	91025	91030	91036	91041	91046	91052	91057	813	3	2
814	91062	91068	91073	91078	91084	91089	91094	91100	91105	91110	814	4	2
815	91116	91121	91126	91132	91137	91142	91148	91153	91158	91164	815	5	3
816	91169	91174	91180	91185	91190	91196	91201	91206	91212	91217	816	6	3
817	91222	91228	91233	91238	91244	91249	91254	91259	91265	91270	817	7	4
818	91275	91281	91286	91291	91297	91302	91307	91313	91318	91323	818	8	4
819	91328	91334	91339	91344	91350	91355	91360	91366	91371	91376	819	9	5
	0	1	2	3	4	5	6	7	8	9			

LOGARITHMS

No. 8200———8799   Log. 91381———94443

	0	1	2	3	4	5	6	7	8	9		5th fig	D
820	91381	91387	91392	91397	91403	91408	91413	91418	91424	91429	820		
821	91434	91440	91445	91450	91456	91461	91466	91471	91477	91482	821	1	1
822	91487	91493	91498	91503	91508	91514	91519	91524	91529	91535	822	2	1
823	91540	91545	91551	91556	91561	91566	91572	91577	91582	91587	823	3	2
824	91593	91598	91603	91609	91614	91619	91624	91630	91635	91640	824	4	2
825	91645	91651	91656	91661	91666	91672	91677	91682	91688	91693	825	5	3
826	91698	91703	91709	91714	91719	91724	91730	91735	91740	91745	826	6	3
827	91751	91756	91761	91766	91772	91777	91782	91787	91793	91798	827	7	4
828	91803	91808	91814	91819	91824	91829	91835	91840	91845	91850	828	8	4
829	91856	91861	91866	91871	91876	91882	91887	91892	91897	91903	829	9	5
830	91908	91913	91918	91924	91929	91934	91939	91944	91950	91955	830		
831	91960	91965	91971	91976	91981	91986	91991	91997	92002	92007	831	1	1
832	92012	92018	92023	92028	92033	92038	92044	92049	92054	92059	832	2	1
833	92065	92070	92075	92080	92085	92091	92096	92101	92106	92111	833	3	2
834	92117	92122	92127	92132	92137	92143	92148	92153	92158	92163	834	4	2
835	92169	92174	92179	92184	92189	92195	92200	92205	92210	92215	835	5	3
836	92221	92226	92231	92236	92241	92247	92252	92257	92262	92267	836	6	3
837	92273	92278	92283	92288	92293	92299	92304	92309	92314	92319	837	7	4
838	92324	92330	92335	92340	92345	92350	92356	92361	92366	92371	838	8	4
839	92376	92381	92387	92392	92397	92402	92407	92412	92418	92423	839	9	5
840	92428	92433	92438	92443	92449	92454	92459	92464	92469	92474	840		
841	92480	92485	92490	92495	92500	92505	92511	92516	92521	92526	841	1	1
842	92531	92536	92542	92547	92552	92557	92562	92567	92572	92578	842	2	1
843	92583	92588	92593	92598	92603	92609	92614	92619	92624	92629	843	3	2
844	92634	92639	92645	92650	92655	92660	92665	92670	92675	92681	844	4	2
845	92686	92691	92696	92701	92706	92711	92717	92722	92727	92732	845	5	3
846	92737	92742	92747	92752	92758	92763	92768	92773	92778	92783	846	6	3
847	92788	92794	92799	92804	92809	92814	92819	92824	92829	92835	847	7	4
848	92840	92845	92850	92855	92860	92865	92870	92875	92881	92886	848	8	4
849	92891	92896	92901	92906	92911	92916	92921	92927	92932	92937	849	9	5
850	92942	92947	92952	92957	92962	92967	92973	92978	92983	92988	850		
851	92993	92998	93003	93008	93013	93019	93024	93029	93034	93039	851	1	1
852	93044	93049	93054	93059	93064	93069	93075	93080	93085	93090	852	2	1
853	93095	93100	93105	93110	93115	93120	93125	93131	93136	93141	853	3	2
854	93146	93151	93156	93161	93166	93171	93176	93181	93186	93192	854	4	2
855	93197	93202	93207	93212	93217	93222	93227	93232	93237	93242	855	5	3
856	93247	93252	93258	93263	93268	93273	93278	93283	93288	93293	856	6	3
857	93298	93303	93308	93313	93318	93323	93329	93334	93339	93344	857	7	3
858	93349	93354	93359	93364	93369	93374	93379	93384	93389	93394	858	8	4
859	93399	93404	93409	93415	93420	93425	93430	93435	93440	93445	859	9	4
860	93450	93455	93460	93465	93470	93475	93480	93485	93490	93495	860		
861	93500	93505	93510	93515	93521	93526	93531	93536	93541	93546	861	1	1
862	93551	93556	93561	93566	93571	93576	93581	93586	93591	93596	862	2	1
863	93601	93606	93611	93616	93621	93626	93631	93636	93641	93646	863	3	2
864	93651	93656	93661	93666	93672	93677	93682	93687	93692	93697	864	4	2
865	93702	93707	93712	93717	93722	93727	93732	93737	93742	93747	865	5	3
866	93752	93757	93762	93767	93772	93777	93782	93787	93792	93797	866	6	3
867	93802	93807	93812	93817	93822	93827	93832	93837	93842	93847	867	7	3
868	93852	93857	93862	93867	93872	93877	93882	93887	93892	93897	868	8	4
869	93902	93907	93912	93917	93922	93927	93932	93937	93942	93947	869	9	4
870	93952	93957	93962	93967	93972	93977	93982	93987	93992	93997	870		
871	94002	94007	94012	94017	94022	94027	94032	94037	94042	94047	871	1	0
872	94052	94057	94062	94067	94072	94077	94082	94087	94092	94096	872	2	1
873	94101	94106	94111	94116	94121	94126	94131	94136	94141	94146	873	3	1
874	94151	94156	94161	94166	94171	94176	94181	94186	94191	94196	874	4	2
875	94201	94206	94211	94216	94221	94226	94231	94236	94241	94245	875	5	2
876	94250	94255	94260	94265	94270	94275	94280	94285	94290	94295	876	6	3
877	94300	94305	94310	94315	94320	94325	94330	94335	94340	94345	877	7	3
878	94349	94354	94359	94364	94369	94374	94379	94384	94389	94394	878	8	4
879	94399	94404	94409	94414	94419	94424	94429	94434	94438	94443	879	9	4

0	1	2	3	4	5	6	7	8	9

LOGARITHMS

No. 8800——9399   Log. 94448——97308

	0	1	2	3	4	5	6	7	8	9		5th fig.	D
880	94448	94453	94458	94463	94468	94473	94478	94483	94488	94493	880		
881	94498	94503	94507	94512	94517	94522	94527	94532	94537	94542	881	1	0
882	94547	94552	94557	94562	94567	94572	94576	94581	94586	94591	882	2	1
883	94596	94601	94606	94611	94616	94621	94626	94631	94636	94640	883	3	1
884	94645	94650	94655	94660	94665	94670	94675	94680	94685	94689	884	4	2
885	94694	94699	94704	94709	94714	94719	94724	94729	94734	94739	885	5	2
886	94743	94748	94753	94758	94763	94768	94773	94778	94783	94788	886	6	3
887	94792	94797	94802	94807	94812	94817	94822	94827	94832	94836	887	7	3
888	94841	94846	94851	94856	94861	94866	94871	94876	94880	94885	888	8	4
889	94890	94895	94900	94905	94910	94915	94920	94924	94929	94934	889	9	4
890	94939	94944	94949	94954	94959	94963	94968	94973	94978	94983	890		
891	94988	94993	94998	95002	95007	95012	95017	95022	95027	95032	891	1	0
892	95037	95041	95046	95051	95056	95061	95066	95071	95075	95080	892	2	1
893	95085	95090	95095	95100	95105	95110	95114	95119	95124	95129	893	3	1
894	95134	95139	95144	95148	95153	95158	95163	95168	95173	95177	894	4	2
895	95182	95187	95192	95197	95202	95207	95211	95216	95221	95226	895	5	2
896	95231	95236	95241	95245	95250	95255	95260	95265	95270	95274	896	6	3
897	95279	95284	95289	95294	95299	95303	95308	95313	95318	95323	897	7	3
898	95328	95333	95337	95342	95347	95352	95357	95362	95366	95371	898	8	4
899	95376	95381	95386	95391	95395	95400	95405	95410	95415	95419	899	9	4
900	95424	95429	95434	95439	95444	95448	95453	95458	95463	95468	900		
901	95473	95477	95482	95487	95492	95497	95501	95506	95511	95516	901	1	0
902	95521	95526	95530	95535	95540	95545	95550	95554	95559	95564	902	2	1
903	95569	95574	95578	95583	95588	95593	95598	95602	95607	95612	903	3	1
904	95617	95622	95626	95631	95636	95641	95646	95651	95655	95660	904	4	2
905	95665	95670	95675	95679	95684	95689	95694	95698	95703	95708	905	5	2
906	95713	95718	95722	95727	95732	95737	95742	95746	95751	95756	906	6	3
907	95761	95766	95770	95775	95780	95785	95789	95794	95799	95804	907	7	3
908	95809	95813	95818	95823	95828	95833	95837	95842	95847	95852	908	8	4
909	95856	95861	95866	95871	95876	95880	95885	95890	95895	95899	909	9	4
910	95904	95909	95914	95918	95923	95928	95933	95938	95942	95947	910		
911	95952	95957	95961	95966	95971	95976	95980	95985	95990	95995	911	1	0
912	96000	96004	96009	96014	96019	96023	96028	96033	96038	96042	912	2	1
913	96047	96052	96057	96061	96066	96071	96076	96080	96085	96090	913	3	1
914	96095	96099	96104	96109	96114	96118	96123	96128	96133	96137	914	4	2
915	96142	96147	96152	96156	96161	96166	96171	96175	96180	96185	915	5	2
916	96190	96194	96199	96204	96209	96213	96218	96223	96228	96232	916	6	3
917	96237	96242	96246	96251	96256	96261	96265	96270	96275	96280	917	7	3
918	96284	96289	96294	96299	96303	96308	96313	96317	96322	96327	918	8	4
919	96332	96336	96341	96346	96350	96355	96360	96365	96369	96374	919	9	4
920	96379	96384	96388	96393	96398	96402	96407	96412	96417	96421	920		
921	96426	96431	96435	96440	96445	96450	96454	96459	96464	96468	921	1	0
922	96473	96478	96483	96487	96492	96497	96501	96506	96511	96516	922	2	1
923	96520	96525	96530	96534	96539	96544	96548	96553	96558	96563	923	3	1
924	96567	96572	96577	96581	96586	96591	96595	96600	96605	96610	924	4	2
925	96614	96619	96624	96628	96633	96638	96642	96647	96652	96656	925	5	2
926	96661	96666	96671	96675	96680	96685	96689	96694	96699	96703	926	6	3
927	96708	96713	96717	96722	96727	96731	96736	96741	96745	96750	927	7	3
928	96755	96760	96764	96769	96774	96778	96783	96788	96792	96797	928	8	4
929	96802	96806	96811	96816	96820	96825	96830	96834	96839	96844	929	9	4
930	96848	96853	96858	96862	96867	96872	96876	96881	96886	96890	930		
931	96895	96900	96904	96909	96914	96918	96923	96928	96932	96937	931	1	0
932	96942	96946	96951	96956	96960	96965	96970	96974	96979	96984	932	2	1
933	96988	96993	96998	97002	97007	97011	97016	97021	97025	97030	933	3	1
934	97035	97039	97044	97049	97053	97058	97063	97067	97072	97077	934	4	2
935	97081	97086	97090	97095	97100	97104	97109	97114	97118	97123	935	5	2
936	97128	97132	97137	97142	97146	97151	97155	97160	97165	97169	936	6	3
937	97174	97179	97183	97188	97193	97197	97202	97206	97211	97216	937	7	3
938	97220	97225	97230	97234	97239	97243	97248	97253	97257	97262	938	8	4
939	97267	97271	97276	97280	97285	97290	97294	97299	97304	97308	939	9	4
	0	1	2	3	4	5	6	7	8	9			

LOGARITHMS

No. 9400———9999 **Log. 97313———99996**

	0	1	2	3	4	5	6	7	8	9		5th fig	D
940	97313	97317	97322	97327	97331	97336	97341	97345	97350	97354	940		
941	97359	97364	97368	97373	97377	97382	97387	97391	97396	97401	941	1	0
942	97405	97410	97414	97419	97424	97428	97433	97437	97442	97447	942	2	1
943	97451	97456	97460	97465	97470	97474	97479	97483	97488	97493	943	3	1
944	97497	97502	97506	97511	97516	97520	97525	97529	97534	97539	944	4	2
945	97543	97548	97552	97557	97562	97566	97571	97575	97580	97585	945	5	2
946	97589	97594	97598	97603	97608	97612	97617	97621	97626	97630	946	6	3
947	97635	97640	97644	97649	97653	97658	97663	97667	97672	97676	947	7	3
948	97681	97685	97690	97695	97699	97704	97708	97713	97718	97722	948	8	4
949	97727	97731	97736	97740	97745	97750	97754	97759	97763	97768	949	9	4
950	97772	97777	97782	97786	97791	97795	97800	97804	97809	97814	950		
951	97818	97823	97827	97832	97836	97841	97845	97850	97855	97859	951	1	0
952	97864	97868	97873	97877	97882	97887	97891	97896	97900	97905	952	2	1
953	97909	97914	97918	97923	97928	97932	97937	97941	97946	97950	953	3	1
954	97955	97959	97964	97969	97973	97978	97982	97987	97991	97996	954	4	2
955	98000	98005	98009	98014	98019	98023	98028	98032	98037	98041	955	5	2
956	98046	98050	98055	98059	98064	98069	98073	98078	98082	98087	956	6	3
957	98091	98096	98100	98105	98109	98114	98118	98123	98128	98132	957	7	3
958	98137	98141	98146	98150	98155	98159	98164	98168	98173	98177	958	8	4
959	98182	98186	98191	98195	98200	98205	98209	98214	98218	98223	959	9	4
960	98227	98232	98236	98241	98245	98250	98254	98259	98263	98268	960		
961	98272	98277	98281	98286	98290	98295	98299	98304	98309	98313	961	1	0
962	98318	98322	98327	98331	98336	98340	98345	98349	98354	98358	962	2	1
963	98363	98367	98372	98376	98381	98385	98390	98394	98399	98403	963	3	1
964	98408	98412	98417	98421	98426	98430	98435	98439	98444	98448	964	4	2
965	98453	98457	98462	98466	98471	98475	98480	98484	98489	98493	965	5	2
966	98498	98502	98507	98511	98516	98520	98525	98529	98534	98538	966	6	3
967	98543	98547	98552	98556	98561	98565	98570	98574	98579	98583	967	7	3
968	98588	98592	98597	98601	98606	98610	98614	98619	98623	98628	968	8	4
969	98632	98637	98641	98646	98650	98655	98659	98664	98668	98673	969	9	4
970	98677	98682	98686	98691	98695	98700	98704	98709	98713	98717	970		
971	98722	98726	98731	98735	98740	98744	98749	98753	98758	98762	971	1	0
972	98767	98771	98776	98780	98785	98789	98793	98798	98802	98807	972	2	1
973	98811	98816	98820	98825	98829	98834	98838	98843	98847	98851	973	3	1
974	98856	98860	98865	98869	98874	98878	98883	98887	98892	98896	974	4	2
975	98901	98905	98909	98914	98918	98923	98927	98932	98936	98941	975	5	2
976	98945	98949	98954	98958	98963	98967	98972	98976	98981	98985	976	6	3
977	98990	98994	98998	99003	99007	99012	99016	99021	99025	99029	977	7	3
978	99034	99038	99043	99047	99052	99056	99061	99065	99069	99074	978	8	4
979	99078	99083	99087	99092	99096	99100	99105	99109	99114	99118	979	9	4
980	99123	99127	99132	99136	99140	99145	99149	99154	99158	99163	980		
981	99167	99171	99176	99180	99185	99189	99193	99198	99202	99207	981	1	0
982	99211	99216	99220	99224	99229	99233	99238	99242	99247	99251	982	2	1
983	99255	99260	99264	99269	99273	99277	99282	99286	99291	99295	983	3	1
984	99300	99304	99308	99313	99317	99322	99326	99330	99335	99339	984	4	2
985	99344	99348	99352	99357	99361	99366	99370	99375	99379	99383	985	5	2
986	99388	99392	99397	99401	99405	99410	99414	99419	99423	99427	986	6	3
987	99432	99436	99441	99445	99449	99454	99458	99463	99467	99471	987	7	3
988	99476	99480	99485	99489	99493	99498	99502	99506	99511	99515	988	8	4
989	99520	99524	99528	99533	99537	99542	99546	99550	99555	99559	989	9	4
990	99564	99568	99572	99577	99581	99585	99590	99594	99599	99603	990		
991	99607	99612	99616	99621	99625	99629	99634	99638	99642	99647	991	1	0
992	99651	99656	99660	99664	99669	99673	99677	99682	99686	99690	992	2	1
993	99695	99699	99704	99708	99712	99717	99721	99726	99730	99734	993	3	1
994	99739	99743	99747	99752	99756	99761	99765	99769	99774	99778	994	4	2
995	99782	99787	99791	99795	99800	99804	99809	99813	99817	99822	995	5	2
996	99826	99830	99835	99839	99843	99848	99852	99856	99861	99865	996	6	3
997	99870	99874	99878	99883	99887	99891	99896	99900	99904	99909	997	7	3
998	99913	99917	99922	99926	99931	99935	99939	99944	99948	99952	998	8	4
999	99957	99961	99965	99970	99974	99978	99983	99987	99991	99996	999	9	4

| | 0 | 1 | 2 | 3 | 4 | 5 | 6 | 7 | 8 | 9 | |

| 0° 180° | LOGS. OF TRIG. FUNCTIONS | | | | | | | | |

'	Sine	Diff.	Cosec.	Tan.	Diff.	Cotan.	Secant	Diff.	Cosine	
00·0	∞		∞	∞		∞	0.(10) 00000		0.(10) 00000	60'
1	$\bar{5}$.(5) 46373	30103	4.(14) 53627	$\bar{5}$.(5) 46373	30103	4.(14) 53627	00000		00000	
·2	76476	17609	23524	76476	17609	23524	00000		00000	
·3	94085	12494	05915	94085	12494	05915	00000		00000	
·4	$\bar{4}$.(6) 06579	9691	3.(13) 93421	$\bar{4}$.(6) 06579	9691	3.(13) 93421	00000		00000	
00·5	16270	7918	83730	16270	7918	83730	00000		00000	
·6	24188	6694	75812	24188	6694	75812	00000		00000	
·7	30882	5800	69118	30882	5800	69118	00000		00000	
·8	36682	5115	63318	36682	5115	63318	00000		00000	
·9	41797	4576	58203	41797	4576	58203	00000		00000	
01·0	46373	4139	53627	46373	4139	53627	00000		00000	59'
·1	50512	3779	49488	50512	3779	49488	00000		00000	
·2	54291	3476	45709	54291	3476	45709	00000		00000	
·3	57767	3218	42233	57767	3218	42233	00000		00000	
·4	60985	2997	39015	60985	2997	39015	00000		00000	
01·5	63982	2803	36018	63982	2803	36018	00000		00000	
·6	66785	2633	33215	66785	2633	33215	00000		00000	
·7	69418	2482	30582	69418	2482	30582	00000		00000	
·8	71900	2348	28100	71900	2348	28100	00000		00000	
·9	74248	2228	25752	74248	2228	25752	00000		00000	
02·0	76476	2119	23524	76476	2119	23524	00000		00000	58'
·1	78595	2020	21405	78595	2020	21405	00000		00000	
·2	80615	1930	19385	80615	1930	19385	00000		00000	
·3	82545	1849	17455	82545	1849	17455	00000		00000	
·4	84394	1773	15606	84394	1773	15606	00000		00000	
02·5	86167	1703	13833	86167	1703	13833	00000		00000	
·6	87870	1639	12130	87870	1639	12130	00000		00000	
·7	89509	1579	10491	89509	1579	10491	00000		00000	
·8	91088	1524	08912	91088	1524	08912	00000		00000	
·9	92612	1473	07388	92612	1473	07388	00000		00000	
03·0	94085	1424	05915	94085	1424	05915	00000		00000	57'
·1	95509	1379	04491	95509	1379	04491	00000		00000	
·2	96888	1336	03112	96888	1336	03112	00000		00000	
·3	98224	1297	01776	98224	1297	01776	00000		00000	
·4	99521	1258	00479	99521	1258	00479	00000		00000	
03·5	$\bar{3}$.(7) 00779	1224	2.(12) 99221	$\bar{3}$.(7) 00779	1224	2.(12) 99221	00000		00000	
·6	02003	1190	97997	02003	1190	97997	00000		00000	
·7	03193	1158	96807	03193	1158	96807	00000		00000	
·8	04351	1128	95649	04351	1128	95649	00000		00000	
·9	05479	1100	94521	05479	1100	94521	00000		00000	
04·0	06579	1072	93421	06579	1072	93421	00000		00000	56'
·1	07651	1047	92349	07651	1047	92349	00000		00000	
·2	08698	1021	91302	08698	1021	91302	00000		00000	
·3	09719	999	90281	09719	999	90281	00000		00000	
·4	10718	976	89282	10718	976	89282	00000		00000	
04·5	11694	954	88306	11694	954	88306	00000		00000	
·6	12648	934	87352	12648	934	87352	00000		00000	
·7	13582	915	86418	13582	915	86418	00000		00000	
·8	14497	895	85503	14497	895	85503	00000		00000	
·9	15392	878	84608	15392	878	84608	00000		00000	
05·0	16270	860	83730	16270	860	83730	00000		00000	55'
·1	17130	843	82870	17130	843	82870	00000		00000	
·2	17973	827	82027	17973	827	82027	00000		00000	
·3	18800	812	81200	18800	812	81200	00000		00000	
·4	19612	797	80388	19612	797	80388	00000		00000	
05·5	20409	782	79591	20409	782	79591	00000		00000	
·6	21191	769	78809	21191	769	78809	00000		00000	
·7	21960	755	78040	21960	755	78040	00000		00000	
·8	22715	743	77285	22715	743	77285	00000		00000	
·9	23458	730	76542	23458	730	76542	00000		00000	
06·0	24188		75812	24188		75812	00000		00000	54'

LOGS. OF TRIG. FUNCTIONS

0°
180°

′	Sine	Diff.	Cosec.	Tan.	Diff.	Cotan.	Secant	Diff.	Cosine	
06·0	3̄.(7) 24188	718	2.(12) 75812	3̄.(7) 24188	718	2.(12) 75812	0.(10) 00000		0.(10) 00000	54′
·1	24906	706	75094	24906	706	75094	00000		00000	
·2	25612	695	74388	25612	695	74388	00000		00000	
·3	26307	684	73693	26307	684	73693	00000		00000	
·4	26991	673	73009	26991	673	73009	00000		00000	
06·5	27664	663	72336	27664	663	72336	00000		00000	
·6	28327	653	71673	28327	653	71673	00000		00000	
·7	28980	644	71020	28980	644	71020	00000		00000	
·8	29624	634	70376	29624	634	70376	00000		00000	
·9	30258	624	69742	30258	625	69742	00000		00000	
07·0	30882	616	69118	30883	615	69118	00000		00000	53′
·1	31498	608	68502	31498	608	68502	00000		00000	
·2	32106	599	67894	32106	599	67894	00000		00000	
·3	32705	591	67295	32705	591	67295	00000		00000	
·4	33296	583	66704	33296	583	66704	00000		00000	
07·5	33879	575	66121	33879	575	66121	00000		00000	
·6	34454	568	65546	34454	568	65546	00000		00000	
·7	35022	560	64978	35022	560	64978	00000		00000	
·8	35582	553	64418	35582	553	64418	00000		00000	
·9	36135	547	63865	36135	547	63865	00000		00000	
08·0	36682	539	63318	36682	539	63318	00000		00000	52′
·1	37221	533	62779	37221	533	62779	00000		00000	
·2	37754	526	62246	37754	526	62246	00000		00000	
·3	38280	521	61720	38280	521	61720	00000		00000	
·4	38801	514	61199	38801	514	61199	00000		00000	
08·5	39315	507	60686	39315	507	60685	00000		00000	
·6	39822	503	60178	39822	503	60178	00000		00000	
·7	40325	496	59675	40325	496	59675	00000		00000	
·8	40821	491	59179	40821	491	59179	00000		00000	
·9	41312	485	58688	41312	485	58688	00000		00000	
09·0	41797	480	58203	41797	480	58203	00000		00000	51′
·1	42277	474	57723	42277	474	57723	00000		00000	
·2	42751	470	57249	42751	470	57249	00000		00000	
·3	43221	464	56779	43221	464	56779	00000		00000	
·4	43685	460	56315	43685	460	56315	00000		00000	
09·5	44145	455	55855	44145	455	55855	00000		00000	
·6	44600	450	55400	44600	450	55400	00000		00000	
·7	45050	445	54950	45050	445	54950	00000		00000	
·8	45495	441	54505	45495	441	54505	00000		00000	
·9	45936	437	54064	45936	437	54064	00000		00000	
10·0	46373	432	53628	46373	432	53627	00000		00000	50′
·1	46805	428	53195	46805	428	53195	00000		00000	
·2	47233	423	52767	47233	423	52767	00000		00000	
·3	47656	420	52344	47656	420	52344	00000		00000	
·4	48076	416	51924	48076	416	51924	00000		00000	
10·5	48492	411	51509	48492	411	51508	00000		00000	
·6	48903	408	51097	48903	408	51097	00000		00000	
·7	49311	404	50689	49311	404	50689	00000		00000	
·8	49715	400	50285	49715	400	50285	00000		00000	
·9	50115	397	49885	50115	397	49885	00000		00000	
11·0	50512	393	49488	50512	393	49488	00000		00000	49′
·1	50905	389	49095	50905	389	49095	00000		00000	
·2	51294	386	48706	51294	386	48706	00000		00000	
·3	51680	383	48320	51680	383	48320	00000		00000	
·4	52063	379	47937	52063	380	47937	00000		00000	
11·5	52442	376	47558	52443	375	47557	00000		00000	
·6	52818	373	47182	52818	373	47182	00000		00000	
·7	53191	370	46809	53191	370	46809	00000		00000	
·8	53561	366	46439	53561	366	46439	00000		00000	
·9	53927	364	46073	53927	364	46073	00000		00000	
12·0	54291		45709	54291		45709	00000		00000	48′

LOGS. OF TRIG. FUNCTIONS

0°
180°

′	Sine	Diff.	Cosec.	Tan.	Diff.	Cotan.	Secant	Diff.	Cosine	
12·0	3̄.(7) 54291		2.(12) 45709	3̄.(7) 54291		2.(12) 45709	0.(10) 00000		0.(10) 00000	48′
·2	55008	717	44992	55008	717	44992	00000		00000	
·4	55715	707	44285	55715	707	44285	00000		00000	
·6	56410	695	43590	56410	695	43590	00000		00000	
·8	57093	683	42917	57093	683	42917	00000		00000	
		674			674					
13·0	57767		42233	57767		42233	00000		00000	47′
·2	58430	663	41570	58430	663	41570	00000		00000	
·4	59083	653	40917	59083	653	40917	00000		00000	
·6	59726	643	40274	59726	643	40274	00000		00000	
·8	60360	634	39640	60360	634	39640	00000		00000	
		625			626					
14·0	60985		39015	60986		39014	00000		00000	46′
·2	61601	616	38399	61601	615	38399	00000		00000	
·4	62209	608	37791	62209	608	37791	00000		00000	
·6	62808	599	37192	62808	599	37192	00000		00000	
·8	63399	591	36601	63399	591	36601	00000		00000	
		583			583					
15·0	63982		36018	63982		36018	00000		00000	45′
·2	64557	575	35443	64557	575	35443	00000		00000	
·4	65124	567	34876	65124	567	34876	00000		00000	
·6	65685	561	34315	65685	561	34315	00000		00000	
·8	66238	553	33762	66238	553	33762	00000		00000	
		546			547					
16·0	66784		33216	66785		33215	00000		00000	44′
·2	67324	540	32676	67324	539	32676	00000		00000	
·4	67857	533	32143	67857	533	32143	00000		00000	
·6	68383	526	31617	68384	527	31616	00001		1̄.(9) 99999	
·8	68903	520	31097	68904	520	31096	00001		99999	
		514			514					
17·0	69417		30583	69418		30582	00001		99999	43′
·2	69925	508	30075	69926	508	30074	00001		99999	
·4	70427	502	29573	70428	502	29572	00001		99999	
·6	70924	497	29076	70925	497	29075	00001		99999	
·8	71414	490	28586	71415	490	28585	00001		99999	
		486			485					
18·0	71900		28100	71900		28100	00001		99999	42′
·2	72379	479	27621	72380	480	27620	00001		99999	
·4	72854	475	27146	72855	475	27145	00001		99999	
·6	73324	470	26676	73325	470	26675	00001		99999	
·8	73788	464	26212	73789	464	26211	00001		99999	
		460			459					
19·0	74248		25752	74248		25752	00001		99999	41′
·2	74702	454	25298	74703	455	25297	00001		99999	
·4	75152	450	24848	75153	450	24847	00001		99999	
·6	75598	446	24402	75599	446	24401	00001		99999	
·8	76039	441	23961	76040	441	23960	00001		99999	
		436			436					
20·0	76475		23525	76476		23524	00001		99999	40′
·2	76907	432	23093	76908	432	23092	00001		99999	
·4	77335	428	22665	77336	428	22664	00001		99999	
·6	77759	424	22241	77760	424	22240	00001		99999	
·8	78179	420	21821	78180	420	21820	00001		99999	
		415			415					
21·0	78594		21406	78595		21405	00001		99999	39′
·2	79006	412	20994	79007	412	20993	00001		99999	
·4	79414	408	20586	79415	408	20585	00001		99999	
·6	79818	404	20182	79819	404	20181	00001		99999	
·8	80218	400	19782	80219	400	19781	00001		99999	
		397			396					
22·0	80615		19385	80616		19385	00001		99999	38′
·2	81008	393	18992	81009	393	18991	00001		99999	
4	81397	389	18603	81398	389	18602	00001		99999	
·6	81783	386	18217	81784	386	18216	00001		99999	
·8	82166	383	17834	82167	383	17833	00001		99999	
		379			379					
23·0	82545		17455	82546		17454	00001		99999	37′
·2	82921	376	17079	82922	376	17078	00001		99999	
·4	83294	373	16706	83295	373	16705	00001		99999	
·6	83663	369	16337	83664	369	16336	00001		99999	
·8	84030	367	15970	84031	367	15969	00001		99999	
		363			363					
24·0	84393		15607	84394		15606	00001		99999	36′

179°
359°

0°
180°

LOGS. OF TRIG. FUNCTIONS

′	Sine	Diff.	Cosec.	Tan.	Diff.	Cotan.	Secant	Diff.	Cosine	
24·0	3̄.(7) 84393	361	2.(12) 15607	3̄.(7) 84394	361	2.(12) 15606	0.(10) 00001		1̄.(9) 99999	36′
·2	84754	357	15246	84755	357	15245	00001		99999	
·4	85111	355	14889	85112	355	14888	00001		99999	
·6	85466	351	14534	85467	351	14533	00001		99999	
·8	85817	349	14183	85818	349	14182	00001		99999	
25·0	86166	346	13834	86167	346	13833	00001		99999	35′
·2	86512	344	13488	86513	344	13487	00001		99999	
·4	86856	340	13144	86857	340	13143	00001		99999	
·6	87196	338	12804	87197	338	12803	00001		99999	
·8	87534	336	12466	87535	336	12465	00001		99999	
26·0	87870	333	12131	87871	332	12129	00001		99999	34′
·2	88202	331	11798	88203	331	11797	00001		99999	
·4	88533	327	11467	88534	327	11466	00001		99999	
·6	88860	326	11140	88861	326	11139	00001		99999	
·8	89186	323	10814	89187	323	10813	00001		99999	
27·0	89509	321	10492	89510	320	10490	00001		99999	33′
·2	89829	318	10171	89830	318	10170	00001		99999	
·4	90147	316	09853	90148	316	09852	00001		99999	
·6	90463	314	09537	90464	314	09536	00001		99999	
·8	90777	311	09223	90778	311	09222	00001		99999	
28·0	91088	309	08912	91089	309	08911	00001		99999	32′
·2	91397	307	08603	91398	307	08602	00001		99999	
·4	91704	305	08296	91705	305	08295	00001		99999	
·6	92009	302	07991	92010	302	07990	00001		99999	
·8	92311	301	07689	92312	301	07688	00001		99999	
29·0	92612	298	07388	92613	299	07387	00001		99999	31′
·2	92910	297	07090	92912	297	07088	00002		99998	
·4	93207	294	06793	93209	294	06791	00002		99998	
·6	93501	293	06499	93503	293	06497	00002		99998	
·8	93794	290	06206	93796	290	06204	00002		99998	
30·0	94084	289	05916	94086	289	05914	00002		99998	30′
·2	94373	286	05627	94375	286	05625	00002		99998	
·4	94659	285	05341	94661	285	05339	00002		99998	
·6	94944	283	05056	94946	283	05054	00002		99998	
·8	95227	281	04773	95229	281	04771	00002		99998	
31·0	95508	279	04492	95510	279	04490	00002		99998	29′
·2	95787	278	04213	95789	278	04211	00002		99998	
·4	96065	276	03935	96067	276	03933	00002		99998	
·6	96341	274	03659	96343	274	03657	00002		99998	
·8	96615	272	03385	96617	272	03383	00002		99998	
32·0	96887	271	03113	96889	271	03111	00002		99998	28′
·2	97158	268	02842	97160	268	02840	00002		99998	
·4	97426	268	02574	97428	268	02572	00002		99998	
·6	97694	265	02306	97696	265	02304	00002		99998	
·8	97959	264	02041	97961	264	02039	00002		99998	
33·0	98223	263	01777	98225	263	01775	00002		99998	27′
·2	98486	261	01514	98488	261	01512	00002		99998	
·4	98747	259	01253	98749	259	01251	00002		99998	
·6	99006	258	00994	99008	258	00992	00002		99998	
·8	99264	256	00736	99266	256	00734	00002		99998	
34·0	99520	254	00480	99522	254	00478	00002		99998	26′
·2	99774	254	00226	99776	254	00224	00002		99998	
·4	2̄.(8) 00028	251	1.(11) 99972	2̄.(8) 00030	251	1.(11) 99970	00002		99998	
·6	00279	251	99721	00281	251	99719	00002		99998	
·8	00530	249	99470	00532	249	99468	00002		99998	
35·0	00779	247	99221	00781	247	99219	00002		99998	25′
·2	01026	246	98974	01028	246	98972	00002		99998	
·4	01272	245	98728	01274	245	98726	00002		99998	
·6	01517	243	98483	01519	243	98481	00002		99998	
·8	01760	242	98240	01762	242	98238	00002		99998	
36·0	02002		97998	02005		97996	00002		99998	24′

LOGS. OF TRIG. FUNCTIONS

0° 180°										
′	Sine	Diff.	Cosec.	Tan.	Diff.	Cotan.	Secant	Diff.	Cosine	
36·0	2̄.(8) 02002	241	1.(11) 97998	2̄.(8) 02005	241	1.(11) 97996	0.(10) 00002		1̄.(9) 99998	24′
·2	02243	239	97757	02245	239	97755	00002		99998	
·4	02482	238	97518	02484	238	97516	00002		99998	
·6	02720	237	97280	02722	237	97278	00002		99998	
·8	02957	235	97043	02959	236	97041	00002		99998	
37·0	03192	234	96808	03195	234	96806	00003		99997	23′
·2	03426	233	96574	03429	233	96571	00003		99997	
·4	03659	231	96341	03662	231	96338	00003		99997	
·6	03890	231	96110	03893	231	96107	00003		99997	
·8	04121	229	95879	04124	229	95876	00003		99997	
38·0	04350	228	95650	04353	228	95647	00003		99997	22′
·2	04578	227	95422	04581	227	95419	00003		99997	
·4	04805	225	95195	04808	225	95192	00003		99997	
·6	05030	225	94970	05033	225	94967	00003		99997	
·8	05255	223	94745	05258	223	94742	00003		99997	
39·0	05478	222	94522	05481	222	94519	00003		99997	21′
·2	05700	221	94300	05703	221	94297	00003		99997	
·4	05921	220	94079	05924	220	94076	00003		99997	
·6	06141	219	93859	06144	219	93856	00003		99997	
·8	06360	218	93640	06363	218	93637	00003		99997	
40·0	06578	216	93422	06581	216	93419	00003		99997	20′
·2	06794	216	93206	06797	216	93203	00003		99997	
·4	07010	214	92990	07013	214	92987	00003		99997	
·6	07224	214	92776	07227	214	92773	00003		99997	
·8	07438	212	92562	07441	212	92559	00003		99997	
41·0	07650	211	92350	07653	211	92347	00003		99997	19′
·2	07861	211	92139	07864	211	92136	00003		99997	
·4	08072	209	91928	08075	209	91925	00003		99997	
·6	08281	208	91719	08284	208	91716	00003		99997	
·8	08489	207	91511	08492	208	91508	00003		99997	
42·0	08696	207	91304	08700	206	91300	00003		99997	18′
·2	08903	205	91097	08906	205	91094	00003		99997	
·4	09108	204	90892	09111	204	90889	00003		99997	
·6	09312	204	90688	09315	204	90685	00003		99997	
·8	09516	202	90484	09519	203	90481	00003		99997	
43·0	09718	202	90282	09722	201	90278	00003		99997	17′
·2	09920	200	90080	09923	200	90077	00003		99997	
·4	10120	200	89880	10123	201	89877	00003		99997	
·6	10320	199	89680	10324	199	89676	00004		99996	
·8	10519	198	89481	10523	197	89477	00004		99996	
44·0	10717	197	89283	10720	198	89280	00004		99996	16′
·2	10914	196	89086	10918	196	89082	00004		99996	
·4	11110	195	88890	11114	195	88886	00004		99996	
·6	11305	194	88695	11309	194	88691	00004		99996	
·8	11499	194	88501	11503	193	88497	00004		99996	
45·0	11693	192	88307	11696	193	88304	00004		99996	15′
·2	11885	192	88115	11889	192	88111	00004		99996	
·4	12077	191	87923	12081	191	87919	00004		99996	
·6	12268	190	87732	12272	190	87728	00004		99996	
·8	12458	189	87542	12462	189	87538	00004		99996	
46·0	12647	188	87353	12651	188	87349	00004		99996	14′
·2	12835	188	87165	12839	188	87161	00004		99996	
·4	13023	187	86977	13027	187	86973	00004		99996	
·6	13210	186	86790	13214	186	87686	00004		99996	
·8	13396	185	86604	13400	185	86600	00004		99996	
47·0	13581	184	86419	13585	184	86415	00004		99996	13′
·2	13765	184	86235	13769	184	86231	00004		99996	
·4	13949	183	86051	13953	183	86047	00004		99996	
·6	14132	182	85868	14136	182	85864	00004		99996	
·8	14314	181	85686	14318	182	85682	00004		99996	
48·0	14495		85505	14500		85500	00004		99996	12′

0°
180°

LOGS. OF TRIG. FUNCTIONS

′	Sine	Diff.	Cosec.	Tan.	Diff.	Cotan.	Secant	Diff.	Cosine	
48·0	$\overline{2}$.(8) 14495	181	1.(11) 85505	$\overline{2}$.(8) 14500	180	1.(11) 85500	0.(10) 00004		$\overline{1}$.(9) 99996	12′
·2	14676	180	85324	14680	180	85320	00004		99996	
·4	14856	179	85144	14860	179	85140	00004		99996	
·6	15035	178	84965	15039	178	84961	00004		99996	
·8	15213	178	84787	15217	178	84783	00004		99996	
49·0	15391	177	84609	15395	177	84605	00004		99996	11′
·2	15568	176	84432	15572	176	84428	00004		99996	
·4	15744	175	84256	15748	176	84252	00004		99996	
·6	15919	175	84081	15924	175	84076	00005		99995	
·8	16094	174	83906	16099	174	83901	00005		99995	
50·0	16268	173	83732	16273	173	83727	00005		99995	10′
·2	16441	173	83559	16446	173	83554	00005		99995	
·4	16614	172	83386	16619	172	83381	00005		99995	
·6	16786	171	83214	16791	171	83209	00005		99995	
·8	16957	171	83043	16962	171	83038	00005		99995	
51·0	17128	170	82872	17133	170	82867	00005		99995	9′
·2	17298	169	82702	17303	169	82697	00005		99995	
·4	17467	169	82533	17472	169	82528	00005		99995	
·6	17636	168	82364	17641	168	82359	00005		99995	
·8	17804	167	82196	17809	167	82191	00005		99995	
52·0	17971	167	82029	17976	167	82024	00005		99995	8′
·2	18138	166	81862	18143	167	81857	00005		99995	
·4	18304	165	81696	18309	165	81691	00005		99995	
·6	18469	165	81531	18474	165	81526	00005		99995	
·8	18634	164	81366	18639	165	81361	00005		99995	
53·0	18798	164	81202	18804	163	81196	00005		99995	7′
·2	18962	163	81038	18967	163	81033	00005		99995	
·4	19125	162	80875	19130	162	80870	00005		99995	
·6	19287	162	80713	19292	162	80708	00005		99995	
·8	19449	161	80551	19454	162	80546	00005		99995	
54·0	19610	161	80390	19616	160	80384	00005		99995	6′
·2	19771	160	80229	19776	160	80224	00005		99995	
·4	19931	159	80069	19936	159	80064	00005		99995	
·6	20090	159	79910	20095	160	79905	00005		99995	
·8	20249	158	79751	20255	158	79745	00006		99994	
55·0	20407	158	79593	20413	158	79587	00006		99994	5′
·2	20565	157	79435	20571	157	79429	00006		99994	
·4	20722	156	79278	20728	156	79272	00006		99994	
·6	20878	156	79122	20884	156	79116	00006		99994	
·8	21034	155	78966	21040	155	78960	00006		99994	
56·0	21189	155	78811	21195	155	78805	00006		99994	4′
·2	21344	155	78656	21350	155	78650	00006		99994	
·4	21499	153	78501	21505	153	78495	00006		99994	
·6	21652	153	78348	21658	153	78342	00006		99994	
·8	21805	153	71895	21811	153	78189	00006		99994	
57·0	21958	152	78042	21964	152	78036	00006		99994	3′
·2	22110	152	77890	22116	152	77884	00006		99994	
·4	22262	151	77738	22268	151	77732	00006		99994	
·6	22413	150	77587	22419	150	77581	00006		99994	
·8	22563	150	77437	22569	150	77431	00006		99994	
58·0	22713	150	77287	22720	150	77281	00006		99994	2′
·2	22863	149	77137	22869	149	77131	00006		99994	
·4	23012	148	76988	23018	148	76982	00006		99994	
·6	23160	148	76840	23166	148	76834	00006		99994	
·8	23308	148	76692	23314	148	76686	00006		99994	
59·0	23456	147	76544	23462	147	76538	00006		99994	1′
·2	23603	146	76397	23609	146	76391	00006		99994	
·4	23749	146	76251	23755	147	76245	00006		99994	
6	23895	146	76105	23902	146	76098	00007		99993	
·8	24041	145	75959	24048	146	75952	00007		99993	
60·0	24186		75815	24192		75808	00007		99993	0′

LOGS. OF TRIG. FUNCTIONS

1°
181°

′	Sine	Diff.	Cosec.	Tan.	Diff.	Cotan.	Secant	Diff.	Cosine	
00·0	2̄.(8) 24186	144	1.(11) 75815	2̄.(8) 24192	145	1.(11) 75808	0.(10) 00007		1̄.(9) 99993	60′
·2	24330	144	75670	24337	144	·75663	00007		99993	
·4	24474	144	75526	24481	144	75519	00007		99993	
·6	24618	143	75382	24625	144	75375	00007		99993	
·8	24761	142	75239	24768	143	75232	00007		99993	
01·0	24903	143	75097	24910	142	75090	00007		99993	59′
·2	25046	141	74954	25053	143	74947	00007		99993	
·4	25187	141	74813	25194	141	74806	00007		99993	
·6	25328	141	74672	25335	141	74665	00007		99993	
·8	25469	140	74531	25476	141	74524	00007		99993	
02·0	25609	140	74391	25617	140	74384	00007		99993	58′
·2	25749	140	74251	25756	140	74244	00007		99993	
·4	25889	139	74111	25896	140	74104	00007		99993	
·6	26028	138	73972	26035	139	73965	00007		99993	
·8	26166	138	73834	26173	138	73827	00007		99993	
03·0	26304	138	73696	26312	138	73689	00007		99993	57′
·2	26442	137	73558	26449	138	73551	00007		99993	
·4	26579	137	73421	26586	137	73414	00007		99993	
·6	26716	136	73284	26724	138	73276	00008		99992	
·8	26852	136	73148	26860	136	73140	00008		99992	
04·0	26988	136	73012	26996	136	73004	00008		99992	56′
·2	27124	135	72876	27132	136	72868	00008		99992	
·4	27259	134	72741	27267	135	72733	00008		99992	
·6	27393	135	72607	27401	134	72599	00008		99992	
·8	27528	133	72472	27536	135	72464	00008		99992	
05·0	27661	134	72339	27669	133	72331	00008		99992	55′
·2	27795	133	72205	27803	134	72197	00008		99992	
·4	27928	132	72072	27936	133	72064	00008		99992	
·6	28060	133	71940	28068	132	71932	00008		99992	
·8	28193	131	71807	28201	133	71799	00008		99992	
06·0	28324	132	71676	28332	131	71668	00008		99992	54′
·2	28456	131	71544	28464	132	71536	00008		99992	
·4	28587	130	71413	28595	131	71405	00008		99992	
·6	28717	130	71283	28725	130	71275	00008		99992	
·8	28847	130	71153	28855	130	71145	00008		99992	
07·0	28977	130	71023	28986	131	71014	00008		99992	53′
·2	29107	129	70893	29115	129	70885	00008		99992	
·4	29236	128	70764	29244	129	70756	00008		99992	
·6	29364	129	70636	29372	128	70628	00008		99992	
·8	29493	128	70507	29501	129	70499	00008		99992	
08·0	29621	127	70379	29629	128	70371	00008		99992	52′
·2	29748	127	70252	29757	128	70243	00009		99991	
·4	29875	127	70125	29884	127	70116	00009		99991	
·6	30002	127	69998	30011	127	69989	00009		99991	
·8	30129	126	69871	30138	127	69862	00009		99991	
09·0	30255	125	69745	30263	125	69737	00009		99991	51′
·2	30380	126	69620	30389	126	69611	00009		99991	
·4	30506	125	69494	30515	126	69485	00009		99991	
·6	30631	124	69369	30640	125	69360	00009		99991	
·8	30755	124	69245	30764	124	69236	00009		99991	
10 0	30879	124	69121	30888	124	69112	00009		99991	50′
·2	31003	124	68997	31012	124	68988	00009		99991	
·4	31127	123	68873	31136	124	68864	00009		99991	
·6	31250	123	68750	31259	123	68741	00009		99991	
·8	31373	122	68627	31382	123	68618	00009		99991	
11·0	31495	122	68505	31505	123	68495	00009		99991	49′
·2	31617	122	68383	31626	121	68374	00009		99991	
·4	31739	122	68261	31748	122	68252	00009		99991	
·6	31861	121	68139	31870	122	68130	00009		99991	
·8	31982	121	68018	31991	121	68009	00009		99991	
12·0	32103		67897	32112	121	67888	00010		99990	48′

178°
358°

LOGS. OF TRIG. FUNCTIONS

1°
181°

′	Sine	Diff.	Cosec.	Tan.	Diff.	Cotan.	Secant	Diff.	Cosine	
12·0	$\overline{2}$.(8) 32103		1.(11) 67897	$\overline{2}$.(8) 32112		1.(11) 67888	0.(10) 00010		$\overline{1}$.(9) 99990	48′
·2	32223	120	67777	32233	121	67767	00010		99990	
·4	32343	120	67657	32353	120	67647	00010		99990	
·6	32463	120	67537	32473	120	67527	00010		99990	
·8	32582	119	67418	32592	119	67408	00010		99990	
		120			119					
13·0	32702		67298	32711		67289	00010		99990	47′
·2	32820	118	67180	32830	119	67170	00010		99990	
·4	32939	119	67061	32949	119	67051	00010		99990	
·6	33057	118	66943	33067	118	66933	00010		99990	
·8	33175	118	66825	33185	118	66815	00010		99990	
		117			117					
14·0	33292		66708	33302		66698	00010		99990	46′
·2	33410	118	66590	33420	118	66580	00010		99990	
·4	33527	117	66473	33537	117	66463	00010		99990	
·6	33643	116	66357	33653	116	66347	00010		99990	
·8	33759	116	66241	33769	116	66231	00010		99990	
		116			117					
15·0	33875		66125	33886		66114	00010		99990	45′
·2	33991	116	66009	34001	115	65999	00010		99990	
·4	34106	115	65894	34116	115	65884	00010		99990	
·6	34221	115	65779	34232	116	65768	00011		99989	
·8	34336	115	65664	34347	115	65653	00011		99989	
		114			114					
16·0	34450		65550	34461		65539	00011		99989	44′
·2	34565	115	65435	34576	115	65424	00011		99989	
·4	34678	113	65322	34689	113	65311	00011		99989	
·6	34792	114	65208	34803	114	65197	00011		99989	
·8	34905	113	65095	34916	113	65084	00011		99989	
		113			113					
17·0	35018		64982	35029		64971	00011		99989	43′
·2	35131	113	64869	35142	113	64858	00011		99989	
·4	35243	112	64757	35254	112	64746	00011		99989	
·6	35355	112	64645	35366	112	64634	00011		99989	
·8	35467	112	64533	35478	112	64522	00011		99989	
		111			112					
18·0	35578		64422	35590		64410	00011		99989	42′
·2	35690	112	64310	35701	111	64299	00011		99989	
·4	35801	111	64199	35812	111	64188	00011		99989	
·6	35911	110	64089	35923	111	64077	00011		99989	
·8	36021	110	63979	36032	109	63968	00011		99989	
		110			111					
19·0	36131		63869	36143		63857	00012		99988	41′
·2	36241	110	63759	36253	110	63747	00012		99988	
·4	36351	110	63649	36363	110	63637	00012		99988	
·6	36460	109	63540	36472	109	63528	00012		99988	
·8	36569	109	63431	36581	109	63419	00012		99988	
		109			109					
20·0	36678		63322	36690		63310	00012		99988	40′
·2	36786	108	63214	36798	108	63202	00012		99988	
·4	36894	108	63106	36906	108	63094	00012		99988	
·6	37002	108	62998	37014	108	62986	00012		99988	
·8	37110	108	62890	37122	108	62878	00012		99988	
		107			107					
21·0	37217		62783	37229		62771	00012		99988	39′
·2	37324	107	62676	37336	107	62664	00012		99988	
·4	37431	107	62569	37443	107	62557	00012		99988	
·6	37538	107	62462	37550	107	62450	00012		99988	
·8	37644	106	62356	37656	106	62344	00012		99988	
		106			106					
22·0	37750		62250	37762		62238	00012		99988	38′
·2	37856	106	62144	37868	106	62132	00012		99988	
·4	37961	105	62039	37973	105	62027	00012		99988	
·6	38066	105	61934	38079	106	61921	00013		99987	
·8	38171	105	61829	38184	105	61816	00013		99987	
		105			105					
23·0	38276		61724	38289		61711	00013		99987	37′
·2	38381	105	61619	38394	105	61606	00013		99987	
·4	38485	104	61515	38498	104	61502	00013		99987	
·6	38589	104	61411	38602	104	61398	00013		99987	
·8	38693	104	61307	38706	104	61294	00013		99987	
		103			103					
24·0	38796		61204	38809		61191	00013		99987	36′

178°
358°

LOGS. OF TRIG. FUNCTIONS

1°
181°

′	Sine	Diff.	Cosec.	Tan.	Diff.	Cotan.	Secant	Diff.	Cosine	
24·0	$\overline{2}$.(8) 38796		1.(11) 61204	$\overline{2}$.(8) 38809		1.(11) 61191	0.(10) 00013		$\overline{1}$.(9) 99987	36′
·2	38899	103	61101	38912	103	61088	00013		99987	
·4	39002	103	60998	39015	103	60985	00013		99987	
·6	39105	103	60895	39118	103	60882	00013		99987	
·8	39208	103	60792	39221	103	60779	00013		99987	
		102			102					
25·0	39310		60690	39323		60677	00013		99987	35′
·2	39412	102	60588	39425	102	60575	00013		99987	
·4	39514	102	60486	39527	102	60473	00013		99987	
·6	39615	101	60385	39628	101	60372	00013		99987	
·8	39717	102	60283	39730	102	60270	00014		99987	
		101			101					
26·0	39818		60182	39832		60169	00014		99986	34′
·2	39919	101	60081	39933	102	60067	00014		99986	
·4	40019	100	59981	40033	100	59967	00014		99986	
·6	40120	101	59880	40134	101	59866	00014		99986	
·8	40220	100	59780	40234	100	59766	00014		99986	
		100			100					
27·0	40320		59680	40334		59666	00014		99986	33′
·2	40420	100	59580	40434	100	59566	00014		99986	
·4	40519	99	59481	40533	99	59467	00014		99986	
·6	40618	99	59382	40632	99	59368	00014		99986	
·8	40717	99	59283	40731	99	59269	00014		99986	
		99			99					
28·0	40816		59184	40830		59170	00014		99986	32′
·2	40915	99	59085	40929	99	59071	00014		99986	
·4	41013	98	58987	41027	98	58973	00014		99986	
·6	41111	98	58889	41125	98	58875	00014		99986	
·8	41209	98	58791	41223	98	58777	00014		99986	
		98			98					
29·0	41307		58693	41321		58679	00015		99985	31′
·2	41404	97	58596	41419	98	58581	00015		99985	
·4	41501	97	58499	41516	97	58484	00015		99985	
·6	41599	98	58401	41614	98	58386	00015		99985	
·8	41695	96	58305	41710	96	58290	00015		99985	
		97			97					
30·0	41792		58208	41807		58193	00015		99985	30′
·2	41888	96	58112	41903	96	58097	00015		99985	
·4	41984	96	58016	41999	96	58001	00015		99985	
·6	42080	96	57920	42095	96	57905	00015		99985	
·8	42176	96	57824	42191	96	57809	00015		99985	
		96			96					
31·0	42272		57728	42287		57713	00015		99985	29′
·2	42367	95	57633	42382	95	57618	00015		99985	
·4	42462	95	57538	42477	95	57523	00015		99985	
·6	42557	95	57443	42572	95	57428	00015		99985	
·8	42652	95	57348	42667	95	57333	00015		99985	
		94			95					
32·0	42746		57254	42762		57238	00016		99984	28′
·2	42841	95	57159	42857	95	57143	00016		99984	
·4	42935	94	57065	42951	94	57049	00016		99984	
·6	43029	93	56971	43045	94	56955	00016		99984	
·8	43122	94	56878	43138	93	56862	00016		99984	
					93					
33·0	43216	93	56784	43232		56769	00016		99984	27′
·2	43309	93	56691	43325	94	56675	00016		99984	
·4	43402	93	56598	43418	93	56582	00016		99984	
·6	43495	93	56505	43511	93	56489	00016		99984	
·8	43588	92	56412	43604	93	56396	00016		99984	
					92					
34·0	43680	92	56320	43696		56304	00016		99984	26′
·2	43772	92	56228	43788	92	56212	00016		99984	
·4	43864	92	56136	43880	92	56120	00016		99984	
·6	43956	92	56044	43972	92	56028	00016		99984	
·8	44048	91	55952	44064	92	55936	00016		99984	
					92					
35·0	44139	92	55861	44156		55844	00017		99983	25′
·2	44231	91	55769	44248	92	55752	00017		99983	
·4	44322	91	55678	44339	91	55661	00017		99983	
·6	44413	91	55587	44430	91	55570	00017		99983	
·8	44504	90	55496	44521	91	55479	00017		99983	
					90					
36·0	44594		55406	44611		55389	00017		99983	24′

178°
358°

LOGS. OF TRIG. FUNCTIONS

1° / **181°**

′	Sine	Diff.	Cosec.	Tan.	Diff.	Cotan.	Secant	Diff.	Cosine	
36·0	$\bar{2}$.(8) 44594	90	1.(11) 55406	$\bar{2}$.(8) 44611	90	1.(11) 55389	0.(10) 00017		$\bar{1}$.(9) 99983	24′
·2	44684	91	55316	44701	91	55299	00017		99983	
·4	44775	90	55225	44792	90	55208	00017		99983	
·6	44865	89	55135	44882	89	55118	00017		99983	
·8	44954	90	55046	44971	90	55029	00017		99983	
37·0	45044	90	54956	45061	90	54939	00017		99983	23′
·2	45134	89	54866	45151	89	54849	00017		99983	
·4	45223	89	54777	45240	90	54760	00017		99983	
·6	45312	89	54688	45330	89	54670	00018		99982	
·8	45401	88	54599	45419	88	54581	00018		99982	
38·0	45489	89	54511	45507	89	54493	00018		99982	22′
·2	45578	88	54422	45596	88	54404	00018		99982	
·4	45666	88	54334	45684	88	54316	00018		99982	
·6	45754	88	54246	45772	88	54228	00018		99982	
·8	45842	88	54158	45860	88	54140	00018		99982	
39·0	45930	88	54070	45948	88	54052	00018		99982	21′
·2	46018	87	53982	46036	87	53964	00018		99982	
·4	46105	88	53895	46123	88	53877	00018		99982	
·6	46193	87	53807	46211	87	53789	00018		99982	
·8	46280	86	53720	46298	87	53702	00018		99982	
40·0	46366	87	53634	46385	86	53615	00018		99982	20′
·2	46453	87	53547	46471	88	53529	00018		99982	
·4	46540	86	53460	46559	86	53441	00019		99981	
·6	46626	86	53374	46645	86	53355	00019		99981	
·8	46712	86	53288	46731	86	53269	00019		99981	
41·0	46799	86	53202	46817	86	53183	00019		99981	19′
·2	46884	86	53116	46903	86	53097	00019		99981	
·4	46970	86	53030	46989	86	53011	00019		99981	
·6	47056	85	52944	47075	85	52925	00019		99981	
·8	47141	85	52859	47160	85	52840	00019		99981	
42·0	47226	85	52774	47245	85	52755	00019		99981	18′
2	47311	85	52689	47330	85	52670	00019		99981	
4	47396	85	52604	47415	85	52585	00019		99981	
·6	47481	85	52519	47500	85	52500	00019		99981	
·8	47566	84	52434	47585	84	52415	00019		99981	
43·0	47650	84	52350	47669	85	52331	00019		99981	17′
·2	47734	84	52266	47754	84	52246	00020		99980	
·4	47818	84	52182	47838	84	52162	00020		99980	
·6	47902	84	52098	47922	84	52078	00020		99980	
·8	47986	83	52014	48006	83	51994	00020		99980	
44·0	48069	84	51931	48089	84	51911	00020		99980	16′
·2	48153	83	51847	48173	83	51827	00020		99980	
·4	48236	83	51764	48256	83	51744	00020		99980	
·6	48319	83	51681	48339	83	51661	00020		99980	
·8	48402	83	51598	48422	83	51578	00020		99980	
45·0	48485	82	51515	48505	82	51495	00020		99980	15′
·2	48567	83	51433	48587	83	51413	00020		99980	
·4	48650	82	51350	48670	83	51330	00020		99980	
·6	48732	82	51268	48753	82	51247	00021		99979	
·8	48814	82	51186	48835	82	51165	00021		99979	
46·0	48896	82	51104	48917	82	51083	00021		99979	14′
·2	48978	82	51022	48999	82	51001	00021		99979	
·4	49060	81	50940	49081	81	50919	00021		99979	
·6	49141	82	50859	49162	82	50838	00021		99979	
·8	49223	81	50777	49244	81	50756	00021		99979	
47·0	49304	81	50696	49325	81	50675	00021		99979	13′
·2	49385	81	50615	49406	81	50594	00021		99979	
·4	49466	81	50534	49487	81	50513	00021		99979	
·6	49547	80	50453	49568	80	50432	00021		99979	
·8	49627	81	50373	49648	81	50352	00021		99979	
48·0	49708		50292	49729		50271	00021		99979	12′

LOGS. OF TRIG. FUNCTIONS

1°
181°

′	Sine	Diff.	Cosec.	Tan.	Diff.	Cotan.	Secant	Diff.	Cosine	
48·0	2̄.(8) 49708		1.(11) 50292	2̄.(8) 49729		1.(11) 50271	0.(10) 00021		1̄.(9) 99979	12′
·2	49788	80	50212	49810	81	50190	00022		99978	
·4	49868	80	50132	49890	80	50110	00022		99978	
·6	49948	80	50052	49970	80	50030	00022		99978	
·8	50028	80	49972	50050	80	49950	00022		99978	
49·0	50108	80	49892	50130	80	49870	00022		99978	11′
·2	50188	80	49812	50210	80	49790	00022		99978	
·4	50267	79	49733	50289	79	49711	00022		99978	
·6	50346	79	49654	50368	79	49632	00022		99978	
·8	50426	80	49574	50448	80	49552	00022		99978	
50·0	50504	78	49496	50527	79	49473	00022		99978	10′
·2	50583	79	49417	50605	78	49395	00022		99978	
·4	50662	79	49338	50684	79	49316	00022		99978	
·6	50741	79	49259	50764	80	49236	00023		99977	
·8	50819	78	49181	50842	78	49158	00023		99977	
51·0	50897	78	49103	50920	78	49080	00023		99977	9′
·2	50976	79	49024	50999	79	49001	00023		99977	
·4	51054	78	48946	51077	78	48923	00023		99977	
·6	51131	77	48869	51154	77	48846	00023		99977	
·8	51209	78	48791	51232	78	48768	00023		99977	
52·0	51287	78	48713	51310	78	48690	00023		99977	8′
·2	51364	77	48636	51387	77	48613	00023		99977	
·4	51442	78	48558	51465	78	48535	00023		99977	
·6	51519	77	48481	51542	77	48458	00023		99977	
·8	51596	77	48404	51619	77	48381	00023		99977	
53·0	51673	77	48327	51696	77	48304	00024		99977	7′
·2	51749	76	48251	51773	77	48227	00024		99976	
·4	51826	77	48174	51850	77	48150	00024		99976	
·6	51902	76	48098	51926	76	48074	00024		99976	
·8	51979	77	48021	52003	77	47997	00024		99976	
54·0	52055	76	47945	52079	76	47921	00024		99976	6′
·2	52131	76	47869	52155	76	47845	00024		99976	
·4	52207	76	47793	52231	76	47769	00024		99976	
·6	52283	76	47717	52307	76	47693	00024		99976	
·8	52359	76	47641	52383	76	47617	00024		99976	
55·0	52434	75	47566	52459	76	47541	00024		99976	5′
·2	52510	76	47490	52534	75	47466	00024		99976	
·4	52585	75	47415	52610	76	47390	00025		99975	
·6	52660	75	47340	52685	75	47315	00025		99975	
·8	52735	75	47265	52760	75	47240	00025		99975	
56·0	52810	75	47190	52835	75	47165	00025		99975	4′
·2	52885	75	47115	52910	75	47090	00025		99975	
·4	52960	75	47040	52985	75	47015	00025		99975	
·6	53034	74	46966	53059	74	46941	00025		99975	
·8	53109	75	46891	53134	75	46866	00025		99975	
57·0	53183	74	46817	53208	74	46792	00025		99975	3′
·2	53257	74	46743	53282	74	46718	00025		99975	
·4	53331	74	46669	53356	74	46644	00025		99975	
·6	53405	74	46595	53430	74	46570	00025		99975	
·8	53479	74	46521	53505	75	46495	00026		99974	
58·0	53552	73	46448	53578	73	46422	00026		99974	2′
·2	53626	74	46374	53652	74	46348	00026		99974	
·4	53699	73	46301	53725	73	46275	00026		99974	
·6	53773	74	46227	53799	74	46201	00026		99974	
·8	53846	73	46154	53872	73	46128	00026		99974	
59·0	53919	73	46081	53945	73	46055	00026		99974	1′
·2	53991	72	46009	54017	72	45983	00026		99974	
·4	54064	73	45936	54090	73	45910	00026		99974	
·6	54137	73	45863	54163	73	45837	00026		99974	
·8	54210	73	45790	54236	73	45764	00026		99974	
60·0	54282	72	45718	54308	72	45692	00027		99974	0′

LOGS. OF TRIG. FUNCTIONS

2°
182°

′	Sine	Diff.	Cosec.	Tan.	Diff.	Cotan.	Secant	Diff.	Cosine	
00·0	$\bar{2}$.(8) 54282	72	1.(11) 45718	$\bar{2}$.(8) 54308	73	1.(11) 45692	0.(10) 00027		$\bar{1}$.(9) 99974	60′
·2	54354	72	45646	54381	72	45619	00027		99973	
·4	54426	72	45574	54453	72	45547	00027		99973	
·6	54498	72	45502	54525	72	45475	00027		99973	
·8	54570	72	45430	54597	72	45403	00027		99973	
01·0	54642	72	45358	54669	72	45331	00027		99973	59′
·2	54714	72	45286	54741	72	45259	00027		99973	
·4	54786	71	45214	54813	71	45187	00027		99973	
·6	54857	71	45143	54884	71	45116	00027		99973	
·8	54928	71	45072	54955	72	45045	00027		99973	
02·0	55000	72	45001	55027	71	44973	00027		99973	58′
·2	55071	71	44929	55098	72	44902	00027		99973	
·4	55142	70	44858	55170	70	44830	00028		99972	
·6	55212	71	44788	55240	71	44760	00028		99972	
·8	55283	71	44717	55311	71	44689	00028		99972	
03·0	55354	70	44646	55382	70	44618	00028		99972	57′
·2	55424	71	44576	55452	71	44548	00028		99972	
·4	55495	70	44505	55523	70	44477	00028		99972	
·6	55565	70	44435	55593	70	44407	00028		99972	
·8	55635	70	44365	55663	71	44337	00028		99972	
04·0	55705	70	44295	55734	69	44266	00028		99972	56′
·2	55775	70	44225	55803	70	44197	00028		99972	
·4	55845	70	44155	55873	71	44127	00028		99972	
·6	55915	69	44085	55944	69	44056	00029		99971	
·8	55984	70	44016	56013	70	43987	00029		99971	
05·0	56054	69	43946	56083	69	43917	00029		99971	55′
·2	56123	70	43877	56152	70	43848	00029		99971	
·4	56193	69	43807	56222	69	43778	00029		99971	
·6	56262	69	43738	56291	69	43709	00029		99971	
·8	56331	69	43669	56360	69	43640	00029		99971	
06·0	56400	69	43600	56429	69	43571	00029		99971	54′
·2	56469	69	43531	56498	69	43502	00029		99971	
·4	56538	68	43462	56567	69	43433	00029		99971	
·6	56606	69	43394	56636	69	43364	00030		99970	
·8	56675	68	43325	56705	68	43295	00030		99970	
07·0	56743	68	43257	56773	68	43227	00030		99970	53′
·2	56811	69	43189	56841	69	43159	00030		99970	
·4	56880	68	43120	56910	68	43090	00030		99970	
·6	56948	68	43052	56978	68	43022	00030		99970	
·8	57016	68	42984	57046	68	42954	00030		99970	
08·0	57084	67	42916	57114	67	42886	00030		99970	52′
·2	57151	68	42849	57181	68	42819	00030		99970	
·4	57219	68	42781	57249	68	42751	00030		99970	
·6	57287	67	42713	57317	68	42683	00030		99970	
·8	57354	67	42646	57385	67	42615	00031		99969	
09·0	57421	68	42579	57452	68	42548	00031		99969	51′
·2	57489	67	42511	57520	67	42480	00031		99969	
·4	57556	67	42444	57587	67	42413	00031		99969	
·6	57623	67	42377	57654	67	42346	00031		99969	
·8	57690	67	42310	57721	67	42279	00031		99969	
10·0	57757	67	42243	57788	66	42212	00031		99969	50′
·2	57823	67	42177	57854	67	42146	00031		99969	
·4	57890	67	42110	57921	67	42079	00031		99969	
·6	57957	66	42043	57988	66	42012	00031		99969	
·8	58023	66	41977	58054	67	41946	00031		99969	
11·0	58089	66	41911	58121	66	41879	00032		99969	49′
·2	58155	67	41845	58187	67	41813	00032		99968	
·4	58222	66	41778	58254	66	41746	00032		99968	
·6	58288	65	41712	58320	65	41680	00032		99968	
·8	58353	66	41647	58385	66	41615	00032		99968	
12·0	58419		41581	58451		41549	00032		99968	48′

177°
357°

LOGS. OF TRIG. FUNCTIONS

2° / *182°*

′	Sine	Diff.	Cosec.	Tan.	Diff.	Cotan.	Secant	Diff.	Cosine	
12·0	$\overline{2}$.(8) 58419		1.(11) 41581	$\overline{2}$.(8) 58451		1.(11) 41549	0.(10) 00032		$\overline{1}$.(9) 99968	48′
·2	58485	66	41515	58517	66	41483	00032		99968	
·4	58551	66	41449	58583	66	41417	00032		99968	
·6	58616	65	41384	58648	65	41352	00032		99968	
·8	58682	66	41318	58714	66	41286	00032		99968	
13·0	58747	65	41253	58780	65	41221	00033		99968	47′
·2	58812	65	41188	58845	66	41155	00033		99967	
·4	58877	65	41123	58910	65	41090	00033		99967	
·6	58942	65	41058	58975	65	41025	00033		99967	
·8	59007	65	40993	59040	65	40960	00033		99967	
14·0	59072	65	40928	59105	65	40895	00033		99967	46′
·2	59137	65	40863	59170	65	40830	00033		99967	
·4	59202	65	40798	59235	65	40765	00033		99967	
·6	59266	64	40734	59299	64	40701	00033		99967	
·8	59330	64	40670	59363	64	40637	00033		99967	
15·0	59395	65	40605	59428	65	40572	00034		99967	45′
·2	59459	64	40541	59493	65	40507	00034		99966	
·4	59523	64	40477	59557	64	40443	00034		99966	
·6	59587	64	40413	59621	64	40379	00034		99966	
·8	59651	64	40349	59685	64	40315	00034		99966	
16·0	59715	64	40285	59749	64	40251	00034		99966	44′
·2	59779	64	40221	59813	64	40187	00034		99966	
·4	59843	64	40157	59877	64	40123	00034		99966	
·6	59906	63	40094	59940	63	40060	00034		99966	
·8	59970	64	40030	60004	64	39996	00034		99966	
17·0	60033	63	39967	60068	64	39932	00035		99966	43′
·2	60097	64	39903	60132	64	39868	00035		99965	
·4	60160	63	39840	60195	63	39805	00035		99965	
·6	60223	63	39777	60258	63	39742	00035		99965	
·8	60286	63	39714	60321	63	39679	00035		99965	
18·0	60349	63	39651	60384	63	39616	00035		99965	42′
·2	60412	63	39588	60447	63	39553	00035		99965	
·4	60475	63	39525	60510	63	39490	00035		99965	
·6	60537	62	39463	60572	62	39428	00035		99965	
·8	60600	63	39400	60635	63	39365	00035		99965	
19·0	60662	62	39338	60698	63	39302	00036		99965	41′
·2	60725	63	39275	60761	63	39239	00036		99964	
·4	60787	62	39213	60823	62	39177	00036		99964	
·6	60849	62	39151	60885	62	39115	00036		99964	
·8	60911	62	39089	60947	62	39053	00036		99964	
20·0	60973	62	39027	61009	62	38991	00036		99964	40′
·2	61035	62	38965	61071	62	38929	00036		99964	
·4	61097	62	38903	61133	62	38867	00036		99964	
·6	61159	62	38841	61195	62	38805	00036		99964	
·8	61221	62	38779	61257	62	38743	00036		99964	
21·0	61282	61	38718	61319	62	38681	00037		99964	39′
·2	61344	62	38656	61381	62	38619	00037		99963	
·4	61405	61	38595	61442	61	38558	00037		99963	
·6	61467	62	38533	61504	62	38496	00037		99963	
·8	61528	61	38472	61565	61	38435	00037		99963	
22·0	61589	61	38411	61626	61	38374	00037		99963	38′
·2	61650	61	38350	61687	61	38313	00037		99963	
·4	61711	61	38289	61748	61	38252	00037		99963	
·6	61772	61	38228	61809	61	38191	00037		99963	
·8	61833	61	38167	61870	61	38130	00037		99963	
23·0	61894	61	38106	61931	61	38069	00038		99962	37′
·2	61954	60	38046	61992	61	38008	00038		99962	
·4	62015	61	37985	62053	61	37947	00038		99962	
·6	62075	60	37925	62113	60	37887	00038		99962	
·8	62136	61	37864	62174	61	37826	00038		99962	
24·0	62196	60	37804	62234	60	37766	00038		99962	36′

2° / 182°

LOGS. OF TRIG. FUNCTIONS

′	Sine	Diff.	Cosec.	Tan.	Diff.	Cotan.	Secant	Diff.	Cosine	
24·0	$\overline{2}$.(8) 62196		1.(11) 37804	$\overline{2}$.(8) 62234		1.(11) 37766	0.(10) 00038		$\overline{1}$.(9) 99962	36′
·2	62256	60	37744	62294	60	37706	00038		99962	
·4	62317	61	37683	62355	61	37645	00038		99962	
·6	62377	60	37623	62415	60	37585	00038		99962	
·8	62437	60	37563	62476	61	37524	00039		99961	
25·0	62497	59	37504	62535	59	37465	00039		99961	35′
·2	62556	60	37444	62595	60	37405	00039		99961	
·4	62616	60	37384	62655	60	37345	00039		99961	
·6	62676	60	37324	62715	60	37285	00039		99961	
·8	62735	59	37265	62774	59	37226	00039		99961	
26·0	62795	60	37205	62834	60	37166	00039		99961	34′
·2	62854	59	37146	62893	59	37107	00039		99961	
·4	62914	60	37086	62953	60	37047	00039		99961	
·6	62973	59	37027	63012	59	36988	00039		99961	
·8	63032	59	36968	63072	60	36928	00040		99960	
27·0	63091	59	36909	63131	59	36869	00040		99960	33′
·2	63150	59	36850	63190	59	36810	00040		99960	
·4	63209	59	36791	63249	59	36751	00040		99960	
·6	63268	59	36732	63308	59	36692	00040		99960	
·8	63327	59	36673	63367	59	36633	00040		99960	
28·0	63385	58	36615	63426	59	36574	00040		99960	32′
·2	63444	59	36556	63484	58	36516	00040		99960	
·4	63503	59	36497	63543	59	36457	00040		99960	
·6	63561	58	36439	63602	59	36398	00041		99959	
·8	63619	58	36381	63660	58	36340	00041		99959	
29·0	63678	59	36322	63718	58	36282	00041		99959	31′
·2	63736	58	36264	63777	59	36223	00041		99959	
·4	63794	58	36206	63835	58	36165	00041		99959	
·6	63852	58	36148	63893	58	36107	00041		99959	
·8	63910	58	36090	63951	58	36049	00041		99959	
30·0	63968	58	36032	64009	58	35991	00041		99959	30′
·2	64026	58	35974	64067	58	35933	00041		99959	
·4	64083	57	35917	64125	58	35875	00042		99958	
·6	64141	58	35859	64183	58	35817	00042		99958	
·8	64199	58	35801	64241	58	35759	00042		99958	
31·0	64256	57	35744	64298	57	35702	00042		99958	29′
·2	64314	58	35686	64356	58	35644	00042		99958	
·4	64371	57	35629	64413	57	35587	00042		99958	
·6	64429	58	35571	64471	58	35529	00042		99958	
·8	64486	57	35514	64528	57	35472	00042		99958	
32·0	64543	57	35457	64585	57	35415	00042		99958	28′
·2	64600	57	35400	64643	58	35357	00043		99957	
·4	64657	57	35343	64700	57	35300	00043		99957	
·6	64714	57	35286	64757	57	35243	00043		99957	
·8	64771	57	35229	64814	57	35186	00043		99957	
33·0	64827	56	35173	64870	56	35130	00043		99957	27′
·2	64884	57	35116	64927	57	35073	00043		99957	
·4	64941	57	35059	64984	57	35016	00043		99957	
·6	64997	56	35003	65040	56	34960	00043		99957	
·8	65054	57	34946	65097	57	34903	00043		99957	
34·0	65110	56	34890	65154	57	34846	00044		99956	26′
·2	65166	56	34834	65210	56	34790	00044		99956	
·4	65223	57	34777	65267	57	34733	00044		99956	
·6	65279	56	34721	65323	56	34677	00044		99956	
·8	65335	56	34665	65379	56	34621	00044		99956	
35·0	65391	56	34609	65435	56	34565	00044		99956	25′
·2	65447	56	34553	65491	56	34509	00044		99956	
·4	65503	56	34497	65547	56	34453	00044		99956	
·6	65559	56	34441	65604	57	34396	00045		99955	
·8	65615	56	34385	65660	56	34340	00045		99955	
36·0	65670	55	34330	65715	55	34285	00045		99955	24′

2°
182°
LOGS. OF TRIG. FUNCTIONS

′	Sine	Diff.	Cosec.	Tan.	Diff.	Cotan.	Secant	Diff.	Cosine	
36·0	2̄.(8) 65670		1.(11) 34330	2̄.(8) 65715		1.(11) 34285	0.(10) 00045		1̄.(9) 99955	24′
·2	65726	56	34274	65771	56	34229	00045		99955	
·4	65781	55	34219	65826	55	34174	00045		99955	
·6	65837	56	34163	65882	56	34118	00045		99955	
·8	65892	55	34108	65937	55	34063	00045		99955	
37·0	65948	55	34053	65993	56	34007	00045		99955	23′
·2	66003	56	33997	66048	55	33952	00045		99955	
·4	66058	55	33942	66104	56	33896	00046		99954	
·6	66113	55	33887	66159	55	33841	00046		99954	
·8	66168	55	33832	66214	55	33786	00046		99954	
38·0	66223	55	33777	66269	55	33731	00046		99954	22′
·2	66278	55	33722	66324	55	33676	00046		99954	
·4	66333	55	33667	66379	55	33621	00046		99954	
·6	66388	55	33612	66434	55	33566	00046		99954	
·8	66442	54	33558	66488	54	33512	00046		99954	
39·0	66497	55	33503	66543	55	33457	00046		99954	21′
·2	66551	54	33449	66598	55	33402	00047		99953	
·4	66606	55	33394	66653	55	33347	00047		99953	
·6	66660	54	33340	66707	54	33293	00047		99953	
·8	66715	55	33285	66762	55	33238	00047		99953	
40·0	66769	54	33231	66816	54	33184	00047		99953	20′
·2	66823	54	33177	66870	54	33130	00047		99953	
·4	66877	54	33123	66924	54	33076	00047		99953	
·6	66931	54	33069	66978	54	33022	00047		99953	
·8	66985	54	33015	67032	54	32968	00047		99953	
41·0	67039	54	32961	67087	55	32913	00048		99952	19′
·2	67093	54	32907	67141	54	32859	00048		99952	
·4	67147	54	32853	67195	54	32805	00048		99952	
·6	67201	54	32799	67249	54	32751	00048		99952	
·8	67254	53	32746	67302	53	32698	00048		99952	
42·0	67308	54	32692	67356	54	32644	00048		99952	18′
·2	67362	54	32638	67410	54	32590	00048		99952	
·4	67415	53	32585	67463	53	32537	00048		99952	
·6	67468	53	32532	67517	54	32483	00049		99951	
·8	67522	54	32478	67571	54	32429	00049		99951	
43·0	67575	53	32425	67624	53	32376	00049		99951	17′
·2	67628	53	32372	67677	53	32323	00049		99951	
·4	67682	54	32318	67731	54	32269	00049		99951	
·6	67735	53	32265	67784	53	32216	00049		99951	
·8	67788	53	32212	67837	53	32163	00049		99951	
44·0	67841	52	32160	67890	53	32110	00049		99951	16′
·2	67893	53	32107	67942	52	32058	00049		99951	
·4	67946	53	32054	67996	54	32004	00050		99950	
·6	67999	53	32001	68049	53	31951	00050		99950	
·8	68052	53	31948	68102	53	31898	00050		99950	
45·0	68104	52	31896	68154	52	31846	00050		99950	15′
·2	68157	53	31843	68207	53	31793	00050		99950	
·4	68209	52	31791	68259	52	31741	00050		99950	
·6	68262	53	31738	68312	53	31688	00050		99950	
·8	68314	52	31686	68364	52	31636	00050		99950	
46·0	68367	52	31634	68417	53	31583	00051		99949	14′
·2	68419	53	31581	68470	53	31530	00051		99949	
·4	68471	52	31529	68522	52	31478	00051		99949	
·6	68523	52	31477	68574	52	31426	00051		99949	
·8	68575	52	31425	68626	52	31374	00051		99949	
47·0	68627	52	31373	68678	52	31322	00051		99949	13′
·2	68679	52	31321	68730	52	31270	00051		99949	
·4	68731	52	31269	68782	52	31218	00051		99949	
·6	68783	52	31217	68835	53	31165	00052		99948	
·8	68835	52	31165	68887	52	31113	00052		99948	
48·0	68886	51	31114	68938	51	31062	00052		99948	12′

LOGS. OF TRIG. FUNCTIONS

2°
182°

′	Sine	Diff.	Cosec.	Tan.	Diff.	Cotan.	Secant	Diff.	Cosine	
48·0	$\overline{2}$.(8) 68886	52	1.(11) 31114	$\overline{2}$.(8) 68938	52	1.(11) 31062	0.(10) 00052		$\overline{1}$.(9) 99948	*12′*
·2	68938	51	31062	68990	51	31010	00052		99948	
·4	68989	52	31011	69041	52	30959	00052		99948	
·6	69041	51	30959	69093	51	30907	00052		99948	
·8	69092	52	30908	69144	52	30856	00052		99948	
49·0	69144	51	30856	69196	52	30804	00053		99948	*11′*
·2	69195	51	30805	69248	51	30752	00053		99947	
·4	69246	52	30754	69299	52	30701	00053		99947	
·6	69298	51	30702	69351	51	30649	00053		99947	
·8	69349	51	30651	69402	51	30598	00053		99947	
50·0	69400	51	30600	69453	51	30547	00053		99947	*10′*
·2	69451	51	30549	69504	52	30496	00053		99947	
·4	69502	51	30498	69556	51	30444	00054		99947	
·6	69553	51	30447	69607	51	30393	00054		99946	
·8	69604	51	30396	69658	50	30342	00054		99946	
51·0	69654	50	30346	69708	51	30292	00054		99946	*9′*
·2	69705	51	30295	69759	51	30241	00054		99946	
·4	69756	51	30244	69810	50	30190	00054		99946	
·6	69806	50	30194	69860	51	30140	00054		99946	
·8	69857	51	30143	69911	51	30089	00054		99946	
52·0	69907	50	30093	69962	51	30038	00054		99946	*8′*
·2	69958	51	30042	70013	50	29987	00055		99945	
·4	70008	50	29992	70063	50	29937	00055		99945	
·6	70058	50	29942	70113	51	29887	00055		99945	
·8	70109	51	29891	70164	50	29836	00055		99945	
53·0	70159	50	29841	70214	50	29786	00055		99945	*7′*
·2	70209	50	29791	70264	50	29736	00055		99945	
·4	70259	50	29741	70314	50	29686	00055		99945	
·6	70309	50	29691	70364	51	29636	00055		99945	
·8	70359	50	29641	70415	50	29585	00056		99944	
54·0	70409	50	29591	70465	50	29535	00056		99944	*6′*
·2	70459	50	29541	70515	50	29485	00056		99944	
·4	70509	50	29491	70565	50	29435	00056		99944	
·6	70559	49	29441	70615	49	29385	00056		99944	
·8	70608	50	29392	70664	50	29336	00056		99944	
55·0	70658	49	29342	70714	49	29286	00056		99944	*5′*
·2	70707	50	29293	70763	51	29237	00056		99944	
·4	70757	49	29243	70814	49	29186	00057		99943	
·6	70806	50	29194	70863	50	29137	00057		99943	
·8	70856	49	29144	70913	49	29087	00057		99943	
56·0	70905	49	29095	70962	49	29038	00057		99943	*4′*
·2	70954	49	29046	71011	49	28989	00057		99943	
·4	71003	50	28997	71060	50	28940	00057		99943	
·6	71053	49	28947	71110	49	28890	00057		99943	
·8	71102	49	28898	71159	49	28841	00057		99943	
57·0	71151	49	28849	71208	50	28791	00058		99942	*3′*
·2	71200	49	28800	71258	49	28742	00058		99942	
·4	71249	49	28751	71307	49	28693	00058		99942	
·6	71298	48	28702	71356	48	28644	00058		99942	
·8	71346	49	28654	71404	49	28596	00058		99942	
58·0	71395	49	28605	71453	49	28547	00058		99942	*2′*
·2	71444	49	28556	71502	49	28498	00058		99942	
·4	71493	48	28507	71551	49	28449	00058		99942	
·6	71541	49	28459	71600	49	28400	00059		99941	
·8	71590	48	28410	71649	48	28351	00059		99941	
59·0	71638	49	28362	71697	49	28303	00059		99941	*1′*
·2	71687	48	28313	71746	48	28254	00059		99941	
·4	71735	49	28265	71794	49	28206	00059		99941	
·6	71784	48	28216	71843	48	28157	00059		99941	
·8	71832	48	28168	71891	49	28109	00059		99941	
60·0	71880		28120	71940		28060	00060		99940	*0′*

177°
357°

3° 183° — LOGS. OF TRIG. FUNCTIONS

'	Sine	Diff.	Cosec.	Tan.	Diff.	Cotan.	Secant	Diff.	Cosine	
00·0	2̄.(8) 71880	48	1.(11) 28120	2̄.(8) 71940	48	1.(11) 28060	0.(10) 00060		1̄.(9) 99940	60'
·2	71928	48	28072	71988	48	28012	00060		99940	
·4	71976	48	28024	72036	48	27964	00060		99940	
·6	72024	48	27976	72084	48	27916	00060		99940	
·8	72072	48	27928	72132	49	27868	00060		99940	
01·0	72120	48	27880	72181	47	27819	00060		99940	59'
·2	72168	48	27832	72228	48	27772	00060		99940	
·4	72216	48	27784	72276	49	27724	00060		99940	
·6	72264	48	27736	72325	48	27675	00061		99939	
·8	72312	48	27688	72373	47	27627	00061		99939	
02·0	72360	47	27641	72420	48	27580	00061		99939	58'
·2	72407	48	27593	72468	48	27532	00061		99939	
·4	72455	47	27545	72516	47	27484	00061		99939	
·6	72502	48	27498	72563	48	27437	00061		99939	
·8	72550	47	27450	72611	48	27389	00061		99939	
03·0	72597	48	27403	72659	48	27341	00062		99938	57'
·2	72645	47	27355	72707	47	27293	00062		99938	
·4	72692	47	27308	72754	47	27246	00062		99938	
·6	72739	47	27261	72801	47	27199	00062		99938	
·8	72786	48	27214	72848	48	27152	00062		99938	
04·0	72834	47	27166	72896	47	27104	00062		99938	56'
·2	71881	47	27119	72943	47	27057	00062		99938	
·4	72928	47	27072	72990	48	27010	00062		99938	
·6	72975	47	27025	73038	47	26962	00063		99937	
·8	73022	47	26978	73085	47	26915	00063		99937	
05·0	73069	47	26931	73132	47	26868	00063		99937	55'
·2	73116	47	26884	73179	47	26821	00063		99937	
·4	73163	46	26837	73226	46	26774	00063		99937	
·6	73209	47	26791	73272	47	26728	00063		99937	
·8	73256	47	26744	73319	47	26681	00063		99937	
06·0	73303	46	26697	73366	47	26634	00064		99936	54'
·2	73349	47	26651	73413	47	26587	00064		99936	
·4	73396	46	26604	73460	46	26540	00064		99936	
·6	73442	47	26558	73506	47	26494	00064		99936	
·8	73489	46	26511	73553	47	26447	00064		99936	
07·0	73535	47	26465	73600	46	26400	00064		99936	53'
·2	73582	46	26418	73646	47	26354	00064		99936	
·4	73628	46	26372	73693	46	26307	00065		99935	
·6	73674	47	26326	73739	47	26261	00065		99935	
·8	73721	46	26279	73786	46	26214	00065		99935	
08·0	73767	46	26233	73732	46	26168	00065		99935	52'
·2	73813	46	26187	73878	46	26122	00065		99935	
·4	73859	46	26141	73924	46	26076	00065		99935	
·6	73905	46	26095	73970	47	26030	00065		99935	
·8	73951	46	26049	74017	46	25983	00066		99934	
09·0	73997	46	26003	74063	46	25937	00066		99934	51'
·2	74043	46	25957	74109	46	25891	00066		99934	
·4	74089	45	25911	74155	45	25845	00066		99934	
·6	74134	46	25866	74200	46	25800	00066		99934	
·8	74180	46	25820	74246	46	25754	00066		99934	
10·0	74226	46	25774	74292	46	25708	00066		99934	50'
·2	74272	45	25728	74338	46	25662	00066		99934	
·4	74317	46	25683	74384	46	25616	00067		99933	
·6	74363	45	25637	74430	45	25570	00067		99933	
·8	74408	46	25592	74475	46	25525	00067		99933	
11·0	74454	45	25546	74521	45	25479	00067		99933	49'
·2	74499	45	25501	74566	45	25434	00067		99933	
·4	74544	46	25456	74611	46	25389	00067		99933	
·6	74590	45	25410	74657	46	25343	00067		99933	
·8	74635	45	25365	74703	45	25297	00068		99932	
12·0	74680		25320	74748		25252	00068		99932	48'

LOGS. OF TRIG. FUNCTIONS

3°
183°

′	Sine	Diff.	Cosec.	Tan.	Diff.	Cotan.	Secant	Diff.	Cosine	
12·0	2̄.(8) 74680		1.(11) 25320	2̄.(8) 74748		1.(11) 25252	0.(10) 00068		1̄.(9) 99932	48′
·2	74725	45	25275	74793	45	25207	00068		99932	
·4	74770	45	25230	74838	45	25162	00068		99932	
·6	74816	46	25184	74884	46	25116	00068		99932	
·8	74861	45	25139	74929	45	25071	00068		99932	
13·0	74906	45	25095	74974	45	25026	00068		99932	47′
·2	74950	44	25050	75019	45	24981	00069		99931	
·4	74995	45	25005	75064	45	24936	00069		99931	
·6	75040	45	24960	75109	45	24891	00069		99931	
·8	75085	45	24915	75154	45	24846	00069		99931	
14·0	75130	45	24870	75199	45	24801	00069		99931	46′
·2	75174	44	24826	75243	44	24757	00069		99931	
·4	75219	45	24781	75288	45	24712	00069		99931	
·6	75264	45	24736	75334	46	24666	00070		99930	
·8	75308	44	24692	75378	44	24622	00070		99930	
15·0	75353	45	24647	75423	45	24577	00070		99930	45′
·2	75397	44	24603	75467	44	24533	00070		99930	
·4	75442	45	24558	75512	45	24488	00070		99930	
·6	75486	44	24514	75556	44	24444	00070		99930	
·8	75530	44	24470	75600	44	24400	00070		99930	
16·0	75575	45	24425	75646	46	24355	00071		99929	44′
·2	75619	44	24381	75690	44	24310	00071		99929	
·4	75663	44	24337	75734	44	24266	00071		99929	
·6	75707	44	24293	75778	44	24222	00071		99929	
·8	75751	44	24249	75822	44	24178	00071		99929	
17·0	75795	44	24205	75866	44	24133	00071		99929	43′
·2	75839	44	24161	75910	44	24090	00071		99929	
·4	75883	44	24117	75955	45	24045	00072		99928	
·6	75927	44	24073	75999	44	24001	00072		99928	
·8	75971	44	24029	76043	44	23957	00072		99928	
18·0	76015	44	23985	76087	44	23913	00072		99928	42′
·2	76559	44	23941	76131	44	23869	00072		99928	
·4	76103	44	23897	76175	44	23825	00072		99928	
·6	76146	43	23854	76218	43	23782	00072		99928	
·8	76190	44	23810	76263	45	23737	00073		99927	
19·0	76234	44	23766	76307	44	23694	00073		99927	41′
·2	76277	43	23723	76350	43	23650	00073		99927	
·4	76321	44	23679	76394	44	23606	00073		99927	
·6	76364	43	23636	76437	43	23563	00073		99927	
·8	76408	44	23592	76481	44	23519	00073		99927	
20·0	76451	43	23549	76525	44	23475	00074		99927	40′
·2	76494	43	23506	76568	43	23432	00074		99926	
·4	76538	44	23462	76612	44	23388	00074		99926	
·6	76581	43	23419	76655	43	23345	00074		99926	
·8	76624	43	23376	76698	43	23302	00074		99926	
21·0	76667	43	23333	76742	44	23258	00074		99926	39′
·2	76711	44	23289	76785	43	23215	00074		99926	
·4	76754	43	23246	76829	44	23171	00075		99925	
·6	76797	43	23203	76872	43	23128	00075		99925	
·8	76840	43	23160	76915	43	23085	00075		99925	
22·0	76883	43	23117	76958	43	23042	00075		99925	38′
·2	76926	43	23074	77001	43	22999	00075		99925	
·4	76969	43	23031	77044	43	22956	00075		99925	
·6	77011	42	22989	77087	43	22913	00076		99924	
·8	77054	43	22946	77130	43	22870	00076		99924	
23·0	77097	43	22903	77173	43	22827	00076		99924	37′
·2	77140	43	22860	77216	43	22784	00076		99924	
·4	77182	42	22818	77258	42	22742	00076		99924	
·6	77225	43	22775	77301	43	22699	00076		99924	
·8	77268	43	22732	77344	43	22656	00076		99924	
24·0	77310	42	22690	77387	43	22613	00077		99924	36′

3°
183°

LOGS. OF TRIG. FUNCTIONS

'	Sine	Diff.	Cosec.	Tan.	Diff.	Cotan.	Secant	Diff.	Cosine	
24·0	2̄.(8) 77310	43	1.(11) 22690	2̄.(8) 77387	43	1.(11) 22613	0.(10) 00077		1̄.(9) 99924	36'
·2	77353	42	22647	77430	42	22570	00077		99923	
·4	77395	43	22605	77472	43	22528	00077		99923	
·6	77438	42	22562	77515	42	22485	00077		99923	
·8	77480	42	22520	77557	43	22443	00077		99923	
25·0	77522	43	22478	77600	42	22401	00077		99923	35'
·2	77565	42	22435	77642	43	22358	00077		99923	
·4	77607	42	22393	77685	42	22315	00078		99922	
·6	77649	42	22351	77727	42	22273	00078		99922	
·8	77691	42	22309	77769	42	22231	00078		99922	
26·0	77733	42	22267	77811	42	22189	00078		99922	34'
·2	77775	42	22225	77853	42	22147	00078		99922	
·4	77817	42	22183	77895	42	22105	00078		99922	
·6	77859	42	22141	77937	43	22063	00078		99922	
·8	77901	42	22099	77980	42	22020	00079		99921	
27·0	77943	42	22057	78022	42	21978	00079		99921	33'
·2	77985	42	22015	78064	42	21936	00079		99921	
·4	78027	42	21973	78106	42	21894	00079		99921	
·6	78069	42	21931	78148	42	21852	00079		99921	
·8	78111	41	21889	78190	42	21810	00079		99921	
28·0	78152	42	21848	78232	42	21768	00080		99921	32'
·2	78194	42	21806	78274	42	21726	00080		99920	
·4	78236	41	21764	78316	41	21684	00080		99920	
·6	78277	42	21723	78357	42	21643	00080		99920	
·8	78319	41	21681	78399	42	21601	00080		99920	
29·0	78361	42	21640	78441	41	21559	00080		99920	31'
·2	78402	41	21598	78482	42	21518	00080		99920	
·4	78443	42	21557	78524	42	21476	00081		99919	
·6	78485	41	21515	78566	41	21434	00081		99919	
·8	78526	42	21474	78607	42	21393	00081		99919	
30·0	78568	41	21433	78649	41	21351	00081		99919	30'
·2	78609	41	21391	78690	41	21310	00081		99919	
·4	78650	41	21350	78731	42	21269	00081		99919	
·6	78691	41	21309	78773	41	21227	00082		99918	
·8	78732	42	21268	78814	41	21186	00082		99918	
31·0	78774	41	21226	78855	42	21145	00082		99918	29'
·2	78815	41	21185	78897	41	21103	00082		99918	
·4	78856	41	21144	78938	41	21062	00082		99918	
·6	78897	41	21103	78979	41	21021	00082		99918	
·8	78938	41	21062	79020	41	20980	00082		99918	
32·0	78979	41	21021	79061	42	20939	00083		99917	28'
·2	79020	40	20980	79103	40	20897	00083		99917	
·4	79060	41	20940	79143	41	20857	00083		99917	
·6	79101	41	20899	79184	41	20816	00083		99917	
·8	79142	41	20858	79225	41	20775	00083		99917	
33·0	79183	41	20817	79266	42	20734	00083		99917	27'
·2	79224	40	20776	79308	40	20692	00084		99916	
·4	79264	41	20736	79348	41	20652	00084		99916	
·6	79305	40	20695	79389	40	20611	00084		99916	
·8	79345	41	20655	79429	41	20571	00084		99916	
34·0	79386	41	20614	79470	41	20530	00084		99916	26'
·2	79427	40	20573	79511	41	20489	00084		99916	
·4	79467	40	20533	79552	40	20448	00085		99915	
·6	79507	41	20493	79592	41	20408	00085		99915	
·8	79548	40	20452	79633	40	20367	00085		99915	
35·0	79588	41	20412	79673	41	20327	00085		99915	25'
·2	79629	40	20371	79714	40	20286	00085		99915	
·4	79669	40	20331	79754	40	20246	00085		99915	
·6	79709	40	20291	79794	41	20206	00085		99915	
·8	79749	40	20251	79835	40	20165	00086		99914	
36·0	79789		20211	79875		20125	00086		99914	24'

LOGS. OF TRIG. FUNCTIONS

3°
183°

′	Sine	Diff.	Cosec.	Tan.	Diff.	Cotan.	Secant	Diff.	Cosine	
36·0	2̄.(8) 79789		1.(11) 20211	2̄.(8) 79875		1.(11) 20125	0.(10) 00086		1̄.(9) 99914	24′
·2	79830	41	20170	79916	41	20084	00086		99914	
·4	79870	40	20130	79956	40	20044	00086		99914	
·6	79910	40	20090	79996	40	20004	00086		99914	
·8	79950	40	20050	80036	40	19964	00086		99914	
37·0	79990	40	20010	80076	40	19924	00087		99913	23′
·2	80030	40	19970	80117	41	19883	00087		99913	
·4	80070	40	19930	80157	40	19843	00087		99913	
·6	80110	40	19890	80197	40	19803	00087		99913	
·8	80149	39	19851	80237	40	19763	00087		99913	
38·0	80189	40	19811	80277	40	19723	00087		99912	22′
·2	80229	40	19771	80317	40	19683	00088		99912	
·4	80269	40	19731	80357	40	19643	00088		99912	
·6	80308	39	19692	80396	39	19604	00088		99912	
·8	80348	40	19652	80436	40	19564	00088		99912	
39·0	80388	40	19612	80476	40	19524	00088		99912	21′
·2	80427	39	19573	80515	39	19485	00088		99912	
·4	80467	40	19533	80555	40	19445	00088		99912	
·6	80506	39	19494	80595	40	19405	00089		99911	
·8	80546	40	19454	80635	40	19365	00089		99911	
40·0	80585	39	19415	80674	39	19326	00089		99911	20′
·2	80625	40	19375	80714	40	19286	00089		99911	
·4	80664	39	19336	80753	39	19247	00089		99911	
·6	80703	39	19297	80793	40	19207	00089		99911	
·8	80743	40	19257	80833	40	19167	00090		99910	
41·0	80782	39	19218	80872	39	19128	00090		99910	19′
·2	80821	39	19179	80911	39	19089	00090		99910	
·4	80860	39	19140	80950	39	19050	00090		99910	
·6	80900	40	19100	80990	40	19010	00090		99910	
·8	80939	39	19061	81029	39	18971	00090		99910	
42·0	80978	39	19022	81068	39	18932	00091		99909	18′
·2	81017	39	18983	81108	40	18892	00091		99909	
·4	81056	39	18944	81147	39	18853	00091		99909	
·6	81095	39	18905	81186	39	18814	00091		99909	
·8	81134	39	18866	81225	39	18775	00091		99909	
43·0	81173	39	18827	81264	39	18736	00091		99909	17′
·2	81211	38	18789	81303	39	18697	00092		99908	
·4	81250	39	18750	81342	39	18658	00092		99908	
·6	81289	39	18711	81381	39	18619	00092		99908	
·8	81328	39	18672	81420	39	18580	00092		99908	
44·0	81367	39	18633	81459	39	18541	00092		99908	16′
·2	81405	38	18595	81498	39	18502	00092		99908	
·4	81444	39	18556	81537	39	18463	00093		99907	
·6	81483	39	18517	81576	39	18424	00093		99907	
·8	81521	38	18479	81614	38	18386	00093		99907	
45·0	81560	39	18440	81653	39	18347	00093		99907	15′
·2	81598	38	18402	81691	38	18309	00093		99907	
·4	81637	39	18363	81730	39	18270	00093		99907	
·6	81675	38	18325	81768	38	18232	00093		99907	
·8	81714	39	18286	81807	39	18193	00094		99906	
46·0	81752	38	18248	81846	39	18154	00094		99906	14′
·2	81790	38	18210	81884	38	18116	00094		99906	
·4	81829	39	18171	81923	39	18077	00094		99906	
·6	81867	38	18133	81961	38	18039	00094		99906	
·8	81905	38	18095	81999	38	18001	00094		99906	
47·0	81944	39	18056	82038	39	17962	00095		99905	13′
·2	81982	38	18018	82077	39	17923	00095		99905	
·4	82020	38	17980	82115	38	17885	00095		99905	
·6	82058	38	17942	82153	38	17847	00095		99905	
·8	82096	38	17904	82191	38	17809	00095		99905	
48·0	82134	38	17866	82230	39	17770	00096		99904	12′

176°
356°

3° 183° LOGS. OF TRIG. FUNCTIONS

′	Sine	Diff.	Cosec.	Tan.	Diff.	Cotan.	Secant	Diff.	Cosine	
48.0	2̄.(8) 82134	38	1.(11) 17866	2̄.(8) 82230	38	1.(11) 17770	0.(10) 00096		1̄.(9) 99904	12′
.2	82172	38	17828	82268	38	17732	00096		99904	
.4	82210	38	17790	82306	38	17694	00096		99904	
.6	82248	38	17752	82344	38	17656	00096		99904	
.8	82286	38	17714	82382	39	17618	00096		99904	
49.0	82324	38	17676	82421	38	17580	00096		99904	11′
.2	82362	38	17638	82459	38	17541	00097		99903	
.4	82400	38	17600	82497	38	17503	00097		99903	
.6	82438	37	17562	82535	37	17465	00097		99903	
.8	82475	38	17525	82572	38	17428	00097		99903	
50.0	82513	38	17487	82610	38	17390	00097		99903	10′
.2	82551	37	17449	82648	38	17352	00097		99903	
.4	82588	38	17412	82686	38	17314	00098		99902	
.6	82626	38	17374	82724	38	17276	00098		99902	
.8	82664	37	17336	82762	37	17238	00098		99902	
51.0	82701	38	17299	82799	38	17201	00098		99902	9′
.2	82739	37	17261	82837	37	17163	00098		99902	
.4	82776	38	17224	82874	38	17126	00098		99902	
.6	82814	37	17186	82912	38	17087	00099		99901	
.8	82851	37	17149	82950	37	17050	00099		99901	
52.0	82888	38	17112	82987	38	17013	00099		99901	8′
.2	82926	37	17074	83025	37	16975	00099		99901	
.4	82963	37	17037	83062	38	16938	00099		99901	
.6	83000	38	17000	83100	38	16901	00100		99901	
.8	83038	37	16962	83138	37	16862	00100		99900	
53.0	83075	37	16925	83175	37	16825	00100		99900	7′
.2	83112	37	16888	83212	37	16788	00100		99900	
.4	83149	38	16851	83249	38	16751	00100		99900	
.6	83187	37	16813	83287	38	16713	00100		99900	
.8	83224	37	16776	83325	36	16675	00101		99899	
54.0	83261	37	16739	83361	38	16639	00101		99899	6′
.2	83298	37	16702	83399	37	16601	00101		99899	
.4	83335	37	16665	83436	37	16564	00101		99899	
.6	83372	37	16628	83473	37	16527	00101		99899	
.8	83409	37	16591	83510	37	16490	00101		99899	
55.0	83446	38	16554	83547	37	16453	00102		99898	5′
.2	83482	37	16518	83584	37	16416	00102		99898	
.4	83519	37	16481	83621	37	16379	00102		99898	
.6	83556	37	16444	83658	37	16342	00102		99898	
.8	83593	37	16407	83695	37	16305	00102		99898	
56.0	83630	36	16370	83732	37	16268	00102		99898	4′
.2	83666	37	16334	83769	37	16231	00103		99897	
.4	83703	37	16297	83806	37	16194	00103		99897	
.6	83740	36	16260	83843	36	16157	00103		99897	
.8	83776	37	16224	83879	37	16121	00103		99897	
57.0	83813	37	16187	83916	37	16083	00103		99897	3′
.2	83850	36	16150	83953	37	16047	00103		99897	
.4	83886	37	16114	83990	37	16010	00104		99896	
.6	83923	36	16077	84027	36	15973	00104		99896	
.8	83959	37	16041	84063	37	15937	00104		99896	
58.0	83996	36	16004	84100	36	15900	00104		99896	2′
.2	84032	36	15968	84136	36	15864	00104		99896	
.4	84068	37	15932	84172	37	15828	00104		99896	
.6	84105	36	15895	84209	37	15790	00105		99895	
.8	84141	36	15859	84246	37	15754	00105		99895	
59.0	84177	37	15823	84283	36	15718	00105		99895	1′
.2	84214	36	15786	84319	36	15681	00105		99895	
.4	84250	36	15750	84355	36	15645	00105		99895	
.6	84286	36	15714	84391	37	15609	00105		99895	
.8	84322	37	15678	84428	36	15572	00106		99894	
60.0	84359		15642	84464		15536	00106		99894	0′

4°
184°

LOGS. OF TRIG. FUNCTIONS

′	Sine	Parts	Cosec.	Tan.	Parts	Cotan.	Secant	Parts	Cosine	
00·0	2̄.(8) 84359	′	1.(11)15642	2̄.(8) 84464	′	1.(11) 15536	0.(10) 00106		1̄.(9) 99894	60′
01·0	84539	·1 18	15461	84646	·1 18	15355	00107		99893	
02·0	84718	·2 35	15282	84826	·2 36	15174	00108		99892	
03·0	84897	·3 53	15103	85006	·3 53	14994	00109		99891	
04·0	85075	·4 71	14925	85185	·4 71	14815	00110		99891	
05·0	85253	·5 88	14748	85363	·5 89	14637	00110		99890	55′
06·0	85429	·6 106	14571	85540	·6 107	14460	00111		99889	
07·0	85605	·7 124	14395	85717	·7 125	14283	00112		99888	
08·0	85780	·8 142	14220	85893	·8 142	14107	00113		99887	
09·0	85955	·9 159	14045	86069	·9 160	13931	00114		99886	
10·0	86128		13872	86243		13757	00115		99885	50′
11·0	86301	·1 17	13699	86417	·1 17	13583	00116		99884	
12·0	86474	·2 34	13526	86591	·2 34	13409	00117		99883	
13·0	86646	·3 51	13355	86763	·3 51	13237	00118		99882	
14·0	86817	·4 68	13184	86935	·4 68	13065	00119		99881	
15·0	86987	·5 85	13013	87106	·5 86	12894	00120		99880	45′
16·0	87157	·6 102	12844	87277	·6 103	12723	00121		99880	
17·0	87326	·7 119	12675	87447	·7 120	12553	00122		99879	
18·0	87494	·8 136	12506	87616	·8 137	12384	00122		99878	
19·0	87662	·9 153	12339	87785	·9 154	12215	00123		99877	
20·0	87829		12172	87953		12047	00124		99876	40′
21·0	87995	·1 16	12005	88120	·1 16	11880	00125		99875	
22·0	88161	·2 33	11839	88287	·2 33	11713	00126		99874	
23·0	88326	·3 49	11674	88453	·3 49	11547	00127		99873	
24·0	88490	·4 65	11510	88619	·4 66	11382	00128		99872	
25·0	88654	·5 82	11346	88783	·5 82	11217	00129		99871	35′
26·0	88817	·6 98	11183	88948	·6 99	11052	00130		99870	
27·0	88980	·7 114	11020	89111	·7 115	10889	00131		99869	
28·0	89142	·8 131	10858	89274	·8 132	10726	00132		99868	
29·0	89304	·9 147	10697	89437	·9 148	10563	00133		99867	
30·0	89464		10536	89598		10402	00134		99866	30′
31·0	89625	·1 16	10375	89760	·1 16	10240	00135		99865	
32·0	89784	·2 32	10216	89920	·2 32	10080	00136		99864	
33·0	89943	·3 47	10057	90080	·3 48	09920	00137		99863	
34·0	90102	·4 63	09898	90240	·4 63	09760	00138		99862	
35·0	90260	·5 79	09740	90399	·5 79	09601	00139		99861	25′
36·0	90417	·6 95	09583	90557	·6 95	09443	00140		99860	
37·0	90574	·7 110	09426	90715	·7 111	09285	00141		99859	
38·0	90730	·8 126	09270	90872	·8 127	09128	00142		99858	
39·0	90885	·9 142	09115	91029	·9 143	08972	00143		99857	
40·0	91040		08960	91185		08815	00144		99856	20′
41·0	91195	·1 15	08805	91340	·1 15	08660	00145		99855	
42·0	91349	·2 30	08651	91495	·2 31	08505	00146		99854	
43·0	91502	·3 46	08498	91650	·3 46	08351	00147		99853	
44·0	91655	·4 61	08345	91803	·4 61	08197	00148		99852	
45·0	91807	·5 76	08193	91957	·5 77	08043	00149		99851	15′
46·0	91959	·6 91	08041	92110	·6 92	07890	00151		99850	
47·0	92110	·7 106	07890	92262	·7 107	07738	00152		99849	
48·0	92261	·8 122	07739	92414	·8 122	07586	00153		99847	
49·0	92411	·9 137	07589	92565	·9 138	07435	00154		99846	
50·0	92561		07439	92716		07284	00155		99845	10′
51·0	92710	·1 15	07290	92866	·1 15	07134	00156		99844	
52·0	92859	·2 29	07141	93016	·2 30	06985	00157		99843	
53·0	93007	·3 44	06993	93165	·3 44	06835	00158		99842	
54·0	93154	·4 59	06846	93313	·4 59	06687	00159		99841	
55·0	93302	·5 73	06699	93462	·5 74	06538	00160		99840	5′
56·0	93448	·6 88	06552	93609	·6 89	06391	00161		99839	
57·0	93594	·7 103	06406	93757	·7 104	06244	00162		99838	
58·0	93740	·8 118	06260	93903	·8 118	06097	00163		99837	
59·0	93885	·9 132	06115	94049	·9 133	05951	00165		99836	
60·0	94030		05970	94195		05805	00166		99834	0′

LOGS. OF TRIG. FUNCTIONS

5°
185°

′	Sine	Parts	Cosec.	Tan.	Parts	Cotan.	Secant	Parts	Cosine	
00·0	2̄.(8) 94030	′	1.(11) 05970	2̄.(8) 94195	′	1.(11) 05805	0.(10) 00166		1̄.(9) 99834	60′
01·0	94174	·1 14	05826	94340	·1 14	05660	00167		99833	
02·0	94317	·2 28	05683	94485	·2 29	05515	00168		99832	
03·0	94461	·3 43	05539	94630	·3 43	05371	00169		99831	
04·0	94603	·4 57	05397	94773	·4 57	05227	00170		99830	
05·0	94746	·5 71	05254	94917	·5 72	05083	00171		99829	55′
06·0	94887	·6 85	05113	95060	·6 86	04940	00172		99828	
07·0	95029	·7 99	04971	95202	·7 100	04798	00173		99827	
08·0	95170	·8 114	04830	95344	·8 115	04656	00175		99826	
09·0	95310	·9 128	04690	95486	·9 129	04514	00176		99824	
10·0	95450	·1 14	04550	95627		04373	00177		99823	50′
11·0	95589	·2 28	04411	95767	·1 14	04233	00178		99822	
12·0	95728	·3 41	04272	95908	·2 28	04093	00179		99821	
13·0	95867	·4 55	04133	96047	·3 42	03953	00180		99820	
14·0	96005	·5 69	03995	96187	·4 55	03813	00181		99819	
15·0	96143	·6 83	03857	96326	·5 69	03675	00183		99817	45′
16·0	96280	·7 96	03720	96464	·6 83	03536	00184		99816	
17·0	96417	·8 110	03583	96602	·7 97	03398	00185		99815	
18·0	96553	·9 124	03447	96739	·8 111	03261	00186		99814	
19·0	96689		03311	96877	·9 125	03123	00187		99813	
20·0	96825		03175	97013		02987	00188		99812	40′
21·0	96960	·1 13	03040	97150	·1 13	02850	00190		99810	
22·0	97095	·2 27	02905	97286	·2 27	02715	00191		99809	
23·0	97229	·3 40	02771	97421	·3 40	02579	00192		99808	
24·0	97363	·4 53	02637	97556	·4 54	02444	00193		99807	
25·0	97496	·5 67	02504	97691	·5 67	02309	00194		99806	35′
26·0	97629	·6 80	02371	97825	·6 81	02175	00196		99804	
27·0	97762	·7 93	02238	97959	·7 94	02041	00197		99803	
28·0	97894	·8 107	02106	98092	·8 108	01908	00198		99802	
29·0	98026	·9 120	01974	98225	·9 121	01775	00199		99801	
30·0	98157		01843	98358		01642	00200		99800	30′
31·0	98288	·1 13	01712	98490	·1 13	01510	00202		99798	
32·0	98419	·2 26	01581	98622	·2 26	01378	00203		99797	
33·0	98549	·3 39	01451	98753	·3 39	01247	00204		99796	
34·0	98679	·4 52	01321	98884	·4 52	01116	00205		99795	
35·0	98808	·5 65	01192	99015	·5 65	00985	00207		99794	25′
36·0	98937	·6 78	01063	99145	·6 78	00855	00208		99792	
37·0	99066	·7 91	00934	99275	·7 91	00725	00209		99791	
38·0	99194	·8 103	00806	99405	·8 104	00596	00210		99790	
39·0	99322	·9 116	00678	99534	·9 117	00466	00212		99789	
40·0	99450		00550	99662		00338	00213		99787	20′
41·0	99577	·1 13	00423	99791	·1 13	00209	00214		99786	
42·0	99704	·2 25	00296	99919	·2 25	00081	00215		99785	
43·0	99830	·3 38	00170	1̄.(9) 00047	·3 38	0.(10) 99954	00217		99784	
44·0	99956	·4 50	00044	00174	·4 51	99826	00218		99782	
45·0	1̄.(9) 00082	·5 63	0.(10) 99918	00301	·5 63	99700	00219		99781	15′
46·0	00207	·6 75	99793	00427	·6 76	99573	00220		99780	
47·0	00332	·7 88	99668	00553	·7 89	99447	00222		99778	
48·0	00456	·8 100	99544	00679	·8 101	99321	00223		99777	
49·0	00581	·9 113	99420	00805	·9 114	99195	00224		99776	
50·0	00704		99296	00930		99070	00226		99775	10′
51·0	00828	·1 12	99172	01055	·1 12	98945	00227		99773	
52·0	00951	·2 24	99049	01179	·2 25	98821	00228		99772	
53·0	01074	·3 37	98926	01303	·3 37	98697	00229		99771	
54·0	01196	·4 49	98804	01427	·4 49	98573	00231		99769	
55·0	01318	·5 61	98682	01550	·5 62	98450	00232		99768	5′
56·0	01440	·6 73	98560	01673	·6 74	98327	00233		99767	
57·0	01561	·7 85	98439	01796	·7 86	98204	00235		99765	
58·0	01682	·8 98	98318	01918	·8 99	98082	00236		99764	
59·0	01803	·9 110	98197	02040	·9 111	97960	00237		99763	
60·0	01924		98077	02162		97838	00239		99761	0′

6°
186°

LOGS. OF TRIG. FUNCTIONS

′	Sine	Parts	Cosec.	Tan.	Parts	Cotan.	Secant	Parts	Cosine	
00·0	1.(9)01924	′	0.(10)98077	1.(9)02162	′	0.(10)97838	0.(10)00239		1.(9)99761	60′
01·0	02044		97957	02283		97717	00240		99760	
02·0	02163	·1 12	97837	02404	·1 12	97596	00241		99759	
03·0	02283	·2 24	97718	02525	·2 24	97475	00243		99757	
04·0	02402	·3 36	97598	02646	·3 36	97355	00244		99756	
05·0	02520	·4 47 ·5 59	97480	02766	·4 48 ·5 60	97235	00245		99755	55′
06·0	02639	·6 71	97361	02885	·6 72	97115	00247		99753	
07·0	02757	·7 83	97243	03005	·7 84	96995	00248		99752	
08·0	02874	·8 95	97126	03124	·8 96	96876	00249		99751	
09·0	02992	·9 107	97008	03243	·9 108	96758	00251		99749	
10·0	03109		96891	03361		96639	00252		99748	50′
11·0	03226	·1 12	96774	03479	·1 12	96521	00253		99747	
12·0	03342	·2 23	96658	03597	·2 23	96403	00255		99745	
13·0	03458	·3 35	96542	03714	·3 35	96286	00256		99744	
14·0	03574	·4 46 ·5 58	96426	03832	·4 47 ·5 58	96168	00258		99743	
15·0	03690	·6 69	96310	03949	·6 70	96052	00259		99741	45′
16·0	03805	·7 81	96195	04065	·7 82	95935	00260		99740	
17·0	03920	·8 92	96080	04181	·8 93	95819	00262		99738	
18·0	04034	·9 104	95966	04297	·9 105	95703	00263		99737	
19·0	04149		95852	04413		95587	00265		99736	
20·0	04263		95738	04528		95472	00266		99734	40′
21·0	04376	·1 11	95624	04643	·1 11	95357	00267		99733	
22·0	04490	·2 22	95511	04758	·2 23	95242	00269		99731	
23·0	04603	·3 34	95397	04873	·3 34	95127	00270		99730	
24·0	04715	·4 45 ·5 56	95285	04987	·4 46 ·5 57	95013	00272		99729	
25·0	04828	·6 67	95172	05101	·6 68	94899	00273		99727	35′
26·0	04940	·7 79	95060	05214	·7 80	94786	00274		99726	
27·0	05052	·8 90	94948	05328	·8 91	94672	00276		99724	
28·0	05164	·9 101	94837	05441	·9 102	94559	00277		99723	
29·0	05275		94725	05554		94447	00279		99721	
30·0	05386		94614	05666		94334	00280		99720	30′
31·0	05497	·1 11	94503	05778	·1 11	94222	00282		99719	
32·0	05607	·2 22	94393	05890	·2 22	94110	00283		99717	
33·0	05717	·3 33	94283	06002	·3 33	93998	00284		99716	
34·0	05827	·4 44 ·5 55	94173	06113	·4 44 ·5 55	93887	00286		99714	
35·0	05937	·6 66	94063	06224	·6 67	93776	00287		99713	25′
36·0	06046	·7 77	93954	06335	·7 78	93665	00289		99711	
37·0	06155	·8 88	93845	06445	·8 89	93555	00290		99710	
38·0	06264	·9 99	93736	06556	·9 100	93444	00292		99708	
39·0	06372		93628	06666		93335	00293		99707	
40·0	06481		93519	06775		93225	00295		99705	20′
41·0	06589	·1 11	93412	06885	·1 11	93115	00296		99704	
42·0	06696	·2 21	93304	06994	·2 22	93006	00298		99702	
43·0	06804	·3 32	93196	07103	·3 32	92897	00299		99701	
44·0	06911	·4 43 ·5 53	93089	07211	·4 43 ·5 54	92789	00301		99699	
45·0	07018	·6 64	92982	07320	·6 65	92680	00302		99698	15′
46·0	07124	·7 75	92876	07428	·7 76	92572	00304		99696	
47·0	07231	·8 85	92769	07536	·8 87	92464	00305		99695	
48·0	07337	·9 96	92663	07643	·9 97	92357	00307		99693	
49·0	07442		92558	07751		92250	00308		99692	
50·0	07548		92452	07858		92142	00310		99690	10′
51·0	07653	·1 10	92347	07964	·1 11	92036	00311		99689	
52·0	07758	·2 21	92242	08071	·2 21	91929	00313		99687	
53·0	07863	·3 31	92137	08177	·3 32	91823	00314		99686	
54·0	07968	·4 42 ·5 52	92032	08283	·4 42 ·5 53	91717	00316		99684	
55·0	08072	·6 62	91928	08389	·6 63	91611	00317		99683	
56·0	08176	·7 73	91824	08495	·7 74	91505	00319		99681	5′
57·0	08280	·8 83	91720	08600	·8 84	91400	00320		99680	
58·0	08383	·9 94	91617	08705	·9 95	91295	00322		99678	
59·0	08486		91514	08810		91190	00323		99677	
60·0	08589		91411	08914		91086	00325		99675	0′

173°
353°

7°
187°

LOGS. OF TRIG. FUNCTIONS

′	Sine	Parts	Cosec.	Tan.	Parts	Cotan.	Secant	Parts	Cosine	
00·0	1̄.(9)08589	′	0.(10)91411	1̄.(9)08914	′	0.(10)91086	0.(10)00325	′	1̄.(9)99675	60′
01·0	08692	·1 10	91308	09019	·1 10	90981	00327	·1 0	99674	
02·0	08795	·2 20	91205	09123	·2 21	90877	00328	·2 0	99672	
03·0	08897	·3 30	91103	09227	·3 31	90773	00330	·3 0	99670	
04·0	08999	·4 41	91001	09330	·4 41	90670	00331	·4 1	99669	
05·0	09101	·5 51	90899	09434	·5 52	90566	00333	·5 1	99667	55′
06·0	09202	·6 61	90798	09537	·6 62	90463	00334	·6 1	99666	
07·0	09304	·7 71	90696	09640	·7 72	90361	00336	·7 1	99664	
08·0	09405	·8 81	90595	09742	·8 83	90258	00338	·8 1	99663	
09·0	09506	·9 92	90494	09845	·9 93	90155	00339	·9 1	99661	
10·0	09606		90394	09947		90053	00341		99659	50′
11·0	09707	·1 10	90294	10049	·1 10	89951	00342	·1 0	99658	
12·0	09807	·2 20	90193	10150	·2 20	89850	00344	·2 0	99656	
13·0	09907	·3 30	90094	10252	·3 30	89748	00345	·3 0	99655	
14·0	10006	·4 40	89994	10353	·4 40	89647	00347	·4 1	99653	
15·0	10106	·5 50	89894	10454	·5 50	89546	00349	·5 1	99651	45′
16·0	10205	·6 60	89795	10555	·6 61	89445	00350	·6 1	99650	
17·0	10304	·7 70	89696	10656	·7 71	89344	89352	·7 1	99648	
18·0	10403	·8 79	89598	10756	·8 81	89244	00354	·8 1	99647	
19·0	10501	·9 89	89499	10856	·9 91	89144	00355	·9 1	99645	
20·0	10599		89401	10956		89044	00357		99643	40′
21·0	10697	·1 10	89303	11056	·1 10	88944	00358	·1 0	99642	
22·0	10795	·2 19	89205	11155	·2 20	88845	00360	·2 0	99640	
23·0	10893	·3 29	89107	11254	·3 30	88746	00362	·3 0	99638	
24·0	10990	·4 39	89010	11353	·4 40	88646	00363	·4 1	99637	
25·0	11087	·5 49	88913	11452	·5 49	88548	00365	·5 1	99635	35′
26·0	11184	·6 58	88816	11551	·6 59	88449	00367	·6 1	99634	
27·0	11281	·7 68	88719	11649	·7 69	88351	00368	·7 1	99632	
28·0	11377	·8 78	88623	11747	·8 79	88253	00370	·8 1	99630	
29·0	11474	·9 87	88526	11845	·9 89	88155	00372	·9 1	99629	
30·0	11570		88430	11943		88057	00373		99627	30′
31·0	11666	·1 9	88334	12040	·1 10	87960	00375	·1 0	99625	
32·0	11761	·2 19	88239	12138	·2 19	87862	00377	·2 0	99624	
33·0	11857	·3 28	88143	12235	·3 29	87765	00378	·3 1	99622	
34·0	11952	·4 38	88048	12332	·4 39	87668	00380	·4 1	99620	
35·0	12047	·5 47	87953	12428	·5 48	87572	00382	·5 1	99619	25′
36·0	12142	·6 57	87858	12525	·6 58	87475	00383	·6 1	99617	
37·0	12236	·7 66	87764	12621	·7 68	87379	00385	·7 1	99615	
38·0	12331	·8 76	87669	12717	·8 77	87283	00387	·8 1	99613	
39·0	12425	·9 85	87575	12813	·9 87	87187	00388	·9 2	99612	
40·0	12519		87481	12909		87091	00390		99610	20′
41·0	12613	·1 9	87388	13004	·1 9	86996	00392	·1 0	99608	
42·0	12706	·2 19	87294	13099	·2 19	86901	00393	·2 0	99607	
43·0	12799	·3 28	87201	13194	·3 28	86806	00395	·3 1	99605	
44·0	12893	·4 37	87108	13289	·4 38	86711	00397	·4 1	99603	
45·0	12985	·5 46	87015	13384	·5 47	86616	00399	·5 1	99602	15′
46·0	13078	·6 56	86922	13478	·6 57	86522	00400	·6 1	99600	
47·0	13171	·7 65	86829	13573	·7 66	86427	00402	·7 1	99598	
48·0	13263	·8 74	86737	13667	·8 76	86333	00404	·8 1	99596	
49·0	13355	·9 84	86645	13761	·9 85	86240	00405	·9 2	99595	
50·0	13447		86553	13854		86146	00407		99593	10′
51·0	13539	·1 9	86461	13948	·1 9	86052	00409	·1 0	99591	
52·0	13630	·2 18	86370	14041	·2 19	85959	00411	·2 0	99589	
53·0	13722	·3 27	86278	14134	·3 28	85866	00412	·3 1	99588	
54·0	13813	·4 36	86187	14227	·4 37	85773	00414	·4 1	99586	
55·0	13904	·5 45	86096	14320	·5 46	85680	00416	·5 1	99584	5′
56·0	13994	·6 55	86006	14412	·6 56	85588	00418	·6 1	99582	
57·0	14085	·7 64	85915	14504	·7 65	85496	00419	·7 1	99581	
58·0	14175	·8 73	85825	14597	·8 74	85403	00421	·8 1	99579	
59·0	14266	·9 82	85735	14689	·9 83	85312	00423	·9 2	99577	
60·0	14356		85645	14780		85220	00425		99575	0′

172°
352°

8°
188°

LOGS. OF TRIG. FUNCTIONS

′	Sine	Parts	Cosec.	Tan.	Parts	Cotan.	Secant	Parts	Cosine	
00·0	1̄.(9)14356	′	0.(10)85645	1̄.(9)14780	′	0.(10)85220	0.(10)00425	′	1̄.(9)99575	60′
01·0	14445	·1 9	85555	14872	·1 9	85128	00427	·1 0	99574	
02·0	14535	·2 18	85465	14963	·2 18	85037	00428	·2 0	99572	
03·0	14624	·3 27	85376	15054	·3 27	84946	00430	·3 1	99570	
04·0	14714	·4 36	85286	15145	·4 36	84855	00432	·4 1	99568	
05·0	14803	·5 44	85197	15236	·5 45	84764	00434	·5 1	99566	55′
06·0	14892	·6 53	85109	15327	·6 54	84673	00435	·6 1	99565	
07·0	14980	·7 62	85020	15417	·7 64	84583	00437	·7 1	99563	
08·0	15069	·8 71	84931	15508	·8 73	84492	00439	·8 1	99561	
09·0	15157	·9 80	84843	15598	·9 82	84402	00441	·9 2	99559	
10·0	15245		84755	15688		84312	00443		99557	50′
11·0	15333	·1 9	84667	15778	·1 9	84223	00445	·1 0	99556	
12·0	15421	·2 17	84579	15867	·2 18	84133	00446	·2 0	99554	
13·0	15508	·3 26	84492	15957	·3 27	84044	00448	·3 1	99552	
14·0	15596	·4 35	84404	16046	·4 36	83954	00450	·4 1	99550	
15·0	15683	·5 44	84317	16135	·5 44	83865	00452	·5 1	99548	45′
16·0	15770	·6 52	84230	16224	·6 53	83776	00454	·6 1	99546	
17·0	15857	·7 61	84143	16312	·7 62	83688	00455	·7 1	99545	
18·0	15944	·8 70	84057	16401	·8 71	83599	00457	·8 1	99543	
19·0	16030	·9 78	83970	16489	·9 80	83511	00459	·9 2	99541	
20·0	16116		83884	16577		83423	00461		99539	40′
21·0	16203	·1 9	83798	16665	·1 9	83335	00463	·1 0	99537	
22·0	16289	·2 17	83712	16753	·2 17	83247	00465	·2 0	99535	
23·0	16374	·3 26	83626	16841	·3 26	83159	00467	·3 1	99533	
24·0	16460	·4 34	83540	16928	·4 35	83072	00468	·4 1	99532	
25·0	16545	·5 43	83455	17016	·5 44	82984	00470	·5 1	99530	35′
26·0	16631	·6 51	83369	17103	·6 52	82897	00472	·6 1	99528	
27·0	16716	·7 60	83284	17190	·7 61	82810	00474	·7 1	99526	
28·0	16801	·8 68	83199	17277	·8 70	82723	00476	·8 2	99524	
29·0	16886	·9 77	83114	17363	·9 79	82637	00478	·9 2	99522	
30·0	16970		83030	17450		82550	00480		99520	30′
31·0	17055	·1 8	82945	17536	·1 9	82464	00482	·1 0	99518	
32·0	17139	·2 17	82861	17622	·2 17	82378	00484	·2 0	99517	
33·0	17223	·3 25	82777	17708	·3 26	82292	00485	·3 1	99515	
34·0	17307	·4 33	82693	17794	·4 34	82206	00487	·4 1	99513	
35·0	17391	·5 42	82609	17880	·5 43	82120	00489	·5 1	99511	25′
36·0	17474	·6 50	82526	17966	·6 51	82035	00491	·6 1	99509	
37·0	17558	·7 59	82442	18051	·7 60	81949	00493	·7 1	99507	
38·0	17641	·8 67	82359	18136	·8 68	81864	00495	·8 2	99505	
39·0	17724	·9 75	82276	18221	·9 77	81779	00497	·9 2	99503	
40·0	17807		82193	18306		81694	00499		99501	20′
41·0	17890	·1 8	82110	18391	·1 8	81609	00501	·1 0	99499	
42·0	17973	·2 16	82027	18475	·2 17	81525	00503	·2 0	99497	
43·0	18055	·3 25	81945	18560	·3 25	81440	00505	·3 1	99496	
44·0	18137	·4 33	81863	18644	·4 34	81356	00507	·4 1	99494	
45·0	18220	·5 41	81780	18728	·5 42	81272	00508	·5 1	99492	15′
46·0	18302	·6 49	81698	18812	·6 50	81188	00510	·6 1	99490	
47·0	18383	·7 57	81617	18896	·7 59	81104	00512	·7 1	99488	
48·0	18465	·8 66	81535	18979	·8 67	81021	00514	·8 2	99486	
49·0	18547	·9 74	81453	19063	·9 76	80937	00516	·9 2	99484	
50·0	18628		81372	19146		80854	00518		99482	10′
51·0	18709	·1 8	81291	19229	·1 8	80771	00520	·1 0	99480	
52·0	18790	·2 16	81210	19312	·2 17	80688	00522	·2 0	99478	
53·0	18871	·3 24	81129	19395	·3 25	80605	00524	·3 1	99476	
54·0	18952	·4 32	81048	19478	·4 33	80522	00526	·4 1	99474	
55·0	19033	·5 40	80968	19561	·5 41	80439	00528	·5 1	99472	5′
56·0	19113	·6 48	80887	19643	·6 50	80357	00530	·6 1	99470	
57·0	19193	·7 56	80807	19725	·7 58	80275	00532	·7 1	99468	
58·0	19273	·8 64	80727	19807	·8 66	80193	00534	·8 2	99466	
59·0	19353	·9 72	80647	19889	·9 74	80111	00536	·9 2	99464	
60·0	19433		80567	19971		80029	00538		99462	0′

9°
189°

LOGS. OF TRIG. FUNCTIONS

′	Sine	Parts	Cosec.	Tan.	Parts	Cotan.	Secant	Parts	Cosine	
00·0	1.(9) 19433		0.(10) 80567	1.(9) 19971		0.(10) 80029	0.(10) 00538		1.(9) 99462	60′
01·0	19513	·1 8	80487	20053	·1 8	79947	00540	·1 0	99460	
02·0	19593	·2 16	80408	20135	·2 16	79866	00542	·2 0	99458	
03·0	19672	·3 24	80328	20216	·3 24	79784	00544	·3 1	99456	
04·0	19751	·4 32	80249	20297	·4 32	79703	00546	·4 1	99454	
05·0	19830	·5 40	80170	20378	·5 41	79622	00548	·5 1	99452	55′
06·0	19909	·6 47	80091	20459	·6 49	79541	00550	·6 1	99450	
07·0	19988	·7 55	80012	20540	·7 57	79460	00552	·7 1	99448	
08·0	20067	·8 63	79933	20621	·8 65	79379	00554	·8 2	99446	
09·0	20145	·9 71	79855	20701	·9 73	79299	00556	·9 2	99444	
10·0	20223		79777	20782		79218	00558		99442	50′
11·0	20302	·1 8	79698	20862	·1 8	79138	00560	·1 0	99440	
12·0	20380	·2 16	79620	20942	·2 16	79058	00562	·2 0	99438	
13·0	20458	·3 23	79542	21022	·3 24	78978	00564	·3 1	99436	
14·0	20535	·4 31	79465	21102	·4 32	78898	00566	·4 1	99434	
15·0	20613	·5 39	79387	21182	·5 40	78819	00568	·5 1	99432	45′
16·0	20691	·6 47	79309	21261	·6 48	78739	00571	·6 1	99430	
17·0	20768	·7 54	79232	21341	·7 56	78660	00573	·7 1	99427	
18·0	20845	·8 62	79155	21420	·8 64	78580	00575	·8 2	99425	
19·0	20922	·9 70	79078	21499	·9 72	78501	00577	·9 2	99423	
20·0	20999		79001	21578		78422	00579		99421	40′
21·0	21076	·1 8	78924	21657	·1 8	78343	00581	·1 0	99419	
22·0	21153	·2 15	78847	21736	·2 16	78264	00583	·2 0	99417	
23·0	21229	·3 23	78771	21814	·3 23	78186	00585	·3 1	99415	
24·0	21306	·4 30	78695	21893	·4 31	78107	00587	·4 1	99413	
25·0	21382	·5 38	78618	21971	·5 39	78029	00589	·5 1	99411	35′
26·0	21458	·6 46	78542	22049	·6 47	77951	00591	·6 1	99409	
27·0	21534	·7 53	78466	22127	·7 55	77873	00593	·7 1	99407	
28·0	21610	·8 61	78390	22205	·8 63	77795	00596	·8 2	99405	
29·0	21685	·9 69	78315	22283	·9 70	77717	00598	·9 2	99402	
30·0	21761		78239	22361		77639	00600		99400	30′
31·0	21836	·1 7	78164	22438	·1 8	77562	00602	·1 0	99398	
32·0	21912	·2 15	78088	22516	·2 15	77484	00604	·2 0	99396	
33·0	21987	·3 22	78013	22593	·3 23	77407	00606	·3 1	99394	
34·0	22062	·4 30	77938	22670	·4 31	77330	00608	·4 1	99392	
35·0	22137	·5 37	77863	22747	·5 38	77253	00610	·5 1	99390	25′
36·0	22211	·6 45	77789	22824	·6 46	77176	00613	·6 1	99388	
37·0	22286	·7 52	77714	22901	·7 54	77099	00615	·7 1	99385	
38·0	22361	·8 60	77639	22977	·8 62	77023	00617	·8 2	99383	
39·0	22435	·9 67	77565	23054	·9 69	76946	00619	·9 2	99381	
40·0	22509		77491	23130		76870	00621		99379	20′
41·0	22583	·1 7	77417	23207	·1 8	76794	00623	·1 0	99377	
42·0	22657	·2 15	77343	23283	·2 15	76717	00625	·2 0	99375	
43·0	22731	·3 22	77269	23359	·3 23	76641	00628	·3 1	99373	
44·0	22805	·4 29	77195	23435	·4 30	76566	00630	·4 1	99370	
45·0	22878	·5 37	77122	23510	·5 38	76490	00632	·5 1	99368	15′
46·0	22952	·6 44	77048	23586	·6 45	76414	00634	·6 1	99366	
47·0	23025	·7 51	76975	23661	·7 53	76339	00636	·7 2	99364	
48·0	23098	·8 59	76902	23737	·8 61	76263	00638	·8 2	99362	
49·0	23172	·9 66	76829	23812	·9 68	76188	00641	·9 2	99359	
50·0	23244		76756	23887		76113	00643		99357	10′
51·0	23317	·1 7	76683	23962	·1 7	76038	00645	·1 0	99355	
52·0	23390	·2 14	76610	24037	·2 15	75963	00647	·2 0	99353	
53·0	23463	·3 22	76538	24112	·3 22	75888	00649	·3 1	99351	
54·0	23535	·4 29	76465	24187	·4 30	75814	00652	·4 1	99348	
55·0	23607	·5 36	76393	24261	·5 37	75739	00654	·5 1	99346	5′
56·0	23680	·6 43	76321	24335	·6 45	75665	00656	·6 1	99344	
57·0	23752	·7 51	76249	24410	·7 52	75590	00658	·7 2	99342	
58·0	23824	·8 58	76177	24484	·8 60	75516	00660	·8 2	99340	
59·0	23895	·9 65	76105	24558	·9 67	75442	00663	·9 2	99337	
60·0	23967		76033	24632		75368	00665		99335	0′

170°
350°

LOGS. OF TRIG. FUNCTIONS

′	Sine	Parts	Cosec.	Tan.	Parts	Cotan.	Secant	Parts	Cosine	
00·0	1.(9) 23967		0.(10) 76033	1.(9) 24632		0.(10) 75368	0.(10) 00665		1.(9) 99335	60′
01·0	24039	·1 7	75961	24706	·1 7	75294	00667	·1 0	99333	
02·0	24110	·2 14	75890	24779	·2 15	75221	00669	·2 0	99331	
03·0	24181	·3 21	75819	24853	·3 22	75147	00672	·3 1	99328	
04·0	24253	·4 28	75747	24926	·4 29	75074	00674	·4 1	99326	
05·0	24324	·5 36	75676	25000	·5 37	75000	00676	·5 1	99324	55′
06·0	24395	·6 43	75605	25073	·6 44	74927	00678	·6 1	99322	
07·0	24466	·7 50	75534	25146	·7 51	74854	00681	·7 2	99320	
08·0	24536	·8 57	75464	25219	·8 59	74781	00683	·8 2	99317	
09·0	24607	·9 64	75393	25292	·9 66	74708	00685	·9 2	99315	
10·0	24678		75323	25365		74635	00687		99313	50′
11·0	24748	·1 7	75252	25437	·1 7	74563	00690	·1 0	99310	
12·0	24818	·2 14	75182	25510	·2 14	74490	00692	·2 0	99308	
13·0	24888	·3 21	75112	25582	·3 22	74418	00694	·3 1	99306	
14·0	24958	·4 28	75042	25655	·4 29	74345	00696	·4 1	99304	
15·0	25028	·5 35	74972	25727	·5 36	74273	00699	·5 1	99301	45′
16·0	25098	·6 42	74902	25799	·6 43	74201	00701	·6 1	99299	
17·0	25168	·7 49	74832	25871	·7 50	74129	00703	·7 2	99297	
18·0	25237	·8 56	74763	25943	·8 58	74057	00706	·8 2	99294	
19·0	25307	·9 63	74693	26015	·9 65	73985	00708	·9 2	99292	
20·0	25376		74624	26086		73914	00710		99290	40′
21·0	25445	·1 7	74555	26158	·1 7	73842	00713	·1 0	99288	
22·0	25514	·2 14	74486	26229	·2 14	73771	00715	·2 0	99285	
23·0	25583	·3 21	74417	26301	·3 21	73700	00717	·3 1	99283	
24·0	25652	·4 27	74348	26372	·4 28	73628	00719	·4 1	99281	
25·0	25721	·5 34	74279	26443	·5 36	73557	00722	·5 1	99278	35′
26·0	25790	·6 41	74210	26514	·6 43	73486	00724	·6 2	99276	
27·0	25858	·7 48	74142	26585	·7 50	73415	00727	·7 2	99274	
28·0	25927	·8 55	74073	26656	·8 57	73345	00729	·8 2	99271	
29·0	25995	·9 62	74005	26726	·9 64	73274	00731		99269	
30·0	26063		73937	26797		73203	00733		99267	30′
31·0	26131	·1 7	73869	26867	·1 7	73133	00736	·1 0	99264	
32·0	26199	·2 14	73801	26938	·2 14	73063	00738	·2 0	99262	
33·0	26267	·3 20	73733	27008	·3 21	72992	00740	·3 1	99260	
34·0	26335	·4 27	73665	27078	·4 28	72922	00743	·4 1	99257	
35·0	26403	·5 34	73597	27148	·5 35	72852	00745	·5 1	99255	25′
36·0	26470	·6 41	73530	27218	·6 42	72782	00748	·6 1	99253	
37·0	26538	·7 47	73462	27288	·7 49	72712	00750	·7 2	99250	
38·0	26605	·8 54	73395	27357	·8 56	72643	00752	·8 2	99248	
39·0	26672	·9 61	73328	27427	·9 63	72573	00755	·9 2	99245	
40·0	26740		73261	27496		72504	00757		99243	20′
41·0	26807	·1 7	73194	27566	·1 7	72434	00759	·1 0	99241	
42·0	26873	·2 13	73127	27635	·2 14	72365	00762	·2 0	99238	
43·0	26940	·3 20	73060	27704	·3 21	72296	00764	·3 1	99236	
44·0	27007	·4 27	72993	27773	·4 28	72227	00767	·4 1	99234	
45·0	27074	·5 33	72927	27842	·5 35	72158	00769	·5 1	99231	15′
46·0	27140	·6 40	72860	27911	·6 41	72089	00771	·6 1	99229	
47·0	27206	·7 47	72794	27980	·7 48	72020	00774	·7 2	99226	
48·0	27273	·8 53	72727	28049	·8 55	71951	00776	·8 2	99224	
49·0	27339	·9 60	72661	28117	·9 62	71883	00779	·9 2	99221	
50·0	27405		72595	28186		71814	00781		99219	10′
51·0	27471	·1 7	72529	28254	·1 7	71746	00783	·1 0	99217	
52·0	27537	·2 13	72463	28323	·2 14	71678	00786	·2 0	99214	
53·0	27603	·3 20	72398	28391	·3 20	71609	00788	·3 1	99212	
54·0	27668	·4 26	72332	28459	·4 27	71541	00791	·4 1	99209	
55·0	27734	·5 33	72266	28527	·5 34	71473	00793	·5 1	99207	5′
56·0	27799	·6 39	72201	28595	·6 41	71405	00796	·6 1	99204	
57·0	27865	·7 46	72136	28662	·7 48	71338	00798	·7 2	99202	
58·0	27930	·8 52	72070	28730	·8 54	71270	00800	·8 2	99200	
59·0	27995	·9 59	72005	28798	·9 61	71202	00803	·9 2	99197	
60·0	28060		71940	28865		71135	00805		99195	0′

11°
191°
LOGS. OF TRIG. FUNCTIONS

′	Sine	Parts	Cosec.	Tan.	Parts	Cotan.	Secant	Parts	Cosine	
00·0	1.(9)28060	′	0.(10)71940	1.(9)28865	′	0.(10)71135	0.(10)00805	′	1.(9)99195	60′
01·0	28125		71875	28933		71067	00808		99192	
02·0	28190	·1 6	71810	29000	·1 7	71000	00810	·1 0	99190	
03·0	28254	·2 13	71746	29067	·2 13	70933	00813	·2 1	99187	
04·0	28319	·3 19	71681	29134	·3 20	70866	00815	·3 1	99185	
05·0	28384	·4 26	71616	29201	·4 27	70799	00818	·4 1	99182	55′
06·0	28448	·5 32	71552	29268	·5 33	70732	00820	·5 1	99180	
07·0	28512	·6 39	71488	29335	·6 40	70665	00823	·6 2	99177	
08·0	28577		71423	29402		70598	00825		99175	
09·0	28641	·7 45	71359	29468	·7 47	70532	00828	·7 2	99172	
10·0	28705		71295	29535		70465	00830		99170	50′
11·0	28769	·8 51	71231	29601	·8 53	70399	00833	·8 2	99167	
12·0	28833	·9 58	71167	29668	·9 60	70332	00835	·9 2	99165	
13·0	28896		71104	29734		70266	00838		99162	
14·0	28960		71040	29800		70200	00840		99160	
15·0	29024		70976	29866		70134	00843		99157	45′
16·0	29087		70913	29932		70068	00845		99155	
17·0	29150	·1 6	70850	29998	·1 7	70002	00848	·1 0	99152	
18·0	29214	·2 13	70786	30064	·2 13	69936	00850	·2 1	99150	
19·0	29277	·3 19	70723	30130	·3 20	69871	00853	·3 1	99147	
20·0	29340		70660	30195		69805	00855		99145	40′
21·0	29403	·4 25	70597	30261	·4 26	69739	00858	·4 1	99142	
22·0	29466	·5 31	70534	30326	·5 33	69674	00860	·5 1	99140	
23·0	29529	·6 38	70471	30391	·6 39	69609	00863	·6 2	99137	
24·0	29591		70409	30457		69543	00865		99135	
25·0	29654	·7 44	70346	30522	·7 46	69478	00868	·7 2	99132	35′
26·0	29716	·8 50	70284	30587	·8 52	69413	00871	·8 2	99130	
27·0	29779	·9 57	70221	30652	·9 59	69348	00873	·9 2	99127	
28·0	29841		70159	30717		69283	00876		99124	
29·0	29903		70097	30781		69218	00878		99122	
30·0	29966		70035	30846		69154	00881		99119	30′
31·0	30028		69972	30911		69089	00883		99117	
32·0	30090	·1 6	69911	30975	·1 6	69025	00886	·1 0	99114	
33·0	30151	·2 12	69849	31040	·2 13	68960	00889	·2 1	99112	
34·0	30213		69787	31104		68896	00891		99109	
35·0	30275	·3 18	69725	31169	·3 19	68832	00894	·3 1	99106	25′
36·0	30336	·4 25	69664	31233	·4 26	68767	00896	·4 1	99104	
37·0	30398	·5 31	69602	31297	·5 32	68703	00899	·5 1	99101	
38·0	30459	·6 37	69541	31361	·6 38	68639	00901	·6 2	99099	
39·0	30521		69479	31425		68575	00904		99096	
40·0	30582	·7 43	69418	31489	·7 45	68512	00907	·7 2	99093	20′
41·0	30643	·8 49	69357	31552	·8 51	68448	00909	·8 2	99091	
42·0	30704	·9 55	69296	31616	·9 58	68384	00912	·9 2	99088	
43·0	30765		69235	31680		68321	00915		99086	
44·0	30826		69174	31743		68257	00917		99083	
45·0	30887		69113	31806		68194	00920		99080	15′
46·0	30947		69053	31870		68130	00922		99078	
47·0	31008	·1 6	68992	31939	·1 6	68067	00925	·1 0	99075	
48·0	31069	·2 12	68932	31996	·2 13	68004	00928	·2 1	99072	
49·0	31129		68871	32059		67941	00930		99070	
50·0	31189	·3 18	68811	32122	·3 19	67878	00933	·3 1	99067	10′
51·0	31250	·4 24	68751	32185	·4 25	67815	00935	·4 1	99065	
52·0	31310	·5 30	68690	32248	·5 31	67752	00938	·5 1	99062	
53·0	31370	·6 36	68630	32311		57689	00941	·6 2	99059	
54·0	31430		68570	32373	·6 38	57627	00944		99057	
55·0	31490	·7 42	68510	32436	·7 44	67564	00946	·7 2	99054	5′
56·0	31550	·8 48	68451	32498	·8 50	67502	00949	·8 2	99051	
57·0	31609		68391	32561		67439	00952		99049	
58·0	31669	·9 54	68331	32623	·9 57	67377	00954	·9 2	99046	
59·0	31728		68272	32685		67315	00957		99043	
60·0	31788		68212	32748		67253	00960		99040	0′

12°
192°

LOGS. OF TRIG. FUNCTIONS

′	Sine	Parts	Cosec.	Tan.	Parts	Cotan.	Secant	Parts	Cosine	
00·0	1.(9) 31788	′	0.(10) 68212	1.(9) 32748	′	0.(10) 67253	0.(10) 00960	′	1.(9) 99040	60′
01·0	31847		68153	32810		67191	00962		99038	
02·0	31907	·1 6	68093	32872	·1 6	67129	00965	·1 0	99035	
03·0	31966	·2 12	68034	32933	·2 12	67067	00968	·2 1	99032	
04·0	32025	·3 18	67975	32995	·3 18	67005	00970	·3 1	99030	
05·0	32084	·4 24	67916	33057	·4 25	66943	00973	·4 1	99027	55′
06·0	32143	·5 29	67857	33119	·5 31	66881	00976	·5 1	99024	
07·0	32202	·6 35	67798	33180	·6 37	66820	00979	·6 2	99022	
08·0	32261	·7 41	67739	33242	·7 43	66758	00981	·7 2	99019	
09·0	32319		67681	33303		66697	00984		99016	
10·0	32378	·8 47	67622	33365	·8 49	66635	00987	·8 2	99013	50′
11·0	32437	·9 53	67563	33426	·9 55	66574	00989	·9 2	99011	
12·0	32495		67505	33487		66513	00992		99008	
13·0	32553		67447	33548		66452	00995		99005	
14·0	32612		67388	33609		66391	00998		99003	
15·0	32670		67330	33670		66330	01000		99000	45′
16·0	32728		67272	33731		66269	01003		98997	
17·0	32786	·1 6	67214	33792	·1 6	66208	01006	·1 0	98994	
18·0	32844	·2 12	67156	33853	·2 12	66147	01009	·2 1	98992	
19·0	32902	·3 17	67098	33913	·3 18	66087	01011	·3 1	98989	
20·0	32960	·4 23	67040	33974	·4 24	66026	01014	·4 1	98986	40′
21·0	33018	·5 29	66982	34034	·5 30	65966	01017	·5 1	98983	
22·0	33075	·6 35	66925	34095	·6 36	65905	01020	·6 2	98980	
23·0	33133	·7 40	66867	34155	·7 42	65845	01022	·7 2	98978	
24·0	33190		66810	34216		65785	01025		98975	
25·0	33248	·8 46	66752	34276	·8 48	65724	01028	·8 2	98972	35′
26·0	33305	·9 52	66695	34336	·9 54	65664	01031	·9 2	98969	
27·0	33362		66638	34396		65604	01034		98967	
28·0	33420		66581	34456		65544	01036		98964	
29·0	33477		66523	34516		65484	01039		98961	
30·0	33534		66466	34576		65425	01042		98958	30′
31·0	33591		66409	34635		65365	01045		98955	
32·0	33648	·1 6	66353	34695	·1 6	65305	01048	·1 0	98953	
33·0	33704	·2 11	66296	34755	·2 12	65246	01050	·2 1	98950	
34·0	33761	·3 17	66239	34814	·3 18	65186	01053	·3 1	98947	
35·0	33818	·4 23	66182	34874	·4 24	65127	01056	·4 1	98944	25′
36·0	33874	·5 28	66126	34933	·5 30	65067	01059	·5 1	98941	
37·0	33931	·6 34	66069	34992	·6 36	65008	01062	·6 2	98939	
38·0	33987	·7 39	66013	35051	·7 41	64949	01064	·7 2	98936	
39·0	34043		65957	35111		64889	01067		98933	
40·0	34100	·8 45	65900	35170	·8 47	64830	01070	·8 2	98930	20′
41·0	34156	·9 51	65844	35229	·9 53	64771	01073	·9 2	98927	
42·0	34212		65788	35288		64712	01076		98924	
43·0	34268		65732	35347		64654	01079		98921	
44·0	34324		65676	35405		64595	01081		98919	
45·0	34380		65620	35464		64536	01084		98916	15′
46·0	34436		65565	35523		64477	01087		98913	
47·0	34491	·1 6	65509	35581	·1 6	64419	01090	·1 0	98910	
48·0	34547	·2 11	65453	35640	·2 12	64360	01093	·2 1	98907	
49·0	34602	·3 17	65398	35698	·3 17	64302	01096	·3 1	98904	
50·0	34658	·4 22	65342	35757	·4 23	64243	01099	·4 1	98901	10′
51·0	34713	·5 28	65287	35815	·5 29	64185	01102	·5 1	98899	
52·0	34769	·6 33	65231	35873	·6 35	64127	01104	·6 2	98896	
53·0	34824	·7 39	65176	35931	·7 41	64069	01107	·7 2	98893	
54·0	34879		65121	35989		64011	01110		98890	
55·0	34934	·8 44	65066	36047	·8 47	63953	01113	·8 2	98887	5′
56·0	34989	·9 50	65011	36105	·9 52	63895	01116	·9 3	98884	
57·0	35044		64956	36163		63837	01119		98881	
58·0	35099		64901	36221		63779	01122		98878	
59·0	35154		64846	36279		63721	01125		98875	
60·0	35209		64791	36336		63664	01128		98872	0′

167°
347°

13°
193°

LOGS. OF TRIG. FUNCTIONS

′	Sine	Parts	Cosec.	Tan.	Parts	Cotan.	Secant	Parts	Cosine	
00·0	1̄.(9) 35209	′	0.(10) 64791	1̄.(9) 36336	′	0.(10) 63664	0.(10) 01128	′	1̄.(9) 98872	60′
01·0	35264		64737	36394		63606	01131		98870	
02·0	35318	·1 5	64682	36452	·1 6	63549	01133	·1 0	98867	
03·0	35373	·2 11	64627	36509	·2 11	63491	01136	·2 1	98864	
04·0	35427	·3 16	64572	36566	·3 17	63434	01139	·3 1	98861	
05·0	35482	·4 22	64519	36624	·4 23	63376	01142	·4 1	98858	55′
06·0	35536	·5 27	64464	36681	·5 29	63319	01145	·5 1	98855	
07·0	35590	·6 33	64410	36738	·6 34	63262	01148	·6 2	98852	
08·0	35644	·7 38	64356	36795	·7 40	63205	01151	·7 2	98849	
09·0	35698	·8 43	64302	36852	·8 46	63148	01154	·8 2	98846	
10·0	35752	·9 49	64248	36909	·9 51	63091	01157	·9 3	98843	50′
11·0	35806		64194	36966		63034	01160		98840	
12·0	35860		64140	37023		62977	01163		98837	
13·0	35914		64086	37080		62920	01166		98834	
14·0	35968		64032	37137		62863	01169		98831	
15·0	36022		63979	37193		62807	01172		98828	45′
16·0	36075		63925	37250		62750	01175		98825	
17·0	36129	·1 5	63871	37306	·1 6	62694	01178	·1 0	98822	
18·0	36182	·2 11	63818	37363	·2 11	62637	01181	·2 1	98819	
19·0	36236	·3 16	63764	37419	·3 17	62581	01184	·3 1	98816	
20·0	36289	·4 21	63711	37476	·4 22	62524	01187	·4 1	98813	40′
21·0	36342	·5 27	63658	37532	·5 28	62468	01190	·5 2	98810	
22·0	36395	·6 32	63605	37588	·6 34	62412	01193	·6 2	98807	
23·0	36449	·7 37	63552	37644	·7 39	62356	01196	·7 2	98804	
24·0	36502	·8 43	63498	37700	·8 45	62300	01199	·8 2	98801	
25·0	36555	·9 48	63445	37756	·9 51	62244	01202	·9 3	98798	35′
26·0	36608		63393	37812		62188	01205		98795	
27·0	36660		63340	37868		62132	01208		98792	
28·0	36713		63287	37924		62076	01211		98789	
29·0	36766		63234	37980		62020	01214		98786	
30·0	36819		63182	38035		61965	01217		98783	30′
31·0	36871		63129	38091		61909	01220		98780	
32·0	36924	·1 5	63076	38147	·1 6	61853	01223	·1 0	98777	
33·0	36976	·2 10	63024	38202	·2 11	61798	01226	·2 1	98774	
34·0	37029	·3 16	62972	38258	·3 17	61743	01229	·3 1	98771	
35·0	37081	·4 21	62919	38313	·4 22	61687	01232	·4 1	98768	25′
36·0	37133	·5 26	62867	38368	·5 28	61632	01235	·5 2	98765	
37·0	37185	·6 31	62815	38423	·6 33	61577	01238	·6 2	98762	
38·0	37237	·7 36	62763	38479	·7 39	61521	01241	·7 2	98759	
39·0	37289	·8 42	62711	38534	·8 44	61466	01244	·8 2	98756	
40·0	37341	·9 47	62659	38589	·9 50	61411	01247	·9 3	98753	20′
41·0	37393		62607	38644		61356	01250		98750	
42·0	37445		62555	38699		61301	01254		98747	
43·0	37497		62503	38754		61246	01257		98743	
44·0	37549		62451	38808		61192	01260		98740	
45·0	37600		62400	38863		61137	01263		98737	15′
46·0	37652		62348	38918		61082	01266		98734	
47·0	37704	·1 5	62297	38972	·1 5	61028	01269	·1 0	98731	
48·0	37755	·2 10	62245	39027	·2 11	60973	01272	·2 1	98728	
49·0	37806	·3 15	62194	39082	·3 16	60919	01275	·3 1	98725	
50·0	37858	·4 20	62142	39136	·4 22	60864	01278	·4 1	98722	10′
51·0	37909	·5 26	62091	39190	·5 27	60810	01281	·5 2	98719	
52·0	37960	·6 31	62040	39245	·6 33	60755	01285	·6 2	98716	
53·0	38011	·7 36	61989	39299	·7 38	60701	01288	·7 2	98712	
54·0	38062	·8 41	61938	39353	·8 43	60647	01291	·8 3	98709	
55·0	38113	·9 46	61887	39407	·9 49	60593	01294	·9 3	98706	5′
56·0	38164		61836	39461		60539	01297		98703	
57·0	38215		61785	39515		60485	01300		98700	
58·0	38266		61734	39569		60431	01303		98697	
59·0	38317		61683	39623		60377	01306		98693	
60·0	38368		61632	39677		60323	01310		98690	0′

LOGS. OF TRIG. FUNCTIONS

14°
194°

'	Sine	Parts	Cosec.	Tan.	Parts	Cotan.	Secant	Parts	Cosine	
00·0	1̄.(9) 38368		0.(10) 61632	1̄.(9) 39677		0.(10) 60323	0.(10) 01310		1̄.(9) 98690	60'
01·0	38418		61582	39731		60269	01313		98687	
02·0	38469	·1 5	61531	39785	·1 5	60215	01316	·1 0	98684	
03·0	38519	·2 10	61481	39838	·2 11	60162	01319	·2 1	98681	
04·0	38570	·3 15	61430	39892	·3 16	60108	01322	·3 1	98678	
05·0	38620	·4 20	61380	39946	·4 21	60055	01325	·4 1	98675	55'
06·0	38670		61330	39999		60001	01329		98671	
07·0	38721	·5 25	61279	40052	·5 27	59948	01332	·5 2	98668	
08·0	38771	·6 30	61229	40106	·6 32	59894	01335	·6 2	98665	
09·0	38821		61179	40159		59841	01338		98662	
10·0	38871	·7 35	61129	40212	·7 37	59788	01341	·7 2	98659	50'
11·0	38921	·8 40	61079	40266	·8 43	59734	01345	·8 3	98656	
12·0	38971	·9 45	61029	40319	·9 48	59681	01348	·9 3	98652	
13·0	39021		60979	40372		59628	01351		98649	
14·0	39071		60929	40425		59575	01354		98646	
15·0	39121		60879	40478		59522	01358		98643	45'
16·0	39170		60830	40531		59469	01361		98640	
17·0	39220	·1 5	60780	40584	·1 5	59416	01364	·1 0	98636	
18·0	39270	·2 10	60731	40636	·2 11	59364	01367	·2 1	98633	
19·0	39319	·3 15	60681	40689	·3 16	59311	01370	·3 1	98630	
20·0	39369	·4 20	60632	40742	·4 21	59258	01373	·4 1	98627	40'
21·0	39418		60582	40795		59206	01377		98623	
22·0	39467	·5 25	60533	40847	·5 26	59153	01380	·5 2	98620	
23·0	39517	·6 30	60483	40900	·6 32	59100	01383	·6 2	98617	
24·0	39566		60434	40952		59048	01386		98614	
25·0	39615	·7 34	60385	41005	·7 37	58996	01390	·7 2	98610	35'
26·0	39664	·8 39	60336	41057	·8 42	58943	01393	·8 3	98607	
27·0	39713	·9 44	60287	41109	·9 47	58891	01396	·9 3	98604	
28·0	39762		60238	41162		58839	01399		98601	
29·0	39811		60189	41214		58786	01403		98597	
30·0	39860		60140	41266		58734	01406		98594	30'
31·0	39909		60091	41318		58682	01409		98591	
32·0	39958	·1 5	60043	41370	·1 5	58630	01412	·1 0	98588	
33·0	40006	·2 10	59994	41422	·2 10	58578	01416	·2 1	98584	
34·0	40055	·3 15	59945	41474	·3 16	58526	01419	·3 1	98581	
35·0	40104	·4 19	59897	41526	·4 21	58474	01422	·4 1	98578	25'
36·0	40152		59848	41578		58423	01426		98575	
37·0	40201	·5 24	59800	41629	·5 26	58371	01429	·5 2	98571	
38·0	40249	·6 29	59751	41681	·6 31	58319	01432	·6 2	98568	
39·0	40297		59703	41733		58267	01435		98565	
40·0	40346	·7 34	59655	41784	·7 36	58216	01439	·7 2	98561	20'
41·0	40394	·8 39	59606	41836	·8 41	58164	01442	·8 3	98558	
42·0	40442	·9 44	59558	41887	·9 47	58113	01445	·9 3	98555	
43·0	40490		59510	41939		58061	01449		98551	
44·0	40538		59462	41990		58010	01452		98548	
45·0	40586		59414	42042		57959	01455		98545	15'
46·0	40634		59366	42093		57907	01459		98541	
47·0	40682	·1 5	59318	42144	·1 5	57856	01462	·1 0	98538	
48·0	40730	·2 10	59270	42195	·2 10	57805	01465	·2 1	98535	
49·0	40778	·3 14	59222	42246	·3 15	57754	01469	·3 1	98531	
50·0	40825	·4 19	59175	42297	·4 20	57703	01472	·4 1	98528	10'
51·0	40873		59127	42348		57652	01475		98525	
52·0	40921	·5 24	59079	42399	·5 25	57601	01479	·5 2	98521	
53·0	40968	·6 29	59032	42450	·6 31	57550	01482	·6 2	98518	
54·0	41016		58984	42501		57499	01485		98515	
55·0	41063	·7 33	58937	42552	·7 36	57448	01489	·7 2	98511	5'
56·0	41111	·8 38	58889	42603	·8 41	57397	01492	·8 3	98508	
57·0	41158	·9 43	58842	42653	·9 46	57347	01496	·9 3	98505	
58·0	41205		58795	42704		57296	01499		98501	
59·0	41252		58748	42755		57245	01502		98498	
60·0	41300		58700	42805		57195	01506		98494	0'

15°
195°

LOGS. OF TRIG. FUNCTIONS

′	Sine	Parts	Cosec.	Tan.	Parts	Cotan.	Secant	Parts	Cosine	
00·0	1̄.(9) 41300	′	0.(10) 58700	1̄.(9) 42805	′	0.(10)57195	0.(10) 01506	′	1̄.(9) 98494	60′
01·0	41347		58653	42856		57144	01509		98491	
02·0	41394		58606	42906		57094	01512		98488	
03·0	41441	·1 5	58559	42957	·1 5	57043	01516	·1 0	98484	
04·0	41488		58512	43007		56993	01519		98481	
05·0	41535	·2 9	58465	43057	·2 10	56943	01523	·2 1	98477	55′
06·0	41582	·3 4	58419	43108	·3 15	56893	01526	·3 1	98474	
07·0	41628		58372	43158		56842	01529		98471	
08·0	41675	·4 19	58325	43208	·4 20	56792	01533	·4 1	98467	
09·0	41722	·5 23	58278	43258	·5 25	56742	01536	·5 2	98464	
10·0	41768		58232	43308		56692	01540		98460	50′
11·0	41815	·6 28	58185	43358	·6 30	56642	01543	·6 2	98457	
12·0	41862		58139	43408		56592	01547		98454	
13·0	41908	·7 33	58092	43458	·7 35	56542	01550	·7 2	98450	
14·0	41954	·8 37	58046	43508	·8 40	56492	01553	·8 3	98447	
15·0	42001		57999	43558		56442	01557		98443	45′
16·0	42047	·9 42	57953	43607	·9 45	56393	01560	·9 3	98440	
17·0	42093		57907	43657		56343	01564		98436	
18·0	42140		57861	43707		56293	01567		98433	
19·0	42186		57814	43756		56244	01571		98429	
20·0	42232		57768	43806		56194	01574		98426	40′
21·0	42278		57722	43855		56145	01578		98422	
22·0	42324		57676	43905		56095	01581		98419	
23·0	42370	·1 5	57630	43954	·1 5	56046	01585	·1 0	98416	
24·0	42416		57584	44004		55996	01588		98412	
25·0	42462	·2 9	57539	44053	·2 10	55947	01592	·2 1	98409	35′
26·0	42507	·3 14	57493	44102	·3 15	55898	01595	·3 1	98405	
27·0	42553		57447	44151		55849	01599		98402	
28·0	42599	·4 18	57401	44201	·4 20	55799	01602	·4 1	98398	
29·0	42644	·5 23	57356	44250	·5 25	55750	01605	·5 2	98395	
30·0	42690		57310	44299		55701	01609		98391	30′
31·0	42735	·6 27	57265	44348	·6 29	55652	01613	·6 2	98388	
32·0	42781		57219	44397		55603	01616		98384	
33·0	42826	·7 32	57174	44446	·7 34	55554	01620	·7 2	98381	
34·0	42872	·8 36	57128	44495	·8 39	55505	01623	·8 3	98377	
35·0	42917		57083	44544		55457	01627		98374	25′
36·0	42962	·9 41	57038	44592	·9 44	55408	01630	·9 3	98370	
37·0	43008		56993	44641		55359	01634		98366	
38·0	43053		56947	44690		55310	01637		98363	
39·0	43098		56902	44738		55262	01641		98359	
40·0	43143		56857	44787		55213	01644		98356	20′
41·0	43188		56812	44836		55164	01648		98352	
42·0	43233		56767	44884		55116	01651		98349	
43·0	43278	·1 4	56722	44933	·1 5	55067	01655	·1 0	98345	
44·0	43323		56677	44981		55019	01658		98342	
45·0	43368	·2 9	56633	45029	·2 10	54971	01662	·2 1	98338	15′
46·0	43412	·3 13	56588	45078	·3 14	54922	01666	·3 1	98335	
47·0	43457		56543	45126		54874	01669		98331	
48·0	43502	·4 18	56498	45174	·4 19	54826	01673	·4 1	98327	
49·0	43546	·5 22	56454	45223	·5 24	54778	01676	·5 2	98324	
50·0	43591		56409	45271		54729	01680		98320	10′
51·0	43635	·6 27	56365	45319	·6 29	54681	01683	·6 2	98317	
52·0	43680		56320	45367		54633	01687		98313	
53·0	43724	·7 31	56276	45415	·7 34	54585	01691	·7 3	98309	
54·0	43769	·8 36	56231	45463	·8 39	54537	01694	·8 3	98306	
55·0	43813		56187	45511		54489	01698		98302	5′
56·0	43857	·9 40	56143	45559	·9 43	54441	01701	·9 3	98299	
57·0	43901		56099	45606		54394	01705		98295	
58·0	43946		56054	45654		54346	01709		98291	
59·0	43990		56010	45702		54298	01712		98288	
60·0	44034		55966	45750		54250	01716		98284	0′

LOGS. OF TRIG. FUNCTIONS

16°
196°

′	Sine	Parts	Cosec.	Tan.	Parts	Cotan.	Secant	Parts	Cosine	
00·0	1̄.(9) 44034		0.(10) 55966	1̄.(9) 45750		0.(10) 54250	0.(10) 01716	′	1̄.(9) 98284	60′
01·0	44078		55922	45797		54203	01720		98281	
02·0	44122	·1 4	55878	45845	·1 5	54155	01723	·1 0	98277	
03·0	44166		55834	45893		54108	01727		98273	
04·0	44210	·2 9	55790	45940	·2 9	54060	01730	·2 1	98270	
05·0	44254		55747	45988		54013	01734		98266	55′
06·0	44297	·3 13	55703	46035	·3 14	53965	01738	·3 1	98262	
07·0	44341		55659	46082		53918	01741		98259	
08·0	44385	·4 17	55615	46130	·4 19	53870	01745	·4 1	98255	
09·0	44428		55572	46177		53823	01749		98251	
10·0	44472	·5 22	55528	46224	·5 24	53776	01752	·5 2	98248	50′
11·0	44516		55485	46272		53729	01756		98244	
12·0	44559	·6 26	55441	46319	·6 28	53681	01760	·6 2	98240	
13·0	44603	·7 30	55398	46366	·7 33	53634	01763	·7 3	98237	
14·0	44646		55354	46413		53587	01767		98233	
15·0	44689	·8 35	55311	46460	·8 38	53540	01771	·8 3	98229	45′
16·0	44733		55267	46507		53493	01774		98226	
17·0	44776	·9 39	55224	46554	·9 43	53446	01778	·9 3	98222	
18·0	44819		55181	46601		53399	01782		98218	
19·0	44862		55138	46648		53352	01785		98215	
20·0	44905		55095	46695		53306	01789		98211	40′
21·0	44949		55052	46741		53259	01793		98207	
22·0	44992	1 4	55009	46788	·1 5	53212	01797	·1 0	98204	
23·0	45035		54966	46835		53165	01800		98200	
24·0	45078	·2 9	54923	46881	·2 9	53119	01804	·2 1	98196	
25·0	45120		54880	46928		53072	01808		98192	35′
26·0	45163	·3 13	54837	46975	·3 14	53025	01811	·3 1	98189	
27·0	45206		54794	47021		52979	01815		98185	
28·0	45249	·4 17	54751	47068	·4 19	52932	01819	·4 2	98181	
29·0	45292		54709	47114		52886	01823		98177	
30·0	45334	·5 21	54666	47161	·5 23	52840	01826	·5 2	98174	30′
31·0	45377	·6 26	54623	47207	·6 28	52793	01830	·6 2	98170	
32·0	45419		54581	47253		52747	01834		98166	
33·0	45462	·7 30	54538	47300	·7 32	52701	01838	·7 3	98163	
34·0	45504		54496	47346		52654	01841		98159	
35·0	45547	·8 34	54453	47392	·8 37	52608	01845	·8 3	98155	25′
36·0	45589		54411	47438		52562	01849		98151	
37·0	45632	·9 38	54368	47484	·9 42	52516	01853	·9 3	98147	
38·0	45674		54326	47530		52470	01856		98144	
39·0	45716		54284	47576		52424	01860		98140	
40·0	45758		54242	47622		52378	01864		98136	20′
41·0	45801		54199	47668		52332	01868		98132	
42·0	45843	·1 4	54157	47714	·1 5	52286	01872	·1 0	98129	
43·0	45885		54115	47760		52240	01875		98125	
44·0	45927	·2 8	54073	47806	·2 9	52194	01879	·2 1	98121	
45·0	45969		54031	47852		52148	01883		98117	15′
46·0	46011	·3 13	53989	47898	·3 14	52103	01887	·3 1	98113	
47·0	46053		53947	47943		52057	01891		98110	
48·0	46095	·4 17	53905	47989	·4 18	52011	01894	·4 2	98106	
49·0	46136		53864	48035		51966	01898		98102	
50·0	46178	·5 21	53822	48080	·5 23	51920	01902	·5 2	98098	10′
51·0	46220	·6 25	53780	48126	·6 27	51874	01906	·6 2	98094	
52·0	46262		53738	48171		51829	01910		98090	
53·0	46303	·7 29	53697	48217	·7 32	51783	01913	·7 3	98087	
54·0	46345		53655	48262		51738	01917		98083	
55·0	46386	·8 33	53614	48308	·8 36	51693	01921	·8 3	98079	5′
56·0	46428		53572	48353		51647	01925		98075	
57·0	46469	·9 38	53531	48398	·9 41	51602	01929	·9 3	98071	
58·0	46511		53489	48444		51557	01933		98067	
59·0	46552		53448	48489		51511	01937		98064	
60·0	46594		53407	48534		51466	01940		98060	0′

163°
343°

17°
197°

LOGS. OF TRIG. FUNCTIONS

′	Sine	Parts	Cosec.	Tan.	Parts	Cotan.	Secant	Parts	Cosine	
00·0	1̄.(9) 46594	′	0.(10) 53407	1̄.(9) 48534	′	0.(10) 51466	0.(10) 01940		1̄.(9) 98060	60′
01·0	46635		53365	48579		51421	01944		98056	
02·0	46676	·1 4	53324	48624	·1 4	51376	01948	·1 0	98052	
03·0	46717		53283	48669		51331	01952		98048	
04·0	46759	·2 8	53242	48714	·2 9	51286	01956	·2 1	98044	
05·0	46800		53200	48759		51241	01960		98040	55′
06·0	46841	·3 12	53159	48804	·3 13	51196	01964	·3 1	98036	
07·0	46882		53118	48849		51151	01968		98033	
08·0	46923	·4 16	53077	48894	·4 18	51106	01971	·4 2	98029	
09·0	46964		53036	48939		51061	01975		98025	
10·0	47005	·5 20	52995	48984	·5 22	51016	01979	·5 2	98021	50′
11·0	47046		52955	49029		50971	01983		98017	
12·0	47086	·6 25	52914	49073	·6 27	50927	01987	·6 2	98013	
13·0	47127	·7 29	52873	49118	·7 31	50882	01991	·7 3	98009	
14·0	47168		52832	49163		50837	01995		98005	
15·0	47209	·8 33	52791	49207	·8 36	50793	01999	·8 3	98001	45′
16·0	47249		52751	49252		50748	02003		97997	
17·0	47290	·9 37	52710	49297	·9 40	50704	02007	·9 4	97993	
18·0	47330		52670	49341		50659	02011		97990	
19·0	47371		52629	49385		50615	02015		97986	
20·0	47412		52589	49430		50570	02018		97982	40′
21·0	47452		52548	49474		50526	02022		97978	
22·0	47492	·1 4	52508	49519	·1 4	50481	02026	·1 0	97974	
23·0	47533		52467	49563		50437	02030		97970	
24·0	47573	·2 8	52427	49607	·2 9	50393	02034	·2 1	97966	
25·0	47613		52387	49652		50349	02038		97962	35′
26·0	47654	·3 12	52346	49696	·3 13	50304	02042	·3 1	97958	
27·0	47694		52306	49740		50260	02046		97954	
28·0	47734	·4 16	52266	49784	·4 18	50216	02050	·4 2	97950	
29·0	47774		52226	49828		50172	02054		97946	
30·0	47814	·5 20	52186	49872	·5 22	50128	02058	·5 2	97942	30′
31·0	47854		52146	49916		50084	02062		97938	
32·0	47894	·6 24	52106	49960	·6 26	50040	02066	·6 2	97934	
33·0	47934	·7 28	52066	50004	·7 31	49996	02070	·7 3	97930	
34·0	47974		52026	50048		49952	02074		97926	
35·0	48014	·8 32	51986	50092	·8 35	49908	02078	·8 3	97922	25′
36·0	48054		51946	50136		49864	02082		97918	
37·0	48094	·9 36	51906	50180	·9 40	49820	02086	·9 4	97914	
38·0	48133		51867	50224		49777	02090		97910	
39·0	48173		51827	50267		49733	02094		97906	
40·0	48213		51787	50311		49689	02098		97902	20′
41·0	48253		51748	50355		49645	02102		97898	
42·0	48292	·1 4	51708	50398	·1 4	49602	02106	·1 0	97894	
43·0	48332		51668	50442		49558	02110		97890	
44·0	48371	·2 8	51629	50485	·2 9	49515	02114	·2 1	97886	
45·0	48411	·3 12	51589	50529	·3 13	49471	02118	·3 1	97882	15′
46·0	48450		51550	50572		49428	02122		97878	
47·0	48490	·4 16	51511	50616	·4 17	49384	02126	·4 2	97874	
48·0	48529		51471	50659		49341	02130		97870	
49·0	48568	·5 20	51432	50703	·5 22	49297	02135	·5 2	97866	
50·0	48608		51393	50746		49254	02139		97862	10′
51·0	48647	·6 24	51353	50789	·6 26	49211	02143	·6 2	97857	
52·0	48686		51314	50833		49167	02147		97853	
53·0	48725	·7 27	51275	50876	·7 30	49124	02151	·7 3	97849	
54·0	48764		51236	50919		49081	02155		97845	
55·0	48803	·8 31	51197	50962	·8 35	49038	02159	·8 3	97841	5′
56·0	48842		51158	51005		48995	02163		97837	
57·0	48881	·9 35	51119	51049	·9 39	48952	02167	·9 4	97833	
58·0	48920		51080	51092		48908	02171		97829	
59·0	48959		51041	51135		48865	02175		97825	
60·0	48998		51002	51178		48822	02179		97821	0′

162°
342°

18°
198°

LOGS. OF TRIG. FUNCTIONS

'	Sine	Parts	Cosec.	Tan.	Parts	Cotan.	Secant	Parts	Cosine	
00·0	1̄.(9) 48998	'	0.(10) 51002	1̄.(9) 51178	'	0.(10) 48822	0.(10) 02179	'	1̄.(9) 97821	60'
01·0	49037		50963	51221		48779	02184		97817	
02·0	49076	·1 4	50924	51264	·1 4	48737	02188	·1 0	97812	
03·0	49115		50885	51306		48694	02192		97808	
04·0	49154	·2 8	50847	51349	·2 9	48651	02196	·2 1	97804	
05·0	49192		50808	51392		48608	02200		97800	55'
06·0	49231	·3 12	50769	51435	·3 13	48565	02204	·3 1	97796	
07·0	49270		50731	51478		48522	02208		97792	
08·0	49308	·4 15	50692	51520	·4 17	48480	02212	·4 2	97788	
09·0	49347		50653	51563		48437	02217		97784	
10·0	49385	·5 19	50615	51606	·5 21	48394	02221	·5 2	97779	50'
11·0	49424		50576	51648		48352	02225		97775	
12·0	49462	·6 23	50538	51691	·6 26	48309	02229	·6 2	97771	
13·0	49501	·7 27	50500	51734	·7 30	48267	02233	·7 3	97767	
14·0	49539		50461	51776		48224	02237		97763	
15·0	49577	·8 31	50423	51819	·8 34	48181	02241	·8 3	97759	45'
16·0	49615		50385	51861		48139	02246		97754	
17·0	49654	·9 35	50346	51903	·9 38	48097	02250	·9 4	97750	
18·0	49692		50308	51946		48054	02254		97746	
19·0	49730		50270	51988		48012	02258		97742	
20·0	49768		50232	52031		47970	02262		97738	40'
21·0	49806		50194	52073		47927	02267		97734	
22·0	49844	·1 4	50156	52115	·1 4	47885	02271	·1 0	97729	
23·0	49883		50118	52157		47843	02275		97725	
24·0	49920	·2 8	50080	52200	·2 8	47801	02279	·2 1	97721	
25·0	49958		50042	52242		47758	02283		97717	35'
26·0	49996	·3 11	50004	52284	·3 13	47716	02288	·3 1	97713	
27·0	50034		49966	52326		47674	02292		97708	
28·0	50072	·4 15	49928	52368	·4 17	47632	02296	·4 2	97704	
29·0	50110		49890	52410		47590	02300		97700	
30·0	50148	·5 19	49852	52452	·5 21	47548	02304	·5 2	97696	30'
31·0	50185	·6 23	49815	52494	·6 25	47506	02309	·6 3	97691	
32·0	50223		49777	52536		47464	02313		97687	
33·0	50261	·7 26	49739	52578	·7 29	47422	02317	·7 3	97683	
34·0	50298		49702	52620		47380	02321		97679	
35·0	50336	·8 30	49664	52662	·8 34	47339	02326	·8 3	97675	25'
36·0	50374		49627	52703		47297	02330		97670	
37·0	50411	·9 34	49589	52745	·9 38	47255	02334	·9 4	97666	
38·0	50449		49552	52787		47213	02338		97662	
39·0	50486		49514	52829		47172	02343		97657	
40·0	50523		49477	52870		47130	02347		97653	20'
41·0	50561		49439	52912		47088	02351		97649	
42·0	50598	·1 4	49402	52954	·1 4	47047	02355	·1 0	97645	
43·0	50635		49365	52995		47005	02360		97640	
44·0	50673	·2 7	49327	53037	·2 8	46963	02364	·2 1	97636	
45·0	50710		49290	53078		46922	02368		97632	15'
46·0	50747	·3 11	49253	53120	·3 12	46880	02373	·3 1	97628	
47·0	50784		49216	53161		46839	02377		97623	
48·0	50821	·4 15	49179	53203	·4 17	46798	02381	·4 2	97619	
49·0	50859		49142	53244		46756	02385		97615	
50·0	50896	·5 19	49104	53285	·5 21	46715	02390	·5 2	97610	10'
51·0	50933	·6 22	49067	53327	·6 25	46673	02394	·6 3	97606	
52·0	50970		49030	53368		46632	02398		97602	
53·0	51007	·7 26	48994	53409	·7 29	46591	02403	·7 3	97597	
54·0	51043		48957	53450		46550	02407		97593	
55·0	51080	·8 30	48920	53492	·8 33	46508	02411	·8 3	97589	5'
56·0	51117		48883	53533		46467	02416		97584	
57·0	51154	·9 33	48846	53574	·9 37	46426	02420	·9 4	97580	
58·0	51191		48809	53615		46385	02424		97576	
59·0	51228		48773	53656		46344	02429		97571	
60·0	51264		48736	53697		46303	02433		97567	0'

161°
341°

19°
199°

LOGS. OF TRIG. FUNCTIONS

′	Sine	Parts	Cosec.	Tan.	Parts	Cotan.	Secant	Parts	Cosine	
00·0	1̄.(9) 51264	′	0.(10) 48736	1̄.(9) 53697	′	0.(10) 46303	0.(10) 02433	′	1̄.(9) 97567	60′
01·0	51301		48699	53738		46262	02437		97563	
02·0	51338	·1 4	48663	53779	·1 4	46221	02442	·1 0	97558	
03·0	51374		48626	53820		46180	02446		97554	
04·0	51411	·2 7	48589	53861	·2 8	46139	02450	·2 1	97550	
05·0	51447		48553	53902		46098	02455		97545	55′
06·0	51484	·3 11	48516	53943	·3 12	46057	02459	·3 1	97541	
07·0	51520		48480	53984		46016	02464		97537	
08·0	51557	·4 15	48443	54025	·4 16	45976	02468	·4 2	97532	
09·0	51593		48407	54065		45935	02472		97528	
10·0	51629	·5 18	48371	54106	·5 20	45894	02477	·5 2	97523	50′
11·0	51666		48334	54147		45853	02481		97519	
12·0	51702	·6 22	48298	54188	·6 24	45813	02486	·6 3	97515	
13·0	51738	·7 25	48262	54228	·7 29	45772	02490	·7 3	97510	
14·0	51775		48226	54269		45731	02494		97506	
15·0	51811	·8 29	48189	54309	·8 33	45691	02499	·8 4	97501	45′
16·0	51847		48153	54350		45650	02503		97497	
17·0	51883	·9 33	48117	54391	·9 37	45610	02508	·9 4	97493	
18·0	51919		48081	54431		45569	02512		97488	
19·0	51955		48045	54472		45529	02516		97484	
20·0	51991		48009	54512		45488	02521		97479	40′
21·0	52027		47973	54552		45448	02525		97475	
22·0	52063	·1 4	47937	54593	·1 4	45407	02530	·1 0	97470	
23·0	52099		47901	54633		45367	02534		97466	
24·0	52135	·2 7	47865	54674	·2 8	45327	02539	·2 1	97461	
25·0	52171		47829	54714		45286	02543		97457	35′
26·0	52207	·3 11	47793	54754	·3 12	45246	02548	·3 1	97453	
27·0	52242		47758	54794		45206	02552		97448	
28·0	52278	·4 14	47722	54835	·4 16	45166	02556	·4 2	97444	
29·0	52314		47686	54875		45125	02561		97439	
30·0	52350	·5 18	47651	54915	·5 20	45085	02565	·5 2	97435	30′
31·0	52385	·6 21	47615	54955	·6 24	45045	02570	·6 3	97430	
32·0	52421		47579	54995		45005	02574		97426	
33·0	52456	·7 25	47544	55035	·7 28	44965	02579	·7 3	97421	
34·0	52492		47508	55075		44925	02583		97417	
35·0	52528	·8 29	47473	55115	·8 32	44885	02588	·8 4	97412	25′
36·0	52563		47437	55155		44845	02592		97408	
37·0	52598	·9 32	47402	55195	·9 36	44805	02597	·9 4	97403	
38·0	52634		47366	55235		44765	02601		97399	
39·0	52669		47331	55275		44725	02606		97394	
40·0	52705		47295	55315		44685	02610		97390	20′
41·0	52740		47260	55355		44645	02615		97385	
42·0	52775	·1 4	47225	55395	·1 4	44605	02619	·1 0	97381	
43·0	52811		47190	55434		44566	02624		97376	
44·0	52846	·2 7	47154	55474	·2 8	44526	02628	·2 1	97372	
45·0	52881		47119	55514		44486	02633		97367	15′
46·0	52916	·3 11	47084	55554	·3 12	44446	02638	·3 1	97363	
47·0	52951		47049	55593		44407	02642		97358	
48·0	52986	·4 14	47014	55633	·4 16	44367	02647	·4 2	97354	
49·0	53022		46979	55673		44328	02651		97349	
50·0	53057	·5 18	46944	55712	·5 20	44288	02656	·5 2	97344	10′
51·0	53092	·6 21	46909	55752	·6 24	44248	02660	·6 3	97340	
52·0	53127		46874	55791		44209	02665		97335	
53·0	53161	·7 25	46839	55831	·7 28	44169	02669	·7 3	97331	
54·0	53196		46804	55870		44130	02674		97326	
55·0	53231	·8 28	46769	55910	·8 32	44090	02679	·8 4	97322	5′
56·0	53266		46734	55949		44051	02683		97317	
57·0	53301	·9 32	46699	55989	·9 36	44012	02688	·9 4	97312	
58·0	53336		46664	56028		43972	02692		97308	
59·0	53370		46630	56067		43933	02697		97303	
60·0	53405		46595	56107		43893	02701		97299	0′

20° 200°   LOGS. OF TRIG. FUNCTIONS

'	Sine	Parts	Cosec.	Tan.	Parts	Cotan.	Secant	Parts	Cosine	
00·0	1.(9) 53405		0.(10) 46595	1.(9) 56107		0.(10) 43893	0.(10) 02701		1.(9) 97299	60'·
01·0	53440		46560	56146		43854	02706		97294	
02·0	53475	·1 3	46526	56185	·1 4	43815	02711	·1 0	97289	
03·0	53509		46491	56224		43776	02715		97285	
04·0	53544		46456	56264		43736	02720		97280	
05·0	53578	·2 7	46422	56303	·2 8	43697	02725	·2 1	97276	55'
06·0	53613		46387	56342		43658	02729		97271	
07·0	53647		46353	56381		43619	02734		97266	
08·0	53682	·3 10	46318	56420	·3 12	43580	02738	·3 1	97262	
09·0	53716		46284	56459		43541	02743		97257	
10·0	53751		46249	56498		43502	02748		97252	50'
11·0	53785	·4 14	46215	56537	·4 16	43463	02752	·4 2	97248	
12·0	53819		46181	56576		43424	02757		97243	
13·0	53854		46146	56615		43385	02762		97239	
14·0	53888		46112	56654		43346	02766		97234	
15·0	53922	·5 17	46078	56693	·5 19	43307	02771	·5 2	97229	45'
16·0	53957		46044	56732		43268	02776		97225	
17·0	53991	·6 21	46009	56771	·6 23	43229	02780	·6 3	97220	
18·0	54025		45975	56810		43190	02785		97215	
19·0	54059		45941	56849		43151	02790		97211	
20·0	54093		45907	56887		43113	02794		97206	40'
21·0	54127	·7 24	45873	56926	·7 27	43074	02799	·7 3	97201	
22·0	54161		45839	56965		43035	02804		97196	
23·0	54195		45805	57004		42997	02808		97192	
24·0	54229	·8 27	45771	57042	·8 31	42958	02813	·8 4	97187	
25·0	54263		45737	57081		42919	02818		97182	35'
26·0	54297		45703	57120		42881	02822		97178	
27·0	54331	·9 31	45669	57158	·9 35	42842	02827	·9 4	97173	
28·0	54365		45635	57197		42803	02832		97168	
29·0	54399		45601	57235		42765	02837		97164	
30·0	54433		45568	57274		42726	02841		97159	30'
31·0	54466		45534	57312		42688	02846		97154	
32·0	54500	·1 3	45500	57351	·1 4	42649	02851	·1 0	97149	
33·0	54534		45466	57389		42611	02855		97145	
34·0	54567		45433	57428		42572	02860		97140	
35·0	54601	·2 7	45399	57466	·2 8	42534	02865	·2 1	97135	25'
36·0	54635		45365	57504		42496	02870		97130	
37·0	54668		45332	57543		42457	02874		97126	
38·0	54702	·3 10	45298	57581	·3 11	42419	02879	·3 1	97121	
39·0	54735		45265	57619		42381	02884		97116	
40·0	54769		45231	57658		42342	02889		97111	20'
41·0	54802	·4 13	45198	57696	·4 15	42304	02893	·4 2	97107	
42·0	54836		45164	57734		42266	02898		97102	
43·0	54869		45131	57772		42228	02903		97097	
44·0	54903		45097	57810		42190	02908		97092	
45·0	54936	·5 17	45064	57849	·5 19	42151	02913	·5 2	97087	15'
46·0	54969		45031	57887		42113	02917		97083	
47·0	55003		44997	57925		42075	02922		97078	
48·0	55036	·6 20	44964	57963	·6 23	42037	02927	·6 3	97073	
49·0	55069		44931	58001		41999	02932		97068	
50·0	55102		44898	58039		41961	02937		97064	10'
51·0	55136	·7 23	44864	58077	·7 27	41923	02941	·7 3	97059	
52·0	55169		44831	58115		41885	02946		97054	
53·0	55202		44798	58153		41847	02951		97049	
54·0	55235	·8 27	44765	58191	·8 31	41809	02956	·8 4	97044	
55·0	55268		44732	58229		41771	02961		97039	5'
56·0	55301		44699	58267		41734	02966		97035	
57·0	55334	·9 30	44666	58304	·9 34	41696	02970	·9 4	97030	
58·0	55367		44633	58342		41658	02975		97025	
59·0	55400		44600	58380		41620	02980		97020	
60·0	55433		44567	58418		41582	02985		97015	0'

21°
201°

LOGS. OF TRIG. FUNCTIONS

′	Sine	Parts	Cosec.	Tan.	Parts	Cotan.	Secant	Parts	Cosine	
00·0	1̄.(9) 55433		0.(10) 44567	1̄.(9) 58418		0.(10) 41582	0.(10) 02985		1̄.(9) 97015	60′
01·0	55466		44534	58456		41545	02990		97010	
02·0	55499	·1 3	44501	58493	·1 4	41507	02995	·1 0	97006	
03·0	55532		44469	58531		41469	02999		97001	
04·0	55564		44436	58569		41431	03004		96996	
05·0	55597	·2 7	44403	58606	·2 7	41394	03009	·2 1	96991	55′
06·0	55630		44370	58644		41356	03014		96986	
07·0	55663		44337	58682		41319	03019		96981	
08·0	55695	·3 10	44305	58719	·3 11	41281	03024	·3 1	96976	
09·0	55728		44272	58757		41243	03029		96971	
10·0	55761		44239	58794		41206	03034		96967	50′
11·0	55793	·4 13	44207	58832	·4 15	41168	03038	·4 2	96962	
12·0	55826		44174	58869		41131	03043		96957	
13·0	55858		44141	58907		41093	03048		96952	
14·0	55891	·5 16	44109	58944	·5 19	41056	03053	·5 2	96947	
15·0	55923		44077	58981		41019	03058		96942	45′
16·0	55956		44044	59019		40981	03063		96937	
17·0	55988		44012	59056		40944	03068		96932	
18·0	56021	·6 20	43979	59094	·6 22	40907	03073	·6 3	96927	
19·0	56053		43947	59131		40869	03078		96922	
20·0	56086		43915	59168		40832	03083		96917	40′
21·0	56118	·7 23	43882	59205	·7 26	40795	03088	·7 3	96912	
22·0	56150		43850	59243		40757	03093		96908	
23·0	56182		43818	59280		40720	03098		96903	
24·0	56215	·8 26	43785	59317	·8 30	40683	03102	·8 4	96898	
25·0	56247		43753	59354		40646	03107		96893	35′
26·0	56279		43721	59391		40609	03112		96888	
27·0	56311	·9 29	43689	59429	·9 34	40572	03117	·9 4	96883	
28·0	56343		43657	59466		40534	03122		96878	
29·0	56376		43625	59503		40497	03127		96873	
30·0	56408		43593	59540		40460	03132		96868	30′
31·0	56440		43560	59577		40423	03137		96863	
32·0	56472	·1 3	43528	59614	·1 4	40386	03142	·1 1	96858	
33·0	56504		43496	59651		40349	03147		96853	
34·0	56536		43464	59688		40312	03152		96848	
35·0	56568	·2 6	43432	59725	·2 7	40275	03157	·2 1	96843	25′
36·0	56600		43401	59762		40238	03162		96838	
37·0	56631		43369	59799		40202	03167		96833	
38·0	56663	·3 10	43337	59835	·3 11	40165	03172	·3 2	96828	
39·0	56695		43305	59872		40128	03177		96823	
40·0	56727		43273	59909		40091	03182		96818	20′
41·0	56759	·4 13	43241	59946	·4 15	40054	03187	·4 2	96813	
42·0	56790		43210	59983		40017	03192		96808	
43·0	56822		43178	60019		39981	03197		96803	
44·0	56854		43146	60056		39944	03202		96798	
45·0	56886	·5 16	43114	60093	·5 18	39907	03207	·5 3	96793	15′
46·0	56917		43083	60130		39870	03212		96788	
47·0	56949		43051	60166		39834	03217		96783	
48·0	56980	·6 19	43020	60203	·6 22	39797	03223	·6 3	96778	
49·0	57012		42988	60240		39761	03228		96773	
50·0	57044		42957	60276		39724	03233		96767	10′
51·0	57075	·7 22	42925	60313	·7 26	39687	03238	·7 4	96762	
52·0	57107		42893	60349		39651	03243		96757	
53·0	57138		42862	60386		39614	03248		96752	
54·0	57170	·8 25	42831	60422	·8 29	39578	03253	·8 4	96747	
55·0	57201		42799	60459		39541	03258		96742	5′
56·0	57232		42768	60495		39505	03263		96737	
57·0	57264	·9 29	42736	60532	·9 33	39468	03268	·9 5	96732	
58·0	57295		42705	60568		39432	03273		96727	
59·0	57326		42674	60605		39395	03278		96722	
60·0	57358		42643	60641		39359	03283		96717	0′

22°
202°

LOGS. OF TRIG. FUNCTIONS

′	Sine	Parts	Cosec.	Tan.	Parts	Cotan.	Secant	Parts	Cosine	
00·0	1.(9) 57358	′	0.(10) 42643	1.(9) 60641	′	0.(10) 39359	0.(10) 03283	′	1.(9) 96717	60′
01·0	57389		42611	60677		39323	03289		96712	
02·0	57420	·1 3	42580	60714	·1 4	39286	03294	·1 1	96706	
03·0	57451		42549	60750		39250	03299		96701	
04·0	57482		42518	60786		39214	03304		96696	
05·0	57514	·2 6	42486	60823	·2 7	39178	03309	·2 1	96691	55′
06·0	57545		42455	60859		39141	03314		96686	
07·0	57576		42424	60895		39105	03319		96681	
08·0	57607	·3 9	42393	60931	·3 11	39069	03324	·3 2	96676	
09·0	57638		42362	60967		39033	03330		96671	
10·0	57669		42331	61004		38996	03335		96665	50′
11·0	57700	·4 12	42300	61040	·4 14	38960	03340	·4 2	96660	
12·0	57731		42269	61076		38924	03345		96655	
13·0	57762		42238	61112		38888	03350		96650	
14·0	57793		42207	61148		38852	03355		96645	
15·0	57824	·5 15	42176	61184	·5 18	38816	03361	·5 3	96640	45′
16·0	57855		42146	61220		38780	03366		96634	
17·0	57885		42115	61256		38744	03371		96629	
18·0	57916	·6 19	42084	61292	·6 22	38708	03376	·6 3	96624	
19·0	57947		42053	61328		38672	03381		96619	
20·0	57978		42022	61364		38636	03386		96614	40′
21·0	58009	·7 22	41992	61400	·7 25	38600	03392	·7 4	96609	
22·0	58039		41961	61436		38564	03397		96603	
23·0	58070		41930	61472		38528	03402		96598	
24·0	58101	·8 25	41900	61508	·8 29	38492	03407	·8 4	96593	
25·0	58131		41869	61544		38457	03412		96588	35′
26·0	58162		41838	61579		38421	03418		96582	
27·0	58192	·9 28	41808	61615	·9 32	38385	03423	·9 5	96577	
28·0	58223		41777	61651		38349	03428		96572	
29·0	58254		41747	61687		38313	03433		96567	
30·0	58284		41716	61722		38277	03439		96562	30′
31·0	58314		41685	61758		38242	03444		96556	
32·0	58345	·1 3	41655	61794	·1 4	38206	03449	·1 1	96551	
33·0	58375		41625	61830		38171	03454		96546	
34·0	58406		41594	61865		38135	03459		96541	
35·0	58436	·2 6	41564	61901	·2 7	38099	03465	·2 1	96535	25′
36·0	58467		41534	61936		38064	03470		96530	
37·0	58497		41503	61972		38028	03475		96525	
38·0	58527	·3 9	41473	62008	·3 11	37992	03481	·3 2	96520	
39·0	58557		41443	62043		37957	03486		96514	
40·0	58588		41412	62079		37921	03491		96509	20′
41·0	58618	·4 12	41382	62114	·4 14	37886	03496	·4 2	96504	
42·0	58648		41352	62150		37850	03502		96498	
43·0	58678		41322	62185		37815	03507		96493	
44·0	58709		41292	62221		37779	03512		96488	
45·0	58739	·5 15	41261	62256	·5 18	37744	03517	·5 3	96483	15′
46·0	58769		41231	62292		37709	03523		96477	
47·0	58799		41201	62327		37673	03528		96472	
48·0	58829	·6 18	41171	62362	·6 21	37638	03533	·6 3	96467	
49·0	58859		41141	62398		37602	03539		96461	
50·0	58889		41111	62433		37567	03544		96456	10′
51·0	58919	·7 21	41081	62468	·7 25	37532	03549	·7 4	96451	
52·0	58949		41051	62504		37496	03555		96445	
53·0	58979		41021	62539		37461	03560		96440	
54·0	59009	·8 24	40991	62574	·8 28	37426	03565	·8 4	96435	
55·0	59039		40961	62609		37391	03571		96429	5′
56·0	59069		40931	62645		37356	03576		96424	
57·0	59098	·9 27	40902	62680	·9 32	37320	03581	·9 5	96419	
58·0	59128		40872	62715		37285	03587		96413	
59·0	59158		40842	62750		37250	03592		96408	
60·0	59188		40812	62785		37215	03597		96403	0′

23°
203°

LOGS. OF TRIG. FUNCTIONS

′	Sine	Parts	Cosec.	Tan.	Parts	Cotan.	Secant	Parts	Cosine	
00·0	1̄.(9) 59188	′	0.(10) 40812	1̄.(9)·62785	′	0.(10) 37215	0.(10) 03597	′	1̄.(9) 96403	60′
01·0	59218		40782	62820		37180	03603		96397	
02·0	59247	·1 3	40753	62855	·1 3	37145	03608	·1 1	96392	
03·0	59277		40723	62891		37110	03614		96387	
04·0	59307		40693	62926		37075	03619		96381	
05·0	59336	·2 6	40664	62961	·2 7	37039	03624	·2 1	96376	55′
06·0	59366		40634	62996		37004	03630		96370	
07·0	59396		40605	63031		36969	03635		96365	
08·0	59425	·3 9	40575	63066	·3 10	36934	03640	·3 2	96360	
09·0	59455		40545	63101		36900	03646		96354	
10·0	59484		40516	63136		36865	03651		96349	50′
11·0	59514	·4 12	40486	63170	·4 14	36830	03657	·4 2	96343	
12·0	59543		40457	63205		36795	03662		96338	
13·0	59573		40427	63240		36760	03668		96333	
14·0	59602		40398	63275		36725	03673		96327	
15·0	59632	·5 15	40369	63310	·5 17	36690	03678	·5 3	96322	45′
16·0	59661		40339	63345		36655	03684		96316	
17·0	59690		40310	63380		36621	03689		96311	
18·0	59720	·6 18	40280	63414	·6 21	36586	03695	·6 3	96305	
19·0	59749		40251	63449		36551	03700		96300	
20·0	59778		40222	63484		36516	03706		96295	40′
21·0	59808	·7 21	40193	63519	·7 24	36482	03711	·7 4	96289	
22·0	59837		40163	63553		36447	03716		96284	
23·0	59866		40134	63588		36412	03722		96278	
24·0	59895	·8 24	40105	63623	·8 28	36377	03727	·8 4	96273	
25·0	59924		40076	63657		36343	03733		96267	35′
26·0	59954		40046	63692		36308	03738		96262	
27·0	59983	·9 26	40017	63727	·9 31	36274	03744	·9 5	96256	
28·0	60012		39988	63761		36239	03749		96251	
29·0	60041		39959	63796		36204	03755		96245	
30·0	60070		39930	63830		36170	03760		96240	30′
31·0	60099		39901	63865		36135	03766		96234	
32·0	60128	·1 3	39872	63899	·1 3	36101	03771	·1 1	96229	
33·0	60157		39843	63934		36066	03777		96223	
34·0	60186		39814	63968		36032	03782		96218	
35·0	60215	·2 6	39785	64003	·2 7	35997	03788	·2 1	96212	25′
36·0	60244		39756	64037		35963	03793		96207	
37·0	60273		39727	64072		35928	03799		96201	
38·0	60302	·3 9	39698	64106	·3 10	35894	03804	·3 2	96196	
39·0	60331		39670	64140		35860	03810		96190	
40·0	60359		39641	64174		35825	03815		96185	20′
41·0	60388	·4 11	39612	64209	·4 14	35791	03821	·4 2	96179	
42·0	60417		39583	64243		35757	03827		96174	
43·0	60446		39554	64278		35722	03832		96168	
44·0	60475		39526	64312		35688	03838		96162	
45·0	60503	·5 14	39497	64346	·5 17	35654	03843	·5 3	96157	15′
46·0	60532		39468	64381		35619	03849		96151	
47·0	60561		39439	64415		35585	03854		96146	
48·0	60589	·6 17	39411	64449	·6 21	35551	03860	·6 3	96140	
49·0	60618		39382	64483		35517	03865		96135	
50·0	60647		39354	64517		35483	03871		96129	10′
51·0	60675	·7 20	39325	64552	·7 24	35448	03877	·7 4	96124	
52·0	60704		39296	64586		35414	03882		96118	
53·0	60732		39268	64620		35380	03888		96112	
54·0	60761	·8 23	39239	64654	·8 27	35346	03893	·8 4	96107	
55·0	60789		39211	64688		35312	03899		96101	5′
56·0	60818		39182	64722		35278	03905		96096	
57·0	60846	·9 26	39154	64756	·9 31	35244	03910	·9 5	96090	
58·0	60875		39126	64790		35210	03916		96084	
59·0	60903		39097	64824		35176	03921		96079	
60·0	60931		39069	64858		35142	03927		96073	0′

LOGS. OF TRIG. FUNCTIONS

24°
204°

′	Sine	Parts	Cosec.	Tan.	Parts	Cotan.	Secant	Parts	Cosine	
00·0	1̄.(9) 60931	′	0.(10) 39069	1̄.(9) 64858	′	0.(10) 35142	0.(10) 03927	′	1̄.(9) 96073	60′
01·0	60960		39040	64892		35108	03933		96067	
02·0	60988	·1 3	39012	64926	·1 3	35074	03938	·1 1	96062	
03·0	61016		38984	64960		35040	03944		96056	
04·0	61045		38955	64994		35006	03950		96051	
05·0	61073	·2 6	38927	65028	·2 7	34972	03955	·2 1	96045	55′
06·0	61101		38899	65062		34938	03961		96039	
07·0	61129		38871	65096		34904	03967		96034	
08·0	61158	·3 8	38842	65130	·3 10	34870	03972	·3 2	96028	
09·0	61186		38814	65164		34836	03978		96022	
10·0	61214		38786	65197		34803	03984		96017	50′
11·0	61242	·4 11	38758	65231	·4 13	34769	03989	·4 2	96011	
12·0	61270		38730	65265		34735	03995		96005	
13·0	61298		38702	65299		34701	04001		96000	
14·0	61326		38674	65333		34667	04006		95994	
15·0	61355	·5 14	38646	65366	·5 17	34634	04012	·5 3	95988	45′
16·0	61383		38618	65400		34600	04018		95983	
17·0	61411		38590	65434		34566	04023		95977	
18·0	61439	·6 17	38562	65467	·6 20	34533	04029	·6 3	95971	
19·0	61467		38534	65501		34499	04035		95965	
20·0	61494		38506	65535		34465	04040		95960	40′
21·0	61522	·7 20	38478	65568	·7 24	34432	04046	·7 4	95954	
22·0	61550		38450	65602		34398	04052		95948	
23·0	61578		38422	65636		34364	04058		95943	
24·0	61606	·8 22	38394	65669	·8 27	34331	04063	·8 5	95937	
25·0	61634		38366	65703		34297	04069		95931	35′
26·0	61662		38338	65736		34264	04075		95925	
27·0	61689	·9 25	38311	65770	·9 30	34230	04081	·9 5	95920	
28·0	61717		38283	65803		34197	04086		95914	
29·0	61745		38255	65837		34163	04092		95908	
30·0	61773		38227	65870		34130	04098		95902	30′
31·0	61800		38200	65904		34096	04104		95897	
32·0	61828	·1 3	38172	65937	·1 3	34063	04109	·1 1	95891	
33·0	61856		38144	65971		34029	04115		95885	
34·0	61883		38117	66004		33996	04121		95879	
35·0	61911	·2 5	38089	66038	·2 7	33962	04127	·2 1	95873	25′
36·0	61939		38061	66071		33929	04132		95868	
37·0	61966		38034	66104		33896	04138		95862	
38·0	61994	·3 8	38006	66138	·3 10	33862	04144	·3 2	95856	
39·0	62021		37979	66171		33829	04150		95850	
40·0	62049		37951	66204		33796	04156		95845	20′
41·0	62076	·4 11	37924	66238	·4 13	33762	04161	·4 2	95839	
42·0	62104		37896	66271		33729	04167		95833	
43·0	62131		37869	66304		33696	04173		95827	
44·0	62159		37841	66338		33663	04179		95821	
45·0	62186	·5 14	37814	66371	·5 17	33629	04185	·5 3	95815	15′
46·0	62214		37787	66404		33596	04190		95810	
47·0	62241		37759	66437		33563	04196		95804	
48·0	62268	·6 16	37732	66470	·6 20	33530	04202	·6 3	95798	
49·0	62296		37704	66504		33497	04208		95792	
50·0	62323		37677	66537		33463	04214		95786	10′
51·0	62350	·7 19	37650	66570	·7 23	33430	04220	·7 4	95780	
52·0	62377		37623	66603		33397	04225		95775	
53·0	62405		37595	66636		33364	04231		95769	
54·0	62432	·8 22	37568	66669	·8 27	33331	04237	·8 5	95763	
55·0	62459		37541	66702		33298	04243		95757	5′
56·0	62486		37514	66735		33265	04249		95751	
57·0	62514	·9 25	37487	66768	·9 30	33232	04255	·9 5	95745	
58·0	62541		37459	66801		33199	04261		95739	
59·0	62568		37432	66834		33166	04267		95734	
60·0	62595		37405	66867		33133	04272		95728	0′

LOGS. OF TRIG. FUNCTIONS

25°
205°

´	Sine	Parts	Cosec.	Tan.	Parts	Cotan.	Secant	Parts	Cosine	
00·0	1̄.(9) 62595		0.(10) 37405	1̄.(9) 66867		0.(10) 33133	0.(10) 04272		1̄.(9) 95728	60´
01·0	62622		37378	66900		33100	04278		95722	
02·0	62649	·1 3	37351	66933	·1 3	33067	04284	·1 1	95716	
03·0	62676		37324	66966		33034	04290		95710	
04·0	62703		37297	66999		33001	04296		95704	
05·0	62730	·2 5	37270	67032	·2 7	32968	04302	·2 1	95698	55´
06·0	62757		37243	67065		32935	04308		95692	
07·0	62784		37216	67098		32902	04314		95686	
08·0	62811	·3 8	37189	67131	·3 10	32869	04320	·3 2	95680	
09·0	62838		37162	67164		32837	04326		95674	
10·0	62865		37135	67196		32804	04332		95668	50´
11·0	62892	·4 11	37108	67229	·4 13	32771	04338	·4 2	95663	
12·0	62919		37082	67262		32738	04343		95657	
13·0	62945		37055	67295		32705	04349		95651	
14·0	62972	·5 13	37028	67327	·5 16	32673	04355	·5 3	95645	
15·0	62999		37001	67360		32640	04361		95639	45´
16·0	63026		36974	67393		32607	04367		95633	
17·0	63052	·6 16	36948	67426	·6 20	32574	04373	·6 4	95627	
18·0	63079		36921	67458		32542	04379		95621	
19·0	63106		36894	67491		32509	04385		95615	
20·0	63133	·7 19	36867	67524	·7 23	32476	04391	·7 4	95609	40´
21·0	63159		36841	67556		32444	04397		95603	
22·0	63186		36814	67589		32411	04403		95597	
23·0	63213		36788	67622		32378	04409		95591	
24·0	63239	·8 21	36761	67654	·8 26	32346	04415	·8 5	95585	
25·0	63266		36734	67687		32313	04421		95579	35´
26·0	63292		36708	67719		32281	04427		95573	
27·0	63319	·9 24	36681	67752	·9 29	32248	04433	·9 5	95567	
28·0	63345		36655	67785		32215	04439		95561	
29·0	63372		36628	67817		32183	04445		95555	
30·0	63398		36602	67850		32150	04451		95549	30´
31·0	63425		36575	67882		32118	04457		95543	
32·0	63451	·1 3	36549	67915	·1 3	32085	04463	·1 1	95537	
33·0	63478		36522	67947		32053	04469		95531	
34·0	63504		36496	67980		32021	04475		95525	
35·0	63531	·2 5	36469	68012	·2 6	31988	04481	·2 1	95519	25´
36·0	63557		36443	68044		31956	04487		95513	
37·0	63583		36417	68077		31923	04494		95507	
38·0	63610	·3 8	36390	68109	·3 10	31891	04500	·3 2	95501	
39·0	63636		36364	68142		31858	04506		95494	
40·0	63662		36338	68174		31826	04512		95488	20´
41·0	63689	·4 10	36311	68206	·4 13	31794	04518	·4 2	95482	
42·0	63715		36285	68239		31761	04524		95476	
43·0	63741		36259	68271		31729	04530		95470	
44·0	63767		36233	68303		31697	04536		95464	
45·0	63794	·5 13	36207	68336	·5 16	31664	04542	·5 3	95458	15´
46·0	63820		36180	68368		31632	04548		95452	
47·0	63846		36154	68400		31600	04554		95446	
48·0	63872	·6 16	36128	68432	·6 19	31568	04560	·6 4	95440	
49·0	63898		36102	68465		31535	04567		95434	
50·0	63924		36076	68497		31503	04573		95427	10´
51·0	63950	·7 18	36050	68529	·7 23	31471	04579	·7 4	95421	
52·0	63976		36024	68561		31439	04585		95415	
53·0	64002		35998	68593		31407	04591		95409	
54·0	64028	·8 21	35972	68626	·8 26	31375	04597	·8 5	95403	
55·0	64054		35946	68658		31342	04603		95397	5´
56·0	64080		35920	68690		31310	04609		95391	
57·0	64106	·9 24	35894	68722	·9 29	31278	04616	·9 5	95385	
58·0	64132		35868	68754		31246	04622		95378	
59·0	64158		35842	68786		31214	04628		95372	
60·0	64184		35816	68818		31182	04634		95366	0´

26°
206°

LOGS. OF TRIG. FUNCTIONS

′	Sine	*Parts*	Cosec.	Tan.	*Parts*	Cotan.	Secant	*Parts*	Cosine	
00·0	1̄.(9) 64184		0.(10) 35816	1̄.(9) 68818		0.(10) 31182	0.(10) 04634		1̄.(9) 95366	60′
01·0	64210		35790	68850		31150	04640		95360	
02·0	64236	·1 3	35764	68882	·1 3	31118	04646	·1 1	95354	
03·0	64262		35738	68914		31086	04653		95348	
04·0	64288		35712	68946		31054	04659		95341	
05·0	64314	·2 5	35687	68978	·2 6	31022	04665	·2 1	95335	55′
06·0	64339		35661	69010		30990	04671		95329	
07·0	64365		35635	69042		30958	04677		95323	
08·0	64391	·3 8	35609	69074	·3 10	30926	04683	·3 2	95317	
09·0	64417		35584	69106		30894	04690		95310	
10·0	64442		35558	69138		30862	04696		95304	50′
11·0	64468	·4 10	35532	69170	·4 13	30830	04702	·4 2	95298	
12·0	64494		35506	69202		30798	04708		95292	
13·0	64519		35481	69234		30766	04715		95286	
14·0	64545	·5 13	35455	69266	·5 16	30734	04721	·5 3	95279	
15·0	64571		35429	69298		30703	04727		95273	45′
16·0	64596		35404	69329		30671	04733		95267	
17·0	64622		35378	69361		30639	04739		95261	
18·0	64647	·6 15	35353	69393	·6 19	30607	04746	·6 4	95254	
19·0	64673		35327	69425		30575	04752		95248	
20·0	64698	·7 18	35302	69457	·7 22	30543	04758	·7 4	95242	40′
21·0	64724		35276	69488		30511	04764		95236	
22·0	64749		35251	69520		30480	04771		95229	
23·0	64775		35225	69552		30448	04777		95223	
24·0	64800	·8 21	35200	69584	·8 25	30416	04783	·8 5	95217	
25·0	64826		35174	69615		30385	04789		95211	35′
26·0	64851		35149	69647		30353	04796		95204	
27·0	64877	·9 23	35123	69679	·9 29	30321	04802	·9 6	95198	
28·0	64902		35098	69710		30290	04808		95192	
29·0	64927		35073	69742		30258	04815		95185	
30·0	64953		35047	69774		30226	04821		95179	30′
31·0	64978		35022	69805		30195	04827		95173	
32·0	65003	·1 2	34997	69837	·1 3	30163	04834	·1 1	95167	
33·0	65029		34971	69869		30132	04840		95160	
34·0	65054		34946	69900		30100	04846		95154	
35·0	65079	·2 5	34921	69932	·2 6	30068	04852	·2 1	95148	25′
36·0	65104		34896	69963		30037	04859		95141	
37·0	65130		34870	69995		30005	04865		95135	
38·0	65155	·3 7	34845	70026	·3 9	29974	04871	·3 2	95129	
39·0	65180		34820	70058		29942	04878		95122	
40·0	65205		34795	70089		29911	04884		95116	20′
41·0	65230	·4 10	34770	70121	·4 13	29879	04890	·4 3	95110	
42·0	65256		34745	70152		29848	04897		95103	
43·0	65281		34719	70184		29816	04903		95097	
44·0	65306		34694	70215		29785	04910		95091	
45·0	65331	·5 12	34669	70247	·5 16	29753	04916	·5 3	95084	15′
46·0	65356		34644	70278		29722	04922		95078	
47·0	65381		34619	70310		29691	04929		95071	
48·0	65406	·6 15	34594	70341	·6 19	29659	04935	·6 4	95065	
49·0	65431		34569	70372		29628	04941		95059	
50·0	65456		34544	70404		29596	04948		95052	10′
51·0	65481	·7 17	34519	70435	·7 22	29565	04954	·7 4	95046	
52·0	65506		34494	70466		29534	04961		95039	
53·0	65531		34469	70498		29502	04967		95033	
54·0	65556	·8 20	34444	70529	·8 25	29471	04973	·8 5	95027	
55·0	65581		34420	70560		29440	04980		95020	5′
56·0	65605		34395	70592		29408	04986		95014	
57·0	65630	·9 22	34370	70623	·9 28	29377	04993	·9 6	95007	
58·0	65655		34345	70654		29346	04999		95001	
59·0	65680		34320	70685		29315	05006		94995	
60·0	65705		34295	70717		29283	05012		94988	0′

27°
207°

LOGS. OF TRIG. FUNCTIONS

′	Sine	*Parts*		Cosec.	Tan.	*Parts*		Cotan.	Secant	*Parts*		Cosine	
00·0	$\overline{1}$.(9) 65705		′	0.(10) 34295	$\overline{1}$.(9) 70717		′	0.(10) 29283	0.(10) 05012		′	$\overline{1}$.(9) 94988	*60′*
01·0	65730			34271	70748			29252	05018			94982	
02·0	65754	·1	2	34246	70779	·1	3	29221	05025	·1	1	94975	
03·0	65779			34221	70810			29190	05031			94969	
04·0	65804			34196	70841			29159	05038			94962	
05·0	65828	·2	5	34172	70873	·2	6	29127	05044	·2	1	94956	*55′*
06·0	65853			34147	70904			29096	05051			94949	
07·0	65878			34122	70935			29065	05057			94943	
08·0	65903	·3	7	34098	70966	·3	9	29034	05064	·3	2	94936	
09·0	65927			34073	70997			29003	05070			94930	
10·0	65952			34048	71028			28972	05077			94924	*50′*
11·0	65976	·4	10	34024	71059	·4	12	28941	05083	·4	3	94917	
12·0	66001			33999	71090			28910	05090			94911	
13·0	66026			33975	71122			28879	05096			94904	
14·0	66050			33950	71153			28848	05103			94898	
15·0	66075	·5	12	33925	71184	·5	16	28816	05109	·5	3	94891	*45′*
16·0	66099			33901	71215			28785	05116			94885	
17·0	66124			33876	71246			28754	05122			94878	
18·0	66148	·6	15	33852	71277	·6	19	28723	05129	·6	4	94872	
19·0	66173			33827	71308			28692	05135			94865	
20·0	66197			33803	71339			28661	05142			94858	*40′*
21·0	66221	·7	17	33779	71370	·7	22	28630	05148	·7	5	94852	
22·0	66246			33754	71401			28600	05155			94845	
23·0	66270			33730	71431			28569	05161			94839	
24·0	66295	·8	20	33705	71462	·8	25	28538	05168	·8	5	94832	
25·0	66319			33681	71493			28507	05174			94826	*35′*
26·0	66343			33657	71524			28476	05181			94819	
27·0	66368	·9	22	33632	71555	·9	28	28445	05187	·9	6	94813	
28·0	66392			33608	71586			28414	05194			94806	
29·0	66416			33584	71617			28383	05201			94800	
30·0	66441			33559	71648			28352	05207			94793	*30′*
31·0	66465			33535	71679			28322	05214			94786	
32·0	66489	·1	2	33511	71709	·1	3	28291	05220	·1	1	94780	
33·0	66513			33487	71740			28260	05227			94773	
34·0	66538			33463	71771			28229	05234			94767	
35·0	66562	·2	5	33438	71802	·2	6	28198	05240	·2	1	94760	*25′*
36·0	66586			33414	71833			28168	05247			94753	
37·0	66610			33390	71863			28137	05253			94747	
38·0	66634	·3	7	33366	71894	·3	9	28106	05260	·3	2	94740	
39·0	66658			33342	71925			28075	05267			94734	
40·0	66682			33318	71956			28045	05273			94727	*20′*
41·0	66707	·4	10	33294	71986	·4	12	28014	05280	·4	3	94720	
42·0	66731			33270	72017			27983	05286			94714	
43·0	66755			33245	72048			27952	05293			94707	
44·0	66779			33221	72078			27922	05300			94700	
45·0	66803	·5	12	33197	72109	·5	15	27891	05306	·5	3	94694	*15′*
46·0	66827			33173	72140			27860	05313			94687	
47·0	66851			33149	72170			27830	05320			94680	
48·0	66875	·6	14	33125	72201	·6	18	27799	05326	·6	4	94674	
49·0	66899			33101	72232			27769	05333			94667	
50·0	66923			33078	72262			27738	05340			94660	*10′*
51·0	66946	·7	17	33054	72293	·7	21	27707	05346	·7	5	94654	
52·0	66970			33030	72323			27677	05353			94647	
53·0	66994			33006	72354			27646	05360			94640	
54·0	67018	·8	19	32982	72384	·8	25	27616	05366	·8	5	94634	
55·0	67042			32958	72415			27585	05373			94627	*5′*
56·0	67066			32934	72445			27555	05380			94620	
57·0	67090	·9	22	32910	72476	·9	28	27524	05386	·9	6	94614	
58·0	67113			32887	72507			27494	05393			94607	
59·0	67137			32863	72537			27463	05400			94600	
60·0	67161			32839	72567			27433	05407			94593	*0′*

152°
332°

28°
208°

LOGS. OF TRIG. FUNCTIONS

′	Sine	Parts	Cosec.	Tan.	Parts	Cotan.	Secant	Parts	Cosine	
00·0	1.(9) 67161		0.(10) 32839	1.(9) 72567		0.(10) 27433	0.(10) 05407		1.(9) 94593	60'
01·0	67185		32815	72598		27402	05413		94587	
02·0	67208	·1 2	32792	72628	·1 3	27372	05420	·1 1	94580	
03·0	67232		32768	72659		27341	05427		94573	
04·0	67256		32744	72689		27311	05433		94567	
05·0	67280	·2 5	32721	72720	·2 6	27280	05440	·2 1	94560	55'
06·0	67303		32697	72750		27250	05447		94553	
07·0	67327		32673	72781		27220	05454		94546	
08·0	67351	·3 7	32650	72811	·3 9	27189	05460	·3 2	94540	
09·0	67374		32626	72841		27159	05467		94533	
10·0	67398		32602	72872		27128	05474		94526	50'
11·0	67421	·4 9	32579	72902	·4 12	27098	05481	·4 3	94519	
12·0	67445		32555	72932		27068	05488		94513	
13·0	67468		32532	72963		27037	05494		94506	
14·0	67492	·5 12	32508	72993	·5 15	27007	05501	·5 3	94499	
15·0	67516		32485	73023		26977	05508		94492	45'
16·0	67539		32461	73054		26947	05515		94485	
17·0	67562		32438	73084		26916	05521		94479	
18·0	67586	·6 14	32414	73114	·6 18	26886	05528	·6 4	94472	
19·0	67609		32391	73144		26856	05535		94465	
20·0	67633		32367	73175		26825	05542		94458	40'
21·0	67656	·7 16	32344	73205	·7 21	26795	05549	·7 5	94451	
22·0	67680		32320	73235		26765	05555		94445	
23·0	67703		32297	73265		26735	05562		94438	
24·0	67726	·8 19	32274	73296	·8 24	26705	05569	·8 5	94431	
25·0	67750		32250	73326		26674	05576		94424	35'
26·0	67773		32227	73356		26644	05583		94417	
27·0	67796	·9 21	32204	73386	·9 27	26614	05590	·9 6	94410	
28·0	67820		32180	73416		26584	05596		94404	
29·0	67843		32157	73446		26554	05603		94397	
30·0	67866		32134	73476		26524	05610		94390	30'
31·0	67890		32111	73507		26493	05617		94383	
32·0	67913	·1 2	32087	73537	·1 3	26463	05624	·1 1	94376	
33·0	67936		32064	73567		26433	05631		94369	
34·0	67959		32041	73597		26403	05638		94362	
35·0	67982	·2 5	32018	73627	·2 6	26373	05645	·2 1	94356	25'
36·0	68006		31994	73657		26343	05651		94349	
37·0	68029		31971	73687		26313	05658		94342	
38·0	68052	·3 7	31948	73717	·3 9	26283	05665	·3 2	94335	
39·0	68075		31925	73747		26253	05672		94328	
40·0	68098		31902	73777		26223	05679		94321	20'
41·0	68121	·4 9	31879	73807	·4 12	26193	05686	·4 3	94314	
42·0	68144		31856	73837		26163	05693		94307	
43·0	68167		31833	73867		26133	05700		94300	
44·0	68191		31810	73897		26103	05707		94293	
45·0	68214	·5 12	31787	73927	·5 15	26073	05714	·5 3	94286	15'
46·0	68237		31764	73957		26043	05721		94280	
47·0	68260		31741	73987		26013	05727		94273	
48·0	68283	·6 14	31718	74017	·6 18	25983	05734	·6 4	94266	
49·0	68306		31695	74047		25953	05741		94259	
50·0	68328		31672	74077		25923	05748		94252	10'
51·0	68351	·7 16	31649	74107	·7 21	25893	05755	·7 5	94245	
52·0	68374		31626	74137		25864	05762		94238	
53·0	68397		31603	74166	·	25834	05769		94231	
54·0	68420	·8 18	31580	74196	·8 24	25804	05776	·8 6	94224	
55·0	68443		31557	74226		25774	05783		94217	5'
56·0	68466		31534	74256		25744	05790		94210	
57·0	68489	·9 21	31511	74286	·9 27	25714	05797	·9 6	94203	
58·0	68512		31489	74316		25684	05804		94196	
59·0	68534		31466	74345		25655	05811		94189	
60·0	68557		31443	74375		25625	05818		1.(9) 94182	0'

151°
331°

29°
209°

LOGS. OF TRIG. FUNCTIONS

′	Sine	Parts	Cosec.	Tan.	Parts	Cotan.	Secant	Parts	Cosine	
00·0	1.(9) 68557	′	0.(10) 31443	1.(9) 74375	′	0.(10) 25625	0.(10) 05818	′	1.(9) 94182	60′
01·0	68580		31420	74405		25595	05825		94175	
02·0	68603	·1 2	31397	74435	·1 3	25565	05832	·1 1	94168	
03·0	68625		31375	74465		25536	05839		94161	
04·0	68648		31352	74494		25506	05846		94154	
05·0	68671	·2 5	31329	74524	·2 6	25476	05853	·2 1	94147	55′
06·0	68694		31306	74554		25446	05860		94140	
07·0	68716		31284	74584		25417	05867		94133	
08·0	68739	·3 7	31261	74613	·3 9	25387	05874	·3 2	94126	
09·0	68762		31238	74643		25357	05881		94119	
10·0	68784		31216	74673		25327	05888		94112	50′
11·0	68807	·4 9	31193	74702	·4 12	25298	05895	·4 3	94105	
12·0	68830		31171	74732		25268	05903		94098	
13·0	68852		31148	74762		25238	05910		94091	
14·0	68875		31125	74791		25209	05917		94083	
15·0	68897	·5 11	31103	74821	·5 15	25179	05924	·5 4	94076	45′
16·0	68920		31080	74851		25150	05931		94069	
17·0	68942		31058	74880		25120	05938		94062	
18·0	68965	·6 14	31035	74910	·6 18	25090	05945	·6 4	94055	
19·0	68987		31013	74939		25061	05952		94048	
20·0	69010		30990	74969		25031	05959		94041	40′
21·0	69032	·7 16	30968	74999	·7 21	25002	05966	·7 5	94034	
22·0	69055		30945	75028		24972	05973		94027	
23·0	69077		30923	75058		24942	05980		94020	
24·0	69100	·8 18	30900	75087	·8 24	24913	05988	·8 6	94013	
25·0	69122		30878	75117		24883	05995		94005	35′
26·0	69144		30856	75146		24854	06002		93998	
27·0	69167	·9 20	30833	75176	·9 27	24824	06009	·9 6	93991	
28·0	69189		30811	75205		24795	06016		93984	
29·0	69212		30789	75235		24765	06023		93977	
30·0	69234		30766	75264		24736	06030		93970	30′
31·0	69256		30744	75294		24706	06038		93963	
32·0	69279	·1 2	30722	75323	·1 3	24677	06045	·1 1	93955	
33·0	69301		30699	75353		24647	06052		93948	
34·0	69323		30677	75382		24618	06059		93941	
35·0	69345	·2 4	30655	75412	·2 6	24589	06066	·2 1	93934	25′
36·0	69368		30632	75441		24559	06073		93927	
37·0	69390		30610	75470		24530	06081		93920	
38·0	69412	·3 7	30588	75500	·3 9	24500	06088	·3 2	93912	
39·0	69434		30566	75529		24471	06095		93905	
40·0	69456		30544	75559		24442	06102		93898	20′
41·0	69479	·4 9	30521	75588	·4 12	24412	06109	·4 3	93891	
42·0	69501		30499	75617		24383	06116		93884	
43·0	69523		30477	75647		24354	06124		93876	
44·0	69545		30455	75676		24324	06131		93869	
45·0	69567	·5 11	30433	75705	·5 15	24295	06138	·5 4	93862	15′
46·0	69589		30411	75735		24266	06145		93855	
47·0	69611		30389	75764		24236	06153		93848	
48·0	69633	·6 13	30367	75793	·6 18	24207	06160	·6 4	93840	
49·0	69655		30345	75822		24178	06167		93833	
50·0	69678		30323	75852		24148	06174		93826	10′
51·0	69700	·7 15	30301	75881	·7 21	24119	06182	·7 5	93819	
52·0	69722		30279	75910		24090	06189		93811	
53·0	69744		30257	75940		24061	06196		93804	
54·0	69765	·8 18	30235	75969	·8 23	24031	06203	·8 6	93797	
55·0	69787		30213	75998		24002	06211		93790	5′
56·0	69809		30191	76027		23973	06218		93782	
57·0	69831	·9 20	30169	76056	·9 26	23944	06225	·9 7	93775	
58·0	69853		30147	76086		23914	06232		93768	
59·0	69875		30125	76115		23885	06240		93760	
60·0	69897		30103	76144		23856	06247		93753	0′

150°
330°

LOGS. OF TRIG. FUNCTIONS

30°
210°

,	Sine	Parts	Cosec.	Tan.	Parts	Cotan.	Secant	Parts	Cosine	
00·0	1.(9) 69897		0.(10) 30103	1.(9) 76144		0.(10) 23856	0.(10) 06247		1.(9) 93753	60'
01·0	69919		30081	76173		23827	06254		93746	
02·0	69941	·1 2	30059	76202	·1 3	23798	06262	·1 1	93739	
03·0	69963		30037	76231		23769	06269		93731	
04·0	69984		30016	76261		23739	06276		93724	
05·0	70006	·2 4	29994	76290	·2 6	23710	06284	·2 1	93717	55'
06·0	70028		29972	76319		23681	06291		93709	
07·0	70050		29950	76348		23652	06298		93702	
08·0	70072	·3 7	29928	76377	·3 9	23623	06305	·3 2	93695	
09·0	70093		29907	76406		23594	06313		93687	
10·0	70115		29885	76435		23565	06320		93680	50'
11·0	70137	·4 9	29863	76464	·4 12	23536	06328	·4 3	93673	
12·0	70159		29842	76493		23507	06335		93665	
13·0	70180		29820	76522		23478	06342		93658	
14·0	70202	·5 11	29798	76551	·5 15	23449	06350	·5 4	93651	
15·0	70224		29776	76581		23420	06357		93643	45'
16·0	70245		29755	76610		23391	06364		93636	
17·0	70267	·6 13	29733	76639	·6 17	23362	06372	·6 4	93628	
18·0	70289		29712	76668		23333	06379		93621	
19·0	70310		29690	76697		23304	06386		93614	
20·0	70332	·7 15	29668	76726	·7 20	23275	06394	·7 5	93606	40'
21·0	70353		29647	76755		23246	06401		93599	
22·0	70375		29625	76783		23217	06409		93591	
23·0	70396		29604	76812		23188	06416		93584	
24·0	70418	·8 17	29582	76841	·8 23	23159	06423	·8 6	93577	
25·0	70440		29561	76870		23130	06431		93569	35'
26·0	70461		29539	76899		23101	06438		93562	
27·0	70483	·9 20	29518	76928	·9 26	23072	06446	·9 7	93554	
28·0	70504		29496	76957		23043	06453		93547	
29·0	70525		29475	76986		23014	06461		93540	
30·0	70547		29453	77015		22985	06468		93532	30'
31·0	70568		29432	77044		22956	06475		93524	
32·0	70590	·1 2	29410	77073	·1 3	22927	06483	·1 1	93517	
33·0	70611		29389	77102		22899	06490		93510	
34·0	70633		29367	77130		22870	06498		93502	
35·0	70654	·2 4	29346	77159	·2 6	22841	06505	·2 2	93495	25'
36·0	70675		29325	77188		22812	06513		93487	
37·0	70697		29303	77217		22783	06520		93480	
38·0	70718	·3 6	29282	77246	·3 9	22754	06528	·3 2	93472	
39·0	70739		29261	77275		22726	06535		93465	
40·0	70761		29239	77303		22697	06543		93457	20'
41·0	70782	·4 8	29218	77332	·4 11	22668	06550	·4 3	93450	
42·0	70803		29197	77361		22639	06558		93442	
43·0	70825		29176	77390		22610	06565		93435	
44·0	70846		29154	77418		22582	06573		93427	
45·0	70867	·5 11	29133	77447	·5 14	22553	06580	·5 4	93420	15'
46·0	70888		29112	77476		22524	06588		93412	
47·0	70909		29091	77505		22495	06595		93405	
48·0	70931	·6 13	29069	77533	·6 17	22467	06603	·6 5	93397	
49·0	70952		29048	77562		22438	06610		93390	
50·0	70973		29027	77591		22409	06618		93382	10'
51·0	70994	·7 15	29006	77620	·7 20	22381	06625	·7 5	93375	
52·0	71015		28985	77648		22352	06633		93367	
53·0	71036		28964	77677		22323	06640		93360	
54·0	71058	·8 17	28943	77706	·8 23	22295	06648	·8 6	93352	
55·0	71079		28921	77734		22266	06656		93345	5'
56·0	71100		28900	77763		22237	06663		93337	
57·0	71121	·9 19	28879	77792	·9 26	22209	06671	·9 7	93329	
58·0	71142		28858	77820		22180	06678		93322	
59·0	71163		28837	77849		22151	06686		93314	
60·0	71184		28816	77877		22123	06693		93307	0'

LOGS. OF TRIG. FUNCTIONS

31°
211°

′	Sine	*Parts*	Cosec.	Tan.	*Parts*	Cotan.	Secant	*Parts*	Cosine	
00·0	1̄.(9) 71184	′	0.(10) 28816	1̄.(9) 77877	′	0.(10) 22123	0.(10) 06693	′	1̄.(9) 93307	60′
01·0	71205		28795	77906		22094	06701		93299	
02·0	71226	·1 2	28774	77935	·1 3	22065	06709	·1 1	93291	
03·0	71247		28753	77963		22037	06716		93284	
04·0	71268		28732	77992		22008	06724		93276	
05·0	71289	·2 4	28711	78020	·2 6	21980	06732	·2 2	93269	55′
06·0	71310		28690	78049		21951	06739		93261	
07·0	71331		28669	78078		21923	06747		93253	
08·0	71352	·3 6	28648	78106	·3 9	21894	06754	·3 2	93246	
09·0	71373		28627	78135		21865	06762		93238	
10·0	71394		28607	78163		21837	06770		93230	50′
11·0	71414	·4 8	28586	78192	·4 11	21808	06777	·4 3	93223	
12·0	71435		28565	78220		21780	06785		93215	
13·0	71456		28544	78249		21751	06793		93208	
14·0	71477	·5 10	28523	78277	·5 14	21723	06800	·5 4	93200	
15·0	71498		28502	78306		21694	06808		93192	45′
16·0	71519		28481	78334		21666	06816		93185	
17·0	71539	·6 12	28461	78363	·6 17	21637	06823	·6 5	93177	
18·0	71560		28440	78391		21609	06831		93169	
19·0	71581		28419	78420		21581	06839		93161	
20·0	71602	·7 15	28398	78448	·7 20	21552	06846	·7 5	93154	40′
21·0	71622		28378	78476		21524	06854		93146	
22·0	71643		28357	78505		21495	06862		93138	
23·0	71664		28336	78533		21467	06869		93131	
24·0	71685	·8 17	28315	78562	·8 23	21438	06877	·8 6	93123	
25·0	71705		28295	78590		21410	06885		93115	35′
26·0	71726		28274	78618		21382	06893		93108	
27·0	71747	·9 19	28253	78647	·9 26	21353	06900	·9 7	93100	
28·0	71767		28233	78675		21325	06908		93092	
29·0	71788		28212	78704		21296	06916		93084	
30·0	71809		28192	78732		21268	06923		93077	30′
31·0	71829		28171	78760		21240	06931		93069	
32·0	71850	·1 2	28150	78789	·1 3	21211	06939	·1 1	93061	
33·0	71870		28130	78817		21183	06947		93053	
34·0	71891		28109	78845		21155	06954		93046	
35·0	71911	·2 4	28089	78874	·2 6	21126	06962	·2 2	93038	25′
36·0	71932		28068	78902		21098	06970		93030	
37·0	71953		28048	78930		21070	06978		93022	
38·0	71973	·3 6	28027	78959	·3 8	21042	06986	·3 2	93015	
39·0	71994		28007	78987		21013	06993		93007	
40·0	72014		27986	79015		20985	07001		92999	20′
41·0	72035	·4 8	27966	79043	·4 11	20957	07009	·4 3	92991	
42·0	72055		27945	79072		20928	07017		92983	
43·0	72075		27925	79100		20900	07025		92976	
44·0	72096		27904	79128		20872	07032		92968	
45·0	72116	·5 10	27884	79156	·5 14	20844	07040	·5 4	92960	15′
46·0	72137		27863	79185		20815	07048		92952	
47·0	72157		27843	79213		20787	07056		92944	
48·0	72177	·6 12	27823	79241	·6 17	20759	07064	·6 5	92936	
49·0	72198		27802	79269		20731	07071		92929	
50·0	72218		27782	79297		20703	07079		92921	10′
51·0	72239	·7 14	27762	79326	·7 20	20674	07087	·7 5	92913	
52·0	72259		27741	79354		20646	07095		92905	
53·0	72279		27721	79382		20618	07103		92897	
54·0	72299	·8 16	27701	79410	·8 23	20590	07111	·8 6	92889	
55·0	72320		27680	79438		20562	07119		92882	5′
56·0	72340		27660	79466		20534	07126		92874	
57·0	72360	·9 18	27640	79495	·9 25	20505	07134	·9 7	92866	
58·0	72381		27620	79523		20477	07142		92858	
59·0	72401		27599	79551		20449	07150		92850	
60·0	72421		27579	79579		20421	07158		92842	0′

LOGS. OF TRIG. FUNCTIONS

32°
212°

′	Sine	*Parts*	Cosec.	Tan.	*Parts*	Cotan.	Secant	*Parts*	Cosine	
00·0	1.(9) 72421	′	0.(10) 27579	1.(9) 79579	′	0.(10) 20421	0.(10) 07158	′	1.(9) 92842	60′
01·0	72441		27559	79607		20393	07166		92834	
02·0	72461	·1 2	27539	79635	·1 3	20365	07174	·1 1	92826	
03·0	72482		27518	79663		20337	07182		92818	
04·0	72502		27498	79691		20309	07190		92810	
05·0	72522	·2 4	27478	79719	·2 6	20281	07198	·2 2	92803	55′
06·0	72542		27458	79748		20253	07205		92795	
07·0	72562		27438	79776		20225	07213		92787	
08·0	72582	·3 6	27418	79804	·3 8	20196	07221	·3 2	92779	
09·0	72602		27398	79832		20168	07229		92771	
10·0	72623		27378	79860		20140	07237		92763	50′
11·0	72643	·4 8	27357	79888	·4 11	20112	07245	·4 3	92755	
12·0	72663		27337	79916		20084	07253		92747	
13·0	72683		27317	79944		20056	07261		92739	
14·0	72703	·5 10	27297	79972	·5 14	20028	07269	·5 4	92731	
15·0	72723		27277	80000		20000	07276		92723	45′
16·0	72743		27257	80028		19972	07285		92715	
17·0	72763	·6 12	27237	80056	·6 17	19944	07293	·6 5	92707	
18·0	72783		27217	80084		19916	07301		92699	
19·0	72803		27197	80112		19888	07309		92691	
20·0	72823	·7 14	27177	80140	·7 20	19860	07317	·7 6	92683	40′
21·0	72843		27157	80168		19833	07325		92675	
22·0	72863		27137	80196		19805	07333		92667	
23·0	72883		27118	80223		19777	07341		92659	
24·0	72902	·8 16	27098	80251	·8 22	19749	07349	·8 6	92651	
25·0	72922		27078	80279		19721	07357		92643	35′
26·0	72942		27058	80307		19693	07365		92635	
27·0	72962	·9 18	27038	80335	·9 25	19665	07373	·9 7	92627	
28·0	72982		27018	80363		19637	07381		92619	
29·0	73002		26998	80391		19609	07389		92611	
30·0	73022		26978	80419		19581	07397		92603	30′
31·0	73042		26959	80447		19553	07405		92595	
32·0	73061	·1 2	26939	80475	·1 3	19526	07413	·1 1	92587	
33·0	73081		26919	80502		19498	07421		92579	
34·0	73101		26899	80530		19470	07429		92571	
35·0	73121	·2 4	26879	80558	·2 6	19442	07437	·2 2	92563	25′
36·0	73140		26860	80586		19414	07446		92555	
37·0	73160		26840	80614		19386	07454		92547	
38·0	73180	·3 6	26820	80642	·3 8	19359	07462	·3 2	92538	
39·0	73200		26800	80669		19331	07470		92530	
40·0	73219		26781	80697		19303	07478		92522	20′
41·0	73239	·4 8	26761	80725	·4 11	19275	07486	·4 3	92514	
42·0	73259		26741	80753		19247	07494		92506	
43·0	73278		26722	80781		19220	07502		92498	
44·0	73298		26702	80808		19192	07510		92490	
45·0	73318	·5 10	26682	80836	·5 14	19164	07518	·5 4	92482	15′
46·0	73337		26663	80864		19136	07527		92474	
47·0	73357		26643	80892		19108	07535		92465	
48·0	73377	·6 12	26624	80919	·6 17	19081	07543	·6 5	92457	
49·0	73396		26604	80947		19053	07551		92449	
50·0	73416		26584	80975		19025	07559		92441	10′
51·0	73435	·7 14	26565	81003	·7 19	18998	07567	·7 6	92433	
52·0	73455		26545	81030		18970	07575		92425	
53·0	73474		26526	81058		18942	07584		92416	
54·0	73494	·8 16	26506	81086	·8 22	18914	07592	·8 7	92408	
55·0	73514		26487	81113		18887	07600		92400	5′
56·0	73533		26467	81141		18859	07608		92392	
57·0	73553	·9 18	26448	81169	·9 25	18831	07616	·9 7	92384	
58·0	73572		26428	81196		18804	07625		92376	
59·0	73591		26409	81224		18776	07633		92367	
60·0	73611		26389	81252		18748	07641		92359	0′

LOGS. OF TRIG. FUNCTIONS

′	Sine	Parts	Cosec.	Tan.	Parts	Cotan.	Secant	Parts	Cosine	
00·0	1̄.(9) 73611	′	0.(10) 26389	1̄.(9) 81252	′	0.(10) 18748	0.(10) 07641	′	1̄.(9) 92359	60′
01·0	73630		26370	81279		18721	07649		92351	
02·0	73650	·1 2	26350	81307	·1 3	18693	07657	·1 1	92343	
03·0	73669		26331	81335		18665	07666		92335	
04·0	73689		26311	81362		18638	07674		92326	
05·0	73708	·2 4	26292	81390	·2 6	18610	07682	·2 2	92318	55′
06·0	73727		26273	81418		18582	07690		92310	
07·0	73747		26253	81445		18555	07698		92302	
08·0	73766	·3 6	26234	81473	·3 8	18527	07707	·3 2	92293	
09·0	73786		26215	81500		18500	07715		92285	
10·0	73805		26195	81528		18472	07723		92277	50′
11·0	73824	·4 8	26176	81556	·4 11	18445	07731	·4 3	92269	
12·0	73843		26157	81583		18417	07740		92260	
13·0	73863		26137	81611		18389	07748		92252	
14·0	73882	·5 10	26118	81638	·5 14	18362	07756	·5 4	92244	
15·0	73901		26099	81666		18334	07765		92236	45′
16·0	73921		26079	81693		18307	07773		92227	
17·0	73940	·6 12	26060	81721	·6 17	18279	07781	·6 5	92219	
18·0	73959		26041	81748		18252	07789		92211	
19·0	73978		26022	81776		18224	07798		92202	
20·0	73998	·7 13	26003	81804	·7 19	18197	07806	·7 6	92194	40′
21·0	74017		25983	81831		18169	07814		92186	
22·0	74036		25964	81859		18142	07823		92177	
23·0	74055		25945	81886		18114	07831		92169	
24·0	74074	·8 15	25926	81914	·8 22	18087	07839	·8 7	92161	
25·0	74093		25907	81941		18059	07848		92152	35′
26·0	74113		25888	81968		18032	07856		92144	
27·0	74132	·9 17	25868	81996	·9 25	18004	07864	·9 7	92136	
28·0	74151		25849	82023		17977	07873		92127	
29·0	74170		25830	82051		17949	07881		92119	
30·0	74189		25811	82078		17922	07889		92111	30′
31·0	74208		25792	82106		17894	07898		92102	
32·0	74227	·1 2	25773	82133	·1 3	17867	07906	·1 1	92094	
33·0	74246		25754	82161		17839	07914		92086	
34·0	74265		25735	82188		17812	07923		92077	
35·0	74284	·2 4	25716	82215	·2 5	17785	07931	·2 2	92069	25′
36·0	74303		25697	82243		17757	07940		92060	
37·0	74322		25678	82270		17730	07948		92052	
38·0	74341	·3 6	25659	82298	·3 8	17702	07956	·3 3	92044	
39·0	74360		25640	82325		17675	07965		92035	
40·0	74379		25621	82352		17648	07973		92027	20′
41·0	74398	·4 8	25602	82380	·4 11	17620	07982	·4 3	92018	
42·0	74417		25583	82407		17593	07990		92010	
43·0	74436		25564	82435		17566	07999		92002	
44·0	74455		25545	82462		17538	08007		91993	
45·0	74474	·5 9	25526	82489	·5 14	17511	08015	·5 4	91985	15′
46·0	74493		25507	82517		17483	08024		91976	
47·0	74512		25488	82544		17456	08032		91968	
48·0	74531	·6 11	25469	82571	·6 16	17429	08041	·6 5	91959	
49·0	74549		25451	82599		17401	08049		91951	
50·0	74568		25432	82626		17374	08058		91942	10′
51·0	74587	·7 13	25413	82653	·7 19	17347	08066	·7 6	91934	
52·0	74606		25394	82681		17320	08075		91925	
53·0	74625		25375	82708		17292	08083		91917	
54·0	74644	·8 15	25356	82735	·8 22	17265	08092	·8 7	91909	
55·0	74662		25338	82762		17238	08100		91900	5′
56·0	74681		25319	82790		17210	08109		91892	
57·0	74700	·9 17	25300	82817	·9 25	17183	08117	·9 8	91883	
58·0	74719		25281	82844		17156	08126		91875	
59·0	74737		25263	82872		17129	08134		91866	
60·0	74756		25244	82899		17101	08143		91857	0′

LOGS. OF TRIG. FUNCTIONS

34°
214°

´	Sine	Parts	Cosec.	Tan.	Parts	Cotan.	Secant	Parts	Cosine	
00·0	1.(9) 74756		0.(10) 25244	1.(9) 82899		0.(10) 17101	0.(10) 08143		1.(9) 91857	60'
01·0	74775		25225	82926		17074	08151		91849	
02·0	74794	·1 2	25206	82953	·1 3	17047	08160	·1 1	91840	
03·0	74812		25188	82981		17020	08168		91832	
04·0	74831		25169	83008		16992	08177		91823	
05·0	74850	·2 4	25150	83035	·2 5	16965	08185	·2 2	91815	55'
06·0	74868		25132	83062		16938	08194		91806	
07·0	74887		25113	83089		16911	08202		91798	
08·0	74906	·3 6	25094	83117	·3 8	16884	08211	·3 3	91789	
09·0	74924		25076	83144		16856	08220		91781	
10·0	74943		25057	83171		16829	08228		91772	50'
11·0	74962	·4 7	25039	83198	·4 11	16802	08237	·4 3	91763	
12·0	74980		25020	83225		16775	08245		91755	
13·0	74999		25001	83253		16748	08254		91746	
14·0	75017	·5 9	24983	83280	·5 14	16720	08262	·5 4	91738	
15·0	75036		24964	83307		16693	08271		91729	45'
16·0	75054		24946	83334		16666	08280		91720	
17·0	75073	·6 11	24927	83361		16639	08288		91712	
18·0	75091		24909	83388	·6 16	16612	08297	·6 5	91703	
19·0	75110		24890	83415		16585	08305		91695	
20·0	75128	·7 13	24872	83443		16558	08314		91686	40'
21·0	75147		24853	83470	·7 19	16530	08323	·7 6	91677	
22·0	75165		24835	83497		16503	08331		91669	
23·0	75184		24816	83524		16476	08340		91660	
24·0	75202	·8 15	24798	83551	·8 22	16449	08349	·8 7	91651	
25·0	75221		24779	83578		16422	08357		91643	35'
26·0	75239		24761	83605		16395	08366		91634	
27·0	75258	·9 17	24742	83632	·9 24	16368	08375	·9 8	91625	
28·0	75276		24724	83659		16341	08383		91617	
29·0	75294		24706	83686		16314	08392		91608	
30·0	75313		24687	83713		16287	08401		91599	30'
31·0	75331		24669	83741		16260	08409		91591	
32·0	75350	·1 2	24651	83768	·1 3	16233	08418	·1 1	91582	
33·0	75368		24632	83795		16205	08427		91573	
34·0	75386		24614	83822		16178	08435		91565	
35·0	75405	·2 4	24595	83849	·2 5	16151	08444	·2 2	91556	25'
36·0	75423		24577	83876		16124	08453		91547	
37·0	75441		24559	83903		16097	08462		91539	
38·0	75460	·3 5	24541	83930	·3 8	16070	08470	·3 3	91530	
39·0	75478		24522	83957		16043	08479		91521	
40·0	75496		24504	83984		16016	08488		91512	20'
41·0	75514	·4 7	24486	84011	·4 11	15989	08497	·4 3	91504	
42·0	75533		24467	84038		15962	08505		91495	
43·0	75551		24449	84065		15935	08514		91486	
44·0	75569	·5 9	24431	84092	·5 14	15908	08523	·5 4	91477	
45·0	75587		24413	84119		15881	08532		91469	15'
46·0	75605		24395	84146		15854	08540		91460	
47·0	75624	·6 11	24376	84173		15827	08549		91451	
48·0	75642		24358	84200	·6 16	15800	08558	·6 5	91442	
49·0	75660		24340	84227		15773	08567		91433	
50·0	75678		24322	84254		15747	08575		91425	10'
51·0	75696	·7 13	24304	84281	·7 19	15720	08584	·7 6	91416	
52·0	75714		24286	84307		15693	08593		91407	
53·0	75733		24267	84334		15666	08602		91398	
54·0	75751	·8 15	24249	84361	·8 22	15639	08611	·8 7	91389	
55·0	75769		24231	84388		15612	08619		91381	5'
56·0	75787		24213	84415		15585	08628		91372	
57·0	75805	·9 16	24195	84442	·9 24	15558	08637	·9 8	91363	
58·0	75823		24177	84469		15531	08646		91354	
59·0	75841		24159	84496		15504	08655		91345	
60·0	75859		24141	84523		15477	08664		91337	0'

145°
325°

35°
215°

LOGS. OF TRIG. FUNCTIONS

′	Sine	Parts	Cosec.	Tan.	Parts	Cotan.	Secant	Parts	Cosine	
00·0	1.(9) 75859	′	0.(10) 24141	1.(9) 84523	′	0.(10) 15477	0.(10) 08664	′	1.(9) 91337	60′
01·0	75877		24123	84550		15450	08672		91328	
02·0	75895	·1 2	24105	84576	·1 3	15424	08681	·1 1	91319	
03·0	75913		24087	84603		15397	08690		91310	
04·0	75931		24069	84630		15370	08699		91301	
05·0	75949	·2 4	24051	84657	·2 5	15343	08708	·2 2	91292	55′
06·0	75967		24033	84684		15316	08717		91283	
07·0	75985		24015	84711		15289	08726		91274	
08·0	76003	·3 5	23997	84798	·3 8	15262	08735	·3 3	91266	
09·0	76021		23979	84764		15236	08743		91257	
10·0	76039		23961	84791		15209	08752		91248	50′
11·0	76057	·4 7	23943	84818	·4 11	15182	08761	·4 4	91239	
12·0	76075		23925	84845		15155	08770		91230	
13·0	76093		23907	84872		15128	08779		91221	
14·0	76111		23889	84899		15101	08788		91212	
15·9	76129	·5 9	23871	84925	·5 13	15075	08797	·5 4	91203	45′
16·0	76146		23854	84952		15048	08806		91194	
17·0	76164		23836	84979		15021	08815		91185	
18·0	76182	·6 11	23818	85006	·6 16	14994	08824	·6 5	91176	
19·0	76200		23800	85033		14968	08833		91167	
20·0	76218		23782	85059		14941	08842		91158	40′
21·0	76236	·7 13	23764	85086	·7 19	14914	08851	·7 6	91150	
22·0	76253		23747	85113		14887	08860		91141	
23·0	76271		23729	85140		14860	08869		91132	
24·0	76289	·8 14	23711	85166	·8 21	14834	08877	·8 7	91123	
25·0	76307		23693	85193		14807	08886		91114	35′
26·0	76325		23676	85220		14780	08895		91105	
27·0	76342	·9 16	23658	85247	·9 24	14753	08904	·9 8	91096	
28·0	76360		23640	85273		14727	08913		91087	
29·0	76378		23622	85300		14700	08922		91078	
30·0	76395		23605	85327		14673	08931		91069	30′
31·0	76413		23587	85354		14647	08940		91060	
32·0	76431	·1 2	23569	85380	·1 3	14620	08949	·1 1	91051	
33·0	76449		23552	85407		14593	08959		91042	
34·0	76466		23534	85434		14566	08968		91033	
35·0	76484	·2 4	23516	85460	·2 5	14540	08977	·2 2	91024	25′
36·0	76502		23499	85487		14513	08986		91014	
37·0	76519		23481	85514		14486	08995		91005	
38·0	76537	·3 5	23463	85540	·3 8	14460	09004	·3 3	90996	
39·0	76554		23446	85567		14433	09013		90987	
40·0	76572		23428	85594		14406	09022		90978	20′
41·0	76590	·4 7	23410	85620	·4 11	14380	09031	·4 4	90969	
42·0	76607		23393	85647		14353	09040		90960	
43·0	76625		23375	85674		14326	09049		90951	
44·0	76642		23358	85700		14300	09058		90942	
45·0	76660	·5 9	23340	85727	·5 13	14273	09067	·5 5	90933	15′
46·0	76677		23323	85754		14246	09076		90924	
47·0	76695		23305	85780		14220	09085		90915	
48·0	76712	·6 11	23288	85807	·6 16	14193	09095	·6 5	90906	
49·0	76730		23270	85834		14166	09104		90896	
50·0	76748		23253	85860		14140	09113		90887	10′
51·0	76765	·7 12	23235	85887	·7 19	14113	09122	·7 6	90878	
52·0	76782		23218	85913		14087	09131		90869	
53·0	76800		23200	85940		14060	09140		90860	
54·0	76817	·8 14	23183	85967	·8 21	14033	09149	·8 7	90851	
55·0	76835		23165	85993		14007	09158		90842	5′
56·0	76852		23148	86020		13980	09168		90832	
57·0	76870	·9 16	23130	86046	·9 24	13954	09177	·9 8	90823	
58·0	76887		23113	86073		13927	09186		90814	
59·0	76905		23096	86100		13901	09195		90805	
60·0	76922		23078	86126		13874	09204		90796	0′

144°
324°

36°
216°

LOGS. OF TRIG. FUNCTIONS

′	Sine	Parts	Cosec.	Tan.	Parts	Cotan.	Secant	Parts	Cosine	
00·0	1̄.(9) 76922	′	0.(10) 23078	1̄.(9) 86126	′	0.(10) 13874	0.(10) 09204	′	1̄.(9) 90796	60′
01·0	76939		23061	86153		13847	09213		90787	
02·0	76957	·1 2	23043	86179	·1 3	13821	09223	·1 1	90777	
03·0	76974		23026	86206		13794	09232		90768	
04·0	76991		23009	86232		13768	09241		90759	
05·0	77009	·2 3	22991	86259	·2 5	13741	09250	·2 2	90750	55′
06·0	77026		22974	86285		13715	09259		90741	
07·0	77043		22957	86312		13688	09269		90731	
08·0	77061	·3 5	22939	86339	·3 8	13662	09278	·3 3	90722	
09·0	77078		22922	86365		13635	09287		90713	
10·0	77095		22905	86392		13609	09296		90704	50′
11·0	77113	·4 7	22888	86418	·4 11	13582	09306	·4 4	90695	
12·0	77130		22870	86445		13556	09315		90685	
13·0	77147		22853	86471		13529	09324		90676	
14·0	77164	·5 9	22836	86498	·5 13	13503	09333	·5 5	90667	
15·0	77182		22819	86524		13476	09343		90658	45′
16·0	77199		22801	86551		13450	09352		90648	
17·0	77216		22784	86577		13423	09361		90639	
18·0	77233	·6 10	22767	86604	·6 16	13397	09370	·6 6	90630	
19·0	77250		22750	86630		13370	09380		90620	
20·0	77268	·7 12	22733	86656	·7 19	13344	09389	·7 6	90611	40′
21·0	77285		22715	86683		13317	09398		90602	
22·0	77302		22698	86709		13291	09408		90593	
23·0	77319		22681	86736		13264	09417		90583	
24·0	77336	·8 14	22664	86762	·8 21	13238	09426	·8 7	90574	
25·0	77353		22647	86789		13211	09436		90565	35′
26·0	77370		22630	86815		13185	09445		90555	
27·0	77388	·9 16	22613	86842	·9 24	13158	09454	·9 8	90546	
28·0	77405		22595	86868		13132	09463		90537	
29·0	77422		22578	86895		13106	09473		90527	
30·0	77439		22561	86921		13079	09482		90518	30′
31·0	77456		22544	86947		13053	09492		90509	
32·0	77473	·1 2	22527	86974	·1 3	13026	09501	·1 1	90499	
33·0	77490		22510	87000		13000	09510		90490	
34·0	77507		22493	87027		12974	09520		90480	
35·0	77524	·2 3	22476	87053	·2 5	12947	09529	·2 2	90471	25′
36·0	77541		22459	87079		12921	09538		90462	
37·0	77558		22442	87106		12894	09548		90452	
38·0	77575	3 5	22425	87132		12868	09557	·3 3	90443	
39·0	77592		22408	87159	·3 8	12841	09567		90434	
40·0	77609		22391	87185		12815	09576		90424	20′
41·0	77626	·4 7	22374	87211	·4 11	12789	09585	·4 4	90415	
42·0	77643		22357	87238		12762	09595		90405	
43·0	77660		22340	87264		12736	09604		90396	
44·0	77677		22323	87290		12710	09614		90386	
45·0	77694	·5 8	22306	87317	·5 13	12683	09623	·5 5	90377	15′
46·0	77711		22289	87343		12657	09632		90368	
47·0	77728		22273	87369		12631	09642		90358	
48·0	77744	·6 10	22256	87396	·6 16	12604	09651	·6 6	90349	
49·0	77761		22239	87422		12578	09661		90339	
50·0	77778		22222	87448		12552	09670		90330	10′
51·0	77795	·7 12	22205	87475	·7 18	12525	09680	·7 7	90320	
52·0	77812		22188	87501		12499	09689		90311	
53·0	77829		22171	87527		12473	09699		90301	
54·0	77846	·8 14	22155	87554	·8 21	12446	09708	·8 8	90292	
55·0	77862		22138	87580		12420	09718		90282	5′
56·0	77879		22121	87606		12394	09727		90273	
57·0	77896	·9 15	22104	87633	·9 24	12367	09737	·9 8	90263	
58·0	77913		22087	87659		12341	09746		90254	
59·0	77930		22071	87685		12315	09756		90244	
60·0	77946		22054	87711		12289	09765		90235	0′

143°
323°

LOGS. OF TRIG. FUNCTIONS

37°
217°

′	Sine	Parts	Cosec.	Tan.	Parts	Cotan.	Secant	Parts	Cosine	
00·0	1.(9) 77946	′	0.(10) 22054	1.(9) 87711	′	0.(10) 12289	0.(10) 09765	′	1.(9) 90235	60′
01·0	77963		22037	87738		12262	09775		90225	
02·0	77980	·1 2	22020	87764	·1 3	12236	09784	·1 1	90216	
03·0	77997		22003	87790		12210	09794		90206	
04·0	78013		21987	87817		12184	09803		90197	
05·0	78030	·2 3	21970	87843	·2 5	12157	09813	·2 2	90187	55′
06·0	78047		21953	87869		12131	09822		90178	
07·0	78063		21937	87895		12105	09832		90168	
08·0	78080	·3 5	21920	87922	·3 8	12078	09842	·3 3	90159	
09·0	78097		21903	87948		12052	09851		90149	
10·0	78113		21887	87974		12026	09861		90139	50′
11·0	78130	·4 7	21870	88000	·4 10	12000	09870	·4 4	90130	
12·0	78147		21853	88027		11974	09880		90120	
13·0	78163		21837	88053		11947	09889		90111	
14·0	78180		21820	88079		11921	09899		90101	
15·0	78197	·5 8	21803	88105	·5 13	11895	09909	·5 5	90091	45′
16·0	78213		21787	88131		11869	09918		90082	
17·0	78230		21770	88158		11842	09928		90072	
18·0	78246	·6 10	21754	88184	·6 16	11816	09937	·6 6	90063	
19·0	78263		21737	88210		11790	09947		90053	
20·0	78280	·7 12	21720	88236	·7 18	11764	09957	·7 7	90043	40′
21·0	78296		21704	88263		11738	09966		90034	
22·0	78313		21687	88289		11711	09976		90024	
23·0	78329		21671	88315		11685	09986		90014	
24·0	78346	·8 13	21654	88341	·8 21	11659	09995	·8 8	90005	
25·0	78362		21638	88367		11633	10005		89995	35′
26·0	78379		21621	88393		11607	10015		89985	
27·0	78395	·9 15	21605	88420	·9 24	11580	10024	·9 9	89976	
28·0	78412		21588	88446		11554	10034		89966	
29·0	78428		21572	88472		11528	10044		89956	
30·0	78445		21555	88498		11502	10053		89947	30′
31·0	78461		21539	88524		11476	10063		89937	
32·0	78478	·1 2	21522	88550	·1 3	11450	10073	·1 1	89927	
33·0	78494		21506	88577		11424	10082		89918	
34·0	78511		21490	88603		11397	10092		89908	
35·0	78527	·2 3	21473	88629	·2 5	11371	10102	·2 2	89898	25′
36·0	78543		21457	88655		11345	10112		89888	
37·0	78560		21440	88681		11319	10121		89879	
38·0	78576	·3 5	21424	88707	·3 8	11293	10131	·3 3	89869	
39·0	78593		21408	88733		11267	10141		89859	
40·0	78609		21391	88759		11241	10151		89849	20′
41·0	78625	·4 7	21375	88786	·4 10	11215	10160	·4 4	89840	
42·0	78642		21358	88812		11188	10170		89830	
43·0	78658		21342	88838		11162	10180		89820	
44·0	78674		21326	88864		11136	10190		89810	
45·0	78691	·5 8	21309	88890	·5 13	11110	10199	·5 5	89801	15′
46·0	78707		21293	88916		11084	10209		89791	
47·0	78723		21277	88942		11058	10219		89781	
48·0	78740	·6 10	21261	88968	·6 16	11032	10229	·6 6	89771	
49·0	78756		21244	88994		11006	10239		89761	
50·0	78772		21228	89020		10980	10248		89752	10′
51·0	78788	·7 11	21212	89047	·7 18	10954	10258	·7 7	89742	
52·0	78805		21196	89073		10928	10268		89732	
53·0	78821		21179	89099		10901	10278		89722	
54·0	78837	·8 13	21163	89125	·8 21	10875	10288	·8 8	89712	
55·0	78853		21147	89151		10849	10298		89703	5′
56·0	78869		21131	89177		10823	10307		89693	
57·0	78886	·9 15	21114	89203	·9 23	10797	10317	·9 9	89683	
58·0	78902		21098	89229		10771	10327		89673	
59·0	78918		21082	89255		10745	10337		89663	
60·0	78934		21066	89281		10719	10347		89653	0′

142°
322°

38°
218°

LOGS. OF TRIG. FUNCTIONS

′	Sine	Parts	Cosec.	Tan.	Parts	Cotan.	Secant	Parts	Cosine	
00·0	1̄.(9) 78934		0.(10) 21066	1̄.(9) 89281		0.(10) 10719	0.(10) 10347		1̄.(9) 89653	60′
01·0	78950		21050	89307		10693	10357		89643	
02·0	78967	·1 2	21034	89333	·1 3	10667	10367	·1 1	89634	
03·0	78983		21017	89359		10641	10376		89624	
04·0	78999		21001	89385		10615	10386		89614	
05·0	79015	·2 3	20985	89411	·2 5	10589	10396	·2 2	89604	55′
06·0	79031		20969	89437		10563	10406		89594	
07·0	79047		20953	89463		10537	10416		89584	
08·0	79063	·3 5	20937	89489	·3 8	10511	10426	·3 3	89574	
09·0	79079		20921	89515		10485	10436		89564	
10·0	79095		20905	89541		10459	10446		89554	50′
11·0	79112	·4 6	20889	89567	·4 10	10433	10456	·4 4	89544	
12·0	79128		20873	89593		10407	10466		89534	
13·0	79144		20856	89619		10381	10476		89524	
14·0	79160	·5 8	20840	89645	·5 13	10355	10486	·5 5	89515	
15·0	79176		20824	89671		10329	10496		89505	45′
16·0	79192		20808	89697		10303	10506		89495	
17·0	79208		20792	89723		10277	10515		89485	
18·0	79224	·6 10	20776	89749	·6 16	10251	10525	·6 6	89475	
19·0	79240		20760	89775		10225	10535		89465	
20·0	79256		20744	89801		10199	10545		89455	40′
21·0	79272	·7 11	20728	89827	·7 18	10173	10555	·7 7	89445	
22·0	79288		20712	89853		10147	10565		89435	
23·0	79304		20697	89879		10121	10575		89425	
24·0	79320	·8 13	20681	89905	·8 21	10095	10585	·8 8	89415	
25·0	79335		20665	89931		10069	10595		89405	35′
26·0	79351		20649	89957		10043	10605		89395	
27·0	79367	·9 14	20633	89983	·9 23	10017	10615	·9 9	89385	
28·0	79383		20617	90009		09991	10626		89375	
29·0	79399		20601	90035		09965	10636		89365	
30·0	79415		20585	90061		09940	10646		89354	30′
31·0	79431		20569	90086		09914	10656		89344	
32·0	79447	·1 2	20553	90112	·1 3	09888	10666	·1 1	89334	
33·0	79463		20537	90138		09862	10676		89324	
34·0	79478		20522	90164		09836	10686		89314	
35·0	79494	·2 3	20506	90190	·2 5	09810	10696	·2 2	89304	25′
36·0	79510		20490	90216		09784	10706		89294	
37·0	79526		20474	90242		09758	10716		89284	
38·0	79542	·3 5	20458	90268	·3 8	09732	10726	·3 3	89274	
39·0	79558		20443	90294		09706	10736		89264	
40·0	79573		20427	90320		09680	10746		89254	20′
41·0	79589	·4 6	20411	90346	·4 10	09654	10757	·4 4	89244	
42·0	79605		20395	90371		09629	10767		89233	
43·0	79621		20379	90397		09603	10777		89223	
44·0	79636	·5 8	20364	90423	·5 13	09577	10787	·5 5	89213	
45·0	79652		20348	90449		09551	10797		89203	15′
46·0	79668		20332	90475		09525	10807		89193	
47·0	79684		20316	90501		09499	10817		89183	
48·0	79699	·6 9	20301	90527	·6 16	09473	10827	·6 6	89173	
49·0	79715		20285	90553		09447	10838		89162	
50·0	79731		20269	90579		09422	10848		89152	10′
51·0	79746	·7 11	20254	90604	·7 18	09396	10858	·7 7	89142	
52·0	79762		20238	90630		09370	10868		89132	
53·0	79778		20222	90656		09344	10878		89122	
54·0	79793	·8 13	20207	90682	·8 21	09318	10889	·8 8	89112	
55·0	79809		20191	90708		09292	10899		89101	5′
56·0	79825		20175	90734		09266	10909		89091	
57·0	79840	·9 14	20160	90759	·9 23	09241	10919	·9 9	89081	
58·0	79856		20144	90785		09215	10929		89071	
59·0	79872		20128	90811		09189	10940		89061	
60·0	79887		20113	90837		09163	10950		89050	0′

141°
321°

LOGS. OF TRIG. FUNCTIONS

′	Sine	Parts	Cosec.	Tan.	Parts	Cotan.	Secant	Parts	Cosine	
00·0	1.(9) 79887	′	0.(10) 20113	1.(9) 90837	′	0.(10) 09163	0.(10) 10950	′	1.(9) 89050	60′
01·0	79903		20097	90863		09137	10960		89040	
02·0	79918	·1 2	20082	90889	·1 3	09111	10970	·1 1	89030	
03·0	79934		20066	90914		09086	10981		89020	
04·0	79950		20051	90940		09060	10991		89009	
05·0	79965	·2 3	20035	90966	·2 5	09034	11001	·2 2	88999	55′
06·0	79981		20019	90992		09008	11011		88989	
07·0	79996		20004	91018		08982	11022		88979	
08·0	80012	·3 5	19988	91044	·3 8	08957	11032	·3 3	88968	
09·0	80027		19973	91069		08931	11042		88958	
10·0	80043		19957	91095		08905	11052		88948	50′
11·0	80058	·4 6	19942	91121	·4 10	08879	11063	·4 4	88937	
12·0	80074		19926	91147		08853	11073		88927	
13·0	80089		19911	91173		08827	11083		88917	
14·0	80105	·5 8	19895	91198	·5 13	08802	11094	·5 5	88906	
15·0	80120		19880	91224		08776	11104		88896	45′
16·0	80136		19864	91250		08750	11114		88886	
17·0	80151		19849	91276		08724	11125		88875	
18·0	80167	·6 9	19834	91301	·6 15	08699	11135	·6 6	88865	
19·0	80182		19818	91327		08673	11145		88855	
20·0	80197		19803	91353		08647	11156		88844	40′
21·0	80213	·7 11	19787	91379	·7 18	08621	11166	·7 7	88834	
22·0	80228		19772	91404		08596	11176		88824	
23·0	80244		19756	91430		08570	11187		88813	
24·0	80259	·8 12	19741	91456	·8 21	08544	11197	·8 8	88803	
25·0	80274		19726	91482		08518	11207		88793	35′
26·0	80290		19710	91508		08493	11218		88782	
27·0	80305	·9 14	19695	91533	·9 23	08467	11228	·9 9	88772	
28·0	80320		19680	91559		08441	11239		88761	
29·0	80336		19664	91585		08415	11249		88751	
30·0	80351		19649	91610		08390	11259		88741	30′
31·0	80366		19634	91636		08364	11270		88730	
32·0	80382	·1 2	19618	91662	·1 3	08338	11280	·1 1	88720	
33·0	80397		19603	91688		08312	11291		88709	
34·0	80412		19588	91713		08287	11301		88699	
35·0	80428	·2 3	19572	91739	·2 5	08261	11312	·2 2	88689	25′
36·0	80443		19557	91765		08235	11322		88678	
37·0	80458		19542	91791		08209	11332		88668	
38·0	80473	·3 5	19527	91816	·3 8	08184	11343	·3 3	88657	
39·0	80489		19511	91842		08158	11353		88647	
40·0	80504		19496	91868		08132	11364		88636	20′
41·0	80519	·4 6	19481	91893	·4 10	08107	11374	·4 4	88626	
42·0	80534		19466	91919		08081	11385		88615	
43·0	80550		19451	91945		08055	11395		88605	
44·0	80565	·5 8	19435	91971	·5 13	08030	11406	·5 5	88594	
45·0	80580		19420	91996		08004	11416		88584	15′
46·0	80595		19405	92022		07978	11427		88573	
47·0	80610		19390	92048		07952	11437		88563	
48·0	80625	·6 9	19375	92073	·6 15	07927	11448	·6 6	88552	
49·0	80641		19359	92099		07901	11458		88542	
50·0	80656		19344	92125		07875	11469		88531	10′
51·0	80671	·7 11	19329	92150	·7 18	07850	11479	·7 7	88521	
52·0	80686		19314	92176		07824	11490		88510	
53·0	80701		19299	92202		07798	11501		88499	
54·0	80716	·8 12	19284	92227	·8 21	07773	11511	·8 8	88489	
55·6	80731		19269	92253		07747	11522		88478	5′
56·0	80747		19254	92279		07721	11532		88468	
57·0	80762	·9 14	19239	92304	·9 23	07696	11543	·9 9	88457	
58·0	80777		19223	92330		07670	11553		88447	
59·0	80792		19208	92356		07644	11564		88436	
60·0	80807		19193	92381		07619	11575		88425	0′

LOGS. OF TRIG. FUNCTIONS

40°
220°

′	Sine	Parts	Cosec.	Tan.	Parts	Cotan.	Secant	Parts	Cosine	
00·0	1.(9) 80807	′	0.(10) 19193	1.(9) 92381	′	0.(10) 07619	0.(10) 11575	′	1.(9) 88425	60′
01·0	80822		19178	92407		07593	11585		88415	
02·0	80837	·1 1	19163	92433	·1 3	07567	11596	·1 1	88404	
03·0	80852		19148	92458		07542	11606		88394	
04·0	80867		19133	92484		07516	11617		88383	
05·0	80882	·2 3	19118	92510	·2 5	07490	11628	·2 2	88372	55′
06·0	80897		19103	92535		07465	11638		88362	
07·0	80912		19088	92561		07439	11649		88351	
08·0	80927	·3 4	19073	92587	·3 8	07414	11660	·3 3	88340	
09·0	80942		19058	92612		07388	11670		88330	
10·0	80957		19043	92638		07362	11681		88319	50′
11·0	80972	·4 6	19028	92663	·4 10	07337	11692	·4 4	88308	
12·0	80987		19013	92689		07311	11702		88298	
13·0	81002		18998	92715		07285	11713		88287	
14·0	81017	·5 7	18983	92740	·5 13	07260	11724	·5 5	88276	
15·0	81032		18968	92766		07234	11734		88266	45′
16·0	81047		18954	92792		07209	11745		88255	
17·0	81061		18939	92817		07183	11756		88244	
18·0	81076	·6 9	18924	92843	·6 15	07157	11766	·6 6	88234	
19·0	81091		18909	92868		07132	11777		88223	
20·0	81106		18894	92894		07106	11788		88212	40′
21·0	81121	·7 10	18879	92920	·7 18	07080	11799	·7 7	88201	
22·0	81136		18864	92945		07055	11809		88191	
23·0	81151		18849	92971		07029	11820		88180	
24·0	81166	·8 12	18835	92996	·8 21	07004	11831	·8 9	88169	
25·0	81180		18820	93022		06978	11842		88158	35′
26·0	81195		18805	93048		06953	11852		88148	
27·0	81210	·9 13	18790	93073	·9 23	06927	11863	·9 10	88137	
28·0	81225		18775	93099		06901	11874		88126	
29·0	81240		18760	93124		06876	11885		88115	
30·0	81254		18746	93150		06850	11895		88105	30′
31·0	81269		18731	93176		06825	11906		88094	
32·0	81284	·1 1	18716	93201	·1 3	06799	11917	·1 1	88083	
33·0	81299		18701	93227		06773	11928		88072	
34·0	81314		18687	93252		06748	11939		88061	
35·0	81328	·2 3	18672	93278	·2 5	06722	11950	·2 2	88051	25′
36·0	81343		18657	93303		06697	11960		88040	
37·0	81358		18642	93329		06671	11971		88029	
38·0	81373	·3 4	18628	93355	·3 8	06646	11982	·3 3	88018	
39·0	81387		18613	93380		06620	11993		88007	
40·0	81402		18598	93406		06594	12004		87996	20′
41·0	81417	·4 6	18583	93431	·4 10	06569	12015	·4 4	87986	
42·0	81431		18569	93457		06543	12025		87975	
43·0	81446		18554	93482		06518	12036		87964	
44·0	81461		18539	93508		06492	12047		87953	
45·0	81475	·5 7	18525	93533	·5 13	06467	12058	·5 5	87942	15′
46·0	81490		18510	93559		06441	12069		87931	
47·0	81505		18495	93584		06416	12080		87920	
48·0	81519	·6 9	18481	93610	·6 15	06390	12091	·6 7	87909	
49·0	81534		18466	93636		06365	12102		87898	
50·0	81549		18452	93661		06339	12113		87888	10′
51·0	81563	·7 10	18437	93687	·7 18	06313	12123	·7 8	87877	
52·0	81578		18422	93712		06288	12134		87866	
53·0	81592		18408	93738		06262	12145		87855	
54·0	81607	·8 12	18393	93763	·8 20	06237	12156	·8 9	87844	
55·0	81622		18379	93789		06211	12167		87833	5′
56·0	81636		18364	93814		06186	12178		87822	
57·0	81651	·9 13	18349	93840	·9 23	06160	12189	·9 10	87811	
58·0	81665		18335	93865		06135	12200		87800	
59·0	81680		18320	93891		06109	12211		87789	
60·0	81694		18306	93916		06084	12222		87778	0′

139°
319°

41°
221°

LOGS. OF TRIG. FUNCTIONS

′	Sine	Parts	Cosec.	Tan.	Parts	Cotan.	Secant	Parts	Cosine	
00·0	1.(9) 81694	′	0.(10) 18306	1.(9) 93916	′	0.(10) 06084	0.(10) 12222	′	1.(9) 87778	60′
01·0	81709		18291	93942		06058	12233		87767	
02·0	81723	·1 1	18277	93967	·1 3	06033	12244	·1 1	87756	
03·0	81738		18262	93993		06007	12255		87745	
04·0	81752		18248	94018		05982	12266		87734	
05·0	81767	·2 3	18233	94044	·2 5	05956	12277	·2 2	87723	55′
06·0	81781		18219	94069		05931	12288		87712	
07·0	81796		18204	94095		05905	12299		87701	
08·0	81810	·3 4	18190	94120	·3 8	05880	12310	·3 3	87690	
09·0	81825		18175	94146		05854	12321		87679	
10·0	81839		18161	94171		05829	12332		87668	50′
11·0	81854	·4 6	18146	94197	·4 10	05803	12343	·4 4	87657	
12·0	81868		18132	94222		05778	12354		87646	
13·0	81883		18118	94248		05752	12365		87635	
14·0	81897	·5 7	18103	94273	·5 13	05727	12376	·5 6	87624	
15·0	81911		18089	94299		05701	12388		87613	45′
16·0	81926		18074	94324		05676	12399		87601	
17·0	81940	·6 9	18060	94350	·6 15	05650	12410	·6 7	87590	
18·0	81955		18046	94375		05625	12421		87579	
19·0	81969		18031	94401		05599	12432		87568	
20·0	81983	·7 10	18017	94426	·7 18	05574	12443	·7 8	87557	40′
21·0	81998		18002	94452		05548	12454		87546	
22·0	82012		17988	94477		05523	12465		87535	
23·0	82026		17974	94503		05497	12476		87524	
24·0	82041	·8 12	17959	94528	·8 20	05472	12487	·8 9	87513	
25·0	82055		17945	94554		05447	12499		87501	35′
26·0	82069		17931	94579		05421	12510		87490	
27·0	82084	·9 13	17916	94605	·9 23	05396	12521	·9 10	87479	
28·0	82098		17902	94630		05370	12532		87468	
29·0	82112		17888	94655		05345	12543		87457	
30·0	82127		17874	94681		05319	12554		87446	30′
31·0	82141		17859	94706		05294	12566		87434	
32·0	82155	·1 1	17845	94732	·1 3	05268	12577	·1 1	87423	
33·0	82169		17831	94757		05243	12588		87412	
34·0	82184		17817	94783		05217	12599		87401	
35·0	82198	·2 3	17802	94808	·2 5	05192	12610	·2 2	87390	25′
36·0	82212		17788	94834		05167	12622		87378	
37·0	82226		17774	94859		05141	12633		87367	
38·0	82240	·3 4	17760	94884	·3 8	05116	12644	·3 3	87356	
39·0	82255		17745	94910		05090	12655		87345	
40·0	82269		17731	94935		05065	12667		87334	20′
41·0	82283	·4 6	17717	94961	·4 10	05039	12678	·4 5	87322	
42·0	82297		17703	94986		05014	12689		87311	
43·0	82311		17689	95012		04988	12700		87300	
44·0	82326		17675	95037		04963	12712		87289	
45·0	82340	·5 7	17660	95063	·5 13	04938	12723	·5 6	87277	15′
46·0	82354		17646	95088		04912	12734		87266	
47·0	82368		17632	95113		04887	12745		87255	
48·0	82382	·6 8	17618	95139	·6 15	04861	12757	·6 7	87243	
49·0	82396		17604	95164		04836	12768		87232	
50·0	82410		17590	95190		04810	12779		87221	10′
51·0	82425	·7 10	17576	95215	·7 18	04785	12791	·7 8	87210	
52·0	82439		17561	95241		04760	12802		87198	
53·0	82453		17547	95266		04734	12813		87187	
54·0	82467	·8 11	17533	95291	·8 20	04709	12825	·8 9	87176	
55·0	82481		17519	95317		04683	12836		87164	5′
56·0	82495		17505	95342		04658	12847		87153	
57·0	82509	·9 13	17491	95368	·9 23	04633	12859	·9 10	87141	
58·0	82523		17477	95393		04607	12870		87130	
59·0	82537		17463	95418		04582	12881		87119	
60·0	82551		17449	95444		04556	12893		87107	0′

138°
318°

42°
222°

LOGS. OF TRIG. FUNCTIONS

′	Sine	Parts		Cosec.	Tan.	Parts		Cotan.	Secant	Parts		Cosine	
00·0	$\overline{1}$.(9) 82551	′		0.(10) 17449	$\overline{1}$.(9) 95444	′		0.(10) 04556	0.(10) 12893	′		$\overline{1}$.(9) 87107	60′
01·0	82565			17435	95469			04531	12904			87096	
02·0	82579	·1	1	17421	95495	·1	3	04505	12915	·1	1	87085	
03·0	82593			17407	95520			04480	12927			87073	
04·0	82607			17393	95545			04455	12938			87062	
05·0	82621	·2	3	17379	95571	·2	5	04429	12950	·2	2	87050	55′
06·0	82635			17365	95596			04404	12961			87039	
07·0	82649			17351	95622			04379	12972			87028	
08·0	82663	·3	4	17337	95647	·3	8	04353	12984	·3	3	87016	
09·0	82677			17323	95672			04328	12995			87005	
10·0	82691			17309	95698			04302	13007			86993	50′
11·0	82705	·4	6	17295	95723	·4	10	04277	13018	·4	5	86982	
12·0	82719			17281	95749			04252	13030			86970	
13·0	82733			17267	95774			04226	13041			86959	
14·0	82747	·5	7	17253	95799	·5	13	04201	13053	·5	6	86947	
15·0	82761			17239	95825			04175	13064			86936	45′
16·0	82775			17226	95850			04150	13076			86925	
17·0	82788			17212	95875			04125	13087			86913	
18·0	82802	·6	8	17198	95901	·6	15	04099	13099	·6	7	86902	
19·0	82816			17184	95926			04074	13110			86890	
20·0	82830	·7	10	17170	95952	·7	18	04048	13122	·7	8	86879	40′
21·0	82844			17156	95977			04023	13133			86867	
22·0	82858			17142	96002			03998	13145			86856	
23·0	82872			17128	96028			03972	13156			86844	
24·0	82886	·8	11	17115	96053	·8	20	03947	13168	·8	9	86832	
25·0	82899			17101	96078			03922	13179			86821	35′
26·0	82913			17087	96104			03896	13191			86809	
27·0	82927	·9	13	17073	96129	·9	23	03871	13202	·9	10	86798	
28·0	82941			17059	96155			03846	13214			86786	
29·0	82955			17046	96180			03820	13225			86775	
30·0	82968			17032	96205			03795	13237			86763	30′
31·0	82982			17018	96231			03769	13249			86752	
32·0	82996	·1	1	17004	86256	·1	3	03744	13260	·1	1	86740	
33·0	83010			16990	96281			03719	13272			86728	
34·0	83023			16977	96307			03693	13283			86717	
35·0	83037	·2	3	16963	96332	·2	5	03668	13295	·2	2	86705	25′
36·0	83051			16949	96357			03643	13307			86694	
37·0	83065			16935	96383			03617	13318			86682	
38·0	83078	·3	4	16922	96408	·3	8	03592	13330	·3	4	86670	
39·0	83092			16908	96434			03567	13341			86659	
40·0	83106			16894	96459			03541	13353			86647	20′
41·0	83120			16881	96484			03516	13365			86635	
42·0	83133	·4	5	16867	96510	·4	10	03491	13376	·4	5	86624	
43·0	83147			16853	96535			03465	13388			86612	
44·0	83161			16839	96560			03440	13400			86600	
45·0	83174	·5	7	16826	96586	·5	13	03415	13411	·5	6	86589	15′
46·0	83188			16812	96611			03389	13423			86577	
47·0	83202			16799	96636			03364	13435			86565	
48·0	83215	·6	8	16785	96662	·6	15	03338	13446	·6	7	86554	
49·0	83229			16771	96687			03313	13458			86542	
50·0	83243			16758	96712			03288	13470			86530	10′
51·0	83256	·7	10	16744	96738	·7	18	03262	13482	·7	8	86519	
52·0	83270			16730	96763			03237	13493			86507	
53·0	83283			16717	96788			03212	13505			86495	
54·0	83297	·8	11	16703	96814	·8	20	03186	13517	·8	9	86483	
55·0	83311			16690	96839			03161	13528			86472	5′
56·0	83324			16676	96864			03136	13540			86460	
57·0	83338	·9	12	16662	96890	·9	23	03110	13552	·9	11	86448	
58·0	83351			16649	96915			03085	13564			86436	
59·0	83365			16635	96940			03060	13576			86425	
60·0	83378			16622	96966			03034	13587			86413	0′

137°
317°

43°
223°

LOGS. OF TRIG. FUNCTIONS

′	Sine	Parts	Cosec.	Tan.	Parts	Cotan.	Secant	Parts	Cosine	
00·0	1.(9) 83378	′	0.(10) 16622	1.(9) 96966	′	0.(10) 03034	0.(10) 13587	′	1.(9) 86413	60′
01·0	83392		16608	96991		03009	13599		86401	
02·0	83405	·1 1	16595	97016	·1 3	02984	13611	·1 1	86389	
03·0	83419		16581	97042		02958	13623		86377	
04·0	83433		16568	97067		.02933	13634		86366	
05·0	83446	·2 3	16554	97092	·2 5	02908	13646	·2 2	86354	55′
06·0	83460		16541	97118		02883	13658		86342	
07·0	83473		16527	97143		02857	13670		86330	
08·0	83487	·3 4	16514	97168	·3 8	02832	13682	·3 4	86318	
09·0	83500		16500	97194		02807	13694		86306	
10·0	83513		16487	97219		02781	13705		86295	50′
11·0	83527	·4 5	16473	97244	·4 10	02756	13717	·4 5	86283	
12·0	83540		16460	97270		02731	13729		86271	
13·0	83554		16446	97295		02705	13741		86259	
14·0	83567	·5 7	16433	97320	·5 13	02680	13753	·5 6	86247	
15·0	83581		16419	97345		02655	13765		86235	45′
16·0	83594		16406	97371		02629	13777		86223	
17·0	83608		16393	97396		02604	13789		86212	
18·0	83621	·6 8	16379	97421	·6 15	02579	13800	·6 7	86200	
19·0	83634		16366	97447		02553	13812		86188	
20·0	83648		16352	97472		02528	13824		86176	40′
21·0	83661	·7 9	16339	97497	·7 18	02503	13836	·7 8	86164	
22·0	83675		16326	97523		02477	13848		86152	
23·0	83688		16312	97548		02452	13860		86140	
24·0	83701	·8 11	16299	97573	·8 20	02427	13872	·8 10	86128	
25·0	83715		16285	97599		02402	13884		86116	35′
26·0	83728		16272	.97624		02376	13896		86104	
27·0	83741	·9 12	16259	97649	·9 23	02351	13908	·9 11	86092	
28·0	83755		16245	97674		02326	13920		86080	
29·0	83768		16232	97700		02300	13932		86068	
30·0	83781		16219	97725		02275	13944		86056	30′
31·0	83795		16206	97750		02250	13956		86044	
32·0	83808	·1 1	16192	97776	·1 3	02224	13968	·1 1	86032	
33·0	83821		16179	97801		02199	13980		86020	
34·0	83834		16166	97826		02174	13992		86008	
35·0	83848	·2 3	16152	97852	·2 5	02149	14004	·2 2	85996	25′
36·0	83861		16139	97877		02123	14016		85984	
37·0	83874		16126	97902		02098	14028		85972	
38·0	83888	·3 4	16113	97927	·3 8	02073	14040	·3 4	85960	
39·0	83901		16099	97953		02047	14052		85948	
40·0	83914		16086	97978		02022	14064		85936	20′
41·0	83927	·4 5	16073	98003	·4 10	01997	14076	·4 5	85924	
42·0	83940		16060	98029		01971	14088		85912	
43·0	83954		16046	98054		01946	14100		85900	
44·0	83967		16033	98079		01921	14112		85888	
45·0	83980	·5 7	16020	98104	·5 13	01896	14124	·5 6	85876	15′
46·0	83993		16007	98130		01870	14137		85864	
47·0	84006		15994	98155		01845	14149		85851	
48·0	84020	·6 8	15980	98180	·6 15	01820	14161	·6 7	85839	
49·0	84033		15967	98206		01794	14173		85827	
50·0	84046		15954	98231		01769	14185		85815	10′
51·0	84059	·7 9	15941	98256	·7 18	01744	14197	·7 8	85803	
52·0	84072		15928	98281		01719	14209		85791	
53·0	84085		15915	98307		01693	14221		85779	
54·0	84099	·8 11	15902	98332	·8 20	01668	14234	·8 10	85767	
55·0	84112		15888	98357		01643	14246		85754	5′
56·0	84125		15875	98383		01617	14258		85742	
57·0	84138	·9 12	15862	98408	·9 23	01592	14270	·9 11	85730	
58·0	84151		15849	98433		01567	14282		85718	
59·0	84164		15836	98458		01542	14294		85706	
60·0	84177		15823	98484		01516	14307		85693	0′

136°
316°

LOGS. OF TRIG. FUNCTIONS

44°
224°

′	Sine	Parts	Cosec.	Tan.	Parts	Cotan.	Secant	Parts	Cosine	
00·0	1̄.(9) 84177	′	0.(10) 15823	1̄.(9) 98484	′	0.(10) 01516	0.(10) 14307	′	1̄.(9) 85693	60′
01·0	84190		15810	98509		01491	14319		85681	
02·0	84203	·1 1	15797	98534	·1 3	01466	14331	·1 1	85669	
03·0	84216		15784	98560		01440	14343		85657	
04·0	84229		15771	98585		01415	14355		85645	
05·0	84242	·2 3	15758	98610	·2 5	01390	14368	·2 2	85632	55′
06·0	84256		15745	98635		01365	14380		85620	
07·0	84269		15732	98661		01339	14392		85608	
08·0	84282	·3 4	15719	98686	·3 8	01314	14404	·3 4	85596	
09·0	84295		15705	98711		01289	14417		85583	
10·0	84308		15692	98737		01264	14429		85571	50′
11·0	84321	·4 5	15679	98762	·4 10	01238	14441	·4 5	85559	
12·0	84334		15666	98787		01213	14454		85547	
13·0	84347		15653	98812		01188	14466		85534	
14·0	84360	·5 6	15641	98838	·5 13	01162	14478	·5 6	85522	
15·0	84373		15628	98863		01137	14490		85510	45′
16·0	84386		15615	98888		01112	14503		85497	
17·0	84398	·6 8	15602	98913	·6 15	01087	14515	·6 7	85485	
18·0	84411		15589	98939		01061	14527		85473	
19·0	84424		15576	98964		01036	14540		85460	
20·0	84437	·7 9	15563	98989	·7 18	01011	14552	·7 9	85448	40′
21·0	84450		15550	99015		00986	14564		85436	
22·0	84463		15537	99040		00960	14577		85423	
23·0	84476		15524	99065		00935	14589		85411	
24·0	84489	·8 10	15511	99090	·8 20	00910	14601	·8 10	85399	
25·0	84502		15498	99116		00884	14614		85386	35′
26·0	84515		15485	99141		00859	14626		85374	
27·0	84528	·9 12	15472	99166	·9 23	00834	14639	·9 11	85361	
28·0	84541		15460	99191		00809	14651		85349	
29·0	84553		15447	99217		00783	14663		85337	
30·0	84566		15434	99242		00758	14676		85324	30′
31·0	84579		15421	99267		00733	14688		85312	
32·0	84592	·1 1	15408	99293	·1 3	00708	14701	·1 1	85299	
33·0	84605		15395	99318		00682	14713		85287	
34·0	84618		15383	99343		00657	14726		85275	
35·0	84630	·2 3	15370	99368	·2 5	00632	14738	·2 3	85262	25′
36·0	84643		15357	99394		00606	14750		85250	
37·0	84656		15344	99419		00581	14763		85237	
38·0	84669	·3 4	15331	99444	·3 8	00556	14775	·3 4	85225	
39·0	84682		15318	99469		00531	14788		85212	
40·0	84694		15306	99495		00505	14800		85200	20′
41·0	84707	·4 5	15293	99520	·4 10	00480	14813	·4 5	85187	
42·0	84720		15280	99545		00455	14825		85175	
43·0	84733		15267	99571		00430	14838		85162	
44·0	84745		15255	99596		00404	14850		85150	
45·0	84758	·5 6	15242	99621	·5 13	00379	14863	·5 6	85137	15′
46·0	84771		15229	99646		00354	14875		85125	
47·0	84784		15216	99672		00329	14888		85112	
48·0	84796	·6 8	15204	99697	·6 15	00303.	14900	·6 8	85100	
49·0	84809		15191	99722		00278	14913		85087	
50·0	84822		15178	99747		00253	14926		85075	10′
51·0	84835	·7 9	15166	99773	·7 18	00227	14938	·7 9	85062	
52·0	84847		15153	99798		00202	14951		85049	
53·0	84860		15140	99823		00177	14963		85037	
54·0	84873	·8 10	15127	99848	·8 20	00152	14976	·8 10	85024	
55 0	84885		15115	99874		00126	14988		85012	5′
56·0	84898		15102	99899		00101	15001		84999	
57·0	84911	·9 11	15089	99924	·9 23	00076	15014	·9 11	84986	
58·0	84923		15077	99950		00051	15026		84974	
59·0	84936		15064	99975		00025	15039		84961	
60·0	84949		15052	0.(10) 00000		00000	15052		84949	0′

135°
315°

45°
225°

LOGS. OF TRIG. FUNCTIONS

′	Sine	Parts	Cosec.	Tan.	Parts	Cotan.	Secant	Parts	Cosine	
00·0	1.(9) 84949	′	0.(10) 15052	0.(10) 00000	′	0.(10) 00000	0.(10) 15052	′	1.(9) 84949	60′
01·0	84961		15039	00025		1.(9) 99975	15064		84936	
02·0	84974	·1 1	15026	00051	·1 3	99950	15077	·1 1	84923	
03·0	84986		15014	00076		99924	15089		84911	
04·0	84999		15001	00101		99899	15102		84898	
05·0	85012	·2 3	14988	00126	·2 5	99874	15115	·2 3	84885	55′
06·0	85024		14976	00152		99848	15127		84873	
07·0	85037		14963	00177		99823	15140		84860	
08·0	85049	·3 4	14951	00202	·3 8	99798	15153	·3 4	84847	
09·0	85062		14938	00227		99773	15166		84835	
10·0	85075		14926	00253		99747	15178		84822	50′
11·0	85087	·4 5	14913	00278	·4 10	99722	15191	·4 5	84809	
12·0	85100		14900	00303		99697	15204		84796	
13·0	85112		14888	00329		99672	15216		84784	
14·0	85125	·5 6	14875	00354	·5 13	99646	15229	·5 6	84771	
15·0	85137		14863	00379		99621	15242		84758	45′
16·0	85150		14850	00404		99596	15255		84745	
17·0	85162		14838	00430		99571	15267		84733	
18·0	85175	·6 8	14825	00455	·6 15	99545	15280	·6 8	84720	
19·0	85187		14813	00480		99520	15293		84707	
20·0	85200		14800	00505		99495	15306		84694	40′
21·0	85212	·7 9	14788	00531	·7 18	99469	15318	·7 9	84682	
22·0	85225		14775	00556		99444	15331		84669	
23·0	85237		14763	00581		99419	15344		84656	
24·0	85250	·8 10	14750	00606	·8 20	99394	15357	·8 10	84643	
25·0	85262		14738	00632		99368	15370		84630	35′
26·0	85275		14726	00657		99343	15383		84618	
27·0	85287	·9 11	14713	00682	·9 23	99318	15395	·9 11	84605	
28·0	85299		14701	00708		99293	15408		84592	
29·0	85312		14688	00733		99267	15421		84579	
30·0	85324		14676	00758		99242	15434		84566	30′
31·0	85337		14663	00783		99217	15447		84553	
32·0	85349	·1 1	14651	00809	·1 3	99191	15460	·1 1	84541	
33·0	85361		14639	00834		99166	15472		84528	
34·0	85374		14626	00859		99141	15485		84515	
35·0	85386	·2 2	14614	00884	·2 5	99116	15498	·2 3	84502	25′
36·0	85399		14601	00910		99090	15511		84489	
37·0	85411		14589	00935		99065	15524		84476	
38·0	85423	·3 4	14577	00960	·3 8	99040	15537	·3 4	84463	
39·0	85436		14564	00986		99015	15550		84450	
40·0	85448		14552	01011		98989	15563		84437	20′
41·0	85460	·4 5	14540	01036	·4 10	98964	15576	·4 5	84424	
42·0	85473		14527	01061		98939	15589		84411	
43·0	85485		14515	01087		98913	15602		84398	
44·0	85497		14503	01112		98888	15615		84386	
45·0	85510	·5 6	14490	01137	·5 13	98863	15628	·5 6	84373	15′
46·0	85522		14478	01162		98838	15641		84360	
47·0	85534		14466	01188		98812	15653		84347	
48·0	85547	·6 7	14454	01213	·6 15	98787	15666	·6 8	84334	
49·0	85559		14441	01238		98762	15679		84321	
50·0	85571		14429	01264		98737	15692		84308	10′
51·0	85583	·7 9	14417	01289	·7 18	98711	15705	·7 9	84295	
52·0	85596		14404	01314		98686	15719		84282	
53·0	85608		14392	01339		98661	15732		84269	
54·0	85620	·8 10	14380	01365	·8 20	98635	15745	·8 10	84256	
55·0	85632		14368	01390		98610	15758		84242	5′
56·0	85645		14355	01415		98585	15771		84229	
57·0	85657	·9 11	14343	01440	·9 23	98560	15784	·9 12	84216	
58·0	85669		14331	01466		98534	15797		84203	
59·0	85681		14319	01491		98509	15810		84190	
60·0	85693		14307	01516		98484	15823		84177	0′

134°
314°

46°

LOGS. OF TRIG. FUNCTIONS

′	Sine	Parts	Cosec.	Tan.	Parts	Cotan.	Secant	Parts	Cosine	
00·0	1.(9) 85693	′	0.(10) 14307	0.(10) 01516	′	1.(9) 98484	0.(10) 15823	′	1.(9) 84177	60′
01·0	85706		14294	01542		98458	15836		84164	
02·0	85718	·1 1	14282	01567	·1 3	98433	15849	·1 1	84151	
03·0	85730		14270	01592		98408	15862		84138	
04·0	85742		14258	01617		98383	15875		84125	
05·0	85754	2 2	14246	01643	2 5	98357	15888	·2 3	84112	55′
06·0	85767		14234	01668		98332	15902		84099	
07·0	85779		14221	01693		98307	15915		84085	
08·0	85791	·3 4	14209	01719	·3 8	98281	15928	·3 4	84072	
09·0	85803		14197	01744		98256	15941		84059	
10·0	85815		14185	01769		98231	15954		84046	50′
11·0	85827	·4 5	14173	01794	·4 10	98206	15967	·4 5	84033	
12·0	85839		14161	01820		98180	15980		84020	
13·0	85851		14149	01845		98155	15994		84006	
14·0	85864	·5 6	14137	01870	·5 13	98130	16007	·5 7	83993	
15·0	85876		14124	01896		98104	16020		83980	45′
16·0	85888		14112	01921		98079	16033		83967	
17·0	85900		14100	01946		98054	16046		83954	
18·0	85912	·6 7	14088	01971	·6 15	98029	16060	·6 8	83940	
19·0	85924		14076	01997		98003	16073		83927	
20·0	85936		14064	02022		97978	16086		83914	40′
21·0	85948	·7 8	14052	02047	·7 18	97953	16099	·7 9	83901	
22·0	85960		14040	02073		97927	16113		83888	
23·0	85972		14028	02098		97902	16126		83874	
24·0	85984	·8 10	14016	02123	·8 20	97877	16139	·8 11	83861	
25·0	85996		14004	02149		97852	16152		83848	35′
26·0	86008		13992	02174		97826	16166		83834	
27·0	86020	·9 11	13980	02199	·9 23	97801	16179	·9 12	83821	
28·0	86032		13968	02224		97776	16192		83808	
29·0	86044		13956	02250		97750	16206		83795	
30·0	86056		13944	02275		97725	16219		83781	30′
31·0	86068		13932	02300		97700	16232		83768	
32·0	86080	·1 1	13920	02326	·1 3	97674	16245	·1 1	83755	
33·0	86092		13908	02351		97649	16259		83741	
34·0	86104		13896	02376		97624	16272		83728	
35·0	86116	·2 2	13884	02402	·2 5	97599	16285	·2 3	83715	25′
36·0	86128		13872	02427		97573	16299		83701	
37·0	86140		13860	02452		97548	16312		83688	
38·0	86152	·3 4	13848	02477	·3 8	97523	16326	·3 4	83675	
39·0	86164		13836	02503		97497	16339		83661	
40·0	86176		13824	02528		97472	16352		83648	20′
41·0	86188	·4 5	13812	02553	·4 10	97447	16366	·4 5	83634	
42·0	86200		13800	02579		97421	16379		83621	
43·0	86212		13789	02604		97396	16393		83608	
44·0	86223		13777	02629		97371	16406		83594	
45·0	86235	·5 6	13765	02655	·5 13	97345	16419	·5 7	83581	15′
46·0	86247		13753	02680		97320	16433		83567	
47·0	86259		13741	02705		97295	16446		83554	
48·0	86271	·6 7	13729	02731	·6 15	97270	16460	·6 8	83540	
49·0	86283		13717	02756		97244	16473		83527	
50·0	86295		13705	02781		97219	16487		83513	10′
51·0	86306	·7 8	13694	02807	·7 18	97194	16500	·7 9	83500	
52·0	86318		13682	02832		97168	16514		83487	
53·0	86330		13670	02857		97143	16527		83473	
54·0	86342	·8 10	13658	02883	·8 20	97118	16541	·8 11	83460	
55·0	86354		13646	02908		97092	16554		83446	5′
56·0	86366		13634	02933		97067	16568		83433	
57·0	86377	·9 11	13623	02958	·9 23	97042	16581	·9 12	83419	
58·0	86389		13611	02984		97016	16595		83405	
59·0	86401		13599	03009		96991	16608		83392	
60·0	86413		13587	03034		96966	16622		83378	0′

47°
227°

LOGS. OF TRIG. FUNCTIONS

'	Sine	Parts	Cosec.	Tan.	Parts	Cotan.	Secant	Parts	Cosine	
00·0	1.(9)86413	'	0.(10)13587	0.(10)03034	'	1.(9)96966	0.(10)16622	'	1.(9)83378	60'
01·0	86425		13576	03060		96940	16635		83365	
02·0	86436	·1 1	13564	03085	·1 3	96915	16649	·1 1	83351	
03·0	86448		13552	03110		96890	16662		83338	
04·0	86460		13540	03136		96864	16676		83324	
05·0	86472	·2 2	13528	03161	·2 5	96839	16690	·2 3	83311	55'
06·0	86483		13517	03186		96814	16703		83297	
07·0	86495		13505	03212		96788	16717		83283	
08·0	86507	·3 4	13493	03237	·3 8	96763	16730	·3 4	83270	
09·0	86519		13482	03262		96738	16744		83256	
10·0	86530		13470	03288		96712	16758		83243	50'
11·0	86542	·4 5	13458	03313	·4 10	96687	16771	·4 5	83229	
12·0	86554		13446	03338		96662	16785		83215	
13·0	86565		13435	03364		96636	16799		83202	
14·0	86577	·5 6	13423	03389	·5 13	96611	16812	·5 7	83188	
15·0	86589		13411	03415		96586	16826		83174	45'
16·0	86600		13400	03440		96560	16839		83161	
17·0	86612		13388	03465		96535	16853		83147	
18·0	86624	·6 7	13376	03491	·6 15	96510	16867	·6 8	83133	
19·0	86635		13365	03516		96484	16881		83120	
20·0	86647	·7 8	13353	03541	·7 18	96459	16894	·7 10	83106	40'
21·0	86659		13341	03567		96434	16908		83092	
22·0	86670		13330	03592		96408	16922		83078	
23·0	86682		13318	03617		96383	16935		83065	
24·0	86694	·8 9	13307	03643	·8 20	96357	16949	·8 11	83051	
25·0	86705		13295	03668		96332	16963		83037	35'
26·0	86717		13283	03693		96307	16977		83023	
27·0	86728	·9 11	13272	03719	·9 23	96281	16990	·9 12	83010	
28·0	86740		13260	03744		96256	17004		82996	
29·0	86752		13249	03769		96231	17018		82982	
30·0	86763		13237	03795		96205	17032		82968	30'
31·0	86775		13225	03820		96180	17046		82955	
32·0	86786	·1 1	13214	03846	·1 3	96155	17059	·1 1	82941	
33·0	86798		13202	03871		96129	17073		82927	
34·0	86809		13191	03896		96104	17087		82913	
35·0	86821	·2 2	13179	03922	·2 5	96078	17101	·2 3	82899	25'
36·0	86832		13168	03947		96053	17115		82886	
37·0	86844		13156	03972		96028	17128		82872	
38·0	86856	·3 3	13145	03998	·3 8	96002	17142	·3 4	82858	
39·0	86867		13133	04023		95977	17156		82844	
40·0	86879		13122	04048		95952	17170		82830	20'
41·0	86890	·4 5	13110	04074	·4 10	95926	17184	·4 6	82816	
42·0	86902		13099	04099		95901	17198		82802	
43·0	86913		13087	04125		95875	17212		82788	
44·0	86925	·5 6	13076	04150	·5 13	95850	17226	·5 7	82775	
45·0	86936		13064	04175		95825	17239		82761	15'
46·0	86947		13053	04201		95799	17253		82747	
47·0	86959	·6 7	13041	04226	·6 15	95774	17267	·6 8	82733	
48·0	86970		13030	04252		95749	17281		82719	
49·0	86982		13018	04277		95723	17295		82705	
50·0	86993	·7 8	13007	04302	·7 18	95698	17309	·7 10	82691	10'
51·0	87005		12995	04328		95672	17323		82677	
52·0	87016		12984	04353		95647	17337		82663	
53·0	87028		12972	04379		95622	17351		82649	
54·0	87039	·8 9	12961	04404	·8 20	95596	17365	·8 11	82635	
55·0	87050		12950	04429		95571	17379		82621	5'
56·0	87062		12938	04455		95545	17393		82607	
57·0	87073	·9 10	12927	04480	·9 23	95520	17407	·9 13	82593	
58·0	87085		12915	04505		95495	17421		82579	
59·0	87096		12904	04531		95469	17435		82565	
60·0	87107		12893	04556		95444	17449		82551	0'

48°
228°

LOGS. OF TRIG. FUNCTIONS

′	Sine	Parts	Cosec.	Tan.	Parts	Cotan.	Secant	Parts	Cosine	
00·0	1̄.(9) 87107	′	0.(10) 12893	0.(10) 04556	′	1̄.(9) 95444	0.(10) 17449	′	1̄.(9) 82551	60′
01·0	87119		12881	04582		95418	17463		82537	
02·0	87130	·1 1	12870	04607	·1 3	95393	17477	·1 1	82523	
03·0	87141		12859	04633		95368	17491		82509	
04·0	87153		12847	04658		95342	17505		82495	
05·0	87164	·2 2	12836	04683	·2 5	95317	17519	·2 3	82481	55′
06·0	87176		12825	04709		95291	17533		82467	
07·0	87187		12813	04734		95266	17547		82453	
08·0	87198	·3 3	12802	04760	·3 8	95241	17561	·3 4	82439	
09·0	87210		12791	04785		95215	17576		82425	
10·0	87221		12779	04810		95190	17590		82410	50′
11·0	87232	·4 5	12768	04836	·4 10	95164	17604	·4 6	82396	
12·0	87243		12757	04861		95139	17618		82382	
13·0	87255		12745	04887		95113	17632		82368	
14·0	87266	·5 6	12734	04912	·5 13	95088	17646	·5 7	82354	
15·0	87277		12723	04938		95063	17660		82340	45′
16·0	87289		12712	04963		95037	17675		82326	
17·0	87300	·6 7	12700	04988	·6 15	95012	17689	·6 8	82311	
18·0	87311		12689	05014		94986	17703		82297	
19·0	87322		12678	05039		94961	17717		82283	
20·0	87334	·7 8	12667	05065	·7 18	94935	17731	·7 10	82269	40′
21·0	87345		12655	05090		94910	17745		82255	
22·0	87356		12644	05116		94884	17760		82240	
23·0	87367		12633	05141		94859	17774		82226	
24·0	87378	·8 9	12622	05167	·8 20	94834	17788	·8 11	82212	
25·0	87390		12610	05192		94808	17802		82198	35′
26·0	87401		12599	05217		94783	17817		82184	
27·0	87412	·9 10	12588	05243	·9 23	94757	17831	·9 13	82169	
28·0	87423		12577	05268		94732	17845		82155	
29·0	87434		12566	05294		94706	17859		82141	
30·0	87446		12554	05319		94681	17874		82127	30′
31·0	87457		12543	05345		94655	17888		82112	
32·0	87468	·1 1	12532	05370	·1 3	94630	17902	·1 1	82098	
33·0	87479		12521	05396		94605	17916		82084	
34·0	87490		12510	05421		94579	17931		82069	
35·0	87501	·2 2	12499	05447	·2 5	94554	17945	·2 3	82055	25′
36·0	87513		12487	05472		94528	17959		82041	
37·0	87524		12476	05497		94503	17974		82026	
38·0	87535	·3 3	12465	05523	·3 8	94477	17988	·3 4	82012	
39·0	87546		12454	05548		94452	18002		81998	
40·0	87557		12443	05574		94426	18017		81983	20′
41·0	87568	·4 4	12432	05599	·4 10	94401	18031	·4 6	81969	
42·0	87579		12421	05625		94375	18046		81955	
43·0	87590		12410	05650		94350	18060		81940	
44·0	87601		12399	05676		94324	18074		81926	
45·0	87613	·5 6	12388	05701	·5 13	94299	18089	·5 7	81911	15′
46·0	87624		12376	05727		94273	18103		81897	
47·0	87635		12365	05752		94248	18118		81883	
48·0	87646	·6 7	12354	05778	·6 15	94222	18132	·6 9	81868	
49·0	87657		12343	05803		94197	18146		81854	
50·0	87668		12332	05829		94171	18161		81839	10′
51·0	87679	·7 8	12321	05854	·7 18	94146	18175	·7 10	81825	
52·0	87690		12310	05880		94120	18190		81810	
53·0	87701		12299	05905		94095	18204		81796	
54·0	87712	·8 9	12288	05931	·8 20	94069	18219	·8 12	81781	
55·0	87723		12277	05956		94044	18233		81767	5′
56·0	87734		12266	05982		94018	18248		81752	
57·0	87745	·9 10	12255	06007	·9 23	93993	18262	·9 13	81738	
58·0	87756		12244	06033		93967	18277		81723	
59·0	87767		12233	06058		93942	18291		81709	
60·0	87778		12222	06084		93916	18306		81694	0′

131°
311°

LOGS. OF TRIG. FUNCTIONS

49°
229°

'	Sine	Parts	Cosec.	Tan.	Parts	Cotan.	Secant	Parts	Cosine	
00·0	1.(9) 87778	'	0.(10) 12222	0.(10) 06084	'	1.(9) 93916	0.(10) 18306	'	1.(9) 81694	60'
01·0	87789		12211	06109		93891	18320		81680	
02·0	87800	·1 1	12200	06135	·1 3	93865	18335	·1 1	81665	
03·0	87811		12189	06160		93840	18349		81651	
04·0	87822		12178	06186		93814	18364		81636	
05·0	87833	·2 2	12167	06211	·2 5	93789	18379	·2 3	81622	55'
06·0	87844		12156	06237		93763	18393		81607	
07·0	87855		12145	06262		93738	18408		81592	
08·0	87866	·3 3	12134	06288	·3 8	93712	18422	·3 4	81578	
09·0	87877		12123	06313		93687	18437		81563	
10·0	87888		12113	06339		93661	18452		81549	50'
11·0	87898	·4 4	12102	06365	·4 10	93636	18466	·4 6	81534	
12·0	87909		12091	06390		93610	18481		81519	
13·0	87920		12080	06416		93584	18495		81505	
14·0	87931	·5 5	12069	06441	·5 13	93559	18510	·5 7	81490	
15·0	87942		12058	06467		93533	18525		81475	45'
16·0	87953		12047	06492		93508	18539		81461	
17·0	87964		12036	06518		93482	18554		81446	
18·0	87975	·6 7	12025	06543	·6 15	93457	18569	·6 9	81431	
19·0	87986		12015	06569		93431	18583		81417	
20·0	87996	·7 8	12004	06594	·7 18	93406	18598	·7 10	81402	40'
21·0	88007		11993	06620		93380	18613		81387	
22·0	88018		11982	06646		93355	18628		81373	
23·0	88029		11971	06671		93329	18642		81358	
24·0	88040	·8 9	11960	06697	·8 20	93303	18657	·8 12	81343	
25·0	88051		11950	06722		93278	18672		81328	35'
26·0	88061		11939	06748		93252	18687		81314	
27·0	88072	·9 10	11928	06773	·9 23	93227	18701	·9 13	81299	
28·0	88083		11917	06799		93201	18716		81284	
29·0	88094		11906	06825		93176	18731		81269	
30·0	88105		11895	06850		93150	18746		81254	30'
31·0	88115		11885	06876		93124	18760		81240	
32·0	88126	·1 1	11874	06901	·1 3	93099	18775	·1 1	81225	
33·0	88137		11863	06927		93073	18790		81210	
34·0	88148		11852	06953		93048	18805		81195	
35·0	88158	·2 2	11842	06978	·2 5	93022	18820	·2 3	81180	25'
36·0	88169		11831	07004		92996	18835		81166	
37·0	88180		11820	07029		92971	18849		81151	
38·0	88191	·3 3	11809	07055	·3 8	92945	18864	·3 4	81136	
39·0	88201		11799	07080		92920	18879		81121	
40·0	88212		11788	07106		92894	18894		81106	20'
41·0	88223	·4 4	11777	07132	·4 10	92868	18909	·4 6	81091	
42·0	88234		11766	07157		92843	18924		81076	
43·0	88244		11756	07183		92817	18939		81061	
44·0	88255	·5 5	11745	07209	·5 13	92792	18954	·5 7	81047	
45·0	88266		11734	07234		92766	18968		81032	15'
46·0	88276		11724	07260		92740	18983		81017	
47·0	88287		11713	07285		92715	18998		81002	
48·0	88298	·6 6	11702	07311	·6 15	92689	19013	·6 9	80987	
49·0	88308		11692	07337		92663	19028		80972	
50·0	98319	·7 7	11681	07362	·7 18	92638	19043	·7 10	80957	10'
51·0	88330		11670	07388		92612	19058		80942	
52·0	88340		11660	07414		92587	19073		80927	
53·0	88351		11649	07439		92561	19088		80912	
54·0	88362	·8 9	11638	07465	·8 21	92535	19103	·8 12	80897	
55·0	88372		11628	07490		92510	19118		80882	5'
56·0	88383		11617	07516		92484	19133		80867	
57·0	88394	·9 10	11606	07542	·9 23	92458	19148	·9 13	80852	
58·0	88404		11596	07567		92433	19163		80837	
59·0	88415		11585	07593		92407	19178		80822	
60·0	88425		11575	07619		92381	19193		80807	0'

130°
310°

LOGS. OF TRIG. FUNCTIONS

50°
230°

′	Sine	Parts		Cosec.	Tan.	Parts		Cotan.	Secant	Parts		Cosine	′
00·0	1.(9) 88425			0.(10) 11575	0.(10) 07619			1.(9) 92381	0.(10) 19193			1.(9) 80807	60′
01·0	88436			11564	07644			92356	19208			80792	
02·0	88447	·1	1	11553	07670	·1	3	92330	19223	·1	2	80777	
03·0	88457			11543	07696			92304	19239			80762	
04·0	88468			11532	07721			92279	19254			80747	
05·0	88478	·2	2	11522	07747	·2	5	92253	19269	·2	3	80731	55′
06·0	88489			11511	07773			92227	19284			80716	
07·0	88499			11501	07798			92202	19299			80701	
08·0	88510	·3	3	11490	07824	·3	8	92176	19314	·3	5	80686	
09·0	88521			11479	07850			92150	19329			80671	
10·0	88531			11469	07875			92125	19344			80656	50′
11·0	88542	·4	4	11458	07901	·4	10	92099	19359	·4	6	80641	
12·0	88552			11448	07927			92073	19375			80625	
13·0	88563			11437	07952			92048	19390			80610	
14·0	88573	·5	5	11427	07978	·5	13	92022	19405	·5	8	80595	
15·0	88584			11416	08004			91996	19420			80580	45′
16·0	88594			11406	08030			91971	19435			80565	
17·0	88605	·6	6	11395	08055	·6	15	91945	19451	·6	9	80550	
18·0	88615			11385	08081			91919	19466			80534	
19·0	88626			11374	08107			91893	19481			80519	
20·0	88636	·7	7	11364	08132	·7	18	91868	19496	·7	10	80504	40′
21·0	88647			11353	08158			91842	19511			80489	
22·0	88657			11343	08184			91816	19527			80473	
23·0	88668			11332	08209			91791	19542			80458	
24·0	88678	·8	8	11322	08235	·8	21	91765	19557	·8	12	80443	
25·0	88689			11312	08261			91739	19572			80428	35′
26·0	88699			11301	08287			91713	19588			80412	
27·0	88709	·9	9	11291	08312	·9	23	91688	19603	·9	14	80397	
28·0	88720			11280	08338			91662	19618			80382	
29·0	88730			11270	08364			91636	19634			80366	
30·0	88741			11259	08390			91610	19649			80351	30′
31·0	88751			11249	08415			91585	19664			80336	
32·0	88761	·1	1	11239	08441	·1	3	91559	19680	·1	2	80320	
33·0	88772			11228	08467			91533	19695			80305	
34·0	88782			11218	08493			91508	19710			80290	
35·0	88793	·2	2	11207	08518	·2	5	91482	19726	·2	3	80274	25′
36·0	88803			11197	08544			91456	19741			80259	
37·0	88813			11187	08570			91430	19756			80244	
38·0	88824	·3	3	11176	08596	·3	8	91404	19772	·3	5	80228	
39·0	88834			11166	08621			91379	19787			80213	
40·0	88844			11156	08647			91353	19803			80197	20′
41·0	88855	·4	4	11145	08673	·4	10	91327	19818	·4	6	80182	
42·0	88865			11135	08699			91301	19834			80167	
43·0	88875			11125	08724			91276	19849			80151	
44·0	88886	·5	5	11114	08750	·5	13	91250	19864	·5	8	80136	
45·0	88896			11104	08776			91224	19880			80120	15′
46·0	88906			11094	08802			91198	19895			80105	
47·0	88917	·6	6	11083	08827	·6	15	91173	19911	·6	9	80089	
48·0	88927			11073	08853			91147	19926			80074	
49·0	88937			11063	08879			91121	19942			80058	
50·0	88948	·7	7	11052	08905	·7	18	91095	19957	·7	11	80043	10′
51·0	88958			11042	08931			91069	19973			80027	
52·0	88968			11032	08957			91044	19988			80012	
53·0	88979			11022	08982			91018	20004			79996	
54·0	88989	·8	8	11011	09008	·8	21	90992	20019	·8	12	79981	
55·0	88999			11001	09034			90966	20035			79965	5′
56·0	89009			10991	09060			90940	20051			79950	
57·0	89020	·9	9	10981	09086	·9	23	90914	20066	·9	14	79934	
58·0	89030			10970	09111			90889	20082			79918	
59·0	89040			10960	09137			90863	20097			79903	
60·0	89050			10950	09163			90837	20113			79887	0′

51° 231° LOGS. OF TRIG. FUNCTIONS

′	Sine	Parts	Cosec.	Tan.	Parts	Cotan.	Secant	Parts	Cosine	
00·0	1.(9) 89050	′	0.(10) 10950	0.(10) 09163	′	1.(9) 90837	0.(10) 20113	′	1.(9) 79887	60′
01·0	89061		10940	09189		90811	20128		79872	
02·0	89071	·1 1	10929	09215	·1 3	90785	20144	·1 2	79856	
03·0	89081		10919	09241		90759	20160		79840	
04·0	89091		10909	09266		90734	20175		79825	
05·0	89101	·2 2	10899	09292	·2 5	90708	20191	·2 3	79809	55′
06·0	89112		10889	09318		90682	20207		79793	
07·0	89122		10878	09344		90656	20222		79778	
08·0	89132	·3 3	10868	09370	·3 8	90630	20238	·3 5	79762	
09·0	89142		10858	09396		90604	20254		79746	
10·0	89152		10848	09422		90579	20269		79731	50′
11·0	89162	·4 4	10838	09447	·4 10	90553	20285	·4 6	79715	
12·0	89173		10827	09473		90527	20301		79699	
13·0	89183		10817	09499		90501	20316		79684	
14·0	89193	·5 5	10807	09535	·5 13	90475	20332	·5 8	79668	
15·0	89203		10797	09551		90449	20348		79652	45′
16·0	89213		10787	09577		90423	20364		79636	
17·0	89223	·6 6	10777	09603	·6 16	90397	20379	·6 9	79621	
18·0	89233		10767	09629		90371	20395		79605	
19·0	89244		10757	09654		90346	20411		79589	
20·0	89254	·7 7	10746	09680	·7 18	90320	20427	·7 11	79573	40′
21·0	89264		10736	09706		90294	20443		79558	
22·0	89274		10726	09732		90268	20458		79542	
23·0	89284		10716	09758		90242	20474		79526	
24·0	89294	·8 8	10706	09784	·8 21	90216	20490	·8 13	79510	
25·0	89304		10696	09810		90190	20506		79494	35′
26·0	89314		10686	09836		90164	20522		79478	
27·0	89324	·9 9	10676	09862	·9 23	90138	20537	·9 14	79463	
28·0	89334		10666	09888		90112	20553		79447	
29·0	89344		10656	09914		90086	20569		79431	
30·0	89354		10646	09940		90061	20585		79415	30′
31·0	89365		10636	09965		90035	20601		79399	
32·0	89375	·1 1	10626	09991	·1 3	90009	20617	·1 2	79383	
33·0	89385		10615	10017		89983	20633		79367	
34·0	89395		10605	10043		89957	20649		79351	
35·0	89405	·2 2	10595	10069	·2 5	89931	20665	·2 3	79335	25′
36·0	89415		10585	10095		89905	20681		79320	
37·0	89425		10575	10121		89879	20697		79304	
38·0	89435	·3 3	10565	10147	·3 8	89853	20712	·3 5	79288	
39·0	89445		10555	10173		89827	20728		79272	
40·0	89455		10545	10199		89801	20744		79256	20′
41·0	89465	·4 4	10535	10225	·4 10	89775	20760	·4 6	79240	
42·0	89475		10525	10251		89749	20776		79224	
43·0	89485		10515	10277		89723	20792		79208	
44·0	89495	·5 5	10506	10303	·5 13	89697	20808	·5 8	79192	
45·0	89505		10496	10329		89671	20824		79176	15′
46·0	89515		10486	10355		89645	20840		79160	
47·0	89524	·6 6	10476	10381	·6 16	89619	20856	·6 10	79144	
48·0	89534		10466	10407		89593	20873		79128	
49·0	89544		10456	10433		89567	20889		79112	
50·0	89554	·7 7	10446	10459	·7 18	89541	20905	·7 11	79095	10′
51·0	89564		10436	10485		89515	20921		79079	
52·0	89574		10426	10511		89489	20937		79063	
53·0	89584		10416	10537		89463	20953		79047	
54·0	89594	·8 8	10406	10563	·8 21	89437	20969	·8 13	79031	
55·0	89604		10396	10589		89411	20985		79015	5′
56·0	89614		10386	10615		89385	21001		78999	
57·0	89624	·9 9	10376	10641	·9 23	89359	21017	·9 14	78983	
58·0	89634		10367	10667		89333	21034		78967	
59·0	89643		10357	10693		89307	21050		78950	
60·0	89653		10347	10719		89281	21066		78934	0′

128° 308°

LOGS. OF TRIG. FUNCTIONS

52°
232°

′	Sine	Parts	Cosec.	Tan.	Parts	Cotan.	Secant	Parts	Cosine	
00·0	1̄.(9) 89653	′	0.(10) 10347	0.(10) 10719	′	1̄.(9) 89281	0.(10) 21066	′	1̄.(9) 78934	60′
01·0	89663		10337	10745		89255	21082		78918	
02·0	89673	·1 1	10327	10771	·1 3	89229	21098	·1 2	78902	
03·0	89683		10317	10797		89203	21114		78886	
04·0	89693		10307	10823		89177	21131		78869	
05·0	89703	·2 2	10298	10849	·2 5	89151	21147	·2 3	78853	55′
06·0	89712		10288	10875		89125	21163		78837	
07·0	89722		10278	10901		89099	21179		78821	
08·0	89732	·3 3	10268	10928	·3 8	89073	21196	·3 5	78805	
09·0	89742		10258	10954		89047	21212		78788	
10·0	89752		10248	10980		89020	21228		78772	50′
11·0	89761	·4 4	10239	11006	·4 10	88994	21244	·4 7	78756	
12·0	89771		10229	11032		88968	21261		78740	
13·0	89781		10219	11058		88942	21277		78723	
14·0	89791	·5 5	10209	11084	·5 13	88916	21293	·5 8	78707	
15·0	89801		10199	11110		88890	21309		78691	45′
16·0	89810		10190	11136		88864	21326		78674	
17·0	89820	·6 6	10180	11162	·6 16	88838	21342	·6 10	78658	
18·0	89830		10170	11188		88812	21358		78642	
19·0	89840		10160	11215		88786	21375		78625	
20·0	89849	·7 7	10151	11241	·7 18	88759	21391	·7 11	78609	40′
21·0	89859		10141	11267		88733	21408		78593	
22·0	89869		10131	11293		88707	21424		78576	
23·0	89879		10121	11319		88681	21440		78560	
24·0	89888	·8 8	10112	11345	·8 21	88655	21457	·8 13	78543	
25·0	89898		10102	11371		88629	21473		78527	35′
26·0	89908		10092	11397		88603	21490		78511	
27·0	89918	·9 9	10082	11424	·9 23	88577	21506	·9 15	78494	
28·0	89927		10073	11450		88550	21522		78478	
29·0	89937		10063	11476		88524	21539		78461	
30·0	89947		10053	11502		88498	21555		78445	30′
31·0	89956		10044	11528		88472	21572		78428	
32·0	89966	·1 1	10034	11554	·1 3	88446	21588	·1 2	78412	
33·0	89976		10024	11580		88420	21605		78395	
34·0	89985		10015	11607		88393	21621		78379	
35·0	89995	·2 2	10005	11633	·2 5	88367	21638	·2 3	78362	25′
36·0	90005		09995	11659		88341	21654		78346	
37·0	90014		09986	11685		88315	21671		78329	
38·0	90024	·3 3	09976	11711	·3 8	88289	21687	·3 5	78313	
39·0	90034		09966	11738		88263	21704		78296	
40·0	90043		09957	11764		88236	21720		78280	20′
41·0	90053	·4 4	09947	11790	·4 10	88210	21737	·4 7	78263	
42·0	90063		09937	11816		88184	21754		78246	
43·0	90072		09928	11842		88158	21770		78230	
44·0	90082		09918	11869		88131	21787		78213	
45·0	90091	·5 5	09909	11895	·5 13	88105	21803	·5 8	78197	15′
46·0	90101		09899	11921		88079	21820		78180	
47·0	90111		09889	11947		88053	21837		78163	
48·0	90120	·6 6	09880	11974	·6 16	88027	21853	·6 10	78147	
49·0	90130		09870	12000		88000	21870		78130	
50·0	90139		09861	12026		87974	21887		78113	10′
51·0	90149	·7 7	09851	12052	·7 18	87948	21903	·7 12	78097	
52·0	90159		09842	12078		87922	21920		78080	
53·0	90168		09832	12105		87895	21937		78063	
54·0	90178	·8 8	09822	12131	·8 21	87869	21953	·8 13	78047	
55·0	90187		09813	12157		87843	21970		78030	5′
56·0	90197		09803	12184		87817	21987		78013	
57·0	90206	·9 9	09794	12210	·9 ·24	87790	22003	·9 15	77997	
58·0	90216		09784	12236		87764	22020		77980	
59·0	90225		09775	12262		87738	22037		77963	
60·0	90235		09765	12289		87711	22054		77946	0′

53°
233°

LOGS. OF TRIG. FUNCTIONS

′	Sine	Parts	Cosec.	Tan.	Parts	Cotan.	Secant	Parts	Cosine	
00·0	1.(9) 90235	′	0.(10) 09765	0.(10) 12289	′	1.(9) 87711	0.(10) 22054	′	1.(9) 77946	60′
01·0	90244		09756	12315		87685	22071		77930	
02·0	90254	·1 1	09746	12341	·1 3	87659	22087	·1 2	77913	
03·0	90263		09737	12367		87633	22104		77896	
04·0	90273		09727	12394		87606	22121		77879	
05·0	90282	·2 2	09718	12420	·2 5	87580	22138	·2 3	77862	55′
06·0	90292		09708	12446		87554	22155		77846	
07·0	90301		09699	12473		87527	22171		77829	
08·0	90311	·3 3	09689	12499	·3 8	87501	22188	·3 5	77812	
09·0	90320		09680	12525		87475	22205		77795	
10·0	90330		09670	12552		87448	22222		77778	50′
11·0	90339	·4 4	09661	12578	·4 11	87422	22239	·4 7	77761	
12·0	90349		09651	12604		87396	22256		77744	
13·0	90358		09642	12631		87369	22273		77728	
14·0	90368		09632	12657		87343	22289		77711	
15·0	90377	·5 5	09623	12683	·5 13	87317	22306	·5 8	77694	45′
16·0	90386		09614	12710		87290	22323		77677	
17·0	90396		09604	12736		87264	22340		77660	
18·0	90405	·6 6	09595	12762	·6 16	87238	22357	·6 10	77643	
19·0	90415		09585	12789		87211	22374		77626	
20·0	90424		09576	12815		87185	22391		77609	40′
21·0	90434	·7 7	09567	12841	·7 18	87159	22408	·7 12	77592	
22·0	90443		09557	12868		87132	22425		77575	
23·0	90452		09548	12894		87106	22442		77558	
24·0	90462	·8 8	09538	12921	·8 21	87079	22459	·8 14	77541	
25·0	90471		09529	12947		87053	22476		77524	35′
26·0	90480		09520	12974		87027	22493		77507	
27·0	90490	·9 8	09510	13000	·9 24	87000	22510	·9 15	77490	
28·0	90499		09501	13026		86974	22527		77473	
29·0	90509		09492	13053		86947	22544		77456	
30·0	90518		09482	13079		86921	22561		77439	30′
31·0	90527		09473	13106		86895	22578		77422	
32·0	90537	·1 1	09463	13132	·1 3	86868	22595	·1 2	77405	
33·0	90546		09454	13158		86842	22613		77388	
34·0	90555		09445	13185		86815	22630		77370	
35·0	90565	·2 2	09436	13211	·2 5	86789	22647	·2 3	77353	25′
36·0	90574		09426	13238		86762	22664		77336	
37·0	90583		09417	13264		86736	22681		77319	
38·0	90593	·3 3	09408	13291	·3 8	86709	22698	·3 5	77302	
39·0	90602		09398	13317		86683	22715		77285	
40·0	90611		09389	13344		86656	22733		77268	20′
41·0	90620	·4 4	09380	13370	·4 11	86630	22750	·4 7	77250	
42·0	90630		09370	13397		86604	22767		77233	
43·0	90639		09361	13423		86577	22784		77216	
44·0	90648		09352	13450		86551	22801		77199	
45·0	90658	·5 5	09343	13476	·5 13	86524	22819	·5 9	77182	15′
46·0	90667		09333	13503		86498	22836		77164	
47·0	90676		09324	13529		86471	22853		77147	
48·0	90685	·6 6	09315	13556	·6 16	86445	22870	·6 10	77130	
49·0	90695		09306	13582		86418	22888		77113	
50·0	90704		09296	13609		86392	22905		77095	10′
51·0	90713	·7 6	09287	13635	·7 19	86365	22922	·7 12	77078	
52·0	90722		09278	13662		86339	22939		77061	
53·0	90731		09269	13688		86312	22957		77043	
54·0	90741	·8 7	09259	13715	·8 21	86285	22974	·8 14	77026	
55·0	90750		09250	13741		86259	22991		77009	5′
56·0	90759		09241	13768		86232	23009		76991	
57·0	90768	·9 8	09232	13794	·9 24	86206	23026	·9 16	76974	
58·0	90777		09223	13821		86179	23043		76957	
59·0	90787		09213	13847		86153	23061		76939	
60·0	90796		09204	13874		86126	23078		76922	0′

54°
234°

LOGS. OF TRIG. FUNCTIONS

′	Sine	Parts	Cosec.	Tan.	Parts	Cotan.	Secant	Parts	Cosine	
00·0	1.(9) 90796	′	0.(10) 09204	0.(10) 13874	′	1.(9) 86126	0.(10) 23078	′	1.(9) 76922	60′
01·0	90805		09195	13901		86100	23096		76905	
02·0	90814	·1 1	09186	13927	·1 3	86073	23113	·1 2	76887	
03·0	90823		09177	13954		86046	23130		76870	
04·0	90832		09168	13980		86020	23148		76852	
05·0	90842	·2 2	09158	14007	·2 5	85993	23165	·2 4	76835	55′
06·0	90851		09149	14033		85967	23183		76817	
07·0	90860		09140	14060		85940	23200		76800	
08·0	90869	·3 3	09131	14087	·3 8	85913	23218	·3 5	76782	
09·0	90878		09122	14113		85887	23235		76765	
10·0	90887		09113	14140		85860	23253		76748	50′
11·0	90896	·4 4	09104	14166	·4 11	85834	23270	·4 7	76730	
12·0	90906		09095	14193		85807	23288		76712	
13·0	90915		09085	14220		85780	23305		76695	
14·0	90924		09076	14246		85754	23323		76677	
15·0	90933	·5 5	09067	14273	·5 13	85727	23340	·5 9	76660	45′
16·0	90942		09058	14300		85700	23358		76642	
17·0	90951		09049	14326		85674	23375		76625	
18·0	90960	·6 5	09040	14353	·6 16	85647	23393	·6 11	76607	
19·0	90969		09031	14380		85620	23410		76590	
20·0	90978		09022	14406		85594	23428		76572	40′
21·0	90987	·7 6	09013	14433	·7 19	85567	23446	·7 12	76554	
22·0	90996		09004	14460		85540	23463		76537	
23·0	91005		08995	14486		85514	23481		76519	
24·0	91014	·8 7	08986	14513	·8 21	85487	23499	·8 14	76502	
25·0	91024		08977	14540		85460	23516		76484	35′
26·0	91033		08968	14566		85434	23534		76466	
27·0	91042	·9 8	08959	14593	·9 24	85407	23552	·9 16	76449	
28·0	91051		08949	14620		85380	23569		76431	
29·0	91060		08940	14647		85354	23587		76413	
30·0	91069		08931	14673		85327	23605		76395	30′
31·0	91078		08922	14700		85300	23622		76378	
32·0	91087	·1 1	08913	14727	·1 3	85273	23640	·1 2	76360	
33·0	91096		08904	14753		85247	23658		76342	
34·0	91105		08895	14780		85220	23676		76325	
35·0	91114	·2 2	08886	14807	·2 5	85193	23693	·2 4	76307	25′
36·0	91123		08877	14834		85166	23711		76289	
37·0	91132		08869	14860		85140	23729		76271	
38·0	91141	·3 3	08860	14887	·3 8	85113	23747	·3 5	76253	
39·0	91150		08851	14914		85086	23764		76236	
40·0	91158		08842	14941		85059	23782		76218	20′
41·0	91167	·4 4	08833	14968	·4 11	85033	23800	·4 7	76200	
42·0	91176		08824	14994		85006	23818		76182	
43·0	91185		08815	15021		84979	23836		76164	
44·0	91194	·5 4	08806	15048		84952	23854		76146	
45·0	91203		08797	15075	·5 13	84925	23871	·5 9	76129	15′
46·0	91212		08788	15101		84899	23889		76111	
47·0	91221	·6 5	08779	15128		84872	23907		76093	
48·0	91230		08770	15155	·6 16	84845	23925	·6 11	76075	
49·0	91239		08761	15182		84818	23943		76057	
50·0	91248	·7 6	08752	15209	·7 19	84791	23961		76039	10′
51·0	91257		08743	15236		84764	23979	·7 13	76021	
52·0	91266		08735	15262		84738	23997		76003	
53·0	91274		08726	15289		84711	24015		75985	
54·0	91283	·8 7	08717	15316	·8 21	84684	24033	·8 14	75967	
55·0	91292		08708	15343		84657	24051		75949	5′
56·0	91301		08699	15370		84630	24069		75931	
57·0	91310	·9 8	08690	15397	·9 24	84603	24087	·9 16	75913	
58·0	91319		08681	15424		84576	24105		75895	
59·0	91328		08672	15450		84550	24123		75877	
60·0	91337		08664	15477		84523	24141		75859	0′

55°

235°

LOGS. OF TRIG. FUNCTIONS

′	Sine	*Parts*		Cosec.	Tan.	*Parts*		Cotan.	Secant	*Parts*		Cosine	
00·0	1̄.(9) 91337	′		0.(10) 08664	0.(10) 15477	′		1̄.(9) 84523	0.(10) 24141	′		1̄.(9) 75859	60′
01·0	91345			08655	15504			84496	24159			75841	
02·0	91354	·1	1	08646	15531	·1	3	84469	24177	·1	2	75823	
03·0	91363			08637	15558			84442	24195			75805	
04·0	91372			08628	15585			84415	24213			75787	
05·0	91381	·2	2	08619	15612	·2	5	84388	24231	·2	4	75769	55′
06·0	91389			08611	15639			84361	24249			75751	
07·0	91398			08602	15666			84334	24267			75733	
08·0	91407	·3	3	08593	15693	·3	8	84307	24286	·3	5	75714	
09·0	91416			08584	15720			84281	24304			75696	
10·0	91425			08575	15747			84254	24322			75678	50′
11·0	91433	·4	3	08567	15773	·4	11	84227	24340	·4	7	75660	
12·0	91442			08558	15800			84200	24358			75642	
13·0	91451			08549	15827			84173	24376			75624	
14·0	91460			08540	15854			84146	24395			75605	
15·0	91469	·5	4	08532	15881	·5	14	84119	24413	·5	9	75587	45′
16·0	91477			08523	15908			84092	24431			75569	
17·0	91486			08514	15935			84065	24449			75551	
18·0	91495	·6	5	08505	15962	·6	16	84038	24467	·6	11	75533	
19·0	91504			08497	15989			84011	24486			75514	
20·0	91512			08488	16016			83984	24504			75496	40′
21·0	91521	·7	6	08479	16043	·7	19	83957	24522	·7	13	75478	
22·0	91530			08470	16070			83930	24541			75460	
23·0	91539			08462	16097			83903	24559			75441	
24·0	91547	·8	7	08453	16124	·8	22	83876	24577	·8	15	75423	
25·0	91556			08444	16151			83849	24595			75405	35′
26·0	91565			08435	16178			83822	24614			75386	
27·0	91573	·9	8	08427	16205	·9	24	83795	24632	·9	16	75368	
28·0	91582			08418	16233			83768	24651			75350	
29·0	91591			08409	16260			83741	24669			75331	
30·0	91599			08401	16287			83713	24687			75313	30′
31·0	91608			08392	16314			83686	24706			75294	
32·0	91617	·1	1	08383	16341	·1	3	83659	24724	·1	2	75276	
33·0	91625			08375	16368			83632	24742			75258	
34·0	91634			08366	16395			83605	24761			75239	
35·0	91643	·2	2	08357	16422	·2	5	83578	24779	·2	4	75221	25′
36·0	91651			08349	16449			83551	24798			75202	
37·0	91660			08340	16476			83524	24816			75184	
38·0	91669	·3	3	08331	16503	·3	8	83497	24835	·3	6	75165	
39·0	91677			08323	16530			83470	24853			75147	
40·0	91686			08314	16558			83443	24872			75128	20′
41·0	91695	·4	3	08305	16585	·4	11	83415	24890	·4	7	75110	
42·0	91703			08297	16612			83388	24909			75091	
43·0	91712			08288	16639			83361	24927			75073	
44·0	91720			08280	16666			83334	24946			75054	
45·0	91729	·5	4	08271	16693	·5	14	83307	24964	·5	9	75036	15′
46·0	91738			08262	16720			83280	24983			75017	
47·0	91746			08254	16748			83253	25001			74999	
48·0	91755	·6	5	08245	16775	·6	16	83225	25020	·6	11	74980	
49·0	91763			08237	16802			83198	25039			74962	
50·0	91772			08228	16829			83171	25057			74943	10′
51·0	91781	·7	6	08220	16856	·7	19	83144	25076	·7	13	74924	
52·0	91789			08211	16884			83117	25094			74906	
53·0	91798			08202	16911			83089	25113			74887	
54·0	91806	·8	7	08194	16938	·8	22	83062	25132	·8	15	74868	
55·0	91815			08185	16965			83035	25150			74850	5′
56·0	91823			08177	16992			83008	25169			74831	
57·0	91832	·9	8	08168	17020	·9	24	82981	25188	·9	17	74812	
58·0	91840			08160	17047			82953	25206			74794	
59·0	91849			08151	17074			82926	25225			74775	
60·0	91857			08143	17101			82899	25244			74756	0′

124°
304°

56°
236°

LOGS. OF TRIG. FUNCTIONS

′	Sine	Parts	Cosec.	Tan.	Parts	Cotan.	Secant	Parts	Cosine	
00·0	1̄.(9) 91857		0.(10) 08143	0.(10) 17101		1̄.(9) 82899	0.(10) 25244		1̄.(9) 74756	60′
01·0	91866		08134	17129		82872	25263		74737	
02·0	91875	·1 1	08126	17156	·1 3	82844	25281	·1 2	74719	
03·0	91883		08117	17183		82817	25300		74700	
04·0	91892		08109	17210		82790	25319		74681	
05·0	91900	·2 2	08100	17238	·2 5	82762	25338	·2 4	74662	55′
06·0	91909		08092	17265		82735	25356		74644	
07·0	91917		08083	17292		82708	25375		74625	
08·0	91925	·3 3	08075	17320	·3 8	82681	25394	·3 6	74606	
09·0	91934		08066	17347		82653	25413		74587	
10·0	91942		08058	17374		82626	25432		74568	50′
11·0	91951	·4 3	08049	17401	·4 11	82599	25451	·4 8	74549	
12·0	91959		08041	17429		82571	25469		74531	
13·0	91968		08032	17456		82544	25488		74512	
14·0	91976	·5 4	08024	17483	·5 14	82517	25507	·5 9	74493	
15·0	91985		08015	17511		82489	25526		74474	45′
16·0	91993		08007	17538		82462	25545		74455	
17·0	92002		07999	17566		82435	25564		74436	
18·0	92010	·6 5	07990	17593	·6 16	82407	25583	·6 11	74417	
19·0	92018		07982	17620		82380	25602		74398	
20·0	92027		07973	17648		82352	25621		74379	40′
21·0	92035	·7 6	07965	17675	·7 19	82325	25640	·7 13	74360	
22·0	92044		07956	17702		82298	25659		74341	
23·0	92052		07948	17730		82270	25678		74322	
24·0	92060	·8 7	07940	17757	·8 22	82243	25697	·8 15	74303	
25·0	92069		07931	17785		82215	25716		74284	35′
26·0	92077		07923	17812		82188	25735		74265	
27·0	92086	·9 8	07914	17839	·9 25	82161	25754	·9 17	74246	
28·0	92094		07906	17867		82133	25773		74227	
29·0	92102		07898	17894		82106	25792		74208	
30·0	92111		07889	17922		82078	25811		74189	30′
31·0	92119		07881	17949		82051	25830		74170	
32·0	92127	·1 1	07873	17977	·1 3	82023	25849	·1 2	74151	
33·0	92136		07864	18004		81996	25868		74132	
34·0	92144		07856	18032		81968	25888		74113	
35·0	92152	·2 2	07848	18059	·2 6	81941	25907	·2 4	74093	25′
36·0	92161		07839	18087		81914	25926		74074	
37·0	92169		07831	18114		81886	25945		74055	
38·0	92177	·3 2	07823	18142	·3 8	81859	25964	·3 6	74036	
39·0	92186		07814	18169		81831	25983		74017	
40·0	92194		07806	18197		81804	26003		73998	20′
41·0	92202	·4 3	07798	18224	·4 11	81776	26022	·4 8	73978	
42·0	92211		07789	18252		81748	26041		73959	
43·0	92219		07781	18279		81721	26060		73940	
44·0	92227	·5 4	07773	18307	·5 14	81693	26079	·5 10	73921	
45·0	92236		07765	18334		81666	26099		73901	15′
46·0	92244		07756	18362		81638	26118		73882	
47·0	92252		07748	18389		81611	26137		73863	
48·0	92260	·6 5	07740	18417	·6 17	81583	26157	·6 12	73843	
49·0	92269		07731	18445		81556	26176		73824	
50·0	92277		07723	18472		81528	26195		73805	10′
51·0	92285	·7 6	07715	18500	·7 19	81500	26215	·7 13	73786	
52·0	92293		07707	18527		81473	26234		73766	
53·0	92302		07698	18555		81445	26253		73747	
54·0	92310	·8 7	07690	18582	·8 22	81418	26273	·8 15	73727	
55·0	92318		07682	18610		81390	26292		73708	5′
56·0	92326		07674	18638		81362	26311		73689	
57·0	92335	·9 7	07666	18665	·9 25	81335	26331	·9 17	73669	
58·0	92343		07657	18693		81307	26350		73650	
59·0	92351		07649	18721		81279	26370		73630	
60·0	92359		07641	18748		81252	26389		73611	0′

123°
303°

LOGS. OF TRIG. FUNCTIONS

57°
237°

′	Sine	Parts	Cosec.	Tan.	Parts	Cotan.	Secant	Parts	Cosine	
00·0	1̄.(9) 92359	′	0.(10) 07641	0.(10) 18748	′	1̄.(9) 81252	0.(10) 26389	′	1̄.(9) 73611	60′
01·0	92367		07633	18776		81224	26409		73591	
02·0	92376	·1 1	07625	18804	·1 3	81196	26428	·1 2	73572	
03·0	92384		07616	18831		81169	26448		73553	
04·0	92392		07608	18859		81141	26467		73533	
05·0	92400	·2 2	07600	18887	·2 6	81113	26487	·2 4	73514	55′
06·0	92408		07592	18914		81086	26506		73494	
07·0	92416		07584	18942		81058	26526		73474	
08·0	92425	·3 2	07575	18970	·3 8	81030	26545	·3 6	73455	
09·0	92433		07567	18998		81003	26565		73435	
10·0	92441		07559	19025		80975	26584		73416	50′
11·0	92449	·4 3	07551	19053	·4 11	80947	26604	·4 8	73396	
12·0	92457		07543	19081		80919	26624		73377	
13·0	92465		07535	19108		80892	26643		73357	
14·0	92474		07527	19136		80864	26663		73337	
15·0	92482	·5 4	07518	19164	·5 14	80836	26682	·5 10	73318	45′
16·0	92490		07510	19192		80808	26702		73298	
17·0	92498		07502	19220		80781	26722		73278	
18·0	92506	·6 5	07494	19247	·6 17	80753	26741	·6 12	73259	
19·0	92514		07486	19275		80725	26761		73239	
20·0	92522		07478	19303		80697	26781		73219	40′
21·0	92530	·7 6	07470	19331	·7 19	80669	26800	·7 14	73200	
22·0	92538		07462	19359		80642	26820		73180	
23·0	92547		07454	19386		80614	26840		73160	
24·0	92555	·8 7	07446	19414	·8 22	80586	26860	·8 16	73140	
25·0	92563		07437	19442		80558	26879		73121	35′
26·0	92571		07429	19470		80530	26899		73101	
27·0	92579	·9 7	07421	19498	·9 25	80502	26919	·9 18	73081	
28·0	92587		07413	19526		80475	26939		73061	
29·0	92595		07405	19553		80447	26959		73042	
30·0	92603		07397	19581		80419	26978		73022	30′
31·0	92611		07389	19609		80391	26998		73002	
32·0	92619	·1 1	07381	19637	·1 3	80363	27018	·1 2	72982	
33·0	92627		07373	19665		80335	27038		72962	
34·0	92635		07365	19693		80307	27058		72942	
35·0	92643	·2 2	07357	19721	·2 6	80279	27078	·2 4	72922	25′
36·0	92651		07349	19749		80251	27098		72902	
37·0	92659		07341	19777		80223	27118		72883	
38·0	92667	·3 2	07333	19805	·3 8	80196	27137	·3 6	72863	
39·0	92675		07325	19833		80168	27157		72843	
40·0	92683		07317	19860		80140	27177		72823	20′
41·0	92691	·4 3	07309	19888	·4 11	80112	27197	·4 8	72803	
42·0	92699		07301	19916		80084	27217		72783	
43·0	92707		07293	19944		80056	27237		72763	
44·0	92715		07285	19972		80028	27257		72743	
45·0	92723	·5 4	07276	20000	·5 14	80000	27277	·5 10	72723	15′
46·0	92731		07269	20028		79972	27297		72703	
47·0	92739		07261	20056		79944	27317		72683	
48·0	92747	·6 5	07253	20084	·6 17	79916	27337	·6 12	72663	
49·0	92755		07245	20112		79888	27357		72643	
50·0	92763		07237	20140		79860	27378		72623	10′
51·0	92771	·7 6	07229	20168	·7 20	79832	27398	·7 14	72602	
52·0	92779		07221	20196		79804	27418		72582	
53·0	92787		07213	20225		79776	27438		72562	
54·0	92795	·8 6	07205	20253	·8 22	79748	27458	·8 16	72542	
55·0	92803		07198	20281		79719	27478		72522	5′
56·0	92810		07190	20309		79691	27498		72502	
57·0	92818	·9 7	07182	20337	·9 25	79663	27518	·9 18	72482	
58·0	92826		07174	20365		79635	27539		72461	
59·0	92834		07166	20393		79607	27559		72441	
60·0	92842		07158	20421		79579	27579		72421	0′

122°
302°

LOGS. OF TRIG. FUNCTIONS

58°
238°

′	Sine	Parts		Cosec.	Tan.	Parts		Cotan.	Secant	Parts		Cosine	
00·0	1̄.(9) 92842		′	0.(10) 07158	0.(10) 20421		′	1̄.(9) 79579	0.(10) 27579		′	1̄.(9) 72421	60′
01·0	92850			07150	20449			79551	27599			72401	
02·0	92858	·1	1	07142	20477	·1	3	79523	27620	·1	2	72381	
03·0	92866			07134	20505			79495	27640			72360	
04·0	92874			07126	20534			79466	27660			72340	
05·0	92882	·2	2	07119	20562	·2	6	79438	27680	·2	4	72320	55′
06·0	92889			07111	20590			79410	27701			72299	
07·0	92897			07103	20618			79382	27721			72279	
08·0	92905	·3	2	07095	20646	·3	8	79354	27741	·3	6	72259	
09·0	92913			07087	20674			79326	27762			72239	
10·0	92921			07079	20703			79297	27782			72218	50′
11·0	92929	·4	3	07071	20731	·4	11	79269	27802	·4	8	72198	
12·0	92936			07064	20759			79241	27823			72177	
13·0	92944			07056	20787			79213	27843			72157	
14·0	92952			07048	20815			79185	27863			72137	
15·0	92960	·5	4	07040	20844	·5	14	79156	27884	·5	10	72116	45′
16·0	92968			07032	20872			79128	27904			72096	
17·0	92976			07025	20900			79100	27925			72075	
18·0	92983	·6	5	07017	20928	·6	17	79072	27945	·6	12	72055	
19·0	92991			07009	20957			79043	27966			72035	
20·0	92999			07001	20985			79015	27986			72014	40′
21·0	93007	·7	5	06993	21013	·7	20	78987	28007	·7	14	71994	
22·0	93015			06986	21042			78959	28027			71973	
23·0	93022			06978	21070			78930	28040			71953	
24·0	93030	·8	6	06970	21098	·8	23	78902	28068	·8	16	71932	
25·0	93038			06962	21126			78874	28089			71911	35′
26·0	93046			06954	21155			78845	28109			71891	
27·0	93053	·9	7	06947	21183	·9	25	78817	28130	·9	18	71870	
28·0	93061			06939	21211			78789	28150			71850	
29·0	93069			06931	21240			78760	28171			71829	
30·0	93077			06923	21268			78732	28192			71809	30′
31·0	93084			06916	21296			78704	28212			71788	
32·0	93092	·1	1	06908	21325	·1	3	78675	28233	·1	2	71767	
33·0	93100			06900	21353			78647	28253			71747	
34·0	93108			06893	21382			78618	28274			71726	
35·0	93115	·2	2	06885	21410	·2	6	78590	28295	·2	4	71705	25′
36·0	93123			06877	21438			78562	28315			71685	
37·0	93131			06869	21467			78533	28336			71664	
38·0	93138	·3	2	06862	21495	·3	9	78505	28357	·3	6	71643	
39·0	93146			06854	21524			78476	28378			71622	
40·0	93154			06846	21552			78448	28398			71602	20′
41·0	93161	·4	3	06839	21581	·4	11	78420	28419	·4	8	71581	
42·0	93169			06831	21609			78391	28440			71560	
43·0	93177			06823	21637			78363	28461			71539	
44·0	93185			06816	21666			78334	28481			71519	
45·0	93192	·5	4	06808	21694	·5	14	78306	28502	·5	10	71498	15′
46·0	93200			06800	21723			78277	28523			71477	
47·0	93208			06793	21751			78249	28544			71456	
48·0	93215	·6	5	06785	21780	·6	17	78220	28565	·6	12	71435	
49·0	93223			06777	21808			78192	28586			71414	
50·0	93230			06770	21837			78163	28607			71394	10′
51·0	93238	·7	5	06762	21865	·7	20	78135	28627	·7	15	71373	
52·0	93246			06754	21894			78106	28648			71352	
53·0	93253			06747	21923			78078	28669			71331	
54·0	93261	·8	6	06739	21951	·8	23	78049	28690	·8	17	71310	
55·0	93269			06732	21980			78020	28711			71289	5′
56·0	93276			06724	22008			77992	28732			71268	
57·0	93284	·9	7	06716	22037	·9	26	77963	28753	·9	19	71247	
58·0	93291			06709	22065			77935	28774			71226	
59·0	93299			06701	22094			77906	28795			71205	
60·0	93307			06693	22123			77877	28816			71184	0′

LOGS. OF TRIG. FUNCTIONS

59°
239°

′	Sine	Parts	Cosec.	Tan.	Parts	Cotan.	Secant	Parts	Cosine	
00·0	1̄.(9) 93307	′	0.(10) 06693	0.(10) 22123	′	1̄.(9) 77877	0.(10) 28816	′	1̄.(9) 71184	60′
01·0	93314		06686	22151		77849	28837		71163	
02·0	93322	·1 1	06678	22180	·1 3	77820	28858	·1 2	71142	
03·0	93329		06671	22209		77792	28879		71121	
04·0	93337		06663	22237		77763	28900		71100	
05·0	93345	·2 2	06656	22266	·2 6	77734	28921	·2 4	71079	55′
06·0	93352		06648	22295		77706	28943		71058	
07·0	93360		06640	22323		77677	28964		71036	
08·0	93367	·3 2	06633	22352	·3 9	77648	28985	·3 6	71015	
09·0	93375		06625	22381		77620	29006		70994	
10·0	93382		06618	22409		77591	29027		70973	50′
11·0	93390	·4 3	06610	22438	·4 11	77562	29048	·4 8	70952	
12·0	93397		06603	22467		77533	29069		70931	
13·0	93405		06595	22495		77505	29091		70909	
14·0	93412	·5 4	06588	22524	·5 14	77476	29112	·5 11	70888	
15·0	93420		06580	22553		77447	29133		70867	45′
16·0	93427		06573	22582		77418	29154		70846	
17·0	93435		06565	22610		77390	29176		70825	
18·0	93442	·6 5	06558	22639	·6 17	77361	29197	·6 13	70803	
19·0	93450		06550	22668		77332	29218		70782	
20·0	93457	·7 5	06543	22697	·7 20	77303	29239	·7 15	70761	40′
21·0	93465		06535	22726		77275	29261		70739	
22·0	93472		06528	22754		77246	29282		70718	
23·0	93480		06520	22783		77217	29303		70697	
24·0	93487	·8 6	06513	22812	·8 23	77188	29325	·8 17	70675	
25·0	93495		06505	22841		77159	29346		70654	35′
26·0	93502		06498	22870		77130	29367		70633	
27·0	93510	·9 7	06490	22899	·9 26	77102	29389	·9 19	70611	
28·0	93517		06483	22927		77073	29410		70590	
29·0	93524		06475	22956		77044	29432		70568	
30·0	93522		06468	22985		77015	29453		70547	30′
31·0	93540		06461	23014		76986	29475		70525	
32·0	93547	·1 1	06453	23043	·1 3	76957	29496	·1 2	70504	
33·0	93554		06446	23072		76928	29518		70483	
34·0	93562		06438	23101		76899	29539		70461	
35·0	93569	·2 1	06431	23130	·2 6	76870	29561	·2 4	70440	25′
36·0	93577		06423	23159		76841	29582		70418	
37·0	93584		06416	23188		76812	29604		70396	
38·0	93591	·3 2	06409	23217	·3 9	76783	29625	·3 7	70375	
39·0	93599		06401	23246		76755	29647		70353	
40·0	93606		06394	23275		76726	29668		70332	20′
41·0	93614	·4 3	06386	23304	·4 12	76697	29690	·4 9	70310	
42·0	93621		06379	23333		76668	29712		70289	
43·0	93628		06372	23362		76639	29733		70267	
44·0	93636		06364	23391		76610	29755		70245	
45·0	93643	·5 4	06357	23420	·5 15	76581	29776	·5 11	70224	15′
46·0	93651		06350	23449		76551	29798		70202	
47·0	93658		06342	23478		76522	29820		70180	
48·0	93665	·6 4	06335	23507	·6 17	76493	29842	·6 13	70159	
49·0	93673		06328	23536		76464	29863		70137	
50·0	93680		06320	23565		76435	29885		70115	10′
51·0	93687	·7 5	06313	23594	·7 20	76406	29907	·7 15	70093	
52·0	93695		06305	23623		76377	29928		70072	
53·0	93702		06298	23652		76348	29950		70050	
54·0	93709	·8 6	06291	23681	·8 23	76319	29972	·8 17	70028	
55·0	93717		06284	23710		76290	29994		70006	5′
56·0	93724		06276	23739		76261	30016		69984	
57·0	93731	·9 7	06269	23769	·9 26	76231	30037	·9 20	69963	
58·0	93739		06262	23798		76202	30059		69941	
59·0	93746		06254	23827		76173	30081		69919	
60·0	93753		06247	23856		76144	30103		69897	0′

120°
300°

60°
240°

LOGS. OF TRIG. FUNCTIONS

′	Sine	Parts		Cosec.	Tan.	Parts		Cotan.	Secant	Parts		Cosine	
00·0	$\overline{1}$.(9) 93753			0.(10) 06247	0.(10) 23856			$\overline{1}$.(9) 76144	0.(10) 30103			$\overline{1}$.(9) 69897	60′
01·0	93760			06240	23885			76115	30125			69875	
02·0	93768	·1	1	06232	23914	·1	3	76086	30147	·1	2	69853	
03·0	93775			06225	23944			76056	30169			69831	
04·0	93782			06218	23973			76027	30191			69809	
05·0	93790	·2	1	06211	24002	·2	6	75998	30213	·2	4	69787	55′
06·0	93797			06203	24031			75969	30235			69765	
07·0	93804			06196	24061			75940	30257			69744	
08·0	93811	·3	2	06189	24090	·3	9	75910	30279	·3	7	69722	
09·0	93819			06182	24119			75881	30301			69700	
10·0	93826			06174	24148			75852	30323			69678	50′
11·0	93833	·4	3	06167	24178	·4	12	75822	30345	·4	9	69655	
12·0	93840			06160	24207			75793	30367			69633	
13·0	93848			06153	24236			75764	30389			69611	
14·0	93855			06145	24266			75735	30411			69589	
15·0	93862	·5	4	06138	24295	·5	15	75705	30433	·5	11	69567	45′
16·0	93869			06131	24324			75676	30455			69545	
17·0	93876			06124	24354			75647	30477			69523	
18·0	93884	·6	4	06116	24383	·6	18	75617	30499	·6	13	69501	
19·0	93891			06109	24412			75588	30521			69479	
20·0	93898			06102	24442			75559	30544			69456	40′
21·0	93905	·7	5	06095	24471	·7	21	75529	30566	·7	15	69434	
22·0	93912			06088	24500			75500	30588			69412	
23·0	93920			06081	24530			75470	30610			69390	
24·0	93927	·8	6	06073	24559	·8	23	75441	30632	·8	18	69368	
25·0	93934			06066	24589			75412	30655			69345	35′
26·0	93941			06059	24618			75382	30677			69323	
27·0	93948	·9	7	06052	24647	·9	26	75353	30699	·9	20	69301	
28·0	93955			06045	24677			75323	30722			69279	
29·0	93963			06038	24706			75294	30744			69256	
30·0	93970			06030	24736			75264	30766			69234	30′
31·0	93977			06023	24765			75235	30789			69212	
32·0	93984	·1	1	06016	24795	·1	3	75205	30811	·1	2	69189	
33·0	93991			06009	24824			75176	30833			69167	
34·0	93998			06002	24854			75146	30856			69144	
35·0	94005	·2	1	05995	24883	·2	6	75117	30878	·2	5	69122	25′
36·0	94013			05988	24913			75087	30900			69100	
37·0	94020			05980	24942			75058	30923			69077	
38·0	94027	·3	2	05973	24972	·3	9	75028	30945	·3	7	69055	
39·0	94034			05966	25002			74999	30968			69032	
40·0	94041			05959	25031			74969	30990			69010	20′
41·0	94048	·4	3	05952	25061	·4	12	74939	31013	·4	9	68987	
42·0	94055			05945	25090			74910	31035			68965	
43·0	94062			05938	25120			74880	31058			68942	
44·0	94069			05931	25150			74851	31080			68920	
45·0	94076	·5	4	05924	25179	·5	15	74821	31103	·5	11	68897	15′
46·0	94083			05917	25209			74791	31125			68875	
47·0	94091			05910	25238			74762	31148			68852	
48·0	94098	·6	4	05903	25268	·6	18	74732	31171	·6	14	68830	
49·0	94105			05895	25298			74702	31193			68807	
50·0	94112	·7	5	05888	25327	·7	21	74673	31216	·7	16	68784	10′
51·0	94119			05881	25357			74643	31238			68762	
52·0	94126			05874	25387			74613	31261			68739	
53·0	94133			05867	25417			74584	31284			68716	
54·0	94140	·8	6	05860	25446	·8	24	74554	31306	·8	18	68694	
55·0	94147			05853	25476			74524	31329			68671	5′
56·0	94154			05846	25506			74494	31352			68648	
57·0	94161	·9	6	05839	25536	·9	27	74465	31375	·9	20	68625	
58·0	94168			05832	25565			74435	31397			68603	
59·0	94175			05825	25595			74405	31420			68580	
60·0	94182			05818	25625			74375	31443			68557	0′

LOGS. OF TRIG. FUNCTIONS

′	Sine	Parts	Cosec.	Tan.	Parts	Cotan.	Secant	Parts	Cosine	
00·0	1.(9) 94182		0.(10) 05818	0.(10) 25625		1.(9) 74375	0.(10) 31443		1.(9) 68557	60′
01·0	94189		05811	25655		74345	31466		68534	
02·0	94196	·1 1	05804	25684	·1 3	74316	31489	·1 2	68512	
03·0	94203		05797	25714		74286	31511		68489	
04·0	94210		05790	25744		74256	31534		68466	
05·0	94217	·2 1	05783	25774	·2 6	74226	31557	·2 5	68443	55′
06·0	94224		05776	25804		74196	31580		68420	
07·0	94231		05769	25834		74166	31603		68397	
08·0	94238	·3 2	05762	25864	·3 9	74137	31626	·3 7	68374	
09·0	94245		05755	25893		74107	31649		68351	
10·0	94252		05748	25923		74077	31672		68328	50′
11·0	94259	·4 3	05741	25953	·4 12	74047	31695	·4 9	68306	
12·0	94266		05734	25983		74017	31718		68283	
13·0	94273		05727	26013		73987	31741		68260	
14·0	94280		05721	26043		73957	31764		68237	
15·0	94286	·5 3	05714	26073	·5 15	73927	31787	·5 12	68214	45′
16·0	94293		05707	26103		73897	31810		68191	
17·0	94300		05700	26133		73867	31833		68167	
18·0	94307	·6 4	05693	26163	·6 18	73837	31856	·6 14	68144	
19·0	94314		05686	26193		73807	31879		68121	
20·0	94321		05679	26223		73777	31902		68098	40′
21·0	94328	·7 5	05672	26253	·7 21	73747	31925	·7 16	68075	
22·0	94335		05665	26283		73717	31948		68052	
23·0	94342		05658	26313		73687	31971		68029	
24·0	94349	·8 6	05651	26343	·8 24	73657	31994	·8 18	68006	
25·0	94356		05645	26373		73627	32018		67982	35′
26·0	94362		05638	26403		73597	32041		67959	
27·0	94369	·9 6	05631	26433	·9 27	73567	32064	·9 21	67936	
28·0	94376		05624	26463		73537	32087		67913	
29·0	94383		05617	26493		73507	32111		67890	
30·0	94390		05610	26524		73476	32134		67866	30′
31·0	94397		05603	26554		73446	32157		67843	
32·0	94404	·1 1	05596	26584	·1 3	73416	32180	·1 2	67820	
33·0	94410		05590	26614		73386	32204		67796	
34·0	94417		05583	26644		73356	32227		67773	
35·0	94424	·2 1	05576	26674	·2 6	73326	32250	·2 5	67750	25′
36·0	94431		05569	26705		73296	32274		67726	
37·0	94438		05562	26735		73265	32297		67703	
38·0	94445	·3 2	05555	26765	·3 9	73235	32320	·3 7	67680	
39·0	94451		05549	26795		73205	32344		67656	
40·0	94458		05542	26825		73175	32367		67633	20′
41·0	94465	·4 3	05535	26856	·4 12	73144	32391	·4 9	67609	
42·0	94472		05528	26886		73114	32414		67586	
43·0	94479		05521	26916		73084	32438		67562	
44·0	94485		05515	26947		73054	32461		67539	
45·0	94492	·5 3	05508	26977	·5 15	73023	32485	·5 12	67516	15′
46·0	94499		05501	27007		72993	32508		67492	
47·0	94506		05494	27037		72963	32532		67468	
48·0	94513	·6 4	05488	27068	·6 18	72932	32555	·6 14	67445	
49·0	94519		05481	27098		72902	32579		67421	
50·0	94526		05474	27128		72872	32602		67398	10′
51·0	94533	·7 5	05467	27159	·7 21	72841	32626	·7 16	67374	
52·0	94540		05460	27189		72811	32650		67351	
53·0	94546		05454	27220		72781	32673		67327	
54·0	94553	·8 5	05447	27250	·8 24	72750	32697	·8 19	67303	
55·0	94560		05440	27290		72720	32721		67280	5′
56·0	94567		05433	27311		72689	32744		67256	
57·0	94573	·9 6	05427	27341	·9 27	72659	32768	·9 21	67232	
58·0	94580		05420	27372		72628	32792		67208	
59·0	94587		05413	27402		72598	32815		67185	
60·0	94593		05407	27433		72567	32839		67161	0′

62°
242°

LOGS. OF TRIG. FUNCTIONS

′	Sine	Diff.	Cosec.	Tan.	Diff.	Cotan.	Secant	Diff.	Cosine	
00·0	1̄.(9) 94593		0.(10) 05407	0.(10) 27433		1̄.(9) 72567	0.(10) 32839		1̄.(9) 67161	60′
01·0	94600		05400	27463		72537	32863		67137	
02·0	94607	·1 1	05393	27494	·1 3	72507	32887	·1 2	67113	
03·0	94614		05386	27524		72476	32910		67090	
04·0	94620		05380	27555		72445	32934		67066	
05·0	94627	·2 1	05373	27585	·2 6	72415	32958	·2 5	67042	55′
06·0	94634		05366	27616		72384	32982		67018	
07·0	94640		05360	27646		72354	33006		66994	
08·0	94647	·3 2	05353	27677	·3 9	72323	33030	·3 7	66970	
09·0	94654		05346	27707		72293	33054		66946	
10·0	94660		05340	27738		72262	33078		66923	50′
11·0	94667	·4 3	05333	27769	·4 12	72232	33101	·4 10	66899	
12·0	94674		05326	27799		72201	33125		66875	
13·0	94680		05320	27830		72170	33149		66851	
14·0	94687	·5 3	05313	27860	·5 15	72140	33173	·5 12	66827	
15·0	94694		05306	27891		72109	33197		66803	45′
16·0	94700		05300	27922		72078	33221		66779	
17·0	94707	·6 4	05293	27952	·6 18	72048	33245	·6 14	66755	
18·0	94714		05286	27983		72017	33270		66731	
19·0	94720		05280	28014		71986	33294		66707	
20·0	94727	·7 5	05273	28045	·7 21	71956	33318	·7 17	66682	40′
21·0	94734		05267	28075		71925	33342		66658	
22·0	94740		05260	28106		71894	33366		66634	
23·0	94747	·8 5	05253	28137	·8 25	71863	33390	·8 19	66610	
24·0	94753		05247	28168		71833	33414		66586	
25·0	94760		05240	28198		71802	33438		66562	35′
26·0	94767		05234	28229		71771	33463		66538	
27·0	94773	·9 6	05227	28260	·9 28	71740	33487	·9 22	66513	
28·0	94780		05220	28291		71709	33511		66489	
29·0	94786		05214	28322		71679	33535		66465	
30·0	94793		05207	28352		71648	33559		66441	30′
31·0	94800		05201	28383		71617	33584		66416	
32·0	94806	·1 1	05194	28414	·1 3	71586	33608	·1 2	66392	
33·0	94813		05187	28445		71555	33632		66368	
34·0	94819		05181	28476		71524	33657		66343	
35·0	94826	·2 1	05174	28507	·2 6	71493	33681	·2 5	66319	25′
36·0	94832		05168	28538		71462	33705		66295	
37·0	94839		05161	28569		71431	33730		66270	
38·0	94845	·3 2	05155	28600	·3 9	71401	33754	·3 7	66246	
39·0	94852		05148	28630		71370	33779		66221	
40·0	94858		05142	28661		71339	33803		66197	20′
41·0	94865	·4 3	05135	28692	·4 12	71308	33827	·4 10	66173	
42·0	94872		05129	28723		71277	33852		66148	
43·0	94878		05122	28754		71246	33876		66124	
44·0	94885		05116	28785		71215	33901		66099	
45·0	94891	·5 3	05109	28816	·5 16	71184	33925	·5 12	66075	15′
46·0	94898		05103	28848		71153	33950		66050	
47·0	94904		05096	28879		71122	33975		66026	
48·0	94911	·6 4	05090	28910	·6 19	71090	33999	·6 15	66001	
49·0	94917		05083	28941		71059	34024		65976	
50·0	94924		05077	28972		71028	34048		65952	10′
51·0	94930	·7 5	05070	29003	·7 22	70997	34073	·7 17	65927	
52·0	94936		05064	29034		70966	34098		65903	
53·0	94943		05057	29065		70935	34122		65878	
54·0	94949	·8 5	05051	29096	·8 25	70904	34147	·8 20	65853	
55·0	94956		05044	29127		70873	34172		65828	5′
56·0	94962		05038	29159		70841	34196		65804	
57·0	94969	·9 6	05031	29190	·9 28	70810	34221	·9 22	65779	
58·0	94975		05025	29221		70779	34246		65754	
59·0	94982		05018	29252		70748	34271		65730	
60·0	94988		05012	29283		70717	34295		65705	0′

117°
297°

63°
243°

LOGS. OF TRIG. FUNCTIONS

′	Sine	Parts		Cosec.	Tan.	Parts		Cotan.	Secant	Parts		Cosine	
00·0	1̄.(9) 94988	′		0.(10) 05012	0.(10) 29283	′		1̄.(9) 70717	0.(10) 34295	′		1̄.(9) 65705	60′
01·0	94995			05006	29315			70685	34320			65680	
02·0	95001	·1	1	04999	29346	·1	3	70654	34345	·1	2	65655	
03·0	95007			04993	29377			70623	34370			65630	
04·0	95014			04986	29408			70592	34395			65605	
05·0	95020	·2	1	04980	29440	·2	6	70560	34420	·2	5	65581	55′
06·0	95027			04973	29471			70529	34444			65556	
07·0	95033			04967	29502			70498	34469			65531	
08·0	95039	·3	2	04961	29534	·3	9	70466	34494	·3	7	65506	
09·0	95046			04954	29565			70435	34519			65481	
10·0	95052			04948	29596			70404	34544			65456	50′
11·0	95059	·4	3	04941	29628	·4	13	70372	34569	·4	10	65431	
12·0	95065			04935	29659			70341	34594			65406	
13·0	95071			04929	29691			70310	34619			65381	
14·0	95078			04922	29722			70278	34644			65356	
15·0	95084	·5	3	04916	29753	·5	16	70247	34669	·5	12	65331	45′
16·0	95091			04910	29785			70215	34694			65306	
17·0	95097			04903	29816			70184	34719			65281	
18·0	95103	·6	4	04897	29848	·6	19	70152	34745	·6	15	65256	
19·0	95110			04890	29879			70121	34770			65230	
20·0	95116			04884	29911			70089	34795			65205	40′
21·0	95122	·7	4	04878	29942	·7	22	70058	34820	·7	17	65180	
22·0	95129			04871	29974			70026	34845			65155	
23·0	95135			04865	30005			69995	34870			65130	
24·0	95141	·8	5	04859	30037	·8	25	69963	34896	·8	20	65104	
25·0	95148			04852	30068			69932	34921			65079	35′
26·0	95154			04846	30100			69900	34946			65054	
27·0	95160	·9	6	04840	30132	·9	28	69869	34971	·9	22	65029	
28·0	95167			04834	30163			69837	34997			65003	
29·0	95173			04827	30195			69805	35022			64978	
30·0	95179			04821	30226			69774	35047			64953	30′
31·0	95185			04815	30258			69742	35073			64927	
32·0	95192	·1	1	04808	30290	·1	3	69710	35098	·1	3	64902	
33·0	95198			04802	30321			69679	35123			64877	
34·0	95204			04796	30353			69647	35149			64851	
35·0	95211	·2	1	04789	30385	·2	6	69615	35174	·2	5	64826	25′
36·0	95217			04783	30416			69584	35200			64800	
37·0	95223			04777	30448			69552	35225			64775	
38·0	95229	·3	2	04771	30480	·3	10	69520	35251	·3	8	64749	
39·0	95236			04764	30511			69488	35276			64724	
40·0	95242			04758	30543			69457	35302			64698	20′
41·0	95248	·4	2	04752	30575	·4	13	69425	35327	·4	10	64673	
42·0	95254			04746	30607			69393	35353			64647	
43·0	95261			04739	30639			69361	35378			64622	
44·0	95267			04733	30671			69329	35404			64596	
45·0	95273	·5	3	04727	30703	·5	16	69298	35429	·5	13	64571	15′
46·0	95279			04721	30734			69266	35455			64545	
47·0	95286			04715	30766			69234	35481			64519	
48·0	95292	·6	4	04708	30798	·6	19	69202	35506	·6	15	64494	
49·0	95298			04702	30830			69170	35532			64468	
50·0	95304			04696	30862			69138	35558			64442	10′
51·0	95310	·7	4	04690	30894	·7	22	69106	35584	·7	18	64417	
52·0	95317			04683	30926			69074	35609			64391	
53·0	95323			04677	30958			69042	35635			64365	
54·0	95329	·8	5	04671	30990	·8	25	69010	35661	·8	21	64339	
55·0	95335			04665	31022			68978	35687			64314	5′
56·0	95341			04659	31054			68946	35712			64288	
57·0	95348	·9	6	04653	31086	·9	29	68914	35738	·9	23	64262	
58·0	95354			04646	31118			68882	35764			64236	
59·0	95360			04640	31150			68850	35790			64210	
60·0	95366			04634	31182			68818	35816			64184	0′

64°
244°

LOGS. OF TRIG. FUNCTIONS

′	Sine	Parts		Cosec.	Tan.	Parts		Cotan.	Secant	Parts		Cosine	
00·0	1̄.(9) 95366		′	0.(10) 04634	0.(10) 31182		′	1̄.(9) 68818	0.(10) 35816		′	1̄.(9) 64184	60′
01·0	95372			04628	31214			68786	35842			64158	
02·0	95378	·1	1	04622	31246	·1	3	68754	35868	·1	3	64132	
03·0	95385			04616	31278			68722	35894			64106	
04·0	95391			04609	31310			68690	35920			64080	
05·0	95397	·2	1	04603	31342	·2	6	68658	35946	·2	5	64054	55′
06·0	95403			04597	31375			68626	35972			64028	
07·0	95409			04591	31407			68593	35998			64002	
08·0	95415	·3	2	04585	31439	·3	10	68561	36024	·3	8	63976	
09·0	95421			04579	31471			68529	36050			63950	
10·0	95427			04573	31503			68497	36076			63924	50′
11·0	95434	·4	2	04567	31535	·4	13	68465	36102	·4	10	63898	
12·0	95440			04560	31568			68432	36128			63872	
13·0	95446			04554	31600			68400	36154			63846	
14·0	95452	·5	3	04548	31632	·5	16	68368	36180	·5	13	63820	
15·0	95458			04542	31664			68336	36207			63794	45′
16·0	95464			04536	31697			68303	36233			63767	
17·0	95470	·6	4	04530	31729	·6	19	68271	36259	·6	16	63741	
18·0	95476			04524	31761			68239	36285			63715	
19·0	95482			04518	31794			68206	36311			63689	
20·0	95488			04512	31826			68174	36338			63662	40′
21·0	95494	·7	4	04506	31858	·7	23	68142	36364	·7	18	63636	
22·0	95501			04500	31891			68109	36390			63610	
23·0	95507			04494	31923			68077	36417			63583	
24·0	95513	·8	5	04487	31956	·8	26	68044	36443	·8	21	63557	
25·0	95519			04481	31988			68012	36469			63531	35′
26·0	95525			04475	32021			67980	36496			63504	
27·0	95531	·9	5	04469	32053	·9	29	67947	36522	·9	24	63478	
28·0	95537			04463	32085			67915	36549			63451	
29·0	95543			04457	32118			67882	36575			63425	
30·0	95549			04451	32150			67850	36602			63398	30′
31·0	95555			04445	32183			67817	36628			63372	
32·0	95561	·1	1	04439	32215	·1	3	67785	36655	·1	3	63345	
33·0	95567			04433	32248			67752	36681			63319	
34·0	95573			04427	32281			67719	36708			63292	
35·0	95579	·2	1	04421	32313	·2	7	67687	36734	·2	5	63266	25′
36·0	95585			04415	32346			67654	36761			63239	
37·0	95591			04409	32378			67622	36788			63213	
38·0	95597	·3	2	04403	32411	·3	10	67589	36814	·3	8	63186	
39·0	95603			04397	32444			67556	36841			63159	
40·0	95609			04391	32476			67524	36867			63133	20′
41·0	95615	·4	2	04385	32509	·4	13	67491	36894	·4	11	63106	
42·0	95621			04379	32542			67458	36921			63079	
43·0	95627			04373	32574			67426	36948			63052	
44·0	95633			04367	32607			67393	36974			63026	
45·0	95639	·5	3	04361	32640	·5	16	67360	37001	·5	13	62999	15′
46·0	95645			04355	32673			67327	37028			62972	
47·0	95651			04349	32705			67295	37055			62945	
48·0	95657	·6	4	04343	32738	·6	20	67262	37082	·6	16	62919	
49·0	95663			04338	32771			67229	37108			62892	
50·0	95668			04332	32804			67196	37135			62865	10′
51·0	95674	·7	4	04326	32837	·7	23	67164	37162	·7	19	62838	
52·0	95680			04320	32869			67131	37189			62811	
53·0	95686			04314	32902			67098	37216			62784	
54·0	95692	·8	5	04308	32935	·8	26	67065	37243	·8	21	62757	
55·0	95698			04302	32968			67032	37270			62730	5′
56·0	95704			04296	33001			66999	37297			62703	
57·0	95710	·9	5	04290	33034	·9	29	66966	37324	·9	24	62676	
58·0	95716			04284	33067			66933	37351			62649	
59·0	95722			04278	33100			66900	37378			62622	
60·0	95728			04272	33133			66867	37405			62595	0′

115°
295°

LOGS. OF TRIG. FUNCTIONS

′	Sine	Parts		Cosec.	Tan.	Parts		Cotan.	Secant	Parts		Cosine	
00·0	1̄.(9) 95728	′		0.(10) 04272	0.(10) 33133	′		1̄.(9) 66867	0.(10) 37405	′		1̄.(9) 62595	60′
01·0	95734			04267	33166			66834	37432			62568	
02·0	95739	·1	1	04261	33199	·1	3	66801	37459	·1	3	62541	
03·0	95745			04255	33232			66768	37487			62514	
04·0	95751			04249	33265			66735	37514			62486	
05·0	95757	·2	1	04243	33298	·2	7	66702	37541	·2	5	62459	55′
06·0	95763			04237	33331			66669	37568			62432	
07·0	95769			04231	33364			66636	37595			62405	
08·0	95775	·3	2	04225	33397	·3	10	66603	37623	·3	8	62377	
09·0	95780			04220	33430			66570	37650			62350	
10·0	95786			04214	33463			66537	37677			62323	50′
11·0	95792	·4	2	04208	33497	·4	13	66504	37704	·4	11	62296	
12·0	95798			04202	33530			66470	37732			62268	
13·0	95804			04196	33563			66437	37759			62241	
14·0	95810			04190	33596			66404	37787			62214	
15·0	95815	·5	3	04185	33629	·5	17	66371	37814	·5	14	62186	45′
16·0	95821			04179	33663			66338	37841			62159	
17·0	95827			04173	33696			66304	37869			62131	
18·0	95833	·6	3	04167	33729	·6	20	66271	37896	·6	16	62104	
19·0	95839			04161	33762			66238	37924			62076	
20·0	95845			04156	33796			66204	37951			62049	40′
21·0	95850	·7	4	04150	33829	·7	23	66171	37979	·7	19	62021	
22·0	95856			04144	33862			66138	38006			61994	
23·0	95862			04138	33896			66104	38034			61966	
24·0	95868	·8	5	04132	33929	·8	27	66071	38061	·8	22	61939	
25·0	95873			04127	33962			66038	38089			61911	35′
26·0	95879			04121	33996			66004	38117			61883	
27·0	95885	·9	5	04115	34029	·9	30	65971	38144	·9	25	61856	
28·0	95891			04109	34063			65937	38172			61828	
29·0	95897			04104	34096			65904	38200			61800	
30·0	95902			04098	34130			65870	38227			61773	30′
31·0	95908			04092	34163			65837	38255			61745	
32·0	95914	·1	1	04086	34197	·1	3	65803	38283	·1	3	61717	
33·0	95920			04081	34230			65770	38311			61689	
34·0	95925			04075	34264			65736	38338			61662	
35·0	95931	·2	1	04069	34297	·2	7	65703	38366	·2	6	61634	25′
36·0	95937			04063	34331			65669	38394			61606	
37·0	95943			04058	34364			65636	38422			61578	
38·0	95948	·3	2	04052	34398	·3	10	65602	38450	·3	8	61550	
39·0	95954			04046	34432			65568	38478			61522	
40·0	95960			04040	34465			65535	38506			61494	20′
41·0	95965	·4	2	04035	34499	·4	13	65501	38534	·4	11	61467	
42·0	95971			04029	34533			65467	38562			61439	
43·0	95977			04023	34566			65434	38590			61411	
44·0	95983			04018	34600			65400	38618			61383	
45·0	95988	·5	3	04012	34634	·5	17	65366	38646	·5	14	61355	15′
46·0	95994			04006	34667			65333	38674			61326	
47·0	96000			04001	34701			65299	38702			61298	
48·0	96005	·6	3	03995	34735	·6	20	65265	38730	·6	17	61270	
49·0	96011			03989	34769			65231	38758			61242	
50·0	96017			03984	34803			65197	38786			61214	10′
51·0	96022	·7	4	03978	34836	·7	24	65164	38814	·7	20	61186	
52·0	96028			03972	34870			65130	38842			61158	
53·0	96034			03967	34904			65096	38871			61129	
54·0	96039	·8	5	03961	34938	·8	27	65062	38899	·8	22	61101	
55·0	96045			03955	34972			65028	38927			61073	5′
56·0	96051			03950	35006			64994	38955			61045	
57·0	96056	·9	5	03944	35040	·9	30	64960	38984	·9	25	61016	
58·0	96062			03938	35074			64926	39012			60988	
59·0	96067			03933	35108			64892	39040			60960	
60·0	96073			03927	35142			64858	39069			60931	0′

LOGS. OF TRIG. FUNCTIONS

′	Sine	*Parts*		Cosec.	Tan.	*Parts*		Cotan.	Secant	*Parts*		Cosine	
00·0	1̄.(9) 96073			0.(10) 03927	0.(10) 35142		′	1̄.(9) 64858	0.(10) 39069		′	1̄.(9) 60931	60′
01·0	96079			03921	35176			64824	39097			60903	
02·0	96084	·1	1	03916	35210	·1	3	64790	39126	·1	3	60875	
03·0	96090			03910	35244			64756	39154			60846	
04·0	96096			03905	35278			64722	39182			60818	
05·0	96101	·2	1	03899	35312	·2	7	64688	39211	·2	6	60789	55′
06·0	96107			03893	35346			64654	39239			60761	
07·0	96112			03888	35380			64620	39268			60732	
08·0	96118	·3	2	03882	35414	·3	10	64586	39296	·3	9	60704	
09·0	96124			03877	35448			64552	39325			60675	
10·0	96129			03871	35483			64517	39354			60647	50′
11·0	96135	·4	2	03865	35517	·4	14	64483	39382	·4	11	60618	
12·0	96140			03860	35551			64449	39411			60589	
13·0	96146			03854	35585			64415	39439			60561	
14·0	96151	·5	3	03849	35619	·5	17	64381	39468	·5	14	60532	
15·0	96157			03843	35654			64346	39497			60503	45′
16·0	96162			03838	35688			64312	39526			60475	
17·0	96168	·6	3	03832	35722	·6	21	64278	39554	·6	17	60446	
18·0	96174			03827	35757			64243	39583			60417	
19·0	96179			03821	35791			64209	39612			60388	
20·0	96185	·7	4	03815	35825	·7	24	64174	39641	·7	20	60359	40′
21·0	96190			03810	35860			64140	39670			60331	
22·0	96196			03804	35894			64106	39698			60302	
23·0	96201	·8	4	03799	35928	·8	27	64072	39727	·8	23	60273	
24·0	96207			03793	35963			64037	39756			60244	
25·0	96212			03788	35997			64003	39785			60215	35′
26·0	96218			03782	36032			63968	39814			60186	
27·0	96223	·9	5	03777	36066	·9	31	63934	39843	·9	26	60157	
28·0	96229			03771	36101			63899	39872			60128	
29·0	96234			03766	36135			63865	39901			60099	
30·0	96240			03760	36170			63830	39930			60070	30′
31·0	96245			03755	36204			63796	39959			60041	
32·0	96251	·1	1	03749	36239	·1	3	63761	39988	·1	3	60012	
33·0	96256			03744	36274			63727	40017			59983	
34·0	96262			03738	36308			63692	40046			59954	
35·0	96267	·2	1	03733	36343	·2	7	63657	40076	·2	6	59924	25′
36·0	96273			03727	36377			63623	40105			59895	
37·0	96278			03722	36412			63588	40134			59866	
38·0	96284	·3	2	03716	36447	·3	10	63553	40163	·3	9	59837	
39·0	96289			03711	36482			63519	40193			59808	
40·0	96295			03706	36516			63484	40222			59778	20′
41·0	96300	·4	2	03700	36551	·4	14	63449	40251	·4	12	59749	
42·0	96305			03695	36586			63414	40280			59720	
43·0	96311			03689	36621			63380	40310			59690	
44·0	96316			03684	36655			63345	40339			59661	
45·0	96322	·5	3	03678	36690	·5	17	63310	40369	·5	15	59632	15′
46·0	96327			03673	36725			63275	40398			59602	
47·0	96333			03668	36760			63240	40427			59573	
48·0	96338	·6	3	03662	36795	·6	21	63205	40457	·6	18	59543	
49·0	96343			03657	36830			63170	40486			59514	
50·0	96349			03651	36865			63136	40516			59484	10′
51·0	96354	·7	4	03646	36900	·7	24	63101	40545	·7	21	59455	
52·0	96360			03640	36934			63066	40575			59425	
53·0	96365			03635	36969			63031	40605			59396	
54·0	96370	·8	4	03630	37004	·8	28	62996	40634	·8	24	59366	
55·0	96376			03624	37039			62961	40664			59336	5′
56·0	96381			03619	37075			62926	40693			59307	
57·0	96387	·9	5	03614	37110	·9	31	62891	40723	·9	26	59277	
58·0	96392			03608	37145			62855	40753			59247	
59·0	96397			03603	37180			62820	40782			59218	
60·0	96403			03597	37215			62785	40812			59188	0′

67°
247°

LOGS. OF TRIG. FUNCTIONS

′	Sine	Parts		Cosec.	Tan.	Parts		Cotan.	Secant	Parts		Cosine	
00·0	1̄.(9) 96403	′		0.(10) 03597	0.(10) 37215	′		1̄.(9) 62785	0.(10) 40812	′		1̄.(9) 59188	60′
01·0	96408			03592	37250			62750	40842			59158	
02·0	96413	·1	1	03587	37285	·1	4	62715	40872	·1	3	59128	
03·0	96419			03581	37320			62680	40902			59098	
04·0	96424			03576	37356			62645	40931			59069	
05·0	96429	·2	1	03571	37391	·2	7	62609	40961	·2	6	59039	55′
06·0	96435			03565	37426			62574	40991			59009	
07·0	96440			03560	37461			62539	41021			58979	
08·0	96445	·3	2	03555	37496	·3	11	62504	41051	·3	9	58949	
09·0	96451			03549	37532			62468	41081			58919	
10·0	96456			03544	37567			62433	41111			58889	50′
11·0	96461	·4	2	03539	37602	·4	14	62398	41141	·4	12	58859	
12·0	96467			03533	37638			62362	41171			58829	
13·0	96472			03528	37673			62327	41201			58799	
14·0	96477			03523	37709			62292	41231			58769	
15·0	96483	·5	3	03517	37744	·5	18	62256	41261	·5	15	58739	45′
16·0	96488			03512	37779			62221	41292			58709	
17·0	96493			03507	37815			62185	41322			58678	
18·0	96498	·6	3	03502	37850	·6	21	62150	41352	·6	18	58648	
19·0	96504			03496	37886			62114	41382			58618	
20·0	96509			03491	37921			62079	41412			58588	40′
21·0	96514	·7	4	03486	37957	·7	25	62043	41443	·7	21	58557	
22·0	96520			03481	37992			62008	41473			58527	
23·0	96525			03475	38028			61972	41503			58497	
24·0	96530	·8	4	03470	38064	·8	28	61936	41534	·8	24	58467	
25·0	96535			03465	38099			61901	41564			58436	35′
26·0	96541			03459	38135			61865	41594			58406	
27·0	96546	·9	5	03454	38171	·9	32	61830	41625	·9	27	58375	
28·0	96551			03449	38206			61794	41655			58345	
29·0	96556			03444	38242			61758	41685			58314	
30·0	96562			03439	38277			61722	41716			58284	30′
31·0	96567			03433	38313			61687	41747			58254	
32·0	96572	·1	1	03428	38349	·1	4	61651	41777	·1	3	58223	
33·0	96577			03423	38385			61615	41808			58192	
34·0	96582			03418	38421			61579	41838			58162	
35·0	96588	·2	1	03412	38457	·2	7	61544	41869	·2	6	58131	25′
36·0	96593			03407	38492			61508	41900			58101	
37·0	96598			03402	38528			61472	41930			58070	
38·0	96603	·3	2	03397	38564	·3	11	61436	41961	·3	9	58039	
39·0	96609			03392	38600			61400	41992			58009	
40·0	96614			03386	38636			61364	42022			57978	20′
41·0	96619	·4	2	03381	38672	·4	14	61328	42053	·4	12	57947	
42·0	96624			03376	38708			61292	42084			57916	
43·0	96629			03371	38744			61256	42115			57885	
44·0	96634			03366	38780			61220	42146			57855	
45·0	96640	·5	3	03361	38816	·5	18	61184	42176	·5	15	57824	15′
46·0	96645			03355	38852			61148	42207			57793	
47·0	96650			03350	38888			61112	42238			57762	
48·0	96655	·6	3	03345	38924	·6	22	61076	42269	·6	19	57731	
49·0	96660			03340	38960			61040	42300			57700	
50·0	96665			03335	38996			61004	42331			57669	10′
51·0	96671	·7	4	03330	39033	·7	25	60967	42362	·7	22	57638	
52·0	96676			03324	39069			60931	42393			57607	
53·0	96681			03319	39105			60895	42424			57576	
54·0	96686	·8	4	03314	39141	·8	29	60859	42455	·8	25	57545	
55·0	96691			03309	39178			60823	42486			57514	5′
56·0	96696			03304	39214			60786	42518			57482	
57·0	96701	·9	5	03299	39250	·9	32	60750	42549	·9	28	57451	
58·0	96706			03294	39286			60714	42580			57420	
59·0	96712			03289	39323			60677	42611			57389	
60·0	96717			03283	39359			60641	42643			57358	0′

112°
292°

LOGS. OF TRIG. FUNCTIONS

68°
248°

′	Sine	Parts	Cosec.	Tan.	Parts	Cotan.	Secant	Parts	Cosine	
00·0	1.(9)96717		0.(10)03283	0.(10)39359		1.(9)60641	0.(10)42643		1.(9)57358	60′
01·0	96722		03278	39395		60605	42674		57326	
02·0	96727	·1 1	03273	39432	·1 4	60568	42705	·1 3	57295	
03·0	96732		03268	39468		60532	42736		57264	
04·0	96737		03263	39505		60495	42768		57232	
05·0	96742	·2 1	03258	39541	·2 7	60459	42799	·2 6	57201	55′
06·0	96747		03253	39578		60422	42831		57170	
07·0	96752		03248	39614		60386	42862		57138	
08·0	96757	·3 2	03243	39651	·3 11	60349	42893	·3 10	57107	
09·0	96762		03238	39687		60313	42925		57075	
10·0	96767		03233	39724		60276	42957		57044	50′
11·0	96773	·4 2	03228	39761	·4 15	60240	42988	·4 13	57012	
12·0	96778		03223	39797		60203	43020		56980	
13·0	96783		03217	39834		60166	43051		56949	
14·0	96788	·5 3	03212	39870	·5 18	60130	43083	·5 16	56917	
15·0	96793		03207	39907		60093	43114		56886	45′
16·0	96798		03202	39944		60056	43146		56854	
17·0	96803		03197	39981		60019	43178		56822	
18·0	96808	·6 3	03192	40017	·6 22	59983	43210	·6 19	56790	
19·0	96813		03187	40054		59946	43241		56759	
20·0	96818		03182	40091		59909	43273		56727	40′
21·0	96823	·7 4	03177	40128	·7 26	59872	43305	·7 22	56695	
22·0	96828		03172	40165		59835	43337		56663	
23·0	96833		03167	40202		59799	43369		56631	
24·0	96838	·8 4	03162	40238	·8 29	59762	43401	·8 25	56600	
25·0	96843		03157	40275		59725	43432		56568	35′
26·0	96848		03152	40312		59688	43464		56536	
27·0	96853	·9 5	03147	40349	·9 33	59651	43496	·9 29	56504	
28·0	96858		03142	40386		59614	43528		56472	
29·0	96863		03137	40423		59577	43560		56440	
30·0	96868		03132	40460		59540	43593		56408	30′
31·0	96873		03127	40497		59503	43625		56376	
32·0	96878	·1 0	03122	40534	·1 4	59466	43657	·1 3	56343	
33·0	96883		03117	40572		59429	43689		56311	
34·0	96888		03112	40609		59391	43721		56279	
35·0	96893	·2 1	03107	40646	·2 7	59354	43753	·2 7	56247	25′
36·0	96898		03102	40683		59317	43785		56215	
37·0	96903		03098	40720		59280	43818		56182	
38·0	96908	·3 1	03093	40757	·3 11	59243	43850	·3 10	56150	
39·0	96912		03088	40795		59205	43882		56118	
40·0	96917		03083	40832		59168	43915		56086	20′
41·0	96922	·4 2	03078	40869	·4 15	59131	43947	·4 13	56053	
42·0	96927		03073	40907		59094	43979		56021	
43·0	96932		03068	40944		59056	44012		55988	
44·0	96937		03063	40981		59019	44044		55956	
45·0	96942	·5 2	03058	41019	·5 19	58981	44077	·5 16	55923	15′
46·0	96947		03053	41056		58944	44109		55891	
47·0	96952		03048	41093		58907	44141		55858	
48·0	96957	·6 3	03043	41131	·6 22	58869	44174	·6 20	55826	
49·0	96962		03038	41168		58832	44207		55793	
50·0	96967		03034	41206		58794	44239		55761	10′
51·0	96971	·7 3	03029	41243	·7 26	58757	44272	·7 23	55728	
52·0	96976		03024	41281		58719	44305		55695	
53·0	96981		03019	41319		58682	44337		55663	
54·0	96986	·8 4	03014	41356	·8 30	58644	44370	·8 26	55630	
55·0	96991		03009	41394		58606	44403		55597	5′
56·0	96996		03004	41431		58569	44436		55564	
57·0	97001	·9 4	02999	41469	·9 34	58531	44469	·9 29	55532	
58·0	97006		02995	41507		58493	44501		55499	
59·0	97010		02990	41545		58456	44534		55466	
60·0	97015		02985	41582		58418	44567		55433	0′

69°
249°

LOGS. OF TRIG. FUNCTIONS

'	Sine	Parts	Cosec.	Tan.	Parts	Cotan.	Secant	Parts	Cosine	
00·0	1.(9)97015		0.(10)02985	0.(10)41582		1.(9)58418	0.(10)44567		1.(9)55433	60'
01·0	97020		02980	41620		58380	44600		55400	
02·0	97025	·1 0	02975	41658	·1 4	58342	44633	·1 3	55367	
03·0	97030		02970	41696		58304	44666		55334	
04·0	97035		02966	41734		58267	44699		55301	
05·0	97039	·2 1	02961	41771	·2 8	58229	44732	·2 7	55268	55'
06·0	97044		02956	41809		58191	44765		55235	
07·0	97049		02951	41847		58153	44798		55202	
08·0	97054	·3 1	02946	41885	·3 11	58115	44831	·3 10	55169	
09·0	97059		02941	41923		58077	44864		55136	
10·0	97064		02937	41961		58039	44898		55102	50'
11·0	97068	·4 2	02932	41999	·4 15	58001	44931	·4 13	55069	
12·0	97073		02927	42037		57963	44964		55036	
13·0	97078		02922	42075		57925	44997		55003	
14·0	97083		02917	42113		57887	45031		54969	
15·0	97087	·5 2	02913	42151	·5 19	57849	45064	·5 17	54936	45'
16·0	97092		02908	42190		57810	45097		54903	
17·0	97097		02903	42228		57772	45131		54869	
18·0	97102	·6 3	02898	42266	·6 23	57734	45164	·6 20	54836	
19·0	97107		02893	42304		57696	45198		54802	
20·0	97111		02889	42342		57658	45231		54769	40'
21·0	97116	·7 3	02884	42381	·7 27	57619	45265	·7 23	54735	
22·0	97121		02879	42419		57581	45298		54702	
23·0	97126		02874	42457		57543	45332		54668	
24·0	97130	·8 4	02870	42496	·8 31	57504	45365	·8 27	54635	
25·0	97135		02865	42534		57466	45399		54601	30'
26·0	97140		02860	42572		57428	45433		54567	
27·0	97145	·9 4	02855	42611	·9 34	57389	45466	·9 30	54534	
28·0	97149		02851	42649		57351	45500		54500	
29·0	97154		02846	42688		57312	45534		54466	
30·0	97159		02841	42726		57274	45568		54433	30'
31·0	97164		02837	42765		57235	45601		54399	
32·0	97168	·1 0	02832	42803	·1 4	57197	45635	·1 3	54365	
33·0	97173		02827	42842		57158	45669		54331	
34·0	97178		02822	42881		57120	45703		54297	
35·0	97182	·2 1	02818	42919	·2 8	57081	45737	·2 7	54263	25'
36·0	97187		02813	42958		57042	45771		54229	
37·0	97192		02808	42997		57004	45805		54195	
38·0	97196		02804	43035		56965	45839		54161	
39·0	97201	·3 1	02799	43074	·3 12	56926	45873	·3 10	54127	
40·0	97206		02794	43113		56887	45907		54093	20'
41·0	97211		02790	43151		56849	45941		54059	
42·0	97215	·4 2	02785	43190	·4 16	56810	45975	·4 14	54025	
43·0	97220		02780	43229		56771	46009		53991	
44·0	97225		02776	43268		56732	46044		53957	
45·0	97229	·5 2	02771	43307	·5 19	56693	46078	·5 17	53922	15'
46·0	97234		02766	43346		56654	46112		53888	
47·0	97239		02762	43385		56615	46146		53854	
48·0	97243	·6 3	02757	43424	·6 23	56576	46181	·6 21	53819	
49·0	97248		02752	43463		56537	46215		53785	
50·0	97252		02748	43502		56498	46249		53751	10'
51·0	97257	·7 3	02743	43541	·7 27	56459	46284	·7 24	53716	
52·0	97262		02738	43580		56420	46318		53682	
53·0	97266		02734	43619		56381	46353		53647	
54·0	97271	·8 4	02729	43658	·8 31	56342	46387	·8 27	53613	
55·0	97276		02725	43697		56303	46422		53578	5'
56·0	97280		02720	43736		56264	46456		53544	
57·0	97285	·9 4	02715	42776	·9 35	56224	46491	·9 31	53509	
58·0	97289		02711	43815		56185	46526		53475	
59·0	97294		02706	43854		56146	46560		53440	0'
60·0	97299		02701	43893		56107	46595		53405	

LOGS. OF TRIG. FUNCTIONS

′	Sine	Parts	Cosec.	Tan.	Parts	Cotan.	Secant	Parts	Cosine	
00·0	1̄.(9) 97299	′	0.(10) 02701	0.(10) 43893	′	1̄.(9) 56107	0.(10) 46595	′	1̄.(9) 53405	60′
01·0	97303		02697	43933		56067	46630		53370	
02·0	97308	·1 0	02692	43972	·1 4	56028	46664	·1 4	53336	
03·0	97312		02688	44012		55989	46699		53301	
04·0	97317	·2 1	02683	44051	·2 8	55949	46734	·2 7	53266	
05·0	97322	·3 1	02679	44090	·3 12	55910	46769	·3 11	53231	55′
06·0	97326		02674	44130		55870	46804		53196	
07·0	97331		02669	44169		55831	46839		53161	
08·0	97335	·4 2	02665	44209	·4 16	55791	46874	·4 14	53127	
09·0	97340	·5 2	02660	44248	·5 20	55752	46909	·5 18	53092	
10·0	97344		02656	44288		55712	46944		53057	50′
11·0	97349	·6 3	02651	44328	·6 24	55673	46979	·6 21	53022	
12·0	97354		02647	44367		55633	47014		52986	
13·0	97358	·7 3	02642	44407	·7 28	55593	47049	·7 25	52951	
14·0	97363		02638	44446		55554	47084		52916	
15·0	97367	·8 4	02633	44486	·8 32	55514	47119	·8 28	52881	45′
16·0	97372		02628	44526		55474	47154		52846	
17·0	97376	·9 4	02624	44566	·9 36	55434	47190	·9 32	52811	
18·0	97381		02619	44605		55395	47225		52775	
19·0	97385		02615	44645		55355	47260		52740	
20·0	97390		02610	44685		55315	47295		52705	40′
21·0	97394		02606	44725		55275	47331		52669	
22·0	97399	·1 0	02601	44765	·1 4	55235	47366	·1 4	52634	
23·0	97403		02597	44805		55195	47402		52598	
24·0	97408	·2 1	02592	44845	·2 8	55155	47437	·2 7	52563	
25·0	97412	·3 1	02588	44885	·3 12	55115	47473	·3 11	52528	35′
26·0	97417		02583	44925		55075	47508		52492	
27·0	97421		02579	44965		55035	47544		52456	
28·0	97426	·4 2	02574	45005	·4 16	54995	47579	·4 14	52421	
29·0	97430	·5 2	02570	45045	·5 20	54955	47615	·5 18	52385	
30·0	97435		02565	45085		54915	47651		52350	30′
31·0	97439	·6 3	02561	45125	·6 24	54875	47686	·6 21	52314	
32·0	97444		02556	45166		54835	47722		52278	
33·0	97448	·7 3	02552	45206	·7 28	54794	47758	·7 25	52242	
34·0	97453		02548	45246		54754	47793		52207	
35·0	97457	·8 4	02543	45286	·8 32	54714	47829	·8 29	52171	25′
36·0	97461		02539	45327		54674	47865		52135	
37·0	97466	·9 4	02534	45367	·9 36	54633	47901	·9 32	52099	
38·0	97470		02530	45407		54593	47937		52063	
39·0	97475		02525	45448		54552	47973		52027	
40·0	97479		02521	45488		54512	48009		51991	20′
41·0	97484		02516	45529		54472	48045		51955	
42·0	97488	·1 0	02512	45569	·1 4	54431	48081	·1 4	51919	
43·0	97493		02508	45610		54391	48117		51883	
44·0	97497	·2 1	02503	45650	·2 8	54350	48153	·2 7	51847	
45·0	97501	·3 1	02499	45691	·3 12	54309	48189	·3 11	51811	15′
46·0	97506		02494	45731		54269	48226		51775	
47·0	97510		02490	45772		54228	48262		51738	
48·0	97515	·4 2	02486	45813	·4 16	54188	48298	·4 15	51702	
49·0	97519	·5 2	02481	45853	·5 20	54147	48334	·5 18	51666	
50·0	97523		02477	45894		54106	48371		51629	10′
51·0	97528	·6 3	02472	45935	·6 24	54065	48407	·6 22	51593	
52·0	97532		02468	45976		54025	48443		51557	
53·0	97537	·7 3	02464	46016	·7 29	53984	48480	·7 25	51520	
54·0	97541		02459	46057		53943	48516		51484	
55·0	97545	·8 4	02455	46098	·8 33	53902	48553	·8 29	51447	5′
56·0	97550		02450	46139		53861	48589		51411	
57·0	97554	·9 4	02446	46180	·9 37	53820	48626	·9 33	51374	
58·0	97558		02442	46221		53779	48663		51338	
59·0	97563		02437	46262		53738	48699		51301	
60·0	97567		02433	46303		53697	48736		51264	0′

LOGS. OF TRIG. FUNCTIONS

71°
251°

′	Sine	Parts	Cosec.	Tan.	Parts	Cotan.	Secant	Parts	Cosine	
00·0	1̄.(9) 97567	′	0.(10) 02433	0.(10) 46303	′	1̄.(9) 53697	0.(10) 48736	′	1̄.(9) 51264	60′
01·0	97571		02429	46344		53656	48773		51228	
02·0	97576	·1 0	02424	46385	·1 4	53615	48809	·1 4	51191	
03·0	97580		02420	46426		53574	48846		51154	
04·0	97584	·2 1	02416	46467	·2 8	53533	48883	·2 7	51117	
05·0	97589		02411	46508		53492	48920		51080	55′
06·0	97593	·3 1	02407	46550	·3 12	53450	48957	·3 11	51043	
07·0	97597		02403	46591		53409	48994		51007	
08·0	97602	·4 2	02398	46632	·4 17	53368	49030	·4 15	50970	
09·0	97606		02394	46673		53327	49067		50933	
10·0	97610	·5 2	02390	46715	·5 21	53285	49104	·5 19	50896	50′
11·0	97615		02385	46756		53244	49142		50859	
12·0	97619	·6 3	02381	46798	·6 25	53203	49179	·6 22	50821	
13·0	97623	·7 3	02377	46839	·7 29	53161	49216	·7 26	50784	
14·0	97628		02373	46880		53120	49253		50747	
15·0	97632	·8 3	02368	46922	·8 33	53078	49290	·8 30	50710	45′
16·0	97636		02364	46963		53037	49327		50673	
17·0	97640	·9 4	02360	47005	·9 37	52995	49365	·9 33	50635	
18·0	97645		02355	47047		52954	49402		50598	
19·0	97649		02351	47088		52912	49439		50561	
20·0	97653		02347	47130		52870	49477		50523	40′
21·0	97657		02343	47172		52829	49514		50486	
22·0	97662	·1 0	02338	47213	·1 4	52787	49552	·1 4	50449	
23·0	97666		02334	47255		52745	49589		50411	
24·0	97670	·2 1	02330	47297	·2 8	52703	49627	·2 8	50374	
25·0	97675	·3 1	02326	47339	·3 13	52662	49664	·3 11	50336	35′
26·0	97679		02321	47380		52620	49702		50298	
27·0	97683	·4 2	02317	47422	·4 17	52578	49739	·4 15	50261	
28·0	97687		02313	47464		52536	49777		50223	
29·0	97691	·5 2	02309	47506	·5 21	52494	49815	·5 19	50185	
30·0	97696		02304	47548		52452	49852		50148	30′
31·0	97700	·6 3	02300	47590	·6 25	52410	49890	·6 23	50110	
32·0	97704		02296	47632		52368	49928		50072	
33·0	97708	·7 3	02292	47674	·7 29	52326	49966	·7 26	50034	
34·0	97713		02288	47716		52284	50004		49996	
35·0	97717	·8 3	02283	47758	·8 34	52242	50042	·8 30	49958	25′
36·0	97721		02279	47801		52200	50080		49920	
37·0	97725	·9 4	02275	47843	·9 38	52157	50118	·9 34	49883	
38·0	97729		02271	47885		52115	50156		49844	
39·0	97734		02267	47927		52073	50194		49806	
40·0	97738		02262	47970		52031	50232		49768	20′
41·0	97742		02258	48012		51988	50270		49730	
42·0	97746	·1 0	02254	48054	·1 4	51946	50308	·1 4	49692	
43·0	97750		02250	48097		51903	50346		49654	
44·0	97754	·2 1	02246	48139	·2 9	51861	50385	·2 8	49615	
45·0	97759	·3 1	02241	48181	·3 13	51819	50423	·3 12	49577	15′
46·0	97763		02237	48224		51776	50461		49539	
47·0	97767	·4 2	02233	48267	·4 17	51734	50500	·4 15	49501	
48·0	97771		02229	48309		51691	50538		49462	
49·0	97775	·5 2	02225	48352	·5 21	51648	50576	·5 19	49424	
50·0	97779		02221	48394		51606	50615		49385	10′
51·0	97784	·6 2	02217	48437	·6 26	51563	50653	·6 23	49347	
52·0	97788		02212	48480		51520	50692		49308	
53·0	97792	·7 3	02208	48522	·7 30	51478	50731	·7 27	49270	
54·0	97796		02204	48565		51435	50769		49231	
55·0	97800	·8 3	02200	48608	·8 34	51392	50808	·8 31	49192	5′
56·0	97804		02196	48651		51349	50847		49154	
57·0	97808	·9 4	02192	48694	·9 38	51306	50885	·9 35	49115	
58·0	97812		02188	48737		51264	50924		49076	
59·0	97817		02184	48779		51221	50963		49037	
60·0	97821		02179	48822		51178	51002		48998	0′

108°
288°

LOGS. OF TRIG. FUNCTIONS

72°
252°

′	Sine	Parts	Cosec.	Tan.	Parts	Cotan.	Secant	Parts	Cosine	
00·0	1.(9) 97821	′	0.(10) 02179	0.(10) 48822	′	1.(9) 51178	0.(10) 51002	′	1.(9) 48998	60′
01·0	97825		02175	48865		51135	51041		48959	
02·0	97829	·1 0	02171	48908	·1 4	51092	51080	·1 4	48920	
03·0	97833		02167	48952		51049	51119		48881	
04·0	97837	·2 1	02163	48995	·2 9	51005	51158	·2 8	48842	
05·0	97841		02159	49038		50962	51197		48803	55′
06·0	97845	·3 1	02155	49081	·3 13	50919	51236	·3 12	48764	
07·0	97849		02151	49124		50876	51275		48725	
08·0	97853	·4 2	02147	49167	·4 17	50833	51314	·4 16	48686	
09·0	97857	·5 2	02143	49211	·5 22	50789	51353	·5 20	48647	
10·0	97862		02139	49254		50746	51393		48608	50′
11·0	97866	·6 2	02135	49297	·6 26	50703	51432	·6 24	48568	
12·0	97870		02130	49341		50659	51471		48529	
13·0	97874	·7 3	02126	49384	·7 30	50616	51511	·7 27	48490	
14·0	97878		02122	49428		50572	51550		48450	
15·0	97882	·8 3	02118	49471	·8 35	50529	51589	·8 31	48411	45′
16·0	97886		02114	49515		50485	51629		48371	
17·0	97890	·9 4	02110	49558	·9 39	50442	51668	·9 35	48332	
18·0	97894		02106	49602		50398	51708		48292	
19·0	97898		02102	49645		50355	51748		48253	
20·0	97902		02098	49689		50311	51787		48213	40′
21·0	97906		02094	49733		50267	51827		48173	
22·0	97910	·1 0	02090	49777	·1 4	50224	51867	·1 4	48133	
23·0	97914		02086	49820		50180	51906		48094	
24·0	97918	·2 1	02082	49864	·2 9	50136	51946	·2 8	48054	
25·0	97922		02078	49908		50092	51986		48014	35′
26·0	97926	·3 1	02074	49952	·3 13	50048	52026	·3 12	47974	
27·0	97930		02070	49996		50004	52066		47934	
28·0	97934	·4 2	02066	50040	·4 18	49960	52106	·4 16	47894	
29·0	97938	·5 2	02062	50084	·5 22	49916	52146	·5 20	47854	
30·0	97942		02058	50128		49872	52186		47814	30′
31·0	97946	·6 2	02054	50172	·6 26	49828	52226	·6 24	47774	
32·0	97950		02050	50216		49784	52266		47734	
33·0	97954	·7 3	02046	50260	·7 31	49740	52306	·7 28	47694	
34·0	97958		02042	50304		49696	52346		47654	
35·0	97962	·8 3	02038	50349	·8 35	49652	52387	·8 32	47613	25′
36·0	97966		02034	50393		49607	52427		47573	
37·0	97970	·9 4	02030	50437	·9 40	49563	52467	·9 36	47533	
38·0	97974		02026	50481		49519	52508		47492	
39·0	97978		02022	50526		49474	52548		47452	
40·0	97982		02018	50570		49430	52589		47412	20′
41·0	97986		02015	50615		49385	52629		47371	
42·0	97990	·1 0	02011	50659	·1 4	49341	52670	·1 4	47330	
43·0	97993		02007	50704		49297	52710		47290	
44·0	97997	·2 1	02003	50748	·2 9	49252	52751	·2 8	47249	
45·0	98001		01999	50793		49207	52791		47209	15′
46·0	98005	·3 1	01995	50837	·3 13	49163	52832	·3 12	47168	
47·0	98009		01991	50882		49118	52873		47127	
48·0	98013	·4 2	01987	50927	·4 18	49073	52914	·4 16	47086	
49·0	98017	·5 2	01983	50971	·5 22	49029	52955	·5 20	47046	
50·0	98021		01979	51016		48984	52995		47005	10′
51·0	98025	·6 2	01975	51061	·6 27	48939	53036	·6 25	46964	
52·0	98029		01971	51106		48894	53077		46923	
53·0	98033	·7 3	01968	51151	·7 31	48849	53118	·7 29	46882	
54·0	98036		01964	51196		48804	53159		46841	
55·0	98040	·8 3	01960	51241	·8 36	48759	53200	·8 33	46800	5′
56·0	98044		01956	51286		48714	53242		46759	
57·0	98048	·9 4	01952	51331	·9 40	48669	53283	·9 37	46717	
58·0	98052		01948	51376		48624	53324		46676	
59·0	98056		01944	51421		48579	53365		46635	
60·0	98060		01940	51466		48534	53407		46594	0′

73°
253°

LOGS. OF TRIG. FUNCTIONS

′	Sine	Parts	Cosec.	Tan.	Parts	Cotan.	Secant	Parts	Cosine	
00·0	1̄.(9) 98060	′	0.(10) 01940	0.(10) 51466	′	1̄.(9) 48534	0.(10) 53407	′	1̄.(9) 46594	60′
01·0	98064		01937	51511		48489	53448		46552	
02·0	98067	·1 0	01933	51557	·1 5	48444	53489	·1 4	46511	
03·0	98071		01929	51602		48398	53531		46469	
04·0	98075	·2 1	01925	51647	·2 9	48353	53572	·2 8	46428	
05·0	98079		01921	51693		48308	53614		46386	55′
06·0	98083	·3 1	01917	51738	·3 14	48262	53655	·3 13	46345	
07·0	98087		01913	51783		48217	53697		46303	
08·0	98090	·4 2	01910	51829	·4 18	48171	53738	·4 17	46262	
09·0	98094		01906	51874		48126	53780		46220	
10·0	98098	·5 2	01902	51920	·5 23	48080	53822	·5 21	46178	50′
11·0	98102	·6 2	01898	51966	·6 27	48035	53864	·6 25	46136	
12·0	98106		01894	52011		47989	53905		46095	
13·0	98110	·7 3	01891	52057	·7 32	47943	53947	·7 29	46053	
14·0	98113		01887	52103		47898	53989		46011	
15·0	98117	·8 3	01883	52148	·8 36	47852	54031	·8 33	45969	45′
16·0	98121		01879	52194		47806	54073		45927	
17·0	98125	·9 3	01875	52240	·9 41	47760	54115	·9 38	45885	
18·0	98129		01872	52286		47714	54157		45843	
19·0	98132		01868	52332		47668	54199		45801	
20·0	98136		01864	52378		47622	54242		45758	40′
21·0	98140		01860	52424		47576	54284		45716	
22·0	98144	·1 0	01856	52470	·1 5	47530	54326	·1 4	45674	
23·0	98147		01853	52516		47484	54368		45632	
24·0	98151	·2 1	01849	52562	·2 9	47438	54411	·2 9	45589	
25·0	98155		01845	52608		47392	54453		45547	35′
26·0	98159	·3 1	01841	52654	·3 14	47346	54496	·3 13	45504	
27·0	98163		01838	52701		47300	54538		45462	
28·0	98166	·4 2	01834	52747	·4 19	47253	54581	4 17	45419	
29·0	98170		01830	52793		47207	54623		45377	
		·5 2			·5 23			·5 21		
30·0	98174		01826	52840		47161	54666		45334	30′
31·0	98177	·6 2	01823	52886	·6 28	47114	54709	·6 26	45292	
32·0	98181		01819	52932		47068	54751		45249	
33·0	98185	·7 3	01815	52979	·7 32	47021	54794	·7 30	45206	
34·0	98189		01811	53025		46975	54837		45163	
35·0	98192	·8 3	01808	53072	·8 37	46928	54880	·8 34	45120	25′
36·0	98196		01804	53119		46881	54923		45078	
37·0	98200	·9 3	01800	53165	·9 42	46835	54966	·9 38	45035	
38·0	98204		01797	53212		46788	55009		44992	
39·0	98207		01793	53259		46741	55052		44949	
40·0	98211		01789	53306		46695	55095		44905	20′
41·0	98215		01785	53352		46648	55138		44862	
42·0	98218	·1 0	01782	53399	·1 5	46601	55181	·1 4	44819	
43·0	98222		01778	53446		46554	55224		44776	
44·0	98226	·2 1	01774	53493	·2 9	46507	55267	·2 9	44733	
45·0	98229		01771	53540		46460	55311		44689	15′
46·0	98233	·3 1	01767	53587	·3 14	46413	55354	·3 13	44646	
47·0	98237		01763	53634		46366	55398		44603	
48·0	98240	·4 1	01760	53681	·4 19	46319	55441	·4 17	44559	
49·0	98244		01756	53729		46272	55485		44516	
		·5 2			·5 24			·5 22		
50·0	98248		01752	53776		46224	55528		44472	10′
51·0	98251	·6 2	01749	53823	·6 28	46177	55572	·6 26	44428	
52·0	98255		01745	53870		46130	55615		44385	
53·0	98258	·7 3	01741	53918	·7 33	46082	55659	·7 30	44341	
54·0	98262		01738	53965		46035	55703		44297	
55·0	98266	·8 3	01734	54013	·8 38	45988	55747	·8 35	44254	5′
56·0	98270		01730	54060		45940	55790		44210	
57·0	98273	·9 3	01727	54108	·9 43	45893	55834	·9 39	44166	
58·0	98277		01723	54155		45845	55878		44122	
59·0	98281		01720	54203		45797	55922		44078	
60·0	98284		01716	54250		45750	55966		44034	0′

LOGS. OF TRIG. FUNCTIONS

74°
254°

′	Sine	Parts	Cosec.	Tan.	Parts	Cotan.	Secant	Parts	Cosine	
00·0	1.(9) 98284	′	0.(10) 01716	0.(10) 54250	′	1.(9) 45750	0.(10) 55966	′	1.(9) 44034	60′
01·0	98288		01712	54298		45702	56010		43990	
02·0	98291	·1 0	01709	54346	·1 5	45654	56054	·1 4	43946	
03·0	98295		01705	54394		45606	56099		43901	
04·0	98299	·2 1	01701	54441	·2 10	45559	56143	·2 9	43857	
05·0	98302		01698	54489		45511	56187		43813	55′
06·0	98306	·3 1	01694	54537	·3 14	45463	56231	·3 13	43769	
07·0	98309		01691	54585		45415	56276		43724	
08·0	98313	·4 1	01687	54633	·4 19	45367	56320	·4 18	43680	
09·0	98317	·5 2	01683	54681	·5 24	45319	56365	·5 22	43635	
10·0	98320		01680	54729		45271	56409		43591	50′
11·0	98324	·6 2	01676	54778	·6 29	45223	56454	·6 27	43546	
12·0	98327		01673	54826		45174	56498		43502	
13·0	98331	·7 3	01669	54874	·7 34	45126	56543	·7 31	43457	
14·0	98335		01666	54922		45078	56588		43412	
15·0	98338	·8 3	01662	54971	·8 39	45029	56633	·8 36	43368	45′
16·0	98342		01658	55019		44981	56677		43323	
17·0	98345	·9 3	01655	55067	·9 43	44933	56722	·9 40	43278	
18·0	98349		01651	55116		44884	56767		43233	
19·0	98352		01648	55164		44836	56812		43188	
20·0	98356		01644	55213		44787	56857		43143	40′
21·0	98359		01641	55262		44738	56902		43098	
22·0	98363	·1 0	01637	55310	·1 5	44690	56947	·1 5	43053	
23·0	98366		01634	55359		44641	56993		43008	
24·0	98370	·2 1	01630	55408	·2 10	44592	57038	·2 9	42962	
25·0	98374	·3 1	01627	55457	·3 15	44544	57083	·3 14	42917	35′
26·0	98377		01623	55505		44495	57128		42872	
27·0	98381	·4 1	01620	55554	·4 20	44446	57174	·4 18	42826	
28·0	98384		01616	55603		44397	57219		42781	
29·0	98388	·5 2	01613	55652	·5 25	44348	57265	·5 23	42735	
30·0	98391		01609	55701		44299	57310		42690	30′
31·0	98395	·6 2	01605	55750	·6 29	44250	57356	·6 27	42644	
32·0	98398		01602	55799		44201	57401		42599	
33·0	98402	·7 2	01599	55849	·7 34	44151	57447	·7 32	42553	
34·0	98405		01595	55898		44102	57493		42507	
35·0	98409	·8 3	01592	55947	·8 39	44053	57539	·8 36	42462	25′
36·0	98412		01588	55996		44004	57584		42416	
37·0	98416	·9 3	01585	56046	·9 44	43954	57630	·9 41	42370	
38·0	98419		01581	56095		43905	57676		42324	
39·0	98422		01578	56145		43855	57722		42278	
40·0	98426		01574	56194		43806	57768		42232	20′
41·0	98429		01571	56244		43756	57814		42186	
42·0	98433	·1 0	01567	56293	·1 5	43707	57861	·1 5	42140	
43·0	98436		01564	56343		43657	57907		42093	
44·0	98440	·2 1	01560	56393	·2 10	43607	57953	·2 9	42047	
45·0	98443	·3 1	01557	56442	·3 15	43558	57999	·3 14	42001	15′
46·0	98447		01553	56492		43508	58046		41954	
47·0	98450	·4 1	01550	56542	·4 20	43458	58092	·4 19	41908	
48·0	98454		01547	56592		43408	58139		41862	
49·0	98457	·5 2	01543	56642	·5 25	43358	58185	·5 23	41815	
50·0	98460		01540	56692		43308	58232		41768	10′
51·0	98464	·6 2	01536	56742	·6 30	43258	58278	·6 28	41722	
52·0	98467		01533	56792		43208	58325		41675	
53·0	98471	·7 2	01529	56842	·7 35	43158	58372	·7 33	41628	
54·0	98474		01526	56893		43108	58419		41582	
55·0	98477	·8 3	01523	56943	·8 40	43057	58465	·8 37	41535	5′
56·0	98481		01519	56993		43007	58512		41488	
57·0	98484	·9 3	01516	57043	·9 45	42957	58559	·9 42	41441	
58·0	98488		01512	57094		42906	58606		41394	
59·0	98491		01509	57144		42856	58653		41347	
60·0	98494		01506	57195		42805	58700		41300	0′

75°
255°

LOGS. OF TRIG. FUNCTIONS

′	Sine	Parts	Cosec.	Tan.	Parts	Cotan.	Secant	Parts	Cosine	
00·0	1̄.(9) 98494	′	0.(10) 01506	0.(10) 57195	′	1̄.(9) 42805	0.(10) 58700	′	1̄.(9) 41300	60′
01·0	98498		01502	57245		42755	58748		41252	
02·0	98501	·1 0	01499	57296	·1 5	42704	58795	·1 5	41205	
03·0	98505	·2 1	01496	57347	·2 10	42653	58842	·2 10	41158	
04·0	98508	·3 1	01492	57397	·3 15	42603	58889	·3 14	41111	
05·0	98511	·4 1	01489	57448	·4 20	42552	58937	·4 19	41063	55′
06·0	98515		01485	57499		42501	58984		41016	
07·0	98518	·5 2	01482	57550	·5 25	42450	59032	·5 24	40968	
08·0	98521	·6 2	01479	57601	·6 31	42399	59079	·6 29	40921	
09·0	98525	·7 2	01475	57652	·7 36	42348	59127	·7 33	40873	
10·0	98528	·8 3	01472	57703	·8 41	42297	59175	·8 38	40825	50′
11·0	98531	·9 3	01469	57754	·9 46	42246	59222	·9 43	40778	
12·0	98535		01465	57805		42195	59270		40730	
13·0	98538		01462	57856		42144	59318		40682	
14·0	98541		01459	57907		42093	59366		40634	
15·0	98545		01455	57959		42042	59414		40586	45′
16·0	98548		01452	58010		41990	59462		40538	
17·0	98551	·1 0	01449	58061	·1 5	41939	59510	·1 5	40490	
18·0	98555	·2 1	01445	58113	·2 10	41887	59558	·2 10	40442	
19·0	98558	·3 1	01442	58164	·3 16	41836	59606	·3 15	40394	
20·0	98561	·4 1	01439	58216	·4 21	41784	59655	·4 19	40346	40′
21·0	98565		01435	58267		41733	59703		40297	
22·0	98568	·5 2	01432	58319	·5 26	41681	59751	·5 24	40249	
23·0	98571	·6 2	01429	58371	·6 31	41629	59800	·6 29	40201	
24·0	98575	·7 2	01426	58423	·7 36	41578	59848	·7 34	40152	
25·0	98578	·8 3	01422	58474	·8 41	41526	59897	·8 39	40104	35′
26·0	98581	·9 3	01419	58526	·9 47	41474	59945	·9 44	40055	
27·0	98584		01416	58578		41422	59994		40006	
28·0	98588		01412	58630		41370	60043		39958	
29·0	98591		01409	58682		41318	60091		39909	
30·0	98594		01406	58734		41266	60140		39860	30′
31·0	98597		01403	58786		41214	60189		39811	
32·0	98601	·1 0	01399	58839	·1 5	41162	60238	·1 5	39762	
33·0	98604	·2 1	01396	58891	·2 11	41109	60287	·2 10	39713	
34·0	98607	·3 1	01393	58943	·3 16	41057	60336	·3 15	39664	
35·0	98610	·4 1	01390	58996	·4 21	41005	60385	·4 20	39615	25′
36·0	98614		01386	59048		40952	60434		39566	
37·0	98617	·5 2	01383	59100	·5 26	40900	60483	·5 25	39517	
38·0	98620	·6 2	01380	59153	·6 32	40847	60533	·6 30	39467	
39·0	98623	·7 2	01377	59206	·7 37	40795	60582	·7 34	39418	
40·0	98627	·8 3	01373	59258	·8 42	40742	60632	·8 39	39369	20′
41·0	98630	·9 3	01370	59311	·9 47	40689	60681	·9 44	39319	
42·0	98633		01367	59364		40636	60731		39270	
43·0	98636		01364	59416		40584	60780		39220	
44·0	98640		01361	59469		40531	60830		39170	
45·0	98643		01358	59522		40478	60879		39121	15′
46·0	98646		01354	59575		40425	60929		39071	
47·0	98649	·1 0	01351	59628	·1 5	40372	60979	·1 5	39021	
48·0	98652	·2 1	01348	59681	·2 11	40319	61029	·2 10	38971	
49·0	98656	·3 1	01345	59734	·3 16	40266	61079	·3 15	38921	
50·0	98659	·4 1	01341	59788	·4 21	40212	61129	·4 20	38871	10′
51·0	98662		01338	59841		40159	61179		38821	
52·0	98665	·5 2	01335	59894	·5 27	40106	61229	·5 25	38771	
53·0	98668	·6 2	01332	59948	·6 32	40052	61279	·6 30	38721	
54·0	98671	·7 2	01329	60001	·7 37	39999	61330	·7 35	38670	
55·0	98675	·8 3	01325	60055	·8 43	39946	61380	·8 40	38620	5′
56·0	98678	·9 3	01322	60108	·9 48	39892	61430	·9 45	38570	
57·0	98681		01319	60162		39838	61481		38519	
58·0	98684		01316	60215		39785	61531		38469	
59·0	98687		01313	60269		39731	61582		38418	
60·0	98690		01310	60323		39677	61632		38368	0′

104°
284°

76°
256°

LOGS. OF TRIG. FUNCTIONS

′	Sine	Parts	Cosec.	Tan.	Parts	Cotan.	Secant	Parts	Cosine	
00·0	1̄.(9) 98690		0.(10) 01310	0.(10) 60323		1̄.(9) 39677	0.(10) 61632		1̄.(9) 38368	60′
01·0	98693		01306	60377		39623	61683		38317	
02·0	98697	·1 0	01303	60431	·1 5	39569	61734	·1 5	38266	
03·0	98700	·2 1	01300	60485	·2 11	39515	61785	·2 10	38215	
04·0	98703	·3 1	01297	60539	·3 16	39461	61836	·3 15	38164	
05·0	98706	·4 1	01294	60593	·4 22	39407	61887	·4 20	38113	55′
06·0	98709		01291	60647		39353	61938		38062	
07·0	98712	·5 2	01288	60701	·5 27	39299	61989	·5 26	38011	
08·0	98716	·6 2	01285	60755	·6 33	39245	62040	·6 31	37960	
09·0	98719	·7 2	01281	60810	·7 38	39190	62091	·7 36	37909	
10·0	98722		01278	60864		39136	62142		37858	50′
11·0	98725	·8 3	01275	60919	·8 43	39082	62194	·8 41	37806	
12·0	98728	·9 3	01272	60973	·9 49	39027	62245	·9 46	37755	
13·0	98731		01269	61028		38972	62297		37704	
14·0	98734		01266	61082		38918	62348		37652	
15·0	98737		01263	61137		38863	62400		37600	45′
16·0	98740		01260	61192		38808	62451		37549	
17·0	98743	·1 0	01257	61246	·1 6	38754	62503	·1 5	37497	
18·0	98747	·2 1	01254	61301	·2 11	38699	62555	·2 10	37445	
19·0	98750	·3 1	01250	61356	·3 17	38644	62607	·3 16	37393	
20·0	98753		01247	61411		38589	62659		37341	40′
21·0	98756	·4 1	01244	61466	·4 22	38534	62711	·4 21	37289	
22·0	98759	·5 2	01241	61521	·5 28	38479	62763	·5 26	37237	
23·0	98762	·6 2	01238	61577	·6 33	38423	62815	·6 31	37185	
24·0	98765		01235	61632		38368	62867		37133	
25·0	98768	·7 2	01232	61687	·7 39	38313	62919	·7 36	37081	35′
26·0	98771	·8 2	01229	61743	·8 44	38258	62972	·8 42	37029	
27·0	98774	·9 3	01226	61798	·9 50	38202	63024	·9 47	36976	
28·0	98777		01223	61853		38147	63076		36924	
29·0	98780		01220	61909		38091	63129		36871	
30·0	98783		01217	61965		38035	63182		36819	30′
31·0	98786		01214	62020		37980	63234		36766	
32·0	98789	·1 0	01211	62076	·1 6	37924	63287	·1 5	36713	
33·0	98792	·2 1	01208	62132	·2 11	37868	63340	·2 11	36660	
34·0	98795	·3 1	01205	62188	·3 17	37812	63393	·3 16	36608	
35·0	98798	·4 1	01202	62244	·4 22	37756	63445	·4 21	36555	25′
36·0	98801		01199	62300		37700	63498		36502	
37·0	98804	·5 2	01196	62356	·5 28	37644	63552	·5 27	36449	
38·0	98807	·6 2	01193	62412	·6 34	37588	63605	·6 32	36395	
39·0	98810	·7 2	01190	62468	·7 39	37532	63658	·7 37	36342	
40·0	98813		01187	62524		37476	63711		36289	20′
41·0	98816	·8 2	01184	62581	·8 45	37419	63764	·8 43	36236	
42·0	98819	·9 3	01181	62637	·9 51	37363	63818	·9 48	36182	
43·0	98822		01178	62694		37306	63871		36129	
44·0	98825		01175	62750		37250	63925		36075	
45·0	98828		01172	62807		37193	63979		36022	15′
46·0	98831		01169	62863		37137	64032		35968	
47·0	98834	·1 0	01166	62920	·1 6	37080	64086	·1 5	35914	
48·0	98837	·2 1	01163	62977	·2 11	37023	64140	·2 11	35860	
49·0	98840	·3 1	01160	63034	·3 17	36966	64194	·3 16	35806	
50·0	98843	·4 1	01157	63091	·4 23	36909	64248	·4 22	35752	10′
51·0	98846		01154	63148		36852	64302		35698	
52·0	98849	·5 1	01151	63205	·5 29	36795	64356	·5 27	35644	
53·0	98852	·6 2	01148	63262	·6 34	36738	64410	·6 33	35590	
54·0	98855		01145	63319		36681	64464		35536	
55·0	98858	·7 2	01142	63376	·7 40	36624	64519	·7 38	35482	5′
56·0	98861	·8 2	01139	63434	·8 46	36566	64572	8 43	35427	
57·0	98864	·9 3	01136	63491	·9 51	36509	64627	·9 49	35373	
58·0	98867		01133	63549		36452	64682		35318	
59·0	98870		01131	63606		36394	64737		35264	
60·0	98872		01128	63664		36336	64791		35209	0′

77°
257°

LOGS. OF TRIG. FUNCTIONS

′	Sine	Parts	Cosec.	Tan.	Parts	Cotan.	Secant	Parts	Cosine	
00·0	1̄.(9) 98872	′	0.(10) 01128	0.(10) 63664	′	1̄.(9) 36336	0.(10) 64791	′	1̄.(9) 35209	60′
01·0	98875		01125	63721		36279	64846		35154	
02·0	98878	·1 0	01122	63779	·1 6	36221	64901	·1 6	35099	
03·0	98881	·2 1	01119	63837	·2 12	36163	64956	·2 11	35044	
04·0	98884	·3 1	01116	63895	·3 17	36105	65011	·3 17	34989	
05·0	98887	·4 1	01113	63953	·4 23	36047	65066	·4 22	34934	55′
06·0	98890	·5 1	01110	64011	·5 29	35989	65121	·5 28	34879	
07·0	98893	·6 2	01107	64069	·6 35	35931	65176	·6 33	34824	
08·0	98896	·7 2	01104	64127	·7 41	35873	65231	·7 39	34769	
09·0	98899		01102	64185		35815	65287		34713	
10·0	98901	·8 2	01099	64243	·8 47	35757	65342	·8 44	34658	50′
11·0	98904	·9 3	01096	64302	·9 52	35698	65398	·9 50	34602	
12·0	98907		01093	64360		35640	65453		34547	
13·0	98910		01090	64419		35581	65509		34491	
14·0	98913		01087	64477		35523	65565		34436	
15·0	98916		01084	64536		35464	65620		34380	45′
16·0	98919		01081	64595		35405	65676		34324	
17·0	98921	·1 0	01079	64654	·1 6	35347	65732	·1 6	34268	
18·0	98924	·2 1	01076	64712	·2 12	35288	65788	·2 11	34212	
19·0	98927	·3 1	01073	64771	·3 18	35229	65844	·3 17	34156	
20·0	98930	·4 1	01070	64830	·4 24	35170	65900	·4 23	34100	40′
21·0	98933	·5 1	01067	64889	·5 30	35111	65957	·5 28	34043	
22·0	98936	·6 2	01064	64949	·6 36	35051	66013	·6 34	33987	
23·0	98939	·7 2	01062	65008	·7 41	34992	66069	·7 39	33931	
24·0	98941		01059	65067		34933	66126		33874	
25·0	98944	·8 2	01056	65127	·8 47	34874	66182	·8 45	33818	35′
26·0	98947	·9 2	01053	65186	·9 53	34814	66239	·9 51	33761	
27·0	98950		01050	65246		34755	66296		33704	
28·0	98953		01048	65305		34695	66353		33648	
29·0	98955		01045	65365		34635	66409		33591	
30·0	98958		01042	65425		34576	66466		33534	30′
31·0	98961		01039	65484		34516	66523		33477	
32·0	98964	·1 0	01036	65544	·1 6	34456	66581	·1 6	33420	
33·0	98967	·2 1	01034	65604	·2 12	34396	66638	·2 12	33362	
34·0	98969	·3 1	01031	65664	·3 18	34336	66695	·3 17	33305	
35·0	98972	·4 1	01028	65724	·4 24	34276	66752	·4 23	33248	25′
36·0	98975	·5 1	01025	65785	·5 30	34216	66810	·5 29	33190	
37·0	98978	·6 2	01022	65845	·6 36	34155	66867	·6 35	33133	
38·0	98980	·7 2	01020	65905	·7 42	34095	66925	·7 40	33075	
39·0	98983		01017	65966		34034	66982		33018	
40·0	98986	·8 2	01014	66026	·8 48	33974	67040	·8 46	32960	20′
41·0	98989	·9 2	01011	66087	·9 54	33913	67098	·9 52	32902	
42·0	98992		01009	66147		33853	67156		32844	
43·0	98994		01006	66208		33792	67214		32786	
44·0	98997		01003	66269		33731	67272		32728	
45·0	99000		01000	66330		33670	67330		32670	15′
46·0	99003		00998	66391		33609	67388		32612	
47·0	99005	·1 0	00995	66452	·1 6	33548	67447	·1 6	32553	
48·0	99008	·2 1	00992	66513	·2 12	33487	67505	·2 12	32495	
49·0	99011	·3 1	00989	66574	·3 18	33426	67563	·3 18	32437	
50·0	99013	·4 1	00987	66635	·4 25	33365	67622	·4 24	32378	10′
51·0	99016	·5 1	00984	66697	·5 31	33303	67681	·5 29	32319	
52·0	99019	·6 2	00981	66758	·6 37	33242	67739	·6 35	32261	
53·0	99022	·7 2	00979	66820	·7 43	33180	67798	·7 41	32202	
54·0	99024		00976	66881		33119	67857		32143	
55·0	99027	·8 2	00973	66943	·8 49	33057	67916	·8 47	32084	5′
56·0	99030	·9 2	00970	67005	·9 55	32995	67975	·9 53	32025	
57·0	99032		00968	67067		32933	68034		31966	
58·0	99035		00965	·67129		32872	68093		31907	
59·0	99038		00962	·67191		32810	·68153		31847	
60·0	99040		00960	·67253		32748	68212		31788	0′

102°
282°

78°
258°

LOGS. OF TRIG. FUNCTIONS

′	Sine	Parts	Cosec.	Tan.	Parts	Cotan.	Secant	Parts	Cosine	
00·0	1̄.(9) 99040	′	0.(10) 00960	0.(10) 67253	′	1̄.(9) 32748	0.(10) 68212	′	1̄.(9) 31788	60′
01·0	99043		00957	67315		32685	68272		31728	
02·0	99046	·1 0	00954	67377	·1 6	32623	68331	·1 6	31669	
03·0	99049	·2 1	00952	67439	·2 13	32561	68391	·2 12	31609	
04·0	99051	·3 1	00949	67502	·3 19	32498	68451	·3 18	31550	
05·0	99054	·4 1	00946	67564	·4 25	32436	68510	·4 24	31490	55′
06·0	99057		00944	67627		32373	68570		31430	
07·0	99059	·5 1	00941	67689	·5 31	32311	68630	·5 30	31370	
08·0	99062	·6 2	00938	67752	·6 38	32248	68690	·6 36	31310	
09·0	99065	·7 2	00935	67815	·7 44	32185	68751	·7 42	31250	
10·0	99067	·8 2	00933	67878	·8 50	32122	68811	·8 48	31189	50′
11·0	99070		00930	67941		32059	68871		31129	
12·0	99072	·9 2	00928	68004	·9 57	31996	68932	·9 54	31069	
13·0	99075		00925	68067		31933	68992		31008	
14·0	99078		00922	68130		31870	69053		30947	
15·0	99080		00920	68194		31806	69113		30887	45′
16·0	99083		00917	68257		31743	69174		30826	
17·0	99086	·1 0	00915	68321	·1 6	31680	69235	·1 6	30765	
18·0	99088	·2 1	00912	68384	·2 13	31616	69296	·2 12	30704	
19·0	99091	·3 1	00909	68448	·3 19	31552	69357	·3 18	30643	
20·0	99093	·4 1	00907	68512	·4 26	31489	69418	·4 25	30582	40′
21·0	99096		00904	68575		31425	69479		30521	
22·0	99099	·5 1	00901	68639	·5 32	31361	69541	·5 31	30459	
23·0	99101	·6 2	00899	68703	·6 38	31297	69602	·6 37	30398	
24·0	99104		00896	68767		31233	69664		30336	
25·0	99106	·7 2	00894	68832	·7 45	31169	69725	·7 43	30275	35′
26·0	99109	·8 2	00891	68896	·8 51	31104	69787	·8 49	30213	
27·0	99112	·9 2	00889	68960	·9 58	31040	69849	·9 55	30151	
28·0	99114		00886	69025		30975	69911		30090	
29·0	99117		00883	69089		30911	69972		30028	
30·0	99119		00881	69154		30846	70035		29966	30′
31·0	99122		00878	69218		30781	70097		29903	
32·0	99124	·1 0	00876	69283	·1 7	30717	70159	·1 6	29841	
33·0	99127	·2 1	00873	69348	·2 13	30652	70221	·2 13	29779	
34·0	99130	·3 1	00871	69413	·3 20	30587	70284	·3 19	29716	
35·0	99132	·4 1	00868	69478	·4 26	30522	70346	·4 25	29654	25′
36·0	99135		00865	69543		30457	70409		29591	
37·0	99137	·5 1	00863	69609	·5 33	30391	70471	·5 31	29529	
38·0	99140	·6 2	00860	69674	·6 39	30326	70534	·6 38	29466	
39·0	99142		00858	69739		30261	70597		29403	
40·0	99145	·7 2	00855	69805	·7 46	30195	70660	·7 44	29340	20′
41·0	99147	·8 2	00853	69871	·8 52	30130	70723	·8 50	29277	
42·0	99150	·9 2	00850	69936	·9 59	30064	70786	·9 57	29214	
43·0	99152		00848	70002		29998	70850		29150	
44·0	99155		00845	70068		29932	70913		29087	
45·0	99157		00843	70134		29866	70976		29024	15′
46·0	99160		00840	70200		29800	71040		28960	
47·0	99162	·1 0	00838	70266	·1 7	29734	71104	·1 6	28896	
48·0	99165	·2 1	00835	70332	·2 13	29668	71167	·2 13	28833	
49·0	99167	·3 1	00833	70399	·3 20	29601	71231	·3 19	28769	
50·0	99170	·4 1	00830	70465	·4 27	29535	71295	·4 26	28705	10′
51·0	99172		00828	70532		29468	71359		28641	
52·0	99175	·5 1	00825	70598	·5 33	29402	71423	·5 32	28577	
53·0	99177	·6 2	00823	70665	·6 40	29335	71488	·6 39	28512	
54·0	99180		00820	70732		29268	71552		28448	
55·0	99182	·7 2	00818	70799	·7 47	29201	71616	·7 45	28384	5′
56·0	99185	·8 2	00815	70866	·8 53	29134	71681	·8 51	28319	
57·0	99187	·9 2	00813	70933	·9 60	29067	71746	·9 58	28254	
58·0	99190		00810	71000		29000	71810		28190	
59·0	99192		00808	71067		28933	71875		28125	
60·0	99195		00805	71135		28865	71940		28060	0′

79°
259°

LOGS. OF TRIG. FUNCTIONS

′	Sine	Parts	Cosec.	Tan.	Parts	Cotan.	Secant	Parts	Cosine	
00·0	1.(9) 99195	′	0.(10) 00805	0.(10) 71135	′	1.(9) 28865	0.(10) 71940	′	1.(9) 28060	60′
01·0	99197	·1 0	00803	71202	·1 7	28798	72005	·1 7	27995	
02·0	99200	·2 0	00800	71270	·2 14	28730	72070	·2 13	27930	
03·0	99202	·3 1	00798	71338	·3 20	28662	72136	·3 20	27865	
04·0	99204	·4 1	00796	71405	·4 27	28595	72201	·4 26	27799	
05·0	99207	·5 1	00793	71473	·5 34	28527	72266	·5 33	27734	55′
06·0	99209	·6 1	00791	71541	·6 41	28459	72332	·6 39	27668	
07·0	99212	·7 2	00788	71609	·7 48	28391	72398	·7 46	27603	
08·0	99214	·8 2	00786	71678	·8 54	28323	72463	·8 52	27537	
09·0	99217	·9 2	00783	71746	·9 61	28254	72529	·9 59	27471	
10·0	99219		00781	71814		28186	72595		27405	50′
11·0	99221	·1 0	00779	71883	·1 7	28117	72661	·1 7	27339	
12·0	99224	·2 0	00776	71951	·2 14	28049	72727	·2 13	27273	
13·0	99226	·3 1	00774	72020	·3 21	27980	72794	·3 20	27206	
14·0	99229	·4 1	00771	72089	·4 28	27911	72860	·4 27	27140	
15·0	99231	·5 1	00769	72158	·5 35	27842	72927	·5 33	27074	45′
16·0	99234	·6 1	00767	72227	·6 41	27773	72993	·6 40	27007	
17·0	99236	·7 2	00764	72296	·7 48	27704	73060	·7 47	26940	
18·0	99238	·8 2	00762	72365	·8 55	27635	73127	·8 53	26873	
19·0	99241	·9 2	00759	72434	·9 62	27566	73194	·9 60	26807	
20·0	99243		00757	72504		27496	73261		26740	40′
21·0	99245	·1 0	00755	72573	·1 7	27427	73328	·1 7	26672	
22·0	99248	·2 0	00752	72643	·2 14	27357	73395	·2 14	26605	
23·0	99250	·3 1	00750	72712	·3 21	27288	73462	·3 20	26538	
24·0	99253	·4 1	00748	72782	·4 28	27218	73530	·4 27	26470	
25·0	99255	·5 1	00745	72852	·5 35	27148	73597	·5 34	26403	35′
26·0	99257	·6 1	00743	72922	·6 42	27078	73665	·6 41	26335	
27·0	99260	·7 2	00740	72992	·7 49	27008	73733	·7 47	26267	
28·0	99262	·8 2	00738	73063	·8 56	26938	73801	·8 54	26199	
29·0	99264	·9 2	00736	73133	·9 63	26867	73869	·9 61	26131	
30·0	99267		00733	73203		26797	73937		26063	30′
31·0	99269	·1 0	00731	73274	·1 7	26726	74005	·1 7	25995	
32·0	99271	·2 0	00729	73345	·2 14	26656	74073	·2 14	25927	
33·0	99274	·3 1	00727	73415	·3 21	26585	74142	·3 21	25858	
34·0	99276	·4 1	00724	73486	·4 28	26514	74210	·4 27	25790	
35·0	99278	·5 1	00722	73557	·5 36	26443	74279	·5 34	25721	25′
36·0	99281	·6 1	00719	73628	·6 43	26372	74348	·6 41	25652	
37·0	99283	·7 2	00717	73700	·7 50	26301	74417	·7 48	25583	
38·0	99285	·8 2	00715	73771	·8 57	26229	74486	·8 55	25514	
39·0	99288	·9 2	00713	73842	·9 64	26158	74555	·9 62	25445	
40·0	99290		00710	73914		26086	74624		25376	20′
41·0	99292	·1 0	00708	73985	·1 7	26015	74693	·1 7	25307	
42·0	99294	·2 0	00706	74057	·2 14	25943	74763	·2 14	25237	
43·0	99297	·3 1	00703	74129	·3 22	25871	74832	·3 21	25168	
44·0	99299	·4 1	00701	74201	·4 29	25799	74902	·4 28	25098	
45·0	99301	·5 1	00699	74273	·5 36	25727	74972	·5 35	25028	15′
46·0	99304	·6 1	00696	74345	·6 43	25655	75042	·6 42	24958	
47·0	99306	·7 2	00694	74418	·7 50	25582	75112	·7 49	24888	
48·0	99308	·8 2	00692	74490	·8 58	25510	75182	·8 56	24818	
49·0	99310	·9 2	00690	74563	·9 65	25437	75252	·9 63	24748	
50·0	99313		00687	74635		25365	75323		24678	10′
51·0	99315	·1 0	00685	74708	·1 7	25292	75393	·1 7	24607	
52·0	99317	·2 0	00683	74781	·2 15	25219	75464	·2 14	24536	
53·0	99320	·3 1	00681	74854	·3 22	25146	75534	·3 21	24466	
54·0	99322	·4 1	00678	74927	·4 29	25073	75605	·4 28	24395	
55·0	99324	·5 1	00676	75000	·5 37	25000	75676	·5 36	24324	5′
56·0	99326	·6 1	00674	75074	·6 44	24926	75747	·6 43	24253	
57·0	99328	·7 2	00672	75147	·7 51	24853	75819	·7 50	24181	
58·0	99331	·8 2	00669	75221	·8 59	24779	75890	·8 57	24110	
59·0	99333	·9 2	00667	75294	·9 66	24706	75961	·9 64	24039	
60·0	99335		00665	75368		24632	76033		23967	0′

80° / 260°
LOGS. OF TRIG. FUNCTIONS

′	Sine	Parts		Cosec.	Tan.	Parts		Cotan.	Secant	Parts		Cosine	
00·0	1̄.(9) 99335	′		0.(10) 00665	0.(10) 75368	′		1̄.(9) 24632	0.(10) 76033	′		1̄.(9) 23967	60′
01·0	99337	·1	0	00663	75442	·1	7	24558	76105	·1	7	23895	
02·0	99340	·2	0	00660	75516	·2	15	24484	76177	·2	14	23824	
03·0	99342	·3	1	00658	75590	·3	22	24410	76249	·3	22	23752	
04·0	99344	·4	1	00656	75665	·4	30	24335	76321	·4	29	23680	
05·0	99346	·5	1	00654	75739	·5	37	24261	76393	·5	36	23607	55′
06·0	99348	·6	1	00652	75814	·6	45	24187	76465	·6	43	23535	
07·0	99351	·7	2	00649	75888	·7	52	24112	76538	·7	51	23463	
08·0	99353	·8	2	00647	75963	·8	60	24037	76610	·8	58	23390	
09·0	99355	·9	2	00645	76038	·9	67	23962	76683	·9	65	23317	
10·0	99357			00643	76113			23887	76756			23244	50′
11·0	99359	·1	0	00641	76188	·1	8	23812	76829	·1	7	23172	
12·0	99362	·2	0	00638	76263	·2	15	23737	76902	·2	15	23098	
13·0	99364	·3	1	00636	76339	·3	23	23661	76975	·3	22	23025	
14·0	99366	·4	1	00634	76414	·4	30	23586	77048	·4	29	22952	
15·0	99368	·5	1	00632	76490	·5	38	23510	77122	·5	37	22878	45′
16·0	99370	·6	1	00630	76566	·6	45	23435	77195	·6	44	22805	
17·0	99373	·7	2	00628	76641	·7	53	23359	77269	·7	51	22731	
18·0	99375	·8	2	00625	76717	·8	61	23283	77343	·8	59	22657	
19·0	99377	·9	2	00623	76794	·9	68	23207	77417	·9	66	22583	
20·0	99379			00621	76870			23130	77491			22509	40′
21·0	99381	·1	0	00619	76946	·1	8	23054	77565	·1	7	22435	
22·0	99383	·2	0	00617	77023	·2	15	22977	77639	·2	15	22361	
23·0	99385	·3	1	00615	77099	·3	23	22901	77714	·3	22	22286	
24·0	99388	·4	1	00613	77176	·4	31	22824	77789	·4	30	22211	
25·0	99390	·5	1	00610	77253	·5	38	22747	77863	·5	37	22137	35′
26·0	99392	·6	1	00608	77330	·6	46	22670	77938	·6	45	22062	
27·0	99394	·7	1	00606	77407	·7	54	22593	78013	·7	52	21987	
28·0	99396	·8	2	00604	77484	·8	62	22516	78088	·8	60	21912	
29·0	99398	·9	2	00602	77562	·9	69	22438	78164	·9	67	2183o	
30·0	99400			00600	77639			22361	78239			21761	30′
31·0	99402	·1	0	00598	77717	·1	8	22283	78315	·1	8	21685	
32·0	99405	·2	0	00596	77795	·2	16	22205	78390	·2	15	21610	
33·0	99407	·3	1	00593	77873	·3	23	22127	78466	·3	23	21534	
34·0	99409	·4	1	00591	77951	·4	31	22049	78542	·4	30	21458	
35·0	99411	·5	1	00589	78029	·5	39	21971	78618	·5	38	21382	25′
36·0	99413	·6	1	00587	78107	·6	47	21893	78695	·6	46	21306	
37·0	99415	·7	1	00585	78186	·7	55	21814	78771	·7	53	21229	
38·0	99417	·8	2	00583	78264	·8	63	21736	78847	·8	61	21153	
39·0	99419	·9	2	00581	78343	·9	70	21657	78924	·9	69	21076	
40·0	99421			00579	78422			21578	79001			20999	20′
41·0	99423	·1	0	00577	78501	·1	8	21499	79078	·1	8	20922	
42·0	99425	·2	0	00575	78580	·2	16	21420	79155	·2	16	20845	
43·0	99427	·3	1	00573	78660	·3	24	21341	79232	·3	23	20768	
44·0	99430	·4	1	00571	78739	·4	32	21261	79309	·4	31	20691	
45·0	99432	·5	1	00568	78819	·5	40	21182	79387	·5	39	20613	15′
46·0	99434	·6	1	00566	78898	·6	48	21102	79465	·6	47	20535	
47·0	99436	·7	1	00564	78978	·7	56	21022	79542	·7	54	20458	
48·0	99438	·8	2	00562	79058	·8	64	20942	79620	·8	62	20380	
49·0	99440	·9	2	00560	79138	·9	72	20862	79698	·9	70	20302	
50·0	99442			00558	79218			20782	79777			20223	10′
51·0	99444	·1	0	00556	79299	·1	8	20701	79855	·1	8	20145	
52·0	99446	·2	0	00554	79379	·2	16	20621	79933	·2	16	20067	
53·0	99448	·3	1	00552	79460	·3	24	20540	80012	·3	24	19988	
54·0	99450	·4	1	00550	79541	·4	32	20459	80091	·4	32	19909	
55·0	99452	·5	1	00548	79622	·5	41	20378	80170	·5	40	19830	5′
56·0	99454	·6	1	00546	79703	·6	49	20297	80249	·6	47	19751	
57·0	99456	·7	1	00544	79784	·7	57	20216	80328	·7	55	19672	
58·0	99458	·8	2	00542	79866	·8	65	20135	80408	·8	63	19593	
59·0	99460	·9	2	00540	79947	·9	73	20053	80487	·9	71	19513	
60·0	99462			00538	80029			19971	80567			19433	0′

81°
LOGS. OF TRIG. FUNCTIONS
261°

′	Sine	Parts	Cosec.	Tan.	Parts	Cotan.	Secant	Parts	Cosine	
00·0	1̄.(9) 99462	′	0.(10) 00538	0.(10) 80029	′	1̄.(9) 19971	0.(10) 80567	′	1̄.(9) 19433	60′
01·0	99464	·1 0	00536	80111	·1 8	19889	80647	·1 8	19353	
02·0	99466	·2 0	00534	80193	·2 17	19807	80727	·2 16	19273	
03·0	99468	·3 1	00532	80275	·3 25	19725	80807	·3 24	19193	
04·0	99470	·4 1	00530	80357	·4 33	19643	80887	·4 32	19113	
05·0	99472	·5 1	00528	80439	·5 41	19561	80968	·5 40	19033	55′
06·0	99474	·6 1	00526	80522	·6 50	19478	81048	·6 48	18952	
07·0	99476	·7 1	00524	80605	·7 58	19395	81129	·7 56	18871	
08·0	99478	·8 2	00522	80688	·8 66	19312	81210	·8 64	18790	
09·0	99480	·9 2	00520	80771	·9 74	19229	81291	·9 72	18709	
10·0	99482		00518	80854		19146	81372		18628	50′
11·0	99484	·1 0	00516	80937	·1 .8	19063	81453	·1 8	18547	
12·0	99486	·2 0	00514	81021	·2 17	18979	81535	·2 16	18465	
13·0	99488	·3 1	00512	81104	·3 25	18896	81617	·3 25	18383	
14·0	99490	·4 1	00510	81188	·4 34	18812	81698	·4 33	18302	
15·0	99492	·5 1	00508	81272	·5 42	18728	81780	·5 41	18220	45′
16·0	99494	·6 1	00507	81356	·6 50	18644	81863	·6 49	18137	
17·0	99496	·7 1	00505	81440	·7 59	18560	81945	·7 57	18055	
18·0	99497	·8 2	00503	81525	·8 67	18475	82027	·8 66	17973	
19·0	99499	·9 2	00501	81609	·9 76	18391	82110	·9 74	17890	
20·0	99501		00499	81694		18306	82193		17807	40′
21·0	99503	·1 0	00497	81779	·1 9	18221	82276	·1 8	17724	
22·0	99505	·2 0	00495	81864	·2 17	18136	82359	·2 17	17641	
23·0	99507	·3 1	00493	81949	·3 26	18051	82442	·3 25	17558	
24·0	99509	·4 1	00491	82035	·4 34	17966	82526	·4 33	17474	
25·0	99511	·5 1	00480	82120	·5 43	17880	82609	·5 42	17391	35′
26·0	99513	·6 1	00487	82206	·6 51	17794	82693	·6 50	17307	
27·0	99515	·7 1	00485	82292	·7 60	17708	82777	·7 59	17223	
28·0	99517	·8 2	00484	82378	·8 68	17622	82861	·8 67	17139	
29·0	99518	·9 2	00482	82464	·9 77	17536	82945	·9 75	17055	
30·0	99520		00480	82550		17450	83030		16970	30′
31·0	99522	·1 0	00478	82637	·1 9	17363	83114	·1 9	16886	
32·0	99524	·2 0	00476	82723	·2 17	17277	83199	·2 17	16801	
33·0	99526	·3 1	00474	82810	·3 26	17190	83284	·3 26	16716	
34·0	99528	·4 1	00472	82897	·4 35	17103	83369	·4 34	16631	
35·0	99530	·5 1	00470	82984	·5 44	17016	83455	·5 43	16545	25′
36·0	99532	·6 1	00468	83072	·6 52	16928	83540	·6 51	16460	
37·0	99533	·7 1	00467	83159	·7 61	16841	83626	·7 60	16374	
38·0	99535	·8 2	00465	83247	·8 70	16753	83712	·8 68	16289	
39·0	99537	·9 2	00463	83335	·9 79	16665	83798	·9 77	16203	
40·0	99539		00461	83423		16577	83884		16116	20′
41·0	99541	·1 0	00459	83511	·1 9	16489	83970	·1 9	16030	
42·0	99543	·2 0	00457	83599	·2 18	16401	84057	·2 17	15944	
43·0	99545	·3 1	00455	83688	·3 27	16312	84143	·3 26	15857	
44·0	99546	·4 1	00454	83776	·4 36	16224	84230	·4 35	15770	
45·0	99548	·5 1	00452	83865	·5 44	16135	84317	·5 44	15683	15′
46·0	99550	·6 1	00450	83954	·6 53	16046	84404	·6 52	15596	
47·0	99552	·7 1	00448	84044	·7 62	15957	84492	·7 61	15508	
48·0	99554	·8 1	00446	84133	·8 71	15867	84579	·8 70	15421	
49·0	99556	·9 2	00445	84223	·9 80	15778	84667	·9 78	15333	
50·0	99557		00443	84312		15688	84755		15245	10′
51·0	99559	·1 0	00441	84402	·1 9	15598	84843	·1 9	15157	
52·0	99561	·2 0	00439	84492	·2 18	15508	84931	·2 18	15069	
53·0	99563	·3 1	00437	84583	·3 27	15417	85020	·3 27	14980	
54·0	99565	·4 1	00435	84673	·4 36	15327	85109	·4 36	14892	
55·0	99566	·5 1	00434	84764	·5 45	15236	85197	·5 44	14803	5′
56·0	99568	·6 1	00432	84855	·6 54	15145	85286	·6 53	14714	
57·0	99570	·7 1	00430	84946	·7 64	15054	85376	·7 62	14624	
58·0	99572	·8 1	00428	85037	·8 73	14963	85465	·8 71	14535	
59·0	99574	·9 2	00427	85128	·9 82	14872	85555	·9 80	14445	
60·0	99575		00425	85220		14780	85645		14356	0′

98°
278°

82°
262°

LOGS. OF TRIG. FUNCTIONS

′	Sine	Parts	Cosec.	Tan.	Parts	Cotan.	Secant	Parts	Cosine	
00·0	1.(9) 99575		0.(10) 00425	0.(10) 85220		1.(9) 14780	0.(10) 85645		1.(9) 14356	60′
01·0	99577	·1 0	00423	85312	·1 9	14689	85735	·1 9	14266	
02·0	99579	·2 0	00421	85403	·2 19	14597	85825	·2 18	14175	
03·0	99581	·3 1	00419	85496	·3 28	14504	85915	·3 27	14085	
04·0	99582	·4 1	00418	85588	·4 37	14412	86006	·4 36	13994	
05·0	99584	·5 1	00416	85680	·5 46	14320	86096	·5 45	13904	55′
06·0	99586	·6 1	00414	85773	·6 56	14227	86187	·6 55	13813	
07·0	99588	·7 1	00412	85866	·7 65	14134	86278	·7 64	13722	
08·0	99589	·8 1	00411	85959	·8 74	14041	86370	·8 73	13630	
09·0	99591	·9 2	00409	86052	·9 83	13948	86461	·9 82	13539	
10·0	99593		00407	86146		13854	86553		13447	50′
11·0	99595	·1 0	00405	86240	·1 9	13761	86645	·1 9	13355	
12·0	99596	·2 0	00404	86333	·2 19	13667	86737	·2 19	13263	
13·0	99598	·3 1	00402	86427	·3 28	13573	86829	·3 28	13171	
14·0	99600	·4 1	00400	86522	·4 38	13478	86922	·4 37	13078	
15·0	99602	·5 1	00399	86616	·5 47	13384	87015	·5 46	12985	45′
16·0	99603	·6 1	00397	86711	·6 57	13289	87108	·6 56	12893	
17·0	99605	·7 1	00395	86806	·7 66	13194	87201	·7 65	12799	
18·0	99607	·8 1	00393	86901	·8 76	13099	87294	·8 74	12706	
19·0	99608	·9 2	00392	86996	·9 85	13004	87388	·9 84	12613	
20·0	99610		00390	87091		12909	87481		12519	40′
21·0	99612	·1 0	00388	87187	·1 10	12813	87575	·1 9	12425	
22·0	99613	·2 0	00387	87283	·2 19	12717	87669	·2 19	12331	
23·0	99615	·3 1	00385	87379	·3 29	12621	87764	·3 28	12236	
24·0	99617	·4 1	00383	87475	·4 39	12525	87858	·4 38	12142	
25·0	99619	·5 1	00382	87572	·5 48	12428	87953	·5 47	12047	35′
26·0	99620	·6 1	00380	87668	·6 58	12332	88048	·6 57	11952	
27·0	99622	·7 1	00378	87765	·7 68	12235	88143	·7 66	11857	
28·0	99624	·8 1	00377	87862	·8 77	12138	88239	·8 76	11761	
29·0	99625	·9 2	00375	87960	·9 87	12040	88334	·9 85	11666	
30·0	99627		00373	88057		11943	88430		11570	30′
31·0	99629	·1 0	00372	88155	·1 10	11845	88526	·1 10	11474	
32·0	99630	·2 0	00370	88253	·2 20	11747	88623	·2 19	11377	
33·0	99632	·3 0	00368	88351	·3 30	11649	88719	·3 29	11281	
34·0	99634	·4 1	00367	88449	·4 40	11551	88816	·4 39	11184	
35·0	99635	·5 1	00365	88548	·5 49	11452	88913	·5 49	11087	25′
36·0	99637	·6 1	00363	88646	·6 59	11353	89010	·6 58	10990	
37·0	99638	·7 1	00362	88746	·7 69	11254	89107	·7 68	10893	
38·0	99640	·8 1	00360	88845	·8 79	11155	89205	·8 78	10795	
39·0	99642	·9 1	00358	88944	·9 89	11056	89303	·9 87	10697	
40·0	99643		00357	89044		10956	89401		10599	20′
41·0	99645	·1 0	00355	89144	·1 10	10856	89499	·1 10	10501	
42·0	99647	·2 0	00354	89244	·2 20	10756	89598	·2 20	10403	
43·0	99648	·3 0	00352	89344	·3 30	10656	89696	·3 30	10304	
44·0	99650	·4 1	00350	89445	·4 40	10555	89795	·4 40	10205	
45·0	99651	·5 1	00349	89546	·5 50	10454	89894	·5 50	10106	15′
46·0	99653	·6 1	00347	89647	·6 61	10353	89994	·6 60	10006	
47·0	99655	·7 1	00345	89748	·7 71	10252	90094	·7 70	09907	
48·0	99656	·8 1	00344	89850	·8 81	10150	90193	·8 79	09807	
49·0	99658	·9 1	00342	89951	·9 91	10049	90294	·9 89	09707	
50·0	99659		00341	90053		09947	90394		09606	10′
51·0	99661	·1 0	00339	90155	·1 10	09845	90494	·1 10	09506	
52·0	99663	·2 0	00338	90258	·2 21	09742	90595	·2 20	09405	
53·0	99664	·3 0	00336	90361	·3 31	09640	90696	·3 30	09304	
54·0	99666	·4 1	00334	90463	·4 41	09537	90798	·4 41	09202	
55·0	99667	·5 1	00333	90566	·5 52	09434	90899	·5 51	09101	5′
56·0	99669	·6 1	00331	90670	·6 62	09330	91001	·6 61	08999	
57·0	99670	·7 1	00330	90773	·7 72	09227	91103	·7 71	08897	
58·0	99672	·8 1	00328	90877	·8 83	09123	91205	·8 81	08795	
59·0	99674	·9 1	00327	90981	·9 93	09019	91308	·9 92	08692	
60·0	99675		00325	91086		08914	91411		08589	0′

97°
277°

83°
263°

LOGS. OF TRIG. FUNCTIONS

′	Sine	Parts	Cosec.	Tan.	Parts	Cotan.	Secant	Parts	Cosine	
00·0	1.(9) 99675		0.(10) 00325	0.(10) 91086	′	1.(9) 08914	0.(10) 91411	′	1.(9) 08589	60′
01·0	99677		00323	91190	·1 11	08810	91514	·1 10	08486	
02·0	99678		00322	91295	·2 21	08705	91617	·2 21	08383	
03·0	99680		00320	91400	·3 32	08600	91720	·3 31	08280	
04·0	99681		00319	91505	·4 42	08495	91824	·4 42	08176	
05·0	99683		00317	91611	·5 53	08389	91928	·5 52	08072	55′
06·0	99684		00316	91717	·6 63	08283	92032	·6 62	07968	
07·0	99686		00314	91823	·7 74	08177	92137	·7 73	07863	
08·0	99687		00313	91929	·8 84	08071	92242	·8 83	07758	
09·0	99689		00311	92036	·9 95	07964	92347	·9 94	07653	
10·0	99690		00310	92142		07858	92452		07548	50′
11·0	99692		00308	92250	·1 11	07751	92558	·1 11	07442	
12·0	99693		00307	92357	·2 22	07643	92663	·2 21	07337	
13·0	99695		00305	92464	·3 32	07536	92769	·3 32	07231	
14·0	99696		00304	92572	·4 43	07428	92876	·4 43	07124	
15·0	99698		00302	92680	·5 54	07320	92982	·5 53	07018	45′
16·0	99699		00301	92789	·6 65	07211	93089	·6 64	06911	
17·0	99701		00299	92897	·7 76	07103	93196	·7 75	06804	
18·0	99702		00298	93006	·8 87	06994	93304	·8 85	06696	
19·0	99704		00296	93115	·9 97	06885	93412	·9 96	06589	
20·0	99705		00295	93225		06775	93519		06481	40′
21·0	99707		00293	93335	·1 11	06666	93628	·1 11	06372	
22·0	99708		00292	93444	·2 22	06556	93736	·2 22	06264	
23·0	99710		00290	93555	·3 33	06445	93845	·3 33	06155	
24·0	99711		00289	93665	·4 44	06335	93954	·4 44	06046	
25·0	99713		00287	93776	·5 55	06224	94063	·5 55	05937	35′
26·0	99714		00286	93887	·6 67	06113	94173	·6 66	05827	
27·0	99716		00284	93998	·7 78	06002	94283	·7 77	05717	
28·0	99717		00283	94110	·8 89	05890	94393	·8 88	05607	
29·0	99719		00282	94222	·9 100	05778	94503	·9 99	05497	
30·0	99720		00280	94334		05666	94614		05386	30′
31·0	99721		00279	94447	·1 11	05554	94725	·1 11	05275	
32·0	99723		00277	94559	·2 23	05441	94837	·2 22	05164	
33·0	99724		00276	94672	·3 34	05328	94948	·3 34	05052	
34·0	99726		00274	94786	·4 46	05214	95060	·4 45	04940	
35·0	99727		00273	94899	·5 57	05101	95172	·5 56	04828	25′
36·0	99729		00272	95013	·6 68	04987	95285	·6 67	04715	
37·0	99730		00270	95127	·7 80	04873	95397	·7 79	04603	
38·0	99731		00269	95242	·8 91	04758	95511	·8 90	04490	
39·0	99733		00267	95357	·9 102	04643	95624	·9 101	04376	
40·0	99734		00266	95472		04528	95738		04263	20′
41·0	99736		00265	95587	·1 12	04413	95852	·1 12	04149	
42·0	99737		00263	95703	·2 23	04297	95966	·2 23	04034	
43·0	99738		00262	95819	·3 35	04181	96080	·3 35	03920	
44·0	99740		00260	95935	·4 47	04065	96195	·4 46	03805	
45·0	99741		00259	96052	·5 58	03949	96310	·5 58	03690	15′
46·0	99743		00258	96168	·6 70	03832	96426	·6 69	03574	
47·0	99744		00256	96286	·7 82	03714	96542	·7 81	03458	
48·0	99745		00255	96403	·8 93	03597	96658	·8 92	03342	
49·0	99747		00253	96521	·9 105	03479	96774	·9 104	03226	
50·0	99748		00252	96639		03361	96891		03109	10′
51·0	99749		00251	96758	·1 12	03243	97008	·1 12	02992	
52·0	99751		00249	96876	·2 24	03124	97126	·2 24	02874	
53·0	99752		00248	96995	·3 36	03005	97243	·3 36	02757	
54·0	99753		00247	97115	·4 48	02885	97361	·4 47	02639	
55·0	99755		00245	97235	·5 60	02766	97480	·5 59	02520	5′
56·0	99756		00244	97355	·6 72	02646	97598	·6 71	02402	
57·0	99757		00243	97475	·7 84	02525	97718	·7 83	02283	
58·0	99759		00241	97596	·8 96	02404	97837	·8 95	02163	
59·0	99760		00240	97717	·9 108	02283	97957	·9 107	02044	
60·0	99761		00239	97838		02162	98077		01924	0′

LOGS. OF TRIG. FUNCTIONS

84° / 264° · 95° / 275°

'	Sine	Parts	Cosec.	Tan.	Parts	Cotan.	Secant	Parts	Cosine	
00·0	1.(9) 99761		0.(10) 00239	0.(10) 97838	'	1.(9) 02162	0.(10) 98077	'	1.(9) 01924	60'
01·0	99763		00237	97960	·1 12	02040	98197	·1 12	01803	
02·0	99764		00236	98082	·2 25	01918	98318	·2 24	01682	
03·0	99765		00235	98204	·3 37	01796	98439	·3 37	01561	
04·0	99767		00233	98327	·4 49	01673	98560	·4 49	01440	
05·0	99768		00232	98450	·5 62	01550	98682	·5 61	01318	55'
06·0	99769		00231	98573	·6 74	01427	98804	·6 73	01196	
07·0	99771		00229	98697	·7 86	01303	98926	·7 85	01074	
08·0	99772		00228	98821	·8 99	01179	99049	·8 98	00951	
09·0	99773		00227	98945	·9 111	01055	99172	·9 110	00828	
10·0	99775		00226	99070		00930	99296		00704	50'
11·0	99776		00224	99195	·1 13	00805	99420	·1 13	00581	
12·0	99777		00223	99321	·2 25	00679	99544	·2 25	00456	
13·0	99778		00222	99447	·3 38	00553	99668	·3 38	00332	
14·0	99780		00220	99573	·4 51	00427	99793	·4 50	00207	
15·0	99781		00219	99700	·5 63	00301	99918	·5 63	00082	45'
16·0	99782		00218	99826	·6 76	00174	1.(11) 00044	·6 75	2.(8) 99956	
17·0	99784		00217	99954	·7 88	00047	00170	·7 88	99830	
18·0	99785		00215	1.(11) 00081	·8 101	2.(8) 99919	00296	·8 100	99704	
19·0	99786		00214	00209	·9 114	99791	00423	·9 113	99577	
20·0	99787		00213	00338		99662	00550		99450	40'
21·0	99789		00212	00466	·1 13	99534	00678	·1 13	99322	
22·0	99790		00210	00596	·2 26	99405	00806	·2 26	99194	
23·0	99791		00209	00725	·3 39	99275	00934	·3 39	99066	
24·0	99792		00208	00855	·4 52	99145	01063	·4 52	98937	
25·0	99794		00207	00985	·5 65	99015	01192	·5 65	98808	35'
26·0	99795		00205	01116	·6 78	98884	01321	·6 78	98679	
27·0	99796		00204	01247	·7 91	98753	01451	·7 91	98549	
28·0	99797		00203	01378	·8 104	98622	01581	·8 103	98419	
29·0	99798		00202	01510	·9 117	98490	01712	·9 116	98288	
30·0	99800		00200	01642		98358	01843		98157	30'
31·0	99801		00199	01775	·1 13	98225	01974	·1 13	98026	
32·0	99802		00198	01908	·2 27	98092	02106	·2 27	97894	
33·0	99803		00197	02041	·3 40	97959	02238	·3 40	97762	
34·0	99804		00196	02175	·4 54	97825	02371	·4 53	97629	
35·0	99806		00194	02309	·5 67	97691	02504	·5 67	97496	25'
36·0	99807		00193	02444	·6 81	97556	02637	·6 80	97363	
37·0	99808		00192	02579	·7 94	97421	02771	·7 93	97229	
38·0	99809		00191	02715	·8 108	97286	02905	·8 107	97095	
39·0	99810		00190	02850	·9 121	97150	03040	·9 120	96960	
40·0	99812		00188	02987		97013	03175		96825	20'
41·0	99813		00187	03123	·1 14	96887	03311	·1 14	96689	
42·0	99814		00186	03261	·2 28	96739	03447	·2 28	96553	
43·0	99815		00185	03398	·3 42	96602	03583	·3 41	96417	
44·0	99816		00184	03536	·4 55	96464	03720	·4 55	96280	
45·0	99817		00183	03675	·5 69	96326	03857	·5 69	96143	15'
46·0	99819		00181	03813	·6 83	96187	03995	·6 83	96005	
47·0	99820		00180	03953	·7 97	96047	04133	·7 96	95867	
48·0	99821		00179	04093	·8 111	95908	04272	·8 110	95728	
49·0	99822		00178	04233	·9 125	95767	04411	·9 124	95589	
50·0	99823		00177	04373		95627	04550		95450	10'
51·0	99824		00176	04514	·1 14	95486	04690	·1 14	95310	
52·0	99826		00175	04656	·2 29	95344	04830	·2 28	95170	
53·0	99827		00173	04798	·3 43	95202	04971	·3 43	95029	
54·0	99828		00172	04940	·4 57	95060	05113	·4 57	94887	
55·0	99829		00171	05083	·5 72	94917	05254	·5 71	94746	5'
56·0	99830		00170	05227	·6 86	94773	05397	·6 85	94603	
57·0	99831		00169	05371	·7 100	94630	05539	·7 99	94461	
58·0	99832		00168	05515	·8 115	94485	05683	·8 114	94317	
59·0	99833		00167	05660	·9 129	94340	05826	·9 128	94174	
60·0	99834		00166	05805		94195	05970		94030	0'

85°
265°

LOGS. OF TRIG. FUNCTIONS

′	Sine	Parts	Cosec.	Tan.	Parts	Cotan.	Secant	Parts	Cosine	
00·0	1.(9) 99834		0.(10) 00166	1.(11) 05805	′	2.(8) 94195	1.(11) 05970	′	2.(8) 94030	60′
01·0	99836		00165	05951	·1 15	94049	06115	·1 15	93885	
02·0	99837		00163	06097	·2 30	93903	06260	·2 29	93740	
03·0	99838		00162	06244	·3 44	93757	06406	·3 44	93594	
04·0	99839		00161	06391	·4 59	93609	06552	·4 59	93448	
05·0	99840		00160	06538	·5 74	93462	06699	·5 73	93302	55′
06·0	99841		00159	06687	·6 89	93313	06846	·6 88	93154	
07·0	99842		00158	06835	·7 104	93165	06993	·7 103	93007	
08·0	99843		00157	06985	·8 118	93016	07141	·8 118	92859	
09·0	99844		00156	07134	·9 133	92866	07290	·9 132	92710	
10·0	99845		00155	07284		92716	07439		92561	50′
11·0	99846		00154	07435	·1 15	92565	07589	·1 15	92411	
12·0	99847		00153	07586	·2 31	92414	07739	·2 30	92261	
13·0	99849		00152	07738	·3 46	92262	07890	·3 46	92110	
14·0	99850		00151	07890	·4 61	92110	08041	·4 61	91959	
15·0	99851		00149	08043	·5 77	91957	08193	·5 76	91807	45′
16·0	99852		00148	08197	·6 92	91803	08345	·6 91	91655	
17·0	99853		00147	08351	·7 107	91650	08498	·7 106	91502	
18·0	99854		00146	08505	·8 122	91495	08651	·8 122	91349	
19·0	99855		00145	08660	·9 138	91340	08805	·9 137	91195	
20·0	99856		00144	08815		91185	08960		91040	40′
21·0	99857		00143	08972	·1 16	91029	09115	·1 16	90885	
22·0	99858		00142	09128	·2 32	90872	09270	·2 32	90730	
23·0	99859		00141	09285	·3 48	90715	09426	·3 47	90574	
24·0	99860		00140	09443	·4 63	90557	09583	·4 63	90417	
25·0	99861		00139	09601	·5 79	90399	09740	·5 79	90260	35′
26·0	99862		00138	09760	·6 95	90240	09898	·6 95	90102	
27·0	99863		00137	09920	·7 111	90080	10057	·7 110	89943	
28·0	99864		00136	10080	·8 127	89920	10216	·8 126	89784	
29·0	99865		00135	10240	·9 143	89760	10375	·9 142	89625	
30·0	99866		00134	10402		89598	10536		89464	30′
31·0	99867		00133	10563	·1 16	89437	10697	·1 16	89304	
32·0	99868		00132	10726	·2 33	89274	10858	·2 33	89142	
33·0	99869		00131	10889	·3 49	89111	11020	·3 49	88980	
34·0	99870		00130	11052	·4 66	88948	11183	·4 65	88817	
35·0	99871		00129	11217	·5 82	88783	11346	·5 82	88654	25′
36·0	99872		00128	11382	·6 99	88619	11510	·6 98	88490	
37·0	99873		00127	11547	·7 115	88453	11674	·7 114	88326	
38·0	99874		00126	11713	·8 132	88287	11839	·8 131	88161	
39·0	99875		00125	11880	·9 148	88120	12005	·9 147	87995	
40·0	99876		00124	12047		87953	12172		87829	20′
41·0	99877		00123	12215	·1 17	87785	12339	·1 17	87662	
42·0	99878		00122	12384	·2 34	87616	12506	·2 34	87494	
43·0	99879		00122	12553	·3 51	87447	12675	·3 51	87326	
44·0	99880		00121	12723	·4 68	87277	12844	·4 68	87157	
45·0	99880		00120	12894	·5 86	87106	13013	·5 85	86987	15′
46·0	99881		00119	13065	·6 103	86935	13184	·6 102	86817	
47·0	99882		00118	13237	·7 120	86763	13355	·7 119	86646	
48·0	99883		00117	13409	·8 137	86591	13526	·8 136	86474	
49·0	99884		00116	13583	·9 154	86417	13699	·9 153	86301	
50·0	99885		00115	13757		86243	13872		86128	10′
51·0	99886		00114	13931	·1 18	86069	14045	·1 18	85955	
52·0	99887		00113	14107	·2 36	85893	14220	·2 35	85780	
53·0	99888		00112	14283	·3 53	85717	14395	·3 53	85605	
54·0	99889		00111	14460	·4 71	85540	14571	·4 71	85429	
55·0	99890		00110	14637	·5 89	85363	14748	·5 88	85253	5′
56·0	99891		00110	14815	·6 107	85185	14925	·6 106	85075	
57·0	99891		00109	14994	·7 125	85006	15103	·7 124	84897	
58·0	99892		00108	15174	·8 142	84826	15282	·8 142	84718	
59·0	99893		00107	15355	·9 160	84646	15461	·9 159	84539	
60·0	99894		00106	15536		84464	15642		84359	0′

94°
274°

86°
266°

LOGS. OF TRIG. FUNCTIONS

′	Sine	Diff.	Cosec.	Tan.	Diff.	Cotan.	Secant	Diff.	Cosine	
00·0	1̄.(9) 99894		0.(10) 00106	1.(11) 15536	36	2̄.(8) 84464	1.(11) 15642	36	2̄.(8) 84359	60′
00·2	99894		00106	15572	37	84428	15678	36	84322	
00·4	99895		00105	15609	36	84391	15714	36	84286	
00·6	99895		00105	15645	36	84355	15750	36	84250	
00·8	99895		00105	15681	37	84319	15786	37	84214	
01·0	99895		00105	15718	36	84283	15823	36	84177	59′
01·2	99895		00105	15754	36	84246	15859	36	84141	
01·4	99895		00105	15790	38	84209	15895	37	84105	
01·6	99896		00104	15828	36	84172	15932	36	84068	
01·8	99896		00104	15864	36	84136	15968	36	84032	
02·0	99896		00104	15900	37	84100	16004	37	83996	58′
02·2	99896		00104	15937	36	84063	16041	36	83959	
02·4	99896		00104	15973	37	84027	16077	37	83923	
02·6	99896		00104	16010	37	83990	16114	36	83886	
02·8	99897		00103	16047	36	83953	16150	37	83850	
03·0	99897		00103	16083	38	83916	16187	37	83813	57′
03·2	99897		00103	16121	36	83879	16224	36	83776	
03·4	99897		00103	16157	37	83843	16260	37	83740	
03·6	99897		00103	16194	37	83806	16297	37	83703	
03·8	99897		00103	16231	37	83769	16334	36	83666	
04·0	99898		00102	16268	37	83732	16370	37	83630	56′
04·2	99898		00102	16305	37	83695	16407	37	83593	
04·4	99898		00102	16342	37	83658	16444	37	83556	
04·6	99898		00102	16379	37	83621	16481	37	83519	
04·8	99898		00102	16416	37	83584	16518	36	83482	
05·0	99898		00102	16453	37	83547	16554	37	83446	55′
05·2	99899		00101	16490	37	83510	16591	37	83409	
05·4	99899		00101	16527	37	83473	16628	37	83372	
05·6	99899		00101	16564	37	83436	16665	37	83335	
05·8	99899		00101	16601	38	83399	16702	37	83298	
06·0	99899		00101	16639	36	83361	16739	37	83261	54′
06·2	99899		00101	16675	38	83325	16776	37	83224	
06·4	99900		00100	16713	38	83287	16813	38	83187	
06·6	99900		00100	16751	37	83249	16851	37	83149	
06·8	99900		00100	16788	37	83212	16888	37	83112	
07·0	99900		00100	16825	37	83175	16925	37	83075	53′
07·2	99900		00100	16862	39	83138	16962	38	83038	
07·4	99901		00100	16901	37	83100	17000	37	83000	
07·6	99901		00099	16938	37	83062	17037	37	82963	
07·8	99901		00099	16975	38	83025	17074	38	82926	
08·0	99901		00099	17013	37	82987	17112	37	82888	52′
08·2	99901		00099	17050	37	82950	17149	37	82851	
08·4	99901		00099	17087	39	82912	17186	38	82814	
08·6	99902		00098	17126	37	82874	17224	37	82776	
08·8	99902		00098	17163	38	82837	17261	38	82739	
09·0	99902		00098	17201	37	82799	17299	37	82701	51′
09·2	99902		00098	17238	38	82762	17336	38	82664	
09·4	99902		00098	17276	38	82724	17374	38	82626	
09·6	99902		00098	17314	38	82686	17412	37	82588	
09·8	99903		00097	17352	38	82648	17449	38	82551	
10·0	99903		00097	17390	38	82610	17487	38	82513	50′
10·2	99903		00097	17428	37	82572	17525	37	82475	
10·4	99903		00097	17465	38	82535	17562	38	82438	
10·6	99903		00097	17503	38	82497	17600	38	82400	
10·8	99903		00097	17541	39	82459	17638	38	82362	
11·0	99904		00096	17580	38	82421	17676	38	82324	49′
11·2	99904		00096	17618	38	82382	17714	38	82286	
11·4	99904		00096	17656	38	82344	17752	38	82248	
11·6	99904		00096	17694	38	82306	17790	38	82210	
11·8	99904		00096	17732	38	82268	17828	38	82172	
12·0	99904		00096	17770		82230	17866		82134	48′

93°
273°

86°
266°

LOGS. OF TRIG. FUNCTIONS

′	Sine	Diff.	Cosec.	Tan.	Diff.	Cotan.	Secant	Diff.	Cosine	
12·0	1̅.(9) 99904		0.(10) 00096	1.(11) 17770	39	2̅.(8) 82230	1.(11) 17866	38	2̅.(8) 82134	48′
·2	99905		00095	17809	38	82191	17904	38	82096	
·4	99905		00095	17847	38	82153	17942	38	82058	
·6	99905		00095	17885	38	82115	17980	38	82020	
·8	99905		00095	17923	39	82077	18018	38	81982	
13·0	99905		00095	17962	39	82038	18056	39	81944	47′
·2	99906		00094	18001	38	81999	18095	38	81905	
·4	99906		00094	18039	38	81961	18133	38	81867	
·6	99906		00094	18077	39	81923	18171	39	81829	
·8	99906		00094	18116	38	81884	18210	38	81790	
14·0	99906		00094	18154	39	81846	18248	38	81752	46′
·2	99906		00094	18193	39	81807	18286	39	81714	
·4	99907		00093	18232	38	81768	18325	38	81675	
·6	99907		00093	18270	39	81730	18363	39	81637	
·8	99907		00093	18309	38	81691	18402	38	81598	
15·0	99907		00093	18347	39	81653	18440	39	81560	45′
·2	99907		00093	18386	38	81614	18479	38	81521	
·4	99907		00093	18424	39	81576	18517	39	81483	
·6	99907		00093	18463	39	81537	18556	39	81444	
·8	99908		00092	18502	39	81498	18595	38	81405	
16·0	99908		00092	18541	39	81459	18633	39	81367	44′
·2	99908		00092	18580	39	81420	18672	39	81328	
·4	99908		00092	18619	39	81381	18711	39	81289	
·6	99908		00092	18658	39	81342	18750	39	81250	
·8	99908		00092	18697	39	81303	18789	38	81211	
17·0	99909		00091	18736	39	81264	18827	39	81173	43′
·2	99909		00091	18775	39	81225	18866	39	81134	
·4	99909		00091	18814	39	81186	18905	39	81095	
·6	99909		00091	18853	39	81147	18944	39	81056	
·8	99909		00091	18892	40	81108	18983	39	81017	
18·0	99909		00091	18932	39	81068	19022	39	80978	42′
·2	99910		00090	18971	39	81029	19061	39	80939	
·4	99910		00090	19010	40	80990	19100	40	80900	
·6	99910		00090	19050	39	80950	19140	39	80860	
·8	99910		00090	19089	39	80911	19179	39	80821	
19·0	99910		00090	19128	39	80872	19218	39	80782	41′
·2	99910		00090	19167	40	80833	19257	40	80743	
·4	99911		00089	19207	40	80793	19297	39	80703	
·6	99911		00089	19247	39	80753	19336	39	80664	
·8	99911		00089	19286	40	80714	19375	40	80625	
20·0	99911		00089	19326	39	80674	19415	39	80585	40′
·2	99911		00089	19365	40	80635	19454	40	80546	
·4	99911		00089	19405	40	80595	19494	39	80506	
·6	99912		00088	19445	40	80555	19533	40	80467	
·8	99912		00088	19485	39	80515	19573	39	80427	
21·0	99912		00088	19524	40	80476	19612	40	80388	39′
·2	99912		00088	19564	40	80436	19652	40	80348	
·4	99912		00088	19604	39	80396	19692	39	80308	
·6	99912		00088	19643	40	80357	19731	40	80269	
·8	99912		00088	19683	40	80317	19771	40	80229	
22·0	99913		00087	19723	40	80277	19811	40	80189	38′
·2	99913		00087	19763	40	80237	19851	39	80149	
·4	99913		00087	19803	40	80197	19890	40	80110	
·6	99913		00087	19843	40	80157	19930	40	80070	
·8	99913		00087	19883	41	80117	19970	40	80030	
23·0	99913		00087	19924	40	80076	20010	40	79990	37′
·2	99914		00086	19964	40	80036	20050	40	79950	
·4	99914		00086	20004	40	79996	20090	40	79910	
·6	99914		00086	20044	40	79956	20130	40	79870	
·8	99914		00086	20084	41	79916	20170	41	79830	
24·0	99914		00086	20125		79875	20211		79789	36′

93°
273°

86°
266°

LOGS. OF TRIG. FUNCTIONS

′	Sine	Diff.	Cosec.	Tan.	Diff.	Cotan.	Secant	Diff.	Cosine	
24·0	1.(9) 99914		0.(10) 00086	1.(11) 20125	40	2.(8) 79875	1.(11) 20211	40	2.(8) 79789	36′
·2	99914		00086	20165	41	79835	20251	40	79749	
·4	99915		00085	20206	40	79794	20291	40	79709	
·6	99915		00085	20246	40	79754	20331	40	79669	
·8	99915		00085	20286	41	79714	20371	41	79629	
25·0	99915		00085	20327	40	79673	20412	40	79588	35′
·2	99915		00085	20367	41	79633	20452	41	79548	
·4	99915		00085	20408	40	79592	20493	40	79507	
·6	99915		00085	20448	41	79552	20533	40	79467	
·8	99916		00084	20489	41	79511	20573	41	79427	
26·0	99916		00084	20530	41	79470	20614	41	79386	34′
·2	99916		00084	20571	40	79429	20655	40	79345	
·4	99916		00084	20611	41	79389	20695	41	79305	
·6	99916		00084	20652	40	79348	20736	40	79264	
·8	99916		00084	20692	42	79308	20776	41	79224	
27·0	99917		00083	20734	41	79266	20817	41	79183	33′
·2	99917		00083	20775	41	79225	20858	41	79142	
·4	99917		00083	20816	41	79184	20899	41	79101	
·6	99917		00083	20857	40	79143	20940	40	79060	
·8	99917		00083	20897	42	79103	20980	41	79020	
28·0	99917		00083	20939	41	79061	21021	41	78979	32′
·2	99918		00082	20980	41	79020	21062	41	78938	
·4	99918		00082	21021	41	78979	21103	41	78897	
·6	99918		00082	21062	41	78938	21144	41	78856	
·8	99918		00082	21103	42	78897	21185	41	78815	
29·0	99918		00082	21145	41	78855	21226	42	78774	31′
·2	99918		00082	21186	41	78814	21268	41	78732	
·4	99918		00082	21227	42	78773	21309	41	78691	
·6	99919		00081	21269	41	78731	21350	41	78650	
·8	99919		00081	21310	41	78690	21391	42	78609	
30·0	99919		00081	21351	42	78649	21433	41	78568	30′
·2	99919		00081	21393	41	78607	21474	41	78526	
·4	99919		00081	21434	42	78566	21515	42	78485	
·6	99919		00081	21476	42	78524	21557	41	78443	
·8	99920		00080	21518	41	78482	21598	42	78402	
31·0	99920		00080	21559	42	78441	21640	41	78361	29′
·2	99920		00080	21601	42	78399	21681	42	78319	
·4	99920		00080	21643	41	78357	21723	41	78277	
·6	99920		00080	21684	42	78316	21764	42	78236	
·8	99920		00080	21726	42	78274	21806	42	78194	
32·0	99921		00080	21768	42	78232	21848	41	78152	28′
·2	99921		00079	21810	42	78190	21889	42	78111	
·4	99921		00079	21852	42	78148	21931	42	78069	
·6	99921		00079	21894	42	78106	21973	42	78027	
·8	99921		00079	21936	42	78064	22015	42	77985	
33·0	99921		00079	21978	42	78022	22057	42	77943	27′
·2	99921		00079	22020	43	77980	22099	42	77901	
·4	99922		00078	22063	42	77937	22141	42	77859	
·6	99922		00078	22105	42	77895	22183	42	77817	
·8	99922		00078	22147	42	77853	22225	42	77775	
34·0	99922		00078	22189	42	77811	22267	42	77733	26′
·2	99922		00078	22231	42	77769	22309	42	77691	
·4	99922		00078	22273	42	77727	22351	42	77649	
·6	99922		00078	22315	43	77685	22393	42	77607	
·8	99923		00077	22358	43	77642	22435	43	77565	
35·0	99923		00077	22401	42	77600	22478	42	77522	25′
·2	99923		00077	22443	42	77557	22520	42	77480	
·4	99923		00077	22485	43	77515	22562	43	77438	
·6	99923		00077	22528	42	77472	22605	42	77395	
·8	99923		00077	22570	43	77430	22647	43	77353	
36·0	99924		00077	22613		77387	22690		77310	24′

86°
266°

LOGS. OF TRIG. FUNCTIONS

′	Sine	Diff.	Cosec.	Tan.	Diff.	Cotan.	Secant	Diff.	Cosine	
36·0	$\bar{1}$.(9) 99924		0.(10) 00077	1.(11) 22613	43	$\bar{2}$.(8) 77387	1.(11) 22690	42	$\bar{2}$.(8) 77310	24′
·2	99924		00076	22656	43	77344	22732	43	77268	
·4	99924		00076	22699	43	77301	22775	43	77225	
·6	99924		00076	22742	42	77258	22818	43	77182	
·8	99924		00076	22784	43	77216	22860	43	77140	
37·0	99924		00076	22827	43	77173	22903	43	77097	23′
·2	99924		00076	22870	43	77130	22946	43	77054	
·4	99924		00076	22913	43	77087	22989	42	77011	
·6	99925		00075	22956	43	77044	23031	43	76969	
·8	99925		00075	22999	43	77001	23074	43	76926	
38·0	99925		00075	23042	43	76958	23117	43	76883	22′
·2	99925		00075	23085	43	76915	23160	43	76840	
·4	99925		00075	23128	43	76872	23203	43	76797	
·6	99925		00075	23171	44	76829	23246	43	76754	
·8	99926		00074	23215	43	76785	23289	44	76711	
39·0	99926		00074	23258	44	76742	23333	43	76667	21′
·2	99926		00074	23302	43	76698	23376	43	76624	
·4	99926		00074	23345	43	76655	23419	43	76581	
·6	99926		00074	23388	44	76612	23462	44	76538	
·8	99926		00074	23432	43	76568	23506	43	76494	
40·0	99927		00074	23475	44	76525	23549	43	76451	20′
·2	99927		00073	23519	44	76481	23592	44	76408	
·4	99927		00073	23563	43	76437	23636	43	76364	
·6	99927		00073	23606	44	76394	23679	44	76321	
·8	99927		00073	23650	44	76350	23723	43	76277	
41·0	99927		00073	23694	43	76307	23766	44	76234	19′
·2	99927		00073	23737	45	76263	23810	44	76190	
·4	99928		00072	23782	43	76218	23854	43	76146	
·6	99928		00072	23825	44	76175	23897	44	76103	
·8	99928		00072	23869	44	76131	23941	44	76059	
42·0	99928		00072	23913	44	76087	23985	44	76015	18′
·2	99928		00072	23957	44	76043	24029	44	75971	
·4	99928		00072	24001	44	75999	24073	44	75927	
·6	99928		00072	24045	45	75955	24117	44	75883	
·8	99928		00072	24090	43	75910	24161	44	75839	
43·0	99929		00071	24133	45	75866	24205	44	75795	17′
·2	99929		00071	24178	44	75822	24249	44	75751	
·4	99929		00071	24222	44	75778	24293	44	75707	
·6	99929		00071	24266	44	75734	24337	44	75663	
·8	99929		00071	24310	45	75690	24381	44	75619	
44·0	99929		00071	24355	45	75646	24425	45	75575	16′
·2	99930		00070	24400	44	75600	24470	44	75530	
·4	99930		00070	24444	44	75556	24514	44	75486	
·6	99930		00070	24488	45	75512	24558	45	75442	
·8	99930		00070	24533	44	75467	24603	44	75397	
45·0	99930		00070	24577	45	75423	24647	45	75353	15′
·2	99930		00070	24622	44	75378	24692	44	75308	
·4	99930		00070	24666	46	75334	24736	45	75264	
·6	99931		00069	24712	45	75288	24781	45	75219	
·8	99931		00069	24757	44	75243	24826	44	75174	
46·0	99931		00069	24801	45	75199	24870	45	75130	14′
·2	99931		00069	24846	45	75154	24915	45	75085	
·4	99931		00069	24891	45	75109	24960	45	75040	
·6	99931		00069	24936	45	75064	25005	45	74995	
·8	99931		00069	24981	45	75019	25050	45	74950	
47·0	99932		00068	25026	45	74974	25095	44	74906	13′
·2	99932		00068	25071	45	74929	25139	45	74861	
·4	99932		00068	25116	46	74884	25184	46	74816	
·6	99932		00068	25162	45	74838	25230	45	74770	
·8	99932		00068	25207	45	74793	25275	45	74725	
48·0	99932		00068	25252		74748	25320		74680	12′

93°
273°

LOGS. OF TRIG. FUNCTIONS

86° / **266°**

′	Sine	Diff.	Cosec.	Tan.	Diff.	Cotan.	Secant	Diff.	Cosine	
48·0	1̄.(9) 99932		0.(10) 00068	1.(11) 25252	45	2̄.(8) 74748	1.(11) 25320	45	2̄.(8) 74680	12′
·2	99932		00068	25297	46	74703	25365	45	74635	
·4	99933		00067	25343	46	74657	25410	46	74590	
·6	99933		00067	25389	45	74611	25456	45	74544	
·8	99933		00067	25434	45	74566	25501	45	74499	
49·0	99933		00067	25479	46	74521	25546	46	74454	11′
·2	99933		00067	25525	45	74475	25592	45	74408	
·4	99933		00067	25570	46	74430	25637	46	74363	
·6	99933		00067	25616	46	74384	25683	45	74317	
·8	99934		00066	25662	46	74338	25728	46	74272	
50·0	99934		00066	25708	46	74292	25774	46	74226	10′
·2	99934		00066	25754	46	74246	25820	46	74180	
·4	99934		00066	25800	45	74200	25866	45	74134	
·6	99934		00066	25845	46	74155	25911	46	74089	
·8	99934		00066	25891	46	74109	25957	46	74043	
51·0	99934		00066	25937	46	74063	26003	46	73997	9′
·2	99934		00066	25983	47	74017	26049	46	73951	
·4	99935		00065	26030	46	73970	26095	46	73905	
·6	99935		00065	26076	46	73924	26141	46	73859	
·8	99935		00065	26122	46	73878	26187	46	73813	
52·0	99935		00065	26168	46	73832	26233	46	73767	8′
·2	99935		00065	26214	47	73786	26279	47	73721	
·4	99935		00065	26261	46	73739	26326	46	73674	
·6	99935		00065	26307	47	73693	26372	47	73628	
·8	99936		00064	26354	46	73646	26418	46	73582	
53·0	99936		00064	26400	47	73600	26465	46	73535	7′
·2	99936		00064	26447	47	73553	26511	47	73489	
·4	99936		00064	26494	46	73506	26558	46	73442	
·6	99936		00064	26540	47	73460	26604	47	73396	
·8	99936		00064	26587	47	73413	26651	46	73349	
54·0	99936		00064	26634	47	73366	26697	47	73303	6′
·2	99937		00063	26681	47	73319	26744	47	73256	
·4	99937		00063	26728	46	73272	26791	46	73209	
·6	99937		00063	26774	47	73226	26837	47	73163	
·8	99937		00063	26821	47	73179	26884	47	73116	
55·0	99937		00063	26868	47	73132	26931	47	73069	5′
·2	99937		00063	26915	47	73085	26978	47	73022	
·4	99937		00063	26962	48	73038	27025	47	72975	
·6	99938		00062	27010	47	72990	27072	47	72928	
·8	99938		00062	27057	47	72943	27119	47	72881	
56·0	99938		00062	27104	48	72896	27166	48	72834	4′
·2	99938		00062	27152	47	72848	27214	47	72786	
·4	99938		00062	27199	47	72801	27261	47	72739	
·6	99938		00062	27246	47	72754	27308	47	72692	
·8	99938		00062	27293	48	72707	27355	48	72645	
57·0	99938		00062	27341	48	72659	27403	47	72597	3′
·2	99939		00061	27389	48	72611	27450	48	72550	
·4	99939		00061	27437	47	72563	27498	47	72502	
·6	99939		00061	27484	48	72516	27545	48	72455	
·8	99939		00061	27532	48	72468	27593	48	72407	
58·0	99939		00061	27580	47	72420	27641	47	72360	2′
·2	99939		00061	27627	48	72373	27688	48	72312	
·4	99939		00061	27675	49	72325	27736	48	72264	
·6	99940		00060	27724	48	72276	27784	48	72216	
·8	99940		00060	27772	47	72228	27832	48	72168	
59·0	99940		00060	27819	49	72181	27880	48	72120	1′
·2	99940		00060	27868	48	72132	27928	48	72072	
·4	99940		00060	27916	48	72084	27976	48	72024	
·6	99940		00060	27964	48	72036	28024	48	71976	
·8	99940		00060	28012	48	71988	28072	48	71928	
60·0	99940		00060	28060		71940	28120		71880	0′

87°
267°

LOGS. OF TRIG. FUNCTIONS

′	Sine	Diff.	Cosec.	Tan.	Diff.	Cotan.	Secant	Diff.	Cosine	
00·0	1̄.(9) 99940		0.(10) 00060	1.(11) 28060		2̄.(8) 71940	1.(11) 28120		2̄.(8) 71880	60′
·2	99941		00059	28109	49	71891	28168	48	71832	
·4	99941		00059	28157	48	71843	28216	48	71784	
·6	99941		00059	28206	49	71794	28265	49	71735	
·8	99941		00059	28254	48	71746	28313	48	71687	
01·0	99941		00059	28303	49	71697	28362	49	71638	59′
·2	99941		00059	28351	48	71649	28410	48	71590	
·4	99941		00059	28400	49	71600	28459	49	71541	
·6	99942		00058	28449	49	71551	28507	48	71493	
·8	99942		00058	28498	49	71502	28556	49	71444	
02·0	99942		00058	28547	49	71453	28605	49	71395	58′
·2	99942		00058	28596	49	71404	28654	49	71346	
·4	99942		00058	28644	48	71356	28702	48	71298	
·6	99942		00058	28693	49	71307	28751	49	71249	
·8	99942		00058	28742	49	71258	28800	49	71200	
03·0	99942		00058	28791	49	71208	28849	49	71151	57′
·2	99943		00057	28841	50	71159	28898	49	71102	
·4	99943		00057	28890	49	71110	28947	49	71053	
·6	99943		00057	28940	50	71060	28997	50	71003	
·8	99943		00057	28989	49	71011	29046	49	70954	
04·0	99943		00057	29038	49	70962	29095	49	70905	56′
·2	99943		00057	29087	49	70913	29144	49	70856	
·4	99943		00057	29137	50	70863	29194	50	70806	
·6	99943		00057	29186	49	70814	29243	49	70757	
·8	99944		00056	29237	51	70763	29293	50	70707	
05·0	99944		00056	29286	49	70714	29342	49	70658	55′
·2	99944		00056	29336	50	70664	29392	50	70608	
·4	99944		00056	29385	49	70615	29441	49	70559	
·6	99944		00056	29435	50	70565	29491	50	70509	
·8	99944		00056	29485	50	70515	29541	50	70459	
06·0	99944		00056	29535	50	70465	29591	50	70409	54′
·2	99944		00056	29585	50	70415	29641	50	70359	
·4	99945		00055	29636	51	70364	29691	50	70309	
·6	99945		00055	29686	50	70314	29741	50	70259	
·8	99945		00055	29736	50	70264	29791	50	70209	
07·0	99945		00055	29786	50	70214	29841	50	70159	53′
·2	99945		00055	29836	50	70164	29891	50	70109	
·4	99945		00055	29887	51	70113	29942	51	70058	
·6	99945		00055	29937	50	70063	29992	50	70008	
·8	99945		00055	29987	50	70013	30042	50	69958	
08·0	99946		00054	30038	51	69962	30093	51	69907	52′
·2	99946		00054	30089	51	69911	30143	50	69857	
·4	99946		00054	30140	51	69860	30194	51	69806	
·6	99946		00054	30190	50	69810	30244	50	69756	
·8	99946		00054	30241	51	69759	30295	51	69705	
09·0	99946		00054	30292	51	69708	30346	51	69654	51′
·2	99946		00054	30342	50	69658	30396	50	69604	
·4	99946		00054	30393	51	69607	30447	51	69553	
·6	99947		00054	30444	51	69556	30498	51	69502	
·8	99947		00053	30496	52	69504	30549	51	69451	
10·0	99947		00053	30547	51	69453	30600	51	69400	50′
·2	99947		00053	30598	51	69402	30651	51	69349	
·4	99947		00053	30649	51	69351	30702	51	69298	
·6	99947		00053	30701	52	69299	30754	52	69246	
·8	99947		00053	30752	51	69248	30805	51	69195	
11·0	99948		00053	30804	52	69196	30856	51	69144	49′
·2	99948		00052	30856	52	69144	30908	52	69092	
·4	99948		00052	30907	51	69093	30959	51	69041	
·6	99948		00052	30959	52	69041	31011	52	68989	
·8	99948		00052	31010	51	68990	31062	51	68938	
12·0	99948		00052	31062	52	68938	31114	52	68886	48′

LOGS. OF TRIG. FUNCTIONS

′	Sine	Diff.	Cosec.	Tan.	Diff.	Cotan.	Secant	Diff.	Cosine	
12·0	1.(9) 99948		0.(10) 00052	1.(11) 31062	51	2.(8) 68938	1.(11) 31114	51	2.(8) 68886	48′
·2	99948		00052	31113	52	68887	31165	52	68835	
·4	99948		00052	31165	53	68835	31217	52	68783	
·6	99949		00051	31218	52	68782	31269	52	68731	
·8	99949		00051	31270	52	68730	31321	52	68679	
13·0	99949		00051	31322	52	68678	31373	52	68627	47′
·2	99949		00051	31374	52	68626	31425	52	68575	
·4	99949		00051	31426	52	68574	31477	52	68523	
·6	99949		00051	31478	52	68522	31529	52	68471	
·8	99949		00051	31530	53	68470	31581	53	68419	
14·0	99949		00051	31583	53	68417	31634	52	68367	46′
·2	99950		00050	31636	52	68364	31686	52	68314	
·4	99950		00050	31688	53	68312	31738	53	68262	
·6	99950		00050	31741	52	68259	31791	52	68209	
·8	99950		00050	31793	53	68207	31843	53	68157	
15·0	99950		00050	31846	52	68154	31896	52	68104	45′
·2	99950		00050	31898	53	68102	31948	53	68052	
·4	99950		00050	31951	53	68049	32001	53	67999	
·6	99950		00050	32004	54	67996	32054	53	67946	
·8	99951		00049	32058	52	67942	32107	53	67893	
16·0	99951		00049	32110	53	67890	32160	52	67841	44′
2	99951		00049	32163	53	67837	32212	53	67788	
·4	99951		00049	32216	53	67784	32265	53	67735	
·6	99951		00049	32269	54	67731	32318	54	67682	
·8	99951		00049	32323	53	67677	32372	53	67628	
17·0	99951		00049	32376	53	67624	32425	53	67575	43′
·2	99951		00049	32429	54	67571	32478	54	67522	
·4	99951		00049	32483	54	67517	32532	53	67468	
·6	99952		00048	32537	53	67463	32585	53	67415	
·8	99952		00048	32590	54	67410	32638	54	67362	
18·0	99952		00048	32644	54	67356	32692	54	67308	42′
·2	99952		00048	32698	53	67302	32746	53	67254	
·4	99952		00048	32751	54	67249	32799	54	67201	
·6	99952		00048	32805	54	67195	32853	54	67147	
·8	99952		00048	32859	54	67141	32907	54	67093	
19·0	99952		00048	32913	55	67087	32961	54	67039	41′
·2	99953		00047	32968	54	67032	33015	54	66985	
·4	99953		00047	33022	54	66978	33069	54	66931	
·6	99953		00047	33076	54	66924	33123	54	66877	
·8	99953		00047	33130	54	66870	33177	54	66823	
20·0	99953		00047	33184	54	66816	33231	54	66769	40′
·2	99953		00047	33238	55	66762	33285	55	66715	
·4	99953		00047	33293	54	66707	33340	54	66660	
·6	99953		00047	33347	55	66653	33394	55	66606	
·8	99953		00047	33402	55	66598	33449	54	66551	
21·0	99954		00046	33457	55	66543	33503	55	66497	39′
·2	99954		00046	33512	54	66488	33558	54	66442	
·4	99954		00046	33566	55	66434	33612	55	66388	
·6	99954		00046	33621	55	66379	33667	55	66333	
·8	99954		00046	33676	55	66324	33722	55	66278	
22·0	99954		00046	33731	55	66269	33777	55	66223	38′
·2	99954		00046	33786	55	66214	33832	55	66168	
·4	99954		00046	33841	55	66159	33887	55	66113	
·6	99954		00046	33896	56	66104	33942	55	66058	
·8	99955		00045	33952	55	66048	33997	56	66003	
23·0	99955		00045	34007	56	65993	34053	55	65948	37′
·2	99955		00045	34063	55	65937	34108	55	65892	
·4	99955		00045	34118	56	65882	34163	56	65837	
·6	99955		00045	34174	55	65826	34219	55	65781	
·8	99955		00045	34229	56	65771	34274	56	65726	
24·0	99955		00045	34285		65715	34330		65670	36′

LOGS. OF TRIG. FUNCTIONS

′	Sine	Diff.	Cosec.	Tan.	Diff.	Cotan.	Secant	Diff.	Cosine	
24·0	1.(9) 99955		0.(10) 00045	1.(11) 34285	55	2.(8) 65715	1.(11) 34330	55	2.(8) 65670	36′
·2	99955		00045	34340	56	65660	34385	56	65615	
·4	99955		00045	34396	57	65604	34441	56	65559	
·6	99956		00044	34453	56	65547	34497	56	65503	
·8	99956		00044	34509	56	65491	34553	56	65447	
25·0	99956		00044	34565	56	65435	34609	56	65391	35′
·2	99956		00044	34621	56	65379	34665	56	65335	
·4	99956		00044	34677	56	65323	34721	56	65279	
·6	99956		00044	34733	57	65267	34777	57	65223	
·8	99956		00044	34790	56	65210	34834	56	65166	
26·0	99956		00044	34846	57	65154	34890	56	65110	34′
·2	99957		00043	34903	57	65097	34946	57	65054	
·4	99957		00043	34960	56	65040	35003	56	64997	
·6	99957		00043	35016	57	64984	35059	57	64941	
·8	99957		00043	35073	57	64927	35116	57	64884	
27·0	99957		00043	35130	56	64870	35173	56	64827	33′
·2	99957		00043	35186	57	64814	35229	57	64771	
·4	99957		00043	35243	57	64757	35286	57	64714	
·6	99957		00043	35300	57	64700	35343	57	64657	
·8	99957		00043	35357	58	64643	35400	57	64600	
28·0	99958		00042	35415	57	64585	35457	57	64543	32′
·2	99958		00042	35472	57	64528	35514	57	64486	
·4	99958		00042	35529	58	64471	35571	58	64429	
·6	99958		00042	35587	57	64413	35629	57	64371	
·8	99958		00042	35644	58	64356	35686	58	64314	
29·0	99958		00042	35702	57	64298	35744	57	64256	31′
·2	99958		00042	35759	58	64241	35801	58	64199	
·4	99958		00042	35817	58	64183	35859	58	64141	
·6	99958		00042	35875	58	64125	35917	57	64083	
·8	99959		00041	35933	58	64067	35974	58	64026	
30·0	99959		00041	35991	58	64009	36032	58	63968	30′
·2	99959		00041	36049	58	63951	36090	58	63910	
·4	99959		00041	36107	58	63893	36148	58	63852	
·6	99959		00041	36165	58	63835	36206	58	63794	
·8	99959		00041	36223	59	63777	36264	58	63736	
31·0	99959		00041	36282	58	63718	36322	59	63678	29′
·2	99959		00041	36340	58	63660	36381	58	63619	
·4	99959		00041	36398	59	63602	36439	58	63561	
·6	99960		00040	36457	59	63543	36497	59	63503	
·8	99960		00040	36516	58	63484	36556	59	63444	
32·0	99960		00040	36574	59	63426	36615	58	63385	28′
·2	99960		00040	36633	59	63367	36673	59	63327	
·4	99960		00040	36692	59	63308	36732	59	63268	
·6	99960		00040	36751	59	63249	36791	59	63209	
·8	99960		00040	36810	59	63190	36850	59	63150	
33·0	99960		00040	36869	59	63131	36909	59	63091	27′
·2	99960		00040	36928	60	63072	36968	59	63032	
·4	99961		00039	36988	59	63012	37027	59	62973	
·6	99961		00039	37047	60	62953	37086	60	62914	
·8	99961		00039	37107	59	62893	37146	59	62854	
34·0	99961		00039	37166	60	62834	37205	60	62795	26′
·2	99961		00039	37226	59	62774	37265	59	62735	
·4	99961		00039	37285	60	62715	37324	60	62676	
·6	99961		00039	37345	60	62655	37384	60	62616	
·8	99961		00039	37405	60	62595	37444	60	62556	
35·0	99961		00039	37465	59	62535	37504	59	62497	25′
·2	99961		00039	37524	61	62476	37563	60	62437	
·4	99962		00038	37585	60	62415	37623	60	62377	
·6	99962		00038	37645	61	62355	37683	61	62317	
·8	99962		00038	37706	60	62294	37744	60	62256	
36·0	99962		00038	37766		62234	37804		62196	24′

LOGS. OF TRIG. FUNCTIONS

87°
267°

′	Sine	Diff.	Cosec.	Tan.	Diff.	Cotan.	Secant	Diff.	Cosine	
36·0	1.(9) 99962	0.(10)	00038	1.(11) 37766	60	2.(8) 62234	1.(11) 37804	60	2.(8) 62196	24′
·2	99962		00038	37826	61	62174	37864	61	62136	
·4	99962		00038	37887	60	62113	37925	60	62075	
·6	99962		00038	37947	61	62053	37985	61	62015	
·8	99962		00038	38008	61	61992	38046	60	61954	
37·0	99962		00038	38069	61	61931	38106	61	61894	23′
·2	99963		00037	38130	61	61870	38167	61	61833	
·4	99963		00037	38191	61	61809	38228	61	61772	
·6	99963		00037	38252	61	61748	38289	61	61711	
·8	99963		00037	38313	61	61687	38350	61	61650	
38·0	99963		00037	38374	61	61626	38411	61	61589	22′
·2	99963		00037	38435	61	61565	38472	61	61528	
·4	99963		00037	38496	62	61504	38533	62	61467	
·6	99963		00037	38558	61	61442	38595	61	61405	
·8	99963		00037	38619	62	61381	38656	62	61344	
39·0	99964		00037	38681	62	61319	38718	61	61282	21′
·2	99964		00036	38743	62	61257	38779	62	61221	
·4	99964		00036	38805	62	61195	38841	62	61159	
·6	99964		00036	38867	62	61133	38903	62	61097	
·8	99964		00036	38929	62	61071	38965	62	61035	
40·0	99964		00036	38991	62	61009	39027	62	60973	20′
·2	99964		00036	39053	62	60947	39089	62	60911	
·4	99964		00036	39115	62	60885	39151	62	60849	
·6	99964		00036	39177	62	60823	39213	62	60787	
·8	99964		00036	39239	63	60761	39275	63	60725	
41·0	99965		00036	39302	63	60698	39338	62	60662	19′
2	99965		00035	39365	63	60635	39400	63	60600	
·4	99965		00035	39428	62	60572	39463	62	60537	
·6	99965		00035	39490	63	60510	39525	63	60475	
·8	99965		00035	39553	63	60447	39588	63	60412	
42·0	99965		00035	39616	63	60384	39651	63	60349	18′
·2	99965		00035	39679	63	60321	39714	63	60286	
·4	99965		00035	39742	63	60258	39777	63	60223	
·6	99965		00035	39805	63	60195	39840	63	60160	
·8	99965		00035	39868	64	60132	39903	64	60097	
43·0	99966		00035	39932	64	60068	39967	63	60033	17′
·2	99966		00034	39996	64	60004	40030	64	59970	
·4	99966		00034	40060	63	59940	40094	63	59906	
·6	99966		00034	40123	64	59877	40157	64	59843	
·8	99966		00034	40187	64	59813	40221	64	59779	
44·0	99966		00034	40251	64	59749	40285	64	59715	16′
·2	99966		00034	40315	64	59685	40349	64	59651	
·4	99966		00034	40379	64	59621	40413	64	59587	
·6	99966		00034	40443	64	59557	40477	64	59523	
·8	99966		00034	40507	65	59493	40541	64	59459	
45·0	99967		00034	40572	65	59428	40605	65	59395	15′
·2	99967		00033	40637	64	59363	40670	64	59330	
·4	99967		00033	40701	64	59299	40734	64	59266	
·6	99967		00033	40765	65	59235	40798	65	59202	
·8	99967		00033	40830	65	59170	40863	65	59137	
46·0	99967		00033	40895	65	59105	40928	65	59072	14′
·2	99967		00033	40960	65	59040	40993	65	59007	
·4	99967		00033	41025	65	58975	41058	65	58942	
·6	99967		00033	41090	65	58910	41123	65	58877	
·8	99967		00033	41155	65	58845	41188	65	58812	
47·0	99968		00033	41221	66	58780	41253	65	58747	13′
·2	99968		00032	41286	66	58714	41318	66	58682	
·4	99968		00032	41352	65	58648	41384	65	58616	
·6	99968		00032	41417	66	58583	41449	66	58551	
·8	99968		00032	41483	66	58517	41515	66	58485	
48·0	99968		00032	41549		58451	41581		58419	12′

92°
272°

87°
267°

LOGS. OF TRIG. FUNCTIONS

′	Sine	Diff.	Cosec.	Tan.	Diff.	Cotan.	Secant	Diff.	Cosine	
48·0	1.(9) 99968		0.(10) 00032	1.(11) 41549	66	2.(8) 58451	1.(11) 41581	66	2.(8) 58419	12′
·2	99968		00032	41615	65	58385	41647	65	58353	
·4	99968		00032	41680	66	58320	41712	66	58288	
·6	99968		00032	41746	67	58254	41778	67	58222	
·8	99968		00032	41813	66	58187	41845	66	58155	
49·0	99969		00032	41879	67	58121	41911	66	58089	11′
·2	99969		00031	41946	66	58054	41977	66	58023	
·4	99969		00031	42012	67	57988	42043	67	57957	
·6	99969		00031	42079	67	57921	42110	67	57890	
·8	99969		00031	42146	66	57854	42177	66	57823	
50·0	99969		00031	42212	67	57788	42243	67	57757	10′
·2	99969		00031	42279	67	57721	42310	67	57690	
·4	99969		00031	42346	67	57654	42377	67	57623	
·6	99969		00031	42413	67	57587	42444	67	57556	
·8	99969		00031	42480	68	57520	42511	68	57489	
51·0	99969		00031	42548	67	57452	42579	67	57421	9′
·2	99969		00031	42615	68	57385	42646	67	57354	
·4	99970		00030	42683	68	57317	42713	68	57287	
·6	99970		00030	42751	68	57249	42781	68	57219	
·8	99970		00030	42819	67	57181	42849	67	57151	
52·0	99970		00030	42886	68	57114	42916	68	57084	8′
·2	99970		00030	42954	68	57046	42984	68	57016	
·4	99970		00030	43022	68	56978	43052	68	56948	
·6	99970		00030	43090	69	56910	43120	69	56880	
·8	99970		00030	43159	68	56841	43189	68	56811	
53·0	99970		00030	43227	68	56773	43257	68	56743	7′
·2	99970		00030	43295	69	56705	43325	69	56675	
·4	99970		00030	43364	69	56636	43394	68	56606	
·6	99971		00029	43433	69	56567	43462	69	56538	
·8	99971		00029	43502	69	56498	43531	69	56469	
54·0	99971		00029	43571	69	56429	43600	69	56400	6′
·2	99971		00029	43640	69	56360	43669	69	56331	
·4	99971		00029	43709	69	56291	43738	69	56262	
·6	99971		00029	43778	70	56222	43807	70	56193	
·8	99971		00029	43848	69	56152	43877	69	56123	
55·0	99971		00029	43917	70	56083	43946	70	56054	5′
·2	99971		00029	43987	69	56013	44016	69	55984	
·4	99971		00029	44056	71	55944	44085	70	55915	
·6	99972		00028	44127	70	55873	44155	70	55845	
·8	99972		00028	44197	69	55803	44225	70	55775	
56·0	99972		00028	44266	71	55734	44295	70	55705	4′
·2	99972		00028	44337	70	55663	44365	70	55635	
·4	99972		00028	44407	70	55593	44435	70	55565	
·6	99972		00028	44477	71	55523	44505	71	55495	
·8	99972		00028	44548	70	55452	44576	70	55424	
57·0	99972		00028	44618	71	55382	44646	71	55354	3′
·2	99972		00028	44689	71	55311	44717	71	55283	
·4	99972		00028	44760	70	55240	44788	70	55212	
·6	99972		00028	44830	72	55170	44858	71	55142	
·8	99973		00027	44902	71	55098	44929	71	55071	
58·0	99973		00027	44973	72	55027	45001	72	55000	2′
·2	99973		00027	45045	71	54955	45072	71	54928	
·4	99973		00027	45116	71	54884	45143	71	54857	
·6	99973		00027	45187	72	54813	45214	72	54786	
·8	99973		00027	45259	72	54741	45286	72	54714	
59·0	99973		00027	45331	72	54669	45358	72	54642	1′
·2	99973		00027	45403	72	54597	45430	72	54570	
·4	99973		00027	45475	72	54525	45502	72	54498	
·6	99973		00027	45547	72	54453	45574	72	54426	
·8	99973		00027	45619	73	54381	45646	72	54354	
60·0	99974		00027	45692		54308	45718		54282	0′

92°
272°

88°
268°

LOGS. OF TRIG. FUNCTIONS

′	Sine	Diff.	Cosec.	Tan.	Diff.	Cotan.	Secant	Diff.	Cosine	
00·0	$\overline{1}$.(9) 99974	0.(10) 00027	1.(11) 45692	72	$\overline{2}$.(8) 54308	1.(11) 45718	72	$\overline{2}$.(8) 54282	60′
·2	99974		00026	45764	73	54236	45790	73	54210	
·4	99974		00026	45837	73	54163	45863	73	54137	
·6	99974		00026	45910	73	54090	45936	73	54064	
·8	99974		00026	45983	72	54017	46009	72	53991	
01·0	99974		00026	46055	73	53945	46081	73	53919	59′
·2	99974		00026	46128	73	53872	46154	73	53846	
·4	99974		00026	46201	74	53799	46227	74	53773	
·6	99974		00026	46275	73	53725	46301	73	53699	
·8	99974		00026	46348	74	53652	46374	74	53626	
02·0	99974		00026	46422	73	53578	46448	73	53552	58′
·2	99974		00026	46495	75	53505	46521	74	53479	
·4	99975		00025	46570	74	53430	46595	74	53405	
·6	99975		00025	46644	74	53356	46669	74	53331	
·8	99975		00025	46718	74	53282	46743	74	53257	
03·0	99975		00025	46792	74	53208	46817	74	53183	57′
·2	99975		00025	46866	75	53134	46891	75	53109	
·4	99975		00025	46941	74	53059	46966	74	53034	
·6	99975		00025	47015	75	52985	47040	75	52960	
·8	99975		00025	47090	75	52910	47115	75	52885	
04·0	99975		00025	47165	75	52835	47190	75	52810	56′
·2	99975		00025	47240	75	52760	47265	75	52735	
·4	99975		00025	47315	75	52685	47340	75	52660	
·6	99975		00025	47390	76	52610	47415	75	52585	
·8	99976		00024	47466	75	52534	47490	76	52510	
05·0	99976		00024	47541	76	52459	47566	75	52434	55′
·2	99976		00024	47617	76	52383	47641	76	52359	
·4	99976		00024	47693	76	52307	47717	76	52283	
·6	99976		00024	47769	76	52231	47793	76	52207	
·8	99976		00024	47845	76	52155	47869	76	52131	
06·0	99976		00024	47921	76	52079	47945	76	52055	54′
·2	99976		00024	47997	77	52003	48021	77	51979	
·4	99976		00024	48074	76	51926	48098	76	51902	
·6	99976		00024	48150	77	51850	48174	77	51826	
·8	99976		00024	48227	77	51773	48251	76	51749	
07·0	99977		00024	48304	77	51696	48327	77	51673	53′
·2	99977		00023	48381	77	51619	48404	77	51596	
·4	99977		00023	48458	77	51542	48481	77	51519	
·6	99977		00023	48535	78	51465	48558	78	51442	
·8	99977		00023	48613	77	51387	48636	77	51364	
08·0	99977		00023	48690	78	51310	48713	78	51287	52′
·2	99977		00023	48768	78	51232	48791	78	51209	
·4	99977		00023	48846	77	51154	48869	77	51131	
·6	99977		00023	48923	78	51077	48946	78	51054	
·8	99977		00023	49001	79	50999	49024	79	50976	
09·0	99977		00023	49080	78	50920	49103	78	50897	51′
·2	99977		00023	49158	78	50842	49181	78	50819	
·4	99977		00023	49236	80	50764	49259	79	50741	
·6	99978		00022	49316	79	50684	49338	79	50662	
·8	99978		00022	49395	78	50605	49417	79	50583	
10·0	99978		00022	49473	79	50527	49496	78	50504	50′
·2	99978		00022	49552	80	50448	49574	80	50426	
·4	99978		00022	49632	79	50368	49654	79	50346	
·6	99978		00022	49711	79	50289	49733	79	50267	
·8	99978		00022	49790	80	50210	49812	80	50188	
11·0	99978		00022	49870	80	50130	49892	80	50108	49′
·2	99978		00022	49950	80	50050	49972	80	50028	
·4	99978		00022	50030	80	49970	50052	80	49948	
·6	99978		00022	50110	80	49890	50132	80	49868	
·8	99978		00022	50190	81	49810	50212	80	49788	
12·0	99979		00021	50271		49729	50292		49708	48′

91°
271°

88°
268°

LOGS. OF TRIG. FUNCTIONS

′	Sine	Diff.	Cosec.	Tan.	Diff.	Cotan.	Secant	Diff.	Cosine	
12·0	1.(9) 99979		0.(10) 00021	1.(11) 50271	81	2.(8) 49729	1.(11) 50292	81	2.(8) 49708	48′
·2	99979		00021	50352	80	49648	50373	80	49627	
·4	99979		00021	50432	81	49568	50453	81	49547	
·6	99979		00021	50513	81	49487	50534	81	49466	
·8	99979		00021	50594	81	49406	50615	81	49385	
13·0	99979		00021	50675	81	49325	50696	81	49304	47′
·2	99979		00021	50756	82	49244	50777	82	49223	
·4	99979		00021	50838	81	49162	50859	81	49141	
·6	99979		00021	50919	82	49081	50940	82	49060	
·8	99979		00021	51001	82	48999	51022	82	48978	
14·0	99979		00021	51083	82	48917	51104	82	48896	46′
·2	99979		00021	51165	82	48835	51186	82	48814	
·4	99979		00021	51247	83	48753	51268	82	48732	
·6	99980		00020	51330	83	48670	51350	83	48650	
·8	99980		00020	51413	82	48587	51433	82	48567	
15·0	99980		00020	51495	83	48505	51515	83	48485	45′
·2	99980		00020	51578	83	48422	51598	83	48402	
·4	99980		00020	51661	83	48339	51681	83	48319	
·6	99980		00020	51744	83	48256	51764	83	48236	
·8	99980		00020	51827	84	48173	51847	84	48153	
16·0	99980		00020	51911	83	48089	51931	83	48069	44′
·2	99980		00020	51994	84	48006	52014	84	47986	
·4	99980		00020	52078	84	47922	52098	84	47902	
·6	99980		00020	52162	84	47838	52182	84	47818	
·8	99980		00020	52246	85	47754	52266	84	47734	
17·0	99981		00019	52331	84	47669	52350	84	47650	43′
·2	99981		00019	52415	85	47585	52434	85	47566	
·4	99981		00019	52500	85	47500	52519	85	47481	
·6	99981		00019	52585	85	47415	52604	85	47396	
·8	99981		00019	52670	85	47330	52689	85	47311	
18·0	99981		00019	52755	85	47245	52774	85	47226	42′
·2	99981		00019	52840	85	47160	52859	85	47141	
·4	99981		00019	52925	86	47075	52944	86	47056	
·6	99981		00019	53011	86	46989	53030	86	46970	
·8	99981		00019	53097	86	46903	53116	85	46884	
19·0	99981		00019	53183	86	46817	53202	87	46799	41′
·2	99981		00019	53269	86	46731	53288	86	46712	
·4	99981		00019	53355	86	46645	53374	86	46626	
·6	99981		00019	53441	88	46559	53460	87	46540	
·8	99982		00018	53529	86	46471	53547	87	46453	
20·0	99982		00018	53615	87	46385	53634	86	46366	40′
·2	99982		00018	53702	87	46298	53720	87	46280	
·4	99982		00018	53789	88	46211	53807	88	46193	
·6	99982		00018	53877	87	46123	53895	87	46105	
·8	99982		00018	53964	88	46036	53982	88	46018	
21·0	99982		00018	54052	88	45948	54070	88	45930	39′
·2	99982		00018	54140	88	45860	54158	88	45842	
·4	99982		00018	54228	88	45772	54246	88	45754	
·6	99982		00018	54316	88	45684	54334	88	45666	
·8	99982		00018	54404	89	45596	54422	89	45578	
22·0	99982		00018	54493	88	45507	54511	88	45489	38′
·2	99982		00018	54581	89	45419	54599	89	45401	
·4	99982		00018	54670	90	45330	54688	89	45312	
·6	99983		00017	54760	89	45240	54777	89	45223	
·8	99983		00017	54849	90	45151	54866	90	45134	
23·0	99983		00017	54939	90	45061	54956	90	45044	37′
·2	99983		00017	55029	89	44971	55046	89	44954	
·4	99983		00017	55118	90	44882	55135	90	44865	
·6	99983		00017	55208	91	44792	55225	91	44775	
·8	99983		00017	55299	90	44701	55316	90	44684	
24·0	99983		00017	55389		44611	55406		44594	36′

91°
271°

LOGS. OF TRIG. FUNCTIONS

88°
268°

′	Sine	Diff.	Cosec.	Tan.	Diff.	Cotan.	Secant	Diff.	Cosine	
24·0	1̄.(9) 99983	0.(10)	00017	1.(11) 55389	90	2̄.(8) 44611	1.(11) 55406	90	2̄.(8) 44594	36′
·2	99983		00017	55479	91	44521	55496	91	44504	
·4	99983		00017	55570	91	44430	55587	91	44413	
·6	99983		00017	55661	91	44339	55678	91	44322	
·8	99983		00017	55752	92	44248	55769	92	44231	
25·0	99983		00017	55844	92	44156	55861	91	44139	35′
·2	99984		00016	55936	92	44064	55952	92	44048	
·4	99984		00016	56028	92	43972	56044	92	43956	
·6	99984		00016	56120	92	43880	56136	92	43864	
·8	99984		00016	56212	92	43788	56228	92	43772	
26·0	99984		00016	56304	92	43696	56320	92	43680	34′
·2	99984		00016	56396	93	43604	56412	93	43588	
·4	99984		00016	56489	93	43511	56505	93	43495	
·6	99984		00016	56582	93	43418	56598	93	43402	
·8	99984		00016	56675	93	43325	56691	93	43309	
27·0	99984		00016	56769	94	43232	56784	94	43216	33′
·2	99984		00016	56862	93	43138	56878	93	43122	
·4	99984		00016	56955	94	43045	56971	94	43029	
·6	99984		00016	57049	94	42951	57065	94	42935	
·8	99984		00016	57143	95	42857	57159	95	42841	
28·0	99984		00016	57238	95	42762	57254	94	42746	32′
·2	99985		00015	57333	95	42667	57348	95	42652	
·4	99985		00015	57428	95	42572	57443	95	42557	
·6	99985		00015	57523	95	42477	57538	95	42462	
·8	99985		00015	57618	95	42382	57633	95	42367	
29·0	99985		00015	57713	96	42287	57728	96	42272	31′
·2	99985		00015	57809	96	42191	57824	96	42176	
·4	99985		00015	57905	96	42095	57920	96	42080	
·6	99985		00015	58001	96	41999	58016	96	41984	
·8	99985		00015	58097	96	41903	58112	96	41888	
30·0	99985		00015	58193	97	41807	58208	97	41792	30′
·2	99985		00015	58290	96	41710	58305	96	41695	
·4	99985		00015	58386	98	41614	58401	98	41599	
·6	99985		00015	58484	97	41516	58499	97	41501	
·8	99985		00015	58581	98	41419	58596	97	41404	
31·0	99985		00015	58679	98	41321	58693	98	41307	29′
·2	99986		00014	58777	98	41223	58791	98	41209	
·4	99986		00014	58875	98	41125	58889	98	41111	
·6	99986		00014	58973	98	41027	58987	98	41013	
·8	99986		00014	59071	99	40929	59085	99	40915	
32·0	99986		00014	59170	99	40830	59184	99	40816	28′
·2	99986		00014	59269	99	40731	59283	99	40717	
·4	99986		00014	59368	99	40632	59382	99	40618	
·6	99986		00014	59467	99	40533	59481	99	40519	
·8	99986		00014	59566	100	40434	59580	100	40420	
33·0	99986		00014	59666	100	40334	59680	100	40320	27′
·2	99986		00014	59766	100	40234	59780	100	40220	
·4	99986		00014	59866	101	40134	59880	100	40120	
·6	99986		00014	59967	100	40033	59981	101	40019	
·8	99986		00014	60067	101	39933	60081	100	39919	
34·0	99986		00014	60169	102	39832	60182	101	39818	26′
·2	99987		00014	60270	102	39730	60283	102	39717	
·4	99987		00013	60372	101	39628	60385	101	39615	
·6	99987		00013	60473	102	39527	60486	102	39514	
·8	99987		00013	60575	102	39425	60588	102	39412	
35·0	99987		00013	60677	102	39323	60690	102	39310	25′
·2	99987		00013	60779	103	39221	60792	103	39208	
·4	99987		00013	60882	103	39118	60895	103	39105	
·6	99987		00013	60985	103	39015	60998	103	39002	
·8	99987		00013	61088	103	38912	61101	103	38899	
36·0	99987		00013	61191		38809	61204		38796	24′

91°
271°

88° / 268° LOGS. OF TRIG. FUNCTIONS

′	Sine	Diff.	Cosec.	Tan.	Diff.	Cotan.	Secant	Diff.	Cosine	
36·0	1̄.(9) 99987		0.(10) 00013	1.(11) 61191		2̄.(8) 38809	1.(11) 61204		2̄.(8) 38796	24′
·2	99987		00013	61294	103	38706	61307	103	38693	
·4	99987		00013	61398	104	38602	61411	104	38589	
·6	99987		00013	61502	104	38498	61515	104	38485	
·8	99987		00013	61606	104	38394	61619	104	38381	
37·0	99987		00013	61711	105	38289	61724	105	38276	23′
·2	99987		00013	61816	105	38184	61829	105	38171	
·4	99987		00013	61921	105	38079	61934	105	38066	
·6	99988		00012	62027	106	37973	62039	105	37961	
·8	99988		00012	62132	105	37868	62144	105	37856	
38·0	99988		00012	62238	106	37762	62250	106	37750	22′
·2	99988		00012	62344	106	37656	62356	106	37644	
·4	99988		00012	62450	106	37550	62462	106	37538	
·6	99988		00012	62557	107	37443	62569	107	37431	
·8	99988		00012	62664	107	37336	62676	107	37324	
39·0	99988		00012	62771	107	37229	62783	107	37217	21′
·2	99988		00012	62878	107	37122	62890	107	37110	
·4	99988		00012	62986	108	37014	62998	108	37002	
·6	99988		00012	63094	108	36906	63106	108	36894	
·8	99988		00012	63202	108	36798	63214	108	36786	
40·0	99988		00012	63310	108	36690	63322	108	36678	20′
·2	99988		00012	63419	109	36581	63431	109	36569	
·4	99988		00012	63528	109	36472	63540	109	36460	
·6	99988		00012	63637	109	36363	63649	109	36351	
·8	99988		00012	63747	110	36253	63759	110	36241	
41·0	99988		00012	63857	110	36143	63869	110	36131	19′
·2	99989		00011	63968	111	36032	63979	110	36021	
·4	99989		00011	64077	109	35923	64089	110	35911	
·6	99989		00011	64188	111	35812	64199	111	35801	
·8	99989		00011	64299	111	35701	64310	112	35690	
42·0	99989		00011	64410	111	35590	64422	111	35578	18′
·2	99989		00011	64522	112	35478	64533	112	35467	
·4	99989		00011	64634	112	35366	64645	112	35355	
·6	99989		00011	64746	112	35254	64757	112	35243	
·8	99989		00011	64858	112	35142	64869	113	35131	
43·0	99989		00011	64971	113	35029	64982	113	35018	17′
·2	99989		00011	65084	113	34916	65095	113	34905	
·4	99989		00011	65197	113	34803	65208	114	34792	
·6	99989		00011	65311	114	34689	65322	113	34678	
·8	99989		00011	65424	113	34576	65435	115	34565	
44·0	99989		00011	65539	115	34461	65550	114	34450	16′
·2	99989		00011	65653	114	34347	65664	115	34336	
·4	99989		00011	65768	115	34232	65779	115	34221	
·6	99990		00010	65884	116	34116	65894	115	34106	
·8	99990		00010	65999	115	34001	66009	115	33991	
45·0	99990		00010	66114	115	33886	66125	116	33875	15′
·2	99990		00010	66231	117	33769	66241	116	33759	
·4	99990		00010	66347	116	33653	66357	116	33643	
·6	99990		00010	66463	116	33537	66473	116	33527	
·8	99990		00010	66580	117	33420	66590	117	33410	
46·0	99990		00010	66698	118	33302	66708	118	33292	14′
·2	99990		00010	66815	117	33185	66825	117	33175	
·4	99990		00010	66933	118	33067	66943	118	33057	
·6	99990		00010	67051	118	32949	67061	118	32939	
·8	99990		00010	67170	119	32830	67180	119	32820	
47·0	99990		00010	67289	119	32711	67298	118	32702	13′
·2	99990		00010	67408	119	32592	67418	120	32582	
·4	99990		00010	67527	119	32473	67537	119	32463	
·6	99990		00010	67647	120	32353	67657	120	32343	
·8	99990		00010	67767	120	32233	67777	120	32223	
48·0	99990		00010	67888	121	32112	67897	120	32103	12′

88°
268°

LOGS. OF TRIG. FUNCTIONS

′	Sine	Diff.	Cosec.	Tan.	Diff.	Cotan.	Secant	Diff.	Cosine	
48·0	$\overline{1}$.(9) 99990		0.(10) 00010	1.(11) 67888	121	$\overline{2}$.(8) 32112	1.(11) 67897	121	$\overline{2}$.(8) 32103	12′
·2	99991		00009	68009	121	31991	68018	121	31982	
·4	99991		00009	68130	122	31870	68139	121	31861	
·6	99991		00009	68252	122	31748	68261	122	31739	
·8	99991		00009	68374	121	31626	68383	122	31617	
49·0	99991		00009	68495	123	31505	68505	122	31495	11′
·2	99991		00009	68618	123	31382	68627	122	31373	
·4	99991		00009	68741	123	31259	68750	123	31250	
·6	99991		00009	68864	124	31136	68873	123	31127	
·8	99991		00009	68988	124	31012	68997	124	31003	
50·0	99991		00009	69112	124	30888	69121	124	30879	10′
·2	99991		00009	69236	124	30764	69245	124	30755	
·4	99991		00009	69360	125	30604	69369	125	30631	
·6	99991		00009	69485	126	30515	69494	126	30506	
·8	99991		00009	69611	126	30389	69620	125	30380	
51·0	99991		00009	69737	125	30263	69745	126	30255	9′
·2	99991		00009	69862	127	30138	69871	127	30129	
·4	99991		00009	69989	127	30011	69998	127	30002	
·6	99991		00009	70116	127	29884	70125	127	29875	
·8	99991		00009	70243	128	29757	70252	127	29748	
52·0	99992		00008	70371	128	29629	70379	128	29621	8′
·2	99992		00008	70499	129	29501	70507	129	29493	
·4	99992		00008	70628	128	29372	70636	128	29364	
·6	99992		00008	70756	129	29244	70764	129	29236	
·8	99992		00008	70885	129	29115	70893	130	29107	
53·0	99992		00008	71014	131	28986	71023	130	28977	7′
·2	99992		00008	71145	130	28855	71153	130	28847	
·4	99992		00008	71275	130	28725	71283	130	28717	
·6	99992		00008	71405	131	28595	71413	131	28587	
·8	99992		00008	71536	132	28464	71544	132	28456	
54·0	99992		00008	71668	131	28332	71676	131	28324	6′
·2	99992		00008	71799	133	28201	71807	133	28193	
·4	99992		00008	71932	132	28068	71940	132	28060	
·6	99992		00008	72064	133	27936	72072	133	27928	
·8	99992		00008	72197	134	27803	72205	134	27795	
55·0	99992		00008	72331	133	27669	72339	133	27661	5′
·2	99992		00008	72464	135	27536	72472	135	27528	
·4	99992		00008	72599	134	27401	72607	134	27393	
·6	99992		00008	72733	135	27267	72741	135	27259	
·8	99992		00008	72868	136	27132	72876	136	27124	
56·0	99992		00008	73004	136	26996	73012	136	26988	4′
·2	99992		00008	73140	136	26860	73148	136	26852	
·4	99992		00008	73276	138	26724	73284	137	26716	
·6	99993		00007	73414	137	26586	73421	137	26579	
·8	99993		00007	73551	137	26449	73558	138	26442	
57·0	99993		00007	73689	139	26312	73696	138	26304	3′
·2	99993		00007	73827	138	26173	73834	138	26166	
·4	99993		00007	73965	139	26035	73972	139	26028	
·6	99993		00007	74104	140	25896	74111	140	25889	
·8	99993		00007	74244	139	25756	74251	140	25749	
58·0	99993		00007	74384	141	25617	74391	140	25609	2′
·2	99993		00007	74524	141	25476	74531	141	25469	
·4	99993		00007	74665	141	25335	74672	141	25328	
·6	99993		00007	74806	141	25194	74813	141	25187	
·8	99993		00007	74947	143	25053	74954	143	25046	
59·0	99993		00007	75090	142	24910	75097	142	24903	1′
·2	99993		00007	75232	143	24768	75239	143	24761	
·4	99993		00007	75375	144	24625	75382	144	24618	
·6	99993		00007	75519	144	24481	75526	144	24474	
·8	99993		00007	75663	145	24337	75670	144	24330	
60·0	99993		00007	75808		24192	75815		24186	0′

89°
269°

LOGS. OF TRIG. FUNCTIONS

′	Sine	Diff.	Cosec.	Tan.	Diff.	Cotan.	Secant	Diff.	Cosine	
00·0	1.(9) 99993		0.(10) 00007	1.(11) 75808	146	2.(8) 24192	1.(11) 75815	145	2.(8) 24186	60′
·2	99993		00007	75952	146	24048	75959	146	24041	
·4	99993		00007	76098	147	23902	76105	146	23895	
·6	99994		00006	76245	146	23755	76251	146	23749	
·8	99994		00006	76391	147	23609	76397	147	23603	
01·0	99994		00006	76538	148	23462	76544	148	23456	59′
·2	99994		00006	76686	148	23314	76692	148	23308	
·4	99994		00006	76834	148	23166	76840	148	23160	
·6	99994		00006	76982	149	23018	76988	149	23012	
·8	99994		00006	77131	149	22869	77137	150	22863	
02·0	99994		00006	77281	151	22720	77287	150	22713	58′
·2	99994		00006	77431	150	22569	77437	150	22563	
·4	99994		00006	77581	151	22419	77587	151	22413	
·6	99994		00006	77732	152	22268	77738	152	22262	
·8	99994		00006	77884	152	22116	77890	152	22110	
03·0	99994		00006	78036	153	21964	78042	153	21958	57′
·2	99994		00006	78189	153	21811	78195	153	21805	
·4	99994		00006	78342	153	21658	78348	153	21652	
·6	99994		00006	78495	155	21505	78501	155	21499	
·8	99994		00006	78650	155	21350	78656	155	21344	
04·0	99994		00006	78805	155	21195	78811	155	21189	56′
·2	99994		00006	78960	156	21040	78966	156	21034	
·4	99994		00006	79116	156	20884	79122	156	20878	
·6	99994		00006	79272	157	20728	79278	157	20722	
·8	99994		00006	79429	158	20571	79435	158	20565	
05·0	99994		00006	79587	158	20413	79593	158	20407	55′
·2	99994		00006	79745	160	20255	79751	159	20249	
·4	99995		00005	79905	159	20095	79910	159	20090	
·6	99995		00005	80064	160	19936	80069	160	19931	
·8	99995		00005	80224	160	19776	80229	161	19771	
06·0	99995		00005	80384	162	19616	80390	161	19610	54′
·2	99995		00005	80546	162	19454	80551	162	19449	
·4	99995		00005	80708	162	19292	80713	162	19287	
·6	99995		00005	80870	163	19130	80875	163	19125	
·8	99995		00005	81033	163	18967	81038	164	18962	
07·0	99995		00005	81196	165	18804	81202	164	18798	53′
·2	99995		00005	81361	165	18639	81366	165	18634	
·4	99995		00005	81526	165	18474	81531	165	18469	
·6	99995		00005	81691	166	18309	81696	166	18304	
·8	99995		00005	81857	167	18143	81862	167	18138	
08·0	99995		00005	82024	167	17976	82029	167	17971	52′
·2	99995		00005	82191	168	17809	82196	168	17804	
·4	99995		00005	82359	169	17641	82364	169	17636	
·6	99995		00005	82528	169	17472	82533	169	17467	
·8	99995		00005	82697	170	17303	82702	170	17298	
09·0	99995		00005	82867	171	17133	82872	171	17128	51′
·2	99995		00005	83038	171	16962	83043	171	16957	
·4	99995		00005	83209	172	16791	83214	172	16786	
·6	99995		00005	83381	173	16619	83386	173	16614	
·8	99995		00005	83554	173	16446	83559	173	16441	
10·0	99995		00005	83727	174	16273	83732	174	16268	50′
·2	99995		00005	83901	175	16099	83906	175	16094	
·4	99995		00005	84076	176	15924	84081	175	15919	
·6	99996		00004	84252	176	15748	84256	176	15744	
·8	99996		00004	84428	177	15572	84432	177	15568	
11·0	99996		00004	84605	178	15395	84609	178	15391	49′
·2	99996		00004	84783	178	15217	84787	178	15213	
·4	99996		00004	84961	179	15039	84965	179	15035	
·6	99996		00004	85140	180	14860	85144	180	14856	
·8	99996		00004	85320	180	14680	85324	181	14676	
12·0	99996		00004	85500		14500	85505		14495	48′

90°
270°

89°
269°

LOGS. OF TRIG. FUNCTIONS

′	Sine	Diff.	Cosec.	Tan.	Diff.	Cotan.	Secant	Diff.	Cosine	
12·0	1̄.(9) 99996		0.(10) 00004	1.(11) 85500		2̄.(8) 14500	1.(11) 85505		2̄.(8) 14495	48′
·2	99996		00004	85682	182	14318	85686	181	14314	
·4	99996		00004	85864	182	14136	85868	182	14132	
·6	99996		00004	86047	183	13953	86051	183	13949	
·8	99996		00004	86231	184	13769	86235	184	13765	
13·0	99996		00004	86415	184	13585	86419	184	13581	47′
·2	99996		00004	86600	185	13400	86604	185	13396	
·4	99996		00004	86786	186	13214	86790	186	13210	
·6	99996		00004	86973	187	13027	86977	187	13023	
·8	99996		00004	87161	188	12839	87165	188	12835	
14·0	99996		00004	87349	188	12651	87353	188	12647	46′
·2	99996		00004	87538	189	12462	87542	189	12458	
·4	99996		00004	87728	190	12272	87732	190	12268	
·6	99996		00004	87919	191	12081	87923	191	12077	
·8	99996		00004	88111	192	11889	88115	192	11885	
15·0	99996		00004	88304	193	11696	88307	192	11693	45′
·2	99996		00004	88497	193	11503	88501	194	11499	
·4	99996		00004	88691	194	11309	88695	194	11305	
·6	99996		00004	88886	195	11114	88890	195	11110	
·8	99996		00004	89082	196	10918	89086	196	10914	
16·0	99996		00004	89280	198	10720	89283	197	10717	44′
·2	99996		00004	89477	197	10523	89481	198	10519	
·4	99996		00004	89676	199	10324	89680	199	10320	
·6	99997		00003	89877	201	10123	89880	200	10120	
·8	99997		00003	90077	200	09923	90080	200	09920	
17·0	99997		00003	90278	201	09722	90282	202	09718	43′
·2	99997		00003	90481	203	09519	90484	202	09516	
·4	99997		00003	90685	204	09315	90688	204	09312	
·6	99997		00003	90889	204	09111	90892	204	09108	
·8	99997		00003	91094	205	08906	91097	205	08903	
18·0	99997		00003	91300	206	08700	91304	207	08696	42′
·2	99997		00003	91508	208	08492	91511	207	08489	
·4	99997		00003	91716	208	08284	91719	208	08281	
·6	99997		00003	91925	209	08075	91928	209	08072	
·8	99997		00003	92136	211	07864	92139	211	07861	
19·0	99997		00003	92347	211	07653	92350	211	07650	41′
·2	99997		00003	92559	212	07441	92562	212	07438	
·4	99997		00003	92773	214	07227	92776	214	07224	
·6	99997		00003	92987	214	07013	92990	214	07010	
·8	99997		00003	93203	216	06797	93206	216	06794	
20·0	99997		00003	93419	216	06581	93422	216	06578	40′
·2	99997		00003	93637	218	06363	93640	218	06360	
·4	99997		00003	93856	219	06144	93859	219	06141	
·6	99997		00003	94076	220	05924	94079	220	05921	
·8	99997		00003	94297	221	05703	94300	221	05700	
21·0	99997		00003	94519	222	05481	94522	222	05478	39′
·2	99997		00003	94742	223	05258	94745	223	05255	
·4	99997		00003	94967	225	05033	94970	225	05030	
·6	99997		00003	95192	225	04808	95195	225	04805	
·8	99997		00003	95419	227	04581	95422	227	04578	
22·0	99997		00003	95647	228	04353	95650	228	04350	38′
·2	99997		00003	95876	229	04124	95879	229	04121	
·4	99997		00003	96107	231	03893	96110	231	03890	
·6	99997		00003	96338	231	03662	96341	231	03659	
·8	99997		00003	96571	233	03429	96574	233	03426	
23·0	99997		00003	96806	234	03195	96808	234	03192	37′
·2	99998		00002	97041	236	02959	97043	235	02957	
·4	99998		00002	97278	237	02722	97280	237	02720	
·6	99998		00002	97516	238	02484	97518	238	02482	
·8	99998		00002	97755	239	02245	97757	239	02243	
24·0	99998		00002	97996	240	02005	97998	241	02002	36′

90°
270°

89°
269°

LOGS. OF TRIG. FUNCTIONS

′	Sine	Diff.	Cosec.	Tan.	Diff.	Cotan.	Secant	Diff.	Cosine	
24·0	1.(9) 99998		0.(10) 00002	1.(11) 97996	242	2.(8) 02005	1.(11) 97998	242	2.(8) 02002	36′
·2	99998		00002	98238	243	01762	98240	243	01760	
·4	99998		00002	98481	245	01519	98483	245	01517	
·6	99998		00002	98726	246	01274	98728	246	01272	
·8	99998		00002	98972	247	01028	98974	247	01026	
25·0	99998		00002	99219	249	00781	99221	249	00779	35′
·2	99998		00002	99468	251	00532	99470	251	00530	
·4	99998		00002	99719	251	00281	99721	251	00279	
·6	99998		00002	99970	254	00030	99972	254	00028	
·8	99998		00002	2.(12) 00224	254	3.(7) 99776	2.(12) 00226	254	3.(7) 99774	
26·0	99998		00002	00478	256	99522	00480	256	99520	34′
·2	99998		00002	00734	258	99266	00736	258	99264	
·4	99998		00002	00992	259	99008	00994	259	99006	
·6	99998		00002	01251	261	98749	01253	261	98747	
·8	99998		00002	01512	263	98488	01514	263	98486	
27·0	99998		00002	01775	264	98225	01777	264	98223	33′
·2	99998		00002	02039	265	97961	02041	265	97959	
·4	99998		00002	02304	268	97696	02306	268	97694	
·6	99998		00002	02572	268	97428	02574	268	97426	
·8	99998		00002	02840	271	97160	02842	271	97158	
28·0	99998		00002	03111	272	96889	03113	272	96887	32′
·2	99998		00002	03383	274	96617	03385	274	96615	
·4	99998		00002	03657	276	96343	03659	276	96341	
·6	99998		00002	03933	278	96067	03935	278	96065	
·8	99998		00002	04211	279	95789	04213	279	95787	
29·0	99998		00002	04490	281	95510	04492	281	95508	31′
·2	99998		00002	04771	283	95229	04773	283	95227	
·4	99998		00002	05054	285	94946	05056	285	94944	
·6	99998		00002	05339	286	94661	05341	286	94659	
·8	99998		00002	05625	289	94375	05627	289	94373	
30·0	99998		00002	05914	290	94086	05916	290	94084	30′
·2	99998		00002	06204	293	93796	06206	293	93794	
·4	99998		00002	06497	294	93503	06499	294	93501	
·6	99998		00002	06791	297	93209	06793	297	93207	
·8	99998		00002	07088	299	92912	07090	298	92910	
31·0	99999		00001	07387	301	92613	07388	301	92612	29′
·2	99999		00001	07688	302	92312	07689	302	92311	
·4	99999		00001	07990	305	92010	07991	305	92009	
·6	99999		00001	08295	307	91705	08296	307	91704	
·8	99999		00001	08602	309	91398	08603	309	91397	
32·0	99999		00001	08911	311	91089	08912	311	91088	28′
·2	99999		00001	09222	314	90778	09223	314	90777	
·4	99999		00001	09536	316	90464	09537	316	90463	
·6	99999		00001	09852	318	90148	09853	318	90147	
·8	99999		00001	10170	320	89830	10171	320	89829	
33·0	99999		00001	10490	323	89510	10492	323	89509	27′
·2	99999		00001	10813	326	89187	10814	326	89186	
·4	99999		00001	11139	327	88861	11140	327	88860	
·6	99999		00001	11466	331	88534	11467	331	88533	
·8	99999		00001	11797	332	88203	11798	332	88202	
34·0	99999		00001	12129	336	87871	12131	336	87870	26′
·2	99999		00001	12465	338	87535	12466	338	87534	
·4	99999		00001	12803	340	87197	12804	340	87196	
·6	99999		00001	13143	344	86857	13144	344	86856	
·8	99999		00001	13487	346	86513	13488	346	86512	
35·0	99999		00001	13833	349	86167	13834	349	86166	25′
·2	99999		00001	14182	351	85818	14183	351	85817	
·4	99999		00001	14533	355	85467	14534	355	85466	
·6	99999		00001	14888	357	85112	14889	357	85111	
·8	99999		00001	15245	361	84755	15246	361	84754	
36·0	99999		00001	15606		84394	15607		84393	24′

90°
270°

LOGS. OF TRIG. FUNCTIONS

89°
269°

′	Sine	Diff.	Cosec.	Tan.	Diff.	Cotan.	Secant	Diff.	Cosine	
36·0	1̄.(9) 99999		0.(10) 00001	2.(12) 15606	363	3̄.(7) 84394	2.(12) 15607	363	3̄.(7) 84393	24′
·2	99999		00001	15969	367	84031	15970	367	84030	
·4	99999		00001	16336	369	83664	16337	369	83663	
·6	99999		00001	16705	373	83295	16706	373	83294	
·8	99999		00001	17078	376	82922	17079	376	82921	
37·0	99999		00001	17454	379	82546	17455	379	82545	23′
·2	99999		00001	17833	383	82167	17834	383	82166	
·4	99999		00001	18216	386	81784	18217	386	81783	
·6	99999		00001	18602	389	81398	18603	389	81397	
·8	99999		00001	18991	393	81009	18992	393	81008	
38·0	99999		00001	19385	396	80616	19385	397	80615	22′
·2	99999		00001	19781	400	80219	19782	400	80218	
·4	99999		00001	20181	404	79819	20182	404	79818	
·6	99999		00001	20585	408	79415	20586	408	79414	
·8	99999		00001	20993	412	79007	20994	412	79006	
39·0	99999		00001	21405	415	78595	21406	415	78594	21′
·2	99999		00001	21820	420	78180	21821	420	78179	
·4	99999		00001	22240	424	77760	22241	424	77759	
·6	99999		00001	22664	428	77336	22665	428	77335	
·8	99999		00001	23092	432	76908	23093	432	76907	
40·0	99999		00001	23524	436	76476	23525	436	76475	20′
·2	99999		00001	23960	441	76040	23961	441	76039	
·4	99999		00001	24401	446	75599	24402	446	75598	
·6	99999		00001	24847	450	75153	24848	450	75152	
·8	99999		00001	25297	455	74703	25298	454	74702	
41·0	99999		00001	25752	459	74248	25752	460	74248	19′
·2	99999		00001	26211	464	73789	26212	464	73788	
·4	99999		00001	26675	470	73325	26676	470	73324	
·6	99999		00001	27145	475	72855	27146	475	72854	
·8	99999		00001	27620	480	72380	27621	479	72379	
42·0	99999		00001	28100	485	71900	28100	486	71900	18′
·2	99999		00001	28585	490	71415	28586	490	71414	
·4	99999		00001	29075	497	70925	29076	497	70924	
·6	99999		00001	29572	502	70428	29573	502	70427	
·8	99999		00001	30074	508	69926	30075	508	69925	
43·0	99999		00001	30582	514	69418	30583	514	69417	17′
·2	99999		00001	31096	520	68904	31097	520	68903	
·4	99999		00001	31616	527	68384	31617	526	68383	
·6	0.(10) 00000		00000	32143	533	67857	32143	533	67857	
·8	00000		00000	32676	539	67324	32676	540	67324	
44·0	00000		00000	33215	547	66785	33216	546	66784	16′
·2	00000		00000	33762	553	66238	33762	553	66238	
·4	00000		00000	34315	561	65685	34315	561	65685	
·6	00000		00000	34876	567	65124	34876	567	65124	
·8	00000		00000	35443	575	64557	35443	575	64557	
45·0	00000		00000	36018	583	63982	36018	583	63982	15′
·2	00000		00000	36601	591	63399	36601	591	63399	
·4	00000		00000	37192	599	62808	37192	599	62808	
·6	00000		00000	37791	608	62209	37791	608	62209	
·8	00000		00000	38399	615	61601	38399	616	61601	
46·0	00000		00000	39014	626	60986	39015	625	60985	14′
·2	00000		00000	39640	634	60360	39640	634	60360	
·4	00000		00000	40274	643	59726	40274	643	59726	
·6	00000		00000	40917	653	59083	40917	653	59083	
·8	00000		00000	41570	663	58430	41570	663	58430	
47·0	00000		00000	42233	674	57767	42233	674	57767	13′
·2	00000		00000	42917	683	57093	42917	683	57093	
·4	00000		00000	43590	695	56410	43590	695	56410	
·6	00000		00000	44285	707	55715	44285	707	55715	
·8	00000		00000	44992	717	55008	44992	717	55008	
48·0	00000		00000	45709		54291	45709		54291	12′

90°
270°

89°
269°

LOGS. OF TRIG. FUNCTIONS

′	Sine	Diff.	Cosec.	Tan.	Diff.	Cotan.	Secant	Diff.	Cosine	
48·0	0.(10) 00000		0.(10) 00000	2.(12) 45709	364	$\overline{3}$.(7) 54291	2.(12) 45709	364	$\overline{3}$.(7) 54291	12′
·1	00000		00000	46073	366	53927	46073	366	53927	
·2	00000		00000	46439	370	53561	46439	370	53561	
·3	00000		00000	46809	373	53191	46809	373	53191	
·4	00000		00000	47182	375	52818	47182	376	52818	
48·5	00000		00000	47557	380	52443	47558	379	52442	
·6	00000		00000	47937	383	52063	47937	383	52063	
·7	00000		00000	48320	386	51680	48320	386	51680	
·8	00000		00000	48706	389	51294	48706	389	51294	
·9	00000		00000	49095	393	50905	49095	393	50905	
49·0	00000		00000	49488	397	50512	49488	397	50512	11′
·1	00000		00000	49885	400	50115	49885	400	50115	
·2	00000		00000	50285	404	49715	50285	404	49715	
·3	00000		00000	50689	408	49311	50689	408	49311	
·4	00000		00000	51097	411	48903	51097	411	48903	
49·5	00000		00000	51508	416	48492	50509	416	48492	
·6	00000		00000	51924	420	48076	51924	420	48076	
·7	00000		00000	52344	423	47656	52344	423	47656	
·8	00000		00000	52767	428	47233	52767	428	47233	
·9	00000		00000	53195	432	46805	53195	432	46805	
50·0	00000		00000	53627	437	46373	53628	437	46373	10′
·1	00000		00000	54064	441	45936	54064	441	45936	
·2	00000		00000	54505	445	45495	54505	445	45495	
·3	00000		00000	54950	450	45050	54950	450	45050	
·4	00000		00000	55400	455	44600	55400	455	44600	
50·5	00000		00000	55855	460	44145	55855	460	44145	
·6	00000		00000	56315	464	43685	56315	464	43685	
·7	00000		00000	56779	470	43221	56779	470	43221	
·8	00000		00000	57249	474	42751	57249	474	42751	
·9	00000		00000	57723	480	42277	57723	480	42277	
51·0	00000		00000	58203	485	41797	58203	485	41797	9′
·1	00000		00000	58688	491	41312	58688	491	41312	
·2	00000		00000	59179	496	40821	59179	496	40821	
·3	00000		00000	59675	503	40325	59675	503	40325	
·4	00000		00000	60178	507	39822	60178	507	39822	
51·5	00000		00000	60685	514	39315	60686	514	39315	
·6	00000		00000	61199	521	38801	61199	521	38801	
·7	00000		00000	61720	526	38280	61720	526	38280	
·8	00000		00000	62246	533	37754	62246	533	37754	
·9	00000		00000	62779	539	37221	62779	539	37221	
52·0	00000		00000	63318	547	36682	63318	547	36682	8′
·1	00000		00000	63865	553	36135	63865	553	36135	
·2	00000		00000	64418	560	35582	64418	560	35582	
·3	00000		00000	64978	568	35022	64978	568	35022	
·4	00000		00000	65546	575	34454	65546	575	34454	
52·5	00000		00000	66121	583	33879	66121	583	33879	
·6	00000		00000	66704	591	33296	66704	591	33296	
·7	00000		00000	67295	599	32705	67295	599	32705	
·8	00000		00000	67894	608	32106	67894	608	32106	
·9	00000		00000	68502	616	31498	68502	616	31498	
53·0	00000		00000	69118	624	30883	69118	624	30882	7′
·1	00000		00000	69742	634	30258	69742	634	30258	
·2	00000		00000	70376	644	29624	70376	644	29624	
·3	00000		00000	71020	653	28980	71020	653	28980	
·4	00000		00000	71673	663	28327	71673	663	28327	
53·5	00000		00000	72336	673	27664	72336	673	27664	
·6	00000		00000	73009	684	26991	73009	684	26991	
·7	00000		00000	73693	695	26307	73693	695	26307	
·8	00000		00000	74388	706	25612	74388	706	25612	
·9	00000		00000	75094	718	24906	75094	718	24906	
54·0	00000		00000	75812		24188	75812		24188	6′

90°
270°

89°
269°

LOGS. OF TRIG. FUNCTIONS

′	Sine	Diff.	Cosec.	Tan.	Diff.	Cotan.	Secant	Diff.	Cosine	
54·0	0.(10) 00000		0.(10) 00000	2.(12) 75812	730	$\overline{3}$.(7) 24188	2.(12) 75812	730	$\overline{3}$.(7) 24188	6′
·1	00000		00000	76542	743	23458	76542	743	23458	
·2	00000		00000	77285	755	22715	77285	755	22715	
·3	00000		00000	78040	769	21960	78040	769	21960	
·4	00000		00000	78809	782	21191	78809	782	21191	
54·5	00000		00000	79591	797	20409	79591	797	20409	
·6	00000		00000	80388	812	19612	80388	812	19612	
·7	00000		00000	81200	827	18800	81200	827	18800	
·8	00000		00000	82027	843	17973	82027	843	17973	
·9	00000		00000	82870	860	17130	82870	860	17130	
55·0	00000		00000	83730	878	16270	83730	878	16270	5′
·1	00000		00000	84608	895	15392	84608	895	15392	
·2	00000		00000	85503	915	14497	85503	915	14497	
·3	00000		00000	86418	934	13582	86418	934	13582	
·4	00000		00000	87352	954	12648	87352	954	12648	
55·5	00000		00000	88306	976	11694	88306	976	11694	
·6	00000		00000	89282	999	10718	89282	999	10718	
·7	00000		00000	90281	1021	09719	90281	1021	09719	
·8	00000		00000	91302	1047	08698	91302	1047	08698	
·9	00000		00000	92349	1072	07651	92349	1072	07651	
56·0	00000		00000	93421	1100	06579	93421	1100	06579	4′
·1	00000		00000	94521	1128	05479	94521	1128	05479	
·2	00000		00000	95649	1158	04351	95649	1158	04351	
·3	00000		00000	96807	1190	03193	96807	1190	03193	
·4	00000		00000	97997	1224	02003	97997	1224	02003	
56·5	00000		00000	99221	1258	00779	99221	1258	00779	
·6	00000		00000	3.(13) 00479	1297	$\overline{4}$.(6) 99521	3.(13) 00479	1297	$\overline{4}$.(6) 99521	
·7	00000		00000	01776	1336	98224	01776	1336	98224	
·8	00000		00000	03112	1379	96888	03112	1379	96888	
·9	00000		00000	04491	1424	95509	04491	1424	95509	
57·0	00000		00000	05915	1473	94085	05915	1473	94085	3′
·1	00000		00000	07388	1524	92612	07388	1524	92612	
·2	00000		00000	08912	1579	91088	08912	1579	91088	
·3	00000		00000	10491	1639	89509	10491	1639	89509	
·4	00000		00000	12130	1703	87870	12130	1703	87870	
57·5	00000		00000	13833	1773	86167	13833	1773	86167	
·6	00000		00000	15606	1849	84394	15606	1849	84394	
·7	00000		00000	17455	1930	82545	17455	1930	82545	
·8	00000		00000	19385	2020	80615	19385	2020	80615	
·9	00000		00000	21405	2119	78595	21405	2119	78595	
58·0	00000		00000	23524	2228	76476	23524	2228	76476	2′
·1	00000		00000	25752	2348	74248	25752	2348	74248	
·2	00000		00000	28100	2482	71900	28100	2482	71900	
·3	00000		00000	30582	2633	69418	30582	2633	69418	
·4	00000		00000	33215	2803	66785	33215	2803	66785	
58·5	00000		00000	36018	2997	63982	36018	2997	63982	
·6	00000		00000	39015	3218	60985	39015	3218	60985	
·7	00000		00000	42233	3476	57767	42233	3476	57767	
·8	00000		00000	45709	3779	54291	45709	3779	54291	
·9	00000		00000	49488	4139	50512	49488	4139	50512	
59·0	00000		00000	53627	4576	46373	53627	4576	46373	1′
·1	00000		00000	58203	5115	41797	58203	5115	41797	
·2	00000		00000	63318	5800	36682	63318	5800	36682	
·3	00000		00000	69118	6694	30882	69118	6694	30882	
·4	00000		00000	75812	7918	24188	75812	7918	24188	
59·5	00000		00000	83730	9691	16270	83730	9691	16270	
·6	00000		00000	93421	12494	06579	93421	12494	06579	
·7	00000		00000	4.(14) 05915	17609	$\overline{5}$.(5) 94085	4.(14) 05915	17609	$\overline{5}$.(5) 94085	
·8	00000		00000	23524	30103	76476	23524	30103	76476	
·9	00000		00000	53627		46373	53627		46373	
60·0	00000		00000	∞		∞	∞		∞	0′

90°
270°

0° HAVERSINES

'	Log .0	Nat .0	Log .2	Nat .2	Log .4	Nat .4	'
00	—̄ —∞	0·00000	0 (0) 92745	0·00000	9̄.(1.) 52951	0·00000	59
01	8̄.(2.) 32539	0·00000	8̄.(2.) 48375	0·00000	8̄.(2.) 61765	0·00000	58
02	92745	0·00000	7̄.(3.) 01024	0·00000	7̄.(3.) 08581	0·00000	57
03	7̄.(3.) 27963	0·00000	33569	0·00000	38835	0·00000	56
04	52951	0·00000	57189	0·00000	61230	0·00000	55
05	72333	0·00000	75740	0·00000	79018	0·00000	54
06	88169	0·00000	91018	0·00000	93775	0·00000	53
07	6̄.(4.) 01559	0·00000	6̄.(4.) 04006	0·00000	06386	0·00000	52
08	13157	0·00000	15302	0·00000	17395	0·00000	51
09	23388	0·00000	25297	0·00000	27165	0·00000	50
10	32539	0·00000	34259	0·00000	35946	0·00000	49
11	40818	0·00000	42383	0·00000	43920	0·00000	48
12	48375	0·00000	49811	0·00000	51224	0·00000	47
13	55328	0·00000	56654	0·00000	57960	0·00000	46
14	61765	0·00000	62997	0·00000	64212	0·00000	45
15	67757	0·00000	68908	0·00000	70043	0·00000	44
16	73363	0·00001	74442	0·00001	75508	0·00001	43
17	78629	0·00001	79645	0·00001	80649	0·00001	42
18	83594	0·00001	84553	0·00001	85503	0·00001	41
19	88290	0·00001	89199	0·00001	90099	0·00001	40
20	92745	0·00001	93609	0·00001	94465	0·00001	39
21	96983	0·00001	97806	0·00001	98622	0·00001	38
22	5̄.(5.) 01024	0·00001	5̄.(5.) 01810	0·00001	5̄.(5.) 02589	0·00001	37
23	04885	0·00001	05637	0·00001	06382	0·00001	36
24	08581	0·00001	09302	0·00001	10017	0·00001	35
25	12127	0·00001	12819	0·00001	13506	0·00001	34
26	15534	0·00001	16199	0·00001	16860	0·00001	33
27	18812	0·00002	19453	0·00002	20089	0·00002	32
28	21971	0·00002	22589	0·00002	23203	0·00002	31
29	25019	0·00002	25616	0·00002	26208	0·00002	30
30	27963	0·00002	28540	0·00002	29114	0·00002	29
31	30811	0·00002	31370	0·00002	31925	0·00002	28
32	33569	0·00002	34110	0·00002	34648	0·00002	27
33	36242	0·00002	36766	0·00002	37288	0·00002	26
34	38835	0·00002	39344	0·00002	39851	0·00003	25
35	41352	0·00003	41847	0·00003	42339	0·00003	24
36	43799	0·00003	44281	0·00003	44759	0·00003	23
37	46179	0·00003	46647	0·00003	47113	0·00003	22
38	48495	0·00003	48951	0·00003	49405	0·00003	21
39	50752	0·00003	51196	0·00003	51638	0·00003	20
40	52951	0·00003	53384	0·00003	53815	0·00003	19
41	55095	0·00004	55518	0·00004	55939	0·00004	18
42	57189	0·00004	57601	0·00004	58012	0·00004	17
43	59232	0·00004	59635	0·00004	60037	0·00004	16
44	61229	0·00004	61623	0·00004	62015	0·00004	15
45	63181	0·00004	63566	0·00004	63950	0·00004	14
46	65090	0·00004	65467	0·00005	65842	0·00005	13
47	66958	0·00005	67327	0·00005	67694	0·00005	12
48	68787	0·00005	69148	0·00005	69508	0·00005	11
49	70578	0·00005	70931	0·00005	71284	0·00005	10
50	72332	0·00005	72679	0·00005	73025	0·00005	09
51	74052	0·00006	74392	0·00006	74731	0·00006	08
52	75739	0·00006	76072	0·00006	76405	0·00006	07
53	77394	0·00006	77721	0·00006	78101	0·00006	06
54	79017	0·00006	79338	0·00006	79658	0·00006	05
55	80611	0·00006	80926	0·00007	81240	0·00007	04
56	82176	0·00007	82486	0·00007	82794	0·00007	03
57	83713	0·00007	84017	0·00007	84321	0·00007	02
58	85224	0·00007	85523	0·00007	85821	0·00007	01
59	86709	0·00007	87002	0·00007	87295	0·00007	00

.8 .6

PARTS for 0'.1: LOGS variable NATURALS negligible

359°

0° HAVERSINES

'	.6 Log.	.6 Nat.	.8 Log.	.8 Nat.	Log.	Nat.	'
00	9̄.(1.) 88169	0·00000	8̄.(2.) 13157	0·00000	8̄.(2.) 32539	0·00000	59
01	8̄.(2.) 73363	0·00000	83594	0·00000	92745	0·00000	58
02	7̄.(3.) 15534	0·00000	7̄.(3.) 21971	0·00000	7̄.(3.) 27963	0·00000	57
03	43800	0·00000	48496	0·00000	52951	0·00000	56
04	65091	0·00000	68787	0·00000	72333	0·00000	55
05	82177	0·00000	85225	0·00000	88169	0·00000	54
06	96448	0·00000	99041	0·00000	6̄.(4.) 01559	0·00000	53
07	6̄.(4.) 08702	0·00000	6̄.(4.) 10958	0·00000	13157	0·00000	52
08	19439	0·00000	21436	0·00000	23388	0·00000	51
09	28993	0·00000	30784	0·00000	32539	0·00000	50
10	37600	0·00000	39224	0·00000	40818	0·00000	49
11	45431	0·00000	46916	0·00000	48375	0·00000	48
12	52613	0·00000	53981	0·00000	55328	0·00000	47
13	59247	0·00000	60515	0·00000	61765	0·00000	46
14	65410	0·00000	66591	0·00000	67757	0·00000	45
15	71164	0·00001	72271	0·00001	73363	0·00001	44
16	76561	0·00001	77601	0·00001	78629	0·00001	43
17	81642	0·00001	82623	0·00001	83594	0·00001	42
18	86442	0·00001	87371	0·00001	88290	0·00001	41
19	90990	0·00001	91872	0·00001	92745	0·00001	40
20	95313	0·00001	96152	0·00001	96983	0·00001	39
21	99430	0·00001	5̄.(5.) 00230	0·00001	5̄.(5.) 01024	0·00001	38
22	5̄.(5.) 03361	0·00001	04126	0·00001	04885	0·00001	37
23	07121	0·00001	07854	0·00001	08581	0·00001	36
24	10726	0·00001	11429	0·00001	12127	0·00001	35
25	14187	0·00001	14863	0·00001	15534	0·00001	34
26	17515	0·00002	18166	0·00002	18812	0·00002	33
27	20721	0·00002	21348	0·00002	21971	0·00002	32
28	23812	0·00002	24417	0·00002	25019	0·00002	31
29	26797	0·00002	27382	0·00002	27963	0·00002	30
30	29683	0·00002	30249	0·00002	30811	0·00002	29
31	32476	0·00002	33024	0·00002	33569	0·00002	28
32	35182	0·00002	35714	0·00002	36242	0·00002	27
33	37807	0·00002	38322	0·00002	38835	0·00002	26
34	40354	0·00003	40855	0·00003	41352	0·00003	25
35	42829	0·00003	43315	0·00003	43799	0·00003	24
36	45235	0·00003	45708	0·00003	46179	0·00003	23
37	47576	0·00003	48037	0·00003	48495	0·00003	22
38	49856	0·00003	50305	0·00003	50752	0·00003	21
39	52078	0·00003	52515	0·00003	52951	0·00003	20
40	54244	0·00004	54671	0·00004	55095	0·00004	19
41	56357	0·00004	56774	0·00004	57189	0·00004	18
42	58421	0·00004	58827	0·00004	59232	0·00004	17
43	60436	0·00004	60833	0·00004	61229	0·00004	16
44	62406	0·00004	62794	0·00004	63181	0·00004	15
45	64332	0·00004	64712	0·00004	65090	0·00004	14
46	66216	0·00005	66588	0·00005	66958	0·00005	13
47	68060	0·00005	68424	0·00005	68787	0·00005	12
48	69866	0·00005	70222	0·00005	70578	0·00005	11
49	71635	0·00005	71984	0·00005	72332	0·00005	10
50	73369	0·00005	73711	0·00005	74052	0·00006	09
51	75068	0·00006	75404	0·00006	75739	0·00006	08
52	76736	0·00006	77065	0·00006	77394	0·00006	07
53	78371	0·00006	78695	0·00006	79017	0·00006	06
54	79977	0·00006	80294	0·00006	80611	0·00006	05
55	81553	0·00007	81865	0·00007	82176	0·00007	04
56	83102	0·00007	83408	0·00007	83713	0·00007	03
57	84623	0·00007	84924	0·00007	85224	0·00007	02
58	86118	0·00007	86414	0·00007	86709	0·00007	01
59	87587	0·00008	87878	0·00008	88168	0·00008	00

| .4 | | .2 | | .0 | | 359° |

PARTS for 0'.1: LOGS variable NATURALS negligible

1° HAVERSINES

,	.0 Log. $\overline{5}.\text{or}(5.)$ / $\overline{\overline{4}}.\text{or}(6.)$	.0 Nat. 0.	.2 Log. $\overline{5}.\text{or}(5.)$ / $\overline{\overline{4}}.\text{or}(6.)$	.2 Nat. 0.	.4 Log. $\overline{5}.\text{or}(5.)$ / $\overline{\overline{4}}.\text{or}(6.)$	.4 Nat. 0.	.6 Log. $\overline{5}.\text{or}(5.)$ / $\overline{\overline{4}}.\text{or}(6.)$	.6 Nat. 0.	.8 Log. $\overline{5}.\text{or}(5.)$ / $\overline{\overline{4}}.\text{or}(6.)$	.8 Nat. 0.	Log. $\overline{5}.\text{or}(5.)$ / $\overline{\overline{4}}.\text{or}(6.)$	Nat. 0.	,
00	88168	00008	88457	00008	88745	00008	89033	00008	89319	00008	89604	00008	59
01	89604	00008	89888	00008	90172	00008	90454	00008	90736	00008	91016	00008	58
02	91016	00008	91296	00008	91575	00008	91853	00008	92130	00008	92406	00008	57
03	92406	00008	92681	00008	92956	00008	93229	00009	93502	00009	93774	00009	56
04	93774	00009	94045	00009	94315	00009	94584	00009	94853	00009	95121	00009	55
05	95121	00009	95387	00009	95653	00009	95919	00009	96183	00009	96447	00009	54
06	96447	00009	96709	00009	96971	00009	97233	00009	97493	00009	97753	00010	53
07	97753	00010	98012	00010	98270	00010	98527	00010	98784	00010	99040	00010	52
08	99040	00010	99295	00010	99549	00010	99803	00010	00055	00010	00308	00010	51
09	00308	00010	00559	00010	00810	00010	01060	00010	01309	00010	01557	00010	50
10	01557	00010	01805	00010	02052	00010	02299	00011	02544	00011	02789	00011	49
11	02789	00011	03034	00011	03277	00011	03520	00011	03763	00011	04004	00011	48
12	04004	00011	04245	00011	04485	00011	04725	00011	04964	00011	05202	00011	47
13	05202	00011	05440	00011	05677	00011	05913	00011	06149	00012	06384	00012	46
14	06384	00012	06618	00012	06852	00012	07085	00012	07318	00012	07550	00012	45
15	07550	00012	07781	00012	08012	00012	08242	00012	08471	00012	08700	00012	44
16	08700	00012	08928	00012	09156	00013	09383	00013	09610	00013	09836	00013	43
17	09836	00013	10061	00013	10286	00013	10510	00013	10733	00013	10956	00013	42
18	10956	00013	11180	00013	11401	00013	11622	00013	11843	00013	12063	00013	41
19	12063	00013	12282	00013	12501	00013	12720	00013	12938	00013	13155	00014	40
20	13155	00014	13372	00014	13588	00014	13804	00014	14019	00014	14234	00014	39
21	14234	00014	14448	00014	14662	00014	14875	00014	15088	00014	15300	00014	38
22	15300	00014	15512	00014	15723	00014	15933	00014	16143	00014	16353	00015	37
23	16353	00015	16562	00015	16770	00015	16978	00015	17186	00015	17393	00015	36
24	17393	00015	17599	00015	17806	00015	18011	00015	18216	00015	18421	00015	35
25	18421	00015	18625	00015	18829	00015	19032	00016	19234	00016	19437	00016	34
26	19437	00016	19638	00016	19840	00016	20040	00016	20241	00016	20441	00016	33
27	20441	00016	20640	00016	20839	00016	21038	00016	21236	00016	21433	00016	32
28	21433	00016	21631	00016	21827	00017	22024	00017	22219	00017	22415	00017	31
29	22415	00017	22610	00017	22804	00017	22998	00017	23192	00017	23385	00017	30
30	23385	00017	23578	00017	23770	00017	23962	00017	24154	00017	24345	00018	29
31	24345	00018	24536	00018	24726	00018	24916	00018	25105	00018	25294	00018	28
32	25294	00018	25483	00018	25671	00018	25859	00018	26046	00018	26233	00018	27
33	26233	00018	26420	00018	26606	00018	26792	00019	26977	00019	27162	00019	26
34	27162	00019	27347	00019	27531	00019	27715	00019	27898	00019	28081	00019	25
35	28081	00019	28264	00019	28446	00019	28628	00019	28810	00019	28991	00019	24
36	28991	00019	29171	00020	29352	00020	29532	00020	29711	00020	29891	00020	23
37	29891	00020	30070	00020	30248	00020	30426	00020	30604	00020	30781	00020	22
38	30781	00020	30959	00020	31135	00020	31312	00021	31470	00021	31663	00021	21
39	31663	00021	31839	00021	32013	00021	32188	00021	32362	00021	32536	00021	20
40	32536	00021	32710	00021	32883	00021	33056	00021	33228	00022	33400	00022	19
41	33400	00022	33572	00022	33744	00022	33915	00022	34086	00022	34256	00022	18
42	34256	00022	34426	00022	34596	00022	34765	00022	34935	00022	35103	00022	17
43	35103	00022	35272	00023	35440	00023	35608	00023	35775	00023	35943	00023	16
44	35943	00023	36109	00023	36276	00023	36442	00023	36608	00023	36774	00023	15
45	36774	00023	36939	00023	37104	00023	37269	00024	37433	00024	37597	00024	14
46	37597	00024	37761	00024	37924	00024	38087	00024	38250	00024	38412	00024	13
47	38412	00024	38575	00024	38737	00024	38898	00024	39059	00025	39220	00025	12
48	39220	00025	39381	00025	39541	00025	39702	00025	39861	00025	40021	00025	11
49	40021	00025	40180	00025	40339	00025	40498	00025	40656	00026	40814	00026	10
50	40814	00026	40972	00026	41129	00026	41287	00026	41443	00026	41600	00026	09
51	41600	00026	41756	00026	41912	00026	42068	00026	42224	00026	42379	00027	08
52	42379	00027	42534	00027	42689	00027	42843	00027	42997	00027	43151	00027	07
53	43151	00027	43305	00027	43458	00027	43611	00027	43764	00027	43916	00027	06
54	43916	00027	44068	00028	44220	00028	44372	00028	44524	00028	44675	00028	05
55	44675	00028	44826	00028	44976	00028	45127	00028	45277	00028	45427	00028	04
56	45427	00028	45576	00029	45726	00029	45875	00029	46024	00029	46172	00029	03
57	46172	00029	46321	00029	46469	00029	46616	00029	46764	00029	46911	00029	02
58	46911	00029	47058	00030	47205	00030	47352	00030	47498	00030	47644	00030	01
59	47644	00030	47790	00030	47936	00030	48081	00030	48226	00030	48371	00030	00
	.8		.6		.4		.2		.0				

PARTS for 0'.1: LOGS variable   NATURALS negligible

358°

2° HAVERSINES

′	.0 Log. $\overline{4}$.or(6.)	.0 Nat. 0.	.2 Log. $\overline{4}$.or(6.)	.2 Nat. 0.	.4 Log. $\overline{4}$.or(6.)	.4 Nat. 0.	.6 Log. $\overline{4}$.or(6.)	.6 Nat. 0.	.8 Log. $\overline{4}$.or(6.)	.8 Nat. 0.	Log. $\overline{4}$.or(6.)	Nat. 0.	′
00	48371	00030	48516	00031	48660	00031	48804	00031	48948	00031	49092	00031	59
01	49092	00031	49235	00031	49378	00031	49521	00031	49664	00031	49807	00031	58
02	49807	00031	49949	00032	50091	00032	50233	00032	50374	00032	50516	00032	57
03	50516	00032	50657	00032	50798	00032	50938	00032	51079	00032	51219	00033	56
04	51219	00033	51359	00033	51499	00033	51638	00033	51777	00033	51916	00033	55
05	51916	00033	52055	00033	52194	00033	52332	00033	52471	00033	52608	00034	54
06	52608	00034	52746	00034	52884	00034	53021	00034	53158	00034	53295	00034	53
07	53295	00034	53432	00034	53568	00034	53704	00034	53840	00035	53976	00035	52
08	53976	00035	54112	00035	54247	00035	54382	00035	54517	00035	54652	00035	51
09	54652	00035	54787	00035	54921	00035	55055	00036	55189	00036	55323	00036	50
10	55323	00036	55456	00036	55590	00036	55723	00036	55856	00036	55988	00036	49
11	55988	00036	56121	00036	56253	00037	56385	00037	56517	00037	56649	00037	48
12	56649	00037	56780	00037	56911	00037	57043	00037	57173	00037	57304	00037	47
13	57304	00037	57435	00038	57565	00038	57695	00038	57825	00038	57955	00038	46
14	57955	00038	58084	00038	58214	00038	58343	00038	58472	00038	58600	00038	45
15	58600	00039	58729	00039	58857	00039	58986	00039	59114	00039	59241	00039	44
16	59241	00039	59369	00039	59496	00039	59624	00039	59751	00040	59878	00040	43
17	59878	00040	60004	00040	60131	00040	60257	00040	60383	00040	60509	00040	42
18	60509	00040	60635	00041	60761	00041	60886	00041	61011	00041	61136	00041	41
19	61136	00041	61261	00041	61386	00041	61510	00041	61635	00041	61759	00041	40
20	61759	00041	61883	00042	62007	00042	62130	00042	62254	00042	62377	00042	39
21	62377	00042	62500	00042	62623	00042	62746	00042	62868	00043	62991	00043	38
22	62991	00043	63113	00043	63235	00043	63357	00043	63479	00043	63600	00043	37
23	63600	00043	63722	00043	63843	00043	63964	00044	64085	00044	64205	00044	36
24	64205	00044	64326	00044	64446	00044	64566	00044	64687	00044	64806	00044	35
25	64806	00044	64926	00045	65046	00045	65165	00045	65284	00045	65403	00045	34
26	65403	00045	65522	00045	65641	00045	65759	00045	65878	00046	65996	00046	33
27	65996	00046	66114	00046	66232	00046	66350	00046	66467	00046	66585	00046	32
28	66585	00046	66702	00046	66819	00047	66936	00047	67053	00047	67170	00047	31
29	67170	00047	67286	00047	67403	00047	67519	00047	67635	00047	67751	00048	30
30	67751	00048	67866	00048	67982	00048	68097	00048	68213	00048	68328	00048	29
31	68328	00048	68443	00048	68557	00048	68672	00049	68787	00049	68901	00049	28
32	68901	00049	69015	00049	69129	00049	69243	00049	69356	00049	69470	00050	27
33	69470	00050	69584	00050	69697	00050	69810	00050	69923	00050	70036	00050	26
34	70036	00050	70149	00050	70261	00050	70374	00051	70486	00051	70598	00051	25
35	70598	00051	70710	00051	70822	00051	70934	00051	71045	00051	71157	00051	24
36	71157	00051	71268	00052	71379	00052	71490	00052	71601	00052	71712	00052	23
37	71712	00052	71822	00052	71933	00052	72043	00053	72153	00053	72263	00053	22
38	72263	00053	72373	00053	72483	00053	72592	00053	72702	00053	72811	00053	21
39	72811	00053	72920	00054	73029	00054	73138	00054	73247	00054	73355	00054	20
40	73355	00054	73464	00054	73572	00054	73680	00055	73789	00055	73896	00055	19
41	73896	00055	74004	00055	74112	00055	74220	00055	74327	00055	74434	00056	18
42	74434	00056	74541	00056	74648	00056	74755	00056	74862	00056	74969	00056	17
43	74969	00056	75075	00056	75181	00056	75288	00057	75394	00057	75500	00057	16
44	75500	00057	75606	00057	75711	00057	75817	00057	75922	00057	76028	00058	15
45	76028	00058	76133	00058	76238	00058	76343	00058	76448	00058	76552	00058	14
46	76552	00058	76657	00058	76761	00059	76866	00059	76970	00059	77074	00059	13
47	77074	00059	77178	00059	77282	00059	77385	00059	77489	00060	77592	00060	12
48	77592	00060	77696	00060	77799	00060	77902	00060	78005	00060	78108	00060	11
49	78108	00060	78211	00061	78313	00061	78416	00061	78518	00061	78620	00061	10
50	78620	00061	78722	00061	78824	00061	78926	00062	79028	00062	79129	00062	09
51	79129	00062	79231	00062	79332	00062	79434	00062	79535	00062	79636	00063	08
52	79636	00063	79737	00063	79838	00063	79938	00063	80039	00063	80139	00063	07
53	80139	00063	80240	00063	80340	00064	80440	00064	80540	00064	80640	00064	06
54	80640	00064	80740	00064	80839	00064	80939	00064	81038	00065	81137	00065	05
55	81137	00065	81237	00065	81336	00065	81435	00065	81534	00065	81632	00066	04
56	81632	00066	81731	00066	81829	00066	81928	00066	82026	00066	82124	00066	03
57	82124	00066	82222	00066	82320	00067	82418	00067	82516	00067	82614	00067	02
58	82614	00067	82711	00067	82808	00067	82906	00067	83003	00068	83100	00068	01
59	83100	00068	83197	00068	83294	00068	83391	00068	83487	00068	83584	00069	00

	.8	.6	.4	.2	.0

PARTS for 0′.1: LOGS variable NATURALS, negligible.

357°

3° HAVERSINES

,	.0 Log. $\overline{4}$.or(6.) $\overline{3}$.or(7.)	.0 Nat. 0.	.2 Log. $\overline{4}$.or(6.) $\overline{3}$.or(7.)	.2 Nat. 0.	.4 Log. $\overline{4}$.or(6.) $\overline{3}$.or(.7)	.4 Nat. 0.	.6 Log. $\overline{4}$.or(6.) $\overline{3}$.or(7.)	.6 Nat. 0.	.8 Log. $\overline{4}$.or(6.) $\overline{3}$.or(7.)	.8 Nat. 0.	Log. $\overline{4}$.or(6.) $\overline{3}$.or(7.)	Nat. 0.	,
00	83584	00069	83680	00069	83777	00069	83873	00069	83969	00069	84065	00069	59
01	84065	00069	84161	00069	84257	00070	84352	00070	84448	00070	84543	00070	58
02	84543	00070	84639	00070	84734	00070	84829	00071	84924	00071	85019	00071	57
03	85019	00071	85114	00071	85209	00071	85303	00071	85398	00071	85492	00072	56
04	85492	00072	85587	00072	85681	00072	85774	00072	85869	00072	85963	00072	55
05	85963	00072	86057	00073	86151	00073	86244	00073	86338	00073	86431	00073	54
06	86431	00073	86525	00073	86618	00073	86711	00074	86804	00074	86897	00074	53
07	86897	00074	86990	00074	87082	00074	87175	00074	87268	00075	87360	00075	52
08	87360	00075	87452	00075	87545	00075	87637	00075	87729	00075	87821	00076	51
09	87821	00076	87912	00076	88004	00076	88096	00076	88187	00076	88279	00076	50
10	88279	00076	88370	00077	88462	00077	88553	00077	88644	00077	88735	00077	49
11	88735	00077	88826	00077	88916	00077	89007	00078	89098	00078	89188	00078	48
12	89188	00078	89279	00078	89369	00078	89459	00078	89549	00079	89639	00079	47
13	89639	00079	89729	00079	89819	00079	89909	00079	89998	00079	90088	00080	46
14	90088	00080	90178	00080	90267	00080	90356	00080	90445	00080	90535	00080	45
15	90535	00080	90624	00081	90712	00081	90801	00081	90890	00081	90979	00081	44
16	90979	00081	91067	00081	91156	00082	91244	00082	91332	00082	91421	00082	43
17	91421	00082	91509	00082	91597	00082	91685	00083	91773	00083	91860	00083	42
18	91860	00083	91948	00083	92036	00083	92123	00083	92210	00084	92298	00084	41
19	92298	00084	92385	00084	92472	00084	92559	00084	92646	00084	92733	00085	40
20	92733	00085	92820	00085	92906	00085	92993	00085	93080	00085	93166	00085	39
21	93166	00085	93252	00086	93339	00086	93425	00086	93511	00086	93597	00086	38
22	93597	00086	93683	00086	93769	00087	93855	00087	93940	00087	94026	00087	37
23	94026	00087	94111	00087	94197	00087	94282	00088	94367	00088	94453	00088	36
24	94453	00088	94538	00088	94623	00088	94708	00089	94792	00089	94877	00089	35
25	94877	00089	94962	00089	95046	00089	95131	00089	95215	00090	95300	00090	34
26	95300	00090	95384	00090	95468	00090	95552	00090	95636	00090	95720	00091	33
27	95720	00091	95804	00091	95888	00091	95972	00091	96055	00091	96139	00091	32
28	96139	00091	96222	00092	96305	00092	96389	00092	96472	00092	96555	00092	31
29	96555	00092	96638	00093	96721	00093	96804	00093	96888	00093	96970	00093	30
30	96970	00093	97052	00093	97135	00094	97217	00094	97300	00094	97382	00094	29
31	97382	00094	97464	00094	97547	00095	97629	00095	97711	00095	97793	00095	28
32	97793	00095	97875	00095	97956	00095	98038	00096	98120	00096	98201	00096	27
33	98201	00096	98283	00096	98364	00096	98446	00096	98527	00097	98608	00097	26
34	98608	00097	98689	00097	98770	00097	98851	00097	98932	00098	99013	00098	25
35	99013	00098	99094	00098	99174	00098	99255	00098	99334	00098	99416	00099	24
36	99416	00099	99496	00099	99576	00099	99657	00099	99737	00099	99817	00100	23
37	99817	00100	99897	00100	99977	00100	00057	00100	00136	00100	00216	00101	22
38	00216	00101	00296	00101	00375	00101	00455	00101	00534	00101	00613	00101	21
39	00613	00101	00693	00102	00772	00102	00851	00102	00930	00102	01009	00102	20
40	01009	00102	01088	00103	01167	00103	01245	00103	01324	00103	01403	00103	19
41	01403	00103	01481	00103	01560	00104	01638	00104	01716	00104	01795	00104	18
42	01795	00104	01873	00104	01951	00105	02029	00105	02107	00105	02185	00105	17
43	02185	00105	02263	00105	02341	00106	02418	00106	02496	00106	02573	00106	16
44	02573	00106	02651	00106	02728	00106	02806	00107	02883	00107	02960	00107	15
45	02960	00107	03037	00107	03114	00107	03191	00108	03268	00108	03345	00108	14
46	03345	00108	03422	00108	03499	00108	03575	00109	03652	00109	03729	00109	13
47	03729	00109	03805	00109	03881	00109	03958	00110	04034	00110	04110	00110	12
48	04110	00110	04186	00110	04262	00110	04338	00111	04414	00111	04490	00111	11
49	04490	00111	04566	00111	04642	00111	04717	00111	04793	00112	04869	00112	10
50	04869	00112	04944	00112	05019	00112	05095	00112	05170	00113	05245	00113	09
51	05245	00113	05320	00113	05396	00113	05471	00113	05545	00114	05620	00114	08
52	05620	00114	05695	00114	05770	00114	05845	00114	05919	00115	05994	00115	07
53	05994	00115	06068	00115	06143	00115	06217	00115	06291	00116	06366	00116	06
54	06366	00116	06440	00116	06514	00116	06588	00116	06662	00117	06736	00117	05
55	06736	00117	06810	00117	06884	00117	06957	00117	07031	00118	07105	00118	04
56	07105	00118	07178	00118	07252	00118	07325	00118	07398	00119	07472	00119	03
57	07472	00119	07545	00119	07618	00119	07691	00119	07764	00120	07837	00120	02
58	07837	00120	07910	00120	07983	00120	08056	00120	08129	00121	08201	00121	01
59	08201	00121	08274	00121	08347	00121	08419	00121	08491	00122	08564	00122	00

.8	.6	.4	.2	.0

PARTS for 0'.1:   LOGS variable   NATURALS. negligible

356°

4° HAVERSINES

′	.0 Log.	.0 Nat.	.2 Log.	.2 Nat.	.4 Log.	.4 Nat.	.6 Log.	.6 Nat.	.8 Log.	.8 Nat.	Log.	Nat.	′
	3̄.or(7.)	0.	3̄.or(7.)	0.	3̄.or(7.)	0.	3̄.or7.)	0.	3̄.or(7.)	0.	3̄.or(7.)	0.	
00	08564	00122	08636	00122	08708	00122	08781	00122	08852	00123	08925	00123	59
01	08925	00123	08997	00123	09069	00123	09141	00123	09213	00124	09284	00124	58
02	09284	00124	09356	00124	09428	00124	09499	00124	09571	00125	09642	00125	57
03	09642	00125	09714	00125	09785	00125	09857	00125	09928	00126	09999	00126	56
04	09999	00126	10070	00126	10141	00126	10212	00127	10283	00127	10354	00127	55
05	10354	00127	10425	00127	10496	00127	10566	00128	10637	00128	10708	00128	54
06	10708	00128	10778	00128	10849	00128	10919	00129	10990	00129	11060	00129	53
07	11060	00129	11130	00129	11200	00129	11271	00130	11341	00130	11411	00130	52
08	11411	00130	11481	00130	11551	00130	11621	00131	11690	00131	11760	00131	51
09	11760	00131	11830	00131	11899	00132	11969	00132	12039	00132	12108	00132	50
10	12108	00132	12178	00132	12247	00133	12316	00133	12385	00133	12455	00133	49
11	12455	00133	12524	00133	12593	00134	12662	00134	12731	00134	12800	00134	48
12	12800	00134	12869	00135	12938	00135	13006	00135	13075	00135	13144	00135	47
13	13144	00135	13212	00136	13281	00136	13349	00136	13418	00136	13486	00136	46
14	13486	00136	13555	00137	13623	00137	13691	00137	13759	00137	13827	00137	45
15	13827	00137	13895	00138	13963	00138	14031	00138	14099	00138	14167	00139	44
16	14167	00139	14235	00139	14303	00139	14370	00139	14438	00139	14506	00140	43
17	14506	00140	14573	00140	14641	00140	14708	00140	14775	00141	14843	00141	42
18	14843	00141	14910	00141	14977	00141	15044	00141	15112	00142	15179	00142	41
19	15179	00142	15246	00142	15313	00142	15380	00143	15446	00143	15513	00143	40
20	15513	00143	15580	00143	15647	00143	15713	00144	15780	00144	15846	00144	39
21	15846	00144	15913	00144	15979	00144	16046	00145	16112	00145	16178	00145	38
22	16178	00145	16245	00145	16311	00146	16377	00146	16443	00146	16509	00146	37
23	16509	00146	16575	00146	16641	00147	16707	00147	16773	00147	16839	00147	36
24	16839	00147	16904	00148	16970	00148	17036	00148	17101	00148	17167	00148	35
25	17167	00148	17232	00149	17298	00149	17363	00149	17429	00149	17494	00150	34
26	17494	00150	17559	00150	17624	00150	17689	00150	17755	00151	17820	00151	33
27	17820	00151	17885	00151	17950	00151	18015	00151	18079	00152	18144	00152	32
28	18144	00152	18209	00152	18274	00152	18338	00153	18403	00153	18468	00153	31
29	18468	00153	18532	00153	18597	00153	18661	00154	18725	00154	18790	00154	30
30	18790	00154	18854	00154	18918	00155	18982	00155	19047	00155	19111	00155	29
31	19111	00155	19175	00156	19239	00156	19303	00156	19367	00156	19430	00156	28
32	19430	00156	19494	00157	19558	00157	19622	00157	19685	00157	19749	00158	27
33	19749	00158	19813	00158	19876	00158	19940	00158	20003	00159	20066	00159	26
34	20066	00159	20130	00159	20193	00159	20256	00159	20319	00160	20383	00160	25
35	20383	00160	20446	00160	20509	00160	20572	00161	20635	00161	20698	00161	24
36	20698	00161	20761	00161	20823	00162	20886	00162	20949	00162	21012	00162	23
37	21012	00162	21074	00162	21137	00163	21200	00163	21262	00163	21325	00163	22
38	21325	00163	21387	00164	21449	00164	21512	00164	21574	00164	21636	00165	21
39	21636	00165	21698	00165	21761	00165	21823	00165	21885	00166	21947	00166	20
40	21947	00166	22009	00166	22071	00166	22133	00166	22195	00167	22256	00167	19
41	22256	00167	22318	00167	22380	00167	22441	00168	22503	00168	22565	00168	18
42	22565	00168	22626	00168	22688	00169	22749	00169	22811	00169	22872	00169	17
43	22872	00169	22933	00170	22995	00170	23056	00170	23117	00170	23178	00171	16
44	23178	00171	23239	00171	23300	00171	23361	00171	23422	00171	23483	00172	15
45	23483	00172	23542	00172	23605	00172	23666	00172	23727	00173	23787	00173	14
46	23787	00173	23848	00173	23909	00173	23969	00174	24030	00174	24090	00174	13
47	24090	00174	24151	00174	24211	00175	24272	00175	24332	00175	24392	00175	12
48	24392	00175	24453	00176	24513	00176	24573	00176	24633	00176	24693	00177	11
49	24693	00177	24753	00177	24813	00177	24873	00177	24933	00178	24993	00178	10
50	24993	00178	25053	00178	25113	00178	25172	00179	25232	00179	25292	00179	09
51	25292	00179	25352	00179	25411	00180	25471	00180	25530	00180	25590	00180	08
52	25590	00180	25649	00181	25709	00181	25768	00181	25827	00181	25886	00181	07
53	25886	00181	25946	00182	26005	00182	26064	00182	26123	00182	26182	00183	06
54	26182	00183	26241	00183	26300	00183	26359	00183	26418	00184	26477	00184	05
55	26477	00184	26536	00184	26595	00184	26653	00185	26712	00185	26771	00185	04
56	26771	00185	26829	00185	26888	00186	26947	00186	27005	00186	27063	00186	03
57	27063	00186	27122	00187	27180	00187	27239	00187	27297	00187	27355	00188	02
58	27355	00188	27414	00188	27472	00188	27530	00188	27588	00189	27646	00189	01
59	27646	00189	27704	00189	27762	00189	27820	00190	27878	00190	27936	00190	00
	.8		.6		4		.2		.0				

PARTS for 0′.1: LOGS variable NATURALS, negligible

355°

5° HAVERSINES

	.0 Log.	.0 Nat.	.2 Log.	.2 Nat.	.4 Log.	.4 Nat.	.6 Log.	.6 Nat.	.8 Log.	.8 Nat.	Log.	Nat.	
′	3̄.or(7.)	0.	3̄.or(7.)	0.	3̄.or(7.)	0.	3̄.or(7.)	0.	3̄.or(7.)	0.	3̄.or(7.)	0.	′
00	27936	00190	27994	00191	28052	00191	28109	00191	28167	00191	28225	00192	59
01	28225	00192	28282	00192	28340	00192	28398	00192	28455	00193	28513	00193	58
02	28513	00193	28570	00193	28628	00193	28685	00194	28742	00194	28800	00194	57
03	28800	00194	28859	00194	28914	00195	28971	00195	29029	00195	29086	00195	56
04	29086	00195	29143	00196	29200	00196	29257	00196	29314	00196	29371	00197	55
05	29371	00197	29428	00197	29484	00197	29541	00197	29598	00198	29655	00198	54
06	29655	00198	29712	00198	29768	00198	29825	00199	29881	00199	29938	00199	53
07	29938	00199	29995	00200	30051	00200	30108	00200	30164	00200	30220	00201	52
08	30220	00201	30277	00201	30333	00201	30389	00201	30445	00202	30502	00202	51
09	30502	00202	30558	00202	30614	00202	30670	00203	30726	00203	30782	00203	50
10	30782	00203	30838	00203	30894	00204	30950	00204	31006	00204	31062	00204	49
11	31062	00204	31117	00205	31173	00205	31229	00205	31285	00206	31340	00206	48
12	31340	00206	31396	00206	31452	00206	31507	00207	31563	00207	31618	00207	47
13	31618	00207	31674	00207	31729	00208	31784	00208	31840	00208	31895	00208	46
14	31895	00208	31950	00209	32005	00209	32061	00209	32116	00209	32171	00210	45
15	32171	00210	32226	00210	32281	00210	32336	00211	32391	00211	32446	00211	44
16	32446	00211	32501	00211	32556	00212	32611	00212	32666	00212	32720	00212	43
17	32720	00212	32775	00213	32830	00213	32884	00213	32939	00213	32994	00214	42
18	32994	00214	33048	00214	33103	00214	33157	00215	33212	00215	33266	00215	41
19	33266	00215	33321	00215	33375	00216	33429	00216	33484	00216	33538	00216	40
20	33538	00216	33592	00217	33646	00217	33700	00217	33755	00218	33809	00218	39
21	33809	00218	33863	00218	33917	00218	33971	00219	34025	00219	34079	00219	38
22	34079	00219	34133	00219	34186	00220	34240	00220	34294	00220	34348	00221	37
23	34348	00221	34402	00221	34455	00221	34509	00221	34562	00222	34616	00222	36
24	34616	00222	34670	00222	34723	00222	34777	00223	34830	00223	34884	00223	35
25	34884	00223	34937	00224	34990	00224	35044	00224	35097	00224	35150	00225	34
26	35150	00225	35203	00225	35257	00225	35310	00225	35363	00226	35416	00226	33
27	35416	00226	35469	00226	35522	00227	35575	00227	35628	00227	35681	00227	32
28	35681	00227	35734	00228	35787	00228	35840	00228	35892	00229	35945	00229	31
29	35945	00229	35998	00229	36051	00229	36103	00230	36156	00230	36209	00230	30
30	36209	00230	36261	00230	36314	00231	36366	00231	36419	00231	36471	00232	29
31	36471	00232	36524	00232	36576	00232	36628	00232	36681	00233	36733	00233	28
32	36733	00233	36785	00233	36838	00234	36890	00234	36942	00234	36994	00234	27
33	36994	00234	37046	00235	37098	00235	37150	00235	37202	00236	37254	00236	26
34	37254	00236	37306	00236	37358	00236	37410	00237	37462	00237	37514	00237	25
35	37514	00237	37566	00237	37617	00238	37669	00238	37721	00238	37772	00239	24
36	37772	00239	37824	00239	37876	00239	37927	00239	37979	00240	38030	00240	23
37	38030	00240	38082	00240	38133	00241	38185	00241	38236	00241	38288	00241	22
38	38288	00241	38339	00242	38390	00242	38442	00242	38493	00243	38544	00243	21
39	38544	00243	38595	00243	38646	00243	38697	00244	38749	00244	38800	00244	20
40	38800	00244	38851	00245	38902	00245	38953	00245	39004	00246	39054	00246	19
41	39054	00246	39105	00246	39156	00246	39207	00247	39258	00247	39309	00247	18
42	39309	00247	39359	00247	39410	00248	39461	00248	39511	00248	39562	00249	17
43	39562	00249	39613	00249	39663	00249	39714	00250	39764	00250	39815	00250	16
44	39815	00250	39865	00250	39916	00251	39966	00251	40016	00251	40067	00252	15
45	40067	00252	40117	00252	40167	00252	40217	00252	40268	00253	40318	00253	14
46	40318	00253	40368	00253	40418	00254	40468	00254	40518	00254	40568	00255	13
47	40568	00255	40618	00255	40668	00255	40718	00255	40768	00256	40818	00256	12
48	40818	00256	40868	00256	40918	00257	40967	00257	41017	00257	41067	00257	11
49	41067	00257	41117	00258	41166	00258	41216	00258	41266	00259	41315	00259	10
50	41315	00259	41365	00259	41414	00259	41464	00260	41513	00260	41563	00260	09
51	41563	00260	41612	00261	41662	00261	41711	00261	41760	00262	41810	00262	08
52	41810	00262	41858	00262	41908	00262	41958	00263	42007	00263	42056	00263	07
53	42056	00263	42105	00264	42154	00264	42203	00264	42252	00265	42301	00265	06
54	42301	00265	42351	00265	42400	00265	42448	00266	42497	00266	42546	00266	05
55	42546	00266	42595	00267	42644	00267	42693	00267	42742	00268	42790	00268	04
56	42790	00268	42839	00268	42888	00268	42937	00269	42985	00269	43034	00269	03
57	43034	00269	43082	00270	43131	00270	43180	00270	43228	00271	43277	00271	02
58	43277	00271	43325	00271	43373	00271	43422	00272	43470	00272	43519	00272	01
59	43519	00272	43567	00273	43615	00273	43664	00273	43712	00274	43760	00274	00

	.8	.6	.4	.2	.0

PARTS for 0′.1:   LOGS variable from 29 to 24   NATURALS negligible

354°

6° HAVERSINES

PARTS for 0'.1:   LOGS variable from 24 to 21   NATURALS negligible

′	.0 Log. 3̄.or(7.)	.0 Nat. 0.	.2 Log. 3̄.or(7.)	.2 Nat. 0.	.4 Log. 3̄.or(7.)	.4 Nat. 0.	.6 Log. 3̄.or(7.)	.6 Nat. 0.	.8 Log. 3̄.or(7.)	.8 Nat. 0.	′
00	43760	00274	43808	00274	43856	00275	43905	00275	43953	00275	44001	00275	59
01	44001	00275	44049	00276	44097	00276	44145	00276	44193	00277	44241	00277	58
02	44241	00277	44289	00277	44337	00278	44385	00278	44432	00278	44480	00278	57
03	44480	00278	44528	00279	44576	00279	44624	00279	44671	00280	44719	00280	56
04	44719	00280	44767	00280	44814	00281	44862	00281	44909	00281	44957	00282	55
05	44957	00282	45005	00282	45052	00282	45100	00282	45147	00283	45194	00283	54
06	45194	00283	45242	00283	45289	00284	45337	00284	45384	00284	45431	00285	53
07	45431	00285	45478	00285	45526	00285	45573	00286	45620	00286	45667	00286	52
08	45667	00286	45714	00287	45762	00287	45809	00287	45856	00287	45903	00288	51
09	45903	00288	45950	00288	45997	00288	46044	00289	46091	00289	46138	00289	50
10	46138	00289	46185	00290	46231	00290	46278	00290	46325	00291	46372	00291	49
11	46372	00291	46419	00291	46465	00292	46512	00292	46559	00292	46605	00292	48
12	46605	00292	46652	00293	46699	00293	46745	00293	46792	00294	46838	00294	47
13	46838	00294	46885	00294	46931	00295	46978	00295	47024	00295	47071	00296	46
14	47071	00296	47117	00296	47163	00296	47210	00297	47256	00297	47302	00297	45
15	47302	00297	47349	00298	47395	00298	47441	00298	47487	00298	47533	00299	44
16	47533	00299	47580	00299	47626	00299	47672	00300	47718	00300	47764	00300	43
17	47764	00300	47810	00301	47856	00301	47902	00301	47948	00302	47994	00302	42
18	47994	00302	48040	00302	48086	00303	48131	00303	48177	00303	48223	00304	41
19	48223	00304	48269	00304	48315	00304	48360	00305	48406	00305	48452	00305	40
20	48452	00305	48497	00305	48543	00306	48589	00306	48634	00306	48680	00307	39
21	48680	00307	48725	00307	48771	00307	48816	00308	48862	00308	48907	00308	38
22	48907	00308	48953	00309	48998	00309	49043	00309	49089	00310	49134	00310	37
23	49134	00310	49179	00310	49225	00311	49270	00311	49315	00311	49360	00312	36
24	49360	00312	49405	00312	49451	00312	49496	00313	49541	00313	49586	00313	35
25	49586	00313	49631	00314	49676	00314	49721	00314	49766	00315	49811	00315	34
26	49811	00315	49856	00315	49901	00316	49946	00316	49991	00316	50036	00316	33
27	50036	00316	50080	00317	50125	00317	50170	00317	50215	00318	50259	00318	32
28	50259	00318	50304	00318	50349	00319	50394	00319	50438	00319	50483	00320	31
29	50483	00320	50527	00320	50572	00320	50617	00321	50661	00321	50706	00321	30
30	50706	00321	50750	00322	50795	00322	50839	00322	50883	00323	50928	00323	29
31	50928	00323	50972	00323	51016	00324	51061	00324	51105	00324	51149	00325	28
32	51149	00325	51194	00325	51238	00325	51282	00326	51326	00326	51370	00326	27
33	51370	00326	51415	00327	51459	00327	51503	00327	51547	00328	51591	00328	26
34	51591	00328	51635	00328	51679	00329	51723	00329	51767	00329	51811	00330	25
35	51811	00330	51855	00330	51899	00330	51943	00331	51986	00331	52030	00331	24
36	52030	00331	52074	00332	52118	00332	52162	00332	52205	00333	52249	00333	23
37	52249	00333	52293	00333	52336	00334	52380	00334	52424	00334	52467	00335	22
38	52467	00335	52511	00335	52554	00335	52598	00336	52642	00336	52685	00336	21
39	52685	00336	52729	00337	52772	00337	52815	00337	52859	00338	52902	00338	20
40	52902	00338	52946	00338	52989	00339	53032	00339	53076	00339	53119	00340	19
41	53119	00340	53162	00340	53205	00340	53249	00341	53292	00341	53335	00341	18
42	53335	00341	53378	00342	53421	00342	53464	00342	53507	00343	53550	00343	17
43	53550	00343	53594	00343	53637	00344	53680	00344	53723	00345	53765	00345	16
44	53765	00345	53808	00345	53851	00346	53894	00346	53939	00346	53980	00347	15
45	53980	00347	54023	00347	54066	00347	54108	00348	54151	00348	54194	00348	14
46	54194	00348	54237	00349	54279	00349	54322	00349	54365	00350	54407	00350	13
47	54407	00350	54450	00350	54493	00351	54535	00351	54578	00351	54620	00352	12
48	54620	00352	54663	00352	54705	00352	54748	00353	54790	00353	54833	00353	11
49	54833	00353	54875	00354	54917	00354	54960	00354	55002	00355	55045	00355	10
50	55045	00355	55087	00356	55129	00356	55171	00356	55214	00357	55256	00357	09
51	55256	00357	55298	00357	55340	00358	55382	00358	55425	00358	55467	00359	08
52	55467	00359	55509	00359	55551	00359	55593	00360	55635	00360	55677	00360	07
53	55677	00360	55719	00361	55761	00361	55803	00361	55845	00362	55887	00362	06
54	55887	00362	55929	00362	55971	00363	56012	00363	56054	00364	56096	00364	05
55	56096	00364	56138	00364	56180	00365	56221	00365	56263	00365	56305	00366	04
56	56305	00366	56347	00366	56388	00366	56430	00367	56472	00367	56513	00367	03
57	56513	00367	56555	00368	56596	00368	56638	00368	56679	00369	56721	00369	02
58	56721	00369	56762	00369	56804	00370	56845	00370	56887	00371	56928	00371	01
59	56928	00371	56970	00371	57011	00372	57052	00372	57094	00372	57135	00373	00

| | .8 | .6 | .4 | .2 | .0 |

353°

7° HAVERSINES

'	.0 Log. $\overline{3}$.or(7.)	.0 Nat. 0.	.2 Log. $\overline{3}$.or(7.)	.2 Nat. 0.	.4 Log. $\overline{3}$.or(7.)	.4 Nat. 0.	.6 Log. $\overline{3}$.or(7.)	.6 Nat. 0.	.8 Log. $\overline{3}$.or(7.)	.8 Nat. 0.	Log. $\overline{3}$.or(7.)	Nat. 0.	'
00	57135	00373	57176	00373	57218	00373	57259	00374	57300	00374	57341	00374	59
01	57341	00374	57383	00375	57424	00375	57465	00376	57506	00376	57547	00376	58
02	57547	00376	57588	00377	57629	00377	57670	00377	57711	00378	57752	00378	57
03	57752	00378	57794	00378	57835	00379	57875	00379	57916	00379	57957	00380	56
04	57957	00380	57998	00380	58039	00381	58080	00381	58121	00381	58162	00382	55
05	58162	00382	58203	00382	58243	00382	58284	00383	58325	00383	58366	00383	54
06	58366	00383	58406	00384	58447	00384	58488	00384	58528	00385	58569	00385	53
07	58569	00385	58609	00386	58650	00386	58691	00386	58731	00387	58772	00387	52
08	58772	00387	58812	00387	58853	00388	58893	00388	58934	00388	58974	00389	51
09	58974	00389	59015	00389	59055	00390	59096	00390	59136	00390	59176	00391	50
10	59176	00391	59217	00391	59257	00391	59297	00392	59338	00392	59378	00392	49
11	59378	00392	59418	00393	59458	00393	59498	00394	59539	00394	59579	00394	48
12	59579	00394	59619	00395	59659	00395	59698	00395	59739	00396	59779	00396	47
13	59779	00396	59819	00396	59859	00397	59900	00397	59940	00398	59979	00398	46
14	59979	00398	60019	00398	60059	00399	60099	00399	60139	00399	60179	00400	45
15	60179	00400	60219	00400	60259	00400	60299	00401	60339	00401	60378	00402	44
16	60378	00402	60418	00402	60458	00402	60498	00403	60537	00403	60577	00403	43
17	60577	00403	60617	00404	60656	00404	60696	00405	60736	00405	60775	00405	42
18	60775	00405	60815	00406	60854	00406	60894	00406	60934	00407	60973	00407	41
19	60973	00407	61013	00408	61052	00408	61092	00408	61131	00409	61170	00409	40
20	61170	00409	61210	00409	61249	00410	61289	00410	61328	00410	61367	00411	39
21	61367	00411	61407	00411	61446	00412	61485	00412	61525	00412	61564	00413	38
22	61564	00413	61603	00413	61642	00413	61682	00414	61721	00414	61760	00415	37
23	61760	00415	61799	00415	61838	00415	61877	00416	61916	00416	61955	00416	36
24	61955	00416	61995	00417	62034	00417	62073	00418	62112	00418	62151	00418	35
25	62151	00418	62190	00419	62229	00419	62267	00419	62306	00420	62345	00420	34
26	62345	00420	62384	00421	62423	00421	62462	00421	62501	00422	62540	00422	33
27	62540	00422	62578	00422	62617	00423	62656	00423	62695	00424	62733	00424	32
28	62733	00424	62772	00424	62811	00425	62849	00425	62888	00425	62927	00426	31
29	62927	00426	62965	00426	63004	00427	63043	00427	63081	00427	63120	00428	30
30	63120	00428	63158	00428	63197	00429	63235	00429	63274	00429	63312	00430	29
31	63312	00430	63351	00430	63389	00430	63428	00431	63466	00431	63504	00432	28
32	63504	00432	63543	00432	63581	00432	63619	00433	63658	00433	63696	00433	27
33	63696	00433	63734	00434	63773	00434	63811	00435	63849	00435	63887	00435	26
34	63887	00435	63925	00436	63964	00436	64002	00437	64040	00437	64078	00437	25
35	64078	00437	64116	00438	64154	00438	64192	00438	64230	00439	64269	00439	24
36	64269	00439	64307	00440	64345	00440	64383	00440	64421	00441	64458	00441	23
37	64458	00441	64496	00442	64534	00442	64572	00442	64610	00443	64648	00443	22
38	64648	00443	64686	00443	64724	00444	64762	00444	64799	00445	64837	00445	21
39	64837	00445	64875	00445	64913	00446	64951	00446	64988	00447	65026	00447	20
40	65026	00447	65064	00447	65101	00448	65139	00448	65177	00449	65214	00449	19
41	65214	00449	65252	00449	65290	00450	65327	00450	65365	00450	65402	00451	18
42	65402	00451	65440	00451	65477	00452	65515	00452	65552	00452	65590	00453	17
43	65590	00453	65627	00453	65665	00454	65702	00454	65739	00454	65777	00455	16
44	65777	00455	65814	00455	65852	00456	65889	00456	65926	00456	65964	00457	15
45	65964	00457	66001	00457	66038	00457	66075	00458	66113	00458	66150	00459	14
46	66150	00459	66187	00459	66224	00459	66261	00460	66299	00460	66336	00461	13
47	66336	00461	66373	00461	66410	00461	66447	00462	66484	00462	66521	00463	12
48	66521	00463	66558	00463	66595	00463	66632	00464	66669	00464	66706	00465	11
49	66706	00465	66743	00465	66780	00465	66817	00466	66854	00466	66891	00467	10
50	66891	00467	66928	00467	66965	00467	67002	00468	67039	00468	67075	00469	09
51	67075	00469	67112	00469	67149	00469	67186	00470	67223	00470	67259	00471	08
52	67259	00471	67296	00471	67333	00471	67370	00472	67406	00472	67443	00473	07
53	67443	00473	67480	00473	67516	00473	67553	00474	67589	00474	67626	00475	06
54	67626	00475	67663	00475	67699	00475	67736	00476	67772	00476	67809	00477	05
55	67809	00477	67845	00477	67882	00477	67918	00478	67955	00478	67991	00479	04
56	67991	00479	68028	00479	68064	00479	68100	00480	68137	00480	68173	00481	03
57	68173	00481	68210	00481	68246	00481	68282	00482	68319	00482	68355	00483	02
58	68355	00483	68391	00483	68427	00483	68464	00484	68500	00484	68536	00485	01
59	68536	00485	68572	00485	68608	00485	68645	00486	68681	00486	68717	00487	00

| | .8 | | .6 | | .4 | | .2 | | .0 | |

PARTS for 0'.1:   LOGS variable from 21 to 18   NATURALS negligible

352°

8° HAVERSINES

′	.0 Log.	.0 Nat.	.2 Log.	.2 Nat.	.4 Log.	.4 Nat.	.6 Log.	.6 Nat.	.8 Log.	.8 Nat.	Log.	Nat.	′
	3̄.or(7.)	0.	3̄.or(7.)	0.	3̄.or(7.)	0.	3̄.or(7.)	0.	3̄.or(7.)	0.	3̄.or(7.)	0.	
00	68717	00487	68753	00487	68789	00487	68825	00488	68861	00488	68897	00489	59
01	68897	00489	68933	00489	68969	00489	69005	00490	69041	00490	69077	00491	58
02	69077	00491	69113	00491	69149	00491	69185	00492	69221	00492	69257	00493	57
03	69257	00493	69293	00493	69329	00494	69365	00494	69401	00494	69437	00495	56
04	69437	00495	69472	00495	69508	00496	69544	00496	69580	00496	69616	00497	55
05	69616	00497	69651	00497	69687	00498	69723	00498	69758	00498	69794	00499	54
06	69794	00499	69830	00499	69865	00500	69901	00500	69937	00500	69972	00501	53
07	69972	00501	70008	00501	70044	00502	70079	00502	70115	00502	70150	00503	52
08	70150	00503	70186	00503	70221	00504	70257	00504	70292	00505	70328	00505	51
09	70328	00505	70363	00505	70399	00506	70434	00506	70470	00507	70505	00507	50
10	70505	00507	70540	00507	70576	00508	70611	00508	70646	00509	70682	00509	49
11	70682	00509	70717	00510	70752	00510	70788	00510	70823	00511	70858	00511	48
12	70858	00511	70893	00512	70929	00512	70964	00512	70999	00513	71034	00513	47
13	71034	00513	71069	00514	71104	00514	71140	00515	71175	00515	71210	00515	46
14	71210	00515	71245	00516	71280	00516	71315	00517	71350	00517	71385	00517	45
15	71385	00517	71420	00518	71455	00518	71490	00519	71525	00519	71560	00520	44
16	71560	00520	71595	00520	71630	00520	71665	00521	71700	00521	71735	00522	43
17	71735	00522	71770	00522	71805	00522	71839	00523	71874	00523	71909	00524	42
18	71909	00524	71944	00524	71979	00525	72013	00525	72048	00525	72083	00526	41
19	72083	00526	72118	00526	72152	00527	72187	00527	72222	00527	72257	00528	40
20	72257	00528	72291	00528	72326	00529	72361	00529	72395	00530	72430	00530	39
21	72430	00530	72464	00530	72499	00531	72534	00531	72568	00532	72603	00532	38
22	72603	00532	72637	00533	72672	00533	72706	00533	72741	00534	72775	00534	37
23	72775	00534	72810	00535	72844	00535	72879	00536	72913	00536	72948	00536	36
24	72948	00536	72982	00537	73016	00537	73051	00538	73085	00538	73119	00539	35
25	73119	00539	73154	00539	73188	00539	73222	00540	73257	00540	73291	00541	34
26	73291	00541	73325	00541	73359	00541	73394	00542	73428	00542	73462	00543	33
27	73462	00543	73496	00543	73530	00544	73564	00544	73598	00544	73633	00545	32
28	73633	00545	73667	00545	73701	00546	73735	00546	73769	00547	73803	00547	31
29	73803	00547	73837	00547	73871	00548	73906	00548	73940	00549	73974	00549	30
30	73974	00549	74008	00550	74042	00550	74075	00550	74109	00551	74143	00551	29
31	74143	00551	74177	00552	74211	00552	74245	00553	74279	00553	74313	00554	28
32	74313	00554	74347	00554	74381	00554	74414	00555	74448	00555	74482	00556	27
33	74482	00556	74516	00556	74550	00557	74583	00557	74617	00557	74651	00558	26
34	74651	00558	74685	00558	74718	00559	74752	00559	74786	00560	74819	00560	25
35	74819	00560	74853	00560	74887	00561	74920	00561	74954	00562	74988	00562	24
36	74988	00562	75021	00563	75055	00563	75088	00563	75122	00564	75155	00564	23
37	75155	00564	75189	00565	75222	00565	75256	00566	75289	00566	75323	00567	22
38	75323	00567	75356	00567	75390	00567	75423	00568	75457	00568	75490	00569	21
39	75490	00569	75524	00569	75557	00570	75590	00570	75624	00570	75657	00571	20
40	75657	00571	75690	00571	75724	00572	75757	00572	75790	00573	75824	00573	19
41	75824	00573	75857	00574	75890	00574	75923	00574	75957	00575	75990	00575	18
42	75990	00575	76023	00576	76056	00576	76089	00577	76123	00577	76156	00578	17
43	76156	00578	76189	00578	76222	00578	76255	00579	76288	00579	76321	00580	16
44	76321	00580	76354	00580	76387	00581	76421	00531	76454	00581	76487	00582	15
45	76487	00582	76520	00582	76553	00583	76586	00583	76619	00584	76652	00584	14
46	76652	00584	76685	00585	76717	00585	76750	00585	76783	00586	76816	00586	13
47	76816	00586	76849	00587	76882	00587	76915	00538	76948	00588	76981	00589	12
48	76981	00589	77013	00589	77046	00589	77079	00590	77112	00590	77145	00591	11
49	77145	00591	77177	00591	77210	00592	77243	00592	77276	00593	77308	00593	10
50	77308	00593	77341	00594	77374	00594	77406	00594	77439	00595	77472	00595	09
51	77472	00595	77504	00596	77537	00596	77570	00597	77602	00597	77635	00598	08
52	77635	00598	77667	00598	77700	00598	77732	00599	77765	00599	77798	00600	07
53	77798	00600	77830	00600	77863	00601	77895	00601	77928	00602	77960	00602	06
54	77960	00602	77993	00602	78025	00603	78058	00603	78090	00604	78122	00604	05
55	78122	00604	78155	00605	78187	00605	78219	00606	78252	00606	78284	00607	04
56	78284	00607	78317	00607	78349	00607	78381	00608	78413	00608	78446	00609	03
57	78446	00609	78478	00609	78510	00610	78543	00610	78575	00611	78607	00611	02
58	78607	00611	78639	00612	78671	00612	78704	00612	78736	00613	78768	00613	01
59	78768	00613	78800	00614	78832	00614	78864	00615	78896	00615	78929	00616	00
	.8		.6		.4		.2		.0 ←				

PARTS for 0′.1:   LOGS variable from 18 to 16   NATURALS negligible

351°

9° HAVERSINES

′	.0 Log. 3.or(7.)	.0 Nat. 0.	.2 Log. 3.or(7.)	.2 Nat. 0.	.4 Log. 3.or(7.)	.4 Nat. 0.	.6 Log. 3.or(7.)	.6 Nat. 0.	.8 Log. 3.or(7.)	.8 Nat. 0.	′
00	78929	00616	78961	00616	78993	00617	79025	00617	79057	00617	79089	00618	59
01	79089	00618	79121	00618	79153	00619	79185	00619	79217	00620	79249	00620	58
02	79249	00620	79281	00621	79313	00621	79345	00622	79377	00622	79409	00622	57
03	79409	00622	79441	00623	79473	00623	79505	00624	79536	00624	79568	00625	56
04	79568	00625	79600	00625	79632	00626	79664	00626	79696	00627	79728	00627	55
05	79728	00627	79759	00627	79791	00628	79823	00628	79855	00629	79886	00629	54
06	79886	00629	79918	00630	79950	00630	79982	00631	80013	00631	80045	00632	53
07	80045	00632	80077	00632	80108	00633	80140	00633	80172	00633	80203	00634	52
08	80203	00634	80235	00634	80267	00635	80298	00635	80330	00636	80361	00636	51
09	80361	00636	80393	00637	80425	00637	80456	00638	80488	00638	80519	00639	50
10	80519	00639	80551	00639	80582	00639	80614	00640	80645	00640	80677	00641	49
11	80677	00641	80708	00641	80739	00642	80771	00642	80802	00643	80834	00643	48
12	80834	00643	80865	00644	80897	00644	80928	00645	80959	00645	80991	00646	47
13	80991	00646	81022	00646	81053	00646	81085	00647	81116	00647	81147	00648	46
14	81147	00648	81178	00648	81210	00649	81241	00649	81272	00650	81303	00650	45
15	81303	00650	81335	00651	81366	00651	81397	00652	81428	00652	81459	00653	44
16	81459	00653	81491	00653	81522	00653	81553	00654	81584	00654	81615	00655	43
17	81615	00655	81646	00655	81677	00656	81708	00656	81740	00657	81771	00657	42
18	81771	00657	81802	00658	81833	00658	81864	00659	81895	00659	81926	00660	41
19	81926	00660	81957	00660	81988	00660	82019	00661	82050	00661	82081	00662	40
20	82081	00662	82112	00662	82143	00663	82174	00663	82204	00664	82235	00664	39
21	82235	00664	82266	00665	82297	00665	82328	00666	82359	00666	82390	00667	38
22	82390	00667	82421	00667	82451	00668	82482	00668	82513	00669	82544	00669	37
23	82544	00669	82575	00669	82605	00670	82636	00670	82667	00671	82698	00671	36
24	82698	00671	82728	00672	82759	00672	82790	00673	82820	00673	82851	00674	35
25	82851	00674	82882	00674	82912	00675	82943	00675	82974	00676	83004	00676	34
26	83004	00676	83035	00677	83066	00677	83096	00678	83127	00678	83157	00679	33
27	83157	00679	83188	00679	83218	00680	83249	00680	83279	00680	83310	00681	32
28	83310	00681	83341	00681	83371	00682	83402	00682	83432	00683	83463	00683	31
29	83463	00683	83493	00684	83523	00684	83554	00685	83584	00685	83615	00686	30
30	83615	00686	83645	00686	83675	00687	83706	00687	83736	00688	83767	00688	29
31	83767	00688	83797	00689	83827	00689	83858	00690	83888	00690	83918	00691	28
32	83918	00691	83948	00691	83979	00692	84009	00692	84039	00692	84070	00693	27
33	84070	00693	84100	00693	84130	00694	84160	00694	84190	00695	84221	00695	26
34	84221	00695	84251	00696	84281	00696	84311	00697	84341	00697	84372	00698	25
35	84372	00698	84402	00698	84432	00699	84462	00699	84492	00700	84522	00700	24
36	84522	00700	84552	00701	84582	00701	84612	00702	84642	00702	84672	00703	23
37	84672	00703	84702	00703	84732	00704	84762	00704	84792	00705	84822	00705	22
38	84822	00705	84852	00706	84882	00706	84912	00707	84942	00707	84972	00707	21
39	84972	00707	85002	00708	85032	00708	85062	00709	85092	00709	85122	00710	20
40	85122	00710	85152	00710	85181	00711	85211	00711	85241	00712	85271	00712	19
41	85271	00712	85301	00713	85331	00713	85360	00714	85390	00714	85420	00715	18
42	85420	00715	85450	00715	85480	00716	85509	00716	85539	00717	85569	00717	17
43	85569	00717	85599	00718	85628	00718	85658	00719	85688	00719	85717	00720	16
44	85717	00720	85747	00720	85777	00721	85806	00721	85836	00722	85866	00722	15
45	85866	00722	85895	00723	85925	00723	85954	00724	85984	00724	86014	00725	14
46	86014	00725	86043	00725	86073	00726	86102	00726	86132	00727	86161	00727	13
47	86161	00727	86191	00728	86220	00728	86250	00729	86279	00729	86309	00730	12
48	86309	00730	86338	00730	86368	C0731	86397	00731	86427	00732	86456	00732	11
49	86456	00732	86485	00733	86515	00733	86544	00734	86574	00734	86603	00735	10
50	86603	00735	86632	00735	86662	00736	86691	00736	86720	00737	86750	00737	09
51	86750	00737	86779	00738	86808	00738	86838	00739	86867	00739	86896	00740	08
52	86896	00740	86925	00740	86955	00741	86984	00741	87013	00742	87042	00742	07
53	87042	00742	87072	00743	87101	00743	87130	00744	87159	00744	87188	00745	06
54	87188	00745	87218	00745	87247	00746	87276	00746	87305	00747	87334	00747	05
55	87334	00747	87363	00748	87392	00748	87421	00749	87451	00749	87480	00750	04
56	87480	00750	87509	00750	87538	00751	87567	00751	87596	00752	87625	00752	03
57	87625	00752	87654	00753	87683	00753	87712	00754	87741	00754	87770	00755	02
58	87770	00755	87799	00755	87828	00756	87857	00756	87886	00757	87915	00757	01
59	87915	00757	87944	00758	87972	00758	88001	00759	88030	00759	88059	00760	00

| | .8 | | .6 | | .4 | | .2 | | .0 | |

PARTS for 0′.1:   LOGS variable from 16 to 14;   NATURALS, negligible.

350°

10° HAVERSINES

′	.0 Log.	.0 Nat.	.2 Log.	.2 Nat.	.4 Log.	.4 Nat.	.6 Log.	.6 Nat.	.8 Log.	.8 Nat.	Log.	Nat.	′
	3̄.or(7.)	0.	3̄.or(7.)	0.	3̄.or(7.)	0.	3̄.or(7.)	0.	3̄.or(7.)	0.	3̄.or(7.)	0.	
00	88059	00760	88088	00760	88117	00761	88146	00761	88175	00762	88203	00762	59
01	88203	00762	88232	00763	88261	00763	88290	00764	88319	00764	88348	00765	58
02	88348	00765	88376	00765	88405	00766	88434	00766	88463	00767	88491	00767	57
03	88491	00767	88520	00768	88549	00768	88577	00769	88606	00769	88635	00770	56
04	88635	00770	88663	00770	88692	00771	88721	00771	88750	00772	88778	00772	55
05	88778	00772	88807	00773	88835	00773	88864	00774	88893	00774	88921	00775	54
06	88921	00775	88950	00775	88978	00776	89007	00776	89036	00777	89064	00777	53
07	89064	00777	89093	00778	89121	00778	89150	00779	89178	00779	89207	00780	52
08	89207	00780	89235	00780	89264	00781	89292	00781	89321	00782	89349	00783	51
09	89349	00783	89377	00783	89406	00784	89434	00784	89463	00785	89491	00785	50
10	89491	00785	89520	00786	89548	00786	89576	00787	89605	00787	89633	00788	49
11	89633	00788	89662	00788	89690	00789	89718	00789	89746	00790	89775	00790	48
12	89775	00790	89803	00791	89831	00791	89860	00792	89888	00792	89916	00793	47
13	89916	00793	89944	00793	89973	00794	90001	00794	90029	00795	90057	00795	46
14	90057	00795	90086	00796	90114	00796	90142	00797	90170	00797	90198	00798	45
15	90198	00798	90227	00798	90255	00799	90283	00800	90311	00800	90339	00801	44
16	90339	00801	90367	00801	90395	00802	90423	00802	90452	00803	90480	00803	43
17	90480	00803	90508	00804	90536	00804	90564	00805	90592	00805	90620	00806	42
18	90620	00806	90648	00806	90676	00807	90704	00807	90732	00808	90760	00808	41
19	90760	00808	90788	00809	90816	00809	90844	00810	90872	00810	90900	00811	40
20	90900	00811	90928	00811	90956	00812	90984	00813	91011	00813	91039	00814	39
21	91039	00814	91067	00814	91095	00815	91123	00815	91151	00816	91179	00816	38
22	91179	00816	91207	00817	91234	00817	91262	00818	91290	00818	91318	00819	37
23	91318	00819	91346	00819	91374	00820	91401	00820	91429	00821	91457	00821	36
24	91457	00821	91485	00822	91512	00822	91540	00823	91568	00824	91596	00824	35
25	91596	00824	91623	00825	91651	00825	91679	00826	91706	00826	91734	00827	34
26	91734	00827	91762	00827	91789	00828	91817	00828	91845	00829	91872	00829	33
27	91872	00829	91900	00830	91928	00830	91955	00831	91983	00831	92010	00832	32
28	92010	00832	92038	00832	92066	00833	92093	00834	92121	00834	92148	00835	31
29	92148	00835	92176	00835	92203	00836	92231	00836	92258	00837	92286	00837	30
30	92286	00837	92313	00838	92341	00838	92368	00839	92396	00839	92423	00840	29
31	92423	00840	92451	00840	92478	00841	92505	00841	92533	00842	92560	00843	28
32	92560	00843	92588	00843	92615	00844	92642	00844	92670	00845	92697	00845	27
33	92697	00845	92725	00846	92752	00846	92779	00847	92807	00847	92834	00848	26
34	92834	00848	92861	00848	92889	00849	92916	00849	92943	00850	92970	00851	25
35	92970	00851	92998	00851	93025	00852	93052	00852	93080	00853	93107	00853	24
36	93107	00853	93134	00854	93161	00854	93188	00855	93216	00855	93243	00856	23
37	93243	00856	93270	00856	93297	00857	93324	00858	93351	00858	93379	00859	22
38	93379	00859	93406	00859	93433	00860	93460	00860	93487	00861	93514	00861	21
39	93514	00861	93541	00862	93569	00862	93596	00863	93623	00863	93650	00864	20
40	93650	00864	93677	00864	93704	00865	93731	00866	93758	00866	93785	00867	19
41	93785	00867	93812	00867	93839	00868	93866	00868	93893	00869	93920	00869	18
42	93920	00869	93947	00870	93974	00870	94001	00871	94028	00872	94055	00872	17
43	94055	00872	94082	00873	94109	00873	94136	00874	94162	00874	94189	00875	16
44	94189	00875	94216	00875	94243	00876	94270	00876	94297	00877	94324	00877	15
45	94324	00877	94351	00878	94377	00879	94404	00879	94431	00880	94458	00880	14
46	94458	00880	94485	00881	94511	00881	94538	00882	94565	00882	94592	00883	13
47	94592	00883	94619	00883	94645	00384	94672	00885	94699	00885	94726	00886	12
48	94726	00886	94752	00886	94779	00887	94806	00887	94832	00888	94859	00888	11
49	94859	00888	94886	00889	94912	00889	94939	00890	94966	00891	94992	00891	10
50	94992	00891	95019	00892	95046	00892	95072	00893	95099	00893	95126	00894	09
51	95126	00894	95152	00894	95179	00895	95205	00895	95232	00896	95259	00897	08
52	95259	00897	95285	00897	95312	00898	95338	00898	95365	00899	95391	00899	07
53	95391	00899	95418	00900	95444	00900	95471	00901	95497	00901	95524	00902	06
54	95524	00902	95550	00903	95577	00903	95603	00904	95630	00904	95656	00905	05
55	95656	00905	95682	00905	95709	00906	95735	00906	95762	00907	95788	00908	04
56	95788	00908	95815	00908	95841	00909	95867	00909	95894	00910	95920	00910	03
57	95920	00910	95946	00911	95973	00911	95999	00912	96025	00913	96052	00913	02
58	96052	00913	96078	00914	96104	00914	96131	00915	96157	00915	96183	00916	01
59	96183	00916	96209	00916	96236	00917	96262	00918	96288	00918	96315	00919	00
		.8		.6		.4		.2		.0			

PARTS for 0′.1: LOGS 14 NATURALS negligible

349°

11° HAVERSINES

′	.0 Log	.0 Nat	.2 Log	.2 Nat	.4 Log	.4 Nat	.6 Log	.6 Nat	.8 Log	.8 Nat	Log	Nat	′
	3.or(7.) / 2.or(8.)	0.	3.or(7.) / 2.or(8.)	0.	3.or(7.) / 2.or(8.)	0.	3.or(7.) / 2.or(8.)	0.	3.or(.7) / 2.or(8.)	0.	3.or(7.) / 2.or(8.)	0.	
00	96315	00919	96341	00919	96367	00920	96393	00920	96419	00921	96446	00921	59
01	96446	00921	96472	00922	96498	00923	96524	00923	96550	00924	96577	00924	58
02	96577	00924	96603	00925	96629	00925	96655	00926	96681	00926	96707	00927	57
03	96707	00927	96733	00928	96759	00928	96786	00929	96812	00929	96838	00930	56
04	96838	00930	96864	00930	96890	00931	96916	00931	96942	00932	96968	00933	55
05	96968	00933	96994	00933	97020	00934	97046	00934	97072	00935	97098	00935	54
06	97098	00935	97124	00936	97150	00936	97176	00937	97202	00938	97228	00938	53
07	97228	00938	97254	00939	97280	00939	97306	00940	97332	00940	97358	00941	52
08	97358	00941	97384	00942	97410	00942	97436	00943	97461	00943	97487	00944	51
09	97487	00944	97513	00944	97539	00945	97565	00945	97591	00946	97617	00947	50
10	97617	00947	97642	00947	97668	00948	97694	00948	97720	00949	97746	00949	49
11	97746	00949	97772	00950	97797	00951	97823	00951	97849	00952	97875	00952	48
12	97875	00952	97901	00953	97926	00953	97952	00954	97978	00954	98003	00955	47
13	98003	00955	98029	00956	98055	00956	98081	00957	98106	00957	98132	00958	46
14	98132	00958	98158	00958	98183	00959	98209	00960	98235	00960	98260	00961	45
15	98260	00961	98286	00961	98312	00962	98337	00962	98363	00963	98389	00964	44
16	98389	00964	98414	00964	98440	00965	98465	00965	98491	00966	98517	00966	43
17	98517	00966	98542	00967	98568	00968	98593	00968	98619	00969	98644	00969	42
18	98644	00969	98670	00970	98695	00970	98721	00971	98746	00972	98772	00972	41
19	98772	00972	98797	00973	98823	00973	98848	00974	98874	00974	98899	00975	40
20	98899	00975	98925	00976	98950	00976	98976	00977	99001	00977	99027	00978	39
21	99027	00978	99052	00978	99077	00979	99103	00980	99128	00980	99154	00981	38
22	99154	00981	99179	00981	99204	00982	99230	00982	99255	00983	99280	00984	37
23	99280	00984	99306	00984	99331	00985	99356	00985	99382	00986	99407	00986	36
24	99407	00986	99432	00987	99458	00988	99483	00988	99508	00989	99534	00989	35
25	99534	00989	99559	00990	99584	00990	99609	00991	99635	00992	99660	00992	34
26	99660	00992	99685	00993	99710	00993	99736	00994	99761	00995	99786	00995	33
27	99786	00995	99811	00996	99836	00996	99862	00997	99887	00997	99912	00998	32
28	99912	00998	99937	00999	99962	00999	99987	01000	00012	01000	00038	01001	31
29	00038	01001	00063	01001	00088	01002	00113	01003	00138	01003	00163	01004	30
30	00163	01004	00188	01004	00213	01005	00238	01005	00264	01006	00289	01007	29
31	00289	01007	00314	01007	00339	01008	00364	01008	00389	01009	00414	01010	28
32	00414	01010	00439	01010	00464	01011	00489	01011	00514	01012	00539	01012	27
33	00539	01012	00564	01013	00589	01014	00614	01014	00639	01015	00664	01015	26
34	00664	01015	00689	01016	00713	01017	00738	01017	00763	01018	00788	01018	25
35	00788	01018	00813	01019	00838	01019	00863	01020	00888	01021	00913	01021	24
36	00913	01021	00937	01022	00962	01022	00987	01023	01012	01024	01037	01024	23
37	01037	01024	01062	01025	01087	01025	01111	01026	01136	01027	01161	01027	22
38	01161	01027	01186	01028	01211	01028	01235	01029	01260	01029	01285	01030	21
39	01285	01030	01310	01031	01335	01031	01359	01032	01384	01032	01409	01033	20
40	01409	01033	01433	01034	01458	01034	01483	01035	01508	01035	01532	01036	19
41	01532	01036	01557	01036	01582	01037	01606	01038	01631	01038	01656	01039	18
42	01656	01039	01680	01039	01705	01040	01730	01041	01754	01041	01779	01042	17
43	01779	01042	01803	01042	01828	01043	01853	01044	01877	01044	01902	01045	16
44	01902	01045	01927	01045	01951	01046	01976	01047	02000	01047	02025	01048	15
45	02025	01048	02049	01048	02074	01049	02098	01050	02123	01050	02147	01051	14
46	02147	01051	02172	01051	02196	01052	02221	01052	02245	01053	02270	01054	13
47	02270	01054	02294	01054	02319	01055	02343	01055	02368	01056	02392	01057	12
48	02392	01057	02417	01057	02441	01058	02466	01058	02490	01059	02514	01060	11
49	02514	01060	02539	01060	02563	01061	02588	01061	02612	01062	02636	01063	10
50	02636	01063	02661	01063	02685	01064	02709	01064	02734	01065	02758	01066	09
51	02758	01066	02783	01066	02807	01067	02831	01067	02856	01068	02880	01069	08
52	02880	01069	02904	01069	02929	01070	02953	01070	02977	01071	03001	01072	07
53	03001	01072	03026	01072	03050	01073	03074	01073	03098	01074	03123	01075	06
54	03123	01075	03147	01075	03171	01076	03195	01076	03220	01077	03244	01078	05
55	03244	01078	03268	01078	03292	01079	03316	01079	03341	01080	03365	01081	04
56	03365	01081	03389	01081	03413	01082	03437	01082	03461	01083	03486	01084	03
57	03486	01084	03510	01084	03534	01085	03558	01085	03582	01086	03606	01087	02
58	03606	01087	03630	01087	03654	01088	03678	01088	03703	01089	03727	01090	01
59	03727	01090	03751	01090	03775	01091	03799	01091	03823	01092	03847	01093	00
		.8		.6		.4		.2		.0			

PARTS for 0′.1: LOGS. 13 NATURALS negligible

348°

HAVERSINES

12°

′	.0 Log. $\overline{2}$.or(8.)	.0 Nat. 0.	.2 Log. $\overline{2}$.or(8.)	.2 Nat. 0.	.4 Log. $\overline{2}$.or(8.)	.4 Nat. 0.	.6 Log. $\overline{2}$.or(8.)	.6 Nat. 0.	.8 Log. $\overline{2}$.or(8.)	.8 Nat. 0.	.8 Log. $\overline{2}$.or(8.)	.8 Nat. 0.	′
00	03847	01093	03871	01093	03895	01094	03919	01094	03943	01095	03967	01096	59
01	03967	01096	03991	01096	04015	01097	04039	01097	04063	01098	04087	01099	58
02	04087	01099	04111	01099	04135	01100	04159	01100	04183	01101	04207	01102	57
03	04207	01102	04231	01102	04255	01103	04279	01104	04302	01104	04326	01105	56
04	04326	01105	04350	01105	04374	01106	04398	01107	04422	01107	04446	01108	55
05	04446	01108	04470	01108	04493	01109	04517	01110	04541	01110	04565	01111	54
06	04565	01111	04589	01111	04613	01112	04637	01113	04660	01113	04684	01114	53
07	04684	01114	04708	01115	04732	01115	04756	01116	04779	01116	04803	01117	52
08	04803	01117	04827	01118	04851	01118	04874	01119	04898	01119	04922	01120	51
09	04922	01120	04946	01121	04969	01121	04993	01122	05017	01122	05041	01123	50
10	05041	01123	05064	01124	05088	01124	05112	01125	05135	01126	05159	01126	49
11	05159	01126	05183	01127	05206	01127	05230	01128	05254	01129	05277	01129	48
12	05277	01129	05301	01130	05324	01130	05348	01131	05372	01132	05395	01132	47
13	05395	01132	05419	01133	05443	01134	05466	01134	05490	01135	05513	01135	46
14	05513	01135	05537	01136	05561	01137	05584	01137	05608	01138	05631	01138	45
15	05631	01138	05655	01139	05678	01140	05702	01140	05725	01141	05749	01142	44
16	05749	01142	05772	01142	05796	01143	05819	01143	05843	01144	05866	01145	43
17	05866	01145	05890	01145	05913	01146	05937	01146	05960	01147	05984	01148	42
18	05984	01148	06007	01148	06030	01149	06054	01150	06077	01150	06101	01151	41
19	06101	01151	06124	01151	06148	01152	06171	01153	06194	01153	06218	01154	40
20	06218	01154	06241	01155	06265	01155	06288	01156	06311	01156	06335	01157	39
21	06335	01157	06358	01158	06381	01158	06405	01159	06428	01160	06451	01160	38
22	06451	01160	06475	01161	06498	01161	06521	01162	06545	01163	06568	01163	37
23	06568	01163	06591	01164	06614	01165	06638	01165	06661	01166	06684	01166	36
24	06684	01166	06707	01167	06731	01168	06754	01168	06777	01169	06800	01170	35
25	06800	01170	06824	01170	06847	01171	06870	01171	06893	01172	06916	01173	34
26	06916	01173	06940	01173	06963	01174	06986	01175	07009	01175	07032	01176	33
27	07032	01176	07056	01176	07079	01177	07102	01178	07125	01178	07148	01179	32
28	07148	01179	07171	01180	07194	01180	07218	01181	07241	01181	07264	01182	31
29	07264	01182	07287	01183	07310	01183	07333	01184	07356	01185	07379	01185	30
30	07379	01185	07402	01186	07425	01186	07448	01187	07471	01188	07494	01188	29
31	07494	01188	07517	01189	07540	01190	07564	01190	07587	01191	07610	01192	28
32	07610	01192	07633	01192	07656	01193	07679	01193	07702	01194	07725	01195	27
33	07725	01195	07748	01195	07771	01196	07793	01197	07816	01197	07839	01198	26
34	07839	01198	07862	01198	07885	01199	07908	01200	07931	01200	07954	01201	25
35	07954	01201	07977	01202	08000	01202	08023	01203	08046	01204	08068	01204	24
36	08068	01204	08091	01205	08114	01205	08137	01206	08160	01207	08183	01207	23
37	08183	01207	08206	01208	08228	01209	08251	01209	08274	01210	08297	01211	22
38	08297	01211	08320	01211	08343	01212	08365	01212	08388	01213	08411	01214	21
39	08411	01214	08434	01214	08457	01215	08479	01216	08502	01216	08525	01217	20
40	08525	01217	08548	01218	08571	01218	08593	01219	08616	01219	08639	01220	19
41	08639	01220	08662	01221	08684	01221	08707	01222	08730	01223	08752	01223	18
42	08752	01223	08775	01224	08798	01225	08820	01225	08843	01226	08866	01226	17
43	08866	01226	08888	01227	08911	01228	08934	01228	08956	01229	08979	01230	16
44	08979	01230	09002	01230	09024	01231	09047	01232	09070	01232	09092	01233	15
45	09092	01233	09115	01234	09137	01234	09160	01235	09183	01235	09205	01236	14
46	09205	01236	09228	01237	09250	01237	09273	01238	09295	01239	09318	01239	13
47	09318	01239	09341	01240	09363	01241	09386	01241	09408	01242	09431	01243	12
48	09431	01243	09453	01243	09476	01244	09498	01244	09521	01245	09543	01246	11
49	09543	01246	09566	01246	09588	01247	09611	01248	09633	01248	09656	01249	10
50	09656	01249	09678	01250	09701	01250	09723	01251	09746	01252	09768	01252	09
51	09768	01252	09790	01253	09813	01254	09835	01254	09858	01255	09880	01255	08
52	09880	01255	09902	01256	09925	01257	09947	01257	09970	01258	09992	01259	07
53	09992	01259	10014	01259	10037	01260	10059	01261	10081	01261	10104	01262	06
54	10104	01262	10126	01263	10149	01263	10171	01264	10193	01265	10216	01265	05
55	10216	01265	10238	01266	10260	01267	10282	01267	10305	01268	10327	01268	04
56	10327	01268	10349	01269	10372	01270	10394	01270	10416	01271	10438	01272	03
57	10438	01272	10461	01272	10483	01273	10505	01274	10528	01274	10550	01275	02
58	10550	01275	10572	01276	10594	01276	10616	01277	10639	01278	10661	01278	01
59	10661	01278	10683	01279	10705	01280	10727	01280	10750	01281	10772	01282	00

| | .8 | .6 | .4 | .2 | .0 ← |

PARTS for 0′.1: LOGS 12 NATURALS negligible

347°

13° HAVERSINES

′	.0 Log. $\overline{2}$.or(8.)	.0 Nat. 0.	.2 Log. $\overline{2}$.or(8.)	.2 Nat. 0.	.4 Log. $\overline{2}$.or(8.)	.4 Nat. 0.	.6 Log. $\overline{2}$.or(8.)	.6 Nat. 0.	.8 Log. $\overline{2}$.or(8.)	.8 Nat. 0.	Log. $\overline{2}$.or(8.)	Nat. 0.	′
00	10772	01282	10794	01282	10816	01283	10838	01283	10860	01284	10883	01285	59
01	10883	01285	10905	01285	10927	01286	10949	01287	10971	01287	10993	01288	58
02	10993	01288	11015	01289	11037	01289	11060	01290	11082	01291	11104	01291	57
03	11104	01291	11126	01292	11148	01293	11170	01293	11192	01294	11214	01295	56
04	11214	01295	11236	01295	11258	01296	11280	01297	11302	01297	11324	01298	55
05	11324	01298	11346	01299	11368	01299	11390	01300	11412	01301	11434	01301	54
06	11434	01301	11456	01302	11478	01303	11500	01303	11522	01304	11544	01305	53
07	11544	01305	11566	01305	11588	01306	11610	01306	11632	01307	11654	01308	52
08	11654	01308	11676	01308	11698	01309	11720	01310	11742	01310	11764	01311	51
09	11764	01311	11786	01312	11808	01312	11830	01313	11852	01314	11873	01314	50
10	11873	01314	11895	01315	11917	01316	11939	01316	11961	01317	11983	01318	49
11	11983	01318	12005	01318	12026	01319	12048	01320	12070	01320	12092	01321	48
12	12092	01321	12114	01322	12136	01322	12158	01323	12179	01324	12201	01324	47
13	12201	01324	12223	01325	12245	01326	12267	01326	12288	01327	12310	01327	46
14	12310	01328	12332	01328	12354	01329	12375	01330	12397	01330	12419	01331	45
15	12419	01331	12441	01332	12463	01332	12484	01333	12506	01334	12528	01334	44
16	12528	01334	12549	01335	12571	01336	12593	01336	12615	01337	12636	01338	43
17	12636	01338	12658	01338	12680	01339	12701	01340	12723	01340	12745	01341	42
18	12745	01341	12766	01342	12788	01342	12810	01343	12831	01344	12853	01344	41
19	12853	01344	12875	01345	12896	01346	12918	01346	12940	01347	12961	01348	40
20	12961	01348	12983	01348	13004	01349	13026	01350	13048	01350	13069	01351	39
21	13069	01351	13091	01352	13112	01352	13134	01353	13155	01354	13177	01354	38
22	13177	01354	13199	01355	13220	01356	13242	01356	13263	01357	13285	01358	37
23	13285	01358	13306	01359	13328	01359	13349	01360	13371	01361	13392	01361	36
24	13392	01361	13414	01362	13435	01363	13457	01363	13478	01364	13500	01365	35
25	13500	01365	13521	01365	13543	01366	13564	01367	13586	01367	13607	01368	34
26	13607	01368	13629	01369	13650	01369	13672	01370	13693	01371	13714	01371	33
27	13714	01371	13736	01372	13757	01373	13779	01373	13800	01374	13821	01375	32
28	13821	01375	13843	01375	13864	01376	13886	01377	13907	01377	13928	01378	31
29	13928	01378	13950	01379	13971	01379	13992	01380	14014	01381	14035	01382	30
30	14035	01382	14057	01382	14078	01383	14099	01384	14120	01384	14142	01385	29
31	14142	01385	14163	01386	14184	01386	14206	01387	14227	01388	14248	01388	28
32	14248	01388	14270	01389	14291	01390	14312	01390	14334	01391	14355	01392	27
33	14355	01392	14376	01392	14397	01393	14419	01394	14440	01394	14461	01395	26
34	14461	01395	14482	01396	14504	01396	14525	01397	14546	01398	14567	01399	25
35	14567	01399	14588	01399	14610	01400	14631	01401	14652	01401	14673	01402	24
36	14673	01402	14694	01403	14716	01403	14737	01404	14758	01405	14779	01405	23
37	14779	01405	14800	01406	14821	01407	14843	01407	14864	01408	14885	01409	22
38	14885	01409	14906	01409	14927	01410	14948	01411	14969	01412	14990	01412	21
39	14990	01412	15012	01413	15033	01414	15054	01414	15075	01415	15096	01416	20
40	15096	01416	15117	01416	15138	01417	15159	01418	15180	01418	15201	01419	19
41	15201	01419	15222	01420	15243	01420	15265	01421	15286	01422	15307	01423	18
42	15307	01423	15328	01423	15349	01424	15370	01425	15391	01425	15412	01426	17
43	15412	01426	15433	01427	15454	01427	15475	01428	15496	01429	15517	01429	16
44	15517	01429	15538	01430	15559	01431	15579	01432	15600	01432	15621	01433	15
45	15621	01433	15642	01434	15663	01434	15684	01435	15705	01436	15726	01436	14
46	15726	01436	15747	01437	15768	01438	15789	01438	15810	01439	15831	01440	13
47	15831	01440	15852	01441	15873	01441	15893	01442	15914	01443	15935	01443	12
48	15935	01443	15956	01444	15977	01445	15998	01445	16019	01446	16040	01447	11
49	16040	01447	16060	01447	16081	01448	16102	01449	16123	01450	16144	01450	10
50	16144	01450	16165	01451	16185	01452	16206	01452	16227	01453	16248	01454	09
51	16248	01454	16269	01454	16289	01455	16310	01456	16331	01457	16352	01457	08
52	16352	01457	16373	01458	16393	01459	16414	01459	16435	01460	16456	01461	07
53	16456	01461	16476	01461	16497	01462	16518	01463	16539	01464	16559	01464	06
54	16559	01464	16580	01465	16601	01466	16621	01466	16642	01467	16663	01468	05
55	16663	01468	16684	01468	16704	01469	16725	01470	16746	01470	16766	01471	04
56	16766	01471	16787	01472	16808	01473	16828	01473	16849	01474	16870	01475	03
57	16870	01475	16890	01475	16911	01476	16932	01477	16952	01478	16973	01478	02
58	16973	01478	16993	01479	17014	01480	17035	01480	17055	01481	17076	01482	01
59	17076	01482	17097	01482	17117	01483	17138	01484	17158	01485	17179	01485	00

	.8		.6		.4		.2		.0	

PARTS for 0′.1: LOGS 11 NATURALS negligible

346°

14° HAVERSINES

'	.0 Log.	.0 Nat.	.2 Log.	.2 Nat.	.4 Log.	.4 Nat.	.6 Log.	.6 Nat.	.8 Log.	.8 Nat.	'
	$\overline{2}$.or(8.)	0.	$\overline{2}$.or(8.)	0.	$\overline{2}$.or(8.)	0.	$\overline{2}$.or(8.)	0.	$\overline{2}$.or(8.)	0.	
00	17179	01485	17199	01486	17220	01487	17241	01487	17261	01488	17282	01489	59
01	17282	01489	17302	01489	17323	01490	17343	01491	17364	01492	17384	01492	58
02	17384	01492	17405	01493	17425	01494	17446	01494	17466	01495	17487	01496	57
03	17487	01496	17507	01497	17528	01497	17548	01498	17569	01499	17589	01499	56
04	17589	01499	17610	01500	17630	01501	17651	01501	17671	01502	17692	01503	55
05	17692	01503	17712	01504	17733	01504	17753	01505	17774	01506	17794	01506	54
06	17794	01506	17814	01507	17835	01508	17855	01509	17876	01509	17896	01510	53
07	17896	01510	17916	01511	17937	01511	17957	01512	17978	01513	17998	01513	52
08	17998	01513	18018	01514	18039	01515	18059	01516	18080	01516	18100	01517	51
09	18100	01517	18121	01518	18141	01518	18161	01519	18181	01520	18202	01521	50
10	18202	01521	18222	01521	18242	01522	18263	01523	18283	01523	18303	01524	49
11	18303	01524	18324	01525	18344	01526	18364	01526	18384	01527	18405	01528	48
12	18405	01528	18425	01528	18445	01529	18466	01530	18486	01531	18506	01531	47
13	18506	01531	18526	01532	18547	01533	18567	01533	18587	01534	18607	01535	46
14	18607	01535	18628	01536	18648	01536	18668	01537	18688	01538	18708	01538	45
15	18708	01538	18729	01539	18749	01540	18769	01541	18789	01541	18809	01542	44
16	18809	01542	18830	01543	18850	01543	18870	01544	18890	01545	18910	01546	43
17	18910	01546	18931	01546	18951	01547	18971	01548	18991	01548	19011	01549	42
18	19011	01549	19031	01550	19051	01551	19072	01551	19092	01552	19112	01553	41
19	19112	01553	19132	01554	19152	01554	19172	01555	19192	01556	19212	01556	40
20	19212	01556	19232	01557	19253	01558	19273	01559	19293	01559	19313	01560	39
21	19313	01560	19333	01561	19353	01561	19373	01562	19393	01563	19413	01564	38
22	19413	01564	19433	01564	19453	01565	19473	01566	19493	01566	19513	01567	37
23	19513	01567	19533	01568	19553	01569	19573	01569	19593	01570	19613	01571	36
24	19613	01571	19633	01572	19653	01572	19673	01573	19693	01574	19713	01574	35
25	19713	01574	19733	01575	19753	01576	19773	01577	19793	01577	19813	01578	34
26	19813	01578	19833	01579	19853	01580	19873	01580	19893	01581	19913	01582	33
27	19913	01582	19933	01582	19953	01583	19973	01584	19992	01585	20012	01585	32
28	20012	01585	20032	01586	20052	01587	20072	01588	20092	01588	20112	01589	31
29	20112	01589	20132	01590	20152	01590	20171	01591	20191	01592	20211	01593	30
30	20211	01593	20231	01593	20251	01594	20271	01595	20291	01596	20310	01596	29
31	20310	01596	20330	01597	20350	01598	20370	01598	20390	01599	20410	01600	28
32	20410	01600	20429	01601	20449	01601	20469	01602	20489	01603	20509	01604	27
33	20509	01604	20528	01604	20548	01605	20568	01606	20588	01606	20607	01607	26
34	20607	01607	20627	01608	20647	01609	20667	01609	20686	01610	20706	01611	25
35	20706	01611	20726	01612	20746	01612	20765	01613	20785	01614	20805	01615	24
36	20805	01615	20825	01615	20844	01616	20864	01617	20884	01617	20903	01618	23
37	20903	01618	20923	01619	20943	01620	20963	01620	20982	01621	21002	01622	22
38	21002	01622	21022	01623	21041	01623	21061	01624	21081	01625	21100	01626	21
39	21100	01626	21120	01626	21139	01627	21159	01628	21179	01629	21198	01629	20
40	21198	01629	21218	01630	21238	01631	21257	01631	21277	01632	21297	01633	19
41	21297	01633	21316	01634	21336	01634	21355	01635	21375	01636	21395	01637	18
42	21395	01637	21414	01637	21434	01638	21453	01639	21473	01640	21492	01640	17
43	21492	01640	21512	01641	21532	01642	21551	01643	21571	01643	21590	01644	16
44	21590	01644	21610	01645	21629	01645	21649	01646	21668	01647	21688	01648	15
45	21688	01648	21707	01648	21727	01649	21746	01650	21766	01651	21785	01651	14
46	21785	01651	21805	01652	21824	01653	21844	01654	21863	01654	21883	01655	13
47	21883	01655	21902	01656	21922	01656	21941	01657	21961	01658	21980	01659	12
48	21980	01659	22000	01660	22019	01660	22039	01661	22058	01662	22077	01663	11
49	22077	01663	22097	01663	22116	01664	22136	01665	22155	01666	22175	01666	10
50	22175	01666	22194	01667	22213	01668	22233	01669	22252	01669	22272	01670	09
51	22272	01670	22291	01671	22310	01671	22330	01672	22349	01673	22368	01674	08
52	22368	01674	22388	01674	22407	01675	22426	01676	22446	01677	22465	01677	07
53	22465	01677	22485	01678	22504	01679	22523	01680	22542	01680	22562	01681	06
54	22562	01681	22581	01682	22600	01683	22620	01683	22639	01684	22658	01685	05
55	22658	01685	22678	01686	22697	01686	22716	01687	22736	01688	22755	01689	04
56	22755	01689	22774	01689	22793	01690	22813	01691	22832	01692	22851	01692	03
57	22851	01692	22870	01693	22890	01694	22909	01695	22928	01695	22947	01696	02
58	22947	01696	22967	01697	22986	01698	23005	01698	23024	01699	23044	01700	01
59	23044	01700	23063	01701	23082	01701	23101	01702	23120	01703	23140	01704	00
	.8		.6		.4		.2		.0		

PARTS for 0'.1: LOGS 10 NATURALS negligible

345°

HAVERSINES

15°

	.0		.2		.4		.6		.8				
	Log.	Nat.	Log.	Nat.	Log.	Nat.	Log.	Nat.	Log.	Nat.	Log.	Nat.	
'	2̄.or(8.)	0.	2̄.or(8.)	0.	2̄.or(8.)	0.	2̄.or(8.)	0.	2̄.or(8.)	0.	2̄.or(8.)	0.	'
00	23140	01704	23159	01704	23178	01705	23197	01706	23216	01707	23235	01707	59
01	23235	01707	23255	01708	23274	01709	23293	01710	23312	01710	23331	01711	58
02	23331	01711	23350	01712	23370	01713	23389	01713	23408	01714	23427	01715	57
03	23427	01715	23446	01716	23465	01717	23484	01717	23503	01718	23523	01719	56
04	23523	01719	23542	01720	23561	01720	23580	01721	23599	01722	23618	01723	55
05	23618	01723	23637	01723	23656	01724	23675	01725	23694	01726	23713	01726	54
06	23713	01726	23732	01727	23751	01728	23771	01729	23790	01729	23809	01730	53
07	23809	01730	23828	01731	23847	01732	23866	01732	23885	01733	23904	01734	52
08	23904	01734	23923	01735	23942	01735	23961	01736	23980	01737	23999	01738	51
09	23999	01738	24018	01739	24037	01739	24056	01740	24075	01741	24094	01742	50
10	24094	01742	24113	01742	24132	01743	24151	01744	24170	01745	24189	01745	49
11	24189	01745	24208	01746	24227	01747	24245	01748	24264	01748	24283	01749	48
12	24283	01749	24302	01750	24321	01751	24340	01751	24359	01752	24378	01753	47
13	24378	01753	24397	01754	24416	01755	24435	01755	24454	01756	24472	01757	46
14	24472	01757	24491	01758	24510	01758	24529	01759	24548	01760	24567	01761	45
15	24567	01761	24586	01761	24605	01762	24624	01763	24642	01764	24661	01764	44
16	24661	01764	24680	01765	24699	01766	24718	01767	24737	01768	24755	01768	43
17	24755	01768	24774	01769	24793	01770	24812	01771	24831	01771	24850	01772	42
18	24850	01772	24868	01773	24887	01774	24906	01774	24925	01775	24944	01776	41
19	24944	01776	24962	01777	24981	01777	25000	01778	25019	01779	25037	01780	40
20	25037	01780	25056	01781	25075	01781	25094	01782	25112	01783	25131	01784	39
21	25131	01784	25150	01784	25169	01785	25187	01786	25206	01787	25225	01788	38
22	25225	01788	25244	01788	25262	01789	25281	01790	25300	01791	25319	01791	37
23	25319	01791	25337	01792	25356	01793	25375	01794	25393	01794	25412	01795	36
24	25412	01795	25431	01796	25449	01797	25468	01798	25487	01798	25505	01799	35
25	25505	01799	25524	01800	25543	01801	25561	01801	25580	01802	25599	01803	34
26	25599	01803	25617	01804	25636	01805	25655	01805	25673	01806	25692	01807	33
27	25692	01807	25710	01808	25729	01808	25748	01809	25766	01810	25785	01811	32
28	25785	01811	25804	01811	25822	01812	25841	01813	25859	01814	25878	01815	31
29	25878	01815	25897	01815	25915	01816	25934	01817	25952	01818	25971	01818	30
30	25971	01818	25989	01819	26008	01820	26026	01821	26045	01822	26064	01822	29
31	26064	01822	26082	01823	26101	01824	26119	01825	26138	01825	26156	01826	28
32	26156	01826	26175	01827	26193	01828	26212	01829	26230	01829	26249	01830	27
33	26249	01830	26267	01831	26286	01832	26304	01832	26323	01833	26341	01834	26
34	26341	01834	26360	01835	26378	01836	26397	01836	26415	01837	26434	01838	25
35	26434	01838	26452	01839	26471	01840	26489	01840	26508	01841	26526	01842	24
36	26526	01842	26544	01843	26563	01843	26581	01844	26600	01845	26618	01846	23
37	26618	01846	26637	01847	26655	01847	26673	01848	26692	01849	26710	01850	22
38	26710	01850	26729	01850	26747	01851	26765	01852	26784	01853	26802	01854	21
39	26802	01854	26821	01854	26839	01855	26857	01856	26876	01857	26894	01858	20
40	26894	01858	26912	01858	26931	01859	26949	01860	26967	01861	26986	01861	19
41	26986	01861	27004	01862	27022	01863	27041	01864	27059	01865	27077	01865	18
42	27077	01865	27096	01866	27114	01867	27132	01868	27151	01869	27169	01869	17
43	27169	01869	27187	01870	27206	01871	27224	01872	27242	01873	27261	01873	16
44	27261	01873	27279	01874	27297	01875	27315	01876	27334	01876	27352	01877	15
45	27352	01877	27370	01878	27388	01879	27407	01880	27425	01880	27443	01881	14
46	27443	01881	27461	01882	27480	01883	27498	01884	27516	01884	27534	01885	13
47	27534	01885	27553	01886	27571	01887	27589	01888	27607	01888	27626	01889	12
48	27626	01889	27644	01890	27662	01891	27680	01891	27698	01892	27717	01893	11
49	27717	01893	27735	01894	27753	01895	27771	01895	27789	01896	27807	01897	10
50	27807	01897	27826	01898	27844	01899	27862	01899	27880	01900	27898	01901	09
51	27898	01901	27916	01902	27934	01903	27953	01903	27971	01904	27989	01905	08
52	27989	01905	28007	01906	28025	01907	28043	01907	28061	01908	28080	01909	07
53	28080	01909	28098	01910	28116	01911	28134	01911	28152	01912	28170	01913	06
54	28170	01913	28188	01914	28206	01915	28224	01915	28242	01916	28260	01917	05
55	28260	01917	28278	01918	28297	01919	28315	01919	28333	01920	28351	01921	04
56	28351	01921	28369	01922	28387	01923	28405	01923	28423	01924	28441	01925	03
57	28441	01925	28459	01926	28477	01927	28495	01927	28513	01928	28531	01929	02
58	28531	01929	28549	01930	28567	01931	28585	01931	28603	01932	28621	01933	01
59	28621	01933	28639	01934	28657	01935	28675	01935	28693	01936	28711	01937	00

	.8		.6		.4		.2		.0	

PARTS for 0'.1:　　LOGS 9　　　　　NATURALS negligible

344°

HAVERSINES

16°

′	.0 Log. 2.or(8.)	.0 Nat. 0.	.2 Log. 2.or(8.)	.2 Nat. 0.	.4 Log. 2.or(8.)	.4 Nat. 0.	.6 Log. 2.or(8.)	.6 Nat. 0.	.8 Log. 2.or(8.)	.8 Nat. 0.	.8 Log. 2.or(8.)	.8 Nat. 0.	′
00	28711	01937	28729	01938	28747	01939	28765	01939	28783	01940	28801	01941	59
01	28801	01941	28819	01942	28837	01943	28855	01943	28873	01944	28891	01945	58
02	28891	01945	28909	01946	28927	01947	28944	01947	28962	01948	28980	01949	57
03	28980	01949	28998	01950	29016	01951	29034	01951	29052	01952	29070	01953	56
04	29070	01953	29088	01954	29106	01955	29124	01955	29141	01956	29159	01957	55
05	29159	01957	29177	01958	29195	01959	29213	01959	29231	01960	29249	01961	54
06	29249	01961	29266	01962	29284	01963	29302	01963	29320	01964	29338	01965	53
07	29338	01965	29356	01966	29374	01967	29392	01968	29409	01968	29427	01969	52
08	29427	01969	29445	01970	29463	01971	29481	01972	29498	01972	29516	01973	51
09	29516	01973	29534	01974	29552	01975	29570	01976	29587	01976	29605	01977	50
10	29605	01977	29623	01978	29641	01979	29659	01980	29676	01980	29694	01981	49
11	29694	01981	29712	01982	29730	01983	29747	01984	29765	01984	29783	01985	48
12	29783	01985	29801	01986	29818	01987	29836	01988	29854	01989	29872	01989	47
13	29872	01989	29889	01990	29907	01991	29925	01992	29943	01993	29960	01993	46
14	29960	01993	29978	01994	29996	01995	30013	01996	30031	01997	30049	01998	45
15	30049	01998	30066	01998	30084	01999	30102	02000	30120	02001	30137	02002	44
16	30137	02002	30155	02002	30173	02003	30190	02004	30208	02005	30226	02006	43
17	30226	02006	30243	02006	30261	02007	30279	02008	30296	02009	30314	02010	42
18	30314	02010	30331	02011	30349	02011	30367	02012	30384	02013	30402	02014	41
19	30402	02014	30420	02015	30437	02015	30455	02016	30473	02017	30490	02018	40
20	30490	02018	30508	02019	30525	02020	30543	02020	30561	02021	30578	02022	39
21	30578	02022	30596	02023	30613	02024	30631	02024	30648	02025	30666	02026	38
22	30666	02026	30684	02027	30701	02028	30719	02029	30736	02029	30754	02030	37
23	30754	02030	30771	02031	30789	02032	30806	02033	30824	02033	30842	02034	36
24	30842	02034	30859	02035	30877	02036	30894	02037	30912	02038	30929	02038	35
25	30929	02038	30947	02039	30964	02040	30982	02041	30999	02042	31017	02043	34
26	31017	02043	31034	02043	31052	02044	31069	02045	31087	02046	31104	02047	33
27	31104	02047	31122	02047	31139	02048	31157	02049	31174	02050	31191	02051	32
28	31191	02051	31209	02052	31226	02052	31244	02053	31261	02054	31279	02055	31
29	31279	02055	31296	02056	31314	02057	31331	02057	31349	02058	31366	02059	30
30	31366	02059	31383	02060	31401	02061	31418	02061	31436	02062	31453	02063	29
31	31453	02063	31470	02064	31488	02065	31505	02066	31523	02066	31540	02067	28
32	31540	02067	31557	02068	31575	02069	31592	02070	31610	02071	31627	02071	27
33	31627	02071	31644	02072	31662	02073	31679	02074	31696	02075	31714	02076	26
34	31714	02076	31731	02076	31748	02077	31766	02078	31783	02079	31800	02080	25
35	31800	02080	31818	02081	31835	02081	31852	02082	31870	02083	31887	02084	24
36	31887	02084	31904	02085	31922	02086	31939	02086	31956	02087	31974	02088	23
37	31974	02088	31991	02089	32008	02090	32026	02091	32043	02091	32060	02092	22
38	32060	02092	32077	02093	32095	02094	32112	02095	32129	02096	32146	02096	21
39	32146	02096	32164	02097	32181	02098	32198	02099	32216	02100	32233	02101	20
40	32233	02101	32250	02101	32267	02102	32285	02103	32302	02104	32319	02105	19
41	32319	02105	32336	02106	32353	02106	32371	02107	32388	02108	32405	02109	18
42	32405	02109	32422	02110	32439	02111	32457	02111	32474	02112	32491	02113	17
43	32491	02113	32508	02114	32526	02115	32543	02116	32560	02116	32577	02117	16
44	32577	02117	32594	02118	32611	02119	32629	02120	32646	02121	32663	02121	15
45	32663	02121	32680	02122	32697	02123	32714	02124	32731	02125	32749	02126	14
46	32749	02126	32766	02126	32783	02127	32800	02128	32817	02129	32834	02130	13
47	32834	02130	32852	02131	32869	02132	32886	02132	32903	02133	32920	02134	12
48	32920	02134	32937	02135	32954	02136	32971	02137	32988	02137	33005	02138	11
49	33005	02138	33022	02139	33040	02140	33057	02141	33074	02142	33091	02142	10
50	33091	02142	33108	02143	33125	02144	33142	02145	33159	02146	33176	02147	09
51	33176	02147	33193	02147	33210	02148	33227	02149	33244	02150	33261	02151	08
52	33261	02151	33278	02152	33295	02153	33313	02153	33330	02154	33347	02155	07
53	33347	02155	33364	02156	33381	02157	33398	02158	33415	02158	33432	02159	06
54	33432	02159	33449	02160	33466	02161	33483	02162	33500	02163	33517	02164	05
55	33517	02164	33534	02164	33551	02165	33568	02166	33585	02167	33602	02168	04
56	33602	02168	33619	02169	33636	02169	33652	02170	33669	02171	33686	02172	03
57	33686	02172	33703	02173	33720	02174	33737	02175	33754	02175	33771	02176	02
58	33771	02176	33788	02177	33805	02178	33822	02179	33839	02180	33856	02181	01
59	33856	02181	33873	02181	33890	02182	33907	02183	33923	02184	33940	02185	00

	.8	.6	.4	.2	.0 ←

PARTS for 0′.1: LOGS 9 NATURALS negligible

343°

HAVERSINES

17°

′	.0 Log. $\overline{2}$.or(8.)	.0 Nat. 0.	.2 Log. $\overline{2}$.or(8.)	.2 Nat. 0.	.4 Log. $\overline{2}$.or(8.)	.4 Nat. 0.	.6 Log. $\overline{2}$.or(8.)	.6 Nat. 0.	.8 Log. $\overline{2}$.or(8.)	.8 Nat. 0.	′
00	33940	02185	33957	02186	33974	02186	33991	02187	34008	02188	34025	02189	59
01	34025	02189	34042	02190	34059	02191	34076	02192	34093	02192	34109	02193	58
02	34109	02193	34126	02194	34143	02195	34160	02196	34177	02197	34194	02198	57
03	34194	02198	34210	02198	34227	02199	34244	02200	34261	02201	34278	02202	56
04	34278	02202	34295	02203	34311	02204	34328	02204	34345	02205	34362	02206	55
05	34362	02206	34379	02207	34396	02208	34412	02209	34429	02209	34446	02210	54
06	34446	02210	34463	02211	34480	02212	34496	02213	34513	02214	34530	02215	53
07	34530	02215	34547	02216	34564	02216	34580	02217	34597	02218	34614	02219	52
08	34614	02219	34631	02220	34648	02221	34664	02221	34681	02222	34698	02223	51
09	34698	02223	34715	02224	34731	02225	34748	02226	34765	02227	34782	02227	50
10	34782	02227	34798	02228	34815	02229	34832	02230	34848	02231	34865	02232	49
11	34865	02232	34882	02233	34899	02234	34915	02234	34932	02235	34949	02236	48
12	34949	02236	34965	02237	34982	02238	34999	02239	35016	02240	35032	02240	47
13	35032	02240	35049	02241	35066	02242	35082	02243	35099	02244	35116	02245	46
14	35116	02245	35132	02246	35149	02246	35166	02247	35182	02248	35199	02249	45
15	35199	02249	35216	02250	35232	02251	35249	02252	35266	02252	35282	02253	44
16	35282	02253	35299	02254	35315	02255	35332	02256	35349	02257	35365	02258	43
17	35365	02258	35382	02259	35399	02259	35415	02260	35432	02261	35448	02262	42
18	35448	02262	35465	02263	35482	02264	35498	02265	35515	02265	35531	02266	41
19	35531	02266	35548	02267	35565	02268	35581	02269	35598	02270	35614	02271	40
20	35614	02271	35631	02271	35648	02272	35664	02273	35681	02274	35697	02275	39
21	35697	02275	35714	02276	35730	02277	35747	02278	35763	02278	35780	02279	38
22	35780	02279	35797	02280	35813	02281	35830	02282	35846	02283	35863	02284	37
23	35863	02284	35879	02285	35896	02285	35912	02286	35929	02287	35945	02288	36
24	35945	02288	35962	02289	35978	02290	35995	02291	36011	02291	36028	02292	35
25	36028	02292	36044	02293	36061	02294	36077	02295	36094	02296	36110	02297	34
26	36110	02297	36127	02298	36143	02298	36160	02299	36176	02300	36193	02301	33
27	36193	02301	36209	02302	36225	02303	36242	02304	36258	02305	36275	02305	32
28	36275	02305	36291	02306	36308	02307	36324	02308	36341	02309	36357	02310	31
29	36357	02310	36373	02311	36390	02312	36406	02312	36423	02313	36439	02314	30
30	36439	02314	36456	02315	36472	02316	36488	02317	36505	02318	36521	02319	29
31	36521	02319	36538	02319	36554	02320	36570	02321	36587	02322	36603	02323	28
32	36603	02323	36620	02324	36636	02325	36652	02326	36669	02326	36685	02327	27
33	36685	02327	36701	02328	36718	02329	36734	02330	36750	02331	36767	02332	26
34	36767	02332	36783	02333	36800	02333	36816	02334	36832	02335	36849	02336	25
35	36849	02336	36865	02337	36881	02338	36898	02339	36914	02340	36930	02340	24
36	36930	02340	36947	02341	36963	02342	36979	02343	36995	02344	37012	02345	23
37	37012	02345	37028	02346	37044	02347	37061	02347	37077	02348	37093	02349	22
38	37093	02349	37110	02350	37126	02351	37142	02352	37158	02353	37175	02354	21
39	37175	02354	37191	02355	37207	02355	37224	02356	37240	02357	37256	02358	20
40	37256	02358	37272	02359	37288	02360	37305	02361	37321	02362	37337	02363	19
41	37337	02363	37353	02363	37370	02364	37386	02365	37402	02366	37418	02367	18
42	37418	02367	37435	02368	37451	02369	37467	02370	37483	02370	37500	02371	17
43	37500	02371	37516	02372	37532	02373	37548	02374	37564	02375	37581	02376	16
44	37581	02376	37597	02377	37613	02378	37629	02378	37645	02379	37662	02380	15
45	37662	02380	37678	02381	37694	02382	37710	02383	37726	02384	37742	02385	14
46	37742	02385	37759	02386	37775	02386	37791	02387	37807	02388	37823	02389	13
47	37823	02389	37839	02390	37855	02391	37872	02392	37888	02393	37904	02394	12
48	37904	02394	37920	02394	37936	02395	37952	02396	37968	02397	37985	02398	11
49	37985	02398	38001	02399	38017	02400	38033	02401	38049	02402	38065	02402	10
50	38065	02402	38081	02403	38097	02404	38113	02405	38129	02406	38146	02407	09
51	38146	02407	38162	02408	38178	02409	38194	02410	38210	02411	38226	02411	08
52	38226	02411	38242	02412	38258	02413	38274	02414	38290	02415	38306	02416	07
53	38306	02416	38322	02417	38338	02418	38355	02419	38371	02419	38387	02420	06
54	38387	02420	38403	02421	38419	02422	38435	02423	38451	02424	38467	02425	05
55	38467	02425	38483	02426	38499	02427	38515	02427	38531	02428	38547	02429	04
56	38547	02429	38563	02430	38579	02431	38595	02432	38611	02433	38627	02434	03
57	38627	02434	38643	02435	38659	02436	38675	02436	38691	02437	38707	02438	02
58	38707	02438	38723	02439	38739	02440	38755	02441	38771	02442	38787	02443	01
59	38787	02443	38803	02444	38819	02444	38835	02445	38851	02446	38867	02447	00
		.8		.6		.4		.2		.0 ←			

PARTS for 0′.1: LOGS 8 NATURALS negligible

342°

18° HAVERSINES

	.0		.2		.4		.6		.8				
	Log.	Nat.	Log.	Nat.	Log.	Nat.	Log.	Nat.	Log.	Nat.	Log.	Nat.	
′	2.or(8.)	0.	2.or(8.)	0.	2.or(8.)	0.	2.or(8.)	0.	2.or(8.)	0.	2.or(8.)	0.	′
00	38867	02447	38882	02448	38898	02449	38914	02450	38930	02451	38946	02452	59
01	38946	02452	38962	02453	38978	02453	38994	02454	39010	02455	39026	02456	58
02	39026	02456	39042	02457	39058	02458	39074	02459	39089	02460	39105	02461	57
03	39105	02461	39121	02462	39137	02463	39153	02463	39169	02464	39185	02465	56
04	39185	02465	39201	02466	39217	02467	39233	02468	39249	02469	39264	02470	55
05	39264	02470	39280	02471	39296	02472	39312	02472	39328	02473	39344	02474	54
06	39344	02474	39360	02475	39375	02476	39391	02477	39407	02478	39423	02479	53
07	39423	02479	39439	02480	39455	02481	39471	02481	39486	02482	39502	02483	52
08	39502	02483	39518	02484	39534	02485	39550	02486	39566	02487	39581	02488	51
09	39581	02488	39597	02489	39613	02490	39629	02491	39645	02491	39660	02492	50
10	39660	02492	39676	02493	39692	02494	39708	02495	39724	02496	39739	02497	49
11	39739	02497	39755	02498	39771	02499	39787	02500	39802	02500	39818	02501	48
12	39818	02501	39834	02502	39850	02503	39866	02504	39881	02505	39897	02506	47
13	39897	02506	39913	02507	39929	02508	39944	02509	39960	02510	39976	02510	46
14	39976	02510	39992	02511	40007	02512	40023	02513	40039	02514	40055	02515	45
15	40055	02515	40070	02516	40086	02517	40102	02518	40117	02519	40133	02520	44
16	40133	02520	40149	02521	40165	02521	40180	02522	40196	02523	40212	02524	43
17	40212	02524	40227	02525	40243	02526	40259	02527	40275	02528	40290	02529	42
18	40290	02529	40306	02530	40322	02531	40337	02531	40353	02532	40369	02533	41
19	40369	02533	40384	02534	40400	02535	40416	02536	40431	02537	40447	02538	40
20	40447	02538	40462	02539	40478	02540	40494	02541	40510	02542	40525	02542	39
21	40525	02542	40541	02543	40556	02544	40572	02545	40588	02546	40603	02547	38
22	40603	02547	40619	02548	40635	02549	40650	02550	40666	02551	40681	02552	37
23	40681	02552	40697	02553	40713	02553	40728	02554	40744	02555	40759	02556	36
24	40759	02556	40775	02557	40791	02558	40806	02559	40822	02560	40837	02561	35
25	40837	02561	40853	02562	40869	02563	40884	02564	40900	02564	40915	02565	34
26	40915	02565	40931	02566	40947	02567	40962	02568	40978	02569	40993	02570	33
27	40993	02570	41009	02571	41024	02572	41040	02573	41055	02574	41071	02575	32
28	41071	02575	41086	02576	41102	02576	41117	02577	41133	02578	41149	02579	31
29	41149	02579	41164	02580	41180	02581	41195	02582	41211	02583	41226	02584	30
30	41226	02584	41242	02585	41257	02586	41273	02587	41288	02588	41304	02588	29
31	41304	02588	41319	02589	41335	02590	41350	02591	41366	02592	41381	02593	28
32	41381	02593	41397	02594	41412	02595	41428	02596	41443	02597	41459	02598	27
33	41459	02598	41474	02599	41489	02600	41505	02600	41520	02601	41536	02602	26
34	41536	02602	41551	02603	41567	02604	41582	02605	41598	02606	41613	02607	25
35	41613	02607	41629	02608	41644	02609	41660	02610	41675	02611	41690	02612	24
36	41690	02612	41706	02613	41721	02613	41737	02614	41752	02615	41767	02616	23
37	41767	02616	41783	02617	41798	02618	41814	02619	41829	02620	41844	02621	22
38	41844	02621	41860	02622	41875	02623	41891	02624	41906	02625	41921	02626	21
39	41921	02626	41937	02626	41952	02627	41968	02628	41983	02629	41998	02630	20
40	41998	02630	42014	02631	42029	02632	42044	02633	42060	02634	42075	02635	19
41	42075	02635	42091	02636	42106	02637	42121	02638	42137	02639	42152	02639	18
42	42152	02639	42167	02640	42183	02641	42198	02642	42213	02643	42229	02644	17
43	42229	02644	42244	02645	42259	02646	42275	02647	42290	02648	42305	02649	16
44	42305	02649	42321	02650	42336	02651	42351	02652	42366	02653	42382	02653	15
45	42382	02653	42397	02654	42412	02655	42428	02656	42443	02657	42458	02658	14
46	42458	02658	42474	02659	42489	02660	42504	02661	42519	02662	42535	02663	13
47	42535	02663	42550	02664	42565	02665	42581	02666	42596	02667	42611	02668	12
48	42611	02668	42626	02668	42642	02669	42657	02670	42672	02671	42687	02672	11
49	42687	02672	42703	02673	42718	02674	42733	02675	42748	02676	42764	02677	10
50	42764	02677	42779	02678	42794	02679	42809	02680	42824	02681	42840	02682	09
51	42840	02682	42855	02683	42870	02683	42885	02684	42901	02685	42916	02686	08
52	42916	02686	42931	02687	42946	02688	42961	02689	42977	02690	42992	02691	07
53	42992	02691	43007	02692	43022	02693	43037	02694	43052	02695	43068	02696	06
54	43068	02696	43083	02697	43098	02698	43113	02699	43128	02700	43144	02700	05
55	43144	02700	43159	02701	43174	02702	43189	02703	43204	02704	43219	02705	04
56	43219	02705	43235	02706	43250	02707	43265	02708	43280	02709	43295	02710	03
57	43295	02710	43310	02711	43325	02712	43340	02713	43356	02714	43371	02715	02
58	43371	02715	43386	02716	43401	02717	43416	02717	43431	02718	43446	02719	01
59	43446	02719	43461	02720	43477	02721	43492	02722	43507	02723	43522	02724	00
	.8		.6		.4		.2		.0				

PARTS for 0′.1: LOGS 8 NATURALS negligible **341°**

19° HAVERSINES

	.0 Log.	.0 Nat.	.2 Log.	.2 Nat.	.4 Log.	.4 Nat.	.6 Log.	.6 Nat.	.8 Log.	.8 Nat.	Log.	Nat.	
′	2̄.or(8.)	0.	2̄.or(8.)	0.	2̄.or(8.)	0.	2̄.or(8.)	0.	2̄.or(8.)	0.	2̄.or(8.)	0.	′
00	43522	02724	43537	02725	43552	02726	43567	02727	43582	02728	43597	02729	59
01	43597	02729	43612	02730	43627	02731	43643	02732	43658	02733	43673	02734	58
02	43673	02734	43688	02735	43703	02735	43718	02736	43733	02737	43748	02738	57
03	43748	02738	43763	02739	43778	02740	43793	02741	43808	02742	43823	02743	56
04	43823	02743	43838	02744	43853	02745	43868	02746	43883	02747	43898	02748	55
05	43898	02748	43913	02749	43928	02750	43944	02751	43959	02752	43974	02753	54
06	43974	02753	43989	02754	44004	02754	44019	02755	44034	02756	44049	02757	53
07	44049	02757	44064	02758	44079	02759	44094	02760	44109	02761	44124	02762	52
08	44124	02762	44139	02763	44154	02764	44169	02765	44185	02766	44199	02767	51
09	44199	02767	44214	02768	44229	02769	44243	02770	44258	02771	44273	02772	50
10	44273	02772	44288	02773	44303	02774	44318	02774	44333	02775	44348	02776	49
11	44348	02776	44363	02777	44378	02778	44393	02779	44408	02780	44423	02781	48
12	44423	02781	44438	02782	44453	02783	44468	02784	44483	02785	44498	02786	47
13	44498	02786	44513	02787	44527	02788	44542	02789	44557	02790	44572	02791	46
14	44572	02791	44587	02792	44602	02793	44617	02794	44632	02795	44647	02796	45
15	44647	02796	44662	02797	44677	02797	44691	02798	44706	02799	44721	02800	44
16	44721	02800	44736	02801	44751	02802	44766	02803	44781	02804	44796	02805	43
17	44796	02805	44810	02806	44825	02807	44840	02808	44855	02809	44870	02810	42
18	44870	02810	44885	02811	44900	02812	44914	02813	44929	02814	44944	02815	41
19	44944	02815	44959	02816	44974	02817	44989	02818	45004	02819	45018	02820	40
20	45018	02820	45033	02821	45048	02821	45063	02822	45078	02823	45092	02824	39
21	45092	02824	45107	02825	45122	02826	45137	02827	45152	02828	45167	02829	38
22	45167	02829	45181	02830	45196	02831	45211	02832	45226	02833	45241	02834	37
23	45241	02834	45255	02835	45270	02836	45285	02837	45300	02838	45315	02839	36
24	45315	02839	45329	02840	45344	02841	45359	02842	45374	02843	45388	02844	35
25	45388	02844	45403	02845	45418	02846	45433	02847	45447	02848	45462	02849	34
26	45462	02849	45477	02850	45492	02850	45506	02851	45521	02852	45536	02853	33
27	45536	02853	45551	02854	45565	02855	45580	02856	45595	02857	45610	02858	32
28	45610	02858	45624	02859	45639	02860	45654	02861	45668	02862	45683	02863	31
29	45683	02863	45698	02864	45713	02865	45727	02866	45742	02867	45757	02868	30
30	45757	02868	45771	02869	45786	02870	45801	02871	45816	02872	45830	02873	29
31	45830	02873	45845	02874	45860	02875	45874	02876	45889	02877	45904	02878	28
32	45904	02878	45918	02879	45933	02880	45948	02881	45962	02882	45977	02883	27
33	45977	02883	45992	02883	46006	02884	46021	02885	46036	02886	46050	02887	26
34	46050	02887	46065	02888	46080	02889	46094	02890	46109	02891	46124	02892	25
35	46124	02892	46138	02893	46153	02894	46168	02895	46182	02896	46197	02897	24
36	46197	02897	46211	02898	46226	02899	46241	02900	46255	02901	46270	02902	23
37	46270	02902	46284	02903	46299	02904	46314	02905	46328	02906	46343	02907	22
38	46343	02907	46358	02908	46372	02909	46387	02910	46401	02911	46416	02912	21
39	46416	02912	46430	02913	46445	02914	46460	02915	46474	02916	46489	02917	20
40	46489	02917	46503	02918	46518	02919	46532	02920	46547	02921	46562	02922	19
41	46562	02922	46576	02923	46591	02924	46605	02924	46620	02925	46634	02926	18
42	46634	02926	46649	02927	46664	02928	46678	02929	46693	02930	46707	02931	17
43	46707	02931	46722	02932	46736	02933	46751	02934	46765	02935	46780	02936	16
44	46780	02936	46794	02937	46809	02938	46823	02939	46838	02940	46852	02941	15
45	46852	02941	46867	02942	46881	02943	46896	02944	46910	02945	46925	02946	14
46	46925	02946	46939	02947	46954	02948	46968	02949	46983	02950	46997	02951	13
47	46997	02951	47012	02952	47026	02953	47041	02954	47055	02955	47070	02956	12
48	47070	02956	47084	02957	47099	02958	47113	02959	47128	02960	47142	02961	11
49	47142	02961	47157	02962	47171	02963	47186	02964	47200	02965	47215	02966	10
50	47215	02966	47229	02967	47243	02968	47258	02969	47272	02970	47287	02971	09
51	47287	02971	47301	02972	47316	02973	47330	02974	47345	02975	47359	02976	08
52	47359	02976	47373	02977	47388	02978	47402	02979	47417	02980	47431	02981	07
53	47431	02981	47445	02982	47460	02983	47474	02984	47489	02985	47503	02986	06
54	47503	02986	47517	02987	47532	02988	47546	02989	47561	02990	47575	02991	05
55	47575	02991	47589	02992	47604	02993	47618	02994	47633	02995	47647	02996	04
56	47647	02996	47661	02996	47676	02997	47690	02998	47704	02999	47719	03000	03
57	47719	03000	47733	03001	47748	03002	47762	03003	47776	03004	47791	03005	02
58	47791	03005	47805	03006	47819	03007	47834	03008	47848	03009	47862	03010	01
59	47862	03010	47877	03011	47891	03012	47905	03013	47920	03014	47934	03015	00
		.8		.6		.4		.2		.0			

PARTS for 0′.1:　　LOGS 7　　　　　　　NATURALS negligible

340°

20° HAVERSINES

	.0		.2		.4		.6		.8		
	Log.	Nat.	Log.	Nat.	Log.	Nat.	Log.	Nat.	Log.	Nat.	
′	2.or(8.)	0.	2.or(8.)	0.	2.or(8.)	0.	2.or(8.)	0.	2.or(8.)	0.	′
00	47934	03015	47948	03016	47963	03017	47977	03018	47991	03019	48006	03020	59
01	48006	03020	48020	03021	48034	03022	48049	03023	48063	03024	48077	03025	58
02	48077	03025	48092	03026	48106	03027	48120	03028	48134	03029	48149	03030	57
03	48149	03030	48163	03031	48177	03032	48192	03033	48206	03034	48220	03035	56
04	48220	03035	48234	03036	48249	03037	48263	03038	48277	03039	48292	03040	55
05	48292	03040	48306	03041	48320	03042	48334	03043	48349	03044	48363	03045	54
06	48363	03045	48377	03046	48391	03047	48406	03048	48420	03049	48434	03050	53
07	48434	03050	48448	03051	48462	03052	48477	03053	48491	03054	48505	03055	52
08	48505	03055	48519	03056	48534	03057	48548	03058	48562	03059	48576	03060	51
09	48576	03060	48591	03061	48605	03062	48619	03063	48633	03064	48647	03065	50
10	48647	03065	48662	03066	48676	03067	48690	03068	48704	03069	48718	03070	49
11	48718	03070	48733	03071	48747	03072	48761	03073	48775	03074	48789	03075	48
12	48789	03075	48804	03076	48818	03077	48832	03078	48846	03079	48860	03080	47
13	48860	03080	48875	03081	48889	03082	48903	03083	48917	03084	48931	03085	46
14	48931	03085	48945	03086	48960	03087	48974	03088	48988	03089	49002	03090	45
15	49002	03090	49016	03091	49030	03092	49044	03093	49058	03094	49073	03095	44
16	49073	03095	49087	03096	49101	03097	49115	03098	49129	03099	49143	03101	43
17	49143	03101	49157	03102	49172	03103	49186	03104	49200	03105	49214	03106	42
18	49214	03106	49228	03107	49242	03108	49256	03109	49270	03110	49284	03111	41
19	49284	03111	49299	03112	49313	03113	49327	03114	49341	03115	49355	03116	40
20	49355	03116	49369	03117	49383	03118	49397	03119	49411	03120	49425	03121	39
21	49425	03121	49439	03122	49453	03123	49468	03124	49482	03125	49496	03126	38
22	49496	03126	49510	03127	49524	03128	49538	03129	49552	03130	49566	03131	37
23	49566	03131	49580	03132	49594	03133	49608	03134	49622	03135	49636	03136	36
24	49636	03136	49650	03137	49664	03138	49678	03139	49692	03140	49706	03141	35
25	49706	03141	49720	03142	49734	03143	49749	03144	49763	03145	49777	03146	34
26	49777	03146	49791	03147	49805	03148	49819	03149	49833	03150	49847	03151	33
27	49847	03151	49861	03152	49875	03153	49889	03154	49903	03155	49917	03156	32
28	49917	03156	49931	03157	49945	03158	49959	03159	49973	03160	49987	03161	31
29	49987	03161	50001	03162	50015	03163	50028	03164	50042	03165	50056	03166	30
30	50056	03166	50070	03167	50084	03168	50098	03169	50112	03170	50126	03171	29
31	50126	03171	50140	03173	50154	03174	50168	03175	50182	03176	50196	03177	28
32	50196	03177	50210	03178	50224	03179	50238	03180	50252	03181	50266	03182	27
33	50266	03182	50280	03183	50294	03184	50308	03185	50321	03186	50335	03187	26
34	50335	03187	50349	03188	50363	03189	50377	03190	50391	03191	50405	03192	25
35	50405	03192	50419	03193	50433	03194	50447	03195	50461	03196	50475	03197	24
36	50475	03197	50488	03198	50502	03199	50516	03200	50530	03201	50544	03202	23
37	50544	03202	50558	03203	50572	03204	50586	03205	50600	03206	50613	03207	22
38	50613	03207	50627	03208	50641	03209	50655	03210	50669	03211	50683	03212	21
39	50683	03212	50697	03213	50711	03214	50724	03215	50738	03216	50752	03218	20
40	50752	03218	50766	03219	50780	03220	50794	03221	50808	03222	50821	03223	19
41	50821	03223	50835	03224	50849	03225	50863	03226	50877	03227	50891	03228	18
42	50891	03228	50904	03229	50918	03230	50932	03231	50946	03232	50960	03233	17
43	50960	03233	50974	03234	50987	03235	51001	03236	51015	03237	51029	03238	16
44	51029	03238	51043	03239	51056	03240	51070	03241	51084	03242	51098	03243	15
45	51098	03243	51112	03244	51126	03245	51139	03246	51153	03247	51167	03248	14
46	51167	03248	51181	03249	51194	03250	51208	03251	51222	03253	51236	03254	13
47	51236	03254	51250	03255	51263	03256	51277	03257	51291	03258	51305	03259	12
48	51305	03259	51318	03260	51332	03261	51346	03262	51360	03263	51373	03264	11
49	51373	03264	51387	03265	51401	03266	51415	03267	51428	03268	51442	03269	10
50	51442	03269	51456	03270	51470	03271	51483	03272	51497	03273	51511	03274	09
51	51511	03274	51525	03275	51538	03276	51552	03277	51566	03278	51580	03279	08
52	51580	03279	51593	03280	51607	03281	51621	03283	51634	03284	51648	03285	07
53	51648	03285	51662	03286	51676	03287	51689	03288	51703	03289	51717	03290	06
54	51717	03290	51730	03291	51744	03292	51758	03293	51771	03294	51785	03295	05
55	51785	03295	51799	03296	51813	03297	51826	03298	51840	03299	51854	03300	04
56	51854	03300	51867	03301	51881	03302	51895	03303	51908	03304	51922	03305	03
57	51922	03305	51935	03306	51949	03307	51963	03308	51977	03310	51990	03311	02
58	51990	03311	52004	03312	52017	03313	52031	03314	52045	03315	52058	03316	01
59	52058	03316	52072	03317	52086	03318	52099	03319	52113	03320	52127	03321	00
			.8		.6		.4		.2		.0	

PARTS for 0′.1: LOGS 7   NATURALS negligible

339°

21° HAVERSINES

′	.0 Log. 2.or(8.)	.0 Nat. 0.	.2 Log. 2.or(8.)	.2 Nat. 0.	.4 Log. 2.or(8.)	.4 Nat. 0.	.6 Log. 2.or(8.)	.6 Nat. 0.	.8 Log. 2.or(8.)	.8 Nat. 0.	′
00	52127	03321	52140	03322	52154	03323	52168	03324	52181	03325	59
01	52195	03326	52208	03327	52222	03328	52236	03329	52249	03330	58
02	52263	03331	52276	03332	52290	03334	52304	03335	52317	03336	57
03	52331	03337	52344	03338	52358	03339	52372	03340	52385	03341	56
04	52399	03342	52412	03343	52426	03344	52440	03345	52453	03346	55
05	52467	03347	52480	03348	52494	03349	52507	03350	52521	03351	54
06	52535	03352	52548	03353	52562	03354	52575	03355	52589	03357	53
07	52602	03358	52616	03359	52630	03360	52643	03361	52657	03362	52
08	52670	03363	52684	03364	52697	03365	52711	03366	52724	03367	51
09	52738	03368	52751	03369	52765	03370	52778	03371	52792	03372	50
10	52805	03373	52819	03374	52832	03375	52846	03376	52859	03378	49
11	52873	03379	52887	03380	52900	03381	52914	03382	52927	03383	48
12	52941	03384	52954	03385	52968	03386	52981	03387	52995	03388	47
13	53008	03389	53021	03390	53035	03391	53048	03392	53062	03393	46
14	53075	03394	53089	03395	53102	03396	53116	03398	53129	03399	45
15	53143	03400	53156	03401	53170	03402	53183	03403	53197	03404	44
16	53210	03405	53224	03406	53237	03407	53251	03408	53264	03409	43
17	53277	03410	53291	03411	53304	03412	53318	03413	53331	03414	42
18	53345	03415	53358	03417	53371	03418	53385	03419	53398	03420	41
19	53412	03421	53425	03422	53439	03423	53452	03424	53466	03425	40
20	53479	03426	53492	03427	53506	03428	53519	03429	53533	03430	39
21	53546	03431	53559	03432	53573	03433	53586	03434	53600	03436	38
22	53613	03437	53626	03438	53640	03439	53653	03440	53666	03441	37
23	53680	03442	53693	03443	53707	03444	53720	03445	53733	03446	36
24	53747	03447	53760	03448	53774	03449	53787	03450	53800	03451	35
25	53814	03453	53827	03454	53840	03455	53854	03456	53867	03457	34
26	53880	03458	53894	03459	53907	03460	53920	03461	53934	03462	33
27	53947	03463	53961	03464	53974	03465	53987	03466	54000	03467	32
28	54014	03468	54027	03470	54040	03471	54054	03472	54067	03473	31
29	54080	03474	54094	03475	54107	03476	54120	03477	54134	03478	30
30	54147	03479	54160	03480	54174	03481	54187	03482	54200	03483	29
31	54213	03484	54227	03486	54240	03487	54253	03488	54267	03489	28
32	54280	03490	54293	03491	54307	03492	54320	03493	54333	03494	27
33	54346	03495	54360	03496	54373	03497	54386	03498	54400	03499	26
34	54413	03500	54426	03502	54439	03503	54453	03504	54466	03505	25
35	54479	03506	54492	03507	54505	03508	54519	03509	54532	03510	24
36	54545	03511	54558	03512	54572	03513	54585	03514	54598	03515	23
37	54611	03517	54625	03518	54638	03519	54651	03520	54664	03521	22
38	54678	03522	54691	03523	54704	03524	54717	03525	54730	03526	21
39	54744	03527	54757	03528	54770	03529	54783	03530	54797	03532	20
40	54810	03533	54823	03534	54836	03535	54849	03536	54863	03537	19
41	54876	03538	54889	03539	54902	03540	54915	03541	54928	03542	18
42	54942	03543	54955	03544	54968	03546	54981	03547	54994	03548	17
43	55008	03549	55021	03550	55034	03551	55047	03552	55060	03553	16
44	55073	03554	55087	03555	55100	03556	55113	03557	55126	03558	15
45	55139	03560	55152	03561	55166	03562	55179	03563	55192	03564	14
46	55205	03565	55218	03566	55231	03567	55244	03568	55257	03569	13
47	55271	03570	55284	03571	55297	03572	55310	03574	55323	03575	12
48	55336	03576	55349	03577	55362	03578	55378	03579	55389	03580	11
49	55402	03581	55415	03582	55428	03583	55441	03584	55454	03585	10
50	55467	03587	55480	03588	55494	03589	55507	03590	55520	03591	09
51	55533	03592	55546	03593	55559	03594	55572	03595	55585	03596	08
52	55598	03597	55611	03598	55624	03600	55637	03601	55651	03602	07
53	55664	03603	55677	03604	55690	03605	55703	03606	55716	03607	06
54	55729	03608	55742	03609	55755	03610	55768	03611	55781	03613	05
55	55794	03614	55807	03615	55820	03616	55833	03617	55846	03618	04
56	55859	03619	55872	03620	55885	03621	55899	03622	55912	03623	03
57	55925	03624	55938	03626	55951	03627	55964	03628	55977	03629	02
58	55990	03630	56003	03631	56016	03632	56029	03633	56042	03634	01
59	56055	03635	56068	03636	56081	03638	56094	03639	56107	03640	00

| | .8 | | .6 | | .4 | | .2 | | .0 | |

PARTS for 0'.1:   LOGS 7   NATURALS negligible

338°

22°   HAVERSINES

′	.0 Log.	.0 Nat.	.2 Log.	.2 Nat.	.4 Log.	.4 Nat.	.6 Log.	.6 Nat.	.8 Log.	.8 Nat.	Log.	Nat.	′
	$\overline{2}$.or(8.)	0.	$\overline{2}$.or(8.)	0.	$\overline{2}$.or(8.)	0.	$\overline{2}$.or(8.)	0.	$\overline{2}$.or(8.)	0.	$\overline{2}$.or(8.)	0.	
00	56120	03641	56133	03642	56146	03643	56159	03644	56172	03645	56185	03646	59
01	56185	03646	56198	03647	56211	03648	56224	03650	56237	03651	56250	03652	58
02	56250	03652	56263	03653	56276	03654	56289	03655	56302	03656	56315	03657	57
03	56315	03657	56328	03658	56341	03659	56353	03660	56366	03662	56379	03663	56
04	56379	03663	56392	03664	56405	03665	56418	03666	56431	03667	56444	03668	55
05	56444	03668	56457	03669	56470	03670	56483	03671	56496	03672	56509	03674	54
06	56509	03674	56522	03675	56535	03676	56548	03677	56560	03678	56573	03679	53
07	56573	03679	56586	03680	56599	03681	56612	03682	56625	03683	56638	03685	52
08	56638	03685	56651	03686	56664	03687	56677	03688	56690	03689	56703	03690	51
09	56703	03690	56716	03691	56728	03692	56741	03693	56754	03694	56767	03695	50
10	56767	03695	56780	03697	56793	03698	56806	03699	56819	03700	56832	03701	49
11	56832	03701	56844	03702	56857	03703	56870	03704	56883	03705	56896	03706	48
12	56896	03706	56909	03708	56922	03709	56935	03710	56948	03711	56960	03712	47
13	56960	03712	56973	03713	56986	03714	56999	03715	57012	03716	57025	03717	46
14	57025	03717	57038	03719	57050	03720	57063	03721	57076	03722	57089	03723	45
15	57089	03723	57102	03724	57115	03725	57128	03726	57140	03727	57153	03728	44
16	57153	03728	57166	03730	57179	03731	57192	03732	57205	03733	57217	03734	43
17	57217	03734	57230	03735	57243	03736	57256	03737	57269	03738	57282	03740	42
18	57282	03740	57294	03741	57307	03742	57320	03743	57333	03744	57346	03745	41
19	57346	03745	57358	03746	57371	03747	57384	03748	57397	03749	57410	03751	40
20	57410	03751	57422	03752	57435	03753	57448	03754	57461	03755	57474	03756	39
21	57474	03756	57486	03757	57499	03758	57512	03759	57525	03761	57538	03762	38
22	57538	03762	57550	03763	57563	03764	57576	03765	57589	03766	57601	03767	37
23	57601	03767	57614	03768	57627	03769	57640	03770	57652	03772	57665	03773	36
24	57665	03773	57678	03774	57691	03775	57703	03776	57716	03777	57729	03778	35
25	57729	03778	57742	03779	57755	03780	57767	03782	57780	03783	57793	03784	34
26	57793	03784	57806	03785	57818	03786	57831	03787	57844	03788	57856	03789	33
27	57856	03789	57869	03790	57882	03792	57895	03793	57907	03794	57920	03795	32
28	57920	03795	57933	03796	57945	03797	57958	03798	57971	03799	57984	03800	31
29	57984	03800	57996	03802	58009	03803	58022	03804	58034	03805	58047	03806	30
30	58047	03806	58060	03807	58073	03808	58085	03809	58098	03810	58111	03812	29
31	58111	03812	58123	03813	58136	03814	58149	03815	58161	03816	58174	03817	28
32	58174	03817	58187	03818	58199	03819	58212	03821	58225	03822	58237	03823	27
33	58237	03823	58250	03824	58263	03825	58275	03826	58288	03827	58301	03828	26
34	58301	03828	58313	03829	58326	03831	58339	03832	58351	03833	58364	03834	25
35	58364	03834	58377	03835	58389	03836	58402	03837	58415	03838	58427	03839	24
36	58427	03839	58440	03841	58453	03842	58465	03843	58478	03844	58491	03845	23
37	58491	03845	58503	03846	58516	03847	58528	03848	58541	03850	58554	03851	22
38	58554	03851	58566	03852	58579	03853	58592	03854	58604	03855	58617	03856	21
39	58617	03856	58629	03857	58642	03859	58655	03860	58667	03861	58680	03862	20
40	58680	03862	58692	03863	58705	03864	58718	03865	58730	03866	58743	03867	19
41	58743	03867	58755	03869	58768	03870	58780	03871	58793	03872	58806	03873	18
42	58806	03873	58818	03874	58831	03875	58844	03876	58856	03878	58869	03879	17
43	58869	03879	58881	03880	58894	03881	58906	03882	58919	03883	58932	03884	16
44	58932	03884	58944	03885	58957	03887	58969	03888	58982	03889	58994	03890	15
45	58994	03890	59007	03891	59020	03892	59032	03893	59045	03894	59057	03896	14
46	59057	03896	59070	03897	59082	03898	59095	03899	59107	03900	59120	03901	13
47	59120	03901	59133	03902	59145	03903	59158	03905	59170	03906	59183	03907	12
48	59183	03907	59195	03908	59208	03909	59220	03910	59233	03911	59245	03912	11
49	59245	03912	59258	03914	59270	03915	59283	03916	59295	03917	59308	03918	10
50	59308	03918	59320	03919	59333	03920	59345	03921	59358	03923	59370	03924	09
51	59370	03924	59383	03925	59395	03926	59408	03927	59420	03928	59433	03929	08
52	59433	03929	59445	03931	59458	03932	59470	03933	59483	03934	59495	03935	07
53	59495	03935	59508	03936	59520	03937	59533	03938	59545	03940	59558	03941	06
54	59558	03941	59570	03942	59583	03943	59595	03944	59608	03945	59620	03946	05
55	59620	03946	59632	03948	59645	03949	59657	03950	59670	03951	59682	03952	04
56	59682	03952	59695	03953	59707	03954	59720	03955	59732	03957	59745	03958	03
57	59745	03958	59757	03959	59769	03960	59782	03961	59794	03962	59807	03963	02
58	59807	03963	59819	03965	59832	03966	59844	03967	59857	03968	59869	03969	01
59	59869	03969	59881	03970	59894	03971	59906	03972	59919	03974	59931	03975	00

	.8		.6		.4		.2		.0	

337°

PARTS for 0′.1:   LOGS 6:   NATURALS 0 or 1 (by inspection)

23° HAVERSINES

′	.0 Log.	.0 Nat.	.2 Log.	.2 Nat.	.4 Log.	.4 Nat.	.6 Log.	.6 Nat.	.8 Log.	.8 Nat.	′
	2.or(8.)	0.	2.or(8.)	0.	2.or(8.)	0.	2.or(8.)	0.	2.or(8.)	0.	
00	59931	03975	59943	03976	59956	03977	59968	03978	59981	03979	59993	03980	59
01	59993	03980	60006	03982	60018	03983	60030	03984	60043	03985	60055	03986	58
02	60055	03986	60068	03987	60080	03988	60092	03990	60105	03991	60117	03992	57
03	60117	03992	60130	03993	60142	03994	60154	03995	60166	03996	60179	03998	56
04	60179	03998	60191	03999	60204	04000	60216	04001	60229	04002	60241	04003	55
05	60241	04003	60253	04004	60266	04006	60278	04007	60290	04008	60303	04009	54
06	60303	04009	60315	04010	60328	04011	60340	04012	60352	04014	60365	04015	53
07	60365	04015	60377	04016	60389	04017	60402	04018	60414	04019	60426	04020	52
08	60426	04020	60439	04021	60451	04023	60463	04024	60476	04025	60488	04026	51
09	60488	04026	60500	04027	60513	04028	60525	04030	60537	04031	60550	04032	50
10	60550	04032	60562	04033	60574	04034	60587	04035	60599	04036	60611	04038	49
11	60611	04038	60624	04039	60636	04040	60648	04041	60661	04042	60673	04043	48
12	60673	04043	60685	04044	60697	04046	60710	04047	60722	04048	60734	04049	47
13	60734	04049	60747	04050	60759	04051	60771	04052	60784	04054	60796	04055	46
14	60796	04055	60808	04056	60820	04057	60833	04058	60845	04059	60857	04060	45
15	60857	04060	60870	04062	60882	04063	60894	04064	60906	04065	60919	04066	44
16	60919	04066	60931	04067	60943	04069	60955	04070	60968	04071	60980	04072	43
17	60980	04072	60992	04073	61005	04074	61017	04075	61029	04077	61041	04078	42
18	61041	04078	61054	04079	61066	04080	61078	04081	61090	04082	61103	04083	41
19	61103	04083	61115	04085	61127	04086	61139	04087	61152	04088	61164	04089	40
20	61164	04089	61176	04090	61188	04092	61201	04093	61213	04094	61225	04095	39
21	61225	04095	61237	04096	61249	04097	61262	04098	61274	04100	61286	04101	38
22	61286	04101	61298	04102	61310	04103	61323	04104	61335	04105	61347	04106	37
23	61347	04106	61359	04108	61372	04109	61384	04110	61396	04111	61408	04112	36
24	61408	04112	61420	04113	61433	04115	61445	04116	61457	04117	61469	04118	35
25	61469	04118	61481	04119	61494	04120	61506	04122	61518	04123	61530	04124	34
26	61530	04124	61542	04125	61554	04126	61567	04127	61579	04128	61591	04130	33
27	61591	04130	61603	04131	61615	04132	61627	04133	61640	04134	61652	04135	32
28	61652	04135	61664	04137	61676	04138	61688	04139	61700	04140	61713	04141	31
29	61713	04141	61725	04142	61737	04144	61749	04145	61761	04146	61773	04147	30
30	61773	04147	61786	04148	61798	04149	61810	04150	61822	04152	61834	04153	29
31	61834	04153	61846	04154	61858	04155	61870	04156	61883	04157	61895	04159	28
32	61895	04159	61907	04160	61919	04161	61931	04162	61943	04163	61955	04164	27
33	61955	04164	61968	04166	61980	04167	61992	04168	62004	04169	62016	04170	26
34	62016	04170	62028	04171	62040	04173	62052	04174	62064	04175	62076	04176	25
35	62076	04176	62089	04177	62101	04178	62113	04180	62125	04181	62137	04182	24
36	62137	04182	62149	04183	62161	04184	62173	04185	62185	04187	62197	04188	23
37	62197	04188	62209	04189	62222	04190	62234	04191	62246	04192	62258	04194	22
38	62258	04194	62270	04195	62282	04196	62294	04197	62306	04198	62318	04199	21
39	62318	04199	62330	04201	62342	04202	62354	04203	62367	04204	62379	04205	20
40	62379	04205	62391	04206	62403	04208	62415	04209	62427	04210	62439	04211	19
41	62439	04211	62451	04212	62463	04213	62475	04215	62487	04216	62499	04217	18
42	62499	04217	62511	04218	62523	04219	62535	04220	62547	04222	62559	04223	17
43	62559	04223	62571	04224	62583	04225	62595	04226	62607	04227	62619	04229	16
44	62619	04229	62631	04230	62643	04231	62655	04232	62667	04233	62679	04234	15
45	62679	04234	62691	04236	62703	04237	62716	04238	62728	04239	62740	04240	14
46	62740	04240	62752	04241	62764	04243	62776	04244	62788	04245	62800	04246	13
47	62800	04246	62812	04247	62824	04248	62835	04250	62847	04251	62859	04252	12
48	62859	04252	62871	04253	62883	04254	62895	04256	62907	04257	62919	04258	11
49	62919	04258	62931	04259	62943	04260	62955	04261	62967	04263	62979	04264	10
50	62979	04264	62991	04265	63003	04266	63015	04267	63027	04268	63039	04270	09
51	63039	04270	63051	04271	63063	04272	63075	04273	63087	04274	63099	04276	08
52	63099	04276	63111	04277	63123	04278	63135	04279	63147	04280	63159	04281	07
53	63159	04281	63171	04283	63183	04284	63194	04285	63206	04286	63218	04287	06
54	63218	04287	63230	04288	63242	04290	63254	04291	63266	04292	63278	04293	05
55	63278	04293	63290	04294	63302	04296	63314	04297	63326	04298	63338	04299	04
56	63338	04299	63350	04300	63362	04301	63373	04303	63385	04304	63397	04305	03
57	63397	04305	63409	04306	63421	04307	63433	04309	63445	04310	63457	04311	02
58	63457	04311	63469	04312	63481	04313	63493	04314	63504	04316	63516	04317	01
59	63516	04317	63528	04318	63540	04319	63552	04320	63564	04322	63576	04323	00
			.8		.6		.4		.2		.0		

PARTS for 0′.1: LOGS 6 NATURALS 0 or 1 (by inspection)

336°

24° HAVERSINES

′	.0 Log.	.0 Nat.	.2 Log.	.2 Nat.	.4 Log.	.4 Nat.	.6 Log.	.6 Nat.	.8 Log.	.8 Nat.	′
	2.or(8.)	0.	2.or(8.)	0.	2.or(8.)	0.	2.or(8.)	0.	2.or(8.)	0.	
00	63576	04323	63588	04324	63600	04325	63611	04326	63623	04327	63635 04329	59
01	63635	04329	63647	04330	63659	04331	63671	04332	63683	04333	63695 04335	58
02	63695	04335	63706	04336	63718	04337	63730	04338	63742	04339	63754 04340	57
03	63754	04340	63766	04342	63778	04343	63789	04344	63801	04345	63813 04346	56
04	63813	04346	63825	04348	63837	04349	63849	04350	63861	04351	63872 04352	55
05	63872	04352	63884	04354	63895	04355	63908	04356	63920	04357	63932 04358	54
06	63932	04358	63943	04359	63955	04361	63967	04362	63979	04363	63991 04364	53
07	63991	04364	64003	04365	64014	04367	64026	04368	64038	04369	64050 04370	52
08	64050	04370	64062	04371	64073	04373	64085	04374	64097	04375	64109 04376	51
09	64109	04376	64121	04377	64133	04379	64144	04380	64156	04381	64168 04382	50
10	64168	04382	64180	04383	64192	04384	64203	04386	64215	04387	64227 04388	49
11	64227	04388	64239	04389	64251	04390	64262	04392	64274	04393	64286 04394	48
12	64286	04394	64298	04395	64310	04396	64321	04398	64333	04399	64345 04400	47
13	64345	04400	64357	04401	64368	04402	64380	04404	64392	04405	64404 04406	46
14	64404	04406	64416	04407	64427	04408	64439	04410	64451	04411	64463 04412	45
15	64463	04412	64474	04413	64486	04414	64498	04415	64510	04417	64521 04418	44
16	64521	04418	64533	04419	64545	04420	64557	04421	64568	04423	64580 04424	43
17	64580	04424	64592	04425	64604	04426	64615	04427	64627	04429	64639 04430	42
18	64639	04430	64651	04431	64662	04432	64674	04433	64686	04435	64697 04436	41
19	64697	04436	64709	04437	64721	04438	64733	04439	64744	04441	64756 04442	40
20	64756	04442	64768	04443	64779	04444	64791	04445	64803	04447	64815 04448	39
21	64815	04448	64826	04449	64838	04450	64850	04451	64861	04453	64873 04454	38
22	64873	04454	64885	04455	64897	04456	64908	04457	64920	04459	64932 04460	37
23	64932	04460	64943	04461	64955	04462	64967	04463	64978	04465	64990 04466	36
24	64990	04466	65002	04467	65013	04468	65025	04469	65037	04471	65049 04472	35
25	65049	04472	65060	04473	65072	04474	65084	04475	65095	04477	65107 04478	34
26	65107	04478	65118	04479	65130	04480	65142	04481	65154	04483	65165 04484	33
27	65165	04484	65177	04485	65188	04486	65200	04487	65212	04489	65223 04490	32
28	65223	04490	65235	04491	65247	04492	65258	04494	65270	04495	65282 04496	31
29	65282	04496	65293	04497	65305	04498	65317	04500	65328	04501	65340 04502	30
30	65340	04502	65352	04503	65363	04504	65375	04506	65387	04507	65398 04508	29
31	65398	04508	65410	04509	65421	04510	65433	04512	65445	04513	65456 04514	28
32	65456	04514	65468	04515	65479	04516	65491	04518	65503	04519	65514 04520	27
33	65514	04520	65526	04521	65538	04522	65549	04524	65561	04525	65572 04526	26
34	65572	04526	65584	04527	65596	04529	65607	04530	65619	04531	65630 04532	25
35	65630	04532	65642	04533	65654	04535	65665	04536	65677	04537	65688 04538	24
36	65688	04538	65700	04539	65712	04541	65723	04542	65735	04543	65746 04544	23
37	65746	04544	65758	04545	65769	04547	65781	04548	65793	04549	65804 04550	22
38	65804	04550	65816	04552	65827	04553	65839	04554	65850	04555	65862 04556	21
39	65862	04556	65874	04558	65885	04559	65897	04560	65908	04561	65920 04562	20
40	65920	04562	65931	04564	65943	04565	65954	04566	65966	04567	65978 04569	19
41	65978	04569	65989	04570	66001	04571	66012	04572	66024	04573	66035 04575	18
42	66035	04575	66047	04576	66058	04577	66070	04578	66081	04579	66093 04581	17
43	66093	04581	66105	04582	66116	04583	66128	04584	66139	04586	66151 04587	16
44	66151	04587	66162	04588	66174	04589	66185	04590	66197	04592	66208 04593	15
45	66208	04593	66220	04594	66231	04595	66243	04597	66254	04598	66266 04599	14
46	66266	04599	66277	04600	66289	04601	66300	04603	66312	04604	66323 04605	13
47	66323	04605	66335	04606	66346	04607	66358	04609	66369	04610	66381 04611	12
48	66381	04611	66392	04612	66404	04614	66415	04615	66427	04616	66438 04617	11
49	66438	04617	66450	04618	66461	04620	66473	04621	66484	04622	66496 04623	10
50	66496	04623	66507	04625	66518	04626	66530	04627	66541	04628	66553 04629	09
51	66553	04629	66564	04631	66576	04632	66587	04633	66599	04634	66610 04636	08
52	66610	04636	66622	04637	66633	04638	66645	04639	66656	04640	66667 04642	07
53	66667	04642	66679	04643	66690	04644	66702	04645	66713	04647	66725 04648	06
54	66725	04648	66736	04649	66748	04650	66759	04651	66771	04653	66782 04654	05
55	66782	04654	66793	04655	66805	04656	66816	04658	66828	04659	66839 04660	04
56	66839	04660	66850	04661	66862	04663	66873	04664	66885	04665	66896 04666	03
57	66896	04666	66908	04667	66919	04669	66931	04670	66942	04671	66953 04672	02
58	66953	04672	66965	04674	66976	04675	66988	04676	66999	04677	67010 04678	01
59	67010	04678	67022	04680	67033	04681	67045	04682	67056	04683	67067 04685	00
	.8		.6		.4		.2		.0		

PARTS for 0′.1:   LOGS 6   NATURALS 0 or 1 (by inspection)

25° HAVERSINES

′	.0 Log.	.0 Nat.	.2 Log.	.2 Nat.	.4 Log.	.4 Nat.	.6 Log.	.6 Nat.	.8 Log.	.8 Nat.	′
	2̄.or(8.)	0.	2̄.or(8.)	0.	2̄.or(8.)	0.	2̄.or(8.)	0.	2̄.or(8.)	0.	2̄.or(8.) 0.	
00	67067	04685	67079	04686	67090	04687	67102	04688	67113	04690	67124 04691	59
01	67124	04691	67136	04692	67147	04693	67158	04694	67170	04696	67181 04697	58
02	67181	04697	67193	04698	67204	04699	67215	04701	67227	04702	67238 04703	57
03	67238	04703	67250	04704	67261	04706	67272	04707	67284	04708	67295 04709	56
04	67295	04709	67306	04710	67318	04712	67329	04713	67340	04714	67352 04715	55
05	67352	04715	67363	04717	67375	04718	67386	04719	67397	04720	67409 04722	54
06	67409	04722	67420	04723	67431	04724	67443	04725	67454	04727	67465 04728	53
07	67465	04728	67477	04729	67488	04730	67499	04731	67511	04733	67522 04734	52
08	67522	04734	67533	04735	67545	04736	67556	04738	67567	04739	67579 04740	51
09	67579	04740	67590	04741	67601	04743	67613	04744	67624	04745	67635 04746	50
10	67635	04746	67647	04747	67658	04749	67669	04750	67680	04751	67692 04752	49
11	67692	04752	67703	04754	67714	04755	67726	04756	67737	04757	67748 04759	48
12	67748	04759	67760	04760	67771	04761	67782	04762	67794	04764	67805 04765	47
13	67805	04765	67816	04766	67827	04767	67839	04769	67850	04770	67861 04771	46
14	67861	04771	67873	04772	67884	04774	67895	04775	67907	04776	67918 04777	45
15	67918	04777	67929	04778	67940	04780	67952	04781	67963	04782	67974 04783	44
16	67974	04783	67985	04785	67997	04786	68008	04787	68019	04788	68030 04790	43
17	68030	04790	68042	04791	68053	04792	68064	04793	68076	04795	68087 04796	42
18	68087	04796	68098	04797	68109	04798	68121	04800	68132	04801	68143 04802	41
19	68143	04802	68154	04803	68165	04805	68177	04806	68188	04807	68199 04808	40
20	68199	04808	68210	04810	68222	04811	68233	04812	68244	04813	68255 04815	39
21	68255	04815	68267	04816	68278	04817	68289	04818	68300	04820	68312 04821	38
22	68312	04821	68323	04822	68334	04823	68345	04825	68357	04826	68368 04827	37
23	68368	04827	68379	04828	68390	04830	68401	04831	68413	04832	68424 04833	36
24	68424	04833	68435	04835	68446	04836	68457	04837	68469	04838	68480 04840	35
25	68480	04840	68491	04841	68502	04842	68513	04843	68525	04844	68536 04846	34
26	68536	04846	68547	04847	68558	04848	68569	04849	68581	04851	68592 04852	33
27	68592	04852	68603	04853	68614	04854	68625	04856	68637	04857	68648 04858	32
28	68648	04858	68659	04859	68670	04861	68681	04862	68692	04863	68704 04864	31
29	68704	04864	68715	04866	68726	04867	68737	04868	68748	04870	68759 04871	30
30	68759	04871	68771	04872	68782	04873	68793	04875	68804	04876	68815 04877	29
31	68815	04877	68826	04878	68838	04880	68849	04881	68860	04882	68871 04883	28
32	68871	04883	68882	04885	68893	04886	68904	04887	68916	04888	68927 04890	27
33	68927	04890	68938	04891	68949	04892	68960	04893	68971	04895	68982 04896	26
34	68982	04896	68994	04897	69005	04898	69016	04900	69027	04901	69038 04902	25
35	69038	04902	69049	04903	69060	04905	69072	04906	69083	04907	69094 04908	24
36	69094	04908	69105	04910	69116	04911	69127	04912	69138	04913	69149 04915	23
37	69149	04915	69160	04916	69172	04917	69183	04918	69194	04920	69205 04921	22
38	69205	04921	69216	04922	69227	04923	69238	04925	69249	04926	69260 04927	21
39	69260	04927	69271	04929	69283	04930	69294	04931	69305	04932	69316 04934	20
40	69316	04934	69327	04935	69338	04936	69349	04937	69360	04939	69371 04940	19
41	69371	04940	69382	04941	69394	04942	69405	04944	69416	04945	69427 04946	18
42	69427	04946	69438	04947	69449	04949	69460	04950	69471	04951	69482 04952	17
43	69482	04952	69493	04954	69504	04955	69515	04956	69526	04957	69537 04959	16
44	69537	04959	69548	04960	69559	04961	69571	04963	69582	04964	69593 04965	15
45	69593	04965	69604	04966	69615	04968	69626	04969	69637	04970	69648 04971	14
46	69648	04971	69659	04973	69670	04974	69681	04975	69692	04976	69703 04978	13
47	69703	04978	69714	04979	69725	04980	69736	04982	69747	04983	69758 04984	12
48	69758	04984	69769	04985	69780	04987	69791	04988	69802	04989	69813 04990	11
49	69813	04990	69824	04992	69835	04993	69847	04994	69858	04995	69869 04997	10
50	69869	04997	69880	04998	69891	04999	69902	05001	69913	05002	69924 05003	09
51	69924	05003	69935	05004	69946	05006	69957	05007	69968	05008	69979 05009	08
52	69979	05009	69990	05011	70001	05012	70012	05013	70023	05014	70034 05016	07
53	70034	05016	70045	05017	70056	05018	70067	05020	70078	05021	70089 05022	06
54	70089	05022	70100	05023	70111	05025	70122	05026	70133	05027	70144 05028	05
55	70144	05028	70155	05030	70166	05031	70176	05032	70187	05034	70198 05035	04
56	70198	05035	70209	05036	70220	05037	70231	05039	70242	05040	70253 05041	03
57	70253	05041	70264	05042	70275	05044	70286	05045	70297	05046	70308 05048	02
58	70308	05048	70319	05049	70330	05050	70341	05051	70352	05053	70363 05054	01
59	70363	05054	70374	05055	70385	05056	70396	05058	70407	05059	70418 05060	00
	.8		.6		.4		.2		.0 ←			

PARTS for 0′.1: LOGS 6   NATURALS 1   **334°**

26° HAVERSINES

′	.0 Log.	.0 Nat.	.2 Log.	.2 Nat.	.4 Log.	.4 Nat.	.6 Log.	.6 Nat.	.8 Log.	.8 Nat.	.0 Log.	.0 Nat.	′
	2.or(8.)	0.	2.or(8.)	0.	2.or(8.)	0.	2.or(8.)	0.	2.or(8.)	0.	2.or(8.)	0.	
00	70418	05060	70429	05062	70440	05063	70450	05064	70461	05065	70472	05067	59
01	70472	05067	70483	05068	70494	05069	70505	05071	70516	05072	70527	05073	58
02	70527	05073	70538	05074	70549	05076	70560	05077	70571	05078	70582	05079	57
03	70582	05079	70593	05081	70603	05082	70614	05083	70625	05085	70636	05086	56
04	70636	05086	70647	05087	70658	05088	70669	05090	70680	05091	70691	05092	55
05	70691	05092	70702	05093	70713	05095	70723	05096	70734	05097	70745	05099	54
06	70745	05099	70756	05100	70767	05101	70778	05102	70789	05104	70800	05105	53
07	70800	05105	70811	05106	70822	05108	70832	05109	70843	05110	70854	05111	52
08	70854	05111	70865	05113	70876	05114	70887	05115	70898	05117	70909	05118	51
09	70909	05118	70919	05119	70930	05120	70941	05122	70952	05123	70963	05124	50
10	70963	05124	70974	05126	70985	05127	70996	05128	71007	05129	71017	05131	49
11	71017	05131	71028	05132	71039	05133	71050	05135	71061	05136	71072	05137	48
12	71072	05137	71082	05138	71093	05140	71104	05141	71115	05142	71126	05144	47
13	71126	05144	71137	05145	71148	05146	71159	05147	71169	05149	71180	05150	46
14	71180	05150	71191	05151	71202	05153	71213	05154	71224	05155	71234	05156	45
15	71234	05156	71245	05158	71256	05159	71267	05160	71278	05162	71289	05163	44
16	71289	05163	71299	05164	71310	05165	71321	05167	71332	05168	71343	05169	43
17	71343	05169	71353	05171	71364	05172	71375	05173	71386	05174	71397	05176	42
18	71397	05176	71408	05177	71418	05178	71429	05180	71440	05181	71451	05182	41
19	71451	05182	71462	05183	71472	05185	71483	05186	71494	05187	71505	05189	40
20	71505	05189	71516	05190	71526	05191	71537	05192	71548	05194	71559	05195	39
21	71559	05195	71570	05196	71580	05198	71591	05199	71602	05200	71613	05201	38
22	71613	05201	71624	05203	71634	05204	71645	05205	71656	05207	71667	05208	37
23	71667	05208	71677	05209	71688	05211	71699	05212	71710	05213	71721	05214	36
24	71721	05214	71731	05216	71742	05217	71753	05218	71764	05220	71774	05221	35
25	71774	05221	71785	05222	71796	05223	71807	05225	71817	05226	71828	05227	34
26	71828	05227	71839	05229	71850	05230	71860	05231	71871	05233	71882	05234	33
27	71882	05234	71893	05235	71903	05236	71914	05238	71925	05239	71936	05240	32
28	71936	05240	71946	05242	71957	05243	71968	05244	71979	05246	71989	05247	31
29	71989	05247	72000	05248	72011	05249	72022	05251	72032	05252	72043	05253	30
30	72043	05253	72054	05255	72065	05256	72075	05257	72086	05258	72097	05260	29
31	72097	05260	72108	05261	72118	05262	72129	05264	72140	05265	72150	05266	28
32	72150	05266	72161	05268	72172	05269	72182	05270	72193	05271	72204	05273	27
33	72204	05273	72215	05274	72225	05275	72236	05277	72247	05278	72257	05279	26
34	72257	05279	72268	05281	72279	05282	72289	05283	72300	05284	72311	05286	25
35	72311	05286	72322	05287	72332	05288	72343	05290	72354	05291	72364	05292	24
36	72364	05292	72375	05294	72386	05295	72396	05296	72407	05298	72418	05299	23
37	72418	05299	72428	05300	72439	05301	72450	05303	72461	05304	72471	05305	22
38	72471	05305	72482	05307	72493	05308	72503	05309	72514	05311	72525	05312	21
39	72525	05312	72535	05313	72546	05314	72557	05316	72567	05317	72578	05318	20
40	72578	05318	72588	05320	72599	05321	72610	05322	72621	05324	72631	05325	19
41	72631	05325	72642	05326	72652	05328	72663	05329	72674	05330	72684	05331	18
42	72684	05331	72695	05333	72706	05334	72716	05335	72727	05337	72738	05338	17
43	72738	05338	72748	05339	72759	05341	72770	05342	72780	05343	72791	05345	16
44	72791	05345	72801	05346	72812	05347	72823	05348	72833	05350	72844	05351	15
45	72844	05351	72855	05352	72865	05354	72876	05355	72886	05356	72897	05358	14
46	72897	05358	72908	05359	72918	05360	72929	05362	72940	05363	72950	05364	13
47	72950	05364	72961	05365	72971	05367	72982	05368	72993	05369	73003	05371	12
48	73003	05371	73014	05372	73024	05373	73035	05375	73046	05376	73056	05377	11
49	73056	05377	73067	05379	73077	05380	73088	05381	73099	05383	73109	05384	10
50	73109	05384	73120	05385	73130	05386	73141	05388	73151	05389	73162	05390	09
51	73162	05390	73173	05392	73183	05393	73194	05394	73204	05396	73215	05397	08
52	73215	05397	73226	05398	73236	05400	73247	05401	73257	05402	73268	05404	07
53	73268	05404	73278	05405	73289	05406	73300	05407	73310	05409	73321	05410	06
54	73321	05410	73331	05411	73342	05413	73352	05414	73363	05415	73374	05417	05
55	73374	05417	73384	05418	73395	05419	73405	05421	73416	05422	73426	05423	04
56	73426	05423	73437	05425	73447	05426	73458	05427	73468	05429	73479	05430	03
57	73479	05430	73490	05431	73500	05433	73511	05434	73521	05435	73532	05436	02
58	73532	05436	73542	05438	73553	05439	73563	05440	73574	05442	73584	05443	01
59	73584	05443	73595	05444	73605	05446	73616	05447	73626	05448	73637	05450	00
	.8		.6		.4		.2		.0				

PARTS for 0′.1: LOGS 5 NATURALS 1.

333°

HAVERSINES

′	.0 Log. $\overline{2}$.or(8.)	.0 Nat. 0.	.2 Log. $\overline{2}$.or(8.)	.2 Nat. 0.	.4 Log. $\overline{2}$.or(8.)	.4 Nat. 0.	.6 Log. $\overline{2}$.or(8.)	.6 Nat. 0.	.8 Log. $\overline{2}$.or(8.)	.8 Nat. 0.	Log. $\overline{2}$.or(8.)	Nat. 0.	′
00	73637	05450	73648	05451	73658	05452	73669	05454	73679	05455	73690	05456	59
01	73690	05456	73700	05458	73711	05459	73721	05460	73732	05462	73742	05463	58
02	73742	05463	73753	05464	73763	05466	73774	05467	73784	05468	73795	05470	57
03	73795	05470	73805	05471	73816	05472	73826	05473	73837	05475	73847	05476	56
04	73847	05476	73858	05477	73868	05479	73879	05480	73889	05481	73900	05483	55
05	73900	05483	73910	05484	73921	05485	73931	05487	73942	05488	73952	05489	54
06	73952	05489	73963	05491	73973	05492	73984	05493	73994	05495	74005	05496	53
07	74005	05496	74015	05497	74026	05499	74036	05500	74047	05501	74057	05503	52
08	74057	05503	74067	05504	74078	05505	74088	05507	74099	05508	74109	05509	51
09	74109	05509	74120	05511	74130	05512	74141	05513	74151	05515	74162	05516	50
10	74162	05516	74172	05517	74182	05519	74193	05520	74203	05521	74214	05523	49
11	74214	05523	74224	05524	74235	05525	74245	05527	74256	05528	74266	05529	48
12	74266	05529	74276	05531	74287	05532	74297	05533	74308	05535	74318	05536	47
13	74318	05536	74329	05537	74339	05539	74350	05540	74360	05541	74370	05542	46
14	74370	05542	74381	05544	74391	05545	74402	05546	74412	05548	74423	05549	45
15	74423	05549	74433	05550	74443	05552	74454	05553	74464	05554	74475	05556	44
16	74475	05556	74485	05557	74495	05558	74506	05560	74516	05561	74527	05562	43
17	74527	05562	74537	05564	74548	05565	74558	05566	74568	05568	74579	05569	42
18	74579	05569	74589	05570	74600	05572	74610	05573	74620	05574	74631	05576	41
19	74631	05576	74641	05577	74652	05578	74662	05580	74672	05581	74683	05582	40
20	74683	05582	74693	05584	74704	05585	74714	05586	74724	05588	74735	05589	39
21	74735	05589	74745	05590	74756	05592	74766	05593	74776	05595	74787	05596	38
22	74787	05596	74797	05597	74807	05599	74818	05600	74828	05601	74838	05603	37
23	74838	05603	74849	05604	74859	05605	74870	05607	74880	05608	74890	05609	36
24	74890	05609	74901	05611	74911	05612	74921	05613	74932	05615	74942	05616	35
25	74942	05616	74953	05617	74963	05619	74973	05620	74984	05621	74994	05623	34
26	74994	05623	75004	05624	75015	05625	75025	05627	75035	05628	75046	05629	33
27	75046	05629	75056	05631	75066	05632	75077	05633	75087	05635	75097	05636	32
28	75097	05636	75108	05637	75118	05639	75128	05640	75139	05641	75149	05643	31
29	75149	05643	75159	05644	75170	05645	75180	05647	75190	05648	75201	05649	30
30	75201	05649	75211	05651	75221	05652	75232	05654	75242	05655	75252	05656	29
31	75252	05656	75263	05658	75273	05659	75283	05660	75293	05662	75304	05663	28
32	75304	05663	75314	05666	75324	05666	75335	05667	75345	05668	75355	05670	27
33	75355	05670	75366	05671	75376	05672	75386	05674	75397	05675	75407	05676	26
34	75407	05676	75417	05678	75428	05679	75438	05680	75448	05682	75458	05683	25
35	75458	05683	75469	05684	75479	05686	75489	05687	75500	05688	75510	05690	24
36	75510	05690	75520	05691	75530	05693	75541	05694	75551	05695	75561	05697	23
37	75561	05697	75571	05698	75582	05699	75592	05701	75602	05702	75613	05703	22
38	75613	05703	75623	05705	75633	05706	75643	05707	75654	05709	75664	05710	21
39	75664	05710	75674	05711	75685	05713	75695	05714	75705	05715	75715	05717	20
40	75715	05717	75726	05718	75736	05720	75746	05721	75756	05722	75767	05724	19
41	75767	05724	75777	05725	75787	05726	75797	05728	75808	05729	75818	05730	18
42	75818	05730	75828	05732	75838	05733	75849	05734	75859	05736	75869	05737	17
43	75869	05737	75879	05738	75890	05740	75900	05741	75910	05743	75920	05744	16
44	75920	05744	75930	05745	75941	05747	75951	05748	75961	05749	75971	05751	15
45	75971	05751	75982	05752	75992	05753	76002	05755	76012	05756	76023	05757	14
46	76023	05757	76033	05759	76043	05760	76053	05761	76063	05763	76074	05764	13
47	76074	05764	76084	05766	76094	05767	76104	05768	76115	05770	76125	05771	12
48	76125	05771	76135	05772	76145	05774	76155	05775	76166	05776	76176	05778	11
49	76176	05778	76186	05779	76196	05780	76206	05782	76217	05783	76227	05785	10
50	76227	05785	76237	05786	76247	05787	76257	05789	76268	05790	76278	05791	09
51	76278	05791	76288	05793	76298	05794	76308	05795	76318	05797	76329	05798	08
52	76329	05798	76339	05799	76349	05801	76359	05802	76369	05804	76380	05805	07
53	76380	05805	76390	05806	76400	05808	76410	05809	76420	05810	76430	05812	06
54	76430	05812	76441	05813	76451	05814	76461	05816	76471	05817	76481	05819	05
55	76481	05819	76491	05820	76502	05821	76512	05823	76522	05824	76532	05825	04
56	76532	05825	76542	05827	76552	05828	76563	05829	76573	05831	76583	05832	03
57	76583	05832	76593	05834	76603	05835	76613	05836	76623	05838	76634	05839	02
58	76634	05839	76644	05840	76654	05842	76664	05843	76674	05844	76684	05846	01
59	76684	05846	76695	05847	76705	05849	76715	05850	76725	05851	76735	05853	00

	.8		.6		.4		.2		.0		←

PARTS for 0′.1:   LOGS 5   NATURALS. 1

28° HAVERSINES

′	.0 Log. 2̄.or(8.)	.0 Nat. 0.	.2 Log. 2̄.or(8.)	.2 Nat. 0.	.4 Log. 2̄.or(8.)	.4 Nat. 0.	.6 Log. 2̄.or(8.)	.6 Nat. 0.	.8 Log. 2̄.or(8.)	.8 Nat. 0.	′
00	76735	05853	76745	05854	76755	05855	76765	05857	76775	05858	76786	05859	59
01	76786	05859	76796	05861	76806	05862	76816	05864	76826	05865	76836	05866	58
02	76836	05866	76847	05868	76857	05870	76867	05870	76877	05872	76887	05873	57
03	76887	05873	76897	05874	76907	05876	76917	05877	76927	05879	76937	05880	56
04	76937	05880	76948	05881	76958	05883	76968	05884	76978	05885	76988	05887	55
05	76988	05887	76998	05888	77008	05890	77018	05891	77028	05892	77038	05894	54
06	77038	05894	77049	05895	77059	05896	77069	05898	77079	05899	77089	05901	53
07	77089	05901	77099	05902	77109	05903	77119	05905	77129	05906	77139	05907	52
08	77139	05907	77149	05909	77160	05910	77170	05911	77180	05913	77190	05914	51
09	77190	05914	77200	05916	77210	05917	77220	05918	77230	05920	77240	05921	50
10	77240	05921	77250	05922	77260	05924	77270	05925	77280	05927	77290	05928	49
11	77290	05928	77300	05929	77311	05931	77321	05932	77331	05933	77341	05935	48
12	77341	05935	77351	05936	77361	05938	77371	05939	77381	05940	77391	05942	47
13	77391	05942	77401	05943	77411	05944	77421	05946	77431	05947	77441	05949	46
14	77441	05949	77451	05950	77461	05951	77472	05953	77482	05954	77492	05955	45
15	77492	05955	77502	05957	77512	05958	77522	05960	77532	05961	77542	05962	44
16	77542	05962	77552	05964	77562	05965	77572	05966	77582	05968	77592	05969	43
17	77592	05969	77602	05971	77612	05972	77622	05973	77632	05975	77642	05976	42
18	77642	05976	77652	05978	77662	05979	77672	05980	77682	05982	77692	05983	41
19	77692	05983	77702	05984	77712	05986	77722	05987	77732	05989	77742	05990	40
20	77742	05990	77752	05991	77762	05993	77772	05994	77782	05995	77792	05997	39
21	77792	05997	77802	05998	77812	06000	77822	06001	77832	06002	77842	06004	38
22	77842	06004	77852	06005	77862	06007	77872	06008	77882	06009	77892	06011	37
23	77892	06011	77902	06012	77912	06013	77922	06015	77932	06016	77942	06018	36
24	77942	06018	77952	06019	77962	06020	77972	06022	77982	06023	77992	06024	35
25	77992	06024	78002	06026	78012	06027	78022	06029	78032	06030	78042	06031	34
26	78042	06031	78052	06033	78062	06034	78072	06036	78082	06037	78092	06038	33
27	78092	06038	78102	06040	78112	06041	78122	06042	78132	06044	78142	06045	32
28	78142	06045	78152	06047	78162	06048	78171	06049	78181	06051	78191	06052	31
29	78191	06052	78201	06054	78211	06055	78221	06056	78231	06058	78241	06059	30
30	78241	06059	78251	06061	78261	06062	78271	06063	78281	06065	78291	06066	29
31	78291	06066	78301	06067	78311	06069	78321	06070	78331	06072	78341	06073	28
32	78341	06073	78351	06074	78360	06076	78370	06077	78380	06079	78390	06080	27
33	78390	06080	78400	06081	78410	06083	78420	06084	78430	06086	78440	06087	26
34	78440	06087	78450	06088	78460	06090	78470	06091	78479	06093	78489	06094	25
35	78489	06094	78499	06095	78509	06097	78519	06098	78529	06099	78539	06101	24
36	78539	06101	78549	06102	78559	06104	78569	06105	78579	06106	78589	06108	23
37	78589	06108	78599	06109	78608	06111	78618	06112	78628	06113	78638	06115	22
38	78638	06115	78648	06116	78658	06118	78668	06119	78678	06120	78688	06122	21
39	78688	06122	78697	06123	78707	06125	78717	06126	78727	06127	78737	06129	20
40	78737	06129	78747	06130	78757	06132	78767	06133	78777	06134	78786	06136	19
41	78786	06136	78796	06137	78806	06139	78816	06140	78826	06141	78836	06143	18
42	78836	06143	78846	06144	78856	06146	78865	06147	78875	06148	78885	06150	17
43	78885	06150	78895	06151	78905	06152	78915	06154	78925	06155	78935	06157	16
44	78935	06157	78944	06158	78954	06159	78964	06161	78974	06162	78984	06164	15
45	78984	06164	78994	06165	79004	06166	79013	06168	79023	06169	79033	06171	14
46	79033	06171	79043	06172	79053	06173	79063	06175	79073	06176	79082	06178	13
47	79082	06178	79092	06179	79102	06180	79112	06182	79122	06183	79132	06185	12
48	79132	06185	79141	06186	79151	06187	79161	06189	79171	06190	79181	06192	11
49	79181	06192	79191	06193	79200	06194	79210	06196	79220	06197	79230	06199	10
50	79230	06199	79240	06200	79250	06202	79259	06203	79269	06204	79279	06206	09
51	79279	06206	79289	06207	79299	06209	79309	06210	79318	06211	79328	06213	08
52	79328	06213	79338	06214	79348	06216	79358	06217	79367	06218	79377	06220	07
53	79377	06220	79387	06221	79397	06223	79407	06224	79417	06225	79426	06227	06
54	79426	06227	79436	06228	79446	06230	79456	06231	79466	06232	79475	06234	05
55	79475	06234	79485	06235	79495	06237	79505	06238	79514	06239	79524	06241	04
56	79524	06241	79534	06242	79544	06244	79554	06245	79563	06246	79573	06248	03
57	79573	06248	79583	06249	79593	06251	79603	06252	79612	06254	79622	06255	02
58	79622	06255	79632	06256	79642	06258	79651	06259	79661	06261	79671	06262	01
59	79671	06262	79681	06263	79691	06265	79700	06266	79710	06268	79720	06269	00

| | | .8 | | .6 | | .4 | | .2 | | .0 ← |

PARTS for 0′.1:   LOGS 5·   NATURALS 1

331°

HAVERSINES

29°

′	.0 Log. 2̄.or(8.)	.0 Nat. 0.	.2 Log. 2̄.or(8.)	.2 Nat. 0.	.4 Log. 2̄.or(8.)	.4 Nat. 0.	.6 Log. 2̄.or(8.)	.6 Nat. 0.	.8 Log. 2̄.or(8.)	.8 Nat. 0.	Log. 2̄.or(8.)	Nat. 0.	′
00	79720	06269	79730	06270	79740	06272	79749	06273	79759	06275	79769	06276	59
01	79769	06276	79779	06277	79788	06279	79798	06280	79808	06282	79818	06283	58
02	79818	06283	79827	06285	79837	06286	79847	06287	79857	06289	79866	06290	57
03	79866	06290	79876	06292	79886	06293	79896	06294	79905	06296	79915	06297	56
04	79915	06297	79925	06299	79935	06300	79944	06301	79954	06303	79964	06304	55
05	79964	06304	79974	06306	79983	06307	79993	06309	80003	06310	80012	06311	54
06	80012	06311	80022	06313	80032	06314	80042	06316	80051	06317	80061	06318	53
07	80061	06318	80071	06320	80081	06321	80090	06323	80100	06324	80110	06326	52
08	80110	06326	80120	06327	80129	06328	80139	06330	80149	06331	80158	06333	51
09	80158	06333	80168	06334	80178	06335	80188	06337	80197	06338	80207	06340	50
10	80207	06340	80217	06341	80226	06343	80236	06344	80246	06345	80255	06347	49
11	80255	06347	80265	06348	80275	06350	80285	06351	80294	06352	80304	06354	48
12	80304	06354	80314	06355	80323	06357	80333	06358	80343	06360	80352	06361	47
13	80352	06361	80362	06362	80372	06364	80382	06365	80391	06367	80401	06368	46
14	80401	06368	80411	06370	80420	06371	80430	06372	80440	06374	80449	06375	45
15	80449	06375	80459	06377	80469	06378	80478	06379	80488	06381	80498	06382	44
16	80498	06382	80507	06384	80517	06385	80527	06387	80537	06388	80546	06389	43
17	80546	06389	80556	06391	80565	06392	80575	06394	80585	06395	80594	06397	42
18	80594	06397	80604	06398	80614	06399	80623	06401	80633	06402	80643	06404	41
19	80643	06404	80652	06405	80662	06407	80672	06408	80681	06409	80691	06411	40
20	80691	06411	80701	06412	80710	06414	80720	06415	80730	06416	80739	06418	39
21	80739	06418	80749	06419	80759	06421	80768	06422	80778	06424	80788	06425	38
22	80788	06425	80797	06426	80807	06428	80817	06429	80826	06431	80836	06432	37
23	80836	06432	80845	06434	80855	06435	80865	06436	80874	06438	80884	06439	36
24	80884	06439	80894	06441	80903	06442	80913	06444	80922	06445	80932	06446	35
25	80932	06446	80942	06448	80951	06449	80961	06451	80971	06452	80980	06454	34
26	80980	06454	80990	06455	80999	06456	81009	06458	81019	06459	81028	06461	33
27	81028	06461	81038	06462	81047	06464	81057	06465	81067	06466	81076	06468	32
28	81076	06468	81086	06469	81096	06471	81105	06472	81115	06474	81124	06475	31
29	81124	06475	81134	06476	81144	06478	81153	06479	81163	06481	81172	06482	30
30	81172	06482	81182	06484	81192	06485	81201	06487	81211	06488	81220	06489	29
31	81220	06489	81230	06491	81240	06492	81249	06494	81259	06495	81268	06497	28
32	81268	06497	81278	06498	81287	06499	81297	06501	81307	06502	81316	06504	27
33	81316	06504	81326	06505	81335	06507	81345	06508	81354	06509	81364	06511	26
34	81364	06511	81374	06512	81383	06514	81393	06515	81402	06517	81412	06518	25
35	81412	06518	81422	06519	81431	06521	81441	06522	81450	06524	81460	06525	24
36	81460	06525	81469	06527	81479	06528	81488	06530	81498	06531	81508	06532	23
37	81508	06532	81517	06534	81527	06535	81536	06537	81546	06538	81555	06540	22
38	81555	06540	81565	06541	81574	06543	81584	06544	81593	06545	81603	06547	21
39	81603	06547	81613	06548	81622	06550	81632	06551	81641	06553	81651	06554	20
40	81651	06554	81660	06555	81670	06557	81679	06558	81689	06560	81698	06561	19
41	81698	06561	81708	06563	81718	06564	81727	06566	81737	06567	81746	06568	18
42	81746	06568	81756	06570	81765	06571	81775	06573	81784	06574	81794	06576	17
43	81794	06576	81803	06577	81813	06579	81822	06580	81832	06581	81841	06583	16
44	81841	06583	81851	06584	81860	06586	81870	06587	81879	06589	81889	06590	15
45	81889	06590	81898	06592	81908	06593	81917	06594	81927	06596	81936	06597	14
46	81936	06597	81946	06599	81955	06600	81965	06602	81974	06603	81984	06605	13
47	81984	06605	81993	06606	82003	06607	82012	06609	82022	06610	82031	06612	12
48	82031	06612	82041	06613	82050	06615	82060	06616	82069	06618	82079	06619	11
49	82079	06619	82088	06620	82098	06622	82107	06623	82117	06625	82126	06626	10
50	82126	06626	82136	06628	82145	06629	82155	06631	82164	06632	82174	06633	09
51	82174	06633	82183	06635	82193	06636	82202	06638	82212	06639	82221	06641	08
52	82221	06641	82231	06642	82240	06644	82250	06645	82259	06646	82269	06648	07
53	82269	06648	82278	06649	82287	06651	82297	06652	82306	06654	82316	06655	06
54	82316	06655	82325	06657	82335	06658	82344	06660	82354	06661	82363	06662	05
55	82363	06662	82373	06664	82382	06665	82392	06667	82401	06668	82410	06670	04
56	82410	06670	82420	06671	82429	06673	82439	06674	82448	06675	82458	06677	03
57	82458	06677	82467	06678	82476	06680	82486	06681	82495	06683	82505	06684	02
58	82505	06684	82514	06686	82524	06687	82533	06689	82543	06690	82552	06691	01
59	82552	06691	82561	06693	82571	06694	82580	06696	82590	06697	82599	06699	00

| | .8 | .6 | .4 | .2 | .0 ← |

PARTS for 0′.1: LOGS 5 NATURALS 1

330°

30° HAVERSINES

′	.0 Log. 2.or(8.)	.0 Nat. 0.	.2 Log. 2.or(8.)	.2 Nat. 0.	.4 Log. 2.or(8.)	.4 Nat. 0.	.6 Log. 2.or(8.)	.6 Nat. 0.	.8 Log. 2.or(8.)	.8 Nat. 0.	Log. 2.or(8.)	Nat. 0.	′
00	82599	06699	82609	06700	82618	06702	82628	06703	82637	06705	82646	06706	59
01	82646	06706	82656	06707	82665	06709	82675	06710	82684	06712	82693	06713	58
02	82693	06713	82703	06715	82712	06716	82722	06718	82731	06719	82741	06721	57
03	82741	06721	82750	06722	82759	06723	82769	06725	82778	06726	82788	06728	56
04	82788	06728	82797	06729	82806	06731	82816	06732	82825	06734	82835	06735	55
05	82835	06735	82844	06737	82853	06738	82863	06740	82872	06741	82882	06742	54
06	82882	06742	82891	06744	82900	06745	82910	06747	82919	06748	82929	06750	53
07	82929	06750	82938	06751	82947	06753	82957	06754	82966	06756	82976	06757	52
08	82976	06757	82985	06758	82994	06760	83004	06761	83013	06763	83022	06764	51
09	83022	06764	83032	06766	83041	06767	83051	06769	83060	06770	83069	06772	50
10	83069	06772	83079	06773	83088	06775	83097	06776	83107	06777	83116	06779	49
11	83116	06779	83126	06780	83135	06782	83144	06783	83154	06785	83163	06786	48
12	83163	06786	83172	06788	83182	06789	83191	06791	83200	06792	83210	06794	47
13	83210	06794	83219	06795	83229	06797	83238	06798	83247	06799	83257	06801	46
14	83257	06801	83266	06802	83275	06804	83285	06805	83294	06807	83303	06808	45
15	83303	06808	83313	06810	83322	06811	83331	06813	83341	06814	83350	06816	44
16	83350	06816	83360	06817	83369	06818	83378	06820	83387	06821	83397	06823	43
17	83397	06823	83406	06824	83415	06826	83425	06827	83434	06829	83443	06830	42
18	83443	06830	83453	06832	83462	06833	83471	06835	83481	06836	83490	06838	41
19	83490	06838	83500	06839	83509	06840	83518	06842	83527	06843	83537	06845	40
20	83537	06845	83546	06846	83555	06848	83565	06849	83574	06851	83583	06852	39
21	83583	06852	83593	06854	83602	06855	83611	06857	83621	06858	83630	06860	38
22	83630	06860	83639	06861	83649	06863	83658	06864	83667	06865	83676	06867	37
23	83676	06867	83686	06868	83695	06870	83704	06871	83714	06873	83723	06874	36
24	83723	06874	83732	06876	83742	06877	83751	06879	83760	06880	83769	06882	35
25	83769	06882	83779	06883	83788	06885	83797	06886	83807	06888	83816	06889	34
26	83816	06889	83825	06891	83834	06892	83844	06893	83853	06895	83862	06896	33
27	83862	06896	83872	06898	83881	06899	83890	06901	83900	06902	83909	06904	32
28	83909	06904	83918	06905	83927	06907	83937	06908	83946	06910	83955	06911	31
29	83955	06911	83964	06913	83974	06914	83983	06916	83992	06917	84001	06919	30
30	84001	06919	84011	06920	84020	06922	84029	06923	84039	06924	84048	06926	29
31	84048	06926	84057	06927	84066	06929	84076	06930	84085	06932	84094	06933	28
32	84094	06933	84103	06935	84113	06936	84122	06938	84131	06939	84140	06941	27
33	84140	06941	84150	06942	84159	06944	84168	06945	84177	06947	84187	06948	26
34	84187	06948	84196	06950	84205	06951	84214	06953	84224	06954	84233	06956	25
35	84233	06956	84242	06957	84251	06958	84261	06960	84270	06961	84279	06963	24
36	84279	06963	84288	06964	84297	06966	84307	06967	84316	06969	84325	06970	23
37	84325	06970	84334	06972	84344	06973	84353	06975	84362	06976	84371	06978	22
38	84371	06978	84381	06979	84390	06981	84399	06982	84408	06984	84417	06985	21
39	84417	06985	84427	06987	84436	06988	84445	06990	84454	06991	84464	06993	20
40	84464	06993	84473	06994	84482	06996	84491	06997	84500	06998	84510	07000	19
41	84510	07000	84519	07001	84528	07003	84537	07004	84546	07006	84556	07007	18
42	84556	07007	84565	07009	84574	07010	84583	07012	84592	07013	84602	07015	17
43	84602	07015	84611	07016	84620	07018	84629	07019	84638	07021	84648	07022	16
44	84648	07022	84657	07024	84666	07025	84675	07027	84684	07028	84694	07030	15
45	84694	07030	84703	07031	84712	07033	84721	07034	84730	07036	84739	07037	14
46	84739	07037	84749	07039	84758	07040	84767	07042	84776	07043	84785	07045	13
47	84785	07045	84795	07046	84804	07048	84813	07049	84822	07051	84831	07052	12
48	84831	07052	84840	07053	84850	07055	84859	07056	84868	07058	84877	07059	11
49	84877	07059	84886	07061	84896	07062	84905	07064	84914	07065	84923	07067	10
50	84923	07067	84932	07068	84941	07070	84950	07071	84960	07073	84969	07074	09
51	84969	07074	84978	07076	84987	07077	84996	07079	85005	07080	85015	07082	08
52	85015	07082	85024	07083	85033	07085	85042	07086	85051	07088	85060	07089	07
53	85060	07089	85069	07091	85079	07092	85088	07094	85097	07095	85106	07097	06
54	85106	07097	85115	07098	85124	07100	85133	07101	85142	07103	85152	07104	05
55	85152	07104	85161	07106	85170	07107	85179	07109	85188	07110	85197	07112	04
56	85197	07112	85207	07113	85216	07115	85225	07116	85234	07118	85243	07119	03
57	85243	07119	85252	07121	85261	07122	85270	07124	85279	07125	85289	07127	02
58	85289	07127	85298	07128	85307	07130	85316	07131	85325	07133	85334	07134	01
59	85334	07134	85343	07136	85352	07137	85362	07139	85371	07140	85380	07142	00

	.8		.6		.4		.2		.0	

PARTS for 0′.1: LOGS 5   NATURALS 1

329°

31° HAVERSINES

′	.0 Log. 2.or(8.)	.0 Nat. 0.	.2 Log. 2.or(8.)	.2 Nat. 0.	.4 Log. 2.or(8.)	.4 Nat. 0.	.6 Log. 2.or(8.)	.6 Nat. 0.	.8 Log. 2.or(8.)	.8 Nat. 0.	Log. 2.or(8.)	Nat. 0.	′
00	85380	07142	85389	07143	85398	07145	85407	07146	85416	07148	85425	07149	59
01	85425	07149	85434	07151	85444	07152	85453	07154	85462	07155	85471	07157	58
02	85471	07157	85480	07158	85489	07160	85498	07161	85507	07163	85516	07164	57
03	85516	07164	85525	07166	85535	07167	85544	07169	85553	07170	85562	07172	56
04	85562	07172	85571	07173	85580	07175	85589	07176	85598	07178	85607	07179	55
05	85607	07179	85616	07181	85625	07182	85634	07184	85644	07185	85653	07187	54
06	85653	07187	85662	07188	85671	07190	85680	07191	85689	07193	85698	07194	53
07	85698	07194	85707	07196	85716	07197	85725	07199	85734	07200	85743	07202	52
08	85743	07202	85752	07203	85762	07205	85771	07206	85780	07208	85789	07209	51
09	85789	07209	85798	07211	85807	07212	85816	07214	85825	07215	85834	07217	50
10	85834	07217	85843	07218	85852	07220	85861	07221	85870	07223	85879	07224	49
11	85879	07224	85888	07226	85897	07227	85907	07229	85916	07230	85925	07232	48
12	85925	07232	85934	07233	85943	07235	85952	07236	85961	07238	85970	07239	47
13	85970	07239	85979	07241	85988	07242	85997	07244	86006	07245	86015	07247	46
14	86015	07247	86024	07248	86033	07250	86042	07251	86051	07253	86060	07254	45
15	86060	07254	86069	07256	86078	07257	86087	07259	86096	07260	86105	07262	44
16	86105	07262	86114	07263	86123	07265	86132	07266	86141	07268	86150	07270	43
17	86150	07270	86159	07271	86168	07273	86178	07274	86187	07276	86196	07277	42
18	86196	07277	86205	07279	86214	07280	86223	07282	86232	07283	86241	07285	41
19	86241	07285	86250	07286	86259	07288	86268	07289	86277	07291	86286	07292	40
20	86286	07292	86295	07294	86304	07295	86313	07297	86322	07298	86331	07300	39
21	86331	07300	86340	07301	86349	07303	86358	07304	86367	07306	86376	07307	38
22	86376	07307	86385	07309	86394	07310	86403	07312	86412	07313	86421	07315	37
23	86421	07315	86430	07316	86439	07318	86448	07319	86457	07321	86466	07322	36
24	86466	07322	86475	07324	86484	07325	86493	07327	86502	07329	86511	07330	35
25	86511	07330	86520	07332	86529	07333	86538	07335	86547	07336	86556	07338	34
26	86556	07338	86565	07339	86574	07341	86582	07342	86591	07344	86600	07345	33
27	86600	07345	86609	07347	86618	07348	86627	07350	86636	07351	86645	07353	32
28	86645	07353	86654	07354	86663	07356	86672	07357	86681	07359	86690	07360	31
29	86690	07360	86699	07362	86708	07363	86717	07365	86726	07366	86735	07368	30
30	86735	07368	86744	07370	86753	07371	86762	07373	86771	07374	86780	07376	29
31	86780	07376	86789	07377	86798	07379	86806	07380	86815	07382	86824	07383	28
32	86824	07383	86833	07385	86842	07386	86851	07388	86860	07389	86869	07391	27
33	86869	07391	86878	07392	86887	07394	86896	07395	86905	07397	86914	07398	26
34	86914	07398	86923	07400	86932	07401	86941	07403	86950	07405	86959	07406	25
35	86959	07406	86968	07408	86976	07409	86985	07411	86994	07412	87003	07414	24
36	87003	07414	87012	07415	87021	07417	87030	07418	87039	07420	87048	07421	23
37	87048	07421	87057	07423	87066	07424	87075	07426	87083	07427	87092	07429	22
38	87092	07429	87101	07430	87110	07432	87119	07433	87128	07435	87137	07437	21
39	87137	07437	87146	07438	87155	07440	87164	07441	87173	07443	87182	07444	20
40	87182	07444	87191	07446	87199	07447	87208	07449	87217	07450	87226	07452	19
41	87226	07452	87235	07453	87244	07455	87253	07456	87262	07458	87271	07459	18
42	87271	07459	87280	07461	87288	07463	87297	07464	87306	07466	87315	07467	17
43	87315	07467	87324	07469	87333	07470	87342	07472	87351	07473	87360	07475	16
44	87360	07475	87368	07476	87377	07478	87386	07479	87395	07481	87404	07482	15
45	87404	07482	87413	07484	87422	07485	87431	07487	87440	07489	87448	07490	14
46	87448	07490	87457	07492	87466	07493	87475	07495	87484	07496	87493	07498	13
47	87493	07498	87502	07499	87511	07501	87519	07502	87528	07504	87537	07505	12
48	87537	07505	87546	07507	87555	07508	87564	07510	87573	07512	87582	07513	11
49	87582	07513	87590	07515	87599	07516	87608	07518	87617	07519	87626	07521	10
50	87626	07521	87635	07522	87644	07524	87652	07525	87661	07527	87670	07528	09
51	87670	07528	87679	07530	87688	07531	87697	07533	87706	07535	87714	07536	08
52	87714	07536	87723	07538	87732	07539	87741	07541	87750	07542	87759	07544	07
53	87759	07544	87767	07545	87776	07547	87785	07548	87794	07550	87803	07551	06
54	87803	07551	87812	07553	87820	07554	87829	07556	87838	07558	87847	07559	05
55	87847	07559	87856	07561	87865	07562	87874	07564	87882	07565	87891	07567	04
56	87891	07567	87900	07568	87909	07570	87918	07571	87927	07573	87935	07575	03
57	87935	07575	87944	07576	87953	07578	87962	07579	87971	07581	87979	07582	02
58	87979	07582	87988	07584	87997	07585	88006	07587	88015	07588	88024	07590	01
59	88024	07590	88032	07591	88041	07593	88050	07595	88059	07596	88068	07598	00

| | .8 | | .6 | | .4 | | .2 | | .0 | |

PARTS for 0′.1:   LOGS 4   NATURALS 1

328°

32° HAVERSINES

′	.0 Log. $\overline{2}$.or(8.)	.0 Nat. 0.	.2 Log. $\overline{2}$.or(8)	.2 Nat. 0.	.4 Log. $\overline{2}$.or(8.)	.4 Nat. 0.	.6 Log. $\overline{2}$.or(8.)	.6 Nat. 0.	.8 Log. $\overline{2}$.or(8.)	.8 Nat. 0.	Log. $\overline{2}$.or(8.)·	Nat. 0.	′
00	88068	07598	88076	07599	88085	07601	88094	07602	88103	07604	88112	07605	59
01	88112	07605	88120	07607	88129	07608	88138	07610	88147	07611	88156	07613	58
02	88156	07613	88164	07615	88173	07616	88182	07618	88191	07619	88200	07621	57
03	88200	07621	88208	07622	88217	07624	88226	07625	88235	07627	88244	07628	56
04	88244	07628	88252	07630	88261	07632	88270	07633	88279	07635	88288	07636	55
05	88288	07636	88296	07638	88305	07639	88314	07641	88323	07642	88332	07644	54
06	88332	07644	88340	07645	88349	07647	88358	07649	88367	07650	88375	07652	53
07	88375	07652	88384	07653	88393	07655	88402	07656	88410	07658	88419	07659	52
08	88419	07659	88428	07661	88437	07662	88446	07664	88454	07666	88463	07667	51
09	88463	07667	88472	07669	88481	07670	88489	07672	88498	07673	88507	07675	50
10	88507	07675	88516	07676	88525	07678	88533	07680	88542	07681	88551	07683	49
11	88551	07683	88560	07684	88568	07686	88577	07687	88586	07689	88595	07690	48
12	88595	07690	88603	07692	88612	07693	88621	07695	88630	07697	88638	07698	47
13	88638	07698	88647	07700	88656	07701	88665	07703	88673	07704	88682	07706	46
14	88682	07706	88691	07707	88700	07709	88708	07711	88717	07712	88726	07714	45
15	88726	07714	88735	07715	88743	07717	88752	07718	88761	07720	88769	07721	44
16	88769	07721	88778	07723	88787	07724	88796	07726	88804	07728	88813	07729	43
17	88813	07729	88822	07731	88831	07732	88839	07734	88848	07735	88857	07737	42
18	88857	07737	88866	07738	88874	07740	88883	07742	88892	07743	88900	07745	41
19	88900	07745	88909	07746	88918	07748	88927	07749	88935	07751	88944	07752	40
20	88944	07752	88953	07754	88961	07756	88970	07757	88979	07759	88988	07760	39
21	88988	07760	88996	07762	89005	07763	89014	07765	89022	07766	89031	07768	38
22	89031	07768	89040	07770	89048	07771	89057	07773	89066	07774	89075	07776	37
23	89075	07776	89083	07777	89092	07779	89101	07780	89109	07782	89118	07784	36
24	89118	07784	89127	07785	89135	07787	89144	07788	89153	07790	89162	07791	35
25	89162	07791	89170	07793	89179	07795	89188	07796	89196	07798	89205	07799	34
26	89205	07799	89214	07801	89222	07802	89231	07804	89240	07805	89248	07807	33
27	89248	07807	89257	07809	89266	07810	89274	07812	89283	07813	89292	07815	32
28	89292	07815	89300	07816	89309	07818	89318	07819	89327	07821	89335	07823	31
29	89335	07823	89344	07824	89353	07826	89361	07827	89370	07829	89379	07830	30
30	89379	07830	89387	07832	89396	07834	89405	07835	89413	07837	89422	07838	29
31	89422	07838	89430	07840	89439	07841	89448	07843	89457	07844	89465	07846	28
32	89465	07846	89474	07848	89482	07849	89491	07851	89500	07852	89508	07854	27
33	89508	07854	89517	07855	89526	07857	89534	07859	89543	07860	89552	07862	26
34	89552	07862	89560	07863	89569	07865	89578	07866	89586	07868	89595	07870	25
35	89595	07870	89604	07871	89612	07873	89621	07874	89630	07876	89638	07877	24
36	89638	07877	89647	07879	89655	07881	89664	07882	89673	07884	89681	07885	23
37	89681	07885	89690	07887	89699	07888	89707	07890	89716	07891	89725	07893	22
38	89725	07893	89733	07895	89742	07896	89750	07898	89759	07899	89768	07901	21
39	89768	07901	89776	07902	89785	07904	89794	07906	89802	07907	89811	07909	20
40	89811	07909	89819	07910	89828	07912	89837	07913	89845	07915	89854	07917	19
41	89854	07917	89862	07918	89871	07920	89880	07921	89888	07923	89897	07924	18
42	89897	07924	89906	07926	89914	07928	89923	07929	89931	07931	89940	07932	17
43	89940	07932	89949	07934	89957	07935	89966	07937	89974	07939	89983	07940	16
44	89983	07940	89992	07942	90000	07943	90009	07945	90017	07946	90026	07948	15
45	90026	07948	90035	07950	90043	07951	90052	07953	90060	07954	90069	07956	14
46	90069	07956	90078	07957	90086	07959	90095	07961	90103	07962	90112	07964	13
47	90112	07964	90121	07965	90129	07967	90138	07969	90146	07970	90155	07972	12
48	90155	07972	90164	07973	90172	07975	90181	07976	90189	07978	90198	07980	11
49	90198	07980	90206	07981	90215	07983	90224	07984	90232	07986	90241	07987	10
50	90241	07987	90249	07989	90258	07991	90266	07992	90275	07994	90284	07995	09
51	90284	07995	90292	07997	90301	07998	90309	08000	90318	08002	90326	08003	08
52	90326	08003	90335	08005	90344	08006	90352	08008	90361	08010	90369	08011	07
53	90369	08011	90378	08013	90386	08014	90395	08016	90403	08017	90412	08019	06
54	90412	08019	90421	08021	90429	08022	90438	08024	90446	08025	90455	08027	05
55	90455	08027	90463	08028	90472	08030	90480	08032	90489	08033	90498	08035	04
56	90498	08035	90506	08036	90515	08038	90523	08040	90532	08041	90540	08043	03
57	90540	08043	90549	08044	90557	08046	90566	08047	90574	08049	90583	08051	02
58	90583	08051	90592	08052	90600	08054	90609	08055	90617	08057	90626	08059	01
59	90626	08059	90634	08060	90643	08062	90651	08063	90660	08065	90668	08066	00

	.8		.6		.4		.2		.0	

327°

PARTS for 0'.1:   LOGS 4   NATURALS 1

33° HAVERSINES

	.0		.2		.4		.6		.8		
	Log.	Nat.	Log.	Nat.	Log.	Nat.	Log.	Nat.	Log.	Nat.	
′	2.or(8.)	0.	2̄.or(8.)	0.	2̄.or(8.)	0.	2̄.or(8.)	0.	2̄.or(8.)	0.	′
00	90668	08066	90677	08068	90685	08070	90694	08071	90702	08073	90711	08074	59
01	90711	08074	90720	08076	90728	08078	90737	08079	90745	08081	90754	08082	58
02	90754	08082	90762	08084	90771	08085	90779	08087	90788	08089	90796	08090	57
03	90796	08090	90805	08092	90813	08093	90822	08095	90830	08097	90839	08098	56
04	90839	08098	90847	08100	90856	08101	90864	08103	90873	08105	90881	08106	55
05	90881	08106	90890	08108	90898	08109	90907	08111	90915	08112	90924	08114	54
06	90924	08114	90932	08116	90941	08117	90949	08119	90958	08120	90966	08122	53
07	90966	08122	90975	08124	90983	08125	90992	08127	91000	08128	91009	08130	52
08	91009	08130	91017	08132	91026	08133	91034	08135	91043	08136	91051	08138	51
09	91051	08138	91060	08139	91068	08141	91077	08143	91085	08144	91094	08146	50
10	91094	08146	91102	08147	91111	08149	91119	08151	91128	08152	91136	08154	49
11	91136	08154	91145	08155	91153	08157	91162	08159	91170	08160	91179	08162	48
12	91179	08162	91187	08163	91195	08165	91204	08167	91212	08168	91221	08170	47
13	91221	08170	91229	08171	91238	08173	91246	08175	91255	08176	91263	08178	46
14	91263	08178	91272	08179	91280	08181	91289	08183	91297	08184	91306	08186	45
15	91306	08186	91314	08187	91322	08189	91331	08190	91339	08192	91348	08194	44
16	91348	08194	91356	08195	91365	08197	91373	08198	91382	08200	91390	08202	43
17	91390	08202	91399	08203	91407	08205	91416	08206	91424	08208	91432	08210	42
18	91432	08210	91441	08211	91449	08213	91458	08214	91466	08216	91475	08218	41
19	91475	08218	91483	08219	91491	08221	91500	08222	91508	08224	91517	08226	40
20	91517	08226	91525	08227	91534	08229	91542	08230	91551	08232	91559	08234	39
21	91559	08234	91567	08235	91576	08237	91584	08238	91593	08240	91601	08242	38
22	91601	08242	91610	08243	91618	08245	91627	08246	91635	08248	91643	08250	37
23	91643	08250	91652	08251	91660	08253	91669	08254	91677	08256	91685	08258	36
24	91685	08258	91694	08259	91702	08261	91711	08262	91719	08264	91728	08266	35
25	91728	08266	91736	08267	91744	08269	91753	08270	91761	08272	91770	08274	34
26	91770	08274	91778	08275	91786	08277	91795	08278	91803	08280	91812	08282	33
27	91812	08282	91820	08283	91828	08285	91837	08286	91845	08288	91854	08290	32
28	91854	08290	91862	08291	91870	08293	91879	08294	91887	08296	91896	08298	31
29	91896	08298	91904	08299	91912	08301	91921	08303	91929	08304	91938	08306	30
30	91938	08306	91946	08307	91954	08309	91963	08311	91971	08312	91980	08314	29
31	91980	08314	91988	08315	91996	08317	92005	08319	92013	08320	92022	08322	28
32	92022	08322	92030	08323	92038	08325	92047	08327	92055	08328	92063	08330	27
33	92063	08330	92072	08331	92080	08333	92089	08335	92097	08336	92105	08338	26
34	92105	08338	92114	08339	92122	08341	92130	08343	92139	08344	92147	08346	25
35	92147	08346	92156	08348	92164	08349	92172	08351	92181	08352	92189	08354	24
36	92189	08354	92198	08356	92206	08357	92214	08359	92223	08360	92231	08362	23
37	92231	08362	92239	08364	92248	08365	92256	08367	92264	08368	92273	08370	22
38	92273	08370	92281	08372	92290	08373	92298	08375	92306	08376	92315	08378	21
39	92315	08378	92323	08380	92331	08381	92340	08383	92348	08385	92356	08386	20
40	92356	08386	92365	08388	92373	08389	92381	08391	92390	08393	92398	08394	19
41	92398	08394	92406	08396	92415	08397	92423	08399	92431	08401	92440	08402	18
42	92440	08402	92448	08404	92456	08406	92465	08407	92473	08409	92481	08410	17
43	92481	08410	92490	08412	92498	08414	92506	08415	92515	08417	92523	08418	16
44	92523	08418	92532	08420	92540	08422	92548	08423	92556	08425	92565	08427	15
45	92565	08427	92573	08428	92581	08430	92590	08431	92598	08433	92606	08435	14
46	92606	08435	92615	08436	92623	08438	92631	08439	92640	08441	92648	08443	13
47	92648	08443	92656	08444	92665	08446	92673	08448	92681	08449	92690	08451	12
48	92690	08451	92698	08452	92706	08454	92715	08456	92723	08457	92731	08459	11
49	92731	08459	92740	08460	92748	08462	92756	08464	92764	08465	92773	08467	10
50	92773	08467	92781	08469	92789	08470	92798	08472	92806	08473	92814	08475	09
51	92814	08475	92823	08477	92831	08478	92839	08480	92848	08482	92856	08483	08
52	92856	08483	92864	08485	92872	08486	92881	08488	92889	08490	92897	08491	07
53	92897	08491	92906	08493	92914	08495	92922	08496	92930	08498	92939	08499	06
54	92939	08499	92947	08501	92955	08503	92964	08504	92972	08506	92980	08508	05
55	92980	08508	92988	08509	92997	08511	93005	08512	93013	08514	93022	08516	04
56	93022	08516	93030	08517	93038	08519	93046	08520	93055	08522	93063	08524	03
57	93063	08524	93071	08525	93080	08527	93088	08529	93096	08530	93104	08532	02
58	93104	08532	93113	08533	93121	08535	93129	08537	93138	08538	93146	08540	01
59	93146	08540	93154	08542	93162	08543	93171	08545	93179	08546	93187	08548	00
		.8		.6		.4		.2		.0	

PARTS for 0′.1: LOGS 4   NATURALS 1

34° HAVERSINES

′	.0 Log. 2.or(8.)	.0 Nat. 0.	.2 Log. 2.or(8.)	.2 Nat. 0.	.4 Log. 2.or(8.)	.4 Nat. 0.	.6 Log. 2.or(8.)	.6 Nat. 0.	.8 Log. 2.or(8.)	.8 Nat. 0.	Log. 2.or(8.)	Nat. 0.	′
00	93187	08548	93195	08550	93204	08551	93212	08553	93220	08555	93228	08556	59
01	93228	08556	93237	08558	93245	08560	93253	08561	93261	08563	93270	08564	58
02	93270	08564	93278	08566	93286	08568	93294	08569	93303	08571	93311	08573	57
03	93311	08573	93319	08574	93327	08576	93336	08577	93344	08579	93352	08581	56
04	93352	08581	93360	08582	93369	08584	93377	08586	93385	08587	93393	08589	55
05	93393	08589	93402	08590	93410	08592	93418	08594	93426	08595	93435	08597	54
06	93435	08597	93443	08599	93451	08600	93459	08602	93468	08604	93476	08605	53
07	93476	08605	93484	08607	93492	08608	93501	08610	93509	08612	93517	08613	52
08	93517	08613	93525	08615	93533	08617	93542	08618	93550	08620	93558	08621	51
09	93558	08621	93566	08623	93574	08625	93583	08626	93591	08628	93599	08630	50
10	93599	08630	93607	08631	93616	08633	93624	08635	93632	08636	93640	08638	49
11	93640	08638	93649	08639	93657	08641	93665	08643	93673	08644	93681	08646	48
12	93681	08646	93690	08648	93698	08649	93706	08651	93714	08653	93722	08654	47
13	93722	08654	93731	08656	93739	08657	93747	08659	93755	08661	93763	08662	46
14	93763	08662	93772	08664	93780	08666	93788	08667	93796	08669	93804	08671	45
15	93804	08671	93813	08672	93821	08674	93829	08675	93837	08677	93845	08679	44
16	93845	08679	93854	08680	93862	08682	93870	08684	93878	08685	93886	08687	43
17	93886	08687	93895	08689	93903	08690	93911	08692	93919	08693	93927	08695	42
18	93927	08695	93936	08697	93944	08698	93952	08700	93960	08702	93968	08703	41
19	93968	08703	93977	08705	93985	08707	93993	08708	94001	08710	94009	08712	40
20	94009	08712	94017	08713	94026	08715	94034	08716	94042	08718	94050	08720	39
21	94050	08720	94058	08721	94067	08723	94075	08725	94083	08726	94091	08728	38
22	94091	08728	94099	08730	94107	08731	94115	08733	94124	08734	94132	08736	37
23	94132	08736	94140	08738	94148	08739	94156	08741	94164	08743	94173	08744	36
24	94173	08744	94181	08746	94189	08748	94197	08749	94205	08751	94213	08753	35
25	94213	08753	94222	08754	94230	08756	94238	08757	94246	08759	94254	08761	34
26	94254	08761	94262	08762	94271	08764	94279	08766	94287	08767	94295	08769	33
27	94295	08769	94303	08771	94311	08772	94319	08774	94328	08776	94336	08777	32
28	94336	08777	94344	08779	94352	08781	94360	08782	94368	08784	94376	08785	31
29	94376	08785	94385	08787	94393	08789	94401	08790	94409	08792	94417	08794	30
30	94417	08794	94425	08795	94433	08797	94442	08799	94450	08800	94458	08802	29
31	94458	08802	94466	08804	94474	08805	94482	08807	94490	08809	94498	08810	28
32	94498	08810	94507	08812	94515	08813	94523	08815	94531	08817	94539	08818	27
33	94539	08818	94547	08820	94556	08822	94563	08823	94571	08825	94580	08827	26
34	94580	08827	94588	08828	94596	08830	94604	08832	94612	08833	94620	08835	25
35	94620	08835	94628	08837	94636	08838	94645	08840	94653	08842	94661	08843	24
36	94661	08843	94669	08845	94677	08847	94685	08848	94693	08850	94701	08851	23
37	94701	08851	94710	08853	94718	08855	94726	08856	94734	08858	94742	08860	22
38	94742	08860	94750	08861	94758	08863	94766	08865	94774	08866	94782	08868	21
39	94782	08868	94791	08870	94799	08871	94807	08873	94815	08875	94823	08876	20
40	94823	08876	94831	08878	94839	08880	94847	08881	94855	08883	94863	08885	19
41	94863	08885	94871	08886	94880	08888	94888	08889	94896	08891	94904	08893	18
42	94904	08893	94912	08894	94920	08896	94928	08898	94936	08899	94944	08901	17
43	94944	08901	94952	08903	94960	08904	94968	08906	94977	08908	94985	08909	16
44	94985	08909	94993	08911	95001	08913	95009	08914	95017	08916	95025	08918	15
45	95025	08918	95033	08919	95041	08921	95049	08923	95057	08924	95065	08926	14
46	95065	08926	95073	08928	95082	08929	95090	08931	95098	08933	95106	08934	13
47	95106	08934	95114	08936	95122	08938	95130	08939	95138	08941	95146	08943	12
48	95146	08943	95154	08944	95162	08946	95170	08948	95178	08949	95186	08951	11
49	95186	08951	95194	08953	95202	08954	95211	08956	95219	08957	95227	08959	10
50	95227	08959	95235	08961	95243	08962	95251	08964	95259	08966	95267	08967	09
51	95267	08967	95275	08969	95283	08971	95291	08972	95299	08974	95307	08976	08
52	95307	08976	95315	08977	95323	08979	95331	08981	95339	08982	95347	08984	07
53	95347	08984	95355	08986	95363	08987	95372	08989	95380	08991	95388	08992	06
54	95388	08992	95396	08994	95404	08996	95412	08997	95420	08999	95428	09001	05
55	95428	09001	95436	09002	95444	09004	95452	09006	95460	09007	95468	09009	04
56	95468	09009	95476	09011	95484	09012	95492	09014	95500	09016	95508	09017	03
57	95508	09017	95516	09019	95524	09021	95532	09022	95540	09024	95548	09026	02
58	95548	09026	95556	09027	95564	09029	95572	09031	95580	09032	95588	09034	01
59	95588	09034	95596	09036	95604	09037	95612	09039	95620	09041	95628	09042	00

	.8	.6	.4	.2	.0 ←

PARTS for 0′.1:   LOGS 4   NATURALS 1

325°

35° HAVERSINES

′	.0 Log. (2.or(8.))	.0 Nat. (0.)	.2 Log. (2.or(8.))	.2 Nat. (0.)	.4 Log. (2.or(8.))	.4 Nat. (0.)	.6 Log. (2.or(8.))	.6 Nat. (0.)	.8 Log. (2.or(8.))	.8 Nat. (0.)	Log. (2.or(8.))	Nat. (0.)	′
00	95628	09042	95636	09044	95644	09046	95652	09047	95660	09049	95668	09051	59
01	95668	09051	95676	09052	95684	09054	95692	09056	95700	09057	95708	09059	58
02	95708	09059	95716	09061	95724	09062	95732	09064	95740	09066	95748	09067	57
03	95748	09067	95756	09069	95764	09071	95772	09072	95780	09074	95788	09076	56
04	95788	09076	95796	09077	95804	09079	95812	09081	95820	09082	95828	09084	55
05	95828	09084	95836	09086	95844	09087	95852	09089	95860	09091	95868	09093	54
06	95868	09093	95876	09094	95884	09096	95892	09098	95900	09099	95908	09101	53
07	95908	09101	95916	09103	95924	09104	95932	09106	95940	09108	95948	09109	52
08	95948	09109	95956	09111	95964	09113	95972	09114	95980	09116	95988	09118	51
09	95988	09118	95996	09119	96004	09121	96012	09123	96020	09124	96028	09126	50
10	96028	09126	96036	09128	96044	09129	96052	09131	96060	09133	96068	09134	49
11	96068	09134	96076	09136	96084	09138	96092	09139	96100	09141	96108	09143	48
12	96108	09143	96116	09144	96124	09146	96132	09148	96140	09149	96148	09151	47
13	96148	09151	96156	09153	96164	09155	96171	09156	96179	09158	96187	09160	46
14	96187	09160	96195	09161	96203	09163	96211	09165	96219	09166	96227	09168	45
15	96227	09168	96235	09170	96243	09171	96251	09173	96259	09175	96267	09176	44
16	96267	09176	96275	09178	96283	09180	96291	09181	96299	09183	96307	09185	43
17	96307	09185	96315	09186	96322	09188	96330	09190	96338	09191	96346	09193	42
18	96346	09193	96354	09195	96362	09196	96370	09198	96378	09200	96386	09202	41
19	96386	09202	96394	09203	96402	09205	96410	09207	96418	09208	96426	09210	40
20	96426	09210	96434	09212	96442	09213	96449	09215	96457	09217	96465	09218	39
21	96465	09218	96473	09220	96481	09222	96489	09223	96497	09225	96505	09227	38
22	96505	09227	96513	09228	96521	09230	96529	09232	96537	09234	96545	09235	37
23	96545	09235	96553	09237	96560	09239	96568	09240	96576	09242	96584	09244	36
24	96584	09244	96592	09245	96600	09247	96608	09249	96616	09250	96624	09252	35
25	96624	09252	96632	09254	96640	09255	96647	09257	96655	09259	96663	09260	34
26	96663	09260	96671	09262	96679	09264	96687	09266	96695	09267	96703	09269	33
27	96703	09269	96711	09271	96719	09272	96727	09274	96734	09276	96742	09277	32
28	96742	09277	96750	09279	96758	09281	96766	09282	96774	09284	96782	09286	31
29	96782	09286	96790	09287	96798	09289	96806	09291	96813	09293	96821	09294	30
30	96821	09294	96829	09296	96837	09298	96845	09299	96853	09301	96861	09303	29
31	96861	09303	96869	09304	96877	09306	96884	09308	96892	09309	96900	09311	28
32	96900	09311	96908	09313	96916	09315	96924	09316	96932	09318	96940	09320	27
33	96940	09320	96947	09321	96955	09323	96963	09325	96971	09326	96979	09328	26
34	96979	09328	96987	09330	96995	09331	97003	09333	97011	09335	97018	09337	25
35	97018	09337	97026	09338	97034	09340	97042	09342	97050	09343	97058	09345	24
36	97058	09345	97066	09347	97073	09348	97081	09350	97089	09352	97097	09353	23
37	97097	09353	97105	09355	97113	09357	97121	09359	97129	09360	97136	09362	22
38	97136	09362	97144	09364	97152	09365	97160	09367	97168	09369	97176	09370	21
39	97176	09370	97184	09372	97191	09374	97199	09375	97207	09377	97215	09379	20
40	97215	09379	97223	09381	97231	09382	97239	09384	97246	09386	97254	09387	19
41	97254	09387	97262	09389	97270	09391	97278	09392	97286	09394	97293	09396	18
42	97293	09396	97301	09398	97309	09399	97317	09401	97325	09403	97333	09404	17
43	97333	09404	97341	09406	97348	09408	97356	09409	97364	09411	97372	09413	16
44	97372	09413	97380	09415	97388	09416	97395	09418	97403	09420	97411	09421	15
45	97411	09421	97419	09423	97427	09425	97435	09426	97442	09428	97450	09430	14
46	97450	09430	97458	09432	97466	09433	97474	09435	97482	09437	97489	09438	13
47	97489	09438	97497	09440	97505	09442	97513	09443	97521	09445	97529	09447	12
48	97529	09447	97536	09449	97544	09450	97552	09452	97560	09454	97568	09455	11
49	97568	09455	97575	09457	97583	09459	97591	09460	97599	09462	97607	09464	10
50	97607	09464	97615	09466	97622	09467	97630	09469	97638	09471	97646	09472	09
51	97646	09472	97654	09474	97661	09476	97669	09477	97677	09479	97685	09481	08
52	97685	09481	97693	09483	97700	09484	97708	09486	97716	09488	97724	09489	07
53	97724	09489	97732	09491	97739	09493	97747	09495	97755	09496	97763	09498	06
54	97763	09498	97771	09500	97778	09501	97786	09503	97794	09505	97802	09506	05
55	97802	09506	97810	09508	97817	09510	97825	09512	97833	09513	97841	09515	04
56	97841	09515	97849	09517	97856	09518	97864	09520	97872	09522	97880	09524	03
57	97880	09524	97888	09525	97895	09527	97903	09529	97911	09530	97919	09532	02
58	97919	09532	97926	09534	97934	09535	97942	09537	97950	09539	97958	09541	01
59	97958	09541	97965	09542	97973	09544	97981	09546	97989	09547	97996	09549	00

	.8	.6	.4	.2	.0

PARTS for 0′.1:   LOGS 4   NATURALS 1

324°

HAVERSINES

36° / **323°**

′	.0 Log. (2.or(8.) / 1.or(9.))	.0 Nat. 0.	.2 Log.	.2 Nat.	.4 Log.	.4 Nat.	.6 Log.	.6 Nat.	.8 Log.	.8 Nat.	′
00	97997	09549	98004	09551	98012	09553	98020	09554	98028	09556	98035	09558	59
01	98035	09558	98043	09559	98051	09561	98059	09563	98066	09565	98074	09566	58
02	98074	09566	98082	09568	98090	09570	98097	09571	98105	09573	98113	09575	57
03	98113	09575	98121	09577	98129	09578	98136	09580	98144	09582	98152	09583	56
04	98152	09583	98160	09585	98167	09587	98175	09589	98183	09590	98191	09592	55
05	98191	09592	98198	09594	98206	09595	98214	09597	98222	09599	98229	09601	54
06	98229	09601	98237	09602	98245	09604	98253	09606	98260	09607	98268	09609	53
07	98268	09609	98276	09611	98284	09613	98291	09614	98299	09616	98307	09618	52
08	98307	09618	98315	09619	98322	09621	98330	09623	98338	09625	98346	09626	51
09	98346	09626	98353	09628	98361	09630	98369	09631	98377	09633	98384	09635	50
10	98384	09635	98392	09637	98400	09638	98408	09640	98415	09642	98423	09643	49
11	98423	09643	98431	09645	98438	09647	98446	09649	98454	09650	98462	09652	48
12	98462	09652	98469	09654	98477	09655	98485	09657	98493	09659	98500	09661	47
13	98500	09661	98508	09662	98516	09664	98524	09666	98531	09667	98539	09669	46
14	98539	09669	98547	09671	98554	09673	98562	09674	98570	09676	98578	09678	45
15	98578	09678	98585	09679	98593	09681	98601	09683	98608	09685	98616	09686	44
16	98616	09686	98624	09688	98632	09690	98639	09692	98647	09693	98655	09695	43
17	98655	09695	98662	09697	98670	09698	98678	09700	98685	09702	98693	09704	42
18	98693	09704	98701	09705	98709	09707	98716	09709	98724	09710	98732	09712	41
19	98732	09712	98739	09714	98747	09716	98755	09717	98763	09719	98770	09721	40
20	98770	09721	98778	09723	98786	09724	98793	09726	98801	09728	98809	09729	39
21	98809	09729	98816	09731	98824	09733	98832	09735	98840	09736	98847	09738	38
22	98847	09738	98855	09740	98863	09742	98870	09743	98878	09745	98886	09747	37
23	98886	09747	98893	09748	98901	09750	98909	09752	98916	09754	98924	09755	36
24	98924	09755	98932	09757	98940	09759	98947	09760	98955	09762	98963	09764	35
25	98963	09764	98970	09766	98978	09767	98986	09769	98993	09771	99001	09773	34
26	99001	09773	99009	09774	99016	09776	99024	09778	99032	09779	99039	09781	33
27	99039	09781	99047	09783	99055	09785	99062	09786	99070	09788	99078	09790	32
28	99078	09790	99085	09792	99093	09793	99101	09795	99108	09797	99116	09799	31
29	99116	09799	99124	09800	99131	09802	99139	09804	99147	09805	99154	09807	30
30	99154	09807	99162	09809	99170	09811	99177	09812	99185	09814	99193	09816	29
31	99193	09816	99200	09818	99208	09819	99216	09821	99223	09823	99231	09824	28
32	99231	09824	99238	09826	99246	09828	99254	09830	99262	09831	99269	09833	27
33	99269	09833	99277	09835	99284	09837	99292	09838	99300	09840	99307	09842	26
34	99307	09842	99315	09844	99323	09845	99330	09847	99338	09849	99346	09850	25
35	99346	09850	99353	09852	99361	09854	99369	09856	99376	09857	99384	09859	24
36	99384	09859	99391	09861	99399	09863	99407	09864	99414	09866	99422	09868	23
37	99422	09868	99430	09870	99437	09871	99445	09873	99453	09875	99460	09877	22
38	99460	09877	99468	09878	99475	09880	99483	09882	99491	09883	99498	09885	21
39	99498	09885	99506	09887	99514	09889	99521	09890	99529	09892	99536	09894	20
40	99536	09894	99544	09896	99552	09897	99559	09899	99567	09901	99575	09903	19
41	99575	09903	99582	09904	99590	09906	99598	09908	99605	09909	99613	09911	18
42	99613	09911	99620	09913	99628	09915	99636	09916	99643	09918	99651	09920	17
43	99651	09920	99658	09922	99666	09923	99674	09925	99681	09927	99689	09929	16
44	99689	09929	99696	09930	99704	09932	99712	09934	99719	09936	99727	09937	15
45	99727	09937	99734	09939	99742	09941	99750	09943	99757	09944	99765	09946	14
46	99765	09946	99773	09948	99780	09949	99788	09951	99795	09953	99803	09955	13
47	99803	09955	99811	09956	99818	09958	99826	09960	99833	09962	99841	09963	12
48	99841	09963	99848	09965	99856	09967	99864	09969	99871	09970	99879	09972	11
49	99879	09972	99886	09974	99894	09976	99902	09977	99909	09979	99917	09981	10
50	99917	09981	99924	09983	99932	09984	99940	09986	99947	09988	99955	09990	09
51	99955	09990	99962	09991	99970	09993	99977	09995	99985	09997	99993	09998	08
52	99993	09998	00000	10000	00008	10002	00015	10004	00023	10005	00031	10007	07
53	00031	10007	00038	10009	00046	10011	00053	10012	00061	10014	00068	10016	06
54	00068	10016	00076	10018	00084	10019	00091	10021	00099	10023	00106	10025	05
55	00106	10025	00114	10026	00121	10028	00129	10030	00137	10032	00144	10033	04
56	00144	10033	00152	10035	00159	10037	00167	10039	00174	10040	00182	10042	03
57	00182	10042	00190	10044	00197	10046	00205	10047	00212	10049	00220	10051	02
58	00220	10051	00227	10052	00235	10054	00242	10056	00250	10058	00258	10059	01
59	00258	10059	00265	10061	00273	10063	00280	10065	00288	10066	00295	10068	00

Bottom scale: .8 | .6 | .4 | .2 | .0

PARTS for 0′.1:   LOGS 4   NATURALS 1

37° HAVERSINES

′	.0 Log. 1.or(9.)	.0 Nat. 0.	.2 Log. 1.or(9.)	.2 Nat. 0.	.4 Log. 1.or(9.)	.4 Nat. 0.	.6 Log. 1.or(9.)	.6 Nat. 0.	.8 Log. 1.or(9.)	.8 Nat. 0.	Log. 1.or(9.)	Nat. 0.	′
00	00295	10068	00303	10070	00310	10072	00318	10073	00325	10075	00333	10077	59
01	00333	10077	00341	10079	00348	10081	00356	10082	00363	10084	00371	10086	58
02	00371	10086	00378	10088	00386	10089	00393	10091	00401	10093	00408	10095	57
03	00408	10095	00416	10096	00424	10098	00431	10100	00439	10102	00446	10103	56
04	00446	10103	00454	10105	00461	10107	00469	10109	00476	10110	00484	10112	55
05	00484	10112	00491	10114	00499	10116	00506	10117	00514	10119	00521	10121	54
06	00521	10121	00529	10123	00537	10124	00544	10126	00552	10128	00559	10130	53
07	00559	10130	00567	10131	00574	10133	00582	10135	00589	10137	00597	10138	52
08	00597	10138	00604	10140	00612	10142	00619	10144	00627	10145	00634	10147	51
09	00634	10147	00642	10149	00649	10151	00657	10152	00664	10154	00672	10156	50
10	00672	10156	00680	10158	00687	10159	00695	10161	00702	10163	00710	10165	49
11	00710	10165	00717	10166	00725	10168	00732	10170	00740	10172	00747	10174	48
12	00747	10174	00755	10175	00762	10177	00770	10179	00777	10181	00785	10182	47
13	00785	10182	00792	10184	00800	10186	00807	10188	00815	10189	00822	10191	46
14	00822	10191	00830	10193	00837	10195	00845	10196	00852	10198	00860	10200	45
15	00860	10200	00867	10202	00875	10203	00882	10205	00890	10207	00897	10209	44
16	00897	10209	00905	10210	00912	10212	00920	10214	00927	10216	00935	10218	43
17	00935	10218	00942	10219	00950	10221	00957	10223	00965	10225	00972	10226	42
18	00972	10226	00979	10228	00987	10230	00994	10232	01002	10233	01009	10235	41
19	01009	10235	01017	10237	01024	10239	01032	10240	01039	10242	01047	10244	40
20	01047	10244	01054	10246	01062	10247	01069	10249	01077	10251	01084	10253	39
21	01084	10253	01092	10255	01099	10256	01107	10258	01114	10260	01122	10262	38
22	01122	10262	01129	10263	01136	10265	01144	10267	01151	10269	01159	10270	37
23	01159	10270	01166	10272	01174	10274	01181	10276	01189	10277	01196	10279	36
24	01196	10279	01204	10281	01211	10283	01219	10285	01226	10286	01234	10288	35
25	01234	10288	01241	10290	01248	10292	01256	10293	01263	10295	01271	10297	34
26	01271	10297	01278	10299	01286	10300	01293	10302	01301	10304	01308	10306	33
27	01308	10306	01316	10308	01323	10309	01331	10311	01338	10313	01345	10315	32
28	01345	10315	01353	10316	01360	10318	01368	10320	01375	10322	01383	10323	31
29	01383	10323	01390	10325	01397	10327	01405	10329	01412	10331	01420	10332	30
30	01420	10332	01427	10334	01435	10336	01442	10338	01450	10339	01457	10341	29
31	01457	10341	01464	10343	01472	10345	01479	10347	01487	10348	01494	10350	28
32	01494	10350	01502	10352	01509	10354	01517	10355	01524	10357	01531	10359	27
33	01531	10359	01539	10361	01546	10362	01554	10364	01561	10366	01569	10368	26
34	01569	10368	01576	10370	01583	10371	01591	10373	01598	10375	01606	10377	25
35	01606	10377	01613	10378	01620	10380	01628	10382	01635	10384	01643	10386	24
36	01643	10386	01650	10387	01658	10389	01665	10391	01673	10393	01680	10394	23
37	01680	10394	01687	10396	01695	10398	01702	10400	01710	10401	01717	10403	22
38	01717	10403	01724	10405	01732	10407	01739	10409	01747	10410	01754	10412	21
39	01754	10412	01761	10414	01769	10416	01776	10417	01784	10419	01791	10421	20
40	01791	10421	01799	10423	01806	10425	01813	10426	01821	10428	01828	10430	19
41	01828	10430	01836	10432	01843	10433	01850	10435	01858	10437	01865	10439	18
42	01865	10439	01873	10441	01880	10442	01887	10444	01895	10446	01902	10448	17
43	01902	10448	01910	10449	01917	10451	01924	10453	01932	10455	01939	10457	16
44	01939	10457	01947	10458	01954	10460	01961	10462	01969	10464	01976	10466	15
45	01976	10466	01983	10467	01991	10469	01998	10471	02006	10473	02013	10474	14
46	02013	10474	02020	10476	02028	10478	02035	10480	02043	10482	02050	10483	13
47	02050	10483	02057	10485	02065	10487	02072	10489	02079	10490	02087	10492	12
48	02087	10492	02094	10494	02102	10496	02109	10498	02116	10499	02124	10501	11
49	02124	10501	02131	10503	02139	10505	02146	10507	02153	10508	02161	10510	10
50	02161	10510	02168	10512	02175	10514	02183	10515	02190	10517	02197	10519	09
51	02197	10519	02205	10521	02212	10523	02220	10524	02227	10526	02234	10528	08
52	02234	10528	02242	10530	02249	10532	02256	10533	02264	10535	02271	10537	07
53	02271	10537	02279	10539	02286	10540	02293	10542	02301	10544	02308	10546	06
54	02308	10546	02315	10548	02323	10549	02330	10551	02337	10553	02345	10555	05
55	02345	10555	02352	10557	02359	10558	02367	10560	02374	10562	02381	10564	04
56	02381	10564	02389	10565	02396	10567	02403	10569	02411	10571	02418	10573	03
57	02418	10573	02426	10574	02433	10576	02440	10578	02448	10580	02455	10582	02
58	02455	10582	02462	10583	02470	10585	02477	10587	02484	10589	02492	10591	01
59	02492	10591	02499	10592	02506	10594	02514	10596	02521	10598	02528	10599	00

| | .8 | | .6 | | .4 | | .2 | | .0 | | |

PARTS for 0′.1:   LOGS 4·   NATURALS 1

322°

38° HAVERSINES

'	.0 Log.	.0 Nat.	.2 Log.	.2 Nat.	.4 Log.	.4 Nat.	.6 Log.	.6 Nat.	.8 Log.	.8 Nat.	'
	1̄.or(9.)	0.	1̄.or(9.)	0.	1̄.or(9.)	0.	1̄.or(9.)	0.	1̄.or(9.)	0.	
00	02528	10599	02536	10601	02543	10603	02550	10605	02558	10607	02565 10608	59
01	02565	10608	02572	10610	02580	10612	02587	10614	02594	10616	02602 10617	58
02	02602	10617	02609	10619	02616	10621	02624	10623	02631	10625	02638 10626	57
03	02638	10626	02646	10628	02653	10630	02660	10632	02668	10634	02675 10635	56
04	02675	10635	02682	10637	02690	10639	02697	10641	02704	10643	02712 10644	55
05	02712	10644	02719	10646	02726	10648	02734	10650	02741	10651	02748 10653	54
06	02748	10653	02756	10655	02763	10657	02770	10659	02777	10660	02785 10662	53
07	02785	10662	02792	10664	02799	10666	02807	10668	02814	10669	02821 10671	52
08	02821	10671	02829	10673	02836	10675	02843	10677	02851	10678	02858 10680	51
09	02858	10680	02865	10682	02872	10684	02880	10686	02887	10687	02894 10689	50
10	02894	10689	02902	10691	02909	10693	02916	10695	02924	10696	02931 10698	49
11	02931	10698	02938	10700	02946	10702	02953	10704	02960	10705	02967 10707	48
12	02967	10707	02975	10709	02982	10711	02989	10713	02997	10714	03004 10716	47
13	03004	10716	03011	10718	03018	10720	03026	10722	03033	10723	03040 10725	46
14	03040	10725	03048	10727	03055	10729	03062	10731	03070	10732	03077 10734	45
15	03077	10734	03084	10736	03091	10738	03099	10740	03106	10741	03113 10743	44
16	03113	10743	03120	10745	03128	10747	03135	10749	03142	10750	03150 10752	43
17	03150	10752	03157	10754	03164	10756	03171	10758	03179	10759	03186 10761	42
18	03186	10761	03193	10763	03201	10765	03208	10767	03215	10768	03222 10770	41
19	03222	10770	03230	10772	03237	10774	03244	10776	03252	10777	03259 10779	40
20	03259	10779	03266	10781	03273	10783	03281	10785	03288	10786	03295 10788	39
21	03295	10788	03302	10790	03310	10792	03317	10794	03324	10795	03331 10797	38
22	03331	10797	03339	10799	03346	10801	03353	10803	03360	10804	03368 10806	37
23	03368	10806	03375	10808	03382	10810	03389	10812	03397	10814	03404 10815	36
24	03404	10815	03411	10817	03418	10819	03426	10821	03433	10823	03440 10824	35
25	03440	10824	03447	10826	03455	10828	03462	10830	03469	10832	03476 10833	34
26	03476	10833	03484	10835	03491	10837	03498	10839	03506	10841	03513 10842	33
27	03513	10842	03520	10844	03527	10846	03535	10848	03542	10850	03549 10851	32
28	03549	10851	03556	10853	03563	10855	03571	10857	03578	10859	03585 10861	31
29	03585	10861	03592	10862	03600	10864	03607	10866	03614	10868	03621 10870	30
30	03621	10870	03629	10871	03636	10873	03643	10875	03650	10877	03657 10879	29
31	03657	10879	03665	10880	03672	10882	03679	10884	03686	10886	03694 10888	28
32	03694	10888	03701	10890	03708	10891	03715	10893	03723	10895	03730 10897	27
33	03730	10897	03737	10899	03744	10900	03751	10902	03759	10904	03766 10906	26
34	03766	10906	03773	10908	03780	10909	03788	10911	03795	10913	03802 10915	25
35	03802	10915	03809	10917	03816	10919	03824	10920	03831	10922	03838 10924	24
36	03838	10924	03845	10926	03852	10928	03860	10929	03867	10931	03874 10933	23
37	03874	10933	03881	10935	03889	10937	03896	10939	03903	10940	03910 10942	22
38	03910	10942	03917	10944	03925	10946	03932	10948	03939	10949	03946 10951	21
39	03946	10951	03953	10953	03961	10955	03968	10957	03975	10958	03982 10960	20
40	03982	10960	03989	10962	03997	10964	04004	10966	04011	10968	04018 10969	19
41	04018	10969	04025	10971	04033	10973	04040	10975	04047	10977	04054 10978	18
42	04054	10978	04061	10980	04069	10982	04076	10984	04083	10986	04090 10988	17
43	04090	10988	04097	10989	04105	10991	04112	10993	04119	10995	04126 10997	16
44	04126	10997	04133	10998	04141	11000	04148	11002	04155	11004	04162 11006	15
45	04162	11006	04169	11008	04176	11009	04184	11011	04191	11013	04198 11015	14
46	04198	11015	04205	11017	04212	11019	04219	11020	04227	11022	04234 11024	13
47	04234	11024	04241	11026	04248	11028	04255	11029	04263	11031	04270 11033	12
48	04270	11033	04277	11035	04284	11037	04291	11039	04298	11040	04306 11042	11
49	04306	11042	04313	11044	04320	11046	04327	11048	04334	11050	04341 11051	10
50	04341	11051	04349	11053	04356	11055	04363	11057	04370	11059	04377 11060	09
51	04377	11060	04385	11062	04392	11064	04399	11066	04406	11068	04413 11070	08
52	04413	11070	04420	11071	04428	11073	04435	11075	04442	11077	04449 11079	07
53	04449	11079	04456	11081	04463	11082	04470	11084	04478	11086	04485 11088	06
54	04485	11088	04492	11090	04499	11092	04506	11093	04513	11095	04520 11097	05
55	04520	11097	04528	11099	04535	11101	04542	11102	04549	11104	04556 11106	04
56	04556	11106	04563	11108	04571	11110	04578	11112	04585	11113	04592 11115	03
57	04592	11115	04599	11117	04606	11119	04613	11121	04620	11123	04628 11124	02
58	04628	11124	04635	11126	04642	11128	04649	11130	04656	11132	04663 11134	01
59	04663	11134	04671	11135	04678	11137	04685	11139	04692	11141	04699 11143	00

	.8		.6		.4		.2		.0	

PARTS for 0'.1: LOGS 4 NATURALS 1

321°

39° HAVERSINES

′	.0 Log. $\overline{1}$.or(9.)	.0 Nat. 0.	.2 Log. $\overline{1}$.or(9.)	.2 Nat. 0.	.4 Log. $\overline{1}$.or(9.)	.4 Nat. 0.	.6 Log. $\overline{1}$.or(9.)	.6 Nat. 0.	.8 Log. $\overline{1}$.or(9.)	.8 Nat. 0.	Log. $\overline{1}$.or(9.)	Nat. 0.	′
00	04699	11143	04706	11145	04713	11146	04720	11148	04728	11150	04735	11152	59
01	04735	11152	04742	11154	04749	11156	04756	11157	04763	11159	04770	11161	58
02	04770	11161	04778	11163	04785	11165	04792	11167	04799	11168	04806	11170	57
03	04806	11170	04813	11172	04820	11174	04827	11176	04834	11178	04842	11179	56
04	04842	11179	04849	11181	04856	11183	04863	11185	04870	11187	04877	11189	55
05	04877	11189	04884	11190	04891	11192	04899	11194	04906	11196	04913	11198	54
06	04913	11198	04920	11200	04927	11201	04934	11203	04941	11205	04948	11207	53
07	04948	11207	04956	11209	04963	11211	04970	11212	04977	11214	04984	11216	52
08	04984	11216	04991	11218	04998	11220	05005	11222	05012	11223	05019	11225	51
09	05019	11225	05027	11227	05034	11229	05041	11231	05048	11233	05055	11234	50
10	05055	11234	05062	11236	05069	11238	05076	11240	05083	11242	05090	11244	49
11	05090	11244	05098	11245	05105	11247	05112	11249	05119	11251	05126	11253	48
12	05126	11253	05133	11255	05140	11256	05147	11258	05154	11260	05161	11262	47
13	05161	11262	05168	11264	05176	11266	05183	11267	05190	11269	05197	11271	46
14	05197	11271	05204	11273	05211	11275	05218	11277	05225	11279	05232	11280	45
15	05232	11280	05239	11282	05247	11284	05254	11286	05261	11288	05268	11290	44
16	05268	11290	05275	11291	05282	11293	05289	11295	05296	11297	05303	11299	43
17	05303	11299	05310	11301	05317	11302	05324	11304	05332	11306	05339	11308	42
18	05339	11308	05346	11310	05353	11312	05360	11314	05367	11315	05374	11317	41
19	05374	11317	05381	11319	05388	11321	05395	11323	05402	11325	05409	11326	40
20	05409	11326	05416	11328	05423	11330	05430	11332	05438	11334	05445	11336	39
21	05445	11336	05452	11337	05459	11339	05466	11341	05473	11343	05480	11345	38
22	05480	11345	05487	11347	05494	11349	05501	11350	05508	11352	05515	11354	37
23	05515	11354	05522	11356	05529	11358	05536	11360	05544	11361	05551	11363	36
24	05551	11363	05558	11365	05565	11367	05572	11369	05579	11371	05586	11373	35
25	05586	11373	05593	11374	05600	11376	05607	11378	05614	11380	05621	11382	34
26	05621	11382	05628	11384	05635	11386	05642	11387	05649	11389	05656	11391	33
27	05656	11391	05663	11393	05670	11395	05678	11397	05685	11398	05692	11400	32
28	05692	11400	05699	11402	05706	11404	05713	11406	05720	11408	05727	11410	31
29	05727	11410	05734	11411	05741	11413	05748	11415	05755	11417	05762	11419	30
30	05762	11419	05769	11421	05776	11422	05783	11424	05790	11426	05797	11428	29
31	05797	11428	05804	11430	05811	11432	05818	11434	05825	11435	05832	11437	28
32	05832	11437	05839	11439	05846	11441	05853	11443	05860	11445	05867	11447	27
33	05867	11447	05874	11448	05881	11450	05889	11452	05896	11454	05903	11456	26
34	05903	11456	05910	11458	05917	11460	05924	11461	05931	11463	05938	11465	25
35	05938	11465	05945	11467	05952	11469	05959	11471	05966	11472	05973	11474	24
36	05973	11474	05980	11476	05987	11478	05994	11480	06001	11482	06008	11484	23
37	06008	11484	06015	11485	06022	11487	06029	11489	06036	11491	06043	11493	22
38	06043	11493	06050	11495	06057	11497	06064	11498	06071	11500	06078	11502	21
39	06078	11502	06085	11504	06092	11506	06099	11508	06106	11510	06113	11511	20
40	06113	11511	06120	11513	06127	11515	06134	11517	06141	11519	06148	11521	19
41	06148	11521	06155	11523	06162	11524	06169	11526	06176	11528	06183	11530	18
42	06183	11530	06190	11532	06197	11534	06204	11536	06211	11537	06218	11539	17
43	06218	11539	06225	11541	06232	11543	06239	11545	06246	11547	06253	11549	16
44	06253	11549	06260	11550	06267	11552	06274	11554	06281	11556	06288	11558	15
45	06288	11558	06295	11560	06302	11562	06309	11563	06316	11565	06323	11567	14
46	06323	11567	06330	11569	06337	11571	06344	11573	06351	11575	06358	11577	13
47	06358	11577	06365	11578	06372	11580	06379	11582	06386	11584	06393	11586	12
48	06393	11586	06400	11588	06407	11590	06414	11591	06421	11593	06428	11595	11
49	06428	11595	06435	11597	06442	11599	06448	11601	06455	11603	06462	11604	10
50	06462	11604	06469	11606	06476	11608	06483	11610	06490	11612	06497	11614	09
51	06497	11614	06504	11616	06511	11617	06518	11619	06525	11621	06532	11623	08
52	06532	11623	06539	11625	06546	11627	06553	11629	06560	11631	06567	11632	07
53	06567	11632	06574	11634	06581	11636	06588	11638	06595	11640	06602	11642	06
54	06602	11642	06609	11644	06616	11645	06623	11647	06630	11649	06637	11651	05
55	06637	11651	06644	11653	06651	11655	06657	11657	06664	11659	06671	11660	04
56	06671	11660	06678	11662	06685	11664	06692	11666	06699	11668	06706	11670	03
57	06706	11670	06713	11672	06720	11673	06727	11675	06734	11677	06741	11679	02
58	06741	11679	06748	11681	06755	11683	06762	11685	06769	11687	06776	11688	01
59	06776	11688	06783	11690	06790	11692	06796	11694	06803	11696	06810	11698	00

.8	.6	.4	.2	.0

PARTS for 0′.1: LOGS 4   NATURALS 1

40° HAVERSINES

′	.0 Log. 1.or(9.)	.0 Nat. 0.	.2 Log. 1.or(9.)	.2 Nat. 0.	.4 Log. 1.or(9.)	.4 Nat. 0.	.6 Log. 1.or(9.)	.6 Nat. 0.	.8 Log. 1.or(9.)	.8 Nat. 0.	′
00	06810	11698	06817	11700	06824	11702	06831	11703	06838	11705	06845 11707	59
01	06845	11707	06852	11709	06859	11711	06866	11713	06873	11715	06880 11716	58
02	06880	11716	06887	11718	06894	11720	06901	11722	06907	11724	06914 11726	57
03	06914	11726	06921	11728	06928	11730	06935	11731	06942	11733	06949 11735	56
04	06949	11735	06956	11737	06963	11739	06970	11741	06977	11743	06984 11745	55
05	06984	11745	06991	11746	06998	11748	07004	11750	07011	11752	07018 11754	54
06	07018	11754	07025	11756	07032	11758	07039	11760	07046	11761	07053 11763	53
07	07053	11763	07060	11765	07067	11767	07074	11769	07081	11771	07088 11773	52
08	07088	11773	07094	11775	07101	11776	07108	11778	07115	11780	07122 11782	51
09	07122	11782	07129	11784	07136	11786	07143	11788	07150	11790	07157 11791	50
10	07157	11791	07164	11793	07170	11795	07177	11797	07184	11799	07191 11801	49
11	07191	11801	07198	11803	07205	11805	07212	11806	07219	11808	07226 11810	48
12	07226	11810	07233	11812	07240	11814	07246	11816	07253	11818	07260 11820	47
13	07260	11820	07267	11821	07274	11823	07281	11825	07288	11827	07295 11829	46
14	07295	11829	07302	11831	07309	11833	07315	11835	07322	11837	07329 11838	45
15	07329	11838	07336	11840	07343	11842	07350	11844	07357	11846	07364 11848	44
16	07364	11848	07371	11850	07377	11852	07384	11853	07391	11855	07398 11857	43
17	07398	11857	07405	11859	07412	11861	07419	11863	07426	11865	07433 11867	42
18	07433	11867	07439	11868	07446	11870	07453	11872	07460	11874	07467 11876	41
19	07467	11876	07474	11878	07481	11880	07488	11882	07495	11884	07501 11885	40
20	07501	11885	07508	11887	07515	11889	07522	11891	07529	11893	07536 11895	39
21	07536	11895	07543	11897	07550	11899	07556	11900	07563	11902	07570 11904	38
22	07570	11904	07577	11906	07584	11908	07591	11910	07598	11912	07605 11914	37
23	07605	11914	07611	11916	07618	11917	07625	11919	07632	11921	07639 11923	36
24	07639	11923	07646	11925	07653	11927	07659	11929	07666	11931	07673 11933	35
25	07673	11933	07680	11934	07687	11936	07694	11938	07701	11940	07708 11942	34
26	07708	11942	07714	11944	07721	11946	07728	11948	07735	11950	07742 11951	33
27	07742	11951	07749	11953	07755	11955	07762	11957	07769	11959	07776 11961	32
28	07776	11961	07783	11963	07790	11965	07797	11966	07804	11968	07810 11970	31
29	07810	11970	07817	11972	07824	11974	07831	11976	07838	11978	07845 11980	30
30	07845	11980	07851	11982	07858	11983	07865	11985	07872	11987	07879 11989	29
31	07879	11989	07886	11991	07892	11993	07899	11995	07906	11997	07913 11999	28
32	07913	11999	07920	12000	07927	12002	07934	12004	07940	12006	07947 12008	27
33	07947	12008	07954	12010	07961	12012	07968	12014	07975	12016	07981 12018	26
34	07981	12018	07988	12019	07995	12021	08002	12023	08009	12025	08016 12027	25
35	03016	12027	08022	12029	08029	12031	08036	12033	08043	12035	08050 12036	24
36	08050	12036	08057	12038	08063	12040	08070	12042	08077	12044	03084 12046	23
37	08084	12046	08091	12048	08098	12050	08104	12052	08111	12053	08118 12055	22
38	08118	12055	08125	12057	08132	12059	08139	12061	08145	12063	08152 12065	21
39	08152	12065	08159	12067	08166	12069	08173	12071	08179	12072	08186 12074	20
40	08186	12074	08193	12076	08200	12078	08207	12080	08214	12082	08220 12084	19
41	08220	12084	08227	12086	08234	12088	08241	12090	08248	12091	08254 12093	18
42	08254	12093	08261	12095	08268	12097	08275	12099	08282	12101	08288 12103	17
43	08288	12103	08295	12105	08302	12107	08309	12108	08316	12110	08323 12112	16
44	08323	12112	08329	12114	08336	12116	08343	12118	08350	12120	08357 12122	15
45	08357	12122	08363	12124	08370	12126	08377	12127	08384	12129	08391 12131	14
46	08391	12131	08397	12133	08404	12135	08411	12137	08418	12139	08425 12141	13
47	08425	12141	08431	12143	08438	12145	08445	12146	08452	12148	08459 12150	12
48	08459	12150	08465	12152	08472	12154	08479	12156	08486	12158	08492 12160	11
49	08492	12160	08499	12162	08506	12164	08513	12165	08520	12167	08526 12169	10
50	08526	12169	08533	12171	08540	12173	08547	12175	08554	12177	08560 12179	09
51	08560	12179	08567	12181	08574	12183	08581	12184	08587	12186	08594 12188	08
52	08594	12188	08601	12190	08608	12192	08615	12194	08621	12196	08628 12198	07
53	08628	12198	08635	12200	08642	12202	08648	12204	08655	12205	08662 12207	06
54	08662	12207	08669	12209	08676	12211	08682	12213	08689	12215	08696 12217	05
55	08696	12217	08703	12219	08710	12221	08716	12223	08723	12224	08730 12226	04
56	08730	12226	08737	12228	08743	12230	08750	12232	08757	12234	08764 12236	03
57	08764	12236	08770	12238	08777	12240	08784	12242	08791	12244	08797 12245	02
58	08797	12245	08804	12247	08811	12249	08818	12251	08824	12253	08831 12255	01
59	08831	12255	08838	12257	08845	12259	08851	12261	08858	12263	08865 12265	00

	.8		.6		.4		.2		.0

PARTS for 0′.1:   LOGS 3   NATURALS 1   319°

41° HAVERSINES

′	.0 Log. $\overline{1}$.or(9.)	.0 Nat. 0.	.2 Log. $\overline{1}$.or(9.)	.2 Nat. 0.	.4 Log. $\overline{1}$.or(9.)	.4 Nat. 0.	.6 Log. $\overline{1}$.or(9.)	.6 Nat. 0.	.8 Log. $\overline{1}$.or(9.)	.8 Nat. 0.	Log. $\overline{1}$.or(9.)	Nat. 0.	′
00	08865	12265	08872	12266	08879	12268	08885	12270	08892	12272	08899	12274	59
01	08899	12274	08906	12276	08912	12278	08919	12280	08926	12282	08933	12284	58
02	08933	12284	08939	12286	08946	12287	08953	12289	08960	12291	08966	12293	57
03	08966	12293	08973	12295	08980	12297	08987	12299	08993	12301	09000	12303	56
04	09000	12303	09007	12305	09014	12307	09020	12308	09027	12310	09034	12312	55
05	09034	12312	09041	12314	09047	12316	09054	12318	09061	12320	09068	12322	54
06	09068	12322	09074	12324	09081	12326	09088	12328	09094	12329	09101	12331	53
07	09101	12331	09108	12333	09115	12335	09121	12337	09128	12339	09135	12341	52
08	09135	12341	09142	12343	09148	12345	09155	12347	09162	12349	09169	12351	51
09	09169	12351	09175	12352	09182	12354	09189	12356	09195	12358	09202	12360	50
10	09202	12360	09209	12362	09216	12364	09222	12366	09229	12368	09236	12370	49
11	09236	12370	09243	12372	09249	12374	09256	12375	09263	12377	09269	12379	48
12	09269	12379	09276	12381	09283	12383	09290	12385	09296	12387	09303	12389	47
13	09303	12389	09310	12391	09316	12393	09323	12395	09330	12396	09337	12398	46
14	09337	12398	09343	12400	09350	12402	09357	12404	09363	12406	09370	12408	45
15	09370	12408	09377	12410	09384	12412	09390	12414	09397	12416	09404	12418	44
16	09404	12418	09411	12420	09417	12421	09424	12423	09431	12425	09437	12427	43
17	09437	12427	09444	12429	09451	12431	09457	12433	09464	12435	09471	12437	42
18	09471	12437	09478	12439	09484	12441	09491	12443	09498	12444	09504	12446	41
19	09504	12446	09511	12448	09518	12450	09524	12452	09531	12454	09538	12456	40
20	09538	12456	09545	12458	09551	12460	09558	12462	09565	12464	09571	12466	39
21	09571	12466	09578	12468	09585	12469	09591	12471	09598	12473	09605	12475	38
22	09605	12475	09611	12477	09618	12479	09625	12481	09632	12483	09638	12485	37
23	09638	12485	09645	12487	09652	12489	09658	12491	09665	12493	09672	12494	36
24	09672	12494	09678	12496	09685	12498	09692	12500	09699	12502	09705	12504	35
25	09705	12504	09712	12506	09719	12508	09725	12510	09732	12512	09739	12514	34
26	09739	12514	09745	12516	09752	12518	09759	12519	09765	12521	09772	12523	33
27	09772	12523	09779	12525	09785	12527	09792	12529	09799	12531	09805	12533	32
28	09805	12533	09812	12535	09819	12537	09825	12539	09832	12541	09839	12543	31
29	09839	12543	09845	12545	09852	12546	09859	12548	09865	12550	09872	12552	30
30	09872	12552	09879	12554	09885	12556	09892	12558	09899	12560	09905	12562	29
31	09905	12562	09912	12564	09919	12566	09925	12568	09932	12570	09939	12572	28
32	09939	12572	09945	12573	09952	12575	09959	12577	09965	12579	09972	12581	27
33	09972	12581	09979	12583	09985	12585	09992	12587	09999	12589	10005	12591	26
34	10005	12591	10012	12593	10019	12595	10025	12597	10032	12599	10039	12600	25
35	10039	12600	10045	12602	10052	12604	10059	12606	10065	12608	10072	12610	24
36	10072	12610	10078	12612	10085	12614	10092	12616	10098	12618	10105	12620	23
37	10105	12620	10112	12622	10118	12624	10125	12626	10132	12627	10138	12629	22
38	10138	12629	10145	12631	10152	12633	10158	12635	10165	12637	10172	12639	21
39	10172	12639	10178	12641	10185	12643	10192	12645	10198	12647	10205	12649	20
40	10205	12649	10211	12651	10218	12653	10225	12655	10231	12656	10238	12658	19
41	10238	12658	10245	12660	10251	12662	10258	12664	10265	12666	10271	12668	18
42	10271	12668	10278	12670	10284	12672	10291	12674	10298	12676	10304	12678	17
43	10304	12678	10311	12680	10317	12682	10324	12684	10331	12686	10337	12687	16
44	10337	12687	10344	12689	10351	12691	10357	12693	10364	12695	10371	12697	15
45	10371	12697	10377	12699	10384	12701	10390	12703	10397	12705	10404	12707	14
46	10404	12707	10410	12709	10417	12711	10424	12713	10430	12715	10437	12717	13
47	10437	12717	10443	12718	10450	12720	10457	12722	10463	12724	10470	12726	12
48	10470	12726	10476	12728	10483	12730	10490	12732	10496	12734	10503	12736	11
49	10503	12736	10510	12738	10516	12740	10523	12742	10529	12744	10536	12746	10
50	10536	12746	10543	12748	10549	12749	10556	12751	10562	12753	10569	12755	09
51	10569	12755	10576	12757	10582	12759	10589	12761	10595	12763	10602	12765	08
52	10602	12765	10609	12767	10615	12769	10622	12771	10629	12773	10635	12775	07
53	10635	12775	10642	12777	10648	12779	10655	12781	10662	12782	10668	12784	06
54	10668	12784	10675	12786	10681	12788	10688	12790	10695	12792	10701	12794	05
55	10701	12794	10708	12796	10714	12798	10721	12800	10727	12802	10734	12804	04
56	10734	12804	10741	12806	10747	12808	10754	12810	10760	12812	10767	12814	03
57	10767	12814	10774	12816	10780	12817	10787	12819	10793	12821	10800	12823	02
58	10800	12823	10807	12825	10813	12827	10820	12829	10826	12831	10833	12833	01
59	10833	12833	10840	12835	10846	12837	10853	12839	10859	12841	10866	12843	00

	.8	.6	.4	.2	.0 ←

PARTS for 0′.1: LOGS 3·   NATURALS 1

318°

42° HAVERSINES

′	.0 Log.	.0 Nat.	.2 Log.	.2 Nat.	.4 Log.	.4 Nat.	.6 Log.	.6 Nat.	.8 Log.	.8 Nat.	Log.	Nat.	′
	1.or(9.)	0.	1.or(9.)	0.	1.or(9.)	0.	1.or(9.)	0.	1.or(9.)	0.	1.or(9.)	0.	
00	10866	12843	10872	12845	10879	12847	10886	12849	10892	12851	10899	12852	59
01	10899	12852	10905	12854	10912	12856	10918	12858	10925	12860	10932	12862	58
02	10932	12862	10938	12864	10945	12866	10951	12868	10958	12870	10964	12872	57
03	10964	12872	10971	12874	10978	12876	10984	12878	10991	12880	10997	12882	56
04	10997	12882	11004	12884	11011	12886	11017	12888	11024	12890	11030	12891	55
05	11030	12891	11037	12893	11043	12895	11050	12897	11056	12899	11063	12901	54
06	11063	12901	11070	12903	11076	12905	11083	12907	11089	12909	11096	12911	53
07	11096	12911	11102	12913	11109	12915	11115	12917	11122	12919	11129	12921	52
08	11129	12921	11135	12923	11142	12925	11148	12927	11155	12929	11161	12930	51
09	11161	12930	11168	12932	11175	12934	11181	12936	11188	12938	11194	12940	50
10	11194	12940	11201	12942	11207	12944	11214	12946	11220	12948	11227	12950	49
11	11227	12950	11234	12952	11240	12954	11247	12956	11253	12958	11260	12960	48
12	11260	12960	11266	12962	11273	12964	11279	12966	11286	12968	11292	12970	47
13	11292	12970	11299	12972	11306	12973	11312	12975	11319	12977	11325	12979	46
14	11325	12979	11332	12981	11338	12983	11345	12985	11351	12987	11358	12989	45
15	11358	12989	11364	12991	11371	12993	11377	12995	11384	12997	11391	12999	44
16	11391	12999	11397	13001	11404	13003	11410	13005	11417	13007	11423	13009	43
17	11423	13009	11430	13011	11436	13013	11443	13015	11449	13016	11456	13018	42
18	11456	13018	11463	13020	11469	13022	11476	13024	11482	13026	11489	13028	41
19	11489	13028	11495	13030	11502	13032	11508	13034	11515	13036	11521	13038	40
20	11521	13038	11528	13040	11534	13042	11541	13044	11547	13046	11554	13048	39
21	11554	13048	11560	13050	11567	13052	11573	13054	11580	13056	11586	13058	38
22	11586	13058	11593	13060	11599	13062	11606	13064	11612	13065	11619	13067	37
23	11619	13067	11626	13069	11632	13071	11639	13073	11645	13075	11652	13077	36
24	11652	13077	11658	13079	11665	13081	11671	13083	11678	13085	11684	13087	35
25	11684	13087	11691	13089	11697	13091	11704	13093	11710	13095	11717	13097	34
26	11717	13097	11723	13099	11730	13101	11736	13103	11743	13105	11749	13107	33
27	11749	13107	11756	13109	11762	13111	11769	13113	11775	13115	11782	13116	32
28	11782	13116	11788	13118	11795	13120	11801	13122	11808	13124	11814	13126	31
29	11814	13126	11821	13128	11827	13130	11834	13132	11840	13134	11847	13136	30
30	11847	13136	11853	13138	11860	13140	11866	13142	11873	13144	11879	13146	29
31	11879	13146	11886	13148	11892	13150	11899	13152	11905	13154	11912	13156	28
32	11912	13156	11918	13158	11925	13160	11931	13162	11938	13164	11944	13166	27
33	11944	13166	11951	13168	11957	13170	11964	13172	11970	13173	11977	13175	26
34	11977	13175	11983	13177	11990	13179	11996	13181	12003	13183	12009	13185	25
35	12009	13185	12015	13187	12022	13189	12028	13191	12035	13193	12041	13195	24
36	12041	13195	12048	13197	12054	13199	12061	13201	12067	13203	12074	13205	23
37	12074	13205	12080	13207	12087	13209	12093	13211	12100	13213	12106	13215	22
38	12106	13215	12113	13217	12119	13219	12126	13221	12132	13223	12139	13225	21
39	12139	13225	12145	13227	12152	13229	12158	13231	12165	13233	12171	13235	20
40	12171	13235	12177	13237	12184	13238	12190	13240	12197	13242	12203	13244	19
41	12203	13244	12210	13246	12216	13248	12223	13250	12229	13252	12236	13254	18
42	12236	13254	12242	13256	12248	13258	12255	13260	12261	13262	12268	13264	17
43	12268	13264	12274	13266	12281	13268	12287	13270	12294	13272	12300	13274	16
44	12300	13274	12307	13276	12313	13278	12320	13280	12326	13282	12332	13284	15
45	12332	13284	12339	13286	12345	13288	12352	13290	12358	13292	12365	13294	14
46	12365	13294	12371	13296	12378	13298	12384	13300	12391	13302	12397	13304	13
47	12397	13304	12403	13306	12410	13308	12416	13310	12423	13312	12429	13314	12
48	12429	13314	12436	13315	12442	13317	12449	13319	12455	13321	12461	13323	11
49	12461	13323	12468	13325	12474	13327	12481	13329	12487	13331	12494	13333	10
50	12494	13333	12500	13335	12506	13337	12513	13339	12519	13341	12526	13343	09
51	12526	13343	12532	13345	12539	13347	12545	13349	12552	13351	12558	13353	08
52	12558	13353	12564	13355	12571	13357	12577	13359	12584	13361	12590	13363	07
53	12590	13363	12597	13365	12603	13367	12610	13369	12616	13371	12622	13373	06
54	12622	13373	12629	13375	12635	13377	12642	13379	12648	13381	12655	13383	05
55	12655	13383	12661	13385	12667	13387	12674	13389	12680	13391	12687	13393	04
56	12687	13393	12693	13395	12699	13397	12706	13399	12712	13401	12719	13403	03
57	12719	13403	12725	13405	12732	13407	12738	13409	12745	13411	12751	13412	02
58	12751	13412	12757	13414	12764	13416	12770	13418	12777	13420	12783	13422	01
59	12783	13422	12789	13424	12796	13426	12802	13428	12809	13430	12815	13432	00
	.8		.6		.4		.2		.0				

PARTS for 0′.1: LOGS 3 NATURALS 1

317°

43° HAVERSINES

′	.0 Log.	.0 Nat.	.2 Log.	.2 Nat.	.4 Log.	.4 Nat.	.6 Log.	.6 Nat.	.8 Log.	.8 Nat.	Log.	Nat.	′
	$\overline{1}$.or(9.)	0.	$\overline{1}$.or(9.)	0.	$\overline{1}$.or(9.)	0.	$\overline{1}$.or(9.)	0.	$\overline{1}$.or(9.)	0.	$\overline{1}$.or(9.)	0.	
00	12815	13432	12821	13434	12828	13436	12834	13438	12841	13440	12847	13442	59
01	12847	13442	12854	13444	12860	13446	12866	13448	12873	13450	12879	13452	58
02	12879	13452	12886	13454	12892	13456	12898	13458	12905	13460	12911	13462	57
03	12911	13462	12918	13464	12924	13466	12930	13468	12937	13470	12943	13472	56
04	12943	13472	12950	13474	12956	13476	12962	13478	12969	13480	12975	13482	55
05	12975	13482	12982	13484	12988	13486	12994	13488	13001	13490	13007	13492	54
06	13007	13492	13014	13494	13020	13496	13026	13498	13033	13500	13039	13502	53
07	13039	13502	13046	13504	13052	13506	13058	13508	13065	13510	13071	13512	52
08	13071	13512	13078	13514	13084	13516	13090	13518	13097	13520	13103	13522	51
09	13103	13522	13110	13524	13116	13526	13122	13528	13129	13530	13135	13532	50
10	13135	13532	13142	13534	13148	13536	13154	13538	13161	13540	13167	13542	49
11	13167	13542	13173	13544	13180	13546	13186	13548	13193	13550	13199	13552	48
12	13199	13552	13205	13554	13212	13556	13218	13558	13224	13560	13231	13562	47
13	13231	13562	13237	13564	13244	13566	13250	13568	13256	13570	13263	13571	46
14	13263	13571	13269	13573	13276	13575	13282	13577	13288	13579	13295	13581	45
15	13295	13581	13301	13583	13307	13585	13314	13587	13320	13589	13326	13591	44
16	13326	13591	13333	13593	13339	13595	13346	13597	13352	13599	13358	13601	43
17	13358	13601	13365	13603	13371	13605	13377	13607	13384	13609	13390	13611	42
18	13390	13611	13397	13613	13403	13615	13409	13617	13416	13619	13422	13621	41
19	13422	13621	13428	13623	13435	13625	13441	13627	13447	13629	13454	13631	40
20	13454	13631	13460	13633	13467	13635	13473	13637	13479	13639	13486	13641	39
21	13486	13641	13492	13643	13498	13645	13505	13647	13511	13649	13517	13651	38
22	13517	13651	13524	13653	13530	13655	13536	13657	13543	13659	13549	13661	37
23	13549	13661	13556	13663	13562	13665	13568	13667	13574	13669	13581	13671	36
24	13581	13671	13587	13673	13594	13675	13600	13677	13606	13679	13613	13681	35
25	13613	13681	13619	13683	13625	13685	13632	13687	13638	13689	13644	13691	34
26	13644	13691	13651	13693	13657	13695	13663	13697	13670	13699	13676	13701	33
27	13676	13701	13682	13703	13689	13705	13695	13707	13701	13709	13708	13711	32
28	13708	13711	13714	13713	13720	13715	13727	13717	13733	13719	13739	13721	31
29	13739	13721	13746	13723	13752	13725	13758	13727	13765	13729	13771	13731	30
30	13771	13731	13778	13733	13784	13735	13790	13737	13796	13739	13803	13741	29
31	13803	13741	13809	13743	13815	13745	13822	13747	13828	13749	13834	13751	28
32	13834	13751	13841	13753	13847	13755	13853	13757	13860	13759	13866	13761	27
33	13866	13761	13872	13763	13879	13765	13885	13767	13891	13769	13898	13771	26
34	13898	13771	13904	13773	13910	13775	13917	13777	13923	13779	13929	13781	25
35	13929	13781	13936	13783	13942	13785	13948	13787	13954	13789	13961	13791	24
36	13961	13791	13967	13793	13973	13795	13980	13797	13986	13799	13992	13801	23
37	13992	13801	13999	13803	14005	13805	14011	13807	14018	13809	14024	13811	22
38	14024	13811	14030	13813	14037	13815	14043	13817	14049	13819	14056	13822	21
39	14056	13822	14062	13824	14068	13826	14074	13828	14081	13830	14087	13832	20
40	14087	13832	14093	13834	14100	13836	14106	13838	14112	13840	14119	13842	19
41	14119	13842	14125	13844	14131	13846	14138	13848	14144	13850	14150	13852	18
42	14150	13852	14156	13854	14163	13856	14169	13858	14175	13860	14182	13862	17
43	14182	13862	14188	13864	14194	13866	14201	13868	14207	13870	14213	13872	16
44	14213	13872	14219	13874	14226	13876	14232	13878	14238	13880	14245	13882	15
45	14245	13882	14251	13884	14257	13886	14263	13888	14270	13890	14276	13892	14
46	14276	13892	14282	13894	14289	13896	14295	13898	14301	13900	14307	13902	13
47	14307	13902	14314	13904	14320	13906	14326	13908	14333	13910	14339	13912	12
48	14339	13912	14345	13914	14352	13916	14358	13918	14364	13920	14370	13922	11
49	14370	13922	14377	13924	14383	13926	14389	13928	14396	13930	14402	13932	10
50	14402	13932	14408	13934	14414	13936	14421	13938	14427	13940	14433	13942	09
51	14433	13942	14439	13944	14446	13946	14452	13948	14458	13950	14465	13952	08
52	14465	13952	14471	13954	14477	13956	14483	13958	14490	13960	14496	13962	07
53	14496	13962	14502	13964	14508	13966	14515	13968	14521	13970	14527	13972	06
54	14527	13972	14533	13974	14540	13976	14546	13979	14552	13981	14559	13983	05
55	14559	13983	14565	13985	14571	13987	14577	13989	14584	13991	14590	13993	04
56	14590	13993	14596	13995	14602	13997	14609	13999	14615	14001	14621	14003	03
57	14621	14003	14627	14005	14634	14007	14640	14009	14646	14011	14653	14013	02
58	14653	14013	14659	14015	14665	14017	14671	14019	14678	14021	14684	14023	01
59	14684	14023	14690	14025	14696	14027	14703	14029	14709	14031	14715	14033	00

| | .8 | | .6 | | .4 | | .2 | | .0 | |

PARTS for 0′.1:   LOGS 3·   NATURALS 1

316°

44° HAVERSINES

′	.0 Log. 1̄.or(9.)	.0 Nat. 0.	.2 Log. 1̄.or(9.)	.2 Nat. 0.	.4 Log. 1̄.or(9.)	.4 Nat. 0.	.6 Log. 1̄.or(9.)	.6 Nat. 0.	.8 Log. 1̄.or(9.)	.8 Nat. 0.	Log. 1̄.or(9.)	Nat. 0.	′
00	14715	14033	14721	14035	14728	14037	14734	14039	14740	14041	14746	14043	59
01	14746	14043	14753	14045	14759	14047	14765	14049	14771	14051	14778	14053	58
02	14778	14053	14784	14055	14790	14057	14796	14059	14803	14061	14809	14063	57
03	14809	14063	14815	14065	14821	14067	14828	14069	14834	14071	14840	14073	56
04	14840	14073	14846	14075	14852	14077	14859	14080	14865	14082	14871	14084	55
05	14871	14084	14877	14086	14884	14088	14890	14090	14896	14092	14902	14094	54
06	14902	14094	14909	14096	14915	14098	14921	14100	14927	14102	14934	14104	53
07	14934	14104	14940	14106	14946	14108	14952	14110	14959	14112	14965	14114	52
08	14965	14114	14971	14116	14977	14118	14984	14120	14990	14122	14996	14124	51
09	14996	14124	15002	14126	15008	14128	15015	14130	15021	14132	15027	14134	50
10	15027	14134	15033	14136	15040	14138	15046	14140	15052	14142	15058	14144	49
11	15058	14144	15064	14146	15071	14148	15077	14150	15083	14152	15089	14154	48
12	15089	14154	15096	14156	15102	14159	15108	14161	15114	14163	15120	14165	47
13	15120	14165	15127	14167	15133	14169	15139	14171	15145	14173	15152	14175	46
14	15152	14175	15158	14177	15164	14179	15170	14181	15176	14183	15183	14185	45
15	15183	14185	15189	14187	15195	14189	15201	14191	15208	14193	15214	14195	44
16	15214	14195	15220	14197	15226	14199	15232	14201	15239	14203	15245	14205	43
17	15245	14205	15251	14207	15257	14209	15263	14211	15270	14213	15276	14215	42
18	15276	14215	15282	14217	15288	14219	15294	14221	15301	14223	15307	14226	41
19	15307	14226	15313	14228	15319	14230	15325	14232	15332	14234	15338	14236	40
20	15338	14236	15344	14238	15350	14240	15356	14242	15363	14244	15369	14246	39
21	15369	14246	15375	14248	15381	14250	15387	14252	15394	14254	15400	14256	38
22	15400	14256	15406	14258	15412	14260	15418	14262	15425	14264	15431	14266	37
23	15431	14266	15437	14268	15443	14270	15449	14272	15456	14274	15462	14276	36
24	15462	14276	15468	14278	15474	14280	15480	14282	15487	14285	15493	14287	35
25	15493	14287	15499	14289	15505	14291	15511	14293	15517	14295	15524	14297	34
26	15524	14297	15530	14299	15536	14301	15542	14303	15548	14305	15555	14307	33
27	15555	14307	15561	14309	15567	14311	15573	14313	15579	14315	15585	14317	32
28	15585	14317	15592	14319	15598	14321	15604	14323	15610	14325	15616	14327	31
29	15616	14327	15623	14329	15629	14331	15635	14333	15641	14335	15647	14337	30
30	15647	14337	15653	14340	15660	14342	15666	14344	15672	14346	15678	14348	29
31	15678	14348	15684	14350	15691	14352	15697	14354	15703	14356	15709	14358	28
32	15709	14358	15715	14360	15721	14362	15727	14364	15734	14366	15740	14368	27
33	15740	14368	15746	14370	15752	14372	15758	14374	15764	14376	15771	14378	26
34	15771	14378	15777	14380	15783	14382	15789	14384	15795	14386	15802	14388	25
35	15802	14388	15808	14391	15814	14393	15820	14395	15826	14397	15832	14399	24
36	15832	14399	15839	14401	15845	14403	15851	14405	15857	14407	15863	14409	23
37	15863	14409	15869	14411	15876	14413	15882	14415	15888	14417	15894	14419	22
38	15894	14419	15900	14421	15906	14423	15912	14425	15918	14427	15925	14429	21
39	15925	14429	15931	14431	15937	14433	15943	14435	15949	14438	15955	14440	20
40	15955	14440	15962	14442	15968	14444	15974	14446	15980	14448	15986	14450	19
41	15986	14450	15992	14452	15999	14454	16005	14456	16011	14458	16017	14460	18
42	16017	14460	16023	14462	16029	14464	16035	14466	16041	14468	16048	14470	17
43	16048	14470	16054	14472	16060	14474	16066	14476	16072	14478	16078	14480	16
44	16078	14480	16085	14483	16091	14485	16097	14487	16103	14489	16109	14491	15
45	16109	14491	16115	14493	16121	14495	16127	14497	16134	14499	16140	14501	14
46	16140	14501	16146	14503	16152	14505	16158	14507	16164	14509	16170	14511	13
47	16170	14511	16177	14513	16183	14515	16189	14517	16195	14519	16201	14521	12
48	16201	14521	16207	14524	16213	14526	16219	14528	16225	14530	16232	14532	11
49	16232	14532	16238	14534	16244	14536	16250	14538	16256	14540	16262	14542	10
50	16262	14542	16269	14544	16275	14546	16281	14548	16287	14550	16293	14552	09
51	16293	14552	16299	14554	16305	14556	16311	14558	16317	14560	16324	14562	08
52	16324	14562	16330	14565	16336	14567	16342	14569	16348	14571	16354	14573	07
53	16354	14573	16360	14575	16366	14577	16373	14579	16379	14581	16385	14583	06
54	16385	14583	16391	14585	16397	14587	16403	14589	16409	14591	16415	14593	05
55	16415	14593	16421	14595	16427	14597	16434	14599	16440	14602	16446	14604	04
56	16446	14604	16452	14606	16458	14608	16464	14610	16470	14612	16476	14614	03
57	16476	14614	16483	14616	16489	14618	16495	14620	16501	14622	16507	14624	02
58	16507	14624	16513	14626	16519	14628	16525	14630	16531	14632	16537	14634	01
59	16537	14634	16544	14636	16550	14639	16556	14641	16562	14643	16568	14645	00

| .8 | .6 | .4 | .2 | .0 ← |

PARTS for 0′.1: LOGS 3   NATURALS 1   315°

45° HAVERSINES

′	.0 Log.	.0 Nat.	.2 Log.	.2 Nat.	.4 Log.	.4 Nat.	.6 Log.	.6 Nat.	.8 Log.	.8 Nat.	Log.	Nat.	′
	$\overline{1}$.or(9.)	0.	$\overline{1}$.or(9.)	0.	$\overline{1}$.or(9.)	0.	$\overline{1}$.or(9.)	0.	$\overline{1}$.or(9.)	0.	$\overline{1}$.or(9.)	0.	
00	16568	14645	16574	14647	16580	14649	16586	14651	16592	14653	16598	14655	59
01	16598	14655	16605	14657	16611	14659	16617	14661	16623	14663	16629	14665	58
02	16629	14665	16635	14667	16641	14669	16647	14671	16653	14673	16659	14676	57
03	16659	14676	16665	14678	16672	14680	16678	14682	16684	14684	16690	14686	56
04	16690	14686	16696	14688	16702	14690	16708	14692	16714	14694	16720	14696	55
05	16720	14696	16726	14698	16732	14700	16739	14702	16745	14704	16751	14706	54
06	16751	14706	16757	14708	16763	14711	16769	14713	16775	14715	16781	14717	53
07	16781	14717	16787	14719	16793	14721	16799	14723	16806	14725	16812	14727	52
08	16812	14727	16818	14729	16824	14731	16830	14733	16836	14735	16842	14737	51
09	16842	14737	16848	14739	16854	14741	16860	14744	16866	14746	16872	14748	50
10	16872	14748	16878	14750	16884	14752	16890	14754	16897	14756	16903	14758	49
11	16903	14758	16909	14760	16915	14762	16921	14764	16927	14766	16933	14768	48
12	16933	14768	16939	14770	16945	14772	16951	14774	16957	14777	16963	14779	47
13	16963	14779	16969	14781	16975	14783	16982	14785	16988	14787	16994	14789	46
14	16994	14789	17000	14791	17006	14793	17012	14795	17018	14797	17024	14799	45
15	17024	14799	17030	14801	17036	14803	17042	14805	17048	14808	17054	14810	44
16	17054	14810	17060	14812	17066	14814	17073	14816	17079	14818	17085	14820	43
17	17085	14820	17091	14822	17097	14824	17103	14826	17109	14828	17115	14830	42
18	17115	14830	17121	14832	17127	14834	17133	14836	17139	14839	17145	14841	41
19	17145	14841	17151	14843	17157	14845	17163	14847	17169	14849	17175	14851	40
20	17175	14851	17181	14853	17187	14855	17194	14857	17200	14859	17206	14861	39
21	17206	14861	17212	14863	17218	14865	17224	14868	17230	14870	17236	14872	38
22	17236	14872	17242	14874	17248	14876	17254	14878	17260	14880	17266	14882	37
23	17266	14882	17272	14884	17278	14886	17284	14888	17290	14890	17296	14892	36
24	17296	14892	17302	14894	17308	14896	17315	14899	17321	14901	17327	14903	35
25	17327	14903	17333	14905	17339	14907	17345	14909	17351	14911	17357	14913	34
26	17357	14913	17363	14915	17369	14917	17375	14919	17381	14921	17387	14923	33
27	17387	14923	17393	14926	17399	14928	17405	14930	17411	14932	17417	14934	32
28	17417	14934	17423	14936	17429	14938	17435	14940	17441	14942	17447	14944	31
29	17447	14944	17453	14946	17459	14948	17465	14950	17471	14952	17477	14955	30
30	17477	14955	17483	14957	17489	14959	17495	14961	17501	14963	17507	14965	29
31	17507	14965	17513	14967	17519	14969	17526	14971	17532	14973	17538	14975	28
32	17538	14975	17544	14977	17550	14979	17556	14982	17562	14984	17568	14986	27
33	17568	14986	17574	14988	17580	14990	17586	14992	17592	14994	17598	14996	26
34	17598	14996	17604	14998	17610	15000	17616	15002	17622	15004	17628	15006	25
35	17628	15006	17634	15009	17640	15011	17646	15013	17652	15015	17658	15017	24
36	17658	15017	17664	15019	17670	15021	17676	15023	17682	15025	17688	15027	23
37	17688	15027	17694	15029	17700	15031	17706	15033	17712	15036	17718	15038	22
38	17718	15038	17724	15040	17730	15042	17736	15044	17742	15046	17748	15048	21
39	17748	15048	17754	15050	17760	15052	17766	15054	17772	15056	17778	15058	20
40	17778	15058	17784	15060	17790	15063	17796	15065	17802	15067	17808	15069	19
41	17808	15069	17814	15071	17820	15073	17826	15075	17832	15077	17838	15079	18
42	17838	15079	17844	15081	17850	15083	17856	15085	17862	15088	17868	15090	17
43	17868	15090	17874	15092	17880	15094	17886	15096	17892	15098	17898	15100	16
44	17898	15100	17904	15102	17910	15104	17916	15106	17922	15108	17928	15110	15
45	17928	15110	17934	15113	17940	15115	17946	15117	17952	15119	17958	15121	14
46	17958	15121	17964	15123	17970	15125	17976	15127	17982	15129	17988	15131	13
47	17988	15131	17994	15133	18000	15135	18006	15138	18012	15140	18018	15142	12
48	18018	15142	18024	15144	18030	15146	18036	15148	18042	15150	18048	15152	11
49	18048	15152	18053	15154	18059	15156	18065	15158	18071	15161	18077	15163	10
50	18077	15163	18083	15165	18089	15167	18095	15169	18101	15171	18107	15173	09
51	18107	15173	18113	15175	18119	15177	18125	15179	18131	15181	18137	15183	08
52	18137	15183	18143	15186	18149	15188	18155	15190	18161	15192	18167	15194	07
53	18167	15194	18173	15196	18179	15198	18185	15200	18191	15202	18197	15204	06
54	18197	15204	18203	15206	18209	15209	18215	15211	18221	15213	18227	15215	05
55	18227	15215	18233	15217	18239	15219	18244	15221	18250	15223	18256	15225	04
56	18256	15225	18262	15227	18268	15229	18274	15232	18280	15234	18286	15236	03
57	18286	15236	18292	15238	18298	15240	18304	15242	18310	15244	18316	15246	02
58	18316	15246	18322	15248	18328	15250	18334	15252	18340	15255	18346	15257	01
59	18346	15257	18352	15259	18358	15261	18364	15263	18370	15265	18376	15267	00
			.8		.6		.4		.2		.0		

PARTS for 0′.1:   LOGS 3   NATURALS 1

314°

46° HAVERSINES

′	.0 Log. 1.or(9.)	.0 Nat. 0.	.2 Log. 1.or(9.)	.2 Nat. 0.	.4 Log. 1.or(9.)	.4 Nat. 0.	.6 Log. 1.or(9.)	.6 Nat. 0.	.8 Log. 1.or(9.)	.8 Nat. 0.	Log. 1.or(9.)	Nat. 0.	′
00	18376	15267	18382	15269	18388	15271	18393	15273	18399	15275	18405	15278	59
01	18405	15278	18411	15280	18417	15282	18423	15284	18429	15286	18435	15288	58
02	18435	15288	18441	15290	18447	15292	18453	15294	18459	15296	18465	15298	57
03	18465	15298	18471	15301	18477	15303	18483	15305	18489	15307	18495	15309	56
04	18495	15309	18501	15311	18506	15313	18512	15315	18518	15317	18524	15319	55
05	18524	15319	18530	15322	18536	15324	18542	15326	18548	15328	18554	15330	54
06	18554	15330	18560	15332	18566	15334	18572	15336	18578	15338	18584	15340	53
07	18584	15340	18590	15342	18596	15345	18601	15347	18607	15349	18613	15351	52
08	18613	15351	18619	15353	18625	15355	18631	15357	18637	15359	18643	15361	51
09	18643	15361	18649	15363	18655	15366	18661	15368	18667	15370	18673	15372	50
10	18673	15372	18679	15374	18684	15376	18690	15378	18696	15380	18702	15382	49
11	18702	15382	18708	15384	18714	15387	18720	15389	18726	15391	18732	15393	48
12	18732	15393	18738	15395	18744	15397	18750	15399	18756	15401	18762	15403	47
13	18762	15403	18767	15405	18773	15408	18779	15410	18785	15412	18791	15414	46
14	18791	15414	18797	15416	18803	15418	18809	15420	18815	15422	18821	15424	45
15	18821	15424	18827	15426	18832	15429	18838	15431	18844	15433	18850	15435	44
16	18850	15435	18856	15437	18862	15439	18868	15441	18874	15443	18880	15445	43
17	18880	15445	18886	15447	18892	15450	18898	15452	18903	15454	18909	15456	42
18	18909	15456	18915	15458	18921	15460	18927	15462	18933	15464	18939	15466	41
19	18939	15466	18945	15469	18951	15471	18957	15473	18963	15475	18968	15477	40
20	18968	15477	18974	15479	18980	15481	18986	15483	18992	15485	18998	15487	39
21	18998	15487	19004	15490	19010	15492	19016	15494	19022	15496	19027	15498	38
22	19027	15498	19033	15500	19039	15502	19045	15504	19051	15506	19057	15509	37
23	19057	15509	19063	15511	19069	15513	19075	15515	19081	15517	19086	15519	36
24	19086	15519	19092	15521	19098	15523	19104	15525	19110	15527	19116	15530	35
25	19116	15530	19122	15532	19128	15534	19134	15536	19140	15538	19145	15540	34
26	19145	15540	19151	15542	19157	15544	19163	15546	19169	15549	19175	15551	33
27	19175	15551	19181	15553	19187	15555	19192	15557	19198	15559	19204	15561	32
28	19204	15561	19210	15563	19216	15565	19222	15568	19228	15570	19234	15572	31
29	19234	15572	19239	15574	19245	15576	19251	15578	19257	15580	19263	15582	30
30	19263	15582	19269	15584	19275	15586	19281	15589	19287	15591	19292	15593	29
31	19292	15593	19298	15595	19304	15597	19310	15599	19316	15601	19322	15603	28
32	19322	15603	19328	15606	19334	15608	19339	15610	19345	15612	19351	15614	27
33	19351	15614	19357	15616	19363	15618	19369	15620	19375	15622	19381	15625	26
34	19381	15625	19386	15627	19392	15629	19398	15631	19404	15633	19410	15635	25
35	19410	15635	19416	15637	19422	15639	19428	15641	19433	15643	19439	15646	24
36	19439	15646	19445	15648	19451	15650	19457	15652	19463	15654	19469	15656	23
37	19469	15656	19474	15658	19480	15660	19486	15663	19492	15665	19498	15667	22
38	19498	15667	19504	15669	19510	15671	19516	15673	19521	15675	19527	15677	21
39	19527	15677	19533	15679	19539	15682	19545	15684	19551	15686	19557	15688	20
40	19557	15688	19562	15690	19568	15692	19574	15694	19580	15696	19586	15699	19
41	19586	15699	19592	15701	19597	15703	19603	15705	19609	15707	19615	15709	18
42	19615	15709	19621	15711	19627	15713	19633	15715	19639	15718	19644	15720	17
43	19644	15720	19650	15722	19656	15724	19662	15726	19668	15728	19674	15730	16
44	19674	15730	19679	15732	19685	15734	19691	15737	19697	15739	19703	15741	15
45	19703	15741	19709	15743	19714	15745	19720	15747	19726	15749	19732	15751	14
46	19732	15751	19738	15754	19744	15756	19750	15758	19755	15760	19761	15762	13
47	19761	15762	19767	15764	19773	15766	19779	15768	19785	15771	19790	15773	12
48	19790	15773	19796	15775	19802	15777	19808	15779	19814	15781	19820	15783	11
49	19820	15783	19825	15785	19831	15787	19837	15790	19843	15792	19849	15794	10
50	19849	15794	19855	15796	19860	15798	19866	15800	19872	15802	19878	15804	09
51	19878	15804	19884	15807	19890	15809	19896	15811	19901	15813	19907	15815	08
52	19907	15815	19913	15817	19919	15819	19925	15821	19930	15824	19936	15826	07
53	19936	15826	19942	15828	19948	15830	19954	15832	19960	15834	19965	15836	06
54	19965	15836	19971	15838	19977	15841	19983	15843	19989	15845	19995	15847	05
55	19995	15847	20000	15849	20006	15851	20012	15853	20018	15855	20024	15858	04
56	20024	15858	20029	15860	20035	15862	20041	15864	20047	15866	20053	15868	03
57	20053	15868	20059	15870	20064	15872	20070	15875	20076	15877	20082	15879	02
58	20082	15879	20088	15881	20093	15883	20099	15885	20105	15887	20111	15889	01
59	20111	15889	20117	15892	20122	15894	20128	15896	20134	15898	20140	15900	00

.8 .6 .4 .2 .0 ←

PARTS for 0′.1:   LOGS 3   NATURALS 1.

313°

HAVERSINES

	.0		.2		.4		.6		.8			
	Log.	Nat.	Log.	Nat.	Log.	Nat.	Log.	Nat.	Log.	Nat.	Log.	Nat.	
′	1̄.or(9.)	0.	1̄.or(9.)	0.	1̄.or(9.)	0.	1̄.or(9.)	0.	1̄.or(9.)	0.	1̄.or(9.)	0.	′
00	20140	15900	20146	15902	20152	15904	20157	15906	20163	15909	20169	15911	59
01	20169	15911	20175	15913	20181	15915	20186	15917	20192	15919	20198	15921	58
02	20198	15921	20204	15923	20210	15926	20215	15928	20221	15930	20227	15932	57
03	20227	15932	20233	15934	20239	15936	20244	15938	20250	15941	20256	15943	56
04	20256	15943	20262	15945	20268	15947	20273	15949	20279	15951	20285	15953	55
05	20285	15953	20291	15955	20297	15958	20302	15960	20308	15962	20314	15964	54
06	20314	15964	20320	15966	20326	15968	20331	15970	20337	15972	20343	15975	53
07	20343	15975	20349	15977	20355	15979	20360	15981	20366	15983	20372	15985	52
08	20372	15985	20378	15987	20384	15990	20389	15992	20395	15994	20401	15996	51
09	20401	15996	20407	15998	20413	16000	20418	16002	20424	16004	20430	16007	50
10	20430	16007	20436	16009	20442	16011	20447	16013	20453	16015	20459	16017	49
11	20459	16017	20465	16019	20470	16022	20476	16024	20482	16026	20488	16028	48
12	20488	16028	20494	16030	20499	16032	20505	16034	20511	16036	20517	16039	47
13	20517	16039	20522	16041	20528	16043	20534	16045	20540	16047	20546	16049	46
14	20546	16049	20551	16051	20557	16054	20563	16056	20569	16058	20574	16060	45
15	20574	16060	20580	16062	20586	16064	20592	16066	20598	16069	20603	16071	44
16	20603	16071	20609	16073	20615	16075	20621	16077	20626	16079	20632	16081	43
17	20632	16081	20638	16083	20644	16086	20649	16088	20655	16090	20661	16092	42
18	20661	16092	20667	16094	20673	16096	20678	16098	20684	16101	20690	16103	41
19	20690	16103	20696	16105	20701	16107	20707	16109	20713	16111	20719	16113	40
20	20719	16113	20725	16116	20730	16118	20736	16120	20742	16122	20748	16124	39
21	20748	16124	20753	16126	20759	16128	20765	16131	20771	16133	20776	16135	38
22	20776	16135	20782	16137	20788	16139	20794	16141	20799	16143	20805	16146	37
23	20805	16146	20811	16148	20817	16150	20822	16152	20828	16154	20834	16156	36
24	20834	16156	20840	16158	20845	16160	20851	16163	20857	16165	20863	16167	35
25	20863	16167	20868	16169	20874	16171	20880	16173	20886	16175	20891	16178	34
26	20891	16178	20897	16180	20903	16182	20909	16184	20914	16186	20920	16188	33
27	20920	16188	20926	16190	20932	16193	20937	16195	20943	16197	20949	16199	32
28	20949	16199	20955	16201	20960	16203	20966	16205	20972	16208	20978	16210	31
29	20978	16210	20983	16212	20989	16214	20995	16216	21001	16218	21006	16220	30
30	21006	16220	21012	16223	21018	16225	21024	16227	21029	16229	21035	16231	29
31	21035	16231	21041	16233	21047	16236	21052	16238	21058	16240	21064	16242	28
32	21064	16242	21070	16244	21075	16246	21081	16248	21087	16251	21092	16253	27
33	21092	16253	21098	16255	21104	16257	21110	16259	21115	16261	21121	16263	26
34	21121	16263	21127	16266	21133	16268	21138	16270	21144	16272	21150	16274	25
35	21150	16274	21156	16276	21161	16278	21167	16281	21173	16283	21178	16285	24
36	21178	16285	21184	16287	21190	16289	21196	16291	21201	16293	21207	16296	23
37	21207	16296	21213	16298	21219	16300	21224	16302	21230	16304	21236	16306	22
38	21236	16306	21242	16309	21247	16311	21253	16313	21259	16315	21264	16317	21
39	21264	16317	21270	16319	21276	16321	21282	16324	21287	16326	21293	16328	20
40	21293	16328	21299	16330	21304	16332	21310	16334	21316	16336	21322	16339	19
41	21322	16339	21327	16341	21333	16343	21339	16345	21344	16347	21350	16349	18
42	21350	16349	21356	16352	21362	16354	21367	16356	21373	16358	21379	16360	17
43	21379	16360	21384	16362	21390	16364	21396	16367	21401	16369	21407	16371	16
44	21407	16371	21413	16373	21419	16375	21424	16377	21430	16380	21436	16382	15
45	21436	16382	21442	16384	21447	16386	21453	16388	21459	16390	21464	16392	14
46	21464	16392	21470	16395	21476	16397	21481	16399	21487	16401	21493	16403	13
47	21493	16403	21499	16405	21504	16408	21510	16410	21516	16412	21521	16414	12
48	21521	16414	21527	16416	21533	16418	21538	16420	21544	16423	21550	16425	11
49	21550	16425	21556	16427	21561	16429	21567	16431	21573	16433	21578	16436	10
50	21578	16436	21584	16438	21590	16440	21595	16442	21601	16444	21607	16446	09
51	21607	16446	21613	16448	21618	16451	21624	16453	21630	16455	21635	16457	08
52	21635	16457	21641	16459	21647	16461	21652	16464	21658	16466	21664	16468	07
53	21664	16468	21669	16470	21675	16472	21681	16474	21687	16477	21692	16479	06
54	21692	16479	21698	16481	21704	16483	21709	16485	21715	16487	21721	16489	05
55	21721	16489	21726	16492	21732	16494	21738	16496	21743	16498	21749	16500	04
56	21749	16500	21755	16502	21760	16505	21766	16507	21772	16509	21777	16511	03
57	21777	16511	21783	16513	21789	16515	21794	16518	21800	16520	21806	16522	02
58	21806	16522	21811	16524	21817	16526	21823	16528	21829	16530	21834	16533	01
59	21834	16533	21840	16535	21846	16537	21851	16539	21857	16541	21863	16543	00
		.8		.6		.4		.2		.0			

PARTS for 0′.1:   LOGS 3   NATURALS 1

48° HAVERSINES

′	.0 Log.	.0 Nat.	.2 Log.	.2 Nat.	.4 Log.	.4 Nat.	.6 Log.	.6 Nat.	.8 Log.	.8 Nat.	1.0 Log.	1.0 Nat.	′
	1̄.or(9.)	0.	1̄.or(9.)	0.	1̄.or(9.)	0.	1̄.or(9.)	0.	1̄.or(9.)	0.	1̄.or(9.)	0.	
00	21863	16543	21868	16546	21874	16548	21880	16550	21885	16552	21891	16554	59
01	21891	16554	21897	16556	21902	16559	21908	16561	21914	16563	21919	16565	58
02	21919	16565	21925	16567	21931	16569	21936	16572	21942	16574	21948	16576	57
03	21948	16576	21953	16578	21959	16580	21965	16582	21970	16585	21976	16587	56
04	21976	16587	21982	16589	21987	16591	21993	16593	21999	16595	22004	16598	55
05	22004	16598	22010	16600	22016	16602	22021	16604	22027	16606	22033	16608	54
06	22033	16608	22038	16611	22044	16613	22050	16615	22055	16617	22061	16619	53
07	22061	16619	22067	16621	22072	16624	22078	16626	22084	16628	22089	16630	52
08	22089	16630	22095	16632	22101	16634	22106	16637	22112	16639	22118	16641	51
09	22118	16641	22123	16643	22129	16645	22135	16647	22140	16650	22146	16652	50
10	22146	16652	22151	16654	22157	16656	22163	16658	22169	16660	22174	16663	49
11	22174	16663	22180	16665	22185	16667	22191	16669	22197	16671	22202	16673	48
12	22202	16673	22208	16676	22214	16678	22219	16680	22225	16682	22231	16684	47
13	22231	16684	22236	16686	22242	16689	22248	16691	22253	16693	22259	16695	46
14	22259	16695	22264	16697	22270	16699	22276	16702	22281	16704	22287	16706	45
15	22287	16706	22293	16708	22298	16710	22304	16712	22310	16715	22315	16717	44
16	22315	16717	22321	16719	22326	16721	22332	16723	22338	16725	22343	16728	43
17	22343	16728	22349	16730	22355	16732	22360	16734	22366	16736	22372	16738	42
18	22372	16738	22377	16741	22383	16743	22389	16745	22394	16747	22400	16749	41
19	22400	16749	22405	16752	22411	16754	22417	16756	22422	16758	22428	16760	40
20	22428	16760	22434	16762	22439	16765	22445	16767	22450	16769	22456	16771	39
21	22456	16771	22462	16773	22467	16775	22473	16778	22479	16780	22484	16782	38
22	22484	16782	22490	16784	22495	16786	22501	16788	22507	16791	22512	16793	37
23	22512	16793	22518	16795	22524	16797	22529	16799	22535	16802	22540	16804	36
24	22540	16804	22546	16806	22552	16808	22557	16810	22563	16812	22569	16815	35
25	22569	16815	22574	16817	22580	16819	22585	16821	22591	16823	22597	16825	34
26	22597	16825	22602	16828	22608	16830	22614	16832	22619	16834	22625	16836	33
27	22625	16836	22630	16839	22636	16841	22642	16843	22647	16845	22653	16847	32
28	22653	16847	22658	16849	22664	16852	22670	16854	22675	16856	22681	16858	31
29	22681	16858	22686	16860	22692	16862	22698	16865	22703	16867	22709	16869	30
30	22709	16869	22715	16871	22720	16873	22726	16876	22731	16878	22737	16880	29
31	22737	16880	22743	16882	22748	16884	22754	16886	22759	16889	22765	16891	28
32	22765	16891	22771	16893	22776	16895	22782	16897	22787	16900	22793	16902	27
33	22793	16902	22799	16904	22804	16906	22810	16908	22815	16910	22821	16913	26
34	22821	16913	22827	16915	22832	16917	22838	16919	22843	16921	22849	16924	25
35	22849	16924	22854	16926	22860	16928	22866	16930	22871	16932	22877	16934	24
36	22877	16934	22883	16937	22888	16939	22894	16941	22899	16943	22905	16945	23
37	22905	16945	22911	16947	22916	16950	22922	16952	22927	16954	22933	16956	22
38	22933	16956	22939	16958	22944	16961	22950	16963	22955	16965	22961	16967	21
39	22961	16967	22966	16969	22972	16972	22978	16974	22983	16976	22989	16978	20
40	22989	16978	22994	16980	23000	16982	23006	16985	23011	16987	23017	16989	19
41	23017	16989	23022	16991	23028	16993	23033	16996	23039	16998	23045	17000	18
42	23045	17000	23050	17002	23056	17004	23061	17006	23067	17009	23073	17011	17
43	23073	17011	23078	17013	23084	17015	23089	17017	23095	17020	23100	17022	16
44	23100	17022	23106	17024	23112	17026	23117	17028	23123	17030	23128	17033	15
45	23128	17033	23134	17035	23140	17037	23145	17039	23151	17041	23156	17044	14
46	23156	17044	23162	17046	23167	17048	23173	17050	23179	17052	23184	17055	13
47	23184	17055	23190	17057	23195	17059	23201	17061	23206	17063	23212	17066	12
48	23212	17066	23218	17068	23223	17070	23229	17072	23234	17074	23240	17076	11
49	23240	17076	23245	17079	23251	17081	23256	17083	23262	17085	23268	17087	10
50	23268	17087	23273	17090	23279	17092	23284	17094	23290	17096	23295	17098	09
51	23295	17098	23301	17101	23307	17103	23312	17105	23318	17107	23323	17109	08
52	23323	17109	23329	17112	23334	17114	23340	17116	23345	17118	23351	17120	07
53	23351	17120	23357	17122	23362	17125	23368	17127	23373	17129	23379	17131	06
54	23379	17131	23384	17133	23390	17136	23395	17138	23401	17140	23407	17142	05
55	23407	17142	23412	17144	23418	17147	23423	17149	23429	17151	23434	17153	04
56	23434	17153	23440	17155	23446	17158	23451	17160	23457	17162	23462	17164	03
57	23462	17164	23468	17166	23473	17169	23479	17171	23484	17173	23490	17175	02
58	23490	17175	23496	17177	23501	17179	23507	17182	23512	17184	23518	17186	01
59	23518	17186	23523	17188	23529	17190	23534	17193	23540	17195	23545	17197	00

| | .8 | | .6 | | .4 | | .2 | | .0 ← | |

PARTS for 0′.1:   LOGS 3   NATURALS 1   **311°**

49° HAVERSINES

'	.0 Log. 1̄.or(9.)	.0 Nat. 0.	.2 Log. 1̄.or(9.)	.2 Nat. 0.	.4 Log. 1̄.or(9.)	.4 Nat. 0.	.6 Log. 1̄.or(9.)	.6 Nat. 0.	.8 Log. 1̄.or(9.)	.8 Nat. 0.	Log. 1̄.or(9.)	Nat. 0.	'
00	23545	17197	23551	17199	23557	17201	23562	17204	23568	17206	23573	17208	59
01	23573	17208	23579	17210	23584	17212	23590	17215	23595	17217	23601	17219	58
02	23601	17219	23606	17221	23612	17223	23617	17226	23623	17228	23629	17230	57
03	23629	17230	23634	17232	23640	17234	23645	17237	23651	17239	23656	17241	56
04	23656	17241	23662	17243	23667	17245	23673	17248	23678	17250	23684	17252	55
05	23684	17252	23689	17254	23695	17256	23700	17259	23706	17261	23712	17263	54
06	23712	17263	23717	17265	23723	17267	23728	17270	23734	17272	23739	17274	53
07	23739	17274	23745	17276	23750	17278	23756	17281	23761	17283	23767	17285	52
08	23767	17285	23772	17287	23778	17289	23783	17292	23789	17294	23794	17296	51
09	23794	17296	23800	17298	23805	17300	23811	17303	23816	17305	23822	17307	50
10	23822	17307	23828	17309	23833	17311	23839	17314	23844	17316	23850	17318	49
11	23850	17318	23855	17320	23861	17322	23866	17325	23872	17327	23877	17329	48
12	23877	17329	23883	17331	23888	17333	23894	17336	23899	17338	23905	17340	47
13	23905	17340	23910	17342	23916	17344	23921	17347	23927	17349	23932	17351	46
14	23932	17351	23938	17353	23943	17355	23949	17358	23954	17360	23960	17362	45
15	23960	17362	23966	17364	23971	17366	23977	17369	23982	17371	23988	17373	44
16	23988	17373	23993	17375	23999	17377	24004	17380	24010	17382	24015	17384	43
17	24015	17384	24021	17386	24026	17388	24032	17391	24037	17393	24043	17395	42
18	24043	17395	24048	17397	24054	17400	24059	17402	24065	17404	24070	17406	41
19	24070	17406	24076	17408	24081	17411	24087	17413	24092	17415	24098	17417	40
20	24098	17417	24103	17419	24109	17422	24114	17424	24120	17426	24125	17428	39
21	24125	17428	24131	17430	24136	17433	24142	17435	24147	17437	24153	17439	38
22	24153	17439	24158	17441	24164	17444	24169	17446	24175	17448	24180	17450	37
23	24180	17450	24186	17452	24191	17455	24197	17457	24202	17459	24208	17461	36
24	24208	17461	24213	17464	24219	17466	24224	17468	24230	17470	24235	17472	35
25	24235	17472	24241	17475	24246	17477	24252	17479	24257	17481	24263	17483	34
26	24263	17483	24268	17486	24274	17488	24279	17490	24285	17492	24290	17494	33
27	24290	17494	24295	17497	24301	17499	24306	17501	24312	17503	24317	17505	32
28	24317	17505	24323	17508	24328	17510	24334	17512	24339	17514	24345	17517	31
29	24345	17517	24350	17519	24356	17521	24361	17523	24367	17525	24372	17528	30
30	24372	17528	24378	17530	24383	17532	24389	17534	24394	17536	24400	17539	29
31	24400	17539	24405	17541	24411	17543	24416	17545	24422	17547	24427	17550	28
32	24427	17550	24432	17552	24438	17554	24443	17556	24449	17559	24454	17561	27
33	24454	17561	24460	17563	24465	17565	24471	17568	24476	17570	24482	17572	26
34	24482	17572	24487	17574	24493	17576	24498	17579	24504	17581	24509	17583	25
35	24509	17583	24515	17585	24520	17587	24526	17590	24531	17592	24536	17594	24
36	24536	17594	24542	17596	24547	17598	24553	17601	24558	17603	24564	17605	23
37	24564	17605	24569	17607	24575	17610	24580	17612	24586	17614	24591	17616	22
38	24591	17616	24597	17618	24602	17621	24608	17623	24613	17625	24618	17627	21
39	24618	17627	24624	17629	24629	17632	24635	17634	24640	17636	24646	17638	20
40	24646	17638	24651	17641	24657	17643	24662	17645	24668	17647	24673	17649	19
41	24673	17649	24678	17652	24684	17654	24689	17656	24695	17658	24700	17661	18
42	24700	17661	24706	17663	24711	17665	24717	17667	24722	17669	24728	17672	17
43	24728	17672	24733	17674	24738	17676	24744	17678	24749	17680	24755	17683	16
44	24755	17683	24760	17685	24766	17687	24771	17689	24777	17692	24782	17694	15
45	24782	17694	24788	17696	24793	17698	24799	17700	24804	17703	24809	17705	14
46	24809	17705	24815	17707	24820	17709	24826	17712	24831	17714	24837	17716	13
47	24837	17716	24842	17718	24847	17720	24853	17723	24858	17725	24864	17727	12
48	24864	17727	24869	17729	24875	17732	24880	17734	24886	17736	24891	17738	11
49	24891	17738	24896	17740	24902	17743	24907	17745	24913	17747	24918	17749	10
50	24918	17749	24924	17752	24929	17754	24935	17756	24940	17758	24945	17760	09
51	24945	17760	24951	17763	24956	17765	24962	17767	24967	17769	24973	17772	08
52	24973	17772	24978	17774	24983	17776	24989	17778	24994	17780	25000	17783	07
53	25000	17783	25005	17785	25011	17787	25016	17789	25022	17792	25027	17794	06
54	25027	17794	25032	17796	25038	17798	25043	17800	25049	17803	25054	17805	05
55	25054	17805	25059	17807	25065	17809	25070	17812	25076	17814	25081	17816	04
56	25081	17816	25087	17818	25092	17821	25098	17823	25103	17825	25108	17827	03
57	25108	17827	25114	17829	25119	17832	25125	17834	25130	17836	25135	17838	02
58	25135	17838	25141	17841	25146	17843	25152	17845	25157	17847	25163	17849	01
59	25163	17849	25168	17852	25173	17854	25179	17856	25184	17858	25190	17861	00

	.8	.6	.4	.2	.0 ←

PARTS for 0'.1: LOGS 3· NATURALS 1

310°

HAVERSINES

50°

	.0		.2		.4		.6		.8		
	Log.	Nat.	Log.	Nat.	Log.	Nat.	Log.	Nat.	Log.	Nat.	
′	$\overline{1}$.or(9.)	0.	$\overline{1}$.or(9.)	0.	$\overline{1}$.or(9.)	0.	$\overline{1}$.or(9.)	0.	$\overline{1}$.or(9.)	0.	′
00	25190	17861	25195	17863	25200	17865	25206	17867	25211	17870	25217	17872	59
01	25217	17872	25222	17874	25228	17876	25233	17878	25238	17881	25244	17883	58
02	25244	17883	25249	17885	25255	17887	25260	17890	25265	17892	25271	17894	57
03	25271	17894	25276	17896	25282	17899	25287	17901	25293	17903	25298	17905	56
04	25293	17905	25303	17907	25309	17910	25314	17912	25320	17914	25325	17916	55
05	25325	17916	25330	17919	25336	17921	25341	17923	25347	17925	25352	17928	54
06	25352	17928	25357	17930	25363	17932	25368	17934	25374	17936	25379	17939	53
07	25379	17939	25384	17941	25390	17943	25395	17945	25401	17948	25406	17950	52
08	25406	17950	25411	17952	25417	17954	25422	17957	25428	17959	25433	17961	51
09	25433	17961	25438	17963	25444	17965	25449	17968	25455	17970	25460	17972	50
10	25460	17972	25465	17974	25471	17977	25476	17979	25482	17981	25487	17983	49
11	25487	17983	25492	17986	25498	17988	25503	17990	25509	17992	25514	17995	48
12	25514	17995	25519	17997	25525	17999	25530	18001	25536	18003	25541	18006	47
13	25541	18006	25546	18008	25552	18010	25557	18012	25563	18015	25568	18017	46
14	25568	18017	25573	18019	25579	18021	25584	18024	25589	18026	25595	18028	45
15	25595	18028	25600	18030	25606	18033	25611	18035	25616	18037	25622	18039	44
16	25622	18039	25627	18041	25633	18044	25638	18046	25643	18048	25649	18050	43
17	25649	18050	25654	18053	25660	18055	25665	18057	25670	18059	25676	18062	42
18	25676	18062	25681	18064	25686	18066	25692	18068	25697	18071	25703	18073	41
19	25703	18073	25708	18075	25713	18077	25719	18080	25724	18082	25729	18084	40
20	25729	18084	25735	18086	25740	18088	25746	18091	25751	18093	25756	18095	39
21	25756	18095	25762	18097	25767	18100	25773	18102	25778	18104	25783	18106	38
22	25783	18106	25789	18109	25794	18111	25799	18113	25805	18115	25810	18118	37
23	25810	18118	25815	18120	25821	18122	25826	18124	25832	18127	25837	18129	36
24	25837	18129	25842	18131	25848	18133	25853	18136	25858	18138	25864	18140	35
25	25864	18140	25869	18142	25875	18144	25880	18147	25885	18149	25891	18151	34
26	25891	18151	25896	18153	25901	18156	25907	18158	25912	18160	25917	18162	33
27	25917	18162	25923	18165	25928	18167	25933	18169	25939	18171	25944	18174	32
28	25944	18174	25950	18176	25955	18178	25960	18180	25966	18183	25971	18185	31
29	25971	18185	25976	18187	25982	18189	25987	18192	25992	18194	25998	18196	30
30	25998	18196	26003	18198	26009	18201	26014	18203	26019	18205	26025	18207	29
31	26025	18207	26030	18210	26035	18212	26041	18214	26046	18216	26051	18219	28
32	26051	18219	26057	18221	26062	18223	26067	18225	26073	18228	26078	18230	27
33	26078	18230	26084	18232	26089	18234	26094	18237	26099	18239	26105	18241	26
34	26105	18241	26110	18243	26116	18246	26121	18248	26126	18250	26132	18252	25
35	26132	18252	26137	18254	26142	18257	26148	18259	26153	18261	26158	18263	24
36	26158	18263	26164	18266	26169	18268	26174	18270	26180	18272	26185	18275	23
37	26185	18275	26190	18277	26196	18279	26201	18281	26206	18284	26212	18286	22
38	26212	18286	26217	18288	26222	18290	26228	18293	26233	18295	26238	18297	21
39	26238	18297	26244	18299	26249	18302	26254	18304	26260	18306	26265	18308	20
40	26265	18308	26271	18311	26276	18313	26281	18315	26286	18317	26292	18320	19
41	26292	18320	26297	18322	26303	18324	26308	18326	26313	18329	26319	18331	18
42	26319	18331	26324	18333	26329	18335	26335	18338	26340	18340	26345	18342	17
43	26345	18342	26351	18344	26356	18347	26361	18349	26366	18351	26372	18353	16
44	26372	18353	26377	18356	26382	18358	26388	18360	26393	18362	26398	18365	15
45	26398	18365	26404	18367	26409	18369	26414	18372	26420	18374	26425	18376	14
46	26425	18376	26430	18378	26436	18381	26441	18383	26446	18385	26452	18387	13
47	26452	18387	26457	18390	26462	18392	26468	18394	26473	18396	26478	18399	12
48	26478	18399	26484	18401	26489	18403	26494	18405	26500	18408	26505	18410	11
49	26505	18410	26510	18412	26516	18414	26521	18417	26526	18419	26532	18421	10
50	26532	18421	26537	18423	26542	18426	26547	18428	26553	18430	26558	18432	09
51	26558	18432	26563	18435	26569	18437	26574	18439	26579	18441	26585	18444	08
52	26585	18444	26590	18446	26595	18448	26601	18450	26606	18453	26611	18455	07
53	26611	18455	26617	18457	26622	18459	26627	18462	26632	18464	26638	18466	06
54	26638	18466	26643	18468	26648	18471	26654	18473	26659	18475	26664	18478	05
55	26664	18478	26670	18480	26675	18482	26680	18484	26686	18487	26691	18489	04
56	26691	18489	26696	18491	26701	18493	26707	18496	26712	18498	26717	18500	03
57	26717	18500	26723	18502	26728	18505	26733	18507	26739	18509	26744	18511	02
58	26744	18511	26749	18514	26754	18516	26760	18518	26765	18520	26770	18523	01
59	26770	18523	26776	18525	26781	18527	26786	18529	26792	18532	26797	18534	00
	.8		.6		.4		.2		.0			

PARTS for 0′.1:   LOGS 3   NATURALS 1

309°

51° HAVERSINES

′	.0 Log	.0 Nat	.2 Log	.2 Nat	.4 Log	.4 Nat	.6 Log	.6 Nat	.8 Log	.8 Nat	′
	$\overline{1}$.or(9.)	0.	$\overline{1}$.or(9.)	0.	$\overline{1}$.or(9.)	0.	$\overline{1}$.or(9.)	0.	$\overline{1}$.or(9.)	0.	
00	26797	18534	26802	18536	26807	18539	26813	18541	26818	18543	26823 18545	59
01	26823	18545	26829	18548	26834	18550	26839	18552	26845	18554	26850 18557	58
02	26850	18557	26855	18559	26860	18561	26866	18563	26871	18566	26876 18568	57
03	26876	18568	26882	18570	26887	18572	26892	18575	26897	18577	26903 18579	56
04	26903	18579	26908	18581	26913	18584	26919	18586	26924	18588	26929 18591	55
05	26929	18591	26934	18593	26940	18595	26945	18597	26950	18600	26956 18602	54
06	26956	18602	26961	18604	26966	18606	26971	18609	26977	18611	26982 18613	53
07	26982	18613	26987	18615	26993	18618	26998	18620	27003	18622	27008 18624	52
08	27008	18624	27014	18627	27019	18629	27024	18631	27030	18634	27035 18636	51
09	27035	18636	27040	18638	27045	18640	27051	18643	27056	18645	27061 18647	50
10	27061	18647	27066	18649	27072	18652	27077	18654	27082	18656	27088 18658	49
11	27088	18658	27093	18661	27098	18663	27103	18665	27109	18668	27114 18670	48
12	27114	18670	27119	18672	27125	18674	27130	18677	27135	18679	27140 18681	47
13	27140	18681	27146	18683	27151	18686	27156	18688	27162	18690	27167 18692	46
14	27167	18692	27172	18695	27177	18697	27183	18699	27188	18702	27193 18704	45
15	27193	18704	27198	18706	27204	18708	27209	18711	27214	18713	27219 18715	44
16	27219	18715	27225	18717	27230	18720	27235	18722	27241	18724	27246 18727	43
17	27246	18727	27251	18729	27256	18731	27262	18733	27267	18736	27272 18738	42
18	27272	18738	27277	18740	27283	18742	27288	18745	27293	18747	27298 18749	41
19	27298	18749	27304	18751	27309	18754	27314	18756	27319	18758	27325 18761	40
20	27325	18761	27330	18763	27335	18765	27340	18767	27346	18770	27351 18772	39
21	27351	18772	27356	18774	27361	18776	27367	18779	27372	18781	27377 18783	38
22	27377	18783	27382	18786	27388	18788	27393	18790	27398	18792	27403 18795	37
23	27403	18795	27409	18797	27414	18799	27419	18801	27424	18804	27430 18806	36
24	27430	18806	27435	18808	27440	18811	27445	18813	27451	18815	27456 18817	35
25	27456	18817	27461	18820	27466	18822	27472	18824	27477	18826	27482 18829	34
26	27482	18829	27487	18831	27493	18833	27498	18836	27503	18838	27508 18840	33
27	27508	18840	27514	18842	27519	18845	27524	18847	27529	18849	27535 18852	32
28	27535	18852	27540	18854	27545	18856	27550	18858	27556	18861	27561 18863	31
29	27561	18863	27566	18865	27571	18867	27577	18870	27582	18872	27587 18874	30
30	27587	18874	27592	18877	27597	18879	27603	18881	27608	18883	27613 18886	29
31	27613	18886	27618	18888	27624	18890	27629	18892	27634	18895	27639 18897	28
32	27639	18897	27645	18899	27650	18902	27655	18904	27660	18906	27666 18908	27
33	27666	18908	27671	18911	27676	18913	27681	18915	27686	18918	27692 18920	26
34	27692	18920	27697	18922	27702	18924	27707	18927	27713	18929	27718 18931	25
35	27718	18931	27723	18933	27728	18936	27734	18938	27739	18940	27744 18943	24
36	27744	18943	27749	18945	27754	18947	27760	18949	27765	18952	27770 18954	23
37	27770	18954	27775	18956	27781	18959	27786	18961	27791	18963	27796 18965	22
38	27796	18965	27801	18968	27807	18970	27812	18972	27817	18975	27822 18977	21
39	27822	18977	27828	18979	27833	18981	27838	18984	27843	18986	27848 18988	20
40	27848	18988	27854	18991	27859	18993	27864	18995	27869	18997	27875 19000	19
41	27875	19000	27880	19002	27885	19004	27890	19006	27895	19009	27901 19011	18
42	27901	19011	27906	19013	27911	19016	27916	19018	27921	19020	27927 19022	17
43	27927	19022	27932	19025	27937	19027	27942	19029	27948	19032	27953 19034	16
44	27953	19034	27958	19036	27963	19038	27968	19041	27974	19043	27979 19045	15
45	27979	19045	27984	19048	27989	19050	27994	19052	28000	19054	28005 19057	14
46	28005	19057	28010	19059	28015	19061	28020	19064	28026	19066	28031 19068	13
47	28031	19068	28036	19070	28041	19073	28046	19075	28052	19077	28057 19080	12
48	28057	19080	28062	19082	28067	19084	28072	19086	28078	19089	28083 19091	11
49	28083	19091	28088	19093	28093	19096	28098	19098	28104	19100	28109 19102	10
50	28109	19102	28114	19105	28119	19107	28124	19109	28130	19112	28135 19114	09
51	28135	19114	28140	19116	28145	19118	28150	19121	28156	19123	28161 19125	08
52	28161	19125	28166	19128	28171	19130	28176	19132	28182	19134	28187 19137	07
53	28187	19137	28193	19139	28197	19141	28202	19144	28208	19146	28213 19148	06
54	28213	19148	28218	19150	28223	19153	28228	19155	28234	19157	28239 19160	05
55	28239	19160	28244	19162	28249	19164	28254	19167	28260	19169	28265 19171	04
56	28265	19171	28270	19173	28275	19176	28280	19178	28285	19180	28291 19183	03
57	28291	19183	28296	19185	28301	19187	28306	19189	28311	19192	28317 19194	02
58	28317	19194	28322	19196	28327	19199	28332	19201	28337	19203	28342 19205	01
59	28342	19205	28348	19208	28353	19210	28358	19212	28363	19215	28368 19217	00

	.8	.6	.4	.2	.0 ←

PARTS for 0′.1:   LOGS 3·   NATURALS 1

308°

52° HAVERSINES

′	.0 Log. 1̄.or(9.)	.0 Nat. 0.	.2 Log. 1̄.or(9.)	.2 Nat. 0.	.4 Log. 1̄.or(9.)	.4 Nat. 0.	.6 Log. 1̄.or(9.)	.6 Nat. 0.	.8 Log. 1̄.or(9.)	.8 Nat. 0.	′
00	28368	19217	28374	19219	28379	19221	28384	19224	28389	19226	28394	19228	59
01	28394	19228	28399	19231	28405	19233	28410	19235	28415	19238	28420	19240	58
02	28420	19240	28425	19242	28431	19244	28436	19247	28441	19249	28446	19251	57
03	28446	19251	28451	19254	28456	19256	28462	19258	28467	19261	28472	19263	56
04	28472	19263	28477	19265	28482	19267	28487	19270	28493	19272	28498	19274	55
05	28498	19274	28503	19277	28508	19279	28513	19281	28518	19283	28524	19286	54
06	28524	19286	28529	19288	28534	19290	28539	19293	28544	19295	28549	19297	53
07	28549	19297	28555	19300	28560	19302	28565	19304	28570	19306	28575	19309	52
08	28575	19309	28581	19311	28586	19313	28591	19316	28596	19318	28601	19320	51
09	28601	19320	28606	19322	28612	19325	28617	19327	28622	19329	28627	19332	50
10	28627	19332	28632	19334	28637	19336	28642	19339	28648	19341	28653	19343	49
11	28653	19343	28658	19345	28663	19348	28668	19350	28673	19352	28679	19355	48
12	28679	19355	28684	19357	28689	19359	28694	19362	28699	19364	28704	19366	47
13	28704	19366	28710	19368	28715	19371	28720	19373	28725	19375	28730	19378	46
14	28730	19378	28735	19380	28740	19382	28745	19385	28751	19387	28756	19389	45
15	28756	19389	28761	19391	28766	19394	28771	19396	28776	19398	28782	19401	44
16	28782	19401	28787	19403	28792	19405	28797	19408	28802	19410	28807	19412	43
17	28807	19412	28813	19414	28818	19417	28823	19419	28828	19421	28833	19424	42
18	28833	19424	28838	19426	28843	19428	28848	19431	28854	19433	28859	19435	41
19	28859	19435	28864	19437	28869	19440	28874	19442	28879	19444	28885	19447	40
20	28885	19447	28890	19449	28895	19451	28900	19454	28905	19456	28910	19458	39
21	28910	19458	28915	19461	28921	19463	28926	19465	28931	19467	28936	19470	38
22	28936	19470	28941	19472	28946	19474	28951	19477	28956	19479	28962	19481	37
23	28962	19481	28967	19484	28972	19486	28977	19488	28982	19490	28987	19493	36
24	28987	19493	28992	19495	28998	19497	29003	19500	29008	19502	29013	19504	35
25	29013	19504	29018	19507	29023	19509	29028	19511	29033	19513	29039	19516	34
26	29039	19516	29044	19518	29049	19520	29054	19523	29059	19525	29064	19527	33
27	29064	19527	29069	19530	29075	19532	29080	19534	29085	19537	29090	19539	32
28	29090	19539	29095	19541	29100	19543	29105	19546	29110	19548	29116	19550	31
29	29116	19550	29121	19553	29126	19555	29131	19557	29136	19560	29141	19562	30
30	29141	19562	29146	19564	29151	19567	29157	19569	29162	19571	29167	19573	29
31	29167	19573	29172	19576	29177	19578	29182	19580	29187	19583	29192	19585	28
32	29192	19585	29198	19587	29203	19590	29208	19592	29213	19594	29218	19597	27
33	29218	19597	29223	19599	29228	19601	29233	19603	29238	19606	29244	19608	26
34	29244	19608	29249	19610	29254	19613	29259	19615	29264	19617	29269	19620	25
35	29269	19620	29274	19622	29279	19624	29285	19627	29290	19629	29295	19631	24
36	29295	19631	29300	19634	29305	19636	29310	19638	29315	19640	29320	19643	23
37	29320	19643	29325	19645	29330	19647	29336	19650	29341	19652	29346	19654	22
38	29346	19654	29351	19657	29356	19659	29361	19661	29366	19664	29371	19666	21
39	29371	19666	29376	19668	29382	19671	29387	19673	29392	19675	29397	19677	20
40	29397	19677	29402	19680	29407	19682	29412	19684	29417	19687	29422	19689	19
41	29422	19689	29428	19691	29433	19694	29438	19696	29443	19698	29448	19701	18
42	29448	19701	29453	19703	29458	19705	29463	19708	29468	19710	29473	19712	17
43	29473	19712	29478	19714	29484	19717	29489	19719	29494	19721	29499	19724	16
44	29499	19724	29504	19726	29509	19728	29514	19731	29519	19733	29524	19735	15
45	29524	19735	29529	19738	29535	19740	29540	19742	29545	19745	29550	19747	14
46	29550	19747	29555	19749	29560	19752	29565	19754	29570	19756	29575	19758	13
47	29575	19758	29580	19761	29586	19763	29591	19765	29596	19768	29601	19770	12
48	29601	19770	29606	19772	29611	19775	29616	19777	29621	19779	29626	19782	11
49	29626	19782	29631	19784	29636	19786	29641	19789	29647	19791	29652	19793	10
50	29652	19793	29657	19796	29662	19798	29667	19800	29672	19802	29677	19805	09
51	29677	19805	29682	19807	29687	19809	29692	19812	29697	19814	29702	19816	08
52	29702	19816	29707	19819	29713	19821	29718	19823	29723	19826	29728	19828	07
53	29728	19828	29733	19830	29738	19833	29743	19835	29748	19837	29753	19840	06
54	29753	19840	29758	19842	29763	19844	29768	19847	29774	19849	29779	19851	05
55	29779	19851	29784	19854	29789	19856	29794	19858	29799	19860	29804	19863	04
56	29804	19863	29809	19865	29814	19867	29819	19870	29824	19872	29829	19874	03
57	29829	19874	29834	19877	29840	19879	29845	19881	29850	19884	29855	19886	02
58	29855	19886	29860	19888	29865	19891	29870	19893	29875	19895	29880	19898	01
59	29880	19898	29885	19900	29890	19902	29895	19905	29900	19907	29905	19909	00

	.8		.6		.4		.2		.0	

307°

PARTS for 0′.1: LOGS 3 NATURALS 1

53° HAVERSINES

′	.0 Log. 1.or(9.)	.0 Nat. 0.	.2 Log. 1.or(9.)	.2 Nat. 0.	.4 Log. 1.or(9.)	.4 Nat. 0.	.6 Log. 1.or(9.)	.6 Nat. 0.	.8 Log. 1.or(9.)	.8 Nat. 0.	Log. 1.or(9.)	Nat. 0.	′
00	29905	19909	29910	19912	29916	19914	29921	19916	29926	19919	29931	19921	59
01	29931	19921	29936	19923	29941	19926	29946	19928	29951	19930	29956	19932	58
02	29956	19932	29961	19935	29966	19937	29971	19939	29976	19942	29981	19944	57
03	29981	19944	29986	19946	29992	19949	29997	19951	30002	19953	30007	19956	56
04	30007	19956	30012	19958	30017	19960	30022	19963	30027	19965	30032	19967	55
05	30032	19967	30037	19970	30042	19972	30047	19974	30052	19977	30057	19979	54
06	30057	19979	30062	19981	30067	19984	30073	19986	30078	19988	30083	19991	53
07	30083	19991	30088	19993	30093	19995	30098	19998	30103	20000	30108	20002	52
08	30108	20002	30113	20005	30118	20007	30123	20009	30128	20012	30133	20014	51
09	30133	20014	30138	20016	30143	20019	30148	20021	30153	20023	30158	20026	50
10	30158	20026	30163	20028	30168	20030	30174	20033	30179	20035	30184	20037	49
11	30184	20037	30189	20040	30194	20042	30199	20044	30204	20046	30209	20049	48
12	30209	20049	30214	20051	30219	20053	30224	20056	30229	20058	30234	20060	47
13	30234	20060	30239	20063	30244	20065	30249	20067	30254	20070	30259	20072	46
14	30259	20072	30264	20074	30269	20077	30275	20079	30280	20081	30285	20084	45
15	30285	20084	30290	20086	30295	20088	30300	20091	30305	20093	30310	20095	44
16	30310	20095	30315	20098	30320	20100	30325	20102	30330	20105	30335	20107	43
17	30335	20107	30340	20109	30345	20112	30350	20114	30355	20116	30360	20119	42
18	30360	20119	30365	20121	30370	20123	30375	20126	30380	20128	30385	20130	41
19	30385	20130	30390	20133	30395	20135	30400	20137	30405	20140	30410	20142	40
20	30410	20142	30415	20144	30420	20147	30426	20149	30431	20151	30436	20154	39
21	30436	20154	30441	20156	30446	20158	30451	20161	30456	20163	30461	20165	38
22	30461	20165	30466	20168	30471	20170	30476	20172	30481	20175	30486	20177	37
23	30486	20177	30491	20179	30496	20182	30501	20184	30506	20186	30511	20189	36
24	30511	20189	30516	20191	30521	20193	30526	20196	30531	20198	30536	20200	35
25	30536	20200	30541	20203	30546	20205	30551	20207	30556	20210	30561	20212	34
26	30561	20212	30566	20214	30571	20217	30576	20219	30581	20221	30586	20224	33
27	30586	20224	30591	20226	30596	20228	30601	20231	30606	20233	30611	20235	32
28	30611	20235	30616	20238	30621	20240	30626	20242	30631	20245	30636	20247	31
29	30636	20247	30641	20249	30646	20252	30652	20254	30657	20257	30662	20259	30
30	30662	20259	30667	20261	30672	20264	30677	20266	30682	20268	30687	20271	29
31	30687	20271	30692	20273	30697	20275	30702	20278	30707	20280	30712	20282	28
32	30712	20282	30717	20285	30722	20287	30727	20289	30732	20292	30737	20294	27
33	30737	20294	30742	20296	30747	20299	30752	20301	30757	20303	30762	20306	26
34	30762	20306	30767	20308	30772	20310	30777	20313	30782	20315	30787	20317	25
35	30787	20317	30792	20320	30797	20322	30802	20324	30807	20327	30812	20329	24
36	30812	20329	30817	20331	30822	20334	30827	20336	30832	20338	30837	20341	23
37	30837	20341	30842	20343	30847	20345	30852	20348	30857	20350	30862	20352	22
38	30862	20352	30867	20355	30872	20357	30877	20360	30882	20362	30887	20364	21
39	30887	20364	30892	20367	30897	20369	30902	20371	30907	20374	30912	20376	20
40	30912	20376	30917	20378	30922	20381	30927	20383	30932	20385	30937	20388	19
41	30937	20388	30942	20390	30947	20392	30952	20395	30957	20397	30962	20399	18
42	30962	20399	30967	20402	30972	20404	30977	20406	30982	20409	30987	20411	17
43	30987	20411	30992	20413	30997	20416	31002	20418	31007	20420	31012	20423	16
44	31012	20423	31017	20425	31022	20427	31026	20430	31031	20432	31036	20435	15
45	31036	20435	31041	20437	31046	20439	31051	20442	31056	20444	31061	20446	14
46	31061	20446	31066	20449	31071	20451	31076	20453	31081	20456	31086	20458	13
47	31086	20458	31091	20460	31096	20463	31101	20465	31106	20467	31111	20470	12
48	31111	20470	31116	20472	31121	20474	31126	20477	31131	20479	31136	20481	11
49	31136	20481	31141	20484	31146	20486	31151	20488	31156	20491	31161	20493	10
50	31161	20493	31166	20496	31171	20498	31176	20500	31181	20503	31186	20505	09
51	31186	20505	31191	20507	31196	20510	31201	20512	31206	20514	31211	20517	08
52	31211	20517	31216	20519	31221	20521	31226	20524	31231	20526	31236	20528	07
53	31236	20528	31241	20531	31246	20533	31250	20536	31255	20538	31260	20540	06
54	31260	20540	31265	20543	31270	20545	31275	20547	31280	20550	31285	20552	05
55	31285	20552	31290	20554	31295	20557	31300	20559	31305	20561	31310	20564	04
56	31310	20564	31315	20566	31320	20568	31325	20571	31330	20573	31335	20575	03
57	31335	20575	31340	20578	31345	20580	31350	20582	31355	20585	31360	20587	02
58	31360	20587	31365	20590	31370	20592	31375	20594	31380	20597	31385	20599	01
59	31385	20599	31390	20601	31395	20604	31399	20606	31404	20608	31409	20611	00
		.8		.6		.4		.2		.0			

PARTS for 0′.1:   LOGS 3 (2 after 53°30′)   NATURALS 1

54° HAVERSINES

′	.0 Log. $\overline{1}$.or(9.)	.0 Nat. 0.	.2 Log. $\overline{1}$.or(9.)	.2 Nat. 0.	.4 Log. $\overline{1}$.or(9.)	.4 Nat. 0.	.6 Log. $\overline{1}$.or(9.)	.6 Nat. 0.	.8 Log. $\overline{1}$.or(9.)	.8 Nat. 0.	Log. $\overline{1}$.or(9.)	Nat. 0.	′
00	31409	20611	31414	20613	31419	20615	31424	20618	31429	20620	31434	20623	59
01	31434	20623	31439	20625	31444	20627	31449	20630	31454	20632	31459	20634	58
02	31459	20634	31464	20637	31469	20639	31474	20641	31479	20644	31484	20646	57
03	31484	20646	31489	20648	31494	20651	31498	20653	31503	20655	31508	20658	56
04	31508	20658	31513	20660	31518	20663	31523	20665	31528	20667	31533	20670	55
05	31533	20670	31538	20672	31543	20674	31548	20677	31553	20679	31558	20681	54
06	31558	20681	31563	20684	31568	20686	31573	20688	31578	20691	31583	20693	53
07	31583	20693	31588	20696	31593	20698	31597	20700	31602	20703	31607	20705	52
08	31607	20705	31612	20707	31617	20710	31622	20712	31627	20714	31632	20717	51
09	31632	20717	31637	20719	31642	20721	31647	20724	31652	20726	31657	20729	50
10	31657	20729	31662	20731	31667	20733	31672	20736	31677	20738	31682	20740	49
11	31682	20740	31687	20743	31691	20745	31696	20747	31701	20750	31706	20752	48
12	31706	20752	31711	20754	31716	20757	31721	20759	31726	20762	31731	20764	47
13	31731	20764	31736	20766	31741	20769	31746	20771	31751	20773	31756	20776	46
14	31756	20776	31761	20778	31765	20780	31770	20783	31775	20785	31780	20788	45
15	31780	20788	31785	20790	31790	20792	31795	20795	31800	20797	31805	20799	44
16	31805	20799	31810	20802	31815	20804	31820	20806	31825	20809	31830	20811	43
17	31830	20811	31835	20814	31839	20816	31844	20818	31849	20821	31854	20823	42
18	31854	20823	31859	20825	31864	20828	31869	20830	31874	20832	31879	20835	41
19	31879	20835	31884	20837	31889	20839	31894	20842	31898	20844	31903	20847	40
20	31903	20847	31908	20849	31913	20851	31918	20854	31923	20856	31928	20858	39
21	31928	20858	31933	20861	31938	20863	31943	20865	31948	20868	31953	20870	38
22	31953	20870	31958	20873	31962	20875	31967	20877	31972	20880	31977	20882	37
23	31977	20882	31982	20884	31987	20887	31992	20889	31997	20891	32002	20894	36
24	32002	20894	32007	20896	32012	20899	32017	20901	32021	20903	32026	20906	35
25	32026	20906	32031	20908	32036	20910	32041	20913	32046	20915	32051	20918	34
26	32051	20918	32056	20920	32061	20922	32066	20925	32071	20927	32076	20929	33
27	32076	20929	32081	20932	32085	20934	32090	20936	32095	20939	32100	20941	32
28	32100	20941	32105	20944	32110	20946	32115	20948	32120	20951	32125	20953	31
29	32125	20953	32130	20955	32134	20958	32139	20960	32144	20962	32149	20965	30
30	32149	20965	32154	20967	32159	20970	32164	20972	32169	20974	32174	20977	29
31	32174	20977	32179	20979	32184	20981	32188	20984	32193	20986	32198	20989	28
32	32198	20989	32203	20991	32208	20993	32213	20996	32218	20998	32223	21000	27
33	32223	21000	32228	21003	32233	21005	32237	21008	32242	21010	32247	21012	26
34	32247	21012	32252	21015	32257	21017	32262	21019	32267	21022	32272	21024	25
35	32272	21024	32277	21026	32282	21029	32286	21031	32291	21034	32296	21036	24
36	32296	21036	32301	21038	32306	21041	32311	21043	32316	21045	32321	21048	23
37	32321	21048	32326	21050	32330	21053	32335	21055	32340	21057	32345	21060	22
38	32345	21060	32350	21062	32355	21064	32360	21067	32365	21069	32370	21072	21
39	32370	21072	32374	21074	32379	21076	32384	21079	32389	21081	32394	21083	20
40	32394	21083	32399	21086	32404	21088	32409	21091	32414	21093	32418	21095	19
41	32418	21095	32423	21098	32428	21100	32433	21102	32438	21105	32443	21107	18
42	32443	21107	32448	21109	32453	21112	32458	21114	32462	21117	32467	21119	17
43	32467	21119	32472	21121	32477	21124	32482	21126	32487	21128	32492	21131	16
44	32492	21131	32497	21133	32502	21136	32506	21138	32511	21140	32516	21143	15
45	32516	21143	32521	21145	32526	21147	32531	21150	32536	21152	32541	21155	14
46	32541	21155	32545	21157	32550	21159	32555	21162	32560	21164	32565	21167	13
47	32565	21167	32570	21169	32575	21171	32580	21174	32584	21176	32589	21178	12
48	32589	21178	32594	21181	32598	21183	32604	21186	32608	21188	32614	21190	11
49	32614	21190	32618	21193	32623	21195	32628	21197	32633	21200	32638	21202	10
50	32638	21202	32643	21205	32648	21207	32653	21209	32658	21212	32662	21214	09
51	32662	21214	32667	21216	32672	21219	32677	21221	32682	21224	32687	21226	08
52	32687	21226	32691	21228	32696	21231	32701	21233	32706	21235	32711	21238	07
53	32711	21238	32716	21240	32721	21243	32726	21245	32731	21247	32735	21250	06
54	32735	21250	32740	21252	32745	21255	32750	21257	32755	21259	32760	21262	05
55	32760	21262	32764	21264	32769	21266	32774	21269	32779	21271	32784	21274	04
56	32784	21274	32789	21276	32794	21278	32799	21281	32803	21283	32808	21285	03
57	32808	21285	32813	21288	32818	21290	32823	21293	32828	21295	32833	21297	02
58	32833	21297	32837	21300	32842	21302	32847	21304	32852	21307	32857	21309	01
59	32857	21309	32862	21312	32867	21314	32871	21316	32876	21319	32881	21321	00

	.8	.6	.4	.2	.0 ←

PARTS for 0′.1:   LOGS 2   NATURALS 1   305°

55° HAVERSINES

	.0		.2		.4		.6		.8				
	Log.	Nat.	Log.	Nat.	Log.	Nat.	Log.	Nat.	Log.	Nat.	Log.	Nat.	
′	$\overline{1}$.or(9.)	0.	$\overline{1}$.or(9.)	0.	$\overline{1}$.or(9.)	0.	$\overline{1}$.or(9.)	0.	$\overline{1}$.or(9.)	0.	$\overline{1}$.or(9.)	0.	′
00	32881	21321	32886	21324	32891	21326	32896	21328	32901	21331	32905	21333	59
01	32905	21333	32910	21335	32915	21338	32920	21340	32925	21343	32930	21345	58
02	32930	21345	32934	21347	32939	21350	32944	21352	32949	21355	32954	21357	57
03	32954	21357	32959	21359	32964	21362	32968	21364	32973	21366	32978	21369	56
04	32978	21369	32983	21371	32988	21374	32993	21376	32998	21378	33002	21381	55
05	33002	21381	33007	21383	33012	21386	33017	21388	33022	21390	33027	21393	54
06	33027	21393	33031	21395	33036	21397	33041	21400	33046	21402	33051	21405	53
07	33051	21405	33056	21407	33060	21409	33065	21412	33070	21414	33075	21417	52
08	33075	21417	33080	21419	33085	21421	33090	21424	33094	21426	33099	21429	51
09	33099	21429	33104	21431	33109	21433	33114	21436	33119	21438	33123	21440	50
10	33123	21440	33128	21443	33133	21445	33138	21448	33143	21450	33148	21452	49
11	33148	21452	33152	21455	33157	21457	33162	21460	33167	21462	33172	21464	48
12	33172	21464	33177	21467	33181	21469	33186	21471	33191	21474	33196	21476	47
13	33196	21476	33201	21479	33205	21481	33210	21483	33215	21486	33220	21488	46
14	33220	21488	33225	21491	33230	21493	33235	21495	33239	21498	33244	21500	45
15	33244	21500	33249	21503	33254	21505	33259	21507	33264	21510	33268	21512	44
16	33268	21512	33273	21514	33278	21517	33283	21519	33288	21522	33292	21524	43
17	33292	21524	33297	21526	33302	21529	33307	21531	33312	21534	33317	21536	42
18	33317	21536	33321	21538	33326	21541	33331	21543	33336	21546	33341	21548	41
19	33341	21548	33345	21550	33350	21553	33355	21555	33360	21558	33365	21560	40
20	33365	21560	33370	21562	33374	21565	33379	21567	33384	21570	33389	21572	39
21	33389	21572	33394	21574	33398	21577	33403	21579	33408	21581	33413	21584	38
22	33413	21584	33418	21586	33423	21589	33427	21591	33432	21593	33437	21596	37
23	33437	21596	33442	21598	33447	21601	33451	21603	33456	21605	33461	21608	36
24	33461	21608	33466	21610	33471	21613	33476	21615	33480	21617	33485	21620	35
25	33485	21620	33490	21622	33495	21625	33500	21627	33504	21629	33509	21632	34
26	33509	21632	33514	21634	33519	21637	33524	21639	33528	21641	33533	21644	33
27	33533	21644	33538	21646	33543	21649	33548	21651	33552	21653	33557	21656	32
28	33557	21656	33562	21658	33567	21661	33572	21663	33576	21665	33581	21668	31
29	33581	21668	33586	21670	33591	21673	33596	21675	33601	21677	33605	21680	30
30	33605	21680	33610	21682	33615	21685	33620	21687	33625	21689	33629	21692	29
31	33629	21692	33634	21694	33639	21696	33644	21699	33649	21701	33653	21704	28
32	33653	21704	33658	21706	33663	21708	33668	21711	33672	21713	33677	21716	27
33	33677	21716	33682	21718	33687	21720	33692	21723	33696	21725	33701	21728	26
34	33701	21728	33706	21730	33711	21732	33716	21735	33720	21737	33725	21740	25
35	33725	21740	33730	21742	33735	21744	33740	21747	33744	21749	33749	21752	24
36	33749	21752	33754	21754	33759	21756	33764	21759	33768	21761	33773	21764	23
37	33773	21764	33778	21766	33783	21768	33788	21771	33792	21773	33797	21776	22
38	33797	21776	33802	21778	33807	21780	33811	21783	33816	21785	33821	21788	21
39	33821	21788	33826	21790	33831	21792	33835	21795	33840	21797	33845	21800	20
40	33845	21800	33850	21802	33855	21804	33859	21807	33864	21809	33869	21812	19
41	33869	21812	33874	21814	33879	21817	33883	21819	33888	21821	33893	21824	18
42	33893	21824	33898	21826	33902	21829	33907	21831	33912	21833	33917	21836	17
43	33917	21836	33922	21838	33926	21841	33931	21843	33936	21845	33941	21848	16
44	33941	21848	33945	21850	33950	21853	33955	21855	33960	21857	33965	21860	15
45	33965	21860	33969	21862	33974	21865	33979	21867	33984	21869	33988	21872	14
46	33988	21872	33993	21874	33998	21877	34003	21879	34007	21881	34012	21884	13
47	34012	21884	34017	21886	34022	21889	34027	21891	34031	21893	34036	21896	12
48	34036	21896	34041	21898	34046	21901	34050	21903	34055	21905	34060	21908	11
49	34060	21908	34065	21910	34070	21913	34074	21915	34079	21917	34084	21920	10
50	34084	21920	34089	21922	34093	21925	34098	21927	34103	21930	34108	21932	09
51	34108	21932	34112	21934	34117	21937	34122	21939	34127	21942	34132	21944	08
52	34132	21944	34136	21946	34141	21949	34146	21951	34151	21954	34155	21956	07
53	34155	21956	34160	21958	34165	21961	34170	21963	34174	21966	34179	21968	06
54	34179	21968	34184	21970	34189	21973	34193	21975	34198	21978	34203	21980	05
55	34203	21980	34208	21983	34213	21985	34217	21987	34222	21990	34227	21992	04
56	34227	21992	34232	21995	34236	21997	34241	21999	34246	22002	34251	22004	03
57	34251	22004	34255	22007	34260	22009	34265	22011	34270	22014	34274	22016	02
58	34274	22016	34279	22019	34284	22021	34289	22023	34292	22026	34298	22028	01
59	34298	22028	34303	22031	34308	22033	34312	22036	34317	22038	34322	22040	00
		.8		.6		.4		.2		.0			

PARTS for 0′.1:   LOGS 2   NATURALS 1

304°

56° HAVERSINES

'	.0 Log. 1.or(9.)	.0 Nat. 0.	.2 Log. 1.or(9.)	.2 Nat. 0.	.4 Log. 1.or(9.)	.4 Nat. 0.	.6 Log. 1.or(9.)	.6 Nat. 0.	.8 Log. 1.or(9.)	.8 Nat. 0.	Log. 1.or(9.)	Nat. 0.	'
00	34322	22040	34327	22043	34331	22045	34336	22048	34341	22050	34346	22052	59
01	34346	22052	34350	22055	34355	22057	34360	22060	34365	22062	34369	22064	58
02	34369	22064	34374	22067	34379	22069	34384	22072	34388	22074	34393	22077	57
03	34393	22077	34398	22079	34403	22081	34407	22084	34412	22086	34417	22089	56
04	34417	22089	34422	22091	34426	22093	34431	22096	34436	22098	34441	22101	55
05	34441	22101	34445	22103	34450	22105	34455	22108	34459	22110	34464	22113	54
06	34464	22113	34469	22115	34474	22118	34478	22120	34483	22122	34488	22125	53
07	34488	22125	34493	22127	34497	22130	34502	22132	34507	22134	34512	22137	52
08	34512	22137	34516	22139	34521	22142	34526	22144	34531	22147	34535	22149	51
09	34535	22149	34540	22151	34545	22154	34550	22156	34554	22159	34559	22161	50
10	34559	22161	34564	22163	34569	22166	34573	22168	34578	22171	34583	22173	49
11	34583	22173	34588	22176	34592	22178	34597	22180	34602	22183	34606	22185	48
12	34606	22185	34611	22188	34616	22190	34621	22192	34625	22195	34630	22197	47
13	34630	22197	34635	22200	34639	22202	34644	22205	34649	22207	34654	22209	46
14	34654	22209	34658	22212	34663	22214	34668	22217	34673	22219	34677	22221	45
15	34677	22221	34682	22224	34687	22226	34692	22229	34696	22231	34701	22234	44
16	34701	22234	34706	22236	34710	22238	34715	22241	34720	22243	34725	22246	43
17	34725	22246	34729	22248	34734	22251	34739	22253	34743	22255	34748	22258	42
18	34748	22258	34753	22260	34758	22263	34762	22265	34767	22267	34772	22270	41
19	34772	22270	34777	22272	34781	22275	34786	22277	34791	22280	34795	22282	40
20	34795	22282	34800	22284	34805	22287	34810	22289	34814	22292	34819	22294	39
21	34819	22294	34824	22297	34828	22299	34833	22301	34838	22304	34843	22306	38
22	34843	22306	34847	22309	34852	22311	34857	22313	34861	22316	34866	22318	37
23	34866	22318	34871	22321	34876	22323	34880	22326	34885	22328	34890	22330	36
24	34890	22330	34894	22333	34899	22335	34904	22338	34908	22340	34913	22343	35
25	34913	22343	34918	22345	34923	22347	34927	22350	34932	22352	34937	22355	34
26	34937	22355	34942	22357	34946	22360	34951	22362	34956	22364	34960	22367	33
27	34960	22367	34965	22369	34970	22372	34974	22374	34979	22376	34984	22379	32
28	34984	22379	34989	22381	34993	22384	34998	22386	35003	22389	35007	22391	31
29	35007	22391	35012	22393	35017	22396	35022	22398	35026	22401	35031	22403	30
30	35031	22403	35036	22406	35040	22408	35045	22410	35050	22413	35054	22415	29
31	35054	22415	35059	22418	35064	22420	35069	22423	35073	22425	35078	22427	28
32	35078	22427	35083	22430	35087	22432	35092	22435	35097	22437	35101	22440	27
33	35101	22440	35106	22442	35111	22444	35115	22447	35120	22449	35125	22452	26
34	35125	22452	35130	22454	35134	22457	35139	22459	35144	22461	35148	22464	25
35	35148	22464	35153	22466	35158	22469	35162	22471	35167	22472	35172	22476	24
36	35172	22476	35176	22478	35181	22481	35186	22483	35191	22486	35195	22488	23
37	35195	22488	35200	22491	35205	22493	35209	22495	35214	22498	35219	22500	22
38	35219	22500	35223	22503	35228	22505	35233	22508	35238	22510	35242	22512	21
39	35242	22512	35247	22515	35252	22517	35256	22520	35261	22522	35266	22525	20
40	35266	22525	35270	22527	35275	22529	35280	22532	35284	22534	35289	22537	19
41	35289	22537	35294	22539	35298	22542	35303	22544	35308	22546	35312	22549	18
42	35312	22549	35317	22551	35322	22554	35326	22556	35331	22559	35336	22561	17
43	35336	22561	35340	22563	35345	22566	35350	22568	35355	22571	35359	22573	16
44	35359	22573	35364	22576	35369	22578	35373	22580	35378	22583	35383	22585	15
45	35383	22585	35387	22588	35392	22590	35397	22593	35401	22595	35406	22598	14
46	35406	22598	35411	22600	35415	22602	35420	22605	35425	22607	35429	22610	13
47	35429	22610	35434	22612	35439	22615	35443	22617	35448	22619	35453	22622	12
48	35453	22622	35457	22624	35462	22627	35467	22629	35472	22632	35476	22634	11
49	35476	22634	35481	22636	35486	22639	35490	22641	35495	22644	35500	22646	10
50	35500	22646	35504	22649	35509	22651	35514	22653	35518	22656	35523	22658	09
51	35523	22658	35527	22661	35532	22663	35537	22666	35542	22668	35546	22671	08
52	35546	22671	35551	22672	35556	22675	35560	22678	35565	22680	35570	22683	07
53	35570	22683	35574	22685	35579	22688	35584	22690	35588	22692	35593	22695	06
54	35593	22695	35597	22697	35602	22700	35607	22702	35611	22705	35616	22707	05
55	35616	22707	35621	22710	35625	22712	35630	22714	35635	22717	35639	22719	04
56	35639	22719	35644	22722	35649	22724	35653	22727	35658	22729	35663	22731	03
57	35663	22731	35667	22734	35672	22736	35677	22739	35681	22741	35686	22744	02
58	35686	22744	35691	22746	35695	22749	35700	22751	35705	22753	35709	22756	01
59	35709	22756	35714	22758	35719	22761	35723	22763	35728	22766	35733	22768	00

| | .8 | | .6 | | .4 | | .2 | | .0 | |

303°

PARTS for 0'.1:   LOGS 2   NATURALS 1

57° HAVERSINES 302°

′	.0 Log. 1.or(9.)	.0 Nat. 0.	.2 Log. 1.or(9.)	.2 Nat. 0.	.4 Log. 1.or(9.)	.4 Nat. 0.	.6 Log. 1.or(9.)	.6 Nat. 0.	.8 Log. 1.or(9.)	.8 Nat. 0.	Log. 1.or(9.)	Nat. 0.	′
00	35733	22768	35737	22770	35742	22773	35747	22775	35751	22778	35756	22780	59
01	35756	22780	35760	22783	35765	22785	35770	22788	35774	22790	35779	22792	58
02	35779	22792	35784	22795	35788	22797	35793	22800	35798	22802	35802	22805	57
03	35802	22805	35807	22807	35812	22810	35816	22812	35821	22814	35826	22817	56
04	35826	22817	35830	22819	35835	22822	35840	22824	35844	22827	35849	22829	55
05	35849	22829	35853	22832	35858	22834	35863	22836	35867	22839	35872	22841	54
06	35872	22841	35877	22844	35881	22846	35886	22849	35891	22851	35895	22853	53
07	35895	22853	35900	22856	35904	22858	35909	22861	35914	22863	35918	22866	52
08	35918	22866	35923	22868	35928	22871	35932	22873	35937	22875	35942	22878	51
09	35942	22878	35946	22880	35951	22883	35956	22885	35960	22888	35965	22890	50
10	35965	22890	35969	22893	35974	22895	35979	22897	35983	22900	35988	22902	49
11	35988	22902	35993	22905	35997	22907	36002	22910	36007	22912	36011	22915	48
12	36011	22915	36016	22917	36020	22919	36025	22922	36030	22924	36034	22927	47
13	36034	22927	36039	22929	36044	22932	36048	22934	36053	22937	36058	22939	46
14	36058	22939	36062	22942	36067	22944	36071	22946	36076	22949	36081	22951	45
15	36081	22951	36085	22954	36090	22956	36095	22959	36099	22961	36104	22964	44
16	36104	22964	36108	22966	36113	22968	36118	22971	36122	22973	36127	22976	43
17	36127	22976	36132	22978	36136	22981	36141	22983	36145	22986	36150	22988	42
18	36150	22988	36155	22990	36159	22993	36164	22995	36169	22998	36173	23000	41
19	36173	23000	36178	23003	36182	23005	36187	23008	36192	23010	36196	23012	40
20	36196	23012	36201	23015	36206	23017	36210	23020	36215	23022	36219	23025	39
21	36219	23025	36224	23027	36229	23030	36233	23032	36238	23035	36243	23037	38
22	36243	23037	36247	23039	36252	23042	36256	23044	36261	23047	36266	23049	37
23	36266	23049	36270	23052	36275	23054	36279	23057	36284	23059	36289	23061	36
24	36289	23061	36293	23064	36298	23066	36303	23069	36307	23071	36312	23074	35
25	36312	23074	36316	23076	36321	23079	36326	23081	36330	23084	36335	23086	34
26	36335	23086	36339	23088	36344	23091	36349	23093	36353	23096	36358	23098	33
27	36358	23098	36362	23101	36367	23103	36372	23106	36376	23108	36381	23110	32
28	36381	23110	36386	23113	36390	23115	36395	23118	36399	23120	36404	23123	31
29	36404	23123	36409	23125	36413	23128	36418	23130	36422	23133	36427	23135	30
30	36427	23135	36432	23137	36436	23140	36441	23142	36445	23145	36450	23147	29
31	36450	23147	36455	23150	36459	23152	36464	23155	36468	23157	36473	23160	28
32	36473	23160	36478	23162	36482	23164	36487	23167	36491	23169	36496	23172	27
33	36496	23172	36501	23174	36505	23177	36510	23179	36514	23182	36519	23184	26
34	36519	23184	36524	23187	36528	23189	36533	23191	36537	23194	36542	23196	25
35	36542	23196	36547	23199	36551	23201	36556	23204	36560	23206	36565	23209	24
36	36565	23209	36570	23211	36574	23214	36579	23216	36583	23218	36588	23221	23
37	36588	23221	36593	23223	36597	23226	36602	23228	36606	23231	36611	23233	22
38	36611	23233	36616	23236	36620	23238	36625	23241	36629	23243	36634	23246	21
39	36634	23246	36639	23248	36643	23250	36648	23253	36652	23255	36657	23258	20
40	36657	23258	36661	23260	36666	23263	36671	23265	36675	23268	36680	23270	19
41	36680	23270	36684	23273	36689	23275	36694	23277	36698	23280	36703	23282	18
42	36703	23282	36707	23285	36712	23287	36716	23290	36721	23292	36726	23295	17
43	36726	23295	36730	23297	36735	23300	36739	23302	36744	23305	36749	23307	16
44	36749	23307	36753	23309	36758	23312	36762	23314	36767	23317	36772	23319	15
45	36772	23319	36776	23322	36781	23324	36785	23327	36790	23329	36794	23332	14
46	36794	23332	36799	23334	36804	23337	36808	23339	36813	23341	36817	23344	13
47	36817	23344	36822	23346	36827	23349	36831	23351	36836	23354	36840	23356	12
48	36840	23356	36845	23359	36849	23361	36854	23364	36858	23366	36863	23368	11
49	36863	23368	36868	23371	36872	23373	36877	23376	36881	23378	36886	23381	10
50	36886	23381	36891	23383	36895	23386	36900	23388	36904	23391	36909	23393	09
51	36909	23393	36913	23396	36918	23398	36922	23401	36927	23403	36932	23405	08
52	36932	23405	36936	23408	36941	23410	36945	23413	36950	23415	36955	23418	07
53	36955	23418	36959	23420	36964	23423	36968	23425	36973	23428	36977	23430	06
54	36977	23430	36982	23433	36987	23435	36991	23437	36996	23440	37000	23442	05
55	37000	23442	37005	23445	37009	23447	37014	23450	37018	23452	37023	23455	04
56	37023	23455	37028	23457	37032	23460	37037	23462	37041	23465	37046	23467	03
57	37046	23467	37050	23470	37055	23472	37059	23474	37064	23477	37069	23479	02
58	37069	23479	37073	23482	37078	23484	37082	23487	37087	23489	37091	23492	01
59	37091	23492	37096	23494	37101	23497	37105	23499	37110	23502	37114	23504	00

.8 .6 .4 .2 .0

PARTS for 0′.1: LOGS 2 NATURALS 1

302°

58° HAVERSINES

′	.0 Log. 1̄.or(9.)	.0 Nat. 0.	.2 Log. 1̄.or(9.)	.2 Nat. 0.	.4 Log. 1̄.or(9.)	.4 Nat. 0.	.6 Log. 1̄.or(9.)	.6 Nat. 0.	.8 Log. 1̄.or(9.)	.8 Nat. 0.	.8 Log. 1̄.or(9.)	.8 Nat. 0.	′
00	37114	23504	37119	23507	37123	23509	37128	23511	37132	23514	37137	23516	59
01	37137	23516	37142	23519	37146	23521	37151	23524	37155	23526	37160	23529	58
02	37160	23529	37164	23531	37169	23534	37173	23536	37178	23539	37183	23541	57
03	37183	23541	37187	23544	37192	23546	37196	23548	37201	23551	37205	23553	56
04	37205	23553	37210	23556	37215	23558	37219	23561	37224	23563	37228	23566	55
05	37228	23566	37233	23568	37237	23571	37242	23573	37246	23576	37251	23578	54
06	37251	23578	37255	23581	37260	23583	37264	23586	37269	23588	37274	23590	53
07	37274	23590	37278	23593	37283	23595	37287	23598	37292	23600	37296	23603	52
08	37296	23603	37301	23605	37305	23608	37310	23610	37314	23613	37319	23615	51
09	37319	23615	37324	23618	37328	23620	37333	23623	37337	23625	37342	23627	50
10	37342	23627	37346	23630	37351	23632	37355	23635	37360	23637	37364	23640	49
11	37364	23640	37369	23642	37374	23645	37378	23647	37383	23650	37387	23652	48
12	37387	23652	37392	23655	37396	23657	37401	23660	37405	23662	37410	23665	47
13	37410	23665	37414	23667	37419	23670	37423	23672	37428	23674	37433	23677	46
14	37433	23677	37437	23679	37442	23682	37446	23684	37451	23687	37455	23689	45
15	37455	23689	37460	23692	37464	23694	37469	23697	37473	23699	37478	23702	44
16	37478	23702	37482	23704	37487	23707	37491	23709	37496	23712	37501	23714	43
17	37501	23714	37505	23717	37510	23719	37514	23721	37519	23724	37523	23726	42
18	37523	23726	37528	23729	37532	23731	37537	23734	37541	23736	37546	23739	41
19	37546	23739	37550	23741	37555	23744	37559	23746	37564	23749	37569	23751	40
20	37569	23751	37573	23754	37578	23756	37582	23759	37587	23761	37591	23764	39
21	37591	23764	37596	23766	37600	23769	37605	23771	37609	23773	37614	23776	38
22	37614	23776	37618	23778	37623	23781	37627	23783	37632	23786	37636	23788	37
23	37636	23788	37641	23791	37645	23793	37650	23796	37654	23798	37659	23801	36
24	37659	23801	37664	23803	37668	23806	37673	23808	37677	23811	37682	23813	35
25	37682	23813	37686	23816	37691	23818	37695	23821	37700	23823	37704	23825	34
26	37704	23825	37709	23828	37713	23830	37718	23833	37722	23835	37727	23838	33
27	37727	23838	37731	23840	37736	23843	37740	23845	37745	23848	37749	23850	32
28	37749	23850	37754	23853	37758	23855	37763	23858	37767	23860	37772	23863	31
29	37772	23863	37776	23865	37781	23868	37785	23870	37790	23873	37794	23875	30
30	37794	23875	37799	23878	37803	23880	37808	23882	37812	23885	37817	23887	29
31	37817	23887	37822	23890	37826	23892	37831	23895	37835	23897	37840	23900	28
32	37840	23900	37844	23902	37849	23905	37853	23907	37858	23910	37862	23912	27
33	37862	23912	37867	23915	37871	23917	37876	23920	37880	23922	37885	23925	26
34	37885	23925	37889	23927	37894	23930	37898	23932	37903	23935	37907	23937	25
35	37907	23937	37912	23940	37916	23942	37921	23945	37925	23947	37930	23950	24
36	37930	23950	37934	23952	37939	23954	37943	23957	37948	23959	37952	23962	23
37	37952	23962	37957	23964	37961	23967	37966	23969	37970	23972	37975	23974	22
38	37975	23974	37979	23977	37984	23979	37988	23982	37993	23984	37997	23987	21
39	37997	23987	38002	23989	38006	23992	38011	23994	38015	23997	38020	23999	20
40	38020	23999	38024	24002	38029	24004	38033	24007	38038	24009	38042	24012	19
41	38042	24012	38047	24014	38051	24017	38056	24019	38060	24022	38065	24024	18
42	38065	24024	38069	24027	38074	24029	38078	24031	38083	24034	38087	24036	17
43	38087	24036	38092	24039	38096	24041	38101	24044	38105	24046	38110	24049	16
44	38110	24049	38114	24051	38119	24054	38123	24056	38128	24059	38132	24061	15
45	38132	24061	38136	24064	38141	24066	38145	24069	38150	24071	38154	24074	14
46	38154	24074	38159	24076	38163	24079	38168	24081	38172	24084	38177	24086	13
47	38177	24086	38181	24089	38186	24091	38190	24094	38195	24096	38199	24099	12
48	38199	24099	38204	24101	38208	24104	38213	24106	38217	24109	38222	24111	11
49	38222	24111	38226	24114	38231	24116	38235	24119	38240	24121	38244	24124	10
50	38244	24124	38248	24126	38253	24129	38257	24131	38262	24134	38267	24136	09
51	38267	24136	38271	24138	38275	24141	38280	24143	38284	24146	38289	24148	08
52	38289	24148	38293	24151	38298	24153	38302	24156	38307	24158	38311	24161	07
53	38311	24161	38316	24163	38320	24166	38325	24168	38329	24171	38334	24173	06
54	38334	24173	38338	24176	38343	24178	38347	24181	38352	24183	38356	24186	05
55	38356	24186	38360	24188	38365	24191	38369	24193	38374	24196	38378	24198	04
56	38378	24198	38383	24201	38387	24203	38392	24206	38396	24208	38401	24211	03
57	38401	24211	38405	24213	38410	24216	38414	24218	38419	24221	38423	24223	02
58	38423	24223	38427	24226	38432	24228	38436	24231	38441	24233	38445	24236	01
59	38445	24236	38450	24238	38454	24241	38459	24243	38463	24246	38468	24248	00

	.8	.6	.4	.2	.0	

PARTS for 0′.1: LOGS 2   NATURALS 1   **301°**

HAVERSINES

′	.0 Log. 1̄.or(9.)	.0 Nat. 0.	.2 Log. 1̄.or(9.)	.2 Nat. 0.	.4 Log. 1̄.or(9.)	.4 Nat. 0.	.6 Log. 1̄.or(9.)	.6 Nat. 0.	.8 Log. 1̄.or(9.)	.8 Nat. 0.	Log. 1̄.or(9.)	Nat. 0.	′
00	38468	24248	38472	24251	38477	24253	38481	24256	38486	24258	38490	24261	59
01	38490	24261	38494	24263	38499	24266	38503	24268	38508	24271	38512	24273	58
02	38512	24273	38517	24276	38521	24278	38526	24281	38530	24283	38535	24286	57
03	38535	24286	38539	24288	38544	24291	38548	24293	38553	24296	38557	24298	56
04	38557	24298	38561	24300	38566	24303	38570	24305	38575	24308	38579	24310	55
05	38579	24310	38584	24313	38588	24315	38593	24318	38597	24320	38602	24323	54
06	38602	24323	38606	24325	38610	24328	38615	24330	38619	24333	38624	24335	53
07	38624	24335	38628	24338	38633	24340	38637	24343	38642	24345	38646	24348	52
08	38646	24348	38651	24350	38655	24353	38660	24355	38664	24358	38668	24360	51
09	38668	24360	38673	24363	38677	24365	38682	24368	38686	24370	38691	24373	50
10	38691	24373	38695	24375	38700	24378	38704	24380	38709	24383	38713	24385	49
11	38713	24385	38717	24388	38722	24390	38726	24393	38731	24395	38735	24398	48
12	38735	24398	38740	24400	38744	24403	38749	24405	38753	24408	38757	24410	47
13	38757	24410	38762	24413	38766	24415	38771	24418	38775	24420	38780	24423	46
14	38780	24423	38784	24425	38788	24428	38793	24430	38797	24433	38802	24435	45
15	38802	24435	38806	24438	38811	24440	38815	24443	38820	24445	38824	24448	44
16	38824	24448	38828	24450	38833	24453	38837	24455	38842	24458	38846	24460	43
17	38846	24460	38851	24463	38855	24465	38860	24468	38864	24470	38868	24473	42
18	38868	24473	38873	24475	38877	24478	38882	24480	38886	24483	38891	24485	41
19	38891	24485	38895	24488	38899	24490	38904	24493	38908	24495	38913	24498	40
20	38913	24498	38917	24500	38922	24503	38926	24505	38931	24508	38935	24510	39
21	38935	24510	38939	24513	38944	24515	38948	24518	38953	24520	38957	24523	38
22	38957	24523	38962	24525	38966	24528	38971	24530	38975	24533	38979	24535	37
23	38979	24535	38984	24538	38988	24540	38993	24543	38997	24545	39001	24548	36
24	39001	24548	39006	24550	39010	24553	39015	24555	39019	24558	39024	24560	35
25	39024	24560	39028	24563	39032	24565	39037	24568	39041	24570	39046	24573	34
26	39046	24573	39050	24575	39055	24578	39059	24580	39063	24583	39068	24586	33
27	39068	24586	39072	24588	39077	24591	39081	24593	39086	24596	39090	24598	32
28	39090	24598	39094	24601	39099	24603	39103	24606	39108	24608	39112	24611	31
29	39112	24611	39117	24613	39121	24616	39125	24618	39130	24621	39134	24623	30
30	39134	24623	39139	24626	39143	24628	39148	24631	39152	24633	39156	24636	29
31	39156	24636	39161	24638	39165	24641	39170	24643	39174	24646	39178	24648	28
32	39178	24648	39183	24651	39187	24653	39192	24656	39196	24658	39201	24661	27
33	39201	24661	39205	24663	39209	24666	39214	24668	39218	24671	39223	24673	26
34	39223	24673	39227	24676	39231	24678	39236	24681	39240	24683	39245	24686	25
35	39245	24686	39249	24688	39253	24691	39258	24693	39262	24696	39267	24698	24
36	39267	24698	39271	24701	39276	24703	39280	24706	39284	24708	39289	24711	23
37	39289	24711	39293	24713	39298	24716	39302	24718	39306	24721	39311	24723	22
38	39311	24723	39315	24726	39320	24728	39324	24731	39328	24733	39333	24736	21
39	39333	24736	39337	24738	39342	24741	39346	24743	39351	24746	39355	24749	20
40	39355	24749	39359	24751	39364	24754	39368	24756	39373	24759	39377	24761	19
41	39377	24761	39381	24764	39386	24766	39390	24769	39395	24771	39399	24774	18
42	39399	24774	39403	24776	39408	24779	39412	24781	39417	24784	39421	24786	17
43	39421	24786	39425	24789	39430	24791	39434	24794	39439	24796	39443	24799	16
44	39443	24799	39447	24801	39452	24804	39456	24806	39461	24809	39465	24811	15
45	39465	24811	39469	24814	39474	24816	39478	24819	39483	24821	39487	24824	14
46	39487	24824	39491	24826	39496	24829	39500	24831	39505	24834	39509	24836	13
47	39509	24836	39513	24839	39518	24841	39522	24844	39526	24846	39531	24849	12
48	39531	24849	39535	24852	39540	24854	39544	24857	39548	24859	39553	24862	11
49	39553	24862	39557	24864	39562	24867	39566	24869	39570	24872	39575	24874	10
50	39575	24874	39579	24877	39584	24879	39588	24882	39592	24884	39597	24887	09
51	39597	24887	39601	24889	39606	24892	39610	24894	39614	24897	39619	24899	08
52	39619	24899	39623	24902	39628	24904	39632	24907	39636	24909	39641	24912	07
53	39641	24912	39645	24914	39649	24917	39654	24919	39658	24922	39663	24924	06
54	39663	24924	39667	24927	39671	24929	39676	24932	39680	24934	39685	24937	05
55	39685	24937	39689	24940	39693	24942	39698	24945	39702	24947	39706	24950	04
56	39706	24950	39711	24952	39715	24955	39720	24957	39724	24960	39728	24962	03
57	39728	24962	39733	24965	39737	24967	39741	24970	39746	24972	39750	24975	02
58	39750	24975	39755	24977	39759	24980	39763	24982	39768	24985	39772	24987	01
59	39772	24987	39777	24990	39781	24992	39785	24995	39790	24997	39794	25000	00

	.8	.6	.4	.2	.0 ←

PARTS for 0′.1:   LOGS 2   NATURALS 1   **300°**

60° HAVERSINES

′	.0 Log. $\overline{1}$.or(9.)	.0 Nat. 0.	.2 Log. $\overline{1}$.or(9.)	.2 Nat. 0.	.4 Log. $\overline{1}$.or(9.)	.4 Nat. 0.	.6 Log. $\overline{1}$.or(9.)	.6 Nat. 0.	.8 Log. 1.or(9.)	.8 Nat. 0.	Log. $\overline{1}$.or(9.)	Nat. 0.	′
00	39794	25000	39798	25003	39803	25005	39807	25008	39811	25010	39816	25013	59
01	39816	25013	39820	25015	39825	25018	39829	25020	39833	25023	39838	25025	58
02	39838	25025	39842	25028	39847	25030	39851	25033	39855	25035	39860	25038	57
03	39860	25038	39864	25040	39868	25043	39873	25045	39877	25048	39881	25050	56
04	39881	25050	39886	25053	39890	25055	39895	25058	39899	25060	39903	25063	55
05	39903	25063	39908	25066	39912	25068	39916	25071	39921	25073	39925	25076	54
06	39925	25076	39930	25078	39934	25081	39938	25083	39943	25086	39947	25088	53
07	39947	25088	39951	25091	39956	25093	39960	25096	39964	25098	39969	25101	52
08	39969	25101	39973	25103	39978	25106	39982	25108	39986	25111	39991	25113	51
09	39991	25113	39995	25116	39999	25118	40004	25121	40008	25124	40012	25126	50
10	40012	25126	40017	25129	40021	25131	40025	25134	40030	25136	40034	25139	49
11	40034	25139	40039	25141	40043	25144	40047	25146	40052	25149	40056	25151	48
12	40056	25151	40060	25154	40065	25156	40069	25159	40073	25161	40078	25164	47
13	40078	25164	40082	25166	40087	25169	40091	25171	40095	25174	40100	25177	46
14	40100	25177	40104	25179	40108	25182	40113	25184	40117	25187	40121	25189	45
15	40121	25189	40126	25192	40130	25194	40134	25197	40139	25199	40143	25202	44
16	40143	25202	40148	25204	40152	25207	40156	25209	40161	25212	40165	25214	43
17	40165	25214	40169	25217	40174	25219	40178	25222	40182	25225	40187	25227	42
18	40187	25227	40191	25230	40195	25232	40200	25235	40204	25237	40208	25240	41
19	40208	25240	40213	25242	40217	25245	40221	25247	40226	25250	40230	25252	40
20	40230	25252	40235	25255	40239	25257	40243	25260	40247	25262	40252	25265	39
21	40252	25265	40256	25268	40261	25270	40265	25273	40269	25275	40274	25278	38
22	40274	25278	40278	25280	40282	25283	40287	25285	40291	25288	40295	25290	37
23	40295	25290	40300	25293	40304	25295	40308	25298	40313	25300	40317	25303	36
24	40317	25303	40321	25305	40326	25308	40330	25310	40334	25313	40339	25316	35
25	40339	25316	40343	25318	40347	25321	40352	25323	40356	25326	40360	25328	34
26	40360	25328	40365	25331	40369	25333	40373	25336	40378	25338	40382	25341	33
27	40382	25341	40387	25343	40391	25346	40395	25348	40399	25351	40404	25354	32
28	40404	25354	40408	25356	40412	25359	40417	25361	40421	25364	40425	25366	31
29	40425	25366	40430	25369	40434	25371	40438	25374	40443	25376	40447	25379	30
30	40447	25379	40452	25381	40456	25384	40460	25386	40464	25389	40469	25391	29
31	40469	25391	40473	25394	40477	25397	40482	25399	40486	25402	40490	25404	28
32	40490	25404	40495	25407	40499	25409	40503	25412	40508	25414	40512	25417	27
33	40512	25417	40517	25419	40521	25422	40525	25424	40529	25427	40534	25429	26
34	40534	25429	40538	25432	40542	25435	40547	25437	40551	25440	40555	25442	25
35	40555	25442	40560	25445	40564	25447	40568	25450	40573	25452	40577	25455	24
36	40577	25455	40581	25457	40586	25460	40590	25462	40594	25465	40599	25467	23
37	40599	25467	40603	25470	40607	25473	40612	25475	40616	25478	40620	25480	22
38	40620	25480	40625	25483	40629	25485	40633	25488	40637	25490	40642	25493	21
39	40642	25493	40646	25495	40650	25498	40655	25500	40659	25503	40663	25506	20
40	40663	25506	40668	25508	40672	25511	40676	25513	40681	25516	40685	25519	19
41	40685	25518	40689	25521	40694	25523	40698	25526	40702	25528	40707	25531	18
42	40707	25531	40711	25533	40715	25536	40720	25538	40724	25541	40728	25544	17
43	40728	25544	40733	25546	40737	25549	40741	25551	40745	25554	40750	25556	16
44	40750	25556	40754	25559	40758	25561	40763	25564	40767	25566	40771	25569	15
45	40771	25569	40776	25571	40780	25574	40784	25577	40788	25579	40793	25582	14
46	40793	25582	40797	25584	40801	25587	40806	25589	40810	25592	40814	25594	13
47	40814	25594	40819	25597	40823	25599	40827	25602	40832	25604	40836	25607	12
48	40836	25607	40840	25610	40844	25612	40849	25615	40853	25617	40858	25620	11
49	40858	25620	40862	25622	40866	25625	40870	25627	40875	25630	40879	25632	10
50	40879	25632	40883	25635	40888	25637	40892	25640	40896	25643	40900	25645	09
51	40900	25645	40905	25648	40909	25650	40913	25653	40918	25655	40922	25658	08
52	40922	25658	40926	25660	40931	25663	40935	25665	40939	25668	40943	25671	07
53	40943	25671	40948	25673	40952	25676	40956	25678	40961	25681	40965	25683	06
54	40965	25683	40969	25686	40974	25688	40978	25691	40982	25693	40986	25696	05
55	40986	25696	40991	25698	40995	25701	40999	25704	41004	25706	41008	25709	04
56	41008	25709	41012	25711	41017	25714	41021	25716	41025	25719	41029	25721	03
57	41029	25721	41034	25724	41038	25726	41042	25729	41047	25732	41051	25734	02
58	41051	25734	41055	25737	41059	25739	41064	25742	41068	25744	41072	25747	01
59	41072	25747	41077	25749	41081	25752	41085	25754	41090	25757	41094	25760	00

	.8		.6		.4		.2		.0	

PARTS for 0′.1: LOGS 2 NATURALS 1 **299°**

61° HAVERSINES

′	.0 Log. $\overline{1}$.or(9.)	.0 Nat. 0.	.2 Log. $\overline{1}$.or(9.)	.2 Nat. 0.	.4 Log. $\overline{1}$.or(9.)	.4 Nat. 0.	.6 Log. $\overline{1}$.or(9.)	.6 Nat. 0.	.8 Log. $\overline{1}$.or.(9.)	.8 Nat. 0.	.8 Log. $\overline{1}$.or.(9.)	.8 Nat. 0.	′
00	41094	25760	41098	25762	41102	25765	41107	25767	41111	25770	41115	25772	59
01	41115	25772	41119	25775	41124	25777	41128	25780	41132	25782	41137	25785	58
02	41137	25785	41141	25788	41145	25790	41149	25793	41154	25795	41158	25798	57
03	41158	25798	41162	25800	41167	25803	41171	25805	41175	25808	41180	25810	56
04	41180	25810	41184	25813	41188	25816	41192	25818	41197	25821	41201	25823	55
05	41201	25823	41205	25826	41210	25828	41214	25831	41218	25833	41222	25836	54
06	41222	25836	41227	25838	41231	25841	41235	25844	41240	25846	41244	25849	53
07	41244	25849	41248	25851	41252	25854	41257	25856	41261	25859	41265	25861	52
08	41265	25861	41269	25864	41274	25866	41278	25869	41282	25872	41287	25874	51
09	41287	25874	41291	25877	41295	25879	41299	25882	41304	25884	41308	25887	50
10	41308	25887	41312	25889	41316	25892	41321	25894	41325	25897	41329	25900	49
11	41329	25900	41333	25902	41338	25905	41342	25907	41346	25910	41351	25912	48
12	41351	25912	41355	25915	41359	25917	41363	25920	41368	25923	41372	25925	47
13	41372	25925	41376	25928	41381	25930	41385	25933	41389	25935	41393	25938	46
14	41393	25938	41398	25940	41402	25943	41406	25945	41410	25948	41415	25951	45
15	41415	25951	41419	25953	41423	25956	41427	25958	41432	25961	41436	25963	44
16	41436	25963	41440	25966	41445	25968	41449	25971	41453	25974	41457	25976	43
17	41457	25976	41462	25979	41466	25981	41470	25984	41474	25986	41479	25989	42
18	41479	25989	41483	25991	41487	25994	41491	25997	41496	25999	41500	26002	41
19	41500	26002	41504	26004	41508	26007	41513	26009	41517	26012	41521	26014	40
20	41521	26014	41525	26017	41530	26019	41534	26022	41538	26025	41543	26027	39
21	41543	26027	41547	26030	41551	26032	41555	26035	41560	26037	41564	26040	38
22	41564	26040	41568	26042	41572	26045	41577	26048	41581	26050	41585	26053	37
23	41585	26053	41589	26055	41594	26058	41598	26060	41602	26063	41606	26065	36
24	41606	26065	41611	26068	41615	26071	41619	26073	41624	26076	41628	26078	35
25	41628	26078	41632	26081	41636	26083	41641	26086	41645	26088	41649	26091	34
26	41649	26091	41653	26094	41657	26096	41662	26099	41666	26101	41670	26104	33
27	41670	26104	41674	26106	41679	26109	41683	26111	41687	26114	41692	26117	32
28	41692	26117	41696	26119	41700	26122	41704	26124	41709	26127	41713	26129	31
29	41713	26129	41717	26132	41721	26134	41726	26137	41730	26140	41734	26142	30
30	41734	26142	41738	26145	41742	26147	41747	26150	41751	26152	41755	26155	29
31	41755	26155	41759	26157	41764	26160	41768	26163	41772	26165	41776	26168	28
32	41776	26168	41781	26170	41785	26173	41789	26175	41793	26178	41798	26180	27
33	41798	26180	41802	26183	41806	26186	41810	26188	41815	26191	41819	26193	26
34	41819	26193	41823	26196	41827	26198	41832	26201	41836	26203	41840	26206	25
35	41840	26206	41844	26209	41848	26211	41853	26214	41857	26216	41861	26219	24
36	41861	26219	41865	26221	41870	26224	41874	26226	41878	26229	41882	26232	23
37	41882	26232	41887	26234	41891	26237	41895	26239	41899	26242	41904	26244	22
38	41904	26244	41908	26247	41912	26250	41916	26252	41921	26255	41925	26257	21
39	41925	26257	41929	26260	41933	26262	41938	26265	41942	26267	41946	26270	20
40	41946	26270	41950	26273	41954	26275	41959	26278	41963	26280	41967	26283	19
41	41967	26283	41971	26285	41976	26288	41980	26290	41984	26293	41988	26296	18
42	41988	26296	41992	26298	41997	26301	42001	26303	42005	26306	42009	26308	17
43	42009	26308	42014	26311	42018	26314	42022	26316	42026	26319	42031	26321	16
44	42031	26321	42035	26324	42039	26326	42043	26329	42048	26331	42052	26334	15
45	42052	26334	42056	26337	42060	26339	42064	26342	42069	26344	42073	26347	14
46	42073	26347	42077	26349	42081	26352	42086	26355	42090	26357	42094	26360	13
47	42094	26360	42098	26362	42102	26365	42107	26367	42111	26370	42115	26372	12
48	42115	26372	42119	26375	42123	26378	42128	26380	42132	26383	42136	26385	11
49	42136	26385	42140	26388	42145	26390	42149	26393	42153	26396	42157	26398	10
50	42157	26398	42161	26401	42166	26403	42170	26406	42174	26408	42178	26411	09
51	42178	26411	42183	26413	42187	26416	42191	26419	42195	26421	42199	26424	08
52	42199	26424	42204	26426	42208	26429	42212	26431	42216	26434	42221	26437	07
53	42221	26437	42225	26439	42229	26442	42233	26444	42237	26447	42242	26449	06
54	42242	26449	42246	26452	42250	26455	42254	26457	42258	26460	42263	26462	05
55	42263	26462	42267	26465	42271	26467	42275	26470	42280	26472	42284	26475	04
56	42284	26475	42288	26478	42292	26480	42296	26483	42301	26485	42305	26488	03
57	42305	26488	42309	26490	42313	26493	42317	26496	42322	26498	42326	26501	02
58	42326	26501	42330	26503	42334	26506	42338	26508	42343	26511	42347	26514	01
59	42347	26514	42351	26516	42355	26519	42359	26521	42364	26524	42368	26526	00

| | .8 | .6 | .4 | .2 | .0 ← |

PARTS for 0′.1: LOGS 2 NATURALS 1

62° HAVERSINES

′	.0 Log. 1̄.or(9.)	.0 Nat. 0.	.2 Log. 1̄.or(9.)	.2 Nat. 0.	.4 Log. 1̄.or(9.)	.4 Nat. 0.	.6 Log. 1̄.or(9.)	.6 Nat. 0.	.8 Log. 1̄.or(9.)	.8 Nat. 0.	Log. 1̄.or(9.)	Nat. 0.	′
00	42368	26526	42372	26529	42376	26532	42380	26534	42385	26537	42389	26539	59
01	42389	26539	42393	26542	42397	26544	42402	26547	42406	26550	42410	26552	58
02	42410	26552	42414	26555	42418	26557	42423	26560	42427	26562	42431	26565	57
03	42431	26565	42435	26568	42439	26570	42444	26573	42448	26575	42452	26578	56
04	42452	26578	42456	26580	42460	26583	42465	26586	42469	26588	42473	26591	55
05	42473	26591	42477	26593	42481	26596	42485	26598	42490	26601	42494	26604	54
06	42494	26604	42498	26606	42502	26609	42506	26611	42511	26614	42515	26616	53
07	42515	26616	42519	26619	42523	26621	42527	26624	42532	26627	42536	26629	52
08	42536	26629	42540	26632	42544	26634	42548	26637	42553	26640	42557	26642	51
09	42557	26642	42561	26645	42565	26647	42569	26650	42574	26652	42578	26655	50
10	42578	26655	42582	26658	42586	26660	42590	26663	42595	26665	42599	26668	49
11	42599	26668	42603	26670	42607	26673	42611	26676	42615	26678	42620	26681	48
12	42620	26681	42624	26683	42628	26686	42632	26688	42636	26691	42641	26694	47
13	42641	26694	42645	26696	42649	26699	42653	26701	42657	26704	42662	26706	46
14	42662	26706	42666	26709	42670	26712	42674	26714	42678	26717	42682	26719	45
15	42682	26719	42687	26722	42691	26724	42695	26727	42699	26730	42703	26732	44
16	42703	26732	42708	26735	42712	26737	42716	26740	42720	26742	42724	26745	43
17	42724	26745	42728	26748	42733	26750	42737	26753	42741	26755	42745	26758	42
18	42745	26758	42749	26760	42754	26763	42758	26766	42762	26768	42766	26771	41
19	42766	26771	42770	26773	42775	26776	42779	26779	42783	26781	42787	26784	40
20	42787	26784	42791	26786	42795	26789	42799	26791	42804	26794	42808	26797	39
21	42808	26797	42812	26799	42816	26802	42820	26804	42825	26807	42829	26809	38
22	42829	26809	42833	26812	42837	26815	42841	26817	42845	26820	42850	26822	37
23	42850	26822	42854	26825	42858	26827	42862	26830	42866	26833	42870	26835	36
24	42870	26835	42875	26838	42879	26840	42883	26843	42887	26846	42891	26848	35
25	42891	26848	42896	26851	42900	26853	42904	26856	42908	26858	42912	26861	34
26	42912	26861	42916	26864	42921	26866	42925	26869	42929	26871	42933	26874	33
27	42933	26874	42937	26876	42941	26879	42945	26882	42950	26884	42954	26887	32
28	42954	26887	42958	26889	42962	26892	42966	26894	42970	26897	42975	26900	31
29	42975	26900	42979	26902	42983	26905	42987	26907	42991	26910	42996	26913	30
30	42996	26913	43000	26915	43004	26918	43008	26920	43012	26923	43016	26925	29
31	43016	26925	43021	26928	43025	26931	43029	26933	43033	26936	43037	26938	28
32	43037	26938	43041	26941	43046	26944	43050	26946	43054	26949	43058	26951	27
33	43058	26951	43062	26954	43066	26956	43070	26959	43075	26962	43079	26964	26
34	43079	26964	43083	26967	43087	26969	43091	26972	43095	26975	43100	26977	25
35	43100	26977	43104	26980	43108	26982	43112	26985	43116	26987	43120	26990	24
36	43120	26990	43125	26993	43129	26995	43133	26998	43137	27000	43141	27003	23
37	43141	27003	43145	27005	43149	27008	43153	27011	43158	27013	43162	27016	22
38	43162	27016	43166	27018	43170	27021	43174	27024	43178	27026	43183	27029	21
39	43183	27029	43187	27031	43191	27034	43195	27037	43199	27039	43203	27042	20
40	43203	27042	43208	27044	43212	27047	43216	27049	43220	27052	43224	27055	19
41	43224	27055	43228	27057	43232	27060	43237	27062	43241	27065	43245	27068	18
42	43245	27068	43249	27070	43253	27073	43257	27075	43261	27078	43266	27080	17
43	43266	27080	43270	27083	43274	27086	43278	27088	43282	27091	43286	27093	16
44	43286	27093	43291	27096	43295	27099	43299	27101	43303	27104	43307	27106	15
45	43307	27106	43311	27109	43315	27111	43319	27114	43324	27117	43328	27119	14
46	43328	27119	43332	27122	43336	27124	43340	27127	43344	27130	43348	27132	13
47	43348	27132	43353	27135	43357	27137	43361	27140	43365	27143	43369	27145	12
48	43369	27145	43373	27148	43377	27150	43382	27153	43386	27155	43390	27158	11
49	43390	27158	43394	27161	43398	27163	43402	27166	43406	27168	43411	27171	10
50	43411	27171	43415	27174	43419	27176	43423	27179	43427	27181	43431	27184	09
51	43431	27184	43435	27186	43439	27189	43444	27192	43448	27194	43452	27197	08
52	43452	27197	43456	27199	43460	27202	43464	27205	43468	27207	43473	27210	07
53	43473	27210	43477	27212	43481	27215	43485	27218	43489	27220	43493	27223	06
54	43493	27223	43497	27225	43501	27228	43506	27231	43510	27233	43514	27236	05
55	43514	27236	43518	27238	43522	27241	43526	27243	43530	27246	43535	27249	04
56	43535	27249	43539	27251	43543	27254	43547	27256	43551	27259	43555	27262	03
57	43555	27262	43559	27264	43563	27267	43568	27269	43572	27272	43576	27275	02
58	43576	27275	43580	27277	43584	27280	43588	27282	43592	27285	43596	27288	01
59	43596	27288	43601	27290	43605	27293	43609	27295	43613	27298	43617	27300	00

	.8		.6		.4		.2		.0 ←	

PARTS for 0′.1: LOGS 2 NATURALS 1

297°

63° HAVERSINES

′	.0 Log. 1̄.or(9.)	.0 Nat. 0.	.2 Log. 1̄.or(9.)	.2 Nat. 0.	.4 Log. 1̄.or(9.)	.4 Nat. 0.	.6 Log. 1̄.or(9.)	.6 Nat. 0.	.8 Log. 1̄.or(9.)	.8 Nat. 0.	.8 Log. 1̄.or(9.)	.8 Nat. 0.	′
00	43617	27300	43621	27303	43625	27306	43629	27308	43633	27311	43638	27313	59
01	43638	27313	43642	27316	43646	27319	43650	27321	43654	27324	43658	27326	58
02	43658	27326	43662	27329	43666	27332	43671	27334	43675	27337	43679	27339	57
03	43679	27339	43683	27342	43687	27345	43691	27347	43695	27350	43699	27352	56
04	43699	27352	43704	27355	43708	27358	43712	27360	43716	27363	43720	27365	55
05	43720	27365	43724	27368	43728	27370	43732	27373	43736	27376	43741	27378	54
06	43741	27378	43745	27381	43749	27383	43753	27386	43757	27389	43761	27391	53
07	43761	27391	43765	27394	43769	27396	43774	27399	43778	27402	43782	27404	52
08	43782	27404	43786	27407	43790	27409	43794	27412	43798	27415	43802	27417	51
09	43802	27417	43806	27420	43810	27422	43815	27425	43819	27428	43823	27430	50
10	43823	27430	43827	27433	43831	27435	43835	27438	43839	27441	43843	27443	49
11	43843	27443	43848	27446	43852	27448	43856	27451	43860	27454	43864	27456	48
12	43864	27456	43868	27459	43872	27461	43876	27464	43880	27467	43884	27469	47
13	43884	27469	43889	27472	43893	27474	43897	27477	43901	27480	43905	27482	46
14	43905	27482	43909	27485	43913	27487	43917	27490	43921	27493	43925	27495	45
15	43925	27495	43930	27498	43934	27500	43938	27503	43942	27505	43946	27508	44
16	43946	27508	43950	27511	43954	27513	43958	27516	43962	27518	43967	27521	43
17	43967	27521	43971	27524	43975	27526	43979	27529	43983	27531	43987	27534	42
18	43987	27534	43991	27537	43995	27539	43999	27542	44003	27544	44008	27547	41
19	44008	27547	44012	27550	44016	27552	44020	27555	44024	27557	44028	27560	40
20	44028	27560	44032	27563	44036	27565	44040	27568	44044	27570	44048	27573	39
21	44048	27573	44053	27576	44057	27578	44061	27581	44065	27583	44069	27586	38
22	44069	27586	44073	27589	44077	27591	44081	27594	44085	27596	44089	27599	37
23	44089	27599	44093	27602	44098	27604	44102	27607	44106	27609	44110	27612	36
24	44110	27612	44114	27615	44118	27617	44122	27620	44126	27622	44130	27625	35
25	44130	27625	44134	27628	44139	27630	44143	27633	44147	27635	44151	27638	34
26	44151	27638	44155	27641	44159	27643	44163	27646	44167	27648	44171	27651	33
27	44171	27651	44175	27654	44179	27656	44183	27659	44188	27661	44192	27664	32
28	44192	27664	44196	27667	44200	27669	44204	27672	44208	27675	44212	27677	31
29	44212	27677	44216	27680	44220	27682	44224	27685	44228	27688	44232	27690	30
30	44232	27690	44236	27693	44241	27695	44245	27698	44249	27701	44253	27703	29
31	44253	27703	44257	27706	44261	27708	44265	27711	44269	27714	44273	27716	28
32	44273	27716	44277	27719	44281	27721	44285	27724	44290	27727	44294	27729	27
33	44294	27729	44298	27732	44302	27734	44306	27737	44310	27740	44314	27742	26
34	44314	27742	44318	27745	44322	27747	44326	27750	44330	27753	44334	27755	25
35	44334	27755	44338	27758	44343	27760	44347	27763	44351	27766	44355	27768	24
36	44355	27768	44359	27771	44363	27773	44367	27776	44371	27779	44375	27781	23
37	44375	27781	44379	27784	44383	27786	44387	27789	44392	27792	44396	27794	22
38	44396	27794	44400	27797	44404	27800	44408	27802	44412	27805	44416	27807	21
39	44416	27807	44420	27810	44424	27813	44428	27815	44432	27818	44436	27820	20
40	44436	27820	44440	27823	44444	27826	44448	27828	44453	27831	44457	27833	19
41	44457	27833	44461	27836	44465	27839	44469	27841	44473	27844	44477	27846	18
42	44477	27846	44481	27849	44485	27852	44489	27854	44493	27857	44497	27859	17
43	44497	27859	44501	27862	44505	27865	44510	27867	44514	27870	44518	27873	16
44	44518	27873	44522	27875	44526	27878	44530	27880	44534	27883	44538	27886	15
45	44538	27886	44542	27888	44546	27891	44550	27893	44554	27896	44558	27899	14
46	44558	27899	44562	27901	44566	27904	44570	27906	44575	27909	44579	27912	13
47	44579	27912	44583	27914	44587	27917	44591	27919	44595	27922	44599	27925	12
48	44599	27925	44603	27927	44607	27930	44611	27933	44615	27935	44619	27938	11
49	44619	27938	44623	27940	44627	27943	44631	27946	44635	27948	44639	27951	10
50	44639	27951	44643	27953	44648	27956	44652	27959	44656	27961	44660	27964	09
51	44660	27964	44664	27966	44668	27969	44672	27972	44676	27974	44680	27977	08
52	44680	27977	44684	27980	44688	27982	44692	27985	44696	27987	44700	27990	07
53	44700	27990	44704	27993	44708	27995	44712	27998	44717	28000	44721	28003	06
54	44721	28003	44725	28006	44729	28008	44733	28011	44737	28013	44741	28016	05
55	44741	28016	44745	28019	44749	28021	44753	28024	44757	28027	44761	28029	04
56	44761	28029	44765	28032	44769	28034	44773	28037	44777	28040	44781	28042	03
57	44781	28042	44785	28045	44789	28047	44793	28050	44797	28053	44801	28055	02
58	44801	28055	44805	28058	44810	28061	44814	28063	44818	28066	44822	28068	01
59	44822	28068	44826	28071	44830	28074	44834	28076	44838	28079	44842	28081	00

	.8	.6	.4	.2	.0 ←

PARTS for 0′.1:   LOGS 2   NATURALS 1   **296°**

64° HAVERSINES

′	.0 Log. 1̄.or(9.)	.0 Nat. 0.	.2 Log. 1̄.or(9.)	.2 Nat. 0.	.4 Log. 1̄.or(9.)	.4 Nat. 0.	.6 Log. 1̄.or(9.)	.6 Nat. 0.	.8 Log. 1̄.or(9.)	.8 Nat. 0.	Log. 1̄.or(9.)	Nat. 0.	′
00	44842	28081	44846	28084	44850	28087	44854	28089	44858	28092	44862	28095	59
01	44862	28095	44866	28097	44870	28100	44874	28102	44878	28105	44882	28108	58
02	44882	28108	44886	28110	44890	28113	44895	28115	44899	28118	44903	28121	57
03	44903	28121	44907	28123	44911	28126	44915	28129	44919	28131	44923	28134	56
04	44923	28134	44927	28136	44931	28139	44935	28142	44939	28144	44943	28147	55
05	44943	28147	44947	28149	44951	28152	44955	28155	44959	28157	44963	28160	54
06	44963	28160	44967	28163	44971	28165	44975	28168	44979	28170	44983	28173	53
07	44983	28173	44987	28176	44991	28178	44995	28181	44999	28183	45003	28186	52
08	45003	28186	45007	28189	45011	28191	45016	28194	45020	28197	45024	28199	51
09	45024	28199	45028	28202	45032	28204	45036	28207	45040	28210	45044	28212	50
10	45044	28212	45048	28215	45052	28217	45056	28220	45060	28223	45064	28225	49
11	45064	28225	45068	28228	45072	28231	45076	28233	45080	28236	45084	28238	48
12	45084	28238	45088	28241	45092	28244	45096	28246	45100	28249	45104	28252	47
13	45104	28252	45108	28254	45112	28257	45116	28259	45120	28262	45124	28265	46
14	45124	28265	45128	28267	45132	28270	45136	28273	45140	28275	45144	28278	45
15	45144	28278	45148	28280	45152	28283	45157	28286	45161	28288	45165	28291	44
16	45165	28291	45169	28293	45173	28296	45177	28299	45181	28301	45185	28304	43
17	45185	28304	45189	28307	45193	28309	45197	28312	45201	28314	45205	28317	42
18	45205	28317	45209	28320	45213	28322	45217	28325	45221	28328	45225	28330	41
19	45225	28330	45229	28333	45233	28335	45237	28338	45241	28341	45245	28343	40
20	45245	28343	45249	28346	45253	28348	45257	28351	45261	28354	45265	28356	39
21	45265	28356	45269	28359	45273	28362	45277	28364	45281	28367	45285	28369	38
22	45285	28369	45289	28372	45293	28375	45297	28377	45301	28380	45305	28383	37
23	45305	28383	45309	28385	45313	28388	45317	28390	45321	28393	45325	28396	36
24	45325	28396	45329	28398	45333	28401	45337	28404	45341	28406	45345	28409	35
25	45345	28409	45349	28411	45353	28414	45357	28417	45361	28419	45365	28422	34
26	45365	28422	45369	28425	45373	28427	45377	28430	45381	28432	45385	28435	33
27	45385	28435	45389	28438	45393	28440	45397	28443	45401	28446	45405	28448	32
28	45405	28448	45409	28451	45413	28453	45418	28456	45422	28459	45426	28461	31
29	45426	28461	45430	28464	45434	28467	45438	28469	45442	28472	45446	28474	30
30	45446	28474	45450	28477	45454	28480	45458	28482	45462	28485	45466	28488	29
31	45466	28488	45470	28490	45474	28493	45478	28495	45482	28498	45486	28501	28
32	45486	28501	45490	28503	45494	28506	45498	28509	45502	28511	45506	28514	27
33	45506	28514	45510	28516	45514	28519	45518	28522	45522	28524	45526	28527	26
34	45526	28527	45530	28530	45534	28532	45538	28535	45542	28537	45546	28540	25
35	45546	28540	45550	28543	45554	28545	45558	28548	45562	28551	45566	28553	24
36	45566	28553	45570	28556	45574	28559	45578	28561	45582	28564	45586	28566	23
37	45586	28566	45590	28569	45594	28572	45597	28574	45601	28577	45605	28580	22
38	45605	28580	45609	28582	45613	28585	45617	28587	45621	28590	45625	28593	21
39	45625	28593	45629	28595	45633	28598	45637	28601	45641	28603	45645	28606	20
40	45645	28606	45649	28608	45653	28611	45657	28614	45661	28616	45665	28619	19
41	45665	28619	45669	28622	45673	28624	45677	28627	45681	28629	45685	28632	18
42	45685	28632	45689	28635	45693	28637	45697	28640	45701	28643	45705	28645	17
43	45705	28645	45709	28648	45713	28651	45717	28653	45721	28656	45725	28658	16
44	45725	28658	45729	28661	45733	28664	45737	28666	45741	28669	45745	28672	15
45	45745	28672	45749	28674	45753	28677	45757	28679	45761	28682	45765	28685	14
46	45765	28685	45769	28687	45773	28690	45777	28693	45781	28695	45785	28698	13
47	45785	28698	45789	28701	45793	28703	45797	28706	45801	28708	45805	28711	12
48	45805	28711	45809	28714	45813	28716	45817	28719	45821	28722	45825	28724	11
49	45825	28724	45829	28727	45833	28729	45837	28732	45841	28735	45845	28737	10
50	45845	28737	45849	28740	45853	28743	45857	28745	45861	28748	45865	28751	09
51	45865	28751	45869	28753	45873	28756	45876	28758	45880	28761	45884	28764	08
52	45884	28764	45888	28766	45892	28769	45896	28772	45900	28774	45904	28777	07
53	45904	28777	45908	28779	45912	28782	45916	28785	45920	28787	45924	28790	06
54	45924	28790	45928	28793	45932	28795	45936	28798	45940	28801	45944	28803	05
55	45944	28803	45948	28806	45952	28808	45956	28811	45960	28814	45964	28816	04
56	45964	28816	45968	28819	45972	28822	45976	28824	45980	28827	45984	28830	03
57	45984	28830	45988	28832	45992	28835	45996	28837	46000	28840	46004	28843	02
58	46004	28843	46008	28845	46012	28848	46015	28851	46019	28853	46023	28856	01
59	46023	28856	46027	28859	46031	28861	46035	28864	46039	28866	46043	28869	00

	.8	.6	.4	.2	.0 ←

PARTS for 0′.1:   LOGS 2   NATURALS 1

295°

HAVERSINES

65°

'	.0 Log.	.0 Nat.	.2 Log.	.2 Nat.	.4 Log.	.4 Nat.	.6 Log.	.6 Nat.	.8 Log.	.8 Nat.	.8 Log.	.8 Nat.	'
	1̄.or(9.)	0.	1̄.or.(9.)	0.	1̄.or(9.)	0.	1̄.or(9.)	0.	1̄.or(9.)	0.	1̄.or(9.)	0.	
00	46043	28869	46047	28872	46051	28874	46055	28877	46059	28880	46063	28882	59
01	46063	28882	46067	28885	46071	28888	46075	28890	46079	28893	46083	28895	58
02	46083	28895	46087	28898	46091	28901	46095	28903	46099	28906	46103	28909	57
03	46103	28909	46107	28911	46111	28914	46115	28917	46119	28919	46123	28922	56
04	46123	28922	46127	28924	46131	28927	46134	28930	46138	28932	46142	28935	55
05	46142	28935	46146	28938	46150	28940	46154	28943	46158	28946	46162	28948	54
06	46162	28948	46166	28951	46170	28953	46174	28956	46178	28959	46182	28961	53
07	46182	28961	46186	28964	46190	28967	46194	28969	46198	28972	46202	28975	52
08	46202	28975	46206	28977	46210	28980	46214	28983	46218	28985	46222	28988	51
09	46222	28988	46226	28990	46229	28993	46233	28996	46237	28998	46241	29001	50
10	46241	29001	46245	29004	46249	29006	46253	29009	46257	29012	46261	29014	49
11	46261	29014	46265	29017	46269	29019	46273	29022	46277	29025	46281	29027	48
12	46281	29027	46285	29030	46289	29033	46293	29035	46297	29038	46301	29041	47
13	46301	29041	46305	29043	46309	29046	46312	29049	46316	29051	46320	29054	46
14	46320	29054	46324	29056	46328	29059	46332	29062	46336	29064	46340	29067	45
15	46340	29067	46344	29070	46348	29072	46352	29075	46356	29078	46360	29080	44
16	46360	29080	46364	29083	46368	29086	46372	29088	46375	29091	46379	29093	43
17	46379	29093	46383	29096	46387	29099	46391	29101	46395	29104	46399	29107	42
18	46399	29107	46403	29109	46407	29112	46411	29115	46415	29117	46419	29120	41
19	46419	29120	46423	29123	46427	29125	46431	29128	46435	29130	46439	29133	40
20	46439	29133	46443	29136	46447	29138	46450	29141	46454	29144	46458	29146	39
21	46458	29146	46462	29149	46466	29152	46470	29154	46474	29157	46478	29160	38
22	46478	29160	46482	29162	46486	29165	46490	29167	46494	29170	46498	29173	37
23	46498	29173	46502	29175	46506	29178	46510	29181	46513	29183	46517	29186	36
24	46517	29186	46521	29189	46525	29191	46529	29194	46533	29197	46537	29199	35
25	46537	29199	46541	29202	46545	29204	46549	29207	46553	29210	46557	29212	34
26	46557	29212	46561	29215	46565	29218	46569	29220	46572	29223	46576	29226	33
27	46576	29226	46580	29228	46584	29231	46588	29234	46592	29236	46596	29239	32
28	46596	29239	46600	29242	46604	29244	46608	29247	46612	29249	46616	29252	31
29	46616	29252	46620	29255	46624	29257	46628	29260	46631	29263	46635	29265	30
30	46635	29265	46639	29268	46643	29271	46647	29273	46651	29276	46655	29279	29
31	46655	29279	46659	29281	46663	29284	46667	29287	46671	29289	46675	29292	28
32	46675	29292	46679	29294	46682	29297	46686	29300	46690	29302	46694	29305	27
33	46694	29305	46698	29308	46702	29310	46706	29313	46710	29316	46714	29318	26
34	46714	29318	46718	29321	46722	29324	46726	29326	46729	29329	46733	29332	25
35	46733	29332	46737	29334	46741	29337	46745	29340	46749	29342	46753	29345	24
36	46753	29345	46757	29347	46761	29350	46765	29353	46769	29355	46773	29358	23
37	46773	29358	46777	29361	46780	29363	46784	29366	46788	29369	46792	29371	22
38	46792	29371	46796	29374	46800	29377	46804	29379	46808	29382	46812	29385	21
39	46812	29385	46816	29387	46820	29390	46824	29392	46827	29395	46831	29398	20
40	46831	29398	46835	29400	46839	29403	46843	29406	46847	29408	46851	29411	19
41	46851	29411	46855	29414	46859	29416	46863	29419	46867	29422	46871	29424	18
42	46871	29424	46875	29427	46878	29430	46882	29432	46886	29435	46890	29438	17
43	46890	29438	46894	29440	46898	29443	46902	29446	46906	29448	46910	29451	16
44	46910	29451	46914	29453	46918	29456	46921	29459	46925	29461	46929	29464	15
45	46929	29464	46933	29467	46937	29469	46941	29472	46945	29475	46949	29477	14
46	46949	29477	46953	29480	46957	29483	46961	29485	46964	29488	46968	29491	13
47	46968	29491	46972	29493	46976	29496	46980	29499	46984	29501	46988	29504	12
48	46988	29504	46992	29507	46996	29509	47000	29512	47003	29514	47007	29517	11
49	47007	29517	47011	29520	47015	29522	47019	29525	47023	29528	47027	29530	10
50	47027	29530	47031	29533	47035	29536	47039	29538	47043	29541	47046	29544	09
51	47046	29544	47050	29546	47054	29549	47058	29552	47062	29554	47066	29557	08
52	47066	29557	47070	29560	47074	29562	47078	29565	47082	29568	47085	29570	07
53	47085	29570	47089	29573	47093	29576	47097	29578	47101	29581	47105	29583	06
54	47105	29583	47109	29586	47113	29589	47117	29591	47121	29594	47124	29597	05
55	47124	29597	47128	29599	47132	29602	47136	29605	47140	29607	47144	29610	04
56	47144	29610	47148	29613	47152	29615	47156	29618	47159	29621	47163	29623	03
57	47163	29623	47167	29626	47171	29629	47175	29631	47179	29634	47183	29637	02
58	47183	29637	47187	29639	47191	29642	47194	29645	47198	29647	47202	29650	01
59	47202	29650	47206	29653	47210	29655	47214	29658	47218	29661	47222	29663	00

	.8	.6	.4	.2	.0

PARTS for 0'.1: LOGS 2 NATURALS 1

294°

HAVERSINES

′	.0 Log. $\overline{1}$.or(9.)	.0 Nat. 0.	.2 Log. $\overline{1}$.or(9.)	.2 Nat. 0.	.4 Log. $\overline{1}$.or(9.)	.4 Nat. 0.	.6 Log. $\overline{1}$.or(9.)	.6 Nat. 0.	.8 Log. $\overline{1}$.or(9.)	.8 Nat. 0.	Log. $\overline{1}$.or(9.)	Nat. 0.	′
00	47222	29663	47226	29666	47230	29668	47233	29671	47237	29674	47241	29676	59
01	47241	29676	47245	29679	47249	29682	47253	29684	47257	29687	47261	29690	58
02	47261	29690	47264	29692	47268	29695	47272	29698	47276	29700	47280	29703	57
03	47280	29703	47284	29706	47288	29708	47292	29711	47296	29714	47300	29716	56
04	47300	29716	47303	29719	47307	29722	47311	29724	47315	29727	47319	29730	55
05	47319	29730	47323	29732	47327	29735	47331	29738	47335	29740	47338	29743	54
06	47338	29743	47342	29746	47346	29748	47350	29751	47354	29754	47358	29756	53
07	47358	29756	47362	29759	47366	29762	47369	29764	47373	29767	47377	29770	52
08	47377	29770	47381	29772	47385	29775	47389	29777	47393	29780	47397	29783	51
09	47397	29783	47400	29785	47404	29788	47408	29791	47412	29793	47416	29796	50
10	47416	29796	47420	29799	47424	29801	47428	29804	47432	29807	47435	29809	49
11	47435	29809	47439	29812	47443	29815	47447	29817	47451	29820	47455	29823	48
12	47455	29823	47459	29825	47463	29828	47466	29831	47470	29833	47474	29836	47
13	47474	29836	47478	29839	47482	29841	47486	29844	47490	29847	47493	29849	46
14	47493	29849	47497	29852	47501	29855	47505	29857	47509	29860	47513	29863	45
15	47513	29863	47517	29865	47521	29868	47524	29871	47528	29873	47532	29876	44
16	47532	29876	47536	29879	47540	29881	47544	29884	47548	29887	47552	29889	43
17	47552	29889	47556	29892	47559	29895	47563	29897	47567	29900	47571	29903	42
18	47571	29903	47575	29905	47579	29908	47583	29911	47586	29913	47590	29916	41
19	47590	29916	47594	29919	47598	29921	47602	29924	47606	29927	47610	29929	40
20	47610	29929	47613	29932	47617	29935	47621	29937	47625	29940	47629	29943	39
21	47629	29943	47633	29945	47637	29948	47641	29951	47644	29953	47648	29956	38
22	47648	29956	47652	29959	47656	29961	47660	29964	47664	29967	47668	29969	37
23	47668	29969	47671	29972	47675	29975	47679	29977	47683	29980	47687	29983	36
24	47687	29983	47691	29985	47695	29988	47698	29991	47702	29993	47706	29996	35
25	47706	29996	47710	29999	47714	30001	47718	30004	47722	30007	47725	30009	34
26	47725	30009	47729	30012	47733	30015	47737	30017	47741	30020	47745	30023	33
27	47745	30023	47749	30025	47752	30028	47756	30031	47760	30033	47764	30036	32
28	47764	30036	47768	30039	47772	30041	47776	30044	47780	30047	47783	30049	31
29	47783	30049	47787	30052	47791	30055	47795	30057	47799	30060	47803	30063	30
30	47803	30063	47806	30065	47810	30068	47814	30071	47818	30073	47822	30076	29
31	47822	30076	47826	30079	47830	30081	47833	30084	47837	30087	47841	30089	28
32	47841	30089	47845	30092	47849	30095	47853	30097	47857	30100	47860	30103	27
33	47860	30103	47864	30105	47868	30108	47872	30111	47876	30113	47880	30116	26
34	47880	30116	47883	30119	47887	30121	47891	30124	47895	30127	47899	30129	25
35	47899	30129	47903	30132	47906	30135	47910	30137	47914	30140	47918	30143	24
36	47918	30143	47922	30145	47926	30148	47930	30151	47934	30153	47937	30156	23
37	47937	30156	47941	30159	47945	30161	47949	30164	47953	30164	47957	30169	22
38	47957	30169	47960	30172	47964	30175	47968	30177	47972	30180	47976	30183	21
39	47976	30183	47980	30185	47983	30188	47987	30191	47991	30193	47995	30196	20
40	47995	30196	47999	30199	48003	30201	48007	30204	48010	30207	48014	30209	19
41	48014	30209	48018	30212	48022	30215	48026	30217	48030	30220	48033	30223	18
42	48033	30223	48037	30225	48041	30228	48045	30231	48049	30233	48053	30236	17
43	48053	30236	48056	30239	48060	30241	48064	30244	48068	30247	48072	30249	16
44	48072	30249	48076	30252	48079	30255	48083	30257	48087	30261	48091	30263	15
45	48091	30263	48095	30265	48099	30268	48102	30271	48106	30273	48110	30276	14
46	48110	30276	48114	30279	48118	30281	48122	30284	48125	30287	48129	30290	13
47	48129	30290	48133	30292	48137	30295	48141	30298	48145	30300	48148	30303	12
48	48148	30303	48152	30306	48156	30308	48160	30311	48164	30314	48168	30316	11
49	48168	30316	48171	30319	48175	30322	48179	30324	48183	30327	48187	30330	10
50	48187	30330	48191	30332	48194	30335	48198	30338	48202	30340	48206	30343	09
51	48206	30343	48210	30346	48213	30348	48217	30351	48221	30354	48225	30356	08
52	48225	30356	48229	30359	48233	30362	48237	30364	48240	30367	48244	30370	07
53	48244	30370	48248	30372	48252	30375	48256	30378	48259	30380	48263	30383	06
54	48263	30383	48267	30386	48271	30388	48275	30391	48279	30394	48282	30397	05
55	48282	30397	48286	30399	48290	30402	48294	30405	48298	30407	48302	30410	04
56	48302	30410	48305	30413	48309	30415	48313	30418	48317	30421	48321	30423	03
57	48321	30423	48324	30426	48328	30429	48332	30431	48336	30434	48340	30437	02
58	48340	30437	48344	30439	48347	30442	48351	30445	48355	30447	48359	30450	01
59	48359	30450	48363	30453	48366	30455	48370	30458	48374	30461	48378	30463	00

	.8	.6	.4	.2	.0

67° HAVERSINES

′	.0 Log. 1.or(9.)	.0 Nat. 0.	.2 Log. 1.or(9.)	.2 Nat. 0.	.4 Log. 1.or(9.)	.4 Nat. 0.	.6 Log. 1.or(9.)	.6 Nat. 0.	.8 Log. 1.or(9.)	.8 Nat. 0.	′
00	48378	30463	48382	30466	48385	30469	48389	30471	48393	30474	48397	30477	59
01	48397	30477	48401	30480	48405	30482	48408	30485	48412	30488	48416	30490	58
02	48416	30490	48420	30493	48424	30496	48428	30498	48431	30501	48435	30504	57
03	48435	30504	48439	30506	48443	30509	48447	30512	48450	30514	48454	30517	56
04	48454	30517	48458	30520	48462	30522	48466	30525	48469	30528	48473	30530	55
05	48473	30530	48477	30533	48481	30536	48485	30538	48489	30541	48492	30544	54
06	48492	30544	48496	30546	48500	30549	48504	30552	48508	30555	48511	30557	53
07	48511	30557	48515	30560	48519	30563	48523	30565	48527	30568	48530	30571	52
08	48530	30571	48534	30573	48538	30576	48542	30579	48546	30581	48549	30584	51
09	48549	30584	48553	30587	48557	30589	48561	30592	48565	30595	48568	30597	50
10	48568	30597	48572	30600	48576	30603	48580	30605	48584	30608	48587	30611	49
11	48587	30611	48591	30613	48595	30616	48599	30619	48603	30622	48607	30624	48
12	48607	30624	48610	30627	48614	30630	48618	30632	48622	30635	48626	30638	47
13	48626	30638	48629	30640	48633	30643	48637	30646	48641	30648	48645	30651	46
14	48645	30651	48648	30654	48652	30656	48656	30659	48660	30662	48664	30664	45
15	48664	30664	48667	30667	48671	30670	48675	30672	48679	30675	48683	30678	44
16	48683	30678	48686	30681	48690	30683	48694	30686	48698	30689	48702	30691	43
17	48702	30691	48705	30694	48709	30697	48713	30699	48717	30702	48720	30705	42
18	48720	30705	48724	30707	48728	30710	48732	30713	48736	30715	48739	30718	41
19	48739	30718	48743	30721	48747	30723	48751	30726	48755	30729	48758	30732	40
20	48758	30732	48762	30734	48766	30737	48770	30740	48774	30742	48777	30745	39
21	48777	30745	48781	30748	48785	30750	48789	30753	48793	30756	48796	30758	38
22	48796	30758	48800	30761	48804	30764	48808	30766	48812	30769	48815	30772	37
23	48815	30772	48819	30774	48823	30777	48827	30780	48830	30783	48834	30785	36
24	48834	30785	48838	30788	48842	30791	48846	30793	48849	30796	48853	30799	35
25	48853	30799	48857	30801	48861	30804	48865	30807	48868	30809	48872	30812	34
26	48872	30812	48876	30815	48880	30817	48883	30820	48887	30823	48891	30826	33
27	48891	30826	48895	30828	48899	30831	48902	30834	48906	30836	48910	30839	32
28	48910	30839	48914	30842	48918	30844	48921	30847	48925	30850	48929	30852	31
29	48929	30852	48933	30855	48936	30858	48940	30860	48944	30863	48948	30866	30
30	48948	30866	48952	30869	48955	30871	48959	30874	48963	30877	48967	30879	29
31	48967	30879	48970	30882	48974	30885	48978	30887	48982	30890	48986	30893	28
32	48986	30893	48989	30895	48993	30898	48997	30901	49001	30904	49004	30906	27
33	49004	30906	49008	30909	49012	30912	49016	30914	49020	30917	49023	30920	26
34	49023	30920	49027	30922	49031	30925	49035	30928	49038	30930	49042	30933	25
35	49042	30933	49046	30936	49050	30938	49054	30941	49057	30944	49061	30946	24
36	49061	30946	49065	30949	49069	30952	49072	30955	49076	30957	49080	30960	23
37	49080	30960	49084	30963	49088	30965	49091	30968	49095	30971	49099	30973	22
38	49099	30973	49103	30976	49106	30979	49110	30981	49114	30984	49118	30987	21
39	49118	30987	49122	30990	49125	30992	49129	30995	49133	30998	49137	31000	20
40	49137	31000	49140	31003	49144	31006	49148	31008	49152	31011	49155	31014	19
41	49155	31014	49159	31016	49163	31019	49167	31022	49170	31025	49174	31027	18
42	49174	31027	49178	31030	49182	31033	49185	31035	49189	31038	49193	31041	17
43	49193	31041	49197	31043	49201	31046	49204	31049	49208	31051	49212	31054	16
44	49212	31054	49216	31057	49220	31059	49223	31062	49227	31065	49231	31068	15
45	49231	31068	49235	31070	49238	31073	49242	31076	49246	31078	49250	31081	14
46	49250	31081	49253	31084	49257	31086	49261	31089	49265	31092	49268	31095	13
47	49268	31095	49272	31097	49276	31100	49280	31103	49283	31105	49287	31108	12
48	49287	31108	49291	31111	49295	31113	49298	31116	49302	31119	49306	31121	11
49	49306	31121	49310	31124	49314	31127	49317	31130	49321	31132	49325	31135	10
50	49325	31135	49329	31138	49332	31140	49336	31143	49340	31146	49344	31148	09
51	49344	31148	49347	31151	49351	31154	49355	31156	49359	31159	49362	31162	08
52	49362	31162	49366	31165	49370	31167	49374	31170	49377	31173	49381	31175	07
53	49381	31175	49385	31178	49389	31181	49392	31183	49396	31186	49400	31189	06
54	49400	31189	49404	31191	49407	31194	49411	31197	49415	31200	49419	31202	05
55	49419	31202	49422	31205	49426	31208	49430	31210	49434	31213	49437	31216	04
56	49437	31216	49441	31218	49445	31221	49449	31224	49452	31227	49456	31229	03
57	49456	31229	49460	31232	49464	31235	49467	31237	49471	31240	49475	31243	02
58	49475	31243	49479	31245	49482	31248	49486	31251	49490	31254	49494	31256	01
59	49494	31256	49497	31259	49501	31262	49505	31264	49509	31267	49512	31270	00

| | .8 | | .6 | | .4 | | .2 | | .0 | |

PARTS for 0′.1: LOGS 2   NATURALS 1

292°

68° HAVERSINES

′	.0 Log.	.0 Nat.	.2 Log.	.2 Nat.	.4 Log.	.4 Nat.	.6 Log.	.6 Nat.	.8 Log.	.8 Nat.	′
	1̄.or(9.)	0.	1̄.or(9.)	0.	1̄.or(9.)	0.	1̄.or(9.)	0.	1̄.or(9.)	0.	
00	49512	31270	49516	31272	49520	31275	49524	31278	49527	31280	59
									49531	31283	
01	49531	31283	49535	31286	49539	31289	49542	31291	49546	31294	58
									49550	31297	
02	49550	31297	49554	31299	49557	31302	49561	31305	49565	31307	57
									49568	31310	
03	49568	31310	49572	31313	49576	31316	49580	31318	49583	31321	56
									49587	31324	
04	49587	31324	49591	31326	49595	31329	49598	31332	49602	31334	55
									49606	31337	
05	49606	31337	49610	31340	49613	31343	49617	31345	49621	31348	54
									49625	31351	
06	49625	31351	49628	31353	49632	31356	49636	31359	49639	31361	53
									49643	31364	
07	49643	31364	49647	31367	49651	31370	49654	31372	49658	31375	52
									49662	31378	
08	49662	31378	49666	31380	49669	31383	49673	31386	49677	31388	51
									49681	31391	
09	49681	31391	49684	31394	49688	31397	49692	31399	49696	31402	50
									49699	31405	
10	49699	31405	49703	31407	49707	31410	49711	31413	49714	31415	49
									49718	31418	
11	49718	31418	49722	31421	49725	31424	49729	31426	49733	31429	48
									49737	31432	
12	49737	31432	49740	31434	49744	31437	49748	31440	49752	31442	47
									49755	31445	
13	49755	31445	49759	31448	49763	31451	49767	31453	49770	31456	46
									49774	31459	
14	49774	31459	49778	31461	49781	31464	49785	31467	49789	31469	45
									49793	31472	
15	49793	31472	49796	31475	49800	31478	49804	31480	49807	31483	44
									49811	31486	
16	49811	31486	49815	31488	49819	31491	49822	31494	49826	31496	43
									49830	31499	
17	49830	31499	49834	31502	49837	31505	49841	31507	49845	31510	42
									49849	31513	
18	49849	31513	49852	31515	49856	31518	49860	31521	49863	31523	41
									49867	31526	
19	49867	31526	49871	31529	49875	31532	49878	31534	49882	31537	40
									49886	31540	
20	49886	31540	49890	31542	49893	31545	49897	31548	49901	31551	39
									49904	31553	
21	49904	31553	49908	31556	49912	31559	49916	31561	49919	31564	38
									49923	31567	
22	49923	31567	49927	31569	49930	31572	49934	31575	49938	31578	37
									49942	31580	
23	49942	31580	49945	31583	49949	31586	49953	31588	49956	31591	36
									49960	31594	
24	49960	31594	49964	31596	49968	31599	49971	31602	49975	31605	35
									49979	31607	
25	49979	31607	49983	31610	49986	31613	49990	31615	49994	31618	34
									49997	31621	
26	49997	31621	50001	31624	50005	31626	50008	31629	50012	31632	33
									50016	31634	
27	50016	31634	50020	31637	50023	31640	50027	31642	50031	31645	32
									50034	31648	
28	50034	31648	50038	31651	50042	31653	50046	31656	50049	31659	31
									50053	31661	
29	50053	31661	50057	31664	50060	31667	50064	31670	50068	31672	30
									50072	31675	
30	50072	31675	50075	31678	50079	31680	50083	31683	50086	31686	29
									50090	31688	
31	50090	31688	50094	31691	50098	31694	50101	31697	50105	31699	28
									50109	31702	
32	50109	31702	50112	31705	50116	31707	50120	31710	50123	31713	27
									50127	31716	
33	50127	31716	50131	31718	50135	31721	50138	31724	50142	31726	26
									50146	31729	
34	50146	31729	50149	31732	50153	31735	50157	31737	50161	31740	25
									50164	31743	
35	50164	31743	50168	31745	50172	31748	50175	31751	50179	31753	24
									50183	31756	
36	50183	31756	50187	31759	50190	31762	50194	31764	50198	31767	23
									50201	31770	
37	50201	31770	50205	31772	50209	31775	50212	31778	50216	31781	22
									50220	31783	
38	50220	31783	50224	31786	50227	31789	50231	31791	50235	31794	21
									50238	31797	
39	50238	31797	50242	31800	50246	31802	50249	31805	50253	31808	20
									50257	31810	
40	50257	31810	50261	31813	50264	31816	50268	31818	50272	31821	19
									50275	31824	
41	50275	31824	50279	31827	50283	31829	50286	31832	50290	31835	18
									50294	31837	
42	50294	31837	50297	31840	50301	31843	50305	31846	50309	31848	17
									50312	31851	
43	50312	31851	50316	31854	50320	31856	50323	31859	50327	31862	16
									50331	31865	
44	50331	31865	50334	31867	50338	31870	50342	31873	50346	31875	15
									50349	31878	
45	50349	31878	50353	31881	50357	31884	50360	31886	50364	31889	14
									50368	31892	
46	50368	31892	50371	31894	50375	31897	50379	31900	50383	31902	13
									50386	31905	
47	50386	31905	50390	31908	50394	31911	50397	31913	50401	31916	12
									50405	31919	
48	50405	31919	50408	31921	50412	31924	50416	31927	50419	31930	11
									50423	31932	
49	50423	31932	50427	31935	50430	31938	50434	31940	50438	31943	10
									50442	31946	
50	50442	31946	50445	31949	50449	31951	50453	31954	50456	31957	09
									50460	31959	
51	50460	31959	50464	31962	50467	31965	50471	31968	50475	31970	08
									50478	31973	
52	50478	31973	50482	31976	50486	31978	50489	31981	50493	31984	07
									50497	31987	
53	50497	31987	50500	31989	50504	31992	50508	31995	50512	31997	06
									50515	32000	
54	50515	32000	50519	32003	50523	32006	50526	32008	50530	32011	05
									50534	32014	
55	50534	32014	50537	32016	50541	32019	50545	32022	50548	32025	04
									50552	32027	
56	50552	32027	50556	32030	50559	32033	50563	32035	50567	32038	03
									50570	32041	
57	50570	32041	50574	32044	50578	32046	50581	32049	50585	32052	02
									50589	32054	
58	50589	32054	50592	32057	50596	32060	50600	32063	50604	32065	01
									50607	32068	
59	50607	32068	50611	32071	50615	32073	50618	32076	50622	32079	00
									50626	32082	
	.8		.6		.4		.2		.0 ←		

PARTS for 0′.1:   LOGS 2   NATURALS 1

291°

69° HAVERSINES

	.0		.2		.4		.6		.8			
	Log.	Nat.	Log.	Nat.	Log.	Nat.	Log.	Nat.	Log.	Nat.	Log.	Nat.
′	1̄.or(9.)	0.	1̄.or(9.)	0.	1̄.or(9.)	0.	1̄.or(9.)	0.	1̄.or(9.)	0.	1̄.or(9.)	0.	′
00	50626	32082	50629	32084	50633	32087	50637	32090	50640	32092	50644	32095	59
01	50644	32095	50648	32098	50651	32101	50655	32103	50659	32106	50662	32109	58
02	50662	32109	50666	32111	50670	32114	50673	32117	50677	32120	50681	32122	57
03	50681	32122	50684	32125	50688	32128	50692	32131	50695	32133	50699	32136	56
04	50699	32136	50703	32139	50706	32141	50710	32144	50714	32147	50717	32150	55
05	50717	32150	50721	32152	50725	32155	50728	32158	50732	32160	50736	32163	54
06	50736	32163	50739	32166	50743	32169	50747	32171	50751	32174	50754	32177	53
07	50754	32177	50758	32179	50761	32182	50765	32185	50769	32188	50772	32190	52
08	50772	32190	50776	32193	50780	32196	50783	32198	50787	32201	50791	32204	51
09	50791	32204	50794	32207	50798	32209	50802	32212	50806	32215	50809	32217	50
10	50809	32217	50813	32220	50816	32223	50820	32226	50824	32228	50827	32231	49
11	50827	32231	50831	32234	50835	32236	50838	32239	50842	32242	50846	32245	48
12	50846	32245	50849	32247	50853	32250	50857	32253	50860	32256	50864	32258	47
13	50864	32258	50868	32261	50871	32264	50875	32266	50879	32269	50882	32272	46
14	50882	32272	50886	32275	50890	32277	50893	32280	50897	32283	50901	32285	45
15	50901	32285	50904	32288	50908	32291	50912	32294	50915	32296	50919	32299	44
16	50919	32299	50923	32302	50926	32304	50930	32307	50934	32310	50937	32313	43
17	50937	32313	50941	32315	50945	32318	50948	32321	50952	32324	50956	32326	42
18	50956	32326	50959	32329	50963	32332	50967	32334	50970	32337	50974	32340	41
19	50974	32340	50977	32343	50981	32345	50985	32348	50988	32351	50992	32353	40
20	50992	32353	50996	32356	50999	32359	51003	32362	51007	32364	51010	32367	39
21	51010	32367	51014	32370	51018	32373	51021	32375	51025	32378	51029	32381	38
22	51029	32381	51032	32383	51036	32386	51040	32389	51043	32392	51047	32394	37
23	51047	32394	51050	32397	51054	32400	51058	32402	51062	32405	51065	32408	36
24	51065	32408	51069	32411	51072	32413	51076	32416	51080	32419	51083	32422	35
25	51083	32422	51087	32424	51091	32427	51094	32430	51098	32432	51102	32435	34
26	51102	32435	51105	32438	51109	32441	51113	32443	51116	32446	51120	32449	33
27	51120	32449	51123	32451	51127	32454	51131	32457	51134	32460	51138	32462	32
28	51138	32462	51142	32465	51145	32468	51149	32471	51153	32473	51156	32476	31
29	51156	32476	51160	32479	51163	32481	51167	32484	51171	32487	51174	32490	30
30	51174	32490	51178	32492	51182	32495	51185	32498	51189	32501	51193	32503	29
31	51193	32503	51196	32506	51200	32509	51204	32511	51207	32514	51211	32517	28
32	51211	32517	51214	32520	51218	32522	51222	32525	51225	32528	51229	32531	27
33	51229	32531	51233	32533	51236	32536	51240	32539	51244	32541	51247	32544	26
34	51247	32544	51251	32547	51254	32550	51258	32552	51262	32555	51265	32558	25
35	51265	32558	51269	32560	51273	32563	51276	32566	51280	32569	51284	32571	24
36	51284	32571	51287	32574	51291	32577	51295	32580	51298	32582	51302	32585	23
37	51302	32585	51305	32588	51309	32590	51313	32593	51316	32596	51320	32599	22
38	51320	32599	51324	32601	51327	32604	51331	32607	51335	32610	51338	32612	21
39	51338	32612	51342	32615	51345	32618	51349	32620	51353	32623	51356	32626	20
40	51356	32626	51360	32629	51363	32631	51367	32634	51371	32637	51374	32640	19
41	51374	32640	51378	32642	51382	32645	51385	32648	51389	32650	51393	32653	18
42	51393	32653	51396	32656	51400	32659	51404	32661	51407	32664	51411	32667	17
43	51411	32667	51414	32670	51418	32672	51422	32675	51425	32678	51429	32681	16
44	51429	32681	51432	32683	51436	32686	51440	32689	51443	32691	51447	32694	15
45	51447	32694	51451	32697	51454	32700	51458	32702	51462	32705	51465	32708	14
46	51465	32708	51469	32711	51472	32713	51476	32716	51480	32719	51483	32721	13
47	51483	32721	51487	32724	51490	32727	51494	32730	51498	32732	51501	32735	12
48	51501	32735	51505	32738	51509	32741	51512	32743	51516	32746	51519	32749	11
49	51519	32749	51523	32751	51527	32754	51530	32757	51534	32760	51538	32762	10
50	51538	32762	51541	32765	51545	32768	51548	32771	51552	32773	51556	32776	09
51	51556	32776	51559	32779	51563	32782	51567	32784	51570	32787	51574	32790	08
52	51574	32790	51577	32792	51581	32795	51585	32798	51588	32801	51592	32803	07
53	51592	32803	51595	32806	51599	32809	51603	32812	51606	32814	51610	32817	06
54	51610	32817	51614	32820	51617	32822	51621	32825	51624	32828	51628	32831	05
55	51628	32831	51632	32833	51635	32836	51639	32839	51642	32842	51646	32844	04
56	51646	32844	51650	32847	51653	32850	51657	32853	51661	32855	51664	32858	03
57	51664	32858	51668	32861	51671	32863	51675	32866	51679	32869	51682	32872	02
58	51682	32872	51686	32874	51689	32877	51693	32880	51697	32883	51700	32885	01
59	51700	32885	51704	32888	51707	32891	51711	32894	51715	32896	51718	32899	00
		.8		.6		.4		.2		.0			

PARTS for 0′.1: LOGS 2   NATURALS 1

290°

70° HAVERSINES

′	.0 Log. $\overline{1}$.or(9.)	.0 Nat. 0.	.2 Log. $\overline{1}$.or(9.)	.2 Nat. 0.	.4 Log. $\overline{1}$.or(9.)	.4 Nat. 0.	.6 Log. $\overline{1}$.or(9.)	.6 Nat. 0.	.8 Log. $\overline{1}$.or(9.)	.8 Nat. 0.	Log. $\overline{1}$.or(9.)	Nat. 0.	′
00	51718	32899	51722	32902	51725	32904	51729	32907	51733	32910	51736	32913	59
01	51736	32913	51740	32915	51743	32918	51747	32921	51751	32924	51754	32926	58
02	51754	32926	51758	32929	51762	32932	51765	32935	51769	32937	51772	32940	57
03	51772	32940	51776	32943	51780	32945	51783	32948	51787	32951	51790	32954	56
04	51790	32954	51794	32956	51798	32959	51801	32962	51805	32965	51808	32967	55
05	51808	32967	51812	32970	51816	32973	51819	32976	51823	32978	51826	32981	54
06	51826	32981	51830	32984	51834	32986	51837	32989	51841	32992	51844	32995	53
07	51844	32995	51848	32997	51852	33000	51855	33003	51859	33006	51862	33008	52
08	51862	33008	51866	33011	51870	33014	51873	33017	51877	33019	51880	33022	51
09	51880	33022	51884	33025	51888	33028	51891	33030	51895	33033	51898	33036	50
10	51898	33036	51902	33038	51906	33041	51909	33044	51913	33047	51916	33049	49
11	51916	33049	51920	33052	51924	33055	51927	33058	51931	33060	51934	33063	48
12	51934	33063	51938	33066	51942	33069	51945	33071	51949	33074	51952	33077	47
13	51952	33077	51956	33080	51960	33082	51963	33085	51967	33088	51970	33090	46
14	51970	33090	51974	33093	51978	33096	51981	33099	51985	33101	51988	33104	45
15	51988	33104	51992	33107	51996	33110	51999	33112	52003	33115	52006	33118	44
16	52006	33118	52010	33121	52014	33123	52017	33126	52021	33129	52024	33132	43
17	52024	33132	52028	33134	52032	33137	52035	33140	52039	33143	52042	33145	42
18	52042	33145	52046	33148	52050	33151	52053	33153	52057	33156	52060	33159	41
19	52060	33159	52064	33162	52068	33164	52071	33167	52075	33170	52078	33173	40
20	52078	33173	52082	33175	52086	33178	52089	33181	52093	33184	52096	33186	39
21	52096	33186	52100	33189	52104	33192	52107	33195	52111	33197	52114	33200	38
22	52114	33200	52118	33203	52122	33205	52125	33208	52129	33211	52132	33214	37
23	52132	33214	52136	33216	52140	33219	52143	33222	52147	33225	52150	33227	36
24	52150	33227	52154	33230	52158	33233	52161	33236	52165	33238	52168	33241	35
25	52168	33241	52171	33244	52175	33247	52178	33249	52182	33252	52185	33255	34
26	52185	33255	52189	33258	52193	33260	52196	33263	52200	33266	52203	33269	33
27	52203	33269	52207	33271	52211	33274	52214	33277	52218	33280	52221	33282	32
28	52221	33282	52225	33285	52228	33288	52232	33290	52236	33293	52239	33296	31
29	52239	33296	52243	33299	52246	33301	52250	33304	52253	33307	52257	33310	30
30	52257	33310	52261	33312	52264	33315	52268	33318	52271	33321	52275	33323	29
31	52275	33323	52278	33326	52282	33329	52286	33332	52289	33334	52293	33337	28
32	52293	33337	52296	33340	52300	33343	52303	33345	52307	33348	52311	33351	27
33	52311	33351	52314	33354	52318	33356	52321	33359	52325	33362	52328	33365	26
34	52328	33365	52332	33367	52336	33370	52339	33373	52343	33376	52346	33378	25
35	52346	33378	52350	33381	52354	33384	52357	33386	52361	33389	52364	33392	24
36	52364	33392	52368	33395	52371	33397	52375	33400	52378	33403	52382	33406	23
37	52382	33406	52386	33408	52389	33411	52393	33414	52396	33417	52400	33419	22
38	52400	33419	52403	33422	52407	33425	52410	33428	52414	33430	52418	33433	21
39	52418	33433	52421	33436	52425	33439	52428	33441	52432	33444	52436	33447	20
40	52436	33447	52439	33450	52443	33452	52446	33455	52450	33458	52453	33461	19
41	52453	33461	52457	33463	52461	33466	52464	33469	52468	33472	52471	33474	18
42	52471	33474	52475	33477	52478	33480	52482	33483	52485	33485	52489	33488	17
43	52489	33488	52493	33491	52496	33494	52500	33496	52503	33499	52507	33502	16
44	52507	33502	52510	33504	52514	33507	52517	33510	52521	33513	52525	33515	15
45	52525	33515	52528	33518	52532	33521	52535	33524	52539	33526	52542	33529	14
46	52542	33529	52546	33532	52550	33535	52553	33537	52557	33540	52560	33543	13
47	52560	33543	52564	33546	52567	33548	52571	33551	52574	33554	52578	33557	12
48	52578	33557	52581	33559	52585	33562	52588	33565	52592	33568	52596	33570	11
49	52596	33570	52599	33573	52603	33576	52606	33579	52610	33581	52613	33584	10
50	52613	33584	52617	33587	52621	33590	52624	33592	52628	33595	52631	33598	09
51	52631	33598	52635	33601	52638	33603	52642	33606	52645	33609	52649	33612	08
52	52649	33612	52653	33614	52656	33617	52660	33620	52663	33623	52667	33625	07
53	52667	33625	52670	33628	52674	33631	52677	33634	52681	33636	52684	33639	06
54	52684	33639	52688	33642	52692	33645	52695	33647	52699	33650	52702	33653	05
55	52702	33653	52706	33656	52709	33658	52713	33661	52716	33664	52720	33667	04
56	52720	33667	52724	33669	52727	33672	52731	33675	52734	33678	52738	33680	03
57	52738	33680	52741	33683	52745	33686	52748	33689	52752	33691	52755	33694	02
58	52755	33694	52759	33697	52762	33700	52766	33702	52769	33705	52773	33708	01
59	52773	33708	52777	33711	52780	33713	52784	33716	52787	33719	52791	33722	00

	.8	.6	.4	.2	.0 ←

PARTS for 0′.1: LOGS 2   NATURALS 1   **289°**

71° HAVERSINES

′	→ .0 Log.	Nat.	.2 Log.	Nat.	.4 Log.	Nat.	.6 Log.	Nat.	.8 Log.	Nat.	Log.	Nat.	′
	1̄.or(9.)	0.	1̄.or(9.)	0.	1̄.or.(9.)	0.	1̄.or(9.)	0.	1̄.or(9.)	0.	1̄.or(9.)	0.	
00	52791	33722	52794	33724	52798	33727	52801	33730	52805	33733	52809	33735	59
01	52809	33735	52812	33738	52816	33741	52819	33744	52823	33746	52826	33749	58
02	52826	33749	52830	33752	52833	33755	52837	33757	52840	33760	52844	33763	57
03	52844	33763	52848	33766	52851	33768	52855	33771	52858	33774	52862	33777	56
04	52862	33777	52865	33779	52869	33782	52872	33785	52876	33788	52879	33790	55
05	52879	33790	52883	33793	52886	33796	52890	33799	52893	33801	52897	33804	54
06	52897	33804	52901	33807	52904	33810	52908	33812	52911	33815	52915	33818	53
07	52915	33818	52918	33821	52922	33823	52925	33826	52929	33829	52932	33832	52
08	52932	33832	52936	33834	52939	33837	52943	33840	52946	33843	52950	33845	51
09	52950	33845	52954	33848	52957	33851	52961	33854	52964	33856	52968	33859	50
10	52968	33859	52971	33862	52975	33865	52978	33867	52982	33870	52985	33873	49
11	52985	33873	52989	33876	52992	33878	52996	33881	52999	33884	53003	33887	48
12	53003	33887	53007	33889	53010	33892	53014	33895	53017	33898	53021	33900	47
13	53021	33900	53024	33903	53028	33906	53031	33909	53035	33912	53038	33914	46
14	53038	33914	53042	33917	53045	33920	53049	33923	53052	33925	53056	33928	45
15	53056	33928	53059	33931	53063	33934	53066	33936	53070	33939	53073	33942	44
16	53073	33942	53077	33945	53081	33947	53084	33950	53088	33953	53091	33956	43
17	53091	33956	53095	33958	53098	33961	53102	33964	53105	33967	53109	33969	42
18	53109	33969	53112	33972	53116	33975	53119	33978	53123	33980	53126	33983	41
19	53126	33983	53130	33986	53133	33989	53137	33991	53140	33994	53144	33997	40
20	53144	33997	53148	34000	53151	34002	53155	34005	53158	34008	53162	34011	39
21	53162	34011	53165	34013	53169	34016	53172	34019	53176	34022	53179	34024	38
22	53179	34024	53183	34027	53186	34030	53190	34033	53193	34035	53197	34038	37
23	53197	34038	53200	34041	53204	34044	53207	34047	53211	34049	53214	34052	36
24	53214	34052	53218	34055	53221	34058	53225	34060	53228	34063	53232	34066	35
25	53232	34066	53235	34069	53239	34071	53242	34074	53246	34077	53249	34080	34
26	53249	34080	53253	34082	53256	34085	53260	34088	53263	34091	53267	34093	33
27	53267	34093	53271	34096	53274	34099	53278	34102	53281	34104	53285	34107	32
28	53285	34107	53288	34110	53292	34113	53295	34115	53299	34118	53302	34121	31
29	53302	34121	53306	34124	53309	34127	53313	34129	53316	34132	53320	34135	30
30	53320	34135	53323	34138	53327	34140	53330	34143	53334	34146	53337	34149	29
31	53337	34149	53341	34151	53344	34154	53348	34157	53351	34160	53355	34162	28
32	53355	34162	53358	34165	53362	34168	53365	34171	53369	34173	53372	34176	27
33	53372	34176	53376	34179	53379	34182	53383	34184	53386	34187	53390	34190	26
34	53390	34190	53393	34193	53397	34195	53400	34198	53404	34201	53407	34204	25
35	53407	34204	53411	34207	53414	34209	53418	34212	53421	34215	53425	34218	24
36	53425	34218	53428	34220	53432	34223	53435	34226	53439	34229	53442	34231	23
37	53442	34231	53446	34234	53449	34237	53453	34240	53456	34242	53460	34245	22
38	53460	34245	53463	34248	53467	34251	53470	34253	53474	34256	53477	34259	21
39	53477	34259	53481	34262	53484	34264	53488	34267	53491	34270	53495	34273	20
40	53495	34273	53498	34276	53502	34278	53505	34281	53509	34284	53512	34287	19
41	53512	34287	53516	34289	53519	34292	53523	34295	53526	34298	53530	34300	18
42	53530	34300	53533	34303	53537	34306	53540	34309	53544	34311	53547	34314	17
43	53547	34314	53551	34317	53554	34320	53558	34322	53561	34325	53565	34328	16
44	53565	34328	53568	34331	53572	34334	53575	34336	53579	34339	53582	34342	15
45	53582	34342	53586	34345	53589	34347	53593	34350	53596	34353	53600	34356	14
46	53600	34356	53603	34358	53607	34361	53610	34364	53614	34367	53617	34369	13
47	53617	34369	53621	34372	53624	34375	53628	34378	53631	34381	53635	34383	12
48	53635	34383	53638	34386	53642	34389	53645	34392	53649	34394	53652	34397	11
49	53652	34397	53656	34400	53659	34403	53663	34405	53666	34408	53670	34411	10
50	53670	34411	53673	34414	53677	34416	53680	34419	53684	34422	53687	34425	09
51	53687	34425	53690	34427	53694	34430	53697	34433	53701	34436	53704	34439	08
52	53704	34439	53708	34441	53711	34444	53715	34447	53718	34450	53722	34452	07
53	53722	34452	53725	34455	53729	34458	53732	34461	53736	34463	53739	34466	06
54	53739	34466	53743	34469	53746	34472	53750	34474	53753	34477	53757	34480	05
55	53757	34480	53760	34483	53764	34486	53767	34488	53771	34491	53774	34494	04
56	53774	34494	53778	34497	53781	34499	53785	34502	53788	34505	53792	34508	03
57	53792	34508	53795	34510	53799	34513	53802	34516	53806	34519	53809	34521	02
58	53809	34521	53812	34524	53816	34527	53819	34530	53823	34533	53826	34535	01
59	53826	34535	53830	34538	53833	34541	53837	34544	53840	34546	53844	34549	00
			.8		.6		.4		.2		.0 ←		

PARTS for 0′.1: LOGS 2 NATURALS 1

288°

72° HAVERSINES

′	.0 Log.	.0 Nat.	.2 Log.	.2 Nat.	.4 Log.	.4 Nat.	.6 Log.	.6 Nat.	.8 Log.	.8 Nat.	′
	1.or(9.)	0.	1.or.(9.)	0.	1.or.(9.)	0.	1.or.(9.)	0.	1.or.(9.)	0.	
00	53844	34549	53847	34552	53851	34555	53854	34557	53858	34560	59
01	53861	34563	53865	34566	53868	34569	53872	34571	53875	34574	58
02	53879	34577	53882	34580	53885	34582	53889	34585	53892	34588	57
03	53896	34591	53899	34593	53903	34596	53906	34599	53910	34602	56
04	53913	34604	53917	34607	53920	34610	53924	34613	53927	34616	55
05	53931	34618	53934	34621	53938	34624	53941	34627	53945	34629	54
06	53948	34632	53951	34635	53955	34638	53958	34640	53962	34643	53
07	53965	34646	53969	34649	53972	34652	53976	34654	53979	34657	52
08	53983	34660	53986	34663	53990	34665	53993	34668	53997	34671	51
09	54000	34674	54003	34676	54007	34679	54010	34682	54014	34685	50
10	54017	34688	54021	34690	54024	34693	54028	34696	54031	34699	49
11	54035	34701	54038	34704	54042	34707	54045	34710	54049	34712	48
12	54052	34715	54055	34718	54059	34721	54062	34724	54066	34726	47
13	54069	34729	54073	34732	54076	34735	54080	34737	54083	34740	46
14	54087	34743	54090	34746	54094	34748	54097	34751	54101	34754	45
15	54104	34757	54107	34760	54111	34762	54114	34765	54118	34768	44
16	54121	34771	54125	34773	54128	34776	54132	34779	54135	34782	43
17	54139	34784	54142	34787	54145	34790	54149	34793	54152	34796	42
18	54156	34798	54159	34801	54163	34804	54166	34807	54170	34809	41
19	54173	34812	54177	34815	54180	34818	54184	34821	54187	34823	40
20	54190	34826	54194	34829	54197	34832	54201	34834	54204	34837	39
21	54208	34840	54211	34843	54215	34845	54218	34848	54222	34851	38
22	54225	34854	54228	34857	54232	34859	54235	34862	54239	34865	37
23	54242	34868	54246	34870	54249	34873	54253	34876	54256	34879	36
24	54260	34882	54263	34884	54266	34887	54270	34890	54273	34893	35
25	54277	34895	54280	34898	54284	34901	54287	34904	54291	34906	34
26	54294	34909	54297	34912	54301	34915	54304	34918	54308	34920	33
27	54311	34923	54315	34926	54318	34929	54322	34931	54325	34934	32
28	54329	34937	54332	34940	54335	34943	54339	34945	54342	34948	31
29	54346	34951	54349	34954	54353	34956	54356	34959	54360	34962	30
30	54363	34965	54366	34967	54370	34970	54373	34973	54377	34976	29
31	54380	34979	54384	34981	54387	34984	54391	34987	54394	34990	28
32	54397	34992	54401	34995	54404	34998	54408	35001	54411	35004	27
33	54415	35006	54418	35009	54421	35012	54425	35015	54428	35017	26
34	54432	35020	54435	35023	54439	35026	54442	35029	54446	35031	25
35	54449	35034	54452	35037	54456	35040	54459	35042	54463	35045	24
36	54466	35048	54470	35051	54473	35054	54477	35056	54480	35059	23
37	54483	35062	54487	35065	54490	35067	54494	35070	54497	35073	22
38	54501	35076	54504	35078	54507	35081	54511	35084	54514	35087	21
39	54518	35090	54521	35092	54525	35095	54528	35098	54532	35101	20
40	54535	35103	54538	35106	54542	35109	54545	35112	54549	35115	19
41	54552	35117	54556	35120	54559	35123	54563	35126	54566	35128	18
42	54569	35131	54573	35134	54576	35137	54580	35140	54583	35142	17
43	54587	35145	54590	35148	54593	35151	54597	35153	54600	35156	16
44	54604	35159	54607	35162	54610	35165	54614	35167	54617	35170	15
45	54621	35173	54624	35176	54628	35178	54631	35181	54635	35184	14
46	54638	35187	54641	35190	54645	35192	54648	35195	54652	35198	13
47	54655	35201	54659	35203	54662	35206	54666	35209	54669	35212	12
48	54672	35215	54676	35217	54679	35220	54683	35223	54686	35226	11
49	54689	35228	54693	35231	54696	35234	54700	35237	54703	35240	10
50	54707	35242	54710	35245	54713	35248	54717	35251	54720	35254	09
51	54724	35256	54727	35259	54730	35262	54734	35265	54737	35267	08
52	54741	35270	54744	35273	54748	35276	54751	35279	54754	35281	07
53	54758	35284	54761	35287	54765	35290	54768	35292	54772	35295	06
54	54775	35298	54778	35301	54782	35304	54785	35306	54789	35309	05
55	54792	35312	54795	35315	54799	35317	54802	35320	54806	35323	04
56	54809	35326	54813	35329	54816	35331	54819	35334	54823	35337	03
57	54826	35340	54830	35342	54833	35345	54837	35348	54840	35351	02
58	54843	35354	54847	35356	54850	35359	54854	35362	54857	35365	01
59	54860	35368	54864	35370	54867	35373	54871	35376	54874	35379	00

| | .8 | | .6 | | .4 | | .2 | | .0 | |

73° HAVERSINES

′	.0 Log.	.0 Nat.	.2 Log.	.2 Nat.	.4 Log.	.4 Nat.	.6 Log.	.6 Nat.	.8 Log.	.8 Nat.	Log.	Nat.	′
	1̄.or.(9.)	0.	1̄.or(9.)	0.	1̄.or(9.)	0.	1̄.or(9.)	0.	1̄.or(9.)	0.	1̄.or(9.)	0.	
00	54878	35381	54881	35384	54884	35387	54888	35390	54891	35393	54895	35395	59
01	54895	35395	54898	35398	54901	35401	54905	35404	54908	35406	54912	35409	58
02	54912	35409	54915	35412	54918	35415	54922	35418	54925	35420	54929	35423	57
03	54929	35423	54932	35426	54936	35429	54939	35431	54942	35434	54946	35437	56
04	54946	35437	54949	35440	54953	35443	54956	35445	54959	35448	54963	35451	55
05	54963	35451	54966	35454	54970	35457	54973	35459	54976	35462	54980	35465	54
06	54980	35465	54983	35468	54987	35470	54990	35473	54994	35476	54997	35479	53
07	54997	35479	55000	35482	55004	35484	55007	35487	55011	35490	55014	35493	52
08	55014	35493	55017	35496	55021	35498	55024	35501	55028	35504	55031	35507	51
09	55031	35507	55034	35509	55038	35512	55041	35515	55045	35518	55048	35521	50
10	55048	35521	55051	35523	55055	35526	55058	35529	55062	35532	55065	35534	49
11	55065	35534	55068	35537	55072	35540	55075	35543	55079	35546	55082	35548	48
12	55082	35548	55085	35551	55089	35554	55092	35557	55096	35560	55099	35562	47
13	55099	35562	55102	35565	55106	35568	55109	35571	55113	35573	55116	35576	46
14	55116	35576	55119	35579	55123	35582	55126	35585	55130	35587	55133	35590	45
15	55133	35590	55136	35593	55140	35596	55143	35599	55147	35601	55150	35604	44
16	55150	35604	55153	35607	55157	35610	55160	35612	55164	35615	55167	35618	43
17	55167	35618	55170	35621	55174	35624	55177	35626	55181	35629	55184	35632	42
18	55184	35632	55187	35635	55191	35638	55194	35640	55198	35643	55201	35646	41
19	55201	35646	55204	35649	55208	35651	55211	35654	55215	35657	55218	35660	40
20	55218	35660	55221	35663	55225	35665	55228	35668	55232	35671	55235	35674	39
21	55235	35674	55238	35677	55242	35679	55245	35682	55248	35685	55252	35688	38
22	55252	35688	55255	35690	55259	35693	55262	35696	55265	35699	55269	35702	37
23	55269	35702	55272	35704	55276	35707	55279	35710	55282	35713	55286	35716	36
24	55286	35716	55289	35718	55293	35721	55296	35724	55299	35727	55303	35730	35
25	55303	35730	55306	35732	55310	35735	55313	35738	55316	35741	55320	35743	34
26	55320	35743	55323	35746	55326	35749	55330	35752	55333	35755	55337	35757	33
27	55337	35757	55340	35760	55343	35763	55347	35766	55350	35769	55354	35771	32
28	55354	35771	55357	35774	55360	35777	55364	35780	55367	35783	55370	35785	31
29	55370	35785	55374	35788	55377	35791	55381	35794	55384	35796	55387	35799	30
30	55387	35799	55391	35802	55394	35805	55397	35808	55401	35810	55404	35813	29
31	55404	35813	55408	35816	55411	35819	55414	35822	55418	35824	55421	35827	28
32	55421	35827	55425	35830	55428	35833	55431	35835	55435	35838	55438	35841	27
33	55438	35841	55442	35844	55445	35847	55448	35849	55452	35852	55455	35855	26
34	55455	35855	55458	35858	55462	35861	55465	35863	55468	35866	55472	35869	25
35	55472	35869	55475	35872	55479	35875	55482	35877	55485	35880	55489	35883	24
36	55489	35883	55492	35886	55496	35889	55499	35891	55502	35894	55506	35897	23
37	55506	35897	55509	35900	55512	35902	55516	35905	55519	35908	55523	35911	22
38	55523	35911	55526	35914	55529	35916	55533	35919	55536	35922	55539	35925	21
39	55539	35925	55543	35928	55546	35930	55549	35933	55553	35936	55556	35939	20
40	55556	35939	55560	35942	55563	35944	55566	35947	55570	35950	55573	35953	19
41	55573	35953	55577	35955	55580	35958	55583	35961	55587	35964	55590	35967	18
42	55590	35967	55593	35969	55597	35972	55600	35975	55603	35978	55607	35981	17
43	55607	35981	55610	35983	55614	35986	55617	35989	55620	35992	55624	35995	16
44	55624	35995	55627	35997	55631	36000	55634	36003	55637	36006	55641	36009	15
45	55641	36009	55644	36011	55647	36014	55651	36017	55654	36020	55657	36023	14
46	55657	36023	55661	36025	55664	36028	55667	36031	55671	36034	55674	36036	13
47	55674	36036	55678	36039	55681	36042	55684	36045	55688	36048	55691	36050	12
48	55691	36050	55694	36053	55698	36056	55701	36059	55704	36062	55708	36064	11
49	55708	36064	55711	36067	55715	36070	55718	36073	55721	36076	55725	36078	10
50	55725	36078	55728	36081	55732	36084	55735	36087	55738	36090	55742	36092	09
51	55742	36092	55745	36095	55748	36098	55752	36101	55755	36104	55758	36106	08
52	55758	36106	55762	36109	55765	36112	55768	36115	55772	36118	55775	36120	07
53	55775	36120	55779	36123	55782	36126	55785	36129	55789	36131	55792	36134	06
54	55792	36134	55795	36137	55799	36140	55802	36143	55805	36145	55809	36148	05
55	55809	36148	55812	36151	55816	36154	55819	36157	55822	36159	55826	36162	04
56	55826	36162	55829	36165	55832	36168	55836	36171	55839	36173	55842	36176	03
57	55842	36176	55846	36179	55849	36182	55852	36185	55856	36187	55859	36190	02
58	55859	36190	55862	36193	55866	36196	55869	36199	55872	36201	55876	36204	01
59	55876	36204	55879	36207	55883	36210	55886	36213	55889	36215	55893	36218	00
			.8		.6		.4		.2		.0	←	

PARTS for 0′.1: LOGS 2 NATURALS 1

286°

74° HAVERSINES

	.0		.2		.4		.6		.8				
	Log.	Nat.	Log.	Nat.	Log.	Nat.	Log.	Nat.	Log.	Nat.	Log.	Nat.	
′	1.or.(9.)	0.	1.or(9.)	0.	1.or(9.)	0.	1.or(9.)	0.	1.or(9.)	0.	1.or.(9.)	0.	′
00	55893	36218	55896	36221	55899	36224	55903	36227	55906	36229	55909	36232	59
01	55909	36232	55913	36235	55916	36238	55919	36241	55923	36243	55926	36246	58
02	55926	36246	55930	36249	55933	36252	55936	36255	55939	36257	55943	36260	57
03	55943	36260	55946	36263	55950	36266	55953	36268	55956	36271	55960	36274	56
04	55960	36274	55963	36277	55966	36280	55970	36282	55973	36285	55976	36288	55
05	55976	36288	55980	36291	55983	36294	55986	36296	55990	36299	55993	36302	54
06	55993	36302	55997	36305	56000	36308	56003	36310	56006	36313	56010	36316	53
07	56010	36316	56013	36319	56017	36322	56020	36324	56023	36327	56027	36330	52
08	56027	36330	56030	36333	56033	36336	56037	36338	56040	36341	56043	36344	51
09	56043	36344	56047	36347	56050	36350	56053	36352	56057	36355	56060	36358	50
10	56060	36358	56063	36361	56067	36364	56070	36366	56073	36369	56077	36372	49
11	56077	36372	56080	36375	56083	36378	56087	36380	56090	36383	56093	36386	48
12	56093	36386	56097	36389	56100	36392	56103	36394	56107	36397	56110	36400	47
13	56110	36400	56114	36403	56117	36406	56120	36408	56123	36411	56127	36414	46
14	56127	36414	56130	36417	56134	36420	56137	36422	56140	36425	56144	36428	45
15	56144	36428	56147	36431	56150	36434	56154	36436	56157	36439	56160	36442	44
16	56160	36442	56164	36445	56167	36448	56170	36450	56173	36453	56177	36456	43
17	56177	36456	56180	36459	56184	36462	56187	36464	56190	36467	56194	36470	42
18	56194	36470	56197	36473	56200	36476	56204	36478	56207	36481	56210	36484	41
19	56210	36484	56214	36487	56217	36490	56220	36492	56223	36495	56227	36498	40
20	56227	36498	56230	36501	56234	36504	56237	36506	56240	36509	56244	36512	39
21	56244	36512	56247	36515	56250	36518	56254	36520	56257	36523	56260	36526	38
22	56260	36526	56264	36529	56267	36532	56270	36534	56273	36537	56277	36540	37
23	56277	36540	56280	36543	56284	36546	56287	36548	56290	36551	56294	36554	36
24	56294	36554	56297	36557	56300	36560	56304	36562	56307	36565	56310	36568	35
25	56310	36568	56314	36571	56317	36574	56320	36576	56323	36579	56327	36582	34
26	56327	36582	56330	36585	56333	36588	56337	36590	56340	36593	56343	36596	33
27	56343	36596	56347	36599	56350	36602	56353	36604	56357	36607	56360	36610	32
28	56360	36610	56363	36613	56367	36616	56370	36618	56373	36621	56377	36624	31
29	56377	36624	56380	36627	56383	36630	56387	36632	56390	36635	56393	36638	30
30	56393	36638	56397	36641	56400	36644	56403	36647	56406	36649	56410	36652	29
31	56410	36652	56413	36655	56416	36658	56420	36661	56423	36663	56426	36666	28
32	56426	36666	56430	36669	56433	36672	56436	36675	56440	36677	56443	36680	27
33	56443	36680	56446	36683	56450	36686	56453	36689	56456	36691	56460	36694	26
34	56460	36694	56463	36697	56466	36700	56470	36703	56473	36705	56476	36708	25
35	56476	36708	56480	36711	56483	36714	56486	36717	56489	36719	56493	36722	24
36	56493	36722	56496	36725	56499	36728	56503	36731	56506	36733	56509	36736	23
37	56509	36736	56513	36739	56516	36742	56519	36745	56523	36747	56526	36750	22
38	56526	36750	56529	36753	56533	36756	56536	36759	56539	36761	56543	36764	21
39	56543	36764	56546	36767	56549	36770	56553	36773	56556	36775	56559	36778	20
40	56559	36778	56563	36781	56566	36784	56569	36787	56572	36790	56576	36792	19
41	56576	36792	56579	36795	56582	36798	56586	36801	56589	36804	56592	36806	18
42	56592	36806	56596	36809	56599	36812	56602	36815	56605	36818	56609	36820	17
43	56609	36820	56612	36823	56615	36826	56619	36829	56622	36832	56625	36834	16
44	56625	36834	56629	36837	56632	36840	56635	36843	56639	36846	56642	36848	15
45	56642	36848	56645	36851	56649	36854	56652	36857	56655	36860	56658	36862	14
46	56658	36862	56662	36865	56665	36868	56668	36871	56672	36874	56675	36877	13
47	56675	36877	56678	36879	56682	36882	56685	36885	56688	36888	56692	36891	12
48	56692	36891	56695	36893	56698	36696	56701	36899	56705	36902	56708	36905	11
49	56708	36905	56711	36907	56715	36910	56718	36913	56721	36916	56725	36919	10
50	56725	36919	56728	36921	56731	36924	56734	36927	56738	36930	56741	36933	09
51	56741	36933	56744	36935	56748	36938	56751	36941	56754	36944	56758	36947	08
52	56758	36947	56761	36950	56764	36952	56767	36955	56771	36958	56774	36961	07
53	56774	36961	56777	36964	56781	36966	56784	36969	56787	36972	56791	36975	06
54	56791	36975	56794	36978	56797	36980	56800	36983	56804	36986	56807	36989	05
55	56807	36989	56810	36992	56814	36994	56817	36997	56820	37000	56824	37003	04
56	56824	37003	56827	37006	56830	37008	56833	37011	56837	37014	56840	37017	03
57	56840	37017	56843	37020	56847	37023	56850	37025	56853	37028	56856	37031	02
58	56856	37031	56860	37034	56863	37037	56866	37039	56870	37042	56873	37045	01
59	56873	37045	56876	37048	56880	37051	56883	37053	56886	37056	56889	37059	00
		.8		.6		.4		.2		.0			

PARTS for 0.1: LOGS 2 NATURALS 1

285°

75° HAVERSINES

′	.0 Log.	.0 Nat.	.2 Log.	.2 Nat.	.4 Log.	.4 Nat.	.6 Log.	.6 Nat.	.8 Log.	.8 Nat.	′
	$\overline{1}$.or(9.)	0.	$\overline{1}$.or(9.)	0.	$\overline{1}$.or(9.)	0.	$\overline{1}$.or(9.)	0.	$\overline{1}$.or(9.)	0.	
00	56889	37059	56893	37062	56896	37065	56899	37067	56903	37070	56906	37073	59
01	56906	37073	56909	37076	56912	37079	56916	37082	56919	37084	56922	37087	58
02	56922	37087	56926	37090	56929	37093	56932	37096	56936	37098	56939	37101	57
03	56939	37101	56942	37104	56945	37107	56949	37110	56952	37112	56955	37115	56
04	56955	37115	56958	37118	56962	37121	56965	37124	56968	37126	56972	37129	55
05	56972	37129	56975	37132	56978	37135	56982	37138	56985	37141	56988	37143	54
06	56988	37143	56991	37146	56995	37149	56998	37152	57001	37155	57005	37157	53
07	57005	37157	57008	37160	57011	37163	57014	37166	57018	37169	57021	37171	52
08	57021	37171	57024	37174	57028	37177	57031	37180	57034	37183	57037	37186	51
09	57037	37186	57041	37188	57044	37191	57047	37194	57051	37197	57054	37200	50
10	57054	37200	57057	37202	57060	37205	57064	37208	57067	37211	57070	37214	49
11	57070	37214	57073	37216	57077	37219	57080	37222	57083	37225	57087	37228	48
12	57087	37228	57090	37231	57093	37233	57096	37236	57100	37239	57103	37242	47
13	57103	37242	57106	37245	57110	37247	57113	37250	57116	37253	57119	37256	46
14	57119	37256	57123	37259	57126	37261	57129	37264	57133	37267	57136	37270	45
15	57136	37270	57139	37273	57142	37276	57146	37278	57149	37281	57152	37284	44
16	57152	37284	57155	37287	57159	37290	57162	37292	57165	37295	57169	37298	43
17	57169	37298	57172	37301	57175	37304	57178	37306	57182	37309	57185	37312	42
18	57185	37312	57188	37315	57192	37318	57195	37321	57198	37323	57201	37326	41
19	57201	37326	57205	37329	57208	37332	57211	37335	57215	37337	57218	37340	40
20	57218	37340	57221	37343	57224	37346	57228	37349	57231	37351	57234	37354	39
21	57234	37354	57237	37357	57241	37360	57244	37363	57247	37366	57250	37368	38
22	57250	37368	57254	37371	57257	37374	57260	37377	57264	37380	57267	37382	37
23	57267	37382	57270	37385	57273	37388	57277	37391	57280	37394	57283	37397	36
24	57283	37397	57286	37399	57290	37402	57293	37405	57296	37408	57299	37411	35
25	57299	37411	57303	37413	57306	37416	57309	37419	57313	37422	57316	37425	34
26	57316	37425	57319	37428	57322	37430	57326	37433	57329	37436	57332	37439	33
27	57332	37439	57335	37442	57339	37444	57342	37447	57345	37450	57348	37453	32
28	57348	37453	57352	37456	57355	37458	57358	37461	57362	37464	57365	37467	31
29	57365	37467	57368	37470	57371	37473	57375	37475	57378	37478	57381	37481	30
30	57381	37481	57384	37484	57388	37487	57391	37489	57394	37492	57397	37495	29
31	57397	37495	57401	37498	57404	37501	57407	37504	57411	37506	57414	37509	28
32	57414	37509	57417	37512	57420	37515	57424	37518	57427	37520	57430	37523	27
33	57430	37523	57433	37526	57437	37529	57440	37532	57443	37535	57446	37537	26
34	57446	37537	57450	37540	57453	37543	57456	37546	57459	37549	57463	37551	25
35	57463	37551	57466	37554	57469	37557	57472	37560	57476	37563	57479	37566	24
36	57479	37566	57482	37568	57485	37571	57489	37574	57492	37577	57495	37580	23
37	57495	37580	57498	37582	57502	37585	57505	37588	57508	37591	57511	37594	22
38	57511	37594	57515	37597	57518	37599	57521	37602	57525	37605	57528	37608	21
39	57528	37608	57531	37611	57534	37613	57538	37616	57541	37619	57544	37622	20
40	57544	37622	57547	37625	57550	37627	57554	37630	57557	37633	57560	37636	19
41	57560	37636	57563	37639	57567	37642	57570	37644	57573	37647	57577	37650	18
42	57577	37650	57580	37653	57583	37656	57586	37659	57590	37661	57593	37664	17
43	57593	37664	57596	37667	57599	37670	57603	37673	57606	37675	57609	37678	16
44	57609	37678	57612	37681	57616	37684	57619	37687	57622	37690	57625	37692	15
45	57625	37692	57629	37695	57632	37698	57635	37701	57638	37704	57642	37706	14
46	57642	37706	57645	37709	57648	37712	57651	37715	57655	37718	57658	37721	13
47	57658	37721	57661	37723	57664	37726	57668	37729	57671	37732	57674	37735	12
48	57674	37735	57677	37737	57680	37740	57684	37743	57687	37746	57690	37749	11
49	57690	37749	57693	37752	57697	37754	57700	37757	57703	37760	57706	37763	10
50	57706	37763	57710	37766	57713	37768	57716	37771	57719	37774	57723	37777	09
51	57723	37777	57726	37780	57729	37783	57732	37785	57736	37788	57739	37791	08
52	57739	37791	57742	37794	57745	37797	57749	37800	57752	37802	57755	37805	07
53	57755	37805	57758	37808	57761	37811	57765	37814	57768	37816	57771	37819	06
54	57771	37819	57774	37822	57778	37825	57781	37828	57784	37831	57787	37833	05
55	57787	37833	57791	37836	57794	37839	57797	37842	57800	37845	57804	37847	04
56	57804	37847	57807	37850	57810	37853	57813	37856	57817	37859	57820	37862	03
57	57820	37862	57823	37864	57826	37867	57830	37870	57833	37873	57836	37876	02
58	57836	37876	57839	37879	57842	37881	57846	37884	57849	37887	57852	37890	01
59	57852	37890	57855	37893	57859	37895	57862	37898	57865	37901	57868	37904	00

| | .8 | | .6 | | .4 | | .2 | | .0 ← | |

PARTS for 0′.1: LOGS 2 NATURALS 1

284°

76° HAVERSINES

′	.0 Log 1.or(9.)	.0 Nat 0.	.2 Log 1.or(9.)	.2 Nat 0.	.4 Log 1.or(9.)	.4 Nat 0.	.6 Log 1.or(9.)	.6 Nat 0.	.8 Log 1.or(9.)	.8 Nat 0.	Log 1.or(9.)	Nat 0.	′
00	57868	37904	57872	37907	57875	37910	57878	37912	57881	37915	57885	37918	59
01	57885	37918	57888	37921	57891	37924	57894	37926	57898	37929	57901	37932	58
02	57901	37932	57904	37935	57907	37938	57910	37941	57914	37943	57917	37946	57
03	57917	37946	57920	37949	57923	37952	57927	37955	57930	37958	57933	37960	56
04	57933	37960	57936	37963	57939	37966	57943	37969	57946	37972	57949	37974	55
05	57949	37974	57952	37977	57956	37980	57959	37983	57962	37986	57965	37989	54
06	57965	37989	57969	37991	57972	37994	57975	37997	57978	38000	57981	38003	53
07	57981	38003	57985	38006	57988	38008	57991	38011	57994	38014	57998	38017	52
08	57998	38017	58001	38020	58004	38022	58007	38025	58011	38028	58014	38031	51
09	58014	38031	58017	38034	58020	38037	58023	38039	58027	38042	58030	38045	50
10	58030	38045	58033	38048	58036	38051	58040	38054	58043	38056	58046	38059	49
11	58046	38059	58049	38062	58052	38065	58056	38068	58059	38071	58062	38073	48
12	58062	38073	58065	38076	58068	38079	58072	38082	58075	38085	58078	38087	47
13	58078	38087	58081	38090	58085	38093	58088	38096	58091	38099	58094	38102	46
14	58094	38102	58097	38104	58101	38107	58104	38110	58107	38113	58110	38116	45
15	58110	38116	58114	38119	58117	38121	58120	38124	58123	38127	58126	38130	44
16	58126	38130	58130	38133	58133	38135	58136	38138	58139	38141	58143	38144	43
17	58143	38144	58146	38147	58149	38150	58152	38152	58155	38155	58159	38158	42
18	58159	38158	58162	38161	58165	38164	58168	38167	58172	38169	58175	38172	41
19	58175	38172	58178	38175	58181	38178	58184	38181	58188	38184	58191	38186	40
20	58191	38186	58194	38189	58197	38192	58200	38195	58204	38198	58207	38200	39
21	58207	38200	58210	38203	58213	38206	58217	38209	58220	38212	58223	38215	38
22	58223	38215	58226	38217	58229	38220	58233	38223	58236	38226	58239	38229	37
23	58239	38229	58242	38232	58245	38234	58249	38237	58252	38240	58255	38243	36
24	58255	38243	58258	38246	58261	38249	58265	38251	58268	38254	58271	38257	35
25	58271	38257	58274	38260	58278	38263	58281	38266	58284	38268	58287	38271	34
26	58287	38271	58290	38274	58294	38277	58297	38280	58300	38282	58303	38285	33
27	58303	38285	58306	38288	58310	38291	58313	38294	58316	38297	58319	38299	32
28	58319	38299	58322	38302	58326	38305	58329	38308	58332	38311	58335	38314	31
29	58335	38314	58338	38316	58342	38319	58345	38322	58348	38325	58351	38328	30
30	58351	38328	58355	38331	58358	38333	58361	38336	58364	38339	58367	38342	29
31	58367	38342	58371	38345	58374	38348	58377	38350	58380	38353	58383	38356	28
32	58383	38356	58387	38359	58390	38362	58393	38364	58396	38367	58399	38370	27
33	58399	38370	58403	38373	58406	38376	58409	38379	58412	38381	58415	38384	26
34	58415	38384	58419	38387	58422	38390	58425	38393	58428	38396	58431	38398	25
35	58431	38398	58435	38401	58438	38404	58441	38407	58444	38410	58447	38413	24
36	58447	38413	58451	38415	58454	38418	58457	38421	58460	38424	58463	38427	23
37	58463	38427	58467	38430	58470	38432	58473	38435	58476	38438	58479	38441	22
38	58479	38441	58483	38444	58486	38447	58489	38449	58492	38452	58495	38455	21
39	58495	38455	58499	38458	58502	38461	58505	38464	58508	38466	58511	38469	20
40	58511	38469	58515	38472	58518	38475	58521	38478	58524	38481	58527	38483	19
41	58527	38483	58530	38486	58534	38489	58537	38492	58540	38495	58543	38498	18
42	58543	38498	58546	38500	58550	38503	58553	38506	58556	38509	58559	38512	17
43	58559	38512	58562	38514	58566	38517	58569	38520	58572	38523	58575	38526	16
44	58575	38526	58578	38529	58582	38531	58585	38534	58588	38537	58591	38540	15
45	58591	38540	58594	38543	58598	38546	58601	38548	58604	38551	58607	38554	14
46	58607	38554	58610	38557	58613	38560	58617	38563	58620	38565	58623	38568	13
47	58623	38568	58626	38571	58629	38574	58633	38577	58636	38580	58639	38582	12
48	58639	38582	58642	38585	58645	38588	58649	38591	58652	38594	58655	38597	11
49	58655	38597	58658	38599	58661	38602	58664	38605	58668	38608	58671	38611	10
50	58671	38611	58674	38614	58677	38616	58680	38619	58684	38622	58687	38625	09
51	58687	38625	58690	38628	58693	38631	58696	38633	58700	38636	58703	38639	08
52	58703	38639	58706	38642	58709	38645	58712	38648	58715	38650	58719	38653	07
53	58719	38653	58722	38656	58725	38659	58728	38662	58731	38665	58735	38667	06
54	58735	38667	58738	38670	58741	38673	58744	38676	58747	38679	58750	38682	05
55	58750	38682	58754	38684	58757	38687	58760	38690	58763	38693	58766	38696	04
56	58766	38696	58770	38699	58773	38701	58776	38704	58779	38707	58782	38710	03
57	58782	38710	58785	38713	58789	38716	58792	38718	58795	38721	58798	38724	02
58	58798	38724	58801	38727	58805	38730	58808	38733	58811	38735	58814	38738	01
59	58814	38738	58817	38741	58820	38744	58824	38747	58827	38750	58830	38752	00

.8 .6 .4 .2 .0 ←

PARTS for 0′.1:   LOGS 2·   NATURALS 1

283°

77° HAVERSINES

′	.0 Log. 1̄.or(9.)	.0 Nat. 0.	.2 Log. 1̄.or(9.)	.2 Nat. 0.	.4 Log. 1̄.or(9.)	.4 Nat. 0.	.6 Log. 1̄.or(9.)	.6 Nat. 0.	.8 Log. 1̄.or(9.)	.8 Nat. 0.	′
00	58830	38752	58833	38755	58836	38758	58839	38761	58843	38764	58846	38767	59
01	58846	38767	58849	38769	58852	38772	58855	38775	58858	38778	58862	38781	58
02	58862	38781	58865	38784	58868	38786	58871	38789	58874	38792	58878	38795	57
03	58878	38795	58881	38798	58884	38801	58887	38803	58890	38806	58893	38809	56
04	58893	38809	58897	38812	58900	38815	58903	38818	58906	38820	58909	38823	55
05	58909	38823	58912	38826	58916	38829	58919	38832	58922	38835	58925	38837	54
06	58925	38837	58928	38840	58932	38843	58935	38846	58938	38849	58941	38852	53
07	58941	38852	58944	38854	58947	38857	58950	38860	58954	38863	58957	38866	52
08	58957	38866	58960	38869	58963	38872	58966	38874	58969	38877	58973	38880	51
09	58973	38880	58976	38883	58979	38886	58982	38889	58985	38891	58988	38894	50
10	58988	38894	58992	38897	58995	38900	58998	38903	59001	38906	59004	38908	49
11	59004	38908	59008	38911	59011	38914	59014	38917	59017	38920	59020	38923	48
12	59020	38923	59023	38925	59027	38928	59030	38931	59033	38934	59036	38937	47
13	59036	38937	59039	38940	59042	38942	59045	38945	59049	38948	59052	38951	46
14	59052	38951	59055	38954	59058	38957	59061	38959	59064	38962	59068	38965	45
15	59068	38965	59071	38968	59074	38971	59077	38974	59080	38976	59083	38979	44
16	59083	38979	59087	38982	59090	38985	59093	38988	59096	38991	59099	38994	43
17	59099	38994	59102	38996	59106	38999	59109	39002	59112	39005	59115	39008	42
18	59115	39008	59118	39011	59121	39013	59124	39016	59128	39019	59131	39022	41
19	59131	39022	59134	39025	59137	39028	59140	39030	59143	39033	59147	39036	40
20	59147	39036	59150	39039	59153	39042	59156	39045	59159	39047	59162	39050	39
21	59162	39050	59166	39053	59169	39056	59172	39059	59175	39062	59178	39064	38
22	59178	39064	59181	39067	59185	39070	59188	39073	59191	39076	59194	39079	37
23	59194	39079	59197	39081	59200	39084	59203	39087	59207	39090	59210	39093	36
24	59210	39093	59213	39096	59216	39099	59219	39101	59222	39104	59225	39107	35
25	59225	39107	59229	39110	59232	39113	59235	39116	59238	39118	59241	39121	34
26	59241	39121	59244	39124	59248	39127	59251	39130	59254	39133	59257	39135	33
27	59257	39135	59260	39138	59263	39141	59266	39144	59270	39147	59273	39150	32
28	59273	39150	59276	39152	59279	39155	59282	39158	59285	39161	59289	39164	31
29	59289	39164	59292	39167	59295	39169	59298	39172	59301	39175	59304	39178	30
30	59304	39178	59307	39181	59311	39184	59314	39187	59317	39189	59320	39192	29
31	59320	39192	59323	39195	59326	39198	59329	39201	59333	39204	59336	39206	28
32	59336	39206	59339	39209	59342	39212	59345	39215	59348	39218	59351	39221	27
33	59351	39221	59355	39223	59358	39226	59361	39229	59364	39232	59367	39235	26
34	59367	39235	59370	39238	59373	39241	59377	39243	59380	39246	59383	39249	25
35	59383	39249	59386	39252	59389	39255	59392	39258	59395	39260	59399	39263	24
36	59399	39263	59402	39266	59405	39269	59408	39272	59411	39275	59414	39277	23
37	59414	39277	59418	39280	59421	39283	59424	39286	59427	39289	59430	39292	22
38	59430	39292	59433	39294	59436	39297	59439	39300	59443	39303	59446	39306	21
39	59446	39306	59449	39309	59452	39312	59455	39314	59458	39317	59461	39320	20
40	59461	39320	59465	39323	59468	39326	59471	39329	59474	39331	59477	39334	19
41	59477	39334	59480	39337	59483	39340	59487	39343	59490	39346	59493	39348	18
42	59493	39348	59496	39351	59499	39354	59502	39357	59505	39360	59508	39363	17
43	59508	39363	59512	39366	59515	39368	59518	39371	59521	39374	59524	39377	16
44	59524	39377	59527	39380	59530	39383	59534	39385	59537	39388	59540	39391	15
45	59540	39391	59543	39394	59546	39397	59549	39400	59552	39403	59556	39405	14
46	59556	39405	59559	39408	59562	39411	59565	39414	59568	39417	59571	39420	13
47	59571	39420	59574	39422	59577	39425	59581	39428	59584	39431	59587	39434	12
48	59587	39434	59590	39437	59593	39439	59596	39442	59599	39445	59602	39448	11
49	59602	39448	59606	39451	59609	39454	59612	39457	59615	39459	59618	39462	10
50	59618	39462	59621	39465	59624	39468	59628	39471	59631	39474	59634	39476	09
51	59634	39476	59637	39479	59640	39482	59643	39485	59646	39488	59649	39491	08
52	59649	39491	59653	39493	59656	39496	59659	39499	59662	39502	59665	39505	07
53	59665	39505	59668	39508	59671	39511	59674	39513	59677	39516	59681	39519	06
54	59681	39519	59684	39522	59687	39525	59690	39528	59693	39530	59696	39533	05
55	59696	39533	59700	39536	59703	39539	59706	39542	59709	39545	59712	39548	04
56	59712	39548	59715	39550	59718	39553	59721	39556	59724	39559	59728	39562	03
57	59728	39562	59731	39565	59734	39567	59737	39570	59740	39573	59743	39576	02
58	59743	39576	59746	39579	59749	39582	59753	39585	59756	39587	59759	39590	01
59	59759	39590	59762	39593	59765	39596	59768	39599	59771	39602	59774	39604	00

| | .8 | .6 | .4 | .2 | .0 |

PARTS for 0′.1: LOGS 2   NATURALS 1

282°

HAVERSINES

′	.0 Log. 1̄.or(9.)	.0 Nat. 0.	.2 Log. 1̄.or(9.)	.2 Nat. 0.	.4 Log. 1̄.or(9.)	.4 Nat. 0.	.6 Log. 1̄.or(9.)	.6 Nat. 0.	.8 Log. 1̄.or(9.)	.8 Nat. 0.	Log. 1̄.or(9.)	Nat. 0.	′
00	59774	39604	59778	39607	59781	39610	59784	39613	59787	39616	59790	39619	59
01	59790	39619	59793	39621	59796	39624	59799	39627	59802	39630	59806	39633	58
02	59806	39633	59809	39636	59812	39639	59815	39641	59818	39644	59821	39647	57
03	59821	39647	59824	39650	59827	39653	59831	39656	59834	39659	59837	39661	56
04	59837	39661	59840	39664	59843	39667	59846	39670	59849	39673	59852	39676	55
05	59852	39676	59855	39678	59859	39681	59862	39684	59865	39687	59868	39690	54
06	59868	39690	59871	39693	59874	39695	59877	39698	59880	39701	59883	39704	53
07	59883	39704	59887	39707	59890	39710	59893	39713	59896	39715	59899	39718	52
08	59899	39718	59902	39721	59905	39724	59908	39727	59911	39730	59915	39732	51
09	59915	39732	59918	39735	59921	39738	59924	39741	59927	39744	59930	39747	50
10	59930	39747	59933	39750	59936	39752	59939	39755	59943	39758	59946	39761	49
11	59946	39761	59949	39764	59952	39767	59955	39770	59958	39772	59961	39775	48
12	59961	39775	59964	39778	59967	39781	59971	39784	59974	39787	59977	39789	47
13	59977	39789	59980	39792	59983	39795	59986	39798	59989	39801	59992	39804	46
14	59992	39804	59995	39807	59999	39809	60002	39812	60005	39815	60008	39818	45
15	60008	39818	60011	39821	60014	39824	60017	39826	60020	39829	60023	39832	44
16	60023	39832	60027	39835	60030	39838	60033	39841	60036	39844	60039	39846	43
17	60039	39846	60042	39849	60045	39852	60048	39855	60051	39858	60054	39861	42
18	60054	39861	60058	39864	60061	39866	60064	39869	60067	39872	60070	39875	41
19	60070	39875	60073	39878	60076	39881	60079	39883	60082	39886	60085	39889	40
20	60085	39889	60089	39892	60092	39895	60095	39898	60098	39901	60101	39903	39
21	60101	39903	60104	39906	60107	39909	60110	39912	60113	39915	60116	39918	38
22	60116	39918	60120	39920	60123	39923	60126	39926	60129	39929	60132	39932	37
23	60132	39932	60135	39935	60138	39938	60141	39940	60144	39943	60147	39946	36
24	60147	39946	60151	39949	60154	39952	60157	39955	60160	39958	60163	39960	35
25	60163	39960	60166	39963	60169	39966	60172	39969	60175	39972	60178	39975	34
26	60178	39975	60181	39977	60185	39980	60188	39983	60191	39986	60194	39989	33
27	60194	39989	60197	39992	60200	39995	60203	39997	60206	40000	60209	40003	32
28	60209	40003	60212	40006	60216	40009	60219	40012	60222	40015	60225	40017	31
29	60225	40017	60228	40020	60231	40023	60234	40026	60237	40029	60240	40032	30
30	60240	40032	60243	40034	60246	40037	60250	40040	60253	40043	60256	40046	29
31	60256	40046	60259	40049	60262	40052	60265	40054	60268	40057	60271	40060	28
32	60271	40060	60274	40063	60277	40066	60280	40069	60284	40072	60287	40074	27
33	60287	40074	60290	40077	60293	40080	60296	40083	60299	40086	60302	40089	26
34	60302	40089	60305	40091	60308	40094	60311	40097	60315	40100	60318	40103	25
35	60318	40103	60321	40106	60324	40109	60327	40111	60330	40114	60333	40117	24
36	60333	40117	60336	40120	60339	40123	60342	40126	60345	40129	60348	40131	23
37	60348	40131	60351	40134	60355	40137	60358	40140	60361	40143	60364	40146	22
38	60364	40146	60367	40149	60370	40151	60373	40154	60376	40157	60379	40160	21
39	60379	40160	60382	40163	60385	40166	60388	40168	60392	40171	60395	40174	20
40	60395	40174	60398	40177	60401	40180	60404	40183	60407	40186	60410	40188	19
41	60410	40188	60413	40191	60416	40194	60419	40197	60423	40200	60426	40203	18
42	60426	40203	60429	40206	60432	40208	60435	40211	60438	40214	60441	40217	17
43	60441	40217	60444	40220	60447	40223	60450	40226	60453	40228	60456	40231	16
44	60456	40231	60459	40234	60463	40237	60466	40240	60469	40243	60472	40245	15
45	60472	40245	60475	40248	60478	40251	60481	40254	60484	40257	60487	40260	14
46	60487	40260	60490	40263	60493	40265	60496	40268	60499	40271	60502	40274	13
47	60502	40274	60505	40277	60509	40280	60512	40283	60515	40285	60518	40288	12
48	60518	40288	60521	40291	60524	40294	60527	40297	60530	40300	60533	40303	11
49	60533	40303	60536	40305	60539	40308	60542	40311	60546	40314	60549	40317	10
50	60549	40317	60552	40320	60555	40323	60558	40325	60561	40328	60564	40331	09
51	60564	40331	60567	40334	60570	40337	60573	40340	60576	40343	60579	40345	08
52	60579	40345	60582	40348	60586	40351	60589	40354	60592	40357	60595	40360	07
53	60595	40360	60598	40362	60601	40365	60604	40368	60607	40371	60610	40374	06
54	60610	40374	60613	40377	60616	40380	60619	40382	60622	40385	60625	40388	05
55	60625	40388	60628	40391	60632	40394	60635	40397	60638	40400	60641	40402	04
56	60641	40402	60644	40405	60647	40408	60650	40411	60653	40414	60656	40417	03
57	60656	40417	60659	40420	60662	40422	60665	40425	60668	40428	60671	40431	02
58	60671	40431	60674	40434	60678	40437	60681	40440	60684	40442	60687	40445	01
59	60687	40445	60690	40448	60693	40451	60696	40454	60699	40457	60702	40460	00

	.8	.6	.4	.2	.0 ←

PARTS for 0′.1:　　LOGS 2　　　　　　NATURALS 1

79° HAVERSINES

′	.0 Log. $\overline{1}$.or(9.)	.0 Nat. 0.	.2 Log. $\overline{1}$.or(9.)	.2 Nat. 0.	.4 Log. $\overline{1}$.or(9.)	.4 Nat. 0.	.6 Log. $\overline{1}$.or(9.)	.6 Nat. 0.	.8 Log. $\overline{1}$.or(9.)	.8 Nat. 0.	Log. $\overline{1}$.or(9.)	Nat. 0.	′
00	60702	40460	60705	40462	60708	40465	60711	40468	60714	40471	60717	40474	59
01	60717	40474	60720	40477	60724	40480	60727	40482	60730	40485	60733	40488	58
02	60733	40488	60736	40491	60739	40494	60742	40497	60745	40500	60748	40502	57
03	60748	40502	60751	40505	60754	40508	60757	40511	60760	40514	60763	40517	56
04	60763	40517	60766	40520	60769	40522	60773	40525	60776	40528	60779	40531	55
05	60779	40531	60782	40534	60785	40537	60788	40540	60791	40542	60794	40545	54
06	60794	40545	60797	40548	60800	40551	60803	40554	60806	40557	60809	40560	53
07	60809	40560	60812	40562	60815	40565	60818	40568	60822	40571	60825	40574	52
08	60825	40574	60828	40577	60831	40580	60834	40582	60837	40585	60840	40588	51
09	60840	40588	60843	40591	60846	40594	60849	40597	60852	40600	60855	40602	50
10	60855	40602	60858	40605	60861	40608	60864	40611	60867	40614	60870	40617	49
11	60870	40617	60873	40620	60876	40622	60880	40625	60883	40628	60886	40631	48
12	60886	40631	60889	40634	60892	40637	60895	40640	60898	40642	60901	40645	47
13	60901	40645	60904	40648	60907	40651	60910	40654	60913	40657	60916	40660	46
14	60916	40660	60919	40662	60922	40665	60925	40668	60928	40671	60931	40674	45
15	60931	40674	60934	40677	60938	40680	60941	40682	60944	40685	60947	40688	44
16	60947	40688	60950	40691	60953	40694	60956	40697	60959	40700	60962	40702	43
17	60962	40702	60965	40705	60968	40708	60971	40711	60974	40714	60977	40717	42
18	60977	40717	60980	40720	60983	40722	60986	40725	60989	40728	60992	40731	41
19	60992	40731	60995	40734	60999	40737	61002	40740	61005	40742	61008	40745	40
20	61008	40745	61011	40748	61014	40751	61017	40754	61020	40757	61023	40760	39
21	61023	40760	61026	40762	61029	40765	61032	40768	61035	40771	61038	40774	38
22	61038	40774	61041	40777	61044	40780	61047	40782	61050	40785	61053	40788	37
23	61053	40788	61056	40791	61059	40794	61063	40797	61066	40800	61069	40802	36
24	61069	40802	61072	40805	61075	40808	61078	40811	61081	40814	61084	40817	35
25	61084	40817	61087	40820	61090	40822	61093	40825	61096	40828	61099	40831	34
26	61099	40831	61102	40834	61105	40837	61108	40840	61111	40842	61114	40845	33
27	61114	40845	61117	40848	61120	40851	61123	40854	61126	40857	61129	40860	32
28	61129	40860	61132	40862	61135	40865	61139	40868	61142	40871	61145	40874	31
29	61145	40874	61148	40877	61151	40880	61154	40882	61157	40885	61160	40888	30
30	61160	40888	61163	40891	61166	40894	61169	40897	61172	40900	61175	40903	29
31	61175	40903	61178	40905	61181	40908	61184	40911	61187	40914	61190	40917	28
32	61190	40917	61193	40920	61196	40923	61199	40925	61202	40928	61205	40931	27
33	61205	40931	61208	40934	61211	40937	61215	40940	61218	40943	61221	40945	26
34	61221	40945	61224	40948	61227	40951	61230	40954	61233	40957	61236	40960	25
35	61236	40960	61239	40963	61242	40965	61245	40968	61248	40971	61251	40974	24
36	61251	40974	61254	40977	61257	40980	61260	40983	61263	40985	61266	40988	23
37	61266	40988	61269	40991	61272	40994	61275	40997	61278	41000	61281	41003	22
38	61281	41003	61284	41006	61287	41008	61290	41011	61293	41014	61296	41017	21
39	61296	41017	61299	41020	61302	41023	61305	41026	61308	41028	61311	41031	20
40	61311	41031	61314	41034	61317	41037	61321	41040	61324	41043	61327	41046	19
41	61327	41046	61330	41048	61333	41051	61336	41054	61339	41057	61342	41060	18
42	61342	41060	61345	41063	61348	41066	61351	41068	61354	41071	61357	41074	17
43	61357	41074	61360	41077	61363	41080	61366	41083	61369	41086	61372	41089	16
44	61372	41089	61375	41091	61378	41094	61381	41097	61384	41100	61387	41103	15
45	61387	41103	61390	41106	61393	41109	61396	41111	61399	41114	61402	41117	14
46	61402	41117	61405	41120	61408	41123	61411	41126	61414	41129	61417	41131	13
47	61417	41131	61420	41134	61423	41137	61427	41140	61430	41143	61433	41146	12
48	61433	41146	61436	41149	61439	41151	61442	41154	61445	41157	61448	41160	11
49	61448	41160	61451	41163	61454	41166	61457	41169	61460	41172	61463	41174	10
50	61463	41174	61466	41177	61469	41180	61472	41183	61475	41186	61478	41189	09
51	61478	41189	61481	41192	61484	41194	61487	41197	61490	41200	61493	41203	08
52	61493	41203	61496	41206	61499	41209	61502	41212	61505	41214	61508	41217	07
53	61508	41217	61511	41220	61514	41223	61517	41226	61520	41229	61523	41232	06
54	61523	41232	61526	41235	61529	41237	61532	41240	61535	41243	61538	41246	05
55	61538	41246	61541	41249	61544	41252	61547	41255	61550	41257	61553	41260	04
56	61553	41260	61556	41263	61559	41266	61562	41269	61565	41272	61568	41275	03
57	61568	41275	61571	41277	61574	41280	61577	41283	61580	41286	61583	41289	02
58	61583	41289	61586	41292	61589	41295	61592	41298	61595	41300	61598	41303	01
59	61598	41303	61601	41306	61604	41309	61607	41312	61610	41315	61613	41318	00

	.8		.6		.4		.2		.0 ←

PARTS for 0′.1: LOGS 2   NATURALS 1

280°

80° HAVERSINES

'	.0 Log. $\overline{1}$.or(9.)	.0 Nat. 0.	.2 Log. $\overline{1}$.or.(9.)	.2 Nat. 0.	.4 Log. $\overline{1}$.or(9.)	.4 Nat. 0.	.6 Log. $\overline{1}$.or(9.)	.6 Nat. 0.	.8 Log. $\overline{1}$.or(9.)	.8 Nat. 0.	Log. $\overline{1}$.or(9.)	Nat. 0.	'
00	61613	41318	61616	41320	61619	41323	61623	41326	61626	41329	61629	41332	59
01	61629	41332	61632	41335	61635	41338	61638	41341	61641	41343	61644	41346	58
02	61644	41346	61647	41349	61650	41352	61653	41355	61656	41358	61659	41361	57
03	61659	41361	61662	41363	61665	41366	61668	41369	61671	41372	61674	41375	56
04	61674	41375	61677	41378	61680	41381	61683	41383	61686	41386	61689	41389	55
05	61689	41389	61692	41392	61695	41395	61698	41398	61701	41401	61704	41404	54
06	61704	41404	61707	41406	61710	41409	61713	41412	61716	41415	61719	41418	53
07	61719	41418	61722	41421	61725	41424	61728	41426	61731	41429	61734	41432	52
08	61734	41432	61737	41435	61740	41438	61743	41441	61746	41444	61749	41447	51
09	61749	41447	61752	41449	61755	41452	61758	41455	61761	41458	61764	41461	50
10	61764	41461	61767	41464	61770	41467	61773	41469	61776	41472	61779	41475	49
11	61779	41475	61782	41478	61785	41481	61788	41484	61791	41487	61794	41490	48
12	61794	41490	61797	41492	61800	41495	61803	41498	61806	41501	61809	41504	47
13	61809	41504	61812	41507	61815	41510	61818	41512	61821	41515	61824	41518	46
14	61824	41518	61827	41521	61830	41524	61833	41527	61836	41530	61839	41533	45
15	61839	41533	61842	41535	61845	41538	61848	41541	61851	41544	61854	41547	44
16	61854	41547	61857	41550	61860	41553	61863	41555	61866	41558	61869	41561	43
17	61869	41561	61872	41564	61875	41567	61878	41570	61881	41573	61884	41576	42
18	61884	41576	61887	41578	61890	41581	61893	41584	61896	41587	61899	41590	41
19	61899	41590	61902	41593	61905	41596	61908	41598	61911	41601	61914	41604	40
20	61914	41604	61917	41607	61920	41610	61923	41613	61926	41616	61929	41619	39
21	61929	41619	61932	41621	61935	41624	61938	41627	61941	41630	61944	41633	38
22	61944	41633	61947	41636	61950	41639	61953	41641	61956	41644	61959	41647	37
23	61959	41647	61962	41650	61965	41653	61968	41656	61971	41659	61974	41662	36
24	61974	41662	61977	41664	61980	41667	61983	41670	61986	41673	61989	41676	35
25	61989	41676	61992	41679	61995	41682	61997	41685	62000	41687	62003	41690	34
26	62003	41690	62006	41693	62009	41696	62012	41699	62015	41702	62018	41705	33
27	62018	41705	62021	41707	62024	41710	62027	41713	62030	41716	62033	41719	32
28	62033	41719	62036	41722	62039	41725	62042	41728	62045	41730	62048	41733	31
29	62048	41733	62051	41736	62054	41739	62057	41742	62060	41745	62063	41748	30
30	62063	41748	62066	41750	62069	41753	62072	41756	62075	41759	62078	41762	29
31	62078	41762	62081	41765	62084	41768	62087	41771	62090	41773	62093	41776	28
32	62093	41776	62096	41779	62099	41782	62102	41785	62105	41788	62108	41791	27
33	62108	41791	62111	41794	62114	41796	62117	41799	62120	41802	62123	41805	26
34	62123	41805	62126	41808	62129	41811	62132	41814	62135	41816	62138	41819	25
35	62138	41819	62141	41822	62144	41825	62147	41828	62150	41831	62153	41834	24
36	62153	41834	62156	41837	62159	41839	62162	41842	62165	41845	62168	41848	23
37	62168	41848	62171	41851	62174	41854	62176	41857	62179	41860	62182	41862	22
38	62182	41862	62185	41865	62188	41868	62191	41871	62194	41874	62197	41877	21
39	62197	41877	62200	41880	62203	41882	62206	41885	62209	41888	62212	41891	20
40	62212	41891	62215	41894	62218	41897	62221	41900	62224	41903	62227	41905	19
41	62227	41905	62230	41908	62233	41911	62236	41914	62239	41917	62242	41920	18
42	62242	41920	62245	41923	62248	41926	62251	41928	62254	41931	62257	41934	17
43	62257	41934	62260	41937	62263	41940	62266	41943	62269	41946	62272	41949	16
44	62272	41949	62275	41951	62278	41954	62281	41957	62284	41960	62287	41963	15
45	62287	41963	62290	41966	62293	41969	62295	41971	62298	41974	62301	41977	14
46	62301	41977	62304	41980	62307	41983	62310	41986	62313	41989	62316	41992	13
47	62316	41992	62319	41994	62322	41997	62325	42000	62328	42003	62331	42006	12
48	62331	42006	62334	42009	62337	42012	62340	42015	62343	42017	62346	42020	11
49	62346	42020	62349	42023	62352	42026	62355	42029	62358	42032	62361	42035	10
50	62361	42035	62364	42038	62367	42040	62370	42043	62373	42046	62376	42049	09
51	62376	42049	62379	42052	62382	42055	62384	42058	62387	42061	62390	42063	08
52	62390	42063	62393	42066	62396	42069	62399	42072	62402	42075	62405	42078	07
53	62405	42078	62408	42081	62411	42083	62414	42086	62417	42089	62420	42092	06
54	62420	42092	62423	42095	62426	42098	62429	42101	62432	42104	62435	42106	05
55	62435	42106	62438	42109	62441	42112	62444	42115	62447	42118	62450	42121	04
56	62450	42121	62453	42124	62456	42127	62458	42129	62461	42132	62464	42135	03
57	62464	42135	62467	42138	62470	42141	62473	42144	62476	42147	62479	42150	02
58	62479	42150	62482	42152	62485	42155	62488	42158	62491	42161	62494	42164	01
59	62494	42164	62497	42167	62500	42170	62503	42173	62506	42175	62509	42178	00

	.8		.6		.4		.2		.0		

PARTS for 0'.1:   LOGS 1   NATURALS 1

81° HAVERSINES

′	.0 Log.	.0 Nat.	.2 Log.	.2 Nat.	.4 Log.	.4 Nat.	.6 Log.	.6 Nat.	.8 Log.	.8 Nat.	Log.	Nat.	′
	$\overline{1}$.or(9.)	0.	$\overline{1}$.or(9.)	0.	$\overline{1}$.or.(9.)	0.	$\overline{1}$.or(9.)	0.	$\overline{1}$.or(9.)	0.	$\overline{1}$.or(9.)	0.	
00	62509	42178	62512	42181	62515	42184	62518	42187	62521	42190	62524	42193	59
01	62524	42193	62527	42196	62530	42198	62532	42201	62535	42204	62538	42207	58
02	62538	42207	62541	42210	62544	42213	62547	42216	62550	42219	62553	42221	57
03	62553	42221	62556	42224	62559	42227	62562	42230	62565	42233	62568	42236	56
04	62568	42236	62571	42239	62574	42241	62577	42244	62580	42247	62583	42250	55
05	62583	42250	62586	42253	62589	42256	62592	42259	62595	42262	62598	42264	54
06	62598	42264	62601	42267	62604	42270	62606	42273	62609	42276	62612	42279	53
07	62612	42279	62615	42282	62618	42285	62621	42287	62624	42290	62627	42293	52
08	62627	42293	62630	42296	62633	42299	62636	42302	62639	42305	62642	42308	51
09	62642	42308	62645	42310	62648	42313	62651	42316	62654	42319	62657	42322	50
10	62657	42322	62660	42325	62663	42328	62665	42331	62668	42333	62671	42336	49
11	62671	42336	62674	42339	62677	42342	62680	42345	62683	42348	62686	42351	48
12	62686	42351	62689	42354	62692	42356	62695	42359	62698	42362	62701	42365	47
13	62701	42365	62704	42368	62707	42371	62710	42374	62713	42377	62716	42379	46
14	62716	42379	62719	42382	62721	42385	62724	42388	62727	42391	62730	42394	45
15	62730	42394	62733	42397	62736	42400	62739	42402	62742	42405	62745	42408	44
16	62745	42408	62748	42411	62751	42414	62754	42417	62757	42420	62760	42423	43
17	62760	42423	62763	42425	62766	42428	62769	42431	62771	42434	62774	42437	42
18	62774	42437	62777	42440	62780	42443	62783	42446	62786	42448	62789	42451	41
19	62789	42451	62792	42454	62795	42457	62798	42460	62801	42463	62804	42466	40
20	62804	42466	62807	42469	62810	42471	62813	42474	62816	42477	62819	42480	39
21	62819	42480	62822	42483	62824	42486	62827	42489	62830	42492	62833	42494	38
22	62833	42494	62836	42497	62839	42500	62842	42503	62845	42506	62848	42509	37
23	62848	42509	62851	42512	62854	42515	62857	42517	62860	42520	62863	42523	36
24	62863	42523	62866	42526	62869	42529	62871	42532	62874	42535	62877	42538	35
25	62877	42538	62880	42540	62883	42543	62886	42546	62889	42549	62892	42552	34
26	62892	42552	62895	42555	62898	42558	62901	42561	62904	42564	62907	42566	33
27	62907	42566	62910	42569	62913	42572	62915	42575	62918	42578	62921	42581	32
28	62921	42581	62924	42584	62927	42587	62930	42589	62933	42592	62936	42595	31
29	62936	42595	62939	42598	62942	42601	62945	42604	62948	42607	62951	42610	30
30	62951	42610	62954	42612	62957	42615	62959	42618	62962	42621	62965	42624	29
31	62965	42624	62968	42627	62971	42630	62974	42633	62977	42635	62980	42638	28
32	62980	42638	62983	42641	62986	42644	62989	42647	62992	42650	62995	42653	27
33	62995	42653	62998	42656	63000	42658	63003	42661	63006	42664	63009	42667	26
34	63009	42667	63012	42670	63015	42673	63018	42676	63021	42679	63024	42681	25
35	63024	42681	63027	42684	63030	42687	63033	42690	63036	42693	63039	42696	24
36	63039	42696	63042	42699	63044	42702	63047	42704	63050	42707	63053	42710	23
37	63053	42710	63056	42713	63059	42716	63062	42719	63065	42722	63068	42725	22
38	63068	42725	63071	42728	63074	42730	63077	42733	63079	42736	63082	42739	21
39	63082	42739	63085	42742	63088	42745	63091	42748	63094	42751	63097	42753	20
40	63097	42753	63100	42756	63103	42759	63106	42762	63109	42765	63112	42768	19
41	63112	42768	63115	42771	63118	42774	63120	42776	63123	42779	63126	42782	18
42	63126	42782	63129	42785	63132	42788	63135	42791	63138	42794	63141	42797	17
43	63141	42797	63144	42799	63147	42802	63150	42805	63153	42808	63156	42811	16
44	63156	42811	63159	42814	63161	42817	63164	42820	63167	42822	63170	42825	15
45	63170	42825	63173	42828	63176	42831	63179	42834	63182	42837	63185	42840	14
46	63185	42840	63188	42843	63191	42846	63193	42848	63196	42851	63199	42854	13
47	63199	42854	63202	42857	63205	42860	63208	42863	63211	42866	63214	42869	12
48	63214	42869	63217	42871	63220	42874	63223	42877	63225	42880	63228	42883	11
49	63228	42883	63231	42886	63234	42889	63237	42892	63240	42894	63243	42897	10
50	63243	42897	63246	42900	63249	42903	63252	42906	63255	42909	63258	42912	09
51	63258	42912	63261	42915	63263	42918	63266	42920	63269	42923	63272	42926	08
52	63272	42926	63275	42929	63278	42932	63281	42935	63284	42938	63287	42941	07
53	63287	42941	63290	42943	63293	42946	63296	42949	63298	42952	63301	42955	06
54	63301	42955	63304	42958	63307	42961	63310	42964	63313	42966	63316	42969	05
55	63316	42969	63319	42972	63322	42975	63325	42978	63327	42981	63330	42984	04
56	63330	42984	63333	42987	63336	42990	63339	42992	63342	42995	63345	42998	03
57	63345	42998	63348	43001	63351	43004	63354	43007	63357	43010	63360	43013	02
58	63360	43013	63362	43015	63365	43018	63368	43021	63371	43024	63374	43027	01
59	63374	43027	63377	43030	63380	43033	63383	43036	63386	43038	63389	43041	00

| | .8 | | .6 | | .4 | | .2 | | .0 | |

PARTS for 0'.1: LOGS 1   NATURALS 1

278°

82° HAVERSINES

'	.0 Log.	.0 Nat.	.2 Log.	.2 Nat.	.4 Log.	.4 Nat.	.6 Log.	.6 Nat.	8 Log.	8 Nat.	Log.	Nat.	'
	1.or(9.)	0.	1.or(9.)	0.	1.or(9.)	0.	1.or(9.)	0.	1.or(9.)	0.	1.or(9.)	0.	
00	63389	43041	63392	43044	63394	43047	63397	43050	63400	43053	63403	43056	59
01	63403	43056	63406	43059	63409	43062	63412	43064	63415	43067	63418	43070	58
02	63418	43070	63421	43073	63423	43076	63426	43079	63429	43082	63432	43085	57
03	63432	43085	63435	43087	63438	43090	63441	43093	63444	43096	63447	43099	56
04	63447	43099	63450	43102	63452	43105	63455	43108	63458	43110	63461	43113	55
05	63461	43113	63464	43116	63467	43119	63470	43122	63473	43125	63476	43128	54
06	63476	43128	63479	43131	63482	43134	63484	43136	63487	43139	63490	43142	53
07	63490	43142	63493	43145	63496	43148	63499	43151	63502	43154	63505	43157	52
08	63505	43157	63508	43159	63511	43162	63513	43165	63516	43168	63519	43171	51
09	63519	43171	63522	43174	63525	43177	63528	43180	63531	43183	63534	43185	50
10	63534	43185	63537	43188	63539	43191	63542	43194	63545	43197	63548	43200	49
11	63548	43200	63551	43203	63554	43206	63557	43208	63560	43211	63563	43214	48
12	63563	43214	63566	43217	63568	43220	63571	43223	63574	43226	63577	43229	47
13	63577	43229	63580	43232	63583	43234	63586	43237	63589	43240	63592	43243	46
14	63592	43243	63594	43246	63597	43249	63600	43252	63603	43255	63606	43257	45
15	63606	43257	63609	43260	63612	43263	63615	43266	63618	43269	63621	43272	44
16	63621	43272	63623	43275	63626	43278	63629	43281	63632	43283	63635	43286	43
17	63635	43286	63638	43289	63641	43292	63644	43295	63647	43298	63649	43301	42
18	63649	43301	63652	43304	63655	43306	63658	43309	63661	43312	63664	43315	41
19	63664	43315	63667	43318	63670	43321	63673	43324	63676	43327	63678	43330	40
20	63678	43330	63681	43332	63684	43335	63687	43338	63690	43341	63693	43344	39
21	63693	43344	63696	43347	63699	43350	63701	43353	63704	43355	63707	43358	38
22	63707	43358	63710	43361	63713	43364	63716	43367	63719	43370	63722	43373	37
23	63722	43373	63725	43376	63728	43379	63730	43381	63733	43384	63736	43387	36
24	63736	43387	63739	43390	63742	43393	63745	43396	63748	43399	63751	43402	35
25	63751	43402	63753	43404	63756	43407	63759	43410	63762	43413	63765	43416	34
26	63765	43416	63768	43419	63771	43422	63774	43425	63777	43428	63779	43430	33
27	63779	43430	63782	43433	63785	43436	63788	43439	63791	43442	63794	43445	32
28	63794	43445	63797	43448	63800	43451	63802	43453	63805	43456	63808	43459	31
29	63808	43459	63811	43462	63814	43465	63817	43468	63820	43471	63823	43474	30
30	63823	43474	63825	43477	63828	43479	63831	43482	63834	43485	63837	43488	29
31	63837	43488	63840	43491	63843	43494	63846	43497	63849	43500	63851	43503	28
32	63851	43503	63854	43505	63857	43508	63860	43511	63863	43514	63866	43517	27
33	63866	43517	63869	43520	63872	43523	63874	43526	63877	43528	63880	43531	26
34	63880	43531	63883	43534	63886	43537	63889	43540	63892	43543	63895	43546	25
35	63895	43546	63897	43549	63900	43552	63903	43554	63906	43557	63909	43560	24
36	63909	43560	63912	43563	63915	43566	63918	43569	63921	43572	63923	43575	23
37	63923	43575	63926	43578	63929	43580	63932	43583	63935	43586	63938	43589	22
38	63938	43589	63941	43592	63944	43595	63946	43598	63949	43601	63952	43603	21
39	63952	43603	63955	43606	63958	43609	63961	43612	63964	43615	63966	43618	20
40	63966	43618	63969	43621	63972	43624	63975	43627	63978	43629	63981	43632	19
41	63981	43632	63984	43635	63987	43638	63989	43641	63992	43644	63995	43647	18
42	63995	43647	63998	43650	64001	43653	64004	43655	64007	43658	64010	43661	17
43	64010	43661	64012	43664	64015	43667	64018	43670	64021	43673	64024	43676	16
44	64024	43676	64027	43678	64030	43681	64033	43684	64035	43687	64038	43690	15
45	64038	43690	64041	43693	64044	43696	64047	43699	64050	43702	64053	43704	14
46	64053	43704	64055	43707	64058	43710	64061	43713	64064	43716	64067	43719	13
47	64067	43719	64070	43722	64073	43725	64076	43728	64078	43730	64081	43733	12
48	64081	43733	64084	43736	64087	43739	64090	43742	64093	43745	64096	43748	11
49	64096	43748	64098	43751	64101	43754	64104	43756	64107	43759	64110	43762	10
50	64110	43762	64113	43765	64116	43768	64119	43771	64121	43774	64124	43777	09
51	64124	43777	64127	43780	64130	43782	64133	43785	64136	43788	64139	43791	08
52	64139	43791	64141	43794	64144	43797	64147	43800	64150	43803	64153	43805	07
53	64153	43805	64156	43808	64159	43811	64161	43814	64164	43817	64167	43820	06
54	64167	43820	64170	43823	64173	43826	64176	43829	64179	43831	64181	43834	05
55	64181	43834	64184	43837	64187	43840	64190	43843	64193	43846	64196	43849	04
56	64196	43849	64199	43852	64201	43855	64204	43857	64207	43860	64210	43863	03
57	64210	43863	64213	43866	64216	43869	64219	43872	64222	43875	64224	43878	02
58	64224	43878	64227	43881	64230	43883	64233	43886	64236	43889	64239	43892	01
59	64239	43892	64241	43895	64244	43898	64247	43901	64250	43904	64253	43907	00

| | .8 | | .6 | | .4 | | .2 | | .0 | | | | |

PARTS for 0'.1:   LOGS 1   NATURALS 1

83° HAVERSINES

′	.0 Log. $\overline{1}$.or(9.)	.0 Nat. 0.	.2 Log. $\overline{1}$.or(9.)	.2 Nat. 0.	.4 Log. $\overline{1}$.or(9.)	.4 Nat. 0.	.6 Log. $\overline{1}$.or(9.)	.6 Nat. 0.	.8 Log. $\overline{1}$.or(9.)	.8 Nat. 0.	Log. $\overline{1}$.or(9.)	Nat. 0.	′
00	64253	43907	64256	43909	64259	43912	64262	43915	64264	43918	64267	43921	59
01	64267	43921	64270	43924	64273	43927	64276	43930	64279	43933	64281	43935	58
02	64281	43935	64284	43938	64287	43941	64290	43944	64293	43947	64296	43950	57
03	64296	43950	64299	43953	64301	43956	64304	43959	64307	43961	64310	43964	56
04	64310	43964	64313	43967	64316	43970	64319	43973	64321	43976	64324	43979	55
05	64324	43979	64327	43982	64330	43984	64333	43987	64336	43990	64339	43993	54
06	64339	43993	64341	43996	64344	43999	64347	44002	64350	44005	64353	44008	53
07	64353	44008	64356	44010	64358	44013	64361	44016	64364	44019	64367	44022	52
08	64367	44022	64370	44025	64373	44028	64376	44031	64378	44034	64381	44036	51
09	64381	44036	64384	44039	64387	44042	64390	44045	64393	44048	64396	44051	50
10	64396	44051	64398	44054	64401	44057	64404	44060	64407	44062	64410	44065	49
11	64410	44065	64413	44068	64415	44071	64418	44074	64421	44077	64424	44080	48
12	64424	44080	64427	44083	64430	44086	64433	44088	64435	44091	64438	44094	47
13	64438	44094	64441	44097	64444	44100	64447	44103	64450	44106	64452	44109	46
14	64452	44109	64455	44112	64458	44114	64461	44117	64464	44120	64467	44123	45
15	64467	44123	64469	44126	64472	44129	64475	44132	64478	44135	64481	44138	44
16	64481	44138	64484	44140	64486	44143	64489	44146	64492	44149	64495	44152	43
17	64495	44152	64498	44155	64501	44158	64504	44161	64506	44164	64509	44166	42
18	64509	44166	64512	44169	64515	44172	64518	44175	64521	44178	64523	44181	41
19	64523	44181	64526	44184	64529	44187	64532	44190	64535	44192	64538	44195	40
20	64538	44195	64540	44198	64543	44201	64546	44204	64549	44207	64552	44210	39
21	64552	44210	64555	44213	64557	44216	64560	44218	64563	44221	64566	44224	38
22	64566	44224	64569	44227	64572	44230	64575	44233	64577	44236	64580	44239	37
23	64580	44239	64583	44242	64586	44244	64589	44247	64592	44250	64594	44253	36
24	64594	44253	64597	44256	64600	44259	64603	44262	64606	44265	64609	44268	35
25	64609	44268	64611	44270	64614	44273	64617	44276	64620	44279	64623	44282	34
26	64623	44282	64626	44285	64628	44288	64631	44291	64634	44294	64637	44296	33
27	64637	44296	64640	44299	64643	44302	64645	44305	64648	44308	64651	44311	32
28	64651	44311	64654	44314	64657	44317	64660	44320	64662	44323	64665	44325	31
29	64665	44325	64668	44328	64671	44331	64674	44334	64677	44337	64679	44340	30
30	64679	44340	64682	44343	64685	44346	64688	44349	64691	44351	64694	44354	29
31	64694	44354	64696	44357	64699	44360	64702	44363	64705	44366	64708	44369	28
32	64708	44369	64711	44372	64713	44375	64716	44377	64719	44380	64722	44383	27
33	64722	44383	64725	44386	64727	44389	64730	44392	64733	44395	64736	44398	26
34	64736	44398	64739	44401	64742	44403	64745	44406	64747	44409	64750	44412	25
35	64750	44412	64753	44415	64756	44418	64759	44421	64761	44424	64764	44427	24
36	64764	44427	64767	44429	64770	44432	64773	44435	64776	44438	64778	44441	23
37	64778	44441	64781	44444	64784	44447	64787	44450	64790	44453	64793	44455	22
38	64793	44455	64795	44458	64798	44461	64801	44464	64804	44467	64807	44470	21
39	64807	44470	64809	44473	64812	44476	64815	44479	64818	44481	64821	44484	20
40	64821	44484	64824	44487	64826	44490	64829	44493	64832	44496	64835	44499	19
41	64835	44499	64838	44502	64840	44505	64843	44508	64846	44510	64849	44513	18
42	64849	44513	64852	44516	64855	44519	64857	44522	64860	44525	64863	44528	17
43	64863	44528	64866	44531	64869	44534	64872	44536	64874	44539	64877	44542	16
44	64877	44542	64880	44545	64883	44548	64886	44551	64888	44554	64891	44557	15
45	64891	44557	64894	44560	64897	44562	64900	44565	64903	44568	64905	44571	14
46	64905	44571	64908	44574	64911	44577	64914	44580	64917	44583	64919	44586	13
47	64919	44586	64922	44588	64925	44591	64928	44594	64931	44597	64934	44600	12
48	64934	44600	64936	44603	64939	44606	64942	44609	64945	44612	64948	44614	11
49	64948	44614	64950	44617	64953	44620	64956	44623	64959	44626	64962	44629	10
50	64962	44629	64964	44632	64967	44635	64970	44638	64973	44641	64976	44643	09
51	64976	44643	64979	44646	64981	44649	64984	44652	64987	44655	64990	44658	08
52	64990	44658	64993	44661	64995	44664	64998	44667	65001	44669	65004	44672	07
53	65004	44672	65007	44675	65009	44678	65012	44681	65015	44684	65018	44687	06
54	65018	44687	65021	44690	65024	44693	65026	44695	65029	44698	65032	44701	05
55	65032	44701	65035	44704	65038	44707	65040	44710	65043	44713	65046	44716	04
56	65046	44716	65049	44719	65052	44722	65054	44724	65057	44727	65060	44730	03
57	65060	44730	65063	44733	65066	44736	65069	44739	65071	44742	65074	44745	02
58	65074	44745	65077	44748	65080	44750	65083	44753	65085	44756	65088	44759	01
59	65088	44759	65091	44762	65094	44765	65097	44768	65099	44771	65102	44774	00

	.8		.6		.4		.2		.0	

PARTS for 0′.1: LOGS 1 NATURALS 1

276°

84° HAVERSINES

′	.0 Log. 1.or(9.)	.0 Nat. 0.	.2 Log. 1.or(9.)	.2 Nat. 0.	.4 Log. 1.or(9.)	.4 Nat. 0.	.6 Log. 1.or(9.)	.6 Nat. 0.	.8 Log. 1.or(9.)	.8 Nat. 0.	Log. 1.or(9.)	Nat. 0.	′
00	65102	44774	65105	44776	65108	44779	65111	44782	65113	44785	65116	44788	59
01	65116	44788	65119	44791	65122	44794	65125	44797	65127	44800	65130	44803	58
02	65130	44803	65133	44805	65136	44808	65139	44811	65141	44814	65144	44817	57
03	65144	44817	65147	44820	65150	44823	65153	44826	65155	44829	65158	44831	56
04	65158	44831	65161	44834	65164	44837	65167	44840	65169	44843	65172	44846	55
05	65172	44846	65175	44849	65178	44852	65181	44855	65183	44837	65186	44860	54
06	65186	44860	65189	44863	65192	44866	65195	44869	65197	44872	65200	44875	53
07	65200	44875	65203	44878	65206	44881	65209	44884	65211	44886	65214	44889	52
08	65214	44889	65217	44892	65220	44895	65223	44898	65225	44901	65228	44904	51
09	65228	44904	65231	44907	65234	44910	65237	44912	65239	44915	65242	44918	50
10	65242	44918	65245	44921	65248	44924	65251	44927	65253	44930	65256	44933	49
11	65256	44933	65259	44936	65262	44939	65265	44941	65267	44944	65270	44947	48
12	65270	44947	65273	44950	65276	44953	65279	44956	65281	44959	65284	44962	47
13	65284	44962	65287	44965	65290	44967	65293	44970	65295	44973	65298	44976	46
14	65298	44976	65301	44979	65304	44982	65307	44985	65309	44988	65312	44991	45
15	65312	44991	65315	44993	65318	44996	65321	44999	65323	45002	65326	45005	44
16	65326	45005	65329	45008	65332	45011	65335	45014	65337	45017	65340	45020	43
17	65340	45020	65343	45022	65346	45025	65348	45028	65351	45031	65354	45034	42
18	65354	45034	65357	45037	65360	45040	65362	45043	65365	45046	65368	45048	41
19	65368	45048	65371	45051	65374	45054	65376	45057	65379	45060	65382	45063	40
20	65382	45063	65385	45066	65388	45069	65390	45072	65393	45075	65396	45077	39
21	65396	45077	65399	45080	65402	45083	65404	45086	65407	45089	65410	45092	38
22	65410	45092	65413	45095	65415	45098	65418	45101	65421	45104	65424	45106	37
23	65424	45106	65427	45109	65429	45112	65432	45115	65435	45118	65438	45121	36
24	65438	45121	65441	45124	65443	45127	65446	45130	65449	45132	65452	45135	35
25	65452	45135	65454	45138	65457	45141	65460	45144	65463	45147	65466	45150	34
26	65466	45150	65468	45153	65471	45156	65474	45159	65477	45161	65480	45164	33
27	65480	45164	65482	45167	65485	45170	65488	45173	65491	45176	65493	45179	32
28	65493	45179	65496	45182	65499	45185	65502	45187	65505	45190	65507	45193	31
29	65507	45193	65510	45196	65513	45199	65516	45202	65518	45205	65521	45208	30
30	65521	45208	65524	45211	65527	45214	65530	45216	65532	45219	65535	45222	29
31	65535	45222	65538	45225	65541	45228	65543	45231	65546	45234	65549	45237	28
32	65549	45237	65552	45240	65555	45242	65557	45245	65560	45248	65563	45251	27
33	65563	45251	65566	45254	65569	45257	65571	45260	65574	45263	65577	45266	26
34	65577	45266	65580	45269	65582	45271	65585	45274	65588	45277	65591	45280	25
35	65591	45280	65594	45283	65596	45286	65599	45289	65602	45292	65605	45295	24
36	65605	45295	65607	45297	65610	45300	65613	45303	65616	45306	65619	45309	23
37	65619	45309	65621	45312	65624	45315	65627	45318	65630	45321	65632	45324	22
38	65632	45324	65635	45326	65638	45329	65641	45332	65643	45335	65646	45338	21
39	65646	45338	65649	45341	65652	45344	65655	45347	65657	45350	65660	45353	20
40	65660	45353	65663	45355	65666	45358	65668	45361	65671	45364	65674	45367	19
41	65674	45367	65677	45370	65680	45373	65682	45376	65685	45379	65688	45381	18
42	65688	45381	65691	45384	65693	45387	65696	45390	65699	45393	65702	45396	17
43	65702	45396	65705	45399	65707	45402	65710	45405	65713	45408	65716	45410	16
44	65716	45410	65718	45413	65721	45416	65724	45419	65727	45422	65729	45425	15
45	65729	45425	65732	45428	65735	45431	65738	45434	65740	45437	65743	45439	14
46	65743	45439	65746	45442	65749	45445	65752	45448	65754	45451	65757	45454	13
47	65757	45454	65760	45457	65763	45460	65765	45463	65768	45465	65771	45468	12
48	65771	45468	65774	45471	65777	45474	65779	45477	65782	45480	65785	45483	11
49	65785	45483	65788	45486	65790	45489	65793	45492	65796	45494	65799	45497	10
50	65799	45497	65801	45500	65804	45503	65807	45506	65810	45509	65812	45512	09
51	65812	45512	65815	45515	65818	45518	65821	45521	65823	45523	65826	45526	08
52	65826	45526	65829	45529	65832	45532	65834	45535	65837	45538	65840	45541	07
53	65840	45541	65843	45544	65846	45547	65848	45550	65851	45552	65854	45555	06
54	65854	45555	65857	45558	65859	45561	65862	45564	65865	45567	65868	45570	05
55	65868	45570	65870	45573	65873	45576	65876	45578	65879	45581	65881	45584	04
56	65881	45584	65884	45587	65887	45590	65890	45593	65892	45596	65895	45599	03
57	65895	45599	65898	45602	65901	45605	65903	45607	65906	45610	65909	45613	02
58	65909	45613	65912	45616	65915	45619	65917	45622	65920	45625	65923	45628	01
59	65923	45628	65926	45631	65928	45634	65931	45636	65934	45639	65937	45642	00

.8   .6   .4   .2   .0 ←

275°

PARTS for 0′.1:   LOGS 1   NATURALS 1

85° HAVERSINES

′	.0 Log. 1̄.or(9.)	.0 Nat. 0.	.2 Log. 1̄.or(9.)	.2 Nat. 0.	.4 Log. 1̄.or(9.)	.4 Nat. 0.	.6 Log. 1̄.or(9.)	.6 Nat. 0.	.8 Log. 1̄.or(9.)	.8 Nat. 0.	Log. 1̄.or(9.)	Nat. 0.	′
00	65937	45642	65939	45645	65942	45648	65945	45651	65948	45654	65950	45657	59
01	65950	45657	65953	45660	65956	45663	65959	45665	65961	45668	65964	45671	58
02	65964	45671	65967	45674	65970	45677	65972	45680	65975	45683	65978	45686	57
03	65978	45686	65981	45689	65984	45691	65986	45694	65989	45697	65992	45700	56
04	65992	45700	65995	45703	65997	45706	66000	45709	66003	45712	66006	45715	55
05	66006	45715	66008	45718	66011	45720	66014	45723	66017	45726	66019	45729	54
06	66019	45729	66022	45732	66025	45735	66028	45738	66030	45741	66033	45744	53
07	66033	45744	66036	45747	66039	45749	66041	45752	66044	45755	66047	45758	52
08	66047	45758	66050	45761	66052	45764	66055	45767	66058	45770	66061	45773	51
09	66061	45773	66063	45776	66066	45778	66069	45781	66072	45784	66074	45787	50
10	66074	45787	66077	45790	66080	45793	66083	45796	66085	45799	66088	45802	49
11	66088	45802	66091	45805	66094	45807	66096	45810	66099	45813	66102	45816	48
12	66102	45816	66105	45819	66107	45822	66110	45825	66113	45828	66116	45831	47
13	66116	45831	66118	45834	66121	45836	66124	45839	66126	45842	66129	45845	46
14	66129	45845	66132	45848	66135	45851	66137	45854	66140	45857	66143	45860	45
15	66143	45860	66146	45863	66149	45865	66151	45868	66154	45871	66157	45874	44
16	66157	45874	66160	45877	66162	45880	66165	45883	66168	45886	66170	45889	43
17	66170	45889	66173	45891	66176	45894	66179	45897	66181	45900	66184	45903	42
18	66184	45903	66187	45906	66190	45909	66192	45912	66195	45915	66198	45918	41
19	66198	45918	66201	45920	66203	45923	66206	45926	66209	45929	66212	45932	40
20	66212	45932	66214	45935	66217	45938	66220	45941	66223	45944	66225	45947	39
21	66225	45947	66228	45949	66231	45952	66234	45955	66236	45958	66239	45961	38
22	66239	45961	66242	45964	66244	45967	66247	45970	66250	45973	66253	45976	37
23	66253	45976	66255	45978	66258	45981	66261	45984	66264	45987	66266	45990	36
24	66266	45990	66269	45993	66272	45996	66275	45999	66277	46002	66280	46005	35
25	66280	46005	66283	46007	66286	46010	66288	46013	66291	46016	66294	46019	34
26	66294	46019	66297	46022	66299	46025	66302	46028	66305	46031	66307	46034	33
27	66307	46034	66310	46036	66313	46039	66316	46042	66318	46045	66321	46048	32
28	66321	46048	66324	46051	66327	46054	66329	46057	66332	46060	66335	46063	31
29	66335	46063	66338	46065	66340	46068	66343	46071	66346	46074	66348	46077	30
30	66348	46077	66351	46080	66354	46083	66357	46086	66359	46089	66362	46092	29
31	66362	46092	66365	46094	66368	46097	66370	46100	66373	46103	66376	46106	28
32	66376	46106	66379	46109	66381	46112	66384	46115	66387	46118	66389	46121	27
33	66389	46121	66392	46123	66395	46126	66398	46129	66400	46132	66403	46135	26
34	66403	46135	66406	46138	66409	46141	66411	46144	66414	46147	66417	46150	25
35	66417	46150	66420	46152	66422	46155	66425	46158	66428	46161	66430	46164	24
36	66430	46164	66433	46167	66436	46170	66439	46173	66441	46176	66444	46179	23
37	66444	46179	66447	46181	66449	46184	66452	46187	66455	46190	66458	46193	22
38	66458	46193	66460	46196	66463	46199	66466	46202	66468	46205	66471	46208	21
39	66471	46208	66474	46210	66477	46213	66479	46216	66482	46219	66485	46222	20
40	66485	46222	66488	46225	66490	46228	66493	46231	66496	46234	66499	46237	19
41	66499	46237	66501	46239	66504	46242	66507	46245	66509	46248	66512	46251	18
42	66512	46251	66515	46254	66518	46257	66520	46260	66523	46263	66526	46266	17
43	66526	46266	66529	46268	66531	46271	66534	46274	66537	46277	66539	46280	16
44	66539	46280	66542	46283	66545	46286	66548	46289	66550	46292	66553	46295	15
45	66553	46295	66556	46298	66558	46300	66561	46303	66564	46306	66567	46309	14
46	66567	46309	66569	46312	66572	46315	66575	46318	66577	46321	66580	46324	13
47	66580	46324	66583	46327	66586	46329	66588	46332	66591	46335	66594	46338	12
48	66594	46338	66597	46341	66599	46344	66602	46347	66605	46350	66607	46353	11
49	66607	46353	66610	46356	66613	46358	66616	46361	66618	46364	66621	46367	10
50	66621	46367	66624	46370	66626	46373	66629	46376	66632	46379	66635	46382	09
51	66635	46382	66637	46385	66640	46387	66643	46390	66645	46393	66648	46396	08
52	66648	46396	66651	46399	66654	46402	66656	46405	66659	46408	66662	46411	07
53	66662	46411	66665	46414	66667	46416	66670	46419	66673	46422	66675	46425	06
54	66675	46425	66678	46428	66681	46431	66683	46434	66686	46437	66689	46440	05
55	66689	46440	66692	46443	66694	46445	66697	46448	66700	46451	66702	46454	04
56	66702	46454	66705	46457	66708	46460	66711	46463	66713	46466	66716	46469	03
57	66716	46469	66719	46472	66721	46474	66724	46477	66727	46480	66730	46483	02
58	66730	46483	66732	46486	66735	46489	66738	46492	66740	46495	66743	46498	01
59	66743	46498	66746	46501	66749	46503	66751	46506	66754	46509	66757	46512	00

| | .8 | .6 | .4 | .2 | .0 ← |

PARTS for 0′.1:   LOGS 1   NATURALS 1

274°

86° HAVERSINES

′	.0 Log. 1.or(9.)	.0 Nat. 0.	.2 Log. 1.or(9.)	.2 Nat. 0.	4 Log. 1.or(9.)	4 Nat. 0.	.6 Log. 1.or(9.)	.6 Nat. 0.	.8 Log. 1.or(9.)	.8 Nat. 0.	.8 Log. 1.or(9.)	.8 Nat. 0.	′
00	66757	46512	66759	46515	66762	46518	66765	46521	66767	46524	66770	46527	59
01	66770	46527	66773	46530	66776	46533	66778	46535	66781	46538	66784	46541	58
02	66784	46541	66786	46544	66789	46547	66792	46550	66795	46553	66797	46556	57
03	66797	46556	66800	46559	66803	46562	66805	46564	66808	46567	66811	46570	56
04	66811	46570	66814	46573	66816	46576	66819	46579	66822	46582	66824	46585	55
05	66824	46585	66827	46588	66830	46591	66832	46593	66835	46596	66838	46599	54
06	66838	46599	66841	46602	66843	46605	66846	46608	66849	46611	66851	46614	53
07	66851	46614	66854	46617	66857	46620	66860	46622	66862	46625	66865	46628	52
08	66865	46628	66868	46631	66870	46634	66873	46637	66876	46640	66878	46643	51
09	66878	46643	66881	46646	66884	46649	66887	46651	66889	46654	66892	46657	50
10	66892	46657	66895	46660	66897	46663	66900	46666	66903	46669	66905	46672	49
11	66905	46672	66908	46675	66911	46678	66914	46681	66916	46683	66919	46686	48
12	66919	46686	66922	46689	66924	46692	66927	46695	66930	46698	66932	46701	47
13	66932	46701	66935	46704	66938	46707	66941	46710	66943	46712	66946	46715	46
14	66946	46715	66949	46718	66951	46721	66954	46724	66957	46727	66959	46730	45
15	66959	46730	66962	46733	66965	46736	66968	46739	66970	46741	66973	46744	44
16	66973	46744	66976	46747	66978	46750	66981	46753	66984	46756	66986	46759	43
17	66986	46759	66989	46762	66992	46765	66994	46767	66997	46770	67000	46773	42
18	67000	46773	67003	46776	67005	46779	67008	46782	67011	46785	67013	46788	41
19	67013	46788	67016	46791	67019	46794	67021	46797	67024	46800	67027	46802	40
20	67027	46802	67029	46805	67032	46808	67035	46811	67038	46814	67040	46817	39
21	67040	46817	67043	46820	67046	46823	67048	46826	67051	46829	67054	46831	38
22	67054	46831	67056	46834	67059	46837	67062	46840	67065	46843	67067	46846	37
23	67067	46846	67070	46849	67073	46852	67075	46855	67078	46858	67081	46860	36
24	67081	46860	67083	46863	67086	46866	67089	46869	67091	46872	67094	46875	35
25	67094	46875	67097	46878	67100	46881	67102	46884	67105	46887	67108	46890	34
26	67108	46890	67110	46892	67113	46895	67116	46898	67118	46901	67121	46904	33
27	67121	46904	67124	46907	67126	46910	67129	46913	67132	46916	67134	46919	32
28	67134	46919	67137	46921	67140	46924	67142	46927	67145	46930	67148	46933	31
29	67148	46933	67151	46936	67153	46939	67156	46942	67159	46945	67161	46948	30
30	67161	46948	67164	46950	67167	46953	67169	46956	67172	46959	67175	46962	29
31	67175	46962	67177	46965	67180	46968	67183	46971	67186	46974	67188	46977	28
32	67188	46977	67191	46980	67194	46982	67196	46985	67199	46988	67202	46991	27
33	67202	46991	67204	46994	67207	46997	67210	47000	67212	47003	67215	47006	26
34	67215	47006	67218	47009	67220	47011	67223	47014	67226	47017	67228	47020	25
35	67228	47020	67231	47023	67234	47026	67236	47029	67239	47032	67242	47035	24
36	67242	47035	67244	47038	67247	47041	67250	47043	67253	47046	67255	47049	23
37	67255	47049	67258	47052	67261	47055	67263	47058	67266	47061	67269	47064	22
38	67269	47064	67271	47067	67274	47070	67277	47072	67279	47075	67282	47078	21
39	67282	47078	67285	47081	67287	47084	67290	47087	67293	47090	67295	47093	20
40	67295	47093	67298	47096	67301	47099	67303	47101	67306	47104	67309	47107	19
41	67309	47107	67311	47110	67314	47113	67317	47116	67320	47119	67322	47122	18
42	67322	47122	67325	47125	67328	47128	67330	47131	67333	47133	67336	47136	17
43	67336	47136	67338	47139	67341	47142	67344	47145	67346	47148	67349	47151	16
44	67349	47151	67352	47154	67354	47157	67357	47160	67360	47162	67362	47165	15
45	67362	47165	67365	47168	67368	47171	67370	47174	67373	47177	67376	47180	14
46	67376	47180	67378	47183	67381	47186	67384	47189	67386	47192	67389	47194	13
47	67389	47194	67392	47197	67394	47200	67397	47203	67400	47206	67402	47209	12
48	67402	47209	67405	47212	67408	47215	67410	47218	67413	47221	67416	47223	11
49	67416	47223	67418	47226	67421	47229	67424	47232	67427	47235	67429	47238	10
50	67429	47238	67432	47241	67434	47244	67437	47247	67440	47250	67442	47252	09
51	67442	47252	67445	47255	67448	47258	67450	47261	67453	47264	67456	47267	08
52	67456	47267	67458	47270	67461	47273	67464	47276	67467	47279	67469	47282	07
53	67469	47282	67472	47284	67474	47287	67477	47290	67480	47293	67482	47296	06
54	67482	47296	67485	47299	67488	47302	67490	47305	67493	47308	67496	47311	05
55	67496	47311	67498	47314	67501	47316	67504	47319	67507	47322	67509	47325	04
56	67509	47325	67512	47328	67514	47331	67517	47334	67520	47337	67522	47340	03
57	67522	47340	67525	47343	67528	47345	67530	47348	67533	47351	67536	47354	02
58	67536	47354	67538	47357	67541	47360	67544	47363	67547	47366	67549	47369	01
59	67549	47369	67552	47372	67554	47375	67557	47377	67560	47380	67562	47383	00

.8 .6 .4 .2 .0 ←

PARTS for 0′.1: LOGS 1 NATURALS 1

273°

87° HAVERSINES

→

	.0		.2		.4		.6		.8			
	Log.	Nat.	Log.	Nat.	Log.	Nat.	Log.	Nat.	Log.	Nat.	Log.	Nat.
′	1̄.or(9.)	0.	1̄.or(9.)	0.	1̄.or(9.)	0.	1̄.or(9.)	0.	1̄.or(9.)	0.	1̄.or(9.)	0.	′
00	67562	47383	67565	47386	67568	47389	67570	47392	67573	47395	67576	47398	59
01	67576	47398	67578	47401	67581	47404	67584	47406	67586	47409	67589	47412	58
02	67589	47412	67592	47415	67594	47418	67597	47421	67600	47424	67602	47427	57
03	67602	47427	67605	47430	67608	47433	67610	47436	67613	47438	67616	47441	56
04	67616	47441	67618	47444	67621	47447	67624	47450	67626	47453	67629	47456	55
05	67629	47456	67632	47459	67634	47462	67637	47465	67640	47467	67642	47470	54
06	67642	47470	67645	47473	67648	47476	67650	47479	67653	47482	67656	47485	53
07	67656	47485	67658	47488	67661	47491	67664	47494	67666	47497	67669	47499	52
08	67669	47499	67671	47502	67674	47505	67677	47508	67679	47511	67682	47514	51
09	67682	47514	67685	47517	67687	47520	67690	47523	67693	47526	67695	47528	50
10	67695	47528	67698	47531	67701	47534	67703	47537	67706	47540	67709	47543	49
11	67709	47543	67711	47546	67714	47549	67717	47552	67719	47555	67722	47558	48
12	67722	47558	67725	47560	67727	47563	67730	47566	67733	47569	67735	47572	47
13	67735	47572	67738	47575	67740	47578	67743	47581	67746	47584	67748	47587	46
14	67748	47587	67751	47589	67754	47592	67756	47595	67759	47598	67762	47601	45
15	67762	47601	67764	47604	67767	47607	67770	47610	67772	47613	67775	47616	44
16	67775	47616	67778	47619	67780	47621	67783	47624	67786	47627	67788	47630	43
17	67788	47630	67791	47633	67793	47636	67796	47639	67799	47642	67801	47645	42
18	67801	47645	67804	47648	67807	47651	67809	47653	67812	47656	67815	47659	41
19	67815	47659	67817	47662	67820	47665	67823	47668	67825	47671	67828	47674	40
20	67828	47674	67831	47677	67833	47680	67836	47682	67839	47685	67841	47688	39
21	67841	47688	67844	47691	67846	47694	67849	47697	67852	47700	67854	47703	38
22	67854	47703	67857	47706	67860	47709	67862	47712	67865	47714	67868	47717	37
23	67868	47717	67870	47720	67873	47723	67876	47726	67878	47719	67881	47732	36
24	67881	47732	67883	47735	67886	47738	67889	47741	67891	47743	67894	47746	35
25	67894	47746	67897	47749	67899	47752	67902	47755	67905	47758	67907	47761	34
26	67907	47761	67910	47764	67912	47767	67915	47770	67918	47773	67920	47775	33
27	67920	47775	67923	47778	67926	47781	67928	47784	67931	47787	67934	47790	32
28	67934	47790	67936	47793	67939	47796	67942	47799	67944	47802	67947	47805	31
29	67947	47805	67949	47807	67952	47810	67955	47813	67957	47816	67960	47819	30
30	67960	47819	67963	47822	67965	47825	67968	47828	67971	47831	67973	47834	29
31	67973	47834	67976	47836	67978	47839	67981	47842	67984	47845	67986	47848	28
32	67986	47848	67989	47851	67992	47854	67994	47857	67997	47860	68000	47863	27
33	68000	47863	68002	47866	68005	47868	68008	47871	68010	47874	68013	47877	26
34	68013	47877	68015	47880	68018	47883	68021	47886	68023	47889	68026	47892	25
35	68026	47892	68029	47895	68031	47898	68034	47900	68037	47903	68039	47906	24
36	68039	47906	68042	47909	68044	47912	68047	47915	68050	47918	68052	47921	23
37	68052	47921	68055	47924	68058	47927	68060	47929	68063	47932	68066	47935	22
38	68066	47935	68068	47938	68071	47941	68073	47944	68076	47947	68079	47950	21
39	68079	47950	68081	47953	68084	47956	68087	47959	68089	47961	68092	47964	20
40	68092	47964	68094	47967	68097	47970	68100	47973	68102	47976	68105	47979	19
41	68105	47979	68108	47982	68110	47985	68113	47988	68116	47991	68118	47993	18
42	68118	47993	68121	47996	68123	47999	68126	48002	68129	48005	68131	48008	17
43	68131	48008	68134	48011	68137	48014	68139	48017	68142	48020	68144	48022	16
44	68144	48022	68147	48025	68150	48028	68152	48031	68155	48034	68158	48037	15
45	68158	48037	68160	48040	68163	48043	68166	48046	68168	48049	68171	48052	14
46	68171	48052	68173	48054	68176	48057	68179	48060	68181	48063	68184	48066	13
47	68184	48066	68186	48069	68189	48072	68192	48075	68194	48078	68197	48081	12
48	68197	48081	68200	48084	68202	48086	68205	48089	68208	48092	68210	48095	11
49	68210	48095	68213	48098	68215	48101	68218	48104	68221	48107	68223	48110	10
50	68223	48110	68226	48113	68228	48116	68231	48118	68234	48121	68236	48124	09
51	68236	48124	68239	48127	68242	48130	68244	48133	68247	48136	68249	48139	08
52	68249	48139	68252	48142	68255	48145	68257	48147	68260	48150	68263	48153	07
53	68263	48153	68265	48156	68268	48159	68270	48162	68273	48165	68276	48168	06
54	68276	48168	68278	48171	68281	48174	68284	48177	68286	48179	68289	48182	05
55	68289	48182	68291	48185	68294	48188	68297	48191	68299	48194	68302	48197	04
56	68302	48197	68304	48200	68307	48203	68310	48206	68312	48209	68315	48211	03
57	68315	48211	68318	48214	68320	48217	68323	48220	68325	48223	68328	48226	02
58	68328	48226	68331	48229	68333	48232	68336	48235	68339	48238	68341	48241	01
59	68341	48241	68344	48243	68346	48246	68349	48249	68352	48252	68354	48255	00
		.8		.6		.4		.2		.0		←	

PARTS for 0′.1: LOGS 1. NATURALS, 1.

272°

HAVERSINES

88°

′	0 Log. $\overline{1}$.or(9.)	0 Nat. 0.	.2 Log. $\overline{1}$.or(9.)	.2 Nat. 0.	.4 Log. $\overline{1}$.or(9.)	.4 Nat. 0.	.6 Log. $\overline{1}$.or(9.)	.6 Nat. 0.	.8 Log. $\overline{1}$.or(9.)	.8 Nat. 0.	Log. $\overline{1}$.or(9.)	Nat. 0.	′
00	68354	48255	68357	48258	68359	48261	68362	48264	68365	48267	68367	48270	59
01	68367	48270	68370	48272	68373	48275	68375	48278	68378	48281	68380	48284	58
02	68380	48284	68383	48287	68386	48290	68388	48293	68391	48296	68393	48299	57
03	68393	48299	68396	48302	68399	48304	68401	48307	68404	48310	68407	48313	56
04	68407	48313	68409	48316	68412	48319	68414	48322	68417	48325	68420	48328	55
05	68420	48328	68422	48331	68425	48334	68427	48336	68430	48339	68433	48342	54
06	68433	48342	68435	48345	68438	48348	68441	48351	68443	48354	68446	48357	53
07	68446	48357	68448	48360	68451	48363	68454	48366	68456	48368	68459	48371	52
08	68459	48371	68461	48374	68464	48377	68467	48380	68469	48383	68472	48386	51
09	68472	48386	68474	48389	68477	48392	68480	48395	68482	48397	68485	48400	50
10	68485	48400	68487	48403	68490	48406	68493	48409	68495	48412	68498	48415	49
11	68498	48415	68501	48418	68503	48421	68506	48424	68508	48427	68511	48429	48
12	68511	48429	68514	48432	68516	48435	68519	48438	68521	48441	68524	48444	47
13	68524	48444	68527	48447	68529	48450	68532	48453	68534	48456	68537	48459	46
14	68537	48459	68540	48461	68542	48464	68545	48467	68547	48470	68550	48473	45
15	68550	48473	68553	48476	68555	48479	68558	48482	68560	48485	68563	48488	44
16	68563	48488	68566	48491	68568	48493	68571	48496	68573	48499	68576	48502	43
17	68576	48502	68579	48505	68581	48508	68584	48511	68587	48514	68589	48517	42
18	68589	48517	68592	48520	68594	48523	68597	48525	68600	48528	68602	48531	41
19	68602	48531	68605	48534	68607	48537	68610	48540	68613	48543	68615	48546	40
20	68615	48546	68618	48549	68620	48552	68623	48554	68626	48557	68628	48560	39
21	68628	48560	68631	48563	68633	48566	68636	48569	68639	48572	68641	48575	38
22	68641	48575	68644	48578	68646	48581	68649	48584	68652	48586	68654	48589	37
23	68654	48589	68657	48592	68659	48595	68662	48598	68665	48601	68667	48604	36
24	68667	48604	68670	48607	68672	48610	68675	48613	68678	48616	68680	48618	35
25	68680	48618	68683	48621	68685	48624	68688	48627	68691	48630	68693	48633	34
26	68693	48633	68696	48636	68698	48639	68701	48642	68703	48645	68706	48648	33
27	68706	48648	68709	48650	68711	48653	68714	48656	68716	48659	68719	48662	32
28	68719	48662	68722	48665	68724	48668	68727	48671	68729	48674	68732	48677	31
29	68732	48677	68735	48680	68737	48682	68740	48685	68742	48688	68745	48691	30
30	68745	48691	68748	48694	68750	48697	68753	48700	68755	48703	68758	48706	29
31	68758	48706	68761	48709	68763	48712	68766	48714	68768	48717	68771	48720	28
32	68771	48720	68774	48723	68776	48726	68779	48729	68781	48732	68784	48735	27
33	68784	48735	68786	48738	68789	48741	68792	48743	68794	48746	68797	48749	26
34	68797	48749	68799	48752	68802	48755	68805	48758	68807	48761	68810	48764	25
35	68810	48764	68812	48767	68815	48770	68818	48773	68820	48775	68823	48778	24
36	68823	48778	68825	48781	68828	48784	68830	48787	68833	48790	68836	48793	23
37	68836	48793	68838	48796	68841	48799	68843	48802	68846	48805	68849	48807	22
38	68849	48807	68851	48810	68854	48813	68856	48816	68859	48819	68862	48822	21
39	68862	48822	68864	48825	68867	48828	68869	48831	68872	48834	63874	48837	20
40	68874	48837	68877	48839	68880	48842	68882	48845	68885	48848	68887	48851	19
41	68887	48851	68890	48854	68893	48857	68895	48860	68898	48863	68900	48866	18
42	68900	48866	68903	48869	68906	48871	68908	48874	68911	48877	68913	48880	17
43	68913	48880	68916	48883	68918	48886	68921	48889	68924	48892	68926	48895	16
44	68926	48895	68929	48898	68931	48901	68934	48903	68937	48906	68939	48909	15
45	68939	48909	68942	48912	68944	48915	68947	48918	68949	48921	68952	48924	14
46	68952	48924	68955	48927	68957	48930	68960	48933	68962	48935	68965	48938	13
47	68965	48938	68968	48941	68970	48944	68973	48947	68975	48950	68978	48953	12
48	68978	48953	68980	48956	68983	48959	68986	48962	68988	48965	68991	48967	11
49	68991	48967	68993	48970	68996	48973	68998	48976	69001	48979	69004	48982	10
50	69004	48982	69006	48985	69009	48988	69011	48991	69014	48994	69017	48997	09
51	69017	48997	69019	48999	69022	49002	69024	49005	69027	49008	69029	49011	08
52	69029	49011	69032	49014	69035	49017	69037	49020	69040	49023	69042	49026	07
53	69042	49026	69045	49029	69047	49031	69050	49034	69053	49037	69055	49040	06
54	69055	49040	69058	49043	69060	49046	69063	49049	69065	49052	69068	49055	05
55	69068	49055	69071	49058	69073	49060	69076	49063	69078	49066	69081	49069	04
56	69081	49069	69084	49072	69086	49075	69089	49078	69091	49081	69094	49084	03
57	69094	49084	69096	49087	69099	49090	69101	49092	69104	49095	69107	49098	02
58	69107	49098	69109	49101	69112	49104	69114	49107	69117	49110	69120	49113	01
59	69120	49113	69122	49116	69125	49119	69127	49122	69130	49124	69132	49127	00

| .8 | .6 | .4 | .2 | .0 |

PARTS for 0′.1: LOGS 1 NATURALS 1

271°

89° HAVERSINES

→

'	.0 Log. $\overline{1}$.or(9.)	.0 Nat. 0.	.2 Log. $\overline{1}$.or(9.)	.2 Nat. 0.	.4 Log. $\overline{1}$.or(9.)	.4 Nat. 0.	.6 Log. $\overline{1}$.or(9.)	.6 Nat. 0.	.8 Log. $\overline{1}$.or(9.)	.8 Nat. 0.	Log. $\overline{1}$.or(9.)	Nat. 0.	'
00	69132	49127	69135	49130	69138	49133	69140	49136	69143	49139	69145	49142	59
01	69145	49142	69148	49145	69150	49148	69153	49151	69155	49154	69158	49156	58
02	69158	49156	69161	49159	69163	49162	69166	49165	69168	49168	69171	49171	57
03	69171	49171	69174	49174	69176	49177	69179	49180	69181	49183	69184	49186	56
04	69184	49186	69186	49188	69189	49191	69191	49194	69194	49197	69197	49200	55
05	69197	49200	69199	49203	69202	49206	69204	49209	69207	49212	69209	49215	54
06	69209	49215	69212	49218	69215	49220	69217	49223	69220	49226	69222	49229	53
07	69222	49229	69225	49232	69227	49235	69230	49238	69232	49241	69235	49244	52
08	69235	49244	69238	49247	69240	49250	69243	49252	69245	49255	69248	49258	51
09	69248	49258	69251	49261	69253	49264	69256	49267	69258	49270	69261	49273	50
10	69261	49273	69263	49276	69266	49279	69268	49282	69271	49284	69274	49287	49
11	69274	49287	69276	49290	69279	49293	69281	49296	69284	49299	69286	49302	48
12	69286	49302	69289	49305	69292	49308	69294	49311	69297	49314	69299	49316	47
13	69299	49316	69302	49319	69304	49322	69307	49325	69309	49328	69312	49331	46
14	69312	49331	69315	49334	69317	49337	69320	49340	69322	49343	69325	49346	45
15	69325	49346	69327	49348	69330	49351	69332	49354	69335	49357	69338	49360	44
16	69338	49360	69340	49363	69343	49366	69345	49369	69348	49372	69350	49375	43
17	69350	49375	69353	49378	69356	49380	69358	49383	69361	49386	69363	49389	42
18	69363	49389	69366	49392	69368	49395	69371	49398	69373	49401	69376	49404	41
19	69376	49404	69379	49407	69381	49410	69384	49412	69386	49415	69389	49418	40
20	69389	49418	69391	49421	69394	49424	69396	49427	69399	49430	69402	49433	39
21	69402	49433	69404	49436	69407	49439	69409	49442	69412	49444	69414	49447	38
22	69414	49447	69417	49450	69419	49453	69422	49456	69424	49459	69427	49462	37
23	69427	49462	69430	49465	69432	49468	69435	49471	69437	49473	69440	49476	36
24	69440	49476	69442	49479	69445	49482	69447	49485	69450	49488	69453	49491	35
25	69453	49491	69455	49494	69458	49497	69460	49500	69463	49503	69465	49506	34
26	69465	49506	69468	49508	69471	49511	69473	49514	69476	49517	69478	49520	33
27	69478	49520	69481	49523	69483	49526	69486	49529	69488	49532	69491	49535	32
28	69491	49535	69493	49538	69496	49540	69498	49543	69501	49546	69504	49549	31
29	69504	49549	69506	49552	69509	49555	69511	49558	69514	49561	69516	49564	30
30	69516	49564	69519	49567	69522	49569	69524	49572	69527	49575	69529	49578	29
31	69529	49578	69532	49581	69534	49584	69537	49587	69539	49590	69542	49593	28
32	69542	49593	69544	49596	69547	49599	69549	49601	69552	49604	69555	49607	27
33	69555	49607	69557	49610	69560	49613	69562	49616	69565	49619	69567	49622	26
34	69567	49622	69570	49625	69572	49628	69575	49631	69577	49633	69580	49636	25
35	69580	49636	69583	49639	69585	49642	69588	49645	69590	49648	69593	49651	24
36	69593	49651	69595	49654	69598	49657	69600	49660	69603	49663	69605	49665	23
37	69605	49665	69608	49668	69611	49671	69613	49674	69616	49677	69618	49680	22
38	69618	49680	69621	49683	69623	49686	69626	49689	69628	49692	69631	49695	21
39	69631	49695	69634	49697	69636	49700	69639	49703	69641	49706	69644	49709	20
40	69644	49709	69646	49712	69649	49715	69651	49718	69654	49721	69656	49724	19
41	69656	49724	69659	49727	69661	49729	69664	49732	69666	49735	69669	49738	18
42	69669	49738	69672	49741	69674	49744	69677	49747	69679	49750	69682	49753	17
43	69682	49753	69684	49756	69687	49759	69689	49761	69692	49764	69694	49767	16
44	69694	49767	69697	49770	69699	49773	69702	49776	69704	49779	69707	49782	15
45	69707	49782	69710	49785	69712	49788	69715	49791	69717	49793	69720	49796	14
46	69720	49796	69722	49799	69725	49802	69727	49805	69730	49808	69732	49811	13
47	69732	49811	69735	49814	69738	49817	69740	49820	69743	49823	69745	49825	12
48	69745	49825	69748	49828	69750	49831	69753	49834	69755	49837	69758	49840	11
49	69758	49840	69760	49843	69763	49846	69765	49849	69768	49852	69770	49855	10
50	69770	49855	69773	49857	69776	49860	69778	49863	69781	49866	69783	49869	09
51	69783	49869	69786	49872	69788	49875	69791	49878	69793	49881	69796	49884	08
52	69796	49884	69798	49887	69801	49889	69803	49892	69806	49895	69808	49898	07
53	69808	49898	69811	49901	69814	49904	69816	49907	69819	49910	69821	49913	06
54	69821	49913	69824	49916	69826	49919	69829	49921	69831	49924	69834	49927	05
55	69834	49927	69836	49930	69839	49933	69841	49936	69844	49939	69846	49942	04
56	69846	49942	69849	49945	69851	49948	69854	49951	69856	49953	69859	49956	03
57	69859	49956	69862	49959	69864	49962	69867	49965	69869	49968	69872	49971	02
58	69872	49971	69874	49974	69877	49977	69879	49980	69882	49983	69884	49985	01
59	69884	49985	69887	49988	69889	49991	69892	49994	69894	49997	69897	50000	00

| | .8 | | .6 | | .4 | | .2 | | .0 ← | | | |

270°

PARTS for 0'.1:   LOGS 1   NATURALS 1

90° HAVERSINES

′	.0 Log. 1̄.or(9.)	.0 Nat. 0.	.2 Log. 1̄.or(9.)	.2 Nat. 0.	.4 Log. 1̄.or(9.)	.4 Nat. 0.	.6 Log. 1̄.or(9.)	.6 Nat. 0.	.8 Log. 1̄.or(9.)	.8 Nat. 0.	Log. 1̄.or(9.)	Nat. 0.	′
00	69897	50000	69900	50003	69902	50006	69905	50009	69907	50012	69910	50015	59
01	69910	50015	69912	50017	69915	50020	69917	50023	69920	50026	69922	50029	58
02	69922	50029	69925	50032	69927	50035	69930	50038	69932	50041	69935	50044	57
03	69935	50044	69937	50047	69940	50049	69942	50052	69945	50055	69948	50058	56
04	69948	50058	69950	50061	69953	50064	69955	50067	69958	50070	69960	50073	55
05	69960	50073	69963	50076	69965	50079	69968	50081	69970	50084	69973	50087	54
06	69973	50087	69975	50090	69978	50093	69980	50096	69983	50099	69985	50102	53
07	69985	50102	69988	50105	69990	50108	69993	50111	69995	50113	69998	50116	52
08	69998	50116	70001	50119	70003	50122	70006	50125	70008	50128	70011	50131	51
09	70011	50131	70013	50134	70016	50137	70018	50140	70021	50143	70023	50145	50
10	70023	50145	70026	50148	70028	50151	70031	50154	70033	50157	70036	50160	49
11	70036	50160	70038	50163	70041	50166	70043	50169	70046	50172	70048	50175	48
12	70048	50175	70051	50177	70053	50180	70056	50183	70058	50186	70061	50189	47
13	70061	50189	70064	50192	70066	50195	70069	50198	70071	50201	70074	50204	46
14	70074	50204	70076	50207	70079	50209	70081	50212	70084	50215	70086	50218	45
15	70086	50218	70089	50221	70091	50224	70094	50227	70096	50230	70099	50233	44
16	70099	50233	70101	50236	70104	50239	70106	50241	70109	50244	70111	50247	43
17	70111	50247	70114	50250	70116	50253	70119	50256	70121	50259	70124	50262	42
18	70124	50262	70126	50265	70129	50268	70131	50271	70134	50273	70136	50276	41
19	70136	50276	70139	50279	70141	50282	70144	50285	70146	50288	70149	50291	40
20	70149	50291	70151	50294	70154	50297	70156	50300	70159	50303	70161	50305	39
21	70161	50305	70164	50308	70166	50311	70169	50314	70171	50317	70174	50320	38
22	70174	50320	70177	50323	70179	50326	70182	50329	70184	50332	70187	50335	37
23	70187	50335	70189	50337	70192	50340	70194	50343	70197	50346	70199	50349	36
24	70199	50349	70202	50352	70204	50355	70207	50358	70209	50361	70212	50364	35
25	70212	50364	70214	50367	70217	50369	70219	50372	70222	50375	70224	50378	34
26	70224	50378	70227	50381	70229	50384	70232	50387	70234	50390	70237	50393	33
27	70237	50393	70239	50396	70242	50399	70244	50401	70247	50404	70249	50407	32
28	70249	50407	70252	50410	70254	50413	70257	50416	70259	50419	70262	50422	31
29	70262	50422	70264	50425	70267	50428	70269	50431	70272	50433	70274	50436	30
30	70274	50436	70277	50439	70279	50442	70282	50445	70284	50448	70287	50451	29
31	70287	50451	70289	50454	70292	50457	70294	50460	70297	50462	70299	50465	28
32	70299	50465	70302	50468	70304	50471	70307	50474	70309	50477	70312	50480	27
33	70312	50480	70314	50483	70317	50486	70319	50489	70322	50492	70324	50495	26
34	70324	50495	70327	50497	70329	50500	70332	50503	70334	50506	70337	50509	25
35	70337	50509	70339	50512	70342	50515	70344	50518	70347	50521	70349	50524	24
36	70349	50524	70352	50527	70354	50529	70357	50532	70359	50535	70362	50538	23
37	70362	50538	70364	50541	70367	50544	70369	50547	70372	50550	70374	50553	22
38	70374	50553	70377	50556	70379	50559	70382	50561	70384	50564	70387	50567	21
39	70387	50567	70389	50570	70392	50573	70394	50576	70397	50579	70399	50582	20
40	70399	50582	70402	50585	70404	50588	70407	50590	70409	50593	70412	50596	19
41	70412	50596	70414	50599	70417	50602	70419	50605	70422	50608	70424	50611	18
42	70424	50611	70427	50614	70429	50617	70432	50620	70434	50622	70437	50625	17
43	70437	50625	70439	50628	70442	50631	70444	50634	70447	50637	70449	50640	16
44	70449	50640	70452	50643	70454	50646	70457	50649	70459	50652	70462	50654	15
45	70462	50654	70464	50657	70467	50660	70469	50663	70472	50666	70474	50669	14
46	70474	50669	70477	50672	70479	50675	70482	50678	70484	50681	70487	50684	13
47	70487	50684	70489	50686	70492	50689	70494	50692	70497	50695	70499	50698	12
48	70499	50698	70502	50701	70504	50704	70507	50707	70509	50710	70512	50713	11
49	70512	50713	70514	50716	70517	50718	70519	50721	70522	50724	70524	50727	10
50	70524	50727	70527	50730	70529	50733	70532	50736	70534	50739	70537	50742	09
51	70537	50742	70539	50745	70542	50748	70544	50750	70547	50753	70549	50756	08
52	70549	50756	70551	50759	70554	50762	70556	50765	70559	50768	70561	50771	07
53	70561	50771	70564	50774	70566	50777	70569	50780	70571	50782	70574	50785	06
54	70574	50785	70576	50788	70579	50791	70581	50794	70584	50797	70586	50800	05
55	70586	50800	70589	50803	70591	50806	70594	50809	70596	50812	70599	50814	04
56	70599	50814	70601	50817	70604	50820	70606	50823	70609	50826	70611	50829	03
57	70611	50829	70614	50832	70616	50835	70619	50838	70621	50841	70624	50844	02
58	70624	50844	70626	50846	70629	50849	70631	50852	70634	50855	70636	50858	01
59	70636	50858	70638	50861	70641	50864	70643	50867	70646	50870	70648	50873	00

| | .8 | | .6 | | .4 | | .2 | | .0 ← | | | |

PARTS for 0′.1: LOGS 1 NATURALS 1

HAVERSINES

Parts for 0'.2. etc.	91° Log.	91° Nat.	92° Log.	92° Nat.	93° Log.	93° Nat.	94° Log.	94° Nat.	95° Log.	95° Nat.	96° Log.	96° Nat.	Parts for 0'.2. etc.
	·2 2 ·2 3 / ·4 5 ·4 6 / ·6 7 ·6 9 / ·8 10 ·8 12		·2 2 ·2 3 / ·4 5 ·4 6 / ·6 7 ·6 9 / ·8 10 ·8 12		·2 2 ·2 3 / ·4 5 ·4 6 / ·6 7 ·6 9 / ·8 10 ·8 12		·2 2 ·2 3 / ·4 5 ·4 6 / ·6 7 ·6 9 / ·8 9 ·8 12		·2 2 ·2 3 / ·4 5 ·4 6 / ·6 7 ·6 9 / ·8 9 ·8 12		·2 2 ·2 3 / ·4 5 ·4 5 / ·6 7 ·6 8 / ·8 9 ·8 ·12		
'	1.or(9.)	0.	1.or(9.)	0.	1.or(9.)	0.	1.or(9.)	0.	1.or(9.)	0.	1.or(9.)	0.	**'**
00	70648	50873	71387	51745	72112	52617	72825	53488	73526	54358	74215	55226	60
01	70661	50887	71399	51760	72124	52631	72837	53502	73538	54372	74226	55241	59
02	70673	50902	71411	51774	72136	52646	72849	53517	73549	54387	74237	55255	58
03	70686	50916	71423	51789	72148	52660	72861	53531	73561	54401	74249	55270	57
04	70698	50931	71436	51803	72160	52675	72873	53546	73572	54416	74260	55284	56
05	70710	50945	71448	51818	72172	52689	72884	53560	73584	54430	74272	55299	55
06	70723	50960	71460	51832	72184	52704	72896	53575	73596	54445	74283	55313	54
07	70735	50974	71472	51847	72196	52718	72908	53589	73607	54459	74294	55328	53
08	70748	50989	71484	51861	72208	52733	72920	53604	73619	54474	74306	55342	52
09	70760	51004	71496	51876	72220	52748	72931	53618	73630	54488	74317	55357	51
10	70772	51018	71509	51890	72232	52762	72943	53633	73642	54503	74328	55371	50
11	70785	51033	71521	51905	72244	52776	72955	53647	73653	54517	74340	55386	49
12	70797	51047	71533	51919	72256	52791	72967	53662	73665	54532	74351	55400	48
13	70809	51062	71545	51934	72268	52806	72978	53676	73676	54546	74362	55414	47
14	70822	51076	71557	51948	72280	52820	72990	53691	73688	54561	74374	55429	46
15	70834	51091	71569	51963	72292	52835	73002	53705	73699	54575	74385	55443	45
16	70847	51105	71582	51978	72304	52849	73014	53720	73711	54590	74396	55458	44
17	70859	51120	71594	51992	72316	52864	73025	53734	73722	54604	74408	55472	43
18	70871	51134	71606	52007	72328	52878	73037	53749	73734	54619	74419	55487	42
19	70884	51149	71618	52021	72340	52893	73049	53763	73746	54633	74430	55501	41
20	70896	51163	71630	52036	72352	52907	73060	53778	73757	54647	74442	55516	40
21	70908	51178	71642	52050	72363	52922	73072	53792	73769	54662	74453	55530	39
22	70921	51193	71654	52065	72375	52936	73084	53807	73780	54676	74464	55545	38
23	70933	51207	71666	52079	72387	52951	73096	53821	73792	54691	74475	55559	37
24	70945	51222	71679	52094	72399	52965	73107	53836	73803	54705	74487	55573	36
25	70958	51236	71691	52108	72411	52980	73119	53850	73815	54720	74498	55588	35
26	70970	51251	71703	52123	72423	52994	73131	53865	73826	54734	74509	55602	34
27	70982	51265	71715	52137	72435	53009	73142	53879	73838	54749	74521	55617	33
28	70995	51280	71727	52152	72447	53023	73154	53894	73849	54763	74532	55631	32
29	71007	51294	71739	52166	72459	53038	73166	53908	73860	54778	74543	55646	31
30	71019	51309	71751	52181	72471	53052	73177	53923	73872	54792	74554	55660	30
31	71032	51323	71763	52196	72482	53067	73189	53937	73883	54807	74566	55675	29
32	71044	51338	71775	52210	72494	53081	73201	53952	73895	54821	74577	55689	28
33	71056	51352	71787	52225	72506	53096	73212	53966	73906	54836	74588	55704	27
34	71068	51367	71800	52239	72518	53110	73224	53981	73918	54850	74600	55718	26
35	71081	51382	71812	52254	72530	53125	73236	53995	73929	54865	74611	55732	25
36	71093	51396	71824	52268	72542	53140	73247	54010	73941	54879	74622	55747	24
37	71105	51411	71836	52283	72554	53154	73259	54024	73952	54894	74633	55761	23
38	71118	51425	71848	52297	72565	53169	73271	54039	73964	54908	74645	55776	22
39	71130	51440	71860	52312	72577	53183	73282	54053	73975	54923	74656	55790	21
40	71142	51454	71872	52326	72589	53198	73294	54068	73987	54937	74667	55805	20
41	71154	51469	71884	52341	72601	53212	73306	54082	73998	54952	74678	55819	19
42	71167	51483	71896	52355	72613	53227	73317	54097	74009	54966	74690	55834	18
43	71179	51498	71908	52370	72625	53241	73329	54111	74021	54980	74701	55848	17
44	71191	51512	71920	52384	72637	53256	73341	54126	74032	54995	74712	55862	16
45	71203	51527	71932	52399	72648	53270	73352	54140	74044	55009	74723	55877	15
46	71216	51541	71944	52413	72660	53285	73364	54155	74055	55024	74734	55891	14
47	71228	51556	71956	52428	72672	53299	73375	54169	74067	55038	74746	55906	13
48	71240	51571	71968	52442	72684	53314	73387	54184	74078	55053	74757	55920	12
49	71252	51585	71980	52457	72696	53328	73399	54198	74089	55067	74768	55935	11
50	71265	51600	71992	52472	72708	53343	73410	54213	74101	55082	74779	55949	10
51	71277	51614	72004	52486	72719	53357	73422	54227	74112	55096	74791	55964	09
52	71289	51629	72016	52501	72731	53372	73433	54242	74124	55111	74802	55978	08
53	71301	51643	72028	52515	72743	53386	73445	54256	74135	55125	74813	55992	07
54	71314	51658	72040	52530	72755	53401	73457	54271	74146	55140	74824	56007	06
55	71326	51672	72052	52544	72767	53415	73468	54285	74158	55154	74835	56021	05
56	71338	51687	72064	52559	72778	53430	73480	54300	74169	55169	74846	56036	04
57	71350	51701	72076	52573	72790	53444	73491	54314	74181	55183	74858	56050	03
58	71362	51716	72088	52588	72802	53459	73503	54329	74192	55197	74869	56065	02
59	71375	51730	72100	52602	72814	53473	73515	54343	74203	55212	74880	56079	01
60	71387	51745	72112	52617	72825	53488	73526	54358	74215	55226	74891	56093	00
	268°		**267°**		**266°**		**265°**		**264°**		**263°**		

HAVERSINES

′	97° Log.	97° Nat.	98° Log.	98° Nat.	99° Log.	99° Nat.	100° Log.	100° Nat.	101° Log.	101° Nat.	102° Log.	102° Nat.	′
	1.or(9.)	0.	1.or(9.)	0.	1.or(9.)	0.	1.or(9.)	0.	1.or(9.)	0.	1.or(9.)	0.	
00	74891	56093	75556	56959	76209	57822	76851	58682	77481	59540	78101	60396	60
01	74902	56108	75567	56973	76220	57836	76861	58697	77492	59555	78111	60410	59
02	74914	56122	75578	56987	76231	57850	76872	58711	77502	59569	78121	60424	58
03	74925	56137	75589	57002	76241	57865	76883	58725	77512	59583	78131	60438	57
04	74936	56151	75600	57016	76252	57879	76893	58740	77523	59598	78141	60452	56
05	74947	56166	75611	57031	76263	57894	76904	58754	77533	59612	78152	60467	55
06	74958	56180	75622	57045	76274	57908	76914	58768	77544	59626	78162	60481	54
07	74969	56195	75633	57059	76285	57922	76925	58783	77554	59640	78172	60495	53
08	74981	56209	75644	57074	76296	57937	76936	58797	77564	59655	78182	60509	52
09	74992	56223	75655	57088	76306	57951	76946	58811	77575	59669	78192	60524	51
10	75003	56238	75666	57103	76317	57965	76957	58826	77585	59683	78203	60538	50
11	75014	56252	75677	57117	76328	57980	76967	58840	77596	59697	78213	60552	49
12	75025	56267	75688	57131	76338	57994	76978	58854	77606	59712	78223	60566	48
13	75036	56281	75698	57146	76349	58008	76988	58869	77616	59726	78233	60580	47
14	75047	56296	75709	57160	76360	58023	76999	58883	77627	59740	78243	60595	46
15	75059	56310	75720	57175	76371	58037	77009	58897	77637	59755	78254	60609	45
16	75070	56324	75731	57189	76381	58051	77020	58911	77647	59769	78264	60623	44
17	75081	56339	75742	57203	76392	58066	77031	58926	77658	59783	78274	60637	43
18	75092	56353	75753	57218	76403	58080	77041	58940	77668	59797	78284	60652	42
19	75103	56368	75764	57232	76414	58095	77052	58954	77679	59812	78294	60666	41
20	75114	56382	75775	57247	76424	58109	77062	58969	77689	59826	78305	60680	40
21	75125	56397	75786	57261	76435	58123	77073	58983	77699	59840	78315	60694	39
22	75136	56411	75797	57275	76446	58138	77083	58997	77710	59854	78325	60708	38
23	75147	56425	75808	57290	76456	58152	77094	59012	77720	59869	78335	60723	37
24	75159	56440	75819	57304	76467	58166	77104	59026	77730	59883	78345	60737	36
25	75170	56454	75830	57318	76478	58181	77115	59040	77741	59897	78355	60751	35
26	75181	56469	75840	57333	76489	58195	77125	59055	77751	59911	78365	60765	34
27	75192	56483	75851	57347	76499	58209	77136	59069	77761	59926	78376	60779	33
28	75203	56497	75862	57362	76510	58224	77146	59083	77772	59940	78386	60794	32
29	75214	56512	75873	57376	76521	58238	77157	59097	77782	59954	78396	60808	31
30	75225	56526	75884	57390	76531	58252	77167	59112	77792	59968	78406	60822	30
31	75236	56541	75895	57405	76542	58267	77178	59126	77803	59983	78416	60836	29
32	75247	56555	75906	57419	76553	58281	77188	59140	77813	59997	78426	60850	28
33	75258	56570	75917	57434	76563	58295	77199	59155	77823	60011	78436	60865	27
34	75269	56584	75927	57448	76574	58310	77209	59169	77834	60025	78447	60879	26
35	75280	56598	75938	57462	76585	58324	77220	59183	77844	60040	78457	60893	25
36	75291	56613	75949	57477	76595	58338	77230	59198	77854	60054	78467	60907	24
37	75303	56627	75960	57491	76606	58353	77241	59212	77864	60068	78477	60921	23
38	75314	56642	75971	57506	76617	58367	77251	59226	77875	60082	78487	60936	22
39	75325	56656	75982	57520	76627	58381	77262	59240	77885	60097	78497	60950	21
40	75336	56670	75993	57534	76638	58396	77272	59255	77895	60111	78507	60964	20
41	75347	56685	76004	57549	76649	58410	77283	59269	77906	60125	78517	60978	19
42	75358	56699	76014	57563	76659	58424	77293	59283	77916	60139	78528	60992	18
43	75369	56714	76025	57577	76670	58439	77304	59298	77926	60154	78538	61007	17
44	75380	56728	76036	57592	76681	58453	77314	59312	77936	60168	78548	61021	16
45	75391	56743	76047	57606	76691	58467	77325	59326	77947	60182	78558	61035	15
46	75402	56757	76058	57621	76702	58482	77335	59340	77957	60196	78568	61049	14
47	75413	56771	76069	57635	76713	58496	77346	59355	77967	60211	78578	61063	13
48	75424	56786	76079	57649	76723	58510	77356	59369	77978	60225	78588	61077	12
49	75435	56800	76090	57664	76734	58525	77366	59383	77988	60239	78598	61092	11
50	75446	56815	76101	57678	76745	58539	77377	59398	77998	60253	78608	61106	10
51	75457	56829	76112	57692	76755	58553	77387	59412	78008	60268	78618	61120	09
52	75468	56843	76123	57707	76766	58568	77398	59426	78019	60282	78628	61134	08
53	75479	56858	76134	57721	76777	58582	77408	59440	78029	60296	78638	61148	07
54	75490	56872	76144	57736	76787	58596	77419	59455	78039	60310	78649	61163	06
55	75501	56887	76155	57750	76798	58611	77429	59469	78049	60324	78659	61177	05
56	75512	56901	76166	57764	76808	58625	77440	59483	78060	60339	78669	61191	04
57	75523	56915	76177	57779	76819	58639	77450	59498	78070	60353	78679	61205	03
58	75534	56930	76188	57793	76830	58654	77460	59512	78080	60367	78689	61219	02
59	75545	56944	76198	57807	76840	58668	77471	59526	78090	60381	78699	61233	01
60	75556	56959	76209	57822	76851	58682	77481	59540	78101	60396	78709	61248	00

| | 262° | | 261° | | 260° | | 259° | | 258° | | 257° | | |

Parts for 0′.2. etc.

97°: ·2 2 ·2 3 / ·4 4 ·4 6 / ·6 7 ·6 9 / ·8 9 ·8 12
98°: ·2 2 ·2 3 / ·4 4 ·4 6 / ·6 7 ·6 9 / ·8 9 ·8 12
99°: ·2 2 ·2 3 / ·6 6 ·6 9 / ·8 9 ·8 11
100°: ·2 2 ·2 3 / ·4 4 ·4 6 / ·6 6 ·6 9 / ·8 8 ·8 11
101°: ·2 2 ·2 3 / ·4 4 ·4 6 / ·6 6 ·6 9 / ·8 8 8 11
102°: ·2 2 ·2 3 / ·4 4 ·4 6 / ·6 6 ·6 9 / ·8 8 ·8 11

336

HAVERSINES

′	103° Log.	103° Nat.	104° Log.	104° Nat.	105° Log.	105° Nat.	106° Log.	106° Nat.	107° Log.	107° Nat.	108° Log.	108° Nat.	′
	1.or(9.)	0.	1.or(9.)	0.	1.or(9.)	0.	1.or(9.)	0.	1.or(9.)	0.	1.or(9.)	0.	
00	78709	61248	79306	62096	79893	62941	80470	63782	81036	64619	81592	65451	60
01	78719	61262	79316	62110	79903	62955	80479	63796	81045	64632	81601	65465	59
02	78729	61276	79326	62124	79913	62969	80489	63810	81054	64646	81610	65479	58
03	78739	61290	79336	62138	79922	62983	80498	63824	81064	64660	81619	65492	57
04	78749	61304	79346	62153	79932	62997	80508	63838	81073	64674	81628	65506	56
05	78759	61318	79356	62167	79942	63011	80517	63852	81082	64688	81637	65520	55
06	78769	61333	79366	62181	79951	63025	80527	63866	81092	64702	81647	65534	54
07	78779	61347	79376	62195	79961	63039	80536	63880	81101	64716	81656	65548	53
08	78789	61361	79385	62209	79971	63053	80546	63894	81110	64730	81665	65561	52
09	78799	61375	79395	62223	79980	63067	80555	63908	81120	64744	81674	65575	51
10	78809	61389	79405	62237	79990	63081	80565	63922	81129	64758	81683	65589	50
11	78819	61403	79415	62251	80000	63095	80574	63936	81138	64772	81692	65603	49
12	78829	61418	79425	62265	80009	63109	80584	63950	81148	64785	81701	65617	48
13	78839	61432	79434	62279	80019	63123	80593	63964	81157	64799	81711	65630	47
14	78849	61446	79444	62294	80029	63138	80603	63977	81166	64813	81720	65644	46
15	78859	61460	79454	62308	80038	63152	80612	63991	81176	64827	81729	65658	45
16	78869	61474	79464	62322	80048	63166	80622	64005	81185	64841	81738	65672	44
17	78879	61488	79474	62336	80058	63180	80631	64019	81194	64855	81747	65686	43
18	78889	61502	79484	62350	80067	63194	80641	64033	81204	64869	81756	65700	42
19	78899	61517	79493	62364	80077	63208	80650	64047	81213	64883	81765	65713	41
20	78909	61531	79503	62378	80087	63222	80660	64061	81222	64897	81775	65727	40
21	78919	61545	79513	62392	80096	63236	80669	64075	81231	64910	81784	65741	39
22	78929	61559	79523	62406	80106	63250	80678	64089	81241	64924	81793	65755	38
23	78939	61573	79533	62420	80116	63264	80688	64103	81250	64938	81802	65769	37
24	78949	61587	79542	62434	80125	63278	80697	64117	81259	64952	81811	65782	36
25	78959	61602	79552	62449	80135	63292	80707	64131	81269	64966	81820	65796	35
26	78969	61616	79562	62463	80144	63306	80716	64145	81278	64980	81829	65810	34
27	78979	61630	79572	62477	80154	63320	80726	64159	81287	64994	81838	65824	33
28	78989	61644	79582	62491	80164	63334	80735	64173	81296	65008	81847	65838	32
29	78999	61658	79591	62505	80173	63348	80745	64187	81306	65021	81857	65851	31
30	79009	61672	79601	62519	80183	63362	80754	64201	81315	65035	81866	65865	30
31	79019	61686	79611	62533	80192	63376	80763	64215	81324	65049	81875	65879	29
32	79029	61701	79621	62547	80202	63390	80773	64229	81333	65063	81884	65893	28
33	79039	61715	79631	62561	80212	63404	80782	64243	81343	65077	81893	65907	27
34	79049	61729	79640	62575	80221	63418	80792	64257	81352	65091	81902	65920	26
35	79059	61743	79650	62589	80231	63432	80801	64270	81361	65105	81911	65934	25
36	79069	61757	79660	62603	80240	63446	80811	64284	81370	65118	81920	65948	24
37	78079	61771	79670	62618	80250	63460	80820	64298	81380	65132	81929	65962	23
38	79089	61785	79679	62632	80260	63474	80829	64312	81389	65146	81938	65976	22
39	79099	61800	79689	62646	80269	63488	80839	64326	81398	65160	81947	65989	21
40	79108	61814	79699	62660	80279	63502	80848	64340	81407	65174	81956	66003	20
41	79118	61828	79709	62674	80288	63516	80858	64354	81417	65188	81965	66017	19
42	79128	61842	79718	62688	80298	63530	80867	64368	81426	65202	81975	66031	18
43	79138	61856	79728	62702	80307	63544	80876	64382	81435	65216	81984	66044	17
44	79148	61870	79738	62716	80317	63558	80886	64396	81444	65229	81993	66058	16
45	79158	61884	79748	62730	80327	63572	80895	64410	81454	65243	82002	66072	15
46	79168	61898	79757	62744	80336	63586	80905	64424	81463	65257	82011	66086	14
47	79178	61913	79767	62758	80346	63600	80914	64438	81472	65271	82020	66100	13
48	79188	61927	79777	62772	80355	63614	80923	64452	81481	65285	82029	66113	12
49	79198	61941	79787	62786	80365	63628	80933	64466	81490	65299	82038	66127	11
50	79208	61955	79796	62800	80374	63642	80942	64479	81500	65312	82047	66141	10
51	79217	61969	79806	62814	80384	63656	80952	64493	81509	65326	82056	66155	09
52	79227	61983	79816	62829	80393	63670	80961	64507	81518	65340	82065	66168	08
53	79237	61997	79825	62843	80403	63684	80970	64521	81527	65354	82074	66182	07
54	79247	62011	79835	62857	80413	63698	80980	64535	81536	65368	82083	66196	06
55	79257	62026	79845	62871	80422	63712	80989	64549	81546	65382	82092	66210	05
56	79267	62040	79855	62885	80432	63726	80998	64563	81555	65396	82101	66223	04
57	79277	62054	79864	62899	80441	63740	81008	64577	81564	65409	82110	66237	03
58	79287	62068	79874	62913	80451	63754	81017	64591	81573	65423	82119	66251	02
59	79297	62082	79884	62927	80460	63768	81026	64605	81582	65437	82128	66265	01
60	79306	62096	79893	62941	80470	63782	81036	64619	81592	65451	82137	66278	00

Left / right margin label: **Parts for 0′.2, etc.**

Parts for 0′.2 etc. (per degree heading):

	103°	104°	105°	106°	107°	108°
	·2 2 / ·2 3	·2 2 / ·2 3	·2 2 / ·2 3	·2 2 / ·2 3	·2 2 / ·2 3	·2 2 / ·2 3
	·4 4 / ·4 6	·4 4 / ·4 6	·4 4 / ·4 6	·4 4 / ·4 6	·4 4 / ·4 6	·4 4 / ·4 6
	·6 6 / ·6 8	·6 6 / ·6 8	·6 6 / ·6 8	·6 6 / ·6 8	·6 6 / ·6 8	·6 5 / ·6 8
	·8 8 / ·8 11	·8 8 / ·8 11	·8 8 / ·8 11	·8 8 / ·8 11	·8 7 / ·8 11	·8 7 / ·8 11

256°	255°	254°	253°	252°	251°

HAVERSINES

Parts for 0'.2 etc.

	109°		110°		111°		112°		113°		114°	
	Log.	Nat.	Log.	Nat.	Log.	Nat.	Log.	Nat.	Log.	Nat.	Log.	Nat.	
	·2 2 ·2 3		·2 2 ·2 3		·2 2 ·2 3		·2 2 ·2 3		·2 2 ·2 3		·2 2 ·2 3		
	·4 4 ·4 5		·4 4 ·4 5		·4 3 ·4 5		·4 3 ·4 5		·4 3 ·4 5		·4 3 ·4 5		
	·6 5 ·6 8		·6 5 ·6 8		·6 5 ·6 8		·6 5 ·6 8		·6 5 ·6 8		·6 5 ·6 8		
	·8 7 ·8 11		·8 7 ·8 11		·8 7 ·8 11		·8 7 ·8 11		·8 7 ·8 11		·8 7 ·8 11		

/	1̄.or(9.)	0.	1̄.or(9.)	0.	1̄.or(9.)	0.	1̄.or(9.)	0.	1̄.or(9.)	0.	1̄.or(9.)	0.	/
00	82137	66278	82673	67101	83199	67918	83715	68730	84221	69537	84718	70337	60
01	82146	66292	82682	67115	83207	67932	83723	68744	84230	69550	84726	70350	59
02	82155	66306	82691	67128	83216	67946	83732	68757	84238	69563	84735	70363	58
03	82164	66320	82699	67142	83225	67959	83740	68771	84246	69577	84743	70377	57
04	82173	66333	82708	67156	83233	67973	83749	68784	84255	69590	84751	70390	56
05	82182	66347	82717	67169	83242	67986	83757	68798	84263	69603	84759	70403	55
06	82191	66361	82726	67183	83251	68000	83766	68811	84271	69617	84767	70417	54
07	82200	66375	82735	67197	83259	68013	83774	68825	84280	69630	84776	70430	53
08	82209	66388	82744	67210	83268	68027	83783	68838	84288	69644	84784	70443	52
09	82218	66402	82752	67224	83277	68041	83791	68852	84296	69657	84792	70456	51
10	82227	66416	82761	67238	83285	68054	83800	68865	84305	69670	84800	70470	50
11	82236	66430	82770	67251	83294	68068	83808	68879	84313	69684	84808	70483	49
12	82245	66443	82779	67265	83303	68081	83817	68892	84321	69697	84817	70496	48
13	82254	66457	82788	67279	83311	68095	83825	68906	84330	69710	84825	70509	47
14	82263	66471	82796	67292	83320	68108	83834	68919	84338	69724	84833	70523	46
15	82272	66485	82805	67306	83329	68122	83842	68932	84346	69737	84841	70536	45
16	82281	66498	82814	67320	83337	68135	83851	68946	84355	69751	84849	70549	44
17	82290	66512	82823	67333	83346	68149	83859	68959	84363	69764	84857	70562	43
18	82299	66526	82832	67347	83355	68163	83868	68973	84371	69777	84866	70576	42
19	82308	66539	82840	67360	83363	68176	83876	68986	84380	69791	84874	70589	41
20	82317	66553	82849	67374	83372	68190	83885	69000	84388	69804	84882	70602	40
21	82326	66567	82858	67388	83380	68203	83893	69013	84396	69817	84890	70615	39
22	82335	66581	82867	67401	83389	68217	83902	69027	84405	69831	84898	70629	38
23	82344	66594	82876	67415	83398	68230	83910	69040	84413	69844	84906	70642	37
24	82353	66608	82884	67429	83406	68244	83919	69054	84421	69857	84914	70655	36
25	82362	66622	82893	67442	83415	68257	83927	69067	84430	69871	84923	70668	35
26	82371	66635	82902	67456	83424	68271	83935	69080	84438	69884	84931	70682	34
27	82380	66649	82911	67469	83432	68284	83944	69094	84446	69897	84939	70695	33
28	82388	66663	82920	67483	83441	68298	83952	69107	84454	69911	84947	70708	32
29	82397	66677	82928	67497	83449	68312	83961	69121	84463	69924	84955	70721	31
30	82406	66690	82937	67510	83458	68325	83969	69134	84471	69937	84963	70735	30
31	82415	66704	82946	67524	83467	68339	83978	69148	84479	69951	84971	70748	29
32	82424	66718	82955	67538	83475	68352	83986	69161	84488	69964	84979	70761	28
33	82433	66731	82963	67551	83484	68366	83995	69174	84496	69977	84988	70774	27
34	82442	66745	82972	67565	83492	68379	84003	69188	84504	69991	84996	70788	26
35	82451	66759	82981	67578	83501	68393	84011	69201	84512	70004	85004	70801	25
36	82460	66773	82990	67592	83510	68406	84020	69215	84521	70017	85012	70814	24
37	82469	66786	82998	67606	83518	68420	84028	69228	84529	70031	85020	70827	23
38	82478	66800	83007	67619	83527	68433	84037	69242	84537	70044	85028	70840	22
39	82487	66814	83016	67633	83535	68447	84045	69255	84545	70057	85036	70854	21
40	82495	66827	83025	67647	83544	68460	84054	69268	84554	70071	85044	70867	20
41	82504	66841	83033	67660	83552	68474	84062	69282	84562	70084	85052	70880	19
42	82513	66855	83042	67674	83561	68487	84070	69295	84570	70097	85061	70893	18
43	82522	66868	83051	67687	83570	68501	84079	69309	84578	70111	85069	70907	17
44	82531	66882	83059	67701	83578	68515	84087	69322	84587	70124	85077	70920	16
45	82540	66896	83068	67715	83587	68528	84096	69336	84595	70137	85085	70933	15
46	82549	66910	83077	67728	83595	68541	84104	69349	84603	70151	85093	70946	14
47	82558	66923	83086	67742	83604	68555	84112	69362	84611	70164	85101	70959	13
48	82567	66937	83094	67755	83612	68568	84121	69376	84620	70177	85109	70973	12
49	82575	66951	83103	67769	83621	68582	84129	69389	84628	70191	85117	70986	11
50	82584	66964	83112	67783	83630	68595	84138	69403	84636	70204	85125	70999	10
51	82593	66978	83120	67796	83638	68609	84146	69416	84644	70217	85133	71012	09
52	82602	66992	83129	67810	83647	68622	84154	69429	84653	70230	85141	71025	08
53	82611	67005	83138	67823	83655	68636	84163	69443	84661	70244	85149	71039	07
54	82620	67019	83147	67837	83664	68649	84171	69456	84669	70257	85158	71052	06
55	82629	67033	83155	67850	83672	68663	84179	69470	84677	70270	85166	71065	05
56	82638	67046	83164	67864	83681	68676	84188	69483	84685	70284	85174	71078	04
57	82646	67060	83173	67878	83689	68690	84196	69496	84694	70297	85182	71091	03
58	82655	67074	83181	67891	83698	68703	84205	69510	84702	70310	85190	71105	02
59	82664	67087	83190	67905	83706	68717	84213	69523	84710	70324	85198	71118	01
60	82673	67101	83199	67918	83715	68730	84221	69537	84718	70337	85206	71131	00

250°	249°	248°	247°	246°	245°

HAVERSINES

′	115° Log.	Nat.	116° Log.	Nat.	117° Log.	Nat.	118° Log.	Nat.	119° Log.	Nat.	120° Log.	Nat.	′
	1̄.or(9.)	0.	1̄.or(9.)	0.	1̄.or(9.)	0.	1̄.or(9.)	0.	1̄.or(9.)	0.	1̄.or(9.)	0.	
00	85206	71131	85684	71919	86153	72700	86613	73474	87064	74240	87506	75000	60
01	85214	71144	85692	71932	86161	72712	86621	73486	87072	74253	87513	75013	59
02	85222	71157	85700	71945	86169	72725	86628	73499	87079	74266	87521	75025	58
03	85230	71170	85708	71958	86176	72738	86636	73512	87086	74279	87528	75038	57
04	85238	71184	85716	71971	86184	72751	86643	73525	87094	74291	87535	75050	56
05	85246	71197	85724	71984	86192	72764	86651	73538	87101	74304	87543	75063	55
06	85254	71210	85731	71997	86200	72777	86659	73551	87109	74317	87550	75075	54
07	85262	71223	85739	72010	86207	72790	86666	73563	87116	74329	87557	75088	53
08	85270	71236	85747	72023	86215	72803	86674	73576	87124	74342	87564	75101	52
09	85278	71249	85755	72036	86223	72816	86681	73589	87131	74355	87572	75113	51
10	85286	71263	85763	72049	86230	72829	86689	73602	87138	74368	87579	75126	50
11	85294	71276	85771	72062	86238	72842	86696	73615	87146	74380	87586	75138	49
12	85302	71289	85779	72075	86246	72855	86704	73628	87153	74393	87593	75151	48
13	85310	71302	85787	72088	86254	72868	86712	73640	87161	74406	87601	75164	47
14	85318	71315	85794	72101	86261	72881	86719	73653	87168	74418	87608	75176	46
15	85326	71328	85802	72114	86269	72894	86727	73666	87175	74431	87615	75189	45
16	85334	71342	85810	72127	86277	72907	86734	73679	87183	74444	87623	75201	44
17	85342	71355	85818	72141	86284	72920	86742	73692	87190	74456	87630	75214	43
18	85350	71368	85826	72154	86292	72932	86749	73704	87198	74469	87637	75226	42
19	85358	71381	85834	72167	86300	72945	86757	73717	87205	74482	87644	75239	41
20	85366	71394	85841	72180	86307	72958	86764	73730	87212	74494	87652	75251	40
21	85374	71407	85849	72193	86315	72971	86772	73743	87220	74507	87659	75264	39
22	85382	71420	85857	72206	86323	72984	86780	73756	87227	74520	87666	75277	38
23	85390	71434	85865	72219	86331	72997	86787	73768	87235	74533	87673	75289	37
24	85398	71447	85873	72232	86338	73010	86795	73781	87242	74545	87680	75302	36
25	85406	71460	85881	72245	86346	73023	86802	73794	87249	74558	87688	75314	35
26	85414	71473	85888	72258	86354	73036	86810	73807	87257	74571	87695	75327	34
27	85422	71486	85896	72271	86361	73049	86817	73820	87264	74583	87702	75339	33
28	85430	71499	85904	72284	86369	73062	86825	73832	87271	74596	87709	75352	32
29	85438	71512	85912	72297	86377	73075	86832	73845	87279	74609	87717	75364	31
30	85446	71526	85920	72310	86384	73087	86840	73858	87286	74621	87724	75377	30
31	85454	71539	85928	72323	86392	73100	86847	73871	87294	74634	87731	75389	29
32	85462	71552	85935	72336	86400	73113	86855	73884	87301	74646	87738	75402	28
33	85470	71565	85943	72349	86407	73126	36862	73896	87308	74659	87745	75415	27
34	85478	71578	85951	72362	86415	73139	86870	73909	87316	74672	87753	75427	26
35	85486	71591	85959	72375	86423	73152	86877	73922	87323	74684	87760	75440	25
36	85494	71604	85967	72388	86430	73165	86885	73935	87330	74697	87767	75452	24
37	85502	71617	85974	72401	86438	73178	86892	73947	87338	74710	87774	75465	23
38	85510	71631	85982	72414	86446	73191	86900	73960	87345	74722	87782	75477	22
39	85518	71644	85990	72427	86453	73203	86907	73973	87352	74735	87789	75490	21
40	85526	71657	85998	72440	86461	73216	86915	73986	87360	74748	87796	75502	20
41	85534	71670	86006	72453	86468	73229	86922	73998	87367	74760	87803	75515	19
42	85542	71683	86013	72466	86476	73242	86930	74011	87374	74773	87810	75527	18
43	85550	71696	86021	72479	86484	73255	86937	74024	87382	74786	87818	75540	17
44	85557	71709	86029	72492	86491	73268	86945	74037	87389	74798	87825	75552	16
45	85565	71722	86037	72505	86499	73281	86952	74049	87396	74811	87832	75565	15
46	85573	71735	86045	72518	86507	73294	86960	74062	87404	74823	87839	75577	14
47	85581	71748	86052	72531	86514	73306	86967	74075	87411	74836	87846	75590	13
48	85589	71762	86060	72544	86522	73319	86975	74088	87418	74849	87853	75602	12
49	85597	71775	86068	72557	86529	73332	86982	74100	87426	74861	87861	75615	11
50	85605	71788	86076	72570	86537	73345	86990	74113	87433	74874	87868	75627	10
51	85613	71801	86083	72583	86545	73358	86997	74126	87440	74887	87875	75640	09
52	85621	71814	86091	72596	86552	73371	87004	74139	87448	74899	87882	75652	08
53	85629	71827	86099	72609	86560	73384	87012	74151	87455	74912	87889	75665	07
54	85637	71840	86107	72622	86568	73396	87019	74164	87462	74924	87896	75677	06
55	85645	71853	86114	72635	86575	73409	87027	74177	87470	74937	87904	75690	05
56	85653	71866	86122	72648	86583	73422	87034	74190	87477	74950	87911	75702	04
57	85660	71879	86130	72661	86590	73435	87042	74202	87484	74962	87918	75714	03
58	85668	71892	86138	72674	86598	73448	87049	74215	87492	74975	87925	75727	02
59	85676	71905	86145	72687	86606	73461	87057	74228	87499	74987	87932	75739	01
60	85684	71919	86153	72700	86613	73474	87064	74240	87506	75000	87939	75752	00

| 244° | 243° | 242° | 241° | 240° | 239° | |

HAVERSINES

Parts for 0'.2 etc.	121°		122°		123°		124°		125°		126°		Parts for 0'.2 etc.
	Log.	Nat.	Log.	Nat.	Log.	Nat.	Log.	Nat.	Log.	Nat.	Log.	Nat.	
	·2 1 ·2 2 ·4 3 ·4 5 ·6 4 ·6 7 ·8 6 ·8 10		·2 1 ·2 2 ·4 3 ·4 5 ·6 4 ·6 7 ·8 6 ·8 10		·2 1 ·2 2 ·4 3 ·4 5 ·6 4 ·6 7 ·8 5 ·8 10		·2 1 ·2 2 ·4 3 ·4 5 ·6 4 ·6 7 ·8 5 ·8 10		·2 1 ·2 2 ·4 3 ·4 5 ·6 4 ·6 7 ·8 5 ·8 9		·2 1 ·2 2 ·4 3 ·4 5 ·6 4 ·6 7 ·8 5 ·8 9		
′	1̄.or(9.)	0.	1̄.or(9.)	0.	1̄.or(9.)	0.	1̄.or(9.)	0.	1̄.or.(9.)	0.	1̄.or(9.)	·0.	′
00	87939	75752	88364	76496	88780	77232	89187	77960	89586	78679	89976	79389	60
01	87947	75764	88371	76508	88787	77244	89194	77972	89592	78691	89983	79401	59
02	87954	75777	88378	76521	88793	77256	89200	77984	89599	78703	89989	79413	58
03	87961	75789	88385	76533	88800	77269	89207	77996	89606	78715	89995	79425	57
04	87968	75802	88392	76545	88807	77281	89214	78008	89612	78726	90002	79436	56
05	87975	75814	88399	76558	88814	77293	89221	78020	89619	78738	90008	79448	55
06	87982	75827	88406	76570	88821	77305	89227	78032	89625	78750	90015	79460	54
07	87989	75839	88413	76582	88828	77317	89234	78044	89632	78762	90021	79471	53
08	87996	75852	88420	76595	88835	77329	89241	78056	89638	78774	90028	79483	52
09	88004	75864	88427	76607	88841	77342	89247	78068	89645	78786	90034	79495	51
10	88011	75876	88434	76619	88848	77354	89254	78080	89651	78798	90040	79507	50
11	88018	75889	88441	76632	88855	77366	89261	78092	89658	78810	90047	79519	49
12	88025	75901	88448	76644	88862	77378	89267	78104	89665	78822	90053	79530	48
13	88032	75914	88455	76656	88869	77390	89274	78116	89671	78834	90060	79542	47
14	88039	75926	88462	76668	88876	77403	89281	78128	89678	78845	90066	79554	46
15	88046	75939	88469	76681	88882	77415	89287	78140	89684	78857	90072	79565	45
16	88053	75951	88476	76693	88889	77427	89294	78152	89691	78869	90079	79577	44
17	88061	75964	88483	76705	88896	77439	89301	78164	89697	78881	90085	79589	43
18	88068	75976	88490	76718	88903	77451	89308	78176	89704	78893	90092	79601	42
19	88075	75988	88496	76730	88910	77463	89314	78188	89710	78905	90098	79612	41
20	88082	76001	88503	76742	88916	77475	89321	78200	89717	78917	90104	79624	40
21	88089	76013	88510	76754	88923	77488	89328	78212	89723	78928	90111	79636	39
22	88096	76026	88517	76767	88930	77500	89334	78224	89730	78940	90117	79648	38
23	88103	76038	88524	76779	88937	77512	89341	78236	89736	78952	90124	79659	37
24	88110	76050	88531	76791	88944	77524	89348	78248	89743	78964	90130	79671	36
25	88117	76063	88538	76804	88950	77536	89354	78260	89749	78976	90136	79683	35
26	88124	76075	88545	76816	88957	77548	89361	78272	89756	78988	90143	79694	34
27	88131	76088	88552	76828	88964	77560	89368	78284	89763	79000	90149	79706	33
28	88139	76100	88559	76840	88971	77573	89374	78296	89769	79011	90156	79718	32
29	88146	76113	88566	76853	88978	77585	89381	78308	89776	79023	90162	79729	31
30	88153	76125	88573	76865	88984	77597	89387	78320	89782	79035	90168	79741	30
31	88160	76137	88580	76877	88991	77609	89394	78332	89789	79047	90175	79753	29
32	88167	76150	88587	76890	88998	77621	89400	78344	89795	79059	90181	79765	28
33	88174	76162	88594	76902	89005	77633	89407	78356	89802	79071	90187	79776	27
34	88181	76175	88600	76914	89012	77645	89414	78368	89808	79082	90194	79788	26
35	88188	76187	88607	76926	89018	77657	89421	78380	89815	79094	90200	79800	25
36	88195	76199	88614	76939	89025	77670	89427	78392	89821	79106	90206	79811	24
37	88202	76212	88621	76951	89032	77682	89434	78404	89828	79118	90213	79823	23
38	88209	76224	88628	76963	89039	77694	89441	78416	89834	79130	90219	79835	22
39	88216	76236	88635	76975	89045	77706	89447	78428	89840	79142	90225	79846	21
40	88223	76249	88642	76988	89052	77718	89454	78440	89847	79153	90232	79858	20
41	88230	76261	88649	77000	89059	77730	89460	78452	89853	79165	90238	79870	19
42	88237	76274	88656	77012	89066	77742	89467	78464	89860	79177	90244	79881	18
43	88244	76286	88663	77024	89072	77754	89474	78476	89866	79189	90251	79893	17
44	88252	76298	88670	77036	89079	77766	89480	78488	89873	79201	90257	79905	16
45	88259	76311	88677	77049	89086	77779	89487	78500	89879	79212	90264	79916	15
46	88266	76323	88683	77061	89093	77791	89493	78512	89886	79224	90270	79928	14
47	88273	76335	88690	77073	89099	77803	89500	78524	89892	79236	90276	79940	13
48	88280	76348	88697	77085	89106	77815	89507	78536	89899	79248	90282	79951	12
49	88287	76360	88704	77098	89113	77827	89513	78548	89905	79260	90289	79963	11
50	88294	76373	88711	77110	89120	77839	89520	78560	89912	79271	90295	79974	10
51	88301	76385	88718	77122	89126	77851	89527	78572	89918	79283	90301	79986	09
52	88308	76397	88725	77134	89133	77863	89533	78583	89925	79295	90308	79998	08
53	88315	76410	88732	77147	89140	77875	89540	78595	89931	79307	90314	80009	07
54	88322	76422	88739	77159	89147	77887	89546	78607	89938	79319	90320	80021	06
55	88329	76434	88745	77171	89153	77899	89553	78619	89944	79330	90327	80033	05
56	88336	76447	88752	77183	89160	77911	89559	78631	89950	79342	90333	80044	04
57	88343	76459	88759	77195	89167	77923	89566	78643	89957	79354	90339	80056	03
58	88350	76471	88766	77208	89174	77936	89573	78655	89963	79366	90346	80068	02
59	88357	76484	88773	77220	89180	77948	89579	78667	89970	79377	90352	80079	01
60	88364	76496	88780	77232	89187	77960	89586	78679	89976	79389	90358	80091	00
	238°		237°		236°		235°		234°		233°		

HAVERSINES

	127°		128°		129°		130°		131°		132°		
	Log.	Nat.	Log.	Nat.	Log.	Nat.	Log.	Nat.	Log.	Nat.	Log.	Nat.	
Parts for 0'·2. etc.	·2 1 ·2 2 ·4 2 ·4 5 ·6 4 ·6 7 ·8 5 ·8 9		·2 1 ·2 2 ·4 2 ·4 5 ·6 4 ·6 7 ·8 5 ·8 9		·2 1 ·2 2 ·4 2 ·4 4 ·6 4 ·6 7 ·8 5 ·8 9		·2 1 ·2 2 ·4 2 ·4 4 ·6 3 ·6 7 ·8 5 ·8 9		·2 1 ·2 2 ·4 2 ·4 4 ·6 3 ·6 7 ·8 5 ·8 9		·2 1 ·2 2 ·4 2 ·4 4 ·6 3 ·6 6 ·8 4 ·8 9		Parts for 0'·2. etc.
′	$\overline{1}$.or(9.)	0.	$\overline{1}$.or(9.)	0.	$\overline{1}$.or(9.)	0.	$\overline{1}$.or(9.)	0.	$\overline{1}$.or(9.)	0.	$\overline{1}$.or(9.)	0.	′
00	90358	80091	90732	80783	91098	81466	91455	82139	91805	82803	92146	83457	60
01	90365	80102	90738	80795	91104	81477	91461	82151	91810	82814	92152	83467	59
02	90371	80114	90744	80806	91110	81489	91467	82162	91816	82825	92157	83478	58
03	90377	80126	90751	80817	91116	81500	91473	82173	91822	82836	92163	83489	57
04	90383	80137	90757	80829	91122	81511	91479	82184	91828	82847	92169	83500	56
05	90390	80149	90763	80840	91128	81523	91485	82195	91833	82858	92174	83511	55
06	90396	80160	90769	80852	91134	81534	91490	82206	91839	82869	92180	83521	54
07	90402	80172	90775	80863	91140	81545	91496	82217	91845	82880	92185	83532	53
08	90409	80184	90781	80875	91146	81556	91502	82228	91851	82891	92191	83543	52
09	90415	80195	90787	80886	91152	81568	91508	82240	91856	82902	92197	83554	51
10	90421	80207	90794	80898	91158	81579	91514	82251	91862	82913	92202	83564	50
11	90428	80218	90800	80909	91164	81590	91520	82262	91868	82924	92208	83575	49
12	90434	80230	90806	80920	91170	81601	91526	82273	91874	82934	92213	83586	48
13	90440	80242	90812	80932	91176	81613	91532	82284	91879	82945	92219	83597	47
14	90446	80253	90818	80943	91182	81624	91537	82295	91885	82956	92225	83608	46
15	90452	80265	90824	80955	91188	81635	91543	82306	91891	82967	92230	83618	45
16	90459	80276	90830	80966	91194	31647	91549	82317	91896	82978	92236	83629	44
17	90465	80288	90836	80978	91200	81658	91555	82328	91902	82989	92241	83640	43
18	90471	80299	90843	80989	91206	81669	91561	82339	91908	83000	92247	83651	42
19	90478	80311	90849	81000	91212	81680	91567	82351	91914	83011	92253	83661	41
20	90484	80323	90855	81012	91218	81692	91573	82362	91919	83022	92258	83672	40
21	90490	80334	90861	81023	91224	81703	91578	82373	91925	83033	92264	83683	39
22	90496	80346	90867	81035	91230	81714	91584	82384	91931	83044	92269	83694	38
23	90503	80357	90873	81046	91236	81725	91590	82395	91936	83055	92275	83704	37
24	90509	80369	90879	81057	91242	81737	91596	82406	91942	83066	92280	83715	36
25	90515	80380	90885	81068	91248	81748	91602	82417	91948	83077	92286	83726	35
26	90521	80392	90892	81080	91254	81759	91608	82428	91954	83087	92292	83737	34
27	90537	80403	90898	81092	91260	81770	91613	82439	91959	83098	92297	83747	33
28	90534	80415	90904	81103	91265	81781	91619	82450	91965	83109	92303	83758	32
29	90540	80427	90910	81114	91271	81793	91625	82461	91971	83120	92308	83769	31
30	90546	80438	90916	81126	91277	81804	91631	82472	91976	83131	92314	83780	30
31	90552	80450	90922	81137	91283	81815	91637	82483	91982	83142	92319	83790	29
32	90559	80461	90928	81148	91289	81826	91643	82495	91988	83153	92325	83801	28
33	90565	80473	90934	81160	91295	81838	91648	82506	91993	83164	92330	83812	27
34	90571	80484	90940	81171	91301	81849	91654	82517	91999	83175	92336	83822	26
35	90577	80496	90946	81183	91307	81860	91660	82528	92005	83185	92342	83833	25
36	90584	80507	90952	81194	91313	81871	91666	82539	92010	83196	92347	83844	24
37	90590	80519	90958	81205	91319	81882	91672	82550	92016	83207	92353	83855	23
38	90596	80530	90965	81217	91325	81894	91677	82561	92022	83218	92358	83865	22
39	90602	80542	90971	81228	91331	81905	91683	82572	92027	83229	92364	83876	21
40	90608	80553	90977	81239	91337	81916	91689	82583	92033	83240	92369	83887	20
41	90615	80565	90983	81251	91343	81927	91695	82594	92039	83251	92375	83897	19
42	90621	80576	90989	81262	91349	81938	91701	82605	92044	83262	92380	83908	18
43	90627	80588	90995	81273	91355	81950	91706	82616	92050	83272	92386	83919	17
44	90633	80599	91001	81285	91361	81961	91712	82627	92056	83283	92391	83929	16
45	90639	80611	91007	81296	91367	81972	91718	82638	92061	83294	92397	83940	15
46	90645	80622	91013	81308	91372	81983	91724	82649	92067	83305	92402	83951	14
47	90652	80634	91019	81319	91378	81994	91730	82660	92073	83316	92408	83961	13
48	90658	80645	91025	81330	91384	82005	91735	82671	92078	83327	92413	83972	12
49	90664	80657	91031	81342	91390	82017	91741	82682	92084	83337	92419	83983	11
50	90670	80668	91037	81353	91396	82028	91747	82693	92090	83348	92425	83993	10
51	90676	80680	91043	81364	91402	82039	91753	82704	92095	83359	92430	84004	09
52	90683	80691	91049	81376	91408	82050	91758	82715	92101	83370	92436	84015	08
53	90689	80703	91055	81387	91414	82061	91764	82726	92107	83381	92441	84025	07
54	90695	80714	91061	81398	91420	82072	91770	82737	92112	83392	92447	84036	06
55	90701	80726	91067	81409	91426	82084	91776	82748	92118	83402	92452	84047	05
56	90707	80737	91074	81421	91432	82095	91782	82759	92124	83413	92458	84057	04
57	90714	80749	91080	81432	91437	82106	91787	82770	92129	83424	92463	84068	03
58	90720	80760	91086	81443	91443	82117	91793	82781	92135	83435	92469	84079	02
59	90726	80772	91092	81455	91449	82128	91799	82792	92140	83446	92474	84089	01
60	90732	80783	91098	81466	91455	82139	91805	82803	92146	83457	92480	84100	00
	232°		231°		230°		229°		228°		227°		

HAVERSINES

	133°		134°		135°		136°		137°		138°		
	Log.	Nat.	Log.	Nat.	Log.	Nat.	Log.	Nat.	Log.	Nat.	Log.	Nat.	
Parts for 0'.2, etc.	·2 1 ·2 2 ·4 2 ·4 4 ·6 3 ·6 6 ·8 4 ·8 8		·2 1 ·2 2 ·4 2 ·4 4 ·6 3 ·6 6 ·8 4 ·8 8		·2 1 ·2 2 ·4 2 ·4 4 ·6 3 ·6 6 ·8 4 ·8 8		·2 1 ·2 2 ·4 2 ·4 4 ·6 3 ·6 6 ·8 4 ·8 8		·2 1 ·2 2 ·4 2 ·4 4 ·6 3 ·6 6 ·8 4 ·8 8		·2 1 ·2 2 ·4 2 ·4 4 ·6 3 ·6 6 ·8 4 ·8 8		Parts for 0'.2, etc.
′	1̄.or(9.)	0.	1̄.or(9.)	0.	1̄.or(9.)	0.	1̄.or(9.)	0.	1̄.or(9.)	0.	1̄.or(9.)	0.	′
00	92480	84100	92805	84733	93123	85355	93433	85967	93736	86568	94030	87157	60
01	92485	84111	92811	84743	93128	85366	93438	85977	93741	86578	94035	87167	59
02	92491	84121	92816	84754	93134	85376	93443	85987	93746	86588	94040	87177	58
03	92496	84132	92821	84764	93139	85386	93448	85997	93751	86597	94045	87186	57
04	92502	84142	92827	84775	93144	85396	93454	86007	93755	86607	94050	87196	56
05	92507	84153	92832	84785	93149	85407	93459	86017	93760	86617	94055	87206	55
06	92512	84164	92837	84796	93154	85417	93464	86028	93765	86627	94059	87216	54
07	92518	84174	92843	84806	93160	85427	93469	86038	93770	86637	94064	87225	53
08	92523	84185	92848	84817	93165	85438	93474	86048	93775	86647	94069	87235	52
09	92529	84196	92853	84827	93170	85448	93479	86058	93780	86657	94074	87245	51
10	92534	84206	92859	84837	93175	85458	93484	86068	93785	86667	94079	87254	50
11	92540	84217	92864	84848	93181	85468	93489	86078	93790	86677	94084	87264	49
12	92545	84227	92869	84858	93186	85479	93494	86088	93795	86686	94088	87274	48
13	92551	84238	92875	84869	93191	85489	93499	86098	93800	86696	94093	87283	47
14	92556	84249	92880	84879	93196	85499	93504	86108	93805	86706	94098	87293	46
15	92562	84259	92885	84890	93201	85509	93509	86118	93810	86716	94103	87303	45
16	92567	84270	92891	84900	93207	85520	93515	86128	93815	86726	94108	87313	44
17	92573	84280	92896	84910	93212	85530	93520	86138	93820	86736	94112	87322	43
18	92578	84291	92901	84921	93217	85540	93525	86148	93825	86746	94117	87332	42
19	92584	84302	92907	84931	93222	85550	93530	86158	93830	86756	94122	87342	41
20	92589	84312	92912	84942	93227	85560	93535	86168	93835	86765	94127	87351	40
21	92594	84323	92917	84952	93232	85571	93540	86178	93840	86775	94132	87361	39
22	92600	84333	92923	84962	93238	85581	93545	86189	93845	86785	94137	87371	38
23	92605	84344	92928	84973	93243	85591	93550	86199	93849	86795	94141	87380	37
24	92611	84354	92933	84983	93248	85601	93555	86209	93854	86805	94146	87390	36
25	92616	84365	92939	84994	93253	85612	93560	86219	93859	86815	94151	87400	35
26	92622	84376	92944	85004	93258	85622	93565	86229	93864	86825	94156	87409	34
27	92627	84386	92949	85014	93264	85632	93570	86239	93869	86834	94161	87419	33
28	92633	84397	92955	85025	93269	85642	93575	86249	93874	86844	94165	87428	32
29	92638	84407	92960	85035	93274	85652	93580	86259	93879	86854	94170	87438	31
30	92643	84418	92965	85045	93279	85663	93585	86269	93884	86864	94175	87448	30
31	92649	84428	92970	85056	93284	85673	93590	86279	93889	86874	94180	87457	29
32	92654	84439	92975	85066	93289	85683	93595	86289	93894	86884	94184	87467	28
33	92660	84449	92981	85077	93295	85693	93600	86299	93899	86893	94189	87477	27
34	92665	84460	92986	85087	93300	85703	93605	86309	93904	86903	94194	87486	26
35	92670	84470	92992	85097	93305	85713	93611	86319	93908	86913	94199	87496	25
36	92676	84481	92997	85108	93310	85724	93616	86329	93913	86923	94204	87505	24
37	92681	84492	93002	85118	93315	85734	93621	86339	93918	86933	94208	87515	23
38	92687	84502	93007	85128	93320	85744	93626	86349	93923	86942	94213	87525	22
39	92692	84513	93013	85139	93326	85754	93631	86359	93928	86952	94218	87534	21
40	92698	84523	93018	85149	93331	85764	93636	86369	93933	86962	94223	87544	20
41	92703	84534	93023	85159	93336	85774	93641	86379	93938	86972	94227	87554	19
42	92708	84544	93029	85170	93341	85785	93646	86389	93943	86982	94232	87563	18
43	92714	84555	93034	85180	93346	85795	93651	86399	93948	86991	94237	87573	17
44	92719	84565	93039	85190	93351	85805	93656	86409	93952	87001	94242	87582	16
45	92725	84576	93044	85201	93356	85815	93661	86419	93957	87011	94246	87592	15
46	92730	84586	93050	85211	93362	85825	93666	86429	93962	87021	94251	87602	14
47	92735	84597	93055	85221	93367	85835	93671	86438	93967	87030	94256	87611	13
48	92741	84607	93060	85232	93372	85846	93676	86448	93972	87040	94261	87621	12
49	92746	84618	93065	85242	93377	85856	93681	86458	93977	87050	94265	87630	11
50	92751	84628	93071	85252	93382	85866	93686	86468	93982	87060	94270	87640	10
51	92757	84639	93076	85263	93387	85876	93691	86478	93987	87070	94275	87649	09
52	92762	84649	93081	85273	93392	85886	93696	86488	93991	87079	94280	87659	08
53	92768	84660	93086	85283	93397	85896	93701	86498	93996	87089	94284	87669	07
54	92773	84670	93092	85294	93403	85906	93706	86508	94001	87099	94289	87678	06
55	92778	84681	93097	85304	93408	85916	93711	86518	94006	87109	94294	87688	05
56	92784	84691	93102	85314	93413	85926	93716	86528	94011	87118	94299	87697	04
57	92789	84702	93107	85324	93418	85937	93721	86538	94016	87128	94303	87707	03
58	92794	84712	93113	85335	93423	85947	93726	86548	94021	87138	94308	87716	02
59	92800	84722	93118	85345	93428	85957	93731	86558	94026	87148	94313	87726	01
60	92805	84733	93123	85355	93433	85967	93736	86568	94030	87157	94318	87735	00

| | 226° | 225° | 224° | 223° | 222° | 221° | |

HAVERSINES

′	139° Log.	139° Nat.	140° Log.	140° Nat.	141° Log.	141° Nat.	142° Log.	142° Nat.	143° Log.	143° Nat.	144° Log.	144° Nat.	′
	1.or(9.)	0.	1.or(9.)	0.	1.or(9.)	0.	1.or(9.)	0.	1.or(9.)	0.	1.or(9.)	0.	
00	94318	87735	94597	88302	94869	88857	95134	89401	95391	89932	95641	90451	60
01	94322	87745	94602	88312	94874	88866	95138	89409	95396	89941	95645	90459	59
02	94327	87755	94606	88321	94878	88876	95143	89418	95400	89949	95649	90468	58
03	94332	87764	94611	88330	94883	88885	95147	89427	95404	89958	95654	90476	57
04	94336	87774	94616	88340	94887	88894	95151	89436	95408	89967	95658	90485	56
05	94341	87783	94620	88349	94892	88903	95156	89445	95412	89976	95662	90494	55
06	94346	87793	94625	88358	94896	88912	95160	89454	95417	89984	95666	90502	54
07	94351	87802	94629	88368	94901	88921	95164	89463	95421	89993	95670	90511	53
08	94355	87812	94634	88377	94905	88930	95169	89472	95425	90002	95674	90519	52
09	94360	87821	94638	88386	94909	88940	95173	89481	95429	90010	95678	90528	51
10	94365	87831	94643	88396	94914	88949	95177	89490	95433	90019	95682	90537	50
11	94369	87840	94648	88405	94918	88958	95182	89499	95438	90028	95686	90545	49
12	94374	87850	94652	88414	94923	88967	95186	89508	95442	90037	95690	90553	48
13	94379	87859	94657	88423	94927	88976	95190	89517	95446	90045	95694	90562	47
14	94383	87869	94661	88433	94932	88985	95195	89526	95450	90054	95699	90570	46
15	94388	87878	94666	88442	94936	88994	95199	89534	95454	90063	95703	90579	45
16	94393	87888	94670	88451	94941	89003	95203	89543	95459	90071	95707	90588	44
17	94398	87897	94675	88461	94945	89012	95208	89552	95463	90080	95711	90596	43
18	94402	87907	94680	88470	94950	89022	95212	89561	95467	90089	95715	90604	42
19	94407	87916	94684	88479	94954	89031	95216	89570	95471	90097	95719	90613	41
20	94412	87926	94689	88489	94958	89040	95221	89579	95475	90106	95723	90621	40
21	94416	87935	94693	88498	94963	89049	95225	89588	95480	90115	95727	90630	39
22	94421	87945	94698	88507	94967	89058	95229	89597	95484	90124	95731	90638	38
23	94426	87954	94702	88516	94972	89067	95234	89606	95488	90132	95735	90647	37
24	94430	87964	94707	88526	94976	89076	95238	89614	95492	90141	95739	90655	36
25	94435	87973	94711	88535	94981	89085	95242	89623	95496	90150	95743	90664	35
26	94440	87983	94716	88544	94985	89094	95246	89632	95501	90158	95747	90672	34
27	94444	87992	94721	88553	94989	89103	95251	89641	95505	90167	95751	90680	33
28	94449	88001	94725	88563	94994	89112	95255	89650	95509	90176	95755	90689	32
29	94454	88011	94730	88572	94998	89121	95259	89659	95513	90184	95759	90697	31
30	94458	88020	94734	88581	95003	89130	95264	89668	95517	90193	95763	90706	30
31	94463	88030	94739	88590	95007	89139	95268	89677	95521	90201	95768	90714	29
32	94468	88039	94743	88600	95011	89149	95272	89685	95526	90210	95772	90723	28
33	94472	88049	94748	88609	95016	89158	95276	89694	95530	90219	95776	90731	27
34	94477	88058	94752	88618	95020	89167	95281	89703	95534	90227	95780	90740	26
35	94482	88068	94757	88627	95025	89176	95285	89712	95538	90236	95784	90748	25
36	94486	88078	94761	88637	95029	89185	95289	89721	95542	90245	95788	90756	24
37	94491	88086	94766	88646	95033	89194	95294	89730	95546	90253	95792	90765	23
38	94496	88096	94770	88655	95038	89203	95298	89738	95550	90262	95796	90773	22
39	94500	88105	94774	88664	95042	89212	95302	89747	95555	90271	95800	90782	21
40	94505	88115	94779	88674	95047	89221	95306	89756	95559	90279	95804	90790	20
41	94509	88124	94784	88683	95051	89230	95311	89765	95563	90288	95808	90798	19
42	94514	88133	94788	88692	95055	89239	95315	89774	95567	90296	95812	90807	18
43	94519	88143	94793	88701	95060	89248	95319	89783	95571	90305	95816	90815	17
44	94523	88152	94797	88710	95064	89257	95323	89791	95575	90314	95820	90824	16
45	94528	88162	94802	88720	95069	89266	95328	89800	95579	90322	95824	90832	15
46	94533	88171	94806	88729	95073	89275	95332	89809	95584	90331	95828	90840	14
47	94537	88180	94811	88738	95077	89284	95336	89818	95588	90339	95832	90849	13
48	94542	88190	94815	88747	95082	89293	95340	89827	95592	90348	95836	90857	12
49	94546	88199	94820	88756	95086	89302	95345	89835	95596	90357	95840	90866	11
50	94551	88209	94824	88766	95090	89311	95349	89844	95600	90365	95844	90874	10
51	94556	88218	94829	88775	95095	89320	95353	89853	95604	90374	95848	90882	09
52	94560	88227	94833	88784	95099	89329	95357	89862	95608	90382	95852	90891	08
53	94565	88237	94838	88793	95104	89338	95362	89870	95613	90391	95856	90899	07
54	94570	88246	94842	88802	95108	89347	95366	89879	95617	90399	95860	90907	06
55	94574	88255	94847	88811	95112	89356	95370	89888	95621	90408	95864	90916	05
56	94579	88265	94851	88821	95117	89365	95374	89897	95625	90417	95868	90924	04
57	94583	88274	94856	88830	95121	89374	95379	89906	95629	90425	95872	90933	03
58	94588	88284	94860	88839	95125	89383	95383	89914	95633	90434	95876	90941	02
59	94593	88293	94865	88848	95130	89392	95387	89923	95637	90442	95880	90949	01
60	94597	88302	94869	88857	95134	89401	95391	89932	95641	90451	95884	90958	00

220°	219°	218°	217°	216°	215°

Parts for 0′.2, etc.

139°	140°	141°	142°	143°	144°
·2 1 ·2 2	·2 1 ·2 2	·2 1 ·2 2	·2 1 ·2 2	·2 1 ·2 2	·2 1 ·2 2
·4 2 ·4 4	·4 2 ·4 4	·4 2 ·4 4	·4 2 ·4 4	·4 2 ·4 3	·4 2 ·4 3
·6 3 ·6 6	·6 3 ·6 6	·6 3 ·6 5	·6 3 ·6 5	·6 3 ·6 5	·6 2 ·6 5
·8 4 ·8 8	·8 4 ·8 8	·8 4 ·8 7	·8 3 ·8 7	·8 3 ·8 7	·8 3 ·8 7

HAVERSINES

Parts for 0'.2 etc	145° Log.	145° Nat.	146° Log.	146° Nat.	147° Log.	147° Nat.	148° Log.	148° Nat.	149° Log.	149° Nat.	150° Log.	150° Nat.	Parts for 0'.2 etc
·2 1 ·2 2 / ·4 2 ·4 3 / ·6 2 ·6 5 / ·8 3 ·8 7	1.or(9.)	0.	1.or(9.)	0.	1.or(9.)	0.	1.or(9.)	0.	1.or(9.)	0.	1.or(9.)	0.	
′													**′**
00	95884	90958	96119	91452	96347	91934	96568	92402	96782	92858	96989	93301	60
01	95888	90966	96123	91460	96351	91941	96572	92410	96786	92866	96992	93309	59
02	95892	90974	96127	91468	96355	91949	96576	92418	96789	92873	96996	93316	58
03	95896	90983	96131	91476	96359	91957	96579	92426	96793	92881	96999	93323	57
04	95900	90991	96135	91484	96362	91965	96583	92433	96796	92888	97002	93330	56
05	95904	90999	96139	91493	96366	91973	96586	92441	96800	92896	97006	93338	55
06	95908	91008	96142	91501	96370	91981	96590	92449	96803	92903	97009	93345	54
07	95912	91016	96146	91509	96374	91989	96594	92456	96807	92911	97012	93352	53
08	95916	91024	96150	91517	96377	91997	96597	92464	96810	92918	97016	93359	52
09	95920	91033	96154	91525	96381	92005	96601	92472	96814	92926	97019	93367	51
10	95924	91041	96158	91533	96385	92013	96604	92479	96817	92933	97022	93374	50
11	95928	91049	96162	91541	96388	92020	96608	92487	96821	92941	97026	93381	49
12	95932	91057	96165	91549	96392	92028	96612	92495	96824	92948	97029	93388	48
13	95936	91066	96169	91557	96396	92036	96615	92502	96827	92955	97033	93395	47
14	95939	91074	96173	91565	96400	92044	96619	92510	96831	92963	97036	93403	46
15	95943	91082	96177	91574	96403	92052	96622	92518	96834	92970	97039	93410	45
16	95947	91091	96181	91582	96407	92060	96626	92525	96837	92978	97043	93417	44
17	95951	91099	96185	91590	96411	92068	96630	92533	96841	92985	97046	93424	43
18	95955	91107	96188	91598	96415	92076	96633	92541	96845	92993	97049	93432	42
19	95959	91115	96192	91606	96418	92083	96637	92548	96848	93000	97052	93439	41
20	95963	91124	96196	91614	96422	92091	96640	92556	96852	93007	97056	93446	40
21	95967	91132	96200	91622	96426	92099	96644	92563	96855	93015	97059	93453	39
22	95971	91140	96204	91630	96429	92107	96648	92571	96859	93022	97063	93460	38
23	95975	91149	96208	91638	96433	92115	96651	92579	96862	93030	97066	93468	37
24	95979	91157	96211	91646	96437	92123	96655	92586	96866	93037	97069	93475	36
25	95983	91165	96215	91654	96440	92130	96658	92594	96869	93045	97073	93482	35
26	95987	91173	96219	91662	96444	92138	96662	92602	96873	93052	97076	93489	34
27	95991	91182	96223	91670	96448	92146	96665	92609	96876	93059	97079	93496	33
28	95995	91190	96227	91678	96451	92154	96669	92617	96879	93067	97083	93503	32
29	95999	91198	96230	91686	96455	92162	96673	92624	96883	93074	97086	93511	31
30	96002	91206	96234	91694	96459	92170	96676	92632	96886	93081	97089	93518	30
31	96006	91215	96238	91702	96462	92177	96680	92640	96890	93089	97093	93525	29
32	96010	91223	96242	91710	96466	92185	96683	92647	96894	93096	97096	93532	28
33	96014	91231	96246	91718	96470	92193	96687	92655	96897	93104	97099	93539	27
34	96018	91239	96249	91726	96473	92201	96690	92662	96900	93111	97103	93546	26
35	96022	91247	96253	91734	96477	92209	96694	92670	96904	93118	97106	93554	25
36	96026	91256	96257	91742	96481	92216	96697	92678	96907	93126	97109	93561	24
37	96030	91264	96261	91750	96484	92224	96701	92685	96910	93133	97113	93568	23
38	96034	91272	96265	91758	96488	92232	96705	92693	96914	93140	97116	93575	22
39	96038	91280	96268	91766	96492	92240	96708	92700	96917	93148	97119	93582	21
40	96042	91289	96272	91774	96495	92248	96712	92708	96921	93155	97123	93589	20
41	96046	91297	96276	91782	96499	92255	96715	92715	96924	93162	97126	93596	19
42	96049	91305	96280	91790	96503	92263	96719	92723	96928	93170	97129	93603	18
43	96053	91313	96283	91798	96506	92271	96722	92731	96931	93177	97132	93611	17
44	96057	91321	96287	91806	96510	92279	96726	92738	96934	93184	97136	93618	16
45	96061	91329	96291	91814	96514	92286	96729	92746	96938	93192	97139	93625	15
46	96065	91338	96295	91822	96517	92294	96733	92753	96941	93199	97142	93632	14
47	96069	91346	96299	91830	96521	92302	96736	92761	96945	93206	97146	93639	13
48	96073	91354	96302	91838	96525	92310	96740	92768	96948	93214	97149	93646	12
49	96077	91362	96306	91846	96528	92317	96743	92776	96951	93221	97152	93653	11
50	96081	91370	96310	91854	96532	92325	96747	92783	96955	93228	97156	93660	10
51	96084	91379	96314	91862	96536	92333	96750	92791	96958	93236	97159	93667	09
52	96088	91387	96317	91870	96539	92341	96754	92798	96962	93243	97162	93674	08
53	96092	91395	96321	91878	96543	92348	96758	92806	96965	93250	97165	93682	07
54	96096	91403	96325	91886	96547	92356	96761	92813	96968	93258	97169	93689	06
55	96100	91411	96329	91894	96550	92364	96765	92821	96972	93265	97172	93696	05
56	96104	91419	96332	91902	96554	92372	96768	92828	96975	93272	97175	93703	04
57	96108	91427	96336	91910	96557	92379	96772	92836	96979	93279	97179	93710	03
58	96112	91436	96340	91918	96561	92387	96775	92843	96982	93287	97182	93717	02
59	96115	91444	96344	91926	96565	92394	96779	92851	96985	93294	97185	93724	01
60	96119	91452	96347	91934	96568	92402	96782	92858	96989	93301	97188	93731	00
	214°		**213°**		**212°**		**211°**		**210°**		**209°**		

HAVERSINES

Parts for 0'.2 etc.

	151°		152°		153°		154°		155°		156°		
	Log.	Nat.	Log.	Nat.	Log.	Nat.	Log.	Nat.	Log.	Nat.	Log.	Nat.	
	·2 1 ·2 1		·2 1 ·2 1		·2 1 ·2 1		·2 1 ·2 1		·2 1 ·2 1		·2 1 ·2 1		
	·4 1 ·4 3		·4 1 ·4 3		·4 1 ·4 3		·4 1 ·4 3		·4 1 ·4 2		·4 1 ·4 2		
	·6 2 ·6 4		·6 2 ·6 4		·6 2 ·6 4		·6 2 ·6 4		·6 2 ·6 4		·6 2 ·6 3		
	·8 3 ·8 6		·8 2 ·8 5		·8 2 ·8 5		·8 2 ·8 5		·8 2 ·8 5		·8 2 ·8 5		
'	1̄.or(9.)	0.	1̄.or(9.)	0.	1̄.or(9.)	0.	1̄.or(9.)	0.	1̄.or(9.)	0.	1̄.or(9.)	0.	**'**
00	97188	93731	97381	94147	97566	94550	97745	94940	97916	95315	98081	95677	60
01	97192	93738	97384	94154	97569	94557	97748	94946	97919	95322	98084	95683	59
02	97195	93745	97387	94161	97572	94564	97751	94952	97922	95328	98086	95689	58
03	97198	93752	97390	94168	97570	94570	97754	94959	97925	95334	98089	95695	57
04	97201	93759	97393	94175	97578	94577	97756	94965	97927	95340	98092	95701	56
05	97205	93766	97397	94181	97581	94583	97759	94972	97930	95346	98094	95707	55
06	97208	93773	97400	94188	97584	94590	97762	94978	97933	95352	98097	95713	54
07	97211	93780	97403	94195	97587	94596	97765	94984	97936	95358	98100	95719	53
08	97214	93787	97406	94202	97591	94603	97768	94991	97939	95364	98102	95724	52
09	97218	93794	97409	94209	97594	94610	97771	94997	97941	95371	98105	95730	51
10	97221	93801	97412	94215	97597	94616	97774	95003	97944	95377	98108	95736	50
11	97224	93808	97415	94222	97600	94623	97777	95010	97947	95383	98110	95742	49
12	97227	93815	97418	94229	97603	94629	97780	95016	97950	95389	98113	95748	48
13	97231	93822	97422	94236	97606	94636	97783	95022	97953	95395	98116	95754	47
14	97234	93829	97425	94243	97609	94642	97785	95029	97955	95401	98118	95760	46
15	97237	93836	97428	94249	97612	94649	97788	95035	97958	95407	98121	95766	45
16	97240	93843	97431	94256	97615	94655	97791	95041	97961	95413	98124	95771	44
17	97244	93850	97434	94263	97618	94662	97794	95048	97964	95419	98126	95777	43
18	97247	93857	97437	94270	97621	94669	97797	95054	97966	95425	98129	95783	42
19	97250	93864	97440	94276	97624	94675	97800	95060	97969	95431	98132	95789	41
20	97253	93871	97443	94283	97627	94682	97803	95066	97972	95438	98134	95795	40
21	97257	93878	97447	94290	97630	94688	97806	95073	97975	95444	98137	95801	39
22	97260	93885	97450	94297	97633	94695	97808	95079	97977	95450	98139	95806	38
23	97263	93892	97453	94303	97636	94701	97811	95085	97980	95456	98142	95812	37
24	97266	93899	97456	94310	97639	94708	97814	95092	97983	95462	98145	95818	36
25	97269	93906	97459	94317	97642	94714	97817	95098	97986	95468	98147	95824	35
26	97273	93913	97462	94324	97645	94721	97820	95104	97988	95474	98150	95830	34
27	97276	93920	97465	94330	97647	94727	97823	95111	97991	95480	98153	95836	33
28	97279	93927	97468	94337	97650	94734	97826	95117	97994	95486	98155	95841	32
29	97282	93934	97471	94344	97653	94740	97829	95123	97997	95492	98158	95847	31
30	97285	93941	97474	94351	97656	94747	97831	95129	97999	95498	98161	95853	30
31	97289	93948	97478	94357	97659	94753	97834	95136	98002	95504	98163	95859	29
32	97292	93955	97481	94364	97662	94760	97837	95142	98005	95510	98166	95865	28
33	97295	93962	97484	94371	97665	94766	97840	95148	98008	95516	98168	95870	27
34	97298	93969	97487	94377	97668	94773	97843	95154	98010	95522	98171	95876	26
35	97301	93976	97490	94384	97671	94779	97846	95161	98013	95528	98174	95882	25
36	97305	93982	97493	94391	97674	94786	97849	95167	98016	95534	98176	95888	24
37	97308	93989	97496	94397	97677	94792	97851	95173	98019	95540	98179	95894	23
38	97311	93996	97499	94404	97680	94799	97854	95179	98021	95546	98182	95899	22
39	97314	94003	97502	94411	97683	94805	97857	95185	98024	95552	98184	95905	21
40	97317	94010	97505	94418	97686	94811	97860	95192	98027	95558	98187	95911	20
41	97321	94017	97508	94424	97689	94818	97863	95198	98030	95564	98189	95917	19
42	97324	94024	97511	94431	97692	94824	97866	95204	98032	95570	98192	95922	18
43	97327	94031	97514	94438	97695	94831	97868	95210	98035	95576	98195	95928	17
44	97330	94038	97518	94444	97698	94837	97871	95217	98038	95582	98197	95934	16
45	97333	94045	97521	94451	97701	94844	97874	95223	98040	95588	98200	95940	15
46	97337	94051	97524	94458	97704	94850	97877	95229	98042	95594	98202	95945	14
47	97340	94058	97527	94464	97707	94857	97880	95235	98046	95600	98205	95951	13
48	97343	94065	97530	94471	97710	94863	97883	95241	98049	95606	98208	95957	12
49	97346	94072	97533	94477	97713	94869	97885	95248	98051	95612	98210	95962	11
50	97349	94079	97536	94484	97716	94876	97888	95254	98054	95618	98213	95968	10
51	97352	94086	97539	94491	97718	94882	97891	95260	98057	95624	98215	95974	09
52	97356	94093	97542	94497	97721	94889	97894	95266	98059	95630	98218	95980	08
53	97359	94099	97545	94504	97724	94895	97897	95272	98062	95636	98221	95985	07
54	97362	94106	97548	94511	97727	94901	97899	95278	98065	95642	98223	95991	06
55	97365	94113	97551	94517	97730	94908	97902	95285	98067	95648	98226	95997	05
56	97368	94120	97554	94524	97733	94914	97905	95291	98070	95654	98228	96002	04
57	97371	94127	97557	94531	97736	94921	97908	95297	98073	95660	98231	96008	03
58	97375	94134	97560	94537	97739	94927	97911	95303	98076	95665	98233	96014	02
59	97378	94141	97563	94544	97742	94933	97914	95309	98078	95671	98236	96020	01
60	97381	94147	97566	94550	97745	94940	97916	95315	98081	95677	98239	96025	00
	208°		207°		206°		205°		204°		203°		

Parts for 0'.2 etc.

HAVERSINES

	157°		158°		159°		160°		161°		162°		
	Log.	Nat.	Log.	Nat.	Log.	Nat.	Log.	Nat.	Log.	Nat.	Log.	Nat.	
Parts for 0'.2 etc.	.2 1 / .4 1 / .6 2 / .8 2	.2 1 / .4 2 / .6 3 / .8 4	.2 0 / .4 1 / .6 1 / .8 2	.2 1 / .4 2 / .6 3 / .8 4	.2 0 / .4 1 / .6 1 / .8 2	.2 1 / .4 2 / .6 3 / .8 4	.2 0 / .4 1 / .6 1 / .8 2	.2 1 / .4 2 / .6 3 / .8 4	.2 0 / .4 1 / .6 1 / .8 2	.2 1 / .4 2 / .6 3 / .8 4	.2 0 / .4 1 / .6 1 / .8 2	.2 1 / .4 2 / .6 3 / .8 3	Parts for 0'.2 etc.
$'$	$\overline{1}$.or(9.)	0.	$\overline{1}$.or(9.)	0.	$\overline{1}$.or(9.)	0.	$\overline{1}$.or(9.)	0.	$\overline{1}$.or(9.)	0.	$\overline{1}$.or(9.)	0.	$'$
00	98239	96025	98389	96359	98533	96679	98670	96985	98801	97276	98924	97553	60
01	98241	96031	98392	96365	98536	96684	98673	96990	98803	97281	98926	97557	59
02	98244	96037	98394	96370	98538	96689	98675	96995	98805	97285	98928	97562	58
03	98246	96042	98397	96376	98540	96695	98677	97000	98807	97290	98930	97566	57
04	98249	96048	98399	96381	98543	96700	98679	97005	98809	97295	98932	97571	56
05	98251	96054	98402	96386	98545	96705	98681	97009	98811	97300	98934	97575	55
06	98254	96059	98404	96392	98547	96710	98684	97014	98813	97304	98936	97580	54
07	98256	96065	98406	96397	98550	96715	98686	97019	98815	97309	98938	97584	53
08	98259	96071	98409	96403	98552	96721	98688	97024	98817	97314	98940	97589	52
09	98262	96076	98411	96408	98554	96726	98690	97029	98819	97318	98942	97593	51
10	98264	96082	98414	96413	98557	96731	98692	97034	98822	97323	98944	97598	50
11	98267	96088	98416	96419	98559	96736	98695	97039	98824	97328	98946	97602	49
12	98269	96093	98419	96424	98561	96741	98697	97044	98826	97332	98948	97606	48
13	98272	96099	98421	96430	98564	96746	98699	97049	98828	97337	98950	97611	47
14	98274	96104	98424	96435	98566	96752	98701	97054	98830	97342	98952	97615	46
15	98277	96110	98426	96440	98568	96757	98703	97059	98832	97347	98954	97620	45
16	98279	96116	98428	96446	98570	96762	98706	97064	98834	97351	98956	97624	44
17	98282	96121	98431	96451	98573	96767	98708	97069	98836	97356	98958	97629	43
18	98285	96127	98433	96457	98575	96772	98710	97074	98838	97361	98960	97633	42
19	98287	96133	98436	96462	98577	96777	98712	97078	98840	97365	98962	97637	41
20	98290	96138	98438	96467	98580	96782	98714	97083	98842	97370	98964	97642	40
21	98292	96144	98440	96473	98582	96788	98717	97088	98845	97374	98966	97646	39
22	98295	96149	98443	96478	98584	96793	98719	97093	98847	97379	98968	97651	38
23	98297	96155	98445	96483	98587	96798	98721	97098	98849	97384	98970	97655	37
24	98300	96161	98448	96489	98589	96803	98723	97103	98851	97388	98971	97660	36
25	98302	96166	98450	96494	98591	96808	98725	97108	98853	97393	98973	97664	35
26	98305	96172	98453	96500	98593	96813	98728	97113	98855	97398	98975	97668	34
27	98307	96177	98455	96505	98596	96818	98730	97117	98857	97402	98977	97673	33
28	98310	96183	98457	96510	98598	96823	98732	97122	98859	97407	98979	97677	32
29	98312	96188	98460	96516	98600	96829	98734	97127	98861	97412	98981	97681	31
30	98315	96194	98462	96521	98603	96834	98736	97132	98863	97416	98983	97686	30
31	98317	96200	98465	96526	98605	96839	98738	97137	98865	97421	98985	97690	29
32	98320	96205	98467	96532	98607	96844	98741	97142	98867	97425	98987	97695	28
33	98322	96211	98469	96537	98609	96849	98743	97147	98869	97430	98989	97699	27
34	98325	96216	98472	96542	98612	96854	98745	97151	98871	97435	98991	97703	26
35	98327	96222	98474	96547	98614	96859	98747	97156	98873	97439	98993	97708	25
36	98330	96227	98476	96553	98616	96864	98749	97161	98875	97444	98995	97712	24
37	98332	96233	98479	96558	98619	96869	98751	97166	98877	97448	98997	97716	23
38	98335	96238	98481	96563	98621	96874	98754	97171	98880	97453	98999	97721	22
39	98337	96244	98484	96569	98623	96879	98756	97176	98882	97458	99001	97725	21
40	98340	96249	98486	96574	98625	96884	98758	97180	98884	97462	99003	97729	20
41	98342	96255	98488	96579	98628	96889	98760	97185	98886	97467	99004	97734	19
42	98345	96260	98491	96585	98630	96894	98762	97190	98888	97471	99006	97738	18
43	98347	96266	98493	96590	98632	96899	98764	97195	98890	97476	99008	97742	17
44	98350	96272	98496	96595	98634	96905	98766	97200	98892	97480	99010	97747	16
45	98352	96277	98498	96600	98637	96910	98769	97204	98894	97485	99012	97751	15
46	98355	96283	98500	96606	98639	96915	98771	97209	98896	97490	99014	97755	14
47	98357	96288	98503	96611	98641	96920	98773	97214	98898	97494	99016	97760	13
48	98360	96294	98505	96616	98643	96925	98775	97219	98900	97499	99018	97764	12
49	98362	96299	98507	96621	98646	96930	98777	97224	98902	97503	99020	97768	11
50	98365	96305	98510	96627	98648	96935	98779	97228	98904	97508	99022	97773	10
51	98367	96310	98512	96632	98650	96940	98781	97233	98906	97512	99024	97777	09
52	98370	96315	98514	96637	98652	96945	98784	97238	98908	97517	99026	97781	08
53	98372	96321	98517	96642	98655	96950	98786	97243	98910	97521	99027	97785	07
54	98375	96326	98519	96648	98657	96955	98788	97247	98912	97526	99029	97790	06
55	98377	96332	98521	96653	98659	96960	98790	97252	98914	97530	99031	97794	05
56	98379	96337	98524	96658	98661	96965	98792	97257	98916	97535	99033	97798	04
57	98382	96343	98526	96663	98664	96970	98794	97262	98918	97539	99035	97802	03
58	98384	96348	98529	96669	98666	96975	98796	97266	98920	97544	99037	97807	02
59	98387	96354	98531	96674	98668	96980	98798	97271	98922	97548	99039	97811	01
60	98389	96359	98533	96679	98670	96985	98801	97276	98924	97553	99041	97815	00
	202°		201°		200°		199°		198°		197°		

HAVERSINES

Parts for 0'.2, etc. (left and right margins):

163°		164°		165°		166°		167°		168°	
.2 0 / .2 1		.2 0 / .2 1		.2 0 / .2 1		.2 0 / .2 1		.2 0 / .2 1		.2 0 / .2 1	
.4 1 / .4 2		.4 1 / .4 2		.4 1 / .4 1		.4 1 / .4 1		.4 1 / .4 1		.4 1 / .4 1	
.6 1 / .6 2		.6 1 / .6 2		.6 1 / .6 2		.6 1 / .6 2		.6 1 / .6 2		.6 1 / .6 2	
.8 1 / .8 3		.8 1 / .8 3		.8 1 / .8 3		.8 1 / .8 3		.8 1 / .8 3		.8 1 / .8 2	

′	163° Log. 1.or(9.)	Nat. 0.	164° Log. 1.or(9.)	Nat. 0.	165° Log. 1.or(9.)	Nat. 0.	166° Log. 1.or(9.)	Nat. 0.	167° Log. 1.or(9.)	Nat. 0.	168° Log. 1.or(9.)	Nat. 0.	′
00	99041	97815	99151	98063	99254	98296	99350	98515	99440	98719	99523	98907	60
01	99043	97819	99152	98067	99255	98300	99352	98518	99441	98722	99524	98910	59
02	99044	97824	99154	98071	99257	98304	99353	98522	99443	98725	99526	98913	58
03	99046	97828	99156	98075	99259	98308	99355	98525	99444	98728	99527	98916	57
04	99048	97832	99158	98079	99260	98311	99356	98529	99446	98732	99528	98919	56
05	99050	97836	99159	98083	99262	98315	99358	98532	99447	98735	99529	98922	55
06	99052	97841	99161	98087	99264	98319	99359	98536	99448	98738	99531	98925	54
07	99054	97845	99163	98091	99265	98323	99361	98539	99450	98741	99532	98928	53
08	99056	97849	99165	98095	99267	98326	99362	98543	99451	98745	99533	98931	52
09	99058	97853	99166	98099	99269	98330	99364	98546	99453	98748	99535	98934	51
10	99059	97858	99168	98103	99270	98334	99366	98550	99454	98751	99536	98937	50
11	99061	97862	99170	98107	99272	98337	99367	98553	99456	98754	99537	98940	49
12	99063	97866	99172	98111	99274	98341	99369	98557	99457	98757	99539	98943	48
13	99065	97870	99173	98115	99275	98345	99370	98560	99458	98761	99540	98946	47
14	99067	97874	99175	98119	99277	98349	99372	98564	99460	98764	99541	98949	46
15	99069	97879	99177	98123	99278	98352	99373	98567	99461	98767	99543	98952	45
16	99071	97883	99179	98127	99280	98356	99375	98571	99463	98770	99544	98955	44
17	99072	97887	99180	98131	98282	98360	99376	98574	99464	98774	99545	98958	43
18	99074	97891	99182	98135	99283	98363	99378	98577	99465	98777	99546	98961	42
19	99076	97895	99184	98139	99285	98367	99379	98581	99467	98780	99548	98964	41
20	99078	97899	99186	98142	99287	98371	99381	98584	99468	98783	99549	98967	40
21	99080	97904	99187	98146	99288	98374	99382	98588	99470	98786	99550	98970	39
22	99082	97908	99189	98150	99290	98378	99384	98591	99471	98789	99552	98973	38
23	99084	97912	99191	98154	99291	98382	99385	98595	99472	98793	99553	98976	37
24	99085	97916	99193	98158	99293	98385	99387	98598	99474	98796	99554	98979	36
25	99087	97920	99194	98162	99295	98389	99388	98601	99475	98799	99555	98982	35
26	99089	97924	99196	98166	99296	98393	99390	98605	99477	98802	99557	98985	34
27	99091	97929	99198	98170	99298	98396	99391	98608	99478	98805	99558	98987	33
28	99093	97933	99200	98174	99300	98400	99393	98611	99479	98809	99559	98990	32
29	99095	97937	99201	98178	99301	98404	99394	98615	99481	98812	99561	98993	31
30	99096	97941	99203	98182	99303	98407	99396	98619	99482	98815	99562	98996	30
31	99098	97945	99205	98185	99304	98411	99397	98622	99484	98818	99563	98999	29
32	99100	97949	99206	98189	99306	98415	99399	98625	99485	98821	99564	99002	28
33	99102	97953	99208	98193	99308	98418	99400	98629	99486	98824	99566	99005	27
34	99104	97957	99210	98197	99309	98422	99402	98632	99488	98827	99567	99008	26
35	99106	97962	99212	98201	99311	98426	99403	98635	99489	98830	99568	99011	25
36	99107	97966	99213	98205	99312	98429	99405	98639	99490	98834	99569	99014	24
37	99109	97970	99215	98209	99314	98433	99406	98642	99492	98837	99571	99016	23
38	99111	97974	99217	98212	99316	98436	99408	98646	99493	98840	99572	99019	22
39	99113	97978	99218	98216	99317	98440	99409	98649	99495	98843	99573	99022	21
40	99115	97982	99220	98220	99319	98444	99411	98652	99496	98846	99575	99025	20
41	99116	97986	99222	98224	99320	98447	99412	98656	99497	98849	99576	99028	19
42	99118	97990	99223	98228	99322	98451	99414	98659	99499	98852	99577	99031	18
43	99120	97994	99225	98232	99324	98454	99415	98662	99500	98855	99578	99034	17
44	99122	97998	99227	98236	99325	98458	99417	98666	99501	98858	99580	99036	16
45	99124	98002	99229	98239	99327	98462	99418	98669	99503	98862	99581	99039	15
46	99126	98007	99230	98243	99328	98465	99420	98672	99504	98865	99582	99042	14
47	99127	98011	99232	98247	99330	98469	99421	98676	99505	98868	99583	99045	13
48	99129	98015	99234	98251	99331	98472	99422	98679	99507	98871	99584	99048	12
49	99131	98019	99235	98255	99333	98476	99424	98682	99508	98874	99586	99051	11
50	99133	98023	99237	98258	99335	98479	99425	98686	99510	98877	99587	99053	10
51	99135	98027	99239	98262	99336	98483	99427	98689	99511	98880	99588	99056	09
52	99136	98031	99240	98266	99338	98487	99429	98692	99512	98883	99589	99059	08
53	99138	98035	99242	98270	99339	98490	99430	98696	99514	98886	99591	99062	07
54	99140	98039	99244	98274	99341	98494	99431	98699	99515	98889	99592	99065	06
55	99142	98043	99245	98277	99342	98497	99433	98702	99516	98892	99593	99067	05
56	99143	98047	99247	98281	99344	98501	99434	98705	99518	98895	99594	99070	04
57	99145	98051	99249	98285	99345	98504	99436	98709	99519	98898	99596	99073	03
58	99147	98055	99250	98289	99347	98508	99437	98712	99520	98901	99597	99076	02
59	99149	98059	99252	98293	99349	98511	99438	98715	99522	98904	99598	99079	01
60	99151	98063	99254	98296	99350	98515	99440	98719	99523	98907	99599	99081	00

| 196° | 195° | 194° | 193° | 192° | 191° |

HAVERSINES

	169°		170°		171°		172°		173°		174°	
	Log.	Nat.	Log.	Nat.	Log.	Nat.	Log.	Nat.	Log.	Nat.	Log.	Nat.	
Parts for 0'2 etc.	·2 0 / ·4 0 / ·6 1 / ·8 1	·2 1 / ·4 1 / ·6 2 / ·8 2	·2 0 / ·4 0 / ·6 1 / ·8 1	·2 0 / ·4 1 / ·6 1 / ·8 2	·2 0 / ·4 0 / ·6 1 / ·8 1	·2 0 / ·4 1 / ·6 1 / ·8 2	·2 0 / ·4 0 / ·6 0 / ·8 1	·2 0 / ·4 1 / ·6 1 / ·8 2	·2 0 / ·4 0 / ·6 0 / ·8 1	·2 0 / ·4 1 / ·6 1 / ·8 1	·2 0 / ·4 0 / ·6 0 / ·8 0	·2 0 / ·4 1 / ·6 1 / ·8 1	Parts for 0'2 etc.
′	1̄.or(9.)	0.	1̄.or(9.)	0.	1̄.or(9.)	0.	1̄.or(9.)	0.	1̄.or(9.)	0.	1̄.or(9.)	0.	′
00	99599	99081	99669	99240	99732	99384	99788	99513	99838	99627	99881	99726	60
01	99600	99084	99670	99243	99733	99387	99789	99515	99839	99629	99882	99728	59
02	99602	99087	99671	99245	99734	99389	99790	99517	99839	99631	99882	99729	58
03	99603	99090	99672	99248	99735	99391	99791	99519	99840	99633	99883	99731	57
04	99604	99092	99673	99250	99736	99393	99792	99521	99841	99634	99884	99732	56
05	99605	99095	99674	99253	99737	99396	99793	99523	99842	99636	99884	99734	55
06	99606	99098	99675	99255	99738	99398	99793	99525	99842	99638	99885	99735	54
07	99608	99101	99677	99258	99739	99400	99794	99527	99843	99640	99885	99737	53
08	99609	99103	99678	99260	99740	99402	99795	99529	99844	99641	99886	99738	52
09	99610	99106	99679	99263	99741	99405	99796	99531	99845	99643	99887	99740	51
10	99611	99109	99680	99265	99742	99407	99797	99533	99845	99645	99887	99741	50
11	99612	99112	99681	99268	99743	99409	99798	99535	99846	99647	99888	99743	49
12	99614	99114	99682	99270	99744	99411	99799	99537	99847	99648	99889	99744	48
13	99615	99117	99683	99273	99745	99414	99800	99539	99848	99650	99889	99746	47
14	99616	99120	99684	99275	99746	99416	99800	99541	99848	99652	99890	99747	46
15	99617	99123	99685	99278	99747	99418	99801	99543	99849	99653	99891	99748	45
16	99618	99125	99686	99280	99748	99420	99802	99545	99850	99655	99891	99750	44
17	99620	99128	99687	99283	99748	99422	99803	99547	99851	99657	99892	99751	43
18	99621	99131	99688	99285	99749	99425	99804	99549	99851	99659	99893	99753	42
19	99622	99133	99690	99288	99750	99427	99805	99551	99852	99660	99893	99754	41
20	99623	99136	99691	99290	99751	99429	99805	99553	99853	99662	99894	99756	40
21	99624	99139	99692	99293	99752	99431	99806	99555	99854	99664	99894	99757	39
22	99626	99141	99693	99295	99753	99433	99807	99557	99854	99665	99895	99759	38
23	99627	99144	99694	99297	99754	99436	99808	99559	99855	99667	99896	99760	37
24	99628	99147	99695	99300	99755	99438	99809	99561	99856	99669	99896	99761	36
25	99629	99149	99696	99302	99756	99440	99810	99563	99857	99670	99897	99763	35
26	99630	99152	99697	99305	99757	99442	99811	99565	99857	99672	99897	99764	34
27	99631	99155	99698	99307	99758	99444	99811	99567	99858	99674	99898	99766	33
28	99633	99157	99699	99309	99759	99446	99812	99568	99859	99675	99899	99767	32
29	99634	99160	99700	99312	99760	99448	99813	99570	99859	99677	99899	99768	31
30	99635	99163	99701	99314	99761	99451	99814	99572	99860	99679	99900	99770	30
31	99636	99165	99702	99317	99762	99453	99815	99574	99861	99680	99901	99771	29
32	99637	99168	99703	99319	99763	99455	99815	99576	99862	99682	99901	99773	28
33	99638	99171	99704	99321	99764	99457	99816	99578	99862	99684	99902	99774	27
34	99639	99173	99705	99324	99765	99459	99817	99580	99863	99685	99902	99775	26
35	99641	99176	99706	99326	99766	99461	99818	99582	99864	99687	99903	99777	25
36	99642	99179	99707	99329	99766	99464	99819	99584	99864	99688	99904	99778	24
37	99643	99181	99708	99331	99767	99466	99820	99585	99865	99690	99904	99780	23
38	99644	99184	99710	99333	99768	99468	99820	99587	99866	99692	99905	99781	22
39	99645	99186	99711	99336	99769	99470	99821	99589	99867	99693	99905	99782	21
40	99646	99189	99712	99338	99770	99472	99822	99591	99867	99695	99906	99784	20
41	99648	99192	99713	99340	99771	99474	99823	99593	99868	99696	99906	99785	19
42	99649	99194	99714	99343	99772	99476	99824	99595	99869	99698	99907	99786	18
43	99650	99197	99715	99345	99773	99478	99824	99597	99869	99700	99908	99788	17
44	99651	99199	99716	99347	99774	99480	99825	99598	99870	99701	99908	99789	16
45	99652	99202	99717	99350	99774	99483	99826	99600	99871	99703	99909	99790	15
46	99653	99205	99718	99352	99775	99485	99827	99602	99871	99704	99909	99792	14
47	99654	99207	99719	99354	99776	99487	99828	99604	99872	99706	99910	99793	13
48	99655	99210	99720	99357	99777	99489	99828	99606	99873	99708	99911	99794	12
49	99657	99212	99721	99359	99778	99491	99829	99608	99874	99709	99911	99796	11
50	99658	99215	99722	99361	99779	99493	99830	99609	99874	99711	99912	99797	10
51	99659	99217	99723	99364	99780	99495	99831	99611	99875	99712	99912	99798	09
52	99660	99220	99724	99366	99781	99497	99832	99613	99876	99714	99913	99799	08
53	99661	99223	99725	99368	99782	99499	99832	99615	99876	99715	99913	99801	07
54	99662	99225	99726	99371	99783	99501	99833	99617	99877	99717	99914	99802	06
55	99663	99228	99727	99373	99784	99503	99834	99618	99878	99719	99915	99803	05
56	99664	99230	99728	99375	99785	99505	99835	99620	99878	99720	99915	99805	04
57	99666	99233	99729	99378	99786	99507	99836	99622	99879	99722	99916	99806	03
58	99667	99235	99730	99380	99786	99509	99836	99624	99880	99723	99916	99807	02
59	99668	99238	99731	99382	99787	99511	99837	99626	99880	99725	99917	99808	01
60	99669	99240	99732	99384	99788	99513	99838	99627	99881	99726	99917	99810	00

190°	189°	188°	187°	186°	185°

HAVERSINES

	175°		176°		177°		178°		179°				
	Log.	Nat.	Log.	Nat.	Log.	Nat.	Log.	Nat.	Log.	Nat.	Log.	Nat.	

Parts for 0'.2, etc.

175°		176°		177°		178°		179°	
·2 0	·2 0	·2 0	·2 0	·2 0	·2 0	·2 0	·2 0	·2 0	·2 0
·4 0	·4 0	·4 0	·4 0	·4 0	·4 0	·4 0	·4 0	·4 0	·4 0
·6 0	·6 1	·6 0	·6 1	·6 0	·6 0	·6 0	·6 0	·6 0	·6 0
·8 1	·8 1	·8 0	·8 1	·8 0	·8 1	·8 0	·8 0	·8 0	·8 0

′	$\overline{1}$.or(9.)	0.	$\overline{1}$.or(9.)	0.	$\overline{1}$.or(9.)	0.	$\overline{1}$.or(9.)	0.	$\overline{1}$.or(9.) / 0.or(10.)	0. / 1.	Log.	Nat.	′
00	99917	99810	99947	99878	99970	99931	99987	99970	99997	99992			60
01	99918	99811	99948	99879	99971	99932	99987	99971	99997	99993			59
02	99918	99812	99948	99880	99971	99933	99987	99971	99997	99993			58
03	99919	99814	99948	99881	99971	99934	99987	99971	99997	99993			57
04	99919	99815	99949	99882	99972	99934	99988	99972	99997	99994			56
05	99920	99816	99949	99883	99972	99935	99988	99972	99997	99994			55
06	99921	99817	99950	99884	99972	99936	99988	99973	99997	99994			54
07	99921	99819	99950	99885	99973	99937	99988	99973	99997	99994			53
08	99922	99820	99951	99886	99973	99937	99988	99973	99998	99994			52
09	99922	99821	99951	99887	99973	99938	99989	99974	99998	99995			51
10	99923	99822	99951	99888	99973	99939	99989	99974	99998	99995			50
11	99923	99823	99952	99889	99974	99940	99989	99975	99998	99995			49
12	99924	99825	99952	99890	99974	99940	99989	99975	99998	99995			48
13	99924	99826	99953	99891	99974	99941	99989	99976	99998	99995			47
14	99925	99827	99953	99892	99975	99942	99990	99976	99998	99996			46
15	99925	99828	99953	99893	99975	99942	99990	99977	99998	99996			45
16	99926	99829	99954	99894	99975	99943	99990	99977	99998	99996			44
17	99926	99831	99954	99895	99976	99944	99990	99978	99998	99996			43
18	99927	99832	99954	99896	99976	99944	99990	99978	99998	99996			42
19	99927	99833	99955	99897	99976	99945	99991	99978	99998	99996			41
20	99928	99834	99955	99898	99976	99946	99991	99979	99999	99997			40
21	99928	99835	99956	99899	99977	99947	99991	99979	99999	99997			39
22	99929	99837	99956	99900	99977	99947	99991	99980	99999	99997			38
23	99929	99838	99957	99900	99977	99948	99991	99980	99999	99997			37
24	99930	99839	99957	99901	99978	99949	99992	99981	99999	99997			36
25	99931	99840	99958	99902	99978	99949	99992	99981	99999	99997			35
26	99931	99841	99958	99903	99978	99950	99992	99981	99999	99998			34
27	99932	99842	99958	99904	99978	99950	99992	99982	99999	99998			33
28	99932	99844	99959	99905	99979	99951	99992	99982	99999	99998			32
29	99933	99845	99959	99906	99979	99952	99992	99982	99999	99998			31
30	99933	99846	99959	99907	99979	99952	99993	99983	99999	99998			30
31	99934	99847	99960	99908	99980	99953	99993	99983	99999	99998			29
32	99934	99848	99960	99909	99980	99954	99993	99984	99999	99998			28
33	99935	99849	99961	99909	99980	99954	99993	99984	99999	99998			27
34	99935	99850	99961	99910	99980	99955	99993	99984	99999	99999			26
35	99935	99851	99961	99911	99981	99956	99993	99985	99999	99999			25
36	99936	99853	99962	99912	99981	99956	99994	99985	99999	99999			24
37	99936	99854	99962	99913	99981	99957	99994	99985	00000	99999			23
38	99937	99855	99963	99914	99981	99957	99994	99986	00000	99999			22
39	99937	99856	99963	99915	99982	99958	99994	99986	00000	99999			21
40	99938	99857	99963	99915	99982	99959	99994	99986	00000	99999			20
41	99938	99858	99964	99916	99982	99959	99994	99987	00000	99999			19
42	99939	99859	99964	99917	99983	99960	99994	99987	00000	99999			18
43	99939	99860	99964	99918	99983	99960	99995	99987	00000	99999			17
44	99940	99861	99965	99919	99983	99961	99995	99988	00000	99999			16
45	99940	99863	99965	99920	99983	99961	99995	99988	00000	00000			15
46	99941	99864	99965	99920	99983	99962	99995	99988	00000	00000			14
47	99941	99865	99966	99921	99984	99963	99995	99989	00000	00000			13
48	99942	99866	99966	99922	99984	99963	99995	99989	00000	00000			12
49	99942	99867	99966	99923	99984	99964	99995	99989	00000	00000			11
50	99943	99868	99967	99924	99984	99964	99996	99990	00000	00000			10
51	99943	99869	99967	99924	99985	99965	99996	99990	00000	00000			09
52	99943	99870	99968	99925	99985	99965	99996	99990	00000	00000			08
53	99944	99871	99968	99926	99985	99966	99996	99991	00000	00000			07
54	99944	99872	99968	99927	99985	99966	99996	99991	00000	00000			06
55	99945	99873	99969	99928	99986	99967	99996	99991	00000	00000			05
56	99945	99874	99969	99928	99986	99967	99996	99991	00000	00000			04
57	99946	99875	99969	99929	99986	99968	99996	99992	00000	00000			03
58	99946	99876	99970	99930	99986	99969	99996	99992	00000	00000			02
59	99947	99877	99970	99931	99987	99969	99997	99992	00000	00000			01
60	99947	99878	99970	99931	99987	99970	99997	99992	00000	00000			00

| 184° | 183° | 182° | 181° | 180° | |

NATURAL FUNCTIONS OF ANGLES

NATURAL SINES

Degrees	0′	6′	12′	18′	24′	30′	36′	42′	48′	54′	Add Mean Difference				
											1′	2′	3′	4′	5′
0	0·00000	00175	00349	00524	00698	00873	01047	01222	01396	01571	29	58	87	117	145
1	·01745	01920	02094	02269	02443	02618	02792	02967	03141	03316	29	58	87	117	145
2	·03490	03664	03839	04013	04188	04362	04536	04711	04885	05059	29	58	87	116	145
3	·05234	05408	05582	05756	05931	06105	06279	06453	06627	06802	29	58	87	116	145
4	·06976	07150	07324	07498	07672	07846	08020	08194	08368	08542	29	58	87	116	145
5	0·08716	08889	09063	09237	09411	09585	09758	09932	10106	10279	29	58	87	116	145
6	·10453	10626	10800	10973	11147	11320	11494	11667	11840	12014	29	58	87	116	145
7	·12187	12360	12533	12706	12880	13053	13226	13399	13572	13744	29	58	87	115	144
8	·13917	14090	14263	14436	14608	14781	14954	15126	15299	15471	29	58	86	115	144
9	·15643	15816	15988	16160	16333	16505	16677	16849	17021	17193	29	57	86	115	144
10	0·17365	17537	17708	17880	18052	18224	18395	18567	18738	18910	29	57	86	114	143
11	·19081	19252	19423	19595	19766	19937	20108	20279	20450	20620	29	57	86	114	143
12	·20791	20962	21132	21303	21474	21644	21814	21985	22155	22325	28	57	85	114	142
13	·22495	22665	22835	23005	23175	23345	23514	23684	23853	24023	28	57	85	113	141
14	·24192	24362	24531	24700	24869	25038	25207	25376	25545	25713	28	56	85	113	141
15	0·25882	26050	26219	26387	26556	26724	26892	27060	27228	27396	28	56	84	112	140
16	·27564	27731	27899	28067	28234	28402	28569	28736	28903	29070	28	56	84	112	139
17	·29237	29404	29571	29737	29904	30071	30237	30403	30570	30736	28	56	83	111	139
18	·30902	31068	31233	31399	31565	31730	31896	32061	32227	32392	28	55	83	110	138
19	·32557	32722	32887	33051	33216	33381	33545	33710	33874	34038	27	55	82	110	137
20	0·34202	34366	34530	34694	34857	35021	35184	35347	35511	35674	27	55	82	109	136
21	·35837	36000	36162	36325	36488	36650	36812	36975	37137	37299	27	54	81	108	135
22	·37461	37622	37784	37946	38107	38268	38430	38591	38752	38912	27	54	81	107	134
23	·39073	39234	39394	39555	39715	39875	40035	40195	40355	40514	27	53	80	107	133
24	·40674	40833	40992	41151	41310	41469	41628	41787	41945	42104	27	53	79	106	132
25	0·42262	42420	42578	42736	42894	43051	43209	43366	43523	43680	26	53	79	105	131
26	·43837	43994	44151	44307	44464	44620	44776	44932	45088	45243	26	52	78	104	130
27	·45399	45554	45710	45865	46020	46175	46330	46484	46639	46793	26	52	77	103	129
28	·46947	47101	47255	47409	47562	47716	47869	48022	48175	48328	26	51	77	102	128
29	·48481	48634	48786	48938	49090	49242	49394	49546	49697	49849	25	51	76	101	126
30	0·50000	50151	50302	50453	50603	50754	50904	51054	51204	51354	25	50	75	100	125
31	·51504	51653	51803	51952	52101	52250	52399	52547	52696	52844	25	50	74	99	124
32	·52992	53140	53288	53435	53583	53730	53877	54024	54171	54317	25	49	74	98	123
33	·54464	54610	54756	54902	55048	55194	55339	55484	55630	55775	24	49	73	97	121
34	·55919	56064	56208	56353	56497	56641	56784	56928	57071	57215	24	48	72	96	120
35	0·57358	57501	57643	57786	57928	58070	58212	58354	58496	58637	24	48	71	95	118
36	·58778	58920	59061	59201	59342	59482	59622	59763	59902	60042	23	47	70	94	117
37	·60181	60321	60460	60599	60738	60876	61015	61153	61291	61429	23	46	69	92	115
38	·61566	61704	61841	61978	62115	62251	62388	62524	62660	62796	23	46	68	91	114
39	·62932	63068	63203	63338	63473	63608	63742	63877	64011	64145	23	45	67	90	112
40	0·64279	64412	64546	64679	64812	64945	65077	65210	65342	65474	22	44	66	88	111
41	·65606	65738	65869	66000	66131	66262	66393	66523	66653	66783	22	44	65	87	109
42	·66913	67043	67172	67301	67430	67559	67688	67816	67944	68072	22	43	64	86	107
43	·68200	68327	68455	68582	68709	68835	68962	69088	69214	69340	21	42	63	84	106
44	·69466	69591	69717	69842	69966	70091	70215	70339	70463	70587	21	41	62	83	104

NATURAL FUNCTIONS OF ANGLES

NATURAL SINES

Degrees	0'	6'	12'	18'	24'	30'	36'	42'	48'	54'	Add Mean Difference				
											1'	2'	3'	4'	5'
45	0·70711	70834	70957	71080	71203	71325	71447	71569	71691	71813	20	41	61	82	102
46	·71934	72055	72176	72297	72417	72537	72657	72777	72897	73016	20	40	60	80	100
47	·73135	73254	73373	73491	73610	73728	73846	73963	74080	74198	20	39	59	79	98
48	·74314	74431	74548	74664	74780	74896	75011	75126	75241	75356	20	39	58	77	96
49	·75471	75585	75700	75813	75927	76041	76154	76267	76380	76492	19	38	57	76	94
50	0·76604	76717	76828	76940	77051	77162	77273	77384	77494	77605	19	37	56	74	93
51	·77715	77824	77934	78043	78152	78261	78369	78478	78586	78694	18	36	54	72	91
52	·78801	78908	79015	79122	79229	79335	79441	79547	79653	79758	18	35	53	71	89
53	·79864	79968	80073	80178	80282	80386	80489	80593	80696	80799	17	35	52	69	87
54	·80902	81004	81106	81208	81310	81412	81513	81614	81714	81815	17	34	51	68	84
55	0·81915	82015	82115	82214	82314	82413	82511	82610	82708	82806	16	33	49	66	82
56	·82904	83001	83098	83195	83292	83389	83485	83581	83676	83772	16	32	48	64	80
57	·83867	83962	84057	84151	84245	84339	84433	84526	84619	84712	16	31	47	62	78
58	·84805	84897	84987	85081	85173	85264	85355	85446	85536	85627	15	31	46	61	76
59	·85717	85806	85896	85985	86074	86163	86251	86340	86427	86515	15	30	44	59	74
60	0·86603	86690	86777	86863	86949	87036	87121	87207	87292	87377	14	29	43	57	72
61	·87462	87546	87631	87715	87798	87882	87965	88048	88130	88213	14	28	42	56	69
62	·88295	88377	88458	88539	88620	88701	88782	88862	88942	89021	14	27	40	54	67
63	·89101	89180	89259	89337	89415	89493	89571	89649	89726	89803	13	26	39	52	65
64	·89879	89956	90032	90108	90183	90259	90334	90408	90483	90557	13	25	38	50	63
65	0·90631	90704	90778	90851	90924	90996	91068	91140	91212	91283	12	24	36	48	60
66	·91355	91425	91496	91566	91636	91706	91775	91845	91914	91982	12	23	35	46	58
67	·92050	92119	92186	92254	92321	92388	92455	92521	92587	92653	11	22	33	45	56
68	·92718	92784	92849	92913	92978	93042	93106	93169	93232	93295	11	21	32	43	54
69	·93358	93420	93483	93544	93606	93667	93728	93789	93849	93909	10	20	31	41	51
70	0·93969	94029	94088	94147	94206	94264	94322	94380	94438	94495	10	19	29	39	49
71	·94552	94609	94665	94721	94777	94832	94888	94943	94997	95052	9	18	28	37	46
72	·95106	95159	95213	95266	95319	95372	95424	95476	95528	95579	9	17	26	35	44
73	·95630	95681	95732	95782	95832	95882	95931	95981	96029	96078	8	17	25	33	41
74	·96126	96174	96222	96269	96316	96363	96410	96456	96502	96547	8	16	23	31	39
75	0·96593	96638	96682	96727	96771	96815	96858	96902	96945	96987	7	16	22	29	36
76	·97030	97072	97113	97155	97196	97237	97278	97318	97358	97398	7	14	20	27	34
77	·97437	97476	97515	97553	97592	97630	97667	97705	97742	97778	6	13	19	25	32
78	·97815	97851	97887	97922	97958	97992	98027	98061	98096	98129	6	12	17	23	29
79	·98163	98196	98229	98261	98294	98325	98357	98388	98420	98450	5	11	16	21	27
80	0·98481	98511	98541	98570	98600	98629	98657	98686	98714	98741	5	10	14	19	24
81	·98769	98796	98823	98849	98876	98902	98927	98953	98978	99002	4	9	13	17	22
82	·99027	99051	99075	99098	99122	99144	99167	99189	99211	99233	4	8	11	15	19
83	·99255	99276	99297	99317	99337	99357	99377	99396	99415	99434	3	7	10	13	16
84	·99452	99470	99488	99506	99523	99540	99556	99572	99588	99604	3	6	8	11	14
85	0·99619	99635	99649	99664	99678	99692	99705	99719	99731	99744	2	5	7	9	11
86	·99756	99768	99780	99792	99803	99813	99824	99834	99844	99854	2	4	5	7	9
87	·99863	99872	99881	99889	99897	99905	99912	99919	99926	99933	1	3	4	5	6
88	·99939	99945	99951	99956	99961	99966	99970	99974	99978	99982	1	2	2	3	4
89	·99985	99988	99990	99993	99995	99996	99998	99999	99999	1·00000	0	1	1	1	1
90	1·00000														

NATURAL FUNCTIONS OF ANGLES

NATURAL COSINES

Degrees	0'	6'	12'	18'	24'	30'	36'	42'	48'	54'	Subtract Mean Differences				
											1'	2'	3'	4'	5'
0	1·00000	1·00000	99999	99999	99998	99996	99995	99993	99990	99988	0	1	1	1	1
1	·99985	99982	99978	99974	99970	99966	99961	99956	99951	99945	1	2	2	3	4
2	·99939	99933	99926	99919	99912	99905	99897	99889	99881	99872	1	3	4	5	6
3	·99863	99854	99844	99834	99824	99813	99803	99792	99780	99768	2	4	5	7	9
4	·99756	99744	99731	99719	99705	99692	99678	99664	99649	99635	2	5	7	9	11
5	0·99619	99604	99588	99572	99556	99540	99523	99506	99488	99470	3	6	8	11	14
6	·99452	99434	99415	99396	99377	99357	99337	99317	99297	99276	3	7	10	13	16
7	·99255	99233	99211	99189	99167	99144	99122	99098	99075	99051	4	8	11	15	19
8	·99027	99002	98978	98953	98927	98902	98876	98849	98823	98796	4	9	13	17	22
9	·98769	98741	98714	98686	98657	98629	98600	98570	98541	98511	5	10	14	19	24
10	0·98481	98450	98420	98388	98357	98325	98294	98261	98229	98196	5	11	16	21	27
11	·98163	98129	98096	98061	98027	97992	97958	97922	97887	97851	6	12	17	23	29
12	·97815	97778	97742	97705	97667	97630	97592	97553	97515	97476	6	13	19	25	32
13	·97437	97398	97358	97318	97278	97237	97196	97155	97113	97072	7	14	20	27	34
14	·97030	96987	96945	96902	96858	96815	96771	96727	96682	96638	7	16	22	29	36
15	0·96593	96547	96502	96456	96410	96363	96316	96269	96222	96174	8	16	23	31	39
16	·96126	96078	96029	95981	95931	95882	95832	95782	95732	95681	8	17	25	33	41
17	·95630	95579	95528	95476	95424	95372	95319	95266	95213	95159	9	17	26	35	44
18	·95106	95052	94997	94943	94888	94832	94777	94721	94665	94609	9	18	28	37	46
19	·94552	94495	94438	94380	94322	94264	94206	94147	94088	94029	10	19	29	39	49
20	0·93969	93909	93849	93789	93728	93667	93606	93544	93483	93420	10	20	31	41	51
21	·93358	93295	93232	93169	93106	93042	92978	92913	92849	92784	10	21	32	43	54
22	·92718	92653	92587	92521	92455	92388	92321	92254	92186	92119	11	22	33	45	56
23	·92050	91982	91914	91845	91775	91706	91636	91566	91496	91425	11	23	35	46	58
24	·91355	91283	91212	91140	91068	90996	90924	90851	90778	90704	12	24	36	48	60
25	0·90631	90557	90483	90408	90334	90259	90183	90108	90032	89956	13	25	38	50	63
26	·89879	89803	89726	89649	89571	89493	89415	89337	89259	89180	13	26	39	52	65
27	·89101	89021	88942	88862	88782	88701	88620	88539	88458	88377	13	27	40	54	67
28	·88295	88213	88130	88048	87965	87882	87798	87715	87631	87546	14	28	42	56	69
29	·87462	87377	87292	87207	87121	87036	86949	86863	86777	86690	14	29	43	57	72
30	0·86603	86515	86427	86340	86251	86163	86074	85985	85896	85806	15	30	44	59	74
31	·85717	85627	85536	85446	85355	85264	85173	85081	84989	84897	16	30	46	61	76
32	·84805	84712	84619	84526	84433	84339	84245	84151	84057	83962	16	31	47	62	78
33	·83867	83772	83676	83581	83485	83389	83292	83195	83098	83001	16	32	48	64	80
34	·82904	82806	82708	82610	82511	82413	82314	82214	82115	82015	16	33	49	66	82
35	0·81915	81815	81714	81614	81513	81412	81310	81208	81106	81004	17	34	51	68	84
36	·80902	80799	80696	80593	80489	80386	80282	80178	80073	79968	17	35	52	69	87
37	·79864	79758	79653	79547	79441	79335	79229	79122	79015	78908	18	35	53	71	89
38	·78801	78693	78586	78478	78369	78261	78152	78043	77934	77824	18	36	54	72	91
39	·77715	77605	77494	77384	77273	77162	77051	76940	76828	76717	18	37	56	74	93
40	0·76604	76492	76380	76267	76154	76041	75927	75813	75700	75585	19	38	57	76	94
41	·75471	75356	75241	75126	75011	74896	74780	74664	74548	74431	19	39	58	77	96
42	·74314	74198	74080	73963	73846	73728	73610	73491	73373	73254	20	39	59	79	98
43	·73135	73016	72897	72777	72657	72537	72417	72297	72176	72055	20	40	60	80	100
44	·71934	71813	71691	71569	71447	71325	71203	71080	70957	70834	20	41	61	82	102

NATURAL FUNCTIONS OF ANGLES

NATURAL COSINES

Degrees	0′	6′	12′	18′	24′	30′	36′	42′	48′	54′	Subtract Mean Differences				
											1′	2′	3′	4′	5′
45	0·70711	70587	70463	70339	70215	70091	69966	69842	69717	69591	21	41	62	83	104
46	·69466	69340	69214	69088	68962	68835	68709	68582	68455	68327	21	42	63	84	106
47	·68200	68072	67944	67816	67688	67559	67430	67301	67172	67043	21	43	64	86	107
48	·66913	66783	66653	66523	66393	66262	66131	66000	65869	65738	22	44	65	87	109
49	·65606	65474	65342	65210	65077	64945	64812	64679	64546	64412	22	44	66	88	111
50	0·64279	64145	64011	63877	63742	63608	63473	63338	63203	63068	22	45	67	90	112
51	·62932	62796	62660	62524	62388	62251	62115	61978	61841	61704	23	45	68	91	114
52	·61566	61429	61291	61153	61015	60876	60738	60599	60460	60321	23	46	69	92	115
53	·60181	60042	59902	59763	59622	59482	59342	59201	59061	58920	23	47	70	94	117
54	·58779	58637	58496	58354	58212	58070	57928	57786	57643	57501	24	47	71	95	118
55	0·57358	57215	57071	56928	56784	56641	56497	56353	56208	56064	24	48	72	96	120
56	·55919	55775	55630	55484	55339	55194	55048	54902	54756	54610	24	49	73	97	121
57	·54464	54317	54171	54024	53877	53730	53583	53435	53288	53140	24	49	74	98	123
58	·52992	52844	52696	52547	52399	52250	52101	51952	51803	51653	25	50	74	99	124
59	·51504	51354	51204	51054	50904	50754	50603	50453	50302	50151	25	50	75	100	125
60	0·50000	49849	49697	49546	49394	49242	49090	48938	48786	48634	25	51	76	101	126
61	·48481	48328	48175	48022	47869	47716	47562	47409	47255	47101	26	51	77	102	128
62	·46947	46793	46639	46484	46330	46175	46020	45865	45710	45554	26	52	77	103	129
63	·45399	45243	45088	44932	44776	44620	44464	44307	44151	43994	26	52	78	104	130
64	·43837	43680	43523	43366	43209	43051	42894	42736	42578	42420	26	53	79	105	131
65	0·42262	42104	41945	41787	41628	41469	41310	41151	40992	40833	26	53	79	106	132
66	·40674	40514	40355	40195	40035	39875	39715	39555	39394	39234	27	53	80	107	133
67	·39073	38912	38752	38591	38430	38268	38107	37946	37784	37622	27	54	81	107	134
68	·37461	37299	37137	36975	36812	36650	36488	36325	36162	36000	27	54	81	108	135
69	·35837	35674	35511	35347	35184	35021	34857	34694	34530	34366	27	54	82	109	136
70	0·34202	34038	33874	33710	33545	33381	33216	33051	32887	32722	27	55	82	110	137
71	·32557	32392	32227	32061	31896	31730	31565	31399	31233	31068	28	55	83	110	138
72	·30902	30736	30570	30403	30237	30071	29904	29737	29571	29404	28	56	83	111	139
73	·29237	29070	28903	28736	28569	28402	28234	28067	27899	27731	28	56	84	112	139
74	·27564	27396	27228	27060	26892	26724	26556	26387	26219	26050	28	56	84	112	140
75	0·25882	25713	25545	25376	25207	25038	24869	24700	24531	24362	28	56	85	113	141
76	·24192	24023	23853	23684	23514	23345	23175	23005	22835	22665	28	57	85	113	141
77	·22495	22325	22155	21985	21814	21644	21474	21303	21132	20962	28	57	85	114	142
78	·20791	20620	20450	20279	20108	19937	19766	19595	19423	19252	29	57	86	114	143
79	·19081	18910	18738	18567	18395	18224	18052	17880	17708	17537	29	57	86	114	143
80	0·17365	17193	17021	16849	16677	16505	16333	16160	15988	15816	29	57	86	115	144
81	·15643	15471	15299	15126	14954	14781	14608	14436	14263	14090	29	58	86	115	144
82	·13917	13744	13572	13399	13226	13053	12880	12706	12533	12360	29	58	87	115	144
83	·12187	12014	11840	11667	11494	11320	11147	10973	10800	10626	29	58	87	116	145
84	·10453	10279	10106	09932	09758	09585	09411	09237	09063	08889	29	58	87	116	145
85	0·08716	08542	08368	08194	08020	07846	07672	07498	07324	07150	29	58	87	116	145
86	·06976	06802	06627	06453	06279	06105	05931	05756	05582	05408	29	58	87	116	145
87	·05234	05059	04885	04711	04536	04362	04188	04013	03839	03664	29	58	87	116	145
88	·03490	03316	03141	02967	02792	02618	02443	02269	02094	01920	29	58	87	117	145
89	·01745	01571	01396	01222	01047	00873	00698	00524	00349	00175	29	58	87	117	145
90	·00000														

NATURAL FUNCTIONS OF ANGLES

NATURAL TANGENTS

Degrees	0'	6'	12'	18'	24'	30'	36'	42'	48'	54'	Add Mean Differences 1'	2'	3'	4'	5'
0	0·00000	00175	00349	00524	00698	00873	01047	01222	01396	01571	29	58	87	116	146
1	·01746	01920	02095	02269	02444	02619	02793	02968	03143	03317	29	58	87	116	146
2	·03492	03667	03842	04016	04191	04366	04541	04716	04891	05066	29	58	87	117	146
3	·05241	05416	05591	05766	05941	06116	06291	06467	06642	06817	29	58	88	117	146
4	·06993	07168	07344	07519	07695	07870	08046	08221	08397	08573	29	59	88	117	146
5	0·08749	08925	09101	09277	09453	09629	09805	09981	10158	10334	29	59	88	117	147
6	·10510	10687	10863	11040	11217	11394	11570	11747	11924	12101	29	59	88	118	147
7	·12278	12456	12633	12810	12988	13165	13343	13521	13698	13876	30	59	89	118	148
8	·14054	14232	14410	14588	14767	14945	15124	15302	15481	15660	30	59	89	119	149
9	·15838	16017	16196	16376	16555	16734	16914	17093	17273	17453	30	60	90	120	150
10	0·17633	17813	17993	18173	18353	18534	18714	18895	19076	19257	30	60	90	120	150
11	·19438	19619	19801	19982	20164	20345	20527	20709	20891	21073	30	60	91	121	152
12	·21256	21438	21621	21804	21986	22169	22353	22536	22719	22903	30	61	92	122	153
13	·23087	23271	23455	23639	23823	24008	24193	24377	24562	24747	31	61	93	124	155
14	·24933	25118	25304	25490	25676	25862	26048	26235	26421	26608	31	62	93	124	155
15	0·26795	26982	27169	27357	27545	27732	27920	28109	28297	28486	31	63	94	125	157
16	·28675	28864	29053	29242	29432	29621	29811	30001	30192	30382	32	63	95	127	158
17	·30573	30764	30955	31147	31338	31530	31722	31914	32106	32299	32	64	96	128	160
18	·32492	32685	32878	33072	33266	33460	33654	33848	34043	34238	32	65	97	129	162
19	·34433	34628	34824	35019	35216	35412	35608	35805	36002	36199	33	66	98	131	164
20	0·36397	36595	36793	36991	37190	37388	37588	37787	37986	38186	33	66	99	133	166
21	·38386	38587	38787	38988	39190	39391	39593	39795	39997	40200	34	67	101	134	168
22	·40403	40606	40809	41013	41217	41421	41626	41831	42036	42242	34	68	102	136	170
23	·42447	42654	42860	43067	43274	43481	43689	43897	44105	44314	34	69	104	138	173
24	·44523	44732	44942	45152	45362	45573	45784	45995	46206	46418	35	70	105	141	176
25	0·46631	46843	47056	47270	47483	47698	47912	48127	48342	48557	36	71	107	143	179
26	·48773	48989	49206	49423	49640	49858	50076	50295	50514	50733	36	73	109	145	182
27	·50953	51173	51393	51614	51835	52057	52279	52501	52724	52947	37	74	111	148	185
28	·53171	53395	53620	53844	54070	54296	54522	54748	54975	55203	38	75	113	151	188
29	·55431	55659	55888	56117	56347	56577	56808	57039	57271	57503	38	77	115	154	192
30	0·57735	57968	58201	58435	58670	58905	59140	59376	59612	59849	39	78	118	157	196
31	·60086	60324	60562	60801	61040	61280	61520	61761	62003	62245	40	79	120	160	200
32	·62487	62730	62973	63217	63462	63707	63953	64199	64446	64693	41	82	123	164	205
33	·64941	65189	65438	65688	65938	66189	66440	66692	66944	67197	42	84	126	167	209
34	·67451	67705	67960	68215	68471	68728	68985	69243	69502	69761	43	86	129	171	214
35	0·70021	70281	70542	70804	71066	71329	71593	71857	72122	72388	44	88	132	176	219
36	·72654	72921	73189	73457	73726	73996	74267	74538	74810	75082	45	90	135	180	225
37	·75355	75629	75904	76180	76456	76733	77010	77289	77568	77848	46	92	139	185	231
38	·78129	78410	78692	78975	79259	79544	79829	80115	80402	80690	47	95	142	190	237
39	·80978	81268	81558	81849	82141	82434	82727	83022	83317	83613	49	98	147	195	244
40	0·83910	84208	84507	84806	85107	85408	85710	86014	86318	86623	50	100	151	201	252
41	·86929	87236	87543	87852	88162	88473	88784	89097	89410	89725	52	103	155	207	259
42	·90040	90357	90674	90993	91313	91633	91955	92277	92601	92926	53	107	160	214	268
43	·93252	93578	93906	94235	94565	94896	95229	95562	95897	96232	55	111	165	221	276
44	·96569	96907	97246	97586	97927	98270	98613	98950	99304	99652	57	114	171	229	286

NATURAL FUNCTIONS OF ANGLES

NATURAL TANGENTS

Degrees	0′	6′	12′	18′	24′	30′	36′	42′	48′	54′	Add Mean Differences				
											1′	2′	3′	4′	5′
45	1·00000	00350	00701	01053	01406	01761	02117	02474	02832	03192	58	118	177	237	296
46	·03553	03915	04279	04644	05010	05378	05747	06117	06489	06862	61	123	184	245	307
47	·07613	07613	07990	08369	08749	09131	09514	09899	10285	10672	63	127	191	255	319
48	·11061	11452	11844	12238	12633	13029	13428	13828	14229	14632	66	132	199	265	331
49	·15037	15443	15851	16261	16672	17085	17500	17916	18334	18754	69	138	207	276	344
50	1·19175	19599	20024	20451	20879	21310	21742	22176	22612	23050	72	143	216	288	359
51	·23490	23931	24375	24820	25268	25717	26169	26622	27077	27535	75	150	225	300	375
52	·27994	28456	28919	29385	29853	30323	30795	31269	31745	32224	78	157	235	314	392
53	·32704	33187	33673	34160	34650	35142	35637	36134	36633	37134	82	164	247	329	411
54	·37638	38145	38653	39165	39679	40195	40714	41235	41759	42286	86	172	259	345	431
55	1·42815	43347	43881	44418	44958	45501	46046	46595	47146	47700	91	181	272	362	453
56	·48256	48816	49378	49944	50512	51084	51658	52235	52816	53400	95	191	286	382	477
57	·53987	54576	55170	55767	56366	56969	57575	58184	58797	59414	100	201	302	403	504
58	·60033	60657	61283	61914	62548	63185	63826	64471	65120	65772	106	213	319	426	533
59	·66428	67088	67752	68419	69091	69766	70446	71129	71817	72509	113	226	339	452	564
60	1·73205	1·73905	1·74610	1·75319	1·76032	1·76749	1·77471	1·78198	1·78929	1·79665	120	240	360	481	600
61	1·80405	1·81150	1·81900	1·82654	1·83413	1·84177	1·84946	185720	1·86500	1·87283	128	255	383	511	639
62	1·88073	1·88867	1·89667	1·90472	1·91282	1·92098	1·92920	1·93746	1·94579	1·95417	136	273	409	546	683
63	1·96261	1·97111	1·97967	1·98828	1·99695	2·00569	2·01449	2·02335	2·03227	2·04125	146	292	438	584	731
64	2·05030	2·05942	2·06860	2·07785	2·08716	2·09654	2·10600	2·11552	2·12511	2·13477	157	314	471	629	786
65	2·14451	2·15432	2·16420	2·17416	2·18419	2·19430	2·20449	2·21475	2·22510	2·23553	169	338	508	677	846
66	2·24604	2·25663	2·26730	2·27806	2·28891	2·29984	2·31086	2·32197	2·33317	2·34447	183	366	549	732	915
67	2·35585	2·36733	2·37891	2·39058	2·40235	2·41421	2·42618	2·43825	2·45043	2·46270	199	397	596	795	994
68	2·47509	2·48758	2·50018	2·51289	2·52571	2·53865	2·55170	2·56487	2·57815	2·59156					
69	2·60509	2·61874	2·63252	2·64642	2·66046	2·67462	2·68892	2·70335	2·71792	2·73263					
70	2·74748	2·76247	2·77761	2·79289	2·80833	2·82391	2·83965	2·85556	2·87161	2·88783					
71	2·90421	2·92076	2·93748	2·95437	2·97144	2·98868	3·00611	3·02372	3·04152	3·05950					
72	3·07768	3·09606	3·11464	3·13341	3·15240	3·17159	3·19100	3·21063	3·23048	3·25055					
73	3·27085	3·29139	3·31216	3·33317	3·35443	3·37594	3·39771	3·41973	3·44202	3·46458					
74	3·48741	3·51053	3·53393	3·55761	3·58160	3·60588	3·63048	3·65538	3·68061	3·70616					
75	3·73205	3·75828	3·78485	3·81177	3·83906	3·86671	3·89474	3·92316	3·95196	3·98117					
76	4·01078	4·04081	4·07127	4·10216	4·13350	4·16530	4·19756	4·23030	4·26352	4·29724					
77	4·33148	4·36623	4·40152	4·43735	4·47374	4·51071	4·54826	4·58641	4·62518	4·66458					
78	4·70463	4·74534	4·78673	4·82882	4·87162	4·91516	4·95945	5·00451	5·05037	5·09704					
79	5·14455	5·19293	5·24218	5·29235	5·34345	5·39552	5·44857	5·50264	5·55777	5·61397					
80	5·67128	5·72974	5·78938	5·85024	5·91236	5·97576	6·04051	6·10664	6·17419	6·24321					
81	6·31375	6·38587	6·45961	6·53503	6·61220	6·69116	6·77199	6·85475	6·93952	7·02637					
82	7·11537	7·20661	7·30018	7·39616	7·49465	7·59575	7·69957	7·80622	7·91582	8·02848					
83	8·14435	8·26356	8·38625	8·51259	8·64275	8·77689	8·91520	9·05789	9·20516	9·35724					
84	9·51436	9·6768	9·8448	10·019	10·199	10·385	10·579	10·780	10·988	11·205					
85	11·430	11·664	11·909	12·163	12·429	12·706	12·996	13·300	13·617	13·951					
86	14·301	14·669	15·056	15·464	15·895	16·350	16·832	17·343	17·886	18·464					
87	19·081	19·740	20·446	21·205	22·022	22·904	23·859	24·898	26·031	27·271					
88	28·636	30·145	31·821	33·694	35·801	38·188	40·917	44·066	47·740	52·081					
89	57·290	63·657	71·615	81·847	95·489	114·60	143·24	190·98	286·48	572·96					
90	∞														

Mean differences no longer sufficiently accurate.

NATURAL FUNCTIONS OF ANGLES

NATURAL COSECANTS

Degrees	0′	6′	12′	18′	24′	30′	36′	42′	48′	54′	Subtract Mean Differences				
											1′	2′	3′	4′	5′
0	∞	572·96	286·48	190·99	143·24	114·59	95·495	81·853	71·622	63·665					
1	57·299	52·090	47·750	44·077	40·930	38·202	35·815	33·708	31·836	30·161					
2	28·654	27·290	26·050	24·918	23·880	22·926	22·044	21·229	20·471	19·766					
3	19·107	18·492	17·914	17·372	16·862	16·380	15·926	15·496	15·089	14·703					
4	14·336	13·987	13·654	13·337	13·035	12·745	12·469	12·204	11·951	11·707					
5	11·474	11·249	11·034	10·826	10·626	10·433	10·248	10·068	9·8955	9·7283					
6	9·5668	9·4105	9·2593	9·1129	8·9711	8·8337	8·7004	8·5711	8·4457	8·3238					
7	8·2055	8·0905	7·9787	7·8700	7·7642	7·6613	7·5611	7·4635	7·3684	7·2757					
8	7·1853	7·0972	7·0112	6·9273	6·8454	6·7655	6·6874	6·6111	6·5366	6·4637					
9	6·3925	6·3228	6·2546	6·1880	6·1227	6·0589	5·9963	5·9351	5·8751	5·8164					
10	5·7588	5·7023	5·6470	5·5928	5·5396	5·4874	5·4362	5·3860	5·3367	5·2883					
11	5·2408	5·1942	5·1484	5·1034	5·0593	5·0159	4·9732	4·9313	4·8901	4·8496					
12	4·8097	4·7706	4·7321	4·6942	4·6569	4·6202	4·5841	4·5486	4·5137	4·4793					
13	4·4454	4·4121	4·3792	4·3469	4·3150	4·2837	4·2527	4·2223	4·1923	4·1627					
14	4·1336	4·1048	4·0765	4·0486	4·0211	3·9939	3·9672	3·9408	3·9147	3·8890					
15	3·86370	3·83871	3·81404	3·78970	3·76568	3·74198	3·71858	3·69549	3·67269	3·65018	Mean Differences no longer sufficiently accurate				
16	3·62796	3·60601	3·58434	3·56294	3·54181	3·52094	3·50032	3·47995	3·45983	3·43995					
17	3·42030	3·40089	3·38171	3·36276	3·34403	3·32551	3·30721	3·28912	3·27123	3·25355					
18	3·23607	3·21878	3·20169	3·18479	3·16808	3·15155	3·13520	3·11903	3·10303	3·08721	274	548	822	1047	1371
19	3·07155	3·05607	3·04075	3·02559	3·01059	2·99574	2·98106	2·96652	2·95213	2·93790	246	492	738	985	1231
20	2·92380	2·90986	2·89605	2·88238	2·86885	2·85545	2·84219	2·82906	2·81605	2·80318	222	445	667	889	1111
21	2·79043	2·77780	2·76530	2·75292	2·74065	2·72850	2·71647	2·70455	2·69275	2·68105	201	403	604	806	1008
22	2·66947	2·65799	2·64662	2·63535	2·62419	2·61313	2·60217	2·59130	2·58054	2·56988	181	367	550	734	918
23	2·55930	2·54883	2·53845	2·52815	2·51795	2·50784	2·49782	2·48789	2·47804	2·46827	168	335	504	671	839
24	2·45859	2·44900	2·43948	2·43005	2·42070	2·41142	2·40222	2·39311	2·38406	2·37509	154	308	462	616	770
25	2·36620	2·35738	2·34863	2·33996	2·33135	2·32282	2·31436	2·30596	2·29763	2·28937	142	283	425	566	708
26	2·28117	2·27304	2·26498	2·25697	2·24903	2·24116	2·23334	2·22559	2·21790	2·21026	130	262	392	523	654
27	2·20269	2·19517	2·18771	2·18031	2·17297	2·16568	2·15845	2·15127	2·14414	2·13707	121	242	363	484	606
28	2·13005	2·12309	2·11617	2·10931	2·10250	2·09574	2·08903	2·08236	2·07575	2·06918	112	225	337	449	561
29	2·06267	2·05619	2·04977	2·04339	2·03706	2·03077	2·02453	2·01833	2·01218	2·00607	104	209	313	417	522
30	2·00000	1·99398	1·98799	1·98205	1·97615	1·97029	1·96448	1·95870	1·95296	1·94726	97	194	292	389	486
31	1·94160	1·93598	1·93040	1·92486	1·91935	1·91388	1·90845	1·90305	1·89769	1·89237	90	182	272	363	454
32	1·88708	1·88183	1·87661	1·87142	1·86627	1·86116	1·85608	1·85103	1·84601	1·84103	85	170	255	340	425
33	1·83608	1·83116	1·82627	1·82142	1·81659	1·81180	1·80704	1·80231	1·79761	1·79293	79	159	239	318	398
34	1·78829	1·78368	1·77910	1·77454	1·77001	1·76552	1·76105	1·75661	1·75219	1·74781	75	149	224	299	374
35	1·74345	73911	73481	73053	72628	72205	71785	71367	70953	70540	70	140	211	281	351
36	·70130	69723	69318	68915	68515	68117	67722	67329	66938	66550	66	132	198	264	331
37	·66164	65780	65399	65020	64643	64268	63895	63525	63157	62791	62	124	187	249	311
38	·62427	62065	61705	61348	60992	60639	60287	59938	59590	59245	59	117	176	235	294
39	·58902	58560	58221	57883	57547	57213	56881	56551	56223	55897	55	111	166	221	278
40	1·55572	55250	54929	54610	54292	53977	53663	53351	53041	52732	52	105	157	210	262
41	·52425	52120	51817	51515	51215	50916	50619	50324	50030	49738	49	99	149	198	248
42	·49448	49159	48871	48586	48301	48019	47738	47458	47180	46903	47	94	141	188	235
43	·46628	46354	46082	45811	45542	45274	45007	44742	44479	44217	44	89	133	178	233
44	·43956	43696	43438	43181	42926	42672	42419	42168	41918	41669	42	84	126	169	211

NATURAL FUNCTIONS OF ANGLES

NATURAL COSECANTS

Degrees	0′	6′	12′	18′	24′	30′	36′	42′	48′	54′	Subtract Mean Differences				
											1′	2′	3′	4′	5′
45	1·41421	41175	40930	40687	40444	40203	39963	39725	39487	39251	40	79	120	160	200
46	·39016	38783	38550	38319	38089	37860	37632	37406	37180	36956	38	76	114	152	190
47	·36733	36511	36290	36070	35852	35634	35418	35203	34988	34775	36	71	108	145	181
48	·34563	34352	34142	33934	33726	33519	33314	33109	32905	32703	34	69	103	137	172
49	·32501	32301	32101	31903	31705	31509	31313	31119	30925	30732	32	65	98	130	163
50	1·30541	30350	30160	29971	29784	29597	29411	29226	29041	28858	31	62	93	124	155
51	·28676	28495	28314	28134	27956	27778	27601	27425	27250	27075	30	59	89	118	148
52	·26902	26729	26557	26387	26216	26047	25879	25711	25545	25379	28	56	84	113	141
53	·25214	25049	24885	24723	24561	24400	24240	24081	23922	23764	27	54	80	107	134
54	·23607	23450	23295	23140	22986	22833	22680	22528	22377	22227	26	51	77	102	128
55	1·22077	21929	21781	21633	21487	21341	21195	21051	20907	20764	24	49	73	97	121
56	·20622	20480	20339	20199	20059	19920	19782	19645	19508	19372	23	46	69	92	116
57	·19236	19102	18967	18834	18701	18569	18437	18307	18176	18047	22	44	66	88	110
58	·17918	17790	17662	17535	17409	17283	17158	17033	16909	16786	21	42	63	84	105
59	·16663	16541	16420	16299	16179	16059	15940	15822	15704	15587	20	40	60	80	99
60	1·15470	15354	15239	15124	15009	14896	14782	14670	14558	14446	19	38	57	76	95
61	·14335	14225	14115	14006	13897	13789	13682	13575	13468	13362	18	36	54	72	90
62	·13257	13152	13048	12944	12841	12738	12636	12534	12433	12333	17	34	51	68	85
63	·12233	12133	12034	11936	11838	11740	11643	11547	11451	11355	16	32	49	65	81
64	·11260	11166	11072	10978	10885	10793	10701	10609	10518	10428	15	31	46	61	77
65	1·10338	10248	10159	10071	09982	09895	09808	09721	09635	09549	15	29	44	58	73
66	·09464	09379	09294	09211	09127	09044	08962	08880	08798	08717	14	28	41	55	69
67	·08636	08556	08476	08397	08318	08239	08161	08084	08006	07930	13	26	39	52	64
68	·07853	07778	07702	07627	07553	07479	07405	07332	07259	07186	12	25	37	49	62
69	·07115	07043	06972	06901	06831	06761	06691	06622	06554	06486	12	23	35	46	58
70	1·06418	06350	06283	06217	06151	06085	06020	05955	05890	05826	11	22	33	44	55
71	·05762	05699	05636	05573	05511	05449	05388	05327	05266	05206	10	21	31	41	51
72	·05146	05087	05028	04969	04911	04853	04795	04738	04682	04625	10	19	29	38	48
73	·04569	04514	04458	04403	04349	04295	04241	04188	04135	04082	9	18	26	34	44
74	·04030	03978	03927	03875	03825	03774	03724	03674	03625	03576	8	17	25	33	42
75	1·03528	03479	03432	03384	03337	03290	03244	03197	03152	03106	8	16	23	31	39
76	·03061	03017	02972	02928	02885	02842	02799	02756	02714	02672	7	14	22	29	36
77	·02630	02589	02548	02508	02468	02428	02388	02349	02311	02272	7	13	20	26	33
78	·02234	02196	02159	02122	02085	02049	02013	01977	01941	01906	6	12	18	24	30
79	·01872	01837	01803	01769	01736	01703	01670	01638	01606	01574	5	11	16	22	27
80	1·01543	01512	01481	01450	01420	01391	01361	01332	01303	01275	5	10	15	20	24
81	·01247	01219	01191	01164	01137	01111	01084	01059	01033	01008	4	9	13	18	22
82	·00983	00958	00934	00910	00886	00863	00840	00817	00795	00773	4	8	12	15	19
83	·00751	00730	00708	00688	00667	00647	00627	00608	00588	00569	3	7	10	13	17
84	·00551	00533	00515	00497	00480	00463	00446	00429	00413	00397	3	6	8	11	14
85	1·00382	00367	00352	00337	00323	00309	00296	00283	00269	00257	2	5	7	9	12
86	·00244	00232	00220	00209	00198	00187	00176	00166	00156	00147	2	4	5	7	9
87	·00137	00128	00120	00111	00103	00095	00088	00081	00074	00067	1	3	4	5	6
88	·00061	00055	00049	00044	00039	00034	00030	00026	00022	00018	1	2	2	3	4
89	·00015	00012	00010	00007	00005	00004	00002	00001	00001	00000	0	1	1	1	1
90	1·00000														

NATURAL FUNCTIONS OF ANGLES

NATURAL SECANTS

Degrees	0′	6′	12′	18′	24′	30′	36′	42′	48′	54′	Add Mean Differences				
											1′	2′	3′	4′	5′
0	1·00000	00000	00001	00001	00002	00004	00005	00007	00010	00012	0	1	1	1	1
1	·00015	00018	00022	00026	00030	00034	00039	00044	00049	00055	1	2	2	3	4
2	·00061	00067	00074	00081	00088	00095	00103	00111	00120	00128	1	3	4	5	6
3	·00137	00147	00156	00166	00176	00187	00198	00209	00220	00232	2	4	5	7	9
4	·00244	00257	00269	00282	00296	00309	00323	00337	00352	00367	2	5	7	9	12
5	1·00382	00397	00413	00429	00446	00463	00480	00497	00515	00533	3	6	8	11	14
6	·00551	00569	00588	00608	00627	00647	00667	00688	00708	00730	3	7	10	13	17
7	·00751	00773	00795	00817	00840	00863	00886	00910	00934	00958	4	8	12	15	19
8	·00983	01008	01033	01059	01084	01111	01137	01164	01191	01219	4	9	13	18	22
9	·01247	01275	01303	01332	01361	01391	01420	01450	01481	01512	5	10	15	20	24
10	1·01543	01574	01606	01638	01670	01703	01736	01769	01803	01837	5	11	16	22	27
11	·01872	01906	01941	01977	02013	02049	02085	02122	02159	02196	6	12	18	24	30
12	·02234	02272	02311	02349	02388	02428	02468	02508	02548	02589	7	13	20	26	33
13	·02630	02672	02714	02756	02799	02842	02885	02928	02972	03017	7	14	22	29	36
14	·03061	03106	03152	03197	03244	03290	03337	03384	03432	03479	8	16	23	31	39
15	1·03528	03576	03625	03674	03724	03774	03825	03875	03927	03978	8	17	25	33	42
16	·04030	04082	04135	04188	04241	04295	04349	04403	04458	04514	9	18	26	34	44
17	·04569	04625	04682	04738	04795	04853	04911	04969	05028	05087	10	19	29	38	48
18	·05146	05206	05266	05327	05388	05449	05511	05573	05636	05699	10	21	31	41	51
19	·05762	05826	05890	05955	06020	06085	06151	06217	06283	06350	11	22	33	44	55
20	1·06418	06486	06554	06622	06691	06761	06831	06901	06972	07043	12	23	35	46	58
21	·07114	07186	07259	07332	07405	07479	07553	07627	07702	07778	12	25	37	49	62
22	·07853	07930	08006	08084	08161	08239	08318	08397	08476	08556	13	26	39	52	64
23	·08636	08717	08798	08880	08962	09044	09127	09211	09294	09379	14	28	41	55	69
24	·09464	09549	09635	09721	09808	09895	09982	10071	10159	10248	15	29	44	58	73
25	1·10338	10428	10518	10609	10701	10793	10885	10978	11072	11166	15	31	46	61	77
26	·11260	11355	11451	11547	11643	11740	11838	11936	12034	12133	16	32	49	65	81
27	·12233	12333	12433	12534	12636	12738	12841	12944	13048	13152	17	34	51	68	85
28	·13257	13362	13468	13575	13682	13789	13897	14006	14115	14225	18	36	54	72	90
29	·14335	14446	14558	14670	14782	14896	15009	15124	15239	15354	19	38	57	76	95
30	1·15470	15587	15704	15822	15940	16059	16179	16299	16420	16541	20	40	60	80	99
31	·16663	16786	16909	17033	17158	17283	17409	17535	17662	17790	21	42	63	84	105
32	·17918	18047	18176	18307	18437	18569	18701	18834	18967	19102	22	44	66	88	110
33	·19236	19372	19508	19645	19782	19920	20059	20199	20339	20480	23	46	69	92	116
34	·20622	20764	20907	21051	21195	21341	21487	21633	21781	21929	24	49	73	97	121
35	1·22077	22227	22377	22528	22680	22833	22986	23140	23295	23450	26	51	77	102	128
36	·23607	23764	23922	24081	24240	24400	24561	24723	24886	25049	27	54	80	107	134
37	·25214	25379	25545	25711	25879	26047	26216	26387	26557	26729	28	56	84	113	141
38	·26902	27075	27250	27425	27601	27778	27956	28134	28314	28495	30	59	89	118	148
39	·28676	28858	29042	29226	29411	29597	29784	29971	30160	30350	31	62	93	124	155
40	1·30541	30732	30925	31119	31313	31509	31705	31903	32101	32301	32	65	98	130	163
41	·32501	32703	32905	33109	33314	33519	33726	33934	34142	34352	34	69	103	137	172
42	·34563	34775	34988	35203	35418	35634	35852	36070	36290	36511	36	71	108	145	181
43	·36733	36956	37180	37406	37632	37860	38089	38319	38550	38783	38	76	114	152	190
44	·39016	39251	39487	39725	39963	40203	40444	40687	40930	41175	40	80	120	160	200

NATURAL FUNCTIONS OF ANGLES

NATURAL SECANTS

Degrees	0′	6′	12′	18′	24′	30′	36′	42′	48′	54′	1′	2′	3′	4′	5′
45	1·41421	41669	41918	42168	42419	42672	42926	43181	43438	43696	42	84	126	169	211
46	·43956	44217	44479	44742	45007	45274	45542	45811	46082	46354	44	89	133	178	223
47	·46628	46903	47180	47458	47738	48019	48301	48586	48871	49159	47	94	141	188	235
48	·49448	49738	50030	50324	50619	50916	51215	51515	51817	52120	49	99	149	198	248
49	·52425	52732	53041	53351	53663	53977	54292	54610	54929	55250	52	105	157	209	262
50	1·55572	55897	56223	56551	56881	57213	57547	57883	58221	58560	55	111	166	222	278
51	·58902	59245	59590	59938	60287	60639	60992	61348	61705	62065	59	117	176	235	294
52	·62427	62791	63157	63525	63895	64268	64643	65020	65399	65780	62	124	187	249	311
53	·66164	66550	66938	67329	67722	68117	68515	68915	69318	69723	66	132	198	264	331
54	·70130	70540	70953	71367	71785	72205	72628	73053	73481	73911	70	140	211	281	351
55	1·74345	74781	75219	75661	76105	76552	77001	77454	77910	78368	75	149	224	299	374
56	·78829	79293	79761	80231	80704	81180	81659	82142	82627	83116	79	159	239	318	398
57	·83608	84103	84601	85103	85608	86116	86627	87142	87661	88183	85	170	253	340	425
58	·88708	89237	89769	90305	90845	91388	91935	92486	93040	93598	90	182	272	363	454
59	·94160	94726	95296	95870	96448	97029	97615	98205	98799	99398	97	194	292	389	486
60	2·00000	00607	01218	01833	02453	03077	03706	04339	04977	05619	104	209	313	417	522
61	·06267	06918	07575	08236	08903	09574	10250	10931	11617	12309	112	225	339	449	561
62	·13005	13707	14414	15127	15845	16568	17297	18031	18772	19517	121	242	363	484	606
63	·20269	21026	21790	22559	23334	24116	24903	25697	26498	27304	130	262	392	523	654
64	·28117	28937	29763	30596	31436	32282	33135	33996	34863	35738	142	283	425	567	709
65	2·36620	37509	38406	39311	40222	41142	42070	43005	43948	44900	154	308	462	616	770
66	·45859	46827	47804	48789	49782	50784	51795	52815	53845	54883	168	335	504	672	839
67	·55930	56988	58054	59130	60217	61313	62419	63535	64662	65799	183	367	550	734	918
68	·66947	68105	69275	70455	71647	72850	74065	75292	76530	77780	200	403	605	806	1008
69	·79043	80318	81605	82906	84219	85545	86885	88238	89605	90986					
70	2·92380	2·93790	2·95213	2·96652	2·98106	2·99574	3·01059	3·02559	3·04075	3·05607					
71	3·07155	3·08721	3·10303	3·11903	3·13520	3·15155	3·16808	3·18479	3·20169	3·21878					
72	3·23607	3·25355	3·27123	3·28912	3·30721	3·32551	3·34403	3·36276	3·38171	3·40089					
73	3·42030	3·43995	3·45983	3·47995	3·50032	3·52094	3·54181	3·56294	3·58434	3·60601					
74	3·62796	3·65018	3·67269	3·69549	3·71858	3·74198	3·76568	3·78970	3·81404	3·83871					
75	3·86370	3·88904	3·91473	3·94076	3·96716	3·99393	4·02107	4·04860	4·07652	4·10484					
76	4·13357	4·16271	4·19228	4·22229	4·25275	4·28366	4·31503	4·34689	4·37923	4·41206					
77	4·44541	4·47928	4·51368	4·54861	4·58414	4·62023	4·65690	4·69417	4·73205	4·77057					
78	4·80973	4·84956	4·89007	4·93128	4·97320	5·01585	5·05926	5·10344	5·14842	5·19421					
79	5·24084	5·28833	5·33671	5·38600	5·43622	5·48740	5·53958	5·59277	5·64701	5·70234					
80	5·75877	5·81635	5·87511	5·93509	5·99633	6·05886	6·12273	6·18797	6·25464	6·32279					
81	6·39245	6·46369	6·53655	6·61110	6·68738	6·76547	6·84542	6·92731	7·01120	7·09717					
82	7·18530	7·27566	7·36835	7·46346	7·56107	7·66130	7·76424	7·87001	7·97873	8·09052					
83	8·20551	8·32384	8·44566	8·57113	8·70041	8·83367	8·97111	9·11292	9·25931	9·41052					
84	9·56677	9·7283	9·8955	10·068	10·248	10·433	10·626	10·826	11·034	11·249					
85	11·474	11·707	11·951	12·204	12·469	12·745	13·035	13·337	13·654	13·987					
86	14·336	14·703	15·089	15·496	15·926	16·380	16·862	17·372	17·914	18·492					
87	19·107	19·766	20·471	21·229	22·044	22·926	23·880	24·918	26·050	27·290					
88	28·654	30·161	31·836	33·708	35·815	38·202	40·930	44·077	47·750	52·090					
89	57·299	63·665	71·622	81·853	95·495	114·59	143·24	190·99	286·48	572·96					
90	∞														

Mean differences no longer sufficiently accurate.

NATURAL FUNCTIONS OF ANGLES

NATURAL COTANGENTS

Degrees	0′	6′	12′	18′	24′	30′	36′	42′	48′	54′	Subtract Mean Differences 1′	2′	3′	4′	5′
0	∞	572·96	286·48	190·98	143·24	114·59	95·489	81·847	71·615	63·657					
1	57·290	52·081	47·740	44·066	40·917	38·188	35·801	33·694	31·821	30·145					
2	28·636	27·271	26·031	24·898	23·859	22·904	22·022	21·205	20·446	19·740					
3	19·081	18·464	17·886	17·343	16·832	16·350	15·895	15·464	15·056	14·669					
4	14·301	13·951	13·617	13·300	12·996	12·706	12·429	12·163	11·909	11·664					
5	11·430	11·205	10·998	10·780	10·579	10·385	10·199	10·019	9·8448	9·6768					
6	9·5144	9·3572	9·2052	9·0579	8·9152	8·7769	8·6427	8·5126	8·3863	8·2636					
7	8·1443	8·0285	7·9158	7·8062	7·6996	7·5958	7·4947	7·3962	7·3002	7·2066					
8	7·1154	7·0264	6·9395	6·8548	6·7720	6·6912	6·6122	6·5350	6·4596	6·3859					
9	6·3138	6·2432	6·1742	6·1066	6·0405	5·9758	5·9124	5·8502	5·7894	5·7297					
10	5·67128	5·61397	5·55777	5·50264	5·44857	5·39552	5·34345	5·29235	5·24218	5·19293					
11	5·14455	5·09704	5·05037	5·00451	4·95945	4·91516	4·87162	4·82882	4·78673	4·74534					
12	4·70463	4·66458	4·62518	4·58641	4·54826	4·51071	4·47374	4·43735	4·40152	4·36623					
13	4·33148	4·29724	4·26352	4·23030	4·19756	4·16530	4·13350	4·10216	4·07127	4·04081					
14	4·01078	3·98117	3·95196	3·92316	3·89474	3·86671	3·83906	3·81177	3·78485	3·75828					
15	3·73205	3·70616	3·68061	3·65538	3·63048	3·60588	3·58160	3·55761	3·53393	3·51053					
16	3·48741	3·46458	3·44202	3·41973	3·39771	3·37594	3·35443	3·33317	3·31216	3·29139					
17	3·27085	3·25055	3·23048	3·21063	3·19100	3·17159	3·15240	3·13341	3·11464	3·09606					
18	3·07768	3·05950	3·04152	3·02372	3·00611	2·98868	2·97144	2·95437	2·93748	2·92076					
19	2·90421	2·88783	2·87161	2·85555	2·83965	2·82391	2·80833	2·79289	2·77761	2·76247	Mean differences no longer sufficiently accurate				
20	2·74748	2·73263	2·71792	2·70335	2·68892	2·67462	2·66046	2·64642	2·63252	2·61874					
21	2·60509	2·59156	2·57815	2·56487	2·55170	2·53865	2·52571	2·51289	2·50018	2·48758					
22	2·47509	2·46270	2·45043	2·43825	2·42618	2·41421	2·40235	2·39058	2·37891	2·36733	199	397	596	795	994
23	2·35585	2·34447	2·33317	2·32197	2·31086	2·29984	2·28891	2·27806	2·26730	2·25663	183	366	549	732	916
24	2·24604	2·23553	2·22510	2·21475	2·20449	2·19430	2·18419	2·17416	2·16420	2·15432	169	338	508	677	846
25	2·14451	2·13477	2·12511	2·11552	2·10600	2·09654	2·08716	2·07785	2·06860	2·05942	157	314	471	629	786
26	2·05030	2·04125	2·03227	2·02335	2·01449	2·00569	1·99695	1·98828	1·97966	1·97111	146	292	438	584	731
27	1·96261	1·95417	1·94579	1·93746	1·92920	1·92098	1·91282	1·90472	1·89667	1·88867	136	273	409	546	683
28	1·88073	1·87283	1·86499	1·85720	1·84946	1·84177	1·83413	1·82654	1·81899	1·81150	128	255	383	511	639
29	1·80405	1·79665	1·78929	1·78198	1·77471	1·76749	1·76032	1·75319	1·74610	1·73905	120	240	360	481	600
30	1·73205	72509	71817	71129	70446	69766	69091	68419	67752	67088	113	226	339	452	564
31	·66428	65772	65120	64471	63826	63185	62548	61914	61283	60657	106	213	319	428	533
32	·60033	59414	58797	58184	57575	56969	56366	55766	55170	54576	101	201	302	403	504
33	·53986	53400	52816	52235	51658	51084	50512	49944	49378	48816	95	191	286	382	477
34	·48256	47699	47146	46595	46046	45501	44958	44418	43881	43347	91	181	272	362	453
35	1·42815	42286	41759	41235	40714	40195	39679	39165	38653	38145	86	172	259	345	431
36	·37638	37134	36633	36134	35637	35142	34650	34160	33673	33187	82	164	247	329	411
37	·32704	32224	31745	31269	30795	30323	29853	29385	28919	28456	78	157	235	314	392
38	·27994	27535	27077	26622	26169	25717	25268	24820	24375	23931	75	150	225	300	375
39	·23490	23050	22612	22176	21742	21310	20879	20451	20024	19599	72	143	216	288	359
40	1·19175	18754	18334	17916	17500	17085	16672	16261	15851	15443	69	138	207	276	343
41	·15037	14632	14229	13828	13428	13029	12633	12238	11844	11452	66	132	199	265	331
42	·11061	10672	10285	09899	09514	09131	08749	08369	07990	07613	63	127	191	255	319
43	·07237	06862	06489	06117	05747	05378	05010	04644	04279	03915	61	123	184	245	307
44	·03553	03192	02832	02474	02117	01761	01406	01053	00701	00350	58	118	177	237	296

NATURAL FUNCTIONS OF ANGLES

NATURAL COTANGENTS

Degrees	0′	6′	12′	18′	24′	30′	36′	42′	48′	54′	Subtract Mean Differences				
											1′	2′	3′	4′	5′
45	1·00000	99652	99304	98958	98613	98270	97927	97586	97246	96907	57	114	171	229	286
46	0·96569	96232	95897	95562	95229	94896	94565	94235	93906	93578	55	111	165	221	276
47	·93252	92926	92601	92277	91955	91633	91313	90993	90674	90357	53	107	160	214	268
48	·90040	89725	89410	89097	88784	88473	88162	87852	87543	87236	52	103	155	207	259
49	·86929	86623	86318	86014	85710	85408	85107	84806	84507	84208	50	100	151	201	252
50	0·83910	83613	83317	83022	82727	82434	82141	81849	81558	81268	49	98	147	195	244
51	·80978	80690	80402	80115	79829	79544	79259	78975	78692	78410	47	95	142	190	237
52	·78129	77848	77568	77289	77010	76733	76456	76180	75904	75629	46	92	139	185	231
53	·75355	75082	74810	74538	74267	73996	73726	73457	73189	72921	45	90	135	180	225
54	·72654	72388	72122	71857	71593	71329	71066	70804	70542	70281	44	88	132	176	219
55	0·70021	69761	69502	69243	68985	68728	68471	68215	67960	67705	43	86	129	171	214
56	·67451	67197	66944	66692	66440	66189	65938	65688	65438	65189	42	84	126	167	209
57	·64941	64693	64446	64199	63953	63707	63462	63217	62973	62730	41	82	123	164	205
58	·62487	62245	62003	61761	61520	61280	61040	60801	60562	60324	40	79	120	160	200
59	·60086	59849	59612	59376	59140	58905	58670	58435	58201	57968	39	78	118	157	196
60	0·57735	57503	57271	57039	56808	56577	56347	56117	55888	55659	38	77	115	154	192
61	·55431	55203	54975	54748	54522	54296	54070	53844	53620	53395	38	75	113	151	188
62	·53171	52947	52724	52501	52279	52057	51835	51614	51393	51173	37	74	111	148	185
63	·50953	50733	50514	50295	50076	49858	49640	49423	49206	48989	36	73	109	145	182
64	·48773	48557	48342	48127	47912	47698	47483	47270	47056	46843	36	71	107	143	179
65	0·46631	46418	46206	45995	45784	45573	45362	45152	44942	44732	35	70	105	141	176
66	·44523	44314	44105	43897	43689	43481	43274	43067	42860	42654	35	69	104	138	173
67	·42447	42242	42036	41831	41626	41421	41217	41013	40809	40606	34	68	102	136	170
68	·40403	40200	39997	39795	39593	39391	39190	38988	38787	38587	34	67	101	134	168
69	·38386	38186	37986	37787	37588	37388	37190	36991	36793	36595	33	66	99	133	166
70	0·36397	36199	36002	35805	35608	35412	35216	35019	34824	34628	33	66	98	131	164
71	·34433	34238	34043	33848	33654	33460	33266	33072	32878	32685	32	65	97	129	162
72	·32492	32299	32106	31914	31722	31530	31338	31147	30955	30764	32	64	96	128	160
73	·30573	30382	30192	30001	29811	29621	29432	29242	29053	28864	32	63	95	127	158
74	·28675	28486	28297	28109	27920	27732	27545	27357	27169	26982	31	63	94	125	157
75	0·26795	26608	26421	26235	26048	25862	25676	25490	25304	25118	31	62	93	124	155
76	·24933	24747	24562	24377	24193	24008	23823	23639	23455	23271	31	61	93	124	155
77	·23087	22903	22719	22536	22353	22169	21986	21804	21621	21438	31	61	92	122	153
78	·21256	21073	20891	20709	20527	20345	20164	19982	19801	19619	30	60	91	121	152
79	·19438	19257	19076	18895	18714	18534	18353	18173	17993	17813	30	60	90	120	150
80	0·17633	17453	17273	17093	16914	16734	16555	16376	16196	16017	30	60	90	120	150
81	·15838	15660	15481	15302	15124	14945	14767	14588	14410	14232	30	59	89	119	149
82	·14054	13876	13698	13521	13343	13165	12988	12810	12633	12456	30	59	89	118	148
83	·12278	12101	11924	11747	11570	11394	11217	11040	10863	10687	29	59	88	118	147
84	·10510	10334	10158	09981	09805	09629	09453	09277	09101	08925	29	59	88	117	147
85	0·08749	08573	08397	08221	08046	07870	07695	07519	07344	07168	29	59	88	117	146
86	·06993	06817	06642	06467	06291	06116	05941	05766	05591	05416	29	58	88	117	146
87	·05241	05066	04891	04716	04541	04366	04191	04016	03842	03667	29	58	87	117	146
88	·03492	03317	03143	02968	02793	02619	02444	02269	02095	01920	29	58	87	116	146
89	·01746	01571	01396	01222	01047	00873	00698	00524	00349	00175	29	58	87	116	146
90	0·00000														

RADIANS TO DEGREES

Radians	·000	·002	·004	·006	·008
	° ′	° ′	° ′	° ′	° ′
·00	0 00	0 06·9	0 13·8	0 20·6	0 27·5
·01	0 34·4	0 41·3	0 48·1	0 55·0	1 01·9
·02	1 08·8	1 15·6	1 22·5	1 29·4	1 36·3
·03	1 43·1	1 50·0	1 56·9	2 03·8	2 10·6
·04	2 17·5	2 24·4	2 31·3	2 38·1	2 45·0
·05	2 51·9	2 58·8	3 05·6	3 12·5	3 19·4
·06	3 26·3	3 33·1	3 40·0	3 46·9	3 53·8
·07	4 00·6	4 07·5	4 14·4	4 21·3	4 28·1
·08	4 35·0	4 41·9	4 48·8	4 55·6	5 02·5
·09	5 09·4	5 16·3	5 23·1	5 30·0	5 36·9
·10	5 43·8	5 50·7	5 57·5	6 04·4	6 11·3
·11	6 18·2	6 25·0	6 31·9	6 38·8	6 45·7
·12	6 52·5	6 59·4	7 06·3	7 13·2	7 20·0
·13	7 26·9	7 33·8	7 40·7	7 47·5	7 54·4
·14	8 01·3	8 08·2	8 15·0	8 21·9	8 28·8
·15	8 35·7	8 42·5	8 49·4	8 56·3	9 03·2
·16	9 10·0	9 16·9	9 23·8	9 30·7	9 37·5
·17	9 44·4	9 51·3	9 58·2	10 05·0	10 11·9
·18	10 18·8	10 25·7	10 32·5	10 39·4	10 46·3
·19	10 53·2	11 00·0	11 06·9	11 13·8	11 20·7
·20	11 27·5	11 34·4	11 41·3	11 48·2	11 55·1
·21	12 01·9	12 08·8	12 15·7	12 22·6	12 29·4
·22	12 36·3	12 43·2	12 50·1	12 56·9	13 03·8
·23	13 10·7	13 17·6	13 24·4	13 31·3	13 38·2
·24	13 45·1	13 51·9	13 58·8	14 05·7	14 12·6
·25	14 19·4	14 26·3	14 33·2	14 40·1	14 46·9
·26	14 53·8	15 00·7	15 07·6	15 14·4	15 21·3
·27	15 28·2	15 35·1	15 41·9	15 48·8	15 55·7
·28	16 02·6	16 09·4	16 16·3	16 23·2	16 30·1
·29	16 36·9	16 43·8	16 50·7	16 57·6	17 04·4
·30	17 11·3	17 18·2	17 25·1	17 32·0	17 38·8
·31	17 45·7	17 52·6	17 59·5	18 06·3	18 13·2
·32	18 20·1	18 27·0	18 33·8	18 40·7	18 47·6
·33	18 54·5	19 01·3	19 08·2	19 15·1	19 22·0
·34	19 28·8	19 35·7	19 42·6	19 49·5	19 56·3
·35	20 03·2	20 10·1	20 17·0	20 23·8	20 30·7
·36	20 37·6	20 44·5	20 51·3	20 58·2	21 05·1
·37	21 12·0	21 18·8	21 25·7	21 32·6	21 39·5
·38	21 46·3	21 53·2	22 00·1	22 07·0	22 13·8
·39	22 20·7	22 27·6	22 34·5	22 41·3	22 48·2
·40	22 55·1	23 02·0	23 08·8	23 15·7	23 22·6
·41	23 29·5	23 36·4	23 43·2	23 50·1	23 57·0
·42	24 03·9	24 10·7	24 17·6	24 24·5	24 31·4
·43	24 38·2	24 45·1	24 52·0	24 58·9	25 05·7
·44	25 12·6	25 19·5	25 26·4	25 33·2	25 40·1
·45	25 47·0	25 53·9	26 00·7	26 07·6	26 14·5
·46	26 21·4	26 28·2	26 35·1	26 42·0	26 48·9
·47	26 55·7	27 02·6	27 09·5	27 16·4	27 23·2
·48	27 30·1	27 37·0	27 43·9	27 50·7	27 57·6
·49	28 04·5	28 11·4	28 18·2	28 25·1	28 32·0
·50	28 38·9				

RADIANS TO DEGREES

Radians	.000		.002		.004		.006		.008	
	°	′	°	′	°	′	°	′	°	′
·50	28	38·9	28	45·7	28	52·6	28	59·5	29	06·4
·51	29	13·3	29	20·1	29	27·0	29	33·9	29	40·8
·52	29	47·6	29	54·5	30	01·4	30	08·3	30	15·1
·53	30	22·0	30	28·9	30	35·8	30	42·6	30	49·5
·54	30	56·4	31	03·3	31	10·1	31	17·0	31	23·9
·55	31	30·8	31	37·6	31	44·5	31	51·4	31	58·3
·56	32	05·1	32	12·0	32	18·9	32	25·8	32	32·6
·57	32	39·5	32	46·4	32	53·3	33	00·1	33	07·0
·58	33	13·9	33	20·8	33	27·6	33	34·5	33	41·4
·59	33	48·3	33	55·1	34	02·0	34	08·9	34	15·8
·60	34	22·6	34	29·5	34	36·4	34	43·3	34	50·2
·61	34	57·0	35	03·9	35	10·8	35	17·7	35	24·5
·62	35	31·4	35	38·3	35	45·2	35	52·0	35	58·9
·63	36	05·8	36	12·7	36	19·5	36	26·4	36	33·3
·64	36	40·2	36	47·0	36	53·9	37	00·8	37	07·7
·65	37	14·5	37	21·4	37	28·3	37	35·2	37	42·0
·66	37	48·9	37	55·8	38	02·7	38	09·5	38	16·4
·67	38	23·3	38	30·2	38	37·0	38	43·9	38	50·8
·68	38	57·7	39	04·5	39	11·4	39	18·3	39	25·2
·69	39	32·0	39	38·9	39	45·8	39	52·7	39	59·5
·70	40	06·4	40	13·3	40	20·2	40	27·0	40	33·9
·71	40	40·8	40	47·7	40	54·6	41	01·4	41	08·3
·72	41	15·2	41	22·1	41	28·9	41	35·8	41	42·7
·73	41	49·6	41	56·4	42	03·3	42	10·2	42	17·1
·74	42	23·9	42	30·8	42	37·7	42	44·6	42	51·4
·75	42	58·3	43	05·2	43	12·1	43	18·9	43	25·8
·76	43	32·7	43	39·6	43	46·4	43	53·3	44	00·2
·77	44	07·1	44	13·9	44	20·8	44	27·7	44	34·6
·78	44	41·4	44	48·3	44	55·2	45	02·1	45	08·9
·79	45	15·8	45	22·7	45	29·6	45	36·4	45	43·3
·80	45	50·2	45	57·1	46	03·9	46	10·8	46	17·7
·81	46	24·6	46	31·5	46	38·3	46	45·2	46	52·1
·82	46	59·0	47	05·8	47	12·7	47	19·6	47	26·5
·83	47	33·3	47	40·2	47	47·1	47	54·0	48	00·8
·84	48	07·7	48	14·6	48	21·5	48	28·3	48	35·2
·85	48	42·1	48	49·0	48	55·8	49	02·7	49	09·6
·86	49	16·5	49	23·3	49	30·2	49	37·1	49	44·0
·87	49	50·8	49	57·7	50	04·6	50	11·5	50	18·3
·88	50	25·2	50	32·1	50	39·0	50	45·8	50	52·7
·89	50	59·6	51	06·5	51	13·3	51	20·2	51	27·1
·90	51	34·0	51	40·8	51	47·7	51	54·6	52	01·5
·91	52	08·3	52	15·2	52	22·1	52	29·0	52	35·9
·92	52	42·7	52	49·6	52	56·5	53	03·4	53	10·2
·93	53	17·1	53	24·0	53	30·9	53	37·7	53	44·6
·94	53	51·5	53	58·4	54	05·2	54	12·1	54	19·0
·95	54	25·9	54	32·7	54	39·6	54	46·5	54	53·4
·96	55	00·2	55	07·1	55	14·0	55	20·9	55	27·7
·97	55	34·6	55	41·5	55	48·4	55	55·2	56	02·1
·98	56	09·0	56	15·9	56	22·7	56	29·6	56	36·5
·99	56	43·4	56	50·2	56	57·1	57	04·0	57	10·9
1·00	57	17·7								

DEGREES TO RADIANS

Degrees	0	1	2	3	4	5	6	7	8	9
					Radians					
0	0·00000	0·01745	0·03491	0·05236	0·06981	0·08727	0·10472	0·12217	0·13963	0·15708
10	·17453	·19199	·20944	·22689	·24435	·26180	·27925	·29671	·31416	·33161
20	·34907	·36652	·38397	·40143	·41888	·43633	·45379	·47124	·48869	·50615
30	·52360	·54105	·55851	·57596	·59341	·61087	·62832	·64577	·66323	·68068
40	·69813	·71558	·73304	·75049	·76794	·78540	·80285	·82030	·83776	·85521
50	0·87266	0·89012	0·90757	0·92502	0·94248	0·95993	0·97738	0·99484	1·01229	1·02974
60	1·04720	1·06465	1·08210	1·09956	1·11701	1·13446	1·15192	1·16937	1·18682	1·20428
70	·22173	·23918	·25664	·27409	·29154	·30900	·32645	·34390	·36136	·37881
80	·39626	·41372	·43117	·44862	·46608	·48353	·50098	·51844	·53589	·55334
90	·57080									

MINUTES OF ARC TO RADIANS

Minutes	0	1	2	3	4	5	6	7	8	9
					Radians					
0	0·00000	0·00029	0·00058	0·00087	0·00116	0·00145	0·00175	0·00204	0·00233	0·00262
10	·00291	·00320	·00349	·00378	·00407	·00436	·00465	·00495	·00524	·00553
20	·00582	·00611	·00640	·00669	·00698	·00727	·00756	·00785	·00814	·00844
30	·00873	·00902	·00931	·00960	·00989	·01018	·01047	·01076	·01105	·01134
40	·01164	·01193	·01222	·01251	·01280	·01309	·01338	·01367	·01396	·01425
50	·01454	·01484	·01513	·01542	·01571	·01600	·01629	·01658	·01687	·01716
60	·01745									

SQUARES OF NUMBERS 1 - 10

	0	1	2	3	4	5	6	7	8	9	Mean Differences								
											1	2	3	4	5	6	7	8	9
1.0	1.000	1.020	1.040	1.061	1.082	1.103	1.124	1.145	1.166	1.188	2	4	6	8	11	13	15	17	19
.1	1.210	1.232	1.254	1.277	1.300	1.323	1.346	1.369	1.392	1.416	2	5	7	9	12	14	16	18	21
.2	1.440	1.464	1.488	1.513	1.538	1.563	1.588	1.613	1.638	1.664	3	5	8	10	13	15	18	20	23
.3	1.690	1.716	1.742	1.769	1.796	1.823	1.850	1.877	1.904	1.932	3	5	8	11	14	16	19	22	24
.4	1.960	1.988	2.016	2.045	2.074	2.103	2.132	2.161	2.190	2.220	3	6	9	12	15	17	20	23	26
1.5	2.250	2.280	2.310	2.341	2.372	2.403	2.434	2.465	2.496	2.528	3	6	9	12	16	19	22	25	28
.6	2.560	2.592	2.624	2.657	2.690	2.723	2.756	2.789	2.822	2.856	3	7	10	13	17	20	23	26	30
.7	2.890	2.924	2.958	2.993	3.028	3.063	3.098	3.133	3.168	3.204	4	7	11	14	18	21	25	28	32
.8	3.240	3.276	3.312	3.349	3.386	3.423	3.460	3.497	3.534	3.572	4	7	11	15	19	22	26	30	33
.9	3.610	3.648	3.686	3.725	3.764	3.803	3.842	3.881	3.920	3.960	4	8	12	16	20	23	27	31	35
2.0	4.000	4.040	4.080	4.121	4.162	4.203	4.244	4.285	4.326	4.368	4	8	12	16	21	25	29	33	37
.1	4.410	4.452	4.494	4.537	4.580	4.623	4.666	4.709	4.752	4.796	4	9	13	17	22	26	30	34	39
.2	4.840	4.884	4.928	4.973	5.018	5.063	5.108	5.153	5.198	5.244	5	9	14	18	23	27	32	36	41
.3	5.290	5.336	5.382	5.429	5.476	5.523	5.570	5.617	5.664	5.712	5	9	14	19	24	28	33	38	42
.4	5.760	5.808	5.856	5.905	5.954	6.003	6.052	6.101	6.150	6.200	5	10	15	20	25	29	34	39	44
2.5	6.250	6.300	6.350	6.401	6.452	6.503	6.554	6.605	6.656	6.708	5	10	15	20	26	31	36	41	46
.6	6.760	6.812	6.864	6.917	6.970	7.023	7.076	7.129	7.182	7.236	5	11	16	21	27	32	37	42	48
.7	7.290	7.344	7.398	7.453	7.508	7.563	7.618	7.673	7.728	7.784	6	11	17	22	28	33	39	44	50
.8	7.840	7.896	7.952	8.009	8.066	8.123	8.180	8.237	8.294	8.352	6	11	17	23	29	34	40	46	51
.9	8.410	8.468	8.526	8.585	8.644	8.703	8.762	8.821	8.880	8.940	6	12	18	24	30	35	41	47	53
3.0	9.000	9.060	9.120	9.181	9.242	9.303	9.364	9.425	9.486	9.548	6	12	18	24	31	37	43	49	55
.1	9.610	9.672	9.734	9.797	9.860	9.923	9.986	10.049	10.112	10.176	6	13	19	25	32	38	44	50	56
.2	10.24	10.30	10.37	10.43	10.50	10.56	10.63	10.69	10.76	10.82	1	1	2	3	3	4	5	5	6
.3	10.89	10.96	11.02	11.09	11.16	11.22	11.29	11.36	11.42	11.49	1	1	2	3	3	4	5	5	6
.4	11.56	11.63	11.70	11.76	11.83	11.90	11.97	12.04	12.11	12.18	1	1	2	3	3	4	5	6	6
3.5	12.25	12.32	12.39	12.46	12.53	12.60	12.67	12.74	12.82	12.89	1	1	2	3	4	4	5	6	6
.6	12.96	13.03	13.10	13.18	13.25	13.32	13.40	13.47	13.54	13.62	1	1	2	3	4	4	5	6	7
.7	13.69	13.76	13.84	13.91	13.99	14.06	14.14	14.21	14.29	14.36	1	2	2	3	4	5	5	6	7
.8	14.44	14.52	14.59	14.67	14.75	14.82	14.90	14.98	15.05	15.13	1	2	2	3	4	5	5	6	7
.9	15.21	15.29	15.37	15.44	15.52	15.60	15.68	15.76	15.84	15.92	1	2	2	3	4	5	6	6	7
4.0	16.00	16.08	16.16	16.24	16.32	16.40	16.48	16.56	16.65	16.73	1	2	2	3	4	5	6	6	7
.1	16.81	16.89	16.97	17.06	17.14	17.22	17.31	17.39	17.47	17.56	1	2	2	3	4	5	6	7	7
.2	17.64	17.72	17.81	17.89	17.98	18.06	18.15	18.23	18.32	18.40	1	2	3	3	4	5	6	7	8
.3	18.49	18.58	18.66	18.75	18.84	18.92	19.01	19.10	19.18	19.27	1	2	3	3	4	5	6	7	8
.4	19.36	19.45	19.54	19.62	19.71	19.80	19.89	19.98	20.07	20.16	1	2	3	4	4	5	6	7	8
4.5	20.25	20.34	20.43	20.52	20.61	20.70	20.79	20.88	20.98	21.07	1	2	3	4	5	5	6	7	8
.6	21.16	21.25	21.34	21.44	21.53	21.62	21.72	21.81	21.90	22.00	1	2	3	4	5	6	7	7	8
.7	22.09	22.18	22.28	22.37	22.47	22.56	22.66	22.75	22.85	22.94	1	2	3	4	5	6	7	8	9
.8	23.04	23.14	23,23	23.33	23.43	23.52	23.62	23.72	23.81	23.91	1	2	3	4	5	6	7	8	9
.9	24.01	24.11	24.21	24.31	24.40	24.50	24.60	24.70	24.80	24.90	1	2	3	4	5	6	7	8	9
5.0	25.00	25.10	25.20	25.30	25.40	25.50	25.60	25.70	25.81	25.91	1	2	3	4	5	6	7	8	9
.1	26.01	26.11	26.21	26.32	26.42	26.52	26.63	26.73	26.83	26.94	1	2	3	4	5	6	7	8	9
.2	27.04	27.14	27.25	27.35	27.46	27.56	27.67	27.77	27.88	27.98	1	2	3	4	5	6	7	8	9
.3	28.09	28.20	28.30	28.41	28.52	28.62	28.73	28.84	28.94	29.05	1	2	3	4	5	6	7	9	10
.4	29.16	29.27	29.38	29.48	29.59	29.70	29.81	29.92	30.03	30.14	1	2	3	4	5	7	8	9	10

SQUARES OF NUMBERS 1 - 10

	0	1	2	3	4	5	6	7	8	9		Mean Differences								
											1	2	3	4	5	6	7	8	9
5.5	30.25	30.36	30.47	30.58	30.69	30.80	30.91	31.02	31.14	31.25	1	2	3	4	6	7	8	9	10
.6	31.36	31.47	31.58	31.70	31.81	31.92	32.04	32.15	32.26	32.38	1	2	3	5	6	7	8	9	10
.7	32.49	32.60	32.72	32.83	32.95	33.06	33.18	33.29	33.41	33.52	1	2	3	5	6	7	8	9	10
.8	33.64	33.76	33.87	33.99	34.11	34.22	34.34	34.46	34.57	34.69	1	2	4	5	6	7	8	9	11
.9	34.81	34.93	35.05	35.16	35.28	35.40	35.52	35.64	35.76	35.88	1	2	4	5	6	7	8	10	11
6.0	36.00	36.10	36.24	36.36	36.48	36.60	36.72	36.84	36.97	37.09	1	2	4	5	6	7	8	10	11
.1	37.21	37.33	37.45	37.58	37.70	37.82	37.95	38.07	38.19	38.32	1	2	4	5	6	7	9	10	11
.2	38.44	38.56	38.69	38.81	38.94	39.06	39.19	39.31	39.44	39.56	1	3	4	5	6	8	9	10	11
.3	39.69	39.82	39.94	40.07	40.20	40.32	40.45	40.58	40.70	40.83	1	3	4	5	6	8	9	10	11
.4	40.96	41.09	41.22	41.34	41.47	41.60	41.73	41.86	41.99	42.12	1	3	4	5	6	8	9	10	12
6.5	42.25	42.38	42.51	42.64	42.77	42.90	43.03	43.16	43.30	43.43	1	3	4	5	7	8	9	10	12
.6	43.56	43.69	43.82	43.96	44.09	44.22	44.36	44.49	44.62	44.76	1	3	4	5	7	8	9	11	12
.7	44.89	45.02	45.16	45.29	45.43	45.56	45.70	45.83	45.97	46.10	1	3	4	5	7	8	9	11	12
.8	46.24	46.38	46.51	46.65	46.79	46.92	47.06	47.20	47.33	47.47	1	3	4	5	7	8	10	11	12
.9	47.61	47.75	47.89	48.02	48.16	48.30	48.44	48.58	48.72	48.86	1	3	4	6	7	8	10	11	13
7.0	49.00	49.14	49.28	49.42	49.56	49.70	49.84	49.98	50.13	50.27	1	3	4	6	7	8	10	11	13
.1	50.41	50.55	50.69	50.84	50.98	51.12	51.27	51.41	51.55	51.70	1	3	4	6	7	9	10	11	13
.2	51.84	51.98	52.13	52.27	52.42	52.56	52.71	52.85	53.00	53.14	1	3	4	6	7	9	10	12	13
.3	53.29	53.44	53.58	53.73	53.88	54.02	54.17	54.32	54.46	54.61	1	3	4	6	7	9	10	12	13
.4	54.76	54.91	55.06	55.20	55.35	55.50	55.65	55.80	55.95	56.10	1	3	4	6	7	9	10	12	13
7.5	56.25	56.40	56.55	56.70	56.85	57.00	57.15	57.30	57.46	57.61	2	3	5	6	8	9	11	12	14
.6	57.76	57.91	58.06	58.22	58.37	58.52	58.68	58.83	58.98	59.14	2	3	5	6	8	9	11	12	14
.7	59.29	59.44	59.60	59.75	59.91	60.06	60.22	60.37	60.53	60.68	2	3	5	6	8	9	11	12	14
.8	60.84	61.00	61.15	61.31	61.47	61.62	61.78	61.94	62.09	62.25	2	3	5	6	8	9	11	13	14
.9	62.41	62.57	62.73	62.88	63.04	63.20	63.36	63.52	63.68	63.84	2	3	5	6	8	10	11	13	14
8.0	64.00	64.16	64.32	64.48	64.64	64.80	64.96	65.12	65.29	65.45	2	3	5	6	8	10	11	13	14
.1	65.61	65.77	65.93	66.10	66.26	66.42	66.59	66.75	66.91	67.08	2	3	5	7	8	10	11	13	15
.2	67.24	67.40	67.57	67.73	67.90	68.06	68.23	68.39	68.56	68.72	2	3	5	7	8	10	12	13	15
.3	68.89	69.06	69.22	69.39	69.56	69.72	69.89	70.06	70.22	70.39	2	3	5	7	8	10	12	13	15
.4	70.56	70.73	70.90	71.06	71.23	71.40	71.57	71.74	71.91	72.08	2	3	5	7	8	10	12	14	15
8.5	72.25	72.42	72.59	72.76	72.93	73.10	73.27	73.44	73.62	73.79	2	3	5	7	9	10	12	14	15
.6	73.96	74.13	74.30	74.48	74.65	74.82	75.00	75.17	75.34	75.52	2	3	5	7	9	10	12	14	16
.7	75.69	75.86	76.04	76.21	76.39	76.56	76.74	76.91	77.09	77.26	2	4	5	7	9	11	12	14	16
.8	77.44	77.62	77.79	77.97	78.15	78.32	78.50	78.68	78.85	79.03	2	4	5	7	9	11	12	14	16
.9	79.21	79.39	79.57	79.74	79.92	80.10	80.28	80.46	80.64	80.82	2	4	5	7	9	11	13	14	16
9.0	81.00	81.18	81.36	81.54	81.72	81.90	82.08	82.26	82.45	82.63	2	4	5	7	9	11	13	14	16
.1	82.81	82.99	83.17	83.36	83.54	83.72	83.91	84.09	84.27	84.46	2	4	5	7	9	11	13	15	16
.2	84.64	84.82	85.01	85.19	85.38	85.56	85.75	85.93	86.12	86.30	2	4	6	7	9	11	13	15	17
.3	86.49	86.68	86.86	87.05	87.24	87.42	87.61	87.80	87.98	88.17	2	4	6	7	9	11	13	15	17
.4	88.36	88.55	88.74	88.92	89.11	89.30	89.49	89.68	89.87	90.06	2	4	6	8	9	11	13	15	17
9.5	90.25	90.44	90.63	90.82	91.01	91.20	91.39	91.58	91.78	91.97	2	4	6	8	10	11	13	15	17
.6	92.16	92.35	92.54	92.74	92.93	93.12	93.32	93.51	93.70	93.90	2	4	6	8	10	12	14	15	17
.7	94.09	94.28	94.48	94.67	94.87	95.06	95.26	95.45	95.65	95.84	2	4	6	8	10	12	14	16	18
.8	96.04	96.24	96.43	96.63	96.83	97.02	97.22	97.42	97.61	97.81	2	4	6	8	10	12	14	16	18
.9	98.01	98.21	98.41	98.60	98.80	99.00	99.20	99.40	99.60	99.80	2	4	6	8	10	12	14	16	18

CUBES OF NUMBERS 1 - 10

	0	1	2	3	4	5	6	7	8	9	Mean Differences 1	2	3	4	5	6	7	8	9
1.0	1.000	1.030	1.061	1.093	1.125	1.158	1.191	1.225	1.260	1.295	3	7	10	13	17	20	23	26	30
.1	1.331	1.368	1.405	1.443	1.482	1.521	1.561	1.602	1.643	1.685	4	8	12	16	20	24	28	32	36
.2	1.728	1.772	1.816	1.861	1.907	1.953	2.000	2.048	2.097	2.147	5	9	14	19	23	28	33	38	42
.3	2.197	2.248	2.300	2.353	2.406	2.460	2.515	2.571	2.628	2.686	5	11	16	22	27	33	38	44	49
.4	2.744	2.803	2.863	2.924	2.986	3.049	3.112	3.177	3.242	3.308	6	13	19	25	32	38	44	50	57
1.5	3.375	3.443	3.512	3.582	3.652	3.724	3.796	3.870	3.944	4.020	7	14	22	29	36	43	50	58	65
.6	4.096	4.173	4.252	4.331	4.411	4.492	4.574	4.657	4.742	4.827	8	16	25	33	41	49	57	65	74
.7	4.913	5.000	5.088	5.178	5.268	5.359	5.452	5.545	5.640	5.735	9	18	28	37	46	55	64	74	83
.8	5.832	5.930	6.029	6.128	6.230	6.332	6.435	6.539	6.645	6.751	10	21	31	41	51	62	72	82	92
.9	6.859	6.968	7.078	7.189	7.301	7.415	7.530	7.645	7.762	7.881	11	23	34	46	57	68	80	91	103
2.0	8.000	8.121	8.242	8.365	8.490	8.615	8.742	8.870	8.999	9.129	13	25	38	50	63	76	88	101	113
.1	9.261	9.394	9.528	9.664	9.800	9.938	10.078	10.218	10.360	10.503	14	27	41	54	68	82	95	109	122
.2	10.65	10.79	10.94	11.09	11.24	11.39	11.54	11.70	11.85	12.01	2	3	5	6	8	9	11	12	14
.3	12.17	12.33	12.49	12.65	12.81	12.98	13.14	13.31	13.48	13.65	2	3	5	7	8	10	12	13	15
.4	13.82	14.00	14.17	14.35	14.53	14.71	14.89	15.07	15.25	15.44	2	4	5	7	9	11	13	14	16
2.5	15.63	15.81	16.00	16.19	16.39	16.58	16.78	16.97	17.17	17.37	2	4	6	8	10	12	14	16	18
.6	17.58	17.78	17.98	18.19	18.40	18.61	18.82	19.03	19.25	19.47	2	4	6	8	11	13	15	17	19
.7	19.68	19.90	20.12	20.35	20.57	20.80	21.02	21.25	21.49	21.72	2	5	7	9	11	14	16	18	20
.8	21.95	22.19	22.43	22.67	22.91	23.15	23.39	23.64	23.89	24.14	2	5	7	10	12	15	17	20	22
.9	24.39	24.64	24.90	25.15	25.41	25.67	25.93	26.20	26.46	26.73	3	5	8	10	13	16	18	21	23
3.0	27.00	27.27	27.54	27.82	28.09	28.37	28.65	28.93	29.22	29.50	3	6	8	11	14	17	20	22	25
.1	29.79	30.08	30.37	30.66	30.96	31.26	31.55	31.86	32.16	32.46	3	6	9	12	15	18	21	24	27
.2	32.77	33.08	33.39	33.70	34.01	34.33	34.65	34.97	35.29	35.61	3	6	10	13	16	19	22	25	29
.3	35.94	36.26	36.59	36.93	37.26	37.60	37.93	38.27	38.61	38.96	3	7	10	13	17	20	24	27	30
.4	39.30	39.65	40.00	40.35	40.71	41.06	41.42	41.78	42.14	42.51	4	7	11	14	18	21	25	29	32
3.5	42.88	43.24	43.61	43.99	44.36	44.74	45.12	45.50	45.88	46.27	4	8	11	15	19	23	26	30	34
.6	46.66	47.05	47.44	47.83	48.23	48.63	49.03	49.43	49.84	50.24	4	8	12	16	20	24	28	32	36
.7	50.65	51.07	51.48	51.90	52.31	52.73	53.16	53.58	54.01	54.44	4	8	13	17	21	25	30	34	38
.8	54.87	55.31	55.74	56.18	56.62	57.07	57.51	57.96	58.41	58.86	4	9	13	18	22	27	31	36	40
.9	59.32	59.78	60.24	60.70	61.16	61.63	62.10	62.57	63.04	63.52	5	9	14	19	23	28	33	37	42
4.0	64.00	64.48	64.96	65.45	65.94	66.43	66.92	67.42	67.92	68.42	5	10	15	20	25	30	34	39	44
.1	68.92	69.43	69.93	70.44	70.96	71.47	71.99	72.51	73.03	73.56	5	10	16	21	26	31	36	41	47
.2	74.09	74.62	75.15	75.69	76.23	76.77	77.31	77.85	78.40	78.95	5	11	16	22	27	33	38	43	49
.3	79.51	80.06	80.62	81.18	81.75	82.31	82.88	83.45	84.03	84.60	6	11	17	23	28	34	40	45	51
.4	85.18	85.77	86.35	86.94	87.53	88.12	88.72	89.31	89.92	90.52	6	12	18	24	30	36	42	48	54
4.5	91.13	91.73	92.35	92.96	93.58	94.20	94.82	95.44	96.07	96.70	6	12	19	25	31	37	43	50	56
.6	97.34	97.97	98.61	99.25	99.90	100.54	101.19	101.85	102.50	103.16	6	13	19	26	32	38	45	51	58
.7	103.8	104.5	105.2	105.8	106.5	107.1	107.9	108.5	109.2	109.9	1	1	2	3	3	4	5	5	6
.8	110.6	111.3	112.0	112.7	113.4	114.1	114.8	115.5	116.2	116.9	1	1	2	3	4	4	5	6	6
.9	117.6	118.4	119.1	119.8	120.6	121.3	122.0	122.8	123.5	124.3	1	1	2	3	4	4	5	6	7
5.0	125.0	125.8	126.5	127.3	128.0	128.8	129.6	130.3	131.1	131.9	1	2	2	3	4	5	5	6	7
.1	132.7	133.4	134.2	135.0	135.8	136.6	137.4	138.2	139.0	139.8	1	2	2	3	4	5	6	6	7
.2	140.6	141.4	142.2	143.1	143.9	144.7	145.5	146.4	147.2	148.0	1	2	2	3	4	5	6	7	7
.3	148.9	149.7	150.6	151.4	152.3	153.1	154.0	154.9	155.7	156.6	1	2	3	3	4	5	6	7	8
.4	157.5	158.3	159.2	160.1	161.0	161.9	162.8	163.7	164.6	165.5	1	2	3	4	4	5	6	7	8

CUBES OF NUMBERS 1 - 10

	0	1	2	3	4	5	6	7	8	9	Mean Differences								
											1	2	3	4	5	6	7	8	9
5.5	166.4	167.3	168.2	169.1	170.0	171.0	171.9	172.8	173.7	174.7	1	2	3	4	5	6	6	7	8
.6	175.6	176.6	177.5	178.5	179.4	180.4	181.3	182.3	183.3	184.2	1	2	3	4	5	6	7	8	9
.7	185.2	186.2	187.1	188.1	189.1	190.1	191.1	192.1	193.1	194.1	1	2	3	4	5	6	7	8	9
.8	195.1	196.1	197.1	198.2	199.2	200.2	201.2	202.3	203.3	204.3	1	2	3	4	5	6	7	8	9
.9	205.4	206.4	207.5	208.5	209.6	210.6	211.7	212.8	213.9	214.9	1	2	3	4	5	6	7	8	10
6.0	216.0	217.1	218.2	219.3	220.3	221.4	222.5	223.6	224.8	225.9	1	2	3	4	6	7	8	9	10
.1	227.0	228.1	229.2	230.3	231.5	232.6	233.7	234.9	236.0	237.2	1	2	3	5	6	7	8	9	10
.2	238.3	239.5	240.6	241.8	243.0	244.1	245.3	246.5	247.7	248.9	1	2	4	5	6	7	8	9	11
.3	250.0	251.2	252.4	253.6	254.8	256.0	257.3	258.5	259.7	260.9	1	2	4	5	6	7	8	10	11
.4	262.1	263.4	264.6	265.9	267.1	268.3	269.6	270.8	272.1	273.4	1	3	4	5	6	8	9	10	11
6.5	274.6	275.9	277.2	278.5	279.7	281.0	282.3	283.6	284.9	286.2	1	3	4	5	6	8	9	10	12
.6	287.5	288.8	290.1	291.4	292.8	294.1	295.4	296.7	298.1	299.4	1	3	4	5	7	8	9	11	12
.7	300.8	302.1	303.5	304.8	306.2	307.5	308.9	310.3	311.7	313.0	1	3	4	5	7	8	10	11	12
.8	314.4	315.8	317.2	318.6	320.0	321.4	322.8	324.2	325.7	327.1	1	3	4	6	7	8	10	11	13
.9	328.5	329.9	331.4	332.8	334.3	335.7	337.2	338.6	340.1	341.5	1	3	4	6	7	9	10	12	13
7.0	343.0	344.5	345.9	347.4	348.9	350.4	351.9	353.4	354.9	356.4	1	3	4	6	7	9	10	12	13
.1	357.9	359.4	360.9	362.5	364.0	365.5	367.1	368.6	370.1	371.7	2	3	5	6	8	9	11	12	14
.2	373.2	374.8	376.4	377.9	379.5	381.1	382.7	384.2	385.8	387.2	2	3	5	6	8	9	11	13	14
.3	389.0	390.6	392.2	393.8	395.4	397.1	398.7	400.3	401.9	403.6	2	3	5	6	8	10	11	13	15
.4	405.2	406.9	408.5	410.2	411.8	413.5	415.2	416.8	418.5	420.2	2	3	5	7	8	10	12	13	15
7.5	421.9	423.6	425.3	427.0	428.7	430.4	432.1	433.8	435.5	437.2	2	3	5	7	9	10	12	14	15
.6	439.0	440.7	442.5	444.2	445.9	447.7	449.5	451.2	453.0	454.8	2	4	5	7	9	11	12	14	16
.7	456.5	458.3	460.1	461.9	463.7	465.5	467.3	469.1	470.9	472.7	2	4	5	7	9	11	13	14	16
.8	474.6	476.4	478.2	480.0	481.9	483.7	485.6	487.4	489.3	491.2	2	4	6	7	9	11	13	15	17
.9	493.0	494.9	496.8	498.7	500.6	502.5	504.4	506.3	508.2	510.1	2	4	6	8	10	11	13	15	17
8.0	512.0	513.9	515.8	517.8	519.7	521.7	523.6	525.6	527.5	529.5	2	4	6	8	10	12	14	16	17
.1	531.4	533.4	535.4	537.4	539.4	541.3	543.3	545.3	547.3	549.4	2	4	6	8	10	12	14	16	18
.2	551.4	553.4	555.4	557.4	559.5	561.5	563.6	565.6	567.7	569.7	2	4	6	8	10	12	14	16	18
.3	571.8	573.9	575.9	578.0	580.1	582.2	584.3	586.4	588.5	590.6	2	4	6	8	10	13	15	17	19
.4	592.7	594.8	596.9	599.1	601.2	603.4	605.5	607.6	609.8	612.0	2	4	6	9	11	13	15	17	19
8.5	614.1	616.3	618.5	620.7	622.8	625.0	627.2	629.4	631.6	633.8	2	4	7	9	11	13	15	18	20
.6	636.1	638.3	640.5	642.7	645.0	647.2	649.5	651.7	654.0	656.2	2	4	7	9	11	13	16	18	20
.7	658.5	660.8	663.1	665.3	667.6	669.9	672.2	674.5	676.8	679.2	2	5	7	9	12	14	16	18	21
.8	681.5	683.8	686.1	688.5	690.8	693.2	695.5	697.9	700.2	702.6	2	5	7	9	12	14	16	19	21
.9	705.0	707.3	709.7	712.1	714.5	716.9	719.3	721.7	724.2	726.6	2	5	7	10	12	14	17	19	22
9.0	729.0	731.4	733.9	736.3	738.8	741.2	743.7	746.1	748.6	751.1	2	5	7	10	12	15	17	20	22
.1	753.6	756.1	758.6	761.0	763.6	766.1	768.6	771.1	773.6	776.2	3	5	8	10	13	15	18	20	23
.2	778.7	781.2	783.8	786.3	788.9	791.5	784.0	796.6	799.2	801.8	3	5	8	10	13	15	18	21	23
.3	804.4	807.0	809.6	812.2	814.8	817.4	820.0	822.7	825.3	827.9	3	5	8	10	13	16	18	21	24
.4	830.6	833.2	835.9	838.6	841.2	843.9	846.6	849.3	852.0	854.7	3	5	8	11	13	16	19	21	24
9.5	857.4	860.1	862.8	865.5	868.3	871.0	873.7	876.5	879.2	882.0	3	5	8	11	14	16	19	22	25
.6	884.7	887.5	890.3	893.1	895.8	898.6	901.4	904.2	907.0	909.9	3	6	8	11	14	17	20	22	25
.7	912.7	915.5	918.3	921.2	924.0	926.9	929.7	932.6	935.4	938.3	3	6	9	11	14	17	20	23	26
.8	941.2	944.1	947.0	949.9	952.8	955.7	958.6	961.5	964.4	967.4	3	6	9	12	15	17	20	23	26
.9	970.3	973.2	976.2	979.1	982.1	985.1	988.0	991.0	994.0	997.0	3	6	9	12	15	18	21	24	27

SQUARE ROOTS OF NUMBERS 1 - 10

	0	1	2	3	4	5	6	7	8	9	Mean Differences								
											1	2	3	4	5	6	7	8	9
1.0	1.000	1.005	1.010	1.015	1.020	1.025	1.030	1.034	1.039	1.044	1	1	2	2	2	3	3	4	4
.1	1.049	1.054	1.058	1.063	1.068	1.072	1.077	1.082	1.086	1.091	1	1	1	2	2	3	3	4	4
.2	1.095	1.100	1.105	1.109	1.114	1.118	1.122	1.127	1.131	1.136	0	1	1	2	2	3	3	4	4
.3	1.140	1.145	1.149	1.153	1.158	1.162	1.166	1.170	1.175	1.179	0	1	1	2	2	3	3	3	4
.4	1.183	1.187	1.192	1.196	1.200	1.204	1.208	1.212	1.217	1.221	0	1	1	2	2	3	3	3	4
1.5	1.225	1.229	1.233	1.237	1.241	1.245	1.249	1.253	1.257	1.261	0	1	1	2	2	2	3	3	4
.6	1.265	1.269	1.273	1.277	1.281	1.285	1.288	1.292	1.296	1.300	0	1	1	2	2	2	3	3	3
.7	1.304	1.308	1.312	1.315	1.319	1.323	1.327	1.330	1.334	1.338	0	1	1	2	2	2	3	3	3
.8	1.342	1.345	1.349	1.353	1.356	1.360	1.364	1.367	1.371	1.375	0	1	1	2	2	2	3	3	3
.9	1.378	1.382	1.386	1.389	1.393	1.396	1.400	1.404	1.407	1.411	0	1	1	1	2	2	3	3	3
2.0	1.414	1.418	1.421	1.425	1.428	1.432	1.435	1.439	1.442	1.446	0	1	1	1	2	2	2	3	3
.1	1.449	1.453	1.456	1.459	1.463	1.466	1.470	1.473	1.476	1.480	0	1	1	1	2	2	2	3	3
.2	1.483	1.487	1.490	1.493	1.497	1.500	1.503	1.507	1.510	1.513	0	1	1	1	2	2	2	3	3
.3	1.517	1.520	1.523	1.526	1.530	1.533	1.536	1.539	1.543	1.546	0	1	1	1	2	2	2	3	3
.4	1.549	1.552	1.556	1.559	1.562	1.565	1.568	1.572	1.575	1.578	0	1	1	1	2	2	2	3	3
2.5	1.581	1.584	1.587	1.591	1.594	1.597	1.600	1.603	1.606	1.609	0	1	1	1	2	2	2	3	3
.6	1.612	1.616	1.619	1.622	1.625	1.628	1.631	1.634	1.637	1.640	0	1	1	1	2	2	2	3	3
.7	1.643	1.646	1.649	1.652	1.655	1.658	1.661	1.664	1.667	1.670	0	1	1	1	2	2	2	2	3
.8	1.673	1.676	1.679	1.682	1.685	1.688	1.691	1.694	1.697	1.700	0	1	1	1	2	2	2	2	3
.9	1.703	1.706	1.709	1.712	1.715	1.718	1.720	1.723	1.726	1.729	0	1	1	1	2	2	2	2	3
3.0	1.732	1.735	1.738	1.741	1.744	1.746	1.749	1.752	1.755	1.758	0	1	1	1	1	2	2	2	3
.1	1.761	1.764	1.766	1.769	1.772	1.775	1.778	1.780	1.783	1.786	0	1	1	1	1	2	2	2	3
.2	1.789	1.792	1.794	1.797	1.800	1.803	1.806	1.808	1.811	1.814	0	1	1	1	1	2	2	2	2
.3	1.817	1.819	1.822	1.825	1.828	1.830	1.833	1.836	1.838	1.841	0	1	1	1	1	2	2	2	2
.4	1.844	1.847	1.849	1.852	1.855	1.857	1.860	1.863	1.865	1.868	0	1	1	1	1	2	2	2	2
3.5	1.871	1.873	1.876	1.879	1.881	1.884	1.887	1.889	1.892	1.895	0	1	1	1	1	2	2	2	2
.6	1.897	1.900	1.903	1.905	1.908	1.910	1.913	1.916	1.918	1.921	0	1	1	1	1	2	2	2	2
.7	1.924	1.926	1.929	1.931	1.934	1.936	1.939	1.942	1.944	1.947	0	1	1	1	1	2	2	2	2
.8	1.949	1.952	1.954	1.957	1.960	1.962	1.965	1.967	1.970	1.972	0	1	1	1	1	2	2	2	2
.9	1.975	1.977	1.980	1.982	1.985	1.987	1.990	1.992	1.995	1.997	0	1	1	1	1	2	2	2	2
4.0	2.000	2.002	2.005	2.007	2.010	2.012	2.015	2.017	2.020	2.022	0	1	1	1	1	2	2	2	2
.1	2.025	2.027	2.030	2.032	2.035	2.037	2.040	2.042	2.045	2.047	0	1	1	1	1	2	2	2	2
.2	2.049	2.052	2.054	2.057	2.059	2.062	2.064	2.066	2.069	2.071	0	1	1	1	1	2	2	2	2
.3	2.074	2.076	2.078	2.081	2.083	2.086	2.088	2.090	2.093	2.095	0	1	1	1	1	1	2	2	2
.4	2.098	2.100	2.102	2.105	2.107	2.110	2.112	2.114	2.117	2.119	0	1	1	1	1	1	2	2	2
4.5	2.121	2.124	2.126	2.128	2.131	2.133	2.135	2.138	2.140	2.142	0	1	1	1	1	1	2	2	2
.6	2.145	2.147	2.149	2.152	2.154	2.156	2.159	2.161	2.163	2.166	0	1	1	1	1	1	2	2	2
.7	2.168	2.170	2.173	2.175	2.177	2.179	2.182	2.184	2.186	2.189	0	1	1	1	1	1	2	2	2
.8	2.191	2.193	2.195	2.198	2.200	2.202	2.205	2.207	2.209	2.211	0	1	1	1	1	1	2	2	2
.9	2.214	2.216	2.218	2.220	2.223	2.225	2.227	2.229	2.232	2.234	0	1	1	1	1	1	2	2	2
5.0	2.236	2.238	2.241	2.243	2.245	2.247	2.249	2.252	2.254	2.256	0	0	1	1	1	1	2	2	2
.1	2.258	2.261	2.263	2.265	2.267	2.269	2.272	2.274	2.276	2.278	0	0	1	1	1	1	2	2	2
.2	2.280	2.283	2.285	2.287	2.289	2.291	2.293	2.296	2.298	2.300	0	0	1	1	1	1	2	2	2
.3	2.302	2.304	2.307	2.309	2.311	2.313	2.315	2.317	2.319	2.322	0	0	1	1	1	1	2	2	2
.4	2.324	2.326	2.328	2.330	2.332	2.335	2.337	2.339	2.341	2.343	0	0	1	1	1	1	2	2	2

SQUARE ROOTS OF NUMBERS 1 - 10

	0	1	2	3	4	5	6	7	8	9
5.5	2.345	2.347	2.349	2.352	2.354	2.356	2.358	2.360	2.362	2.364
.6	2.366	2.369	2.371	2.373	2.375	2.377	2.379	2.381	2.383	2.385
.7	2.387	2.390	2.392	2.394	2.396	2.398	2.400	2.402	2.404	2.406
.8	2.408	2.410	2.412	2.415	2.417	2.419	2.421	2.423	2.425	2.427
.9	2.429	2.431	2.433	2.435	2.437	2.439	2.441	2.443	2.445	2.447
6.0	2.449	2.452	2.454	2.456	2.458	2.460	2.462	2.464	2.466	2.468
.1	2.470	2.472	2.474	2.476	2.478	2.480	2.482	2.484	2.486	2.488
.2	2.490	2.492	2.494	2.496	2.498	2.500	2.502	2.504	2.506	2.508
.3	2.510	2.512	2.514	2.516	2.518	2.520	2.522	2.524	2.526	2.528
.4	2.530	2.532	2.534	2.536	2.538	2.540	2.542	2.544	2.546	2.548
6.5	2.550	2.553	2.553	2.555	2.557	2.559	2.561	2.563	2.565	2.567
.6	2.569	2.571	2.573	2.575	2.577	2.579	2.581	2.583	2.585	2.587
.7	2.588	2.590	2.592	2.594	2.596	2.598	2.600	2.602	2.604	2.606
.8	2.608	2.610	2.612	2.613	2.615	2.617	2.619	2.621	2.623	2.625
.9	2.627	2.629	2.631	2.632	2.634	2.636	2.638	2.640	2.642	2.644
7.0	2.646	2.648	2.650	2.651	2.653	2.655	2.657	2.659	2.661	2.663
.1	2.665	2.668	2.668	2.670	2.672	2.674	2.676	2.678	2.680	2.681
.2	2.683	2.685	2.687	2.689	2.691	2.693	2.964	2.696	2.698	2.700
.3	2.702	2.704	2.706	2.707	2.709	2.711	2.713	2.715	2.717	2.718
.4	2.720	2.722	2.724	2.726	2.728	2.729	2.731	2.733	2.735	2.737
7.5	2.739	2.740	2.742	2.744	2.746	2.748	2.750	2.751	2.753	2.755
.6	2.757	2.759	2.760	2.762	2.764	2.766	2.768	2.769	2.771	2.773
.7	2.775	2.777	2.778	2.780	2.782	2.784	2.786	2.787	2.789	2.791
.8	2.793	2.795	2.796	2.798	2.800	2.802	2.804	2.805	2.807	2.809
.9	2.811	2.813	2,814	2.816	2.818	2.820	2.821	2.823	2.825	2.827
8.0	2.828	2.830	2.832	2.834	2.835	2.837	2.839	2.841	2.843	2.844
.1	2.846	2.848	2.850	2.851	2.853	2.855	2.857	2.858	2.860	2.862
.2	2.864	2.865	2.867	2.869	2.871	2.872	8.874	2.876	2.877	2.879
.3	2.881	2.883	2.884	2.886	2.888	2.890	2.891	2.893	2.895	2.897
.4	2.898	2.900	2.902	2.903	2.905	2.907	2.909	2.910	2.912	2.914
8.5	2.915	2.917	2.919	2.921	2.922	2.924	2.926	2.927	2.929	2.931
.6	2.933	2.934	2.936	2.938	2.939	2.941	2.943	2.944	2.946	2.948
.7	2.950	2.951	2.953	2.955	2.956	2.958	2.960	2.961	2.963	2.965
.8	2.966	2.968	2.970	2.972	2.973	2.975	2.977	2.978	2.980	2.982
.9	2.983	2.985	2.987	2.988	2.990	2.992	2.993	2.995	2.997	2.998
9.0	3.000	3.002	3.003	3.005	3.007	3.008	3.010	3.012	3.013	3.015
.1	3.017	3.018	3.020	3.022	3.023	3.025	3.027	3.028	3.030	3.032
.2	3.033	3.035	3.036	3.038	3.040	3.041	3.043	3.045	3.046	3.048
.3	3.050	3.051	3.053	3.055	3.056	3.058	3.059	3.061	3.063	3.064
.4	3.066	3.068	3.069	3.071	3.072	3.074	3.076	3.077	3.079	3.081
9.5	3.082	3.084	3.085	3.087	3.089	3.090	3.092	3.094	3.095	3.097
.6	3.098	3.100	3.102	3.103	3.105	3.106	3.108	3.110	3.111	3.113
.7	3.115	3.116	3.118	3.119	3.121	3.122	3.124	3.126	3.127	3.129
.8	3.130	3.132	3.134	3.135	3.137	3.138	3.140	3.142	3.143	3.145
9.9	3.146	3.148	3.150	3.151	3.153	3.154	3.156	3.158	3.159	3.161

SQUARE ROOTS OF NUMBERS 10 - 100

	0	1	2	3	4	5	6	7	8	9	Mean Differences								
											1	2	3	4	5	6	7	8	9
10	3.162	3.178	3.194	3.209	3.225	3.240	3.256	3.271	3.286	3.302	2	3	5	6	8	9	11	12	14
11	3.317	3.332	3.347	3.362	3.376	3.391	3.406	3.421	3.435	3.450	1	3	4	6	7	9	10	12	13
12	3.464	3.479	3.493	3.507	3.521	3.536	3.550	3.564	3.578	3.592	1	3	4	6	7	8	10	11	13
13	3.606	3.619	3.633	3.647	3.661	3.674	3.688	3.701	3.715	3.728	1	3	4	5	7	8	10	11	12
14	3.742	3.755	3.768	3.782	3.795	3.808	3.821	3.834	3.847	3.860	1	3	4	5	7	8	9	11	12
15	3.873	3.886	3.899	3.912	3.924	3.937	3.950	3.962	3.975	3.987	1	3	4	5	6	8	9	10	11
16	4.000	4.012	4.025	4.037	4.050	4.062	4.074	4.087	4.099	4.111	1	2	4	5	6	7	9	10	11
17	4.123	4.135	4.147	4.159	4.171	4.183	4.195	4.207	4.219	4.231	1	2	4	5	6	7	8	10	11
18	4.243	4.254	4.266	4.278	4.290	4.301	4.313	4.324	4.336	4.347	1	2	3	5	6	7	8	9	10
19	4.359	4.370	4.382	4.393	4.405	4.416	4.427	4.438	4.450	4.461	1	2	3	5	6	7	8	9	10
20	4.472	4.483	4.494	4.506	4.517	4.528	4.539	4.550	4.561	4.572	1	2	3	4	5	7	8	9	10
21	4.583	4.593	4.604	4.615	4.626	4.637	4.648	4.658	4.669	4.680	1	2	3	4	5	6	8	9	10
22	4.690	4.701	4.712	4.722	4.733	4.743	4.754	4.764	4.775	4.785	1	2	3	4	5	6	7	8	9
23	4.796	4.806	4.817	4.827	4.837	4.848	4.858	4.868	4.879	4.889	1	2	3	4	5	6	7	8	9
24	4.899	4.909	4.919	4.930	4.940	4.950	4.960	4.970	4.980	4.990	1	2	3	4	5	6	7	8	9
25	5.000	5.010	5.020	5.030	5.040	5.050	5.060	5.070	5.079	5.089	1	2	3	4	5	6	7	8	9
26	5.099	5.109	5.119	5.128	5.138	5.148	5.158	5.167	5.177	5.187	1	2	3	4	5	6	7	8	9
27	5.196	5.206	5.215	5.225	5.235	5.244	5.254	5.263	5.273	5.282	1	2	3	4	5	6	7	8	9
28	5.292	5.301	5.310	5.320	5.329	5.339	5.348	5.357	5.367	5.376	1	2	3	4	5	6	7	7	8
29	5.385	5.394	5.404	5.413	5.422	5.431	5.441	5.450	5.459	5.468	1	2	3	4	5	5	6	7	8
30	5.477	5.486	5.495	5.505	5.514	5.523	5.532	5.541	5.550	5.559	1	2	3	4	4	5	6	7	8
31	5.568	5.577	5.586	5.595	5.604	5.612	5.621	5.630	5.639	5.648	1	2	3	3	4	5	6	7	8
32	5.657	5.666	5.675	5.683	5.692	5.701	5.710	5.718	5.727	5.736	1	2	3	3	4	5	6	7	8
33	5.745	5.753	5.762	5.771	5.779	5.788	5.797	5.805	5.814	5.822	1	2	3	3	4	5	6	7	8
34	5.831	5.840	5.848	5.857	5.865	5.874	5.882	5.891	5.899	5.908	1	2	3	3	4	5	6	7	8
35	5.916	5.925	5.933	5.941	5.950	5.958	5.967	5.975	5.983	5.992	1	2	2	3	4	5	6	7	8
36	6.000	6.008	6.017	6.025	6.033	6.042	6.050	6.058	6.066	6.075	1	2	2	3	4	5	6	7	7
37	6.083	6.091	6.099	6.107	6.116	6.124	6.132	6.140	6.148	6.156	1	2	2	3	4	5	6	7	7
38	6.164	6.173	6.181	6.189	6.197	6.205	6.213	6.221	6.229	6.237	1	2	2	3	4	5	6	6	7
39	6.245	6.253	6.261	6.269	6.277	6.285	6.293	6.301	6.309	6.317	1	2	2	3	4	5	6	6	7
40	6.325	6.332	6.340	6.348	6.356	6.364	6.372	6.380	6.38	6.395	1	2	2	3	4	5	6	6	7
41	6.403	6.411	6.419	6.427	6.434	6.442	6.450	6.458	6.465	6.473	1	2	2	3	4	5	5	6	7
42	6.481	6.488	6.496	6.504	6.512	6.519	6.527	6.535	6.542	6.550	1	2	2	3	4	5	5	6	7
43	6.557	6.565	6.573	6.580	6.588	6.595	6.603	6.611	6.618	6.626	1	2	2	3	4	5	5	6	7
44	6.633	6.641	6.648	6.656	6.663	6.671	6.678	6.686	6.693	6.701	1	2	2	3	4	4	5	6	7
45	6.708	6.716	6.723	6.731	6.738	6.745	6.753	6.760	6.768	6.775	1	1	2	3	4	4	5	6	7
46	6.782	6.790	6.797	6.804	6.812	6.819	6.826	6.834	6.841	6.848	1	1	2	3	4	4	5	6	7
47	6.856	6.863	6.870	6.877	6.885	6.892	6.899	6.907	6.914	6.921	1	1	2	3	4	4	5	6	7
48	6.928	6.935	6.943	6.950	6.957	6.964	6.971	6.979	6.986	6.993	1	1	2	3	4	4	5	6	6
49	7.000	7.007	7.014	7.021	7.029	7.036	7.043	7.050	7.057	7.064	1	1	2	3	4	4	5	6	6
50	7.071	7.078	7.085	7.092	7.099	7.106	7.113	7.120	7.127	7.134	1	1	2	3	4	4	5	6	6
51	7.141	7.148	7.155	7.162	7.169	7.176	7.183	7.190	7.197	7.204	1	1	2	3	4	4	5	6	6
52	7.211	7.218	7.225	7.232	7.239	7.246	7.253	7.259	7.266	7.273	1	1	2	3	3	4	5	6	6
53	7.280	7.287	7.294	7.301	7.308	7.314	7.321	7.328	7.335	7.342	1	1	2	3	3	4	5	5	6
54	7.348	7.355	7.362	7.369	7.376	7.382	7.389	7.396	7.403	7.409	1	1	2	3	3	4	5	5	6

SQUARE ROOTS OF NUMBERS 10 - 100

	0	1	2	3	4	5	6	7	8	9	Mean Differences								
											1	2	3	4	5	6	7	8	9
55	7.416	7.423	7.430	7.436	7.443	7.450	7.457	7.463	7.470	7.477	1	1	2	3	3	4	5	5	6
56	7.483	7.490	7.497	7.503	7.510	7.517	7.523	7.530	7.537	7.543	1	1	2	3	3	4	5	5	6
57	7.550	7.556	7.563	7.570	7.576	7.583	7.5xx	7.596	7.603	7.609	1	1	2	3	3	4	5	5	6
58	7.616	7.622	7.629	7.635	7.642	7.649	7.655	7.662	7.668	7.675	1	1	2	3	3	4	5	5	6
59	7.681	7.688	7.694	7.701	7.707	7.714	7.720	7.727	7.733	7.740	1	1	2	3	3	4	5	5	6
60	7.746	7.752	7.759	7.765	7.772	7.778	7.785	7.791	7.797	7.804	1	1	2	3	3	4	4	5	6
61	7.810	7.817	7.823	7.829	7.836	7.842	7.849	7.855	7.861	7.868	1	1	2	3	3	4	4	5	6
62	7.874	7.880	7.887	7.893	7.899	7.906	7.912	7.918	7.925	7.931	1	1	2	3	3	4	4	5	6
63	7.937	7.944	7.950	7.956	7.962	7.969	7.975	7.981	7.987	7.994	1	1	2	3	3	4	4	5	6
64	8.000	8.006	8.012	8.019	8.025	8.031	8.037	8.044	8.050	8.056	1	1	2	2	3	4	4	5	6
65	8.062	8.068	8.075	8.081	8.087	8.093	8.099	8.106	8.112	8.118	1	1	2	2	3	4	4	5	5
66	8.124	8.130	8.136	8.142	8.149	8.155	8.161	8.167	8.173	8.179	1	1	2	2	3	4	4	5	5
67	8.185	8.191	8.198	8.204	8.210	8.216	8.222	8.228	8.234	8.240	1	1	2	2	3	4	4	5	5
68	8.246	8.252	8.258	8.264	8.270	8.276	8.283	8.289	8.295	8.301	1	1	2	2	3	4	4	5	5
69	8.307	8.313	8.319	8.325	8.331	8.337	8.343	8.349	8.355	8.361	1	1	2	2	3	4	4	5	5
70	8.367	8.373	8.379	8.385	8.390	8.396	8.402	8.408	8.414	8.420	1	1	2	2	3	4	4	5	5
71	8.426	8.432	8.438	8.444	8.450	8.456	8.462	8.468	8.473	8.479	1	1	2	2	3	3	4	5	5
72	8.485	8.491	8.497	8.503	8.509	8.515	8.521	8.526	8.532	8.538	1	1	2	2	3	3	4	5	5
73	8.544	8.550	8.556	8.562	8.567	8.573	8.579	8.585	8.591	8.597	1	1	2	2	3	3	4	5	5
74	8.602	8.608	8.614	8.620	8.626	8.631	8.637	8.643	8.649	8.654	1	1	2	2	3	3	4	5	5
75	8.660	8.666	8.672	8.678	8.683	8.689	8.695	8.701	8.706	8.712	1	1	2	2	3	3	4	5	5
76	8.718	8.724	8.729	8.735	8.741	8.746	8.752	8.758	8.764	8.769	1	1	2	2	3	3	4	5	5
77	8.775	8.781	8.786	8.792	8.798	8.803	8.809	8.815	8.820	8.826	1	1	2	2	3	3	4	4	5
78	8.832	8.837	8.843	8.849	8.854	8.860	8.866	8.871	8.877	8.883	1	1	2	2	3	3	4	4	5
79	8.888	8.894	8.899	8.905	8.911	8.916	8.922	8.927	8.933	8.939	1	1	2	2	3	3	4	4	5
80	8.944	8.950	8.955	8.961	8.967	8.972	8.978	8.983	8.989	8.994	1	1	2	2	3	3	4	4	5
81	9.000	9.006	9.011	9.017	9.022	9.028	9.033	9.039	9.044	9.050	1	1	2	2	3	3	4	4	5
82	9.055	9.061	9.066	9.072	9.077	9.083	9.088	9.094	9.099	9.105	1	1	2	2	3	3	4	4	5
83	9.110	9.116	9.121	9.127	9.132	9.138	9.143	9.149	9.154	9.160	1	1	2	2	3	3	4	4	5
84	9.165	9.171	9.176	9.182	9.187	9.192	9.198	9.203	9.209	9.214	1	1	2	2	3	3	4	4	5
85	9.220	9.225	9.230	9.236	9.241	9.247	9.252	9.257	9.263	9.268	1	1	2	2	3	3	4	4	5
86	9.274	9.279	9.284	9.290	9.295	9.301	9.306	9.311	9.317	9.322	1	1	2	2	3	3	4	4	5
87	9.327	9.333	9.338	9.343	9.349	9.354	9.359	9.365	9.370	9.375	1	1	2	2	3	3	4	4	5
88	9.381	9.386	9.391	9.397	9.402	9.407	9.413	9.418	9.423	9.429	1	1	2	2	3	3	4	4	5
89	9.434	9.439	9.445	9.450	9.455	9.460	9.466	9.471	9.476	9.482	1	1	2	2	3	3	4	4	5
90	9.487	9.492	9.497	9.503	9.508	9.513	9.518	9.524	9.529	9.534	1	1	2	2	3	3	4	4	5
91	9.539	9.545	9.550	9.555	9.560	9.566	9.571	9.576	9.581	9.586	1	1	2	2	3	3	4	4	5
92	9.592	9.597	9.602	9.607	9.612	9.618	9.623	9.628	9.633	9.638	1	1	2	2	3	3	4	4	5
93	9.644	9.649	9.654	9.659	9.664	9.670	9.675	9.680	9.685	9.690	1	1	2	2	3	3	4	4	5
94	9.695	9.701	9.706	9.711	9.716	9.721	9.726	9.731	9.737	9.742	1	1	2	2	3	3	4	4	5
95	9.747	9.752	9.757	9.762	9.767	9.772	9.778	9.783	9.788	9.793	1	1	2	2	3	3	4	4	5
96	9.798	9.803	9.808	9.813	9.818	9.823	9.829	9.834	9.839	9.844	1	1	2	2	3	3	4	4	5
97	9.849	9.854	9.859	9.864	9.869	9,874	9,879	9,884	9.889	9.894	1	1	2	2	3	3	4	4	5
98	9.899	9.905	9.910	9.915	9.920	9.925	9.930	9.935	9.940	9.945	0	1	1	2	2	3	3	4	4
99	9.950	9.955	9.960	9.965	9.970	9.975	9.980	9.985	9.990	9.995	0	1	1	2	2	3	3	4	4

CUBE ROOTS OF NUMBERS 1 - 10

	0	1	2	3	4	5	6	7	8	9
1.0	1.000	1.003	1.007	1.010	1.013	1.016	1.020	1.023	1.026	1.029
.1	1.032	1.035	1.038	1.042	1.045	1.048	1.051	1.054	1.057	1.060
.2	1.063	1.066	1.069	1.071	1.074	1.077	1.080	1.083	1.086	1.089
.3	1.091	1.094	1.097	1.100	1.102	1.105	1.108	1.111	1.113	1.116
.4	1.119	1.121	1.124	1.127	1.129	1.132	1.134	1.137	1.140	1.142
1.5	1.145	1.147	1.150	1.152	1.155	1.157	1.160	1.162	1.165	1.167
.6	1.170	1.172	1.174	1.177	1.179	1.182	1.184	1.186	1.189	1.191
.7	1.193	1.196	1.198	1.200	1.203	1.205	1.207	1.210	1.212	1.214
.8	1.216	1.219	1.221	1.223	1.225	1.228	1.230	1.232	1.234	1.236
.9	1.239	1.241	1.243	1.245	1.247	1.249	1.251	1.254	1.256	1.258
2.0	1.260	1.262	1.264	1.266	1.268	1.270	1.272	1.274	1.277	1.279
.1	1.281	1.283	1.285	1.287	1.289	1.291	1.293	1.295	1.297	1.299
.2	1.301	1.303	1.305	1.306	1.308	1.310	1.312	1.314	1.316	1.318
.3	1.320	1.322	1.324	1.326	1.328	1.330	1.331	1.333	1.335	1.337
.4	1.339	1.341	1.343	1.344	1.346	1.348	1.350	1.352	1.354	1.355
2.5	1.357	1.359	1.361	1.363	1.364	1.366	1.368	1.370	1.372	1.373
.6	1.375	1.377	1.379	1.380	1.382	1.384	1.386	1.387	1.389	1.391
.7	1.392	1.394	1.396	1.398	1.399	1.401	1.403	1.404	1.406	1.408
.8	1.409	1.411	1.413	1.414	1.416	1.418	1.419	1.421	1.423	1.424
.9	1.426	1.428	1.429	1.431	1.433	1.434	1.436	1.437	1.439	1.441
3.0	1.442	1.444	1.445	1.447	1.449	1.450	1.452	1.453	1.455	1.457
.1	1.458	1.460	1.461	1.463	1.464	1.466	1.467	1.469	1.471	1.472
.2	1.474	1.475	1.477	1.478	1.480	1.481	1.483	1.484	1.486	1.487
.3	1.489	1.490	1.492	1.493	1.495	1.496	1.498	1.499	1.501	1.502
.4	1.504	1.505	1.507	1.508	1.510	1.511	1.512	1.514	1.515	1.517
3.5	1.518	1.520	1.521	1.523	1.524	1.525	1.527	1.528	1.530	1.531
.6	1.533	1.534	1.535	1.537	1.538	1.540	1.541	1.542	1.544	1.545
.7	1.547	1.548	1.549	1.551	1.552	1.554	1.555	1.556	1.558	1.559
.8	1.560	1.562	1.563	1.565	1.566	1.567	1.569	1.570	1.571	1.573
.9	1.574	1.575	1.577	1.578	1.579	1.581	1.582	1.583	1.585	1.586
4.0	1.587	1.589	1.590	1.591	1.593	1.594	1.595	1.597	1.598	1.599
.1	1.601	1.602	1.603	1.604	1.606	1.607	1.608	1.610	1.611	1.612
.2	1.613	1.615	1.616	1.617	1.619	1.620	1.621	1.622	1.624	1.625
.3	1.626	1.627	1.629	1.630	1.631	1.632	1.634	1.635	1.636	1.637
.4	1.639	1.640	1.641	1.642	1.644	1.645	1.646	1.647	1.649	1.650
4.5	1.651	1.652	1.653	1.655	1.656	1.657	1.658	1.659	1.661	1.662
.6	1.663	1.664	1.666	1.667	1.668	1.669	1.670	1.671	1.673	1.674
.7	1.675	1.676	1.677	1.679	1.680	1.681	1.682	1.683	1.685	1.686
.8	1.687	1.688	1.689	1.690	1.692	1.693	1.694	1.695	1.696	1.697
.9	1.698	1.700	1.701	1.702	1.703	1.704	1.705	1.707	1.708	1.709
5.0	1.710	1.711	1.712	1.713	1.715	1.716	1.717	1.718	1.719	1.720
.1	1.721	1.722	1.724	1.725	1.726	1.727	1.728	1.729	1.730	1.731
.2	1.732	1.734	1.735	1.736	1.737	1.738	1.739	1.740	1.741	1.742
.3	1.744	1.745	1.746	1.747	1.748	1.749	1.750	1.751	1.752	1.753
.4	1.754	1.755	1.757	1.758	1.759	1.760	1.761	1.762	1.763	1.764

CUBE ROOTS OF NUMBERS 1 - 10

	0	1	2	3	4	5	6	7	8	9
5.5	1.765	1.766	1.767	1.768	1.769	1.771	1.772	1.773	1.774	1.775
.6	1.776	1.777	1.778	1.779	1.780	1.781	1.782	1.783	1.784	1.785
.7	1.786	1.787	1.788	1.789	1.790	1.792	1.793	1.794	1.795	1.796
.8	1.797	1.798	1.799	1.800	1.801	1.802	1.803	1.804	1.805	1.806
.9	1.807	1.808	1.809	1.810	1.811	1.812	1.813	1.814	1.815	1.816
6.0	1.817	1.818	1.819	1.820	1.821	1.822	1.823	1.824	1.825	1.826
.1	1.827	1.828	1.829	1.830	1.831	1.832	1.833	1.834	1.835	1.836
.2	1.837	1.838	1.839	1.840	1.841	1.842	1.843	1.844	1.845	1.846
.3	1.847	1.848	1.849	1.850	1.851	1.852	1.853	1.854	1.855	1.856
.4	1.857	1.858	1.859	1.860	1.860	1.861	1.862	1.863	1.864	1.865
6.5	1.866	1.867	1.868	1.869	1.870	1.871	1.872	1.873	1.874	1.875
.6	1.876	1.877	1.878	1.879	1.880	1.881	1.881	1.882	1.883	1.884
.7	1.885	1.886	1.887	1.888	1.889	1.890	1.891	1.892	1.893	1.894
.8	1.895	1.895	1.896	1.897	1.898	1.899	1.900	1.901	1.902	1.903
.9	1.904	1.905	1.906	1.907	1.907	1.908	1.909	1.910	1.911	1.912
7.0	1.913	1.914	1.915	1.916	1.917	1.917	1.918	1.919	1.920	1.921
.1	1.922	1.923	1.924	1.925	1.926	1.926	1.927	1.928	1.929	1.930
.2	1.931	1.932	1.933	1.934	1.935	1.935	1.936	1.937	1.938	1.939
.3	1.940	1.941	1.942	1.943	1.943	1.944	1.945	1.946	1.947	1.948
.4	1.949	1.950	1.950	1.951	1.952	1.953	1.954	1.955	1.956	1.957
7.5	1.957	1.958	1.959	1.960	1.961	1.962	1.963	1.964	1.964	1.965
.6	1.966	1.967	1.968	1.969	1.970	1.970	1.971	1.972	1.973	1.974
.7	1.975	1.976	1.976	1.977	1.978	1.979	1.980	1.981	1.981	1.982
.8	1.983	1.984	1.985	1.986	1.987	1.987	1.988	1.989	1.990	1.991
.9	1.992	1.992	1.993	1.994	1.995	1.996	1.997	1.997	1.998	1.999
8.0	2.000	2.001	2.002	2.002	2.003	2.004	2.005	2.006	2.007	2.007
.1	2.008	2.009	2.010	2.011	2.012	2.012	2.013	2.014	2.015	2.016
.2	2.017	2.017	2.018	2.019	2.020	2.021	2.021	2.022	2.023	2.024
.3	2.025	2.026	2.026	2.027	2.028	2.029	2.030	2.030	2.031	2.032
.4	2.033	2.034	2.034	2.035	2.036	2.037	2.038	2.038	2.039	2.040
8.5	2.041	2.042	2.042	2.043	2.044	2.045	2.046	2.046	2.047	2.048
.6	2.049	2.050	2.050	2.051	2.052	2.053	2.054	2.054	2.055	2.056
.7	2.057	2.057	2.058	2.059	2.060	2.061	2.061	2.062	2.063	2.064
.8	2.065	2.065	2.066	2.067	2.068	2.068	2.069	2.070	2.071	2.072
.9	2.072	2.073	2.074	2.075	2.075	2.076	2.077	2.078	2.079	2.079
9.0	2.080	2.081	2.082	2.082	2.083	2.084	2.085	2.085	2.086	2.087
.1	2.088	2.089	2.089	2.090	2.091	2.092	2.092	2.093	2.094	2.095
.2	2.095	2.096	2.097	2.098	2.098	2.099	2.100	2.101	2.101	2.102
.3	2.103	2.104	2.104	2.105	2.106	2.107	2.107	2.108	2.109	2.110
.4	2.110	2.111	2.112	2.113	2.113	2.114	2.115	2.116	2.116	2.117
9.5	2.118	2.119	2.119	2.120	2.121	2.122	2.122	2.123	2.124	2.125
.6	2.125	2.126	2.127	2.128	2.128	2.129	2.130	2.130	2.131	2.132
.7	2.133	2.133	2.134	2.135	2.136	2.136	2.137	2.138	2.139	2.139
.8	2.140	2.141	2.141	2.142	2.143	2.144	2.144	2.145	2.146	2.147
.9	2.147	2.148	2.149	2.149	2.150	2.151	2.152	2.152	2.153	2.154

CUBE ROOTS OF NUMBERS 10 - 100

	0	.1	.2	.3	.4	.5	.6	.7	.8	.9	Mean Differences								
											1	2	3	4	5	6	7	8	9
10	2.154	2.162	2.169	2.176	2.183	2.190	2.197	2.204	2.210	2.217	1	1	2	3	4	4	5	6	6
11	2.224	2.231	2.237	2.244	2.251	2.257	2.264	2.270	2.277	2.283	1	1	2	3	3	4	5	5	6
12	2.289	2.296	2.302	2.308	2.315	2.321	2.327	2.333	2.339	2.345	1	1	2	2	3	4	4	5	5
13	2.351	2.357	2.363	2.369	2.375	2.381	2.387	2.393	2.399	2.404	1	1	2	2	3	4	4	5	5
14	2.410	2.416	2.422	2.427	2.433	2.438	2.444	2.450	2.455	2.461	1	1	2	2	3	3	4	4	5
15	2.466	2.472	2.477	2.483	2.488	2.493	2.499	2.504	2.509	2.515	1	1	2	2	3	3	4	4	5
16	2.520	2.525	2.530	2.535	2.541	2.546	2.551	2.556	2.561	2.566	1	1	2	2	3	3	4	4	5
17	2.571	2.576	2.581	2.586	2.591	2.596	2.601	2.606	2.611	2.616	1	1	2	2	3	3	4	4	4
18	2.621	2.626	2.630	2.635	2.640	2.645	2.650	2.654	2.659	2.664	1	1	1	2	2	3	3	4	4
19	2.668	2.673	2.678	2.682	2.687	2.692	2.696	2.701	2.705	2.710	1	1	1	2	2	3	3	4	4
20	2.714	2.719	2.723	2.728	2.732	2.737	2.741	2.746	2.750	2.755	0	1	1	2	2	3	3	4	4
21	2.759	2.763	2.768	2.772	2.776	2.781	2.785	2.789	2.794	2.798	0	1	1	2	2	3	3	3	4
22	2.802	2.806	2.811	2.815	2.819	2.823	2.827	2.831	2.836	2.840	0	1	1	2	2	2	3	3	4
23	2.844	2.848	2.852	2.856	2.860	2.864	2.868	2.872	2.876	2.880	0	1	1	2	2	2	3	3	4
24	2.884	2.888	2.892	2.896	2.900	2.904	2.908	2.912	2.916	2.920	0	1	1	2	2	2	3	3	3
25	2.924	2.928	2.932	2.936	2.940	2.943	2.947	2.951	2.955	2.959	0	1	1	2	2	2	3	3	3
26	2.962	2.966	2.970	2.974	2.978	2.981	2.985	2.989	2.993	2.996	0	1	1	2	2	2	3	3	3
27	3.000	3.004	3.007	3.011	3.015	3.018	3.022	3.026	3.029	3.033	0	1	1	2	2	2	3	3	3
28	3.037	3.040	3.044	3.047	3.051	3.055	3.058	3.062	3.065	3.069	0	1	1	1	2	2	2	3	3
29	3.072	3.076	3.079	3.083	3.086	3.090	3.093	3.097	3.100	3.104	0	1	1	1	2	2	2	3	3
30	3.107	3.111	3.114	3.118	3.121	3.124	3.128	3.131	3.135	3.138	0	1	1	1	2	2	2	3	3
31	3.141	3.145	3.148	3.151	3.155	3.158	3.162	3.165	3.168	3.171	0	1	1	1	2	2	2	3	3
32	3.175	3.178	3.181	3.185	3.188	3.191	3.195	3.198	3.201	3.204	0	1	1	1	2	2	2	3	3
33	3.208	3.211	3.214	3.217	3.220	3.224	3.227	3.230	3.233	3.236	0	1	1	1	2	2	2	3	3
34	3.240	3.243	3.246	3.249	3.252	3.255	3.259	3.262	3.265	3.268	0	1	1	1	2	2	2	2	3
35	3.271	3.274	3.277	3.280	3.283	3.287	3.290	3.293	3.296	3.299	0	1	1	1	2	2	2	2	3
36	3.302	3.305	3.308	3.311	3.314	3.317	3.320	3.323	3.326	3.329	0	1	1	1	2	2	2	2	3
37	3.332	3.335	3.338	3.341	3.344	3.347	3.350	3.353	3.356	3.359	0	1	1	1	2	2	2	2	3
38	3.362	3.365	3.368	3.371	3.374	3.377	3.380	3.382	3.385	3.388	0	1	1	1	2	2	2	2	3
39	3.391	3.394	3.397	3.400	3.403	3.406	3.409	3.411	3.414	3.417	0	1	1	1	1	2	2	2	3
40	3.420	3.423	3.426	3.428	3.431	3.434	3.437	3.440	3.443	3.445	0	1	1	1	1	2	2	2	2
41	3.448	3.451	3.454	3.457	3.459	3.462	3.465	3.468	3.471	3.473	0	1	1	1	1	2	2	2	2
42	3.476	3.479	3.482	3.484	3.487	3.490	3.493	3.495	3.498	3.501	0	1	1	1	1	2	2	2	2
43	3.503	3.506	3.509	3.512	3.514	3.517	3.520	3.522	3.525	3.528	0	1	1	1	1	2	2	2	2
44	3.530	3.533	3.536	3.538	3.541	3.544	3.546	3.549	3.552	3.554	0	1	1	1	1	2	2	2	2
45	3.557	3.560	3.562	3.565	3.567	3.570	3.573	3.575	3.578	3.580	0	0	1	1	1	2	2	2	2
46	3.583	3.586	3.588	3.591	3.593	3.596	3.599	3.601	3.604	3.606	0	0	1	1	1	2	2	2	2
47	3.609	3.611	3.614	3.616	3.619	3.622	3.624	3.627	3.629	3.632	0	0	1	1	1	1	2	2	2
48	3.634	3.637	3.639	3.642	3.644	3.647	3.649	3.652	3.654	3.657	0	0	1	1	1	1	2	2	2
49	3.659	3.662	3.664	3.667	3.669	3.672	3.674	3.677	3.679	3.682	0	0	1	1	1	1	2	2	2
50	3.684	3.686	3.689	3.691	3.694	3.696	3.699	3.701	3.704	3.706	0	0	1	1	1	1	2	2	2
51	3.708	3.711	3.713	3.716	3.718	3.721	3.723	3.725	3.278	3.730	0	0	1	1	1	1	2	2	2
52	3.733	3.735	3.737	3.740	3.742	3.744	3.747	3.749	3.752	3.754	0	0	1	1	1	1	2	2	2
53	3.756	3.759	3.761	3.763	3.766	3.768	3.770	3.773	3.775	3.777	0	0	1	1	1	1	2	2	2
54	3.780	3.782	3.784	3.787	3.789	3.791	3.794	3.796	3.798	3.801	0	0	1	1	1	1	2	2	2

CUBE ROOTS OF NUMBERS 10 - 100

	0	.1	.2	.3	.4	.5	.6	.7	.8	.9
55	3.803	3.805	3.808	3.810	3.812	3.814	3.817	3.819	3.821	3.824
56	3.826	3.828	3.830	3.833	3.835	3.837	3.839	3.842	3.844	3.846
57	3.849	3.851	3.853	3.855	3.857	3.860	3.862	3.864	3.866	3.869
58	3.871	3.873	3.875	3.878	3.880	3.882	3.884	3.886	3.889	3.891
59	3.893	3.895	3.897	3.900	3.902	3.904	3.906	3.908	3.911	3.913
60	3.915	3.917	3.919	3.921	3.924	3.926	3.928	3.930	3.932	3.934
61	3.936	3.939	3.941	3.943	3.945	3.947	3.949	3.951	3.954	3.956
62	3.958	3.960	3.962	3.964	3.966	3.969	3.971	3.973	3.975	3.977
63	3.979	3.981	3.983	3.985	3.987	3.990	3.992	3.994	3.996	3.998
64	4.000	4.002	4.004	4.006	4.008	4.010	4.012	4.015	4.017	4.019
65	4.021	4.023	4.025	4.027	4.029	4.031	4.033	4.035	4.037	4.039
66	4.041	4.043	4.045	4.047	4.049	4.051	4.053	4.055	4.058	4.060
67	4.062	4.064	4.066	4.068	4.070	4.072	4.074	4.076	4.078	4.080
68	4.082	4.084	4.086	4.088	4.090	4.092	4.094	4.096	4.098	4.100
69	4.102	4.104	4.106	4.108	4.109	4.111	4.113	4.115	4.117	4.119
70	4.121	4.123	4.125	4.127	4.129	4.131	4.133	4.135	4.137	4.139
71	4.141	4.143	4.145	4.147	4.149	4.151	4.152	4.154	4.156	4.158
72	4.160	4.162	4.164	4.166	4.168	4.170	4.172	4.174	4.176	4.177
73	4.179	4.181	4.183	4.185	4.187	4.189	4.191	4.193	4.195	4.196
74	4.198	4.200	4.202	4.204	4.206	4.208	4.210	4.212	4.213	4.215
75	4.217	4.219	4.221	4.223	4.225	4.227	4.228	4.230	4.232	4.234
76	4.236	4.238	4.240	4.241	4.243	4.245	4.247	4.249	4.251	4.252
77	4.254	4.256	4.258	4.260	4.262	4.264	4.265	4.267	4.269	4.271
78	4.273	4.274	4.276	4.278	4.280	4.282	4.284	4.285	4.287	4.289
79	4.291	4.293	4.294	4.296	4.298	4.300	4.302	4.303	4.305	4.307
80	4.309	4.311	4.312	4.314	4.316	4.318	4.320	4.321	4.323	4.325
81	4.327	4.329	4.330	4.332	4.334	4.336	4.337	4.339	4.341	4.343
82	4.344	4.346	4.348	4.350	4.352	4.353	4.355	4.357	4.359	4.360
83	4.362	4.364	4.366	4.367	4.369	4.371	4.373	4.374	4.376	4.378
84	4.380	4.381	4.383	4.385	4.386	4.388	4.390	4.392	4.393	4.395
85	4.397	4.399	4.400	4.402	4.404	4.405	4.407	4.409	4.411	4.412
86	4.414	4.416	4.417	4.419	4.421	4.423	4.424	4.426	4.428	4.429
87	4.431	4.433	4.434	4.436	4.438	4.440	4.441	4.443	4.445	4.446
88	4.448	4.450	4.451	4.453	4.455	4.456	4.458	4.460	4.461	4.463
89	4.465	4.466	4.468	4.470	4.471	4.473	4.475	4.476	4.478	4.480
90	4.481	4.483	4.485	4.486	4.488	4.490	4.491	4.493	4.495	4.496
91	4.498	4.500	4.501	4.503	4.505	4.506	4.508	4.509	4.511	4.513
92	4.514	4.516	4.518	4.519	4.521	4.523	4.524	4.526	4.527	4.529
93	4.531	4.532	4.534	4.536	4.537	4.539	4.540	4.542	4.544	4.545
94	4.547	4.548	4.550	4.552	4.553	4.555	4.556	4.558	4.560	4.561
95	4.563	4.565	4.566	4.568	4.569	4.571	4.572	4.574	4.576	4.577
96	4.579	4.580	4.582	4.584	4.585	4.587	4.588	4.590	4.592	4.593
97	4.595	4.596	4.598	4.599	4.601	4.603	4.604	4.606	4.607	4.609
98	4.610	4.612	4.614	4.615	4.617	4.618	4.620	4.621	4.623	4.625
99	4.626	4.628	4.629	4.631	4.632	4.634	4.635	4.638	4.638	4.640

CUBE ROOTS OF NUMBERS 100 - 1000

	0	1	2	3	4	5	6	7	8	9	.1	.2	.3	.4	.5	.6	.7	.8	.9
10	4.642	4.657	4.672	4.688	4.703	4.718	4.733	4.747	4.762	4.777	2	3	5	6	8	9	11	12	14
11	4.791	4.806	4.820	4.835	4.849	4.863	4.877	4.891	4.905	4.919	1	3	4	6	7	9	10	11	13
12	4.932	4.946	4.960	4.973	4.987	5.000	5.013	5.027	5.040	5.053	1	3	4	5	7	8	9	11	12
13	5.066	5.079	5.092	5.104	5.117	5.130	5.143	5.155	5.168	5.180	1	3	4	5	6	8	9	10	11
14	5.192	5.205	5.217	5.229	5.241	5.254	5.266	5.278	5.290	5.301	1	2	4	5	6	7	9	10	11
15	5.313	5.325	5.337	5.348	5.360	5.372	5.383	5.395	5.406	5.418	1	2	4	5	6	7	8	9	10
16	5.429	5.440	5.451	5.463	5.474	5.485	5.496	5.507	5.518	5.529	1	2	3	4	6	7	8	9	10
17	5.540	5.550	5.561	5.572	5.583	5.593	5.604	5.615	5.625	5.636	1	2	3	4	5	6	8	9	10
18	5.646	5.657	5.667	5.677	5.688	5.698	5.708	5.718	5.729	5.739	1	2	3	4	5	6	7	8	9
19	5.749	5.759	5.769	5.779	5.789	5.799	5.809	5.819	5.828	5.838	1	2	3	4	5	6	7	8	9
20	5.848	5.858	5.867	5.877	5.887	5.896	5.906	5.915	5.925	5.934	1	2	3	4	5	6	7	8	9
21	5.944	5.953	5.963	5.972	5.981	5.991	6.000	6.009	6.019	6.028	1	2	3	4	5	6	6	7	8
22	6.037	6.046	6.055	6.064	6.073	6.082	6.091	6.100	6.109	6.118	1	2	3	4	5	5	6	7	8
23	6.127	6.136	6.145	6.153	6.162	6.171	6.180	6.188	6.197	6.206	1	2	3	4	4	5	6	7	8
24	6.214	6.223	6.232	6.240	6.249	6.257	6.266	6.274	6.283	6.291	1	2	3	3	4	5	6	7	8
25	6.300	6.308	6.316	6.325	6.333	6.341	6.350	6.358	6.366	6.374	1	2	2	3	4	5	6	7	7
26	6.383	6.391	6.399	6.407	6.415	6.423	6.431	6.439	6.447	6.455	1	2	2	3	4	5	6	7	7
27	6.463	6.471	6.479	6.487	6.495	6.503	6.511	6.519	6.527	6.534	1	2	2	3	4	5	6	6	7
28	6.542	6.550	6.558	6.565	6.573	6.581	6.589	6.596	6.604	6.611	1	2	2	3	4	5	5	6	7
29	6.619	6.627	6.634	6.642	6.649	6.657	6.664	6.672	6.679	6.687	1	2	2	3	4	4	5	6	7
30	6.694	6.702	6.709	6.717	6.724	6.731	6.739	6.746	6.753	6.761	1	1	2	3	4	4	5	6	7
31	6.768	6.775	6.782	6.790	6.797	6.804	6.811	6.818	6.826	6.833	1	1	2	3	4	4	5	6	7
32	6.840	6.847	6.854	6.861	6.868	6.875	6.882	6.889	6.896	6.903	1	1	2	3	4	4	5	6	6
33	6.910	6.917	6.924	6.931	6.938	6.945	6.952	6.959	6.966	6.973	1	1	2	3	4	4	5	6	6
34	6.980	6.986	6.993	7.000	7.007	7.014	7.020	7.027	7.034	7.041	1	1	2	3	3	4	5	5	6
35	7.047	7.054	7.061	7.067	7.074	7.081	7.087	7.094	7.101	7.107	1	1	2	3	3	4	5	5	6
36	7.114	7.120	7.127	7.133	7.140	7.147	7.153	7.160	7.166	7.173	1	1	2	3	3	4	5	5	6
37	7.179	7.186	7.192	7.198	7.205	7.211	7.218	7.224	7.230	7.237	1	1	2	3	3	4	4	5	6
38	7.243	7.250	7.256	7.262	7.268	7.275	7.281	7.287	7.294	7.300	1	1	2	3	3	4	4	5	6
39	7.306	7.312	7.319	7.325	7.331	7.337	7.343	7.350	7.356	7.362	1	1	2	2	3	4	4	5	6
40	7.368	7.374	7.380	7.386	7.393	7.399	7.405	7.411	7.417	7.423	1	1	2	2	3	4	4	5	5
41	7.429	7.435	7.441	7.447	7.453	7.459	7.465	7.471	7.477	7.483	1	1	2	2	3	4	4	5	5
42	7.489	7.495	7.501	7.507	7.513	7.518	7.524	7.530	7.536	7.542	1	1	2	2	3	4	4	5	5
43	7.548	7.554	7.560	7.565	7.571	7.577	7.583	7.589	7.594	7.600	1	1	2	2	3	3	4	5	5
44	7.606	7.612	7.617	7.623	7.629	7.635	7.640	7.646	7.652	7.657	1	1	2	2	3	3	4	5	5
45	7.663	7.669	7.674	7.680	7.686	7.691	7.697	7.703	7.708	7.714	1	1	2	2	3	3	4	4	5
46	7.719	7.725	7.731	7.736	7.742	7.747	7.753	7.758	7.764	7.769	1	1	2	2	3	3	4	4	5
47	7.775	7.780	7.786	7.791	7.797	7.802	7.808	7.813	7.819	7.824	1	1	2	2	3	3	4	4	5
48	7.830	7.835	7.841	7.846	7.851	7.857	7.862	7.868	7.873	7.878	1	1	2	2	3	3	4	4	5
49	7.884	7.889	7.894	7.900	7.905	7.910	7.916	7.921	7.926	7.932	1	1	2	2	3	3	4	4	5
50	7.937	7.942	7.948	7.953	7.958	7.963	7.969	7.974	7.979	7.984	1	1	2	2	3	3	4	4	5
51	7.990	7.995	8.000	8.005	8.010	8.016	8.021	8.026	8.031	8.036	1	1	2	2	3	3	4	4	5
52	8.041	8.047	8.052	8.057	8.062	8.067	8.072	8.077	8.082	8.088	1	1	2	2	3	3	4	4	5
53	8.093	8.098	8.103	8.108	8.113	8.118	8.123	8.128	8.133	8.138	1	1	2	2	3	3	4	4	5
54	8.143	8.148	8.153	8.158	8.163	8.168	8.173	8.178	8.183	8.188	1	1	2	2	3	3	4	4	5

CUBE ROOTS OF NUMBERS 100 - 1000

	0	1	2	3	4	5	6	7	8	9	Mean Differences								
											.1	.2	.3	.4	.5	.6	.7	.8	.9
55	8.193	8.198	8.203	8.208	8.213	8.218	8.223	8.228	8.233	8.238	1	1	2	2	3	3	3	4	4
56	8.243	8.247	8.252	8.257	8.262	8.267	8.272	8.277	8.282	8.286	0	1	1	2	2	3	3	4	4
57	8.291	8.296	8.301	8.306	8.311	8.316	8.320	8.325	8.330	8.335	0	1	1	2	2	3	3	4	4
58	8.340	8.344	8.349	8.354	8.359	8.363	8.368	8.373	8.378	8.382	0	1	1	2	2	3	3	4	4
59	8.387	8.392	8.397	8.401	8.406	8.411	8.416	8.420	8.425	8.430	0	1	1	2	2	3	3	4	4
60	8.434	8.439	8.444	8.448	8.453	8.458	8.462	8.467	8.472	8.476	0	1	1	2	2	3	3	4	4
61	8.481	8.486	8.490	8.495	8.499	8.504	8.509	8.513	8.518	8.522	0	1	1	2	2	3	3	4	4
62	8.527	8.532	8.536	8.541	8.545	8.550	8.554	8.559	8.564	8.568	0	1	1	2	2	3	3	4	4
63	8.573	8.577	8.582	8.586	8.591	8.595	8.600	8.604	8.609	8.613	0	1	1	2	2	3	3	4	4
64	8.618	8.622	8.627	8.631	8.636	8.460	8.645	8.649	8.653	8.658	0	1	1	2	2	3	3	4	4
65	8.662	8.667	8.671	8.676	8.680	8.685	8.689	8.693	8.698	8.702	0	1	1	2	2	3	3	4	4
66	8.707	8.711	8.715	8.720	8.724	8.729	8.733	8.737	8.742	8.746	0	1	1	2	2	3	3	3	4
67	8.750	8.755	8.759	8.763	8.768	8.772	8.776	8.781	8.785	8.789	0	1	1	2	2	3	3	3	4
68	8.794	8.798	8.802	8.807	8.811	8.815	8.819	8.824	8.828	8.832	0	1	1	2	2	3	3	3	4
69	8.837	8.841	8.845	8.849	8.854	8.858	8.862	8.866	8.871	8.875	0	1	1	2	2	3	3	3	4
70	8.879	8.883	8.887	8.892	8.896	8.900	8.904	8.909	8.913	8.917	0	1	1	2	2	3	3	3	4
71	8.921	8.925	8.929	8.934	8.938	8.942	8.946	8.950	8.955	8.959	0	1	1	2	2	3	3	3	4
72	8.963	8.967	8.971	8.975	8.979	8.984	8.988	8.992	8.996	9.000	0	1	1	2	2	2	3	3	4
73	9.004	9.008	9.012	9.016	9.021	9.025	9.029	9.033	9.037	9.041	0	1	1	2	2	2	3	3	4
74	9.045	9.049	9.053	9.057	9.061	9.065	9.069	9.073	9.078	9.082	0	1	1	2	2	2	3	3	4
75	9.086	9.090	9.094	9.098	9.102	9.106	9.110	9.114	9.118	9.122	0	1	1	2	2	2	3	3	4
76	9.126	9.130	9.134	9.138	9.142	9.146	9.150	9.154	9.158	9.162	0	1	1	2	2	2	3	3	4
77	9.166	9.170	9.174	9.178	9.182	9.185	9.189	9.193	9.197	9.201	0	1	1	2	2	2	3	3	4
78	9.205	9.209	9.213	9.217	9.221	9.225	9.229	9.233	9.237	9.240	0	1	1	2	2	2	3	3	4
79	9.244	9.248	9.252	9.256	9.260	9.264	9.268	9.272	9.275	9.279	0	1	1	2	2	2	3	3	4
80	9.283	9.287	9.291	9.295	9.299	9.302	9.306	9.310	9.314	9.318	0	1	1	2	2	2	3	3	3
81	9.322	9.326	9.329	9.333	9.337	9.341	9.345	9.348	9.352	9.356	0	1	1	2	2	2	3	3	3
82	9.360	9.364	9.368	9.371	9.375	9.379	9.383	9.386	9.390	9.394	0	1	1	2	2	2	3	3	3
83	9.398	9.402	9.405	9.409	9.413	9.417	9.420	9.424	9.428	9.432	0	1	1	1	2	2	3	3	3
84	9.435	9.439	9.443	9.447	9.450	9.454	9.458	9.462	9.465	9.469	0	1	1	1	2	2	3	3	3
85	9.473	9.476	9.480	9.484	9.488	9.491	9.495	9.499	9.502	9.506	0	1	1	1	2	2	3	3	3
86	9.510	9.513	9.517	9.521	9.524	9.528	9.532	9.535	9.539	9.543	0	1	1	1	2	2	3	3	3
87	9.546	9.550	9.554	9.557	9.561	9.565	9.568	9.572	9.576	9.579	0	1	1	1	2	2	3	3	3
88	9.583	9.586	9.590	9.594	9.597	9.601	9.605	9.608	9.612	9.615	0	1	1	1	2	2	3	3	3
89	9.619	9.623	9.626	9.630	9.633	9.637	9.641	9.644	9.648	9.651	0	1	1	1	2	2	3	3	3
90	9.655	9.658	9.662	9.666	9.669	9.673	9.676	9.680	9.683	9.687	0	1	1	1	2	2	3	3	3
91	9.691	9.694	9.698	9.701	9.705	9.708	9.712	9.715	9.719	9.722	0	1	1	1	2	2	2	3	3
92	9.726	9.729	9.733	9.736	9.740	9.743	9.747	9.751	9.754	9.758	0	1	1	1	2	2	2	3	3
93	9.761	9.764	9.768	9.771	9.775	9.778	9.781	9.785	9.789	9.792	0	1	1	1	2	2	2	3	3
94	9.796	9.799	9.803	9.806	9.810	9.813	9.817	9.820	9.824	9.827	0	1	1	1	2	2	2	3	3
95	9.830	9.834	9.837	9.841	9.844	9.848	8.851	9.855	9.858	9.861	0	1	1	1	2	2	2	3	3
96	9.865	9.868	9.872	9.875	9.879	9.882	9.885	9.889	9.892	9.896	0	1	1	1	2	2	2	3	3
97	9.899	9.902	9.906	9.909	9.913	9.916	9.919	9.923	9.926	9.930	0	1	1	1	2	2	2	3	3
98	9.933	9.936	9.940	9.943	9.946	9.950	9.953	9.956	9.960	9.963	0	1	1	1	2	2	2	3	3
99	9.967	9.970	9.973	9.977	9.980	9.983	9.987	9.990	9.993	9.997	0	1	1	1	2	2	2	3	3

II TABLES FOR USE IN CELESTIAL NAVIGATION

TABLE A HOUR ANGLE

Lat.°	0° 15' / 359° 45'	0° 30' / 359° 30'	0° 45' / 359° 15'	1° 00' / 359° 00'	1° 15' / 358° 45'	1° 30' / 358° 30'	1° 45' / 358° 15'	2° 00' / 358° 00'	2° 15' / 357° 45'	2° 30' / 357° 30'	2° 45' / 357° 15'	3° 00' / 357° 00'	3° 15' / 356° 45'	3° 30' / 356° 30'	3° 45' / 356° 15'	Lat.°
0	·00	·00	·00	·00	·00	·00	·00	·00	·00	·00	·00	·00	·00	·00	·00	0
1	4·00	2·00	1·33	1·00	·80	·67	·57	·50	·44	·40	·36	·33	·31	·29	·27	1
2	8·00	4·00	2·67	2·00	1·60	1·33	1·14	1·00	·89	·80	·73	·67	·61	·57	·53	2
3	12·0	6·01	4·00	3·00	2·40	2·00	1·72	1·50	1·33	1·20	1·09	1·00	·92	·86	·80	3
4	16·0	8·01	5·34	4·01	3·21	2·67	2·29	2·00	1·78	1·60	1·46	1·33	1·23	1·14	1·07	4
5	20·1	10·0	6·68	5·01	4·01	3·34	2·86	2·51	2·23	2·00	1·82	1·67	1·54	1·43	1·33	5
6	24·1	12·0	8·03	6·02	4·82	4·01	3·44	3·01	2·68	2·41	2·19	2·01	1·85	1·72	1·60	6
7	28·1	14·1	9·38	7·03	5·63	4·69	4·02	3·52	3·13	2·81	2·56	2·34	2·16	2·01	1·87	7
8	32·2	16·1	10·7	8·05	6·44	5·37	4·60	4·02	3·58	3·22	2·93	2·68	2·48	2·30	2·14	8
9	36·3	18·1	12·1	9·07	7·26	6·05	5·18	4·54	4·03	3·63	3·30	3·02	2·79	2·59	2·42	9
10	40·4	20·2	13·5	10·1	8·08	6·73	5·77	5·05	4·49	4·04	3·67	3·36	3·10	2·88	2·69	10
11	44·5	22·3	14·9	11·1	8·91	7·42	6·36	5·57	4·95	4·45	4·05	3·71	3·42	3·18	2·97	11
12	48·7	24·4	16·2	12·2	9·74	8·12	6·96	6·09	5·41	4·87	4·43	4·06	3·74	3·48	3·24	12
13	52·9	26·5	17·6	13·2	10·6	8·82	7·56	6·61	5·88	5·29	4·81	4·41	4·07	3·78	3·52	13
14	57·1	28·6	19·1	14·3	11·4	9·52	8·16	7·14	6·35	5·71	5·19	4·76	4·39	4·08	3·80	14
15	61·4	30·7	20·5	15·4	12·3	10·2	8·77	7·67	6·82	6·14	5·58	5·11	4·72	4·38	4·09	15
16	65·7	32·9	21·9	16·4	13·1	11·0	9·39	8·21	7·30	6·57	5·97	5·47	5·05	4·69	4·37	16
17	70·1	35·0	23·4	17·5	14·0	11·7	10·0	8·75	7·78	7·00	6·36	5·83	5·38	5·00	4·66	17
18	74·5	37·2	24·8	18·6	14·9	12·4	10·6	9·30	8·27	7·44	6·76	6·20	5·72	5·31	4·96	18
19	78·9	39·5	26·3	19·7	15·8	13·1	11·3	9·86	8·76	7·89	7·17	6·57	6·06	5·63	5·25	19
20	83·4	41·7	27·8	20·9	16·7	13·9	11·9	10·4	9·26	8·34	7·58	6·94	6·41	5·95	5·55	20
21	88·0	44·0	29·3	22·0	17·6	14·7	12·6	11·0	9·77	8·79	7·99	7·32	6·76	6·28	5·86	21
22	92·6	46·3	30·9	23·1	18·5	15·4	13·2	11·6	10·3	9·25	8·41	7·71	7·12	6·61	6·16	22
23	97·3	48·6	32·4	24·3	19·5	16·2	13·9	12·2	10·8	9·72	8·84	8·10	7·48	6·94	6·48	23
24	102	51·0	34·0	25·5	20·4	17·0	14·6	12·7	11·3	10·2	9·27	8·50	7·84	7·28	6·79	24
25	107	53·4	35·6	26·7	21·4	17·8	15·3	13·4	11·9	10·7	9·71	8·90	8·21	7·62	7·11	25
26	112	55·9	37·3	27·9	22·4	18·6	16·0	14·0	12·4	11·2	10·2	9·31	8·59	7·97	7·44	26
27	117	58·4	38·9	29·2	23·4	19·5	16·7	14·6	13·0	11·7	10·6	9·72	8·97	8·33	7·77	27
28	122	60·9	40·6	30·5	24·4	20·3	17·4	15·2	13·5	12·2	11·1	10·1	9·36	8·69	8·11	28
29	127	63·5	42·3	31·8	25·4	21·2	18·1	15·9	14·1	12·7	11·5	10·6	9·76	9·06	8·46	29
30	132	66·2	44·1	33·1	26·5	22·0	18·9	16·5	14·7	13·2	12·0	11·0	10·2	9·44	8·81	30
31	138	68·9	45·9	34·4	27·5	22·9	19·7	17·2	15·3	13·8	12·5	11·5	10·6	9·82	9·17	31
32	143	71·6	47·7	35·8	28·6	23·9	20·5	17·9	15·9	14·3	13·0	11·9	11·0	10·2	9·53	32
33	149	74·4	49·6	37·2	29·8	24·8	21·3	18·6	16·5	14·9	13·5	12·4	11·4	10·6	9·91	33
34	155	77·3	51·5	38·6	30·9	25·8	22·1	19·3	17·2	15·4	14·0	12·9	11·9	11·0	10·3	34
35	160	80·2	53·5	40·1	32·1	26·7	22·9	20·1	17·8	16·0	14·6	13·4	12·3	11·4	10·7	35
36	167	83·3	55·5	41·6	33·3	27·7	23·8	20·8	18·5	16·6	15·1	13·9	12·8	11·9	11·1	36
37	173	86·3	57·6	43·2	34·5	28·8	24·7	21·6	19·2	17·3	15·7	14·4	13·3	12·3	11·5	37
38	179	89·5	59·7	44·8	35·8	29·8	25·6	22·4	19·9	17·9	16·3	14·9	13·8	12·8	11·9	38
39	186	92·8	61·9	46·4	37·1	30·9	26·5	23·2	20·6	18·6	16·9	15·5	14·3	13·2	12·4	39
40	192	96·2	64·1	48·1	38·5	32·0	27·5	24·0	21·4	19·2	17·5	16·0	14·8	13·7	12·8	40
41	199	99·6	66·4	49·8	39·8	33·2	28·5	24·9	22·1	19·9	18·1	16·6	15·3	14·2	13·3	41
42	206	103	68·8	51·6	41·3	34·4	29·5	25·8	22·9	20·6	18·8	17·2	15·9	14·7	13·7	42
43	214	107	71·2	53·4	42·7	35·6	30·5	26·7	23·7	21·4	19·4	17·8	16·4	15·2	14·2	43
44	221	111	73·8	55·3	44·3	36·9	31·6	27·7	24·6	22·1	20·1	18·4	17·0	15·8	14·7	44
45	229	115	76·4	57·3	45·8	38·2	32·7	28·6	25·5	22·9	20·8	19·1	17·6	16·4	15·3	45
46	237	119	79·1	59·3	47·5	39·6	33·9	29·7	26·4	23·7	21·6	19·8	18·2	16·9	15·8	46
47	246	123	31·9	61·4	49·2	41·0	35·1	30·7	27·3	24·6	22·3	20·5	18·9	17·5	16·4	47
48	255	127	84·8	63·6	50·9	42·4	36·4	31·8	28·3	25·4	23·1	21·2	19·6	18·2	16·9	48
49	264	132	87·9	65·9	52·7	43·9	37·7	32·9	29·3	26·4	24·0	22·0	20·3	18·8	17·6	49
50	273	137	91·0	68·3	54·6	45·5	39·0	34·1	30·3	27·3	24·8	22·7	21·0	19·5	18·2	50
51	283	142	94·3	70·8	56·6	47·2	40·4	35·4	31·4	28·3	25·7	23·6	21·8	20·2	18·8	51
52	293	147	97·8	73·3	58·7	48·9	41·9	36·7	32·6	29·3	26·7	24·4	22·5	20·9	19·5	52
53	304	152	101	76·0	60·8	50·7	43·4	38·0	33·8	30·4	27·6	25·3	23·4	21·7	20·3	53
54	315	158	105	78·9	63·1	52·6	45·1	39·4	35·0	31·5	28·7	26·3	24·2	22·5	21·0	54
55	327	164	109	81·8	65·5	54·5	46·7	40·9	36·4	32·7	29·7	27·3	25·2	23·4	21·8	55
56	340	170	113	84·9	67·9	56·6	48·5	42·5	37·7	34·0	30·9	28·3	26·1	24·2	22·6	56
57	353	176	118	88·2	70·6	58·8	50·4	44·1	39·2	35·3	32·1	29·4	27·1	25·2	23·5	57
58	367	183	122	91·7	73·3	61·1	52·4	45·8	40·7	36·7	33·3	30·5	28·2	26·2	24·4	58
59	381	191	127	95·4	76·3	63·6	54·5	47·7	42·4	38·1	34·7	31·8	29·3	27·2	25·4	59
60	397	198	132	99·2	79·4	66·1	56·7	49·6	44·1	39·7	36·1	33·0	30·5	28·3	26·4	60
Lat.	179° 45' / 180° 15'	179° 30' / 180° 30'	179° 15' / 180° 45'	179° 00' / 181° 00'	178° 45' / 181° 15'	178° 30' / 181° 30'	178° 15' / 181° 45'	178° 00' / 182° 00'	177° 45' / 182° 15'	177° 30' / 182° 30'	177° 15' / 182° 45'	177° 00' / 183° 00'	176° 45' / 183° 15'	176° 30' / 183° 30'	176° 15' / 183° 45'	Lat.

A

HOUR ANGLE

TABLE B HOUR ANGLE

B - Always named the **same** as Declination

Dec. °	0° 15' / 359° 45'	0° 30' / 359° 30'	0° 45' / 359° 15'	1° 00' / 359° 00'	1° 15' / 358° 45'	1° 30' / 358° 30'	1° 45' / 358° 15'	2° 00' / 358° 00'	2° 15' / 357° 45'	2° 30' / 357° 30'	2° 45' / 357° 15'	3° 00' / 357° 00'	3° 15' / 356° 45'	3° 30' / 356° 30'	3° 45' / 356° 15'	Dec. °
0	·00	·00	·00	·00	·00	·00	·00	·00	·00	·00	·00	·00	·00	·00	·00	0
1	4·00	2·00	1·33	1·00	·80	·67	·57	·50	·45	·40	·36	·33	·31	·29	·27	1
2	8·00	4·00	2·67	2·00	1·60	1·33	1·14	1·00	·89	·80	·73	·67	·62	·57	·53	2
3	12·0	6·01	4·00	3·00	2·40	2·00	1·72	1·50	1·34	1·20	1·09	1·00	·92	·86	·80	3
4	16·0	8·01	5·34	4·01	3·21	2·67	2·29	2·00	1·78	1·60	1·46	1·34	1·23	1·15	1·07	4
5	20·1	10·0	6·68	5·01	4·01	3·34	2·87	2·51	2·23	2·01	1·82	1·67	1·54	1·43	1·34	5
6	24·1	12·0	8·03	6·02	4·82	4·02	3·44	3·01	2·68	2·41	2·19	2·01	1·85	1·72	1·61	6
7	28·1	14·1	9·38	7·04	5·63	4·69	4·02	3·52	3·13	2·81	2·56	2·35	2·17	2·01	1·88	7
8	32·2	16·1	10·7	8·05	6·44	5·37	4·60	4·03	3·58	3·22	2·93	2·69	2·48	2·30	2·15	8
9	36·3	18·1	12·1	9·08	7·26	6·05	5·19	4·54	4·03	3·63	3·30	3·03	2·79	2·59	2·42	9
10	40·4	20·2	13·5	10·1	8·08	6·74	5·77	5·05	4·49	4·04	3·68	3·37	3·11	2·89	2·70	10
11	44·5	22·3	14·9	11·1	8·91	7·43	6·37	5·57	4·95	4·46	4·05	3·71	3·43	3·18	2·97	11
12	48·7	24·4	16·2	12·2	9·74	8·12	6·96	6·09	5·41	4·87	4·43	4·06	3·75	3·48	3·25	12
13	52·9	26·5	17·6	13·2	10·6	8·82	7·56	6·62	5·88	5·29	4·81	4·41	4·07	3·78	3·53	13
14	57·1	28·6	19·1	14·3	11·4	9·53	8·16	7·14	6·35	5·72	5·20	4·76	4·40	4·08	3·81	14
15	61·4	30·7	20·5	15·4	12·3	10·2	8·77	7·68	6·83	6·14	5·58	5·12	4·73	4·39	4·10	15
16	65·7	32·9	21·9	16·4	13·1	11·0	9·39	8·22	7·30	6·57	5·98	5·48	5·06	4·70	4·38	16
17	70·1	35·0	23·4	17·5	14·0	11·7	10·0	8·76	7·79	7·01	6·37	5·84	5·39	5·01	4·67	17
18	74·5	37·2	24·8	18·6	14·9	12·4	10·6	9·31	8·28	7·45	6·77	6·21	5·73	5·32	4·97	18
19	78·9	39·5	26·3	19·7	15·8	13·2	11·3	9·87	8·77	7·89	7·18	6·58	6·07	5·64	5·26	19
20	83·4	41·7	27·8	20·9	16·7	13·9	11·9	10·4	9·27	8·34	7·59	6·95	6·42	5·96	5·57	20
21	88·0	44·0	29·3	22·0	17·6	14·7	12·6	11·0	9·78	8·80	8·00	7·33	6·77	6·29	5·87	21
22	92·6	46·3	30·9	23·2	18·5	15·4	13·2	11·6	10·3	9·26	8·42	7·72	7·13	6·62	6·18	22
23	97·3	48·6	32·4	24·3	19·5	16·2	13·9	12·2	10·8	9·73	8·85	8·11	7·49	6·95	6·49	23
24	102	51·0	34·0	25·5	20·4	17·0	14·6	12·8	11·3	10·2	9·28	8·51	7·85	7·29	6·81	24
25	107	53·4	35·6	26·7	21·4	17·8	15·3	13·4	11·9	10·7	9·72	8·91	8·23	7·64	7·13	25
26	112	55·9	37·3	27·9	22·4	18·6	16·0	14·0	12·4	11·2	10·2	9·32	8·60	7·99	7·46	26
27	117	58·4	38·9	29·2	23·4	19·5	16·7	14·6	13·0	11·7	10·6	9·74	8·99	8·35	7·79	27
28	122	60·9	40·6	30·5	24·4	20·3	17·4	15·2	13·5	12·2	11·1	10·2	9·38	8·71	8·13	28
29	127	63·5	42·4	31·8	25·4	21·2	18·2	15·9	14·1	12·7	11·6	10·6	9·78	9·08	8·48	29
30	132	66·2	44·1	33·1	26·5	22·1	18·9	16·5	14·7	13·2	12·0	11·0	10·2	9·46	8·83	30
31	138	68·9	45·9	34·4	27·5	23·0	19·7	17·2	15·3	13·8	12·5	11·5	10·6	9·84	9·19	31
32	143	71·6	47·7	35·8	28·6	23·9	20·5	17·9	15·9	14·3	13·0	11·9	11·0	10·2	9·55	32
33	149	74·4	49·6	37·2	29·8	24·8	21·3	18·6	16·5	14·9	13·5	12·4	11·5	10·6	9·93	33
34	155	77·3	51·5	38·6	30·9	25·8	22·1	19·3	17·2	15·5	14·1	12·9	11·9	11·0	10·3	34
35	160	80·2	53·5	40·1	32·1	26·7	22·9	20·1	17·8	16·1	14·6	13·4	12·4	11·5	10·7	35
36	167	83·3	55·5	41·6	33·3	27·8	23·8	20·8	18·5	16·7	15·1	13·9	12·8	11·9	11·1	36
37	173	86·4	57·6	43·2	34·5	28·8	24·7	21·6	19·2	17·3	15·7	14·4	13·3	12·3	11·5	37
38	179	89·5	59·7	44·8	35·8	29·8	25·6	22·4	19·9	17·9	16·3	14·9	13·8	12·8	12·0	38
39	186	92·8	61·9	46·4	37·1	30·9	26·5	23·2	20·6	18·6	16·9	15·5	14·3	13·3	12·4	39
40	192	96·2	64·1	48·1	38·5	32·1	27·5	24·0	21·4	19·2	17·5	16·0	14·8	13·7	12·8	40
41	199	99·6	66·4	49·8	39·9	33·2	28·5	24·9	22·1	19·9	18·1	16·6	15·3	14·2	13·3	41
42	206	103	68·8	51·6	41·3	34·4	29·5	25·8	22·9	20·6	18·8	17·2	15·9	14·7	13·8	42
43	214	107	71·2	53·4	42·8	35·6	30·5	26·7	23·8	21·4	19·4	17·8	16·5	15·3	14·3	43
44	221	111	73·8	55·3	44·3	36·9	31·6	27·7	24·6	22·1	20·1	18·5	17·0	15·8	14·8	44
45	229	115	76·4	57·3	45·8	38·2	32·8	28·7	25·5	22·9	20·9	19·1	17·6	16·4	15·3	45
46	237	119	79·1	59·3	47·5	39·6	33·9	29·7	26·4	23·7	21·6	19·8	18·3	17·0	15·8	46
47	246	123	81·9	61·4	49·2	41·0	35·1	30·7	27·3	24·6	22·4	20·5	18·9	17·6	16·4	47
48	255	127	84·9	63·6	50·9	42·4	36·4	31·8	28·3	25·5	23·2	21·2	19·6	18·2	17·0	48
49	264	132	87·9	65·9	52·7	43·9	37·7	33·0	29·3	26·4	24·0	22·0	20·3	18·8	17·6	49
50	273	137	91·1	68·3	54·6	45·5	39·0	34·1	30·4	27·3	24·8	22·7	21·0	19·5	18·2	50
51	283	142	94·3	70·8	56·6	47·2	40·4	35·4	31·5	28·3	25·7	23·6	21·8	20·2	18·9	51
52	293	147	97·8	73·3	58·7	48·9	41·9	36·7	32·6	29·3	26·7	24·5	22·6	21·0	19·6	52
53	304	152	101	76·0	60·8	50·7	43·5	38·0	33·8	30·4	27·7	25·4	23·4	21·7	20·3	53
54	315	158	105	78·9	63·1	52·6	45·1	39·4	35·1	31·6	28·7	26·3	24·3	22·5	21·0	54
55	327	164	109	81·8	65·5	54·6	46·8	40·9	36·4	32·7	29·8	27·3	25·2	23·4	21·8	55
56	340	170	113	84·9	68·0	56·6	48·6	42·5	37·8	34·0	30·9	28·3	26·2	24·3	22·7	56
57	353	176	118	88·2	70·6	58·8	50·4	44·1	39·2	35·3	32·1	29·4	27·2	25·2	23·5	57
58	367	183	122	91·7	73·4	61·1	52·4	45·9	40·8	36·7	33·4	30·6	28·2	26·2	24·5	58
59	381	191	127	95·4	76·3	63·6	54·5	47·7	42·4	38·2	34·7	31·8	29·4	27·3	25·5	59
60	397	198	132	99·2	79·4	66·2	56·7	49·6	44·1	39·7	36·1	33·1	30·6	28·4	26·5	60
Dec.	179° 45' / 180° 15'	179° 30' / 180° 30'	179° 15' / 180° 45'	179° 00' / 181° 00'	178° 45' / 181° 15'	178° 30' / 181° 30'	178° 15' / 181° 45'	178° 00' / 182° 00'	177° 45' / 182° 15'	177° 30' / 182° 30'	177° 15' / 182° 45'	177° 00' / 183° 00'	176° 45' / 183° 15'	176° 30' / 183° 30'	176° 15' / 183° 45'	Dec.

B - Always named the **same** as Declination

HOUR ANGLE

B

TABLE A HOUR ANGLE

Lat. °	3°45' / 356°15'	4°00' / 356°00'	4°15' / 355°45'	4°30' / 355°30'	4°45' / 355°15'	5°00' / 355°00'	5°15' / 354°45'	5°30' / 354°30'	5°45' / 354°15'	6°00' / 354°00'	6°15' / 353°45'	6°30' / 353°30'	6°45' / 353°15'	7°00' / 353°00'	7°15' / 352°45'	7°30' / 352°30'	Lat. °
0	·00	·00	·00	·00	·00	·00	·00	·00	·00	·00	·00	·00	·00	·00	·00	·00	0
1	·27	·25	·23	·22	·21	·20	·19	·18	·17	·17	·16	·15	·15	·14	·14	·13	1
2	·53	·50	·47	·44	·42	·40	·38	·36	·35	·33	·32	·31	·30	·28	·27	·27	2
3	·80	·75	·71	·67	·63	·60	·57	·54	·52	·50	·48	·46	·44	·43	·41	40	3
4	1·07	1·00	·94	·89	·84	·80	·76	·73	·69	·67	·64	·61	·59	·57	·55	·53	4
5	1·33	1·25	1·18	1·11	1·05	1·00	·95	·91	·87	·83	·80	·77	·74	·71	·69	66	5
6	1·60	1·50	1·41	1·34	1·26	1·20	1·14	1·09	1·04	1·00	·96	·92	·89	·86	·83	·80	6
7	1·87	1·76	1·65	1·56	1·48	1·40	1·34	1·28	1·22	1·17	1·12	1·08	1·04	1·00	·97	·93	7
8	2·14	2·01	1·89	1·79	1·69	1·61	1·53	1·46	1·40	1·34	1·28	1·23	1·19	1·14	1·10	1·07	8
9	2·42	2·27	2·13	2·01	1·91	1·81	1·72	1·65	1·57	1·51	1·45	1·39	1·34	1·29	1·25	1·20	9
10	2·69	2·52	2·37	2·24	2·12	2·02	1·92	1·83	1·75	1·68	1·61	1·55	1·49	1·44	1·39	1·34	10
11	2·97	2·78	2·62	2·47	2·34	2·22	2·12	2·02	1·93	1·85	1·77	1·71	1·64	1·58	1·53	1·48	11
12	3·24	3·04	2·86	2·70	2·56	2·43	2·31	2·21	2·11	2·02	1·94	1·87	1·80	1·73	1·67	1·61	12
13	3·52	3·30	3·11	2·93	2·78	2·64	2·51	2·40	2·29	2·20	2·11	2·03	1·95	1·88	1·81	1·75	13
14	3·80	3·57	3·35	3·17	3·00	2·85	2·71	2·59	2·48	2·37	2·28	2·19	2·11	2·03	1·96	1·89	14
15	4·09	3·83	3·61	3·40	3·22	3·06	2·92	2·78	2·66	2·55	2·45	2·35	2·26	2·18	2·11	2·04	15
16	4·37	4·10	3·86	3·64	3·45	3·28	3·12	2·98	2·85	2·73	2·62	2·52	2·42	2·34	2·25	2·18	16
17	4·66	4·37	4·11	3·88	3·68	3·49	3·33	3·18	3·04	2·91	2·79	2·68	2·58	2·49	2·40	2·32	17
18	4·96	4·65	4·37	4·13	3·91	3·71	3·54	3·38	3·23	3·09	2·97	2·85	2·75	2·65	2·55	2·47	18
19	5·25	4·92	4·63	4·38	4·14	3·94	3·75	3·58	3·42	3·28	3·14	3·02	2·91	2·80	2·71	2·62	19
20	5·55	5·21	4·90	4·62	4·38	4·16	3·96	3·78	3·61	3·46	3·32	3·19	3·08	2·96	2·86	2·76	20
21	5·86	5·49	5·17	4·88	4·62	4·39	4·18	3·99	3·81	3·65	3·51	3·37	3·24	3·13	3·02	2·92	21
22	6·16	5·78	5·44	5·13	4·86	4·62	4·40	4·20	4·01	3·84	3·69	3·55	3·41	3·29	3·18	3·07	22
23	6·48	6·07	5·71	5·39	5·11	4·85	4·62	4·41	4·22	4·04	3·88	3·73	3·59	3·46	3·34	3·22	23
24	6·79	6·37	5·99	5·66	5·36	5·09	4·85	4·62	4·42	4·24	4·07	3·91	3·76	3·63	3·50	3·38	24
25	7·11	6·67	6·27	5·92	5·61	5·33	5·08	4·84	4·63	4·44	4·26	4·09	3·94	3·80	3·67	3·54	25
26	7·44	6·98	6·56	6·20	5·87	5·57	5·31	5·07	4·84	4·64	4·45	4·28	4·12	3·97	3·83	3·70	26
27	7·77	7·29	6·86	6·47	6·13	5·82	5·55	5·29	5·06	4·85	4·65	4·47	4·30	4·15	4·01	3·87	27
28	8·11	7·60	7·15	6·76	6·40	6·08	5·79	5·52	5·28	5·06	4·85	4·67	4·49	4·33	4·18	4·04	28
29	8·46	7·93	7·46	7·04	6·67	6·34	6·03	5·76	5·50	5·27	5·06	4·87	4·68	4·52	4·36	4·21	29
30	8·81	8·26	7·77	7·34	6·95	6·60	6·28	6·00	5·73	5·49	5·27	5·07	4·88	4·70	4·54	4·39	30
31	9·17	8·59	8·09	7·63	7·23	6·87	6·54	6·24	5·97	5·72	5·49	5·27	5·08	4·89	4·72	4·56	31
32	9·53	8·94	8·41	7·94	7·52	7·14	6·80	6·49	6·21	5·95	5·71	5·48	5·28	5·09	4·91	4·75	32
33	9·91	9·29	8·74	8·25	7·82	7·42	7·07	6·74	6·45	6·18	5·93	5·70	5·49	5·29	5·10	4·93	33
34	10·3	9·65	9·08	8·57	8·12	7·71	7·34	7·01	6·70	6·42	6·16	5·92	5·70	5·49	5·30	5·12	34
35	10·7	10·0	9·42	8·90	8·43	8·00	7·62	7·27	6·95	6·66	6·39	6·15	5·92	5·70	5·50	5·32	35
36	11·1	10·4	9·78	9·23	8·74	8·30	7·91	7·55	7·22	6·91	6·63	6·38	6·14	5·92	5·71	5·52	36
37	11·5	10·8	10·1	9·57	9·07	8·61	8·20	7·83	7·48	7·17	6·88	6·61	6·37	6·14	5·92	5·72	37
38	11·9	11·2	10·5	9·93	9·40	8·93	8·50	8·11	7·76	7·43	7·13	6·86	6·60	6·36	6·14	5·93	38
39	12·4	11·6	10·9	10·3	9·75	9·26	8·81	8·41	8·04	7·70	7·39	7·11	6·84	6·60	6·37	6·15	39
40	12·8	12·0	11·3	10·7	10·1	9·59	9·13	8·71	8·33	7·98	7·66	7·36	7·09	6·83	6·60	6·37	40
41	13·3	12·4	11·7	11·0	10·5	9·94	9·46	9·03	8·63	8·27	7·94	7·63	7·34	7·08	6·83	6·60	41
42	13·7	12·9	12·1	11·4	10·8	10·3	9·80	9·35	8·94	8·57	8·22	7·90	7·61	7·33	7·08	6·84	42
43	14·2	13·3	12·5	11·8	11·2	10·7	10·1	9·68	9·26	8·87	8·51	8·18	7·88	7·59	7·33	7·08	43
44	14·7	13·8	13·0	12·3	11·6	11·0	10·5	10·0	9·59	9·19	8·82	8·48	8·16	7·86	7·59	7·34	44
45	15·3	14·3	13·5	12·7	12·0	11·4	10·9	10·4	9·93	9·51	9·13	8·78	8·45	8·14	7·86	7·60	45
46	15·8	14·8	13·9	13·2	12·5	11·8	11·3	10·8	10·3	9·85	9·46	9·09	8·75	8·43	8·14	7·87	46
47	16·4	15·3	14·4	13·6	12·9	12·3	11·7	11·1	10·6	10·2	9·79	9·41	9·06	8·73	8·43	8·15	47
48	16·9	15·9	14·9	14·1	13·4	12·7	12·1	11·5	11·0	10·6	10·1	9·75	9·38	9·05	8·73	8·44	48
49	17·6	16·5	15·5	14·6	13·8	13·1	12·5	11·9	11·4	10·9	10·5	10·1	9·72	9·37	9·04	8·74	49
50	18·2	17·0	16·0	15·1	14·3	13·6	13·0	12·4	11·8	11·3	10·9	10·5	10·1	9·71	9·37	9·05	50
51	18·8	17·7	16·6	15·7	14·9	14·1	13·4	12·8	12·3	11·7	11·3	10·8	10·4	10·1	9·71	9·38	51
52	19·5	18·3	17·2	16·3	15·4	14·6	13·9	13·3	12·7	12·2	11·7	11·2	10·8	10·4	10·1	9·72	52
53	20·2	19·0	17·9	16·9	16·0	15·2	14·4	13·8	13·2	12·6	12·1	11·6	11·2	10·8	10·4	10·1	53
54	21·0	19·7	18·5	17·5	16·6	15·7	15·0	14·3	13·7	13·1	12·6	12·1	11·6	11·2	10·8	10·5	54
55	21·8	20·4	19·2	18·1	17·2	16·3	15·5	14·8	14·2	13·6	13·0	12·5	12·1	11·6	11·2	10·8	55
56	22·6	21·2	20·0	18·8	17·8	16·9	16·1	15·4	14·7	14·1	13·5	13·0	12·5	12·1	11·7	11·3	56
57	23·5	22·0	20·7	19·6	18·5	17·6	16·8	16·0	15·3	14·7	14·1	13·5	13·0	12·5	12·1	11·7	57
58	24·4	22·9	21·5	20·3	19·3	18·3	17·4	16·6	15·9	15·2	14·6	14·0	13·5	13·0	12·6	12·2	58
59	25·4	23·8	22·4	21·1	20·0	19·0	18·1	17·3	16·5	15·8	15·2	14·6	14·1	13·6	13·1	12·6	59
60	26·4	24·8	23·3	22·0	20·8	19·8	18·8	18·0	17·2	16·5	15·8	15·2	14·6	14·1	13·6	13·2	60
Lat.	176°15' / 183°45'	176°00' / 184°00'	175°45' / 184°15'	175°30' / 184°30'	175°15' / 184°45'	175°00' / 185°00'	174°45' / 185°15'	174°30' / 185°30'	174°15' / 185°45'	174°00' / 186°00'	173°45' / 186°15'	173°30' / 186°30'	173°15' / 186°45'	173°00' / 187°00'	172°45' / 187°15'	172°30' / 187°30'	Lat.

HOUR ANGLE

A

TABLE B HOUR ANGLE

Dec.°	3°45' 356°15'	4°00' 356°00'	4°15' 355°45'	4°30' 355°30'	4°45' 355°15'	5°00' 355°00'	5°15' 354°45'	5°30' 354°30'	5°45' 354°15'	6°00' 354°00'	6°15' 353°45'	6°30' 353°30'	6°45' 353°15'	7°00' 353°00'	7°15' 352°45'	7°30' 352°30'	Dec.°
0	·00	·00	·00	·00	·00	·00	·00	·00	·00	·00	·00	·00	·00	·00	·00	·00	0
1	·27	·25	·24	·22	·21	·20	·19	·18	·17	·17	·16	·15	·15	·14	·14	·13	1
2	·53	·50	·47	·45	·42	·40	·38	·36	·35	·33	·32	·31	·30	·29	·28	·27	2
3	·80	·75	·71	·67	·63	·60	·57	·55	·52	·50	·48	·46	·45	·43	·42	·40	3
4	1·07	1·00	·94	·89	·84	·80	·76	·73	·70	·67	·64	·62	·60	·57	·55	·54	4
5	1·34	1·25	1·18	1·12	1·06	1·00	·9€	·91	·87	·84	·80	·77	·74	·72	·69	·67	5
6	1·61	1·51	1·42	1·34	1·27	1·21	1·15	1·10	1·05	1·01	·97	·93	·89	·86	·83	·81	6
7	1·88	1·76	1·66	1·56	1·48	1·41	1·34	1·28	1·23	1·17	1·13	1·08	1·04	1·01	·97	·94	7
8	2·15	2·01	1·90	1·79	1·70	1·61	1·54	1·47	1·40	1·34	1·29	1·24	1·20	1·15	1·11	1·08	8
9	2·42	2·27	2·14	2·02	1·91	1·82	1·73	1·65	1·58	1·52	1·45	1·40	1·35	1·30	1·26	1.21	9
10	2·70	2·53	2·38	2·25	2·13	2·02	1·93	1·84	1·76	1·69	1·62	1·56	1·50	1·45	1·40	1·35	10
11	2·97	2·79	2·62	2·48	2·35	2·23	2·12	2·03	1·94	1·86	1·79	1·72	1·65	1·59	1·54	1·49	11
12	3·25	3·05	2·87	2·71	2·57	2·44	2·32	2·22	2·12	2·03	1·95	1·88	1·81	1·74	1·68	1·63	12
13	3·53	3·31	3·12	2·94	2·79	2·65	2·52	2·41	2·30	2·21	2·12	2·04	1·96	1·89	1·83	1·77	13
14	3·81	3·57	3·36	3·18	3·01	2·86	2·72	2·60	2·49	2·39	2·29	2·20	2·12	2·05	1·98	1·91	14
15	4·10	3·84	3·62	3·41	3·24	3·07	2·93	2·80	2·67	2·56	2·46	2·37	2·28	2·20	2·12	2·05	15
16	4·38	4·11	3·87	3·65	3·46	3·29	3·13	2·99	2·86	2·74	2·63	2·53	2·44	2·35	2·27	2·20	16
17	4·67	4·38	4·13	3·90	3·69	3·51	3·34	3·19	3·05	2·92	2·81	2·70	2·60	2·51	2·42	2·34	17
18	4·97	4·66	4·38	4·14	3·92	3·73	3·55	3·39	3·24	3·11	2·98	2·87	2·76	2·67	2·57	2·49	18
19	5·26	4·94	4·65	4·39	4·16	3·95	3·76	3·59	3·44	3·29	3·16	3·04	2·93	2·83	2·73	2·64	19
20	5·57	5·22	4·91	4·64	4·40	4·18	3·98	3·80	3·63	3·48	3·34	3·22	3·10	2·99	2·88	2·79	20
21	5·87	5·50	5·18	4·89	4·64	4·40	4·20	4·01	3·83	3·67	3·53	3·39	3·27	3·15	3·04	2·94	21
22	6·18	5·79	5·45	5·15	4·88	4·64	4·42	4·22	4·03	3·87	3·71	3·57	3·44	3·32	3·20	3·10	22
23	6·49	6·09	5·73	5·41	5·13	4·87	4·64	4·43	4·24	4·06	3·90	3·75	3·61	3·48	3·36	3·25	23
24	6·81	6·38	6·01	5·67	5·38	5·11	4·87	4·65	4·44	4·26	4·09	3·93	3·79	3·65	3·53	3·41	24
25	7·13	6·68	6·29	5·94	5·63	5·35	5·10	4·87	4·65	4·46	4·28	4·12	3·97	3·83	3·70	3·57	25
26	7·46	6·99	6·58	6·22	5·89	5·60	5·33	5·09	4·87	4·67	4·48	4·31	4·15	4·00	3·86	3·74	26
27	7·79	7·30	6·88	6·49	6·15	5·85	5·57	5·32	5·09	4·87	4·68	4·50	4·34	4·18	4·04	3·90	27
28	8·13	7·62	7·17	6·78	6·42	6·10	5·81	5·55	5·31	5·09	4·88	4·70	4·52	4·36	4·21	4·07	28
29	8·48	7·95	7·48	7·06	6·69	6·36	6·06	5·78	5·53	5·30	5·09	4·90	4·72	4·55	4·39	4·25	29
30	8·83	8·28	7·79	7·36	6·97	6·62	6·31	6·02	5·76	5·52	5·30	5·10	4·91	4·74	4·57	4·42	30
31	9·19	8·61	8·11	7·66	7·26	6·89	6·57	6·27	6·00	5·75	5·52	5·31	5·11	4·93	4·76	4·60	31
32	9·55	8·96	8·43	7·96	7·55	7·17	6·83	6·52	6·24	5·98	5·74	5·52	5·32	5·13	4·95	4·79	32
33	9·93	9·31	8·76	8·28	7·84	7·45	7·10	6·78	6·48	6·21	5·97	5·74	5·53	5·33	5·15	4·98	33
34	10·3	9·67	9·10	8·60	8·15	7·74	7·37	7·04	6·73	6·45	6·20	5·96	5·74	5·54	5·34	5·17	34
35	10·7	10·0	9·45	8·92	8·46	8·03	7·65	7·31	6·99	6·70	6·43	6·19	5·96	5·75	5·55	5·36	35
36	11·1	10·4	9·80	9·26	8·77	8·34	7·94	7·58	7·25	6·95	6·67	6·42	6·18	5·96	5·76	5·57	36
37	11·5	10·8	10·2	9·60	9·10	8·65	8·24	7·86	7·52	7·21	6·92	6·66	6·41	6·18	5·97	5·77	37
38	11·9	11·2	10·5	9·96	9·43	8·96	8·54	8·15	7·80	7·47	7·18	6·90	6·65	6·41	6·19	5·99	38
39	12·4	11·6	10·9	10·3	9·78	9·29	8·85	8·45	8·08	7·75	7·44	7·15	6·89	6·65	6·42	6·20	39
40	12·8	12·0	11·3	10·7	10·1	9·63	9·17	8·75	8·38	8·03	7·71	7·41	7·14	6·89	6·65	6·43	40
41	13·3	12·5	11·7	11·1	10·5	9·97	9·50	9·07	8·68	8·32	7·98	7·68	7·40	7·13	6·89	6·66	41
42	13·8	12·9	12·1	11·5	10·9	10·3	9·84	9·39	8·99	8·61	8·27	7·95	7·66	7·39	7·13	6·90	42
43	14·3	13·4	12·6	11·9	11·3	10·7	10·2	9·73	9·31	8·92	8·57	8·24	7·93	7·65	7·39	7·14	43
44	14·8	13·8	13·0	12·3	11·7	11·1	10·6	10·1	9·64	9·24	8·87	8·53	8·22	7·92	7·65	7·40	44
45	15·3	14·3	13·5	12·7	12·1	11·5	10·9	10·4	9·98	9·57	9·19	8·83	8·51	8·21	7·92	7·66	45
46	15·8	14·8	14·0	13·2	12·5	11·9	11·3	10·8	10·3	9·91	9·51	9·15	8·81	8·50	8·21	7·93	46
47	16·4	15·4	14·5	13·7	13·0	12·3	11·7	11·2	10·7	10·3	9·85	9·47	9·12	8·80	8·50	8·22	47
48	17·0	15·9	15·0	14·2	13·4	12·7	12·1	11·6	11·1	10·6	10·2	9·81	9·45	9·11	8·80	8·51	48
49	17·6	16·5	15·5	14·7	13·9	13·2	12·6	12·0	11·5	11·0	10·6	10·2	9·79	9·44	9·12	8·81	49
50	18·2	17·1	16·1	15·2	14·4	13·7	13·0	12·4	11·9	11·4	10·9	10·5	10·1	9·78	9·44	9·13	50
51	18·9	17·7	16·7	15·7	14·9	14·2	13·5	12·9	12·3	11·8	11·3	10·9	10·5	10·1	9·79	9·46	51
52	19·6	18·3	17·3	16·3	15·5	14·7	14·0	13·4	12·8	12·2	11·8	11·3	10·9	10·5	10·1	9·81	52
53	20·3	19·0	17·9	16·9	16·0	15·2	14·5	13·8	13·2	12·7	12·2	11·7	11·3	10·9	10·5	10·2	53
54	21·0	19·7	18·6	17·5	16·6	15·8	15·0	14·4	13·7	13·2	12·6	12·2	11·7	11·3	10·9	10·5	54
55	21·8	20·5	19·3	18·2	17·2	16·4	15·6	14·9	14·3	13·7	13·1	12·6	12·2	11·7	11·3	10·9	55
56	22·7	21·3	20·0	18·9	17·9	17·0	16·2	15·5	14·8	14·2	13·6	13·1	12·6	12·2	11·7	11·4	56
57	23·5	22·1	20·8	19·6	18·6	17·7	16·8	16·1	15·4	14·7	14·1	13·6	13·1	12·6	12·2	11·8	57
58	24·5	22·9	21·6	20·4	19·3	18·4	17·5	16·7	16·0	15·3	14·7	14·1	13·6	13·1	12·7	12·3	58
59	25·4	23·9	22·5	21·2	20·1	19·1	18·2	17·4	16·6	15·9	15·3	14·7	14·2	13·7	13·2	12·8	59
60	26·5	24·8	23·4	22·1	20·9	19·8	18·9	18·1	17·3	16·6	15·9	15·3	14·7	14·2	13·7	13·3	60
Dec.	176°15' 183°45'	176°00' 184°00'	175°45' 184°15'	175°30' 184°30'	175°15' 184°45'	175°00' 185°00'	174°45' 185°15'	174°30' 185°30'	174°15' 185°45'	174°00' 186°00'	173°45' 186°15'	173°30' 186°30'	173°15' 186°45'	173°00' 187°00'	172°45' 187°15'	172°30' 187°30'	Dec.

HOUR ANGLE

B - Always named the **same** as Declination

B

TABLE A HOUR ANGLE

A - Named opposite to Latitude, except when Hour Angle is between 90° and 270°

Lat.°	7°30' / 352°30'	7°45' / 352°15'	8°00' / 352°00'	8°15' / 351°45'	8°30' / 351°30'	8°45' / 351°15'	9°00' / 351°00'	9°15' / 350°45'	9°30' / 350°30'	9°45' / 350°15'	10°00' / 350°00'	10°15' / 349°45'	10°30' / 349°30'	10°45' / 349°15'	11°00' / 349°00'	11°15' / 348°45'	Lat.°
0	·00	·00	·00	·00	·00	·00	·00	·00	·00	·00	·00	·00	·00	·00	·00	·00	0
1	·13	·13	·12	·12	·12	·11	·11	·11	·10	·10	·10	·10	·09	·09	·09	·09	1
2	·27	·26	·25	·24	·23	·23	·22	·21	·21	·20	·20	·19	·19	·18	·18	·18	2
3	·40	·39	·37	·36	·35	·34	·33	·32	·31	·30	·30	·29	·28	·28	·27	·26	3
4	·53	·51	·50	·48	·47	·45	·44	·43	·42	·41	·40	·39	·38	·37	·36	·35	4
5	·66	·64	·62	·60	·59	·57	55	·54	·52	·51	·50	·48	·47	·46	·45	·44	5
6	·80	·77	·75	·72	·70	·68	·66	·65	·63	·61	·60	·58	·57	·55	·54	·53	6
7	·93	·90	·87	·85	·82	·80	·78	·75	·73	·72	·70	·68	·66	·65	·63	·62	7
8	1·07	1·03	1·00	·97	·94	·91	·89	·86	·84	·82	·80	·78	·76	·74	·72	·71	8
9	1·20	1·16	1·13	1·09	1·06	1·03	1·00	·97	·95	·92	·90	·88	·85	·83	·81	·80	9
10	1·34	1·30	1·25	1·22	1·18	1·15	1·11	1·08	1·05	1·03	1·00	·98	·95	·93	·91	·89	10
11	1·48	1·43	1·38	1·34	1·30	1·26	1·23	1·19	1·16	1·13	1·10	1·07	1·05	1·02	1·00	·98	11
12	1·61	1·56	1·51	1·47	1·42	1·38	1·34	1·31	1·27	1·24	1·21	1·18	1·15	1·12	1·09	1·07	12
13	1·75	1·70	1·64	1·59	1·54	1·50	1·46	1·42	1·38	1·34	1·31	1·28	1·25	1·22	1·19	1·16	13
14	1·89	1·83	1·77	1·72	1·67	1·62	1·57	1·53	1·49	1·45	1·41	1·38	1·35	1·31	1·28	1·25	14
15	2·04	1·97	1·91	1·85	1·79	1·74	1·69	1·64	1·60	1·56	1·52	1·48	1·45	1·41	1·38	1·35	15
16	2·18	2·11	2·04	1·98	1·92	1·86	1·81	1·76	1·71	1·67	1·63	1·59	1·55	1·51	1·48	1·44	16
17	2·32	2·25	2·18	2·11	2·05	1·99	1·93	1·88	1·83	1·78	1·73	1·69	1·65	1·61	1·57	1·54	17
18	2·47	2·39	2·31	2·24	2·17	2·11	2·05	2·00	1·94	1·89	1·84	1·80	1·75	1·71	1·67	1·63	18
19	2·62	2·53	2·45	2·37	2·30	2·24	2·17	2·11	2·06	2·00	1·95	1·90	1·86	1·81	1·77	1·73	19
20	2·76	2·67	2·59	2·51	2·44	2·36	2·30	2·23	2·18	2·12	2·06	2·01	1·96	1·92	1·87	1·83	20
21	2·92	2·82	2·73	2·65	2·57	2·49	2·42	2·36	2·29	2·23	2·18	2·12	2·07	2·02	1·97	1·93	21
22	3·07	2·97	2·87	2·79	2·70	2·63	2·55	2·48	2·41	2·35	2·29	2·23	2·18	2·13	2·08	2·03	22
23	3·22	3·12	3·02	2·93	2·84	2·76	2·68	2·61	2·54	2·47	2·41	2·35	2·29	2·24	2·18	2·13	23
24	3·38	3·27	3·17	3·07	2·98	2·89	2·81	2·73	2·66	2·59	2·53	2·46	2·40	2·35	2·29	2·24	24
25	3·54	3·43	3·32	3·22	3·12	3·03	2·94	2·86	2·79	2·71	2·64	2·58	2·52	2·46	2·40	2·34	25
26	3·70	3·58	3·47	3·36	3·26	3·17	3·08	2·99	2·91	2·84	2·77	2·70	2·63	2·57	2·51	2·45	26
27	3·87	3·74	3·63	3·51	3·41	3·31	3·22	3·13	3·04	2·97	2·89	2·82	2·75	2·68	2·62	2·56	27
28	4·04	3·91	3·78	3·67	3·56	3·45	3·36	3·26	3·18	3·09	3·02	2·94	2·87	2·80	2·74	2·67	28
29	4·21	4·07	3·94	3·82	3·71	3·60	3·50	3·40	3·31	3·23	3·14	3·07	2·99	2·92	2·85	2·79	29
30	4·39	4·24	4·11	3·98	3·86	3·75	3·65	3·55	3·45	3·36	3·27	3·19	3·12	3·04	2·97	2·90	30
31	4·56	4·42	4·28	4·14	4·02	3·90	3·79	3·69	3·59	3·50	3·41	3·32	3·24	3·16	3·09	3·02	31
32	4·75	4·59	4·45	4·31	4·18	4·06	3·95	3·84	3·73	3·64	3·54	3·46	3·37	3·29	3·21	3·14	32
33	4·93	4·77	4·62	4·48	4·35	4·22	4·10	3·99	3·88	3·78	3·68	3·59	3·50	3·42	3·34	3·26	33
34	5·12	4·96	4·80	4·65	4·51	4·38	4·26	4·14	4·03	3·93	3·83	3·73	3·64	3·55	3·47	3·39	34
35	5·32	5·15	4·98	4·83	4·69	4·55	4·42	4·30	4·18	4·08	3·97	3·87	3·78	3·69	3·60	3·52	35
36	5·52	5·34	5·17	5·01	4·86	4·72	4·59	4·46	4·34	4·23	4·12	4·02	3·92	3·83	3·74	3·65	36
37	5·72	5·54	5·36	5·20	5·04	4·90	4·76	4·63	4·50	4·39	4·27	4·17	4·07	3·97	3·88	3·79	37
38	5·93	5·74	5·56	5·39	5·23	5·08	4·93	4·80	4·67	4·55	4·43	4·32	4·22	4·12	4·02	3·93	38
39	6·15	5·95	5·76	5·58	5·42	5·26	5·11	4·97	4·84	4·71	4·59	4·48	4·37	4·27	4·17	4·07	39
40	6·37	6·17	5·97	5·79	5·61	5·45	5·30	5·15	5·01	4·88	4·76	4·64	4·53	4·42	4·32	4·22	40
41	6·60	6·39	6·19	6·00	5·82	5·65	5·49	5·34	5·19	5·06	4·93	4·81	4·69	4·58	4·47	4·37	41
42	6·84	6·62	6·41	6·21	6·02	5·85	5·69	5·53	5·38	5·24	5·11	4·98	4·86	4·74	4·63	4·53	42
43	7·08	6·85	6·64	6·43	6·24	6·06	5·89	5·73	5·57	5·43	5·29	5·16	5·03	4·91	4·80	4·69	43
44	7·34	7·10	6·87	6·66	6·46	6·27	6·10	5·93	5·77	5·62	5·48	5·34	5·21	5·09	4·97	4·85	44
45	7·60	7·35	7·12	6·90	6·69	6·50	6·31	6·14	5·98	5·82	5·67	5·53	5·40	5·27	5·15	5·03	45
46	7·87	7·61	7·37	7·14	6·93	6·73	6·54	6·36	6·19	6·03	5·87	5·73	5·59	5·46	5·33	5·21	46
47	8·15	7·88	7·63	7·40	7·18	6·97	6·77	6·59	6·41	6·24	6·08	5·93	5·79	5·65	5·52	5·39	47
48	8·44	8·16	7·90	7·66	7·43	7·22	7·01	6·82	6·64	6·46	6·30	6·14	5·99	5·85	5·71	5·58	48
49	8·74	8·45	8·19	7·93	7·70	7·47	7·26	7·06	6·87	6·69	6·52	6·36	6·21	6·06	5·92	5·78	49
50	9·05	8·76	8·48	8·22	7·97	7·74	7·52	7·32	7·12	6·94	6·76	6·59	6·43	6·28	6·13	5·99	50
51	9·38	9·07	8·79	8·52	8·26	8·02	7·80	7·58	7·38	7·19	7·00	6·83	6·66	6·50	6·35	6·21	51
52	9·72	9·40	9·11	8·83	8·56	8·32	8·08	7·86	7·65	7·45	7·26	7·08	6·91	6·74	6·58	6·43	52
53	10·1	9·75	9·44	9·15	8·88	8·62	8·38	8·15	7·93	7·72	7·53	7·34	7·16	6·99	6·83	6·67	53
54	10·5	10·1	9·79	9·49	9·21	8·94	8·69	8·45	8·23	8·01	7·81	7·61	7·43	7·25	7·08	6·92	54
55	10·8	10·5	10·2	9·85	9·56	9·28	9·02	8·77	8·53	8·31	8·10	7·90	7·71	7·52	7·35	7·18	55
56	11·3	10·9	10·5	10·2	9·92	9·63	9·36	9·10	8·86	8·63	8·41	8·20	8·00	7·81	7·63	7·45	56
57	11·7	11·3	11·0	10·6	10·3	10·0	9·72	9·46	9·20	8·96	8·73	8·52	8·31	8·11	7·92	7·74	57
58	12·2	11·8	11·4	11·0	10·7	10·4	10·1	9·83	9·56	9·31	9·08	8·85	8·64	8·43	8·23	8·05	58
59	12·6	12·2	11·8	11·5	11·1	10·8	10·5	10·2	9·95	9·69	9·44	9·20	8·98	8·77	8·56	8·37	59
60	13·2	12·7	12·3	11·9	11·6	11·3	10·9	10·6	10·4	10·1	9·82	9·58	9·35	9·12	8·91	8·71	60
Lat.	172°30' / 187°30'	172°15' / 187°45'	172°00' / 188°00'	171°45' / 188°15'	171°30' / 188°30'	171°15' / 188°45'	171°00' / 189°00'	170°45' / 189°15'	170°30' / 189°30'	170°15' / 189°45'	170°00' / 190°00'	169°45' / 190°15'	169°30' / 190°30'	169°15' / 190°45'	169°00' / 191°00'	168°45' / 191°15'	Lat.

A - Named opposite to Latitude, except when Hour Angle is between 90° and 270°

HOUR ANGLE

A

TABLE B HOUR ANGLE

Dec. °	7° 30' 352° 30'	7° 45' 352° 15'	8° 00' 352° 00'	8° 15' 351° 45'	8° 30' 351° 30'	8° 45' 351° 15'	9° 00' 351° 00'	9° 15' 350° 45'	9° 30' 350° 30'	9° 45' 350° 15'	10° 00' 350° 00'	10° 15' 349° 45'	10° 30' 349° 30'	10° 45' 349° 15'	11° 00' 349° 00'	11° 15' 348° 45'	Dec. °
0	·00	·00	·00	·00	·00	·00	·00	·00	·00	·00	·00	·00	·00	·00	·00	·00	0
1	·13	·13	·13	·12	·12	·12	·11	·11	·11	·10	·10	·10	·10	·09	·09	·09	1
2	·27	·26	·25	·24	·24	·23	·22	·22	·21	·21	·20	·20	·19	·19	·18	·18	2
3	·40	·39	·38	·37	·36	·35	·34	·33	·32	·31	·30	·30	·29	·28	·27	·27	3
4	·54	·52	·50	·49	·47	·46	·45	·44	·42	·41	·40	·39	·38	·38	·37	·36	4
5	·67	·65	·63	·61	·59	·58	·56	·54	·53	·52	·50	·49	·48	·47	·46	·45	5
6	·81	·78	·76	·73	·71	·69	·67	·65	·64	·62	·61	·59	·58	·56	·55	·54	6
7	·94	·91	·88	·86	·83	·81	·79	·76	·74	·73	·71	·69	·67	·66	·64	·63	7
8	1·08	1·04	1·01	·98	·95	·92	·90	·87	·85	·83	·81	·79	·77	·75	·74	·72	8
9	1·21	1·17	1·14	1·10	1·07	1·04	1·01	·99	·96	·94	·91	·89	·87	·85	·83	·81	9
10	1·35	1·31	1·27	1·23	1·19	1·16	1·13	1·10	1·07	1·04	1·02	·99	·97	·95	·92	·90	10
11	1·49	1·44	1·40	1·35	1·32	1·28	1·24	1·21	1·18	1·15	1·12	1·09	1·07	1·04	1·02	1·00	11
12	1·63	1·58	1·53	1·48	1·44	1·40	1·36	1·32	1·29	1·26	1·22	1·19	1·17	1·14	1·11	1·09	12
13	1·77	1·71	1·66	1·61	1·56	1·52	1·48	1·44	1·40	1·36	1·33	1·30	1·27	1·24	1·21	1·18	13
14	1·91	1·85	1·79	1·74	1·69	1·64	1·59	1·55	1·51	1·47	1·44	1·40	1·37	1·34	1·31	1·28	14
15	2·05	1·99	1·93	1·87	1·81	1·76	1·71	1·67	1·62	1·58	1·54	1·51	1·47	1·44	1·40	1·37	15
16	2·20	2·13	2·06	2·00	1·94	1·88	1·83	1·78	1·74	1·69	1·65	1·61	1·57	1·54	1·50	1·47	16
17	2·34	2·27	2·20	2·13	2·07	2·01	1·95	1·90	1·85	1·80	1·76	1·72	1·68	1·64	1·60	1·57	17
18	2·49	2·41	2·33	2·26	2·20	2·14	2·08	2·02	1·97	1·92	1·87	1·83	1·78	1·74	1·70	1·67	18
19	2·64	2·55	2·47	2·40	2·33	2·26	2·20	2·14	2·09	2·03	1·98	1·94	1·89	1·85	1·80	1·76	19
20	2·79	2·70	2·62	2·54	2·46	2·39	2·33	2·26	2·21	2·15	2·10	2·05	2·00	1·95	1·91	1·87	20
21	2·94	2·85	2·76	2·68	2·60	2·52	2·45	2·39	2·33	2·27	2·21	2·16	2·11	2·06	2·01	1·97	21
22	3·10	3·00	2·90	2·82	2·73	2·66	2·58	2·51	2·45	2·39	2·33	2·27	2·22	2·17	2·12	2·07	22
23	3·25	3·15	3·05	2·96	2·87	2·79	2·71	2·64	2·57	2·51	2·44	2·39	2·33	2·28	2·22	2·18	23
24	3·41	3·30	3·20	3·10	3·01	2·93	2·85	2·77	2·70	2·63	2·56	2·50	2·44	2·39	2·33	2·28	24
25	3·57	3·46	3·35	3·25	3·15	3·07	2·98	2·90	2·83	2·75	2·69	2·62	2·56	2·50	2·44	2·39	25
26	3·74	3·62	3·50	3·40	3·30	3·21	3·12	3·03	2·96	2·88	2·81	2·74	2·68	2·61	2·56	2·50	26
27	3·90	3·78	3·66	3·55	3·45	3·35	3·26	3·17	3·09	3·01	2·93	2·86	2·80	2·73	2·67	2·61	27
28	4·07	3·94	3·82	3·71	3·60	3·50	3·40	3·31	3·22	3·14	3·06	2·99	2·92	2·85	2·79	2·73	28
29	4·25	4·11	3·98	3·86	3·75	3·64	3·54	3·45	3·36	3·27	3·19	3·12	3·04	2·97	2·91	2·84	29
30	4·42	4·28	4·15	4·02	3·91	3·80	3·69	3·59	3·50	3·41	3·32	3·24	3·17	3·10	3·03	2·96	30
31	4·60	4·46	4·32	4·19	4·07	3·95	3·84	3·74	3·64	3·55	3·46	3·38	3·30	3·22	3·15	3·08	31
32	4·79	4·63	4·49	4·35	4·23	4·11	3·99	3·89	3·79	3·69	3·60	3·51	3·43	3·35	3·27	3·20	32
33	4·98	4·82	4·67	4·53	4·39	4·27	4·15	4·04	3·93	3·83	3·74	3·65	3·56	3·48	3·40	3·33	33
34	5·17	5·00	4·85	4·70	4·56	4·43	4·31	4·20	4·09	3·98	3·88	3·79	3·70	3·62	3·53	3·46	34
35	5·36	5·19	5·03	4·88	4·74	4·60	4·48	4·36	4·24	4·13	4·03	3·93	3·84	3·75	3·67	3·59	35
36	5·57	5·39	5·22	5·06	4·92	4·78	4·64	4·52	4·40	4·29	4·18	4·08	3·99	3·90	3·81	3·72	36
37	5·77	5·59	5·41	5·25	5·10	4·95	4·82	4·69	4·57	4·45	4·34	4·23	4·14	4·04	3·95	3·86	37
38	5·99	5·79	5·61	5·44	5·29	5·14	5·00	4·86	4·73	4·61	4·50	4·39	4·29	4·19	4·09	4·00	38
39	6·20	6·01	5·82	5·64	5·48	5·32	5·18	5·04	4·91	4·78	4·66	4·55	4·44	4·34	4·24	4·15	39
40	6·43	6·22	6·03	5·85	5·68	5·52	5·36	5·22	5·08	4·95	4·83	4·72	4·60	4·50	4·40	4·30	40
41	6·66	6·45	6·25	6·06	5·88	5·71	5·56	5·41	5·27	5·13	5·01	4·89	4·77	4·66	4·56	4·46	41
42	6·90	6·68	6·47	6·27	6·09	5·92	5·76	5·60	5·46	5·32	5·19	5·06	4·94	4·83	4·72	4·62	42
43	7·14	6·92	6·70	6·50	6·31	6·13	5·96	5·80	5·65	5·51	5·37	5·24	5·12	5·00	4·89	4·78	43
44	7·40	7·16	6·94	6·73	6·53	6·35	6·17	6·01	5·85	5·70	5·56	5·43	5·30	5·18	5·06	4·95	44
45	7·66	7·42	7·19	6·97	6·77	6·57	6·39	6·22	6·06	5·90	5·76	5·62	5·49	5·36	5·24	5·13	45
46	7·93	7·68	7·44	7·22	7·01	6·81	6·62	6·44	6·27	6·11	5·96	5·82	5·68	5·55	5·43	5·31	46
47	8·22	7·95	7·71	7·47	7·26	7·05	6·86	6·67	6·50	6·33	6·18	6·03	5·88	5·75	5·62	5·50	47
48	8·51	8·24	7·98	7·74	7·51	7·30	7·10	6·91	6·73	6·56	6·40	6·24	6·09	5·95	5·82	5·69	48
49	8·81	8·53	8·27	8·02	7·78	7·56	7·35	7·16	6·97	6·79	6·62	6·46	6·31	6·17	6·03	5·90	49
50	9·13	8·84	8·56	8·31	8·06	7·83	7·62	7·41	7·22	7·04	6·86	6·70	6·54	6·39	6·25	6·11	50
51	9·46	9·16	8·87	8·61	8·35	8·12	7·89	7·68	7·48	7·29	7·11	6·94	6·78	6·62	6·47	6·33	51
52	9·81	9·49	9·20	8·92	8·66	8·41	8·18	7·96	7·75	7·56	7·37	7·19	7·02	6·86	6·71	6·56	52
53	10·2	9·84	9·54	9·25	8·98	8·72	8·48	8·26	8·04	7·84	7·64	7·46	7·28	7·11	6·95	6·80	53
54	10·5	10·2	9·89	9·59	9·31	9·05	8·80	8·56	8·34	8·13	7·93	7·73	7·55	7·38	7·21	7·06	54
55	10·9	10·6	10·3	9·95	9·66	9·39	9·13	8·88	8·65	8·43	8·22	8·03	7·84	7·66	7·48	7·32	55
56	11·4	11·0	10·7	10·3	10·0	9·75	9·48	9·22	8·98	8·75	8·54	8·33	8·14	7·95	7·77	7·60	56
57	11·8	11·4	11·1	10·7	10·4	10·1	9·84	9·58	9·33	9·09	8·87	8·65	8·45	8·26	8·07	7·89	57
58	12·3	11·9	11·5	11·2	10·8	10·5	10·2	9·96	9·70	9·45	9·22	8·99	8·78	8·58	8·39	8·20	58
59	12·8	12·3	12·0	11·6	11·3	10·9	10·6	10·4	10·1	9·83	9·58	9·35	9·13	8·92	8·72	8·53	59
60	13·3	12·8	12·4	12·1	11·7	11·4	11·1	10·8	10·5	10·2	9·97	9·73	9·50	9·29	9·08	8·88	60
Dec.	172° 30' 187° 30'	172° 15' 187° 45'	172° 00' 188° 00'	171° 45' 188° 15'	171° 30' 188° 30'	171° 15' 188° 45'	171° 00' 189° 00'	170° 45' 189° 15'	170° 30' 189° 30'	170° 15' 189° 45'	170° 00' 190° 00'	169° 45' 190° 15'	169° 30' 190° 30'	169° 15' 190° 45'	169° 00' 191° 00'	168° 45' 191° 15'	Dec.

B - Always named the same as Declination

B - Always named the same as Declination

HOUR ANGLE

B

TABLE A HOUR ANGLE

A - Named opposite to Latitude, except when Hour Angle is between 90° and 270°

A - Named opposite to Latitude, except when Hour Angle is between 90° and 270°

Lat.°	11°15' 348°45'	11°30' 348°30'	11°45' 348°15'	12°00' 348°00'	12°15' 347°45'	12°30' 347°30'	12°45' 347°15'	13°00' 347°00'	13°15' 346°45'	13°30' 346°30'	13°45' 346°15'	14°00' 346°00'	14°15' 345°45'	14°30' 345°30'	14°45' 345°15'	15°00' 345°00'	Lat.°
0	·00	·00	·00	·00	·00	·00	·00	·00	·00	·00	·00	·00	·00	·00	·00	·00	0
1	·09	·09	·08	·08	·08	·08	·08	·08	·07	·07	·07	·07	·07	·07	·07	·07	1
2	·18	·17	·17	·16	·16	·16	·15	·15	·15	·15	·14	·14	·14	·14	·13	·13	2
3	·26	·26	·25	·24	·24	·23	·23	·22	·22	·21	·21	·21	·20	·20	·20	·20	3
4	·35	·34	·34	·33	·32	·32	·31	·30	·30	·29	·29	·28	·28	·27	·27	·26	4
5	·44	·43	·42	·41	·40	·39	·39	·38	·37	·36	·36	·35	·34	·34	·33	·33	5
6	·53	·52	·51	·49	·48	·47	·46	·46	·45	·44	·43	·42	·41	·41	·40	·39	6
7	·62	·60	·59	·58	·57	·55	·54	·53	·52	·51	·50	·49	·48	·47	·47	·46	7
8	·71	·69	·68	·66	·65	·63	·62	·61	·60	·59	·57	·56	·55	·54	·53	·52	8
9	·80	·78	·76	·75	·73	·71	·70	·69	·67	·66	·65	·64	·62	·61	·60	·59	9
10	·89	·87	·85	·83	·81	·80	·78	·76	·75	·73	·72	·71	·69	·68	·67	·66	10
11	·98	·96	·94	·91	·90	·88	·86	·84	·83	·81	·79	·78	·77	·75	·74	·73	11
12	1·07	1·04	1·02	1·00	·98	·96	·94	·92	·90	·89	·87	·85	·84	·82	·81	·79	12
13	1·16	1·13	1·11	1·09	1·06	1·04	1·02	1·00	·98	·96	·94	·93	·91	·89	·88	·86	13
14	1·25	1·23	1·20	1·17	1·15	1·12	1·10	1·08	1·06	1·04	1·02	1·00	·98	·96	·95	·93	14
15	1·35	1·32	1·29	1·26	1·23	1·21	1·18	1·16	1·14	1·12	1·10	1·07	1·06	1·04	1·02	1·00	15
16	1·44	1·41	1·38	1·35	1·32	1·29	1·27	1·24	1·22	1·19	1·17	1·15	1·13	1·11	1·09	1·07	16
17	1·54	1·50	1·47	1·44	1·41	1·38	1·35	1·32	1·30	1·27	1·25	1·23	1·20	1·18	1·16	1·14	17
18	1·63	1·59	1·56	1·53	1·50	1·47	1·44	1·41	1·38	1·35	1·33	1·30	1·28	1·26	1·23	1·21	18
19	1·73	1·69	1·66	1·62	1·59	1·55	1·52	1·49	1·46	1·43	1·41	1·38	1·36	1·33	1·31	1·29	19
20	1·83	1·79	1·75	1·71	1·68	1·64	1·61	1·58	1·55	1·52	1·49	1·46	1·43	1·41	1·38	1·36	20
21	1·93	1·89	1·85	1·81	1·77	1·73	1·70	1·66	1·63	1·60	1·57	1·54	1·51	1·48	1·46	1·43	21
22	2·03	1·99	1·94	1·90	1·86	1·82	1·79	1·75	1·72	1·68	1·65	1·62	1·59	1·56	1·53	1·51	22
23	2·13	2·09	2·04	2·00	1·96	1·91	1·88	1·84	1·80	1·77	1·73	1·70	1·67	1·64	1·61	1·58	23
24	2·24	2·19	2·14	2·09	2·05	2·01	1·97	1·93	1·89	1·85	1·82	1·79	1·75	1·72	1·69	1·66	24
25	2·34	2·29	2·24	2·19	2·15	2·10	2·06	2·02	1·98	1·94	1·91	1·87	1·84	1·80	1·77	1·74	25
26	2·45	2·40	2·34	2·29	2·25	2·20	2·16	2·11	2·07	2·03	1·99	1·96	1·92	1·89	1·85	1·82	26
27	2·56	2·50	2·45	2·40	2·35	2·30	2·25	2·21	2·16	2·12	2·08	2·04	2·01	1·97	1·94	1·90	27
28	2·67	2·61	2·56	2·50	2·45	2·40	2·35	2·30	2·26	2·21	2·17	2·13	2·09	2·06	2·02	1·98	28
29	2·79	2·73	2·66	2·61	2·55	2·50	2·45	2·40	2·35	2·31	2·27	2·22	2·18	2·14	2·11	2·07	29
30	2·90	2·84	2·78	2·72	2·66	2·60	2·55	2·50	2·45	2·40	2·36	2·32	2·27	2·23	2·19	2·15	30
31	3·02	2·95	2·89	2·83	2·77	2·71	2·66	2·60	2·55	2·50	2·46	2·41	2·37	2·32	2·28	2·24	31
32	3·14	3·07	3·00	2·94	2·88	2·82	2·76	2·71	2·65	2·60	2·55	2·51	2·46	2·42	2·37	2·33	32
33	3·26	3·19	3·12	3·06	2·99	2·93	2·87	2·81	2·76	2·71	2·66	2·61	2·56	2·51	2·47	2·42	33
34	3·39	3·32	3·24	3·17	3·11	3·04	2·98	2·92	2·86	2·81	2·76	2·71	2·66	2·61	2·56	2·52	34
35	3·52	3·44	3·37	3·29	3·22	3·16	3·09	3·03	2·97	2·92	2·86	2·81	2·76	2·71	2·66	2·61	35
36	3·65	3·57	3·49	3·42	3·35	3·28	3·21	3·15	3·09	3·03	2·97	2·91	2·86	2·81	2·76	2·71	36
37	3·79	3·70	3·62	3·55	3·47	3·40	3·33	3·26	3·20	3·14	3·08	3·02	2·97	2·91	2·86	2·81	37
38	3·93	3·84	3·76	3·68	3·60	3·52	3·45	3·38	3·32	3·25	3·19	3·13	3·08	3·02	2·97	2·92	38
39	4·07	3·98	3·89	3·81	3·73	3·65	3·58	3·51	3·44	3·37	3·31	3·25	3·19	3·13	3·08	3·02	39
40	4·22	4·12	4·03	3·95	3·86	3·78	3·71	3·63	3·56	3·50	3·43	3·37	3·30	3·24	3·19	3·13	40
41	4·37	4·27	4·18	4·09	4·00	3·92	3·84	3·77	3·69	3·62	3·55	3·49	3·42	3·36	3·30	3·24	41
42	4·53	4·43	4·33	4·24	4·15	4·06	3·98	3·90	3·82	3·75	3·68	3·61	3·55	3·48	3·42	3·36	42
43	4·69	4·58	4·48	4·39	4·30	4·21	4·12	4·04	3·96	3·88	3·81	3·74	3·67	3·61	3·54	3·48	43
44	4·85	4·75	4·64	4·54	4·45	4·36	4·27	4·18	4·10	4·02	3·95	3·87	3·80	3·73	3·67	3·60	44
45	5·03	4·92	4·81	4·70	4·61	4·51	4·42	4·33	4·25	4·17	4·09	4·01	3·94	3·87	3·80	3·73	45
46	5·21	5·09	4·98	4·87	4·77	4·67	4·58	4·49	4·40	4·31	4·23	4·15	4·08	4·00	3·93	3·86	46
47	5·39	5·27	5·16	5·05	4·94	4·84	4·74	4·65	4·56	4·47	4·38	4·30	4·22	4·15	4·07	4·00	47
48	5·58	5·46	5·34	5·23	5·12	5·01	4·91	4·81	4·72	4·63	4·54	4·45	4·37	4·29	4·22	4·14	48
49	5·78	5·65	5·53	5·41	5·30	5·19	5·08	4·98	4·89	4·79	4·70	4·61	4·53	4·45	4·37	4·29	49
50	5·99	5·86	5·73	5·61	5·49	5·38	5·27	5·16	5·06	4·96	4·87	4·78	4·69	4·61	4·53	4·45	50
51	6·21	6·07	5·94	5·81	5·69	5·57	5·46	5·35	5·24	5·14	5·05	4·95	4·86	4·77	4·69	4·61	51
52	6·43	6·29	6·15	6·02	5·90	5·77	5·66	5·55	5·44	5·33	5·23	5·13	5·04	4·95	4·86	4·78	52
53	6·67	6·52	6·38	6·24	6·11	5·99	5·86	5·75	5·64	5·53	5·42	5·32	5·23	5·13	5·04	4·95	53
54	6·92	6·77	6·62	6·48	6·34	6·21	6·08	5·96	5·85	5·73	5·62	5·52	5·42	5·32	5·23	5·14	54
55	7·18	7·02	6·87	6·72	6·58	6·44	6·31	6·19	6·07	5·95	5·84	5·73	5·62	5·52	5·42	5·33	55
56	7·45	7·29	7·13	6·97	6·83	6·69	6·55	6·42	6·30	6·18	6·06	5·95	5·84	5·73	5·63	5·53	56
57	7·74	7·57	7·40	7·24	7·09	6·95	6·81	6·67	6·54	6·41	6·29	6·18	6·06	5·95	5·85	5·75	57
58	8·05	7·87	7·69	7·53	7·37	7·22	7·07	6·93	6·80	6·67	6·54	6·42	6·30	6·19	6·08	5·97	58
59	8·37	8·18	8·00	7·83	7·67	7·51	7·36	7·21	7·07	6·93	6·80	6·68	6·55	6·44	6·32	6·21	59
60	8·71	8·51	8·33	8·15	7·98	7·81	7·65	7·50	7·36	7·21	7·08	6·95	6·82	6·70	6·58	6·46	60
Lat.	168°45' 191°15'	168°30' 191°30'	168°15' 191°45'	168°00' 192°00'	167°45' 192°15'	167°30' 192°30'	167°15' 192°45'	167°00' 193°00'	166°45' 193°15'	166°30' 193°30'	166°15' 193°45'	166°00' 194°00'	165°45' 194°15'	165°30' 194°30'	165°15' 194°45'	165°00' 195°00'	Lat.

A HOUR ANGLE

TABLE B HOUR ANGLE

Dec.°	11°15' 348°45'	11°30' 348°30'	11°45' 348°15'	12°00' 348°00'	12°15' 347°45'	12°30' 347°30'	12°45' 347°15'	13°00' 347°00'	13°15' 346°45'	13°30' 346°30'	13°45' 346°15'	14°00' 346°00'	14°15' 345°45'	14°30' 345°30'	14°45' 345°15'	15°00' 345°00'	Dec.°
0	·00	·00	·00	·00	·00	·00	·00	·00	·00	·00	·00	·00	·00	·00	·00	·00	0
1	·09	·09	·09	·08	·08	·08	·08	·08	·08	·08	·07	·07	·07	·07	·07	·07	1
2	·18	·18	·17	·17	·17	·16	·16	·16	·15	·15	·15	·14	·14	·14	·14	·13	2
3	·27	·26	·26	·25	·25	·24	·24	·23	·23	·22	·22	·22	·21	·21	·21	·20	3
4	·36	·35	·34	·34	·33	·32	·32	·31	·31	·30	·29	·29	·28	·28	·28	·27	4
5	·45	·44	·43	·42	·41	·40	·40	·39	·38	·38	·37	·36	·36	·35	·34	·34	5
6	·54	·53	·52	·51	·50	·49	·48	·47	·46	·45	·44	·43	·43	·42	·41	·41	6
7	·63	·62	·60	·59	·58	·57	·56	·55	·54	·53	·52	·51	·50	·49	·48	·47	7
8	·72	·71	·69	·68	·66	·65	·64	·62	·61	·60	·59	·58	·57	·56	·55	·54	8
9	·81	·79	·78	·76	·75	·73	·72	·70	·69	·68	·67	·65	·64	·63	·62	·61	9
10	·90	·88	·87	·85	·83	·82	·80	·78	·77	·76	·74	·73	·72	·70	·69	·68	10
11	1·00	·98	·96	·93	·92	·90	·88	·86	·85	·83	·82	·80	·79	·78	·76	·75	11
12	1·09	1·07	1·04	1·02	1·00	·98	·96	·94	·93	·91	·89	·88	·86	·85	·84	·82	12
13	1·18	1·16	1·13	1·11	1·09	1·07	1·05	1·03	1·01	·99	·97	·95	·94	·92	·91	·89	13
14	1·28	1·25	1·22	1·20	1·18	1·15	1·13	1·11	1·09	1·07	1·05	1·03	1·01	1·00	·98	·96	14
15	1·37	1·34	1·32	1·29	1·26	1·24	1·21	1·19	1·17	1·15	1·13	1·11	1·09	1·07	1·05	1·04	15
16	1·47	1·44	1·41	1·38	1·35	1·32	1·30	1·27	1·25	1·23	1·21	1·19	1·16	1·15	1·13	1·11	16
17	1·57	1·53	1·50	1·47	1·44	1·41	1·39	1·36	1·33	1·31	1·29	1·26	1·24	1·22	1·20	1·18	17
18	1·67	1·63	1·60	1·56	1·53	1·50	1·47	1·44	1·42	1·39	1·37	1·34	1·32	1·30	1·28	1·26	18
19	1·76	1·73	1·69	1·66	1·62	1·59	1·56	1·53	1·50	1·47	1·45	1·42	1·40	1·38	1·35	1·33	19
20	1·87	1·83	1·79	1·75	1·72	1·68	1·65	1·62	1·59	1·56	1·53	1·50	1·48	1·45	1·43	1·41	20
21	1·97	1·93	1·89	1·85	1·81	1·77	1·74	1·71	1·67	1·64	1·62	1·59	1·56	1·53	1·51	1·48	21
22	2·07	2·03	1·98	1·94	1·90	1·87	1·83	1·80	1·76	1·73	1·70	1·67	1·64	1·61	1·59	1·56	22
23	2·18	2·13	2·08	2·04	2·00	1·96	1·92	1·89	1·85	1·82	1·79	1·75	1·72	1·70	1·67	1·64	23
24	2·28	2·23	2·19	2·14	2·10	2·06	2·02	1·98	1·94	1·91	1·87	1·84	1·81	1·78	1·75	1·72	24
25	2·39	2·34	2·29	2·24	2·20	2·15	2·11	2·07	2·03	2·00	1·96	1·93	1·89	1·86	1·83	1·80	25
26	2·50	2·45	2·40	2·35	2·30	2·25	2·21	2·17	2·13	2·09	2·05	2·02	1·98	1·95	1·92	1·88	26
27	2·61	2·56	2·50	2·45	2·40	2·35	2·31	2·27	2·22	2·18	2·14	2·11	2·07	2·04	2·00	1·97	27
28	2·73	2·67	2·61	2·56	2·51	2·46	2·41	2·36	2·32	2·28	2·24	2·20	2·16	2·12	2·09	2·05	28
29	2·84	2·78	2·72	2·67	2·61	2·56	2·51	2·46	2·42	2·37	2·33	2·29	2·25	2·21	2·18	2·14	29
30	2·96	2·90	2·84	2·78	2·72	2·67	2·62	2·57	2·52	2·47	2·43	2·39	2·35	2·31	2·27	2·23	30
31	3·08	3·01	2·95	2·89	2·83	2·78	2·72	2·67	2·62	2·57	2·53	2·48	2·44	2·40	2·36	2·32	31
32	3·20	3·13	3·07	3·01	2·95	2·89	2·83	2·78	2·73	2·68	2·63	2·58	2·54	2·50	2·45	2·41	32
33	3·33	3·26	3·19	3·12	3·06	3·00	2·94	2·89	2·83	2·78	2·73	2·68	2·64	2·59	2·55	2·51	33
34	3·46	3·38	3·31	3·24	3·18	3·12	3·06	3·00	2·94	2·89	2·84	2·79	2·74	2·69	2·65	2·61	34
35	3·59	3·51	3·44	3·37	3·30	3·24	3·17	3·11	3·06	3·00	2·95	2·89	2·84	2·80	2·75	2·71	35
36	3·72	3·64	3·57	3·49	3·42	3·36	3·29	3·23	3·17	3·11	3·06	3·00	2·95	2·90	2·85	2·81	36
37	3·86	3·78	3·70	3·62	3·55	3·48	3·41	3·35	3·29	3·23	3·17	3·11	3·06	3·01	2·96	2·91	37
38	4·00	3·92	3·84	3·76	3·68	3·61	3·54	3·47	3·41	3·35	3·29	3·23	3·17	3·12	3·07	3·02	38
39	4·15	4·06	3·98	3·90	3·82	3·74	3·67	3·60	3·53	3·47	3·41	3·35	3·29	3·23	3·18	3·13	39
40	4·30	4·21	4·12	4·04	3·95	3·88	3·80	3·73	3·66	3·59	3·53	3·47	3·41	3·35	3·30	3·24	40
41	4·46	4·36	4·27	4·18	4·10	4·02	3·94	3·86	3·79	3·72	3·66	3·59	3·53	3·47	3·41	3·36	41
42	4·62	4·52	4·42	4·33	4·24	4·16	4·08	4·00	3·93	3·86	3·79	3·72	3·66	3·60	3·54	3·48	42
43	4·78	4·68	4·58	4·49	4·39	4·31	4·23	4·15	4·07	3·99	3·92	3·85	3·79	3·72	3·66	3·60	43
44	4·95	4·84	4·74	4·64	4·55	4·46	4·38	4·29	4·21	4·14	4·06	3·99	3·92	3·86	3·79	3·73	44
45	5·13	5·02	4·91	4·81	4·71	4·62	4·53	4·45	4·36	4·28	4·21	4·13	4·06	3·99	3·93	3·86	45
46	5·31	5·19	5·09	4·98	4·88	4·78	4·69	4·60	4·52	4·44	4·36	4·28	4·21	4·14	4·07	4·00	46
47	5·50	5·38	5·27	5·16	5·05	4·96	4·86	4·77	4·68	4·59	4·51	4·43	4·36	4·28	4·21	4·14	47
48	5·69	5·57	5·45	5·34	5·23	5·13	5·03	4·94	4·85	4·76	4·67	4·59	4·51	4·44	4·36	4·29	48
49	5·90	5·77	5·65	5·53	5·42	5·31	5·21	5·11	5·02	4·93	4·84	4·76	4·67	4·59	4·52	4·44	49
50	6·11	5·98	5·85	5·73	5·62	5·51	5·40	5·30	5·20	5·11	5·01	4·93	4·84	4·76	4·68	4·60	50
51	6·33	6·19	6·06	5·94	5·82	5·71	5·60	5·49	5·39	5·29	5·20	5·10	5·02	4·93	4·85	4·77	51
52	6·56	6·42	6·29	6·16	6·03	5·91	5·80	5·69	5·58	5·48	5·39	5·29	5·20	5·11	5·03	4·95	52
53	6·80	6·66	6·52	6·38	6·25	6·13	6·01	5·90	5·79	5·68	5·58	5·49	5·39	5·30	5·21	5·13	53
54	7·06	6·90	6·76	6·62	6·49	6·36	6·24	6·12	6·01	5·90	5·79	5·69	5·59	5·50	5·41	5·32	54
55	7·32	7·16	7·01	6·87	6·73	6·60	6·47	6·35	6·23	6·12	6·01	5·90	5·80	5·70	5·61	5·52	55
56	7·60	7·44	7·28	7·13	6·99	6·85	6·72	6·59	6·47	6·35	6·24	6·13	6·02	5·92	5·82	5·73	56
57	7·89	7·72	7·56	7·41	7·26	7·12	6·98	6·85	6·72	6·60	6·48	6·37	6·26	6·15	6·05	5·95	57
58	8·20	8·03	7·86	7·70	7·54	7·39	7·25	7·11	6·98	6·86	6·73	6·62	6·50	6·39	6·29	6·18	58
59	8·53	8·35	8·17	8·00	7·84	7·69	7·54	7·40	7·26	7·13	7·00	6·88	6·76	6·65	6·54	6·43	59
60	8·88	8·69	8·51	8·33	8·16	8·00	7·85	7·70	7·56	7·42	7·29	7·16	7·04	6·92	6·82	6·69	60
Dec.	168°45' 191°15'	168°30' 191°30'	168°15' 191°45'	168°00' 192°00'	167°45' 192°15'	167°30' 192°30'	167°15' 192°45'	167°00' 193°00'	166°45' 193°15'	166°30' 193°30'	166°15' 193°45'	166°00' 194°00'	165°45' 194°15'	165°30' 194°30'	165°15' 194°45'	165°00' 195°00'	Dec.

HOUR ANGLE

B

TABLE A HOUR ANGLE

Left margin: A - Named opposite to Latitude, **except** when **Hour Angle** is between 90° and 270°

Right margin: A - Named opposite to Latitude, **except** when **Hour Angle** is between 90° and 270°

Lat. °	15° 00' 345° 00'	15° 30' 344° 30'	16° 00' 344° 00'	16° 30' 343° 30'	17° 00' 343° 00'	17° 30' 342° 30'	18° 00' 342° 00'	18° 30' 341° 30'	19° 00' 341° 00'	19° 30' 340° 30'	20° 00' 340° 00'	20° 30' 339° 30'	21° 00' 339° 00'	21° 30' 338° 30'	22° 00' 338° 00'	22° 30' 337° 30'	Lat. °
0	·00	·00	·00	·00	·00	·00	·00	·00	·00	·00	·00	·00	·00	·00	·00	·00	0
1	·07	·06	·06	·06	·06	·06	·05	·05	·05	·05	·05	·05	·05	·04	·04	·04	1
2	·13	·13	·12	·12	·11	·11	·11	·10	·10	·10	·10	·09	·09	·09	·09	·08	2
3	·20	·19	·18	·18	·17	·17	·16	·16	·15	·15	·14	·14	·14	·13	·13	·13	3
4	·26	·25	·24	·24	·23	·22	·22	·21	·20	·20	·19	·19	·18	·18	·17	·17	4
5	·33	·32	·31	·30	·29	·28	·27	·26	·25	·25	·24	·23	·23	·22	·22	·21	5
6	·39	·38	·37	·35	·34	·33	·32	·31	·31	·30	·29	·28	·27	·27	·26	·25	6
7	·46	·44	·43	·41	·40	·39	·38	·37	·36	·35	·34	·33	·32	·31	·30	·30	7
8	·52	·51	·49	·47	·46	·45	·43	·42	·41	·40	·39	·38	·37	·36	·35	·34	8
9	·59	·57	·55	·53	·52	·50	·49	·47	·46	·45	·44	·42	·41	·40	·39	·38	9
10	·66	·64	·61	·60	·58	·56	·54	·53	·51	·50	·48	·47	·46	·45	·44	·43	10
11	·73	·70	·68	·66	·64	·62	·60	·58	·56	·55	·53	·52	·51	·49	·48	·47	11
12	·79	·77	·74	·72	·70	·67	·65	·64	·62	·60	·58	·57	·55	·54	·53	·51	12
13	·86	·83	·81	·78	·76	·73	·71	·69	·67	·65	·63	·62	·60	·59	·57	·56	13
14	·93	·90	·87	·84	·82	·79	·77	·75	·72	·70	·69	·67	·65	·63	·62	·60	14
15	1·00	·97	·93	·90	·88	·85	·82	·80	·78	·76	·74	·72	·70	·68	·66	·65	15
16	1·07	1·03	1·00	·97	·94	·91	·88	·86	·83	·81	·79	·77	·75	·73	·71	·69	16
17	1·14	1·10	1·07	1·03	1·00	·97	·94	·91	·89	·86	·84	·82	·80	·78	·76	·74	17
18	1·21	1·17	1·13	1·10	1·06	1·03	1·00	·97	·94	·92	·89	·87	·85	·82	·80	·78	18
19	1·29	1·24	1·20	1·16	1·13	1·09	1·06	1·03	1·00	·97	·95	·92	·90	·87	·85	·83	19
20	1·36	1·31	1·27	1·23	1·19	1·15	1·12	1·09	1·06	1·03	1·00	·97	·95	·92	·90	·88	20
21	1·43	1·38	1·34	1·30	1·26	1·22	1·18	1·15	1·11	1·08	1·05	1·03	1·00	·97	·95	·93	21
22	1·51	1·46	1·41	1·36	1·32	1·28	1·24	1·21	1·17	1·14	1·11	1·08	1·05	1·03	1·00	·97	22
23	1·58	1·53	1·48	1·43	1·39	1·35	1·31	1·27	1·23	1·20	1·17	1·14	1·11	1·08	1·05	1·02	23
24	1·66	1·61	1·55	1·50	1·46	1·41	1·37	1·33	1·29	1·26	1·22	1·19	1·16	1·13	1·10	1·07	24
25	1·74	1·68	1·63	1·57	1·53	1·48	1·44	1·39	1·35	1·32	1·28	1·25	1·21	1·18	1·15	1·13	25
26	1·82	1·76	1·70	1·65	1·60	1·55	1·50	1·46	1·42	1·38	1·34	1·30	1·27	1·24	1·21	1·18	26
27	1·90	1·84	1·78	1·72	1·67	1·62	1·57	1·52	1·48	1·44	1·40	1·36	1·33	1·29	1·26	1·23	27
28	1·98	1·92	1·85	1·79	1·74	1·69	1·64	1·59	1·54	1·50	1·46	1·42	1·39	1·35	1·32	1·28	28
29	2·07	2·00	1·93	1·87	1·81	1·76	1·71	1·66	1·61	1·57	1·52	1·48	1·44	1·41	1·37	1·34	29
30	2·15	2·08	2·01	1·95	1·89	1·83	1·78	1·73	1·68	1·63	1·59	1·54	1·50	1·47	1·43	1·39	30
31	2·24	2·17	2·10	2·03	1·97	1·91	1·85	1·80	1·75	1·70	1·65	1·61	1·57	1·53	1·49	1·45	31
32	2·33	2·25	2·18	2·11	2·04	1·98	1·92	1·87	1·81	1·76	1·72	1·67	1·63	1·59	1·55	1·51	32
33	2·42	2·34	2·26	2·19	2·12	2·06	2·00	1·94	1·89	1·83	1·78	1·74	1·69	1·65	1·61	1·57	33
34	2·52	2·43	2·35	2·28	2·21	2·14	2·08	2·02	1·96	1·90	1·85	1·80	1·76	1·71	1·67	1·63	34
35	2·61	2·52	2·44	2·36	2·29	2·22	2·16	2·09	2·03	1·98	1·92	1·87	1·82	1·78	1·73	1·69	35
36	2·71	2·62	2·53	2·45	2·38	2·30	2·24	2·17	2·11	2·05	2·00	1·94	1·89	1·84	1·80	1·75	36
37	2·81	2·72	2·63	2·54	2·46	2·39	2·32	2·25	2·19	2·13	2·07	2·02	1·96	1·91	1·87	1·82	37
38	2·92	2·82	2·72	2·64	2·56	2·48	2·40	2·34	2·27	2·21	2·15	2·09	2·04	1·98	1·93	1·89	38
39	3·02	2·92	2·82	2·73	2·65	2·57	2·49	2·42	2·35	2·29	2·23	2·17	2·11	2·06	2·00	1·95	39
40	3·13	3·03	2·93	2·83	2·74	2·66	2·58	2·51	2·44	2·37	2·31	2·25	2·19	2·13	2·08	2·03	40
41	3·24	3·13	3·03	2·93	2·84	2·76	2·68	2·60	2·52	2·45	2·39	2·33	2·27	2·21	2·15	2·10	41
42	3·36	3·25	3·14	3·04	2·95	2·86	2·77	2·69	2·61	2·54	2·47	2·41	2·35	2·29	2·23	2·17	42
43	3·48	3·36	3·25	3·15	3·05	2·96	2·87	2·79	2·71	2·63	2·56	2·49	2·43	2·37	2·31	2·25	43
44	3·60	3·48	3·37	3·26	3·16	3·06	2·97	2·89	2·80	2·73	2·65	2·58	2·52	2·45	2·39	2·33	44
45	3·73	3·61	3·49	3·38	3·27	3·17	3·08	2·99	2·90	2·82	2·75	2·67	2·61	2·54	2·48	2·41	45
46	3·86	3·73	3·61	3·50	3·39	3·28	3·19	3·09	3·01	2·92	2·85	2·77	2·70	2·63	2·56	2·50	46
47	4·00	3·87	3·74	3·62	3·51	3·40	3·30	3·21	3·11	3·03	2·95	2·87	2·79	2·72	2·65	2·59	47
48	4·14	4·00	3·87	3·75	3·63	3·52	3·42	3·32	3·23	3·14	3·05	2·97	2·89	2·82	2·75	2·68	48
49	4·29	4·15	4·01	3·88	3·76	3·65	3·54	3·44	3·34	3·25	3·16	3·08	3·00	2·92	2·85	2·78	49
50	4·45	4·30	4·16	4·02	3·90	3·78	3·67	3·56	3·46	3·37	3·27	3·19	3·10	3·03	2·95	2·88	50
51	4·61	4·45	4·31	4·17	4·04	3·92	3·80	3·69	3·59	3·49	3·39	3·30	3·22	3·14	3·06	2·98	51
52	4·78	4·62	4·46	4·32	4·19	4·06	3·94	3·83	3·72	3·62	3·52	3·42	3·33	3·25	3·17	3·09	52
53	4·95	4·79	4·63	4·48	4·34	4·21	4·08	3·97	3·86	3·75	3·65	3·55	3·46	3·37	3·28	3·20	53
54	5·14	4·96	4·80	4·65	4·50	4·37	4·24	4·11	4·00	3·89	3·78	3·68	3·59	3·49	3·41	3·32	54
55	5·33	5·15	4·98	4·82	4·67	4·53	4·40	4·27	4·15	4·03	3·92	3·82	3·72	3·63	3·53	3·45	55
56	5·53	5·35	5·17	5·01	4·85	4·70	4·56	4·43	4·31	4·19	4·07	3·97	3·86	3·76	3·67	3·58	56
57	5·75	5·55	5·37	5·20	5·04	4·88	4·74	4·60	4·47	4·35	4·23	4·12	4·01	3·91	3·81	3·72	57
58	5·97	5·77	5·58	5·40	5·23	5·08	4·93	4·78	4·65	4·52	4·40	4·28	4·17	4·06	3·96	3·86	58
59	6·21	6·00	5·80	5·62	5·44	5·28	5·12	4·97	4·83	4·70	4·57	4·45	4·34	4·23	4·12	4·02	59
60	6·46	6·25	6·04	5·85	5·67	5·49	5·33	5·18	5·03	4·89	4·76	4·63	4·51	4·40	4·29	4·18	60
Lat.	165° 00' 195° 00'	164° 30' 195° 30'	164° 00' 196° 00'	163° 30' 196° 30'	163° 00' 197° 00'	162° 30' 197° 30'	162° 00' 198° 00'	161° 30' 198° 30'	161° 00' 199° 00'	160° 30' 199° 30'	160° 00' 200° 00'	159° 30' 200° 30'	159° 00' 201° 00'	158° 30' 201° 30'	158° 00' 202° 00'	157° 30' 202° 30'	Lat.

A

HOUR ANGLE

TABLE B HOUR ANGLE

B - Always named the **same** as Declination

Dec.°	15°00' 345°00'	15°30' 344°30'	16°00' 344°00'	16°30' 343°30'	17°00' 343°00'	17°30' 342°30'	18°00' 342°00'	18°30' 341°30'	19°00' 341°00'	19°30' 340°30'	20°00' 340°00'	20°30' 339°30'	21°00' 339°00'	21°30' 338°30'	22°00' 338°00'	22°30' 337°30'	Dec.°
0	·00	·00	·00	·00	·00	·00	·00	·00	·00	·00	·00	·00	·00	·00	·00	·00	0
1	·07	·07	·06	·06	·06	·06	·06	·06	·05	·05	·05	·05	·05	·05	·05	·05	1
2	·13	·13	·13	·12	·12	·12	·11	·11	·11	·10	·10	·10	·10	·10	·09	·09	2
3	·20	·20	·19	·19	·18	·17	·17	·17	·16	·16	·15	·15	·15	·14	·14	·14	3
4	·27	·26	·25	·25	·24	·23	·23	·22	·21	·21	·20	·20	·20	·19	·19	·18	4
5	·34	·33	·32	·31	·30	·29	·28	·28	·27	·26	·26	·25	·24	·24	·23	·23	5
6	·41	·39	·38	·37	·36	·35	·34	·33	·32	·31	·31	·30	·29	·29	·28	·27	6
7	·47	·46	·45	·43	·42	·41	·40	·39	·38	·37	·36	·35	·34	·34	·33	·32	7
8	·54	·53	·51	·49	·48	·47	·45	·44	·43	·42	·41	·40	·39	·38	·38	·37	8
9	·61	·59	·57	·56	·54	·53	·51	·50	·49	·47	·46	·45	·44	·43	·42	·41	9
10	·68	·66	·64	·62	·60	·59	·57	·56	·54	·53	·52	·50	·49	·48	·47	·46	10
11	·75	·73	·71	·68	·66	·65	·63	·61	·60	·58	·57	·55	·54	·53	·52	·51	11
12	·82	·80	·77	·75	·73	·71	·69	·67	·65	·64	·62	·61	·59	·58	·57	·56	12
13	·89	·86	·84	·81	·79	·77	·75	·73	·71	·69	·68	·66	·64	·63	·62	·60	13
14	·96	·93	·90	·88	·85	·83	·81	·79	·77	·75	·73	·71	·70	·68	·67	·65	14
15	1·04	1·00	·97	·94	·92	·89	·87	·84	·82	·80	·78	·77	·75	·73	·72	·70	15
16	1·11	1·07	1·04	1·01	·98	·95	·93	·90	·88	·86	·84	·82	·80	·78	·77	·75	16
17	1·18	1·14	1·11	1·08	1·05	1·02	·99	·96	·94	·92	·89	·87	·85	·83	·82	·80	17
18	1·26	1·22	1·18	1·14	1·11	1·08	1·05	1·02	1·00	·97	·95	·93	·91	·89	·87	·85	18
19	1·33	1·29	1·25	1·21	1·18	1·15	1·11	1·09	1·06	1·03	1·01	·98	·96	·94	·92	·90	19
20	1·41	1·36	1·32	1·28	1·24	1·21	1·18	1·15	1·12	1·09	1·06	1·04	1·02	·99	·97	·95	20
21	1·48	1·44	1·39	1·35	1·31	1·28	1·24	1·21	1·18	1·15	1·12	1·10	1·07	1·05	1·02	1·00	21
22	1·56	1·51	1·47	1·42	1·38	1·34	1·31	1·27	1·24	1·21	1·18	1·15	1·13	1·10	1·08	1·06	22
23	1·64	1·59	1·54	1·49	1·45	1·41	1·37	1·34	1·30	1·27	1·24	1·21	1·18	1·16	1·13	1·11	23
24	1·72	1·67	1·62	1·57	1·52	1·48	1·44	1·40	1·37	1·33	1·30	1·27	1·24	1·21	1·19	1·16	24
25	1·80	1·74	1·69	1·64	1·59	1·55	1·51	1·47	1·43	1·40	1·36	1·33	1·30	1·27	1·24	1·22	25
26	1·88	1·83	1·77	1·72	1·67	1·62	1·58	1·54	1·50	1·46	1·43	1·39	1·36	1·33	1·30	1·27	26
27	1·97	1·91	1·85	1·79	1·74	1·69	1·65	1·61	1·57	1·53	1·49	1·45	1·42	1·39	1·36	1·33	27
28	2·05	1·99	1·93	1·87	1·82	1·77	1·72	1·68	1·63	1·59	1·55	1·52	1·48	1·45	1·42	1·39	28
29	2·14	2·07	2·01	1·95	1·90	1·84	1·79	1·75	1·70	1·66	1·62	1·58	1·55	1·51	1·48	1·45	29
30	2·23	2·16	2·09	2·03	1·97	1·92	1·87	1·82	1·77	1·73	1·69	1·65	1·61	1·58	1·54	1·51	30
31	2·32	2·25	2·18	2·12	2·06	2·00	1·94	1·89	1·85	1·80	1·76	1·72	1·68	1·64	1·60	1·57	31
32	2·41	2·34	2·27	2·20	2·14	2·08	2·02	1·97	1·92	1·87	1·83	1·78	1·74	1·70	1·67	1·63	32
33	2·51	2·43	2·36	2·29	2·22	2·16	2·10	2·05	1·99	1·95	1·90	1·85	1·81	1·77	1·73	1·70	33
34	2·61	2·52	2·45	2·37	2·31	2·24	2·18	2·13	2·07	2·02	1·97	1·93	1·88	1·84	1·80	1·76	34
35	2·71	2·62	2·54	2·46	2·39	2·33	2·27	2·21	2·15	2·10	2·05	2·00	1·95	1·91	1·87	1·83	35
36	2·81	2·72	2·64	2·56	2·48	2·42	2·35	2·29	2·23	2·18	2·12	2·07	2·03	1·98	1·94	1·90	36
37	2·91	2·82	2·73	2·65	2·58	2·51	2·44	2·37	2·31	2·26	2·20	2·15	2·10	2·06	2·01	1·97	37
38	3·02	2·92	2·83	2·75	2·67	2·60	2·53	2·46	2·40	2·34	2·28	2·23	2·18	2·13	2·09	2·04	38
39	3·13	3·03	2·94	2·85	2·77	2·69	2·62	2·55	2·49	2·43	2·37	2·31	2·26	2·21	2·16	2·12	39
40	3·24	3·14	3·04	2·95	2·87	2·79	2·72	2·64	2·58	2·51	2·45	2·40	2·34	2·29	2·24	2·19	40
41	3·36	3·25	3·15	3·06	2·97	2·89	2·81	2·74	2·67	2·60	2·54	2·48	2·43	2·37	2·32	2·27	41
42	3·48	3·37	3·27	3·17	3·08	2·99	2·91	2·84	2·77	2·70	2·63	2·57	2·51	2·46	2·40	2·35	42
43	3·60	3·49	3·38	3·28	3·19	3·10	3·02	2·94	2·86	2·79	2·73	2·66	2·60	2·54	2·49	2·44	43
44	3·73	3·61	3·50	3·40	3·30	3·21	3·13	3·04	2·97	2·90	2·83	2·76	2·69	2·63	2·58	2·52	44
45	3·86	3·74	3·63	3·52	3·42	3·33	3·24	3·15	3·07	3·00	2·92	2·86	2·79	2·73	2·67	2·61	45
46	4·00	3·87	3·76	3·65	3·54	3·44	3·35	3·26	3·18	3·10	3·03	2·96	2·89	2·83	2·76	2·71	46
47	4·14	4·01	3·89	3·78	3·67	3·57	3·47	3·38	3·29	3·21	3·14	3·06	2·99	2·93	2·86	2·80	47
48	4·29	4·16	4·03	3·91	3·80	3·69	3·59	3·50	3·41	3·33	3·25	3·17	3·10	3·03	2·96	2·90	48
49	4·44	4·30	4·17	4·05	3·93	3·83	3·72	3·63	3·53	3·45	3·36	3·28	3·21	3·14	3·07	3·01	49
50	4·60	4·46	4·32	4·20	4·08	3·96	3·86	3·76	3·66	3·57	3·48	3·40	3·33	3·25	3·18	3·11	50
51	4·77	4·62	4·48	4·35	4·22	4·11	4·00	3·89	3·79	3·70	3·61	3·53	3·45	3·37	3·30	3·23	51
52	4·95	4·79	4·64	4·51	4·38	4·26	4·14	4·03	3·93	3·83	3·74	3·65	3·57	3·49	3·42	3·35	52
53	5·13	4·97	4·81	4·67	4·54	4·42	4·29	4·18	4·08	3·98	3·88	3·79	3·70	3·62	3·54	3·47	53
54	5·32	5·15	4·99	4·85	4·71	4·58	4·45	4·34	4·23	4·12	4·02	3·93	3·84	3·76	3·67	3·60	54
55	5·52	5·34	5·18	5·03	4·88	4·75	4·62	4·50	4·39	4·28	4·18	4·08	3·99	3·90	3·81	3·73	55
56	5·73	5·55	5·38	5·22	5·07	4·93	4·80	4·67	4·55	4·44	4·34	4·23	4·14	4·05	3·96	3·87	56
57	5·95	5·76	5·59	5·42	5·27	5·12	4·98	4·85	4·73	4·61	4·50	4·40	4·30	4·20	4·11	4·02	57
58	6·18	5·99	5·81	5·63	5·47	5·32	5·18	5·04	4·92	4·79	4·68	4·57	4·47	4·37	4·27	4·18	58
59	6·43	6·23	6·04	5·86	5·69	5·54	5·39	5·25	5·11	4·99	4·87	4·75	4·64	4·54	4·44	4·35	59
60	6·69	6·48	6·28	6·10	5·92	5·76	5·61	5·46	5·32	5·19	5·06	4·95	4·83	4·73	4·62	4·53	60
Dec.	165°00' 195°00'	164°30' 195°30'	164°00' 196°00'	163°30' 196°30'	163°00' 197°00'	162°30' 197°30'	162°00' 198°00'	161°30' 198°30'	161°00' 199°00'	160°30' 199°30'	160°00' 200°00'	159°30' 200°30'	159°00' 201°00'	158°30' 201°30'	158°00' 202°00'	157°30' 202°30'	Dec.

B - Always named the **same** as Declination

HOUR ANGLE

B

TABLE A HOUR ANGLE

Lat.°	22°30′ 337°30′	23°00′ 337°00′	23°30′ 336°30′	24°00′ 336°00′	24°30′ 335°30′	25°00′ 335°00′	25°30′ 334°30′	26°00′ 334°00′	26°30′ 333°30′	27°00′ 333°00′	27°30′ 332°30′	28°00′ 332°00′	28°30′ 331°30′	29°00′ 331°00′	29°30′ 330°30′	30°00′ 330°00′	Lat.°
0	·00	·00	·00	·00	·00	·00	·00	·00	·00	·00	·00	·00	·00	·00	·00	·00	0
1	·04	·04	·04	·04	·04	·04	·04	·04	·04	·03	·03	·03	·03	·03	·03	·03	1
2	·08	·08	·08	·08	·08	·08	·07	·07	·07	·07	·07	·07	·06	·06	·06	·06	2
3	·13	·12	·12	·12	·12	·11	·11	·11	·11	·10	·10	·10	·10	·09	·09	·09	3
4	·17	·16	·16	·16	·15	·15	·15	·14	·14	·14	·13	·13	·13	·13	·12	·12	4
5	·21	·21	·20	·20	·19	·19	·18	·18	·18	·17	·17	·16	·16	·16	·16	·15	5
6	·25	·25	·24	·24	·23	·23	·22	·22	·21	·21	·20	·20	·19	·19	·19	·18	6
7	·30	·29	·28	·28	·27	·26	·26	·25	·25	·24	·24	·23	·23	·22	·22	·21	7
8	·34	·33	·32	·32	·31	·30	·29	·29	·28	·28	·27	·26	·26	·25	·25	·24	8
9	·38	·37	·36	·36	·35	·34	·33	·32	·32	·31	·30	·30	·29	·29	·28	·27	9
10	·43	·42	·41	·40	·39	·38	·37	·36	·35	·35	·34	·33	·33	·32	·31	·31	10
11	·47	·46	·45	·44	·43	·42	·41	·40	·39	·38	·37	·37	·36	·35	·34	·34	11
12	·51	·50	·49	·48	·47	·46	·45	·44	·43	·42	·41	·40	·39	·38	·38	·37	12
13	·56	·54	·53	·52	·51	·50	·48	·47	·46	·45	·44	·43	·43	·42	·41	·40	13
14	·60	·59	·57	·56	·55	·53	·52	·51	·50	·49	·48	·47	·46	·45	·44	·43	14
15	·65	·63	·62	·60	·59	·57	·56	·55	·54	·53	·51	·50	·49	·48	·47	·46	15
16	·69	·68	·66	·64	·63	·61	·60	·59	·58	·56	·55	·54	·53	·52	·51	·50	16
17	·74	·72	·70	·69	·67	·66	·64	·63	·61	·60	·59	·58	·56	·55	·54	·53	17
18	·78	·77	·75	·73	·71	·70	·68	·67	·65	·64	·62	·61	·60	·59	·57	·56	18
19	·83	·81	·79	·77	·76	·74	·72	·71	·69	·68	·66	·65	·63	·62	·61	·60	19
20	·88	·86	·84	·82	·80	·78	·76	·75	·73	·71	·70	·68	·67	·66	·64	·63	20
21	·93	·90	·88	·86	·84	·82	·81	·79	·77	·75	·74	·72	·71	·69	·68	·66	21
22	·97	·95	·93	·91	·89	·87	·85	·83	·81	·79	·78	·76	·74	·73	·71	·70	22
23	1·02	1·00	·98	·95	·93	·91	·89	·87	·85	·83	·82	·80	·78	·77	·75	·74	23
24	1·07	1·05	1·02	1·00	·98	·95	·93	·91	·89	·87	·85	·84	·82	·80	·79	·77	24
25	1·13	1·10	1·07	1·05	1·02	1·00	·98	·96	·94	·92	·90	·88	·86	·84	·82	·81	25
26	1·18	1·15	1·12	1·10	1·07	1·05	1·02	1·00	·98	·96	·94	·92	·90	·88	·86	·84	26
27	1·23	1·20	1·17	1·14	1·12	1·09	1·07	1·04	1·02	1·00	·98	·96	·94	·92	·90	·88	27
28	1·28	1·25	1·22	1·19	1·17	1·14	1·11	1·09	1·07	1·04	1·02	1·00	·98	·96	·94	·92	28
29	1·34	1·31	1·27	1·25	1·22	1·19	1·16	1·14	1·11	1·09	1·06	1·04	1·02	1·00	·98	·96	29
30	1·39	1·36	1·33	1·30	1·27	1·24	1·21	1·18	1·16	1·13	1·11	1·09	1·06	1·04	1·02	1·00	30
31	1·45	1·42	1·38	1·35	1·32	1·29	1·26	1·23	1·21	1·18	1·15	1·13	1·11	1·08	1·06	1·04	31
32	1·51	1·47	1·44	1·40	1·37	1·34	1·31	1·28	1·25	1·23	1·20	1·18	1·15	1·13	1·10	1·08	32
33	1·57	1·53	1·49	1·46	1·42	1·39	1·36	1·33	1·30	1·27	1·25	1·22	1·20	1·17	1·15	1·12	33
34	1·63	1·59	1·55	1·51	1·48	1·45	1·41	1·38	1·35	1·32	1·30	1·27	1·24	1·22	1·19	1·17	34
35	1·69	1·65	1·61	1·57	1·54	1·50	1·47	1·44	1·40	1·37	1·35	1·32	1·29	1·26	1·24	1·21	35
36	1·75	1·71	1·67	1·63	1·59	1·56	1·52	1·49	1·46	1·43	1·40	1·37	1·34	1·31	1·28	1·26	36
37	1·82	1·78	1·73	1·69	1·65	1·62	1·58	1·55	1·51	1·48	1·45	1·42	1·39	1·36	1·33	1·31	37
38	1·89	1·84	1·80	1·75	1·71	1·68	1·64	1·60	1·57	1·53	1·50	1·47	1·44	1·41	1·38	1·35	38
39	1·95	1·91	1·86	1·82	1·78	1·74	1·70	1·66	1·62	1·59	1·56	1·52	1·49	1·46	1·43	1·40	39
40	2·03	1·98	1·93	1·88	1·84	1·80	1·76	1·72	1·68	1·65	1·61	1·58	1·55	1·51	1·48	1·45	40
41	2·10	2·05	2·00	1·95	1·91	1·86	1·82	1·78	1·74	1·71	1·67	1·63	1·60	1·57	1·54	1·51	41
42	2·17	2·12	2·07	2·02	1·98	1·93	1·89	1·85	1·81	1·77	1·73	1·69	1·66	1·62	1·59	1·56	42
43	2·25	2·20	2·14	2·09	2·05	2·00	1·96	1·91	1·87	1·83	1·79	1·75	1·72	1·68	1·65	1·62	43
44	2·33	2·28	2·22	2·17	2·12	2·07	2·02	1·98	1·94	1·90	1·86	1·82	1·78	1·74	1·71	1·67	44
45	2·41	2·36	2·30	2·25	2·19	2·14	2·10	2·05	2·01	1·96	1·92	1·88	1·84	1·80	1·77	1·73	45
46	2·50	2·44	2·38	2·33	2·27	2·22	2·17	2·12	2·08	2·03	1·99	1·95	1·91	1·87	1·83	1·79	46
47	2·59	2·53	2·47	2·41	2·35	2·30	2·25	2·20	2·15	2·10	2·06	2·02	1·98	1·93	1·90	1·86	47
48	2·68	2·62	2·55	2·49	2·44	2·38	2·33	2·28	2·23	2·18	2·13	2·09	2·05	2·00	1·96	1·92	48
49	2·78	2·71	2·65	2·58	2·52	2·47	2·41	2·36	2·31	2·26	2·21	2·16	2·12	2·08	2·03	1·99	49
50	2·88	2·81	2·74	2·68	2·62	2·56	2·50	2·44	2·39	2·34	2·29	2·24	2·19	2·15	2·11	2·06	50
51	2·98	2·91	2·84	2·77	2·71	2·65	2·59	2·53	2·48	2·42	2·37	2·32	2·27	2·23	2·18	2·14	51
52	3·09	3·02	2·94	2·87	2·81	2·74	2·68	2·62	2·57	2·51	2·46	2·41	2·36	2·31	2·26	2·22	52
53	3·20	3·13	3·05	2·98	2·91	2·85	2·78	2·72	2·66	2·60	2·55	2·50	2·44	2·39	2·35	2·30	53
54	3·32	3·24	3·17	3·09	3·02	2·95	2·88	2·82	2·76	2·70	2·64	2·59	2·53	2·48	2·43	2·38	54
55	3·45	3·36	3·28	3·21	3·13	3·06	2·99	2·93	2·86	2·80	2·74	2·69	2·63	2·58	2·52	2·47	55
56	3·58	3·49	3·41	3·33	3·25	3·18	3·11	3·04	2·97	2·91	2·85	2·79	2·73	2·67	2·62	2·57	56
57	3·72	3·63	3·54	3·46	3·38	3·30	3·23	3·16	3·09	3·02	2·96	2·90	2·84	2·78	2·72	2·67	57
58	3·86	3·77	3·68	3·59	3·51	3·43	3·36	3·28	3·21	3·14	3·07	3·01	2·95	2·89	2·83	2·77	58
59	4·02	3·92	3·83	3·74	3·65	3·57	3·49	3·41	3·34	3·27	3·20	3·13	3·07	3·00	2·94	2·88	59
60	4·18	4·08	3·98	3·89	3·80	3·71	3·63	3·55	3·47	3·40	3·33	3·26	3·19	3·12	3·06	3·00	60
Lat.	157°30′ 202°30′	157°00′ 203°00′	156°30′ 203°30′	156°00′ 204°00′	155°30′ 204°30′	155°00′ 205°00′	154°30′ 205°30′	154°00′ 206°00′	153°30′ 206°30′	153°00′ 207°00′	152°30′ 207°30′	152°00′ 208°00′	151°30′ 208°30′	151°00′ 209°00′	150°30′ 209°30′	150°00′ 210°00′	Lat.

HOUR ANGLE

A - Named opposite to Latitude, **except** when **Hour Angle** is between 90° and 270°

A - Named opposite to Latitude, **except** when **Hour Angle** is between 90° and 270°

A

TABLE B HOUR ANGLE

Left margin: B - Always named the **same** as Declination

Right margin: B - Always named the **same** as Declination

Dec.°	22°30' / 337°30'	23°00' / 337°00'	23°30' / 336°30'	24°00' / 336°00'	24°30' / 335°30'	25°00' / 335°00'	25°30' / 334°30'	26°00' / 334°00'	26°30' / 333°30'	27°00' / 333°00'	27°30' / 332°30'	28°00' / 332°00'	28°30' / 331°30'	29°00' / 331°00'	29°30' / 330°30'	30°00' / 330°00'	Dec.°
0	·00	·00	·00	·00	·00	·00	·00	·00	·00	·00	·00	·00	·00	·00	·00	·00	0
1	·05	·04	·04	·04	·04	·04	·04	·04	·04	·04	·04	·04	·04	·04	·04	·03	1
2	·09	·09	·09	·09	·08	·08	·08	·08	·08	·08	·08	·07	·07	·07	·07	·07	2
3	·14	·13	·13	·13	·13	·12	·12	·12	·12	·12	·11	·11	·11	·11	·11	·10	3
4	·18	·18	·18	·17	·17	·17	·16	·16	·16	·15	·15	·15	·15	·14	·14	·14	4
5	·23	·22	·22	·22	·21	·21	·20	·20	·20	·19	·19	·19	·18	·18	·18	·17	5
6	·27	·27	·26	·26	·25	·25	·24	·24	·24	·23	·23	·22	·22	·22	·21	·21	6
7	·32	·31	·31	·30	·30	·29	·29	·28	·28	·27	·27	·26	·26	·25	·25	·25	7
8	·37	·36	·35	·35	·34	·33	·33	·32	·31	·31	·30	·30	·29	·29	·29	·28	8
9	·41	·41	·40	·39	·38	·37	·37	·36	·35	·35	·34	·34	·33	·33	·32	·32	9
10	·46	·45	·44	·43	·43	·42	·41	·40	·40	·39	·38	·38	·37	·36	·36	·35	10
11	·51	·50	·49	·48	·47	·46	·45	·44	·44	·43	·42	·41	·41	·40	·39	·39	11
12	·56	·54	·53	·52	·51	·50	·49	·48	·48	·47	·46	·45	·45	·44	·43	·43	12
13	·60	·59	·58	·57	·56	·55	·54	·53	·52	·51	·50	·49	·48	·48	·47	·46	13
14	·65	64	·63	·61	6C	·59	·58	·57	·56	·55	·54	·53	·52	·51	·51	·50	14
15	·70	·69	·67	·66	·65	·63	·62	·61	·60	·59	·58	·57	·56	·55	·54	·54	15
16	·75	·73	·72	·71	·69	·68	·67	·65	·64	·63	·62	·61	·60	·59	·58	·57	16
17	·80	·78	·77	·75	·74	·72	·71	·70	·69	·67	·66	·65	·64	·63	·62	·61	17
18	·85	·83	·81	·80	·78	·77	·75	·74	·73	·72	·70	·69	·68	·67	·66	·65	18
19	·90	·88	·86	·85	·83	·81	·80	·79	·77	·76	·75	·73	·72	·71	·70	·69	19
20	·95	·93	·91	·89	·88	·86	·85	·83	·82	·80	·79	·78	·76	·75	·74	·73	20
21	1·00	·98	·96	·94	·93	·91	·89	·88	·86	·85	·83	·82	·80	·79	·78	·77	21
22	1·06	1·03	1·01	·99	·97	·96	·94	·92	·91	·89	·87	·86	·85	·83	·82	·81	22
23	1·11	1·09	1·06	1·04	1·02	1·00	·99	·97	·95	·93	·92	·90	·89	·88	·86	·85	23
24	1·16	1·14	1·12	1·09	1·07	1·05	1·03	1·02	1·00	·98	·96	·95	·93	·92	·90	·89	24
25	1·22	1·19	1·17	1·15	1·12	1·10	1·08	1·06	1·05	1·03	1·01	·99	·98	·96	·95	·93	25
26	1·27	1·25	1·22	1·20	1·18	1·15	1·13	1·11	1·09	1·07	1·06	1·04	1·02	1·01	·99	·98	26
27	1·33	1·30	1·28	1·25	1·23	1·21	1·18	1·16	1·14	1·12	1·10	1·09	1·07	1·05	1·03	1·02	27
28	1·39	1·36	1·33	1·31	1·28	1·26	1·24	1·21	1·19	1·17	1·15	1·13	1·11	1·10	1·08	1·06	28
29	1·45	1·42	1·39	1·36	1·34	1·31	1·29	1·26	1·24	1·22	1·20	1·18	1·16	1·14	1·13	1·11	29
30	1·51	1·48	1·45	1·42	1·39	1·37	1·34	1·32	1·29	1·27	1·25	1·23	1·21	1·19	1·17	1·15	30
31	1·57	1·54	1·51	1·48	1·45	1·42	1·40	1·37	1·35	1·32	1·30	1·28	1·26	1·24	1·22	1·20	31
32	1·63	1·60	1·57	1·54	1·51	1·48	1·45	1·43	1·40	1·38	1·35	1·33	1·31	1·29	1·27	1·25	32
33	1·70	1·66	1·63	1·60	1·57	1·54	1·51	1·48	1·46	1·43	1·41	1·38	1·36	1·34	1·32	1·30	33
34	1·76	1·73	1·69	1·66	1·63	1·60	1·57	1·54	1·51	1·49	1·46	1·44	1·41	1·39	1·37	1·35	34
35	1·83	1·79	1·76	1·72	1·69	1·66	1·63	1·60	1·57	1·54	1·52	1·49	1·47	1·44	1·42	1·40	35
36	1·90	1·86	1·82	1·79	1·75	1·72	1·69	1·66	1·63	1·60	1·57	1·55	1·52	1·50	1·48	1·45	36
37	1·97	1·93	1·89	1·85	1·82	1·78	1·75	1·72	1·69	1·66	1·63	1·61	1·58	1·55	1·53	1·51	37
38	2·04	2·00	1·96	1·92	1·88	1·85	1·81	1·78	1·75	1·72	1·69	1·66	1·64	1·61	1·59	1·56	38
39	2·12	2·07	2·03	1·99	1·95	1·92	1·88	1·85	1·81	1·78	1·75	1·72	1·70	1·67	1·64	1·62	39
40	2·19	2·15	2·10	2·06	2·02	1·99	1·95	1·91	1·88	1·85	1·82	1·79	1·76	1·73	1·70	1·68	40
41	2·27	2·22	2·18	2·14	2·10	2·06	2·02	1·98	1·95	1·91	1·88	1·85	1·82	1·79	1·77	1·74	41
42	2·35	2·30	2·26	2·21	2·17	2·13	2·09	2·05	2·02	1·98	1·95	1·92	1·89	1·86	1·83	1·80	42
43	2·44	2·39	2·34	2·29	2·25	2·21	2·17	2·13	2·09	2·05	2·02	1·99	1·95	1·92	1·89	1·87	43
44	2·52	2·47	2·42	2·37	2·33	2·29	2·24	2·20	2·16	2·13	2·09	2·06	2·02	1·99	1·96	1·93	44
45	2·61	2·56	2·51	2·46	2·41	2·37	2·32	2·28	2·24	2·20	2·17	2·13	2·10	2·06	2·03	2·00	45
46	2·71	2·65	2·60	2·55	2·50	2·45	2·41	2·36	2·32	2·28	2·24	2·21	2·17	2·14	2·10	2·07	46
47	2·80	2·74	2·69	2·64	2·59	2·54	2·49	2·45	2·40	2·36	2·32	2·28	2·25	2·21	2·18	2·14	47
48	2·90	2·84	2·79	2·73	2·68	2·63	2·58	2·53	2·49	2·45	2·41	2·37	2·33	2·29	2·26	2·22	48
49	3·01	2·94	2·88	2·83	2·77	2·72	2·67	2·62	2·58	2·53	2·49	2·45	2·41	2·37	2·34	2·30	49
50	3·11	3·05	2·99	2·93	2·87	2·82	2·77	2·72	2·67	2·63	2·58	2·54	2·50	2·46	2·42	2·38	50
51	3·23	3·16	3·10	3·04	2·98	2·92	2·87	2·82	2·77	2·72	2·67	2·63	2·59	2·55	2·51	2·47	51
52	3·35	3·28	3·21	3·15	3·09	3·03	2·97	2·92	2·87	2·82	2·77	2·73	2·68	2·64	2·60	2·56	52
53	3·47	3·40	3·33	3·26	3·20	3·14	3·08	3·03	2·97	2·92	2·87	2·83	2·78	2·74	2·69	2·65	53
54	3·60	3·52	3·45	3·38	3·32	3·26	3·20	3·14	3·08	3·03	2·98	2·93	2·88	2·84	2·80	2·75	54
55	3·73	3·66	3·58	3·51	3·44	3·38	3·32	3·26	3·20	3·15	3·09	3·04	2·99	2·95	2·90	2·86	55
56	3·87	3·79	3·72	3·65	3·58	3·51	3·44	3·38	3·32	3·27	3·21	3·16	3·11	3·06	3·01	2·97	56
57	4·02	3·94	3·86	3·79	3·71	3·64	3·58	3·51	3·45	3·39	3·34	3·28	3·23	3·18	3·13	3·08	57
58	4·18	4·10	4·01	3·93	3·86	3·79	3·72	3·65	3·59	3·53	3·47	3·41	3·35	3·30	3·25	3·20	58
59	4·35	4·26	4·17	4·09	4·01	3·94	3·87	3·80	3·73	3·67	3·60	3·55	3·49	3·43	3·38	3·33	59
60	4·53	4·43	4·34	4·26	4·18	4·10	4·02	3·95	3·88	3·82	3·75	3·69	3·63	3·57	3·52	3·46	60
Dec.	157°30' / 202°30'	157°00' / 203°00'	156°30' / 203°30'	156°00' / 204°00'	155°30' / 204°30'	155°00' / 205°00'	154°30' / 205°30'	154°00' / 206°00'	153°30' / 206°30'	153°00' / 207°00'	152°30' / 207°30'	152°00' / 208°00'	151°30' / 208°30'	151°00' / 209°00'	150°30' / 209°30'	150°00' / 210°00'	Dec.

HOUR ANGLE

B

TABLE A HOUR ANGLE

Lat. °	30° 330°	31° 329°	32° 328°	33° 327°	34° 326°	35° 325°	36° 324°	37° 323°	38° 322°	39° 321°	40° 320°	41° 319°	42° 318°	43° 317°	44° 316°	45° 315°	Lat. °
0	·00	·00	·00	·00	·00	·00	·00	·00	·00	·00	·00	·00	·00	·00	·00	·00	0
1	·03	·03	·03	·03	·03	·02	·02	·02	·02	·02	·02	·02	·02	·02	·02	·02	1
2	·06	·06	·06	·05	·05	·05	·05	·05	·04	·04	·04	·04	·04	·04	·04	·04	2
3	·09	·09	·08	·08	·08	·07	·07	·07	·07	·06	·06	·06	·06	·06	·05	·05	3
4	·12	·12	·11	·11	·10	·10	·10	·09	·09	·09	·08	·08	·08	·07	·07	·07	4
5	·15	·15	·14	·13	·13	·12	·12	·12	·11	·11	·10	·10	·10	·09	·09	·09	5
6	·18	·17	·17	·16	·16	·15	·14	·14	·13	·13	·13	·12	·12	·11	·11	·11	6
7	·21	·20	·20	·19	·18	·18	·17	·16	·16	·15	·15	·14	·14	·13	·13	·12	7
8	·24	·23	·22	·22	·21	·20	·19	·19	·18	·17	·17	·16	·16	·15	·15	·14	8
9	·27	·26	·25	·24	·23	·23	·22	·21	·20	·20	·19	·18	·18	·17	·16	·16	9
10	·31	·29	·28	·27	·26	·25	·24	·23	·23	·22	·21	·20	·20	·19	·18	·18	10
11	·34	·32	·31	·30	·29	·28	·27	·26	·25	·24	·23	·22	·22	·21	·20	·19	11
12	·37	·35	·34	·33	·32	·30	·29	·28	·27	·26	·25	·24	·24	·23	·22	·21	12
13	·40	·38	·37	·36	·34	·33	·32	·31	·30	·29	·28	·27	·26	·25	·24	·23	13
14	·43	·41	·40	·38	·37	·36	·34	·33	·32	·31	·30	·29	·27	·27	·26	·25	14
15	·46	·45	·43	·41	·40	·38	·37	·36	·34	·33	·32	·31	·30	·29	·28	·27	15
16	·50	·48	·46	·44	·43	·41	·39	·38	·37	·35	·34	·33	·32	·31	·30	·29	16
17	·53	·51	·49	·47	·45	·44	·42	·41	·39	·38	·36	·35	·34	·33	·32	·31	17
18	·56	·54	·52	·50	·48	·46	·45	·43	·42	·40	·39	·37	·36	·35	·34	·32	18
19	·60	·57	·55	·53	·51	·49	·47	·46	·44	·43	·41	·40	·38	·37	·36	·34	19
20	·63	·61	·58	·56	·54	·52	·50	·48	·47	·45	·43	·42	·40	·39	·38	·36	20
21	·66	·64	·61	·59	·57	·55	·53	·51	·49	·47	·46	·44	·43	·41	·40	·38	21
22	·70	·67	·65	·62	·60	·58	·56	·54	·52	·50	·48	·46	·45	·43	·42	·40	22
23	·74	·71	·68	·65	·63	·61	·58	·56	·54	·52	·51	·49	·47	·45	·44	·42	23
24	·77	·74	·71	·69	·66	·64	·61	·59	·57	·55	·53	·51	·49	·48	·46	·45	24
25	·81	·78	·75	·72	·69	·67	·64	·62	·60	·58	·56	·54	·52	·50	·48	·47	25
26	·84	·81	·78	·75	·72	·70	·67	·65	·62	·60	·58	·56	·54	·52	·51	·49	26
27	·88	·85	·82	·78	·76	·73	·70	·68	·65	·63	·61	·59	·57	·55	·53	·51	27
28	·92	·88	·85	·82	·79	·76	·73	·71	·68	·66	·63	·61	·59	·57	·55	·53	28
29	·96	·92	·89	·85	·82	·79	·76	·74	·71	·68	·66	·64	·62	·59	·57	·55	29
30	1·00	·96	·92	·89	·86	·82	·79	·77	·74	·71	·69	·66	·64	·62	·60	·58	30
31	1·04	1·00	·96	·93	·89	·86	·83	·80	·77	·74	·72	·69	·67	·64	·62	·60	31
32	1·08	1·04	1·00	·96	·93	·89	·86	·83	·80	·77	·74	·72	·69	·67	·65	·62	32
33	1·12	1·08	1·04	1·00	·96	·93	·89	·86	·83	·80	·77	·75	·72	·70	·67	·65	33
34	1·17	1·12	1·08	1·04	1·00	·96	·93	·90	·86	·83	·80	·78	·75	·72	·70	·67	34
35	1·21	1·17	1·12	1·08	1·04	1·00	·96	·93	·90	·86	·83	·81	·78	·75	·73	·70	35
36	1·26	1·21	1·16	1·12	1·08	1·04	1·00	·96	·93	·90	·87	·84	·81	·78	·75	·73	36
37	1·31	1·25	1·21	1·16	1·12	1·08	1·04	1·00	·96	·93	·90	·87	·84	·81	·78	·75	37
38	1·35	1·30	1·25	1·20	1·16	1·12	1·08	1·04	1·00	·96	·93	·90	·87	·84	·81	·78	38
39	1·40	1·35	1·30	1·25	1·20	1·16	1·11	1·07	1·04	1·00	·97	·93	·90	·87	·84	·81	39
40	1·45	1·40	1·34	1·29	1·24	1·20	1·15	1·11	1·07	1·04	1·00	·97	·93	·90	·87	·84	40
41	1·51	1·45	1·39	1·34	1·29	1·24	1·20	1·15	1·11	1·07	1·04	1·00	·97	·93	·90	·87	41
42	1·56	1·50	1·44	1·39	1·33	1·29	1·24	1·19	1·15	1·11	1·07	1·04	1·00	·97	·93	·90	42
43	1·62	1·55	1·49	1·44	1·38	1·33	1·28	1·24	1·19	1·15	1·11	1·07	1·04	1·00	·97	·93	43
44	1·67	1·61	1·55	1·49	1·43	1·38	1·33	1·28	1·24	1·19	1·15	1·11	1·07	1·04	1·00	·97	44
45	1·73	1·66	1·60	1·54	1·48	1·43	1·38	1·33	1·28	1·23	1·19	1·15	1·11	1·07	1·04	1·00	45
46	1·79	1·72	1·66	1·59	1·54	1·48	1·43	1·37	1·33	1·28	1·23	1·19	1·15	1·11	1·07	1·04	46
47	1·86	1·78	1·72	1·65	1·59	1·53	1·48	1·42	1·37	1·32	1·28	1·23	1·19	1·15	1·11	1·07	47
48	1·92	1·85	1·78	1·71	1·65	1·59	1·53	1·47	1·42	1·37	1·32	1·28	1·23	1·19	1·15	1·11	48
49	1·99	1·91	1·84	1·77	1·71	1·64	1·58	1·53	1·47	1·42	1·37	1·32	1·28	1·23	1·19	1·15	49
50	2·06	1·98	1·91	1·84	1·77	1·70	1·64	1·58	1·53	1·47	1·42	1·37	1·32	1·28	1·23	1·19	50
51	2·14	2·06	1·98	1·90	1·83	1·76	1·70	1·64	1·58	1·52	1·47	1·42	1·37	1·32	1·28	1·23	51
52	2·22	2·13	2·05	1·97	1·90	1·83	1·76	1·70	1·64	1·58	1·52	1·47	1·42	1·37	1·33	1·28	52
53	2·30	2·21	2·12	2·04	1·97	1·90	1·83	1·76	1·70	1·64	1·58	1·52	1·47	1·42	1·37	1·33	53
54	2·38	2·29	2·20	2·12	2·04	1·97	1·89	1·83	1·76	1·70	1·64	1·58	1·53	1·48	1·43	1·38	54
55	2·47	2·38	2·29	2·20	2·12	2·04	1·97	1·90	1·83	1·76	1·70	1·64	1·59	1·53	1·48	1·43	55
56	2·57	2·47	2·37	2·28	2·20	2·12	2·04	1·97	1·90	1·83	1·77	1·71	1·65	1·59	1·54	1·48	56
57	2·67	2·56	2·46	2·37	2·28	2·20	2·12	2·04	1·97	1·90	1·84	1·77	1·71	1·65	1·59	1·54	57
58	2·77	2·66	2·56	2·46	2·37	2·29	2·20	2·12	2·05	1·98	1·91	1·84	1·78	1·72	1·66	1·60	58
59	2·88	2·77	2·66	2·56	2·47	2·38	2·29	2·21	2·13	2·06	1·98	1·91	1·85	1·78	1·72	1·66	59
60	3·00	2·88	2·77	2·67	2·57	2·47	2·38	2·30	2·22	2·14	2·06	1·99	1·92	1·86	1·79	1·73	60
Lat.	150° 210°	149° 211°	148° 212°	147° 213°	146° 214°	145° 215°	144° 216°	143° 217°	142° 218°	141° 219°	140° 220°	139° 221°	138° 222°	137° 223°	136° 224°	135° 225°	Lat.

A - Named opposite to Latitude, except when Hour Angle is between 90° and 270°

A - Named opposite to Latitude, except when Hour Angle is between 90° and 270°

A   **HOUR ANGLE**

TABLE B HOUR ANGLE

Dec. °	30° 330°	31° 329°	32° 328°	33° 327°	34° 326°	35° 325°	36° 324°	37° 323°	38° 322°	39° 321°	40° 320°	41° 319°	42° 318°	43° 317°	44° 316°	45° 315°	Dec. °
0	·00	·00	·00	·00	·00	·00	·00	·00	·00	·00	·00	·00	·00	·00	·00	·00	**0**
1	·03	·03	·03	·03	·03	·03	·03	·03	·03	·03	·03	·03	·03	·03	·03	·02	**1**
2	·07	·07	·07	·06	·06	·06	·06	·06	·06	·06	·05	·05	·05	·05	·05	·05	**2**
3	·10	·10	·10	·10	·09	·09	·09	·09	·09	·08	·08	·08	·08	·08	·08	·07	**3**
4	·14	·14	·13	·13	·13	·12	·12	·12	·11	·11	·11	·11	·10	·10	·10	·10	**4**
5	·17	·17	·17	·16	·16	·15	·15	·15	·14	·14	·14	·13	·13	·13	·13	·12	**5**
6	·21	·20	·20	·19	·19	·18	·18	·17	·17	·17	·16	·16	·16	·15	·15	·15	**6**
7	·25	·24	·23	·23	·22	·21	·21	·20	·20	·20	·19	·19	·18	·18	·18	·17	**7**
8	·28	·27	·27	·26	·25	·25	·24	·23	·23	·22	·22	·21	·21	·21	·20	·20	**8**
9	·32	·31	·30	·29	·28	·28	·27	·26	·26	·25	·25	·24	·24	·23	·23	·22	**9**
10	·35	·34	·33	·32	·32	·31	·30	·29	·29	·28	·27	·27	·26	·26	·25	·25	**10**
11	·39	·38	·37	·36	·35	·34	·33	·32	·32	·31	·30	·30	·29	·29	·28	·27	**11**
12	·43	·41	·40	·39	·38	·37	·36	·35	·35	·34	·33	·32	·32	·31	·31	·30	**12**
13	·46	·45	·44	·42	·41	·40	·39	·38	·37	·37	·36	·35	·35	·34	·33	·33	**13**
14	·50	·48	·47	·46	·45	·43	·42	·41	·40	·40	·39	·38	·37	·37	·36	·35	**14**
15	·54	·52	·51	·49	·48	·47	·46	·45	·44	·43	·42	·41	·40	·39	·39	·38	**15**
16	·57	·56	·54	·53	·51	·50	·49	·48	·47	·46	·45	·44	·43	·42	·41	·41	**16**
17	·61	·59	·58	·56	·55	·53	·52	·51	·50	·49	·48	·47	·46	·45	·44	·43	**17**
18	·65	·63	·61	·60	·58	·57	·55	·54	·53	·52	·51	·50	·49	·48	·47	·46	**18**
19	·69	·67	·65	·63	·62	·60	·59	·57	·56	·55	·54	·52	·51	·50	·50	·49	**19**
20	·73	·71	·69	·67	·65	·63	·62	·60	·59	·58	·57	·55	·54	·53	·52	·51	**20**
21	·77	·75	·72	·70	·69	·67	·65	·64	·62	·61	·60	·59	·57	·56	·55	·54	**21**
22	·81	·78	·76	·74	·72	·70	·69	·67	·66	·64	·63	·62	·60	·59	·58	·57	**22**
23	·85	·82	·80	·78	·76	·74	·72	·71	·69	·67	·66	·65	·63	·62	·61	·60	**23**
24	·89	·86	·84	·82	·80	·78	·76	·74	·72	·71	·69	·68	·67	·65	·64	·63	**24**
25	·93	·91	·88	·86	·83	·81	·79	·77	·76	·74	·73	·71	·70	·68	·67	·66	**25**
26	·98	·95	·92	·90	·87	·85	·83	·81	·79	·78	·76	·74	·73	·72	·70	·69	**26**
27	1·02	·99	·96	·94	·91	·89	·87	·85	·83	·81	·79	·78	·76	·75	·73	·72	**27**
28	1·06	1·03	1·00	·98	·95	·93	·90	·88	·86	·84	·83	·81	·79	·78	·77	·75	**28**
29	1·11	1·08	1·05	1·02	·99	·97	·94	·92	·90	·88	·86	·84	·83	·81	·80	·78	**29**
30	1·15	1·12	1·09	1·06	1·03	1·01	·98	·96	·94	·92	·90	·88	·86	·85	·83	·82	**30**
31	1·20	1·17	1·13	1·10	1·07	1·05	1·02	1·00	·98	·95	·93	·92	·90	·88	·87	·85	**31**
32	1·25	1·21	1·18	1·15	1·12	1·09	1·06	1·04	1·01	·99	·97	·95	·93	·92	·90	·88	**32**
33	1·30	1·26	1·23	1·19	1·16	1·13	1·11	1·08	1·05	1·03	1·01	·99	·97	·95	·93	·92	**33**
34	1·35	1·31	1·27	1·24	1·21	1·18	1·15	1·12	1·10	1·07	1·05	1·03	1·01	·99	·97	·96	**34**
35	1·40	1·36	1·32	1·29	1·25	1·22	1·19	1·16	1·14	1·11	1·09	1·07	1·05	1·03	1·01	·99	**35**
36	1·45	1·41	1·37	1·33	1·30	1·27	1·24	1·21	1·18	1·15	1·13	1·11	1·09	1·07	1·05	1·03	**36**
37	1·51	1·46	1·42	1·38	1·35	1·31	1·28	1·25	1·22	1·20	1·17	1·15	1·13	1·10	1·08	1·07	**37**
38	1·56	1·52	1·47	1·43	1·40	1·36	1·33	1·30	1·27	1·24	1·22	1·19	1·17	1·15	1·12	1·11	**38**
39	1·62	1·57	1·53	1·49	1·45	1·41	1·38	1·35	1·32	1·29	1·26	1·23	1·21	1·19	1·17	1·15	**39**
40	1·68	1·63	1·58	1·54	1·50	1·46	1·43	1·39	1·36	1·33	1·31	1·28	1·25	1·23	1·21	1·19	**40**
41	1·74	1·69	1·64	1·60	1·55	1·52	1·48	1·44	1·41	1·38	1·35	1·33	1·30	1·27	1·25	1·23	**41**
42	1·80	1·75	1·70	1·65	1·61	1·57	1·53	1·50	1·46	1·43	1·40	1·37	1·35	1·32	1·30	1·28	**42**
43	1·87	1·81	1·76	1·71	1·67	1·63	1·59	1·55	1·51	1·48	1·45	1·42	1·39	1·37	1·34	1·32	**43**
44	1·93	1·87	1·82	1·77	1·73	1·68	1·64	1·60	1·57	1·53	1·50	1·47	1·44	1·42	1·39	1·37	**44**
45	2·00	1·94	1·89	1·84	1·79	1·74	1·70	1·66	1·62	1·59	1·56	1·52	1·49	1·47	1·44	1·41	**45**
46	2·07	2·01	1·95	1·90	1·85	1·81	1·76	1·72	1·68	1·65	1·61	1·58	1·55	1·52	1·49	1·47	**46**
47	2·14	2·08	2·02	1·97	1·92	1·87	1·82	1·78	1·74	1·70	1·67	1·63	1·60	1·57	1·54	1·52	**47**
48	2·22	2·16	2·10	2·04	1·99	1·94	1·89	1·85	1·80	1·76	1·73	1·69	1·66	1·63	1·60	1·57	**48**
49	2·30	2·23	2·17	2·11	2·06	2·01	1·96	1·91	1·87	1·83	1·79	1·75	1·72	1·69	1·66	1·63	**49**
50	2·38	2·31	2·25	2·19	2·13	2·08	2·03	1·98	1·94	1·89	1·85	1·82	1·78	1·75	1·72	1·69	**50**
51	2·47	2·40	2·33	2·27	2·21	2·15	2·10	2·05	2·01	1·96	1·92	1·88	1·85	1·81	1·78	1·75	**51**
52	2·56	2·49	2·42	2·35	2·29	2·23	2·18	2·13	2·08	2·03	1·99	1·95	1·91	1·88	1·84	1·81	**52**
53	2·65	2·58	2·50	2·44	2·37	2·31	2·26	2·21	2·16	2·11	2·06	2·02	1·98	1·95	1·91	1·88	**53**
54	2·75	2·67	2·60	2·53	2·46	2·40	2·34	2·29	2·24	2·19	2·14	2·10	2·06	2·02	1·98	1·95	**54**
55	2·86	2·77	2·70	2·62	2·55	2·49	2·43	2·37	2·32	2·27	2·22	2·18	2·13	2·09	2·06	2·02	**55**
56	2·97	2·88	2·80	2·72	2·65	2·58	2·52	2·46	2·41	2·36	2·31	2·26	2·22	2·17	2·13	2·10	**56**
57	3·08	2·99	2·91	2·83	2·75	2·68	2·62	2·56	2·50	2·45	2·40	2·35	2·30	2·26	2·22	2·18	**57**
58	3·20	3·11	3·02	2·94	2·86	2·79	2·72	2·66	2·60	2·54	2·49	2·44	2·39	2·35	2·30	2·27	**58**
59	3·33	3·23	3·14	3·06	2·98	2·90	2·83	2·77	2·70	2·64	2·59	2·54	2·49	2·44	2·40	2·36	**59**
60	3·46	3·36	3·27	3·18	3·10	3·02	2·95	2·88	2·81	2·75	2·69	2·64	2·59	2·54	2·49	2·45	**60**
Dec.	150° 210°	149° 211°	148° 212°	147° 213°	146° 214°	145° 215°	144° 216°	143° 217°	142° 218°	141° 219°	140° 220°	139° 221°	138° 222°	137° 223°	136° 224°	135° 225°	Dec.

HOUR ANGLE

B - Always named the **same** as Declination

B - Always named the **same** as Declination

B

TABLE A HOUR ANGLE

Lat.°	45° 315°	46° 314°	47° 313°	48° 312°	49° 311°	50° 310°	51° 309°	52° 308°	53° 307°	54° 306°	55° 305°	56° 304°	57° 303°	58° 302°	59° 301°	60° 300°	Lat.°
0	·00	·00	·00	·00	·00	·00	·00	·00	·00	·00	·00	·00	·00	·00	·00	·00	0
1	·02	·02	·02	·02	·02	·01	·01	·01	·01	·01	·01	·01	·01	·01	·01	·01	1
2	·03	·03	·03	·03	·03	·03	·03	·03	·03	·03	·02	·02	·02	·02	·02	·02	2
3	·05	·05	·05	·05	·05	·04	·04	·04	·04	·04	·04	·04	·03	·03	·03	·03	3
4	·07	·07	·07	·06	·06	·06	·06	·05	·05	·05	·05	·05	·05	·04	·04	·04	4
5	·09	·08	·08	·08	·08	·07	·07	·07	·07	·06	·06	·06	·06	·05	·05	·05	5
6	·11	·10	·10	·09	·09	·09	·09	·08	·08	·08	·07	·07	·07	·07	·06	·06	6
7	·12	·12	·11	·11	·11	·10	·10	·10	·09	·09	·09	·08	·08	·08	·07	·07	7
8	·14	·14	·13	·13	·12	·12	·11	·11	·11	·10	·10	·09	·09	·09	·08	·08	8
9	·16	·15	·15	·14	·14	·13	·13	·12	·12	·12	·11	·11	·10	·10	·10	·09	9
10	·18	·17	·16	·16	·15	·15	·14	·14	·13	·13	·12	·12	·11	·11	·11	·10	10
11	·19	·19	·18	·18	·17	·16	·16	·15	·15	·14	·14	·13	·13	·12	·12	·11	11
12	·21	·21	·20	·19	·18	·18	·17	·17	·16	·15	·15	·14	·14	·13	·13	·12	12
13	·23	·22	·22	·21	·20	·19	·19	·18	·17	·17	·16	·16	·15	·14	·14	·13	13
14	·25	·24	·23	·22	·22	·21	·20	·19	·19	·18	·17	·17	·16	·16	·15	·14	14
15	·27	·26	·25	·24	·23	·22	·22	·21	·20	·19	·19	·18	·17	·17	·16	·15	15
16	·29	·28	·27	·26	·25	·24	·23	·22	·22	·21	·20	·19	·19	·18	·17	·17	16
17	·31	·30	·29	·28	·27	·26	·25	·24	·23	·22	·21	·21	·20	·19	·18	·18	17
18	·32	·31	·30	·29	·28	·27	·26	·25	·24	·24	·23	·22	·21	·20	·20	·19	18
19	·34	·33	·32	·31	·30	·29	·28	·27	·26	·25	·24	·23	·22	·22	·21	·20	19
20	·36	·35	·34	·33	·32	·31	·29	·28	·27	·26	·25	·25	·24	·23	·22	·21	20
21	·38	·37	·36	·35	·33	·32	·31	·30	·29	·28	·27	·26	·25	·24	·23	·22	21
22	·40	·39	·38	·36	·35	·34	·33	·32	·30	·29	·28	·27	·26	·25	·24	·23	22
23	·42	·41	·40	·38	·37	·36	·34	·33	·32	·31	·30	·29	·28	·27	·26	·25	23
24	·45	·43	·42	·40	·39	·37	·36	·35	·34	·32	·31	·30	·29	·28	·27	·26	24
25	·47	·45	·44	·42	·41	·39	·38	·36	·35	·34	·33	·31	·30	·29	·28	·27	25
26	·49	·47	·46	·44	·42	·41	·39	·38	·37	·35	·34	·33	·32	·30	·29	·28	26
27	·51	·49	·48	·46	·44	·43	·41	·40	·38	·37	·36	·34	·33	·32	·31	·29	27
28	·53	·51	·50	·48	·46	·45	·43	·42	·40	·39	·37	·36	·35	·33	·32	·31	28
29	·55	·54	·52	·50	·48	·47	·45	·43	·42	·40	·39	·37	·36	·35	·33	·32	29
30	·58	·56	·54	·52	·50	·48	·47	·45	·44	·42	·40	·39	·37	·36	·35	·33	30
31	·60	·58	·56	·54	·52	·50	·49	·47	·45	·44	·42	·40	·39	·38	·36	·35	31
32	·62	·60	·58	·56	·54	·52	·51	·49	·47	·45	·44	·42	·41	·39	·38	·36	32
33	·65	·63	·61	·58	·56	·55	·53	·51	·49	·47	·45	·44	·42	·41	·39	·37	33
34	·67	·65	·63	·61	·59	·57	·55	·53	·51	·49	·47	·46	·44	·42	·41	·39	34
35	·70	·68	·65	·63	·61	·59	·57	·55	·53	·51	·49	·47	·45	·44	·42	·40	35
36	·73	·70	·68	·65	·63	·61	·59	·57	·55	·53	·51	·49	·47	·45	·44	·42	36
37	·75	·73	·70	·68	·66	·63	·61	·59	·57	·55	·53	·51	·49	·47	·45	·44	37
38	·78	·75	·73	·70	·68	·66	·63	·61	·59	·57	·55	·53	·51	·49	·47	·45	38
39	·81	·78	·76	·73	·70	·68	·66	·63	·61	·59	·57	·55	·53	·51	·49	·47	39
40	·84	·81	·78	·76	·73	·70	·68	·66	·63	·61	·59	·57	·55	·52	·50	·48	40
41	·87	·84	·81	·78	·76	·73	·70	·68	·66	·63	·61	·59	·56	·54	·52	·50	41
42	·90	·87	·84	·81	·78	·76	·73	·70	·68	·65	·63	·61	·58	·56	·54	·52	42
43	·93	·90	·87	·84	·81	·78	·76	·73	·70	·68	·65	·63	·61	·58	·56	·54	43
44	·97	·93	·90	·87	·84	·81	·78	·75	·73	·70	·68	·65	·63	·60	·58	·56	44
45	1·00	·97	·93	·90	·87	·84	·81	·78	·75	·73	·70	·68	·65	·63	·60	·58	45
46	1·04	1·00	·97	·93	·90	·87	·84	·81	·78	·75	·73	·70	·67	·65	·62	·60	46
47	1·07	1·04	1·00	·97	·93	·90	·87	·84	·81	·78	·75	·72	·70	·67	·64	·62	47
48	1·11	1·07	1·04	1·00	·97	·93	·90	·87	·84	·81	·78	·75	·72	·69	·67	·64	48
49	1·15	1·11	1·07	1·04	1·00	·97	·93	·90	·87	·84	·81	·78	·75	·72	·69	·66	49
50	1·19	1 15	1·11	1·07	1·04	1·00	·97	·93	·90	·87	·83	·80	·77	·75	·72	·69	50
51	1·23	1·19	1·15	1·11	1·07	1·04	1·00	·97	·93	·90	·86	·83	·80	·77	·74	71	51
52	1·28	1·24	1·19	1·15	1·11	1·07	1·04	1·00	·96	·93	·90	·86	·83	·80	·77	·74	52
53	1·33	1·28	1·24	1·19	1·15	1·11	1·07	1·04	1·00	·96	·93	·90	·86	·83	·80	·77	53
54	1·38	1·33	1·28	1·24	1·20	1·15	1·11	1·08	1·04	1·00	·96	·93	·89	·86	·83	·79	54
55	1·43	1·38	1·33	1·29	1·24	1·20	1·16	1·12	1·08	1·04	1·00	·96	·93	·89	·86	·82	55
56	1·48	1·43	1·38	1·34	1·29	1·24	1·20	1·16	1·12	1·08	1·04	1·00	·96	·93	·89	·86	56
57	1·54	1·49	1·44	1·39	1·34	1·29	1·25	1·20	1·16	1·12	1·08	1·04	1·00	·96	·93	·89	57
58	1·60	1·55	1·49	1·44	1·39	1·34	1·30	1·25	1·21	1·16	1·12	1·08	1·04	1·00	·96	·92	58
59	1·66	1·61	1·55	1·50	1·45	1·40	1·35	1·30	1·25	1·21	1·17	1·12	1·08	1·04	1·00	·96	59
60	1·73	1·67	1·62	1·56	1·51	1·45	1·40	1·35	1·31	1·26	1·21	1·17	1·12	1·08	1·04	1·00	60

| Lat. | 135° 225° | 134° 226° | 133° 227° | 132° 228° | 131° 229° | 130° 230° | 129° 231° | 128° 232° | 127° 233° | 126° 234° | 125° 235° | 124° 236° | 123° 237° | 122° 238° | 121° 239° | 120° 240° | Lat. |

HOUR ANGLE

A - Named opposite to Latitude, except when Hour Angle is between 90° and 270°

A - Named opposite to Latitude, except when Hour Angle is between 90° and 270°

A

TABLE B HOUR ANGLE

Dec.°	45° / 315°	46° / 314°	47° / 313°	48° / 312°	49° / 311°	50° / 310°	51° / 309°	52° / 308°	53° / 307°	54° / 306°	55° / 305°	56° / 304°	57° / 303°	58° / 302°	59° / 301°	60° / 300°	Dec.°
0	·00	·00	·00	·00	·00	·00	·00	·00	·00	·00	·00	·00	·00	·00	·00	·00	0
1	·02	·02	·02	·02	·02	·02	·02	·02	·02	·02	·02	·02	·02	·02	·02	·02	1
2	·05	·05	·05	·05	·05	·05	·04	·04	·04	·04	·04	·04	·04	·04	·04	·04	2
3	·07	·07	·07	·07	·67	·07	·07	·07	·07	·06	·06	·06	·06	·06	·06	·06	3
4	·10	·10	·10	·09	·09	·09	·09	·09	·09	·09	·09	·08	·08	·08	·08	·08	4
5	·12	·12	·12	·12	·12	·11	·11	·11	·11	·11	·11	·11	·10	·10	·10	·10	5
6	·15	·15	·14	·14	·14	·14	·14	·13	·13	·13	·13	·13	·13	·12	·12	·12	6
7	·17	·17	·17	·17	·16	·16	·16	·16	·15	·15	·15	·15	·15	·14	·14	·14	7
8	·20	·20	·19	·19	·19	·18	·18	·18	·18	·17	·17	·17	·17	·17	·16	·16	8
9	·22	·22	·22	·21	·21	·21	·20	·20	·20	·20	·19	·19	·19	·19	·18	·18	9
10	·25	·25	·24	·24	·23	·23	·23	·22	·22	·22	·22	·21	·21	·21	·21	·20	10
11	·27	·27	·27	·26	·26	·25	·25	·25	·24	·24	·24	·23	·23	·23	·23	·22	11
12	·30	·30	·29	·29	·28	·28	·27	·27	·27	·26	·26	·26	·25	·25	·25	·24	12
13	·33	·32	·32	·31	·31	·30	·30	·29	·29	·29	·28	·28	·28	·27	·27	·27	13
14	·35	·35	·34	·34	·33	·33	·32	·32	·31	·31	·30	·30	·30	·29	·29	·29	14
15	·38	·37	·37	·36	·36	·35	·34	·34	·34	·33	·33	·32	·32	·32	·31	·31	15
16	·41	·40	·39	·39	·38	·37	·37	·36	·36	·35	·35	·35	·34	·34	·33	·33	16
17	·43	·43	·42	·41	·41	·40	·39	·39	·38	·38	·37	·37	·36	·36	·36	·35	17
18	·46	·45	·44	·44	·43	·42	·42	·41	·41	·40	·40	·39	·39	·38	·38	·38	18
19	·49	·48	·47	·46	·46	·45	·44	·44	·43	·43	·42	·42	·41	·41	·40	·40	19
20	·51	·51	·50	·49	·48	·48	·47	·46	·46	·45	·44	·44	·43	·43	·42	·42	20
21	·54	·53	·52	·52	·51	·50	·49	·49	·48	·47	·47	·46	·46	·45	·45	·44	21
22	·57	·56	·55	·54	·54	·53	·52	·51	·51	·50	·49	·49	·48	·48	·47	·47	22
23	·60	·59	·58	·57	·56	·55	·55	·54	·53	·52	·52	·51	·51	·50	·50	·49	23
24	·63	·62	·61	·60	·59	·58	·57	·57	·56	·55	·54	·54	·53	·53	·52	·51	24
25	·66	·65	·64	·63	·62	·61	·60	·59	·58	·58	·57	·56	·56	·55	·54	·54	25
26	·69	·68	·67	·66	·65	·64	·63	·62	·61	·60	·60	·59	·58	·58	·57	·56	26
27	·72	·71	·70	·69	·68	·67	·66	·65	·64	·63	·62	·61	·61	·60	·59	·59	27
28	·75	·74	·73	·72	·70	·69	·68	·67	·67	·66	·65	·64	·63	·63	·62	·61	28
29	·78	·77	·76	·75	·73	·72	·71	·70	·69	·69	·68	·67	·66	·65	·65	·64	29
30	·82	·80	·79	·78	·76	·75	·74	·73	·72	·71	·70	·70	·69	·68	·67	·67	30
31	·85	·84	·82	·81	·80	·78	·77	·76	·75	·74	·73	·72	·72	·71	·70	·69	31
32	·88	·87	·85	·84	·83	·82	·80	·79	·78	·77	·76	·75	·75	·74	·73	·72	32
33	·92	·90	·89	·87	·86	·85	·84	·82	·81	·80	·79	·78	·77	·77	·76	·75	33
34	·96	·94	·92	·91	·89	·88	·87	·86	·84	·83	·82	·81	·80	·80	·79	·78	34
35	·99	·97	·96	·94	·93	·91	·90	·89	·88	·87	·85	·84	·83	·83	·82	·81	35
36	1·03	1·01	·99	·98	·96	·95	·93	·92	·91	·90	·89	·88	·87	·86	·85	·84	36
37	1·07	1·05	1·03	1·01	1·00	·98	·97	·96	·94	·93	·92	·91	·90	·89	·88	·87	37
38	1·11	1·09	1·07	1·05	1·04	1·02	1·00	·99	·98	·97	·95	·94	·93	·92	·91	·90	38
39	1·15	1·13	1·11	1·09	1·07	1·06	1·04	1·03	1·01	1·00	·99	·98	·97	·95	·94	·94	39
40	1·19	1·17	1·15	1·13	1·11	1·10	1·08	1·06	1·05	1·04	1·02	1·01	1·00	·99	·98	·97	40
41	1·23	1·21	1·19	1·17	1·15	1·13	1·12	1·10	1·09	1·07	1·06	1·05	1·04	1·03	1·01	1·00	41
42	1·28	1·25	1·23	1·21	1·19	1·18	1·16	1·14	1·13	1·11	1·10	1·09	1·07	1·06	1·05	1·04	42
43	1·32	1·30	1·28	1·25	1·24	1·22	1·20	1·18	1·17	1·15	1·14	1·12	1·11	1·10	1·09	1·08	43
44	1·37	1·34	1·32	1·30	1·28	1·26	1·24	1·23	1·21	1·19	1·18	1·16	1·15	1·14	1·13	1·12	44
45	1·41	1·39	1·37	1·35	1·33	1·31	1·29	1·27	1·25	1·24	1·22	1·21	1·19	1·18	1·17	1·15	45
46	1·47	1·44	1·42	1·39	1·37	1·35	1·33	1·31	1·30	1·28	1·26	1·25	1·23	1·22	1·21	1·20	46
47	1·52	1·49	1·47	1·44	1·42	1·40	1·38	1·36	1·34	1·33	1·31	1·29	1·28	1·26	1·25	1·24	47
48	1·57	1·54	1·52	1·49	1·47	1·45	1·43	1·41	1·39	1·37	1·36	1·34	1·32	1·31	1·30	1·28	48
49	1·63	1·60	1·57	1·55	1·52	1·50	1·48	1·46	1·44	1·42	1·40	1·39	1·37	1·36	1·34	1·33	49
50	1·69	1·66	1·63	1·60	1·58	1·56	1·53	1·51	1·49	1·47	1·45	1·44	1·42	1·41	1·39	1·38	50
51	1·75	1·72	1·69	1·66	1·64	1·61	1·59	1·57	1·55	1·53	1·51	1·49	1·47	1·46	1·44	1·43	51
52	1·81	1·78	1·75	1·72	1·70	1·67	1·65	1·62	1·60	1·58	1·56	1·54	1·53	1·51	1·49	1·48	52
53	1·88	1·84	1·81	1·79	1·76	1·73	1·71	1·68	1·66	1·64	1·62	1·60	1·58	1·56	1·55	1·53	53
54	1·95	1·91	1·88	1·85	1·82	1·80	1·77	1·75	1·72	1·70	1·68	1·66	1·64	1·62	1·61	1·59	54
55	2·02	1·99	1·95	1·92	1·89	1·86	1·84	1·81	1·79	1·77	1·74	1·72	1·70	1·68	1·67	1·65	55
56	2·10	2·06	2·03	2·00	1·96	1·94	1·91	1·88	1·86	1·83	1·81	1·79	1·77	1·75	1·73	1·71	56
57	2·18	2·14	2·11	2·07	2·04	2·01	1·98	1·95	1·93	1·90	1·88	1·86	1·84	1·82	1·80	1·78	57
58	2·27	2·22	2·19	2·15	2·12	2·09	2·06	2·03	2·00	1·98	1·95	1·93	1·91	1·89	1·87	1·85	58
59	2·36	2·31	2·28	2·24	2·21	2·17	2·14	2·11	2·08	2·06	2·03	2·01	1·98	1·96	1·94	1·92	59
60	2·45	2·41	2·37	2·33	2·29	2·26	2·23	2·20	2·17	2·14	2·11	2·09	2·07	2·04	2·02	2·00	60
Dec.	135° / 225°	134° / 226°	133° / 227°	132° / 228°	131° / 229°	130° / 230°	129° / 231°	128° / 232°	127° / 233°	126° / 234°	125° / 235°	124° / 236°	123° / 237°	122° / 238°	121° / 239°	120° / 240°	Dec.

B - Always named the same as Declination

HOUR ANGLE

B

TABLE A HOUR ANGLE

Lat. °	60°	61°	62°	63°	64°	65°	66°	67°	68°	69°	70°	71°	72°	73°	74°	75°	Lat. °
	300°	299°	298°	297°	296°	295°	294°	293°	292°	291°	290°	289°	288°	287°	286°	285°	
0	·00	·00	·00	·00	·00	·00	·00	·00	·00	·00	·00	·00	·00	·00	·00	·00	0
1	·01	·01	·01	·01	·01	·01	·01	·01	·01	·01	·01	·01	·01	·01	·01	·01	1
2	·02	·02	·02	·02	·02	·02	·02	·02	·02	·02	·01	·01	·01	·01	·01	·01	2
3	·03	·03	·03	·03	·03	·02	·02	·02	·02	·02	·02	·02	·02	·02	·02	·01	3
4	·04	·04	·04	·04	·03	·03	·03	·03	·03	·03	·03	·02	·02	·02	·02	·02	4
5	·05	·05	·05	·04	·04	·04	·04	·04	·04	·03	·03	·03	·03	·03	·03	·02	5
6	·06	·06	·06	·05	·05	·05	·05	·05	·04	·04	·04	·04	·03	·03	·03	·03	6
7	·07	·07	·07	·06	·06	·06	·06	·05	·05	·05	·05	·04	·04	·04	·04	·03	7
8	·08	·08	·07	·07	·07	·07	:06	·06	·06	·05	·05	·05	·05	·04	·04	·04	8
9	·09	·09	·08	·08	·08	·07	·07	·07	·06	·06	·06	·06	·05	·05	·05	·04	9
10	·10	·10	·09	·09	·09	·08	·08	·08	·07	·07	·06	·06	·06	·05	·05	·05	10
11	·11	·11	·10	·10	·10	·09	·09	·08	·08	·08	·07	·07	·06	·06	·06	·05	11
12	·12	·12	·11	·11	·10	·10	·10	·09	·09	·08	·08	·07	·07	·07	·06	·06	12
13	·13	·13	·12	·12	·11	·11	·10	·10	·09	·09	·08	·08	·08	·07	·07	·06	13
14	·14	·14	·13	·13	·12	·12	·11	·11	·10	·10	·09	·09	·08	·08	·07	·07	14
15	·15	·15	·14	·14	·13	·12	·12	·11	·11	·10	·10	·09	·09	·08	·08	·07	15
16	·17	·16	·15	·15	·14	·13	·13	·12	·12	·11	·10	·10	·09	·09	·08	·08	16
17	·18	·17	·16	·16	·15	·14	·14	·13	·12	·12	·11	·11	·10	·09	·09	·08	17
18	·19	·18	·17	·17	·16	·15	·15	·14	·13	·13	·12	·11	·11	·10	·09	·09	18
19	·20	·19	·18	·18	·17	·16	·15	·15	·14	·13	·13	·12	·11	·11	·10	·09	19
20	·21	·20	·19	·19	·18	·17	·16	·15	·15	·14	·13	·13	·12	·11	·10	·10	20
21	·22	·21	·20	·20	·19	·18	·17	·16	·16	·15	·14	·13	·13	·12	·11	·10	21
22	·23	·22	·21	·21	·20	·19	·18	·17	·16	·16	·15	·14	·13	·12	·12	·11	22
23	·25	·24	·23	·22	·21	·20	·19	·18	·17	·16	·15	·15	·14	·13	·12	·11	23
24	·26	·25	·24	·23	·22	·21	·20	·19	·18	·17	·16	·15	·15	·14	·13	·12	24
25	·27	·26	·25	·24	·23	·22	·21	·20	·19	·18	·17	·16	·15	·14	·13	·13	25
26	·28	·27	·26	·25	·24	·23	·22	·21	·20	·19	·18	·17	·16	·15	·14	·13	26
27	·29	·28	·27	·26	·25	·24	·23	·22	·21	·20	·19	·18	·17	·16	·15	·14	27
28	·31	·29	·28	·27	·26	·25	·24	·23	·22	·20	·19	·18	·17	·16	·15	·14	28
29	·32	·31	·29	·28	·27	·26	·25	·24	·22	·21	·20	·19	·18	·17	·16	·15	29
30	·33	·32	·31	·29	·28	·27	·26	·25	·23	·22	·21	·20	·19	·18	·17	·16	30
31	·35	·33	·32	·31	·29	·28	·27	·26	·24	·23	·22	·21	·20	·18	·17	16	31
32	·36	·35	·33	·32	·31	·29	·28	·27	·25	·24	·23	·22	·20	·19	·18	·17	32
33	·37	·36	·35	·33	·32	·30	·29	·28	·26	·25	·24	·22	·21	·20	·19	·17	33
34	·39	·37	·36	·34	·33	·31	·30	·29	·27	·26	·25	·23	·22	·21	·19	·18	34
35	·40	·39	·37	·36	·34	·33	·31	·30	·28	·27	·26	·24	·23	·21	·20	·19	35
36	·42	·40	·39	·37	·35	·34	·32	·31	·29	·28	·26	·25	·24	·22	·21	·20	36
37	·44	·42	·40	·38	·37	·35	·34	·32	·30	·29	·27	·26	·25	·23	·22	·20	37
38	·45	·43	·42	·40	·38	·36	·35	·33	·32	·30	·28	·27	·25	·24	·22	·21	38
39	·47	·45	·43	·41	·40	·38	·36	·34	·33	·31	·30	·28	·26	·25	·23	·22	39
40	·48	·47	·45	·43	·41	·39	·37	·36	·34	·32	·31	·29	·27	·26	·24	·23	40
41	·50	·48	·46	·44	·42	·41	·39	·37	·35	·33	·32	·30	·28	·27	·25	·23	41
42	·52	·50	·48	·46	·44	·42	·40	·38	·36	·35	·33	·31	·29	·28	·26	·24	42
43	·54	·52	·50	·48	·46	·43	·42	·40	·38	·36	·34	·32	·30	·29	·27	·25	43
44	·56	·54	·51	·49	·47	·45	·43	·41	·39	·37	·35	·33	·31	·30	·28	·26	44
45	·58	·55	·53	·51	·49	·47	·45	·42	·40	·38	·36	·34	·33	·31	·29	·27	45
46	·60	·57	·55	·53	·51	·48	·46	·44	·42	·40	·38	·36	·34	·32	·30	·28	46
47	·62	·59	·57	·55	·52	·50	·48	·45	·43	·41	·39	·37	·35	·33	·31	·29	47
48	·64	·62	·59	·57	·54	·52	·49	·47	·45	·43	·40	·38	·36	·34	·32	·30	48
49	·66	·64	·61	·59	·56	·54	·51	·49	·47	·44	·42	·40	·37	·35	·33	·31	49
50	·69	·66	·63	·61	·58	·56	·53	·51	·48	·46	·43	·41	·39	·36	·34	·32	50
51	·71	·68	·66	·63	·60	·58	·55	·52	·50	·47	·45	·43	·40	·38	·35	·33	51
52	·74	·71	·68	·65	·62	·60	·57	·54	·52	·49	·47	·44	·42	·39	·37	·34	52
53	·77	·74	·71	·68	·65	·62	·59	·56	·54	·51	·48	·46	·43	·41	·38	·36	53
54	·79	·76	·73	·70	·67	·64	·61	·58	·56	·53	·50	·47	·45	·42	·40	·37	54
55	·82	·79	·76	·73	·70	·67	·64	·61	·58	·55	·52	·49	·46	·44	·41	·38	55
56	·86	·82	·79	·76	·72	·69	·66	·63	·60	·57	·54	·51	·48	·45	·43	·40	56
57	·89	·85	·82	·78	·75	·72	·69	·65	·62	·59	·56	·53	·50	·47	·44	·41	57
58	·92	·89	·85	·81	·78	·75	·71	·68	·65	·61	·58	·55	·52	·49	·46	·43	58
59	·96	·92	·88	·85	·81	·78	·74	·71	·67	·64	·61	·57	·54	·51	·48	·45	59
60	1·00	·96	·92	·88	·85	·81	·77	·74	·70	·67	·63	·60	·56	·53	·50	·46	60
Lat.	120°	119°	118°	117°	116°	115°	114°	113°	112°	111°	110°	109°	108°	107°	106°	105°	Lat.
	240°	241°	242°	243°	244°	245°	246°	247°	248°	249°	250°	251°	252°	253°	254°	255°	

A - Named opposite to Latitude, except when Hour Angle is between 90° and 270°

A - Named opposite to Latitude, except when Hour Angle is between 90° and 270°

HOUR ANGLE

A

TABLE B HOUR ANGLE

Dec. °	60°	61°	62°	63°	64°	65°	66°	67°	68°	69°	70°	71°	72°	73°	74°	75°	Dec. °
	300°	299°	298°	297°	296°	295°	294°	293°	292°	291°	290°	289°	288°	287°	286°	285°	
0	·00	·00	·00	·00	·00	·00	·00	·00	·00	·00	·00	·00	·00	·00	·00	·00	0
1	·02	·02	·02	·02	·02	·02	·02	·02	·02	·02	·02	·02	·02	·02	·02	·02	1
2	·04	·04	·04	·04	·04	·04	·04	·04	·04	·04	·04	·04	·04	·04	·04	·04	2
3	·06	·06	·06	·06	·06	·06	·06	·06	·06	·06	·06	·06	·06	·06	·06	·05	3
4	·08	·08	·08	·08	·08	·08	·08	·08	·08	·08	·07	·07	·07	·07	·07	·07	4
5	·10	·10	·10	·10	·10	·10	·10	·10	·09	·09	·09	·09	·09	·09	·09	·09	5
6	·12	·12	·12	·12	·12	·12	·12	·11	·11	·11	·11	·11	·11	·11	·11	·11	6
7	·14	·14	·14	·14	·14	·14	·13	·13	·13	·13	·13	·13	·13	·13	·13	·13	7
8	·16	·16	·16	·16	·16	·16	·15	·15	·15	·15	·15	·15	·15	·15	·15	·15	8
9	·18	·18	·18	·18	·18	·18	·17	·17	·17	·17	·17	·17	·17	·17	·16	·16	9
10	·20	·20	·20	·20	·20	·19	·19	·19	·19	·19	·19	·19	·19	·18	·18	·18	10
11	·22	·22	·22	·22	·22	·21	·21	·21	·21	·21	·21	·21	·20	·20	·20	·20	11
12	·25	·24	·24	·24	·24	·23	·23	·23	·23	·23	·23	·23	·22	·22	·22	·22	12
13	·27	·26	·26	·26	·26	·25	·25	·25	·25	·25	·25	·24	·24	·24	·24	·24	13
14	·29	·29	·28	·28	·28	·28	·27	·27	·27	·27	·27	·26	·26	·26	·26	·26	14
15	·31	·31	·30	·30	·30	·30	·29	·29	·29	·29	·29	·28	·28	·28	·28	·28	15
16	·33	·33	·32	·32	·32	·32	·31	·31	·31	·31	·31	·30	·30	·30	30	·30	16
17	·35	·35	·35	·34	·34	·34	·33	·33	·33	·33	·33	·32	·32	·32	·32	·32	17
18	·38	·37	·37	·36	·36	·36	·36	·35	·35	·35	·35	·34	·34	·34	·34	·34	18
19	·40	·39	·39	·39	·38	·38	·38	·37	·37	·37	·37	·36	·36	·36	·36	·36	19
20	·42	·42	·41	·41	·41	·40	·40	·40	·39	·39	·39	·39	·38	·38	·38	·38	20
21	·44	·44	·43	·43	·43	·42	·42	·42	·41	·41	·41	·41	·40	·40	·40	·40	21
22	·47	·46	·46	·45	·45	·45	·44	·44	·44	·43	·43	·43	·43	·42	·42	·42	22
23	·49	·49	·48	·48	·47	·47	·46	·46	·46	·46	·45	·45	·45	·44	·44	·44	23
24	·51	·51	·50	·50	·50	·49	·49	·48	·48	·48	·47	·47	·47	·47	·46	·46	24
25	·54	·53	·53	·52	·52	·52	·51	·51	·50	·50	·49	·49	·49	·49	·49	·48	25
26	·56	·56	·55	·55	·54	·54	·53	·53	·53	·52	·52	·52	·51	·51	·51	·50	26
27	·59	·58	·58	·57	·57	·56	·56	·55	·55	·55	·54	·54	·54	·53	·53	·53	27
28	·61	·61	·60	·60	·59	·59	·58	·58	·57	·57	·57	·56	·56	·56	·55	·55	28
29	·64	·63	·63	·62	·62	·61	·61	·60	·60	·59	·59	·59	·58	·58	·58	·57	29
30	·67	·66	·65	·65	·64	·64	·63	·63	·62	·62	·62	·61	·61	·60	·60	·60	30
31	·69	·69	·68	·67	·67	·66	·66	·65	·65	·64	·64	·64	·63	·63	·63	·62	31
32	·72	·71	·71	·70	·70	·69	·68	·68	·67	·67	·67	·66	·66	·65	·65	·65	32
33	·75	·74	·74	·73	·72	·72	·71	·71	·70	·70	·69	·69	·68	·68	·68	·67	33
34	·78	·77	·76	·76	·75	·75	·74	·73	·73	·72	·72	·71	·71	·71	·70	·70	34
35	·81	·80	·79	·79	·78	·77	·77	·76	·76	·75	·74	·74	·74	·73	·73	·72	35
36	·84	·83	·82	·82	·81	·80	·80	·79	·78	·78	·77	·77	·76	·76	·76	·75	36
37	·87	·86	·85	·85	·84	·83	·82	·82	·81	·81	·80	·80	·79	·79	·78	·78	37
38	·90	·89	·88	·88	·87	·86	·86	·85	·84	·84	·83	·83	·82	·82	·81	·81	38
39	·94	·93	·92	·91	·90	·89	·89	·88	·87	·87	·86	·86	·85	·85	·84	·84	39
40	·97	·96	·95	·94	·93	·93	·92	·91	·91	·90	·89	·89	·88	·88	·87	·87	40
41	1·00	·99	·98	·98	·97	·96	·95	·94	·94	·93	·92	·92	·91	·91	·90	·90	41
42	1·04	1·03	1·02	1·01	1·00	·99	·99	·98	·97	·96	·96	·95	·95	·94	·94	·93	42
43	1·08	1·07	1·06	1·05	1·04	1·03	1·02	1·01	1·01	1·00	·99	·99	·98	·98	·97	·97	43
44	1·11	1·10	1·09	1·08	1·07	1·06	1·06	1·05	1·04	1·04	1·03	1·02	1·02	1·01	1·00	1·00	44
45	1·15	1·14	1·13	1·12	1·11	1·10	1·10	1·09	1·08	1·07	1·06	1·06	1·05	1·05	1·04	1·04	45
46	1·20	1·18	1·17	1·16	1·15	1·14	1·13	1·12	1·12	1·11	1·10	1·10	1·09	1·08	1·08	1·07	46
47	1·24	1·23	1·22	1·20	1·19	1·18	1·17	1·16	1·16	1·15	1·14	1·13	1·13	1·12	1·12	1·11	47
48	1·28	1·27	1·26	1·25	1·24	1·22	1·22	1·21	1·20	1·19	1·18	1·17	1·17	1·16	1·16	1·15	48
49	1·33	1·32	1·30	1·29	1·28	1·27	1·26	1·25	1·24	1·23	1·22	1·22	1·20	1·20	1·20	1·19	49
50	1·38	1·36	1·35	1·34	1·33	1·31	1·31	1·29	1·29	1·28	1·27	1·26	1·25	1·25	1·24	1·23	50
51	1·43	1·41	1·40	1·39	1·37	1·36	1·35	1·34	1·33	1·32	1·31	1·31	1·30	1·29	1·28	1·28	51
52	1·48	1·46	1·45	1·44	1·42	1·41	1·40	1·39	1·38	1·37	1·36	1·35	1·35	1·34	1·33	1·33	52
53	1·53	1·52	1·50	1·49	1·48	1·46	1·45	1·44	1·43	1·42	1·41	1·40	1·40	1·39	1·38	1·37	53
54	1·59	1·57	1·56	1·55	1·53	1·52	1·51	1·50	1·48	1·47	1·46	1·46	1·45	1·44	1·43	1·42	54
55	1·65	1·63	1·62	1·60	1·59	1·58	1·56	1·55	1·54	1·53	1·52	1·51	1·50	1·49	1·49	1·48	55
56	1·71	1·70	1·68	1·66	1·65	1·64	1·62	1·61	1·60	1·59	1·58	1·57	1·56	1·55	1·54	1·54	56
57	1·78	1·76	1·74	1·73	1·71	1·70	1·69	1·67	1·66	1·65	1·64	1·63	1·62	1·61	1·60	1·60	57
58	1·85	1·83	1·81	1·80	1·78	1·77	1·75	1·74	1·73	1·71	1·71	1·69	1·68	1·67	1·66	1·66	58
59	1·92	1·90	1·89	1·87	1·85	1·84	1·82	1·81	1·79	1·78	1·77	1·76	1·75	1·74	1·73	1·72	59
60	2·00	1·98	1·96	1·94	1·93	1·91	1·89	1·88	1·87	1·86	1·84	1·83	1·82	1·81	1·80	1·79	60
Dec.	120°	119°	118°	117°	116°	115°	114°	113°	112°	111°	110°	109°	108°	107°	106°	105°	Dec.
	240°	241°	242°	243°	244°	245°	246°	247°	248°	249°	250°	251°	252°	253°	254°	255°	

B - Always named the same as Declination

B - Always named the same as Declination

HOUR ANGLE

B

TABLE A HOUR ANGLE

A - Named opposite to Latitude, except when Hour Angle is between 90° and 270°

Lat. °	75° 285°	76° 284°	77° 283°	78° 282°	79° 281°	80° 280°	81° 279°	82° 278°	83° 277°	84° 276°	85° 275°	86° 274°	87° 273°	88° 272°	89° 271°	90° 270°	Lat. °
0	·00	·00	·00	·00	·00	·00	·00	·00	·00	·00	·00	·00	·00	·00	·00	·00	0
1	·01	·00	·00	·00	·00	·00	·00	·00	·00	·00	·00	·00	·00	·00	·00	·00	1
2	·01	·01	·01	·01	·01	·01	·01	·01	·00	·00	·00	·00	·00	·00	·00	·00	2
3	·01	·01	·01	·01	·01	·01	·01	·01	·01	·01	·01	·01	·00	·00	·00	·00	3
4	·02	·02	·02	·02	·01	·01	·01	·01	·01	·01	·01	·01	·00	·00	·00	·00	4
5	·02	·02	·02	·02	·02	·02	·01	·01	·01	·01	·01	·01	·01	·00	·00	·00	5
6	·03	·03	·02	·02	·02	·02	·02	·02	·01	·01	·01	·01	·01	·00	·00	·00	6
7	·03	·03	·03	·03	·02	·02	·02	·02	·02	·01	·01	·01	·01	·00	·00	·00	7
8	·04	·04	·03	·03	·03	·03	·02	·02	·02	·02	·01	·01	·01	·01	·00	·00	8
9	·04	·04	·04	·03	·03	·03	·03	·02	·02	·02	·01	·01	·01	·00	·00	·00	9
10	·05	·04	·04	·04	·03	·03	·03	·03	·02	·02	·02	·01	·01	·01	·00	·00	10
11	·05	·05	·05	·04	·04	·03	·03	·03	·02	·02	·02	·01	·01	·01	·00	·00	11
12	·06	·05	·05	·05	·04	·04	·03	·03	·03	·02	·02	·02	·01	·01	·00	·00	12
13	·06	·06	·05	·05	·05	·04	·04	·03	·03	·02	·02	·02	·01	·01	·00	·00	13
14	·07	·06	·06	·05	·05	·04	·04	·03	·03	·03	·02	·02	·01	·01	·00	·00	14
15	·07	·07	·06	·06	·05	·05	·04	·04	·03	·03	·02	·02	·01	·01	·01	·00	15
16	·08	·07	·07	·06	·06	·05	·05	·04	·04	·03	·03	·02	·02	·01	·01	·00	16
17	·08	·08	·07	·07	·06	·05	·05	·04	·04	·03	·03	·02	·02	·01	·01	·00	17
18	·09	·08	·08	·07	·06	·06	·05	·05	·04	·03	·03	·02	·02	·01	·01	·00	18
19	·09	·09	·08	·07	·07	·06	·06	·05	·04	·04	·03	·02	·02	·01	·01	·00	19
20	·10	·09	·08	·08	·07	·06	·06	·05	·05	·04	·03	·03	·02	·01	·01	·00	20
21	·10	·10	·09	·08	·07	·07	·06	·05	·05	·04	·03	·03	·02	·01	·01	·00	21
22	·11	·10	·09	·09	·08	·07	·06	·06	·05	·04	·04	·03	·02	·01	·01	·00	22
23	·11	·11	·10	·09	·08	·08	·07	·06	·05	·05	·04	·03	·02	·02	·01	·00	23
24	·12	·11	·10	·10	·09	·08	·07	·06	·06	·05	·04	·03	·02	·02	·01	·00	24
25	·13	·12	·11	·10	·09	·08	·07	·07	·06	·05	·04	·03	·02	·02	·01	·00	25
26	·13	·12	·11	·10	·10	·09	·08	·07	·06	·05	·04	·03	·03	·02	·01	·00	26
27	·14	·13	·12	·11	·10	·09	·08	·07	·06	·05	·05	·04	·03	·02	·01	·00	27
28	·14	·13	·12	·11	·10	·09	·08	·08	·07	·06	·05	·04	·03	·02	·01	·00	28
29	·15	·14	·13	·12	·11	·10	·09	·08	·07	·06	·05	·04	·03	·02	·01	·00	29
30	·16	·14	·13	·12	·11	·10	·09	·08	·07	·06	·05	·04	·03	·02	·01	·00	30
31	·16	·15	·14	·13	·12	·11	·10	08	·07	·06	·05	·04	·03	·02	·01	·00	31
32	·17	·16	·14	·13	·12	·11	·10	09	·08	·07	·06	·04	·03	·02	·01	·00	32
33	·17	·16	·15	·14	·13	·11	·10	·09	·08	·07	·06	·05	·03	·02	·01	·00	33
34	·18	·17	·16	·14	·13	·12	·11	·10	·08	·07	·06	·05	·04	·02	·01	·00	34
35	·19	·18	·16	·15	·14	·12	·11	·10	·09	·07	·06	·05	·04	·02	·01	·00	35
36	·20	·18	·17	·15	·14	·13	·12	·10	·09	·08	·06	·05	·04	·03	·01	·00	36
37	·20	·19	·17	·16	·15	·13	·12	·11	·09	·08	·07	·05	·04	·03	·01	·00	37
38	·21	·20	·18	·17	·15	·14	·12	·11	·10	·08	·07	·06	·04	·03	·01	·00	38
39	·22	·20	·19	·17	·16	·14	·13	·11	·10	·09	·07	·06	·04	·03	·01	·00	39
40	·23	·21	·19	·18	·16	·15	·13	·12	·10	·09	·07	·06	·04	·03	·02	·00	40
41	·23	·22	·20	·19	·17	·15	·14	·12	·11	·09	·08	·06	·05	·03	·02	·00	41
42	·24	·22	·21	·19	·18	·16	·14	·13	·11	·10	·08	·06	·05	·03	·02	·00	42
43	·25	·23	·22	·20	·18	·16	·15	·13	·11	·10	·08	·07	·05	·03	·02	·00	43
44	·26	·24	·22	·21	·19	·17	·15	·14	·12	·10	·09	·07	·05	·03	·02	·00	44
45	·27	·25	·23	·21	·19	·18	·16	·14	·12	·11	·09	·07	·05	·04	·02	·00	45
46	·28	·26	·24	·22	·20	·18	·16	·15	·13	·11	·09	·07	·05	·04	·02	·00	46
47	·29	·27	·25	·23	·21	·19	·17	·15	·13	·11	·09	·08	·06	·04	·02	·00	47
48	·30	·28	·26	·24	·22	·20	·18	·16	·14	·12	·10	·08	·06	·04	·02	·00	48
49	·31	·29	·27	·25	·22	·20	·18	·16	·14	·12	·10	·08	·06	·04	·02	·00	49
50	·32	·30	·28	·25	·23	·21	·19	·17	·15	·13	·10	·08	·06	·04	·02	·00	50
51	·33	·31	·29	·26	·24	·22	·20	·17	·15	·13	·11	·09	·07	·04	·02	·00	51
52	·34	·32	·30	·27	·25	·23	·20	·18	·16	·14	·11	·09	·07	·05	·02	·00	52
53	·36	·33	·31	·28	·26	·23	·21	·19	·16	·14	·12	·09	·07	·05	·02	·00	53
54	·37	·34	·32	·29	·27	·24	·22	·19	·17	·15	·12	·10	·07	·05	·02	·00	54
55	·38	·36	·33	·30	·28	·25	·23	·20	·18	·15	·13	·10	·08	·05	·03	·00	55
56	·40	·37	·34	·32	·29	·26	·24	·21	·18	·16	·13	·10	·08	·05	·03	·00	56
57	·41	·38	·36	·33	·30	·27	·24	·22	·19	·16	·14	·11	·08	·05	·03	·00	57
58	·43	·40	·37	·34	·31	·28	·25	·23	·20	·17	·14	·11	·08	·06	·03	·00	58
59	·45	·42	·38	·35	·32	·29	·26	·23	·20	·18	·15	·12	·09	·06	·03	·00	59
60	·46	·43	·40	·37	·34	·31	·27	·24	·21	·18	·15	·12	·09	·06	·03	·00	60
Lat.	105° 255°	104° 256°	103° 257°	102° 258°	101° 259°	100° 260°	99° 261°	98° 262°	97° 263°	96° 264°	95° 265°	94° 266°	93° 267°	92° 268°	91° 269°	90° 270°	Lat.

A - Named opposite to Latitude, except when Hour Angle is between 90° and 270°

HOUR ANGLE

A

TABLE B HOUR ANGLE

Dec.°	75° 285°	76° 284°	77° 283°	78° 282°	79° 281°	80° 280°	81° 279°	82° 278°	83° 277°	84° 276°	85° 275°	86° 274°	87° 273°	88° 272°	89° 271°	90° 270°	Dec.°
0	·00	·00	·00	·00	·00	·00	·00	·00	·00	·00	·00	·00	·00	·00	·00	·00	0
1	·02	·02	·02	·02	·02	·02	·02	·02	·02	·02	·02	·02	·02	·02	·02	·02	1
2	·04	·04	·04	·04	·04	·04	·04	·04	·04	·04	·04	·04	·04	·04	·03	·03	2
3	·05	·05	·05	·05	·05	·05	·05	·05	·05	·05	·05	·05	·05	·05	·05	·05	3
4	·07	·07	·07	·07	·07	·07	·07	·07	·07	·07	·07	·07	·07	·07	·07	·07	4
5	·09	·09	·09	·09	·09	·09	·09	·09	·09	·09	·09	·09	·09	·09	·09	·09	5
6	·11	·11	·11	·11	·11	·11	·11	·11	·11	·11	·11	·11	·11	·11	·11	·11	6
7	·13	·13	·13	·13	·13	·12	·12	·12	·12	·12	·12	·12	·12	·12	·12	·12	7
8	·15	·15	·14	·14	·14	·14	·14	·14	·14	·14	·14	·14	·14	·14	·14	·14	8
9	·16	·16	·16	·16	·16	·16	·16	·16	·16	·16	·16	·16	·16	·16	·16	·16	9
10	·18	·18	·18	·18	·18	·18	·18	·18	·18	·18	·18	·18	·18	·18	·18	·18	10
11	·20	·20	·20	·20	·20	·20	·20	·20	·20	·20	·20	·20	·20	·19	·19	·19	11
12	·22	·22	·22	·22	·22	·22	·22	·22	·21	·21	·21	·21	·21	·21	·21	·21	12
13	·24	·24	·24	·24	·24	·23	·23	·23	·23	·23	·23	·23	·23	·23	·23	·23	13
14	·26	·26	·26	·26	·25	·25	·25	·25	·25	·25	·25	·25	·25	·25	·25	·25	14
15	·28	·28	·28	·27	·27	·27	·27	·27	·27	·27	·27	·27	·27	·27	·27	·27	15
16	·30	·30	·29	·29	·29	·29	·29	·29	·29	·29	·29	·29	·29	·29	·29	·29	16
17	·32	·32	·31	·31	·31	·31	·31	·31	·31	·31	·31	·31	·31	·31	·31	·31	17
18	·34	·34	·33	·33	·33	·33	·33	·33	·33	·33	·33	·33	·33	·33	·33	·32	18
19	·36	·36	·35	·35	·35	·35	·35	·35	·35	·35	·35	·35	·35	·35	·34	·34	19
20	·38	·38	·37	·37	·37	·37	·37	·37	·37	·37	·37	·37	·36	·36	·36	·36	20
21	·40	·40	·39	·39	·39	·39	·39	·39	·39	·39	·39	·39	·38	·38	·38	·38	21
22	·42	·42	·42	·41	·41	·41	·41	·41	·41	·41	·41	·41	·41	·40	·40	·40	22
23	·44	·44	·44	·43	·43	·43	·43	·43	·43	·43	·43	·43	·43	·43	·43	·42	23
24	·46	·46	·46	·46	·45	·45	·45	·45	·45	·45	·45	·45	·45	·45	·45	·45	24
25	·48	·48	·48	·48	·48	·47	·47	·47	·47	·47	·47	·47	·47	·47	·47	·47	25
26	·50	·50	·50	·50	·50	·50	·49	·49	·49	·49	·49	·49	·49	·49	·49	·49	26
27	·53	·53	·52	·52	·52	·52	·52	·52	·51	·51	·51	·51	·51	·51	·51	·51	27
28	·55	·55	·55	·54	·54	·54	·54	·54	·54	·54	·53	·53	·53	·53	·53	·53	28
29	·57	·57	·57	·57	·57	·56	·56	·56	·56	·56	·56	·56	·56	·56	·55	·55	29
30	·60	·60	·59	·59	·59	·59	·59	·58	·58	·58	·58	·58	·58	·58	·58	·58	30
31	·62	·62	·62	·61	·61	·61	·61	·61	·61	·60	·60	·60	·60	·60	·60	·60	31
32	·65	·64	·64	·64	·64	·63	·63	·63	·63	·63	·63	·63	·63	·63	·63	·62	32
33	·67	·67	·67	·66	·66	·66	·66	·66	·65	·65	·65	·65	·65	·65	·65	·65	33
34	·70	·70	·69	·69	·69	·69	·68	·68	·68	·68	·68	·68	·68	·68	·68	·67	34
35	·72	·72	·72	·72	·71	·71	·71	·71	·71	·70	·70	·70	·70	·70	:70	·70	35
36	·75	·75	·75	·74	·74	·74	·74	·73	·73	·73	·73	·73	·73	·73	·73	·73	36
37	·78	·78	·77	·77	·77	·77	·76	·76	·76	·76	·75	·76	·76	·75	·75	·75	37
38	·81	·81	·80	·80	·80	·79	·79	·79	·79	·79	·78	·78	·78	·78	·78	·78	38
39	·84	·84	·83	·83	·83	·82	·82	·82	·82	·81	·81	·81	·81	·81	·81	·81	39
40	·87	·87	·86	·86	·86	·85	·85	·85	·85	·84	·84	·84	·84	·84	·84	·84	40
41	·90	·90	·89	·89	·89	·88	·88	·88	·88	·87	·87	87	·87	·87	·87	·87	41
42	·93	·93	·92	·92	·92	·91	·91	·91	·91	·91	·90	·90	·90	·90	·90	·90	42
43	·97	·96	·96	·95	·95	·95	·94	·94	·94	·94	·94	·94	·93	·93	·93	·93	43
44	1·00	1·00	·99	·99	·99	·98	·98	·98	·97	·97	·97	·97	·97	·97	·97	·97	44
45	1·04	1·03	1·03	1·02	1·02	1·02	1·01	1·01	1·01	1·01	1·00	1·00	1·00	1·00	1·00	1·00	45
46	1·07	1·07	1·06	1·06	1·05	1·05	1·05	1·05	1·04	1·04	1·04	1·04	1·04	1·04	1·04	1·04	46
47	1·11	1·11	1·10	1·10	1·09	1·09	1·09	1·08	1·08	1·08	1·08	1·07	1·07	1·07	1·07	1·07	47
48	1·15	1·14	1·14	1·14	1·13	1·13	1·12	1·12	1·12	1·12	1·11	1·11	1·11	1·11	1·11	1·11	48
49	1·19	1·19	1·18	1·18	1·17	1·17	1·16	1·16	1·16	1·16	1·15	1·15	1·15	1·15	1·15	1·15	49
50	1·23	1·23	1·22	1·22	1·21	1·21	1·21	1·20	1·20	1·20	1·20	1·19	1·19	1·19	1·19	1·19	50
51	1·28	1·27	1·27	1·26	1·26	1·25	1·25	1·25	1·24	1·24	1·24	1·24	1·24	1·24	1·24	1·23	51
52	1·33	1·32	1·31	1·31	1·30	1·30	1·30	1·29	1·29	1·29	1·28	1·28	1·28	1·28	1·28	1·28	52
53	1·37	1·37	1·36	1·36	1·35	1·35	1·34	1·34	1·34	1·33	1·33	1·33	1·33	1·33	1·33	1·33	53
54	1·42	1·42	1·41	1·41	1·40	1·40	1·39	1·39	1·39	1·38	1·38	1·38	1·38	1·38	1·38	1·38	54
55	1·48	1·47	1·47	1·46	1·46	1·45	1·45	1·44	1·44	1·44	1·43	1·43	1·43	1·43	1·43	1·43	55
56	1·54	1·53	1·52	1·52	1·51	1·51	1·50	1·50	1·49	1·49	1·49	1·49	1·48	1·48	1·48	1·48	56
57	1·60	1·59	1·58	1·57	1·57	1·57	1·56	1·55	1·55	1·55	1·55	1·54	1·54	1·54	1·54	1·54	57
58	1·66	1·65	1·64	1·64	1·63	1·63	1·62	1·62	1·61	1·61	1·61	1·60	1·60	1·60	1·60	1·60	58
59	1·72	1·72	1·71	1·70	1·70	1·69	1·69	1·68	1·68	1·67	1·67	1·67	1·67	1·67	1·66	1·66	59
60	1·79	1·79	1·78	1·77	1·76	1·76	1·75	1·75	1·75	1·74	1·74	1·74	1·73	1·73	1·73	1·73	60
Dec.	105° 255°	104° 256°	103° 257°	102° 258°	101° 259°	100° 260°	99° 261°	98° 262°	97° 263°	96° 264°	95° 265°	94° 266°	93° 267°	92° 268°	91° 269°	90° 270°	Dec.

B - Always named the **same** as Declination

HOUR ANGLE

B

TABLE A HOUR ANGLE

Lat. °	0° 15' / 359° 45'	0° 30' / 359° 30'	0° 45' / 359° 15'	1° 00' / 359° 00'	1° 15' / 358° 45'	1° 30' / 358° 30'	1° 45' / 358° 15'	2° 00' / 358° 00'	2° 15' / 357° 45'	2° 30' / 357° 30'	2° 45' / 357° 15'	3° 00' / 357° 00'	3° 15' / 356° 45'	3° 30' / 356° 30'	3° 45' / 356° 15'	Lat. °
60	397	198	132	99·2	79·4	66·1	56·7	49·6	44·1	39·7	36·1	33·0	30·5	28·3	26·4	60
61	414	207	138	103	82·7	68·9	59·0	51·7	45·9	41·3	37·6	34·4	31·8	29·5	27·5	61
62	431	216	144	108	86·2	71·8	61·6	53·9	47·9	43·1	39·2	35·9	33·1	30·8	28·7	62
63	450	225	150	112	89·9	74·9	64·2	56·2	50·0	45·0	40·9	37·4	34·6	32·1	29·9	63
64	470	235	157	117	94·0	78·3	67·1	58·7	52·2	47·0	42·7	39·1	36·1	33·5	31·3	64
65	491	246	164	123	98·3	81·9	70·2	61·4	54·6	49·1	44·6	40·9	37·8	35·1	32·7	65
66	515	257	172	129	103	85·8	73·5	64·3	57·2	51·4	46·8	42·9	39·6	36·7	34·3	66
67	540	270	180	135	108	90·0	77·1	67·5	60·0	54·0	49·0	45·0	41·5	38·5	35·9	67
68	567	284	189	142	113	94·5	81·0	70·9	63·0	56·7	51·5	47·2	43·6	40·5	37·8	68
69	597	299	199	149	119	99·5	85·3	74·6	66·3	59·7	54·2	49·7	45·9	42·6	39·7	69
70	630	315	210	157	126	105	89·9	78·7	69·9	62·9	57·2	52·4	48·4	44·9	41·9	70
71	666	333	222	166	133	111	95·1	83·2	73·9	66·5	60·5	55·4	51·2	47·5	44·3	71
72	705	353	235	176	141	118	101	88·1	78·3	70·5	64·1	58·7	54·2	50·3	47·0	72
73	750	375	250	187	150	125	107	93·7	83·3	74·9	68·1	62·4	57·6	53·5	49·9	73
74	799	400	266	200	160	133	114	99·9	88·8	79·9	72·6	66·6	61·4	57·0	53·2	74
75	855	428	285	215	171	143	122	107	95·0	85·5	77·7	71·3	65·7	61·0	56·9	75
76	919	460	306	230	184	153	131	115	102	91·9	83·5	76·5	70·6	65·6	61·2	76
77	993	496	331	248	199	165	142	124	110	99·2	90·2	82·7	76·3	70·8	66·1	77
78	1078	539	359	270	216	180	154	135	120	108	97·9	89·7	82·9	76·9	71·8	78
79	1179	590	393	295	236	197	168	147	131	118	107	98·2	90·6	84·1	78·5	79
80	1300	650	433	325	260	217	186	162	144	130	118	108	100	92·7	86·5	80
81	1447	724	482	362	289	241	207	181	161	145	131	121	111	103	96·3	81
82	1631	815	544	408	326	272	233	204	181	163	148	136	125	116	109	82
83	1867	933	622	467	373	311	267	233	207	187	170	155	143	133	124	83
Lat.	179° 45' / 180° 15'	179° 30' / 180° 30'	179° 15' / 180° 45'	179° 00' / 181° 00'	178° 45' / 181° 15'	178° 30' / 181° 30'	178° 15' / 181° 45'	178° 00' / 182° 00'	177° 45' / 182° 15'	177° 30' / 182° 30'	177° 15' / 182° 45'	177° 00' / 183° 00'	176° 45' / 183° 15'	176° 30' / 183° 30'	176° 15' / 183° 45'	Lat.

HOUR ANGLE

TABLE A HOUR ANGLE

Lat. °	4° 00' / 356° 00'	4° 15' / 355° 45'	4° 30' / 355° 30'	4° 45' / 355° 15'	5° 00' / 355° 00'	5° 15' / 354° 45'	5° 30' / 354° 30'	5° 45' / 354° 15'	6° 00' / 354° 00'	6° 15' / 353° 45'	6° 30' / 353° 30'	6° 45' / 353° 15'	7° 00' / 353° 00'	7° 15' / 352° 45'	7° 30' / 352° 30'	Lat. °
60	24·8	23·3	22·0	20·8	19·8	18·8	18·0	17·2	16·5	15·8	15·2	14·6	14·1	13·6	13·2	60
61	25·8	24·3	22·9	21·7	20·6	19·6	18·7	17·9	17·2	16·5	15·8	15·2	14·7	14·2	13·7	61
62	26·9	25·3	23·9	22·6	21·5	20·5	19·5	18·7	17·9	17·2	16·5	15·9	15·3	14·8	14·3	62
63	28·1	26·4	24·9	23·6	22·4	21·4	20·4	19·5	18·7	17·9	17·2	16·6	16·0	15·4	14·9	63
64	29·3	27·6	26·1	24·7	23·4	22·3	21·3	20·4	19·5	18·7	18·0	17·3	16·7	16·1	15·6	64
65	30·7	28·9	27·2	25·8	24·5	23·3	22·3	21·3	20·4	19·6	18·8	18·1	17·5	16·9	16·3	65
66	32·1	30·2	28·5	27·0	25·7	24·4	23·3	22·3	21·4	20·5	19·7	19·0	18·3	17·7	17·1	66
67	33·7	31·7	29·9	28·4	26·9	25·6	24·5	23·4	22·4	21·5	20·7	19·9	19·2	18·5	17·9	67
68	35·4	33·3	31·4	29·8	28·3	26·9	25·7	24·6	23·5	22·6	21·7	20·9	20·2	19·5	18·8	68
69	37·3	35·1	33·1	31·4	29·8	28·4	27·1	25·9	24·8	23·8	22·9	22·0	21·2	20·5	19·8	69
70	39·3	37·0	34·9	33·1	31·4	29·9	28·5	27·3	26·1	25·1	24·1	23·2	22·4	21·6	20·9	70
71	41·5	39·1	36·9	35·0	33·2	31·6	30·2	28·9	27·6	26·5	25·5	24·5	23·7	22·8	22·1	71
72	44·0	41·4	39·1	37·0	35·2	33·5	32·0	30·6	29·3	28·1	27·0	26·0	25·1	24·2	23·4	72
73	46·8	44·0	41·6	39·4	37·4	35·6	34·0	32·5	31·1	30·0	28·7	27·6	26·6	25·7	24·8	73
74	50·0	46·9	44·3	42·0	39·9	38·0	36·2	34·6	33·2	31·9	30·6	29·5	28·4	27·4	26·5	74
75	53·4	50·2	47·4	44·9	42·7	40·6	38·8	37·1	35·5	34·1	32·8	31·5	30·4	29·3	28·4	75
76	57·4	54·0	51·0	48·3	45·8	43·7	41·7	39·8	38·2	36·6	35·2	33·9	32·7	31·5	30·5	76
77	62·0	58·3	55·0	52·1	49·5	47·1	45·0	43·0	41·2	39·6	38·0	36·6	35·2	34·1	32·9	77
78	67·3	63·3	59·8	56·6	53·8	51·2	48·9	46·7	44·8	43·0	41·3	39·8	38·3	37·0	35·7	78
79	73·6	69·2	65·4	61·9	58·8	56·0	53·4	51·1	49·0	47·0	45·2	43·5	41·9	40·0	39·1	79
80	81·1	76·3	72·1	68·3	64·8	61·7	58·9	56·3	54·0	51·8	49·8	47·9	46·2	44·6	43·1	80
81	90·3	85·0	80·2	76·0	72·2	68·7	65·6	62·7	60·1	57·7	55·4	53·3	51·4	49·6	48·0	81
82	102	96·0	90·4	85·6	81·3	77·4	73·9	70·7	67·7	65·0	62·5	60·1	58·0	55·9	54·0	82
83	117	110	104	98·0	93·1	88·6	84·6	80·9	77·5	74·4	71·5	68·8	66·3	64·0	61·9	83
Lat.	176° 00' / 184° 00'	175° 45' / 184° 15'	175° 30' / 184° 30'	175° 15' / 184° 45'	175° 00' / 185° 00'	174° 45' / 185° 15'	174° 30' / 185° 30'	174° 15' / 185° 45'	174° 00' / 186° 00'	173° 45' / 186° 15'	173° 30' / 186° 30'	173° 15' / 186° 45'	173° 00' / 187° 00'	172° 45' / 187° 15'	172° 30' / 187° 30'	Lat.

HOUR ANGLE

Left margin: A - Named opposite to Latitude, **except** when Hour Angle is between 90° and 270°

Right margin: A - Named opposite to Latitude, **except** when Hour Angle is between 90° and 270°

A

TABLE B HOUR ANGLE

Dec. °	0°15' 359°45'	0°30' 359°30'	0°45' 359°15'	1°00' 359°00'	1°15' 358°45'	1°30' 358°30'	1°45' 358°15'	2°00' 358°00'	2°15' 357°45'	2°30' 357°30'	2°45' 357°15'	3°00' 357°00'	3°15' 356°45'	3°30' 356°30'	3°45' 356°15'	Dec. °
60	397	198	132	99.2	79.4	66.2	56.7	49.6	44.1	39.7	36.1	33.1	30.6	28.4	26.5	60
61	414	207	138	103	82.7	68.9	59.1	51.7	46.0	41.4	37.6	34.5	31.8	29.6	27.6	61
62	431	216	144	108	86.2	71.8	61.6	53.9	47.9	43.1	39.2	35.9	33.2	30.8	28.8	62
63	450	225	150	112	90.0	75.0	64.3	56.2	50.0	45.0	40.9	37.5	34.6	32.1	30.0	63
64	470	235	157	117	94.0	78.3	67.1	58.7	52.2	47.0	42.7	39.2	36.2	33.6	31.4	64
65	491	246	164	123	98.3	81.9	70.2	61.4	54.6	49.2	44.7	41.0	37.8	35.1	32.8	65
66	515	257	172	129	103	85.8	73.5	64.4	57.2	51.5	46.8	42.9	39.6	36.8	34.3	66
67	540	270	180	135	108	90.0	77.1	67.5	60.0	54.0	49.1	45.0	41.6	38.6	36.0	67
68	567	284	189	142	113	94.6	81.0	70.9	63.0	56.7	51.6	47.3	43.7	40.5	37.8	68
69	597	299	199	149	119	99.5	85.3	74.6	66.4	59.7	54.3	49.8	46.0	42.7	39.8	69
70	630	315	210	157	126	105	90.0	78.7	70.0	63.0	57.3	52.5	48.5	45.0	42.0	70
71	666	333	222	166	133	111	95.1	83.2	74.0	66.6	60.5	55.5	51.2	47.6	44.4	71
72	705	353	235	176	141	118	101	88.2	78.4	70.6	64.2	58.8	54.3	50.4	47.1	72
73	750	375	250	187	150	125	107	93.7	83.3	75.0	68.2	62.5	57.7	53.6	50.0	73
74	799	400	266	200	160	133	114	100	88.8	80.0	72.7	66.6	61.5	57.1	53.3	74
75	855	428	285	214	171	143	122	107	95.1	85.6	77.8	71.3	65.8	61.1	57.1	75
Dec.	179°45' 180°15'	179°30' 180°30'	179°15' 180°45'	179°00' 181°00'	178°45' 181°15'	178°30' 181°30'	178°15' 181°45'	178°00' 182°00'	177°45' 182°15'	177°30' 182°30'	177°15' 182°45'	177°00' 183°00'	176°45' 183°15'	176°30' 183°30'	176°15' 183°45'	Dec.

HOUR ANGLE

TABLE B - HOUR ANGLE

Dec. °	3°45' 356°15'	4°00' 356°00'	4°15' 355°45'	4°30' 355°30'	4°45' 355°15'	5°00' 355°00'	5°15' 354°45'	5°30' 354°30'	5°45' 354°15'	6°00' 354°00'	6°15' 353°45'	6°30' 353°30'	6°45' 353°15'	7°00' 353°00'	7°15' 352°45'	7°30' 352°30'	Dec. °
60	26.5	24.8	23.4	22.1	20.9	19.9	18.9	18.1	17.3	16.6	15.9	15.3	14.7	14.2	13.7	13.3	60
61	27.6	25.9	24.3	23.0	21.8	20.7	19.7	18.8	18.0	17.3	16.6	15.9	15.3	14.8	14.3	13.8	61
62	28.8	27.0	25.4	24.0	22.7	21.6	20.6	19.6	18.8	18.0	17.3	16.6	16.0	15.4	14.9	14.4	62
63	30.0	28.1	26.5	25.0	23.7	22.5	21.4	20.5	19.6	18.8	18.0	17.3	16.7	16.1	15.6	15.0	63
64	31.3	29.4	27.7	26.1	24.8	23.5	22.4	21.4	20.5	19.6	18.8	18.1	17.4	16.8	16.2	15.7	64
65	32.8	30.7	28.9	27.3	25.9	24.6	23.4	22.4	21.4	20.5	19.7	18.9	18.2	17.6	17.0	16.4	65
66	34.3	32.2	30.3	28.6	27.1	25.8	24.5	23.4	22.4	21.5	20.6	19.8	19.1	18.4	17.8	17.2	66
67	36.0	33.8	31.8	30.0	28.4	27.0	25.7	24.6	23.5	22.5	21.6	20.8	20.1	19.3	18.7	18.0	67
68	37.8	35.5	33.4	31.5	29.9	28.4	27.0	25.8	24.7	23.7	22.7	21.9	21.1	20.3	19.6	19.0	68
69	39.8	37.3	35.2	33.2	31.5	29.9	28.5	27.2	26.0	24.9	23.9	23.0	22.2	21.4	20.6	20.0	69
70	42.0	39.4	37.1	35.0	33.2	31.5	30.0	28.7	27.4	26.3	25.2	24.3	23.4	22.5	21.8	21.1	70
71	44.4	41.6	39.2	37.0	35.1	33.3	31.7	30.3	29.0	27.8	26.7	25.7	24.7	23.8	23.0	22.6	71
72	47.1	44.1	41.5	39.2	37.2	35.3	33.6	32.1	30.7	29.4	28.3	27.2	26.2	25.3	24.4	23.3	72
73	50.0	46.9	44.1	41.7	39.5	37.5	35.8	34.1	32.7	31.3	30.0	28.9	27.8	26.8	25.9	25.1	73
74	53.3	50.0	47.1	44.5	42.1	40.0	38.1	36.4	34.8	33.4	32.0	30.8	29.7	28.6	27.6	26.7	74
75	57.1	53.5	50.4	47.6	45.1	42.8	40.8	38.9	37.3	35.7	34.3	33.0	31.8	30.6	29.6	28.6	75
Dec.	176°15' 183°45'	176°00' 184°00'	175°45' 184°15'	175°30' 184°30'	175°15' 184°45'	175°00' 185°00'	174°45' 185°15'	174°30' 185°30'	174°15' 185°45'	174°00' 186°00'	173°45' 186°15'	173°30' 186°30'	173°15' 186°45'	173°00' 187°00'	172°45' 187°15'	172°30' 187°30'	Dec.

HOUR ANGLE

B - Always named the same as Declination

B

TABLE A - HOUR ANGLE

A - Named opposite to Latitude, **except** when **Hour Angle** is between 90° and 270°

Lat.°	7° 30' 352° 30'	7° 45' 352° 15'	8° 00' 352° 00'	8° 15' 351° 45'	8° 30' 351° 30'	8° 45' 351° 15'	9° 00' 351° 00'	9° 15' 350° 45'	9° 30' 350° 30'	9° 45' 350° 15'	10° 00' 350° 00'	10° 15' 349° 45'	10° 30' 349° 30'	10° 45' 349° 15'	11° 00' 349° 00'	11° 15' 348° 45'	Lat.°
60	13.2	12.7	12.3	11.9	11.6	11.3	10.9	10.6	10.4	10.1	9.82	9.58	9.35	9.12	8.91	8.71	60
61	13.7	13.3	12.8	12.4	12.1	11.7	11.4	11.1	10.8	10.5	10.2	9.98	9.73	9.50	9.28	9.07	61
62	14.3	13.8	13.4	13.0	12.6	12.2	11.9	11.5	11.2	10.9	10.7	10.4	10.1	9.91	9.68	9.46	62
63	14.9	14.4	14.0	13.5	13.1	12.8	12.4	12.1	11.7	11.4	11.1	10.9	10.6	10.3	10.1	9.87	63
64	15.6	15.1	14.6	14.1	13.7	13.3	12.9	12.6	12.3	11.9	11.6	11.3	11.1	10.8	10.5	10.3	64
65	16.3	15.8	15.3	14.8	14.3	13.9	13.5	13.2	12.8	12.5	12.2	11.9	11.6	11.3	11.0	10.8	65
66	17.1	16.5	16.0	15.5	15.0	14.6	14.2	13.8	13.4	13.1	12.7	12.4	12.1	11.8	11.6	11.3	66
67	17.9	17.3	16.8	16.2	15.8	15.3	14.9	14.5	14.1	13.7	13.4	13.0	12.7	12.4	12.1	11.8	67
68	18.8	18.2	17.6	17.1	16.6	16.1	15.6	15.2	14.8	14.4	14.0	13.7	13.4	13.0	12.7	12.4	68
69	19.8	19.1	18.5	18.0	17.4	16.9	16.5	16.0	15.6	15.2	14.8	14.4	14.1	13.7	13.4	13.1	69
70	20.9	20.2	19.6	19.0	18.4	17.9	17.4	16.9	16.4	16.0	15.6	15.2	14.8	14.5	14.1	13.8	70
71	22.1	21.3	20.7	20.0	19.4	18.9	18.3	17.8	17.4	16.9	16.5	16.1	15.7	15.3	14.9	14.6	71
72	23.4	22.6	21.9	21.2	20.6	20.0	19.4	18.9	18.4	17.9	17.5	17.0	16.6	16.2	15.8	15.5	72
73	24.8	24.0	23.3	22.6	21.9	21.3	20.6	20.1	19.5	19.0	18.6	18.1	17.7	17.2	16.8	16.4	73
74	26.5	25.6	24.8	24.1	23.3	22.7	22.0	21.4	20.8	20.3	19.8	19.3	18.8	18.4	17.9	17.5	74
75	28.4	27.4	26.6	25.7	25.0	24.3	23.6	22.9	22.3	21.7	21.2	20.6	20.1	19.7	19.2	18.8	75
76	30.5	29.5	28.5	27.7	26.8	26.1	25.3	24.6	24.0	23.3	22.8	22.2	21.6	21.1	20.6	20.2	76
77	32.9	31.8	30.8	29.9	29.0	28.1	27.4	26.6	25.9	25.2	24.6	24.0	23.4	22.8	22.3	21.8	77
78	35.7	34.6	33.5	32.5	31.5	30.6	29.7	28.9	28.1	27.4	26.7	26.0	25.4	24.8	24.2	23.7	78
79	39.1	37.8	36.6	35.5	34.4	33.4	32.5	31.6	30.7	29.9	29.2	28.5	27.8	27.1	26.5	25.9	79
80	43.1	41.7	40.4	39.1	38.0	36.9	35.8	34.8	33.9	33.0	32.2	31.4	30.6	29.9	29.2	28.5	80
81	48.0	46.4	44.9	43.6	42.2	41.0	39.9	38.8	37.7	36.7	35.8	34.9	34.1	33.3	32.5	31.7	81
82	54.0	52.3	50.6	49.1	47.6	46.2	44.9	43.7	42.5	41.4	40.4	39.4	38.4	37.5	36.6	35.8	82
83	61.9	59.9	58.0	56.2	54.5	52.9	51.4	50.0	48.7	47.4	46.2	45.0	43.9	42.9	41.9	41.0	83
Lat.	172° 30' 187° 30'	172° 15' 187° 45'	172° 00' 188° 00'	171° 45' 188° 15'	171° 30' 188° 30'	171° 15' 188° 45'	171° 00' 189° 00'	170° 45' 189° 15'	170° 30' 189° 30'	170° 15' 189° 45'	170° 00' 190° 00'	169° 45' 190° 15'	169° 30' 190° 30'	169° 15' 190° 45'	169° 00' 191° 00'	168° 45' 191° 15'	Lat.

HOUR ANGLE

TABLE A - HOUR ANGLE

A - Named opposite to Latitude, **except** when **Hour Angle** is between 90° and 270°

Lat.°	11° 15' 348° 45'	11° 30' 348° 30'	11° 45' 348° 15'	12° 00' 348° 00'	12° 15' 347° 45'	12° 30' 347° 30'	12° 45' 347° 15'	13° 00' 347° 00'	13° 15' 346° 45'	13° 30' 346° 30'	13° 45' 346° 15'	14° 00' 346° 00'	14° 15' 345° 45'	14° 30' 345° 30'	14° 45' 345° 15'	15° 00' 345° 00'	Lat.°
60	8.71	8.51	8.33	8.15	7.98	7.81	7.65	7.50	7.36	7.21	7.08	6.95	6.82	6.70	6.58	6.46	60
61	9.07	8.87	8.67	8.49	8.31	8.14	7.97	7.81	7.66	7.51	7.37	7.24	7 10	6.98	6.85	6.73	61
62	9.46	9.24	9.04	8.85	8.66	8.48	8.31	8.15	7.99	7.83	7.69	7.54	7.41	7.27	7.14	7.02	62
63	9.87	9.65	9.44	9.23	9.04	8.85	8.67	8.50	8.33	8.17	8.02	7.87	7.73	7.59	7.45	7.32	63
64	10.3	10.1	9.86	9.65	9.44	9.25	9.06	8.88	8.71	8.54	8.38	8.22	8.07	7.93	7.79	7.65	64
65	10.8	10.5	10.3	10.1	9 88	9.67	9.48	9.29	9.11	8.93	8.76	8.60	8.44	8.29	8.15	8.00	65
66	11.3	11.0	10.8	10.6	10.3	10.1	9.93	9.73	9.54	9.36	9.18	9.01	8.84	8.68	8.53	8.38	66
67	11.8	11.6	11.3	11.1	10.9	10.6	10.4	10.2	10.0	9.81	9.63	9.45	9.28	9.11	8.95	8.79	67
68	12.4	12.2	11.9	11.6	11.4	11.2	10.9	10.7	10.5	10.3	10.1	9 93	9.75	9.57	9.40	9.24	68
69	13.1	12.8	12.5	12.3	12.0	11.8	11.5	11.3	11.1	10.9	10.7	10.5	10.3	10.1	9.90	9.72	69
70	13.8	13.5	13.2	12.9	12.7	12.4	12.1	11.9	11.7	11.4	11.2	11.0	10.8	10.6	10.4	10.3	70
71	14.6	14.3	14.0	13.7	13.4	13.1	12.8	12.6	12.3	12.1	11.9	11.7	11.4	11.2	11.0	10.8	71
72	15.5	15.1	14.8	14.5	14.2	13.9	13.6	13.3	13.1	12.8	12.6	12.3	12.1	11.9	11.7	11.5	72
73	16.4	16.1	15.7	15.4	15.1	14.8	14.5	14.2	13.9	13.6	13.4	13.1	12.9	12.7	12.4	12.2	73
74	17.5	17.1	16.8	16.4	16.1	15.7	15.4	15.1	14.8	14.5	14.3	14.0	13.7	13.5	13.3	13.0	74
75	18.8	18.3	17.9	17.6	17.2	16.8	16.5	16.2	15.9	15.6	15.3	15.0	14.7	14.4	14.2	13.9	75
76	20.2	19.7	19.3	18.9	18.5	18.1	17.7	17.4	17.0	16.7	16.4	16.1	15.8	15.5	15.2	15.0	76
77	21.8	21.3	20.8	20.4	20.0	19.5	19.2	18.8	18.4	18.0	17.7	17.4	17.1	16.8	16.5	16.2	77
78	23.7	23.1	22.6	22.1	21.7	21.2	20.8	20.4	20.0	19.6	19.2	18.9	18.5	18.2	17.9	17.6	78
79	25.9	25.3	24.7	24.2	23.7	23.2	22.7	22.3	21.9	21.4	21.0	20.6	20.3	19.9	19.5	19.2	79
80	28.5	27.9	27.3	26.7	26.1	25.6	25.1	24.5	24.1	23.6	23.2	22.8	22.3	21.9	21.5	21.2	80
81	31.7	31.0	30.4	29.7	29.1	28.5	27.9	27.4	26.8	26.3	25.8	25.3	24.9	24.4	24.0	23.6	81
82	35.8	35.0	34.2	33.5	32.8	32.1	31.5	30.8	30.2	29.6	29.1	28.5	28.0	27.5	27.0	26.6	82
83	41.0	40.0	39.2	38.3	37.5	36.7	36.0	35.3	34.6	33.9	33.3	32.7	32.1	31.5	30.9	30.4	83
Lat.	168° 45' 191° 15'	168° 30' 191° 30'	168° 15' 191° 45'	168° 00' 192° 00'	167° 45' 192° 15'	167° 30' 192° 30'	167° 15' 192° 45'	167° 00' 193° 00'	166° 45' 193° 15'	166° 30' 193° 30'	166° 15' 193° 45'	166° 00' 194° 00'	165° 45' 194° 15'	165° 30' 194° 30'	165° 15' 194° 45'	165° 00' 195° 00'	Lat.

HOUR ANGLE

A - Named opposite to Latitude, **except** when **Hour Angle** is between 90° and 270°

A

TABLE B HOUR ANGLE

Dec.°	7°30' / 352°30'	7°45' / 352°15'	8°00' / 352°00'	8°15' / 351°45'	8°30' / 351°30'	8°45' / 351°15'	9°00' / 351°00'	9°15' / 350°45'	9°30' / 350°30'	9°45' / 350°15'	10°00' / 350°00'	10°15' / 349°45'	10°30' / 349°30'	10°45' / 349°15'	11°00' / 349°00'	11°15' / 348°45'	Dec.°
60	13·3	12·8	12·4	12·1	11·7	11·4	11·1	10·8	10·5	10·2	9·97	9·73	9·50	9·29	9·08	8·88	60
61	13·8	13·4	13·0	12·6	12·2	11·9	11·6	11·2	10·9	10·7	10·4	10·1	9·90	9·67	9·45	9·25	61
62	14·4	13·9	13·5	13·1	12·7	12·4	12·0	11·7	11·4	11·1	10·8	10·6	10·3	10·1	9·86	9·64	62
63	15·0	14·6	14·1	13·7	13·3	12·9	12·5	12·2	11·9	11·6	11·3	11·0	10·8	10·5	10·3	10·1	63
64	15·7	15·2	14·7	14·3	13·9	13·5	13·1	12·8	12·4	12·1	11·8	11·5	11·3	11·0	10·7	10·5	64
65	16·4	15·9	15·4	14·9	14·5	14·1	13·7	13·3	13·0	12·7	12·3	12·1	11·8	11·5	11·2	11·0	65
66	17·2	16·7	16·1	15·7	15·2	14·8	14·4	14·0	13·6	13·3	12·9	12·6	12·3	12·0	11·8	11·5	66
67	18·0	17·5	16·9	16·4	15·9	15·5	15·1	14·7	14·3	13·9	13·6	13·2	12·9	12·6	12·3	12·1	67
68	19·0	18·4	17·8	17·2	16·7	16·3	15·8	15·4	15·0	14·6	14·3	13·9	13·6	13·3	13·0	12·7	68
69	20·0	19·3	18·7	18·2	17·6	17·1	16·7	16·2	15·8	15·4	15·0	14·6	14·3	14·0	13·7	13·4	69
70	21·1	20·4	19·7	19·1	18·6	18·1	17·6	17·1	16·6	16·2	15·8	15·4	15·1	14·7	14·4	14·1	70
71	22·3	21·5	20·9	20·2	19·6	19·1	18·6	18·1	17·6	17·1	16·7	16·3	15·9	15·6	15·2	14·9	71
72	23·6	22·8	22·1	21·4	20·8	20·2	19·7	19·1	18·6	18·2	17·7	17·3	16·9	16·5	16·1	15·8	72
73	25·1	24·3	23·5	22·8	22·1	21·5	20·9	20·3	19·8	19·3	18·8	18·4	18·0	17·5	17·1	16·8	73
74	26·7	25·9	25·1	24·3	23·6	22·9	22·3	21·7	21·1	20·6	20·1	19·6	19·1	18·7	18·3	17·9	74
75	28·6	27·7	26·8	26·0	25·3	24·5	23·9	23·2	22·6	22·0	21·5	21·0	20·5	20·0	19·6	19·1	75
Dec.	172°30' / 187°30'	172°15' / 187°45'	172°00' / 188°00'	171°45' / 188°15'	171°30' / 188°30'	171°15' / 188°45'	171°00' / 189°00'	170°45' / 189°15'	170°30' / 189°30'	170°15' / 189°45'	170°00' / 190°00'	169°45' / 190°15'	169°30' / 190°30'	169°15' / 190°45'	169°00' / 191°00'	168°45' / 191°15'	Dec.

HOUR ANGLE

B - Always named the **same** as Declination

TABLE B - HOUR ANGLE

Dec.°	11°15' / 348°45'	11°30' / 348°30'	11°45' / 348°15'	12°00' / 348°00'	12°15' / 347°45'	12°30 / 347°30'	12°45' / 347°15'	13°00' / 347°00'	13°15' / 346°45'	13°30' / 346°30'	13°45' / 346°15'	14°00' / 346°00'	14°15' / 345°45'	14°30' / 345°30'	14°45' / 345°15'	15°00' / 345°00'	Dec.°
60	8·88	8·69	8·51	8·33	8·16	8·00	7·85	7·70	7·56	7·42	7·29	7·16	7·04	6·92	6·80	6·69	60
61	9·25	9·05	8·86	8·68	8·50	8·34	8·17	8·02	7·87	7·73	7·59	7·46	7·33	7·21	7·09	6·97	61
62	9·64	9·43	9·24	9·05	8·86	8·69	8·52	8·36	8·21	8·06	7·91	7·77	7·64	7·51	7·39	7·27	62
63	10·1	9·84	9·64	9·44	9·25	9·07	8·89	8·72	8·56	8·41	8·26	8·11	7·97	7·84	7·71	7·58	63
64	10·5	10·3	10·1	9·86	9·66	9·47	9·29	9·11	8·95	8·78	8·63	8·48	8·33	8·19	8·05	7·92	64
65	11·0	10·8	10·5	10·3	10·1	9·91	9·72	9·53	9·36	9·19	9·02	8·86	8·71	8·57	8·42	8·29	65
66	11·5	11·3	11·0	10·8	10·6	10·4	10·2	9·98	9·80	9·62	9·45	9·28	9·12	8·97	8·82	8·68	66
67	12·1	11·8	11·6	11·3	11·1	10·9	10·7	10·5	10·3	10·1	9·91	9·74	9·57	9·41	9·25	9·10	67
68	12·7	12·4	12·2	11·9	11·7	11·4	11·2	11·0	10·8	10·6	10·4	10·2	10·1	9·89	9·72	9·56	68
69	13·4	13·1	12·8	12·5	12·3	12·0	11·8	11·6	11·4	11·2	11·0	10·8	10·6	10·4	10·2	10·1	69
70	14·1	13·8	13·5	13·2	12·9	12·7	12·4	12·2	12·0	11·8	11·6	11·4	11·2	11·0	10·8	10·6	70
71	14·9	14·6	14·3	14·0	13·7	13·4	13·2	12·9	12·7	12·4	12·2	12·0	11·8	11·6	11·4	11·2	71
72	15·8	15·4	15·1	14·8	14·5	14·2	13·9	13·7	13·4	13·2	12·9	12·7	12·5	12·3	12·1	11·9	72
73	16·8	16·4	16·1	15·7	15·4	15·1	14·8	14·5	14·3	14·0	13·8	13·5	13·3	13·1	12·8	12·6	73
74	17·9	17·5	17·1	16·8	16·4	16·1	15·8	15·5	15·2	14·9	14·7	14·4	14·2	13·9	13·7	13·5	74
75	19·1	18·7	18·3	18·0	17·6	17·2	16·9	16·6	16·3	16·0	15·7	15·4	15·2	14·9	14·7	14·4	75
Dec.	168°45' / 191°15'	168°30' / 191°30'	168°15' / 191°45'	168°00' / 192°00'	167°45' / 192°15'	167°30' / 192°30'	167°15' / 192°45'	167°00' / 193°00'	166°45' / 193°15'	166°30' / 193°30'	166°15' / 193°45'	166°00' / 194°00'	165°45' / 194°15'	165°30' / 194°30'	165°15' / 194°45'	165°00' / 195°00'	Dec.

HOUR ANGLE

B - Always named the **same** as Declination

B

TABLE A HOUR ANGLE

Lat. °	15°00'	15°30'	16°00'	16°30'	17°00'	17°30'	18°00'	18°30'	19°00'	19°30'	20°00'	20°30'	21°00'	21°30'	22°00'	22°30'	Lat. °
	345°00'	344°30'	344°00'	343°30'	343°00'	342°30'	342°00'	341°30'	341°00'	340°30'	340°00'	339°30'	339°00'	338°30'	338°00'	337°30'	
60	6·46	6·25	6·04	5·85	5·67	5·49	5·33	5·18	5·03	4·89	4·76	4·63	4·51	4·40	4·29	4·18	60
61	6·73	6·51	6·29	6·09	5·90	5·72	5·55	5·39	5·24	5·09	4·96	4·83	4·70	4·58	4·47	4·36	61
62	7·02	6·78	6·56	6·35	6·15	5·96	5·79	5·62	5·46	5·31	5·17	5·03	4·90	4·77	4·65	4·54	62
63	7·32	7·08	6·84	6·63	6·42	6·23	6·04	5·87	5·70	5·54	5·39	5·25	5·11	4·98	4·86	4·74	63
64	7·65	7·39	7·15	6·92	6·71	6·50	6·31	6·13	5·95	5·79	5·63	5·48	5·34	5·21	5·08	4·95	64
65	8·00	7·73	7·48	7·24	7·01	6·80	6·60	6·41	6·23	6·06	5·89	5·74	5·59	5·44	5·31	5·18	65
66	8·38	8·10	7·83	7·58	7·35	7·12	6·91	6·71	6·52	6·34	6·17	6·01	5·85	5·70	5·56	5·42	66
67	8·79	8·50	8·22	7·95	7·71	7·47	7·25	7·04	6·84	6·65	6·47	6·30	6·14	5·98	5·83	5·69	67
68	9·24	8·92	8·63	8·36	8·10	7·85	7·62	7·40	7·19	6·99	6·80	6·62	6·45	6·28	6·13	5·98	68
69	9·72	9·39	9·09	8·80	8·52	8·26	8·02	7·79	7·57	7·36	7·16	6·97	6·79	6·61	6·45	6·29	69
70	10·3	9·91	9·58	9·28	8·99	8·71	8·46	8·21	7·98	7·76	7·55	7·35	7·16	6·98	6·80	6·63	70
71	10·8	10·5	10·1	9·81	9·50	9·21	8·94	8·68	8·43	8·20	7·98	7·77	7·57	7·37	7·19	7·01	71
72	11·5	11·1	10·7	10·4	10·1	9·76	9·47	9·20	8·94	8·69	8·46	8·23	8·02	7·81	7·62	7·43	72
73	12·2	11·8	11·4	11·1	10·7	10·4	10·1	9·78	9·50	9·24	8·99	8·75	8·52	8·30	8·10	7·90	73
74	13·0	12·6	12·2	11·8	11·4	11·1	10·7	10·4	10·1	9·85	9·58	9·33	9·09	8·85	8·63	8·42	74
75	13·9	13·5	13·0	12·6	12·2	11·8	11·5	11·2	10·8	10·5	10·3	9·98	9·72	9·47	9·24	9·01	75
76	15·0	14·5	14·0	13·5	13·1	12·7	12·4	12·0	11·7	11·3	11·1	10·7	10·5	10·2	9·93	9·68	76
77	16·2	15·6	15·1	14·6	14·2	13·7	13·3	13·0	12·6	12·2	11·9	11·6	11·3	11·0	10·7	10·5	77
78	17·6	17·0	16·4	15·9	15·4	14·9	14·5	14·1	13·7	13·3	12·9	12·6	12·3	11·9	11·7	11·4	78
79	19·2	18·6	17·9	17·4	16·8	16·3	15·8	15·4	14·9	14·5	14·1	13·8	13·4	13·1	12·7	12·4	79
80	21·2	20·5	19·8	19·2	18·6	18·0	17·5	17·0	16·5	16·0	15·6	15·2	14·8	14·4	14·0	13·7	80
81	23·6	22·8	22·0	21·3	20·7	20·0	19·4	18·9	18·3	17·8	17·4	16·9	16·5	16·0	15·6	15·2	81
82	26·6	25·7	24·8	24·0	23·3	22·6	21·9	21·3	20·7	20·1	19·6	19·0	18·5	18·1	17·6	17·2	82
83	30·4	29·4	28·4	27·5	26·6	25·8	25·1	24·3	23·7	23·0	22·4	21·8	21·2	20·7	20·2	19·7	83
Lat.	165°00'	164°30'	164°00'	163°30'	163°00'	162°30'	162°00'	161°30'	161°00'	160°30'	160°00'	159°30'	159°00'	158°30'	158°00'	157°30'	Lat.
	195°00'	195°30'	196°00'	196°30'	197°00'	197°30'	198°00'	198°30'	199°00'	199°30'	200°00'	200°30'	201°00'	201°30'	202°00'	202°30'	

HOUR ANGLE

TABLE A - HOUR ANGLE

Lat. °	22°30'	23°00'	23°30'	24°00'	24°30'	25°00'	25°30'	26°00'	26°30'	27°00'	27°30'	28°00'	28°30'	29°00'	29°30'	30°00'	Lat. °
	337°30'	337°00'	336°30'	336°00'	335°30'	335°00'	334°30'	334°00'	333°30'	333°00'	332°30'	332°00'	331°30'	331°00'	330°30'	330°00'	
60	4·18	4·08	3·98	3·89	3·80	3·71	3·63	3·55	3·47	3·40	3·33	3·26	3·19	3·12	3·06	3·00	60
61	4·36	4·25	4·15	4·05	3·96	3·87	3·78	3·70	3·62	3·54	3·47	3·39	3·32	3·25	3·18	3·12	61
62	4·54	4·43	4·33	4·22	4·13	4·03	3·94	3·86	3·77	3·69	3·61	3·54	3·46	3·39	3·32	3·26	62
63	4·74	4·62	4·51	4·41	4·31	4·21	4·11	4·02	3·94	3·85	3·77	3·69	3·61	3·54	3·47	3·40	63
64	4·95	4·83	4·72	4·61	4·50	4·40	4·30	4·20	4·11	4·02	3·94	3·86	3·78	3·70	3·62	3·55	64
65	5·18	5·05	4·93	4·82	4·71	4·60	4·50	4·40	4·30	4·21	4·12	4·03	3·95	3·87	3·79	3·71	65
66	5·42	5·29	5·17	5·04	4·93	4·82	4·71	4·61	4·51	4·41	4·31	4·22	4·13	4·05	3·97	3·89	66
67	5·69	5·55	5·42	5·29	5·17	5·05	4·94	4·83	4·73	4·62	4·53	4·43	4·34	4·25	4·16	4·08	67
68	5·98	5·83	5·69	5·56	5·43	5·31	5·19	5·07	4·97	4·86	4·75	4·65	4·56	4·47	4·38	4·29	68
69	6·29	6·14	5·99	5·85	5·72	5·59	5·46	5·34	5·23	5·11	5·00	4·90	4·80	4·70	4·60	4·51	69
70	6·63	6·47	6·32	6·17	6·03	5·89	5·76	5·63	5·51	5·39	5·28	5·17	5·06	4·96	4·86	4·76	70
71	7·01	6·84	6·68	6·52	6·37	6·23	6·09	5·96	5·83	5·70	5·58	5·46	5·35	5·24	5·13	5·03	71
72	7·43	7·25	7·08	6·91	6·75	6·60	6·45	6·31	6·17	6·04	5·91	5·79	5·67	5·55	5·44	5·33	72
73	7·90	7·71	7·52	7·35	7·18	7·01	6·86	6·71	6·56	6·42	6·28	6·15	6·03	5·90	5·78	5·67	73
74	8·42	8·22	8·02	7·83	7·65	7·48	7·31	7·15	6·99	6·84	6·70	6·56	6·42	6·29	6·16	6·04	74
75	9·01	8·79	8·58	8·38	8·19	8·00	7·82	7·65	7·49	7·32	7·17	7·02	6·87	6·73	6·60	6·46	75
76	9·68	9·45	9·22	9·01	8·80	8·60	8·41	8·22	8·04	7·87	7·71	7·54	7·39	7·24	7·09	6·95	76
77	10·5	10·2	9·96	9·73	9·51	9·29	9·08	8·88	8·69	8·50	8·32	8·15	7·98	7·81	7·66	7·50	77
78	11·4	11·1	10·8	10·6	10·3	10·1	9·86	9·65	9·44	9·23	9·04	8·85	8·67	8·49	8·32	8·15	78
79	12·4	12·1	11·8	11·6	11·3	11·0	10·8	10·6	10·3	10·1	9·88	9·68	9·48	9·28	9·09	8·91	79
80	13·7	13·4	13·0	12·7	12·4	12·2	11·9	11·6	11·4	11·1	10·9	10·7	10·4	10·3	10·0	9·82	80
81	15·2	14·9	14·5	14·2	13·9	13·5	13·2	13·0	12·7	12·4	12·1	11·9	11·6	11·4	11·2	10·9	81
82	17·2	16·8	16·4	16·0	15·6	15·3	14·9	14·6	14·3	14·0	13·7	13·4	13·1	12·8	12·6	12·3	82
83	19·7	19·2	18·7	18·3	17·9	17·5	17·1	16·7	16·3	16·0	15·7	15·3	15·0	14·7	14·4	14·1	83
Lat.	157°30'	157°00'	156°30'	156°00'	155°30'	155°00'	154°30'	154°00'	153°30'	153°00'	152°30'	152°00'	151°30'	151°00'	150°30'	150°00'	Lat.
	202°30'	203°00'	203°30'	204°00'	204°30'	205°00'	205°30'	206°00'	206°30'	207°00'	207°30'	208°00'	208°30'	209°00'	209°30'	210°00'	

HOUR ANGLE

A

A - Named opposite to Latitude, except when Hour Angle is between 90° and 270°

A - Named opposite to Latitude, except when Hour Angle is between 90° and 270°

TABLE B HOUR ANGLE

Dec. °	15° 00' 345° 00'	15° 30' 344° 30'	16° 00' 344° 00'	16° 30' 343° 30'	17° 00' 343° 00'	17° 30' 342° 30'	18° 00' 342° 00'	18° 30' 341° 30'	19° 00' 341° 00'	19° 30' 340° 30'	20° 00' 340° 00'	20° 30' 339° 30'	21° 00' 339° 00'	21° 30' 338° 30'	22° 00' 338° 00'	22° 30' 337° 30'	Dec. °
60	6·69	6·48	6·28	6·10	5·92	5·76	5·61	5·46	5·32	5·19	5·06	4·95	4·83	4·73	4·62	4·53	60
61	6·97	6·75	6·55	6·35	6·17	6·00	5·84	5·69	5·54	5·40	5·27	5·15	5·03	4·92	4·82	4·71	61
62	7·27	7·04	6·82	6·62	6·43	6·25	6·09	5·93	5·78	5·63	5·50	5·37	5·25	5·13	5·02	4·91	62
63	7·58	7·34	7·12	6·91	6·71	6·53	6·35	6·19	6·03	5·88	5·74	5·60	5·48	5·36	5·24	5·13	63
64	7·92	7·67	7·44	7·22	7·01	6·82	6·63	6·46	6·30	6·14	5·99	5·85	5·72	5·59	5·47	5·36	64
65	8·29	8·02	7·78	7·55	7·33	7·13	6·94	6·76	6·59	6·42	6·27	6·12	5·98	5·85	5·72	5·60	65
66	8·68	8·40	8·15	7·91	7·68	7·47	7·27	7·08	6·90	6·73	6·57	6·41	6·27	6·13	6·00	5·87	66
67	9·10	8·82	8·55	8·29	8·06	7·83	7·62	7·42	7·24	7·06	6·89	6·73	6·57	6·43	6·29	6·16	67
68	9·56	9·26	8·98	8·72	8·47	8·23	8·01	7·80	7·60	7·41	7·24	7·07	6·91	6·75	6·61	6·47	68
69	10·1	9·75	9·45	9·17	8·91	8·66	8·43	8·21	8·00	7·80	7·62	7·44	7·27	7·11	6·95	6·81	69
70	10·6	10·3	9·97	9·67	9·40	9·14	8·89	8·66	8·44	8·23	8·03	7·85	7·67	7·50	7·33	7·18	70
71	11·2	10·9	10·5	10·2	9·93	9·66	9·40	9·15	8·92	8·70	8·49	8·29	8·10	7·92	7·75	7·59	71
72	11·9	11·5	11·2	10·8	10·5	10·2	9·96	9·70	9·45	9·22	9·00	8·79	8·59	8·40	8·22	8·04	72
73	12·6	12·2	11·9	11·5	11·2	10·9	10·6	10·3	10·0	9·80	9·57	9·34	9·13	8·93	8·73	8·55	73
74	13·5	13·1	12·7	12·3	11·9	11·6	11·3	11·0	10·7	10·4	10·2	9·96	9·73	9·52	9·31	9·11	74
75	14·4	14·0	13·5	13·1	12·8	12·4	12·1	11·8	11·5	11·2	10·9	10·7	10·4	10·2	9·96	9·75	75
Dec.	165° 00' 195° 00'	164° 30' 195° 30'	164° 00' 196° 00'	163° 30' 196° 30'	163° 00' 197° 00'	162° 30' 197° 30'	162° 00' 198° 00'	161° 30' 198° 30'	161° 00' 199° 00'	160° 30' 199° 30'	160° 00' 200° 00'	159° 30' 200° 30'	159° 00' 201° 00'	158° 30' 201° 30'	158° 00' 202° 00'	157° 30' 202° 30'	Dec.

HOUR ANGLE

B - Always named the **same** as Declination

B - Always named the **same** as Declination

TABLE B - HOUR ANGLE

Dec. °	22° 30' 337° 30'	23° 00' 337° 00'	23° 30' 336° 30'	24° 00' 336° 00'	24° 30' 335° 30'	25° 00' 335° 00'	25° 30' 334° 30'	26° 00' 334° 00'	26° 30' 333° 30'	27° 00' 333° 00'	27° 30' 332° 30'	28° 00' 332° 00'	28° 30' 331° 30'	29° 00' 331° 00'	29° 30' 330° 30'	30° 00' 330° 00'	Dec. °
60	4·53	4·43	4·34	4·26	4·18	4·10	4·02	3·95	3·88	3·82	3·75	3·69	3·63	3·57	3·52	3·46	60
61	4·71	4·62	4·52	4·44	4·35	4·27	4·19	4·12	4·04	3·97	3·91	3·84	3·78	3·72	3·66	3·61	61
62	4·91	4·81	4·72	4·62	4·54	4·45	4·37	4·29	4·22	4·14	4·07	4·01	3·94	3·88	3·82	3·76	62
63	5·13	5·02	4·92	4·83	4·73	4·64	4·56	4·48	4·40	4·32	4·25	4·18	4·11	4·05	3·99	3·93	63
64	5·36	5·25	5·14	5·04	4·94	4·85	4·76	4·68	4·60	4·52	4·44	4·37	4·30	4·23	4·16	4·10	64
65	5·60	5·49	5·38	5·27	5·17	5·07	4·98	4·89	4·81	4·72	4·64	4·57	4·49	4·42	4·35	4·29	65
66	5·87	5·75	5·63	5·52	5·42	5·31	5·22	5·12	5·03	4·95	4·86	4·78	4·71	4·63	4·56	4·49	66
67	6·16	6·03	5·91	5·79	5·68	5·57	5·47	5·37	5·28	5·19	5·10	5·02	4·94	4·86	4·78	4·71	67
68	6·47	6·33	6·21	6·09	5·97	5·86	5·75	5·65	5·55	5·45	5·36	5·27	5·19	5·11	5·03	4·95	68
69	6·81	6·67	6·53	6·40	6·28	6·16	6·05	5·94	5·84	5·74	5·64	5·55	5·46	5·37	5·29	5·21	69
70	7·18	7·03	6·89	6·75	6·63	6·50	6·38	6·27	6·16	6·05	5·95	5·85	5·76	5·67	5·58	5·49	70
71	7·59	7·43	7·28	7·14	7·00	6·87	6·75	6·63	6·51	6·40	6·29	6·19	6·08	5·99	5·90	5·81	71
72	8·04	7·88	7·72	7·57	7·42	7·28	7·15	7·02	6·90	6·78	6·67	6·56	6·45	6·35	6·25	6·15	72
73	8·55	8·37	8·20	8·04	7·89	7·74	7·60	7·46	7·33	7·21	7·08	6·97	6·86	6·75	6·64	6·54	73
74	9·11	8·93	8·75	8·57	8·41	8·25	8·10	7·96	7·82	7·68	7·55	7·43	7·31	7·19	7·08	6·97	74
75	9·75	9·55	9·36	9·18	9·00	8·83	8·67	8·52	8·37	8·22	8·08	7·95	7·82	7·70	7·58	7·46	75
Dec.	157° 30' 202° 30'	157° 00' 203° 00'	156° 30' 203° 30'	156° 00' 204° 00'	155° 30' 204° 30'	155° 00' 205° 00'	154° 30' 205° 30'	154° 00' 206° 00'	153° 30' 206° 30'	153° 00' 207° 00'	152° 30' 207° 30'	152° 00' 208° 00'	151° 30' 208° 30'	151° 00' 209° 00'	150° 30' 209° 30'	150° 00' 210° 00'	Dec.

HOUR ANGLE

B

TABLE A HOUR ANGLE

Lat. °	30° 330°	31° 329°	32° 328°	33° 327°	34° 326°	35° 325°	36° 324°	37° 323°	38° 322°	39° 321°	40° 320°	41° 319°	42° 318°	43° 317°	44° 316°	45° 315°	Lat. °
60	3·00	2·88	2·77	2·67	2·57	2·47	2·38	2·30	2·22	2·14	2·06	1·99	1·92	1·86	1·79	1·73	60
61	3·12	3·00	2·89	2·78	2·67	2·58	2·48	2·39	2·31	2·23	2·15	2·08	2·00	1·93	1·87	1·80	61
62	3·26	3·13	3·01	2·90	2·79	2·69	2·59	2·50	2·41	2·32	2·24	2·16	2·09	2·02	1·95	1·88	62
63	3·40	3·27	3·14	3·02	2·91	2·80	2·70	2·60	2·51	2·42	2·34	2·26	2·18	2·10	2·03	1·96	63
64	3·55	3·41	3·28	3·16	3·04	2·93	2·82	2·72	2·62	2·53	2·44	2·36	2·28	2·20	2·12	2·05	64
65	3·71	3·57	3·43	3·30	3·18	3·06	2·95	2·85	2·74	2·65	2·56	2·47	2·38	2·30	2·22	2·14	65
66	3·89	3·74	3·59	3·46	3·33	3·21	3·09	2·98	2·87	2·77	2·68	2·58	2·49	2·41	2·33	2·25	66
67	4·08	3·92	3·77	3·63	3·49	3·36	3·24	3·13	3·02	2·91	2·81	2·71	2·62	2·53	2·44	2·36	67
68	4·29	4·12	3·96	3·81	3·67	3·53	3·41	3·28	3·17	3·06	2·95	2·85	2·75	2·65	2·56	2·48	68
69	4·51	4·34	4·17	4·01	3·86	3·72	3·59	3·46	3·34	3·22	3·11	3·00	2·89	2·79	2·70	2·61	69
70	4·76	4·57	4·40	4·23	4·07	3·92	3·78	3·65	3·52	3·39	3·27	3·16	3·04	2·95	2·85	2·75	70
71	5·03	4·83	4·65	4·47	4·31	4·15	4·00	3·85	3·72	3·59	3·46	3·34	3·23	3·11	3·01	2·90	71
72	5·33	5·12	4·93	4·74	4·56	4·40	4·24	4·08	3·94	3·80	3·67	3·54	3·42	3·30	3·19	3·08	72
73	5·67	5·44	5·23	5·04	4·85	4·67	4·50	4·34	4·19	4·04	3·90	3·76	3·63	3·51	3·39	3·27	73
74	6·04	5·80	5·58	5·37	5·17	4·98	4·80	4·63	4·46	4·31	4·16	4·01	3·87	3·74	3·61	3·49	74
75	6·46	6·21	5·97	5·75	5·53	5·33	5·14	4·95	4·78	4·61	4·45	4·29	4·15	4·00	3·87	3·73	75
76	6·95	6·68	6·42	6·18	5·95	5·73	5·52	5·32	5·13	4·95	4·78	4·61	4·45	4·30	4·15	4·01	76
77	7·50	7·21	6·93	6·67	6·42	6·19	5·96	5·75	5·54	5·35	5·16	4·98	4·81	4·65	4·49	4·33	77
78	8·15	7·83	7·53	7·25	6·98	6·72	6·48	6·24	6·02	5·81	5·61	5·41	5·23	5·05	4·87	4·70	78
79	8·91	8·56	8·23	7·92	7·63	7·35	7·08	6·83	6·59	6·35	6·13	5·92	5·71	5·52	5·33	5·14	79
80	9·82	9·44	9·08	8·73	8·41	8·10	7·81	7·53	7·26	7·00	6·76	6·52	6·30	6·08	5·87	5·67	80
81	10·9	10·5	10·1	9·72	9·36	9·02	8·69	8·38	8·08	7·80	7·52	7·26	7·01	6·77	6·54	6·31	81
82	12·3	11·8	11·4	11·0	10·6	10·2	9·79	9·44	9·11	8·79	8·48	8·19	7·90	7·63	7·37	7·12	82
83	14·1	13·6	13·0	12·5	12·1	11·6	11·2	10·8	10·4	10·1	9·71	9·37	9·05	8·73	8·43	8·14	83
Lat.	150° 210°	149° 211°	148° 212°	147° 213°	146° 214°	145° 215°	144° 216°	143° 217°	142° 218°	141° 219°	140° 220°	139° 221°	138° 222°	137° 223°	136° 224°	135° 225°	Lat.

HOUR ANGLE

TABLE A HOUR ANGLE

Lat. °	45° 315°	46° 314°	47° 313°	48° 312°	49° 311°	50° 310°	51° 309°	52° 308°	53° 307°	54° 306°	55° 305°	56° 304°	57° 303°	58° 302°	59° 301°	60° 300°	Lat. °
60	1·73	1·67	1·62	1·56	1·51	1·45	1·40	1·35	1·31	1·26	1·21	1·17	1·12	1·08	1·04	1·00	60
61	1·80	1·74	1·68	1·62	1·57	1·51	1·46	1·41	1·36	1·31	1·26	1·22	1·17	1·13	1·08	1·04	61
62	1·88	1·82	1·75	1·69	1·63	1·58	1·52	1·47	1·42	1·37	1·32	1·27	1·22	1·18	1·13	1·09	62
63	1·96	1·90	1·83	1·77	1·71	1·65	1·59	1·53	1·48	1·43	1·37	1·32	1·27	1·23	1·18	1·13	63
64	2·05	1·98	1·91	1·85	1·78	1·72	1·66	1·60	1·55	1·49	1·44	1·38	1·33	1·28	1·23	1·18	64
65	2·14	2·07	2·00	1·93	1·86	1·80	1·74	1·68	1·62	1·56	1·50	1·45	1·39	1·34	1·29	1·24	65
66	2·25	2·17	2·09	2·02	1·95	1·88	1·82	1·75	1·69	1·63	1·57	1·52	1·46	1·40	1·35	1·30	66
67	2·36	2·28	2·20	2·12	2·05	1·98	1·91	1·84	1·78	1·71	1·65	1·59	1·53	1·47	1·42	1·36	67
68	2·48	2·39	2·31	2·23	2·15	2·08	2·00	1·93	1·87	1·80	1·73	1·67	1·61	1·55	1·49	1·43	68
69	2·61	2·52	2·43	2·35	2·26	2·19	2·11	2·04	1·96	1·89	1·82	1·76	1·69	1·63	1·57	1·50	69
70	2·75	2·65	2·56	2·47	2·39	2·31	2·23	2·15	2·07	2·00	1·92	1·85	1·78	1·72	1·65	1·59	70
71	2·90	2·80	2·71	2·62	2·52	2·44	2·35	2·27	2·19	2·11	2·03	1·96	1·89	1·82	1·75	1·68	71
72	3·08	2·97	2·87	2·77	2·68	2·58	2·49	2·41	2·32	2·24	2·16	2·08	2·00	1·92	1·85	1·78	72
73	3·27	3·16	3·05	2·95	2·84	2·74	2·65	2·56	2·47	2·38	2·29	2·21	2·12	2·04	1·97	1·89	73
74	3·49	3·37	3·25	3·14	3·03	2·93	2·82	2·73	2·63	2·53	2·44	2·35	2·27	2·18	2·10	2·01	74
75	3·73	3·60	3·48	3·36	3·24	3·13	3·02	2·92	2·81	2·71	2·61	2·52	2·42	2·33	2·24	2·16	75
76	4·01	3·87	3·74	3·61	3·49	3·37	3·25	3·13	3·02	2·91	2·81	2·71	2·61	2·51	2·41	2·32	76
77	4·33	4·18	4·04	3·90	3·77	3·64	3·51	3·38	3·26	3·15	3·03	2·92	2·81	2·71	2·60	2·50	77
78	4·70	4·54	4·39	4·24	4·09	3·95	3·81	3·68	3·55	3·42	3·29	3·17	3·06	2·94	2·83	2·72	78
79	5·14	4·97	4·80	4·63	4·47	4·32	4·17	4·02	3·88	3·74	3·60	3·47	3·34	3·22	3·09	2·97	79
80	5·67	5·48	5·29	5·11	4·93	4·76	4·59	4·43	4·27	4·12	3·97	3·83	3·68	3·54	3·41	3·27	80
81	6·31	6·10	5·89	5·69	5·49	5·30	5·11	4·93	4·76	4·59	4·42	4·26	4·10	3·95	3·79	3·65	81
82	7·12	6·87	6·64	6·41	6·19	5·97	5·76	5·56	5·36	5·17	4·98	4·80	4·62	4·45	4·28	4·11	82
83	8·14	7·86	7·60	7·33	7·08	6·83	6·60	6·36	6·14	5·92	5·70	5·49	5·29	5·09	4·89	4·70	83
Lat.	135° 225°	134° 226°	133° 227°	132° 228°	131° 229°	130° 230°	129° 231°	128° 232°	127° 233°	126° 234°	125° 235°	124° 236°	123° 237°	122° 238°	121° 239°	120° 240°	Lat.

HOUR ANGLE

A - Named opposite to Latitude, except when Hour Angle is between 90° and 270°

A - Named opposite to Latitude, except when Hour Angle is between 90° and 270°

A

TABLE B HOUR ANGLE

Dec.°	30°	31°	32°	33°	34°	35°	36°	37°	38°	39°	40°	41°	42°	43°	44°	45°	Dec.°
	330°	329°	328°	327°	326°	325°	324°	323°	322°	321°	320°	319°	318°	317°	316°	315°	
60	3·46	3·36	3·27	3·18	3·10	3·02	2·95	2·88	2·81	2·75	2·69	2·64	2·59	2·54	2·49	2·45	60
61	3·61	3·50	3·40	3·31	3·23	3·15	3·07	3·00	2·93	2·87	2·81	2·75	2·70	2·65	2·60	2·55	61
62	3·76	3·65	3·55	3·45	3·36	3·28	3·20	3·13	3·05	2·99	2·93	2·87	2·81	2·76	2·71	2·66	62
63	3·93	3·81	3·70	3·60	3·51	3·42	3·34	3·26	3·19	3·12	3·05	2·99	2·93	2·88	2·83	2·78	63
64	4·10	3·98	3·87	3·76	3·67	3·57	3·49	3·41	3·33	3·26	3·19	3·13	3·06	3·01	2·95	2·90	64
65	4·29	4·16	4·05	3·94	3·84	3·74	3·65	3·56	3·48	3·41	3·34	3·27	3·20	3·14	3·09	3·03	65
66	4·49	4·36	4·24	4·12	4·02	3·92	3·82	3·73	3·65	3·57	3·49	3·42	3·36	3·29	3·23	3·18	66
67	4·71	4·57	4·45	4·33	4·21	4·11	4·01	3·91	3·83	3·74	3·67	3·59	3·52	3·45	3·39	3·33	67
68	4·95	4·81	4·67	4·54	4·43	4·32	4·21	4·11	4·02	3·93	3·85	3·77	3·70	3·63	3·56	3·50	68
69	5·21	5·06	4·92	4·78	4·66	4·54	4·43	4·33	4·23	4·14	4·05	3·97	3·89	3·82	3·75	3·68	69
70	5·49	5·33	5·18	5·04	4·91	4·79	4·67	4·56	4·46	4·37	4·27	4·19	4·11	4·03	3·95	3·89	70
71	5·81	5·64	5·48	5·33	5·19	5·06	4·94	4·83	4·72	4·61	4·52	4·43	4·34	4·26	4·18	4·11	71
72	6·15	5·98	5·81	5·65	5·50	5·37	5·24	5·11	5·00	4·89	4·79	4·69	4·60	4·51	4·43	4·35	72
73	6·54	6·35	6·17	6·01	5·85	5·70	5·57	5·44	5·31	5·20	5·09	4·99	4·89	4·80	4·71	4·63	73
74	6·97	6·77	6·58	6·40	6·24	6·08	5·93	5·79	5·67	5·54	5·43	5·32	5·21	5·11	5·02	4·93	74
75	7·46	7·25	7·04	6·85	6·67	6·51	6·35	6·20	6·06	5·93	5·81	5·69	5·58	5·47	5·37	5·28	75
Dec.	150°	149°	148°	147°	146°	145°	144°	143°	142°	141°	140°	139°	138°	137°	136°	135°	Dec.
	210°	211°	212°	213°	214°	215°	216°	217°	218°	219°	220°	221°	222°	223°	224°	225°	

HOUR ANGLE

TABLE B - HOUR ANGLE

Dec.°	45°	46°	47°	48°	49°	50°	51°	52°	53°	54°	55°	56°	57°	58°	59°	60°	Dec.°
	315°	314°	313°	312°	311°	310°	309°	308°	307°	306°	305°	304°	303°	302°	301°	300°	
60	2·45	2·41	2·37	2·33	2·29	2·26	2·23	2·20	2·17	2·14	2·11	2·09	2·07	2·04	2·02	2·00	60
61	2·55	2·51	2·47	2·43	2·39	2·36	2·32	2·29	2·26	2·23	2·20	2·18	2·15	2·13	2·10	2·08	61
62	2·66	2·62	2·57	2·53	2·49	2·46	2·42	2·39	2·35	2·32	2·30	2·27	2·24	2·22	2·19	2·17	62
63	2·78	2·73	2·68	2·64	2·60	2·56	2·53	2·49	2·46	2·43	2·40	2·36	2·34	2·31	2·29	2·27	63
64	2·90	2·85	2·80	2·76	2·72	2·68	2·64	2·60	2·57	2·53	2·50	2·47	2·44	2·42	2·39	2·37	64
65	3·03	2·98	2·93	2·89	2·84	2·80	2·76	2·72	2·69	2·65	2·62	2·59	2·56	2·53	2·50	2·48	65
66	3·18	3·12	3·07	3·02	2·98	2·93	2·89	2·85	2·81	2·78	2·74	2·71	2·68	2·65	2·62	2·59	66
67	3·33	3·28	3·22	3·17	3·12	3·08	3·03	2·99	2·95	2·91	2·88	2·84	2·81	2·78	2·75	2·72	67
68	3·50	3·44	3·38	3·33	3·28	3·23	3·18	3·14	3·10	3·06	3·02	2·99	2·95	2·92	2·89	2·86	68
69	3·68	3·62	3·56	3·51	3·45	3·40	3·35	3·31	3·26	3·22	3·18	3·14	3·11	3·07	3·04	3·01	69
70	3·89	3·82	3·76	3·70	3·64	3·59	3·54	3·49	3·44	3·40	3·35	3·31	3·28	3·24	3·20	3·17	70
71	4·11	4·04	3·97	3·91	3·85	3·79	3·74	3·68	3·64	3·59	3·54	3·50	3·46	3·42	3·39	3·35	71
72	4·35	4·28	4·21	4·14	4·08	4·02	3·96	3·91	3·85	3·80	3·76	3·71	3·67	3·63	3·59	3·55	72
73	4·63	4·55	4·47	4·40	4·33	4·27	4·21	4·15	4·10	4·04	3·99	3·95	3·90	3·86	3·82	3·78	73
74	4·93	4·85	4·77	4·69	4·62	4·55	4·49	4·43	4·37	4·31	4·26	4·21	4·16	4·11	4·07	4·03	74
75	5·28	5·19	5·10	5·02	4·95	4·87	4·80	4·74	4·67	4·61	4·56	4·50	4·45	4·40	4·35	4·31	75
Dec.	135°	134°	133°	132°	131°	130°	129°	128°	127°	126°	125°	124°	123°	122°	121°	120°	Dec.
	225°	226°	227°	228°	229°	230°	231°	232°	233°	234°	235°	236°	237°	238°	239°	240°	

HOUR ANGLE

B - Always named the same as Declination

B - Always named the same as Declination

B

TABLE A HOUR ANGLE

Lat. °	60° / 300°	61° / 299°	62° / 298°	63° / 297°	64° / 296°	65° / 295°	66° / 294°	67° / 293°	68° / 292°	69° / 291°	70° / 290°	71° / 289°	72° / 288°	73° / 287°	74° / 286°	75° / 285°	Lat. °
60	1·00	·96	·92	·88	·85	·81	·77	·74	·70	·67	·63	·60	·56	·53	·50	·46	60
61	1·04	1·00	·96	·92	·88	·84	·80	·77	·73	·69	·66	·62	·59	·55	·52	·48	61
62	1·09	1·04	1·00	·96	·92	·88	·84	·80	·76	·72	·68	·65	·61	·58	·54	·50	62
63	1·13	1·09	1·04	1·00	·96	·92	·87	·83	·79	·75	·71	·68	·64	·60	·56	·53	63
64	1·18	1·14	1·09	1·05	1·00	·96	·91	·87	·83	·79	·75	·71	·67	·63	·59	·55	64
65	1·24	1·19	1·14	1·09	1·05	1·00	·96	·91	·87	·82	·78	·74	·70	·66	·62	·57	65
66	1·30	1·25	1·19	1·14	1·10	1·05	1·00	·95	·91	·86	·82	·77	·73	·69	·64	·60	66
67	1·36	1·31	1·25	1·20	1·15	1·10	1·05	1·00	·95	·90	·86	·81	·77	·72	·68	·63	67
68	1·43	1·37	1·32	1·26	1·21	1·15	1·09	1·05	1·00	·95	·90	·85	·80	·76	·71	·66	68
69	1·50	1·44	1·39	1·33	1·27	1·22	1·16	1·11	1·05	1·00	·95	·90	·85	·80	·75	·70	69
70	1·59	1·52	1·46	1·40	1·34	1·28	1·22	1·17	1·11	1·05	1·00	·95	·89	·84	·79	·74	70
71	1·68	1·61	1·54	1·48	1·42	1·35	1·29	1·23	1·17	1·11	1·06	1·00	·94	·89	·83	·78	71
72	1·78	1·71	1·64	1·57	1·50	1·44	1·37	1·31	1·24	1·18	1·12	1·06	1·00	·94	·88	·82	72
73	1·89	1·81	1·74	1·67	1·60	1·53	1·46	1·39	1·32	1·26	1·19	1·13	1·06	1·00	·94	·88	73
74	2·01	1·93	1·85	1·78	1·70	1·63	1·55	1·48	1·41	1·34	1·27	1·20	1·13	1·07	1·00	·93	74
75	2·16	2·07	1·98	1·90	1·82	1·74	1·66	1·58	1·51	1·43	1·36	1·29	1·21	1·14	1·07	1·00	75
76	2·32	2·22	2·13	2·04	1·96	1·87	1·79	1·70	1·62	1·54	1·46	1·38	1·30	1·23	1·15	1·07	76
77	2·50	2·40	2·30	2·21	2·11	2·02	1·93	1·84	1·75	1·66	1·58	1·49	1·41	1·32	1·24	1·16	77
78	2·72	2·61	2·50	2·40	2·29	2·19	2·09	2·00	1·90	1·81	1·71	1·62	1·53	1·44	1·35	1·26	78
79	2·97	2·85	2·74	2·62	2·51	2·40	2·29	2·18	2·08	1·97	1·87	1·77	1·67	1·57	1·48	1·37	79
80	3·27	3·14	3·02	2·89	2·77	2·64	2·53	2·41	2·29	2·18	2·06	1·95	1·84	1·73	1·63	1·52	80
81	3·65	3·50	3·36	3·22	3·08	2·94	2·81	2·68	2·55	2·42	2·30	2·17	2·05	1·93	1·81	1·69	81
82	4·11	3·94	3·78	3·63	3·47	3·32	3·17	3·02	2·87	2·73	2·59	2·45	2·31	2·18	2·04	1·91	82
83	4·70	4·51	4·33	4·15	3·97	3·80	3·63	3·46	3·29	3·13	2·96	2·80	2·65	2·49	2·34	2·18	83
Lat.	120° / 240°	119° / 241°	118° / 242°	117° / 243°	116° / 244°	115° / 245°	114° / 246°	113° / 247°	112° / 248°	111° / 249°	110° / 250°	109° / 251°	108° / 252°	107° / 253°	106° / 254°	105° / 255°	Lat.

HOUR ANGLE

A - Named opposite to Latitude, **except** when **Hour Angle** is between 90° and 270°

TABLE A HOUR ANGLE

Lat. °	75° / 285°	76° / 284°	77° / 283°	78° / 282°	79° / 281°	80° / 280°	81° / 279°	82° / 278°	83° / 277°	84° / 276°	85° / 275°	86° / 274°	87° / 273°	88° / 272°	89° / 271°	90° / 270°	Lat. °
60	·46	·43	·40	·37	·34	·31	·27	·24	·21	·18	·15	·12	·09	·06	·03	·00	60
61	·48	·45	·42	·38	·35	·32	·29	·25	·22	·19	·16	·13	·10	·06	·03	·00	61
62	·50	·47	·43	·40	·37	·33	·30	·26	·23	·20	·16	·13	·10	·07	·03	·00	62
63	·53	·49	·45	·42	·38	·35	·31	·28	·24	·21	·17	·14	·10	·07	·03	·00	63
64	·55	·51	·47	·44	·40	·36	·33	·29	·25	·22	·18	·14	·11	·07	·04	·00	64
65	·57	·54	·50	·46	·42	·38	·34	·30	·26	·23	·19	·15	·11	·08	·04	·00	65
66	·60	·56	·52	·48	·44	·40	·36	·32	·28	·24	·20	·16	·12	·08	·04	·00	66
67	·63	·59	·54	·50	·46	·42	·37	·33	·29	·25	·21	·17	·12	·08	·04	·00	67
68	·66	·62	·57	·53	·48	·44	·39	·35	·30	·26	·22	·17	·13	·09	·04	·00	68
69	·70	·65	·60	·55	·51	·46	·41	·37	·32	·27	·23	·18	·14	·09	·05	·00	69
70	·74	·69	·63	·58	·53	·48	·44	·39	·34	·29	·24	·19	·14	·10	·05	·00	70
71	·78	·72	·67	·62	·57	·51	·46	·41	·36	·31	·25	·20	·15	·10	·05	·00	71
72	·82	·77	·71	·65	·60	·54	·49	·43	·38	·32	·27	·22	·16	·11	·05	·00	72
73	·88	·82	·78	·70	·64	·58	·52	·46	·40	·34	·29	·23	·17	·11	·06	·00	73
74	·93	·87	·81	·74	·68	·61	·55	·49	·43	·37	·31	·24	·18	·12	·06	·00	74
75	1·00	·93	·86	·79	·73	·66	·59	·53	·46	·39	·33	·26	·20	·13	·07	·00	75
76	1·07	1·00	·93	·85	·78	·71	·64	·56	·49	·42	·35	·28	·21	·14	·07	·00	76
77	1·16	1·08	1·00	·92	·84	·76	·69	·61	·53	·46	·38	·30	·23	·15	·08	·00	77
78	1·26	1·17	1·09	1·00	·91	·83	·75	·66	·58	·49	·41	·33	·25	·16	·08	·00	78
79	1·37	1·28	1·19	1·09	1·00	·91	·82	·72	·63	·54	·45	·36	·27	·18	·09	·00	79
80	1·52	1·41	1·31	1·21	1·10	1·00	·90	·80	·70	·60	·50	·40	·30	·20	·10	·00	80
81	1·69	1·57	1·46	1·34	1·23	1·11	1·00	·89	·78	·66	·55	·44	·33	·22	·11	·00	81
82	1·91	1·77	1·64	1·51	1·38	1·26	1·13	1·00	·87	·75	·62	·50	·37	·25	·12	·00	82
83	2·18	2·03	1·88	1·73	1·58	1·44	1·29	1·15	1·00	·86	·71	·57	·43	·28	·14	·00	83
Lat.	105° / 255°	104° / 256°	103° / 257°	102° / 258°	101° / 259°	100° / 260°	99° / 261°	98° / 262°	97° / 263°	96° / 264°	95° / 265°	94° / 266°	93° / 267°	92° / 268°	91° / 269°	90° / 270°	Lat.

A - Named opposite to Latitude, **except** when **Hour Angle** is between 90° and 270°

A - Named opposite to Latitude, **except** when **Hour Angle** is between 90° and 270°

HOUR ANGLE

A

TABLE B HOUR ANGLE

Dec. °	60° 300°	61° 299°	62° 298°	63° 297°	64° 296°	65° 295°	66° 294°	67° 293°	68° 292°	69° 291°	70° 290°	71° 289°	72° 288°	73° 287°	74° 286°	75° 285°	Dec. °
60	2·00	1·98	1·96	1·94	1·93	1·91	1·89	1·88	1·87	1·86	1·84	1·83	1·82	1·81	1·80	1·79	60
61	2·08	2·06	2·04	2·03	2·01	1·99	1·98	1·96	1·95	1·93	1·92	1·91	1·90	1·89	1·88	1·87	61
62	2·17	2·15	2·13	2·11	2·09	2·08	2·06	2·04	2·03	2·01	2·00	1·99	1·98	1·97	1·96	1·95	62
63	2·27	2·24	2·22	2·20	2·18	2·17	2·15	2·13	2·12	2·10	2·09	2·08	2·06	2·05	2·04	2·03	63
64	2·37	2·34	2·32	2·30	2·28	2·26	2·24	2·23	2·21	2·20	2·18	2·16	2·16	2·14	2·13	2·12	64
65	2·48	2·45	2·43	2·41	2·39	2·37	2·35	2·33	2·31	2·30	2·28	2·27	2·25	2·24	2·23	2·22	65
66	2·59	2·57	2·54	2·52	2·50	2·48	2·46	2·44	2·42	2·41	2·39	2·38	2·36	2·35	2·34	2·33	66
67	2·72	2·69	2·67	2·64	2·62	2·60	2·58	2·56	2·54	2·52	2·51	2·49	2·48	2·46	2·45	2·44	67
68	2·86	2·83	2·80	2·78	2·75	2·73	2·71	2·69	2·67	2·65	2·63	2·62	2·60	2·59	2·57	2·56	68
69	3·01	2·98	2·95	2·92	2·90	2·87	2·85	2·83	2·81	2·79	2·77	2·76	2·74	2·72	2·71	2·70	69
70	3·17	3·14	3·11	3·08	3·06	3·03	3·01	2·98	2·96	2·94	2·92	2·91	2·89	2·87	2·86	2·84	70
71	3·35	3·32	3·29	3·26	3·23	3·20	3·18	3·16	3·13	3·11	3·09	3·07	3·05	3·04	3·02	3·01	71
72	3·55	3·52	3·49	3·45	3·42	3·40	3·37	3·34	3·32	3·30	3·28	3·26	3·24	3·22	3·20	3·19	72
73	3·78	3·74	3·70	3·67	3·64	3·61	3·58	3·55	3·53	3·50	3·48	3·46	3·44	3·42	3·40	3·39	73
74	4·03	3·99	3·95	3·91	3·88	3·85	3·82	3·79	3·76	3·74	3·71	3·69	3·67	3·65	3·63	3·61	74
75	4·31	4·27	4·23	4·19	4·15	4·12	4·09	4·05	4·03	4·00	3·97	3·95	3·92	3·90	3·88	3·86	75
Dec.	120° 240°	119° 241°	118° 242°	117° 243°	116° 244°	115° 245°	114° 246°	113° 247°	112° 248°	111° 249°	110° 250°	109° 251°	108° 252°	107° 253°	106° 254°	105° 255°	Dec.

HOUR ANGLE

B - Always named the **same** as Declination

TABLE B - HOUR ANGLE

Dec. °	75° 285°	76° 284°	77° 283°	78° 282°	79° 281°	80° 280°	81° 279°	82° 278°	83° 277°	84° 276°	85° 275°	86° 274°	87° 273°	88° 272°	89° 271°	90° 270°	Dec. °
60	1·79	1·79	1·78	1·77	1·76	1·76	1·75	1·75	1·75	1·74	1·74	1·74	1·73	1·73	1·73	1·73	60
61	1·87	1·86	1·85	1·84	1·84	1·83	1·83	1·82	1·82	1·81	1·81	1·81	1·81	1·80	1·80	1·80	61
62	1·95	1·94	1·93	1·92	1·92	1·91	1·90	1·90	1·89	1·89	1·89	1·89	1·88	1·88	1·88	1·88	62
63	2·03	2·02	2·01	2·01	2·00	1·99	1·99	1·98	1·98	1·97	1·97	1·97	1·97	1·96	1·96	1·96	63
64	2·12	2·11	2·10	2·10	2·09	2·08	2·08	2·07	2·07	2·06	2·06	2·06	2·05	2·05	2·05	2·05	64
65	2·22	2·21	2·20	2·19	2·18	2·18	2·17	2·17	2·16	2·16	2·15	2·15	2·15	2·14	2·14	2·14	65
66	2·33	2·31	2·31	2·30	2·29	2·28	2·27	2·27	2·26	2·26	2·25	2·25	2·25	2·25	2·25	2·25	66
67	2·44	2·43	2·42	2·41	2·40	2·39	2·39	2·38	2·37	2·37	2·36	2·36	2·36	2·36	2·36	2·36	67
68	2·56	2·55	2·54	2·53	2·52	2·51	2·51	2·50	2·49	2·49	2·48	2·48	2·48	2·48	2·48	2·48	68
69	2·70	2·68	2·67	2·66	2·65	2·65	2·64	2·63	2·62	2·62	2·62	2·61	2·61	2·61	2·61	2·61	69
70	2·84	2·83	2·82	2·81	2·80	2·79	2·78	2·78	2·77	2·76	2·76	2·75	2·75	2·75	2·75	2·75	70
71	3·01	2·99	2·98	2·97	2·96	2·95	2·94	2·93	2·93	2·92	2·92	2·91	2·91	2·90	2·90	2·90	71
72	3·19	3·17	3·16	3·15	3·14	3·13	3·12	3·11	3·10	3·09	3·09	3·09	3·08	3·08	3·08	3·08	72
73	3·39	3·37	3·36	3·34	3·33	3·32	3·31	3·30	3·30	3·29	3·28	3·28	3·28	3·27	3·27	3·27	73
74	3·61	3·59	3·58	3·57	3·55	3·54	3·53	3·52	3·51	3·51	3·50	3·50	3·49	3·49	3·49	3·49	74
75	3·86	3·85	3·83	3·82	3·80	3·79	3·78	3·77	3·76	3·75	3·75	3·74	3·74	3·73	3·73	3·73	75
Dec.	105° 255°	104° 256°	103° 257°	102° 258°	101° 259°	100° 260°	99° 261°	98° 262°	97° 263°	96° 264°	95° 265°	94° 266°	93° 267°	92° 268°	91° 269°	90° 270°	Dec.

HOUR ANGLE

B - Always named the **same** as Declination

B

TABLE C

A & B CORRECTION.

A±B=	·00′	·01′	·02′	·03′	·04′	·05′	·06′	·07′	·08′	·09′	·10′	·11′	·12′	·13′	·14′	·15′	=A±B
Lat.°							AZIMUTHS										Lat.°
0	90·0	89·4	88·9	88·3	87·7	87·1	86·6	86·0	85·4	84·9	84·3	83·7	83·2	82·6	82·0	81·5	0
5	90·0	89·4	88·9	88·3	87·7	87·1	86·6	86·0	85·4	84·9	84·3	83·7	83·2	82·6	82·1	81·5	5
10	90·0	89·4	88·9	88·3	87·7	87·2	86·6	86·1	85·5	84·9	84·4	83·8	83·3	82·7	82·1	81·6	10
14	90·0	89·5	88·9	88·3	87·8	87·2	86·7	86·1	85·6	85·0	84·4	83·9	83·4	82·8	82·3	81·7	14
18	90·0	89·5	88·9	88·4	87·8	87·3	86·7	86·2	85·6	85·1	84·5	84·0	83·5	83·0	82·4	81·9	18
20	90·0	89·5	88·9	88·4	87·8	87·3	86·8	86·2	85·7	85·2	84·6	84·1	83·6	83·0	82·5	82·0	20
22	90·0	89·5	88·9	88·4	87·9	87·3	86·8	86·3	85·8	85·2	84·7	84·2	83·7	83·1	82·6	82·1	22
24	90·0	89·5	89·0	88·4	87·9	87·4	86·9	86·3	85·8	85·3	84·8	84·3	83·7	83·2	82·7	82·2	24
26	90·0	89·5	89·0	88·5	87·9	87·4	86·9	86·4	85·9	85·4	84·9	84·4	83·8	83·3	82·8	82·3	26
28	90·0	89·5	89·0	88·5	88·0	87·5	87·0	86·5	86·0	85·5	85·0	84·5	84·0	83·5	83·0	82·5	28
30	90·0	89·5	89·0	88·5	88·0	87·5	87·0	86·5	86·0	85·5	85·1	84·6	84·1	83·6	83·1	82·6	30
31	90·0	89·5	89·0	88·5	88·0	87·5	87·1	86·6	86·1	85·6	85·1	84·6	84·1	83·6	83·2	82·7	31
32	90·0	89·5	89·0	88·5	88·1	87·6	87·1	86·6	86·1	85·6	85·2	84·7	84·2	83·7	83·2	82·8	32
33	90·0	89·5	89·0	88·6	88·1	87·6	87·1	86·6	86·2	85·7	85·2	84·7	84·3	83·8	83·3	82·8	33
34	90·0	89·5	89·1	88·6	88·1	87·6	87·2	86·7	86·2	85·7	85·3	84·8	84·3	83·8	83·4	82·9	34
35	90·0	89·5	89·1	88·6	88·1	87·7	87·2	86·7	86·3	85·8	85·3	84·9	84·4	83·9	83·5	83·0	35
36	90·0	89·5	89·1	88·6	88·1	87·7	87·2	86·8	86·3	85·8	85·4	84·9	84·5	84·0	83·5	83·1	36
37	90·0	89·5	89·1	88·6	88·2	87·7	87·3	86·8	86·3	85·9	85·4	85·0	84·5	84·1	83·6	83·2	37
38	90·0	89·5	89·1	88·6	88·2	87·7	87·3	86·8	86·4	85·9	85·5	85·0	84·6	84·2	83·7	83·3	38
39	90·0	89·6	89·1	88·7	88·2	87·8	87·3	86·9	86·4	86·0	85·6	85·1	84·7	84·2	83·8	83·4	39
40	90·0	89·6	89·1	88·7	88·2	87·8	87·4	86·9	86·5	86·1	85·6	85·2	84·7	84·3	83·9	83·4	40
41	90·0	89·6	89·1	88·7	88·3	87·8	87·4	87·0	86·5	86·1	85·7	85·3	84·8	84·4	84·0	83·5	41
42	90·0	89·6	89·1	88·7	88·3	87·9	87·4	87·0	86·6	86·2	85·7	85·3	84·9	84·5	84·1	83·6	42
43	90·0	89·6	89·2	88·7	88·3	87·9	87·5	87·1	86·7	86·2	85·8	85·4	85·0	84·6	84·2	83·7	43
44	90·0	89·6	89·2	88·8	88·4	87·9	87·5	87·1	86·7	86·3	85·9	85·5	85·1	84·7	84·2	83·8	44
45	90·0	89·6	89·2	88·8	88·4	88·0	87·6	87·2	86·8	86·4	86·0	85·6	85·1	84·7	84·3	83·9	45
46	90·0	89·6	89·2	88·8	88·4	88·0	87·6	87·2	86·8	86·4	86·0	85·6	85·2	84·8	84·4	84·1	46
47	90·0	89·6	89·2	88·8	88·4	88·0	87·7	87·3	86·9	86·5	86·1	85·7	85·3	84·9	84·5	84·2	47
48	90·0	89·6	89·2	88·9	88·5	88·1	87·7	87·3	86·9	86·6	86·2	85·8	85·4	85·0	84·6	84·3	48
49	90·0	89·6	89·2	88·9	88·5	88·1	87·7	87·4	87·0	86·6	86·2	85·9	85·5	85·1	84·8	84·4	49
50	90·0	89·6	89·3	88·9	88·5	88·2	87·8	87·4	87·1	86·7	86·3	86·0	85·6	85·2	84·9	84·5	50
51	90·0	89·6	89·3	88·9	88·6	88·2	87·8	87·5	87·1	86·8	86·4	86·0	85·7	85·3	85·0	84·6	51
52	90·0	89·6	89·3	88·9	88·6	88·2	87·9	87·5	87·2	86·8	86·5	86·1	85·8	85·4	85·1	84·7	52
53	90·0	89·7	89·3	89·0	88·6	88·3	87·9	87·6	87·2	86·9	86·6	86·2	85·9	85·5	85·2	84·8	53
54	90·0	89·7	89·3	89·0	88·7	88·3	88·0	87·6	87·3	87·0	86·6	86·3	86·0	85·6	85·3	85·0	54
55	90·0	89·7	89·3	89·0	88·7	88·4	88·0	87·7	87·4	87·0	86·7	86·4	86·1	85·7	85·4	85·1	55
56	90·0	89·7	89·4	89·0	88·7	88·4	88·1	87·8	87·4	87·1	86·8	86·5	86·2	85·8	85·5	85·2	56
57	90·0	89·7	89·4	89·1	88·8	88·4	88·1	87·8	87·5	87·2	86·9	86·6	86·3	86·0	85·6	85·3	57
58	90·0	89·7	89·4	89·1	88·8	88·5	88·2	87·9	87·6	87·3	87·0	86·7	86·4	86·1	85·8	85·5	58
59	90·0	89·7	89·4	89·1	88·8	88·5	88·2	87·9	87·6	87·3	87·1	86·8	86·5	86·2	85·9	85·6	59
60	90·0	89·7	89·4	89·1	88·9	88·6	88·3	88·0	87·7	87·4	87·1	86·9	86·6	86·3	86·0	85·7	60
61	90·0	89·7	89·4	89·2	88·9	88·6	88·3	88·0	87·8	87·5	87·2	86·9	86·7	86·4	86·1	85·8	61
62	90·0	89·7	89·5	89·2	88·9	88·7	88·4	88·1	87·8	87·6	87·3	87·0	86·8	86·5	86·2	86·0	62
63	90·0	89·7	89·5	89·2	89·0	88·7	88·4	88·2	87·9	87·7	87·4	87·1	86·9	86·6	86·4	86·1	63
64	90·0	89·7	89·5	89·2	89·0	88·7	88·5	88·2	88·0	87·7	87·5	87·2	87·0	86·7	86·5	86·2	64
65	90·0	89·8	89·5	89·3	89·0	88·8	88·5	88·3	88·1	87·8	87·6	87·3	87·1	86·9	86·6	86·4	65
66	90·0	89·8	89·5	89·3	89·1	88·8	88·6	88·4	88·1	87·9	87·7	87·4	87·2	87·0	86·7	86·5	66
67	90·0	89·8	89·6	89·3	89·1	88·9	88·7	88·4	88·2	88·0	87·8	87·5	87·3	87·1	86·9	86·6	67
68	90·0	89·8	89·6	89·4	89·1	88·9	88·7	88·5	88·3	88·1	87·9	87·6	87·4	87·2	87·0	86·8	68
A±B=	·00′	·01′	·02′	·03′	·04′	·05′	·06′	·07′	·08′	·09′	·10′	·11′	·12′	·13′	·14′	·15′	=A±B

A & B **S**ame Names } RULE TO FIND { A & B **D**ifferent names
take **S**um, (add). } **C CORRECTION** { take **D**ifference (Sub.)
C CORRECTION, (A ± B) is named the same as the greater of these quantities.
AZIMUTH takes combined names of **C** Correction and Hour Angle

C

TABLE C

A & B CORRECTION.

AZIMUTHS

Lat.°	·15'	·16'	·17'	·18'	·19'	·20'	·21'	·22'	·23'	·24'	·25'	·26'	·27'	·28'	·29'	·30'	Lat.°
0	81·5	80·9	80·4	79·8	79·2	78·7	78·1	77·6	77·0	76·5	76·0	75·4	74·9	74·4	73·8	73·3	0
5	81·5	80·9	80·4	79·8	79·3	78·7	78·2	77·6	77·1	76·6	76·0	75·5	74·9	74·4	73·9	73·4	5
10	81·6	81·0	80·5	79·9	79·4	78·9	78·3	77·8	77·2	76·7	76·2	75·6	75·1	74·6	74·1	73·5	10
14	81·7	81·2	80·6	80·1	79·6	79·1	78·5	78·0	77·4	76·9	76·4	75·8	75·3	74·8	74·3	73·7	14
18	81·9	81·3	80·8	80·3	79·8	79·2	78·7	78·2	77·7	77·1	76·6	76·1	75·6	75·1	74·6	74·1	18
20	82·0	81·4	80·9	80·4	79·9	79·4	78·8	78·3	77·8	77·3	76·8	76·3	75·8	75·3	74·8	74·3	20
22	82·1	81·6	81·0	80·5	80·0	79·5	79·0	78·5	78·0	77·5	76·9	76·4	75·9	75·4	75·0	74·5	22
24	82·2	81·7	81·2	80·7	80·2	79·6	79·1	78·6	78·1	77·6	77·1	76·6	76·1	75·7	75·2	74·7	24
26	82·3	81·8	81·3	80·8	80·3	79·8	79·3	78·8	78·3	77·8	77·3	76·8	76·4	75·9	75·4	74·9	26
28	82·5	82·0	81·5	81·0	80·5	80·0	79·5	79·0	78·5	78·0	77·6	77·1	76·6	76·1	75·6	75·2	28
30	82·6	82·1	81·6	81·1	80·7	80·2	79·7	79·2	78·7	78·3	77·8	77·3	76·8	76·4	75·9	75·4	30
31	82·7	82·2	81·7	81·2	80·7	80·3	79·8	79·3	78·8	78·4	77·9	77·4	77·0	76·5	76·0	75·6	31
32	82·8	82·3	81·8	81·3	80·8	80·4	79·9	79·4	79·0	78·5	78·0	77·6	77·1	76·6	76·2	75·7	32
33	82·8	82·4	81·9	81·4	80·9	80·5	80·0	79·5	79·1	78·6	78·2	77·7	77·2	76·8	76·3	75·9	33
34	82·9	82·4	82·0	81·5	81·0	80·6	80·1	79·7	79·2	78·7	78·3	77·8	77·4	76·9	76·5	76·0	34
35	83·0	82·5	82·1	81·6	81·2	80·7	80·2	79·8	79·3	78·9	78·4	78·0	77·5	77·1	76·6	76·2	35
36	83·1	82·6	82·2	81·7	81·3	80·8	80·4	79·9	79·5	79·0	78·6	78·1	77·7	77·2	76·8	76·4	36
37	83·2	82·7	82·3	81·8	81·4	80·9	80·5	80·0	79·6	79·1	78·7	78·3	77·8	77·4	77·0	76·5	37
38	83·3	82·8	82·4	81·9	81·5	81·0	80·6	80·2	79·7	79·3	78·9	78·4	78·0	77·6	77·1	76·7	38
39	83·4	82·9	82·5	82·0	81·6	81·2	80·7	80·3	79·9	79·4	79·0	78·6	78·1	77·7	77·3	76·9	39
40	83·4	83·0	82·6	82·1	81·7	81·3	80·9	80·4	80·0	79·6	79·2	78·7	78·3	77·9	77·5	77·1	40
41	83·5	83·1	82·7	82·3	81·8	81·4	81·0	80·6	80·2	79·7	79·3	78·9	78·5	78·1	77·7	77·2	41
42	83·6	83·2	82·8	82·4	82·0	81·5	81·1	80·7	80·3	79·9	79·5	79·1	78·7	78·2	77·8	77·4	42
43	83·7	83·3	82·9	82·5	82·1	81·7	81·3	80·9	80·5	80·0	79·6	79·2	78·8	78·4	78·0	77·6	43
44	83·8	83·4	83·0	82·6	82·2	81·8	81·4	81·0	80·6	80·2	79·8	79·4	79·0	78·6	78·2	77·8	44
45	83·9	83·5	83·1	82·7	82·3	82·0	81·6	81·2	80·8	80·4	80·0	79·6	79·2	78·8	78·4	78·0	45
46	84·1	83·7	83·3	82·9	82·5	82·1	81·7	81·3	80·9	80·5	80·1	79·8	79·4	79·0	78·6	78·2	46
47	84·2	83·8	83·4	83·0	82·6	82·2	81·8	81·5	81·1	80·7	80·3	79·9	79·6	79·2	78·8	78·4	47
48	84·3	83·9	83·5	83·1	82·8	82·4	82·0	81·6	81·3	80·9	80·5	80·1	79·8	79·4	79·0	78·6	48
49	84·4	84·0	83·6	83·3	82·9	82·5	82·2	81·8	81·4	81·1	80·7	80·3	80·0	79·6	79·2	78·9	49
50	84·5	84·1	83·8	83·4	83·0	82·7	82·3	82·0	81·6	81·2	80·9	80·5	80·2	79·8	79·4	79·1	50
51	84·6	84·3	83·9	83·5	83·2	82·8	82·5	82·1	81·8	81·4	81·1	80·7	80·4	80·0	79·7	79·3	51
52	84·7	84·4	84·0	83·7	83·3	83·0	82·6	82·3	81·9	81·6	81·2	80·9	80·6	80·2	79·9	79·5	52
53	84·8	84·5	84·2	83·8	83·5	83·1	82·8	82·5	82·1	81·8	81·4	81·1	80·8	80·4	80·1	79·8	53
54	85·0	84·6	84·3	84·0	83·6	83·3	83·0	82·6	82·3	82·0	81·6	81·3	81·0	80·7	80·3	80·0	54
55	85·1	84·8	84·4	84·1	83·8	83·5	83·1	82·8	82·5	82·2	81·8	81·5	81·2	80·9	80·6	80·2	55
56	85·2	84·9	84·6	84·3	83·9	83·6	83·3	83·0	82·7	82·4	82·0	81·7	81·4	81·1	80·8	80·5	56
57	85·3	85·0	84·7	84·4	84·1	83·8	83·5	83·2	82·9	82·6	82·2	81·9	81·6	81·3	81·0	80·7	57
58	85·5	85·2	84·9	84·6	84·3	84·0	83·7	83·4	83·1	82·8	82·5	82·2	81·9	81·6	81·3	81·0	58
59	85·6	85·3	85·0	84·7	84·4	84·1	83·8	83·5	83·2	83·0	82·7	82·4	82·1	81·8	81·5	81·2	59
60	85·7	85·4	85·1	84·9	84·6	84·3	84·0	83·7	83·4	83·2	82·9	82·6	82·3	82·0	81·7	81·5	60
61	85·8	85·6	85·3	85·0	84·7	84·5	84·2	83·9	83·6	83·4	83·1	82·8	82·5	82·3	82·0	81·7	61
62	86·0	85·7	85·4	85·2	84·9	84·6	84·4	84·1	83·8	83·6	83·3	83·0	82·8	82·5	82·2	82·0	62
63	86·1	85·8	85·6	85·3	85·1	84·8	84·6	84·3	84·0	83·8	83·5	83·3	83·0	82·8	82·5	82·2	63
64	86·2	86·0	85·7	85·5	85·2	85·0	84·7	84·5	84·2	34·0	83·7	83·5	83·2	83·0	82·8	82·5	64
65	86·4	86·1	85·9	85·6	85·4	85·2	84·9	84·7	84·4	84·2	84·0	83·7	83·5	83·3	83·0	82·8	65
66	86·5	86·3	86·0	85·8	85·6	85·3	85·1	84·9	84·7	84·4	84·2	84·0	83·7	83·5	83·3	83·0	66
67	86·6	86·4	86·2	86·0	85·8	85·5	85·3	85·1	84·9	84·6	84·4	84·2	84·0	83·8	83·5	83·3	67
68	86·8	86·6	86·4	86·1	85·9	85·7	85·5	85·3	85·1	84·9	84·6	84·4	84·2	84·0	83·8	83·6	68

A±B= ·15' ·16' ·17' ·18' ·19' ·20' ·21' ·22' ·23' ·24' ·25' ·26' ·27' ·28' ·29' ·30' =A±B

A & B **S**ame Names take **S**um, (add). } RULE TO FIND **C** CORRECTION { A & B take **D**ifferent names **D**ifference (Sub.)

C CORRECTION, (A ± B) is named the same as the greater of these quantities.

AZIMUTH takes combined names of **C** Correction and Hour Angle

C

TABLE C

A. & B. CORRECTION.

AZIMUTHS

A±B=	·30'	·31'	·32'	·33'	·34'	·35'	·36'	·37'	·38'	·39'	·40'	·41'	·42'	·43'	·44'	·45'=A±B	Lat.°
0	73·3	72·8	72·3	71·7	71·2	70·7	70·2	69·7	69·2	68·7	68·2	67·7	67·3	66·7	66·3	65·8	0
5	73·4	72·8	72·3	71·8	71·3	70·8	70·3	69·8	69·3	68·8	68·3	67·8	67·3	66·8	66·4	65·9	5
10	73·5	73·0	72·5	72·0	71·5	71·0	70·5	70·0	69·5	69·0	68·5	68·0	67·5	67·0	66·6	66·1	10
14	73·7	73·2	72·7	72·2	71·7	71·2	70·7	70·2	69·7	69·3	68·8	68·3	67·8	67·4	66·9	66·4	14
18	74·1	73·6	73·1	72·6	72·1	71·6	71·1	70·6	70·1	69·6	69·2	68·7	68·2	67·8	67·3	66·8	18
20	74·3	73·8	73·3	72·8	72·3	71·8	71·3	70·8	70·3	69·9	69·4	68·9	68·5	68·0	67·5	67·1	20
22	74·5	74·0	73·5	73·0	72·5	72·0	71·5	71·1	70·6	70·1	69·7	69·2	68·7	68·3	67·8	67·4	22
24	74·7	74·2	73·7	73·2	72·7	72·3	71·8	71·3	70·9	70·4	69·9	69·5	69·0	68·6	68·1	67·7	24
26	74·9	74·4	74·0	73·5	73·0	72·5	72·1	71·6	71·1	70·7	70·2	69·8	69·3	68·9	68·4	68·0	26
28	75·2	74·7	74·2	73·8	73·3	72·8	72·4	71·9	71·5	71·0	70·5	70·1	69·7	69·2	68·8	68·3	28
30	75·4	75·0	74·5	74·1	73·6	73·1	72·7	72·2	71·8	71·3	70·9	70·5	70·0	69·6	69·1	68·7	30
31	75·6	75·1	74·7	74·2	73·8	73·3	72·9	72·4	72·0	71·5	71·1	70·6	70·2	69·8	69·3	68·9	31
32	75·7	75·3	74·8	74·4	73·9	73·5	73·0	72·6	72·1	71·7	71·3	70·8	70·4	70·0	69·5	69·1	32
33	75·9	75·4	75·0	74·5	74·1	73·6	73·2	72·8	72·3	71·9	71·5	71·0	70·6	70·2	69·7	69·3	33
34	76·0	75·6	75·1	74·7	74·3	73·8	73·4	72·9	72·5	72·1	71·7	71·2	70·8	70·4	70·0	69·5	34
35	76·2	75·8	75·3	74·9	74·4	74·0	73·6	73·1	72·7	72·3	71·9	71·4	71·0	70·6	70·2	69·8	35
36	76·4	75·9	75·5	75·1	74·6	74·2	73·8	73·3	72·9	72·5	72·1	71·6	71·2	70·8	70·4	70·0	36
37	76·5	76·1	75·7	75·2	74·8	74·4	74·0	73·5	73·1	72·7	72·3	71·9	71·5	71·0	70·6	70·2	37
38	76·7	76·3	75·8	75·4	75·0	74·6	74·2	73·7	73·3	72·9	72·5	72·1	71·7	71·3	70·9	70·5	38
39	76·9	76·5	76·0	75·6	75·2	74·8	74·4	74·0	73·5	73·1	72·7	72·3	71·9	71·5	71·1	70·7	39
40	77·1	76·6	76·2	75·8	75·4	75·0	74·6	74·2	73·8	73·4	73·0	72·6	72·2	71·8	71·4	71·0	40
41	77·2	76·8	76·4	76·0	75·6	75·2	74·8	74·4	74·0	73·6	73·2	72·8	72·4	72·0	71·6	71·2	41
42	77·4	77·0	76·6	76·2	75·8	75·4	75·0	74·6	74·2	73·8	73·4	73·1	72·7	72·3	71·9	71·5	42
43	77·6	77·2	76·8	76·4	76·0	75·6	75·2	74·9	74·5	74·1	73·7	73·3	72·9	72·5	72·2	71·8	43
44	77·8	77·4	77·0	76·6	76·3	75·9	75·5	75·1	74·7	74·3	73·9	73·6	73·2	72·8	72·4	72·1	44
45	78·0	77·6	77·3	76·9	76·5	76·1	75·7	75·3	75·0	74·6	74·2	73·8	73·5	73·1	72·7	72·3	45
46	78·2	77·8	77·5	77·1	76·7	76·3	76·0	75·6	75·2	74·8	74·5	74·1	73·7	73·4	73·0	72·6	46
47	78·4	78·1	77·7	77·3	76·9	76·6	76·2	75·8	75·5	75·1	74·7	74·4	74·0	73·7	73·3	72·9	47
48	78·6	78·3	77·9	77·5	77·2	76·8	76·5	76·1	75·7	75·4	75·0	74·7	74·3	73·9	73·6	73·2	48
49	78·9	78·5	78·1	77·8	77·4	77·1	76·7	76·4	76·0	75·6	75·3	74·9	74·6	74·2	73·9	73·6	49
50	79·1	78·7	78·4	78·0	77·7	77·3	77·0	76·6	76·3	75·9	75·6	75·2	74·9	74·5	74·2	73·9	50
51	79·3	79·0	78·6	78·3	77·9	77·6	77·2	76·9	76·6	76·2	75·9	75·5	75·2	74·9	74·5	74·2	51
52	79·5	79·2	78·9	78·5	78·2	77·8	77·5	77·2	76·8	76·5	76·2	75·8	75·5	75·2	74·8	74·5	52
53	79·8	79·4	79·1	78·8	78·4	78·1	77·8	77·4	77·1	76·8	76·5	76·1	75·8	75·5	75·2	74·8	53
54	80·0	79·7	79·3	79·0	78·7	78·4	78·1	77·7	77·4	77·1	76·8	76·5	76·1	75·8	75·5	75·2	54
55	80·2	79·9	79·6	79·3	79·0	78·6	78·3	78·0	77·7	77·4	77·1	76·8	76·5	76·1	75·8	75·5	55
56	80·5	80·2	79·9	79·5	79·2	78·9	78·6	78·3	78·0	77·7	77·4	77·1	76·8	76·5	76·2	75·9	56
57	80·7	80·4	80·1	79·8	79·5	79·2	78·9	78·6	78·3	78·0	77·7	77·4	77·1	76·8	76·5	76·2	57
58	81·0	80·7	80·4	80·1	79·8	79·5	79·2	78·9	78·6	78·3	78·0	77·7	77·5	77·2	76·9	76·6	58
59	81·2	80·9	80·6	80·4	80·1	79·8	79·5	79·2	78·9	78·6	78·4	78·1	77·8	77·5	77·2	77·0	59
60	81·5	81·2	80·9	80·6	80·4	80·1	79·8	79·5	79·2	79·0	78·7	78·4	78·1	77·9	77·6	77·3	60
61	81·7	81·5	81·2	80·9	80·6	80·4	80·1	79·8	79·6	79·3	79·0	78·8	78·5	78·2	78·0	77·7	61
62	82·0	81·7	81·5	81·2	80·9	80·7	80·4	80·1	79·9	79·6	79·4	79·1	78·8	78·6	78·3	78·1	62
63	82·2	82·0	81·7	81·5	81·2	81·0	80·7	80·5	80·2	80·0	79·7	79·5	79·2	79·0	78·7	78·5	63
64	82·5	82·3	82·0	81·8	81·5	81·3	81·0	80·8	80·5	80·3	80·1	79·8	79·6	79·3	79·1	78·8	64
65	82·8	82·5	82·3	82·1	81·8	81·6	81·3	81·1	80·9	80·6	80·4	80·2	79·9	79·7	79·5	79·2	65
66	83·0	82·8	82·6	82·4	82·1	81·9	81·7	81·4	81·2	81·0	80·8	80·5	80·3	80·1	79·9	79·6	66
67	83·3	83·1	82·9	82·7	82·4	82·2	82·0	81·8	81·6	81·3	81·1	80·9	80·7	80·5	80·2	80·0	67
68	83·6	83·4	83·2	83·0	82·7	82·5	82·3	82·1	81·9	81·7	81·5	81·3	81·1	80·8	80·6	80·4	68

| A±B= | ·30' | ·31' | ·32' | ·33' | ·34' | ·35' | ·36' | ·37' | ·38' | ·39' | ·40' | ·41' | ·42' | ·43' | ·44' | ·45'=A±B |

A & B **S**ame Names take **S**um, (add). } RULE TO FIND { A & B take **D**ifferent names **D**ifference (Sub.)

C CORRECTION

C CORRECTION, (A ± B) is named the same as the greater of these quantities.

AZIMUTH takes combined names of **C** Correction and Hour Angle

C

TABLE C

A & B CORRECTION.

AZIMUTHS

Lat.°	·45′	·46′	·47′	·48′	·49′	·50′	·51′	·52′	·53′	·54′	·55′	·56′	·57′	·58′	·59′	·60′	Lat.°
0	65·8	65·3	64·8	64·4	63·9	63·4	63·0	62·5	62·1	61·6	61·2	60·8	60·3	59·9	59·5	59·0	0
5	65·9	65·4	64·9	64·4	64·0	63·5	63·1	62·6	62·2	61·7	61·3	60·8	60·4	60·0	59·6	59·1	5
10	66·1	65·6	65·2	64·7	64·2	63·8	63·3	62·9	62·4	62·0	61·6	61·1	60·7	60·3	59·8	59·4	10
14	66·4	65·9	65·5	65·0	64·6	64·1	63·7	63·2	62·8	62·3	61·9	61·5	61·1	60·6	60·2	59·8	14
18	66·8	66·4	65·9	65·5	65·0	64·6	64·1	63·7	63·2	62·8	62·4	62·0	61·5	61·1	60·7	60·3	18
20	67·1	66·6	66·2	65·7	65·3	64·8	64·4	64·0	63·5	63·1	62·7	62·2	61·8	61·4	61·0	60·6	20
22	67·4	66·9	66·5	66·0	65·6	65·1	64·7	64·3	63·8	63·4	63·0	62·6	62·1	61·7	61·3	60·9	22
24	67·7	67·2	66·8	66·3	65·9	65·5	65·0	64·6	64·2	63·7	63·3	62·9	62·5	62·1	61·7	61·3	24
26	68·0	67·5	67·1	66·7	66·2	65·8	65·4	64·9	64·5	64·1	63·7	63·3	62·9	62·5	62·1	61·7	26
28	68·3	67·9	67·5	67·0	66·6	66·2	65·8	65·3	64·9	64·5	64·1	63·7	63·3	62·9	62·5	62·1	28
30	68·7	68·3	67·9	67·4	67·0	66·6	66·2	65·8	65·3	64·9	64·5	64·1	63·7	63·3	62·9	62·5	30
31	68·9	68·5	68·1	67·6	67·2	66·8	66·4	66·0	65·6	65·2	64·8	64·4	64·0	63·6	63·2	62·8	31
32	69·1	68·7	68·3	67·9	67·4	67·0	66·6	66·2	65·8	65·4	65·0	64·6	64·2	63·8	63·4	63·0	32
33	69·3	68·9	68·5	68·1	67·7	67·2	66·8	66·4	66·0	65·6	65·2	64·8	64·5	64·1	63·7	63·3	33
34	69·5	69·1	68·7	68·3	67·9	67·5	67·1	66·7	66·3	65·9	65·5	65·1	64·7	64·3	63·9	63·6	34
35	69·8	69·4	68·9	68·5	68·1	67·7	67·3	66·9	66·5	66·1	65·7	65·4	65·0	64·6	64·2	63·8	35
36	70·0	69·6	69·2	68·8	68·4	68·0	67·6	67·2	66·8	66·4	66·0	65·6	65·2	64·9	64·5	64·1	36
37	70·2	69·8	69·4	69·0	68·6	68·2	67·8	67·4	67·1	66·7	66·3	65·9	65·5	65·1	64·8	64·4	37
38	70·5	70·1	69·7	69·3	68·9	68·5	68·1	67·7	67·3	66·9	66·6	66·2	65·8	65·4	65·1	64·7	38
39	70·7	70·3	69·9	69·5	69·2	68·8	68·4	68·0	67·6	67·2	66·9	66·5	66·1	65·7	65·4	65·0	39
40	71·0	70·6	70·2	69·8	69·4	69·0	68·7	68·3	67·9	67·5	67·2	66·8	66·4	66·0	65·7	65·3	40
41	71·2	70·9	70·5	70·1	69·7	69·3	68·9	68·6	68·2	67·8	67·5	67·1	66·7	66·4	66·0	65·6	41
42	71·5	71·1	70·7	70·4	70·0	69·6	69·2	68·9	68·5	68·1	67·8	67·4	67·0	66·7	66·3	66·0	42
43	71·8	71·4	71·0	70·7	70·3	69·9	69·5	69·2	68·8	68·4	68·1	67·7	67·4	67·0	66·7	66·3	43
44	72·1	71·7	71·3	71·0	70·6	70·2	69·9	69·5	69·1	68·8	68·4	68·1	67·7	67·4	67·0	66·7	44
45	72·3	72·0	71·6	71·3	70·9	70·5	70·2	69·8	69·5	69·1	68·7	68·4	68·0	67·7	67·4	67·0	45
46	72·6	72·3	71·9	71·6	71·2	70·8	70·5	70·1	69·8	69·4	69·1	68·7	68·4	68·1	67·7	67·4	46
47	72·9	72·6	72·2	71·9	71·5	71·2	70·8	70·5	70·1	69·8	69·4	69·1	68·8	68·4	68·1	67·7	47
48	73·2	72·9	72·5	72·2	71·8	71·5	71·2	70·8	70·5	70·1	69·8	69·5	69·1	68·8	68·5	68·1	48
49	73·6	73·2	72·9	72·5	72·2	71·8	71·5	71·2	70·8	70·5	70·2	69·8	69·5	69·2	68·8	68·5	49
50	73·9	73·5	73·2	72·9	72·5	72·2	71·8	71·5	71·2	70·9	70·5	70·2	69·9	69·6	69·2	68·9	50
51	74·2	73·9	73·5	73·2	72·9	72·5	72·2	71·9	71·6	71·2	70·9	70·6	70·3	69·9	69·6	69·3	51
52	74·5	74·2	73·9	73·5	73·2	72·9	72·6	72·2	71·9	71·6	71·3	71·0	70·7	70·3	70·0	69·7	52
53	74·8	74·5	74·2	73·9	73·6	73·3	72·9	72·6	72·3	72·0	71·7	71·4	71·1	70·8	70·5	70·1	53
54	75·2	74·9	74·6	74·2	73·9	73·6	73·3	73·0	72·7	72·4	72·1	71·8	71·5	71·2	70·9	70·6	54
55	75·5	75·2	74·9	74·6	74·3	74·0	73·7	73·4	73·1	72·8	72·5	72·2	71·9	71·6	71·3	71·0	55
56	75·9	75·6	75·3	75·0	74·7	74·4	74·1	73·8	73·5	73·2	72·9	72·6	72·3	72·0	71·7	71·5	56
57	76·2	75·9	75·6	75·3	75·1	74·8	74·5	74·2	73·9	73·6	73·3	73·0	72·8	72·5	72·2	71·9	57
58	76·6	76·3	76·0	75·7	75·4	75·2	74·9	74·6	74·3	74·0	73·8	73·5	73·2	72·9	72·6	72·4	58
59	77·0	76·7	76·4	76·1	75·8	75·6	75·3	75·0	74·7	74·5	74·2	73·9	73·6	73·4	73·1	72·8	59
60	77·3	77·0	76·8	76·5	76·2	76·0	75·7	75·4	75·2	74·9	74·6	74·4	74·1	73·8	73·6	73·3	60
61	77·7	77·4	77·2	76·9	76·6	76·4	76·1	75·9	75·6	75·3	75·1	74·8	74·6	74·3	74·0	73·8	61
62	78·1	77·8	77·6	77·3	77·0	76·8	76·5	76·3	76·0	75·8	75·5	75·3	75·0	74·8	74·5	74·3	62
63	78·5	78·2	78·0	77·7	77·5	77·2	77·0	76·7	76·5	76·2	76·0	75·7	75·5	75·2	75·0	74·8	63
64	78·8	78·6	78·4	78·1	77·9	77·6	77·4	77·2	76·9	76·7	76·4	76·2	76·0	75·7	75·5	75·3	64
65	79·2	79·0	78·8	78·5	78·3	78·1	77·8	77·6	77·4	77·1	76·9	76·7	76·5	76·2	76·0	75·8	65
66	79·6	79·4	79·2	79·0	78·7	78·5	78·3	78·1	77·8	77·6	77·4	77·2	76·9	76·7	76·5	76·3	66
67	80·0	79·8	79·6	79·4	79·2	78·9	78·7	78·5	78·3	78·1	77·9	77·7	77·4	77·2	77·0	76·8	67
68	80·4	80·2	80·0	79·8	79·6	79·4	79·2	79·0	78·8	78·6	78·4	78·2	77·9	77·7	77·5	77·3	68

A±B= ·45′ ·46′ ·47′ ·48′ ·49′ ·50′ ·51′ ·52′ ·53′ ·54′ ·55′ ·56′ ·57′ ·58′ ·59′ ·60′ =A±B

A & B **S**ame Names take **S**um, (add). } RULE TO FIND { A & B **D**ifferent names take **D**ifference (Sub.).
} C CORRECTION {

C CORRECTION, (A ± B) is named the same as the greater of these quantities.

AZIMUTH takes combined names of C Correction and Hour Angle

C

TABLE C

A & B CORRECTION.

A±B=	·60'	·62'	·64'	·66'	·68'	·70'	·72'	·74'	·76'	·78'	·80'	·82'	·84'	·86'	·88'	·90'=	A±B
Lat.°							**AZIMUTHS**										**Lat.°**
0	59·0	58·2	57·4	56·6	55·8	55·0	54·2	53·5	52·8	52·0	51·3	50·6	50·0	49·3	48·7	48·0	0
5	59·1	58·3	57·5	56·7	55·9	55·1	54·3	53·6	52·9	52·2	51·5	50·8	50·1	49·4	48·8	48·1	5
10	59·4	58·6	57·8	57·0	56·2	55·4	54·7	53·9	53·2	52·5	51·8	51·1	50·4	49·7	49·1	48·4	10
14	59·8	59·0	58·2	57·4	56·6	55·8	55·1	54·3	53·6	52·9	52·2	51·5	50·8	50·2	49·5	48·9	14
18	60·3	59·5	58·7	57·9	57·1	56·3	55·6	54·9	54·1	53·4	52·7	52·1	51·4	50·7	50·1	49·4	18
20	60·6	59·8	59·0	58·2	57·4	56·7	55·9	55·2	54·5	53·8	53·1	52·4	51·7	51·1	50·4	49·8	20
22	60·9	60·1	59·3	58·5	57·8	57·0	56·3	55·5	54·8	54·1	53·4	52·8	52·1	51·4	50·8	50·2	22
24	61·3	60·5	59·7	58·9	58·2	57·4	56·7	55·9	55·2	54·5	53·8	53·2	52·5	51·8	51·2	50·6	24
26	61·7	60·9	60·1	59·3	58·6	57·8	57·1	56·4	55·7	55·0	54·3	53·6	52·9	52·3	51·7	51·0	26
28	62·1	61·3	60·5	59·8	59·0	58·3	57·6	56·8	56·1	55·4	54·8	54·1	53·4	52·8	52·2	51·5	28
30	62·5	61·8	61·0	60·2	59·5	58·8	58·1	57·3	56·6	56·0	55·3	54·6	54·0	53·3	52·7	52·1	30
31	62·8	62·0	61·3	60·5	59·8	59·0	58·3	57·6	56·9	56·2	55·6	54·9	54·2	53·6	53·0	52·4	31
32	63·0	62·3	61·5	60·8	60·0	59·3	58·6	57·9	57·2	56·5	55·8	55·2	54·5	53·9	53·3	52·7	32
33	63·3	62·5	61·8	61·0	60·3	59·6	58·9	58·2	57·5	56·8	56·1	55·5	54·8	54·2	53·6	53·0	33
34	63·6	62·8	62·1	61·3	60·6	59·9	59·2	58·5	57·8	57·1	56·4	55·8	55·1	54·5	53·9	53·3	34
35	63·8	63·1	62·3	61·6	60·9	60·2	59·5	58·8	58·1	57·4	56·8	56·1	55·5	54·8	54·2	53·6	35
36	64·1	63·4	62·6	61·9	61·2	60·5	59·8	59·1	58·4	57·7	57·1	56·4	55·8	55·2	54·6	53·9	36
37	64·4	63·7	62·9	62·2	61·5	60·8	60·1	59·4	58·7	58·1	57·4	56·8	56·1	55·5	54·9	54·3	37
38	64·7	64·0	63·2	62·5	61·8	61·1	60·4	59·8	59·1	58·4	57·8	57·1	56·5	55·9	55·3	54·7	38
39	65·0	64·3	63·6	62·8	62·1	61·5	60·8	60·1	59·4	58·8	58·1	57·5	56·9	56·2	55·6	55·0	39
40	65·3	64·6	63·9	63·2	62·5	61·8	61·1	60·5	59·8	59·1	58·5	57·9	57·2	56·6	56·0	55·4	40
41	65·6	64·9	64·2	63·5	62·8	62·2	61·5	60·8	60·2	59·5	58·9	58·2	57·6	57·0	56·4	55·8	41
42	66·0	65·3	64·6	63·9	63·2	62·5	61·9	61·2	60·5	59·9	59·3	58·6	58·0	57·4	56·8	56·2	42
43	66·3	65·6	64·9	64·2	63·6	62·9	62·2	61·6	60·9	60·3	59·7	59·0	58·4	57·8	57·2	56·6	43
44	66·7	66·0	65·3	64·6	63·9	63·3	62·6	62·0	61·3	60·7	60·1	59·5	58·9	58·3	57·7	57·1	44
45	67·0	66·3	65·7	65·0	64·3	63·7	63·0	62·4	61·7	61·1	60·5	59·9	59·3	58·7	58·1	57·6	45
46	67·4	66·7	66·0	65·4	64·7	64·1	63·4	62·8	62·2	61·5	60·9	60·3	59·7	59·1	58·6	58·0	46
47	67·7	67·1	66·4	65·8	65·1	64·5	63·8	63·2	62·6	62·0	61·4	60·8	60·2	59·6	59·0	58·5	47
48	68·1	67·5	66·8	66·2	65·5	64·9	64·3	63·7	63·0	62·4	61·8	61·2	60·7	60·1	59·5	58·9	48
49	68·5	67·9	67·2	66·6	66·0	65·3	64·7	64·1	63·5	62·9	62·3	61·7	61·1	60·6	60·0	59·4	49
50	68·9	68·3	67·6	67·0	66·4	65·8	65·2	64·6	64·0	63·4	62·8	62·2	61·6	61·1	60·5	60·0	50
51	69·3	68·7	68·1	67·4	66·8	66·2	65·6	65·0	64·4	63·9	63·3	62·7	62·1	61·6	61·0	60·5	51
52	69·7	69·1	68·5	67·9	67·3	66·7	66·1	65·5	64·9	64·4	63·8	63·2	62·7	62·1	61·6	61·0	52
53	70·1	69·5	68·9	68·3	67·7	67·2	66·6	66·0	65·4	64·9	64·3	63·7	63·2	62·6	62·1	61·6	53
54	70·6	70·0	69·4	68·8	68·2	67·6	67·1	66·5	65·9	65·4	64·8	64·3	63·7	63·2	62·6	62·1	54
55	71·0	70·4	69·8	69·3	68·7	68·1	67·6	67·0	66·4	65·9	65·4	64·8	64·3	63·7	63·2	62·7	55
56	71·5	70·9	70·3	69·7	69·2	68·6	68·1	67·5	67·0	66·4	65·9	65·4	64·9	64·3	63·8	63·3	56
57	71·9	71·3	70·8	70·2	69·7	69·1	68·6	68·0	67·5	67·0	66·5	65·9	65·4	64·9	64·4	63·9	57
58	72·4	71·8	71·3	70·7	70·2	69·6	69·1	68·6	68·1	67·5	67·0	66·5	66·0	65·5	65·0	64·5	58
59	72·8	72·3	71·8	71·2	70·7	70·2	69·7	69·1	68·6	68·1	67·6	67·1	66·6	66·1	65·6	65·1	59
60	73·3	72·8	72·3	71·7	71·2	70·7	70·2	69·7	69·2	68·7	68·2	67·7	67·2	66·7	66·3	65·8	60
61	73·8	73·3	72·8	72·3	71·8	71·3	70·8	70·3	69·8	69·3	68·8	68·3	67·8	67·4	66·9	66·4	61
62	74·3	73·8	73·3	72·8	72·3	71·8	71·3	70·8	70·4	69·9	69·4	68·9	68·5	68·0	67·6	67·1	62
63	74·8	74·3	73·8	73·3	72·8	72·4	71·9	71·4	71·0	70·5	70·0	69·6	69·1	68·7	68·2	67·8	63
64	75·3	74·8	74·3	73·9	73·4	72·9	72·5	72·0	71·6	71·1	70·7	70·2	69·8	69·3	68·9	68·5	64
65	75·8	75·3	74·9	74·4	74·0	73·5	73·1	72·6	72·2	71·8	71·3	70·9	70·5	70·0	69·6	69·2	65
66	76·3	75·8	75·4	75·0	74·5	74·1	73·7	73·2	72·8	72·4	72·0	71·6	71·1	70·7	70·3	69·9	66
67	76·8	76·4	76·0	75·5	75·1	74·7	74·3	73·9	73·5	73·1	72·6	72·2	71·8	71·4	71·0	70·6	67
68	77·3	76·9	76·5	76·1	75·7	75·3	74·9	74·5	74·1	73·7	73·3	72·9	72·5	72·1	71·8	71·4	68

A±B=	·60'	·62'	·64'	·66'	·68'	·70'	·72'	·74'	·76'	·78'	·80'	·82'	·84'	·86'	·88'	·90'=	A±B

A & B **S**ame Names } take **S**um, (add) } RULE TO FIND { A & B **D**ifferent names C CORRECTION { take **D**ifference (Sub.)

C CORRECTION, (A ± B) is named the same as the greater of these quantities.

AZIMUTH takes combined names of **C** Correction and Hour Angle

C

TABLE C

Lat.	·90′	·92′	·94′	·96′	·98′	1·00′	1·02′	1·04′	1·06′	1·08′	1·10′	1·12′	1·14′	1·16′	1·18′	1·20′	Lat.
0	48·0	47·4	46·8	46·2	45·6	45·0	44·4	43·9	43·3	42·8	42·3	41·8	41·3	40·8	40·3	39·8	**0**
5	48·1	47·5	46·9	46·3	45·7	45·1	44·5	44·0	43·4	42·9	42·4	41·9	41·4	40·9	40·4	39·9	**5**
10	48·4	47·8	47·2	46·6	46·0	45·4	44·9	44·3	43·8	43·2	42·7	42·2	41·7	41·2	40·7	40·2	**10**
14	48·9	48·3	47·7	47·1	46·5	45·9	45·3	44·7	44·2	43·7	43·1	42·6	42·1	41·6	41·2	40·7	**14**
18	49·4	48·8	48·2	47·6	47·0	46·4	45·9	45·3	44·8	44·2	43·7	43·2	42·7	42·2	41·7	41·2	**18**
20	49·8	49·2	48·5	47·9	47·4	46·8	46·2	45·7	45·1	44·6	44·1	43·5	43·0	42·5	42·0	41·6	**20**
22	50·2	49·5	48·9	48·3	47·7	47·2	46·6	46·0	45·5	45·0	44·4	43·9	43·4	42·9	42·4	41·9	**22**
24	50·6	50·0	49·3	48·7	48·2	47·6	47·0	46·5	45·9	45·4	44·9	44·3	43·8	43·3	42·9	42·4	**24**
26	51·0	50·4	49·8	49·2	48·6	48·1	47·5	46·9	46·4	45·9	45·3	44·8	44·3	43·8	43·3	42·8	**26**
28	51·5	50·9	50·3	49·7	49·1	48·6	48·0	47·4	46·9	46·4	45·8	45·3	44·8	44·3	43·8	43·3	**28**
30	52·1	51·5	50·9	50·3	49·7	49·1	48·5	48·0	47·4	46·9	46·4	45·9	45·4	44·9	44·4	43·9	**30**
31	52·4	51·7	51·1	50·6	50·0	49·4	48·8	48·3	47·7	47·2	46·7	46·2	45·7	45·2	44·7	44·2	**31**
32	52·7	52·0	51·4	50·9	50·3	49·7	49·1	48·6	48·0	47·5	47·0	46·5	46·0	45·5	45·0	44·5	**32**
33	53·0	52·3	51·7	51·2	50·6	50·0	49·5	48·9	48·4	47·8	47·3	46·8	46·3	45·8	45·3	44·8	**33**
34	53·3	52·7	52·1	51·5	50·9	50·3	49·8	49·2	48·7	48·2	47·6	47·1	46·6	46·1	45·6	45·1	**34**
35	53·6	53·0	52·4	51·8	51·2	50·7	50·1	49·6	49·0	48·5	48·0	47·5	47·0	46·5	46·0	45·5	**35**
36	53·9	53·3	52·7	52·2	51·6	51·0	50·5	49·9	49·4	48·9	48·3	47·8	47·3	46·8	46·3	45·8	**36**
37	54·3	53·7	53·1	52·5	52·0	51·4	50·8	50·3	49·8	49·2	48·7	48·2	47·7	47·2	46·7	46·2	**37**
38	54·7	54·1	53·5	52·9	52·3	51·8	51·2	50·7	50·1	49·6	49·1	48·6	48·1	47·6	47·1	46·6	**38**
39	55·0	54·4	53·9	53·3	52·7	52·1	51·6	51·1	50·5	50·0	49·5	49·0	48·5	48·0	47·5	47·0	**39**
40	55·4	54·8	54·2	53·7	53·1	52·5	52·0	51·5	50·9	50·4	49·9	49·4	48·9	48·4	47·9	47·4	**40**
41	55·8	55·2	54·6	54·1	53·5	53·0	52·4	51·9	51·3	50·8	50·3	49·8	49·3	48·8	48·3	47·8	**41**
42	56·2	55·6	55·1	54·5	53·9	53·4	52·8	52·3	51·8	51·2	50·7	50·2	49·7	49·2	48·8	48·3	**42**
43	56·6	56·1	55·5	54·9	54·4	53·8	53·3	52·7	52·2	51·7	51·2	50·7	50·2	49·7	49·2	48·7	**43**
44	57·1	56·5	55·9	55·4	54·8	54·3	53·7	53·2	52·7	52·2	51·6	51·1	50·6	50·2	49·7	49·2	**44**
45	57·5	57·0	56·4	55·8	55·3	54·7	54·2	53·7	53·1	52·6	52·1	51·6	51·1	50·6	50·2	49·7	**45**
46	58·0	57·4	56·9	56·3	55·8	55·2	54·7	54·2	53·6	53·1	52·6	52·1	51·6	51·1	50·7	50·2	**46**
47	58·5	57·9	57·3	56·8	56·2	55·7	55·2	54·7	54·1	53·6	53·1	52·6	52·1	51·7	51·2	50·7	**47**
48	58·9	58·4	57·8	57·3	56·7	56·2	55·7	55·2	54·7	54·1	53·6	53·2	52·7	52·2	51·7	51·2	**48**
49	59·4	58·9	58·3	57·8	57·3	56·7	56·2	55·7	55·2	54·7	54·2	53·7	53·2	52·7	52·3	51·8	**49**
50	60·0	59·4	58·9	58·3	57·8	57·3	56·7	56·2	55·7	55·2	54·7	54·2	53·8	53·3	52·8	52·4	**50**
51	60·5	59·9	59·4	58·9	58·3	57·8	57·3	56·8	56·3	55·8	55·3	54·8	54·3	53·9	53·4	52·9	**51**
52	61·0	60·5	59·9	59·4	58·9	58·4	57·9	57·4	56·9	56·4	55·9	55·4	54·9	54·5	54·0	53·5	**52**
53	61·6	61·0	60·5	60·0	59·5	59·0	58·5	58·0	57·5	57·0	56·5	56·0	55·5	55·1	54·6	54·2	**53**
54	62·1	61·6	61·1	60·6	60·1	59·6	59·1	58·6	58·1	57·6	57·1	56·6	56·2	55·7	55·3	54·8	**54**
55	62·7	62·2	61·7	61·2	60·7	60·2	59·7	59·2	58·7	58·2	57·8	57·3	56·8	56·4	55·9	55·5	**55**
56	63·3	62·8	62·3	61·8	61·3	60·8	60·3	59·8	59·3	58·9	58·4	57·9	57·5	57·0	56·6	56·1	**56**
57	63·9	63·4	62·9	62·4	61·9	61·4	60·9	60·5	60·0	59·5	59·1	58·6	58·2	57·7	57·3	56·8	**57**
58	64·5	64·0	63·5	63·0	62·6	62·1	61·6	61·1	60·7	60·2	59·8	59·3	58·9	58·4	58·0	57·5	**58**
59	65·1	64·6	64·2	63·7	63·2	62·7	62·3	61·8	61·4	60·9	60·5	60·0	59·6	59·1	58·7	58·3	**59**
60	65·8	65·3	64·8	64·4	63·9	63·4	63·0	62·5	62·1	61·6	61·2	60·8	60·3	59·9	59·5	59·0	**60**
61	66·4	66·0	65·5	65·0	64·6	64·1	63·7	63·2	62·8	62·4	61·9	61·5	61·1	60·6	60·2	59·8	**61**
62	67·1	66·6	66·2	65·7	65·3	64·9	64·4	64·0	63·5	63·1	62·7	62·3	61·8	61·4	61·0	60·6	**62**
63	67·8	67·3	66·9	66·5	66·0	65·6	65·2	64·7	64·3	63·9	63·5	63·0	62·6	62·2	61·8	61·4	**63**
64	68·5	68·0	67·6	67·2	66·8	66·3	65·9	65·5	65·1	64·7	64·3	63·9	63·4	63·0	62·6	62·3	**64**
65	69·2	68·8	68·3	67·9	67·5	67·1	66·7	66·3	65·9	65·5	65·1	64·7	64·3	63·9	63·5	63·1	**65**
66	69·9	69·5	69·1	68·7	68·3	67·9	67·5	67·1	66·7	66·3	65·9	65·5	65·1	64·7	64·4	64·0	**66**
67	70·6	70·2	69·8	69·4	69·0	68·7	68·3	67·9	67·5	67·1	66·7	66·4	66·0	65·6	65·2	64·9	**67**
68	71·4	71·0	70·6	70·2	69·8	69·5	69·1	68·7	68·3	68·0	67·6	67·2	66·9	66·5	66·2	65·8	**68**

A & B CORRECTION. — AZIMUTHS

A ± B = ·90′ ·92′ ·94′ ·96′ ·98′ 1·00′ 1·02′ 1·04′ 1·06′ 1·08′ 1·10′ 1·12′ 1·14′ 1·16′ 1·18′ 1·20′ = A ± B

A & B **S**ame Names } RULE TO FIND { A & B **D**ifferent names
take **S**um, (add). } **C** CORRECTION { take **D**ifference (Sub.)

C CORRECTION, (A ± B) is named the same as the greater of these quantities.

AZIMUTH takes combined names of **C** Correction and Hour Angle

C

TABLE C

A & B CORRECTION.

A±B=1·20'	1·24'	1·28'	1·32'	1·36'	1·40'	1·44'	1·48'	1·52'	1·56'	1·60'	1·64'	1·68'	1·72'	1·76'	1·80'=A±B

AZIMUTHS

Lat.°																Lat.°
0	39·8	38·9	38·0	37·1	36·3	35·5	34·8	34·0	33·3	32·7	32·0	31·4	30·8	30·2	29·6	29·1	0
5	39·9	39·0	38·1	37·3	36·4	35·6	34·9	34·1	33·4	32·8	32·1	31·5	30·9	30·3	29·7	29·2	5
10	40·2	39·3	38·4	37·6	36·8	36·0	35·2	34·5	33·8	33·1	32·4	31·8	31·2	30·6	30·0	29·4	10
14	40·7	39·7	38·8	38·0	37·2	36·4	35·6	34·9	34·2	33·5	32·8	32·1	31·5	30·9	30·4	29·8	14
18	41·2	40·3	39·4	38·5	37·7	36·9	36·1	35·4	34·7	34·0	33·3	32·7	32·0	31·4	30·9	30·3	18
20	41·6	40·6	39·7	38·9	38·0	37·2	36·5	35·7	35·0	34·3	33·6	33·0	32·4	31·8	31·2	30·6	20
22	42·0	41·0	40·1	39·3	38·4	37·6	36·8	36·1	35·4	34·7	34·0	33·3	32·7	32·1	31·5	30·9	22
24	42·4	41·4	40·5	39·7	38·8	38·0	37·2	36·5	35·8	35·1	34·4	33·7	33·1	32·5	31·9	31·3	24
26	42·8	41·9	41·0	40·1	39·3	38·5	37·7	36·9	36·2	35·5	34·8	34·2	33·5	32·9	32·3	31·7	26
28	43·3	42·4	41·5	40·6	39·8	39·0	38·2	37·4	36·7	36·0	35·3	34·6	34·0	33·4	32·8	32·2	28
30	43·9	43·0	42·1	41·2	40·3	39·5	38·7	38·0	37·2	36·5	35·8	35·1	34·5	33·9	33·3	32·7	30
31	44·2	43·3	42·4	41·5	40·6	39·8	39·0	38·2	37·5	36·8	36·1	35·4	34·8	34·1	33·5	32·9	31
32	44·5	43·6	42·7	41·8	40·9	40·1	39·3	38·5	37·8	37·1	36·4	35·7	35·1	34·4	33·8	33·2	32
33	44·8	43·9	43·0	42·1	41·2	40·4	39·6	38·9	38·1	37·4	36·7	36·0	35·4	34·7	34·1	33·5	33
34	45·1	44·2	43·3	42·4	41·6	40·7	39·9	39·2	38·4	37·7	37·0	36·3	35·7	35·0	34·4	33·8	34
35	45·5	44·6	43·7	42·8	41·9	41·1	40·3	39·5	38·8	38·0	37·3	36·7	36·0	35·4	34·7	34·1	35
36	45·8	44·9	44·0	43·1	42·3	41·4	40·6	39·9	39·1	38·4	37·7	37·0	36·3	35·7	35·1	34·5	36
37	46·2	45·3	44·4	43·5	42·6	41·8	41·0	40·2	39·5	38·8	38·1	37·4	36·7	36·1	35·4	34·8	37
38	46·6	45·7	44·8	43·9	43·0	42·2	41·4	40·6	39·9	39·1	38·4	37·7	37·1	36·4	35·8	35·2	38
39	47·0	46·1	45·2	44·3	43·4	42·6	41·8	41·0	40·3	39·5	38·8	38·1	37·4	36·8	36·2	35·6	39
40	47·4	46·5	45·6	44·7	43·8	43·0	42·2	41·4	40·7	39·9	39·2	38·5	37·8	37·2	36·6	36·0	40
41	47·8	46·9	46·0	45·1	44·3	43·4	42·6	41·8	41·1	40·3	39·6	33·9	38·3	37·6	37·0	36·4	41
42	48·3	47·3	46·4	45·6	44·7	43·9	43·1	42·3	41·5	40·8	40·1	39·4	38·7	38·0	37·4	36·8	42
43	48·7	47·8	46·9	46·0	45·2	44·3	43·5	42·7	42·0	41·2	40·5	39·8	39·1	38·5	37·8	37·2	43
44	49·2	48·3	47·4	46·5	45·6	44·8	44·0	43·2	42·4	41·7	41·0	40·3	39·6	38·9	38·3	37·7	44
45	49·7	48·8	47·9	47·0	46·1	45·3	44·5	43·7	42·9	42·2	41·5	40·8	40·1	39·4	38·8	38·2	45
46	50·2	49·3	48·4	47·5	46·6	45·8	45·0	44·2	43·4	42·7	42·0	41·3	40·6	39·9	39·3	38·7	46
47	50·7	49·8	48·9	48·0	47·2	46·3	45·5	44·7	44·0	43·2	42·5	41·8	41·1	40·4	39·8	39·2	47
48	51·2	50·3	49·4	48·5	47·7	46·9	46·1	45·3	44·5	43·8	43·0	42·3	41·7	41·0	40·3	39·7	48
49	51·8	50·9	50·0	49·1	48·3	47·4	46·6	45·8	45·1	44·3	43·6	42·9	42·2	41·5	40·9	40·3	49
50	52·4	51·5	50·6	49·7	48·8	48·0	47·2	46·4	45·7	44·9	44·2	43·5	42·8	42·1	41·5	40·8	50
51	52·9	52·0	51·2	50·3	49·4	48·6	47·8	47·0	46·3	45·5	44·8	44·1	43·4	42·7	42·1	41·4	51
52	53·5	52·6	51·8	50·9	50·1	49·2	48·4	47·7	46·9	46·2	45·4	44·7	44·0	43·4	42·7	42·1	52
53	54·2	53·3	52·4	51·5	50·7	49·9	49·1	48·3	47·5	46·8	46·1	45·4	44·7	44·0	43·4	42·7	53
54	54·8	53·9	53·0	52·2	51·4	50·6	49·8	49·0	48·2	47·5	46·8	46·1	45·4	44·7	44·0	43·4	54
55	55·5	54·6	53·7	52·9	52·0	51·2	50·5	49·7	48·9	48·2	47·5	46·8	46·1	45·4	44·7	44·1	55
56	56·1	55·3	54·4	53·6	52·7	51·9	51·2	50·4	49·6	48·9	48·2	47·5	46·8	46·1	45·5	44·8	56
57	56·8	56·0	55·1	54·3	53·5	52·7	51·9	51·1	50·4	49·7	48·9	48·2	47·5	46·9	46·2	45·6	57
58	57·5	56·7	55·9	55·0	54·2	53·4	52·7	51·9	51·1	50·4	49·7	49·0	48·3	47·7	47·0	46·4	58
59	58·3	57·4	56·6	55·8	55·0	54·2	53·4	52·7	51·9	51·2	50·5	49·8	49·1	48·5	47·8	47·2	59
60	59·0	58·2	57·4	56·6	55·8	55·0	54·2	53·5	52·8	52·0	51·3	50·6	50·0	49·3	48·7	48·0	60
61	59·8	59·0	58·2	57·4	56·6	55·8	55·1	54·3	53·6	52·9	52·2	51·5	50·8	50·2	49·5	48·9	61
62	60·6	59·8	59·0	58·2	57·4	56·7	55·9	55·2	54·5	53·8	53·1	52·4	51·7	51·1	50·4	49·8	62
63	61·4	60·6	59·8	59·1	58·3	57·6	56·8	56·1	55·4	54·7	54·0	53·3	52·7	52·0	51·4	50·7	63
64	62·3	61·5	60·7	59·9	59·2	58·5	57·7	57·0	56·3	55·6	55·0	54·3	53·6	53·0	52·4	51·7	64
65	63·1	62·3	61·6	60·8	60·1	59·4	58·7	58·0	57·3	56·6	55·9	55·3	54·6	54·0	53·4	52·7	65
66	64·0	63·2	62·5	61·8	61·1	60·3	59·6	59·0	58·3	57·6	56·9	56·3	55·7	55·0	54·4	53·8	66
67	64·9	64·1	63·4	62·7	62·0	61·3	60·6	60·0	59·3	58·6	58·0	57·3	56·7	56·1	55·5	54·9	67
68	65·8	65·1	64·4	63·7	63·0	62·3	61·7	61·0	60·3	59·7	59·1	58·4	57·8	57·2	56·6	56·0	68

A±B=1·20'	1·24'	1·28'	1·32'	1·36'	1·40'	1·44'	1·48'	1·52'	1·56'	1·60'	1·64'	1·68'	1·72'	1·76'	1·80'=A±B

A & B **S**ame Names } RULE TO FIND { A & B **D**ifferent names
take **S**um, (add). } **C** CORRECTION { take **D**ifference (Sub.)
C CORRECTION, (A ± B) is named the same as the greater of these quantities.
AZIMUTH takes combined names of **C** Correction and Hour Angle

C

TABLE C

A±B=	1·80'	1·84'	1·88'	1·92'	1·96'	2·00'	2·04'	2·08'	2·12'	2·16'	2·20'	2·24'	2·28'	2·32'	2·36'	2·40'	=A±B
Lat.								AZIMUTHS									Lat.
0	29·1	28·5	28·0	27·5	27·0	26·6	26·1	25·7	25·2	24·8	24·4	24·0	23·7	23·3	23·0	22·6	0
5	29·1	28·6	28·1	27·6	27·1	26·7	26·2	25·8	25·3	24·9	24·5	24·1	23·8	23·4	23·0	22·7	5
10	29·4	28·9	28·4	27·9	27·4	26·9	26·5	26·0	25·6	25·2	24·8	24·4	24·0	23·6	23·3	22·9	10
14	29·8	29·3	28·7	28·2	27·7	27·3	26·8	26·4	25·9	25·5	25·1	24·7	24·3	24·0	23·6	23·2	14
18	30·3	29·7	29·2	28·7	28·2	27·7	27·3	26·8	26·4	26·0	25·6	25·2	24·8	24·4	24·0	23·7	18
20	30·6	30·0	29·5	29·0	28·5	28·0	27·6	27·1	26·7	26·2	25·8	25·4	25·0	24·6	24·3	23·9	20
22	30·9	30·4	29·8	29·3	28·8	28·3	27·9	27·4	27·0	26·5	26·1	25·7	25·3	24·9	24·6	24·2	22
24	31·3	30·8	30·2	29·7	29·2	28·7	28·2	27·8	27·3	26·9	26·5	26·1	25·7	25·3	24·9	24·5	24
26	31·7	31·2	30·6	30·1	29·6	29·1	28·6	28·2	27·7	27·3	26·8	26·4	26·0	25·6	25·2	24·9	26
28	32·2	31·6	31·1	30·5	30·0	29·5	29·0	28·6	28·1	27·7	27·2	26·8	26·4	26·0	25·6	25·3	28
30	32·7	32·1	31·6	31·0	30·5	30·0	29·5	29·0	28·6	28·1	27·7	27·3	26·9	26·5	26·1	25·7	30
31	32·9	32·4	31·8	31·3	30·8	30·3	29·8	29·3	28·8	28·4	27·9	27·5	27·1	26·7	26·3	25·9	31
32	33·2	32·7	32·1	31·6	31·0	30·5	30·0	29·6	29·1	28·6	28·2	27·8	27·3	26·9	26·5	26·2	32
33	33·5	32·9	32·4	31·8	31·3	30·8	30·3	29·8	29·4	28·9	28·5	28·0	27·6	27·2	26·8	26·4	33
34	33·8	33·2	32·7	32·1	31·6	31·1	30·6	30·1	29·6	29·2	28·7	28·3	27·9	27·5	27·1	26·7	34
35	34·1	33·6	33·0	32·4	31·9	31·4	30·9	30·4	29·9	29·5	29·0	28·6	28·2	27·8	27·4	27·0	35
36	34·5	33·9	33·3	32·8	32·2	31·7	31·2	30·7	30·3	29·8	29·3	28·9	28·5	28·1	27·7	27·3	36
37	34·8	34·2	33·7	33·1	32·6	32·1	31·6	31·1	30·6	30·1	29·6	29·2	28·8	28·4	28·0	27·6	37
38	35·2	34·6	34·0	33·5	32·9	32·4	31·9	31·4	30·9	30·4	30·0	29·5	29·1	28·7	28·3	27·9	38
39	35·6	35·0	34·4	33·8	33·3	32·8	32·3	31·8	31·3	30·8	30·3	29·9	29·4	29·0	28·6	28·2	39
40	36·0	35·4	34·8	34·2	33·7	33·1	32·6	32·1	31·6	31·2	30·7	30·2	29·8	29·4	28·9	28·5	40
41	36·4	35·8	35·2	34·6	34·1	33·5	33·0	32·5	32·0	31·5	31·1	30·6	30·2	29·7	29·3	28·9	41
42	36·8	36·2	35·6	35·0	34·5	33·9	33·4	32·9	32·4	31·9	31·5	31·0	30·5	30·1	29·7	29·3	42
43	37·2	36·6	36·0	35·5	34·9	34·4	33·8	33·3	32·8	32·3	31·9	31·4	31·0	30·5	30·1	29·7	43
44	37·7	37·1	36·5	35·9	35·3	34·8	34·3	33·8	33·3	32·8	32·3	31·8	31·4	30·9	30·5	30·1	44
45	38·2	37·6	37·0	36·4	35·8	35·3	34·7	34·2	33·7	33·2	32·7	32·3	31·8	31·4	30·9	30·5	45
46	38·7	38·1	37·5	36·9	36·3	35·7	35·2	34·7	34·2	33·7	33·2	32·7	32·3	31·8	31·4	31·0	46
47	39·2	38·6	38·0	37·4	36·8	36·2	35·7	35·2	34·7	34·2	33·7	33·2	32·7	32·3	31·9	31·4	47
48	39·7	39·1	38·5	37·9	37·3	36·8	36·2	35·7	35·2	34·7	34·2	33·7	33·2	32·8	32·4	31·9	48
49	40·3	39·6	39·0	38·4	37·9	37·3	36·8	36·2	35·7	35·2	34·7	34·2	33·8	33·3	32·9	32·4	49
50	40·8	40·2	39·6	39·0	38·4	37·9	37·3	36·8	36·3	35·8	35·3	34·8	34·3	33·8	33·4	33·0	50
51	41·4	40·8	40·2	39·6	39·0	38·4	37·9	37·4	36·9	36·3	35·8	35·3	34·9	34·4	34·0	33·5	51
52	42·1	41·4	40·8	40·2	39·6	39·1	38·5	38·0	37·5	36·9	36·4	35·9	35·5	35·0	34·5	34·1	52
53	42·7	42·1	41·5	40·9	40·3	39·7	39·2	38·6	38·1	37·6	37·1	36·6	36·1	35·6	35·1	34·7	53
54	43·4	42·8	42·1	41·5	41·0	40·4	39·8	39·3	38·7	38·2	37·7	37·2	36·7	36·3	35·8	35·3	54
55	44·1	43·5	42·8	42·2	41·7	41·1	40·5	40·0	39·4	38·9	38·4	37·9	37·4	36·9	36·5	36·0	55
56	44·8	44·2	43·6	43·0	42·4	41·8	41·2	40·7	40·1	39·6	39·1	38·6	38·1	37·6	37·2	36·7	56
57	45·6	44·9	44·3	43·7	43·1	42·6	42·0	41·4	40·9	40·4	39·8	39·3	38·8	38·4	37·9	37·4	57
58	46·4	45·7	45·1	44·5	43·9	43·4	42·8	42·2	41·7	41·2	40·6	40·1	39·6	39·1	38·6	38·2	58
59	47·2	46·5	45·9	45·3	44·7	44·2	43·6	43·0	42·5	42·0	41·4	40·9	40·4	39·9	39·4	39·0	59
60	48·0	47·4	46·8	46·2	45·6	45·0	44·4	43·9	43·3	42·8	42·3	41·8	41·3	40·8	40·3	39·8	60
61	48·9	48·3	47·7	47·1	46·5	45·9	45·3	44·8	44·2	43·7	43·2	42·7	42·2	41·7	41·2	40·7	61
62	49·8	49·2	48·6	48·0	47·4	46·8	46·2	45·7	45·1	44·6	44·1	43·6	43·1	42·6	42·1	41·6	62
63	50·7	50·1	49·5	48·9	48·3	47·8	47·2	46·6	46·1	45·6	45·0	44·5	44·0	43·5	43·0	42·5	63
64	51·7	51·1	50·5	49·9	49·3	48·8	48·2	47·6	47·1	46·6	46·0	45·5	45·0	44·5	44·0	43·5	64
65	52·7	52·1	51·5	50·9	50·4	49·8	49·2	48·7	48·1	47·6	47·1	46·6	46·1	45·6	45·1	44·6	65
66	53·8	53·2	52·6	52·0	51·4	50·9	50·3	49·8	49·2	48·7	48·2	47·7	47·2	46·7	46·2	45·7	66
67	54·9	54·3	53·7	53·1	52·6	52·0	51·4	50·9	50·4	49·8	49·3	48·8	48·3	47·8	47·3	46·8	67
68	56·0	55·4	54·8	54·3	53·7	53·2	52·6	52·1	51·5	51·0	50·5	50·0	49·5	49·0	48·5	48·0	68
A±B=	1·80'	1·84'	1·88'	1·92'	1·96'	2·00'	2·04'	2·08'	2·12'	2·16'	2·20'	2·24'	2·28'	2·32'	2·36'	2·40'	=A±B

A & B **S**ame Names } RULE TO FIND { A & B **D**ifferent names
take **S**um, (add). } **C** CORRECTION { take **D**ifference (Sub.)
C CORRECTION, (A ± B) is named the same as the greater of these quantities.
AZIMUTH takes combined names of **C** Correction and Hour Angle

C

TABLE C

A & B CORRECTION.

AZIMUTHS

A±B=	2·40'	2·45'	2·50'	2·55'	2·60'	2·65'	2·70'	2·75'	2·80'	2·90'	3·00'	3·10'	3·20'	3·30'	3·40'	3·50'=	A±B
Lat.																	**Lat.**
0	22·6	22·2	21·8	21·4	21·0	20·7	20·3	20·0	19·7	19·0	18·4	17·9	17·4	16·9	16·4	15·9	0
5	22·7	22·3	21·9	21·5	21·1	20·8	20·4	20·1	19·7	19·1	18·5	17·9	17·4	16·9	16·4	16·0	5
10	22·9	22·5	22·1	21·7	21·3	21·0	20·6	20·3	19·9	19·3	18·7	18·1	17·6	17·1	16·6	16·2	10
14	23·2	22·8	22·4	22·0	21·6	21·3	20·9	20·5	20·2	19·6	19·0	18·4	17·9	17·4	16·9	16·4	14
18	23·7	23·2	22·8	22·4	22·0	21·6	21·3	20·9	20·6	19·9	19·3	18·7	18·2	17·7	17·2	16·7	18
20	23·9	23·5	23·1	22·7	22·3	21·9	21·5	21·2	20·8	20·2	19·5	18·9	18·4	17·9	17·4	16·9	20
22	24·2	23·8	23·3	22·9	22·5	22·2	21·8	21·4	21·1	20·4	19·8	19·2	18·6	18·1	17·6	17·1	22
24	24·5	24·1	23·6	23·2	22·8	22·5	22·1	21·7	21·4	20·7	20·0	19·4	18·9	18·4	17·8	17·4	24
26	24·9	24·4	24·0	23·6	23·2	22·8	22·4	22·0	21·7	21·0	20·3	19·7	19·2	18·6	18·1	17·6	26
28	25·3	24·8	24·4	23·9	23·5	23·1	22·8	22·4	22·0	21·3	20·7	20·1	19·5	18·9	18·4	17·9	28
30	25·7	25·2	24·8	24·4	23·9	23·5	23·2	22·8	22·4	21·7	21·1	20·4	19·8	19·3	18·8	18·3	30
31	25·9	25·5	25·0	24·6	24·2	23·8	23·4	23·0	22·6	21·9	21·2	20·6	20·0	19·5	18·9	18·4	31
32	26·2	25·7	25·3	24·8	24·4	24·0	23·6	23·2	22·8	22·1	21·5	20·8	20·2	19·7	19·1	18·6	32
33	26·4	26·0	25·5	25·1	24·6	24·2	23·8	23·4	23·1	22·4	21·7	21·0	20·4	19·9	19·3	18·8	33
34	26·7	26·2	25·8	25·3	24·9	24·5	24·1	23·7	23·3	22·6	21·9	21·3	20·7	20·1	19·5	19·0	34
35	27·0	26·5	26·0	25·6	25·2	24·7	24·3	23·9	23·6	22·8	22·1	21·5	20·9	20·3	19·8	19·2	35
36	27·3	26·8	26·3	25·9	25·4	25·0	24·6	24·2	23·8	23·1	22·4	21·7	21·1	20·5	20·0	19·5	36
37	27·6	27·1	26·6	26·2	25·7	25·3	24·9	24·5	24·1	23·4	22·7	22·0	21·4	20·8	20·2	19·7	37
38	27·9	27·4	26·9	26·5	26·0	25·6	25·2	24·8	24·4	23·6	22·9	22·3	21·6	21·0	20·5	19·9	38
39	28·2	27·7	27·2	26·8	26·3	25·9	25·5	25·1	24·7	23·9	23·2	22·5	21·9	21·3	20·7	20·2	39
40	28·5	28·1	27·6	27·1	26·7	26·2	25·8	25·4	25·0	24·2	23·5	22·8	22·2	21·6	21·0	20·5	40
41	28·9	28·4	27·9	27·5	27·0	26·6	26·1	25·7	25·3	24·6	23·8	23·1	22·5	21·9	21·3	20·7	41
42	29·3	28·8	28·3	27·8	27·4	26·9	26·5	26·1	25·7	24·9	24·2	23·5	22·8	22·2	21·6	21·0	42
43	29·7	29·2	28·7	28·2	27·7	27·3	26·9	26·4	26·0	25·2	24·5	23·8	23·1	22·5	21·9	21·3	43
44	30·1	29·6	29·1	28·6	28·1	27·7	27·2	26·8	26·4	25·6	24·9	24·2	23·5	22·8	22·2	21·7	44
45	30·5	30·0	29·5	29·0	28·5	28·1	27·6	27·2	26·8	26·0	25·2	24·5	23·8	23·2	22·6	22·0	45
46	31·0	30·4	29·9	29·5	29·0	28·6	28·1	27·6	27·2	26·4	25·6	24·9	24·2	23·6	22·9	22·4	46
47	31·4	30·9	30·4	29·9	29·4	29·0	28·5	28·1	27·6	26·8	26·0	25·3	24·6	24·0	23·3	22·7	47
48	31·9	31·4	30·9	30·4	29·9	29·4	29·0	28·5	28·1	27·3	26·5	25·7	25·0	24·4	23·7	23·1	48
49	32·4	31·9	31·4	30·9	30·4	29·9	29·4	29·0	28·6	27·7	26·9	26·2	25·5	24·8	24·1	23·5	49
50	33·0	32·4	31·9	31·4	30·9	30·4	30·0	29·5	29·1	28·2	27·4	26·6	25·9	25·2	24·6	24·0	50
51	33·5	33·0	32·4	31·9	31·4	30·9	30·5	30·0	29·6	28·7	27·9	27·1	26·4	25·7	25·0	24·4	51
52	34·1	33·5	33·0	32·5	32·0	31·5	31·0	30·6	30·1	29·3	28·5	27·7	26·9	26·2	25·5	24·9	52
53	34·7	34·1	33·6	33·1	32·6	32·1	31·6	31·1	30·7	29·8	29·0	28·2	27·4	26·7	26·0	25·4	53
54	35·3	34·8	34·2	33·7	33·2	32·7	32·2	31·7	31·3	30·4	29·6	28·8	28·0	27·3	26·6	25·9	54
55	36·0	35·4	34·9	34·4	33·8	33·4	32·9	32·4	31·9	31·0	30·2	29·4	28·6	27·9	27·1	26·5	55
56	36·7	36·1	35·6	35·1	34·5	34·0	33·5	33·1	32·6	31·7	30·8	30·0	29·2	28·5	27·7	27·1	56
57	37·4	36·8	36·3	35·8	35·2	34·7	34·2	33·8	33·3	32·4	31·5	30·6	29·8	29·1	28·4	27·7	57
58	38·2	37·6	37·0	36·5	36·0	35·5	35·0	34·5	34·0	33·1	32·2	31·3	30·5	29·8	29·0	28·3	58
59	39·0	38·4	37·8	37·3	36·8	36·3	35·7	35·2	34·7	33·8	32·9	32·1	31·2	30·5	29·7	29·0	59
60	39·8	39·2	38·7	38·1	37·6	37·1	36·5	36·0	35·5	34·6	33·7	32·8	32·0	31·2	30·5	29·8	60
61	40·7	40·1	39·5	39·0	38·4	37·9	37·3	36·9	36·4	35·4	34·5	33·6	32·8	32·0	31·2	30·5	61
62	41·6	41·0	40·4	39·9	39·3	38·8	38·3	37·8	37·3	36·3	35·4	34·5	33·6	32·8	32·1	31·3	62
63	42·5	42·0	41·4	40·8	40·3	39·7	39·2	38·7	38·2	37·2	36·3	35·4	34·5	33·7	32·9	32·2	63
64	43·5	43·0	42·4	41·8	41·3	40·7	40·2	39·7	39·2	38·2	37·3	36·4	35·5	34·7	33·9	33·1	64
65	44·6	44·0	43·4	42·9	42·3	41·8	41·2	40·7	40·2	39·2	38·3	37·4	36·5	35·7	34·9	34·1	65
66	45·7	45·1	44·5	44·0	43·4	42·9	42·3	41·8	41·3	40·3	39·3	38·4	37·6	36·7	35·9	35·1	66
67	46·8	46·2	45·7	45·1	44·6	44·0	43·5	42·9	42·4	41·4	40·5	39·5	38·7	37·8	37·0	36·2	67
68	48·0	47·4	46·9	46·3	45·8	45·2	44·7	44·1	43·6	42·6	41·7	40·7	39·8	39·0	38·1	37·3	68
Lat.																	**Lat.**
A±B=	2·40'	2·45'	2·50'	2·55'	2·60'	2·65'	2·70'	2·75'	2·80'	2·90'	3·00'	3·10'	3·20'	3·30'	3·40'	3·50'=	A±B

A & B **S**ame Names } RULE TO FIND { A & B **D**ifferent names
take **S**um, (add). } **C** CORRECTION { take **D**ifference (Sub.)

C CORRECTION, (A ± B) is named the same as the greater of these quantities.

AZIMUTH takes combined names of **C** Correction and Hour Angle

C

TABLE C

A & B CORRECTION.

AZIMUTHS

A±B=3.50'	3.60'	3.70'	3.80'	3.90'	4.00'	4.10'	4.20'	4.30'	4.40'	4.50'	4.60'	4.70'	4.80'	4.90'	5.00'=A±B
Lat.															**Lat.**
0 15.9	15.5	15.1	14.7	14.4	14.0	13.7	13.4	13.1	12.8	12.5	12.3	12.0	11.8	11.5	11.3 **0**
5 16.0	15.6	15.2	14.8	14.4	14.1	13.8	13.5	13.2	12.9	12.6	12.3	12.1	11.8	11.6	11.4 **5**
10 16.2	15.8	15.4	15.0	14.6	14.2	13.9	13.6	13.3	13.0	12.7	12.4	12.2	11.9	11.7	11.5 **10**
14 16.4	16.0	15.6	15.2	14.8	14.4	14.1	13.8	13.5	13.2	12.9	12.6	12.4	12.1	11.9	11.6 **14**
18 16.7	16.3	15.9	15.5	15.1	14.7	14.4	14.1	13.7	13.4	13.1	12.9	12.6	12.4	12.1	11.9 **18**
20 16.9	16.5	16.0	15.6	15.3	14.9	14.6	14.2	13.9	13.6	13.3	13.0	12.8	12.5	12.3	12.0 **20**
22 17.1	16.7	16.3	15.8	15.5	15.1	14.7	14.4	14.1	13.8	13.5	13.2	12.9	12.7	12.4	12.2 **22**
24 17.4	16.9	16.5	16.1	15.7	15.3	14.9	14.6	14.3	14.0	13.7	13.4	13.1	12.9	12.6	12.3 **24**
26 17.6	17.2	16.7	16.3	15.9	15.5	15.2	14.8	14.5	14.2	13.9	13.6	13.3	13.1	12.8	12.5 **26**
28 17.9	17.5	17.0	16.6	16.2	15.8	15.4	15.1	14.8	14.4	14.1	13.8	13.5	13.3	13.0	12.8 **28**
30 18.3	17.8	17.3	16.9	16.5	16.1	15.7	15.4	15.0	14.7	14.4	14.1	13.8	13.5	13.3	13.0 **30**
31 18.4	18.0	17.5	17.1	16.7	16.3	15.9	15.5	15.2	14.9	14.5	14.2	13.9	13.7	13.4	13.1 **31**
32 18.6	18.1	17.7	17.2	16.8	16.4	16.0	15.7	15.3	15.0	14.7	14.4	14.1	13.8	13.5	13.3 **32**
33 18.8	18.3	17.9	17.4	17.0	16.6	16.2	15.8	15.5	15.2	14.9	14.5	14.2	14.0	13.7	13.4 **33**
34 19.0	18.5	18.1	17.6	17.2	16.8	16.4	16.0	15.7	15.3	15.0	14.7	14.4	14.1	13.8	13.6 **34**
35 19.2	18.7	18.3	17.8	17.4	17.0	16.6	16.2	15.9	15.5	15.2	14.9	14.6	14.3	14.0	13.7 **35**
36 19.5	19.0	18.5	18.0	17.6	17.2	16.8	16.4	16.1	15.7	15.4	15.0	14.7	14.4	14.2	13.9 **36**
37 19.7	19.2	18.7	18.2	17.7	17.4	17.0	16.6	16.3	15.9	15.6	15.2	14.9	14.6	14.3	14.1 **37**
38 19.9	19.4	18.9	18.5	18.0	17.6	17.2	16.8	16.5	16.1	15.8	15.4	15.1	14.8	14.5	14.2 **38**
39 20.2	19.7	19.2	18.7	18.3	17.8	17.4	17.0	16.7	16.3	16.0	15.6	15.3	15.0	14.7	14.4 **39**
40 20.5	19.9	19.4	19.0	18.5	18.1	17.7	17.3	16.9	16.5	16.2	15.8	15.5	15.2	14.9	14.6 **40**
41 20.7	20.2	19.7	19.2	18.8	18.3	17.9	17.5	17.1	16.8	16.4	16.1	15.7	15.4	15.1	14.8 **41**
42 21.0	20.5	20.0	19.5	19.0	18.6	18.2	17.8	17.4	17.0	16.7	16.3	16.0	15.7	15.4	15.1 **42**
43 21.3	20.8	20.3	19.8	19.3	18.9	18.4	18.0	17.6	17.3	16.9	16.6	16.2	15.9	15.6	15.3 **43**
44 21.7	21.1	20.6	20.1	19.6	19.2	18.7	18.3	17.9	17.5	17.2	16.8	16.5	16.2	15.8	15.5 **44**
45 22.0	21.4	20.9	20.4	19.9	19.5	19.0	18.6	18.2	17.8	17.5	17.1	16.8	16.4	16.1	15.8 **45**
46 22.4	21.8	21.3	20.8	20.3	19.8	19.3	18.9	18.5	18.1	17.8	17.4	17.1	16.7	16.4	16.1 **46**
47 22.7	22.2	21.6	21.1	20.6	20.1	19.7	19.2	18.8	18.4	18.1	17.7	17.4	17.0	16.7	16.3 **47**
48 23.1	22.5	22.0	21.5	21.0	20.5	20.0	19.6	19.2	18.8	18.4	18.0	17.7	17.3	17.0	16.6 **48**
49 23.5	22.9	22.4	21.9	21.4	20.9	20.4	19.9	19.5	19.1	18.7	18.3	18.0	17.6	17.3	17.0 **49**
50 24.0	23.4	22.8	22.3	21.8	21.3	20.8	20.3	19.9	19.5	19.1	18.7	18.3	18.0	17.6	17.3 **50**
51 24.4	23.8	23.3	22.7	22.2	21.7	21.2	20.7	20.3	19.9	19.5	19.1	18.7	18.3	18.0	17.6 **51**
52 24.9	24.3	23.7	23.1	22.6	22.1	21.6	21.1	20.7	20.3	19.9	19.5	19.1	18.7	18.3	18.0 **52**
53 25.4	24.8	24.2	23.6	23.1	22.6	22.1	21.6	21.2	20.7	20.3	19.9	19.5	19.1	18.7	18.4 **53**
54 25.9	25.3	24.7	24.1	23.6	23.1	22.6	22.1	21.6	21.1	20.7	20.3	19.9	19.5	19.1	18.8 **54**
55 26.5	25.8	25.2	24.6	24.1	23.6	23.1	22.6	22.1	21.6	21.2	20.8	20.4	20.0	19.6	19.2 **55**
56 27.1	26.4	25.8	25.2	24.6	24.1	23.6	23.1	22.6	22.1	21.7	21.3	20.8	20.4	20.1	19.7 **56**
57 27.7	27.0	26.4	25.8	25.2	24.7	24.1	23.6	23.1	22.7	22.2	21.8	21.3	20.9	20.6	20.2 **57**
58 28.3	27.7	27.0	26.4	25.8	25.3	24.7	24.2	23.7	23.2	22.8	22.3	21.9	21.5	21.1	20.7 **58**
59 29.0	23.4	27.7	27.1	26.5	25.9	25.3	24.8	24.3	23.8	23.4	22.9	22.5	22.0	21.6	21.2 **59**
60 29.8	29.1	28.4	27.8	27.2	26.6	26.0	25.5	24.9	24.4	24.0	23.5	23.1	22.6	22.2	21.8 **60**
61 30.5	29.8	29.1	28.5	27.9	27.3	26.7	26.2	25.6	25.1	24.6	24.2	23.7	23.3	22.8	22.4 **61**
62 31.3	30.6	29.9	29.3	28.7	28.0	27.5	26.9	26.4	25.8	25.3	24.8	24.4	23.9	23.5	23.1 **62**
63 32.2	31.5	30.8	30.1	29.5	28.8	28.2	27.7	27.1	26.6	26.1	25.6	25.1	24.6	24.2	23.8 **63**
64 33.1	32.4	31.7	31.0	30.3	29.7	29.1	28.5	27.9	27.4	26.9	26.4	25.9	25.4	25.0	24.5 **64**
65 34.1	33.3	32.6	31.9	31.2	30.6	30.0	29.4	28.8	28.3	27.8	27.2	26.7	26.2	25.8	25.3 **65**
66 35.1	34.3	33.6	32.9	32.2	31.6	30.9	30.3	29.8	29.2	28.7	28.1	27.6	27.1	26.7	26.2 **66**
67 36.2	35.4	34.7	34.0	33.3	32.6	32.0	31.4	30.8	30.2	29.6	29.1	28.6	28.1	27.6	27.1 **67**
68 37.3	36.6	35.8	35.1	34.4	33.7	33.1	32.4	31.8	31.2	30.7	30.1	29.6	29.1	28.6	28.1 **68**

| A±B=3.50' | 3.60' | 3.70' | 3.80' | 3.90' | 4.00' | 4.10' | 4.20' | 4.30' | 4.40' | 4.50' | 4.60' | 4.70' | 4.80' | 4.90' | 5.00'=A±B |

A & B **S**ame Names take **S**um, (add). } RULE TO FIND { A & B **D**ifferent names **C** CORRECTION take **D**ifference (Sub.)

C CORRECTION, (A ± B) is named the same as the greater of these quantities.

AZIMUTH takes combined names of **C** Correction and Hour Angle

C

TABLE C

A & B CORRECTION.

Lat.°	5·00'	5·20'	5·40'	5·60'	5·80'	6·00'	6·20'	6·40'	6·60'	6·80'	7·00'	7·20'	7·40'	7·60'	7·80'	8·00'	Lat.°
							AZIMUTHS										
0	11·3	10·9	10·5	10·1	9·8	9·5	9·2	8·9	8·6	8·4	8·1	7·9	7·7	7·5	7·3	7·1	0
5	11·4	10·9	10·5	10·2	9·8	9·5	9·2	8·9	8·6	8·4	8·2	7·9	7·7	7·5	7·3	7·2	5
10	11·5	11·0	10·6	10·3	9·9	9·6	9·3	9·0	8·7	8·5	8·3	8·0	7·8	7·6	7·4	7·2	10
14	11·6	11·2	10·8	10·4	10·1	9·7	9·4	9·1	8·9	8·7	8·4	8·1	7·9	7·7	7·5	7·3	14
18	11·9	11·4	11·0	10·6	10·3	9·9	9·6	9·3	9·1	8·8	8·5	8·3	8·1	7·9	7·7	7·5	18
20	12·0	11·6	11·1	10·8	10·4	10·1	9·7	9·4	9·2	8·9	8·6	8·4	8·2	8·0	7·8	7·6	20
22	12·2	11·7	11·3	10·9	10·5	10·2	9·9	9·6	9·3	9·0	8·8	8·5	8·3	8·1	7·9	7·7	22
24	12·3	11·9	11·5	11·1	10·7	10·3	10·0	9·7	9·4	9·1	8·9	8·6	8·4	8·2	8·0	7·8	24
26	12·5	12·1	11·6	11·2	10·9	10·5	10·2	9·9	9·6	9·3	9·0	8·8	8·6	8·3	8·1	7·9	26
28	12·8	12·3	11·8	11·4	11·0	10·7	10·4	10·0	9·7	9·5	9·2	8·9	8·7	8·5	8·3	8·1	28
30	13·0	12·5	12·1	11·7	11·3	10·9	10·5	10·2	9·9	9·6	9·4	9·1	8·9	8·6	8·4	8·2	30
31	13·1	12·6	12·2	11·8	11·4	11·0	10·7	10·3	10·0	9·7	9·5	9·2	9·0	8·7	8·5	8·3	31
32	13·3	12·8	12·3	11·9	11·5	11·1	10·8	10·4	10·1	9·8	9·6	9·3	9·1	8·8	8·6	8·4	32
33	13·4	12·9	12·5	12·0	11·6	11·2	10·9	10·6	10·2	9·9	9·7	9·4	9·2	8·9	8·7	8·5	33
34	13·6	13·1	12·6	12·2	11·7	11·4	11·0	10·7	10·4	10·1	9·8	9·5	9·3	9·0	8·8	8·6	34
35	13·7	13·2	12·7	12·3	11·9	11·5	11·1	10·8	10·5	10·2	9·9	9·6	9·4	9·1	8·9	8·7	35
36	13·9	13·4	12·9	12·4	12·0	11·6	11·3	10·9	10·6	10·3	10·0	9·7	9·5	9·2	9·0	8·8	36
37	14·1	13·5	13·1	12·6	12·2	11·8	11·4	11·1	10·7	10·4	10·1	9·9	9·6	9·4	9·1	8·9	37
38	14·2	13·7	13·2	12·8	12·3	11·9	11·6	11·2	10·9	10·6	10·3	10·0	9·7	9·5	9·2	9·0	38
39	14·4	13·9	13·4	12·9	12·5	12·1	11·7	11·4	11·0	10·7	10·4	10·1	9·9	9·6	9·4	9·1	39
40	14·6	14·1	13·6	13·1	12·7	12·3	11·9	11·5	11·2	10·9	10·6	10·3	10·0	9·7	9·5	9·3	40
41	14·8	14·3	13·8	13·3	12·9	12·5	12·1	11·7	11·4	11·0	10·7	10·4	10·2	9·9	9·6	9·4	41
42	15·1	14·5	14·0	13·5	13·1	12·6	12·2	11·9	11·5	11·2	10·9	10·6	10·3	10·0	9·8	9·5	42
43	15·3	14·7	14·2	13·7	13·3	12·8	12·4	12·1	11·7	11·4	11·1	10·8	10·5	10·2	9·9	9·7	43
44	15·5	15·0	14·4	13·9	13·5	13·0	12·6	12·3	11·9	11·6	11·2	10·9	10·6	10·4	10·1	9·9	44
45	15·8	15·2	14·7	14·2	13·7	13·3	12·8	12·5	12·1	11·7	11·4	11·1	10·8	10·5	10·3	10·0	45
46	16·1	15·5	14·9	14·4	13·9	13·5	13·1	12·7	12·3	12·0	11·6	11·3	11·0	10·7	10·5	10·2	46
47	16·3	15·7	15·2	14·7	14·2	13·7	13·3	12·9	12·5	12·2	11·8	11·5	11·2	10·9	10·6	10·4	47
48	16·6	16·0	15·5	14·9	14·4	14·0	13·6	13·1	12·8	12·4	12·1	11·7	11·4	11·1	10·8	10·6	48
49	17·0	16·3	15·8	15·2	14·7	14·3	13·8	13·4	13·0	12·6	12·3	12·0	11·6	11·3	11·1	10·8	49
50	17·3	16·7	16·1	15·5	15·0	14·5	14·1	13·7	13·3	12·9	12·5	12·2	11·9	11·6	11·3	11·0	50
51	17·6	17·0	16·4	15·8	15·3	14·8	14·4	13·9	13·5	13·2	12·8	12·4	12·1	11·8	11·5	11·2	51
52	18·0	17·3	16·7	16·2	15·6	15·1	14·7	14·2	13·8	13·4	13·1	12·7	12·4	12·1	11·8	11·5	52
53	18·4	17·7	17·1	16·5	16·0	15·5	15·0	14·6	14·1	13·7	13·4	13·0	12·7	12·3	12·0	11·7	53
54	18·8	18·1	17·5	16·9	16·3	15·8	15·3	14·9	14·5	14·1	13·7	13·3	13·0	12·6	12·3	12·0	54
55	19·2	18·5	17·9	17·3	16·7	16·2	15·7	15·2	14·8	14·4	14·0	13·6	13·3	12·9	12·6	12·3	55
56	19·7	19·0	18·3	17·7	17·1	16·6	16·1	15·6	15·2	14·7	14·3	13·9	13·6	13·2	12·9	12·6	56
57	20·2	19·5	18·8	18·2	17·6	17·0	16·5	16·0	15·5	15·1	14·7	14·3	13·9	13·6	13·2	12·9	57
58	20·7	20·0	19·3	18·6	18·0	17·5	16·9	16·4	16·0	15·5	15·1	14·7	14·3	13·9	13·6	13·3	58
59	21·2	20·5	19·8	19·1	18·5	17·9	17·4	16·9	16·4	15·9	15·5	15·1	14·7	14·3	14·0	13·6	59
60	21·8	21·0	20·3	19·7	19·0	18·4	17·9	17·4	16·9	16·4	15·9	15·5	15·1	14·7	14·4	14·0	60
61	22·4	21·6	20·9	20·2	19·6	19·0	18·4	17·9	17·4	16·9	16·4	16·0	15·6	15·2	14·8	14·5	61
62	23·1	22·3	21·5	20·8	20·2	19·6	19·0	18·4	17·9	17·4	16·9	16·5	16·1	15·7	15·3	14·9	62
63	23·8	23·0	22·2	21·5	20·8	20·2	19·6	19·0	18·5	18·0	17·5	17·0	16·6	16·2	15·8	15·4	63
64	24·5	23·7	22·9	22·2	21·5	20·8	20·2	19·6	19·1	18·6	18·1	17·6	17·1	16·7	16·3	15·9	64
65	25·3	24·5	23·7	23·0	22·2	21·5	20·9	20·3	19·7	19·2	18·7	18·2	17·7	17·3	16·9	16·5	65
66	26·2	25·3	24·5	23·7	23·0	22·3	21·6	21·0	20·4	19·9	19·4	18·9	18·4	17·9	17·5	17·1	66
67	27·1	26·2	25·4	24·6	23·8	23·1	22·4	21·8	21·2	20·6	20·1	19·6	19·1	18·6	18·2	17·8	67
68	28·1	27·2	26·3	25·5	24·7	24·0	23·3	22·6	22·0	21·4	20·9	20·3	19·8	19·4	18·9	18·5	68

A±B=5·00' 5·20' | 5·40' 5·60' | 5·80' 6·00' | 6·20' 6·40' | 6·60' 6·80' | 7·00' 7·20' | 7·40' 7·60' | 7·80' 8·00'=A±B

A & B **S**ame Names } take **S**um, (add). } RULE TO FIND { A & B **D**ifferent names C CORRECTION { take **D**ifference (Sub.)

C CORRECTION, (A ± B) is named the same as the greater of these quantities.

AZIMUTH takes combined names of **C** Correction and Hour Angle

C

TABLE C

A & B CORRECTION.

AZIMUTHS

Lat.°	8·00′	8·20′	8·40′	8·60′	8·80′	9·00′	9·20′	9·40′	9·60′	9·80′	10·0′	10·3′	10·6′	11·0′	11·5′	12·0′	Lat.°
0	7·1	7·0	6·8	6·6	6·5	6·3	6·2	6·1	5·9	5·8	5·7	5·5	5·4	5·2	5·0	4·8	0
5	7·2	7·0	6·8	6·7	6·5	6·4	6·2	6·1	6·0	5·8	5·7	5·6	5·4	5·2	5·0	4·8	5
10	7·2	7·1	6·9	6·7	6·6	6·4	6·3	6·2	6·0	5·9	5·8	5·6	5·5	5·3	5·0	4·8	10
14	7·3	7·2	7·0	6·8	6·7	6·5	6·4	6·3	6·1	6·0	5·9	5·7	5·6	5·4	5·1	4·9	14
18	7·5	7·3	7·1	7·0	6·8	6·7	6·5	6·4	6·3	6·1	6·0	5·8	5·7	5·5	5·2	5·0	18
20	7·6	7·4	7·2	7·1	6·9	6·7	6·6	6·5	6·3	6·2	6·1	5·9	5·7	5·5	5·3	5·1	20
22	7·7	7·5	7·3	7·1	7·0	6·8	6·7	6·5	6·4	6·3	6·2	6·0	5·8	5·6	5·4	5·1	22
24	7·8	7·6	7·4	7·3	7·1	6·9	6·8	6·6	6·5	6·4	6·2	6·1	5·9	5·7	5·4	5·2	24
26	7·9	7·7	7·5	7·4	7·2	7·0	6·9	6·7	6·6	6·5	6·3	6·2	6·0	5·8	5·5	5·3	26
28	8·1	7·9	7·7	7·5	7·3	7·2	7·0	6·9	6·7	6·6	6·5	6·3	6·1	5·9	5·6	5·4	28
30	8·2	8·0	7·8	7·6	7·5	7·3	7·2	7·0	6·9	6·7	6·6	6·4	6·2	6·0	5·7	5·5	30
31	8·3	8·1	7·9	7·7	7·6	7·4	7·2	7·1	6·9	6·8	6·7	6·5	6·3	6·1	5·8	5·6	31
32	8·4	8·2	8·0	7·8	7·6	7·5	7·3	7·2	7·0	6·9	6·7	6·5	6·3	6·1	5·9	5·6	32
33	8·5	8·3	8·1	7·9	7·7	7·5	7·4	7·2	7·1	6·9	6·8	6·6	6·4	6·2	5·9	5·7	33
34	8·6	8·4	8·2	8·0	7·8	7·6	7·5	7·3	7·2	7·0	6·9	6·7	6·5	6·3	6·0	5·7	34
35	8·7	8·5	8·3	8·1	7·9	7·7	7·6	7·4	7·2	7·1	7·0	6·8	6·6	6·3	6·1	5·8	35
36	8·8	8·6	8·4	8·2	8·0	7·8	7·7	7·5	7·3	7·2	7·0	6·8	6·7	6·4	6·1	5·9	36
37	8·9	8·7	8·5	8·3	8·1	7·9	7·8	7·6	7·4	7·3	7·1	6·9	6·7	6·5	6·2	6·0	37
38	9·0	8·8	8·6	8·4	8·2	8·0	7·9	7·7	7·5	7·4	7·2	7·0	6·9	6·6	6·3	6·0	38
39	9·1	8·9	8·7	8·5	8·3	8·1	8·0	7·8	7·6	7·5	7·3	7·1	6·9	6·7	6·4	6·1	39
40	9·3	9·0	8·8	8·6	8·4	8·3	8·1	7·9	7·7	7·6	7·4	7·2	7·0	6·8	6·5	6·2	40
41	9·4	9·2	9·0	8·8	8·6	8·4	8·2	8·0	7·9	7·7	7·5	7·3	7·1	6·9	6·6	6·3	41
42	9·5	9·3	9·1	8·9	8·7	8·5	8·3	8·1	8·0	7·8	7·7	7·4	7·2	7·0	6·7	6·4	42
43	9·7	9·5	9·2	9·0	8·8	8·6	8·5	8·3	8·1	7·9	7·8	7·6	7·4	7·1	6·8	6·5	43
44	9·9	9·6	9·4	9·2	8·9	8·8	8·6	8·4	8·2	8·1	7·9	7·7	7·5	7·2	6·9	6·6	44
45	10·0	9·8	9·6	9·3	9·1	8·9	8·7	8·6	8·4	8·2	8·0	7·8	7·6	7·3	7·0	6·7	45
46	10·2	10·0	9·7	9·5	9·3	9·1	8·9	8·7	8·5	8·4	8·2	8·0	7·7	7·5	7·1	6·8	46
47	10·4	10·1	9·9	9·7	9·5	9·3	9·1	8·9	8·7	8·5	8·3	8·1	7·9	7·6	7·3	7·0	47
48	10·6	10·3	10·1	9·9	9·6	9·4	9·2	9·0	8·8	8·7	8·5	8·3	8·0	7·7	7·4	7·1	48
49	10·8	10·5	10·3	10·1	9·8	9·6	9·4	9·2	9·0	8·8	8·7	8·4	8·2	7·9	7·6	7·2	49
50	11·0	10·7	10·5	10·3	10·0	9·8	9·6	9·4	9·2	9·0	8·8	8·6	8·3	8·0	7·7	7·4	50
51	11·2	11·0	10·7	10·5	10·2	10·0	9·8	9·6	9·4	9·2	9·0	8·8	8·5	8·2	7·9	7·5	51
52	11·5	11·2	10·9	10·7	10·5	10·2	10·0	9·8	9·6	9·4	9·2	9·0	8·7	8·4	8·0	7·7	52
53	11·7	11·5	11·2	10·9	10·7	10·5	10·2	10·0	9·8	9·6	9·4	9·2	8·9	8·6	8·2	7·9	53
54	12·0	11·7	11·4	11·2	10·9	10·7	10·5	10·3	10·0	9·8	9·7	9·4	9·1	8·8	8·4	8·1	54
55	12·3	12·0	11·7	11·5	11·2	11·0	10·7	10·5	10·3	10·1	9·9	9·6	9·3	9·0	8·6	8·3	55
56	12·6	12·3	12·0	11·7	11·5	11·2	11·0	10·8	10·6	10·3	10·1	9·8	9·6	9·2	8·8	8·5	56
57	12·9	12·6	12·3	12·1	11·8	11·5	11·3	11·1	10·8	10·6	10·4	10·1	9·8	9·5	9·1	8·7	57
58	13·3	13·0	12·7	12·4	12·1	11·8	11·6	11·4	11·1	10·9	10·7	10·4	10·1	9·7	9·3	8·9	58
59	13·6	13·3	13·0	12·7	12·4	12·2	11·9	11·7	11·4	11·2	11·0	10·7	10·4	10·0	9·6	9·2	59
60	14·0	13·7	13·4	13·1	12·8	12·5	12·3	12·0	11·8	11·5	11·3	11·0	10·7	10·3	9·9	9·5	60
61	14·5	14·1	13·8	13·5	13·2	12·9	12·6	12·4	12·1	11·9	11·7	11·3	11·0	10·6	10·2	9·8	61
62	14·9	14·6	14·2	13·9	13·6	13·3	13·0	12·8	12·5	12·3	12·0	11·7	11·4	11·0	10·5	10·1	62
63	15·4	15·0	14·7	14·4	14·1	13·8	13·5	13·2	12·9	12·7	12·4	12·1	11·7	11·3	10·8	10·4	63
64	15·9	15·5	15·2	14·9	14·5	14·2	13·9	13·6	13·4	13·1	12·9	12·5	12·1	11·7	11·2	10·8	64
65	16·5	16·1	15·7	15·4	15·1	14·7	14·4	14·1	13·8	13·6	13·3	12·9	12·6	12·1	11·6	11·2	65
66	17·1	16·7	16·3	16·0	15·6	15·3	15·0	14·7	14·4	14·1	13·8	13·4	13·1	12·6	12·1	11·6	66
67	17·8	17·3	16·9	16·6	16·2	15·9	15·5	15·2	14·9	14·6	14·4	14·0	13·6	13·1	12·5	12·0	67
68	18·5	18·0	17·6	17·2	16·9	16·5	16·2	15·9	15·5	15·2	14·9	14·6	14·2	13·6	13·1	12·5	68

A±B = 8·00′ 8·20′ | 8·40′ 8·60′ | 8·80′ 9·00′ | 9·20′ 9·40′ | 9·60′ 9·80′ | 10·0′ 10·3′ | 10·6′ 11·0′ | 11·5′ 12·0′ = A±B

A & B **S**ame Names take **S**um, (add). } RULE TO FIND { A & B **D**ifferent names take **D**ifference (Sub.)
C CORRECTION

C CORRECTION, (A ± B) is named the same as the greater of these quantities.

AZIMUTH takes combined names of **C** Correction and Hour Angle

C

TABLE C

A & B CORRECTION.

Lat.°	12·0'	12·5'	13·0'	13·5'	14·0'	14·5'	15·0'	16·0'	17·0'	18·0'	19·0'	20·0'	21·0'	22·0'	23·0'	25·0'	Lat.°
							AZIMUTHS										
0	4·8	4·6	4·4	4·2	4·1	3·9	3·8	3·6	3·4	3·2	3·0	2·9	2·7	2·6	2·5	2·3	0
5	4·8	4·6	4·4	4·3	4·1	4·0	3·8	3·6	3·4	3·2	3·0	2·9	2·7	2·6	2·5	2·3	5
10	4·8	4·6	4·5	4·3	4·1	4·0	3·9	3·6	3·4	3·2	3·1	2·9	2·8	2·6	2·5	2·3	10
14	4·9	4·7	4·5	4·4	4·2	4·1	3·9	3·7	3·5	3·3	3·1	2·9	2·8	2·7	2·6	2·4	14
18	5·0	4·8	4·6	4·4	4·3	4·1	4·0	3·8	3·5	3·3	3·2	3·0	2·9	2·7	2·6	2·4	18
20	5·1	4·9	4·7	4·5	4·3	4·2	4·1	3·8	3·6	3·4	3·2	3·0	2·9	2·8	2·6	2·4	20
22	5·1	4·9	4·7	4·6	4·4	4·3	4·1	3·9	3·6	3·4	3·3	3·1	2·9	2·8	2·7	2·5	22
24	5·2	5·0	4·8	4·6	4·5	4·3	4·2	3·9	3·7	3·5	3·3	3·1	3·0	2·8	2·7	2·5	24
26	5·3	5·1	4·9	4·7	4·5	4·4	4·2	4·0	3·7	3·5	3·4	3·2	3·0	2·9	2·8	2·5	26
28	5·4	5·2	5·0	4·8	4·6	4·5	4·3	4·0	3·8	3·6	3·4	3·2	3·1	2·9	2·8	2·6	28
30	5·5	5·3	5·1	4·9	4·7	4·6	4·4	4·1	3·9	3·7	3·5	3·3	3·1	3·0	2·9	2·6	30
31	5·6	5·3	5·1	4·9	4·8	4·6	4·4	4·2	3·9	3·7	3·5	3·3	3·2	3·0	2·9	2·7	31
32	5·6	5·4	5·2	5·0	4·8	4·6	4·5	4·2	4·0	3·7	3·6	3·4	3·2	3·1	2·9	2·7	32
33	5·7	5·4	5·2	5·0	4·9	4·7	4·5	4·3	4·0	3·8	3·6	3·4	3·2	3·1	3·0	2·7	33
34	5·7	5·5	5·3	5·1	4·9	4·8	4·6	4·3	4·1	3·8	3·6	3·5	3·3	3·1	3·0	2·8	34
35	5·8	5·6	5·4	5·2	5·0	4·8	4·7	4·4	4·1	3·9	3·7	3·5	3·3	3·2	3·0	2·8	35
36	5·9	5·7	5·4	5·2	5·0	4·9	4·7	4·4	4·2	3·9	3·7	3·5	3·4	3·2	3·1	2·8	36
37	6·0	5·7	5·5	5·3	5·1	4·9	4·8	4·5	4·2	4·0	3·8	3·6	3·4	3·3	3·1	2·9	37
38	6·0	5·8	5·6	5·4	5·2	5·0	4·8	4·5	4·3	4·0	3·8	3·6	3·5	3·3	3·2	2·9	38
39	6·1	5·9	5·7	5·5	5·3	5·1	4·9	4·6	4·3	4·1	3·9	3·7	3·5	3·3	3·2	2·9	39
40	6·2	6·0	5·7	5·5	5·3	5·2	5·0	4·7	4·4	4·1	3·9	3·7	3·6	3·4	3·2	3·0	40
41	6·3	6·1	5·8	5·6	5·4	5·2	5·0	4·7	4·5	4·2	4·0	3·8	3·6	3·4	3·3	3·0	41
42	6·4	6·1	5·9	5·7	5·5	5·3	5·1	4·8	4·5	4·3	4·1	3·8	3·7	3·5	3·3	3·1	42
43	6·5	6·2	6·0	5·8	5·6	5·4	5·2	4·9	4·6	4·3	4·1	3·9	3·7	3·6	3·4	3·1	43
44	6·6	6·3	6·1	5·9	5·7	5·5	5·3	5·0	4·7	4·4	4·2	4·0	3·8	3·6	3·5	3·2	44
45	6·7	6·5	6·2	6·0	5·8	5·6	5·4	5·1	4·8	4·5	4·3	4·0	3·9	3·7	3·5	3·2	45
46	6·8	6·6	6·3	6·1	5·9	5·7	5·5	5·1	4·8	4·6	4·3	4·1	3·9	3·7	3·6	3·3	46
47	7·0	6·7	6·4	6·2	6·0	5·8	5·6	5·2	4·9	4·7	4·4	4·2	4·0	3·8	3·6	3·4	47
48	7·1	6·8	6·6	6·3	6·1	5·9	5·7	5·3	5·0	4·7	4·5	4·3	4·1	3·9	3·7	3·4	48
49	7·2	7·0	6·7	6·4	6·2	6·0	5·8	5·4	5·1	4·8	4·6	4·4	4·2	4·0	3·8	3·5	49
50	7·4	7·1	6·8	6·6	6·3	6·1	5·9	5·6	5·2	4·9	4·7	4·4	4·2	4·0	3·9	3·6	50
51	7·5	7·2	7·0	6·7	6·5	6·2	6·0	5·7	5·3	5·0	4·8	4·5	4·3	4·1	4·0	3·6	51
52	7·7	7·4	7·1	6·9	6·6	6·4	6·2	5·8	5·5	5·2	4·9	4·6	4·4	4·2	4·0	3·7	52
53	7·9	7·6	7·3	7·0	6·8	6·5	6·3	5·9	5·6	5·3	5·0	4·7	4·5	4·3	4·1	3·8	53
54	8·1	7·8	7·5	7·2	6·9	6·7	6·5	6·1	5·7	5·4	5·1	4·9	4·6	4·4	4·2	3·9.	54
55	8·3	7·9	7·6	7·4	7·1	6·9	6·6	6·2	5·9	5·5	5·2	5·0	4·7	4·5	4·3	4·0	55
56	8·5	8·1	7·8	7·5	7·3	7·0	6·8	6·4	6·0	5·7	5·4	5·1	4·9	4·6	4·4	4·1	56
57	8·7	8·4	8·0	7·7	7·5	7·2	7·0	6·5	6·2	5·8	5·5	5·2	5·0	4·8	4·6	4·2	57
58	8·9	8·6	8·3	8·0	7·7	7·4	7·2	6·7	6·3	6·0	5·7	5·4	5·1	4·9	4·7	4·3	58
59	9·2	8·8	8·5	8·2	7·9	7·6	7·4	6·9	6·5	6·2	5·8	5·5	5·3	5·0	4·8	4·4	59
60	9·5	9·1	8·7	8·4	8·1	7·9	7·6	7·1	6·7	6·3	6·0	5·7	5·4	5·2	5·0	4·6	60
61	9·8	9·4	9·0	8·7	8·4	8·1	7·8	7·3	6·9	6·5	6·2	5·9	5·6	5·4	5·1	4·7	61
62	10·1	9·7	9·3	9·0	8·7	8·4	8·1	7·6	7·1	6·7	6·4	6·1	5·8	5·5	5·3	4·9	62
63	10·4	10·0	9·6	9·3	8·9	8·6	8·4	7·8	7·4	7·0	6·6	6·3	6·0	5·7	5·5	5·0	63
64	10·8	10·3	10·0	9·6	9·3	8·9	8·6	8·1	7·6	7·2	6·8	6·5	6·2	5·9	5·7	5·2	64
65	11·2	10·7	10·3	9·9	9·6	9·3	9·0	8·4	7·9	7·5	7·1	6·7	6·4	6·1	5·9	5·4	65
66	11·6	11·1	10·7	10·3	10·0	9·6	9·3	8·7	8·2	7·8	7·4	7·0	6·7	6·4	6·1	5·6	66
67	12·0	11·6	11·1	10·7	10·4	10·0	9·7	9·1	8·6	8·1	7·7	7·3	6·9	6·6	6·3	5·8	67
68	12·5	12·1	11·6	11·2	10·8	10·4	10·1	9·5	8·9	8·4	8·0	7·6	7·2	6·9	6·6	6·1	68

| A±B= | 12·0' | 12·5' | 13·0' | 13·5' | 14·0' | 14·5' | 15·0' | 16·0' | 17·0' | 18·0' | 19·0' | 20·0' | 21·0' | 22·0' | 23·0' | 25·0' | =A±B |

A & B **S**ame Names } RULE TO FIND { A & B **D**ifferent names
take **S**um, (add). } **C** CORRECTION { take **D**ifference (Sub.)
C CORRECTION, (A ± B) is named the same as the greater of these quantities.
AZIMUTH takes combined names of **C** Correction and Hour Angle

C

TABLE C

A±B=	25.0′	27.0′	30.0′	33.0′	36.0′	40.0′	45.0′	50.0′	60.0	70.0′	80.0′	100′	150′	200′	400′	800′=A±B	Lat.°
Lat.°	°	°	°	°	°	°	°	°	°	°	°	°	°	°	°	°	
0	2.3	2.1	1.9	1.7	1.6	1.4	1.3	1.1	1.0	0.8	0.7	0.6	0.4	0.3	0.1	0.1	0
5	2.3	2.1	1.9	1.7	1.6	1.4	1.3	1.2	1.0	0.8	0.7	0.6	0.4	0.3	0.1	0.1	5
10	2.3	2.2	1.9	1.8	1.6	1.5	1.3	1.2	1.0	0.8	0.7	0.6	0.4	0.3	0.1	0.1	10
14	2.4	2.2	2.0	1.8	1.6	1.5	1.3	1.2	1.0	0.8	0.7	0.6	0.4	0.3	0.1	0.1	14
18	2.4	2.2	2.0	1.8	1.7	1.5	1.3	1.2	1.0	0.9	0.8	0.6	0.4	0.3	0.2	0.1	18
20	2.4	2.2	2.0	1.8	1.7	1.5	1.4	1.2	1.0	0.9	0.8	0.6	0.4	0.3	0.2	0.1	20
22	2.5	2.3	2.1	1.9	1.7	1.5	1.4	1.2	1.0	0.9	0.8	0.6	0.4	0.3	0.2	0.1	22
24	2.5	2.3	2.1	1.9	1.7	1.6	1.4	1.3	1.0	0.9	0.8	0.6	0.4	0.3	0.2	0.1	24
26	2.5	2.4	2.1	1.9	1.8	1.6	1.4	1.3	1.1	0.9	0.8	0.6	0.4	0.3	0.2	0.1	26
28	2.6	2.4	2.2	2.0	1.8	1.6	1.4	1.3	1.1	0.9	0.8	0.6	0.4	0.3	0.2	0.1	28
30	2.6	2.4	2.2	2.0	1.8	1.7	1.5	1.3	1.1	0.9	0.8	0.7	0.4	0.3	0.2	0.1	30
31	2.7	2.5	2.2	2.0	1.9	1.7	1.5	1.3	1.1	1.0	0.8	0.7	0.4	0.3	0.2	0.1	31
32	2.7	2.5	2.3	2.0	1.9	1.7	1.5	1.4	1.1	1.0	0.8	0.7	0.5	0.3	0.2	0.1	32
33	2.7	2.5	2.3	2.1	1.9	1.7	1.5	1.4	1.1	1.0	0.9	0.7	0.5	0.3	0.2	0.1	33
34	2.8	2.6	2.3	2.1	1.9	1.7	1.5	1.4	1.2	1.0	0.9	0.7	0.5	0.3	0.2	0.1	34
35	2.8	2.6	2.3	2.1	2.0	1.7	1.6	1.4	1.2	1.0	0.9	0.7	0.5	0.3	0.2	0.1	35
36	2.8	2.6	2.4	2.1	2.0	1.8	1.6	1.4	1.2	1.0	0.9	0.7	0.5	0.4	0.2	0.1	36
37	2.9	2.7	2.4	2.2	2.0	1.8	1.6	1.4	1.2	1.0	0.9	0.7	0.5	0.4	0.2	0.1	37
38	2.9	2.7	2.4	2.2	2.0	1.8	1.6	1.5	1.2	1.0	0.9	0.7	0.5	0.4	0.2	0.1	38
39	2.9	2.7	2.5	2.2	2.0	1.8	1.6	1.5	1.2	1.0	0.9	0.7	0.5	0.4	0.2	0.1	39
40	3.0	2.8	2.5	2.3	2.1	1.9	1.7	1.5	1.2	1.1	0.9	0.7	0.5	0.4	0.2	0.1	40
41	3.0	2.8	2.5	2.3	2.1	1.9	1.7	1.5	1.3	1.1	1.0	0.8	0.5	0.4	0.2	0.1	41
42	3.1	2.9	2.6	2.3	2.1	1.9	1.7	1.5	1.3	1.1	1.0	0.8	0.5	0.4	0.2	0.1	42
43	3.1	2.9	2.6	2.4	2.2	2.0	1.7	1.6	1.3	1.1	1.0	0.8	0.5	0.4	0.2	0.1	43
44	3.2	2.9	2.7	2.4	2.2	2.0	1.8	1.6	1.3	1.1	1.0	0.8	0.5	0.4	0.2	0.1	44
45	3.2	3.0	2.7	2.5	2.2	2.0	1.8	1.6	1.4	1.2	1.0	0.8	0.5	0.4	0.2	0.1	45
46	3.3	3.1	2.7	2.5	2.3	2.1	1.8	1.6	1.4	1.2	1.0	0.8	0.5	0.4	0.2	0.1	46
47	3.4	3.1	2.8	2.5	2.3	2.1	1.9	1.7	1.4	1.2	1.1	0.8	0.6	0.4	0.2	0.1	47
48	3.4	3.2	2.9	2.6	2.4	2.1	1.9	1.7	1.4	1.2	1.1	0.9	0.6	0.4	0.2	0.1	48
49	3.5	3.2	2.9	2.6	2.4	2.2	1.9	1.7	1.5	1.2	1.1	0.9	0.6	0.4	0.2	0.1	49
50	3.6	3.3	3.0	2.7	2.5	2.2	2.0	1.8	1.5	1.3	1.1	0.9	0.6	0.4	0.2	0.1	50
51	3.6	3.4	3.0	2.8	2.5	2.3	2.0	1.8	1.5	1.3	1.2	0.9	0.6	0.5	0.2	0.1	51
52	3.7	3.4	3.1	2.8	2.6	2.3	2.1	1.9	1.6	1.3	1.2	0.9	0.6	0.5	0.2	0.1	52
53	3.8	3.5	3.2	2.9	2.6	2.4	2.1	1.9	1.6	1.4	1.2	1.0	0.6	0.5	0.2	0.1	53
54	3.9	3.6	3.2	3.0	2.7	2.4	2.2	1.9	1.6	1.4	1.2	1.0	0.6	0.5	0.2	0.1	54
55	4.0	3.7	3.3	3.0	2.8	2.5	2.2	2.0	1.7	1.4	1.2	1.0	0.7	0.5	0.2	0.1	55
56	4.1	3.8	3.4	3.1	2.8	2.6	2.3	2.0	1.7	1.5	1.3	1.0	0.7	0.5	0.3	0.1	56
57	4.2	3.9	3.5	3.2	2.9	2.6	2.3	2.1	1.8	1.5	1.3	1.1	0.7	0.5	0.3	0.1	57
58	4.3	4.0	3.6	3.3	3.0	2.7	2.4	2.2	1.8	1.5	1.4	1.1	0.7	0.5	0.3	0.1	58
59	4.4	4.1	3.7	3.4	3.1	2.8	2.5	2.2	1.9	1.6	1.4	1.1	0.7	0.6	0.3	0.1	59
60	4.6	4.2	3.8	3.5	3.2	2.9	2.5	2.3	1.9	1.6	1.4	1.1	0.8	0.6	0.3	0.1	60
61	4.7	4.4	3.9	3.6	3.3	3.0	2.6	2.4	2.0	1.7	1.5	1.2	0.8	0.6	0.3	0.1	61
62	4.9	4.5	4.1	3.7	3.4	3.0	2.7	2.4	2.0	1.7	1.5	1.2	0.8	0.6	0.3	0.2	62
63	5.0	4.7	4.2	3.8	3.5	3.2	2.8	2.5	2.1	1.8	1.6	1.3	0.8	0.6	0.3	0.2	63
64	5.2	4.8	4.3	4.0	3.6	3.3	2.9	2.6	2.2	1.9	1.6	1.3	0.9	0.7	0.3	0.2	64
65	5.4	5.0	4.5	4.1	3.8	3.4	3.0	2.7	2.3	1.9	1.7	1.4	0.9	0.7	0.3	0.2	65
66	5.6	5.2	4.7	4.3	3.9	3.5	3.1	2.8	2.3	2.0	1.8	1.4	0.9	0.7	0.4	0.2	66
67	5.8	5.4	4.9	4.4	4.1	3.7	3.3	2.9	2.4	2.1	1.8	1.5	1.0	0.7	0.4	0.2	67
68	6.1	5.6	5.1	4.6	4.2	3.8	3.4	3.1	2.5	2.2	1.9	1.5	1.0	0.8	0.4	0.2	68

A & B CORRECTION. — **AZIMUTHS**

| A±B= | 25.0′ | 27.0 | 30.0′ | 33.0′ | 36.0′ | 40.0′ | 45.0′ | 50.0′ | 60.0′ | 70.0′ | 80.0′ | 100′ | 150′ | 200′ | 400′ | 800′=A±B |

A & B **S**ame Names take **S**um, (add). } RULE TO FIND { A & B take **D**ifferent names **C** CORRECTION difference (Sub.)

C CORRECTION, (A±B) is named the same as the greater of these quantities.

AZIMUTH takes combined names of **C** Correction and Hour Angle

C

TABLE C

A & B CORRECTION

AZIMUTHS

A±B =	·00′	·01′	·02′	·03′	·04′	·05′	·06′	·07′	·08′	·09′	·10′	·11′	·12′	·13′	·14′	·15′ = A±B
Lat.°	°	°	°	°	°	°	°	°	°	°	°	°	°	°	°	**Lat.°**
68	90·0	89·8	89·6	89·4	89·1	88·9	88·7	88·5	88·3	88·1	87·9	87·6	87·4	87·2	87·0	86·8	68
69	90·0	89·8	89·6	89·4	89·2	89·0	88·8	88·6	88·4	88·2	88·0	87·7	87·5	87·3	87·1	86·9	69
70	90·0	89·8	89·6	89·4	89·2	89·0	88·8	88·6	88·4	88·2	88·0	87·8	87·7	87·5	87·3	87·1	70
71	90·0	89·8	89·6	89·4	89·3	89·1	88·9	88·7	88·5	88·3	88·1	87·9	87·8	87·6	87·4	87·2	71
72	90·0	89·8	89·6	89·5	89·3	89·1	88·9	88·8	88·6	88·4	88·2	88·1	87·9	87·7	87·5	87·3	72
73	90·0	89·8	89·7	89·5	89·3	89·2	89·0	88·8	88·7	88·5	88·3	88·2	88·0	87·8	87·7	87·5	73
74	90·0	89·8	89·7	89·5	89·4	89·2	89·0	88·9	88·7	88·6	88·4	88·3	88·1	87·9	87·8	87·6	74
75	90·0	89·9	89·7	89·6	89·4	89·3	89·1	89·0	88·8	88·7	88·5	88·4	88·2	88·1	87·9	87·8	75
76	90·0	89·9	89·7	89·6	89·4	89·3	89·2	89·0	88·9	88·8	88·6	88·5	88·3	88·2	88·1	87·9	76
77	90·0	89·9	89·7	89·6	89·5	89·4	89·2	89·1	89·0	88·8	88·7	88·6	88·5	88·3	88·2	88·1	77
78	90·0	89·9	89·8	89·6	89·5	89·4	89·3	89·2	89·0	88·9	88·8	88·6	88·5	88·4	88·3	88·2	78
79	90·0	89·9	89·8	89·7	89·6	89·5	89·4	89·2	89·1	89·0	88·9	88·8	88·7	88·6	88·5	88·4	79
80	90·0	89·9	89·8	89·7	89·6	89·5	89·4	89·3	89·2	89·1	89·0	88·9	88·8	88·7	88·6	88·5	80

TABLE C

A & B CORRECTION

AZIMUTHS

A±B =	·15′	·16′	·17′	·18′	·19′	·20′	·21′	·22′	·23′	·24′	·25′	·26′	·27′	·28′	·29′	·30′ = A±B
Lat.°	°	°	°	°	°	°	°	°	°	°	°	°	°	°	°	**Lat.°**
68	86·8	86·6	86·4	86·1	85·9	85·7	85·5	85·3	85·1	84·9	84·6	84·4	84·2	84·0	83·8	83·6	68
69	86·9	86·7	86·5	86·3	86·1	85·9	85·7	85·5	85·3	85·1	84·9	84·7	84·5	84·3	84·1	83·9	69
70	87·1	86·9	86·7	86·5	86·3	86·1	85·9	85·7	85·5	85·3	85·1	84·9	84·7	84·5	84·3	84·1	70
71	87·2	87·0	86·8	86·6	86·5	86·3	86·1	85·9	85·7	85·5	85·3	85·2	85·0	84·8	84·6	84·4	71
72	87·3	87·2	87·0	86·8	86·6	86·5	86·3	86·1	85·9	85·8	85·6	85·4	85·2	85·1	84·9	84·7	72
73	87·5	87·3	87·2	87·0	86·8	86·7	86·5	86·3	86·2	86·0	85·8	85·6	85·5	85·3	85·2	85·0	73
74	87·6	87·5	87·3	87·2	87·0	86·8	86·7	86·5	86·4	86·2	86·1	85·9	85·7	85·6	85·4	85·3	74
75	87·8	87·6	87·5	87·3	87·2	87·0	86·9	86·7	86·6	86·4	86·3	86·2	86·0	85·9	85·7	85·6	75
76	87·9	87·8	87·6	87·5	87·4	87·2	87·1	87·0	86·8	86·7	86·5	86·4	86·3	86·1	86·0	85·9	76
77	88·1	87·9	87·8	87·7	87·6	87·4	87·3	87·2	87·0	86·9	86·8	86·7	86·5	86·4	86·3	86·1	77
78	88·2	88·1	88·0	87·9	87·7	87·6	87·5	87·4	87·3	87·1	87·0	86·9	86·8	86·7	86·6	86·4	78
79	88·4	88·3	88·1	88·0	87·9	87·8	87·7	87·6	87·5	87·4	87·3	87·2	87·1	86·9	86·8	86·7	79
80	88·5	88·4	88·3	88·2	88·1	88·0	87·9	87·8	87·7	87·6	87·5	87·4	87·3	87·2	87·1	87·0	80

TABLE C

A & B CORRECTION

AZIMUTHS

A±B =	·30′	·31′	·32′	·33′	·34′	·35′	·36′	·37′	·38′	·39′	·40′	·41′	·42′	·43′	·44′	·45′ = A±B
Lat.°	°	°	°	°	°	°	°	°	°	°	°	°	°	°	°	**Lat.°**
68	83·6	83·4	83·2	83·0	82·7	82·5	82·3	82·1	81·9	81·7	81·5	81·3	81·1	80·8	80·6	80·4	68
69	83·9	83·7	83·5	83·3	83·1	82·9	82·7	82·5	82·3	82·0	81·8	81·6	81·4	81·2	81·0	80·8	69
70	84·1	83·9	83·7	83·6	83·4	83·2	83·0	82·8	82·6	82·4	82·2	82·0	81·8	81·6	81·4	81·3	70
71	84·4	84·2	84·0	83·9	83·7	83·5	83·3	83·1	83·0	82·8	82·6	82·4	82·2	82·0	81·9	81·7	71
72	84·7	84·5	84·4	84·2	84·0	83·8	83·7	83·5	83·3	83·1	83·0	82·8	82·6	82·4	82·3	82·1	72
73	85·0	84·8	84·7	84·5	84·3	84·2	84·0	83·8	83·7	83·5	83·3	83·2	83·0	82·8	82·7	82·5	73
74	85·3	85·1	85·0	84·8	84·6	84·5	84·3	84·2	84·0	83·9	83·7	83·6	83·4	83·2	83·1	82·9	74
75	85·6	85·4	85·3	85·1	85·0	84·8	84·7	84·5	84·4	84·2	84·1	83·9	83·8	83·7	83·5	83·4	75
76	85·9	85·7	85·6	85·4	85·3	85·2	85·0	84·9	84·8	84·6	84·5	84·3	84·2	84·1	83·9	83·8	76
77	86·1	86·0	85·9	85·8	85·6	85·5	85·4	85·2	85·1	85·0	84·9	84·7	84·6	84·5	84·4	84·2	77
78	86·4	85·3	86·2	86·1	86·0	85·8	85·7	85·6	85·5	85·4	85·3	85·1	85·0	84·9	84·8	84·7	78
79	86·7	86·6	86·5	86·4	86·3	86·2	86·1	86·0	85·9	85·7	85·6	85·5	85·4	85·3	85·2	85·1	79
80	87·0	86·9	86·8	86·7	86·6	86·5	86·4	86·3	86·2	86·1	86·0	85·9	85·8	85·7	85·6	85·5	80

C

TABLE C

A±B=	·45′	·46′	·47′	·48′	·49′	·50′	·51′	·52′	·53′	·54′	·55′	·56′	·57′	·58′	·59′	·60′=A±B
Lat. °							AZIMUTHS									Lat. °
68	80·4	80·2	80·0	79·8	79·6	79·4	79·2	79·0	78·8	78·6	78·4	78·2	77·9	77·7	77·5	77·3 68
69	80·8	80·6	80·4	80·2	80·0	79·8	79·6	79·5	79·3	79·1	78·9	78·7	78·5	78·3	78·1	77·9 69
70	81·3	81·1	80·9	80·7	80·5	80·3	80·1	79·9	79·7	79·5	79·4	79·2	79·0	78·8	78·6	78·4 70
71	81·7	81·5	81·3	81·1	80·9	80·8	80·6	80·4	80·2	80·0	79·9	79·7	79·5	79·3	79·1	79·0 71
72	82·1	81·9	81·7	81·6	81·4	81·2	81·0	80·9	80·7	80·5	80·4	80·2	80·0	79·8	79·7	79·5 72
73	82·5	82·3	82·2	82·0	81·9	81·7	81·5	81·4	81·2	81·0	80·9	80·7	80·5	80·4	80·2	80·1 73
74	82·9	82·8	82·6	82·5	82·3	82·2	82·0	81·9	81·7	81·5	81·4	81·2	81·1	80·9	80·8	80·6 74
75	83·4	83·2	83·1	83·0	82·8	82·6	82·5	82·3	82·2	82·1	81·9	81·8	81·6	81·5	81·3	81·2 75
76	83·8	83·7	83·5	83·4	83·2	83·1	83·0	82·8	82·7	82·6	82·4	82·3	82·2	82·0	81·9	81·8 76
77	84·2	84·1	84·0	83·8	83·7	83·6	83·5	83·3	83·2	83·1	83·0	82·8	82·7	82·6	82·4	82·3 77
78	84·7	84·5	84·4	84·3	84·2	84·1	84·0	83·8	83·7	83·6	83·5	83·4	83·2	83·1	83·0	82·9 78
79	85·1	85·0	84·9	84·8	84·7	84·6	84·5	84·4	84·2	84·1	84·0	83·9	83·8	83·7	83·6	83·5 79
80	85·5	85·4	85·3	85·2	85·1	85·0	84·9	84·8	84·7	84·6	84·5	84·5	84·4	84·3	84·2	84·1 80

A & B CORRECTION

TABLE C

A±B=	·60′	·62′	·64′	·66′	·68′	·70′	·72′	·74′	·76′	·78′	·80′	8 2′	·84′	·86′	·88′	·90′=A±B
Lat. °							AZIMUTHS									Lat. °
68	77·3	76·9	76·5	76·1	75·7	75·3	74·9	74·5	74·1	73·7	73·3	72·9	72·5	72·1	71·8	71·4 68
69	77·9	77·5	77·1	76·7	76·3	75·9	75·5	75·2	74·8	74·4	74·0	73·6	73·3	72·9	72·5	72·1 69
70	78·4	78·0	77·7	77·3	76·9	76·5	76·2	75·8	75·4	75·1	74·7	74·3	74·0	73·6	73·3	72·9 70
71	79·0	78·6	78·2	77·9	77·5	77·2	76·8	76·5	76·1	75·8	75·4	75·1	74·7	74·4	74·0	73·7 71
72	79·5	79·2	78·8	78·5	78·1	77·8	77·5	77·1	76·8	76·5	76·1	75·8	75·5	75·1	74·8	74·5 72
73	80·1	79·7	79·4	79·1	78·8	78·4	78·1	77·8	77·5	77·2	76·8	76·5	76·2	75·9	75·6	75·3 73
74	80·6	80·3	80·0	79·7	79·4	79·1	78·8	78·5	78·2	77·9	77·6	77·3	77·0	76·7	76·4	76·1 74
75	81·2	80·9	80·6	80·3	80·0	79·7	79·4	79·2	78·9	78·6	78·3	78·0	77·7	77·5	77·2	76·9 75
76	81·8	81·5	81·2	80·9	80·7	80·4	80·1	79·9	79·6	79·3	79·0	78·8	78·5	78·3	78·0	77·7 76
77	82·3	82·1	81·8	81·6	81·3	81·1	80·8	80·6	80·3	80·1	79·8	79·6	79·3	79·1	78·8	78·5 77
78	82·9	82·7	82·4	82·2	82·0	81·7	81·5	81·3	81·0	80·8	80·6	80·3	80·1	79·9	79·6	79·4 78
79	83·5	83·3	83·0	82·8	82·6	82·4	82·2	82·0	81·8	81·5	81·3	81·1	80·9	80·7	80·5	80·3 79
80	84·1	83·9	83·7	83·5	83·3	83·1	82·9	82·7	82·5	82·3	82·1	81·9	81·7	81·5	81·3	81·1 80

A & B CORRECTION

TABLE C

A±B=	·90′	·92′	·94′	·96′	·98′	1·00′	1·02′	1·04′	1·06′	1·08′	1·10′	1·12′	1·14′	1·16′	1·18′	1·20′=A±B
Lat. °							AZIMUTHS									Lat. °
68	71·4	71·0	70·6	70·2	69·8	69·5	69·1	68·7	68·3	68·0	67·6	67·2	66·9	66·5	66·2	65·8 68
69	72·1	71·8	71·4	71·0	70·6	70·3	69·9	69·5	69·2	68·9	68·5	68·1	67·8	67·4	67·1	66·7 69
70	72·9	72·5	72·2	71·8	71·5	71·1	70·8	70·4	70·1	69·7	69·4	69·0	68·7	68·4	68·0	67·7 70
71	73·7	73·3	73·0	72·6	72·3	72·0	71·6	71·3	71·0	70·6	70·3	70·0	69·6	69·3	69·0	68·7 71
72	74·5	74·1	73·8	73·5	73·2	72·8	72·5	72·2	71·9	71·5	71·2	70·9	70·6	70·3	70·0	69·7 72
73	75·3	74·9	74·6	74·3	74·0	73·7	73·4	73·1	72·8	72·5	72·2	71·9	71·6	71·3	71·0	70·7 73
74	76·1	75·8	75·5	75·2	74·9	74·6	74·3	74·0	73·7	73·4	73·1	72·8	72·6	72·3	72·0	71·7 74
75	76·9	76·6	76·3	76·0	75·8	75·5	75·2	74·9	74·7	74·4	74·1	73·8	73·6	73·3	73·0	72·7 75
76	77·7	77·5	77·2	76·9	76·7	76·4	76·1	75·9	75·6	75·4	75·1	74·8	74·6	74·3	74·1	73·8 76
77	78·5	78·3	78·1	77·8	77·6	77·3	77·1	76·8	76·6	76·4	76·1	75·9	75·6	75·4	75·1	74·9 77
78	79·4	79·2	78·9	78·7	78·5	78·3	78·0	77·8	77·6	77·4	77·1	76·9	76·7	76·4	76·2	76·0 78
79	80·3	80·0	79·8	79·6	79·4	79·2	79·0	78·8	78·6	78·4	78·1	77·9	77·7	77·5	77·3	77·1 79
80	81·1	80·9	80·7	80·5	80·3	80·1	80·0	79·8	79·6	79·4	79·2	79·0	78·8	78·6	78·4	78·2 80

A & B CORRECTION

C

TABLE C

A±B=	1·20'	1·24'	1·28'	1·32'	1·36'	1·40'	1·44'	1·48'	1·52'	1·56'	1·60'	1·64'	1·68'	1·72'	1·76'	1·80'	=A±B
							A & B CORRECTION										
Lat.°							**AZIMUTHS**										Lat.°
68	65·8	65·1	64·4	63·7	63·0	62·3	61·7	61·0	60·3	59·7	59·1	58·4	57·8	57·2	56·6	56·0	68
69	66·7	66·0	65·4	64·7	64·0	63·4	62·7	62·1	61·4	60·8	60·2	59·6	59·0	58·4	57·8	57·2	69
70	67·7	67·0	66·4	65·7	65·0	64·4	63·8	63·2	62·5	61·9	61·3	60·7	60·1	59·5	58·9	58·4	70
71	68·7	68·0	67·4	66·7	66·1	65·5	64·9	64·3	63·7	63·1	62·5	61·9	61·3	60·7	60·2	59·6	71
72	69·7	69·0	68·4	67·8	67·2	66·6	66·0	65·4	64·9	64·3	63·7	63·1	62·6	62·0	61·4	60·9	72
73	70·7	70·1	69·5	68·9	68·3	67·7	67·2	66·6	66·0	65·5	64·9	64·4	63·8	63·3	62·8	62·2	73
74	71·7	71·1	70·6	70·0	69·5	68·9	68·4	67·8	67·2	66·7	66·2	65·7	65·2	64·6	64·1	63·6	74
75	72·7	72·2	71·7	71·1	70·6	70·1	69·6	69·0	68·5	68·0	67·5	67·0	66·5	66·0	65·5	65·0	75
76	73·8	73·3	72·8	72·3	71·8	71·3	70·8	70·3	69·8	69·3	68·8	68·4	67·9	67·4	66·9	66·5	76
77	74·9	74·4	73·9	73·5	73·0	72·5	72·0	71·6	71·1	70·7	70·2	69·8	69·3	68·8	68·4	68·0	77
78	76·0	75·5	75·1	74·7	74·2	73·8	73·3	72·9	72·5	72·0	71·6	71·2	70·7	70·3	69·9	69·5	78
79	77·1	76·7	76·3	75·9	75·5	75·1	74·6	74·2	73·8	73·4	73·0	72·6	72·2	71·8	71·4	71·0	79
80	78·2	77·9	77·5	77·1	76·7	76·4	75·9	75·6	75·2	74·8	74·5	74·1	73·7	73·4	73·0	72·6	80

TABLE C

A±B=	1·80'	1·84'	1·88'	1·92'	1·96'	2·00'	2·04'	2·08'	2·12'	2·16'	2·20'	2·24'	2·28'	2·32'	2·36'	2·40'	=A±B
							A & B CORRECTION										
Lat.°							**AZIMUTHS**										Lat.°
68	56·0	55·4	54·8	54·3	53·7	53·2	52·6	52·1	51·5	51·0	50·5	50·0	49·5	49·0	48·5	48·0	68
69	57·2	56·6	56·0	55·5	54·9	54·4	53·8	53·3	52·8	52·2	51·8	51·3	50·8	50·3	49·8	49·3	69
70	58·4	57·8	57·2	56·7	56·2	55·6	55·1	54·6	54·0	53·5	53·0	52·5	52·1	51·6	51·1	50·5	70
71	59·6	59·1	58·5	58·0	57·5	56·9	56·4	55·9	55·4	54·9	54·4	53·9	53·4	52·9	52·5	52·0	71
72	60·9	60·4	59·8	59·3	58·8	58·3	57·8	57·3	56·8	56·3	55·8	55·3	54·8	54·4	53·9	53·4	72
73	62·2	61·7	61·2	60·7	60·2	59·7	59·2	58·7	58·2	57·7	57·3	56·8	56·3	55·9	55·4	54·9	73
74	63·6	63·1	62·6	62·1	61·6	61·1	60·6	60·2	59·7	59·2	58·8	58·3	57·9	57·4	56·9	56·5	74
75	65·0	64·5	64·0	63·6	63·1	62·6	62·2	61·7	61·2	60·8	60·3	59·9	59·5	59·0	58·6	58·1	75
76	66·5	66·0	65·6	65·1	64·6	64·2	63·7	63·3	62·8	62·4	62·0	61·6	61·1	60·7	60·3	59·8	76
77	68·0	67·5	67·1	66·6	66·2	65·8	65·4	64·9	64·5	64·1	63·7	63·2	62·8	62·5	62·0	61·6	77
78	69·5	69·1	68·7	68·2	67·8	67·4	67·0	66·6	66·2	65·8	65·4	65·0	64·6	64·3	63·9	63·5	78
79	71·0	70·7	70·3	69·9	69·5	69·1	68·7	68·4	68·0	67·6	67·2	66·9	66·5	66·1	65·8	65·4	79
80	72·6	72·3	71·9	71·6	71·2	70·8	70·5	70·1	69·8	69·4	69·1	68·8	68·4	68·1	67·7	67·4	80

TABLE C

A±B=	2·40'	2·45'	2·50'	2·55'	2·60'	2·65'	2·70'	2·75'	2·80'	2·90'	3·00'	3·10'	3·20'	3·30'	3·40'	3·50'	=A±B
							A & B CORRECTION										
Lat.°							**AZIMUTHS**										Lat.°
68	48·0	47·4	46·9	46·3	45·8	45·2	44·7	44·1	43·6	42·6	41·7	40·7	39·8	39·0	38·1	37·3	68
69	49·3	48·7	48·2	47·6	47·0	46·5	45·9	45·4	44·9	43·9	42·9	42·0	41·1	40·2	39·4	38·6	69
70	50·5	50·0	49·5	48·9	48·4	47·8	47·3	46·8	46·2	45·2	44·3	43·3	42·4	41·5	40·7	39·9	70
71	52·0	51·4	50·9	50·3	49·8	49·2	48·8	48·3	47·7	46·7	45·7	44·7	43·8	42·9	42·1	41·3	71
72	53·4	52·9	52·4	51·8	51·2	50·7	50·2	49·7	49·2	48·2	47·2	46·2	45·3	44·4	43·6	42·7	72
73	54·9	54·4	53·9	53·3	52·8	52·2	51·7	51·2	50·7	49·7	48·8	47·8	46·9	46·0	45·2	44·3	73
74	56·5	56·0	55·5	54·9	54·4	53·9	53·4	52·8	52·3	51·4	50·4	49·5	48·6	47·7	46·9	46·0	74
75	58·1	57·6	57·1	56·6	56·1	55·6	55·1	54·6	54·1	53·1	52·2	51·3	50·4	49·5	48·7	47·8	75
76	59·8	59·3	58·8	58·3	57·8	57·3	56·8	56·4	55·9	54·9	54·0	53·1	52·3	51·4	50·6	49·8	76
77	61·6	61·1	60·7	60·2	59·7	59·2	58·7	58·3	57·8	56·9	56·0	55·1	54·3	53·4	52·6	51·8	77
78	63·5	63·0	62·5	62·1	61·6	61·1	60·7	60·3	59·8	58·9	58·1	57·2	56·4	55·5	54·7	53·9	78
79	65·4	64·9	64·5	64·1	63·6	63·2	62·7	62·3	61·9	61·0	60·2	59·4	58·6	57·8	57·0	56·3	79
80	67·4	67·0	66·6	66·1	65·7	65·3	64·9	64·5	64·1	63·3	62·5	61·7	60·9	60·2	59·5	58·8	80

C

TABLE C

A & B CORRECTION

A±B=	3·50'	3·60'	3·70'	3·80'	3·90'	4·00'	4·10'	4·20'	4·30'	4·40'	4·50'	4·60'	4·70'	4·80'	4·90'	5·00'	=A±B
Lat. °							AZIMUTHS										Lat. °
68	37·3	36·6	35·8	35·1	34·4	33·7	33·1	32·4	31·8	31·2	30·7	30·1	29·6	29·1	28·6	28·1	68
69	38·6	37·8	37·0	36·3	35·6	34·9	34·2	33·6	32·9	32·4	31·8	31·2	30·7	30·2	29·7	29·2	69
70	39·9	39·1	38·3	37·6	36·8	36·2	35·5	34·8	34·2	33·6	33·0	32·4	31·8	31·3	30·8	30·3	70
71	41·3	40·5	39·8	38·9	38·2	37·5	36·8	36·2	35·5	34·9	34·3	33·7	33·2	32·6	32·1	31·5	71
72	42·7	41·9	41·2	40·4	39·7	38·9	38·3	37·6	36·9	36·3	35·7	35·1	34·5	33·9	33·4	32·9	72
73	44·3	43·4	42·7	41·9	41·2	40·5	39·8	39·2	38·5	37·8	37·2	36·6	36·0	35·5	34·9	34·4	73
74	46·0	45·2	44·4	43·7	42·9	42·2	41·5	40·8	40·1	39·5	38·9	38·3	37·7	37·1	36·5	35·9	74
75	47·8	47·0	46·2	45·5	44·8	44·0	43·3	42·6	41·9	41·3	40·6	40·0	39·4	38·8	38·2	37·7	75
76	49·8	48·9	48·2	47·4	46·7	45·9	45·2	44·6	43·9	43·2	42·6	41·9	41·3	40·7	40·1	39·6	76
77	51·8	51·0	50·2	49·5	48·7	48·0	47·3	46·6	45·9	45·3	44·6	44·0	43·4	42·8	42·2	41·6	77
78	53·9	53·2	52·4	51·7	50·9	50·2	49·5	48·9	48·2	47·6	46·9	46·3	45·7	45·1	44·5	43·9	78
79	56·3	55·5	54·8	54·1	53·3	52·6	51·9	51·3	50·6	49·9	49·3	48·7	48·1	47·5	46·9	46·3	79
80	58·8	58·0	57·3	56·6	55·9	55·2	54·5	53·9	53·2	52·6	52·0	51·4	50·8	50·2	49·6	49·0	80

TABLE C

A & B CORRECTION

A±B=	5·00'	5·20'	5·40'	5·60'	5·80'	6·00'	6·20'	6·40'	6·60'	6·80'	7·00'	7·20'	7·40'	7·60'	7·80'	8·00'	=A±B
Lat. °							AZIMUTHS										Lat. °
68	28·1	27·2	26·3	25·5	24·7	24·0	23·3	22·6	22·0	21·4	20·9	20·3	19·8	19·4	18·9	18·5	68
69	29·2	28·2	27·3	26·5	25·7	24·9	24·2	23·5	22·9	22·3	21·7	21·2	20·7	20·2	19·7	19·2	69
70	30·3	29·3	28·4	27·6	26·8	25·9	25·2	24·5	23·9	23·3	22·7	22·1	21·6	21·0	20·5	20·1	70
71	31·5	30·6	29·6	28·7	27·9	27·1	26·3	25·6	24·9	24·3	23·7	23·1	22·5	22·0	21·5	21·0	71
72	32·9	31·9	30·9	30·0	29·1	28·3	27·5	26·8	26·1	25·4	24·8	24·2	23·6	23·1	22·6	22·0	72
73	34·4	33·3	32·3	31·4	30·5	29·7	28·9	28·1	27·4	26·7	26·1	25·4	24·8	24·2	23·7	23·1	73
74	35·9	34·9	33·9	32·9	32·0	31·2	30·3	29·6	28·8	28·1	27·4	26·7	26·1	25·5	25·0	24·4	74
75	37·7	36·6	35·6	34·6	33·7	32·8	31·9	31·1	30·3	29·6	28·9	28·2	27·6	27·0	26·4	25·8	75
76	39·6	38·5	37·4	36·4	35·5	34·6	33·7	32·8	32·1	31·3	30·6	29·8	29·2	28·5	27·9	27·3	76
77	41·6	40·5	39·4	38·4	37·5	36·5	35·6	34·8	33·9	33·2	32·4	31·7	30·9	30·3	29·7	29·0	77
78	43·9	42·8	41·7	40·7	39·7	38·7	37·8	36·9	36·1	35·3	34·5	33·7	33·0	32·3	31·6	31·0	78
79	46·3	45·2	44·1	43·1	42·1	41·1	40·2	39·3	38·4	37·6	36·8	36·1	35·3	34·6	33·9	33·2	79
80	49·0	47·9	46·8	45·8	44·8	43·8	42·9	41·9	41·1	40·3	39·4	38·6	37·9	37·2	36·5	35·8	80

TABLE C

A & B CORRECTION

A±B=	8·00'	8·20'	8·40'	8·60'	8·80'	9·00'	9·20'	9·40'	9·60'	9·80'	10·0'	10·3'	10·6'	11·0'	11·5'	12·0'	=A±B
Lat. °							AZIMUTHS										Lat. °
68	18·5	18·0	17·6	17·2	16·9	16·5	16·2	15·9	15·5	15·2	14·9	14·6	14·2	13·6	13·1	12·5	68
69	19·2	18·8	18·4	18·0	17·6	17·2	16·9	16·5	16·2	15·8	15·5	15·2	14·8	14·2	13·6	13·1	69
70	20·1	19·6	19·2	18·8	18·4	18·0	17·6	17·2	16·9	16·6	16·3	15·9	15·5	14·9	14·2	13·7	70
71	21·0	20·5	20·1	19·6	19·2	18·8	18·5	18·1	17·8	17·4	17·1	16·6	16·1	15·6	15·0	14·4	71
72	22·0	21·5	21·1	20·6	20·2	19·8	19·4	19·0	18·6	18·2	17·9	17·5	17·0	16·4	15·7	15·1	72
73	23·1	22·6	22·2	21·7	21·2	20·8	20·4	20·0	19·6	19·2	18·9	18·4	17·9	17·3	16·6	15·9	73
74	24·4	23·9	23·4	22·9	22·4	21·9	21·5	21·1	20·7	20·3	19·9	19·4	18·9	18·3	17·5	16·8	74
75	25·8	25·2	24·7	24·2	23·7	23·2	22·8	22·3	21·9	21·5	21·1	20·6	20·1	19·4	18·6	17·9	75
76	27·3	26·7	26·2	25·7	25·2	24·7	24·2	23·7	23·3	22·9	22·5	21·9	21·3	20·6	19·8	19·0	76
77	29·0	28·4	27·9	27·3	26·8	26·3	25·8	25·3	24·8	24·4	24·0	23·4	22·8	22·0	21·1	20·3	77
78	31·0	30·4	29·8	29·2	28·7	28·1	27·6	27·1	26·6	26·1	25·7	25·0	24·3	23·6	22·7	21·9	78
79	33·2	32·5	31·9	31·3	30·8	30·2	29·7	29·1	28·6	28·1	27·7	27·0	26·3	25·5	24·5	23·7	79
80	35·8	35·1	34·4	33·8	33·2	32·6	32·0	31·5	31·0	30·4	29·9	29·2	28·5	27·6	26·6	25·7	80

C

TABLE C

A±B=	12.0'	12.5'	13.0'	13.5'	14.0'	14.5'	A & B CORRECTION 15.0'	16.0'	17.0'	18.0'	19.0'	20.0'	21.0'	22.0'	23.0'	25.0' =A±B
Lat. °	°	°	°	°	°	°	AZIMUTHS °	°	°	°	°	°	°	°	°	Lat. °
68	12.5	12.1	11.6	11.2	10.8	10.4	10.1	9.5	8.9	8.4	8.0	7.6	7.2	6.9	6.6	6.1	68
69	13.1	12.6	12.1	11.7	11.3	10.9	10.5	9.9	9.4	8.8	8.4	7.9	7.6	7.2	6.9	6.4	69
70	13.7	13.2	12.7	12.2	11.8	11.4	11.0	10.4	9.8	9.2	8.7	8.3	7.9	7.6	7.3	6.7	70
71	14.4	13.8	13.3	12.8	12.4	12.0	11.6	10.9	10.2	9.7	9.2	8.7	8.3	7.9	7.6	7.0	71
72	15.1	14.5	14.0	13.5	13.0	12.6	12.2	11.4	10.8	10.2	9.7	9.2	8.8	8.4	8.0	7.4	72
73	15.9	15.3	14.7	14.2	13.7	13.3	12.8	12.1	11.4	10.8	10.2	9.7	9.3	8.8	8.5	7.8	73
74	16.8	16.2	15.6	15.0	14.5	14.1	13.6	12.8	12.1	11.4	10.8	10.3	9.8	9.4	9.0	8.3	74
75	17.9	17.2	16.6	16.0	15.4	14.9	14.5	13.6	12.8	12.1	11.5	10.9	10.4	10.0	9.6	8.8	75
76	19.0	18.3	17.6	17.0	16.3	15.6	15.4	14.5	13.7	12.9	12.3	11.7	11.1	10.7	10.2	9.4	76
77	20.3	19.6	18.9	18.2	17.6	17.0	16.5	15.5	14.7	13.9	13.2	12.5	11.9	11.4	10.9	10.1	77
78	21.9	21.1	20.3	19.6	19.0	18.4	17.8	16.7	15.8	15.0	14.2	13.5	12.9	12.3	11.9	10.9	78
79	23.7	22.8	22.0	21.2	20.5	19.9	19.7	18.1	17.1	16.2	15.4	14.7	14.0	13.4	12.9	11.8	79
80	25.7	24.7	23.9	23.1	22.4	21.7	21.0	19.8	18.7	17.8	16.9	16.1	15.3	14.7	14.0	13.0	80

TABLE C

A±B=	25.0'	27.0'	30.0'	33.0'	36.0'	40.0'	A & B CORRECTION 45.0'	50.0'	60.0'	70.0'	80.0'	100'	150'	200'	400'	800' =A±B
Lat. °	°	°	°	°	°	°	AZIMUTHS °	°	°	°	°	•	•	°	°	Lat. °
68	6.1	5.6	5.1	4.6	4.2	3.8	3.4	3.1	2.5	2.2	1.9	1.5	1.0	0.8	0.4	0.2	68
69	6.4	5.9	5.3	4.8	4.4	4.0	3.5	3.2	2.7	2.3	2.0	1.6	1.1	0.8	0.4	0.2	69
70	6.7	6.2	5.6	5.1	4.6	4.2	3.7	3.4	2.8	2.4	2.1	1.7	1.1	0.8	0.4	0.2	70
71	7.0	6.5	5.9	5.3	4.9	4.4	3.9	3.5	2.9	2.5	2.2	1.8	1.2	0.9	0.4	0.2	71
72	7.4	6.8	6.2	5.6	5.1	4.6	4.1	3.7	3.1	2.6	2.3	1.9	1.2	0.9	0.5	0.2	72
73	7.8	7.3	6.5	5.9	5.4	4.9	4.4	3.9	3.3	2.8	2.4	2.0	1.3	1.0	0.5	0.2	73
74	8.3	7.7	6.9	6.3	5.8	5.2	4.6	4.2	3.5	3.0	2.6	2.1	1.4	1.0	0.5	0.3	74
75	8.8	8.1	7.3	6.7	6.1	5.5	4.9	4.4	3.7	3.2	2.8	2.2	1.5	1.1	0.6	0.3	75
76	9.4	8.7	7.8	7.1	6.6	5.9	5.3	4.7	3.9	3.4	3.0	2.4	1.6	1.2	0.6	0.3	76
77	10.1	9.4	8.4	7.7	7.0	6.3	5.6	5.1	4.2	3.6	3.2	2.6	1.7	1.3	0.6	0.3	77
78	10.9	10.1	9.1	8.3	7.6	6.9	6.1	5.5	4.6	3.9	3.4	2.8	1.8	1.4	0.7	0.3	78
79	11.8	11.0	9.9	9.0	8.3	7.5	6.7	6.0	5.0	4.3	3.8	3.0	2.0	1.5	0.7	0.4	79
80	13.0	12.0	10.9	9.9	9.1	8.2	7.3	6.6	5.5	4.7	4.1	3.3	2.2	1.7	0.8	0.4	80

C

TRUE AMPLITUDES

Lat.	1°	2°	3°	4°	5°	6°	7°	8°	9°	10°	11°	12°	13°	14°	15°
2	1·0	2·0	3·0	4·0	5·0	6·0	7·0	8·0	9·0	10·0	11·0	12·0	13·0	14·0	15·0
4	1·0	2·0	3·0	4·0	5·0	6·0	7·0	8·0	9·0	10·0	11·0	12·0	13·0	14·0	15·0
6	1·0	2·0	3·0	4·0	5·0	6·0	7·1	8·1	9·1	10·1	11·1	12·1	13·1	14·1	15·1
8	1·0	2·0	3·0	4·1	5·1	6·1	7·1	8·1	9·1	10·1	11·1	12·1	13·1	14·1	15·2
10	1·0	2·0	3·1	4·1	5·1	6·1	7·1	8·1	9·2	10·2	11·2	12·2	13·2	14·2	15·3
12	1·0	2·1	3·1	4·1	5·1	6·1	7·2	8·2	9·2	10·2	11·3	12·3	13·3	14·3	15·4
14	1·0	2·1	3·1	4·1	5·2	6·2	7·2	8·3	9·3	10·3	11·3	12·4	13·4	14·4	15·5
16	1·1	2·1	3·1	4·2	5·2	6·2	7·3	8·3	9·4	10·4	11·5	12·5	13·5	14·6	15·6
18	1·1	2·1	3·2	4·2	5·3	6·3	7·4	8·4	9·5	10·5	11·6	12·6	13·7	14·7	15·8
20	1·1	2·1	3·2	4·3	5·3	6·4	7·5	8·5	9·6	10·7	11·7	12·8	13·9	14·9	15·9
22	1·1	2·2	3·2	4·3	5·4	6·5	7·6	8·6	9·7	10·8	11·9	13·0	14·1	15·1	16·2
24	1·1	2·2	3·3	4·4	5·5	6·6	7·7	8·8	9·9	11·0	12·1	13·2	14·3	15·4	16·5
26	1·1	2·2	3·4	4·5	5·6	6·7	7·8	8·9	10·0	11·2	12·3	13·4	14·5	15·6	16·8
28	1·1	2·3	3·4	4·5	5·7	6·8	7·9	9·1	10·2	11·4	12·5	13·6	14·8	15·9	17·1
30	1·2	2·3	3·5	4·6	5·8	6·9	8·1	9·3	10·4	11·6	12·7	13·9	15·1	16·2	17·4
31	1·2	2·3	3·5	4·7	5·8	7·0	8·2	9·4	10·5	11·7	12·9	14·0	15·2	16·4	17·6
32	1·2	2·4	3·6	4·7	5·9	7·1	8·3	9·5	10·6	11·8	13·0	14·2	15·4	16·6	17·8
33	1·2	2·4	3·6	4·8	6·0	7·2	8·4	9·6	10·8	12·0	13·2	14·4	15·6	16·8	18·0
34	1·2	2·4	3·6	4·8	6·0	7·3	8·5	9·7	10·9	12·1	13·3	14·5	15·8	17·0	18·2
35	1·2	2·5	3·7	4·9	6·1	7·3	8·6	9·8	11·0	12·2	13·5	14·7	16·0	17·2	18·4
36	1·2	2·5	3·7	5·0	6·2	7·4	8·7	9·9	11·2	12·4	13·7	14·9	16·2	17·4	18·7
37	1·3	2·5	3·8	5·0	6·3	7·5	8·8	10·0	11·3	12·6	13·8	15·1	16·3	17·6	18·9
38	1·3	2·5	3·8	5·1	6·4	7·6	8·9	10·2	11·4	12·7	14·0	15·3	16·6	17·9	19·2
39	1·3	2·6	3·9	5·2	6·4	7·7	9·0	10·3	11·6	12·9	14·2	15·5	16·8	18·1	19·5
40	1·3	2·6	3·9	5·2	6·5	7·9	9·2	10·5	11·8	13·1	14·4	15·8	17·1	18·4	19·8
41	1·3	2·7	4·0	5·3	6·6	8·0	9·3	10·6	12·0	13·3	14·7	16·0	17·4	18·7	20·1
42	1·4	2·7	4·0	5·4	6·7	8·1	9·4	10·8	12·2	13·5	14·9	16·3	17·6	19·0	20·4
43	1·4	2·7	4·1	5·5	6·9	8·2	9·6	11·0	12·4	13·7	15·1	16·5	17·9	19·3	20·7
44	1·4	2·8	4·2	5·6	7·0	8·4	9·8	11·2	12·6	14·0	15·4	16·8	18·2	19·7	21·1
45	1·4	2·8	4·3	5·7	7·1	8·5	9·9	11·4	12·8	14·2	15·7	17·1	18·6	20·0	21·5
46	1·4	2·9	4·3	5·8	7·2	8·7	10·1	11·6	13·0	14·5	16·0	17·4	18·9	20·4	21·9
47	1·5	2·9	4·4	5·9	7·4	8·8	10·3	11·8	13·3	14·8	16·3	17·8	19·3	20·8	22·3
48	1·5	3·0	4·5	6·0	7·5	9·0	10·5	12·0	13·5	15·1	16·6	18·1	19·7	21·2	22·8
49	1·5	3·1	4·6	6·1	7·6	9·2	10·7	12·3	13·8	15·4	16·9	18·5	20·1	21·6	23·2
50	1·6	3·1	4·7	6·2	7·8	9·4	10·9	12·5	14·1	15·7	17·3	18·9	20·5	22·1	23·8
50½	1·6	3·1	4·7	6·3	7·9	9·5	11·0	12·6	14·2	15·8	17·5	19·1	20·7	22·4	24·0
51	1·6	3·1	4·8	6·4	8·0	9·6	11·2	12·8	14·4	16·0	17·7	19·3	21·0	22·6	24·3
51½	1·6	3·2	4·8	6·4	8·0	9·7	11·3	12·9	14·6	16·2	17·8	19·5	21·2	22·9	24·6
52	1·6	3·3	4·9	6·5	8·1	9·8	11·4	13·1	14·7	16·4	18·1	19·7	21·4	23·2	24·9
52½	1·6	3·3	4·9	6·6	8·2	9·9	11·5	13·2	14·9	16·6	18·3	20·0	21·7	23·4	25·2
53	1·7	3·3	5·0	6·7	8·3	10·0	11·7	13·4	15·1	16·8	18·5	20·2	22·0	23·7	25·5
53½	1·7	3·4	5·0	6·7	8·4	10·1	11·8	13·5	15·2	17·0	18·7	20·5	22·2	24·0	25·8
54	1·7	3·4	5·1	6·8	8·5	10·3	12·0	13·7	15·4	17·2	19·0	20·7	22·5	24·3	26·1
54½	1·7	3·4	5·2	6·9	8·6	10·4	12·2	13·9	15·6	17·4	19·2	21·0	22·8	24·6	26·5
55	1·8	3·5	5·2	7·0	8·7	10·5	12·3	14·1	15·8	17·6	19·4	21·3	23·1	25·0	26·8
55½	1·8	3·5	5·3	7·1	8·9	10·6	12·4	14·2	16·0	17·9	19·7	21·5	23·4	25·3	27·2
56	1·8	3·6	5·4	7·2	9·0	10·8	12·6	14·4	16·3	18·1	20·0	21·8	23·7	25·6	27·6
56½	1·8	3·6	5·4	7·3	9·1	10·9	12·8	14·6	16·5	18·3	20·2	22·1	24·1	26·0	28·0
57	1·8	3·7	5·5	7·4	9·2	11·1	12·9	14·8	16·7	18·6	20·5	22·4	24·4	26·4	28·4
57½	1·9	3·7	5·6	7·5	9·3	11·2	13·1	15·0	16·9	18·9	20·8	22·8	24·8	26·8	28·9
58	1·9	3·8	5·7	7·6	9·5	11·4	13·3	15·2	17·2	19·1	21·1	23·1	25·1	27·2	29·2
58½	1·9	3·8	5·7	7·7	9·6	11·5	13·5	15·4	17·4	19·4	21·4	23·4	25·4	27·6	29·7
59	2·0	3·9	5·8	7·8	9·8	11·7	13·7	15·7	17·7	19·7	21·8	23·8	25·9	28·0	30·2
59½	2·0	3·9	5·9	7·9	9·9	11·9	13·9	15·9	18·0	20·0	22·1	24·2	26·3	28·5	30·7
60	2·0	4·0	6·0	8·0	10·0	12·1	14·1	16·2	18·2	20·3	22·4	24·6	26·7	28·9	31·2
60½	2·0	4·1	6·1	8·1	10·2	12·3	14·3	16·4	18·5	20·6	22·8	25·0	27·2	29·4	31·7
61	2·1	4·1	6·2	8·3	10·4	12·5	14·6	16·7	18·8	21·0	23·2	25·4	27·7	29·9	32·3
61½	2·1	4·2	6·3	8·4	10·5	12·7	14·8	17·0	19·1	21·3	23·6	25·8	28·1	30·5	32·8
62	2·1	4·3	6·4	8·6	10·7	12·9	15·1	17·3	19·5	21·7	24·0	26·3	28·6	31·0	33·5
62½	2·2	4·3	6·5	8·7	10·9	13·1	15·3	17·5	19·8	22·1	24·4	26·8	29·2	31·6	34·1

TRUE AMPLITUDES

Declination

Lat.	16°	17°	18°	19°	20°	20½°	21°	21½°	22°	22½°	23°	23½°	24°	24½°	25°
°	°	°	°	°	°	°	°	°	°	°	°	°	°	°	°
2	16·0	17·0	18·0	19·0	20·0	20·5	21·0	21·5	22·0	22·5	23·0	23·5	24·0	24·5	25·0
4	16·0	17·1	18·1	19·1	20·1	20·6	21·1	21·6	22·1	22·6	23·1	23·6	24·1	24·6	25·1
6	16·1	17·1	18·1	19·1	20·1	20·6	21·1	21·6	22·1	22·6	23·1	23·6	24·1	24·6	25·1
8	16·2	17·2	18·2	19·2	20·2	20·7	21·2	21·7	22·2	22·7	23·2	23·7	24·3	24·8	25·3
10	16·3	17·3	18·3	19·3	20·3	20·8	21·4	21·8	22·4	22·9	23·4	23·9	24·4	24·9	25·4
12	16·4	17·4	18·4	19·4	20·5	21·0	21·5	22·0	22·5	23·0	23·6	24·1	24·6	25·1	25·6
14	16·5	17·5	18·6	19·6	20·6	21·2	21·7	22·2	22·7	23·2	23·8	24·3	24·8	25·3	25·8
16	16·7	17·7	18·8	19·8	20·9	21·4	21·9	22·4	22·9	23·5	24·0	24·5	25·0	25·6	26·1
18	16·9	17·9	19·0	20·0	21·1	21·6	22·1	22·7	23·2	23·7	24·3	24·8	25·3	25·9	26·4
20	17·1	18·1	19·2	20·3	21·4	21·9	22·4	23·0	23·5	24·0	24·6	25·1	25·7	26·2	26·7
22	17·3	18·4	19·5	20·6	21·7	22·2	22·7	23·3	23·8	24·4	24·9	25·5	26·0	26·6	27·1
24	17·6	18·7	19·8	20·9	22·0	22·5	23·1	23·7	24·2	24·8	25·3	25·9	26·4	27·0	27·6
26	17·9	19·0	20·1	21·2	22·4	22·9	23·5	24·1	24·6	25·2	25·8	26·3	27·5	27·5	28·0
28	18·2	19·3	20·5	21·6	22·8	23·4	24·0	24·5	25·1	25·7	26·3	26·8	27·4	28·0	28·6
30	18·6	19·7	20·9	22·1	23·3	23·9	24·5	25·0	25·6	26·2	26·8	27·4	28·0	28·6	29·2
31	18·8	20·0	21·1	22·3	23·5	24·1	24·7	25·3	25·9	26·5	27·1	27·7	28·3	28·9	29·5
32	19·0	20·2	21·4	22·6	23·8	24·4	25·0	25·6	26·2	26·8	27·4	28·0	28·7	29·3	29·9
33	19·2	20·4	21·6	22·9	24·1	24·7	25·3	25·9	26·5	27·1	27·8	28·4	29·0	29·6	30·3
34	19·4	20·6	21·9	23·1	24·4	25·0	25·6	26·2	26·9	27·5	28·1	28·7	29·4	29·9	30·7
35	19·7	20·9	22·2	23·4	24·7	25·3	26·0	26·6	27·2	27·9	28·5	29·1	29·8	30·4	31·1
36	19·9	21·2	22·5	23·7	25·0	25·7	26·3	26·9	27·6	28·2	28·9	29·5	30·2	30·8	31·5
37	20·2	21·5	22·8	24·1	25·4	26·0	26·7	27·3	28·0	28·6	29·3	30·0	30·6	31·3	31·9
38	20·5	21·8	23·1	24·4	25·7	26·4	27·1	27·7	28·4	29·1	29·7	30·4	31·1	31·8	32·4
39	20·8	22·1	23·4	24·8	26·1	26·8	27·5	28·1	28·8	29·5	30·2	30·9	31·6	32·3	32·9
40	21·1	22·4	23·8	25·2	26·5	27·2	27·9	28·6	29·3	30·0	30·7	31·4	32·1	32·8	33·5
41	21·4	22·8	24·2	25·6	27·0	27·6	28·4	29·1	29·8	30·5	31·2	31·9	32·6	33·3	34·1
42	21·8	23·2	24·6	26·0	27·4	28·1	28·8	29·6	30·3	31·0	31·7	32·5	33·2	33·9	34·7
43	22·1	23·6	25·0	26·4	27·9	28·6	29·3	30·1	30·8	31·6	32·3	33·0	33·8	34·5	35·3
44	22·5	24·0	25·4	26·9	28·4	29·1	29·9	30·6	31·4	32·1	32·9	33·7	34·4	35·2	36·0
45	23·0	24·4	25·9	27·4	28·9	29·7	30·5	31·3	32·0	32·8	33·6	34·3	35·1	35·9	36·7
46	23·4	24·9	26·4	28·0	29·5	30·3	31·1	31·8	32·6	33·4	34·2	35·0	35·8	36·7	37·5
47	23·8	25·4	27·0	28·5	30·1	30·9	31·7	32·5	33·3	34·1	35·0	35·8	36·6	37·5	38·3
48	24·3	25·9	27·5	29·1	30·7	31·6	32·4	33·2	34·1	34·9	35·7	36·6	37·4	38·3	39·2
49	24·9	26·5	28·1	29·8	31·4	32·3	33·1	34·0	34·8	35·7	36·6	37·4	38·3	39·2	40·1
50	25·4	27·1	28·7	30·4	32·2	33·0	33·9	34·8	35·6	36·5	37·4	38·3	39·3	40·2	41·1
50½	25·7	27·4	29·1	30·8	32·5	33·4	34·3	35·2	36·1	37·0	37·9	38·8	39·8	40·7	41·6
51	26·0	27·7	29·4	31·2	32·9	33·8	34·7	35·6	36·5	37·5	38·4	39·3	40·3	41·2	42·2
51½	26·3	28·0	29·8	31·5	33·3	34·2	35·1	36·1	37·0	37·9	38·9	39·8	40·8	41·8	42·8
52	26·6	28·4	30·1	31·9	33·8	34·7	35·6	36·5	37·5	38·4	39·4	40·4	41·4	42·3	43·4
52½	26·9	28·7	30·5	32·3	34·2	35·1	36·1	37·0	38·0	38·9	39·9	40·9	41·9	42·9	44·0
53	27·3	29·1	30·9	32·8	34·6	35·6	36·6	37·5	38·5	39·5	40·5	41·5	42·5	43·6	44·6
53½	27·6	29·4	31·3	33·2	35·1	36·1	37·0	38·0	39·0	40·0	41·1	42·1	43·1	44·2	45·3
54	28·0	29·8	31·7	33·6	35·6	36·6	37·6	38·6	39·6	40·6	41·7	42·7	43·8	44·9	46·0
54½	28·3	30·2	32·2	34·1	36·1	37·1	38·1	39·1	40·1	41·2	42·3	43·4	44·5	45·6	46·7
55	28·7	30·7	32·6	34·6	36·6	37·6	38·7	39·7	40·8	41·9	42·9	44·0	45·2	46·3	47·5
55½	29·1	31·1	33·1	35·1	37·1	38·2	39·3	40·3	41·4	42·5	43·6	44·7	45·9	46·9	48·3
56	29·5	31·5	33·6	35·6	37·7	38·8	39·9	41·0	42·1	43·2	44·3	45·5	46·7	47·9	49·1
56½	30·0	32·0	34·0	36·1	38·3	39·4	40·5	41·6	42·6	43·9	45·1	46·3	47·5	48·7	50·0
57	30·4	32·5	34·6	36·7	38·9	40·0	41·2	42·3	43·5	44·6	45·9	47·1	48·3	49·6	50·9
57½	30·9	33·0	35·1	37·3	39·5	40·7	41·8	43·0	44·2	45·4	46·7	47·9	49·2	50·5	51·9
58	31·3	33·5	35·7	37·9	40·2	41·4	42·6	43·8	45·0	46·2	47·5	48·8	50·1	51·5	52·9
58½	31·8	34·0	36·3	38·5	40·9	42·1	43·3	44·5	45·8	47·1	48·4	49·7	51·1	52·5	54·0
59	32·4	34·6	36·9	39·2	41·6	42·8	44·1	45·4	46·7	48·0	49·4	50·7	52·2	53·6	55·1
59½	32·9	35·2	37·5	39·9	42·4	43·6	44·9	46·2	47·6	48·9	50·3	51·8	53·3	54·8	56·4
60	33·5	35·8	38·2	40·6	43·2	44·5	45·8	47·1	48·5	49·9	51·4	52·9	54·4	56·0	57·7
60½	34·0	36·4	38·8	41·4	44·0	45·3	46·7	48·1	49·5	51·0	52·5	54·1	55·7	57·4	59·1
61	34·7	37·1	39·6	42·2	44·9	46·3	47·7	49·1	50·6	52·1	53·7	55·3	57·0	58·8	60·6
61½	35·3	37·8	40·4	43·0	45·8	47·2	48·7	50·2	51·7	53·3	55·0	56·7	58·5	60·4	62·3
62	36·0	38·5	41·2	43·9	46·8	48·2	49·8	51·3	52·9	54·6	56·3	58·1	60·0	62·0	64·2
62½	36·7	39·3	42·0	44·8	47·8	49·3	50·9	52·5	54·2	56·0	57·8	59·7	61·7	63·9	66·2

TRUE AMPLITUDES

Lat.	25½°	26°	26½°	27°	27½°	28°	28½°	29°
2	25.5	26.0	26.5	27.0	27.5	28.0	28.5	29.0
4	25.6	26.1	26.6	27.1	27.6	28.1	28.6	29.1
6	25.7	26.2	26.7	27.2	27.7	28.2	28.7	29.2
8	25.8	26.3	26.8	27.3	27.8	28.3	28.8	29.3
10	25.9	26.4	26.9	27.5	28.0	28.5	29.0	29.5
12	26.1	26.6	27.1	27.7	28.2	28.7	29.2	29.7
14	26.3	26.9	27.4	27.9	28.4	28.9	29.5	30.0
16	26.6	27.1	27.7	28.2	28.7	29.2	29.8	30.3
18	26.9	27.5	28.0	28.5	29.0	29.6	30.1	30.7
20	27.3	27.8	28.3	28.9	29.4	30.0	30.5	31.1
22	27.7	28.2	28.8	29.3	29.9	30.4	31.0	31.5
24	28.1	28.7	29.2	29.8	30.4	30.9	31.5	32.1
26	28.6	29.2	29.8	30.3	30.9	31.5	32.1	32.6
28	29.2	29.8	30.4	30.9	31.5	32.1	32.7	33.3
30	29.8	30.4	31.0	31.6	32.2	32.8	33.4	34.1
31	30.1	30.8	31.4	32.0	32.6	33.2	33.8	34.5
32	30.5	31.1	31.7	32.4	33.0	33.6	34.2	34.9
33	30.9	31.5	32.1	32.8	33.4	34.0	34.7	35.3
34	31.3	31.9	32.6	33.2	33.8	34.5	35.1	35.8
35	31.7	32.4	33.0	33.7	34.3	35.0	35.6	36.3
36	32.2	32.8	33.5	34.1	34.8	35.5	36.1	36.8
37	32.6	33.3	34.0	34.6	35.3	36.0	36.7	37.4
38	33.1	33.8	34.5	35.2	35.9	36.6	37.3	38.0
39	33.6	34.3	35.0	35.8	36.5	37.2	37.9	38.6
40	34.2	34.9	35.6	36.4	37.1	37.8	38.5	39.3
41	34.8	35.5	36.2	37.0	37.7	38.5	39.2	40.0
42	35.4	36.2	36.9	37.7	38.4	39.2	39.9	40.7
43	36.1	36.8	37.6	38.4	39.2	39.9	40.7	41.5
44	36.8	37.5	38.3	39.2	39.9	40.7	41.6	42.4
45	37.5	38.3	39.1	39.9	40.8	41.6	42.4	43.3
46	38.3	39.1	40.0	40.8	41.7	42.5	43.4	44.3
47	39.1	40.0	40.9	41.7	42.6	43.5	44.4	45.3
48	40.0	40.9	41.8	42.7	43.6	44.5	45.5	46.4
49	41.0	41.9	42.9	43.8	44.7	45.7	46.7	47.7
50	42.0	43.0	44.0	44.9	45.9	46.9	47.9	49.0
50½	42.6	43.6	44.5	45.5	46.5	47.6	48.6	49.7
51	43.2	44.2	45.2	46.2	47.2	48.2	49.3	50.4
51½	43.8	44.8	45.8	46.8	47.9	49.0	50.0	51.2
52	44.4	45.4	46.4	47.5	48.6	49.7	50.8	52.0
52½	45.0	46.0	47.1	48.2	49.3	50.5	51.6	52.8
53	45.7	46.7	47.9	49.0	50.1	51.3	52.5	53.7
53½	46.4	47.5	48.6	49.8	50.9	52.1	53.3	54.6
54	47.1	48.2	49.4	50.6	51.8	53.0	54.3	55.6
54½	47.8	49.0	50.2	51.4	52.7	53.9	55.3	56.6
55	48.6	49.8	51.1	52.3	53.6	54.9	56.3	57.7
55½	49.5	50.7	52.0	53.3	54.6	56.0	57.4	58.9
56	50.3	51.6	52.9	54.3	55.7	57.1	58.6	60.1
56½	51.3	52.6	53.9	55.4	56.8	58.3	59.8	61.4
57	52.2	53.6	55.0	56.5	58.0	59.6	61.2	62.9
57½	53.2	54.7	56.1	57.7	59.2	60.7	62.6	65.0
58	54.3	55.8	57.4	58.9	60.6	62.4	64.2	66.2
58½	55.5	57.0	58.6	60.3	62.1	64.0	66.0	68.1
59	56.7	58.3	60.0	61.8	63.7	65.7	67.9	70.3
59½	58.0	59.7	61.5	63.4	65.5	67.7	70.1	72.8
60	59.4	61.2	63.2	65.2	67.4	69.9	72.6	75.8
60½	61.0	62.9	65.0	67.2	69.7	72.4	75.7	79.9
61	62.6	64.7	67.0	69.4	72.3	75.5	79.8	90.0
61½	64.5	66.7	69.3	72.1	75.4	79.7	90.0	—
62	66.2	69.0	71.9	75.2	79.6	90.0	—	—
62½	68.8	71.7	75.1	79.5	90.0	—	—	—

Amplitude Corrections

Lat.	0°	5°	10°	15°	20°	25°
0	0.0	0.0	0.0	0.0	0.0	0.0
5	0.1	0.1	0.1	0.1	0.1	0.1
10	0.1	0.1	0.1	0.1	0.1	0.1
15	0.2	0.2	0.2	0.2	0.2	0.2
20	0.2	0.2	0.2	0.2	0.2	0.3
25	0.3	0.3	0.3	0.3	0.3	0.3
30	0.4	0.4	0.4	0.4	0.4	0.4
35	0.4	0.5	0.5	0.5	0.5	0.5
40	0.5	0.6	0.6	0.6	0.6	0.7
42	0.6	0.6	0.6	0.6	0.7	0.7
44	0.6	0.6	0.7	0.7	0.7	0.7
46	0.7	0.7	0.7	0.7	0.8	0.8
48	0.7	0.8	0.8	0.8	0.9	0.9
50	0.8	0.8	0.8	0.9	0.9	1.0
52	0.8	0.9	0.9	0.9	1.0	1.1
54	0.9	0.9	1.0	1.0	1.1	1.3
56	0.9	0.9	1.0	1.0	1.2	1.5
58	1.0	1.0	1.1	1.2	1.3	1.7
60	1.1	1.2	1.2	1.3	1.5	2.1
62	1.2	1.2	1.3	1.4	1.8	2.9

COMPASS ERROR BY AMPLITUDE

The true amplitudes given in the main table are calculated for the instant when the true altitude of the body is precisely 0° 00′. In the case of the sun (owing to the effects of dip, refraction and parallax) the lower limb at this instant will appear to be approximately half a diameter above the visible horizon. If the compass bearing is taken at that moment there will be no need to apply any correction.

However, should the bearing be observed when the sun's centre appears to be in the visible horizon, the correction obtained from the subsidiary table should be applied by being added to the observed azimuth reckoned from the elevated pole as shown in the example below. (Lat. 62° N., decl. 20° S.).

Obs'd. Azi.	S. 41°.5 E.
From elev. pole	N. 138°.5 E.
Corr'n.	+ 1°.8
Sum	N. 140°.3 E.
Corr'd. obs'd. Amp.	E. 50°.3 S.
T. Amp. from table	E. 46°.8 S.
Comp. Error	3°.5 W.

Observations of rising or setting stars and planets are seldom practicable but, if obtained, should be treated in the same way as those of the sun's centre.

In the case of the moon that body will be approximately one-third of a degree below the horizon at the moment when its true altitude is 0° 00′. If observed when its centre appears in the visible horizon, two-thirds of the correction from the subsidiary table should be subtracted from the observed azimuth reckoned from the elevated pole.

EX-MERIDIAN TABLE I
Latitude and Declination SAME NAME
Change of Altitude in one minute from Meridian Passage = A

Lat. °	0°	1°	2°	3°	4°	5°	6°	7°	8°	9°	10°	11°	12°	13°	14°	Lat. °
0					28.1	22.4	18.7	16.0	14.0	12.4	11.1	10.1	9.2	8.5	7.9	0
1						28.0	22.4	186	16.0	13.9	12.4	11.1	10.1	9.2	8.5	1
2							28.0	22.3	18.6	15.9	13.9	12.3	11.1	10.0	9.2	2
3								27.9	22.3	18.5	15.8	13.8	12.3	11.0	10.0	3
4	28.1								27.8	22.2	18.5	15.8	13.8	12.2	10.9	4
5	22.4	28.0								27.7	22.1	18.4	15.7	13.7	12.1	5
6	18.7	22.4	28.0								27.6	22.0	18.3	15.6	13.6	6
7	16.0	18.6	22.3	27.9								27.4	21.9	18.2	15.5	7
8	14.0	16.0	18.6	22.3	27.8								27.3	21.7	18.0	8
9	12.4	13.9	15.9	18.5	22.2	27.7								27.1	21.6	9
10	11.1	12.4	13.9	15.8	18.5	22.1	27.6								26.9	10
11	10.1	11.1	12.3	13.8	15.8	18.4	22.0	27.4								11
12	9.2	10.1	11.1	12.3	13.8	15.7	18.3	21.9	27.3							12
13	8.5	9.2	10.0	11.0	12.2	13.7	15.6	18.2	21.7	27.1						13
14	7.9	8.5	9.2	10.0	10.9	12.1	13.6	15.5	18.0	21.6	26.9					14
15	7.3	7.8	8.4	9.1	9.9	10.0	12.1	13.5	15.4	17.9	21.4	26.7				15
16	6.8	7.3	7.8	8.4	9.1	9.8	10.8	12.0	13.4	15.3	17.8	21.3	26.5			16
17	6.4	6.8	7.2	7.8	8.3	9.0	9.8	10.7	11.9	13.3	15.2	17.6	21.1	26.2		17
18	6.0	6.4	6.8	7.2	7.7	8.3	8.9	9.7	10.6	11.8	13.2	15.0	17.5	20.9	26.0	18
19	5.7	6.0	6.3	6.7	7.2	7.6	8.2	8.9	9.6	10.6	11.7	13.1	14.9	17.3	20.7	19
20	5.4	5.7	6.0	6.3	6.7	7.1	7.6	8.1	8.8	9.5	10.5	11.6	13.0	14.8	17.1	20
21	5.1	5.4	5.6	5.9	6.3	6.6	7.0	7.5	8.1	8.7	9.5	10.4	11.5	12.8	14.6	21
22	4.9	5.1	5.3	5.6	5.9	6.2	6.6	7.0	7.5	8.0	8.6	9.4	10.3	11.3	12.7	22
23	4.6	4.8	5.0	5.3	5.5	5.8	6.1	6.5	6.9	7.4	7.9	8.5	9.3	10.1	11.2	23
24	4.4	4.6	4.8	5.0	5.2	5.5	5.8	6.1	6.4	6.8	7.3	7.8	8.4	9.2	10.0	24
25	4.2	4.4	4.6	4.7	5.0	5.2	5.4	5.7	6.0	6.4	6.8	7.2	7.7	8.3	9.0	25
26	4.0	4.2	4.3	4.5	4.7	4.9	5.1	5.4	5.7	6.0	6.3	6.7	7.1	7.6	8.2	26
27	3.9	4.0	4.1	4.3	4.5	4.7	4.9	5.1	5.3	5.6	5.9	6.2	6.6	7.0	7.5	27
28	3.7	3.8	4.0	4.1	4.3	4.4	4.6	4.8	5.0	5.3	5.5	5.8	6.2	6.5	7.0	28
29	3.5	3.7	3.8	3.9	4.1	4.2	4.4	4.6	4.7	5.0	5.2	5.5	5.7	6.1	6.4	29
30	3.4	3.5	3.6	3.7	3.9	4.0	4.2	4.3	4.5	4.7	4.9	5.1	5.4	5.7	6.0	30
31	3.3	3.4	3.5	3.6	3.7	3.8	4.0	4.1	4.3	4.4	4.6	4.8	5.1	5.3	5.6	31
32	3.1	3.2	3.3	3.4	3.5	3.7	3.8	3.9	4.1	4.2	4.4	4.6	4.8	5.0	5.2	32
33	3.0	3.1	3.2	3.3	3.4	3.5	3.6	3.7	3.9	4.0	4.2	4.3	4.5	4.7	4.9	33
34	2.9	3.0	3.1	3.2	3.2	3.3	3.4	3.6	3.7	3.8	3.9	4.1	4.3	4.4	4.6	34
35	2.8	2.9	3.0	3.0	3.1	3.2	3.3	3.4	3.5	3.6	3.7	3.9	4.0	4.2	4.4	35
36	2.7	2.8	2.8	2.9	3.0	3.1	3.2	3.3	3.4	3.5	3.6	3.7	3.8	4.0	4.1	36
37	2.6	2.7	2.7	2.8	2.9	2.9	3.0	3.1	3.2	3.3	3.4	3.5	3.6	3.8	3.9	37
38	2.5	2.6	2.6	2.7	2.8	2.8	2.9	3.0	3.0	3.2	3.2	3.3	3.4	3.6	3.7	38
39	2.4	2.5	2.5	2.6	2.7	2.7	2.8	2.9	2.9	3.0	3.1	3.2	3.3	3.4	3.5	39
40	2.3	2.4	2.4	2.5	2.6	2.6	2.7	2.7	2.8	2.9	3.0	3.0	3.1	3.2	3.3	40
41	2.3	2.3	2.4	2.4	2.5	2.5	2.6	2.6	2.7	2.8	2.8	2.9	3.0	3.1	3.2	41
42	2.2	2.2	2.3	2.3	2.4	2.4	2.5	2.5	2.6	2.6	2.7	2.8	2.9	2.9	3.0	42
43	2.1	2.1	2.2	2.2	2.3	2.3	2.4	2.4	2.5	2.5	2.6	2.7	2.7	2.8	2.9	43
44	2.0	2.1	2.1	2.1	2.2	2.2	2.3	2.3	2.4	2.4	2.5	2.5	2.6	2.7	2.7	44
45	2.0	2.0	2.0	2.1	2.1	2.2	2.2	2.2	2.3	2.3	2.4	2.4	2.5	2.6	2.6	45
46	1.9	1.9	2.0	2.0	2.0	2.1	2.1	2.2	2.2	2.2	2.3	2.3	2.4	2.4	2.5	46
47	1.8	1.9	1.9	1.9	2.0	2.0	2.0	2.1	2.1	2.1	2.2	2.2	2.3	2.3	2.4	47
48	1.8	1.8	1.8	1.9	1.9	1.9	2.0	2.0	2.0	2.1	2.1	2.1	2.2	2.2	2.3	48
49	1.7	1.7	1.8	1.8	1.8	1.8	1.9	1.9	1.9	2.0	2.0	2.1	2.1	2.1	2.2	49
50	1.6	1.7	1.7	1.7	1.8	1.8	1.8	1.8	1.9	1.9	1.9	2.0	2.0	2.0	2.1	50
51	1.6	1.6	1.6	1.7	1.7	1.7	1.7	1.8	1.8	1.8	1.9	1.9	1.9	2.0	2.0	51
52	1.5	1.6	1.6	1.6	1.6	1.6	1.7	1.7	1.7	1.8	1.8	1.8	1.8	1.9	1.9	52
53	1.5	1.5	1.5	1.5	1.6	1.6	1.6	1.6	1.7	1.7	1.7	1.7	1.8	1.8	1.8	53
54	1.4	1.4	1.5	1.5	1.5	1.5	1.5	1.6	1.6	1.6	1.6	1.7	1.7	1.7	1.7	54
55	1.4	1.4	1.4	1.4	1.5	1.5	1.5	1.5	1.5	1.6	1.6	1.6	1.6	1.6	1.7	55
56	1.3	1.3	1.4	1.4	1.4	1.4	1.4	1.4	1.5	1.5	1.5	1.5	1.5	1.6	1.6	56
57	1.3	1.3	1.3	1.3	1.3	1.4	1.4	1.4	1.4	1.4	1.4	1.5	1.5	1.5	1.5	57
58	1.2	1.2	1.3	1.3	1.3	1.3	1.3	1.3	1.3	1.4	1.4	1.4	1.4	1.4	1.5	58
59	1.2	1.2	1.2	1.2	1.2	1.3	1.3	1.3	1.3	1.3	1.3	1.3	1.4	1.4	1.4	59
60	1.1	1.1	1.2	1.2	1.2	1.2	1.2	1.2	1.2	1.2	1.3	1.3	1.3	1.3	1.3	60

EX-MERIDIAN TABLE I
Latitude and Declination SAME NAME
Change of Altitude in one minute from Meridian Passage = A

Lat.°	15°	16°	17°	18°	19°	20°	21°	22°	23°	24°	25°	26°	27°	28°	29°	30°	Lat.°
0	7.3	6.8	6.4	6.0	5.7	5.4	5.1	4.9	4.6	4.4	4.2	4.0	3.9	3.7	3.5	3.4	0
1	7.8	7.3	6.8	6.4	6.0	5.7	5.4	5.1	4.8	4.6	4.4	4.2	4.0	3.8	3.7	3.5	1
2	8.4	7.8	7.2	6.8	6.3	6.0	5.6	5.3	5.0	4.8	4.6	4.3	4.1	4.0	3.8	3.6	2
3	9.1	8.4	7.8	7.2	6.7	6.3	5.9	5.6	5.3	5.0	4.7	4.5	4.3	4.1	3.9	3.7	3
4	9.9	9.1	8.3	7.7	7.2	6.7	6.3	5.9	5.5	5.2	5.0	4.7	4.5	4.3	4.1	3.9	4
5	10.9	9.8	9.0	8.3	7.6	7.1	6.6	6.2	5.8	5.5	5.2	4.9	4.7	4.4	4.2	4.0	5
6	12.1	10.8	9.8	8.9	8.2	7.6	7.0	6.6	6.1	5.8	5.4	5.1	4.9	4.6	4.4	4.2	6
7	13.5	12.0	10.7	9.7	8.9	8.1	7.5	7.0	6.5	6.1	5.7	5.4	5.1	4.8	4.6	4.3	7
8	15.4	13.4	11.9	10.6	9.6	8.8	8.1	7.5	6.9	6.4	6.0	5.7	5.3	5.0	4.8	4.5	8
9	17.9	15.3	13.3	11.8	10.6	9.5	8.7	8.0	7.4	6.8	6.4	6.0	5.6	5.3	5.0	4.7	9
10	21.4	17.8	15.2	13.2	11.7	10.5	9.5	8.6	7.9	7.3	6.8	6.3	5.9	5.5	5.2	4.9	10
11	26.7	21.3	17.6	15.0	13.1	11.6	10.4	9.4	8.5	7.8	7.2	6.7	6.2	5.8	5.5	5.1	11
12		26.5	21.1	17.5	14.9	13.0	11.5	10.3	9.3	8.4	7.7	7.1	6.6	6.2	5.8	5.4	12
13			26.2	20.9	17.3	14.8	12.8	11.3	10.1	9.2	8.3	7.6	7.1	6.5	6.1	5.7	13
14				26.0	20.7	17.1	14.6	12.7	11.2	10.0	9.1	8.2	7.6	7.0	6.4	6.0	14
15					25.7	20.4	16.9	14.4	12.5	11.1	9.9	8.9	8.1	7.4	6.9	6.4	15
16						25.4	20.2	16.7	14.3	12.4	10.9	9.8	8.8	8.0	7.3	6.8	16
17							25.1	20.0	16.5	14.1	12.2	10.8	9.6	8.7	7.9	7.2	17
18								24.8	19.7	16.3	13.9	12.1	10.6	9.5	8.6	7.8	18
19	25.7								24.5	19.5	16.1	13.7	11.9	10.5	9.4	8.4	19
20	20.4	25.4								24.2	19.2	15.9	13.5	11.7	10.3	9.2	20
21	16.9	20.2	25.1								23.8	18.9	15.6	13.3	11.5	10.2	21
22	14.4	16.7	20.0	24.8								23.5	18.6	15.4	13.1	11.3	22
23	12.5	14.3	16.5	19.7	24.5								23.1	18.3	15.1	12.8	23
24	11.1	12.4	14.1	16.3	19.5	24.2								22.7	18.0	14.9	24
25	9.9	10.9	12.2	13.9	16.1	19.2	23.8								22.3	17.7	25
26	8.9	9.8	10.8	12.1	13.7	15.9	18.9	23.5								21.9	26
27	8.1	8.8	9.6	10.6	11.9	13.5	15.6	18.6	23.1								27
28	7.4	8.0	8.7	9.5	10.5	11.7	13.3	15.4	18.3	22.7							28
29	6.9	7.3	7.9	8.6	9.4	10.3	11.5	13.1	15.1	18.0	22.3						29
30	6.4	6.8	7.2	7.8	8.4	9.2	10.1	11.3	12.8	14.9	17.7	21.9					30
31	5.9	6.3	6.7	7.1	7.7	8.3	9.0	10.0	11.1	12.6	14.6	17.4	21.5				31
32	5.5	5.8	6.2	6.5	7.0	7.5	8.1	8.9	9.8	10.9	12.4	14.3	17.0	21.1			32
33	5.1	5.4	5.7	6.1	6.4	6.9	7.4	8.0	8.7	9.6	10.7	12.1	14.0	16.7	20.6		33
34	4.8	5.1	5.3	5.6	5.9	6.3	6.8	7.3	7.8	8.6	9.4	10.5	11.9	13.8	16.3	20.2	34
35	4.5	4.7	5.0	5.2	5.5	5.8	6.2	6.6	7.1	7.7	8.4	9.2	10.3	11.7	13.5	16.0	35
36	4.3	4.5	4.7	4.9	5.1	5.4	5.7	6.1	6.5	7.0	7.5	8.2	9.1	10.1	11.4	13.2	36
37	4.0	4.2	4.4	4.6	4.8	5.0	5.3	5.6	6.0	6.4	6.8	7.4	8.1	8.9	9.9	11.1	37
38	3.8	4.0	4.1	4.3	4.5	4.7	4.9	5.2	5.5	5.8	6.2	6.7	7.2	7.9	8.7	9.6	38
39	3.6	3.8	3.9	4.0	4.2	4.4	4.6	4.8	5.1	5.4	5.7	6.1	6.5	7.1	7.7	8.5	39
40	3.4	3.6	3.7	3.8	4.0	4.1	4.3	4.5	4.7	5.0	5.3	5.6	6.0	6.4	6.9	7.5	40
41	3.3	3.4	3.5	3.6	3.7	3.9	4.0	4.2	4.4	4.6	4.9	5.2	5.5	5.8	6.2	6.7	41
42	3.1	3.2	3.3	3.4	3.5	3.7	3.8	4.0	4.1	4.3	4.5	4.8	5.0	5.3	5.7	6.1	42
43	3.0	3.0	3.1	3.2	3.3	3.5	3.6	3.7	3.9	4.0	4.2	4.4	4.6	4.9	5.2	5.5	43
44	2.8	2.9	3.0	3.1	3.2	3.3	3.4	3.5	3.6	3.8	3.9	4.1	4.3	4.5	4.8	5.1	44
45	2.7	2.8	2.8	2.9	3.0	3.1	3.2	3.3	3.4	3.5	3.7	3.8	4.0	4.2	4.4	4.7	45
46	2.6	2.6	2.7	2.8	2.8	2.9	3.0	3.1	3.2	3.3	3.5	3.6	3.7	3.9	4.1	4.3	46
47	2.4	2.5	2.6	2.6	2.7	2.8	2.9	2.9	3.0	3.1	3.3	3.4	3.5	3.6	3.8	4.0	47
48	2.3	2.4	2.4	2.5	2.6	2.6	2.7	2.8	2.9	3.0	3.1	3.2	3.3	3.4	3.5	3.7	48
49	2.2	2.3	2.3	2.4	2.4	2.5	2.6	2.6	2.7	2.8	2.9	3.0	3.1	3.2	3.3	3.4	49
50	2.1	2.2	2.2	2.3	2.3	2.4	2.4	2.5	2.6	2.6	2.7	2.8	2.9	3.0	3.1	3.2	50
51	2.0	2.1	2.1	2.2	2.2	2.3	2.3	2.4	2.4	2.5	2.6	2.6	2.7	2.8	2.9	3.0	51
52	1.9	2.0	2.0	2.1	2.1	2.1	2.2	2.2	2.3	2.4	2.4	2.5	2.6	2.6	2.7	2.8	52
53	1.9	1.9	1.9	2.0	2.0	2.0	2.1	2.1	2.2	2.2	2.3	2.3	2.4	2.5	2.5	2.6	53
54	1.8	1.8	1.8	1.9	1.9	1.9	2.0	2.0	2.1	2.1	2.2	2.2	2.3	2.3	2.4	2.5	54
55	1.7	1.7	1.8	1.8	1.8	1.9	1.9	1.9	2.0	2.0	2.0	2.1	2.1	2.2	2.3	2.3	55
56	1.6	1.6	1.7	1.7	1.7	1.8	1.8	1.8	1.9	1.9	1.9	2.0	2.0	2.1	2.1	2.2	56
57	1.5	1.6	1.6	1.6	1.6	1.7	1.7	1.7	1.8	1.8	1.8	1.9	1.9	2.0	2.0	2.0	57
58	1.5	1.5	1.5	1.5	1.6	1.6	1.6	1.6	1.7	1.7	1.7	1.8	1.8	1.8	1.9	1.9	58
59	1.4	1.4	1.5	1.5	1.5	1.5	1.5	1.6	1.6	1.6	1.6	1.7	1.7	1.7	1.8	1.8	59
60	1.3	1.4	1.4	1.4	1.4	1.4	1.5	1.5	1.5	1.5	1.6	1.6	1.6	1.6	1.7	1.7	60

EX-MERIDIAN TABLE I
Latitude and Declination SAME NAME
Change of Altitude in one minute from Meridian Passage = A

Lat.°	31°	32°	33°	34°	35°	36°	37°	38°	39°	40°	41°	42°	43°	44°	45°	46°	Lat.°
0	3.3	3.1	3.0	2.9	2.8	2.7	2.6	2.5	2.4	2.3	2.3	2.2	2.1	2.0	2.0	1.9	0
1	3.4	3.2	3.1	3.0	2.9	2.8	2.7	2.6	2.5	2.4	2.3	2.2	2.2	2.1	2.0	1.9	1
2	3.5	3.3	3.2	3.1	3.0	2.8	2.7	2.6	2.5	2.4	2.4	2.3	2.2	2.1	2.0	2.0	2
3	3.6	3.4	3.3	3.2	3.0	2.9	2.8	2.7	2.6	2.5	2.4	2.3	2.2	2.2	2.1	2.0	3
4	3.7	3.5	3.4	3.3	3.1	3.0	2.9	2.8	2.7	2.6	2.5	2.4	2.3	2.2	2.1	2.0	4
5	3.3	3.7	3.5	3.3	3.2	3.1	3.0	2.8	2.7	2.6	2.5	2.4	2.3	2.2	2.2	2.1	5
6	4.0	3.8	3.6	3.5	3.3	3.2	3.0	2.9	2.8	2.7	2.6	2.5	2.4	2.3	2.2	2.1	6
7	4.1	3.9	3.7	3.6	3.4	3.3	3.1	3.0	2.9	2.7	2.6	2.5	2.4	2.3	2.2	2.2	7
8	4.3	4.1	3.9	3.7	3.5	3.4	3.2	3.1	2.9	2.8	2.7	2.6	2.5	2.4	2.3	2.2	8
9	4.4	4.2	4.0	3.8	3.6	3.5	3.3	3.2	3.0	2.9	2.8	2.7	2.5	2.4	2.3	2.2	9
10	4.6	4.4	4.2	3.9	3.8	3.6	3.4	3.3	3.1	3.0	2.8	2.7	2.6	2.5	2.4	2.3	10
11	4.8	4.6	4.3	4.1	3.9	3.7	3.5	3.4	3.2	3.1	2.9	2.8	2.7	2.6	2.4	2.3	11
12	5.1	4.8	4.5	4.3	4.0	3.8	3.6	3.5	3.3	3.1	3.0	2.9	2.7	2.6	2.5	2.4	12
13	5.3	5.0	4.7	4.4	4.2	4.0	3.8	3.6	3.4	3.2	3.1	2.9	2.8	2.7	2.6	2.4	13
14	5.6	5.2	4.9	4.6	4.4	4.1	3.9	3.7	3.5	3.3	3.2	3.0	2.9	2.7	2.6	2.5	14
15	5.9	5.5	5.2	4.8	4.5	4.3	4.0	3.8	3.6	3.4	3.3	3.1	3.0	2.8	2.7	2.6	15
16	6.3	5.8	5.4	5.1	4.8	4.5	4.2	4.0	3.8	3.6	3.4	3.2	3.0	2.9	2.8	2.6	16
17	6.7	6.2	5.7	5.3	5.0	4.7	4.4	4.1	3.9	3.7	3.5	3.3	3.1	3.0	2.8	2.7	17
18	7.1	6.6	6.1	5.6	5.2	4.9	4.6	4.3	4.1	3.8	3.6	3.4	3.2	3.1	2.9	2.8	18
19	7.7	7.0	6.4	6.0	5.5	5.1	4.8	4.5	4.2	4.0	3.7	3.5	3.3	3.2	3.0	2.8	19
20	8.3	7.5	6.9	6.3	5.8	5.4	5.0	4.7	4.4	4.1	3.9	3.7	3.5	3.3	3.1	2.9	20
21	9.1	8.2	7.4	6.8	6.2	5.7	5.3	4.9	4.6	4.3	4.0	3.8	3.6	3.4	3.2	3.0	21
22	10.0	8.9	8.0	7.3	6.6	6.1	5.6	5.2	4.8	4.5	4.2	4.0	3.7	3.5	3.3	3.1	22
23	11.1	9.8	8.7	7.9	7.1	6.5	6.0	5.5	5.1	4.7	4.4	4.1	3.9	3.6	3.4	3.2	23
24	12.6	10.9	9.6	8.6	7.7	7.0	6.4	5.8	5.4	5.0	4.6	4.3	4.0	3.8	3.5	3.3	24
25	14.6	12.4	10.7	9.4	8.4	7.5	6.8	6.2	5.7	5.3	4.9	4.5	4.2	3.9	3.7	3.5	25
26	17.4	14.3	12.1	10.5	9.2	8.2	7.4	6.7	6.1	5.6	5.2	4.8	4.4	4.1	3.8	3.6	26
27	21.5	17.0	14.0	11.9	10.3	9.1	8.1	7.2	6.5	6.0	5.5	5.0	4.6	4.3	4.0	3.7	27
28		21.1	16.7	13.8	11.7	10.1	8.9	7.9	7.1	6.4	5.8	5.3	4.9	4.5	4.2	3.9	28
29			20.6	16.3	13.5	11.4	9.9	8.7	7.7	6.9	6.2	5.7	5.2	4.8	4.4	4.1	29
30				20.2	16.0	13.2	11.1	9.6	8.5	7.5	6.7	6.1	5.5	5.1	4.7	4.3	30
31					19.8	15.6	12.9	10.9	9.4	8.2	7.3	6.6	5.9	5.4	4.9	4.5	31
32						19.3	15.3	12.6	10.6	9.2	8.0	7.1	6.4	5.8	5.2	4.8	32
33							18.9	14.9	12.2	10.4	8.9	7.8	6.9	6.2	5.6	5.1	33
34								18.4	14.5	11.9	10.1	8.7	7.6	6.7	6.0	5.4	34
35	19.8								17.9	14.1	11.6	9.8	8.5	7.4	6.6	5.9	35
36	15.6	19.3								17.4	13.8	11.3	9.5	8.2	7.2	6.4	36
37	12.9	15.3	18.9								17.0	13.4	11.0	9.3	8.0	7.0	37
38	10.9	12.6	14.9	18.4								16.5	13.0	10.7	9.0	7.7	38
39	9.4	10.6	12.2	14.5	17.9								16.0	12.6	10.3	8.7	39
40	8.2	9.2	10.4	11.9	14.1	17.4								15.5	12.2	10.0	40
41	7.3	8.0	8.9	10.1	11.6	13.8	17.0								15.0	11.8	41
42	6.6	7.1	7.8	8.7	9.8	11.3	13.4	16.5								14.5	42
43	5.9	6.4	6.9	7.6	8.5	9.5	11.0	13.0	16.0								43
44	5.4	5.8	6.2	6.7	7.4	8.2	9.3	10.7	12.6	15.5							44
45	4.9	5.2	5.6	6.0	6.6	7.2	8.0	9.0	10.3	12.2	15.0						45
46	4.5	4.8	5.1	5.4	5.9	6.4	7.0	7.7	8.7	10.0	11.8	14.5					46
47	4.2	4.4	4.6	4.9	5.3	5.7	6.2	6.8	7.5	8.4	9.7	11.4	14.0				47
48	3.9	4.0	4.3	4.5	4.8	5.1	5.5	6.0	6.5	7.2	8.1	9.3	11.0	13.6			48
49	3.6	3.7	3.9	4.1	4.4	4.6	5.0	5.3	5.8	6.3	7.0	7.9	9.0	10.6	13.1		49
50	3.3	3.5	3.6	3.8	4.0	4.2	4.5	4.8	5.1	5.6	6.1	6.7	7.6	8.7	10.2	12.6	50
51	3.1	3.2	3.4	3.5	3.7	3.9	4.1	4.3	4.6	5.0	5.4	5.9	6.5	7.3	8.4	9.9	51
52	2.9	3.0	3.1	3.2	3.4	3.6	3.7	3.9	4.2	4.5	4.8	5.2	5.7	6.3	7.0	8.0	52
53	2.7	2.8	2.9	3.0	3.1	3.3	3.4	3.6	3.8	4.0	4.3	4.6	5.0	5.4	6.0	6.7	53
54	2.5	2.6	2.7	2.8	2.9	3.0	3.2	3.3	3.5	3.7	3.9	4.1	4.4	4.8	5.2	5.8	54
55	2.4	2.4	2.5	2.6	2.7	2.8	2.9	3.0	3.2	3.3	3.5	3.7	4.0	4.3	4.6	5.0	55
56	2.2	2.3	2.4	2.4	2.5	2.6	2.7	2.8	2.9	3.1	3.2	3.4	3.6	3.8	4.1	4.4	56
57	2.1	2.2	2.2	2.3	2.3	2.4	2.5	2.6	2.7	2.8	2.9	3.1	3.2	3.4	3.6	3.9	57
58	2.0	2.0	2.1	2.1	2.2	2.3	2.3	2.4	2.5	2.6	2.7	2.8	2.9	3.1	3.3	3.5	58
59	1.9	1.9	1.9	2.0	2.0	2.1	2.2	2.2	2.3	2.4	2.5	2.6	2.7	2.8	3.0	3.1	59
60	1.7	1.8	1.8	1.9	1.9	2.0	2.0	2.1	2.1	2.2	2.3	2.4	2.5	2.6	2.7	2.8	60

EX-MERIDIAN TABLE I

Latitude and Declination SAME NAME

Change of Altitude in one minute from Meridian Passage = A

Lat. °	47°	48°	49°	50°	51°	52°	53°	54°	55°	56°	57°	58°	59°	60°	61°	62°	63°	Lat. °
0	1.8	1.8	1.7	1.7	1.6	1.5	1.5	1.4	1.4	1.3	1.3	1.2	1.2	1.1	1.1	1.0	1.0	0
1	1.9	1.8	1.7	1.7	1.6	1.6	1.5	1.4	1.4	1.3	1.3	1.2	1.2	1.2	1.1	1.1	1.0	1
2	1.9	1.8	1.8	1.7	1.6	1.6	1.5	1.5	1.4	1.4	1.3	1.3	1.2	1.2	1.1	1.1	1.0	2
3	1.9	1.9	1.8	1.7	1.7	1.6	1.5	1.5	1.4	1.4	1.3	1.3	1.2	1.2	1.1	1.1	1.0	3
4	2.0	1.9	1.8	1.8	1.7	1.6	1.6	1.5	1.5	1.4	1.3	1.3	1.2	1.2	1.1	1.1	1.0	4
5	2.0	1.9	1.9	1.8	1.7	1.7	1.6	1.5	1.5	1.4	1.4	1.3	1.3	1.2	1.1	1.1	1.1	5
6	2.0	2.0	1.9	1.8	1.7	1.7	1.6	1.5	1.5	1.4	1.4	1.3	1.3	1.2	1.2	1.1	1.1	6
7	2.1	2.0	1.9	1.8	1.8	1.7	1.6	1.6	1.5	1.4	1.4	1.3	1.3	1.2	1.2	1.1	1.1	7
8	2.1	2.0	1.9	1.9	1.8	1.7	1.7	1.6	1.5	1.5	1.4	1.4	1.3	1.2	1.2	1.1	1.1	8
9	2.2	2.1	2.0	1.9	1.8	1.8	1.7	1.6	1.6	1.5	1.4	1.4	1.3	1.3	1.2	1.1	1.1	9
10	2.2	2.1	2.0	1.9	1.9	1.8	1.7	1.6	1.6	1.5	1.4	1.4	1.3	1.3	1.2	1.2	1.1	10
11	2.2	2.1	2.1	2.0	1.9	1.8	1.7	1.7	1.6	1.5	1.5	1.4	1.3	1.3	1.2	1.2	1.1	11
12	2.3	2.2	2.1	2.0	1.9	1.8	1.8	1.7	1.6	1.6	1.5	1.4	1.4	1.3	1.2	1.2	1.1	12
13	2.3	2.2	2.1	2.0	2.0	1.9	1.8	1.7	1.6	1.6	1.5	1.4	1.4	1.3	1.3	1.2	1.1	13
14	2.4	2.3	2.2	2.1	2.0	1.9	1.8	1.7	1.7	1.6	1.5	1.5	1.4	1.3	1.3	1.2	1.2	14
15	2.4	2.3	2.2	2.1	2.0	1.9	1.9	1.8	1.7	1.6	1.5	1.5	1.4	1.3	1.3	1.2	1.2	15
16	2.5	2.4	2.3	2.2	2.1	2.0	1.9	1.8	1.7	1.6	1.6	1.5	1.4	1.4	1.3	1.2	1.2	16
17	2.6	2.4	2.3	2.2	2.1	2.0	1.9	1.8	1.8	1.7	1.6	1.5	1.5	1.4	1.3	1.3	1.2	17
18	2.6	2.5	2.4	2.3	2.2	2.1	2.0	1.9	1.8	1.7	1.6	1.5	1.5	1.4	1.3	1.3	1.2	18
19	2.7	2.6	2.4	2.3	2.2	2.1	2.0	1.9	1.8	1.7	1.6	1.6	1.5	1.4	1.4	1.3	1.2	19
20	2.8	2.6	2.5	2.4	2.3	2.1	2.0	1.9	1.9	1.8	1.7	1.6	1.5	1.4	1.4	1.3	1.2	20
21	2.9	2.7	2.6	2.4	2.3	2.2	2.1	2.0	1.9	1.8	1.7	1.6	1.5	1.5	1.4	1.3	1.2	21
22	2.9	2.8	2.6	2.5	2.4	2.2	2.1	2.0	1.9	1.8	1.7	1.6	1.6	1.5	1.4	1.3	1.3	22
23	3.0	2.9	2.7	2.6	2.4	2.3	2.2	2.1	2.0	1.9	1.8	1.7	1.6	1.5	1.4	1.4	1.3	23
24	3.1	3.0	2.8	2.6	2.5	2.4	2.2	2.1	2.0	1.9	1.8	1.7	1.6	1.5	1.5	1.4	1.3	24
25	3.3	3.1	2.9	2.7	2.6	2.4	2.3	2.2	2.0	1.9	1.8	1.7	1.6	1.6	1.5	1.4	1.3	25
26	3.4	3.2	3.0	2.8	2.6	2.5	2.3	2.2	2.1	2.0	1.9	1.8	1.7	1.6	1.5	1.4	1.3	26
27	3.5	3.3	3.1	2.9	2.7	2.6	2.4	2.3	2.1	2.0	1.9	1.8	1.7	1.6	1.5	1.4	1.4	27
28	3.6	3.4	3.2	3.0	2.8	2.6	2.5	2.3	2.2	2.1	2.0	1.8	1.7	1.6	1.5	1.5	1.4	28
29	3.8	3.5	3.3	3.1	2.9	2.7	2.5	2.4	2.3	2.1	2.0	1.9	1.8	1.7	1.6	1.5	1.4	29
30	4.0	3.7	3.4	3.2	3.0	2.8	2.6	2.5	2.3	2.2	2.0	1.9	1.8	1.7	1.6	1.5	1.4	30
31	4.2	3.9	3.6	3.3	3.1	2.9	2.7	2.5	2.4	2.2	2.1	2.0	1.9	1.7	1.6	1.5	1.4	31
32	4.4	4.0	3.7	3.5	3.2	3.0	2.8	2.6	2.4	2.3	2.2	2.0	1.9	1.8	1.7	1.6	1.5	32
33	4.6	4.3	3.9	3.6	3.4	3.1	2.9	2.7	2.5	2.4	2.2	2.1	1.9	1.8	1.7	1.6	1.5	33
34	4.9	4.5	4.1	3.8	3.5	3.2	3.0	2.8	2.6	2.4	2.3	2.1	2.0	1.9	1.7	1.6	1.5	34
35	5.3	4.8	4.4	4.0	3.7	3.4	3.1	2.9	2.7	2.5	2.3	2.2	2.0	1.9	1.8	1.7	1.6	35
36	5.7	5.1	4.6	4.2	3.9	3.6	3.3	3.0	2.8	2.6	2.4	2.3	2.1	2.0	1.8	1.7	1.6	36
37	6.2	5.5	5.0	4.5	4.1	3.7	3.4	3.2	2.9	2.7	2.5	2.3	2.2	2.0	1.9	1.7	1.6	37
38	6.8	6.0	5.3	4.8	4.3	3.9	3.6	3.3	3.0	2.8	2.6	2.4	2.2	2.1	1.9	1.8	1.7	38
39	7.5	6.5	5.8	5.1	4.6	4.2	3.8	3.5	3.2	2.9	2.7	2.5	2.3	2.1	2.0	1.8	1.7	39
40	8.4	7.2	6.3	5.6	5.0	4.5	4.0	3.7	3.3	3.1	2.8	2.6	2.4	2.2	2.0	1.9	1.8	40
41	9.7	8.1	7.0	6.1	5.4	4.8	4.3	3.9	3.5	3.2	2.9	2.7	2.5	2.3	2.1	1.9	1.8	41
42	11.4	9.3	7.9	6.7	5.9	5.2	4.6	4.1	3.7	3.4	3.1	2.8	2.6	2.4	2.2	2.0	1.9	42
43	14.0	11.0	9.0	7.6	6.5	5.7	5.0	4.4	4.0	3.6	3.2	2.9	2.7	2.5	2.3	2.1	1.9	43
44		13.6	10.6	8.7	7.3	6.3	5.4	4.8	4.3	3.8	3.4	3.1	2.8	2.6	2.3	2.2	2.0	44
45			13.1	10.2	8.4	7.0	6.0	5.2	4.6	4.1	3.6	3.3	3.0	2.7	2.4	2.2	2.0	45
46				12.6	9.9	8.0	6.7	5.8	5.0	4.4	3.9	3.5	3.1	2.8	2.6	2.3	2.1	46
47					12.1	9.5	7.7	6.5	5.5	4.8	4.2	3.7	3.3	3.0	2.7	2.4	2.2	47
48						11.6	9.1	7.4	6.2	5.3	4.6	4.0	3.6	3.2	2.8	2.6	2.3	48
49							11.1	8.7	7.1	5.9	5.0	4.4	3.8	3.4	3.0	2.7	2.4	49
50								10.6	8.3	6.8	5.6	4.8	4.2	3.6	3.2	2.9	2.6	50
51	12.1								10.2	7.0	6.4	5.4	4.6	4.0	3.5	3.0	2.7	51
52	9.5	11.6								9.7	7.6	6.1	5.1	4.3	3.8	3.3	2.9	52
53	7.7	9.1	11.1								9.2	7.2	5.9	4.9	4.1	3.6	3.1	53
54	6.5	7.4	8.7	10.6								8.8	6.8	5.5	4.6	3.9	3.4	54
55	5.5	6.2	7.1	8.3	10.2								8.3	6.5	5.3	4.3	3.7	55
56	4.8	5.3	5.9	6.8	7.9	9.7								7.9	6.1	5.0	4.1	56
57	4.2	4.6	5.0	5.6	6.4	7.6	9.2								7.4	5.8	4.7	57
58	3.7	4.0	4.4	4.8	5.4	6.1	7.2	8.8								7.0	5.4	58
59	3.3	3.6	3.8	4.2	4.6	5.1	5.9	6.8	8.3								6.6	59
60	3.0	3.2	3.4	3.6	4.0	4.3	4.9	5.5	6.5	7.9								60

EX-MERIDIAN TABLE I

Supplementary Table to 83°

Latitude and Declination SAME NAME

Change of Altitude in one minute from Meridian Passage = A

DECLINATION

Lat.	0°	1°	2°	3°	4°	5°	6°	7°	8°	9°	10°	11°	12°	13°	14°	Lat.
60	1·13	1·15	1·16	1·17	1·18	1·19	1·21	1·22	1·23	1·25	1·26	1·28	1·29	1·31	1·33	60
61	1·09	1·10	1·11	1·12	1·13	1·14	1·16	1·17	1·18	1·20	1·21	1·22	1·23	1·25	1·26	61
62	1·04	1·05	1·06	1·07	1·08	1·09	1·11	1·12	1·13	1·14	1·15	1·16	1·17	1·19	1·20	62
63	1·00	1·01	1·02	1·03	1·04	1·05	1·06	1·07	1·08	1·09	1·10	1·11	1·12	1·13	1·14	63
64	0·96	0·97	0·97	0·98	0·99	1·00	1·01	1·02	1·03	1·04	1·05	1·06	1·07	1·08	1·09	64
65	0·92	0·92	0·93	0·94	0·94	0·95	0·96	0·97	0·98	0·99	1·00	1·01	1·02	1·03	1·04	65
66	0·87	0·88	0·89	0·89	0·90	0·91	0·92	0·92	0·93	0·94	0·95	0·96	0·97	0·97	0·98	66
67	0·83	0·84	0·85	0·85	0·86	0·86	0·87	0·88	0·89	0·90	0·90	0·91	0·92	0·92	0·93	67
68	0·79	0·80	0·80	0·81	0·81	0·82	0·83	0·83	0·84	0·85	0·85	0·86	0·87	0·88	0·88	68
69	0·75	0·76	0·76	0·77	0·77	0·78	0·79	0·79	0·80	0·80	0·81	0·81	0·82	0·83	0·83	69
70	0·71	0·72	0·72	0·73	0·73	0·74	0·74	0·74	0·75	0·75	0·76	0·76	0·77	0·78	0·78	70
71	0·67	0·68	0·68	0·69	0·69	0·70	0·70	0·71	0·71	0·71	0·72	0·72	0·73	0·73	0·74	71
72	0·64	0·64	0·64	0·65	0·65	0·66	0·66	0·66	0·67	0·67	0·68	0·68	0·68	0·68	0·69	72
73	0·60	0·60	0·61	0·61	0·61	0·62	0·62	0·62	0·63	0·63	0·63	0·64	0·64	0·64	0·65	73
74	0·56	0·56	0·57	0·57	0·57	0·58	0·58	0·58	0·59	0·59	0·59	0·60	0·60	0·60	0·60	74
75	0·52	0·53	0·53	0·53	0·54	0·54	0·54	0·54	0·55	0·55	0·55	0·55	0·56	0·56	0·56	75
76	0·49	0·49	0·49	0·50	0·50	0·50	0·50	0·51	0·51	0·51	0·51	0·51	0·52	0·52	0·52	76
77	0·45	0·45	0·46	0·46	0·46	0·46	0·46	0·47	0·47	0·47	0·47	0·47	0·48	0·48	0·48	77
78	0·42	0·42	0·42	0·42	0·42	0·43	0·43	0·43	0·43	0·43	0·43	0·43	0·44	0·44	0·44	78
79	0·38	0·38	0·38	0·39	0·39	0·39	0·39	0·39	0·39	0·39	0·39	0·40	0·40	0·40	0·40	79
80	0·35	0·35	0·35	0·35	0·35	0·35	0·36	0·36	0·36	0·36	0·36	0·36	0·36	0·36	0·36	80
81	0·31	0·31	0·31	0·31	0·31	0·32	0·32	0·32	0·32	0·32	0·32	0·32	0·32	0·32	0·32	81
82	0·28	0·28	0·28	0·28	0·28	0·28	0·28	0·28	0·28	0·28	0·28	0·28	0·28	0·29	0·29	82
83	0·24	0·24	0·24	0·24	0·24	0·24	0·24	0·24	0·25	0·25	0·25	0·25	0·25	0·25	0·25	83
	0°	1°	2°	3°	4°	5°	6°	7°	8°	9°	10°	11°	12°	13°	14°	

DECLINATION

DECLINATION

Lat.	15°	16°	17°	18°	19°	20°	21°	22°	23°	24°	25°	26°	27°	28°	29°	30°	Lat.
60	1·34	1·36	1·38	1·40	1·42	1·44	1·46	1·48	1·50	1·53	1·55	1·58	1·61	1·64	1·67	1·70	60
61	1·28	1·29	1·31	1·33	1·35	1·36	1·38	1·40	1·43	1·45	1·47	1·49	1·52	1·54	1·57	1·60	61
62	1·21	1·23	1·25	1·26	1·28	1·29	1·31	1·33	1·35	1·36	1·38	1·40	1·43	1·46	1·48	1·51	62
63	1·16	1·17	1·19	1·20	1·21	1·22	1·24	1·26	1·27	1·29	1·30	1·32	1·35	1·37	1·39	1·42	63
64	1·10	1·12	1·13	1·14	1·15	1·16	1·18	1·19	1·20	1·21	1·24	1·25	1·27	1·29	1·31	1·33	64
65	1·05	1·06	1·07	1·08	1·09	1·10	1·11	1·13	1·14	1·15	1·17	1·18	1·20	1·21	1·23	1·24	65
66	0·99	1·00	1·01	1·02	1·03	1·04	1·05	1·07	1·08	1·09	1·10	1·11	1·13	1·14	1·16	1·17	66
67	0·93	0·94	0·95	0·96	0·97	0·98	1·00	1·01	1·02	1·03	1·04	1·05	1·06	1·08	1·09	1·10	67
68	0·89	0·89	0·90	0·91	0·92	0·93	0·94	0·95	0·96	0·97	0·98	0·99	1·00	1·01	1·03	1·04	68
69	0·84	0·84	0·85	0·86	0·87	0·88	0·89	0·89	0·90	0·91	0·92	0·93	0·94	0·95	0·96	0·97	69
70	0·79	0·79	0·80	0·81	0·82	0·83	0·83	0·84	0·85	0·85	0·86	0·87	0·88	0·89	0·90	0·91	70
71	0·74	0·74	0·75	0·76	0·77	0·78	0·78	0·79	0·79	0·80	0·80	0·81	0·82	0·83	0·84	0·84	71
72	0·70	0·70	0·71	0·71	0·72	0·73	0·73	0·74	0·74	0·75	0·75	0·75	0·76	0·77	0·78	0·79	72
73	0·65	0·66	0·66	0·67	0·67	0·68	0·68	0·69	0·69	0·70	0·70	0·70	0·71	0·71	0·72	0·73	73
74	0·61	0·61	0·61	0·62	0·62	0·63	0·63	0·64	0·64	0·65	0·65	0·65	0·66	0·66	0·66	0·67	74
75	0·56	0·57	0·57	0·58	0·58	0·58	0·58	0·58	0·59	0·60	0·60	0·61	0·61	0·61	0·61	0·62	75
76	0·52	0·52	0·53	0·53	0·54	0·54	0·54	0·54	0·54	0·55	0·55	0·56	0·56	0·56	0·57	0·57	76
77	0·48	0·48	0·49	0·49	0·49	0·49	0·50	0·50	0·50	0·50	0·50	0·51	0·51	0·52	0·52	0·52	77
78	0·44	0·44	0·45	0·45	0·45	0·45	0·45	0·46	0·46	0·46	0·46	0·46	0·47	0·47	0·47	0·48	78
79	0·40	0·40	0·41	0·41	0·41	0·41	0·41	0·41	0·41	0·42	0·42	0·42	0·42	0·42	0·42	0·43	79
80	0·36	0·36	0·37	0·37	0·37	0·37	0·37	0·37	0·37	0·38	0·38	0 38	0·38	0·38	0·38	0·39	80
81	0·32	0·33	0·33	0·33	0·33	0·33	0·33	0·33	0·33	0·33	0·34	0 34	0·34	0·34	0·34	0·34	81
82	0·29	0·29	0·29	0·29	0·29	0·29	0·29	0·29	0·29	0·29	0·30	0·30	0·30	0·30	0·30	0·30	82
83	0·25	0·25	0·25	0·25	0·25	0·25	0·25	0·25	0·25	0·26	0·26	0·26	0·26	0·26	0·26	0·26	83
	15°	16°	17°	18°	19°	20°	21°	22°	23°	24°	25°	26°	27°	28°	29°	30°	

DECLINATION

EX-MERIDIAN TABLE I

Supplementary Table to 83°

Latitude and Declination SAME NAME

Change of Altitude in one minute from Meridian Passage = A

Lat.	DECLINATION																Lat.
	31°	32°	33°	34°	35°	36°	37°	38°	39°	40°	41°	42°	43°	44°	45°	46°	
°	"	"	"	"	"	"	"	"	"	"	"	"	"	"	"	"	°
60	1·74	1·77	1·81	1·86	1·90	1·95	2·01	2·07	2·13	2·20	2·28	2·36	2·46	2·56	2·68	2·82	60
61	1·63	1·67	1·70	1·74	1·78	1·82	1·87	1·92	1·97	2·03	2·10	2·17	2·25	2·34	2·44	2·56	61
62	1·53	1·56	1·59	1·63	1·66	1·70	1·74	1·78	1·83	1·88	1·94	2·01	2·08	2·15	2·24	2·32	62
63	1·44	1·47	1·49	1·53	1·56	1·59	1·62	1·66	1·71	1·75	1·79	1·85	1·91	1·97	2·05	2·12	63
64	1·35	1·37	1·40	1·44	1·46	1·49	1·51	1·55	1·59	1·63	1·67	1·71	1·76	1·81	1·87	1·94	64
65	1·26	1·28	1·31	1·34	1·36	1·38	1·41	1·44	1·47	1·50	1·53	1·57	1·62	1·67	1·72	1·77	65
66	1·19	1·20	1·22	1·24	1·27	1·29	1·32	1·34	1·37	1·40	1·42	1·46	1·49	1·53	1·57	1·62	66
67	1·12	1·13	1·14	1·16	1·18	1·20	1·22	1·24	1·26	1·29	1·32	1·34	1·37	1·41	1·45	1·49	67
68	1·05	1·06	1·07	1·09	1·10	1·12	1·14	1·15	1·17	1·19	1·22	1·25	1·27	1·30	1·33	1·36	68
69	0·98	0·99	1·00	1·01	1·02	1·04	1·06	1·08	1·09	1·11	1·13	1·15	1·17	1·19	1·22	1·24	69
70	0·92	0·93	0·94	0·95	0·96	0·97	0·99	1·00	1·01	1·03	1·05	1·06	1·08	1·10	1·12	1·14	70
71	0·85	0·86	0·87	0·88	0·89	0·90	0·92	0·93	0·94	0·95	0·96	0·97	0·99	1·01	1·03	1·05	71
72	0·79	0·80	0·81	0·82	0·83	0·84	0·85	0·86	0·87	0·88	0·89	0·90	0·91	0·92	0·94	0·96	72
73	0·73	0·74	0·75	0·76	0·76	0·77	0·78	0·79	0·80	0·81	0·82	0·83	0·84	0·85	0·86	0·88	73
74	0·67	0·68	0·69	0·70	0·70	0·71	0·72	0·73	0·74	0·75	0·75	0·76	0·77	0·78	0·79	0·80	74
75	0·62	0·63	0·64	0·64	0·64	0·65	0·65	0·66	0·67	0·67	0·68	0·69	0·70	0·71	0·72	0·73	75
76	0·57	0·58	0·59	0·59	0·59	0·59	0·60	0·60	0·61	0·62	0·62	0·63	0·63	0·64	0·65	0·66	76
77	0·53	0·53	0·54	0·54	0·54	0·54	0·55	0·55	0·55	0·56	0·57	0·57	0·57	0·58	0·59	0·60	77
78	0·48	0·48	0·49	0·49	0·49	0·49	0·50	0·50	0·50	0·51	0·51	0·52	0·52	0·53	0·53	0·53	78
79	0·43	0·43	0·44	0·44	0·44	0·44	0·45	0·45	0·45	0·46	0·46	0·46	0·46	0·47	0·47	0·47	79
80	0·39	0·39	0·39	0·39	0·39	0·40	0·40	0·40	0·40	0·41	0·41	0·42	0·42	0·42	0·42	0·42	80
81	0·34	0·35	0·35	0·35	0·35	0·35	0·35	0·35	0·36	0·36	0·36	0·36	0·36	0·37	0·37	0·37	81
82	0·30	0·30	0·30	0·30	0·31	0·31	0·31	0·31	0·31	0·31	0·31	0·32	0·32	0·32	0·32	0·32	82
83	0·26	0·26	0·26	0·26	0·26	0·26	0·27	0·27	0·27	0·27	0·27	0·27	0·27	0·27	0·27	0·28	83
	31°	32°	33°	34°	35°	36°	37°	38°	39°	40°	41°	42°	43°	44°	45°	46°	

DECLINATION

DECLINATION

Lat.	DECLINATION																	Lat.
	47°	48°	49°	50°	51°	52°	53°	54°	55°	56°	57°	58°	59°	60°	61°	62°	63°	
°	"	"	"	"	"	"	"	"	"	"	"	"		"	"	"	"	°
60	2·98	3·16	3·38	3·63	3·95	4·34	4·85	5·52	6·46	7·87								60
61	2·68	2·83	3·00	3·21	3·45	3·75	4·12	4·59	5·22	6·11	7·43							61
62	2·44	2·56	2·70	2·85	3·04	3·27	3·55	3·89	4·34	4·93	5·76	7·00						62
63	2·21	2·29	2·41	2·55	2·70	2·88	3·09	3·35	3·67	4·09	4·65	5·42	6·58					63
64	2·01	2·09	2·19	2·29	2·41	2·55	2·72	2·91	3·16	3·46	3·85	4·36	5·09	6·17				64
65	1·83	1·89	1·98	2·06	2·16	2·27	2·40	2·56	2·74	2·97	3·25	3·61	4·09	4·76	5·77			65
66	1·67	1·73	1·79	1·86	1·94	2·03	2·14	2·26	2·40	2·57	2·78	3·04	3·38	3·82	4·44	5·38		66
67	1·53	1·58	1·63	1·69	1·75	1·83	1·91	2·01	2·12	2·25	2·41	2·60	2·84	3·15	3·56	4·13	4·99	67
68	1·40	1·44	1·48	1·53	1·58	1·64	1·71	1·79	1·88	1·98	2·10	2·24	2·42	2·64	2·93	3·30	3·83	68
69	1·27	1·31	1·35	1·39	1·43	1·48	1·54	1·60	1·67	1·75	1·85	1·95	2·09	2·25	2·45	2·71	3·06	69
70	1·16	1·19	1·23	1·26	1·30	1·34	1·38	1·43	1·49	1·56	1·63	1·71	1·81	1·93	2·08	2·27	2·50	70
71	1·07	1·09	1·12	1·15	1·18	1·21	1·25	1·29	1·33	1·39	1·45	1·52	1·59	1·68	1·79	1·92	2·09	71
72	0·97	0·99	1·01	1·04	1·07	1·10	1·13	1·16	1·19	1·23	1·28	1·33	1·39	1·46	1·54	1·64	1·76	72
73	0·89	0·91	0·93	0·95	0·97	0·99	1·01	1·04	1·07	1·10	1·13	1·17	1·21	1·27	1·32	1·40	1·50	73
74	0·81	0·83	0·84	0·85	0·87	0·89	0·91	0·93	0·95	0·98	1·01	1·04	1·08	1·12	1·16	1·21	1·27	74
75	0·74	0·75	0·76	0·77	0·78	0·80	0·81	0·83	0·86	0·88	0·91	0·93	0·95	0·98	1·02	1·06	1·10	75
76	0·67	0·68	0·69	0·70	0·71	0·72	0·73	0·74	0·76	0·78	0·80	0·82	0·84	0·86	0·89	0·92	0·95	76
77	0·60	0·61	0·62	0·63	0·63	0·64	0·65	0·66	0·67	0·69	0·70	0·72	0·74	0·76	0·78	0·81	0·83	77
78	0·54	0·55	0·55	0·56	0·56	0·57	0·58	0·59	0·60	0·61	0·62	0·63	0·65	0·67	0·68	0·70	0·71	78
79	0·48	0·49	0·49	0·50	0·50	0·51	0·51	0·51	0·52	0·53	0·54	0·55	0·57	0·58	0·59	0·60	0·61	79
80	0·43	0·43	0·43	0·44	0·44	0·45	0·45	0·46	0·46	0·47	0·48	0·48	0·49	0·50	0·51	0·52	0·53	80
81	0·37	0·38	0·38	0·38	0·39	0·39	0·39	0·40	0·40	0·41	0·41	0·42	0·42	0·43	0·44	0·44	0·45	81
82	0·32	0·33	0·33	0·33	0·33	0·34	0·34	0·34	0·35	0·35	0·35	0·36	0·36	0·36	0·37	0·37	0·38	82
83	0·28	0·28	0·28	0·28	0·28	0·29	0·29	0·29	0·29	0·29	0·30	0·30	0·30	0·31	0·31	0·31	0·32	83
	47°	48°	49°	50°	51°	52°	53°	54°	55°	56°	57°	58°	59°	60°	61°	62°	63°	

DECLINATION

EX-MERIDIAN TABLE I
Latitude and Declination DIFFERENT NAME
Change of Altitude in one minute from Meridian Passage = A

Lat. °	0°	1°	2°	3°	4°	5°	6°	7°	8°	9°	10°	11°	12°	13°	14°	Lat. °
0					28.1	22.4	18.7	16.0	14.0	12.4	11.1	10.1	9.2	8.5	7.9	0
1				28.1	22.4	18.7	16.0	14.0	12.4	11.2	10.1	9.3	8.5	7.9	7.4	1
2			28.1	22.4	18.7	16.0	14.0	12.5	11.2	10.2	9.3	8.6	7.9	7.4	6.9	2
3		28.1	22.4	18.7	16.0	14.0	12.5	11.2	10.2	9.3	8.6	8.0	7.4	6.9	6.5	3
4	28.1	22.4	18.7	16.0	14.0	12.5	11.2	10.2	9.3	8.6	8.0	7.4	7.0	6.5	6.2	4
5	22.4	18.7	16.0	14.0	12.5	11.2	10.2	9.3	8.6	8.0	7.4	7.0	6.5	6.2	5.8	5
6	18.7	16.0	14.0	12.5	11.2	10.2	9.3	8.6	8.0	7.5	7.0	6.6	6.2	5.8	5.5	6
7	16.0	14.0	12.4	11.2	10.2	9.3	8.6	8.0	7.5	7.0	6.6	6.2	5.9	5.6	5.3	7
8	14.0	12.4	11.2	10.2	9.3	8.6	8.0	7.5	7.0	6.6	6.2	5.9	5.6	5.3	5.0	8
9	12.4	11.2	10.2	9.3	8.6	8.0	7.5	7.0	6.6	6.2	5.9	5.6	5.3	5.0	4.8	9
10	11.1	10.1	9.3	8.6	8.0	7.4	7.0	6.6	6.2	5.9	5.6	5.3	5.0	4.8	4.6	10
11	10.1	9.3	8.6	8.0	7.4	7.0	6.6	6.2	5.9	5.6	5.3	5.1	4.8	4.6	4.4	11
12	9.2	8.5	7.9	7.4	7.0	6.5	6.2	5.9	5.6	5.3	5.0	4.8	4.6	4.4	4.3	12
13	8.5	7.9	7.4	6.9	6.5	6.2	5.8	5.6	5.3	5.0	4.8	4.6	4.4	4.3	4.1	13
14	7.9	7.4	6.9	6.5	6.2	5.8	5.5	5.3	5.0	4.8	4.6	4.4	4.2	4.1	3.9	14
15	7.3	6.9	6.5	6.1	5.8	5.5	5.3	5.0	4.8	4.6	4.4	4.2	4.1	3.9	3.8	15
16	6.8	6.5	6.1	5.8	5.5	5.2	5.0	4.8	4.6	4.4	4.2	4.1	3.9	3.8	3.7	16
17	6.4	6.1	5.8	5.5	5.2	5.0	4.8	4.6	4.4	4.2	4.1	3.9	3.8	3.7	3.5	17
18	6.0	5.7	5.5	5.2	5.0	4.8	4.6	4.4	4.2	4.1	3.9	3.8	3.7	3.5	3.4	18
19	5.7	5.4	5.2	4.9	4.7	4.5	4.4	4.2	4.0	3.9	3.8	3.6	3.5	3.4	3.3	19
20	5.4	5.1	4.9	4.7	4.5	4.3	4.2	4.0	3.9	3.8	3.6	3.5	3.4	3.3	3.2	20
21	5.1	4.9	4.7	4.5	4.3	4.2	4.0	3.9	3.7	3.6	3.5	3.4	3.3	3.2	3.1	21
22	4.9	4.7	4.5	4.3	4.1	4.0	3.9	3.7	3.6	3.5	3.4	3.3	3.2	3.1	3.0	22
23	4.6	4.4	4.3	4.1	4.0	3.8	3.7	3.6	3.5	3.4	3.3	3.2	3.1	3.0	2.9	23
24	4.4	4.2	4.1	3.9	3.8	3.7	3.6	3.5	3.4	3.3	3.2	3.1	3.0	2.9	2.8	24
25	4.2	4.1	3.9	3.8	3.7	3.5	3.4	3.3	3.2	3.1	3.1	3.0	2.9	2.8	2.7	25
26	4.0	3.9	3.8	3.6	3.5	3.4	3.3	3.2	3.1	3.0	3.0	2.9	2.8	2.7	2.7	26
27	3.9	3.7	3.6	3.5	3.4	3.3	3.2	3.1	3.0	2.9	2.9	2.8	2.7	2.7	2.6	27
28	3.7	3.6	3.5	3.4	3.3	3.2	3.1	3.0	2.9	2.8	2.8	2.7	2.6	2.6	2.5	28
29	3.5	3.4	3.3	3.2	3.1	3.1	3.0	2.9	2.8	2.8	2.7	2.6	2.6	2.5	2.4	29
30	3.4	3.3	3.2	3.1	3.0	3.0	2.9	2.8	2.7	2.7	2.6	2.5	2.5	2.4	2.4	30
31	3.3	3.2	3.1	3.0	2.9	2.9	2.8	2.7	2.6	2.6	2.5	2.5	2.4	2.4	2.3	31
32	3.2	3.1	3.0	2.9	2.8	2.8	2.7	2.6	2.6	2.5	2.5	2.4	2.3	2.3	2.2	32
33	3.0	2.9	2.9	2.8	2.7	2.7	2.6	2.5	2.5	2.4	2.4	2.3	2.3	2.2	2.2	33
34	2.9	2.8	2.8	2.7	2.6	2.6	2.5	2.5	2.4	2.4	2.3	2.3	2.2	2.2	2.1	34
35	2.8	2.7	2.7	2.6	2.5	2.5	2.4	2.4	2.3	2.3	2.2	2.2	2.2	2.1	2.1	35
36	2.7	2.6	2.6	2.5	2.5	2.4	2.4	2.3	2.3	2.2	2.2	2.1	2.1	2.1	2.0	36
37	2.6	2.5	2.5	2.4	2.4	2.3	2.3	2.2	2.2	2.2	2.1	2.1	2.0	2.0	2.0	37
38	2.5	2.5	2.4	2.4	2.3	2.3	2.2	2.2	2.1	2.1	2.1	2.0	2.0	1.9	1.9	38
39	2.4	2.4	2.3	2.3	2.2	2.2	2.1	2.1	2.1	2.0	2.0	2.0	1.9	1.9	1.9	39
40	2.3	2.3	2.2	2.2	2.2	2.1	2.1	2.0	2.0	2.0	1.9	1.9	1.9	1.8	1.8	40
41	2.3	2.2	2.2	2.1	2.1	2.1	2.0	2.0	1.9	1.9	1.9	1.8	1.8	1.8	1.8	41
42	2.2	2.1	2.1	2.1	2.0	2.0	2.0	1.9	1.9	1.9	1.8	1.8	1.8	1.7	1.7	42
43	2.1	2.1	2.0	2.0	2.0	1.9	1.9	1.9	1.8	1.8	1.8	1.7	1.7	1.7	1.7	43
44	2.0	2.0	2.0	1.9	1.9	1.9	1.8	1.8	1.8	1.7	1.7	1.7	1.7	1.6	1.6	44
45	2.0	1.9	1.9	1.9	1.8	1.8	1.8	1.7	1.7	1.7	1.7	1.6	1.6	1.6	1.6	45
46	1.9	1.9	1.8	1.8	1.8	1.7	1.7	1.7	1.7	1.6	1.6	1.6	1.6	1.6	1.5	46
47	1.8	1.8	1.8	1.7	1.7	1.7	1.7	1.6	1.6	1.6	1.6	1.6	1.5	1.5	1.5	47
48	1.8	1.7	1.7	1.7	1.7	1.6	1.6	1.6	1.6	1.6	1.5	1.5	1.5	1.5	1.4	48
49	1.7	1.7	1.7	1.6	1.6	1.6	1.6	1.5	1.5	1.5	1.5	1.5	1.4	1.4	1.4	49
50	1.6	1.6	1.6	1.6	1.6	1.5	1.5	1.5	1.5	1.5	1.4	1.4	1.4	1.4	1.4	50
51	1.6	1.6	1.6	1.5	1.5	1.5	1.5	1.5	1.4	1.4	1.4	1.4	1.4	1.3	1.3	51
52	1.5	1.5	1.5	1.5	1.5	1.4	1.4	1.4	1.4	1.4	1.4	1.3	1.3	1.3	1.3	52
53	1.5	1.5	1.4	1.4	1.4	1.4	1.4	1.4	1.3	1.3	1.3	1.3	1.3	1.3	1.3	53
54	1.4	1.4	1.4	1.4	1.4	1.3	1.3	1.3	1.3	1.3	1.3	1.3	1.2	1.2	1.2	54
55	1.4	1.4	1.3	1.3	1.3	1.3	1.3	1.3	1.3	1.2	1.2	1.2	1.2	1.2	1.2	55
56	1.3	1.3	1.3	1.3	1.3	1.3	1.2	1.2	1.2	1.2	1.2	1.2	1.2	1.1	1.1	56
57	1.3	1.3	1.3	1.2	1.2	1.2	1.2	1.2	1.2	1.2	1.1	1.1	1.1	1.1	1.1	57
58	1.2	1.2	1.2	1.2	1.2	1.2	1.2	1.1	1.1	1.1	1.1	1.1	1.1	1.1	1.1	58
59	1.2	1.2	1.2	1.2	1.1	1.1	1.1	1.1	1.1	1.1	1.1	1.1	1.1	1.0	1.0	59
60	1.1	1.1	1.1	1.1	1.1	1.1	1.1	1.1	1.0	1.0	1.0	1.0	1.0	1.0	1.0	60

EX-MERIDIAN TABLE I
Latitude and Declination DIFFERENT NAME
Change of Altitude in one minute from Meridian Passage = A

Lat. °	15°	16°	17°	18°	19°	20°	21°	22°	23°	24°	25°	26°	27°	28°	29°	30°	Lat. °
0	7.3	6.8	6.4	6.0	5.7	5.4	5.1	4.9	4.6	4.4	4.2	4.0	3.9	3.7	3.5	3.4	0
1	6.9	6.5	6.1	5.7	5.4	5.1	4.9	4.7	4.4	4.2	4.1	3.9	3.7	3.6	3.4	3.3	1
2	6.5	6.1	5.8	5.5	5.2	4.9	4.7	4.5	4.3	4.1	3.9	3.8	3.6	3.5	3.3	3.2	2
3	6.1	5.8	5.5	5.2	4.9	4.7	4.5	4.3	4.1	3.9	3.8	3.6	3.5	3.4	3.2	3.1	3
4	5.8	5.5	5.2	5.0	4.7	4.5	4.3	4.1	4.0	3.8	3.7	3.5	3.4	3.3	3.2	3.0	4
5	5.5	5.2	5.0	4.8	4.5	4.3	4.2	4.0	3.8	3.7	3.6	3.4	3.3	3.2	3.1	3.0	5
6	5.3	5.0	4.8	4.6	4.4	4.2	4.0	3.9	3.7	3.6	3.4	3.3	3.2	3.1	3.0	2.9	6
7	5.0	4.8	4.6	4.4	4.2	4.0	3.9	3.7	3.6	3.5	3.3	3.2	3.1	3.0	2.9	2.8	7
8	4.8	4.6	4.4	4.2	4.0	3.9	3.7	3.6	3.5	3.4	3.2	3.1	3.0	2.9	2.8	2.7	8
9	4.6	4.4	4.2	4.1	3.9	3.8	3.6	3.5	3.4	3.3	3.1	3.0	2.9	2.9	2.8	2.7	9
10	4.4	4.2	4.1	3.9	3.8	3.6	3.5	3.4	3.3	3.2	3.1	3.0	2.9	2.8	2.7	2.6	10
11	4.2	4.1	3.9	3.8	3.6	3.5	3.4	3.3	3.2	3.1	3.0	2.9	2.8	2.7	2.6	2.5	11
12	4.1	3.9	3.8	3.7	3.5	3.4	3.3	3.2	3.1	3.0	2.9	2.8	2.7	2.6	2.6	2.5	12
13	3.9	3.8	3.7	3.5	3.4	3.3	3.2	3.1	3.0	2.9	2.8	2.7	2.7	2.6	2.5	2.4	13
14	3.8	3.7	3.5	3.4	3.3	3.2	3.1	3.0	2.9	2.8	2.7	2.7	2.6	2.5	2.4	2.4	14
15	3.7	3.5	3.4	3.3	3.2	3.1	3.0	2.9	2.8	2.8	2.7	2.6	2.5	2.5	2.4	2.3	15
16	3.5	3.4	3.3	3.2	3.1	3.0	2.9	2.8	2.8	2.7	2.6	2.5	2.5	2.4	2.3	2.3	16
17	3.4	3.3	3.2	3.1	3.0	2.9	2.8	2.8	2.7	2.6	2.5	2.5	2.4	2.3	2.3	2.2	17
18	3.3	3.2	3.1	3.0	2.9	2.9	2.8	2.7	2.6	2.5	2.5	2.4	2.4	2.3	2.2	2.2	18
19	3.2	3.1	3.0	2.9	2.9	2.8	2.7	2.6	2.6	2.5	2.4	2.4	2.3	2.2	2.2	2.1	19
20	3.1	3.0	2.9	2.9	2.8	2.7	2.6	2.6	2.5	2.4	2.4	2.3	2.3	2.2	2.1	2.1	20
21	3.0	2.9	2.8	2.8	2.7	2.6	2.6	2.5	2.4	2.4	2.3	2.3	2.2	2.1	2.1	2.0	21
22	2.9	2.8	2.8	2.7	2.6	2.6	2.5	2.4	2.4	2.3	2.3	2.2	2.2	2.1	2.1	2.0	22
23	2.8	2.8	2.7	2.6	2.6	2.5	2.4	2.4	2.3	2.3	2.2	2.2	2.1	2.1	2.0	2.0	23
24	2.8	2.7	2.6	2.5	2.5	2.4	2.4	2.3	2.3	2.2	2.2	2.1	2.1	2.0	2.0	1.9	24
25	2.7	2.6	2.5	2.5	2.4	2.4	2.3	2.3	2.2	2.2	2.1	2.1	2.0	2.0	1.9	1.9	25
26	2.6	2.5	2.5	2.4	2.4	2.3	2.3	2.2	2.1	2.1	2.1	2.0	2.0	1.9	1.9	1.9	26
27	2.5	2.5	2.4	2.4	2.3	2.2	2.2	2.1	2.1	2.1	2.0	2.0	1.9	1.9	1.9	1.8	27
28	2.5	2.4	2.3	2.3	2.2	2.2	2.1	2.1	2.1	2.0	2.0	1.9	1.9	1.9	1.8	1.8	28
29	2.4	2.3	2.3	2.2	2.2	2.1	2.1	2.0	2.0	2.0	1.9	1.9	1.9	1.8	1.8	1.7	29
30	2.3	2.3	2.2	2.2	2.1	2.1	2.0	2.0	2.0	1.9	1.9	1.8	1.8	1.8	1.7	1.7	30
31	2.3	2.2	2.2	2.1	2.1	2.0	2.0	2.0	1.9	1.9	1.8	1.8	1.8	1.7	1.7	1.7	31
32	2.2	2.2	2.1	2.1	2.0	2.0	1.9	1.9	1.9	1.8	1.8	1.8	1.7	1.7	1.7	1.6	32
33	2.1	2.1	2.1	2.0	2.0	1.9	1.9	1.9	1.8	1.8	1.8	1.7	1.7	1.7	1.6	1.6	33
34	2.1	2.0	2.0	2.0	1.9	1.9	1.9	1.8	1.8	1.8	1.7	1.7	1.7	1.6	1.6	1.6	34
35	2.0	2.0	2.0	1.9	1.9	1.8	1.8	1.8	1.7	1.7	1.7	1.7	1.6	1.6	1.6	1.5	35
36	2.0	1.9	1.9	1.9	1.8	1.8	1.8	1.7	1.7	1.7	1.6	1.6	1.6	1.5	1.5	1.5	36
37	1.9	1.9	1.9	1.8	1.8	1.8	1.7	1.7	1.7	1.6	1.6	1.6	1.6	1.5	1.5	1.5	37
38	1.9	1.8	1.8	1.8	1.8	1.7	1.7	1.7	1.6	1.6	1.6	1.5	1.5	1.5	1.5	1.5	38
39	1.8	1.8	1.8	1.7	1.7	1.7	1.6	1.6	1.6	1.6	1.5	1.5	1.5	1.5	1.4	1.4	39
40	1.8	1.7	1.7	1.7	1.7	1.6	1.6	1.6	1.6	1.5	1.5	1.5	1.5	1.4	1.4	1.4	40
41	1.7	1.7	1.7	1.6	1.6	1.6	1.6	1.5	1.5	1.5	1.5	1.4	1.4	1.4	1.4	1.4	41
42	1.7	1.7	1.6	1.6	1.6	1.6	1.5	1.5	1.5	1.5	1.4	1.4	1.4	1.4	1.4	1.3	42
43	1.6	1.6	1.6	1.6	1.5	1.5	1.5	1.5	1.4	1.4	1.4	1.4	1.4	1.3	1.3	1.3	43
44	1.6	1.6	1.5	1.5	1.5	1.5	1.5	1.4	1.4	1.4	1.4	1.4	1.3	1.3	1.3	1.3	44
45	1.5	1.5	1.5	1.5	1.5	1.4	1.4	1.4	1.4	1.4	1.3	1.3	1.3	1.3	1.3	1.2	45
46	1.5	1.5	1.5	1.4	1.4	1.4	1.4	1.4	1.3	1.3	1.3	1.3	1.3	1.3	1.2	1.2	46
47	1.5	1.4	1.4	1.4	1.4	1.4	1.3	1.3	1.3	1.3	1.3	1.3	1.2	1.2	1.2	1.2	47
48	1.4	1.4	1.4	1.4	1.4	1.3	1.3	1.3	1.3	1.3	1.2	1.2	1.2	1.2	1.2	1.2	48
49	1.4	1.4	1.3	1.3	1.3	1.3	1.3	1.3	1.2	1.2	1.2	1.2	1.2	1.2	1.2	1.1	49
50	1.3	1.3	1.3	1.3	1.3	1.3	1.3	1.2	1.2	1.2	1.2	1.2	1.2	1.1	1.1	1.1	50
51	1.3	1.3	1.3	1.3	1.2	1.2	1.2	1.2	1.2	1.2	1.2	1.1	1.1	1.1	1.1	1.1	51
52	1.3	1.3	1.3	1.2	1.2	1.2	1.2	1.2	1.1	1.1	1.1	1.1	1.1	1.1	1.1	1.1	52
53	1.2	1.2	1.2	1.2	1.2	1.2	1.2	1.1	1.1	1.1	1.1	1.1	1.1	1.1	1.0	1.0	53
54	1.2	1.2	1.2	1.2	1.1	1.1	1.1	1.1	1.1	1.1	1.1	1.0	1.0	1.0	1.0	1.0	54
55	1.2	1.1	1.1	1.1	1.1	1.1	1.1	1.1	1.1	1.1	1.0	1.0	1.0	1.0	1.0		55
56	1.1	1.1	1.1	1.1	1.1	1.1	1.1	1.0	1.0	1.0	1.0	1.0	1.0	1.0			56
57	1.1	1.1	1.1	1.1	1.0	1.0	1.0	1.0	1.0	1.0	1.0	1.0	1.0				57
58	1.1	1.0	1.0	1.0	1.0	1.0	1.0	1.0	1.0	1.0	1.0	0.9					58
59	1.0	1.0	1.0	1.0	1.0	1.0	1.0	1.0	0.9	0.9	0.9						59
60	1.0	1.0	1.0	1.0	0.9	0.9	0.9	0.9	0.9	0.9							60

EX-MERIDIAN TABLE I
Latitude and Declination DIFFERENT NAME
Change of Altitude in one minute from Meridian Passage = A

Lat.°	31°	32°	33°	34°	35°	36°	37°	38°	39°	40°	41°	42°	43°	44°	45°	46°	Lat.°
0	3.3	3.1	3.0	2.9	2.8	2.7	2.6	2.5	2.4	2.3	2.3	2.2	2.1	2.0	2.0	1.9	0
1	3.2	3.1	2.9	2.8	2.7	2.6	2.6	2.5	2.4	2.3	2.2	2.1	2.1	2.0	1.9	1.9	1
2	3.1	3.0	2.9	2.8	2.7	2.6	2.5	2.4	2.3	2.3	2.2	2.1	2.0	2.0	1.9	1.8	2
3	3.0	2.9	2.8	2.7	2.6	2.5	2.4	2.4	2.3	2.2	2.1	2.1	2.0	1.9	1.9	1.8	3
4	2.9	2.8	2.7	2.6	2.6	2.5	2.4	2.3	2.2	2.2	2.1	2.0	2.0	1.9	1.8	1.8	4
5	2.9	2.8	2.7	2.6	2.5	2.4	2.3	2.3	2.2	2.1	2.1	2.0	1.9	1.9	1.8	1.8	5
6	2.8	2.7	2.6	2.5	2.4	2.4	2.3	2.2	2.2	2.1	2.0	2.0	1.9	1.8	1.8	1.7	6
7	2.7	2.6	2.5	2.5	2.4	2.3	2.2	2.2	2.1	2.0	2.0	1.9	1.9	1.8	1.8	1.7	7
8	2.7	2.6	2.5	2.4	2.3	2.3	2.2	2.1	2.1	2.0	1.9	1.9	1.8	1.8	1.7	1.7	8
9	2.6	2.5	2.4	2.4	2.3	2.2	2.2	2.1	2.0	2.0	1.9	1.9	1.8	1.8	1.7	1.6	9
10	2.5	2.5	2.4	2.3	2.2	2.2	2.1	2.1	2.0	1.9	1.9	1.8	1.8	1.7	1.7	1.6	10
11	2.5	2.4	2.3	2.3	2.2	2.1	2.1	2.0	2.0	1.9	1.8	1.8	1.7	1.7	1.6	1.6	11
12	2.4	2.3	2.3	2.2	2.2	2.1	2.0	2.0	1.9	1.9	1.8	1.8	1.7	1.7	1.6	1.6	12
13	2.4	2.3	2.2	2.2	2.1	2.1	2.0	1.9	1.9	1.8	1.8	1.7	1.7	1.6	1.6	1.6	13
14	2.3	2.3	2.2	2.1	2.1	2.0	2.0	1.9	1.9	1.8	1.8	1.7	1.7	1.6	1.6	1.5	14
15	2.3	2.2	2.1	2.1	2.0	2.0	1.9	1.9	1.8	1.8	1.7	1.7	1.6	1.6	1.6	1.5	15
16	2.2	2.2	2.1	2.0	2.0	1.9	1.9	1.8	1.8	1.7	1.7	1.7	1.6	1.6	1.5	1.5	16
17	2.2	2.1	2.1	2.0	2.0	1.9	1.9	1.8	1.8	1.7	1.7	1.6	1.6	1.5	1.5	1.5	17
18	2.1	2.1	2.0	2.0	1.9	1.9	1.8	1.8	1.7	1.7	1.6	1.6	1.6	1.5	1.5	1.4	18
19	2.1	2.0	2.0	1.9	1.9	1.8	1.8	1.7	1.7	1.7	1.6	1.6	1.5	1.5	1.5	1.4	19
20	2.0	2.0	1.9	1.9	1.9	1.8	1.8	1.7	1.7	1.6	1.6	1.6	1.5	1.5	1.4	1.4	20
21	2.0	2.0	1.9	1.9	1.8	1.8	1.7	1.7	1.6	1.6	1.6	1.5	1.5	1.5	1.4	1.4	21
22	2.0	1.9	1.9	1.8	1.8	1.7	1.7	1.7	1.6	1.6	1.5	1.5	1.5	1.4	1.4	1.4	22
23	1.9	1.9	1.8	1.8	1.8	1.7	1.7	1.6	1.6	1.6	1.5	1.5	1.4	1.4	1.4	1.3	23
24	1.9	1.8	1.8	1.8	1.7	1.7	1.6	1.6	1.6	1.5	1.5	1.5	1.4	1.4	1.3	1.3	24
25	1.8	1.8	1.8	1.7	1.7	1.6	1.6	1.6	1.5	1.5	1.5	1.4	1.4	1.4	1.3	1.3	25
26	1.8	1.8	1.7	1.7	1.7	1.6	1.6	1.6	1.5	1.5	1.5	1.4	1.4	1.4	1.3	1.3	26
27	1.8	1.7	1.7	1.7	1.6	1.6	1.6	1.5	1.5	1.5	1.4	1.4	1.4	1.3	1.3	1.3	27
28	1.7	1.7	1.7	1.6	1.6	1.6	1.5	1.5	1.5	1.4	1.4	1.4	1.3	1.3	1.3	1.3	28
29	1.7	1.7	1.6	1.6	1.6	1.5	1.5	1.5	1.4	1.4	1.4	1.4	1.3	1.3	1.3	1.2	29
30	1.7	1.6	1.6	1.6	1.5	1.5	1.5	1.5	1.4	1.4	1.4	1.3	1.3	1.3	1.2	1.2	30
31	1.6	1.6	1.6	1.5	1.5	1.5	1.5	1.4	1.4	1.4	1.3	1.3	1.3	1.3	1.2	1.2	31
32	1.6	1.6	1.5	1.5	1.5	1.5	1.4	1.4	1.4	1.3	1.3	1.3	1.3	1.2	1.2	1.2	32
33	1.6	1.5	1.5	1.5	1.5	1.4	1.4	1.4	1.4	1.3	1.3	1.3	1.2	1.2	1.2	1.2	33
34	1.5	1.5	1.5	1.5	1.4	1.4	1.4	1.4	1.3	1.3	1.3	1.3	1.2	1.2	1.2	1.2	34
35	1.5	1.5	1.5	1.4	1.4	1.4	1.4	1.3	1.3	1.3	1.3	1.2	1.2	1.2	1.2	1.1	35
36	1.5	1.5	1.4	1.4	1.4	1.4	1.3	1.3	1.3	1.3	1.2	1.2	1.2	1.2	1.1	1.1	36
37	1.5	1.4	1.4	1.4	1.4	1.3	1.3	1.3	1.3	1.2	1.2	1.2	1.2	1.2	1.1	1.1	37
38	1.4	1.4	1.4	1.4	1.3	1.3	1.3	1.3	1.2	1.2	1.2	1.2	1.2	1.1	1.1	1.1	38
39	1.4	1.4	1.4	1.3	1.3	1.3	1.3	1.2	1.2	1.2	1.2	1.2	1.1	1.1	1.1		39
40	1.4	1.3	1.3	1.3	1.3	1.3	1.2	1.2	1.2	1.2	1.2	1.1	1.1	1.1			40
41	1.3	1.3	1.3	1.3	1.3	1.2	1.2	1.2	1.2	1.2	1.1	1.1	1.1				41
42	1.3	1.3	1.3	1.2	1.2	1.2	1.2	1.2	1.2	1.1	1.1	1.1					42
43	1.3	1.3	1.2	1.2	1.2	1.2	1.2	1.2	1.1	1.1	1.1						43
44	1.3	1.2	1.2	1.2	1.2	1.2	1.2	1.1	1.1	1.1							44
45	1.2	1.2	1.2	1.2	1.2	1.1	1.1	1.1	1.1								45
46	1.2	1.2	1.2	1.2	1.1	1.1	1.1	1.1									46
47	1.2	1.2	1.1	1.1	1.1	1.1	1.1										47
48	1.1	1.1	1.1	1.1	1.1	1.1											48
49	1.1	1.1	1.1	1.1	1.1												49
50	1.1	1.1	1.1	1.1											0.9		50
51	1.1	1.1	1.0												0.9	0.9	51
52	1.0	1.0												0.9	0.9	0.9	52
53	1.0												0.9	0.9	0.8	0.8	53
54												0.9	0.9	0.8	0.8	0.8	54
55											0.9	0.8	0.8	0.8	0.8	0.8	55
56										0.8	0.8	0.8	0.8	0.8	0.8	0.8	56
57									0.8	0.8	0.8	0.8	0.8	0.8	0.8	0.8	57
58								0.8	0.8	0.8	0.8	0.8	0.8	0.8	0.8	0.8	58
59							0.8	0.8	0.8	0.8	0.8	0.8	0.8	0.8	0.7	0.7	59
60						0.8	0.8	0.8	0.8	0.8	0.8	0.8	0.7	0.7	0.7	0.7	60

The values of 'A' printed below are for circumpolar bodies near to their Lower Meridian Transit. Latitude and Declination SAME NAME.

EX-MERIDIAN TABLE I
Latitude and Declination DIFFERENT NAME
Change of Altitude in one minute from Meridian Passage = A

DECLINATION

Lat. °	47°	48°	49°	50°	51°	52°	53°	54°	55°	56°	57°	58°	59°	60°	61°	62°	63°	Lat. °
0	1.8	1.8	1.7	1.7	1.6	1.5	1.5	1.4	1.4	1.3	1.3	1.2	1.2	1.1	1.1	1.0	1.0	0
1	1.8	1.7	1.7	1.6	1.6	1.5	1.5	1.4	1.4	1.3	1.3	1.2	1.2	1.1	1.1	1.0	1.0	1
2	1.8	1.7	1.7	1.6	1.5	1.5	1.4	1.4	1.3	1.3	1.3	1.2	1.2	1.1	1.1	1.0	1.0	2
3	1.8	1.7	1.6	1.6	1.5	1.5	1.4	1.4	1.3	1.3	1.2	1.2	1.1	1.1	1.1	1.0	1.0	3
4	1.7	1.7	1.6	1.6	1.5	1.5	1.4	1.4	1.3	1.3	1.2	1.2	1.1	1.1	1.1	1.0	1.0	4
5	1.7	1.6	1.6	1.5	1.5	1.4	1.4	1.3	1.3	1.3	1.2	1.2	1.1	1.1	1.0	1.0	1.0	5
6	1.7	1.6	1.6	1.5	1.5	1.4	1.4	1.3	1.3	1.2	1.2	1.2	1.1	1.1	1.0	1.0	1.0	6
7	1.6	1.6	1.5	1.5	1.4	1.4	1.4	1.3	1.3	1.2	1.2	1.1	1.1	1.1	1.0	1.0	0.9	7
8	1.6	1.6	1.5	1.5	1.4	1.4	1.3	1.3	1.3	1.2	1.2	1.1	1.1	1.1	1.0	1.0	0.9	8
9	1.6	1.6	1.5	1.5	1.4	1.4	1.3	1.3	1.2	1.2	1.2	1.1	1.1	1.0	1.0	1.0	0.9	9
10	1.6	1.5	1.5	1.4	1.4	1.4	1.3	1.3	1.2	1.2	1.1	1.1	1.1	1.0	1.0	1.0	0.9	10
11	1.6	1.5	1.5	1.4	1.4	1.3	1.3	1.3	1.2	1.2	1.1	1.1	1.1	1.0	1.0	1.0	0.9	11
12	1.5	1.5	1.4	1.4	1.4	1.3	1.3	1.2	1.2	1.2	1.1	1.1	1.1	1.0	1.0	0.9	0.9	12
13	1.5	1.5	1.4	1.4	1.3	1.3	1.3	1.2	1.2	1.2	1.1	1.1	1.0	1.0	1.0	0.9	0.9	13
14	1.5	1.4	1.4	1.4	1.3	1.3	1.3	1.2	1.2	1.1	1.1	1.1	1.0	1.0	1.0	0.9	0.9	14
15	1.5	1.4	1.4	1.4	1.3	1.3	1.2	1.2	1.2	1.1	1.1	1.1	1.0	1.0	1.0	0.9	0.9	15
16	1.4	1.4	1.4	1.3	1.3	1.3	1.2	1.2	1.1	1.1	1.1	1.0	1.0	1.0	0.9	0.9	0.9	16
17	1.4	1.4	1.4	1.3	1.3	1.2	1.2	1.2	1.1	1.1	1.1	1.0	1.0	1.0	0.9	0.9	0.9	17
18	1.4	1.4	1.3	1.3	1.3	1.2	1.2	1.2	1.1	1.1	1.1	1.0	1.0	1.0	0.9	0.9	0.9	18
19	1.4	1.4	1.3	1.3	1.2	1.2	1.2	1.1	1.1	1.1	1.0	1.0	1.0	1.0	0.9	0.9	0.9	19
20	1.4	1.3	1.3	1.3	1.2	1.2	1.2	1.1	1.1	1.1	1.0	1.0	1.0	0.9	0.9	0.9	0.8	20
21	1.4	1.3	1.3	1.3	1.2	1.2	1.2	1.1	1.1	1.1	1.0	1.0	1.0	0.9	0.9	0.9	0.8	21
22	1.3	1.3	1.3	1.2	1.2	1.2	1.1	1.1	1.1	1.0	1.0	1.0	1.0	0.9	0.9	0.9		22
23	1.3	1.3	1.3	1.2	1.2	1.2	1.1	1.1	1.1	1.0	1.0	1.0	0.9	0.9	0.9			23
24	1.3	1.3	1.2	1.2	1.2	1.1	1.1	1.1	1.1	1.0	1.0	1.0	0.9	0.9				24
25	1.3	1.2	1.2	1.2	1.2	1.1	1.1	1.1	1.0	1.0	1.0	1.0	0.9					25
26	1.3	1.2	1.2	1.2	1.1	1.1	1.1	1.1	1.0	1.0	1.0	0.9						26
27	1.2	1.2	1.2	1.2	1.1	1.1	1.1	1.0	1.0	1.0	1.0							27
28	1.2	1.2	1.2	1.1	1.1	1.1	1.1	1.0	1.0	1.0								28
29	1.2	1.2	1.2	1.1	1.1	1.1	1.0	1.0	1.0									29
30	1.2	1.2	1.1	1.1	1.1	1.1	1.0	1.0										30
31	1.2	1.2	1.1	1.1	1.1	1.0	1.0											31
32	1.2	1.1	1.1	1.1	1.1	1.0												32
33	1.1	1.1	1.1	1.1	1.1												0.8	33
34	1.1	1.1	1.1	1.1												0.8	0.7	34
35	1.1	1.1	1.1												0.8	0.8	0.7	35
36	1.1	1.1												0.8	0.8	0.8	0.7	36
37	1.1												0.8	0.8	0.8	0.7	0.7	37
38												0.8	0.8	0.8	0.8	0.7	0.7	38
39											0.8	0.8	0.8	0.8	0.8	0.7	0.7	39
40										0.8	0.8	0.8	0.8	0.8	0.8	0.7	0.7	40
41									0.9	0.8	0.8	0.8	0.8	0.8	0.7	0.7	0.7	41
42								0.9	0.8	0.8	0.8	0.8	0.8	0.8	0.7	0.7	0.7	42
43							0.9	0.9	0.8	0.8	0.8	0.8	0.8	0.7	0.7	0.7	0.7	43
44						0.9	0.9	0.8	0.8	0.8	0.8	0.8	0.8	0.7	0.7	0.7	0.7	44
45					0.9	0.9	0.8	0.8	0.8	0.8	0.8	0.8	0.7	0.7	0.7	0.7	0.7	45
46				0.9	0.9	0.9	0.8	0.8	0.8	0.8	0.8	0.8	0.7	0.7	0.7	0.7	0.7	46
47			0.9	0.9	0.9	0.8	0.8	0.8	0.8	0.8	0.8	0.7	0.7	0.7	0.7	0.7	0.6	47
48		0.9	0.9	0.9	0.8	0.8	0.8	0.8	0.8	0.8	0.7	0.7	0.7	0.7	0.7	0.7	0.6	48
49	0.9	0.9	0.9	0.8	0.8	0.8	0.8	0.8	0.8	0.7	0.7	0.7	0.7	0.7	0.7	0.6	0.6	49
50	0.9	0.9	0.8	0.8	0.8	0.8	0.8	0.8	0.7	0.7	0.7	0.7	0.7	0.7	0.7	0.6	0.6	50
51	0.9	0.8	0.8	0.8	0.8	0.8	0.8	0.8	0.7	0.7	0.7	0.7	0.7	0.7	0.7	0.6	0.6	51
52	0.8	0.8	0.8	0.8	0.8	0.8	0.8	0.7	0.7	0.7	0.7	0.7	0.7	0.7	0.6	0.6	0.6	52
53	0.8	0.8	0.8	0.8	0.8	0.7	0.7	0.7	0.7	0.7	0.7	0.7	0.7	0.6	0.6	0.6	0.6	53
54	0.8	0.8	0.8	0.8	0.8	0.7	0.7	0.7	0.7	0.7	0.7	0.7	0.6	0.6	0.6	0.6	0.6	54
55	0.8	0.8	0.8	0.7	0.7	0.7	0.7	0.7	0.7	0.7	0.7	0.7	0.6	0.6	0.6	0.6	0.6	55
56	0.8	0.8	0.7	0.7	0.7	0.7	0.7	0.7	0.7	0.7	0.7	0.6	0.6	0.6	0.6	0.6	0.6	56
57	0.8	0.7	0.7	0.7	0.7	0.7	0.7	0.7	0.7	0.7	0.6	0.6	0.6	0.6	0.6	0.6	0.6	57
58	0.7	0.7	0.7	0.7	0.7	0.7	0.7	0.7	0.7	0.6	0.6	0.6	0.6	0.6	0.6	0.6	0.6	58
59	0.7	0.7	0.7	0.7	0.7	0.7	0.7	0.6	0.6	0.6	0.6	0.6	0.6	0.6	0.6	0.6	0.5	59
60	0.7	0.7	0.7	0.7	0.7	0.7	0.6	0.6	0.6	0.6	0.6	0.6	0.6	0.6	0.6	0.6	0.5	60

The values of 'A' printed below are for circumpolar bodies near to their Lower Meridian Transit. Latitude and Declination SAME NAME.

EX-MERIDIAN TABLE I
Latitude and Declination DIFFERENT NAME
Change of Altitude in one minute from Meridian Passage = A

DECLINATION

Lat.	0°	1°	2°	3°	4°	5°	6°	7°	8°	9°	10°	11°	12°	13°	14°	Lat.
60	1·13	1·12	1·11	1·10	1·09	1·08	1·07	1·06	1·05	1·04	1·03	1·02	1·01	1·00	0·99	60
61	1·09	1·08	1·07	1·06	1·05	1·04	1·03	1·02	1·01	1·00	0·99	0·98	0·97	0·96	0·96	61
62	1·04	1·03	1·03	1·02	1·01	1·00	0·99	0·98	0·97	0·96	0·95	0·94	0·94	0·93	0·92	62
63	1·00	0·99	0·98	0·97	0·97	0·96	0·95	0·94	0·93	0·92	0·91	0·90	0·90	0·90	0·89	63
64	0·96	0·95	0·94	0·93	0·93	0·92	0·91	0·90	0·89	0·89	0·88	0·87	0·87	0·86	0·85	64
65	0·92	0·91	0·90	0·89	0·89	0·88	0·87	0·86	0·86	0·85	0·85	0·84	0·83	0·82	0·81	65
66	0·87	0·87	0·86	0·85	0·85	0·84	0·84	0·83	0·82	0·81	0·81	0·80	0·80	0·79	0·78	66
67	0·83	0·83	0·82	0·81	0·81	0·80	0·80	0·79	0·79	0·78	0·78	0·77	0·76	0·76	0·75	67
68	0·79	0·79	0·78	0·78	0·77	0·76	0·76	0·75	0·75	0·75	0·74	0·74	0·73	0·73	0·72	68
69	0·75	0·75	0·74	0·74	0·73	0·73	0·72	0·72	0·71	0·71	0·71	0·71	0·70	0·70	0·69	69
70	0·71	0·71	0·70	0·70	0·69	0·69	0·69	0·68	0·68	0·67	0·67	0·67	0·67	0·67	0·66	70
71	0·67	0·67	0·66	0·66	0·66	0·65	0·65	0·64	0·63	0·63	0·63	0·63	0·63	0·63	0·62	71
72	0·64	0·63	0·63	0·62	0·62	0·61	0·61	0·61	0·61	0·61	0·60	0·60	0·60	0·59		72
73	0·60	0·60	0·59	0·59	0·59	0·58	0·58	0·58	0·58	0·57	0·57	0·57	0·56			73
74	0·56	0·56	0·55	0·55	0·55	0·54	0·54	0·54	0·54	0·54	0·53	0·53				74
75	0·52	0·52	0·52	0·52	0·51	0·51	0·51	0·51	0·51	0·50	0·50					75
76	0·49	0·49	0·49	0·48	0·48	0·48	0·48	0·47	0·47	0·47						76
77	0·45	0·45	0·45	0·45	0·44	0·44	0·44	0·44	0·44							77
78	0·42	0·42	0·41	0·41	0·41	0·41	0·41	0·40								78
79	0·38	0·38	0·37	0·37	0·37	0·37	0·37									79
80	0·35	0·35	0·34	0·34	0·34	0·34										80
81	0·31	0·31	0·31	0·31	0·31										0·30	81
82	0·28	0·28	0·27	0·27										0·27	0·27	82
83	0·24	0·24	0·24										0·23	0·23	0·23	83

The values of 'A' printed below are for circumpolar bodies near to their Lower Meridian Transit. Latitude and Declination SAME NAME

DECLINATION — 0° 1° 2° 3° 4° 5° 6° 7° 8° 9° 10° 11° 12° 13° 14°

Different Name — **DECLINATION**

Lat.	15°	16°	17°	18°	19°	20°	21°	22°	23°	24°	25°	26°	27°	28°	29°	30°	Lat.
60	0·98	0·97	0·96	0·95	0·95	0·94	0·93	0·92	0·91	0·90	0·89						60
61	0·95	0·94	0·93	0·92	0·91	0·91	0·90	0·89	0·88	0·87							61
62	0·91	0·90	0·90	0·89	0·88	0·87	0·87	0·86	0·85								62
63	0·88	0·87	0·86	0·86	0·85	0·84	0·84	0·83									63
64	0·84	0·83	0·83	0·82	0·82	0·81	0·81										64
65	0·81	0·80	0·80	0·79	0·78	0·78										0·72	65
66	0·78	0·78	0·77	0·76	0·76										0·70	0·70	66
67	0·75	0·74	0·74	0·73										0·68	0·68	0·67	67
68	0·72	0·71	0·71									0·66	0·65	0·65	0·65	0·64	68
69	0·68	0·68									0·63	0·63	0·62	0·62	0·62	0·61	69
70	0·65									0·61	0·60	0·60	0·60	0·60	0·59	0·59	70
71									0·59	0·58	0·57	0·57	0·57	0·57	0·57	0·56	71
72								0·56	0·56	0·55	0·54	0·54	0·54	0·53	0·53	0·53	72
73							0·53	0·53	0·53	0·52	0·51	0·51	0·51	0·50	0·50	0·50	73
74						0·51	0·51	0·50	0·50	0·50	0·49	0·49	0·49	0·49	0·48	0·48	74
75					0·48	0·48	0·48	0·47	0·47	0·47	0·47	0·46	0·46	0·46	0·46	0·45	75
76				0·45	0·45	0·45	0·44	0·44	0·44	0·44	0·44	0·43	0·43	0·43	0·43	0·42	76
77			0·42	0·42	0·42	0·42	0·41	0·41	0·41	0·41	0·41	0·40	0·40	0·40	0·40	0·40	77
78		0·39	0·39	0·39	0·39	0·39	0·38	0·38	0·38	0·38	0·38	0·38	0·37	0·37	0·37	0·37	78
79		0·36	0·36	0·36	0·36	0·36	0·36	0·35	0·35	0·35	0·35	0·35	0·35	0·35	0·35	0·34	79
80	0·33	0·33	0·33	0·33	0·32	0·32	0·32	0·32	0·32	0·32	0·32	0·32	0·32	0·32	0·32	0·31	80
81	0·30	0·30	0·30	0·30	0·29	0·29	0·29	0·29	0·29	0·29	0·29	0·29	0·29	0·29	0·29	0·28	81
82	0·27	0·27	0·26	0·26	0·26	0·26	0·26	0·26	0·26	0·26	0·26	0·26	0·26	0·26	0·26	0·26	82
83	0·23	0·23	0·23	0·23	0·23	0·23	0·23	0·23	0·23	0·23	0·23	0·23	0·23	0·23	0·23	0·23	83

The values of 'A' printed below are for circumpolar bodies near to their Lower Meridian Transit. Latitude and Declination SAME NAME

DECLINATION — 15° 16° 17° 18° 19° 20° 21° 22° 23° 24° 25° 26° 27° 28° 29 30°

EX-MERIDIAN TABLE I

Supplementary Table to 83°

Latitude and Declination SAME NAME, near Lower Transit.
Change of Altitude in one minute from Meridian Passage = A

DECLINATION

Lat.	31°	32°	33°	34°	35°	36°	37°	38°	39°	40°	41°	42°	43°	44°	45°	46°	Lat.
60					0·81	0·80	0·79	0·78	0·77	0·76	0·75	0·75	0·74	0·73	0·72	0·71	60
61				0·79	0·79	0·78	0·77	0·76	0·75	0·74	0·73	0·72	0·72	0·71	0·70	0·69	61
62			0·78	0·77	0·76	0·76	0·75	0·74	0·73	0·72	0·71	0·70	0·70	0·69	0·68	0·67	62
63		0·76	0·75	0·75	0·74	0·74	0·73	0·72	0·71	0·70	0·69	0·68	0·68	0·67	0·66	0·65	63
64	0·74	0·74	0·73	0·73	0·71	0·71	0·70	0·70	0·69	0·68	0·67	0·66	0·66	0·65	0·64	0·63	64
65	0·72	0·71	0·70	0·70	0·69	0·68	0·68	0·67	0·66	0·66	0·65	0·64	0·64	0·63	0·62	0·62	65
66	0·69	0·68	0·68	0·67	0·67	0·66	0·65	0·65	0·64	0·64	0·63	0·62	0·62	0·61	0·60	0·60	66
67	0·66	0·65	0·65	0·64	0·64	0·64	0·63	0·63	0·62	0·62	0·61	0·60	0·60	0·59	0·58	0·58	67
68	0·63	0·63	0·63	0·62	0·62	0·61	0·61	0·60	0·60	0·60	0·59	0·58	0·58	0·57	0·56	0·56	68
69	0·61	0·61	0·61	0·60	0·60	0·59	0·59	0·58	0·58	0·58	0·57	0·56	0·56	0·55	0·54	0·54	69
70	0·59	0·58	0·58	0·57	0·57	0·57	0·56	0·56	0·55	0·55	0·54	0·54	0·53	0·53	0·52	0·52	70
71	0·56	0·56	0·55	0·55	0·54	0·54	0·53	0·53	0·52	0·52	0·51	0·51	0·51	0·50	0·50	0·50	71
72	0·53	0·53	0·52	0·52	0·52	0·51	0·51	0·51	0·50	0·50	0·49	0·49	0·49	0·48	0·48	0·48	72
73	0·50	0·50	0·50	0·50	0·50	0·49	0·49	0·49	0·48	0·48	0·47	0·47	0·47	0·46	0·46	0·46	73
74	0·48	0·47	0·47	0·47	0·47	0·47	0·46	0·46	0·46	0·46	0·45	0·45	0·45	0·44	0·44	0·43	74
75	0·45	0·45	0·45	0·45	0·44	0·44	0·44	0·44	0·43	0·43	0·43	0·42	0·42	0·42	0·42	0·41	75
76	0·42	0·42	0·42	0·42	0·41	0·41	0·41	0·41	0·40	0·40	0·40	0·40	0·40	0·40	0·39	0·39	76
77	0·40	0·39	0·39	0·39	0·39	0·38	0·38	0·38	0·38	0·38	0·38	0·38	0·38	0·38	0·37	0·37	77
78	0·37	0·37	0·37	0·36	0·36	0·36	0·36	0·35	0·35	0·35	0·35	0·35	0·35	0·35	0·35	0·35	78
79	0·34	0·34	0·34	0·34	0·34	0·34	0·33	0·33	0·33	0·33	0·33	0·33	0·33	0·33	0·32	0·32	79
80	0·31	0·31	0·31	0·31	0·31	0·31	0·31	0·30	0·30	0·30	0·30	0·30	0·30	0·30	0·29	0·29	80
81	0·28	0·28	0·28	0·28	0·28	0·28	0·28	0·28	0·28	0·27	0·27	0·27	0·27	0·27	0·27	0·27	81
82	0·25	0·25	0·25	0·25	0·25	0·25	0·25	0·25	0·25	0·25	0·25	0·25	0·24	0·24	0·24	0·24	82
83	0·22	0·22	0·22	0·22	0·22	0·22	0·22	0·22	0·22	0·22	0·22	0·22	0·22	0·22	0·21	0·21	83
	31°	32°	33°	34°	35°	36°	37°	38°	39°	40°	41°	42°	43°	44°	45°	46°	

DECLINATION

DECLINATION

Lat.	47°	48°	49°	50°	51°	52°	53°	54°	55°	56°	57°	58°	59°	60°	61°	62°	63°	Lat.
60	0·70	0·69	0·68	0·67	0·66	0·65	0·64	0·63	0·62	0·61	0·60	0·59	0·58	0·57	0·56	0·54	0·53	60
61	0·69	0·68	0·67	0·66	0·65	0·64	0·63	0·62	0·61	0·60	0·59	0·58	0·57	0·56	0·54	0·53	0·52	61
62	0·67	0·66	0·65	0·64	0·63	0·62	0·61	0·61	0·60	0·59	0·58	0·57	0·56	0·55	0·53	0·52	0·51	62
63	0·65	0·64	0·63	0·62	0·61	0·60	0·60	0·59	0·58	0·57	0·56	0·55	0·54	0·53	0·52	0·51	0·50	63
64	0·63	0·62	0·61	0·60	0·59	0·59	0·58	0·57	0·56	0·55	0·54	0·54	0·53	0·52	0·51	0·50	0·49	64
65	0·61	0·60	0·60	0·59	0·58	0·57	0·57	0·56	0·55	0·54	0·53	0·52	0·52	0·51	0·50	0·49	0·48	65
66	0·59	0·58	0·58	0·57	0·56	0·55	0·55	0·54	0·53	0·53	0·52	0·51	0·51	0·50	0·49	0·48	0·47	66
67	0·57	0·56	0·56	0·55	0·55	0·54	0·54	0·53	0·52	0·52	0·51	0·50	0·50	0·49	0·48	0·47	0·46	67
68	0·55	0·54	0·54	0·53	0·53	0·52	0·52	0·51	0·51	0·50	0·50	0·49	0·48	0·47	0·46	0·45	0·44	68
69	0·53	0·52	0·52	0·51	0·51	0·50	0·50	0·49	0·49	0·48	0·48	0·47	0·46	0·45	0·44	0·44	0·43	69
70	0·51	0·51	0·50	0·50	0·49	0·49	0·48	0·48	0·47	0·46	0·46	0·45	0·45	0·44	0·43	0·42	0·42	70
71	0·49	0·49	0·48	0·48	0·47	0·47	0·46	0·46	0·46	0·45	0·45	0·44	0·43	0·43	0·42	0·41	0·40	71
72	0·47	0·47	0·46	0·46	0·45	0·45	0·44	0·44	0·44	0·43	0·43	0·42	0·41	0·41	0·40	0·39	0·38	72
73	0·45	0·45	0·44	0·44	0·43	0·43	0·42	0·42	0·42	0·42	0·41	0·41	0·40	0·39	0·38	0·38	0·37	73
74	0·43	0·43	0·42	0·42	0·41	0·41	0·40	0·40	0·40	0·40	0·39	0·38	0·38	0·37	0·37	0·36	0·35	74
75	0·41	0·41	0·40	0·40	0·40	0·39	0·39	0·38	0·38	0·38	0·37	0·37	0·36	0·36	0·35	0·35	0·34	75
76	0·39	0·39	0·38	0·38	0·38	0·37	0·37	0·36	0·36	0·36	0·35	0·35	0·34	0·34	0·34	0·33	0·33	76
77	0·37	0·37	0·36	0·36	0·36	0·35	0·35	0·34	0·34	0·34	0·33	0·33	0·32	0·32	0·32	0·31	0·31	77
78	0·34	0·34	0·33	0·33	0·33	0·33	0·32	0·32	0·32	0·32	0·31	0·31	0·30	0·30	0·30	0·29	0·29	78
79	0·32	0·32	0·31	0·31	0·31	0·30	0·30	0·30	0·30	0·30	0·29	0·29	0·28	0·28	0·28	0·27	0·27	79
80	0·29	0·29	0·29	0·29	0·28	0·28	0·28	0·28	0·28	0·27	0·27	0·27	0·27	0·27	0·26	0·26	0·26	80
81	0·27	0·26	0·26	0·26	0·26	0·26	0·26	0·26	0·25	0·25	0·25	0·25	0·25	0·24	0·24	0·24	0·24	81
82	0·24	0·24	0·23	0·23	0·23	0·23	0·23	0·23	0·23	0·23	0·23	0·23	0·22	0·22	0·22	0·22	0·22	82
83	0·21	0·21	0·21	0·21	0·21	0·21	0·21	0·21	0·21	0·20	0·20	0·20	0·20	0·20	0·20	0·20	0·19	83
	47°	48°	49°	50°	51°	52°	53°	54°	55°	56°	57°	58°	59°	60°	61°	62°	63°	

DECLINATION

EX-MERIDIAN TABLE II

Reduction Plus to True Altitude at Upper Transit

HOUR ANGLE

A	0° 5' 359°55'	0° 10' 359°50'	0° 15' 359°45'	0° 20' 359°40'	0° 25' 359°35'	0° 30' 359°30'	0° 35' 359°25'	0° 40' 359°20'	0° 45' 359°15'	0° 50' 359°10'	0° 55' 359° 5'	1° 0' 359° 0'	A
1	0·0	0·0	0·0	0·0	0·0	0·1	0·1	0·1	0·2	0·2	0·2	0·3	1
2	0·0	0·0	0·0	0·1	0·1	0·1	0·2	0·2	0·3	0·4	0·4	0·5	2
3	0·0	0·0	0·1	0·1	0·1	0·2	0·3	0·4	0·5	0·6	0·7	0·8	3
4	0·0	0·0	0·1	0·1	0·2	0·3	0·4	0·5	0·6	0·7	0·9	1·1	4
5	0·0	0·0	0·1	0·1	0·2	0·3	0·5	0·6	0·8	0·9	1·1	1·3	5
6	0·0	0·0	0·1	0·2	0·3	0·4	0·5	0·7	0·9	1·1	1·3	1·6	6
7	0·0	0·1	0·1	0·2	0·3	0·5	0·6	0·8	1·1	1·3	1·6	1·9	7
8	0·0	0·1	0·1	0·2	0·4	0·5	0·7	0·9	1·2	1·5	1·8	2·1	8
9	0·0	0·1	0·2	0·3	0·4	0·6	0·8	1·1	1·4	1·7	2·0	2·4	9

A	1° 5' 358°55'	1° 10' 358°50'	1° 15' 358°45'	1° 20' 358°40'	1° 25' 358°35'	1° 30' 358°30'	1° 35' 358°25'	1° 40' 358°20'	1° 45' 358°15'	1° 50' 358° 10'	1° 55' 358° 5'	2° 0' 358° 0'	A
1	0·3	0·4	0·4	0·5	0·5	0·6	0·7	0·7	0·8	0·9	1·0	1·1	1
2	0·6	0·7	0·8	0·9	1·0	1·2	1·3	1·5	1·6	1·8	1·9	2·1	2
3	0·9	1·1	1·3	1·5	1·7	1·8	2·0	2·2	2·5	2·7	3·0	3·2	3
4	1·2	1·4	1·7	1·9	2·2	2·4	2·7	3·0	3·3	3·6	3·9	4·3	4
5	1·6	1·8	2·1	2·4	2·7	3·0	3·4	3·7	4·1	4·5	4·9	5·3	5
6	1·9	2·2	2·5	2·9	3·2	3·6	4·0	4·4	4·9	5·4	5·9	6·4	6
7	2·2	2·5	2·9	3·3	3·7	4·2	4·7	5·2	5·7	6·3	6·9	7·5	7
8	2·5	2·9	3·3	3·8	4·3	4·8	5·4	5·9	6·5	7·1	7·8	8·5	8
9	2·8	3·3	3·8	4·3	4·9	5·4	6·0	6·7	7·4	8·1	8·8	9·6	9

A	2° 5' 357°55'	2° 10' 357°50'	2° 15' 357°45'	2° 20' 357°40'	2° 25' 357°35'	2° 30' 357°30'	2° 35' 357°25'	2° 40' 357°20'	2° 45' 357°15'	2° 50' 357°10'	2° 55' 357° 5'	3° 0' 357° 0'	A
1	1·2	1·3	1·4	1·5	1·6	1·7	1·8	1·9	2·0	2·1	2·3	2·4	1
2	2·3	2·5	2·7	2·9	3·1	3·3	3·5	3·8	4·0	4·2	4·5	4·8	2
3	3·5	3·8	4·1	4·4	4·7	5·0	5·3	5·7	6·1	6·5	6·9	7·2	3
4	4·7	5·0	5·4	5·8	6·2	6·7	7·1	7·6	8·1	8·6	9·1	9·6	4
5	5·8	6·3	6·8	7·3	7·8	8·3	8·9	9·5	10·1	10·7	11·4	12·0	5
6	6·9	7·5	8·1	8·7	9·3	10·0	10·7	11·4	12·1	12·8	13·6	14·4	6
7	8·1	8·8	9·5	10·2	10·9	11·7	12·5	13·3	14·1	14·9	15·8	16·8	7
8	9·2	10·0	10·8	11·6	12·5	13·3	14·2	15·1	16·1	17·1	18·1	19·2	8
9	10·4	11·3	12·2	13·1	14·1	15·0	16·0	17·1	18·2	19·3	20·5	21·6	9

A	3° 5' 356°55'	3° 10' 356°50'	3° 15' 356°45'	3° 20' 356°40'	3° 25' 356°35'	3° 30' 356°30'	3° 35' 356°25'	3° 40' 356°20'	3° 45' 356°15'	3° 50' 356°10'	3° 55' 356° 5'	4° 0' 356° 0'	A
1	2·5	2·7	2·8	2·9	3·1	3·3	3·5	3·6	3·8	4·0	4·1	4·3	1
2	5·1	5·3	5·6	5·9	6·2	6·5	6·8	7·1	7·5	7·8	8·2	8·5	2
3	7·6	8·0	8·5	8·9	9·4	9·8	10·3	10·8	11·3	11·8	12·3	12·8	3
4	10·1	10·7	11·3	11·9	12·5	13·1	13·7	14·4	15·0	15·7	16·4	17·1	4
5	12·7	13·4	14·1	14·8	15·6	16·3	17·1	17·9	18·8	19·6	20·5	21·3	5
6	15·2	16·0	16·9	17·8	18·7	19·6	20·5	21·5	22·5	23·5	24·5	25·6	6
7	17·7	18·7	19·7	20·7	21·8	22·9	24·0	25·1	26·3	27·5	28·7	29·9	7
8	20·3	21·4	22·5	23·7	24·9	26·1	27·4	28·7	30·0	31·3	32·7	34·1	8
9	22·8	24·1	25·4	26·7	28·0	29·4	30·8	32·3	33·8	35·3	36·9	38·4	9

Reduction Minus to True Altitude at Lower Transit

EX-MERIDIAN TABLE II

Reduction Plus to True Altitude at Upper Transit

HOUR ANGLE

A	4° 5' 355°55'	4° 10' 355°50'	4° 15' 355°45'	4° 20' 355°40'	4° 25' 355°35'	4° 30' 355°30'	4° 35' 355°25'	4° 40' 355°20'	4° 45' 355°15'	4° 50' 355°10'	4° 55' 355° 5'	5° 0' 355° 0'	A
1	4·5	4·7	4·8	5·0	5·2	5·4	5·6	5·8	6·0	6·2	6·4	6·7	1
2	8·9	9·2	9·6	10·0	10·4	10·8	11·2	11·6	12·0	12·4	12·9	13·3	2
3	13·3	13·9	14·5	15·1	15·7	16·2	16·8	17·4	18·1	18·7	19·4	20·0	3
4	17·8	18·5	19·3	20·1	20·8	21·6	22·4	23·2	24·1	24·9	25·7	26·7	4
5	22·2	23·1	24·1	25·1	26·0	27·0	28·0	29·9	30·1	31·2	32·3	33·3	5
6	26·7	27·8	28·9	30·0	31·2	32·4	33·6	34·8	36·1	37·4	38·7	40·0	6
7	31·2	32·4	33·7	35·0	36·4	37·8	39·2	40·6	42·1	43·6	45·1	46·7	7
8	35·5	37·0	38·5	40·0	41·6	43·2	44·8	46·5	48·1	49·8	51·5	53·3	8
9	40·0	41·7	43·4	45·1	46·9	48·6	50·4	52·3	54·2	56·1	58·1	60·0	9

A	5° 5' 354°55'	5° 10' 354°50'	5° 15' 354°45'	5° 20' 354°40'	5° 25' 354°35'	5° 30' 354°30'	5° 35' 354°25'	5° 40' 354°20'	5° 45' 354°15'	5° 50' 354°10'	5° 55' 354° 5'	6° 0' 354° 0'	A
1	6·9	7·2	7·4	7·6	7·9	8·1	8·3	8·6	8·8	9·1	9·3	9·6	1
2	13·7	14·2	14·7	15·2	15·6	16·1	16·6	17·1	17·6	18·1	18·6	19·2	2
3	20·7	21·4	22·1	22·8	23·5	24·2	24·9	25·7	26·5	27·3	28·1	28·8	3
4	27·6	28·5	29·4	30·3	31·3	32·3	33·3	34·3	35·3	36·3	37·4	38·4	4
5	34·4	35·6	36·8	38·0	39·2	40·3	41·5	42·8	44·1	45·4	46·7	48·0	5
6	41·3	42·7	44·1	45·5	46·9	48·4	49·9	51·4	52·9	54·4	56·0	57·6	6
7	48·3	49·9	51·5	53·1	54·8	56·5	58·2	60·0	61·7	63·5	65·3	67·2	7
8	55·1	56·9	58·8	60·7	62·6	64·5	66·5	68·5	70·5	72·6	74·7	76·8	8
9	62·0	64·1	66·2	68·3	70·5	72·6	74·8	77·1	79·4	81·7	84·1	86·4	9

A	6° 5' 353°55'	6° 10' 353°50'	6° 15' 353°45'	6° 20' 353°40'	6° 25' 353°35'	6° 30' 353°30'	6° 35' 353°25'	6° 40' 353°20'	6° 45' 353°15'	6° 50' 353°10'	6° 55' 353° 5'	7° 0' 353° 0'	A
1	9·9	10·1	10·4	10·7	11·0	11·3	11·6	11·9	12·2	12·5	12·8	13·1	1
2	19·7	20·3	20·8	21·4	21·9	22·5	23·1	23·7	24·3	24·9	25·5	26·1	2
3	29·6	30·4	31·3	32·1	33·0	33·8	34·7	35·6	36·5	37·4	38·3	39·2	3
4	39·5	40·6	41·7	42·8	44·0	45·1	46·3	47·4	48·6	49·8	51·0	52·3	4
5	49·3	50·7	52·1	53·5	54·9	56·3	57·8	59·3	60·8	62·3	63·8	65·3	5
6	59·2	60·8	62·5	64·2	65·9	67·6	69·3	71·1	72·9	74·7	76·5	78·4	6
7	69·1	71·0	72·9	74·9	76·9	78·9	80·9	83·0	85·1	87·2	89·4	91·5	7
8	78·9	81·1	83·3	85·5	87·8	90·1	92·4	94·8	97·2	99·6	102	105	8
9	88·8	91·3	93·8	96·3	98·9	101	104	107	109	112	115	118	9

A	7° 5' 352°55'	7° 10' 352°50'	7° 15' 352°45'	7° 20' 352°40'	7° 25' 352°35'	7° 30' 352°30'	7° 35' 352°25'	7° 40' 352°20'	7° 45' 352°15'	7° 50' 352°10'	7° 55' 352° 5'	8° 0' 352° 0'	A
1	13·4	13·7	14·0	14·3	14·7	15·0	15·3	15·7	16·0	16·3	16·7	17·1	1
2	26·7	27·4	28·0	28·6	29·3	30·0	30·7	31·3	32·0	32·7	33·4	34·1	2
3	40·1	41·1	42·1	43·1	44·1	45·0	46·0	47·0	48·1	49·1	50·2	51·2	3
4	53·6	54·8	56·1	57·4	58·7	60·0	61·3	62·7	64·1	65·5	66·9	68·3	4
5	66·9	68·5	70·1	71·7	73·4	75·0	76·7	78·4	80·1	81·8	83·6	85·8	5
6	80·3	82·2	84·1	86·0	88·0	90·0	92·0	94·0	96·1	98·2	100	102	6
7	93·7	95·9	98·1	100	103	105	107	110	112	115	117	120	7
8	107	110	112	115	117	120	123	125	128	131	134	137	8
9	120	123	126	129	132	135	138	141	144	147	151	154	9

Reduction Minus to True Altitude at Lower Transit

EX-MERIDIAN TABLE II

Reduction Plus to True Altitude at Upper Transit

HOUR ANGLE

A	8° 5'	8° 10'	8° 15'	8° 20'	8° 25'	8° 30'	8° 35'	8° 40'	8° 45'	8° 50'	8° 55'	9° 0'	A
	351°55'	351°50'	351°45'	351°40'	351°35'	351°30'	351°25'	351°20'	351°15'	351°10'	351° 5'	351° 0'	
1	17·5	17·8	18·2	18·6	18·9	19·3	19·7	20·1	20·4	20·8	21·2	21·6	1
2	34·8	35·5	36·3	37·0	37·8	38·5	39·3	40·0	40·8	41·6	42·4	43·2	2
3	52·3	53·4	54·5	55·6	56·7	57·8	58·9	60·1	61·3	62·5	63·7	64·8	3
4	69·7	71·2	72·6	74·1	75·6	77·1	78·6	80·2	81·7	83·3	84·8	86·4	4
5	87·1	88·9	90·8	92·6	94·5	96·3	98·2	100	102	104	106	108	5
6	105	107	109	111	113	116	118	120	123	125	127	130	6
7	122	125	127	130	132	135	138	140	143	146	148	151	7
8	139	142	145	148	151	154	157	160	163	166	170	173	8
9	157	160	163	167	170	173	177	180	184	187	191	194	9

A	9° 5'	9° 10'	9° 15'	9° 20'	9° 25'	9° 30'	9° 35'	9° 40'	9 45'°	9° 50'	9° 55'	10° 0'	A
	350°55'	350°50'	350°45'	350°40'	350°35'	350°30'	350°25'	350°20'	350°15'	350°10'	350° 5'	350° 0'	
1	22·0	22·4	22·8	23·2	23·6	24·1	24·5	25·0	25·4	25·8	26·3	26·7	1
2	44·0	44·8	45·6	46·4	47·3	48·1	48·9	49·8	50·7	51·6	52·4	53·3	2
3	66·0	67·2	68·5	69·7	71·0	72·2	73·5	74·8	76·1	77·4	78·7	80·0	3
4	88·0	89·6	91·3	93·0	94·5	96·3	98·0	99·7	101	103	105	107	4
5	110	112	114	116	118	120	122	125	127	129	131	133	5
6	132	134	137	139	142	144	147	150	152	155	157	160	6
7	154	157	160	163	166	169	172	175	178	181	184	187	7
8	176	179	183	186	189	193	196	199	203	206	210	213	8
9	198	202	205	209	213	217	220	224	228	232	236	240	9

A	10° 5'	10° 10'	10° 15'	10° 20'	10° 25'	10° 30'	10° 35'	10° 40'	10° 45'	10° 50'	10° 55'	11° 0'	A
	349°55'	349°50'	349°45'	349°40'	349°35'	349°30'	349°25	349°20'	349°15'	349°10'	349°5'	349° 0'	
1	27·1	27·6	28·0	28·5	28·9	29·4	29·9	30·3	30·8	31·3	31·8	32·3	1
2	54·2	55·1	56·0	56·9	57·8	58·8	59·7	60·7	61·6	62·6	63·5	64·5	2
3	81·3	82·7	84·1	85·5	86·9	88·2	89·6	91·0	92·5	93·9	95·4	96·8	3
4	109	110	112	114	116	118	120	121	123	125	127	129	4
5	136	138	140	142	145	147	149	152	154	157	159	161	5
6	163	165	168	171	174	176	179	182	185	188	191	194	6
7	190	193	196	199	203	206	209	212	216	219	222	226	7
8	217	221	224	228	232	235	239	243	247	250	254	258	8
9	244	248	252	256	261	265	269	273	277	282	286	290	9

A	11° 5'	11° 10'	11° 15'	11° 20'	11° 25'	11° 30'	11° 35'	11° 40'	11° 45'	11° 50'	11° 55'	12° 0'	A
	348°55'	348°50'	348°45'	348°40'	348°35'	348°30'	348°25'	348°20'	348°15'	348°10'	348° 5'	348° 0'	
1	32·8	33·3	33·8	34·3	34·8	35·3	35·8	36·3	36·8	37·3	37·9	38·4	1
2	65·5	66·5	67·5	68·5	69·5	70·5	71·5	72·6	73·6	74·6	75·7	76·8	2
3	98·3	99·8	101	103	104	106	107	109	111	112	114	115	3
4	131	133	135	137	139	141	143	145	147	149	152	154	4
5	164	166	169	171	174	176	179	182	184	187	189	192	5
6	197	200	203	206	209	212	215	218	221	224	227	230	6
7	229	233	236	240	243	247	251	254	258	261	265	269	7
8	262	266	270	274	278	282	286	290	295	299	303	307	8
9	295	299	304	308	313	317	322	327	331	336	341	346	9

Reduction Minus to True Altitude at Lower Transit

EX-MERIDIAN TABLE II

Reduction Plus to True Altitude at Upper Transit

HOUR ANGLE

A	12° 5'	12° 10'	12° 15'	12° 20'	12° 25'	12° 30'	12° 35'	12° 40'	12° 45'	12° 50'	12° 55'	13° 0'	A
	347°55'	347°50'	347°45'	347°40'	347°35'	347°30'	347°25'	347°20'	347°15'	347°10'	347°5'	347° 0'	
"	'	'	'	'	'	'	'	'	'	'	'	'	"
1	38·9	39·5	40·0	40·5	41·1	41·7	42·3	42·8	43·4	44·0	44·5	45·1	1
2	77·9	78·9	80·0	81·1	82·2	83·3	84·4	85·5	86·7	87·8	89·0	90·1	2
3	117	118	120	122	123	125	127	128	130	132	134	135	3
4	156	158	160	162	165	167	169	171	173	176	178	180	4
5	195	197	200	203	206	208	211	214	217	220	223	225	5
6	234	237	240	243	247	250	253	257	260	264	267	270	6
7	273	276	280	284	288	292	296	300	304	308	312	316	7
8	312	316	320	325	329	333	338	342	347	351	356	361	8
9	350	355	3€0	365	370	375	380	385	390	395	401	406	9

A	13° 5'	13° 10'	13° 15'	13° 20'	13° 25'	13° 30'	13° 35'	13° 40'	13° 45'	13° 50'	13° 55'	14° 0'	A
	346°55'	346°50'	346°45'	346°40'	346°35'	346°30'	346°25'	346°20'	346°15'	346°10'	346° 5'	346° 0'	
"	'	'	'	'	'	'	'	'	'	'	'	'	"
1	45·7	46·3	46·8	47·4	48·0	48·6	49·2	49·8	50·4	51·0	51·6	52·3	1
2	91·3	92·4	93·6	94·8	96·0	97·2	98·4	99·6	101	102	103	105	2
3	137	139	141	142	144	146	148	149	151	153	155	157	3
4	183	185	187	190	192	194	197	199	202	204	207	209	4
5	228	231	234	237	240	243	246	249	252	255	258	261	5
6	274	277	281	284	288	292	295	299	303	306	310	314	6
7	320	324	328	332	336	340	344	349	353	357	362	366	7
8	365	370	375	379	384	389	394	399	404	408	413	418	8
9	411	416	421	427	432	437	443	448	454	459	465	470	9

A	14° 5'	14° 10'	14° 15'	14° 20'	14° 25'	14° 30'	14° 35'	14° 40'	14° 45'	14° 50'	14° 55'	15° 0'	A
	345°55'	345°50'	345°45'	345°40'	345°35'	345°30'	345°25'	345°20'	345°15'	345°10'	345° 5'	345° 0'	
"	'	'	'	'	'	'	'	'	'	'	'	'	"
1	52·9	53·6	54·2	54·8	55·5	56·1	56·7	57·4	58·0	58·7	59·3	60·0	1
2	106	107	108	110	111	112	113	115	116	117	119	120	2
3	159	161	163	164	166	168	170	172	174	176	178	180	3
4	212	214	217	219	222	224	227	230	232	235	237	240	4
5	264	268	271	274	277	280	284	287	290	293	297	300	5
6	317	321	325	329	333	336	340	344	348	352	356	360	6
7	370	375	379	384	388	393	397	402	406	411	415	420	7
8	423	428	433	438	443	449	454	459	464	469	475	480	8
9	476	482	487	493	499	505	510	516	522	528	534	540	9

A	15° 5'	15° 10'	15° 15'	15° 20'	15° 25'	15° 30'	15° 35'	15° 40'	15° 45'	15° 50'	15° 55'	16° 0'	A
	344°55'	344°50'	344°45'	344°40'	344°35'	344°30'	344°25'	344°20'	344°15'	344°10'	344° 5'	344° 0'	
"	'	'	'	'	'	'	'	'	'	'	'	'	"
1	60·7	61·3	62·0	62·7	63·4	64·1	64·8	65·4	66·2	66·9	67·6	68·3	1
2	121	123	124	125	127	128	130	131	132	134	135	137	2
3	182	184	186	188	190	192	194	197	199	201	203	205	3
4	243	245	248	251	254	256	259	262	265	268	270	273	4
5	304	307	310	314	317	320	324	328	331	335	338	341	5
6	364	368	372	376	380	384	389	393	397	401	406	410	6
7	425	429	434	439	444	448	454	459	463	468	473	478	7
8	486	490	496	502	507	513	519	524	530	535	541	546	8
9	546	552	558	564	571	577	583	590	596	502	608	614	9

Reduction Minus to True Altitude at Lower Transit

EX-MERIDIAN TABLE III
Second Correction Subtractive from First Correction

First Corr '	Altitude																First Corr '
	15°	30°	35°	40°	45°	50°	53°	56°	59°	62°	65°	68°	71°	74°	77°	80°	
	'	'	'	'	'	'	'	'	'	'	'	'	'	'	'	'	
15	0.0	0.0	0.0	0.0	0.0	0.0	0.0	0.1	0.1	0.1	0.1	0.1	0.1	0.1	0.1	0.2	15
30	0.0	0.1	0.1	0.1	0.1	0.2	0.2	0.2	0.2	0.2	0.3	0.3	0.4	0.5	0.6	0.7	30
35	0.1	0.1	0.1	0.2	0.2	0.2	0.2	0.3	0.3	0.3	0.4	0.4	0.5	0.6	0.8	1.0	35
40	0.1	0.1	0.2	0.2	0.2	0.3	0.3	0.3	0.4	0.4	0.5	0.6	0.7	0.8	1.0	1.3	40
45	0.1	0.2	0.2	0.3	0.3	0.4	0.4	0.4	0.5	0.6	0.6	0.7	0.9	1.0	1.3	1.7	45
50	0.1	0.2	0.3	0.3	0.4	0.4	0.5	0.5	0.6	0.7	0.8	0.9	1.1	1.3	1.6	2.1	50
55	0.1	0.3	0.3	0.4	0.4	0.5	0.6	0.7	0.7	0.8	0.9	1.1	1.3	1.5	1.9	2.5	55
60	0.1	0.3	0.4	0.4	0.5	0.6	0.7	0.7	0.9	1.0	1.1	1.3	1.5	1.8	2.3	3.0	60
65	0.2	0.4	0.4	0.5	0.6	0.7	0.8	0.9	1.0	1.2	1.3	1.5	1.8	2.1	2.7	3.5	65
70	0.2	0.4	0.5	0.6	0.7	0.9	0.9	1.1	1.2	1.3	1.5	1.8	2.1	2.5	3.1	4.0	70
75	0.2	0.5	0.6	0.7	0.8	1.0	1.1	1.2	1.4	1.5	1.8	2.0	2.4	2.9	3.5	4.6	75
80	0.3	0.5	0.7	0.8	0.9	1.1	1.2	1.4	1.6	1.8	2.0	2.3	2.7	3.3	4.0	5.3	80
85	0.3	0.6	0.7	0.9	1.1	1.3	1.4	1.6	1.8	2.0	2.3	2.6	3.1	3.7	4.5	6.0	85
90	0.3	0.7	0.8	1.0	1.2	1.4	1.6	1.8	2.0	2.2	2.5	2.9	3.4	4.1	5.1	6.7	90
93	0.3	0.7	0.9	1.1	1.3	1.5	1.7	1.9	2.1	2.4	2.7	3.1	3.7	4.4	5.5	7.1	93
96	0.4	0.8	0.9	1.1	1.3	1.6	1.8	2.0	2.2	2.5	2.9	3.3	3.9	4.7	5.8	7.6	96
99	0.4	0.8	1.0	1.2	1.4	1.7	1.9	2.1	2.4	2.7	3.1	3.5	4.1	5.0	6.2	8.1	99
102	0.4	0.9	1.1	1.3	1.5	1.8	2.0	2.2	2.5	2.9	3.2	3.7	4.4	5.3	6.6	8.6	102
105	0.4	0.9	1.1	1.4	1.6	1.9	2.1	2.4	2.7	3.0	3.4	4.0	4.7	5.6	7.0	9.1	105
108	0.5	1.0	1.2	1.4	1.7	2.0	2.3	2.5	2.8	3.2	3.6	4.2	4.9	5.9	7.3	9.6	108
111	0.5	1.0	1.3	1.5	1.8	2.1	2.4	2.7	3.0	3.4	3.8	4.4	5.2	6.3	7.8	10.2	111
114	0.5	1.1	1.3	1.6	1.9	2.3	2.5	2.8	3.2	3.6	4.1	4.7	5.5	6.6	8.2	10.7	114
117	0.5	1.1	1.4	1.7	2.0	2.4	2.6	3.0	3.3	3.7	4.3	4.9	5.8	6.9	8.6	11.3	117
120	0.6	1.2	1.5	1.8	2.1	2.5	2.8	3.1	3.5	3.9	4.5	5.2	6.1	7.3	9.1	11.9	120
123	0.6	1.3	1.5	1.8	2.2	2.6	2.9	3.3	3.7	4.1	4.7	5.5	6.4	7.6	9.5	12.5	123
126	0.6	1.3	1.6	1.9	2.3	2.8	3.1	3.4	3.8	4.3	5.0	5.7	6.7	8.0	10.0	13.1	126
129	0.7	1.4	1.7	2.0	2.4	2.9	3.2	3.6	4.0	4.6	5.2	6.0	7.0	8.4	10.5	13.7	129
132	0.7	1.5	1.8	2.1	2.5	3.0	3.4	3.8	4.2	4.8	5.4	6.3	7.4	8.8	11.0	14.4	132
135	0.7	1.5	1.9	2.2	2.6	3.2	3.5	3.9	4.4	5.0	5.7	6.6	7.7	9.2	11.5	15.0	135
138	0.7	1.6	1.9	2.3	2.8	3.3	3.7	4.1	4.6	5.2	5.9	6.9	8.0	9.7	12.0	15.7	138
141	0.8	1.7	2.0	2.4	2.9	3.5	3.8	4.3	4.8	5.4	6.2	7.2	8.4	1.0	12.5	16.4	141

EX-MERIDIAN TABLE IV
Limits of Hour Angle or Time 'before or after' Meridian Passage

A "	Hour Angle m	A "	Hour Angle m	A "	Hour Angle m	A "	Hour Angle m	A "	Hour Angle m
52·2	4	7·54	17	3·37	30	1·92	43	1·21	56
40·2	5	6·94	18	3·20	31	1·85	44	1·17	57
31·4	6	6·44	19	3·05	32	1·78	45	1·13	58
25·4	7	6·00	20	2·92	33	1·72	46	1·09	59
21·2	8	5·64	21	2·79	34	1·66	47	1·06	60
18·0	9	5·26	22	2·67	35	1·60	48	1·02	61
15·7	10	4·94	23	2·55	36	1·54	49	0·99	62
13·8	11	4·60	24	2·45	37	1·49	50	0·96	63
12·2	12	4·40	25	2·35	38	1·43	51	0·93	64
10·9	13	4·17	26	2·25	39	1·38	52	0·90	65
9·90	14	3·94	27	2·16	40	1·34	53	0·87	66
9·02	15	3·73	28	2·08	41	1·29	54		
8·22	16	3·54	29	2·00	42	1·25	55		

CHANGE of HOUR ANGLE with ALTITUDE

AZIMUTH	0°	3°	6°	9°	12°	15°	18°	21°	24°	27°	30°	33°	36°
°	′	′	′	′	′	′	′	′	′	′	′	′	′
1	57·30	57·38	57·61	58·01	58·58	59·32	60·25	61·38	62·72	64·31	66·16	68·32	70·83
2	28·65	28·69	28·81	29·01	29·29	29·66	30·13	30·69	31·37	32·16	33·09	34·17	35·42
3	19·11	19·13	19·21	19·35	19·53	19·78	20·09	20·47	20·92	21·44	22·06	22·78	23·62
4	14·34	14·36	14·41	14·51	14·66	14·84	15·07	15·36	15·69	16·09	16·55	17·09	17·72
5	11·47	11·49	11·54	11·62	11·73	11·88	12·06	12·29	12·56	12·88	13·25	13·68	14·18
6	9·57	9·58	9·62	9·69	9·78	9·90	10·06	10·25	10·47	10·74	11·05	11·41	11·83
7	8·21	8·22	8·25	8·31	8·39	8·50	8·63	8·79	8·98	9·21	9·48	9·78	10·14
8	7·19	7·20	7·23	7·28	7·35	7·44	7·56	7·70	7·87	8·06	8·30	8·57	8·88
9	6·39	6·40	6·43	6·47	6·54	6·62	6·72	6·85	7·00	7·17	7·38	7·62	7·90
10	5·76	5·77	5·79	5·83	5·89	5·96	6·06	6·17	6·30	6·46	6·65	6·87	7·12
11	5·24	5·25	5·27	5·31	5·36	5·43	5·51	5·61	5·74	5·88	6·05	6·25	6·48
12	4·81	4·82	4·84	4·87	4·92	4·98	5·06	5·15	5·27	5·40	5·55	5·74	5·95
13	4·45	4·45	4·47	4·50	4·55	4·60	4·67	4·76	4·87	4·99	5·13	5·30	5·50
14	4·13	4·14	4·16	4·19	4·23	4·28	4·35	4·43	4·53	4·64	4·77	4·93	5·11
15	3·86	3·87	3·89	3·91	3·95	4·00	4·06	4·14	4·23	4·34	4·46	4·61	4·78
16	3·63	3·63	3·65	3·67	3·71	3·76	3·82	3·89	3·97	4·07	4·19	4·33	4·48
17	3·42	3·43	3·44	3·46	3·50	3·54	3·60	3·66	3·74	3·84	3·95	4·08	4·23
18	3·24	3·24	3·25	3·28	3·31	3·35	3·40	3·47	3·54	3·63	3·74	3·86	4·00
19	3·07	3·08	3·09	3·11	3·14	3·18	3·23	3·29	3·36	3·45	3·55	3·66	3·80
20	2·92	2·93	2·94	2·96	2·99	3·03	3·07	3·13	3·20	3·28	3·38	3·49	3·61
21	2·79	2·79	2·81	2·83	2·85	2·89	2·93	2·99	3·06	3·13	3·22	3·33	3·45
22	2·67	2·67	2·68	2·70	2·73	2·76	2·81	2·86	2·92	3·00	3·08	3·18	3·30
24	2·46	2·46	2·47	2·49	2·51	2·55	2·59	2·63	2·69	2·76	2·84	2·93	3·04
26	2·28	2·28	2·29	2·31	2·33	2·36	2·40	2·44	2·50	2·56	2·63	2·72	2·82
28	2·13	2·13	2·14	2·16	2·18	2·21	2·24	2·28	2·33	2·39	2·46	2·54	2·63
30	2·00	2·00	2·01	2·03	2·05	2·07	2·10	2·14	2·19	2·25	2·31	2·39	2·47
32	1·89	1·89	1·90	1·91	1·93	1·95	1·98	2·02	2·07	2·12	2·18	2·25	2·33
34	1·79	1·79	1·80	1·81	1·83	1·85	1·88	1·92	1·96	2·01	2·07	2·13	2·21
36	1·70	1·70	1·71	1·72	1·74	1·76	1·79	1·82	1·86	1·91	1·96	2·03	2·10
38	1·62	1·63	1·63	1·65	1·66	1·68	1·71	1·74	1·78	1·82	1·88	1·94	2·01
40	1·56	1·56	1·56	1·58	1·59	1·61	1·64	1·67	1·70	1·75	1·80	1·86	1·92
42	1·49	1·50	1·50	1·51	1·53	1·55	1·57	1·60	1·64	1·68	1·73	1·78	1·85
44	1·44	1·44	1·45	1·46	1·47	1·49	1·51	1·54	1·58	1·62	1·66	1·72	1·78
46	1·39	1·39	1·40	1·41	1·42	1·44	1·46	1·49	1·52	1·56	1·61	1·66	1·72
48	1·35	1·35	1·35	1·36	1·38	1·40	1·42	1·44	1·47	1·51	1·55	1·60	1·66
50	1·31	1·31	1·31	1·32	1·34	1·35	1·37	1·40	1·43	1·47	1·51	1·56	1·61
52	1·27	1·27	1·28	1·29	1·30	1·31	1·33	1·36	1·39	1·42	1·47	1·51	1·57
55	1·22	1·22	1·23	1·24	1·25	1·26	1·28	1·31	1·34	1·37	1·41	1·46	1·51
60	1·16	1·16	1·16	1·17	1·18	1·20	1·21	1·24	1·26	1·30	1·33	1·38	1·43
65	1·10	1·11	1·11	1·12	1·13	1·14	1·16	1·18	1·21	1·24	1·27	1·32	1·36
70	1·06	1·07	1·07	1·08	1·09	1·10	1·12	1·14	1·17	1·19	1·23	1·27	1·32
75	1·04	1·04	1·04	1·05	1·06	1·07	1·09	1·11	1·13	1·16	1·19	1·23	1·28
80	1·02	1·02	1·02	1·03	1·04	1·05	1·07	1·09	1·11	1·14	1·17	1·21	1·26
85	1·00	1·01	1·01	1·02	1·03	1·04	1·06	1·08	1·10	1·13	1·16	1·20	1·24
90	1·00	1·00	1·01	1·01	1·02	1·04	1·05	1·07	1·09	1·12	1·15	1·19	1·24

CHANGE OF HOUR ANGLE
with ALTITUDE

AZIMUTH	LATITUDE											
°	39°	42°	45°	48°	51°	54°	57°	60°	63°	66°	69°	72°
	′	′	′	′	′	′	′	′	′	′	′	′
1	73·73	77·10	81·03	85·63	91·05	97·48	105·2(	114·60	126·21	140·88	159·89	185·43
2	36·87	38·56	40·52	42·82	45·53	48·75	52·61	57·31	63·11	70·45	79·96	92·73
3	24·59	25·71	27·02	28·56	30·36	32·51	35·08	38·21	42·09	46·98	53·32	61·83
4	18·45	19·29	20·27	21·42	22·78	24·39	26·32	28·67	31·58	35·25	40·00	46·39
5	14·76	15·44	16·23	17·15	18·23	19·52	21·07	22·95	25·27	28·21	32·02	37·13
6	12·31	12·87	13·53	14·30	15·20	16·28	17·57	19·13	21·04	23·48	26·65	30·91
7	10·56	11·04	11·60	12·26	13·04	13·96	15·07	16·41	18·07	20·17	22·90	26·55
8	9·25	9·67	10·16	10·74	11·42	12·22	13·19	14·37	15·83	17·67	20·05	23·25
9	8·23	8·60	9·04	9·55	10·16	10·88	11·74	12·78	14·08	15·72	17·84	20·69
10	7·41	7·75	8·14	8·61	9·15	9·80	10·57	11·52	12·68	14·16	16·07	18·64
11	6·74	7·05	7·41	7·83	8·33	8·92	9·62	10·48	11·54	12·89	14·63	16·96
12	6·19	6·47	6·80	7·19	7·64	8·18	8·83	9·62	10·59	11·83	13·42	15·56
13	5·72	5·98	6·29	6·64	7·06	7·56	8·16	8·89	9·79	10·93	12·40	14·39
14	5·32	5·56	5·85	6·18	6·57	7·03	7·59	8·27	9·11	10·16	11·53	13·38
15	4·97	5·20	5·4€	5·77	6·14	6·57	7·09	7·73	8·51	9·50	10·78	12·50
16	4·67	4·88	5·13	5·42	5·77	6·17	6·66	7·26	7·99	8·92	10·12	11·74
17	4·40	4·60	4·84	5·11	5·44	5·82	6·28	6·84	7·53	8·41	9·54	11·07
18	4·16	4·36	4·58	4·84	5·14	5·51	5·94	6·47	7·13	7·96	9·03	10·47
19	3·95	4·13	4·34	4·59	4·88	5·23	5·64	6·14	6·77	7·55	8·57	9·94
20	3·76	3·93	4·14	4·37	4·65	4·97	5·37	5·85	6·44	7·19	8·16	9·46
21	3·59	3·76	3·95	4·17	4·43	4·75	5·12	5·58	6·15	6·86	7·79	9·03
22	3·44	3·59	3·78	3·99	4·24	4·54	4·90	5·34	5·88	6·56	7·45	8·64
24	3·16	3·31	3·48	3·67	3·91	4·18	4·51	4·92	5·42	6·04	6·86	7·96
26	2·94	3·07	3·23	3·41	3·63	3·88	4·19	4·56	5·02	5·61	6·37	7·38
28	2·74	2·87	3·01	3·18	3·39	3·62	3·91	4·26	4·69	5·24	5·94	6·89
30	2·57	2·69	2·83	2·99	3·18	3·40	3·67	4·00	4·41	4·92	5·58	6·47
32	2·43	2·54	2·67	2·82	3·00	3·21	3·47	3·77	4·16	4·64	5·27	6·11
34	2·30	2·41	2·53	2·67	2·84	3·04	3·28	3·58	3·94	4·40	4·99	5·79
36	2·19	2·29	2·41	2·54	2·70	2·89	3·12	3·40	3·75	4·18	4·75	5·51
38	2·09	2·19	2·30	2·43	2·58	2·76	2·98	3·25	3·58	3·99	4·53	5·26
40	2·00	2·09	2·20	2·33	2·47	2·65	2·86	3·11	3·43	3·82	4·34	5·03
42	1·92	2·01	2·11	2·23	2·38	2·54	2·74	2·99	3·29	3·67	4·17	4·84
44	1·85	1·94	2·04	2·15	2·29	2·45	2·64	2·88	3·17	3·54	4·02	4·66
46	1·79	1·87	1·97	2·08	2·21	2·37	2·55	2·78	3·06	3·42	3·88	4·50
48	1·73	1·81	1·90	2·01	2·14	2·29	2·47	2·69	2·96	3·31	3·75	4·35
50	1·68	1·76	1·85	1·95	2·07	2·22	2·40	2·61	2·88	3·21	3·64	4·22
52	1·63	1·71	1·80	1·90	2·02	2·16	2·33	2·54	2·80	3·12	3·54	4·11
55	1·57	1·64	1·73	1·82	1·94	2·08	2·24	2·44	2·69	3·00	3·41	3·95
60	1·49	1·55	1·63	1·73	1·84	1·96	2·12	2·31	2·54	2·84	3·22	3·74
65	1·42	1·49	1·56	1·65	1·75	1·88	2·03	2·21	2·43	2·71	3·08	3·57
70	1·37	1·43	1·51	1·59	1·69	1·81	1·95	2·13	2·34	2·62	2·97	3·44
75	1·33	1·39	1·46	1·55	1·65	1·76	1·90	2·07	2·28	2·55	2·89	3·35
80	1·31	1·37	1·44	1·52	1·61	1·73	1·86	2·03	2·24	2·50	2·83	3·29
85	1·29	1·35	1·42	1·50	1·60	1·71	1·84	2·01	2·21	2·47	2·80	3·25
90	1·29	1·35	1·41	1·49	1·59	1·70	1·84	2·00	2·20	2·46	2·79	3·24

CHANGE OF ALTITUDE IN ONE MINUTE OF TIME

AZIMUTH

Lat.	0°	2½°	5°	7½°	10°	12½°	15°	17½°	20°	22½°	25°	27½°	30°	32½°	35°	37½°	Lat.
0°	0	0.7	1.3	1.9	2.6	3.2	3.9	4.5	5.1	5.7	6.3	6.9	,7.5	8.0	8.6	9.1	0°
4°	0	0.7	1.3	1.9	2.6	3.2	3.9	4.5	5.1	5.7	6.3	6.9	7.5	8.0	8.6	9.1	4°
8°	0	0.7	1.3	1.9	2.6	3.2	3.8	4.4	5.1	5.7	6.3	6.8	7.4	7.9	8.5	9.0	8°
12°	0	0.7	1.3	1.9	2.5	3.1	3.8	4.4	5.0	5.6	6.2	6.7	7.3	7.8	8.4	8.9	12°
16°	0	0.7	1.3	1.9	2.5	3.1	3.7	4.3	4.9	5.5	6.1	6.6	7.2	7.7	8.3	8.8	16°
20°	0	0.6	1.2	1.8	2.4	3.0	3.6	4.2	4.8	5.4	6.0	6.5	7.0	7.5	8.1	8.6	20°
24°	0	0.6	1.2	1.8	2.4	3.0	3.5	4.1	4.7	5.3	5.8	6.3	6.9	7.4	7.9	8.4	24°
26°	0	0.6	1.2	1.7	2.3	2.9	3.5	4.0	4.6	5.1	5.7	6.2	6.7	7.2	7.7	8.2	26°
28°	0	0.6	1.2	1.7	2.3	2.8	3.4	4.0	4.5	5.0	5.6	6.1	6.6	7.1	7.6	8.0	28°
30°	0	0.5	1.1	1.7	2.3	2.8	3.4	3.9	4.4	5.0	5.5	6.0	6.5	7.0	7.4	7.8	30°
32°	0	0.5	1.1	1.6	2.2	2.7	3.3	3.8	4.4	4.9	5.4	5.9	6.4	6.9	7.3	7.7	32°
34°	0	0.5	1.1	1.6	2.2	2.7	3.2	3.7	4.3	4.8	5.3	5.8	6.2	6.6	7.1	7.5	34°
36°	0	0.5	1.1	1.6	2.1	2.6	3.1	3.6	4.2	4.6	5.1	5.6	6.1	6.5	7.0	7.4	36°
38°	0	0.5	1.0	1.5	2.1	2.6	3.1	3.5	4.0	4.5	5.0	5.4	5.9	6.3	6.8	7.2	38°
40°	0	0.5	1.0	1.5	2.0	2.5	3.0	3.5	3.9	4.4	4.9	5.3	5.7	6.1	6.6	7.0	40°
42°	0	0.5	1.0	1.4	1.9	2.4	2.9	3.4	3.8	4.3	4.7	5.1	5.6	6.0	6.4	6.8	42°
44°	0	0.4	0.9	1.4	1.9	2.4	2.8	3.3	3.7	4.2	4.6	5.0	5.4	5.8	6.2	6.5	44°
46°	0	0.4	0.9	1.3	1.8	2.3	2.7	3.2	3.6	4.0	4.4	4.8	5.2	5.6	6.0	6.3	46°
48°	0	0.4	0.9	1.3	1.7	2.2	2.6	3.0	3.4	3.8	4.3	4.6	5.0	5.4	5.8	6.1	48°
49°	0	0.4	0.8	1.3	1.7	2.2	2.5	2.9	3.4	3.8	4.2	4.5	4.9	5.3	5.7	6.0	49°
50°	0	0.4	0.8	1.2	1.7	2.1	2.5	2.9	3.3	3.7	4.1	4.4	4.8	5.1	5.5	5.8	50°
51°	0	0.4	0.8	1.2	1.6	2.0	2.4	2.8	3.2	3.6	4.0	4.3	4.7	5.0	5.4	5.7	51°
52°	0	0.4	0.8	1.2	1.6	2.0	2.4	2.8	3.2	3.5	3.9	4.2	4.6	5.0	5.3	5.6	52°
53°	0	0.4	0.8	1.2	1.6	2.0	2.3	2.7	3.1	3.4	3.8	4.1	4.5	4.9	5.2	5.5	53°
54°	0	0.4	0.8	1.2	1.5	1.9	2.3	2.6	3.0	3.4	3.7	4.0	4.4	4.8	5.1	5.4	54°
55°	0	0.4	0.7	1.1	1.5	1.8	2.2	2.5	2.9	3.2	3.5	3.9	4.3	4.6	4.9	5.2	55°
56°	0	0.4	0.7	1.1	1.5	1.8	2.2	2.5	2.9	3.2	3.5	3.8	4.2	4.5	4.8	5.1	56°
57°	0	0.3	0.7	1.1	1.4	1.7	2.1	2.5	2.8	3.1	3.5	3.8	4.1	4.4	4.7	5.0	57°
58°	0	0.3	0.7	1.0	1.4	1.7	2.0	2.4	2.7	3.0	3.4	3.7	4.0	4.3	4.6	4.8	58°
59°	0	0.3	0.7	1.0	1.3	1.6	2.0	2.3	2.6	3.0	3.3	3.6	3.9	4.2	4.4	4.7	59°
60°	0	0.3	0.7	1.0	1.3	1.6	1.9	2.3	2.6	2.9	3.2	3.6	3.8	4.1	4.3	4.6	60°
61°	0	0.3	0.7	1.0	1.3	1.6	1.9	2.3	2.6	2.9	3.2	3.6	3.8	4.1	4.3	4.6	61°
62°	0	0.3	0.6	0.9	1.2	1.5	1.8	2.1	2.4	2.7	3.0	3.3	3.5	3.8	4.0	4.2	62°
63°	0	0.3	0.6	0.9	1.2	1.5	1.7	2.0	2.3	2.6	2.9	3.1	3.4	3.6	3.8	4.0	63°
64°	0	0.3	0.6	0.9	1.2	1.4	1.7	2.0	2.3	2.5	2.8	3.0	3.3	3.5	3.7	3.9	64°
65°	0	0.3	0.6	0.9	1.1	1.4	1.6	1.9	2.2	2.5	2.7	2.9	3.2	3.4	3.6	3.8	65°
66°	0	0.3	0.5	0.8	1.0	1.3	1.5	1.8	2.1	2.4	2.6	2.8	3.0	3.3	3.5	3.7	66°
67°	0	0.2	0.5	0.8	1.0	1.2	1.5	1.7	2.0	2.3	2.5	2.7	2.9	3.2	3.4	3.6	67°
68°	0	0.2	0.5	0.8	1.0	1.2	1.5	1.7	1.9	2.1	2.4	2.6	2.8	3.0	3.2	3.4	68°
69°	0	0.2	0.5	0.7	0.9	1.1	1.4	1.6	1.8	2.0	2.3	2.5	2.7	2.9	3.1	3.3	69°
70°	0	0.2	0.5	0.7	0.9	1.1	1.4	1.6	1.8	2.0	2.2	2.4	2.6	2.8	3.0	3.1	70°
71°	0	0.2	0.4	0.6	0.9	1.1	1.3	1.5	1.7	1.9	2.1	2.3	2.4	2.6	2.8	2.9	71°
72°	0	0.2	0.4	0.6	0.8	1.0	1.2	1.4	1.6	1.8	2.0	2.1	2.3	2.5	2.6	2.8	72°
73°	0	0.2	0.4	0.6	0.8	0.9	1.1	1.3	1.5	1.7	1.9	2.0	2.2	2.4	2.5	2.7	73°
74°	0	0.2	0.4	0.6	0.8	0.9	1.1	1.2	1.4	1.6	1.8	1.9	2.0	2.2	2.4	2.5	74°
75°	0	0.1	0.3	0.5	0.7	0.8	1.0	1.1	1.3	1.5	1.6	1.8	1.9	2.0	2.2	2.3	75°
Lat.	0°	2½°	5°	7½°	10°	12°	15°	17½°	20°	22½°	25°	27½°	30°	32½°	35°	37½°	Lat.

CHANGE OF ALTITUDE IN ONE MINUTE OF TIME
AZIMUTH

Lat.	40°	42½°	45°	47½°	50°	52½°	55°	57½°	60°	62½°	65°	67½°	70°	75°	80°	90°	Lat.
0°	9.6	10.1	10.6	11.0	11.5	11.9	12.3	12.7	13.0	13.3	13.6	13.8	14.1	14.5	14.8	15.0	0°
4°	9.6	10.1	10.6	11.0	11.5	11.9	12.3	12.6	13.0	13.3	13.6	13.8	14.1	14.5	14.7	15.0	4°
8°	9.5	10.0	10.5	11.0	11.4	11.8	12.2	12.5	12.9	13.2	13.5	13.7	14.0	14.4	14.6	14.9	8°
12°	9.4	9.9	10.4	10.8	11.2	11.6	12.0	12.3	12.7	13.0	13.3	13.5	13.8	14.2	14.4	14.7	12°
16°	9.3	9.8	10.2	10.6	11.0	11.4	11.8	12.1	12.5	12.8	13.1	13.3	13.5	13.9	14.2	14.4	16°
20°	9.1	9.5	10.0	10.4	10.8	11.1	11.5	11.8	12.2	12.5	12.8	13.0	13.2	13.6	13.9	14.1	20°
24°	8.8	9.2	9.7	10.2	10.5	10.8	11.2	11.5	11.9	12.2	12.4	12.6	12.9	13.2	13.5	13.7	24°
26°	8.7	9.1	9.5	9.9	10.3	10.6	11.0	11.3	11.7	12.0	12.2	12.5	12.7	13.0	13.3	13.5	26°
28°	8.5	9.0	9.4	9.7	10.1	10.4	10.8	11.1	11.5	11.7	12.0	12.2	12.4	12.8	13.1	13.2	28°
30°	8.3	8.8	9.2	9.6	9.9	10.2	10.6	10.9	11.2	11.5	11.8	12.0	12.2	12.5	12.8	13.0	30°
32°	8.2	8.6	9.0	9.4	9.7	10.0	10.4	10.7	11.0	11.3	11.5	11.8	12.0	12.3	12.5	12.7	32°
34°	8.0	8.4	8.8	9.2	9.5	9.8	10.2	10.5	10.8	11.0	11.3	11.5	11.7	12.0	12.3	12.4	34°
36°	7.8	8.2	8.6	9.0	9.3	9.6	9.9	10.2	10.5	10.7	11.0	11.2	11.4	11.7	12.0	12.1	36°
38°	7.6	8.0	8.4	8.7	9.1	9.4	9.7	10.0	10.2	10.5	10.7	10.9	11.1	11.4	11.6	11.8	38°
40°	7.4	7.7	8.1	8.5	8.8	9.1	9.4	9.7	10.0	10.2	10.4	10.6	10.8	11.1	11.3	11.5	40°
42°	7.2	7.5	7.9	8.2	8.5	8.8	9.1	9.4	9.7	9.9	10.1	10.3	10.5	10.8	11.0	11.1	42°
44°	6.9	7.2	7.6	8.0	8.3	8.6	8.8	9.0	9.3	9.6	9.8	10.0	10.1	10.4	10.6	10.8	44°
46°	6.7	7.0	7.4	7.7	8.0	8.3	8.5	8.7	9.0	9.2	9.4	9.6	9.8	10.1	10.3	10.4	46°
48°	6.5	6.8	7.1	7.4	7.7	8.0	8.2	8.5	8.7	8.9	9.1	9.3	9.4	9.7	9.9	10.0	48°
49°	6.3	6.6	6.9	7.2	7.6	7.8	8.0	8.3	8.5	8.7	8.9	9.1	9.2	9.5	9.7	9.8	49°
50°	6.2	6.5	6.8	7.1	7.4	7.6	7.9	8.1	8.3	8.5	8.7	8.9	9.1	9.3	9.5	9.6	50°
51°	6.0	6.3	6.6	6.8	7.2	7.5	7.7	7.9	8.1	8.3	8.5	8.7	8.9	9.1	9.3	9.4	51°
52°	5.9	6.2	6.5	6.8	7.1	7.4	7.6	7.8	8.0	8.2	8.4	8.6	8.7	8.9	9.1	9.2	52°
53°	5.8	6.1	6.4	6.7	7.0	7.3	7.5	7.7	7.9	8.1	8.3	8.4	8.5	8.7	8.9	9.0	53°
54°	5.7	6.0	6.2	6.5	6.8	7.0	7.2	7.4	7.6	7.8	8.0	8.2	8.3	8.5	8.7	8.8	54°
55°	5.5	5.8	6.1	6.3	6.6	6.8	7.0	7.2	7.5	7.6	7.8	8.0	8.1	8.3	8.5	8.6	55°
56°	5.4	5.7	5.9	6.2	6.4	6.7	6.9	7.1	7.3	7.4	7.6	7.8	7.9	8.1	8.3	8.4	56°
57°	5.2	5.5	5.8	6.0	6.3	6.5	6.7	6.9	7.1	7.2	7.4	7.6	7.7	7.9	8.0	8.2	57°
58°	5.1	5.3	5.6	5.8	6.1	6.3	6.5	6.7	6.9	7.0	7.2	7.4	7.5	7.7	7.8	8.0	58°
59°	5.0	5.2	5.5	5.7	5.9	6.1	6.3	6.5	6.7	6.9	7.0	7.2	7.3	7.5	7.6	7.7	59°
60°	4.8	5.1	5.3	5.5	5.7	5.9	6.1	6.3	6.5	6.7	6.8	6.9	7.0	7.2	7.4	7.5	60°
61°	4.8	5.1	5.3	5.5	5.7	5.9	6.1	6.3	6.5	6.6	6.7	6.8	6.9	7.0	7.2	7.3	61°
62°	4.5	4.7	5.0	5.2	5.4	5.6	5.8	5.9	6.1	6.2	6.4	6.5	6.6	6.7	6.9	7.0	62°
63°	4.3	4.5	4.8	5.0	5.2	5.4	5.6	5.7	5.9	6.0	6.2	6.3	6.4	6.5	6.7	6.8	63°
64°	4.2	4.4	4.7	4.9	5.1	5.2	5.4	5.5	5.7	5.8	6.0	6.1	6.2	6.3	6.4	6.5	64°
65°	4.1	4.3	4.5	4.7	4.9	5.0	5.2	5.3	5.5	5.6	5.8	5.9	6.0	6.1	6.2	6.3	65°
66°	4.0	4.1	4.3	4.5	4.7	4.9	5.0	5.1	5.3	5.4	5.5	5.6	5.7	5.9	6.0	6.1	66°
67°	3.8	4.0	4.1	4.3	4.5	4.7	4.8	5.0	5.1	5.2	5.3	5.4	5.5	5.7	5.8	5.9	67°
68°	3.6	3.8	4.0	4.1	4.3	4.5	4.6	4.8	4.9	5.0	5.1	5.1	5.2	5.4	5.5	5.6	68°
69°	3.5	3.6	3.8	4.0	4.1	4.3	4.4	4.6	4.7	4.8	4.9	5.0	5.0	5.1	5.3	5.4	69°
70°	3.3	3.5	3.6	3.7	3.9	4.1	4.2	4.3	4.5	4.6	4.7	4.7	4.8	4.9	5.0	5.1	70°
71°	3.1	3.3	3.5	3.6	3.7	3.9	4.0	4.1	4.2	4.3	4.4	4.5	4.6	4.7	4.8	4.9	71°
72°	2.9	3.1	3.3	3.4	3.5	3.7	3.8	3.9	4.0	4.1	4.2	4.2	4.3	4.4	4.5	4.6	72°
73°	2.8	3.0	3.1	3.3	3.4	3.5	3.6	3.7	3.8	3.9	4.0	4.1	4.1	4.2	4.3	4.4	73°
74°	2.6	2.8	2.9	3.1	3.2	3.3	3.4	3.5	3.6	3.7	3.8	3.9	3.9	3.9	4.0	4.1	74°
75°	2.5	2.6	2.7	2.9	3.0	3.1	3.2	3.3	3.4	3.4	3.5	3.5	3.6	3.7	3.8	3.9	75°
Lat.	40°	42½°	45°	47½°	50°	52½°	55°	57½°	60°	62½°	65°	67½°	70°	75°	80°	90°	Lat.

AUGMENTATION OF THE MOON'S SEMI - DIAMETER

App. Alt.	Moon's Semi-Diameter					
	14.5 ′	15.0 ′	15.5 ′	16.0 ′	16.5 ′	17.0 ′
°	′	′	′	′	′	′
10	0.0	0.0	0.1	0.1	0.1	0.1
20	0.1	0.1	0.1	0.1	0.1	0.1
30	0.1	0.1	0.1	0.1	0.2	0.2
40	0.1	0.2	0.2	0.2	0.2	0.2
50	0.2	0.2	0.2	0.2	0.2	0.2
60	0.2	0.2	0.2	0.2	0.3	0.3
70	0.2	0.2	0.3	0.3	0.3	0.3
80	0.2	0.2	0.3	0.3	0.3	0.3
90	0.2	0.2	0.3	0.3	0.3	0.3

REDUCTION OF THE MOON'S HORIZONTAL PARALLAX

Lat.	Horizontal Parallax		
	54 ′	58 ′	62 ′
°	′	′	′
10	0.0	0.0	0.0
20	0.0	0.0	0.0
30	0.0	0.0	0.1
40	0.1	0.1	0.1
50	0.1	0.1	0.1
60	0.1	0.2	0.2
70	0.2	0.2	0.2
80	0.2	0.2	0.2

DIP OF THE SEA HORIZON

m	ft	Dip ′	m	ft	Dip ′
0.5	1.5	−1.2	20.5	67	−8.0
1.0	3	−1.8	21.0	69	−8.1
1.5	5	−2.2	21.5	71	−8.2
2.0	7	−2.5	22.0	72	−8.3
2.5	8	−2.8	22.5	74	−8.3
3.0	10	−3.0	23.0	75	−8.4
3.5	11	−3.3	23.5	77	−8.5
4.0	13	−3.5	24.0	79	−8.6
4.5	15	−3.7	24.5	80	−8.7
5.0	16	−3.9	25.0	82	−8.8
5.5	18	−4.1	25.5	84	−8.9
6.0	20	−4.3	26.0	85	−9.0
6.5	21	−4.5	26.5	87	−9.1
7.0	23	−4.7	27.0	89	−9.1
7.5	25	−4.8	27.5	90	−9.2
8.0	26	−5.0	28.0	92	−9.3
8.5	28	−5.1	28.5	94	−9.4
9.0	30	−5.3	29.0	95	−9.5
9.5	31	−5.4	29.5	97	−9.6
10.0	33	−5.6	30.0	98	−9.6
10.5	34	−5.7	31	102	−9.8
11.0	36	−5.8	32	105	−10.0
11.5	38	−6.0	33	108	−10.1
12.0	39	−6.1	34	112	−10.3
12.5	41	−6.2	35	115	−10.4
13.0	43	−6.3	36	118	−10.6
13.5	44	−6.5	37	121	−10.7
14.0	46	−6.6	38	125	−10.8
14.5	48	−6.7	39	128	−11.0
15.0	49	−6.8	40	131	−11.1
15.5	51	−6.9	41	135	−11.3
16.0	52	−7.0	42	138	−11.4
16.5	54	−7.1	43	141	−11.5
17.0	56	−7.3	44	144	−11.7
17.5	57	−7.4	45	148	−11.8
18.0	59	−7.5	46	151	−11.9
18.5	61	−7.6	47	154	−12.1
19.0	62	−7.7	48	157	−12.2
19.5	64	−7.8	49	161	−12.3
20.0	66	−7.9	50	164	−12.4

SUN

Parallax in Altitude		Mean Semi Diameter	
App. Alt.	Parlx.	Month	Mean S.D.
°	′		′
		Jan.	16.3
0	+ 0.2	Feb.	16.2
10	+ 0.2	March	16.1
20	+ 0.1	April	16.0
30	+ 0.1	May	15.8
40	+ 0.1	June	15.8
50	+ 0.1	July	15.8
60	+ 0.1	Aug.	15.8
70	+ 0.1	Sept.	15.9
80	+ 0.0	Oct.	16.1
90	+ 0.0	Nov.	16.2
		Dec.	16.3

MEAN REFRACTION

Atmospheric Pressure 1000mbs (29.5ins)
Temperature 10°C (50°F)

App. Alt.	Refr.	App. Alt.	Refr.	App. Alt.	Refr.
° ′	′	° ′	′	° ′	′
0 00	−33.9	4 00	−11.5	12 00	−4.4
05	32.8	10	11.1	20	4.3
10	31.8	20	10.8	40	4.2
15	30.8	30	10.5	13 00	4.0
20	29.9	40	10.2	20	3.9
25	29.0	50	9.9	40	3.9
0 30	−23.2	5 00	−9.7	14 00	−3.8
35	27.4	10	9.4	20	3.7
40	26.6	20	9.2	40	3.6
45	25.9	30	8.9	15 00	3.5
50	25.2	40	8.7	20	3.4
55	24.6	50	8.5	40	3.4
1 00	−23.9	6 00	−8.3	16 00	−3.3
05	23.3	10	8.1	17 00	3.1
10	22.7	20	7.9	18 00	2.9
15	22.1	30	7.7	19 00	2.7
20	21.5	40	7.5	20 00	2.6
25	21.0	50	7.4	21 00	2.5
1 30	−20.5	7 00	−7.2	22 00	−2.3
35	20.1	10	7.0	23 00	2.2
40	19.6	20	6.9	24 00	2.1
45	19.1	30	6.8	25 00	2.0
50	18.7	40	6.6	26 00	1.9
55	18.3	50	6.5	27 00	1.8
2 00	−17.9	8 00	−6.4	28 00	−1.8
05	17.5	10	6.3	29 00	1.7
10	17.1	20	6.2	30 00	1.7
15	16.8	30	6.1	31 00	1.6
20	16.4	40	6.0	32 00	1.5
25	16.1	50	5.9	33 00	1.5
2 30	−15.8	9 00	−5.8	34 00	−1.4
35	15.5	10	5.7	35 00	1.4
40	15.2	20	5.6	36 00	1.3
45	14.8	30	5.5	37 00	1.2
50	14.6	40	5.4	38 00	1.2
55	14.4	50	5.3	39 00	1.2
3 00	−14.1	10 00	−5.2	40 00	−1.1
05	13.8	10	5.2	45 00	0.9
10	13.6	20	5.1	50 00	0.8
15	13.4	30	5.0	55 00	0.7
20	13.1	40	4.9	60 00	0.5
25	12.9	50	4.9	65 00	0.4
3 30	−12.7	11 00	−4.8	70 00	−0.3
35	12.4	10	4.7	75 00	0.3
40	12.2	20	4.7	80 00	0.2
45	12.1	30	4.6	85 00	0.1
50	11.9	40	4.5	90 00	0.0
55	11.7	50	4.5		
4 00	−11.5	12 00	−4.4		

ADDITIONAL REFRACTION CORRECTIONS FOR AIR TEMPERATURE

To be applied to the Apparent Altitude

App. Alt.	Air Temperature - °C								
	−5°	0°	5°	10°	15°	20°	25°	30°	35°
° ′	′	′	′	′	′	′	′	′	′
0 00	−3.4	−2.0	−1.0	0.0	+1.0	+1.9	+2.8	+3.7	+4.7
20	2.7	1.8	0.9	0.0	0.9	1.5	2.2	3.1	3.7
40	2.4	1.6	0.8	0.0	0.8	1.3	2.0	2.7	3.3
1 00	2.0	1.4	0.7	0.0	0.7	1.2	1.8	2.4	2.9
20	1.8	1.2	0.6	0.0	0.6	1.0	1.5	2.0	2.6
40	1.5	1.0	0.5	0.0	0.5	0.9	1.3	1.8	2.2
2 00	−1.3	−0.9	−0.4	0.0	+0.4	+0.8	+1.2	+1.5	+1.9
20	1.2	0.8	0.4	0.0	0.4	0.7	1.1	1.4	1.7
40	1.1	0.7	0.4	0.0	0.4	0.7	1.0	1.2	1.6
3 00	1.0	0.7	0.3	0.0	0.3	0.6	1.0	1.2	1.5
20	1.0	0.6	0.3	0.0	0.3	0.6	0.9	1.1	1.4
40	0.9	0.6	0.3	0.0	0.3	0.6	0.8	1.0	1.3
4 00	−0.8	−0.6	−0.3	0.0	+0.3	+0.5	+0.8	+1.0	+1.2
5	0.7	0.5	0.2	0.0	0.2	0.4	0.7	0.8	1.0
6	0.6	0.4	0.2	0.0	0.2	0.4	0.6	0.7	0.9
7	0.5	0.4	0.2	0.0	0.2	0.3	0.5	0.6	0.8
8	0.5	0.3	0.2	0.0	0.1	0.3	0.4	0.5	0.7
9	0.4	0.3	0.1	0.0	0.1	0.3	0.4	0.5	0.6
10 00	−0.4	−0.3	−0.1	0.0	+0.1	+0.2	+0.4	+0.4	+0.5
20	0.2	0.1	0.1	0.0	0.1	0.1	0.2	0.2	0.3
30	0.1	0.1	0.0	0.0	0.0	0.1	0.1	0.1	0.2
40	0.1	0.1	0.0	0.0	0.0	0.1	0.1	0.1	0.1
50	0.1	0.0	0.0	0.0	0.0	0.0	0.0	0.1	0.1
60	0.0	0.0	0.0	0.0	0.0	0.0	0.0	0.0	0.0

ADDITIONAL REFRACTION CORRECTIONS FOR ATMOSPHERIC PRESSURE

To be applied to the Apparent Altitude

App. Alt.	Atmospheric Pressure - millibars				
	960	980	1000	1020	1030
° ′	′	′	′	′	′
0 00	+1.7	+0.8	0.0	−0.8	−1.7
30	1.4	0.7	0.0	0.7	1.4
1 00	1.2	0.6	0.0	0.6	1.2
30	1.0	0.5	0.0	0.5	1.0
2 00	+0.9	+0.4	0.0	−0.4	−0.9
4	0.6	0.3	0.0	0.3	0.6
6	0.4	0.2	0.0	0.2	0.4
8	0.3	0.2	0.0	0.2	0.3
10	0.3	0.1	0.0	0.1	0.3
15 00	+0.2	+0.1	0.0	−0.1	−0.2
20	0.1	0.1	0.0	0.1	0.1
25	0.1	0.1	0.0	0.1	0.1
30	0.1	0.0	0.0	0.0	0.1
35	0.1	0.0	0.0	0.0	0.1
40 00	0.0	0.0	0.0	0.0	0.0

CORRECTION OF MOON'S MER. PASS.
Corr. Plus to Mer. Pass. in West Long.

Long.	39 m.	42 m.	45 m.	48 m.	51 m.	54 m.	57 m.	60 m.	63 m.	66 m.	Long.
°	m.	m.	m.	m.	m.	m.	m.	m.	m.	m.	°
3	0·3	0·4	0·4	0·4	0·4	0·4	0·5	0·5	0·5	0·6	3
6	0·6	0·7	0·8	0·8	0·8	0·9	1·0	1·0	1·0	1·1	6
9	1·0	1·0	1·1	1·2	1·3	1·4	1·4	1·5	1·6	1·6	9
12	1·3	1·4	1·5	1·6	1·7	1·8	1·9	2·0	2·1	2·2	12
15	1·6	1·8	1·9	2·0	2·1	2·2	2·4	2·5	2·6	2·8	15
18	2·0	2·1	2·2	2·4	2·6	2·7	2·8	3·0	3·2	3·3	18
21	2·3	2·4	2·6	2·8	3·0	3·2	3·3	3·5	3·7	3·8	21
24	2·6	2·8	3·0	3·2	3·4	3·6	3·8	4·0	4·2	4·4	24
27	2·9	3·2	3·4	3·6	3·8	4·0	4·3	4·5	4·7	5·0	27
30	3·2	3·5	3·8	4·0	4·2	4·5	4·8	5·0	5·2	5·5	30
33	3·6	3·8	4·1	4·4	4·7	5·0	5·2	5·5	5·8	6·0	33
36	3·9	4·2	4·5	4·8	5·1	5·4	5·7	6·0	6·3	6·6	36
39	4·2	4·6	4·9	5·2	5·5	5·8	6·2	6·5	6·8	7·2	39
42	4·6	4·9	5·2	5·6	6·0	6·3	6·6	7·0	7·4	7·7	42
45	4·9	5·2	5·6	6·0	6·4	6·8	7·1	7·5	7·9	8·2	45
48	5·2	5·6	6·0	6·4	6·8	7·2	7·6	8·0	8·4	8·8	48
51	5·5	6·0	6·4	6·8	7·2	7·6	8·1	8·5	8·9	9·4	51
54	5·8	6·3	6·8	7·2	7·6	8·1	8·6	9·0	9·4	9·9	54
57	6·2	6·6	7·1	7·6	8·1	8·6	9·0	9·5	10·0	10·4	57
60	6·5	7·0	7·5	8·0	8·5	9·0	9·5	10·0	10·5	11·0	60
63	6·8	7·4	7·9	8·4	8·9	9·4	10·0	10·5	11·0	11·6	63
66	7·2	7·7	8·2	8·8	9·4	9·9	10·4	11·0	11·6	12·1	66
69	7·5	8·0	8·6	9·2	9·8	10·4	10·9	11·5	12·1	12·6	69
72	7·8	8·4	9·0	9·6	10·2	10·8	11·4	12·0	12·6	13·2	72
75	8·1	8·8	9·4	10·0	10·6	11·2	11·9	12·5	13·2	13·8	75
78	8·4	9·1	9·8	10·4	11·0	11·7	12·4	13·0	13·6	14·3	78
81	8·8	9·4	10·1	10·8	11·5	12·2	12·8	13·5	14·2	14·8	81
84	9·1	9·8	10·5	11·2	11·9	12·6	13·3	14·0	14·7	15·4	84
87	9·4	10·2	10·9	11·6	12·3	13·0	13·8	14·5	15·2	16·0	87
90	9·8	10·5	11·2	12·0	12·8	13·5	14·2	15·0	15·8	16·5	90
93	10·1	10·8	11·6	12·4	13·2	14·0	14·7	15·5	16·3	17·0	93
96	10·4	11·2	12·0	12·8	13·6	14·4	15·2	16·0	16·8	17·6	96
99	10·7	11·6	12·4	13·2	14·0	14·8	15·7	16·5	17·3	18·2	99
102	11·0	11·9	12·8	13·6	14·4	15·3	16·2	17·0	17·8	18·7	102
105	11·4	12·2	13·1	14·0	14·9	15·8	16·6	17·5	18·4	19·2	105
108	11·7	12·6	13·5	14·4	15·3	16·2	17·1	18·0	18·9	19·8	108
111	12·0	13·0	13·9	14·8	15·7	16·6	17·6	18·5	19·4	20·4	111
114	12·4	13·3	14·2	15·2	16·2	17·1	18·0	19·0	20·0	20·9	114
117	12·7	13·6	14·6	15·6	16·6	17·6	18·5	19·5	20·5	21·4	117
120	13·0	14·0	15·0	16·0	17·0	18·0	19·0	20·0	21·0	22·0	120
123	13·3	14·4	15·4	16·4	17·4	18·4	19·5	20·5	21·5	22·6	123
126	13·6	14·7	15·8	16·8	17·8	18·9	20·0	21·0	22·0	23·1	126
129	14·0	15·0	16·1	17·2	18·3	19·4	20·4	21·5	22·6	23·6	129
132	14·3	15·4	16·5	17·6	18·7	19·8	20·9	22·0	23·1	24·2	132
135	14·6	15·8	16·9	18·0	19·1	20·2	21·4	22·5	23·6	24·8	135
138	15·0	16·1	17·2	18·4	19·6	20·7	21·8	23·0	24·2	25·3	138
141	15·3	16·4	17·6	18·8	20·0	21·2	22·3	23·5	24·7	25·8	141
144	15·6	16·8	18·0	19·2	20·4	21·6	22·8	24·0	25·2	26·4	144
147	15·9	17·2	18·4	19·6	20·8	22·0	23·3	24·5	25·7	27·0	147
150	16·2	17·5	18·8	20·0	21·2	22·5	23·8	25·0	26·2	27·5	150
153	16·6	17·8	19·1	20·4	21·7	23·0	24·2	25·5	26·8	28·0	153
156	16·9	18·2	19·5	20·8	22·1	23·4	24·7	26·0	27·3	28·6	156
159	17·2	18·6	19·9	21·2	22·5	23·8	25·2	26·5	27·8	29·2	159
162	17·6	18·9	20·2	21·6	23·0	24·3	25·6	27·0	28·4	29·7	162
165	17·9	19·2	20·6	22·0	23·4	24·8	26·1	27·5	28·9	30·2	165
168	18·2	19·6	21·0	22·4	23·8	25·2	26·6	28·0	29·4	30·8	168
171	18·5	20·0	21·4	22·8	24·2	25·6	27·1	28·5	29·9	31·4	171
174	18·8	20·3	21·8	23·2	24·6	26·1	27·6	29·0	30·4	31·9	174
177	19·2	20·6	22·1	23·6	25·1	26·6	28·0	29·5	31·0	32·4	177
180	19·5	21·0	22·5	24·0	25·5	27·0	28·5	30·0	31·5	33·0	180

Corr. Minus to Mer. Pass. in East Long.

SUN'S TOTAL CORRECTION

To be applied to the Observed Altitude of the Sun's Lower (L) or Upper (U) Limb

	2.0m (7ft)		2.3m (8ft)		2.7m (9ft)		3.1m (10ft)		3.5m (11ft)		3.9m (13ft)		4.4m (15ft)		4.9m (16ft)	
Obs. Alt.	L	U	L	U	L	U	L	U	L	U	L	U	L	U	L	U
06 00	+5.1	−26.9	+4.9	−27.1	+4.7	−27.3	+4.5	−27.5	+4.3	−27.7	+4.1	−27.9	+3.9	−28.1	+3.7	−28.3
10	5.3	26.7	5.1	26.9	4.9	27.1	4.7	27.3	4.5	27.5	4.3	27.7	4.1	27.9	3.9	28.1
20	5.5	26.5	5.3	26.7	5.1	26.9	4.9	27.1	4.7	27.3	4.5	27.5	4.3	27.7	4.1	27.9
30	5.7	26.3	5.5	26.5	5.3	26.7	5.1	26.9	4.9	27.1	4.7	27.3	4.5	27.5	4.3	27.7
40	5.9	26.1	5.7	26.3	5.5	26.5	5.3	26.7	5.1	26.9	4.9	27.1	4.7	27.3	4.5	27.5
50	6.1	25.9	5.9	26.1	5.7	26.3	5.5	26.5	5.3	26.7	5.1	26.9	4.9	27.1	4.7	27.3
07 00	+6.3	−25.7	+6.1	−25.9	+5.9	−26.1	+5.7	−26.3	+5.5	26.5	+5.3	−26.7	+5.1	−26.9	+4.9	−27.1
15	6.5	25.5	6.3	25.7	6.1	25.9	5.9	26.1	5.7	26.3	5.5	26.5	5.3	26.7	5.1	26.9
30	6.7	25.3	6.5	25.5	6.3	25.7	6.1	25.9	5.9	26.1	5.7	26.3	5.5	26.5	5.3	26.7
45	6.9	25.1	6.7	25.3	6.5	25.5	6.3	25.7	6.1	25.9	5.9	26.1	5.7	26.3	5.5	26.5
08 00	7.1	24.9	6.9	25.1	6.7	25.3	6.5	25.5	6.3	25.7	6.1	25.9	5.9	26.1	5.7	26.3
15	7.3	24.7	7.1	24.9	6.9	25.1	6.7	25.3	6.5	25.5	6.3	25.7	6.1	25.9	5.9	26.1
30	7.5	24.5	7.3	24.7	7.1	24.9	6.9	25.1	6.7	25.3	6.5	25.5	6.3	25.7	6.1	25.9
45	7.7	24.3	7.5	24.5	7.3	24.7	7.1	24.9	6.9	25.1	6.7	25.3	6.5	25.5	6.3	25.7
09 00	+7.9	−24.1	+7.7	−24.3	+7.5	−24.5	+7.3	−24.7	+7.1	24.9	+6.9	−25.1	+6.7	−25.3	+6.5	−25.5
20	8.1	23.9	7.9	24.1	7.7	24.3	7.5	24.5	7.3	24.7	7.1	24.9	6.9	25.1	6.7	25.3
40	8.3	23.7	8.1	23.9	7.9	24.1	7.7	24.3	7.5	24.5	7.3	24.7	7.1	24.9	6.9	25.1
10 00	8.5	23.5	8.3	23.7	8.1	23.9	7.9	24.1	7.7	24.3	7.5	24.5	7.3	24.7	7.1	24.9
30	8.7	23.3	8.5	23.5	8.3	23.7	8.1	23.9	7.9	24.1	7.7	24.3	7.5	24.5	7.3	24.7
11 00	8.9	23.1	8.7	23.3	8.5	23.5	8.3	23.7	8.1	23.9	7.9	24.1	7.7	24.3	7.5	24.5
30	9.1	22.9	8.9	23.1	8.7	23.3	8.5	23.5	8.3	23.7	8.1	23.9	7.9	24.1	7.7	24.3
12 00	9.3	22.7	9.1	22.9	8.9	23.1	8.7	23.3	8.5	23.5	8.3	23.7	8.1	23.9	7.9	24.1
30	9.5	22.5	9.3	22.7	9.1	22.9	8.9	23.1	8.7	23.3	8.5	23.5	8.3	23.7	8.1	23.9
13 00	+9.7	−22.3	+9.5	−22.5	+9.3	−22.7	+9.1	−22.9	+8.9	−23.1	+8.7	−23.3	+8.5	−27.5	+8.3	−23.7
14 00	9.9	22.1	9.7	22.3	9.5	22.5	9.3	22.7	9.1	22.9	8.9	23.1	8.7	23.3	8.5	23.5
15 00	10.1	21.9	9.9	22.1	9.7	22.3	9.5	22.5	9.3	22.7	9.1	22.9	8.9	23.1	8.7	23.3
16 00	10.3	21.7	10.1	21.9	9.9	22.1	9.7	22.3	9.5	22.5	9.3	22.7	9.1	22.9	8.9	23.1
17 00	10.5	21.5	10.3	21.7	10.1	21.9	9.9	22.1	9.7	22.3	9.5	22.5	9.3	22.7	9.1	22.9
18 00	10.7	21.3	10.5	21.5	10.3	21.7	10.1	21.9	9.9	22.1	9.7	22.3	9.5	22.5	9.3	22.7
19 00	10.9	21.1	10.7	21.3	10.5	21.5	10.3	21.7	10.1	21.9	9.9	22.1	9.7	22.3	9.5	22.5
20 00	+11.1	−20.9	+10.9	−21.1	+10.7	−21.3	+10.5	−21.5	+10.3	−21.7	+10.1	−21.9	+9.9	−22.1	+9.7	−22.3
22 00	11.3	20.7	11.1	20.9	10.9	21.1	10.7	21.3	10.5	21.5	10.3	21.7	10.1	21.9	9.9	22.1
24 00	11.5	20.5	11.3	20.7	11.1	20.9	10.9	21.1	10.7	21.3	10.5	21.5	10.3	21.7	10.1	21.9
26 00	11.7	20.3	11.5	20.5	11.3	20.7	11.1	20.9	10.9	21.1	10.7	21.3	10.5	21.5	10.3	21.7
29 00	11.9	20.1	11.7	20.3	11.5	20.5	11.3	20.7	11.1	20.9	10.9	21.1	10.7	21.3	10.5	21.5
32 00	12.1	19.9	11.9	20.1	11.7	20.3	11.5	20.5	11.3	20.7	11.1	20.9	10.9	21.1	10.7	21.3
36 00	12.3	19.7	12.1	19.9	11.9	20.1	11.7	20.3	11.5	20.5	11.3	20.7	11.1	20.9	10.9	21.1
40 00	+12.5	−19.5	+12.3	−19.7	+12.1	−19.9	+11.9	−20.1	+11.7	−20.3	+11.5	−20.7	+11.3	−20.7	+11.1	−20.9
45 00	12.7	19.3	12.5	19.5	12.3	19.7	12.1	19.9	11.9	20.1	11.7	20.3	11.5	20.5	11.3	20.7
52 00	12.9	19.1	12.7	19.3	12.5	19.5	12.3	19.7	12.1	19.9	11.9	20.1	11.7	20.3	11.5	20.5
60 00	13.1	18.9	12.9	19.1	12.7	19.3	12.5	19.5	12.3	19.7	12.1	19.9	11.9	20.1	11.7	20.3
75 00	13.3	18.7	13.1	18.9	12.9	19.1	12.7	19.3	12.5	19.5	12.3	19.7	12.1	19.9	11.9	20.1
90 00	13.5	18.5	13.3	18.7	13.1	18.9	12.9	19.1	12.7	19.3	12.5	19.5	12.3	19.7	12.1	19.9

SUN'S TOTAL CORRECTION

To be applied to the Observed Altitude of the Sun's Lower (L) or Upper (U) Limb

Obs. Alt.	5.4m (18ft)		5.9m (20ft)		6.5m (21ft)		7.1m (23ft)		7.7m (25ft)		8.4m (28ft)		9.1m (30ft)		9.8m (32ft)	
	L	U	L	U	L	U	L	U	L	U	L	U	L	U	L	U
06 00	+3.5	−28.5	+3.3	−28.7	+3.1	−28.9	+2.9	−29.1	+2.7	−29.3	+2.5	−29.5	+2.3	−29.7	+2.1	−29.9
10	3.7	28.3	3.5	28.5	3.3	28.7	3.1	28.9	2.9	29.1	2.7	29.3	2.5	29.5	2.3	29.7
20	3.9	28.1	3.7	28.3	3.5	28.5	3.3	28.7	3.1	28.9	2.9	29.1	2.7	29.3	2.5	29.5
30	4.1	27.9	3.9	28.1	3.7	28.3	3.5	28.5	3.3	28.7	3.1	28.9	2.9	29.1	2.7	29.3
40	4.3	27.7	4.1	27.9	3.9	28.1	3.7	28.3	3.5	28.5	3.3	28.7	3.1	28.9	2.9	29.1
50	4.5	27.5	4.3	27.7	4.1	27.9	3.9	28.1	3.7	28.3	3.5	28.5	3.3	28.7	3.1	28.9
07 00	+4.7	−27.3	+4.5	−27.5	+4.3	−27.7	+4.1	−27.9	+3.9	−28.1	+3.7	−28.3	+3.5	−28.5	+3.3	−28.7
15	4.9	27.1	4.7	27.3	4.5	27.5	4.3	27.7	4.1	27.9	3.9	28.1	3.7	28.3	3.5	28.5
30	5.1	26.9	4.9	27.1	4.7	27.3	4.5	27.5	4.3	27.7	4.1	27.9	3.9	28.1	3.7	28.3
45	5.3	26.7	5.1	26.9	4.9	27.1	4.7	27.3	4.5	27.5	4.3	27.7	4.1	27.9	3.9	28.1
08 00	5.5	26.5	5.3	26.7	5.1	26.9	4.9	27.1	4.7	27.3	4.5	27.5	4.3	27.7	4.1	27.9
15	5.7	26.3	5.5	26.5	5.3	26.7	5.1	26.9	4.9	27.1	4.7	27.3	4.5	27.5	4.3	27.7
30	5.9	26.1	5.7	26.3	5.5	26.5	5.3	26.7	5.1	26.9	4.9	27.1	4.7	27.3	4.5	27.5
45	6.1	25.9	5.9	26.1	5.7	26.3	5.5	26.5	5.3	26.7	5.1	26.9	4.9	27.1	4.7	27.3
09 00	+6.3	−25.7	+6.1	−25.9	+5.9	−26.1	+5.7	−26.3	+5.5	−26.5	+5.3	−26.7	+5.1	−26.9	+4.9	−27.1
20	6.5	25.5	6.3	25.7	6.1	25.9	5.9	26.1	5.7	26.3	5.5	26.5	5.3	26.7	5.1	26.9
40	6.7	25.3	6.5	25.5	6.3	25.7	6.1	25.9	5.9	26.1	5.7	26.3	5.5	26.5	5.3	26.7
10 00	6.9	25.1	6.7	25.3	6.5	25.5	6.1	25.7	6.1	25.9	5.9	26.1	5.7	26.3	5.5	26.5
30	7.1	24.9	6.9	25.1	6.7	25.3	6.5	25.5	6.3	25.7	6.1	25.9	5.9	26.1	5.7	26.3
11 00	7.3	24.7	7.1	24.9	6.9	25.1	6.7	25.3	6.5	25.5	6.3	25.7	6.1	25.9	5.9	26.1
30	7.5	24.5	7.3	24.7	7.1	24.9	6.9	25.1	6.7	25.3	6.5	25.5	6.3	25.7	6.1	25.9
12 00	7.7	24.3	7.5	24.5	7.3	24.7	7.1	24.9	6.9	25.1	6.7	25.3	6.5	25.5	6.3	25.7
30	7.9	24.1	7.7	24.3	7.5	24.5	7.3	24.7	7.1	24.9	6.9	25.1	6.7	25.3	6.5	25.5
13 00	+8.1	−23.9	+7.9	−24.1	+7.7	−24.3	+7.5	−24.5	+7.3	−24.7	+7.1	−24.9	+6.9	−25.1	+6.7	−25.3
14 00	8.3	23.7	8.1	23.9	7.9	24.1	7.7	24.3	7.5	24.5	7.3	24.7	7.1	24.9	6.9	25.1
15 00	8.5	23.5	8.3	23.7	8.1	23.9	7.9	24.1	7.7	24.3	7.5	24.5	7.3	24.7	7.1	24.9
16 00	8.7	23.3	8.5	23.5	8.3	23.7	8.1	23.9	7.9	24.1	7.7	24.3	7.5	24.5	7.3	24.7
17 00	8.9	23.1	8.7	23.3	8.5	23.5	8.3	23.7	8.1	23.9	7.9	24.1	7.7	24.3	7.5	24.5
18 00	9.1	22.9	8.9	23.1	8.7	23.3	8.5	23.5	8.3	23.7	8.1	23.9	7.9	24.1	7.7	24.3
19 00	9.3	22.7	9.1	22.9	8.9	23.1	8.7	23.3	8.5	23.5	8.3	23.7	8.1	23.9	7.9	24.1
20 00	+9.5	−22.5	+9.3	−22.7	+9.1	−22.9	+8.9	−23.1	+8.7	−23.3	+8.5	−23.5	+8.3	−23.7	+8.1	−23.9
22 00	9.7	22.3	9.5	22.5	9.3	22.7	9.1	22.9	8.9	23.1	8.7	23.3	8.5	23.5	8.3	23.7
24 00	9.9	22.1	9.7	22.3	9.5	22.5	9.3	22.7	9.1	22.9	8.9	23.1	8.7	23.3	8.5	23.5
26 00	10.1	21.9	9.9	22.1	9.7	22.3	9.5	22.5	9.3	22.7	9.1	22.9	8.9	23.1	8.7	23.3
29 00	10.3	21.7	10.1	21.9	9.9	22.1	9.7	22.3	9.5	22.5	9.3	22.7	9.1	22.9	8.9	23.1
32 00	10.5	21.5	10.3	21.7	10.1	21.9	9.9	22.1	9.7	22.3	9.5	22.5	9.3	22.7	9.1	22.9
36 00	10.7	21.3	10.5	21.5	10.3	21.7	10.1	21.9	9.9	22.1	9.7	22.3	9.5	22.5	9.3	22.7
40 00	+10.9	−21.1	+10.7	−21.3	+10.5	−21.5	+10.3	−21.7	+10.1	−21.9	+9.9	−22.1	+9.7	−22.3	+9.5	−22.5
45 00	11.1	20.9	10.9	21.1	10.7	21.3	10.5	21.5	10.3	21.7	10.1	21.9	9.9	22.1	9.7	22.3
52 00	11.3	20.7	11.1	20.9	10.9	21.1	10.7	21.3	10.5	21.5	10.3	21.7	10.1	21.9	9.9	22.1
60 00	11.5	20.5	11.3	20.7	11.1	20.9	10.9	21.1	10.7	21.3	10.5	21.5	10.3	21.7	10.1	21.9
75 00	11.7	20.3	11.5	20.5	11.3	20.7	11.1	20.9	10.9	21.1	10.7	21.3	10.5	21.5	10.3	21.7
90 00	11.9	20.1	11.7	20.3	11.5	20.5	11.3	20.7	11.1	20.9	10.9	21.1	10.7	21.3	10.5	21.5

ADDITIONAL MONTHLY CORRECTION

	Jan	Feb	Mar	Apr	May	June	July	Aug	Sept	Oct	Nov	Dec
LL	+0.2	+0.2	+0.1	0.0	−0.1	−0.2	−0.2	−0.2	−0.1	0.0	+0.2	+0.2
UL	−0.2	−0.2	−0.1	0.0	+0.1	+0.2	+0.2	+0.2	+0.1	0.0	−0.2	−0.2

SUN'S TOTAL CORRECTION

To be applied to the Observed Altitude of the Sun's Lower (L) or Upper (U) Limb

Obs. Alt.	10.5m (34ft) L	U	11.2m (37ft) L	U	12.0m (39ft) L	U	12.8m 42ft) L	U	13.6m (45ft) L	U	14.5M (48ft) L	U	15.4m (50ft) L	U	16.3m (53ft) L	U
06 00	+1.9	−30.1	+1.7	−30.3	+1.5	−30.5	+1.3	−30.7	+1.1	−30.9	+0.9	−31.1	+0.7	−31.3	+0.5	−31.5
10	2.1	29.9	1.9	30.1	1.7	30.3	1.5	30.5	1.3	30.7	1.1	30.9	0.9	31.1	0.7	31.3
20	2.3	29.7	2.1	29.9	1.9	30.1	1.7	30.3	1.5	30.5	1.3	30.7	1.1	30.9	0.9	31.1
30	2.5	29.5	2.3	29.7	2.1	29.9	1.9	30.1	1.7	30.3	1.5	30.5	1.3	30.7	1.1	30.9
40	2.7	29.3	2.5	29.5	2.3	29.7	2.1	29.9	1.9	30.1	1.7	30.3	1.5	30.5	1.3	30.7
50	2.9	29.1	2.7	29.3	2.5	29.5	2.3	29.7	2.1	29.9	1.9	30.1	1.7	30.3	1.5	30.5
07 00	+3.1	−28.9	+2.9	−29.1	+2.7	−29.3	+2.5	−29.5	+2.3	−29.7	+2.1	−29.9	+1.9	−30.1	+1.7	−30.3
15	3.3	28.7	3.1	28.9	2.9	29.1	2.7	29.3	2.5	29.5	2.3	29.7	2.1	29.9	1.9	30.1
30	3.5	28.5	3.3	28.7	3.1	28.9	2.9	29.1	2.7	29.3	2.5	29.5	2.3	29.7	2.1	29.9
45	3.7	28.3	3.5	28.5	3.3	28.7	3.1	28.9	2.9	29.1	2.7	29.3	2.5	29.5	2.3	29.7
08 00	3.9	28.1	3.7	28.3	3.5	28.5	3.3	28.7	3.1	28.9	2.9	29.1	2.7	29.3	2.5	29.5
15	4.1	27.9	3.9	28.1	3.7	28.3	3.5	28.5	3.3	28.7	3.1	28.9	2.9	29.1	2.7	29.3
30	4.3	27.7	4.1	27.9	3.9	28.1	3.7	28.3	3.5	28.5	3.3	28.7	3.1	28.9	2.9	29.1
45	4.5	27.5	4.3	27.7	4.1	27.9	3.9	28.1	3.7	28.3	3.5	28.5	3.3	28.7	3.1	28.9
09 00	+4.7	−27.3	+4.5	−27.5	+4.3	−27.7	+4.1	−27.9	+3.9	−28.1	+3.7	−28.3	+3.5	−28.5	+3.3	−28.7
20	4.9	27.1	4.7	27.3	4.5	27.5	4.3	27.7	4.1	27.9	3.9	28.1	3.7	28.3	3.5	28.5
40	5.1	26.9	4.9	27.1	4.7	27.3	4.5	27.5	4.3	27.7	4.1	27.9	3.9	28.1	3.7	28.3
10 00	5.3	26.7	5.1	26.9	4.9	27.1	4.7	27.3	4.5	27.5	4.3	27.7	4.1	27.9	3.9	28.1
30	5.5	26.5	5.3	26.7	5.1	26.9	4.9	27.1	4.7	27.3	4.5	27.5	4.3	27.7	4.1	27.9
11 00	5.7	26.3	5.5	26.5	5.3	26.7	5.1	26.9	4.9	27.1	4.7	27.3	4.5	27.5	4.3	27.7
30	5.9	26.1	5.7	26.3	5.5	26.5	5.3	26.7	5.1	26.9	4.9	27.1	4.7	27.3	4.5	27.5
12 00	6.1	25.9	5.9	26.1	5.7	26.3	5.5	26.5	5.3	26.7	5.1	26.9	4.9	27.1	4.7	27.3
30	6.3	25.7	6.1	25.9	5.9	26.1	5.7	26.3	5.5	26.5	5.3	26.7	5.1	26.9	4.9	27.1
13 00	+6.5	−25.5	+6.3	−25.7	+6.1	−25.9	+5.9	−26.1	+5.7	−26.3	+5.5	−26.5	+5.3	−26.7	+5.1	−26.9
14 00	6.7	25.3	6.5	25.5	6.3	25.7	6.1	25.9	5.9	26.1	5.7	26.3	5.5	26.5	5.3	26.7
15 00	6.9	25.1	6.7	25.3	6.5	25.5	6.3	25.7	6.1	25.9	5.9	26.1	5.7	26.3	5.5	26.5
16 00	7.1	24.9	6.9	25.1	6.7	25.3	6.5	25.5	6.3	25.7	6.1	25.9	5.9	26.1	5.7	26.3
17 00	7.3	24.7	7.1	24.9	6.9	25.1	6.7	25.3	6.5	25.5	6.3	25.7	6.1	25.9	5.9	26.1
18 00	7.5	24.5	7.3	24.7	7.1	24.9	6.9	25.1	6.7	25.3	6.5	25.5	6.3	25.7	6.1	25.9
19 00	7.7	24.3	7.5	24.5	7.3	24.7	7.1	24.9	6.9	25.1	6.7	25.3	6.5	25.5	6.3	25.7
20 00	+7.9	−24.1	+7.7	−24.3	+7.5	−24.5	+7.3	−24.7	+7.1	−24.9	+6.9	−25.1	+6.7	−25.3	+6.5	−25.5
22 00	8.1	23.9	7.9	24.1	7.7	24.3	7.5	24.5	7.3	24.7	7.1	24.9	6.9	25.1	6.7	25.3
24 00	8.3	23.7	8.1	23.9	7.9	24.1	7.7	24.3	7.5	24.5	7.3	24.7	7.1	24.9	6.9	25.1
26 00	8.5	23.5	8.3	23.7	8.1	23.9	7.9	24.1	7.7	24.3	7.5	24.5	7.3	24.7	7.1	24.9
29 00	8.7	23.3	8.5	23.5	8.3	23.7	8.1	23.9	7.9	24.1	7.7	24.3	7.5	24.5	7.3	24.7
32 00	8.9	23.1	8.7	23.3	8.5	23.5	8.3	23.7	8.1	23.9	7.9	24.1	7.7	24.3	7.5	24.5
36 00	9.1	22.9	8.9	23.1	8.7	23.3	8.5	23.5	8.3	23.7	8.1	23.9	7.9	24.1	7.7	24.3
40 00	+9.3	−22.7	+9.1	−22.9	+8.9	−23.1	+8.7	−23.3	+8.5	−23.5	+8.3	−23.7	+8.1	−23.9	+7.9	−24.1
45 00	9.5	22.5	9.3	22.7	9.1	22.9	8.9	23.1	8.7	23.3	8.5	23.5	8.3	23.7	8.1	23.9
52 00	9.7	22.3	9.5	22.5	9.3	22.7	9.1	22.9	8.9	23.1	8.7	23.3	8.5	23.5	8.3	23.7
60 00	9.9	22.1	9.7	22.3	9.5	22.5	9.3	22.7	9.1	22.9	8.9	23.1	8.7	23.3	8.5	23.5
75 00	10.1	21.9	9.9	22.1	9.7	22.3	9.5	22.5	9.3	22.7	9.1	22.9	8.9	23.1	8.7	23.3
90 00	10.3	21.7	10.1	21.9	9.9	22.1	9.7	22.3	9.5	22.5	9.3	22.7	9.1	22.9	8.9	23.1

ADDITIONAL MONTHLY CORRECTION

	Jan	Feb	Mar	Apr	May	June	July	Aug	Sept	Oct	Nov	Dec
LL	+0.2	+0.2	+0.1	0.0	−0.1	−0.2	−0.2	−0.2	−0.1	0.0	+0.2	+0.2
UL	−0.2	−0.2	−0.1	0.0	+0.1	+0.2	+0.2	+0.2	+0.1	0.0	−0.2	−0.2

SUN'S TOTAL CORRECTION

To be applied to the Observed Altitude of the Sun's Lower (L) or Upper (U) Limb

Height of Eye

Obs. Alt	17.2m (56ft) L	U	18.2m (60ft) L	U	19.2m (63ft) L	U	20.2m (66ft) L	U	21.2m (70ft) L	U	22.2m (73ft) L	U	23.3m (77ft) L	U	24.4m (80ft) L	U
06 00	+0.3	−31.7	+0.1	−31.9	−0.1	−32.1	−0.3	−32.3	−0.5	−32.5	−0.7	−32.7	−0.9	−32.9	−1.1	−33.1
10	0.5	31.5	0.3	31.7	+0.1	31.9	0.1	32.1	0.3	32.3	0.5	32.5	0.7	32.7	0.9	32.9
20	0.7	31.3	0.5	31.5	0.3	31.7	+0.1	31.9	0.1	32.1	0.3	32.3	0.5	32.5	0.7	32.7
30	0.9	31.1	0.7	31.3	0.5	31.5	0.3	31.7	+0.1	31.9	0.1	32.1	0.3	32.3	0.5	32.5
40	1.1	30.9	0.9	31.1	0.7	31.3	0.5	31.5	0.3	31.7	+0.1	31.9	0.1	32.1	0.3	32.3
50	1.3	30.7	1.1	20.9	0.9	31.1	0.7	31.3	0.5	31.5	0.3	31.7	+0.1	31.9	0.1	32.1
07 00	+1.5	−30.5	+1.3	−30.7	+1.1	−30.9	+0.9	−31.1	+0.7	−31.3	+0.5	−31.5	+0.3	−31.7	+0.1	−31.9
15	1.7	30.3	1.5	30.5	1.3	30.7	1.1	30.9	0.9	31.1	0.7	31.3	0.5	31.5	0.3	31.7
30	1.9	30.1	1.7	30.3	1.5	30.5	1.3	30.7	1.1	30.9	0.9	31.1	0.7	31.3	0.5	31.5
45	2.1	29.9	1.9	30.1	1.7	30.3	1.5	30.5	1.3	30.7	1.1	30.9	0.9	31.1	0.7	31.3
08 00	2.3	29.7	2.1	29.9	1.9	30.1	1.7	30.3	1.5	30.5	1.3	30.7	1.1	30.9	0.9	31.1
15	2.5	29.5	2.3	29.7	2.1	29.9	1.9	30.1	1.7	30.3	1.5	30.5	1.3	30.7	1.1	30.9
30	2.7	29.3	2.5	29.5	2.3	29.7	2.1	29.9	1.9	30.1	1.7	30.3	1.5	30.5	1.3	30.7
45	2.9	29.1	2.7	29.3	2.5	29.5	2.3	29.7	2.1	29.9	1.9	30.1	1.7	30.3	1.5	30.5
09 00	+3.1	−28.9	+2.9	−29.1	+2.7	−29.3	+2.5	29.5	+2.3	29.7	+2.1	−29.9	+1.9	−30.1	+1.7	−03.3
20	3.3	28.7	3.1	28.9	2.9	29.1	2.7	29.3	2.5	29.5	2.3	29.7	2.1	29.9	1.9	30.1
40	3.5	28.5	3.3	28.7	3.1	28.9	2.9	29.1	2.7	29.3	2.5	29.5	2.3	29.7	2.1	29.9
10 00	3.7	28.3	3.5	28.5	3.3	28.7	3.1	28.9	2.9	29.1	2.7	29.3	2.5	29.5	2.3	29.7
30	3.9	28.1	3.7	28.3	3.5	28.5	3.3	28.7	3.1	28.9	2.9	29.1	2.7	29.3	2.5	29.5
11 00	4.1	27.9	3.9	28.1	3.7	28.3	3.5	28.5	3.3	28.7	3.1	28.9	2.9	29.1	2.7	29.3
30	4.3	27.7	4.1	27.9	3.9	28.1	3.7	28.3	3.5	28.5	3.3	28.7	3.1	28.9	2.9	29.1
12 00	4.5	27.5	4.3	27.7	4.1	27.9	3.9	28.1	3.7	28.3	3.5	28.5	3.3	28.7	3.1	28.9
30	4.7	27.3	4.5	27.5	4.3	27.7	4.1	27.9	3.9	28.1	3.7	28.3	3.5	28.5	3.3	28.7
13 00	+4.9	−27.1	+4.7	−27.3	+4.5	−37.5	+4.3	−27.7	+4.1	−27.9	+3.9	−28.1	+3.7	−28.3	+3.5	−28.5
14 00	5.1	26.9	4.9	27.1	4.7	27.3	4.5	27.5	4.3	27.7	4.1	27.9	3.9	28.1	3.7	28.3
15 00	5.3	26.7	5.1	26.9	4.9	27.1	4.7	27.3	4.5	27.5	4.3	27.7	4.1	27.9	3.9	28.1
16 00	5.5	26.5	5.3	26.7	5.1	26.9	4.9	27.1	4.7	27.3	4.5	27.5	4.3	27.7	4.1	27.9
17 00	5.7	26.3	5.5	26.5	5.3	26.7	5.1	26.9	4.9	27.1	4.7	27.3	4.5	27.5	4.3	27.7
18 00	5.9	26.1	5.7	26.3	5.5	26.5	5.3	26.7	5.1	26.9	4.9	27.1	4.7	27.3	4.5	27.5
19 00	6.1	25.9	5.9	26.1	5.7	26.3	5.5	26.5	5.3	26.7	5.1	26.9	4.9	27.1	4.7	27.3
20 00	+6.3	−25.7	+6.1	−25.9	+5.9	−26.1	+5.7	−26.3	+5.5	−26.5	+5.3	−26.7	+5.1	−26.9	+4.9	−27.1
22 00	6.5	25.5	6.3	25.7	6.1	25.9	5.9	26.1	5.7	26.3	5.5	26.5	5.3	26.7	5.1	26.9
24 00	6.3	25.3	6.5	25.5	6.3	25.7	6.1	25.9	5.9	26.1	5.7	26.3	5.5	26.5	5.3	26.7
26 00	6.9	25.1	6.7	25.3	6.5	25.5	6.3	25.7	6.1	25.9	5.9	26.1	5.7	26.3	5.5	26.5
29 00	7.1	24.9	6.9	25.1	6.7	25.3	6.5	25.5	6.3	25.7	6.1	25.9	5.9	26.1	5.7	26.3
32 00	7.3	24.7	7.1	24.9	6.9	25.1	6.7	25.3	6.5	25.5	6.3	25.7	6.1	25.9	5.9	26.1
36 00	7.5	24.5	7.3	24.7	7.1	24.9	6.9	25.1	6.7	25.3	6.5	25.5	6.3	25.7	6.1	25.9
40 00	+7.7	−24.3	+7.5	−24.7	+7.3	24.7	+7.1	−24.9	+6.9	−25.1	+6.7	−25 3	6.5	−25.5	6.3	−25.7
45 00	7.9	24.1	7.7	24.3	7.5	24.5	7.3	24.7	7.1	24.9	6.9	25.1	6.7	25.3	6.5	25.5
52 00	8.1	23.9	7.9	24.1	7.7	24.3	7.5	24.5	7.3	24.7	7.1	24.9	6.9	25.1	6.7	25.3
60 00	8.3	23.7	8.1	23.9	7.9	24.1	7.7	24.3	7.5	24.5	7.3	24.7	7.1	24.9	6.9	25.1
75 00	8.5	23.5	8.3	23.7	8.1	23.9	7.9	24.1	7.7	24.3	7.5	24.5	7.3	24.7	7.1	24.9
90 00	8.7	23.3	8.5	23.5	8.3	23.7	8.1	23.9	7.9	24.1	7.7	24.3	7.5	24.5	7.3	24.7

ADDITIONAL MONTHLY CORRECTION

	Jan	Feb	Mar	Apr	May	June	July	Aug	Sept	Oct	Nov	Dec
LL	+0.2	+0.2	+0.1	0.0	−0.1	−0.2	−0.2	−0.2	−0.1	0.0	+0.2	+0.2
UL	−0.2	−0.2	−0.1	0.0	+0.1	+0.2	+0.2	+0.2	+0.1	0.0	−0.2	−0.2

SUN'S TOTAL CORRECTION

To be applied to the Observed Altitude of the Sun's Lower (L) or Upper (U) Limb

Height of Eye

Obs. Alt.	25.5m (84ft)		26.7m (88ft)		27.9m (92ft)		29.1m (96ft)		30.3m (100ft)		31.6m (104ft)		32.9m (108ft)		34.0m (112ft)		35.5m (117ft)	
	L	U	L	U	L	U	L	U	L	U	L	U	L	U	L	U	L	U
	′	′	′	′	′	′	′	′	′	′	′	′	′	′	′	′	′	′
06 00	−1.3	−33.3	−1.5	−33.5	−1.7	−33.7	−1.9	−33.9	−2.1	−34.1	−2.3	−34.3	−2.5	−34.5	−2.7	−34.7	−2.9	−34.9
10	1.1	33.1	1.3	33.3	1.5	33.5	1.7	33.7	1.9	33.9	2.1	34.1	2.3	34.3	2.5	34.5	2.7	34.7
20	0.9	32.9	1.1	33.1	1.3	33.3	1.5	33.5	1.7	33.7	1.9	33.9	2.1	34.1	2.3	34.3	2.5	34.5
30	0.7	32.7	0.9	32.9	1.1	33.1	1.3	33.3	1.5	33.5	1.7	33.7	1.9	33.9	2.1	34.1	2.3	34.3
40	0.5	32.5	0.7	32.7	0.9	32.9	1.1	33.1	1.3	33.3	1.5	33.5	1.7	33.7	1.9	33.9	2.1	34.1
50	0.3	32.3	0.5	32.5	0.7	32.7	0.9	32.9	1.1	33.1	1.3	33.3	1.5	33.5	1.7	33.7	1.9	33.9
07 00	−0.1	−32.1	−0.3	−32.3	−0.5	−32.5	−0.7	−32.7	−0.9	−32.9	−1.1	−33.1	−1.3	−33.3	−1.5	−33.5	−1.7	−33.7
15	+0.1	31.9	0.1	32.1	0.3	32.3	0.5	32.5	0.7	32.7	0.9	32.9	1.1	33.1	1.3	33.3	1.5	33.5
30	0.3	31.7	+0.1	31.9	0.1	32.1	0.3	32.3	0.5	32.5	0.7	32.7	0.9	32.9	1.1	33.1	1.3	33.3
45	0.5	31.5	0.3	31.7	+0.1	31.9	0.1	32.1	0.3	32.3	0.5	32.5	0.7	32.7	0.9	32.9	1.1	33.1
08 00	0.7	31.3	0.5	31.5	0.3	31.7	+0.1	31.9	0.1	32.1	0.3	32.3	0.5	32.5	0.7	32.7	0.9	32.9
15	0.9	31.1	0.7	31.3	0.5	31.5	0.3	31.7	+0.1	31.9	0.1	32.1	0.3	32.3	0.5	32.5	0.7	32.7
30	1.1	30.9	0.9	31.1	0.7	31.3	0.5	31.5	0.3	31.7	+0.1	31.9	0.1	32.1	0.3	32.3	0.5	32.5
45	1.3	30.7	1.1	30.9	0.9	31.1	0.7	31.3	0.5	31.5	0.3	31.7	+0.1	31.9	0.1	32.1	0.3	32.3
09 00	+1.5	−30.5	+1.3	−30.7	+1.1	−30.9	+0.9	−31.1	+0.7	−31.3	+0.5	−31.5	+0.3	−31.7	+0.1	−31.9	−0.1	−32.2
20	1.7	30.3	1.5	30.5	1.3	30.7	1.1	30.9	0.9	31.1	0.7	31.3	0.5	31.5	0.3	31.7	+0.1	31.9
40	1.9	30.1	1.7	30.3	1.5	30.5	1.3	30.7	1.1	30.9	0.9	31.1	0.7	31.3	0.5	31.5	0.3	31.7
10 00	2.1	29.9	1.9	30.1	1.7	30.3	1.5	30.5	1.3	30.7	1.1	30.9	0.9	31.1	0.7	31.3	0.5	31.5
30	2.3	29.7	2.1	29.9	1.9	30.1	1.7	30.3	1.5	30.5	1.3	30.7	1.1	30.9	0.9	31.1	0.7	31.4
11 00	2.5	29.5	2.3	29.7	2.1	29.9	1.9	30.1	1.7	30.3	1.5	30.5	1.3	30.7	1.1	30.9	0.9	31.1
30	2.7	29.3	2.5	29.5	2.3	29.7	2.1	29.9	1.9	30.1	1.7	30.3	1.5	30.5	1.3	30.7	1.1	30.9
12 00	2.9	29.1	2.7	29.3	2.5	29.5	2.3	29.7	2.1	29.9	1.9	30.1	1.7	30.3	1.5	30.5	1.3	30.7
30	3.1	28.9	2.9	29.1	2.7	29.3	2.5	29.5	2.3	29.7	2.1	29.9	1.9	30.1	1.7	30.3	1.5	30.5
13 00	+3.3	−28.7	+3.1	−28.9	+2.9	−29.1	+2.7	−29.3	+2.5	−29.5	+2.3	−29.7	+2.1	−29.9	+1.9	−30.1	+1.7	−30.3
14 00	3.5	28.5	3.3	28.7	3.1	28.9	2.9	29.1	2.7	29.3	2.5	29.5	2.3	29.7	2.1	29.9	1.9	30.0
15 00	3.7	28.3	3.5	28.5	3.3	28.7	3.1	28.9	2.9	29.1	2.7	29.3	2.5	29.5	2.3	29.7	2.1	29.9
16 00	3.9	28.1	3.7	28.3	3.5	28.5	3.3	28.7	3.1	28.9	2.9	29.1	2.7	29.3	2.5	29.5	2.3	29.
17 00	4.1	27.9	3.9	28.1	3.7	28.3	3.5	28.5	3.3	28.7	3.1	28.9	2.9	29.1	2.7	29.3	2.5	29.
18 00	4.3	27.7	4.1	27.9	3.9	28.1	3.7	28.3	3.5	28.5	3.3	28.7	3.1	28.9	2.9	29.1	2.7	29.
19 00	4.5	27.5	4.3	27.7	4.1	27.9	3.9	28.1	3.7	28.3	3.5	28.5	3.3	28.7	3.1	28.9	2.9	29.
20 00	+4.7	−27.3	+4.5	−27.5	+4.3	−27.7	+4.1	−27.9	+3.9	−28.1	+3.7	−28.3	+3.5	−28.5	+3.3	−28.7	+3.1	−28.
22 00	4.9	27.1	4.7	27.3	4.5	27.5	4.3	27.7	4.1	27.9	3.9	28.1	3.7	28.3	3.5	28.5	3.3	28.
24 00	5.1	26.9	4.9	27.1	4.7	27.3	4.5	27.5	4.3	27.7	4.1	27.9	3.9	28.1	3.7	28.3	3.5	28.
26 00	5.3	26.7	5.1	26.9	4.9	27.1	4.7	27.3	4.5	27.5	4.3	27.7	4.1	27.9	3.9	28.1	3.7	28.
29 00	5.5	26.5	5.3	26.7	5.1	26.9	4.9	27.1	4.7	27.3	4.5	27.5	4.3	27.7	4.1	27.9	3.9	28.
32 00	5.7	26.3	5.5	26.5	5.3	26.7	5.1	26.9	4.9	27.1	4.7	27.3	4.5	27.5	4.3	27.7	4.1	27.
36 00	5.9	26.1	5.7	26.3	5.5	26.5	5.3	26.7	5.1	26.9	4.9	27.1	4.7	27.3	4.5	27.5	4.3	27.
40 00	6.1	−25.9	5.9	−26.1	+5.7	−26.3	+5.5	−26.5	+5.3	−26.7	+5.1	−26.9	+4.9	−27.1	+4.7	27.3	+4.5	−27.
45 00	6.3	25.7	6.1	25.9	5.9	26.1	5.7	26.3	5.5	26.5	5.3	26.7	5.1	26.9	4.9	27.1	4.7	27.
52 00	6.5	25.5	6.3	25.7	6.1	25.9	5.9	26.1	5.7	26.3	5.5	26.5	5.3	26.7	5.1	26.9	4.9	27.
60 00	6.7	25.3	6.5	25.5	6.3	25.7	6.1	25.9	5.9	26.1	5.7	26.3	5.5	26.5	5.3	26.7	5.1	26.
75 00	6.9	25.1	6.7	25.3	6.5	25.5	6.3	25.7	6.1	25.9	5.9	26.1	5.7	26.3	5.5	26.5	5.3	26.
90 00	7.1	24.9	6.9	25.1	6.7	25.3	6.5	25.5	6.3	25.7	6.1	25.9	5.9	26.1	5.7	26.3	5.5	26.

ADDITIONAL MONTHLY CORRECTION

	Jan	Feb	Mar	Apr	May	June	July	Aug	Sept	Oct	Nov	Dec
LL	+0.2	+0.2	+0.1	0.0	−0.1	−0.2	−0.2	−0.2	−0.1	0.0	+0.2	+0.2
UL	−0.2	−0.2	−0.1	0.0	+0.1	+0.2	+0.2	+0.2	+0.1	0.0	−0.2	−0.2

SUN'S TOTAL CORRECTION

To be applied to the Observed Altitude of the Sun's Lower (L) or Upper (U) Limb

Height of Eye

Obs. Alt.	37.0m (121ft) L	U	38.5m (126ft) L	U	40.0m (131ft) L	U	41.5m (135ft) L	U	43.0m (140ft) L	U	44.5m (145ft) L	U	46.0m (150ft) L	U	47.5m (155ft) L	U	49.0m (160ft) L	U
06 00	−3.1	−35.1	−3.3	−35.3	−3.5	−35.5	−3.7	−35.7	−3.9	−35.9	−4.1	−36.1	−4.3	−36.3	−4.5	−36.5	−4.7	−36.7
10	2.9	34.9	3.1	35.1	3.3	35.3	3.5	35.5	3.7	35.7	3.9	35.9	4.1	36.1	4.3	36.3	4.5	36.5
20	2.7	34.7	2.9	34.9	3.1	35.1	3.3	35.3	3.5	35.5	3.7	35.7	3.9	35.9	4.1	36.1	4.3	36.3
30	2.5	34.5	2.7	34.7	2.9	34.9	3.1	35.1	3.3	35.3	3.5	35.5	3.7	35.7	3.9	35.9	4.1	36.1
40	2.3	34.3	2.5	34.5	2.7	34.7	2.9	34.9	3.1	35.1	3.3	35.3	3.5	35.5	3.7	35.7	3.9	35.9
50	2.1	34.1	2.3	34.3	2.5	34.5	2.7	34.7	2.9	34.9	3.1	35.1	3.3	35.3	3.5	35.5	3.7	35.7
07 00	−1.9	−33.9	−2.1	−34.1	−2.3	−34.3	−2.5	−34.5	−2.7	−34.7	−2.9	−34.9	−3.1	−35.1	−3.3	−35.3	−3.5	−35.5
15	1.7	33.7	1.9	33.9	2.1	34.1	2.3	34.3	2.5	34.5	2.7	34.7	2.9	34.9	3.1	35.1	3.3	35.3
30	1.5	33.5	1.7	33.7	1.9	33.9	2.1	34.1	2.3	34.3	2.5	34.5	2.7	34.7	2.9	34.9	3.1	35.1
45	1.3	33.3	1.5	33.5	1.7	33.7	1.9	33.9	2.1	34.1	2.3	34.3	2.5	34.5	2.7	34.7	2.9	34.9
08 00	1.1	33.1	1.3	33.3	1.5	33.5	1.7	33.7	1.9	33.9	2.1	34.1	2.3	34.3	2.5	34.5	2.7	34.7
15	0.9	32.9	1.1	33.1	1.3	33.3	1.5	33.5	1.7	33.7	1.9	33.9	2.1	34.1	2.3	34.3	2.5	34.5
30	0.7	32.7	0.9	32.9	1.1	33.1	1.3	33.3	1.5	33.5	1.7	33.7	1.9	33.9	2.1	34.1	2.3	34.3
45	0.5	32.5	0.7	32.7	0.9	32.9	1.1	33.1	1.3	33.3	1.5	33.5	1.7	33.7	1.9	33.9	2.1	34.1
09 00	−0.3	−32.3	−0.5	−32.5	−0.7	−32.7	−0.9	−32.9	−1.1	−33.1	−1.3	−33.3	−1.5	−33.5	−1.7	−33.7	−1.9	−33.9
20	0.1	32.1	0.3	32.3	0.5	32.5	0.7	32.7	0.9	32.9	1.1	33.1	1.3	33.3	1.5	33.5	1.7	33.7
40	+0.1	31.9	0.1	32.1	0.3	32.3	0.5	32.5	0.7	32.7	0.9	32.9	1.1	33.1	1.3	33.3	1.5	33.5
10 00	0.3	31.7	+0.1	31.9	0.1	32.1	0.3	32.3	0.5	32.5	0.7	32.7	0.9	32.9	1.1	33.1	1.3	33.3
30	0.5	31.5	0.3	31.7	+0.1	31.9	0.1	32.1	0.3	32.3	0.5	32.5	0.7	32.7	0.9	32.9	1.1	33.1
11 00	0.7	31.3	0.5	31.5	0.3	31.7	+0.1	31.9	0.1	32.1	0.3	32.3	0.5	32.5	0.7	32.7	0.9	32.9
30	0.9	31.1	0.7	31.3	0.5	31.5	0.3	31.7	+0.1	31.9	0.1	32.1	0.3	32.3	0.5	32.5	0.7	32.7
12 00	1.1	30.9	0.9	31.1	0.7	31.3	0.5	31.5	0.3	31.7	+0.1	31.9	0.1	32.1	0.3	32.3	0.5	32.5
30	1.3	30.7	1.1	30.9	0.9	31.1	0.7	31.3	0.5	31.5	0.3	31.7	+0.1	31.9	0.1	32.1	0.3	32.3
13 00	+1.5	−30.5	+1.3	−30.7	+1.1	−30.9	+0.9	−31.1	+0.7	−31.3	+0.5	−31.5	+0.3	−31.7	+0.1	−31.9	−0.1	−32.1
14 00	1.7	30.3	1.5	30.5	1.3	30.7	1.1	30.9	0.9	31.1	0.7	31.3	0.5	31.5	0.3	31.7	+0.1	31.9
15 00	1.9	30.1	1.7	30.3	1.5	30.5	1.3	30.7	1.1	30.9	0.9	31.1	0.7	31.3	0.5	31.5	0.3	31.7
16 00	2.1	29.9	1.9	30.1	1.7	30.3	1.5	30.5	1.3	30.7	1.1	30.9	0.9	31.1	0.7	31.3	0.5	31.5
17 00	2.3	29.7	2.1	29.9	1.9	30.1	1.7	30.3	1.5	30.5	1.3	30.7	1.1	30.9	0.9	31.1	0.7	31.3
18 00	2.5	29.5	2.3	29.7	2.1	29.9	1.9	30.1	1.7	30.3	1.5	30.5	1.3	30.7	1.1	30.9	0.9	31.1
19 00	2.7	29.3	2.5	29.5	2.3	29.7	2.1	29.9	1.9	30.1	1.7	30.3	1.5	30.5	1.3	30.7	1.1	30.9
20 00	+2.9	−29.1	+2.7	−29.3	+2.5	−29.5	+2.3	−29.7	+2.1	−29.9	+1.9	−30.1	+1.7	−30.3	+1.5	−30.5	+1.3	−30.7
22 00	3.1	28.9	2.9	29.1	2.7	29.3	2.5	29.5	2.3	29.7	2.1	29.9	1.9	30.1	1.7	30.3	1.5	30.5
24 00	3.3	28.7	3.1	28.9	2.9	29.1	2.7	29.3	2.5	29.5	2.3	29.7	2.1	29.9	1.9	30.1	1.7	30.3
26 00	3.5	28.5	3.3	28.7	3.1	28.9	2.9	29.1	2.7	29.3	2.5	29.5	2.3	29.7	2.1	29.9	1.9	30.1
29 00	3.7	28.3	3.5	28.5	3.3	28.7	3.1	28.9	2.9	29.1	2.7	29.3	2.5	29.5	2.3	29.7	2.1	29.9
32 00	3.9	28.1	3.7	28.3	3.5	28.5	3.3	28.7	3.1	28.9	2.9	29.1	2.7	29.3	2.5	29.5	2.3	29.7
36 00	4.1	27.9	3.9	28.1	3.7	28.3	3.5	28.5	3.3	28.7	3.1	28.9	2.9	29.1	2.7	29.3	2.5	29.5
40 00	+4.3	−27.7	+4.1	−27.9	+3.9	−28.1	+3.7	−28.3	+3.5	−28.5	+3.3	−28.7	+3.1	−28.9	+2.9	−29.1	+2.7	−29.3
45 00	4.5	27.5	4.3	27.7	4.1	27.9	3.9	28.1	3.7	28.3	3.5	28.5	3.3	28.7	3.1	28.9	2.9	29.1
52 00	4.7	27.3	4.5	27.5	4.3	27.7	4.1	27.9	3.9	28.1	3.7	28.3	3.5	28.5	3.3	28.7	3.1	28.9
60 00	4.9	27.1	4.7	27.3	4.5	27.5	4.3	27.7	4.1	27.9	3.9	28.1	3.7	28.3	3.5	28.5	3.3	28.7
75 00	5.1	26.9	4.9	27.1	4.7	27.3	4.5	27.5	4.3	27.7	4.1	27.9	3.9	28.1	3.7	28.3	3.5	28.5
90 00	5.3	26.7	5.1	26.9	4.9	27.1	4.7	27.3	4.5	27.5	4.3	27.7	4.1	27.9	3.9	28.1	3.7	28.3

ADDITIONAL MONTHLY CORRECTION

	Jan	Feb	Mar	Apr	May	June	July	Aug	Sept	Oct	Nov	Dec
LL	+0.2	+0.2	+0.1	0.0	−0.1	−0.2	−0.2	−0.2	−0.1	0.0	+0.2	+0.2
UL	−0.2	−0.2	−0.1	0.0	+0.1	+0.2	+0.2	+0.2	+0.1	0.0	−0.2	−0.2

STAR'S TOTAL CORRECTION

To be SUBTRACTED from the Observed Altitude of the Star

Height of Eye														
Metres 2.0	2.3	2.7	3.1	3.5	3.9	4.4	4.9	5.4	5.9	6.5	7.1	7.7	8.4	9.1
Feet 7	8	9	10	11	13	14	16	18	19	21	23	25	28	30
Obs. Alt. ′	′	′	′	′	′	′	′	′	′	′	′	′	′	′
6° 00 10.8	11.0	11.2	11.4	11.6	11.8	12.0	12.2	12.4	12.6	12.8	13.0	13.2	13.4	13.6
12 10.6	10.8	11.0	11.2	11.4	11.6	11.8	12.0	12.2	12.4	12.6	12.8	13.0	13.2	13.4
24 10.4	10.6	10.8	11.0	11.2	11.4	11.6	11.8	12.0	12.2	12.4	12.6	12.8	13.0	13.2
36 10.2	10.4	10.6	10.8	11.0	11.2	11.4	11.6	11.8	12.0	12.2	12.4	12.6	12.8	13.0
48 10.0	10.2	10.4	10.6	10.8	11.0	11.2	11.4	11.6	11.8	12.0	12.2	12.4	12.6	12.8
7 00 9.8	10.0	10.2	10.4	10.6	10.8	11.0	11.2	11.4	11.6	11.8	12.0	12.2	12.4	12.6
15 9.6	9.8	10.0	10.2	10.4	10.6	10.8	11.0	11.2	11.4	11.6	11.8	12.0	12.2	12.4
30 9.4	9.6	9.8	10.0	10.2	10.4	10.6	10.8	11.0	11.2	11.4	11.6	11.8	12.0	12.2
45 9.2	9.4	9.6	9.8	10.0	10.2	10.4	10.6	10.8	11.0	11.2	11.4	11.6	11.8	12.0
8 00 9.0	9.2	9.4	9.6	9.8	10.0	10.2	10.4	10.6	10.8	11.0	11.2	11.4	11.6	11.8
20 8.8	9.0	9.2	9.4	9.6	9.8	10.0	10.2	10.4	10.6	10.8	11.0	11.2	11.4	11.6
40 8.6	8.8	9.0	9.2	9.4	9.6	9.8	10.0	10.2	10.4	10.6	10.8	11.0	11.2	11.4
9 00 8.4	8.6	8.8	9.0	9.2	9.4	9.6	9.8	10.0	10.2	10.4	10.6	10.8	11.0	11.2
20 8.2	8.4	8.6	8.8	9.0	9.2	9.4	9.6	9.8	10.0	10.2	10.4	10.6	10.8	11.0
40 8.0	8.2	8.4	8.6	8.8	9.0	9.2	9.4	9.6	9.8	10.0	10.2	10.4	10.6	10.8
10 00 7.8	8.0	8.2	8.4	8.6	8.8	9.0	9.2	9.4	9.6	9.8	10.0	10.2	10.4	10.6
30 7.6	7.8	8.0	8.2	8.4	8.6	8.8	9.0	9.2	9.4	9.6	9.8	10.0	10.2	10.4
11 00 7.4	7.6	7.8	8.0	8.2	8.4	8.6	8.8	9.0	9.2	9.4	9.6	9.8	10.0	10.2
30 7.2	7.4	7.6	7.8	8.0	8.2	8.4	8.6	8.8	9.0	9.2	9.4	9.6	9.8	10.0
12 00 7.0	7.2	7.4	7.6	7.8	8.0	8.2	8.4	8.6	8.8	9.0	9.2	9.4	9.6	9.8
30 6.8	7.0	7.2	7.4	7.6	7.8	8.0	8.2	8.4	8.6	8.8	9.0	9.2	9.4	9.6
13 00 6.6	6.8	7.0	7.2	7.4	7.6	7.8	8.0	8.2	8.4	8.6	8.8	9.0	9.2	9.4
30 6.4	6.6	6.8	7.0	7.2	7.4	7.6	7.8	8.0	8.2	8.4	8.6	8.8	9.0	9.2
14 00 6.2	6.4	6.6	6.8	7.0	7.2	7.4	7.6	7.8	8.0	8.2	8.4	8.6	8.8	9.0
15 00 6.0	6.2	6.4	6.6	6.8	7.0	7.2	7.4	7.6	7.8	8.0	8.2	8.4	8.6	8.8
16 00 5.8	6.0	6.2	6.4	6.6	6.8	7.0	7.2	7.4	7.6	7.8	8.0	8.2	8.4	8.6
17 00 5.6	5.8	6.0	6.2	6.4	6.6	6.8	7.0	7.2	7.4	7.6	7.8	8.0	8.2	8.4
18 00 5.4	5.6	5.8	6.0	6.2	6.4	6.6	6.8	7.0	7.2	7.4	7.6	7.8	8.0	8.2
19 00 5.2	5.4	5.6	5.8	6.0	6.2	6.4	6.6	6.8	7.0	7.2	7.4	7.6	7.8	8.0
21 00 5.0	5.2	5.4	5.6	5.8	6.0	6.2	6.4	6.6	6.8	7.0	7.2	7.4	7.6	7.8
23 00 4.8	5.0	5.2	5.4	5.6	5.8	6.0	6.2	6.4	6.6	6.8	7.0	7.2	7.4	7.6
25 00 4.6	4.8	5.0	5.2	5.4	5.6	5.8	6.0	6.2	6.4	6.6	6.8	7.0	7.2	7.4
27 00 4.4	4.6	4.8	5.0	5.2	5.4	5.6	5.8	6.0	6.2	6.4	6.6	6.8	7.0	7.2
29 00 4.2	4.4	4.6	4.8	5.0	5.2	5.4	5.6	5.8	6.0	6.2	6.4	6.6	6.8	7.0
33 00 4.0	4.2	4.4	4.6	4.8	5.0	5.2	5.4	5.6	5.8	6.0	6.2	6.4	6.6	6.8
36 00 3.8	4.0	4.2	4.4	4.6	4.8	5.0	5.2	5.4	5.6	5.8	6.0	6.2	6.4	6.6
41 00 3.6	3.8	4.0	4.2	4.4	4.6	4.8	5.0	5.2	5.4	5.6	5.8	6.0	6.2	6.4
48 00 3.4	3.6	3.8	4.0	4.2	4.4	4.6	4.8	5.0	5.2	5.4	5.6	5.8	6.0	6.2
55 00 3.2	3.4	3.6	3.8	4.0	4.2	4.4	4.6	4.8	5.0	5.2	5.4	5.6	5.8	6.0
65 00 3.0	3.2	3.4	3.6	3.8	4.0	4.2	4.4	4.6	4.8	5.0	5.2	5.4	5.6	5.8
75 00 2.8	3.0	3.2	3.4	3.6	3.8	4.0	4.2	4.4	4.6	4.8	5.0	5.2	5.4	5.6
85 00 2.6	2.8	3.0	3.2	3.4	3.6	3.8	4.0	4.2	4.4	4.6	4.8	5.0	5.2	5.4
90 00 2.5	2.7	2.9	3.1	3.3	3.5	3.7	3.9	4.1	4.3	4.5	4.7	4.9	5.1	5.3

A shortened table of the Star's Total Correction is given inside the back cover

STAR'S TOTAL CORRECTION

To be SUBTRACTED from the Observed Altitude of the Star

Height of Eye

Metres	9.1	9.8	10.5	11.2	12.0	12.8	13.6	14.5	15.4	16.3	17.2	18.2	19.2	20.2	21.2
Feet	30	32	34	37	39	42	45	48	51	53	56	60	63	66	70
Obs. Alt.	′	′	′	′	′	′	′	′	′	′	′	′	′	′	′
6° 00	13.6	13.8	14.0	14.2	14.4	14.6	14.8	15.0	15.2	15.4	15.6	15.8	16.0	16.2	16.4
12	13.4	13.6	13.8	14.0	14.2	14.4	14.6	14.8	15.0	15.2	15.4	15.6	15.8	16.0	16.2
24	13.2	13.4	13.6	13.8	14.0	14.2	14.4	14.6	14.8	15.0	15.2	15.4	15.6	15.8	16.0
36	13.0	13.2	13.4	13.6	13.8	14.0	14.2	14.4	14.6	14.8	15.0	15.2	15.4	15.6	15.8
48	12.8	13.0	13.2	13.4	13.6	13.8	14.0	14.2	14.4	14.6	14.8	15.0	15.2	15.4	15.6
7 00	12.6	12.8	13.0	13.2	13.4	13.6	13.8	14.0	14.2	14.4	14.6	14.8	15.0	15.2	15.4
15	12.4	12.6	12.8	13.0	13.2	13.4	13.6	13.8	14.0	14.2	14.4	14.6	14.8	15.0	15.2
30	12.2	12.4	12.6	12.8	13.0	13.2	13.4	13.6	13.8	14.0	14.2	14.4	14.6	14.8	15.0
45	12.0	12.2	12.4	12.6	12.8	13.0	13.2	13.4	13.6	13.8	14.0	14.2	14.4	14.6	14.8
8 00	11.8	12.0	12.2	12.4	12.6	12.8	13.0	13.2	13.4	13.6	13.8	14.0	14.2	14.4	14.6
20	11.6	11.8	12.0	12.2	12.4	12.6	12.8	13.0	13.2	13.4	13.6	13.8	14.0	14.2	14.4
40	11.4	11.6	11.8	12.0	12.2	12.4	12.6	12.8	13.0	13.2	13.4	13.6	13.8	14.0	14.2
9 00	11.2	11.4	11.6	11.8	12.0	12.2	12.4	12.6	12.8	13.0	13.2	13.4	13.6	13.8	14.0
20	11.0	11.2	11.4	11.6	11.8	12.0	12.2	12.4	12.6	12.8	13.0	13.2	13.4	13.6	13.8
40	10.8	11.0	11.2	11.4	11.6	11.8	12.0	12.2	12.4	12.6	12.8	13.0	13.2	13.4	13.6
10 00	10.6	10.8	11.0	11.2	11.4	11.6	11.8	12.0	12.2	12.4	12.6	12.8	13.0	13.2	13.4
30	10.4	10.6	10.8	11.0	11.2	11.4	11.6	11.8	12.0	12.2	12.4	12.6	12.8	13.0	13.2
11 00	10.2	10.4	10.6	10.8	11.0	11.2	11.4	11.6	11.8	12.0	12.2	12.4	12.6	12.8	13.0
30	10.0	10.2	10.4	10.6	10.8	11.0	11.2	11.4	11.6	11.8	12.0	12.2	12.4	12.6	12.8
12 00	9.8	10.0	10.2	10.4	10.6	10.8	11.0	11.2	11.4	11.6	11.8	12.0	12.2	12.4	12.6
30	9.6	9.8	10.0	10.2	10.4	10.6	10.8	11.0	11.2	11.4	11.6	11.8	12.0	12.2	12.4
13 00	9.4	9.6	9.8	10.0	10.2	10.4	10.6	10.8	11.0	11.2	11.4	11.6	11.8	12.0	12.2
30	9.2	9.4	9.6	9.8	10.0	10.2	10.4	10.6	10.8	11.0	11.2	11.4	11.6	11.8	12.0
14 00	9.0	9.2	9.4	9.6	9.8	10.0	10.2	10.4	10.6	10.8	11.0	11.2	11.4	11.6	11.8
15 00	8.8	9.0	9.2	9.4	9.6	9.8	10.0	10.2	10.4	10.6	10.8	11.0	11.2	11.4	11.6
16 00	8.6	8.8	9.0	9.2	9.4	9.6	9.8	10.0	10.2	10.4	10.6	10.8	11.0	11.2	11.4
17 00	8.4	8.6	8.8	9.0	9.2	9.4	9.6	9.8	10.0	10.2	10.4	10.6	10.8	11.0	11.2
18 00	8.2	8.4	8.6	8.8	9.0	9.2	9.4	9.6	9.8	10.0	10.2	10.4	10.6	10.8	11.0
19 00	8.0	8.2	8.4	8.6	8.8	9.0	9.2	9.4	9.6	9.8	10.0	10.2	10.4	10.6	10.8
21 00	7.8	8.0	8.2	8.4	8.6	8.8	9.0	9.2	9.4	9.6	9.8	10.0	10.2	10.4	10.6
23 00	7.6	7.8	8.0	8.2	8.4	8.6	8.8	9.0	9.2	9.4	9.6	9.8	10.0	10.2	10.4
25 00	7.4	7.6	7.8	8.0	8.2	8.4	8.6	8.8	9.0	9.2	9.4	9.6	9.8	10.0	10.2
27 00	7.2	7.4	7.6	7.8	8.0	8.2	8.4	8.6	8.8	9.0	9.2	9.4	9.6	9.8	10.0
29 00	7.0	7.2	7.4	7.6	7.8	8.0	8.2	8.4	8.6	8.8	9.0	9.2	9.4	9.6	9.8
33 00	6.8	7.0	7.2	7.4	7.6	7.8	8.0	8.2	8.4	8.6	8.8	9.0	9.2	9.4	9.6
36 00	6.6	6.8	7.0	7.2	7.4	7.6	7.8	8.0	8.2	8.4	8.6	8.8	9.0	9.2	9.4
41 00	6.4	6.6	6.8	7.0	7.2	7.4	7.6	7.8	8.0	8.2	8.4	8.6	8.8	9.0	9.2
48 00	6.2	6.4	6.6	6.8	7.0	7.2	7.4	7.6	7.8	8.0	8.2	8.4	8.6	8.8	9.0
55 00	6.0	6.2	6.4	6.6	6.8	7.0	7.2	7.4	7.6	7.8	8.0	8.2	8.4	8.6	8.8
65 00	5.8	6.0	6.2	6.4	6.6	6.8	7.0	7.2	7.4	7.6	7.8	8.0	8.2	8.4	8.6
75 00	5.6	5.8	6.0	6.2	6.4	6.6	6.8	7.0	7.2	7.4	7.6	7.8	8.0	8.2	8.4
85 00	5.4	5.6	5.8	6.0	6.2	6.4	6.6	6.8	7.0	7.2	7.4	7.6	7.8	8.0	8.2
90 00	5.3	5.5	5.7	5.9	6.1	6.3	6.5	6.7	6.9	7.1	7.3	7.5	7.7	7.9	8.1

A shortened table of the Star's Total Correction is given inside the back cover

STAR'S TOTAL CORRECTION

To be SUBTRACTED from the Observed Altitude of the Star

Height of Eye

Metres	21.2	22.2	23.3	24.4	25.5	26.7	27.9	29.1	30.3	31.6	32.9	34.0	35.5	37.0	38.5
Feet	70	73	76	80	84	88	92	95	99	104	108	112	116	121	126
Obs. Alt.	′	′	′	′	′	′	′	′	′	′	′	′	′	′	′
6° 00	16.4	16.6	16.8	17.0	17.2	17.4	17.6	17.8	18.0	18.2	18.4	18.6	18.8	19.0	19.2
12	16.2	16.4	16.6	16.8	17.0	17.2	17.4	17.6	17.8	18.0	18.2	18.4	18.6	18.8	19.0
24	16.0	16.2	16.4	16.6	16.8	17.0	17.2	17.4	17.6	17.8	18.0	18.2	18.4	18.6	18.8
36	15.8	16.0	16.2	16.4	16.6	16.8	17.0	17.2	17.4	17.6	17.8	18.0	18.2	18.4	18.6
48	15.6	15.8	16.0	16.2	16.4	16.6	16.8	17.0	17.2	17.4	17.6	17.8	18.0	18.2	18.4
7 00	15.4	15.6	15.8	16.0	16.2	16.4	16.6	16.8	17.0	17.2	17.4	17.6	17.8	18.0	18.2
15	15.2	15.4	15.6	15.8	16.0	16.2	16.4	16.6	16.8	17.0	17.2	17.4	17.6	17.8	18.0
30	15.0	15.2	15.4	15.6	15.8	16.0	16.2	16.4	16.6	16.8	17.0	17.2	17.4	17.6	17.8
45	14.8	15.0	15.2	15.4	15.6	15.8	16.0	16.2	16.4	16.6	16.8	17.0	17.2	17.4	17.6
8 00	14.6	14.8	15.0	15.2	15.4	15.6	15.8	16.0	16.2	16.4	16.6	16.8	17.0	17.2	17.4
20	14.4	14.6	14.8	15.0	15.2	15.4	15.6	15.8	16.0	16.2	16.4	16.6	16.8	17.0	17.2
40	14.2	14.4	14.6	14.8	15.0	15.2	15.4	15.6	15.8	16.0	16.2	16.4	16.6	16.8	17.0
9 00	14.0	14.2	14.4	14.6	14.8	15.0	15.2	15.4	15.6	15.8	16.0	16.2	16.4	16.6	16.8
20	13.8	14.0	14.2	14.4	14.6	14.8	15.0	15.2	15.4	15.6	15.8	16.0	16.2	16.4	16.6
40	13.6	13.8	14.0	14.2	14.4	14.6	14.8	15.0	15.2	15.4	15.6	15.8	16.0	16.2	16.4
10 00	13.4	13.6	13.8	14.0	14.2	14.4	14.6	14.8	15.0	15.2	15.4	15.6	15.8	16.0	16.2
30	13.2	13.4	13.6	13.8	14.0	14.2	14.4	14.6	14.8	15.0	15.2	15.4	15.6	15.8	16.0
11 00	13.0	13.2	13.4	13.6	13.8	14.0	14.2	14.4	14.6	14.8	15.0	15.2	15.4	15.6	15.8
30	12.8	13.0	13.2	13.4	13.6	13.8	14.0	14.2	14.4	14.6	14.8	15.0	15.2	15.4	15.6
12 00	12.6	12.8	13.0	13.2	13.4	13.6	13.8	14.0	14.2	14.4	14.6	14.8	15.0	15.2	15.4
30	12.4	12.6	12.8	13.0	13.2	13.4	13.6	13.8	14.0	14.2	14.4	14.6	14.8	15.0	15.2
13 00	12.2	12.4	12.6	12.8	13.0	13.2	13.4	13.6	13.8	14.0	14.2	14.4	14.6	14.8	15.0
30	12.0	12.2	12.4	12.6	12.8	13.0	13.2	13.4	13.6	13.8	14.0	14.2	14.4	14.6	14.8
14 00	11.8	12.0	12.2	12.4	12.6	12.8	13.0	13.2	13.4	13.6	13.8	14.0	14.2	14.4	14.6
15 00	11.6	11.8	12.0	12.2	12.4	12.6	12.8	13.0	13.2	13.4	13.6	13.8	14.0	14.2	14.4
16 00	11.4	11.6	11.8	12.0	12.2	12.4	12.6	12.8	13.0	13.2	13.4	13.6	13.8	14.0	14.2
17 00	11.2	11.4	11.6	11.8	12.0	12.2	12.4	12.6	12.8	13.0	13.2	13.4	13.6	13.8	14.0
18 00	11.0	11.2	11.4	11.6	11.8	12.0	12.2	12.4	12.6	12.8	13.0	13.2	13.4	13.6	13.8
19 00	10.8	11.0	11.2	11.4	11.6	11.8	12.0	12.2	12.4	12.6	12.8	13.0	13.2	13.4	13.6
21 00	10.6	10.8	11.0	11.2	11.4	11.6	11.8	12.0	12.2	12.4	12.6	12.8	13.0	13.2	13.4
23 00	10.4	10.6	10.8	11.0	11.2	11.4	11.6	11.8	12.0	12.2	12.4	12.6	12.8	13.0	13.2
25 00	10.2	10.4	10.6	10.8	11.0	11.2	11.4	11.6	11.8	12.0	12.2	12.4	12.6	12.8	13.0
27 00	10.0	10.2	10.4	10.6	10.8	11.0	11.2	11.4	11.6	11.8	12.0	12.2	12.4	12.6	12.8
29 00	9.8	10.0	10.2	10.4	10.6	10.8	11.0	11.2	11.4	11.6	11.8	12.0	12.2	12.4	12.6
33 00	9.6	9.8	10.0	10.2	10.4	10.6	10.8	11.0	11.2	11.4	11.6	11.8	12.0	12.2	12.4
36 00	9.4	9.6	9.8	10.0	10.2	10.4	10.6	10.8	11.0	11.2	11.4	11.6	11.8	12.0	12.2
41 00	9.2	9.4	9.6	9.8	10.0	10.2	10.4	10.6	10.8	11.0	11.2	11.4	11.6	11.8	12.0
48 00	9.0	9.2	9.4	9.6	9.8	10.0	10.2	10.4	10.6	10.8	11.0	11.2	11.4	11.6	11.8
55 00	8.8	9.0	9.2	9.4	9.6	9.8	10.0	10.2	10.4	10.6	10.8	11.0	11.2	11.4	11.6
65 00	8.6	8.8	9.0	9.2	9.4	9.6	9.8	10.0	10.2	10.4	10.6	10.8	11.0	11.2	11.4
75 00	8.4	8.6	8.8	9.0	9.2	9.4	9.6	9.8	10.0	10.2	10.4	10.6	10.8	11.0	11.2
85 00	8.2	8.4	8.6	8.8	9.0	9.2	9.4	9.6	9.8	10.0	10.2	10.4	10.6	10.8	11.0
90 00	8.1	8.3	8.5	8.7	8.9	9.1	9.3	9.5	9.7	9.9	10.1	10.3	10.5	10.7	10.9

A shortened table of the Star's Total Correction is given inside the back cover

STAR'S TOTAL CORRECTION

				Height of Eye				
Metres	38.5	40.0	41.5	43.0	44.5	46.0	47.5	49.0
Feet	126	131	136	141	146	151	156	161
Obs. Alt.	′	′	′	′	′	′	′	′
6° 00	19.2	19.4	19.6	19.8	20.0	20.2	20.4	20.6
12	19.0	19.2	19.4	19.6	19.8	20.0	20.2	20.4
24	18.8	19.0	19.2	19.4	19.6	19.8	20.0	20.2
36	18.6	18.8	19.0	19.2	19.4	19.6	19.8	20.0
48	18.4	18.6	18.8	19.0	19.2	19.4	19.6	19.8
7 00	18.2	18.4	18.6	18.8	19.0	19.2	19.4	19.6
15	18.0	18.2	18.4	18.6	18.8	19.0	19.2	19.4
30	17.8	18.0	18.2	18.4	18.6	18.8	19.0	19.2
45	17.6	17.8	18.0	18.2	18.4	18.6	18.8	19.0
8 00	17.4	17.6	17.8	18.0	18.2	18.4	18.6	18.8
20	17.2	17.4	17.6	17.8	18.0	18.2	18.4	18.6
40	17.0	17.2	17.4	17.6	17.8	18.0	18.2	18.4
9 00	16.8	17.0	17.2	17.4	17.6	17.8	18.0	18.2
20	16.6	16.8	17.0	17.2	17.4	17.6	17.8	18.0
40	16.4	16.6	16.8	17.0	17.2	17.4	17.6	17.8
10 00	16.2	16.4	16.6	16.8	17.0	17.2	17.4	17.6
30	16.0	16.2	16.4	16.6	16.8	17.0	17.2	17.4
11 00	15.8	16.0	16.2	16.4	16.6	16.8	17.0	17.2
30	15.6	15.8	16.0	16.2	16.4	16.6	16.8	17.0
12 00	15.4	15.6	15.8	16.0	16.2	16.4	16.6	16.8
30	15.2	15.4	15.6	15.8	16.0	16.2	16.4	16.6
13 00	15.0	15.2	15.4	15.6	15.8	16.0	16.2	16.4
30	14.8	15.0	15.2	15.4	15.6	15.8	16.0	16.2
14 00	14.6	14.8	15.0	15.2	15.4	15.6	15.8	16.0
15 00	14.4	14.6	14.8	15.0	15.2	15.4	15.6	15.8
16 00	14.2	14.4	14.6	14.8	15.0	15.2	15.4	15.6
17 00	14.0	14.2	14.4	14.6	14.8	15.0	15.2	15.4
18 00	13.8	14.0	14.2	14.4	14.6	14.8	15.0	15.2
19 00	13.6	13.8	14.0	14.2	14.4	14.6	14.8	15.0
21 00	13.4	13.6	13.8	14.0	14.2	14.4	14.6	14.8
23 00	13.2	13.4	13.6	13.8	14.0	14.2	14.4	14.6
25 00	13.0	13.2	13.4	13.6	13.8	14.0	14.2	14.4
27 00	12.8	13.0	13.2	13.4	13.6	13.8	14.0	14.2
29 00	12.6	12.8	13.0	13.2	13.4	13.6	13.8	14.0
33 00	12.4	12.6	12.8	13.0	13.2	13.4	13.6	13.8
36 00	12.2	12.4	12.6	12.8	13.0	13.2	13.4	13.6
41 00	12.0	12.2	12.4	12.6	12.8	13.0	13.2	13.4
48 00	11.8	12.0	12.2	12.4	12.6	12.8	13.0	13.2
55 00	11.6	11.8	12.0	12.2	12.4	12.6	12.8	13.0
65 00	11.4	11.6	11.8	12.0	12.2	12.4	12.6	12.8
75 00	11.2	11.4	11.6	11.8	12.0	12.2	12.4	12.6
85 00	11.0	11.2	11.4	11.6	11.8	12.0	12.2	12.4
90 00	10.9	11.1	11.3	11.5	11.7	11.9	12.1	12.3

A shortened table of the Star's Total Correction is given inside the back cover

MOON'S TOTAL CORRECTION – LOWER LIMB

Add to the Observed Altitude of the Moon's Lower limb

Observed Altitude

H.P.	6°00'	6°10'	6°20'	6°30'	6°40'	6°50'	7°00'	7°15'	7°30'	7°45'	8°00'	8°30'	9°00'	9°30'	10°00'
54.0	47.8	48.0	48.2	48.4	48.5	48.7	48.9	49.1	49.2	49.4	49.7	50.0	50.2	50.4	50.5
54.2	48.1	48.3	48.5	48.6	48.8	49.0	49.2	49.3	49.5	49.6	50.0	50.2	50.4	50.6	50.8
54.4	48.3	48.5	48.7	48.9	49.0	49.2	49.4	49.6	49.7	49.9	50.2	50.5	50.7	50.9	51.0
54.6	48.6	48.8	49.0	49.1	49.3	49.5	49.7	49.8	50.0	50.1	50.5	50.7	50.9	51.1	51.3
54.8	48.8	49.0	49.2	49.4	49.6	49.7	49.9	50.1	50.2	50.4	50.7	51.0	51.2	51.4	51.5
55.0	49.1	49.3	49.5	49.6	49.8	50.0	50.2	50.3	50.5	50.7	51.0	51.2	51.4	51.6	51.8
55.2	49.3	49.5	49.7	49.9	50.1	50.2	50.4	50.6	50.7	50.9	51.2	51.5	51.7	51.9	52.0
55.4	49.6	49.8	50.0	50.1	50.3	50.5	50.7	50.8	51.0	51.2	51.5	51.7	51.9	52.1	52.3
55.6	49.8	50.0	50.2	50.4	50.6	50.7	50.9	51.1	51.2	51.4	51.7	52.0	52.2	52.4	52.5
55.8	50.1	50.3	50.5	50.6	50.8	51.0	51.2	51.3	51.5	51.7	52.0	52.2	52.4	52.6	52.8
56.0	50.3	50.5	50.7	50.9	51.1	51.2	51.4	51.6	51.8	51.9	52.2	52.5	52.7	52.9	53.0
56.2	50.6	50.8	51.0	51.1	51.3	51.5	51.7	51.8	52.0	52.2	52.5	52.7	52.9	53.1	53.3
56.4	50.8	51.0	51.2	51.4	51.6	51.7	51.9	52.1	52.3	52.4	52.7	53.0	53.2	53.4	53.5
56.6	51.1	51.3	51.5	51.6	51.8	52.0	52.2	52.3	52.5	52.7	53.0	53.2	53.4	53.6	53.8
56.8	51.3	51.5	51.7	51.9	52.1	52.2	52.4	52.6	52.8	52.9	53.2	53.5	53.7	53.9	54.0
57.0	51.6	51.8	52.0	52.1	52.3	52.5	52.7	52.8	53.0	53.2	53.5	53.7	53.9	54.1	54.3
57.2	51.8	52.0	52.2	52.4	52.6	52.7	52.9	53.1	53.3	53.4	53.7	54.0	54.2	54.4	54.5
57.4	52.1	52.3	52.5	52.7	52.8	53.0	53.2	53.3	53.5	53.7	54.0	54.2	54.4	54.6	54.8
57.6	52.4	52.5	52.7	52.9	53.1	53.2	53.4	53.6	53.8	53.9	54.2	54.5	54.7	54.9	55.0
57.8	52.6	52.8	53.0	53.2	53.3	53.5	53.7	53.8	54.0	54.2	54.5	54.7	54.9	55.1	55.3
58.0	52.9	53.0	53.2	53.4	53.6	53.7	53.9	54.1	54.3	54.4	54.7	55.0	55.2	55.4	55.5
58.2	53.1	53.3	53.5	53.7	53.8	54.0	54.2	54.4	54.5	54.7	55.0	55.2	55.4	55.6	55.8
58.4	53.4	53.5	53.7	53.9	54.1	54.2	54.4	54.6	54.8	54.9	55.2	55.5	55.7	55.9	56.0
58.6	53.6	53.8	54.0	54.2	54.3	54.5	54.7	54.9	55.0	55.2	55.5	55.7	55.9	56.1	56.3
58.8	53.9	54.1	54.2	54.4	54.6	54.7	54.9	55.1	55.3	55.4	55.7	56.0	56.2	56.4	56.5
59.0	54.1	54.3	54.5	54.7	54.8	55.0	55.2	55.4	55.5	55.7	56.0	56.2	56.4	56.6	56.8
59.2	54.4	54.6	54.7	54.9	55.1	55.2	55.4	55.6	55.8	55.9	56.2	56.5	56.7	56.9	57.0
59.4	54.6	54.8	55.0	55.2	55.3	55.5	55.7	55.9	56.0	56.2	56.5	56.7	56.9	57.1	57.3
59.6	54.9	55.1	55.2	55.4	55.6	55.7	55.9	56.1	56.3	56.4	56.7	57.0	57.2	57.4	57.5
59.8	55.1	55.3	55.5	55.7	55.8	56.0	56.2	56.4	56.5	56.7	57.0	57.2	57.4	57.6	57.8
60.0	55.4	55.6	55.7	55.9	56.1	56.2	56.4	56.6	56.8	56.9	57.2	57.5	57.7	57.9	58.0
60.2	55.6	55.8	56.0	56.2	56.3	56.5	56.7	56.9	57.0	57.2	57.5	57.7	57.9	58.1	58.3
60.4	55.9	56.1	56.2	56.4	56.6	56.7	56.9	57.1	57.3	57.4	57.7	58.0	58.2	58.3	58.5
60.6	56.1	56.3	56.5	56.7	56.8	57.0	57.2	57.4	57.5	57.7	58.0	58.2	58.4	58.6	58.7
60.8	56.4	56.6	56.7	56.9	57.1	57.2	57.4	57.6	57.8	57.9	58.2	58.5	58.7	58.8	59.0
61.0	56.6	56.8	57.0	57.2	57.3	57.5	57.7	57.9	58.0	58.2	58.5	58.7	58.9	59.1	59.2
61.2	56.9	57.1	57.3	57.4	57.6	57.8	57.9	58.1	58.3	58.4	58.7	59.0	59.2	59.3	59.5
61.4	57.1	57.3	57.5	57.7	57.8	58.0	58.2	58.4	58.5	58.7	59.0	59.2	59.4	59.6	59.7
61.5	57.3	57.5	57.7	57.8	58.0	58.2	58.3	58.5	58.7	58.8	59.1	59.4	59.6	59.8	59.9

Height of Eye Correction Always ADDED to the Observed Altitude

Metres	2	2.3	2.7	3.1	3.5	3.9	4.4	4.9	5.4	5.9	6.5
Feet	7	8	9	10	11	13	14	16	18	19	21
Corrn '	9.8	9.6	9.4	9.2	9.0	8.8	8.6	8.4	8.2	8.0	7.8

MOON'S TOTAL CORRECTION – LOWER LIMB

Add to the Observed Altitude of the Moon's Lower limb

Observed Altitude °

H.P. '	10°00'	30'	11°00'	30'	12°00'	30'	13°00'	30'	14°00'	30'	15°00'	30'	16°00'	30'	17°00'
54.0	50.5	50.6	50.8	50.9	50.9	51.0	51.1	51.1	51.1	51.1	51.1	51.1	51.1	51.0	51.0
54.2	50.8	50.9	51.0	51.1	51.2	51.3	51.3	51.3	51.4	51.4	51.4	51.3	51.3	51.3	51.2
54.4	51.0	51.1	51.3	51.4	51.4	51.5	51.5	51.6	51.6	51.6	51.6	51.6	51.6	51.5	51.5
54.6	51.3	51.4	51.5	51.6	51.7	51.7	51.8	51.8	51.8	51.9	51.8	51.8	51.8	51.8	51.7
54.8	51.5	51.6	51.8	51.9	51.9	52.0	52.0	52.1	52.1	52.1	52.1	52.1	52.1	52.0	52.0
55.0	51.8	51.9	52.0	52.1	52.2	52.2	52.3	52.3	52.3	52.3	52.3	52.3	52.3	52.3	52.2
55.2	52.0	52.1	52.3	52.4	52.4	52.5	52.5	52.6	52.6	52.6	52.6	52.6	52.8	52.7	52.5
55.4	52.3	52.4	52.5	52.6	52.7	52.7	52.8	52.8	52.8	52.8	52.8	52.8	52.8	52.7	52.7
55.6	52.5	52.6	52.8	52.9	52.9	53.0	53.0	53.1	53.1	53.1	53.1	53.1	53.0	53.0	52.9
55.8	52.8	52.9	53.0	53.1	53.2	53.2	53.3	53.3	53.3	53.3	53.3	53.3	53.3	53.2	53.2
56.0	53.0	53.1	53.3	53.3	53.4	53.5	53.5	53.6	53.6	53.6	53.6	53.5	53.5	53.5	53.4
56.2	53.3	53.4	53.5	53.6	53.7	53.7	53.8	53.8	53.8	53.8	53.8	53.8	53.8	53.7	53.7
56.4	53.5	53.6	53.8	53.8	53.9	54.0	54.0	54.0	54.1	54.1	54.1	54.0	54.0	54.0	53.9
56.6	53.8	53.9	54.0	54.1	54.2	54.2	54.3	54.3	54.3	54.3	54.3	54.3	54.3	54.2	54.2
56.8	54.0	54.1	54.3	54.3	54.4	54.5	54.5	54.5	54.6	54.6	54.6	54.5	54.5	54.5	54.4
57.0	54.3	54.4	54.5	54.6	54.7	54.7	54.8	54.8	54.8	54.8	54.8	54.8	54.7	54.7	54.7
57.2	54.5	54.6	54.7	54.8	54.9	55.0	55.0	55.0	55.1	55.1	55.0	55.0	55.0	54.9	54.9
57.4	54.8	54.9	55.0	55.1	55.2	55.2	55.3	55.3	55.3	55.3	55.3	55.3	55.2	55.2	55.1
57.6	55.0	55.1	55.2	55.3	55.4	55.5	55.5	55.5	55.5	55.5	55.5	55.5	55.5	55.4	55.4
57.8	55.3	55.4	55.5	55.6	55.7	55.7	55.8	55.8	55.8	55.8	55.8	55.8	55.7	55.7	55.6
58.0	55.5	55.6	55.7	55.8	55.9	56.0	56.0	56.0	56.0	56.0	56.0	56.0	56.0	55.9	55.9
58.2	55.8	55.9	56.0	56.1	56.2	56.2	56.2	56.3	56.3	56.3	56.3	56.2	56.2	56.2	56.1
58.4	56.0	56.1	56.2	56.3	56.4	56.5	56.5	56.5	56.5	56.5	56.5	56.5	56.5	56.4	56.4
58.6	56.3	56.4	56.5	56.6	56.7	56.7	56.7	56.8	56.8	56.8	56.8	56.7	56.7	56.7	56.6
58.8	56.5	56.6	56.7	56.8	56.9	57.0	57.0	57.0	57.0	57.0	57.0	57.0	56.9	56.9	56.8
59.0	56.8	56.9	57.0	57.1	57.1	57.2	57.2	57.3	57.3	57.3	57.3	57.2	57.2	57.1	57.1
59.2	57.0	57.1	57.2	57.3	57.4	57.4	57.5	57.5	57.5	57.5	57.5	57.5	57.4	57.4	57.3
59.4	57.3	57.4	57.5	57.6	57.6	57.7	57.7	57.8	57.8	57.8	57.7	57.7	57.7	57.6	57.6
59.6	57.5	57.6	57.7	57.8	57.9	57.9	58.0	58.0	58.0	58.0	58.0	58.0	57.9	57.9	57.8
59.8	57.8	57.9	58.0	58.1	58.1	58.2	58.2	58.2	58.3	58.3	58.2	58.2	58.2	58.1	58.1
60.0	58.0	58.1	58.2	58.3	58.4	58.4	58.5	58.5	58.5	58.5	58.5	58.5	58.4	58.4	58.3
60.2	58.3	58.4	58.5	58.6	58.6	58.7	58.7	58.7	58.8	58.7	58.7	58.7	58.7	58.6	58.6
60.4	58.5	58.6	58.7	58.8	58.9	58.9	59.0	59.0	59.0	59.0	59.0	58.9	58.9	58.9	58.8
60.6	58.7	58.9	59.0	59.1	59.1	59.2	59.2	59.2	59.2	59.2	59.2	59.2	59.2	59.1	59.0
60.8	59.0	59.1	59.2	59.3	59.4	59.4	59.5	59.5	59.5	59.5	59.5	59.4	59.4	59.3	59.3
61.0	59.2	59.4	59.5	59.6	59.6	59.7	59.7	59.7	59.7	59.7	59.7	59.7	59.6	59.6	59.5
61.2	59.5	59.6	59.7	59.8	59.9	59.9	60.0	60.0	60.0	60.0	60.0	59.9	59.9	59.8	59.8
61.5	59.9	60.0	60.1	60.2	60.3	60.3	60.4	60.4	60.4	60.4	60.4	60.3	60.3	60.2	60.2

Height of Eye Correction Always ADDED to the Observed Altitude

Metres	6.5	7.1	7.7	8.4	9.1	9.8	10.5	11.2	12	12.8	13.6
Feet	21	23	25	28	30	32	34	37	39	42	45
Corrn '	7.8	7.6	7.4	7.2	7.0	6.8	6.6	6.4	6.2	6.0	5.8

MOON'S TOTAL CORRECTION – LOWER LIMB

Add to the Observed Altitude of the Moon's Lower limb

Observed Altitude

H.P.	17°00'	30'	18°00'	30'	19°00'	30'	20°00'	30'	21°00'	30'	22°00'	30'	23°00'	30'	24°00'
54.0	51.0	50.9	50.9	50.8	50.7	50.7	50.6	50.5	50.4	50.3	50.1	50.0	49.9	49.8	49.6
54.2	51.2	51.2	51.1	51.1	51.0	50.9	50.8	50.7	50.6	50.5	50.4	50.3	50.1	50.0	49.8
54.4	51.5	51.4	51.4	51.3	51.2	51.1	51.0	50.9	50.8	50.7	50.6	50.5	50.4	50.2	50.1
54.6	51.7	51.7	51.6	51.5	51.5	51.4	51.3	51.2	51.1	51.0	50.9	50.7	50.6	50.5	50.3
54.8	52.0	51.9	51.9	51.8	51.7	51.6	51.5	51.4	51.3	51.2	51.1	51.0	50.8	50.7	50.6
55.0	52.2	52.2	52.1	52.0	51.9	51.9	51.8	51.7	51.6	51.4	51.3	51.2	51.1	50.9	50.8
55.2	52.5	52.4	52.3	52.3	52.2	52.1	52.0	51.9	51.8	51.7	51.6	51.4	51.3	51.2	51.0
55.4	52.7	52.6	52.6	52.5	52.4	52.3	52.3	52.1	52.0	51.9	51.8	51.7	51.5	51.4	51.3
55.6	52.9	52.9	52.8	52.8	52.7	52.6	52.5	52.4	52.3	52.2	52.0	51.9	51.8	51.6	51.5
55.8	53.2	53.1	53.1	53.0	52.9	52.8	52.7	52.6	52.5	52.4	52.3	52.2	52.0	51.9	51.7
56.0	53.4	53.4	53.3	53.2	53.2	53.1	53.0	52.9	52.8	52.6	52.5	52.4	52.3	52.1	52.0
56.2	53.7	53.6	53.6	53.5	53.4	53.3	53.2	53.1	53.0	52.9	52.8	52.6	52.5	52.3	52.2
56.4	53.9	53.9	53.8	53.7	53.6	53.6	53.5	53.3	53.2	53.1	53.0	52.9	52.7	52.6	52.4
56.6	54.2	54.1	54.0	54.0	53.9	53.8	53.7	53.6	53.5	53.4	53.2	53.1	53.0	52.8	52.7
56.8	54.4	54.4	54.3	54.2	54.1	54.0	53.9	53.8	53.7	53.6	53.5	53.3	53.2	53.1	52.9
57.0	54.7	54.6	54.5	54.4	54.4	54.3	54.2	54.1	54.0	53.8	53.7	53.6	53.4	53.3	53.1
57.2	54.9	54.8	54.8	54.7	54.6	54.5	54.4	54.3	54.2	54.1	53.9	53.8	53.7	53.5	53.4
57.4	55.1	55.1	55.0	54.9	54.8	54.8	54.7	54.5	54.4	54.3	54.2	54.1	53.9	53.8	53.6
57.6	55.4	55.3	55.3	55.2	55.1	55.0	54.9	54.8	54.7	54.6	54.4	54.3	54.1	54.0	53.8
57.8	55.6	55.6	55.5	55.4	55.3	55.2	55.1	55.0	54.9	54.8	54.7	54.5	54.4	54.2	54.1
58.0	55.9	55.8	55.7	55.7	55.6	55.5	55.4	55.3	55.2	55.0	54.9	54.8	54.6	54.5	54.3
58.2	56.1	56.1	56.0	55.9	55.8	55.7	55.6	55.5	55.4	55.3	55.1	55.0	54.9	54.7	54.6
58.4	56.4	56.3	56.2	56.1	56.1	56.0	55.9	55.7	55.6	55.5	55.4	55.2	55.1	54.9	54.8
58.6	56.6	56.5	56.5	56.4	56.3	56.2	56.1	56.0	55.9	55.7	55.6	55.5	55.3	55.2	55.0
58.8	56.8	56.8	56.7	56.6	56.5	56.4	56.3	56.2	56.1	56.0	55.9	55.7	55.6	55.4	55.3
59.0	57.1	57.0	57.0	56.9	56.8	56.7	56.6	56.5	56.3	56.2	56.1	56.0	55.8	55.7	55.5
59.2	57.3	57.3	57.2	57.1	57.0	56.9	56.8	56.7	56.6	56.5	56.3	56.2	56.0	55.9	55.7
59.4	57.6	57.5	57.4	57.4	57.3	57.2	57.1	56.9	56.8	56.7	56.6	56.4	56.3	56.1	56.0
59.6	57.8	57.8	57.7	57.6	57.5	57.4	57.3	57.2	57.1	56.9	56.8	56.7	56.5	56.4	56.2
59.8	58.1	58.0	57.9	57.8	57.8	57.7	57.5	57.4	57.3	57.2	57.0	56.9	56.8	56.6	56.4
60.0	58.3	58.2	58.2	58.1	58.0	57.9	57.8	57.7	57.5	57.4	57.3	57.1	57.0	56.8	56.7
60.2	58.6	58.5	58.4	58.3	58.2	58.1	58.0	57.9	57.8	57.7	57.5	57.4	57.2	57.1	56.9
60.4	58.8	58.7	58.7	58.6	58.5	58.4	58.3	58.1	58.0	57.9	57.8	57.6	57.5	57.3	57.1
60.6	59.0	59.0	58.9	58.8	58.7	58.6	58.5	58.4	58.3	58.1	58.0	57.8	57.7	57.5	57.4
60.8	59.3	59.2	59.1	59.1	59.0	58.9	58.7	58.6	58.5	58.4	58.2	58.1	57.9	57.8	57.6
61.0	59.5	59.5	59.4	59.3	59.2	59.1	59.0	58.9	58.7	58.6	58.5	58.3	58.2	58.0	57.8
61.2	59.8	59.7	59.6	59.5	59.4	59.3	59.2	59.1	59.0	58.8	58.7	58.6	58.4	58.2	58.1
61.4	60.0	59.9	59.9	59.8	59.7	59.6	59.5	59.3	59.2	59.1	58.9	58.8	58.6	58.5	58.3
61.5	60.2	60.1	60.0	59.9	59.8	59.7	59.6	59.5	59.4	59.2	59.1	58.9	58.8	58.6	58.5

Height of Eye Correction Always ADDED to the Observed Altitude

Metres	13.6	14.5	15.4	16.3	17.2	18.2	19.2	20.2	21.2	22.2	23.3
Feet	45	48	51	53	56	60	63	66	70	73	76
Corrn '	5.8	5.6	5.4	5.2	5.0	4.8	4.6	4.4	4.2	4.0	3.8

MOON'S TOTAL CORRECTION – LOWER LIMB

Add to the Observed Altitude of the Moon's Lower limb

Observed Altitude

H.P. '	24°00'	30'	25°00'	30'	26°00'	30'	27°00'	30'	28°00'	30'	29°00'	30'	30°00'	30'	31°00'
54.0	49.6	49.5	49.3	49.2	49.0	48.8	48.7	48.5	48.3	48.1	47.9	47.7	47.5	47.3	47.1
54.2	49.8	49.7	49.5	49.4	49.2	49.1	48.9	48.7	48.5	48.3	48.1	47.9	47.7	47.5	47.3
54.4	50.1	49.9	49.8	49.6	49.5	49.3	49.1	48.9	48.8	48.6	48.4	48.2	48.0	47.8	47.6
54.6	50.3	50.2	50.0	49.9	49.7	49.5	49.3	49.2	49.0	48.8	48.6	48.4	48.2	48.0	47.8
54.8	50.6	50.4	50.2	50.1	49.9	49.8	49.6	49.4	49.2	49.0	48.8	48.6	48.4	48.2	48.0
55.0	50.8	50.6	50.5	50.3	50.2	50.0	49.8	49.6	49.4	49.3	49.1	48.9	48.7	48.4	48.2
55.2	51.0	50.9	50.7	50.6	50.4	50.2	50.0	49.9	49.7	49.5	49.3	49.1	48.9	48.7	48.5
55.4	51.3	51.1	51.0	50.8	50.6	50.4	50.3	50.1	49.9	49.7	49.5	49.3	49.1	48.9	48.7
55.6	51.5	51.3	51.2	51.0	50.9	50.7	50.5	50.3	50.1	49.9	49.7	49.5	49.3	49.1	48.9
55.8	51.7	51.6	51.4	51.3	51.1	50.9	50.7	50.5	50.4	50.2	50.0	49.8	49.6	49.3	49.1
56.0	52.0	51.8	51.7	51.5	51.3	51.1	51.0	50.8	50.6	50.4	50.2	50.0	49.8	49.6	49.3
56.2	52.2	52.0	51.9	51.7	51.6	51.4	51.2	51.0	50.8	50.6	50.4	50.2	50.0	49.8	49.6
56.4	52.4	52.3	52.1	52.0	51.8	51.6	51.4	51.2	51.0	50.9	50.6	50.4	50.2	50.0	49.8
56.6	52.7	52.5	52.4	52.2	52.0	51.8	51.7	51.5	51.3	51.1	50.9	50.7	50.5	50.2	50.0
56.8	52.9	52.8	52.6	52.4	52.2	52.1	51.9	51.7	51.5	51.3	51.1	50.9	50.7	50.5	50.2
57.0	53.1	53.0	52.8	52.7	52.5	52.3	52.1	51.9	51.7	51.5	51.3	51.1	50.9	50.7	50.5
57.2	53.4	53.2	53.1	52.9	52.7	52.5	52.3	52.2	52.0	51.8	51.6	51.3	51.1	50.9	50.7
57.4	53.6	53.5	53.3	53.1	52.9	52.8	52.6	52.4	52.2	52.0	51.8	51.6	51.4	51.1	50.9
57.6	53.8	53.7	53.5	53.4	53.2	53.0	52.8	52.6	52.4	52.2	52.0	51.8	51.6	51.4	51.1
57.8	54.1	53.9	53.8	53.6	53.4	53.2	53.0	52.8	52.7	52.4	52.2	52.0	51.8	51.6	51.4
58.0	54.3	54.2	54.0	53.8	53.6	53.5	53.3	53.1	52.9	52.7	52.5	52.3	52.0	51.8	51.6
58.2	54.6	54.4	54.2	54.1	53.9	53.7	53.5	53.3	53.1	52.9	52.7	52.5	52.3	52.0	51.8
58.4	54.8	54.6	54.5	54.3	54.1	53.9	53.7	53.5	53.3	53.1	52.9	52.7	52.5	52.3	52.0
58.6	55.0	54.9	54.7	54.5	54.3	54.2	54.0	53.8	53.6	53.4	53.2	52.9	52.7	52.5	52.3
58.8	55.3	55.1	54.9	54.8	54.6	54.4	54.2	54.0	53.8	53.6	53.4	53.2	52.9	52.7	52.5
59.0	55.5	55.3	55.2	55.0	54.8	54.6	54.4	54.2	54.0	53.8	53.6	53.4	53.2	52.9	52.7
59.2	55.7	55.6	55.4	55.2	55.0	54.9	54.7	54.5	54.3	54.0	53.8	53.6	53.4	53.2	52.9
59.4	56.0	55.8	55.6	55.5	55.3	55.1	54.9	54.7	54.5	54.3	54.1	53.8	53.6	53.4	53.2
59.6	56.2	56.0	55.9	55.7	55.5	55.3	55.1	54.9	54.7	54.5	54.3	54.1	53.8	53.6	53.4
59.8	56.4	56.3	56.1	55.9	55.7	55.5	55.4	55.1	54.9	54.7	54.5	54.3	54.1	53.8	53.6
60.0	56.7	56.5	56.3	56.2	56.0	55.8	55.6	55.4	55.2	55.0	54.7	54.5	54.3	54.1	53.8
60.2	56.9	56.7	56.6	56.4	56.2	56.0	55.8	55.6	55.4	55.2	55.0	54.8	54.5	54.3	54.1
60.4	57.1	57.0	56.8	56.6	56.4	56.2	56.0	55.8	55.6	55.4	55.2	55.0	54.7	54.5	54.3
60.6	57.4	57.2	57.0	56.9	56.7	56.5	56.3	56.1	55.9	55.6	55.4	55.2	55.0	54.7	54.5
60.8	57.6	57.4	57.3	57.1	56.9	56.7	56.5	56.3	56.1	55.9	55.7	55.4	55.2	55.0	54.7
61.0	57.8	57.7	57.5	57.3	57.1	56.9	56.7	56.5	56.3	56.1	55.9	55.7	55.4	55.2	54.9
61.2	58.1	57.9	57.7	57.6	57.4	57.2	57.0	56.8	56.5	56.3	56.1	55.9	55.7	55.4	55.2
61.4	58.3	58.1	58.0	57.8	57.6	57.4	57.2	57.0	56.8	56.6	56.3	56.1	55.9	55.6	55.4
61.5	58.5	58.3	58.1	57.9	57.7	57.5	57.3	57.1	56.9	56.7	56.5	56.2	56.0	55.8	55.5

Height of Eye Correction Always ADDED to the Observed Altitude

Metres	23.3	24.4	25.5	26.7	27.9	29.1	30.3	31.6	32.9	34	35.5
Feet	76	80	84	88	92	95	99	104	108	112	116
Corrn '	3.8	3.6	3.4	3.2	3.0	2.8	2.6	2.4	2.2	2.0	1.8

MOON'S TOTAL CORRECTION – LOWER LIMB

Add to the Observed Altitude of the Moon's Lower limb

Observed Altitude

H.P.	31°00'	30'	32°00'	30'	33°00'	30'	34°00'	30'	35°00'	30'	36°00'	30'	37°00'	30'	38°00'
54.0	47.1	46.9	46.7	46.5	46.2	46.0	45.8	45.5	45.3	45.0	44.8	44.5	44.3	44.0	43.7
54.2	47.3	47.1	46.9	46.7	46.4	46.2	46.0	45.7	45.5	45.2	45.0	44.7	44.5	44.2	43.9
54.4	47.6	47.3	47.1	46.9	46.7	46.4	46.2	46.0	45.7	45.5	45.2	44.9	44.7	44.4	44.2
54.6	47.8	47.6	47.3	47.1	46.9	46.7	46.4	46.2	45.9	45.7	45.4	45.2	44.9	44.6	44.4
54.8	48.0	47.8	47.6	47.3	47.1	46.9	46.6	46.4	46.1	45.9	45.6	45.4	45.1	44.8	44.6
55.0	48.2	48.0	47.8	47.6	47.3	47.1	46.9	46.6	46.4	46.1	45.8	45.6	45.3	45.1	44.8
55.2	48.5	48.2	48.0	47.8	47.5	47.3	47.1	46.8	46.6	46.3	46.1	45.8	45.5	45.3	45.0
55.4	48.7	48.5	48.2	48.0	47.8	47.5	47.3	47.0	46.8	46.5	46.3	46.0	45.7	45.5	45.2
55.6	48.9	48.7	48.5	48.2	48.0	47.7	47.5	47.3	47.0	46.8	46.5	46.2	46.0	45.7	45.4
55.8	49.1	48.9	48.7	48.4	48.2	48.0	47.7	47.5	47.2	47.0	46.7	46.4	46.2	45.9	45.6
56.0	49.3	49.1	48.9	48.7	48.4	48.2	47.9	47.7	47.4	47.2	46.9	46.7	46.4	46.1	45.8
56.2	49.6	49.3	49.1	48.9	48.6	48.4	48.2	47.9	47.7	47.4	47.1	46.9	46.6	46.3	46.0
56.4	49.8	49.6	49.3	49.1	48.9	48.6	48.4	48.1	47.9	47.6	47.3	47.1	46.8	46.5	46.3
56.6	50.0	49.8	49.6	49.3	49.1	48.8	48.6	48.3	48.1	47.8	47.6	47.3	47.0	46.7	46.5
56.8	50.2	50.0	49.8	49.5	49.3	49.1	48.8	48.6	48.3	48.0	47.8	47.5	47.2	47.0	46.7
57.0	50.5	50.2	50.0	49.8	49.5	49.3	49.0	48.8	48.5	48.3	48.0	47.7	47.4	47.2	46.9
57.2	50.7	50.5	50.2	50.0	49.8	49.5	49.3	49.0	48.7	48.5	48.2	47.9	47.7	47.4	47.1
57.4	50.9	50.7	50.5	50.2	50.0	49.7	49.5	49.2	49.0	48.7	48.4	48.1	47.9	47.6	47.3
57.6	51.1	50.9	50.7	50.4	50.2	49.9	49.7	49.4	49.2	48.9	48.6	48.4	48.1	47.8	47.5
57.8	51.4	51.1	50.9	50.7	50.4	50.2	49.9	49.7	49.4	49.1	48.9	48.6	48.3	48.0	47.7
58.0	51.6	51.4	51.1	50.9	50.6	50.4	50.1	49.9	49.6	49.3	49.1	48.8	48.5	48.2	47.9
58.2	51.8	51.6	51.3	51.1	50.9	50.6	50.3	50.1	49.8	49.6	49.3	49.0	48.7	48.4	48.1
58.4	52.0	51.8	51.6	51.3	51.1	50.8	50.6	50.3	50.0	49.8	49.5	49.2	48.9	48.6	48.4
58.6	52.3	52.0	51.8	51.5	51.3	51.0	50.8	50.5	50.3	50.0	49.7	49.4	49.1	48.9	48.6
58.8	52.5	52.2	52.0	51.8	51.5	51.3	51.0	50.7	50.5	50.2	49.9	49.6	49.4	49.1	48.8
59.0	52.7	52.5	52.2	52.0	51.7	51.5	51.2	51.0	50.7	50.4	50.1	49.9	49.6	49.3	49.0
59.2	52.9	52.7	52.5	52.2	52.0	51.7	51.4	51.2	50.9	50.6	50.4	50.1	49.8	49.5	49.2
59.4	53.2	52.9	52.7	52.4	52.2	51.9	51.7	51.4	51.1	50.8	50.6	50.3	50.0	49.7	49.4
59.6	53.4	53.1	52.9	52.6	52.4	52.1	51.9	51.6	51.3	51.1	50.8	50.5	50.2	49.9	49.6
59.8	53.6	53.4	53.1	52.9	52.6	52.4	52.1	51.8	51.6	51.3	51.0	50.7	50.4	50.1	49.8
60.0	53.8	53.6	53.3	53.1	52.8	52.6	52.3	52.0	51.8	51.5	51.2	50.9	50.6	50.3	50.0
60.2	54.1	53.8	53.6	53.3	53.1	52.8	52.5	52.3	52.0	51.7	51.4	51.1	50.8	50.6	50.3
60.4	54.3	54.0	53.8	53.5	53.3	53.0	52.7	52.5	52.2	51.9	51.6	51.4	51.1	50.8	50.5
60.6	54.5	54.3	54.0	53.8	53.5	53.2	53.0	52.7	52.4	52.1	51.9	51.6	51.3	51.0	50.7
60.8	54.7	54.5	54.2	54.0	53.7	53.5	53.2	52.9	52.6	52.4	52.1	51.8	51.5	51.2	50.9
61.0	54.9	54.7	54.5	54.2	53.9	53.7	53.4	53.1	52.9	52.6	52.3	52.0	51.7	51.4	51.1
61.2	55.2	54.9	54.7	54.4	54.2	53.9	53.6	53.3	53.1	52.8	52.5	52.2	51.9	51.6	51.3
61.4	55.4	55.1	54.9	54.6	54.4	54.1	53.8	53.6	53.3	53.0	52.7	52.4	52.1	51.8	51.5
61.5	55.5	55.3	55.0	54.8	54.5	54.2	54.0	53.7	53.4	53.1	52.8	52.6	52.3	52.0	51.6

Height of Eye Correction Always ADDED to the Observed Altitude

Metres	35.5	37	38.5	40	41.5	43	44.5	46	47.5	49
Feet	116	121	126	131	136	141	146	151	156	161
Corrn '	1.8	1.6	1.4	1.2	1.0	0.8	0.6	0.4	0.2	0.0

71

MOON'S TOTAL CORRECTION – LOWER LIMB

Add to the Observed Altitude of the Moon's Lower limb

Observed Altitude

H.P.	38°00'	30'	39°00'	30'	40°00'	30'	41°00'	30'	42°00'	30'	43°00'	30'	44°00'	30'	45°00'
54.0	43.7	43.5	43.2	42.9	42.6	42.3	42.1	41.8	41.5	41.2	40.9	40.6	40.3	39.9	39.6
54.2	43.9	43.7	43.4	43.1	42.8	42.6	42.3	42.0	41.7	41.4	41.1	40.8	40.5	40.1	39.8
54.4	44.2	43.9	43.6	43.3	43.0	42.8	42.5	42.2	41.9	41.6	41.3	41.0	40.6	40.3	40.0
54.6	44.4	44.1	43.8	43.5	43.2	43.0	42.7	42.4	42.1	41.8	41.5	41.2	40.8	40.5	40.2
54.8	44.6	44.3	44.0	43.7	43.5	43.2	42.9	42.6	42.3	42.0	41.7	41.4	41.0	40.7	40.4
55.0	44.8	44.5	44.2	43.9	43.7	43.4	43.1	42.8	42.5	42.2	41.9	41.6	41.2	40.9	40.6
55.2	45.0	44.7	44.4	44.2	43.9	43.6	43.3	43.0	42.7	42.4	42.1	41.8	41.4	41.1	40.8
55.4	45.2	44.9	44.6	44.4	44.1	43.8	43.5	43.2	42.9	42.6	42.3	41.9	41.6	41.3	41.0
55.6	45.4	45.1	44.9	44.6	44.3	44.0	43.7	43.4	43.1	42.8	42.5	42.1	41.8	41.5	41.2
55.8	45.6	45.3	45.1	44.8	44.5	44.2	43.9	43.6	43.3	43.0	42.7	42.3	42.0	41.7	41.4
56.0	45.8	45.6	45.3	45.0	44.7	44.4	44.1	43.8	43.5	43.2	42.9	42.5	42.2	41.9	41.6
56.2	46.0	45.8	45.5	45.2	44.9	44.6	44.3	44.0	43.7	43.4	43.1	42.7	42.4	42.1	41.8
56.4	46.3	46.0	45.7	45.4	45.1	44.8	44.5	44.2	43.9	43.6	43.3	42.9	42.6	42.3	42.0
56.6	46.5	46.2	45.9	45.6	45.3	45.0	44.7	44.4	44.1	43.8	43.5	43.1	42.8	42.5	42.2
56.8	46.7	46.4	46.1	45.8	45.5	45.2	44.9	44.6	44.3	44.0	43.7	43.3	43.0	42.7	42.3
57.0	46.9	46.6	46.3	46.0	45.7	45.4	45.1	44.8	44.5	44.2	43.9	43.5	43.2	42.9	42.5
57.2	47.1	46.8	46.5	46.2	45.9	45.6	45.3	45.0	44.7	44.4	44.1	43.7	43.4	43.1	42.7
57.4	47.3	47.0	46.7	46.4	46.1	45.8	45.5	45.2	44.9	44.6	44.3	43.9	43.6	43.3	42.9
57.6	47.5	47.2	46.9	46.6	46.3	46.0	45.7	45.4	45.1	44.8	44.5	44.1	43.8	43.5	43.1
57.8	47.7	47.4	47.1	46.8	46.5	46.2	45.9	45.6	45.3	45.0	44.6	44.3	44.0	43.7	43.3
58.0	47.9	47.6	47.4	47.1	46.7	46.4	46.1	45.8	45.5	45.2	44.8	44.5	44.2	43.9	43.5
58.2	48.1	47.9	47.6	47.3	47.0	46.6	46.3	46.0	45.7	45.4	45.0	44.7	44.4	44.0	43.7
58.4	48.4	48.1	47.8	47.5	47.2	46.8	46.5	46.2	45.9	45.6	45.2	44.9	44.6	44.2	43.9
58.6	48.6	48.3	48.0	47.7	47.4	47.1	46.7	46.4	46.1	45.8	45.4	45.1	44.8	44.4	44.1
58.8	48.8	48.5	48.2	47.9	47.6	47.3	46.9	46.6	46.3	46.0	45.6	45.3	45.0	44.6	44.3
59.0	49.0	48.7	48.4	48.1	47.8	47.5	47.1	46.8	46.5	46.2	45.8	45.5	45.2	44.8	44.5
59.2	49.2	48.9	48.6	48.3	48.0	47.7	47.4	47.0	46.7	46.4	46.0	45.7	45.4	45.0	44.7
59.4	49.4	49.1	48.8	48.5	48.2	47.9	47.6	47.2	46.9	46.6	46.2	45.9	45.6	45.2	44.9
59.6	49.6	49.3	49.0	48.7	48.4	48.1	47.8	47.4	47.1	46.8	46.4	46.1	45.8	45.4	45.1
59.8	49.8	49.5	49.2	48.9	48.6	48.3	48.0	47.6	47.3	47.0	46.6	46.3	46.0	45.6	45.3
60.0	50.0	49.7	49.4	49.1	48.8	48.5	48.2	47.8	47.5	47.2	46.8	46.5	46.2	45.8	45.5
60.2	50.3	49.9	49.6	49.3	49.0	48.7	48.4	48.0	47.7	47.4	47.0	46.7	46.3	46.0	45.6
60.4	50.5	50.2	49.8	49.5	49.2	48.9	48.6	48.2	47.9	47.6	47.2	46.9	46.5	46.2	45.8
60.6	50.7	50.4	50.1	49.7	49.4	49.1	48.8	48.4	48.1	47.8	47.4	47.1	46.7	46.4	46.0
60.8	50.9	50.6	50.3	49.9	49.6	49.3	49.0	48.6	48.3	48.0	47.6	47.3	46.9	46.6	46.2
61.0	51.1	50.8	50.5	50.2	49.8	49.5	49.2	48.9	48.5	48.2	47.8	47.5	47.1	46.8	46.4
61.2	51.3	51.0	50.7	50.4	50.0	49.7	49.4	49.1	48.7	48.4	48.0	47.7	47.3	47.0	46.6
61.4	51.5	51.2	50.9	50.6	50.2	49.9	49.6	49.3	48.9	48.6	48.2	47.9	47.5	47.2	46.8
61.5	51.6	51.3	51.0	50.7	50.4	50.0	49.7	49.4	49.0	48.7	48.4	48.0	47.7	47.3	46.9

Height of Eye Correction Always ADDED to the Observed Altitude

Metres	2	2.3	2.7	3.1	3.5	3.9	4.4	4.9	5.4	5.9	6.5
Feet	7	8	9	10	11	13	14	16	18	19	21
Corrn '	9.8	9.6	9.4	9.2	9.0	8.8	8.6	8.4	8.2	8.0	7.8

472

MOON'S TOTAL CORRECTION – LOWER LIMB

Add to the Observed Altitude of the Moon's Lower limb

Observed Altitude

H.P.	45°00'	30'	46°00'	30'	47°00'	30'	48°00'	30'	49°00'	30'	50°00'	30'	51°00'	30'	52°00'
54.0	39.6	39.3	39.0	38.7	38.3	38.0	37.7	37.3	37.0	36.7	36.3	36.0	35.6	35.3	34.9
54.2	39.8	39.5	39.2	38.9	38.5	38.2	37.9	37.5	37.2	36.8	36.5	36.1	35.8	35.4	35.1
54.4	40.0	39.7	39.4	39.0	38.7	38.4	38.0	37.7	37.4	37.0	36.7	36.3	36.0	35.6	35.3
54.6	40.2	39.9	39.6	39.2	38.9	38.6	38.2	37.9	37.5	37.2	36.9	36.5	36.1	35.8	35.4
54.8	40.4	40.1	39.8	39.4	39.1	38.8	38.4	38.1	37.7	37.4	37.0	36.7	36.3	36.0	35.6
55.0	40.6	40.3	39.9	39.6	39.3	38.9	38.6	38.3	37.9	37.6	37.2	36.9	36.5	36.1	35.8
55.2	40.8	40.5	40.1	39.8	39.5	39.1	38.8	38.4	38.1	37.8	37.4	37.0	36.7	36.3	36.0
55.4	41.0	40.7	40.3	40.0	39.7	39.3	39.0	38.6	38.3	37.9	37.6	37.2	36.9	36.5	36.1
55.6	41.2	40.9	40.5	40.2	39.9	39.5	39.2	38.8	38.5	38.1	37.8	37.4	37.0	36.7	36.3
55.8	41.4	41.0	40.7	40.4	40.0	39.7	39.4	39.0	38.7	38.3	37.9	37.6	37.2	36.9	36.5
56.0	41.6	41.2	40.9	40.6	40.2	39.9	39.5	39.2	38.8	38.5	38.1	37.8	37.4	37.0	36.7
56.2	41.8	41.4	41.1	40.8	40.4	40.1	39.7	39.4	39.0	38.7	38.3	37.9	37.6	37.2	36.8
56.4	42.0	41.6	41.3	40.9	40.6	40.3	39.9	39.6	39.2	38.8	38.5	38.1	37.8	37.4	37.0
56.6	42.2	41.8	41.5	41.1	40.8	40.4	40.1	39.7	39.4	39.0	38.7	38.3	37.9	37.6	37.2
56.8	42.3	42.0	41.7	41.3	41.0	40.6	40.3	39.9	39.6	39.2	38.8	38.5	38.1	37.7	37.4
57.0	42.5	42.2	41.9	41.5	41.2	40.8	40.5	40.1	39.8	39.4	39.0	38.7	38.3	37.9	37.5
57.2	42.7	42.4	42.1	41.7	41.4	41.0	40.7	40.3	39.9	39.6	39.2	38.8	38.5	38.1	37.7
57.4	42.9	42.6	42.2	41.9	41.6	41.2	40.8	40.5	40.1	39.8	39.4	39.0	38.6	38.3	37.9
57.6	43.1	42.8	42.4	42.1	41.7	41.4	41.0	40.7	40.3	39.9	39.6	39.2	38.8	38.4	38.1
57.8	43.3	43.0	42.6	42.3	41.9	41.6	41.2	40.9	40.5	40.1	39.8	39.4	39.0	38.6	38.2
58.0	43.5	43.2	42.8	42.5	42.1	41.8	41.4	41.0	40.7	40.3	39.9	39.6	39.2	38.8	38.4
58.2	43.7	43.4	43.0	42.7	42.3	42.0	41.6	41.2	40.9	40.5	40.1	39.7	39.4	39.0	38.6
58.4	43.9	43.6	43.2	42.9	42.5	42.1	41.8	41.4	41.0	40.7	40.3	39.9	39.5	39.2	38.8
58.6	44.1	43.7	43.4	43.0	42.7	42.3	42.0	41.6	41.2	40.9	40.5	40.1	39.7	39.3	38.9
58.8	44.3	43.9	43.6	43.2	42.9	42.5	42.1	41.8	41.4	41.0	40.7	40.3	39.9	39.5	39.1
59.0	44.5	44.1	43.8	43.4	43.1	42.7	42.3	42.0	41.6	41.2	40.8	40.5	40.1	39.7	39.3
59.2	44.7	44.3	44.0	43.6	43.3	42.9	42.5	42.2	41.8	41.4	41.0	40.6	40.3	39.9	39.5
59.4	44.9	44.5	44.2	43.8	43.4	43.1	42.7	42.3	42.0	41.6	41.2	40.8	40.4	40.0	39.6
59.6	45.1	44.7	44.4	44.0	43.6	43.3	42.9	42.5	42.1	41.8	41.4	41.0	40.6	40.2	39.8
59.8	45.3	44.9	44.5	44.2	43.8	43.5	43.1	42.7	42.3	41.9	41.6	41.2	40.8	40.4	40.0
60.0	45.5	45.1	44.7	44.4	44.0	43.6	43.3	42.9	42.5	42.1	41.7	41.4	41.0	40.6	40.2
60.2	45.6	45.3	44.9	44.6	44.2	43.8	43.5	43.1	42.7	42.3	41.9	41.5	41.1	40.7	40.3
60.4	45.8	45.5	45.1	44.8	44.4	44.0	43.6	43.3	42.9	42.5	42.1	41.7	41.3	40.9	40.5
60.6	46.0	45.7	45.3	44.9	44.6	44.2	43.8	43.4	43.1	42.7	42.3	41.9	41.5	41.1	40.7
60.8	46.2	45.9	45.5	45.1	44.8	44.4	44.0	43.6	43.2	42.9	42.5	42.1	41.7	41.3	40.9
61.0	46.4	46.1	45.7	45.3	45.0	44.6	44.2	43.8	43.4	43.0	42.7	42.3	41.9	41.5	41.1
61.2	46.6	46.3	45.9	45.5	45.1	44.8	44.4	44.0	43.6	43.2	42.8	42.4	42.0	41.6	41.2
61.4	46.8	46.4	46.1	45.7	45.3	45.0	44.6	44.2	43.8	43.4	43.0	42.6	42.2	41.8	41.4
61.5	46.9	46.6	46.2	45.8	45.5	45.1	44.7	44.3	43.9	43.5	43.1	42.7	42.3	41.9	41.5

Height of Eye Correction Always ADDED to the Observed Altitude

Metres	6.5	7.1	7.7	8.4	9.1	9.8	10.5	11.2	12	12.8	13.6
Feet	21	23	25	28	30	32	34	37	39	42	45
Corrn '	7.8	7.6	7.4	7.2	7.0	6.8	6.6	6.4	6.2	6.0	5.8

MOON'S TOTAL CORRECTION – LOWER LIMB

Add to the Observed Altitude of the Moon's Lower limb

Observed Altitude

H.P. '	52°00'	30'	53°00'	30'	54°00'	30'	55°00'	30'	56°00'	30'	57°00'	30'	58°00'	30'	59°00'
54.0	34.9	34.5	34.2	33.8	33.4	33.1	32.7	32.3	32.0	31.6	31.2	30.8	30.4	30.0	29.6
54.2	35.1	34.7	34.4	34.0	33.6	33.2	32.9	32.5	32.1	31.7	31.4	31.0	30.6	30.2	29.8
54.4	35.3	34.9	34.5	34.2	33.8	33.4	33.0	32.7	32.3	31.9	31.5	31.1	30.7	30.3	30.0
54.6	35.4	35.1	34.7	34.3	34.0	33.6	33.2	32.8	32.4	32.1	31.7	31.3	30.9	30.5	30.1
54.8	35.6	35.2	34.9	34.5	34.1	33.8	33.4	33.0	32.6	32.2	31.8	31.4	31.1	30.7	30.3
55.0	35.8	35.4	35.0	34.7	34.3	33.9	33.5	33.2	32.8	32.4	32.0	31.6	31.2	30.8	30.4
55.2	36.0	35.6	35.2	34.8	34.5	34.1	33.7	33.3	32.9	32.6	32.2	31.8	31.4	31.0	30.6
55.4	36.1	35.8	35.4	35.0	34.6	34.3	33.9	33.5	33.1	32.7	32.3	31.9	31.5	31.1	30.7
55.6	36.3	35.9	35.6	35.2	34.8	34.4	34.0	33.7	33.3	32.9	32.5	32.1	31.7	31.3	30.9
55.8	36.5	36.1	35.7	35.4	35.0	34.6	34.2	33.8	33.4	33.0	32.6	32.2	31.8	31.4	31.0
56.0	36.7	36.3	35.9	35.5	35.1	34.8	34.4	34.0	33.6	33.2	32.8	32.4	32.0	31.6	31.2
56.2	36.8	36.5	36.1	35.7	35.3	34.9	34.5	34.2	33.8	33.4	33.0	32.6	32.2	31.8	31.4
56.4	37.0	36.6	36.3	35.9	35.5	35.1	34.7	34.3	33.9	33.5	33.1	32.7	32.3	31.9	31.5
56.6	37.2	36.8	36.4	36.0	35.7	35.3	34.9	34.5	34.1	33.7	33.3	32.9	32.5	32.1	31.7
56.8	37.4	37.0	36.6	36.2	35.8	35.4	35.0	34.7	34.3	33.9	33.5	33.0	32.6	32.2	31.8
57.0	37.5	37.2	36.8	36.4	36.0	35.6	35.2	34.8	34.4	34.0	33.6	33.2	32.8	32.4	32.0
57.2	37.7	37.3	36.9	36.6	36.2	35.8	35.4	35.0	34.6	34.2	33.8	33.4	33.0	32.5	32.1
57.4	37.9	37.5	37.1	36.7	36.3	35.9	35.6	35.2	34.7	34.3	33.9	33.5	33.1	32.7	32.3
57.6	38.1	37.7	37.3	36.9	36.5	36.1	35.7	35.3	34.9	34.5	34.1	33.7	33.3	32.9	32.4
57.8	38.2	37.9	37.5	37.1	36.7	36.3	35.9	35.5	35.1	34.7	34.3	33.8	33.4	33.0	32.6
58.0	38.4	38.0	37.6	37.2	36.9	36.5	36.1	35.6	35.2	34.8	34.4	34.0	33.6	33.2	32.8
58.2	38.6	38.2	37.8	37.4	37.0	36.6	36.2	35.8	35.4	35.0	34.6	34.2	33.8	33.3	32.9
58.4	38.8	38.4	38.0	37.6	37.2	36.8	36.4	36.0	35.6	35.2	34.7	34.3	33.9	33.5	33.1
58.6	38.9	38.6	38.2	37.8	37.4	37.0	36.6	36.1	35.7	35.3	34.9	34.5	34.1	33.6	33.2
58.8	39.1	38.7	38.3	37.9	37.5	37.1	36.7	36.3	35.9	35.5	35.1	34.6	34.2	33.8	33.4
59.0	39.3	38.9	38.5	38.1	37.7	37.3	36.9	36.5	36.1	35.6	35.2	34.8	34.4	34.0	33.5
59.2	39.5	39.1	38.7	38.3	37.9	37.5	37.1	36.6	36.2	35.8	35.4	35.0	34.5	34.1	33.7
59.4	39.6	39.2	38.9	38.4	38.0	37.6	37.2	36.8	36.4	36.0	35.6	35.1	34.7	34.3	33.8
59.6	39.8	39.4	39.0	38.6	38.2	37.8	37.4	37.0	36.6	36.1	35.7	35.3	34.9	34.4	34.0
59.8	40.0	39.6	39.2	38.8	38.4	38.0	37.6	37.1	36.7	36.3	35.9	35.5	35.0	34.6	34.2
60.0	40.2	39.8	39.4	39.0	38.6	38.1	37.7	37.3	36.9	36.5	36.0	35.6	35.2	34.7	34.3
60.2	40.3	39.9	39.5	39.1	38.7	38.3	37.9	37.5	37.1	36.6	36.2	35.8	35.3	34.9	34.5
60.4	40.5	40.1	39.7	39.3	38.9	38.5	38.1	37.6	37.2	36.8	36.4	35.9	35.5	35.1	34.6
60.6	40.7	40.3	39.9	39.5	39.1	38.6	38.2	37.8	37.4	37.0	36.5	36.1	35.7	35.2	34.8
60.8	40.9	40.5	40.1	39.6	39.2	38.8	38.4	38.0	37.5	37.1	36.7	36.3	35.8	35.4	34.9
61.0	41.1	40.6	40.2	39.8	39.4	39.0	38.6	38.1	37.7	37.3	36.8	36.4	36.0	35.5	35.1
61.2	41.2	40.8	40.4	40.0	39.6	39.2	38.7	38.3	37.9	37.4	37.0	36.6	36.1	35.7	35.2
61.4	41.4	41.0	40.6	40.2	39.7	39.3	38.9	38.5	38.0	37.6	37.2	36.7	36.3	35.8	35.4
61.5	41.5	41.1	40.7	40.3	39.9	39.4	39.0	38.6	38.1	37.7	37.3	36.8	36.4	36.0	35.5

Height of Eye Correction Always ADDED to the Observed Altitude

Metres	13.6	14.5	15.4	16.3	17.2	18.2	19.2	20.2	21.2	22.2	23.3
Feet	45	48	51	53	56	60	63	66	70	73	76
Corrn '	5.8	5.6	5.4	5.2	5.0	4.8	4.6	4.4	4.2	4.0	3.8

MOON'S TOTAL CORRECTION – LOWER LIMB

Add to the Observed Altitude of the Moon's Lower limb

Observed Altitude

H.P. '	59°00'	30'	60°00'	30'	61°00'	30'	62°00'	30'	63°00'	30'	64°00'	30'	65°00'	30'	66°00'
54.0	29.6	29.2	28.9	28.5	28.1	27.7	27.2	26.8	26.4	26.0	25.6	25.2	24.8	24.4	23.9
54.2	29.8	29.4	29.0	28.6	28.2	27.8	27.4	27.0	26.6	26.2	25.7	25.3	24.9	24.5	24.1
54.4	30.0	29.6	29.2	28.8	28.4	27.9	27.5	27.1	26.7	26.3	25.9	25.5	25.1	24.6	24.2
54.6	30.1	29.7	29.3	28.9	28.5	28.1	27.7	27.3	26.9	26.4	26.0	25.6	25.2	24.8	24.3
54.8	30.3	29.9	29.5	29.1	28.7	28.2	27.8	27.4	27.0	26.6	26.2	25.7	25.3	24.9	24.5
55.0	30.4	30.0	29.6	29.2	28.8	28.4	28.0	27.6	27.1	26.7	26.3	25.9	25.5	25.0	24.6
55.2	30.6	30.2	29.8	29.4	28.9	28.5	28.1	27.7	27.3	26.9	26.5	26.0	25.6	25.2	24.7
55.4	30.7	30.3	29.9	29.5	29.1	28.7	28.3	27.9	27.4	27.0	26.6	26.2	25.7	25.3	24.9
55.6	30.9	30.5	30.1	29.7	29.2	28.8	28.4	28.0	27.6	27.2	26.7	26.3	25.9	25.4	25.0
55.8	31.0	30.6	30.2	29.8	29.4	29.0	28.6	28.1	27.7	27.3	26.9	26.4	26.0	25.6	25.1
56.0	31.2	30.8	30.4	30.0	29.5	29.1	28.7	28.3	27.9	27.4	27.0	26.6	26.2	25.7	25.3
56.2	31.4	30.9	30.5	30.1	29.7	29.3	28.9	28.4	28.0	27.6	27.2	26.7	26.3	25.9	25.4
56.4	31.5	31.1	30.7	30.3	29.8	29.4	29.0	28.6	28.2	27.7	27.3	26.9	26.4	26.0	25.5
56.6	31.7	31.3	30.8	30.4	30.0	29.6	29.2	28.7	28.3	27.9	27.4	27.0	26.6	26.1	25.7
56.8	31.8	31.4	31.0	30.6	30.1	29.7	29.3	28.9	28.4	28.0	27.6	27.1	26.7	26.3	25.8
57.0	32.0	31.6	31.1	30.7	30.3	29.9	29.4	29.0	28.6	28.1	27.7	27.3	26.8	26.4	26.0
57.2	32.1	31.7	31.3	30.9	30.4	30.0	29.6	29.2	28.7	28.3	27.9	27.4	27.0	26.5	26.1
57.4	32.3	31.9	31.4	31.0	30.6	30.2	29.7	29.3	28.9	28.4	28.0	27.6	27.1	26.7	26.2
57.6	32.4	32.0	31.6	31.2	30.7	30.3	29.9	29.4	29.0	28.6	28.1	27.7	27.2	26.8	26.4
57.8	32.6	32.2	31.8	31.3	30.9	30.5	30.0	29.6	29.2	28.7	28.3	27.8	27.4	26.9	26.5
58.0	32.8	32.3	31.9	31.5	31.0	30.6	30.2	29.7	29.3	28.9	28.4	28.0	27.5	27.1	26.6
58.2	32.9	32.5	32.1	31.6	31.2	30.8	30.3	29.9	29.4	29.0	28.6	28.1	27.7	27.2	26.8
58.4	33.1	32.6	32.2	31.8	31.3	30.9	30.5	30.0	29.6	29.1	28.7	28.2	27.8	27.3	26.9
58.6	33.2	32.8	32.4	31.9	31.5	31.1	30.6	30.2	29.7	29.3	28.8	28.4	27.9	27.5	27.0
58.8	33.4	32.9	32.5	32.1	31.6	31.2	30.8	30.3	29.9	29.4	29.0	28.5	28.1	27.6	27.2
59.0	33.5	33.1	32.7	32.2	31.8	31.4	30.9	30.5	30.0	29.6	29.1	28.7	28.2	27.8	27.3
59.2	33.7	33.3	32.8	32.4	31.9	31.5	31.1	30.6	30.2	29.7	29.3	28.8	28.3	27.9	27.4
59.4	33.8	33.4	33.0	32.5	32.1	31.6	31.2	30.8	30.3	29.9	29.4	28.9	28.5	28.0	27.6
59.6	34.0	33.6	33.1	32.7	32.2	31.8	31.3	30.9	30.4	30.0	29.5	29.1	28.6	28.2	27.7
59.8	34.2	33.7	33.3	32.8	32.4	31.9	31.5	31.0	30.6	30.1	29.7	29.2	28.8	28.3	27.8
60.0	34.3	33.9	33.4	33.0	32.5	32.1	31.6	31.2	30.7	30.3	29.8	29.4	28.9	28.4	28.0
60.2	34.5	34.0	33.6	33.1	32.7	32.2	31.8	31.3	30.9	30.4	30.0	29.5	29.0	28.6	28.1
60.4	34.6	34.2	33.7	33.3	32.8	32.4	31.9	31.5	31.0	30.6	30.1	29.6	29.2	28.7	28.2
60.6	34.8	34.3	33.9	33.4	33.0	32.5	32.1	31.6	31.2	30.7	30.2	29.8	29.3	28.8	28.4
60.8	34.9	34.5	34.0	33.6	33.1	32.7	32.2	31.8	31.3	30.8	30.4	29.9	29.4	29.0	28.5
61.0	35.1	34.6	34.2	33.7	33.3	32.8	32.4	31.9	31.5	31.0	30.5	30.1	29.6	29.1	28.6
61.2	35.2	34.8	34.3	33.9	33.4	33.0	32.5	32.1	31.6	31.1	30.7	30.2	29.7	29.2	28.8
61.4	35.4	34.9	34.5	34.0	33.6	33.1	32.7	32.2	31.7	31.3	30.8	30.3	29.9	29.4	28.9
61.5	35.5	35.1	34.6	34.1	33.7	33.2	32.8	32.3	31.8	31.4	30.9	30.4	29.9	29.5	29.0

Height of Eye Correction Always ADDED to the Observed Altitude

Metres	23.3	24.4	25.5	26.7	27.9	29.1	30.3	31.6	32.9	34	35.5
Feet	76	80	84	88	92	95	99	104	108	112	116
Corrn '	3.8	3.6	3.4	3.2	3.0	2.8	2.6	2.4	2.2	2.0	1.8

MOON'S TOTAL CORRECTION – LOWER LIMB

Add to the Observed Altitude of the Moon's Lower limb

Observed Altitude

H.P. '	66°00'	30'	67°00'	30'	68°00'	30'	69°00'	30'	70°00'	30'	71°00'	30'	72°00'	30'	73°00'
54.0	23.9	23.5	23.1	22.7	22.2	21.8	21.4	21.0	20.5	20.1	19.7	19.2	18.8	18.3	17.9
54.2	24.1	23.7	23.2	22.8	22.4	21.9	21.5	21.1	20.6	20.2	19.8	19.3	18.9	18.5	18.0
54.4	24.2	23.8	23.4	22.9	22.5	22.1	21.6	21.2	20.8	20.3	19.9	19.5	19.0	18.6	18.1
54.6	24.3	23.9	23.5	23.1	22.6	22.2	21.8	21.3	20.9	20.4	20.0	19.6	19.1	18.7	18.2
54.8	24.5	24.0	23.6	23.2	22.8	22.3	21.9	21.4	21.0	20.6	20.1	19.7	19.2	18.8	18.3
55.0	24.6	24.2	23.8	23.3	22.9	22.4	22.0	21.6	21.1	20.7	20.2	19.8	19.4	18.9	18.5
55.2	24.7	24.3	23.9	23.4	23.0	22.6	22.1	21.7	21.3	20.8	20.4	19.9	19.5	19.0	18.6
55.4	24.9	24.4	24.0	23.6	23.1	22.7	22.3	21.8	21.4	20.9	20.5	20.0	19.6	19.1	18.7
55.6	25.0	24.6	24.1	23.7	23.3	22.8	22.4	21.9	21.5	21.0	20.6	20.1	19.7	19.2	18.8
55.8	25.1	24.7	24.3	23.8	23.4	23.0	22.5	22.1	21.6	21.2	20.7	20.3	19.8	19.4	18.9
56.0	25.3	24.8	24.4	24.0	23.5	23.1	22.6	22.2	21.7	21.3	20.8	20.4	19.9	19.5	19.0
56.2	25.4	25.0	24.5	24.1	23.6	23.2	22.8	22.3	21.9	21.4	21.0	20.5	20.0	19.6	19.1
56.4	25.5	25.1	24.7	24.2	23.8	23.3	22.9	22.4	22.0	21.5	21.1	20.6	20.2	19.7	19.2
56.6	25.7	25.2	24.8	24.4	23.9	23.5	23.0	22.6	22.1	21.6	21.2	20.7	20.3	19.8	19.3
56.8	25.8	25.4	24.9	24.5	24.0	23.6	23.1	22.7	22.2	21.8	21.3	20.8	20.4	19.9	19.5
57.0	26.0	25.5	25.1	24.6	24.2	23.7	23.3	22.8	22.3	21.9	21.4	21.0	20.5	20.0	19.6
57.2	26.1	25.6	25.2	24.7	24.3	23.8	23.4	22.9	22.5	22.0	21.5	21.1	20.6	20.1	19.7
57.4	26.2	25.8	25.3	24.9	24.4	24.0	23.5	23.0	22.6	22.1	21.7	21.2	20.7	20.3	19.8
57.6	26.4	25.9	25.5	25.0	24.5	24.1	23.6	23.2	22.7	22.2	21.8	21.3	20.8	20.4	19.9
57.8	26.5	26.0	25.6	25.1	24.7	24.2	23.8	23.3	22.8	22.4	21.9	21.4	21.0	20.5	20.0
58.0	26.6	26.2	25.7	25.3	24.8	24.3	23.9	23.4	22.9	22.5	22.0	21.5	21.1	20.6	20.1
58.2	26.8	26.3	25.8	25.4	24.9	24.5	24.0	23.5	23.1	22.6	22.1	21.7	21.2	20.7	20.2
58.4	26.9	26.4	26.0	25.5	25.1	24.6	24.1	23.7	23.2	22.7	22.2	21.8	21.3	20.8	20.3
58.6	27.0	26.6	26.1	25.6	25.2	24.7	24.2	23.8	23.3	22.8	22.4	21.9	21.4	20.9	20.5
58.8	27.2	26.7	26.2	25.8	25.3	24.8	24.4	23.9	23.4	23.0	22.5	22.0	21.5	21.0	20.6
59.0	27.3	26.8	26.4	25.9	25.4	25.0	24.5	24.0	23.6	23.1	22.6	22.1	21.6	21.2	20.7
59.2	27.4	27.0	26.5	26.0	25.6	25.1	24.6	24.1	23.7	23.2	22.7	22.2	21.8	21.3	20.8
59.4	27.6	27.1	26.6	26.2	25.7	25.2	24.7	24.3	23.8	23.3	22.8	22.4	21.9	21.4	20.9
59.6	27.7	27.2	26.8	26.3	25.8	25.3	24.9	24.4	23.9	23.4	23.0	22.5	22.0	21.5	21.0
59.8	27.8	27.4	26.9	26.4	25.9	25.5	25.0	24.5	24.0	23.6	23.1	22.6	22.1	21.6	21.1
60.0	28.0	27.5	27.0	26.5	26.1	25.6	25.1	24.6	24.2	23.7	23.2	22.7	22.2	21.7	21.2
60.2	28.1	27.6	27.2	26.7	26.2	25.7	25.2	24.8	24.3	23.8	23.3	22.8	22.3	21.8	21.3
60.4	28.2	27.8	27.3	26.8	26.3	25.8	25.4	24.9	24.4	23.9	23.4	22.9	22.4	21.9	21.5
60.6	28.4	27.9	27.4	26.9	26.5	26.0	25.5	25.0	24.5	24.0	23.5	23.0	22.6	22.1	21.6
60.8	28.5	28.0	27.5	27.1	26.6	26.1	25.6	25.1	24.6	24.2	23.7	23.2	22.7	22.2	21.7
61.0	28.6	28.2	27.7	27.2	26.7	26.2	25.7	25.3	24.8	24.3	23.8	23.3	22.8	22.3	21.8
61.2	28.8	28.3	27.8	27.3	26.8	26.4	25.9	25.4	24.9	24.4	23.9	23.4	22.9	22.4	21.9
61.4	28.9	28.4	27.9	27.5	27.0	26.5	26.0	25.5	25.0	24.5	24.0	23.5	23.0	22.5	22.0
61.5	29.0	28.5	28.0	27.5	27.1	26.6	26.1	25.6	25.1	24.6	24.1	23.6	23.1	22.6	22.1

Height of Eye Correction Always ADDED to the Observed Altitude

Metres	35.5	37	38.5	40	41.5	43	44.5	46	47.5	49
Feet	116	121	126	131	136	141	146	151	156	161
Corrn '	1.8	1.6	1.4	1.2	1.0	0.8	0.6	0.4	0.2	0.0

MOON'S TOTAL CORRECTION – LOWER LIMB

Add to the Observed Altitude of the Moon's Lower limb

Observed Altitude

H.P. '	73°00'	30'	74°00'	30'	75°00'	30'	76°00'	30'	77°00'	30'	78°00'	30'	79°00'	30'	80°00'
54.0	17.9	17.5	17.0	16.6	16.1	15.7	15.2	14.8	14.3	13.9	13.4	13.0	12.5	12.1	11.6
54.2	18.0	17.6	17.1	16.7	16.2	15.8	15.3	14.9	14.4	14.0	13.5	13.1	12.6	12.2	11.7
54.4	18.1	17.7	17.2	16.8	16.3	15.9	15.4	15.0	14.5	14.1	13.6	13.2	12.7	12.2	11.8
54.6	18.2	17.8	17.3	16.9	16.4	16.0	15.5	15.1	14.6	14.2	13.7	13.3	12.8	12.3	11.9
54.8	18.3	17.9	17.4	17.0	16.5	16.1	15.6	15.2	14.7	14.3	13.8	13.3	12.9	12.4	12.0
55.0	18.5	18.0	17.6	17.1	16.6	16.2	15.7	15.3	14.8	14.4	13.9	13.4	13.0	12.5	12.1
55.2	18.6	18.1	17.7	17.2	16.8	16.3	15.8	15.4	14.9	14.5	14.0	13.5	13.1	12.6	12.1
55.4	18.7	18.2	17.8	17.3	16.9	16.4	15.9	15.5	15.0	14.6	14.1	13.6	13.2	12.7	12.2
55.6	18.8	18.3	17.9	17.4	17.0	16.5	16.0	15.6	15.1	14.6	14.2	13.7	13.2	12.8	12.3
55.8	18.9	18.4	18.0	17.5	17.1	16.6	16.1	15.7	15.2	14.7	14.3	13.8	13.3	12.9	12.4
56.0	19.0	18.6	18.1	17.6	17.2	16.7	16.2	15.8	15.3	14.8	14.4	13.9	13.4	13.0	12.5
56.2	19.1	18.7	18.2	17.7	17.3	16.8	16.3	15.9	15.4	14.9	14.5	14.0	13.5	13.0	12.6
56.4	19.2	18.8	18.3	17.8	17.4	16.9	16.4	16.0	15.5	15.0	14.6	14.1	13.6	13.1	12.7
56.6	19.3	18.9	18.4	17.9	17.5	17.0	16.5	16.1	15.6	15.1	14.7	14.2	13.7	13.2	12.8
56.8	19.5	19.0	18.5	18.1	17.6	17.1	16.6	16.2	15.7	15.2	14.7	14.3	13.8	13.3	12.8
57.0	19.6	19.1	18.6	18.2	17.7	17.2	16.7	16.3	15.8	15.3	14.8	14.4	13.9	13.4	12.9
57.2	19.7	19.2	18.7	18.3	17.8	17.3	16.8	16.4	15.9	15.4	14.9	14.5	14.0	13.5	13.0
57.4	19.8	19.3	18.8	18.4	17.9	17.4	16.9	16.5	16.0	15.5	15.0	14.5	14.1	13.6	13.1
57.6	19.9	19.4	19.0	18.5	18.0	17.5	17.0	16.6	16.1	15.6	15.1	14.6	14.2	13.7	13.2
57.8	20.0	19.5	19.1	18.6	18.1	17.6	17.1	16.7	16.2	15.7	15.2	14.7	14.2	13.8	13.3
58.0	20.1	19.6	19.2	18.7	18.2	17.7	17.3	16.8	16.3	15.8	15.3	14.8	14.3	13.9	13.4
58.2	20.2	19.8	19.3	18.8	18.3	17.8	17.4	16.9	16.4	15.9	15.4	14.9	14.4	13.9	13.4
58.4	20.3	19.9	19.4	18.9	18.4	17.9	17.5	17.0	16.5	16.0	15.5	15.0	14.5	14.0	13.5
58.6	20.5	20.0	19.5	19.0	18.5	18.0	17.6	17.1	16.6	16.1	15.6	15.1	14.6	14.1	13.6
58.8	20.6	20.1	19.6	19.1	18.6	18.1	17.7	17.2	16.7	16.2	15.7	15.2	14.7	14.2	13.7
59.0	20.7	20.2	19.7	19.2	18.7	18.2	17.8	17.3	16.8	16.3	15.8	15.3	14.8	14.3	13.8
59.2	20.8	20.3	19.8	19.3	18.8	18.3	17.9	17.4	16.9	16.4	15.9	15.4	14.9	14.4	13.9
59.4	20.9	20.4	19.9	19.4	18.9	18.5	18.0	17.5	17.0	16.5	16.0	15.5	15.0	14.5	14.0
59.6	21.0	20.5	20.0	19.5	19.0	18.6	18.1	17.6	17.1	16.6	16.1	15.6	15.1	14.6	14.1
59.8	21.1	20.6	20.1	19.6	19.2	18.7	18.2	17.7	17.2	16.7	16.2	15.7	15.2	14.7	14.1
60.0	21.2	20.7	20.2	19.8	19.3	18.8	18.3	17.8	17.3	16.8	16.3	15.8	15.2	14.7	14.2
60.2	21.3	20.9	20.4	19.9	19.4	18.9	18.4	17.9	17.4	16.9	16.4	15.8	15.3	14.8	14.3
60.4	21.5	21.0	20.5	20.0	19.5	19.0	18.5	18.0	17.5	17.0	16.4	15.9	15.4	14.9	14.4
60.6	21.6	21.1	20.6	20.1	19.6	19.1	18.6	18.1	17.6	17.0	16.5	16.0	15.5	15.0	14.5
60.8	21.7	21.2	20.7	20.2	19.7	19.2	18.7	18.2	17.7	17.1	16.6	16.1	15.6	15.1	14.6
61.0	21.8	21.3	20.8	20.3	19.8	19.3	18.8	18.3	17.7	17.2	16.7	16.2	15.7	15.2	14.7
61.2	21.9	21.4	20.9	20.4	19.9	19.4	18.9	18.4	17.8	17.3	16.8	16.3	15.8	15.3	14.8
61.4	22.0	21.5	21.0	20.5	20.0	19.5	19.0	18.5	17.9	17.4	16.9	16.4	15.9	15.4	14.8
61.5	22.1	21.6	21.1	20.6	20.1	19.6	19.0	18.5	18.0	17.5	17.0	16.5	16.0	15.4	14.9

Height of Eye Correction Always ADDED to the Observed Altitude

Metres	2	2.3	2.7	3.1	3.5	3.9	4.4	4.9	5.4	5.9	6.5
Feet	7	8	9	10	11	13	14	16	18	19	21
Corrn '	9.8	9.6	9.4	9.2	9.0	8.8	8.6	8.4	8.2	8.0	7.8

MOON'S TOTAL CORRECTION – LOWER LIMB

Add to the Observed Altitude of the Moon's Lower limb

Observed Altitude

H.P.	80°00'	30'	81°00'	30'	82°00'	30'	83°00'	30'	84°00'	30'	85°00'	30'	86°00'	30'	87°00'
54.0	11.6	11.2	10.7	10.2	9.8	9.3	8.9	8.4	8.0	7.5	7.0	6.6	6.1	5.6	5.2
54.2	11.7	11.2	10.8	10.3	9.9	9.4	8.9	8.5	8.0	7.6	7.1	6.6	6.2	5.7	5.2
54.4	11.8	11.3	10.9	10.4	9.9	9.5	9.0	8.6	8.1	7.6	7.2	6.7	6.2	5.8	5.3
54.6	11.9	11.4	11.0	10.5	10.0	9.6	9.1	8.6	8.2	7.7	7.2	6.8	6.3	5.8	5.4
54.8	12.0	11.5	11.0	10.6	10.1	9.6	9.2	8.7	8.2	7.8	7.3	6.8	6.4	5.9	5.4
55.0	12.1	11.6	11.1	10.7	10.2	9.7	9.3	8.8	8.3	7.8	7.4	6.9	6.4	6.0	5.5
55.2	12.1	11.7	11.2	10.7	10.3	9.8	9.3	8.9	8.4	7.9	7.5	7.0	6.5	6.0	5.6
55.4	12.2	11.8	11.3	10.8	10.4	9.9	9.4	8.9	8.5	8.0	7.5	7.0	6.6	6.1	5.6
55.6	12.3	11.8	11.4	10.9	10.4	10.0	9.5	9.0	8.5	8.1	7.6	7.1	6.6	6.2	5.7
55.8	12.4	11.9	11.5	11.0	10.5	10.0	9.6	9.1	8.6	8.1	7.7	7.2	6.7	6.2	5.8
56.0	12.5	12.0	11.5	11.1	10.6	10.1	9.6	9.2	8.7	8.2	7.7	7.3	6.8	6.3	5.8
56.2	12.6	12.1	11.6	11.1	10.7	10.2	9.7	9.2	8.8	8.3	7.8	7.3	6.8	6.4	5.9
56.4	12.7	12.2	11.7	11.2	10.8	10.3	9.8	9.3	8.8	8.4	7.9	7.4	6.9	6.4	5.9
56.6	12.8	12.3	11.8	11.3	10.8	10.4	9.9	9.4	8.9	8.4	7.9	7.5	7.0	6.5	6.0
56.8	12.8	12.4	11.9	11.4	10.9	10.4	9.9	9.5	9.0	8.5	8.0	7.5	7.0	6.6	6.1
57.0	12.9	12.4	12.0	11.5	11.0	10.5	10.0	9.5	9.1	8.6	8.1	7.6	7.1	6.6	6.1
57.2	13.0	12.5	12.0	11.6	11.1	10.6	10.1	9.6	9.1	8.6	8.2	7.7	7.2	6.7	6.2
57.4	13.1	12.6	12.1	11.6	11.2	10.7	10.2	9.7	9.2	8.7	8.2	7.7	7.2	6.7	6.3
57.6	13.2	12.7	12.2	11.7	11.2	10.7	10.3	9.8	9.3	8.8	8.3	7.8	7.3	6.8	6.3
57.8	13.3	12.8	12.3	11.8	11.3	10.8	10.3	9.8	9.3	8.9	8.4	7.9	7.4	6.9	6.4
58.0	13.4	12.9	12.4	11.9	11.4	10.9	10.4	9.9	9.4	8.9	8.4	7.9	7.4	6.9	6.4
58.2	13.4	13.0	12.5	12.0	11.5	11.0	10.5	10.0	9.5	9.0	8.5	8.0	7.5	7.0	6.5
58.4	13.5	13.0	12.5	12.1	11.6	11.1	10.6	10.1	9.6	9.1	8.6	8.1	7.6	7.1	6.6
58.6	13.6	13.1	12.6	12.1	11.6	11.1	10.6	10.1	9.6	9.1	8.6	8.1	7.6	7.1	6.6
58.8	13.7	13.2	12.7	12.2	11.7	11.2	10.7	10.2	9.7	9.2	8.7	8.2	7.7	7.2	6.7
59.0	13.8	13.3	12.8	12.3	11.8	11.3	10.8	10.3	9.8	9.3	8.8	8.3	7.8	7.3	6.8
59.2	13.9	13.4	12.9	12.4	11.9	11.4	10.9	10.4	9.9	9.4	8.9	8.3	7.8	7.3	6.8
59.4	14.0	13.5	13.0	12.5	12.0	11.5	10.9	10.4	9.9	9.4	8.9	8.4	7.9	7.4	6.9
59.6	14.1	13.6	13.1	12.5	12.0	11.5	11.0	10.5	10.0	9.5	9.0	8.5	8.0	7.5	7.0
59.8	14.1	13.6	13.1	12.6	12.1	11.6	11.1	10.6	10.1	9.6	9.1	8.6	8.0	7.5	7.0
60.0	14.2	13.7	13.2	12.7	12.2	11.7	11.2	10.7	10.2	9.6	9.1	8.6	8.1	7.6	7.1
60.2	14.3	13.8	13.3	12.8	12.3	11.8	11.3	10.7	10.2	9.7	9.2	8.7	8.2	7.7	7.1
60.4	14.4	13.9	13.4	12.9	12.4	11.8	11.3	10.8	10.3	9.8	9.3	8.8	8.2	7.7	7.2
60.6	14.5	14.0	13.5	13.0	12.4	11.9	11.4	10.9	10.4	9.9	9.3	8.8	8.3	7.8	7.3
60.8	14.6	14.1	13.6	13.0	12.5	12.0	11.5	11.0	10.5	9.9	9.4	8.9	8.4	7.9	7.3
61.0	14.7	14.2	13.6	13.1	12.6	12.1	11.6	11.0	10.5	10.0	9.5	9.0	8.4	7.9	7.4
61.2	14.8	14.2	13.7	13.2	12.7	12.2	11.6	11.1	10.6	10.1	9.6	9.0	8.5	8.0	7.5
61.4	14.8	14.3	13.8	13.3	12.8	12.2	11.7	11.2	10.7	10.1	9.6	9.1	8.6	8.0	7.5
61.5	14.9	14.4	13.9	13.4	12.8	12.3	11.8	11.3	10.7	10.2	9.7	9.2	8.6	8.1	7.6

Height of Eye Correction Always ADDED to the Observed Altitude

Metres	6.5	7.1	7.7	8.4	9.1	9.8	10.5	11.2	12	12.8	13.6
Feet	21	23	25	28	30	32	34	37	39	42	45
Corrn '	7.8	7.6	7.4	7.2	7.0	6.8	6.6	6.4	6.2	6.0	5.8

MOON'S TOTAL CORRECTION – LOWER LIMB

Add to the Observed Altitude of the Moon's Lower limb

Observed Altitude

H.P.	87°00′	30′	88°00′	30′	89°00′	30′	90°00′
54.0	5.2	4.7	4.3	3.8	3.3	2.9	2.4
54.2	5.2	4.8	4.3	3.9	3.4	2.9	2.5
54.4	5.3	4.8	4.4	3.9	3.4	3.0	2.5
54.6	5.4	4.9	4.4	4.0	3.5	3.0	2.6
54.8	5.4	5.0	4.5	4.0	3.6	3.1	2.6
55.0	5.5	5.0	4.6	4.1	3.6	3.1	2.7
55.2	5.6	5.1	4.6	4.1	3.7	3.2	2.7
55.4	5.6	5.2	4.7	4.2	3.7	3.3	2.8
55.6	5.7	5.2	4.7	4.3	3.8	3.3	2.8
55.8	5.8	5.3	4.8	4.3	3.8	3.4	2.9
56.0	5.8	5.3	4.9	4.4	3.9	3.4	2.9
56.2	5.9	5.4	4.9	4.4	4.0	3.5	3.0
56.4	5.9	5.5	5.0	4.5	4.0	3.5	3.0
56.6	6.0	5.5	5.0	4.5	4.1	3.6	3.1
56.8	6.1	5.6	5.1	4.6	4.1	3.6	3.1
57.0	6.1	5.6	5.2	4.7	4.2	3.7	3.2
57.2	6.2	5.7	5.2	4.7	4.2	3.7	3.2
57.4	6.3	5.8	5.3	4.8	4.3	3.8	3.3
57.6	6.3	5.8	5.3	4.8	4.3	3.9	3.3
57.8	6.4	5.9	5.4	4.9	4.4	3.9	3.4
58.0	6.4	5.9	5.5	5.0	4.5	4.0	3.5
58.2	6.5	6.0	5.5	5.0	4.5	4.0	3.5
58.4	6.6	6.1	5.6	5.1	4.6	4.1	3.6
58.6	6.6	6.1	5.6	5.1	4.6	4.1	3.6
58.8	6.7	6.2	5.7	5.2	4.7	4.2	3.7
59.0	6.8	6.3	5.7	5.2	4.7	4.2	3.7
59.2	6.8	6.3	5.8	5.3	4.8	4.3	3.8
59.4	6.9	6.4	5.9	5.4	4.8	4.3	3.8
59.6	7.0	6.4	5.9	5.4	4.9	4.4	3.9
59.8	7.0	6.5	6.0	5.5	5.0	4.4	3.9
60.0	7.1	6.6	6.0	5.5	5.0	4.5	4.0
60.2	7.1	6.6	6.1	5.6	5.1	4.6	4.0
60.4	7.2	6.7	6.2	5.6	5.1	4.6	4.1
60.6	7.3	6.7	6.2	5.7	5.2	4.7	4.1
60.8	7.3	6.8	6.3	5.8	5.2	4.7	4.2
61.0	7.4	6.9	6.3	5.8	5.3	4.8	4.2
61.2	7.5	6.9	6.4	5.9	5.4	4.8	4.3
61.4	7.5	7.0	6.5	5.9	5.4	4.9	4.3
61.5	7.6	7.0	6.5	6.0	5.5	4.9	4.4

Height of Eye Correction Always ADDED to the Observed Altitude

Metres	13.6	14.5	15.4	16.3	17.2	18.2	19.2	20.2	21.2	22.2	23.3
Feet	45	48	51	53	56	60	63	66	70	73	76
Corrn′	5.8	5.6	5.4	5.2	5.0	4.8	4.6	4.4	4.2	4.0	3.8

MOON'S TOTAL CORRECTION – UPPER LIMB

ADD to the Observed Altitude of the Moon's Upper Limb then SUBTRACT 30'

Observed Altitude °

H.P. '	6°00'	6°10'	6°20'	6°30'	6°40'	6°50'	7°00'	7°15'	7°30'	7°45'	8°00'	8°30'	9°00'	9°30'	10°00'
54.0	48.4	48.6	48.8	49.0	49.1	49.3	49.5	49.7	49.8	50.0	50.3	50.6	50.8	51.0	51.1
54.2	48.6	48.8	48.9	49.1	49.3	49.5	49.6	49.8	50.0	50.1	50.5	50.7	50.9	51.1	51.3
54.4	48.7	48.9	49.1	49.3	49.4	49.6	49.8	50.0	50.1	50.3	50.6	50.8	51.1	51.2	51.4
54.6	48.9	49.1	49.2	49.4	49.6	49.7	49.9	50.1	50.3	50.4	50.7	51.0	51.2	51.4	51.5
54.8	49.0	49.2	49.4	49.6	49.7	49.9	50.1	50.3	50.4	50.6	50.9	51.1	51.3	51.5	51.7
55.0	49.2	49.3	49.5	49.7	49.9	50.0	50.2	50.4	50.6	50.7	51.0	51.3	51.5	51.7	51.8
55.2	49.3	49.5	49.7	49.9	50.0	50.2	50.4	50.6	50.7	50.9	51.2	51.4	51.6	51.8	52.0
55.4	49.4	49.6	49.8	50.0	50.2	50.3	50.5	50.7	50.9	51.0	51.3	51.6	51.8	52.0	52.1
55.6	49.6	49.8	50.0	50.1	50.3	50.5	50.7	50.8	51.0	51.2	51.5	51.7	51.9	52.1	52.3
55.8	49.7	49.9	50.1	50.3	50.5	50.6	50.8	51.0	51.2	51.3	51.6	51.9	52.1	52.3	52.4
56.0	49.9	50.1	50.3	50.4	50.6	50.8	51.0	51.1	51.3	51.5	51.8	52.0	52.2	52.4	52.6
56.2	50.0	50.2	50.4	50.6	50.8	50.9	51.1	51.3	51.4	51.6	51.9	52.2	52.4	52.5	52.7
56.4	50.2	50.4	50.6	50.7	50.9	51.1	51.3	51.4	51.6	51.7	52.1	52.3	52.5	52.7	52.8
56.6	50.3	50.5	50.7	50.9	51.0	51.2	51.4	51.6	51.7	51.9	52.2	52.4	52.7	52.8	53.0
56.8	50.5	50.7	50.8	51.0	51.2	51.4	51.5	51.7	51.9	52.0	52.3	52.6	52.8	53.0	53.1
57.0	50.6	50.8	51.0	51.2	51.3	51.5	51.7	51.9	52.0	52.2	52.5	52.7	52.9	53.1	53.3
57.2	50.8	51.0	51.1	51.3	51.5	51.6	51.8	52.0	52.2	52.3	52.6	52.9	53.1	53.3	53.4
57.4	50.9	51.1	51.3	51.5	51.6	51.8	52.0	52.2	52.3	52.5	52.8	53.0	53.2	53.4	53.6
57.6	51.1	51.2	51.4	51.6	51.8	51.9	52.1	52.3	52.5	52.6	52.9	53.2	53.4	53.6	53.7
57.8	51.2	51.4	51.6	51.8	51.9	52.1	52.3	52.4	52.6	52.8	53.1	53.3	53.5	53.7	53.9
58.0	51.3	51.5	51.7	51.9	52.1	52.2	52.4	52.6	52.8	52.9	53.2	53.5	53.7	53.8	54.0
58.2	51.5	51.7	51.9	52.0	52.2	52.4	52.6	52.7	52.9	53.1	53.4	53.6	53.8	54.0	54.1
58.4	51.6	51.8	52.0	52.2	52.4	52.5	52.7	52.9	53.0	53.2	53.5	53.7	54.0	54.1	54.3
58.6	51.8	52.0	52.2	52.3	52.5	52.7	52.9	53.0	53.2	53.3	53.7	53.9	54.1	54.3	54.4
58.8	51.9	52.1	52.3	52.5	52.7	52.8	53.0	53.2	53.3	53.5	53.8	54.0	54.2	54.4	54.6
59.0	52.1	52.3	52.5	52.6	52.8	53.0	53.2	53.3	53.5	53.6	53.9	54.2	54.4	54.6	54.7
59.2	52.2	52.4	52.6	52.8	52.9	53.1	53.3	53.5	53.6	53.8	54.1	54.3	54.5	54.7	54.9
59.4	52.4	52.6	52.7	52.9	53.1	53.2	53.4	53.6	53.8	53.9	54.2	54.5	54.7	54.9	55.0
59.6	52.5	52.7	52.9	53.1	53.2	53.4	53.6	53.8	53.9	54.1	54.4	54.6	54.8	55.0	55.2
59.8	52.7	52.9	53.0	53.2	53.4	53.5	53.7	53.9	54.1	54.2	54.5	54.8	55.0	55.1	55.3
60.0	52.8	53.0	53.2	53.4	53.5	53.7	53.9	54.1	54.2	54.4	54.7	54.9	55.1	55.3	55.4
60.2	53.0	53.1	53.3	53.5	53.7	53.8	54.0	54.2	54.4	54.5	54.8	55.1	55.3	55.4	55.6
60.4	53.1	53.3	53.5	53.7	53.8	54.0	54.2	54.3	54.5	54.7	55.0	55.2	55.4	55.6	55.7
60.6	53.3	53.4	53.6	53.8	54.0	54.1	54.3	54.5	54.6	54.8	55.1	55.3	55.5	55.7	55.9
60.8	53.4	53.6	53.8	53.9	54.1	54.3	54.5	54.6	54.8	54.9	55.3	55.5	55.7	55.9	56.0
61.0	53.5	53.7	53.9	54.1	54.3	54.4	54.6	54.8	54.9	55.1	55.4	55.6	55.8	56.0	56.2
61.2	53.7	53.9	54.1	54.2	54.4	54.6	54.8	54.9	55.1	55.2	55.5	55.8	56.0	56.2	56.3
61.4	53.8	54.0	54.2	54.4	54.5	54.7	54.9	55.1	55.2	55.4	55.7	55.9	56.1	56.3	56.5
61.5	53.9	54.1	54.3	54.4	54.6	54.8	54.9	55.1	55.3	55.4	55.7	56.0	56.2	56.4	56.5

Height of Eye Correction Always ADDED to the Observed Altitude

Metres	2	2.3	2.7	3.1	3.5	3.9	4.4	4.9	5.4	5.9	6.5
Feet	7	8	9	10	11	13	14	16	18	19	21
Corrn '	9.8	9.6	9.4	9.2	9.0	8.8	8.6	8.4	8.2	8.0	7.8

MOON'S TOTAL CORRECTION – UPPER LIMB

ADD to the Observed Altitude of the Moon's Upper Limb then SUBTRACT 30'

Observed Altitude °

H.P. '	10°00'	30'	11°00'	30'	12°00'	30'	13°00'	30'	14°00'	30'	15°00'	30'	16°00	30'	17°00'
54.0	51.1	51.2	51.4	51.5	51.5	51.6	51.7	51.7	51.7	51.7	51.7	51.7	51.7	51.6	51.6
54.2	51.3	51.4	51.5	51.6	51.7	51.7	51.8	51.8	51.8	51.9	51.8	51.8	51.8	51.8	51.7
54.4	51.4	51.5	51.7	51.7	51.8	51.9	51.9	52.0	52.0	52.0	52.0	52.0	52.0	51.9	51.9
54.6	51.5	51.7	51.8	51.9	52.0	52.0	52.1	52.1	52.1	52.1	52.1	52.1	52.1	52.1	52.0
54.8	51.7	51.8	51.9	52.0	52.1	52.2	52.2	52.3	52.3	52.3	52.3	52.3	52.2	52.2	52.1
55.0	51.8	52.0	52.1	52.2	52.3	52.3	52.4	52.4	52.4	52.4	52.4	52.4	52.4	52.3	52.3
55.2	52.0	52.1	52.2	52.3	52.4	52.5	52.5	52.5	52.6	52.6	52.6	52.5	52.5	52.5	52.4
55.4	52.1	52.3	52.4	52.5	52.5	52.6	52.6	52.7	52.7	52.7	52.7	52.7	52.6	52.6	52.6
55.6	52.3	52.4	52.5	52.6	52.7	52.7	52.8	52.8	52.8	52.8	52.8	52.8	52.8	52.8	52.7
55.8	52.4	52.5	52.7	52.8	52.8	52.9	52.9	53.0	53.0	53.0	53.0	53.0	52.9	52.9	52.8
56.0	52.6	52.7	52.8	52.9	53.0	53.0	53.1	53.1	53.1	53.1	53.1	53.1	53.1	53.0	53.0
56.2	52.7	52.8	52.9	53.0	53.1	53.2	53.2	53.2	53.3	53.3	53.3	53.2	53.2	53.2	53.1
56.4	52.8	53.0	53.1	53.2	53.3	53.3	53.4	53.4	53.4	53.4	53.4	53.4	53.3	53.3	53.3
56.6	53.0	53.1	53.2	53.3	53.4	53.5	53.5	53.5	53.5	53.5	53.5	53.5	53.5	53.4	53.4
56.8	53.1	53.3	53.4	53.5	53.5	53.6	53.6	53.7	53.7	53.7	53.7	53.7	53.6	53.6	53.5
57.0	53.3	53.4	53.5	53.6	53.7	53.7	53.8	53.8	53.8	53.8	53.8	53.8	53.8	53.7	53.7
57.2	53.4	53.6	53.7	53.8	53.8	53.9	53.9	54.0	54.0	54.0	54.0	53.9	53.9	53.9	53.8
57.4	53.6	53.7	53.8	53.9	54.0	54.0	54.1	54.1	54.1	54.1	54.1	54.1	54.0	54.0	54.0
57.6	53.7	53.8	54.0	54.0	54.1	54.2	54.2	54.2	54.2	54.3	54.2	54.2	54.2	54.1	54.1
57,8	53.9	54.0	54.1	54.2	54.3	54.3	54.4	54.4	54.4	54.4	54.4	54.4	54.3	54.3	54.2
58.0	54.0	54.1	54.2	54.3	54.4	54.5	54.5	54.5	54.5	54.5	54.5	54.5	54.5	54.4	54.4
58.2	54.1	54.3	54.4	54.5	54.5	54.6	54.6	54.7	54.7	54.7	54.7	54.6	54.6	54.6	54.5
58.4	54.3	54.4	54.5	54.6	54.7	54.7	54.8	54.8	54.8	54.8	54.8	54.8	54.7	54.7	54.6
58.6	54.4	54.6	54.7	54.8	54.8	54.9	54.9	54.9	55.0	55.0	54.9	54.9	54.9	54.8	54.8
58.8	54.6	54.7	54.8	54.9	55.0	55.0	55.1	55.1	55.1	55.1	55.1	55.1	55.0	55.0	54.9
59.0	54.7	54.9	55.0	55.0	55.1	55.2	55.2	55.2	55.2	55.2	55.2	55.2	55.2	55.1	55.1
59.2	54.9	55.0	55.1	55.2	55.3	55.3	55.3	55.4	55.4	55.4	55.4	55.3	55.3	55.3	55.2
59.4	55.0	55.1	55.2	55.3	55.4	55.5	55.5	55.5	55.5	55.5	55.5	55.5	55.4	55.4	55.3
59.6	55.2	55.3	55.4	55.5	55.5	55.6	55.6	55.7	55.7	55.7	55.6	55.6	55.6	55.5	55.5
59.8	55.3	55.4	55.5	55.6	55.7	55.7	55.8	55.8	55.8	55.8	55.8	55.8	55.7	55.7	55.6
60.0	55.4	55.6	55.7	55.8	55.8	55.9	55.9	55.9	55.9	55.9	55.9	55.9	55.9	55.8	55.8
60.2	55.6	55.7	55.8	55.9	56.0	56.0	56.1	56.1	56.1	56.1	56.1	56.0	56.0	56.0	55.9
60.4	55.7	55.9	56.0	56.0	56.1	56.2	56.2	56.2	56.2	56.2	56.2	56.2	56.1	56.1	56.0
60.6	55.9	56.0	56.1	56.2	56.3	56.3	56.3	56.4	56.4	56.4	56.3	56.3	56.3	56.2	56.2
60.8	56.0	56.1	56.3	56.3	56.4	56.5	56.5	56.5	56.5	56.5	56.5	56.5	56.4	56.4	56.3
61.0	56.2	56.3	56.4	56.5	56.5	56.6	56.6	56.6	56.7	56.6	56.6	56.6	56.6	56.5	56.4
61.2	56.3	56.4	56.5	56.6	56.7	56.7	56.8	56.8	56.8	56.8	56.8	56.7	56.7	56.6	56.6
61.4	56.5	56.6	56.7	56.8	56.8	56.9	56.9	56.9	56.9	56.9	56.9	56.9	56.8	56.8	56.7
61.5	56.5	56.6	56.7	56.8	56.9	56.9	57.0	57.0	57.0	57.0	57.0	56.9	56.9	56.8	56.8

Height of Eye Correction Always ADDED to the Observed Altitude

Metres	6.5	7.1	7.7	8.4	9.1	9.8	10.5	11.2	12	12.8	13.6
Feet	21	23	25	28	30	32	34	37	39	42	45
Corrn '	7.8	7.6	7.4	7.2	7.0	6.8	6.6	6.4	6.2	6.0	5.8

MOON'S TOTAL CORRECTION – UPPER LIMB

ADD to the Observed Altitude of the Moon's Upper Limb then SUBTRACT 30'

Observed Altitude °

H.P. '	17°00'	30'	18°00'	30'	19°00'	30'	20°00'	30'	21°00'	30'	22°00'	30'	23°00'	30'	24°00'
54.0	51.6	51.5	51.5	51.4	51.3	51.3	51.2	51.1	51.0	50.9	50.7	50.6	50.5	50.4	50.2
54.2	51.7	51.7	51.6	51.6	51.5	51.4	51.3	51.2	51.1	51.0	50.9	50.7	50.6	50.5	50.3
54.4	51.9	51.8	51.8	51.7	51.6	51.5	51.4	51.3	51.2	51.1	51.0	50.9	50.7	50.6	50.5
54.6	52.0	52.0	51.9	51.8	51.7	51.7	51.6	51.5	51.4	51.3	51.1	51.0	50.9	50.7	50.6
54.8	52.1	52.1	52.0	52.0	51.9	51.8	51.7	51.6	51.5	51.4	51.3	51.1	51.0	50.9	50.7
55.0	52.3	52.2	52.2	52.1	52.0	51.9	51.8	51.7	51.6	51.5	51.4	51.3	51.1	51.0	50.9
55.2	52.4	52.4	52.3	52.2	52.2	52.1	52.0	51.9	51.8	51.7	51.5	51.4	51.3	51.1	51.0
55.4	52.6	52.5	52.4	52.4	52.3	52.2	52.1	52.0	51.9	51.8	51.7	51.5	51.4	51.3	51.1
55.6	52.7	52.6	52.6	52.5	52.4	52.3	52.2	52.1	52.0	51.9	51.8	51.7	51.5	51.4	51.3
55.8	52.8	52.8	52.7	52.6	52.6	52.5	52.4	52.3	52.2	52.1	51.9	51.8	51.7	51.5	51.4
56.0	53.0	52.9	52.9	52.8	52.7	52.6	52.5	52.4	52.3	52.2	52.1	51.9	51.8	51.7	51.5
56.2	53.1	53.1	53.0	52.9	52.8	52.8	52.7	52.6	52.4	52.3	52.2	52.1	51.9	51.8	51.6
56.4	53.3	53.2	53.1	53.1	53.0	52.9	52.8	52.7	52.6	52.5	52.3	52.2	52.1	51.9	51.8
56.6	53.4	53.3	53.3	53.2	53.1	53.0	52.9	52.8	52.7	52.6	52.5	52.3	52.2	52.1	51.9
56.8	53.5	53.5	53.4	53.3	53.3	53.2	53.1	53.0	52.8	52.7	52.6	52.5	52.3	52.2	52.0
57.0	53.7	53.6	53.5	53.5	53.4	53.3	53.2	53.1	53.0	52.9	52.7	52.6	52.5	52.3	52.2
57.2	53.8	53.8	53.7	53.6	53.5	53.4	53.3	53.2	53.1	53.0	52.9	52.7	52.6	52.4	52.3
57.4	54.0	53.9	53.8	53.7	53.7	53.6	53.5	53.4	53.2	53.1	53.0	52.9	52.7	52.6	52.4
57.6	54.1	54.0	54.0	53.9	53.8	53.7	53.6	53.5	53.4	53.3	53.1	53.0	52.9	52.7	52.6
57.8	54.2	54.2	54.1	54.0	53.9	53.8	53.7	53.6	53.5	53.4	53.3	53.1	53.0	52.8	52.7
58.0	54.4	54.3	54.2	54.2	54.1	54.0	53.9	53.8	53.6	53.5	53.4	53.3	53.1	53.0	52.8
58.2	54.5	54.4	54.4	54.3	54.2	54.1	54.0	53.9	53.8	53.7	53.5	53.4	53.2	53.1	52.9
58.4	54.6	54.6	54.5	54.4	54.3	54.2	54.1	54.0	53.9	53.8	53.7	53.5	53.4	53.2	53.1
58.6	54.8	54.7	54.6	54.6	54.5	54.4	54.3	54.2	54.0	53.9	53.8	53.7	53.5	53.4	53.2
58.8	54.9	54.9	54.8	54.7	54.6	54.5	54.4	54.3	54.2	54.1	53.9	53.8	53.6	53.5	53.3
59.0	55.1	55.0	54.9	54.8	54.8	54.7	54.5	54.4	54.3	54.2	54.1	53.9	53.8	53.6	53.5
59.2	55.2	55.1	55.1	55.0	54.9	54.8	54.7	54.6	54.5	54.3	54.2	54.1	53.9	53.8	53.6
59.4	55.3	55.3	55.2	55.1	55.0	54.9	54.8	54.7	54.6	54.5	54.3	54.2	54.0	53.9	53.7
59.6	55.5	55.4	55.3	55.3	55.2	55.1	55.0	54.8	54.7	54.6	54.5	54.3	54.2	54.0	53.9
59.8	55.6	55.5	55.5	55.4	55.3	55.2	55.1	55.0	54.9	54.7	54.6	54.4	54.3	54.1	54.0
60.0	55.8	55.7	55.6	55.5	55.4	55.3	55.2	55.1	55.0	54.9	54.7	54.6	54.4	54.3	54.1
60.2	55.9	55.8	55.7	55.7	55.6	55.5	55.4	55.2	55.1	55.0	54.9	54.7	54.6	54.4	54.2
60.4	56.0	56.0	55.9	55.8	55.7	55.6	55.5	55.4	55.3	55.1	55.0	54.8	54.7	54.5	54.4
60.6	56.2	56.1	56.0	55.9	55.8	55.7	55.6	55.5	55.4	55.3	55.1	55.0	54.8	54.7	54.5
60.8	56.3	56.2	56.2	56.1	56.0	55.9	55.8	55.6	55.5	55.4	55.3	55.1	55.0	54.8	54.6
61.0	56.4	56.4	56.3	56.2	56.1	56.0	55.9	55.8	55.7	55.5	55.4	55.2	55.1	54.9	54.8
61.2	56.6	56.5	56.4	56.3	56.3	56.1	56.0	55.9	55.8	55.7	55.5	55.4	55.2	55.1	54.9
61.4	56.7	56.7	56.6	56.5	56.4	56.3	56.2	56.1	55.9	55.8	55.7	55.5	55.4	55.2	55.0
61.5	56.8	56.7	56.6	56.5	56.4	56.3	56.2	56.1	56.0	55.8	55.7	55.5	55.4	55.2	55.1

Height of Eye Correction Always ADDED to the Observed Altitude

Metres	13.6	14.5	15.4	16.3	17.2	18.2	19.2	20.2	21.2	22.2	23.3
Feet	45	48	51	53	56	60	63	66	70	73	76
Corrn '	5.8	5.6	5.4	5.2	5.0	4.8	4.6	4.4	4.2	4.0	3.8

MOON'S TOTAL CORRECTION – UPPER LIMB

ADD to the Observed Altitude of the Moon's Upper Limb then SUBTRACT 30'

Observed Altitude °

H.P.	24°00'	30'	25°00'	30'	26°00'	30'	27°00'	30'	28°00'	30'	29°00'	30'	30°00'	30'	31°00'
54.0	50.2	50.1	49.9	49.8	49.6	49.4	49.3	49.1	48.9	48.7	48.5	48.3	48.1	47.9	47.7
54.2	50.3	50.2	50.0	49.9	49.7	49.6	49.4	49.2	49.0	48.8	48.6	48.4	48.2	48.0	47.8
54.4	50.5	50.3	50.2	50.0	49.8	49.7	49.5	49.3	49.1	49.0	48.8	48.6	48.4	48.2	47.9
54.6	50.6	50.5	50.3	50.1	50.0	49.8	49.6	49.5	49.3	49.1	48.9	48.7	48.5	48.3	48.1
54.8	50.7	50.6	50.4	50.3	50.1	49.9	49.8	49.6	49.4	49.2	49.0	48.8	48.6	48.4	48.2
55.0	50.9	50.7	50.6	50.4	50.2	50.1	49.9	49.7	49.5	49.3	49.1	48.9	48.7	48.5	48.3
55.2	51.0	50.8	50.7	50.5	50.4	50.2	50.0	49.8	49.6	49.4	49.3	49.1	48.8	48.6	48.4
55.4	51.1	51.0	50.8	50.7	50.5	50.3	50.1	50.0	49.8	49.6	49.4	49.2	49.0	48.8	48.5
55.6	51.3	51.1	50.9	50.8	50.6	50.4	50.3	50.1	49.9	49.7	49.5	49.3	49.1	48.9	48.7
55.8	51.4	51.2	51.1	50.9	50.7	50.6	50.4	50.2	50.0	49.8	49.6	49.4	49.2	49.0	48.8
56.0	51.5	51.4	51.2	51.0	50.9	50.7	50.5	50.3	50.1	49.9	49.7	49.5	49.3	49.1	48.9
56.2	51.6	51.5	51.3	51.2	51.0	50.8	50.6	50.5	50.3	50.1	49.9	49.7	49.4	49.2	49.0
56.4	51.8	51.6	51.5	51.3	51.1	50.9	50.8	50.6	50.4	50.2	50.0	49.8	49.6	49.4	49.1
56.6	51.9	51.7	51.6	51.4	51.2	51.1	50.9	50.7	50.5	50.3	50.1	49.9	49.7	49.5	49.3
56.8	52.0	51.9	51.7	51.5	51.4	51.2	51.0	50.8	50.6	50.4	50.2	50.0	49.8	49.6	49.4
57.0	52.2	52.0	51.8	51.7	51.5	51.3	51.1	51.0	50.8	50.6	50.4	50.1	49.9	49.7	49.5
57.2	52.3	52.1	52.0	51.8	51.6	51.4	51.3	51.1	50.9	50.7	50.5	50.3	50.1	49.8	49.6
57.4	52.4	52.3	52.1	51.9	51.8	51.6	51.4	51.2	51.0	50.8	50.6	50.4	50.2	50.0	49.7
57.6	52.6	52.4	52.2	52.1	51.9	51.7	51.5	51.3	51.1	50.9	50.7	50.5	50.3	50.1	49.8
57.8	52.7	52.5	52.4	52.2	52.0	51.8	51.6	51.4	51.3	51.0	50.8	50.6	50.4	50.2	50.0
58.0	52.8	52.7	52.5	52.3	52.1	52.0	51.8	51.6	51.4	51.2	51.0	50.8	50.5	50.3	50.1
58.2	52.9	52.8	52.6	52.4	52.3	52.1	51.9	51.7	51.5	51.3	51.1	50.9	50.7	50.4	50.2
58.4	53.1	52.9	52.7	52.6	52.4	52.2	52.0	51.8	51.6	51.4	51.2	51.0	50.8	50.5	50.3
58.6	53.2	53.0	52.9	52.7	52.5	52.3	52.1	51.9	51.7	51.5	51.3	51.1	50.9	50.7	50.4
58.8	53.3	53.2	53.0	52.8	52.6	52.5	52.3	52.1	51.9	51.7	51.5	51.2	51.0	50.8	50.6
59.0	53.5	53.3	53.1	53.0	52.8	52.6	52.4	52.2	52.0	51.8	51.6	51.4	51.1	50.9	50.7
59.2	53.6	53.4	53.3	53.1	52.9	52.7	52.5	52.3	52.1	51.9	51.7	51.5	51.3	51.0	50.8
59.4	53.7	53.6	53.4	53.2	53.0	52.8	52.6	52.4	52.2	52.0	51.8	51.6	51.4	51.1	50.9
59.6	53.9	53.7	53.5	53.3	53.2	53.0	52.8	52.6	52.4	52.2	51.9	51.7	51.5	51.3	51.0
59.8	54.0	53.8	53.6	53.5	53.3	53.1	52.9	52.7	52.5	52.3	52.1	51.8	51.6	51.4	51.2
60.0	54.1	53.9	53.8	53.6	53.4	53.2	53.0	52.8	52.6	52.4	52.2	52.0	51.7	51.5	51.3
60.2	54.2	54.1	53.9	53.7	53.5	53.3	53.1	52.9	52.7	52.5	52.3	52.1	51.9	51.6	51.4
60.4	54.4	54.2	54.0	53.8	53.7	53.5	53.3	53.1	52.9	52.7	52.4	52.2	52.0	51.7	51.5
60.6	54.5	54.3	54.2	54.0	53.8	53.6	53.4	53.2	53.0	52.8	52.6	52.3	52.1	51.9	51.6
60.8	54.6	54.5	54.3	54.1	53.9	53.7	53.5	53.3	53.1	52.9	52.7	52.5	52.2	52.0	51.7
61.0	54.8	54.6	54.4	54.2	54.0	53.9	53.7	53.4	53.2	53.0	52.8	52.6	52.3	52.1	51.9
61.2	54.9	54.7	54.5	54.4	54.2	54.0	53.8	53.6	53.4	53.1	52.9	52.7	52.5	52.2	52.0
61.4	55.0	54.9	54.7	54.5	54.3	54.1	53.9	53.7	53.5	53.3	53.0	52.8	52.6	52.3	52.1
61.5	55.1	54.9	54.7	54.5	54.3	54.1	53.9	53.7	53.5	53.3	53.1	52.8	52.6	52.4	52.1

Height of Eye Correction Always ADDED to the Observed Altitude

Metres	23.3	24.4	25.5	26.7	27.9	29.1	30.3	31.6	32.9	34	35.5
Feet	76	80	84	88	92	95	99	104	108	112	116
Corrn '	3.8	3.6	3.4	3.2	3.0	2.8	2.6	2.4	2.2	2.0	1.8

MOON'S TOTAL CORRECTION – UPPER LIMB

ADD to the Observed Altitude of the Moon's Upper Limb then SUBTRACT 30'

Observed Altitude °

H.P. '	31°00'	30'	32°00'	30'	33°00'	30'	34°00'	30'	35°00'	30'	36°00'	30'	37°00'	30'	38°00'
54.0	47.7	47.5	47.3	47.1	46.8	46.6	46.4	46.1	45.9	45.6	45.4	45.1	44.9	44.6	44.3
54.2	47.8	47.6	47.4	47.2	46.9	46.7	46.5	46.2	46.0	45.7	45.5	45.2	45.0	44.7	44.4
54.4	47.9	47.7	47.5	47.3	47.1	46.8	46.6	46.3	46.1	45.8	45.6	45.3	45.1	44.8	44.5
54.6	48.1	47.8	47.6	47.4	47.2	46.9	46.7	46.5	46.2	46.0	45.7	45.4	45.2	44.9	44.6
54.8	48.2	48.0	47.7	47.5	47.3	47.0	46.8	46.6	46.3	46.1	45.8	45.6	45.3	45.0	44.8
55.0	48.3	48.1	47.9	47.6	47.4	47.2	46.9	46.7	46.4	46.2	45.9	45.7	45.4	45.1	44.9
55.2	48.4	48.2	48.0	47.7	47.5	47.3	47.0	46.8	46.5	46.3	46.0	45.8	45.5	45.2	45.0
55.4	48.5	48.3	48.1	47.9	47.6	47.4	47.2	46.9	46.7	46.4	46.1	45.9	45.6	45.3	45.1
55.6	48.7	48.4	48.2	48.0	47.7	47.5	47.3	47.0	46.8	46.5	46.3	46.0	45.7	45.4	45.2
55.8	48.8	48.6	48.3	48.1	47.9	47.6	47.4	47.1	46.9	46.6	46.4	46.1	45.8	45.6	45.3
56.0	48.9	48.7	48.4	48.2	48.0	47.7	47.5	47.2	47.0	46.7	46.5	46.2	45.9	45.7	45.4
56.2	49.0	48.8	48.6	48.3	48.1	47.8	47.6	47.4	47.1	46.8	46.6	46.3	46.0	45.8	45.5
56.4	49.1	48.9	48.7	48.4	48.2	48.0	47.7	47.5	47.2	47.0	46.7	46.4	46.1	45.9	45.6
56.6	49.3	49.0	48.8	48.6	48.3	48.1	47.8	47.6	47.3	47.1	46.8	46.5	46.3	46.0	45.7
56.8	49.4	49.1	48.9	48.7	48.4	48.2	47.9	47.7	47.4	47.2	46.9	46.6	46.4	46.1	45.8
57.0	49.5	49.3	49.0	48.8	48.6	48.3	48.1	47.8	47.5	47.3	47.0	46.7	46.5	46.2	45.9
57.2	49.6	49.4	49.1	48.9	48.7	48.4	48.2	47.9	47.7	47.4	47.1	46.9	46.6	46.3	46.0
57.4	49.7	49.5	49.3	49.0	48.8	48.5	48.3	48.0	47.8	47.5	47.2	47.0	46.7	46.4	46.1
57.6	49.8	49.6	49.4	49.1	48.9	48.6	48.4	48.1	47.9	47.6	47.3	47.1	46.8	46.5	46.2
57.8	50.0	49.7	49.5	49.3	49.0	48.8	48.5	48.3	48.0	47.7	47.5	47.2	46.9	46.6	46.3
58.0	50.1	49.9	49.6	49.4	49.1	48.9	48.6	48.4	48.1	47.8	47.6	47.3	47.0	46.7	46.4
58.2	50.2	50.0	49.7	49.5	49.2	49.0	48.7	48.5	48.2	47.9	47.7	47.4	47.1	46.8	46.5
58.4	50.3	50.1	49.8	49.6	49.4	49.1	48.8	48.6	48.3	48.1	47.8	47.5	47.2	46.9	46.6
58.6	50.4	50.2	50.0	49.7	49.5	49.2	49.0	48.7	48.4	48.2	47.9	47.6	47.3	47.0	46.7
58.8	50.6	50.3	50.1	49.8	49.6	49.3	49.1	48.8	48.5	48.3	48.0	47.7	47.4	47.1	46.9
59.0	50.7	50.4	50.2	50.0	49.7	49.4	49.2	48.9	48.7	48.4	48.1	47.8	47.5	47.3	47.0
59.2	50.8	50.6	50.3	50.1	49.8	49.6	49.3	49.0	48.8	48.5	48.2	47.9	47.6	47.4	47.1
59.4	50.9	50.7	50.4	50.2	49.9	49.7	49.4	49.1	48.9	48.6	48.3	48.0	47.8	47.5	47.2
59.6	51.0	50.8	50.5	50.3	50.0	49.8	49.5	49.3	49.0	48.7	48.4	48.1	47.9	47.6	47.3
59.8	51.2	50.9	50.7	50.4	50.2	49.9	49.6	49.4	49.1	48.8	48.5	48.3	48.0	47.7	47.4
60.0	51.3	51.0	50.8	50.5	50.3	50.0	49.8	49.5	49.2	48.9	48.7	48.4	48.1	47.8	47.5
60.2	51.4	51.1	50.9	50.6	50.4	50.1	49.9	49.6	49.3	49.0	48.8	48.5	48.2	47.9	47.6
60.4	51.5	51.3	51.0	50.8	50.5	50.2	50.0	49.7	49.4	49.2	48.9	48.6	48.3	48.0	47.7
60.6	51.6	51.4	51.1	50.9	50.6	50.4	50.1	49.8	49.5	49.3	49.0	48.7	48.4	48.1	47.8
60.8	51.7	51.5	51.3	51.0	50.7	50.5	50.2	49.9	49.7	49.4	49.1	48.8	48.5	48.2	47.9
61.0	51.9	51.6	51.4	51.1	50.9	50.6	50.3	50.0	49.8	49.5	49.2	48.9	48.6	48.3	48.0
61.2	52.0	51.7	51.5	51.2	51.0	50.7	50.4	50.2	49.9	49.6	49.3	49.0	48.7	48.4	48.1
61.4	52.1	51.9	51.6	51.3	51.1	50.8	50.5	50.3	50.0	49.7	49.4	49.1	48.8	48.5	48.2
61.5	52.1	51.9	51.6	51.4	51.1	50.8	50.6	50.3	50.0	49.7	49.4	49.2	48.9	48.6	48.2

Height of Eye Correction Always ADDED to the Observed Altitude

Metres	35.5	37	38.5	40	41.5	43	44.5	46	47.5	49
Feet	116	121	126	131	136	141	146	151	156	161
Corrn '	1.8	1.6	1.4	1.2	1.0	0.8	0.6	0.4	0.2	0.0

MOON'S TOTAL CORRECTION – UPPER LIMB

ADD to the Observed Altitude of the Moon's Upper Limb then SUBTRACT 30'

Observed Altitude °

H.P.'	38°00'	30'	39°00'	30'	40°00'	30'	41°00'	30'	42°00'	30'	43°00'	30'	44°00'	30'	45°00'
54.0	44.3	44.1	43.8	43.5	43.2	42.9	42.7	42.4	42.1	41.8	41.5	41.2	40.9	40.5	40.2
54.2	44.4	44.2	43.9	43.6	43.3	43.0	42.8	42.5	42.2	41.9	41.6	41.3	40.9	40.6	40.3
54.4	44.5	44.3	44.0	43.7	43.4	43.1	42.9	42.6	42.3	42.0	41.7	41.4	41.0	40.7	40.4
54.6	44.6	44.4	44.1	43.8	43.5	43.2	43.0	42.7	42.4	42.1	41.8	41.4	41.1	40.8	40.5
54.8	44.8	44.5	44.2	43.9	43.6	43.3	43.1	42.8	42.5	42.2	41.8	41.5	41.2	40.9	40.6
55.0	44.9	44.6	44.3	44.0	43.7	43.4	43.1	42.9	42.6	42.2	41.9	41.6	41.3	41.0	40.7
55.2	45.0	44.7	44.4	44.1	43.8	43.5	43.2	42.9	42.6	42.3	42.0	41.7	41.4	41.1	40.8
55.4	45.1	44.8	44.5	44.2	43.9	43.6	43.3	43.0	42.7	42.4	42.1	41.8	41.5	41.2	40.9
55.6	45.2	44.9	44.6	44.3	44.0	43.7	43.4	43.1	42.8	42.5	42.2	41.9	41.6	41.3	40.9
55.8	45.3	45.0	44.7	44.4	44.1	43.8	43.5	43.2	42.9	42.6	42.3	42.0	41.7	41.4	41.0
56.0	45.4	45.1	44.8	44.5	44.2	43.9	43.6	43.3	43.0	42.7	42.4	42.1	41.8	41.4	41.1
56.2	45.5	45.2	44.9	44.6	44.3	44.0	43.7	43.4	43.1	42.8	42.5	42.2	41.9	41.5	41.2
56.4	45.6	45.3	45.0	44.7	44.4	44.1	43.8	43.5	43.2	42.9	42.6	42.3	42.0	41.6	41.3
56.6	45.7	45.4	45.1	44.8	44.5	44.2	43.9	43.6	43.3	43.0	42.7	42.4	42.0	41.7	41.4
56.8	45.8	45.5	45.2	44.9	44.6	44.3	44.0	43.7	43.4	43.1	42.8	42.5	42.1	41.8	41.5
57.0	45.9	45.6	45.3	45.0	44.7	44.4	44.1	43.8	43.5	43.2	42.9	42.6	42.2	41.9	41.6
57.2	46.0	45.7	45.4	45.1	44.8	44.5	44.2	43.9	43.6	43.3	43.0	42.6	42.3	42.0	41.7
57.4	46.1	45.8	45.5	45.2	44.9	44.6	44.3	44.0	43.7	43.4	43.1	42.7	42.4	42.1	41.7
57.6	46.2	45.9	45.6	45.3	45.0	44.7	44.4	44.1	43.8	43.5	43.2	42.8	42.5	42.2	41.8
57.8	46.3	46.0	45.7	45.4	45.1	44.8	44.5	44.2	43.9	43.6	43.2	42.9	42.6	42.3	41.9
58.0	46.4	46.1	45.8	45.5	45.2	44.9	44.6	44.3	44.0	43.7	43.3	43.0	42.7	42.3	42.0
58.2	46.5	46.2	45.9	45.6	45.3	45.0	44.7	44.4	44.1	43.8	43.4	43.1	42.8	42.4	42.1
58.4	46.6	46.3	46.1	45.7	45.4	45.1	44.8	44.5	44.2	43.9	43.5	43.2	42.9	42.5	42.2
58.6	46.7	46.5	46.2	45.9	45.5	45.2	44.9	44.6	44.3	44.0	43.6	43.3	43.0	42.6	42.3
58.8	46.9	46.6	46.3	46.0	45.6	45.3	45.0	44.7	44.4	44.0	43.7	43.4	43.0	42.7	42.4
59.0	47.0	46.7	46.4	46.1	45.7	45.4	45.1	44.8	44.5	44.1	43.8	43.5	43.1	42.8	42.4
59.2	47.1	46.8	46.5	46.2	45.8	45.5	45.2	44.9	44.6	44.2	43.9	43.6	43.2	42.9	42.6
59.4	47.2	46.9	46.6	46.3	45.9	45.6	45.3	45.0	44.7	44.3	44.0	43.7	43.3	43.0	42.6
59.6	47.3	47.0	46.7	46.4	46.0	45.7	45.4	45.1	44.8	44.4	44.1	43.8	43.4	43.1	42.7
59.8	47.4	47.1	46.8	46.5	46.1	45.8	45.5	45.2	44.9	44.5	44.2	43.8	43.5	43.2	42.8
60.0	47.5	47.2	46.9	46.6	46.2	45.9	45.6	45.3	45.0	44.6	44.3	43.9	43.6	43.2	42.9
60.2	47.6	47.3	47.0	46.7	46.3	46.0	45.7	45.4	45.0	44.7	44.4	44.0	43.7	43.3	43.0
60.4	47.7	47.4	47.1	46.8	46.4	46.1	45.8	45.5	45.1	44.8	44.5	44.1	43.8	43.4	43.1
60.6	47.8	47.5	47.2	46.9	46.5	46.2	45.9	45.6	45.2	44.9	44.6	44.2	43.9	43.5	43.2
60.8	47.9	47.6	47.3	47.0	46.7	46.3	46.0	45.7	45.3	45.0	44.7	44.3	44.0	43.6	43.2
61.0	48.0	47.7	47.4	47.1	46.8	46.4	46.1	45.8	45.4	45.1	44.7	44.4	44.1	43.7	43.3
61.2	48.1	47.8	47.5	47.2	46.9	46.5	46.2	45.9	45.5	45.2	44.8	44.5	44.1	43.8	43.4
61.4	48.2	47.9	47.6	47.3	47.0	46.6	46.3	46.0	45.6	45.3	44.9	44.6	44.2	43.9	43.5
61.5	48.2	47.9	47.6	47.3	47.0	46.6	46.3	46.0	45.6	45.3	45.0	44.6	44.3	43.9	43.5

Height of Eye Correction Always ADDED to the Observed Altitude

Metres	2	2.3	2.7	3.1	3.5	3.9	4.4	4.9	5.4	5.9	6.5
Feet	7	8	9	10	11	13	14	16	18	19	21
Corrn '	9.8	9.6	9.4	9.2	9.0	8.8	8.6	8.4	8.2	8.0	7.8

MOON'S TOTAL CORRECTION – UPPER LIMB

ADD to the Observed Altitude of the Moon's Upper Limb then SUBTRACT 30'

Observed Altitude °

H.P.	45°00'	30'	46°00'	30'	47°00'	30'	48°00'	30'	49°00'	30'	50°00'	30'	51°00'	30'	52°00'
54.0	40.2	39.9	39.6	39.3	38.9	38.6	38.3	37.9	37.6	37.3	36.9	36.6	36.2	35.9	35.5
54.2	40.3	40.0	39.7	39.4	39.0	38.7	38.4	38.0	37.7	37.3	37.0	36.6	36.3	35.9	35.6
54.4	40.4	40.1	39.8	39.4	39.1	38.8	38.4	38.1	37.8	37.4	37.1	36.7	36.4	36.0	35.6
54.6	40.5	40.2	39.8	39.5	39.2	38.9	38.5	38.2	37.8	37.5	37.1	36.8	36.4	36.1	35.7
54.8	40.6	40.3	39.9	39.6	39.3	38.9	38.6	38.3	37.9	37.6	37.2	36.9	36.5	36.1	35.8
55.0	40.7	40.3	40.0	39.7	39.4	39.0	38.7	38.3	38.0	37.6	37.3	36.9	36.6	36.2	35.9
55.2	40.8	40.4	40.1	39.8	39.4	39.1	38.8	38.4	38.1	37.7	37.4	37.0	36.7	36.3	35.9
55.4	40.9	40.5	40.2	39.9	39.5	39.2	38.8	38.5	38.1	37.8	37.4	37.1	36.7	36.4	36.0
55.6	40.9	40.6	40.3	39.9	39.6	39.3	38.9	38.6	38.2	37.9	37.5	37.2	36.8	36.4	36.1
55.8	41.0	40.7	40.4	40.0	39.7	39.4	39.0	38.7	38.3	38.0	37.6	37.2	36.9	36.5	36.1
56.0	41.1	40.8	40.5	40.1	39.8	39.4	39.1	38.7	38.4	38.0	37.7	37.3	36.9	36.6	36.2
56.2	41.2	40.9	40.5	40.2	39.9	39.5	39.2	38.8	38.5	38.1	37.7	37.4	37.0	36.6	36.3
56.4	41.3	41.0	40.6	40.3	39.9	39.6	39.2	38.9	38.5	38.2	37.8	37.5	37.1	36.7	36.3
56.6	41.4	41.1	40.7	40.4	40.0	39.7	39.3	39.0	38.6	38.3	37.9	37.5	37.2	36.8	36.4
56.8	41.5	41.1	40.8	40.5	40.1	39.8	39.4	39.1	38.7	38.3	38.0	37.6	37.2	36.9	36.5
57.0	41.6	41.2	40.9	40.5	40.2	39.8	39.5	39.1	38.8	38.4	38.0	37.7	37.3	36.9	36.6
57.2	41.7	41.3	41.0	40.6	40.3	39.9	39.6	39.2	38.9	38.5	38.1	37.8	37.4	37.0	36.6
57.4	41.7	41.4	41.1	40.7	40.4	40.0	39.7	39.3	38.9	38.6	38.2	37.8	37.5	37.1	36.7
57.6	41.8	41.5	41.1	40.8	40.4	40.1	39.7	39.4	39.0	38.6	38.3	37.9	37.5	37.2	36.8
57.8	41.9	41.6	41.2	40.9	40.5	40.2	39.8	39.5	39.1	38.7	38.4	38.0	37.6	37.2	36.8
58.0	42.0	41.7	41.3	41.0	40.6	40.3	39.9	39.5	39.2	38.8	38.4	38.1	37.7	37.3	36.9
58.2	42.1	41.8	41.4	41.1	40.7	40.3	40.0	39.6	39.2	38.9	38.5	38.1	37.7	37.4	37.0
58.4	42.2	41.8	41.5	41.1	40.8	40.4	40.1	39.7	39.3	39.0	38.6	38.2	37.8	37.4	37.1
58.6	42.3	41.9	41.6	41.2	40.9	40.5	40.1	39.8	39.4	39.0	38.7	38.3	37.9	37.5	37.1
58.8	42.4	42.0	41.7	41.3	40.9	40.6	40.2	39.9	39.5	39.1	38.7	38.4	38.0	37.6	37.2
59.0	42.4	42.1	41.7	41.4	41.0	40.7	40.3	39.9	39.6	39.2	38.8	38.4	38.0	37.7	37.3
59.2	42.5	42.2	41.8	41.5	41.1	40.8	40.4	40.0	39.6	39.3	38.9	38.5	38.1	37.7	37.3
59.4	42.6	42.3	41.9	41.6	41.2	40.8	40.5	40.1	39.7	39.3	39.0	38.6	38.2	37.8	37.4
59.6	42.7	42.4	42.0	41.6	41.3	40.9	40.5	40.2	39.8	39.4	39.0	38.7	38.3	37.9	37.5
59.8	42.8	42.5	42.1	41.7	41.4	41.0	40.6	40.3	39.9	39.5	39.1	38.7	38.3	37.9	37.5
60.0	42.9	42.5	42.2	41.8	41.5	41.1	40.7	40.3	40.0	39.6	39.2	38.8	38.4	38.0	37.6
60.2	43.0	42.6	42.3	41.9	41.5	41.2	40.8	40.4	40.0	39.7	39.3	38.9	38.5	38.1	37.7
60.4	43.1	42.7	42.4	42.0	41.6	41.2	40.9	40.5	40.1	39.7	39.3	38.9	38.6	38.2	37.8
60.6	43.2	42.8	42.4	42.1	41.7	41.3	41.0	40.6	40.2	39.8	39.4	39.0	38.6	38.2	37.8
60.8	43.2	42.9	42.5	42.2	41.8	41.4	41.0	40.7	40.3	39.9	39.5	39.1	38.7	38.3	37.9
61.0	43.3	43.0	42.6	42.2	41.9	41.5	41.1	40.7	40.3	40.0	39.6	39.2	38.8	38.4	38.0
61.2	43.4	43.1	42.7	42.3	42.0	41.6	41.2	40.8	40.4	40.0	39.6	39.2	38.8	38.4	38.0
61.4	43.5	43.2	42.8	42.4	42.0	41.7	41.3	40.9	40.5	40.1	39.7	39.3	38.9	38.5	38.1
61.5	43.5	43.2	42.8	42.4	42.1	41.7	41.3	40.9	40.5	40.1	39.7	39.3	38.9	38.5	38.1

Height of Eye Correction Always ADDED to the Observed Altitude

Metres	6.5	7.1	7.7	8.4	9.1	9.8	10.5	11.2	12	12.8	13.6
Feet	21	23	25	28	30	32	34	37	39	42	45
Corrn '	7.8	7.6	7.4	7.2	7.0	6.8	6.6	6.4	6.2	6.0	5.8

MOON'S TOTAL CORRECTION – UPPER LIMB

ADD to the Observed Altitude of the Moon's Upper Limb then SUBTRACT 30'

Observed Altitude °

H.P. '	52°00'	30'	53°00'	30'	54°00'	30'	55°00'	30'	56°00'	30'	57°00'	30'	58°00'	30'	59°00'
54.0	35.5	35.1	34.8	34.4	34.0	33.7	33.3	32.9	32.6	32.2	31.8	31.4	31.0	30.6	30.2
54.2	35.6	35.2	34.8	34.5	34.1	33.7	33.4	33.0	32.6	32.2	31.8	31.5	31.1	30.7	30.3
54.4	35.6	35.3	34.9	34.5	34.2	33.8	33.4	33.1	32.7	32.3	31.9	31.5	31.1	30.7	30.3
54.6	35.7	35.3	35.0	34.6	34.2	33.9	33.5	33.1	32.7	32.3	32.0	31.6	31.2	30.8	30.4
54.8	35.8	35.4	35.1	34.7	34.3	33.9	33.6	33.2	32.8	32.4	32.0	31.6	31.2	30.8	30.4
55.0	35.9	35.5	35.1	34.7	34.4	34.0	33.6	33.2	32.8	32.5	32.1	31.7	31.3	30.9	30.5
55.2	35.9	35.6	35.2	34.8	34.4	34.1	33.7	33.3	32.9	32.5	32.1	31.7	31.3	30.9	30.5
55.4	36.0	35.6	35.3	34.9	34.5	34.1	33.7	33.4	33.0	32.6	32.2	31.8	31.4	31.0	30.6
55.6	36.1	35.7	35.3	34.9	34.6	34.2	33.8	33.4	33.0	32.6	32.2	31.8	31.4	31.0	30.6
55.8	36.1	35.8	35.4	35.0	34.6	34.2	33.9	33.5	33.1	32.7	32.3	31.9	31.5	31.1	30.7
56.0	36.2	35.8	35.5	35.1	34.7	34.3	33.9	33.5	33.1	32.8	32.4	32.0	31.6	31.2	30.7
56.2	36.3	35.9	35.5	35.1	34.8	34.4	34.0	33.6	33.2	32.8	32.4	32.0	31.6	31.2	30.8
56.4	36.3	36.0	35.6	35.2	34.8	34.4	34.1	33.7	33.3	32.9	32.5	32.1	31.7	31.3	30.8
56.6	36.4	36.0	35.7	35.3	34.9	34.5	34.1	33.7	33.3	32.9	32.5	32.1	31.7	31.3	30.9
56.8	36.5	36.1	35.7	35.3	35.0	34.6	34.2	33.8	33.4	33.0	32.6	32.2	31.8	31.4	30.9
57.0	36.6	36.2	35.8	35.4	35.0	34.6	34.2	33.8	33.4	33.0	32.6	32.2	31.8	31.4	31.0
57.2	36.6	36.2	35.9	35.5	35.1	34.7	34.3	33.9	33.5	33.1	32.7	32.3	31.9	31.5	31.0
57.4	36.7	36.3	35.9	35.5	35.2	34.8	34.4	34.0	33.6	33.2	32.7	32.3	31.9	31.5	31.1
57.6	36.8	36.4	36.0	35.6	35.2	34.8	34.4	34.0	33.6	33.2	32.8	32.4	32.0	31.6	31.1
57.8	36.8	36.5	36.1	35.7	35.3	34.9	34.5	34.1	33.7	33.3	32.9	32.4	32.0	31.6	31.2
58.0	36.9	36.5	36.1	35.7	35.3	34.9	34.5	34.1	33.7	33.3	32.9	32.5	32.1	31.7	31.2
58.2	37.0	36.6	36.2	35.8	35.4	35.0	34.6	34.2	33.8	33.4	33.0	32.6	32.1	31.7	31.3
58.4	37.1	36.7	36.3	35.9	35.5	35.1	34.7	34.3	33.9	33.4	33.0	32.6	32.2	31.8	31.3
58.6	37.1	36.7	36.3	35.9	35.5	35.1	34.7	34.3	33.9	33.5	33.1	32.7	32.2	31.8	31.4
58.8	37.2	36.8	36.4	36.0	35.6	35.2	34.8	34.4	34.0	33.6	33.1	32.7	32.3	31.9	31.4
59.0	37.3	36.9	36.5	36.1	35.7	35.3	34.9	34.4	34.0	33.6	33.2	32.8	32.4	31.9	31.5
59.2	37.3	36.9	36.5	36.1	35.7	35.3	34.9	34.5	34.1	33.7	33.3	32.8	32.4	32.0	31.5
59.4	37.4	37.0	36.6	36.2	35.8	35.4	35.0	34.6	34.2	33.7	33.3	32.9	32.5	32.0	31.6
59.6	37.5	37.1	36.7	36.3	35.9	35.5	35.0	34.6	34.2	33.8	33.4	32.9	32.5	32.1	31.7
59.8	37.5	37.1	36.7	36.3	35.9	35.5	35.1	34.7	34.3	33.8	33.4	33.0	32.6	32.1	31.7
60.0	37.6	37.2	36.8	36.4	36.0	35.6	35.2	34.8	34.3	33.9	33.5	33.1	32.6	32.2	31.8
60.2	37.7	37.3	36.9	36.5	36.1	35.6	35.2	34.8	34.4	34.0	33.5	33.1	32.7	32.2	31.8
60.4	37.8	37.4	36.9	36.5	36.1	35.7	35.3	34.9	34.4	34.0	33.6	33.2	32.7	32.3	31.9
60.6	37.8	37.4	37.0	36.6	36.2	35.8	35.4	34.9	34.5	34.1	33.6	33.2	32.8	32.3	31.9
60.8	37.9	37.5	37.1	36.7	36.3	35.8	35.4	35.0	34.6	34.1	33.7	33.3	32.8	32.4	32.0
61.0	38.0	37.6	37.2	36.7	36.3	35.9	35.5	35.1	34.6	34.2	33.8	33.3	32.9	32.4	32.0
61.2	38.0	37.6	37.2	36.8	36.4	36.0	35.5	35.1	34.7	34.3	33.8	33.4	32.9	32.5	32.1
61.4	38.1	37.7	37.3	36.9	36.5	36.0	35.6	35.2	34.7	34.3	33.9	33.4	33.0	32.6	32.1
61.5	38.1	37.7	37.3	36.9	36.5	36.0	35.6	35.2	34.7	34.3	33.9	33.4	33.0	32.6	32.1

Height of Eye Correction Always ADDED to the Observed Altitude

Metres	13.6	14.5	15.4	16.3	17.2	18.2	19.2	20.2	21.2	22.2	23.3
Feet	45	48	51	53	56	60	63	66	70	73	76
Corrn '	5.8	5.6	5.4	5.2	5.0	4.8	4.6	4.4	4.2	4.0	3.8

MOON'S TOTAL CORRECTION – UPPER LIMB

ADD to the Observed Altitude of the Moon's Upper Limb then SUBTRACT 30'

Observed Altitude °

H.P.	59°00'	30'	60°00'	30'	61°00'	30'	62°00'	30'	63°00'	30'	64°00'	30'	65°00'	30'	66°00'
54.0	30.2	29.8	29.5	29.1	28.7	28.3	27.8	27.4	27.0	26.6	26.2	25.8	25.4	25.0	24.5
54.2	30.3	29.9	29.5	29.1	28.7	28.3	27.9	27.5	27.1	26.7	26.2	25.8	25.4	25.0	24.6
54.4	30.3	29.9	29.5	29.1	28.7	28.3	27.9	27.5	27.1	26.7	26.3	25.9	25.4	25.0	24.6
54.6	30.4	30.0	29.6	29.2	28.8	28.4	28.0	27.6	27.1	26.7	26.3	25.9	25.5	25.1	24.6
54.8	30.4	30.0	29.6	29.2	28.8	28.4	28.0	27.6	27.2	26.8	26.3	25.9	25.5	25.1	24.7
55.0	30.5	30.1	29.7	29.3	28.9	28.5	28.1	27.6	27.2	26.8	26.4	26.0	25.5	25.1	24.7
55.2	30.5	30.1	29.7	29.3	28.9	28.5	28.1	27.7	27.3	26.8	26.4	26.0	25.6	25.1	24.7
55.4	30.6	30.2	29.8	29.4	29.0	28.5	28.1	27.7	27.3	26.9	26.5	26.0	25.6	25.2	24.7
55.6	30.6	30.2	29.8	29.4	29.0	28.6	28.2	27.8	27.3	26.9	26.5	26.1	25.6	25.2	24.8
55.8	30.7	30.3	29.9	29.5	29.1	28.6	28.2	27.8	27.4	27.0	26.5	26.1	25.7	25.2	24.8
56.0	30.7	30.3	29.9	29.5	29.1	28.7	28.3	27.8	27.4	27.0	26.6	26.1	25.7	25.3	24.8
56.2	30.8	30.4	30.0	29.6	29.1	28.7	28.3	27.9	27.5	27.0	26.6	26.2	25.7	25.3	24.9
56.4	30.8	30.4	30.0	29.6	29.2	28.8	28.4	28.0	27.5	27.1	26.6	26.2	25.8	25.3	24.9
56.6	30.9	30.5	30.1	29.6	29.3	28.8	28.4	28.0	27.6	27.1	26.7	26.2	25.8	25.4	24.9
56.8	30.9	30.5	30.1	29.7	29.3	28.9	28.5	28.0	27.6	27.2	26.7	26.3	25.9	25.4	25.0
57.0	31.0	30.6	30.2	29.8	29.4	28.9	28.5	28.1	27.6	27.2	26.8	26.3	25.9	25.4	25.0
57.2	31.0	30.6	30.2	29.8	29.4	29.0	28.5	28.1	27.7	27.2	26.8	26.4	25.9	25.5	25.0
57.4	31.1	30.7	30.3	29.8	29.4	29.0	28.5	28.1	27.7	27.2	26.8	26.4	25.9	25.5	25.0
57.6	31.1	30.7	30.3	29.9	29.5	29.0	28.6	28.2	27.7	27.3	26.8	26.4	26.0	25.5	25.1
57.8	31.2	30.8	30.4	29.9	29.5	29.1	28.6	28.2	27.8	27.3	26.9	26.4	26.0	25.5	25.1
58.0	31.2	30.8	30.4	30.0	29.5	29.1	28.7	28.2	27.8	27.4	26.9	26.5	26.0	25.6	25.1
58.2	31.3	30.9	30.4	30.0	29.6	29.1	28.7	28.3	27.8	27.4	26.9	26.5	26.0	25.6	25.1
58.4	31.3	30.9	30.5	30.1	29.6	29.2	28.8	28.3	27.9	27.4	27.0	26.5	26.1	25.6	25.2
58.6	31.4	31.0	30.5	30.1	29.7	29.2	28.8	28.4	27.9	27.5	27.0	26.6	26.1	25.7	25.2
58.8	31.4	31.0	30.6	30.2	29.7	29.3	28.8	28.4	27.9	27.5	27.0	26.6	26.1	25.7	25.2
59.0	31.5	31.1	30.6	30.2	29.8	29.3	28.9	28.4	28.0	27.5	27.1	26.6	26.2	25.7	25.3
59.2	31.5	31.1	30.7	30.2	29.8	29.4	28.9	28.5	28.0	27.6	27.1	26.7	26.2	25.7	25.3
59.4	31.6	31.2	30.7	30.3	29.8	29.4	29.0	28.5	28.1	27.6	27.2	26.7	26.2	25.8	25.3
59.6	31.7	31.2	30.8	30.3	29.9	29.4	29.0	28.6	28.1	27.6	27.2	26.7	26.3	25.8	25.3
59.8	31.7	31.3	30.8	30.4	29.9	29.5	29.0	28.6	28.1	27.7	27.2	26.8	26.3	25.8	25.4
60.0	31.8	31.3	30.9	30.4	30.0	29.5	29.1	28.6	28.2	27.7	27.3	26.8	26.3	25.9	25.4
60.2	31.8	31.4	30.9	30.5	30.0	29.6	29.1	28.7	28.2	27.8	27.3	26.8	26.4	25.9	25.4
60.4	31.9	31.4	31.0	30.5	30.1	29.6	29.2	28.7	28.3	27.8	27.3	26.9	26.4	25.9	25.5
60.6	31.9	31.5	31.0	30.6	30.1	29.7	29.2	28.8	28.3	27.8	27.4	26.9	26.4	26.0	25.5
60.8	32.0	31.5	31.1	30.6	30.2	29.7	29.2	28.8	28.3	27.9	27.4	26.9	26.5	26.0	25.5
61.0	32.0	31.6	31.1	30.7	30.2	29.7	29.3	28.8	28.4	27.9	27.4	27.0	26.5	26.0	25.5
61.2	32.1	31.6	31.2	30.7	30.2	29.8	29.3	28.9	28.4	27.9	27.5	27.0	26.5	26.1	25.6
61.4	32.1	31.7	31.2	30.7	30.3	29.8	29.4	28.9	28.4	28.0	27.5	27.0	26.6	26.1	25.6
61.5	32.1	31.7	31.2	30.7	30.3	29.8	29.4	28.9	28.4	28.0	27.5	27.0	26.5	26.1	25 6

Height of Eye Correction Always ADDED to the Observed Altitude

Metres	23.3	24.4	25.5	26.7	27.9	29.1	30.3	31.6	32.9	34	35.5
Feet	76	80	84	88	92	95	99	104	108	112	116
Corrn'	3.8	3.6	3.4	3.2	3.0	2.8	2.6	2.4	2.2	2.0	1.8

MOON'S TOTAL CORRECTION – UPPER LIMB

ADD to the Observed Altitude of the Moon's Upper Limb then SUBTRACT 30'

Observed Altitude °

H.P.	66°00'	30'	67°00'	30'	68°00'	30'	69°00'	30'	70°00'	30'	71°00'	30'	72°00'	30'	73°00'
54.0	24.5	24.1	23.7	23.3	22.8	22.4	22.0	21.6	21.1	20.7	20.3	19.8	19.4	18.9	18.5
54.2	24.6	24.1	23.7	23.3	22.9	22.4	22.0	21.6	21.1	20.7	20.3	19.8	19.4	18.9	18.5
54.4	24.6	24.2	23.7	23.3	22.9	22.5	22.0	21.6	21.2	20.7	20.3	19.8	19.4	19.0	18.5
54.6	24.6	24.2	23.8	23.3	22.9	22.5	22.0	21.6	21.2	20.7	20.3	19.9	19.4	19.0	18.5
54.8	24.7	24.2	23.8	23.4	22.9	22.5	22.1	21.6	21.2	20.7	20.3	19.9	19.4	19.0	18.5
55.0	24.7	24.3	23.8	23.4	23.0	22.5	22.1	21.6	21.2	20.8	20.3	19.9	19.4	19.0	18.5
55.2	24.7	24.3	23.9	23.4	23.0	22.5	22.1	21.7	21.2	20.8	20.3	19.9	19.4	19.0	18.5
55.4	24.7	24.3	23.9	23.4	23.0	22.6	22.1	21.7	21.2	20.8	20.3	19.9	19.4	19.0	18.5
55.6	24.8	24.3	23.9	23.5	23.0	22.6	22.1	21.7	21.3	20.8	20.4	19.9	19.5	19.0	18.5
55.8	24.8	24.4	23.9	23.5	23.0	22.6	22.2	21.7	21.3	20.8	20.4	19.9	19.5	19.0	18.6
56.0	24.8	24.4	24.0	23.5	23.1	22.6	22.2	21.7	21.3	20.8	20.4	19.9	19.5	19.0	18.6
56.2	24.9	24.4	24.0	23.5	23.1	22.6	22.2	21.7	21.3	20.8	20.4	19.9	19.5	19.0	18.6
56.4	24.9	24.4	24.0	23.6	23.1	22.7	22.2	21.8	21.3	20.9	20.4	19.9	19.5	19.0	18.6
56.6	24.9	24.5	24.0	23.6	23.1	22.7	22.2	21.8	21.3	20.9	20.4	20.0	19.5	19.0	18.6
56.8	24.9	24.5	24.1	23.6	23.2	22.7	22.3	21.8	21.3	20.9	20.4	20.0	19.5	19.0	18.6
57.0	25.0	24.5	24.1	23.6	23.2	22.7	22.3	21.8	21.4	20.9	20.4	20.0	19.5	19.1	18.6
57.2	25.0	24.6	24.1	23.7	23.2	22.7	22.3	21.8	21.4	20.9	20.5	20.0	19.5	19.1	18.6
57.4	25.0	24.6	24.1	23.7	23.2	22.8	22.3	21.9	21.4	20.9	20.5	20.0	19.5	19.1	18.6
57.6	25.1	24.6	24.2	23.7	23.2	22.8	22.3	21.9	21.4	20.9	20.5	20.0	19.5	19.1	18.6
57.8	25.1	24.6	24.2	23.7	23.3	22.8	22.4	21.9	21.4	21.0	20.5	20.0	19.6	19.1	18.6
58.0	25.1	24.7	24.2	23.8	23.3	22.8	22.4	21.9	21.4	21.0	20.5	20.0	19.6	19.1	18.6
58.2	25.1	24.7	24.2	23.8	23.3	22.9	22.4	21.9	21.5	21.0	20.5	20.0	19.6	19.1	18.6
58.4	25.2	24.7	24.3	23.8	23.3	22.9	22.4	21.9	21.5	21.0	20.5	20.1	19.6	19.1	18.6
58.6	25.2	24.7	24.3	23.8	23.4	22.9	22.4	22.0	21.5	21.0	20.5	20.1	19.6	19.1	18.6
58.8	25.2	24.8	24.3	23.8	23.4	22.9	22.4	22.0	21.5	21.0	20.6	20.1	19.6	19.1	18.6
59.0	25.3	24.8	24.3	23.9	23.4	22.9	22.5	22.0	21.5	21.0	20.6	20.1	19.6	19.1	18.6
59.2	25.3	24.8	24.4	23.9	23.4	23.0	22.5	22.0	21.5	21.1	20.6	20.1	19.6	19.1	18.7
59.4	25.3	24.9	24.4	23.9	23.4	23.0	22.5	22.0	21.6	21.1	20.6	20.1	19.6	19.1	18.7
59.6	25.3	24.9	24.4	23.9	23.5	23.0	22.5	22.0	21.6	21.1	20.6	20.1	19.6	19.2	18.7
59.8	25.4	24.9	24.4	24.0	23.5	23.0	22.5	22.1	21.6	21.1	20.6	20.1	19.6	19.2	18.7
60.0	25.4	24.9	24.5	24.0	23.5	23.0	22.6	22.1	21.6	21.1	20.6	20.1	19.7	19.2	18.7
60.2	25.4	25.0	24.5	24.0	23.5	23.1	22.6	22.1	21.6	21.1	20.6	20.2	19.7	19.2	18.7
60.4	25.5	25.0	24.5	24.0	23.6	23.1	22.6	22.1	21.6	21.1	20.7	20.2	19.7	19.2	18.7
60.6	25.5	25.0	24.5	24.1	23.6	23.1	22.6	22.1	21.6	21.2	20.7	20.2	19.7	19.2	18.7
60.8	25.5	25.0	24.6	24.1	23.6	23.1	22.6	22.1	21.7	21.2	20.7	20.2	19.7	19.2	18.7
61.0	25.5	25.1	24.6	24.1	23.6	23.1	22.7	22.2	21.7	21.2	20.7	20.2	19.7	19.2	18.7
61.2	25.6	25.1	24.6	24.1	23.6	23.2	22.7	22.2	21.7	21.2	20.7	20.2	19.7	19.2	18.7
61.4	25.6	25.1	24.6	24.2	23.7	23.2	22.7	22.2	21.7	21.2	20.7	20.2	19.7	19.2	18.7
61.5	25.6	25.1	24.6	24.1	23.7	23.2	22.7	22.2	21.7	21.2	20.7	20.2	19.7	19.2	18.7

Height of Eye Correction Always ADDED to the Observed Altitude

Metres	35.5	37	38.5	40	41.5	43	44.5	46	47.5	49
Feet	116	121	126	131	136	141	146	151	156	161
Corrn '	1.8	1.6	1.4	1.2	1.0	0.8	0.6	0.4	0.2	0.0

MOON'S TOTAL CORRECTION – UPPER LIMB

ADD to the Observed Altitude of the Moon's Upper Limb then SUBTRACT 30'

Observed Altitude °

H.P. '	73°00'	30'	74°00'	30'	75°00'	30'	76°00'	30'	77°00'	30'	78°00'	30'	79°00'	30'	80°00'
54.0	18.5	18.1	17.6	17.2	16.7	16.3	15.8	15.4	14.9	14.5	14.0	13.6	13.1	12.7	12.2
54.2	18.5	18.1	17.6	17.2	16.7	16.3	15.8	15.4	14.9	14.5	14.0	13.6	13.1	12.7	12.2
54.4	18.5	18.1	17.6	17.2	16.7	16.3	15.8	15.4	14.9	14.5	14.0	13.6	13.1	12.6	12.2
54.6	18.5	18.1	17.6	17.2	16.7	16.3	15.8	15.4	14.9	14.5	14.0	13.5	13.1	12.6	12.2
54.8	18.5	18.1	17.6	17.2	16.7	16.3	15.8	15.4	14.9	14.4	14.0	13.5	13.1	12.6	12.1
55.0	18.5	18.1	17.6	17.2	16.7	16.3	15.8	15.4	14.9	14.4	14.0	13.5	13.1	12.6	12.1
55.2	18.5	18.1	17.6	17.2	16.7	16.3	15.8	15.3	14.9	14.4	14.0	13.5	13.0	12.6	12.1
55.4	18.5	18.1	17.6	17.2	16.7	16.3	15.8	15.3	14.9	14.4	14.0	13.5	13.0	12.6	12.1
55.6	18.5	18.1	17.6	17.2	16.7	16.3	15.8	15.3	14.9	14.4	13.9	13.5	13.0	12.5	12.1
55.8	18.6	18.1	17.6	17.2	16.7	16.3	15.8	15.3	14.9	14.4	13.9	13.5	13.0	12.5	12.1
56.0	18.6	18.1	17.6	17.2	16.7	16.3	15.8	15.3	14.9	14.4	13.9	13.4	13.0	12.5	12.0
56.2	18.6	18.1	17.6	17.2	16.7	16.3	15.8	15.3	14.8	14.4	13.9	13.4	13.0	12.5	12.0
56.4	18.6	18.1	17.6	17.2	16.7	16.2	15.8	15.3	14.8	14.4	13.9	13.4	12.9	12.5	12.0
56.6	18.6	18.1	17.6	17.2	16.7	16.2	15.8	15.3	14.8	14.4	13.9	13.4	12.9	12.5	12.0
56.8	18.6	18.1	17.6	17.2	16.7	16.2	15.8	15.3	14.8	14.4	13.9	13.4	12.9	12.4	12.0
57.0	18.6	18.1	17.7	17.2	16.7	16.2	15.8	15.3	14.8	14.3	13.9	13.4	12.9	12.4	11.9
57.2	18.6	18.1	17.7	17.2	16.7	16.2	15.8	15.3	14.8	14.3	13.9	13.4	12.9	12.4	11.9
57.4	18.6	18. '	17.7	17.2	16.7	16.2	15.8	15.3	14.8	14.3	13.8	13.4	12.9	12.4	11.9
57.6	18.6	18.1	17.7	17.2	16.7	16.2	15.8	15.3	14.8	14.3	13.8	13.3	12.9	12.4	11.9
57.8	18.6	18.1	17.7	17.2	16.7	16.2	15.7	15.3	14.8	14.3	13.8	13.3	12.8	12.4	11.9
58.0	18.6	18.1	17.7	17.2	16.7	16.2	15.7	15.3	14.8	14.3	13.8	13.3	12.8	12.3	11.9
58.2	18.6	18.1	17.7	17.2	16.7	16.2	15.7	15.3	14.8	14.3	13.8	13.3	12.8	12.3	11.8
58.4	18.6	18.2	17.7	17.2	16.7	16.2	15.7	15.3	14.8	14.3	13.8	13.3	12.8	12.3	11.8
58.6	18.6	18.2	17.7	17.2	16.7	16.2	15.7	15.2	14.8	14.3	13.8	13.3	12.8	12.3	11.8
58.8	18.6	18.2	17.7	17.2	16.7	16.2	15.7	15.2	14.7	14.3	13.8	13.3	12.8	12.3	11.8
59.0	18.6	18.2	17.7	17.2	16.7	16.2	15.7	15.2	14.7	14.2	13.8	13.3	12.8	12.3	11.8
59.2	18.7	18.2	17.7	17.2	16.7	16.2	15.7	15.2	14.7	14.2	13.7	13.2	12.7	12.2	11.7
59.4	18.7	18.2	17.7	17.2	16.7	16.2	15.7	15.2	14.7	14.2	13.7	13.2	12.7	12.2	11.7
59.6	18.7	18.2	17.7	17.2	16.7	16.2	15.7	15.2	14.7	14.2	13.7	13.2	12.7	12.2	11.7
59.8	18.7	18.2	17.7	17.2	16.7	16.2	15.7	15.2	14.7	14.2	13.7	13.2	12.7	12.2	11.7
60.0	18.7	18.2	17.7	17.2	16.7	16.2	15.7	15.2	14.7	14.2	13.7	13.2	12.7	12.2	11.7
60.2	18.7	18.2	17.7	17.2	16.7	16.2	15.7	15.2	14.7	14.2	13.7	13.2	12.7	12.2	11.7
60.4	18.7	18.2	17.7	17.2	16.7	16.2	15.7	15.2	14.7	14.2	13.7	13.2	12.7	12.2	11.6
60.6	18.7	18.2	17.7	17.2	16.7	16.2	15.7	15.2	14.7	14.2	13.7	13.2	12.6	12.1	11.6
60.8	18.7	18.2	17.7	17.2	16.7	16.2	15.7	15.2	14.7	14.2	13.7	13.1	12.6	12.1	11.6
61.0	18.7	18.2	17.7	17.2	16.7	16.2	15.7	15.2	14.7	14.2	13.6	13.1	12.6	12.1	11.6
61.2	18.7	18.2	17.7	17.2	16.7	16.2	15.7	15.2	14.7	14.1	13.6	13.1	12.6	12.1	11.6
61.4	18.7	18.2	17.7	17.2	16.7	16.2	15.7	15.2	14.6	14.1	13.6	13.1	12.6	12.1	11.6
61.5	18.7	18.2	17.7	17.2	16.7	16.2	15.6	15.1	14.6	14.1	13.6	13.1	12.6	12.0	11.5

Height of Eye Correction Always ADDED to the Observed Altitude

Metres	2	2.3	2.7	3.1	3.5	3.9	4.4	4.9	5.4	5.9	6.5
Feet	7	8	9	10	11	13	14	16	18	19	21
Corrn '	9.8	9.6	9.4	9.2	9.0	8.8	8.6	8.4	8.2	8.0	7.8

MOON'S TOTAL CORRECTION – UPPER LIMB

ADD to the Observed Altitude of the Moon's Upper Limb then SUBTRACT 30′

Observed Altitude °

H.P.′	80°00′	30′	81°00′	30′	82°00′	30′	83°00′	30′	84°00′	30′	85°00′	30′	86°00′	30′	87°00′
54.0	12.2	11.8	11.3	10.8	10.4	9.9	9.5	9.0	8.6	8.1	7.6	7.2	6.7	6.2	5.8
54.2	12.2	11.7	11.3	10.8	10.4	9.9	9.4	9.0	8.5	8.1	7.6	7.1	6.7	6.2	5.7
54.4	12.2	11.7	11.3	10.8	10.3	9.9	9.4	9.0	8.5	8.0	7.6	7.1	6.6	6.2	5.7
54.6	12.2	11.7	11.2	10.8	10.3	9.8	9.4	8.9	8.5	8.0	7.5	7.1	6.6	6.1	5.7
54.8	12.1	11.7	11.2	10.8	10.3	9.8	9.4	8.9	8.4	8.0	7.5	7.0	6.6	6.1	5.6
55.0	12.1	11.7	11.2	10.7	10.3	9.8	9.3	8.9	8.4	7.9	7.5	7.0	6.5	6.0	5.6
55.2	12.1	11.6	11.2	10.7	10.2	9.8	9.3	8.8	8.4	7.9	7.4	6.9	6.5	6.0	5.5
55.4	12.1	11.6	11.2	10.7	10.2	9.7	9.3	8.8	8.3	7.9	7.4	6.9	6.4	6.0	5.5
55.6	12.1	11.6	11.1	10.7	10.2	9.7	9.2	8.8	8.3	7.8	7.3	6.9	6.4	5.9	5.4
55.8	12.1	11.6	11.1	10.6	10.2	9.7	9.2	8.7	8.3	7.8	7.3	6.8	6.4	5.9	5.4
56.0	12.0	11.6	11.1	10.6	10.1	9.7	9.2	8.7	8.2	7.8	7.3	6.8	6.3	5.8	5.4
56.2	12.0	11.5	11.1	10.6	10.1	9.6	9.2	8.7	8.2	7.7	7.2	6.8	6.3	5.8	5.3
56.4	12.0	11.5	11.0	10.6	10.1	9.6	9.1	8.7	8.2	7.7	7.2	6.7	6.2	5.8	5.3
56.6	12.0	11.5	11.0	10.5	10.1	9.6	9.1	8.6	8.1	7.7	7.2	6.7	6.2	5.7	5.2
56.8	12.0	11.5	11.0	10.5	10.0	9.6	9.1	8.6	8.1	7.6	7.1	6.7	6.2	5.7	5.2
57.0	11.9	11.5	11.0	10.5	10.0	9.5	9.0	8.6	8.1	7.6	7.1	6.6	6.1	5.6	5.2
57.2	11.9	11.4	11.0	10.5	10.0	9.5	9.0	8.5	8.0	7.6	7.1	6.6	6.1	5.6	5.1
57.4	11.9	11.4	10.9	10.5	10.0	9.5	9.0	8.5	8.0	7.5	7.0	6.5	6.0	5.6	5.1
57.6	11.9	11.4	10.9	10.4	9.9	9.5	9.0	8.5	8.0	7.5	7.0	6.5	6.0	5.5	5.0
57.8	11.9	11.4	10.9	10.4	9.9	9.4	8.9	8.4	7.9	7.5	7.0	6.5	6.0	5.5	5.0
58.0	11.9	11.4	10.9	10.4	9.9	9.4	8.9	8.4	7.9	7.4	6.9	6.4	5.9	5.4	4.9
58.2	11.8	11.3	10.9	10.4	9.9	9.4	8.9	8.4	7.9	7.4	6.9	6.4	5.9	5.4	4.9
58.4	11.8	11.3	10.8	10.3	9.8	9.3	8.8	8.4	7.9	7.4	6.9	6.4	5.9	5.4	4.9
58.6	11.8	11.3	10.8	10.3	9.8	9.3	8.8	8.3	7.8	7.3	6.8	6.3	5.8	5.3	4.8
58.8	11.8	11.3	10.8	10.3	9.8	9.3	8.8	8.3	7.8	7.3	6.8	6.3	5.8	5.3	4.8
59.0	11.8	11.3	10.8	10.3	9.8	9.3	8.8	8.3	7.8	7.3	6.7	6.2	5.7	5.2	4.7
59.2	11.7	11.2	10.7	10.2	9.7	9.2	8.7	8.2	7.7	7.2	6.7	6.2	5.7	5.2	4.7
59.4	11.7	11.2	10.7	10.2	9.7	9.2	8.7	8.2	7.7	7.2	6.7	6.2	5.7	5.2	4.6
59.6	11.7	11.2	10.7	10.2	9.7	9.2	8.7	8.2	7.7	7.2	6.6	6.1	5.6	5.1	4.6
59.8	11.7	11.2	10.7	10.2	9.7	9.2	8.7	8.1	7.6	7.1	6.6	6.1	5.6	5.1	4.6
60.0	11.7	11.2	10.7	10.2	9.6	9.1	8.6	8.1	7.6	7.1	6.6	6.1	5.5	5.0	4.5
60.2	11.7	11.2	10.6	10.1	9.6	9.1	8.6	8.1	7.6	7.1	6.5	6.0	5.5	5.0	4.5
60.4	11.6	11.1	10.6	10.1	9.6	9.1	8.6	8.1	7.5	7.0	6.5	6.0	5.5	5.0	4.4
60.6	11.6	11.1	10.6	10.1	9.6	9.1	8.5	8.0	7.5	7.0	6.5	5.9	5.4	4.9	4.4
60.8	11.6	11.1	10.6	10.1	9.5	9.0	8.5	8.0	7.5	7.0	6.4	5.9	5.4	4.9	4.4
61.0	11.6	11.1	10.6	10.0	9.5	9.0	8.5	8.0	7.4	6.9	6.4	5.9	5.4	4.8	4.3
61.2	11.6	11.1	10.5	10.0	9.5	9.0	8.5	7.9	7.4	6.9	6.4	5.8	5.3	4.8	4.3
61.4	11.6	11.0	10.5	10.0	9.5	8.9	8.4	7.9	7.4	6.9	6.3	5.8	5.3	4.8	4.2
61.5	11.5	11.0	10.5	10.0	9.4	8.9	8.4	7.9	7.3	6.8	6.3	5.8	5.2	4.7	4.2

Height of Eye Correction Always ADDED to the Observed Altitude

Metres	6.5	7.1	7.7	8.4	9.1	9.8	10.5	11.2	12	12.8	13.6
Feet	21	23	25	28	30	32	34	37	39	42	45
Corrn ′	7.8	7.6	7.4	7.2	7.0	6.8	6.6	6.4	6.2	6.0	5.8

MOON'S TOTAL CORRECTION – UPPER LIMB

ADD to the Observed Altitude of the Moon's Upper Limb then SUBTRACT 30'

Observed Altitude °

H.P.	87°00'	30'	88°00'	30'	89°00'	30'	90°00'
54.0	5.8	5.3	4.9	4.4	3.9	3.5	3.0
54.2	5.7	5.3	4.8	4.3	3.9	3.4	2.9
54.4	5.7	5.2	4.8	4.3	3.8	3.4	2.9
54.6	5.7	5.2	4.7	4.3	3.8	3.3	2.8
54.8	5.6	5.1	4.7	4.2	3.7	3.3	2.8
55.0	5.6	5.1	4.6	4.2	3.7	3.2	2.7
55.2	5.5	5.1	4.6	4.1	3.6	3.2	2.7
55.4	5.5	5.0	4.5	4.1	3.6	3.1	2.6
55.6	5.4	5.0	4.5	4.0	3.5	3.1	2.6
55.8	5.4	4.9	4.4	4.0	3.5	3.0	2.5
56.0	5.4	4.9	4.4	3.9	3.4	3.0	2.5
56.2	5.3	4.8	4.4	3.9	3.4	2.9	2.4
56.4	5.3	4.8	4.3	3.8	3.3	2.9	2.4
56.6	5.2	4.8	4.3	3.8	3.3	2.8	2.3
56.8	5.2	4.7	4.2	3.7	3.2	2.8	2.3
57.0	5.2	4.7	4.2	3.7	3.2	2.7	2.2
57.2	5.1	4.6	4.1	3.6	3.1	2.7	2.2
57.4	5.1	4.6	4.1	3.6	3.1	2.6	2.1
57.6	5.0	4.5	4.0	3.5	3.0	2.6	2.1
57.8	5.0	4.5	4.0	3.5	3.0	2.5	2.0
58.0	4.9	4.4	3.9	3.4	3.0	2.5	1.9
58.2	4.9	4.4	3.9	3.4	2.9	2.4	1.9
58.4	4.9	4.4	3.9	3.4	2.9	2.4	1.8
58.6	4.8	4.3	3.8	3.3	2.8	2.3	1.8
58.8	4.8	4.3	3.8	3.3	2.8	2.2	1.7
59.0	4.7	4.2	3.7	3.2	2.7	2.2	1.7
59.2	4.7	4.2	3.7	3.2	2.7	2.1	1.6
59.4	4.6	4.1	3.6	3.1	2.6	2.1	1.6
59.6	4.6	4.1	3.6	3.1	2.6	2.0	1.5
59.8	4.6	4.0	3.5	3.0	2.5	2.0	1.5
60.0	4.5	4.0	3.5	3.0	2.5	1.9	1.4
60.2	4.5	4.0	3.4	2.9	2.4	1.9	1.4
60.4	4.4	3.9	3.4	2.9	2.4	1.8	1.3
60.6	4.4	3.9	3.4	2.8	2.3	1.8	1.3
60.8	4.4	3.8	3.3	2.8	2.3	1.7	1.2
61.0	4.3	3.8	3.3	2.7	2.2	1.7	1.2
61.2	4.3	3.7	3.2	2.7	2.2	1.6	1.1
61.4	4.2	3.7	3.2	2.6	2.1	1.6	1.1
61.5	4.2	3.6	3.1	2.6	2.1	1.5	1.0

Height of Eye Correction Always ADDED to the Observed Altitude

Metres	13.6	14.5	15.4	16.3	17.2	18.2	19.2	20.2	21.2	22.2	23.3
Feet	45	48	51	53	56	60	63	66	70	73	76
Corrn '	5.8	5.6	5.4	5.2	5.0	4.8	4.6	4.4	4.2	4.0	3.8

III TABLES FOR USE IN COASTAL NAVIGATION

DAY'S RUN - AVERAGE SPEED TABLE

STEAMING TIME

Distance in Nautical Miles	h. m. 21 59	h. m. 22 00	h. m. 22 01	h. m. 22 02	h. m. 22 03	h. m. 22 04	h. m. 22 05	h. m. 22 06	h. m. 22 07
	Knots	Knots	Knots	Knots	Knots	Knots	Knots	Knots	Knots
900	40·940	40·909	40·878	40·846	40·816	40·785	40·754	40·724	40·693
800	36·391	36·364	36·336	36·307	36·281	36·254	36·226	36·199	36·172
700	31·842	31·818	31·794	31·769	31·746	31·722	31·698	31·674	31·650
600	27·293	27·274	27·252	27·231	27·211	27·190	27·170	27·149	27·129
500	22·745	22·727	22·710	22·692	22·676	22·659	22·641	22·624	22·607
400	18·196	18·182	18·168	18·154	18·141	18·127	18·113	18·100	18·086
300	13·647	13·636	13·626	13·615	13·605	13·595	13·585	13·575	13·564
200	9·098	9·091	9·084	9·077	9·070	9·063	9·057	9·050	9·043
100	4·549	4·545	4·542	4·538	4·535	4·532	4·528	4·525	4·521

Distance in Nautical Miles	h. m. 22 08	h. m. 22 09	h. m. 22 10	h. m. 22 11	h. m. 22 12	h. m. 22 13	h. m. 22 14	h. m. 22 15	h. m. 22 16
900	40·663	40·632	40·602	40·571	40·541	40·510	40·480	40·449	40·419
800	36·145	36·117	36·090	36·063	36·036	36·009	35·982	35·955	35·928
700	31·626	31·603	31·579	31·555	31·532	31·508	31·484	31·461	31·437
600	27·108	27·088	27·068	27·047	27·027	27·007	26·987	26·966	26·946
500	22·590	22·573	22·566	22·539	22·523	22·506	22·489	22·472	22·455
400	18·072	18·059	18·045	18·032	18·018	18·005	17·991	17·978	17·964
300	13·554	13·544	13·534	13·524	13·514	13·504	13·493	13·483	13·473
200	9·036	9·029	9·023	9·016	9·009	9·002	8·996	8·989	8·982
100	4·518	4·515	4·511	4·508	4·505	4·501	4·498	4·494	4·491

Distance in Nautical Miles	h. m. 22 17	h. m. 22 18	h. m. 22 19	h. m. 22 20	h. m. 22 21	h. m. 22 22	h. m. 22 23	h. m. 22 24	h. m. 22 25
900	40·389	40·359	40·329	40·299	40·268	40·238	40·208	40·179	40·149
800	35·901	35·874	35·848	35·821	35·794	35·768	35·741	35·714	35·688
700	31·414	31·390	31·367	31·343	31·320	31·297	31·273	31·250	31·227
600	26·926	26·906	26·886	26·866	26·846	26·826	26·806	26·786	26·766
500	22·438	22·422	22·405	22·388	22·371	22·355	22·338	22·321	22·305
400	17·951	17·937	17·924	17·910	17·898	17·884	17·870	17·857	17·844
300	13·463	13·453	13·443	13·433	13·423	13·413	13·403	13·393	13·383
200	8·975	8·969	8·962	8·955	8·949	8·942	8·9³5	8·929	8·922
100	4·488	4·484	4·481	4·478	4·474	4·471	4·468	4·464	4·461

Distance in Nautical Miles	h. m. 22 26	h. m. 22 27	h. m. 22 28	h. m. 22 29	h. m. 22 30	h. m. 22 31	h. m. 22 32	h. m. 22 33	h. m. 22 34
900	40·119	40·089	40·059	40·030	40·000	39·970	39·941	39·911	39·882
800	35·661	35·635	35·608	35·582	35·556	35·529	35·503	35·477	35·450
700	31·204	31·180	31·157	31·134	31·111	31·088	31·065	31·042	31·019
600	26·746	26·726	26·706	26·686	26·667	26·647	26·627	26·608	26·588
500	22·288	22·272	22·255	22·239	22·222	22·206	22·189	22·173	22·157
400	17·831	17·817	17·804	17·791	17·778	17·765	17·751	17·739	17·725
300	13·373	13·363	13·353	13·343	13·333	13·323	13·314	13·304	13·294
200	8·915	8·909	8·902	8·895	8·889	8·882	8·876	8·869	8·863
100	4·458	4·454	4·451	4·448	4·444	4·441	4·438	4·435	4·431

DAY'S RUN - AVERAGE SPEED TABLE

STEAMING TIME

Distance in Nautical Miles	h. m. 22 35	h. m. 22 36	h. m. 22 37	h. m. 22 38	h. m. 22 39	h. m. 22 40	h. m. 22 41	h. m. 22 42	h. m. 22 43
	Knots	Knots	Knots	Knots	Knots	Knots	Knots	Knots	Knots
900	39·852	39·823	29·794	39·764	39·735	29·706	39·677	39·648	39·618
800	35·424	35·398	35·372	35·346	35·320	35·294	35·268	35·242	35·216
700	30·996	30·973	30·951	30·928	30·905	30·882	30·860	30·837	30·814
600	26·568	26·549	26·529	26·510	26·490	26·471	26·451	26·432	26·412
500	22·140	22·124	22·108	22·091	22·075	22·059	22·043	22·026	22·010
400	17·712	17·699	17·686	17·673	17·660	17·647	17·634	17·621	17·608
300	13·284	13·274	13·265	13·255	13·245	13·235	13·226	13·216	13·206
200	8·856	8·850	8·843	8·837	8·830	8·824	8·817	8·811	8·804
100	4·428	4·425	4·422	4·418	4·415	4·412	4·409	4·405	4·402

Distance in Nautical Miles	h. m. 22 44	h. m. 22 45	h. m. 22 46	h. m. 22 47	h. m. 22 48	h. m. 22 49	h. m. 22 50	h. m. 22 51	h. m. 22 52
900	39·589	39·560	39·532	39·503	39·474	39·445	39·416	39·387	39·359
800	35·191	35·165	35·139	35·113	35·088	35·062	35·036	35·011	34·985
700	30·792	30·769	30·747	30·724	30·702	30·679	30·657	30·635	30·612
600	26·393	26·374	26·354	26·335	26·316	26·297	26·277	26·258	26·239
500	21·994	21·978	21·962	21·946	21·930	21·914	21·898	21·882	21·866
400	17·595	17·582	17·570	17·557	17·544	17·531	17·518	17·505	17·493
300	13·196	13·187	13·177	13·168	13·158	13·148	13·139	13·129	13·120
200	8·798	8·791	8·785	8·778	8·772	8·766	8·759	8·753	8·746
100	4·399	4·396	4·392	4·389	4·386	4·383	4·380	4·376	4·373

Distance in Nautical Miles	h. m. 22 53	h. m. 22 54	h. m. 22 55	h. m. 22 56	h. m. 22 57	h. m. 22 58	h. m. 22 59	h. m. 23 00	h. m. 23 01
900	39·330	39·301	39·273	39·244	39·216	39·187	39·159	39·130	39·102
800	34·960	34·934	34·909	34·884	34·858	34·833	34·808	34·783	34·757
700	30·590	30·568	30·545	30·523	30·501	30·479	30·457	30·435	30·413
600	26·220	26·201	26·182	26·163	26·144	26·125	26·106	26·087	26·068
500	21·850	21·834	21·818	21·802	21·787	21·771	21·755	21·739	21·723
400	17·480	17·467	17·455	17·442	17·429	17·417	17·404	17·391	17·379
300	13·110	13·100	13·091	13·081	13·072	13·062	13·053	13·043	13·034
200	8·740	8·734	8·727	8·721	8·715	8·708	8·702	8·696	8·689
100	4·370	4·367	4·364	4·360	4·357	4·354	4·351	4·348	4·345

Distance in Nautical Miles	h. m. 23 02	h. m 23 03	h. m. 23 04	h. m. 23 05	h. m. 23 06	h. m. 23 07	h. m. 23 08	h. m. 23 09	h. m. 23 10
900	39·074	39·046	39·017	38·989	38·961	38·933	38·905	38·877	38·849
800	34·732	34·707	34·682	34·657	34·632	34·607	34·582	34·557	34·532
700	30·391	30·369	30·347	30·325	30·303	30·281	30·259	30·238	30·216
600	26·049	26·030	26·012	25·993	25·974	25·955	25·937	25·918	25·899
500	21·708	21·692	21·676	21·661	21·645	21·629	21·614	21·598	21·583
400	17·366	17·354	17·341	17·329	17·316	17·304	17·291	17·279	17·266
300	13·025	13·015	13·006	12·996	12·987	12·978	12·968	12·959	12·950
200	8·683	8·677	8·671	8·664	8·658	8·652	8·646	8·639	8·633
100	4·342	4·338	4·335	4·332	4·329	4·326	4·323	4·320	4·317

DAY'S RUN - AVERAGE SPEED TABLE

Distance in Nautical Miles	STEAMING TIME								
	h. m. 23 11	h. m. 23 12	h. m. 23 13	h. m. 23 14	h. m. 23 15	h. m. 23 16	h. m. 23 17	h. m. 23 18	h. m. 23 19
	Knots	Knots	Knots	Knots	Knots	Knots	Knots	Knots	Knots
900	38·821	38·793	38·765	38·737	38·710	38·682	38·654	38·627	38·599
800	34·508	34·483	34·458	34·433	34·409	34·384	34·359	34·335	34·310
700	30·194	30·172	30·151	30·129	30·108	30·086	30·064	30·043	30·021
600	25·881	25·862	25·844	25·825	25·806	25·788	25·770	25·751	25·733
500	21·567	21·552	21·536	21·521	21·505	21·490	21·475	21·459	21·444
400	17·254	17·241	17·229	17·217	17·204	17·192	17·180	17·167	17·155
300	12·940	12·931	12·922	12·912	12·903	12·894	12·885	12·876	12·866
200	8·627	8·621	8·615	8·608	8·602	8·596	8·590	8·584	8·578
100	4·313	4·310	4·307	4·304	4·301	4·298	4·295	4·292	4·289

Distance	h. m. 23 20	h. m. 23 21	h. m. 23 22	h. m. 23 23	h. m. 23 24	h. m. 23 25	h. m. 23 26	h. m. 23 27	h. m. 23 28
900	38·571	38·544	38·516	38·489	38·462	38·434	38·407	38·380	38·352
800	34·296	34·261	34·237	34·212	34·188	34·164	34·139	34·115	34·091
700	30·000	29·979	29·957	29·936	29·915	29·893	29·872	29·851	29·830
600	25·714	25·696	25·678	25·660	25·641	25·623	25·605	25·586	25·568
500	21·429	21·413	21·398	21·383	21·368	21·352	21·337	21·322	21·307
400	17·143	17·131	17·118	17·106	17·094	17·082	17·070	17·058	17·045
300	12·857	12·848	12·839	12·830	12·821	12·811	12·802	12·793	12·784
200	8·571	8·565	8·559	8·553	8·547	8·541	8·535	8·529	8·523
100	4·286	4·283	4·280	4·277	4·274	4·270	4·267	4·264	4·261

Distance	h. m. 23 29	h. m. 23 30	h. m. 23 31	h. m. 23 32	h. m. 23 33	h. m. 23 34	h. m. 23 35	h. m. 23 36	h. m. 23 37
900	38·324	38·298	38·271	38·244	38·217	38·190	38·163	38·136	38·109
800	34·066	34·043	34·018	33·994	33·970	33·946	33·922	33·898	33·874
700	29·808	29·787	29·766	29·745	29·724	29·703	29·682	29·661	29·640
600	25·550	25·532	25·514	25·496	25·478	25·460	25·442	25·424	25·406
500	21·291	21·277	21·262	21·246	21·231	21·216	21·201	21·186	21·172
400	17·033	17·021	17·009	16·997	16·985	16·973	16·961	16·949	16·937
300	12·775	12·766	12·757	12·748	12·739	12·730	12·721	12·712	12·703
200	8·517	8·511	8·505	8·499	8·493	8·487	8·481	8·475	8·469
100	4·258	4·255	4·252	4·249	4·246	4·243	4·240	4·237	4·234

Distance	h. m. 23 38	h. m. 23 39	h. m. 23 40	h. m. 23 41	h. m. 23 42	h. m. 23 43	h. m. 23 44	h. m. 23 45	h. m. 23 46
900	38·082	38·055	38·028	38·001	37·975	37·948	37·921	37·895	37·868
800	33·850	33·827	33·803	33·779	33·755	33·732	33·708	33·684	33·661
700	29·619	29·598	29·577	29·557	29·536	29·515	29·494	29·474	29·453
600	25·388	25·370	25·352	25·334	25·316	25·299	25·281	25·263	25·245
500	21·157	21·142	21·127	21·112	21·097	21·082	21·067	21·053	21·038
400	16·925	16·913	16·901	16·890	16·878	16·866	16·854	16·842	16·830
300	12·694	12·685	12·676	12·667	12·658	12·649	12·640	12·632	12·623
200	8·463	8·457	8·451	8·445	8·439	8·433	8·427	8·421	8·415
100	4·231	4·228	4·225	4·222	4·219	4·216	4·213	4·211	4·208

DAY'S RUN - AVERAGE SPEED TABLE

Distance in Nautical Miles	STEAMING TIME								
	h. m. 23 47	h. m. 23 48	h. m. 23 49	h. m. 23 50	h. m. 23 51	h. m. 23 52	h. m. 23 53	h. m. 23 54	h. m. 23 55
	Knots	Knots	Knots	Knots	Knots	Knots	Knots	Knots	Knots
900	37·842	37·815	37·789	37·762	37·736	37·709	37·683	37·657	37·631
800	33·637	33·613	33·590	33·566	33·543	33·520	33·496	33·473	33·449
700	29·432	29·412	29·391	29·371	29·350	29·330	39·309	29·289	29·268
600	25·228	25·210	25·192	25·175	25·157	25·140	25·122	25·105	25·087
500	21·023	21·008	20·994	20·979	20·964	20·950	20·935	20·921	20·906
400	16·819	16·807	16·795	16·783	16·771	16·760	16·748	16·736	16·725
300	12·614	12·605	12·596	12·587	12·579	12·570	12·561	12·552	12·544
200	8·409	8·403	8·397	8·392	8·386	8·380	8·374	8·368	8·362
100	4·205	4·202	4·199	4·196	4·193	4·190	4·187	4·184	4·181
	h. m. 23 56	h. m. 23 57	h. m. 23 58	h. m. 23 59	h. m. 24 00	h. m. 24 01	h. m. 24 02	h. m. 24 03	h. m. 24 04
900	37·604	37·578	37·552	37·526	37·500	37·474	37·448	37·422	37·396
800	33·426	33·403	33·380	33·356	33·333	33·310	33·287	33·264	33·241
700	29·248	29·228	29·207	29·187	29·167	29·146	29·126	29·106	29·086
600	25·070	25·052	25·035	25·017	25·000	24·983	24·965	24·948	24·931
500	20·891	20·877	20·862	20·848	20·833	20·819	20·804	20·790	20·776
400	16·713	16·701	16·690	16·678	16·667	16·655	16·644	16·632	16·620
300	12·535	12·526	12·517	12·509	12·500	12·491	12·483	12·474	12·465
200	8·357	8·351	8·345	8·339	8·333	8·328	8·322	8·316	8·310
100	4·178	4·175	4·172	4·170	4·167	4·164	4·161	4·158	4·155
	h. m. 24 05	h. m. 24 06	h. m. 24 07	h. m. 24 08	h. m. 24 09	h. m. 24 10	h. m. 24 11	h. m. 24 12	h. m. 24 13
900	37·370	37·344	37·319	37·293	37·267	37·241	37·216	37·190	37·165
800	33·218	33·195	33·172	33·149	33·126	33·103	33·081	33·058	33·035
700	29·066	29·046	29·026	29·006	28·986	28·966	28·946	28·926	28·906
600	24·914	24·896	24·879	24·862	24·845	24·828	24·810	24·793	24·776
500	20·761	20·747	20·733	20·718	20·704	20·690	20·675	20·661	20·647
400	16·609	16·598	16·586	16·575	16·563	16·552	16·540	16·529	16·518
300	12·457	12·448	12·440	12·431	12·422	12·414	12·405	12·397	12·388
200	8·305	8·299	8·293	8·287	8·282	8·276	8·270	8·264	8·259
100	4·152	4·149	4·147	4·144	4·141	4·138	4·135	4·132	4·129
	h. m. 24 14	h. m. 24 15	h. m. 24 16	h. m. 24 17	h. m. 24 18	h. m. 24 19	h. m. 24 20	h. m. 24 21	h. m. 24 22
900	37·139	37·113	37·088	37·062	37·037	37·012	36·986	36·961	36·936
800	33·012	32·990	32·967	32·944	32·922	32·899	32·877	32·854	32·832
700	28·886	28·866	28·846	28·826	28·807	28·787	28·767	28·747	28·728
600	24·759	24·742	24·725	24·708	24·691	24·674	24·658	24·641	24·624
500	20·633	20·619	20·604	20·590	20·576	20·562	20·548	20·534	20·520
400	16·506	16·495	16·484	16·472	16·461	16·450	16·438	16·427	16·416
300	12·380	12·371	12·363	12·354	12·346	12·337	12·329	12·320	12·312
200	8·253	8·247	8·242	8·236	8·230	8·225	8·219	8·214	8·208
100	4·127	4·124	4·121	4·118	4·115	4·112	4·110	4·107	4·104

DAY'S RUN - AVERAGE SPEED TABLE

STEAMING TIME

Distance in Nautical Miles	h. m. 24 23	h. m. 24 24	h. m. 24 25	h. m. 24 26	h. m. 24 27	h. m. 24 28	h. m. 24 29	h. m. 24 30	h. m. 24 31
	Knots	Knots	Knots	Knots	Knots	Knots	Knots	Knots	Knots
900	36·910	36·885	36·860	36·835	36·810	36·785	36·760	36·735	36·710
800	32·809	32·787	32·764	32·742	32·720	32·698	32·675	32·653	32·631
700	28·708	28·689	28·669	28·649	28·630	28·610	28·591	28·571	28·552
600	24·607	24·590	24·573	24·557	24·540	24·523	24·506	24·490	24·473
500	20·506	20·492	20·478	20·464	20·450	20·436	20·422	20·408	20·394
400	16·405	16·393	16·382	16·371	16·360	16·349	16·338	16·327	16·315
300	12·303	12·295	12·287	12·278	12·270	12·262	12·253	12·245	12·237
200	8·202	8·197	8·191	8·186	8·180	8·174	8·169	8·163	8·158
100	4·101	4·098	4·096	4·093	4·090	4·087	4·084	4·082	4·079

Distance in Nautical Miles	h. m. 24 32	h. m. 24 33	h. m. 24 34	h. m. 24 35	h. m. 24 36	h. m. 24 37	h. m. 24 38	h. m. 24 39	h. m. 24 40
900	36·685	36·660	36·635	36·610	36·585	36·561	36·536	36·511	36·486
800	32·609	32·587	32·564	32·542	32·520	32·498	32·476	32·454	32·432
700	28·533	28·513	28·494	28·475	28·455	28·436	28·417	28·398	28·378
600	24·457	24·440	24·423	24·407	24·390	24·374	24·357	24·341	24·324
500	20·380	20·367	20·353	20·339	20 325	20·312	20·298	20·284	20·270
400	16·304	16·293	16·282	16·271	16·260	16·249	16·238	16·227	16·216
300	12·228	12·220	12·212	12·203	12·195	12·187	12·179	12·170	12·162
200	8·152	8·147	8·141	8·136	8·130	8·125	8·119	8·114	8·108
100	4·076	4·073	4·071	4·068	4·065	4·062	4·060	4·057	4·054

Distance in Nautical Miles	h. m. 24 41	h. m. 24 42	h. m. 24 43	h. m. 24 44	h. m. 24 45	h. m. 24 46	h. m. 24 47	h. m. 24 48	h. m. 24 49
900	36·462	36·438	36·413	36·388	36·364	36·339	36·315	36·290	36·266
800	32·411	32·389	32·367	32·345	32·323	32·302	32·280	32·258	32·236
700	28·359	28·341	28·321	28·302	28·283	28·264	28·245	28·226	28·207
600	24·308	24·292	24·275	24·259	24·242	24·226	24·210	24·194	24·177
500	20·257	20·243	20·229	20·216	20·202	20·188	20·175	20·161	20·148
400	16·205	16·195	16·183	16·173	16·162	16·151	16·140	16·129	16·118
300	12·154	12·146	12·138	12·129	12·121	12·113	12·105	12·097	12·089
200	8·103	8·097	8·092	8·086	8·081	8·075	8·070	8·065	8·059
100	4·051	4·049	4·046	4·043	4·040	4·038	4·035	4·032	4·030

Distance in Nautical Miles	h. m. 24 50	h. m. 24 51	h. m. 24 52	h. m. 24 53	h. m. 24 54	h. m. 24 55	h. m. 24 56	h. m. 24 57	h. m. 24 58
900	36·241	36·217	36·193	36·169	36·145	36·120	36·096	36·072	36·048
800	32·215	32·193	32·172	32·150	32·128	32·107	32·086	32·064	32·043
700	28·188	28·169	28·150	28·131	28·112	28·094	28·075	28·056	28·037
600	24·161	24·145	24·129	24·113	24·096	24·080	24·064	24·048	24·032
500	20·134	20·121	20·107	20·094	20·080	20·067	20·054	20·040	20·027
400	16·107	16·097	16·086	16·075	16·064	16·054	16·043	16·032	16·021
300	12·080	12·072	12·064	12·056	12·048	12·040	12·032	12·024	12·016
200	8·054	8·048	8·043	8·038	8·032	8·027	8·021	8·016	8·011
100	4·027	4·024	4·021	4·019	4·016	4·013	4·011	4·008	4·005

DAY'S RUN - AVERAGE SPEED TABLE

Distance in Nautical Miles	STEAMING TIME								
	h. m. 24 59	h. m. 25 00	h. m. 25 01	h. m. 25 02	h. m. 25 03	h. m. 25 04	h. m. 25 05	h. m. 25 06	h. m. 25 07
	Knots	Knots	Knots	Knots	Knots	Knots	Knots	Knots	Knots
900	36·024	36·000	35·976	35·952	35·928	35·904	35·880	35·857	35·833
800	32·021	32·000	31·979	31·957	31·936	31·915	31·894	31·872	31·851
700	28·019	28·000	27·981	27·963	27·944	27·926	27·908	27·888	27·870
600	24·016	24·000	23·984	23·968	23·952	23·936	23·920	23·904	23·889
500	20·013	20·000	19·987	19·973	19·960	19·947	19·934	19·920	19·907
400	16·011	16·000	15·989	15·979	15·968	15·957	15·947	15·936	15·926
300	12·008	12·000	11·992	11·984	11·976	11·968	11·960	11·952	11·944
200	8·005	8·000	7·995	7·989	7·984	7·979	7·973	7·968	7·963
100	4·003	4·000	3·997	3·995	3·992	3·989	3·987	3·984	3·981
	h. m. 25 08	h. m. 25 09	h. m. 25 10	h. m. 25 11	h. m. 25 12	h. m. 25 13	h. m. 25 14	h. m. 25 15	h. m. 25 16
900	35·809	35·785	35·762	35·738	35·714	35·691	35·667	35·644	35·620
800	31·830	31·809	31·788	31·767	31·746	31·725	31·704	31·683	31·662
700	27·851	27·833	27·815	27·796	27·778	27·759	27·741	27·723	27·704
600	23·873	23·857	23·841	23·825	23·810	23·794	23·778	23·762	23·747
500	19·894	19·881	19·868	19·854	19·841	19·828	19·815	19·802	19·789
400	15·915	15·905	15·894	15·884	15·873	15·863	15·852	15·842	15·831
300	11·936	11·928	11·921	11·913	11·905	11·897	11·889	11·881	11·873
200	7·958	7·952	7·947	7·942	7·937	7·931	7·926	7·921	7·916
100	3·979	3·976	3·974	3·971	3·968	3·966	3·963	3·960	3·958
	h. m. 25 17	h. m. 25 18	h. m. 25 19	h. m. 25 20	h. m. 25 21	h. m. 25 22	h. m. 25 23	h. m. 25 24	h. m. 25 25
900	35·597	35·573	35·550	35·526	35·503	35·480	35·456	35·433	35·410
800	31·641	31·621	31·600	31·579	31·558	31·537	31·517	31·496	31·475
700	27·686	27·668	27·650	27·632	27·613	27·595	27·577	27·559	27·541
600	23·731	23·715	23·700	23·684	23·669	23·653	23·638	23·622	23·607
500	19·776	19·763	19·750	19·737	19·724	19·711	19·698	19·685	19·672
400	15·821	15·810	15·800	15·789	15·779	15·769	15·758	15·748	15·738
300	11·866	11·858	11·850	11·842	11·834	11·827	11·819	11·811	11·803
200	7·910	7·905	7·900	7·895	7·890	7·884	7·879	7·874	7·869
100	3·955	3·953	3·950	3·947	3·945	3·942	3·940	3·937	3·934
	h. m. 25 26	h. m. 25 27	h. m. 25 28	h. m. 25 29	h. m. 25 30	h. m. 25 31	h. m. 25 32	h. m. 25 33	h. m. 25 34
900	35·387	35·363	35·340	35·317	35·294	35·271	35·248	35·225	35·202
800	31·455	31·434	31·414	31·393	31·373	31·352	31·332	31·311	31·291
700	27·523	27·505	27·487	27·469	27·451	27·433	27·415	27·397	27·379
600	23·591	23·576	23·560	23·545	23·529	23·514	23·499	23·483	23·468
500	19·659	19·646	19·634	19·621	19·608	19·595	19·582	19·569	19·557
400	15·727	15·717	15·707	15·697	15·686	15·676	15·666	15·656	15·645
300	11·796	11·788	11·780	11·772	11·765	11·757	11·749	11·742	11·734
200	7·864	7·859	7·853	7·848	7·843	7·838	7·833	7·828	7·823
100	3·932	3·929	3·927	3·924	3·922	3·919	3·916	3·914	3·911

DAY'S RUN - AVERAGE SPEED TABLE

STEAMING TIME

Distance in Nautical Miles	h. m. 25 35	h. m. 25 36	h. m. 25 37	h. m. 25 38	h. m. 25 39	h. m. 25 40	h. m. 25 41	h. m. 25 42	h. m. 25 43
	Knots	Knots	Knots	Knots	Knots	Knots	Knots	Knots	Knots
900	35·179	35·156	35·133	35·111	35·088	35·065	35·042	35·019	34·997
800	31·270	31·250	31·230	31·209	31·189	31·169	31·149	31·128	31·108
700	27·362	27·344	27·326	27·308	27·290	27·273	27·255	27·237	27·220
600	23·453	23·438	23·422	23·407	23·392	23·377	23·361	23·346	23·331
500	19·544	19·531	19·519	19·506	19·493	19·481	19·468	19·455	19·443
400	15·635	15·625	15·615	15·605	15·595	15·584	15·574	15·564	15·554
300	11·726	11·719	11·711	11·704	11·696	11·688	11·681	11·673	11·666
200	7·818	7·813	7·807	7·802	7·797	7·792	7·787	7·782	7·777
100	3·909	3·906	3·904	3·901	3·899	3·896	3·894	3·891	3·889

Distance	h. m. 25 44	h. m. 25 45	h. m. 25 46	h. m. 25 47	h. m. 25 48	h. m. 25 49	h. m. 25 50	h. m. 25 51	h. m. 25 52
900	34·974	34·952	34·929	34·906	34·884	34·861	34·838	34·816	34·794
800	31·088	31·068	31·048	31·028	31·008	30·988	30·968	30·948	30·928
700	27·202	27·185	27·167	27·149	27·132	27·114	27·097	27·079	27·062
600	23·316	23·301	23·286	23·271	23·256	23·241	23·226	23·211	23·196
500	19·430	19·418	19·405	19·392	19·380	19·367	19·355	19·342	19·330
400	15·544	15·534	15·524	15·514	15·504	15·494	15·484	15·474	15·464
300	11·658	11·651	11·643	11·635	11·628	11·620	11·613	11·605	11·598
200	7·772	7·767	7·762	7·757	7·752	7·747	7·742	7·737	7·732
100	3·886	3·884	3·881	3·878	3·876	3·873	3·871	3·868	3·866

Distance	h. m. 25 53	h. m. 25 54	h. m. 25 55	h. m. 25 56	h. m. 25 57	h. m. 25 58	h. m. 25 59	h. m. 26 00	h. m. 26 01
900	34·771	34·749	34·726	34·704	34·682	34·660	34·638	34·615	34·593
800	30·908	30·888	30·868	30·848	30·828	30·809	30·789	30·769	30·750
700	27·044	27·027	27·010	26·992	26·975	26·958	26·940	26·923	26·906
600	23·181	23·166	23·151	23·136	23·121	23·107	23·092	23·077	23·062
500	19·317	19·305	19·293	19·280	19·268	19·255	19·243	19·231	19·218
400	15·454	15·444	15·434	15·424	15·414	15·404	15·394	15·385	15·375
300	11·590	11·583	11·576	11·568	11·561	11·553	11·546	11·538	11·531
200	7·727	7·722	7·717	7·712	7·707	7·702	7·697	7·692	7·687
100	3·863	3·861	3·858	3·856	3·854	3·851	3·849	3·846	3·844

HALF HOUR INTERVAL SUMMARY

Distance	h. m. 22 00	h. m. 22 30	h. m. 23 00	h. m. 23 30	h. m. 24 00	h. m. 24 30	h. m. 25 00	h. m. 25 30	h. m. 26 00
900	40·909	40·000	39·130	38·298	37·500	36·735	36·000	35·294	34·615
800	36·364	35·556	34·783	34·043	33·333	32·653	32·000	31·373	30·769
700	31·818	31·111	30·435	29·787	29·167	28·571	28·000	27·451	26·923
600	27·274	26·667	26·087	25·532	25·000	24·490	24·000	23·529	23·077
500	22·727	22·222	21·739	21·277	20·833	20·408	20·000	19·608	19·231
400	18·182	17·778	17·391	17·021	16·667	16·327	16·000	15·686	15·385
300	13·636	13·333	13·043	12·766	12·500	12·245	12·000	11·765	11·538
200	9·091	8·889	8·696	8·511	8·333	8·163	8·000	7·843	7·692
100	4·545	4·444	4·348	4·255	4·167	4·082	4·000	3·922	3·846

RADAR RANGE TABLE

The accompanying table gives the approximate distance of the 'radar horizon' corresponding to different heights of the radar aerial or target from which an echo is returned, and is based on the formula:—

horizon dist. in n.mls = $2.21\sqrt{h}$
where h = height of aerial or target in metres

In similar manner to light waves, radio waves are refracted in passing through the atmosphere. This has the effect of making the distance of the radar horizon for 3cm. waves, under certain standard conditions of the atmosphere, about 15 per cent. greater than the distance of the geometrical horizon. Hence, taking the latter in nautical miles to be $1.92\sqrt{h}$, the distance of the radar horizon becomes $2.21\sqrt{h}$. This will be correct only under the standard conditions, and every departure from such standard will cause the distances to vary somewhat. The standard referred to is as follows:—

Atmospheric *pressure* 1013mb. decreasing with height at the rate of approximately 100mb. per 1000m.

Air *temperature* at sea level 30°C. decreasing with height at the rate of 6.5°C per 1000m.

60 per cent. *relative humidity* remaining constant with height.

Apart from variations from the above standard, the range at which target echoes can be seen on the P.P.I. screen will depend to a considerable extent on the characteristics of the particular radar installation and on the echoing qualities of the target.

Used with discretion, however, the information given in the table can be of much value to the radar observer.

Note: — The sum of the radar horizon distances of aerial and target respectively gives the maximum distance from which that target can return an echo.

Examples:—

1. A target of height 120m (390ft) should begin to appear on the P.P.I. of an installation with an aerial mounted 10m (33ft) above sea level at a range of approximately 24 + 7 = 31 miles

2. If an echo first appears on the P.P.I. (aerial 10m (33ft) above sea level) at a range of 26 miles, the probable height of the target is of the order of about 70m (230ft). This may assist in identifying it.

CAUTION: — TO BE USED WITH 3cm. WAVE RADAR ONLY.

m	ft.	Range Mls	m.	ft.	Range Mls
2	7	3.1	110	360	23
4	13	4.4	120	390	24
6	20	5.4	130	430	25
8	26	6.3	140	460	26
10	33	7.0	150	490	27
15	49	8.6	160	530	28
20	66	9.9	170	560	29
25	82	11.1	180	590	30
30	98	12.1	190	620	31
35	115	13.1	200	660	31
40	131	14.0	220	720	33
45	148	14.8	240	790	34
50	164	15.6	260	850	36
55	180	16.0	280	920	37
60	197	17.1	300	980	38
70	230	18.5	320	1050	40
80	262	19.8	340	1120	41
90	295	21.0	360	1180	42
100	328	22.1	380	1250	43
110	360	23.0	400	1310	44

RADAR PLOTTER'S
SPEED AND DISTANCE TABLE

SPEED IN KNOTS	Miles in 1 min.	Miles in 2 min.	Miles in 2½ min.	Miles in 3 min.	Miles in 4 min.	Miles in 5 min.	Miles in 6 min.	SPEED IN KNOTS
4·0	0·07	0·13	0·17	0·20	0·27	0·33	0·40	4·0
4·5	0·08	0·15	0·19	0·23	0·30	0·38	0·45	4·5
5·0	0·08	0·17	0·21	0·25	0·33	0·42	0·50	5·0
5·5	0·10	0·18	0·23	0·28	0·37	0·46	0·55	5·5
6·0	0·10	0·20	0·25	0·30	0·40	0·50	0·60	6·0
6·5	0·11	0·22	0·27	0·33	0·43	0·54	0·65	6·5
7·0	0·12	0·23	0·29	0·35	0·47	0·58	0·70	7·0
7·5	0·13	0·25	0·31	0·38	0·50	0·63	0·75	7·5
8·0	0·13	0·27	0·33	0·40	0·53	0·67	0·80	8·0
8·5	0·14	0·28	0·35	0·43	0·57	0·71	0·85	8·5
9·0	0·15	0·30	0·38	0·45	0·60	0·75	0·90	9·0
9·5	0·16	0·32	0·40	0·48	0·63	0·80	0·95	9·5
10·0	0·17	0·33	0·42	0·50	0·67	0·83	1·00	10·0
10·5	0·18	0·35	0·44	0·53	0·70	0·88	1·05	10·5
11·0	0·18	0·37	0·46	0·55	0·73	0·91	1·10	11·0
11·5	0·19	0·38	0·48	0·58	0·77	0·96	1·15	11·5
12·0	0·20	0·40	0·50	0·60	0·80	1·00	1·20	12·0
12·5	0·21	0·42	0·52	0·63	0·83	1·04	1·25	12·5
13·0	0·22	0·43	0·54	0·65	0·87	1·08	1·30	13·0
13·5	0·23	0·45	0·56	0·68	0·90	1·13	1·35	13·5
14·0	0·23	0·47	0·58	0·70	0·93	1·17	1·40	14·0
14·5	0·24	0·48	0·60	0·73	0·97	1·21	1·45	14·5
15·0	0·25	0·50	0·63	0·75	1·00	1·25	1·50	15·0
15·5	0·26	0·52	0·65	0·78	1·03	1·29	1·55	15·5
16·0	0·27	0·53	0·67	0·80	1·07	1·33	1·60	16·0
16·5	0·28	0·55	0·69	0·83	1·10	1·38	1·65	16·5
17·0	0·28	0·57	0·71	0·85	1·13	1·42	1·70	17·0
17·5	0·29	0·58	0·73	0·88	1·17	1·46	1·75	17·5
18·0	0·30	0·60	0·75	0·90	1·20	1·50	1·80	18·0
18·5	0·31	0·62	0·77	0·93	1·23	1·54	1·85	18·5
19·0	0·32	0·63	0·79	0·95	1·27	1·58	1·90	19·0
19·5	0·33	0·65	0·81	0·98	1·30	1·63	1·95	19·5
20·0	0·33	0·67	0·83	1·00	1·33	1·67	2·00	20·0
20·5	0·34	0·68	0·85	1·03	1·37	1·71	2·05	20·5
21·0	0·35	0·70	0·88	1·05	1·40	1·75	2·10	21·0
21·5	0·36	0·72	0·90	1·08	1·43	1·79	2·15	21·5
22·0	0·37	0·73	0·92	1·10	1·47	1·83	2·20	22·0
22·5	0·38	0·75	0·94	1·13	1·50	1·88	2·25	22·5
23·0	0·38	0·77	0·96	1·15	1·53	1·92	2·30	23·0
23·5	0·39	0·78	0·98	1·18	1·57	1·96	2·35	23·5
24·0	0·40	0·80	1·00	1·20	1·60	2·00	2·40	24·0
24·5	0·41	0·82	1·02	1·23	1·63	2·04	2·45	24·5
25·0	0·42	0·83	1·04	1·25	1·67	2·08	2·50	25·0
25·5	0·43	0·85	1·06	1·28	1·70	2·13	2·55	25·5
26·0	0·43	0·87	1·08	1·30	1·73	2·17	2·60	26·0
26·5	0·44	0·88	1·10	1·33	1·77	2·21	2·65	26·5
27·0	0·45	0·90	1·13	1·35	1·80	2·25	2·70	27·0
27·5	0·46	0·92	1·15	1·38	1·83	2·29	2·75	27·5
28·0	0·47	0·93	1·17	1·40	1·87	2·33	2·80	28·0
28·5	0·48	0·95	1·19	1·43	1·90	2·38	2·85	28·5
29·0	0·48	0·97	1·21	1·45	1·93	2·42	2·90	29·0
29·5	0·49	0·98	1·23	1·48	1·97	2·46	2·95	29·5
30·0	0·50	1·00	1·25	1·50	2·00	2·50	3·00	30·0
30·5	0·51	1·02	1·27	1·53	2·03	2·54	3·05	30·5
31·0	0·52	1·03	1·29	1·55	2·07	2·58	3·10	31·0
31·5	0·53	1·05	1·31	1·58	2·10	2·63	3·15	31·5
32·0	0·53	1·07	1·33	1·60	2·13	2·67	3·20	32·0
32·5	0·54	1·08	1·35	1·63	2·17	2·71	3·25	32·5
33·0	0·55	1·10	1·38	1·65	2·20	2·75	3·30	33·0
33·5	0·56	1·12	1·40	1·68	2·23	2·79	3·35	33·5
34·0	0·57	1·13	1·42	1·70	2·27	2·83	3·40	34·0

MEASURED MILE SPEED TABLE

Time to Steam One Mile in Minutes and Seconds

Speed in Knots

12 00·7	11 19·9	10 43·4	10 10·7	9 41·1	9 14·3	8 49·8	8 27·4	8 06·8	7 47·8	7 30·3
5·00	*5·30*	*5·60*	*5·90*	*6·20*	*6·50*	*6·80*	*7·10*	*7·40*	*7·70*	*8·00*
11 59·3	11 18·6	10 42·3	10 09·7	9 40·2	9 13·4	8 49·0	8 26·7	8 06·2	7 47·2	7 29·7
5·01	*5·31*	*5·61*	*5·91*	*6·21*	*6·51*	*6·81*	*7·11*	*7·41*	*7·71*	*8·01*
11 57·9	11 17·3	10 41·1	10 08·6	9 39·2	9 12·6	8 48·2	8 26·0	8 05·5	7 46·6	7 29·2
5·02	*5·32*	*5·62*	*5·92*	*6·22*	*6·52*	*6·82*	*7·12*	*7·42*	*7·72*	*8·02*
11 56·4	11 16·1	10 40·0	10 07·6	9 38·3	9 11·7	8 47·5	8 25·3	8 04·8	7 46·0	7 28·6
5·03	*5·33*	*5·63*	*5·93*	*6·23*	*6·53*	*6·83*	*7·13*	*7·43*	*7·73*	*8·03*
11 55·0	11 14·8	10 38·9	10 06·6	9 37·4	9 10·9	8 46·7	8 24·6	8 04·2	7 45·4	7 28·0
5·04	*5·34*	*5·64*	*5·94*	*6·24*	*6·54*	*6·84*	*7·14*	*7·44*	*7·74*	*8·04*
11 53·6	11 13·5	10 37·7	10 05·6	9 36·5	9 10·0	8 45·9	8 23·8	8 03·5	7 44·8	7 27·5
5·05	*5·35*	*5·65*	*5·95*	*6·25*	*6·55*	*6·85*	*7·15*	*7·45*	*7·75*	*8·05*
11 52·2	11 12·3	10 36·6	10 04·5	9 35·5	9 09·2	8 45·2	8 23·1	8 02·9	7 44·2	7 26·9
5·06	*5·36*	*5·66*	*5·96*	*6·26*	*6·56*	*6·86*	*7·16*	*7·46*	*7·76*	*8·06*
11 50·8	11 11·0	10 35·5	10 03·5	9 34·6	9 08·4	8 44·4	8 22·4	8 02·3	7 43·6	7 26·4
5·07	*5·37*	*5·67*	*5·97*	*6·27*	*6·57*	*6·87*	*7·17*	*7·47*	*7·77*	*8·07*
11 49·4	11 09·8	10 34·4	10 02·5	9 33·7	9 07·5	8 43·6	8 21·7	8 01·6	7 43·0	7 25·8
5·08	*5·38*	*5·68*	*5·98*	*6·28*	*6·58*	*6·88*	*7·18*	*7·48*	*7·78*	*8·08*
11 48·0	11 08·5	10 33·2	10 01·5	9 32·8	9 06·7	8 42·9	8 21·0	8 01·0	7 42·4	7 25·3
5·09	*5·39*	*5·69*	*5·99*	*6·29*	*6·59*	*6·89*	*7·19*	*7·49*	*7·79*	*8·09*
11 46·6	11 07·3	10 32·1	10 00·5	9 31·9	9 05·9	8 42·1	8 20·3	8 00·3	7 41·8	7 24·7
5·10	*5·40*	*5·70*	*6·00*	*6·30*	*6·60*	*6·90*	*7·20*	*7·50*	*7·80*	*8·10*
11 45·2	11 06·1	10 31·0	9 59·5	9 31·0	9 05·0	8 41·4	8 19·7	7 59·7	7 41·2	7 24·2
5·11	*5·41*	*5·71*	*6·01*	*6·31*	*6·61*	*6·91*	*7·21*	*7·51*	*7·81*	*8·11*
11 43·8	11 04·8	10 29·9	9 58·5	9 30·1	9 04·2	8 40·6	8 19·0	7 59·0	7 40·7	7 23·6
5·12	*5·42*	*5·72*	*6·02*	*6·32*	*6·62*	*6·92*	*7·22*	*7·52*	*7·82*	*8·12*
11 42·4	11 03·6	10 28·8	9 57·5	9 29·2	9 03·4	8 39·9	8 18·3	7 58·4	7 40·1	7 23·1
5·13	*5·43*	*5·73*	*6·03*	*6·33*	*6·63*	*6·93*	*7·23*	*7·53*	*7·83*	*8·13*
11 41·1	11 02·4	10 27·7	9 56·5	9 28·3	9 02·6	8 39·1	8 17·6	7 57·8	7 39·5	7 22·5
5·14	*5·44*	*5·74*	*6·04*	*6·34*	*6·64*	*6·94*	*7·24*	*7·54*	*7·84*	*8·14*
11 39·7	11 01·2	10 26·6	9 55·5	9 27·4	9 01·8	8 38·4	8 16·9	7 57·1	7 38·9	7 22·0
5·15	*5·45*	*5·75*	*6·05*	*6·35*	*6·65*	*6·95*	*7·25*	*7·55*	*7·85*	*8·15*
11 38·4	10 59·9	10 25·5	9 54·6	9 26·5	9 00·9	8 37·6	8 16·2	7 56·5	7 38·3	7 21·4
5·16	*5·46*	*5·76*	*6·06*	*6·36*	*6·66*	*6·96*	*7·26*	*7·56*	*7·86*	*8·16*
11 37·0	10 58·7	10 24·5	9 53·6	9 25·6	9 00·1	8 36·9	8 15·5	7 55·9	7 37·7	7 20·9
5·17	*5·47*	*5·77*	*6·07*	*6·37*	*6·67*	*6·97*	*7·27*	*7·57*	*7·87*	*8·17*
11 35·7	10 57·5	10 23·4	9 52·6	9 24·7	8 59·3	8 36·1	8 14·8	7 55·2	7 37·1	7 20·4
5·18	*5·48*	*5·78*	*6·08*	*6·38*	*6·68*	*6·98*	*7·28*	*7·58*	*7·88*	*8·18*
11 34·3	10 56·3	10 22·3	9 51·6	9 23·8	8 58·5	8 35·4	8 14·2	7 54·6	7 36·6	7 19·8
5·19	*5·49*	*5·79*	*6·09*	*6·39*	*6·69*	*6·99*	*7·29*	*7·59*	*7·89*	*8·19*
11 33·0	10 55·1	10 21·2	9 50·7	9 22·9	8 57·7	8 34·7	8 13·5	7 54·0	7 36·0	7 19·3
5·20	*5·50*	*5·80*	*6·10*	*6·40*	*6·70*	*7·00*	*7·30*	*7·60*	*7·90*	*8·20*
11 31·6	10 54·0	10 20·1	9 49·7	9 22·1	8 56·9	8 33·9	8 12·8	7 53·4	7 35·4	7 18·8
5·21	*5·51*	*5·81*	*6·11*	*6·41*	*6·71*	*7·01*	*7·31*	*7·61*	*7·91*	*8·21*
11 30·3	10 52·8	10 19·1	9 48·7	9 21·2	8 56·1	8 33·2	8 12·1	7 52·8	7 34·8	7 18·2
5·22	*5·52*	*5·82*	*6·12*	*6·42*	*6·72*	*7·02*	*7·32*	*7·62*	*7·92*	*8·22*
11 29·0	10 51·6	10 18·0	9 47·8	9 20·3	8 55·3	8 32·5	8 11·5	7 52·1	7 34·3	7 17·7
5·23	*5·53*	*5·83*	*6·13*	*6·43*	*6·73*	*7·03*	*7·33*	*7·63*	*7·93*	*8·23*
11 27·7	10 50·4	10 17·0	9 46·8	9 19·4	8 54·5	8 31·7	8 10·8	7 51·5	7 33·7	7 17·2
5·24	*5·54*	*5·84*	*6·14*	*6·44*	*6·74*	*7·04*	*7·34*	*7·64*	*7·94*	*8·24*
11 26·4	10 49·2	10 15·9	9 45·8	9 18·6	8 53·7	8 31·0	8 10·1	7 50·9	7 33·1	7 16·6
5·25	*5·55*	*5·85*	*6·15*	*6·45*	*6·75*	*7·05*	*7·35*	*7·65*	*7·95*	*8·25*
11 25·1	10 48·1	10 14·8	9 44·9	9 17·7	8 52·9	8 30·3	8 09·5	7 50·3	7 32·5	7 16·1
5·26	*5·56*	*5·86*	*6·16*	*6·46*	*6·76*	*7·06*	*7·36*	*7·66*	*7·96*	*8·26*
11 23·8	10 46·9	10 13·8	9 43·9	9 16·8	8 52·2	8 29·6	8 08·8	7 49·7	7 32·0	7 15·6
5·27	*5·57*	*5·87*	*6·17*	*6·47*	*6·77*	*7·07*	*7·37*	*7·67*	*7·97*	*8·27*
11 22·5	10 45·7	10 12·8	9 43·0	9 16·0	8 51·4	8 28·8	8 08·1	7 49·1	7 31·4	7 15·0
5·28	*5·58*	*5·88*	*6·18*	*6·48*	*6·78*	*7·08*	*7·38*	*7·68*	*7·98*	*8·28*
11 21·2	10 44·6	10 11·8	9 42·1	9 15·1	8 50·6	8 28·1	8 07·5	7 48·4	7 30·8	7 14·5
5·29	*5·59*	*5·89*	*6·19*	*6·49*	*6·79*	*7·09*	*7·39*	*7·69*	*7·99*	*8·29*
11 19·9	10 43·4	10 10·7	9 41·1	9 14·3	8 49·8	8 27·4	8 06·8	7 47·8	7 30·3	7 14·0
5·30	*5·60*	*5·90*	*6·20*	*6·50*	*6·80*	*7·10*	*7·40*	*7·70*	*8·00*	*8·30*
11 18·6	10 42·3	10 09·7	9 40·2	9 13·4	8 49·0	8 26·7	8 06·2	7 47·2	7 29·7	7 13·5

MEASURED MILE SPEED TABLE

Time to Steam One Mile in Minutes and Seconds

Speed in Knots

7 14·0	6 58·8	6 44·7	6 31·5	6 19·1	6 07·5	5 56·6	5 46·3	5 36·6	5 27·4	5 18·7
8·30	*8·60*	*8·90*	*9·20*	*9·50*	*9·80*	*10·10*	*10·40*	*10·70*	*11·00*	*11·30*
7 13·5	6 58·4	6 44·3	6 31·1	6 18·7	6 07·2	5 56·3	5 46·0	5 36·3	5 27·1	5 18·4
8·31	*8·61*	*8·91*	*9·21*	*9·51*	*9·81*	*10·11*	*10·41*	*10·71*	*11·01*	*11·31*
7 13·0	6 57·9	6 43·8	6 30·7	6 18·3	6 06·8	5 55·9	5 45·7	5 36·0	5 26·8	5 18·2
8·32	*8·62*	*8·92*	*9·22*	*9·52*	*9·82*	*10·12*	*10·42*	*10·72*	*11·02*	*11·32*
7 12·4	6 57·4	6 43·4	6 30·2	6 18·0	6 06·4	5 55·6	5 45·3	5 35·7	5 26·5	5 17·9
8·33	*8·63*	*8·93*	*9·23*	*9·53*	*9·83*	*10·13*	*10·43*	*10 73*	*11·03*	*11·33*
7 11·9	6 56·9	6 42·9	6 29·8	6 17·6	6 06·0	5 55·2	5 45·0	5 35·4	5 26·2	5 17·6
8·34	*8·64*	*8·94*	*9·24*	*9·54*	*9·84*	*10·14*	*10·44*	*10·74*	*11·04*	*11·34*
7 11·4	6 56·4	6 42·5	6 29·4	6 17·2	6 05·7	5 54·9	5 44·7	5 35·0	5 25·9	5 17·3
8·35	*8·65*	*8·95*	*9·25*	*9·55*	*9·85*	*10·15*	*10·45*	*10·75*	*11·05*	*11·35*
7 10·9	6 55·9	6 42·0	6 29·0	6 16·8	6 05·3	5 54·5	5 44·3	5 34·7	5 25·6	5 17·0
8·36	*8·66*	*8·96*	*9·26*	*9·56*	*9·86*	*10·16*	*10·46*	*10·76*	*11·06*	*11·36*
7 10·4	6 55·4	6 41·6	6 28·6	6 16·4	6 04·9	5 54·2	5 44·0	5 34·4	5 25·4	5 16·8
8·37	*8·67*	*8·97*	*9·27*	*9·57*	*9·87*	*10·17*	*10·47*	*10·77*	*11·07*	*11·37*
7 09·9	6 55·0	6 41·1	6 28·1	6 16·0	6 04·6	5 53·8	5 43·7	5 34·1	5 25·1	5 16·5
8·38	*8·68*	*8·98*	*9·28*	*9·58*	*9·88*	*10·18*	*10·48*	*10·78*	*11·08*	*11·38*
7 09·3	6 54·5	6 40·7	6 27·7	6 15·6	6 04·2	5 53·5	5 43·3	5 33·8	5 24·8	5 16·2
8·39	*8·69*	*8·99*	*9·29*	*9·59*	*9·89*	*10·19*	*10·49*	*10·79*	*11·09*	*11·39*
7 08·8	6 54·0	6 40·2	6 27·3	6 15·2	6 03·8	5 53·1	5 43·0	5 33·5	5 24·5	5 15·9
8·40	*8·70*	*9·00*	*9·30*	*9·60*	*9·90*	*10·20*	*10·50*	*10·80*	*11·10*	*11·40*
7 08·3	6 53·6	6 39·8	6 26·9	6 14·8	6 03·5	5 52·8	5 42·7	5 33·2	5 24·2	5 15·7
8·41	*8·71*	*9·01*	*9·31*	*9·61*	*9·91*	*10·21*	*10·51*	*10·81*	*11·11*	*11·41*
7 07·8	6 53·1	6 39·3	6 26·5	6 14·4	6 03·1	5 52·4	5 42·4	5 32·9	5 23·9	5 15·4
8·42	*8·72*	*9·02*	*9·32*	*9·62*	*9·92*	*10·22*	*10·52*	*10·82*	*11·12*	*11·42*
7 07·3	6 52·6	6 38·8	6 26·1	6 14·0	6 02·7	5 52·1	5 42·0	5 32·6	5 23·6	5 15·1
8·43	*8·73*	*9·03*	*9·33*	*9·63*	*9·93*	*10·23*	*10·53*	*10·83*	*11·13*	*11·43*
7 06·8	6 52·1	6 38·5	6 25·6	6 13·6	6 02·4	5 51·7	5 41·7	5 32·3	5 23·3	5 14·8
8·44	*8·74*	*9·04*	*9·34*	*9·64*	*9·94*	*10·24*	*10·54*	*10·84*	*11·14*	*11·44*
7 06·3	6 51·7	6 38·0	6 25·2	6 13·3	6 02·0	5 51·4	5 41·4	5 32·0	5 23·0	5 14·5
8·45	*8·75*	*9·05*	*9·35*	*9·65*	*9·95*	*10·25*	*10·55*	*10·85*	*11·15*	*11·45*
7 05·8	6 51·2	6 37·6	6 24·8	6 12·9	6 01·6	5 51·0	5 41·1	5 31·6	5 22·7	5 14·3
8·46	*8·76*	*9·06*	*9·36*	*9·66*	*9·96*	*10·26*	*10·56*	*10·86*	*11·16*	*11·46*
7 05·3	6 50·7	6 37·1	6 24·4	6 12·5	6 01·3	5 50·7	5 40·7	5 31·3	5 22·4	5 14·0
8·47	*8·77*	*9·07*	*9·37*	*9·67*	*9·97*	*10·27*	*10·57*	*10·87*	*11·17*	*11·47*
7 04·8	6 50·3	6 36·7	6 24·0	6 12·1	6 00·9	5 50·4	5 40·4	5 31·0	5 22·1	5 13·7
8·48	*8·78*	*9·08*	*9·38*	*9·68*	*9·98*	*10·28*	*10·58*	*10·88*	*11·18*	*11·48*
7 04·3	6 49·8	6 36·3	6 23·6	6 11·7	6 00·5	5 50·0	5 40·1	5 30·7	5 21·9	5 13·5
8·49	*8·79*	*9·09*	*9·39*	*9·69*	*9·99*	*10·29*	*10·59*	*10·89*	*11·19*	*11·49*
7 03·8	6 49·3	6 35·8	6 23·2	6 11·3	6 00·2	5 49·7	5 39·8	5 30·4	5 21·6	5 13·2
8·50	*8·80*	*9·10*	*9·40*	*9·70*	*10·00*	*10·30*	*10·60*	*10·90*	*11·20*	*11·50*
7 03·3	6 48·9	6 35·4	6 22·8	6 10·9	5 59·8	5 49·3	5 39·5	5 30·1	5 21·3	5 12·9
8·51	*8·81*	*9·11*	*9·41*	*9·71*	*10·01*	*10·31*	*10·61*	*10·91*	*11·21*	*11·51*
7 02·8	6 48·4	6 35·0	6 22·4	6 10·6	5 59·5	5 49·0	5 39·1	5 29·8	5 21·0	5 12·6
8·52	*8·82*	*9·12*	*9·42*	*9·72*	*10·02*	*10·32*	*10·62*	*10·92*	*11·22*	*11·52*
7 02·3	6 47·9	6 34·5	6 22·0	6 10·2	5 59·1	5 48·7	5 38·8	5 29·5	5 20·7	5 12·4
8·53	*8·83*	*9·13*	*9·43*	*9·73*	*10·03*	*10·33*	*10·63*	*10·93*	*11·23*	*11·53*
7 01·8	6 47·5	6 34·1	6 21·6	6 09·8	5 58·7	5 48·3	5 38·5	5 29·2	5 20·4	5 12·1
8·54	*8·84*	*9·14*	*9·44*	*9·74*	*10·04*	*10·34*	*10·64*	*10·94*	*11·24*	*11·54*
7 01·3	6 47·0	6 33·7	6 21·2	6 09·4	5 58·4	5 48·0	5 38·2	5 28·9	5 20·1	5 11·8
8·55	*8·85*	*9·15*	*9·45*	*9·75*	*10·05*	*10·35*	*10·65*	*10·95*	*11·25*	*11·55*
7 00·8	6 46·6	6 33·2	6 20·8	6 09·0	5 58·0	5 47·7	5 37·9	5 28·6	5 19·9	5 11·6
8·56	*8·86*	*9·16*	*9·46*	*9·76*	*10·06*	*10·36*	*10·66*	*10·96*	*11·26*	*11·56*
7 00·3	6 46·1	6 32·8	6 20·3	6 08·7	5 57·7	5 47·3	5 37·6	5 28·3	5 19·6	5 11·3
8·57	*8·87*	*9·17*	*9·47*	*9·77*	*10·07*	*10·37*	*10·67*	*10·97*	*11·27*	*11·57*
6 59·8	6 45·6	6 32·4	6 19·9	6 08·3	5 57·3	5 47·0	5 37·2	5 28·0	5 19·3	5 11·0
8·58	*8·88*	*9·18*	*9·48*	*9·78*	*10·08*	*10·38*	*10·68*	*10·98*	*11·28*	*11·58*
6 59·3	6 45·2	6 31·9	6 19·5	6 07·9	5 57·0	5 46·7	5 36·9	5 27·7	5 19·0	5 10·7
8·59	*8·89*	*9·19*	*9·49*	*9·79*	*10·09*	*10·39*	*10·69*	*10·99*	*11·29*	*11·59*
6 58·8	6 44·7	6 31·5	6 19·1	6 07·5	5 56·6	5 46·3	5 36·6	5 27·4	5 18·7	5 10·5
8·60	*8·90*	*9·20*	*9·50*	*9·80*	*10·10*	*10·40*	*10·70*	*11·00*	*11·30*	*11·60*
6 58·4	6 44·3	6 31·1	6 18·7	6 07·2	5 56·3	5 46·0	5 36·3	5 27·1	5 18·4	5 10·2

MEASURED MILE SPEED TABLE

Time to Steam One Mile in Minutes and Seconds

Speed in Knots

5 10·5	**5 02·6**	**4 55·2**	**4 48·1**	**4 41·4**	**4 34·9**	**4 28·8**	**4 22·9**	**4 17·2**	**4 11·8**	**4 06·7**
11·60	*11·90*	*12·20*	*12·50*	*12·80*	*13·10*	*13·40*	*13·70*	*14·00*	*14·30*	*14·60*
5 10·2	**5 02·4**	**4 55·0**	**4 47·9**	**4 41·1**	**4 34·7**	**4 28·6**	**4 22·7**	**4 17·1**	**4 11·7**	**4 06·5**
11·61	*11·91*	*12·21*	*12·51*	*12·81*	*13·11*	*13·41*	*13·71*	*14·01*	*14·31*	*14·61*
5 09·9	**5 02·1**	**4 54·7**	**4 47·7**	**4 40·9**	**4 34·5**	**4 28·4**	**4 22·5**	**4 16·9**	**4 11·5**	**4 06·3**
11·62	*11·92*	*12·22*	*12·52*	*12·82*	*13·12*	*13·42*	*13·72*	*14·02*	*14·32*	*14·62*
5 09·7	**5 01·9**	**4 54·5**	**4 47·4**	**4 40·7**	**4 34·3**	**4 28·2**	**4 22·3**	**4 16·7**	**4 11·3**	**4 06·2**
11·63	*11·93*	*12·23*	*12·53*	*12·83*	*13·13*	*13·43*	*13·73*	*14·03*	*14·33*	*14·63*
5 09·4	**5 01·6**	**4 54·2**	**4 47·2**	**4 40·5**	**4 34·1**	**4 28·0**	**4 22·1**	**4 16·5**	**4 11·1**	**4 06·0**
11·64	*11·94*	*12·24*	*12·54*	*12·84*	*13·14*	*13·44*	*13·74*	*14·04*	*14·34*	*14·64*
5 09·1	**5 01·4**	**4 54·0**	**4 47·0**	**4 40·3**	**4 33·9**	**4 27·8**	**4 21·9**	**4 16·3**	**4 11·0**	**4 05·8**
11·65	*11·95*	*12·25*	*12·55*	*12·85*	*13·15*	*13·45*	*13·75*	*14·05*	*14·35*	*14·65*
5 08·9	**5 01·1**	**4 53·8**	**4 46·7**	**4 40·0**	**4 33·7**	**4 27·6**	**4 21·7**	**4 16·1**	**4 10·8**	**4 05·6**
11·66	*11·96*	*12·26*	*12·56*	*12·86*	*13·16*	*13·46*	*13·76*	*14·06*	*14·36*	*14·66*
5 08·6	**5 00·9**	**4 53·5**	**4 46·5**	**4 39·8**	**4 33·5**	**4 27·4**	**4 21·5**	**4 16·0**	**4 10·6**	**4 05·5**
11·67	*11·97*	*12·27*	*12·57*	*12·87*	*13·17*	*13·47*	*13·77*	*14·07*	*14·37*	*14·67*
5 08·4	**5 00·6**	**4 53·3**	**4 46·3**	**4 39·6**	**4 33·2**	**4 27·2**	**4 21·3**	**4 15·8**	**4 10·4**	**4 05·3**
11·68	*11·98*	*12·28*	*12·58*	*12·88*	*13·18*	*13·48*	*13·78*	*14·08*	*14·38*	*14·68*
5 08·1	**5 00·4**	**4 53·0**	**4 46·1**	**4 39·4**	**4 33·0**	**4 27·0**	**4 21·2**	**4 15·6**	**4 10·3**	**4 05·1**
11·69	*11·99*	*12·29*	*12·59*	*12·89*	*13·19*	*13·49*	*13·79*	*14·09*	*14·39*	*14·69*
5 07·8	**5 00·1**	**4 52·8**	**4 45·8**	**4 39·2**	**4 32·8**	**4 26·8**	**4 21·0**	**4 15·4**	**4 10·1**	**4 05·0**
11·70	*12·00*	*12·30*	*12·60*	*12·90*	*13·20*	*13·50*	*13·80*	*14·10*	*14·40*	*14·70*
5 07·6	**4 59·9**	**4 52·6**	**4 45·6**	**4 39·0**	**4 32·6**	**4 26·6**	**4 20·8**	**4 15·2**	**4 09·9**	**4 04·8**
11·71	*12·01*	*12·31*	*12·61*	*12·91*	*13·21*	*13·51*	*13·81*	*14·11*	*14·41*	*14·71*
5 07·3	**4 59·6**	**4 52·3**	**4 45·4**	**4 38·8**	**4 32·4**	**4 26·4**	**4 20·6**	**4 15·0**	**4 09·7**	**4 04·6**
11·72	*12·02*	*12·32*	*12·62*	*12·92*	*13·22*	*13·52*	*13·82*	*14·12*	*14·42*	*14·72*
5 07·0	**4 59·4**	**4 52·1**	**4 45·1**	**4 38·5**	**4 32·2**	**4 26·2**	**4 20·4**	**4 14·9**	**4 09·6**	**4 04·5**
11·73	*12·03*	*12·33*	*12·63*	*12·93*	*13·23*	*13·53*	*13·83*	*14·13*	*14·43*	*14·73*
5 06·8	**4 59·1**	**4 51·9**	**4 44·9**	**4 38·3**	**4 32·0**	**4 26·0**	**4 20·2**	**4 14·7**	**4 09·4**	**4 04·3**
11·74	*12·04*	*12·34*	*12·64*	*12·94*	*13·24*	*13·54*	*13·84*	*14·14*	*14·44*	*14·74*
5 06·5	**4 58·9**	**4 51·6**	**4 44·7**	**4 38·1**	**4 31·8**	**4 25·8**	**4 20·0**	**4 14·5**	**4 09·2**	**4 04·2**
11·75	*12·05*	*12·35*	*12·65*	*12·95*	*13·25*	*13·55*	*13·85*	*14·15*	*14·45*	*14·75*
5 06·3	**4 58·6**	**4 51·4**	**4 44·5**	**4 37·9**	**4 31·6**	**4 25·6**	**4 19·8**	**4 14·3**	**4 09·0**	**4 04·0**
11·76	*12·06*	*12·36*	*12·66*	*12·96*	*13·26*	*13·56*	*13·86*	*14·16*	*14·46*	*14·76*
5 06·0	**4 58·4**	**4 51·1**	**4 44·2**	**4 37·7**	**4 31·4**	**4 25·4**	**4 19·6**	**4 14·1**	**4 08·9**	**4 03·8**
11·77	*12·07*	*12·37*	*12·67*	*12·97*	*13·27*	*13·57*	*13·87*	*14·17*	*14·47*	*14·77*
5 05·7	**4 58·1**	**4 50·9**	**4 44·0**	**4 37·5**	**4 31·2**	**4 25·2**	**4 19·5**	**4 14·0**	**4 08·7**	**4 03·7**
11·78	*12·08*	*12·38*	*12·68*	*12·98*	*13·28*	*13·58*	*13·88*	*14·18*	*14·48*	*14·78*
5 05·5	**4 57·9**	**4 50·7**	**4 43·8**	**4 37·2**	**4 31·0**	**4 25·0**	**4 19·3**	**4 13·8**	**4 08·5**	**4 03·5**
11·79	*12·09*	*12·39*	*12·69*	*12·99*	*13·29*	*13·59*	*13·89*	*14·19*	*14·49*	*14·79*
5 05·2	**4 57·6**	**4 50·4**	**4 43·6**	**4 37·0**	**4 30·8**	**4 24·8**	**4 19·1**	**4 13·6**	**4 08·4**	**4 03·3**
11·80	*12·10*	*12·40*	*12·70*	*13·00*	*13·30*	*13·60*	*13·90*	*14·20*	*14·50*	*14·80*
5 05·0	**4 57·4**	**4 50·2**	**4 43·4**	**4 36·8**	**4 30·6**	**4 24·6**	**4 18·9**	**4 13·4**	**4 08·2**	**4 03·2**
11·81	*12·11*	*12·41*	*12·71*	*13·01*	*13·31*	*13·61*	*13·91*	*14·21*	*14·51*	*14·81*
5 04·7	**4 57·2**	**4 50·0**	**4 43·1**	**4 36·6**	**4 30·4**	**4 24·4**	**4 18·7**	**4 13·3**	**4 08·0**	**4 03·0**
11·82	*12·12*	*12·42*	*12·72*	*13·02*	*13·32*	*13·62*	*13·92*	*14·22*	*14·52*	*14·82*
5 04·4	**4 56·9**	**4 49·7**	**4 42·9**	**4 36·4**	**4 30·2**	**4 24·2**	**4 18·5**	**4 13·1**	**4 07·8**	**4 02·8**
11·83	*12·13*	*12·43*	*12·73*	*13·03*	*13·33*	*13·63*	*13·93*	*14·23*	*14·53*	*14·83*
5 04·2	**4 56·7**	**4 49·5**	**4 42·7**	**4 36·2**	**4 30·0**	**4 24·0**	**4 18·3**	**4 12·9**	**4 07·7**	**4 02·7**
11·84	*12·14*	*12·44*	*12·74*	*13·04*	*13·34*	*13·64*	*13·94*	*14·24*	*14·54*	*14·84*
5 03·9	**4 56·4**	**4 49·3**	**4 42·5**	**4 36·0**	**4 29·8**	**4 23·8**	**4 18·2**	**4 12·7**	**4 07·5**	**4 02·5**
11·85	*12·15*	*12·45*	*12·75*	*13·05*	*13·35*	*Knots*	*13·95*	*14·25*	*14·55*	*14·85*
5 03·7	**4 56·2**	**4 49·0**	**4 42·2**	**4 35·8**	**4 29·6**	**4 23·6**	**4 18·0**	**4 12·5**	**4 07·3**	**4 02·3**
11·86	*12·16*	*12·46*	*12·76*	*13·06*	*13·36*	*13·66*	*13·96*	*14·26*	*14·56*	*14·86*
5 03·4	**4 55·9**	**4 48·8**	**4 42·0**	**4 35·5**	**4 29·4**	**4 23·4**	**4 17·8**	**4 12·4**	**4 07·2**	**4 02·2**
11·87	*12·17*	*12·47*	*12·77*	*13·07*	*13·37*	*13·67*	*13·97*	*14·27*	*14·57*	*14·87*
5 03·2	**4 55·7**	**4 48·6**	**4 41·8**	**4 35·3**	**4 29·2**	**4 23·3**	**4 17·6**	**4 12·2**	**4 07·0**	**4 02·0**
11·88	*12·18*	*12·48*	*12·78*	*13·08*	*13·38*	*13·68*	*13·98*	*14·28*	*14·58*	*14·88*
5 02·9	**4 55·4**	**4 48·3**	**4 41·6**	**4 35·1**	**4 29·0**	**4 23·1**	**4 17·4**	**4 12·0**	**4 06·8**	**4 01·9**
11·89	*12·19*	*12·49*	*12·79*	*13·09*	*13·39*	*13·69*	*13·99*	*14·29*	*14·59*	*14·89*
5 02·6	**4 55·2**	**4 48·1**	**4 41·4**	**4 34·9**	**4 28·8**	**4 22·9**	**4 17·2**	**4 11·8**	**4 06·7**	**4 01·7**
11·90	*12·20*	*12·50*	*12·80*	*13·10*	*13·40*	*13·70*	*14·00*	*14·30*	*14·60*	*14·90*
5 02·4	**4 55·0**	**4 47·9**	**4 41·1**	**4 34·7**	**4 28·6**	**4 22·7**	**4 17·1**	**4 11·7**	**4 06·5**	**4 01·5**

MEASURED MILE SPEED TABLE

Time to Steam One Mile in Minutes and Seconds

Speed in Knots

4 01·7	3 56·9	3 52·3	3 47·9	3 43·7	3 39·6	3 35·6	3 31·8	3 28·2	3 24·6	3 21·2
14·90	*15·20*	*15·50*	*15·80*	*16·10*	*16·40*	*16·70*	*17·00*	*17·30*	*17·60*	*17·90*
4 01·5	3 56·8	3 52·2	3 47·8	3 43·5	3 39·4	3 35·5	3 31·7	3 28·0	3 24·5	3 21·1
14·91	*15·21*	*15·51*	*15·81*	*16·11*	*16·41*	*16·71*	*17·01*	*17·31*	*17·61*	*17·91*
4 01·4	3 56·6	3 52·0	3 47·6	3 43·4	3 39·3	3 35·4	3 31·6	3 27·9	3 24·4	3 20·9
14·92	*15·22*	*15·52*	*15·82*	*16·12*	*16·42*	*16·72*	*17·02*	*17·32*	*17·62*	*17·92*
4 01·2	3 56·5	3 51·9	3 47·5	3 43·3	3 39·2	3 35·2	3 31·5	3 27·8	3 24·3	3 20·8
14·93	*15·23*	*15·53*	*15·83*	*16·13*	*16·43*	*16·73*	*17·03*	*17·33*	*17·63*	*17·93*
4 01·0	3 56·3	3 51·7	3 47·3	3 43·1	3 39·0	3 35·1	3 31·3	3 27·7	3 24·1	3 20·7
14·94	*15·24*	*15·54*	*15·84*	*16·14*	*16·44*	*16·74*	*17·04*	*17·34*	*17·64*	*17·94*
4 00·9	3 56·1	3 51·6	3 47·2	3 43·0	3 38·9	3 35·0	3 31·2	3 27·6	3 24·0	3 20·6
14·95	*15·25*	*15·55*	*15·85*	*16·15*	*16·45*	*16·75*	*17·05*	*17·35*	*17·65*	*17·95*
4 00·7	3 56·0	3 51·4	3 47·1	3 42·8	3 38·8	3 34·9	3 31·1	3 27·4	3 23·9	3 20·5
14·96	*15·26*	*15·56*	*15·86*	*16·16*	*16·46*	*16·76*	*17·06*	*17·36*	*17·66*	*17·96*
4 00·6	3 55·8	3 51·3	3 46·9	3 42·7	3 38·6	3 34·7	3 31·0	3 27·3	3 23·8	3 20·4
14·97	*15·27*	*15·57*	*15·87*	*16·17*	*16·47*	*16·77*	*17·07*	*17·37*	*17·67*	*17·97*
4 00·4	3 55·7	3 51·1	3 46·8	3 42·6	3 38·5	3 34·6	3 30·8	3 27·2	3 23·7	3 20·3
14·98	*15·28*	*15·58*	*15·88*	*16·18*	*16·48*	*16·78*	*17·08*	*17·38*	*17·68*	*17·98*
4 00·2	3 55·5	3 51·0	3 46·6	3 42·4	3 38·4	3 34·5	3 30·7	3 27·1	3 23·6	3 20·2
14·99	*15·29*	*15·59*	*15·89*	*16·19*	*16·49*	*16·79*	*17·09*	*17·39*	*17·69*	*17·99*
4 00·1	3 55·4	3 50·8	3 46·5	3 42·3	3 38·2	3 34·3	3 30·6	3 27·0	3 23·4	3 20·1
15·00	*15·30*	*15·60*	*15·90*	*16·20*	*16·50*	*16·80*	*17·10*	*17·40*	*17·70*	*18·00*
3 59·9	3 55·2	3 50·7	3 46·3	3 42·2	3 38·1	3 34·2	3 30·5	3 26·8	3 23·3	3 19·9
15·01	*15·31*	*15·61*	*15·91*	*16·21*	*16·51*	*16·81*	*17·11*	*17·41*	*17·71*	*18·01*
3 59·8	3 55·1	3 50·5	3 46·2	3 42·0	3 38·0	3 34·1	3 30·3	3 26·7	3 23·2	3 19·8
15·02	*15·32*	*15·62*	*15·92*	*16·22*	*16·52*	*16·82*	*17·12*	*17·42*	*17·72*	*18·02*
3 59·6	3 54·9	3 50·4	3 46·1	3 41·9	3 37·9	3 34·0	3 30·2	3 26·6	3 23·1	3 19·7
15·03	*15·33*	*15·63*	*15·93*	*16·23*	*16·53*	*16·83*	*17·13*	*17·43*	*17·73*	*18·03*
3 59·4	3 54·8	3 50·3	3 45·9	3 41·7	3 37·7	3 33·8	3 30·1	3 26·5	3 23·0	3 19·6
15·04	*15·34*	*15·64*	*15·94*	*16·24*	*16·54*	*16·84*	*17·14*	*17·44*	*17·74*	*18·04*
3 59·3	3 54·6	3 50·1	3 45·8	3 41·6	3 37·6	3 33·7	3 30·0	3 26·4	3 22·9	3 19·5
15·05	*15·35*	*15·65*	*15·95*	*16·25*	*16·55*	*16·85*	*17·15*	*17·45*	*17·75*	*18·05*
3 59·1	3 54·5	3 50·0	3 45·6	3 41·5	3 37·5	3 33·6	3 29·9	3 26·2	3 22·8	3 19·4
15·06	*15·36*	*15·66*	*15·96*	*16·26*	*16·56*	*16·86*	*17·16*	*17·46*	*17·76*	*18·06*
3 59·0	3 54·3	3 49·8	3 45·5	3 41·3	3 37·3	3 33·5	3 29·7	3 26·1	3 22·6	3 19·3
15·07	*15·37*	*15·67*	*15·97*	*16·27*	*16·57*	*16·87*	*17·17*	*17·47*	*17·77*	*18·07*
3 58·8	3 54·1	3 49·7	3 45·4	3 41·2	3 37·2	3 33·3	3 29·6	3 26·0	3 22·5	3 19·2
15·08	*15·38*	*15·68*	*15·98*	*16·28*	*16·58*	*16·88*	*17·18*	*17·48*	*17·78*	*18·08*
3 58·6	3 54·0	3 49·5	3 45·2	3 41·1	3 37·1	3 33·2	3 29·5	3 25·9	3 22·4	3 19·1
15·09	*15·39*	*15·69*	*15·99*	*16·29*	*16·59*	*16·89*	*17·19*	*17·49*	*17·79*	*18·09*
3 58·5	3 53·8	3 49·4	3 45·1	3 40·9	3 36·9	3 33·1	3 29·4	3 25·8	3 22·3	3 18·9
15·10	*15·40*	*15·70*	*16·00*	*16·30*	*16·60*	*16·90*	*17·20*	*17·50*	*17·80*	*18·10*
3 58·3	3 53·7	3 49·2	3 44·9	3 40·8	3 36·8	3 33·0	3 29·2	3 25·7	3 22·2	3 18·8
15·11	*15·41*	*15·71*	*16·01*	*16·31*	*16·61*	*16·91*	*17·21*	*17·51*	*17·81*	*18·11*
3 58·2	3 53·5	3 49·1	3 44·8	3 40·7	3 36·7	3 32·8	3 29·1	3 25·5	3 22·1	3 18·7
15·12	*15·42*	*15·72*	*16·02*	*16·32*	*16·62*	*16·92*	*17·22*	*17·52*	*17·82*	*18·12*
3 58·0	3 53·4	3 48·9	3 44·6	3 40·5	3 36·5	3 32·7	3 29·0	3 25·4	3 22·0	3 18·6
15·13	*15·43*	*15·73*	*16·03*	*16·33*	*16·63*	*16·93*	*17·23*	*17·53*	*17·83*	*18·13*
3 57·9	3 53·2	3 48·8	3 44·5	3 40·5	3 36·4	3 32·6	3 28·9	3 25·3	3 21·9	3 18·5
15·14	*15·44*	*15·74*	*16·04*	*16·34*	*16·64*	*16·94*	*17·24*	*17·54*	*17·84*	*18·14*
3 57·7	3 53·1	3 48·6	3 44·4	3 40·3	3 36·3	3 32·5	3 28·8	3 25·2	3 21·7	3 18·4
15·15	*15·45*	*15·75*	*16·05*	*16·35*	*16·65*	*16·95*	*17·25*	*17·55*	*17·85*	*18·15*
3 57·5	3 52·9	3 48·5	3 44·2	3 40·1	3 36·2	3 32·3	3 28·6	3 25·1	3 21·6	3 18·3
15·16	*15·46*	*15·76*	*16·06*	*16·36*	*16·66*	*16·96*	*17·26*	*17·56*	*17·86*	*18·16*
3 57·4	3 52·8	3 48·4	3 44·1	3 40·0	3 36·0	3 32·2	3 28·5	3 25·0	3 21·5	3 18·2
15·17	*15·47*	*15·77*	*16·07*	*16·37*	*16·67*	*16·97*	*17·27*	*17·57*	*17·87*	*18·17*
3 57·2	3 52·6	3 48·2	3 44·0	3 39·8	3 35·9	3 32·1	3 28·4	3 24·8	3 21·4	3 18·1
15·18	*15·48*	*15·78*	*16·08*	*16·38*	*16·68*	*16·98*	*17·28*	*17·58*	*17·88*	*18·18*
3 57·1	3 52·5	3 48·1	3 43·8	3 39·7	3 35·8	3 32·0	3 28·3	3 24·7	3 21·3	3 18·0
15·19	*15·49*	*15·79*	*16·09*	*16·39*	*16·69*	*16·99*	*17·29*	*17·59*	*17·89*	*18·19*
3 56·9	3 52·3	3 47·9	3 43·7	3 39·6	3 35·6	3 31·8	3 28·2	3 24·6	3 21·2	3 17·9
15·20	*15·50*	*15·80*	*16·10*	*16·40*	*16·70*	*17·00*	*17·30*	*17·60*	*17·90*	*18·20*
3 56·8	3 52·2	3 47·8	3 43·5	3 39·4	3 35·5	3 31·7	3 28·0	3 24·5	3 21·1	**3 17·7**

MEASURED MILE SPEED TABLE

Time to Steam One Mile in Minutes and Seconds

Speed in Knots

3 17·9	**3 14·6**	**3 11·5**	**3 08·5**	**3 05·6**	**3 02·8**	**—**	**2 57·4**	**2 54·8**	**2 52·3**	**2 49·9**
18·20	*18·50*	*18·80*	*19·10*	*19·40*	*19·70*	*20·00*	*20·30*	*20·60*	*20·90*	*21·20*
3 17·7	**3 14·5**	**3 11·4**	**3 08·4**	**3 05·5**	**3 02·7**	**—**	**2 57·3**	**2 54·7**	**2 52·2**	**2 49·8**
18·21	*18·51*	*18·81*	*19·11*	*19·41*	*19·71*	*20·01*	*20·31*	*20·61*	*20·91*	*21·21*
3 17·6	**3 14·4**	**3 11·3**	**3 08·3**	**3 05·4**	**3 02·6**	**2 59·9**	**2 57·2**	**2 54·6**	**2 52·1**	**2 49·7**
18·22	*18·52*	*18·82*	*19·12*	*19·42*	*19·72*	*20·02*	*20·32*	*20·62*	*20·92*	*21·22*
3 17·5	**3 14·3**	**3 11·2**	**3 08·2**	**3 05·3**	**3 02·5**	**2 59·8**	**2 57·1**	**2 54·5**	**2 52·0**	**2 49·6**
18·23	*18·53*	*18·83*	*19·13*	*19·43*	*19·73*	*20·03*	*20·33*	*20·63*	*20·93*	*21·23*
3 17·4	**3 14·2**	**3 11·1**	**3 08·1**	**3 05·2**	**3 02·4**	**2 59·7**	**2 57·0**	**—**	**—**	**2 49·5**
18·24	*18·54*	*18·84*	*19·14*	*19·44*	*19·74*	*20·04*	*20·34*	*20·64*	*20·94*	*21·24*
3 17·3	**3 14·1**	**3 11·0**	**3 08·0**	**3 05·1**	**3 02·3**	**2 59·6**	**2 56·9**	**2 54·4**	**2 51·9**	**—**
18·25	*18·55*	*18·85*	*19·15*	*19·45*	*19·75*	*20·05*	*20·35*	*20·65*	*20·95*	*21·25*
3 17·2	**3 14·0**	**3 10·9**	**3 07·9**	**3 05·0**	**3 02·2**	**2 59·5**	**—**	**2 54·3**	**2 51·8**	**2 49·4**
18·26	*18·56*	*18·86*	*19·16*	*19·46*	*19·76*	*20·06*	*20·36*	*20·66*	*20·96*	*21·26*
3 17·1	**3 13·9**	**3 10·8**	**3 07·8**	**3 04·9**	**3 02·1**	**2 59·4**	**2 56·8**	**2 54·2**	**2 51·7**	**2 49·3**
18·27	*18·57*	*18·87*	*19·17*	*19·47*	*19·77*	*20·07*	*20·37*	*20·67*	*20·97*	*21·27*
3 17·0	**3 13·8**	**3 10·7**	**3 07·7**	**—**	**3 02·0**	**2 59·3**	**2 56·7**	**2 54·1**	**2 51·6**	**2 49·2**
18·28	*18·58*	*18·88*	*19·18*	*19·48*	*19·78*	*20·08*	*20·38*	*20·68*	*20·98*	*21·28*
3 16·9	**3 13·7**	**3 10·6**	**3 07·6**	**3 04·8**	**—**	**2 59·2**	**2 56·6**	**2 54·0**	**—**	**2 49·1**
18·29	*18·59*	*18·89*	*19·19*	*19·49*	*19·79*	*20·09*	*20·39*	*20·69*	*20·99*	*21·29*
3 16·8	**3 13·6**	**3 10·5**	**3 07·5**	**3 04·7**	**3 01·9**	**2 59·1**	**2 56·5**	**—**	**2 51·5**	**—**
18·30	*18·60*	*18·90*	*19·20*	*19·50*	*19·80*	*20·10*	*20·40*	*20·70*	*21·00*	*21·30*
3 16·7	**3 13·5**	**3 10·4**	**—**	**3 04·6**	**3 01·8**	**—**	**2 56·4**	**2 53·9**	**2 51·4**	**2 49·0**
18·31	*18·61*	*18·91*	*19·21*	*19·51*	*19·81*	*20·11*	*20·41*	*20·71*	*21·01*	*21·31*
3 16·6	**3 13·4**	**3 10·3**	**3 07·4**	**3 04·5**	**3 01·7**	**2 59·0**	**2 56·3**	**2 53·8**	**2 51·3**	**2 48·9**
18·32	*18·62*	*18·92*	*19·22*	*19·52*	*19·82*	*20·12*	*20·42*	*20·72*	*21·02*	*21·32*
3 16·5	**3 13·3**	**3 10·2**	**3 07·3**	**3 04·4**	**3 01·6**	**2 58·9**	**—**	**2 53·7**	**2 51·2**	**2 48·8**
18·33	*18·63*	*18·93*	*19·23*	*19·53*	*19·83*	*20·13*	*20·43*	*20·73*	*21·03*	*21·33*
3 16·3	**3 13·2**	**3 10·1**	**3 07·2**	**3 04·3**	**3 01·5**	**2 58·8**	**2 56·2**	**2 53·6**	**2 51·1**	**2 48·7**
18·34	*18·64*	*18·94*	*19·24*	*19·54*	*19·84*	*20·14*	*20·44*	*20·74*	*21·04*	*21·34*
3 16·2	**3 13·1**	**3 10·0**	**3 07·1**	**3 04·2**	**3 01·4**	**2 58·7**	**2 56·1**	**2 53·5**	**—**	**—**
18·35	*18·65*	*18·95*	*19·25*	*19·55*	*19·85*	*20·15*	*20·45*	*20·75*	*21·05*	*21·35*
3 16·1	**3 13·0**	**3 09·9**	**3 07·0**	**3 04·1**	**3 01·3**	**2 58·6**	**2 56·0**	**—**	**2 51·0**	**2 48·6**
18·36	*18·66*	*18·96*	*19·26*	*19·56*	*19·86*	*20·16*	*20·46*	*20·76*	*21·06*	*21·36*
3 16·0	**3 12·9**	**3 09·8**	**3 06·9**	**3 04·0**	**3 01·2**	**2 58·5**	**2 55·9**	**2 53·4**	**2 50·9**	**2 48·5**
18·37	*18·67*	*18·97*	*19·27*	*19·57*	*19·87*	*20·17*	*20·47*	*20·77*	*21·07*	*21·37*
3 15·9	**3 12·8**	**3 09·7**	**3 06·8**	**3 03·9**	**3 01·1**	**2 58·4**	**2 55·8**	**2 53·3**	**2 50·8**	**2 48·4**
18·38	*18·68*	*18·98*	*19·28*	*19·58*	*19·88*	*20·18*	*20·48*	*20·78*	*21·08*	*21·38*
3 15·8	**3 12·7**	**3 09·6**	**3 06·7**	**3 03·8**	**3 01·0**	**—**	**2 55·7**	**2 53·2**	**2 50·7**	**2 48·3**
18·39	*18·69*	*18·99*	*19·29*	*19·59*	*19·89*	*20·19*	*20·49*	*20·79*	*21·09*	*21·39*
3 15·7	**3 12·6**	**3 09·5**	**3 06·6**	**3 03·7**	**3 00·9**	**2 58·3**	**—**	**2 53·1**	**—**	**—**
18·40	*18·70*	*19·00*	*19·30*	*19·60*	*19·90*	*20·20*	*20·50*	*20·80*	*21·10*	*21·40*
3 15·6	**3 12·5**	**3 09·4**	**3 06·5**	**3 03·6**	**—**	**2 58·2**	**2 55·6**	**2 53·0**	**2 50·6**	**2 48·2**
18·41	*18·71*	*19·01*	*19·31*	*19·61*	*19·91*	*20·21*	*20·51*	*20·81*	*21·11*	*21·41*
3 15·5	**3 12·4**	**3 09·3**	**3 06·4**	**3 03·5**	**3 00·8**	**2 58·1**	**2 55·5**	**—**	**2 50·5**	**2 48·1**
18·42	*18·72*	*19·02*	*19·32*	*19·62*	*19·92*	*20·22*	*20·52*	*20·82*	*21·12*	*21·42*
3 15·4	**3 12·3**	**3 09·2**	**3 06·3**	**3 03·4**	**3 00·7**	**2 58·0**	**2 55·4**	**2 52·9**	**2 50·4**	**2 48·0**
18·43	*18·73*	*19·03*	*19·33*	*19·63*	*19·93*	*20·23*	*20·53*	*20·83*	*21·13*	*21·43*
3 15·3	**3 12·2**	**3 09·1**	**3 06·2**	**3 03·3**	**3 00·6**	**2 57·9**	**2 55·3**	**2 52·8**	**2 50·3**	**2 47·9**
18·44	*18·74*	*19·04*	*19·34*	*19·64*	*19·94*	*20·24*	*20·54*	*20·84*	*21·14*	*21·44*
3 15·2	**3 12·1**	**3 09·0**	**3 06·1**	**—**	**3 00·5**	**2 57·8**	**2 55·2**	**2 52·7**	**—**	**—**
18·45	*18·75*	*19·05*	*19·35*	*19·65*	*19·95*	*20·25*	*20·55*	*20·85*	*21·15*	*21·45*
3 15·1	**3 11·9**	**3 08·9**	**3 06·0**	**3 03·2**	**3 00·4**	**2 57·7**	**2 55·1**	**2 52·6**	**2 50·2**	**2 47·8**
18·46	*18·76*	*19·06*	*19·36*	*19·66*	*19·96*	*20·26*	*20·56*	*20·86*	*21·16*	*21·46*
3 15·0	**3 11·8**	**3 08·8**	**3 05·9**	**3 03·1**	**3 00·3**	**2 57·6**	**—**	**2 52·5**	**2 50·1**	**2 47·7**
18·47	*18·77*	*19·07*	*19·37*	*19·67*	*19·97*	*20·27*	*20·57*	*20·87*	*21·17*	*21·47*
3 14·9	**3 11·7**	**3 08·7**	**3 05·8**	**3 03·0**	**3 00·2**	**—**	**2 55·0**	**—**	**2 50·0**	**2 47·6**
18·48	*18·78*	*19·08*	*19·38*	*19·68*	*19·98*	*20·28*	*20·58*	*20·88*	*21·18*	*21·48*
3 14·8	**3 11·6**	**3 08·6**	**3 05·7**	**3 02·9**	**3 00·1**	**2 57·5**	**2 54·9**	**2 52·4**	**2 49·9**	**—**
18·49	*18·79*	*19·09*	*19·39*	*19·69*	*19·99*	*20·29*	*20·59*	*20·89*	*21·19*	*21·49*
3 14·6	**3 11·5**	**3 08·5**	**3 05·6**	**3 02·8**	**3 00·0**	**2 57·4**	**2 54·8**	**2 52·3**	**—**	**2 47·5**
18·50	*18·80*	*19·10*	*19·40*	*19·70*	*20·00*	*20·30*	*20·60*	*20·90*	*21·20*	*21·50*
3 14·5	**3 11·4**	**3 08·4**	**3 05·5**	**3 02·7**	**—**	**2 57·3**	**2 54·7**	**2 52·2**	**2 49·8**	**2 47·4**

MEASURED MILE SPEED TABLE

Time to Steam One Mile in Minutes and Seconds

Speed in Knots

2 47·5	**2 45·2**	**2 42·9**	**2 40·8**	**2 38·6**	**2 36·6**	**2 34·5**	**2 32·6**	**2 30·7**	**2 28·8**	**2 27·0**
21·50	*21·80*	*22·10*	*22·40*	*22·70*	*23·00*	*23·30*	*23·60*	*23·90*	*24·20*	*24·50*
2 47·4	**2 45·1**	—	**2 40·7**	—	**2 36·5**	—	**2 32·5**	**2 30·6**	**2 28·7**	**2 26·9**
21·51	*21·81*	*22·11*	*22·41*	*22·71*	*23·01*	*23·31*	*23·61*	*23·91*	*24·21*	*24·51*
2 47·3	**2 45·0**	**2 42·8**	**2 40·6**	**2 38·5**	**2 36·4**	**2 34·4**	**2 32·4**	**2 30·5**	—	**2 26·8**
21·52	*21·82*	*22·12*	*22·42*	*22·72*	*23·02*	*23·32*	*23·62*	*23·92*	*24·22*	*24·52*
2 47·2	**2 44·9**	**2 42·7**	**2 40·5**	**2 38·4**	—	**2 34·3**	—	—	**2 28·6**	—
21·53	*21·83*	*22·13*	*22·43*	*22·73*	*23·03*	*23·33*	*23·63*	*23·93*	*24·23*	*24·53*
—	—	**2 42·6**	—	**2 38·3**	**2 36·3**	—	**2 32·3**	**2 30·4**	**2 28·5**	**2 26·7**
21·54	*21·84*	*22·14*	*22·44*	*22·74*	*23·04*	*23·34*	*23·64*	*23·94*	*24·24*	*34·54*
2 47·1	**2 44·8**	—	**2 40·4**	—	**2 36·2**	**2 34·2**	—	**2 30·3**	—	—
21·55	*21·85*	*22·15*	*22·45*	*22·75*	*23·05*	*23·35*	*23·65*	*23·95*	*24·25*	*24·55*
2 47·0	**2 44·7**	**2 42·5**	**2 40·3**	**2 38·2**	**2 36·1**	**2 34·1**	**2 32·2**	—	**2 28·4**	**2 26·6**
21·56	*21·86*	*22·16*	*22·46*	*22·76*	*23·06*	*23·36*	*23·66*	*23·96*	*24·26*	*24·56*
2 46·9	**2 44·6**	**2 42·4**	**2 40·2**	**2 38·1**	—	—	**2 32·1**	**2 30·2**	—	**2 26·5**
21·57	*21·87*	*22·17*	*22·47*	*22·77*	*23·07*	*23·37*	*23·67*	*23·97*	*24·27*	*24·57*
—	—	**2 42·3**	— ·	—	**2 36·0**	**2 34·0**	—	—	**2·28·3**	—
21·58	*21·88*	*22·18*	*22·48*	*22·78*	*23·08*	*23·38*	*23·68*	*23·98*	*24·28*	*24·58*
2 46·8	**2 44·5**	—	**2 40·1**	**2 38·0**	**2 35·9**	**2 33·9**	**2 32·0**	**2 30·1**	**2 28·2**	**2 26·4**
21·59	*21·89*	*22·19*	*22·49*	*22·79*	*23·09*	*23·39*	*23·69*	*23·99*	*24·29*	*24·59*
2 46·7	**2 44·4**	**2 42·2**	**2 40·0**	**2 37·9**	**2 35·8**	—	**2 31·9**	**2 30·0**	—	—
21·60	*21·90*	*22·20*	*22·50*	*22·80*	*23·10*	*23·40*	*23·70*	*24·00*	*24·30*	*24·60*
2 46·6	**2 44·3**	**2 42·1**	—	—	—	**2 33·8**	—	—	**2 28·1**	**2 26·3**
21·61	*21·91*	*22·21*	*22·51*	*22·81*	*23·11*	*23·41*	*23·71*	*24·01*	*24·31*	*24·61*
—	—	—	**2 39·9**	**2 37·8**	**2 35·7**	**2 33·7**	**2 31·8**	**2 29·9**	—	—
21·62	*21·92*	*22·22*	*22·52*	*22·82*	*23·12*	*23·42*	*23·72*	*24·02*	*24·32*	*24·62*
2 46·5	**2 44·2**	**2 42·0**	**2 39·8**	**2 37·7**	—	—	**2 31·7**	**2 29·8**	**2 28·0**	**2 26·2**
21·63	*21·93*	*22·23*	*22·53*	*22·83*	*23·13*	*23·43*	*23·73*	*24·03*	*24·33*	*24·63*
2 46·4	**2 44·1**	**2 41·9**	—	—	**2 35·6**	**2 33·6**	—	—	**2 27·9**	**2 26·1**
21·64	*21·94*	*22·24*	*22·54*	*22·84*	*23·14*	*23·44*	*23·74*	*24·04*	*24·34*	*24·64*
2 46·3	**2 44·0**	**2 41·8**	**2 39·7**	**2 37·6**	**2 35·5**	—	**2 31·6**	**2 29·7**	—	—
21·65	*21·95*	*22·25*	*22·55*	*22·85*	*23·15*	*23·45*	*23·75*	*24·05*	*24·35*	*24·65*
2 46·2	—	—	**2 39·6**	**2 37·5**	—	**2 33·5**	**2 31·5**	—	**2 27·8**	**2 26·0**
21·66	*21·96*	*22·26*	*22·56*	*22·86*	*23·16*	*23·46*	*23·76*	*24·06*	*24·36*	*24·66*
—	**2 43·9**	**2 41·7**	**2 39·5**	**2 37·4**	**2 35·4**	**2 33·4**	—	**2 29·6**	—	—
21·67	*21·97*	*22·27*	*22·57*	*22·87*	*23·17*	*23·47*	*23·77*	*24·07*	*24·37*	*24·67*
2 46·1	**2 43·8**	**2 41·6**	—	—	**2 35·3**	—	**2 31·4**	**2 29·5**	**2 27·7**	**2 25·9**
21·68	*21·98*	*22·28*	*22·58*	*22·88*	*23·18*	*23·48*	*23·78*	*24·08*	*24·38*	*24·68*
2 46·0	**2 43·7**	**2 41·5**	**2 39·4**	**2 37·3**	—	**2 33·3**	—	—	**2 27·6**	**2 25·8**
21·69	*21·99*	*22·29*	*22·59*	*22·89*	*23·19*	*23·49*	*23·79*	*24·09*	*24·39*	*24·69*
2 45·9	—	—	**2 39·3**	**2 37·2**	**2 35·2**	**2 33·2**	**2 31·3**	**2 29·4**	—	—
21·70	*22·00*	*22·30*	*22·60*	*22·90*	*23·20*	*23·50*	*23·80*	*24·10*	*24·40*	*24·70*
—	**2 43·6**	**2 41·4**	—	—	**2 35·1**	—	**2 31·2**	**2 29·3**	**2 27·5**	**2 25·7**
21·71	*22·01*	*22·31*	*22·61*	*22·91*	*23·21*	*23·51*	*23·81*	*24·11*	*24·41*	*24·71*
2 45·8	**2 43·5**	**2 41·3**	**2 39·2**	**2 37·1**	—	**2 33·1**	—	—	—	—
21·72	*22·02*	*22·32*	*22·62*	*22·92*	*23·22*	*23·52*	*23·82*	*24·12*	*24·42*	*24·72*
2 45·7	—	—	**2 39·1**	**2 37·0**	**2 35·0**	**2 33·0**	**2 31·1**	**2 29·2**	**2 27·4**	**2 25·6**
21·73	*22·03*	*22·33*	*22·63*	*22·93*	*23·23*	*23·53*	*23·83*	*24·13*	*24·43*	*24·73*
2 45·6	**2 43·4**	**2 41·2**	**2 39·0**	—	**2 34·9**	—	**2 31·0**	—	**2 27·3**	**2 25·5**
21·74	*22·04*	*22·34*	*22·64*	*22·94*	*23·24*	*23·54*	*23·84*	*24·14*	*24·44*	*24·74*
—	**2 43·3**	**2 41·1**	—	**2 36·9**	—	**2 32·9**	—	**2 29·1**	—	—
21·75	*22·05*	*22·35*	*22·65*	*22·95*	*23·25*	*23·55*	*23·85*	*24·15*	*24·45*	*24·75*
2 45·5	**2 43·2**	**2 41·0**	**2 38·9**	**2 36·8**	**2 34·8**	**2 32·8**	**2 30·9**	**2 29·0**	**2 27·2**	**2 25·4**
21·76	*22·06*	*22·36*	*22·66*	*22·96*	*23·26*	*23·56*	*23·86*	*24·16*	*24·46*	*24·76*
2 45·4	—	—	**2 38·8**	—	**2 34·7**	—	**2 30·8**	—	**2 27·1**	—
21·77	*22·07*	*22·37*	*22·67*	*22·97*	*23·27*	*23·57*	*23·87*	*24·17*	*24·47*	*24·77*
2 45·3	**2 43·1**	**2 40·9**	—	**2 36·7**	—	**2 32·7**	—	**2 28·9**	—	**2 25·3**
21·78	*22·08*	*22·38*	*22·68*	*22·98*	*23·28*	*23·58*	*23·88*	*24·18*	*24·48*	*24·78*
—	**2 43·0**	**2 40·8**	**2 38·7**	**2 36·6**	**2 34·6**	**2 32·6**	**2 30·7**	—	**2 27·0**	**2 25·2**
21·79	*22·09*	*22·39*	*22·69*	*22·99*	*23·29*	*23·59*	*23·89*	*24·19*	*24·49*	*24·79*
2 45·2	**2 42·9**	—	**2 38·6**	—	**2 34·5**	—	—	**2 28·8**	—	—
21·80	*22·10*	*22·40*	*22·70*	*23·00*	*23·30*	*23·60*	*23·90*	*24·20*	*24·50*	*24·80*
2 45·1	—	**2 40·7**	—	**2 36·5**	—	**2 32·5**	**2 30·6**	**2 28·7**	**2 26·9**	**2 25·1**

MEASURED MILE SPEED TABLE

Time to Steam One Mile in Minutes and Seconds

Speed in Knots

2 25·2	2 23·5	2 21·8	2 20·1	2 18·5	2 16·9	2 15·4	2 13·9	2 12·4	2 10·9	2 09·5
24·80	25·10	25·40	25·70	26·00	26·30	26·60	26·90	27·20	27·50	27·80
2 25·1	2 23·4	2 21·7	—	2 18·4	—	2 15·3	2 13·8	2 12·3	—	—
24·81	25·11	25·41	25·71	26·01	26·31	26·61	26·91	27·21	27·51	27·81
—	2 23·3	2 21·6	2 20·0	—	2 16·8	—	—	—	2 10·8	2 09·4
24·82	25·12	25·42	25·72	26·02	26·32	26·62	26·92	27·22	27·52	27·82
2 25·0	—	—	2 19·9	2 18·3	—	2 15·2	2 13·7	2 12·2	—	—
24·83	25·13	25·43	25·73	26·03	26·33	26·63	26·93	27·23	27·53	27·83
—	2 23·2	2 21·5	—	—	2 16·7	—	—	—	2 10·7	2 09·3
24·84	25·14	25·44	25·74	26·04	26·34	26·64	26·94	27·24	27·54	27·84
2 24·9	—	—	2 19·8	2 18·2	2 16·6	2 15·1	2 13·6	2 12·1	—	—
24·85	25·15	25·45	25·75	26·05	26·35	26·65	26·95	27·25	27·55	27·85
2 24·8	2 23·1	2 21·4	—	—	—	—	—	—	2 10·6	2 09·2
24·86	25·16	25·46	25·76	26·06	26·36	26·66	26·96	27·26	27·56	27·86
—	—	—	2 19·7	2 18·1	2 16·5	2 15·0	2 13·5	2 12·0	—	—
24·87	25·17	25·47	25·77	26·07	26·37	26·67	26·97	27·27	25·57	27·87
2 24·7	2 23·0	2 21·3	—	—	—	—	—	—	—	2 09·1
24·88	25·18	25·48	25·78	26·08	26·38	26·68	26·98	27·28	27·58	27·88
—	2 22·9	—	2 19·6	2 18·0	2 16·4	2 14·9	2 13·4	2 11·9	2 10·5	—
24·89	25·19	25·49	25·79	26·09	26·39	26·69	26·99	27·29	27·59	27·89
2 24·6	—	2 21·2	—	—	—	—	—	—	—	—
24·90	25·20	25·50	25·80	26·10	26·40	26·70	27·00	27·30	27·60	27·90
2 24·5	2 22·8	2 21·1	2 19·5	2 17·9	2 16·3	2 14·8	2 13·3	2 11·8	2 10·4	2 09·0
24·91	25·21	25·51	25·81	26·11	26·41	26·71	27·01	27·31	27·61	27·91
24·92	25·22	25·52	25·82	26·12	26·42	26·72	27·02	27·32	27·62	27·92
2 24·4	2 22·7	2 21·0	2 19·4	2 17·8	2 16·2	2 14·7	2 13·2	2 11·7	2 10·3	2 08·9
24·93	25·23	25·53	25·83	26·13	26·43	26·73	27·03	27·33	27·63	27·93
—	—	—	2 19·3	2 17·7	—	—	—	—	—	—
24·94	25·24	25·54	25·84	26·14	26·44	26·74	27·04	27·34	27·64	27·94
2 24·3	2 22·6	2 20·9	—	—	2 16·1	2 14·6	2 13·1	—	2 10·2	2 08·8
24·95	25·25	25·55	25·85	26·15	26·45	26·75	27·05	27·35	27·65	27·95
—	2 22·5	—	2 19·2	2 17·6	—	—	—	2 11·6	—	—
24·96	25·26	25·56	25·86	26·16	26·46	26·76	27·06	27·36	27·66	27·96
2 24·2	—	2 20·8	—	—	2 16·0	2 14·5	2 13·0	—	2 10·1	2 08·7
24·97	25·27	25·57	25·87	26·17	26·47	26·77	27·07	27·37	27·67	27·97
2 24·1	2 22·4	—	2 19·1	2 17·5	—	—	—	2 11·5	—	—
24·98	25·28	25·58	25·88	26·18	26·48	26·78	27·08	27·38	27·68	27·98
—	—	2 20·7	—	—	2 15·9	2 14·4	2 12·9	—	2 10·0	2 08·6
24·99	25·29	25·59	25·89	26·19	26·49	26·79	27·09	27·39	27·69	27·99
2 24·0	2 22·3	—	2 19·0	2 17·4	—	—	—	2 11·4	—	—
25·00	25·30	25·60	25·90	26·20	26·50	26·80	27·10	27·40	27·70	28·00
—	—	2 20·6	—	—	2 15·8	2 14·3	2 12·8	—	2 09·9	2 08·5
25·01	25·31	25·61	25·91	26·21	26·51	26·81	27·11	27·41	27·71	28·01
2 23·9	2 22·2	2 20·5	2 18·9	2 17·3	—	—	—	2 11·3	—	—
25·02	25·32	25·62	25·92	26·22	26·52	26·82	27·12	27·42	27·72	28·02
—	—	—	—	—	2 15·7	2 14·2	2 12·7	—	2 09·8	—
25·03	25·33	25·63	25·93	26·23	26·53	26·83	27·13	27·43	27·73	28·03
2 23·8	2 22·1	2 20·4	2 18·8	2 17·2	—	—	—	2 11·2	—	2 08·4
25·04	25·34	25·64	25·94	26·24	26·54	26·84	27·14	27·44	27·74	28·04
2 23·7	2 22·0	—	—	—	2 15·6	2 14·1	2 12·6	—	—	—
25·05	25·35	25·65	25·95	26·25	26·55	26·85	27·15	27·45	27·75	28·05
—	—	2 20·3	2 18·7	2 17·1	—	—	—	2 11·1	2 09·7	2 08·3
25·06	25·36	25·66	25·96	26·26	26·56	26·86	27·16	27·46	27·76	28·06
2 23·6	2 21·9	—	2 18·6	—	2 15·5	2 14·0	2 12·5	—	—	—
25·07	25·37	25·67	25·97	26·27	26·57	26·87	27·17	27·47	27·77	28·07
—	—	2 20·2	—	2 17·0	—	—	—	2 11·0	2 09·6	2 08·2
25·08	25·38	25·68	25·98	26·28	26·58	26·88	27·18	27·48	27·78	28·08
2 23·5	2 21·8	—	2 18·5	—	2 15·4	2 13·9	2 12·4	—	—	—
25·09	25·39	25·69	25·99	26·29	26·59	26·89	27·19	27·49	27·79	28·09
—	—	2 20·1	—	2 16·9	—	—	—	2 10·9	2 09·5	2 08·1
25·10	25·40	25·70	26·00	26·30	26·60	26·90	27·20	27·50	27·80	28·10
2 23·4	2 21·7	—	2 18·4	—	2 15·3	2 13·8	2 12·3	—	—	—

DISTANCE BY VERTICAL ANGLE

Height of Object

Values are given as degrees and minutes (° '). Column headers show Height of Object in metres (m) and feet (ft).

Distance mls	m 7 / ft 23	8.5 / 28	10 / 33	11.5 / 38	13 / 43	14.5 / 48	16 / 52	17.5 / 57	19 / 62	20.5 / 67	22' / 72	23.5 / 77	25 / 82	26.5 / 87
0.1	2 10	2 38	3 05	3 33	4 01	4 12	4 56	5 24	5 51	6 19	6 46	7 14	7 41	8 09
.2	1 05	1 19	1 33	1 47	2 01	2 14	2 28	2 44	2 56	3 10	3 24	3 38	3 52	4 06
.3	0 43	0 53	1 02	1 11	1 20	1 17	1 39	1 48	1 58	2 07	2 16	2 25	2 35	2 44
.4	0 33	0 39	0 46	0 53	1 03	1 07	1 14	1 21	1 28	1 35	1 42	1 49	1 56	2 03
0.5	0 26	0 32	0 37	0 43	0 48	0 54	0 59	1 05	1 11	1 16	1 22	1 27	1 33	1 38
.6	0 22	0 26	0 31	0 36	0 40	0 45	0 49	0 54	0 59	1 03	1 08	1 13	1 17	1 22
.7	0 19	0 23	0 27	0 30	0 34	0 38	0 42	0 46	0 50	0 54	0 58	1 02	1 06	1 10
.8	0 16	0 20	0 23	0 27	0 30	0 34	0 37	0 41	0 44	0 47	0 51	0 55	0 58	1 01
.9	0 14	0 18	0 21	0 24	0 27	0 30	0 33	0 36	0 39	0 42	0 45	0 48	0 52	0 55
1.0	0 13	0 16	0 19	0 21	0 24	0 27	0 30	0 32	0 35	0 38	0 41	0 44	0 46	0 49
.1	0 12	0 14	0 17	0 19	0 22	0 24	0 27	0 30	0 32	0 34	0 37	0 40	0 42	0 45
.2	0 11	0 13	0 15	0 18	0 20	0 22	0 25	0 27	0 29	0 32	0 34	0 36	0 39	0 41
.3	0 10	0 12	0 14	0 16	0 19	0 21	0 23	0 25	0 27	0 29	0 31	0 34	0 36	0 38
.4	0 9	0 11	0 13	0 15	0 17	0 19	0 21	0 23	0 25	0 27	0 29	0 31	0 33	0 35
1.5	0 9	0 11	0 12	0 14	0 16	0 18	0 20	0 21	0 24	0 25	0 27	0 29	0 31	0 33
.6	0 8	0 10	0 12	0 13	0 15	0 17	0 19	0 20	0 22	0 24	0 26	0 27	0 29	0 31
.7		0 9	0 11	0 13	0 14	0 16	0 17	0 19	0 21	0 22	0 24	0 26	0 27	0 29
.8		0 9	0 10	0 12	0 13	0 15	0 16	0 18	0 20	0 21	0 23	0 24	0 26	0 27
.9		0 8	0 10	0 11	0 13	0 14	0 16	0 17	0 19	0 20	0 21	0 23	0 24	0 26
2.0			0 9	0 11	0 12	0 13	0 15	0 16	0 18	0 19	0 20	0 22	0 23	0 25
.1			0 9	0 10	0 11	0 13	0 14	0 15	0 17	0 18	0 19	0 21	0 22	0 23
.2			0 8	0 10	0 11	0 12	0 13	0 15	0 16	0 17	0 19	0 20	0 21	0 22
.3				0 9	0 10	0 12	0 13	0 14	0 15	0 17	0 18	0 19	0 20	0 21
.4				0 9	0 10	0 11	0 12	0 14	0 15	0 16	0 17	0 18	0 19	0 20
2.5					0 10	0 11	0 12	0 13	0 14	0 15	0 16	0 17	0 19	0 20
.6					0 9	0 10	0 11	0 12	0 14	0 15	0 16	0 17	0 18	0 19
.7					0 9	0 10	0 11	0 12	0 13	0 14	0 15	0 16	0 17	0 18
.8						0 10	0 11	0 12	0 13	0 14	0 15	0 16	0 17	0 18
.9						0 9	0 10	0 11	0 12	0 13	0 14	0 15	0 16	0 17
3.0							0 10	0 11	0 12	0 13	0 14	0 15	0 15	0 16
.2							0 9	0 10	0 11	0 12	0 13	0 14	0 14	0 15
.4								0 10	0 10	0 11	0 12	0 13	0 14	0 14
.6								0 9	0 10	0 11	0 11	0 12	0 13	0 14
.8								0 9	0 9	0 10	0 11	0 11	0 12	0 13
4.0								0 8	0 9	0 10	0 10	0 11	0 12	0 12
.2									0 8	0 9	0 10	0 10	0 11	0 12
.4										0 9	0 9	0 10	0 11	0 11
.6										0 8	0 9	0 9	0 10	0 11
.8												0 9	0 10	0 10
5.0													0 9	0 10

Tan. $\theta = \dfrac{h}{d}$. Where θ = vertical angle, h = height of object, and d = distance.

DISTANCE BY VERTICAL ANGLE

Height of Object

Distance mls	m 26.5 / ft 87	28 / 92	29.5 / 97	31 / 102	32.5 / 107	34 / 112	35.5 / 116	37 / 121	38.5 / 126	40 / 131	41.5 / 136	43 / 141	44.5 / 146	46 / 151
	° ′	° ′	° ′	° ′	° ′	° ′	° ′	° ′	° ′	° ′	° ′	° ′	° ′	° ′
0.1	8 09	8 36	9 03	9 30	9 57	10 24	10 51	11 18	11 45	12 11	12 38	13 04	13 31	13 57
.2	4 06	4 19	4 33	4 47	5 09	5 15	5 28	5 42	5 56	6 10	6 24	6 37	6 51	7 05
.3	2 44	2 53	3 02	3 12	3 21	3 30	3 39	3 49	3 58	4 07	4 16	4 26	4 35	4 44
.4	2 03	2 10	2 17	2 24	2 31	2 38	2 45	2 52	2 59	3 05	3 12	3 19	3 26	3 33
0.5	1 38	1 44	1 49	1 55	2 01	2 06	2 12	2 17	2 23	2 28	2 34	2 40	2 45	2 51
.6	1 22	1 27	1 31	1 36	1 41	1 45	1 50	1 54	1 59	2 04	2 08	2 13	2 18	2 22
.7	1 10	1 14	1 18	1 22	1 26	1 30	1 34	1 38	1 42	1 46	1 50	1 54	1 58	2 02
.8	1 01	1 05	1 08	1 12	1 15	1 19	1 22	1 26	1 29	1 33	1 36	1 40	1 43	1 47
.9	0 55	0 58	1 01	1 04	1 07	1 10	1 13	1 16	1 19	1 22	1 26	1 29	1 32	1 35
1.0	0 49	0 52	0 55	0 58	1 00	1 03	1 06	1 09	1 11	1 14	1 17	1 20	1 23	1 25
.1	0 45	0 47	0 50	0 52	0 55	0 57	1 00	1 02	1 05	1 07	1 10	1 13	1 15	1 18
.2	0 41	0 43	0 46	0 48	0 50	0 53	0 55	0 57	1 00	1 02	1 04	1 07	1 09	1 11
.3	0 38	0 40	0 42	0 44	0 46	0 49	0 51	0 53	0 55	0 57	0 59	1 01	1 04	1 06
.4	0 35	0 37	0 39	0 41	0 43	0 45	0 47	0 49	0 51	0 53	0 55	0 57	0 59	1 01
1.5	0 33	0 35	0 37	0 38	0 40	0 42	0 44	0 46	0 48	0 49	0 51	0 53	0 55	0 57
.6	0 31	0 33	0 34	0 36	0 38	0 39	0 41	0 43	0 45	0 46	0 48	0 50	0 52	0 53
.7	0 29	0 31	0 32	0 34	0 35	0 37	0 39	0 40	0 40	0 41	0 45	0 47	0 49	0 50
.8	0 27	0 29	0 30	0 32	0 34	0 35	0 37	0 38	0 40	0 41	0 43	0 44	0 46	0 47
.9	0 26	0 27	0 29	0 30	0 32	0 33	0 35	0 36	0 38	0 39	0 41	0 42	0 43	0 45
2.0	0 25	0 26	0 27	0 29	0 30	0 32	0 33	0 34	0 36	0 37	0 39	0 40	0 41	0 43
.1	0 23	0 25	0 26	0 27	0 29	0 30	0 31	0 33	0 34	0 35	0 37	0 38	0 39	0 41
.2	0 22	0 24	0 25	0 26	0 27	0 29	0 30	0 31	0 32	0 34	0 35	0 36	0 38	0 39
.3	0 21	0 23	0 24	0 25	0 26	0 27	0 29	0 30	0 31	0 32	0 33	0 35	0 36	0 37
.4	0 20	0 22	0 23	0 24	0 25	0 26	0 27	0 29	0 30	0 31	0 32	0 33	0 34	0 36
2.5	0 20	0 21	0 22	0 23	0 24	0 25	0 26	0 27	0 29	0 30	0 31	0 32	0 33	0 34
.6	0 19	0 20	0 21	0 22	0 23	0 24	0 25	0 26	0 27	0 29	0 30	0 31	0 32	0 33
.7	0 18	0 19	0 20	0 21	0 22	0 23	0 24	0 25	0 26	0 27	0 29	0 30	0 31	0 32
.8	0 18	0 19	0 20	0 21	0 22	0 23	0 24	0 25	0 26	0 27	0 28	0 29	0 30	0 30
.9	0 17	0 18	0 19	0 20	0 21	0 22	0 23	0 24	0 25	0 26	0 27	0 28	0 28	0 29
3.0	0 16	0 17	0 18	0 19	0 20	0 21	0 22	0 23	0 24	0 25	0 26	0 27	0 28	0 28
.2	0 15	0 16	0 17	0 18	0 19	0 20	0 21	0 21	0 22	0 23	0 24	0 26	0 26	0 27
.4	0 14	0 15	0 16	0 17	0 18	0 19	0 19	0 20	0 21	0 22	0 23	0 23	0 24	0 25
.6	0 14	0 14	0 15	0 16	0 17	0 18	0 18	0 19	0 20	0 21	0 21	0 22	0 23	0 24
.8	0 13	0 14	0 14	0 15	0 16	0 17	0 17	0 18	0 19	0 20	0 20	0 21	0 22	0 22
4.0	0 12	0 13	0 14	0 14	0 15	0 16	0 16	0 17	0 18	0 19	0 19	0 20	0 21	0 21
.2	0 12	0 12	0 13	0 14	0 14	0 15	0 16	0 16	0 17	0 18	0 18	0 19	0 20	0 20
.4	0 11	0 12	0 12	0 13	0 14	0 14	0 15	0 16	0 16	0 17	0 18	0 18	0 19	0 19
.6	0 11	0 11	0 12	0 13	0 13	0 14	0 14	0 15	0 16	0 16	0 17	0 17	0 18	0 19
.8	0 10	0 11	0 11	0 12	0 13	0 13	0 14	0 14	0 15	0 15	0 16	0 17	0 17	0 18
5.0	0 10	0 10	0 11	0 12	0 12	0 13	0 13	0 14	0 14	0 15	0 15	0 16	0 17	0 17

$$\text{Tan. } \theta = \frac{h}{d}.$$

Where θ = vertical angle, h = height of object, and d = distance.

DISTANCE BY VERTICAL ANGLE

Height of Object

Distance mls	m 46 / ft 151	47.5 / 156	49 / 161	50.5 / 166	52 / 171	53.5 / 176	55 / 180	56.5 / 185	58 / 190	59.5 / 195	61 / 200	62.5 / 205	64 / 210	65.5 / 215
0.1	13 57	14 23	14 49	15 15	15 41	16 07	16 32	16 58	17 23	17 49	18 14	18 39	19 04	19 29
.2	7 05	7 18	7 32	7 45	7 59	8 13	8 27	8 40	8 54	9 08	9 21	9 35	9 48	10 02
.3	4 44	4 53	5 02	5 12	5 21	5 30	5 39	5 48	5 58	6 07	6 16	6 25	6 34	6 43
.4	3 33	3 40	3 47	3 54	4 01	4 08	4 15	4 22	4 29	4 36	4 42	4 49	5 49	5 03
0.5	2 51	2 56	3 02	3 07	3 13	3 18	3 24	3 29	3 35	3 41	3 46	3 52	3 57	4 03
.6	2 22	2 27	2 31	2 36	2 41	2 45	2 50	2 55	2 59	3 04	3 09	3 13	3 18	3 22
.7	2 02	2 06	2 10	2 14	2 18	2 22	2 26	2 30	2 34	2 38	2 42	2 46	2 50	2 54
.8	1 47	1 51	1 54	1 57	2 01	2 04	2 08	2 11	2 15	2 18	2 21	2 25	2 28	2 32
.9	1 35	1 38	1 41	1 44	1 47	1 50	1 53	1 56	2 00	2 03	2 06	2 09	2 12	2 15
1.0	1 25	1 28	1 31	1 34	1 36	1 39	1 42	1 45	1 48	1 50	1 53	1 56	1 59	2 02
.1	1 18	1 20	1 23	1 25	1 28	1 30	1 33	1 35	1 38	1 40	1 43	1 45	1 48	1 50
.2	1 11	1 13	1 16	1 18	1 20	1 23	1 25	1 27	1 30	1 32	1 34	1 37	1 39	1 41
.3	1 06	1 08	1 10	1 12	1 14	1 16	1 18	1 21	1 23	1 24	1 27	1 29	1 31	1 34
.4	1 01	1 03	1 05	1 07	1 09	1 11	1 13	1 15	1 17	1 19	1 21	1 23	1 25	1 27
1.5	0 57	0 59	1 01	1 02	1 04	1 06	1 08	1 10	1 12	1 14	1 15	1 17	1 19	1 21
.6	0 53	0 55	0 57	0 59	1 00	1 02	1 04	1 06	1 08	1 09	1 11	1 12	1 14	1 16
.7	0 50	0 52	0 53	0 55	0 57	0 58	1 00	1 02	1 03	1 05	1 07	1 08	1 10	1 12
.8	0 47	0 49	0 50	0 52	0 54	0 55	0 56	0 58	1 00	1 01	1 03	1 04	1 06	1 08
.9	0 45	0 46	0 48	0 49	0 51	0 52	0 54	0 55	0 57	0 58	1 00	1 01	1 03	1 04
2.0	0 43	0 44	0 45	0 47	0 48	0 50	0 51	0 52	0 54	0 55	0 57	0 58	0 59	1 01
.1	0 41	0 42	0 43	0 45	0 46	0 47	0 49	0 50	0 51	0 53	0 54	0 55	0 57	0 58
.2	0 39	0 40	0 41	0 43	0 44	0 45	0 46	0 48	0 49	0 50	0 51	0 53	0 54	0 55
.3	0 37	0 38	0 39	0 41	0 42	0 43	0 44	0 46	0 47	0 48	0 49	0 50	0 52	0 53
.4	0 36	0 37	0 38	0 39	0 40	0 41	0 43	0 44	0 45	0 46	0 47	0 48	0 49	0 51
2.5	0 34	0 35	0 36	0 37	0 39	0 40	0 41	0 42	0 43	0 44	0 45	0 46	0 48	0 49
.6	0 33	0 34	0 35	0 36	0 37	0 38	0 39	0 40	0 41	0 42	0 44	0 45	0 46	0 47
.7	0 32	0 33	0 34	0 35	0 36	0 37	0 38	0 39	0 40	0 41	0 42	0 43	0 44	0 45
.8	0 30	0 31	0 32	0 33	0 34	0 35	0 36	0 37	0 38	0 39	0 40	0 41	0 42	0 43
.9	0 29	0 30	0 31	0 32	0 33	0 34	0 35	0 36	0 37	0 38	0 39	0 40	0 41	0 42
3.0	0 28	0 29	0 30	0 31	0 32	0 33	0 34	0 35	0 36	0 37	0 38	0 39	0 40	0 41
.2	0 27	0 28	0 29	0 29	0 30	0 31	0 32	0 33	0 34	0 35	0 35	0 36	0 37	0 38
.4	0 25	0 26	0 27	0 28	0 28	0 29	0 30	0 31	0 32	0 32	0 33	0 34	0 35	0 36
.6	0 24	0 24	0 25	0 26	0 27	0 28	0 28	0 29	0 30	0 31	0 31	0 32	0 33	0 34
.8	0 22	0 23	0 24	0 25	0 25	0 26	0 27	0 28	0 28	0 29	0 30	0 31	0 31	0 32
4.0	0 21	0 22	0 23	0 23	0 24	0 25	0 26	0 26	0 27	0 28	0 28	0 29	0 30	0 30
.2	0 20	0 21	0 22	0 22	0 23	0 24	0 24	0 25	0 26	0 26	0 27	0 28	0 28	0 29
.4	0 19	0 20	0 21	0 21	0 22	0 23	0 23	0 24	0 24	0 25	0 26	0 26	0 27	0 28
.6	0 19	0 19	0 20	0 20	0 21	0 22	0 22	0 23	0 23	0 24	0 25	0 25	0 26	0 26
.8	0 18	0 18	0 19	0 20	0 20	0 21	0 21	0 22	0 22	0 23	0 24	0 24	0 25	0 25
5.0	0 17	0 18	0 18	0 19	0 19	0 20	0 20	0 21	0 22	0 22	0 23	0 23	0 24	0 24
.2	0 16	0 17	0 17	0 18	0 19	0 19	0 20	0 20	0 21	0 21	0 22	0 22	0 23	0 23
.4	0 16	0 16	0 17	0 17	0 18	0 18	0 19	0 19	0 20	0 20	0 21	0 21	0 22	0 23
.6	0 15	0 16	0 16	0 17	0 17	0 18	0 18	0 19	0 19	0 20	0 20	0 21	0 21	0 22
.8	0 15	0 15	0 16	0 16	0 17	0 17	0 18	0 18	0 19	0 19	0 20	0 20	0 20	0 21
6.0	0 14	0 15	0 15	0 16	0 16	0 17	0 17	0 17	0 18	0 18	0 19	0 19	0 20	0 20

$$\text{Tan. } \theta = \frac{h}{d}$$

Where θ = vertical angle, h = height of object, and d = distance.

DISTANCE BY VERTICAL ANGLE

Height of Object

Distance mls	m 65.5 / ft 215	67 / 220	68.5 / 225	70 / 230	75 / 246	80 / 262	85 / 279	90 / 295	95 / 312	100 / 328	105 / 344	110 / 361	120 / 394	130 / 427
	° ′	° ′	° ′	° ′	° ′	° ′	° ′	° ′	° ′	° ′	° ′	° ′	° ′	° ′
0.1	19 29	19 53	20 18											
.2	10 02	10 15	10 29	10 42	11 27	12 11	12 55	13 39	14 23	15 07	15 50	16 32	17 57	19 20
.3	6 43	6 53	7 02	7 11	7 41	8 12	8 42	9 12	9 42	10 12	10 42	11 12	12 11	13 10
.4	5 03	5 10	5 17	5 24	5 47	6 10	6 33	6 56	7 18	7 41	8 04	8 27	9 12	9 57
0.5	4 03	4 08	4 14	4 19	4 38	4 56	5 15	5 33	5 51	6 10	6 28	6 46	7 23	7 59
.6	3 22	3 27	3 32	3 36	3 52	4 07	4 22	4 38	4 53	5 08	5 24	5 39	6 10	6 40
.7	2 54	2 58	3 01	3 05	3 19	3 32	3 45	3 58	4 11	4 25	4 38	4 51	5 17	5 44
.8	2 32	2 35	2 39	2 42	2 54	3 05	3 17	3 29	3 40	3 52	4 03	4 15	4 38	5 01
.9	2 15	2 18	2 21	2 24	2 35	2 45	2 55	3 05	3 16	3 26	3 36	3 47	4 07	4 28
1.0	2 02	2 04	2 07	2 10	2 19	2 28	2 38	2 47	2 56	3 05	3 15	3 24	3 42	4 01
.1	1 50	1 53	1 56	1 58	2 07	2 15	2 23	2 32	2 40	2 49	2 57	3 05	3 22	3 49
.2	1 41	1 44	1 46	1 48	1 56	2 04	2 11	2 19	2 27	2 35	2 42	2 50	3 05	3 21
.3	1 34	1 36	1 38	1 40	1 47	1 54	2 01	2 08	2 16	2 23	2 30	2 37	2 51	3 05
.4	1 27	1 29	1 31	1 33	1 39	1 46	1 53	1 59	2 06	2 13	2 19	2 26	2 39	2 52
1.5	1 21	1 23	1 25	1 27	1 33	1 39	1 45	1 51	1 58	2 04	2 10	2 16	2 28	2 41
.6	1 16	1 18	1 19	1 21	1 27	1 33	1 39	1 44	1 50	1 56	2 02	2 08	2 19	2 31
.7	1 12	1 13	1 15	1 16	1 22	1 27	1 33	1 38	1 44	1 49	1 55	2 00	2 11	2 22
.8	1 08	1 09	1 11	1 12	1 17	1 22	1 28	1 33	1 38	1 43	1 48	1 53	2 04	2 14
.9	1 04	1 05	1 07	1 08	1 13	1 18	1 23	1 28	1 33	1 38	1 42	1 47	1 57	2 07
2.0	1 01	1 02	1 04	1 05	1 10	1 14	1 19	1 24	1 28	1 33	1 37	1 42	1 51	2 01
.1	0 58	0 59	1 01	1 02	1 06	1 11	1 15	1 20	1 24	1 28	1 33	1 37	1 46	1 55
.2	0 55	0 57	0 58	0 59	1 03	1 07	1 12	1 16	1 20	1 24	1 29	1 33	1 41	1 50
.3	0 53	0 54	0 55	0 56	1 01	1 05	1 09	1 13	1 17	1 21	1 25	1 29	1 37	1 45
.4	0 51	0 52	0 53	0 54	0 58	1 02	1 06	1 10	1 14	1 17	1 21	1 25	1 33	1 41
2.5	0 49	0 50	0 51	0 52	0 56	0 59	1 03	1 07	1 11	1 14	1 18	1 22	1 29	1 36
.6	0 47	0 48	0 49	0 50	0 54	0 57	1 01	1 04	1 08	1 11	1 15	1 19	1 26	1 33
.7	0 45	0 46	0 47	0 48	0 52	0 55	0 58	1 02	1 05	1 09	1 12	1 16	1 22	1 29
.8	0 43	0 44	0 45	0 46	0 50	0 53	0 56	1 00	1 03	1 06	1 10	1 13	1 20	1 26
.9	0 42	0 43	0 44	0 45	0 48	0 51	0 54	0 58	1 01	1 04	1 07	1 10	1 17	1 23
3.0	0 41	0 41	0 42	0 43	0 46	0 49	0 53	0 56	0 59	1 02	1 05	1 08	1 14	1 20
.2	0 38	0 39	0 40	0 41	0 44	0 46	0 49	0 52	0 55	0 58	1 01	1 04	1 10	1 15
.4	0 36	0 37	0 38	0 38	0 41	0 44	0 46	0 49	0 52	0 55	0 57	1 00	1 06	1 11
.6	0 34	0 35	0 36	0 36	0 39	0 41	0 44	0 46	0 49	0 52	0 54	0 57	1 02	1 07
.8	0 32	0 33	0 34	0 34	0 37	0 39	0 42	0 44	0 46	0 49	0 51	0 54	0 59	1 03
4.0	0 30	0 31	0 32	0 32	0 35	0 37	0 39	0 42	0 44	0 46	0 49	0 51	0 56	1 00
.2	0 29	0 30	0 30	0 31	0 33	0 35	0 38	0 40	0 42	0 44	0 46	0 49	0 53	0 57
.4	0 28	0 28	0 29	0 30	0 32	0 34	0 36	0 38	0 40	0 42	0 44	0 46	0 51	0 55
.6	0 26	0 27	0 28	0 28	0 30	0 32	0 34	0 36	0 38	0 40	0 42	0 44	0 48	0 52
.8	0 25	0 26	0 26	0 27	0 29	0 31	0 33	0 35	0 37	0 39	0 41	0 43	0 46	0 50
5.0	0 24	0 25	0 25	0 26	0 28	0 30	0 32	0 33	0 35	0 37	0 39	0 41	0 45	0 48
.2	0 23	0 24	0 24	0 25	0 27	0 29	0 30	0 32	0 34	0 36	0 37	0 39	0 43	0 46
.4	0 23	0 23	0 24	0 24	0 26	0 27	0 29	0 31	0 33	0 34	0 36	0 38	0 41	0 45
.6	0 22	0 22	0 23	0 23	0 25	0 27	0 28	0 30	0 32	0 33	0 35	0 36	0 40	0 43
.8	0 21	0 21	0 22	0 22	0 24	0 26	0 27	0 29	0 30	0 32	0 34	0 35	0 38	0 42
6.0	0 20	0 21	0 21	0 22	0 23	0 25	0 26	0 28	0 29	0 31	0 32	0 34	0 37	0 40

Tan. $\theta = \dfrac{h}{d}$. Where θ = vertical angle, h = height of object, and d = distance.

DISTANCE BY VERTICAL ANGLE

Height of Object

Distance mls	m 130	140	150	160	170	180	190	200	210	220	230	240	250	260
	ft 427	459	492	525	558	591	623	656	689	722	755	787	820	853
	° ′	° ′	° ′	° ′	° ′	° ′	° ′	° ′	° ′	° ′	° ′	° ′	° ′	° ′
0.1														
.2	19 20	20 42	22 03	23 22	24 39									
.3	13 10	14 09	15 07	16 04	17 01	17 57	18 53	19 48	20 42	21 36	22 29	23 22	24 14	
.4	9 57	10 42	11 27	12 11	12 55	13 39	14 23	15 07	15 50	16 32	17 15	17 57	18 39	19 20
0.5	7 59	8 36	9 12	9 48	10 24	11 00	11 36	12 11	12 47	13 22	13 57	14 32	15 07	15 41
.6	6 40	7 11	7 41	8 12	8 42	9 12	9 42	10 12	10 42	11 12	11 42	12 11	12 41	13 10
.7	5 44	6 10	6 36	7 02	7 28	7 54	8 20	8 46	9 12	9 38	10 04	10 29	10 55	11 20
.8	5 01	5 24	5 47	6 10	6 33	6 56	7 18	7 41	8 04	8 27	8 49	9 12	9 35	9 57
.9	4 28	4 48	5 09	5 29	5 49	6 10	6 30	6 51	7 11	7 31	7 51	8 12	8 32	8 52
1.0	4 01	4 19	4 38	4 56	5 15	5 33	5 51	6 10	6 28	6 46	7 05	7 23	7 41	7 59
.1	3 49	3 56	4 13	4 29	4 46	5 03	5 20	5 36	5 53	6 10	6 26	6 43	7 00	7 16
.2	3 21	3 36	3 52	4 07	4 26	4 38	4 53	5 09	5 24	5 39	5 55	6 10	6 25	6 40
.3	3 05	3 20	3 34	3 48	4 02	4 17	4 31	4 45	4 59	5 13	5 27	5 42	5 56	6 10
.4	2 52	3 05	3 19	3 32	3 45	3 58	4 11	4 25	4 38	4 51	5 04	5 17	5 30	5 44
1.5	2 41	2 53	3 05	3 18	3 30	3 42	3 55	4 07	4 19	4 32	4 44	4 56	5 09	5 21
.6	2 31	2 42	2 54	3 05	3 17	3 29	3 40	3 52	4 03	4 15	4 26	4 38	4 49	5 01
.7	2 22	2 33	2 44	2 55	3 05	3 16	3 27	3 38	3 49	4 00	4 11	4 22	4 32	4 43
.8	2 14	2 24	2 35	2 45	2 55	3 05	3 16	3 26	3 36	3 47	3 57	4 07	4 17	4 28
.9	2 07	2 17	2 26	2 36	2 46	2 56	3 05	3 15	3 25	3 35	3 44	3 54	4 04	4 14
2.0	2 01	2 10	2 19	2 28	2 38	2 47	2 56	3 05	3 15	3 24	3 33	3 42	3 52	4 01
.1	1 55	2 04	2 13	2 21	2 30	2 39	2 48	2 57	3 05	3 14	3 23	3 32	3 41	3 49
.2	1 50	1 58	2 07	2 15	2 23	2 32	2 40	2 49	2 57	3 05	3 14	3 22	3 31	3 39
.3	1 45	1 53	2 01	2 09	2 17	2 25	2 33	2 41	2 49	2 57	3 05	3 13	3 22	3 30
.4	1 41	1 48	1 56	2 04	2 11	2 19	2 27	2 35	2 42	2 50	2 58	3 05	3 13	3 21
2.5	1 36	1 44	1 51	1 59	2 06	2 14	2 21	2 28	2 36	2 43	2 51	2 58	3 05	3 13
.6	1 33	1 40	1 47	1 54	2 01	2 08	2 16	2 23	2 30	2 37	2 44	2 51	2 58	3 05
.7	1 29	1 36	1 43	1 50	1 57	2 04	2 11	2 17	2 24	2 31	2 38	2 45	2 52	2 59
.8	1 26	1 33	1 39	1 46	1 53	1 59	2 06	2 13	2 19	2 26	2 32	2 39	2 46	2 52
.9	1 23	1 30	1 36	1 42	1 49	1 55	2 02	2 08	2 14	2 21	2 27	2 34	2 40	2 46
3.0	1 20	1 27	1 33	1 39	1 45	1 51	1 58	2 04	2 10	2 16	2 22	2 28	2 35	2 41
.2	1 15	1 21	1 27	1 33	1 39	1 44	1 50	1 56	2 02	2 08	2 13	2 19	2 25	2 31
.4	1 11	1 16	1 22	1 27	1 33	1 38	1 44	1 49	1 55	2 00	2 06	2 11	2 16	2 22
.6	1 07	1 12	1 17	1 22	1 28	1 33	1 38	1 43	1 48	1 53	1 59	2 04	2 09	2 14
.8	1 03	1 08	1 13	1 18	1 23	1 28	1 33	1 38	1 43	1 47	1 52	1 57	2 02	2 07
4.0	1 00	1 05	1 10	1 14	1 19	1 24	1 28	1 33	1 37	1 42	1 47	1 51	1 56	2 01
.2	0 57	1 02	1 06	1 11	1 15	1 20	1 24	1 28	1 33	1 37	1 42	1 46	1 50	1 55
.4	0 55	0 59	1 03	1 07	1 12	1 16	1 20	1 24	1 29	1 33	1 37	1 41	1 45	1 50
.6	0 52	0 56	1 01	1 05	1 09	1 13	1 17	1 21	1 25	1 29	1 33	1 37	1 41	1 45
.8	0 50	0 54	0 58	1 02	1 06	1 10	1 13	1 17	1 21	1 25	1 29	1 33	1 37	1 41
5.0	0 48	0 52	0 56	0 59	1 03	1 07	1 11	1 14	1 18	1 22	1 25	1 29	1 33	1 36
.2	0 46	0 50	0 54	0 57	1 01	1 04	1 08	1 11	1 15	1 19	1 22	1 26	1 29	1 33
.4	0 45	0 48	0 52	0 55	0 58	1 02	1 05	1 09	1 12	1 16	1 19	1 22	1 26	1 29
.6	0 43	0 46	0 50	0 53	0 56	1 00	1 03	1 06	1 10	1 13	1 16	1 20	1 23	1 26
.8	0 42	0 45	0 47	0 51	0 54	0 58	1 01	1 04	1 07	1 10	1 14	1 17	1 20	1 23
6.0	0 40	0 43	0 46	0 49	0 53	0 56	0 59	1 02	1 05	1 08	1 11	1 14	1 17	1 20
.2	0 39	0 42	0 45	0 48	0 51	0 54	0 57	1 00	1 03	1 06	1 09	1 12	1 15	1 18
.4	0 38	0 41	0 44	0 46	0 49	0 52	0 55	0 58	1 01	1 04	1 07	1 10	1 12	1 15
.6	0 37	0 39	0 42	0 45	0 48	0 51	0 53	0 56	0 59	1 02	1 05	1 08	1 10	1 13
.8	0 35	0 38	0 41	0 44	0 46	0 49	0 52	0 55	0 57	1 00	1 03	1 06	1 08	1 11
7.0	0 34	0 37	0 40	0 42	0 45	0 48	0 50	0 53	0 56	0 58	1 01	1 04	1 06	1 09

$\text{Tan. } \theta = \dfrac{h}{d}$. Where θ = vertical angle, h = height of object, and d = distance.

DISTANCE BY VERTICAL ANGLE

Height of Object

Distance mls	m 260 ft 853	270 886	280 919	290 951	300 984	320 1050	340 1115	360 1181	380 1247	400 1312	450 1476	500 1640	550 1805	600 1969
	° ′	° ′	° ′	° ′	° ′	° ′	° ′	° ′	° ′	° ′	° ′	° ′	° ′	° ′
0.1														
.2														
.3														
.4	19 20	20 02	20 42	21 23	22 03	23 22	24 39	25 55	27 09					
0.5	15 41	16 15	16 49	17 23	17 57	19 04	20 10	21 15	22 19	23 22				
.6	13 10	13 39	14 09	14 38	15 07	16 04	17 01	17 57	18 52	19 48	22 03	24 14	26 20	28 22
.7	11 20	11 46	12 11	12 37	13 02	13 52	14 42	15 31	16 20	17 09	19 09	21 05	22 59	24 50
.8	9 57	10 20	10 42	11 04	11 27	12 11	12 55	13 39	14 23	15 07	16 54	18 39	20 22	22 03
.9	8 52	9 12	9 32	9 52	10 12	10 52	11 32	12 11	12 51	13 30	15 07	16 42	18 16	19 48
1.0	7 59	8 18	8 36	8 54	9 12	9 48	10 24	11 00	11 36	12 11	13 39	15 07	16 32	17 57
.1	7 16	7 33	7 50	8 06	8 23	8 56	9 29	10 01	10 34	11 07	12 27	13 47	15 07	16 25
.2	6 40	6 56	7 11	7 26	7 41	8 12	8 42	9 12	9 42	10 12	11 27	12 41	13 54	15 07
.3	6 10	6 24	6 38	6 52	7 06	7 34	8 02	8 30	8 58	9 26	10 35	11 44	12 52	14 00
.4	5 44	5 57	6 10	6 23	6 36	7 02	7 28	7 54	8 20	8 46	9 51	10 55	11 59	13 02
1.5	5 21	5 33	5 45	5 58	6 10	6 34	6 59	7 23	7 47	8 12	9 12	10 12	11 12	12 11
.6	5 01	5 12	5 24	5 35	5 47	6 10	6 33	6 56	7 18	7 41	8 38	9 35	10 31	11 27
.7	4 43	4 54	5 05	5 16	5 27	5 48	6 10	6 31	6 53	7 14	8 08	9 01	9 55	10 47
.8	4 28	4 38	4 48	4 58	5 09	5 29	5 49	6 10	6 30	6 51	7 41	8 32	9 22	10 12
.9	4 14	4 23	4 33	4 43	4 52	5 12	5 31	5 50	6 10	6 29	7 17	8 05	8 53	9 41
2.0	4 01	4 10	4 19	4 29	4 38	4 56	5 15	5 33	5 51	6 10	6 56	7 41	8 27	9 12
.1	3 49	3 58	4 07	4 16	4 25	4 42	5 00	5 17	5 35	5 52	6 36	7 20	8 03	8 46
.2	3 39	3 47	3 56	4 04	4 13	4 29	4 46	5 03	5 20	5 36	6 18	7 00	7 41	8 23
.3	3 30	3 38	3 46	3 54	4 02	4 18	4 34	4 50	5 06	5 22	6 02	6 42	7 21	8 01
.4	3 21	3 29	3 36	3 44	3 52	4 07	4 22	4 38	4 53	5 09	5 47	6 25	7 03	7 41
2.5	3 13	3 20	3 28	3 35	3 42	3 57	4 12	4 27	4 42	4 56	5 33	6 10	6 46	7 23
.6	3 05	3 13	3 20	3 27	3 34	3 48	4 02	4 17	4 31	4 45	5 20	5 56	6 31	7 06
.7	2 59	3 05	3 12	3 19	3 26	3 40	3 53	4 07	4 21	4 34	5 09	5 43	6 17	6 51
.8	2 52	2 59	3 05	3 12	3 19	3 32	3 45	3 58	4 12	4 25	4 58	5 30	6 03	6 36
.9	2 46	2 53	2 59	3 05	3 12	3 25	3 37	3 50	4 03	4 16	4 47	5 19	5 51	6 22
3.0	2 41	2 47	2 53	2 59	3 05	3 18	3 30	3 42	3 55	4 07	4 38	5 09	5 39	6 10
.2	2 31	2 37	2 42	2 48	2 54	3 05	3 17	3 29	3 40	3 52	4 21	4 49	5 18	5 47
.4	2 22	2 27	2 33	2 38	2 44	2 55	3 05	3 16	3 27	3 38	4 05	4 37	5 00	5 27
.6	2 14	2 19	2 24	2 29	2 35	2 45	2 55	3 05	3 16	3 26	3 52	4 17	4 43	5 09
.8	2 07	2 12	2 17	2 22	2 26	2 36	2 46	2 56	3 05	3 15	3 40	4 04	4 28	4 52
4.0	2 01	2 05	2 10	2 15	2 19	2 28	2 38	2 47	2 56	3 05	3 29	3 52	4 15	4 38
.2	1 55	1 59	2 04	2 08	2 13	2 21	2 30	2 39	2 48	2 57	3 19	3 41	4 03	4 25
.4	1 50	1 54	1 58	2 02	2 07	2 15	2 23	2 32	2 40	2 49	3 10	3 31	3 52	4 13
.6	1 45	1 49	1 53	1 57	2 01	2 09	2 17	2 25	2 33	2 41	3 01	3 22	3 42	4 02
.8	1 41	1 44	1 48	1 52	1 56	2 04	2 11	2 19	2 27	2 35	2 54	3 13	3 32	3 52
5.0	1 36	1 40	1 44	1 48	1 51	1 59	2 06	2 14	2 21	2 28	2 47	3 05	3 24	3 42
.2	1 33	1 36	1 40	1 43	1 47	1 54	2 01	2 08	2 16	2 23	2 41	2 58	3 16	3 34
.4	1 29	1 33	1 36	1 40	1 43	1 50	1 57	2 04	2 11	2 17	2 35	2 52	3 09	3 26
.6	1 26	1 29	1 33	1 36	1 39	1 46	1 53	1 59	2 06	2 13	2 29	2 46	3 02	3 19
.8	1 23	1 26	1 30	1 33	1 36	1 42	1 49	1 55	2 02	2 08	2 24	2 40	2 56	3 12
6.0	1 20	1 24	1 27	1 30	1 33	1 39	1 45	1 51	1 58	2 04	2 19	2 35	2 50	3 05
.2	1 18	1 21	1 24	1 27	1 30	1 36	1 42	1 48	1 54	2 00	2 15	2 30	2 45	2 59
.4	1 15	1 18	1 21	1 24	1 27	1 33	1 39	1 44	1 50	1 56	2 10	2 25	2 39	2 54
.6	1 13	1 16	1 19	1 22	1 24	1 30	1 36	1 41	1 47	1 52	2 07	2 21	2 35	2 49
.8	1 11	1 14	1 16	1 19	1 22	1 27	1 33	1 38	1 44	1 49	2 03	2 16	2 30	2 44
7.0	1 09	1 12	1 14	1 17	1 20	1 25	1 30	1 35	1 41	1 46	1 59	2 13	2 26	2 39

Tan. $\theta = \dfrac{h}{d}$. Where θ = vertical angle, h = height of object, and d = distance.

EXTREME RANGE TABLE

Elevation		Height of Eye											
	m	1.5	3	4.5	6	8	10	12	14	16	18	20	22
m	ft	5	10	15	20	26	33	39	46	52	59	66	72
0	0	2.6	3.6	4.4	5.1	5.9	6.6	7.3	7.8	8.4	8.9	9.4	9.8
2	7	5.5	6.6	7.4	8.1	8.9	9.6	10.2	10.8	11.3	11.9	12.3	12.8
4	13	6.8	7.8	8.6	9.3	10.1	10.8	11.4	12.0	12.6	13.1	13.6	14.0
6	20	7.7	8.8	9.6	10.3	11.1	11.8	12.4	13.0	13.5	14.0	14.5	15.0
8	26	8.5	9.6	10.4	11.1	11.9	12.6	13.2	13.8	14.3	14.8	15.3	15.8
10	33	9.2	10.3	11.1	11.8	12.6	13.3	13.9	14.5	15.0	15.5	16.0	16.5
12	39	9.8	10.9	11.7	12.4	13.2	13.9	14.5	15.1	15.6	16.1	16.6	17.1
14	46	10.4	11.5	12.3	13.0	13.8	14.5	15.1	15.7	16.2	16.7	17.2	17.7
16	52	10.9	12.0	12.8	13.5	14.3	15.0	15.6	16.2	16.8	17.3	17.7	18.2
18	59	11.4	12.5	13.3	14.0	14.8	15.5	16.1	16.7	17.3	17.8	18.3	18.7
20	66	11.9	13.0	13.8	14.5	15.3	16.0	16.6	17.2	17.7	18.3	18.7	19.2
22	72	12.4	13.5	14.3	15.0	15.8	16.5	17.1	17.7	18.2	18.7	19.2	19.7
24	79	12.8	13.9	14.7	15.4	16.2	16.9	17.5	18.1	18.6	19.2	19.6	20.1
26	85	13.2	14.3	15.1	15.8	16.6	17.3	17.9	18.5	19.1	19.6	20.1	20.5
28	92	13.7	14.7	15.5	16.2	17.0	17.7	18.3	18.9	19.5	20.0	20.5	20.9
30	98	14.0	15.1	15.9	16.6	17.4	18.1	18.7	19.3	19.9	20.4	20.8	21.3
35	115	15.0	16.0	16.8	17.5	18.3	19.0	19.7	20.2	20.8	21.3	21.8	22.2
40	131	15.8	16.9	17.7	18.4	19.2	19.9	20.5	21.1	21.6	22.1	22.6	23.1
45	148	16.6	17.7	18.5	19.2	20.0	20.7	21.3	21.9	22.4	22.9	23.4	23.9
50	164	17.4	18.4	19.2	19.9	20.7	21.4	22.1	22.7	23.2	23.7	24.2	24.6
55	180	18.1	19.2	20.0	20.7	21.5	22.2	22.8	23.4	23.9	24.4	24.9	25.4
60	197	18.8	19.9	20.7	21.4	22.2	22.9	23.5	24.1	24.6	25.1	25.6	26.1
65	213	19.5	20.5	21.3	22.0	22.8	23.5	24.1	24.7	25.3	25.8	26.3	26.7
70	230	20.1	21.1	21.9	22.7	23.5	24.2	24.8	25.4	25.9	26.4	26.9	27.4
75	246	20.7	21.7	22.5	23.3	24.1	24.8	25.4	26.0	26.5	27.0	27.5	28.0
80	262	21.3	22.4	23.2	23.9	24.7	25.4	26.0	26.6	27.1	27.6	28.1	28.6
85	279	21.9	22.9	23.7	24.4	25.2	25.9	26.6	27.2	27.7	28.2	28.7	29.1
90	295	22.4	23.5	24.3	25.0	25.8	26.5	27.1	27.7	28.3	28.8	29.2	29.7
95	312	23.0	24.0	24.8	25.6	26.3	27.0	27.7	28.3	28.8	29.3	29.8	30.2
100	328	23.5	24.6	25.4	26.1	26.9	27.6	28.2	28.8	29.3	29.8	30.3	30.8
110	361	24.5	25.6	26.4	27.1	27.9	28.6	29.2	29.8	30.4	30.9	31.3	31.8
120	394	25.5	26.6	27.4	28.1	28.9	29.6	30.2	30.8	31.3	31.8	32.3	32.8
130	427	26.5	27.5	28.3	29.0	29.8	30.5	31.1	31.7	32.3	32.8	33.3	33.7
140	459	27.4	28.4	29.2	29.9	30.7	31.4	32.0	32.6	33.2	33.7	34.2	34.6
150	492	28.2	29.3	30.1	30.8	31.6	32.3	32.9	33.5	34.0	34.5	35.0	35.5
160	525	29.1	30.1	30.9	31.6	32.4	33.1	33.8	34.3	34.9	35.4	35.9	36.3
170	558	29.9	30.9	31.7	32.4	33.2	33.9	34.6	35.2	35.7	36.2	36.7	37.1
180	591	30.7	31.7	32.5	33.2	34.0	34.7	35.4	35.9	36.5	37.0	37.5	37.9
190	623	31.4	32.5	33.3	34.0	34.8	35.5	36.1	36.7	37.3	37.8	38.2	38.7
200	656	32.2	33.3	34.1	34.8	35.6	36.3	36.9	37.5	38.0	38.5	39.0	39.5
210	689	32.9	34.0	34.8	35.5	36.3	37.0	37.6	38.2	38.7	39.2	39.7	40.2
220	722	33.6	34.7	35.5	36.2	37.0	37.7	38.3	38.9	39.5	40.0	40.4	40.9
230	755	34.3	35.4	36.2	36.9	37.7	38.4	39.0	39.6	40.1	40.7	41.1	41.6
240	787	35.0	36.1	36.9	37.6	38.4	39.1	39.7	40.3	40.8	41.3	41.8	42.3
250	820	35.7	36.8	37.6	38.3	39.1	39.8	40.4	41.0	41.5	42.0	42.5	43.0
260	853	36.3	37.4	38.2	38.9	39.7	40.4	41.0	41.6	42.2	42.7	43.2	43.6
270	886	37.0	38.1	38.9	39.6	40.4	41.0	41.7	42.3	42.8	43.3	43.8	44.3
280	919	37.6	38.7	39.5	40.2	41.0	41.7	42.3	42.9	43.4	43.9	44.4	44.9
290	951	38.2	39.3	40.1	40.8	41.6	42.3	42.9	43.5	44.1	44.6	45.0	45.5
300	984	38.9	39.9	40.7	41.4	42.2	42.9	43.5	44.1	44.7	45.2	45.7	46.1

EXTREME RANGE TABLE

Elevation							Height of Eye						
	m	22	24	26	28	30	32	34	36	38	40	45	50
m	ft	72	79	85	92	98	105	112	118	125	131	148	164
0	0	9.8	10.3	10.7	11.1	11.5	11.9	12.2	12.6	12.9	13.3	14.1	14.8
2	7	12.8	13.2	13.6	14.0	14.4	14.8	15.2	15.5	15.9	16.2	17.0	17.8
4	13	14.0	14.5	14.9	15.3	15.7	16.0	16.4	16.8	17.1	17.4	18.2	19.0
6	20	15.0	15.4	15.8	16.2	16.6	17.0	17.3	17.7	18.0	18.4	19.2	19.9
8	26	15.8	16.2	16.6	17.0	17.4	17.8	18.1	18.5	18.8	19.2	20.0	20.7
10	33	16.5	16.9	17.3	17.7	18.1	18.5	18.8	19.2	19.5	19.9	20.7	21.4
12	39	17.1	17.5	17.9	18.3	18.7	19.1	19.5	19.8	20.2	20.5	21.3	22.1
14	46	17.7	18.1	18.5	18.9	19.3	19.7	20.1	20.4	20.8	21.1	21.9	22.7
16	52	18.2	18.6	19.1	19.5	19.9	20.2	20.6	21.0	21.3	21.6	22.4	23.2
18	59	18.7	19.2	19.6	20.0	20.4	20.7	21.1	21.5	21.8	22.1	22.9	23.7
20	66	19.2	19.6	20.0	20.5	20.8	21.2	21.6	21.9	22.3	22.6	23.4	24.2
22	72	19.7	20.1	20.5	20.9	21.3	21.7	22.0	22.4	22.7	23.1	23.9	24.6
24	79	20.1	20.5	20.9	21.3	21.7	22.1	22.5	22.8	23.2	23.5	24.3	25.1
26	85	20.5	20.9	21.4	21.8	22.2	22.5	22.9	23.3	23.6	23.9	24.7	25.5
28	92	20.9	21.3	21.8	22.2	22.6	22.9	23.3	23.7	24.0	24.3	25.1	25.9
30	98	21.3	21.7	22.2	22.6	23.0	23.3	23.7	24.0	24.4	24.7	25.8	26.3
35	115	22.2	22.7	23.1	23.5	23.9	24.2	24.6	25.0	25.3	25.6	26.4	27.2
40	131	23.1	23.5	23.9	24.3	24.7	25.1	25.5	25.8	26.2	26.5	27.3	28.1
45	148	23.9	24.3	24.7	25.1	25.5	25.9	26.3	26.6	27.0	27.3	28.1	28.9
50	164	24.6	25.1	25.5	25.9	26.3	26.7	27.0	27.4	27.7	28.1	28.9	29.6
55	180	25.4	25.8	26.2	26.6	27.0	27.4	27.8	28.1	28.5	28.8	29.6	30.4
60	197	26.1	26.5	26.9	27.3	27.7	28.1	28.4	28.8	29.1	29.5	30.3	31.0
65	213	26.7	27.2	27.6	28.0	28.4	28.7	29.1	29.5	29.8	30.1	30.9	31.7
70	230	27.4	27.8	28.2	28.6	29.0	29.4	29.7	30.1	30.4	30.8	31.6	32.3
75	246	28.0	28.4	28.8	29.2	29.6	30.0	30.4	30.7	31.1	31.4	32.2	33.0
80	262	28.6	29.0	29.4	29.8	30.2	30.6	31.0	31.3	31.7	32.0	32.8	33.6
85	279	29.1	29.6	30.0	30.4	30.8	31.2	31.5	31.9	32.2	32.6	33.4	34.1
90	295	29.7	30.1	30.6	31.0	31.4	31.7	32.1	32.4	32.8	33.1	33.9	34.7
95	312	30.2	30.7	31.1	31.5	31.9	32.3	32.6	33.0	33.3	33.7	34.5	35.2
100	328	30.8	31.2	31.6	32.0	32.4	32.8	33.2	33.5	33.9	34.2	35.0	35.8
110	361	31.8	32.2	32.7	33.1	33.4	33.8	34.2	34.5	34.9	35.2	36.0	36.8
120	394	32.8	33.2	33.6	34.0	34.4	34.8	35.2	35.5	35.9	36.2	37.0	37.8
130	427	33.7	34.2	34.6	35.0	35.4	35.7	36.1	36.5	36.8	37.1	37.9	38.7
140	459	34.6	35.1	35.5	35.9	36.3	36.6	37.0	37.4	37.7	38.0	38.8	39.6
150	492	35.5	35.9	36.3	36.7	37.1	37.5	37.9	38.2	38.6	38.9	39.7	40.5
160	525	36.3	36.8	37.2	37.6	38.0	38.4	38.7	39.1	39.4	39.8	40.6	41.3
170	558	37.1	37.6	38.0	38.4	38.8	39.2	39.5	39.9	40.2	40.6	41.4	42.1
180	591	37.9	38.4	38.8	39.2	39.6	40.0	40.3	40.7	41.0	41.4	42.2	42.9
190	623	38.7	39.1	39.6	40.0	40.4	40.7	41.1	41.4	41.8	42.1	42.9	43.7
200	656	39.5	39.9	40.3	40.7	41.1	41.5	41.8	42.2	42.5	42.9	43.7	44.4
210	689	40.2	40.6	41.0	41.4	41.8	42.2	42.6	42.9	43.3	43.6	44.4	45.2
220	722	40.9	41.3	41.8	42.2	42.5	42.9	43.3	43.6	44.0	44.3	45.1	45.9
230	755	41.6	42.0	42.5	42.9	43.2	43.6	44.0	44.3	44.7	45.0	45.8	46.6
240	787	42.3	42.7	43.1	43.5	43.9	44.3	44.7	45.0	45.4	45.7	46.5	47.3
250	820	43.0	43.4	43.8	44.2	44.6	45.0	45.3	45.7	46.0	46.4	47.2	47.9
260	853	43.6	44.0	44.5	44.9	45.3	45.6	46.0	46.4	46.7	47.0	47.8	48.6
270	886	44.3	44.7	45.1	45.5	45.9	46.3	46.6	47.0	47.3	47.7	48.5	49.2
280	919	44.9	45.3	45.7	46.1	46.5	46.9	47.3	47.6	48.0	48.3	49.1	49.9
290	951	45.5	45.9	46.4	46.8	47.2	47.5	47.9	48.2	48.6	48.9	49.7	50.5
300	984	46.1	46.5	47.0	47.4	47.8	48.1	48.5	48.9	49.2	49.5	50.3	51.1

DISTANCE OF THE SEA HORIZON

Height m	ft	Dist. mls
0.5	1.6	1.5
1.0	3	2.1
1.5	5	2.6
2.0	7	3.0
2.5	8	3.3
3.0	10	3.6
3.5	11	3.9
4.0	13	4.2
4.5	15	4.4
5.0	16	4.7
5.5	18	4.9
6.0	20	5.1
6.5	21	5.3
7.0	23	5.5
7.5	25	5.7
8.0	26	5.9
8.5	28	6.1
9.0	30	6.3
9.5	31	6.5
10.0	33	6.6
11	36	6.9
12	39	7.3
13	43	7.6
14	46	7.8
15	49	8.1
16	52	8.4
17	56	8.6
18	59	8.9
19	62	9.1
20	66	9.4
21	69	9.6
22	72	9.8
23	75	10.0
24	79	10.3
25	82	10.5
26	85	10.7
27	89	10.9
28	92	11.1
29	95	11.3
30	98	11.5
31	102	11.7
32	105	11.9
33	108	12.0
34	112	12.2
35	115	12.4
36	118	12.6
37	121	12.7
38	125	12.9
39	128	13.1
40	131	13.3

Height m	ft	Dist. Miles
40	131	13.3
42	138	13.6
44	144	13.9
46	151	14.2
48	157	14.5
50	164	14.8
52	171	15.1
54	177	15.4
56	184	15.7
58	190	16.0
60	197	16.2
62	203	16.5
64	210	16.8
66	217	17.0
68	223	17.3
70	230	17.5
72	236	17.8
74	243	18.0
76	249	18.3
78	256	18.5
80	262	18.7
82	269	19.0
84	276	19.2
86	282	19.4
88	289	19.7
90	295	19.9
92	302	20.1
94	308	20.3
96	315	20.5
98	322	20.7
100	328	21.0
105	344	21.5
110	361	22.0
115	377	22.5
120	394	23.0
125	410	23.4
130	427	23.9
135	443	24.3
140	459	24.8
145	476	25.2
150	492	25.7
155	509	26.1
160	525	26.5
165	541	26.9
170	558	27.3
175	574	27.7
180	591	28.1
185	607	28.5
190	623	28.9
195	640	29.3
200	656	29.6

Height m	ft	Dist Miles
200	656	29.6
205	673	30.0
210	689	30.4
215	705	30.7
220	722	31.1
225	738	31.4
230	755	31.8
235	771	32.1
240	787	32.5
245	804	32.8
250	820	33.1
260	853	33.8
270	886	34.4
280	919	35.1
290	951	35.7
300	984	36.3
310	1017	36.9
320	1050	37.5
330	1083	38.1
340	1115	38.6
350	1148	39.2
360	1181	39.8
370	1214	40.3
380	1247	40.8
390	1280	41.4
400	1312	41.9
410	1345	42.4
420	1378	42.9
430	1411	43.4
440	1444	43.9
450	1476	44.4
460	1509	44.9
470	1542	45.4
480	1575	45.9
490	1608	46.4
500	1640	46.8
510	1673	47.3
520	1706	47.8
530	1739	48.2
540	1772	48.7
550	1804	49.1
560	1837	49.6
570	1870	50.0
580	1903	50.5
590	1936	50.9
600	1969	51.3
610	2001	51.7
620	2034	52.2
630	2067	52.6
640	2100	53.0
650	2133	53.4

DIP OF THE SHORE HORIZON or Dip at Different Ranges

Height of Eye

Miles	m 1.5 / ft 5	3 / 10	4.5 / 15	6 / 20	7.5 / 25	9 / 30	10.5 / 36	12 / 39	13.5 / 44	15 / 49	17.5 / 57	20 / 66
	° ′	° ′	° ′	° ′	° ′	° ′	° ′	° ′	° ′	° ′	° ′	° ′
0.1	−27.9	−55.7	−1 23.5	−1 51.3	−2 19.1	−2 46.9	−3 14.7	−3 42.5	−4 10.3	−4 38.1	−5 24.5	−6 10.8
.2	14.0	27.9	41.8	55.7	1 09.6	1 23.5	1 37.4	1 51.3	2 05.2	2 19.1	2 42.3	3 05.5
.3	9.4	18.7	27.9	37.2	46.5	55.8	1 05.0	1 14.3	1 23.6	1 32.8	1 48.3	2 03.7
.4	7.1	14.1	21.0	28.0	34.9	41.9	48.8	55.8	1 02.7	1 09.7	1 21.3	1 32.9
.5	5.8	11.3	16.9	22.4	28.0	33.6	39.1	44.7	50.3	55.8	1 05.1	1 14.4
0.6	−4.9	−9.5	−14.2	−18.8	−23.4	−28.1	−32.7	−37.3	−42.0	−46.6	−54.3	−1 02.1
.7	4.3	8.2	12.2	16.2	20.2	24.1	28.1	32.1	36.1	40.0	46.7	53.3
.8	3.8	7.3	10.8	14.2	17.7	21.2	24.7	28.2	31.6	35.1	40.9	46.7
.9	3.5	6.6	9.7	12.7	15.8	18.9	22.0	25.1	28.2	31.3	36.4	41.6
1.0	3.2	6.0	8.8	11.5	14.3	17.1	19.9	22.7	25.4	28.2	32.9	37.5
1.2	−2.8	−5.1	−7.5	−9.8	−12.1	−14.4	−16.7	−19.0	−21.4	−23.7	−27.6	−31.4
.4	2.6	4.6	6.5	8.5	10.5	12.5	14.5	16.5	18.5	20.5	23.8	27.1
.6	2.4	4.1	5.9	7.6	9.4	11.1	12.9	14.7	16.3	18.1	21.0	23.9
.8	2.3	3.9	5.4	6.9	8.5	10.0	11.6	13.1	14.7	16.2	18.8	21.4
2.0	2.2	3.6	5.0	6.4	7.8	9.2	10.6	12.0	13.4	14.8	17.1	19.4
2.5		−3.3	−4.4	−5.5	−6.6	−7.7	−8.8	−10.0	−11.1	−12.2	−14.0	−15.9
3.0		3.1	4.1	5.0	5.9	6.8	7.8	8.7	9.6	10.5	12.1	13.6
.5			3.9	4.7	5.5	6.2	7.0	7.8	8.6	9.4	10.8	12.1
4.0			3.8	4.5	5.2	5.9	6.6	7.3	7.9	8.6	9.8	11.0
.5				4.4	5.0	5.6	6.2	6.8	7.5	8.1	9.1	10.1
5.0					4.9	5.5	6.1	6.6	7.2	7.7	8.6	9.6
6.0						5.3	5.8	6.2	6.7	7.2	7.9	8.7
7.0								6.1	6.5	6.9	7.6	8.3
8.0											7.4	8.0
9.0												7.9

Height of Eye

Miles	m 20 / ft 66	22.5 / 74	25 / 82	27.5 / 90	30 / 98	32.5 / 107	35 / 115	37.5 / 123	40 / 131	42.5 / 139	45 / 148	47.5 / 156
	° ′	° ′	° ′	° ′	° ′	° ′	° ′	° ′	° ′	° ′	° ′	° ′
0.1	−6 10.8	−6 57.2	−7 43.5	−8 29.9	−9 16.2	−10 02.6	−10 48.9	−11 35.3	−12 21.6	−13 08.0	−13 54.3	−14 40.7
.2	3 05.5	3 28.6	3 51.8	4 15.0	4 38.2	5 01.4	5 24.5	5 47.7	6 10.9	6 34.0	6 57.2	7 20.4
.3	2 03.7	2 19.2	2 34.6	2 50.1	3 05.5	3 21.0	3 36.3	3 51.9	4 07.3	4 22.8	4 38.2	4 53.7
.4	1 32.9	1 44.5	1 56.0	2 07.6	2 19.2	2 30.8	2 42.4	2 54.0	3 05.6	3 17.2	3 28.7	3 40.3
.5	1 14.4	1 23.6	1 32.9	1 42.2	1 51.4	2 00.7	2 10.0	2 19.3	2 28.5	2 37.8	2 47.1	2 56.3
0.6	−1 02.1	−1 09.8	−1 17.5	−1 25.2	−1 33.0	−1 40.7	−1 48.4	−1 56.1	−2 03.9	−2 11.6	−2 19.3	−2 27.0
.7	53.3	59.9	1 06.5	1 13.1	1 19.8	1 26.4	1 33.0	1 39.6	1 46.2	1 52.8	1 59.4	2 06.1
.8	46.7	52.5	58.3	1 04.1	1 09.9	1 15.7	1 21.5	1 27.2	1 33.0	1 38.8	1 44.6	1 50.4
.9	41.6	46.7	51.9	57.0	1 02.2	1 07.3	1 12.5	1 17.6	1 22.8	1 27.9	1 33.1	1 38.2
1.0	37.5	42.1	46.8	51.4	56.0	1 00.7	1 05.3	1 09.9	1 14.6	1 19.2	1 23.9	1 28.5
1.2	−31.4	−35.3	−39.1	−43.0	−46.9	−50.7	−54.6	−58.4	−1 02.3	−1 06.2	−1 10.0	−1 13.9
.4	27.1	30.4	33.7	37.0	40.3	43.6	46.9	50.3	53.9	56.9	1 00.2	1 03.5
.6	23.9	26.8	29.7	32.6	35.4	38.3	41.2	44.1	47.0	49.9	52.8	55.7
.8	21.4	23.9	26.5	29.1	31.7	34.2	36.8	39.4	42.0	44.5	47.1	49.7
2.0	19.4	21.7	24.0	26.3	28.7	31.0	33.3	35.6	37.9	40.2	42.6	44.9
2.5	−15.9	−17.8	−19.6	−21.5	−23.3	−25.2	−27.0	−28.9	−30.7	−32.6	−34.4	−36.3
3.0	13.6	15.2	16.7	18.3	19.8	21.4	22.9	24.4	26.0	27.5	29.1	30.6
3.5	12.1	13.4	14.7	16.0	17.4	18.7	20.0	21.3	22.7	24.0	25.3	26.6
4.0	11.0	12.1	13.3	14.4	15.6	16.8	17.9	19.1	20.2	21.4	22.5	23.7
4.5	10.1	11.2	12.2	13.2	14.3	15.3	16.3	17.4	18.4	19.5	20.4	21.5
5.0	−9.6	−10.5	−11.4	−12.4	−13.3	−14.2	−15.1	−16.1	−17.0	−17.9	−18.8	−19.8
6.0	8.7	9.5	10.3	11.0	11.8	12.6	13.4	14.1	14.9	15.7	16.4	17.2
7.0	8.3	8.9	9.6	10.2	10.9	11.6	12.2	12.9	13.6	14.2	14.9	15.5
8.0	8.0	8.6	9.2	9.8	10.3	10.9	11.5	12.1	12.6	13.2	13.8	14.4
9.0	7.9	8.4	9.0	9.5	10.0	10.5	11.0	11.5	12.1	12.6	13.1	13.6
10.0			−8.9	−9.3	−9.8	−10.3	−10.7	−11.2	−11.6	−12.1	−12.6	−13.0
11.0					9.7	10.1	10.5	11.0	11.4	11.8	12.2	12.7
12.0								10.9	11.3	11.6	12.0	12.4
13.0									11.2	11.6	11.9	12.3
14.0												12.2

CORRECTION REQUIRED to CONVERT a RADIO GREAT CIRCLE BEARING to MERCATORIAL BEARING

Mean Lat.	DIFFERENCE OF LONGITUDE OF SHIP AND RADIO STATION															Mean Lat.
	2°	4°	6°	8°	10°	12°	14°	16°	18°	20°	22°	24°	26°	28°	30°	
84	1·0	2·0	3·0	4·0	5·0	6·0	7·0	8·0	9·0	9·9	10·9	11·9	12·9	13·9	14·9	84
81	1·0	2·0	2·9	4·0	4·9	5·9	6·9	7·9	8·9	9·9	10·9	11·9	12·8	13·8	14·8	81
78	1·0	2·0	2·9	3·9	4·9	5·9	6·8	7·8	8·8	9·8	10·8	11·7	12·7	13·7	14·7	78
75	1·0	1·9	2·9	3·9	4·8	5·8	6·8	7·7	8·7	9·7	10·7	11·6	12·6	13·5	14·4	75
72	1·0	1·9	2·9	3·8	4·8	5·7	6·7	7·6	8·6	9·5	10·5	11·4	12·4	13·3	14·3	72
69	0·9	1·9	2·8	3·7	4·7	5·6	6·5	7·5	8·4	9·3	10·3	11·2	12·1	13·1	14·0	69
66	0·9	1·8	2·8	3·7	4·6	5·5	6·4	7·3	8·2	9·1	10·0	11·0	11·9	12·8	13·7	66
63	0·9	1·8	2·7	3·6	4·5	5·4	6·3	7·1	8·0	8·9	9·8	10·7	11·6	12·5	13·3	63
60	0·9	1·7	2·6	3·5	4·3	5·2	6·1	6·9	7·8	8·6	9·5	10·4	11·2	12·1	12·9	60
57	0·8	1·7	2·5	3·4	4·2	5·0	5·9	6·7	7·5	8·4	9·2	10·0	10·9	11·7	12·5	57
54	0·8	1·6	2·4	3·3	4·1	4·9	5·7	6·5	7·3	8·1	8·9	9·7	10·5	11·3	12·1	54
51	0·8	1·6	2·3	3·1	3·9	4·7	5·5	6·2	7·0	7·8	8·5	9·3	10·1	10·8	11·6	51
48	0·8	1·5	2·2	3·0	3·7	4·5	5·2	5·9	6·7	7·4	8·2	8·9	9·6	10·4	11·1	48
45	0·7	1·4	2·1	2·8	3·5	4·2	4·9	5·6	6·3	7·1	7·8	8·5	9·2	9·9	10·6	45
42	0·7	1·4	2·0	2·7	3·4	4·0	4·7	5·4	6·0	6·7	7·4	8·0	8·7	9·4	10·0	42
39	0·6	1·3	1·9	2·5	3·2	3·8	4·4	5·0	5·7	6·3	6·9	7·5	8·1	8·8	9·4	39
36	0·6	1·2	1·8	2·4	3·0	3·5	4·1	4·7	5·3	5·9	6·4	7·0	7·6	8·2	8·7	36
33	0·5	1·1	1·6	2·2	2·7	3·3	3·8	4·4	4·9	5·4	6·0	6·5	7·1	7·6	8·1	33
30	0·5	1·0	1·5	2·0	2·5	3·0	3·5	4·0	4·5	5·0	5·5	6·0	6·5	7·0	7·4	30
27	0·5	0·9	1·4	1·8	2·3	2·7	3·2	3·6	4·1	4·5	5·0	5·4	5·9	6·3	6·8	27
24	0·4	0·8	1·2	1·6	2·1	2·4	2·9	3·3	3·6	4·0	4·4	4·8	5·2	5·6	6·0	24
21	0·3	0·7	1·1	1·4	1·8	2·2	2·5	2·9	3·2	3·6	3·9	4·3	4·6	5·0	5·3	21
18	0·3	0·6	0·9	1·2	1·6	1·9	2·2	2·5	2·8	3·1	3·4	3·7	4·0	4·3	4·6	18
15	0·3	0·5	0·8	1·0	1·3	1·6	1·8	2·1	2·3	2·6	2·8	3·1	3·3	3·6	3·8	15
12	0·2	0·4	0·6	0·8	1·0	1·3	1·5	1·7	1·9	2·1	2·3	2·5	2·7	2·9	3·1	12
9	0·2	0·3	0·5	0·6	0·8	1·0	1·1	1·2	1·4	1·6	1·7	1·9	2·0	2·2	2·3	9
6	0·1	0·2	0·3	0·4	0·5	0·6	0·7	0·8	0·9	1·0	1·1	1·2	1·3	1·5	1·6	6
3	0·1	0·1	0·2	0·2	0·3	0·3	0·4	0·4	0·5	0·5	0·6	0·6	0·7	0·7	0·8	3
	2°	4°	6°	8°	10°	12°	14°	16°	18°	20°	22°	24°	26°	28°	30°	

In both North and South latitudes always allow the above corrections towards the Equator from the Radio Great Circle bearing to obtain the corresponding Mercatorial line of bearing.

N.B.—The Bearings must always be laid off, on the chart, from the Radio Station.

EXAMPLE I. A ship in D.R. position Lat. 39° 37′ N., Long. 56° 25′ W., receives from a Radio Station in Lat. 35° 14′ N., Long. 75° 32′ W., the Radio bearing 074°. Find the correction and the corresponding Mercatorial bearing.

Mean Lat. is ½ (39° 37′+35° 14′) or ½ (74° 51′) =37°·4.

D. Long. is 75° 32′—56° 25′ =19°·1.

For Mean Lat. 37°·4 and D. Long. 19°·1 the Table gives a correction of 6° (approx.).

Allowing this correction towards the Equator the corresponding Mercatorial bearing is found to be 074°+6° =080°.

EXAMPLE 2. A ship in D.R. position Lat. 37° 26′ S., Long. 84° 35′ W., finds, with her own apparatus, the Radio bearing of a station in Lat. 36° 37′ S., Long. 73° 03′ W., to be 089°. Find the correction and the corresponding Mercatorial bearing.

For Mean Lat. 37° and D. Long. 11°·5 the Table gives a correction of 3°·5 (approx.).

Allowing this correction towards the Equator the corresponding Mercatorial bearing is found to be 089°—3°·5 =085°·5.

IV   PHYSICAL AND CONVERSION TABLES

CONVERSION OF ARC TO TIME

Arc °	Time h.m. m.s.	Arc °	Time h.m.	Arc °	Time h.m.	Arc °	Time h.m.	Arc °	Time h.m.	Arc °	Time h.m.	Parts of 1′	s.	Arc ″	Time s.
0	0 00	60	4 00	120	8 00	180	12 00	240	16 00	300	20 00	0·1	0·4	0	0·00
1	0 04	61	4 04	121	8 04	181	12 04	241	16 04	301	20 04			1	0·07
2	0 08	62	4 08	122	8 08	182	12 08	242	16 08	302	20 08	0·2	0·8	2	0·13
3	0 12	63	4 12	123	8 12	183	12 12	243	16 12	303	20 12			3	0·20
4	0 16	64	4 16	124	8 16	184	12 16	244	16 16	304	20 16	0·3	1·2	4	0·27
5	0 20	65	4 20	125	8 20	185	12 20	245	16 20	305	20 20			5	0·33
6	0 24	66	4 24	126	8 24	186	12 24	246	16 24	306	20 24	0·4	1·6	6	0·40
7	0 28	67	4 28	127	8 28	187	12 28	247	16 28	307	20 28			7	0·47
8	0 32	68	4 32	128	8 32	188	12 32	248	16 32	308	20 32	0·5	2·0	8	0·53
9	0 36	69	4 36	129	8 36	189	12 36	249	16 36	309	20 36			9	0·60
10	0 40	70	4 40	130	8 40	190	12 40	250	16 40	310	20 40	0·6	2·4	10	0·67
11	0 44	71	4 44	131	8 44	191	12 44	251	16 44	311	20 44	0·7	2·8	11	0·73
12	0 48	72	4 48	132	8 48	192	12 48	252	16 48	312	20 48			12	0·80
13	0 52	73	4 52	133	8 52	193	12 52	253	16 52	313	20 52	0·8	3·2	13	0·87
14	0 56	74	4 56	134	8 56	194	12 56	254	16 56	314	20 56			14	0·93
15	1 00	75	5 00	135	9 00	195	13 00	255	17 00	315	21 00	0·9	3·6	15	1·00
16	1 04	76	5 04	136	9 04	196	13 04	256	17 04	316	21 04			16	1·07
17	1 08	77	5 08	137	9 08	197	13 08	257	17 08	317	21 08			17	1·13
18	1 12	78	5 12	138	9 12	198	13 12	258	17 12	318	21 12			18	1·20
19	1 16	79	5 16	139	9 16	199	13 16	259	17 16	319	21 16			19	1·27
20	1 20	80	5 20	140	9 20	200	13 20	260	17 20	320	21 20			20	1·33
21	1 24	81	5 24	141	9 24	201	13 24	261	17 24	321	21 24			21	1·40
22	1 28	82	5 28	142	9 28	202	13 28	262	17 28	322	21 28			22	1·47
23	1 32	83	5 32	143	9 32	203	13 32	263	17 32	323	21 32			23	1·53
24	1 36	84	5 36	144	9 36	204	13 36	264	17 36	324	21 36			24	1·60
25	1 40	85	5 40	145	9 40	205	13 40	265	17 40	325	21 40			25	1·67
26	1 44	86	5 44	146	9 44	206	13 44	266	17 44	326	21 44			26	1·73
27	1 48	87	5 48	147	9 48	207	13 48	267	17 48	327	21 48			27	1·80
28	1 52	88	5 52	148	9 52	208	13 52	268	17 52	328	21 52			28	1·87
29	1 56	89	5 56	149	9 56	209	13 56	269	17 56	329	21 56			29	1·93
30	2 00	90	6 00	150	10 00	210	14 00	270	18 00	330	22 00			30	2·00
31	2 04	91	6 04	151	10 04	211	14 04	271	18 04	331	22 04			31	2·07
32	2 08	92	6 08	152	10 08	212	14 08	272	18 08	332	22 08			32	2·13
33	2 12	93	6 12	153	10 12	213	14 12	273	18 12	333	22 12			33	2·20
34	2 16	94	6 16	154	10 16	214	14 16	274	18 16	334	22 16			34	2·27
35	2 20	95	6 20	155	10 20	215	14 20	275	18 20	335	22 20			35	2·33
36	2 24	96	6 24	156	10 24	216	14 24	276	18 24	336	22 24			36	2·40
37	2 28	97	6 28	157	10 28	217	14 28	277	18 28	337	22 28			37	2·47
38	2 32	98	6 32	158	10 32	218	14 32	278	18 32	338	22 32			38	2·53
39	2 36	99	6 36	159	10 36	219	14 36	279	18 36	339	22 36			39	2·60
40	2 40	100	6 40	160	10 40	220	14 40	280	18 40	340	22 40			40	2·67
41	2 44	101	6 44	161	10 44	221	14 44	281	18 44	341	22 44			41	2·73
42	2 48	102	6 48	162	10 48	222	14 48	282	18 48	342	22 48			42	2·80
43	2 52	103	6 52	163	10 52	223	14 52	283	18 52	343	22 52			43	2·87
44	2 56	104	6 56	164	10 56	224	14 56	284	18 56	344	22 56			44	2·93
45	3 00	105	7 00	165	11 00	225	15 00	285	19 00	345	23 00			45	3·00
46	3 04	106	7 04	166	11 04	226	15 04	286	19 04	346	23 04			46	3·07
47	3 08	107	7 08	167	11 08	227	15 08	287	19 08	347	23 08			47	3·13
48	3 12	108	7 12	168	11 12	228	15 12	288	19 12	348	23 12			48	3·20
49	3 16	109	7 16	169	11 16	229	15 16	289	19 16	349	23 16			49	3·27
50	3 20	110	7 20	170	11 20	230	15 20	290	19 20	350	23 20			50	3·33
51	3 24	111	7 24	171	11 24	231	15 24	291	19 24	351	23 24			51	3·40
52	3 28	112	7 28	172	11 28	232	15 28	292	19 28	352	23 28			52	3·47
53	3 32	113	7 32	173	11 32	233	15 32	293	19 32	353	23 32			53	3·53
54	3 36	114	7 36	174	11 36	234	15 36	294	19 36	354	23 36			54	3·60
55	3 40	115	7 40	175	11 40	235	15 40	295	19 40	355	23 40			55	3·67
56	3 44	116	7 44	176	11 44	236	15 44	296	19 44	356	23 44			56	3·73
57	3 48	117	7 48	177	11 48	237	15 48	297	19 48	357	23 48			57	3·80
58	3 52	118	7 52	178	11 52	238	15 52	298	19 52	358	23 52			58	3·87
59	3 56	119	7 56	179	11 56	239	15 56	299	19 56	359	23 56			59	3·93
60	4 00	120	8 00	180	12 00	240	16 00	300	20 00	360	24 00			60	4·00

CONVERSION OF TIME TO ARC

Time h. m. (m. s.)	Arc ° (′)	Time h. m.	Arc °	Time h. m.	Arc °	Time h. m.	Arc °	Time h. m.	Arc °	Time h. m.	Arc °	Time m. (s.)	Arc ° ′ (′ ″)
0 00	0	4 00	60	8 00	120	12 00	180	16 00	240	20 00	300	0	0 00
0 04	1	4 04	61	8 04	121	12 04	181	16 04	241	20 04	301	1	0 15
0 08	2	4 08	62	8 08	122	12 08	182	16 08	242	20 08	302	2	0 30
0 12	3	4 12	63	8 12	123	12 12	183	16 12	243	20 12	303	3	0 45
0 16	4	4 16	64	8 16	124	12 16	184	16 16	244	20 16	304	4	1 00
0 20	5	4 20	65	8 20	125	12 20	185	16 20	245	20 20	305	5	1 15
0 24	6	4 24	66	8 24	126	12 24	186	16 24	246	20 24	306	6	1 30
0 28	7	4 28	67	8 28	127	12 28	187	16 28	247	20 28	307	7	1 45
0 32	8	4 32	68	8 32	128	12 32	188	16 32	248	20 32	308	8	2 00
0 36	9	4 36	69	8 36	129	12 36	189	16 36	249	20 36	309	9	2 15
0 40	10	4 40	70	8 40	130	12 40	190	16 40	250	20 40	310	10	2 30
0 44	11	4 44	71	8 44	131	12 44	191	16 44	251	20 44	311	11	2 45
0 48	12	4 48	72	8 48	132	12 48	192	16 48	252	20 48	312	12	3 00
0 52	13	4 52	73	8 52	133	12 52	193	16 52	253	20 52	313	13	3 15
0 56	14	4 56	74	8 56	134	12 56	194	16 56	254	20 56	314	14	3 30
1 00	15	5 00	75	9 00	135	13 00	195	17 00	255	21 00	315	15	3 45
1 04	16	5 04	76	9 04	136	13 04	196	17 04	256	21 04	316	16	4 00
1 08	17	5 08	77	9 08	137	13 08	197	17 08	257	21 08	317	17	4 15
1 12	18	5 12	78	9 12	138	13 12	198	17 12	258	21 12	318	18	4 30
1 16	19	5 16	79	9 16	139	13 16	199	17 16	259	21 16	319	19	4 45
1 20	20	5 20	80	9 20	140	13 20	200	17 20	260	21 20	320	20	5 00
1 24	21	5 24	81	9 24	141	13 24	201	17 24	261	21 24	321	21	5 15
1 28	22	5 28	82	9 28	142	13 28	202	17 28	262	21 28	322	22	5 30
1 32	23	5 32	83	9 32	143	13 32	203	17 32	263	21 32	323	23	5 45
1 36	24	5 36	84	9 36	144	13 36	204	17 36	264	21 36	324	24	6 00
1 40	25	5 40	85	9 40	145	13 40	205	17 40	265	21 40	325	25	6 15
1 44	26	5 44	86	9 44	146	13 44	206	17 44	266	21 44	326	26	6 30
1 48	27	5 48	87	9 48	147	13 48	207	17 48	267	21 48	327	27	6 45
1 52	28	5 52	88	9 52	148	13 52	208	17 52	268	21 52	328	28	7 00
1 56	29	5 56	89	9 56	149	13 56	209	17 56	269	21 56	329	29	7 15
2 00	30	6 00	90	10 00	150	14 00	210	18 00	270	22 00	330	30	7 30
2 04	31	6 04	91	10 04	151	14 04	211	18 04	271	22 04	331	31	7 45
2 08	32	6 08	92	10 08	152	14 08	212	18 08	272	22 08	332	32	8 00
2 12	33	6 12	93	10 12	153	14 12	213	18 12	273	22 12	333	33	8 15
2 16	34	6 16	94	10 16	154	14 16	214	18 16	274	22 16	334	34	8 30
2 20	35	6 20	95	10 20	155	14 20	215	18 20	275	22 20	335	35	8 45
2 24	36	6 24	96	10 24	156	14 24	216	18 24	276	22 24	336	36	9 00
2 28	37	6 28	97	10 28	157	14 28	217	18 28	277	22 28	337	37	9 15
2 32	38	6 32	98	10 32	158	14 32	218	18 32	278	22 32	338	38	9 30
2 36	39	6 36	99	10 36	159	14 36	219	18 36	279	22 36	339	39	9 45
2 40	40	6 40	100	10 40	160	14 40	220	18 40	280	22 40	340	40	10 00
2 44	41	6 44	101	10 44	161	14 44	221	18 44	281	22 44	341	41	10 15
2 48	42	6 48	102	10 48	162	14 48	222	18 48	282	22 48	342	42	10 30
2 52	43	6 52	103	10 52	163	14 52	223	18 52	283	22 52	343	43	10 45
2 56	44	6 56	104	10 56	164	14 56	224	18 56	284	22 56	344	44	11 00
3 00	45	7 00	105	11 00	165	15 00	225	19 00	285	23 00	345	45	11 15
3 04	46	7 04	106	11 04	166	15 04	226	19 04	286	23 04	346	46	11 30
3 08	47	7 08	107	11 08	167	15 08	227	19 08	287	23 08	347	47	11 45
3 12	48	7 12	108	11 12	168	15 12	228	19 12	288	23 12	348	48	12 00
3 16	49	7 16	109	11 16	169	15 16	229	19 16	289	23 16	349	49	12 15
3 20	50	7 20	110	11 20	170	15 20	230	19 20	290	23 20	350	50	12 30
3 24	51	7 24	111	11 24	171	15 24	231	19 24	291	23 24	351	51	12 45
3 28	52	7 28	112	11 28	172	15 28	232	19 28	292	23 28	352	52	13 00
3 32	53	7 32	113	11 32	173	15 32	233	19 32	293	23 32	353	53	13 15
3 36	54	7 36	114	11 36	174	15 36	234	19 36	294	23 36	354	54	13 30
3 40	55	7 40	115	11 40	175	15 40	235	19 40	295	23 40	355	55	13 45
3 44	56	7 44	116	11 44	176	15 44	236	19 44	296	23 44	356	56	14 00
3 48	57	7 48	117	11 48	177	15 48	237	19 48	297	23 48	357	57	14 15
3 52	58	7 52	118	11 52	178	15 52	238	19 52	298	23 52	358	58	14 30
3 56	59	7 56	119	11 56	179	15 56	239	19 56	299	23 56	359	59	14 45
4 00	60	8 00	120	12 00	180	16 00	240	20 00	300	24 00	360	60	15 00

Critical Table *

s.	′
0·0	
	0·0
0·2	
	0·1
0·5	
	0·2
1·0	
	0·3
1·3	
	0·4
1·8	
	0·5
2·1	
	0·6
2·6	
	0·7
2·9	
	0·8
3·4	
	0·9
3·7	
	1·0
4·0	

* For use when quantity is required only to nearest 0′.1. In critical cases use upper value.

HOURS AND MINUTES TO DECIMAL OF A DAY

Min.	0	1	2	3	4	5	6	7	8	9	10	11
						Hours						
0	·0000	·0417	·0833	·1250	·1667	·2083	·2500	·2917	·3333	·3750	·4167	·4583
1	·0007	·0424	·0840	·1257	·1674	·2090	·2507	·2924	·3340	·3757	·4174	·4590
2	·0014	·0431	·0847	·1264	·1681	·2097	·2514	·2931	·3347	·3764	·4181	·4597
3	·0021	·0438	·0854	·1271	·1688	·2104	·2521	·2938	·3354	·3771	·4188	·4604
4	·0028	·0444	·0861	·1278	·1694	·2111	·2528	·2944	·3361	·3778	·4194	·4611
5	·0035	·0451	·0868	·1285	·1701	·2118	·2535	·2951	·3368	·3785	·4201	·4618
6	·0042	·0458	·0875	·1292	·1708	·2125	·2542	·2958	·3375	·3792	·4208	·4625
7	·0049	·0465	·0882	·1299	·1715	·2132	·2549	·2965	·3382	·3799	·4215	·4632
8	·0056	·0472	·0889	·1306	·1722	·2139	·2556	·2972	·3389	·3806	·4222	·4639
9	·0063	·0479	·0896	·1313	·1729	·2146	·2563	·2979	·3396	·3813	·4229	·4646
10	·0069	·0486	·0903	·1319	·1736	·2153	·2569	·2986	·3403	·3819	·4236	·4653
11	·0076	·0493	·0910	·1326	·1743	·2160	·2576	·2993	·3410	·3826	·4243	·4660
12	·0083	·0500	·0917	·1333	·1750	·2167	·2583	·3000	·3417	·3833	·4250	·4667
13	·0090	·0507	·0924	·1340	·1757	·2174	·2590	·3007	·3424	·3840	·4257	·4674
14	·0097	·0514	·0931	·1347	·1764	·2181	·2597	·3014	·3431	·3847	·4264	·4681
15	·0104	·0521	·0938	·1354	·1771	·2188	·2604	·3021	·3438	·3854	·4271	·4688
16	·0111	·0528	·0944	·1361	·1778	·2194	·2611	·3028	·3444	·3861	·4278	·4694
17	·0118	·0535	·0951	·1368	·1785	·2201	·2618	·3035	·3451	·3868	·4285	·4701
18	·0125	·0542	·0958	·1375	·1792	·2208	·2625	·3042	·3458	·3875	·4292	·4708
19	·0132	·0549	·0965	·1382	·1799	·2215	·2632	·3049	·3465	·3882	·4299	·4715
20	·0139	·0556	·0972	·1389	·1806	·2222	·2639	·3056	·3472	·3889	·4306	·4722
21	·0146	·0563	·0979	·1396	·1813	·2229	·2646	·3063	·3479	·3896	·4313	·4729
22	·0153	·0569	·0986	·1403	·1819	·2236	·2653	·3069	·3486	·3903	·4319	·4736
23	·0160	·0576	·0993	·1410	·1826	·2243	·2660	·3076	·3493	·3910	·4326	·4743
24	·0167	·0583	·1000	·1417	·1833	·2250	·2667	·3083	·3500	·3917	·4333	·4750
25	·0174	·0590	·1007	·1424	·1840	·2257	·2674	·3090	·3507	·3924	·4340	·4757
26	·0181	·0597	·1014	·1431	·1847	·2264	·2681	·3097	·3514	·3931	·4347	·4764
27	·0188	·0604	·1021	·1438	·1854	·2271	·2688	·3104	·3521	·3938	·4354	·4771
28	·0194	·0611	·1028	·1444	·1861	·2278	·2694	·3111	·3528	·3944	·4361	·4778
29	·0201	·0618	·1035	·1451	·1868	·2285	·2701	·3118	·3535	·3951	·4368	·4785
30	·0208	·0625	·1042	·1458	·1875	·2292	·2708	·3125	·3542	·3958	·4375	·4792
31	·0215	·0632	·1049	·1465	·1882	·2299	·2715	·3132	·3549	·3965	·4382	·4799
32	·0222	·0639	·1056	·1472	·1889	·2306	·2722	·3139	·3556	·3972	·4389	·4806
33	·0229	·0646	·1063	·1479	·1896	·2313	·2729	·3146	·3563	·3979	·4396	·4813
34	·0236	·0653	·1069	·1486	·1903	·2319	·2736	·3153	·3569	·3986	·4403	·4819
35	·0243	·0660	·1076	·1493	·1910	·2326	·2743	·3160	·3576	·3993	·4410	·4826
36	·0250	·0667	·1083	·1500	·1917	·2333	·2750	·3167	·3583	·4000	·4417	·4833
37	·0257	·0674	·1090	·1507	·1924	·2340	·2757	·3174	·3590	·4007	·4424	·4840
38	·0264	·0681	·1097	·1514	·1931	·2347	·2764	·3181	·3597	·4014	·4431	·4847
39	·0271	·0688	·1104	·1521	·1938	·2354	·2771	·3188	·3604	·4021	·4438	·4854
40	·0278	·0694	·1111	·1528	·1944	·2361	·2778	·3194	·3611	·4028	·4444	·4861
41	·0285	·0701	·1118	·1535	·1951	·2368	·2785	·3201	·3618	4035	·4451	·4868
42	·0292	·0708	·1125	·1542	·1958	·2375	·2792	·3208	·3625	·4042	·4458	·4875
43	·0299	·0715	·1132	·1549	·1965	·2382	·2799	·3215	·3632	·4049	·4465	·4882
44	·0306	·0722	·1139	·1556	·1972	·2389	·2806	·3222	·3639	·4056	·4472	·4889
45	·0313	·0729	·1146	·1563	·1979	·2396	·2813	·3229	·3646	·4063	·4479	·4896
46	·0319	·0736	·1153	·1569	·1986	·2403	·2819	·3236	·3653	·4069	·4486	·4903
47	·0326	·0743	·1160	·1576	·1993	·2410	·2826	·3243	·3660	·4076	·4493	·4910
48	·0333	·0750	·1167	·1583	·2000	·2417	·2833	·3250	·3667	·4083	·4500	·4917
49	·0340	·0757	·1174	·1590	·2007	·2424	·2840	·3257	·3674	·4090	·4507	·4924
50	·0347	·0764	·1181	·1597	·2014	·2431	·2847	·3264	·3681	·4097	·4514	·4931
51	·0354	·0771	·1188	·1604	·2021	·2438	·2854	·3271	·3688	·4104	·4521	·4938
52	·0361	·0778	·1194	·1611	·2028	·2444	·2861	·3278	·3694	·4111	·4528	·4944
53	·0368	·0785	·1201	·1618	·2035	·2451	·2868	·3285	·3701	·4118	·4535	·4951
54	·0375	·0792	·1208	·1625	·2042	·2458	·2875	·3292	·3708	·4125	·4542	·4958
55	·0382	·0799	·1215	·1632	·2049	·2465	·2882	·3299	·3715	·4132	·4549	·4965
56	·0389	·0806	·1222	·1639	·2056	·2472	·2889	·3306	·3722	·4139	·4556	·4972
57	·0396	·0813	·1229	·1646	·2063	·2479	·2896	·3313	·3729	·4146	·4563	·4979
58	·0403	·0819	·1236	·1653	·2069	·2486	·2903	·3319	·3736	·4153	·4569	·4986
59	·0410	·0826	·1243	·1660	·2076	·2493	·2910	·3326	·3743	·4160	·4576	·4993
60	·0417	·0833	·1250	·1667	·2083	·2500	·2917	·3333	·3750	·4167	·4583	·5000

For an additional 12 hours, increase the tabulated value by 0.5.,
e.g., 14h. 38m. = 12h. + 2h. 38m. = 0.5 + .1097 = 0.6097 of a day.
Similarly, .8972 of a day = 0.5 + .3972 = 12h. + 9h. 32m. = 21h.32m.

ATMOSPHERIC PRESSURE CONVERSION TABLES

MERCURY INCHES TO MILLIBARS

In.	Mb.	In.	Mb.	In.	Mb.
28·0	948·2	29·1	985·4	30·2	1022·7
28·1	951·6	29·2	988·8	30·3	1026·1
28·2	954·9	29·3	992·2	30·4	1029·4
28·3	958·3	29·4	995·6	30·5	1032·8
28·4	961·7	29·5	999·0	30·6	1036·2
28·5	965·1	29·6	1002·4	30·7	1039·6
28·6	968·5	29·7	1005·7	30·8	1043·0
28·7	971·9	29·8	1009·1	30·9	1046·4
28·8	975·3	29·9	1012·5	31·0	1049·8
28·9	978·6	30·0	1015·9	31·1	1053·1
29·0	982·0	30·1	1019·3	31·2	1056·5

For { Lat. 45°
Temp. 32°F 0°C

1 lb/in² = 6.894 76 kN/m²
1 kN/m² = 0.145 038 lb/in²
1 mb = 100 N/m²
1 inch mercury = 3.386 39 kN/m²
1 kN/m² = 0.295 300 inches mercury

The Standard Atmosphere is:

101 325 N/m²
1013.25 mb
760 mm mercury

MILLIBARS TO MERCURY INCHES

Mb.	In.	Mb..	In.	Mb.	In.
948	28·00	984	29·06	1020	30·12
949	28·02	985	29·09	1021	30·15
950	28·05	986	29·12	1022	30·18
951	28·08	987	29·15	1023	30·21
952	28·11	988	29·18	1024	30·24
953	28·14	989	29·21	1025	30·27
954	28·17	990	29·24	1026	30·30
955	28·20	991	29·26	1027	30·33
956	28·23	992	29·29	1028	30·36
957	28·26	993	29·32	1029	30·39
958	28·29	994	29·35	1030	30·42
959	28·32	995	29·38	1031	30·45
960	28·35	996	29·41	1032	30·48
961	28·38	997	29·44	1033	30·50
962	28·41	998	29·47	1034	30·53
963	28·44	999	29·50	1035	30·56
964	28·47	1000	29·53	1036	30·59
965	28·50	1001	29·56	1037	30·62
966	28·53	1002	29·59	1038	30·65
967	28·56	1003	29·62	1039	30·68
968	28·59	1004	29·65	1040	30·71
969	28·62	1005	29·68	1041	30·74
970	28·64	1006	29:71	1042	30·77
971	28·67	1007	29·74	1043	30·80
972	28·70	1008	29·77	1044	30·83
973	28·73	1009	29·80	1045	30·86
974	28·76	1010	29·83	1046	30·89
975	28·79	1011	29·86	1047	30·92
976	28·82	1012	29·88	1048	30·95
977	28·85	1013	29·91	1049	30·98
978	28·88	1014	29·94	1050	31·01
979	28·91	1015	29·97	1051	31·04
980	28·94	1016	30·00	1052	31·07
981	28·97	1017	30·03	1053	31·10
982	29·00	1018	30·06	1054	31·13
983	29·03	1019	30·09	1055	31·15

°FAHRENHEIT - °CELSIUS - °FAHRENHEIT

Temp. °F	0	1	2	3	4	5	6	7	8	9
					°Celsius					
0	−17.8	−17.2	−16.7	−16.1	−15.6	−15.0	−14.4	−13.9	−13.3	−12.8
10	−12.2	−11.7	−11.1	−10.6	−10.0	−9.4	−8.9	−8.3	−7.8	−7.2
20	−6.7	−6.1	−5.6	−5.0	−4.4	−3.9	−3.3	−2.8	−2.2	−1.7
30	−1.1	−0.6	0.0	0.6	1.1	1.7	2.2	2.8	3.3	3.9
40	4.4	5.0	5.6	6.1	6.7	7.2	7.8	8.3	8.9	9.4
50	10.0	10.6	11.1	11.7	12.2	12.8	13.3	13.9	14.4	15.0
60	15.6	16.1	16.7	17.2	17.8	18.3	18.9	19.4	20.0	20.6
70	21.1	21.7	22.2	22.8	23.3	23.9	24.4	25.0	25.6	26.1
80	26.7	27.2	27.8	28.3	28.9	29.4	30.0	30.6	31.1	31.7
90	32.2	32.8	33.3	33.9	34.4	35.0	35.6	36.1	36.7	37.2
100	37.8	38.3	38.9	39.4	40.0	40.6	41.1	41.7	42.2	42.8
110	43.3	43.9	44.4	45.0	45.6	46.1	46.7	47.2	47.8	48.3
120	48.9	49.4	50.0	50.6	51.1	51.7	52.2	52.8	53.3	53.9
130	54.4	55.0	55.6	56.1	56.7	57.2	57.8	58.3	58.9	59.4
140	60.0	60.6	61.1	61.7	62.2	62.8	63.3	63.9	64.4	65.0

Examples: 22°F = -5.6°C; 126°F = 52.2 °C

°CELSIUS - °FAHRENHEIT - °CELSIUS

Temp. °C	0	1	2	3	4	5	6	7	8	9
					°Fahrenheit					
−10	14.0	12.2	10.4	8.6	6.8	5.0	3.2	1.4	−0.4	−2.2
−0	32.0	30.2	28.4	26.6	24.8	23.0	21.2	19.4	17.6	15.8
0	32.0	33.8	35.6	37.4	39.2	41.0	42.8	44.6	46.4	48.2
10	50.0	51.8	53.6	55.4	57.2	59.0	60.8	62.6	64.4	66.2
20	68.0	69.8	71.6	73.4	75.2	77.0	78.8	80.6	82.4	84.2
30	86.0	87.8	89.6	91.4	93.2	95.0	96.8	98.6	100.4	102.2
40	104.0	105.8	107.6	109.4	111.2	113.0	114.8	116.6	118.4	120.2
50	122.0	123.9	125.6	127.4	129.2	131.0	132.8	134.6	136.4	138.2

Examples: -15°C = 5.0°F; -9°C ≑ 15.8°F; 54°C = 129.2°F

S.I. - BRITISH UNITS

S.I. recommended and recognised Units	Conversion Factors	
	British Units to S.I.	S.I. Units to British
LENGTH		
millimetre (mm)	1 in = 25.4 mm*	1 mm = 0.039 370 in
centimetre (cm)	1 ft = 0.3048 m*	1 m = 3.280 83 ft
metre (m)	1 yd = 0.9144 m*	1 m = 1.093 61 yd
kilometre (km)	1 fathom = 1.8288 m*	1 m = 0.546 807 fathom
International nautical mile	1 mile = 1.609 34 km	1 km = 0.621 371 mile
(n mile) = 1,852.0 m	1 n mile (British) = 1.000 64 n mile (Inter.)	1 n mile (Inter.) = 0.999 36 n mile (British)
AREA		
square millimetres (mm²)	1 in² = 645.16 mm² *	1 mm² = 0.001 550 in²
square centimetre (cm²)	1 ft² = 0.092 903 m²	1 m² = 10.7639 ft²
square metre (m²)	1 yd² = 0.836 127 m²	1 m² = 1.195 99 yd²
square kilometre (km²)	1 acre = 4046.86 m²	
hectare (ha) = 10000 m²	1 acre = 0.404 686 ha	1 ha = 2.471 05 acre
VOLUME		
cubic millimetre (mm³)	1 in³ = 16387.1 mm³	1 mm³ = 0.000 061 0237 in³
cubic centimetre (cm³)	1 ft³ = 0.028 3168 m³	1 m³ = 35.3147 ft³
cubic metre (m³)	1 yd³ = 0.764 555 m³	1 m³ = 1.307 95 yd³
litre (l) = 0.001 m³	1 pint = 0.000 568 261 m³	
	1 gal = 0.004 546 09 m³	1 m³ = 219.969 gal
	1 pint = 0.568 261 l	1 l = 1.759 75 pint
	1 gal = 4.546 09 l	1 l = 0.219 969 gal
	1 Freight ton (40 ft³) = 1.1327 m³	
MASS		
gramme (g)	1 oz (avdp) = 28.3495 g	1 g = 0.035 274 oz (avdp)
kilogramme (kg)	1 lb = 0.453 592 37 kg*	1 kg = 2.204 62 lb
tonne (t) = 1000 kg	1 cwt = 50.8023 kg	1 t (tonne) = 0.984 207 ton
	1 ton = 1016.05 kg	1 t (tonne) = 2204.62 lb
	1 ton = 1.016 05 t (tonne)	
DENSITY		
kilogramme/cubic metre (kg/m³)	1 lb/ft³ = 16.0185 kg/m³	1 kg/m³ = 0.062 428 lb/ft³
gramme/cubic centimetre (g/cm³)	1 lb/in³ = 27.6799 g/cm³	1 g/cm³ = 0.036 127 lb/in³
tonne/cubic metre (t/m³)	1 ton/yd³ = 1.328 94 t/m³	1 t/m³ = 0.752 479 ton/yd³
FORCE		
newton (N)	1 tonf = 9.964 02 kN	1 kN = 0.100 361 tonf
kilonewton (kN)	1 lbf = 4.448 22 N	1 N = 0.224 809 lbf
meganewton (MN)	1 poundal = 0.138 255 N	1 N = 7.233 01 poundal
VELOCITY		
metre/second (m/s)	1 in/s = 25.4 mm/s*	1 mm/s = 0.039 3701 in/s
kilometre/second (km/s)	1 ft/min = 5.08 mm/s	1 mm/s = 0.196 85 ft/min
knot International = 1,852.0 m/h	1 ft/s = 0.3048 m/s*	1 m/s = 3.280 84 ft/s
	1 mph = 0.447 040 m/s	1 m/s = 2.236 94 mph
	1 mph = 1.609 34 km/h	1 km/h = 0.621 371 mph
	1 knot (British) = 1.000 64 knot (Inter.)	1 knot (Inter.) = 0.999 36 knot (British)
VOLUME FLOW RATE		
cubic metres/second (m³/s)	1 ft³/s = 0.028 3168 m³/s	1 m³/s = 35.3147 ft³/s
cubic metres/hour (m³/h)	1 gal/h = 0.004 546 09 m³/h	1 m³/h = 219.969 gal/h
litres/hour (l/h)	1 gal/h = 4.546 09 l/h	1 l/h = 0.219 969 gal/h
litres/second (l/s)	1 gal/min = 0.272 765 m³/h	1 m³/h = 3.666 16 gal/min
	1 gal/min = 0.075 768 2 l/s	1 l/s = 13.1981 gal/min
ENERGY		
joule (J)	1 kWh = 3.6 MJ*	1 MJ = 0.277 778 kWh
kilojoule (kJ)	1 ftlbf = 1.355 82 J	1 J = 0.737 562 ftlbf
megajoule (MJ)	1 ftpdl = 0.042 1401 J	1 J = 23.7304 ftpdl
	1 therm = 105.506 MJ	1 MJ = 0.009 478 13 therm
	1 Btu = 1.055 06 kJ	1 kJ = 0.947 813 Btu
POWER		
watt (W)	1 hp = 745.700 W	1 W = 0.001 341 02 hp
kilowatt (kW)	1 ftlbf/s = 1.355 82 W	1 W = 0.737 561 ftlbf/s
megawatt (MW)		

* Indicates a conversion factor which is exact.

S.I. UNITS - PREFIXES

The prefixes for forming multiples and sub-multiples of S.I. units are:

Prefix name	Prefix symbol	Factor by which the unit is multiplied	
tera	T	10^{12} =	1 000 000 000 000
giga	G	10^{9} =	1 000 000 000
mega	M	10^{6} =	1 000 000
kilo	k	10^{3} =	1 000
hecto	h	10^{2} =	100
deca	da	10^{1} =	10
deci	d	10^{-1} =	0.1
centi	c	10^{-2} =	0.01
milli	m	10^{-3} =	0.001
micro	μ	10^{-6} =	0.000 001
nano	n	10^{-9} =	0.000 000 001
pico	p	10^{-12} =	0.000 000 000 001
femto	f	10^{-15} =	0.000 000 000 000 001
atto	a	10^{-18} =	0.000 000 000 000 000 001

For example:

megawatt (MW)	=	1 000 000 watts
kilogramme (kg)	=	1 000 grammes
millivolt (mV)	=	0.001 volt
microsecond (μs)	=	0.000 001 second
picofarad (pF)	=	0.000 000 000 001 farad

BRITISH GALLONS - LITRES - BRITISH GALLONS

British Gallons	0	1	2	3	4	5	6	7	8	9
					Litres					
0	—	4.55	9.09	13.64	18.18	22.73	27.28	31.82	36.37	40.92
10	45.46	50.01	54.55	59.10	63.65	68.19	72.74	77.28	81.83	86.38
20	90.92	95.47	100.01	104.56	109.11	113.65	118.20	122.74	127.29	131.84
30	136.38	140.93	145.48	150.02	154.57	159.11	163.66	168.21	172.75	177.30
40	181.84	186.39	190.94	195.48	200.03	204.57	209.12	213.67	218.21	222.76
50	227.31	231.85	236.40	240.94	245.49	250.04	254.58	259.13	263.67	268.22
60	272.77	277.31	281.86	286.40	290.95	295.50	300.04	304.59	309.13	313.68
70	318.23	322.77	327.32	331.86	336.41	340.96	345.50	350.05	354.60	359.14
80	363.69	368.23	372.78	377.33	381.87	386.42	390.96	395.51	400.06	404.60
90	409.15	413.69	418.24	422.79	427.33	431.88	436.42	440.97	445.52	450.06

British Gallons	0	100	200	300	400	500	600	700	800	900
					Litres					
0	—	454.6	909.2	1363.8	1818.4	2273.0	2727.7	3182.3	3636.9	4091.5
1000	4546.1	5000.7	5455.3	5909.9	6364.5	6819.1	7273.7	7728.4	8183.0	8637.6
2000	9092.2	9546.8	10001.4	10456.0	10910.6	11365.2	11819.8	12274.4	12729.1	13183.7
3000	13638.3	14092.9	14547.5	15002.1	15456.7	15911.3	16365.9	16820.5	17275.1	17729.8
4000	18184.4	18639.0	19093.6	19548.2	20002.8	20457.4	20912.0	21366.6	21821.2	22275.9
5000	22730.5	23185.1	23639.7	24094.3	24548.9	25003.5	25458.1	25912.7	26367.3	26821.9

Examples: 23 British gallons = 104.56 litres;   4189 British gallons = 18639.0 + 404.60 = 19043.6 litres

Litres	0	1	2	3	4	5	6	7	8	9
					British Gallons					
0	—	0.22	0.44	0.66	0.88	1.10	1.32	1.54	1.76	1.98
10	2.20	2.42	2.64	2.86	3.08	3.30	3.52	3.74	3.96	4.18
20	4.40	4.62	4.84	5.06	5.28	5.50	5.72	5.94	6.16	6.38
30	6.60	6.82	7.04	7.26	7.48	7.70	7.92	8.14	8.36	8.58
40	8.80	9.02	9.24	9.46	9.68	9.90	10.12	10.34	10.56	10.78
50	11.00	11.22	11.44	11.66	11.88	12.10	12.32	12.54	12.76	12.98
60	13.20	13.42	13.64	13.86	14.08	14.30	14.52	14.74	14.96	15.18
70	15.40	15.62	15.84	16.06	16.28	16.50	16.72	16.94	17.16	17.38
80	17.60	17.82	18.04	18.26	18.48	18.70	18.92	19.14	19.36	19.58
90	19.80	20.02	20.24	20.46	20.68	20.90	21.12	21.34	21.56	21.78

Litres	0	100	200	300	400	500	600	700	800	900
					British Gallons					
0	—	22.0	44.0	66.0	88.0	110.0	132.0	154.0	176.0	198.0
1000	220.0	242.0	264.0	286.0	308.0	330.0	352.0	373.9	395.9	417.9
2000	439.9	461.9	483.9	505.9	527.9	549.9	571.9	593.9	615.9	637.9
3000	659.9	681.9	703.9	725.9	747.9	769.9	791.9	813.9	835.9	857.9
4000	879.9	901.9	923.9	945.9	967.9	989.9	1011.9	1033.9	1055.9	1077.8
5000	1099.8	1121.8	1143.8	1165.8	1187.8	1209.8	1231.8	1253.8	1275.8	1297.8

Examples: 82 litres = 18.04 British gallons;   3945 litres = 857.9 +9.9 = 867.8 British gallons

BRITISH GALLONS - U.S.GALLONS - BRITISH GALLONS

British Gallons	0	1	2	3	4	5	6	7	8	9
					U.S. Gallons					
0	—	1.20	2.40	3.60	4.80	6.00	7.21	8.41	9.61	10.81
10	12.01	13.21	14.41	15.61	16.81	18.01	19.22	20.42	21.62	22.82
20	24.02	25.22	26.42	27.62	28.82	30.02	31.23	32.43	33.63	34.83
30	36.03	37.23	38.43	39.63	40.83	42.03	43.23	44.44	45.64	46.84
40	48.04	49.24	50.44	51.64	52.84	54.04	55.24	56.45	57.65	58.85
50	60.05	61.25	62.45	63.65	64.85	66.05	67.25	68.45	69.66	70.86
60	72.06	73.26	74.46	75.66	76.86	78.06	79.26	80.46	81.66	82.87
70	84.07	85.27	86.47	87.67	88.87	90.07	91.27	92.47	93.67	94.88
80	96.08	97.28	98.48	99.68	100.88	102.08	103.28	104.48	105.68	106.88
90	108.09	109.29	110.49	111.69	112.89	114.09	115.29	116.49	117.69	118.89

British Gallons	0	100	200	300	400	500	600	700	800	900
					U.S. Gallons					
0	—	120.1	240.2	360.3	480.4	600.5	720.6	840.7	960.8	1080.9
1000	1201.0	1321.0	1441.1	1561.2	1681.3	1801.4	1921.5	2041.6	2161.7	2281.8
2000	2401.9	2522.0	2642.1	2762.2	2882.3	3002.4	3122.5	3242.6	3362.7	3482.8
3000	3602.9	3722.9	3843.0	3963.1	4083.2	4203.3	4323.4	4443.5	4563.6	4683.7
4000	4803.8	4923.9	5044.0	5164.1	5284.2	5404.3	5524.4	5644.5	5764.6	5884.7
5000	6004.8	6124.8	6244.9	6365.0	6485.1	6605.2	6725.3	6845.4	6965.5	7085.6

Examples: 24 British gallons = 28.82 U.S. gallons; 1343 British gallons = 1561.2 + 51.64 = 1612.84 U.S. gallons

U.S. Gallons	0	1	2	3	4	5	6	7	8	9
					British Gallons					
0	—	0.83	1.67	2.50	3.33	4.16	5.00	5.83	6.66	7.49
10	8.33	9.16	9.99	10.82	11.66	12.49	13.32	14.16	14.99	15.82
20	16.65	17.49	18.32	19.15	19.98	20.82	21.65	22.48	23.31	24.15
30	24.98	25.81	26.65	27.48	28.31	29.14	29.98	30.81	31.64	32.47
40	33.31	34.14	34.97	35.81	36.64	37.47	38.30	39.14	39.97	40.80
50	41.63	42.47	43.30	44.13	44.96	45.80	46.63	47.46	48.30	49.13
60	49.96	50.79	51.63	52.46	53.29	54.12	54.96	55.79	56.62	54.45
70	58.29	59.12	59.95	60.79	61.62	62.45	63.28	64.12	64.95	65.78
80	66.61	67.45	68.28	69.11	69.94	70.78	71.61	72.44	73.28	74.11
90	74.94	75.77	76.61	77.44	78.27	79.10	79.94	80.77	81.60	82.43

U.S. Gallons	0	100	200	300	400	500	600	700	800	900
					British Gallons					
0	—	83.3	166.5	249.8	333.1	416.3	499.6	582.9	666.1	749.4
1000	832.7	915.9	999.2	1082.5	1165.7	1249.0	1332.3	1415.5	1498.8	1582.1
2000	1665.4	1748.6	1831.9	1915.2	1998.4	2081.7	2165.0	2248.2	2331.5	2414.8
3000	2498.0	2581.3	2664.6	2747.8	2831.1	2914.4	2997.6	3080.9	3164.2	3247.4
4000	3330.7	3414.0	3497.2	3580.5	3663.8	3747.0	3830.3	3913.6	3996.8	4080.1
5000	4163.4	4246.6	4329.9	4413.2	4496.4	4579.7	4663.0	4746.2	4829.5	4912.8

Examples: 44 U.S. gallons = 36.64 British gallons; 2896 U.S. gallons = 2331.5 + 79.94 = 2411.44 British gallons

U.S. GALLONS - LITRES - U.S. GALLONS

U.S. Gallons	0	1	2	3	4	5	6	7	8	9
					Litres					
0	—	3.79	7.57	11.36	15.14	18.93	22.71	26.50	30.28	34.07
10	37.85	41.64	45.43	49.21	53.00	56.78	60.57	64.35	68.14	71.92
20	75.71	79.49	83.28	87.06	90.85	94.64	98.42	102.21	105.99	109.78
30	113.56	117.35	121.13	124.92	128.70	132.49	136.28	140.06	143.85	147.63
40	151.42	155.20	158.99	162.77	166.56	170.34	174.13	177.91	181.70	185.49
50	189.27	193.06	196.84	200.63	204.41	208.20	211.98	215.77	219.55	223.34
60	227.12	230.91	234.70	238.48	242.27	246.05	249.84	253.62	257.41	261.19
70	264.98	268.76	272.55	276.34	280.12	283.91	287.69	291.48	295.26	299.05
80	302.83	306.62	310.40	314.19	317.97	321.76	325.55	329.33	333.12	336.90
90	340.69	344.47	348.26	352.04	355.83	359.61	363.40	367.18	370.97	374.76

U.S. Gallons	0	100	200	300	400	500	600	700	800	900
					Litres					
0	—	378.5	757.1	1135.6	1514.2	1892.7	2271.2	2649.8	3028.3	3406.9
1000	3785.4	4164.0	4542.5	4921.0	5299.6	5678.1	6056.7	6435.2	6813.7	7192.3
2000	7570.8	7949.4	8327.9	8706.4	9085.0	9463.5	9842.1	10220.6	10599.2	10977.7
3000	11356.2	11734.8	12113.3	12491.9	12870.4	13248.9	13627.5	14006.0	14384.6	14763.1
4000	15141.6	15520.2	15898.7	16277.3	16655.8	17034.4	17412.9	17791.4	18170.0	18548.5
5000	18927.1	19305.6	19684.1	20062.7	20441.2	20819.8	21198.3	21576.8	21955.4	22333.9

Examples: 28 U.S. gallons = 105.99 litres;   641 U.S. gallons = 2271.2 + 155.20 = 2426.40 litres

Litres	0	1	2	3	4	5	6	7	8	9
					U.S. Gallons					
0	—	0.26	0.53	0.79	1.06	1.32	1.59	1.85	2.11	2.38
10	2.64	2.91	3.17	3.43	3.70	3.96	4.23	4.49	4.76	5.02
20	5.28	5.55	5.81	6.08	6.34	6.60	6.87	7.13	7.40	7.66
30	7.93.	8.19	8.45	8.72	8.98	9.25	9.51	9.77	10.04	10.30
40	10.57	10.83	11.10	11.36	11.62	11.89	12.15	12.42	12.68	12.94
50	13.21	13.47	13.74	14.00	14.27	14.53	14.79	15.06	15.32	15.59
60	15.85	16.11	16.38	16.64	16.91	17.17	17.44	17.70	17.96	18.23
70	18.49	18.76	19.02	19.28	19.55	19.81	20.08	20.34	20.61	20.87
80	21.13	21.40	21.66	21.93	22.19	22.45	22.72	22.98	23.25	23.51
90	23.78	24.04	24.30	24.57	24.83	25.10	25.36	25.62	25.89	26.15

Litres	0	100	200	300	400	500	600	700	800	900
					U.S. Gallons					
0	—	26.4	52.8	79.3	105.7	132.1	158.5	184.9	211.3	237.8
1000	264.2	290.6	317.0	343.4	369.8	396.3	422.7	449.1	475.5	501.9
2000	528.3	554.8	581.2	607.6	634.0	660.4	686.8	713.3	739.7	766.1
3000	792.5	818.9	845.4	871.8	898.2	924.6	951.0	977.4	1003.9	1030.3
4000	1056.7	1083.1	1109.5	1135.9	1162.4	1188.8	1215.2	1241.6	1268.0	1294.4
5000	1320.9	1347.3	1373.7	1400.1	1426.5	1452.9	1479.4	1505.8	1532.2	1558.6

Examples: 53 litres = 14.00 U.S. gallon;   5119 litres = 1347.3 + 5.02 = 1352.32 U.S. Gallons

INT. NAUTICAL MILES - KILOMETRES - INT. NAUTICAL MILES

Internat. N. Miles	0	1	2	3	4	5	6	7	8	9
					Kilometres					
0	—	1.85	3.70	5.56	7.41	9.26	11.11	12.96	14.82	16.67
10	18.52	20.37	22.22	24.08	25.93	27.78	29.63	31.48	33.34	35.19
20	37.04	38.89	40.74	42.60	44.45	46.30	48.15	50.00	51.86	53.71
30	55.56	57.41	59.26	61.12	62.97	64.82	66.67	68.52	70.38	72.23
40	74.08	75.93	77.78	79.64	81.49	83.34	85.19	87.04	88.90	90.75
50	92.60	94.45	96.30	98.16	100.01	101.86	103.71	105.56	107.42	109.27
60	111.12	112.97	114.82	116.68	118.53	120.38	122.23	124.08	125.94	127.79
70	129.64	131.49	133.34	135.20	137.05	138.90	140.75	142.60	144.46	146.31
80	148.16	150.01	151.86	153.72	155.57	157.42	159.27	161.12	162.98	164.83
90	166.68	168.53	170.38	172.24	174.09	175.94	177.79	179.64	181.50	183.35

Internat. N. Miles	0	100	200	300	400	500	600	700	800	900
					Kilometres					
0	—	185.2	370.4	555.6	740.8	926.0	1111.2	1296.4	1481.6	1666.8
1000	1852.0	2037.2	2222.4	2407.6	2592.8	2778.0	2963.2	3148.4	3333.6	3518.8
2000	3704.0	3889.2	4074.4	4259.6	4444.8	4630.0	4815.2	5000.4	5185.6	5370.8
3000	5556.0	5741.2	5926.4	6111.6	6296.8	6482.0	6667.2	6852.4	7037.6	7222.8
4000	7408.0	7593.2	7778.4	7963.6	8148.8	8334.0	8519.2	8704.4	8889.6	9074.8
5000	9260.0	9445.2	9630.4	9815.6	10000.8	10186.0	10371.2	10556.4	10741.6	10926.8

Examples: 30 Inter. n. miles = 55.56 kilometres;   1584 Inter. n. miles = 2778.0 + 155.57 = 2933.57 kilometres

Kilo- metres	0	1	2	3	4	5	6	7	8	9
					International Nautical Miles					
0	—	0.54	1.08	1.62	2.16	2.70	3.24	3.78	4.32	4.86
10	5.40	5.94	6.48	7.02	7.56	8.10	8.64	9.18	9.72	10.26
20	10.80	11.34	11.88	12.42	12.96	13.50	14.04	14.58	15.12	15.66
30	16.20	16.74	17.28	17.82	18.36	18.90	19.44	19.98	20.52	21.06
40	21.60	22.14	22.68	23.22	23.76	24.30	24.84	25.38	25.92	26.46
50	27.00	27.54	28.08	28.62	29.16	29.70	30.24	30.78	31.32	31.86
60	32.40	32.94	33.48	34.02	34.56	35.10	35.64	36.18	36.72	37.26
70	37.80	38.34	38.88	39.42	39.96	40.50	41.04	41.58	42.12	42.66
80	43.20	43.74	44.28	44.82	45.36	45.90	46.44	46.98	47.52	48.06
90	48.60	49.14	49.68	50.22	50.76	51.30	51.84	52.38	52.92	53.46

Kilo- metres	0	100	200	300	400	500	600	700	800	900
					International Nautical Miles					
0	—	54.0	108.0	162.0	216.0	270.0	324.0	378.0	432.0	486.0
1000	540.0	594.0	647.9	701.9	755.9	809.9	863.9	917.9	971.9	1025.9
2000	1079.9	1133.9	1187.9	1241.9	1295.9	1349.9	1403.9	1457.9	1511.9	1565.9
3000	1619.9	1673.9	1727.9	1781.9	1835.9	1889.8	1943.8	1997.8	2051.8	2105.8
4000	2159.8	2213.8	2267.8	2321.8	2375.8	2429.8	2483.8	2537.8	2591.8	2645.8
5000	2699.8	2753.8	2807.8	2861.8	2915.8	2969.8	3023.8	3077.8	3131.7	3185.7

Examples: 66 kilometres = 35.64 Inter. n. miles;   4422 kilometres = 2375.8 + 11.88 = 2387.68 Inter. n. miles

INT. NAUTICAL MILES - STATUTE MILES - INT. NAUTICAL MILES

Internat. N. Miles	0	1	2	3	4	5	6	7	8	9
					Statute Miles					
0	—	1.15	2.30	3.45	4.60	5.75	6.91	8.06	9.21	10.36
10	11.51	12.66	13.81	14.96	16.11	17.26	18.41	19.56	20.71	21.87
20	23.02	24.17	25.32	26.47	27.62	28.77	29.92	31.07	32.22	33.37
30	34.52	35.67	36.83	37.98	39.13	40.28	41.43	42.58	43.73	44.88
40	46.03	47.18	48.33	49.48	50.63	51.79	52.94	54.09	55.24	56.39
50	57.54	58.69	59.84	60.99	62.14	63.29	64.44	65.59	66.75	67.90
60	69.05	70.20	71.35	72.50	73.65	74.80	75.95	77.10	78.25	79.40
70	80.55	81.71	82.86	84.01	85.16	86.31	87.46	88.61	89.76	90.91
80	92.06	93.21	94.36	95.51	96.67	97.82	98.97	100.12	101.27	102.42
90	103.57	104.72	105.87	107.02	108.17	109.32	110.47	111.63	112.78	113.93

Internat. N. Miles	0	100	200	300	400	500	600	700	800	900
					Statute Miles					
0	—	115.1	230.2	345.2	460.3	575.4	690.5	805.5	920.6	1035.7
1000	1150.8	1265.9	1380.9	1496.0	1611.1	1726.2	1841.2	1956.3	2071.4	2186.5
2000	2301.6	2416.6	2531.7	2646.8	2761.9	2876.9	2992.0	3107.1	3222.2	3337.3
3000	3452.3	3567.4	3682.5	3797.6	3912.7	4027.7	4142.8	4257.9	4373.0	4488.0
4000	4603.1	4718.2	4833.3	4948.4	5063.4	5178.5	5293.6	5408.7	5523.7	5638.8
5000	5753.9	5869.0	5984.1	6099.1	6214.2	6329.3	6444.4	6559.4	6674.5	6789.6

Examples: 9 Inter. n. miles = 10.36 statute miles; 1009 Inter. n. miles = 1150.8 + 10.36 = 1161.16 statute miles

Statute Miles	0	1	2	3	4	5	6	7	8	9
					International Nautical Miles					
0	—	0.87	1.74	2.61	3.48	4.35	5.21	6.08	6.95	7.82
10	8.69	9.56	10.43	11.30	12.17	13.04	13.90	14.77	15.64	16.51
20	17.38	18.25	19.12	19.99	20.86	21.72	22.59	23.46	24.33	25.20
30	26.07	26.94	27.81	28.68	29.55	30.41	31.28	32.15	33.02	33.89
40	34.76	35.63	36.50	37.37	38.24	39.10	39.97	40.84	41.71	42.58
50	43.45	44.32	45.19	46.06	46.93	47.79	48.66	49.53	50.40	51.27
60	52.14	53.01	53.88	54.75	55.61	56.48	57.35	58.22	59.09	59.96
70	60.83	61.70	62.57	63.44	64.30	65.17	66.04	66.91	67.78	68.65
80	69.52	70.39	71.26	72.13	72.99	73.86	74.73	75.60	76.47	77.34
90	78.21	79.08	79.95	80.81	81.68	82.55	83.42	84.29	85.16	86.03

Statute Miles	0	100	200	300	400	500	600	700	800	900
					International Nautical Miles					
0	—	86.90	173.8	260.7	347.6	434.5	521.4	608.3	695.2	782.1
1000	869.0	955.9	1042.8	1129.7	1216.6	1303.5	1390.4	1477.3	1564.2	1651.1
2000	1738.0	1824.8	1911.7	1998.6	2085.5	2172.4	2259.3	2346.2	2433.1	2520.0
3000	2606.9	2693.8	2780.7	2867.6	2954.5	3041.4	3128.3	3215.2	3302.1	3389.0
4000	3475.9	3562.8	3649.7	3736.6	3823.5	3910.4	3997.3	4084.2	4171.1	4258.0
5000	4344.9	4431.8	4518.7	4605.6	4692.5	4779.4	4866.3	4953.2	5040.1	5127.0

Examples: 26 Statute miles = 22.59 Inter. n. miles; 2641 statute miles = 2259.3 + 35.63 = 2294.93 Inter. n. miles

STATUTE MILES -KILOMETRES - STATUTE MILES

Statute Miles	0	1	2	3	4	5	6	7	8	9
					Kilometres					
0	—	1.61	3.22	4.83	6.44	8.05	9.66	11.27	12.88	14.48
10	16.09	17.70	19.31	20.92	22.53	24.14	25.75	27.36	28.97	30.58
20	32.19	33.80	35.41	37.02	38.62	40.23	41.84	43.45	45.06	46.67
30	48.28	49.89	51.50	53.11	54.72	56.33	57.94	59.55	61.16	62.76
40	64.37	65.98	67.59	69.20	70.81	72.42	74.03	75.64	77.25	78.86
50	80.47	82.08	83.69	85.30	86.91	88.51	90.12	91.73	93.34	94.95
60	96.56	98.17	99.78	101.39	103.0	104.61	106.22	107.83	109.44	111.04
70	112.65	114.26	115.87	117.48	119.09	120.70	122.31	123.92	125.53	127.14
80	128.75	130.36	131.97	133.58	135.18	136.79	138.40	140.01	141.62	143.23
90	144.84	146.45	148.06	149.67	151.28	152.89	154.50	156.11	157.72	159.33

Statute Miles	0	100	200	300	400	500	600	700	800	900
					Kilometres					
0	—	160.9	321.9	482.8	643.7	804.7	965.6	1126.5	1287.5	1448.4
1000	1609.3	1770.3	1931.2	2092.1	2253.1	2414.0	2575.0	2735.9	2896.8	3057.8
2000	3218.7	3379.6	3540.6	3701.5	3862.4	4023.4	4184.3	4345.2	4506.2	4667.1
3000	4828.0	4989.0	5149.9	5310.8	5471.8	5632.7	5793.6	5954.6	6115.5	6276.4
4000	6437.4	6598.3	6759.2	6920.2	7081.1	7242.0	7403.0	7563.9	7724.9	7885.8
5000	8046.7	8207.7	8368.6	8529.5	8690.5	8851.4	9012.3	9173.3	9334.2	9495.1

Examples: 32 statute miles = 51.50 kilometres;   2992 statute miles = 4667.1 + 148.06 = 4815.16 kilometres

Kilo-metres	0	1	2	3	4	5	6	7	8	9
					Statute Miles					
0	—	0.62	1.24	1.86	2.49	3.11	3.73	4.35	4.97	5.59
10	6.21	6.84	7.46	8.08	8.70	9.32	9.94	10.56	11.19	11.81
20	12.43	13.05	13.67	14.29	14.91	15.53	16.16	16.78	17.40	18.02
30	18.64	19.26	19.88	20.51	21.13	21.75	22.37	22.99	23.61	24.23
40	24.85	25.48	26.10	26.72	27.34	27.96	28.58	29.20	29.83	30.45
50	31.07	31.69	32.31	32.93	33.55	34.18	34.80	35.42	36.04	36.66
60	37.28	37.90	38.53	39.15	39.77	40.39	41.01	41.63	42.25	42.87
70	43.50	44.12	44.74	45.36	45.98	46.60	47.22	47.85	48.47	49.09
80	49.71	50.33	50.95	51.57	52.20	52.82	53.44	54.06	54.68	55.30
90	55.92	56.54	57.17	57.79	58.41	59.03	59.65	60.27	60.89	61.52

Kilo-Metres	0	100	200	300	400	500	600	700	800	900
					Statute Miles					
0	—	62.1	124.3	186.4	248.5	310.7	372.8	435.0	497.1	559.2
1000	621.4	683.5	745.6	807.8	869.9	932.1	994.2	1056.3	1118.5	1180.6
2000	1242.7	1304.9	1367.0	1429.2	1491.3	1553.4	1615.6	1677.7	1739.8	1802.0
3000	1864.1	1926.3	1988.4	2050.5	2112.7	2174.8	2236.9	2299.1	2361.2	2423.3
4000	2485.5	2547.6	2609.8	2671.9	2734.0	2796.2	2858.3	2920.4	2982.6	3044.7
5000	3106.9	3169.0	3231.1	3293.3	3355.4	3417.5	3479.7	3541.8	3604.0	3666.1

Examples: 42 kilometres = 26.10 statute miles;   5073 kilometres = 3106.9 + 45.36 = 3152.26 statute miles

FATHOMS - METRES - FATHOMS

Fathoms	0	1	2	3	4	5	6	7	8	9
					Metres					
0	—	1.83	3.66	5.49	7.32	9.14	10.97	12.80	14.63	16.46
10	18.29	20.12	21.95	23.77	25.60	27.43	29.26	31.09	32.92	34.75
20	36.58	38.40	40.23	42.06	43.89	45.72	47.55	49.38	51.21	53.04
30	54.86	56.69	58.52	60.35	62.18	64.01	65.84	67.67	69.49	71.32
40	73.15	74.98	76.81	78.64	80.47	82.30	84.12	85.95	87.78	89.61
50	91.44	93.27	95.10	96.93	98.76	100.58	102.41	104.24	106.07	107.90
60	109.73	111.56	113.39	115.21	117.04	118.87	120.70	122.53	124.36	126.19
70	128.02	129.84	131.67	133.50	135.33	137.16	138.99	140.82	142.65	144.48
80	146.30	148.13	149.96	151.79	153.62	155.45	157.28	159.11	160.93	162.76
90	164.59	166.42	168.25	170.08	171.91	173.74	175.56	177.39	179.22	181.05

Fathoms	0	100	200	300	400	500	600	700	800	900
					Metres					
0	—	182.9	365.8	548.6	731.5	914.4	1097.3	1280.2	1463.0	1645.9
1000	1828.8	2011.7	2194.6	2377.4	2560.3	2743.2	2926.1	3109.0	3291.8	3474.7
2000	3657.6	3840.5	4023.4	4206.2	4389.1	4572.0	4754.9	4937.8	5120.6	5303.5
3000	5486.4	5669.3	5852.2	6035.0	6217.9	6400.8	6583.7	6766.6	6949.4	7132.3
4000	7315.2	7498.1	7681.0	7863.8	8046.7	8229.6	8412.5	8595.4	8778.2	8961.1
5000	9144.0	9326.9	9509.8	9692.6	9875.5	10058.4	10241.3	10424.2	10607.0	10789.9

Examples: 31 fathoms = 56.69 metres;   4867 fathoms = 8778.2 + 122.53 = 8900.73 metres

Metres	0	1	2	3	4	5	6	7	8	9
					Fathoms					
0	—	0.55	1.09	1.64	2.19	2.73	3.28	3.83	4.37	4.92
10	5.47	6.01	6.56	7.10	7.66	8.20	8.74	9.30	9.84	10.39
20	10.94	11.48	12.03	12.58	13.12	13.67	14.22	14.76	15.31	15.86
30	16.40	16.95	17.50	18.04	18.59	19.14	19.69	20.23	20.78	21.33
40	21.87	22.42	22.97	23.51	24.06	24.61	25.15	25.70	26.25	26.79
50	27.34	27.89	28.43	28.98	29.53	30.07	30.62	31.17	31.71	32.26
60	32.81	33.36	33.90	34.45	35.00	35.54	36.09	36.64	37.18	37.73
70	38.28	38.82	39.37	39.92	40.46	41.01	41.56	42.10	42.65	43.20
80	43.74	44.29	44.84	45.38	45.93	46.48	47.03	47.57	48.12	48.67
90	49.21	49.76	50.31	50.85	51.40	51.95	52.49	53.04	53.59	54.13

Metres	0	100	200	300	400	500	600	700	800	900
					Fathoms					
0	—	54.7	109.4	164.0	218.7	273.4	328.1	382.8	437.4	492.1
1000	546.8	601.5	656.2	710.8	765.5	820.2	874.9	929.6	984.3	1038.9
2000	1093.6	1148.3	1203.0	1257.7	1312.3	1367.0	1421.7	1476.4	1531.1	1585.7
3000	1640.4	1695.1	1749.8	1804.5	1859.1	1913.8	1968.5	2023.2	2077.9	2132.5
4000	2187.2	2241.9	2296.6	2351.3	2406.0	2460.6	2515.3	2570.0	2624.7	2679.4
5000	2734.0	2788.7	2843.4	2898.1	2952.8	3007.4	3062.1	3116.8	3171.5	3226.2

Examples: 35 metres = 19.14 fathoms;   1982 metres = 1038.9 + 44.84 = 1083.74 fathoms

DECIMALS OF THE DEGREE

′	.0	.2	.4	.6	.8
0	0.000	0.003	0.007	0.010	0.013
1	.017	.020	.023	.027	.030
2	.033	.037	.040	.043	.047
3	.050	.053	.057	.060	.063
4	.067	.070	.073	.077	.080
5	0.083	0.087	0.090	0.093	0.097
6	.100	.103	.107	.110	.113
7	.117	.120	.123	.127	.130
8	.133	.137	.140	.143	.147
9	.150	.153	.157	.160	.163
10	0.167	0.170	0.173	0.177	0.180
11	.183	.187	.190	.193	.197
12	.200	.203	.207	.210	.213
13	.217	.220	.223	.227	.230
14	.233	.237	.240	.243	.247
15	0.250	0.253	0.257	0.260	0.263
16	.267	.270	.273	.277	.280
17	.283	.287	.290	.293	.297
18	.300	.303	.307	.310	.313
19	.317	.320	.323	.327	.330
20	0.333	0.337	0.340	0.343	0.347
21	.350	.353	.357	.360	.363
22	.367	.370	.373	.377	.380
23	.383	.387	.390	.393	.397
24	.400	.403	.407	.410	.413
25	0.417	0.420	0.423	0.427	0.430
26	.433	.437	.440	.443	.447
27	.450	.453	.457	.460	.463
28	.467	.470	.473	.477	.480
29	.483	.487	.490	.493	.497
30	0.500	0.503	0.507	0.510	0.513
31	.517	.520	.523	.527	.530
32	.533	.537	.540	.543	.547
33	.550	.553	.557	.560	.563
34	.567	.570	.573	.577	.580
35	0.583	0.587	0.590	0.593	0.597
36	.600	.603	.607	.610	.613
37	.617	.620	.623	.627	.630
38	.633	.637	.640	.643	.647
39	.650	.653	.657	.660	.663
40	0.667	0.670	0.673	0.677	0.680
41	.683	.687	.690	.693	.697
42	.700	.703	.707	.710	.713
43	.717	.720	.723	.727	.730
44	.733	.737	.740	.743	.747
45	0.750	0.753	0.757	0.760	0.763
46	.767	.770	.773	.777	.780
47	.783	.787	.790	.793	.797
48	.800	.803	.807	.810	.813
49	.817	.820	.823	.827	.830
50	0.833	0.837	0.840	0.843	0.847
51	.850	.853	.857	.860	.863
52	.867	.870	.873	.877	.880
53	.883	.887	.890	.893	.897
54	.900	.903	.907	.910	.913
55	0.917	0.920	0.923	0.927	0.930
56	.933	.937	.940	.943	.947
57	.950	.953	.957	.960	.963
58	.967	.970	.973	.977	.980
59	.983	.987	.990	.993	.997

V   PORTS OF THE WORLD

Aabenraa Jylland, Denmark 55 03N 09 25E
Aaiun (El Aaiun) (Laayoune) (Fosbucraa) Morocco
27 04N 13 28W
Aalborg Limfjord, Jylland, Denmark
57 03N 09 55E
Aalesund (Alesund) Norway 62 28N 06 10E
Aalvik (Alvik) Hardangerfjord, Norway 60 26N 06 24E
Aaraich, El (El Arish) (Larache) Morocco 35 12N 06 09W
Aardalstangen (Ardalstangen) Sognefjord, Norway
61 14N 07 43E
Aarhus (Arhus) Jylland, Denmark 56 10N 10 14E
Aarosund (Arosund) Jylland, Denmark 55 15N 09 43E
Abadan Shatt al Arab, Iran 30 20N 48 16E

Abashiri Hokkaido, Japan 44 01N 144 17E
Abbas, Bandar Iran 27 14N 56 16E
Abd al Aziz (Damman) Saudi Arabia 26 30N 50 12E
Abd Allah, Mina (Mina Abdulla) Kuwait 29 02N 48 10E
Abdallah, Sidi Tunisia 37 10N 09 48E
Abdulla, Mina (Mina Abd Allah) Kuwait
29 02N 48 10E
Abeltoft (Ebeltoft) Jylland, Denmark 56 12N 10 42E
Aberdeen Scotland, UK 57 09N 02 05W
Aberdeen Grays Harbour, Washington, USA
46 58N 123 50W
Aberdovey Wales, UK 52 33N 04 03W
Abidjan Ivory Coast 05 15N 04 01W
Abo (Turku) Finland 60 27N 22 16E
Abonnema Nigeria 04 44N 06 49E
Aboshi Honshu, Japan 34 46N 134 36E
Abu al Bu'Khoosh United Arab Emirates 25 26N 53 08E
Abu Dhabi (Abu Zabi) (Mina Zayed) United Arab
Emirates 24 29N 54 22E
Abu el Flus, Nahr (Abu Flus) Shatt al Arab, Iraq
30 27N 48 02E
Abu Flus (Nahr Abu el Flus) Shatt al Arab, Iraq
30 27N 48 02E
Abu Kammash Libya 33 04N 11 49E
Abu Sultan Buheirat-Murat-el-Kubra, Suez Canal, Egypt
30 25N 32 18E
Abu Zabi (Abu Dhabi) (Mina Zayed) United Arab
Emirates 24 29N 54 22E
Abu Zenima Sinai, Egypt 29 02N 33 06E
Acajutla El Salvador 13 34N 89 51W
Acapulco Mexico 16 51N 99 56W
Accra Ghana 05 32N 00 13W
Acevedo, Puerto R Parana, Argentina 33 15S 60 18W
Acquacalda Lipari, Italy 38 31N 14 56E
Acton Grange Manchester Ship Canal, England, UK
53 21N 02 38W
Adabiya Gulf of Suez, Egypt 29 52N 32 29E
Adamas Milos, Greece 36 45N 24 25E
Adams, Port Houston Ship Canal, Texas, USA
29 45N 95 11W
Ad Dawhah (Doha) Qatar 25 18N 51 33E
Adelaide, Port St Vincent Gulf, South Australia, Australia
34 51S 138 30E
Aden South Yemen 12 47N 44 59E
Aden, Little South Yemen 12 46N 44 55E
Advent Bay (Adventfjorden) Spitsbergen, Svalbard
78 15N 15 26E
Adventfjorden (Advent Bay) Spitsbergen, Svalbard
78 15N 15 26E
Advocate Harbour Minas Channel, Nova Scotia, Canada
45 20N 64 47W
Aegion (Vostizza) (Aiyion) Korinthiakos Kolpos, Greece
38 15N 22 05E
Aeroskobing (Aroskobing) Aero, Denmark 54 53N 10 25E
Afrida (Ashkelon) (Ashqelon) Israel 31 39N 34 32E
Agadir Morocco 30 25N 09 38W

Aggersund Limfjord, Jylland, Denmark 57 00N 09 18E
Agotnes Sotra, Norway 60 24N 05 02E
Agua Amarga Spain 36 56N 01 56W
Aguadilla Puerto Rico 18 26N 67 10W
Agua Dulce Parida Is., Panama 08 06N 82 20W
Aguilas Spain 37 24N 01 35W
Aguirre Bahia de Jobos, Puerto Rico 17 57N 66 13W
Ahmadi, Mina al (Fahaheel) Kwait 29 04N 48 09E
Ahmedi Khor Kathib, Yemen 14 50N 42 56E
Ahmed, Kassr (Qasr Ahmed) (Misurata) Libya
32 22N 15 12E
Ahmed, Qasr (Kassr Ahmed) (Misurata) Libya
32 22N 15 12E
Ahus Sweden 55 56N 14 19E
Ainoura Kyushu, Japan 33 11N 129 39E
Ain Sukhna Gulf of Suez, Egypt 29 35N 32 23E
Aioi Honshu, Japan 34 47N 134 28E
Aires, Buenos R. de la Plata, Argentina 34 36S 58 22W
Aitape New Guinea, Papua New Guinea 03 09S 142 22E
Aitutaki Cook Is. 18 50S 159 47W
Aivaly (Ayvalik) Turkey 39 19N 26 38E
Aiyion (Aegion) (Vostizza) Korinthiakos Kolpos, Greece
38 15N 22 05E
Ajaccio Corse, France 41 55N 08 44E
Ajman United Arab Emirates 25 24N 55 26E
Ajos Finland 65 40N 24 31E
Akaba (Aqaba) Jordan 29 31N 35 01E
Akassa Nigeria 04 16N 06 02E
Akcaabat (Polathane) Turkey 41 02N 39 35E
Akhomten Kamchatka, USSR 52 28N 158 31E
Akishi (Akkeshi) Hokkaido, Japan 43 02N 144 49E
Akita Honshu, Japan 39 45N 140 04E
Akkeshi (Akishi) Hokkaido, Japan 43 02N 144 49E
Akranes, Iceland 64 19N 22 03W
Akureyri Eyjafjordhur, Iceland 65 41N 18 05W
Akyab (Sittwe) Burma 20 09N 92 56E
Ala Sweden 61 13N 17 10E
Al Ahmadi, Mina (Fahaheel) Kuwait 29 04N 48 09E
Al Amaya, Khawr (Mina al Amaya) Iraq 29 47N 48 49E
Alameda San Francisco Bay, California, USA
37 47N 122 15W
Alamein, El (Marsa el Hamra) Egypt 30 58N 28 51E
Alanya (Alaya) Turkey 36 32N 32 03E
Alaya (Alanya) Turkey 36 32N 32 03E
Al Aziz, Abd (Damman) Saudi Arabia 26 30N 50 12E
Albaek Jylland, Denmark 57 35N 10 26E
Al Bakr, Mina (Albakr Terminal) (Khawr al Kafka) (Khor
al Kafka), Iraq 29 41N 48 49E
Albakr Terminal (Mina al Bakr) (Khawr al Kafta)
(Khor al Kafta), Iraq 29 41N 48 49E
Albany Western Australia, Australia 35 02S 117 54E
Albany Hudson R., New York, USA 42 39N 73 46W
Alba Terminal Bahrain 26 09N 50 40E
Albatross Bay Gulf of Carpentaria, Queensland, Australia
12 42S 141 40E
Alberni, Port Vancouver Is., British Columbia, Canada
49 14N 124 49W
Alberton Prince Edward Is., Canada 46 48N 64 03W
Albert, Port Victoria, Australia 38 40S 146 41E
Albina Marowijne R., Surinam 05 29N 54 03W
Al Bu'Khoosh, Abu United Arab Emirates 25 26N 53 08E
Alcanar Spain 40 34N 00 33E
Alcochete R. Tejo, Portugal 38 45N 08 58W
Alderney Channel Is., UK 49 43N 02 12W
Alegre, Porto R. Guaiba, Brazil 30 03S 51 13W
Aleksandrovsk-Sakhalinskiy (Alexandrovsk-Sakhalinskiy)
Sakhalin, USSR 50 54N 142 10E
Alen, Castro (Castro Urdiales) Spain 43 24N 03 13W
Alert Bay Broughton Passage, British Columbia, Canada
50 35N 126 56W

Alesund (Aalesund) Norway 62 28N 06 10E
Alexandre, Porto Angola 15 48N 11 51E
Alexandretta (Iskenderun) Iskenderun Korfezi, Turkey
36 36N 36 10E
Alexandria (El Iskandariya) Egypt 31 09N 29 52E
Alexandria Virginia, USA 38 48N 77 02W
Alexandroupolis (Dedeagach) Greece 40 51N 25 53E
Alexandrovski (De Kastri) Tartarskiy Proliv, USSR
51 29N 140 47E
Alexandrovsk-Sakhalinskiy (Aleksandrovsk-Sakhalinskiy)
Sakhalin, USSR 50 54N 142 10E
Al Fahal, Mina Oman 23 38N 58 31E
Al Faw (Fao) Shatt al Arab, Iraq 29 58N 48 29E
Alfred, Port Saguenay R., Quebec Province, Canada
48 20N 70 53W
Alfredshem Ornskoldsvik, Sweden 63 16N 18 43E
Alfueca, Lobos de Peru 06 56S 80 42W
Algeciras Spain 36 07N 0527W
Alger (Algiers) Algeria 36 47N 03 04E
Al Ghardaqah (Hurghada) Egypt 27 14N 33 50E
Al Ghar, Ras Saudi Arabia 26 52N 49 52E
Alghero Sardegna, Italy 40 34N 08 19E
Algiers (Alger) Algeria 36 47N 03 04E
Algoa Bay South Africa 33 55S 25 40E
Al Hariga, Marsa (Tobruk Terminal) Libya
32 04N 24 00E
Alholmen Finland 63 42N 22 42E
Al Hudayday (Hodeidah) (Hudaida) Yemen
14 49N 42 55E
Aliaga Candarli Korfezi, Turkey 38 50N 26 57E
Alicante Spain 38 22N 00 28W
Alice, Port Vancouver Is., British Columbia, Canada
50 23N 127 27W
Alice, Port Heceta Is., Alaska, USA 55 48N 133 38W
Alice, Punta Golfo di Taranto, Italy 39 24N 17 09E
Ali, Mina Jebel United Arab Emirates 25 03N 55 01E
Ali, Tobo Banka, Indonesia 03 00S 106 27E
Aliverion Evvoia, Greece 38 23N 24 03E
Al Ju'aymah Terminal Saudi Arabia 26 56N 50 02E
Al Jabayl (Jubail) Saudi Arabia 27 02N 49 41E
Al Kafka, Khawr (Mina al Bakr) (Albakr Terminal) Iraq
29 41N 48 49E
Al Katheeb, Ras (Ras Kathib) Yemen 14 56N 42 54E
Al Khafji, Ras Saudi Arabia 28 25N 48 32E
Al Khaimah, Ras (Ras al Khaimah) United Arab Emirates
25 48N 56 01E
Al Khaymah, Ras (Ras al Khaymah) United Arab
Emirates 25 48N 56 01E
Al Khobar (Al Khubar) Saudi Arabia 26 17N 50 13E
Al Khubar (Al Khobar) Saudi Arabia 26 17N 50 13E
Alkmaar Noordhollands Kanaal, Netherlands
52 38N 04 44E
Al Kuwayt (Kuwait) (Koweit) Kuwait
29 23N 47 59E
Allah, Mina Abd (Mina Abdulla) Kuwait 29 02N 48 10E
Allardyce Harbour Santa Isabel, Solomon Is.
07 49S 158 39E
Allen, Port Kauai, Hawaiian Is., USA 21 54N 159 36W
Allen, Port Mississippi R., Louisiana, USA
30 28N 91 12W
Alleppey India 09 29N 76 20E
Alliford Bay Skidegate Inlet, British Columbia, Canada
53 12N 132 01W
Allinge Bornholm, Denmark 55 17N 14 48E
Al Manamah (Manama) Bahrain 26 14N 50 35E
Alma, Port Queensland, Australia 23 35S 150 52E
Al Masirah Oman 20 10N 58 40E
Almeria Spain 36 51N 02 30W
Almirante Panama 09 17N 82 23W
Almirante Barrosso Terminal (Tebar Terminal) Brazil
23 48S 45 23W

Almirante Soares Dutra Terminal Tramandi, Brazil
30 01S 50 06W
Al Mishab, Ras Saudi Arabia 28 10N 48 41E
Al Mubarras, Halat (Mubarras Terminal) Abu Dhabi
24 27N 53 42E
Al Mufatta, Khawr (Khor al Mufatta) Kuwait
28 39N 48 24E
Alotau Milne Bay, Papua, Papua New Guinea
10 19S 150 27E
Alpena Lake Huron, Michigan, USA 45 04N 83 26W
Al Quadayama (Quadheema) Saudi Arabia
22 19N 39 06E
Al Qaiwain, Umm United Arab Emirates 25 35N 55 35E
Al Ruwais (Ar Ru'ais) United Arab Emirates
24 08N 52 44E
Alsancak Izmir Korfezi, Turkey 38 27N 27 09E
Al Shuaiba (Ash Shu'aybah) Kuwait 29 02N 48 09E
Altagracia Lago de Maracaibo, Venezuela 10 43N 71 32W
Althrope River Trent, England, UK 53 35N 00 43W
Altona Die Elbe, West Germany 53 34N 09 56E
Alucroix, Port (Port Harvey) (Port Martin Marietta)
St. Croix, Virgin Is. 17 42N 64 46W
Alvarado Golfo de Campeche, Mexico 18 46N 95 46W
Alvaro Obregon, Puerto (Frontera) Golfo de Campeche,
Mexico 18 36N 92 39W
Alvik (Aalvik) Hardangerfjord, Norway 60 26N 06 24E
Alvik, Indre Hardangerfjord, Norway 60 26N 06 26E
Alvik Alno, R., Sweden 62 26N 17 25E
Alvim Glomma R., Norway 59 16N 11 02E
Al Yadida (El Jadida (Mazagan) Morocco 33 14N 08 28W
Amagasaki Honshu, Japan 34 42N 135 24E
Amahai, Teluk Seram Indonesia 03 20S 128 55E
Amal Vanern, Sweden 59 03N 12 42E
Amamapare, Port Irian Jaya, Indonesia 04 49S 136 52E
Amapala Tigre Is., Honduras 13 18N 87 40W
Amarga, Agua Spain 36 56N 01 56W
Amarracao (Luis Correia) R. Igaracu de Sao Jose, Brazil
02 53S 41 40W
Amasra (Amastra) Turkey 41 45N 32 24E
Amastra (Amasra) Turkey 41 45N 32 24E
Amaya, Mena Al (Khawr al Amayah) Iraq 29 47N 48 49E
Ambarchik Vostochno Sibirskoye More, USSR
69 39N 162 27E
Ambelaki (Ambelakion) Salamis, Greece 37 57N 23 33E
Ambelakion (Ambelaki) Salamis, Greece 37 57N 23 33E
Ambes, Bec d' La Dordogne, France 45 02N 00 34W
Amble (Warkworth) England, UK 55 20N 01 35W
Ambodifototra Ile Ste. Marie, Malagasy Republic
17 00S 49 51E
Amboim, Porto (Benguela Velha) Angola 10 44S 13 46E
Amboina (Ambon) Ambon, Indonesia 03 41S 128 07E
Ambon (Amboina) Ambon, Indonesia 03 41S 128 07E
Amboy, Perth Raritan Bay, New Jersey, USA
40 30N 74 16W
Amboy, South Raritan R., New Jersey, USA
40 29N 74 16W
Ambriz Angola 07 51S 13 07E
Ambrizete (N'zeto) Angola 07 15S 12 52E
Amelia, Porto (Pemba) Mozambique 12 58S 40 29E
Amesville Mississippi R., Louisiana USA
29 54N 90 07W
Amherstburg Detroit R., Ontario, Canada 42 06N 83 08W
Amherst Harbour (Havre Aubert) Madeleine Is., Quebec
Province, Canada 47 14N 61 50W
Amlwch Anglesey, Wales, UK 53 25N 04 20W
Amoy (Hsia-men) China 24 27N 118 04E
Ampenan Lombok, Indonesia 08 33S 116 04E
Amsterdam Noordzeekanaal, Netherlands 52 22N 04 54E
Amsterdam, New Berbice R., Guyana 06 16N 57 31W
Amsterdam, Nieuw Surinam 05 53N 55 05W

Amuay, Bahia de Peninsula de Paraguana, Venezuela
11 45N 70 13W

Ana Chaves, Baia de Sao Tome Is., Sao Tome and
Principe 00 21N 06 44E

Anacortes Washington, USA 48 31N 122 37W

Anadyrskiy Liman USSR 64 44N 177 32E

Anaheim Bay California, USA 33 44N 118 05W

Anakan Mindanao, Philippines 08 51N 125 09E

Analalava Malagasy Republic 14 38S 47 46E

Anan (Tachibana) Kii Suido, Shikoku, Japan
33 52N 134 39E

Anawa Bay Bougainville, Papua New Guinea
06 12S 153 33E

Anchorage Cook Inlet, Alaska, USA 61 13N 149 54W

Ancon Peru 11 47S 77 12W

Ancona Italy 43 37N 13 31E

Ancud Chiloe Is., Chile 41 52S 73 50W

Andalsnes Romsdalsfjord, Norway 62 34N 07 41E

Andres Dominican Republic 18 27N 69 37W

Aneityum, Port Aneitum Is., New Hebrides
20 14S 169 47E

Angel, Puerto Mexico 15 39N 96 30W

Angeles, Los California USA 33 44N 118 16W

Angeles, Port Juan de Fuca Strait, Washington, USA
48 07N 123 26W

Angermanalven Sweden 62 52N 17 53E

Angle Bay Miford Haven, Wales, UK 51 42N 05 03W

Anglesey Oil Terminal Wales, UK 53 27N 04 20W

Angmagssalik Greenland 65 35N 37 34W

Ango Ango R.Zaire, Zaire 05 51S 13 26E

Angoche (Antonio Enes) Mozambique 16 14S 39 55E

Angra (Angra do Heroismo) Terceira, Acores
38 38N 27 13W

Angra do Heroismo (Angra) Terceira, Acores
38 38N 27 13W

Angra dos Reis Brazil 23 01S 44 19W

Animas, Chanaral de Las Chile 26 21S 70 38W

Anjouan Island Republic of the Comoros 12 10S 44 23E

Ankarsvik Alno, Sweden 62 23N 17 25E

Anking (Huai-ning) Ch'ang Chiang, China
30 31N 117 02E

Anklam Die Peene, East Germany 53 51N 13 41E

Annaba (Bona) (Bone) Algeria 36 54N 07 45E

Annan Solway Firth, Scotland, UK 54 59N 03 16W

Annapolis Annapolis Basin, Nova Scotia, Canada
44 45N 65 31W

Annotto Bay Jamaica 18 17N 76 48W

Annunziata, Torre Golfo di Napoli, Italy 40 45N 14 27E

An-P'ing Taiwan 23 00N 120 09E

Anson, Telok Malaya, Malaysia 04 01N 101 01E

Antalaha Malagasy Republic 14 53S 50 18E

Antalya (Attalia) Turkey 36 50N 30 43E

Antibes (Port Vauban) Côte d'Azur, France
43 34N 07 08E

Antifer Baie de la Seine, France 49 40N 00 10E

Antigonish St George's Bay, Nova Scotia, Canada
45 41N 62 00W

Antigua 17 07N 61 50W

Antilla Bahia Nipe, Cuba 20 50N 75 44W

Antimonan Luzon, Philippines 14 01N 121 56E

Antioch San Joaquin R., California, USA
38 01N 121 48W

Antivari (Bar) Yugoslavia 42 05N 19 05E

Antofagasta Chile 23 39S 70 25W

Antonina (Barao de Tefee) Brazil 25 26S 48 42W

Antonio Enes (Angoche) Mozambique 16 14S 39 55E

Antonio, Port Jamaica 18 11N 76 27W

Antsiranana (Diego Suarez) Malagasy Republic
12 16S 49 17E

An-Tung (Dandong) Yalu Chiang, China 40 08N 124 23E

Antwerp (Antwerpen) (Anvers) Schelde R., Belgium
51 14N 04 25E

Antwerpen (Antwerp) (Anvers) Schelde R., Belgium
51 14N 04 25E

Anvers (Antwerp) (Antwerpen) Schelde R., Belgium
51 14N 04 25E

Anzio, Porto d' Italy 41 27N 12 38E

Ao Chumphon Thailand 10 25N 99 18E

Aomori Honshu, Japan 40 49N 140 45E

Ao Sattahip Thailand 12 40N 100 54E

Ao Trat Thailand 12 06N 102 38E

Ao Udom Thailand 13 07N 100 53E

Apapa Lagos Harbour, Nigeria 06 27N 03 24E

Aparri Luzon, Philippines 18 22N 121 38E

Apia Upolu, Samoa 13 49S 171 46W

Api Api, Bagan Si Sumatera, Indonesia 02 09N 100 48E

Appledore R. Torridge, England, UK 51 03N 04 12W

Apra, Port Guam, Marianas (Ladrones) Is.
13 27N 144 39E

Aqaba (Akaba) Jordan 29 31N 35 01E

Aquin Haiti 18 16N 73 23W

Aracaju R. Sergipe, Brazil 10 56S 37 02W

Aracati Brazil 04 31S 37 46W

Aranci, Golfo Sardegna, Italy 40 57N 09 37E

Aratu Brazil 12 47S 38 30W

Araya Venezuela 10 34N 64 16W

Arbatax Sardegna, Italy 39 56N 09 42E

Arboga Malaren, Sweden 59 25N 15 51E

Arbroath Scotland, UK 56 33N 02 35W

Arcachon France 44 37N 01 15W

Archangel (Arkhangel'sk) R. Severnaya Dvina, USSR
64 33N 40 31E

Ardalstangen (Aardalstangen) Sognefjord, Norway
61 14N 07 43E

Ardesen Turkey 41 15N 41 02E

Ardglass Ulster, UK 54 16N 05 36W

Ardjuna Terminal Jawa, Indonesia 05 56S 107 45E

Ardrishaig Loch Fyne, Scotland, UK 56 01N 05 27W

Ardrossan South Australia, Australia 34 26S 137 55E

Ardrossan Firth of Clyde, Scotland, UK 55 38N 04 49W

Arecibo Puerto Rico 18 29N 66 43W

Areia Branca Brazil 04 57S 37 09W

Arenas, Punta Estrecho de Magallenes, Chile
53 10S 70 54W

Arendal Norway 58 27N 08 46E

Argentia Newfoundland, Canada 47 18N 53 59W

Argostoli (Argostolion) Kefallinia, Greece 38 11N 20 29E

Argostolion Kefallinia, Greece 38 11N 20 29E

Arguineguin Grand Canary, Canary Is. 27 47N 15 42W

Argyle Terminal Scotland, UK 56 10N 02 48E

Arhus (Aarhus) Jylland, Denmark 56 10N 10 14E

Arica Chile 18 28S 70 19W

Arichat Isle Madame, Nova Scotia, Canada
45 31N 61 02W

Arida Kii-suido, Honshu, Japan 34 06N 135 07E

Arios, Puerto Honduras 15 49N 87 57W

Arish, El (El Aaraiche) (Larache) Morocco
35 12N 06 09W

Arkhangel'sk (Archangel) R. Severnaya Dvina, USSR
64 33N 40 31E

Arklow R. Avoca, Republic of Ireland 52 48N 06 09W

Armuelles, Puerto Panama 08 16N 82 51W

Arosa, Villagarcia de Spain 42 36N 08 46W

Aroskobing (Aeroskobing) Aero, Denmark
54 53N 10 25E

Arosund (Aarosund) Jylland, Denmark 55 15N 09 43E

Arrecife Lanzarote, Canary Is 28 57N 13 33W

Arrega, La Lago de Maracaibo, Venezuela 10 36N 71 36W

Arroyo, Puerto Puerto Rico 17 57W 66 05W

Ar Ru'ays (Al Ruwais) United Arab Emirates
24 08N 52 44E

Arsa (Rasa) Kvarner, Yugoslavia 45 03N 14 04E
Arthur Kill River New Jersey, USA 40 35N 74 13W
Arthur, Port Tasmania, Australia 43 09S 147 51E
Arthur, Port Lake Superior, Ontario, Canada
 48 27N 89 12W
Arthur, Port (Ryojun) (Lushun) China 38 48N 121 15E
Arthur, Port Sabine Lake, Texas, USA 29 53N 93 57W
Aruba Island Caribbean Sea, 12 30N 70 00W
Arun Terminal Sumatera, Indonesia 05 14N 97 07E
Arzanah, Jazirat United Arab Emirates 24 46N 52 33E
Arzew Algeria 35 52N 00 18W
Asahan Sumatera, Indonesia 02 58N 99 48E
Ascension Island 07 55S 14 22W
Ashdod Israel 31 49N 34 39E
Ashkelon (Afrida) (Ashqelon) Israel 31 39N 34 32E
Ashland Lake Superior, Wisconsin, USA 46 35N 90 53E
Ashqelon (Ashkelon) (Afrida) Israel 31 39N 34 32E
Ash Shariqah (Sharjah) (Mina Khalid) United Arab
 Emirates 25 22N 55 24E
Ash Shu'Aybah (Al Shuaiba) Kuwait 29 02N 48 09E
Ash Shuwaykh (Shuwaikh) Kuwait 29 21N 47 56E
Ashtabula Lake Erie, Ohio, USA 41 53N 80 48W
Ashtart Tunisia 34 15N 10 24E
Ashtart Terminal Tunisia 34 17N 11 24E
Askaig, Port Islay, Scotland, UK 55 50N 06 05W
Askersund Vattern, Sweden 58 53N 14 55E
Askja Sweden 63 01N 18 13E
Asnaes Sjaeland, Denmark 55 40N 11 05E
Aspropyrgos Kolpos Elevsinos, Greece 38 02N 23 38E
Assab Ethiopia 13 01N 42 44E
Assens Fyn, Denmark 55 16N 09 54E
Astakos (Dragamestre) Greece 38 32N 21 05E
Astillero Spain 43 24N 03 49W
Astoria Columbia R., Oregon USA 46 12N 123 50W
Asuncion R. Paraguay, Paraguay 25 16S 57 41W
Atlantic Highlands Lower Bay, New Jersey, USA
 40 25N 74 01W
Atreco Neches R., Texas, USA 29 59N 93 53W
Atsumi Honshu, Japan 34 39N 137 04E
Attaka (Santan Terminal) Kalimantan, Indonesia
 00 06S 117 32E
Attalia (Antalya) Turkey 36 50N 30 43E
Aubert, Harve (Amherst Harbour) Madaleine Is., Quebec
 Province, Canada 47 14N 61 50W
Auckland North Is., New Zealand 36 51S 174 47E
Auckland Point Gladstone, Queensland, Australia
 23 50S 151 15E
Audierne France 48 01N 04 33W
Augusta Sicilia, Italy 37 13N 15 14E
Augusta, Port Spencer Gulf, South Australia, Australia
 32 30S 137 46E
Auk Terminal Scotland, UK 56 24N 02 04E
Aultbea Loch Ewe, Scotland, UK 57 50N 05 35W
Aux Cayes Haiti 18 11N 73 44W
Avalon Santa Catalina Is., California, USA
 33 21N 118 20W
Avarua Rarotonga, Cook Is 12 12S 159 47W
Avatiu Rarotonga, Cook Is 21 12S 159 47W
Aveiro Portugal 40 38N 08 45W
Avernakke Fyn, Denmark 55 18N 10 48E
Aviles Spain 43 35N 05 57W
Avola Sicilia, Italy 36 54N 15 10E
Avon Suisun Bay, California, USA 38 02N 122 05W
Avondale Mississippi R., Louisiana, USA 29 55N 90 11W
Avonmouth Bristol Channel, England, UK
 51 30N 02 43W
Axelsvik Sweden 65 46N 23 23E
Axim Ghana 04 52N 02 15W
Ayamonte R. Guadiana, Spain 37 13N 07 25W
Ayas Iskenderun Korfezi, Turkey 36 41N 35 47E

Ayer Chawan, Pulau Singapore 01 17N 103 42E
Ayios Giorgios (St George's Harbour) Piraievs, Greece
 37 57N 23 36E
Ayios Nikolas (St. Nicholas) Kriti, Greece
 35 11N 25 43E
Ayios Nikolas (St. Nicholas) Kea, Greece 37 40N 24 19E
Ayr Firth of Clyde, Scotland, UK 55 28N 04 38W
Aysen, Puerto Seno Aysen, Chile 45 25S 72 49W
Ayvalik (Aivaly) Turkey 39 19N 26 38E
Azhikal India 11 57N 75 18E
Aziz, Abd al (Damman) Saudi Arabia 26 30N 50 12E
Aznalfarache, San Juan de R. Guadalquivir, Spain
 37 21N 06 01W
Azov R. Don, USSR 47 07N 39 25E
Azqostal Zhdanov, Azovskoye More, USSR
 47 05N 37 35E
Azua, Puerto Viejo de Dominican Republic
 18 19N 70 49W
Azul, Cerro Peru 13 02S 76 31W
Az Zannah, Jabal (Jebel Dhanna) United Arab Emirates
 24 12N 52 34E
Az Zawiya, (Zawia Terminal) Libya 32 49N 12 42E
Az Zubayr, Khawr (khor az Zubayr) Iraq 30 24N 47 45E
Azzurro, Porto Elba, Italy 42 46N 10 24E
Az Zuwaytinah (Zueitina) Libya 50 57N 20 11E

Babitonga (Tefran Terminal) Brazil 26 13S 48 25W
Bachaquero Lago de Maracaibo, Venezuelá
 09 57N 71 09W
Bacolod Negros, Philippines 10 40N 122 56E
Badagara India 11 35N 75 34E
Badalona Spain 41 27N 02 15E
Baddeck Bras d'Or Lake, Cape Breton Is., Nova Scotia,
 Canada 46 07N 60 44W
Bado Uddevallah Hamn, Sweden 58 21N 11 56E
Bagan Si Api Api Sumatera, Indonesia 02 09N 100 48E
Bagfas Jetty Marmara Denizi, Turkey 40 25N 27 56E
Bagnoli Golfo di Napoli, Italy 40 48N 14 10E
Bagotville Saguenay R., Quebec Province, Canada
 48 21N 70 53W
Bahar, Chah (Chahbar) Iran 25 16N 60 37E
Bahia (Salvador) Brazil 12 58S 38 31W
Bahia Blanca Argentina 38 45S 62 16W
Bahia Caldera Dominican Republic 18 13N 70 32W
Bahia de Amuay Peninsula de Paraguana, Venezuela
 11 45N 70 13W
Bahia de Caraquez Ecuador 00 36S 80 24W
Bahia de Guantanamo Cuba 20 00N 75 10W
Bahia de Tallaboa Puerto Rico 17 59N 66 45W
Bahia Gente Grande Estrecho de Magallanes, Chile
 53 00S 70 20W
Bahia Gregorio Estrecho de Magallanes, Chile
 52 38S 70 12W
Bahia Honda Cuba 22 58N 83 09W
Bahia las Minas Panama 09 24N 79 50W
Bahia Moin Costa Rica 10 01N 83 05W
Bahia Nombre de Dios Panama 09 36N 79 29W
Bahia Porvenir Estrecho de Magallanes, Chile
 53 19S 70 25W
Bahia San Sebastian Tiera del Fuego, Argentina
 53 09S 68 15W
Bahrain Island 26 10N 50 40E
Bahregan, Ras (Nowruz Terminal) Iran 29 43N 50 10E
Baia de Ana Chaves Sao Tome Is., Sao Tome and Principe
 00 21N 06 44E
Baia di Muggia Golfo di Trieste, Italy 45 37N 13 46E
Baia dos Tigres Angola 16 36S 11 46E
Baie Comeau (Comeau Bay) Quebec Province, Canada
 49 14N 68 08W

Baie de Jeremie (Jeromio) Haiti 18 39N 74 07W
Baie de Ream Kampuchea 10 33N 103 36E
Baie des Dames New Caledonia 22 14S 166 24E
Baie de Vun Chao Vietnam 13 26N 109 14E
Baie Faanui Bora-Bora, Society Is. 16 30S 151 45W
Baie Verte Newfoundland, Canada 49 56N 56 12W
Baile Atha Claith (Dublin) Republic of Ireland
   53 21N 06 13W
Bais Negros, Philippines 09 36N 123 08E
Bajada Grande R. Parana, Argentina 31 43S 60 35W
Bajo Grande Lago de Maracaibo, Venezuela
   10 31N 71 36W
Bajur, Teluk (Padang) Sumatera, Indonesia 00 59S 100 23E
Bakapit Sabah, Malaysia 04 57N 118 35E
Bakar Rijecki Zaliv, Yugoslavia 45 18N 14 32E
Bakr, Mina al (Albakr Terminal) (Khawr al Kafka) Iraq
   29 41N 48 49E
Balai, Tanjung Sungai Asahan, Sumatera, Indonesia
   02 58N 99 48E
Balam, Pangkal Bangka, Indonesia 02 06S 106 08E
Balancan, Port Marinduque, Philippines 13 32N 121 52E
Balao Terminal Ecuador 01 02N 79 42W
Balboa Panama Canal Zone 08 57N 79 34W
Balchik (Baljik) Bulgaria 43 24N 28 10E
Baler Luzon, Philippines 15 46N 121 34E
Baliango Mindanao, Philippines 08 40N 123 36E
Balikpapan Kalimantan, Indonesia 01 16S 116 49E
Balingian Sarawak, Malaysia 03 00N 112 35E
Baliwasan Mindanao, Philippines 06 55N 122 03E
Baljik (Balchik) Bulgaria 43 24N 28 10E
Ballangen Ofotfjord, Norway 68 21N 16 50E
Ballast Head Kangaroo Is., South Australia, Australia
   35 46S 137 48E
Ballen Samso, Denmark 55 49N 10 39E
Ballina R. Moy, Republic of Ireland 54 07N 09 09W
Ballina New South Wales, Australia 28 52S 153 34E
Ballybricken Corcaigh, Republic of Ireland
   51 50N 08 20W
Ballykissane (Killorglin) Dingle Bay, Republic of Ireland
   52 07N 09 47W
Balmain Sydney, New South Wales, Australia
   33 52S 151 11E
Balongan Terminal Jawa, Indonesia 06 17S 108 27E
Balsta Malaren, Sweden 59 33N 17 33E
Balticport (Paldiski) Finskiy Zaliv, USSR 59 21N 24 04E
Baltimore Republic of Ireland 51 28N 09 24W
Baltimore Maryland, USA 39 16N 76 34W
Baltiysk (Pillau) Gdanskiy Zaliv, USSR 54 39N 19 54E
Baluarte Luzon, Philippines 15 45N 119 53E
Bamberton Vancouver Is., British Columbia, Canada
   48 35N 123 31E
Bamfield Vancouver Is., British Columbia, Canada
   48 50N 125 08W
Banaba (Ocean Is.) 00 54S 169 33E
Banana Zaire 06 01S 12 25E
Banatica R. Tejo, Portugal 38 40N 09 13W
Bandar Abbas Iran 27 14N 56 16E
Bandar e Lengeh (Lingah) Iran 26 33N 54 53E
Bandar Khomeini (Bandar Shahpour) Iran 30 27N 49 05E
Bandar Mahshahr (Bandar Mashahr) (Bandar Ma'shur)
   Iran 30 28N 49 11E
Bandar Mashahr (Bandar Ma'shur) (Bandar Mahshahr)
   Iran 30 28N 49 11E
Bandar Ma'shur (Bandar Mashahr) (Bandar Mahshahr)
   Iran 30 28N 49 11E
Bandar Qasim (Port Muhammad Bin Qasim) Phitti Creek,
   Pakistan 24 46N 67 19E
Bandar Rayzut (Mina Raysut) (Salalah) Oman
   16 56N 54 01E
Bandar Seri Begawan (Brunei) Brunei 04 53N 114 56E

Bandar Shahpour (Bandar Khomeini) Iran 30 27N 49 05E
Bandholm Lolland, Denmark 54 50N 11 29W
Bandirma (Panderma) Marmara Denizi, Turkey
   40 21N 27 59E
Ban Don (Surat Thani) Thailand 09 09N 99 20E
Bandon Oregon, USA 43 07N 124 25W
Banes, Puerto Cuba 20 54N 75 43W
Banghazi (Benghazi) Libya 32 07N 20 03E
Bangkahulu (Bengkulu) (Benkulen) Sumatera, Indonesia
   03 47S 102 15E
Bangkok Thailand 13 45N 100 30E
Bangor Belfast Lough, Ulster, UK 54 40N 05 39W
Bangor Maine, USA 44 48N 68 46W
Banias (Banias) Syria 35 14N 35 56E
Baniyas (Baniyas) Syria 35 14N 35 56E
Banjarmasin Sungai Barito, Kalimantan, Indonesia
   03 20S 114 35E
Banjul (Bathurst) Gambia 13 27N 16 35W
Bank, Grand Newfoundland, Canada 47 06N 55 45W
Bantry Republic of Ireland 51 41N 09 27W
Banyuwanga (Port Meneng) Jawa, Indonesia
   08 13S 114 23E
Bar (Antivari) Yugoslavia 42 05N 19 05E
Baracoa Cuba 20 22N 74 30W
Baradero R.Parana, Argentina 33 48S 59 31W
Barahona Dominican Republic 18 12N 71 04W
Baram, Kuala Sarawak, Malaysia 04 35N 113 59E
Barao de Tefee (Antonina) Brazil 25 26S 48 42W
Barawe (Brava) Somalia 01 06N 44 03E
Barbate de Franco (Barbate) Spain 36 11N 05 56W
Barbers Point Oahu, Hawaiian Is USA 21 18N 158 07W
Barbours Cut Texas, USA 29 41N 94 59W
Barcadera, Haven Aruba 12 29N 70 01W
Barcelona Spain 41 22N 02 10E
Bardia (Bardiyah) Libya 31 46N 25 07E
Bardiyah (Bardia) Libya 31 46N 25 07E
Barentsburg Gronfjorden, Spitsbergen, Svalbard,
   78 05N 14 15E
Bares (Barquero) Spain 43 44N 07 42W
Barfleur France 49 40N 01 16W
Bar Harbour Maine, USA 44 24W 68 13W
Bari Italy 41 08N 16 53E
Barking R.Thames, England, UK 51 30N 00 06E
Barletta Italy 41 19N 16 17E
Barmouth Wales, UK 52 43N 04 03W
Barnabe, Isla Brazil 23 55S 46 20W
Barney Point Gladstone, Queensland, Australia
   23 50S 151 15E
Barnstaple R.Taw, England, UK 51 05N 04 04W
Barquero (Bares) Spain 43 44N 07 42W
Barquito, Caleta Chile 26 21S 70 39W
Barra do Riacho (Portocel) Brazil 19 51S 40 03W
Barrancas R. Orinoco, Venezuela 08 42N 62 11W
Barranquilla R. Magdalena, Colombia 10 58N 74 46W
Barra Seco Brazil 19 05N 39 40W
Barreiro R. Tejo, Portugal 38 39N 09 05W
Barrier, Port Baie de St. Brieuc, France 48 38N 02 25W
Barrios, Puerto Bahia de Amatique, Guatemala
   15 43N 88 35W
Barrosso Terminal, Almirante (Tebar Terminal) Brazil
   23 48S 45 23W
Barrow-in-Furness England, UK 54 06N 03 14W
Barrow Island Western Australia, Australia
   20 45S 115 27E
Barry Bristol Channel, Wales, UK 51 24N 03 17W
Barth East Germany 54 22N 12 44E
Bartica Essequibo R., Guyana 06 24N 58 37W
Bartlett Cove Glacier Bay, Alaska, USA 58 27N 135 55W
Barton Manchester Ship Canal, England, UK
   53 28N 02 23W

Baru, Kota Pulo Laut, Indonesia 03 14S 116 13E
Basbeck Die Oste, West Germany 53 41N 09 11E
Basques, Port aux Newfoundland, Canada
47 35N 59 08W
Basrah (Busreh) Shatt al Arab, Iraq 30 31N 47 51E
Bassa, Grand Liberia 05 52N 10 04W
Bassein Bassien R., Burma 16 47N 94 45E
Basse Indre La Loire, France 47 13N 01 41W
Bassens La Garonne, France 44 54N 00 32W
Basse Terre Guadeloupe 16 00N 61 43W
Basseterre St Kitts 17 17N 62 42W
Bastia Corse, France 42 41N 09 27E
Bata Rio Muni, Guinea Equatorial 01 51N 09 47E
Bataan Luzon, Philippines 14 32N 120 36E
Batabano Golfo de Batabano, Cuba 22 41N 82 18W
Batangas Luzon, Philippines 13 46N 121 02E
Batang Lupar Sarawak, Malaysia 01 31N 110 56E
Batan, Port Panay, Philippines 11 35N 122 30E
Bath Maine, USA 43 55N 69 49W
Bathurst (Banjul) Gambia 13 27N 16 35W
Bathurst Baie des Chaleurs, New Brunswick,
Canada 47 37N 65 39W
Baton Rouge Mississippi R., Louisiana, USA
30 27N 91 12W
Batu, Tanjong Sabah, Malaysia 04 15N 117 52E
Batum (Batumi) USSR 41 39N 41 38E
Batumi (Batum) USSR 41 39N 41 38E

Baybay Leyte, Philippines 10 41N 124 49E
Bay of Islands Newfoundland, Canada 49 15N 58 10W
Bayonne France 43 30N 01 29W
Bayonne New Jersey, USA 40 39N 74 08W
Bayou Casotte Pascagoula, Mississippi, USA
30 21N 88 34W
Bayovar, Puerto Peru 05 49S 81 00W
Bayport Texas, USA 29 37N 94 59W
Bay Roberts Newfoundland, Canada 47 36N 53 16W
Baytown Houston Ship Canal, Texas, USA
29 44N 95 01W
Beaufort South Carolina, USA 32 26N 80 40W
Beaufort Inlet North Carolina, USA 34 43N 76 40W
Beaumont Neches R., Texas, USA 30 05N 94 06W
Beauty Point R. Tamar, Tasmania, Australia
41 10S 146 49E
Beaver Cove Vancouver Is., British Columbia, Canada
50 33N 126 52W
Beaver Harbour Bay of Fundy, New Brunswick, Canada
45 04N 66 44W
Beaver Harbour Nova Scotia, Canada 44 53N 62 25W
Bec d' Ambes La Dordogne, France 45 02N 00 34W
Bedford Basin Nova Scotia, Canada 44 42N 63 37W
Bedford, New Buzzards Bay, Massachusetts, USA
41 38N 70 55W
Bedi (Bedi Bandar) India 22 31N 70 02E
Bedi Bandar (Bedi) India 22 31N 70 02E
Bee Ness R. Medway, England, UK 51 25N 00 39E
Befu Seto Naikai, Honshu, Japan 34 42N 134 52E
Begawan, Bandar Seri (Brunei) Brunei 04 53N 114 56E
Beida, Dar el (Casablanca) Morocco 33 37N 07 36W
Beira Mozambique 19 50S 34 50E
Beirut (Beyrouth) Lebanon 33 54N 35 31E
Bejaia (Bougie) Algeria 36 45N 05 05E
Bekapai Terminal Kalimantan, Indonesia 00 59S 117 31E
Belait, Kuala Brunei 04 35N 114 11E
Belawan Sungei Bila, Sumatera, Indonesia 03 47N 98 41E
Belekeri India 14 43N 74 15E
Belem (Para) R. Para, Brazil 01 27S 48 30W
Belem R.Tejo, Portugal 38 41N 09 13W
Belfast Ulster, UK 54 36N 05 55W
Belfast Maine, USA 44 25N 69 00W

Belgorod Dnestrovskiy Liman, USSR 46 12N 30 21E
Belgrano, Puerto Bahia Blanca, Argentina 38 54S 62 06W
Belize City Belize 17 30N 88 11W
Bella Bella Lama Passage, British Columbia, Canada
52 09N 128 07W
Bella Coola North Bentinct Arm, British Columbia, Canada
52 23N 126 47W
Bella Vista R. Parana, Argentina 32 41S 60 44W
Bell Bay R. Tamar, Tasmania, Australia 41 08S 146 52E
Belledune Baie des Chaleurs, New Brunswick, Canada
47 55N 65 50W
Belleville Lake Ontario, Ontario, Canada 44 08N 77 22W
Bellingham Washington, USA 48 45N 122 29W
Belliveau Cove St. Mary's Bay, Nova Scotia, Canada
44 24N 66 03W
Bellport R. Usk, Wales, UK 51 34N 02 58W
Belmonte Brazil 15 51S 38 52W
Belomorsk (Soroka) Onezhskaya Guba, USSR
64 32N 34 49E
Belwaarde Surinam River, Surinam 05 51N 55 05W
Bend, North Coos Bay, Oregon, USA 43 24N 124 13W
Bend, South Willapa R., Washington, USA
46 40N 123 48W
Bender Eregli (Heraklea) Turkey 41 18N 31 26E

Benghazi (Banghazi) Libya 32 07N 20 03E
Bengkalis (Benkalis) Sumatera, Indonesia
01 27N 102 06E
Bengkulu (Benkulen) (Bangkahulu) Sumetra, Indonesia
03 47S 102 15E
Benguela Angola 12 34S 13 24E
Benguela Velha (Porto Amboim) Angola 10 44S 13 46E
Be, Nha Song Sai Gon, Vietnam 10 42N 106 45E
Benicarlo Spain 40 25N 00 26E
Benicia San Pablo Bay, California, USA 38 03N 122 09W
Beni Saf Algeria 35 18N 01 24E
Benito, Rio Rio Muni, Guinea Equatorial 01 36N 09 37E
Benjamin Constant R. Javari, Brazil 04 23S 69 59W
Benkalis (Bengkalis) Sumatera, Indonesia 01 27N 102 06E
Benkulen (Bengkulu) (Bangkahulu) Sumatera, Indonesia
03 47S 102 15E
Benoa Bali, Indonesia 08 46S 115 12E
Benodet France 47 52N 04 06W
Be,Nossi (Nosy Be) Malagasy Republic 13 12S 48 11E
Bensersiel West Germany 53 41N 07 35E
Beppu Kyushu, Japan 33 16N 131 31E
Berbera Somalia 10 26N 45 01E
Berbice (New Amsterdam) Guyana 06 16N 57 31W
Berdiansk (Berdyanskiy Port) Azovskoye More, USSR
46 45N 36 48E
Berdyanskiy Port (Berdiansk) Azovskoye More, USSR
46 45N 36 48E
Bere Haven (Castletown Bere) Bantry Bay, Republic of
Ireland 51 39N 09 54W
Bergen Norway 60 24N 05 19E
Berghamn Aland, Finland 60 14N 19 33E
Berhala, Tanjong Malaya, Malaysia 01 15N 103 28E
Berlayer, Tanjong Singapore 01 16N 103 48E
Berre, Etang de Golfe du Lion, France 43 28N 05 10E
Berwick R. Tweed, England, UK 55 46N 02 00W
Bessin, Port en Baie de la Seine, France 49 21N 00 46W
Bethioua, Port de Golfe d'Arzew, Algeria
35 49N 00 16W
Betio Tarawa, Kiribati Republic 01 21N 172 56E
Beypore India 11 10N 75 49E
Beyrouth (Beirut) Lebanon 33 54N 35 31E
Bhatkal India 13 58N 74 31E
Bhavnagar New Port India 21 45N 72 14E
Bhavnagar Old Port India 21 47N 72 08E
Bheemunipatnam (Bhimunipatnam) (Bimlipatam) India
17 54N 83 29E

Bhimunipatnam (Bheemunipatnam) (Bimlipatam) India 17 54N 83 29E

Biawak Sarawak, Malaysia 01 34N 110 24E

Bideford R. Torridge, England, UK 51 01N 04 12W

Bilbao Spain 43 21N 03 02W

Bildudalur Arnarfjordhur, Iceland 65 41N 23 36W

Billingham R. Tees, England, UK 54 35N 01 16W

Biloxi Mississippi, USA 30 24N 88 53W

Bima Sumbawa, Indonesia 08 27S 118 43E

Bimlipatam (Bhimunipatnam) (Bheemunipatnam) India 17 54N 83 29E

Binanga, Port Luzon, Philippines 14 44N 120 16E

Binatang Sarawak, Malaysia 02 10N 111 37E

Binic France 48 36N 02 49W

Bintulu Sarawak, Malaysia 03 10N 113 03E

Birkenhead R. Mersey, England, UK 53 24N 03 01W

Bislig Mindanao, Philippines 08 12N 126 22E

Bissao (Bissau) R.Geba, Guinea Bissau 11 52N 15 35W

Bissau (Bissao) R. Geba, Guinea Bissau 11 52N 15 35W

Bisserup Sjaelland, Denmark 55 12N 11 29E

Bitung Sulawesi, Indonesia 01 26N 125 12E

Bizerta (Bizerte) Tunisia 37 16N 09 53E

Bizerte (Bizerta) Tunisia 37 16N 09 53E

Bjorneborg (Pori) Finland 61 28N 21 48E

Bjuroklubb Sweden 64 29N 21 35E

Black Cape Baie des Chaleurs, Quebec Province, Canada 48 08N 65 49W

Black River Jamaica 18 01N 77 53W

Blacks Harbour Bay of Fundy, New Brunswick, Canada 45 03N 66 49W

Blackwater River England, UK 51 45N 00 55E

Blaine Washington, USA 48 59N 122 45W

Blair, Port Andaman Is., India 11 41N 92 46E

Blanca, Bahia Argentina 38 45S 62 16W

Blanco, Cabo Peru 04 15S 81 15W

Blanes Spain 41 41N 02 47E

Blankaholm Sweden 57 35N 16 31E

Blaye La Gironde, France 45 08N 00 40W

Blexen Die Weser, West Germany 53 32N 08 32E

Bloscon France 48 43N 03 58W

Blount Island Jacksonville, Florida, USA 30 24N 81 33W

Blubber Bay Texada Is., British Columbia, Canada 49 48N 124 37W

Bluefields (El Bluff) Nicaragua 11 59N 83 44W

Bluff South Is., New Zealand 46 36S 168 20E

Bluff, El (Bluefields) Nicaragua 11 59N 83 44W

Bluff, Smith's Neches R., Texas, USA 30 00N 93 59W

Blumenthal Die Weser, West Germany 53 12N 08 34E

Blyth England, UK 55 08N 01 30W

Boa, Fonte R. Amazonas, Brazil 02 33S 65 59W

Bobergshamn Finland 62 10N 21 21E

Boca Chica Bahia Andres, Dominican Republic 18 27N 69 36W

Boca Grande Cuba 21 33N 78 40W

Boca Grande, Port Florida, USA 26 43N 82 15W

Bocas del Toro Panama 09 20N 82 15W

Bodo Saltfjord, Norway 67 17N 14 24E

Bodrum (Budrum) Mandalya Korfezi, Turkey 37 02N 27 26E

Boeleleng (Buleleng) Bali, Indonesia 08 06S 115 06E

Boeton (Buton) Butung, Indonesia 05 27S 122 38E

Bogense Fyn, Denmark 55 34N 10 05E

Bohayan, Pulau Sabah, Malaysia 04 48N 118 18E

Boisdale, Loch South Uist, Scotland, UK 57 09N 07 18W

Boke R. Nunez, Guinea 10 57N 14 13W

Bolama Bissagos Is., Guinea-Bissau 11 34N 15 27W

Bole R. Skien, Norway 59 11N 09 38E

Bolivar, Ciudad R. Orinoco, Venezuela 08 05N 63 35W

Bolivar, Puerto Ecuador 03 16S 80 00W

Bollsta Sweden 62 59N 17 42E

Bol'shaya Pir'ya, Guba Kandakshskaya Guba, USSR 66 40N 34 21E

Bolungavik Isafjardjup, Iceland 66 09N 23 14W

Boma R. Zaire, Zaire 05 51S 13 03E

Bombay India 18 55N 72 50E

Bona (Annaba) (Bone) Algeria 36 54N 07 45E

Bonaberi Cameroon 04 05N 09 41E

Bonaire Island 12 10N 68 25W

Bonaire Terminal Bonaire 12 13N 68 23W

Bonanza R. Guadalquivir, Spain 36 48N 06 21W

Bone (Bona) (Annaba) Algeria 36 54N 07 45E

Bo'ness R. Forth, Scotland, UK 56 01N 03 37W

Bongabong Mindoro, Philippines 12 45N 121 29E

Bonifacio Corse, France 41 23N 09 10E

Bonny Bonny R., Nigeria 04 26N 07 12E

Bonthe Sherbro Is., Sierra Leone 07 32N 12 30W

Boqueron Bahia de Guantanamo, Cuba 19 59N 75 07W

Bora Bora Island Society Is., 16 30S 151 45W

Borburata Venezuela 10 29N 68 01W

Borco Terminal Grand Bahama, Bahamas 26 30N 78 46W

Bordeaux La Garonne, France 44 50N 00 34W

Borga (Porvoo) Finland 60 24N 25 40E

Borgarnes Borgarfjordhur, Iceland 64 33N 21 55W

Borgeskov Sjaelland, Denmark 55 22N 12 25E

Borghi, Puerto R. Parana, Argentina 32 48S 60 43W

Borgholm Oland, Sweden 56 51N 16 39E

BorjIslam Syria 35 40N 35 48E

Borkum Ostfriesischen, West Germany 53 34N 06 39E

Borongan Samar, Philippines 11 37N 125 27E

Borot Cove Mindanao, Philippines 06 36N 126 05E

Borsele Westerschelde, Netherlands 51 25N 03 44E

Borstahusen Sweden 55 54N 12 48E

Boskamp Coppename R., Surinam 05 47N 55 53W

Boston R. Witham, England, UK 52 58N 00 01W

Boston Massachusetts, USA 42 22N 71 04W

Boston, East Massachusetts, USA 42 23N 71 02W

Boston, South Massachusetts, USA 42 20N 71 02W

Botado, El Bahia Samana, Dominican Republic 19 12N 69 26W

Botany Bay New South Wales, Australia 34 00S 151 12E

Botas Terminal Ceyhan Limani, Iskenderun Korfezi, Turkey 36 53N 35 56E

Botwood Exploits Bay, Newfoundland, Canada 49 09N 55 19W

Boucau France 43 32N 01 29W

Bouc, Port de France 43 24N 04 59E

Bouet, Port Ivory Coast 05 14N 03 56W

Bougie (Bejaia) Algeria 36 45N 05 05E

Boulogne sur Mer France 50 44N 01 35E

Bourail New Caledonia 21 36S 165 26E

Bourgas (Burghaz) Bulgaria 42 29N 27 29E

Bourguiba, Menzel Tunisia 37 10N 09 48E

Bowden Wharf (Port Morant) Jamaica 17 53N 76 19W

Bowen (Port Denison) Queensland, Australia 20 01S 148 15E

Bowling R. Clyde, Scotland, UK 55 56N 29 29W

Braakmanhaven Westerschelde, Netherlands 51 21N 03 46E

Brac, Cayman Cayman Is. 19 45N 79 45W

Brahestad (Raahe) Finland 64 42N 24 28E

Braila R.Dunarea, Romania 45 15N 27 59E

Brake Die Weser, West Germany 53 20N 08 29E

Branca, Areia Brazil 04 57S 37 09W

Brandohamn (Merikarvia) Finland 61 50N 21 28E

Brannfors Sweden 65 02N 21 23E

Branthallsredd Sweden 61 16N 17 14E

Brass Nigeria 04 20N 06 14E

Brass Terminal Brass R., Nigeria 04 04N 06 19E

Brattvag Samsfjord, Norway 62 36N 06 27E

Brava (Barawe) Somalia 01 06N 44 03E

Braviken Sweden 58 38N 16 16E

Brayton Point Narragansett Bay, Rhode Island, USA 41 42N 71 11W

Brazos Texas, USA 28 57N 95 19W

Brea, La (Brighton) Trinidad 10 15N 61 38W

Breeze, Point Delaware R., Pennsylvania, USA 39 55N 75 12W

Brega, Marsa el Libya 30 25N 19 34E

Breira, Port Algeria 36 32N 01 35E

Breivika Tromso, Norway 69 40N 18 58E

Bremen Die Weser, West Germany 53 05N 08 47E

Bremerhaven Die Weser, West Germany 53 33N 08 34E

Bremerton Puget Sound, Washington, USA 47 34N 122 37W

Bremervorde Die Oste, West Germany 53 29N 09 09E

Breskens Westerschelde, Netherlands 51 24N 03 34E

Brest France 48 23N 04 29W

Breves R. Para, Brazil 01 42S 50 29W

Brevik Norway 59 03N 09 41E

Brewer, South Penobscot R., Maine, USA 44 47N 68 46W

Bridgeport Connecticut, USA 41 10N 73 11W

Bridgetown Barbados 13 05N 59 36W

Bridgewater La Have R., Nova Scotia, Canada 44 23N 64 31W

Bridgewater R. Parret, England, UK 51 08N 03 00W

Bridlington England, UK 54 05N 00 11W

Bridport Lyme Bay, England, UK 50 42N 02 46W

Brightlingsea R. Colne, England, UK 51 48N 01 01E

Brighton (La Brea) Trinidad 10 15N 61 38W

Brindisi Italy 40 39N 17 57E

Brisbane Queensland, Australia 27 28S 153 03E

Bristol R. Avon, England, UK 51 27N 02 37W

Bristol Narragansett Bay, Rhode Island, USA 41 40N 71 17W

Britannia Howe Sound, British Columbia, Canada 39 38N 123 12W

Briton Ferry R. Neath, Wales, UK 51 38N 03 49W

Brixham Tor Bay, England, UK 50 24N 03 31W

Brockville St. Lawrence Seaway, Ontario, Canada 44 35N 75 42W

Brofjorden Sweden 58 21N 11 26E

Bromborough Dock R. Mersey, England, UK 53 21N 02 59W

Bronnoysund Norway 65 29N 12 13E

Brook, Corner Bay of Islands, Newfoundland, Canada 48 58N 57 57W

Brooklyn New York, USA 40 42N 74 00W

Brook, Main Hare Bay, Newfoundland, Canada 51 11N 56 01W

Broome Western Australia, Australia 17 59S 122 15E

Brouwershaven Schouwen, Netherlands 51 44N 03 55E

Brownies Taing Mainland, Shetland Is., Scotland, UK 59 59N 01 14W

Brownsville Rio Grande, Texas 25 54N 97 25W

Brsica Kvarner, Yugoslavia 45 02N 14 03E

Bruges (Brugge) Boudewijnkanaal, Belgium 51 13N 03 13E

Brugge (Bruges) Boudewijnkanaal, Belgium 51 13N 03 13E

Brunei (Bandar Seri Begawan) Brunei 04 53N 114 56E

Brunsbuttel Die Elbe, West Germany 53 54N 09 08E

Brunswick Georgia, USA 31 09N 81 32W

Brussels (Bruxelles) Belgium 50 50N 04 21E

Bruxelles (Brussels) Belgium 50 50N 04 21E

Buaun Batangas Bay, Luzon, Philippines 13 47N 121 00E

Buchanan Liberia 05 52N 10 03W

Buckie Scotland, UK 57 41N 02 57W

Buckner Bay (Nakagusuku-Wan) Okinawa, Nansei Shoto, Japan 26 15N 127 49E

Bucksport Penobscot River, Maine, USA 44 34N 68 47W

Buctouche Northumberland Strait, New Brunswick, Canada 46 28N 64 43W

Budge Budge (Buj Buj) R. Hugli, India 22 29N 88 11E

Budhir Faskrudhsfjordhur, Iceland 64 56N 14 01W

Budrum (Bodrum) Mandalya Korfezi, Turkey 37 02N 27 26E

Buena, Rio Jamaica 18 29N 77 29W

Buenaventura Colombia 03 54N 77 02W

Buenos Aires R. de la Plata, Argentina 34 36S 58 22W

Bufadero Bahia Nuevitas, Cuba 21 34N 77 14W

Buffalo Lake Erie, New York, USA 42 52N 78 52W

Buffington Lake Michigan, Indiana, USA 41 38N 87 25W

Bugo Macalajar Bay, Mindanao, Philippines 08 31N 124 46E

Buitagro, Puerto R.Parana, Argentina 33 21S 60 11W

Buj Buj (Budge Budge) R. Hugli, India 22 29N 88 11E

Buka Island Papua New Guinea 05 26S 154 40E

Bu'khoosh, Abu al United Arab Emirates 25 26N 53 08E

Bukhta Provideniya Anadyrskiy Zaliv, USSR 64 21N 173 19W

Bukhta Tiksi Guba Buorkhaya, USSR 71 40N 128 45E

Bukom, Pulau Singapore 01 14N 103 46E

Bukpyong Mukho, South Korea 37 30N 129 08E

Buleleng (Boeleleng) Bali, Indonesia 08 06S 115 06E

Buli, Teluk Halmahera, Indonesia 00 52N 128 14E

Bullen Baai Curacao 12 11N 69 02W

Bulwer Island Brisbane R., Queensland, Australia 27 25S 153 08E

Bunbury Koombana Bay, Western Australia, Australia 33 18S 115 39E

Buncrana Lough Swilly, Republic of Ireland 55 08N 07 28W

Bundaberg Burnett R., Queensland, Australia 24 52S 152 21E

Burea Sweden 64 37N 21 15E

Burela Spain 43 39N 07 20W

Burghaz (Bourgas) Bulgaria 42 29N 27 29E

Burghead Scotland, UK 57 42N 03 30W

Burgstaaken Fehmarn, West Germany 54 25N 11 12E

Burgsvik Gotland, Sweden 57 02N 18 17E

Burin Newfoundland, Canada 47 02N 55 11W

Burnie Emu Bay, Tasmania, Australia 41 03S 145 55E

Burns Harbour Lake Michigan, Indiana, USA 41 37N 87 11W

Burnside Mississippi R., Louisiana, USA 30 06N 90 55W

Burntisland Firth of Forth, Scotland, UK 56 03N 03 14W

Burriana Spain 39 51N 00 04W

Bur Sa'id (Port Said) Egypt 31 15N 32 19E

Bur Taufiq (Port Tewfik) Gulf of Suez, Egypt 29 56N 32 34E

Burton-upon-Stather R. Trent, England, UK 53 39N 00 40W

Burutu Nigeria 05 21N 05 31E

Burvik Sweden 64 35N 21 20E

Busan (Pusan) South Korea 35 07N 129 02E

Bushehr (Bushire) (Khowr e Soltani) Iran 29 59N 50 47E

Bushire (Bushehr) (Khowr e Soltani) Iran 28 59N 50 47E

Busreh (Basrah) Shatt al Arab, Iraq 30 31N 47 51E

Busselton Western Australia, Australia 33 37S 115 20E

Butartari Island Kiribati Republic 03 02N 172 48E

Butcher Island Bombay, India 18 57N 72 54E

Butedale Fraser Reach, British Columbia, Canada 53 10N 128 42W

Buton (Boeton) Butung, Indonesia 05 27S 122 38E

Butterworth Malaya, Malaysia 05 24N 100 22E

Butuan Mindanao, Philippines 08 57N 125 33E

Butuku-Luba (San Carlos) Macias Nguema Biyogo (Fernando Poo Is.) Guinea Equatorial 03 29N 08 36E

Butzfleth Die Elbe, West Germany 53 39N 09 31E

Buxtehude Die Este, West Germany 53 28N 09 42E
Buyan City (Dadiangas) (General Santos City) Mindanao, Philippines 06 06N 125 09E
Buyukdere Karadeniz Bogazi, Turkey 41 09N 29 03E

Caballo, Salta Spain 43 22N 03 11W
Cabanas Cuba 23 00N 82 56W
Cabedello Brazil 06 57S 34 50W
Cabello, Puerto Venezuela 10 29N 68 00W
Cabezas, Puerto Nicaragua 14 01N 83 24W
Cabimas Lago de Maracaibo, Venezuela 10 23N 71 28W
Cabinda (Kabinda) Angola 05 33S 12 12E
Cabo Blanco Peru 04 15S 81 15W
Cabo Frio Brazil 22 54S 42 00W
Cabo Negro Estrecho de Magallanes, Chile 52 58S 70 48W
Cabo Rojo Dominican Republic 17 54N 71 39W
Cabo Ruivo R. Tejo, Portugal 38 46N 09 05W
Cabo San Agustin Spain 43 34N 06 44W
Cacheu (Cachew) Guinea-Bissau 12 17N 16 10W
Cachew (Cacheu) Guinea-Bissau 12 17N 16 10W
Cachoeira Ilheus, Brazil 14 48S 39 02W
Cacouna St Lawrence R., Quebec Province, Canada 47 56N 69 31W
Cadiz Spain 36 31N 06 19W
Caen France 49 12N 00 22W
Caernarvon (Carnarvon) Wales, UK 53 09N 04 16W
Cagayan de Oro Mindanao, Philippines 08 31N 124 39E
Cagliari Sardegna, Italy 39 13N 09 07E
Cahersiveen (Cahirciveen) Republic of Ireland 51 57N 10 13W
Cahirciveen (Cahersiveen) Republic of Ireland 51 57N 10 13W
Caibarien (Caybarien) Bahia de Buena Vista, Cuba 22 32N 79 27W
Caimanera Bahia de Guantanamo, Cuba 19 58N 75 09W
Cairn Ryan Scotland, UK 54 58N 05 01W
Cairns Queensland, Australia 16 56S 145 47E
Cais do Pico Pico, Acores 38 32N 28 19W
Calabar Nigeria 04 59N 08 20E
Calabria, Reggio (Reggio) Italy 38 07N 15 39E
Calais France 50 58N 01 51E
Calais St Croix R., Maine, USA 45 11W 67 17W
Calamar R. Magdalena, Colombia 10 15N 74 57W
Calamata (Kalamata) (Kalamai) Messiniakos Kolpos, Greece 37 27N 22 09E
Calapan Mindoro, Philippines 13 25N 121 11E
Calcutta Hugli R., India 22 33N 88 20E
Caldera Chile 27 04S 70 50W
Caldera Golfo de Nicoya, Costa Rica 09 55N 84 43W
Caldera, Bahia Dominican Republic 18 13N 70 32W
Caldera Point Mindanao, Philippines 06 57N 121 58E
Calderilla Chile 27 05S 70 52W
Caleta Barquito Chile 26 21S 70 39W
Caleta Clarencia (Clarence Cove) Bahia Gente Grande, Chile 52 55S 70 08W
Caleta Cordova Golfo de San Jorge, Argentina 45 45S 67 22W
Caleta la Chimba Chile 23 34S 70 25W
Caleta Mansa Chile 40 34S 73 46W
Caleta Olivares Golfo de San Jorge, Argentina 45 47S 67 23W
Caleta Olivia Golfo de San Jorge, Argentina 46 26S 67 30W
Caleta Patillos Chile 20 45S 70 12W
Caleta Percy Bahia Gente Grande, Chile 52 54S 70 15W
Calicut (Kozhikode) India 11 15N 75 46E
Calingapatnam (Kalingapatam) India 18 19N 84 07E
Callao Peru 12 03S 77 09W
Calumet Chicago, Lake Michigan, Illinois, USA 41 44N 87 31W

Calvi Corse, France 42 34N 08 46E
Camacho, Punta Lago de Maracaibo, Venezuela 10 33N 71 32W
Camarinas Spain 43 07N 09 12W
Cama, Sette Gabon 02 37S 09 44E
Cambridge Chesapeake Bay, Maryland, USA 38 35N 76 04W
Camden Deleware R., New Jersey, USA 39 56N 75 08W
Cameta R. Tocantins, Brazil 02 13S 49 29W
Camocim Brazil 02 54S 40 52W
Campachuela Golfo de Guacanayabo, Cuba 20 14N 77 17W
Campana R. Parana, Argentina 34 10S 58 57W
Campbell River Vancouver Is., British Columbia, Canada 50 01N 125 16W
Campbellton Baie des Chaleurs, New Brunswick, Canada 47 59N 66 40W
Campbeltown Firth of Clyde, Scotland, UK 55 26N 05 36W
Campeche Bahia de Campeche, Mexico 19 50N 90 32W
Cam-pha, Port Vietnam 21 02N 107 21E
Camp Lloyd Sondre Stromfjord, Greenland 66 58N 50 57W
Camp Overton Mindanao, Philippines 08 12N 124 13E
Cam Ranh, Vinh Vietnam 11 53N 109 12E
Canakkale (Chanak) Canakkale Bogazi, Turkey 40 09N 26 24E
Canamay Point Negros, Philippines 09 33N 123 08E
Canaport Bay of Fundy, New Brunswick, Canada 45 12N 65 59W
Canaveral, Port Florida, USA 28 25N 80 36W
Cancale Golfe de St. Malo, France 48 40N 01 51W
Candarli (Chandarly) Candarli Korfezi, Turkey 38 52N 26 54E
Candia (Irakleous) (Iraklion) (Heraklion) Kriti, Greece 35 21N 25 09E
Canea (Khania) Kriti, Greece 35 32N 24 01E
Cannanore India 11 52N 75 23E
Cannes Cote d'Azur, France 43 33N 07 01E
Canoan, Port Siquijor, Philippines 09 15N 123 35E
Canso Harbour Nova Scotia, Canada 45 20N 61 00W
Canso Strait Nova Scotia, Canada 45 33N 61 20W
Canton (Kwangchow) (Kuang-chou Kan) (Guangzhou) Chou Chiang, China 23 07N 113 14E
Canton Island 02 49S 171 42W
Canvey Island R. Thames, England, UK 51 31N 00 34E
Cap d'Antifer France 49 41N 00 09E
Cape Cod Canal Massachusetts, USA
East Entrance 41 47N 70 30W
West Entrance 41 44N 70 41W
Cape Cove Quebec Province, Canada 48 26N 64 19W
Cape Cuvier Western Australia, Australia 24 13S 113 25E
Cape Lambert Port Walcott, Western Australia, Australia 20 35S 117 12E
Cape Lopez Gabon 00 38S 08 43E
Cape Palmas Liberia 04 22N 07 44W
Cape Tormentine Northumberland Strait, New Brunswick, Canada 46 08N 63 47W
Cape Town South Africa 33 54S 18 25E
Cape Verde Islands 17 00N 24 00W
Cap Haitien Haiti 19 46N 72 12W
Cap Lopez Gabon 00 38S 08 43E
Caracas Baai Curacao 12 04N 68 52W
Caraga Mindanao, Philippines 07 19N 126 34E
Caraminal, Puebla del Spain 42 36N 08 56W
Caraquet Baie des Chaleurs, New Brunswick, Canada 47 48N 64 56W
Caraquez, Bahia de Ecuador 00 36S 80 24W
Caravellas Brazil 17 43 3S 39 16W
Carbonear Newfoundland, Canada 47 44N 53 14W

Cardenas Cuba 23 03N 81 12W
Cardenas, Lazaro Mexico 17 54N 102 11W
Cardiff Bristol Channel, Wales, UK 51 29N 03 10W
Cardigan Wales, UK 52 05N 04 40W
Cardon, Punta Peninsula de Paraguana, Venezuela
11 37N 70 14W
Carentan France 49 18N 01 15W
Carino Spain 43 44N 07 51W
Caripito R. San Juan, Venezuela 10 09N 63 05W
Carleton Baie des Chaleurs, Quebec Province, Canada
48 06N 66 08W
Carlingford Republic of Ireland 54 03N 06 11W
Carloforte San Pietro Is., Sardegna, Italy 39 08N 08 19E
Carlsborg Vattern, Sweden 58 32N 14 32E
Carlsborg (Karlsborg) Sweden 65 48N 23 16E
Carlsvik (Karlsvik) Sweden 65 36N 22 06E
Carmanville Newfoundland, Canada 49 25N 54 14W
Carmelo, Puerto de R. Uruguay, Uruguay 34 01S 58 18W
Carmen, Ciudad del Laguna de Terminos, Mexico
18 39N 91 50W
Carmen, Puerto Is.,de Chiloe, Chile 43 09S 73 46W
Carmopolis Brazil 11 02S 37 02W
Carnarvon Western Australia, Australia 24 53S 113 42E
Carnarvon (Caernarvon) Wales, UK 53 09N 04 16W
Carnlough Ulster, UK 54 59N 06 00W
Caronte Golfe de Fos, France 43 24N 05 02E
Carranza, Venustiano Laguna de Guerrero Negra, Mexico
28 02N 114 07W
Carrara, Marina di Italy 44 02N 10 03E
Carrickfergus Belfast Lough, Ulster, UK 54 43N 05 48W
Carrizal Bajo Chile 28 05S 71 12W
Cartagena Colombia 10 24N 75 32W
Cartagena Spain 37 35N 00 59W
Carteret Arthur Kill R., New Jersey, USA
40 35N 74 13W
Cartier, Port St. Lawrence R., Quebec Province, Canada
50 02N 66 47W
Cartwright Labrador, Canada 53 42N 57 01W
Carupano Venezuela 10 41N 63 15W
Carupano, Puerto Puerto Padre, Cuba 21 18N 76 32W
Casablanca (Dar el Beida) Morocco 33 37N 07 36W
Casas, Las Isla Quiriquina, Chile 36 38S 73 03W
Cascade Bay Norfolk Is. 29 01S 167 58E
Casilda Cuba 21 45N 79 59W
Casma Peru 09 28S 78 24W
Casotte, Bayou Pascagoula, Mississippi, USA
30 21N 88 34W
Castanas Luzon, Philippines 13 52N 121 33E
Castellammare del Golfo Sicilia, Italy 38 01N 12 53E
Castellammare di Stabia Golfo di Napoli, Italy
40 42N 14 28E
Castellon de la Plana, Puerto del Grao de Spain
39 58N 00 01E
Castellon Refinery Spain 39 57N 00 01E
Castelnuovo (Herceg-Novi) Boka Kotorska, Yugoslavia
42 27N 18 34E
Castilla, Puerto Honduras 15 59N 86 00W
Castilla, Santo Tomas de Guatemala 15 41N 88 37W
Castle Harbour Bermuda 32 21N 64 41W
Castle Island Duncan Canal, Alaska, USA
56 39N 133 10W
Castletown Isle of Man, UK 54 04N 04 39W
Castletown Bere (Bere Haven) Bantry Bay, Republic of
Ireland 51 39N 09 54W
Castries, Port St. Lucia 14 01N 61 00W
Castro Isla de Chiloe, Chile 42 29S 73 47W
Castro Alen (Castro Urdiales) Spain 43 24N 03 13W
Castro Urdiales (Castro Alen) Spain 43 24N 03 13W
Catacolo (Katakolo) (Katakolon) Greece 37 39N 21 20E
Catalina Harbour Newfoundland, Canada 48 30N 53 05W

Cantania Sicilia, Italy 37 29N 15 06E
Catbalogan Samar, Philippines 11 46N 125 53E
Catia la Mar Venezuela 10 36N 67 02W
Cattaro (Kotor) Boka Kotorska, Yugoslavia
42 25N 18 46E
Caudebec La Seine, France 49 31N 00 42E
Cavalla (Kavalla) Greece 40 55N 24 25E
Cavite Luzon, Philippines 14 29N 120 55E
Caybarien (Caibarien) Bahia de Buena Vista, Cuba
22 32N 79 27W
Cayenne French Guiana 04 56N 52 21W
Cayes, Aux Haiti 18 11N 73 44W
Cayman Brac Cayman Is., 19 45N 79 45E
Cayman, Grand Cayman Is. 19 20N 81 20W
Cayman, Little Cayman Is. 19 42N 80 00N
Cayo Frances Cuba 22 38N 79 13W
Cayo Juan Claro Cuba 21 18N 76 32W
Cayo Mambi Puerto Tanamo, Cuba 20 40N 75 17W
Cayo Moa, Puerto Cuba 20 40N 74 55W
Ceara (Fortaleza) Brazil 03 44S 38 31W
Cebu Cebu Is., Philippines 10 17N 123 54E
Cedeira Spain 43 39N 08 03W
Cedros, Isla Mexico 28 10N 115 10W
Cee Spain 42 56N 09 11W
Ceiba Hueca Golfo de Guacanayabo, Cuba
20 14N 77 19W
Ceiba, La Honduras 15 47N 86 52W
Ceiba, La Lago de Maracaibo, Venezuela 09 29N 71 05W
Cemaes Bay Anglesey, Wales, UK 53 25N 04 27W
Central, Point Mauritania 20 49N 17 02W
Cephalonia (Kefallinia) Greece 38 11N 20 28E
Cerro Azul Peru 13 02S 76 31W
Cesme (Chesme) Turkey 38 20N 26 16E
Cette (Sete) Golfe du Lion, France 43 24N 03 41E
Ceuta Spanish North Africa 35 54N 05 18W
Ceyhan Terminal Iskenderun Korfezi, Turkey
36 53N 35 57E
Chabang, Laem Thailand 13 05N 100 53E
Chacabuco Puerto Seno Aysen, Chile 45 28S 72 50W
Chaguaramas Trinidad 10 40N 61 38W
Chah Bahar (Chahbar) Iran 25 16N 60 37E
Chahbar (Chah Bahar) Iran 25 16N 60 37E
Chake Chake Pemba Is., Tanzania 05 14S 39 46E
Chala Peru 15 51S 74 14W
Chalkis (Khalkis) Evvoia, Greece 38 27N 23 36E
Chalmers, Port Otago Harbour, South Is., New Zealand
45 49S 170 38E
Chalmette Mississippi R., Louisiana, USA
29 56N 90 00W
Chalna Anchorage (Mongla) Pussur R., Bangladesh
22 27N 89 34E
Champerico Guatemala 14 18N 91 56W
Chanak (Canakkale) Canakkale Bogazi, Turkey
40 09N 26 24E
Chanaral de Las Animas Chile 26 21S 70 38W
Chancay Peru 11 35S 77 17W
Chan-Chiang (Tsamkong) Kuang-chow Wan, China
21 12N 110 24E
Chandarly (Candarli) Candarli Korfezi, Turkey
38 52N 26 54E
Chandbali R. Dhawra, India 20 46N 86 45E
Chandler Baie des Chaleurs, Quebec Province, Canada
48 22N 64 40W
Changhang South Korea 36 01N 126 42E
Chantenay La Loire, France 47 12N 01 36W
Chanthaburi Thailand 12 37N 102 07E
Chao, Baie de Vung Vietnam 13 26N 109 14E
Charente, Tonnay La Ccarente, France 45 57N 00 53W
Charles, Lake Louisiana, USA 30 13N 93 14W
Charleston South Carolina, USA 32 47N 79 56W

Charleston, North South Carolina, USA 32 53N 79 58W

Charlestown Nevis 17 08N 62 37W

Charlestown St Austel Bay, England, UK
50 20N 04 45W

Charlestown Boston, Massachusetts, USA 42 23N 71 03E

Charlotte-Amalie St Thomas, Virgin Is. 18 21N 64 56W

Charlottetown Prince Edward Is., Canada 46 14N 63 08W

Chateau, Le Ile d'Oleron, France 45 53N 01 11W

Chatham Miramichi Bay, New Brunswick, Canada
47 02N 65 28W

Chatham R. Medway, England, UK 51 24N 00 33E

Chatham Sitka Bay, Alaska, USA 57 31N 134 57W

Chaure, El Bahia Bergantin, Venezuela 10 15N 64 37W

Chavez, Punta Golfo de Triste, Venezuela 10 30N 68 07W

Chawan, Pulau Ayer Singapore 01 17N 103 42E

Cheboygan Straits of Mackinac, Michigan, USA
45 40N 84 28W

Ch'e-Ch'eng Taiwan 22 04N 120 42E

Chefoo (Yen-t'ai) China 37 33N 121 23E

Cheju Saishu To, South Korea 33 31N 126 32E

Chekaa (Chekka) (Shiq'a) Lebanon 34 20N 35 43E

Chekka (Chekaa) (Shiq'a) Lebanon 34 20N 35 43E

Chekov Sakhalin, USSR 47 26N 141 58E

Chelsea Massachusetts, USA 42 23N 71 02W

Chelsea Hudson R., New York, USA 41 32N 73 57W

Chemainus Vancouver Is., British Columbia, Canada
48 56N 123 42W

Chemulpo (Inchon) (Jinsen) South Korea 37 28N 126 37E

Cheng-Chiang (Chinkiang) Ch'ang Kiang, China
32 13N 119 26E

Chepstow R. Wye, Wales, UK 51 38N 02 40W

Cherbourg France 49 39N 01 37W

Cherchel Algeria 36 37N 02 11E

Cheribon (Tjirebon) (Cirebon) Jawa, Indonesia
06 42S 108 35E

Cherry Point Washington, USA 48 52N 122 45W

Chesapeake Bay Virginia, USA 36 58N 76 20W

Chesapeake City Maryland, USA 39 28N 75 51W

Chesme (Cesme) Turkey 38 20N 26 16E

Chester Mahone Bay, Nova Scotia, Canada
44 32N 64 14W

Chester Delaware R., Pennsylvania, USA 39 49N 75 22W

Chester, Port (Metlakatla) Annette Is., Alaska, USA
55 08N 131 34W

Cheticamp Cape Breton Is., Nova Scotia, Canada
46 40N 60 57W

Chevire La Loire, France 47 12N 01 36W

Chiba Tokyo Wan, Honshu, Japan 35 36N 140 06E

Chica, Boca Dominican Republic 18 27N 69 36W

Chicago Lake Michigan, Illinois, USA 41 50N 87 42W

Chicago, Port Suisan Bay, California, USA
38 03N 122 01W

Chicama, Puerto Peru 07 42S 79 26W

Chicoutimi Saguenay R., Quebec Province, Canada
48 25N 71 06W

Chilca, Puerto de Peru 12 30S 76 50W

Chilia (Kiliya) Kiliyskiy Rukav, R. Dunay, USSR
45 26N 29 17E

Chiltepec Golfo de Campeche, Mexico 18 26N 93 05W

Chi-Lung (Keelung) Taiwan 25 08N 121 44E

Chimba, Caleta La Chile 23 34S 70 25W

Chimbote Peru 09 05S 78 36W

Chim Wan (Kin Wan) Okinawa, Nansei Shoto, Japan
26 22N 127 58E

Chinde Mozambique 18 36S 36 28E

Ch'ing-Lan Chiang Hai-Nan Tao, China 19 32N 110 51E

Ch'ing-Tao (Tsingtao) China 36 05N 120 19E

Chinhae (Jinhae) South Korea 35 06N 128 47E

Ch'in-Huang-Tao (Chinwangtao) Liao-Tung Wan, China
39 54N 119 37E

Chinkiang (Cheng-chiang) Ch'ang Chiang, China
32 13N 119 26E

Chinnampo (Nampo) (Chonsu Man) Taedong Gang, North
Korea 38 44N 125 24E

Chinwangtao (Ch'in-huang-tao) Liao-Tung, Wan,, China
39 54N 119 37E

Chioggia Golfo di Venezia, Italy 45 14N 12 17E

Chios (Khios) Greece 38 22N 26 08E

Chisimaio (Kismayu) Somalia 00 22S 42 33E

Chittagong Bangladesh 22 20N 91 50E

Chiu-Chiang (Kiukiang) Ch'ang Chiang, China
29 44N 116 02E

Cho-Lon Vietnam 10 45N 106 39E

Ch'ongjin (Chungjin) (Seishin) North Korea
41 46N 129 50E

Chonsu Man (Chinnampo) (Nampo) Taedong Gang, North
Korea 38 44N 125 24E

Christiansand (Kristiansand) Norway 58 09N 07 59E

Christianshaab Davis Strait, Greenland 68 49N 51 12W

Christiansted St. Croix, Virgin Is. 17 45N 64 42W

Christiansund (Kristiansund) Norway 63 07N 07 44E

Christi, Corpus Texas, USA 27 48N 97 23W

Christi, Monte Dominican Republic 19 51N 71 41W

Christmas Island Indian Ocean 10 25S 105 43E

Christmas Island (Kiritimati) Pacific Ocean
01 59N 157 28W

Chuanchou (Tsinkiang) Chin-chiang, China
24 54N 118 35E

Chumphon, Ao Thailand 10 25N 99 18E

Chungjin (Seishin) (Chongjin) North Korea
41 46N 129 50E

Churchill Hudson Bay, Manitoba, Canada 58 47N 94 13W

Chyoda Island Terminal Jiddah, Saudi Arabia
21 26N 39 09E

Cienfuegos Cuba 22 08N 80 28W

Cilacap (Tjilatjap) Jawa, Indonesia 07 46S 109 01E

Cillero Spain 43 41N 07 36W

Cinta Terminal Sumatera, Indoneisa 05 27S 106 16E

Ciotat, La Golfe du Lion, France 43 11N 05 39E

Cirebon (Tjirebon) (Cheribon) Jawa, Indonesia
06 42S 108 35E

Ciro Marina Italy 39 22N 17 08E

Cisneros, Villa (Dakhla) Mauretania 23 42N 15 56W

Cisnes, Puerto Canal Phyuguapi, Chile 44 46S 72 40W

Ciudad Bolivar R. Orinoco, Venezuela 08 05N 63 35W

Ciudad del Carmen Laguna de Terminos, Mexico
18 39N 91 50W

Ciudad Trujillo (Santo Domingo) Dominican Republic
18 28N 69 53W

Civitavecchia Italy 42 05N 11 48E

Clairette, Pointe Gabon 00 39S 08 43E

Clarecastle R. Shannon, Republic of Ireland
52 49N 08 58W

Claremont Upper Bay, New Jersey, USA 40 41N 74 05W

Clarence Cove (Caleta Clarencia) Bahia Gente Grande,
Chile 52 55S 70 08W

Clarence River New South Wales, Australia
29 25S 153 23E

Clarencia, Caleta (Clarence Cove) Bahia Gente Grande,
Chile 52 55S 70 08W

Clarenville Newfoundland, Canada 48 10N 53 57W

Clarke City St. Lawrence R., Quebec Province, Canada
50 12N 66 38W

Claveria Luzon, Philippines 18 37N 121 05E

Claxton Bay Trinidad 10 21N 61 28W

Clayoquot Vancouver Is., British Columbia, Canada
49 09N 125 56W

Clements, Port Graham Is., British Columbia, Canada
53 41N 132 11W

Cleveland Lake Erie, Ohio, USA 41 30N 81 40W

Clifden Republic of Ireland 53 29N 10 02W
Clifton Pier New Providence, Bahamas 25 01N 77 33W
Clydebank R. Clyde, Scotland, UK 55 54N 04 24W
Coal Bay Spitsbergen, Svalbard 78 10N 15 10E
Coari R. Amazonas, Brazil 04 08S 63 07W
Coatzacoalcos (Puerto Mexico) Golfo de Campeche,
　Mexico 18 08N 94 25W
Cobh Corcaigh, Republic of Ireland 51 51N 08 19W
Cobourg Lake Ontario, Ontario, Canada 43 57N 78 11W
Cocanada (Kakinada) India 16 56N 82 15E
Cochin India 09 58N 76 15E
Cockatoo Harbour Sidney, New South Wales, Australia
　33 51S 151 10E
Cockatoo Island Western Australia, Australia
　16 06S 123 36E
Cockburn Sound Western Australia, Australia
　32 10S 115 45E
Cockburn Town Grand Turk, Turks Is. 21 29N 71 08W
Cockenzie Firth of Forth, Scotland, UK 55 58N 02 57W
Cocos Island (Keeling Islands) 12 06S 96 52E
Cocos, Los Bahia Pozuelos, Venezuela 10 13N 64 39W
Codajas R. Amazonas, Brazil 03 55S 62 00W
Codrington Barbuda 17 38N 61 46W
Coff's Harbour New South Wales, Australia
　30 18S 153 08E
Cogo (Kogo) (Puerto Iradier) Rio Muni, Guinea Equatorial
　01 05N 09 42E
Colachel (Kolachel) India 08 11N 77 14E
Colborne, Port Welland Canal, Ontario, Canada
　42 53N 79 14W
Colchester R. Colne, England, UK 51 54N 00 55E
Cold Bay Alaska Peninsula, Alaska, USA
　USA 55 10N 162 35W
Coleraine R. Bann, Ulster, UK 55 09N 06 41W
Collingwood Lake Huron, Ontario, Canada
　44 30N 80 16W
Collingwood South Is., New Zealand 40 41S 172 41E
Collo Algeria 37 00N 06 34E
Coloma, La Golfo de Batabano, Cuba 22 17N 83 38W
Colombia, Puerto Colombia 10 59N 74 58W
Colombo Sri Lanka 06 56N 79 51E
Colon R. Uruguay, Argentina 32 13S 58 07W
Colon Panama 09 22N 79 54W
Colon, Fabrica (Fabrica Liebigs) R. Uruguay, Argentina
　32 09S 58 12W
Coloncha Lago de Maracaibo, Venezuela 09 13N 71 41N
Colonia R. de la Plata, Uruguay 34 29S 57 51W
Colorada, Punta Golfo San Matias, Argentina
　41 41S 65 01W
Colorados, Pozos Colombia 11 10N 74 14W
Comeau Bay (Baie Comeau) Quebec Province, Canada
　49 14N 68 08W
Come-by-Chance Newfoundland, Canada 47 49N 54 01W
Comfort, Point Texas, USA 28 39N 96 34W
Commodores Point Jacksonville, Florida, USA
　30 19N 81 38W
Comodoro Rivadavia Golfo de San Jorge, Argentina
　45 51S 67 28W
Comoro Islands Republic of the Comoros 12 00S 44 00E
Comox Vancouver Is., British Columbia, Canada
　49 40N 124 55W
Conakry (Konakri) Guinea 09 31N 13 43W
Concarneau France 47 52N 03 54W
Concepcion del Uruguay R. Uruguay, Argentina
　32 29S 58 14W
Conchan Beach Peru 12 10S 77 02W
Concordia R. Uruguay, Argentina 31 24S 58 01W
Connah's Quay R. Dee, England, UK 53 13N 03 03W
Conneaut Harbour Lake Erie, Ohio, USA
　41 57N 80 32W

Constable Hook New Jersey, USA 40 39N 74 05W
Constanta Romania 44 11N 28 40E
Constant, Benjamin R. Javari, Brazil 04 23S 69 59W
Constantine Harbour Aleutian Is., Alaska, USA
　51 24N 179 19W
Constitucion, Villa R. Parana, Argentina 33 17S 60 20W
Contrecoeur St Lawrence R., Quebec Province, Canada
　45 54N 73 12W
Cooktown Queensland, Australia 15 28S 145 15E
Coola, Bella North Bentinct Arm, British Columbia, Canada
　52 23N 126 47W
Coolkeeragh Lough Foyle, Ulster, UK 55 04N 07 08W
Coondapoor India 13 37N 74 40E
Coos Bay Oregon, USA 43 23N 124 13W
Copenhagen (Kobenhavn) Sjaelland, Denmark
　55 42N 12 36E
Coppename Coppename R., Surinam 05 46N 55 54W
Couqimbo Chile 29 57S 71 21W
Corcaigh (Cork) Republic of Ireland 51 54N 08 28W
Corcubion Spain 42 57N 09 11W
Cordemais R. Loire, France 47 18N 01 52W
Cordova Prince William Sound, Alaska, USA
　60 33N 145 46W
Cordova, Caleta Golfo de San Jorge, Argentina
　45 45S 67 22W
Corfu (Kerkira) Greece 39 37N 19 56E
Corinth (Korinthos) Kolpos Korinthiakos, Greece
　37 57N 22 56E
Corinto Nicaragua 12 28N 87 11W
Cork (Corcaigh) Republic of Ireland 51 54N 08 28W
Corkbeg (Whitegate) Corcaigh, Republic of Ireland
　51 50N 08 14W
Corme Spain 43 16N 08 58W
Corner Brook Bay of Islands, Newfoundland, Canada
　48 58N 57 57W
Corniquel R. Odet, France 47 57N 04 07W
Cornwall St Lawrence Seaway, Ontario, Canada
　45 03N 74 44W
Cornwallis North Is., New Zealand 37 01S 174 36E
Coron Calamian, Philippines 11 59N 120 12E
Coronel Chile 37 02S 73 09W
Corosal (Corozal) Belize 18 22N 88 27W
Corozal (Corosal) Belize 18 22N 88 27W
Corpach Loch Linnhe, Scotland, UK 56 50N 05 08W
Corpus Christi Texas, USA 27 48N 97 23W
Corral Chile 39 52S 73 26W
Correia, Luis (Amarracao) R. Igaracu de Sao Jose, Brazil
　02 53S 41 40W
Corsini, Porto Italy 44 29N 12 17E
Cortes, Puerto Honduras 15 49N 87 57W
Cortes, Puerto Is. Santa Margarita, Mexico
　24 28N 111 49W
Corunna, La Spain 43 22N 08 24W
Coryton R. Thames, England, UK 51 30N 00 33E
Costelo, Vianna do (Vianna) Portugal 41 41N 08 50W
Cotabato (Kotabato) Illana Bay, Mindanao, Philippines
　07 13N 124 15E
Cotonou (Kotonu) Benin 06 21N 02 26E
Coueron La Loire, France 47 12N 01 44W
Coulport Loch Long, Scotland, UK 55 59N 04 51W
Country Harbour Nova Scotia, Canada 45 10N 61 42W
Couronne, Petit La Seine, France 49 23N 01 01E
Courselles-sur-mer Baie de la Seine, France
　49 20N 00 27W
Courtenay Bay Bay of Fundy, New Brunswick, Canada
　45 15N 66 03W
Cove, Cape Quebec Province, Canada 48 26N 64 19W
Covenas Colombia 09 25N 75 41W
Covington, Port Baltimore, Maryland, USA
　39 16N 76 36W

Cowes Isle of Wight, England, UK 50 45N 01 18W
Cowichan Bay Vancouver Is., British Columbia, Canada
48 45N 123 37W
Cox's Bazaar Bangladesh 21 26N 91 59E
Cozumel, Isla Mexico 20 25N 86 55W
Crabbs Point Antigua 17 08N 61 52W
Craig Klawock Inlet, Alaska, USA 55 28N 133 09W
Creosote Puget Sound, Washington, USA
47 37N 122 31W
Crescent City California, USA 41 45N 124 12W
Crib Point Westernport, Victoria, Australia
38 21S 145 14E
Cristi, Monte Dominican Republic 19 51N 71 41W
Cristina, Isla Spain 37 12N 07 19W
Cristobal Panama Canal Zone 09 21N 79 55W
Cristobal Colon, Puerto Golfo de Paria, Venezuela
10 39N 61 56W
Crockett Carquinez Strait, California, USA
38 03N 122 13W
Crofton Vancouver Is., British Columbia, Canada
48 52N 123 38W
Croisic, Le France 47 18N 02 31W
Cromarty Firth Scotland, UK 57 41N 04 03W
Cronstadt Island Trinidad 10 39N 61 38W
Crotone Italy 39 05N 17 08E
Cruz Grande Chile 29 27S 71 20W
Cruz, Puerto la Bahia de Pozuelos, Venezuela
10 13N 64 38W
Cruz, Salina Mexico 16 10N 95 12W
Cruz, Vera Golfo de Campeche, Mexico 19 12N 96 08W
Cuchillo, Punta R. Orinoco, Venezuela 08 20N 62 47W
Cuddalore India 11 43N 79 47E
Culasi Panay, Philippines 11 37N 122 42E
Cul de Sac Bay, Grand St. Lucia 13 59N 61 02W
Culebra, Puerto Costa Rica 10 37N 85 39W
Culion, Port Culion Is., Philippines 11 53N 120 01E
Cullen Bay Scotland, UK 57 42N 02 49W
Cullera Spain 39 09N 00 14W
Cumana Venezuela 10 28N 64 12W
Cumarebo Venezuela 11 31N 69 20W
Curacao 12 05N 68 50W
Curtis Bay Maryland, USA 39 13N 76 35W
Curtis, Port Queensland, Australia 23 50S 151 15E
Cutuco Golfo de Fonseca, El Salvador 13 19N 87 49W
Cuvier, Cape Western Australia, Australia 24 13S 113 25E
Cuxhaven Die Elbe, West Germany 53 52N 08 43E
Cyrus Terminal Iran 29 01N 49 28E

Dabhol India 17 34N 73 09E
Dabo Singkep, Indonesia 00 30S 104 28E
Dadiangas (Buyan City) (General Santos City) Mindanao,
Philippines 06 06N 125 14E
Daepo (Daipori) (Sokch'o) South Korea 38 11N 128 36E
Dagenham R. Thames, England, UK 51 31N 00 09E
Dahouet Golfe de St. Malo, France 48 35N 02 35W
Daipori (Daepo) (Sokch'o) South Korea 38 11N 128 36E
Daiquiri Cuba 19 55N 75 38W
Dairen (Ta-lien) China 38 56N 121 39E
Dakar Senegal 14 41N 17 26W
Dakhla (Villa Cisneros) Mauritania 23 42N 15 56W
Dakliyat, Khor Ethiopia 15 38N 39 29E
Dalaro Sweden 59 08N 18 25E
Dale Dalsfjord, Norway 61 22N 05 24E
Dalen Langsundsfjord, Norway 59 04N 09 42E
Dalhousie Baie des Chaleurs, New Brunswick, Canada
48 04N 66 22W
Dalhousie, Port Lake Ontario, Ontario, Canada
43 12N 79 15W
Dalles Columbia R., Oregon, USA 45 36N 121 11W

Dal'nyaya Finskiy Zaliv, USSR 60 32N 28 10E
Dalsbruk (Taalintehdas) Finland 60 02N 22 31E
Daman India 20 25N 72 47E
Damas, Playa de Panama 09 36N 79 29W
Dames, Baie des New Caledonia 22 14S 166 24E
Damietta (Dumyat) Egypt 31 31N 31 51E
Damman (Adb al Aziz) Saudi Arabia 26 30N 50 12E
Dampier Western Australia, Australia 20 40S 116 42E
Da-Nang (Touraine) Vietnam 16 05N 108 12E
Dandong (An-tung) Yalu Chiang, China 40 07N 124 24E
Dangrida (Stann Creek) Belize 16 56N 88 14W
Daniel, Port Baie des Chaleurs, Quebec Province, Canada
48 09N 64 57W
Danischburg Die Trave, West Germany 53 55N 10 44E
Danmark Havn Greenland 76 46N 18 46W
Dante (Ras Hafun) Somalia 10 26N 51 16E
D'Antifer, Cap France 49 41N 00 09E
Danzig (Gdansk) Poland 54 21N 18 41E
Dapa Siargao, Philippines 09 45N 126 03E
Dar el Beida (Casablanca) Morocco 33 37N 07 36W
Dar-es-Salaam Tanzania 06 49S 39 19E
Darien Georgia, USA 31 21N 81 26W
Darius Terminal Iran 29 15N 50 21E
Darling Harbour Sydney, New South Wales, Australia
33 52S 151 12E
Darlowo (Rugenwalde) Poland 54 26N 16 25E
Darna (Derna) Libya 32 45N 22 39E
Dartmouth Halifax, Nova Scotia, Canada
44 40N 63 34W
Dartmouth R. Dart, England, UK 50 21N 03 34W
Daru Island Papua, Papua New Guinea 09 04S 143 12E
Darwin Northern Territory, Australia 12 28S 130 51E
Das Island United Arab Emirates 25 09N 52 52E
Datu, Lahad Telok Darvel, Sabah, Malaysia
05 02N 118 20E
Dauphin, Fort (Tolagnaro) Malagasy Republic
52 02S 47 00E
Davao Mindanao, Philippines 07 04N 125 38E
Davis Point San Pablo Bay, California, USA
38 03N 122 15W
Davisville Narragansett Bay, Rhode Island, USA
41 37N 71 24W
Dawhah, Ad (Doha) Qatar 25 18N 51 33E
Dealgan, Dun (Dundalk) Republic of Ireland
54 01N 06 22W
Deauville Baie de la Seine, France 49 22N 00 04E
Deception Bay Hudson Strait, Quebec Province, Canada
62 08N 74 42W
Dedeagach (Alexandropoulis) Greece 40 51N 25 53E
Deer Park Houston Ship Canal, Texas, USA
29 45N 95 08W
Degema Nigeria 04 45N 06 49E
Degerby Finland 60 20N 20 36E
Degerhamn Oland, Sweden 56 21N 16 25E
De Kastri (Alexandrovski) Tartarskiy Proliv, USSR
51 29N 140 47E
Delair Delaware R., Pennsylvania, USA 39 59N 75 05W
Delaware Breakwater Delaware, USA 38 47N 75 06W
Delaware City Delaware R., Delaware, USA
39 35N 75 35W
Delfzijl (Delfzyl) De Eems, Netherlands 53 20N 06 55E
Delfzyl (Delfzijl) De Eems, Netherlands 53 20N 06 55E
Delgada, Ponta Sao Miguel, Acores 37 44N 25 41W
Dellys Algeria 36 55N 03 55E
Demerara (Georgetown) Guyana 06 49N 58 06W
Den Helder Netherlands 52 58N 04 46E
Denia (Denja) Spain 38 50N 00 07E
Denison, Fort Sydney, New South Wales, Australia
33 51S 151 13E
Denison, Port (Bowen) Queensland, Australia
20 01S 148 15E

Denja (Denia) Spain 38 50N 00 07E
Derby King Sound, Western Australia, Australia 17 20S 123 36E
Derince (Derindje) Izmit Korfezi, Marmara Denizi, Turkey 40 45N 29 50E
Derindje (Derince) Izmit Korfezi, Marmara Denizi, Turkey 40 45N 29 50E
Derna (Darna) Libya 32 45N 22 39E
Deseado, Puerto Argentina 47 44S 65 53W
Dernish Oil Fuel Jetty R. Shannon, Republic of Ireland 52 41N 08 55W
Destrahan Mississippi R., Louisiana, USA 29 56N 90 21W
Detroit Detroit R., Michigan, USA 42 22N 83 05W
Deus, Madre de Brazil 12 45S 38 38W
Devgarh India 16 23N 73 22E
Devonport Tasmania, Australia 41 11S 146 22E
Devonport England, UK 50 23N 04 11W
Dhabi, Abu (Abu Zabi) (Mina Zayed) United Arab Emirates 24 29N 54 22E
Dhana, Jebel (Jabal az Zannah) United Arab Emirates 24 12N 52 34E
Dhrapetsonas, Ormos (Drapetzona) Greece 37 56N 23 37E
Diamante R. Parana Medio, Argentina 32 04S 60 39W
Diamond Harbour R. Hugli, India 22 11N 88 11E
Dicido Spain 43 23N 03 12W
Dickson, Port Malaya, Malaysia 02 31N 101 47E
Diego Garcia 07 19S 72 28E
Diego Suarez (Antsiranana) Malagasy Republic 12 16S 49 17E
Dielette France 49 33N 01 52W
Dieppe France 49 56N 01 05E
Digby Annapolis Basin, Nova Scotia, Canada 44 38N 65 45W
Dikhelia Cyprus 34 58N 33 44E
Dikili Midilli Kanali, Turkey 39 04N 26 53E
Dili (Dilly) Timor, Indonesia 08 33S 125 34E
Dilly (Dili) Timor, Indonesia 08 33S 125 34E
Dingle R. Mersey, England, UK 53 22N 02 58W
Dingwall Cape Breton Is., Nova Scotia, Canada 46 54N 60 27W
Dinorwic, Port Menai Strait, Wales, UK 53 11N 04 12W
Direction Island Cocos (Keeling) Is. 12 06S 96 52E
Discovery Bay Jamaica 18 28N 77 26W
Djakarta (Jakarta) Jawa, Indonesia 06 07S 106 49E
Djeno Terminal Congo Republic 04 55S 11 55E
Djibouti (Jibuti) Republic of Djibouti 11 35N 43 09E
Djidjelli (Jizella) (Jijel) Algeria 36 50N 05 47E
Djuphamn Sweden 57 45N 16 41E
Djupivogur Iceland 64 39N 14 17W
Djupvik Sweden 63 44N 20 22E
Djuron Braiviken, Sweden 58 38N 16 20E
Docksta Sweden 63 03N 18 19E
Doha (Ad Dawhah) Qatar 25 18N 51 33E
Dokai Kyushu, Japan 33 56N 130 57E
Dolores Samar, Philippines 12 02N 125 29E
Domiaza Poland 53 33N 14 36E
Domsjo Sweden 63 16N 18 44E
Donaghadee Ulster, UK 54 39N 05 32W
Donaldsonville Mississippi R., Louisiana, USA 30 05N 91 00W
Donges La Loire, France 47 18N 02 03W
Donggala Sulawesi, Indonesia 00 40S 119 45E
Donsol Luzon, Philippines 12 54N 123 35E
Dordrecht Oud Maas, Netherlands 51 49N 04 40E
Dortyol Iskenderun Korfezi, Turkey 36 51N 36 08E
Douala (Duala) Cameroon R., Cameroon 04 03N 09 43E
Douarnenez France 48 06N 04 20W
Douglas Isle of Man, UK 54 09N 04 28W

Douglastown Miramichi R., New Brunswick, Canada 47 01N 65 32W
Dougoufissa Rio Nunez, Guinea 10 40N 14 35W
Douiambo New Caledonia 22 16S 166 26E
Douro, Rio Portugal 41 10N 08 37W
Dover England, UK 51 07N 01 19E
Dragamestre (Astakos) Greece 38 32N 21 05E
Drammen Dramsfjord, Norway 59 44N 10 11E
Drapetzona (Ormos Dhrapetsonas) Greece 37 56N 23 37E
Drift River Terminal Cook Inlet, Alaska, USA 60 33N 152 07W
Drobak Oslofjord, Norway 59 40N 10 39E
Drogheda Boyne R., Republic of Ireland 53 43N 06 20W
Druif Aruba 12 32N 70 04W
Drujba (Druzba) Burgaski Zaliv, Bulgaria 42 27N 27 32E
Druzba (Drujba) Burgaski Zaliv, Bulgaria 42 27N 27 32E
Duala (Douala) Cameroon R., Cameroon 04 03N 09 43E
Dubai (Dubayy) United Arab Emirates 25 16N 55 18E
Dubayy (Dubai) United Arab Emirates 25 16N 55 18E
Dublin (Baile Atha Cliath) Republic of Ireland 53 21N 06 13W
Dubrovnik (Ragusa) Yugoslavia 42 38N 18 07E
Dubrovnik 2 (Gruz) (Gravosa) Yugoslavia 42 40N 18 05E
Duclair La Seine, France 49 29N 00 52E
Dudinka R. Yenisey, USSR 69 27N 86 13E
Due (Makarevsk) Sakhalin, USSR 50 51N 142 05E
Dulce, Agua Parida Is., Panama 08 06N 82 20W
Duluth Lake Superior, Minnesota, USA 46 49N 92 10W
Dumaguete Negros, Philippines 09 19N 123 19E
Dumai Sumatera, Indonesia 01 41N 101 27E
Dumbarton R. Clyde, Scotland, UK 55 56N 04 34W
Dumfries R. Nith, Scotland, UK 55 04N 03 37W
Dumyat (Damietta) Egypt 31 31N 31 51E
Duncan Bay Vancouver Is., British Columbia, Canada 50 04N 125 18W
Dundalk (Dun Dealgan) Republic of Ireland 54 01N 06 22W
Dundalk Maryland, USA 39 15N 76 32W
Dun Dealgan (Dundalk) Republic of Ireland 54 01N 06 22W
Dundee Firth of Tay, Scotland, UK 56 28N 02 57W
Dundrum Ulster, UK 54 15N 05 50W
Dunedin Otago Harbour, South Is., New Zealand 45 53S 170 31E
Dungarvan Republic of Ireland 52 05N 07 37W
Dunglass River Clyde, Scotland, UK 55 56N 04 29W
Dungun, Kuala Malaya, Malaysia 04 47N 103 26E
Dunkerque (Dunkirk) France 51 03N 02 23E
Dunkirk (Dunkerque) France 51 03N 02 23E
Dun Laoghaire Republic of Ireland 53 18N 06 07W
Dumore East Port Lairge, Republic of Ireland 52 09N 06 59W
Dunoon Firth of Clyde, Scotland, UK 55 57N 04 55W
Dunston R. Tyne, England, UK 54 57N 01 39W
Duran Ecuador 02 10S 79 51W
Durazzo (Durres) Albania 41 19N 19 28E
Durban South Africa 29 52S 31 03E
Durres (Durazzo) Albania 41 19N 19 28E
Dusavik Norway 59 00N 05 40E
Dutch Harbour Unalaska Is., Alaska, USA 53 54N 166 32W
Dyke, Jost van Virgin Is. 18 27N 64 45W
Dynas Sweden 62 58N 17 46E
Dyrafjordhur Iceland 65 55N 23 51W
Dzaoudzi Mayotte, Republic of the Comoros 12 47S 45 15E
Dzilam (Silan) Yucatan, Mexico 21 23N 88 54W

Eagle Harbour Puget Sound, Washington, USA
47 37N 122 31W
Eagle Point Delaware R., New Jersey, USA
39 53N 75 11W
East Boston Massachusetts, USA 42 23N 71 02W
Eastham Manchester Ship Canal, England, UK
53 19N 02 57W
East Howdon R. Tyne, England, UK 54 59N 01 29W
East Intercourse Island Western Australia, Australia
20 39S 116 40E
East London South Africa 33 02S 27 55E
Easton Chesapeake Bay, Maryland, USA 38 44N 76 04W
Eastport Maine, USA 44 54N 66 59W
East Side Coos Bay, Oregon, USA 43 18N 124 10W
Ebeltoft (Abeltoft) Jylland, Denmark 56 12N 10 42E
Eccles Manchester Ship Canal, England, UK
53 29N 02 21W
Eckernford West Germany 54 29N 09 50E
Eckero Aland, Finland 60 12N 19 36E
Ecopetrol Terminal Isla Brujas,Colombia 10 21N 75 31W
Eden Twofold Bay, New South Wales, Australia
37 05S 149 54E
Edgartown Massachusetts, USA 41 24N 70 31W
Edgewater Hudson R., New Jersey, USA 40 49N 73 59W
Edincik Erdek Korfezi, Marmara Denizi, Turkey
40 21N 27 52E
Edward, Point Cape Breton Is., Nova Scotia, Canada
46 12N 60 14W
Edward, Port Prince Rupert, British Columbia, Canada
54 14N 130 18W
Edwards' Point Puget Sound, Washington, USA
47 48N 122 24W
Eemshaven Westerems, Netherlands 53 27N 06 50E
Efate Island New Hebrides 17 40S 168 20E
Egedesminde Davis Strait, Greenland 68 42N 52 53W
Egersund Norway 58 28N 06 00E
Eilat (Elath) Gulf of Aqaba, Israel 29 33N 34 56E
Einso Finland 60 01N 23 58E
Einswarden Die Weser, West Germany 53 31N 08 31E
Eitreim Sorfjorden, Norway 60 06N 06 32E
Ekenas (Tammisaari) Finland 59 59N 23 27E
Ekofisk Terminal Norway 56 31N 03 12E
Ekonomiya R. Severnaya Dvina, USSR 64 42N 40 31E
Ekonrod Skein R., Norway 59 12N 09 38E
El Aaiun (Laayoune) (Aaiun) Fosbucraa) Morocco
27 04N 13 28W
El Aaraich (El Arish) (Larache) Morocco 35 12N 06 09W
El Akaba (Aqaba) Gulf of Aqaba, Jordan 29 31N 35 01E
El Alamein (Marsa el Hamra) Egypt 30 58N 28 51E
El Arish (Larrache) (El Aaraich) Morocco 35 12N 06 09W
Elath (Eilat) Gulf of Aqaba, Israel 29 33N 34 56E
Elbehafen Die Elbe, West Germany 53 53N 09 10E
El Bieda, Dar (Casablanca) Morocco 33 37N 07 36W
Elbing (Elblag) Zalew Wislany, Poland 54 09N 19 24E
Elblag (Elbing) Zalew Wislany, Poland 54 09N 19 24E
El Bluff (Bluefields) Nicaragua 11 59N 83 44E
El Botado Bahia Samana, Dominican Republic
19 12N 69 26W
El Brega, Marsa Libya 30 25N 19 34E
El Chaure Bahia Bergantin, Venezuela
10 15N 64 37W
Electrona North West Bay, Tasmania, Australia
43 04S 147 16E
Eleuthera Island Bahamas 25 10N 76 15W
Elevsis Kolpos Elevsinos, Greece 38 02N 23 32E
El Fallah, Marsa Egypt 31 21N 27 21E
El Ferrol del Caudillo (Ferrol) Spain 43 28N 08 14W
El Flus, Nahr Abu (Abu Flus) Shatt al Arab, Iraq
30 27N 48 02E
El-Gedida, El-Mina Suez Canal, Egypt 30 58N 32 33E

El Grao Spain 39 28N 00 18W
El Hamra, Marsa (El Alemain) Egypt 30 58N 28 51E
El Hamrawein (Hamrawein Port) Egypt 26 15N 34 12E
El Iskandariya (Alexandria) Egypt 31 09N 29 52E
Elizabeth, Port Algoa Bay, South Africa 33 58S 25 38E
Elizabethport New Jersey, USA 40 39N 74 11W
Elizabeth Terminal New Jersey, USA 40 41N 74 08W
El Jadida (Mazagan) (Al Yadida) Morocco
33 14N 08 28W
Ellen, Port Islay, Scotland, UK 55 38N 06 11W
Ellesmere Port Manchester Ship Canal, England, UK
53 17N 02 54W
Ellington Viti Levu, Fiji 17 20S 178 13E
El-Marakib, Qad (Marakeb) Suez Canal, Egypt
29 55N 32 34E
El-Mina el-Gedida Suez Canal, Egypt 29 58N 32 33E
El Palito Venezuela 10 28N 68 06W
El Puerto (Musel) Concha de Gijon, Spain
43 34N 05 43W
El Quseir (Kosseir) Egypt 26 07N 34 17E
El Rincon Chile 29 28S 71 20W
El Salif, Ras (Saleef) Yemen 15 19N 42 41E
El Segundo California, USA 33 55N 118 26W
Elsfleth Die Weser, West Germany 53 15N 08 28E
Elsinore (Helsingor) Sjaelland, Denmark 56 02N 12 38E
El Sudr, Ras Sinai, Egypt 29 35N 32 41E
El Suweis (Suez) Egypt 29 58N 32 34E
El Triunfo Bahia Jiquilisco, El Salvador 13 15N 88 33W
El Tur (Tor) Sinai, Egypt 28 14N 33 37E
El Wejh Saudi Arabia 26 13N 36 27E
Emden Die Ems, West Germany 53 22N 07 12E
Emmastad Curacao 12 08N 68 56W
Empedocle, Porto Sicilia, Italy 37 17N 13 32E
Empire Coos Bay, Oregon, USA 43 24N 124 16W
Emu Bay Tasmania, Australia 41 00S 145 55E
Enanger Sweden 61 33N 17 04E
Endau, Kuala Malaya, Malaysia 02 39N 103 38E
English Bay Ascension 07 53S 14 23W
English Harbour Antigua 17 00N 61 46W
Enkhuizen Ijsselmeer, Netherlands 52 42N 05 18E
Enkoping Malaren, Sweden 59 38N 17 05E
Ensenada Bahia de Todos Santos, Baja California, Mexico
31 52N 116 38W
Ensenada Bahia de Guanica, Puerto Rico 17 58N 64 56W
Ensenada de Mora (Pilon) Cuba 19 54N 77 18W
Ensenada Honda Puerto Rico 18 14N 65 38W
Ensenada, La Lago de Maracaibo, Venezuela
10 26N 71 39W
Ensenada san Martin Chile 18 31S 70 19W
Enstedvaerket Aabenraa Fjord, Jylland, Denmark
55 01N 09 25E
Eregli (Heraklea) Turkey 41 18N 31 26E
Ergasteria (Lavrion) (Laurium) Greece 37 43N 24 04E
Erie Lake Erie, Pennsylvania, USA 42 08N 80 06W
Erith R. Thames, England, UK 51 29N 00 11E
Ermoupolis (Siros) Siros, Greece 37 26N 24 57E
Ernakulam India 09 59N 76 15E
Ernholm Finland 60 12N 21 56E
Esashi Hokkaido, Japan 41 52N 140 08E
Esashi Hokkaido, Japan 44 58N 142 35E
Esbjerg Jylland, Denmark 55 29N 08 28E
Escombreras, Puerto de Spain 37 34N 00 58W
Escoumins St Lawrence R., Quebec Province, Canada
48 21N 69 23W
Escravos Nigeria 05 30N 05 00E
Eskifjordhur Iceland 65 04N 14 00W
Esmeraldas Ecuador 00 59N 79 39W
Esperance Western Australia, Australia 33 52S 121 54E
Espiritu Santo Island New Hebrides 15 20S 167 00E
Esquimalt Vancouver Is., British Columbia, Canada
48 26N 123 27W

Esquina R. Parana, Argentina 29 58S 59 30W
Esquivel, Port Portland Bight, Jamaica 17 53N 77 08W
Essaouira (Mogador) Morocco 31 31N 09 47W
Essequibo River Guyana 06 24N 58 40W
Es Sider, Ras Libya 30 39N 18 22E
Essvik Sundsvall, Sweden 62 19N 17 24E
Estacada, La Lago de Maracaibo, Venezuela
  10 42N 71 32W
Estaque Golfe de Marseille, France 43 22N 05 19E
Estepona Spain 36 25N 05 09W
Este, Punta del Uruguay 34 58S 54 57W
Etajima Hiroshima Bay, Honshu, Japan 34 12N 132 29E
Etang de Berre Golfe du Lion, France 43 28N 05 10E
Etang Harbour Bay of Fundy, New Brunswick, Canada
  45 04N 66 49W
Eten, Puerto de Peru 06 56S 79 52W
Etienne, Port (Nouadhibou) Baie de Levrier, Mauritania
  20 54N 17 03W
Eureka Humboldt Bay, California, USA 40 48N 124 10W
Europoort Nieuwe Waterweg, Netherlands 51 58N 04 08E
Evans Bay Elrington Passage, Alaska, USA
  60 03N 148 00W
Everett Boston, Massachusetts, USA 42 24N 71 03W
Everett Washington, USA 47 59N 122 13W
Everglades, Port Florida, USA 26 06N 80 07W
Everton Berbice R., Guyana 06 14N 57 33W
Ewe, Loch Scotland, UK 57 50N 05 35W
Exeter R. Exe, England, UK 50 43N 03 31W
Exmouth Western Australia, Australia 21 49S 114 11E
Exmouth R. Exe, England, UK 50 37N 03 26W
Eydehamn Norway 58 30N 08 53E
Eymouth Scotland, UK 55 52N 02 05W

Faaborg Fyn, Denmark 55 07N 10 14E
Faanui, Baie Bora Bora, Society Is. 16 30S 151 45W
Fabrica Colon (Fabrica Liebigs) R Uruguay, , Argentina
  32 09S 58 12W
Fabrica Liebigs (Fabrica Colon) R Uruguay, Argentina
  32 09S 58 12W
Faeringehavn Greenland 63 42N 51 33E
Fagerstrand Oslofjord, Norway 59 44N 10 36E
Fagervik Finland 60 02N 23 50E
Fagervik Sundsval, Sweden 62 29N 17 23E
Fagerviken Gavlebukten, Sweden 60 33N 17 45E
Fahaheel (Mina al Ahmedi) Kuwait 29 04N 48 09E
Fahal, Mina al Oman 23 38N 58 31E
Faial (Fayal) Acores 38 30N 28 40W
Fairlie Firth of Clyde, Scotland, UK 55 46N 04 53W
Fairymead Burnett R., Queensland, Australia
  24 48S 152 22E
Fairy, Port Victoria, Australia 38 23S 142 15E
Fajardo Puerto Rico 18 20N 65 38W
Fak Fak Irian Jaya, Indonesia 02 56S 132 18E
Fakkan, Khawr (Khor Fakkan) Gulf of Oman, United Arab
  Emirates 25 21N 56 22E
Fakse Ladeplads Sjaelland, Denmark 55 13N 12 10E
Falaises, Les Algeria 36 39N 05 25E
Falconara Italy 43 39N 13 24E
Faldsled Fyn, Denmark 55 09N 10 10E
Falkenberg Sweden 56 55N 12 30E
Fallah, Marsa el Egypt 31 21N 27 21E
Fall River Narragansett Bay, Massachusetts, USA
  41 42N 71 10W
Falmouth England, UK 50 09N 05 04W
Famagusta (Magosa) Cyprus 35 08N 33 58E
Fanara Buheirat-Murat-el-Kubra, Suez Canal, Egypt
  30 17N 32 23E
Fanning Island (Teraina) 03 51N 159 22W

Fao (Al Faw) Shatt al Arab, Iraq 29 58N 48 29E
Farge Die Weser, West Germany 53 12N 08 32E
Farjestaden Oland, Sweden 56 39N 16 28E
Faro Portugal 37 01N 07 54W
Farosund Gotland, Sweden 57 52N 19 04E
Farsund Norway 58 05N 06 48E
Faskrudhsfjordhur Iceland 64 53N 13 44W
Faslane Gareloch, Scotland, UK 56 03N 04 49W
Fateh Terminal United Arab Emirates 25 35N 54 25E
Father Point (Pointe-au-Pere) St Lawrence R., Quebec
  Province, Canada 48 31N 68 28W
Fatsa Turkey 41 03N 37 29E
Fauske Saltfjord, Norway 67 15N 15 24E
Faw, Al (Fao) Shatt al Arab, Iraq 29 58N 48 29E
Fawley Southampton Water, England, UK 50 51N 01 20W
Fayal (Faial) Acores 38 30N 28 40W
Fecamp France 49 46N 00 21E
Fedalah (Mohammedia) Morocco 33 45N 07 22W
Fehmarnsund West Germany 54 24N 11 07E
Feiran, Wadi Sinai, Egypt 28 44N 33 13E
Felixstowe England, UK 51 57N 01 20E
Felton Bahia Nipe, Cuba 20 45N 75 36W
Fenit Tralee Bay, Republic of Ireland 52 17N 09 52W
Feodosiya (Theodosia) Feodosiyskiy Zaliv, Krym, USSR
  45 03N 35 24E
Fernandina Florida, USA 30 40N 81 28W
Fernando Poo Island (Macias Nguema Biyogo) Guinea
  Equatorial 03 30N 08 40E
Ferndale Washington, USA 48 49N 122 43W
Ferrol (El Ferrol del Caudillo) Spain 43 28N 08 14W
Fethiye (Megri) Turkey 36 39N 29 08E
Figeholm Sweden 57 22N 16 35E
Figueira da Foz (Figueira) Portugal 40 09N 08 52W
Fila (Port Vila) Efate, New Hebrides 17 44S 168 18E
Filipsburg (Philipsbourg) St. Martin 18 01N 63 03W
Finike Turkey 36 17N 30 09E
Finkenwerder Die Elbe, West Germany 53 32N 09 51E
Finnart Loch Long, Scotland, UK 56 07N 04 50W
Finschaven (Finsch Harbour) New Guinea, Papua New
  Guinea 06 34S 147 51E
Finsch Harbour (Finschaven) New Guinea, Papua New
  Guinea 06 34S 147 51E
Fisherman's Island Brisbane R., Queensland, Australia
  27 23S 153 10E
Fishguard Wales, UK 52 01N 04 58W
Fiume (Rijeka) Rijecki Zaliv, Yugoslavia 45 20N 14 26E
Fiumicino Italy 41 46N 12 13E
Fjallbacka Sweden 58 36N 11 17E
Flateyri Onundarfjordhur, Iceland 66 03N 23 31W
Flattery Harbour Queensland, Australia 14 57S 145 21E
Flaxenvik Sweden 59 28N 18 24E
Fleetwood R. Wyre, England, UK 53 55N 03 01W
Flekkefjord Norway 58 18N 06 40E
Flensburg West Germany 54 47N 09 25E
Flivik Gasfjarden, Sweden 57 33N 16 35E
Flixborough R. Trent, England, UK 53 37N 00 41W
Florence Oregon, USA 43 58N 124 06W
Flores Acores 39 30N 31 10W
Florianopolis Santa Catarina, Brazil 27 36S 48 34W
Floro Norway 61 36N 05 02E
Flotta Terminal Orkney Is., Scotland, UK 58 51N 03 07W
Flow, Scapa Orkney Is., Scotland, UK 58 55N 03 00W
Flus, Abu (Nahr Abu el Flus) Shatt al Arab, Iraq
  30 27N 48 02E
Flushing (Vlissingen) Westerschelde, Netherlands
  51 28N 03 36E
Flushing East (Sloehaven) Westerschelde, Netherlands
  51 27N 03 40E
Flus, Nahr Abu el (Abu Flus) Shatt al Arab, Iraq
  30 27N 48 02E

Foca Nemrut Limani, Turkey 38 43N 26 55E
Fogo Island Newfoundland, Canada 49 44N 54 15W
Foldafos (Follafos) Trondheimsfjord, Norway
63 59N 11 02E
Folkestone England, UK 51 05N 01 11E
Follafos (Foldafos) Trondheimsfjord, Norway
63 59N 11 02E
Follonica Italy 42 55N 10 45E
Fomboni (Foumbouni) Moheli, Republic of the Comoros
12 16S 43 44E
Fondeadero Monypenny Golfo de Fonesca, Nicaragua
13 05N 87 33W
Fonte Boa R. Amazonas, Brazil 02 33S 65 59W
Foochow (Fuzhou) Min Chiang, China 26 03N 119 18E
Forari Metensa Bay, Efate, New Hebrides 17 41S 168 32E
Forcados Nigeria 05 22N 05 21E
Forcados Terminal Nigeria 05 10N 05 10E
Forestville St Lawrence R., Quebec Province, Canada
48 44N 69 04W
Formosa, Praia Maderia 32 37N 16 57W
Fornelos Spain 42 57N 09 11W
Foron, Ormos Piraievs, Greece 37 56N 23 37E
Forsmark Sweden 60 25N 18 13E
Fortaleza (Ceara) Brazil 03 44S 38 31W
Fort Dauphin (Tolagnaro) Malagasy Republic
25 02S 47 00E
Fort de France Martinique 14 36N 61 05W
Fort Denison Sydney, New South Wales, Australia
33 51S 151 13E
Fortin, Point Trinidad 10 12N 61 42W
Fort Liberte Haiti 19 41N 71 51W
Fort Mifflin Delaware R., Philadelphia, Pennsylvania, USA
39 52N 75 13W
Fort Pierce Florida, USA 27 28N 80 19W
Fortune Newfoundland, Canada 47 05N 55 50W
Fort, Vieux St Lucia 13 44N 60 58W
Fort William Lake Superior, Ontario, Canada
48 26N 89 13W
Fort William Loch Linnhe, Scotland, UK
56 49N 05 07W
Fos France 43 24N 04 52E
Fosbaek (Fossbekk) Norway 58 15N 08 23E
Fosbucraa (El Aaiun) (Laayoune) Morocco
27 04N 13 28W
Fosdyke R. Welland, England, UK 52 52N 00 02W
Foso, Rade de Haiti 18 42N 72 21W
Fossbekk (Fosbaek) Norway 58 15N 08 23E
Foumboini (Fomboni) Moheli, Republic of the Comoros
12 16N 43 44E
Fowey England, UK 50 20N 04 39W
Foxi, Porto (Sarroch) Sardegna, Italy 39 05N 09 01E
Foynes R. Shannon, Republic of Ireland 52 37N 09 07W
Frafjord Ryfylkefjordene, Norway 58 51N 06 17E
Francais Port au Kerguelen Is. 49 21S 70 13E
France, Fort de Martinique 14 36N 61 05W
Frances, Cayo Cuba 22 38N 79 13W
Franco, Barbate de (Barbate) Spain 36 11N 05 56W
Franklin Harbour South Australia, Australia
33 44S 136 58E
Fraserburgh Scotland, UK 57 42N 02 00W
Fray Bentos R. Uruguay, Uruguay 33 06S 58 19W
Fredericia Jylland, Denmark 58 35N 09 45E
Frederiksdal Greenland 60 00N 44 40W
Frederikshaab Greenland 62 00N 49 42W
Frederikshamn (Hamina) Finland 60 34N 27 11E
Frederiks-Havn Jylland, Denmark 57 27N 10 32E
Frederiksnas Orrenfjard, Sweden 58 15N 16 45E
Frederiksskans Gavlebukten, Sweden 60 41N 17 14E
Frederikssund Sjaelland, Denmark 55 50N 12 05E
Frederikstad Glomma R., Norway 59 12N 10 58E

Frederiksted St. Croix, Virgin Is. 17 43N 64 53W
Frederiksvaerk Sjaelland, Denmark 55 58N 12 01E
Freeport Grand Bahama, Bahamas 26 31N 78 46W
Freeport Ireland Is., Bermuda 32 19N 64 50W
Freeport Brazos R., Texas, USA 28 57N 95 21W
Freetown Sierra Leone 08 30N 13 13W
Fremantle Western Australia, Australia 32 03S 115 45E
Fremington R. Taw, England, UK 51 05N 04 07W
Frenchman Bay Albany, Western Australia, Australia
35 05S 117 56E
Freshwater Bay Juan de Fuca Strait, Washington, USA
48 09N 123 36W
Friedrichstadt Die Eider, West Germany 54 22N 09 05E
Frihamnen Goteborg, Sweden 57 43N 11 57E
Frio, Cabo Brazil 22 54S 42 00W
Frobisher Bay Baffin Is., North West Territory, Canada
63 44N 68 32W
Frontera (Puerto Alvaro Obregon) Golfo de Campeche,
Mexico 18 36N 92 39W
Frontignan Golfe du Lion, France 43 27N 03 45E
Fruglot Gropviken, Sweden 58 21N 16 38E
Fuglefjord Eysturoy, Faroe Is. 62 15N 06 48W
Fuik Baai Curacao 12 03N 68 50W
Fujairah (Fujayrah) Gulf of Oman, United Arab Emirates
25 09N 56 19E
Fujayrah (Fujairah) Gulf of Oman, United Arab Emirates
25 09N 56 19E
Fukuoka Kyushu, Japan 33 36N 130 23E
Fukuyama Seto Naikai, Honshu, Japan 34 27N 133 25E
Funabashi Tokyo Wan, Honshu, Japan 35 41N 140 00E
Funafuti Island Tuvalu 08 31S 179 13E
Funakawa Honshu, Japan 39 52N 139 51E
Funchal Madeira 32 39N 16 55W
Fur Denmark 56 50N 09 01E
Furuogrund Sweden 64 56N 21 14E
Fushiki Toyama Wan, Honshu, Japan 36 47N 137 04E
Futami Chichishima Retto, Nanpo Shoto, Japan
27 05N 142 11E
Fuzhou (Foochow) Min Chiang, China 26 03N 119 18E

Gabense Falster, Denmark 54 57N 11 53E
Gabes Tunisia 33 53N 10 07E
Gaboto, Puerto R. Parana, Argentina 32 26S 60 49W
Gaeta Italy 41 12N 13 34E
Gager Griefswald Bodden, East Germany 54 19N 13 41E
Gainsborough R. Trent, England, UK 53 24N 00 46W
Galata Istanbul, Karadeniz Bogazi, Turkey 41 01N 28 57E
Galati (Galatz) R. Dunarea, Romania 45 25N 28 05E
Galatz (Galati) R. Dunarea, Romania 45 25N 28 05E
Galena Park Houston Ship Canal, Texas, USA
29 44N 95 16W
Galeota Point Trinidad 10 07N 60 59W
Galets, Pointe des La Reunion 20 55S 55 17E
Galle Sri Lanka 06 01N 80 13E
Gallegos, Rio Argentina 51 36S 69 12W
Gallipoli Golfo di Taranto, Italy 40 03N 17 59E
Gallipoli (Gelibolu) Canakkale Bogazi, Turkey
40 24N 26 41E
Galvan, Puerto Bahia Blanca, Argentina 38 47S 62 18W
Galveston Texas, USA 29 18N 94 47W
Galway Galway Bay, Republic of Ireland 53 16N 09 04W
Gamba Terminal Gabon 02 48S 09 59E
Gamble, Port Hood Canal, Washington, USA
47 51N 122 35W
Gamla Karleby (Kokkola) Finland 63 50N 23 08E
Gamleby Sweden 57 53N 16 25E
Gand (Ghent) Oostende-Gent Canal, Belgium
51 03N 03 42E

Gandia Spain 38 59N 00 09W
Garcia, Diego 07 19S 72 28E
Garden Reach Hugli R., India 22 33N 88 18E
Gardiner Upqua R., Oregon, USA 43 44N 124 07W
Garlieston Scotland, UK 54 47N 04 22W
Garrucha Spain 37 10N 01 49W
Garston R. Mersey, England, UK 53 21N 02 54W
Gashaga Sweden 59 21N 18 14E
Gasmata New Britain, Papua New Guinea 06 19S 150 19E
Gaspe Baie de Gaspe, Quebec Province, Canada
48 50N 64 29W
Gastgivarehagen Braviken, Sweden 58 36N 16 13E
Gateshead R. Tyne, England, UK 54 58N 01 36W
Gavilian Point Mindanao, Philippines 06 54N 122 03E
Gavle (Gefle) Sweden 60 40N 17 10E
Gdansk (Danzig) Zatoka Gdanska, Poland 54 21N 18 41E
Gdynia Zatoke Gdanska, Poland 54 32N 18 33E
Gebe Island Indonesia 00 03S 129 21E
Gedida, El Mina el Suez Canal, Egypt 29 58N 32 33E
Geelong Port Phillip Bay, Victoria, Australia
38 06S 144 22E
Geestemunde Die Weser, West Germany 53 32N 08 35E
Gefle (Gavle) Sweden 60 40N 17 10E
Geismar Mississippi R., Louisiana, USA 30 13N 91 01W
Gela Sicilia, Italy 37 04N 14 16E
Gelibolu (Gallipoli) Canakkale Bogazi, Turkey
40 24N 26 41E
Gemikonagi (Karavostassi) Cyprus 35 08N 32 49E
Gemlik Marmara Denizi, Turkey 40 25N 29 09E
Gemsa Gulf of Suez, Egypt 27 39N 33 36E
General San Martin Peru 13 48S 76 17W
Gerneral Santos City (Buyan City) (Dadiangas) Mindanao,
Philippines 06 06N 125 09E
General Uribura (Zarate) R. Parana, Argentina
34 06S 59 02W
Genicheskiy Utlyukskiy Liman, Azovskoye More, USSR
46 11N 34 48E
Gennevilliers R. Seine, France 48 57N 02 17E
Genoa (Genova) Italy 44 24N 08 56E
Genova (Genoa) Italy 44 24N 08 56E
Gensan (Wonsan) Yonghung Man, North Korea
39 10N 127 26E
Gente Grande, Bahia Estrecho de Magallanes, Chile
53 00S 70 20W
Gentil, Port Gabon 00 43S 08 48E
Gent, Sas van Gent-Terneuzen Kanaal, Netherlands
51 14N 03 48E
Georgetown Ascension Is. 07 55S 14 25W
Georgetown Prince Edward Is., Canada 46 10N 62 31W
Georgetown Grand Cayman, Cayman Is., 19 19N 81 23W
Georgetown (Demerara) Guyana 06 49N 58 06W
Georgetown Penang Is., Malaya, Malaysia
05 25N 100 21E
Georgetown South Carolina, USA 33 22N 79 17W
Geradra Baia de Setubal, Portugal 38 29N 08 54W
Geraldton Champion Bay, Western Australia, Australia
28 47S 114 36E
Gerona, Nueva Isla de Pinos, Cuba 21 54N 82 47W
Gerong, Sungei Sumetra, Indonesia 02 59S 104 52E
Gersik (Gresik) Jawa, Indonesia 07 10S 112 39E
Ghannouche Tunisia 33 55N 10 06E
Ghardaqah, Al (Hurghada)Egypt 27 14N 33 50E
Gharib, Ras Gulf of Suez, Egypt 28 21N 33 07E
Ghar, Ras al Saudi Arabia 26 52N 49 52E
Ghazaouet (Nemours) Algeria 35 06N 01 52W

Ghent (Gand) Oostende-Gent Canal, Belgium
51 03N 03 42E
Gibara Cuba 21 07N 76 09W
Gibraltar 36 08N 05 22W

Gibraltar, Refineria Algeciras, Spain 36 11N 05 24W
Gibson Island Brisbane R., Queensland, Australia
27 26S 153 07E
Gijon Spain 43 34N 05 40W
Giles, Port St Vincent Gulf, South Australia, Australia
35 05S 137 46E
Giles Quay Port Lairge, Republic of Ireland
52 15N 07 04W
Gillingham R. Medway, England, UK 51 24N 00 34E
Girard Point Philadelphia, Delaware R., Pennsylvania,
USA 39 53N 75 12W
Giresun (Kerasunda) Turkey 40 56N 38 23E
Girne (Kyrenia) Cyprus 35 20N 33 20E
Girvan Scotland, UK 55 15N 04 52W
Gisborne North Is., New Zealand 38 41S 178 02E
Gizan (Jizan) Saudi Arabia 16 54N 42 31E
Gizo Island Solomon Is., 08 05S 156 51E
Glace Bay Cape Breton Is., Nova Scotia, Canada
46 12N 59 55W
Gladstone Queensland, Australia 23 50S 151 15E
Glasgow R. Clyde, Scotland, UK 55 52N 04 18W
Glasgow, New Nova Scotia, Canada 45 36N 62 38W
Glasgow, Port Firth of Clyde, Scotland, UK
55 56N 04 41W
Glasson Dock R. Lune, England, UK 54 00N 02 51W
Glebe Island Sydney, New South Wales, Australia
33 52S 151 11E
Glenarm Ulster, UK 54 58N 05 57W
Glencaple R. Nith, Scotland, UK 55 01N 03 35W
Glengarriff Bantry Bay, Republic of Ireland
51 44N 09 32W
Glomfjord Norway 66 49N 13 59E
Gloucester R. Severn, England, UK 51 53N 02 13W
Gloucester Massachusetts, USA 42 37N 70 39W
Gloucester Delaware R., New Jersey, USA
39 54N 75 08W
Gluckstadt Die Elbe, West Germany 53 47N 09 25E
Gocek (Kocek) Turkey 36 45N 28 57E
Goderich Lake Huron, Ontario, Canada 43 44N 81 44W
Godhavn Disko, Greenland 69 15N 53 31W
Godthaab Greenland 64 11N 51 44W
Golcuk (Gueldjuk) Izmit Korfezi, Marmara Denizi, Turkey
40 44N 29 49E
Gold River Vancouver Is., British Columbia, Canada
49 41N 126 07W
Golfito Costa Rica 08 37N 83 12W
Golfo Aranci Sardegna, Italy 40 57N 09 37E
Golfo, Castellammare del Sicilia, Italy 38 01N 12 53E
Golluk (Kolluk) (Gulluk) Maadalya Korfezi, Turkey
37 15N 27 38E
Golovasi Iskenderun Korfezi, Turkey 36 53N 35 56E
Gonaives Haiti 19 27N 72 42W
Gonfreville l'Orcher La Seine, France 49 29N 00 14E
Good Hope Mississippi R., Louisiana, USA
29 59N 90 24W
Goole R. Ouse, England, UK 53 42N 00 51W
Goose Bay Hamilton Inlet, Labrador, Canada
53 21N 60 25W
Gopalpur India 19 16N 84 54E
Gorda, Punta Cuba 20 38N 74 51W
Gorda, Punta Belize 16 06N 88 48W
Gore Bay Sidney, New South Wales, Australia
33 50S 151 11E
Gorele Turkey 41 04N 38 59E
Gorey Jersey, Channel Is., UK 49 12N 02 01W
Gorontalo Sulawesi, Indonesia 00 30N 123 03E
Gotay, Punta Puerto Rico 17 59N 66 46W
Goteborg (Gothenburg) Sweden 57 42N 11 58E
Gothenburg (Goteborg) Sweden 57 42N 11 58E
Gouave, Petit Haiti 18 26N 72 52W
Goulette, La Tunisia 36 49N 10 18E

Gourock Firth of Clyde, Scotland, UK 55 58N 04 49W
Gove Melville Bay, Northern Territory, Australia
12 12S 136 38E
Graasten (Gravenstein) Jylland, Denmark 54 55N 09 36E
Gracias a Dios, Puerto Nicaragua 15 00N 83 12W
Graciosa Island Acores 39 05N 28 00W
Grafton Clarence R., New South Wales, Australia
29 42S 152 57E
Graham, Port Cook Inlet, Alaska, USA 59 22N 151 52W
Grain, Isle of R. Medway, England, UK 51 26N 00 42E
Gramercy Mississippi R., Louisiana, USA 30 01N 90 41W
Granaderos, Puerto R. Parana, Argentina 32 46S 60 44W
Grand Bank Newfoundland, Canada 47 06N 55 45W
Grand Bassa Liberia 05 52N 10 04W
Grand Cayman Cayman Is., 19 20N 81 20W
Grand Cul de Sac Bay St. Lucia 13 59N 61 02W
Grande, Bajada R. Parana, Argentina 31 43S 60 35W
Grande, Bajo Lago de Maracaibo, Venezuela
10 31N 71 36W
Grande, Boca Cuba 21 33N 78 40W
Grande, Porto Sao Vicente, Republic of Cape Verde
16 53N 25 00W
Grande, Rio Tierra del Fuego, Argentina 53 47S 67 42W
Grande, Rio Brazil 32 04S 52 04W
Grand Harbour Grand Manan Is., New Brunswick, Canada
44 41N 66 46W
Grand Haven Lake Michigan, Michigan, USA
43 04N 86 14W
Grand Turk Turks Is. 21 29N 71 08W
Granerudstoa Oslofjord, Norway 59 47N 10 36E
Grangemouth R. Forth, Scotland, UK 56 02N 03 42W
Grankullaviken Oland, Sweden 57 21N 17 06E
Granton Firth of Forth, Scotland, UK 55 59N 03 13W
Granudden Terminal Gavlebukten, Sweden
60 42N 17 14E
Granville Golfe de St. Malo, France 48 50N 01 36W
Grao de Castellon de la Palma, Puerto del Spain
39 58N 00 01E
Grao, El Spain 39 28N 00 18W
Grassy King Is., Bass Strait, Australia 40 03S 144 04E
Gravelines France 51 00N 02 07E
Gravenstein (Graasten) Jylland, Denmark 54 55N 09 36E
Gravesend R. Thames, England, UK 51 27N 00 23E
Gravosa (Dubrovnik 2) (Gruz) Yugoslavia 42 40N 18 05E
Grays Harbour Washington, USA 46 59N 123 57W
Greaker Glomma R., Norway 59 16N 11 02E
Great Yarmouth R. Yare, England, UK 52 34N 01 44E
Greco, Torre del Golfo di Napoli, Italy 40 47N 14 22E
Green Bay Lake Michigan, Wisconsin, USA
44 32N 88 01W
Green Harbour (Gronfjorden) Spitsbergen, Svalbard
78 03N 14 14E
Greenhithe R. Thames, England, UK 51 28N 00 17E
Greenock R. Clyde, Scotland, UK 55 57N 04 46W
Greenore Carlingford Lough, Republic of Ireland
54 02N 06 08W
Greenport Harbour Long Is., New York, USA
41 06N 72 21W
Greenville Liberia 04 59N 09 02W
Greenwich Point Philadelphia, Delaware R., Pennsylvania,
USA 39 55N 75 08W
Gregorio, Bahia Estrecho de Magallanes, Chile
52 38S 70 12W
Greifswald East Germany 54 05N 13 22E
Grenaa Jylland, Denmark 56 25N 10 55E
Gresik (Gersik) Jawa, Indonesia 07 10S 112 39E
Gretna Mississippi R., Louisiana, USA 29 55N 90 03W
Greymouth South Is., New Zealand 42 26S 171 13E
Greytown (San Juan del Norte) Nicaragua 10 56N 83 43W
Grigor'yevka USSR 46 36N 31 01E

Grimsby R. Humber, England, UK 53 34N 00 04W
Grimstad Norway 58 21N 08 35E
Grindstone Madeleine Is., Quebec Province, Canada
47 23N 61 51W
Grisslehamn Sweden 60 06N 18 49E
Grogot, Tanah Sungai Pasir, Kalimantan, Indonesia
01 55S 116 11E
Gronfjorden (Green Harbour) Spitsbergen
78 03N 14 14E
Gronhogen Oland, Sweden 56 16N 16 24E
Groningen Eems Kanaal, Netherlands 53 13N 06 35E
Gronnedal Greenland 61 14N 48 06W
Groote Eylandt Gulf of Carpentaria, Northern Territory,
Australia 14 00S 136 30E
Grossendorf (Wladyslawowo) Zatoka Gdanska, Poland
54 47N 18 26E
Groton Connecticut, USA 41 21N 72 05W
Grovehurst Jetty The Swale, England, UK 51 22N 00 46E
Grumantbyen Spitzbergen, Svalbard 78 10N 15 12E
Gruvon Vanern, Sweden 59 20N 13 07E
Gruz (Dubrovnik 2) (Gravosa) Yugoslavia 42 40N 18 05E
Grytviken South Georgia 54 16S 36 30W
Guacolda Huasco, Chile 28 27S 71 14W
Guadalcanal Solomon Is. 09 25S 160 00E
Guaiba Island Brazil 23 01S 44 02W
Guairi, La Venezuela 10 36N 66 56W
Gualeguaychu R. Uruguay, Argentina 33 01S 58 31W
Guam Marianas (Ladrones) Is. 13 30N 144 40E
Guanabara Terminal Rio de Janeiro, Brazil
22 49S 43 09W
Guangzhou (Canton) (Kuang-chou Kan) (Kwangchow) Chu
Chiang, China 23 07N 113 14E
Guanica Puerto Rico 17 58N 66 54W
Guanta Venezuela 10 15N 64 34W
Guantanamo, Bahia de Cuba 20 00N 75 10W
Guaraguao Venezuela 10 14N 64 38W
Guaranao, Salina Peninsula de Paraguana, Venezuela
11 40N 70 13W
Guaricema Terminal Brazil 11 09S 37 03W
Guatemala (Preston) Bahia Nipe, Cuba 20 46N 75 39W
Guayabal Golfo de Guacanayabo, Cuba 20 41N 77 37W
Guayacan Chile 29 58S 71 22W
Guayama Puerto Rico 17 55N 66 04W
Guayanilla Puerto Rico 18 00N 66 46W
Guayaquil Ecuador 02 12S 79 53W
Guayaquil, Puerto Maritima De Ecuador 02 17S 79 54W
Guayas River Ecuador 02 40S 79 55W
Guaymas Golfo de California, Mexico 27 55N 110 52W
Guba Bol'shaya Pir'ya Kandalakshskaya Guba, Beloye
More, USSR 66 40N 34 21E
Guba Keret Kandalakshskaya Guba, Beloye More, USSR
66 16N 33 35E
Guba Kovda Kandalakshskaya Guba, Beloye More, USSR
66 44N 32 51E
Guba Pechenga (Petsamo Gulf) USSR 69 40N 31 22E
Guba Vayenga Kol'skiy Zaliv USSR 69 05N 33 25E
Gubre Terminal, Toros Iskenderun Korfezi, Turkey
36 55N 36 59E
Gudang, Pasir Selat Tebrau, Malaya, Malaysia
01 26N 103 54E
Guedjuk (Golcuk) Izmit Korfezi, Marmara Denizi, Turkey
40 44N 29 49E
Guetaria Spain 43 18N 02 12W
Guildo, Le Golfe de St. Malo, France 48 34N 02 13W
Guimaras Island Philippines 10 40N 122 39E
Guindulman Bohol, Philippines 09 46N 124 29E
Guiria Golfo de Paria, Venezuela 10 34N 62 18W
Guiuan Harbour Samar, Philippines 11 02N 125 43E
Guixols, San Feliu de Spain 41 46N 03 02E
Gulfhavn Sjaelland, Denmark 55 12N 11 16E

Gulfport Mississippi, USA 30 21N 89 05W
Gulfport Arthur Kill R., New York, USA 40 38N 74 12W
Gullsmedvik Ranenfjord, Norway 66 20N 14 09E
Gulluk (Kulluk) (Golluk) Mandalya Korfezi, Turkey
   37 15N 27 38E
Gumaining Luzon, Philippines 16 15N 122 04E
Gumbodahamn Sweden 64 14N 21 04E
Gunnebo Sweden 57 42N 16 33E
Gunness R. Trent, England, UK 53 36N 00 43W
Gunung Sitoli Nias, Indonesia 01 19N 97 36E
Gunza Kabolo (Novo Redondo) Angola 11 11S 13 52E
Gunzan (Kunsan) South Korea 35 59N 126 43E
Gustafsvik Angermanalven, Sweden 62 50N 17 52E
Gustavsberg Alno, Sweden 62 24N 17 25E
Gustavsberg Sweden 59 20N 18 23E
Guysborough Chedabucto Bay, Nova Scotia, Canada
   45 23N 61 30W
Gythion (Yithion) Lakonikos Kolpos, Greece
   36 45N 22 34E

Ha'apai Tonga Is., 19 50S 174 20W
Haapsalu (Hapsal) USSR 58 57N 23 34E
Habana (Havana) Cuba 23 08N 82 21W
Habu Innoshima, Seto Naikai, Japan 34 17N 133 11E
Hachinohe Honshu, Japan 40 32N 141 31E
Haderslev Jylland, Denmark 55 16N 09 30E
Hadsund Mariager Fjord, Jylland, Denmark
   56 44N 10 07E
Haeju (Haijuube) North Korea 37 59N 125 42E
Hafnafjordhur Iceland 64 04N 21 56W
Hafun, Ras (Dante) Somalia 10 26N 51 16E
Ha Ha Bay Saguenay R., Quebec Province, Canada
   48 21N 70 53W
Haidar Pacha (Haydarpasa) Karadeniz Bogazi, Turkey
   41 00N 29 04E
Haifa (Kaifa) Israel 32 49N 35 00E
Haijuube (Haeju) North Korea 37 59N 125 42E
Hai-K'ou (Hoihow) Hai-Nan Tao, China 20 03N 110 21E
Hai-K'ou Taiwan 22 05N 124 42E
Haina, Rio Dominican Republic 18 25N 70 01W
Haines Lynn canal, Alaska, USA 59 14N 135 26W
Haiphong Vietnam 20 52N 106 41E
Haitien, Cap Haiti 19 46N 72 12W
Hakansvik Finland 60 10N 25 25 01E
Hakata Kyushu, Japan 33 37N 130 24E
Hakodate Hokkaido, Japan 41 47N 140 43E
Halat al Mubarras (Mubarras Terminal) Abu Dhabi
   24 27N 53 42E
Halden Idefjord, Norway 59 08N 11 23E
Haldia Hugli R., India 22 01N 88 05E
Halifax Nova Scotia, Canada 44 38W 63 34W
Halla Finland 60 29N 26 57E
Hallstavik Sweden 60 03N 18 36E
Halmstad Sweden 56 40N 12 51E
Halsskov Sjaelland, Denmark 55 21N 11 08E
Halteneau Nord-Ostsee Kanal, West Germany
   54 22N 10 09E
Halul, Jazirat Qatar 25 39N 52 26E
Hamada Honshu, Japan 34 53N 132 04E
Hamburg Die Elbe, West Germany 53 33N 09 58E
Hamilton Brisbane R., Queensland, Australia
   27 27S 153 05E
Hamilton Bermuda 32 17N 64 48W
Hamilton Lake Ontario, Ontario, Canada 43 15N 79 51W
Hamina (Fredrikshamn) Finland 60 34N 27 11E
Hammerfest Norway 70 40N 23 44E
Hampton Roads Chesapeake Bay, Virginia, USA
   36 58N 76 20W

Hamra, Marsa El (El Alamein) Egypt 30 58N 28 51E
Hamrawein, El (Hamrawein Port) Egypt 26 15N 34 12E
Hamrawein Port (El Hamrawein) Egypt 26 15N 34 12E
Hamriya United Arab Emirates 25 29N 55 32E
Handa Chita Wan, Honshu, Japan 34 53N 136 57E
Hangam, Jazireh-Ye (Henjam Is.) Iran 26 41N 55 53E
Hango (Hanko) Finland 59 49N 22 58E
Hanko (Hango) Finland 59 49N 22 58E
Han-K'ou (Hankow) Ch'ang Chiang, China
   30 35N 114 17E
Hankow (Han-K'ou) Ch'ang Chiang, China
   30 35N 114 17E
Hannan Osaka Wan, Honshu, Japan 34 27N 135 23E
Hanstholm Jylland, Denmark 57 08N 08 36E
Hansweert R. Schelde, Netherlands 51 26N 04 00E
Hantsport Minas Basin, Nova Scotia, Canada
   45 04N 64 10W
Haparanda Sweden 65 50N 24 08E
Hapsal (Haapsalu) USSR 58 57N 23 34E
Haraholmen Sweden 65 15N 21 35E
Harami Dere Marmara Denizi, Turkey 40 58N 28 49E
Harbour Grace Newfoundland, Canada 47 42N 53 14W
Harburg Die Elbe, West Germany 53 28N 09 59E
Harcourt, Port Bonny R., Nigeria 04 46N 07 01E
Hardy, Port Vancouver Is., British Columbia, Canada
   50 43N 127 29W
Hare Bay Newfoundland, Canada 51 16N 56 00W
Harfleur R. Seine, France 49 31N 00 12E
Hargshamn Sweden 60 11N 18 29E
Hariga, Marsa al (Tobruk Terminal) Libya
   32 04N 24 00E
Harlingen Netherlands 53 10N 05 25E
Harmac Vancouver Is., British Columbia, Canada
   49 08N 123 52W
Harmon, Port Newfoundland, Canada 48 31N 58 33W
Harnas Sweden 60 39N 17 23E
Harnosand (Hernosand) Sweden 62 38N 17 58E
Harstad Hinno, Vesteralen, Norway 68 48N 16 37E
Harta Point Shatt al Arab, Iran 30 22N 48 11E
Hartlepool England, UK 54 42N 01 11W
Hartlepool, West England, UK 54 41N 01 12W
Harton R. Tyne, England, UK 55 00N 01 26W
Harvey, Port (Port Martin Marietta) (Port Alucroix)
   St. Croix, Virgin Is. 17 42N 64 46W
Harwich R. Stour, England, UK 51 57N 01 15E
Harwood Clarence R., New South Wales, Australia
   29 26S 153 16E
Hashihama Seto Naikai, Shikoku, Japan 34 06N 132 58E
Hasle Bornholm, Denmark 55 11N 14 42E
Hastings Lake Ontario, New York, USA
   43 20N 76 10W
Hastings, Port Strait of Canso, Nova Scotia, Canada
   45 39N 61 24W
Ha Tien Vietnam 10 23N 104 28E
Haugesund Norway 59 25N 05 16E
Haulbowline Island Corcaigh, Republic of Ireland
   51 51N 08 18W
Haute Indre La Loire, France 47 12N 01 38W
Havana (Havana) Cuba 23 08N 82 21W
Havannah Harbour Efate, New Hebrides 17 37S 168 14E
Have, La Nova Scotia, Canada 44 17N 64 21W
Haven Barcadera Aruba 12 29N 70 01W
Haven, New Connecticut, USA 41 18N 72 55W
Havre-Antifer France 49 41N 00 09E
Havre Aubert (Amherst Harbour) Madeleine Is., Quebec
   Province, Canada 47 14N 61 50W
Havre, Le La Seine, France 49 28N 00 06E
Havre St Pierre St Lawrence R., Quebec Province, Canada
   50 14N 63 36W
Hawkes Bay Newfoundland, Canada 50 37N 57 16W

Hawkesbury, Port Strait of Canso, Nova Scotia, Canada
45 37N 61 22W
Hawkins Point Baltimore, Maryland, USA
39 13N 76 32W
Haydarpasa (Haidar Pacha) Karadeniz Bogazi, Turkey
41 00N 29 04E
Hayle St. Ives Bay, England, UK 50 11N 05 25W
Hay Point Queensland, Australia 21 16S 149 19E
Hebburn R. Tyne, England, UK 54 59N 01 31W
Hedland, Port Western Australia, Australia
20 19S 118 35E
Hechthausen Die Oste, West Germany 53 39N 09 15E
Heherr Point (Tanjong Heherr) Sabah, Malaysia
04 17N 117 48E
Heianza Shima Okinawa Gunto, Nansei Shoto, Japan
26 21N 127 57E
Heiligenhafen West Germany 54 22N 11 01E
Heimaey Vestmannaeyjar, Iceland 63 27N 20 15W
Hel (Hela) Zatoka Gdanska, Poland 54 36N 18 48E
Hela (Hel) Zatoka Gdanska, Poland 54 36N 18 48E
Helder, Den Netherlands 52 58N 04 46E
Helgenas Sweden 58 00N 16 31E
Hellevoetsluis Voorne, Netherlands 51 49N 04 08E
Hellville Malagasy Republic 13 24S 48 17E
Helmi Finland 64 41N 24 25E
Helmsdale Scotland, UK 58 07N 03 38W
Helsingborg Sweden 56 03N 12 42E
Helsingfors (Helsinki) Finland 60 10N 24 58E
Helsingor (Elsinore) Sjaelland, Denmark 56 02N 12 38E
Helsinki (Helsingfors) Finland 60 10N 24 58E
Hemiksen (Hemixen) R. Schelde, Belgium 51 09N 04 20E
Hemixen (Hemiksen) R. Schelde, Belgium 51 09N 04 20E
Henecan Golfo de Fonseca, Honduras 13 24N 87 25W
Henjam Island (Jazireh-ye Hangam) Iran 26 41N 55 53E
Hennebont France 47 48N 03 16W
Henry, Point Geelong, Victoria, Australia
38 08S 144 26E
Hepokari Uuskiaupunki (Nystad) Finland 60 48N 21 23E
Heraklea (Eregli) Turkey 41 18N 31 26E
Heraklion (Iraklion) (Candia) Kriti, Greece
35 21N 25 09E
Herceg-Novi (Castelnuovo) Boka Kotorska, Yugoslavia
42 27N 18 34E
Hercules California, USA 38 01N 122 18W
Hereke Izmit Korfezi, Turkey 40 45N 29 45E
Hernosand (Harnosand) Sweden 62 38N 17 58E
Heroen (Heroya) R. Skien, Norway 59 07N 09 38E
Heroismo, Angra do (Angra) Terceira, Acores
38 38N 27 13W
Heroya (Heroen) R. Skien, Norway 59 07N 09 38E
Herrenwyk Die Trave, West Germany 53 54N 10 48E
Herring Cove Bay of Fundy, New Brunswick, Canada
45 34N 64 58W
Hertonas (Herttoniemi) Finland 60 11N 25 02E
Herttoniemi (Hertonas) Finland 60 11N 25 02E
Heysham England, UK 54 02N 02 55W
Hibi Seto Naikai, Honshu, Japan 34 27N 133 56E
Hierro, Puerto de Golfo de Paria, Venezuela
10 38N 62 06W
Higashi-Harima Seto Naikai, Honshu, Japan
34 43N 134 50E
Higashi Ku Seto Naikai, Honshu, Japan 34 46N 134 41E
Hillskar Sweden 63 41N 20 21E
Hilo Hawaii, Hawaiian Is., USA 19 44N 155 05W
Himango (Himanka) Finland 64 03N 23 39E
Himanka (Himango) Finland 64 03N 23 39E
Himeji Seto Naikai, Honshu, Japan 34 47N 134 38E
Himugaan Negros, Philippines 10 58N 123 24E
Hinchinbrook Queensland, Australia 18 29S 146 15E
Hirakata Honshu, Japan 36 51N 140 50E

Hirao Seto Naikai, Honshu, Japan 33 54N 132 03E
Hirohata Seto Naikai, Honshu, Japan 34 46N 134 38E
Hiroshima Seto Naikai, Honshu, Japan 34 20N 132 28E
Hirtshals Jylland, Denmark 57 36N 09 57E
Hitachi Honshu, Japan 36 34N 140 37E
Hjartholmen Sweden 57 41N 11 48E
Hobart R. Derwent, Tasmania, Australia 42 53S 147 20E
Hoboken Hudson R., New Jersey, USA 40 45N 74 02W
Hobro Mariager Fjord, Jylland, Denmark 56 39N 09 48E
Ho Chi Minh City (Saigon) Vietnam 10 46N 106 44E
Hodeidah (Hudaida) (Al Hudaydah) Yemen
14 49N 42 55E
Hoek van Holland (Hook of Holland) Nieuwe Waterweg,
Netherlands 51 59N 04 07E
Hofn Hornafjordhur, Iceland 64 16N 15 10W
Hoganas Sweden 56 13N 12 33E
Hoggarn, Stora Sweden 59 22N 18 17E
Hog Island Delaware R., Pennsylvania, USA
39 52N 75 16W
Hoihow (Hai-k'ou) Hai-Nan Tao, China 20 03N 110 21E
Holbaek Sjaelland, Denmark 55 42N 11 43E
Hollandia (Teluk Jayapura) (Sukarnapura) Irian Jaya,
Indonesia 02 32S 140 43E
Holland, Port Basilan, Philippines 06 33N 121 52E
Hollen Norway 58 05N 07 49E
Holmavick Hunafloi, Iceland 65 42N 21 41W
Holmstrand Oslofjord, Norway 59 29N 10 19E
Holmsund Sweden 63 42N 20 21E
Holsteinborg Davis Strait, Greenland 66 56N 53 42W
Holtenau Nord-Ostsee Kanal, West Germany
54 22N 10 09E
Holyhead Anglesey, Wales, UK 53 19N 04 37W
Holy Loch Firth of Clyde, Scotland, UK 55 59N 04 55W
Holyrood Newfoundland, Canada 47 24N 53 08W
Homer Kachemack Bay, Alaska, USA 59 39N 151 33W
Hommelvik Trondheimsfjord, Norway 63 25N 10 49E
Honavar India 14 16N 74 26E
Honda, Bahia Cuba 22 58N 83 09W
Honda, Ensenada Puerto Rico 18 14N 65 38W
Hondagua Lamon Bay, Luzon, Philippines
13 56N 122 14E
Hondura, Puerto de la Tenerife, Canary Is.
28 27N 16 16W
Honfleur La Seine, France 49 25N 00 14E
Hon Gay Baie d'Along Vietnam 20 57N 107 04E
Hong Kong 22 18N 144 10E
Honiara Guadacanal, Solomon Is. 09 25S 159 58E
Honningsvaag Mageroyo, Norway 70 59N 25 59E
Honolulu Oahu, Hawaiian Is., USA 21 19N 157 52W
Honto (Nevelsk) Sakhalin, USSR 46 40N 141 51E
Honuapo Hawaii, Hawaiian Is., USA 19 05N 155 33W
Honura Naoshima, Seto Naikai, Japan 34 27N 134 00E
Hood, Port Cape Breton Is., Nova Scotia, Canada
46 01N 61 31W
Hook R. Ouse, England, UK 53 43N 00 51W
Hook of Holland (Hoek van Holland) Nieuwe Waterweg,
Netherlands 51 59N 04 07E
Hooksiel Innenjade, West Germany 53 38N 08 02E
Hoonah Harbour Icy Strait, Alaska, USA
58 07N 135 27W
Hoorn Ijsselmeer, Netherlands 52 39N 05 03E
Hopa (Khoppa) Turkey 41 25N 41 24E
Hopedale Labrador, Canada 55 27N 60 12W
Hope, Port Lake Ontario, Ontario, Canada
43 57N 78 17W
Hope Simpson, Port Labrador, Canada 52 33N 56 16W
Hopewell James R., Virginia, USA 37 16N 77 17W
Hoquiam Grays Harbour, Washington, USA
46 58N 123 53W
Horie Seto Naikai, Shikoku, Japan 33 54N 132 45E

Horli (Khorly) Dzharylgachskiy Zaliv, USSR 46 04N 33 16E
Hormoz, Jazireh-Ye (Hormuz Is.) Iran 27 04N 56 27E
Hormuz Island (Jazireh-ye Hormoz) Iran 27 04N 56 27E
Hornafjordur Iceland 64 14W 15 02W
Horneborg Sweden 63 17N 18 43E
Hornefors Sweden 63 38N 19 55E
Hornum Sylt, West Germany 54 45N 08 18E
Horsens Jylland, Denmark 55 52N 09 52E
Horta Faial, Acores 38 32N 28 38W
Horten Oslofjord, Norway 59 25N 10 29E
Hortonville Minas Basin, Nova Scotia, Canada 45 06N 64 18W
Hososhima Kyushu, Japan 32 26N 131 40E
Hound Point Firth of Forth, Scotland, UK 56 00N 03 22W
Houston Houston Ship Canal, Texas, USA 29 44N 95 20W
Hout Bay South Africa 34 03S 18 22E
Hovic (Limetree Bay) St Croix, Virgin Is. 17 42N 64 45W
Howard, Point Wellington, North Is., New Zealand 41 15S 174 54E
Howdon, East R. Tyne, England, UK 54 59N 01 29W
Howland Hook Staten Is., New York, USA 40 39N 74 11W
Howth Republic of Ireland 53 24N 06 04W
Hoyanger Sognefjord, Norway 61 11N 06 03E
Hsia-Men (Amoy) China 24 27N 118 04E
Hsinkang (T'ang-ku) (Tongku) Hai Ho, China 38 59N 117 44E
Huacho Peru 11 08S 77 37W
Huai-Ning (Anking) Ch'ang Chiang, China 30 31N 117 02E
Hua-Lien (Karenko) Taiwan 23 59N 121 36E
Huang-Pu (Whampoa) Chu Chiang, China 23 06N 113 24E
Huarmey Peru 10 06S 78 11W
Huasco Chile 28 28S 71 14W
Hubberston Terminal Milford Haven, Wales, UK 51 42N 05 03W
Hudaida (Hodeidah) (Al Hudaydah) Yemen 14 49N 42 55E
Hudaydah, Al (Hodeidah) (Hudaida) Yemen 14 49N 42 55E
Hudiksvall Sweden 61 44N 17 08E
Hueca, Ceiba Golfo de Guacananyabo, Cuba 20 14N 77 19W
Huelva Spain 37 15N 06 55W
Hueneme, Port California, USA 34 09N 119 12W
Hull (Kingston-upon-Hull) R. Humber, England, UK 53 45N 00 17W
Humacao Puerto Rico 18 07N 65 46W
Humbermouth Corner Brook, Bay of Islands, Newfoundland, Canada 48 57N 57 55W
Humboldt Bay California, USA 40 46N 124 13W
Hunnebostrand Sweden 58 27N 11 18E
Hunterston Firth of Clyde, Scotland, UK 55 45N 04 53W
Huon, Port Tasmania, Australia 43 10S 146 58E
Hurghada (Al Ghardaqah) Egypt 27 14N 33 50E
Huron Lake Erie, Ohio, USA 41 24N 82 35W
Huron, Port St. Clair R., Michigan, USA 43 00N 82 28W
Husavik Eyjafjordhur, Iceland 66 03N 17 21W
Husnes Hardangerfjord, Norway 59 52N 05 46E
Husum Die Hever, West Germany 54 29N 09 03E
Husum Sweden 63 20N 19 09E
Husvik Harbour South Georgia 54 10S 36 42W
Hvalfjordhur Iceland 64 24N 21 28W
Hvammstangi Midfjordhur, Iceland 65 24N 20 57W
Hvar Island (Lesina) Yugoslavia 43 12E 16 27E

Hvidovre Sjaelland, Denmark 55 38N 12 30E

Ibicuy R. Parana, Argentina 33 45S 59 11W
Ibiza (Iviza) Islas Baleares, Spain 38 54N 01 28E
Iboe, Qua (Kwa Ibo) Nigeria 04 20N 08 00E
Ibo, Kwa (Qua Iboe) Nigeria 04 20N 08 00E
Ibrahim, Port Suez Canal, Egypt 29 56N 32 33E
Ica, Santo Antonio Do R. Amazonas, Brazil 03 05S 76 56W
I-Chang Ch'ang Chiang, China 30 42N 111 17E
Icoraci R. Para, Brazil 01 18S 48 29W
Ifni, Sidi Morocco 29 22N 10 12W
Igarka R. Yenisey, Karskoye More, USSR 67 30N 86 28E
Iggesund Sweden 61 37N 17 06E
Iguela Gabon 01 56S 09 19E
Iho Seto Naikai, Honshu, Japan 34 45N 134 46E
Ijmuiden (Ymuiden) Noordzeekanaal, Netherlands 52 28N 04 34E
Ilanin Bay Subic Bay, Luzon, Philippines 14 46N 120 15E
Ile Rousse Corse, France 42 38N 08 56E
Ilfracombe Bristol Channel, England, UK 51 13N 04 07W
Ilha Barnabe Brazil 23 55S 46 20W
Ilheus Brazil 14 48S 39 01W
Il'Ichevsk Sukhoy Liman, USSR 46 19N 30 39E
Iligan Mindanao, Philippines 08 14N 124 14E
Il'Insk Sakhalin, USSR 47 59N 142 12E
Ilo Peru 17 38S 71 20W
Iloilo Panay, Philippines 10 42N 122 34E
Imabari Seto Naikai, Shikoku, Japan 34 04N 133 00E
Imari Kyushu, Japan 33 17N 129 52E
Imatra Saimaa Canal, Finland 61 12N 28 50E
Imbituba Brazil 28 13S 48 41W
Imerese, Termini Sicilia, Italy 37 59N 13 43E
Immingham R. Humber, England, UK 53 38N 00 12W
Imperia (Oneglia) (Porto Maurizio) Italy 43 53N 08 02E
Inamucan Bay Mindanao, Philippines 08 36N 123 44E
Ince Manchester Ship Canal, England, UK 53 17N 02 50W
Inchon (Chemulpo) (Jinsen) South Korea 37 28N 126 37E
Indre Alvik Hardangerfjord, Norway 60 26N 06 26E
Indre, Basse La Loire, France 47 13N 01 41W
Indre, Haute La Loire, France 47 12N 01 38W
Indret La Loire, France 47 12N 01 42W
Inebolu Turkey 41 58N 33 46E
Inga (Inkoo) Finland 60 03N 24 01E
Ingeneiro White Bahia Blanca, Argentina 38 48S 62 16W
Ingleside Texas, USA 27 51N 97 14W
Inhambane Mozambique 23 51S 35 24E
Inkoo (Inga) Finland 60 03N 24 01E
Innisfail Queensland, Australia 17 32S 146 02E
Innoshima Seto Naikai, Japan 34 17N 133 11E
Inokuchi Omishima, Seto Naikai, Japan 34 16N 133 03E
Inspection Head R. Tamar, Tasmania, Australia 41 09S 146 49E
Intercourse Island, East Western Australia, Australia 20 39S 116 40E
Invercargill Buff Harbour, South Is., New Zealand 46 25S 168 21E
Invergordon Cromarty Firth, Scotland, UK 57 41N 04 10W
Inverkeithing Firth of Forth, Scotland, UK 56 01N 03 24W
Inverkip Firth of Clyde, Scotland, UK 55 54N 04 52W
Inverness British Columbia, Canada 54 12N 130 15W
Inverness Scotland, UK 57 29N 04 14W
Iona Bras d'Or Lake, Cape Breton Is., Nova Scotia, Canada 45 58N 60 48W
Ipswich R. Orwell, England, UK 52 03N 01 10E

Iquique Chile 20 13S 70 10W
Iquitos R. Amazonas, Peru 03 45S 73 11W
Iradier, Puerto (Cogo) (Kogo) Rio Muni, Guinea
　Equatorial 01 05N 09 42E
Iraklion (Candia) (Heraklion) Kriti, Greece
　35 21N 25 09E
Ireland Island Bermuda 32 19N 64 50W
Irene, Port Luzon, Philippines 18 26N 122 06E
Irlam Manchester Ship Canal, England, UK
　53 26N 02 23W
Irvine Firth of Clyde, Scotland, UK 55 37N 04 41W
Isaac's Harbour Nova Scotia, Canada 45 10N 61 41W
Isabela Basilan, Philippines 06 43N 121 58E
Isabela de Sagua R. Sagua la Grande, Cuba
　22 56N 80 01W
Isabel, Port Texas, USA 26 04N 97 12W
Isafjordhur Iceland 66 05N 23 07W
Ishigaki Ishigaki Shima, Sakishima Gunto, Japan
　24 20N 124 09E
Ishikawa Okinawa, Nansei Shoto, Japan 26 26N 127 50E
Ishinomaki Honshu, Japan 38 25N 141 20E
Isigny-sur-Mer France 49 19N 01 07W
Iskandariya, El (Alexandria) Egypt 31 09N 29 52E
Iskenderun (Alexandretta) Iskenderun Korfezi, Turkey
　36 36N 36 10E
Isla Barnabe Brazil 23 55S 46 20W
Isla Cedros Mexico 28 10N 115 10W
Isla Cozumel Mexico 20 55N 86 55W
Isla Cristina Spain 37 12N 07 19W
Isla de Pinos Cuba 21 40N 82 40W
Islam, Borj Syria 35 40N 35 48E
Isla Payardi Bahia las Minas, Panama 09 24N 79 50W
Isle of Grain R. Medway, England, UK 51 26N 00 42E
Ismail (Izmail) Kiliyskiy Rukav, R. Dunay, USSR
　45 20N 28 51E
Ismailia (Isma'iliya) Suez Canal, Egypt 30 36N 32 17E
Isma'iliya (Ismailia) Suez Canal, Egypt 30 36N 32 17E
Ismit (Izmit) Izmit Korfezi, Marmara Denizi, Turkey
　40 46N 29 55E
Isnas Finland 60 24N 26 01E
Isola, Porto Sicilia, Italy 37 02N 14 15E
Istanbul Karadeniz Bogazi, Turkey 41 01N 28 58E
Isthmia Dhiorix Korinthou, Greece 37 55N 23 00E
Istinye Karadeniz Bogazi, Turkey 41 08N 29 04E
Itajai Brazil 26 54S 48 39W
Itaqui Brazil 02 34S 44 22W
Itea Kolpos Korinthiakos, Greece 38 26N 22 25E
Ithaki Greece 38 20N 20 42E
Itozaki Seto Naikai, Honshu, Japan 34 23N 133 06E
Itzehoe Die Stor, West Germany 53 56N 09 32E
Ivigtut Greenland 61 12N 48 10W
Iviza (Ibiza) Islas Baleares, Spain 38 54N 01 28E
Ivory, Port Staten Is., New York, USA 40 38N 74 11W
Iwanai Hokkaido, Japan 42 59N 140 31E
Iwakuni Hiroshima Bay, Honshu, Japan 34 11N 132 14E
Iyo-Mishima (Mishima) Seto Naikai, Shikoku, Japan
　33 59N 133 33E
Izmail (Ismail) Kiliyskiy Rukav, R. Dunay, USSR
　45 20N 28 51E
Izmir (Smyrna) Turkey 38 24N 27 09E
Izmit (Ismit) Izmit Korfezi, Marmara Denizi, Turkey
　40 46N 29 55E
Izola Golfo di Trieste, Italy 45 33N 13 39E
Izuhara Tsushima, Japan 34 11N 129 18E

Jaagurahu Saaremaa, USSR 58 23N 21 56E
Jabal Az Zannah (Jebel Dhanna) United Arab Emirates
　24 12N 52 34E
Jackhau (Jakhau) India 23 14N 68 36E
Jackson, Port New South Wales, Australia
　33 50S 151 17E

Jacksonville St. John's R., Florida, USA 30 19N 81 38W
Jacmel Haiti 18 13N 72 31W
Jacobshavn (Jakobshavn) Greenland 69 13N 51 06W
Jacobstad (Pietarsaari) Finland 63 41N 22 43E
Jadida, El (Mazagan) (Al Yadida) Morocco
　33 14N 08 28W
Jaffna Sri Lanka 09 40N 79 59E
Jagna Bohol, Philippines 09 39N 124 22E
Jakarta (Djakarta) Jawa, Indonesia 06 07S 106 49E
Jakhau (Jackhau) India 23 14N 68 36E
Jakobshavn (Jacobshavn) 69 13N 51 06W
Jakobstad (Pietarsaari) Finland 63 41N 22 43E
Jaluit Marshall Is. 05 55N 169 39E
Jambi (Telanaipura) Sungai Jambi, Sumatera, Indonesia
　01 35S 103 37E
Jamestown St Helena 15 55S 05 43W
Janeiro, Rio de Brazil 23 54S 43 12W
Janjira, Murud India 18 18N 72 57E
Jaragua Maceio, Brazil 09 41S 35 43W
Jarrow R. Tyne, England, UK 54 59N 01 28W
Jarved Sweden 63 17N 18 45E
Jary, Point Guadeloupe 16 13N 61 37W
Jask Gulf of Oman, Iran 25 38N 57 46E
Jastarnia Zatoka Gdanska, Poland 54 42N 18 41E
Javea Spain 38 48N 00 11E
Jayapura, Teluk (Hollandia) (Sukarnapura) Irian Jaya,
　Indonesia 02 32S 104 43E
Jazirat Arzanah United Arab Emirates 24 46N 52 33E
Jazirat Halul Qatar 25 39N 52 26E
Jazirat Zarakkuh (Zirku Is.) United Arab Emirates
　24 52N 53 04E
Jazireh Sheykh Sho'eyb (Lavan Is.) (Jazireh-ye Lavan)
　Iran 26 47N 53 22E
Jazireh Sirri (Sirri Is.) Iran 25 54N 54 33E
Jazireh-Ye Hangam (Henjam Is.) Iran 26 41N 55 53E
Jazireh-Ye Hormoz (Hormuz Is.) Iran 27 04N 56 27E
Jazireh-Ye Khark (Kharg Is.) Iran 29 14N 50 19E
Jazireh-Ye Lavan (Jazireh Sheykh Sho'eyb) (Lavan Is.)
　Iran 26 47N 53 22E

Jebel Ali, Mina United Arab Emirates 25 03N 55 01E
Jebel Dhanna, Mina (Jabal az Zannah) United Arab
　Emirates 24 12N 52 34E
Jeddah (Jidda) Saudi Arabia 21 28N 39 11E
Jefferson, Port Long Is., New York, USA 40 57N 73 04W
Jeremie, Baie de (Jeromio) Haiti 18 39N 74 07W
Jerome, Port La Seine, France 49 29N 00 32E
Jeromio (Baie de Jeremie) Haiti 18 39N 74 07W
Jersey Channel Is., UK 49 15N 02 05W
Jersey City New Jersey, USA 40 42N 74 02W
Jervis Bay New South Wales, Australia 35 05S 150 45E
Jesselton (Kota Kinabalu) Sabah, Malaysia
　06 00N 116 05E
Jibouti (Djibouti) Republic of Djibouti 11 35N 43 09E
Jidda (Jeddah) Saudi Arabia 21 28N 39 11E
Jijel (Jizella) (Djidjelli) Algeria 36 50N 05 47E
Jimenez Iligan Bay, Mindanao, Philippines
　08 20N 123 52E
Jinhae (Chinhae) South Korea 35 06N 128 47E
Jinsen (Inchon) (Chemulpo) South Korea 37 28N 126 37E
Jizan (Gizan) Saudi Arabia 16 54N 42 31E
Jizella (Jijel) (Djidjelli) Algeria 36 50N 05 47E
Joa Pessoa R. Parraiba, Brazil 07 06S 34 53W
Jobos Puerto Rico 17 57N 66 11W
Joensuu Saimaa Canal, Finland 62 36N 29 45E
Johannedal Sundsvall, Sweden 62 26N 17 24E
Johnston Atoll 16 45N 169 31N
Johore Bahru Malaya, Malaysia 01 28N 103 46E
Jolo (Sulu) Jolo Is., Philippines 06 03N 121 00E
Jonesport Maine, USA 44 32N 67 36W

Jonkoping Vattern, Sweden 57 46N 14 10E
Jordan Panay, Philippines 10 40N 122 34E
Jose Ignacio Terminal Uruguay 34 54S 54 43W
Jose Panganiban (Mambulao) Luzon, Philippines
14 17N 122 42E
Jost Van Dyke Virgin Is. 18 27N 64 45W
Jounieh (Juniye) Lebanon 33 59N 35 37E
Juana, Tia Lago de Maracaibo, Venezuela 10 15N 71 22W
Juan Claro, Cayo Cuba 21 18N 76 32W
Ju'aymah Terminal Saudi Arabia 26 56N 50 02E
Jubail (Al Jubayl) Saudi Arabia 27 02N 49 41E
Jubayl, Al (Jubail) Saudi Arabia 27 02N 49 41E
Jucaro Cuba 21 37N 78 52W
Juelsminde Jylland, Denmark 55 43N 10 01E
Julianehaab Greenland 60 43N 46 01W
Juneau Alaska, USA 58 18N 134 24W
Juniye (Jounieh) Lebanon 33 59N 35 37E
Jurong Singapore 01 18N 103 43E

Kabinda (Cabinda) Angola 05 33S 12 12E
Kabolo, Gunza (Novo Redondo) Angola 11 11S 13 52E
Kafka, Khawr al (Mina al Bakr) (Albakr Terminal) Iraq
29 41N 48 49E
Kaganjuan (Panabo) Mindanao, Philippines
07 18N 125 44E
Kage (Kagefjarden) Sweden 64 50N 21 01E
Kagefjarden (Kage) Sweden 64 50N 21 01E
Kagoshima Kyushu, Japan 31 35N 130 34E
Kahului Maui, Hawaiian Is., USA 20 54N 156 28W
Kaifa (Haifa) Israel 32 49N 35 00E
Kailua Hawaii, Hawaiian Is., USA 19 39N 156 00W
Kainan Honshu, Japan 34 09N 135 12E
Kaiser, Port (Little Pedro) Jamaica 17 52N 77 36W
Kaituma, Port Guyana 07 44N 59N 52W
Kakande, Port (Port Kamsar) R. Nunez, Guinea
10 39N 14 37W
Kake Keku Strait, Alaska, USA 56 59N 133 57W
Kakinada (Cocanada) India 16 56N 82 15E
Kalajoki Finland 64 16N 23 57E
Kalama Columbia R., Washington, USA 46 01N 122 49W
Kalamai (Kalamata) (Calamata) Messiniakos Kolpos,
Greece 37 02N 22 09E
Kalamaki Greece 37 55N 23 01E
Kalamata (Kalamai) (Calamata) Messiniakos Kolpos,
Greece 37 02N 22 09E
Kalaranta Finland 60 29N 26 57E
Kalba, Khawr (Khor Kalba) United Arab Emirates
25 02N 56 22E
Kalianget Madura, Indonesia 07 03S 113 56E
Kali Limenes (Kalon Limenon) Kriti, Greece
34 56N 24 51E
Kalingapatam (Calingapatnam) India 18 19N 84 07E
Kaliningrad (Konigsberg) Kaliningradskiy Zaliv, USSR
54 42N 20 31E
Kalix (Neder Kalix) Sweden 65 52N 23 08E
Kallholmen Sweden 64 41N 21 17E
Kallviken Sweden 64 20N 21 24E
Kalmar Sweden 56 40N 16 21E
Kalon Limenon (Kali Limenes) Kriti, Greece
34 56N 24 51E
Kalundborg Sjaelland, Denmark 55 41N 11 07E
Kamaishi Honshu, Japan 39 16N 141 54E
Kamalo Harbour Molokai, Hawaiian Is., USA
21 03N 156 53W
Kambo Oslofjord, Norway 59 29N 10 42E
Kamenka Mezenskaya Guba, USSR 65 53N 44 05E
Kammash, Abu Libya 33 04N 11 49E
Kampong Saom (Kompong Som) Kampuchea
10 38N 103 30E

Kampong Sebuyau Sarawak, Malaysia 01 31N 110 56E
Kampot Kampuchea 10 34N 104 09E
Kamsar, Port (Port Kakande) R. Nunez, Guinea
10 39N 14 37W
Kanda Suo Nada, Kyushu, Japan 33 48N 131 00E
Kandalaksha Kandalakshaya Guba, Beloye More, USSR
67 08N 32 25E
Kandla Gulf of Kutch, India 23 01N 70 12E
Kangaroo Island South Australia, Australia
35 40S 137 30E
Kankesanturai Sri Lanka 09 49N 80 03E
Kanmon-Ko Kyushu, Japan 33 54N 130 55E
Kanokawa Hiroshima Wan, Seto Naikai, Honshu, Japan
34 11N 132 26E
Kantvik (Porkkala) Finland 60 05N 24 23E
Kaohsiung (Takao) Taiwan 22 37N 120 16E
Kaolack R. Saloum, Senegal 14 09N 16 06W
Kappeln Die Schlie, West Germany 54 40N 09 56E
Kappelshamn Gotland, Sweden 57 51N 18 48E
Karaagac Limani Turkey 36 51N 28 25E
Karabiga (Karabogha) Erdek Korfezi, Marmara Denizi,
Turkey 40 24N 27 20E
Karabogha (Karabiga) Erdek Korfezi, Marmara Denizi,
Turkey 40 24N 27 20E
Karachi Pakistan 24 51N 67 00E
Karamanli Libya 32 54N 13 12E
Karamunting Sabah, Malaysia 05 49N 118 05E
Karatsu Kyushu, Japan 33 27N 129 59E
Karavani Finskiy Zaliv, USSR 59 28N 24 44E
Karavostassi (Gemikonagi) Cyprus 35 08N 32 49E
Kardeljevo (Ploce) Yugoslavia 43 02N 17 26E
Karenko (Hua-lien) Taiwan 24 59N 121 36E
Karikal India 10 55N 79 50E
Karleby, Gamla (Kokkola) Finland 63 50N 23 08E
Karlholm Sweden 60 31N 17 38E
Karlovassi Samos, Greece 37 48N 26 42E
Karlsborg (Carlsborg) Sweden 65 48N 23 16E
Karlsborgverken Sweden 65 48N 23 17E
Karlshagen East Germany 54 08N 13 46E
Karlshamn Sweden 56 11N 14 52E
Karlskrona Sweden 56 11N 15 37E
Karlstad Vanern, Sweden 59 23N 13 30E
Karlsvik (Carlsvik) Sweden 65 36N 22 06E
Karmakuly, Malyy Novaya Zemlaya, USSR
72 23N 52 42E
Karrebaeksminde (Karrebak) Sjaelland, Denmark
55 11N 11 39E
Karrebak (Karrebaeksminde) Sjaelland, Denmark
55 11N 11 39E
Karskar Gavlebukten, Sweden 60 41N 17 16E
Karsnes Skerjafjordhur, Iceland 64 07N 21 56W
Karumba Gulf of Carpentaria, Queensland, Australia
17 29S 140 51E
Karwar India 14 48N 74 06E
Kasennuma Honshu, Japan 38 54N 141 36E
Kashima Honshu, Japan 35 58N 140 38E
Kasim Marine Terminal Irian Jaya, Indonesia
01 18S 131 01E
Kaskinen (Kasko) Finland 62 23N 12 14E
Kasko (Kaskinen) Finland 62 23N 12 14E
Kassr Ahmed Port (Qasr Ahmed Port) (Misurata) Libya
32 22N 15 12E
Kastelli (Kastellion) Kriti, Greece 35 31N 23 38E
Kastellion (Kastelli) Kriti, Greece 35 31N 23 38E
Kastet Gavlebukten, Sweden 60 41N 17 16E
Kastri, De (Alexandrovski) Tartarskiy Proliv, USSR
51 29N 140 47E
Kastrup Sjaelland, Denmark 55 38N 12 39E
Katakolo (Katakolon) (Catacolo) Greece 37 39N 21 20E
Katakolon (Katakolo) (Catacolo) Greece 37 39N 21 20E

Katheeb, Ras al (Ras Kathib) Yemen 14 56N 42 54E
Kathib, Ras (Ras al Katheeb) Yemen 14 56N 42 54E
Kaukas Saimaa Canal, Finland 61 04N 28 13E
Kaukopaa Saimaa Canal, Finland 61 15N 28 52E
Kaur Gambia 13 42N 15 19W
Kavalla (Cavalla) Greece 40 55N 24 25E
Kavieng New Ireland, Papua New Guinea 02 34S 150 49E
Kawaihae Hawaii, Hawaiian Is., USA 20 03N 155 50W
Kawanoe Seto Naikai, Shikoku, Japan 34 01N 133 34E
Kawasaki Tokyo Wan, Honshu, Japan 35 29N 139 43E
Kawthaung (Victoria Point Harbour) Burma
    09 59N 98 33E
Kawhia North Is., New Zealand 38 05S 174 49E
Kayts Sri Lanka 09 42N 79 50E
Keadby R. Trent, England, UK 53 36N 00 43W
Keauhou Bay Hawaii, Hawaiian Is., USA
    19 36N 155 58W
Keeling Islands (Cocos Islands) 12 06S 96 52W
Keelung (Chi-lung) Taiwan 25 08N 121 44E
Keffalinia (Cephalonia) Greece 38 11N 20 28E
Keflavik Iceland 64 01N 22 33W
Keihin Tokyo Wan, Honshu, Japan 35 28N 139 42E
Kelah, Port Algeria 35 06N 02 08W
Kelang, Port (Port Swettenham) Malaya, Malaysia
    03 00N 101 24E
Kemaman Malaya, Malaysia 04 14N 103 27E
Kemano Bay British Columbia, Canada
    53 29N 128 08W
Kembla, Port New South Wales, Australia
    34 28S 150 54E
Kemi Finland 65 44N 24 34E
Kempo Sumbawa, Indonesia 08 35S 118 15E
Kem', Port Onezhskaya Guba, Beloye More, USSR
    64 59N 34 45E
Kenai Cook Inlet, Alaska, USA 60 34N 151 17W
Kenitra (Port Lyautey) Wadi Sebou, Morocco
    34 17N 06 41W
Kenosha Lake Michigan, Wisconsin, USA
    42 35N 87 49W
Keppel Harbour Singapore 01 16N 103 50E
Kerasunda (Giresun) Turkey 40 56N 38 23E
Kerch (Kertch) Krym, USSR 45 21N 36 29E
Keret, Guba Kandalakshskaya Guba, Beloye More, USSR
    66 16N 33 35E
Kerguelen Island 49 30S 69 30E
Kerir, Sidi Egypt 31 06N 29 37E
Kerkira (Corfu) Greece 39 37N 19 56E
Kertch (Kerch) Krym, USSR 45 21N 36 29E
Kerteminde (Kjertminde) Fyn, Denmark 55 27N 10 40E
Kesennuma Honshu, Japan 38 54N 141 36E
Ketapang Sungai Pawan, Kalimantan, Indonesia
    01 50S 109 55E
Ketchikan Clarence Strait, Alaska, USA 55 21N 131 38W
Key West Florida, USA 24 33N 81 48W
Khafji, Ras Al Saudi Arabia 28 25N 48 32E
Khaimah, Ras Al (Ras al Khaymah) United Arab Emirates
    25 48N 56 01E
Khalid, Mina (Sharjah) (Ash Shariqah) United Arab
    Emirates 25 22N 55 24E
Khalkis (Chalkis) Evvoia, Greece 38 27N 23 36E
Khania (Canea) Kriti, Greece 35 32N 24 01E
Kharg Island (Jazireh-ye Khark) Iran 29 14N 50 19E
Khark, Jazireh-Ye (Kharg Island) Iran 29 14N 50 19E
Khawr al Amaya (Mena al Amaya) (Khor al Amaya) Iraq
    29 47N 48 49E
Khawr al Kafka (Khor al Kafka) (Mina al Bakr) (Albakr
    Terminal) Iraq 29 41N 48 49E
Khawr al Mufatta (Khor al Mufatta) Kuwait
    28 39N 48 24E
Khawr az Zubayr (Khor az Zubayr) Iraq 30 24N 47 45E
Khawr Dubai (Khor Dubai) Dubai 25 16N 55 18E

Khawr Fakkan (Khor Fakkan) Gulf of Oman, United Arab
    Emirates 25 21N 56 22E
Khawr Kalba (Khor Kalba) United Arab Emirates
    25 02N 56 22E
Khawr Khuwain (Khor Khuwain) (Mina Saqr) United
    Arab Emirates 25 59N 56 03E
Khawr Musa (Khor Musa) (Khowr-e Musa) Iran
    29 56N 49 04E
Khaymah, Ras al (Ras al Khaimah) United Arab Emirates
    25 48N 56 01E
Khemco Terminal Jazireh-ye Khark, Iran 29 13N 50 20E
Kherson R. Dnepr, USSR 46 38N 32 37E
Khios (Chios) Greece 38 22N 26 08E
Khiri Khan, Prachuap Thailand 11 47N 99 49E
Khobar, Al (Al Khubar) Saudi Arabia 26 17N 50 13E
Kholmsk (Maoka) Sakhalin, USSR 47 02N 142 03E
Khomeini, Bandar (Bandar Shahpour) Iran
    30 27N 49 05E
Khoppa (Hopa) Turkey 41 25N 41 24E
Khor al-Amaya (Khawr al Amaya) (Mina al Amaya) Iraq
    29 47N 48 49E
Khor al Kafka (Khawr al Kafka) (Mina al Bakr)
    (Albakr Terminal) Iraq 29 41N 48 48E
Khor al Mufatta (Khawr al Mufatta) Kuwait
    28 39N 48 24E
Khor az Zubayr (Khawr az Zubayr) Iraq 30 24N 47 45E
Khor Dakliyat Ethiopia 15 38N 39 29E
Khor Dubai (Khawr Dubai) Dubai 25 16N 55 18E
Khor Fakkan (Khawr Fakkan) Gulf of Oman, United Arab
    Emirates 25 21N 56 22E
Khor Kalba (Khawr Kalba) United Arab Emirates
    25 02N 56 22E
Khor Khuwain (Khawr Khuwain) (Mina Saqr) United
    Arab Emirates 25 59N 56 03E
Khorly (Horli) Dzharylgachskiy Zaliv, USSR
    46 04N 33 16E
Khor Musa (Khawr Musa) (Khowr-e Musa) Iran
    29 56N 49 04E
Khorramshahr Shatt al Arab, Iran 30 26N 48 10E
Khowr-e Musa (Khor Musa) (Khawr Musa) Iran
    29 56N 49 04E
Khowr-e Soltani (Bushire) (Bushehr) Iran 28 59N 50 47E
Khrysokhou Bay Cyprus 35 03N 32 27E
Khubar, Al (Al Khobar) Saudi Arabia 26 17N 50 13E
Khulna Bangladesh 22 48N 89 35E
Khuwain, Khawr (Mina Saqr) United Arab Emirates
    25 59N 56 03E
Kidjang Strait (Selat Kijang) Bintan, Indonesia
    00 51N 104 37E
Kiel Kieler Forde, West Germany 54 19N 10 10E
Kieta Bougainville, Papua New Guinea 06 13S 155 39E
Kiire Kyushu, Japan 31 23W 130 34E
Kijang, Selat (Kidjang Strait) Bintan, Indonesia
    00 51N 104 37E
Kikone (Kilwa Masoko) Tanzania 08 57S 39 31E
Kikuma Seto Naikai, Shikoku, Japan 34 02N 132 50E
Kilindini (Mombassa) Kenya 04 04S 39 40E
Kiliya (Chilia) Kiliyskiy Rukav, R. Dunay, USSR
    45 26N 29 17E
Kilkeel Ulster, UK 54 03N 05 59W
Killala Republic of Ireland 54 13N 09 13W
Killingholme R. Humber, England, UK 53 39N 00 13W
Killorglin (Ballykissane) Dingle Bay, Republic of Ireland
    52 07N 09 47W
Kill Van Kull River New Jersey, USA 40 39N 74 07E
Killybegs Donegal Bay, Republic of Ireland
    54 38N 08 26W
Kilmokea Point Port Lairge, Republic of Ireland
    52 17N 06 59W
Kilpatrick, Old R. Clyde, Scotland, UK 55 55N 04 27W

Kilroot Belfast Lough, Ulster, UK 54 43N 05 45W
Kilrush R. Shannon, Republic of Ireland 52 38N 09 29W
Kilwa Kisiwani Tanzania 06 57S 39 32E
Kilwa Kivinje Tanzania 08 45S 39 25E
Kilwa Masoko (Kikone) Tanzania 08 57S 39 31E
Kimbe Stettin Bay, New Britain, Papua New Guinea
05 33S 150 10E
Kimch'aek (Songjin) North Korea 40 40N 129 12E
Kimitsu (Kisarazu) Tokyo-Wan, Honshu, Japan
35 22N 139 54E
Kinabalu, Kota (Jesselton) Sabah, Malaysia
06 00N 116 05E
King Cove Alaska Peninsula, Alaska, USA
55 01N 162 15W
Kings Bay Georgia, USA 30 45N 81 29W
Kingscote Kangaroo Is., South Australia, Australia
35 39S 137 39E
King's Lynn R. Ouse, England, UK 52 46N 00 24E
Kingsnorth R. Medway, England, UK 51 25N 00 36E
Kingsport Minas Basin, Nova Scotia, Canada
45 10N 64 21W
Kingston Lake Ontario, Ontario, Canada 44 14N 76 30W
Kingston Jamacia 17 58N 76 49W
Kingston Hudson R., New York, USA 41 54W 73 59W
Kingston-upon-Hull (Hull) R. Humber, England, UK
53 45N 00 17W
Kingstown St Vincent 13 09N 61 13W
Kinlochleven Loch Linnhe, Scotland, UK 56 43N 04 59W
Kinsale R. Bandon, Republic of Ireland 51 42N 08 31W
Kinuura (Taketoyo) Chita Wan, Honshu, Japan
34 52N 136 57E
Kin Wan (Chim Wan) Okinawa, Nansei Shoto, Japan
26 22N 127 58E
Kipevu Kenya 04 02S 39 38E
Kiritimati (Christmas Is.) Pacific Ocean 01 59N 157 28W
Kirkaldy Firth of Forth, Scotland, UK 56 07N 03 09W
Kirkcudbright Scotland, UK 54 50N 04 03W
Kirkehamn Norway 58 14N 06 31E
Kirkenes Norway 69 44N 30 03E
Kirkwall Mainland, Orkney Is., Scotland, UK
58 59N 02 58W
Kisarazu (Kimitsu) Tokyo Wan, Honshu, Japan
35 22N 139 54E
Kishon Port (Qishon) Israel 32 49N 35 01E
Kisiwani, Kilwa Tanzania 08 57S 39 32E
Kiska Harbour Aleutian Is., Alaska, USA
51 59N 177 34E
Kismayu (Chisimaio) Somalia 00 22S 42 33E
Kissy Sierra Leone 08 29N 13 12W
Kita-Kyushu Kyushu, Japan 33 54N 130 58E
Kitimat Douglas Channel, British Columbia, Canada
53 59N 128 41W
Kiukiang (Chiu-chiang) Ch'ang Chiang, China
29 44N 116 02E
Kivinje, Kilwa Tanzania 08 45S 39 25E
Kjerteminde (Kertmind) Fyn, Denmark 55 27N 10 40E
Kjoge (Koge) Sjaelland, Denmark 55 26W 12 12E
Klagshamn Sweden 55 31N 12 53E
Klaipeda (Memel) USSR 55 43N 21 07E
Klaksvig (Klaksvik) Bordoy, Faero Is., 62 14N 06 35W
Klaksvik (Klaksvig) Bordoy, Faero Is. 62 14N 06 35W
Klawak (Klawock) Prince of Wales Is., Alaska, USA
55 33N 133 06W
Klawock (Klawak) Prince of Wales Is., Alaska, USA
55 33N 133 06W
Kleven Norway 58 01N 07 29E
Kliktsoatli Harbour British Columbia, Canada
52 09N 128 05W
Klintebjerg Odensefjord, Fyn, Denmark 55 29N 10 27E
Klintehamn Gotland, Sweden 57 23N 18 11E

Knysna South Africa 34 04S 23 03E
Kobe Osaka Wan, Honshu, Japan 34 41N 135 12E
Kobenhavn (Copenhagen) Sjaelland, Denmark
55 42N 12 36E
Kocek (Gocek) Turkey 36 45N 28 57E
Kochi Shikoku, Japan 33 33N 133 33E
Kodiak Alaska, USA 57 47N 152 24W
Koeberg Harbour South Africa 33 41S 18 24E
Koepang (Kupang) Timor, Indonesia 10 10S 123 34E
Koge (Kjoge) Sjaelland, Denmark 55 26N 12 12E
Kogo (Cogo) (Puerto Iradier) Rio Muni, Guinea Equatorial
01 05N 09 42E
Kokkola (Gamla Karleby) Finland 63 50N 23 08E
Koko Benin R., Nigeria 06 01N 05 29E
Kokura Kyushu, Japan 33 53N 130 53E
Kolachel (Colachel) India 08 11N 77 14E
Kolak, Sungei Bintan, Indonesia 00 51N 104 37E
Kolberg (Kolobrzeg) Poland 54 11N 15 34E
Kolby Kaas Samso, Denmark 55 48N 10 32E
Kolding Jylland, Denmark 55 29N 09 29E
Kole Terminal Cameroon 04 15N 08 33E
Kolobrzeg (Kolberg) Poland 54 11N 15 34E
Kolohamnen Sweden 56 09N 14 50E
Koltrepynten Karmsundet, Norway 59 19N 05 19E
Komatsushima Shikoku, Japan 34 00N 134 36E
Kompong Som (Kampon Saom) Kampuchea
10 38N 103 30E
Komsomol'sk-na-Amur Amur R., USSR
50 33N 136 58E
Konakri (Conakry) Guinea 09 31N 13 43W
Kongsdal Mariager Fjord, Jylland, Denmark
56 41N 10 04E
Kongshavn Eysturoy, Faero Is. 62 07N 06 44E
Kongsmoen Indre Foldenfjord, Norway 64 53N 12 26E
Konigsberg (Kaliningrad) Kaliningradskiy Zaliv, USSR
54 42N 20 31E
Konstantin Harbour New Guinea, Papua New Guinea
05 29S 145 49E
Koolan Island Western Australia, Australia
16 08S 123 45E
Kopar (Koper) Trscanski Zaliv, Yugoslavia 45 33N 13 44E
Koper (Kopar) Trscanski Zaliv, Yugoslavia 45 33N 13 44E
Kopervik Karmoy, Norway 59 17N 05 18E
Koping Malern, Sweden 59 31N 16 00E
Kopmanholmen Natrafjarden, Sweden 63 11N 18 36E
Kopparverkshamn Sweden 56 01N 12 43E
Korcula Yugoslavia 42 57N 17 08E
Korfa, Zaliv Kamchatka, USSR 60 20N 165 45E
Korinthos (Corinth) Kolpos Korinthiakos, Greece
37 57N 22 56E
Koror Palau, Caroline Is. 07 16N 134 29E
Korsor Sjaelland, Denmark 55 19N 11 08E
Ko Si-Chang Thailand 13 09N 100 49E
Kosseir (El Quseir) Egypt 26 07N 34 17E
Kota Baru Pulo Laut, Indonesia 03 14S 116 13E
Kotabato (Cotabato) Illana Bay, Mindanao, Philippines
07 13N 124 15E
Kota Kinabalu (Jesselton) Sabah, Malaysia
06 00N 116 05E
Kota Raja (Olee Lheue) Sumatera, Indonesia
05 33N 95 19E
Kotka Finland 60 28N 26 57E
Kotonu (Cotonou) Benin 06 21N 02 26E
Kotor (Cattaro) Boka Kotorska, Yugoslavia
42 25N 18 46E
Kouaoua New Caledonia 21 24S 165 50E
Kouilou Congo Republic 04 29S 11 41E
Koutala Serifos, Greece 37 07N 24 28E
Kovda, Guba Kandalakshskaya Guba, Beloye More, USSR
66 44N 32 51E

Koverhar Finland 59 53N 23 13E
Koweit (Kuwait) (Al Kuwayt) Kuwait 29 23N 47 59E
Kowloon Hong Kong 22 18N 114 10E
Kozhikode (Calicut) India 11 15N 75 46E
Kozlu Turkey 41 27N 31 46E
Kpeme Togo 06 12N 01 31E
Kragero Norway 58 52N 09 24E
Kralendijk Bonaire 12 09N 68 17W
Kramfors Sweden 62 56N 17 49E
Krause Lagoon St Croix, Virgin Is. 17 42N 64 46W
Kribi Cameroon 02 56N 09 55E
Krishnapatam India 14 18N 80 05E
Kristiansand (Christiansand) Norway 58 09N 07 59E
Kristiansund (Christiansund) Norway 63 07N 07 44E
Kristiina (Kristinestad) Finland 62 16N 21 23E
Kristiina Oil Harbour Finland 62 16N 21 19E
Kristinehamn Vanern, Sweden 59 18N 14 07E
Kristinestad (Kristiina) Finland 62 16N 21 23E
Kronshtadt Finskiy Zaliv, USSR 59 59N 29 43E
Kronvik Finland 63 06N 21 31E
Kryugera Kamchatka, USSR 56 01N 161 58E
Kuala Baram Sarawak, Malaysia 04 35N 113 59E
Kuala Belait Brunei 04 35N 114 11E
Kuala Dungun Malaya, Malaysia 04 47N 103 26E
Kuala Endau Malaya, Malaysia 02 39N 103 38E
Kuala Pahang Malaya, Malaysia 03 32N 103 28E
Kuala Rompin Malaya, Malaysia 02 49N 103 29E
Kuala Sibuti Sarawak, Malaysia 03 59N 113 44E
Kuala Similajau Sarawak, Malaysia 03 31N 113 18E
Kuala Suai Sarawak, Malaysia 03 48N 113 29E
Kuala Trengganu Malaya, Malaysia 05 20N 103 08E
Kuanakakai Molokai Hawaiian Is USA 21 05N 157 02W
Kuang-Chou Kan (Canton) (Guangzhou) (Kwangchow) Chu Chiang, China 23 07N 113 14E
Kuang-Chou Wan (Kwangchow Wan) China 21 10N 110 25E
Kuantan Malaya, Malaysia 03 58N 103 26E
Kuantan New Port Malaya, Malaysia 03 48N 103 21E
Kubikenborg Sundsvall, Sweden 62 23N 17 21E
Kuching Sarawak, Malaysia 01 34N 110 21E
Kuchinotsu Kyushu, Japan 32 36N 130 11E
Kudamatsu Suo-nada, Honshu, Japan 34 00N 131 52E
Kudat Sabah, Malaysia 06 53N 116 48E
Kulluk (Gulluk) (Golluk) Mandalya Korfezi, Turkey 37 15N 27 38E
Kunak Darvel Bay, Sabah, Malaysia 04 42N 118 15E
Kundzin Riga, Rizhskiy Zaliv, USSR 57 01N 24 06E
Kungsor Malaren, Sweden 59 26N 16 06E
Kunsan (Gunzan) South Korea 35 59N 126 43E
Kuntaur Gambia 13 40N 14 53W
Kuopio Saimaa Canal, Finland 62 52N 27 35E
Kupang (Koepang) Timor, Indonesia 10 10S 123 34E
Kure Seto Naikai, Honshu, Japan 34 14N 132 33E
Kurnell Botany Bay, New South Wales, Australia 34 00S 151 14E
Kusadasi (Scalanova) Turkey 37 52N 27 17E
Kushiro Hokkaido, Japan 42 59N 144 22E
Kuwait (Koweit) (Al Kuwayt) Kuwait 29 23N 47 59E
Kuwayt, Al (Kuwait) (Koweit) Kuwait 29 23N 47 59E
Kvarnholmen Sweden 59 19N 18 09E
Kwa Ibo (Qua Iboe) Nigeria 04 20N 08 00E
Kwangchow (Canton) (Kuang-chou Kan) (Guangzhou) Chu Chiang, China 23 07N 113 14E
Kwangchow Wan (Kuangchow Wan) China 21 10N 110 25E
Kwinana Western Australia, Australia 32 14S 115 46E
Kyle of Lochalsh Scotland, UK 57 17N 05 43W
Kymassi Evvoia, Greece 38 49N 23 28E
Kyndby Sjaelland, Denmark 55 49N 11 53E
Kyrenia (Girne) Cyprus 35 20N 33 20E
Kyrkebyn Vanern, Sweden 59 16N 13 04E

Laajasalo Harbour Finland 60 10N 25 01E
La Arrega Lago de Maracaibo, Venezuela 10 36N 71 36W
Laayoune (El Aaiun) (Aaiun) (Fosbucraa) Morocco 27 04N 13 28W
Labasa (Lambasa) Vanau Levu, Fiji 16 26S 179 23E
L'Abbe, Pont France 47 52N 04 13W
Laboe Kieler Forde, West Germany 54 24N 10 13E
La Brea (Brighton) Trinidad 10 15N 61 38W
Labuan, Pulau Sabah, Malaysia 05 17N 115 15E
Labuantring Bay (Labuhan Tereng) Lombok, Indonesia 08 44S 116 04E
Labuha Bacan, Indonesia 00 38S 127 29E
Labuhan Tereng (Labuantring Bay) Lombok, Indonesia 08 44S 116 04E
La Ceiba Honduras 15 47N 86 52W
La Ceiba Lago de Maracaibo, Venezuela 09 29N 71 05W
Lacertus (La Salina) Lago de Maracaibo, Venezuela 10 22N 71 28W
La Chimba, Caleta Chile 23 34S 70 25W
La Ciotat Golfe du Lion, France 43 11N 05 39E
La Coloma Golfo de Batabano, Cuba 22 17N 83 38W
La Corunna Spain 43 22N 08 24W
La Cruz, Puerto Bahia de Pozuelos, Venezuela 10 13N 64 38W
Ladhiqiya, El (Latakia) (Lattiquie) Syria 35 31N 35 46E
Ladysmith Vancouver Is., British Columbia, Canada 48 59N 123 49W
Lae New Guinea, Papua New Guinea 06 45S 147 01E
Laem Chabang Thailand 13 05N 100 53E
La Ensenada Lago de Maracaibo, Venezuela 10 26N 71 39W
La Estacada Lago de Maracaibo, Venezuela 10 42N 71 32W
Lage Spain 43 13N 09 00W
Lagos Nigeria 06 27N 03 24E
Lagos Portugal 37 06N 08 40W
Lago Sea Berth Aruba 12 26N 69 56W
La Goulette Tunisia 36 49N 10 18E
La Guaira Venezuela 10 36N 66 56W
Laguna de Terminos Golfo de Campeche, Mexico 18 39N 91 50W
Laguna, Porto Brazil 28 31S 48 47W
Lagunillas Lago de Maracaibo, Venezuela 10 07N 71 16W
Lahad Datu Darvel Bay, Sabah, Malaysia 05 02N 118 20E
La Have Nova Scotia, Canada 44 17N 64 21W
La Hondura, Puerto de Tenerife, Canary Is. 28 27N 16 16W
Lairge, Port (Waterford) Republic of Ireland 52 15N 07 07W
Lake Charles Louisiana, USA 30 13N 93 14W
Lakehead Harbour Lake Superior, Ontario, Canada 48 27N 89 13W
La Libertad Ecuador 02 13S 80 55W
La Libertad El Salvador 13 29N 89 20W
La Maddalena Sardegna, Italy 41 13N 09 24E
La Mailleraye La Seine, France 49 29N 00 47E
La Malbaie (Murray Bay) St Lawrence R., Quebec Province, Canada 47 37N 70 09W
La Mar, Catia Venezuela 10 36N 67 02W
La Mar, Savanna Jamaica 18 12N 78 08W
Lambasa (Labasa) Vanau Levu, Fiji 16 26S 179 23E
Lambert, Cape Port Walcott, Western Australia, Australia 20 35S 117 12E
Lambert's Bay South Africa 32 05S 18 18E
Lamberts Point Chesapeake Bay, Virginia, USA 37 53N 76 20W
La Mede, Port de Etang de Berre, France 43 24N 05 07E

Lamitan Basilan, Philippines 06 39N 122 09E
Lampon, Port Luzon, Philippines 14 40N 121 37E
Lamu Kenya 02 17S 40 55E
Lanang Point Mindanao, Philippines 07 07N 125 40E
Lancaster R. Lune, England, UK 54 03N 02 48W
Landana Angola 05 15S 12 10E
Landerneau France 48 27N 04 15W
Landskrona Sweden 55 53N 12 49E
Landugan Basilan, Philippines 06 35N 121 49E
Langeoog Ostfriesischen, West Germany 53 44N 07 30E
Langesund Norway 59 00N 09 43E
Langevag Borgundfjord, Norway 62 26N 06 12E
Langor Samso, Denmark 55 55N 10 38E
Langror Sweden 61 16N 17 11E
Lang Suan Thailand 09 56N 99 09E
La Nouvelle Golfe du Lion, France 43 01N 03 04E
Lanuf, Ras (Sirtica Terminal) Libya 30 31N 18 35E
Laoang Samar, Philippines 12 34N 125 01E
Laoghaire, Dun Republic of Ireland 53 18N 06 07W
Lao-Yao (Lien-yun) China 34 44N 119 27E
La Pallice France 46 10N 01 13W
Lapaluoto Finland 64 40N 24 25E
La Pampilla Peru 11 55S 77 09W
La Paz R. Parana Superior, Argentina 30 46S 59 38W
La Paz Baja California, Mexico 24 10N 110 19W
La Plata R. de la Plata, Argentina 34 52S 57 54W
Lappeenranta Saimaa Canal, Finalnd 61 04N 28 15E
Lapu Lapu Mactan, Philippines 10 19N 123 57E
Larache (El Arish) (El Aaraich) Morocco
  35 12N 06 09W
La Reunion 21 00S 55 20E
Larnaca Cyprus 34 55N 33 39E
Larne Ulster, UK 54 51N 05 48W
La Rochelle La Charente, France 46 09N 01 09W
La Romana Dominican Republic 18 25N 68 57W
Larvik Norway 59 03N 10 03E
La Salina (Lacertus) Lago de Maracaibo, Venezuela
  10 22N 71 28W
La Salineta Grand Canary, Canary Is. 27 59N 15 22W
Las Animas, Chanarel de Chile 26 21S 70 38W
Las Casas Isla Quiriquina, Chile 36 38S 73 03W
La Seyne Toulon, France 43 06N 05 53E
La Skhirra Tunisia 34 18N 10 09E
Las Mareas, Puerto Puerto Rico 17 55N 66 04W
Las Minas, Bahia Panama 09 24N 79 50W
Las Palmas Grand Canary, Canary Is. 28 07N 15 25W
La Spezia Italy 44 06N 09 49E
Las Piedras Venezuela 11 42N 70 13W
Latakia (Lattaquie) (El Ladhiqiya) Syria 35 31N 35 46E
Latchford Manchester Ship Canal, England, UK
  53 23N 02 33W
Latchi (Latzi) Cyprus 35 02N 32 24E
La Trinite Martinique 14 45N 60 58W
Latta, Port Tasmania, Australia 40 50S 145 23E
Lattaquie (Latakia) (El Ladhiqiya) Syria 35 31N 35 46E
Latzi (Latchi) Cyprus 35 02N 32 24E
Laudania, Port Florida, USA 26 04N 80 06W
Launay, Port France 48 13N 04 06W
Launceston R. Tamar, Tasmania, Australia
  41 24S 147 07E
La Union Golfo de Fonseca, El Salvador 13 20N 87 51W
Laurium (Lavrion) (Ergasteria) Greece 37 43N 24 04E
Lauterbach Rugen, East Germany 54 21N 13 30E
Lautoka Viti Levu, Fiji 17 36S 177 27E
Laut, Pulo Indonesia 03 15S 166 15E
Lavaca, Port Texas, USA 28 37N 96 37W
Lavan, Jazireh-Ye (Lavan Is.) Jazireh Sheykh Sho'eyb)
  Iran 26 47N 53 22E
Lavera, Port de Golfe de Marseille, France
  43 23N 05 00E

Lavezares Harbour Samar, Philippines 12 32N 124 20E
Lavrion (Ergasteria) (Laurium) Greece 37 43N 24 04E
Lawes Sarawak, Malaysia 04 51N 115 24E
Lazaret Toulon, France 43 04N 05 55E
Lazaro Cardenas Mexico 17 54N 102 11W
Leba Poland 54 46N 17 33E
Lebak, Port Mindanao, Philippines 06 33N 124 03E
Lebbin (Lubin) Zalew Szczecinski, Poland
  53 52N 14 26E
Lebu Chile 37 36S 73 40W
Le Chateau Ile d'Oleron, France 45 53N 01 11W
Le Croisic France 47 18N 02 31W
Leer Die Ems, West Germany 53 13N 07 27E
Legaspi (Legazpi) Luzon, Philippines 13 09N 123 45E
Legazpi (Legaspi) Luzon, Philippines 13 09N 123 45E
Leghorn (Livorno) Italy 43 33N 10 20E
Legue, Le (St Brieuc) Golfe de St. Malo, France
  48 32N 02 43W
Le Guildo Golfe de St. Malo, France 48 36N 02 13W
Le Havre La Seine, France 49 28N 00 06E
Lehe Die Weser, West Germany 53 34N 08 35E
Leirvik (Lervik) Feddefjord, Norway 58 16N 06 53E
Leirvik Stordoy, Norway 59 47N 05 31E
Leith Firth of Forth, Scotland, UK 55 59N 03 11W
Leith Harbour South Georgia 54 08S 36 41W
Leixoes Portugal 41 11N 08 42W
Le Legue (St Brieuc) Golfe de St. Malo, France
  48 32N 02 43W
Le Marquis La Garonne, France 45 00N 00 33W
Lemvig Jylland, Denmark 56 32N 08 18E
Lenadura Estrecho de Magallanes, Chile 53 12S 70 54W
Lengeh, Bandar e (Lingah) Iran 26 33N 54 53E
Leningrad Finskiy Zaliv, USSR 59 57N 30 19E
Lepee, Tanjung Sulawesi, Indonesia 04 13S 121 33E
Lervik (Leirvik) Feddefjord, Norway 58 16N 06 53E
Lerwick Mainland, Shetland Is., Scotland, UK
  60 09N 01 08W
Les Escoumins St Lawrence R., Quebec Province, Canada
  48 21N 69 23W
Les Falaises Algeria 36 39N 05 25E
Lesina (Hvar) Yugoslavia 43 12N 16 27E
Les Sables d'Olonne France 46 30N 01 48W
L'Etang Harbour Bay of Fundy, New Brunswick, Canada
  45 04N 66 49W
Le Trait La Seine, France 49 29N 00 47E
Le Treport France 50 04N 01 23E
Letterkenny Lough Swilly, Republic of Ireland
  54 57N 07 44W
Levanger Trondheimsfjord, Norway 63 45N 11 18E
Le Verdon La Gironde, France 45 33N 01 05W
Lever Harbour New Georgia, Solomon Is.
  08 01S 157 36E
Levis St Lawrence R., Quebec Province, Canada
  46 49N 71 12W
Levuka Ovalau, Fiji 17 41S 178 51E
Lewisporte Newfoundland, Canada 49 15N 55 03W
Lezardrieux R. de Pontrieux, France 48 47N 03 06W
Lheue, Olee (Kota Raja) Sumatera, Indonesia
  05 33N 95 19E
Lho Seumawe Sumatera, Indonesia 05 08N 97 10E
Libas, Port Samar, Philippines 11 46N 125 27E
Libau (Liepaja) USSR 56 33N 21 01E
Libertad, La Ecuador 02 13S 80 55W
Libertad, La El Salvador 13 29N 89 20W
Libertador, Puerto (Manzanillo) Dominican Republic
  19 43N 71 44W
Liberte, Fort Haiti 19 41N 71 51W
Libog Luzon, Philippines 13 14N 123 47E
Libourne La Dordogne, France 44 55N 00 14W
Libreville R. Gaboon, Gabon 00 23N 09 27E

Licata Sicilia, Italy 37 06N 13 56E
Lidkoping Vanern, Sweden 58 30N 13 11E
Lido Golfo di Venezia, Italy 45 25N 12 26E
Liebigs, Fabrica R. Uruguay, Argentina 32 09S 58 21W
Lien-Yun (Lao-yao) China 34 44N 119 27E
Liepaja (Libau) USSR 56 33N 21 01E
Ligure, Vado Golfo di Genova, Italy 44 16N 08 27E
Liinahamari (Linakhamari) Guba Pechenga, USSR 69 39N 31 23E
Lilla Saltvik Oskarhamn, Sweden 57 18N 16 31E
Lillesand Norway 58 15N 08 23E
Lilljungfrunaredd Sweden 61 15N 17 16E
Limassol Cyprus 34 39N 33 03E
Limay Luzon, Philippines 14 31N 120 37E
Limbang Sarawak, Malaysia 04 48N 115 01E
Limerick (Luimneach) R. Shannon, Republic of Ireland 52 40N 08 37W
Limetree Bay (Hovic) St Croix, Virgin Is. 17 42N 64 45W
Limhamn Sweden 55 35N 12 56E
Limin Sirou Greece 37 26N 24 56E
Limni Mines Cyprus 35 03N 32 27E
Limon, Puerto Costa Rica 09 59N 83 01W
Linakhamari (Liinahamari) Guba Pechenga, USSR 69 39N 31 23E
Lincoln, Port Spencer Gulf, South Australia, Australia 34 43S 136 52E
Linden Arthur Kill R., New Jersey, USA 40 37N 74 12W
Lindholm Alborg, Limfjord, Jylland, Denmark 57 04N 09 52E
Lindi Tanzania 10 00S 39 44E
Lindo Fyn, Denmark 55 28N 10 32E
Lingah (Bandar e Lengah) Iran 26 33N 54 53E
Lingaro Sweden 61 43N 17 15E
Lingga Batang Lupar, Sarawak, Malaysia 01 20N 111 10E
Lingkas Kalimantan, Indonesia 03 17N 117 36E
Lirquen Chile 36 43S 72 59W
Lisahally R. Foyle, Ulster, UK 55 01N 07 17W
Lisas, Point Trinidad 10 22N 61 29W
Lisboa (Lisbon) R. Tejo, Portugal 38 42N 09 08W
Lisbon (Lisboa) R. Tejo, Portugal 38 42N 09 08W
Liscomb Nova Scotia, Canada 45 00N 62 00W
List Sylt, West Germany 55 01N 08 26E
Little Aden South Yemen 12 46N 44 55E
Little Cayman Cayman Is. 19 42N 80 00W
Littlehampton England, UK 50 48N 00 32W
Little Narrows Cape Breton Is., Nova Scotia, Canada 45 59N 60 59W
Little Pedro (Port Kaiser) Jamaica 17 52N 77 36W
Little Placentia Newfoundland, Canada 47 17N 54 00W
Little Wick Terminal Milford Haven, Wales, UK 51 42N 05 05W
Livadhi Serifos, Greece 37 09N 24 31E
Liverpool Nova Scotia, Canada 44 02N 64 42W
Liverpool R. Mersey, England, UK 53 25N 03 00W
Livingston Guatamala 15 49N 88 47W
Livorno (Leghorn) Italy 43 33N 10 20E
Lixourion (Lixuri) Kefallinia, Greece 38 12N 20 27E
Lixuri (Lixourion) Kefallinia, Greece 38 12N 20 27E
Ljusne Sweden 61 12N 17 08E
Llanddulas Wales, UK 53 18N 03 38W
Llanelli Burry Inlet, Wales, UK 51 40N 04 10W
Lloyd, Camp Sondre Stomfjord, Greenland 66 58N 50 57W
Loanda (St Paul de Loanda) (Luanda) Angola 08 47S 13 14E
Loango Congo Republic 04 39S 11 48E
Loay Bohol, Philippines 09 36N 124 01E
Lobito Angola 12 20S 13 35E
Lobitos Peru 04 27S 81 17W
Lobos de Alfueca Peru 06 56S 80 42W

Lobos de Tierra Peru 06 27S 08 51W
Lochaline Sound of Mull, Scotland, UK 56 32N 05 47W
Lochalsh, Kyle of Scotland, UK 57 17N 05 43W
Loch Boisdale South Uist, Scotland, UK 57 09N 07 18W
Loch Ewe Scotland, UK 57 50N 05 35W
Lochmaddy North Uist, Scotland, UK 57 36N 07 11W
Loctudy France 47 50N 04 10W
Locust Point Baltimore, Maryland, USA 39 17N 76 36W
Lodingen Hinnoy, Lofoten, Norway 68 24N 16 01E
Lofudden (Lovudden) Sweden 62 36N 17 56E
Logstor Limsfjord, Jylland, Denmark 56 58N 09 16E
Lohals Langeland, Denmark 55 08N 10 54E
Lokanin Point Luzon, Philippines 14 29N 120 37E
Loksa Finskiy Zaliv, USSR 59 35N 25 43E
Lomas Peru 15 33S 74 52W
Lome Togo 06 09N 01 20E
Lomma Sweden 55 40N 13 04E
Lomonosov Neveskaya Guba, USSR 59 55N 29 46E
London R. Thames, England, UK 51 30N 00 05W
Londonderry R. Foyle, Ulster, UK 55 00N 07 19W
Londond, East South Africa 33 02S 27 55E
London, New Connecticut, USA 41 21N 72 06W
Long Beach San Pedro Bay, California, USA 33 45N 118 11W
Long Harbour Newfoundland, Canada 47 25N 53 49W
Long Island Terminal Westernport, Victoria, Australia 38 18S 145 14E
Long Pond Newfoundland, Canada 47 31N 52 59W
Longview Columbia R., Washington, USA 46 08N 122 57W
Longyearbyen Adventfjorden, Spitsbergen, Svalbard 78 14N 15 38E
Looe England, UK 50 21N 04 27W
L.O.O.P. Terminal (Louisiana Offshore Oil Port Terminal) USA 28 53N 90 01W
Lopez, Cap Gabon 00 38S 08 43E
Lorain Lake Erie, Ohio, USA 41 28N 82 12W
Lorengau Manus, Papua New Guinea 02 01S 147 17E
Loreto, Puerto Baja California, Mexico 26 01N 111 20W
Lorient France 47 45N 03 21W
Los Angeles California, USA 33 44N 118 16W
Los Cocos Pozuelos Bay, Venezuela 10 13N 64 39W
Los Organos Peru 04 10S 81 08W
Lossiemouth Moray Firth, Scotland, UK 57 43N 03 17W
Los Vilos Chile 31 54S 71 32W
Lota Chila 37 06S 73 09W
Loudden Sweden 59 20N 18 08E
Louisburg Cape Breton Is., Nova Scotia, Canada 45 55N 59 58W
Louisiana Offshore Oil Port (L.O.O.P.) USA 28 53N 90 01W
Louis, Mont St. Lawrence R., Quebec Province, Canada 49 14N 65 44W
Louis, Port Mauritius 20 09S 57 30E
Lourenco Marques (Maputo) Mozambique 25 59S 32 36E
Loviisa (Lovisa) Finland 60 27N 26 16E
Lovisa (Loviisa) Finland 60 27N 26 16E
Lovudden (Lofudden) Sweden 62 36N 17 56E
Lowestoft England, UK 52 28N 01 45E
Loyang Singapore 01 23N 103 58E
Luanda (Loanda) (St Paul de Loanda) Angola 08 47S 13 14E
Luarca Spain 43 33N 06 32W
Luba, Butuku (San Carlos) Macias Nguema Biyogo (Fernando Poo Is.) Guinea Equatorial 03 29N 08 36E
Lubeck Die Trave, West Germany 53 52N 10 40E
Lubin (Lebbin) Zalew Szczecinski, Poland 53 52N 14 26E
Lucea Jamaica 18 27N 78 11W
Lucero, Punta Spain 43 23N 03 05W
Lucina Terminal Gabon 03 40S 10 46E

Lucinda Queensland, Australia 18 32S 146 20E
Luderitz Namibia 26 38S 15 08E
Luganville Bay Espiritu Santo, New Hebrides
   15 31S 167 09E
Luga, Reka Finskiy Zaliv, USSR 59 40N 28 18E
Lugnvik Angermanalven, Sweden 62 56N 17 56E
Luimneach (Limerick) R. Shannon, Republic of Ireland
   52 40N 08 37W
Luis Correia (Amarracao) R. Igaracu de Sao Jose, Brazil
   02 53S 41 40W
Lulea Sweden 65 35N 22 08E
Lumut Brunei 04 43N 114 26E
Lumut Malaya, Malaysia 04 14N 100 38E
Luna, Media Golfo de Guacanayabo, Cuba
   20 09N 77 27W
Lunde Angermanalven, Sweden 62 53N 17 53E
Lundevagen Norway 58 05N 06 48E
Lundu Sarawak, Malaysia 01 41N 109 41E
Lunenburg Nova Scotia, Canada 44 23N 64 18W
Lupar, Batang Sarawak, Malaysia 01 31N 110 56E
Lushun (Ryojun) (Port Arthur) China 38 48N 121 15E
Lutak Inlet Lynn Canal, Alaska, USA 59 18N 135 27W
Lutong Sarawak, Malaysia 04 29N 113 57E
Luvia Finland 61 22N 21 35E
Lyautey, Port (Kentira) Wadi Sebou, Morocco
   34 17N 06 41W
Lybster Scotland, UK 58 18N 03 17W
Lyness Hoy, Orkney Is., Scotland, UK 58 50N 03 11W
Lygnor Norway 58 38N 09 09E
Lyngsbaek Jylland, Denmark 56 14N 10 37E
Lynn, King's R. Ouse, England, UK 52 46N 00 24E
Lysaker Oslofjord, Norway 59 55N 10 39E
Lysekil Sweden 58 17N 11 27E
Lyttleton, Port South Is., New Zealand 43 37S 172 43E
Lytton Brisbane R., Queensland, Australia 27 25S 153 09E

Maaloy (Maloy) Vaagsoy, Norway 61 56N 05 07E
Maarianhamina (Mariehamn) Aland, Finland
   60 06N 19 56E
Maarup Samso, Denmark 55 56N 10 33E
Maasin Leyte, Philippines 10 08N 124 50E
Maassluis Nieuwe Waterweg, Netherlands 51 55N 04 15E
Mabou Cape Breton Is., Nova Scotia, Canada
   46 05N 61 24W
Macabi (Nicaragua) Bahia Banes, Cuba 20 54N 75 44W
Macacos, Sao Miguel dos Os Estreitos, Brazil
   01 07S 50 28W
Macao (Macau) 22 12N 113 33E
Macapa R. Amazonas, Brazil 00 02N 51 03W
Macassar (Makassar) (Ujung Pandang) Sulawesi, Indonesia
   05 07S 119 24E
Macau (Macao) 22 12N 113 33E
Macau Brazil 05 06S 36 38W
Macduff Scotland, UK 57 40N 02 30W
Maceio Brazil 09 41S 35 44W
Machilapatnam (Masulipatam) (Masulipatnam) India
   16 10N 81 12E
Macias Nguema Biyogo (Fernando Poo Is.) Guinea
   Equatorial 03 30N 08 40E
Macias, Puerto (Puerto Nuevo) Rio Muni, Guinea
   Equatorial 01 50N 09 44E
Mackay Queensland, Australia 21 06S 149 14E
Mackenzie Demerara R., Guyana 05 59N 58 18W
McNeill, Port Vancouver Is., British Columbia, Canada
   50 36N 127 05W
Macoris, San Pedro de Dominican Republic
   18 26N 69 18W

Macquarie Harbour Tasmania, Australia 42 10S 145 20E
Madang New Guinea, Papua New Guinea
   05 13S 145 48E
Maddalena, La Sardegna, Italy 41 13N 09 24E
Madden Point Strait of Canso, Nova Scotia Canada
   45 36N 61 22W
Madeira Island 32 40N 17 00W
Madeleine, Is. de la (Magdalen Is.) Quebec Province,
   Canada 47 30N 61 50W
Madero, Puerto (Puerto San Benito) Mexico
   14 43N 92 27W
Madison Port Puget Sound, Washington, USA
   47 42N 122 34W
Madras India 13 05N 80 17E
Madre de Deus Brazil 12 45S 38 38W
Madryn, Puerto Golfo Nuevo, Argentina 42 47S 65 02W
Magallanes Mindanao, Philippines 09 01N 125 31E
Magazine Point Mobile, Alabama, USA 30 43N 88 03W
Magdalen Island (Is. de la Madeleine) Quebec Province,
   Canada 47 30N 61 50W
Mago R. Amur, USSR 53 15N 109 06E
Magosa (Famagusta) Cyprus 35 08N 33 58E
Magpetco Neches R., Texas, USA 30 02N 93 59W
Mahajanga (Majunga) Malagasy Republic 15 44S 46 19E
Mahdia Tunisia 35 30N 11 05E
Mahe India 11 42N 75 32E
Mahe Island Seychelle Islands 04 35S 55 30E
Mahon Menorca, Islas Baleares, Spain 39 52N 04 18E
Mahone Nova Scotia, Canada 44 27N 64 22W
Mahshahr, Bandar (Bandar Ma'shur) (Bandar Mashahr)
   Iran 30 28N 49 11E
Mahukona Hawaii, Hawaiian Is., USA 20 11N 155 54W
Mailleraye, La La Seine, France 49 29N 00 47E
Mainaga Cove Luzon, Philippines 13 46N 120 57E
Main Brook Hare Bay, Newfoundland, Canada
   51 11N 56 01W
Maintirano Malagasy Republic 18 03S 44 01E
Maizuru Honshu, Japan 35 27N 135 20E
Majene Sulawesi, Indonesia 03 33S 118 58E
Majunga (Mahajanga) Malagasy Republic 15 44S 46 19E
Majuro Atoll Marshall Is. 07 07N 171 10E
Makar Sarangani Bay, Mindanao, Philippines
   06 06N 125 10E
Makarevsk (Due) Sakhalin, USSR 50 51N 142 05E
Makarov (Shirutoru) Sakhalin, USSR 48 37N 142 47E
Makassar (Macassar) (Ujung Pandang) Sulaweisi, Indonesia
   05 07S 119 24E
Makiyama Wakamatsu Ku, Kyushu, Japan
   33 53N 130 49E
Malabo, Rey (Santa Isabel) Macias Nguema Biyogo
   (Fernando Poo Is.) Guinea Equatorial 03 46N 08 47E
Malacca (Melaka) Malaya, Malaysia 02 12N 102 15E
Malaga Spain 36 44N 04 23W
Malakal Palau, Caroline Is. 07 20N 134 28E
Malalag Davao Gulf, Mindanao, Philippines
   06 37N 125 25E
Malamocco Golfo de Venezia, Italy 45 20N 12 19E
Malangas Mindanao, Philippines 07 37N 123 02E
Malbaie, La (Murray Bay) St. Lawrence R., Quebec
   Province, Canada 47 37N 70 09W
Maldon R. Blackwater, England, UK 51 44N 00 42E
Maldonado Uruguay 34 55S 54 58W
Malhado Brazil 14 47S 39 02W
Malili Sulawesi, Indonesia 02 38S 121 04E
Malindi Kenya 03 14S 40 09E
Malitbog Leyte, Philippines 10 10N 125 01E
Mallaig Scotland, UK 57 00N 05 50W
Malm Beitstadfjord, Norway 64 04N 11 13E
Malmo Sweden 55 37N 13 01E
Malongo Terminal Angola 05 24S 12 12E

Maloy (Maaloy) Vaagsoy, NOrway 61 56N 05 07E

Malpe India 13 21N 74 41E

Malyy Karmakuly Novaya Zemlaya, USSR
72 23N 52 42E

Mambi, Cayo Puerto Tanamo, Cuba 20 40N 75 17W

Mambulao (Jose Panganiban) Luzon, Philippines
14 17N 122 42E

Mamonal Colombia 10 19N 75 31W

Manakara Malagasy Republic 22 08S 48 01E

Manama (Al Manamah) Bahrain 26 14N 50 35E

Manamah, Al (Manama) Bahrain 26 14N 50 35E

Mananjary Malagasy Republic 21 13S 48 21E

Mananara Malagasy Republic 16 09S 49 45E

Manatee, Port Florida, USA 27 30N 82 34W

Manati Cuba 21 22N 76 49W

Manaus, R. Negro, Brazil 03 08S 60 01W

Manchester Manchester Ship Canal, England, UK
53 29N 02 14W

Manchester Ship Canal Eastham Entrance, R. Mersey,
England UK 53 19N 02 57W

Manchioneal Harbour Jamaica 18 02N 76 17W

Mandal Norway 58 02N 07 28E

Mandvi India 22 49N 69 20E

Manfredonia Italy 41 37N 15 56E

Mangalia Bulgaria 43 49N 28 35E

Mangalore India 12 51N 74 49E

Mangalore, New (Panamburu) India 12 56N 74 48E

Mangarin Mindoro, Philippines 12 19N 121 03E

Mangkasa Sulawesi, Indonesia 02 44S 121 04E

Manila Luzon, Philippines 14 36N 120 57E

Manistee Lake Michigan, Michigan, USA 44 15N 86 20W

Mani, Tanjong Sarawak, Malaysia 02 09N 111 21E

Manitowoc Lake Michigan, Wisconsin, USA
44 06N 87 39W

Manokwari Irian Jaya, Indonesia 00 52S 134 04E

Manopla Golfo de Guacanay, Cuba 20 39N 77 52W

Mansa Caleta Chile 40 34S 73 46W

Manta Ecuador 00 56S 80 43W

Mantyluoto Finland 61 36N 21 29E

Manukau Harbour North Is., New Zealand
37 03S 174 30E

Manus Island Admiralty Is., Papua New Guinea
02 00S 147 20E

Manzanillo Golfo de Guacanay, Cuba 20 21N 77 07W

Manzanillo (Puerto Libertador) Dominican Republic
19 43N 71 44W

Manzanillo Mexico 19 04N 104 19W

Maoka (Kholmsk) Sakhalin, USSR 47 02N 142 03E

Maputo (Lourenco Marques) Mozambique 25 59S 32 36E

Maracaibo Venezuela 10 38N 71 36W

Marakeb (Qad el Marakib) Suez Canal, Egypt
29 55N 32 34E

Marakib, Qad el (Marakeb) Suez Canal, Egypt
29 55N 32 34E

Maranhao, Sao Luis de Brazil 02 31S 44 18W

Marans France 46 19N 01 01W

Mara, Palmarejo de Canal de Maracaibo, Venezuela
10 48N 71 40W

Marbella Spain 36 31N 04 53W

Mar, Catia la Venezuela 10 36N 67 02W

March Point Washington, USA 48 30N 122 34W

Marchwood R. Test, England, UK 50 54N 01 26W

Marcus Hook Delaware R., Pennsylvania, USA
39 49N 75 25W

Mar del Plata Argentina 38 03S 57 32W

Mareas, Puerto Las Puerto Rico 17 55N 66 04W

Mare Island San Pablo Bay, California, USA
38 06N 122 15W

Marghera, Porto Golfo di Venezia, Italy 45 27N 12 17E

Margosatubig Mindanao, Philippines 07 35N 123 10E

Mariager Mariager Fjord, Jylland, Denmark
56 39N 09 59E

Marieberg Sweden 63 00N 17 48E

Mariehamn (Maarianhamina) Aland, Finland
60 06N 19 56E

Mariel Cuba 23 00N 82 45W

Mariestad Vanern, Sweden 58 44N 13 50E

Marietta, Port Martin (Port Harvey) (Port Alucroix)
St. Croix, Virgin Is. 17 42N 64 46W

Marigot St Martin 18 04N 63 06W

Marin Martinique 14 29N 60 53W

Marin (Pontevedra) Spain 42 24N 08 42W

Marina di Carrara Italy 44 02N 10 03E

Marina, Rio Elba, Italy 42 49N 10 26E

Marino Point Corcaigh, Republic of Ireland
51 53N 08 20W

Mariupol (Zhdanov) Azovskoye More, USSR
47 05N 37 32E

Mariveles Luzon, Philippines 14 26N 120 29E

Marmagoa (Mormugao) India 15 25N 73 48E

Marmarice (Marmaris) Turkey 36 51N 28 16E

Marmaris (Marmarice) Turkey 36 51N 28 16E

Marmorilik Greenland 71 08N 51 18W

Maroantsetra Malagasy Republic 15 26S 49 44E

Marquette Lake Superior, Michigan, USA 46 33N 87 23W

Marquis, Le La Garonne, France 45 00N 00 33W

Marrero Mississippi R., Louisiana, USA 29 54N 90 06W

Marsa al Hariga (Tobruk Terminal) Libya 32 04N 24 00E

Marsa el Brega Libya 30 25N 19 34E

Marsa el Fallah Egypt 31 21N 27 21E

Marsa el Hamra (El Alamein) Egypt 30 58N 28 51E

Marsala Sicilia, Italy 37 47N 12 26E

Mar, Savanna la Jamaica 18 12N 78 08W

Marsden Point Whangarei, North Is., New Zealand
35 50S 174 30E

Marseille France 43 18N 05 23E

Marshall Liberia 06 08N 10 22W

Marsholm Sweden 57 11N 16 28E

Marstal Aero, Denmark 54 51N 10 32E

Marstrand Sweden 57 53N 11 35E

Marsviken Sweden 58 41N 16 58E

Martinez Carquinez Strait, California, USA
38 02N 122 08W

Martin Marietta, Port (Port Harvey) (Port Alucroix)
St. Croix, Virgin Is. 17 42N 64 46W

Martinniemi Finland 65 13N 25 17E

Martinscica Rijeka, Yugoslavia 45 19N 14 29E

Marugame Seto Naikai, Shikoku, Japan 34 18N 133 47E

Maryborough Mary R., Queensland, Australia
25 31S 152 43E

Marystown Newfoundland, Canada 47 10N 55 09W

Masachapa Nicaragua 11 47N 86 32W

Masan South Korea 35 12N 128 34E

Masao Mindanao, Philippines 09 01N 125 30E

Masbate Masbate Is., Philippines 12 22N 123 37E

Mashahr, Bandar (Bandar Ma'Shur) (Bandar Mahshahr)
Iran 30 28N 49 11E

Mashike Hokkaido, Japan 43 51N 141 31E

Ma'Shur, Bandar (Banda Mahshahr) (Bandar Mashahr)
Iran 30 28N 49 11E

Masinlok Luzon, Philippines 15 32N 119 57E

Masirah, Al Oman 20 10N 58 40E

Maslinica Solta, Yugoslavia 44 24N 16 12E

Masnedoevaerket Sjaelland, Denmark 55 00N 11 53E

Masnedsund Sjaelland, Denmark 55 00N 11 54E

Masoko, Kilwa (Kikone) Tanzania 08 57S 39 31E

Massawa (Massowah) Ethiopia 15 37N 39 28E

Masset Harbour Graham Is., British Columbia, Canada
54 01N 132 09W

Massowah (Massawa) Ethiopia 15 37N 39 28E

Masulipatam (Machilipatnam) (Masulipatnam) India 16 10N 81 12E
Masulipatnam (Masulipatam) (Machilipatnam) India 16 10N 81 12E
Matadi Zaire R., Zaire 05 48S 13 28E
Matagorda Texas, USA 28 41N 95 59W
Matalvi, Port Luzon, Philippines 15 29N 119 56E
Matanzas Cuba 23 04N 81 32W
Mata, Puerto de Cuba 20 18N 74 23W
Matanzas (Puerto de Sidor en Matanzas) R. Orinoco, Venezuela 08 17N 62 51W
Matarani Peru 17 00S 72 06W
Mathew Town Great Inagua Is., Bahamas 20 57N 73 40W
Mati Mindanao. Philippines 06 57N 126 13E
Matola Mozambique 25 58S 32 31E
Matrah (Muttrah) Oman 23 38N 58 34E
Matruh, Mersa Egypt 31 22N 27 14E
Matsunaga Seto Naikai, Honshu, Japan 34 26N 133 15E
Matsuyama Seto Naikai, Shikoku, Japan 33 51N 132 42E
Maulmain (Moulmein) Burma 16 29N 97 38E
Maumere Flores, Indonesia 08 37S 122 13E
Mauganui, Mount North Is., New Zealand 37 38S 176 11E
Maurizio Porto (Imperia) (Oneglia) Italy 43 53N 08 02E
Maya Bandar (Mayabunder) Stewart Sound, Andaman Is., India 12 56N 92 54E
Mayabunder (Maya Bandar) Stewart Sound, Andaman Is., India 12 56N 92 54E
Mayaguez Puerto Rico 18 13N 67 10W
Mayotte Island Republic of the Comoros 12 47S 45 15E
Mayport St Johns R., Florida, USA 30 24N 81 25W
Mayumba Gabon 03 23S 10 38E
Mazagan (El Jadida) (Al Yadida) Morocco 33 14N 08 28W
Mazara del Vallo Sicilia, Italy 37 39N 12 36E
Mazatlan Mexico 23 12N 106 26W
M'Bao Terminal Senegal 14 43N 17 22W
Mede, Port de la Etang de Berre, France 43 24N 05 07E
Media Luna Golfo de Guacanayabo, Cuba 20 09N 77 27W
Medina Mindanao, Philippines 08 55N 125 01E
Medway, Port Nova Scotia, Canada 44 08N 64 36W
Medway River England, UK 51 25N 00 40E
Mega Seto Naikai, Honshu, Japan 34 46N 134 41E
Megara Saronikos Kolpos Greece 38 00N 23 21E
Megri (Fethiye) Turkey 36 39N 29 08E
Mehdia Morocco 34 16N 06 39W
Mejillones del Sur Chile 23 06S 70 28W
Melaka (Malacca) Malaya, Malaysia 02 12N 102 15E
Melbourne Victoria, Australia 37 49S 144 57E
Meldorf West Germany 54 05N 09 03E
Melilla Spanish North Africa 35 18N 02 56W
Melilli Sicilia, Italy 37 07N 15 17E
Mellon, Port Howe Sound, British Columbia, Canada 49 31N 123 29W
Mem Gota Kanal, Sweden 58 29N 16 25E
Memel (Klaipeda) USSR 55 43N 21 07E
Menado Sulawesi, Indonesia 01 31N 124 51E
Meneng, Port (Banyuwanga) Jawa, Indonesia 08 13S 114 23E
Menstad R. Skien, Norway 59 10N 09 39E
Menzel Bourguiba Tunisia 37 10N 09 48E
Merah Batang Igan, Sarawak, Malaysia 02 20N 111 49E
Merak Jawa, Indonesia 05 56S 106 00E
Merauke Irian Jaya, Indonesia 08 29S 140 22E
Merca (Merka) Somalia 01 43S 44 46E
Mergui Burma 12 26N 98 36E
Merikarvia (Brandohamn) Finland 61 50N 21 28E
Merka (Merca) Somalia 01 43S 44 46E
Merlimau, Pulau Singapore 01 17N 103 43E

Mersa Matruh Egypt 31 22N 27 14E
Mers-el-Kebir Algeria 35 44N 00 42W
Mersin Turkey 36 47N 34 38E
Mersing Malaya, Malaysia 02 26N 103 51E
Mesane (Mezen) R. Mezen, USSR 65 51N 44 16E
Messina Sicilia, Italy 38 11N 15 34E
Meteghan Nova Scotia, Canada 44 14N 66 09W
Metensa Bay (Forari) Efate, New Hebrides 07 41S 168 32E
Methil Firth of Forth, Scotland, UK 56 11N 03 00W
Metis St. Lawrence R., Quebec Province. Canada 48 41N 67 58W
Metlakatla (Port Chester) Annette Is., Alaska, USA 55 08N 131 34W
Mexico, Puerto (Coatzacoalcos) Golfo de Campeche, Mexico 18 08N 94 25W
Mezen (Mesane) R. Mezen, USSR 65 51N 44 16E
Miami Florida, USA 25 46N 80 11W
Michipicoten Lake Superior, Ontario, Canada 47 58N 84 53W
Middleburg Walcheren, Netherlands 51 30N 03 37E
Middlefart Fyn, Denmark 55 30N 09 44E
Middlesborough R. Tees, England,UK 54 35N 01 14W
Midland Lake Huron, Ontario, Canada 44 45N 79 53W
Midvaag (Midvagur) Vagar, Faero Is. 62 03N 07 11W
Midvagur (Midvaag) Vagar, Faero Is. 62 03N 07 11W
Midway Islands 28 13N 177 21W
Mifflin, Fort Philadelphia, Delaware R., Pennsylvania, USA 39 52N 75 13W
Miike Kyushu, Japan 33 00N 130 25E
Mikindani Tanzania 10 16S 40 08E
Mikonos Greece 37 27N 25 20E
Milazzo Sicilia, Italy 38 12N 15 15E
Milbuk Mindanao, Philippines 06 09N 124 17E
Milford Milford Haven, Wales, UK 51 43N 05 02W
Milford Haven Wales, UK 51 42N 05 08W
Milford, Port Mulroy Bay, Republic of Ireland 55 06N 07 42W
Milgravis (Muhlgraben) R. Daugava, USSR 57 02N 24 07E
Millom England, UK 54 13N 03 15W
Milner Bay Groote Eylandt, Northern Territory, Australia 13 52S 136 25E
Milos Greece 36 45N 24 30E
Milwaukee Lake Michigan, Wisconsin, USA 43 03N 87 55W
Mina Abd Allah (Mina Abdulla) Kuwait 29 02N 48 10E
Mina Abdulla (Mina Abd Allah) Kuwait 29 02N 48 10E
Mina al Ahmadi (Fahaheel) Kuwait 29 04N 48 09E
Mina al Amaya (Khawr al Amaya) Iraq 29 47N 48 49E
Mina al Bakr (Albakr Terminal) (Khawr al Kafka) Iraq 29 41N 48 49E
Mina al Fahal Oman 23 38N 58 31E
Mina Jebel Ali United Arab Emirates 25 03N 55 01E
Mina Jebel Dhanna (Jabal az Zannah) United Arab Emirates 24 12N 52 34E
Mina Khalid (Sharjah) (Ash Shariqah) United Arab Emirates 25 22N 55 24E
Minamata Kyushu, Japan 32 13N 130 24E
Mina Qaboos (Muscat) Oman 23 37N 58 36E
Mina Rashid United Arab Emirates 25 16N 55 17E
Mina Raysut (Bandar Rayzut) (Salalah) Oman 16 56N 54 01E
Mina Saqr (Khawr Khuwain) United Arab Emirates 25 59N 56 03E
Mina Saud Kuwait 28 45N 48 24E
Minas, Bahia Las Panama 09 24N 79 50W
Mina Sulman Bahrain 26 12N 50 37E
Minatitlan Mexico 17 59N 94 32W
Mina Zayed (Abu Dhabi) (Abu Zabi) United Arab Emirates 24 29N 54 22E

Mineralier, Port Baie du Levrier, Mauritania
20 46N 17 03W
Miragoane Haiti 18 28N 73 05W
Miramar R. Para, Brazil 01 24S 48 30W
Miramichi Bay New Brunswick, Canada 47 05N 65 10W
Miranda, Puerto Lago de Maracaibo, Venezuela
10 46N 71 33W
Miri Sarawak, Malaysia 04 25N 113 59E
Miroline, Poste La Seine, France 49 26N 00 17E
Mirya Bay India 17 00N 73 16E
Misamis (Ozamiz) Mindanao, Philippines 08 09N 123 51E
Mishab, Ras al Saudi Arabia 28 10N 48 41E
Mishima (Iyo-Mishima) Seto Naikai, Shikoku, Japan
33 59N 133 33E
Mispec Point St John, New Brunswick, Canada
45 12N 65 59W
Mistaken Island Western Australia, Australia
20 39S 116 40E
Mistley R. Stour, England, UK 51 57N 01 05E
Misumi Kyushu, Japan 32 37N 130 27E
Misurata (Qasr Ahmed Port) (Kassr Ahmed Port) Libya
32 22N 15 12E
Mitajiri Suo Nada, Honshu, Japan 34 02N 131 35E
Mitilini (Mitylene) Lesvos, Greece 39 06N 26 35E
Mitylene (Mitilini) Lesvos, Greece 39 06N 26 35E
Miyako Honshu, Japan 39 38N 141 58E
Mizushima Seto Naikai, Honshu, Japan 34 29N 133 45E
Mjimwema Bay Tanzania 06 49N 39 22E
Mkoani Pemba Is., Tanzania 05 21S 39 38E
Mo Ranfjord, Norway 66 19N 14 08E
Moa, Puerto Cayo Cuba 20 40N 74 55W
Moanda Terminal Zaire 05 58S 12 08E
Mobile Alabama, USA 30 41N 88 02W
Mobile Terminal Singapore 01 18N 103 41E
Mocambique, Porto de (Porto de Mozambique)
Mozambique 15 02S 40 46E
Mocamedes (Mossamedes) Angola 15 12S 12 09E
Mocha (Mokha) Yemen 13 19N 43 15E
Mocimboa de Praia Mozambique 11 20S 40 22E
Moengo Cottica R., Surinam 05 38N 54 24W
Mogadiscio (Mogadishu) Somalia 02 01N 45 21E
Mogadishu (Mogadiscio) Somalia 02 01N 45 21E
Mogador (Essaouira) Morocco 31 31N 09 47W
Mogpo (Mokp'o) South Korea 34 47N 126 23E
Mohammedia (Fedalah) Morocco 33 45N 07 22W
Moheli Island Republic of the Comoros 12 18S 43 46E
Moin, Bahia Costa Rica 10 01N 83 05W
Mo-i-Rana Ranfjord, Norway 66 19N 14 08E
Moji Kyushu, Japan 33 57N 130 58E
Mokha (Mocha) Yemen 13 19N 43 15E
Mokmer Biak, Indonesia 01 12S 136 09E
Mokp'o (Mogpo) South Korea 34 47N 126 23E
Molate, Point San Pablo Bay, California, USA
37 55N 122 22W
Molde Norway 62 44N 07 09E
Molfetta Italy 41 13N 16 37E
Molle Sweden 56 17N 12 30E
Mollendo Peru 17 01S 72 02W
Molotovsk (Port Severodvinsk) Dvinskaya Guba, Beloye
More, USSR 64 33N 39 49E
Mombasa (Kilindini) Kenya 04 04S 39 40E
Mombetsu Hokkaido, Japan 44 21N 143 22E
Monaco Principality of Monaco 43 44N 07 25E
Monastir Tunisia 35 46N 10 50E
Moncton Peticodiak R., New Brunswick, Canada
46 05N 64 47W
Monfalcone Golfo di Trieste, Italy 45 47N 13 32E
Mongla (Chalna Anchorage) Bangladesh 22 27N 89 34E
Mongstad Norway 60 49N 05 02E
Moni Cyprus 34 42N 33 11E

Monopoli Italy 40 57N 17 18E
Monroe Lake Erie, Michigan, USA 41 55N 83 20W
Monrovia Liberia 06 21N 10 48W
Montague Prince Edward Is., Canada 46 10N 62 38W
Monte Cristi Dominican Republic 19 51N 71 41W
Montego Bay Jamaica 18 29N 77 57W
Monterey California, USA 36 36N 121 53W
Montevideo R. de la Plata, Uruguay 34 54S 56 14W
Montijo R. Tejo, Portugal 38 42N 09 00W
Mont Louis St Lawrence R., Quebec Province, Canada
49 14N 65 44W
Montoir de Bretagne La Loire, France 47 20N 02 08W
Montreal St Lawrence R., Quebec Province, Canada
45 31N 73 32W
Montrose Scotland, UK 56 42N 02 28W
Montt, Puerto Chile 41 29S 72 59W
Montu Saaremaa, USSR 57 57N 22 08E
Monypenny, Fondeadero Golfo de Fonesco, Nicaragua
13 05N 87 33W
Moody, Port Burrard Inlet, British Columbia, Canada
49 17N 122 52W
Moonta Spencer Gulf, South Australia, Australia
34 04S 137 33E
Moorea Tahiti, Society Is. 17 29S 149 48W
Moosonee James Bay, Ontario, Canada 51 18N 80 39W
Mora, Ensenada de (Pilon) Cuba 19 54N 77 18W
Morant, Port (Bowden Wharf) Jamaica 17 53N 76 19W
Mora, Tambo de Peru 13 28S 76 12W
Morazan, Puerto Estero Real, Nicaragua 12 53N 87 16W
Morbylanga Oland, Sweden 56 32N 16 23E
Morehead City North Carolina, USA 34 43N 76 43W
Moresby, Port Papua, Papua New Guinea 09 29S 147 09E
Morien, Port Cape Breton Is., Nova Scotia, Canada
46 09N 59 52W
Morlaix France 48 36N 03 50W
Mormugao (Marmagoa) India 15 25N 73 48E
Morobe Papua, Papua New Guinea 07 45S 147 36E
Morombe Malagasy Republic 21 45S 43 21E
Moron Venezuela 10 32N 68 16W
Morondava Malagasy Republic 20 18S 44 17E
Moroni Grand Comoro, Republic of the Comoros
11 42S 43 14E
Morphou Bay Cyprus 35 08N 32 50E
Morro Redondo Isla Cedros, Mexico 28 03N 115 11W
Mort Bay Sydney, New South Wales, Australia
33 51S 151 11E
Mosjoen Vefsnfjord, Norway 65 51N 13 11E
Moskal'vo Sakhalin, USSR 53 36N 142 33E
Moss Oslofjord, Norway 59 26N 10 40E
Mossamedes (Mocamedes) Angola 15 12S 12 09E
Mossel Bay South Africa 34 11S 22 09E
Mostaganem Algeria 35 56N 00 05E
Mostyn R. Dee, Wales, UK 53 19N 03 16W
Motala Vattern, Sweden 58 33N 15 04E
Motril Spain 36 44N 03 31W
Moudhros (Mudros) Limnos, Greece 39 51N 25 16E
Mouettes, Pointe des Baie du Levrier, Mauritania
20 49N 17 02W
Moulmein (Maulmain) Burma 16 29N 97 38E
Mount Maunganui North Is., New Zealand
37 38S 176 11E
Mourilyan Queensland, Australia 17 36S 146 08E
Mozambique, Porto do (Porto de Mocambique)
Mozambique 15 02S 40 46E
Mtwara Tanzania 10 16N 40 12E
Muara Harbour Brunei 05 01N 115 04E
Mubarek Terminal United Arab Emirates 25 49N 55 11E
Mubarras, Halat al (Mubarras Terminal) Abu Dhabi
24 27N 53 42E
Mubarras Terminal (Halat al Mubarras) Abu Dhabi
24 27N 53 42E

Mucuripe Brazil 03 42S 38 29W
Mudania (Mudanya) Gemlik Korfezi, Marmara Denizi, Turkey 40 23N 28 54E
Mudanya (Mudania) Gemlik Korfezi, Marmara Denizi, Turkey 40 23N 28 54E
Mudros (Moudhros) Limnos, Greece 39 51N 25 16E
Mueo, Port de New Caledonia 21 19S 165 00E
Mufatta, Khawr al (Khor al Mufatta) Kuwait 28 39N 48 24E
Mugia Spain 43 06N 09 13W
Muggia, Baia di Golfo di Trieste, Italy 45 37N 13 46E
Mugho (Mukho) South Korea 37 33N 129 07E
Muhammad Bin Qasim, Port (Bandar Qasim) Phitti Creek, Pakistan 24 46N 67 19E
Muhlgraben (Milgravis) R. Daugava, USSR 57 02N 24 07E
Mukalla South Yemem 14 32N 49 07E
Mukho (Mugho) South Korea 37 33N 129 07E
Mulas, Porto Is. de Vieques, Puerto Rico 18 09N 65 25W
Mulgrave, Port Strait of Canso, Nova Scotia, Canada 45 36N 61 23W
Mullerup Sjaelland, Denmark 55 30N 11 11E
Multedo Golfo di Genova, Italy 44 25N 08 50E
Mundra India 22 46N 69 42E
Munkedal Sweden 58 26N 11 40E
Muntok Bangka, Indonesia 02 04S 105 10E
Murat, Point Exmouth Gulf, Western Australia, Australia 21 49S 114 11E
Murmansk Kol'skiy Zaliv, USSR 68 58N 33 04E
Muroan Hokkaido, Japan 42 20N 140 59E
Muros Spain 42 47N 09 03W
Murray Bay (La Malbaie) St Lawrence R., Quebec Province, Canada 47 37N 70 09W
Murray's Anchorage Bermuda 32 22N 64 43W
Murud Janjira India 18 18N 72 57E
Murwick Flensburger Forde, West Germany 54 49N 09 28E
Musa, Khawr (Khowr-e-Musa) Iran 29 56N 49 04E
Musay'id (Umm Said) Qatar 24 54N 51 34E
Muscat (Mina Qaboos) Oman 23 37N 58 36E
Musel (El Puerto) Concha de Gijon, Spain 43 34N 05 43W
Muskegon Lake Michigan, Michigan, USA 43 15N 86 15W
Mustola Saimaa Canal, Finland 61 04N 28 18E
Mutsamudu Anjouan, Republic of the Comoros 12 10S 44 23E
Mutsure Shima Honshu, Japan 33 58N 130 52E
Muttrah (Matrah) Oman 23 38N 58 34E
Muturi Terminal Irian Jaya, Indonesia 02 12S 133 41E
Myrtle Grove Mississippi R., Louisiana, USA 29 38N 89 57W

Naantali (Nadendal) Finland 60 28N 22 01E
Nacala Mozambique 14 31S 40 39E
Nadendal (Naantali) Finland 60 28N 22 01E
Nador, Port Morocco 35 17N 02 56W
Naersnes Oslofjord, Norway 59 46N 10 31E
Naestved Sjaelland, Denmark 55 14N 11 45E
Naga Cebu, Philippines 10 12N 123 38E
Nagahama Seto Naikai, Shikoku, Japan 33 36N 132 29E
Nagapattinam (Negapatam) India 10 46N 79 51E
Nagasaki Kyushu, Japan 32 44N 129 52E
Nagayeva Tauyskaya Guba, USSR 59 29N 150 31E
Nagoya Ise Wan, Honshu, Japan 35 04N 136 52E
Naha Okinawa, Nansei Shoto, Japan 26 12N 127 40E
Nahr Abu el Flus (Abu Flus) Shatt al Arab, Iraq 30 27N 48 02E

Najin (Rashin) North Korea 42 13N 130 17E
Nakanoseki Suo Nada, Honshu, Japan 34 01N 131 33E
Nakagusuku-Wan (Buckner Bay) Okinawa, Nansei Shoto, Japan 26 15N 127 49E
Nakhodka Zaliv Nakhodka, USSR 42 48N 132 53E
Nakskov Lolland, Denmark 54 50N 11 08E
Nampo (Chinnampo) (Chonsu Man) Taedong Gang, North Korea 38 44N 125 24E
Namsos Namsenfjorden, Norway 64 28N 11 30E
Namu Fitzhugh Sound, British Columbia, Canada 51 51N 127 51W
Nanaimo Vancouver Is., British Columbia, Canada 49 10N 123 56W
Nanao Honshu, Japan 37 03N 136 59E
Nan-Ching (Nanking) Ch'ang Chiang, China 32 05N 118 43E
Nanchital Golfo de Campeche, Mexico 18 03N 94 26W
Nancowry Nicobar Is., India 08 02N 93 33E
Nanisivik Baffin Is., North West Territory, Canada 73 04N 84 34W
Nanking (Nan-ching) Ch'ang Chiang, China 32 05N 118 43E
Nanortalik Greenland 60 09N 45 14W
Nantes La Loire, France 47 13N 01 34W
Nantucket Massachusetts, USA 41 17N 70 05W
Naoetsu Honshu, Japan 37 11N 138 15E
Nao Shima Seto Naikai, Japan 34 28N 133·59E
Napier North Is., New Zealand 39 29S 176 55E
Naples (Naploi) Italy 40 50N 14 17E
Napoli (Naples) Golfo di Napoli, Italy 40 50N 14 17E
Napoopoo Hawaii, Hawaiian Is., USA 19 28N 155 56W
Narian Mar (Nar'yan-Mar) Pechora R., USSR 67 38N 53 02E
Narrows, Little Cape Breton Is., Nova Scotia, Canada 45 59N 60 59W
Narrsaq Greenland 60 55N 46 04W
Narssarssuak Greenland 61 09N 45 26W
Narva Finskiy Zaliv, USSR 59 23N 28 12E
Narvik Ofotfjord, Norway 68 26N 17 25E
Nar'yan-Mar (Narian Mar) Pechora R., USSR 67 38N 53 02E
Na Savu Savu Vanau Levu, Fiji 16 46S 179 19E
Nasipit Mindanao, Philippines 08 59N 125 20E
Nassau New Providence, Bahamas 25 05N 77 21W
Nasugbu (Wawa) Luzon, Philippines 14 05N 120 37E
Nataji Subhas Docks Hugli R., India 22 33N 88 17E
Natal Brazil 05 47S 35 12W
Natales, Puerto Chile 51 44S 72 32W
Nauplia (Navplion) Argolikos Kolpos, Greece 37 34N 22 49E
Nauru Island 00 31S 165 54E
Navlakhi India 22 58N 70 27E
Navplion (Nauplia) Argolikos Kolpos, Greece 37 34N 22 49E
Nawiliwili Kauai, Hawaiian Is., USA 21 58N 159 21W
Naze Ko Anami O Shima, Nansei Shoto, Japan 28 23N 129 30E
Neah Bay Washington, USA 48 22N 124 36W
Neap House R. Trent, England, UK 53 37N 00 41W
Neath Wales, UK 51 39N 03 49W
Neches, Port Neches R., Texas, USA 29 59N 93 56W
Necochea Argentina 38 34S 58 43W
Neder Kalix (Kalix) Sweden 65 52N 23 08E
Neendakara (Nindakara) India 08 57N 76 33E
Negapatam (Nagapittinam) India 10 46N 79 51E
Negishi Tokyo Wan, Honshu, Japan 35 24N 139 39E
Negro, Cabo Estrecho de Magallanes, Chile 52 58S 70 48W
Neguac Miramichi R., New Brunswick, Canada 47 15N 65 04W

Neiafu Vavau, Tonga Is., 18 39S 173 59W
Nekso (Nexo) Bornholm, Denmark 55 04N 15 09E
Nelson Miramichi R., New Brunswick, Canada
46 59N 65 33W
Nelson South Is., New Zealand 41 16S 173 16E
Nemours (Ghazaouet) Algeria 35 06N 01 52W
Nemrut Limani Candarli Korfezi, Turkey 38 46N 26 56E
Nemuro Hokkaido, Japan 43 20N 145 33E
Nenseth R. Skien, Norway 59 10N 09 39E
Nesebur Burgaski Zaliv, Bulgaria 42 40N 27 44E
Neskaupstadur Iceland 65 09N 13 41W
Neufahrwasser (Nowy Port Zatoka Gdanska, Poland
54 24N 18 40E
Neuhaus Die Oste, West Germany 53 48N 09 02E
Neustadt Lubecker Bucht, West Germany 54 07N 10 49E
Nevelsk (Honto) Sakhalin, USSR 46 40N 141 51W
Neville, Port Johnstone Strait, British Columbia, Canada
50 29N 126 05W
New Amsterdam Berbice R., Guyana 06 16N 57 31W
Newark New Jersey, USA 40 44N 74 10W
Newark, Port New Jersey, USA 40 42N 74 08W
New Bedford Buzzards Bay, Massachusetts, USA
41 38N 70 55W
Newburgh R. Tay, Scotland, UK 56 21N 03 15W
Newburgh R. Ythan, Scotland, UK 57 19N 02 00W
Newburgh Hudson R., New York, USA 41 30N 74 05W
Newcastle New South Wales, Australia 32 56S 151 46E
Newcastle Miramichi R., New Brunswick, Canada
47 00N 65 33W
Newcastle R. Tyne, England, UK 54 58N 01 36W
Newchwang (Yingk'ou) Liao Ho, China 40 41N 122 14E
New Glasgow Nova Scotia, Canada 45 36N 62 38W
Newhaven England, UK 50 47N 00 04E
New Haven Connecticut, USA 41 18N 72 55W
New London Connecticut, USA 41 21N 72 06W
Newlyn Mounts Bay, England, UK 50 06N 05 33W
New Mangalore (Panamburu) India 12 56N 74 48E
New Nickerie (Nieuw Nickerie) R. Nickerie, Surinam
05 57N 56 59W
New Orleans Mississippi R., Louisana, USA
29 56N 90 05W
Newport Isle of Wight, England, UK 50 42N 01 17W
Newport Bristol Channel, Wales, UK 51 34N 02 59W
Newport Oregon, USA 44 38N 124 03W
Newport Narragansett Bay, Rhode Is., USA
41 29N 71 19W
Newport News Virginia, USA 36 58N 76 26W
New Quay Cardigan Bay, Wales, UK 52 13N 04 21W
New Richmond Baie des Chaleurs, Quebec Province,
Canada 48 08N 65 52W
New Ross R. Barrow, Republic of Ireland 52 24N 06 57W
Newry Carlingford Lough, Ulster, UK 54 10N 06 20W
New Tuticorin India 08 42N 78 20E
New Washington Panay, Philippines 11 40N 122 26E
New Westminster British Columbia, Canada
49 12N 122 55W
New York New York, USA 40 40N 74 00W
Nexo (Nekso) Bornholm, Denmark 55 04N 15 09E
Nha Be Song Sai Gon, Vietnam 10 42N 106 45E
Nha Trang Vietnam 12 14N 109 13E
Niah Sarawak, Malaysia 03 58N 113 42E
Nibung, Teluk Sungai Asahan, Sumatera, Indonesia
03 00N 99 48E
Nicaragua (Macabi) Bahia Banes, Cuba 20 54N 75 44W
Nicaro Bahia Levisa, Cuba 20 43N 75 33W
Nice France 43 42N 07 17E
Nickerie, Nieuw (New Nickerie) Nickerie R., Surinam
05 57N 56 59W
Niedersachsenbrucke Die Innenjade, West Germany
53 35N 08 09E

Nieuport Belgium 51 09N 02 44E
Nieuw Amsterdam Surinam 05 53N 55 05W
Nieuwediep Netherlands 52 58N 04 47E
Nieuw Nickerie (New Nickerie) Nickerie R., Surinam
05 57N 56 59W
Nieuwe Waterweg Netherlands 51 59N 04 08E
Nieva, San Juan de Spain 43 35N 05 56W
Nigg Bay Cromarty Firth, Scotland, UK 57 42N 04 02W
Niigata Seto Naikai, Shikoku, Japan 33 59N 133 16E
Niihama Seto Naikai, Shikoku, Japan 33 59N 133 16E
Nikiski Cook Inlet, Alaska, USA 60 44N 151 24W
Nikolaistad (Vaasa) (Vasa) Finland 36 06N 21 36E
Nikolayev Yuzhnyy Bug, USSR 46 58N 31 59E
Nikolayev Amur R., USSR 53 08N 140 43E
Nima Nima Cuba 19 57N 75 59W
Nindakara (Neendakara) India 08 57N 76 33E
Ning-Po (Yin-Hsien) Yung Chiang, China
29 53N 121 33E
Ninilchik Cook Inlet, Alaska, USA 60 03N 151 43W
Nipa, Suba Olutanga, Philippines 07 18N 122 51E
Niquero Golfo de Guacanayabo, Cuba 20 03N 77 35W
Nishihara Okinawa, Nansei Shoto, Japan 26 14N 127 50E
Nishi Ku Seto Naikai, Honshu, Japan 34 46N 134 36E
Nishinomiya Osaka Wan, Honshu, Japan 34 43N 135 20E
Niteroi Brazil 22 53S 43 07W
Niue Island 19 02S 169 55W
Njardhvik Iceland 65 34N 13 54W
Noire, Pointe St Lawrence R., Quebec Province Canada
50 10N 66 28W
Noire, Pointe Congo Republic 04 47S 11 50E
Noirmoitier, Port de R. Loire, France 47 01N 02 15W
Nolloth, Port South Africa 29 15S 16 52E
Nombre de Dios, Bahia Panama 09 36N 79 29W
Nome Alaska, USA 64 31N 165 25W
Nonopapa Niihau, Hawaiian Is., USA 21 52N 160 14W
Nordby Jylland, Denmark 55 27N 08 24E
Norddeich Ostfriesischen West Germany 53 38N 07 09E
Nordenham Die Weser, West Germany 53 30N 08 29E
Norderney Ostfriesischen, West Germany 53 42N 07 11E
Nordfjordeid Eidsfjord, Norway 61 54N 06 00E
Nordfjordhur Iceland 65 09N 13 39W
Normaling Sweden 63 34N 19 29E
Norfolk Elizabeth R., Virginia, USA 36 52N 76 19W
Noro New Georgia, Solomon Is., 08 13S 157 12E
Norra Nyhamn Sundsvall, Sweden 62 20N 17 25E
Norrbyskar Orefjarden, Sweden 63 33N 19 53E
Norresundby Limfjord, Jylland, Denmark 57 04N 09 55E
Norrfjarden Sweden 63 52N 20 45E
Norrkoping Sweden 58 36N 16 12E
Norrsundet Sweden 60 56N 17 09E
Norrtalje Sweden 59 46N 18 41E
North Bend Coos Bay, Oregon, USA 43 24N 124 13W
North Charleston South Carolina, USA 32 53N 79 58W
Northfleet Hope R. Thames, England, UK 51 27N 00 20E
North Shields R. Tyne, England, UK 55 00N 01 27W
North Star Bugt Baffin Bay, Greenland 76 33N 68 52W
North Sunderland (Seahouses) England, UK
55 35N 01 39W
North Sydney Cape Breton Is., Nova Scotia, Canada
46 12N 60 14W
Northville Long Is., New York, USA 41 00N 72 39W
North Weymouth Massachusetts, USA 42 15N 70 55W
Northwich R. Weaver, England, UK 53 16N 02 30W
Norwich R. Yare, England, UK 52 38N 01 19E
Noshiro Honshu, Japan 40 13N 140 00E
Nossi Be (Nosy Be) Malagasy Republic 13 12S 48 11E
Nosy Be (Nossi Be) Malagasy Republic, 13 12S 48 11E
Notholmen Sweden 63 34N 19 29E
Nouadhibou (Port Etienne) Mauritania 20 54N 17 03W
Nouakchott Mauritania 18 02N 16 02W

Noumea New Caledonia 22 16S 166 26E
Nouvelle, La Golfe du Lion, France 43 01N 03 04E
Nova Vicosa R. Peruipe, Brazil 17 54S 39 21W
Novitskogo Zaliv Nakhodka, USSR 42 46N 132 53E
Novo, Porto Benin 06 27N 02 38E
Novo, Porto Santo Antao, Republic of Cape Verde
17 01N 23 04W
Novo Redondo (Gunza Kabolo) Angolo 11 11S 13 52E
Novorossiysk Chernoye More, USSR 44 43N 37 47E
Novyy Port Obskaya Guba, USSR 67 38N 72 49E
Nowruz Terminal (Ras Bahregan) Iran 29 43N 50 10E
Nowy Port (Neufahrwasser) Zatoka Gdanska, Poland
54 24N 18 40E
Noya, Villa De Spain 42 47N 08 53W
Noyo California, USA 39 25N 123 49W
Nueva Gerona Isla de Pinos, Cuba 21 54N 82 47W
Nueva Palmira R. Uruguay, Uruguay 33 53S 58 25W
Nueva, Puerto (Puerto Macias) Rio Muni, Guinea
Equatorial 01 50N 09 44E
Nuevitas Cuba 21 34N 77 15W
Nuku'alofa Tongatapu, Tonga Is., 21 09S 175 13W
Nuottasaari Finland 65 00N 25 26E
Ny-Alesund Kongsfjorden, Spitzbergen, Svalbard
78 56N 11 57E
Nyborg Fyn, Denmark 55 19N 10 48E
Nyhamn, Norra Sundsvall, Sweden 62 20N 17 25E
Nyhamn, Sodra Sundsvall, Sweden 62 19N 17 24E
Nykobing Falster, Denmark 54 46N 11 52E
Nykobing Mors, Denmark 56 48N 08 52E
Nykobing Sjaelland, Denmark 55 55N 11 41E
Nykoping Sweden 58 45N 17 01E
Nyland Angermanalven, Sweden 63 00N 17 46E
Nynashamn Sweden 58 54N 17 58E
Nystad (Uusikaupunki) Finland 60 48N 21 24E
Nysted Lolland, Denmark 54 39N 11 44E
N'Zeto (Ambrizete) Angola 07 15S 12 52E

Oakham Ness R. Medway, England, UK 51 25N 00 39E
Oakland San Francisco Bay, California, USA
37 49N 122 19W
Oamaru South Is., New Zealand 45 07S 170 59E
Oaxen Sweden 58 58N 17 43E
Oban Scotland, UK 56 25N 05 28W
Obbola Sweden 63 42N 20 19E
Obidos R. Amazonas, Brazil 01 52S 55 31W
Obligado, Puerto R. Parana, Argentina 33 36S 59 49W
Ocean Cay Bahamas 25 25N 79 12W
Ocean Falls Cousins Inlet, British Columbia, Canada
52 21N 127 42W
Ocean Island (Banaba) 00 54S 169 33E
Ochakov Dneprovskiy Liman, USSR 46 37N 31 33E
Ochio Rios Bay Jamaica 18 25N 77 08W
Odda Hardangerfjord, Norway 60 04N 06 33E
Odderoya Kristiansand, Norway 58 08N 08 01E
Odense Fyn, Denmark 55 25N 10 24E
Odessa (Odesskiy Port) USSR 46 29N 30 46E
Odesskiy Port (Odessa) USSR 46 29N 30 46E
Ofunato Honshu, Japan 39 04N 141 44E
Ogdensburg St Lawrence Seaway, New York, USA
44 42N 75 29W
Oita Seto Naikai, Kyushu, Japan 33 15N 131 36E
Okha, Port India 22 28N 69 05E
Okhotsk Okhotskoye More, USSR 59 22N 143 12E
Okrika Bonny R., Nigeria 04 43N 07 04E
Oktyabr'skiy Kamchatka, USSR 52 39N 156 13E
Ola Okhotskoye More, USSR 59 34N 151 18E
Olafsfjordhur Eyjafjordhur, Iceland 66 04N 18 39W
Olbia Sardegna, Italy 40 55N 09 31E
Oldenburg Die Weser, West Germany 53 08N 08 13E

Old Kilpatrick R. Clyde, Scotland, UK 55 55N 04 27W
Olee Lheue (Kota Raja) Sumatera, Indonesia
05 33N 95 19E
Oleum San Pablo Bay, California, USA 38 03N 122 16W
Olhao Portugal 37 01N 07 50W
Olivares, Caleta Golfo de San Jorge, Argentina
45 47S 67 23W
Olivia, Caleta Golfo de San Jorge, Argentina
46 26S 67 30W
Olivos, Puerto de Canal Costanero, Argentina
34 31S 58 29W
Olongapo, Port Subic Bay, Luzon, Philippines
14 49N 120 17E
Olonne, Les Sables d' France 46 30N 01 48W
Olutanga Island Philippines 07 17N 122 51E
Olympia Puget Sound, Washington, USA
47 03N 122 53W
Omisalj Rijecki Zaliv, Yugoslavia 45 13N 14 33E
Omishima Seto Naikai, Japan 34 16N 133 00E
Omoa Golfo de Honduras, Honduras 15 42N 88 04W
Omuta Ariake-Kai, Kyushu, Japan 33 01N 130 25E
Onahama Honshu, Japan 36 56N 140 55E
Onega Onezhskaya Guba, Beloye More, USSR
63 54N 38 06E
Oneglia (Imperia) (Porto Maurizio) Italy 43 53N 08 02E
Onehunga North Is., New Zealand 36 56S 174 47E
Onodo Suo Nada, Honshu, Japan 33 58N 131 11E
Onomichi Seto Naikai, Honshu, Japan 34 24N 133 12E
Onslow Western Australia, Australia 21 38S 115 07E
Onton Spain 43 22N 03 11W
Oostende (Ostend) Belgium 51 14N 02 55E
O Porto (Porto) R. Douro, Portugal 41 09N 08 37W
Opotiki North Is., New Zealand 37 59S 177 17E
Opua North Is., New Zealand 35 19S 174 07E
Oracabessa Bay Jamacia 18 25N 76 58W
Oran Algeria 35 43N 00 39W
Orange Sabine R., Texas, USA 30 05N 93 44W
Orange Town (Oranjestad) St. Eustatius 17 29N 62 59W
Oranjestad Aruba 12 31N 70 02W
Oranjestad (Orange Town) St. Eustatius 17 29N 62 59W
Ordaz, Puerto R. Orinoco, Venezuela 08 21N 62 43W
Ordu Turkey 41 00N 37 53E
Oreby Lolland, Denmark 54 50N 11 36E
Oregrund Sweden 60 20N 18 26E
Orehoved Falster, Denmark 54 58N 11 51E
Organos, Los Peru 04 10S 81 08W
Orient, Point San Pablo Bay, California, USA
37 57N 122 26W
Oristano Sardegna Italy 39 52N 08 33E
Oritkari Finland 65 00N 25 26E
Orjaku Kassaar, USSR 58 47N 22 48E
Orleans, New Mississippi R., Louisiana, USA
29 56N 90 05W
Ormos Dhrapetsonas (Drapetzona) Greece
37 56N 23 37E
Ormos Soudhas (Suda Bay) Kriti, Greece 35 29N 24 04E
Ormos Foron Piraievs, Greece 37 56N 23 37E
Ornskoldsvik Sweden 63 17N 18 42E
Oro Bay Papua, Papua New Guinea 08 53S 148 29E
Oro, Cagayan de Mindanao, Philippines 08 31N 124 39E
Orrskarhamnen Sweden 61 13N 17 10E
Orth Fehmarn, West Germany 54 27N 11 03E
Ortona Italy 42 21N 14 25E
Ortviken Sundsvall, Sweden 62 24N 17 22E
Orviken Sweden 64 41N 21 18E
Osaka Honshu, Japan 34 39N 135 27E
Oshawa Lake Ontario, Ontario, Canada 43 52N 78 51W
Oskarshamn Sweden 57 16N 16 27E
Oslo Oslofjord, Norway 59 54N 10 45E
Osten Die Oste, West Germany 53 42N 09 12E

Ostend (Oostende) Belgium 51 14N 02 55E
Ostermoor Nord-Ostsee Kanal, West Germany
53 55N 09 12E
Ostrand Sundsvall, Sweden 62 29N 17 20E
Ostrica Mississippi R., Louisiana, USA 29 22N 89 32W
Oswego Lake Ontario, New York, USA 43 28N 76 30W
Otago Harbour South Is., New Zealand 45 46S 170 44E
Otaru Hokkaido, Japan 43 12N 141 01E
Otterbacken Vanern, Sweden 58 57N 14 03E
Otterham Quay R. Medway, England, UK 51 23N 00 38E
Ouistreham Baie de la Seine, France 49 17N 00 15W
Oulu (Uleaborg) Finland 65 01N 25 28E
Ovendo (Owendo) R. Gaboon, Gabon 00 17N 09 31E
Overton, Camp Mindanao, Philippines 08 12N 124 13E
Owase Honshu, Japan 34 04N 136 12E
Owendo (Ovendo) R. Gaboon, Gabon 00 17N 09 31E
Owen Sound Georgia Bay, Lake Huron, Ontario, Canada
44 35N 80 56W
Oxelosund Sweden 58 40N 17 06E
Oye Fedafjord, Norway 58 16N 06 54E
Ozamiz (Misamis) Mindanao, Philippines 08 09N 123 51E
Ozol Carquinez Strait, California, USA 38 02N 122 10W

Pacasmayo Peru 07 24S 79 35W
Pacocha Peru 17 38S 71 22W
Padang (Teluk Bajur) Sumatera, Indonesia
00 59S 100 23E
Padre, Puerto Cuba 21 12N 76 36W
Padstow R. Camel, England, UK 50 32N 04 56W
Pagadian Illana Bay, Mindanao, Philippines
07 49N 123 26E
Pagar, Tanjong Singapore 01 16N 103 51E
Pago Pago Tutuila, Samoa 14 17S 170 41W
Pahang, Kuala Malaya, Malaysia 03 32N 103 28E
Paimboeuf La Loire, France 47 17N 02 02W
Paimpol France 48 47N 03 02W
Paita Peru 05 05S 81 07W
Paix, Port de Haiti 19 57N 72 52W
Pajaritos Golfo de Campeche, Mexico 18 07N 94 24W
Pakhi Terminal Saronikos Kolpos, Greece 37 58N 23 23E
Pakhoi (Pei-hai) Gulf of Tonkin, China 21 29N 109 06E
Pakning Sungei Sumatera, Indonesia, 01 21N 102 10E
Palamos Spain 41 50N 03 08E
Palau Islands Caroline Is. 07 16N 134 28E
Paldski (Balticport) Finskiy Zaliv, USSR 59 21N 24 04E
Palembang Sungei Palembang, Sumatera, Indonesia
03 00S 104 45E
Palenque, Puerto Dominican Republic 18 14N 70 09W
Palenque Terminal, Punta Dominican Republic
18 13N 70 11W
Palermo Sicilia, Italy 38 07N 13 21E
Palito, El Venezuela 10 28N 68 06W
Pallice, La France 46 10N 01 14W
Palma Mallorca, Islas Baleares, Spain 39 34N 02 38E
Palmarejo De Mara Canal de Maracaibo, Venezuela
10 48N 71 40W
Palmas, Cape Liberia 04 22N 07 44W
Palmas del sur, Punta de Lago de Maracaibo, Venezuela
10 24N 71 34W
Palmas, Las Grand Canary, Canary Is. 28 07N 15 25W
Palm Beach Florida, USA 26 46N 80 03W
Palmira, Nueva R. Uruguay, Uruguay 33 53S 58 25W
Palmyra Island 05 52N 162 06W
Palnackie R. Urr. Scotland, UK 54 54N 03 50W
Palo Alto Cuba 21 36N 78 58W
Paloh, Sungei Kalimantan, Indonesia 01 45N 109 17E
Palompon, Port Leyte, Philippines 11 02N 124 23E
Palua R. Orinoco, Venezuela 08 21N 62 42W

Palupandam Negros, Philippines 10 31N 122 48E
Pamatacual Bahia Pertigalete, Venezuela 10 15N 64 34W
Pamatacualito Bahia Pertigalete, Venezuela
10 15N 64 35W
Pamintayan Point Mindanao, Philippines 07 40N 123 05E
Pampatar Isla de Margarita, Venezuela 11 00N 63 48W
Pampilla, La Peru 11 55S 77 09W
Pampushamnen Braviken, Sweden 58 37N 16 15E
Panabo (Kaganjuan) Mindanao, Philippines
07 18N 125 44E
Panabutan Mindanao, Philippines 07 35N 122 07E
Panama City St Andrew's Bay, Florida, USA
30 09N 85 40W
Panamburu (New Mangalore) India 12 56N 74 48E
Panarukan Jawa, Indonesia 07 41S 113 57E
Pandang, Ujung (Macassar) (Makassar) Sulawesi,
Indonesia 05 07S 119 24E
Pandan, Tanjung Belitung, Indonesia 02 44S 107 38E
Panderma (Bandirma Marmara Denizi, Turkey
40 21N 27 59E
Pangai Island Tonga Is. 19 48S 174 21W
Pangani Tanzania 05 24S 38 59E
Pangasahan River Basilan, Philippines 06 37N 121 48E
Pangkalan Susu Teluk Aru, Sumatera, Indonesia
04 07N 98 13E
Pangkal Balam Bangka, Indonesia 02 06S 106 08E
Panjang Sumatera, Indonesia 05 28S 105 19E
Pansio Oil Harbour Finland 60 27N 20 11E
Papeete Tahiti, Society Is., 17 33S 149 34W
Papenburg Die Ems, West Germany 53 06N 07 23E
Paphos Cyprus 34 45N 32 25E
Par England, UK 50 21N 04 42W
Para (Belem) R. Para, Brazil 01 27S 48 30W
Parachuap Khiri Khan Thailand 11 47N 99 49E
Paradip Mahanadi R., India 20 16N 86 41E
Paraguana, Puerto de Venezuela 11 40N 70 13W
Parainen (Pargas) Finland 60 18N 22 18E
Paramaribo Surinam R., Surinam 05 50N 55 09W
Parana R. Parana Medio, Argentina 31 43S 60 31W
Paranagua Brazil 25 30S 48 31W
Paranam Surinam R., Surinam 05 36N 55 05W
Parang Illana Bay, Mindanao, Philippines
07 22N 124 15E
Pare Pare Sulawesi, Indonesia 04 01S 119 37E
Pargas (Parainen) Finland 60 18N 22 18E
Parinas, Punta Peru 04 35S 81 18W
Parintins R. Amazonas, Brazil 02 38S 56 45W
Paris La Seine, France 48 52N 02 20E
Parker Point Western Australia, Australia
20 38S 11 43E
Parkeston Quay R. Stour, England, UK 51 57N 01 15E
Parnahyba (Parnaiba) R. Igaracu de Sao Jose, Brazil
02 54S 41 44W
Parnaiba (Parnahyba) R. Igaracu de Sao Jose, Brazil
02 54S 41 44W
Parnu (Pyarnu) (Pernau) Rizhskiy Zaliv, USSR
58 23N 24 30E
Parrsboro Minas Basin, Nova Scotia, Canada
45 23N 64 19W
Parry Sound Lake Huron, Ontario, Canada
45 20N 80 03W
Partington Manchester Ship Canal, England, UK
53 26N 02 25W
Pasacao Ragay Gulf, Luzon, Philippines 13 30N 123 02E
Pasadena Houston Ship Canal, Texas, USA
29 43N 95 14W
Pasajes Spain 43 21N 01 55W
Pascagoula Mississippi, USA 30 22N 88 34W
Pasir Gudang Selat Tebrau, Malaya, Malaysia
01 26N 103 54E

Paskallavik Kalmar Sound, Sweden 57 10N 16 28E
Pasni Pakistan 25 12N 63 30E
Paspebiac Baie des Chaleurs, Quebec Province, Canada
48 02N 65 14W
Passage West Corcaigh, Republic of Ireland
51 52N 08 20W
Pastelillo Bahia Nuevitas, Cuba 21 33N 77 13W
Pasuruan Jawa, Indonesia 07 38S 112 55E
Pataholm Sweden 56 55N 16 26E
Patani Halmahera, Indonesia 00 16N 128 45E
Pateniemi Finland 65 05N 25 23E
Patillos, Caleta Chile 20 45S 70 12W
Patrai (Patras) Patraikos Kolpos, Greece 38 14N 21 45E
Patras (Patrai) Patraikos Kolpos, Greece 38 14N 21 45E
Patreksfjordhur Iceland 65 37N 24 20W
Patrick, Port Aneityum, New Hebrides 20 09S 169 47W
Pattani Thailand 06 56N 101 18E
Pauillac La Gironde, France 45 12N 00 45W
Paulauan, Port Mindanao, Philippines 08 38N 123 23E
Pauline Mississippi R., Louisiana, USA 30 07N 90 41W
Paulsboro Delaware R., New Jersey, USA
39 51N 75 15W
Pau, Pir Bombay Harbour, India 19 01N 72 55E
Pavilosta USSR 56 54N 21 11E
Pavitt Point Sabah, Malaysia 05 49N 118 05E
Payardi, Isla Bahia Las Minas, Panama 09 24N 79 50E
Paysandu R. Uruguay, Uruguay 32 18S 58 07W
Paz, La R. Parana Superior, Argentina 30 46S 59 38W
Paz, La Baja California, Mexico 24 10N 110 19W
Pearl Harbour Oahu, Hawaiian Is., USA
21 19N 157 58W
Pechenga, Guba (Petsamo Gulf) USSR 69 40N 31 22E
Pechora, Reka Pechorskoye More, USSR 67 39N 53 02E
Pedernales Gulf of Paria, Venezuela 09 58N 62 16W
Pedro, Little (Port Kaiser) Jamaica 17 52N 77 36W
Peebles Point Strait of Canso, Nova Scotia, Canada
45 35N 61 21W
Peel Isle of Man, UK 54 13N 04 42W
Pei-Hai (Pakhoi) Gulf of Tonkin, China 21 29N 109 06E
Pelabuhan Piru Seram, Indonesia 03 04S 128 12E
Pelabuhan Saumlaki Tanimbar, Indonesia 07 58S 131 17E
Pelican Lisianski Inlet, Alaska, USA 57 57N 136 14W
Pelotas R. Sao Goncalo, Brazil 31 47S 52 19W
Pemangkat Kalimantan, Indonesia 01 11N 108 59E
Pemba (Porto Amelia) Mozambique 12 58S 40 29E
Pemba Island Tanzania 15 15S 39 45E
Pembroke Dock Milford Haven, Wales, UK
51 42N 04 56W
Penang Island (Pulau Pinang) Malaya, Malaysia
05 25N 100 21E
Panasco, Puerto Golfo de California, Mexico
31 19N 113 34W
Penco, Puerto de Chile 36 44S 73 00W
Pendam, Tanjong Batang Rajang, Sarawak, Malaysia
02 17N 111 40E
Pending Sarawak, Malaysia 01 33N 110 24E
Penetanguishene Lake Huron, Ontario, Canada
44 46N 79 56W
Penjuru, Tanjong Singapore 01 18N 103 45E
Penmaenmawr Conway Bay, Wales, UK 53 16N 03 55W
Pennington Terminal Nigeria 04 15N 05 37E
Pennsauken Delaware R., New Jersey, USA
40 00N 75 03W
Penrhyn, Port Conway Bay, Wales, UK 53 14N 04 07W
Penryn Falmouth, England, UK 50 10N 05 06W
Pensacola Florida, USA 30 24N 87 13W
Penazance Mounts Bay, England, UK 50 07N 05 32W
Pepel Sierra Leone 08 34N 13 03W
Perai (Prai) Malaya, Malaysia 05 23N 100 22E
Perak, Tanjung (Surabaya) Jawa, Indonesia
07 12S 112 44E

Perama Piraievs, Greece 37 58N 23 35E
Percy, Caleta Bahia Gente Grande, Chile 52 54S 70 15W
Pernaja (Pernoviken) Finland 60 26N 26 02E
Pernambuco (Recife) Brazil 08 04S 34 52W
Pernau (Parnu) (Pyarnu) Rizhskiy Zaliv, USSR
58 23N 24 39E
Pernis Nieuwe Waterweg, Netherlands 51 54N 04 23E
Pernoviken (Pernaja) Finland 60 26N 26 02E
Perros-Guirec France 48 48N 03 26W
Perth R. Tay, Scotland, UK 56 24N 03 26W
Perth Amboy Raritan Bay, New Jersey, USA
40 30N 74 16W
Pertigalete Venezuela 10 15N 64 34W
Pesaro Italy 43 55N 12 55E
Pessoa, Joao R. Parraiba, Brazil 07 06S 34 53W
Peterhead Scotland, UK 57 30N 01 46W
Petersburg Mitkof Is., Alaska, USA 56 49N 132 57W
Petit Couronne La Seine, France 49 23N 01 01E
Petit Gouave Haiti 18 26N 72 52W
Petropavlovsk Kamchatka, USSR 53 01N 158 39E
Petsamo Gulf (Guba Pechenga) USSR 69 40N 31 22E
Pevek Chaun Gulf, USSR 69 43N 170 18E
Philadelphia Delaware R., Pennsylvania, USA
39 57N 75 10W
Philippeville (Skikda) Algeria 36 53N 06 55E
Philipsbourg (Filipsburg) St Martin 18 01N 63 03W
Phnom-Penh Mekong R., Kampuchea 11 36N 104 56E
Phuket Thailand 07 54N 98 23E
Pichilinque Golfo de California, Mexico 24 16N 110 19W
Picton South Is., New Zealand 41 17S 174 01E
Pictou Nova Scotia, Canada 45 41N 62 43W
Piedras, Las Venezuela 11 42N 70 13W
Piedras, Punta Lago de Maracaibo, Venezuela
10 35N 71 36W
Pierce, Fort Florida, USA 27 28N 80 19W
Pierre, Pointe A Trinidad 10 19N 61 28W
Pietarsaari (Jacobstad) Finland 63 41N 22 43E
Pillau (Baltiysk) Gdanskiy Zaliv, USSR
54 39N 19 54E
Pilon Esenada de Mora Cuba 19 54N 77 18W
Pilos (Pylos) Ormos Navarinou, Greece 36 55N 21 42E
Pimentel Peru 06 50S 79 56W
Pinamalayan Mindoro, Philippines 13 02N 121 30E
Pinang, Pulau (Penang Is.) Malaya, Malaysia
05 25N 100 21E
Pinan, Tanjung Bintan, Indonesia 00 55N 104 26E
Piney Point Potomac R., Maryland, USA 38 08N 76 32W
Pinos, Isla de Cuba 21 40N 82 40W
Piombino, Porto Vecchio Di (Piombino) Italy
42 56N 10 33E
Piraeus (Piraievs) Greece 37 56N 23 40E
Piraievs (Piraeus) Greece 37 56N 23 40E
Piran (Pirano) Trscanski Zaliv, Yugoslavia 45 13N 13 34E
Pirano (Piran) Trscanski Zaliv, Yugoslavia 45 13N 13 34E
Pirie, Port Spencer Gulf, South Australia, Australia
33 10S 138 01E
Pir Pau Bombay Harbour, India 19 01N 72 55E
Piru, Pelabuhan Seram, Indonesia 03 04S 128 12E
Pir'ya, Guba Bol'shaya Kandalakshskaya Guba, Beloye
More, USSR 66 40N 34 21E
Pisagua Chile 19 35S 70 14W
Pisco Peru 13 43S 76 14W
Pitch Point (Sobo) Trinidad 10 16N 61 37W
Pitea Sweden 65 19N 21 29E
Pitre, Pointe a Guadeloupe 16 14N 61 32W
Pittsburg Suisun Bay, California, USA 38 02N 121 53W
Placentia Newfoundland, Canada 47 14N 54 00W
Placentia, Little Newfoundland, Canada 47 17N 54 00W
Plaju Sungai Palembang, Sumatera, Indonesia
02 59S 104 48E

Plata, La R. de la Plata, Argentina 34 52S 57 54W

Plata, Mar del Argentina 38 03S 57 32W

Plata, Puerto Dominican Republic 19 49N 70 42W

Playa de Damas Panama 09 36N 79 29W

Pleasant Bay Cape Breton Is., Nova Scotia, Canada
46 50N 60 49W

Ploce (Kardeljevo) Yugoslavia 43 02N 17 26E

Plymouth Montserrat 16 42N 62 13W

Plymouth England, UK 50 22N 04 09W

Plymouth Massachusetts, USA 41 57N 70 40W

P'Ohang South Korea 36 01N 129 24E

Point Breeze Delaware R., Pennsylvania, USA
39 55N 75 12W

Point Central Mauritania 20 49N 17 02W

Point Comfort Texas, USA 28 39N 96 34W

Pointe a Pierre Trinidad 10 19N 61 28W

Pointe a Pitre Guadeloupe 16 14N 61 32W

Pointe-au-Pere (Father Point) St Lawrence R., Quebec
Province, Canada 48 31N 68 28W

Pointe Clairette Gabon 00 39S 08 43E

Pointe des Galets La Reunion 20 55S 55 17E

Pointe des Mouettes Baie du Levrier, Mauritania
20 49N 17 02W

Point Edward Cape Breton Is., Nova Scotia, Canada
46 12N 60 14W

Pointe Noire St Lawrence R., Quebec Province, Canada
50 10N 66 28W

Pointe Noire Congo Republic 04 47S 11 50E

Point Fortin Trinidad 10 12N 61 42W

Point Henry Geelong, Victoria, Australia
38 08S 144 26E

Point Howard Wellington, North Is., New Zealand
41 15S 174 54E

Point Jary Guadeloupe 16 13N 61 37W

Point Lisas Trinidad 10 22N 61 29W

Point, Molate San Pablo Bay, California, USA
37 57N 122 26W

Point Murat Exmouth Gulf, Western Australia, Australia
21 49S 114 11E

Point Orient San Pablo Bay, California, USA
37 57N 122 26W

Point Samson Port Walcott, Western Australia, Australia
20 38S 117 12E

Point Tupper Strait of Canso, Nova Scotia, Canada
45 36N 61 22W

Point Wells Puget Sound, Washington, USA
47 47N 122 24W

Pola (Pula) Yugoslavia 44 53N 13 51E

Polathane (Akcaabaat) Turkey 41 02N 39 35E

Polillo Polillo Is., Philippines 14 43N 121 56E

Polnocny, Port Zatoka Gdanska, Poland 54 24N 18 42E

Polyarnyy Kol'skiy Zaliv, USSR 69 13N 33 28E

Pomalaa Sulawesi, Indonesia 04 10S 121 36E

Pomarao R. Guadiana, Portugal 37 34N 07 32W

Ponape Caroline Is. 07 01N 158 12E

Ponce Puerto Rico 17 58N 66 37W

Pondicherry India 11 56N 79 50E

Pond, Long Newfoundland, Canada 47 31N 52 59W

Pon'goma Beloye More, USSR 65 19N 34 31E

Ponnani India 10 47N 75 54E

Ponta Delgada Sao Miguel, Acores 37 44N 25 41W

Ponta do Ubu Brazil 20 46S 40 34W

Pontevedra (Marin) Spain 42 24N 08 42W

Pontianak Kalimantan, Indonesia 00 01S 109 16E

Pont l'Abbe France 47 52N 04 13W

Pontrieux R. De Pontrieux, France 48 43N 03 09W

Poole England, UK 50 43N 01 59W

Porbandar India 21 37N 69 36E

Porfida, Punta Golfo San Matias, Argentina
41 41S 65 01W

Pori (Bjornborg) Finland 61 28N 21 48E

Porkkala (Kantvik) Finland 60 05N 24 23E

Porlamar Isla de Margarita, Venezuela 10 57N 63 51W

Poro New Caledonia 21 18S 165 43E

Poro Luzon, Philippines 16 36N 120 17E

Poronaysk Sakhalin, USSR 49 13N 143 07E

Porpoise Harbour Prince Rupert, British Columbia, Canada
54 14N 130 18W

Porsgrunn R. Skien, Norway 59 08N 09 38E

Port Adams Houston Ship Canal, Texas, USA
29 45N 95 11W

Port Adelaide St Vincent Gulf, South Australia, Australia
34 51S 138 30E

Port Alberni Vancouver Is., British Columbia, Canada
49 14N 124 49W

Port Albert Victoria, Australia 38 40S 146 41E

Port Alfred Saguenay R., Quebec Province, Canada
48 20N 70 53W

Port Alice Vancouver Is., British Columbia, Canada
50 23N 127 27W

Port Alice Heceta Is., Alaska, USA 55 48N 133 38W

Port Allen Kauai, Hawaiian Is., USA 21 54N 159 36W

Port Allen Mississippi R., Louisiana, USA
30 28N 91 12W

Port Alma Queensland, Australia 23 35S 150 52E

Port Alucroix (Port Harvey) (Port Martin Marietta)
St Croix, Virgin Is. 17 42N 64 46W

Port Amamapare Irian Jaya, Indonesia 04 49S 136 52E

Port Aneityum Aneityum New Hebrides 20 14S 169 47E

Port Angeles Juan de Fuca Strait, Washington, USA
48 07N 123 26W

Port Antonio Jamaica 18 11N 76 27W

Portapique Cobequid Bay, Nova Scotia, Canada
45 25N 63 43W

Port Apra Guam, Marianas (Ladrones) Is.
13 27N 144 39E

Port Arthur Tasmania, Australia 43 09S 147 51E

Port Arthur Lake Superior, Ontario, Canada
48 27N 89 12W

Port Arthur (Ryojun) (Lushun) China 38 48N 121 15E

Port Arthur Sabine Lake, Texas, USA 29 53N 93 57W

Port Askaig Islay, Scotland, UK 55 50N 06 05W

Port au Francais Kerguelen Is. 49 21S 70 13E

Port Augusta Spencer Gulf, South Australia, Australia
32 30S 137 46E

Port au Prince Haiti 18 33N 72 21W

Port aux Basques Newfoundland, Canada 47 35N 59 08W

Port Balancan Marinduque, Philippines 13 32N 121 52E

Port Barrier Baie de St. Brieuc, France 48 38N 02 25W

Port Batan Panay, Philippines 14 44N 120 16E

Port Binanga Luzon, Philippines 14 44N 120 16E

Port Blair Andaman Is., India 11 41N 92 46E

Port Boca Grande Florida, USA 26 43N 82 15W

Port Bouet Ivory Coast 05 14N 03 56W

Port Breira Algeria 36 32N 01 35E

Port Cam Pha Vietnam 21 02N 107 21E

Port Canaveral Florida, USA 28 25N 80 36W

Port Canoan Siquijor, Philippines 09 15N 123 35E

Port Cartier St Lawrence R., Quebec Province, Canada
50 02N 66 47W

Port Castries St Lucia 14 01N 61 00W

Port Chalmers Otago Harbour, South Is., New Zealand
45 49S 170 38E

Port Chester (Metlakatla) Annette Is., Alaska, USA
55 08N 131 34W

Port Chicago Suisan Bay, California, USA
38 03N 122 01W

Port Clements Graham Is., British Columbia, Canada
53 41N 132 11W

Port Colborne Welland Canal, Ontario, Canada
42 53N 79 14W

Port Covington Baltimore, Maryland, USA
39 16N 76 36W

Port Culion Culion Is., Philippines 11 53N 120 01E

Port Curtis Queensland, Australia 23 50S 151 15E

Port Dalhousie Lake Ontario, Ontario, Canada
43 12N 79 15W

Port Daniel Baie des Chaleurs, Quebec Province, Canada
48 09N 64 57W

Port Darwin Northern Territory, Australia 12 28S 130 51E

Port de Berre France 43 28N 05 10E

Port de Bethioua Golfe d'Arzew, Algeria 35 49N 00 16W

Port de Bouc France 43 24N 04 59E

Port de la Mede Etang de Berre, France 43 24N 05 07E

Port de Lavera Port de Bouc, France 43 23N 05 00E

Port de Mueo New Caledonia 21 19S 165 00E

Port Denison (Bowen) Queensland, Australia
20 01S 148 15E

Port de Noirmoitier La Loire, France 47 01N 02 15W

Port de Paix Haiti 19 57N 72 52W

Port Dickson Malaya, Malaysia 02 31N 101 47E

Port Dinorwic Menai Strait, Wales, UK 53 11N 04 12W

Port d'Uturoa Raiatea, Society Is. 16 44S 151 26W

Port Edward Prince Rupert, British Columbia, Canada
54 14N 130 18W

Port Elizabeth Algoa Bay, South Africa 33 58S 25 38E

Port Ellen Islay, Scotland, UK 55 38N 06 11W

Port en Bessin Baie de la Seine, France 49 21N 00 46W

Port Esquivel Portland Bight, Jamaica 17 53N 77 08W

Port Etienne (Nouadhibou) Baie du Levrier, Mauritania
20 54N 17 03W

Port Everglades Florida, USA 26 06N 80 07W

Port Fairy Victoria, Australia 38 23S 142 15E

Port Gamble Hood Canal, Washington, USA
47 51N 122 35W

Port Gentil Gabon 00 43S 08 48E

Port Giles St Vincent Gulf, South Australia, Australia
35 05S 137 46E

Port Glasgow R. Clyde, Scotland, UK 55 56N 04 41W

Port Graham Cook Inlet, Alaska, USA 59 22N 151 52W

Port Harcourt Bonny R., Nigeria 04 46N 07 01E

Port Hardy Vancouver Is., British Columbia, Canada
50 43N 127 29W

Port Harmon Newfoundland, Canada 48 31N 58 33W

Port Harvey (Port Martin Marietta) (Port Alucroix)
St Croix, Virgin Is. 17 42N 64 46W

Port Hastings Strait of Canso, Nova Scotia, Canada
45 39N 61 24W

Port Hawkesbury Strait of Canso, Nova Scotia, Canada
45 37N 61 22W

Porthcawl Bristol Channel, Wales, UK 51 28N 03 42W

Port Hedland Western Australia, Australia
20 19S 118 35E

Porthleven Mounts Bay, England, UK 50 05N 05 19W

Porthmadog (Portmadoc) Wales, UK 52 55N 04 08W

Port Holland Basilan, Philippines 06 33N 121 52E

Port Hood Cape Breton Is., Nova Scotia, Canada
46 01N 61 31W

Port Hope Lake Ontario, Ontario, Canada 43 57N 78 17W

Port Hope Simpson Labrador, Canada 52 33N 56 16W

Port Hueneme California, USA 34 09N 119 12W

Port Huon Tasmania, Australia 43 10S 146 58E

Port Huron St Clair R., Michigan, USA 43 00N 82 28W

Port Ibrahim Suez Canal, Egypt 29 56N 32 33E

Porticello Lipari Italy 38 31N 14 58E

Portici Golfo de Napoli, Italy 40 47N 14 21E

Portiglione Italy 42 53N 10 47E

Portimao, Vila Nova de (Portimao) Portugal
37 08N 08 31W

Port Irene Luzon, Philippines 18 26N 122 06E

Port Isabel Texas, USA 26 04N 97 12W

Portishead Bristol Channel, England UK 51 29N 02 46W

Port Ivory Staten Is., New York, USA 40 38N 74 11W

Port Jackson New South Wales, Australia 33 50S 151 17E

Port Jefferson Long Is., New York, USA 40 57N 73 04W

Port Jerome La Seine, France 49 29N 00 32E

Port Kaiser (Little Pedro) Jamaica 17 52N 77 36W

Port Kaituma Guyana 07 44N 59 52W

Port Kakande (Port Kamsar) R. Nunez, Guinea
10 39N 14 37W

Port Kamsa (Port Kakande) R. Nunez, Guinea
10 39N 14 37W

Port Kelah Algeria 35 06N 02 08W

Port Kelang (Port Swettenham) Malaya, Malaysia
03 00N 101 24E

Port Kem' Onezhskaya Guba, Beloye More, USSR
64 59N 34 45E

Port Kembla New South Wales, Australia
34 28S 150 54E

Port Lairge (Waterford) Republic of Ireland
52 15N 07 07W

Port Lampon Luzon, Philippines 14 40N 121 37E

Portland Victoria, Australia 38 21S 141 37E

Portland Whangarei, North Is., New Zealand
35 48S 174 21E

Portland England, UK 50 34N 02 26W

Portland Maine, USA 43 39N 70 15W

Portland Columbia R., Oregon, USA 45 32N 122 43W

Port-la-Nouvelle Golfe du Lion, France 43 01N 03 04E

Port Latta Tasmania, Australia 40 50S 145 23E

Port Laudania Florida, USA 26 04N 80 06W

Port Launay France 43 13N 04 06W

Pot Lavaca Texas, USA 28 37N 96 37W

Port Lebak Mindanao, Philippines 06 33N 124 03E

Port Libas Samar, Philippines 11 46N 125 27E

Port Lincoln Spencer Gulf, South Australia, Australia
34 43S 136 52E

Port Louis Mauritius 20 09S 57 30E

Port Lyautey (Kentira) Wadi Sebou, Morocco
34 17N 06 41W

Port Lyttleton South Is., New Zealand 43 37S 172 43E

Port McNeill Vancouver Is., British Columbia, Canada
50 36N 127 05W

Port Madison Puget Sound, Washington, USA
47 42N 122 34W

Portmadoc (Porthmadog) Wales, UK 52 55N 04 08W

Port Manatee Florida, USA 27 30N 82 34W

Port Matalvi Luzon, Philippines 15 29N 119 56E

Port Martin Marietta (Port Harvey) (Port Alucroix)
St Croix, Virgin Is. 17 42N 64 46W

Port Medway Nova Scotia, Canada 44 08N 64 36W

Port Mellon Howe Sound, British Columbia, Canada
49 31N 123 29W

Port Meneng (Banyuwanga) Jawa, Indonesia
08 13S 114 23E

Port Milford Mulroy Bay, Republic of Ireland
55 06N 07 42W

Port Mineralier Baie du Levrier, Mauritania
20 46N 17 03W

Port Moody Burrard Inlet, British Columbia, Canada
49 17N 122 52W

Port Morant (Bowden Wharf) Jamaica 17 53N 76 19W

Port Moresby Papua, Papua New Guinea 09 29S 147 09E

Port Morien Cape Breton Is., Nova Scotia, Canada
46 09N 59 52W

Port Muhammad Bin Qasim (Bandar Qasim) Phitti Creek,
Pakistan 24 46N 67 19E

Port Mulgrave Strait of Casno, Nova Scotia, Canada
45 36N 61 23W

Port Nador Morocco 35 17N 02 56W

Port Neches Neches R., Texas, USA 29 59N 93 56W

Port Nesebur Burgaski Zaliv, Bulgaria 42 40N 27 44E
Portneuf St Lawrence R., Quebec Province, Canada
  48 37N 69 06W
Port Neville Johnstone Strait, British Columbia, Canada
  50 29N 126 05W
Port Newark New Jersey, USA 40 42N 74 08W
Port Nolloth South Africa 29 15S 16 52E
Porto (O Porto) R. Douro, Portugal 41 09N 08 37W
Porto Alegre R. Guaiba, Brazil 30 03S 51 13W
Porto Alexandre Angola 15 48S 11 51E
Porto Amboim (Benguela Velha) Angola 10 44S 13 46E
Porto Amelia (Pemba) Mozambique 12 58S 40 29E
Porto Azzurro Elba, Italy 42 46N 10 24E
Portocel (Barra do Riacho) Brazil 19 51S 40 03W
Porto Corsini Italy 44 29N 12 17E
Porto d'Anzio (Anzio) Italy 41 27N 12 38E
Porto de Mocambique (Porto de Mozambique)
  Mozambique 15 02S 40 46E
Porto de Mozambique (Porto de Mocambique)
  Mozambique 15 02S 40 46E
Porto Empedocle Sicilia, Italy 37 17N 13 32E
Portoferraio Elba, Italy 42 49N 10 20E
Porto Foxi (Sarroch) Sardegna, Italy 39 05N 09 01E
Port of Spain Trinidad 10 39N 61 32W
Porto Grande Sao Vicente, Republic of Cape Verde
  16 53N 25 00W
Porto Isola Sicilia, Italy 37 02N 14 15E
Porto Okha India 22 28N 69 05E
Porto Laguna Brazil 28 31S 48 47W
Port Olongapo Subic Bay, Luzon, Philippines
  14 49N 120 17E
Porto Marghera Golfo di Venezia, Italy 45 27N 12 17E
Porto Maurizio (Imperia) (Oneglia) Italy 43 53N 08 02E
Porto Mulas Is. de Vieques, Puerto Rico 18 09N 65 25W
Porto Novo Benin 06 27N 02 38E
Porto Novo Santo Antao, Republic of Cape Verde
  17 01N 25 04W
Porto Praia Sao Tiago, Republic of Cape Verde
  14 55N 23 31W
Porto, Puent del Spain 43 07N 09 10W
Porto Romano Sardegna, Italy 40 57N 09N 31E
Portoroz Trscanski Zaliv, Yugoslavia 45 31N 13 35E
Porto Saco (Porto Salazar) Angola 15 08S 12 07E
Porto Salazar (Porto Saco) Angola 15 08S 12 07E
Porto Santo Stefano Italy 42 26N 11 07E
Porto Torres Sardegna, Italy 40 51N 08 24E
Porto Trombetas R. Trombetas, Brazil 01 28S 56 23W
Porto Vecchio Corse, France 41 35N 09 17E
Porto Vecchio di Piombino (Piombino) Italy
  42 56N 10 33E
Porto Velho R. Madeira, Brazil 08 45S 63 54W
Porto Vesme Sardegna, Italy 39 12N 08 24E
Porto, Vila do Santa Maria, Acores 36 56N 25 09W
Port Palompon Leyte, Philippines 11 02N 124 23E
Port Patrick Aneityum, New Hebrides 20 09S 169 47E
Port Paulauan Mindanao, Philippines 08 38N 123 23E
Port Penrhyn Conway Bay, Wales, UK 53 14N 04 07W
Port Pirie Spencer Gulf, South Australia, Australia
  33 10S 138 01E
Port Polnocny Zatoka Gdanska, Poland 54 24N 18 42E
Port Purcell Tortola, Virgin Is. 18 25N 64 37W
Port Qaboos-Matrah (Mina Qaboos-Matrah) Oman
  23 37N 58 35E
Port Ragay Luzon, Philippines 13 52N 122 38E
Port Raritan Lower Bay, New Jersey, USA
  40 29N 74 16W
Port Rashid (Mina Rashid) Dubai, United Arab Emirates
  25 16N 55 16E
Port Reading Arthur Kill R., New Jersey, USA
  40 34N 74 14W

Port Redi (Rairi) India 15 44N 73 39E
Portree Skye, Scotland, UK 57 24N 06 11W
Port Refuge Cocos (Keeling) Is. 12 06S 96 52E
Port Reitz Kilindini, Kenya 04 03S 39 38E
Port Rhoades Discovery Bay, Jamaica 18 28N 77 26W
Port Richmond Staten Is., New York, USA
  40 38N 74 08W
Port Richmond Delaware R., Pennsylvania, USA
  39 58N 75 07W
Portrieux France 48 39N 02 49W
Port Romblon Romblon Is., Philippines 12 35N 122 16E
Port Romilly Papua, Papua New Guinea 07 41S 144 50E
Port Royal Jamaica 17 56N 76 51W
Port Royal South Carolina, USA 32 23N 80 41W
Port Royal Bay Hamilton, Bermuda 32 16N 64 47W
Portrush Ulster, UK 55 13N 06 40W
Port Said (Bur Sa'id) Egypt 31 15N 32 19E
Port St Joe Florida, USA 29 49N 85 19W
Port St Louis Malagasy Republic 13 05S 48 50E
Port St Mary Isle of Man, UK 54 04N 04 44W
Port Sandwich Malekula, New Hebrides 16 26S 167 46E
Port San Esteban Luzon, Philippines 17 21N 120 27E
Port San Luis San Luis Obisbo Bay, California, USA
  35 10N 12 44W
Port Santa Maria Mindanao, Philippines 07 46N 122 07W
Port Saunders Ingornachoix Bay, Newfoundland, Canada
  50 38N 57 18W
Port Severodvinsk (Molotovsk) Dvinskaya Guba, Beloye
  More, USSR 64 33N 39 49E
Port Sharma Saudi Arabia 27 56N 35 16E
Port Simpson British Columbia, Canada 54 34N 130 25W
Port Skoldvik (Porvoo Oil Harbour) Finland
  60 18N 25 33E
Portsmouth England, UK 50 48N 01 06W
Portsmouth New Hampshire, USA 43 05N 70 45W
Portsmouth Elizabeth R., Virginia, USA 36 51N 76 19W
Port Socony Staten Is., New York, USA 40 33N 74 15W
Port Stanley Falkland Is. 51 42S 57 51W
Port Stanvac St Vincent Gulf, South Australia, Australia
  35 07S 138 28E
Port Stephens New South Wales, Australia
  32 43S 152 12E
Port Sudan Sudan 19 37N 37 14E
Port Sulphur Mississippi R., Louisiana, USA
  29 28N 89 41W
Port Suriago Mindanao, Philippines 09 48N 125 29E
Port Sutton Tampa Bay, Florida, USA 27 54N 82 25W
Port Swettenham (Port Kelang) Malaya, Malaysia
  03 00N 101 24E
Port Talbot Bristol Channel, Wales, UK 51 35N 03 47W
Port Tampa Florida, USA 27 52N 82 33W
Port Taranaki North Is., New Zealand 39 03S 174 02E
Port Tewfik (Bur Taufiq) Gulf of Suez, Egypt
  29 56N 32 34E
Port Tilic Lubang, Philippines 13 49N 120 12E
Port Townsend Washington, USA 48 07N 122 46W
Port Tudy I. de Groix, France 47 39N 03 27W
Portugalete Spain 43 19N 03 01W
Port Union Catalina Harbour, Newfoundland, Canada
  48 30N 53 05W
Port Vauban (Antibes) Cote d'Azur, France
  43 34N 07 08E
Port Vendres France 42 31N 03 07E
Port Victoria Mahe, Seychelles 04 37S 55 28E
Port Vila (Fila) Efate, New Hebrides 17 44S 168 18E
Port Vincent South Australia, Australia
  34 47S 137 52E
Port Vladimir Motoviskiy Zaliv, USSR 69 25N 33 09E
Port Wade Annapolis Basin, Nova Scotia, Canada
  44 41N 65 42W

Port Wakefield St Vincent Gulf, South Australia, Australia
34 12S 138 09E
Port Walcott Western Australia, Australia
20 38S 117 12E
Port Walter Baranof Is., Alaska, USA 56 23N 134 39W
Port Weller Welland Canal, Ontario, Canada
43 14N 79 12W
Port Welshpool Victoria, Australia 38 42S 146 28E
Port Wentworth Georgia, USA 32 08N 81 09W
Port Whangarei North Is., New Zealand 35 47S 174 21E
Port Williams Minas Basin, Nova Scotia, Canada
45 06N 64 24W
Porvenir, Bahia Estrecho de Magallanes, Chile
53 19S 70 25W
Porvoo (Borga) Finland 60 24N 25 40E
Porvoo Oil Harbour (Port Skoldvik) Finland
60 18N 25 33E
Poseidonia (Posidhonia) Dhiorix Korinthou, Greece
37 57N 22 57E
Posidhonia (Poseidonia) Dhiorix Korinthou, Greece
37 57N 22 57E
Poste Miroline La Seine, France 49 26N 00 17E
Poti USSR 42 09N 41 39E
Poughkeepsie Hudson R., New York, USA
41 42N 73 55W
Powell River Desolation Sound, British Columbia, Canada
49 52N 124 33W
Pozos Colorados Colombia 11 10N 74 14W
Pozzuoli Golfo di Napoli, Italy 40 49N 14 07E
Prachuap Khiri Khan Thailand 11 47N 99 49E
Praesto Sjaelland, Denmark 55 08N 12 02E
Prai (Perai) Malaya, Malaysia 05 23N 100 22E
Praia da Vitoria (Praia) Terceira, Acores 38 44N 27 04W
Praia Formosa Madeira Is. 32 37N 16 57W
Praia, Mocimboa de Mozambique 11 20S 40 22E
Praia, Porto Sao Tiago, Republic of Cape Verde
14 55N 23 31W
Prainha R. Amazonas, Brazil 01 48S 53 29W
Pravia, San Esteban de Spain 43 34N 06 05W
Prescott St Lawrence Seaway, Ontario, Canada
44 44N 75 31W
Preston (Guatemala) Bahia Nipe, Cuba 20 46N 75 39W
Preston R. Ribble, England, UK 53 46N 02 42W
Primorsk Vislinskiy Zaliv, USSR 54 44N 20 00E
Prince, Port au Haiti 18 33N 72 21W
Prince Rupert British Columbia, Canada
54 19N 130 22W
Princesa, Puerto Palawan, Philippines 09 44N 118 45E
Priok, Tanjung Jawa, Indonesia 06 06S 106 53E
Probolinggo Jawa, Indonesia 07 43S 113 13E
Progreso Yucatan, Mexico 21 18N 89 40W
Proper Bay South Australia, Australia 34 45S 135 53E
Provestens Sjaelland, Denmark 55 41N 12 38E
Providence Narragansett Bay, Rhode Is., USA
41 48N 71 23W
Provideniya, Bukhta Anadyrskiy Zaliv, USSR
64 21N 173 19W
Psakhna Terminal Evvoikos Kolpos, Greece
38 33N 23 29E
Puebla del Caraminal Spain 42 36N 08 56W
Pueblo del Rio R. Guadalquivir, Spain 37 16N 06 04W
Puent del Porto Spain 43 07N 09 10W
Puerto Acevedo R. Parana, Argentina 33 15S 60 18W
Puerto Alvaro Obregon (Frontera) Golfo de Campeche,
Mexico 18 36N 92 39W
Puerto Angel Mexico 15 39N 96 30W
Puerto Arios Honduras 15 49N 87 57W
Puerto Armuelles Panama 08 16N 82 51W
Puerto Arroyo Puerto Rico 17 57N 66 05W
Puerto Aysen Seno Aysen, Chile 45 25S 72 49W

Puerto Banes Cuba 20 54N 75 43W
Puerto Barrios Bahia de Amatique, Guatemala
15 43N 88 35W
Puerto Bayovar Peru 05 49S 81 00W
Puerto Belgrano Bahia Blanca, Argentina 38 54S 62 06W
Puerto Bolivar Ecuador 03 16S 80 00W
Puerto Borghi R. Parana, Argentina 32 48S 60 48W
Puerto Buitagro R. Parana, Argentina 33 21S 60 11W
Puerto Cabello Venezuela 10 29N 68 00W
Puerto Cabezas Nicaragua 14 01N 83 24W
Puerto Carmen Is. de Chiloe, Chile 43 09S 73 46W
Puerto Carupano Puerto Padre, Cuba 21 18N 76 32W
Puerto Castilla Honduras 15 59N 86 00W
Puerto Cayo Moa (Moa) Cuba 20 40N 74 55W
Puerto Chacabuco Seno Aysen, Chile 45 28S 72 50W
Puerto Chicama Peru 07 42S 79 26W
Puerto Cisnes Canal Phyuguapi, Chile 44 46S 72 40W
Puerto Colombia Colombia 10 59N 74 58W
Puerto Cortes Honduras 15 49N 87 57W
Puerto Cortes Is. Santa Margarita, Mexico
24 28N 111 49W
Puerto Cristobal Colon Golfo de Paria, Venezuela
10 39N 61 56W
Puerto Culebra Costa Rica 10 37N 85 39W
Puerto de Carmello R. Uruguay, Uruguay 34 01S 58 18W
Puerto de Chilca Peru 12 30S 76 50W
Puerto de Escombreras Spain 37 34N 00 58W
Puerto de Eten Peru 06 56S 79 52W
Puerto de Hierro Golfo de Paria, Venezuela
10 38N 62 06W
Puerto de la Honduras Tenerife, Canary Is.
28 27N 16 16W
Puerto del Grao de Castellon de la Plana Spain
39 58N 00 01E
Puerto Del Rosario Fuerteventura, Canary Is.
28 30N 13 52W
Puerto de Mata Cuba 20 18N 74 23W
Puerto de Olivos Canal Costanero, Argentina
34 31S 58 29W
Puerto de Paraguana Venezuela 11 40N 70 13W
Puerto de Penco Chile 36 44S 73 00W
Puerto de San Carlos Bahia Magdalena, Mexico
24 48N 112 06W
Puerto de Santa Maria Spain 36 36N 06 13W
Puerto Deseado Argentina 47 44S 65 53W
Puerto de Sidor En Matanzas (Matanzas) R. Orinoco,
Venezuela, 08 17N 62 51W
Puerto de Soller Mallorca, Islas Balleares, Spain
39 47N 02 42E
Puerto de Yucalpeten Mexico 21 17N 89 42W
Puerto, El (Musel) Concha de Gijon, Spain
43 34N 05 43W
Puerto Gaboto R. Parana, Argentina 32 26S 60 49W
Puerto Galvan Bahia Blanca, Argentina 38 47S 62 18W
Puerto Gracias a Dios Nicaragua 15 00N 83 12W
Puerto Granaderos R. Parana, Argentina 32 46S 60 44W
Puerto Iradier (Kogo) (Cogo) Rio Muni, Guinea Equatorial
01 05N 09 42E
Puerto la Cruz Bahia de Pozuelos, Venezuela
10 13N 64 38W
Puerto las Mareas Puerto Rico 17 55N 66 04W
Puerto Libertador (Manzanillo) Dominican Republic
19 43N 71 44W
Puerto Limon Costa Rica 09 59N 83 01W
Puerto Loreto Baja California, Mexico 26 01N 111 20W
Puerto Macias (Puerto Nuevo) Rio Muni, Guinea
Equatorial 01 50N 09 44E
Puerto Madero (Puerto San Benito) Mexico
14 43N 92 27W
Puerto Madryn Golfo Nuevo, Argentina 42 47S 65 02W

Puerto Maritima de Guayaquil Ecuador 02 17S 79 54W
Puerto Mexico (Coatzacoalcos) Golfo de Campeche, Mexico 18 08N 94 25W
Puerto Miranda Lago de Maracaibo, Venezuela 10 46N 71 33W
Puerto Montt Chile 41 29S 72 59W
Puerto Morazan Estero Real, Nicaragua 12 53N 87 16W
Puerto Natales Chile 51 44S 72 32W
Puerto Nuevo (Puerto Macias) Rio Muni, Guinea Equatorial 01 50N 09 44E
Puerto Obligada R. Parana, Argentina 33 36S 59 49W
Puerto Ordaz R. Orinoco, Venezuela 08 21N 62 43W
Puerto Padre Cuba 21 12N 76 36W
Puerto Palenque Dominican Republic 18 14N 70 09W
Puerto Penasco Golfo de California, Mexico 31 19N 113 34W
Puerto Plata Dominican Republic 19 49N 70 42W
Puerto Princesa Palawan, Philippines 09 44N 118 45E
Puerto Real Spain 36 31N 06 10W
Puerto Rosales Bahia Blanca, Argentina 38 56S 62 04W
Puerto Sama Cuba 21 08N 75 46W
Puerto San Benito (Puerto Madero) Mexico 14 43N 92 27W
Puerto San Blas Argentina 40 33S 62 13W
Puerto San Julian Argentina 49 19S 67 42W
Puerto San Martin R. Parana, Argentina 32 43S 60 44W
Puerto Santa Cruz (Punta Quilla) Argentina 50 08S 68 24W
Puerto Santiago R. de la Plata, Argentina 34 51S 57 54W
Puerto Sara Bahia Gregorio, Estrecho de Magallanes, Chile 52 38S 70 12W
Puerto Somoza Nicaragua 12 11N 86 47W
Puerto Sucre Golfo de Cariaco, Venezuela 10 28N 64 12W
Puerto Tarafa Bahia Nuevitas, Cuba 21 34N 77 15W
Puerto Vallarta Mexico 20 37N 105 15W
Puerto Viejo de Azua Dominican Republic 18 19N 70 49W
Puerto Zorritos Peru 03 40S 80 40W
Pugwash Nova Scotia, Canada 45 52N 63 40W
Pukoo Harbour Molokai, Hawaiian Is., USA 21 04N 156 48W
Pula (Pola) Yugoslavia 44 53N 13 51E
Pulau Ayer Chawan Singapore 01 17N 103 42E
Pulau Bohayan Sabah, Malaysia 04 48N 118 18E
Pulau Bukom Singapore 01 14N 103 46E
Pulau Labuan Sabah, Malaysia 05 17N 115 15E
Pulau Merlimau Singapore 01 17N 103 43E
Pulau Pinang (Penang Is.) Malaya, Malaysia 05 25N 100 21E
Pulau Sebarok Singapore 01 12N 103 48E
Pulau Tarakan Kalimantan, Indonesia 03 17N 117 36E
Pulmoddai Sri Lanka 08 57N 81 00E
Pulo Laut Indonesia 03 15S 116 15E
Pulo Sambu Indonesia 01 09N 103 54E
Pulo We Indonesia 05 50N 95 20E
Pulupandan Negros, Philippines 10 31N 122 48E
Puna Ecuador 02 44S 79 55W
Punta Alice Golfo di Taranto, Italy 39 24N 17 09E
Punta Arenas Estrecho de Magallanes, Chile 53 10S 70 54W
Punta Camacho Lago de Maracaibo, Venezuela 10 33N 71 32W
Punta Cardon Peninsula de Paraguana, Venezuela 11 37N 70 14W
Punta Chavez Golfa de Triste, Venezuela 10 30N 68 07W
Punta Colorada Golfo San Martin, Argentina 41 41S 65 01W
Punta Cuchillo R. Orinoco, Venezuela 08 20N 62 47W
Punta del Este Uruguay 34 58S 54 57W

Punta de Palmas del Sur Lago de Maracaibo, Venezuela 10 24N 71 34W
Punta Gorda Belize 16 06N 88 48W
Punta Gorda Cuba 20 38N 74 51W
Punta Gotay Puerto Rico 17 59N 66 46W
Punta Lucero Spain 43 23N 03 05W
Punta Palenque Terminal Dominican Republic 18 13N 70 11W
Punta Parinas Peru 04 35S 81 18W
Punta Piedras Lago de Maracaibo, Venezuela 10 35N 71 36W
Punta Porfida Golfo San Matias, Argentina 41 41S 65 01W
Punta Quilla (Puerto Santa Cruz) Argentina 50 08S 68 24W
Puntarenas Costa Rica 09 59N 84 48W
Punta Tablones Peru 17 36S 71 20W
Purcell, Port Totola, Virgin Is. 18 25N 64 37W
Purfleet R. Thames, England, UK 51 29N 00 14E
Pusan (Busan) South Korea 35 07N 129 02E
Puteh, Tanah Sarawak, Malaysia 01 33N 110 23E
Puttgarden Fehmarn, West Germany 54 30N 11 14E
Pyarnu (Parnu) (Pernau) Rizhskiy Zaliv, USSR 58 23N 24 3E
Pylos (Pilos) Ormos Navarinou, Greece 36 55N 21 42E
Pyrgos Greece 37 40N 21 27E
Pyrmont Sydney, New South Wales, Australia 33 52S 151 12E

Qaboos, Mina (Muscat) Oman 23 37N 58 36E
Qad el-Marakib (Marakeb) Suez Canal, Egypt 29 55N 32 34E
Qaiwain, Umm al United Arab Emirates 25 35N 55 35E
Qasim, Bandar (Port Muhammad Bin Qasim) Phitti Creek, Pakistan 24 46N 67 19E
Qasim, Port Muhammad Bin (Bandar Qasim) Phitti Creek, Pakistan 24 46N 67 19E
Qasr Ahmed Port (Misurata) (Kassr Ahmed Port) Libya 32 22N 15 12E
Qasr, Umm Khawr 'Abd Allah, Iraq 30 01N 47 57E
Qishon (Kishon Port) Israel 32 49N 35 01E

Quaco Bay Bay of Fundy, New Brunswick, Canada 45 20N 65 34W
Quadayama, Al (Quadheema) Saudi Arabia 22 19N 39 06E
Quadheema (Al Quadayama) Saudi Arabia 22 19N 39 06E
Qua Iboe (Kwa Ibo) Nigeria 04 20N 08 00E
Quatsino Vancouver Is., British Columbia, Canada 50 32N 127 37W
Quebec St Lawrence R., Quebec Province, Canada 46 49N 71 12W
Queenborough The Swale, England, UK 51 25N 00 44E
Queen Charlotte Skidegate Inlet, British Columbia, Canada 53 15N 132 04W
Quelimane (Quilimane) Mozambique 17 53S 36 54E
Quellon Chile 43 07N 73 33W
Quepos Costa Rica 09 21N 84 09W
Quequen Argentina 38 34S 58 42W
Quiliano Terminal Golfo di Genova, Italy 44 17N 08 28E
Quilimane (Quelimane) Mozambique 17 53S 36 54E
Quilla, Punta (Puerto Santa Cruz) Argentina 50 08S 68 24W
Quilon India 08 53N 76 35E
Quimper R. Odet, France 47 59N 04 07W
Quincy Massachusetts, USA 42 15N 70 58W
Quinfuquena Angola 06 20S 12 14E

Qui-Nhon, Vung Vietnam 13 46N 109 14E
Quintero Chile 32 47S 71 31W
Quoile Quay Strangford Lough, Ulster, UK
54 24N 05 39W
Quseir, El (Kosseir) Egypt 26 07N 34 17E

Raa Sweden 56 00N 12 45E
Raahe (Brahestad) Finland 64 42N 24 28E
Rabat Morocco 34 03N 06 46W
Rabaul New Britain, Papua New Gunea 04 13S 152 12E
Rabegh (Sharm Rabigh) Saudi Arabia 22 45N 38 59E
Rabigh, Sharm (Rabegh) Saudi Arabia 22 45N 38 59E
Racha, Si (Siracha) Thailand 13 10N 100 55E
Racine Lake Michigan, Wisconsin, USA 42 42N 87 49W
Rade de Foso Haiti 18 42N 72 21W
Radicatel La Seine, France 49 29N 00 31E
Rafso (Reposaari) Finland 61 37N 21 27E
Ragay, Port Luzon Philippines 13 52N 122 38E
Raglan North Is. New Zealand 37 46S 174 54E
Ragusa (Dubrovnik) Yugoslavia 42 38N 18 07E
Rahja Finland 64 12N 23 44E
Rainham R. Medway, England, UK 51 23N 00 37E
Rairi (Port Redi) India 15 44N 73 39E
Raja, Kota (Olee Lheue) Sumatera, Indonesia
05 33N 95 19E
Rajang Sarawak, Malaysia 02 09N 111 15E
Ramallo R. Parana, Argentina 33 31S 59 59W
Ramree Burma 18 55N 94 00E
Ramsey Isle of Man, UK 54 19N 04 22W
Ramsgate England, UK 51 20N 01 25E
Ramshall Braviken, Sweden 58 36N 16 12E
Ramsund Ototfjord, Norway 68 30N 16 30E
Ramunia, Telok Malaya, Malaysia 01 20N 104 14E
Ramvik Sweden 62 49N 17 52E
Rande Spain 42 17N 08 37W
Randers Jylland, Denmark 56 29N 10 03E
Rangoon Irrawaddy R., Burma 16 47N 96 12E
Rankin Inlet Hudson Bay, North West Territory, Canada
62 50N 92 00W
Rapasaari Saimaa Canal, Finland 61 04N 28 15E
Rapid Bay St Vincent Gulf, South Australia, Australia
35 32S 138 11E
Rapita, San Carlos de la Spain 40 37N 00 36E
Raritan, Port Lower Bay, New Jersey, USA
40 29N 74 16W
Rarotonga Cook Is. 21 12S 159 47W
Rasa (Arsa) Kvarner, Yugoslavia 45 03N 14 04E
Ras al Ghar Saudi Arabia 26 52N 49 52E
Ras al Ju'Aymah Terminal Saudi Arabia 26 56N 50 02E
Ras al Katheeb (Ras Kathib) Yemen 14 56N 42 54E
Ras al Khafji Saudi Arabia 28 25N 48 32E
Ras al Khaimah (Ras al Khaymah) United Arab Emirates
25 48N 56 01E
Ras al Khaymah (Ras al Khaimah) United Arab Emirates
25 48N 56 01E
Ras al Mishab Saudi Arabia 28 10N 48 41E
Ras as Saffaniya Saudi Arabia 28 00N 48 48E
Ras Bahregan (Nowruz Terminal) Iran 29 43N 50 10E
Ras el Saliff (Saleef) Yemen 15 19N 42 41E
Ras el Sudr Sinai, Egypt 29 35N 32 41E
Ras es Sider Libya 30 39N 18 22E
Ras Gharib Gulf of Suez, Egypt 28 21N 33 07E
Ras Hafun (Dante) Somalia 10 26N 51 16E
Rashid, Mina United Arab Emirates 25 16N 55 17E
Rashin (Najin) North Korea 42 13N 130 17E
Ras Kathib (Ras al Katheeb) Yemen 14 56N 42 54E
Ras Lanuf (Sirtica Terminal) Libya 30 31N 18 35E
Ras Sel'ata Lebanon 34 17N 35 39E

Ras Shukheir Gulf of Suez, Egypt 28 08N 33 17E
Rasta Hustegafjarden, Sweden 59 21N 18 13E
Ras Tannurah (Ras Tanura) Saudi Arabia 26 38N 50 10E
Ras Tanura (Ras Tannurah) Saudi Arabia 26 38N 50 10E
Ratan Sweden 64 00N 20 54E
Rathmullen Lough Swilly, Republic of Ireland
55 06N 07 32W
Ratnagiri India 16 59N 73 17E
Raufarhofn Iceland 66 27N 15 55W
Rauma (Raumo) Finland 61 08N 21 30E
Raumo (Rauma) Finland 61 08N 21 30E
Rautaruukki Finland 64 39N 24 25E
Ravenna Italy 44 25N 12 12E
Ravenna Terminal Italy 44 28N 12 26E
Ravensbourne Otago Harbour, South Is., New Zealand
45 52S 170 33E
Rawson Argentina 43 18S 65 04W
Raymond Willapa R., Washington, USA 46 38N 123 47W
Raysut, Mina (Bandar Rayzut) (Salalah) Oman
16 56N 54 01E
Rayzut, Bandar (Mina Raysut) (Salalah) Oman
16 56N 54 01E
Reading, Port Arthur Kill R., New Jersey, USA
40 34N 74 14W
Real, Puerto Spain 36 31N 06 10W
Ream, Baie de Kampuchea 10 33N 103 36E
Recife (Pernambuco) Brazil 08 04S 34 52W
Redcliffe Bay Bristol Channel, England, UK
51 29N 02 49W
Redi, Port (Rairi) India 15 44N 73 39E
Redondo, Morro Isla Cedros, Mexico 28 03N 115 11W
Redondo, Novo (Gunza Kabolo) Angola 11 11S 13 52E
Redwood City San Francisco Bay, California, USA
37 31N 122 13W
Reedsport Umpqua R., Oregon, USA 43 42N 124 07W
Refineria Gibraltar Algeciras, Spain 36 11N 05 24W
Refuge, Port Cocos (Keeling) Is. 12 06S 96 52E
Reggio Calabria (Reggio) Italy 38 07N 15 39E
Regla Cuba 23 08N 82 20W
Reis, Angra Dos Brazil 23 01S 44 19W
Reisui (Yosu) (Yeosu) South Korea 34 45N 127 44E
Reitz, Port Kilindini, Kenya 04 03S 39 38E
Rejaie Port, Shahid Iran 27 07N 56 03E
Reka Luga Finskiy Zaliv, USSR 59 40N 28 18E
Reka Pechora Pechorskoye More, USSR 67 39N 53 02E
Rendsburg Nord-Ostee Kanal, West Germany
54 19N 09 41E
Renfrew R. Clyde, Scotland, UK 55 53N 04 23W
Reni R. Dunay, USSR 45 26N 28 18E
Renteria Spain 43 20N 01 53W
Repola Rauma, Finland 61 07N 21 27E
Reposaari (Rafso) Finland 61 37N 21 27E
Rethimnon Kriti, Greece 35 22N 24 29E
Reunion, La 21 00S 55 20E
Reval (Tallinn) Finskiy Zaliv, USSR 59 26N 24 45E
Revere Boston, Massachusetts, USA 42 25N 70 59W
Reydharfjordhur Iceland 64 58N 13 40W
Reykjavik Iceland 64 09N 21 56W
Rey Malabo (Santa Isabel) Macias Nguema Biyogo
(Fernando Poo Is.) Guinea Equatorial 03 46N 08 47E
Rhoades, Port Discovery Bay, Jamaica 18 28N 77 26W
Rhodes (Rodhos) Greece 36 27N 28 14E
Riacho, Barra de (Portocel) Brazil 19 51S 40 03W
Ribadeo (Rivadeo) Spain 43 32N 07 02W
Ribadesella (Rivadesella) Spain 43 28N 05 04W
Richards Bay South Africa 28 48S 32 06E
Richborough R. Stour, England, UK 51 18N 01 21E
Richibucto New Brunswick, Canada 46 41N 64 52W
Richmond Halifax, Nova Scotia, Canada 44 40N 63 35W
Richmond San Francisco Bay, California, USA
37 55N 122 22W

Richmond James R., Virginia, USA 37 32N 77 25W
Richmond, New Baie des Chaleurs, Quebec Province,
　Canada 48 08N 65 52W
Richmond, Port Staten Is., New York, USA
　40 38N 74 08W
Richmond, Port Delaware R., Pennsylvania, USA
　39 58N 75 07W
Ridham Dock The Swale, England, UK 51 23N 00 46E
Riding Point, South Grand Bahama, Bahamas
　26 36N 78 14W
Riga Rizhskiy Zaliv, USSR 56 57N 24 06E
Rijeka (Fiume) Rijecki Zaliv, Yugoslavia
　45 20N 14 26E
Rikitea Iles Gambier 23 07S 134 58W
Rimini Italy 44 05N 12 35E
Rimouski St Lawrence R., Quebec Province, Canada
　48 29N 68 31W
Rincon, El Chile 29 28S 71 20W
Ringi Cove Kolombangara, Solomon Is. 08 07S 157 07E
Ringkobing Jylland, Denmark 56 05N 08 15E
Rio Benito Rio Muni, Guinea Equatorial 01 36N 09 37E
Rio Buena Jamaica 18 29N 77 29W
Rio de Janeiro Brazil 22 54S 43 12W
Rio Douro Portugal 41 10N 08 37W
Rio Gallegos Argentina 51 36S 69 12W
Rio Grande Tierra del Fuego, Argentina 53 47S 67 42W
Rio Grande Brazil 32 04S 52 04W
Rio Haina Dominican Republic 18 25N 70 01W
Rio Marina Elba, Italy 42 49N 10 26E
Rio, Pueblo del R. Guadalquivir, Spain 37 16N 06 04W
Rio Sagua la Grande Cuba 22 52N 80 01W
Riposto Sicilia, Italy 37 44N 15 13E
Risavika Norway 58 55N 05 36E
Risdon R. Derwent, Tasmania, Australia 42 48S 147 19E
Risobank Mandal, Norway 58 00N 07 26E
Risor Norway 58 43N 09 14E
Ristiina Saimaa Canal, Finland 61 32N 27 20E
Rivadavia, Comodoro Golfo de San Jorge, Argentina
　45 51S 67 28W
Rivadeo (Ribadeo) Spain 43 32N 07 02W
Rivadesella (Ribadesella) Spain 43 28N 05 04W
Riversdale Belize 16 42N 82 20W
Riviere du Loup Quebec Province, Canada
　47 51N 69 34W
Rize (Rizeh) Turkey 41 04N 40 33E
Rizeh (Rize) Turkey 41 04N 40 33E
Road Harbour Tortola, Virgin Is. 18 25N 64 37E
Roatam Island Honduras 16 20N 86 30W
Roberts Bank British Columbia, Canada 49 01N 123 09W
Roberts, Bay Newfoundland, Canada 47 36N 53 16W
Robertsport Liberia 06 44N 11 22W
Rochefort La Charente, France 45 56N 00 57W
Rochelle, La La Charente, France 46 09N 01 09W
Rochester R. Medway, England, UK 51 23N 00 30E
Rochester Lake Ontario, New York, USA 43 12N 77 36W
Rock Ferry R. Mersey, England, UK 53 22N 03 00W
Rockhampton Queensland, Australia 23 23S 150 31E
Rockland Maine, USA 44 06N 69 06W
Rocky Point Jamaica 17 49N 77 09W
Rodbyhavn Lolland, Denmark 54 39N 11 22E
Roddicton Canada Bay, Newfoundland, Canada
　50 52N 56 08W
Rodhos (Rhodes) Greece 36 27N 28 14E
Rodosto (Tekirdag) Marmara Denizi, Turkey
　40 58N 27 32E
Rodrigues Island 19 40S 63 25E
Rodvig Sjaelland, Denmark 55 15N 12 23E
Rohukula USSR 58 55N 23 26E
Rojo, Cabo Dominican Republic 17 54N 71 39W
Romana, La Dominican Republic 18 25N 68 57W

Romano, Porto Sardegna, Italy 40 57N 09 31E
Romblon, Port Romblon Is., Philippines 12 35N 122 16E
Romilly, Port Papua, Papua New Guinea 07 41S 144 50E
Romohavn Romo, Denmark 55 05N 08 34E
Rompin, Kuala Malaya, Malaysia 02 49N 103 29E
Rondeau Lake Erie, Ontario, Canada 42 21N 18 58W
Ronehamn Gotland, Sweden 57 10N 18 31E
Ronne Bornholm, Denmark 55 06N 14 42E
Ronnebyhamn Sweden 56 10N 15 18E
Ronnskar Hornefors, Sweden 63 36N 19 54E
Ronnskar Skeleftea, Sweden 64 40N 21 17E
Rordal Limfjord, Jylland, Denmark 57 04N 09 58E
Rorvik Norway 64 52N 11 14E
Rosales, Puerto Bahia Blanca, Argentine 38 56S 62 04W
Rosario R. Parana, Argentina 32 57S 60 38W
Rosario Luzon, Philippines 14 24N 120 51E
Rosario, Puerto del Fuerteventura, Canary Is.
　28 30N 13 52W
Rosarito Terminal Mexico 32 21N 117 04W
Rosas Spain 42 15N 03 11E
Roscoff France 48 43N 03 59W
Roseau Dominica 15 18N 61 23W
Roska Finland 64 42N 24 24E
Roskilde Sjaelland, Denmark 55 39N 12 05E
Rosslare Republic of Ireland 52 15N 06 20W
Ross, New R. Barrow, Republic of Ireland
　52 24N 06 57W
Rosta Kol'skiy Zaliv, USSR 69 01N 33 06E
Rostock East Germany 54 05N 12 08E
Rostov R. Don, USSR 47 10N 39 42E
Rosyth Firth of Forth, Scotland, UK 56 01N 03 27W
Rota Bahia de Cadiz, Spain 36 37N 06 21W
Rothesay Bute, Scotland, UK 55 50N 05 03W
Rotterdam Nieuwe Waterweg, Netherlands
　51 55N 04 30E
Rottnest Island Western Australia, Australia
　32 00S 115 30E
Rouen La Seine, France 49 28N 01 04E
Rousse, Ile Corse, France 42 38N 08 56E
Rovigno (Rovinj) Yugoslavia 45 05N 13 38E
Rovinj (Rovigno) Yugoslavia 45 05N 13 38E
Ro, Vung Vietnam 12 52N 109 26E
Rowhedge R. Colne, England, UK 51 51N 00 57E
Royal Bay, Port Hamilton, Bermuda 32 16N 64 47W
Royal, Port Jamaica 17 56N 76 51W
Royal, Port South Carolina, USA 32 23N 80 41W
Roytta Finland 65 46N 24 09E
Rozelle Bay Sydney, New South Wales, Australia
　33 52S 151 11E
Rozi Gulf of Kutch, India 22 33N 70 03E
Ru'ays, Ar (Al Ruwais) United Arab Emirates
　24 08N 52 44E
Rudkobing Langeland, Denmark 54 56N 10 42E
Rugenwalde (Darlowo) Poland 54 26N 16 25E
Ruivo, Cabo R. Tejo, Portugal 38 46N 09 05W
Rumoi Hokkaido, Japan 43 57N 141 38E
Runcorn Manchester Ship Canal, England, UK
　53 21N 02 44W
Rundvik Sweden 63 32N 19 27E
Rushbrooke Corcaigh, Republic of Ireland 51 51N 08 19W
Ruwais, Al (Ar Ru'ays) United Arab Emirates
　24 08N 52 44E
Rye England, UK 50 57N 00 44E
Ryojun (Port Arthur) (Lushun) China 38 48N 121 15E

Sabang Pulo We, Indonesia 05 53N 95 19E
Sabine Texas, USA 29 43N 93 52W
Sabine Pass Texas, USA 29 44N 93 53W
Sablayan Mindoro, Philippines 12 50N 120 46E
Sables d'Olonne, Les France 46 30N 01 48W
Saby (Saeby) Jylland, Denmark 57 20N 10 31E
Saco, Porto (Porto Salazar) Angola 15 08S 12 07E
Sacramento Sacramento R., California, USA
    38 35N 121 25W
Saeby (Saby) Jylland, Denmark 57 20N 10 31E
Saeki (Saiki) Kyushu, Japan 32 59N 131 54E
Saelvig Samso, Denmark 55 52N 10 33E
Saevareid Bjornafjorden, Norway 60 11N 05 46E
Safaga (Safaja) Egypt 26 44N 33 56E
Safaja (Safaga) Egypt 26 44N 33 56E
Saf, Beni Algeria 35 18N 01 24W
Saffaniya, Ras as Saudi Arabia 28 00N 48 48E
Safi Morocco 32 19N 09 15W
Saganoseki Kyushu, Japan 33 15N 131 52E
Saginaw Lake Huron, Michigan, USA 43 25N 83 54W
Sagua de Tanamo Cuba 20 43N 75 19W
Sagua la Grande, Rio Cuba 22 52N 80 01W
Sagua, Isabela de R. Sagua la Grande, Cuba
    22 56N 80 01W
Saida (Sidon) Lebanon 33 34N 35 22E
Sagunto Spain 39 39N 00 13W
Sa'Id, Bur (Port Said) Egypt 31 15N 32 19E
Said, Port (Bur Sa'id) Egypt 31 15N 32 19E
Said, Umm (Musay'id) Qatar 24 54N 51 34E
Saigon (Ho Chi Minh City) Vietnam 10 46N 106 44E
Saiki (Saeki) Kyushu, Japan 32 59N 131 54E
Saimaa Canal Vyborg Entrance, Gulf of Finland
    60 43N 28 46E
St Andrews New Brunswick, Canada 45 04N 67 03W
St Ann's Bay Jamaica 18 26N 77 13W
St Ann's Harbour Cape Breton Is., Nova Scotia, Canada
    46 15N 60 36W
St Barbe Harbour Newfoundland, Canada
    51 12N 56 46W
St Brieuc (Le Legue) Golfe de St. Malo 48 32N 02 43W
St Catherines Welland Canal, Ontario, Canada
    43 11N 79 16W
St Christopher Island (St Kitts) 17 15N 64 45W
St Croix Virgin Islands 17 45N 64 50W
Ste Anne des Monts St Lawrence R., Quebec Province,
    Canada 49 08N 66 29W
Ste Marie, Sault St Mary's R., Ontario, Canada
    46 29N 84 21W
St George Grenada 12 03N 61 44W
St George's Harbour Newfoundland, Canada
    48 26N 58 29W
St George's Harbour (Ayios Giorgios) Piraievs, Greece
    37 57N 23 36E
St George's Island Bermuda 32 23N 64 41W
St Helena Island 15 55S 05 40W
St Helens Columbia R., Oregon, USA 45 51N 122 48W
St Helier Jersey, Channel Is., UK 49 11N 02 07W
St Ives England, UK 50 13N 05 29W
St Joe, Port Florida, USA 29 49N 85 19W
St John Bay of Fundy, New Brunswick, Canada
    45 16N 66 04W
St Johns Antigua 17 06N 61 51W
St John's Newfoundland, Canada 47 34N 52 42W
St Kitts Island (St Christopher) 17 15N 62 45W
St Laurent Maroni R., French Guiana 05 29N 54 01W
St Lawrence Harbours Newfoundland, Canada
    46 54N 55 21W
St Louis Senegal 16 02N 16 31W
St Louis du Rhone France 42 23N 04 48E
St Louis, Port Malagasy Republic 15 05S 48 50E
St Lucia Island 13 50N 61 00W

St Maarten Island (St Martin) 18 00N 63 05W
St Malo France 48 39N 02 02W
St Marc Haiti 19 07N 72 42W
St Margaret's Hope South Ronaldsay, Orkney Is., Scotland
    UK 58 50N 02 57W
St Martin Ile de Re, France 46 12N 01 22W
St Martin Island (St Maarten) 18 00N 63 05W
St Mary, Port Isle of Man, UK 54 04N 04 44W
St Mary's Island Scilly Is., England, UK 49 55N 06 19W
St Michael Norton Sound, Alaska, USA 63 29N 162 02W
St Michael's Island (Sao Miguel) Acores 37 45N 25 40W
St Michiel's Baai Curacao 12 09N 69 00W
St Nazaire La Loire, France 47 17N 02 12W
St Nicholas (Ayios Nikolaos) Kriti, Greece 35 11N 25 43E
St Nicholas (Ayios Nikolaos) Kea, Greece 37 40N 24 19E
St Nicolaas Haven Aruba 12 26N 69 55W
St Paul de Loanda (Luanda) Angola 08 47S 13 14E
St Peter Port Guernsey, Channel Is., UK 49 27N 02 32W
St Petersburg Tampa Bay, Florida, USA 27 46N 82 37W
St Pierre St Pierre and Miquelon Is. 46 47N 56 10W
St Pierre, Harve St Lawrence R., Quebec Province, Canada
    50 14N 63 36W
St Raphael Cote d'Azur, France 43 25N 06 46E
St Rose Mississippi R., Louisiana, USA 29 56N 90 20W
St Sampson's Guernsey, Channel Is., UK 49 29N 02 31W
St Stephen New Brunswick, Canada 45 12N 67 17W
St Thomas Island Virgin Is. 18 20N 64 55W
St Valery en Caux France 49 52N 00 42E
St Valery sur Somme France 50 11N 01 37E
St Vincent (Sao Vicente) Republic of Cape Verde
    16 53N 25 00W
St Vincent Island 13 10N 61 15W
St Wandrille La Seine, France 49 31N 00 46E
Saipan Island Marianas (Ladrones) Is. 15 14N 145 44E
Sakai Osaka Wan, Honshu, Japan 34 35N 135 27E
Sakaide Seto Naikai, Shikoku, Japan 34 20N 133 51E
Sakai-Minato Honshu, Japan 35 33N 133 14E
Sakata Honshu, Japan 38 55N 139 49E
Sakito Kyushu, Japan 33 01N 129 34E
Sakskobing (Saxbobing) Lolland, Denmark 54 47N 11 39E
Salalah (Bandar Rayzut) (Mina Raysut) Oman
    16 56N 54 01E
Salaverry Peru 08 13S 78 59W
Salawati Irian Jaya, Indonesia 01 21S 130 59E
Salazar, Porto (Porto Saco) Angola 15 08S 12 07E
Saldanha Bay South Africa 33 02S 17 56E
Saleef (Ras el Saliff) Yemen 15 19N 42 41E
Salem Massachusetts, USA 42 31N 70 52W
Salerno Italy 40 40N 14 45E
Salif, Ras el (Saleef) Yemen 15 19N 42 41E
Salina Cruz Mexico 16 10N 95 12W
Salina Guaranao Peninsula de Paraguana, Venezuela
    11 40N 70 13W
Salina, La (Lacertus) Lago de Maracaibo, Venezuela
    10 22N 71 28W
Salinas Ecuador 02 12S 80 58W
Salineta, La Grand Canary, Canary Is. 27 59N 15 22W
Salirong, Tanjong Brunei 04 54N 115 06E
Salo Finland 60 22N 23 05E
Salomague Harbour Luzon, Philippines 17 46N 120 25E
Salona (Solin) Yugoslavia 43 32N 16 28E
Saloniki (Thessaloniki) Thermaikos Kolpos, Greece
    40 38N 22 56E
Salta Caballo Spain 43 22N 03 11W
Salt End R. Humber, England, UK 53 44N 00 15W
Salto R. Uruguay, Uruguay 31 23S 57 58W
Salt River Portland Bight, Jamaica 17 50N 77 10W
Saltvik, Lilla Oskarhamn, Sweden 57 18N 16 31E
Salum Egypt 31 34N 25 10E
Salvador (Bahia) Brazil 12 58S 38 31W

Samana, Santa Barbara de Dominican Republic
19 13N 69 19W
Samanco Peru 09 17S 78 32W
Sama, Puerto Cuba 21 08N 75 46W
Samarai Papua, Papua New Guinea 10 37S 150 40E
Samar Jawa, Indonesia 06 56S 110 25E
Samarinda Kalimantan, Indonesia 00 29S 117 09E
Sambas Kalimantan, Indonesia 01 21N 109 18E
Sambu, Pulo Indonesia 01 09N 103 54E
Sami (Samos) Kefallinia, Greece 38 15N 20 39E
Samos (Sami) Kefallinia, Greece 38 15N 20 39E
Samos (Vathi) Samos, Greece 37 45N 26 59E
Sampit Kalimantan, Indonesia 02 32S 112 57E
Samson, Point Port Walcott, Western Australia, Australia
20 38S 117 12E
Samsun Turkey 41 18N 36 21E
San Antonio Chile 33 35S 71 38W
San Antonio do Zaire (Soyo) Angola 06 07N 12 22E
San Antonio Oeste Golfo de San Matias, Argentina
40 48S 64 54W
San Augistin, Cabo Spain 43 34N 06 44W
San Benito, Puerto (Puerto Madero) Mexico
14 43N 92 27W
San Blas, Puerto Argentina 40 33S 62 13W
San Blas Mexico 21 33N 105 18W
San Carlos (Butuku-Luba) Macias Nguema Biyogo
(Fernando Poo Is.) Guinea Equatorial 03 29N 08 36E
San Carlos Negros, Phillipines 10 29N 123 25E
San Carlos de la Rapita Spain 40 37N 00 36E
San Carlos, Puerto de Bahia Magdalena, Mexico
24 48N 112 06W
Sanchez Bahia de Samand, Dominican Republic
19 14N 69 36W
San Cipran Spain 43 42N 07 28W
Sand Sandsfjord, Norway 59 29N 06 15E
Sandakan Sabah, Malaysia 05 50N 118 08E
Sandarne Sweden 61 16N 17 11E
Sanday Island Orkney Is., Scotland, UK 59 14N 02 36W
Sandefjord Norway 59 08N 10 15E
San Diego California, USA 32 42N 117 10W
Sandnes Norway 58 51N 05 45E
Sandnessjoen Alsten, Norway 66 01N 12 38E
Sandoway Burma 18 29N 94 23E
Sandusky Lake Erie, Ohio, USA 41 26N 82 42W
Sandvik Seskaro, Sweden 65 44N 23 45E
Sandvik Umeafjarden, Sweden 63 43N 20 23E
Sandviken Angermanakven, Sweden 62 58N 17 47E
Sandviken Braviken, Sweden 58 39N 16 24E
Sandviken Oland, Sweden 57 04N 16 52E
Sandwich, Port Malekula, New Hebrides 16 26S 167 00E
Sandy Beach Gaspe Harbour, Quebec Province, Canada
48 49N 64 26W
Sandy Hook Terminal New Jersey, USA 40 27N 74 03W
San Esteban de Pravia Spain 43 34N 06 05W
San Esteban, Port Luzon, Philippines 17 21N 120 27E
San Felieu de Guixols Spain 41 46N 03 02E
San Felix R. Orinoco, Venezuela 08 22N 62 40W
San Fernando Luzon, Philippines 16 37N 120 19E
San Fernando Spain 36 28N 06 12W
San Fernando Trinidad 10 17N 61 28W
San Francisco California, USA 37 48N 122 24W
Sangi Cebu, Philippines 10 24N 123 38E
San Giovanni di Medua (Shengjin) Albania
41 49N 19 35E
Sangkulirang Kalimantan, Indonesia 00 54N 118 02E
San Isidro R. de la Plata, Argentina 34 28S 58 31W
San Jose Guatemala 13 55N 90 50W
San Jose del Cabo Baja California, Mexico
23 03N 109 40W

San Juan Peru 15 20S 75 11W
San Juan Puerto Rico 18 28N 66 07W
San Juan de Aznalfarache R. Guadalquivir, Spain
37 21N 06 01W
San Juan del Norte (Greytown) Nicaragua
10 56N 83 43W
San Juan del Sur Nicaragua 11 15N 85 54W
San Juan de Nieva Spain 43 35N 05 56W
San Juan de Ulua Golfo de Campeche, Mexico
19 12N 96 08W
San Julian, Puerto Argentina 49 19S 67 42W
San Lorenzo R. Parana, Argentina 32 45S 60 44W
San Lorenzo Ecuador 01 17N 78 54W
San Lorenzo Honduras 13 23N 87 26W
San Lorenzo Lago de Maracaibo, Venezuela
09 47N 71 05W
San Luis, Port San Luis Obispo Bay, California, USA
35 10N 120 44W
San Martin, Ensenada Chile 18 31S 70 19W
San Martin, General Peru 13 48S 76 17W
San Martin, Puerto R. Parana, Argentina 32 43S 60 44W
San Nicolas R. Parana, Argentina 33 20S 60 12W
San Nicolas Aruba 12 26N 69 55W
San Nicolas Peru 15 14S 75 14W
San Pedro R. Parana, Argentina 33 42S 59 39W
San Pedro Ivory Coast 04 44N 06 37W
San Pedro California, USA 33 44N 118 17W
San Pedro de Macoris Dominican Republic
18 26N 69 18W
San Ramon Golfo de Guacanayabo, Cuba 20 13N 77 22W
San Remo Italy 43 49N 07 47E
San Sebastian Spain 43 19N 01 59W
San Sebastian, Bahia Tierra del Fuego, Argentina
53 09S 68 15W
Santa Ana Mindanao, Philippines 07 05N 125 37E
Santa Barbara Chile 28 28S 71 15W
Santa Barbara de Samana Dominican Republic
19 13N 69 19W
Santa Cruz Flores, Acores 39 27N 31 08W
Santa Cruz Graciosa, Acores 39 05N 28 01W
Santa Cruz Palma, Canary Is. 28 40N 17 45W
Santa Cruz Tenerife, Canary Is. 28 29N 16 13W
Santa Cruz Luzon, Philippines 15 46N 119 54E
Santa Cruz Marinduque, Philippines 13 32N 122 03E
Santa Cruz del Sur Golfo de Guacanayabo, Cuba
20 42N 77 59W
Santa Cruz, Puerto (Punta Quilla) Argentina
50 08S 68 24W
Santa Fe R. Parana, Argentina 31 40S 60 42W
Santa Isabel (Rey Malabo) Macias Nguema Biyogo
(Fernando Poo Is.) Guinea-Equatorial 03 46N 08 47E
Santa Lucia Cuba 22 41N 83 58W
Santa Maria Cuba 21 17N 78 32W
Santa Maria Ilha Acores 36 55N 25 10W
Santa Maria, Port Mindanao, Philippines 07 46N 122 07E
Santa Maria, Puerto de Spain 36 36N 06 13W
Santa Marta Colombia 11 15N 74 13W
Santana R. Amazonas, Brazil 00 03S 51 11W
Santander Spain 43 28N 03 47W
Santan Terminal (Attaka) Kalimantan, Indonesia
00 06S 117 34E
Santa Pola Spain 38 11N 00 34W
Santa Panagia Sicilia, Italy 37 06N 15 17E
Santa Rita Batangas Bay, Luzon, Philippines
13 46N 121 02E
Santarem R. Amazonas, Brazil 02 26S 54 42W
Santa Rosalia Golfo de California, Mexico
27 20N 112 16W
Santiago de Cuba Cuba 20 01N 75 50W
Santiago, Puerto Argentina 34 51S 57 54W

Santi Quaranta (Sarande) Albania 39 52N 20 01E
Santo Espiritu Santo, New Hebrides 15 31S 167 10E
Santo Antonio Principe, Sao Thorne & Principe
  01 39N 07 27E
Santo Antonio do Ica R. Amazonas, Brazil
  03 05S 67 56W
Santo Antonio, Vila Real de R. Guadiana, Portugal
  37 11N 07 26W
Santo Domingo (Ciudad Trujillo) Dominican Republic
  18 28N 69 53W
Santonia Spain 43 27N 03 27W
Santo Nino Negros, Philippines 10 41N 122 56E
Santos Brazil 23 56S 46 19W
Santos City, General (Buyan City) (Dadiangas) Mindanao,
  Philippines 06 06N 125 09E
Santo Stefano, Porto Italy 42 26N 11 07E
Santo Tomas de Castilla Guatemala 15 41N 88 37W
Santucre Spain 43 19N 03 02W
San Vicente Chile 36 44S 73 08W
San Vicente Luzon, Philippines 18 31N 122 08E
Sao Francisco do Sul Brazil 26 14S 48 37W
Sao Luis de Maranhao Brazil 02 31S 44 18W
Sao Miguel, Ilha (St Michael's Is.) Acores 37 45N 25 40W
Sao Miguel dos Macacos Os Estreitos, Brazil
  01 07S 50 28W
Saom, Kampong (Kompong Som) Kampuchea
  10 38N 103 30E
Sao Sebastiao Brazil 23 48S 45 23W
Sao Tome Sao Tome & Principe 00 20N 06 45E
Sao Vicente (St Vincente) Republic of Cape Verde
  16 53N 25 00W
Sapec Setubal, Portugal 38 30N 08 50W
Sapele Benin R., Nigeria 05 55N 05 42E
Sapurara (Tabatinga) R. Amazonas, Brazil 04 15S 69 44W
Saqr, Mina (Khawr Khuwain) United Arab Emirates
  25 59N 56 03E
Sarande (Santi Quaranta) Albania 39 52N 20 01E
Sara, Puerto Bahia Gregorio, Estrecho de Magallanes,
  Chile 52 38S 70 12W
Sarikei Sungai Rejang, Sarawak, Malaysia
  02 09N 111 32E
Sarnia St Clair R., Ontario, Canada 42 58N 82 24W
Sarpsborg Glomma R., Norway 59 16N 11 06E
Sarroch (Porto Foxi) Sardegna, Italy 39 05N 09 01E
Sasa Mindanao, Philippines 07 07N 125 40E

Sasebo Kyushu, Japan 33 10N 129 43E
Sassandra Ivory Coast 04 57N 06 05W
Sassnitz (Zassnitz) Rugen, East Germany 54 31N 13 39E
Sas Van Gent Gent-Terneuzen Kanaal, Netherlands
  51 14N 03 48E
Sattahip, Ao Thailand 12 40N 100 54E
Sauce R. de la Plata, Uruguay 34 27S 57 27W
Sauda Saudafjord, Norway 59 39N 06 22E
Saudarkrokur Skagafjordhur, Iceland 65 45N 19 39W
Sauda, Mina Kuwait 28 45N 48 24E
Sault Sainte Marie St Mary's R., Ontario, Canada
  46 29N 84 21W
Saumlaki, Pelabuhan Tanimbar, Indonesia
  07 58S 131 17E
Saunders, Port Ingornachoix Bay, Newfoundland, Canada
  50 38N 57 18W
Savannah Georgia, USA 32 05N 81 06W
Savanna la Mar Jamaica 18 12N 78 08W
Savenas Skelleftehamn, Sweden 64 41N 21 14E
Savona Golfo di Genova, Italy 44 18N 08 29E
Savonlinna Saimaa Canal, Finland 61 53N 28 54E
Savu Savu, Na Vanau Levu, Fiji 16 46S 179 19E
Sawmill Cove Sitka Sound, Alaska, USA
  57 03N 135 12W

Saxkobing (Sakskobing) Lolland, Denmark 54 47N 11 39E
Scalanova (Kusadasi) Turkey 37 52N 27 17E
Scalloway Mainland, Shetland Is., Scotland, UK
  60 08N 01 17W
Scanraff Terminal Brofjord, Sweden 58 21N 11 24E
Scapa Flow Orkney Is., Scotland, UK 58 55N 03 00W
Scarborough Tobago 11 11N 60 44W
Scarborough England, UK 54 17N 00 23W
Scheveningen Netherlands 52 06N 04 16E
Schiedam Nieuwe Waterweg, Netherlands 51 55N 04 24E
Schillig Reede Die Jade, West Germany 53 41N 08 03E
Schleswig Die Schlei, West Germany 54 31N 09 34E
Schlutup Die Trave, West Germany 53 53N 10 47
Schulau Die Pinnau, West Germany 53 34 09 42E
Schwarzenhutten Die Oste, West Germany
  53 43N 09 10E
Sciacca Sicilia, Italy 37 30N 13 05E
Scrabster Scotland, UK 58 37N 03 33W
Seaforth R. Mersey, England, UK 53 28N 03 01W
Seaham England, UK 54 50N 01 20W
Seahouses (North Sunderland) England, UK
  55 35N 01 39W
Sea Island Kuwait 29 06N 48 17E
Searsport Maine, USA 44 27N 68 56W
Seattle Puget Sound, Washington, USA 47 36N 122 20W
Sebarok, Pulau Singapore 01 12N 103 48E
Sebatic (Wallace Bay) Sebatic Is., Sabah, Malaysia
  04 15N 117 39E
Sebuyau, Kampong Sarawak, Malaysia 01 31N 110 56E
Seca, Barra Brazil 19 05S 39 40W
Seddon Island Tampa Bay, Florida, USA 27 56N 82 27W
Seeadler Harbour Manus, Papua New Guinea
  02 00S 147 18E
Segundo, El California, USA 33 55N 118 26E
Seikoshin (Sohojin) North Korea 39 49N 127 40E
Seishin (Ch'ongjin) (Chungjin) North Korea
  41 46N 129 50E
Sejinkat Sarawak, Malaysia 01 35N 110 26E
Sekondi Ghana 04 56N 01 42W
Sel'ata, Ras Lebanon 34 17N 35 39E
Selat Kijang (Kidjang Strait) Bintan, Indonesia
  00 51N 104 37E
Selby R. Ouse, England, UK 53 47N 01 04W
Seldom Harbour Newfoundland, Canada 49 37N 54 11W
Seldovia Alaska, USA 59 26N 151 43W
Selfs Point Tasmania, Australia 42 51S 147 20E
Selzate (Zelzate) Gent-Terneuzen Canal, Belgium
  51 12N 03 49E
Semarang (Samarang) Jawa, Indonesia 06 56S 110 25E
Sematan, Sungei Sarawak, Malaysia 01 49N 109 47E
Sembawang Singapore 01 28N 103 50E
Semporna Sabah, Malaysia 04 29N 118 37E
Senboku Osaka Wan, Honshu, Japan 34 36N 135 26E
Senipah Terminal Kalimantan, Indonesia 01 03S 117 13E
Senj Yugoslavia 45 00N 14 54E
Sepetiba Terminal Guaiba Is., Brazil 23 01S 44 02W
Sept Iles (Seven Islands) St Lawrence R., Quebec Province
  Canada 50 11N 66 26W
Serangoon Harbour Pulau Ubin, Singapore
  01 24N 103 57E
Seria Brunei 04 37N 114 20E
Seri Begawan, Bandar (Brunei) Brunei 04 53N 114 56E
Serifos Greece 37 08N 24 27E
Seskaro Sweden 65 43N 23 45E
Sestroretsk Finskiy Zaliv, USSR 60 07N 29 58E
Sete (Cette) Golfe du Lion, France 43 24N 03 41E
Setoda Ikuchi Shima, Seto Naikai, Japan 34 18N 133 05E
Sette Cama Gabon 02 37S 09 44E
Seumawe, Lho Sumatera, Indonesia 05 08N 97 10E
Sevastopol (Sevastopol'skaya Bukhta) Krym, USSR
  44 37N 33 30E

Sevastopol'skaya Bukhta (Sevastopol) Krym, USSR 44 37N 33 30E

Seven Islands (Sept Iles) St Lawrence R., Quebec Province; Canada 50 11N 66 26W

Severodvinsk, Port (Molotovsk) Dvinskaya Guba, Beloye More, USSR 64 33N 39 49E

Severomorsk Guba Vayenga, Barentsova More, USSR 69 04N 33 28E

Seville R. Guadalquivir, Spain 37 23N 05 59W

Seward Resurrection Bay, Alaska, USA 60 07N 149 26W

Sewaren Arthur Kill R., New Jersey, USA 40 33N 74 15W

Sewells Point Chesapeake Bay, Virginia, USA 36 57N 76 19W

Seydisfjordhur Iceland 65 16N 14 00W

Seyne, La Toulon, France 43 06N 05 53E

Sfaktiria Ormos Navarinou, Greece 36 54N 21 40E

Sfax Tunisia 34 44N 10 46E

Shahid Rejaie Port Iran 27 07N 56 03E

Shahpour, Bandar (Bandar Khomeini) Iran 30 27N 49 05E

Shanghai Huang-p'u Chiang, China 31 15N 121 30E

Shannon Airport Fuel Depot R. Shannon, Republic of Ireland 52 41N 08 55W

Shan-T'ou (Swatow) Shan-t'ou Chiang, China 23 21N 116 40E

Shariqah, Ash (Sharjah) (Mina Khalid) United Arab Emirates 25 22N 55 24E

Sharjah (Ash Shariqah) (Mina Khalid) United Arab Emirates 25 22N 55 24E

Shark Bay Western Australia, Australia 26 05S 113 35E

Sharma, Port Saudi Arabia 27 56N 35 16E

Sharm Rabigh (Rabegh) Saudi Arabia 22 45N 38 59E

Sharpness R. Severn, England, UK 51 43N 02 29W

Sheboygan Lake Michigan, Wisconsin, USA 43 46N 87 43W

Shediac Northumberland Strait, New Brunswick, Canada 46 14N 64 32W

Sheerness R. Medway, England, UK 51 27N 00 45E

Sheerwater Halifax, Nova Scotia, Canada 44 37N 63 31W

Sheet Harbour Nova Scotia, Canada 44 53N 62 30W

Shellburne Nova Scotia, Canada 43 45N 65 19W

Shell Haven R. Thames, England, UK 51 30N 00 29E

Shengjin (San Giovanni di Medua) Albania 41 49N 19 35E

Sherbro Island Sierra Leone 07 30N 12 40W

Sheskharis Novorissisk Bukhta, USSR 44 42N 37 50E

Sheva Bombay, India 18 56N 72 51E

Sheykh Sho'eyb, Jazireh (Lavan Is.) (Jazireh-ye Lavan) Iran 26 47N 53 22E

Shibushi Kyushu, Japan 31 28N 131 07E

Shields, North R. Tyne, England, UK 55 00N 01 27W

Shields, South R. Tyne, England, UK 55 00N 01 26W

Shikama Seto Naikai, Honshu, Japan 34 47N 134 40E

Shima Shipyard Kyushu, Japan 33 03N 129 38E

Shimizu Suruga Wan, Honshu, Japan 35 01N 138 30E

Shimonoseki Honshu, Japan 33 56N 130 56E

Shimotsu Kii-Suido, Honshu, Japan 34 06N 135 08E

Shingle Bay Skidegate Inlet, British Colombia, Canada 53 16N 131 53W

Shiogama Honshu, Japan 38 19N 141 02E

Ship Harbour Nova Scotia, Canada 44 47N 62 50W

Shippigan New Brunswick, Canada 47 54N 64 42W

Shiq'a (Chekaa) (Chekka) Lebanon 34 20N 35 43E

Shirutoru (Makarov) Sakhalin, USSR 48 37N 142 47E

Sho'eyb Jazireh Sheykh (Lavan Is.) (Jazireh-ye Lavan) Iran 26 47N 53 22E

Shoreham England, UK 50 50N 00 15W

Shuaiba, Al (Ash Shu'aybah) Kuwait 29 02N 48 09E

Shu'aybah, Ash (Al Shuaiba) Kuwait 29 02N 48 09E

Shukheir, Ras Gulf of Suez, Egypt 28 08N 33 17E

Shuwaikh (Ash Shuwaykh) Kuwait 29 21N 47 56E

Shuwaykh, Ash (Shuwaikh) Kuwait 29 21N 47 56E

Siain Luzon Philippines 13 57N 122 01E

Si Api Api, Bagan Sumatera, Indonesia 02 09N 100 48E

Siasi Siasi Is., Philippines 05 33N 120 49E

Sibenico (Sibenik) Yugoslavia 43 43N 15 35E

Sibenik (Sibenico) Yugoslavia 43 43N 15 53E

Sibolga Sumatera, Indonesia 01 43N 98 48E

Sibu Sarawak, Malaysia 02 18N 111 53E

Sibuti, Kuala Sarawak, Malaysia 03 59N 113 44E

Si-Chang, Ko Thailand 13 09N 100 49E

Sider, Ras es Libya 30 39N 18 22E

Sidi Abdallah Tunisia 37 10N 09 48E

Sidi Ifni Morocco 29 22N 10 12W

Sidi Kerir Egypt 31 06N 29 37E

Sidney Vancouver Is., British Columbia, Canada 48 39N 123 24W

Sidon (Saida) Lebanon 33 34N 35 22E

Sidor en Matanzas, Puerto de (Matanzas) R. Orinoco, Venezuela 08 17N 62 51W

Siems Die Trave, West Germany 53 53N 10 45E

Sigerslev Sjaelland, Denmark 55 19N 12 27E

Siglufjordhur Iceland 66 09N 18 54W

Sikea Sweden 64 09N 20 59E

Sikka Gulf of Kutch, India 22 27N 69 50E

Silan (Dzilam) Yucatan, Mexico 21 23N 88 54W

Silloth Solway Firth, England, UK 54 52N 03 24W

Similajau, Kuala Sarawak, Malaysia 03 31N 113 18E

Simonstown South Africa 34 11S 18 26E

Simpson, Port British Columbia, Canada 54 34N 130 25W

Simrishamn Sweden 55 33N 14 22E

Simunjan Sarawak, Malaysia 01 24N 110 44E

Sines Portugal 37 57N 08 53W

Singapore 01 16N 103 50E

Singkawang Kalimantan, Indonesia 00 55N 108 58E

Singora (Songkhla) Thailand 07 12N 100 38E

Sinoe Bay (Sinu Bay) Liberia 04 59N 09 02W

Sinop (Sinub) Turkey 42 01N 35 09E

Sinub (Sinop) Turkey 42 01N 35 09E

Sinu Bay (Sinoe Bay) Liberia 04 59N 09 02W

Siracha (Si Racha) Thailand 13 10N 100 55E

Siracusa (Syracuse) Sicilia, Italy 37 03N 15 18E

Siros (Ermoupolis) Siros, Greece 37 26N 24 57E

Sirou, Limin Siros, Greece 37 26N 24 56E

Sirri Island (Jazireh-ye Sirri) Iran 25 54N 54 33E

Sirtica Terminal (Ras Lanuf) Libya 30 31N 18 35E

Sisiman Bay Luzon, Philippines 14 26N 120 31E

Sitia Kriti, Greece 35 13E 26 07E

Sitka Sitka Sound, Alaska, USA 57 03N 135 20W

Sitoli, Gunung Nias, Indonesia 01 19N 97 36E

Sitra Bahrain 26 09N 50 40E

Sittwe (Akyab) Burma 20 09N 92 56E

Skadovsk Dzharylgachskiy Zaliv, USSR 46 06N 32 55E

Skaelskor Sjaelland, Demark 55 15N 11 16E

Skaerbaek Jylland, Denmark 55 31N 09 37E

Skagastrond Hunafloi, Iceland 65 49N 20 18W

Skagen Jylland, Denmark 57 43N 10 36E

Skagway Taiyu Inlet, Alaska, USA 59 27N 135 19W

Skandiahamnen Gothenburg, Sweden 57 41N 11 52E

Skaramanga Greece 37 59N 23 34E

Skarhamn Sweden 57 59N 11 33E

Skeldon Corentyn R., Guyana 05 54N 57 07W

Skelleftea Sweden 64 44N 20 57E

Skelleftehamn Sweden 64 41N 21 15E

Skerjafjordhur Iceland 64 07N 21 56W

Skhirra, La Tunisia 34 18N 10 09E

Skidegate Queen Charlotte Is., British Columbia, Canada 53 16N 132 04W

Skien Norway 59 13N 09 36E

Skikda (Phillippeville) Algeria 36 53N 06 55E
Skive Limfjord, Jylland, Denmark 56 34N 09 03E
Skoghall Vanern, Sweden 59 19N 13 28E
Skoldvik Finland 60 19N 25 33E
Skoldvik, Port (Porvoo Oil Harbour) Finland
   60 18N 25 33E
Skonvik Sundsvall, Sweden 62 28N 17 20E
Skudenes Karmoy, Norway 59 08N 05 16E
Skuru Finland 60 06N 23 33E
Skuthamn Pitea, Sweden 65 16N 21 31E
Skutskar Sweden 60 39N 17 24E
Slagen Oslofjord, Norway 59 19N 10 32E
Sligo Republic of Ireland 54 17N 08 27W
Slite Gotland, Sweden 57 42N 18 49E
Sloehaven (Flushing East) Westerschelde, Netherlands
   51 27N 03 40E
Slottsbron Vanern, Sweden 59 20N 13 06E
Sluiskil Gent-Terneuzen Canal, Netherlands
   51 17N 03 50E
Smalkalden Surinam R., Surinam 05 38N 55 05W
Smith's Bluff Neches R., Texas, USA 30 00N 93 59W
Smogen Sweden 58 21N 11 14E
Smojen Gotland, Sweden 57 44N 18 57E
Smyrna (Izmir) Turkey 38 24N 27 09E
Snails Bay Sydney, New South Wales, Australia
   33 51S 151 11E
Soares Dutra Terminal, Almirante Tramandi, Brazil
   30 01S 50 06W
Sobo (Pitch Point) Trinidad 10 16N 61 37W
Soby Aero, Denmark 54 57N 10 16E
Socel Setubal, Portugal 38 29N 08 49W
Sochi USSR 43 35N 39 43E
Soconusco Mexico 15 09N 92 56W
Socony, Port Staten Is., New York, USA
   40 33N 74 15W
Soderhamn Sweden 61 18N 17 06E
Soderkoping Gota Kanal, Sweden 58 28N 16 20E
Sodertalje Sweden 59 12N 17 38E
Sodra Nyhamn Sundsvall, Sweden 62 19N 17 24E
Sogndal Sogndalfjord, Norway 61 14N 07 06E
Sogud Leyte, Philippines 10 23N 124 59E
Sohojin (Seikoshin) North Korea 39 49N 127 40E
Sokch'o (Daepo) (Daipori) South Korea 38 11N 128 36E
Solin (Salona) Yugoslavia 43 32N 16 28E
Soller, Puerto de Mallorca, Islas Baleares, Spain
   39 47N 02 42E
Solombala R. Severnaya Dvina, Beloye More, USSR
   64 35N 40 30E
Soltani, Khowr e (Bushire) (Bushehr) Iran 29 59N 50 47E
Solvesborg Sweden 56 03N 14 35E
Som, Kompong (Kampong Saom) Kampuchea
   10 38N 103 30E
Somoza, Puerto Nicaragua 12 11N 86 47W
Sonderborg Jylland, Denmark 54 55N 09 47E
Sondre Stromfjord (South Stromfjord) Greenland
   66 01N 53 31W
Songjin (Kimch'aek) North Korea 40 40N 129 12E
Songkhla (Singora) Thailand 07 12N 100 38E
Sonora Nova Scotia, Canada 45 04N 61 55W
Soraker Sundsvall, Sweden 62 31N 17 30E
Sorel St Lawrence R., Quebec Province, Canada
   46 02N 73 09W
Sorido Biak, Indonesia 01 10S 136 03E
Sornainen (Sornas) Finland 60 11N 24 59E
Sornas (Sornainen) Finland 60 11N 24 59E
Soroka (Belomorsk) Onezhskaya Guba, Beloye More,
   USSR 64 32N 34 48E
Sorong Irian Jaya, Indonesia 00 51S 131 14E
Sorvaag (Sorvagur) Vagar, Faero Is. 62 04N 07 18W
Sorvagur (Sorvaag) Vagar, Faero Is. 62 04N 07 18W

Soudhas, Ormos (Suda Bay) Kriti, Greece 35 29N 24 04E
Souris Prince Edward Is., Canada 46 21N 62 14W
Sousse (Susa) Tunisia 35 50N 10 38E
South Amboy Raritan R., New Jersey, USA
   40 29N 74 16W
Southampton England, UK 50 54N 01 24W
South Bend Willapa R., Washington, USA
   46 40N 123 48W
South Boston Massachusetts, USA 42 20N 71 02W
South Brewer Penobscot R., Maine, USA 44 47N 68 46W
South Riding Point Grand Bahama, Bahamas
   26 36N 78 14W
South Shields R. Tyne, England, UK 55 00N 01 26W
South Stromfjord (Sondre Stromfjord) Greenland
   66 01N 53 31W
South-Trees Point Queensland, Australia 23 51S 151 19E
Sovetskaya Gavan Tartarskiy Proliv, USSR
   48 58N 140 13E
Soyo (San Antonio do Zaire) Angola 06 07N 12 22E
Spain, Port of Trinidad 10 39N 61 32W
Spalato (Split) Yugoslavia 43 31N 16 26E
Sparrows Point Baltimore, Maryland, USA
   39 13N 76 29W
Spesshult Vanern, Sweden 59 04N 12 55E
Spezia, La Italy 44 06N 09 49E
Split (Spalato) Yugoslavia 43 31N 16 26E
Spring Bay Tasmania, Australia 42 33S 147 56E
Springdale Hall Bay, Newfoundland, Canada
   49 30N 56 04W
Squamish Howe Sound, British Columbia, Canada
   49 41N 123 10W
Stabia, Castellammare di Golfo di Napoli, Italy
   40 42N 14 28E
Stade Die Schwinge, West Germany 53 36N 09 28E
Stadersand Die Elbe, West Germany 53 37N 09 32E
Stalin (Varna) Bulgaria 43 11N 27 57E
Stanley Tasmania, Australia 40 46S 145 18E
Stanley, Port Falkland Is. 51 42S 57 51W
Stanleytown Berbice R., Guyana 06 13N 57 30W
Stanlow Manchester Ship Canal, England, UK
   53 17N 02 52W
Stann Creek (Dangriga) Belize 16 56N 88 14W
Stansbury South Australia, Australia 34 54S 137 48E
Stanvac, Port St Vincent Gulf, South Australia, Australia
   35 07S 138 28E
Stapleton Staten Is., New York, USA 40 38N 74 04W
Staten Island New York, USA 40 35N 74 10W
Stavanger Norway 58 58N 05 44E
Staveren Ijsselmeer, Netherlands 52 53N 05 22E
Stavern Norway 59 00N 10 03E
Stege Mon, Denmark 54 59N 12 17E
Steinkjer Trondheimsfjord, Norway 64 01N 11 29E
Stenhouse Bay South Australia, Australia 35 17S 136 57E
Stenungsund Sweden 58 04N 11 48E
Stephens, Port New South Wales, Australia
   32 43S 152 12E
Stephenville Newfoundland, Canada 48 31N 58 32W
Stettin (Szczecin) Poland 53 25N 14 33E
Stewart Portland Inlet, British Columbia, Canada
   55 55N 130 01W
Stigsnaes Sjaelland, Denmark 55 12N 11 16E
Stilleryd Sweden 56 09N 14 49E
Stocka Sweden 61 54N 17 21E
Stockholm Sweden 59 19N 18 04E
Stockton San Joaquin R., California, USA
   37 58N 121 17W
Stockvik Sundsvall, Sweden 62 20N 17 22E
Stolpmunde (Ustka) Poland 54 35N 16 52E
Stonehaven Scotland, UK 56 58N 02 12W
Stonington Connecticut, USA 41 20N 71 54W

Stora Hoggarn Sweden 59 22N 18 17E
Stora Vika Sweden 58 57N 17 47E
Storkage Sweden 64 50N 21 01E
Stormskar Sweden 63 42N 20 21E
Stornoway Lewis, Scotland, UK 58 12N 06 23W
Storugns Gotland, Sweden 57 50N 18 47E
Strahan Macquarie Harbour, Tasmania, Australia
    42 09S 145 20E
Stralsund East Germany 54 19N 13 06E
Strangford Ulster, UK 54 22N 05 33W
Strangnas Malern, Sweden 59 23N 17 02E
Stranraer Loch Ryan, Scotland, UK 54 54N 05 02W
Strathcona Sound North West Territory, Canada
    73 13N 85 11W
Stratoni Kolpos Ierissou, Greece 40 31N 23 50E
Strib Fyn, Denmark 55 33N 09 46E
Stromfjord, Sondre (South Stromfjord) Greenland
    66 01N 53 31W
Stromness Orkney Is., Scotland, UK 58 58N 03 18W
Stromness Harbour South Georgia 54 09S 36 42W
Stromskar Terminal Sweden 63 41N 20 21E
Stromstad Sweden 58 56N 11 10E
Strood R. Medway, England, UK 51 24N 00 30E
Struerhavn Limfjord, Jylland, Denmark 56 29N 08 36E
Stubbekoping Falster, Denmark 54 53N 12 02E
Studstrup Jylland, Denmark 56 15N 10 21E
Stugsund Sweden 61 18N 17 08E
Stykkisholmur Iceland 65 04N 22 44W
Suai, Kuala Sarawak, Malaysia 03 48N 113 29E
Suakin Sudan 19 07N 37 18E
Suances Spain 43 25N 04 03W
Suan, Lang Thailand 09 56N 99 09E
Su-Ao (Suo Wan) Taiwan 24 36N 121 51E
Suarez, Diego (Antsiranana) Malagasy Republic
    12 16S 49 17E
Suba Nipa Olutanga, Philippines 07 18N 122 51E
Subhas Docks, Nataji Hugli R., India 22 33N 88 17E
Subic Luzon, Philippines 14 52N 120 14E
Sucre, Puerto Golfo de Cariaco, Venezuela
    10 28N 64 12W
Suda Bay (Ormos Soudhas) Kriti, Greece 35 29N 24 04E
Sudan, Port Sudan 19 37N 37 14E
Sudhureyri Sugandafjordhur, Iceland 66 08N 23 31W
Sudr, Ras el Sinai, Egypt 29 35N 32 41E
Suez (El Suweis) Egypt 29 58N 32 34E
Sukarnapura (Hollandia) (Teluk Jayapura) Irian Jaya,
    Indonesia 02 32S 104 43E
Sukhna, Ain Gulf of Suez, Egypt 29 35N 32 23E
Sukhumi USSR 42 59N 41 02E
Sukkertoppen Davis Strait, Greenland 65 25N 52 55W
Sulina Gura Sulina, R. Dunarea, USSR 45 09N 29 39E
Sullom Voe Mainland, Shetland Is., Scotland, UK
    60 27N 01 17W
Sulman, Mina Bahrain 26 12N 50 37E
Sulphur, Port Mississippi R., Louisiana, USA
    29 28N 89 41W
Sultan, Abu Buheirat-Murat-el-Kubra, Suez Canal, Egypt
    30 25N 32 18E
Sulu (Jolo) Jolo Is., Philippines 06 03N 121 00E
Suminoe Kyushu, Japan 33 11N 130 13E
Sumiyoshi Kyushu, Japan 33 15N 131 36E
Summa Finland 60 32N 27 07E
Summerside Bedeque Bay, Prince Edward Is., Canada
    43 23N 63 48W
Summerville Minas Basin, Nova Scotia, Canada
    45 08N 64 11W
Sundahofn Iceland 64 09N 21 52W
Sundbyberg Ballstaviken, Sweden 59 21N 17 58E
Sunderland R. Wear, England, UK 54 55N 01 21W
Sunderland, North (Seahouses) England, UK
    55 35N 01 39W

Sundsvall Sweden 62 24N 17 19E
Sungei Gerong Sumatera, Indonesia 02 59N 104 52E
Sungei Kolak Bintan, Indonesia 00 51N 104 37E
Sungei Pakning Sumatera, Indonesia 01 21N 102 10E
Sungei Paloh Kalimantan, Indonesia 01 45N 109 17E
Sungei Sematan Sarawak, Malaysia 01 49N 109 47E
Sunila Finland 60 30N 26 57E
Sunndalsora Norway 62 40N 08 35E
Sunny Point North Carolina, USA 33 59N 77 57W
Suo Wan (Su-ao) Taiwan 24 36N 121 51E
Supe Peru 10 50S 77 44W
Superior Lake Superior, Wisconsin, USA 46 43N 92 04W
Surabaya (Tanjung Perak) Jawa, Indonesia
    07 12S 112 44E
Surat Thani (Ban Don) Thailand 09 09N 99 20E
Suriago, Port Mindanao, Philippines 09 48N 125 29E
Surigao Mindanao, Philippines 09 47N 125 30E
Suroc (Tignabon) Samar, Philippines 10 59N 125 48E
Susa (Sousse) Tunisia 35 50N 10 38E
Susak Kvarner, Yugoslavia 45 19N 14 27E
Susaki (Suzaki) Shikoku, Japan 33 23N 133 18E
Susu, Pankalan Teluk Aru, Sumatera, Indonesia
    04 07N 98 13E
Sutton, Port Tampa Bay, Florida, USA 27 54N 82 25W
Suva Viti Levu, Fiji 18 08S 178 26E
Suweis, El (Suez) Egypt 29 58N 32 34E
Suzaki (Susaki) Shikoku, Japan 33 23N 133 18E
Svaneke Bornholm, Denmark 55 08N 15 09E
Svarton Sweden 65 33N 22 14E
Svartvik Sundsvall, Sweden 62 19N 17 22E
Svelgen Norway 61 46N 05 18E
Svelvik Drammenfjord, Norway 59 37N 10 25E
Svendborg Fyn, Denmark 55 03N 10 38E
Svolvaer Austvagoy, Lofoten, Norway 68 14N 14 35E
Swansea Bristol Channel, Wales, UK 51 37N 03 56W
Swatow (Shan-t'ou) Shan-t'ou Chiang, China
    23 21N 116 40E
Sweeper Cove Adak Is., Alaska, USA 51 51N 176 38W
Swettenham, Port (Port Kelang) Malaya, Malaysia
    03 00N 101 24E
Swinemunde (Swinoujscie) Poland 53 56N 14 17E
Swinoujscie (Swinemunde) Poland 53 56N 14 17E
Sydhavnen Greenland 63 41N 51 31W
Sydney New South Wales, Australia 33 51S 151 12E
Sydney Cape Breton Is., Nova Scotia, Canada
    46 09N 60 12W
Sydney Bay Norfolk Is. 29 04S 167 57E
Sydney, North Cape Breton Is., Nova Scotia, Canada
    46 12N 60 14W
Syracuse (Siracusa) Sicilia, Italy 37 03N 15 18E
Szczecin (Stettin) Poland 53 25N 14 33E

Taalintehadas (Dalsbruk) Finland 60 02N 22 31E
Tabaco Luzon, Philippines 13 22N 123 44E
Tabangao Luzon, Philippines 13 43N 121 04E
Tabarka Tunisia 36 58N 08 46E
Tabatinga R. Amazonas, Brazil 04 15S 69 44W
Tablones, Punta Peru 17 36S 71 20W
Tabou Ivory Coast 04 25N 07 21W
Tachibana (Anan) Kii Suido, Shikoku, Japan
    33 52N 134 39E
Tachudju (Tasucu) Turkey 36 14N 33 54E
Tacloban Leyte, Philippines 11 14N 125 01E
Tacoma Puget Sound, Washington, USA 47 16N 122 25W
Taconite Harbour Lake Superior, Minnesota, USA
    47 31N 90 53W
Tadotsu Seto Naikai, Shikoku, Japan 34 16N 133 45E
Tadoussac Saguenay R., Quebec Province, Canada
    48 08N 69 43W

Tadri India 14 31N 74 21E
Taganrog Tagonrogskiy Zaliv, Azovskoye More, USSR
47 12N 37 57E
Tagbilaran Bohol, Philippines 09 39N 123 51E
Tagudin Luzon, Philippines 16 56N 120 27E
Taharoa Terminal North Is., New Zealand
38 11S 174 42E
Tahkolouto Finland 61 38N 21 25E
Tahsis Vancouver Is., British Columbia, Canada
49 55N 126 40W
Taichung Taiwan 24 17N 120 31E
Takamatsu Seto Naikai, Shikoku, Japan 34 21N 134 03E
Takao (Kaohsiung) Taiwan 22 37N 120 16E
Takasago Seto Naikai, Honshu, Japan 34 44N 134 48E
Takehara Seto Naikai, Honshu, Japan 34 20N 132 55E
Taketoyo (Kinuura) Chita Wan, Honshu, Japan
34 51N 136 56E
Takoradi Ghana 04 53N 01 45W
Taku Bar Hai Ho, China 38 59N 117 41E
Takuma Seto Naikai, Shikoku, Japan 34 15N 133 41E
Talamone Italy 42 33N 11 08E
Talara Peru 04 34S 81 17W
Talbot, Port Bristol Channel, England, UK
51 35N 03 47W
Talcahuano Chile 36 41S 73 06W
Ta-Lien (Dairen) China 38 56N 121 39E
Talisayan Gingoog Bay, Mindanao, Philippines
09 00N 124 53E
Tallaboa, Bahia de Puerto Rico 17 59N 66 45W
Tallbacken Braviken, Sweden 58 37N 16 12E
Talleyrand Docks Jacksonville, Florida, USA
30 22N 81 38W
Tallinn (Reval) Finskiy Zaliv, USSR 59 26N 24 45E
Taltal Chile 25 24S 70 29W
Tamano Seto Naikai, Honshu, Japan 34 28N 133 57E
Tamatave (Taomasina) Malagasy Republic 18 08S 49 26E
Tambo de Mora Peru 13 28S 76 12W
Tambongon Mindanao, Philippines 07 15N 125 40E
Tammisaari (Ekenas) Finland 59 59N 23 27E
Tampa Florida, USA 27 57N 82 27W
Tampa, Port Florida, USA 27 52N 82 33W
Tampico Mexico 22 13N 97 51W
Tanabe Kii Suido, Honshu, Japan 33 43N 135 23E
Tanah Grogot Sungai Pasir, Kalimantan, Indonesia
01 55S 116 11E
Tanah Puteh Sarawak, Malaysia 01 33N 110 23E
Tanamo, Sagua de Cuba 20 43N 75 19W
Tananger Norway 58 56N 05 35E
Tanauan Leyte, Philippines 11 07N 125 01E
Tancarville La Seine, France 49 29N 00 28E
Tandoc Luzon, Philippines 14 03N 123 18E
Tanga Tanzania 05 04S 39 07E
Tanger (Tangier) Morocco 35 46N 05 49W
Tangier (Tanger) Morocco 35 46N 05 49W
T'ang-Ku (Tongku) (Hsinkang) Hai Ho, China
38 59N 117 44E
Tanjong Batu Sabah, Malaysia 04 15N 117 52E
Tanjong Berlayer Singapore 01 16N 103 48E
Tanjong Heherr (Heherr Point) Sabah, Malaysia
04 17N 117 48E
Tanjong Mani Sarawak, Malaysia 02 09N 111 21E
Tanjong Pagar Singapore 01 16N 103 51E
Tanjong Pendam Batang Rajang, Sarawak, Malaysia
02 17N 111 40E
Tanjong Penjuru Singapore 01 18N 103 45E
Tanjong Salirong Brunei 04 54N 115 06E
Tanjung Balai Sungai Asahan, Sumatera, Indonesia
02 58N 99 48E
Tanjung Lepee Sulawesi, Indonesia 04 13S 121 33E
Tanjung Pandan Belitung, Indonesia 02 44S 104 38E

Tanjung Perak (Surabaya) Jawa, Indonesia
07 12S 112 44E
Tanjung Pinang Bintan, Indonesia 00 55N 104 26E
Tanjung Priok Jawa, Indonesia 06 06S 106 53E
Tanjung Uban Bintan, Indonesia 01 04N 104 13E
Tannurah, Ras (Ras Tanura) Saudi Arabia 26 38N 50 10E
Tanoura Kyushu, Japan 33 57N 131 01E
Tan-Shui Taiwan 25 10N 121 26E
Tanura, Ras (Ras Tannurah) Saudi Arabia 26 38N 50 10E
Taomasina (Tamatave) Malagasy Republic 18 08S 49 26E
Tapaktuan (Tapa Tuan) Sumatera, Indonesia
03 16N 97 11E
Tapal Bohol, Philippines 10 03N 124 32E
Tapa Tuan (Tapaktuan) Sumatera, Indonesia
03 16N 97 11E
Tapis Marine Terminal Malaya, Malaysia
05 31N 105 01E
Tarabulus al Gharb (Tripoli) Libya 32 54N 13 12E
Tarabulus ash Sham (Tripoli) Lebanon 34 28N 35 49E
Tarafa, Puerto Bahia Nuevitas, Cuba 21 34N 77 15W
Tarakan, Pulau Kalimantan, Indonesia 03 17N 117 36E
Taranaki, Port North Is., New Zealand 39 03S 174 02E
Taranto Italy 40 28N 17 13E
Tarawa Island Kiribati Republic 01 23N 172 55E
Tarbert R. Shannon, Republic of Ireland 52 34N 09 22W
Tarbert Island Terminal R. Shannon, Republic of Ireland
52 35N 09 22W
Tarifa Spain 36 00N 05 37W
Tarragona Spain 41 06N 01 14E
Tartous (Tartus) Syria 34 54N 35 51E
Tartus (Tartous) Syria 34 54N 35 51E
Tasu Bay Queen Charlotte Is., British Columbia, Canada
52 46N 132 03W
Tasucu (Tachudju) Turkey 36 14N 33 54E
Tateyama Honshu, Japan 34 59N 139 52E
Tau (Tou) Norway 59 04N 05 55E
Taufiq, Bur (Port Tewfik) Gulf of Suez, Egypt
29 56N 32 34E
Taunton Narragansett Bay, Massachusetts, USA
41 45N 71 08W
Taupse USSR 44 06N 39 04E
Tauranga Harbour North Is., New Zealand
37 40S 176 10E
Tavoy Burma 14 04N 98 12E
Tawau Sabah, Malaysia 04 14N 117 53E
Taynabo Point Mindanao, Philippines 07 46N 122 41E
Tayport Firth of Tay, Scotland, UK 56 27N 02 53W
Tebar Terminal (Almirante Barrosso Terminal) Brazil
23 48S 45 23W
Teesport R. Tees, England, UK 54 36N 01 10W
Tefe R. Amazonas, Brazil 03 24S 64 45W
Tefee, Barao de (Antonina) Brazil 25 26S 48 42W
Tefran Terminal Babitonga, Brazil 26 13S 48 25W
Tegal Jawa, Indonesia 06 51S 109 08E
Teignmouth Lyme Bay, England, UK 50 33N 03 30W
Tekirdag (Rodosto) Marmara Denizi, Turkey
40 58N 27 32E
Tela Honduras 15 47N 87 30W
Telanaipura (Jambi) Sungai Jambi, Sumatera, Indonesia
01 35S 103 37E
Telegrafberget Halvkakssundet, Sweden 59 21N 18 14E
Tellicherry India 11 45N 75 29E
Telok Anson Malaya, Malaysia 04 01N 101 01E
Telok Ramunia Malaya, Malaysia 01 20N 104 14E
Teluk Amahai Seram, Indonesia 03 20S 128 55E
Teluk Bajur (Padang) Sumatera, Indonesia
00 59S 100 23E
Teluk Buli Halmahera Indonesia 00 52N 128 14E
Teluk Jayapura (Holandia) (Sukarnapura) Irian Jaya,
Indonesia 02 32S 104 43E

Teluk Nibung Sungai Asahan, Sumatera, Indonesia
03 00N 99 48E

Teluk Wahai Seram, Indonesia 02 47S 129 30E

Tema Ghana 05 38N 00 01E

Tembladora Trinidad 10 41N 61 36W

Temriuk (Temryuk) Azovskoye More, USSR
45 18N 37 22E

Temryuk (Temriuk) Azovskoye More, USSR
45 18N 37 22E

Tenerife Canary Is. 28 30N 16 15W

Tenes Algeria 36 32N 01 20E

Teraina (Fanning Is.) 03 51N 159 22W

Terceira Island Acores 38 40N 27 10W

Tereboli (Tirebolu) Turkey 41 01N 38 49E

Tereng, Labuhan (Labuantring Bay) Lombok, Indonesia
08 44S 116 04E

Teriberka Barentsovo More, USSR 69 09N 35 10E

Termini Imerese Sicilia, Italy 37 59N 13 43E

Terminos, Laguna de Golfo de Campeche, Mexico
18 39N 91 50W

Ternate Indonesia 00 47N 127 17E

Terneuzen Westerschelde, Netherlands 51 20N 03 49E

Terre, Basse Guadeloupe 16 00N 61 43W

Tetney Terminal R. Humber, England, UK 53 34N 00 05E

Tewfik, Port (Bur Taufiq) Gulf of Suez, Egypt
29 56N 32 34E

Texada Island Vancouver Is., British Columbia, Canada
49 40N 124 30W

Texas City Texas, USA 29 22N 94 53W

Thames Firth of Thames, North Is., New Zealand
37 08S 175 32E

Thames Haven R. Thames, England, UK 51 31N 00 31E

Thamshamn (Thamshavn) Trondheimsfjord, Norway
63 19N 09 52E

Thamshavn (Thamshamn) Trondheimsfjord, Norway
63 19N 09 52E

Thani, Surat (Ban Don) Thailand 09 09N 99 20E

Theodosia (Feodosiya) Feodosiyskiy Zaliv, Krym, USSR
45 03N 35 24E

Thessaloniki (Saloniki) Thermaikos Kolpos, Greece
40 38N 22 56E

Thevenard Denial Bay, South Australia, Australia
32 09S 133 39E

Thingeyri Dyrafjordhur, Iceland 65 53N 23 30W

Thio New Caledonia 21 36S 166 14E

Thisted (Tisted) Limfjord, Jylland, Denmark
56 57N 08 42E

Thorlakshofn Iceland 63 51N 21 21W

Thorold Welland Canal, Ontario, Canada 43 07N 79 14W

Thorshavn (Torshavn) Stremoy, Faero Is. 62 01N 06 46W

Three Rivers (Trois Rivieres) St Lawrence R., Quebec
Province, Canada 46 22N 72 34W

Thule Baffin Bay, Greenland 77 28N 69 12W

Thunder Bay Lake Superior, Ontario, Canada
48 24N 89 14W

Thursday Island Queensland, Australia 10 35S 142 13E

Thurso Scotland, UK 58 36N 03 30W

Thyboron Jylland, Denmark 56 42N 08 13E

Tia Juana Lago de Maracaibo, Venezuela 10 15N 71 22W

Tianjin (Tientsin) Hai Ho, China 39 09N 117 12E

Tien, Ha Vietnam 10 23N 104 28E

Tientsin (Tianjin) Hai Ho, China 39 09N 117 12E

Tierra, Lobos de Peru 06 27S 80 51W

Tignabon (Suroc) Samar, Philippines 10 59N 125 48E

Tignish Prince Edward Is., Canada 46 58N 64 00W

Tigres, Baia dos Angola 16 36S 11 46E

Tiko Cameroon 04 03N 09 24E

Tiksi, Bukhta Guba Buorkhaya, USSR 71 40N 128 45E

Tilbury R. Thames, England, UK 51 27N 00 22E

Tilic, Port Lubang, Philippines 13 49N 120 12E

Tillingenabben Sweden 56 58N 16 26E

Tilt Cove Newfoundland, Canada 49 53N 55 37W

Timaru South Is., New Zealand 44 24S 171 16E

Timmernabben Sweden 56 59N 16 27E

Tinian Islands Marianas (Ladrones) Is. 14 58N 145 37E

Tioga Terminal Delaware R., Pennsylvania, USA
39 58N 75 05W

Tirebolu (Tereboli) Turkey 41 01N 38 49E

Tisted (Thisted) Limfjord, Jylland, Denmark
56 57N 08 42E

Tivat Boka Kotorska, Yugoslavia 42 26N 18 42E

Tiverton Nova Scotia, Canada 44 24N 66 13E

Tivoli Corcaigh, Republic of Ireland 51 54N 08 26W

Tivoli Hudson R., New York, USA 42 04N 73 56W

Tjilatjap (Cilacap) Jawa, Indonesia 07 46S 109 01E

Tjirebon (Cirebon) (Cheribon) Jawa, Indonesia
06 42N 108 35E

Tobata Kyushu, Japan 33 54N 130 51E

Tobermory Mull, Scotland, UK 56 37N 06 04W

Tobo Ali Bangka, Indonesia 03 00S 106 27E

Tobruch (Tobruk) (Tubruq) Libya 32 05N 23 59E

Tobruk (Tobruch) (Tubruq) Libya 32 05N 23 59E

Tobruk Terminal (Marsa al Hariga) Libya
32 04N 24 00E

Tocopilla Chile 22 04S 70 14W

Toeban (Tuban) Jawa, Indonesia 06 54S 112 04E

Tokushima Kii Suido, Shikoku, Japan 34 03N 134 35E

Tokuyama Seto Naikai, Honshu, Japan 34 03N 131 48E

Tokyo Honshu, Japan 35 39N 139 47E

Tolagnaro (Fort Dauphin) Malagasy Republic
52 02S 47 00E

Toleary (Tulear) Malagasy Republic 23 23S 43 39E

Toledo Cebu, Philippines 10 23N 123 38E

Toledo Lake Erie, Ohio, USA 41 36N 83 34W

Toli Toli Sulawesi, Indonesia 01 02N 120 49E

Tolkis (Tolkkinen) Finland 60 20N 25 34E

Tolkkinen (Tolkis) Finland 60 20N 25 34E

Tollare Sweden 59 18N 18 14E

Tomakomai Hokkaido, Japan 42 37N 141 35E

Tomari Sakhalin, USSR 47 46N 142 03E

Tome Chile 36 38S 72 57W

Tongatapu Island Tonga Islands 21 10S 175 15W

Tongku (T'ang-ku) (Hsinkang) Hai Ho, China
38 59N 117 44E

Tongoy Chile 30 15S 71 31W

Tonnay Charente La Charente, France 45 57N 00 53W

Tonning West Germany 54 19N 08 57E

Tonsberg Norway 59 16N 10 25E

Topolly Bulgaria 43 12N 27 39E

Topolobampo Golfo de California, Mexico
25 33N 109 07W

Toppila Finland 65 03N 25 26E

Topsham R. Exe, England, UK 50 41N 03 28W

Tor (El Tur) Sinai, Egypt 28 14N 33 37E

Tor Bay England, UK 50 25N 03 30W

Tore Sweden 65 54N 22 40E

Torfyanovka Finskiy Zaliv, USSR 60 34N 27 51E

Tormentine, Cape Northumberland Strait, New Brunswick,
Canada 46 08N 63 47W

Tornea (Tornio) Finland 65 51N 24 10E

Tornio (Tornea) Finland 65 51N 24 10E

Toro, Bocas del Panama 09 20N 82 15W

Toronto Lake Ontario, Ontario, Canada 43 39N 79 24W

Toros Gubre Terminal Iskenderun Korfezi, Turkey
36 55N 36 59E

Torquay England, UK 50 27N 03 32W

Torre Annunziata Golfo di Napoli, Italy 40 45N 14 27E

Torrecilla Dominican Republic 18 28N 69 52W

Torre del Greco Golfo di Napoli, Italy 40 47N 14 22E

Torres, Porto Sardegna, Italy 40 51N 08 24E

Torrevieja Spain 37 58N 00 41W
Torshamnen Sweden 57 41N 11 47E
Torshavn (Thorshavn) Stremoy, Faero Is. 62 01N 06 46W
Torskholmen Sweden 58 56N 11 10E
Tortola Virgin Is. 18 25N 64 37W
Totnes R. Dart, England, UK 50 26N 03 41W
Tou (Tau) Norway 59 04N 05 55E
Toulcha (Tulcea) Bratul Sulina, R. Dunarea, Romania 45 11N 28 49E
Toulon France 43 07N 05 55E
Touraine (Da-Nang) Vietnam 16 05N 108 12E
Towartit Anchorage Sudan 19 30N 37 20E
Townsend, Port Washington, USA 48 07N 122 46W
Townsville Cleveland Bay, Queensland, Australia 19 16S 146 49E
Toyama Toyama Wan, Honshu, Japan 36 45N 137 14E
Toyama-Shinko Toyama Wan, Honshu, Japan 36 47N 137 07E
Trabzon (Trebizond) Turkey 41 00N 39 44E
Trait, Le La Seine, France 49 29N 00 47E
Tralee Republic of Ireland 52 16N 09 43W
Tramandai Brazil 30 00S 50 08W
Trangisvaag (Trongisvagur) Suderoy, Faero Is. 61 33N 06 49W
Trang, Nha Vietnam 12 14N 109 13E
Tranmere R. Mersey, England, UK 53 23N 03 00W
Trapani Sicilia, Italy 38 01N 12 30E
Trat, Ao Thailand 12 06N 102 38E
Travemunde Die Trave, West Germany 53 58N 10 53E
Trebizond (Trabzon) Turkey 41 00N 39 44E
Treguier R. Jaudy, France 48 47N 03 14W
Trelleborg Sweden 55 21N 13 09E
Trengganu, Kuala Malaya, Malaysia 05 20N 103 08E
Trenton Delaware R., New Jersey, USA 40 12N 74 46W
Treport, Le France 50 04N 01 23E
Triboa Bay Luzon, Philippines 14 47N 120 16E
Trieste Golfo di Trieste, Italy 45 39N 13 45E
Triigi Saaremaa, USSR 58 36N 22 45E
Trincomalee (Trincomali) Sri Lanka 08 34N 81 13E
Trincomali (Trincomalee) Sri Lanka 08 34N 81 13E
Trinite, La Martinique 14 45N 60 58W
Tripoli (Tarabulus ash Sham) Lebanon 34 28N 35 49E
Tripoli (Tarbulus Gharb) Libya 32 54N 13 12E
Triunfo, El Bahia Jiquilisco, El Salvador 13 15N 88 33W
Trivandrum India 08 31N 76 59E
Trois Rivieres (Three Rivers) St Lawrence R., Quebec Province, Canada 46 22N 72 34W
Trombetas, Porto R. Trombetas, Brazil 01 28S 56 23W
Tromso Norway 69 39N 18 58E
Trondheim Trondheimsfjord, Norway 63 26N 10 24E
Trongisvagur (Trangisvaag) Suderoy, Faero Is. 61 33N 06 49W
Troon Firth of Clyde, Scotland, UK 55 33N 04 41W
Trosvik Langsundsfjord, Norway 59 03N 09 42E
Trouville Baie de la Seine, France 49 23N 00 05E
Trujillo Honduras 15 56N 85 59W
Trujillo, Ciudad (Santo Domingo) Dominican Republic 18 28N 69 53W
Truk Caroline Is. 07 20N 151 50E
Truro R. Fal, England, UK 50 16N 05 03W
Trzebiez Zalew Szczecinski, Poland 53 40N 14 31E
Tsamkong (Chan-chiang) Kuang-Chow Wan, China 21 12N 110 24E
Tsingtao (Ch'ing-tao) China 36 05N 120 19E
Tsinkiang (Chuanchou) Chin-chiang, China 24 54N 118 35E
Tsu Ise Wan, Honshu, Japan 34 42N 136 31E
Tsukumi Bungo Suido, Kyushu, Japan 33 05N 131 52E
Tsuruga Honshu, Japan 35 40N 136 04E

Tsurumi Tokyo Wan, Honshu, Japan 35 28N 139 41E
Tsurusaki Seto Naikai, Kyushu, Japan 33 16N 131 41E
Tuapse USSR 44 06N 39 04E
Tuban (Toeban) Jawa, Indonesia 06 54S 112 04E
Tubarao Brazil 20 17S 40 15W
Tubigon Bohol, Philippines 09 57N 123 58E
Tuborg Havn Sjaelland, Denmark 55 43N 12 35E
Tubruq (Tobruk) (Tobruch) Libya 32 05N 23 59E
Tudy, Port Ile de Groix, France 47 39N 03 27W
Tufi Harbour Papua, Papua New Guinea 09 04S 149 18E
Tuktoyaktuk Beaufort Sea, North West Territory, Canada 69 25N 133 03W
Tulagi Florida Is., Solomon Is. 09 06S 160 09E
Tulcea (Toulcha) Bratul Sulina, R. Dunarea, Romania 45 11N 28 49E
Tulear (Toleary) Malagasy Republic 23 23S 43 39E
Tumaco Colombia 01 51N 78 42W
Tumpat Malaya, Malaysia 06 13N 102 09E
Tunadal Alnosundet, Sweden 62 26N 17 23E
Tunas de Zaza Cuba 21 38N 79 33W
T'ung-Hai-T'an Hai-nan Tao, China 19 06N 108 36E
Tunis Tunisia 36 46N 10 13E
Tupavuori Oil Harbour Finland 60 27N 22 04E
Tupper, Point Strait of Canso, Nova Scotia, Canada 45 36N 61 22W
Turbo Golfo de Uraba, Colombia 08 05N 76 43W
Tur, El (Tur) Sinai, Egypt 28 14N 33 37E
Turiamo Venezuela 10 28N 67 51W
Turk, Grand Turk Is. 21 29N 71 08W
Turku (Abo) Finland 60 27N 22 16E
Tuticorin India 08 48N 78 10E
Tuticorin, New India 08 42N 78 20E
Tutoia Brazil 02 46S 42 16W
Tutuila Island Samoa 14 20S 170 45W
Tutun Ciftlik Izmit Korfezi, Marmara Denizi, Turkey 40 45N 29 47E
Tuxpan Golfo de Campeche, Mexico 20 59N 97 19W
Tvedestrand Oksefjorden, Norway 58 37N 08 56E
Twillingate Newfoundland, Canada 49 40N 54 46W
Tyne Dock R. Tyne, England, UK 54 59N 01 27W
Tynemouth R. Tyne, England, UK 55 01N 01 24W
Tyssedal Sorfjorden, Norway 60 07N 06 34E

Uban, Tanjung Bintan, Indonesia 01 04N 104 13E
Ube Seto Naikai, Honshu, Japan 33 57N 131 15E
Ubu, Ponta do Brazil 20 46S 40 34W
Ucluelet Vancouver Is. British Columbia, Canada 48 57N 125 33W
Uddevalla Sweden 58 21N 11 56E
Udom, Ao Thailand 13 07N 100 53E
Ueckermunde Stettiner Haff, East Germany 53 44N 14 03E
Uetersen Die Pinnnau, West Germany 53 41N 09 40E
Uglegorsk Sakhalin, USSR 49 04N 142 01E
Uig Skye, Scotland, UK 57 34N 06 22W
Ujung Pandang (Macassar) (Makassar) Sulawesi, Indonesia 05 07S 119 24E
Uleaborg (Oulu) Finland 65 01N 25 28E
Ulfvik (Ulvvik) Alandsfjarden, Sweden 62 41N 17 53E
Ulladulla New South Wales, Australia 35 22S 150 29E
Ullapool Loch Broom, Scotland, UK 57 54N 05 09W
Ulsan South Korea 35 33N 129 19E
Ulua, San Juan de Golfo de Campeche, Mexico 19 12N 96 08W
Ulvvik (Ulfvik) Alandsfjarden, Sweden 62 41N 17 53E
Umba Kandalakshskaya Guba, Bekoye More, USSR 66 39N 34 16E

Umea Umea Alv, Sweden 63 49N 20 17E
Umea Uthamn Sweden 63 42N 20 21E
Umm al Qaiwain United Arab Emirates 25 35N 55 35E
Umm Qasr Khawr 'Abd Allah, Iraq 30 01N 47 57E
Umm Said (Musay'id) Qatar 24 54N 51 34E
Unga Shumagin Is., Alaska, USA 55 10N 160 35W
Unggi (Yuki) North Korea 42 19N 130 23E
Union, La Golfo de Fonseca, El Salvador 13 20N 87 51W
Union, Port Catalina Harbour, Newfoundland, Canada 48 30N 53 05W
Uno Seto Naikai, Honshu, Japan 34 29N 133 57E
Unten Okinawa, Nansei Shoto, Japan 26 41N 128 01E
Unye Turkey 41 08N 37 18E
Upnor R. Medway, England, UK 51 25N 00 32E
Urangan Hervey Bay, Queensland, Australia 25 17S 152 55E
Urdiales, Castro (Castro Alen) Spain 43 24N 03 13W
Uribura, General (Zarate) R. Parana, Argentina 34 06S 59 02W
Urk Ijsselmeer, Netherlands 52 40N 05 36E
Ursviken Skelleftea, Sweden 64 42N 21 12E
Uruguay, Concepcion del R. Uruguay, Argentina 32 29S 58 14W
Useless Loop Shark Bay, Western Australia, Australia 26 09S 113 24E
Ushuaia Tierra del Fuego, Argentina 54 48S 68 19W
Usimanas Vitoria, Brazil 20 18S 40 20W
Ustka (Stolpmunde) Poland 54 35N 16 52E
Ust-Kamchatsk Kamchatka, USSR 56 13N 162 28E
Ust' Port Yenisey R., USSR 69 40N 84 25E
Usuki Bungo Suido, Kyushu, Japan 33 07N 131 48E
Usunoura Kyushu, Japan 33 12N 129 37E
Utansjo Angermanalven, Sweden 62 46N 17 55E
Utersen Die Pinnau, West Germany 53 41N 09 39E
Uturoa, Port d' Raiatea, Society Is. 16 44S 151 26W
Uusikaupunki (Nystad) Finland 60 48N 21 24E
Uwajima Bungo Suido, Shikoku, Japan 33 13N 132 33E
Uzunkum Turkey 41 16N 31 25E

Vaag (Vagur) Suderoy, Faero Is. 61 28N 06 48W
Vaasa (Vasa) (Nikolaistad) Finland 63 06N 21 36E
Vacamonte Golfo de Panama, Panama 08 52N 79 40W
Vago Ligure Golfo di Genova, Italy 44 16N 08 27E
Vadso Varangerfjord, Norway 70 05N 29 45E
Vagur (Vaag) Suderoy, Faero Is. 61 28N 06 48W
Vaitape Borabora, Society Is. 16 30S 151 45W
Vaja (Waija) Angermanalven, Sweden 62 59N 17 42E
Vaksdal Sorfjorden, Norway 60 29N 05 45E
Valdemarsvik Sweden 58 12N 16 36E
Valdez Prince William Sound, Alaska, USA 61 08N 146 19W
Valdez Marine Terminal Prince William Sound, Alaska USA 61 05N 146 23W
Valdivia Chile 39 48S 73 14W
Valencia Spain 39 27N 00 19W
Valentia Marina Italy 38 43N 16 08E
Valetta (Valletta) Malta 35 54N 14 31E
Valko (Walkom) (Valkom) Finland 60 25N 26 16E
Valkom (Walkom) (Valko) Finland 60 25N 26 16E
Vallarta, Puerto Mexico 20 37N 105 15W
Vallcara Spain 41 14N 01 52E
Vallejo San Pablo Bay, California, USA 38 06N 122 15W
Valletta (Valetta) Malta 35 54N 14 31E
Vallo (Valloy) Oslofjord, Norway 59 16N 10 30E
Vallo, Mazara del Sicilia, Italy 37 39N 12 36E
Valloy (Vallo) Oslofjord, Norway 59 16N 10 30E
Vallvik (Wallvik) Sweden 61 08N 17 11E

Valona (Vlore) Gji i Vlores, Albania 40 27N 19 29E
Valparaiso Chile 33 02S 71 37W
Vanada Texada Is., British Columbia, Canada 49 46N 124 33W
Vancouver British Columbia, Canada 49 20N 123 06W
Vancouver Columbia R., Washington, USA 45 37N 122 40W
Van Dyke, Jost Virgin Is. 18 27N 64 45W
Vanersborg (Venersborg) Vanern, Sweden 58 23N 12 19E
Vange Bornholm, Denmark 55 15N 14 44E
Van Gent, Sas Gent-Terneuzen Kanaal, Netherlands 51 14N 03 48E
Vanimo New Guinea, Papua New Guinea 02 41S 141 18E
Vanino Tartarskiy Proliv, USSR 49 04N 140 17E
Van Kull River, Kill New Jersey, USA 40 39N 74 07W
Vannes Morbihan, France 47 39N 02 46W
Varberg Sweden 57 07N 12 15E
Vardo Norway 70 23N 31 10E
Varel Die Jade, West Germany 53 24N 08 08E
Varkaus Saimaa Canal, Finland 62 17N 27 47E
Varna (Stalin) Bulgaria 43 11N 27 57E
Vartan Sweden 59 21N 18 11E
Vasa (Vaasa) (Nikolaistad) Finland 63 06N 21 36E
Vasilikos Cyprus 34 43N 33 19E
Vaskiluoto (Wasklot) Finland 63 05N 21 34E
Vasteras (Vesteras) Malaren, Sweden 59 36N 16 32E
Vastervik (Westervik) Sweden 57 45N 16 37E
Vasto Italy 42 07N 14 43E
Vathi Ithaki, Greece 38 23N 20 42E
Vathi (Samos) Samos, Greece 37 45N 26 59E
Vatia Point Viti Levu, Fiji 17 25N 177 46E
Vatneyri Patreksfjordhur, Iceland 65 36N 24 00W
Vauban, Port (Antibes) Cote d'Azur, France 43 34N 07 08E
Vaxholm Sweden 59 24N 18 22E
Vayenga, Guba Kol'skiy Zaliv, USSR 69 05N 33 25E
Vecchio di Piombino, Porto (Piombino) Italy 42 56N 10 33E
Vecchio, Porto Corse, France 41 35N 09 17E
Vegesack Die Weser, West Germany 53 10N 08 38E
Veitsiluoto Finland 65 42N 24 37E
Vejle Jylland, Denmark 55 42N 09 33E
Velha, Benguela (Porto Amboim) Angola 10 44S 13 46E
Velho, Porto R. Madeira, Brazil 08 45S 63 54W
Velsen Noordzeekanaal, Netherlands 52 28N 04 38E
Venadillo Nicaragua 11 55N 86 39W
Vendres, Port France 42 31N 03 07E
Venersborg (Vanersborg) Vanern, Sweden 58 23N 12 19E
Venezia (Venice) Golfo di Venezia, Italy 45 26N 12 20E
Vengurla India 15 51N 73 37E
Venice (Venezia) Golfo di Venezia, Italy 45 26N 12 20E
Ventspils (Windau) USSR 57 24N 21 32E
Ventura California, USA 34 16N 119 18W
Venustiano Carranza Laguna del Guerrero Negra, Mexico 28 02N 114 07W
Vera Cruz Golfo de Campeche, Mexico 19 12N 96 08W
Veraval India 20 54N 70 28E
Verdal Havn Trondheimsfjord, Norway 63 47N 11 26E
Verdon, Le La Gironde, France 45 33N 01 05W
Verkeback Sweden 57 44N 16 32E
Verte, Baie Newfoundland, Canada 49 56N 56 12W
Vesique Bahia Samanco, Peru 09 13S 78 29W
Vesme, Porto Sardegna, Italy 39 12N 08 24E
Vesteras (Vasteras) Malaren, Sweden 59 36N 16 32E
Vesterohavn Laeso, Denmark 57 18N 10 55E
Vestmanhavn (Vestmanna) Stremoy, Faero Is. 62 09N 07 09W
Vestmanna (Vestmanhavn) Stermoy, Faero Is. 62 09N 07 09W

Vestmannaeyjar (Vestmann Is.) Iceland 63 25N 20 20W
Vestmann Islands (Vestmannaeyjar) Iceland
63 25N 20 20W
Vianna (Vianna do Costelo) Portugal 41 41N 08 50W
Vianna do Costelo (Vianna) Portugal 41 41N 08 50W
Vicosa, Nova R. Peruipe, Brazil 17 54S 39 21W
Victor Harbour South Australia, Australia
35 33S 138 38E
Victoria (Vitoria) Brazil 20 19S 40 20W
Victoria Cameroon 04 00N 09 12E
Victoria Vancouver Is., British Columbia, Canada
48 25N 123 22W
Victoria Labuan, Sabah, Malaysia 05 17N 115 14E
Victoria Point Harbour (Kawthaung) Burma
09 59N 98 33E
Victoria, Port Mahe, Seychelle Is. 04 37S 55 28E
Viejo de Azua, Puerto Dominican Republic
18 19N 70 19W
Vieux Fort St. Lucia 13 44N 60 58W
Vifstavarf Sundsvall, Sweden 62 29N 17 23E
Vigo Spain 42 14N 08 44W
Vihreasaari Finland 65 00N 25 25E
Viipuri (Wiborg) (Vyborg) Vyborgskiy Zaliv, USSR
60 43N 28 46E
Vijayadurg India 16 33N 73 20E
Vika, Stora Sweden 58 57N 17 47E
Vila do Porto Santa Maria, Acores 36 56N 25 09W
Vila Nova de Portimao (Portimao) Portugal
37 08N 08 31W
Vila, Port (Fila) Efate, New Hebrides 17 44S 168 18E
Vila Real de Santo Antonio R. Gudiana, Portugal
37 11N 07 26W
Villa Cisneros (Dakhla) Mauritania 23 42N 15 56W
Villa Constitucion R. Parana, Argentina 33 17S 60 20W
Villa de Noya Spain 42 47N 08 53W
Villagarcia de Arosa Spain 42 36N 08 46W
Villanueva Mindanao, Philippines 08 35N 124 46E
Villaricos Spain 37 13N 01 47W
Villefranche Cote d'Azur, France 43 42N 07 19E
Vilos, Los Chile 31 54S 71 32W
Vilvoorde R. Senne, Belgium 50 56N 04 23E
Vinaroz Spain 40 28N 00 29E
Vincent, Port South Australia, Australia
34 47S 137 52E
Vindskarsvarv Sundsvall, Sweden 62 24N 17 21E
Vinh Cam-Ranh Vietnam 11 53N 109 12E
Virac Catanduanes, Philippines 13 34N 124 14E
Virolahti Finland 60 33N 27 45E
Virpiniemi Oil Jetty Finland 65 08N 25 15E
Viru Harbour New Georgia, Solomon Is. 08 30S 157 44E
Visakhapatnam (Vizagapatam) India 17 42N 83 18E
Visby Gotland, Sweden 57 39N 18 17E
Vita Cuba 21 05N 75 57W
Vitoria (Victoria) Brazil 20 19S 40 20W
Vitoria, Praia da Terceira, Acores 38 44N 27 04W
Vivero Spain 43 40N 07 36W
Vivstavarv-Fagervik Sundsvall, Sweden 62 29N 17 23E
Vizagapatam (Visakhapatnam) India 17 42N 83 18E
Vlaardingen Nieuwe Waterweg, Netherlands
51 54N 04 20E
Vladimir, Port Motoviskiy Zaliv, USSR 69 25N 33 09E
Vladivostock Ostroy Ruskiy Zaliv, USSR 43 06N 131 54E
Vlissingen (Flushing) Westerschelde, Netherlands
51 28N 03 36E
Vlore (Valona) Gji i Vlores, Albania 40 27N 19 29E
Vohemar Malagasy Republic 13 21S 50 00E
Volda Voldafjord, Norway 62 09N 06 04E
Volos Pagastikos Kolpos, Greece 39 21N 22 59E
Voltri Golfo di Genova, Italy 44 26N 08 45E
Vopnafjordhur Iceland 65 45N 14 50W

Vordingborg Sjaelland, Denmark 55 00N 11 54E
Vostizza (Aegion) (Aiyion) Korinthiakos Kolpos, Greece
38 15N 22 05E
Vostochny Bukhta Vrangelya, USSR 42 44N 133 03E
Vostochnyy Sakhalin, USSR 48 16N 142 38E
Voudhia (Voudia) Milos, Greece 36 45N 24 32E
Voudia (Voudhia) Milos, Greece 36 45N 24 32E
Vragnizza (Vranjic) Yugoslavia 43 32N 16 28E
Vranjic (Vragnizza) Yugoslavia 43 32N 16 28E
Vridi Abidjan, Ivory Coast 05 15N 04 00W
Vunda Point Viti Levu, Fiji 17 41S 177 24E
Vung Chao, Baie de Vietnam 13 26N 109 14E
Vung Qui-Nhon Vietman 13 46N 109 14E
Vung Ro Vietnam 12 52N 109 26E
Vuosaari Finland 60 13N 25 11E
Vyborg (Viipuri) (Wiborg) Vyborgskiy Zaliv, USSR
60 43N 28 46E
Vys'otsk Vyborgskiy Zaliv, USSR 60 38N 28 34E

Wabana Bell Is., Newfoundland, Canada 47 38N 52 55W
Wade, Port Annapolis Basin, Nova Scotia, Canada
44 41N 65 42W
Wadi Feiran Sinai, Egypt 28 44N 33 13E
Wageningen Nickerie R., Surinam 05 46N 56 41W
Wahai, Teluk Seram, Indonesia 02 47S 129 30E
Waija (Vaja) Angermanalven, Sweden 62 59N 17 42E
Waikawa South Is., New Zealand 46 38S 169 08E
Waingapu Sumba, Indonesia 09 39S 120 16E
Wajima Honshu, Japan 37 24N 136 54E
Wakamatsu Kyushu, Japan 33 54N 130 48E
Wakayama Kii Suido, Honshu, Japan 34 13N 135 09E
Wakefield, Port St. Vincent Gulf, South Australia, Australia
34 12S 138 09E
Wake Island 19 18N 166 36E
Walcott, Port Western Australia, Australia
20 38S 117 12E
Walkom (Valkom) (Valko) Finland 60 25N 26 16E
Wallace Bay (Sebatic) Sebatic Is., Sabah, Malaysia
04 15N 117 39E
Wallaceburg Lake St. Clair, Ontario, Canada
42 36N 82 24W
Wallaroo Spencer Gulf, South Australia, Australia
33 56S 137 37E
Wallhamn Tjorn, Sweden 58 01N 11 42E
Wallsend R. Tyne, England, UK 54 59N 01 30W
Wallvik (Vallvik) Sweden 61 08N 17 11E
Walsh Bay Sydney, New South Wales, Australia
33 51S 151 12E
Walsoorden Westerschelde, Netherlands 51 23N 04 02E
Walter, Port Baranof Is., Alaska USA 56 23N 134 39W
Walton Minas Basin, Nova Scotia, Canada
45 14N 64 01W
Walvisbaai (Walvis Bay) Namibia 22 57S 14 30E
Walvis Bay (Walvisbaai) Namibia 22 57S 14 30E
Wanganui North Is., New Zealand 39 57S 175 00E
Wapnica Zalew Szczecinski, Poland 53 52N 14 26E
Warkworth (Amble) England, UK 55 20N 01 35W
Warnemunde Mecklenburger Bucht, East Germany
54 11N 12 05E
Warrenpoint Carlingford Lough, Ulster, UK
54 06N 06 15W
Warri Forcados R., Nigeria 05 31N 05 45E
Warrington Manchester Ship Canal, England, UK
53 24N 02 37W
Warrnambool Victoria, Australia 38 24S 142 29E
Washington, New Panay, Philippines 11 40N 122 26E
Wasklot (Vaskiluoto) Finland 63 05N 21 34E
Watchet Bristol Channel, England, UK 51 11N 03 20W

Waterfall Ulloa Channel, Alaska, USA 55 18N 133 14W
Waterford (Port Lairge) Republic of Ireland
52 15N 07 07W
Waterloo R. Skien, Norway 59 10N 09 38E
Watson Island British Columbia, Canada 54 14N 130 18W
Waverley North Is., New Zealand 39 50S 174 36E
Wawa (Nasugbu) Luzon, Philippines 14 05N 120 37E
Wear Point Milford Haven, Wales, UK 51 42N 04 59W
Wedel Die Elbe, West Germany 53 34N 09 43E
Weehawken Hudson R., New Jersey, USA
40 46N 74 01W
Wei-Hai-Wei China 37 30N 122 07E
Weipa Albatross Bay, Queensland, Australia
12 40S 141 53E
Wejh, El Saudi Arabia 26 13N 36 27E
Welland Welland Canal, Ontario, Canada
42 59N 79 12W
Weller, Port Welland Canal, Ontario, Canada
43 14N 79 12W
Welles Harbor Midway Is. 28 12N 177 22W
Wellington North Is., New Zealand 41 17S 174 47E
Wells England, UK 52 57N 00 51E
Wells Point Puget Sound, Washington, USA
47 47N 122 24W
Welshpool Bay of Fundy, New Brunswick, Canada
44 53N 66 57W
Welshpool, Port Victoria, Australia 38 42S 146 28E
Wentworth, Port Georgia, USA 32 08N 81 09W
We, Pulo Indonesia 05 50N 95 20E
Wesermunde Die Weser, West Germany 53 32N 08 35E
Westernport Victoria, Australia 38 21S 145 14E
Westervik (Vastervik) Sweden 57 45N 16 37E
West Hartlepool England, UK 54 41N 01 12W
Westminster, New British Columbia, Canada
49 12N 122 55W
Weston Point Manchester Ship Canal, England, UK
53 20N 02 46W
West Point Hudson R., New York, USA 41 24N 73 57W
Westport Clew Bay, Republic of Ireland 53 48N 09 32W
Westport South Is., New Zealand 41 45S 171 36E
Westray Orkney Is., Scotland, UK 59 19N 02 58W
Westview Malaspina Strait, British Columbia, Canada
49 50N 124 32W
Westville Delaware R., New Jersey, USA 39 52N 75 08W
Westwego Mississippi R., Louisiana, USA 29 55N 90 09W
Westzaan Noordzeekanaal, Netherlands 52 27N 04 46E
Wete Pemba Is., Tanzania 05 04S 39 43E
Wewak New Guinea, Papua New Guinea 03 33S 143 39E
Wexford Republic of Ireland 52 20N 06 27W
Weymouth St. Mary's Bay, Nova Scotia, Canada
44 27N 66 01W
Weymouth England, UK 50 36N 02 27W
Weymouth, North Massachusetts, USA 42 15N 70 55W
Whampoa (Huang-pu) Chu Chiang, China
23 06N 113 24E
Whangarei North Is., New Zealand 35 47S 174 21E
Whangaroa North Is., New Zealand 34 59S 173 47E
Whiddy Island Bantry Bay, Republic of Ireland
51 41N 09 31W
Whitby England, UK 54 29N 00 37W
White Bay Sydney, New South Wales, Australia
33 52S 151 11E
Whitegate (Corkbeg) Corcaigh, Republic of Ireland
51 50N 08 14W
Whitehall Stronsay, Orkney Is., Scotland, UK
59 09N 02 36W
Whitehaven England, UK 54 33N 03 36W
White, Ingeniero Bahia Blanca, Argentina 38 48S 62 16W
Whiteness Sand Moray Firth, Scotland, UK
57 36N 04 00W

Whitstable England, UK 51 22N 01 02E
Whittier Prince William Sound, Alaska, USA
60 47N 148 40W
Whyalla Spencer Gulf, South Australia, Australia
33 02S 137 36E
Wiborg (Vyborg) (Viipuri) Vyborgskiy Zaliv, USSR
60 43N 28 46E
Wick Scotland, UK 58 26N 03 05W
Wick, Little Milford Haven, Wales, UK 51 42N 05 05W
Wicklow Republic of Ireland 52 59N 06 02W
Widnes R. Mersey, England, UK 53 22N 02 45W
Wieckhafen Greifswald Bodden, East Germany
54 06N 13 28E
Wilhelmsburg Die Elbe, West Germany 53 27N 09 57E
Wilhelmshaven Die Jade, West Germany 53 31N 08 10E
Willapa Willapa R., Washington, USA 46 40N 123 46W
Willemstad Curacao 12 06N 68 56W
William, Fort Lake Superior, Ontario, Canada
48 26N 89 13W
William, Fort Loch Linnhe, Scotland, UK 56 49N 05 07W
Williams, Port Minas Basin, Nova Scotia, Canada
45 06N 64 24W
Williamstown R. Yarra, Victoria, Australia
37 52S 144 55E
Willington R. Tyne, England, UK 54 59N 01 30W
Wilmington California, USA 33 46N 118 16W
Wilmington Delaware R., Delaware, USA
39 46N 75 29W
Wilmington North Carolina, USA 34 14N 77 57W
Windau (Ventspils) USSR 57 24N 21 32E
Windsor Minas Basin, Nova Scotia, Canada
44 59N 64 09W
Windsor Detroit R., Ontario, Canada 42 20N 83 04W
Winneba Ghana 05 20N 00 38W
Wisbech R. Nene, England, UK 52 39N 00 09E
Wismar Wismarbucht, East Germany 53 54N 11 27E
Wivenhoe R. Colne, England, UK 51 51N 00 58W
Wladyslawowo (Grossendorf) Zatsoka Gdanska, Poland
54 47N 18 26E
Wolgast East Germany 54 03N 13 47E
Wolin Zalew Szczecinski. Poland 53 51N 14 37E
Womens Bay Kodiak Is., Alaska, USA 57 43N 152 31W
Wonsan (Gensan) Yonghung Man, North Korea
39 10N 127 26E
Woodbridge Bay Dominica 15 19N 61 24W
Woodfibre Howe Sound, British Columbia, Canada
49 40N 123 15W
Woods Hole Massachusetts, USA 41 31N 70 40W
Wooloomooloo Sydney, New South Wales, Australia
33 52S 151 13E
Woosung Ch'ang Chiang, China 31 22N 121 29E
Workington England, UK 54 39N 03 34W
Wormerveer Noordzeekanaal, Netherlands 52 29N 04 47E
Wrangell Alaska, USA 56 27N 132 23W
Wright Point Strait of Canso, Nova Scotia, Canada
45 34N 61 21W
Wu-Hu Ch'ang Chiang, China 31 20N 118 21E
Wyk Fohr, West Germany 54 42N 08 35E
Wyndham Canbridge Gulf, Western Australia, Australia
15 29S 128 05E

Xcalak Mexico 18 15N 87 49W
Xeros Pier Cyprus 35 08N 32 49E

Yabucoa Puerto Rico 18 03N 65 50W
Yadida, Al (El Jadida) (Mazagan) Morocco
33 14N 08 28W
Yainville La Seine, France 49 28N 00 49E

Yakacik Iskenderun Korfezi, Turkey 36 43N 36 12E
Yakutat Bay Alaska, USA 59 33N 139 45W
Yali (Yiali) Greece 36 38N 27 07E
Yalova Marmara Denizi, Turkey 40 39N 29 16E
Yalta (Yaltinskiy Port) Krym, USSR 44 30N 34 10E
Yaltinskiy Port (Yalta) Krym, USSR 44 30N 34 10E
Yamagawa Kagoshima Wan, Kyushu, Japan
  31 12N 130 38E
Yamba New South Wales, Australia 29 26S 153 21E
Yampi Sound Western Australia, Australia
  16 09S 123 39E
Yanbo el Bahr (Yanbu) (Yenbo) Saudi Arabia
  24 06N 38 03E
Yanbu (Yanbo el Bahr) (Yenbo) Saudi Arabia
  24 06N 38 03E
Yanbu as Sinaiyah (Yanbu Industrial Port) Saudi Arabia
  23 57N 38 13E
Yanbu Construction Support Port Saudi Arabia
  23 55N 38 19E
Yanbu Industrial Port (Yanbu as Sinaiyah) Saudi Arabia
  23 57N 38 13E
Yandina Russel, Solomon Is. 09 04S 159 13E
Yap Caroline Is. 09 30N 138 10E
Yaquina Bay Oregon, USA 44 36N 124 03W
Yaremdji (Yarimca) Izmit Korfezi, Marmara Denizi,
  Turkey 40 44N 29 44E
Yarimca (Yaremdji) Izmit Korfezi, Marmara Denizi, Turkey
  40 44N 29 44E
Yarmouth Nova Scotia, Canada 43 50N 66 07W
Yarmouth, Great R. Yare, England, UK 52 34N 01 44E
Yarraville Yarra R., Victoria, Australia 37 49S 144 54E
Yatsushiro Yatsushiro Kai, Kyushu, Japan
  32 30N 130 34E
Yavaros Golfo de California, Mexico 26 41N 109 31W
Yawata Kyushu, Japan 33 52N 130 49E
Yelland R. Taw, England, UK 51 04N 04 10W
Yeisk (Yeysk) Azovskoye More, USSR 46 44N 38 16E
Yenbo (Yanbu) (Yanbo el Bahr) Saudi Arabia
  24 06N 38 03E
Yen-T'ai (Chefoo) China 37 33N 121 23E
Yeosu (Yosu) (Reisui) South Korea 34 45N 127 44E
Yerakini Toronaios Kolpos, Greece 40 16N 23 27E
Yeysk (Yeisk) Azovskoye More USSR 46 44N 38 16E
Yiali (Yali) Greece 36 38N 27 07E
Yingk'ou (Newchwang) Liao Ho, China 40 41N 122 14E
Yin-Hsien (Ning-Po) Yung Chiang, China 29 53N 121 33E
Yithion (Gythion) Lakonikos Kolpos, Greece
  36 45N 22 34E
Ykspihlaja (Yxpila) Finland 63 51N 23 01E
Ymuiden (Ijmuiden) Noordzeekanaal, Netherlands
  52 28N 04 34E
Yokkaichi Ise Wan, Honshu, Japan 34 58N 136 39E
Yokohama Tokyo Wan, Honshu, Japan 35 27N 139 39E
Yokosuka Tokyo Wan, Honshu, Japan 35 17N 139 40E
Yonkers Hudson R., New York, USA 40 57N 73 54W
Yosu (Reisui) (Yeosu) South Korea 34 45N 127 44E
Youghal Republic of Ireland 51 57N 07 50W
Ystad Sweden 55 26N 13 50E
Yucalpeten, Puerto De Mexico 21 17N 89 42W
Yuki (Unggi) North Korea 42 19N 130 23E
Yu-Lin Hai-Nan Tao, China 18 13N 109 32E
Yura Kii Suido, Honshu, Japan 33 58N 135 07E
Yurimaguas R. Huallaga, Peru 05 55S 76 08W
Yxpila (Ykspihlaja) Finland 63 51N 23 01E

Zaandam Noordzeekanaal, Netherlands 52 26N 04 50E
Zabi, Abu (Abu Dhabi) (Mina Zayed) United Arab
  Emirates 24 29N 54 22E
Zadar (Zara) Yugoslavia 44 07N 15 13E

Zahrani Lebanon 33 30N 35 20E
Zakinthos (Zante) Greece 37 47N 20 54E
Zaliv Korfa Kamchatka, USSR 60 20N 165 45E
Zamboanga Mindanao, Philippines 06 54N 122 04E
Zannah, Jabal az (Jebel Dhanna) United Arab Emirates
  24 12N 52 34E
Zante (Zakinthos) Greece 37 47N 20 54E
Zanzibar Island Tanzania 06 09S 39 11E
Zara (Zadar) Yugoslavia 44 07N 15 13E
Zarakkuh, Jazirat (Zirku Is.) United Arab Emirates
  24 52N 52 04E
Zarate (General Uriburu) R. Parana, Argentina
  34 06S 59 02W
Zassnitz (Sassnitz) Rugen, East Germany 54 31N 13 39E
Zawia Terminal (Az Zawiya) Libya 32 49N 12 42E
Zawiya, Az (Zawia Terminal) Libya 32 49N 12 42E
Zayed, Mina (Abu Dhabi) (Abu Zabi) United Arab
  Emirates 24 29N 54 22E
Zaza, Tunas de Cuba 21 38N 79 33W
Zeballos Vancouver Is., British Columbia, Canada
  49 59N 126 51W
Zeebrugge Belgium 51 20N 03 12E
Zelenika Boka Kotorska, Yugoslavia 42 27N 18 35E
Zelzate (Selzaete) Gent-Terneuzen Canal, Belgium
  51 12N 03 48E
Zenima, Abu Sinai, Egypt 29 02N 33 06E
Zhdanov (Mariupol) Azovskoye More, USSR
  47 05N 37 32E
Zierikzee Schouwen, Netherlands 51 38N 03 53E
Zighinkor (Ziguinchor) Casamance R., Senegal
  12 34N 16 20W
Ziguinchor (Zighinkor) Casamance R., Senegal
  12 34N 16 20W
Zirku Island (Jazirat Zarakkuh) United Arab Emirates
  24 52N 52 04E
Zonguldak Turkey 41 28N 31 47E
Zorritos, Puerto Peru 03 40S 80 40W
Zuara (Zuwara) Libya 32 55N 12 07E
Zubayr, Khawr al (Khor az Zubayr) Iraq 30 24N 47 45E
Zueitina (Az Zuwaytinah) Libya 30 57N 20 11E
Zulayfayn Saudi Arabia 26 53N 49 55E
Zuwara (Zuara) Libya 32 55N 12 07E
Zuwaytinah, Az (Zuetina) Libya 30 57N 20 11E
Zwijndrecht (Zwyndrecht) Oud Maas, Netherlands
  51 49N 04 39E
Zwolle Netherlands 52 31N 06 07E
Zwyndrecht (Zwijndrecht) Oud Maas, Netherlands
  51 49N 04 39E
Zyyi Cyprus 34 43N 33 21E

INDEX

DECIMALS OF THE DEGREE

'	.0	.2	.4	.6	.8
0	0.000	0.003	0.007	0.010	0.013
1	.017	.020	.023	.027	.030
2	.033	.037	.040	.043	.047
3	.050	.053	.057	.060	.063
4	.067	.070	.073	.077	.080
5	0.083	0.087	0.090	0.093	0.097
6	.100	.103	.107	.110	.113
7	.117	.120	.123	.127	.130
8	.133	.137	.140	.143	.147
9	.150	.153	.157	.160	.163
10	0.167	0.170	0.173	0.177	0.180
11	.183	.187	.190	.193	.197
12	.200	.203	.207	.210	.213
13	.217	.220	.223	.227	.230
14	.233	.237	.240	.243	.247
15	0.250	0.253	0.257	0.260	0.263
16	.267	.270	.273	.277	.280
17	.283	.287	.290	.293	.297
18	.300	.303	.307	.310	.313
19	.317	.320	.323	.327	.330
20	0.333	0.337	0.340	0.343	0.347
21	.350	.353	.357	.360	.363
22	.367	.370	.373	.377	.380
23	.383	.387	.390	.393	.397
24	.400	.403	.407	.410	.413
25	0.417	0.420	0.423	0.427	0.430
26	.433	.437	.440	.443	.447
27	.450	.453	.457	.460	.463
28	.467	.470	.473	.477	.480
29	.483	.487	.490	.493	.497
30	0.500	0.503	0.507	0.510	0.513
31	.517	.520	.523	.527	.530
32	.533	.537	.540	.543	.547
33	.550	.553	.557	.560	.563
34	.567	.570	.573	.577	.580
35	0.583	0.587	0.590	0.593	0.597
36	.600	.603	.607	.610	.613
37	.617	.620	.623	.627	.630
38	.633	.637	.640	.643	.647
39	.650	.653	.657	.660	.663
40	0.667	0.670	0.673	0.677	0.680
41	.683	.687	.690	.693	.697
42	.700	.703	.707	.710	.713
43	.717	.720	.723	.727	.730
44	.733	.737	.740	.743	.747
45	0.750	0.753	0.757	0.760	0.763
46	.767	.770	.773	.777	.780
47	.783	.787	.790	.793	.797
48	.800	.803	.807	.810	.813
49	.817	.820	.823	.827	.830
50	0.833	0.837	0.840	0.843	0.847
51	.850	.853	.857	.860	.863
52	.867	.870	.873	.877	.880
53	.883	.887	.890	.893	.897
54	.900	.903	.907	.910	.913
55	0.917	0.920	0.923	0.927	0.930
56	.933	.937	.940	.943	.947
57	.950	.953	.957	.960	.963
58	.967	.970	.973	.977	.980
59	.983	.987	.990	.993	.997

STAR'S TOTAL CORRECTION

Metres	2.0	2.3	2.7	3.1	3.5	3.9	4.4	4.9	5.4	5.9	6.5	7.1
Feet	7	8	9	10	11	13	14	16	18	19	21	23
Obs. Alt.	'	'	'	'	'	'	'	'	'	'	'	'
10 00	7.8	8.0	8.2	8.4	8.6	8.8	9.0	9.2	9.4	9.6	9.8	10.0
30	7.6	7.8	8.0	8.2	8.4	8.6	8.8	9.0	9.2	9.4	9.6	9.8
11 00	7.4	7.6	7.8	8.0	8.2	8.4	8.6	8.8	9.0	9.2	9.4	9.6
30	7.2	7.4	7.6	7.8	8.0	8.2	8.4	8.6	8.8	9.0	9.2	9.4
12 00	7.0	7.2	7.4	7.6	7.8	8.0	8.2	8.4	8.6	8.8	9.0	9.2
30	6.8	7.0	7.2	7.4	7.6	7.8	8.0	8.2	8.4	8.6	8.8	9.0
13 00	6.6	6.8	7.0	7.2	7.4	7.6	7.8	8.0	8.2	8.4	8.6	8.8
30	6.4	6.6	6.8	7.0	7.2	7.4	7.6	7.8	8.0	8.2	8.4	8.6
14 00	6.2	6.4	6.6	6.8	7.0	7.2	7.4	7.6	7.8	8.0	8.2	8.4
15 00	6.0	6.2	6.4	6.6	6.8	7.0	7.2	7.4	7.6	7.8	8.0	8.2
16 00	5.8	6.0	6.2	6.4	6.6	6.8	7.0	7.2	7.4	7.6	7.8	8.0
17 00	5.6	5.8	6.0	6.2	6.4	6.6	6.8	7.0	7.2	7.4	7.6	7.8
18 00	5.4	5.6	5.8	6.0	6.2	6.4	6.6	6.8	7.0	7.2	7.4	7.6
19 00	5.2	5.4	5.6	5.8	6.0	6.2	6.4	6.6	6.8	7.0	7.2	7.4
21 00	5.0	5.2	5.4	5.6	5.8	6.0	6.2	6.4	6.6	6.8	7.0	7.2
23 00	4.8	5.0	5.2	5.4	5.6	5.8	6.0	6.2	6.4	6.6	6.8	7.0
25 00	4.6	4.8	5.0	5.2	5.4	5.6	5.8	6.0	6.2	6.4	6.6	6.8
27 00	4.4	4.6	4.8	5.0	5.2	5.4	5.6	5.8	6.0	6.2	6.4	6.6
29 00	4.2	4.4	4.6	4.8	5.0	5.2	5.4	5.6	5.8	6.0	6.2	6.4
33 00	4.0	4.2	4.4	4.6	4.8	5.0	5.2	5.4	5.6	5.8	6.0	6.2
36 00	3.8	4.0	4.2	4.4	4.6	4.8	5.0	5.2	5.4	5.6	5.8	6.0
41 00	3.6	3.8	4.0	4.2	4.4	4.6	4.8	5.0	5.2	5.4	5.6	5.8
48 00	3.4	3.6	3.8	4.0	4.2	4.4	4.6	4.8	5.0	5.2	5.4	5.6
55 00	3.2	3.4	3.6	3.8	4.0	4.2	4.4	4.6	4.8	5.0	5.2	5.4
65 00	3.0	3.2	3.4	3.6	3.8	4.0	4.2	4.4	4.6	4.8	5.0	5.2
75 00	2.8	3.0	3.2	3.4	3.6	3.8	4.0	4.2	4.4	4.6	4.8	5.0
85 00	2.6	2.8	3.0	3.2	3.4	3.6	3.8	4.0	4.2	4.4	4.6	4.8
90 00	2.5	2.7	2.9	3.1	3.3	3.5	3.7	3.9	4.1	4.3	4.5	4.7

Metres	22.2	23.3	24.4	25.5	26.7	27.9	29.1	30.3	31.6	32.9	34.0	35.5
Feet	73	76	80	84	88	92	95	99	104	108	112	116
Obs. Alt.	'	'	'	'	'	'	'	'	'	'	'	'
10 00	13.6	13.8	14.0	14.2	14.4	14.6	14.8	15.0	15.2	15.4	15.6	15.8
30	13.4	13.6	13.8	14.0	14.2	14.4	14.6	14.8	15.0	15.2	15.4	15.6
11 00	13.2	13.4	13.6	13.8	14.0	14.2	14.4	14.6	14.8	15.0	15.2	15.4
30	13.0	13.2	13.4	13.6	13.8	14.0	14.2	14.4	14.6	14.8	15.0	15.2
12 00	12.8	13.0	13.2	13.4	13.6	13.8	14.0	14.2	14.4	14.6	14.8	15.0
30	12.6	12.8	13.0	13.2	13.4	13.6	13.8	14.0	14.2	14.4	14.6	14.8
13 00	12.4	12.6	12.8	13.0	13.2	13.4	13.6	13.8	14.0	14.2	14.4	14.6
30	12.2	12.4	12.6	12.8	13.0	13.2	13.4	13.6	13.8	14.0	14.2	14.4
14 00	12.0	12.2	12.4	12.6	12.8	13.0	13.2	13.4	13.6	13.8	14.0	14.2
15 00	11.8	12.0	12.2	12.4	12.6	12.8	13.0	13.2	13.4	13.6	13.8	14.0
16 00	11.6	11.8	12.0	12.2	12.4	12.6	12.8	13.0	13.2	13.4	13.6	13.8
17 00	11.4	11.6	11.8	12.0	12.2	12.4	12.6	12.8	13.0	13.2	13.4	13.6
18 00	11.2	11.4	11.6	11.8	12.0	12.2	12.4	12.6	12.8	13.0	13.2	13.4
19 00	11.0	11.2	11.4	11.6	11.8	12.0	12.2	12.4	12.6	12.8	13.0	13.2
21 00	10.8	11.0	11.2	11.4	11.6	11.8	12.0	12.2	12.4	12.6	12.8	13.0
23 00	10.6	10.8	11.0	11.2	11.4	11.6	11.8	12.0	12.2	12.4	12.6	12.8
25 00	10.4	10.6	10.8	11.0	11.2	11.4	11.6	11.8	12.0	12.2	12.4	12.6
27 00	10.2	10.4	10.6	10.8	11.0	11.2	11.4	11.6	11.8	12.0	12.2	12.4
29 00	10.0	10.2	10.4	10.6	10.8	11.0	11.2	11.4	11.6	11.8	12.0	12.2
33 00	9.8	10.0	10.2	10.4	10.6	10.8	11.0	11.2	11.4	11.6	11.8	12.0
36 00	9.6	9.8	10.0	10.2	10.4	10.5	10.8	11.0	11.2	11.4	11.6	11.8
41 00	9.4	9.6	9.8	10.0	10.2	10.4	10.6	10.8	11.0	11.2	11.4	11.6
48 00	9.2	9.4	9.6	9.8	10.0	10.2	10.4	10.6	10.8	11.0	11.2	11.4
55 00	9.0	9.2	9.4	9.6	9.8	10.0	10.2	10.4	10.6	10.8	11.0	11.2
65 00	8.8	9.0	9.2	9.4	9.6	9.8	10.0	10.2	10.4	10.6	10.8	11.0
75 00	8.6	8.8	9.0	9.2	9.4	9.6	9.8	10.0	10.2	10.4	10.6	10.8
85 00	8.4	8.6	8.8	9.0	9.2	9.4	9.6	9.8	10.0	10.2	10.4	10.6
90 00	8.3	8.5	8.7	8.9	9.1	9.3	9.5	9.7	9.9	10.1	10.3	10.5